The Good Pub Guide 2011

The Good Pub Guide 2011

Edited by

Alisdair Aird and Fiona Stapley

Managing Editor: Karen Fick
Associate Editors: Patrick Stapely, Tim Locke
Editorial Assistance: Fiona Wright

EBURY PRESS
LONDON

Please send reports on pubs to

The Good Pub Guide
FREEPOST TN1569
WADHURST
East Sussex
TN5 7BR

or feedback@goodguides.com

or visit our website:
www.thegoodpubguide.co.uk

Good Guide publications are available at special discounts for bulk purchases
or for sales promotions or premiums. Special editions, including personalised
covers, excerpts of existing Guides and corporate imprints, can be created in
large quantities for special needs. Enquiries should be sent to the Sales
Development Department, Random House, 20 Vauxhall Bridge Road, London
SW1V 2SA (020 7840 8400).

Published in 2010 by Ebury Press, an imprint of Ebury Publishing

A Random House Group Company

Text © 2010 Random House Group Ltd
Maps © 2010 Perrott Cartographics
Cover design by Two Associates
Cover photograph of the Trout Inn in Lower Wolvercote, Oxfordshire © Richard Harris

The Random House Group Limited Reg. No. 954009

Addresses for companies within the Random House Group can be found at
www.randomhouse.co.uk

A CIP catalogue record for this book is available from the British Library

Typeset from authors' files by Clive Dorman
Edited by Nicky Thompson and Jacqueline Krendel
Project managed by Nicky Thompson

Printed in the UK by CPI Cox & Wyman, Reading, RG1 8EX

ISBN 9780091930264

To buy books by your favourite authors and register for offers visit www.rbooks.co.uk

Contents

Introduction

This year, besides the 1,600 new entries in our small print Lucky Dip sections, 134 pubs have made it as new Main Entries. Some of these strike us as very special: the Flying Childers at Stanton in Peak (Derbyshire), Coventry Arms at Corfe Mullen (Dorset), Kings Arms in Tring (Hertfordshire), Castle in Bradford-on-Avon (Wiltshire), Swan at Birlingham (Worcestershire), Anderson in Fortrose (Scotland), Crown at Pantygelli and Ship at Tresaith (Wales). The Ship at Tresaith, in its superb spot above a magnificent beach, is **New Pub of the Year 2011**.

Several hundred of our best pubs are in appealing countryside or nice little villages, with the relaxed and informal character and atmosphere to match. Top examples are the White Horse at Hedgerley (Buckinghamshire), Bear at Alderwasley (Derbyshire), Grove at King's Nympton and London at Molland (Devon), Brace of Pheasants at Plush (Dorset), Royal Oak at Fritham (Hampshire), Royal Oak at Ramsden (Oxfordshire), George at Alstonefield (Staffordshire), Duke of Cumberland Arms at Henley (Sussex), Royal Oak at Bishopstone, Horseshoe at Ebbesbourne Wake, Malet Arms at Newton Tony and Cross Keys at Upper Chute (all in Wiltshire), Swan at Birlingham (Worcestershire), Cresselly Arms at Cresswell Quay (Wales) and Stein Inn on Skye (Scotland). The Royal Oak at Ramsden, cosy, friendly and unpretentious, is **Country Pub of the Year 2011**.

Some of our best big-town pubs have won their place on the strength of a great beer offering, others through good value food. In cities, it's much rarer to find a pub that's really good for the broader virtues of real character and a genuinely warm and personal welcome. Outstanding contenders are the Albion and Old Harkers Arms, both in Chester (Cheshire), Britons Protection in Manchester (Lancashire chapter), Turf Tavern in Oxford (Oxfordshire), Nags Head in Malvern (Worcestershire), Black Friar and Olde Mitre, both in Central London, Market Porter in South London and Café Royal in Edinburgh (Scotland). The ancient Turf Tavern hidden away beneath Oxford's medieval walls, a heart-warming oasis, is **Town Pub of the Year 2011**.

FOR CHEAP BEER, HEAD FOR THE WEST MIDLANDS

Our annual survey of beer prices compares what individual pubs are charging this year with what those same pubs charged last year. This is the longest-running survey of beer prices, comparing like with like. This year's survey, covering 1,110 pubs, shows that the price of a pint has gone up by 4%, and now averages £2.80.

This year, Berkshire and Surrey join London in the infamous £3-a-pint bracket. Even outside these areas, nearly one in four pubs now also charges as much. But there are significant regional variations in the prices pubs charge, as the table overleaf shows.

You can save money on beer by finding one of the many pubs brewing their own, on the premises. About one in 30 good pubs now does this, often producing delicious beers, usually at great savings for their customers, and often very rewarding in taste. Own-brew pubs typically save you 35p a pint. Current favourites are the Brewery Tap in Peterborough (Cambridgeshire), Flower Pots at Cheriton (Hampshire), Church Inn at Uppermill (Lancashire), Grainstore on the edge of Oakham (Leicestershire and Rutland), Six Bells and Three Tuns, both in Bishop's Castle (Shropshire), Masons Arms at Odcombe (Somerset), Burton Bridge Inn in Burton upon Trent (Staffordshire) and Beacon in Sedgley (Warwickshire chapter). The Grainstore beers travel well and are found in many pubs elsewhere, but it's really worth tracking them down at their source; the Grainstore at Oakham is **Own-Brew Pub of the Year 2011**.

Some breweries stand out for their customer-friendly pricing. Brewers giving much the same savings as own-brew pubs – or even better – are, starting with the best value, Sam Smiths, Wyre Piddle, Hydes, Donnington and Robinsons. We found each of these offered as the cheapest beer in several pubs in our survey (we have not listed the 20 or so breweries as cheap as these which did crop up but less frequently).

HOW BEER PRICES VARY	£/pint
extraordinarily cheap	
West Midlands	2.45
very cheap	
Staffordshire	2.54
Nottinghamshire, Shropshire	2.59
Derbyshire	2.60
Cheshire, Lancashire, Worcestershire	2.61
quite cheap	
Cumbria	2.67
Herefordshire	2.68
Yorkshire	2.69
Northumbria	2.72
Cornwall	2.74
Gloucestershire, Northamptonshire, Somerset	2.75
average	
Wales	2.76
Devon, Dorset	2.77
Wiltshire	2.78
Lincolnshire	2.80
Warwickshire	2.82
Cambridgeshire	2.83
Essex, Leicestershire and Rutland, Norfolk, Suffolk	2.85
quite expensive	
Hertfordshire, Isle of Wight, Oxfordshire	2.88
Hampshire, Scotland	2.90
Bedfordshire	2.91
Kent	2.94
Sussex	2.96
very expensive	
Buckinghamshire	2.98
Berkshire	3.02
London	3.07
Surrey	3.08

Our top ten breweries – the ones which most often supply good pubs with their cheapest beer – are Adnams, Black Sheep, Fullers, Greene King, Harveys, Hook Norton, Otter, Sharps, Wadworths and Wells & Youngs. Of these, family-run Adnams stands out, with its interesting and seasonally changing range of splendid ales (good wines, too), now very widely available. What's more, this year in their own tied pubs Adnams have held any increase in beer prices down to about half the national average. Adnams is **Brewery of the Year 2011.**

Most well run pubs keep real ale in top condition. Many landlords now go that extra length, serving beer of outstanding quality, and often hunting down a really interesting choice – nearly 400 pubs have now qualified for our Beer Award. For a beer lover's national tour, we'd suggest starting over at the Tom Cobley at Spreyton (Devon), then going north via the Crown at Churchill and Halfway House at Pitney (Somerset), Nags Head in Malvern (Worcestershire), Bhurtpore at Aston (Cheshire) and Watermill at Ings (Cumbria) to the Bon Accord up in Glasgow (Scotland), then heading back down via the Kelham Island Tavern in Sheffield (Yorkshire) to the Fat Cat in Norwich (Norfolk) and Fat Cat in Ipswich (Suffolk). From these outstanding pubs, each of them a paradise for beer drinkers, we name the Watermill at Ings **Beer Pub of the Year 2011.**

WINE, WHISKY AND A BEEF ABOUT GLASS SIZES
One in three Main Entries now holds a Wine Award, and decent quality is now the general rule. No pub can afford to neglect wine quality, as so many customers drink it in preference to beer – one in ten of the thousands of reports which readers send us now mentions wine. However, almost all pubs insist on selling wine only in big glasses, refusing to use the standard 125ml measure even as an option. This is crazy, when all the guidance on sensible drinking uses 125ml as the standard unit. The best system is as used by the Inn at West End (Surrey), where the wine-merchant landlord offers his splendid range in a choice of 125, 175 or 250ml glass sizes. Commendably, the Wetherspoons pub chain also offers these three glass sizes.

Other pubs with an excellent wine list are the Old Bridge Hotel in Huntingdon (Cambridgeshire), Harris Arms at Portgate (Devon), Caunton Beck at Caunton (Lincolnshire), Yew Tree at Clifford's Mesne (excellent pricing too – Gloucestershire), Crown at Stoke-by-Nayland (Suffolk) and Vine Tree at Norton (Wiltshire). None of these can compare with Woods in Dulverton (Somerset), which will open any of its 400 listed wines for you to have just a glass – and the quality is superb. Woods in Dulverton is **Wine Pub of the Year 2011.**

It's a surprise to find that several pubs in the north-west of England actually rival Scotland's very best pubs, in their fantastic collections of a hundred or more interesting malt whiskies: the Britons Protection in Manchester and Fishermans Retreat out near Ramsbottom (Lancashire chapter), Bhurtpore at Aston, Combermere Arms at Burleydam and Old Harkers Arms in Chester (Cheshire). However, drinking whisky on its home ground always seems to add a touch of magic to the drink itself, in such pubs as the Bon Accord in Glasgow, Port Charlotte Hotel on Islay (an unrivalled range of the island's own whiskies) and the Sligachan Hotel on Skye. Sampling a different malt each day in the Sligachan Hotel, in its perfect spot below the looming Black Cuillin, would take you the best part of a year; it is **Whisky Pub of the Year 2011.**

NO SHORTAGE OF UNSPOILT PUBS
There are more truly unspoilt pubs in this *Guide* than there were in its first edition, nearly 30 years ago. So many dozen to choose from, in fact, that it was not easy to whittle the numbers down to this shortlist of outstanding examples: the Bell at Aldworth (Berkshire), White Lion in Barthomley (Cheshire), Olde Gate at Brassington, Barley Mow at Kirk Ireton and Flying Childers at Stanton in Peak (Derbyshire), Bridge in Topsham (Devon), Vine at Pamphill and Square & Compass at Worth Matravers (Dorset), Viper at Mill Green (Essex), Harrow at Steep (Hampshire), Royal Oak at Wineham (Sussex), Turf in Bloxwich and Case is Altered (Warwickshire chapter). The Harrow at Steep, little changed since the family took it on over 80 years ago, is **Unspoilt Pub of the Year 2011.**

HOTEL COMFORTS WITH THE FRIENDLY INFORMALITY OF A PUB
Nearly a quarter of the Main Entries have bedrooms, and around half of these hold a Stay Award. The style varies from the simplest walkers' taverns to civilised country restaurants-

with-rooms and comfortable old coaching inns – some now bang up to date with a touch of contemporary luxury. The *Guide* also includes quite a few hotels, particularly in Scotland, where the bar does duty as a pub, attracting locals and passers-by much as a proper pub does. Occasionally, these bars have great character, a thriving atmosphere and a good mix of customers. Some favourites are the Old Bridge Hotel in Huntingdon (Cambridgeshire), Pheasant at Bassenthwaite Lake (Cumbria), Seaview Hotel on the Isle of Wight and White Swan in Pickering (Yorkshire). Other inns particularly enjoyed this year are the Punch Bowl at Crosthwaite and Kirkstile Inn at Loweswater (Cumbria), Brace of Pheasants at Plush (Dorset), Bathurst Arms at North Cerney (Gloucestershire), Cartwright at Aynho (Northamptonshire), Crown at Stoke-by-Nayland (Suffolk) and Black Swan at Oldstead (Yorkshire). Particularly after recent improvements on the accommodation side, the bustling Bathurst Arms at North Cerney is **Inn of the Year 2011**.

Pub food – prices are higher this year, but we've found plenty of bargains and some superb cooking. Our price survey shows that on average pub food costs 5% more this year than last. However, most good pubs have worked very hard indeed to keep prices down, despite their own running costs rising. We found that a few (one in 20) have actually cut the price of their most popular dishes. Another one in five have adjusted their menus so that their bestselling dishes this year are different from last year's – cheaper, and just as appealing, despite the difference. So for example we found one pub's most popular dish changing from fish and chips to mussels, and quite a few pub chefs concentrating on pork rather than lamb, say.

Good value pub lunches have always been a particular lure for many of our readers. These days, value counts for even more. One in 11 Main Entries has our Bargain Award. Some of these do straightforward pubby dishes at rock-bottom prices: the Digby Tap in Sherborne (Dorset), George in Kilsby (Northamptonshire), Red Lion at Steeple Aston (Oxfordshire), George & Dragon in Much Wenlock (Shropshire), Six Bells at Chiddingly (Sussex) and Farmers Arms at Birtsmorton (Worcestershire). It's rarer to find interesting food at such reasonable prices, but it can be done. The Lincolnshire Poacher in Nottingham (Nottinghamshire), Stiperstones Inn (Shropshire), Queens Head in Lichfield (Staffordshire), Basketmakers Arms in Brighton and Lewes Arms in Lewes (Sussex) all brighten up their very cheap menus with thoughtful proper home cooking. With dishes such as goat curry and venison burger served alongside staples like steak and kidney pie and pork in cider, as well as a terrific cheeseboard, readers from the south tell us that the prices at the Queens Head bring tears to their eyes; the Queens Head in Lichfield is **Bargain Pub of the Year 2011**.

The current economic downturn has stimulated pub chefs to inject a strong dose of common sense into their menus. We have been struck this year by the way that even the most ambitious dining pubs have been serving good food that's less fanciful without being any less delicious. So there are more old favourites around these days, but supercharged by top-quality ingredients and a chef's personal ingenuity. Good old ham, eggs and chips becomes home-reared rare-breed gammon with free-range eggs from their own hens, and triple-cooked chips. All sorts of interesting sausages are teamed with unusual mash, perhaps gravy made with caramelised red onions and beer or red wine. Those triple-cooked chips turn up again with beer- or tempura-battered fresh haddock with home-made tartare sauce, as boosters behind the regained popularity of fish and chips in pubs.

Dining pubs which show this trend at its best, alongside a full offering of imaginative contemporary food, include the Cock at Hemingford Grey (Cambridgeshire), Gate Inn at Yanwath (Cumbria), Stagg at Titley (Herefordshire), Olive Branch at Clipsham (Leicestershire and Rutland), Wildebeest Arms in Stoke Holy Cross (Norfolk), Plough at Kingham (Oxfordshire), Jolly Sportsman at East Chiltington (Sussex), Potting Shed at Crudwell (Wiltshire), Star at Harome and Pipe & Glass at South Dalton (Yorkshire). Excitingly inventive cooking, a warm welcome for all, and a slightly quirky relaxed pubby atmosphere combine to make the Potting Shed at Crudwell hugely popular with readers; it is **Dining Pub of the Year 2011**.

SERVICE WITH A SMILE – OR A SNEER?
Readers kindly send us many thousands of reports on pubs each year. As we are *The Good Pub Guide*, the overwhelming majority of these are favourable – people telling us what

they like about each pub. But inevitably there are pubs which used to be good but fall from grace, usually after a change of management. And there are other pubs which have never been in the *Guide*, which people feel they simply must warn us against.

This year there have been 381 pubs on our blacklist, excluded from the *Guide* after serious criticism from their customers. When we checked on exactly how these pubs fell short, we found all sorts of reasons, varying from a very smelly roaming dog through grubby or cheerless surroundings, overpowering TVs or piped music and a poor choice of beers to a whole load of shortcomings in food. The biggest single problem was bad service, reported by four in ten disappointed customers. This is a higher proportion than the three in ten that we found in our last survey.

Unacceptably slow service is a problem in one in seven or eight of the pubs denounced as bad by readers. It has become twice as common as it was in our last survey. Often, short staffing is the culprit. In our own anonymous inspections this year, we have noticed that some pubs do seem to be over-economising on staff, leading to service delays and related problems. In the last two years, the hospitality industry generally (including pubs) has cut back jobs by 4% – and it shows.

Another common complaint – in one in nine bad pubs – is of unwelcoming and uncaring staff. A further one in 15 of the thumbs-down reports describe surly, insulting or even aggressive publicans or staff. It's quite clear from their reports that something which really rankles with readers is staff reacting badly or unsympathetically to a complaint (the absolute opposite of what good publicans do). But occasional managers seem to get a kick out of turning on mild-mannered customers in an unforgivable display of gratuitous rudeness, right out of the blue:

> Manager: *'That table's reserved.'*
> My wife: *'It doesn't say so.'*
> Manager: *'Well it should.'* Manager goes behind the bar, grabs a plastic Reserved sign and slams it down on the table next to me. *'It does now.'*
> Wife: *'You are not exactly making us feel welcome in your establishment.'*
> Manager: *'It's a pleasure.'*
> Me: *'I don't think "it's a pleasure" is quite the phrase to be using in the circumstances.'*
> Manager: *'I'm not in the mood for this. You can finish your drinks and leave.'*
> We didn't finish our drinks, but we did leave. My father (who was with us) has been marvelling at the fact it has taken him 86 years to get barred from a pub.

By contrast, quite a few favourite pubs owe their appeal almost entirely to the caring and welcoming personalities of their hard-working landlords and landladies. Outstanding among these are Julie and Justin Satur of the Church Inn at Chelmorton and Bob, Cynthia and Elliott Emery of the Plough in Hathersage (Derbyshire), Tim Gray of the Yew Tree, Lower Wield (Hampshire), Peter and Assumpta Golding of the Chequers, Churchill and Jon Oldham of the Royal Oak, Ramsden (Oxfordshire), Peter and Veryan Graham of the George, Croscombe (Somerset), Emily Hammond of the George at Alstonefield (Staffordshire), Gerry and Ann Price of the Inn at West End (Surrey), Chris Gibbs of the Red Lion at Kilmington (Wiltshire), Eamon and Kathy Scott of the Olde Mitre, Central London, and Norman and Jonathan Nunn of the Colton Arms (Norman has been the landlord there since 1963) and Gerry O'Brien of the Churchill Arms, both in West London. Running his 15th-c National Trust pub in such an exemplary way for some 30 years now, Chris Gibbs of the Red Lion at Kilmington is **Landlord of the Year 2011**.

THE TOP TEN PUBS

This year's ten top pubs are the Bell at Aldworth (Berkshire), Sun in Kirkby Lonsdale (Cumbria), Five Mile House at Duntisbourne Abbots and Bathurst Arms at North Cerney (Gloucestershire), Highwayman at Nether Burrow (Lancashire), the George of Stamford (Lincolnshire), Running Horses in Mickleham (Surrey), Malet Arms at Newton Tony (Wiltshire), Nags Head in Malvern (Worcestershire) and Tempest Arms at Elslack (Yorkshire). With good food and drink, great atmosphere and comfortable bedrooms, the Tempest Arms at Elslack is **Pub of the Year 2011**.

What is a Good Pub?

The Main Entries in this *Guide* have been through a two-stage sifting process. First of all, some 2,000 regular correspondents keep in touch with us about the pubs they visit, and double that number report occasionally. We also get a flow of reports sent to us at **feedback@goodguides.com**. This keeps us up to date about pubs included in previous editions – it's their alarm signals that warn us when a pub's standards have dropped (after a change of management, say), and it's their continuing approval that reassures us about keeping a pub as a Main Entry for another year. Very important, though, are the reports they send us on pubs we don't know at all. It's from these new discoveries that we make up a shortlist, to be considered for possible inclusion as new Main Entries. The more people who report favourably on a new pub, the more likely it is to win a place on this shortlist – especially if some of the reporters belong to our hard core of about 600 trusted correspondents whose judgement we have learned to rely on. These are people who have each given us detailed comments on dozens of pubs, and shown that (when we ourselves know some of those pubs, too) their judgement is closely in line with our own.

This brings us to the acid test. Each pub, before inclusion as a Main Entry, is inspected anonymously by one of the editorial team. They have to find some special quality that would make strangers enjoy visiting it. What often marks the pub out for special attention is good value food (and that might mean anything from a well made sandwich, with good fresh ingredients at a low price, to imaginative cooking outclassing most restaurants in the area). The drinks may be out of the ordinary – maybe several hundred whiskies, remarkable wine lists, interesting ciders or a wide range of well kept real ales possibly with some home-brewed or bottled beers from all over the world. Perhaps there's a special appeal about it as a place to stay, with good bedrooms and obliging service. Maybe it's the building itself (from centuries-old parts of monasteries to extravagant Victorian gin-palaces), or its surroundings (lovely countryside, attractive waterside, extensive well kept garden), or what's in it (charming furnishings, extraordinary collections of bric-a-brac).

Above all, though, what makes a good pub is its atmosphere – you should be able to feel at home there, and feel not just that *you're* glad you've come but that *they're* glad you've come. A good landlord or landlady makes a huge difference here – they can make or break a pub.

It follows from this that a great many ordinary locals, perfectly good in their own right, don't earn a place in the *Guide*. What makes them attractive to their regular customers (an almost clubby chumminess) may even make strangers feel rather out-of-place.

Another important point is that there's not necessarily any link between charm and luxury. A basic unspoilt village tavern, with hard seats and a flagstone floor, may be worth travelling miles to find, while a deluxe pub-restaurant may not be worth crossing the street for. Landlords can't buy the *Good Pub* accolade by spending thousands on refits, soft music and elaborate menus – they can only win it, by having a genuinely personal concern for both their customers and their pub.

Using the *Guide*

THE COUNTIES
England has been split alphabetically into counties. Each chapter starts by picking out the pubs that are currently doing best in the area, or are specially attractive for one reason or another.

The county boundaries we use are those for the administrative counties (not the old traditional counties, which were changed back in 1976). We have left the new unitary authorities within the counties that they formed part of until their creation in the most recent local government reorganisation. Metropolitan areas have been included in the counties around them – for example, Merseyside in Lancashire. And occasionally we have grouped counties together – for example, Rutland with Leicestershire, and Durham with Northumberland to make Northumbria. If in doubt, check the Contents.

Scotland, Wales and London have each been covered in single chapters. Pubs are listed alphabetically (except in London which is split into Central, East, North, South and West), under the name of the town or village where they are. If the village is so small that you probably wouldn't find it on a road map, we've listed it under the name of the nearest sizeable village or town. The maps use the same town and village names, and additionally include a few big cities that don't have any listed pubs – for orientation.

We list pubs in their true county, not their postal county. Just once or twice, when the village itself is in one county but the pub is just over the border in the next-door county, we have used the village county, not the pub one.

STARS ★
Really outstanding pubs are awarded a star, and in a few cases two: these are the aristocrats among pubs. The stars do NOT signify extra luxury or specially good food – in fact some of the pubs which appeal most distinctively and strongly of all are decidedly basic in terms of food and surroundings. The detailed description of each pub shows what its particular appeal is, and this is what the stars refer to.

FOOD AWARD 🍴
Pubs where food is quite outstanding.

STAY AWARD ⇥
Pubs that are good as places to stay at (obviously you can't expect the same level of luxury at £60 a head as you'd get for £100 a head). Pubs with bedrooms are marked on the maps as a dot within a square.

WINE AWARD ♀
Pubs with particularly enjoyable wines by the glass – often a good choice.

BEER AWARD 🍺
Pubs where the quality of the beer is quite exceptional, or pubs which keep a particularly interesting range of beers in good condition.

BARGAIN AWARD £
Pubs with decent snacks at £3.75 or less, or worthwhile main dishes at £7 or under.

RECOMMENDERS
At the end of each Main Entry we include the names of readers who have recently recommended that pub (unless they've asked us not to).

Important note: the description of the pub and the comments on it are our own and not the recommenders'; they are based on our own personal inspections and on later verification of facts with each pub. A good pub which has no reader recommenders, or one that we judge deserves to stay in the Main Entries despite a very recent management change, may have BB, BOB or LYM as a recommender.

LUCKY DIPS
The Lucky Dip section at the end of each county chapter includes brief descriptions of pubs that have been recommended by readers in the year before the *Guide* goes to print and that we feel are worthy of inclusion. We do not include a pub unless readers' descriptions make the nature of the pub quite clear, and give us good grounds for trusting that other readers would be glad to know of the pub. A bare mention that food is served shouldn't be taken to imply a recommendation of the food. The same is true of accommodation and so forth. At the end of the entry we print the recommender's names. BB means we have inspected a pub and found nothing against it and LYM means the pub was a Main Entry in a previous edition of the *Guide*. In both these cases, the description is our own; in others, it's based on the readers' reports. This year, we have deleted many previously highly rated pubs from the *Guide* simply because we have no very recent reports on them. This may well mean that we have left out some favourites – please tell us if we have!

LUCKY DIPS WITH ☆
Roughly speaking these pubs are as much worth considering as some of the Main Entries themselves.

The Lucky Dips, particularly the starred ones, are under consideration for inspection for a future edition so please let us have any comments you can make on them using the report forms in this *Guide*, by writing to us at The Good Pub Guide, FREEPOST TN1569, WADHURST, East Sussex TN5 7BR or by emailing us at **feedback@goodguides.com**.

LOCATING PUBS
To help readers who use digital mapping systems we include a **postcode** for every pub.

Pubs outside London are given a British Grid four-figure **map reference**. Where a pub is exceptionally difficult to find, we include a six-figure reference in the directions. The map number (Main Entries only) refers to the map in our *Guide*.

MOTORWAY PUBS
If a pub is within four or five miles of a motorway junction, we give special directions for finding it from the motorway. You will find a list of these pubs, motorway by motorway, on page 959.

PRICES AND OTHER FACTUAL DETAILS
The *Guide* went to press during the summer of 2010, after each pub was sent a checking sheet to get up-to-date food, drink and bedroom prices and other factual information. By the summer of 2011 prices are bound to have increased, but if you find a significantly different price please let us know.

Breweries or independent chains to which pubs are 'tied' are named at the beginning of the italic-print rubric after each Main Entry. That generally means the pub has to get most if not all of its drinks from that brewery or chain. If the brewery is not an independent one but just part of a combine, we name the combine in brackets. When the pub is tied, we have spelled out whether the landlord is a tenant, has the pub on a lease or is a manager. Tenants and leaseholders of breweries generally have considerably greater freedom to do things their own way, and in particular are allowed to buy drinks including a beer from sources other than their tied brewery.

Free houses are pubs not tied to a brewery. In theory they can shop around but in practice many free houses have loans from the big brewers, on terms that bind them to sell those breweries' beers. So don't be too surprised to find that so-called free houses may be stocking a range of beers restricted to those from a single brewery.

Real ale is used by us to mean beer that has been maturing naturally in its cask. We do not count as real ale beer which has been pasteurised or filtered to remove its natural yeasts. If it is kept under a blanket of carbon dioxide to preserve it, we still generally mention it – as long as the pressure is too light for you to notice any extra fizz, it's hard to tell the difference. (For brevity, we use the expression 'under light blanket pressure' to cover such pubs; we do not include among them pubs where the blanket pressure is high enough to force the beer up from the cellar, as this does make it unnaturally fizzy.)

Other drinks: we've also looked out particularly for pubs doing enterprising non-alcoholic drinks (including good tea or coffee), interesting spirits (especially malt whiskies), freshly squeezed juices and good farm ciders.

Bar food usually refers to what is sold in the bar; we do not describe menus that are restricted to a separate restaurant. If we know that a pub serves sandwiches we say so – if you don't see them mentioned, assume you can't get them. Food listed is an example of the sort of thing you'd find served in the bar on a normal day and we try to indicate any difference we know of between lunchtime and evening.

Children If we don't mention children at all, assume that they are not welcome. All but one or two pubs allow children in their garden if they have one. 'Children welcome' means the pub has told us that it lets them in with no special restrictions. In other cases we report exactly what arrangements pubs say they make for children. However, we have to note that in readers' experience some pubs make restrictions that they haven't told us about (children only if eating, for example). If you come across this, please let us know, so that we can clarify with the pub concerned for the next edition. The absence of any reference to children in a Lucky Dip entry means we don't know either way. Children's Certificates exist, but in practice children are allowed into some part of most pubs in this *Guide* (there is no legal restriction on the movement of children over 14 in any pub). Children under 16 cannot have alcoholic drinks. Children aged 16 and 17 can drink beer, wine or cider with a meal if it is bought by an adult and they are accompanied by an adult.

Dogs If Main Entry licensees have told us they allow dogs in their pub or bedrooms we say so. Absence of reference to dogs means dogs are not welcome. If you take a dog into a pub you should have it on a lead. We also mention in the text any pub dogs or cats (or indeed other animals) that we've come across ourselves, or heard about from readers.

Parking If we know there is a problem with parking we say so; otherwise assume there is a car park.

Credit cards We say if a pub does not accept them; some which do may put a surcharge on credit card bills, to cover charges made by the card company. We also say if we know that a pub tries to retain customers' credit cards while they are eating. This is a reprehensible practice, and if a pub tries it on you, please tell them that all banks and card companies frown on it – and please let us know the pub's name, so that we can warn readers in future editions.

Telephone numbers are given for all Main Entries that are not ex-directory.

Opening hours are for summer; we say if we know of differences in winter, or on particular days of the week. In the country, many pubs may open rather later and close earlier than their details show (if you come across this, please let us know – with details). Pubs are allowed to stay open all day if licensed to do so. However, outside cities many pubs in England and Wales close during the afternoon. We'd be grateful to hear of any differences from the hours we quote.

Bedroom prices normally include full english breakfasts (if available), VAT and any automatic service charge. If we give just one price, it is the total price for two people sharing a double or twin-bedded room for one night. Otherwise, prices before the / are for single occupancy, prices after it for double. A capital B against the price means that it includes a private bathroom, a capital S a private shower. As all this coding packs in quite a lot of information, some examples may help to explain it:

£60   on its own means that's the total bill for two people sharing a twin or double room without private bath; the pub has no rooms with private bath, and a single person might have to pay that full price

£60B   means exactly the same – but all the rooms have private bath

£60(£90B)   means rooms with private baths cost £30 extra

£35/£60(£90B)   means the same as the last example, but also shows that there are single rooms for £35, none of which has a private bathroom

If there's a choice of rooms at different prices, we normally give the cheapest. If there are seasonal price variations, we give the summer price (the highest), but during the winter there may be all sorts of cheaper rates and bargain breaks.

Meal times Bar food is commonly served from 12-2 and 7-9, at least from Monday to Saturday. If we don't give a time, assume you can get bar food at those times. However, we do spell out the times if they are significantly different. To be sure of a table it's best to book before you go. Sunday hours vary considerably from pub to pub so it's best to ring before you leave.

Disabled access Deliberately, we do not ask pubs about this, as their answers would not give a reliable picture of how easy access is. Instead, we depend on readers' direct experience. If you are able to give us help about this, we would be particularly grateful for your reports.

SAT NAV AND ELECTRONIC ROUTE PLANNING
In conjunction with Garmin *The Good Pub Guide* is available for your Sat Nav. Available as an SD card or download, it integrates quickly and easily into your Garmin Sat Nav and gives you access to all recommended pubs in the *Guide*. The Sat-Nav guide will tell you the nearest pubs to your current location, or you can get it to track down a particular pub. Microsoft® AutoRoute™, a route-finding software package, shows the location of *Good Pub Guide* pubs on detailed maps and shows our text entries for those pubs on screen.

OUR WEBSITE (www.thegoodpubguide.co.uk)
Our website includes every pub in this *Guide* plus many more. It shows the location of every pub on detailed maps.

CHANGES DURING THE YEAR – PLEASE TELL US
Changes are inevitable during the course of the year. Landlords change, and so do their policies. We hope that you will find everything just as we say but if not please let us know. You can use the tear-out card in the middle of the book, the report forms at the back of the book, or just a letter. You don't need a stamp: the freepost address is The Good Pub Guide, FREEPOST TN1569, WADHURST, East Sussex, TN5 7BR. You can also send us reports at **feedback@goodguides.com**.

Authors' Acknowledgements

We could not produce this *Guide* without the huge help we have from the many thousands of readers who report to us on the pubs they visit, often in great detail. Particular thanks to these greatly valued correspondents: Jeremy King, LM, Chris and Angela Buckell, N R White, the Didler, George Atkinson, Michael Doswell, Tracey and Stephen Groves, Phil and Jane Hodson, Paul Humphreys, Michael and Jenny Back, Tony and Wendy Hobden, Phil Bryant, Alan and Eve Harding, Clive and Fran Dutson, Guy Vowles, Michael Dandy, Joan and Michel Hooper-Immins, Gerry and Rosemary Dobson, Ian Phillips, Martin and Karen Wake, Ann and Colin Hunt, Andy and Jill Kassube, Susan and John Douglas, Brian and Anna Marsden, Phyl and Jack Street, Dennis Jenkin, Alan Thwaite, Peter Meister, David and Sue Smith, John Wooll, Barry and Anne, Gordon and Margaret Ormondroyd, Steve Whalley, Donna and Roger, Barbarrick, Val and Alan Green, Rob and Catherine Dunster, Martin and Pauline Jennings, Dennis Jones, Mike and Eleanor Anderson, Richard Fendick, Reg Fowle, Helen Rickwood, JJW, CMW, Simon and Mandy King, John Prescott, Terry Buckland, Sheila Topham, Ross Balaam, Sara Fulton, Roger Baker, John Saville, Ann and Tony Bennett-Hughes, Edward Mirzoeff, Dr Kevan Tucker, Tina and David Woods-Taylor, Bob and Margaret Holder, Peter F Marshall, Michael Butler, Jeff and Wendy Williams, Bruce and Sharon Eden, John Beeken, Tony and Jill Radnor, R L Borthwick, Liz Bell, Simon Collett-Jones, Neil and Anita Christopher, Sue and Mike Todd, Phil and Sally Gorton, Comus and Sarah Elliott, Giles and Annie Francis, Richard and Jean Green, John Branston, Dave Braisted, Tom McLean, Dave Irving, Jenny Huggins, Ewan and Moira McCall, Roy Hoing, Mike Proctor, Pat and Tony Martin, Chris Evans, Margaret Dickinson, R T and J C Moggridge, Ian Herdman, Terry and Nickie Williams, Ryta Lyndley, Joe Green, Mike and Mary Carter, Bruce Bird, Charles and Pauline Stride, Eithne Dandy, Dr and Mrs A K Clarke, Ian Malone, Brian Glozier, Colin and Louise English, Chris Flynn, Wendy Jones, JPR, C and R Bromage, Derek and Sylvia Stephenson, Richard Tilbrook, MDN, B and M Kendall, Tom Evans, KC, Adrian and Dawn Collinge, MLR, Brian and Janet Ainscough, Graham and Toni Sanders, Nigel Espley, Dennis and Doreen Haward, D and M T Ayres-Regan, David and Sue Atkinson, Jerry Brown, J F M and M West, R C Vincent, Chris and Val Ramstedt, John and Eleanor Holdsworth, Henry Pursehouse-Tranter, G Wordsworth, Marlene and Jim Godfrey, Jill and Julian Tasker, Karen Eliot, David and Gill Carrington, Mr and Mrs Maurice Thompson, Roger and Lesley Everett, MP, Robert Lorimer, Malc Newton, Ron and Sheila Corbett, John and Gloria Isaacs, WW, John and Helen Rushton, M G Hart, David M Smith, Eric Thomas Yarwood, Mrs Margo Finlay, Jörg Kasprowski, Tony and Maggie Harwood, Nick Lawless, Sylvia and Tony Birbeck, Anthony Longden, Caroline and Michael Abbey, Stanley and Annie Matthews, Howard and Margaret Buchanan, James Stretton, Chris and Jeanne Downing, Doug Kennedy, Mike Gorton, Bill Adie, W A Evershed and Nick Wallis.

Warm thanks, too, to John Holliday of Trade Wind Technology, who built and looks after our database.

Alisdair Aird and Fiona Stapley

England

Bedfordshire

Our Bedfordshire pubs are a good solid set of enjoyably useful places. Not many of this little county's pubs hold our Food Award but the Plough at Bolnhurst stands out for its delicious food and carefully annotated wine list (it's our Bedfordshire Dining Pub 2011) and other pubs here offer enjoyable meals – particularly the well run Hare and Hounds in Old Warden. With its ten or so interesting real ales, the Engineers Arms in Henlow deserves special mention for its cheery atmosphere and reasonable prices, and back in these pages after a break is the riverside Falcon in Bletsoe (imaginative food). If you enjoy really traditional old pubs, don't miss the Cock at Broom.

AMPTHILL   TL0338   MAP 5
Prince of Wales
Bedford Street (B540 N from central crossroads); MK45 2NB

Civilised lunch pub with contemporary décor and menu; bedrooms

A pleasant place for an enjoyable lunch, the neatly modernised interior of this open-plan L-shaped bar-brasserie is on two levels, with big leather deco-style armchairs and sofas at low tables on wood strip flooring as you come in. It then angles around past a slightly sunken flagstoned bit, with an exposed brick fireplace, to a partly ply-panelled dining area with comfortable dark leather dining chairs set around a mixed set of sturdy tables. Modern prints decorate the mainly cream walls (dark green and maroon accents at either end), it's all nicely lit and the piped music is quite well reproduced. They have Wells & Youngs Bombardier and Eagle on handpump, good coffee, and service is brisk and helpful. There are picnic-sets out on a nicely planted two-level lawn, and a terrace by the car park.

🍴 **As well as lunchtime snacks such as tortilla wraps, baked potatoes and filled baguettes, bar food might include toad in the hole, chilli, steak and kidney pudding, lamb shank with rosemary and red wine reduction, moroccan-style stuffed peppers and grilled pollack with king prawns and citrus butter, with puddings such as wild berry eton mess and apple crumble and custard. On Monday evenings they offer a 'taste of England' menu.**
Starters/Snacks: £5.00 to £10.00. Main Courses: £7.00 to £15.00. Puddings: £5.00

Charles Wells ~ Lease Richard and Neia Heathorn ~ Real ale ~ Bar food (12-2.30(3 Sun), 7-9.30) ~ Restaurant ~ (01525) 840504 ~ Children welcome ~ Dogs allowed in bar ~ Open 12-midnight(5 Sun); closed Sun evening ~ Bedrooms: £55S/£70S
Recommended by Michael Butler, Michael Dandy, Dave Hollins, David and Diane Young, Ross Balaam

---

BLETSOE   TL0157   MAP 5
Falcon ♀
Rushden Road (A6 N of Bedford); MK44 1QN

Thoughtfully cared-for beamed old place with cheerful attentive service, imaginative food, a decent range of drinks, and extensive riverside garden

French doors lead from this 17th-c building to a sheltered terrace and then to a lovely big grassed area, which works its way down to the slow River Ouse, and has plenty of trees and shrubs, perhaps strolling peafowl. The welcoming bar is comfortably traditional with low beams and joists, bistro tables, seating that ranges from cushioned wall/window seats to high-backed settles, and in winter a couple of open fires – look out for the wild-tongued gargoyles around the one by the front door. A little side snug on the right has sofas and a skittles table, and through on the left there's an attractive panelled dining room. They have Wells & Youngs Eagle and Bombardier on handpump, with a guest such as Everards Tiger, a decent choice of around a dozen wines by the glass, over a dozen malt whiskies and good coffee; daily papers and unobtrusive piped music.

〚¶〛 The tempting menu might include deli plates, imaginative sandwiches, prepared with home-made bread, such as tuna with purple basil jam, black olives and tomato, twice-baked cheese soufflé, thai mussels, filo wrapped haggis with whisky and plum dipping sauce, pumpkin and mushroom risotto in sweet potato cream, beef bourguignon, serrano-wrapped chicken breast with bacon and pâté, stuffing and mushroom sauce and beef fillet on a giant croûton with bacon and mushroom sauce. Puddings might include chocolate truffle torte and treacle tart, and they've a thoughtfully annotated english cheeseboard. *Starters/Snacks: £5.00 to £7.00. Main Courses: £5.00 to £15.00. Puddings: £5.00 to £6.00*

Charles Wells ~ Tenant Brendan Brokenshaw ~ Real ale ~ Bar food (12-2.45, 6-9.15; 12-9 Sun) ~ Restaurant ~ (01234) 781222 ~ Children welcome ~ Dogs welcome ~ Open 11-11 ~ Bedrooms: /£49.95S

Recommended by Meg and Colin Hamilton, Peter Martin, O K Smyth, Dennis and Doreen Haward, Bruce and Sharon Eden, D C Poulton, G Jennings

BOLNHURST

Plough 〚🍴〛 〚🍷〛   TL0858   MAP 5

Kimbolton Road; MK44 2EX

BEDFORDSHIRE DINING PUB OF THE YEAR

Stylish conversion of ancient building with thriving atmosphere, charming staff, top-notch food and drinks, and lovely garden

We can always be sure of good reader reports on this well run ship with its views into the busy kitchen and cheery helpful staff coping admirably in the chatty atmosphere. It's a strikingly beautiful old building, with impressive timbers set off nicely by light and airy contemporary décor. Sourced with care, the range of drinks here includes local Potton Village Bike and a couple of guests such as Adnams and Buntingford on handpump, a very good carefully annotated wine list (inluding organic vintages), with well over a dozen by the glass, home-made lemonade (in summer) and tomato juice, and local apple juice; board games. The attractive tree-shaded garden overlooks a pond, where you can still see the remains of the moat that used to surround the pub.

〚¶〛 Beautifully presented food, from a well balanced changing menu, is prepared using carefully sourced ingredients, some from named producers. Served with complimentary home-made bread and olive oil, dishes work their way up from a few simple dishes such as good fish and chips and rib-eye steak sandwich to tasty canapés such as devils on horseback, starters such as beetroot and cumin soup with garlic yoghurt, confit duck terrine with marinated baby onions and celeriac rémoulade, with main courses such as roast butternut squash with ricotta, cavalo nero and pine nut, garlic and marjoram dressing, chicken with thyme puy lentils and braised savoy cabbage and roast ox cheeks. Puddings might be rhubarb brûlée and honey and Grand Marnier nougat glace with orange compote and sugared almonds, and they've a very good cheese platter; reasonably priced set lunch menu. *Starters/Snacks: £5.75 to £10.95. Main Courses: £11.95 to £18.50. Puddings: £5.00 to £6.95*

Free house ~ Licensees Martin and Jayne Lee and Michael Moscrop ~ Real ale ~ Bar food (12-2, 6.30-9.30) ~ (01234) 376274 ~ Children welcome ~ Dogs allowed in bar ~ Open 12-3, 6.30-11; closed Sun evening, Mon, first two weeks in Jan

Recommended by Ryta Lyndley, Michael Sargent, Carol Beeby, G Jennings, R T and J C Moggridge, J Woodgate

You can send reports directly to us at feedback@goodguides.com

BROOM   TL1743   MAP 5

Cock ★ £

High Street; from A1 opposite northernmost Biggleswade turn-off follow Old Warden 3, Aerodrome 2 signpost, and take first left signposted Broom; SG18 9NA

Friendly village green pub with straightforward tasty food, beers tapped from the cask, and caravanning and camping facilities

The Greene King IPA, Abbot and Ruddles County served at this much-loved traditional little house are tapped straight from casks by the cellar steps off the central corridor – there's no bar counter. Original latch doors lead from one quietly cosy little room to the next (four in all), with warming winter fires, low ochre ceilings, stripped panelling and farmhouse tables and chairs on antique tiles; piped (perhaps classical) music, darts, bar skittles and board games. There are picnic-sets and flower tubs on the terrace by the back lawn.

🍴 **Food is down-to-earth but reasonably priced and tasty; sandwiches, soup, ploughman's, scampi, vegetarian curry and filled yorkshire puddings.** *Starters/Snacks: £3.85 to £6.95. Main Courses: £8.95 to £9.95. Puddings: £3.55 to £3.85*

Greene King ~ Tenants Gerry and Jean Lant ~ Real ale ~ Bar food ~ Restaurant ~ (01767) 314411 ~ Children welcome ~ Dogs welcome ~ Open 12-3(4 Sat, 6 Sun), 6-11; closed Sun evening
Recommended by the Didler

HENLOW   TL1738   MAP 5

Engineers Arms 🍺 £

A6001 S of Biggleswade; High Street; SG16 6AA

Fabulous range of beautifully kept beers and other drinks and snacks (all day) at charmingly spick and span village pub; no smoking garden

Besides their house beers (Caledonian Deuchars IPA and Oakham), guests on the eight to ten handpumps at this traditional local come from a terrific range of smaller, often far-flung brewers such as Buntingford, Cotswold Spring and Potbelly. They also stock five ciders, a perry, many belgian bottled beers and decent wines by the glass. Helpful staff are very knowledgeable about the range, and the pub holds quarterly bank holiday beer festivals, and a bigger one in mid-October; Tyrrells crisps and good coffee. The comfortable green-carpeted front room has lots of old local photographs on its green fleur-de-lys wallpaper, tidily kept and interesting bric-a-brac collections, traditional green-cushioned wall seats, other dark seats, armchair-style bar stools, daily papers and a good log fire. A small tiled inner area has wide-screen TV, and beyond is a step up to another comfortable carpeted area, with a second TV, juke box, silenced fruit machine and board games; the good-natured spaniel is called Chico. The no smoking back terrace has picnic-sets and heaters (smokers have an area in front); more reports please.

🍴 **A limited range of good value snacks, including sausage rolls, pies and pizzas, are served most of the time they are open.** *Starters/Snacks: £1.20 to £5.00*

Free house ~ Licensees Kevin Machin and Claire Sturgeon ~ Real ale ~ Bar food (snacks when open) ~ (01462) 812284 ~ Dogs allowed in bar ~ Occasional music Fri, Sat ~ Open 12-midnight (1am Sat, 10.30 Sun)
Recommended by Michael and Deborah Ethier, Howard Galloway, Andy Lickfold, R T and J C Moggridge

> Post Office address codings confusingly give the impression that some pubs are in Bedfordshire, when they're really in Buckinghamshire or Cambridgeshire (which is where we list them).

IRELAND

Black Horse

Village signposted off A600 Shefford—Bedford; SG17 5QL

Contemporary décor in old building, imaginative food, good wine list, and lovely garden with attractive terraces; bedrooms

Still feeling a little cottagey with its low ceilings and little windows, this picturesque dining pub (in a nice peaceful rural setting) has a gently contemporary style to its furnishings, with stripped wood or stone flooring, ceiling spotlights, a comfortable mix of modern banquettes, bucket chairs and low tables and simple ornaments and lamps, all giving a pleasing feel of spreading spaciousness. Attentive staff serve Adnams and Fullers London Pride, over a dozen wines by the glass and good coffee from the long black bar counter. Outside, the various terraces give a clever sense of garden rooms, with their individual furnishings and mature topiary. One terrace is prettily surrounded by white wicket fencing and gives on to a neatly kept garden with a play area. We'd love to hear from readers about the bedrooms here.

🍴 As well as filled ciabattas, the changing menu might include twice-baked crab soufflé, devilled whitebait, fresh fish of the day, suet pie of the day, herb tagliatelle with chicken and chorizo, mushroom, hazelnut and tarragon strudel, fried duck breast with braised fennel and redcurrant jus and well hung steaks, and puddings such as black forest trifle and raspberry and Drambuie soufflé with clotted cream ice-cream, lavender syrup and oatmeal crisp. *Starters/Snacks: £4.95 to £7.95. Main Courses: £6.50 to £10.95. Puddings: £5.95 to £6.50*

Free house ~ Licensee Jim Campbell ~ Real ale ~ Bar food (12-2.30, 6.30-9.30; 12-5 Sun) ~ Restaurant ~ (01462) 811398 ~ Children welcome ~ Open 11-3, 6-11; 12-5 Sun; closed Sun evening ~ Bedrooms: /£55S

Recommended by Michael Dandy, Eleanor Dandy, Peter and Margaret Glenister, Geoff and Carol Thorp, Michael Sargent, Eithne Dandy, Howard Galloway

NORTHILL

Crown

Ickwell Road; village signposted from B658 W of Biggleswade; SG18 9AA

Prettily situated village pub with nice old interior, inviting atmosphere, enjoyable food, and big child-friendly garden

At this attractive old building, you can choose between the cosy bar (snugly traditional with a big open fire, flagstones, heavy low beams and comfortable bay window seats) and the more formal light walled main dining room with its elegantly laid tables on bare boards. The atmosphere throughout is warm and relaxed with friendly service and fairly unobtrusive piped music. Greene King IPA and Abbot and a guest or two from a brewer such as Holdens on handpump, nine wines by the glass and over 30 malt whiskies are served from the copper-topped counter. A sheltered side terrace (with picnic-sets) opens up into a very large back garden with well spaced canopied tables, plenty of trees and shrubs, a good play area, and masses of room for children to run around. Big tables under cocktail parasols out in front look over the village pond and across to the church, in a green and peaceful village.

🍴 All home made, and where possible prepared with locally sourced ingredients such as free-range meat from a nearby farm, the nicely pubby bar menu includes a good choice of lunchtime sandwiches, tortillas and ciabattas, as well as ploughman's, beef stew, scampi, battered pollack and mushy peas, home-made burger, and daily specials such as breaded chicken breast, and puddings like bread and butter or summer pudding; elaborate restaurant menu. *Starters/Snacks: £3.95 to £6.95. Main Courses: £4.75 to £10.95. Puddings: £4.50*

Greene King ~ Tenant Kevin Blois ~ Real ale ~ Bar food (12-2.30, 6.30-9.30; 12-8 Sun; 12-9.30 Sat in summer) ~ Restaurant ~ (01767) 627337 ~ Children welcome ~ Dogs allowed in bar ~ Open 11.30-3, 6-11; 11.30-11 Sat; 12-11 Sun

Recommended by Michael Dandy, Mrs Margo Finlay, Jörg Kasprowski, Robert Turnham, M and GR, Andy Lickfold, D C Poulton

OLD WARDEN   TL1343   MAP 5

Hare & Hounds 🍴 🍷

Village signposted off A600 S of Bedford and B658 W of Biggleswade; SG18 9HQ

Popular but comfortably elegant dining pub with emphasis on good food served by welcoming well turned-out staff; lovely gardens

Four beautifully kept beamed rooms, with dark standing timbers, work their way around the central servery at this carefully run dining pub. Cleverly blending contemporary styling with the attractive old structure, décor is in cosy reds and creams, with upholstered armchairs and sofas on stripped flooring, light wood tables and coffee tables, a woodburning stove in an inglenook fireplace and fresh flowers on the bar. Prints and photographs depict historic aircraft in the famous Shuttleworth Collection just up the road. Wells & Youngs Eagle IPA and Youngs are on handpump, with a dozen or so wines by the glass including some from a local vineyard; piped music. The pub is part of the 200-year-old swiss-styled Shuttleworth Estate, and the glorious sloping garden (with tables on a terrace and which stretches up to pine woods behind the pub) dates back to the same period and was designed in the same style. Though there's an ample car park, you may need to use the village hall parking as an overflow. There are some substantial walks nearby.

🍴 Food here is thoughtfully prepared and presented. Breads and ice-cream are home made and they make an effort to use local and organic ingredients (such as pork from the Shuttleworth Estate). The changing menus might include tempura squid, goats cheese and potato terrine with red onion marmalade, ploughman's, pie of the day, sausage and mash and battered haddock, spiced chickpea, potato and tomato curry, well-hung steak, and puddings such as warm strawberry bakewell tart or caramelised lemon tart, and a british cheeseboard. *Starters/Snacks: £6.00 to £10.95. Main Courses: £10.95 to £12.95. Puddings: £6.00 to £6.95*

Charles Wells ~ Lease Jane Hurt ~ Real ale ~ Bar food (till 3.30 Sun, not Sun evening) ~ Restaurant ~ (01767) 627225 ~ Children welcome ~ Dogs allowed in bar ~ Open 11.30-3, 6-11; 12-10.30 Sun; closed Mon (except bank hol lunchtimes)

Recommended by Peter and Margaret Glenister, Michael Dandy, P Waterman, Robert Turnham, R T and J C Moggridge, Michael Sargent, Nick Turner, Eithne Dandy, David and Ruth Shillitoe

RAVENSDEN   TL0754   MAP 5

Horse & Jockey 🍷

Village signed off B660 N of Bedford; pub at Church End, off village road; MK44 2RR

Contemporary comfort, with old-fashioned virtues on the food and drinks side

Readers enjoy a drink in the bar before dining at this comfortably refurbished place. Careful lighting, hardwood venetian blinds, modern leather easy chairs in the bar, the quiet colour scheme of olive greys and dark red, the meticulous layout of one wall of old local photographs, and the pleasing chunky tables and high-backed seats in the bright dining room, with its well lit prints and contemporary etched glass screen, all tell you that this is a place where trouble is taken to get things just so. Service is charming, they have a good choice of wines by the glass, guest ales from brewers such as Potbelly and Potton as well as St Austell Tribute and Wells & Youngs on handpump, over 20 wines by the glass, nicely served coffee, and a rack of recent *Country Life* issues as well as daily papers. The dining room overlooks a sheltered terrace with smart modern tables and chairs under cocktail parasols, with a few picnic-sets on the grass beside, and the handsome medieval church in its churchyard just beyond; there is a heated smokers' shelter.

🍴 Sensibly priced enjoyable food includes starters such as devilled whitebait, muffin topped with smoked salmon, a poached egg and hollandaise sauce, main courses such as club sandwich, chicken caesar salad, seafood linguine with creamy white wine sauce, rocket and parmesan, steak and kidney pudding, battered haddock, aberdeen angus burger, and puddings such as pear, fig and pecan frangipane tart or lemon curd tart. *Starters/Snacks: £4.50 to £8.25. Main Courses: £8.75 to £13.95. Puddings: £4.95 to £5.95*

Free house ~ Licensees Darron and Sarah Smith ~ Real ale ~ Bar Food (12-2(3 Sun), 6-9.30
(8 Sun)); ~ (01234) 772319 ~ Children welcome ~ Dogs welcome ~ Open 12-3, 6-11;
12-midnight Sat; 12-11 Sun; 12-3, 6-12 Sat in winter
Recommended by Michael Dandy, Sarah Flynn, Michael Sargent, D C Poulton, Eithne Dandy

RISELEY

TL0462 MAP 5

Fox & Hounds

High Street; village signposted off A6 and B660 N of Bedford; MK44 1DT

Relaxing old pub with emphasis on good steaks; pleasant garden

It's worth arriving here early at peak times (when they don't take bookings) as there may
be a wait for a table. Generally quite traditional, this cheery establishment has timber
uprights under heavy low beams and unobtrusive piped classical or big band music. The
clubby lounge area has comfortable leather chesterfields, low tables and wing chairs. A
decent range of drinks takes in Wells & Youngs Eagle and Bombardier with a guest such
as Youngs on handpump, bin-end wines and a range of malts and cognacs. The
attractively decked terrace has wooden tables and chairs under outside heaters, and the
pleasant garden has shrubs and a pergola.

🍴 The speciality here is steaks. You choose your piece, you pay by weight and you can
watch it being cooked on an open grill. Other good food might include french onion soup,
whitebait, ploughman's, mushroom risotto, grilled dover sole, steak and mushroom pie and
chilli, and puddings such as spotted dick and jam roly-poly; Sunday roast. Even if you don't
see anything you like on the menu it's worth asking as they will try to cope with particular
food requests. *Starters/Snacks: £2.95 to £6.25. Main Courses: £6.95 to £14.75. Puddings: £3.95*

Charles Wells ~ Lease Jan and Lynne Zielinski ~ Real ale ~ Bar food (11.30-1.45, 6.30-9.30
(10 Sat); 12-2, 7-9 Sun) ~ Restaurant ~ (01234) 708240 ~ Children welcome ~ Dogs allowed in
bar ~ Open 11.30-2.30, 6.30-11(11.30 Fri, Sat); 12-3, 7-10.30 Sun
Recommended by John Cook, Michael Sargent, Michael Dandy, Susan and Jeremy Arthern

SOULDROP

SP9861 MAP 4

Bedford Arms 🍺

Village signposted off A6 Rushden—Bedford; High Street; MK44 1EY

Cosy and friendly proper country tavern with good value food in cottagey dining area

With a few regulars settled into the bar chairs by the counter (which has Black Sheep
and Phipps Red Star on handpump alongside a couple of guests such as Greene King IPA
and Elgoods Cambridge and several wines by the glass), there is no doubting the
pubbiness of this place. It's given real heart by its lively welcoming licensee, and is
relaxed and chatty at lunchtime. There are just a few more seats in this small low-beamed
area, including a couple of tables in one very low-ceilinged snug hutch of an alcove. The
cottagey dining area has more low beams (one way through is a real head-cracker if
you're careless) and a central fireplace – and, like the rest of the pub, broad floorboards,
shelves of china, and country prints. In the evenings and at weekends the roomy
mansard-ceilinged public area (once a brew house) perks into life, with well placed hood
skittles, darts and board games; it has a big inglenook fireplace, and opens on to a neat
garden with pretty flower borders. The landlady is fond of her pets – look out for Poky
the cat and out in the garden, JD and Gin and Tonic the rabbits.

🍴 Straightforward bar food includes sandwiches, baguettes and ciabatta, prawn cocktail,
garlic mushrooms, battered cod, cottage pie, chilli, leek and stilton bread and butter
pudding, curries, mixed grill and steaks; Sunday roasts. *Starters/Snacks: £3.50 to £4.95.
Main Courses: £7.25 to £14.95. Puddings: £3.95*

Free house ~ Licensees Sally Rushworth and Fred and Caroline Rich ~ Real ale ~ Bar food (12-2,
6.30-9; 12-4 Sun) ~ (01234) 781384 ~ Children welcome ~ Dogs welcome ~ Open 12-3, 6-11;
12-(11 Sun) midnight Fri, Sat; closed Mon except bank hols when open all day
Recommended by D C Poulton, Richard Tingle

WOBURN   SP9433   MAP 4

Birch ♀

3.5 miles from M1 junction 13; follow Woburn signs via A507 and A4012, then in village turn right and head out on A5130 (Newport Road); MK17 9HX

Well run dining establishment with focus on good imaginative food, good wines and attentive service

There are modern furnishings throughout the extensive linked areas of this neatly kept refurbished pub. You'll find brown leather-dining chairs and sofas on dark hardwood flooring, modern prints on deep red or cream walls, splashes of bright blue dotted around, and a snazzy new West End-style counter. Window blinds keep it all cosy. At the back, an airy conservatory feels a little continental with its ceramic tile floor, light furnishings and glazed pitched roof; unobtrusive piped music and daily papers. They keep a good range of interesting wines by the glass, and Adnams and Fullers London Pride on handpump. There are tables out on a sheltered deck.

🍴 Food is well prepared and nicely presented. **The changing menu might include filled ciabatta, battered fish, fried haloumi, pork belly, local venison, cod and steak, and puddings such as berry meringue soufflé and sticky toffee pudding.** *Starters/Snacks: £7.95 to £9.95. Main Courses: £9.95 to £12.95. Puddings: £5.50 to £6.95*

Free house ~ Licensee Mark Campbell ~ Real ale ~ Bar food (12-2.30, 6-10; 12-5 Sun) ~ Restaurant ~ (01525) 290295 ~ Children welcome ~ Open 12-3, 6-11; 12-5 Sun; closed Sun evening

Recommended by John Saville, Mrs Jane Kingsbury, Geoff and Carol Thorp, Michael Sargent, Eithne Dandy, Ross Balaam

---

LUCKY DIP

Besides the fully inspected pubs, you might like to try these Lucky Dips recommended to us and described by readers (if you do, please send us reports: feedback@goodguides.com).

BEDFORD [TL0549]
Embankment MK40 3PD [The Embankment]: Airy L-shaped bar in refurbished mock-Tudor hotel adjacent to river, mix of modern furniture on wood floor, Wells & Youngs ales, good choice of food inc deli boards and daily roast, nice coffee, cheerful helpful service, back restaurant; piped music; seats out at front, 20 bedrooms (best ones with river views), good breakfast *(Michael Dandy, Eithne Dandy, Martin and Clare Warne)*
Park MK40 2PF [Park Ave/Kimbolton Rd]: Large comfortably modernised pub with mix of furnishings inc leather sofas in partly flagstoned linked areas, enjoyable food from good sandwiches up, good friendly service, well kept Wells & Youngs and guests, decent wines by the glass, daily papers, conservatory eating area (best to book Sun lunch); piped music; garden with tables on decking, open all day *(Eithne Dandy, Andy Lickfold, Revd R P Tickle)*
Wellington Arms MK40 2JX [Wellington St]: Traditional friendly corner local with Adnams, B&T and up to eight guest ales (beer festivals), also bottled continentals, real cider and perry, interesting décor, darts, dominoes, hood skittles, lunchtime rolls (not Sun); no children or mobile phones; back yard, open all day *(S Holder)*
White Horse MK41 9PX [Newnham Ave]:

Welcoming landlord and staff, large open-plan dining area and bar, wide choice of enjoyable sensibly priced food, Wells & Youngs and guests in good condition, beer festivals and other well organised events; garden *(S Holder, Sarah Flynn)*
BIDDENHAM [TL0249]
☆ *Three Tuns* MK40 4BD [off A428]: Straightforward extended village pub under new management, traditionally furnished low-beamed lounge, fairly priced food, Greene King and guests, skittles and darts; piped music, TV; children in dining area, dogs welcome, spacious garden with good play area, picnic-sets on decked terrace *(Paul Dunne, LYM)*
BROMHAM [TL0050]
Swan MK43 8LS [Bridge End; nr A428, 2 miles W of Bedford]: Popular recently refurbished beamed dining pub, wide food choice inc meal deals, good separate restaurant menu, quick friendly service, well kept Greene King ales and a guest, good choice of wines by the glass, log fire, lots of pictures, locals' bar; children welcome, disabled access, picnic-sets out by car park *(Peter Wiser, Howard Galloway)*
CARDINGTON [TL0847]
Kings Arms MK44 3SP [The Green; off A603 E of Bedford]: Comfortably refurbished M&B village dining pub with contemporary rustic

feel, well cooked food inc standard and more enterprising dishes, good choice of wines by the glass, good coffee, well kept Fullers London Pride, Greene King IPA and Timothy Taylors Landlord, helpful friendly staff, attractive linked areas with nice mix of varying-sized tables on bare boards and coir matting, log fire, interesting local airship photographs; well behaved children and dogs welcome, disabled facilities, good tables and chairs out on peaceful front terrace, open all day *(Michael Dandy, D C Poulton, Eithne Dandy, Peter Martin)*

CLOPHILL [TL0837]

Flying Horse MK45 4AD [2 The Green]: Refurbished dining pub with good choice of food inc fixed-price menu (Mon-Thurs till 6), Wells & Youngs Bombardier, several wines by the glass, split level bar with mix of contemporary furniture on wood and stone floors, beams and inglenook log fire, spacious dining areas inc raftered room; open all day *(Michael Dandy)*

Stone Jug MK45 4BY [N on A6 from A507 roundabout, after 200 yds 2nd turn on right into Back St]: Secluded stone-built local, cosy and welcoming, with enjoyable bargain pubby lunchtime food from sandwiches up, good service, well kept ales such as Everards, Fullers, Oldershaws and Skinners, pleasantly unpretentious comfortable bar with family area and darts in small games extension; piped music; small pretty back terrace, roadside picnic-sets *(Howard Galloway, Ross Balaam)*

DUNSTABLE [TL0221]

Victoria LU6 1ST [West St]: Neatly kept little local, comfortable and welcoming, with well kept ales, simple food inc all-day breakfast; darts and cribbage; terrace tables *(David M Smith)*

EATON BRAY [SP9620]

White Horse LU6 2DG [Market Sq]: Wide choice of good fresh food in well run and relaxing old low-beamed and timbered dining pub, suit of armour in one room, well kept ales, decent wines, reasonable prices, friendly helpful staff; ranks of tables on back lawn, good walking nearby *(Stuart Turner)*

FLITTON [TL0535]

☆ *White Hart* MK45 5EJ [Brook Lane]: Simple village pub opp church, leather seating in front bar with well kept ales such as B&T Two Brewers and Youngs, good choice of wines; steps down to good-sized modern dining area with chef-landlord's enterprising food changing daily; TV; good-sized garden with neat shrub borders and well furnished terrace shaded by cedars and weeping willows *(Peter Martin, Eithne Dandy, Michael Dandy, BB)*

HARROLD [SP9456]

Oakley Arms MK43 7BH [between A6 and A428, E of Northampton; High St]: Friendly beamed village local, cosy and comfortable, with several linked areas around central bar, welcoming new landlord, enjoyable pub food, well kept Wells & Youngs and guests;

piped music; quiet garden tables, bedrooms *(Revd R P Tickle, D C Poulton)*

HENLOW [TL1738]

Crown SG16 6BS [High St]: Small inviting pub with good choice of enjoyable all-day food and of wines by the glass, well kept Adnams Broadside and Greene King IPA, good coffee, nice log fire, daily papers; piped music, games machine; terrace and small garden, open all day *(Michael and Deborah Ethier)*

HOUGHTON CONQUEST [TL0441]

☆ *Knife & Cleaver* MK45 3LA [Between B530 (old A418) and A6, S of Bedford]: 17th-c dining pub with cosy dark-panelled bar, drawings and old documents, comfortable seating and a blazing fire, airy conservatory restaurant with hanging plants, family room, seasonal food inc greek dishes and separate seafood menu, cheerful staff, well kept Potton and a guest ale, Stowford Press cider, good choice of wines by the glass and of well aged malt whiskies; unobtrusive piped music; neatly kept garden with terrace, nine bedrooms *(LYM, Robert Turnham, John Branston, Dave Braisted, JCW, Rod Weston, R T and J C Moggridge)*

KEYSOE [TL0763]

☆ *Chequers* MK44 2HR [Pertenhall Rd, Brook End (B660)]: Good value tasty home-made food from sandwiches to blackboard specials in down-to-earth village local with long-serving licensees, two homely comfortably worn-in beamed rooms divided by stone-pillared fireplace, beers such as Boddingtons and Hook Norton, reasonably priced wines; piped music/radio, no credit cards; seats on front lawn and on terrace behind, play area, cl Mon evening, Tues *(Michael and Jenny Back, D C Poulton, LYM)*

LINSLADE [SP9126]

Globe LU7 2TA [off A4146 nr bridge on outskirts]: Refurbished 19th-c pub very popular for nice setting below Grand Union Canal, lots of rooms, beams and flagstones, log and coal fires, several well kept Greene King ales and guests, good winter hot drinks, enjoyable usual food (all day wknds), friendly efficient service; piped music; children welcome in eating areas, disabled facilities, tables up on embankment and in garden, open all day *(Ross Balaam, Michael Dandy, LYM)*

MAULDEN [TL0538]

☆ *Dog & Badger* MK45 2AD [Clophill Rd E of village, towards A6/A507 junction]: Neatly comfortable family pub with welcoming licensees, good home-made pubby food from snacks up inc good value Mon-Sat lunches, Wells & Youngs and guest ales, friendly staff, bare-boards bar with log fire, beams and exposed brickwork, steps down to two carpeted areas and restaurant; piped music; tables out at front (with smart smokers' shelter) and in back garden with sturdy play area *(D C Poulton, B R and M F Arnold, Michael Dandy, Dudley and Moira Cockroft, BB)*

MILLBROOK [TL0138]
Chequers MK45 2JB: Two-room village pub opp golf club, log fire and plate collection in small low-beamed carpeted bar, changing seasonal ales, good coffee, reasonably priced food inc lunch deals, chatty landlord and quick service, back restaurant; piped music *(David and Ruth Shillitoe)*

MILTON BRYAN [SP9730]
Red Lion MK17 9HS [Toddington Rd, off B528 S of Woburn]: Greene King pub between managers as we went to press – news please; beamed traditional interior, dark pub furniture on polished wood, flagstones and red carpets; pretty views from seats on terrace and lawn, has been closed Sun evening *(Peter Serlin, LYM, Gerry and Rosemary Dobson, Michael Dandy)*

OAKLEY [TL0053]
Bedford Arms MK43 7RH [High St]: Large refurbished village pub under new management, pleasant contemporary feel, well kept Wells & Youngs ales, wide choice of good food (especially fish), attentive service *(Peter Martin, Colin and Janet Roe)*

ODELL [SP9657]
Bell MK43 7AS [off A6 S of Rushden, via Sharnbrook; High St]: Popular thatched village pub with several low-beamed rooms around central servery, mix of old settles and neat modern furniture, log or coal fires, good service under friendly licensees, Greene King ales, good choice of generous usual food (not Sun evening) from sandwiches and baked potatoes up; children welcome away from counter, delightful big garden backing on to River Ouse, handy for Harrold-Odell country park *(LYM, Ross Balaam, Anthony Barnes)*

PAVENHAM [SP9955]
Cock MK43 7NJ [High St]: Simple welcoming village pub with well kept real ales and good value tasty food served piping hot *(Peter Martin)*

PEGSDON [TL1130]
☆ ***Live & Let Live*** SG5 3JX [B655 W of Hitchin]: Neatly kept dining pub with wide choice of generous enjoyable food, friendly staff, well kept Adnams, Greene King IPA, Fullers London Pride and Marstons Pedigree, good wine choice, snug traditional tiled and panelled core; piped music; nice terrace and garden below Deacon Hill, great show of hanging baskets and flower tubs, open all day *(LYM, Michael Dandy)*

SALFORD [SP9338]
Red Lion MK17 8AZ [Wavendon Rd]: Small simply decorated red-brick country pub, Wells & Youngs Eagle and Bombardier, good choice of wines, soft drinks and fresh food, log fire, dining room; piped music; hanging baskets and tubs in front, garden tables, six bedrooms *(Gwyn and Anne Wake, Michael Dandy)*
Swan MK17 8BD [not far from M1 junction 13 – left off A5140]: Modernised Peach gastropub doing modest choice of food and wine, Greene King IPA and Wells & Youngs Bombardier, drinking area to right of central servery with sofas and leather chairs,

restaurant to left with contemporary furniture on wood floor; seats outside *(Michael Dandy)*

SHEFFORD [TL1439]
Brewery Tap SG17 5DH [North Bridge St]: No-nonsense L-shaped bar notable for its well kept B&T ales brewed nearby and guest beers; bare-boards and low ceiling, beer bottle collection filling all the ledges, brewery posters and advertisements, chatty staff, no food, live music; picnic-sets out behind, open all day *(Peter Mahaffey)*

STEPPINGLEY [TL0135]
French Horn MK45 5AU [off A507 just N of Flitwick; Church End]: Reopened beamed dining pub, a previous main entry, good food, Greene King ales, more reports please *(LYM, Dave Hollins)*

STUDHAM [TL0215]
Red Lion LU6 2QA [Church Rd]: Open-plan pub in attractive setting below grassy common, bright and cheerful décor in bare-boards front bar, roaring fire, back carpeted dining area, well kept Adnams, Fullers London Pride, Greene King IPA and a guest ale, decent wines, pubby food from sandwiches to steaks, friendly service, darts in small side area; quiet piped music; some garden tables, handy for Whipsnade *(LYM, David Gurr, Ross Balaam)*

TODDINGTON [TL0028]
☆ ***Sow & Pigs*** LU5 6AA [a mile from M1 junction 12; A5120 (Church Sq)]: Greene King and guest ales in traditional town-style bar with mixed furnishings from ecclesiastical-look chairs to button-back leather on worn tiles and boards, open fire, lots of breweriana, food running up to hot-rock steaks and Sun roasts, chatty newish landlord, two log fires, restaurant; children welcome, picnic-sets in small garden, open all day wknds, cl wkdy lunchtimes *(Andy and Jill Kassube, Conor McGaughey, BB)*

TOTTERNHOE [SP9721]
☆ ***Cross Keys*** LU6 2DA [off A505 W of A5; Castle Hill Rd]: Well restored thatched and timbered two-bar pub below remains of a motte and bailey fort, low beams, cosy furnishings, good straightforward food, several real ales inc well kept Adnams Broadside, friendly service, dining room; big-screen TV; good views from large attractive garden *(Ross Balaam, LYM)*

TURVEY [SP9352]
Three Fyshes MK43 8ER [A428 NW of Bedford; Bridge St, W end of village]: Recently refurbished early 17th-c beamed pub, big inglenook with woodburner, mix of easy chairs and upright chairs around tables on tiles or ancient flagstones, enjoyable interesting home-made food (all day wknds), good friendly service, Adnams, Caledonian Deuchars IPA, Courage Best and a local ale, good coffee, daily paper, newly extended restaurant; piped music; dogs welcome, children in eating areas, decking and canopy in charming garden overlooking bridge and mill on Great Ouse, open all day *(Susan and Jeremy Arthern, George Atkinson, Eithne Dandy, LYM)*

Berkshire

You can find quite a choice of pubs here ranging from delightfully unspoilt taverns to cheerful town-centre pubs with a great selection of real ales to civilised dining places for that special meal out. Those doing especially well here this year include the unspoilt and unchanging Bell in Aldworth, the Sun in the Wood in Ashmore Green (enjoyed by customers of all ages), the Hinds Head in Bray (owned by Heston Blumenthal of the nearby Fat Duck restaurant), the Chequers in Cookham Dean (a smashing choice of drinks), the Royal Oak at Paley Street (run by Sir Michael Parkinson's son), and the Winterbourne Arms at Winterbourne (a popular stop from the busy nearby M4). New to the *Guide* this year are the Olde Bell in Hurley (a charming hotel and restaurant with a proper drinkers' bar), the Bull at Sonning (a fine old building close to the Thames), and the Red Lion in Upper Basildon (a Victorian village pub with a smart new makeover and good food). Our Award for Berkshire Dining Pub 2011 goes to the Royal Oak in Paley Street.

ALDWORTH

SU5579   MAP 2

Bell ★ ♀ ◖ £

A329 Reading—Wallingford; left on to B4009 at Streatley; RG8 9SE

Exceptional unspoilt pub, super value snacks, very well kept beers, good quality house wines, lovely friendly atmosphere and nice garden; tends to be busy at weekends

'Just one of the best places on the planet' says one of our readers – and hundreds agree with him. It's a special pub that remains quite unspoilt and unchanging and has been run by the same family for over 250 years – they continue to ban mobile phones, piped music and games machines. The rooms have benches around the panelled walls, beams in the shiny ochre ceiling, an ancient one-handed clock and a woodburning stove. Rather than a bar counter for service, there's a glass-panelled hatch from which they serve the very well kept Arkells BBB and Kingsdown and local West Berkshire Old Tyler, Mild and a monthly guest; also, Upton farm cider, good house wines and maybe winter mulled wine. No draught lager. As you might expect, the pub games here are traditional: darts, shove-ha'penny and dominoes. The quiet, old-fashioned cottagey garden is by the village cricket ground and behind the pub there's a paddock with farm animals. In summer there may be occasional morris dancers, while at Christmas local mummers perform in the road by the ancient well-head (the shaft is sunk 365 feet through the chalk). It tends to get very busy at weekends with a happy mix of customers; dogs must be kept on leads.

🍴 **Excellent value bar food is limited to filled hot crusty rolls and a variety of ploughman's; in winter they also do home-made soup.** *Starters/Snacks: £2.80. Puddings: £3.50*

Free house ~ Licensee H E Macaulay ~ Real ale ~ Bar food (11-2.30, 6(7 Sun)-10) ~ No credit cards ~ (01635) 578272 ~ Children welcome if well behaved ~ Dogs welcome ~ Open 11-3, 6-11; 12-3, 7-10.30 Sun; closed Mon (except bank hol lunchtimes)

Recommended by Michael B Griffith, Samantha McGahan, Michael and Deborah Ethier, the Didler, Mr Ray J Carter, Rob Winstanley, Richard Endacott, Dick and Madeleine Brown, Mr and Mrs H J Langley

ASHMORE GREEN   SU4969   MAP 2

Sun in the Wood ♀

B4009 (Shaw Road) off A339, then right on to Kiln Road, then left on to Stoney Lane. Pub 1 mile on left; RG18 9HF

Cheery family pub with a genuine mix of customers, plenty of room, tasty food, beer and wine, and friendly licensees; big garden

There's a loyal following from regular customers of all ages plus plenty of visitors too in this very well run country pub – and after 14 years, the hard-working licensees and their attentive staff remain just as enthusiastic. The high-beamed front bar is comfortable and unimposing and has bare boards on the left, carpet on the right, and a mix of nice old chairs, padded dining chairs and stripped pews around sturdy tables. It opens into a big back dining area which has the same informal feel, candles on tables, and some interesting touches like the big stripped bank of apothecary's drawers. There's a small conservatory sitting area by the side entrance. Wadworths IPA, 6X and a guest beer are well kept on handpump, and they offer a fine choice of wines by the glass. Outside, the attractive decked terrace has seats under green parasols, heaters, plenty of flowering tubs, and old-fashioned street lights, and there's a big woodside garden with lots of picnic-sets, a small child-free area, and a popular nine-hole woodland crazy golf pitch. It's hard to believe the pub is only a few minutes away from the centre of Newbury.

🍴 **Popular and enjoyable, the bar food includes soup, garlic mushrooms in creamy white wine sauce, salmon and haddock fishcake with a dill and lime crème fraîche dressing, butternut squash stuffed with mushroom, spinach and goats cheese, steak and kidney or fish pies, fresh haddock in crispy beer batter, lambs liver with crispy bacon and onion gravy, venison on smoky bacon mash with port and cranberry sauce, and puddings like dark chocolate and Bailey's cappuccino mousse and fresh fruit salad with a slash of vodka and pink grapefruit ice-cream. Thursday is steak night and they offer two- and three-course Sunday lunches.** *Starters/Snacks: £4.50 to £6.00. Main Courses: £8.95 to £10.95. Puddings: £4.95 to £5.50*

Wadworths ~ Tenant Philip Davison ~ Real ale ~ Bar food (12-2, 6-9.30; 12-4 Sun; not Mon) ~ Restaurant ~ (01635) 42377 ~ Children welcome ~ Open 12-3, 6-11; 12-11 Sat; 12-5 Sun; closed Sun evening and Mon

Recommended by Mary Dyke, Evelyn and Derek Walter, Douglas and Ann Hare, Ian Herdman, R T and J C Moggridge, Dave Braisted

BRAY   SU9079   MAP 2

Crown

1.75 miles from M4 junction 9; A308 towards Windsor, then left at Bray signpost on to B3028; High Street; SL6 2AH

Low-beamed, busy pub with roaring log fires in knocked-through rooms, real ales and popular food

Although many customers are here to enjoy the bar food, some tables in this 14th-c dining pub are set aside for drinkers. The partly panelled main bar has oak tables and leather-backed armchairs, and one dining area has photographs of World War II aeroplanes. Some of its heavy old beams are so low you may have to mind your head, and there are plenty of timbers handily left at elbow height where walls have been knocked through. The three roaring winter log fires are extremely cosy. Courage Best and Directors on handpump are served alongside a guest such as Wadworths 6X and a decent choice of wines. There are tables and benches out in a sheltered flagstoned front courtyard (which has a flourishing grape vine) and in the large back garden. More reports please.

Post Office address codings confusingly give the impression that some pubs are in Berkshire, when they're really in Buckinghamshire, Oxfordshire or Hampshire (which is where we list them).

🍴 **Popular bar food includes soup, home-made pâté, moules marinière, grilled goats cheese on peppered pineapple with raspberry vinaigrette, oriental warm chicken salad, tagliatelle with fresh tomatoes, mushrooms, basil and chilli sauce, wild boar sausages, beef in Guinness pie, fresh fish of the day, slow-cooked lamb shoulder with mint gravy, and king prawns in garlic butter.** *Starters/Snacks: £5.50 to £11.50. Main Courses: £8.95 to £19.95. Puddings: £3.50 to £4.95*

Scottish Courage ~ Lease John and Carole Noble ~ Real ale ~ Bar food (not Sun or Mon evenings) ~ Restaurant ~ (01628) 621936 ~ Children welcome ~ Dogs allowed in bar ~ Open 11-3, 6-11; 12-3, 7-10.30 Sun; closed 25 and 26 Dec, 1 Jan
Recommended by Ron and Sheila Corbett

Hinds Head 🍴 ⛾

High Street; car park opposite (exit rather tricky); SL6 2AB

Top-notch gastropub with excellent british food, traditional surroundings, a fine choice of drinks, and efficient service

As we went to press a new licensee was due to take over this handsome old pub. The excellent food has been quite a draw and given that the renowned Fat Duck restaurant nearby is under the same ownership, we would not expect that to change. But if all you want is a drink and chat then you will be made just as welcome. The thoroughly traditional L-shaped bar has dark beams and panelling, polished oak parquet, blazing log fires, red-cushioned built-in wall seats and studded leather carving chairs around small round tables, and latticed windows. Fullers London Pride, Greene King St Edmunds and Rebellion IPA on handpump, 14 interesting wines by the glass from an extensive list, quite a few malt whiskies and a fine choice of teas and coffees. More reports please.

🍴 **Extremely good, the popular food includes snacks like devils on horseback or scotch egg, sandwiches, soup, duck and smoked guinea fowl terrine with spiced apples, tea-smoked salmon with soda bread, potted shrimps with watercress salad, oxtail and kidney pudding, venison cheeseburger, whole lemon sole roasted with garlic and thyme, specials such as grilled cuttlefish salad with pickled lemon, and puddings like sussex pond pudding and chocolate wine slush with millionaire shortbread.** *Starters/Snacks: £6.35 to £9.50. Main Courses: £11.95 to £29.50. Puddings: £6.50 to £8.95*

Free house ~ Real ale ~ Bar food (12-2.30, 6.30-9.30; 12-4 Sun; not Sun evening) ~ Restaurant ~ (01628) 626151 ~ Children welcome ~ Dogs allowed in bar ~ Open 11-11; 12-10.30 Sun; closed 25 and 26 Dec
Recommended by Andy and Claire Barker, Mr Ray J Carter, Simon Rodway, Les Scott-Maynard

COOKHAM DEAN   SU8785   MAP 2

Chequers 🍴 ⛾

Dean Lane; from Cookham follow signpost Cookham Dean, Marlow (unsuitable for heavy vehicles); SL6 9BQ

Restauranty pub with well liked food, fine choice of drinks, friendly staff and cosy bar

This is a friendly dining pub run by professional, helpful staff and, although much emphasis is on the imaginative food, you will be welcome if it's just a chatty drink you want. The compact bar has beams and flagstones and comfortable old sofas, and on the mixed dining tables on either side of the bar there are fresh flowers and crisp white linen; a relaxed atmosphere and maybe piped music. The area on the left, with an open stove in its big brick fireplace, leads back into a conservatory that looks on to the neat slope of the lawn. Adnams Bitter, Marlow Rebellion IPA and St Austells Tribute on handpump, quite a few wines by the glass, smashing bloody mary's with ten infused vodkas to choose from, all sorts of cocktails, ten single malt whiskies, and good coffees and teas. There are picnic-sets outside, some on a front terrace.

🍴 **Interesting bar food might includes soup, spiced potted shrimps, tempura beef strips with sweet chilli sauce, roasted butternut squash, mascarpone and toasted pine nut** risotto, beer-battered fish, cumberland spiced sausages with ham hock, cheddar mash and onion gravy, calves liver and smoked bacon with red wine jus, gressingham duck breast with blood orange and redcurrant jus, and puddings such as cambridge burnt cream and treacle sponge and custard. *Starters/Snacks: £4.95 to £7.95. Main Courses: £10.95 to £22.95. Puddings: £4.95 to £6.95*

Free house ~ Licensee Peter Roehrig ~ Real ale ~ Bar food (12-2.30, 6.30-9.30(10 Fri and Sat); 12-6 Sun; not Sun evening) ~ Restaurant ~ (01628) 481232 ~ Children welcome ~ Open 11-3, 5.30-11; 11-11.30 Sat; 11-6.30 Sun; closed Sun evening

Recommended by Paul Humphreys, Chris Sale, Hugh Roberts, P Waterman, Humphry and Angela Crum Ewing, Hunter and Christine Wright, David A Hammond

FRILSHAM   SU5573   MAP 2

Pot Kiln 🍽 🍺

From Yattendon take turning S, opposite church, follow first Frilsham signpost, but just after crossing motorway go straight on towards Bucklebury ignoring Frilsham signposted right; pub on right after about half a mile; RG18 0XX

Country dining pub, bustling little bar, local beers, and imaginative bar and restaurant dishes; suntrap garden and nearby walks

Despite its surprisingly isolated position, this well run country pub fills up quickly with customers keen to enjoy the good interesting food. But there are also plenty of friendly locals who gather in the little bar where they offer West Berkshire Brick Kiln Bitter, Mr Chubbs Lunchtime Bitter and Maggs Magnificent Mild, and a weekly changing guest beer on handpump. The main bar area has dark wooden tables and chairs on bare boards, and a good winter log fire, and the extended lounge is open plan at the back and leads into a large, pretty dining room with a nice jumble of old tables and chairs, and an old-looking stone fireplace; darts and board games. This is a charming rural spot, and seats in the big suntrap garden have good views of forest and meadows; nearby walks.

🍽 Using home-made bread, some home-grown vegetables, and venison shot by the landlord, the imaginative food includes soup, filled rolls, ploughman's, game sausages, a sharing platter of pig cheeks, muntjac cutlets, ham hock terrine and truffled duck egg, caramelised red onion and Montgomery cheese tart, venison burger with celeriac remoulade, saddleback pork chop marinated in oregano and lemon with white beans and spinach, monkfish with black butter, capers and anchovies, and puddings like hazelnut brownie with amaretto cream or sticky toffee pudding with cardamom ice-cream; they also offer two- and three-course lunchtime options. *Starters/Snacks: £3.00 to £6.00. Main Courses: £6.00 to £10.00. Puddings: £5.50*

Free house ~ Licensees Mr and Mrs Michael Robinson ~ Real ale ~ Bar food (12-2.30, 6.30-8.30; 12-2.30 Sun; not Sun evening, not Tues) ~ Restaurant ~ (01635) 201366 ~ Children welcome ~ Dogs allowed in bar ~ Open 12-3, 6-11; 12-11 Sat; 12-10.30 Sun; closed 6pm Sun in winter; closed Tues

Recommended by Robert Watt, Ben Andrews, Samantha McGahan, the Didler, Graham and Toni Sanders, Neil and Karen Dignan, N R White, Paul Humphreys

HENLEY   SU7682   MAP 2

Little Angel 🍷

Remenham Lane (A4130, just over bridge E of Henley); RG9 2LS

Relaxed linked contemporary areas plus attractive conservatory, modern bar food, helpful service, real ales, and several wines by the glass

There's a good mix of both drinkers and diners in this civilised and rather smart place and this creates an informal, chatty atmosphere. It's all very attractive and more or less open-plan but with several clearly distinct seating areas. There's a mix of well spaced dining and wooden chairs and tables on the bare, light boards, comfortable bar chairs, tub chairs and sofas, and quite a bit of artwork on the creamy yellow walls. In one corner a case of art books and the like helps to set the tone. There's a winter woodburning stove, fresh flowers, and an airy conservatory. The attractive curved bar counter has a good choice of wines by the glass (plus champagne), cocktails, and Brakspears Bitter, Special and Oxford Gold on handpump; board games, unobtrusive piped music, TV, and prompt, attentive service. A sheltered floodlit back terrace has tables under cocktail parasols, looking over to the local cricket ground.

🍴 Using local seasonal produce and game from the Hambledon Estate, the bar food includes lunchtime sandwiches and ploughman's, eggs benedict, salt and pepper squid with coriander and lime dressing, cumberland sausages with red onion gravy, risotto of mediterranean vegetables with goats cheese, steak and kidney suet pudding, slow-cooked pork belly with crackling and madeira jus, salmon with a crayfish and chive vanilla beurre blanc, and puddings like tamarind rice pudding with grilled white peach and vanilla and bay leaf crème brûlée with their own shortbread. *Starters/Snacks: £4.95 to £8.95. Main Courses: £9.95 to £17.95. Puddings: £5.50*

Brakspears ~ Lease Douglas and Lolly Green ~ Real ale ~ Bar food ~ Restaurant ~ (01491) 411008 ~ Children allowed but must be well behaved ~ Dogs allowed in bar ~ Open 11-11(midnight Sat); 12-10 Sun
Recommended by Roy Hoing, Simon Collett-Jones, Neil and Karen Dignan, Chris Glasson, Peter and Judy Frost, Ian Phillips

HUNGERFORD

SU3368   MAP 2

Plume of Feathers

High Street; street parking opposite; RG17 0NB

An oasis in this appealing small town, with good home cooking and a relaxed family atmosphere

Well liked by chatty regulars but with a welcome for visitors too, this open-plan place stretches from its smallish bow-windowed façade around the island bar to an open fire in the stripped fireplace right at the back. There are armchairs and a black leather sofa around low tables under lowish beams on the left at the front and a mix of tables with padded chairs or cushioned small pews on the bare boards elsewhere. They have a fair choice of wines by the glass alongside Greene King IPA and Ruddles Best on handpump and good coffee, and the scottish landlord and staff are friendly and helpful. The sheltered back courtyard isn't large but is well worth knowing on a warm day: prettily planted, and with a swing seat as well as green-painted metal tables and chairs.

🍴 Carefully cooked bar food includes lunchtime filled panini and a sandwich of the day, filled baked potatoes, ploughman's, soup, ham hock terrine with home-made chutney, crab with avocado purée and a mango and chilli salsa, home-made burger with cheese, seafood pie, liver and bacon, spatchcocked poussin with a changing sauce, gammon and free-range eggs, and puddings like banana toffee pudding or lemon cheesecake; Sunday roasts. *Starters/Snacks: £4.95 to £5.95. Main Courses: £7.95 to £16.95. Puddings: £5.25*

Greene King ~ Lease Haley and Jimmy Weir ~ Real ale ~ Bar food (12-2.30(4 Sun), 7-9; not Sun evening) ~ (01488) 682154 ~ Children welcome ~ Dogs welcome ~ Open 11-3, 5.30(6 Sat)-11(midnight Fri and Sat); 12-4 Sun; closed Sun evening
Recommended by Anne Morton, I D Barnett, Chris and Martin Taylor, Richard Tilbrook, Clive and Fran Dutson

HURLEY

SU8283   MAP 2

Olde Bell 🛏

High Street; village signposted from A4130; SL6 5LX

Charming hotel with informal, relaxed bar, good choice of drinks, bistro-style cooking, and big garden; bedrooms

Dating from the 12th century and attractively timbered, this is a charming hotel and restaurant but with a thriving bar at its heart. This properly old-fashioned little bar has massive beams, simple but elegant seats and rustic tables on quarry tiles, with a rocking chair and tall farmhouse ones by the log fire, Rebellion IPA on handpump, good malt whiskies, vintage ports and properly mixed cocktails. The dignified communicating lounge has comfortable chintz armchairs and sofas and several smaller seats, and there are various nooks and crannies, bare floorboards, and more open fires. The carefully thought-out, shabby-chic style and straightforward furnishings add to the informal and relaxed feel of the place – though by contrast the dining room is clean-cut and modern. There's a large back terrace with sturdy oak furniture and a big barbecue that leads to a meadow garden with a flower-arbour walk and a dining tent on the lawn (flooring and heaters are added in cooler weather). The Thames-side village is attractive to walk through, and has a regatta on the middle Saturday in August.

📋 As well as sandwiches, soup, ploughman's and a house terrine, the enjoyable bistro-style food includes deep-fried squid and aioli, potato and stinking bishop (cheese) pie, coq au vin, rare roast venison with duck fat potato cake and red cabbage, calves liver, seven-hour shoulder of lamb, lemon sole with caper butter, and puddings like raspberry queen of puddings and banana and chocolate cake. *Starters/Snacks: £3.00 to £7.50. Main Courses: £7.50 to £14.00. Puddings: £5.00 to £8.00*

Dhillon ~ Manager Salim Shaik ~ Real ale ~ Bar food (10am-10pm; restaurant shut 3-6.30 and Sun evening) ~ Restaurant ~ (01628) 825881 ~ Children welcome ~ Dogs welcome ~ Open 10am-11.30pm(11pm Sun) ~ Bedrooms: /£99B

Recommended by Susan and John Douglas

INKPEN   SU3764   MAP 2

Crown & Garter 🍺 🛏

Inkpen Common: Inkpen signposted with Kintbury off A4; in Kintbury turn left into Inkpen Road, then keep on into Inkpen Common; RG17 9QR

Remote-feeling pub with appealing layout, lovely garden and nearby walks, local ales, nicely lit bars, and especially friendly landlady

You can be sure of a friendly welcome from the helpful landlady of this attractive old 16th-c brick pub. The low-ceilinged and relaxed panelled bar has West Berkshire Mr Chubbs Lunchtime Bitter and Good Old Boy and a guest such as Arkells Moonlight on handpump, decent wines by the glass and several malt whiskies. Three areas radiate from here; our pick is the parquet-floored part by the raised woodburning stove which has a couple of substantial old tables and a huge old-fashioned slightly curved settle. Other parts are slate and wood with a good mix of well spaced tables and chairs, and nice lighting. There's a front terrace for outside eating, a lovely long side garden with picnic-sets, and plenty of good downland walks nearby. In a separate single-storey building, the bedrooms (many have been redecorated recently) form an L around a pretty garden. James II is reputed to have used the pub on his way to visit his mistress locally.

📋 Bar food includes filled baguettes, soup, devilled whitebait, shepherd's pie, vegetable curry, haddock and chips with mushy peas, local sausages, and steak and kidney pudding. *Starters/Snacks: £4.95 to £7.95. Main Courses: £9.95 to £19.95. Puddings: £4.95 to £6.95*

Free house ~ Licensee Gill Hern ~ Real ale ~ Bar food (not Sun evening or Mon/Tues lunchtimes) ~ Restaurant ~ (01488) 668325 ~ Children allowed in bar only but must be over 7 evenings and in bedrooms ~ Dogs allowed in bar ~ Open 12-3, 5.30-11; 12-5, 7-10.30 Sun; closed Mon and Tues lunchtimes ~ Bedrooms: £69.50B/£99B

Recommended by Michael and Deborah Ethier, Paul Boot, I H G Busby, Julia and Richard Tredgett, Mr and Mrs H J Langley, Mr and Mrs P D Titcomb

> If a service charge is mentioned prominently on a menu or accommodation terms, you must pay it if service was satisfactory. If service is really bad, you are legally entitled to refuse to pay some or all of the service charge as compensation for not getting the service you might reasonably have expected.

PALEY STREET

SU8676 MAP 2

Royal Oak 🍽 🍷
B3024 W; SL6 3JN

BERKSHIRE DINING PUB OF THE YEAR

Friendly pub with informal bar, good choice of wines, excellent british cooking in smarter dining areas, and helpful service

Although there is a little bar, most people come to this attractively modernised 17th-c pub to enjoy the excellent food. It's very stylish and popular and owned by Sir Michael Parkinson and his son Nick. The atmosphere is relaxed and friendly and the smallish bar is informal, with beams, an open fire, leather sofas, Fullers London Pride on handpump and a wide choice of wines (and champagne) by the glass; helpful service. The dining room stretches back with a mix of well spaced wooden tables and leather dining chairs on bare boards or flagstones, and brick pillars and timbering split the room into different areas; piped jazz.

First-rate british cooking using seasonal produce includes scotch eggs, soup, potted crab with rosemary and sea salt toast, lasagne of rabbit with wild mushrooms and chervil, rosary cheese pasty with buttered leeks and pumpkin seed salad, halibut with samphire, cockles and mussels, haunch of venison with creamed spinach and pepper sauce, and puddings like chocolate fondant with toffee sauce and pistachio ice-cream or baked alaska. They also offer a good value two- and three-course set lunch. *Starters/Snacks: £3.50 to £14.00. Main Courses: £12.50 to £24.00. Puddings: £6.00 to £8.50*

Fullers ~ Lease N D Parkinson ~ Real ale ~ Bar food (12-2.30, 6-9.30 (10 Fri and Sat); 12-3.30 Sun; not Sun evening) ~ Restaurant ~ (01628) 620541 ~ Children welcome but no pushchairs in restaurant ~ Open 12-3, 6-11(midnight Sat); 12-5 Sun; closed Sun evening and 1-5 Jan

Recommended by David and Sue Smith, David Tindal, Peter Sampson

READING

SU7173 MAP 2

Hobgoblin
2 Broad Street; RG1 2BH

No-frills pub with small panelled rooms, cheerful atmosphere and quickly changing ales

Not surprisingly, this cheerfully basic town pub does get very busy – especially at weekends. It's the fine range of up to eight real ales that draws in the customers and on handpump these might include West Berkshire Gibbet, Good Old Boy, and Maggs Magnificent Mild, plus Allgates Unhinged, Pilgrim Weald Ale, Red Squirrel IPA and Storm Pale Ale. Pump clips cover practically every inch of the walls and ceiling of the simple bare-boards bar – a testament to the enormous number of brews that have passed through the pumps over the years (now over 6,000). They've also lots of different bottled beers, czech lager on tap, Weston's farm cider, perry and country wines. Up a step is a small seating area, but the best places to sit are the three or four tiny panelled rooms reached by a narrow corridor leading from the bar; cosy and intimate, each has barely enough space for one table and a few chairs or wall seats, but they're very appealing if you're able to bag one; the biggest also manages to squeeze in a fireplace; piped music and TV.

No food.

Community Taverns ~ Manager Katrina Fletcher ~ Real ale ~ No credit cards ~ (0118) 950 8119 ~ Open 11-11; 12-10.30 Sun

Recommended by the Didler, Simon Collett-Jones, Dr and Mrs A K Clarke

SU7976   MAP 2

Royal Oak

Ruscombe Lane (B3024 just E of Twyford); RG10 9JN

Wide choice of popular food at welcoming pub with interesting furnishings and paintings and adjoining antiques and collectables shop

Run by licensees who care about their customers and their pub, this is a welcoming and interestingly decorated place. The open-plan carpeted interior is well laid out so that each bit is fairly snug, but still manages to keep the overall feel of a lot of people enjoying themselves. A good variety of furniture runs from dark oak tables to big chunky pine ones with mixed seating to match – the two sofas facing one another are popular. Contrasting with the old exposed ceiling joists, mostly unframed modern paintings and prints decorate the walls – mainly dark terracotta over a panelled dado. Fullers London Pride and a couple of guests from breweries such as Hogs Back and Rebellion on handpump and a dozen nicely chosen wines (including champagne) by the glass. Picnic-sets are ranged around a venerable central hawthorn in the garden behind (where there are ducks and chickens); summer barbecues. The landlady's antiques and collectables shop is open during pub hours. The pub is on the Henley Arts Trail.

[] Using their own eggs and some local produce, the good, popular bar food includes sandwiches and panini, soup, ploughman's, ham and egg, stilton and bacon burger, and sausages and mash with caramelised onion gravy, with more elaborate choices such as cured meats with olives, black pudding stack with wholegrain mustard mash and peppered sauce, fillet of salmon with a prawn and chive sauce, leek and mushroom stroganoff, lamb shank with rosemary jus, and puddings such as pancakes filled with ice-cream and chocolate sauce. *Starters/Snacks: £3.00 to £9.95. Main Courses: £6.50 to £9.95. Puddings: £4.95 to £5.95*

Enterprise ~ Lease Jenny and Stefano Buratta ~ Real ale ~ Bar food (12-2.30, 5.30-9.30; 12-3 Sun; not Sun or Mon evenings) ~ Restaurant ~ (0118) 934 5190 ~ Children welcome ~ Dogs welcome ~ Open 12-3, 6-11; 12-5 Sun; closed Sun and Mon evenings
Recommended by Miss A Hawkes, Paul Humphreys, John Branston

SU7367   MAP 2

Magpie & Parrot ◀

2.6 miles from M4 junction 11, via B3270; A327 just SE of Shinfield – heading out on Arborfield Road, keep eyes skinned for small hand-painted green Nursery sign on left, and Fullers 'bar open' blackboard; RG2 9EA

Unusual homely little roadside cottage with warm fire, lots of bric-a-brac in cosy small bars and hospitable landlady

You enter this homely and unusual little cottage through a lobby with its antiquated telephone equipment and will probably be greeted by Aitch the pub dog. A cosy and inviting high-raftered room has a handful of small polished tables and a comfortable mix of individualistic seats from Georgian oak thrones to a red velveteen sofa, not to mention the armchair with the paw-printed cushion reserved for Aitch. Everything is spic and span, from the brightly patterned carpet to the plethora of interesting bric-a-brac covering the walls: miniature and historic bottles, dozens of model cars, veteran AA badges and automotive instruments, and mementoes of a pranged Spitfire (do ask about its story – they love to chat here). Fullers London Pride and Timothy Taylors Landlord on handpump at the small corner counter. There are teak tables on the back terrace and an immaculate lawn beyond where there is now a purpose-built marquee; they may have hog roasts and morris men at various summer events and two beer festivals in June and December with 22 real ales; aunt sally. Note the unusual opening hours.

[] Lunchtime bar food includes toasties, pies, ham and egg, and so forth, and on Thursday and Friday evenings they offer fish and chips. *Starters/Snacks: £3.95 to £7.50*

Free house ~ Licensee Mrs Carole Headland ~ Real ale ~ Bar food (12-2 but they also offer Thurs and Fri early evening fish and chips; not Sat or Sun) ~ No credit cards ~ (0118) 988 4130 ~ Dogs welcome ~ Open 12-7.30; 12-4 Sun; closed evenings

Recommended by Susan and John Douglas, the Didler, Dr and Mrs A K Clarke, Simon Collett-Jones

SONNING   SU7575   MAP 2

Bull 🛏️

Off B478, by church; village signed off A4 E of Reading; RG4 6UP

Pretty timbered inn in attractive spot near Thames, plenty of character in old-fashioned bars, Fullers beers, friendly staff and good food; bedrooms

When the wisteria is out, this 16th-c black and white timbered inn looks especially pretty, and the courtyard is bright with tubs of flowers; plenty of outside seating. Inside, the two old-fashioned bar rooms have low ceilings and heavy beams, cosy alcoves, leather armchairs and sofas, cushioned antique settles and low wooden chairs on bare boards, and open fireplaces. The dining room has a mix of wooden chairs and tables, rugs on parquet flooring, and shelves of books. Fullers Chiswick, Discovery, HSB, London Pride and a couple of guests on handpump served by friendly staff. If you bear left through the ivy-clad churchyard opposite, then turn left along the bank of the River Thames, you come to a very pretty lock.

🍴 **Good bar food includes sandwiches and light bites such as duck liver parfait with onion and cranberry chutney, a seafood basket and a plate of cured meats (these are served all day), as well as soup, potted rabbit and pheasant, ham with poached egg and dauphinoise potatoes, spinach and ricotta cannelloni, cumberland sausage with beer and onion gravy, steak and venison or fish pies, duck cassoulet, and puddings like sticky toffee pudding with white chocolate ice-cream.** *Starters/Snacks: £5.95 to £9.50. Main Courses: £10.00 to £18.00. Puddings: £5.50 to £8.00*

Gales (Fullers) ~ Manager Dennis Mason ~ Real ale ~ Bar food (all day) ~ Restaurant ~ (0118) 969 3901 ~ Children welcome ~ Dogs allowed in bar ~ Open 11-11(11.30 Fri and Sat); 12-10.30 Sun ~ Bedrooms: /£99S(£125B)

Recommended by Jennifer Banks, Simon Collett-Jones, Susan and John Douglas

STANFORD DINGLEY   SU5771   MAP 2

Old Boot

Off A340 via Bradfield, coming from A4 just W of M4 junction 12; RG7 6LT

Neat pub with emphasis on imaginative food; country furnishings and rural garden views

An interesting choice of popular food is the main draw to this stylish 18th-c pub and many of the tables are laid for dining. But the beamed bar has two welcoming fires (one in an inglenook), fine old pews, settles, old country chairs and polished tables, as well as some striking pictures and hunting prints, boot ornaments and fresh flowers. Three real ales might include West Berkshire Good Old Boy, Wadworths 6X, and a changing guest on handpump; several wines by the glass. There are seats in the quiet sloping back garden or on the terrace, and pleasant rural views; more tables out in front.

🍴 **Good, interesting bar food includes filled baguettes, soup, grilled sardines on warm potato salad with anchovy vinaigrette, deep-fried brie with mango salsa, pork stir fry with noodles, fresh haddock in tempura batter, wild mushroom risotto with broad beans, popular tiger prawn and smoked salmon linguine, duck leg confit with red berry veal jus, ostrich fillet with caramelised onions and red wine jus, and puddings like bread and butter pudding with crème anglaise and apple tarte tatin with vanilla pod ice-cream.** *Starters/Snacks: £5.95 to £8.95. Main Courses: £8.95 to £11.95. Puddings: £5.95*

Free house ~ Licensee John Haley ~ Real ale ~ Bar food ~ Restaurant ~ (0118) 974 4292 ~ Children welcome ~ Dogs allowed in bar ~ Open 11-3, 6-11; 12-11 Sun ~ Bedrooms: /£50B

Recommended by T R and B C Jenkins, Neil and Karen Dignan

UPPER BASILDON
SU5976   MAP 2

Red Lion ♀ ◖
Off A329 NW of Pangbourne; Aldworth Road; RG8 8NG

Laid-back country pub with friendly family atmosphere, some inventive food, good drinks

The informal gastropub makeover here features chapel chairs, a few pews and miscellaneous stripped tables on the bare boards, a green leather chesterfield and armchair, and pale blue-grey paintwork throughout – even on the beams, ceiling, some of the top-stripped tables, and the wicker bar stools where the regulars hang out with their dogs. Beyond a double-sided woodburning stove, a pitched-ceiling area has much the same furniture on cord carpet, but a big cut-glass chandelier and large mirror give it a slightly more formal dining feel. Changing ales such as Brakspears, Otter, Timothy Taylors Landlord and West Berkshire Good Old Boy on handpump, and an extensive wine list; the *Independent* and *Racing Post*, occasional piped music, regular live – usually jazz-related. There are sturdy picnic-sets in the sizeable enclosed garden, where they have summer barbecues and hog roasts.

🍴 **Using local produce, the enjoyable food might include a good rare roast beef sandwich, soup, rabbit, black pudding and pistachio terrine with apricot and ginger, various platters, a pie of the week, egg and sausages with bubble and squeak and red wine gravy, home-made burgers with onions, bacon or melted cheese, marinated chicken with aioli, specials such as a warm pigeon, chorizo and duck egg starter salad and butternut squash, spinach and courgette curry, and puddings like coffee crème brûlée and sticky toffee pudding with toffee sauce; bar nibbles, Sunday roasts.** *Starters/Snacks: £4.50 to £8.50. Main Courses: £8.50 to £16.50. Puddings: £5.50*

Enterprise ~ Lease Alison Green ~ Real ale ~ Bar food (12-2.30, 6-9.30(10 Fri and Sat); 12-3, 6-9 Sun) ~ Restaurant ~ (01491) 671234 ~ Children welcome ~ Dogs allowed in bar ~ Open 11-3, 5-11; 12-10.30 Sun
Recommended by Julia and Richard Tredgett, I H G Busby, Gene and Kitty Rankin

WHITE WALTHAM
SU8477   MAP 2

Beehive ◖
Waltham Road (B3024 W of Maidenhead); SL6 3SH

Honest bar food and welcoming staff at traditional village pub

You can be sure of a friendly welcome from the landlord and his staff in this solidly run country local, and although food is important, this is very much a proper pub. To the right, several comfortably and recently redecorated spacious areas have leather chairs around sturdy tables, and there's a conservatory. The neat bar to the left is brightened up by cheerful scatter cushions on its comfortable built-in wall seats and captain's chairs. Brakspears Bitter, Fullers London Pride, Greene King Abbot and a changing guest from Loddon on handpump, with a good choice of soft drinks; piped music, board games and a quiz evening on the last Thursday of the month. Picnic-sets and teak seats out in front on the terrace take in the pub's rather fine topiary, and there are more seats on a good-sized sheltered back lawn; disabled access and facilities.

🍴 **Well liked honest bar food includes sandwiches, soup, chicken liver pâté, seared scallops and shrimps with chorizo, filled baked potatoes, burgers, home-baked ham and eggs, steak and kidney pie, home-made fishcakes, lamb rump on a field mushroom with parsnip and parmesan rösti, medallions of venison with red wine and rosemary jus, and puddings like fruit crumble; Sunday roasts.** *Starters/Snacks: £2.00 to £6.95. Main Courses: £8.95 to £10.95. Puddings: £2.95 to £6.95*

Enterprise ~ Lease Guy Martin ~ Real ale ~ Bar food (12-2.30, 5-9.30; 12-9.30(8.30 Sun) Sat) ~ Restaurant ~ (01628) 822877 ~ Children welcome ~ Dogs allowed in bar ~ Open 10.30-3.30, 5-11; 10.30-12 Sat; 12-11 Sun
Recommended by Stan Edwards, Paul Humphreys, June and Robin Savage, Miss A Hawkes, Richard and Liz Thorne, Dr and Mrs A K Clarke, Tracey and Stephen Groves, D and M T Ayres-Regan

WINTERBOURNE

Winterbourne Arms ♀

3.7 miles from M4 junction 13; at A34 turn into Chievley Services and follow Donnington signs to Arlington Lane, then follow Winterbourne signs; RG20 8BB

Popular village pub just a few miles from M4 with good bar food, real ales, lots of wines by the glass and large landscaped garden

Friendly and relaxed, this pretty black and white village pub is very popular with our readers. The traditionally furnished bars have stools along the counter, a mix of pine dining chairs and tables, a collection of old irons around the big fireplace with its warming winter log fire, and early prints and old photographs of the village on the pale washed or exposed stone walls; piped music. Big windows take in peaceful views over rolling fields. Ramsbury Gold and a beer brewed by them for the pub called Winterbourne Whistle Wetter on handpump and 20 wines by the glass including sparkling and sweet wines. There are seats outside in the large landscaped side garden and pretty flowering tubs and hanging baskets. The surrounding countryside here is lovely, with nearby walks to Snelsmore Common and Donnington Castle.

🍴 Well liked bar food includes filled baguettes, ploughman's, soup, chicken liver pâté with red onion marmalade, home-made burger, gammon and eggs, a home-made pie of the week, butternut squash, sweet potato and spinach risotto with crème fraîche and parmesan, daily specials such as duck leg confit on asian-style noodles, tuna loin with niçoise salad or ham hock with a light grain mustard sauce, and puddings like warm chocolate brownie with ice-cream and apple and blackberry crumble; roast Sunday lunches. *Starters/Snacks: £3.95 to £8.25. Main Courses: £6.95 to £21.95. Puddings: £3.95 to £6.95*

Free house ~ Licensee Frank Adams ~ Real ale ~ Bar food (12-2.30, 6-10; 12-3.30, 6-9.30 Sun) ~ Restaurant ~ (01635) 248200 ~ Children welcome ~ Dogs allowed in bar ~ Open 12-3, 6-11; 12-10.30 Sun

Recommended by Martin and Pauline Jennings, Peter Sampson, Rev W R Fillery, Dr and Mrs J D Abell, Samantha McGahan, Mike and Sue Loseby, John Saville, Tracey and Stephen Groves, Humphry and Angela Crum Ewing, Adele Summers, Alan Black, Phyl and Jack Street, Peter Meister, Rob and Catherine Dunster, Andy and Claire Barker, Dr and Mrs A K Clarke, George and Maureen Roby, N R White, George Atkinson, John Robertson, Brian and Rosalie Laverick, Annette Tress, Gary Smith

LUCKY DIP

Besides the fully inspected pubs, you might like to try these Lucky Dips recommended to us and described by readers (if you do, please send us reports: feedback@goodguides.com).

ALDERMASTON [SU5865]
☆ **Hinds Head** RG7 4LX [Wasing Lane]: Creeper-clad red brick 17th-c inn at heart of attractive old village and doing well under newish management; spacious contemporary-feel bar, pews, old tables and sofas on wood floor, log fire, Fullers ale, plenty of wines by the glass, several malt whiskies, enjoyable home-made food (all day Sun), neat staff, restaurant; piped music and some live, quiz nights (2nd Tues of month); children welcome, dogs in one area, seats in back garden, 17 boutique bedrooms, open all day (*David and Sue Smith, LYM, Dr and Mrs A K Clarke, Neil and Karen Dignan, Sara Fulton, Roger Baker*)

ASTON [SU7884]
☆ **Flower Pot** RG9 3DG [small signpost off A4130 Henley—Maidenhead at top of Remenham Hill]: Roomy popular country pub with nice local feel, roaring log fire, array of stuffed fish and fishing prints on dark green walls of attractively done airy country dining area, enjoyable food from baguettes to fish and game, Brakspears, Hook Norton and Wychwood ales, quick friendly service, snug traditional bar with more fishing memorabilia; very busy with walkers and families wknds; lots of picnic-sets giving quiet country views from nice big dog-friendly orchard garden, side field with poultry, crocodile on roof, bedrooms (*BB, DHV, Susan and John Douglas, Roy Hoing, Paul Humphreys, Michael Dandy*)

BAGNOR [SU4569]
☆ **Blackbird** RG20 8AQ [quickest approach is from Speen on edge of Newbury]: Chatty country pub in peaceful setting nr Watermill Theatre (pre-show menu, discount for actors and stage hands), well kept changing ales inc West Berkshire, enjoyable reasonably priced home-made pubby food, friendly efficient service, simple unfussy traditional bar with good log fire, old farm tools and firearms, more formal eating area off; children welcome, tables in pleasant side

garden and on green in front *(Ann Whatley, Kevin Brown, David and Judy Robison, BB)*

BEECH HILL [SU6964]

Elm Tree RG7 2AZ [3.3 miles from M4 junction 11: A33 towards Basingstoke, turning off into Beech Hill Rd after about 2 miles]: Five carefully furnished and decorated rooms, one with dozens of clocks, Hollywood photographs and blazing fire, nice views especially from simply furnished more modern barn-style restaurant and conservatory, quick friendly staff, enjoyable if not cheap food (all day wknds) from hearty baguettes up inc some unusual dishes, well kept Fullers, Greene King and a guest beer, good choice of wines by the glass; amazing ladies'; children welcome away from bar, benches and tables on front decking in nice setting, open all day *(Martin and Karen Wake, LYM, Stan Edwards)*

BEENHAM [SU5868]

Six Bells RG7 5NX: Welcoming village pub, nicely furnished and comfortable, with enjoyable food inc imaginative additions to standard pub menu, well kept ales such as West Berkshire, separate sizeable dining room, conservatory *(I H G Busby)*

CHADDLEWORTH [SU4177]

Ibex RG20 7ER [Main St]: Homely village pub with friendly attentive staff, enjoyable food from good baguettes up, some bargain prices, good choice of beers and soft drinks, good coffee, games in public bar, post office in back room; wheelchair access, dogs and walkers welcome, tables out on sheltered lawn and floodlit terrace *(Paul Humphreys, LYM)*

CHAPEL ROW [SU5769]

Bladebone RG7 6PD: Large pub doing reliable well cooked food (local meats from butcher next door), cheerful helpful staff, well kept ales inc West Berkshire, dining room with conservatory; tables in big garden *(I H G Busby)*

CHIEVELEY [SU4773]

☆ *Olde Red Lion* RG20 8XB [handy for M4 junction 13 via A34 N-bound; Green Lane]: Attractive red-brick village pub, friendly landlord and helpful staff, well kept Arkells, wide choice of generously served food from good sandwiches and baguettes up, low-beamed carpeted L-shaped bar with panelling and hunting prints, log fire, extended back restaurant, piped music, games machine, TV; wheelchair accessible throughout, small garden, bedrooms *(BB, Chris and Angela Buckell, J V Dadswell)*

COOKHAM [SU8985]

☆ *Bel & the Dragon* SL6 9SQ [High St (B4447)]: Smart old dining pub with panelling and heavy Tudor beams, log fires, bare boards and simple country furnishings in two-room front bar and dining area, more formal back restaurant, helpful friendly staff (but service can slow when busy), enjoyable food at prices you might expect for the area, Greene King ales, good choice of wines; children welcome, well kept garden with

terrace tables, Stanley Spencer Gallery almost opposite, open all day *(N R White, LYM)*

Ferry SL6 9SN [Sutton Rd]: Splendidly placed riverside pub with relaxing contemporary décor, Rebellion IPA and Timothy Taylors Landlord, some interesting lagers and good wine range, decent food (popular Sun lunchtime), light and airy Thames-view dining areas upstairs and down, sofas and coffee tables by fireplace, small servery in beamed core; piped music; children welcome, extensive decking overlooking river *(BB, Mrs June Wilmers, Mrs Ann Gray, David Tindal)*

White Oak SL6 9QE [The Pound]: Airy busy pub doing fairly priced food inc good two-course set menu and specials, competent cooking, fast friendly service; big garden, good Thames walks *(John Urquhart)*

COOKHAM DEAN [SU8785]

☆ *Jolly Farmer* SL6 9PD [Church Rd, off Hills Lane]: Traditional pub owned by village consortium, old-fashioned unspoilt bars with open fires, prompt friendly service, well kept ales, farm cider, decent wines and coffee, good choice of sensibly priced food from nice baguettes up, good-sized more modern eating area and small dining room, old and new local photographs, pub games, no music or machines, friendly black lab called Czar; well behaved children welcome, tables out in front and in good garden with play area *(Paul Humphreys, R K Phillips, LYM, David and Sue Smith)*

Uncle Toms Cabin SL6 9NT [off A308 Maidenhead—Marlow; Hills Lane, towards Cookham Rise and Cookham]: Welcoming small-roomed local nicely redone by new landlord, decent pubby food from sandwiches and baguettes up, low beams, wood floors and half panelling, coal fire; children in eating areas, sheltered sloping back garden *(LYM, Paul Humphreys)*

CRAZIES HILL [SU7980]

Horns RG10 8LY [Warren Row Rd off A4 towards Cockpole Green, then follow Crazies Hill signs]: Comfortable and individual beamed pub under new licensees, enjoyable reasonably priced generous food inc bargain OAP lunches, well kept Brakspears ales, good wines by the glass, friendly helpful service (landlord runs mini-bus for local customers), stripped furniture and open fires, raftered barn dining room; children welcome, seats in big informal garden with ponies, rabbits and guinea pigs *(LYM, Paul Humphreys, Roy and Jean Russell)*

EAST GARSTON [SU3676]

☆ *Queens Arms* RG17 7ET [3.5 miles from M4 junction 14; A338 and village signposted Gt Shefford]: Smart country dining pub under new licensees – reports please; roomy opened-up bare-boards bar with lighter dining area off; sheltered terrace, good downland walks, bedrooms *(LYM, Phyl and Jack Street, BOB)*

EAST ILSLEY [SU4981]

Swan RG20 7LF [just off A34 Newbury—

Abingdon; High St]: Refurbished Greene King pub with their beers and enjoyable well priced food from sandwiches up, good Sun carvery, cheerful helpful staff, comfortable seating by log fire; well behaved children and dogs welcome, tables in courtyard and walled garden, good bedrooms (LYM, Edward and Ava Williams, Sue Shaw, Val and Alan Green, Sylvia van der Plas)

FINCHAMPSTEAD [SU7963]

Queens Oak RG40 4LS [Church Lane, off B3016]: Relaxed country local under newish management, largely open-plan, with mix of simple seats and tables, some in airy parquet-floored area on right, well kept Brakspears ales and a guest, good value food from baguettes up, separate dining room where children allowed; picnic-sets, some sheltered, in good-sized garden with aunt sally, play area, has been open all day at least in summer (BB, Paul Humphreys, David and Sue Smith)

GREAT SHEFFORD [SU3875]

☆ *Swan* RG17 7DS [2 miles from M4 junction 14 – A338 towards Wantage (Newbury Rd)]: Low-ceilinged bow-windowed pub, nicely redecorated, with good log fire, real ales such as local Butts and Fullers London Pride, good wine choice, baguettes and hot dishes inc pubby favourites, daily papers, nice river-view dining room; soft piped music; good wheelchair access, children in eating areas, tables on attractive waterside lawn and terrace (Colin and Janet Roe, Dr and Mrs A K Clarke, LYM)

HOLYPORT [SU8977]

☆ *Belgian Arms* SL6 2JR [1.5 miles from M4 junction 8/9 via A308(M), A330; in village turn left on to big green, then left again at war memorial]: Bustling village-green pub, well kept Brakspears and Oxford Gold, several wines by the glass, generally enjoyable if not cheap food, friendly service, low-ceilinged bar with well spaced tables on stripped-wood, interesting cricketing memorabilia, hot woodburner, old cellar dining area; piped music, TV; children welcome, dogs in bar, good furniture on terrace overlooking pond, open all day Fri-Sun (Ian Wilson, LYM, Ian Barker, Peter Barton, June and Robin Savage)

Sun & Stars SL6 2NN [Forest Green Rd]: Welcoming place popular for its food from pub favourites to more upmarket dishes, good vegetarian options too, small cosy bar and several linked eating rooms, well kept Greene King ales (June and Robin Savage)

HUNGERFORD [SU3468]

Downgate RG17 0ED [Down View, Park St]: Prettily placed and relaxing old country local, decent well priced food inc good Sun roast, friendly efficient licensees, well kept Arkells, two compact linked areas overlooking common, small lower room with open fire, coin/currency collection, model aircraft overhead, old tankards; picnic-sets out at front (Phil Bryant)

HURLEY [SU8281]

Dew Drop SL6 6RB [small yellow sign to pub off A4130 just W]: Flint and brick pub in nice rustic setting, continuing well under friendly new licensees, enjoyable good value traditional food from baguettes up, Brakspears ales; children and dogs welcome, french windows to terrace, landscaped back garden with views, good walks, open all day Sat, cl Sun evening, Mon lunchtime (Paul Humphreys, LYM)

HURST [SU8074]

☆ *Green Man* RG10 0BP [off A321 just outside village]: Partly 17th-c pub with new licensees taking over as we went to press; old-fashioned bar with dark beams and standing timbers, cosy alcoves, cushioned wall seats and built-in settles, hot little fire in one fireplace, old iron stove in another, dining area with modern sturdy wooden tables and high-backed chairs on solid oak floor; sheltered terrace, picnic-sets under big oak trees in large garden with play area (BB, LYM, Dr and Mrs A K Clarke, Paul Humphreys)

INKPEN [SU3564]

☆ *Swan* RG17 9DX [Lower Inkpen; coming from A338 in Hungerford, take Park St (first left after railway bridge, coming from A4)]: Popular rambling beamed country pub with strong organic leanings in its wines, beers and home-made food from sandwiches and pubby things to more upscale dishes (farming owners have interesting organic shop next door), cosy corners, eclectic bric-a-brac, three log fires, friendly helpful staff, good Butts and West Berkshire ales, local farm cider, pleasant restaurant, flagstoned games area; piped music; well behaved children welcome in eating areas, picnic-sets out in front tiered garden, good bedrooms and breakfast, open all day in summer (LYM, Michael and Deborah Ethier, N R White, John Robertson, CP)

KINTBURY [SU3866]

☆ *Dundas Arms* RG17 9UT [Station Rd]: Fine summer pub, with tables out on deck above Kennet & Avon Canal and pleasant walks; well kept Adnams, Ramsbury, West Berkshire and a guest ale, good coffee and wines by the glass, good reasonably priced home-made pub food (not Sun), evening restaurant; they may try to keep your credit card while you eat outside; children welcome, comfortable bedrooms with own secluded waterside terrace, good breakfast, cl Sun evening (Jeff and Wendy Williams, LYM, T R and B C Jenkins, J C Burgis)

KNOWL HILL [SU8178]

☆ *Bird in Hand* RG10 9UP [A4, quite handy for M4 junction 8/9]: Relaxed, civilised and roomy, with cosy alcoves, heavy beams, panelling and splendid log fire in tartan-carpeted main area with leather chairs, wide choice of enjoyable home-made food even Sun evening inc occasional good value set menus, well kept Brakspears and local guests such as Ascot and West Berkshire, good choice of other drinks, attentive prompt service, much older side bar, smart restaurant; soft piped music; tables out on front terrace, Sun summer barbecues, 15 tidy modern bedrooms *(DHV, Andy and Jill Kassube, Richard Endacott, Susan and John Douglas, LYM, June and Robin Savage)*

☆ **Old Devil** RG10 9UU [Bath Rd (A4)]: Roomy and popular beamed roadhouse, leather sofas and chairs in bar, well spaced tables with fresh flowers in dining areas each side, chintzy feel, wide choice of decent food, Fullers London Pride, good range of wines by the glass; pleasant verandah above attractive lawn *(David and Sue Smith, Paul Humphreys, Miss A Hawkes)*

LAMBOURN [SU3180]
Malt Shovel RG17 8QN [Upper Lambourn]: Décor and customers reflecting race-stables surroundings, traditional locals' bar, enjoyable home-made food in smart modern dining extension inc good Sun carvery, good choice of wines by the glass, real ales, helpful staff; racing TV *(Michael Sargent, Mrs Jane Kingsbury)*

LITTLEWICK GREEN [SU8379]
Cricketers SL6 3RA [not far from M4 junction 9; A404(M) then left on to A4 – village signed on left; Coronation Rd]: Proper old-fashioned welcoming country pub with newish landlord, well kept Badger and Wells & Youngs ales, good choice of wines by the glass, enjoyable reasonably priced food from lunchtime baguettes to blackboard specials, huge clock above brick fireplace; piped music; charming spot opp cricket green, bedrooms, open all day wknds *(Paul Humphreys, Andy and Jill Kassube, Richard Endacott, Roger and Anne Newbury, Ian Barker, Susan and John Douglas, LYM)*

MAIDENHEAD [SU8682]
☆ **Robin Hood** SL6 6PR [Furze Platt Rd, Pinkneys Green (A308N)]: Well run Greene King dining pub with their ales and good choice of wines by the glass, extensive series of well divided and varied eating areas off oak-boarded bar, enjoyable good value food from sandwiches up, you can pick your own fish/meat (inc kangaroo and ostrich) and they'll cook it for you, friendly helpful service, feature fireplace; piped music; broad picnic-sets on big front terrace and lawn, sheltered bower with awning, open all day *(BB, Ron Clementson, Paul Humphreys, DHV)*

OAKLEY GREEN [SU9276]
Olde Red Lion SL4 4PZ [4 miles from M4 junctions 8 and 6; B3024]: Beamed dining pub under newish ownership, low-ceilinged bar with leather sofas and chairs, Black Sheep, Fullers London Pride and John Smiths, good choice of enjoyable food (not Sun evening) from sandwiches and baguettes up, extensive wood-floored dining area with woodburner, friendly atmosphere; piped music; children and dogs welcome, good-sized sheltered back garden with play area, open all day *(June and Robin Savage, Craig Bulman, LYM)*

PALEY STREET [SU8675]
Bridge House SL6 3JS: Extended beamed cottage with comfortably refurbished traditional log-fire bar, friendly helpful landlady, well kept Brakspears and Fullers London Pride, decent pubby food at reasonable prices from lunchtime baguettes up, also wkdy breakfast from 8am, pleasant back dining room; darts, Weds quiz night, soft piped music, TV; children welcome, big garden, smokers' shelter *(June and Robin Savage, Paul Humphreys)*

PANGBOURNE [SU6376]
Cross Keys RG8 7AR [Church Rd, opp church]: Good bar and restaurant food (not Sun evening) from baguettes to steaks inc good value set lunches, own-baked bread, Greene King ales, good wine choice, linked beamed rooms with simple bar on right, neat dining area on left; service can be slow, piped pop music may obtrude, paid parking some way off; nice back streamside terrace with sizeable heated marquee, open all day *(BB, Bob and Angela Brooks, David Rule)*

READING [SU7273]
Eldon Arms RG1 4DX [Eldon Terr]: Two-room backstreet pub well run by long-serving licensees, well kept Wadworths, cosy lounge, lots of bric-a-brac *(the Didler)*

☆ **Fishermans Cottage** RG1 3DW [Kennet Side – easiest to walk from Orts Rd, off Kings Rd]: Nice spot by canal lock and towpath, good value lunches especially sandwiches (very busy then but service quick and friendly), full Fullers beer range, small choice of wines, modern furnishings, pleasant stone snug behind woodburning range, light and airy conservatory, small darts room; influx of regulars evenings, Sky TV; dogs allowed (not in garden), waterside tables, lovely big back garden *(DM, the Didler, Susan and John Douglas)*

Nags Head RG1 7XD [Russell St]: Friendly local with good mix of customers, a dozen well kept changing ales, wkdy lunchtime baguettes and bargain early evening meal (lunchtime food only wknds inc Sun roasts), open fire, live music Sun; garden with hops, open all day *(John Slade, the Didler)*

☆ **Sweeney & Todd** RG1 7RD [Castle St]: Pie shop with popular pub/restaurant behind, warren of private little period-feel alcoves and other areas on various levels, good home-made food all day inc wide choice of pies such as venison and wild boar, cheery knowledgeable service, small bar with four well kept ales such as Wadworths 6X, Weston's cider, children welcome in restaurant area, open all day (cl Sun and bank hols) *(John Branston, the Didler, Susan and John Douglas, Ewan and Moira McCall, Paul Humphreys, LYM, D J and P M Taylor)*

SHEFFORD WOODLANDS [SU3673]
☆ **Pheasant** RG17 7AA [less than 0.5 miles from M4 junction 14 – A338 towards Wantage then 1st left on to B4000]: Tucked-away horse-racing inn with large bedroom

extension, welcoming old-school landlord and friendly staff, good regularly changing traditional food, well kept ales, log fires and stone floors, four rooms inc end dining area with burgundy décor and bistro atmosphere, public bar with games inc ring the bull; attractive views from garden, 11 bedrooms (*LYM, Colin and Janet Roe, Tony and Tracy Constance*)

SHURLOCK ROW [SU8374]

Shurlock Inn RG10 0PS [The Street]: Recently bought and refurbished by village consortium, friendly service, good choice of enjoyable food at reasonable prices, beams, panelling and inglenook log fire; children welcome till 8pm, dogs in bar, picnic-sets in courtyard and good-sized garden with play area, cl Sun evening (*Alan and Catherine Turner*)

SUNNINGHILL [SU9367]

Dog & Partridge SL5 7AQ [Upper Village Rd]: Modern feel under hard-working owners with emphasis on the enjoyable reasonably priced food, friendly helpful staff, real ales, good range of wines; piped music; children and dogs welcome, nice garden (*Chris Sale, Mary McSweeney, Paul Nickson*)

SWALLOWFIELD [SU7364]

☆ *George & Dragon* RG7 1TJ [Church Rd, towards Farley Hill]: Restaur+ty pub, relaxed and cottagey, with thriving atmosphere, interesting generous food (best to book wknds), several real ales, good reasonably priced wines, pleasant service, big log fire, stripped beams, red walls, rugs on flagstones, lit candles, plenty of character; very popular with business diners, piped music; well behaved children welcome, open all day (*LYM, Dr and Mrs R E S Tanner*)

TIDMARSH [SU6374]

Greyhound RG8 8ER [A340 S of Pangbourne]: Prettily restored thatched pub, warm and friendly, with good choice of enjoyable food, pleasant service, Fullers ales, two carpeted bars, woodburner, back dining extension; good walks nearby (*Paul Humphreys, Roy Hoing*)

WALTHAM ST LAWRENCE [SU8376]

☆ *Bell* RG10 0JJ [B3024 E of Twyford; The Street]: Heavy-beamed and timbered village local with cheerful landlord and chatty regulars, good log fires, efficient service, good value pubby bar food (not Sun evening) from good sandwich range up inc interesting pizzas, small choice of main dishes (may ask to keep your credit card while you eat), well kept changing local ales such as Loddon and West Berkshire, plenty of malt whiskies, good wine, daily papers, compact panelled lounge; children and dogs welcome, tables in back garden with extended terrace, open all day wknds (*LYM, Paul Humphreys*)

WARGRAVE [SU7878]

St George & Dragon RG10 8HY [High St]: Large smartly refurbished M&B dining pub with decking overlooking Thames, good range of enjoyable food inc some unusual

dishes and lunchtime deals, friendly helpful staff, central fire giving cosy feel (*David and Sue Smith, Hunter and Christine Wright, Paul Humphreys*)

WARREN ROW [SU8180]

Old House RG10 8QS: Attractive old rambling dining pub with lots of bric-a-brac, newish chef-landlord, good choice of wines by the glass, real ales inc Loddon; bedrooms planned, cl Mon, Tues and lunchtime exc Sun (*Paul Humphreys*)

WASH COMMON [SU4563]

Woodpeckers RG20 0LU [just off A343 S of Newbury, signposted to East Woodhay]: very friendly team in this old village pub – an Arkells pub for the last 20 years; TV and music are intrusive but the atmosphere is relaxing and welcoming; lovely timbers in ceiling; modern dining area at the back (*Giles and Annie Francis*)

WINDSOR [SU9676]

☆ *Carpenters Arms* SL4 1PB [Market St]: Town pub ambling around central servery with ales such as Everards, Fullers, Harveys, Pilgrim and Sharps Doom Bar, good value pubby food all day from sandwiches up inc good range of pies, friendly helpful service (can be slow when busy), good choice of wines by the glass (and bargain bottles), sturdy pub furnishings and Victorian-style décor inc two pretty fireplaces, family areas up a few steps, also downstairs beside former tunnel entrance with suits of armour; piped music, no nearby parking; tables out on cobbled pedestrian alley opp castle, handy for Legoland bus stop, open all day (*Andy and Jill Kassube, David M Smith, Terry Buckland, N R White, BB, D J and P M Taylor*)

☆ *Two Brewers* SL4 1LB [Park St]: In the shadow of Windsor Castle with three compact unchanging bare-board rooms, well kept Fullers, Wadworths and Wells & Youngs ales, good choice of wines by the glass, enjoyable food (not wknd evenings), thriving old-fashioned pub atmosphere, open fire, daily papers; piped music, no children inside; tables out by pretty Georgian street next to Windsor Park's Long Walk, open all day (*Simon Collett-Jones, John Saville, Conor McGaughey, Tom and Ruth Rees, Andy and Jill Kassube, Peter Barton, LYM*)

WINNERSH [SU7871]

Wheelwrights Arms RG10 0TR [off A329 Reading—Wokingham at Winnersh crossroads by Sainsburys, signed Hurst, Twyford; then right into Davis Way]: Cheerfully bustling beamed local, straightforward food from baguettes up (they may ask to keep a credit card while you eat), friendly attentive service, Wadworths ales, good value wines, cafetière coffee, big woodburner, bare blackboards and flagstones, daily papers, newer cottagey dining area; soft piped music, machines; children welcome, disabled parking and facilities, picnic-sets in garden with terrace (some motorway noise), opp Dinton Pastures, open all day wknds (*Paul Humphreys, Ian and Barbara Rankin,*

BB, June and Robin Savage)
WOODSIDE [SU9270]
☆ *Rose & Crown* SL4 2DP [Woodside Rd, Winkfield, off A332 Ascot—Windsor]: Welcoming pub with low-beamed bar and extended dining area, good attentive service, enjoyable food (not Sun or Mon evening) using good ingredients from lunchtime sandwiches and baguettes to more elaborate evening restaurant dishes and popular Sun lunch, well kept Greene King ales, interesting affordable wines; piped music, games machine; children in eating areas, tables and swing in side garden backed by woodland, bedrooms, open all day, cl Sun evening *(LYM, Gerry and Rosemary Dobson)*
WOOLHAMPTON [SU5766]
Angel RG7 5RT [Bath Rd]: Friendly pub/restaurant in former 18th-c coaching inn, good well presented food; cl Sun evening *(J C Burgis)*
YATTENDON [SU5574]
☆ *Royal Oak* RG18 0UG [The Square; B4009 NE from Newbury; turn right at Hampstead Norreys, village signposted on left]: Appealing civilised old-world inn with panelled and prettily decorated brasserie/bar, good if pricey food (not Sun evening) with cheaper wkdy set lunch, nice log fire and striking flower arrangements, well kept West Berkshire beers, several wines by the glass, friendly unhurried service; well behaved children welcome, tables in lovely walled garden, more in front by peaceful village square, five attractive bedrooms, open all day *(Anne Morton, the Didler, Ray Carter, LYM)*

A very few pubs try to make you leave a credit card at the bar, as a sort of deposit if you order food. They are not entitled to do this. The credit card firms and banks which issue them warn you not to let credit cards out of your sight. If someone behind the counter used your card fraudulently, the card company or bank could in theory hold you liable, because of your negligence in letting a stranger hang on to your card. Suggest instead that if they feel the need for security, they 'swipe' your card and give it back to you. And do name and shame the pub to us.

Buckinghamshire

Whatever your mood, there's bound to be a pub to suit it here. As well as simple, unspoilt places in pretty walking country there are some smart hotels with proper little bars and some fine dining pubs, too. Those pubs doing particularly well this year include the Kings Head in Aylesbury (such a surprise to find a lovely old building in a modern town), the Royal Oak in Bovingdon Green (a terrific dining pub), the Pheasant in Brill (new to the *Guide* this year and doing terribly well), the Red Lion in Chenies (much loved by loyal regulars), the Chequers in Fingest (a smashing country pub), the Red Lion in Great Kingshill (super brasserie food but a welcome for drinkers also), the White Horse in Hedgerley (a country gem with lots of real ales), the Queens Head in Little Marlow (thoroughly enjoyable all round), the Crown in Little Missenden (spotlessly kept and in the same family for 90 years), the Polecat in Prestwood (professionally run and nicely old-fashioned), and the Chequers at Wooburn Common (a delightful bustling bar in a smart hotel). New entries this year include the Harte & Magpies at Coleshill (under the same ownership as the Royal Standard of England, at Forty Green, another Main Entry in this county), the Black Horse in Fulmer (another success for the small Salisbury Pubs group), the Red Lion in Little Missenden (an unchanging little cottage with friendly licensees) and the Hit or Miss at Penn Street (an enjoyable small local with friendly irish landlords). For that special meal out, our Buckinghamshire Dining Pub 2011 is the Royal Oak in Bovingdon Green.

AYLESBURY

SP8113   MAP 4

Kings Head 🍺

Kings Head Passage (narrow passage off Bourbon Street), also entrance off Temple Street; no nearby parking except for disabled; HP20 2RW

Handsome town centre pub with civilised atmosphere, good local ales (used in the food too) and friendly service

The National Trust owns this rather special 15th-c building and the pub is just one part – the others being a coffee shop, arts and crafts shop, Tourist Information Office, and conference rooms. It's such a surprise, tucked away as it is in a modern town centre, with its particularly beautiful early Tudor windows and stunning 15th-c stained glass in the former Great Hall showing the Royal Arms of Henry VI and Margaret of Anjou. Three truly timeless rooms have been restored with careful and unpretentious simplicity – stripped boards, cream walls with little decoration, gentle lighting, a variety of seating which includes upholstered sofas and armchairs, cushioned high-backed settles and some simple modern pale dining tables and chairs dotted around. Most of the bar tables are of round glass, supported on low cask tops. It's all nicely low-key – not smart, but thoroughly civilised. The neat corner bar has Chiltern Ale, Beechwood Bitter, and a couple of guests on handpump and some interesting bottled beers. Service is friendly and there's no piped music or machines; disabled access and facilities. The atmospheric medieval cobbled courtyard has teak seats and tables, some under cover of a pillared roof, and a second-hand bookshop.

🍽 **Using Chiltern beer in quite a few of the recipes, the bar food includes soup, ploughman's, crab pâté, cornish sardines on toast with tomato compote, home-made burger, ham and egg, steak in ale pie, sausages of the day, calves liver, and puddings like apple pie or caramelised rice pudding.** *Starters/Snacks: £3.95 to £6.95. Main Courses: £7.50 to £11.00. Puddings: £3.50 to £6.50*

Chiltern ~ Manager Neil Pickles ~ Real ale ~ Bar food (12-2(3 Sat), 6-9; not Sun-Tues evenings) ~ (01296) 718812 ~ Open 11-11; 12-10.30 Sun; closed 25 Dec, Easter Sun

Recommended by Roger Shipperley, Tracey and Stephen Groves, Doug Kennedy, Tim and Ann Newell

BENNETT END
SU7897   MAP 4

Three Horseshoes

Horseshoe Road; from Radnage follow unclassified road towards Princes Risborough and turn left into Bennett End Road, then right into Horseshoe Road; HP14 4EB

Quietly set country pub with quite an emphasis on interesting meals, real ales and wines by the glass; seats in the garden; bedrooms

This is a lovely spot – seemingly off the beaten track but close to the M40 – and if you are lucky you should spot red kites soaring overhead. It's a nicely converted old country inn and you can opt to sit in one of the small traditional rooms or in the more spacious modern restaurant. To the left of the entrance (mind your head) is the flagstoned and darkly lit snug bar with a log fire in the raised stone fireplace with original brickwork and bread oven. To the right of the entrance are two further sitting areas, one with a long wooden winged settle, and the other enclosed by standing timbers with wooden flooring and a woodburning stove. Big windows in the light and airy dining room overlook seats in the garden, a red telephone box endearingly half submerged in the middle of one of the duck ponds, and the valley beyond. Smartly uniformed staff are friendly and attentive, and drinks include Rebellion IPA and a guest beer on handpump, quite a few wines by the glass, summer Pimms and winter mulled wine.

🍽 **Good bar food includes lunchtime sandwiches, soup, pork, smoked bacon and green peppercorn terrine with fig chutney, sautéed tiger prawns and chorizo with garlic and herb butter, home-made burger with red onion compote, ham and eggs, wild mushroom risotto, natural smoked haddock and leek tart with poached egg and hollandaise, suckling pig with dauphinoise potatoes, and puddings like baked chocolate and stem ginger cheesecake with rhubarb ice-cream and sticky toffee pudding with caramel sauce and toffee ice-cream; they offer a two- and three-course Sunday lunch menu, and the breakfasts are good.** *Starters/Snacks: £4.75 to £11.50. Main Courses: £9.50 to £14.50. Puddings: £5.75 to £7.00*

Free house ~ Licensee Simon Crawshaw ~ Real ale ~ Bar food (12-2.30, 7-9.30; not Sun evening or Mon lunchtime) ~ Restaurant ~ (01494) 483273 ~ Children welcome but not after 9pm Sat ~ Dogs allowed in bar and bedrooms ~ Open 12-3, 6-11; 12-11 Sat; 12-6 Sun; closed Sun evening and Mon lunchtime ~ Bedrooms: £80B/£120S(£110B)

Recommended by Dick Vardy, Torrens Lyster, Kevin Thomas, Nina Randall, Roy Hoing, Di and Mike Gillam, Howard Dell

BOVINGDON GREEN
SU8386   MAP 2

Royal Oak 🍽 ☿

0.75 miles N of Marlow, on back road to Frieth signposted off West Street (A4155) in centre; SL7 2JF

BUCKINGHAMSHIRE DINING PUB OF THE YEAR

Civilised dining pub with nice little bar, excellent choice of wines by the glass, real ales, good service and extremely popular, interesting food

'A really terrific dining pub with friendly, professional staff ' is how one of our readers describes this pub – and many agree with him. But there are still regulars who drop in for a chat and a pint and who tend to head for the low-beamed cosy snug, closest to the car park, which has three small tables, a woodburning stove in an exposed brick fireplace, and a big pile of logs. Several attractively decorated areas open off the central bar; the half-panelled walls variously painted in pale blue, green or cream (though the dining room ones are red).Throughout there's a mix of church chairs, stripped wooden tables and chunky wall seats, with rugs on the partly wooden, partly flagstoned floors, co-ordinated cushions and curtains, and a very bright, airy feel; thoughtful extra touches enhance the tone: a bowl of olives on the bar, carefully laid out newspapers and fresh flowers or candles on the tables. Brakspears Bitter, Rebellion IPA and Smuggler on handpump, nearly two dozen wines by the glass (all european), nine pudding wines and a good choice of liqueurs; board games and piped music. A terrace with good solid tables leads to an appealing garden, and there's a smaller side garden; pétanque.

🍴 Consistently good, interesting food includes lunchtime sandwiches, soup, popular crispy chilli squid with romesco sauce, home-smoked pigeon breast with soused root vegetables and burgundy mayonnaise, twice-baked oxford blue and watercress soufflé with spiced apricot and raisin dressing, beef bourguignon with dauphinoise potatoes, slow-roasted gressingham duck leg with champ and manuka honey jus, crispy skinned bass fillet with caramelised fennel, sweet potato purée and béarnaise sauce, and puddings like dark chocolate sludge cake with chilli and caramelised apple tarte tatin with cinnamon ice-cream. *Starters/Snacks: £3.75 to £6.75. Main Courses: £11.50 to £17.50. Puddings: £4.50 to £6.75*

Salisbury Pubs ~ Lease James Penlington ~ Real ale ~ Bar food (12-2.30(3 Sat, 4 Sun), 6.30-9.30(10 Fri, Sat)) ~ Restaurant ~ (01628) 488611 ~ Children welcome ~ Dogs allowed in bar ~ Open 11-11; 12-10.30 Sun; closed 25 and 26 Dec

Recommended by T R and B C Jenkins, Roger and Anne Newbury, Gary Ingram, Simon Rodway, Serkan Ibrahim, Chris Smith, Jeff and Wendy Williams, Tracey and Stephen Groves, C and R Bromage, Doug Kennedy, Neil and Karen Dignan, Lee Fathers, T A R Curran, David Tindal, Andy Ingle

BRILL
SP6514   MAP 4

Pheasant

Off B4011 Bicester—Long Crendon; Windmill Street; HP18 9TG

Carefully refurbished under new licensees, good mix of customers, real ales, highly rated food, and smashing views; bedrooms

The new licensees have completely refurbished this bustling pub and our readers are delighted with the results. It's more or less open-plan with beams here and there, a chatty bar with smart high-backed bar chairs by the counter, leather tub chairs in front of the woodburning stove, Vale Best Bitter and a guest beer on handpump, and several wines by the glass; piped music. The dining areas have a mix of high-backed leather or dark wooden dining chairs around shiny tables, attractively framed prints, and books on shelves. It's all very relaxed and friendly and there's a good mix of both locals and visitors. There are plenty of seats outside on the decked area and in the garden, and marvellous views over the windmill opposite (it's one of the oldest post windmills still in working order) and into the distance across five different counties. Roald Dahl used to drink here, and some of the tales the locals told him were worked into his short stories. We have not heard from people who have stayed here, but expect it to be very comfortable.

🍴 First-rate bar food includes sandwiches, soup, satay chicken with sweet chilli, scallops wrapped in smoked bacon skewered with black pudding, spaghetti carbonara, field mushroom stuffed with risotto and parmesan, fillet of plaice with citrus sauce, chicken breast stuffed with dolcelatte and tomatoes bound with parma ham, duck breast with a brandy and peppercorn sauce, and puddings. *Starters/Snacks: £4.50 to £8.95. Main Courses: £8.95 to £15.95. Puddings: £5.00*

Free house ~ Licensee Marilyn Glover ~ Real ale ~ Bar food (12-2, 6-9(7 Sun)) ~ (01844) 239370 ~ Children welcome ~ Dogs allowed in bar ~ Open 12-11(midnight Sat) ~ Bedrooms: £65B/£85B

Recommended by Ross Balaam, Doug Kennedy

CHENIES

TQ0298   MAP 3

Red Lion ★ 🍺

2 miles from M25 junction 18; A404 towards Amersham, then village signposted on right; Chesham Road; WD3 6ED

Delightful pub with long-serving licensees, a bustling atmosphere, real ales and popular food

Thankfully for their many loyal customers, this splendid little village pub is as good as ever and still run by the friendly licensees who have been here for well over 20 years now. The L-shaped bar is very traditional and unpretentious (no games machines or piped music) and has comfortable built-in wall benches by the front windows, other straightforward seats and tables, and original photographs of the village and traction engines. There's also a small back snug and a neat dining extension with more modern décor. Well kept Lion Pride is brewed for the pub by Rebellion and served on handpump alongside Vale Best Bitter, a changing guest and Wadworths 6X, and they have a dozen wines by the glass and some nice malt whiskies. The hanging baskets and window boxes are pretty in summer, there are picnic-sets on a small side terrace, and good local walks. No children.

🍽 **Well liked bar food includes sandwiches, soup, home-made pâté, bangers and mash with red wine gravy, a changing curry, mushroom and mixed pepper stroganoff, their very popular lamb pie, pork belly with crackling on leek and potato mash, chicken breast stuffed with stilton, wrapped in bacon with a creamy sauce, daily specials, and puddings.** *Starters/Snacks: £4.95 to £7.95. Main Courses: £9.50 to £13.75. Puddings: £4.50 to £4.95*

Free house ~ Licensee Mike Norris ~ Real ale ~ Bar food (12-2,7-10(6.30–9.30 Sun)) ~ Restaurant ~ (01923) 282722 ~ Dogs allowed in bar ~ Open 11-2.30, 5.30-11; 12-3, 6.30-10.30 Sun

Recommended by N R White, Roy Hoing, Tracey and Stephen Groves, J V Dadswell, John and Victoria Fairley, Tim Maddison

COLESHILL

SU9594   MAP 4

Harte & Magpies

E of village on A355 Amersham—Beaconsfield, by junction with Magpie Lane; HP7 0LU

Good, friendly, new roadside dining pub with enjoyable food all day, well kept local ales; big garden

This was reopened in 2009 by the landlord of the Royal Standard of England over at Forty Green, and inside is not unlike an uncluttered version of that distinctive pub, especially in its profusion of vigorously patriotic antique prints. It's a big place, open-plan, but its rambling collection of miscellaneous pews, high-backed booths and some quite distinctive tables and chairs, and the candles in bottles, give it a pleasantly snug feeling. Scrumpy Jick, the self-possessed young labrador, adds a relaxed country touch, as does the jar of dog treats. They have well kept Chiltern Ale and Rebellion Smuggler on handpump, and take a lot of care over their other drinks; service is friendly and civilised. Outside, a terrace has picnic-sets by a tree picturesquely draped with wisteria, and service; a big sloping informal garden has more trees and more tables on wood chippings.

🍽 **Bar food includes filled baguettes, soup, garlic mushrooms on toast, welsh rarebit, hummus and pitta bread, sausages with onion gravy, fish pie, vegetable risotto, gammon and egg, rack of lamb with ratatouille, rib-eye steak, and puddings such as sticky toffee pudding and crème brûlée.** *Starters/Snacks: £3.50 to £5.00. Main Courses: £9.50 to £18.00. Puddings: £5.00*

Free house ~ Licensee Stephen Lever ~ Real ale ~ Bar food (10-9.45; 12-8 Sun) ~ (01494) 726754 ~ Children welcome ~ Dogs welcome ~ Open mike night every second Fri evening ~ Open 10am-11pm; 11-10.30 Sun

Recommended by Tracey and Stephen Groves, Mrs Ann Gray

CUDDINGTON

SP7311 MAP 4

Crown 🍺

Village signposted off A418 Thame—Aylesbury; Spurt Street; HP18 0BB

Convivial low-beamed thatched cottage with inglenook bar and popular dining area

There's a good chatty atmosphere and plenty of cheerful drinkers in this friendly local. The two very low-beamed linked rooms of the tiled-floor front bar have a comfortable mix of pubby furnishings including capacious housekeeper's chairs and cushioned settles, and there's a winter log fire burning in the big inglenook on the right. Fullers London Pride and ESB and a guest like Adnams Bitter on handpump, and 20 wines by the glass. The carpeted back area, with dark red walls above its panelled dado, is also more or less divided into two rooms with country-kitchen chairs around a nice variety of stripped or polished tables. This part opens on to a neat side terrace with contemporary garden furniture and planters, and there are some picnic-sets under cocktail parasols out in front.

🍽 Bar food includes sandwiches, soup, chicken caesar salad, spaghetti carbonara, smoked haddock with welsh rarebit topping on tomato and basil salad, fish and chips, gnocchi and spinach bake, duck breast with sweet chilli sauce and stir-fried vegetables, bass fillet with celeriac purée, steaks, and puddings; Sunday roasts. *Starters/Snacks: £4.50 to £7.95. Main Courses: £8.95 to £15.95. Puddings: £4.50 to £5.95.*

Fullers ~ Tenants David and Heather Berry ~ Real ale ~ Bar food (12-2(3 Sun), 7-9; not Sun evening) ~ Restaurant ~ (01844) 292222 ~ Children welcome ~ Open 12-3, 6-11; 12-10.30 Sun
Recommended by Ian Herdman, Dennis and Doreen Haward, Roy Hoing

DORNEY

SU9279 MAP 2

Pineapple

2.4 miles from M4 junction 7; turn left on to A4, then left on B3026 (or take first left off A4 at traffic lights, into Huntercombe Lane S, then left at T junction on main road – shorter but slower); Lake End Road; SL4 6QS

Extraordinary choice of sandwiches in popular refurbished pub with real ales and plenty of outside seating

Nicely old-fashioned, this popular pub does get especially busy at weekend lunchtimes when it might be best to book a table in advance. As well as shiny low Anaglypta ceilings, black-panelled dados and new leather chairs around sturdy country tables (one very long and another in a big bow window), there's a woodburning stove at one end and a pretty little fireplace in a second room. China pineapples join other decorations on a set of shelves in one of three cottagey carpeted linked rooms on the left. It's bare boards on the right where the bar counter has Black Sheep Bitter, Fullers London Pride and Marstons Pedigree on handpump, and several wines (and champagne) by the glass; piped music and games machine. A roadside verandah has some rustic tables and there are plenty of round picnic-sets out in the garden, some on fairy-lit decking under an oak tree; the nearby motorway can be heard out here.

🍽 A remarkable selection of up to 1,000 varieties of sandwiches in five different fresh breads come with your choice of hearty vegetable soup, salad or chips, and run from cream cheese with beetroot, smoked salmon and cream cheese to chicken, avocado, crispy bacon and lettuce with honey and mustard dressing and spicy 'passage to India'; Sunday roasts. They may ask you to leave your credit card behind the bar. *Starters/Snacks: £6.95. Puddings: £3.95*

Punch ~ Lease Stuart Jones ~ Real ale ~ Bar food (12-9) ~ (01628) 662353 ~ Children welcome ~ Dogs welcome ~ Open 11-11; 12-10.30 Sun
Recommended by Charles Harvey, Steve and Claire Harvey, Paul Humphreys, Piotr Chodzko-Zajko, LM

Pubs close to motorway junctions are listed at the back of the book.

EASINGTON

SP6810 MAP 4

Mole & Chicken 🍽 ⍩ 🛏

From B4011 in Long Crendon follow Chearsley, Waddesdon signpost into Carters Lane opposite indian restaurant, then turn left into Chilton Road; HP18 9EY

Lovely views from deck and garden, inviting interior, real ales, and much emphasis on restaurant food; nice bedrooms

This is very much a dining pub with upmarket food and prices to match, but they do still keep Hook Norton Bitter and Vale Best Bitter on handpump, lots of wines by the glass and quite a few malt whiskies. The opened-up interior is arranged so that its different parts seem quite snug and self-contained without being cut off from the relaxed sociable atmosphere. The beamed bar curves around the serving counter in a sort of S-shape, and there are cream-cushioned chairs and high-backed leather dining chairs at oak and pine tables on flagstones or tiles, a couple of dark leather sofas, and fabric swatches stylishly hung as decorations on creamy walls, lit candles and good winter log fires; piped music. The attractive raised terrace, with views over fine rolling countryside, is a lovely place for a summer's lunch or sunset drink. More reports please.

🍴 Using carefully sourced ingredients, the interesting food includes lunchtime snacks such as open sandwiches, pork and leek sausages, chicken caesar salad and linguine carbonara, as well as soup, chilli fried squid, potted ham hock, flaked duck salad with thai herbs and cashews, beer-battered cod with tartare sauce, gnocchi with creamed wild mushrooms, pork belly with apple and black pudding, braised steak and mushroom pudding, wild bass fillet with mussels, leeks and tomatoes, and puddings like pear and plum crumble with honeycomb ice-cream and vanilla panna cotta; they also offer a two- and three-course set menu. *Starters/Snacks: £6.00 to £12.00. Main Courses: £9.50 to £18.00. Puddings: £5.95*

Free house ~ Licensees Alan Heather and Steve Bush ~ Real ale ~ Bar food (12-2.30, 6.30-9.30; 12-4, 6-9 Sun) ~ Restaurant ~ (01844) 208387 ~ Children welcome ~ Occasional jazz evenings ~ Open 12-3(4 Sat), 6-11; 12-10 Sun ~ Bedrooms: £70B/£95B

Recommended by M and GR, Rich Read, Richard and Sissel Harris, John Wheeler, David and Lexi Young, Di and Mike Gillam, John Rodgers, Felicity Davies, Dennis and Doreen Haward

FINGEST

SU7791 MAP 2

Chequers

Village signposted off B482 Marlow—Stokenchurch; RG9 6QD

Friendly, spotlessly kept old pub with big garden and good reasonably priced food

With a friendly landlord and an unaffected public bar with real country charm, this 15th-c pub is a great favourite with our readers. The several neatly kept old-fashioned rooms are warm, cosy and traditional, with large open fires, horsebrasses, pewter tankards, and pub team photographs on the walls. Brakspears Bitter and Oxford Gold, Marstons Bitter, and a seasonal ale from Ringwood are served on handpump alongside a dozen wines by the glass, jugs of Pimms and several malt whiskies; board games. French doors from the smart back dining extension open to a terrace (plenty of picnic-sets), which leads on to the big garden with fine views over the Hambleden valley. Over the road is a unique Norman twin-roofed church tower – probably the nave of the original church. This is good walking country with quiet pastures sloping up to beechwoods and you can make your way on foot from here to other pubs in this chapter.

🍴 Wholesome and satisfying bar food includes smoked salmon, ploughman's, home-made sausages, popular shepherd's pie with cheddar crust, braised oxtail stew, crispy battered haddock, chicken and tarragon pie, and traditional puddings. *Starters/Snacks: £5.75 to £6.95. Main Courses: £9.25 to £14.75. Puddings: £4.75 to £5.75*

Brakspears ~ Tenants Ray Connelly and Christian Taubert ~ Real ale ~ Bar food (not Sun evening) ~ Restaurant ~ (01491) 638335 ~ Children welcome away from dining room ~ Dogs allowed in bar ~ Open 12-3, 6-11; 12-4 Sun; closed Sun evening

Recommended by Noel Grundy, Paul Humphreys, the Didler, Susan and John Douglas, Roy Hoing, Martin and Karen Wake, Tracey and Stephen Groves, Doug Kennedy, Dr Kevan Tucker

FORTY GREEN   SU9291   MAP 2

Royal Standard of England 🍺

3.5 miles from M40 junction 2, via A40 to Beaconsfield, then follow sign to Forty Green, off B474 0.75 miles N of New Beaconsfield; keep going through village; HP9 1XT

Ancient place with fascinating antiques in rambling rooms and good choice of drinks

As popular as ever and deservedly so – this is not a pub that rests on its laurels. You can be sure of a friendly welcome; and the rambling rooms have huge black ship's timbers, lovely worn floors, finely carved old oak panelling, roaring winter fires with handsomely decorated iron firebacks and cluttered mantelpieces, and there's a massive settle apparently built to fit the curved transom of an Elizabethan ship. Nooks and crannies are filled with a fascinating collection of antiques, including rifles, powder-flasks and bugles, ancient pewter and pottery tankards, lots of tarnished brass and copper, needlework samplers and richly coloured stained glass. Brakspears, Chiltern Ale, Rebellion IPA and Mild, Theakstons Old Peculier and Timothy Taylors Landlord are well kept on handpump, there's a great, carefully annotated list of bottled beers and malt whiskies, farm ciders, perry, somerset brandy and around a dozen wines by the glass; shove-ha'penny. You can sit outside in a neatly hedged front rose garden or under the shade of a tree. This is a genuinely historic place that evolved from a Saxon dwelling into an alehouse and has therefore been trading for nearly 900 years.

🍴 **Traditional bar food includes lunchtime sandwiches and ploughman's, onion soup, pork terrine, devilled lambs kidneys, moules marinière, vegetable risotto, chicken caesar salad, ham and eggs, beer-battered fish and chips, sausages with onion sauce, shepherd's pie, steak and kidney pudding, lambs liver and bacon, and puddings like spotted dick and hot chocolate fondant; Sunday roasts.** *Starters/Snacks: £3.50 to £6.00. Main Courses: £8.00 to £16.00. Puddings: £3.00 to £5.00*

Free house ~ Licensee Matthew O'Keeffe ~ Real ale ~ Bar food (12-10) ~ Restaurant ~ (01494) 673382 ~ Children welcome ~ Dogs welcome ~ Open 11-11(10.30 Sun)

Recommended by Paul Humphreys, Richard and Liz Thorne, Dr and Mrs A K Clarke, the Didler, Roy Hoing, Tracey and Stephen Groves, D and M T Ayres-Regan, June and Robin Savage, Susan and John Douglas, Peter Martin

FULMER   SU9985   MAP 2

Black Horse

Village signposted off A40 in Gerrards Cross, W of its junction with A413; Windmill Road; SL3 6HD

Appealingly reworked dining pub, friendly and relaxed, with enjoyable up-to-date food, exemplary service and pleasant garden

The latest success for the small local Salisbury Pubs group, this again scores with their good service and attention to detail. Fresh and light throughout, it does have a proper bar area on the left – three smallish rooms, low black beams, parquet floor or a rug on bare boards, very mixed tables. They have Greene King IPA, Abbot and Ruddles County on handpump, a good wine range (about 20 by the glass), and service is prompt, friendly and efficient. The main area on the right is set for dining, with comfortable discreetly modern dining chairs on a beige carpet, and the pub has a warm, relaxed and contented atmosphere throughout. There may be faint piped music. Like the rest of this attractive village, the pub has a tiled roof and crisp white paintwork. Its good-sized back terrace, below the church, has teak and wrought-iron tables and chairs, with picnic-sets on the sheltered grass beyond.

🍴 **As well as an open sandwich of the day, bar food includes starters such as spicy salt and pepper squid with watercress and wasabi mayonnaise, salted lambs kidneys with roasted** red onion and crispy nettles, goats cheese and caramelised onion tart with garlic aioli, main courses such as pork belly with sticky onions and black pudding roly-poly, crispy skinned bass fillets on niçoise salad, butternut squash gnocchi with roast beetroot, mushrooms and watercress and walnut pesto, and puddings such as chocolate fondant with crème fraîche and white chocolate ice-cream and fruited brioche bread and butter pudding. *Starters/Snacks: £4.50 to £7.50. Main Courses: £11.75 to £17.50. Puddings: £5.00 to £6.00*

Salisbury Pubs ~ Manager Richard Coletta ~ Real ale ~ Bar food (12-2.30(3 Sat, 4 Sun), 6.30-9.30(10 Fri, Sat)) ~ (01753) 663183 ~ Children welcome ~ Dogs allowed in bar ~ Open 11-11; 12-10.30 Sun
Recommended by BOB

GREAT KINGSHILL
SU8798   MAP 4

Red Lion 🍴 ♀
A4128 N of High Wycombe; HP15 6EB

Carefully refurbished pub with contemporary décor, interesting brasserie-style pub food, local beers and friendly licensees

Although this bustling, well run pub has a deservedly good reputation for its fine food, the dedicated licensees and their obliging staff are just as happy to welcome customers only wanting a drink and a chat. There's plenty of space in the 'lobby' and the cosy little bar has brown leather sofas and tub armchairs, low tables and an open log fire. To its left, a spacious dining room has a contemporary brown colour scheme with modern paintings on striped brown wallpaper, candles on tables, and some original flagstones. The atmosphere is relaxed and comfortable. Rebellion IPA and a seasonal Rebellion guest are well kept on handpump and the wine list is good.

🍴 Using seasonal local produce, the popular brasserie-style food at lunchtime includes filled baguettes, ploughman's, soup, eggs benedict, pork and leek sausages with onion gravy, pasta of the day, steak pie with chantenay carrots, and king prawns in tomato and garlic; with evening dishes such as king scallops with spinach and bacon, farmhouse terrine with whisky-soaked prunes and pistachios, a plate of vegetarian tapas, venison loin and venison pie, roast cod with clams, chorizo and tomato, and puddings like knickerbocker glory and pumpkin custard with praline, cocoa crumble and coffee ice-cream; they also offer a two- and three-course set menu. *Starters/Snacks: £4.00 to £9.00. Main Courses: £9.00 to £23.00. Puddings: £5.00 to £7.00*

Pubmaster ~ Managers Kim and Chris O'Brien ~ Real ale ~ Bar food (12-3, 5-9(9.30 Fri, Sat)) ~ Restaurant ~ (01494) 711262 ~ Well behaved children welcome ~ Open 12-3, 5-11.30; 12-5 Sun; closed Sun evening, Mon
Recommended by Tracey and Stephen Groves

GROVE
SP9122   MAP 4

Grove Lock ♀ 🍺
Pub signed off B488, on left just S of A505 roundabout (S of Leighton Buzzard); LU7 0QU

By Grand Union Canal Lock 28, with plenty of room inside, good food and real ales, and lots of seats overlooking the water

Overlooking the Grand Union Canal and usefully open all day, this open-plan pub has plenty of seats and picnic-sets in the terraced waterside garden and on the canopied decking area. Inside, the bar has a lofty high-raftered pitched roof and it's all warm and comfortable with terracotta and wallpapered walls, squishy brown leather sofas on diagonal oak floor boarding, an eclectic mix of tables and chairs, a couple of butchers' block tables by the bar, a big open-standing winter log fire and canal-themed artwork. Steps take you up to the original lock-keeper's cottage (now a three-room restaurant area) which is partly flagstoned, has more winter log fires and looks down on the narrow canal lock. Fullers London Pride and a couple of Fullers seasonal beers on handpump, several wines by the glass, and friendly staff; piped music and newspapers. More reports please.

🍴 Enjoyable bar food includes sandwiches, wraps and baps, soup, crab and smoked haddock fishcakes with lemon mayo, butternut squash and goats cheese risotto, treacle-glazed ham with eggs, coq au vin suet pudding, beer-battered cod, popular slow-cooked braised blade of beef with caramelised onion sauce, chicken breast filled with pork sausage and sage and onion stuffing wrapped in bacon, salmon fillet with a white wine sauce, daily specials, and puddings. *Starters/Snacks: £3.95 to £6.95. Main Courses: £8.95 to £15.95. Puddings: £4.95*

Fullers ~ Managers Gregg and Angela Worrall ~ Real ale ~ Bar food (12-9(7 Sun)) ~ (01525) 380940 ~ Children welcome ~ Open 11-11; 12-10.30 Sun; closed evenings 25 and 26 Dec

Recommended by Ross Balaam, Susan and John Douglas, Mr and Mrs John Taylor, Anthony and Marie Lewis

HEDGERLEY

SU9687   MAP 2

White Horse ★ 🍺

2.4 miles from M40 junction 2; at exit roundabout take Slough turn-off then take Hedgerley Lane (immediate left) following alongside M40; after 1.5 miles turn right at T junction into Village Lane; SL2 3UY

Old-fashioned drinkers' pub with lots of beers tapped straight from the cask, regular beer festivals and a cheery mix of customers

You can be sure of a friendly welcome – and a fine pint of beer – in this unchanging country gem. The cottagey main bar has plenty of unspoilt character, with lots of beams, brasses and exposed brickwork, low wooden tables, standing timbers, jugs, ballcocks and other bric-a-brac, a log fire, and a good few leaflets and notices about village events. A little flagstoned public bar on the left has darts and board games. As well as Rebellion IPA they keep up to seven daily changing guests, sourced from all over the country and tapped straight from casks kept in a room behind the tiny hatch counter. Their Easter, May, Spring and August bank holiday beer festivals (they can get through about 130 beers during the May one) are a highlight of the local calendar. This fine range of drinks extends to three farm ciders, still apple juice, a perry, belgian beers, ten or so wines by the glass and winter mulled wine. A canopy extension leads out to the garden where there are tables and occasional barbecues, and there are lots of hanging baskets and a couple more tables in front of the building overlooking the quiet road. Good walks nearby, and the pub is handy for the Church Wood RSPB reserve and popular with walkers and cyclists; it can get crowded at weekends.

🍴 Lunchtime bar food such as sandwiches, ploughman's, cold meats and quiches, and changing straightforward hot dishes. *Starters/Snacks: £4.25 to £6.00. Main Courses: £5.50 to £7.95. Puddings: £3.50*

Free house ~ Licensees Doris Hobbs and Kevin Brooker ~ Real ale ~ Bar food (lunchtime only) ~ (01753) 643225 ~ Children in canopy extension area ~ Dogs allowed in bar ~ Open 11-2.30, 5-11; 11-11 Sat; 12-10.30 Sun; closed evenings 25 and 26 Dec

Recommended by Anthony Longden, N R White, Mike and Eleanor Anderson, LM, the Didler, Susan and John Douglas, Roy Hoing, D and M T Ayres-Regan, Tracey and Stephen Groves, Nigel and Sue Foster, Gavin Robinson

LACEY GREEN

SP8201   MAP 4

Pink & Lily 🍷 🍺

From A4010 High Wycombe—Princes Risborough follow Loosley sign, then Gt Hampden, Gt Missenden one; HP27 ORJ

Well run and friendly pub with several real ales, good choice of wines, popular food and big garden

There's a really good mix of customers in this extended and modernised dining pub – plenty of locals mixing happily with families and their dogs. The airy main bar has typical pub furniture, an open fire and some cosier side areas, and there's a conservatory-style extension with big arches decorated in various shades of brown, beige and cream. The

36 • BUCKINGHAMSHIRE

little tap room has been well preserved with built-in wall benches on the red flooring tiles, an old wooden ham-rack hanging from the ceiling and a broad inglenook with a low mantelpiece (there's always a fire in winter). Framed on a wall is a Rupert Brooke poem (there's a room dedicated to him too) that begins with a mention of this pub. The atmosphere is relaxed and friendly and the staff are polite and helpful. Brakspears Bitter, Red Squirrel RSB and Tring Royal Poacher on handpump and lots of wines by the glass; piped music and board games. The big garden has lots of wooden tables and seats and the hanging baskets are very pretty.

🍴 Generous helpings of bar food includes sandwiches and filled ciabattas, filled baked potatoes, ploughman's, soup, pâté of the day with fruit chutney, beef or spicy bean burgers with cheese and red onion marmalade, fishcakes of the day with horseradish crème fraîche, cider and sugar-roasted ham with free-range eggs, beer-battered haddock, steak in ale pie and wild bass fillet with garlic potatoes and a creamed red chard sauce; Sunday roasts. *Starters/Snacks: £4.75 to £6.25. Main Courses: £8.95 to £16.95. Puddings: £5.25*

Enterprise ~ Lease Shakira Englefield ~ Real ale ~ Bar food (12-2.30, 6.15-9(9.15 Fri, Sat); 12-8(4 winter) Sun) ~ Restaurant ~ (01494) 488308 ~ Children welcome ~ Dogs welcome ~ Open 11-11; 12-8(4 winter) Sun

Recommended by the Didler, Roy Hoing, Ryta Lyndley, Tim and Ann Newell, Doug Kennedy, Tracey and Stephen Groves

LEY HILL   SP9901   MAP 4
Swan 🍺
Village signposted off A416 in Chesham; HP5 1UT

Charming, old-fashioned pub with chatty customers, five real ales and quite a choice of popular food

Everything here is kept spic and span by the friendly licensees and the atmosphere is relaxed and chatty. The main bar is cosily old-fashioned with black beams (mind your head) and standing timbers, an old range, a log fire, a nice mix of old furniture and a collection of old local photographs. Adnams Bitter, Brakspears Bitter, Timothy Taylors Landlord and guests such as St Austell Tribute and York Guzzler on handpump and several wines by the glass. The dining area is light and airy with a raftered ceiling, cream walls and curtains and a mix of old tables and chairs on timber floors. It's worth wandering over the common (there's a cricket pitch and a nine-hole golf course here) opposite this little timbered 16th-c pub to turn back and take a look at the very pretty picture it makes with its picnic-sets amongst flower tubs and hanging baskets (there are more in the large back garden). More reports please.

🍴 As well as lunchtime sandwiches, the changing bar menu might include soup, pork and apple sausages, home-roast honey ham with eggs, vegetable tagliatelle and corn-fed chicken and ham pie, with more elaborate dishes such as pigeon breast with pomegranate dressing, tiger prawns with garlic, chilli and ginger, risotto with goats cheese and pine nuts, sea bream with crayfish and herb sauce, 28-day-aged sirloin steak with café de paris butter, and puddings like sticky toffee and date pudding with toffee sauce and banana ice-cream and raspberry and white chocolate cheesecake. *Starters/Snacks: £4.50 to £6.95. Main Courses: £6.95 to £16.95. Puddings: £4.95 to £5.95*

Free house ~ Licensee Nigel Byatt ~ Real ale ~ Bar food (12-2.30(3 Sun), 6.30-9.30; not Sun or Mon evenings) ~ Restaurant ~ (01494) 783075 ~ Children welcome ~ Open 12-3, 5.30-11; 12-10.30 Sun

Recommended by C R Cann, Roy Hoing, LM, John and Elisabeth Cox

---

Real ale may be served from handpumps, electric pumps (not just the on-off switches used for keg beer) or – common in Scotland – tall taps called founts (pronounced 'fonts') where a separate pump pushes the beer up under air pressure.

LITTLE MARLOW
SU8787 MAP 2

Queens Head

Village signposted off A4155 E of Marlow near Kings Head; bear right into Pound Lane cul de sac; SL7 3RZ

Charmingly tucked away, with enjoyable food and appealing garden

On a summer's day, the garden of this pretty tiled cottage – though not large – is a decided plus, sheltered and neatly planted, with some teak tables, some quite close-set picnic-sets, and some white-painted metal furniture in a little wickerwork bower. Inside, the style is that of an unpretentious country pub, and the main bar, with a table of magazines by the door, has simple but comfortable furniture on its polished boards, and leads back to a sizeable squarish carpeted dining extension with good solid tables. Throughout are old local photographs on the cream or maroon walls, panelled dados painted brown or sage, and lit candles. On the right is a small, quite separate, low-ceilinged public bar with Brakspears Bitter, Fullers London Pride and a weekly changing guest like Greene King Old Speckled Hen on handpump, quite a range of whiskies and good coffee; neatly dressed efficient staff and unobtrusive piped music.

Ⓜ Enjoyable bar food includes sandwiches, ploughman's, smoked salmon and scrambled eggs on toast, crayfish pâté, linguine with squid, chilli, lemon and garlic, roasted leg and breast of guinea fowl on chasseur garnish, roasted lamb rump with confit garlic and rosemary potatoes, 10oz rib-eye steak, and puddings like lime brûlée with apple sorbet and chocolate and praline mousse with home-made shortbread. *Starters/Snacks: £4.95 to £8.50. Main Courses: £9.95 to £15.95. Puddings: £5.75*

Punch ~ Lease Daniel O'Sullivan and Chris Rising ~ Real ale ~ Bar food (12-2.30(4 Sat, Sun), 6.30-9.30) ~ Restaurant ~ (01628) 482927 ~ Children welcome ~ Open 11-11; 12-10.30 Sun; closed 25 and 26 Dec

Recommended by D J and P M Taylor, D and M T Ayres-Regan, Roy Hoing, Doug Kennedy, Martin and Karen Wake, Tracey and Stephen Groves

LITTLE MISSENDEN
SU9298 MAP 4

Crown 🏠 £

Crown Lane, SE end of village, which is signposted off A413 W of Amersham; HP7 0RD

Long-serving licensees and pubby feel in little brick cottage, with several real ales and traditional food; attractive garden

A favourite with many customers, this is a small brick cottage that has been in the same family for over 90 years and the friendly landlord proudly keeps it spotless. It's all very traditional, with old red flooring tiles on the left, oak parquet on the right, built-in wall seats, studded red leatherette chairs, and a few small tables. A good mix of customers, including a loyal bunch of regulars, adds to the cheerfully chatty atmosphere. Adnams Bitter, Hook Norton Bitter, St Austell Tribute, and a guest or two, such as Butcombe Gold or Cotswold Spring Codrington Codger on handpump or tapped from the cask, farm cider, summer Pimms and several malt whiskies; darts, bar billiards and board games. The large attractive sheltered garden behind has picnic-sets and other tables, and there are also seats out in front. The interesting church in the pretty village is well worth a visit. Bedrooms are in a converted barn (continental breakfasts in your room only).

Ⓜ Straightforward bar food such as good fresh sandwiches, soup, buck's bite (a special home-made pizza-like dish), filled baked potatoes, ploughman's, and steak and kidney pie. *Starters/Snacks: £3.75 to £6.50. Main Courses: £4.95 to £6.95*

Free house ~ Licensees Trevor and Carolyn How ~ Real ale ~ Bar food (12-2; not evenings, not Sun) ~ (01494) 862571 ~ Open 11-2.30, 6-11; 12-3, 7-10.30 Sun ~ Bedrooms: £65S/£75S

Recommended by Tracey and Stephen Groves, Anthony Longden, Dick Vardy, N R White, Patrick and Daphne Darley, Roy Hoing

Red Lion

Village signposted just off A413 Amersham—Great Missenden; HP7 0QZ

Country food, fair prices and cheery family service in small unspoilt two-room local; good-sized waterside garden

Dating from the 15th c, this pretty little cottage seems hardly changed in generations inside, though it needed some rebuilding after a 2007 fire. The small black-beamed bar has plain seats around elm pub tables, a piano squashed into the big inglenook beside a black kitchen range packed with copper pots and kettles, and a rack of old guns. Off to one side is an even smaller country dining room with just a few good heavy tables and a pheasant-dominated décor. They have well kept Greene King IPA, Marstons Pedigree and Wadworths 6X on handpump, nicely served coffee and very reasonably priced wines; the family give good service. In front by the quiet village lane are tables and picnic-sets, some on grass behind a little wall, and a sheltered garden behind has many more tables (one huge) by a biggish pond with various fancy waterfowl; in the meadow beyond are aviaries with more foreign birds.

🍴 **They do a good range of cold or hot sandwiches at fair prices, as well as ploughman's, soup, smoked salmon roulade, salads and mainly simple country cooking from a cheap basket of sausage and chips to hearty things like home-made burgers, liver and bacon, steak and mushroom pie or shoulder of lamb.** *Starters/Snacks: £4.50 to £6.95. Main Courses: £7.00 to £10.00. Puddings: £3.95*

Free house ~ Licensee Alan How ~ Real ale ~ Bar food (11-2.30, 5.30-9) ~ Restaurant ~ (01494) 862876 ~ Children welcome ~ Dogs allowed in bar ~ Open mike Tues evening, live band Sat evening ~ Open 11-3, 5.30-11; 11(12 Sun)-midnight Fri, Sat and Sun ~ Bedrooms: /£60S

Recommended by Susan and John Douglas, Roy Hoing

PENN   SU9093   MAP 4

Old Queens Head 🍷

Hammersley Lane/Church Road, off B474 between Penn and Tylers Green; HP10 8EY

Smartly updated pub with new licensee, good choice of drinks and interesting modern cooking

A new licensee has taken over this bustling open-plan pub but luckily little seems to have changed. It's decorated in a stylish mix of contemporary and chintz and has well spaced tables in a variety of linked areas, with a modicum of old prints, and comfortably varied seating on flagstones or broad dark boards. Stairs take you up to an attractive (and popular) two-level dining room, part carpeted, with stripped rafters. The active bar side has Greene King IPA and Ruddles County on handpump, good fresh juices and nearly two dozen old-world wines by the glass. Once tired of the display behind the counter, the turntable-top bar stools let you swivel to face the log fire in the big nearby fireplace; lots of daily papers and well reproduced piped music. The L-shaped lawn, sheltered by shrubs, has picnic-sets, some under cocktail parasols; St Margaret's church is just across the quiet road. More reports please.

🍴 **Enjoyable modern food includes weekday lunchtime sandwiches, soup, local game terrine with elderberry and apple jam, steamed mussels with chilli, lemon grass and coconut, creamy wild mushroom and baby spinach vol-au-vent, slow-cooked ox cheeks with pan haggerty potatoes, pancetta-wrapped chicken breast with onion bread pudding and truffle cream, venison and pearl barley stew with rosemary dumplings, and puddings such as dark chocolate truffle cake with pistachio ice-cream and prune and armagnac crème brûlée; additional side orders are extra.** *Starters/Snacks: £3.75 to £9.25. Main Courses: £11.50 to £17.50. Puddings: £4.50 to £6.75*

Salisbury Pubs ~ Lease Tina Brown ~ Real ale ~ Bar food (12-2.30(3 Sat, 4 Sun), 6.30-9.30(10 Fri, Sat)) ~ Restaurant ~ (01494) 813371 ~ Children welcome ~ Dogs allowed in bar ~ Open 11-11; 12-10.30 Sun; closed 25 and 26 Dec

Recommended by Tracey and Stephen Groves

PENN STREET   SU9295   MAP 4

Hit or Miss

off A404 SW of Amersham, then keep on towards Winchmore Hill; HP7 0PX

Traditional pub with friendly licensees, cheerful linked bar rooms, real ales and interesting food

Run by a friendly irish couple, this wisteria-covered brick-built pub is much enjoyed by our readers. The three linked rooms are well laid out and traditional with a cheerful atmosphere; Badger K&B Sussex Bitter, First Gold and a seasonal beer on handpump. The busy, little, heavily beamed main bar has leather sofas and armchairs on the parquet flooring, an open fire and quite a few brass items and horsebrasses; piped music. The other two carpeted rooms have interesting cricket and chair-making memorabilia on the walls, more sofas and wheelback and other wooden dining chairs around pine tables. There are picnic-sets on the terrace overlooking the pub's cricket pitch.

🍴 Interesting – if not cheap – bar food includes sandwiches, filled baked potatoes, soup, duck liver pâté with rhubarb chutney, an antipasti plate, goats cheese filo parcel with a roast fennel and walnut salad and beetroot dressing, calves liver with caramelised red onions and a pink peppercorn and sage sauce, herb-roasted poussin with herb gravy, grilled bass fillets with smoked bacon and crushed peas and a carrot vinaigrette, and puddings such as vanilla crème brûlée and bakewell tart; Sunday roasts. *Starters/Snacks: £4.95 to £6.95. Main Courses: £10.50 to £15.95. Puddings: £4.95*

Badger ~ Tenants Mike and Mary Macken ~ Real ale ~ Bar food (12-2.30, 6.45-9.30; 12-8 Sun) ~ (01494) 713109 ~ Children welcome ~ Dogs allowed in bar ~ Open 11-11; 12-10.30 Sun

Recommended by J C Upshall, H Wainman, Tracey and Stephen Groves, D and M T Ayres-Regan, Mrs Ann Gray

PRESTWOOD   SP8799   MAP 4

Polecat

170 Wycombe Road (A4128 N of High Wycombe); HP16 0HJ

Enjoyable food, real ales and a chatty atmosphere in several smallish civilised rooms; attractive sizeable garden

Run with a light but professional touch this is a smart country pub with a civilised feel. Several smallish rooms, opening off the low-ceilinged bar, have a slightly chintzy décor: an assortment of tables and chairs, various stuffed birds, stuffed white polecats in one big cabinet, small country pictures, rugs on bare boards or red tiles, and a couple of antique housekeeper's chairs by a good open fire. Brakspears Bitter, Flowers IPA, Greene King Old Speckled Hen and Marstons Pedigree on handpump, 16 wines by the glass and 20 malt whiskies; piped music. The garden is most attractive with lots of spring bulbs and colourful summer hanging baskets and tubs, and herbaceous plants; quite a few picnic-sets under parasols on neat grass out in front beneath a big fairy-lit pear tree, with more on a big well kept back lawn. They don't take bookings at lunchtime (except for tables of six or more) so you do need to arrive promptly at weekends to be sure of a table.

🍴 Well liked bar food includes lunchtime sandwiches and ploughman's, as well as crab cakes rolled in lemon crumbs with chilli jam, house pâté with red onion marmalade, chickpea, sweet potato and apricot tagine, steak and kidney pie, chicken curry, salmon fishcakes with tomato and basil sauce, braised lamb shank, daily specials like venison and rabbit pie, and puddings such as sherry trifle and chocolate and hazelnut torte. *Starters/Snacks: £4.20 to £6.50. Main Courses: £10.20 to £13.90. Puddings: £4.80*

Free house ~ Licensee John Gamble ~ Real ale ~ Bar food (12-2, 6.30-9 (not Sun evening)) ~ (01494) 862253 ~ Children in gallery or drovers' bar only ~ Dogs welcome ~ Open 11.30-2.30, 6-11.30; 12-3 Sun; closed Sun evening; 25 and 26 Dec, evening 31 Dec, 1 Jan

Recommended by Peter and Jan Humphreys, Ken Richards, Howard and Margaret Buchanan, Tracey and Stephen Groves, Simon Collett-Jones, Gordon Tong, Roy Hoing

SKIRMETT

SU7790 MAP 2

Frog ⓣ ♀ ⇌

From A4155 NE of Henley take Hambleden turn and keep on; or from B482 Stokenchurch—Marlow take Turville turn and keep on; RG9 6TG

Bustling pub with modern cooking in traditional atmosphere, fine choice of drinks, lovely garden and nearby walks; bedrooms

Extremely busy with both regulars and visitors, this country pub still has its heart in the public bar – despite the emphasis on the good, interesting food. There's a winter log fire in the brick fireplace with lots of little framed prints above it, a cushioned sofa and leather-seated bar stools around a low circular table on the wooden floor, and high bar chairs by the counter; piped music. Fullers London Pride, Rebellion IPA and Wadworths JCB on handpump, with a dozen wines by the glass (including champagne), and about two dozen carefully sourced malt whiskies. The two dining rooms are quite different in style. Outside, a side gate leads to a lovely garden with a large tree in the middle and the unusual five-sided tables are well placed for attractive valley views. Plenty of nearby hikes (Henley is close by) and just down the road is the delightful Ibstone windmill. There's a purpose-built outdoor heated area for smokers. The breakfasts are good.

Ⓜ **Imaginative food includes soup, potted shrimp and watercress salad, rabbit and asparagus terrine with baby pickles, venison cheeseburger, baked stuffed marrow with ratatouille and goats cheese, hake with chorizo, sweet pepper sauce and balsamic reduction, calves liver and bacon with black pudding and red wine jus, guinea fowl breast stuffed with oxtail with a Grand Marnier sauce and confit leg, daily specials such as assorted smoked fish plate with dill and orange dressing, beer-battered haddock and duck breast with honey and black pepper, and puddings.** *Starters/Snacks: £4.95 to £7.25. Main Courses: £11.95 to £16.50. Puddings: £5.50*

Free house ~ Licensees Jim Crowe and Noelle Greene ~ Real ale ~ Bar food (12-2.30, 6.30-9.30; 12-4, 6-9 Sun) ~ Restaurant ~ (01491) 638996 ~ Children welcome ~ Dogs allowed in bar ~ Open 11.30-3, 6-11; 12-10.30 Sun; closed Sun evening Oct-Apr ~ Bedrooms: £60B/£80B

Recommended by Tracey and Stephen Groves, Richard and Liz Thorne, T R and B C Jenkins, Martin and Karen Wake, Ian Wilson, Noel Grundy, Paul Humphreys

WOOBURN COMMON

SU9187 MAP 2

Chequers

From A4094 N of Maidenhead at junction with A4155 Marlow road keep on A4094 for another 0.75 miles, then at roundabout turn off right towards Wooburn Common, and into Kiln Lane; if you find yourself in Honey Hill, Hedsor, turn left into Kiln Lane at the top of the hill; OS Sheet 175 map reference 910870; HP10 0JQ

Busy and friendly hotel with bustling bar and restaurant

The atmosphere in the friendly main bar of this busy hotel seems more like that of a bustling, rustic local. It feels nicely pubby with low beams, standing timbers and alcoves, characterful rickety furniture and comfortably lived-in sofas on bare boards, a bright log-effect gas fire, pictures, plates, a two-man saw and tankards. In contrast, the bar to the left, with its dark brown leather sofas at low tables, on new wood floors, feels plain and modern. They have a good sizeable wine list (with a dozen by the glass), a fair range of malt whiskies and brandies, and Greene King IPA and Old Speckled Hen and Rebellion Smuggler on handpump; piped music. The spacious garden, set away from the road, has seats around cast-iron tables and summer barbecues.

Ⓜ **Pubby bar food includes quite a choice of sandwiches, toasties and open ciabattas as well as soup, nibbles such as spicy meatballs, whitebait and a tapas sharing plate, linguine with carbonara sauce, burger with bacon and cheese, beer-battered haddock, chilli con carne, cumberland sausage with onion gravy, steak and kidney pie, fillet of salmon with pea risotto, and puddings like sticky toffee pudding and chocolate fondant.** *Starters/Snacks: £3.95 to £8.95. Main Courses: £8.95 to £16.95. Puddings: £4.95 to £5.95*

Free house ~ Licensee Peter Roehrig ~ Real ale ~ Bar food (12-2.30, 6-9.30(10 Fri);
12-10(9.30 Sun) Sat) ~ Restaurant ~ (01628) 529575 ~ Children welcome ~ Open 11-12.30
(midnight Sun); closed evenings 25 Dec and 1 Jan ~ Bedrooms: £99.50B/£107.50B
Recommended by Peter and Giff Bennett, Simon Collett-Jones, Tracey and Stephen Groves

LUCKY DIP

Besides the fully inspected pubs, you might like to try these Lucky Dips recommended to us and
described by readers (if you do, please send us reports: feedback@goodguides.com).

ADSTOCK [SP7330]
☆ *Old Thatched Inn* MK18 2JN [Main St, off
A413]: Restaurantly place doing good home-
made food (all day Sun) from own filled
focaccia breads up, well kept Greene King
ales and a guest like Silverstone Pitstop,
good choice of wines by the glass,
enthusiastic landlord and friendly helpful
service; beams and flagstones, cosy corners
and open fires, part comfortably pubby, and
part with easy chairs and settees leading to
modern back conservatory restaurant;
children in eating areas, dogs in bar, tables
in garden with sheltered terrace, open all day
Weds-Sun *(Sue Vincent, Michael Dandy, LYM)*
AMERSHAM [SU9597]
Crown HP7 0DH [Market Sq]: Spotless
modernised hotel bar, leather, polished wood
and beams, interesting 16th-c features in
comfortable lounge, pleasant formal dining
area, enjoyable food from sandwiches to
some interesting dishes, young helpful staff,
Bass, good range of wines by the glass;
attractive split-level outside area inc
cobbled courtyard, bedrooms *(BB, Phyl and
Jack Street, Mrs Ann Gray)*
Swan HP7 0ED [High St]: Refurbished M&B
pub-restaurant on two floors, contemporary
bar with comfortable chairs and low tables,
enterprising food all day inc children's, good
choice of wines by the glass, well kept
Adnams and Timothy Taylors Landlord, fast
friendly service; picnic-sets in pleasant
garden behind, open all day *(John Faircloth)*
ASKETT [SP8105]
☆ *Three Crowns* HP27 9LT: Well run pub
producing wide range of good food at
sensible prices, beamed and boarded dining
rooms either side of small bar, fresh modern
décor, comfortable leather chairs *(Peter and
Jan Humphreys, Doug Kennedy)*
ASTWOOD [SP9547]
☆ *Old Swan* MK16 9JS [Main Rd]: Stylish low-
beamed pub with helpful friendly service,
well kept Adnams Bitter and Broadside,
enjoyable food, fair prices, gleaming
flagstones, inglenook woodburner, nice china
collection, two attractive dining areas,
warm cosy atmosphere; large garden *(LYM,
Howard Galloway, Jeremy King)*
AYLESBURY [SP8114]
Hop Pole HP19 9AZ [Bicester Rd]: Friendly
open-plan pub tied to Vale, their ales and
lots of guest beers (tasters offered), good
value food; open all day *(Kevin Brown,
Roger Shipperley)*

BEACHAMPTON [SP7736]
Bell MK19 6DX [Main St]: Good choice of
ales inc local ones in big low-beamed pub
with pleasant view down attractive
streamside village street, log fire dividing
bar from lounge and attractive refurbished
dining area, nice range of home-made pubby
food, decent wines, good friendly service,
pool in small separate games room; piped
music; open all day, terrace and play area in
big garden *(George Atkinson, Michael Dandy)*
BLEDLOW [SP7702]
Lions of Bledlow HP27 9PE [off B4009
Chinnor—Princes Risborough; Church End]:
Great views from bay windows of relaxed
take-us-as-you-find-us Chilterns pub with
low 16th-c beams, ancient floor tiles,
inglenook log fires and a woodburner, well
kept ales such as Rebellion and Wadworths,
good choice of food inc vegetarian, games
room; well behaved children allowed, dogs
welcome, picnic-sets out in peaceful sloping
garden with sheltered terrace; nice setting,
good walks *(LYM, the Didler, Susan and
John Douglas, Doug Kennedy, Roy Hoing,
Paul Humphreys)*
CADMORE END [SU7892]
Old Ship HP14 3PN [B482 Stokenchurch—
Marlow (Marlow Rd)]: Tiny, carefully restored
old cottage, two little low-beamed rooms
separated by standing timbers, simple
furnishings (one chair still has a hole for
game called five-farthings), coal fire, beers
tapped straight from the cask down in cellar,
wines by the glass; children and dogs
welcome, seats in sheltered garden and on
terrace, parking on other side of road, cl Sun
evening, Mon, *(the Didler, LYM)*
CADSDEN [SP8204]
Plough HP27 0NB [Cadsden Rd]: Welcoming
extended and refurbished pub with airy
open-plan bar/dining area, well spaced
tables on wood floor, very popular with
families and Chilterns ramblers, good choice
of real ales and of hearty food, cherry pie
festival (1st Sun in Aug), friendly efficient
service; lots of tables in delightful quiet
front and back garden, pretty spot on
Ridgeway Path, bedrooms, open all day
wknds *(Paul Humphreys, Torrens Lyster,
Roy Hoing, Doug Kennedy)*
CHALFONT ST GILES [SU9893]
Fox & Hounds HP8 4PS [Silver Hill]: Small
quietly set 16th-c local with well kept ales
such as Adnams and St Austell, enjoyable
good value pubby food, friendly staff, open

fire in simple unspoilt interior, darts and pool; pleasant garden behind with play area *(R K Phillips, Ross Balaam)*

☆ *Ivy House* HP8 4RS [A413 S]: Open-plan dining pub tied to Fullers, their ales include Gales, good if not cheap food, friendly young staff, good wines by the glass, espresso coffee, comfortable fireside armchairs in carefully lit and elegantly cosy L-shaped tiled bar, lighter flagstoned dining extension; pleasant terrace and sloping garden (can be traffic noise), five bedrooms *(Roy Hoing, Mrs Ann Gray, BB)*

White Hart HP8 4LP [Three Households, Main St]: Under new italian owner keeping emphasis on good imaginative cooking (not cheap – but doing lunchtime deals), good service, well kept Greene King ales, several wines by the glass, modern furnishings in bar and bare-boards dining room, newspapers; soft piped music; well behaved children welcome, picnic-sets on sheltered back terrace and in garden beyond, 11 barn bedrooms, open all day Sun *(LYM, Roy Hoing, Phyl and Jack Street, Karen Eliot)*

CHESHAM [SP9604]

Black Horse HP5 3NS [Vale Rd, N off A416 in Chesham]: Neatly extended popular black-beamed country pub with good choice of enjoyable food inc OAP lunch Weds, real ales, decent wines, good service; tables on back grass *(LYM, Roy Hoing, Joan Baillie)*

CHICHELEY [SP9045]

☆ *Chester Arms* MK16 9JE [quite handy for M1 junction 14]: Cosy and pretty, with low-beamed rooms off semicircular bar, log fire, comfortable settles and chairs, helpful friendly service; wide choice of good popular home-made food at fair prices, children's helpings, Greene King ales, decent wines, good coffee, daily papers, interesting back dining room down steps; picnic-sets in small back garden and out in front *(Michael Dandy, Graeme Manson, BB)*

COLESHILL [SU9495]

☆ *Red Lion* HP7 0LH [Village Rd]: Small popular local with welcoming long-serving landlord, generous good value pubby food (not Sun evening) from sandwiches up, Vale Wychert and guest ales, quick service, two open fires, thriving darts and dominoes teams; TV for racing, games machine; front and back gardens, sturdy climbing frames, good walks, open all day wknds *(N R White, BB, Roy Hoing)*

COLNBROOK [TQ0277]

Ostrich SL3 0JZ [1.25 miles from M4 junction 5 via A4/B3378, then 'village only' road; High St]: Spectacular timbered Elizabethan building (with even longer gruesome history) given contemporary makeover; comfortable sofas on stripped wood and a startling red plastic and stainless steel bar counter, blazing log fires, real ales such as Courage Directors and Sharps Doom Bar, enjoyable upscale food inc good vegetarian choice, attractive restaurant; soft piped

music, comedy nights and live music upstairs *(LYM, A Darroch Harkness, Sally Norman, Terry Buckland)*

DENHAM [TQ0487]

☆ *Swan* UB9 5BH [village signed from M25 exit 16]: Civilised pub/restaurant in lovely village, good imaginative food (not Sun, Mon evenings and quite pricey), Courage Best, Rebellion IPA and Wadworths 6X, good wine choice, stylish mix of old chairs and solid tables, heavily draped curtains, open fires, fresh flowers, daily papers; piped music; children welcome, extensive floodlit garden with sheltered terrace, open all day Sun *(Susan and John Douglas, Brian Glozier, LYM, Kevin Thomas, Nina Randall)*

DORNEY [SU9279]

☆ *Palmer Arms* SL4 6QW [2.7 miles from M4 junction 7, via B3026; Village Rd]: Smartly modernised extended dining pub in attractive conservation village, all-day fresh food from pub favourites up, lots of wines by the glass, well kept Greene King ales, pleasant attentive service, open fires, daily papers, civilised front bar, elegant back dining room; soft piped music; children welcome, dogs in certain areas, disabled facilities, stylish terrace overlooking mediterranean-feel garden, enclosed play area, open all day *(Simon Collett-Jones, Nigel and Sue Foster, I D Barnett, Susan and John Douglas, LYM, Peter Price)*

FORD [SP7709]

☆ *Dinton Hermit* HP17 8XH [SW of Aylesbury]: Extended 17th-c stone inn, scrubbed tables and comfortable chairs on old tiled floor, huge working inglenook, real ales inc Badger, decent choice of wines, good value food, back dining area; well behaved children allowed, disabled access, terrace seating and garden, 13 bedrooms in barn conversion, open all day *(LYM, J A Snell)*

FRIETH [SU7990]

Prince Albert RG9 6PY [off B482 SW of High Wycombe]: Friendly cottagey Chilterns local with low black beams and joists, high-backed settles, big black stove in inglenook, log fire in larger area on the right, decent food (mainly lunchtime) from sandwiches up, well kept Brakspears; children and dogs welcome, nicely planted informal side garden with views of woods and fields, open all day *(R K Phillips, Ross Balaam, Paul Humphreys, the Didler, Tracey and Stephen Groves, Peter Dandy, LYM, Noel Grundy)*

GREAT HAMPDEN [SP8401]

☆ *Hampden Arms* HP16 9RQ [off A4010 N and S of Princes Risborough]: Nicely placed dining pub opp village cricket pitch, reasonably priced food made by landlord from lunchtime sandwiches to substantial main dishes, friendly service, Adnams, a seasonal Vale ale and Addlestone's cider from small corner bar, good choice of wines by the glass, big woodburner in more spacious back room; children and dogs welcome, nice tree-sheltered garden, good walks nearby *(LYM, John and Eileen Kent, Roy Hoing)*

GREAT HORWOOD [SP7731]
Crown MK17 0RH [off B4033 N of Winslow; The Green]: Small comfortable Georgian pub with striking inglenook fireplace, well kept real ales, good choice of wines by the glass, friendly service, good value home-made food, dining room; piped music; tables on neat front lawn, pretty village, very handy for Winslow Hall *(Sue Vincent, BB)*

GREAT MISSENDEN [SP8901]
☆ *Cross Keys* HP16 0AU [High St]: Relaxed village pub, unspoilt beamed bar divided by standing timbers, traditional furnishings inc high-backed settle, log-effect gas fire in huge fireplace, well kept Fullers ales, decent food from sandwiches up inc Sun roasts, spacious beamed restaurant, cheerful helpful staff; children and dogs welcome, back terrace with picnic-sets, open all day *(Jill Bickerton, N R White, Roy Hoing, Mrs Ann Gray, LYM)*

☆ *Nags Head* HP16 0DG [old London road, E – beyond Abbey]: Civilised and neatly revamped by licensees of Bricklayers Arms, Flaunden (see Herts Main Entries), similar good if pricey food using local produce and own smoked fish and meat, good service, Fullers London Pride, Rebellion and Tring, fine armagnac range and wines by the glass, unusual bar counter (windows behind face road), carpet throughout, low beams on left, loftier on right, log fire in handsome fireplace, relaxed atmosphere, Roald Dahl links; garden picnic-sets, seven comfortably redone bedrooms, open all day *(Kevin Thomas, Nina Randall, Tracey and Stephen Groves, D and M T Ayres-Regan, BB, Mrs Shirley Hughes)*

HADDENHAM [SP7408]
Green Dragon HP17 8AA [village signposted off A418 and A4129, E/NE of Thame; then follow Church End signs into Churchway]: Shuttered cottagey front with neat window boxes, contrasting open-plan modernised interior with mix of old tables and chairs and leather sofas, two log fires, Sharps Doom Bar, Timothy Taylors Landlord and a guest, over a dozen wines by the glass, straightforward food; dogs and children welcome, big sheltered gravel terrace, picnic-sets under parasols in appealing garden, open all day *(Nina Bell, John Branston, LYM, Gerry and Rosemary Dobson)*

HAMBLEDEN [SU7886]
☆ *Stag & Huntsman* RG9 6RP [off A4155 Henley—Marlow]: Handsome brick and flint pub in pretty Chilterns village, congenial old-fashioned front public bar with masses of beer mats, big fireplace in low-ceilinged partly panelled lounge bar, Loddon Hoppit, Rebellion IPA, Wadworths 6X and a guest beer, farm cider and good wines, friendly efficient staff, good reasonably priced pubby food (not Sun evening), secluded dining room; darts, TV, piped music; children welcome, dogs in bar, good garden with some raised areas and decking, nice walks, bedrooms; refurbishments planned for spring

2011, when there will be a very limited service *(Ross Balaam, LYM, Roy Hoing, Simon Collett-Jones, John Saul, Anthony Longden)*

HAWRIDGE COMMON [SP9406]
☆ *Full Moon* HP5 2UH [Hawridge Common; left fork off A416 N of Chesham, then follow for 3.5 miles towards Cholesbury]: Low-beamed bar with ancient flagstones and chequered floor tiles, built-in floor-to-ceiling oak settles, hunting prints, inglenook; Adnams, Bass, Fullers London Pride, Timothy Taylors Landlord and changing guests, several wines by the glass, popular standard food from sandwiches up, restaurant; piped music; children and dogs welcome, country views from pleasant garden with heated covered terrace, paddock for hitching horses, good walks on common *(Roy Hoing, Ross Balaam, LYM, John and Victoria Fairley, Susan and John Douglas)*

HIGH WYCOMBE [SU8792]
Belle Vue HP13 6EQ [Gordon Rd]: Unpretentious traditional backstreet local with well kept regularly changing ales, enthusiastic staff, characterful friendly locals, well worn but not tatty; handy for station *(Tracey and Stephen Groves)*

HOLMER GREEN [SU9097]
Old Oak HP15 6SX [New Pond Rd]: Recently refurbished and improved under new management; children welcome *(Teri Doubtfire)*

HUGHENDEN VALLEY [SU8697]
☆ *Harrow* HP14 4LX [Warrendene Rd, off A4128 N of High Wycombe]: Roadside pub doing well under newish owners, good spot by Chilterns walking valley, popular food inc some bargains, just roasts on Sun, nice staff, real ales such as Fullers London Pride, Rebellion and Wells & Youngs, cosy traditional bar on left, bigger dining area, beams and tiled or brick floors, log fire; tables out on terraces and in garden with swings and slides, open all day, food all day Fri and Sat *(Tracey and Stephen Groves, Mike and Eleanor Anderson, BB)*

HYDE HEATH [SU9300]
Plough HP6 5RW [off B485 Great Missenden—Chesham]: Prettily placed pub overlooking village green, good value food in bar and evening restaurant extension, friendly landlord, real ales such as Adnams, Fullers London Pride and Wells & Youngs, open fires *(LYM, Roy Hoing)*

ICKFORD [SP6407]
Rising Sun HP18 9JD [E of Thame; Worminghall Rd]: Carefully restored pretty thatched local, cosy low-beamed bar, friendly staff and locals, good range of reasonably priced home-made food inc occasional game, real ales such as Black Sheep *(David Lamb)*

LACEY GREEN [SP8200]
Black Horse HP27 0QU [Main Rd]: Friendly little beamed country local very popular for good value home-made food (not Sun evening, Mon), four real ales,

good choice of wines by the glass, big open fire; sports TV; picnic-sets in garden with play area, cl Mon lunchtime, open all day Thurs-Sun *(Graham Middleton)*

LANE END [SU8091]
Grouse & Ale HP14 3JG [High St]: Enjoyable food from standards to some unusual things, Sun carvery, great range of wines by the glass, well kept changing ales such as Adnams Broadside, Courage Best and Shepherd Neame Spitfire, friendly helpful staff, fresh flowers, newspapers; soft piped music *(Simon Collett-Jones, Mrs Margo Finlay, Jörg Kasprowski)*

LAVENDON [SP9153]
Green Man MK46 4HA [A428 Bedford—Northampton]: Handsome 17th-c thatched pub in pretty village, friendly attentive staff, good value reliable food from soup and sandwiches up, Greene King ales, good choice of wines by the glass, nice coffee; roomy and relaxed open-plan wood-floored area with two raised sections, beams, lots of stripped stone and open woodburner, big carpeted evening/wknd restaurant; piped music; children welcome, tables and heaters outside, open all day *(George Atkinson, Bruce and Sharon Eden)*

LITTLE KINGSHILL [SU8999]
Full Moon HP16 0EE [Hare Lane]: Picturesque country pub with new landlord, good choice of popular food, Adnams, Fullers London Pride and Wells & Youngs, pleasantly traditional beamed bar with open fire, bigger carpeted dining room; attractive garden *(Roy Hoing, Mike and Eleanor Anderson)*

LITTLE MARLOW [SU8788]
☆ ***Kings Head*** SL7 3RZ [A4155 about 2 miles E of Marlow; Church Rd]: Long flower-covered pub with open-plan low-beamed bar, wide blackboard choice of enjoyable food from plenty of sandwiches to popular Sun roasts, smart dining room, several well kept ales inc Adnams, Fullers and Timothy Taylors Landlord, quick cheerful service even when busy, open fires, Sun bar nibbles, cricket memorabilia; children welcome; big attractive walled garden behind popular with families *(D and M T Ayres-Regan, Chris Glasson, Paul Humphreys, BB, Roy Hoing, Doug Kennedy)*

LITTLE TINGEWICK [SP6432]
Red Lion MK18 4AG [off A421 SW of Buckingham; pub towards Finmere, over the Oxon border]: Nicely renovated 16th-c stone and thatch pub, some emphasis on good gently upmarket food inc fresh fish, also interesting sandwiches and pub favourites, bar nibbles, Fullers ales and a guest, decent wines by the glass, helpful service; inglenook log fire, low beams, mixed simple new furniture on wood floor; piped music; tables out in front and in small garden behind with aunt sally, open all day wknds *(Caroline and Michael Abbey)*

LITTLEWORTH COMMON [SU9386]
Jolly Woodman SL1 8PF [2 miles from M40 junction 2; off A355]: Welcoming red-brick

country pub doing well under present licensees, good home-made food from extensive varied menu, five well kept changing ales, rambling multilevel beamed and timbered areas inc a snug, central woodburner, jazz Mon evening (can get busy); small front terrace and nice garden, good site by Burnham Beeches, open all day *(LYM, Les and Sandra Brown, Brian Glozier, D Crook, LM, Phil Bryant)*

LONG CRENDON [SP6908]
Eight Bells HP18 9AL [High St]: Unassuming old timbered pub with cheerful service and good landlady, well kept Wadworths and interesting guests (several tapped from the cask), short choice of enjoyable home-made pubby food (pies recommended), simple wooden furniture on long airy main room's tiled floor, open fire, darts; charming garden with aunt sally, lovely village *(Doug Kennedy)*

LUDGERSHALL [SP6617]
☆ ***Bull & Butcher*** HP18 9NZ [off A41 Aylesbury—Bicester; bear left to The Green]: Nicely old-fashioned low-beamed country pub, tiles, flagstones and inglenook fireplace, good choice of enjoyable reasonably priced food, popular breakfast (1st Sat of month), Greene King IPA and Vale VPA, back dining room, exemplary ladies'; picnic-sets on pleasant front terrace overlooking green, cl Mon and lunchtimes Tues and Thurs, open all day wknds *(David Lamb, BB)*

MARLOW [SU8586]
☆ ***Two Brewers*** SL7 1NQ [St Peter St, first right off Station Rd from double roundabout]: Busy low-beamed pub with shiny black woodwork, nautical pictures, gleaming brassware and interesting layout, most tables, inc upstairs and downstairs overflows, set for good food (wide evening choice), Brakspears, Fullers, Hop Back and Rebellion, nice wines and coffee, good friendly service, relaxed atmosphere; children in eating area, may be unobtrusive piped music; tables in sheltered back courtyard with covered area, front seats with glimpse of the Thames – pub right on Thames Path *(Robert Kibble, LYM)*

MARLOW BOTTOM [SU8588]
Three Horseshoes SL7 3RA [signed from Handy Cross roundabout, off M40 junction 4]: Tied to nearby Rebellion brewery and usually their full range, knowledgeable staff, wide choice of popular food (not Sun evening), good value wines by the glass; open all day Fri and Sat *(Tracey and Stephen Groves)*

MARSH GIBBON [SP6423]
Plough OX27 0HQ [Church St]: Old stone-built beamed village pub with plenty of tables, good choice of reasonably priced food, friendly helpful staff, several real ales; pleasant back garden *(David Lamb)*

MARSWORTH [SP9114]
☆ ***Red Lion*** HP23 4LU [village signed off B489 Dunstable—Aylesbury; Vicarage Rd]: Low-

beamed partly thatched village pub with well kept Fullers London Pride and guests such as Rebellion and Vale, cheerful efficient service, enjoyable good value pubby food from sandwiches up, decent wines, main quarry-tiled bar with pews and open fire, snug, steps up to lounge and dining area; games area with bar billiards, darts and juke box; children and dogs on leads welcome, sheltered garden with heated smokers' gazebo, not far from impressive flight of canal locks, open all day Sun *(LYM, Roy Hoing, Ross Balaam, Tracey and Stephen Groves)*

MEDMENHAM [SU8084]

Dog & Badger SL7 2HE [Bockmer (A4155)]: Spacious low-beamed pub, nice décor with good mix of old furniture on polished boards, open fire, enjoyable food in bar and restaurant, charming service, Rebellion ales; piped music and some live; children welcome, terrace tables, open all day *(T A R Curran, LYM)*

MILTON KEYNES [SP9137]

Wavendon Arms MK17 8LJ [not far from M1 junctions 13 and 14]: Pleasant front bar with mix of modern furniture, airy contemporary tiled-floor restaurant, Timothy Taylors Landlord, good choice of wines by the glass, popular up-to-date food, good service; piped music; tables out in back garden with terrace, more in front *(Eithne Dandy, Michael Dandy)*

NEWTON BLOSSOMVILLE [SP9251]

Old Mill Burnt Down MK43 8AN [4 miles from M1 junction 14; off A428 at Turvey — Clifton road]: Smart old stone-built beamed pub, three linked areas on two levels, mixed furnishings on stone floor, three real ales inc Timothy Taylors Landlord, welcoming efficient staff, good food; courtyard seating, three comfortable bedrooms *(Michael Sargent)*

OAKLEY [SP6312]

Chandos Arms HP18 9QB [The Turnpike]: Small welcoming 16th-c village local, with chef/landlord doing good reasonably priced food inc some unusual choices in bar and end restaurant, well kept Adnams and Greene King *(David Lamb, Malcolm Lock, Sharon Oldham)*

OLNEY [SP8851]

Bull MK46 4EA [Market Pl/High St]: Former coaching inn smartened up by present licensees, sofas and other seats in three smallish front rooms, big airy eating area on the right, popular food (not Sun evening) from bar snacks up inc mussels done in six ways and interesting vegetarian choices; good service, well kept Wells & Youngs and guests, Aug bank hol beer festival, good coffee, open and log-effect gas fires; courtyard, big back garden (no dogs) with climbing frame; start of the famous Shrove Tuesday pancake race; open all day from 10am *(George Atkinson)*

☆ *Swan* MK46 4AA [High St S]: Friendly beamed and timbered linked rooms, wide choice of reasonably priced generous food (not Mon)

from sandwiches up, good range of well kept ales, good value wines by the glass, quick helpful service, daily papers, attractive flowers, rather close-set pine tables, log fires, small back bistro dining room (booking advised for this); back courtyard tables, some cover *(Michael Sargent, Jim Lyon, Gerry and Rosemary Dobson, BB)*

OVING [SP7821]

☆ *Black Boy* HP22 4HN [off A413 N of Aylesbury]: Extended 16th-c timbered pub nr church, low heavy beams, log fire in enormous inglenook, steps up to snug stripped-stone area, well kept ales such as Batemans, Brakspears and Rebellion, lots of wines by the glass, pubby bar food and more elaborate restaurant menu, modern dining room with good-sized pine tables and picture windows, prompt friendly service; piped music; children and dogs welcome, tables on spacious sloping lawns and terrace (music here summer Suns), expansive Vale of Aylesbury views, cl Sun evening, Mon *(John Beeken, LYM, Dick Vardy, Andy Dobbing, J A Snell, John Faircloth, Stephen Castle)*

PENN [SU9193]

☆ *Crown* HP10 8NY [B474 Beaconsfield—High Wycombe]: Busy Chef & Brewer opp 14th-c church on high ridge with distant views, interesting décor and attractive furnishings in linked areas around low-ceilinged medieval core, wide range of generous food all day inc fixed-price bargains (Mon-Thurs) and Sun roasts, friendly service, well kept Fullers London Pride and guest ales, good choice of wines by the glass, interesting summer cocktails, two roaring log fires; piped music (outside too), games machine; children very welcome, lots of tables in attractive split-level garden, open all day *(Tracey and Stephen Groves, Roy Hoing, Mrs Ann Gray, Susan and John Douglas, LYM)*

PENN STREET [SU9295]

Squirrel HP7 0PX: Family-friendly sister pub to nearby Hit or Miss (see Main Entries), open-plan bar with flagstones, log fire, comfortable sofas as well as tables and chairs, good value home-made traditional food from baguettes up (not Sun evening), good children's meals, well kept changing ales, good service, free coffee refills; bric-a-brac and cricketing memorabilia, darts; big garden with good play area and village cricket view, lovely walks, open all day wknds *(Roy Hoing, David Lamb, C and R Bromage, Tracey and Stephen Groves)*

PITSTONE GREEN [SP9216]

Duke of Wellington LU7 9AD [Pitstone Wharf]: Unpretentious country pub with two traditional rooms divided by log fire, black beams, brasses, copper and decorative china, Fullers and Marstons, limited but good food; nr Grand Union Canal *(Roy Hoing)*

PRESTON BISSETT [SP6529]

White Hart MK18 4LX [off A421 or A4421 SW of Buckingham; Pound Lane]: Thatched, timbered and low-beamed 18th-c village pub run by chinese family, three cosy rooms, log fire, enjoyable good value home-made pubby food (there's also a monthly chinese evening), real ales; children welcome, garden *(Andrew Bagnell, John Stowe, LYM)*

PRINCES RISBOROUGH [SP8104]
Red Lion HP27 0LL [Whiteleaf, off A4010; OS Sheet 165 map ref 817043]: Simple comfortably worn-in village pub with welcoming landlady, good generous home-made bar food at reasonable prices, well kept beer, log fire, traditional games; garden tables, charming village, good Chilterns walks *(LYM, Roy Hoing, Peter Donaghy)*

SEER GREEN []
Jolly Cricketers HP9 2YG: Two-bar refurbished pub doing well under newish management, three changing local ales, decent home cooking, cricketing odds and ends, woodburner; live jazz and beer festivals; dogs welcome, small garden, good walks *(anon)*

SHERINGTON [SP8946]
White Hart MK16 9PE [off A509; Gun Lane]: Good changing ales such as Archers, Greene King, Purity and Rebellion, helpful landlord and friendly staff, good pub food (not Sun evening) from sandwiches and tapas up, bright fire, two-room bar, contemporary flagstoned dining room; children and dogs welcome, picnic-sets in garden with terrace, pretty hanging baskets, bedrooms in adjacent building *(Peter Martin, Colin and Janet Roe, Gerry and Rosemary Dobson)*

ST LEONARDS [SP9107]
White Lion HP23 6NW [Jenkins Lane, by Buckland Common; off A4011 Wendover—Tring]: Neat open-plan pub, highest in the Chilterns, with old black beams, well kept ales such as Batemans and Greene King, good value pub food, friendly service, log-effect gas fire; children and dogs welcome, attractive sheltered garden, good walks *(BB, Roy Hoing, Susan and John Douglas)*

STOKE GOLDINGTON [SP8348]
☆ ***Lamb*** MK16 8NR [High St (B526 Newport Pagnell—Northampton)]: Chatty village pub with friendly helpful licensees, up to four interesting changing ales, Weston's farm cider, good range of wines and soft drinks, good generous home-made food (all day Sat, not Sun evening) from baguettes to bargain Sun roasts; public bar with table skittles, two small pleasant dining rooms, quiet lounge with log fire and sheep decorations; may be soft piped music, TV; dogs welcome, terrace and sheltered garden behind, open all day wknds *(BB, JJW, CMW)*

STOKE MANDEVILLE [SP8310]
☆ ***Woolpack*** HP22 5UP [Risborough Rd (A4010 S of Aylesbury)]: Popular 16th-c partly thatched pub reopened after 2009 fire; stylish contemporary refurbishment keeping original beams and timbers and massive inglenook fireplace, knocked-through front bar and big busy extended dining room, wide choice of food with some italian influences (should book wknds), Brakspears, Purity and

Timothy Taylors Landlord, good choice of wines by the glass; no dogs inside; well behaved children allowed, tables in back garden and heated front terrace, open all day *(John Faircloth, LYM)*

STONE [SP7912]
Bugle Horn HP17 8QP [Oxford Rd, Hartwell (A418 SW of Aylesbury)]: Long low 17th-c stone-built Vintage Inn, friendly and comfortable linked rooms, good choice of modestly priced food, friendly service; Brakspears and Hook Norton, lots of wines by the glass, several log fires, prettily planted well furnished conservatory; attractive terrace, lovely trees in big pretty garden, pastures beyond, open all day *(Tim and Ann Newell)*

THE LEE [SP8904]
☆ ***Cock & Rabbit*** HP16 9LZ [back roads 2.5 miles N of Great Missenden, E of A413]: Warmly welcoming italian-run dining pub, stylish and comfortable, with enjoyable home-made food (not Sun or Mon evenings) from nice lunchtime baps to good pasta and fresh fish, real ales such as Fullers and Greene King, decent wines, panelled locals' bar, charming back dining areas welcoming children; big garden with tables on verandah, terraces and lawn *(Paul Humphreys, Roy Hoing, David Lamb, LYM)*

☆ ***Old Swan*** HP16 9NU [Swan Bottom, back road 0.75 miles N of The Lee]: Welcoming tucked-away 16th-c dining pub, three attractively furnished linked rooms, low beams and flagstones, cooking-range log fire in inglenook, good choice of enjoyable food, Brakspears; big back garden with play area, good walks *(LYM, Paul Humphreys, Doug Kennedy)*

TURVILLE [SU7691]
☆ ***Bull & Butcher*** RG9 6QU [valley road off A4155 Henley—Marlow at Mill End, past Hambleden and Skirmett]: Black and white pub in pretty village (famous as film and TV setting), two traditional low-beamed rooms with inglenooks, wall settles in tiled-floor bar, deep well incorporated into a glass-topped table, Brakspears and Hook Norton ales, several wines by the glass, pricey bar food; piped and monthly live music, TV; children (away from bar) and dogs welcome, seats by fruit trees in attractive garden, good walks, open all day *(Ross Balaam, Anthony and Pam Stamer, Simon Collett-Jones, Doug Kennedy, LYM, Dr Kevan Tucker, Noel Grundy, Laurence Smith)*

WENDOVER [SP8607]
Firecrest HP22 6QG [London Rd (A413 about 2 miles S)]: Popular roadside Vintage Inn, good value food all day inc smaller dishes, neat efficient staff, Wells & Youngs Bombardier, civilised eating areas, old fireplace, pictures on stripped brickwork; disabled parking *(David Lamb)*
Red Lion HP22 6DU [High St]: Spacious 17th-c inn doing enjoyable food in refurbished oak-beamed flagstoned bar and

adjacent restaurant, well kept Marstons; walker-friendly (on Ridgeway Path), tables out behind, bedrooms *(Mike and Jayne Bastin, BB)*

WEST WYCOMBE [SU8394]

George & Dragon HP14 3AB [High St; A40 W of High Wycombe]: Popular rambling hotel bar in preserved Tudor village, massive beams and sloping walls, dim lighting, big log fire, Courage Best, Brakspears, St Austell Tribute and a guest, fairly priced food, friendly staff, small family dining room; dogs welcome, garden with fenced play area, character bedrooms (magnificent oak staircase), handy for West Wycombe Park, open all day wknds *(Doug Kennedy, LYM)*

WHITCHURCH [SP8020]

White Swan HP22 4JT [High St]: Thatched two-bar Fullers local with friendly landlady, some imaginative cooking by landlord as well as quickly served bargain two-course meals; picnic-sets in big rambling back garden looking over fields to distant Chilterns *(David Lamb, John and Elisabeth Cox, LYM)*

Post Office address codings confusingly give the impression that some pubs are in Buckinghamshire, when they're really in Bedfordshire or Berkshire (which is where we list them).

Cambridgeshire

The pubs in this county seem to be extremely well run and enjoyable and it makes no difference whether they are town-centre alehouses, civilised dining pubs or smart hotels with proper pubby bars. Town-centre pubs doing well this year include the three quite different Cambridge ones – the Cambridge Blue (a dozen real ales), the Eagle (some fine architectural features) and the Free Press (quiet and unspoilt) and in Peterborough, the Brewery Tap (super own-brew beers, thai food and live music) and Charters (a fine range of real ales, pan-asian food and a big pub garden). Both the George in Buckden and the Old Bridge in Huntingdon are smart hotels with relaxed, informal bars – not an easy thing to achieve – and they both have a really wide mix of customers. Other pubs on a high at the moment are the John Barleycorn in Duxford (new to the *Guide* this year and carefully and interestingly refurbished recently), the Blue Bell in Helpston (always busy and popular for its good value food), the Cock in Hemingford Grey (pretty and friendly with excellent food), the Red Lion at Hinxton (enjoyed for its bar food and cheerful atmosphere), the Red Lion at Histon (another new entry and serving seven interesting real ales), the New Sun in Kimbolton (village pub liked for both food and drink), the Hole in the Wall at Little Wilbraham (tucked away and with interesting food), the Queens Head in Newton (unspoilt and unchanging), the Chequers in Pampisford (traditional and warmly welcoming) and the Anchor in Sutton Gault (excellent food and a nice relaxed atmosphere). For being such a well run all-rounder as well as having delicious food, our Cambridgeshire Dining Pub 2011 is the Cock in Hemingford Grey.

BUCKDEN

George 🍽 🍷 🛏
High Street; PE19 5XA

Stylish refurbishment of handsome coaching inn, bustling bar, friendly staff, first-rate modern cooking, real ales and fine choice of wines; bedrooms

---

Although this is a handsome and stylish Georgian-faced hotel with contemporary furnishings throughout, it does have a bustling bar that is a comfortable and informal place for a drink. It has some wonderful fan beamwork, leather and chrome bar chairs, a log fire, Adnams Best and a changing guest on handpump from a chrome-topped counter, 20 wines (including champagne) by the glass and a good choice of teas and coffees; hospitable staff and piped music. The bustling brasserie has smart cream dining chairs around carefully polished tables set with proper white napkins and pretty foliage arrangements. In fine weather you can sit outside at seats and tables under large parasols on the pretty sheltered terrace with its box hedging and flowering plants. The charming bedrooms are all named after a famous George.

🍴 **Excellent modern food might include sandwiches, soup, hand-dived scallops with truffle sauce and pancetta salad, duck rillette with pine nuts, raisins and orange dressing,** gnocchi with roasted butternut squash and pesto, stuffed chicken breast wrapped in pancetta with shi-itake mushroom sauce, peppered rare-grilled yellow-fin tuna with warm spicy lentil salsa, venison loin with caramelised red cabbage and casserole sauce, and puddings like peanut butter and chocolate cheesecake with strawberry jelly and rhubarb panna cotta. They also serve afternoon tea. *Starters/Snacks: £5.50 to £10.00. Main Courses: £7.50 to £19.50. Puddings: £5.50 to £6.00*

Free house ~ Licensee Cynthia Schaeffer ~ Real ale ~ Bar food ~ Restaurant ~ (01480) 812300 ~ Children welcome ~ Dogs welcome ~ Open 12-11 ~ Bedrooms: £90S/£110B

Recommended by Michael Sargent, Ryta Lyndley, Michael Dandy, Stuart Turner, R T and J C Moggridge

CAMBRIDGE

TL4658   MAP 5

Cambridge Blue 🍺 £

85 Gwydir Street; CB1 2LG

Friendly backstreet pub, simply decorated with lots to look at, and interesting ales

Run by knowledgeable licensees, this backstreet pub is extremely popular with our readers. You can be sure of a friendly welcome and a fantastic choice of up to a dozen real ales on handpump or tapped from the cask. As well as Nethergate Dewdrop and Woodfordes Wherry, there are ten changing guests from an endless list, and quite a choice of bottled beers and malt whiskies as well; they hold a beer festival every February and June. There's an attractive little conservatory and two peaceful rooms that are simply decorated with old-fashioned bare-boards style furnishings, candles on the tables, and a big collection of breweriana; board games, cards and dominoes. The big back garden is surprisingly rural feeling. It does get very busy at weekends.

🍴 Traditional bar food includes filled ciabattas and baked potatoes, soup, sausage and mash, home-made nut roast, vegetable or chicken stir fry, curry of the day, steak and mushroom pie, and puddings like chocolate brownie or sticky toffee pudding with butterscotch sauce. *Starters/Snacks: £4.00 to £6.00. Main Courses: £7.00 to £12.50. Puddings: £3.25*

Free house ~ Licensees Jethro and Terri Scotcher-Littlechild ~ Real ale ~ Bar food (12-10(9 Sun)) ~ (01223) 471680 ~ Children welcome ~ Dogs welcome ~ Open 12(11 Sat)-11; 12-10.30 Sun

Recommended by the Didler, Chris and Angela Buckell, Geoff Reynolds, Jerry Brown, Lawrence R Cotter, Ralph Holland

Eagle 🍺 £

Bene't Street; CB2 3QN

Some fine architectural features in former coaching inn, open fires, seven real ales, popular pubby food, and seats outside

This was once the city's most important coaching inn and there are quite a few original architectural features to look at. The rambling rooms have two medieval mullioned windows and the remains of two possibly medieval wall paintings, two fireplaces dating back to around 1600, lovely worn wooden floors and plenty of pine panelling. Don't miss the high dark red ceiling which has been left unpainted since World War II to preserve the signatures of British and American airmen worked in with Zippo lighters, candle smoke and lipstick; the creaky old furniture is nicely in keeping with it all. Greene King IPA, Abbot, Old Speckled Hen, H & H Olde Trip and Bitter and guests like Hook Norton Old Hookey and O'Hanlons Yellowhammer on handpump. An attractive cobbled and galleried courtyard, screened from the street, has heavy wooden seats and tables, heaters and pretty hanging baskets.

🍴 As well as lunchtime sandwiches and filled baked potatoes, the fairly priced (especially at lunchtime) bar food includes soup, sausage and mash, red pesto linguine, very popular fish and chips with mushy peas, steak in ale pie, slow-cooked lamb shank with minted gravy, chicken with bacon, cheese and barbecue sauce, and puddings like apple pie or sticky toffee pudding with toffee sauce; Sunday roasts. *Starters/Snacks: £6.95 to £8.95. Main Courses: £6.95 to £14.95. Puddings: £2.95 to £3.95*

Greene King ~ Manager Karl Storey ~ Real ale ~ Bar food (10am-10pm) ~ (01223) 505020 ~ Children welcome ~ Open 10am-11pm; 12-10.30 Sun

Recommended by Michael Dandy, Michael Sargent, the Didler, John and Gloria Isaacs, Chris and Angela Buckell, David and Sue Atkinson, Simon Watkins, David and Gill Carrington, Peter and Giff Bennett, Ian Phillips

Free Press £

Prospect Row; CB1 1DU

Quiet and unspoilt with interesting local décor, several real ales, and good value food

This is a warm and cosy little pub and just the place for a quiet drink. You can enjoy a pint and a newspaper by the warm log fire and the unspoilt atmosphere is undisturbed by mobile phones, piped music or games machines. In a nod to the building's history as home to a local newspaper, the walls of its characterful bare-floorboarded rooms are hung with old newspaper pages and printing memorabilia, as well as old printing trays that local customers are encouraged to top up with little items. Greene King IPA, Abbot and Mild and regularly changing guests such as Holdens Golden Glow and Okells Olde Skipper on handpump, 24 malt whiskies, a dozen wines by the glass, and lots of different fruit juices; assorted board games. There are seats in the suntrap sheltered and paved garden and perhaps summer morris men. Wheelchair access.

🍴 **Home-made pubby food includes lunchtime sandwiches and toasted ciabatta, ploughman's, spicy tuscan bean soup, pasta dishes, and salads, with evening meals such as gammon and pineapple with bubble and squeak, sausage and mash, and chunky beef chilli; daily specials, puddings like brioche bread and butter pudding with orange custard, and a very good value three-course meal Mon-Weds evenings.** *Starters/Snacks: £1.50 to £4.50. Main Courses: £4.50 to £12.95. Puddings: £3.95 to £4.25*

Greene King ~ Lease Craig Bickley ~ Real ale ~ Bar food (12-2(2.30 Sat and Sun), 6(7 Sun)-9) ~ (01223) 368337 ~ Children welcome ~ Dogs welcome ~ Open 12-2.30, 6-11; 12-11 Sat; 12-3, 7-10.30 Sun

Recommended by D Miles, Giles and Annie Francis, the Didler, Chris and Angela Buckell, R T and J C Moggridge, John Wooll, David and Gill Carrington, Ralph Holland

DUXFORD   TL4746   MAP 5

John Barleycorn 🛏

Handy for M11 junction 10; signed off A505 E at Volvo junction; CB2 4PP

Pretty pub with welcoming landlord and staff, attractive beamed interior, real ales and good wines, enjoyable food; seats on terrace and in garden; bedrooms in converted barn

The friendly and professional landlord has re-thatched the roof and completely refurbished the interior of this charming village pub – and opened up bedrooms in the converted barn. It's all extremely attractive with hops on heavy beams and standing timbers and brick pillars creating alcoves and different drinking and dining areas. Old floor tiles have been exposed, there are log fires, all manner of seating from rustic blue-painted cushioned settles through white-painted and plain wooden dining chairs to some rather fine antique farmhouse chairs, a mix of wooden tables, and lots of things to look at: china plates, copper pans, old clocks, a butterchurn, a large stuffed fish, and lots of pictures on the blue or pale yellow walls. Greene King Abbot and IPA, Hook Norton Bitter, a changing guest and a beer named after the pub on handpump, and a large wine list; piped music. There are blue-painted picnic-sets beside pretty baskets on the front terrace and more picnic-sets among flowering tubs and shrubs in the back garden. This is a comfortable place to stay. The pub was used by the young airmen of Douglas Bader's Duxford Wing during World War II. The Air Museum is close by.

> Post Office address codings confusingly give the impression that some pubs are in Cambridgeshire, when they're really in Bedfordshire, Lincolnshire, Norfolk or Northamptonshire (which is where we list them).

⌕ Enjoyable bar food includes lunchtime sandwiches, soup, smoked trout pâté, burger with smoked bacon, cheese and caramelised onions, wild boar and apple sausages with stout gravy, a changing home-made pie, butternut squash and thyme risotto with pine nuts and parmesan, salmon with peach salsa and citrus-dressed salad topped with dill crème fraîche, roasted rack of lamb with red onion marmalade and redcurrant jus, and puddings such as brioche white chocolate and apricot pudding with crème anglaise and banana and butterscotch fool. *Starters/Snacks: £4.99 to £9.99. Main Courses: £7.90 to £20.00. Puddings: £4.99 to £7.00*

Greene King ~ Tenant Bernard Lee ~ Real ale ~ Bar food (12-2.30, 6-9.30) ~ (01223) 832699 ~ Children welcome ~ Open 11-midnight(10.30 Sun) ~ Bedrooms: £69.50B/£89.50B

Recommended by Caroline and Michael Abbey, Mr and Mrs T B Staples, Ross Balaam

ELSWORTH   TL3163   MAP 5
George & Dragon
Off A14 NW of Cambridge, via Boxworth, or off A428; CB3 8JQ

Busy dining pub with quite a choice of food inc fresh fish from Lowestoft served by efficient staff

Extremely popular and well run by polite, helpful staff, this brick-built dining pub is spotlessly kept. A pleasant panelled main bar, decorated with a fishy theme, opens on the left to a slightly elevated dining area with comfortable tables and a good woodburning stove. From here, steps lead down to a newly refurbished garden room behind with tables overlooking attractive garden terraces. On the right is a more formal restaurant. To be sure of a table, it's best to book in advance. Greene King IPA and Old Speckled Hen and a guest beer on handpump and decent wines. The Rose at Stapleford (see the Lucky Dip section) is under the same ownership.

⌕ As well as lunchtime sandwiches, filled baguettes and ploughman's, a large choice of food might include chicken liver pâté with plum and apple chutney, smoked salmon and crab fishcake with sweet chilli dip, ham and eggs, vegetable curry, fresh cod fillet in beer batter, fresh haddock topped with prawns and baked in a cheese and lobster sauce, chicken breast and half a rack of pork ribs with barbecue sauce, aberdeen angus steaks, and a fish mixed grill; they also offer a good value two- and three-course weekday lunchtime set menu. *Starters/Snacks: £4.50 to £9.00. Main Courses: £10.00 to £18.00. Puddings: £4.50 to £4.75*

Free house ~ Licensees Paul and Karen Beer ~ Real ale ~ Bar food ~ Restaurant ~ (01954) 267236 ~ Children welcome ~ Dogs allowed in bar ~ Open 11-2.30, 6-11; 12-10.30 Sun

Recommended by Michael and Jenny Back, Gordon and Margaret Ormondroyd, Peter Martin, Simon Watkins, Dr Peter Andrews, R T and J C Moggridge

ELTON   TL0893   MAP 5
Black Horse ♀
B671 off A605 W of Peterborough and A1(M); Overend; PE8 6RU

Well run dining pub with country furnishings and super views from big garden

Although much emphasis is placed on the good food in this handsome honey-stone dining pub, regulars do still drop in for a pint and a chat. There are roaring log fires, hop-strung beams, a homely and comfortable mix of furniture (no two tables and chairs seem the same), antique prints, and lots of ornaments and bric-a-brac including an intriguing ancient radio set. Dining areas at each end of the bar have parquet flooring and tiles, and the stripped-stone back lounge towards the restaurant has an interesting fireplace. Daleside Spring Frenzy, Digfield Barnwell Bitter, Everards Tiger and Oakham JHB on handpump, and quite a few wines by the glass. The big garden has super views across to Elton Hall park and the village church, there are seats on the terrace, and a couple of acres of grass for children to play. More reports please.

🍴 They grow their own herbs and much of their own fruit, salad and vegetables (including asparagus) for the popular bar food: filled baguettes, soup, chicken liver pâté, spicy haddock and salmon fishcakes, thai chicken curry, ham and eggs, home-made burger, a changing pie, fish and chips with mushy peas, slow-cooked pork belly, generous goats cheese salad, a fish dish of the day, steaks, and puddings like chocolate torte and fruit crumbles; well liked Sunday roasts and in winter they offer a two- and three-course set menu. *Starters/Snacks: £4.95 to £7.95. Main Courses: £8.95 to £19.00. Puddings: £4.95*

Free house ~ Licensee John Clennell ~ Real ale ~ Bar food (12-2(2.30 Fri and Sat, 3 Sun), 6.30-9; all day in summer school hols) ~ Restaurant ~ (01832) 280240 ~ Children welcome ~ Dogs allowed in bar ~ Open 12-11(midnight Sat); 12-7 Sun; closed Sun evening

Recommended by R T and J C Moggridge, George Atkinson, Peter Meister

Crown 🍴 ⏥ 🛏

Off B671 S of Wansford (A1/A47), and village signposted off A605 Peterborough—Oundle; Duck Street; PE8 6RQ

Lovely thatched pub in charming village, interesting food, five real ales, well chosen wines, and friendly atmosphere; bedrooms

With a good mix of both locals and visitors, this lovely thatched stone inn is just the place for a drink or an especially good meal. It's run by a friendly young chef/landlord and his wife and the layout inside is most attractive. It's been stylishly refurbished and the softly lit beamed bar has an open fire in the stone fireplace, good pictures and pubby ornaments on pastel walls, and cushioned settles and chunky farmhouse furniture on the tartan carpet. The beamed main dining area has fresh flowers and candles and similar tables and chairs on its stripped boards; a more formal, circular, conservatory-style restaurant is open at weekends. Greene King IPA, a beer named for the pub and guests like Digfield March Hare, Oakham JHB and Shepherd Neame Spitfire on handpump, besides well chosen wines by the glass. There are tables outside on the front terrace. Elton Mill and Lock are a short walk away. More reports please.

🍴 Cooked by the landlord, the enjoyable food includes sandwiches, soup, chicken liver parfait with home-made chutney, caesar salad, three-egg omelette, home-made burger, beer-battered haddock, breaded slow-braised pork belly, ham and apple cake, risotto of shi-itake mushrooms, spinach, brandy and cream with white truffle, beef and mushroom pie, chicken breast in honey and lime, and loin of tuna with szechuan pepper and oriental stir fry. *Starters/Snacks: £5.50 to £9.50. Main Courses: £10.50 to £18.00. Puddings: £5.95*

Free house ~ Licensee Marcus Lamb ~ Real ale ~ Bar food (12-2(3 Sun), 6.30-9; not Sun evening, not Mon) ~ Restaurant ~ (01832) 280232 ~ Children welcome ~ Dogs allowed in bar ~ Open 12-11 (Mon 5-11); closed Mon lunchtime ~ Bedrooms: £60B/£90B

Recommended by Michael Doswell

FEN DITTON   TL4860   MAP 5

Ancient Shepherds

Off B1047 at Green End, The River signpost, just NE of Cambridge; CB5 8ST

Beamed and comfortable with coal fires and well liked food

This is a friendly old beamed pub with a welcome for all. Perhaps the nicest room is the softly lit central lounge where you can't fail to be comfortable on one of the big fat dark red button-back leather settees or armchairs which are grouped round low dark wood tables. The warm coal fire and heavy drapes around the window seat with its big scatter cushions add to the cosiness. Above a black dado, the walls (and ceiling) are dark pink and decorated with comic fox and policeman prints plus little steeplechasing and equestrian ones. On the right the smallish more pubby bar, with its coal fire, serves Adnams Bitter and Greene King IPA and maybe Old Speckled Hen on handpump, while on the left is a pleasant restaurant. The licensee's west highland terrier, Billie, might be around outside food service times. More reports please.

🍴 Enjoyable bar food includes soup, chicken liver pâté, ham and egg, lasagne, beef in ale pie, smoked haddock and spring onion fishcakes, pork loin with a cream and mustard sauce, duck with brandy and oranges, peppered fillet steak, and puddings such as cheesecake and crumbles; Sunday roasts. *Starters/Snacks: £4.95 to £7.00. Main Courses: £7.96 to £10.95. Puddings: £4.95*

Punch ~ Tenant J M Harrington ~ Real ale ~ Bar food (not Sun or Mon evenings) ~ Restaurant ~ (01223) 293280 ~ Children welcome ~ Dogs allowed in bar ~ Open 12-2.30, 6-11; 12-5 Sun; closed Sun and Mon evenings

Recommended by Peter Martin, D Miles, John and Elisabeth Cox, Mrs Carolyn Dixon, Paul and Margaret Baker, M and GR

HELPSTON
TF1205   MAP 5

Blue Bell 🍺
Woodgate; off B1443; PE6 7ED

Bustling pub with friendly landlord and cheerful staff, fine choice of beers and tasty food including good value lunches

No matter how busy this particularly well run and popular pub is, you can be sure of a warm welcome from the hard-working landlord and his cheerful staff; it's best to book a table in advance. The lounge, parlour and snug have comfortable cushioned chairs and settles, plenty of pictures, ornaments, mementoes and cartwheel displays, and a homely atmosphere. The dining extension is light and airy with a sloping glass roof. Grainstore Ten Fifty and (exclusive to this pub) John Clare, and quickly changing guests such as Adnams Bitter and Extra and Everards Tiger on handpump, and summer scrumpy cider. They may have marmalade and jam for sale; piped music, pool and TV. A sheltered and heated terrace has cafe-style chairs and tables and an awning; pretty hanging baskets and wheelchair access. The poet John Clare lived in the cottage next door which is open to the public.

🍴 Generous helpings of enjoyable food at fair prices includes sandwiches, soup, duck and port pâté, garlic mushrooms, steak in ale pie, stilton and vegetable crumble, gammon and egg or pineapple, fish pie, lamb curry, liver and bacon, pork hotpot, sirloin steak, daily specials, and good puddings; they also offer good value two-course lunches. *Starters/Snacks: £3.95 to £4.75. Main Courses: £6.95 to £10.95. Puddings: £3.95*

Free house ~ Licensee Aubrey Sinclair Ball ~ Real ale ~ Bar food (12-2, 6.30-9; 12-5 Sun; not Mon, not Sun or Tues evenings) ~ Restaurant ~ (01733) 252394 ~ Children welcome away from bar ~ Dogs allowed in bar ~ Open 11.30-2.30, 5(6 Sat)-11(midnight Sat); 12-6 Sun

Recommended by Michael and Jenny Back, Roy Bromell, George Atkinson, R T and J C Moggridge, Henry Paulinski

HEMINGFORD GREY
TL2970   MAP 5

Cock 🍴 🍷 🍺
Village signposted off A14 eastbound, and (via A1096 St Ives road) westbound; High Street; PE28 9BJ

CAMBRIDGESHIRE DINING PUB OF THE YEAR

Imaginative food in pretty pub, extensive wine list plus other drinks including four real ales, bustling atmosphere, and smart restaurant

'It has all that one could wish for' says one of our readers about this pretty little pub – and many agree with him. There's a friendly welcome from the helpful staff, excellent food, real ales, and a happy mix of both locals and visitors. The bar rooms have dark or white-painted beams, lots of contemporary pale yellow and cream paintwork, artwork here and there, fresh flowers and church candles, and throughout, a really attractive mix of old wooden dining chairs, settles and tables. They've sensibly kept the traditional public bar on the left for drinkers only: an open woodburning stove on the raised hearth, bar stools, wall seats and a carver, steps that lead down to more seating, Nethergate IPA, Tydd

Steam Barn Ale, Wolf Golden Jackal and a changing guest on handpump, 14 wines by the glass and local farm cider. In marked contrast, the stylishly simple spotless restaurant on the right – you must book to be sure of a table – is set for dining with flowers on each table, pale wooden floorboards and another woodburning stove. There are seats and tables among stone troughs and flowers in the neat garden, and lovely hanging baskets.

⊞ **First-class modern food includes sandwiches, soup, rabbit, orange and hazelnut terrine with piccalilli, duck parcel with sweet and sour cucumber, smoked cheese, apple and leek pasty with leek vinaigrette, chickpea, olive and fennel cakes with aioli, chicken breast with chicken and sage cake and onion gravy, steak, Guinness and mushroom pie, smoked haddock with grain mustard and dill tagliatelle and poached egg, lamb chump with caper sauce and crispy sweet bread, and puddings like cardamom crème brûlée with orange biscuit and rhubarb and ginger snap crumble with custard; they also offer a popular two- and three-course lunch menu.** *Starters/Snacks: £5.00 to £7.00. Main Courses: £11.00 to £16.00. Puddings: £5.00 to £7.00*

Free house ~ Licensees Oliver Thain and Richard Bradley ~ Real ale ~ Bar food (12-2.30(3 Sun), 6.30-9(6.15-9.30 Fri and Sat; 8.30 Sun)) ~ Restaurant ~ (01480) 463609 ~ Children allowed but must be over 5 in evening restaurant ~ Dogs allowed in bar ~ Open 11.30-3, 6-11; 12-4, 6.30-10.30 Sun; closed 26 Dec

Recommended by Jeff and Wendy Williams, Gordon and Margaret Ormonroyd, Michael Sargent, Jamie May, Howard and Margaret Buchanan, Moira and John Cole, M Mossman, Jane Hudson, Sarah Flynn, George and Maureen Roby, John Wooll

HEYDON
TL4339   MAP 5

King William IV
Off A505 W of M11 junction 10; SG8 8PW

Rambling rooms with fascinating rustic jumble, real ales and pretty garden

The nooks and crannies in the rambling beamed rooms of this neat pub are full of interest: ploughshares, yokes and iron tools, cowbells, beer steins, samovars, brass or black wrought-iron lamps, copper-bound casks and milk ewers, harness, horsebrasses and smith's bellows – as well as decorative plates, cut-glass and china ornaments. Fullers London Pride, Greene King IPA and Timothy Taylors Landlord on handpump, a dozen wines by the glass, several malt whiskies, and helpful staff; warming log fire and piped music. There are teak seats and tables and outdoor heaters on the terrace as well as seats in the pretty garden. More reports please.

⊞ **Bar food includes sandwiches, filled baked potatoes, soup, moules marinière, chicken tikka masala, sausages with onion gravy, beef in ale pie, chinese-style duck, beef wellington, and puddings like chocolate bread and butter pudding and toffee pecan cheesecake.** *Starters/Snacks: £4.95 to £6.95. Main Courses: £11.95 to £16.95. Puddings: £5.95*

Free house ~ Licensee Elizabeth Nicholls ~ Real ale ~ Bar food (12-2, 7-9; all day weekends) ~ Restaurant ~ (01763) 838773 ~ Children welcome ~ Dogs allowed in bar ~ Open 12-2.30, 6-11; 12-midnight(10.30 Sun) Sat

Recommended by Anthony Barnes, Mrs Margo Finlay, Jörg Kasprowski

HINXTON
TL4945   MAP 5

Red Lion
2 miles off M11 junction 9 northbound; take first exit off A11, A1301 N, then left turn into village – High Street; a little further from junction 10, via A505 E and A1301 S; CB10 1QY

Pink-washed and handy for Imperial War Museum Duxford, friendly staff, interesting bar food, real ales and big landscaped garden; bedrooms

Handy for the M11, this extended pinkwashed 16th-c inn is much enjoyed by our readers. The low-beamed bar is mainly open-plan, with a bustling and convivial atmosphere, leather chesterfields on wooden floors, an old wall clock, a dark green fireplace, Adnams Bitter, Greene King IPA, Woodfordes Wherry and a guest such as Nethergate Augustinian

Ale on handpump, 12 wines by the glass and Aspall's cider; there are some unusual foreign insects in glass cases. An informal dining area has high-backed settles and the smart restaurant is decorated with various pictures and assorted clocks. The neatly kept big garden has a pleasant terrace with picnic-sets, a dovecote and views of the village church. The bedrooms are in a separate flint and brick building.

❚❚ Good interesting bar food includes sandwiches and filled baguettes, soup, ham hock and petit pois terrine with piccalilli cups and pork broth, a trio of beef (carpaccio, tartare and bresaola) with chilli oil, ham and free-range eggs, home-made burger, globe artichoke risotto with white truffle foam and pea sprouts, steak in ale pie, beer-battered cod, bass fillets with thai salad, trumpet mushrooms and coconut foam, and puddings like poached pear with brandy snap baskets, strawberry jelly and lemon grass granita and bakewell tart with custard. *Starters/Snacks: £4.50 to £7.00. Main Courses: £9.00 to £15.00. Puddings: £2.00 to £6.00.*

Free house ~ Licensee Alex Clarke ~ Real ale ~ Bar food (12-2, 6.45-9; 12-2.30, 6.45-9.30 Fri and Sat; 12-2.30, 7-9 Sun) ~ Restaurant ~ (01799) 530601 ~ Well behaved children welcome ~ Dogs allowed in bar ~ Open 11-3, 6-11; 12-4, 7-10.30 Sun; closed evenings 25 and 26 Dec and 1 Jan ~ Bedrooms: £80B/£120S(£99B)

Recommended by M and GR, Mrs Margo Finlay, Jörg Kasprowski, Edward Mirzoeff, Gordon Stevenson, Jenny and Brian Seller, Jerry Brown, Adele Summers, Alan Black, Peter and Heather Elliott, Dave Braisted

HISTON

TL4363   MAP 5

Red Lion 🍺

3.7 miles from M11 junction 1; village signposted off A14 E via B1049; High Street, off Station Road; CB4 9JD

Great changing beer choice and enjoyable lunchtime food in cheerful and distinctive village pub with good-sized garden

The L-shaped main bar on the right is a shrine to beer, its ceiling joists packed with hundreds of often esoteric beer mats and pump clips among the hop vines and whisky-water jugs, the walls housing a fine collection of old brewery advertisements and a rack of real ale campaign literature, and the brick bar counter topped by an impressive row of handpumps. On our early summer inspection visit the changing choice consisted of Everards Tiger, Grainstore Triple B, Mighty Oak Oscar Wilde, Oakham Bishops Farewell, Stonehenge Eye Opener, Theakstons Best and Tring Blonde, with Pickled Pig farm cider and Weston's perry, as well as a splendid range of bottled beers. They mount well organised beer festivals in spring and early autumn. All is spic and span, with comfortable brocaded wall seats and matching mate's chairs around polished pub tables on the red carpet, and service is cheerful and efficient; winter log fires, and a nice antique one-arm bandit. They open sensibly early – popular with people dropping in for a civilised morning coffee. The left-hand bar has windsor chairs around chunky tables on its composition floor, darts and TV, and an eye-opening collection of beer bottles. The neat garden, hedged off from the back car park, has black picnic-sets, swings, a slide, and a small water feature.

❚❚ The landlord tell us that emphasis on the lunchtime bar food is limited: sandwiches, soup, dressed prawns with tomatoes, broccoli and stilton bake and lamb casserole with dumplings. Wednesday is fish day; no puddings. *Starters/Snacks: £3.95 to £5.25. Main Courses: £6.25 to £8.50*

Free house ~ Licensees Mark Donachy and Louise Simpson ~ Real ale ~ Bar food (12-2; 10.30-2 Sat; no food evenings or Sun) ~ (01223) 564437 ~ Well behaved children in one bar only ~ Open 10.30am-11pm(midnight Sat); 12-11 Sun

Recommended by Jerry Brown

HUNTINGDON   TL2471 MAP 5

Old Bridge Hotel 🍴 🍷 🛏️

1 High Street; ring road just off B1044 entering from easternmost A14 slip road; PE29 3TQ

Georgian hotel with smartly pubby bar, splendid range of drinks, first-class service and excellent food

The professional and friendly staff in this civilised Georgian hotel manage to deal effortlessly with a really wide range of customers here and cope admirably with the needs of all. The hotel side of things clearly dominates but not at the expense of the more traditional pubby bar which has a log fire, comfortable sofas and low wooden tables on polished floorboards and Adnams Bitter, City of Cambridge Hobsons Choice and Fullers London Pride on handpump. They also have an exceptional wine list (a dozen by the glass in the bar) and a wine shop. You can eat in the big airy Terrace (an indoor room, but with beautifully painted verdant murals suggesting the open air) or in the slightly more formal panelled restaurant. This is a very nice place to stay.

🍴 **Excellent modern food includes sandwiches and various smart nibbles as well as soup, salad of dorset crab with fennel, red pepper and pomegranate dressing, chicken, leek and jerusalem artichoke terrine with shallot and hazelnut salad, saddleback pork sausages, braised pork cheek and onion gravy, fish and chips with pease pudding, wild brill with chorizo, crab and cockle broth and saffron potatoes, saddle of lamb with a mini lamb suet pudding, potato purée and lamb sauce, and puddings such as baked lemon and sultana cheesecake with caramelised banana and chocolate fondant with parsnip ice-cream; they also offer a two- and three-course set lunch (not Sunday) and afternoon tea.**
Starters/Snacks: £4.95 to £7.95. Main Courses: £9.95 to £12.95. Puddings: £3.95 to £6.95

Huntsbridge ~ Licensee John Hoskins ~ Real ale ~ Bar food (12-2, 6.30-10) ~ Restaurant ~ (01480) 424300 ~ Children welcome ~ Dogs welcome ~ Open 11-11 ~ Bedrooms: £99B/£135B
Recommended by Martin and Pauline Jennings, Michael Sargent, Phil Bryant, Bruce and Sharon Eden, R T and J C Moggridge, Dr A B Clayton, Michael Dandy

KIMBOLTON   TL0967 MAP 5

New Sun 🍴 🍷

High Street; PE28 0HA

Interesting bars and rooms, tapas menu plus other good food and pleasant back garden

Whether it's just a pint and a chat or a full meal in the restaurant, this pleasant old pub fits in well with the village's delightfully harmonious high street. The cosiest room is perhaps the low-beamed front lounge with a couple of comfortable armchairs and a sofa beside the log fire, standing timbers and exposed brickwork, and books, pottery and brasses. This leads into a narrower locals' bar with Wells & Youngs Bombardier and Eagle and a weekly changing guest on handpump, and over a dozen wines (including champagne) by the glass; piped music and quiz machine. The traditionally furnished dining room opens off here. The airy conservatory with high-backed wicker dining chairs has doors opening on to the terrace where there are smart seats and tables under giant umbrellas. Do note that some of the nearby parking spaces have a 30-minute limit.

🍴 **Using local game and meat, the well liked bar food includes a range of tapas, lunchtime sandwiches, ploughman's and filled baked potatoes, king prawns in garlic and chilli, home-cooked ham and free-range egg, smoked haddock with bubble and squeak, spinach, poached egg and grain mustard sauce, steak and kidney pudding, butternut squash, sage and garlic risotto, honey-roast duck breast with leek and bacon rösti and wild mushroom and port jus, daily specials including Friday beer-battered cod and chicken breast on chorizo cassoulet, and puddings like mascarpone and vanilla panna cotta with poached rhubarb and steamed chocolate sponge with chocolate fudge sauce.**
Starters/Snacks: £4.50 to £7.25. Main Courses: £10.25 to £18.00. Puddings: £4.25 to £5.50

Charles Wells ~ Lease Stephen and Elaine Rogers ~ Real ale ~ Bar food (12-2.15(2.30 Sun), 7-9.30; not Sun or Mon evenings) ~ Restaurant ~ (01480) 860052 ~ Children allowed but not in main bar ~ Dogs allowed in bar ~ Open 11.30-2.30, 6-11; 11.30-11 Fri and Sat; 12-10.30 Sun

LITTLE WILBRAHAM

TL5458 MAP 5

Hole in the Wall ⚒️ 🍷 ☕

Take A1303 Newmarket Road to Stow cum Quy off A14, then turn left at The Wilbrahams signpost, then right at Little Wilbraham signpost; High Street; CB1 5JY

Charming tucked-away dining pub – quite a find

The food in this enjoyable country pub is extremely popular and very good, so to be sure of a table it's best to get here early or book in advance. The carpeted ochre-walled bar on the right is a cosy place for a robust no-nonsense pub lunch, with its logs burning in the big brick fireplace, 15th-c beams and timbers, snug little window seats and other mixed seating around scrubbed kitchen tables. For more of an occasion, either the similar middle room (with another fire in its open range) or the rather plusher main dining room (yet another fire here) are the places to head for. Old Cannon Best Bitter, Woodfordes Wherry and a changing guest on handpump, ten wines by the glass, and unusual soft drinks such as pomegranate and elderflower pressé. Helpful service. The neat side garden has good teak furniture and a little verandah. It's a very quiet hamlet, with an interesting walk to nearby unspoilt Little Wilbraham Fen.

🍴 **Popular bar food includes ploughman's, soup, mackerel, bacon and whisky pâté with horseradish cream, haggis fritters in beer batter with pickled red cabbage and sour cream, potted prawns and brown shrimps with spiced lemon butter, smoked salmon with free-range scrambled eggs, sausages with wholegrain mustard mash and caper mayonnaise, wild mushroom and spinach risotto, calves liver with pancetta and peppercorn and brandy cream, pork tenderloin with black pudding mash and cider sauce, and puddings like dark chocolate torte with black cherry ice-cream and griottine cherries and lemon posset with home-made shortbread.** *Starters/Snacks: £4.00 to £7.50. Main Courses: £7.50 to £17.25. Puddings: £5.95*

Free house ~ Licensees Stephen Bull, Jenny and Chris Leeton ~ Real ale ~ Bar food ~ Restaurant ~ (01223) 812282 ~ Well behaved children welcome ~ Dogs allowed in bar ~ Open 11.30-3, 6.30-11; 12-3 Sun; closed Sun evening, all day Mon; two weeks Jan, two weeks Sept

MADINGLEY

TL3960 MAP 5

Three Horseshoes ⚒️ 🍷

Off A1303 W of Cambridge; High Street; CB3 8AB

Civilised dining pub, outstanding wine list, sophisticated italian meals and efficient service

There's a small and pleasantly relaxed bar in this civilised thatched dining pub but there's no doubt that most customers are here to eat the imaginative italian food – and certainly for some, this place stretches the line between whether it's pub or a restaurant. There's an open fire, simple wooden tables and chairs on bare floorboards, stools at the bar counter and pictures on green walls; it can be a bit of a crush here at peak times. The dining conservatory is pretty and leads out into the garden where there are picnic-sets under parasols. Adnams Bitter and Jennings Cumberland on handpump and an outstanding wine list with 23 by the glass, plus sweet wines and ports. More reports please.

🍴 **The interesting – if not cheap – italian food includes smart nibbles, antipasti such as chargrilled squid with chilli and lemon, napoli and milano salami, cured wild boar, and pigs head with lemon and spices, as well as soup, pasta with red mullet, clams, garlic, chilli and crème fraîche, roast lamb with braised borlotti beans, bass with black olives,** cherry tomatoes, spinach and pine nuts, smoked haddock with vermouth and a deep-fried poached egg, 21-day dry-aged aberdeenshire steaks, and puddings like lemon tart with raspberry sorbet and chocolate truffle cake with vin santo ice-cream. *Starters/Snacks: £6.00 to £10.00. Main Courses: £13.00 to £20.00. Puddings: £5.00 to £10.00*

Free house ~ Licensee Richard Stokes ~ Real ale ~ Bar food (12-2(2.30 Sat and Sun), 6-9.30) ~ Restaurant ~ (01954) 210221 ~ Children welcome ~ Open 11.30-3, 6-11; 12-2.30, 6-9.30 Sun
Recommended by P and D Carpenter, Peter and Eleanor Kenyon, Dr Kevan Tucker

NEWTON
TL4349 MAP 5

Queens Head ★ ◧ £

2.5 miles from M11 junction 11; A10 towards Royston, then left on to B1368; CB2 5PG

Lovely traditional old pub in the same family for many years, simple popular food and fair choice of drinks

Many customers have been coming to this unspoilt and staunchly traditional old pub for years and they tell us that nothing has changed – thankfully. It's still run by the third generation of the same genuinely welcoming family and the peaceful main bar has a low ceiling and crooked beams, bare wooden benches and seats built into the cream walls, paintings and bow windows. A curved high-backed settle stands on yellow tiles, there's a lovely big log fire, and Adnams Bitter and Broadside and a seasonal guest tapped from the cask, farm cider and several wines by the glass. The little carpeted saloon is similar but even cosier. Darts, shove-ha'penny, table skittles, dominoes, cribbage and nine men's morris. There are seats in front of the pub, and there's a vine trellis. This is a popular place so you will need to get here early for a seat during peak times, and there may be a queue of people waiting for the doors to open on a Sunday.

⑪ **A limited range of basic but well liked food comes in hearty and very fairly priced helpings: toast and beef dripping, lunchtime sandwiches (including things like banana with sugar and lemon), a mug of their famous home-made soup and filled Aga-baked potatoes; evening and Sunday lunchtime plates of excellent cold meat, smoked salmon, and cheeses.** *Starters/Snacks: £2.70 to £3.50. Main Courses: £3.50 to £6.00*

Free house ~ Licensees David and Robert Short ~ Real ale ~ Bar food (12-2.15, 7-9.30) ~ No credit cards ~ (01223) 870436 ~ Very well behaved children welcome in games room only ~ Dogs welcome ~ Open 11.30-2.30, 6-11; 12-2.30, 7-10.30 Sun; closed 25 and 26 Dec
Recommended by Jerry Brown, Simon Watkins, John Walker, Mrs J Ekins-Daukes

PAMPISFORD
TL4948 MAP 5

Chequers ◧ £

2.6 miles from M11 junction 10: A505 E, then village and pub signed off; Town Lane; CB2 4ER

Cosy and civilised proper traditional pub with good value food – a nice find so close to the motorway

'Faultless' and 'a joy' are just two of the comments we've received over the year about this neatly kept old place. It's run by friendly, hard-working licensees and their helpful staff; there are comfortably pubby old-fashioned furnishings under the low beams in the ochre ceiling, booth seating on the pale ceramic tiles of the cream-walled main area, and a low step down to a floorboarded part with dark pink walls (and a television). Fullers London Pride, Greene King IPA, Timothy Taylors Landlord, and Woodfordes Wherry on handpump, a good choice of wines by the glass, and nicely served coffee. The prettily planted simple garden has picnic-sets and is lit by traditional black streetlamps; the resident collie is called Snoopy.

⑪ **The enjoyable bar food includes lunchtime filled baguettes and baked potatoes, soup, chicken liver pâté with sweet onion marmalade, smoked haddock and leek or steak and Guinness pie, gorgonzola and walnut tortellini with tomato and basil sauce, home-made beefburger with cheese, honey-roast crispy duck with chilli, plum and stem ginger sauce,** slow-roasted belly pork with veal jus and apple and onion velouté, and tiger prawns stir-fried in a thai curry sauce; they also offer a good value two-course menu. *Starters/Snacks: £4.00 to £8.00. Main Courses: £8.50 to £9.90. Puddings: £4.25*

Free house ~ Licensee Maureen Hutton ~ Real ale ~ Bar food (all day (restricted between 2-6); 12-2.30 Sun) ~ (01223) 833220 ~ Children welcome ~ Dogs welcome ~ Open 11-11(10 Sun)
Recommended by Christopher Roberts, D and M T Ayres-Regan, Dave Braisted, James Morrell, Jerry Brown, JPR

PETERBOROUGH

TL1899   MAP 5

Brewery Tap 🍺 £

Opposite Queensgate car park; PE1 2AA

Fantastic range of real ales including own brews and popular thai food in huge conversion of old labour exchange

It may be an unusual combination, but the popular thai food and the particularly good own-brewed real ales in this striking modern conversion of an old labour exchange continue to draw in the crowds. There's an easy-going relaxed feel to the open-plan contemporary interior, with an expanse of light wood and stone floors and blue-painted iron pillars holding up a steel-corded mezzanine level. It's stylishly lit by a giant suspended steel ring with bulbs running around the rim and steel-meshed wall lights. A band of chequered floor tiles traces the path of the long sculpted light wood bar counter, which is boldly backed by an impressive display of bottles in a ceiling-high wall of wooden cubes. A comfortable downstairs area has a surprisingly mixed bunch of customers of all ages; there's a big screen TV for sporting events, piped music and games machines and regular live bands and comedy nights. A vast two-storey glass wall divides the bar and the new brewery, giving fascinating views of the newly installed 10 hectolitre microbrewing plant. From here they produce their own Oakham beers (Bishops Farewell, Inferno, JHB and White Dwarf) and also keep up to eight guests; quite a few whiskies and several wines by the glass. It gets very busy in the evening. The pub is owned by the same people as Charters (see below).

🍴 The thai food is very good and extremely popular and runs from snacks such as chicken satay or tempura vegetables to soups like aromatic crispy duck noodle or tom yum and to main courses such as curries, noodle and rice dishes, salads and stir fries. *Starters/Snacks: £3.20 to £4.95. Main Courses: £6.95 to £14.95. Puddings: £3.65 to £3.95*

Own brew ~ Licensee Jessica Loock ~ Real ale ~ Bar food (12-2.30, 6-9.30; 12-10.30 Fri, Sat) ~ Restaurant ~ (01733) 358500 ~ Children welcome during food service times only ~ Dogs allowed in bar ~ Live bands and comedy Fri and Sat evenings ~ Open 12-11(10.30 Sun); closed 25 and 26 Dec, 1 Jan
Recommended by R T and J C Moggridge, Andy and Jill Kassube, Mike and Sue Loseby, the Didler, Roger Fox, Ian and Helen Stafford, David Warren

Charters 🍺 £

Town Bridge, S side; PE1 1FP

Remarkable conversion of dutch grain barge with impressive real ales and good value pan-asian food

As busy as ever, this unusual place was once a barge working on the rivers and canals of Holland, Belgium and Germany and is now moored on the River Nene. It houses a sizeable timbered bar on the lower deck and an oriental restaurant on the upper deck, and there are old wooden tables and pews that provide plenty of seating, an impressive range of real ales that includes four Oakham beers and around eight quickly changing guests from an interesting variety of brewers. They also keep around 30 foreign bottled beers, and hold regular beer festivals; piped music, games machines and darts. It also has one of the biggest pub gardens in the city and is extremely popular in fine weather.

If we know a pub has an outdoor play area for children, we mention it.

🍴 As well as lunchtime panini, the pan-asian food includes lots of good value set-course meals, starters such as mixed tempura, penang chicken skewers and various parcels and rolls, and main courses that include noodle, rice and wok dishes, curries and seafood; they do a takeaway menu, too. *Starters/Snacks: £2.95. Main Courses: £4.95 to £5.95*

Free house ~ Licensee Paul Hook ~ Real ale ~ Bar food (12-2.30(3.30 Sun), 5.30-10.30) ~ Restaurant ~ (01733) 315700 ~ Children welcome ~ Dogs allowed in bar ~ Live bands occasionally Fri and Sat after 11pm ~ Open 12-11(later Fri, Sat)

Recommended by the Didler, R T and J C Moggridge, Barry Collett, Steve Nye

STILTON   TL1689   MAP 5

Bell ♀ 🛏

High Street; village signposted from A1 S of Peterborough; PE7 3RA

Fine coaching inn with several civilised rooms including a residents' bar, bar food using the famous cheese, and seats in the very pretty courtyard; bedrooms

Rather elegant and full of history, this fine 17th-c coaching inn has a relaxed, friendly atmosphere and a good mix of customers. There are two neatly kept bars (the front one is used for drinking) with bow windows, sturdy upright wooden seats on flagstone floors as well as plush button-back built-in banquettes, and a good big log fire in one handsome stone fireplace; one bar has a large cheese press. The partly stripped walls have big prints of sailing and winter coaching scenes, and there's a giant pair of blacksmith's bellows hanging in the middle of the front bar. Crouch Vale Brewers Gold, Digfield Barnwell Bitter, Fullers London Pride, Greene King IPA and Abbot and Hop Back Crop Circle on handpump or tapped from the cask, a dozen malt whiskies, and 20 wines by the glass. Also, a bistro, restaurant and residents' bar. Through the fine coach arch is a very pretty sheltered courtyard with tables and a well which dates back to Roman times.

🍴 As well as sandwiches, the bistro-style food includes soup, chicken liver pâté, stilton and roast shallot risotto, corned beef hash with poached egg, chicken breast with spring onion mash and chorizo and mushroom sauce, escalope of salmon with creamy leek sauce, braised pork belly with truffled mash, venison goulash with sour cream, and puddings like banana and maple syrup crème brûlée and dark chocolate torte with mascarpone sorbet and orange caramel sauce. *Starters/Snacks: £5.00 to £7.00. Main Courses: £9.00 to £17.00. Puddings: £5.00 to £6.00*

Free house ~ Licensee Liam McGivern ~ Real ale ~ Bar food (12-2(2.30 Sat), 6-9.30; all day Sun) ~ Restaurant ~ (01733) 241066 ~ Children allowed away from bar areas ~ Open 12-2.30(3 Sat), 6-11(midnight Fri and Sat); 12-11 Sun ~ Bedrooms: £73.50B/£100.50B

Recommended by Mrs P Bishop, Kevin Thomas, Nina Randall, N R White, Ian and Nita Cooper, Phil and Jane Hodson, Jeremy King, Gordon and Margaret Ormondroyd, R T and J C Moggridge, Blaise Vyner

SUTTON GAULT   TL4279   MAP 5

Anchor 🍽 ♀

Village signed off B1381 in Sutton; CB6 2BD

Tucked-away inn with charming candlelit rooms, good modern food, real ale and thoughtful wine list; bedrooms

Before or after a lunchtime visit to this popular dining pub, you can enjoy a walk along the high embankment – and the bird-watching is said to be good, too; pleasant seats outside. Drinkers do pop in for a pint of City of Cambridge Hobson's Choice or Old Cannon Best Bitter but most are here to enjoy the very popular interesting food. The four heavily timbered rooms are stylishly simple with two log fires, antique settles and wooden dining chairs around well spaced candlelit scrubbed pine tables on gently undulating old floors, and good lithographs and big prints on the walls. A dozen wines by the glass (including champagne) and helpful, friendly service.

🍴 Excellent, imaginative food includes soup, ham hock and chicken terrine with apple and sultana chutney, seared king scallops with chorizo and a parsley salad, baked butternut squash stuffed with pearl barley, goats cheese, red onion and parmesan risotto, fillet of bass on warm pumpkin, pine nut and watercress salad with red pepper essence, corn-fed chicken suprême stuffed with dates and spinach, haunch of venison with parsnip purée and port jus, and puddings like spiced mulled wine jelly with ginger and cinnamon cream and ginger sticky toffee pudding with butterscotch sauce and vanilla ice-cream; they also offer a weekday two- and three-course menu and Sunday roasts. *Starters/Snacks: £4.50 to £6.95. Main Courses: £10.50 to £21.50. Puddings: £4.95 to £6.50*

Free house ~ Licensees Carlene Bunten and Adam Pickup ~ Real ale ~ Bar food (12-2, 7-9(6.30-9.30 Sat evening; 12-2.30, 6.30-8.30 Sun) ~ (01353) 778537 ~ Children welcome ~ Open 12-3, 7(6.30 weekends)-10(10.30 Sat, 9.30 Sun) ~ Bedrooms: £59.50(£75B)/ £79.50S(£115B)

Recommended by Mrs Margo Finlay, Jörg Kasprowski, Mr and Mrs B Murray, Peter J and Avril Hanson, M and GR, B R and M F Arnold, John Redfern, Jeff and Wendy Williams, Geoff and Carol Thorp, Mrs Carolyn Dixon, David and Sharon Collison, Graeme Manson, Jane Hudson, Malcolm and Kate Dowty, P and D Carpenter

THRIPLOW
TL4346   MAP 5

Green Man

3 miles from M11 junction 10; A505 towards Royston, then first right; Lower Street; SG8 7RJ

Comfortable and cheery with pubby food and changing ales

Handy for the Imperial War Museum Duxford, this is a bustling Victorian pub with plenty of customers. It's comfortably laid out with modern tables and attractive high-backed dining chairs and pews, there are beer mats on the ceiling and champagne bottles on high shelves, and two arches lead through to a restaurant on the left. The regularly changing real ales might be from breweries such as Buntingford, Milton, Nethergate, Oakham and Woodfordes. There are tables in the pleasant garden and the vivid blue paintwork makes an excellent backdrop for the floral displays.

🍴 Well liked bar food includes filled baguettes, sausages with whole-grain mustard mash and onion gravy, beer-battered cod and chips, chilli con carne, roast butternut squash and pine nut risotto, pork loin with cider gravy, slow-roasted lamb shoulder, and puddings. *Starters/Snacks: £5.00 to £7.00. Main Courses: £7.50 to £14.00. Puddings: £4.50*

Free house ~ Licensee Mary Lindgren ~ Real ale ~ Bar food (not Sun evening or Mon) ~ (01763) 208855 ~ Children welcome away from the bar ~ Open 12-3, 7-11; closed Sun evening, all day Mon, Christmas week, Easter weekend

Recommended by Roger and Lesley Everett

LUCKY DIP

Besides the fully inspected pubs, you might like to try these Lucky Dips recommended to us and described by readers (if you do, please send us reports: feedback@goodguides.com).

ABINGTON PIGOTTS [TL3044]
Pig & Abbot SG8 0SD: Popular Queen Anne local, two small traditional bars and restaurant, good choice of food from bar meals up inc vegetarian and ample Sun lunch, friendly attentive staff, Adnams, Fullers London Pride and two guest beers, open woodburner in inglenook, quiz night 2nd Weds; garden, pretty village with good walks, open all day wknds *(Lucien Perring, David Billings, Steve Nye)*
ALWALTON [TL1396]
Cuckoo PE7 3UP [Oundle Rd, just off A1 at A605 junction]: Attractively refurbished well divided Vintage Inn, beams and open fires, well kept changing ales, good wine choice, food all day, quick friendly service, some nice cosy corners; garden picnic-sets

(C and R Bromage)
ARRINGTON [TL3250]
☆ *Hardwicke Arms* SG8 0AH [Ermine Way (A1198)]: Handsome 18th-c coaching inn with 13th-c origins and 1792 work by Sir John Soane, enjoyable food from sandwiches and pub favourites up inc bargain wkdy lunch and Sun carvery, Greene King IPA and two interesting guests, good friendly service, dark-panelled dining room, huge central fireplace, daily papers; piped music; 12 bedrooms, handy for Wimpole Hall, open all day *(LYM, Michael Dandy)*
BABRAHAM [TL5150]
George CB22 3AG [High St; just off A1307]: Restauranty beamed and timbered dining pub, well presented food inc fixed-price wkdy lunch, Greene King ales, bar area with

comfortable seating (separate menu), efficient service; children welcome, terrace tables, nice setting on quiet road *(Jeremy King)*

BALSHAM [TL5850]

Black Bull CB21 4DJ [High St]: Attractive 16th-c beamed and thatched pub, four well kept changing ales (July beer festival), enjoyable food from sandwiches to Sun roasts, takeaway service, open fires, restaurant; tables outside, five bedrooms, appealing village *(Jerry Brown)*

BARNACK [TF0704]

☆ *Millstone* PE9 3ET [off B1443 SE of Stamford; Millstone Lane]: Timbered bar in stone-built pub with clean contemporary feel, open fires, cosy corner, Adnams, Greene King Old Speckled Hen and Everards Tiger, several well priced wines by the glass, good home-made food (not Sun evening, Mon or Tues), friendly service; piped music; sheltered courtyard, pretty village nr Burghley House *(G Jennings, LYM, Roy Bromell, Susan and Nigel Brookes, Ian and Helen Stafford)*

BARRINGTON [TL3849]

Royal Oak CB22 7RZ [turn off A10 about 3.7 miles SW of M11 junction 11, in Foxton; West Green]: Rambling thatched Tudor pub with tables out overlooking classic village green, heavy low beams and timbers, mixed furnishings, beers from Adnams, Potton and Wells & Youngs, light and airy dining conservatory, enjoyable if not particularly cheap food; piped music; children welcome *(Michael Dandy, DC, LYM)*

BUCKDEN [TL1967]

☆ *Lion* PE19 5XA [High St]: Partly 15th-c coaching inn, black beams and big inglenook log fire in airy and civilised bow-windowed entrance bar with plush bucket seats, wing armchairs and settees, good food from lunchtime sandwiches up, good choice of wines, Adnams and Caledonian Deuchars IPA, prompt friendly staff, no music or machines, panelled back restaurant beyond latticed window partition; children welcome, bedrooms *(BB, Lois Dyer, Gerry and Rosemary Dobson, Michael Dandy)*

CAMBRIDGE [TL4458]

Bath House CB2 3QN [Bene't St]: Unpretentious panelled pub with Greene King ales, sensibly priced food (as Eagle next door); sports TV, piped music, games machine *(Michael Dandy, David and Gill Carrington)*

Castle CB3 0AJ [Castle St]: Full Adnams beer range and several guests in big airy bare-boards bar, several pleasantly simple rooms, wide range of good value quick pubby food from sandwiches up, quick friendly staff, peaceful upstairs (downstairs can be louder, with piped pop music – live jazz Sun night); picnic-sets in good walled back courtyard *(J K Parry, the Didler, Ralph Holland, Jerry Brown)*

Clarendon Arms CB1 1JX [Clarendon St]: Partly flagstoned, with interesting wall

hangings and other collectables, friendly attentive service, bustling local atmosphere, Greene King ales, reasonably priced food (credit card surcharge), carpeted dining area, books and daily papers, darts, cribbage; piped music, TV; simple good value bedrooms, open all day *(John Marsh, P and D Carpenter)*

Elm Tree CB1 1JT [Orchard St]: Traditional one-bar backstreet pub, nice unspoilt interior, ten well kept real ales and good range of continental bottled beers, friendly knowledgeable staff, breweriana; some outside tables at side *(Giles and Annie Francis, Jerry Brown)*

Granta CB3 9EX [Newnham Terr]: Early 19th-c pub with balcony and heated terrace taking full advantage of view over mill pond, ducks and weeping-willow meadow, good value pub food from sandwiches up, Greene King ales with a guest such as Everards, pleasant helpful service; punt hire *(Ian Phillips, John Wooll)*

Green Dragon CB4 1NZ [Water St, Chesterton]: Attractive late medieval beamed and timber-framed building, friendly and popular, with well kept changing ales, real cider, substantial bargain basic food all day, comfortable linked areas, huge inglenook fireplace; dogs welcome, waterside green *(Steve Turner)*

☆ *Kingston Arms* CB1 2NU [Kingston St]: Well kept interesting changing ales from a dozen or so handpumps, good fresh lunchtime food inc bargains, companionably big plain tables and basic seating, thriving chatty largely studenty atmosphere, good choice of wines by the glass, friendly service, no music or children inside, two internet points; small pretty back yard, torch-lit, heated and partly covered, open all day Fri-Sun *(Jerry Brown, Chris and Angela Buckell, David Miles-Dinham, Ralph Holland, BB)*

Live & Let Live CB1 2EA [Mawson Rd]: Popular backstreet alehouse, friendly and relaxed, with Tring Jack O'Legs, Nethergate Umbel Magna and six changing guests tapped from the cask, lots of bottled belgian beers, local ciders, bargain bar food, heavily timbered brickwork rooms with sturdy varnished pine tables on bare boards, country bric-a-brac and some steam railway and brewery memorabilia, gas lighting (not always lit), cribbage and dominoes; children and dogs welcome, disabled access *(Revd R P Tickle, Dave Braisted, Chris and Angela Buckell, R T and J C Moggridge, Ralph Holland, LYM)*

Mitre CB2 1UF [Bridge St, opp St John's College]: Welcoming M&B pub close to the river, rambling bar on several levels with soft lighting and old-fashioned tavern décor, tasty bargain food inc speciality fish and chips, good friendly service, well priced wines by the glass, well kept ales such as Greene King IPA and Timothy Taylors Landlord, farm cider, log-effect fire; disabled access *(Mrs Hazel Rainer, Revd R P Tickle,*

Chris and Angela Buckell, Michael Dandy, D W Stokes, J K Parry)

☆ *Old Spring* CB4 1HB [Ferry Path; car park on Chesterton Rd]: Extended Victorian pub, roomy and airy, with smartly old-fashioned scrubbed-wood décor, bare boards, lots of old pictures, enjoyable home-made food inc enterprising dishes and Sun roasts, efficient pleasant service, well kept Greene King IPA, Abbot and three guests, good coffee and choice of wines by the glass, two log fires, long bank conservatory; piped music, no under-21s evenings, dogs outside only; disabled facilities, large heated well planted terrace, open all day *(Mrs Hazel Rainer, LYM, P and D Carpenter, Andrew Watson)*

Punter CB3 0AE [Pound Hill]: Attractive dining pub with enterprising food from burgers to good changing continental dishes, good value lunch offers, prompt friendly service, good choice of wines by the glass, Adnams and Wells & Youngs Bombardier, continental lagers, Addlestone's cider, leather sofas, log fire, several areas inc adjoining barn; courtyard *(John Wooll)*

Red Bull CB3 9JZ [Barton Rd, Newnham; A603 SW edge]: Four well kept local ales, enjoyable good value food inc takeaway pizzas, friendly service even when very busy (nr rugby ground); sports TV *(Jerry Brown, Giles and Annie Francis)*

CASTOR [TL1298]
☆ *Prince of Wales Feathers* PE5 7AL [off A47]: Friendly stone-built local with well kept Castor Oil, Woodfordes and interesting guests, farm cider and perry, landlady doing good value lunchtime food inc Sun roasts, friendly setter, side dining area; Sky TV, games machines, pool (free Thurs), Sat live music; children and dogs welcome, attractive front terrace, back one with shelters, open all day and till late wknds *(Ian and Helen Stafford, Phil and Jane Hodson, BB)*

CLAYHITHE [TL5064]
☆ *Bridge Hotel* CB5 9HZ [Clayhithe Rd]: Popular Chef & Brewer with good choice of enjoyable sensibly priced food, plenty of tables inside and out, friendly attentive staff, small bar area, well kept ales, beams and timbers; pretty spot by River Cam with waterside garden *(LYM, M and GR)*

CROYDON [TL3149]
☆ *Queen Adelaide* SG8 0DN [off A1198 or B1042; High St]: Spreading open-plan carpeted local with wide range of enjoyable food inc Mon-Weds OAP lunches, friendly prompt service, real ales such as Badger and Elgoods, several wines by the glass, lots of spirits, big low-beamed main area with standing timbers dividing off part with settees, banquettes and stools, games area with pool, conservatory extension, daily papers; piped music (even in gents' – a shrine to Marilyn Monroe), TV, machines; heated terrace with smokers' shelter, lawn with play area, bedrooms, open all day Fri-Sun *(R T and J C Moggridge, BB, Michael Dandy, Simon Watkins)*

DRY DRAYTON [TL3862]
Black Horse CB3 8DA [signed off A428 (was A45) W of Cambridge; Park St, opp church]: Low-beamed village pub reopened under enthusiastic new management, central woodburner in compact bar, good-sized restaurant, four well kept ales such as Milton and Buntingford, enjoyable food (not Sun evening); tables on back terrace and sheltered lawn; open all day, cl Mon *(Jerry Brown, BB)*

ELTISLEY [TL2759]
Eltisley PE19 6TG [signed off A428; The Green]: Attractive dining areas inc stylish barn room, flagstoned bar with beams, timbering, some zinc-topped cast-iron tables and big log fire, good carefully sourced home-made food, friendly service, Wells & Youngs ales and guests like Hop Back Summer Lightning, good choice of wines by the glass; piped music and live jazz (1st Sun of month); children welcome, dogs in bar, nice garden behind, six good value bedrooms, cl Sun evening, Mon *(Eithne Dandy, Michael Dandy, Michael Sargent, Nick Turner, LYM, Maggie Oliver)*

ELY [TL5479]
☆ *Cutter* CB7 4BN [Annesdale, off Station Rd (or walk S along Riverside Walk from Maltings)]: Beautifully placed contemporary riverside pub, enjoyable promptly served food from sandwiches up inc good value Sun roasts in carpeted dining bar and smart restaurant, Greene King, Shepherd Neame Spitfire and Woodfordes Wherry, nice wines by the glass, good coffee; terrace tables popular with smokers *(Mr and Mrs T B Staples, John Saville, Michael Butler, Ryta Lyndley, D Goodger, Robert Turnham, LYM, DF, NF)*

☆ *Fountain* CB7 4JF [corner of Barton Square and Silver Street]: Simple town pub close to cathedral, old cartoons, local photographs, regional maps and mementos of neighbouring King's School, big windows, stuffed pike above fireplace and a few antlers dotted about, back extension providing much needed additional seating, Adnams Broadside, Fullers London Pride, Woodfordes Wherry and a guest, no food or credit cards; dogs welcome, children till 8pm away from bar, cl wkdy lunchtimes *(the Didler, LYM)*

Lamb CB7 4EJ [Brook St (Lynn rd)]: Wide choice of good locally sourced food in hotel's panelled lounge bar inc Sun roasts and OAP deals (Mon), friendly welcoming staff, good choice of wines by the glass, Greene King ales; close to cathedral, bedrooms *(John Wooll, David Greene)*

Royal Standard CB7 4AF [Forehill]: Part early 17th-c, some beams, large bar with rooms off, Greene King Abbot and Old Speckled Hen, decent wines, bargain food, friendly licensees, live music wknds; pool, darts, machines; a few tables out behind *(John Wooll)*

ETTON [TF1406]

Golden Pheasant PE6 7DA [just off B1443 N of Peterborough, signed from nr N end of A15 bypass]: Refurbished by friendly landlady, restaurant next to comfortable bar, enjoyable food inc early-evening bargains, good service, well kept Fullers London Pride and two other beers, good choice of wines and spirits; children welcome, good-sized tree-sheltered garden *(Michael and Jenny Back, Phil and Jane Hodson, Ian and Helen Stafford, BB)*

EYNESBURY [TL1859]

Cambridgeshire Hunter PE19 2NF [Berkley St]: Proper unspoilt beamed local with friendly landlord, generous simple food; children welcome, garden *(JPR)*

FEN DITTON [TL4860]

Plough CB5 8SX [Green End]: Big refurbished M&B dining pub with wide choice of food all day inc good Sun roasts, pleasant prompt service even though busy, well kept Adnams and Timothy Taylors Landlord, rowing décor; children welcome, lots of tables on decking and riverside lawns, nice walk from town *(LYM, Jeremy King, P and D Carpenter)*

FEN DRAYTON [TL3468]

☆ **Three Tuns** CB4 5SJ [off A14 NW of Cambridge at Fenstanton; High St]: Friendly well preserved thatched pub in charming village, heavy Tudor beams and timbers, inglenook fireplaces, tiled-floor bar, comfortable settles and other seats, well laid out dining end (children welcome), Greene King ales, good value usual bar food (not Sun evening) from lunchtime sandwiches to steaks, sensibly placed darts; piped music; tables on covered terrace and neat back lawn, good play area, open all day *(LYM, Celia Jones)*

FORDHAM [TL6270]

☆ **White Pheasant** CB7 5LQ [off A142/B1102 N of Newmarket; Market St]: Light and airy open-plan dining pub, generally good if pricey food, well kept beers such as Brandon Saxon Gold and Woodfordes Wherry, good wines by the glass inc champagne, quite a few malt whiskies, log fire, some stripped brickwork, rugs on bare boards, nice mix of mismatched furniture inc big farmhouse tables; well behaved children welcome, nice garden behind *(George Cowie, Frances Gosnell, Dave Braisted, John Saville, Mr and Mrs W W Burke, BB, LYM)*

FOWLMERE [TL4245]

☆ **Chequers** SG8 7SR [B1368]: Civilised and gently refurbished 16th-c country dining pub, two comfortable downstairs rooms with log fire, room upstairs with beams, timbers and some interesting moulded plasterwork above one fireplace, good if pricey upscale food, good choice of ales, wines and whiskies, conservatory (children allowed here); piped music; terrace with smart dark green furniture, neat floodlit garden *(John Robertson, David and Valerie Mort, Roy Hoing, M R D Foot, LYM)*

GRANTCHESTER [TL4355]

☆ **Blue Ball** CB3 9NQ [Broadway]: Particularly well kept Adnams and a guest ale in character bare-boards village local, said to be the area's oldest, proper hands-on landlord, good log fire, Aspall's cider, cards and traditional games inc shut the box and ring the bull, lots of books; dogs welcome, tables on small terrace with lovely views to Grantchester meadows, nice village *(Simon Watkins, Jerry Brown)*

Green Man CB3 9NF [High St]: Friendly pub reopened and brightened up after year's closure; heavy beams, mix of old tables and chairs on bare boards, leather sofa and armchairs, log fire, well cooked traditional food from shortish menu, good range of local ales, separate dining room; children welcome, dogs in bar, disabled facilities, tables in big back garden with own bar, views of Granchester Meadows, open all day *(DC, LYM)*

Rupert Brooke CB3 9NQ [Broadway; junction Coton rd with Cambridge—Trumpington rd]: Tidy open-plan pub with enjoyable food from good lunchtime sandwiches and light dishes up, well kept Adnams, Harveys and Woodfordes Wherry, good choice of wines by the glass, friendly young staff, central log fire in small comfortable bar, simple extended family dining area *(P and D Carpenter, Jerry Brown)*

GREAT ABINGTON [TL5348]

Three Tuns CB21 6AB [off A1307 Cambridge—Haverhill, and A11]: Peacefully set low-beamed 16th-c village local with open fires, low-backed settles on stripped wood floors, authentic thai food, three changing ales; garden picnic-sets, five well appointed bedrooms in new block, open all day wknds *(Jerry Brown)*

GREAT CHISHILL [TL4239]

☆ **Pheasant** SG8 8SR [follow Heydon signpost from B1039 in village]: Good freshly made food using local produce in popular split-level flagstoned pub with beams, open fires, timbering and some elaborately carved though modern seats and settles, welcoming landlady and friendly service, real ales such as Adnams, Courage Best and Directors and Theakstons, good choice of wines by the glass, small dining room (best to book), darts, cribbage, dominoes; children welcome, charming secluded back garden with small play area *(LYM, Mrs Margo Finlay, Jörg Kasprowski, Nick Wooder, Marion and Bill Cross)*

GREAT SHELFORD [TL4652]

Square & Compass CB22 5EH [High St]: Small well kept village local with friendly welcoming staff, enjoyable food inc evening bargains (steak Thurs, fish Fri), Greene King ales, Aspall's cider *(Jerry Brown)*

GUYHIRN [TF3903]

☆ **Oliver Twist** PE13 4EA [follow signs from A47/A141 junction S of Wisbech]: Comfortable open-plan lounge with buoyant local atmosphere, good generous inexpensive home-made food from sandwiches to steaks, cheerful attentive service, interesting changing ales kept well, big open fires, neat sturdy furnishings, restaurant; may be piped music; six bedrooms *(BB, Ginny Smith, Phil and Jane Hodson, Barry Collett, Malcolm M Stewart)*

HARDWICK [TL3758]

Blue Lion CB23 7QU [signed off A428 (was A45) W of Cambridge; Main St]: Friendly and attractive old local with lots of beams, inglenook log fire and woodburner, good food from lunchtime sandwiches and baguettes to wide choice of home-made dishes in bar, extended air-conditioned dining area with pleasant conservatory (evening booking recommended), children's helpings, cheerful helpful staff, Greene King ales tapped from the cask, old farm tools, games and TV on lower level; may be piped music; pretty roadside front garden, play area and pets corner, handy for Wimpole Way walkers *(David and Gill Carrington, BB)*

HOLYWELL [TL3370]

Old Ferry Boat PE27 4TG [signed off A1123]: Welcoming partly thatched Greene King pub in lovely peaceful setting, low beams, open fires and interesting side areas, window seats overlooking Great Ouse, well kept beer, good coffee, but mixed reports on food; quiet piped music, games; children welcome, plenty of tables and cocktail parasols on front terrace and riverside lawn, moorings, seven good bedrooms, open all day wknds *(Lois Dyer, David and Sue Atkinson, LYM)*

HORSEHEATH [TL6147]

Old Red Lion CB1 6QF [Linton Rd]: Well refurbished and neatly kept Greene King pub, good value food, efficient staff; 12 comfortable bedroom cabins *(Mrs Jane Kingsbury, Mr and Mrs T B Staples, Simon Watkins)*

KEYSTON [TL0475]

Pheasant PE28 0RE [Just off A14 SE of Thrapston; village loop road, off B663]: Attractive long, low thatched dining pub, spacious oak-beamed bar with civilised atmosphere, open fires, simple wooden tables and chairs and country paintings on pale walls, three distinct dining areas, Digfield, Grainstore, Potbelly and a guest ale, 16 wines by the glass inc champagne, restaurant-style food, helpful prompt service; children and dogs welcome, seats out at front and on back terrace, cl Sun evening and Mon, otherwise open all day *(David Gunn, LYM, Martin and Pauline Jennings, Paul and Margaret Baker)*

LINTON [TL5546]

☆ *Crown* CB21 4HS [High St]: Friendly traditional local, comfortable and well run, enjoyable enterprising food from sandwiches up prepared by chef/landlord, up to four well kept beers, decent wines, big log fire and close-set seating areas in bar, brasserie-style restaurant with conservatory wing; games machine, piped music; five bedrooms, covered back decking, open all day Sun

till 8pm *(Jerry Brown, BB, Mrs Margo Finlay, Jörg Kasprowski)*

LITTLE SHELFORD [TL4551]

Navigator CB2 5ES [2.5 miles from M11 junction 11: A10 towards Royston, then left at Hauxton, The Shelfords signpost]: Friendly attractive 16th-c village local with pews, beams, pine panelling and a hot coal fire, good generous authentic thai food (not Sat lunchtime or Sun evening), Greene King and a guest ale, Aspall's cider, decent wines, quick obliging service; children welcome, some picnic-sets outside *(LYM, Jerry Brown)*

LONGSTOWE [TL3154]

☆ *Red House* CB3 7UT [Old North Road; A1198 Royston—Huntingdon, S of village]: Creeper-covered pub with dark red décor and sporting theme, red-tiled bar with big log fire, lower part with chintzy easy chairs and settees, well kept ales such as Church End and Woodfordes, several wines by glass, straightforward food; piped music; children and dogs welcome, sheltered little garden with picnic-sets, open all day wknds *(Simon Watkins, LYM)*

MEPAL [TL4481]

Three Pickerels CB6 2AR [Bridge Rd]: Modernised old riverside inn, popular good value pub food, Greene King ales and a guest, interesting old local photographs; garden and decking overlooking New Bedford river and grassland, four bedrooms, open all day Fri-Sun *(Terry Mizen, Mr and Mrs T B Staples)*

NEEDINGWORTH [TL3571]

☆ *Pike & Eel* PE27 4TW [pub signed from A1123; Overcote Rd]: Peacefully placed riverside hotel with spacious lawns and small marina; plush bar opening into room with easy chairs, settees and big open fire, civilised eating area (also separate smart restaurant) in light and airy glass-walled block overlooking water, boats and swans, good food and service, Adnams Broadside, Black Sheep and Greene King IPA, good coffee and wines; piped music; children welcome, 12 clean simple bedrooms, good breakfast *(LYM, David and Sue Atkinson, Ryta Lyndley, Jane Hudson)*

NORTHBOROUGH [TF1407]

Packhorse PE6 9BL [Lincoln Rd]: Smartly reworked as dining pub, enjoyable reasonably priced food in cosy restaurant, bar snacks and takeaway pizzas too, good wines with emphasis on new world, Adnams and Theakstons, polite helpful staff, stripped boards and log fire *(Ian and Helen Stafford, C D Morris)*

PETERBOROUGH [TL1897]

Coalheavers Arms PE2 9BH [Park St, Woodston]: Friendly old-fashioned flagstoned local, well kept Milton and guest beers, farm cider, good range of continental imports and malt whiskies; pleasant garden, cl Mon-Weds lunchtimes, open all day wknds *(the Didler)*

Drapers Arms PE1 1LZ [Cowgate]: Roomy relaxed open-plan Wetherspoons in sympathetically converted draper's, fine ale range, bargain food all day; can get very busy Fri and Sat evenings; children welcome, open all day from 9am *(Roger Fox, JPR, Ian and Helen Stafford)*

Palmerston Arms PE2 9PA [Oundle Rd]: Refurbished open-plan stone pub, partly 17th-c, Batemans and up to 12 changing guests tapped from the cask, real cider, good choice of malt whiskies, good pork pies, welcoming service, large jug collection, no music or machines; picnic-sets in small garden, open all day wknds *(the Didler)*

Wortley Almshouses PE1 1QA [Westgate]: Attractive conversion of old stone-built almshouses (among modern buildings), well kept bargain Sam Smiths, lunchtime food only, pleasant staff, appropriately robust furnishings and simple décor in several appealing rooms off corridor, prints, drawings and old photographs, dominoes; open all day *(the Didler, Jeremy King)*

REACH [TL5666]
☆ *Dyke's End* CB5 0JD [From B1102 follow signpost to Swaffham Prior and Upware; village signposted]: Welcoming 17th-c farmhouse with own-brewed beers and guests, simply decorated ochre-walled bar with high-backed settle, heavy pine tables and kitchen chairs on dark boards, panelled section with a few smarter dining tables, steps down to red-carpeted part with small servery, decent wine list and bar food (not Sun evening, Mon), darts and board games; well behaved children and dogs welcome, front picnic-sets under big parasols on grass, attractive spot next to church and green, open all day wknds, cl Mon lunchtime *(John Wooll, LYM, Jeremy King)*

SPALDWICK [TL1372]
☆ *George* PE28 0TD [just off A14 W of Huntingdon]: Friendly 16th-c pub with good individual up-to-date food, stylish décor, sofas in bar, larger bistro area, lots of wines by the glass, local real ales, good coffee; children welcome *(Charman family, Michael Sargent, LYM)*

ST IVES [TL3171]
Oliver Cromwell PE27 5AZ [Wellington St]: Friendly traditional two-bar pub with good value lunchtime food (not Sun) inc good homely dishes, half a dozen well kept changing ales such as Adnams, Oakham JHB and Woodfordes Wherry; pleasant garden with stylish terrace, open all day *(Barry Collett)*

STAPLEFORD [TL4651]
☆ *Rose* CB22 5DG [London Rd]: Comfortable sister pub to George & Dragon at Elsworth (see Main Entries), good choice of well cooked reasonably priced food, pleasant staff, well kept Greene King IPA, St Austell Tribute and Woodfordes Wherry, small low-ceilinged lounge with inglenook woodburner, roomy dining area; faint piped music; picnic-sets on back grass *(Gordon and Margaret Ormondroyd, BB)*

STOW CUM QUY [TL5160]
Wheatsheaf CB25 9AD [Stow Rd (B1102), off A1303 E of Cambridge]: Warmly

welcoming, with enjoyable home-made food inc lunchtime deals, Greene King ales, helpful service; handy for Anglesey Abbey (NT) *(R L Borthwick)*

STRETHAM [TL5072]
Lazy Otter CB6 3LU [Elford Closes, off A10 S of Stretham roundabout]: Big rambling family pub on Great Ouse, good views from waterside conservatory and big garden, cheerful staff, good value enjoyable food, good wine choice, interesting guest ales such as Bull Box, clean and nicely furnished, warm fire; piped music can be obtrusive; bedroom annexe, open all day *(Adele Summers, Alan Black, Mrs Hazel Rainer, LYM, Ian and Nita Cooper, DF, NF)*

SUTTON [TL4478]
Chequers CB6 2NW [(B1381 W of Ely); High St]: Welcoming down-to-earth local with bright attractive L-shaped bar and dining room, enjoyable food from generous sandwiches up, well kept Greene King ales, log fire, comfortable wall banquettes, World War II local bomber photographs, lots of decorative china; may be piped music, month folk night 4th Weds of month; small garden, a few tables out in front *(R T and J C Moggridge)*

SWAFFHAM PRIOR [TL5663]
Red Lion CB5 0LD [B1102 NE of Cambridge; High St]: Attractive old building with L-shaped bar, ales such as Timothy Taylors Landlord and Woodfordes Wherry, food reasonably priced and can be good; brick fireplace, framed drawings and old local photographs, separate room with TV; children welcome, picnic-sets in big raised orchard behind, interesting church and priory, open all day wknds *(P and D Carpenter, Jeremy King)*

TILBROOK [TL0769]
White Horse PE28 0JP [High St]: Relaxed two-room country pub, decent reasonably priced food (not Sun evening, Mon), cosy bar with traditional games, Wells & Youngs ales, some low beams, conservatory; big garden with play equipment, goats, chickens and ducks, cl Mon lunchtime *(JPR)*

TRUMPINGTON [TL4455]
Green Man CB2 9HZ [High St]: Comfortably refurbished pub/restaurant, wide choice of food all day inc set-price menu, friendly service, well kept ales such as Adnams and Greene King, bare-boards raftered dining area; children welcome, garden picnic-sets, open all day *(Ian Wilson)*

UFFORD [TF0904]
☆ *White Hart* PE9 3BH [back rd Peterborough—Stamford, just S of B1443; Main St]: 17th-c village pub with good food all day using local organic supplies and their own free-range eggs, nice coffee and wines by the glass, welcoming service, own good Ufford ales (brewed here) and guests, comfortable seating, log fire and railway/farming memorabilia in busy stripped-stone and flagstoned bar, rustic back dining area and conservatory; children

welcome, nice big garden with terrace and play area, bedroom block, open all day *(Ray and Winifred Halliday, the Didler, Max Williams, Phil and Jane Hodson, LYM)*

UPWARE [TL5372]

Five Miles From Anywhere, No Hurry CB7 5ZR: Aptly named spacious modern pub in fine riverside site with extensive moorings and public slipway (day boats for hire, riverboat stop), picnic-sets on heated waterside terrace and on lawns by weeping willows, elaborate play area; friendly prompt service, real ales such as Caledonian Deuchars IPA, Elgoods Mild, Greene King Old Speckled Hen and St Austell Tribute, good choice of pubby food inc Mon bargains, open fire, restaurant, pool room; may be piped music, games machines; children welcome, disabled facilities, open all day in summer *(LYM, David and Sue Atkinson, Dudley and Moira Cockroft)*

WANSFORD [TL0799]

Paper Mills PE8 6JB [London Rd]: Recently refurbished and welcoming, good choice of local ales such as Digfield, enjoyable food, good service, conservatory; dogs welcome, garden tables *(Mr and Mrs D Gipson)*

WARESLEY [TL2454]

Duncombe Arms SG19 3BS [Eltisley Rd (B1040, 5 miles S of A428)]: Comfortable welcoming old pub, long main bar with fire one end, good value wholesome food cooked

to order, well kept Greene King ales, friendly service, back room and restaurant; occasional live music; picnic-sets in small shrub-sheltered garden *(Denise Edwards, BB)*

WHITTLESFORD [TL4648]

Bees in the Wall CB2 4NZ [North Rd; handy for M11 junction 10]: Comfortably worn-in split-level timbered lounge with flowers on polished tables and country prints, small tiled public bar with old wall settles, darts, decent good value food (not Sun and Mon evenings) from sandwiches up inc good fish and chips, well kept Fullers London Pride, Timothy Taylors Landlord and a guest beer, open fires; may be piped classical music, games machine, no dogs; picnic-sets in big paddock-style garden with terrace, bees' nest visible in wall, handy for Imperial War Museum Duxford, open all day wknds *(Noel Young, Ruth Whitehead, David and Gill Carrington, Nigel Dawson, Kevin Thorpe)*

Red Lion CB22 4NL [Station Rd]: Dating from 16th c and handy for Imperial War Museum Duxford, character bar with well kept Adnams, enjoyable reasonably priced home-made food, friendly helpful staff, warm fires; bedrooms, adjacent to Duxford Chapel (EH) *(Rita Scarratt)*

WISBECH [TF4609]

Royal Standard PE13 2TB [Elm Rd]: Enjoyable good value food, well kept beer, obliging service, clean *(D and D G Humpherson)*

Cheshire

This is a particularly good county for reasonably priced beer and over a third of the Main Entries have one of our Beer Awards. The Bhurtpore at Aston has a tremendous selection of 11 real ales, the Mill in Chester has a remarkable 16 and the Old Harkers Arms in Chester has ten. Nearly a quarter of the Main Entries in this county are run by the small Brunning & Price chain – each has its own individual character and all of them doing particularly well at the moment. Out of a completely different mould, both the timelessly traditional White Lion at Barthomley and the quirky Albion at Chester generate warm praise for their genuine character and old-fashioned atmosphere. The Old Harkers Arms in Chester and Sutton Hall in Macclesfield (both Brunning & Price) stand out as contenders for County Dining Pub of the Year, but with its slightly more inventive menu and splendid interior – just the place for a special night out – the Sutton Hall is our Cheshire Dining Pub 2011.

ALDFORD
SJ4259 MAP 7

Grosvenor Arms ★

B5130 Chester—Wrexham; CH3 6HJ

Spacious place with buoyantly chatty atmosphere, impressive range of drinks, well balanced sensibly imaginative menu, good service; lovely big terrace and gardens

With over two decades of successful trading under its belt, this substantial building was one of Brunning & Price's first pubs and very much a prototype. Spacious cream-painted areas are sectioned by big knocked-through arches with a variety of wood, quarry tile, flagstone and black and white tiled floor finishes – some attractive richly coloured turkey rugs look well against these natural materials. Good solid pieces of traditional furniture, plenty of interesting pictures and attractive lighting keep it all intimate enough. A big panelled library room has tall bookshelves lining one wall and a handsomely boarded floor; good selection of board games. Lovely on summer evenings, the airy terracotta-floored conservatory has lots of gigantic low-hanging flowering baskets and chunky pale wood garden furniture. This opens out to a large elegant suntrap terrace, and a neat lawn with picnic-sets, young trees and a characterful old tractor. Attentive staff dispense a very wide array of drinks here from a fine-looking bar counter, including an impressive range of over 60 whiskies, distinctive soft drinks such as peach and elderflower cordial and Willington Fruit Farm pressed apple juice, as well as seven real ales including Brunning & Price Original (brewed for them by Phoenix), Thwaites Original and Weetwood Eastgate and interesting guests such as Hawkshead Red.

Food here is very good. A well balanced changing menu includes something to please most tastes. As well as sandwiches, there might be spiced celeriac and onion soup, chilli beef and pak choi salad, thai-style mussels, battered haddock with mushy peas, steak burger, chicken satay with mango and cashew salad, roast pork belly with herb and pine nut crust on chorizo, pepper and butter bean stew and rump steak, and puddings such as lemon tart with raspberry meringue ice-cream and chocolate brownie with Baileys panna cotta. *Starters/Snacks: £4.50 to £8.85. Main Courses: £8.95 to £17.50. Puddings: £4.50 to £5.75*

Brunning & Price ~ Manager Tracey Varley ~ Real ale ~ Bar food (12-9.30(10 Fri, Sat; 9 Sun)) ~
(01244) 620228 ~ Children welcome ~ Dogs allowed in bar ~ Open 11.30-11; 12-10.30 Sun

Recommended by Gerry and Rosemary Dobson, Paul Boot, J S Burn, Clive Watkin, Bruce and Sharon Eden

ASTBURY
SJ8461   MAP 7

Egerton Arms 🛏

Village signposted off A34 S of Congleton; CW12 4RQ

Cheery village pub with straightforward bar food, large garden and nice bedrooms

Handy for Little Moreton Hall (National Trust), parts of this friendly farmhouse date back
to the 16th c. Rambling around the bar, its pubby cream-painted rooms are decorated
with the odd piece of armour and shelves of books. Mementoes of the Sandow Brothers
who performed as 'the World's Strongest Youths' are particularly interesting as one of
them was the landlady's father. In summer, dried flowers replace the fire in the big
fireplace. Three Robinsons ales are on handpump, in addition to Pimms and a range of
malt whiskies. Well placed tables outside enjoy pleasant views of the church, and a play
area has a wooden fort. Despite the large car park you might struggle for a place Sunday
lunchtime; more reports please.

🍴 As well as sandwiches, bar food might include fig and goats cheese parcels with
rhubarb chutney, steak and mushroom pudding, halibut steak grilled with sage butter,
steak burger, vegetable balti and steaks, with puddings such as honeycomb and
butterscotch sundae and chocolate sponge in orange and chocolate sauce. Other than light
snacks, a similar menu is available in the restaurant. *Starters/Snacks: £3.95 to £4.95. Main
Courses: £8.75 to £14.95. Puddings: £3.85 to £3.95*

Robinsons ~ Tenants Alan and Grace Smith ~ Real ale ~ Bar food (11.30-2, 6-9; 12-8 Sun) ~
Restaurant ~ (01260) 273946 ~ Children welcome ~ Open 11.30-11(10.30 Sun) ~
Bedrooms: £50S/£80S(£70B)

Recommended by Mike Proctor, David Rutter, Joan and Tony Walker, John Branston

ASTON
SJ6146   MAP 7

Bhurtpore ★ ♀ 🍺

Off A530 SW of Nantwich; in village follow Wrenbury signpost; CW5 8DQ

**Fantastic range of drinks (especially real ales) and tasty curries in this warm-hearted pub
with some unusual artefacts; big garden**

The 11 taps at this well cared-for place usually run through over 1,000 different superbly
kept real ales a year, all drawn from an enterprising range of nationally sourced brewers
such as Abbeydale, Acorn, Copper Dragon, Phoenix, Salopian and Wincle. They also stock
dozens of unusual bottled beers and fruit beers, a great many bottled ciders and perries,
over 100 different whiskies, carefully selected soft drinks and a good wine list; summer
beer festival. The pub takes its unusual name from the town in India where a local
landowner by the name of Lord Combermere won a battle. The indian connection also
explains some of the exotic artefacts in the carpeted lounge bar – look out for the
turbaned statue behind the counter, proudly sporting any sunglasses left behind by
customers; also good local period photographs and some attractive furniture. Tables in
the comfortable public bar are reserved for people not eating; board games, pool, TV and
games machine. At lunchtime and early weekday evenings the atmosphere is cosy and
civilised, and cheery staff usually cope superbly with the busy weekends.

🍴 The enjoyably varied menu has bar nibbles, sandwiches and panini (not Fri or Sat
evenings), a choice of around half a dozen tasty curries, battered haddock, steak and ale
pie, mutton pie, braised pig cheeks with star anise, honey and tomato, rabbit loin with
pork and black pudding stuffing and whisky sauce, and puddings such as baked blueberry
cheesecake, ginger and black pepper pudding with toffee sauce and local ice-creams.
Starters/Snacks: £4.25 to £5.25. Main Courses: £7.95 to £15.95. Puddings: £4.75 to £4.95

Free house ~ Licensee Simon George ~ Real ale ~ Bar food (12-2, 7-9; 12-9.30 Sat (9 Sun)) ~ Restaurant ~ (01270) 780917 ~ Children welcome (until 8.30pm Fri, Sat) ~ Dogs allowed in bar ~ Folk third Tues of the month ~ Open 12-2.30, 6.30-11.30; 12-(11 Sun) midnight Fri and Sat

Recommended by Malcolm and Pauline Pellatt, Mike Proctor, R T and J C Moggridge, Dr D J and Mrs S C Walker, the Didler, Mr and Mrs P R Thomas, Tony and Wendy Hobden, Brian and Anna Marsden, Martin Grosberg

BARTHOMLEY   SJ7752   MAP 7

White Lion ★ £

A mile from M6 junction 16; from exit roundabout take B5078 N towards Alsager, then Barthomley signposted on left; CW2 5PG

Charming 17th-c thatched village tavern with classic period interior and good value, straightforward, tasty lunchtime food

With its locals, bikers, cheery dogs and travellers (possibly all seeking respite from the motorway), the friendly main bar at this unpretentious place is timelessly informal with well worn paintwork, a blazing open fire, heavy low oak beams dating back to Stuart times, attractively moulded black panelling, Cheshire history and prints on the walls, latticed windows and uneven wobbly old tables. Up some steps, a second room has another welcoming open fire, more oak panelling, a high-backed winged settle and a paraffin lamp hinged to the wall; shove-ha'penny; local societies make good use of a third room. Five real ales include Mansfield, Marstons Bitter, usually Jennings Cocker Hoop and Snecklifter, and a true guest such as Wychwood Hobgoblin. In the summer, seats on the cobbles outside, taking in the view of the attractive old village and the early 15th-c red sandstone church of St Bertiline (where you can learn about the Barthomley massacre), can be quite idyllic.

🍴 **Tasty food from the short good value traditional menu includes enjoyable sandwiches and baguettes (some made with hot beef, ham or pork), ploughman's, staffordshire oatcakes with bacon, cheese, onions, tomatoes and beans, steak pie and hotpot with french bread.** *Starters/Snacks: £4.25 to £6.95*

Marstons ~ Tenant Laura Condliffe ~ Real ale ~ Bar food (lunchtime only 12-2) ~ (01270) 882242 ~ Children welcome away from bar ~ Dogs welcome ~ Open 11.30-11; 12-10.30 Sun

Recommended by Paul J Robinshaw, the Didler, Dr and Mrs A K Clarke, Mike Proctor, Joe Green, Mr and Mrs P R Thomas, Edward Mirzoeff

BICKLEY MOSS   SJ5550   MAP 7

Cholmondeley Arms ♀

Cholmondeley; A49 5.5 miles N of Whitchurch; the owners would like us to list them under Cholmondeley Village, but as this is rarely located on maps we have mentioned the nearest village which appears more often; SY14 8HN

Imaginatively converted high-ceilinged schoolhouse with decent range of real ales and wines, well presented food and sizeable garden

This clever schoolhouse conversion (handily placed for Cholmondeley Castle Gardens) is thoroughly good fun and makes a memorable setting for a meal or a drink. The cross-shaped lofty bar, high gothic windows, huge old radiators and old school desks on a gantry above the bar are all testament to its former identity. Well used chairs in all shapes and forms – some upholstered, some bentwood, some with ladderbacks and some with wheelbacks – are set in groups round an equally eclectic mix of tables, all on comfy carpets. There's a stag's head over one of the side arches, an open fire and lots of Victorian portraits and military pictures on colourwashed walls; piped music and board games. Salopian Shropshire Gold and Weetwood Eastgate, and a couple of guests from brewers such as Brakspear and Slaters, are served from a pine-clad bar, alongside around ten interesting and reasonably priced wines by the glass which are listed on a blackboard, and a growing selection of whiskies. There are seats outside on the sizeable lawn and more in front overlooking the quiet road.

⑪ Readers very much enjoy the food here. As well as lunchtime sandwiches (not Sun), there might be home-cured salt beef hash with brown sauce and crispy poached egg, seared scallops with pea purée and crispy pancetta, ploughman's, devilled kidneys, battered haddock, bass fillet with pea and crayfish risotto and samphire, lamb rump with smoked pancetta and flageolet bean ragoût and sirloin steak, and puddings such as white chocolate and rhubarb brûlée and bakewell tart. *Starters/Snacks: £3.95 to £7.50. Main Courses: £7.75 to £17.95. Puddings: £4.75*

Free house ~ Licensee Carolyn Ross-Lowe ~ Real ale ~ Bar food (12-2.30, 7-9; 12-9.30(9 Sun) Sat, bank hols) ~ (01829) 720300 ~ Children welcome ~ Dogs welcome ~ Open 11-11(10.30 Sun) ~ Bedrooms: £55B/£70S(£80B)

Recommended by Mr and Mrs James Freund, Guy Vowles, Mike Proctor, J S Burn, Alan and Eve Harding, Paul and Gaynor Heath, Ray and Winifred Halliday

BUNBURY

SJ5658   MAP 7

Dysart Arms

Bowes Gate Road; village signposted off A51 NW of Nantwich; and from A49 S of Tarporley – coming this way, coming in on northernmost village access road, bear left in village centre; CW6 9PH

Civilised chatty dining pub attractively filled with good furniture in thoughtfully laid-out rooms; very enjoyable food, lovely garden with pretty views

The knocked-through opened-up rooms at this comfortable Brunning & Price country pub have an easy-going sociable atmosphere. Neatly kept, they ramble gently around the pleasantly lit central bar. Cream walls keep it light, clean and airy, with deep venetian-red ceilings adding cosiness, and each room (some with good winter fires) is cleverly furnished with an appealing variety of well spaced sturdy wooden tables and chairs, a couple of tall filled bookcases and just the right amount of carefully chosen bric-a-brac, properly lit pictures and plants. Flooring ranges from red and black tiles, to stripped boards and some carpet. Service is efficient and friendly. Phoenix Brunning & Price Original, Weetwood Cheshire Cat and two or three guests such as Crouch Vale Brewers Gold and Hop Back Summer Lightning are very well kept on handpump, alongside a good selection of 15 wines by the glass and just over 20 malts. Sturdy wooden tables on the terrace and picnic-sets on the lawn in the neatly kept slightly elevated garden are lovely in summer, with views of the splendid church at the end of this pretty village, and the distant Peckforton Hills beyond.

⑪ From a changing menu, food is tasty, just imaginative enough, attractively presented and fairly priced. As well as sandwiches, there might be crayfish cocktail, home-smoked pigeon and walnut salad, ploughman's, roast pork belly with chorizo and mixed bean cassoulet, sweet potato and blue cheese frittata with tomato relish, steak and kidney pie, fried bass with saffron, pea and roast pepper risotto, caerphilly cheese and leek sausages with lentils and tomato and roast garlic sauce, steak burger, and puddings such as iced chocolate parfait with caramelised orange and chocolate sauce and Baileys and white chocolate cheesecake with chocolate sauce; good british cheeseboard. *Starters/Snacks: £4.50 to £8.95. Main Courses: £8.25 to £15.95. Puddings: £4.25 to £5.50*

Brunning & Price ~ Manager Greg Williams ~ Real ale ~ Bar food (12-9.30(9 Sun)) ~ (01829) 260183 ~ Children welcome ~ Dogs allowed in bar ~ Open 11.30-11; 12-10.30 Sun

Recommended by C R Taylor, Mike Proctor, Paul Boot, J S Burn, John Cook, Peter Webb, Gerry and Rosemary Dobson, Clive Watkin, Sian Davies, Dr and Mrs Michael Smith, Bruce and Sharon Eden

---

Stars after the name of a pub show exceptional quality. One star means most people (after reading the report to see just why the star has been won) would think a special trip worth while. Two stars mean that the pub is really outstanding – for its particular qualities it could hardly be bettered.

BURLEYDAM   SJ6042   MAP 7

Combermere Arms

A525 Whitchurch—Audlem; SY13 4AT

Roomy and attractive beamed pub successfully mixing good drinking side with imaginative all-day food; rear and front garden

Trademark Brunning & Price furnishings and décor at this spreading pub take in an eclectic mix of dark wood furniture and rugs on wood (some old and some new oak) or stone floors, print-covered cream walls, deep red ceilings, panelling and open fires. Friendly staff extend an equally nice welcome to drinkers and diners, with both aspects of the business seeming to do well here. Alongside Phoenix Brunning & Price Original and Weetwood Cheshire Cat, three or four guests might be from brewers such as Acorn, Brains, Greene King and Salopian. They also stock around 100 whiskies and a dozen wines by the glass from an extensive list; a few board games. During summer evenings they put candles on the good solid wood tables in the pretty, well tended garden.

As well as interesting sandwiches and ploughman's, the enjoyable daily-changing menu might include pork, apricot and sage pie, roasted fig, red onion and blue cheese tart, battered haddock, fried bream with mild curried mussel sauce and bombay potatoes, roast butternut squash and sage risotto with grilled artichokes, fried venison rump with colcannon cake, roasted root vegetables and juniper gravy, and puddings such as white chocolate cheesecake with raspberry compote and rhubarb jelly and custard panna cotta with ginger shortbread, and a british cheeseboard. *Starters/Snacks: £4.50 to £8.95. Main Courses: £9.25 to £16.50. Puddings: £4.75 to £5.25*

Brunning & Price ~ Manager Lisa Hares ~ Real ale ~ Bar food (12-9.30; 12-10 Fri, Sat; 12-9 Sun) ~ (01948) 871223 ~ Children welcome ~ Dogs allowed in bar ~ Open 11.30-11(10.30 Sun)

Recommended by Paul and Margaret Baker, R T and J C Moggridge, Tom and Jill Jones

BURWARDSLEY   SJ5256   MAP 7

Pheasant

Higher Burwardsley; signposted from Tattenhall (which itself is signposted off A41 S of Chester) and from Harthill (reached by turning off A534 Nantwich—Holt at the Copper Mine); follow pub's signpost on up hill from Post Office; OS Sheet 117 map reference 523566; CH3 9PF

Fantastic views, local beer and good range of enjoyable food at this roomily fresh conversion of an old heavily beamed inn; open all day

There are stunning views right across the Cheshire plains from nice hardwood furniture on the terrace at this half-timbered sandstone 17th-c pub and on a clear day the telescope sees as far as the pier head and cathedrals in Liverpool. Divided into separate areas and almost circling the bar, the beamed interior (great views from here too), quite airy and modern feeling in parts, has wooden floors, well spaced furniture, including comfy leather armchairs and some nice old chairs. They say the see-through fireplace houses the largest log fire in the county. Local Weetwood Best and Eastgate beers are served alongside a couple of guests such as Phoenix Pale Moonlight and Weetwood Mad Hatter, as well as local farm cider and apple juice; quiet piped music, daily newspapers. This is a great stop if you are walking the scenic Sandstone Trail along the Peckforton Hills.

Besides sandwiches (served until 6pm), the changing menu might include ginger and chilli prawns, chicken liver pâté, several deli boards, chilli, baked sole, chicken breast with creamed leeks and bourguignon sauce, steak burger, five-spice duck breast with stir-fried vegetables, fried lambs liver with lyonnaise potatoes, creamed oatmeal cabbage and crispy bacon, well hung rib-eye steak, and puddings such as warm chocolate fudge cake and lemon posset; summer weekend barbecues. *Starters/Snacks: £2.95 to £8.50. Main Courses: £8.95 to £17.95. Puddings: £3.75 to £5.25*

Free house ~ Licensee Andrew Nelson ~ Real ale ~ Bar food (12-3, 6-9.30 Mon, 12-9.30 Tues-Thurs, 12-10 Fri, Sat; 12-8.30 Sun) ~ (01829) 770434 ~ Children welcome ~ Dogs welcome ~ Open 11-11; 12-10.30 Sun ~ Bedrooms: £65B/£85B

Recommended by Noel Woods, Dave Irving, Jenny Huggins, John and Verna Aspinall, Val Carter, Maurice and Gill McMahon, Gerry and Rosemary Dobson, Jeremy King, Jill and Julian Tasker

CHESTER

SJ4066   MAP 7

Albion ★

Albion Street; CH1 1RQ

Strongly traditional pub with comfortable Edwardian décor and captivating World War I memorabilia; pubby food and good drinks

There is something inimitably genuine about this firmly run, peaceful Victorian haunt with its long-standing friendly licensees of nearly 40 years now. Uniquely in Chester for a pub of this period it has kept its original layout, and its homely interior is entirely dedicated to the Great War of 1914-18; most unusually it's also the officially listed site of four war memorials to soldiers from the Cheshire Regiment. Throughout its tranquil rooms you'll find an absorbing collection of World War I memorabilia, from big engravings of men leaving for war, and similarly moving prints of wounded veterans, to flags, advertisements and so on. You might even be lucky enough to hear the vintage 1928 Steck pianola being played. The post-Edwardian décor is appealingly muted, with dark floral William Morris wallpaper (designed on the first day of World War I), a cast-iron fireplace, appropriate lamps, leatherette and hoop-backed chairs and cast-iron-framed tables; there's an attractive side dining room too. Service is friendly though groups of race-goers are discouraged (opening times may be limited during meets), and they don't like people rushing in just before closing time. Three real ales might be from brewers such as Adnams, Jennings and Shepherd Neame. They stock new world wines, fresh orange juice, organic bottled cider and fruit juice, over 25 malt whiskies and a good selection of rums and gins. Dog owners can request a water bowl and cold sausage for their pets. Bedrooms are small but comfortable and furnished in keeping with the pub's style.

🍴 **As well as doorstep sandwiches and filled staffordshire oatcakes, generous helpings of good homely food might include boiled gammon and pease pudding with parsley sauce, lambs liver, bacon and onions with cider gravy, fish pie, haggis, tatties and vegetables, with puddings such as chocolate torte or bread and butter pudding with marmalade.** *Starters/Snacks: £1.90 to £6.20. Main Courses: £9.70 to £10.90. Puddings: £4.20*

Punch ~ Lease Michael Edward Mercer ~ Real ale ~ Bar food (12-1.45, 5-7.45(8.15 Sat); not Sun evening) ~ No credit cards ~ (01244) 340345 ~ Dogs allowed in bar ~ Open 12-3, 5(6 Sat)-11; 12-3, 7-10 Sun ~ Bedrooms: £70B/£80B

Recommended by Margaret White, Steve Narey, Roger and Anne Newbury, J S Burn, Joe Green, Colin Moore, Mrs M Smith, Alan and Eve Harding, Martin and Sue Radcliffe, Philip and Jan Medcalf, Keith Sale, Dennis Jones, Kim Mackay, Mary Mackay, the Didler, Barry Collett, Maurice and Gill McMahon, Neil Whitehead, Victoria Anderson

Mill 🍺 £

Milton Street; CH1 3NF

Big hotel with huge range of real ales, good value food and cheery service in sizeable bar

It's quite unusual for a modern hotel like this to carry such an impressive range of beers: Cornmill (brewed for them by Phoenix), Mill Premium (brewed for them by Coach House), Copper Dragon Golden Pippin and Weetwood Best are well kept alongside up to a dozen guests from brewers such as Marstons, RCH and Whim; also a dozen wines by the glass and two farm ciders. Converted from an old mill, the building straddles either side of the Shropshire Union Canal, with a glassed-in bridge connecting its two halves. The very neatly kept bar has stripped light wood flooring throughout, marble-topped tables, some exposed brickwork and supporting pillars, and local photographs and cigarette cards framed on cream-papered walls. One comfortable area is reminiscent of a bar on a cruise liner. Service here is very friendly and you'll find a real mix of customers; quiet piped music and unobtrusively placed big-screen sports TV. Readers say the bedrooms are comfortable and make a handy base for exploring the city.

🍴 Very reasonably priced pubby food includes sandwiches, ciabattas and enjoyable hot dishes such as curry and rice, scampi, fish and chips and their popular steak and ale pie. *Starters/Snacks: £1.20 to £4.95. Main Courses: £5.50 to £7.50. Puddings: £3.95*

Free house ~ Licensees Gary and Gordon Vickers ~ Real ale ~ Bar food (11.30(12 Sun)-10) ~ Restaurant ~ (01244) 350035 ~ Children welcome ~ Live jazz Mon ~ Open 10am-midnight; 11-11 Sun ~ Bedrooms: £73B/£91B

Recommended by Colin Moore, Ben Williams, Alan Johnson, Joe Green, Dennis Jones

Old Harkers Arms ♀ 🍺

Russell Street, down steps off City Road where it crosses canal – under Mike Melody antiques; CH3 5AL

Well run spacious canalside building with great range of drinks (including lots of changing real ales) and good tasty food

Even a rainy day can work out well here as you while away time watching drops of water splashing on to the Shropshire Union Canal, just feet away from the tall windows of this high-ceilinged converted early Victorian warehouse. Huge brick pillars cleverly divide the big airy interior into some intimate places, and cheery staff spread a happy bustle. Mixed dark wood furniture is intimately grouped on stripped wood floors, walls are covered with frame-to-frame old prints, and the usual Brunning & Price wall of bookshelves is to be found above a leather banquette at one end. Attractive lamps add cosiness, and the bar counter is apparently constructed from salvaged doors; selection of board games. You'll find a very wide range of drinks with around nine real ales on handpump including Phoenix Brunning & Price, Flowers Original and Weetwood Cheshire Cat, and regularly changing guests from brewers such as Abbeydale, BrewDog, Roosters and Wincle, more than 100 malt whiskies, 50 well described wines (with around half of them by the glass), eight or so farmhouse ciders and local apple juice.

🍴 As well as a good range of interesting sandwiches, nicely presented, carefully sourced bar food – a good balance of homely dishes and more imaginative ones – might include snacks and starters such as black pudding fritters with cider apple sauce, stilton and Guinness pâté with grape and pear salad, crab linguini with ginger, lime and chilli, ploughman's, sausage and mash, lamb casserole, butternut squash, chickpea and spinach curry with onion bhaji, fried salmon fillet with sweet and sour peppers, steak burger, rump steak, and puddings such as chocolate brownie and blackberry parfait with pear compote, and a british cheeseboard. *Starters/Snacks: £4.50 to £7.50. Main Courses: £8.95 to £16.95. Puddings: £4.75 to £5.85*

Brunning & Price ~ Manager Paul Jeffery ~ Real ale ~ Bar food (12-9.30) ~ (01244) 344525 ~ Older children welcome until 5pm if well behaved ~ Dogs allowed in bar ~ Open 11.30-11; 12-10.30 Sun

Recommended by Bruce and Sharon Eden, Dr Kevan Tucker, Ian and Nita Cooper, Joe Green, Dennis Jones, Charles and Pauline Stride, Simon J Barber, Clive Watkin, the Didler

EATON   SJ8765   MAP 7

Plough 🛏

A536 Congleton—Macclesfield; CW12 2NH

Neat and cosy village pub with up to four interesting beers, bar food, views from big attractive garden; good bedrooms

With a fairly traditional feel, the carefully converted bar at this tidy red-brick 17th-c pub has plenty of beams and exposed brickwork, a couple of snug little alcoves, comfortable armchairs and cushioned wooden wall seats on red patterned carpets, long red curtains, leaded windows and a big stone fireplace. Attentive service is friendly and readers have been given highchairs and a little table with crayons and paper for children. Beers include Hydes Bitter (very reasonably priced), Storm PGA, Wells & Youngs Bombardier, an occasional guest, and a decent wine list offers ten by the glass; piped music and occasional TV. Moved here piece by piece from its original home in Wales, the heavily raftered barn at the back makes a striking restaurant and the appealingly designed bedrooms are in a converted stable block. Being not far from the fringes of the Peak District, you get good views of its nearby hills from the big tree-filled garden which has picnic-sets on the lawn and a covered decked terrace with outdoor heaters.

🍴 **It's advisable to book if you are eating. Food includes lunchtime sandwiches as well as soup, prawns in garlic butter, steak and kidney pudding, thai green curry, 10oz rib-eye steak and some interesting daily specials such as roast duck breast on sweet potato rösti with ginger-fried pineapple and red wine jus, mushroom stroganoff, and puddings such as fruit crumble and crème brûlée; three-course Sunday lunch.** *Starters/Snacks: £3.95 to £6.75. Main Courses: £7.95 to £15.95. Puddings: £4.25*

Free house ~ Licensee Mujdat Karatas ~ Real ale ~ Bar food (12-2.30, 6-9.30; 12-9.30(8 Sun)Fri, Sat) ~ Restaurant ~ (01260) 280207 ~ Children welcome ~ Open 11am-midnight(1am Sat, 11 Sun) ~ Bedrooms: £60B/£75B

Recommended by Paul and Margaret Baker, Pam and John Smith, Phil Merrin, Rob and Catherine Dunster, John Ashford

LACH DENNIS
SJ7072   MAP 7

Duke of Portland 🍴 ♀
Holmes Chapel Road (B5082, off A556 SE of Northwich); CW9 7SY

Good food in stylish upscale dining pub which doesn't neglect the beer side

This civilised pub is an inviting place for a relaxed meal but you are equally welcome to sink into one of their comfortable leather sofas for a drink. The bar area is gently decorated in beige, grey and cream, with square leather pouffes opposite the sofas and chunky low tables on neutral carpets, and nicely framed prints above its panelled dado. Friendly young staff behind its handsomely carved counter serve four ales from handpump, including Marstons Pedigree and guests from brewers such as Batemans, Brakspear, Jennings and Wychwood. The interesting changing choice of about a dozen wines by the glass is fairly priced; daily papers. The main dining room, with its lofty ceiling, sturdy balustrades and big pictures, gives quite a sense of occasion, but keeps a fairly relaxed feel – perhaps because of the friendly mixture of styles in the comfortable dining chairs on its floorboards; piped music, TV. Outside, a neat terrace has alloy tables and chairs among modernist planters and lovely countryside views. The family also own the locally famous Belle Epoque restaurant in Knutsford.

🍴 **They take great care over sourcing really good ingredients from named local suppliers, showing justifiable pride in their meats and cheeses; even the chips come in for admiration and are cooked in beef dripping and bread is home-baked. Dishes might include welsh brie and roast ham toastie, crispy bread, black pudding and crumbled gloucester old spot pork belly with apple and mustard sauce, mushroom risotto with truffle oil, crispy oriental duck salad, fish and chips, steak burger, baked bass with pesto and grilled mediterranean vegetables, venison bourguignon, and puddings such as chocolate brownie and Baileys cheesecake.** *Starters/Snacks: £3.95 to £6.95. Main Courses: £9.95 to £14.95. Puddings: £5.95*

Marstons ~ Lease Matthew Mooney ~ Real ale ~ Bar food (12-2.30, 5.30-10; 12-8 Sun) ~ Restaurant ~ (01606) 46264 ~ Children welcome (only if dining after 7pm) ~ Open 12-11; 12-3, 5.30-11 in winter

Recommended by Paul and Margaret Baker, Dr and Mrs A K Clarke, Alan Poole

LANGLEY
SJ9569   MAP 7

Hanging Gate ♀
Meg Lane, Higher Sutton; follow Langley signpost from A54 beside Fourways Motel, and that road passes the pub; from Macclesfield, heading S from centre on A523 turn left into Byrons Lane at Langley, Wincle signpost; in Sutton (0.5 miles after going under canal bridge, ie before Langley) fork right at Church House Inn, following Wildboarclough signpost, then 2 miles later turning sharp right at steep hairpin bend; OS Sheet 118 map reference 952696; SK11 0NG

Remotely set old place with fires in traditional cosy rooms; lovely views from airy extension and terrace

Traditional pubby little rooms or an airy dining room with panoramic views over a patchwork of valley pastures to distant moors and the tall Sutton Common transmitter are the choice at this low-beamed old drovers' pub (first licensed in 1621 but built earlier) high up in the Peak District. Still in their original layout, the three cosy little low-beamed rooms are simply furnished. The tiny little snug bar, at its pubbiest at lunchtime, has a welcoming log fire in a big brick fireplace, a single table, plain chairs and cushioned wall seats, a few old pub pictures and seasonal photographs on its creamy walls. Beers are served in here and include well kept Hydes Original, Jekylls Gold and Over A Barrel and a guest such as Fullers London Pride on handpump, quite a few malt whiskies and ten wines by the glass. The second room, with just a section of bar counter in the corner, has only five tables, and there's a third appealing little oak-beamed blue room. Seats out on the crazy-paved terrace are a great place to take in the views and sunset; piped music, board games, dominoes, books. It does get busy so it's best to book on weekends. Walkers are made to feel welcome with tap water and there's a dog bowl outside.

As well as good sandwiches and ploughman's, made with home-baked bread, tasty bar food might include black pudding, duck and chicken liver pâté, slow-braised lamb shoulder, venison pie, fish and chips, roast wild boar with plums and well hung rib-eye steak, with puddings such as parkin with extra treacle, dark chocolate sponge pudding and apple crumble. *Starters/Snacks: £3.95 to £6.95. Main Courses: £6.95 to £12.95. Puddings: £3.95 to £4.95*

Hydes ~ Tenants Ian and Luda Rottenbury ~ Real ale ~ Bar food (12-2.30(4 Sun), 6-9) ~ Restaurant ~ (01260) 252238 ~ Children welcome until 7pm ~ Dogs allowed in bar ~ Open 12-3, 5.30-11.30; 12-11.30 Sat; 10am–10pm Sun

Recommended by Rob and Catherine Dunster, David and Katharine Cooke, the Haytons, Mike Proctor, Hilary Forrest, the Didler, Lesley and Peter Barrett

MACCLESFIELD   SJ9271   MAP 7

Sutton Hall

Leaving Macclesfield southwards on A523, turn left into Byrons Lane signposted Langley, Wincle, then just before canal viaduct fork right into Bullocks Lane; OS Sheet 118 map reference 925715; SK11 0HE

CHESHIRE DINING PUB OF THE YEAR

Recently refurbished historic building set in attractive grounds; fine range of drinks and good food

Brunning & Price have done an admirable job in the conversion of this splendid 16th-c manor house. The original hall that forms the heart of the building is beautifully impressive, particularly in its entrance space. Delightful bar areas, some divided by tall oak timbers have plenty of character with antique squared oak panelling, warmly coloured rugs on broad flagstones, board floor and tiled floors, frame-to-frame pictures and a raised open fire – all very Brunning & Price. Kind efficient staff serve six real ales including Flowers Original, Phoenix Brunning & Price, Weetwood Cheshire Cat and three guests from brewers such as Storm, Titanic and Wincle, plus several wines by the glass. Pleasant gardens have good solid wood tables on terraces surrounded by a tree-sheltered lawn.

Bar food includes imaginative sandwiches, interestingly turned out pub staples like ploughman's and beer-battered haddock, more imaginative dishes such as citrus marinated king scallops or potted rabbit and belly pork, smoked haddock and watercress tart or rump steak sandwich, slow-roasted pork with apple fritters and parsnip, chicken leek and bacon pie or tandoori monkfish with onion fritter, spiced potato and mango and crème fraîche salad, with puddings such as passion fruit panna cotta with passion fruit jelly and coconut biscuit and rum baba and white chocolate tart with roast pineapple; good cheeseboard. *Starters/Snacks: £4.50 to £8.95. Main Courses: £6.95 to £16.25. Puddings: £4.50 to £5.30*

Brunning & Price ~ Manager Sid Foster ~ Real ale ~ Bar food (12-10(9.30 Sun)) ~
(01260) 253211 ~ Children welcome ~ Dogs allowed in bar ~ Open 11.30-11; 12-10.30 Sun

*Recommended by Noel Grundy, Beryl and David Sowter, Brian and Anna Marsden, Susan and Nigel Brookes,
R T and J C Moggridge, Bruce and Sharon Eden, Michael Butler, Maurice and Gill McMahon, Steve Whalley*

MOBBERLEY

SJ7879   MAP 7

Roebuck ⊗ ☂

Mill Lane; down hill from sharp bend on B5085 at E edge of 30mph limit; WA16 7HX

**Stylishly simple country interior, warm welcome and very helpful service, good food, good
wine list, courtyard and garden**

With an airy interior that quietly makes the most of its original features, this discerningly
laid out place is much liked by both drinkers and diners, and readers find a warm
welcome from the attentive staff. Old tiled and boarded floors carry a comfortable mix of
country furnishings, from cushioned long wood pews (rescued from a welsh chapel) to
scrubbed pine farmhouse tables and a mix of old chairs. The wine list (well over a dozen
by the glass) is short but well chosen and very reasonably priced, and beers are Black
Sheep, Tetleys, Timothy Taylors Landlord and a guest from local Storm; piped music.
Outside you'll find picnic-sets on a cobbled courtyard, metal café furniture on a wooden
deck, and picnic-sets in an enclosed and well manicured beer garden.

⊞ **The enjoyable food is thoughtfully prepared and features traditional dishes with an
appealing twist. As well as upmarket sandwiches (not evenings), dishes might include
duck liver parfait with spiced plum chutney, glazed poached pear with cheshire brie
fritter and fig jam, battered haddock with mushy peas, braised steak and onions with
horseradish mash, goats cheese and shallot tart, well hung rib-eye steak, fried bass with
roast garlic and chive cream sauce, and puddings such as eton mess, chocolate brownie
with white chocolate ice-cream or rhubarb and ginger crumble; british cheeseboard. Side
orders are extra so you might want to add a couple of pounds to the prices below, and you
will probably need to book.** *Starters/Snacks: £4.25 to £5.95. Main Courses: £8.95 to £12.95.
Puddings: £3.95 to £5.25*

Free house ~ Licensee Jane Kerr ~ Real ale ~ Bar food (12-2.30, 5.30-9.30; 12-9.30 Sat(8 Sun)
~ (01565) 873322 ~ Children welcome ~ Open 12-3, 5-11; 12-11 Sat; 12-10.30 Sun

*Recommended by Noel Grundy, Neil and Karen Dignan, Mrs P J Carroll, Dr and Mrs A K Clarke, P J and R D Greaves,
Gerry and Rosemary Dobson*

PEOVER HEATH

SJ7973   MAP 7

Dog ◖

*Off A50 N of Holmes Chapel at the Whipping Stocks, keep on past Parkgate into Wellbank
Lane; OS Sheet 118 map reference 794735; note that this village is called Peover Heath on
the OS map and shown under that name on many road maps, but the pub is often listed
under Over Peover instead; WA16 8UP*

Homely pub with interesting range of beers and generously served food; bedrooms

Gently old-fashioned with a comfortably cottagey feel, the neatly kept bar at this
unpretentious pub has neat tied-back floral curtains at little windows, a curved
cushioned banquette built into a bay window and mostly traditional dark wheelbacks
arranged on a patterned carpet. A coal fire, copper pieces and pot plants add to the
homely feel. A games room has a games machine, darts, pool, dominoes, board games
and TV; piped music. Hydes (very good value at £2 a pint) and two beers from Weetwood
are on handpump alongside a guest such as Slaters Top Totty. They also have a good
range of malt whiskies and wines by the glass. Friendly efficient staff cope well when it
gets busy. There are picnic-sets beneath colourful hanging baskets on the peaceful lane,
and more out in a pretty back garden. It's a pleasant walk from here to the Jodrell Bank
Centre and Arboretum.

🍴 As well as soup and sandwiches, bar food might include battered mushrooms, smoked salmon salad, sautéed chicken liver salad with brandy and cream, seared lamb chops with red wine jus, steak and ale pie, oatcakes stuffed with leeks, mushrooms and cheese and cod and chips, with puddings such as baked lemon cheesecake, bread and butter pudding and chocolate fudge cake. *Starters/Snacks: £4.00 to £8.00. Main Courses: £9.95 to £17.95. Puddings: £4.50*

Free house ~ Licensee Steven Wrigley ~ Real ale ~ Bar food (12-2.30, 6-9; 12-8.30 Sun) ~ Restaurant ~ (01625) 861421 ~ Children welcome ~ Dogs allowed in bar ~ Occasional live music Fri ~ Open 11.30-3, 4.30-11.30; 11.30-11.30 Sat; 12-11.30 Sun ~ Bedrooms: £60B/£80B

Recommended by Gerry and Rosemary Dobson, John Cook, Sylvia and Tony Birbeck, S Bloomfield, Peter Dowd

PLUMLEY   SJ7075   MAP 7

Smoker

2.5 miles from M6 junction 19: A556 towards Northwich and Chester; WA16 0TY

Spotlessly kept comfortable lounges and a breakfast menu; handy for M6

This neatly kept old pub makes a handy break from the nearby M6. Look out for the Edwardian print of a hunt meeting outside (tucked in among the military prints), which shows how little the pub's appearance has changed over the centuries. Popular with an older set, its three connecting rooms have dark panelling, open fires in impressive period fireplaces, deep sofas, other comfortable seats and settles, and a sweet collection of copper kettles; piped music. Three Robinsons beers are on handpump and they've a good choice of wines and whiskies. The sizeable garden has roses, flower beds and a children's play area.

🍴 Breakfast is served till midday, followed by sandwiches, starters such as crispy duck pancake and warm goats cheese salad, main courses such as steak burger, red thai curry, roast shoulder of lamb with redcurrant and port sauce and steak, mushroom and ale pie, battered haddock and bass with ginger and spring onions, and puddings such as apple crumble and warm chocolate fudge cake. *Starters/Snacks: £4.50 to £6.95. Main Courses: £8.95 to £16.95. Puddings: £5.25*

Robinsons ~ Tenants John and Diana Bailey ~ Real ale ~ Bar food (10-2.15, 6-9.15; 10-9 Sun) ~ Restaurant ~ (01565) 722338 ~ Children welcome ~ Open 10-3, 6-11; 10am-10.30pm Sun

Recommended by Dennis Jones, Peter Webb, John and Helen Rushton, David and Sue Atkinson

PRESTBURY   SJ8976   MAP 7

Legh Arms 🛏️

A538, village centre; SK10 4DG

Immaculately kept hotel with good food, appealingly individual bar and walled garden; beautiful bedrooms

The bar and lounge areas at this upmarket hotel are smartly traditional with plenty of elegant soft furnishings. Though opened up, it is well divided into several intimate areas, with muted tartan fabric over a panelled dado on the right, ladderback dining chairs, good solid dark tables, stylish french steam train prints, italian costume engravings and a glass case of china and books. On the left there are brocaded bucket seats around more solid tables, antique steeplechase prints, and staffordshire dogs on the stone mantelpiece, all warmed by a good coal fire; a snug panelled back part has cosy wing armchairs and a grand piano (sometimes played) and a narrow side offshoot has pairs of art deco leather armchairs around small granite tables and antique costume prints of french tradesmen. The bar, towards the back on the left, has well kept Robinsons Hatters Mild and Unicorn on handpump and nice house wines (seven by the glass), a good range of malts and cognacs, good coffee, and maybe genial regulars perched on the comfortable leather bar stools; this part looks up to an unusual balustraded internal landing. There are daily papers on a coffee table and magazines on an antique oak dresser; piped music. A garden behind has a terrace with outdoor heating.

🍴 Very tasty bar food might include soup, sandwiches, spicy fishcakes with sweet chilli sauce, thai chicken curry, chicken and mushroom pie, grilled bass, sweet chilli beef noodles, tomato and roasted red pepper cannelloni, and puddings such as chocolate torte and sticky toffee pudding. The pricier menu in the sumptuous restaurant is more elaborate. *Starters/Snacks: £3.75 to £7.95. Main Courses: £7.95 to £13.95. Puddings: £4.50 to £6.50*

Robinsons ~ Tenant Peter Myers ~ Real ale ~ Bar food (12-2, 6-10; 12-10 Sat, Sun) ~ Restaurant ~ (01625) 829130 ~ Children welcome ~ Dogs welcome ~ Open 11-midnight ~ Bedrooms: £70S/£95B

Recommended by Susan and Nigel Brookes, Pam and John Smith

TARPORLEY
SJ5562   MAP 7

Rising Sun
High Street; village signposted off A51 Nantwich—Chester; CW6 0DX

Friendly, bustling and quaint, with pubby food

The low-ceilinged characterful interior of this brick-fronted family-run pub is cosily furnished with well chosen tables surrounded by eye-catching old seats (including creaky 19th-c mahogany and oak settles), an attractively blacked iron kitchen range, and sporting and other old-fashioned prints on the walls. Accommodating staff serve Robinsons Dizzy Blonde, Unicorn and a seasonal ale from handpumps. There are one or two seats and a TV for sporting events in a tiny side bar; piped music. More reports please.

🍴 Alongside pub standards such as soup, sandwiches and toasties, a surprisingly extensive menu lists more than half a dozen tasty pies, wide choices of fish, poultry, casserole and grilled meat dishes (such as seafood pancake, chicken maryland, beef bourguignon, braised rabbit and mixed grill), as well as spicy indian and oriental food and a dozen vegetarian items. Puddings might include home-made sherry trifle, raspberry meringue roulade, ice-creams and sorbets. *Starters/Snacks: £3.25 to £5.35. Main Courses: £6.50 to £15.95. Puddings: £3.95 to £4.15*

Robinsons ~ Tenant David Robertson ~ Real ale ~ Bar food (11.30-2, 5.30-9.30(9 Mon); 12-9 Sun) ~ Restaurant (evening) ~ (01829) 732423 ~ Children welcome away from bar ~ Open 11.30-3, 5.30-11; 11.30-11 Sat; 12-10.30 Sun

Recommended by the Didler, Alistair Stanier

WILLINGTON
SJ5367   MAP 7

Boot
Boothsdale, off A54 at Kelsall; CW6 0NH

Friendly and attractive dining pub (you may need to book at weekends) with suntrap terrace

The interior of this converted row of cottages has been opened up around a central bar, leaving small unpretentiously furnished room areas, with lots of original features; woodburning stove in the bar. Friendly staff serve Greene King IPA and a guest or two from Weetwood brewery (which is just down the road) from handpumps, 30 malt whiskies and a decent wine list. An extension with french windows overlooks the garden where you might find Jessie the donkey, Sooty and Sweep the cats and Harvey the dog. Picnic-sets in front on the raised stone terrace are an idyllic suntrap in summer; more reports please.

🍴 Besides regularly changing specials such as spicy crab fishcakes and smoked haddock with rarebit topping, the menu includes soup, olives and bread, sandwiches and baguettes, starters or light dishes such as warm rösti or smoked haddock fishcakes, and main courses such as steak and ale or fisherman's pie, 10oz rump or rib-eye steaks, moroccan curried chicken and cumberland sausage, followed by puddings such as chocolate brownies with chocolate sauce and baked raspberry cheesecake. *Starters/Snacks: £3.75 to £6.95. Main Courses: £9.50 to £14.95. Puddings: £4.95*

Punch ~ Tenant Mike Gollings ~ Real ale ~ Bar food (11-2.30, 6-9; 11-9.30 Fri-Sun and bank hols) ~ (01829) 751375 ~ Well behaved children welcome, no pushchairs ~ Open 10am-midnight
Recommended by Paul Boot, Roger and Anne Newbury

WRENBURY   SJ5947   MAP 7
Dusty Miller
Village signposted from A530 Nantwich—Whitchurch; Cholmondeley Road; CW5 8HG

Generous food and views of busy canal from bars and terrace of big mill conversion

The gravel terrace with picnic-sets among rose bushes outside this well converted 19th-c corn mill and indoor tables by a series of tall glazed arches are great vantage points for the comings and goings of craft along the Shropshire Union Canal, which runs immediately outside, and passes beneath a weighted drawbridge. Inside, you can still see the old lift hoist up under the rafters. The atmosphere is low-key restauranty, with some emphasis on the generously served food, though drinkers are welcome. The very spacious modern-feeling main bar area is comfortably furnished with a mixture of seats (including tapestried banquettes, oak settles and wheelback chairs) round rustic tables. Further in, a quarry-tiled part by the bar counter has an oak settle and refectory table. Friendly staff serve four well kept Robinsons beers on handpump and straight from the cask, as well as farm cider; eclectic piped music. More reports please.

🍴 As well as soup and sandwiches, the monthly changing menu might include morecambe bay shrimps, rarebit with red onion marmalade, grilled chicken fillet with creamy mustard sauce, grilled bream fillet with crab butter, roast pork belly with crackling and garlic mash, grilled lamb steak with redcurrant gravy, and puddings such as crumble of the day and sticky toffee pudding. Their free-range pork comes from 1.5 miles away in Wrenbury, and seasonal vegetables are supplied by the hobby market gardener next door to the pub. *Starters/Snacks: £3.45 to £6.95. Main Courses: £8.95 to £14.95. Puddings: £3.95 to £4.95*

Robinsons ~ Tenant Mark Sumner ~ Real ale ~ Bar food (12-2, 6.30-9.30(7-9 Sun)) ~ Restaurant ~ (01270) 780537 ~ Children welcome ~ Dogs allowed in bar ~ Folk last Fri of the month ~ Open 12-3, 6.30(7 Sun)-11; closed Mon in winter
Recommended by Bob and Laura Brock

LUCKY DIP

Besides the fully inspected pubs, you might like to try these Lucky Dips recommended to us and described by readers (if you do, please send us reports: feedback@goodguides.com).

ALLOSTOCK [SJ7572]
Drovers Arms WA16 9JD [A50 Knutsford—Holmes Chapel]: Cosy log-fire lounge, public bar and dining room, good choice of food all day inc children's menu, OAP lunchtime buffet (Mon-Thurs) and Sun carvery, Black Sheep and Boddingtons; garden picnic-sets, bowling green, open all day *(Edward Leetham)*

ALPRAHAM [SJ5759]
Travellers Rest CW6 9JA [A51 Nantwich—Chester]: Unspoilt four-room country local in same friendly family for three generations, well kept Caledonian Deuchars IPA, Tetleys Bitter and Mild and wknd guests, low prices; leatherette, wicker and Formica, some flock wallpaper, fine old brewery mirrors, darts and dominoes, back bowling green; no machines, piped music or food (apart from crisps and nuts), cl wkdy lunchtimes *(the Didler)*

ANDERTON [SJ6475]
Stanley Arms CW9 6AG [just NW of Northwich; Old Rd]: Busy friendly local by Trent & Mersey Canal overlooking amazing restored Anderton boat lift, wide choice of good value well presented pubby food from sandwiches up, well kept ales inc Greene King, John Smiths and Tetleys, nice family dining area; tables on decked terrace, play area, overnight mooring *(Tom and Jill Jones, Mr and Mrs A Curry, Ben Williams)*

AUDLEM [SJ6543]
Shroppie Fly CW3 0DX [Shropshire St]: Popular three-room former warehouse by Locks 12/13 of Shropshire Union Canal, friendly staff, five ales, good value pub food inc basket meals; bar made from original barge, canal memorabilia, mainly modern furnishings, central fire, pool in public bar; piped music, live Sat; children welcome, waterside terrace, open almost all day

summer *(LYM, Charles and Pauline Stride, Ben Williams)*

BICKERTON [SJ5254]

Bickerton Poacher SY14 8BE [A534 E of junction with A41]: Rambling 17th-c poacher-theme pub, linked beamed rooms with open fires, glass-covered well, copper-mining memorabilia and talkative parrot; good choice of enjoyable reasonably priced food inc wknd carvery, cheerful attentive staff, four well kept ales inc Wells & Youngs Bombardier, selection of wines, skittle alley; sheltered partly covered courtyard, play area *(LYM, Alan and Eve Harding)*

BOLLINGTON [SJ9377]

Vale SK10 5JT [Adlington Rd]: Friendly village pub with several ales inc own good Bollington beers, enjoyable reasonably priced pubby food all day from sandwiches up; nice outside area behind looking over cricket pitch, nr Middlewood Way and Macclesfield Canal *(Andy and Jill Kassube, Brian and Anna Marsden, the Didler, Ludo McGurk)*

BOLLINGTON CROSS [SJ9177]

Cock & Pheasant SK10 5EJ [Bollington Rd]: Smart 18th-c dining pub at edge of village, wide choice of enjoyable good value food inc children's menu, well kept Copper Dragon, Storm, Theakstons and guests, conservatory; disabled facilities, garden with tables in heated pergola, good local walks, open all day *(Andy and Jill Kassube, Dr D J and Mrs S C Walker)*

BOTTOM OF THE OVEN [SJ9872]

Stanley Arms SK11 0AR [A537 Buxton—Macclesfield, 1st left past Cat & Fiddle]: Isolated moorland pub, small, friendly and cosy, lots of shiny black woodwork, plush seats, dimpled copper tables, good coal fires in all rooms inc dining room, generous well cooked traditional food, well kept Marstons and guest beers, good unhurried service; piped music; children welcome, picnic-sets on grass behind, bedrooms, may close Mon in winter if weather bad *(LYM, Pete Yearsley, Dr D J and Mrs S C Walker)*

CHELFORD [SJ8175]

Egerton Arms SK11 9BB [A537 Macclesfield—Knutsford]: Rambling village pub dating from 16th c, low beams and big fireplaces, good choice of enjoyable food from pub favourites up inc popular Sun lunch, friendly attentive service; three well kept ales from old brass pumps, restaurant, some live music; garden picnic-sets, open all day *(Roger and Anne Newbury, Dr D J and Mrs S C Walker)*

CHESTER [SJ4065]

☆ *Bear & Billet* CH1 1RU [Lower Bridge St]: Handsome timbered 17th-c Okells pub with four changing guest ales such as Copper Dragon Best Bill, belgian and US imports, nice range of wines by the glass and of reasonably priced home-made pubby food; interesting features and some attractive furnishings in friendly and comfortable open-plan bar with fire, sitting and dining

rooms upstairs; sports TV; pleasant courtyard, open all day *(the Didler, BB)*

Brewery Tap CH1 1RU [Lower Bridge St]: Tap for Spitting Feathers brewery in interesting Jacobean building with 18th-c brick façade, steps up to hall-like bar serving their ales and guests (mainly local), real cider, good home-made food all day using local suppliers *(Edward Leetham, Rosalyn Thomas)*

Coach House CH1 2HQ [Northgate St]: Refurbished 19th-c coaching inn by town hall and cathedral, comfortable lounge with central bar, Shepherd Neame Spitfire, Spitting Feathers Thirstquencher and Thwaites, good choice of food from semi-open kitchen, prompt friendly service; nine bedrooms *(Gerry and Rosemary Dobson)*

Olde Boot CH1 1LQ [Eastgate Row N]: Good value in lovely 17th-c Rows building, heavy beams, dark woodwork, oak flooring, flagstones, some exposed Tudor wattle and daub, old kitchen range in lounge beyond, old-fashioned settles and oak panelling in upper area popular with families; standard food, bargain Sam Smiths OB kept well, good cheerful service, bustling atmosphere; piped music *(Colin Moore, Joe Green, Tom and Jill Jones, Eric Larkham, the Didler, George Atkinson, LYM)*

Ship Victory CH1 3EQ [George St]: Friendly old local with chatty landlord, low beams and simple décor, well kept Tetleys and changing guest beers, music nights *(the Didler, Dave Braisted, Joe Green)*

Telfords Warehouse CH1 4EZ [Tower Wharf, behind Northgate St nr railway]: Well kept interesting ales in large converted canal building, generous fresh up-to-date food, efficient staff, bare brick and boards, high pitched ceiling, big wall of windows overlooking water, massive iron winding gear in bar, some old enamel signs, steps to heavy-beamed area with sofas, artwork and restaurant; late-night live music, bouncers on door; tables out by water, open all day *(BB, the Didler)*

☆ *Union Vaults* CH1 3ND [Francis St/Egerton St]: Friendly old-fashioned street-corner local, well kept Caledonian Deuchars IPA and two changing guests, three separate dining areas, friendly staff, old local photographs, back games room; piped music, sports TV; good outside seating for smokers, open all day *(the Didler)*

CHRISTLETON [SJ4565]

Plough CH3 7PT [Plough Lane]: Popular 18th-c country local, three linked areas, up to nine ales inc Spitting Feathers and Theakstons, enjoyable home-made local food (not Sun); garden with play area, nice setting *(the Didler)*

CHURCH LAWTON [SJ8255]

Red Bull ST7 3AJ [Congleton Rd S (A34)]: Welcoming three-room pub by Trent & Mersey Canal, good value home-made food with emphasis on fish, well kept Robinsons and guest ales, beams and open fire, old photographs of canal barges, upstairs lounge and eating area; no credit cards; outside grassy area by lock (Ben Williams, Peter and Vivienne Shilston)

COMBERBACH [SJ6477]

☆ *Spinner & Bergamot* CW9 6AY [Warrington Rd]: Comfortably plush beamed 18th-c village pub (named after two racehorses), good freshly prepared bar and restaurant food (12-7.30 Sun) inc fresh fish, Robinsons ales, good wines; log fires, hunting prints and lots of toby jugs and brasses, daily papers, softly lit back dining room with country-kitchen furniture and big inglenook, tiled family room with TV (dogs welcome here); piped music; picnic-sets on sloping lawn, lots of flowers, bowling green, open all day (Quentin Spratt, Mark Sowery, Simon J Barber, Dr and Mrs D Scott)

CONGLETON [SJ8663]

Beartown Tap CW12 1RL [Willow St (A54)]: Friendly tap for small nearby Beartown brewery, their interesting beers well priced and perhaps a guest microbrew, farm cider and belgian beers; bare boards in down-to-earth bar and two light airy rooms off, no food, games or music; upstairs lavatories; open all day Fri-Sun (the Didler)

COTEBROOK [SJ5765]

☆ *Fox & Barrel* CW6 9DZ [A49 NE of Tarporley]: Old beamed pub-restaurant, well kept Caledonian Deuchars IPA, Weetwood and two guests in bar with big log fireplace, good choice of wines by the glass, interesting food in uncluttered dining area with rugs and an eclectic mix of period tables on polished oak boards, extensive panelling, lots of old prints; children welcome (no pushchairs – highchairs provided), dogs in bar, tables on terrace and in garden with old fruit trees and tractor, open all day (Paul Boot, Bruce and Sharon Eden, Lionel Townsend, LYM, Jackie Jones)

DISLEY [SJ9784]

Rams Head SK12 2AE [A6]: Enjoyable food all day inc fixed-price menu and children's meals, well kept Timothy Taylors Landlord and Thwaites Lancaster Bomber, good choice of wines by the glass, unusual gothic-arched interior; large enclosed garden behind; open all day (Murtagh David, Gerry and Rosemary Dobson)

FRODSHAM [SJ5277]

☆ *Ring o' Bells* WA6 6BS [Bellemonte Rd, Overton – off B5152 at Parish Church sign; M56 junction 12 not far]: Charming early 17th-c pub with unpretentious bargain lunchtime food, good long-serving landlady and friendly staff, locals and cats; little rambling rooms, beams, dark oak panelling and stained glass, changing ales from central servery, games room; children in eating areas, lovely secluded and interesting back garden with pond (LYM, J S Burn, Eric Eustance, Sue and Alex Crooks)

GAWSWORTH [SJ8869]

☆ *Harrington Arms* SK11 9RJ [Church Lane]: Rustic 17th-c farm pub, well run and now doing food, Robinsons Hatters Mild, Unicorn and a guest ale, two small gently updated rooms (children allowed in one), bare boards and panelling, fine carved oak bar counter; sunny benches on small front cobbled terrace (the Didler, LYM, Dr D J and Mrs S C Walker)

GRAPPENHALL [SJ6386]

Parr Arms WA4 3EP [nr M6 junction 20; A50 towards Warrington, left after 1.5 miles; Church Lane]: Charming pub in picture-postcard setting with tables out on cobbles by church, well kept Robinsons ales, decent food from sandwiches up, several different areas off central bar, fire (Andy West)

HUXLEY [SJ5061]

Farmers Arms CH3 9BG [off A51 SE of Chester]: Long low white building with bar and separate restaurant, small cosy rooms with bric-a-brac and open fires, good food (not Sun evening) inc speciality steaks and lunchtime/early evening set deals, good choice of beers, over 90 wines (own wine shop), friendly staff and locals, real ales; tables outside, sumptuous hanging baskets and wisteria, open all day Sun, cl Mon lunchtime (Ann and Tony Bennett-Hughes)

KNUTSFORD [SJ7776]

Dun Cow WA16 8RH [Chelford Rd (A537 SE of Knutsford)]: Cosy beamed country pub given contemporary refurbishment by new licensees, good inventive cooking using locally sourced produce, Robinsons ales, newspapers, two open fires (Anne Wareing, Tim Chapman)

Rose & Crown WA16 6DT [King St]: 17th-c inn refurbished by new owners, traditional food, local ales and ciders, good wine list; nine bedrooms (anon)

LANGLEY [SJ9471]

☆ *Leather's Smithy* SK11 0NE [off A523 S of Macclesfield, OS Sheet 118 map ref 952715]: Isolated stone-built pub up in fine walking country next to reservoir; four well kept ales inc Black Sheep and Wells & Youngs Bombardier, lots of whiskies, enjoyable food from sandwiches and bloomers up, good welcoming service, pleasant relaxing atmosphere, beams and log fire, flagstoned bar, carpeted dining areas, interesting local prints and photographs; unobtrusive piped music, no dogs; picnic-sets in garden behind and on grass opposite, open all day wknds (LYM, Malcolm and Pauline Pellatt, Dave Irving, Jenny Huggins)

LITTLE BUDWORTH [SJ5965]

Red Lion CW6 9BY [Vicarage Lane]: Traditional local in unspoilt spot, good choice of generous food, well kept Robinsons, bright interior with nice fire; good bedrooms, country walks (Roger and Anne Newbury)

LITTLE LEIGH [SJ6076]

Leigh Arms CW8 4QT [A49 by swing bridge]: Welcoming riverside pub next to Acton swing bridge, beams and flagstoned, tiled or wooden floors, interesting pictures, leather chesterfields and armchairs, country kitchen tables and chairs; wide choice of good pub food, Robinsons and guest ales, music nights Thurs; waterside garden with play area *(Charles and Pauline Stride)*

☆ **Bells of Peover** WA16 9PZ [just off B5081; The Cobbles]: Lovely old refurbished building in charming spot, panelling, beams, open fires and antiques, three well kept Robinsons ales, good food from sandwiches up inc Sun roasts, dining room; piped music, children till 8pm, disabled facilities; terrace tables, big side lawn with trees, rose pergolas and little stream, on quiet cobbled lane with fine black and white 14th-c church, open all day *(Mrs P J Carroll, LYM, Tom and Jill Jones)*

Crown WA16 9QB [B5081, off A50]: Comfortable and attractive L-shaped bar with two rooms off, consistently good food (all day Sun), freshly cooked so can take a while, up to seven real ales inc Caledonian Deuchars IPA, Courage Directors and local guests; quick friendly service, low beams and flagstones, lots of bric-a-brac inc interesting gooseberry championship memorabilia, darts and dominoes; tables outside, open all day Sun *(Tom and Jill Jones)*

LYMM [SJ6787]

Church Green WA13 0AP [Higher Lane]: Newish chef/landlord doing good if pricey seasonal food in refurbished bar and restaurant, Caledonian Deuchars IPA and Greene King Old Speckled Hen; piped music; disabled facilities, heated side terrace, open all day *(W K Wood)*

MACCLESFIELD [SJ9272]

Railway View SK11 7JW [Byrons Lane (off A523)]: Pair of 1700 knocked-through cottages under new owners, attractive snug corners, six or more changing ales, good value food, friendly service, remarkably shaped gents'; back terrace overlooking railway, open all day wknds *(the Didler)*

Waters Green Tavern SK11 6LH [Waters Green, opp station]: Seven quickly changing and interesting largely northern ales in roomy L-shaped open-plan local, good value home-made lunchtime food (not Sun), friendly staff and locals, back pool room *(the Didler)*

MARBURY [SJ5645]

Swan SY13 4LS [NNE of Whitchurch; OS Sheet 117 map ref 562457]: Change of licensee at this farmhouse pub, three ales such as Weetwood, Wem and Woodlands, good choice of wines by the glass, food from well filled baguettes up, (service can be slow); roomy partly panelled lounge with upholstered banquettes and country furniture, copper-canopied log fire, candlelit cottagey dining room with another inglenook; piped music; garden picnic-sets, attractive village with lakeside church, not far from Llangollen Canal (Bridges 23/24), cl Mon *(LYM, Alan and Eve Harding, Tony and Wendy Hobden)*

MOULDSWORTH [SJ5170]

Goshawk CH3 8AJ [Station Rd (B5393)]: Comfortable family dining pub with masses of pictures and nice mix of largely pine furniture in extensive series of rooms inc small 'library' area, large double-sided log fire, attentive cheerful uniformed staff, good food from sandwiches to upscale restaurant dishes (all day; free rail travel from Chester if you eat), enterprising wines by the glass, four well kept ales such as Black Sheep, Greene King Old Speckled Hen, Timothy Taylors Landlord and Weetwood; piped music, no dogs; disabled facilities, good spot nr Delamere Forest with big outdoor space inc good play area and bowling green, open all day *(Gerry and Rosemary Dobson, Tom and Jill Jones)*

NANTWICH [SJ6452]

☆ **Black Lion** CW5 5ED [Welsh Row]: Old black and white building smartened up but keeping beams, timbered brickwork and open fire, enjoyable reasonably priced food, two Weetwood ales and four regularly changing guests; upstairs rooms with old wooden tables and sumptuous leather sofas; open all day *(Phil Merrin, Edward Leetham, BB, Alun Jones)*

Vine CW5 5RP [Hospital St]: Dates from 17th c, sympathetically modernised and stretching far back with old prints, books and dimly lit quiet corners, well kept Hydes and maybe a guest, friendly service and locals, lunchtime sandwiches, baguettes, wraps, baked potatoes and simple hot dishes, raised sitting areas; unobtrusive piped music and TV; children welcome, small outside area behind, open all day *(Martin Grosberg, Charles and Pauline Stride, BB)*

NESTON [SJ2976]

☆ **Harp** CH64 0TB [Quayside, SW of Little Neston; keep on along track at end of Marshlands Rd]: Tucked-away two-room country local, well kept interesting changing ales inc local Betwixt, good malt whiskies, basic good value home-made lunchtime food, woodburner in pretty fireplace, pale quarry tiles and simple furnishings, hatch servery in one room; children allowed in room on right; garden behind, picnic-sets up on front grassy bank facing Dee marshes and Wales, glorious sunsets with wild calls of wading birds, open all day *(BB, Roger and Anne Newbury, Maurice and Gill McMahon, Ann and Tony Bennett-Hughes)*

PARKGATE [SJ2778]

Boathouse CH64 6RN [village signed off A540]: Black and white timbered pub with well spaced tables in attractively refurbished linked rooms, enjoyable food from bar food to restaurant meals, cheerful staff, good value wines, Timothy Taylors Landlord, tea and coffee, big conservatory with great views to Wales over silted Dee estuary *(Maurice and Gill McMahon, Paul Humphreys)*

☆ **Red Lion** CH64 6SB [The Parade (B5135)]:
Comfortable neatly kept Victorian local with
views over silted grassy estuary to Wales;
pleasant chatty landlord, typical pub
furnishings, shiny brown beams hung with
china, copper and brass, standard food inc
sandwiches, OAP lunches and other bargain
offers, Adnams, Tetleys and Wells & Youngs
Bombardier on the glass, decent wines by the
glass, flame-effect fire in pretty fireplace,
good games room off public bar; picnic-sets
on small front terrace, open all day *(BB,
Tom and Jill Jones)*
RAINOW [SJ9678]

☆ **Highwayman** SK10 5UU [A5002 Whaley
Bridge—Macclesfield, NE of village]:
Welcoming 17th-c moorside pub with good
interesting locally sourced food, cheerful
efficient service, Thwaites Lancaster
Bomber, cosy low-beamed rooms with lovely
log fires, separate restaurant; outside
seating, grand views *(the Didler, LYM,
Robert and Ann Lees)*
RAVENSMOOR [SJ6250]

Farmers Arms CW5 8PN [Barracks Lane]:
Popular and welcoming with wide range of
good fairly priced food in big dining lounge,
Timothy Taylors Landlord and local
Woodlands, separate bar, pool room; garden
with terrace and play area *(Edward Leetham)*
SHOCKLACH [SJ4349]

Bull SY14 7BL [off B5069 W of Malpas]:
Welcoming and comfortable village pub,
contemporary feel with beams, open fire and
mixed furniture on stone and wood floors,
nice range of interesting fresh food from
changing menu, good choice of wines and of
well kept local ales (summer beer festival),
friendly informal service, conservatory; back
terrace and garden *(Noel Woods, Alun Jones,
Mr and Mrs J Palmer)*
STOAK [SJ4273]

Bunbury Arms CH2 4HW [Little Stanney
Lane; a mile from M53 junction 10, A5117
W, then first left]: Small snug and big but
cosy beamed lounge with antique furniture,
pictures and books, enjoyable food (all day
Sun) from sandwiches to interesting specials,
good changing ales, extensive wine list,
jovial landlord and friendly staff, open fires,
board games; can get busy; garden tables
(some motorway noise), short walk for canal
users from Bridge 136 or 138, handy for
Cheshire Oaks shopping outlet, open all day
(Jack Spratt)

STRETTON [SJ6282]

Stretton Fox WA4 4NU [Spark Hall Close,
Tarporley Rd, just off M56 junction 10 exit
roundabout]: Good Vintage Inn in spaciously
converted farmhouse, surprisingly rural
setting, interesting variety of rooms
pleasantly done in their usual faux-old style,
extensive choice of generous well priced
food, cheerful young staff (service can be
slow when busy), varying number of ales but
good choice of wines *(Simon J Barber)*
TIVERTON [SJ5360]

Shady Oak CW6 9UE [Bates Mill Lane]:
Canalside family pub looking up to Beeston
Castle, reasonably priced food all day from
good sandwiches to enjoyable blackboard
dishes, good friendly service, well kept
Theakstons and Greene King Ruddles,
comfortable timbered bar, airy lounge with
leather chesterfields, small carpeted
conservatory, games room; plenty of tables
in waterside garden with covered decking,
good play area, summer barbecues, moorings
and boat trips, campsite, open all day *(LYM,
Charles and Pauline Stride)*
WILMSLOW [SJ8781]

Unicorn SK9 2LN [Adlington Rd (B5358 E)]:
Large open-plan pub with stripped brick
walls, old local photographs and shelves of
books, beers inc Black Sheep and Timothy
Taylors Landlord, decent standard food
(E McCall, T McLean, D Irving)
WINCLE [SJ9665]

☆ **Ship** SK11 0QE [Village signposted off
A54 Congleton—Buxton]: Change of tenants
for this 16th-c stone-built country pub, bare
boards bar leading to carpeted dining room,
old stables area (children welcome here)
with flagstones, beams, woodburner and
open fire, locally sourced food (not Sun
evening) from sandwiches to steaks, up to
five Lees ales; dogs very welcome, tables in
small garden, good Dane Valley walks (own
guide book for sale), open all day wknds,
cl Mon *(Malc Newton, LYM)*
WRENBURY [SJ5947]

Cotton Arms CW5 8HG [Cholmondeley Rd]:
Beamed and timbered village pub in
popular spot by canal locks and boatyard,
good value pub food in two large
comfortable dining areas, friendly staff,
well kept ales, lots of brass, open fire, side
games room, Fri quiz; dogs welcome,
bowling green, camping *(Rachael Keith,
Charles and Pauline Stride)*

Post Office address codings give the impression that some pubs are in Cheshire, when
they're really in Derbyshire (and therefore included in this book under that chapter)
or in Greater Manchester (see the Lancashire chapter).

As it's such a popular holiday destination, it's important that pubs here can cope with – and genuinely welcome – the seasonal crowds; many of these pubs are in lovely spots surrounded by fine walks. Doing well this year are the Trengilly Wartha at Constantine (a much enjoyed all-rounder), the newly opened Finnygook at Crafthole (civilised but informal and interestingly re-styled), the Gurnards Head Hotel (back in these pages again with warm praise from our readers), the Halzephron near Helston (long-standing landlady and good food and beer), the Globe in Lostwithiel (cheerful town pub with fine a range of drinks and interesting food), the Miners Arms in Mithian (traditional and with a friendly young landlady), the Port Gaverne Inn near Port Isaac (not a traditional pub but with a smashing little bar), the New Inn on Tresco (smashing position, good food and nice to stay in), the Driftwood Spars at Trevaunance Cove (own-brew beers plus guests, enjoyable food and just up from the beach) and the Tinners Arms at Zennor (well run and popular with tasty food and beers). Not many of the pubs here hold our Food Award but the title of Cornwall Dining Pub 2011 goes to the Gurnards Head Hotel.

ALTARNUN

SX2083   MAP 1

Rising Sun 🍺

Village signposted off A39 just W of A395 junction; pub itself NW of village, so if coming instead from A30 go through Treween and turn left at T junction; PL15 7SN

Tucked-away pub with local ales, quite a choice of bar food and seats in suntrap garden; camping field

In fine weather the suntrap terrace at the back of this tucked-away pub is a lovely spot for a drink; there are more seats in the garden opposite and they have a pétanque pitch. Inside, the low-beamed L-shaped main bar has plain traditional furnishings, bare boards and polished delabole slate flagstones, some stripped stone and a couple of coal fires. From the nearby Penpont Brewery there might be Cornish Arvor, St Nonnas and Roughtor on handpump and a guest like Skinners Betty Stogs, several wines by the glass and local cider; piped music. There's a field for camping (and a smart shower block) screened off by high evergreens. The village itself is well worth a look and the church is beautiful. Dogs are allowed in the bar if on a lead. They are hoping to open bedrooms.

🍴 Using local produce the lunchtime bar food may include sandwiches, moules marinière and fries, crab, mango and avocado salad, bangers and mash with onion gravy, ham and free-range eggs and baked cod in parsley sauce, with evening choices such as scallops with a warm lemon and elderflower dressing, a charcuterie plate, crispy duck leg confit with sherry sauce, cider-braised and pressed pork belly, sea trout with horseradish lemon cream, and puddings. *Starters/Snacks: £4.00 to £8.00. Main Courses: £6.00 to £15.00. Puddings: £4.95*

Free house ~ Licensee Andy Mason ~ Real ale ~ Bar food (12-2(2.30 weekends), 6-9) ~ Restaurant ~ (01566) 86636 ~ Well behaved children allowed in bar but not in restaurant ~ Dogs allowed in bar ~ Open 11-2.30, 5.30-11; 11-11 Sat; 12-10.30 Sun

Recommended by David Hoare, the Didler, Reg Fowle, Helen Rickwood, Penny Lang, Jacquie Jones, David Heath, Mr and Mrs P D Titcomb, Tracey and Stephen Groves, Dennis Jenkin, Comus and Sarah Elliott, Colin McKerrow, Susan Lang, John and Bernadette Elliott

BLISLAND   SX1073   MAP 1

Blisland Inn ◀

Village signposted off A30 and B3266 NE of Bodmin; PL30 4JF

Village local with fine choice of real ales, beer-related memorabilia, pubby food and seats outside

In a pretty village, this is a bustling small local with up to eight real ales on handpump and some interesting beer-related memorabilia. Every inch of the beams and ceiling is covered with beer badges (or their particularly wide-ranging collection of mugs), and the walls are similarly filled with beer-related posters and such like. Tapped from the cask or on handpump, the ales might include two brewed for the pub by Sharps – Blisland Special and Bulldog – as well as Bass, Cottage Puffing Billy, Geene King Abbot, Sharps Own and Wooden Hand Black Pearl. They also have a changing farm cider, fruit wines and real apple juice; good service. The carpeted lounge has a number of barometers on the walls, a rack of daily newspapers for sale, and a few standing timbers, and the family room has pool, table skittles, euchre, cribbage and dominoes; piped music. Plenty of picnic-sets outside. The popular Camel Trail cycle path is close by – though the hill up to Blisland is pretty steep. As with many pubs in this area, it's hard to approach without negotiating several single-track roads.

🍴 **Straightforward pubby food includes filled lunchtime baps and ploughman's, soup, burgers, fish or egg and chips, scampi, and daily specials like leek and mushroom crumble or beef curry.** *Starters/Snacks: £3.95 to £5.95. Main Courses: £6.95 to £15.95. Puddings: £4.25*

Free house ~ Licensees Gary and Margaret Marshall ~ Real ale ~ Bar food ~ (01208) 850739 ~ Children in family room only ~ Dogs welcome ~ Live music most Sat evenings ~ Open 11.30-11; 12-10.30 Sun

Recommended by R J Herd, David Heath, John and Bernadette Elliott, the Didler, Michael B Griffith, Andrea Rampley, Joe Green, R K Phillips, Henry Fryer, Dr and Mrs M W A Haward, Comus and Sarah Elliott, R T and J C Moggridge, Chris and Sheila Smith, Reg Fowle, Helen Rickwood

BODINNICK   SX1352   MAP 1

Old Ferry

Across the water from Fowey; coming by road, to avoid the ferry queue turn left as you go down the hill – car park on left before pub; PL23 1LX

Bustling local across the water from Fowey, simple little rooms with nautical bits and pieces and lots of summer customers

To make the most of the pretty river views here you must arrive early to bag a seat on the front terrace or by the window in the homely little restaurant. Three simply furnished small rooms have quite a few bits of nautical memorabilia, a couple of half model ships mounted on the wall and several old photographs, as well as wheelback chairs, built-in plush pink wall seats and an old high-backed settle. The family room at the back is actually hewn into the rock; piped music, darts and TV. Sharps Own and in summer, Sharps Coaster, on handpump, several wines by the glass and a farm cider. Mobile phones are banned and a 50p fine goes to the RNLI. Most of the bedrooms have waterside views. The pub is best reached by parking in the public car park in Fowey and taking the small ferry across the water. The lane beside the pub, in front of the ferry slipway, is extremely steep and parking is limited. There are lovely circular walks from here. As we went to press, we heard that the pub is up for sale; more reports please.

Every entry includes a postcode for use in Sat-Nav devices.

🍴 **Bar food includes sandwiches, ploughman's, filled baked potatoes, pasties, soup, home-cooked ham and egg, various burgers, steak in ale pie, vegetable or chicken curry, specials such as cottage pie, vegetable lasagne and braised lamb shank, and puddings like syrup sponge cake or apple pie.** *Starters/Snacks: £4.95 to £6.50. Main Courses: £7.25 to £16.95. Puddings: £4.25 to £5.00*

Free house ~ Licensees Royce and Patricia Smith ~ Real ale ~ Bar food (12-3, 6-9; 12-2.30, 6.30-8.30 in winter) ~ Restaurant ~ (01726) 870237 ~ Children welcome ~ Dogs allowed in bar and bedrooms ~ Open 11-11; 12-10(10.30 Sat) in winter ~ Bedrooms: £90S(£95B)/£105B

Recommended by Suzy Miller

BOSCASTLE

SX0991   MAP 1

Cobweb

B3263, just E of harbour; PL35 0HE

Heavy beams, flagstones, lots of old jugs and bottles, a cheerful atmosphere, real ales, enjoyable pubby food and friendly staff

Just up from the tiny steeply cut harbour in a pretty village, this is a friendly old pub. The two bars have heavy beams that are hung with hundreds of bottles and jugs, the walls are covered with lots of pictures of bygone years, and there's a cheerful, chatty atmosphere created by a good mix of customers. As well as a cosy log fire, there are comfortable high-backed winged settles, a couple of venerable carved chairs, flagstones, and St Austells Tribute and Harbour Special, Sharps Doom Bar and a local guest on handpump. There's a second winter fire and more conventional seats and tables, too. Games machine, darts, pool and juke box. The upstairs restaurant has been refurbished; they have self-catering apartments.

🍴 **Generous helpings of bar food at lunchtime include sandwiches, soup, local fish or steak in ale pies, honeyed beef casserole and lamb curry, with evening choices like devilled kidneys, fillets of bass and beef wellington, and puddings such as white chocolate and Baileys cheesecake and sticky toffee pudding.** *Starters/Snacks: £4.50 to £5.75. Main Courses: £5.50 to £18.00. Puddings: £3.95*

Free house ~ Licensees Ivor and Adrian Bright ~ Real ale ~ Bar food (11.30-2.30, 6-9.30) ~ Restaurant ~ (01840) 250278 ~ Children welcome ~ Dogs welcome ~ Live entertainment Sat evenings ~ Open 10.30am-11pm(midnight Sat); 11-11 Sun in winter

Recommended by Irene and Derek Flewin, Ross Balaam, the Didler, Steve and Liz Tilley, Ted George, David Eagles, Barry and Anne

CADGWITH

SW7214   MAP 1

Cadgwith Cove Inn

Down very narrow lane off A3083 S of Helston; no nearby parking; TR12 7JX

Fine walks in either direction from old-fashioned inn at the bottom of fishing cove; bedrooms

The position of this small local is one of the main draws here. It's in a fishing cove at the bottom of a charming village and there are fine coastal walks in either direction. Inside, there are two snugly dark front rooms with plain pub furnishings on their mainly parquet flooring, a log fire in one stripped-stone end wall, lots of local photographs including some of gig races, cases of naval hat ribands and of fancy knot-work and a couple of compass binnacles. Some of the dark beams have ships' shields and others have spliced blue rope hand-holds. Otter Bitter, Sharps Doom Bar, Skinners Betty Stogs and a guest beer on handpump. A back bar has a huge and colourful fish mural; piped music. There are green-painted picnic-sets on the good-sized front terrace, some under a fairy-lit awning, looking down to the fish sheds by the bay. The bedrooms overlook the sea and they make their own jams and marmalades for breakfast. While it's best to park at the top of the village and meander down through the thatched cottages, it's quite a steep hike back up again.

🍴 Using local produce, bar food includes sandwiches, soup, duck liver or crab pâté, ham and eggs, spinach and feta or steak and kidney pies, fish and chips, chicken curry, daily specials like pheasant breast with hazelnut stuffing and game jus and monkfish with bacon and garlic, and puddings such as chocolate mousse with spiced pear or fruit crumble with clotted cream. *Starters/Snacks: £3.75 to £6.95. Main Courses: £7.95 to £11.00. Puddings: £4.50 to £5.00*

Punch ~ Lease David and Lynda Trivett ~ Real ale ~ Bar food ~ (01326) 290513 ~ Well behaved children welcome away from main bar ~ Dogs welcome ~ Open 12-11 (1am Fri; 10.30 Sun); 12-3, 7-11 in winter ~ Bedrooms: £30.25(£47.50S)/£60.50(£82.50S)

Recommended by Adrian Johnson, Dr and Mrs M E Wilson, Dave Webster, Sue Holland, Mayur Shah, Comus and Sarah Elliott, Ewan and Moira McCall

CONSTANTINE   SW7328   MAP 1

Trengilly Wartha ♀ ⛏

Simplest approach is from A3083 S of Helston, signposted Gweek near RNAS Culdrose, then fork right after Gweek; coming instead from Penryn (roads narrower), turn right in Constantine just before mini-market (towards Gweek), then pub signposted left in nearly a mile; at Nancenoy, OS Sheet 204 map reference 731282; TR11 5RP

Bustling friendly inn in several acres of gardens, real ales, lots of wines and whiskies and popular bar food; bedrooms

Our readers very much enjoy staying at this friendly and well run inn and the breakfasts are especially good. But it's also an extremely popular place for a drink and a chat or a leisurely meal, and both children and dogs are welcome. The long low-beamed main bar has a mix of tables and chairs, a woodburning stove, Dartmoor Legend, Skinners Heligan Honey and a beer named for the pub on handpump, 16 wines by the glass, and 50 malt whiskies. Leading off the bar is the conservatory family room and there's also a cosy bistro; table football. Plenty of seats under large parasols in the six acres of gardens; boules. Lots of surrounding walks. They have an active cricket team.

🍴 Using local fish and shellfish and other local produce, the generous helpings of enjoyable bar food include lunchtime sandwiches, ploughman's, soup, pâté with home-made chutney, thai pork burger with chilli mayonnaise, sausages of the day with onion gravy, daily specials like mussels with white wine, garlic and cream, scallops with a leek and wholegrain mustard sauce, lamb shank with rosemary and garlic jus, sea bream with a roast cherry tomato sauce, chicken curry, and duck breast with a plum and chilli sauce, and puddings. *Starters/Snacks: £2.20 to £9.60. Main Courses: £8.50 to £22.00. Puddings: £3.60 to £4.75*

Free house ~ Licensees Will and Lisa Lea ~ Real ale ~ Bar food (12-2.15, 6-9.30) ~ Restaurant ~ (01326) 340332 ~ Children welcome away from bar area ~ Dogs allowed in bar and bedrooms ~ Folk evening every other Weds ~ Open 11-3.15, 6-11 ~ Bedrooms: £50B/£80B

Recommended by Anthony Rogers, John and Bryony Coles, Peter Randell, Mark Evans, M Mossman, Rupert Sligh, Chris and Angela Buckell, Eamonn and Natasha Skyrme, Richard Stanfield, Julie Callow, Bernard and Ruth Chudley, John and Victoria Fairley, Dr and Mrs M E Wilson, Andy and Claire Barker

CRAFTHOLE   SX3654   MAP 1

Finnygook ♀

B3247, off A374 Torpoint road; PL11 3BQ

Carefully renovated and rather civilised former coaching inn, good mix of drinkers and diners, interesting furniture and décor in bar and dining room, enjoyable food, real ales and friendly service; bedrooms

Under the same ownership as the good Turtley Corn Mill at Avonwick (see our Devon Main Entries), this 15th-c coaching inn has been totally renovated. It's a civilised place with a happy mix of diners and drinkers, an informal atmosphere and friendly helpful staff. The bar has beams and joists, a central log fire that warms both sides of the room, really long pews set against the walls with attractive cushions and carved cushioned dining chairs around various wooden tables on the stripped floorboards. There's also a couple of high wooden tables with chairs to match near the bar counter, big bowls of lilies, black and white local photographs, big warship and other prints on the walls and in one large window, an old compass. St Austell Tribute and Sharps Doom Bar on handpump and a decent choice of wines by the glass. The carefully lit dining room on the other side of the building has all manner of dining chairs and tables, rugs on floorboards, an unusual log-effect gas fire in a big glass cabinet, church candles and plants, black and white photographs of local people, houses and beaches, and some vinyl records on the walls; at one end, there's a library. Through the hop-hung windows are fine views across the Lynher and Tamar rivers.

🍴 Good bistro-style bar food includes sandwiches, ploughman's, soup, duck rillette with toasted brioche, crayfish and crab salad, local beer-battered haddock and chips, ham and eggs, stir-fried noodles with chicken or sweet and sour pork, mixed vegetable and lentil dahl curry, local scallops topped with crispy bacon, lamb shank with creamy mash, brill with a mediterranean crust on wilted spinach, and puddings. *Starters/Snacks: £4.50 to £8.50. Main Courses: £8.95 to £17.95. Puddings: £5.95*

Free house ~ Licensee David Colton ~ Real ale ~ Bar food (12-9.30(9 Sun)) ~ Restaurant ~ (01503) 230338 ~ Children welcome until 7pm ~ Dogs allowed in bar ~ Open 11-11; 12-10.30 Sun ~ Bedrooms: £55B/£75B

Recommended by Dennis Jenkin, Dr and Mrs M W A Haward

GURNARDS HEAD

SW4337   MAP 1

Gurnards Head Hotel 🍴 ♀ 🛏

B3306 Zennor—St Just; TR26 3DE

CORNWALL DINING PUB OF THE YEAR

Interestingly renovated inn close to the sea with real ales, lots of wines by the glass and very good food; comfortable bedrooms and fine surrounding walks

Our readers have been warm in their enthusiasm about this handsome building and all customers are made welcome. It's just 500 yards from the Atlantic in outstanding bleak National Trust scenery and surrounded by glorious walks – both inland and along the cliffy coast. The bar rooms are painted in bold, strong colours, there's an interesting mix of furniture, paintings by local artists, open fires, and an informal, friendly atmosphere. Skinners Betty Stogs and Ginger Tosser, St Austell Tribute and Tomos Watkin Cwrw Braf on handpump and 20 wines by the glass or carafe; piped music and darts. Seats in the large garden behind and the comfortable bedrooms either have views of the rugged moors or of the sea. This is under the same ownership as the civilised Griffin at Felinfach (see our Wales chapter).

🍴 First-rate food using local produce at lunchtime includes open sandwiches, soup, home-made pork pie with pickles, sardines on toast with gribiche sauce, ham and egg, smoked haddock fishcakes with lemon mayonnaise, beer-battered fish and beef in ale pie with evening choices such as scallop risotto with cucumber and tarragon, braised lamb with fresh pea purée, pea shoots and pancetta, duck breast with spiced puy lentils and apricots and beef rump with braised little gem, boulangère potatoes, red wine and béarnaise, and puddings like rhubarb streusel tart, crème pâtissière and ginger ice-cream and rosemary panna cotta with poached peaches. *Starters/Snacks: £5.00 to £8.00. Main Courses: £9.50 to £16.50. Puddings: £5.00*

Free house ~ Licensees Charles and Edmund Inkin ~ Real ale ~ Bar food (12-2.30, 6-9) ~ Restaurant ~ (01736) 796928 ~ Children welcome ~ Dogs allowed in bar and bedrooms ~ Live folk Mon evenings ~ Open 11.30-11; closed 24 and 25 Dec and four days in Jan ~ Bedrooms: £75B/£95B

Recommended by Mr and Mrs Richard Osborne, Tim Sanders, Hannah Barlow, Peter Monk, S J and C C Davidson, Nicky Pallot

---

If you're planning a long journey, it might help you to look at the list of pubs near motorway junctions at the end of the book.

HELSTON   SW6522   MAP 1

Halzephron ♀ ⇐

Gunwalloe, village about 4 miles S but not marked on many road maps; look for brown sign on A3083 alongside perimeter fence of RNAS Culdrose; TR12 7QB

Popular pub in lovely spot with well liked food, local beers and bedrooms; good nearby walks

You can be sure of a friendly welcome in this much enjoyed inn with its relaxed and informal atmosphere; it's best to book in advance to be sure of a table at peak times. The neatly kept rooms have comfortable seating, copper on the walls and mantelpiece, a warm winter fire in the woodburning stove and Chough Halzephron Gold, St Austell Tribute, Sharps Doom Bar and Skinners Betty Stogs on handpump; also, eight wines by the glass and 40 malt whiskies. The dining Gallery seats up to 30 people; darts and board games. There are lots of fine surrounding unspoilt walks with views of Mount's Bay. Gunwalloe fishing cove is just 300 yards away and Church Cove with its sandy beach is a mile away – as is the church of St Winwaloe (built into the dunes on the seashore).

🍽 As well as lunchtime sandwiches and ploughman's, the good bar food includes soup, fishcake with pea purée and fennel salad, medley of mushrooms and leeks in a white wine mustard cream layered with filo pastry and spinach, spicy cinnamon lamb, marinated and breadcrumbed chicken in herbs and dijon mustard, venison and beef stroganoff, fish pie, pork tenderloin wrapped in bacon with a mushroom and herb duxelles, a filo basket of wild mushrooms and café au lait sauce, and puddings such as white chocolate cheesecake and crème brûlée. *Starters/Snacks: £5.00 to £7.95. Main Courses: £8.50 to £18.50. Puddings: £3.90 to £5.50*

Free house ~ Licensee Angela Thomas ~ Real ale ~ Bar food ~ Restaurant ~ (01326) 240406 ~ Children in family room ~ Open 11-2.30, 6-11; 12-2.30, 6-10.30 Sun; 6.30 opening time in winter ~ Bedrooms: £50S/£90S

Recommended by Ewan and Moira McCall, Jacquie Jones, John and Gloria Isaacs, P J Checksfield, J B Taylor, Mr Ray J Carter, M and L Towers, Mayur Shah, Barry Collett, Chris and Val Ramstedt, Marianne and Peter Stevens, R and S Bentley, Dr and Mrs M W A Haward, Edna Jones, Andy and Claire Barker

LANLIVERY   SX0759   MAP 1

Crown ◀

Signposted off A390 Lostwithiel—St Austell (tricky to find from other directions); PL30 5BT

Chatty atmosphere in nice old pub, traditional rooms, and well liked food and drink; the Eden Project is close by; bedrooms

A new landlord has taken over this ancient inn – it's one of Cornwall's oldest pubs and has some real character. The main bar has a warming log fire in the huge fireplace, traditional settles on the big flagstones, some cushioned farmhouse chairs, a mix of wooden chairs and tables and Sharps Doom Bar and 6 Hop, Skinners Betty Stogs and Cornish Knocker on handpump. A couple of other rooms are similarly furnished and there's another open fire; darts. There is a huge lit-up well with a glass top by the porch and plenty of picnic-sets in the quiet garden. The Eden Project is only ten minutes away.

🍽 Well liked bar food includes sandwiches, crab salad, ham and free-range eggs, apple and cider sausages with wholegrain mustard mash and caramelised onion gravy, braised pork belly, steak in ale pie, local steaks, and puddings. *Starters/Snacks: £3.95 to £7.95. Main Courses: £8.95 to £16.95. Puddings: £4.95*

Wagtail Inns ~ Licensee Graham Hill ~ Real ale ~ Bar food (12-9; may stop afternoon food service in winter) ~ Restaurant ~ (01208) 872707 ~ Children welcome but must be away from bar ~ Dogs allowed in bar and bedrooms ~ Open 12-11 ~ Bedrooms: /£79.95S

Recommended by Mr and Mrs Gravener, Andy and Claire Barker, Dr and Mrs M W A Haward, T R and B C Jenkins, Mr and Mrs W D Borthwick, Simon Le Fort, Nick Lawless

---

If we know a pub does summer barbecues, we say so.

LOSTWITHIEL

Globe ♀ ◖

North Street (close to medieval bridge); PL22 0EG

Unassuming bar in traditional local, interesting food and drinks and friendly staff; suntrap back courtyard with outside heaters

Cheerful and very well run, this 13th-c town local is somewhere customers tend to return to again and again. There's a warm welcome for both visitors and locals and the unassuming bar is long and somewhat narrow with a bustling atmosphere and a good mix of pubby tables and seats. There are customers' photographs on pale green plank panelling at one end, nice more or less local prints (for sale) on canary walls above a coal-effect stove at the snug inner end and a small red-walled front alcove. The ornately carved bar counter, with comfortable chrome and leatherette stools, dispenses Sharps Doom Bar, Skinners Betty Stog, Otter Ale and a changing guest from handpump, with a dozen reasonably priced wines by the glass, 20 malt whiskies and two farm ciders. Piped music, darts, board games and TV. The sheltered back courtyard is not large, but has some attractive and unusual plants, and is a real suntrap (with an extendable overhead awning and outside heaters). You can park in several of the nearby streets. The 13th-c church is worth a look and the ancient river bridge, a few yards aways is lovely.

🍴 As well as lunchtime sandwiches, filled baguettes and baked potatoes and ploughman's, the enjoyable bar food might include soup, chilli and ginger butterflied prawns, chicken and chardonnay pâté, moules marinière, beef in ale pie, vegetarian roast with port and mushroom sauce, pork and leek sausages with onion gravy, pasta carbonara, veal burger with coleslaw and chips, venison, rabbit, pheasant and pigeon pie, honey-roast duck, fresh local fish of the day, and puddings like raspberry cheesecake and ginger and black treacle sponge; Sunday roasts. *Starters/Snacks: £4.00 to £7.00. Main Courses: £6.00 to £14.00. Puddings: £3.50 to £4.95*

Free house ~ Licensee William Erwin ~ Real ale ~ Bar food ~ Restaurant ~ (01208) 872501 ~ Children welcome ~ Dogs allowed in bar ~ Live music Weds evening ~ Open 12-2.30, 6-11(5-midnight Fri); 12-midnight(11 Sun) Sat ~ Bedrooms: /£70B

Recommended by Dave Braisted, Tracey and Stephen Groves, Peter Salmon, B and M Kendall, Mike and Monnie Jefferies, Evelyn and Derek Walter, John and Joan Calvert

MALPAS

Heron

Trenhaile Terrace, off A39 S of Truro; TR1 1SL

Lovely creekside spot, attractively decorated pub, friendly service and good food

You must arrive early if you want to bag one of the seats on the heated terrace in front of this idyllically placed creekside pub; there are a few window tables inside that share the same view. The long, narrow bar has several areas leading off and a raised part at one end – it's all very light and airy with blue and white décor and furnishings throughout. There are two gas fires, mainly wooden floors with flagstones by the bar, modern yacht paintings on the wood-planked walls, some brass nautical items, heron pictures, a stuffed heron in a cabinet and a chatty atmosphere. St Austell IPA and Tribute and a guest like Proper Job on handpump; piped music, darts and a Tuesday evening quiz. Parking is difficult in high season.

🍴 Enjoyable bar food includes lunchtime filled rolls, wraps and toasted panini, ploughman's, spicy crab cakes with sweet chilli, pork and ale sausages with onion gravy, ham and egg, chickpea and sweet potato curry, beer-battered haddock, chicken with creamy mushroom and crispy pancetta, lamb cutlets with redcurrant and red wine sauce, a trio of fish in lemon and parsley butter sauce, and puddings. *Starters/Snacks: £4.50 to £5.50. Main Courses: £7.25 to £13.95. Puddings: £4.95*

St Austell ~ Tenants Jonathan and Karen Berg ~ Real ale ~ Bar food ~ (01872) 272773 ~ Children welcome ~ Open 11.30-11; 11am-11.30pm Fri and Sat; 12-11 Sun; 11.30-3, 6-10.30 Mon-Thurs in winter

Recommended by Ian Phillips, John Marsh, Andrea Rampley, Comus and Sarah Elliott, W N F Boughey, Norman and Sarah Keeping, Mr and Mrs P D Titcomb, Chris and Angela Buckell, Adrian Johnson, Mark Flynn

MITCHELL   SW8554   MAP 1

Plume of Feathers 🛏

Just off A30 Bodmin—Redruth, by A3076 junction; take the southwards road then turn first right; TR8 5AX

Contemporary décor in several rooms, friendly welcome, enjoyable food, real ales and seats outside; comfortable bedrooms

A new conservatory has been added to this friendly dining pub which will give additional space for eating – and there's a new licensee, too. As well as a public bar, there are other rooms with appealing and contemporary décor, Farrow & Ball pastel-coloured walls, paintings by local artists, stripped old beams, painted wooden dado and two fireplaces. Sharps Doom Bar, a changing ale from Skinners and St Austell Tribute on handpump and several wines by the glass; piped music. The well planted garden areas have plenty of seats and the bedrooms are comfortable.

🍴 **Good bar food includes sandwiches, soup, wild game terrine, pigeon breast with prosciutto and port reduction, warm spanish omelette, ham and free-range eggs, sausages with bacon and herb mash and caramelised onions, beer-battered fish, jerusalem and wild mushroom risotto, loin of pork with roasted sweet potato and cider sauce, bass with pea purée, and puddings like sticky toffee pudding with butterscotch sauce and pear and plum crumble with custard.** *Starters/Snacks: £5.00 to £10.00. Main Courses: £9.00 to £17.00. Puddings: £5.00 to £6.00*

Free house ~ Licensee Paul Partridge ~ Real ale ~ Bar food (9am-10pm) ~ Restaurant ~ (01872) 510387/511125 ~ Children welcome but must be away from bar ~ Dogs allowed in bar and bedrooms ~ Open 9am-midnight ~ Bedrooms: £66.25S(£73.75B)/£80S(£90B)

Recommended by Nick and Meriel Cox, Dennis Jenkin, R J Herd, John Marsh, Michelle and Graeme Voss, W N F Boughey, M Mossman, Steve and Liz Tilley, Andy and Claire Barker

MITHIAN   SW7450   MAP 1

Miners Arms

Just off B3285 E of St Agnes; TR5 0QF

Cosy pub with open fires in several smallish rooms, friendly staff and popular food

Our readers are very much enjoying their visits to this well run cosy old pub and the young landlady and her staff are sure to make you welcome. Several traditional little rooms and passages are warmed by winter open fires, there are pubby furnishings on the patterned carpet and the small back bar has an irregular beam and plank ceiling, a wood block floor and bulging squint walls (one with a fine old wall painting of Elizabeth I). Another small room has a decorative low ceiling and lots of books. Sharps Doom Bar and perhaps Skinners Betty Stogs on handpump; piped music, board games and darts. There are seats outside on the back terrace and in the garden, with more on the sheltered front cobbled forecourt. More reports please.

🍴 **As well as some sort of sandwiches, filled baked potatoes and ploughman's, the popular bar food includes soup, prawn and pineapple kebab with honey and ginger, ham and egg, a burger with home-made relish, mushroom, brie and cranberry wellington, steak in ale pie, chicken wrapped in bacon and stuffed with apricots in a creamy mustard sauce, a trio of fish in a white wine and asparagus sauce, and puddings.** *Starters/Snacks: £4.00 to £6.00. Main Courses: £6.00 to £12.00. Puddings: £4.00 to £5.00*

Punch ~ Lease Anouska House ~ Real ale ~ Bar food (12-2, 6-9) ~ Restaurant ~ (01872) 552375 ~ Children allowed away from bar ~ Dogs allowed in bar ~ Open 12-midnight

Recommended by Dennis Jenkin, John Marsh, Ted George, Mr and Mrs Gravener

MORWENSTOW

Bush

Signed off A39 N of Kilkhampton; Crosstown; EX23 9SR

Friendly, ancient pub in fine spot, character bar and airy dining rooms, real ales, carefully sourced produce for well liked food and seats outside; bedrooms

In lovely walking country, this 13th-c pub was once a monastic rest house on a pilgrim route between Wales and Spain. It's a ten-minute walk to Vicarage Cliff, one of the grandest parts of the Cornish coast (with 400-ft precipices) and just off the South West Coast Path; one reader tells us the circular walk from the pub is well worth trying, too. The bar has real character with old built-in settles, flagstones, a woodburning stove in a big stone fireplace, lots of brass and copper knick-knacks, some horse tack and St Austell HSD and Tribute and Skinners Betty Stogs on handpump. Other rooms are set for dining with pale wooden dining chairs and tables, pictures on creamy yellow walls, beams and fresh flowers; the dining room has big windows overlooking the picnic-sets on the grass outside. As well as bedrooms, they offer self-catering, too.

🍴 **Using beef from their own farm and other local produce, bar food includes sandwiches, ploughman's, soup, chicken liver parfait with onion jam, garlic mushrooms on toasted brioche, smoked salmon with horseradish cream, sausages with onion gravy, home-made burger, red wine and blue cheese risotto, beer-battered pollack, pork chops with chorizo cassoulet, wild bass with caramelised onions, good steaks, and puddings like warm treacle tart with clotted cream and chocolate brownie.** *Starters/Snacks: £4.80 to £7.00. Main Courses: £9.00 to £19.00. Puddings: £5.25 to £7.00*

Free house ~ Licensees Rob and Edwina Tape ~ Real ale ~ Bar food (all day) ~ Restaurant ~ (01288) 331242 ~ Children welcome ~ Dogs allowed in bar and bedrooms ~ Occasional live music ~ Open 11-11 ~ Bedrooms: £49S/£85S

Recommended by John and Fiona Merritt, Quentin and Carol Williamson, the Didler, Christian Mole, Barry and Anne, Anthony Bradbury, Dr and Mrs M W A Haward, Mike and Sue Losey, Geoffrey and Karen Berrill, Jean and David Lewis

MYLOR BRIDGE

Pandora ★★ ♀

Restronguet Passage: from A39 in Penryn, take turning signposted Mylor Church, Mylor Bridge, Flushing and go straight through Mylor Bridge following Restronguet Passage signs; or from A39 further N, at or near Perranarworthal, take turning signposted Mylor, Restronguet, then follow Restronguet Weir signs, but turn left down hill at Restronguet Passage sign; TR11 5ST

Beautifully placed waterside inn with seats on long floating pontoon, lots of atmosphere in beamed and flagstoned rooms, and some sort of food all day

On a quiet day at high tide, it would be hard to beat this medieval thatched pub's sheltered waterfront position – best enjoyed from the picnic-table sets in front or on the long floating jetty. Inside, several rambling, interconnecting rooms have low wooden ceilings (mind your head on some of the beams), beautifully polished big flagstones, cosy alcoves with leatherette benches built into the walls, old race posters, model boats in glass cabinets, and three large log fires in high hearths (to protect them against tidal floods). St Austell HSD, Tinners and Tribute and a guest such as Bass on handpump and a dozen wines by the glass. It does get very crowded and parking is extremely difficult at peak times; there is wheelchair access.

🍴 **Bar food includes ciabatta sandwiches, soup, cornish yarg fritters with coriander salsa, chicken liver terrine with fig relish, beer-battered fish and chips, sausages with red onion and thyme gravy, local scallops with lemon mustard sauce and parmesan, sunblush tomato and basil pasta, rib-eye steak, and puddings.** *Starters/Snacks: £5.00 to £8.00. Main Courses: £8.00 to £16.00. Puddings: £5.00 to £7.00*

St Austell ~ Tenant John Milan ~ Real ale ~ Bar food (all day) ~ Restaurant ~ (01326) 372678 ~ Children welcome away from bar area ~ Dogs allowed in bar ~ Open 10.30am-midnight (11pm in winter)

Recommended by Adrian Johnson, Kelvin and Carol Butcher, Mrs Mary Woods, the Didler, Mr and Mrs Gravener, John and Bernadette Elliott, John and Fiona McIlwain, Peter Salmon, John Marsh, Andrea Rampley, Jim Lyon, DFL, Miss K Hunt, Mr M Smith, M Mossman, Chris and Angela Buckell, Gene and Tony Freemantle, Guy Vowles, David Rule, Roger and Pauline Pearce, Maurice and Gill McMahon, Mr and Mrs Powers, R T and J C Moggridge, Mrs P Sumner, Stuart Turner, Andy and Claire Barker

PENZANCE   SW4730   MAP 1

Turks Head

At top of main street, by big domed building (Lloyds TSB), turn left down Chapel Street; TR18 4AF

Cheerfully run pub, the oldest in town, with a good, bustling atmosphere and decent food and beer

Although this bustling old town pub is popular locally, you can be sure of a friendly welcome as a visitor, too. The bar has old flat irons, jugs and so forth hanging from the beams, pottery above the wood-effect panelling, wall seats and tables and a couple of elbow-rests around central pillars; piped music. Sharps Doom Bar, Skinners Betty Stogs and Shepherd Neame Spitfire on handpump served by helpful staff. The suntrap back garden has big urns of flowers. There has been a Turks Head here for over 700 years – though most of the original building was destroyed by a Spanish raiding party in the 16th century.

▥ **Popular bar food includes lunchtime sandwiches, filled ciabatta and filled baked potatoes, soup, omelettes, smoked haddock kedgeree with a soft boiled egg, home-roasted honey and mustard glazed ham and egg, butternut squash, spinach and sweet potato curry, pork and leek sausages with caramelised onion gravy, local fish and chips, beef stew with herb dumplings, and sizzling tandoori monkfish.** *Starters/Snacks: £3.95 to £7.95. Main Courses: £6.95 to £13.95. Puddings: £3.95 to £4.95*

Punch ~ Lease Jonathan and Helen Gibbard ~ Real ale ~ Bar food ~ Restaurant ~ (01736) 363093 ~ Children welcome ~ Dogs welcome ~ Open 11(12 Sun)-11

Recommended by David Crook, Jerry Brown, Michael and Alison Sandy, Neil and Anita Christopher, Alan Johnson, Dave Webster, Sue Holland, Richard Stanfield, B and M Kendall, Giles and Annie Francis, Dr and Mrs R E S Tanner, Tim and Ann Newell, R J Herd

PERRANUTHNOE   SW5329   MAP 1

Victoria 🍽

Signed off A394 Penzance—Helston; TR20 9NP

Carefully refurbished inn close to Mounts Bay beaches, friendly welcome, local beers, interesting fresh food and seats in pretty garden; bedrooms

The heart of the local community, this village pub has a good mix of both regulars and visitors. There's a relaxed atmosphere and exposed joists in the L-shaped bar, various cosy corners, a woodburning stove, an attractive array of dining chairs around wooden tables on the oak flooring, china plates, all sorts of artwork on the walls and fresh flowers. The restaurant is separate. Sharps Doom Bar and St Austell Tribute on handpump and several wines by the glass; piped music. The pub labrador is called Bailey. The pretty tiered garden has white metal furniture under green parasols and the beaches of Mounts Bay are a couple of minutes' stroll away.

▥ **Well presented bar food includes lunchtime sandwiches, soup, duck liver and port pâté with spiced pear chutney, crab and potato salad with curry spices, mango and lime chutney, tagliatelle with mushrooms, leeks, cep sauce, parmesan and truffle oil, slow-roasted pork belly with black pudding, onion marmalade and apple sauce, chicken with bubble and squeak potato cake, cabbage and bacon and rosemary sauce, and puddings like sticky toffee pudding with caramelised banana and banana ice-cream and dark chocolate and orange pot with Grand Marnier ice-cream and chocolate shortbread; some interesting cheeses, too.** *Starters/Snacks: £4.95 to £7.50. Main Courses: £9.95 to £17.50. Puddings: £5.25*

Pubfolio ~ Lease Anna and Stewart Eddy ~ Real ale ~ Bar food (12-2(2.30 Sun), 6.30-9; not Sun evening or winter Mon) ~ Restaurant ~ (01736) 710309 ~ Children welcome ~ Dogs allowed in bar ~ Open 12-11; 12-2.30 Sun; closed Sun evening, winter Mon, 25 and 26 Dec, 1 Jan, one week in Jan ~ Bedrooms: £45S/£70S

Recommended by Nigel Long, Catherine and Richard Preston, James Sturtridge, Bryan and Mary Blaxall, Jan Taplin, Dave Webster, Sue Holland, Clifford Blakemore, Ian Herdman

PERRANWELL
SW7739 MAP 1
Royal Oak ♀
Village signposted off A393 Redruth—Falmouth and A39 Falmouth—Truro; TR3 7PX

Welcoming and relaxed with well presented food, real ales and thoughtful wines

There's a gently upmarket but relaxed atmosphere in this pretty and quietly set village pub and most customers are here to enjoy the popular food – but they do keep Bass, Sharps Atlantic IPA and Skinners Betty Stogs on handpump, as well as good wines by the glass, summer sangria and winter mulled wine. The roomy, carpeted bar has horsebrasses and pewter and china mugs on its black beams and joists, plates and country pictures on the cream-painted stone walls and cosy wall and other seats around candlelit tables. It rambles around beyond a big stone fireplace (with a winter log fire) into a snug little nook of a room behind, with just a couple more tables.

🍴 Listed on wooden boards in the shape of an oak tree, the good, interesting food includes lunchtime sandwiches and filled baguettes, ploughman's, soup, grilled figs with prosciutto and goats cheese, mussels in white wine and cream, their much-ordered tapas and meze plates (for sharing), artichoke and saffron risotto, a pie of the day (their fish one is popular), crispy beer-battered cod, coconut chicken curry, rack of lamb with mint and redcurrant sauce, and puddings like vanilla cheesecake and hot chocolate fudge brownie; lobster nights on summer Thursdays. *Starters/Snacks: £3.60 to £9.75. Main Courses: £6.95 to £18.50. Puddings: £2.95 to £5.95*

Free house ~ Licensee Richard Rudland ~ Real ale ~ Bar food (12-2.30, 7-9.30) ~ Restaurant ~ (01872) 863175 ~ Children welcome ~ Dogs allowed in bar ~ Open 11-3, 6-11(midnight Sat); 11.30-3.30, 6-11 Sun

Recommended by John and Susan Miln, John Marsh, Gene and Tony Freemantle, J B Taylor, Mr and Mrs Powers, David Crook, John and Fiona McIlwain

PHILLEIGH
SW8739 MAP 1
Roseland 🍺
Between A3078 and B3289, NE of St Mawes just E of King Harry Ferry; TR2 5NB

Popular pub near King Harry ferry, real ales including an own-brew, bustling atmosphere and well liked food

There's always a good mix of both locals and holidaymakers in this popular pub and it's best to book in advance if you want to be sure of a table. The two bar rooms (one with flagstones and the other carpeted) have wheelback chairs and built-in red-cushioned seats, open fires, old photographs and some giant beetles and butterflies in glass cases. The tiny lower area is liked by regulars and there's a back restaurant. As well as their own-brewed Roseland Cornish Shag, they keep Skinners Betty Stogs and Sharps Doom Bar on handpump. There are seats on a pretty paved front courtyard and to the side of this, a shop selling local produce and locally made gifts; the King Harry ferry and Trelissick Gardens are close by.

🍴 Bar food includes lunchtime sandwiches, soup, local mussels in cider and cream, crab risotto, lambs liver with bacon, horseradish mash and red wine, beer-battered cod, smoked haddock and leek pie, steaks, and puddings like fruit crumble and white chocolate and raspberry cheesecake. *Starters/Snacks: £5.50 to £7.50. Main Courses: £9.95 to £13.50. Puddings: £5.50*

Free house ~ Licensee Philip Heslip ~ Real ale ~ Bar food (12-2.30, 6(6.30 in winter)-9.30) ~ Restaurant ~ (01872) 580254 ~ Children welcome ~ Dogs allowed in bar ~ Open 11-11

Recommended by Mr and Mrs W D Borthwick, Donna and Roger, R K Phillips, Chris and Angela Buckell, Mrs Sheena Killick, R and S Bentley, John and Susan Miln

POLKERRIS

SX0952   MAP 1

Rashleigh ⬗

Signposted off A3082 Fowey—St Austell; PL24 2TL

Fine beach-side spot, heaters on sizeable sun terrace, several real ales and good bar food

Although there's a good bustling atmosphere inside this former fisherman's tavern, the big front terrace with its heaters and awning (handy for less clement weather) remains quite a draw – as does the adjacent splendid beach with its restored jetty and far-reaching views. The bar is cosy and the front part has comfortably cushioned seats and up to five real ales on handpump: Otter Bitter, Sharps Doom Bar, Timothy Taylors Landlord and a couple of guests like St Austell HAD and Skinners Betty Stogs. They also have several wines by the glass, farm cider and organic soft drinks. The more basic back area has local photographs on the brown panelling and a winter log fire, and in the restaurant, every table has a sea view. There's plenty of parking either in the pub's own car park or the large village one. The local section of the Cornish Coast Path is renowned for its striking scenery.

📖 Well liked bar food includes sandwiches (the summer crab are popular), ploughman's, soup, white crab and prawn cocktail, scallops in garlic butter, a tapas platter, beer-battered cod, steak in ale pie, mushroom and vegetable strudel with three-cheese sauce, chicken stew with herb dumplings and parsnip and apple mash, brill in a prawn and cream sauce, and puddings such as plum crumble and Baileys crème brûlée. *Starters/Snacks: £4.20 to £6.50. Main Courses: £7.50 to £16.50. Puddings: £2.95 to £3.95*

Free house ~ Licensees Jon and Samantha Spode ~ Real ale ~ Bar food (12-2, 6-9; cream teas and snacks during the afternoon) ~ Restaurant ~ (01726) 813991 ~ Children welcome ~ Piano player Sat evening ~ Open 11-11; 12-11 Sun; may close at 10pm in winter

Recommended by Kelvin and Carol Butcher, Peter Martin, the Didler, Roy Hoing, Tracey and Stephen Groves, Andy and Claire Barker

POLPERRO

SX2050   MAP 1

Blue Peter

Quay Road; PL13 2QZ

Friendly pub overlooking pretty harbour with fishing paraphernalia and paintings by local artists

The cosy low-beamed bar in this bustling and friendly little pub is popular with both locals and visitors; families must use the upstairs room (try to get a window seat overlooking the harbour if you can). There are traditional furnishings including a small winged settle and a polished pew on the wooden floor, fishing regalia, photographs and pictures by local artists, lots of candles, a solid wood bar counter and a simple old-fashioned atmosphere. One window seat looks down on the harbour, another looks out past rocks to the sea. St Austell Tribute and Sharps Doom Bar and guests like Bays Gold and Otter Ale on handpump and local cider; board games and TV. There are a few seats outside on the terrace and more in an upstairs amphitheatre-style area. The pub is quite small, so it does get crowded at peak times. They have a cash machine as there is no bank in the village.

📖 Using carefully sourced produce, the well liked bar food includes sandwiches, soup, pâté with red onion chutney, crab linguine with garlic, parsley and chilli, vegetable and feta wraps with hummus, free-range egg omelettes, goujons of fish and chips, gammon with egg and pineapple, daily specials such as scallops in garlic butter with bacon and beef in ale pie, and puddings. *Starters/Snacks: £3.95 to £6.95. Main Courses: £6.95 to £14.95. Puddings: £4.25 to £4.50*

Free house ~ Licensees Steve and Caroline Steadman ~ Real ale ~ Bar food (12-2.30, 6.30-8.30(6-9 in summer)) ~ Restaurant ~ (01503) 272743 ~ Children in upstairs family room only ~ Dogs welcome ~ Live music Fri and Sat evenings ~ Open 11-11(10.30 Sun)

Recommended by the Didler, the Brewers, Suzy Miller, Gordon Briggs, Barry Collett, Evelyn and Derek Walter

PORT ISAAC

SX0080   MAP 1

Port Gaverne Inn ♀ 🛏

Port Gaverne signposted from Port Isaac and from B3314 E of Pendoggett; PL29 3SQ

Lively bar with plenty of chatty locals in popular small hotel near sea and fine cliff walks

You are instantly made to feel welcome in the bustling small bar of this popular 17th-c inn by both the landlord and the regulars and many of our readers have been happily coming here for years – either for a just drink before a walk or to stay overnight. The cheerful bar has a relaxed atmosphere, low beams, flagstones as well as carpeting, a big log fire, some exposed stone and helpful staff; the lounge has some interesting antique local photographs. You can eat in the bar or the 'Captain's Cabin' – a little room where everything is shrunk to scale (old oak chest, model sailing ship, even the prints on the white stone walls. St Austell Tribute and Sharps Doom Bar and Cornish Coaster on handpump, a good wine list and several whiskies; cribbage and board games. There are seats in the terraced garden and splendid clifftop walks all around.

🍽 **Bar food includes sandwiches, ploughman's, soup, grilled goats cheese croûte, home-cooked ham and eggs, local crab salad, mediterranean vegetable lasagne, and battered fish of the day; evening meals such as chicken breast with sherry, cream and red peppers, medallions of monkfish with a citrus marmalade coulis, and fillet steak with a red wine, parsley and mushroom sauce.** *Starters/Snacks: £4.95 to £7.95. Main Courses: £8.95 to £14.95. Puddings: £4.95*

Free house ~ Licensee Graham Sylvester ~ Real ale ~ Bar food (12-2.30, 6.30-9) ~ Restaurant ~ (01208) 880244 ~ Children welcome ~ Dogs allowed in bar and bedrooms ~ Open 11-11; 12-10.30 Sun ~ Bedrooms: £65B/£110B

Recommended by Barry and Anne, Susan Lang, J L Wedel, Anne McCarthy, Sam Ward, Jeremy and Ruth Preston-Hoar, John and Susan Miln, Mr and Mrs Richard Osborne

PORTHLEVEN

SW6225   MAP 1

Ship

Village on B3304 SW of Helston; pub perched on edge of harbour; TR13 9JS

Fisherman's pub built into cliffs, fine views from seats on terrace and tasty bar food

If you get to this friendly old fisherman's pub early enough, you might be able to bag a seat by the window inside or at one of the tables out in the terraced garden – they give a marvellous view over the pretty working harbour and out to sea; at night, the harbour is interestingly floodlit. The knocked-through bar has a relaxed atmosphere, welcoming log fires in big stone fireplaces and some genuine individuality. The family room is a conversion of an old smithy with logs burning in a huge open fireplace; the candlelit dining room also looks over the sea. Courage Best and Sharps Doom Bar on handpump; piped music and games machine.

🍽 **Honest bar food includes sandwiches and toasties, filled baked potatoes, ploughman's, moules marinière, grilled goats cheese on a pesto croûton with gooseberry sauce, half a barbecue chicken, crab and prawn mornay, mediterranean vegetable bake, a daily changing fish dish, and puddings like caramel apple pie or syrup sponge.** *Starters/Snacks: £4.95 to £6.95. Main Courses: £9.95 to £21.95. Puddings: £4.95*

Free house ~ Licensee Colin Oakden ~ Real ale ~ Bar food ~ (01326) 564204 ~ Children in family room ~ Dogs allowed in bar ~ Open 11.30-11; 12-10.30 Sun

Recommended by the Didler, Andy and Claire Barker, Andrea Rampley, John and Gloria Isaacs, Miss K Hunt, Mr M Smith, Adrian Johnson, Ewan and Moira McCall, Kelvin and Carol Butcher, Mr and Mrs Gravener, Bryan and Mary Blaxall

PORTHTOWAN

Blue

Beach Road, East Cliff; use the car park (fee in season), not the slippery sand; TR4 8AW

Informal, busy bar – not a traditional pub – right by wonderful beach with modern food and drinks; lively staff and customers

This is certainly not a traditional pub. It's a cheerful bar right by a fantastic beach which makes it incredibly popular with customers of all ages – and their dogs. The atmosphere is easy and informal – and huge picture windows look across the terrace to the huge expanse of sand and sea. The front bays have built-in pine seats and the rest of the large room has chrome and wicker chairs around plain wooden tables on the stripped wood floor, quite a few high-legged chrome and wooden bar stools and plenty of standing space around the bar counter; powder blue-painted walls, ceiling fans, some big ferny plants and fairly quiet piped music; pool table. St Austell Tribute and Admirals Ale on handpump, several wines by the glass, cocktails and shots, and giant cups of coffee all served by perky, helpful young staff. More reports please.

🍽 Good modern bar food using local, seasonal produce includes daily specials like pea, lemon and mint risotto, halloumi fajitas, salad of chilli beetroot, goats cheese and rocket, and various falafels as well as lunchtime filled baps, soup, tasty home-made burgers, nice pizzas, beer-battered pollack, mussels steamed with bacon, leeks, cider and cream, and chargrilled mackerel with tomato, black olives and red onion salad. *Starters/Snacks: £4.50 to £6.00. Main Courses: £8.00 to £13.50. Puddings: £4.00 to £5.00*

Free house ~ Licensees Tara Roberts and Luke Morris ~ Real ale ~ Bar food (12-9 though menu reduced between 3-6) ~ (01209) 890329 ~ Children welcome ~ Dogs welcome ~ Live bands Sat evening ~ Open 10am-11pm(midnight Sat; 10.30 Sun); closed 6pm winter Mon and Tues; closed two weeks in Jan

Recommended by Jonathon Bunt, John Marsh, Andy and Claire Barker, David Crook

RUAN LANIHORNE

Kings Head

Village signposted off A3078 St Mawes road; TR2 5NX

Country pub in quiet hamlet, small bar, two dining areas, real ales and seats outside

Off the beaten track and enjoyed by our readers, this is a neatly kept pub with real ales and well liked food. The small right-hand bar has an informal, relaxed atmosphere, a winter log fire, comfortable sofas and seats around a low table or two, a few high bar chairs used by locals, and Skinners Betty Stogs and a beer named for the pub on handpump; several wines by the glass and farm cider. Further to the right are two dining rooms with lots of china cups hanging from ceiling joists, plenty of copper and brass, hunting prints, a glass cabinet filled with old glass bottles and an aquarium. There's also a restaurant; piped music. Across the road is a terrace with seats and tables under trees and outdoor heaters and below that is a sunken beer garden. The nearby church is interesting and you can walk along the Fal Estuary below the pub.

🍽 Popular food using carefully sourced local ingredients includes sandwiches, ploughman's, soup, tiger prawns in sweet chilli, crab pâté, sausages with red onion marmalade, wild mushroom and parmesan risotto and chicken with chorizo, butter beans and a spicy tomato sauce, with evening dishes like bass with garlic and rosemary, local scallops in garlic and lemon, their speciality slow-cooked duckling off the bone with a warm pepper sauce, and puddings such as bitter chocolate mousse and sticky toffee pudding. *Starters/Snacks: £5.15 to £7.95. Main Courses: £9.95 to £17.95. Puddings: £5.40 to £5.60*

Free house ~ Licensees Andrew and Niki Law ~ Real ale ~ Bar food (not winter Sun evening or Mon) ~ Restaurant ~ (01872) 501263 ~ Well behaved children welcome in dining areas only ~ Dogs allowed in bar ~ Open 12-2.30, 6-11; closed Sun evening and all day Mon in winter

Recommended by Jennifer Sheridan, Comus and Sarah Elliott, Donna and Roger, R K Phillips, Nick Lawless, Mr and Mrs P D Titcomb, Philip and Jan Medcalf, Stephen and Jean Curtis

ST KEW

St Kew Inn ▯▯

Village signposted from A39 NE of Wadebridge; PL30 3HB

Grand-looking 15th-c pub with neat bar and dining areas, first-rate food and big garden

You can be sure of a warm welcome from the friendly, knowledgeable staff in this handsome stone inn and although there's much emphasis on the excellent food, there's also a proper pubby and informal atmosphere. The neatly kept bar has beams, stone walls, winged high-backed settles and wheelback chairs around varnished rustic tables on the tartan carpet, all sorts of jugs here and there, a woodburner in the stone fireplace and St Austell HSD, Proper Job, Tinners and Tribute tapped from wooden casks behind the counter; several wines by the glass. There are also three dining areas. The flowering tubs and baskets are very pretty in summer.

▯ Using carefully sourced produce (including that grown by locals in their gardens and allotments), the exceptionally good food at lunchtime includes sandwiches, dishes on toast such as home-made Boston baked beans with a fried free-range hens egg or hand-made fennel salami with a free-range duck egg, soup, free-range pork sausages with caramelised shallot gravy, cottage pie and minute steak with french fries, with evening choices like crispy fried squid with basil mayonnaise, house terrine with pickles and chutney, steamed steak and mushroom suet pudding, belly and cutlet of pork with sage and cider sauce, roast cod fillet with brandade, trompettes, salsify and grain mustard sauce, and puddings such as chocolate torte with rum-marinated raisins and cornish ale cake with warm caramel sauce and clotted cream; good Sunday lunches. *Starters/Snacks: £4.50 to £7.95. Main Courses: £9.50 to £18.95. Puddings: £5.50 to £6.50*

St Austell ~ Tenants Paul Ripley and Sarah Allen ~ Real ale ~ Bar food (no food winter Sun evenings) ~ Restaurant ~ (01208) 841259 ~ Children welcome away from main bar ~ Dogs allowed in bar ~ Live music every other Friday ~ Open 11-11; 12-10.30 Sun

Recommended by David Eberlin, Christopher Scott, the Didler, Andrea Rampley, W N F Boughey, Anthony Barnes, Henry Fryer, David Hoult

TRESCO

New Inn ▯ ▯ ▯

New Grimsby; Isles of Scilly; TR24 0QG

Attractive inn close to quay and ferries, with chatty bar and light dining extension, enjoyable food and drinks; sunny terrace; bedrooms

Very popular with visitors and handy for the famous gardens, this is a well run inn with cheerful, friendly staff. There is a little locals' bar but most customers tend to head for the main bar room or the light, airy dining extension: comfortable old sofas, banquettes, planked partition seating and farmhouse chairs and tables, a few standing timbers, boat pictures, a large model sailing boat, a collection of old telescopes and plates on the delft shelf. The Pavilion extension has cheerful yellow walls and plenty of seats and tables on the blue wooden floors and looks over the flower-filled terrace with its teak furniture, huge umbrellas and views of the sea. Ales of Scilly Scuppered, St Austell Tribute and Skinners Tresco Tipple on handpump, 13 good wines by the glass, quite a choice of spirits and several coffees; piped music, darts and pool.

▯ As well as lunchtime sandwiches, good bar food includes soup, tempura tiger prawns and calamari with a sweet chilli dip, wild mushroom risotto with mascarpone and truffle oil, burgers with bacon and cheese or onions and gherkin, beer-battered pollack, parsley and parmesan-baked chicken breast with gnocchi dumpling and ratatouille, crayfish, crab, chilli and pak choi linguine, and puddings such as hot chocolate tart with chocolate ice-cream and lemon grass crème brûlée with a coconut biscuit. *Starters/Snacks: £4.95 to £8.00. Main Courses: £9.00 to £16.00. Puddings: £5.50*

Free house ~ Licensee Robin Lawson ~ Real ale ~ Bar food (12-2, 6.30-9) ~ (01720) 422844 ~ Children welcome ~ Dogs allowed in bar ~ Live music every two weeks ~ Open 11-11; 12-10.30 Sun; 11-2.30, 6-11 in winter ~ Bedrooms: £100B/£200B

Recommended by R J Herd, Michael Sargent, Bernard Stradling, Bob Potter, Neil and Anita Christopher

TREVAUNANCE COVE

SW7251 MAP 1

Driftwood Spars 🍺 🛏

Off B3285 in St Agnes; Quay Road; TR5 ORT

Friendly old inn, plenty of history, own-brew beers and wide range of other drinks, popular food and beach nearby; attractive bedrooms

The fine choice of real ales and the fact that it's just up the road from the beach and its dramatic cove are two big draws to this 17th-c inn; plenty of surrounding coastal walks, too. They have their own Driftwood brewery and always keep two of their own-brew beers plus St Austell Dartmoor Best, Tribute and Proper Job, Sharps Doom Bar and Skinners Heligan Honey on handpump; also, 35 malt whiskies, 11 rums, several wines by the glass and sometimes their own alcoholic ginger beer. The bustling bars are timbered with massive ships' spars – the masts of great sailing ships, many of which were wrecked along this coast – and there are dark wooden farmhouse chairs, tub chairs and settles around a mix of tables, padded bar stools by the bar counter, old ship prints and lots of nautical and wreck memorabilia, and a winter log fire; there's said to be an old smugglers' tunnel leading from behind the bar, up through the cliff. The modern dining room overlooks the cove; service is friendly and helpful. The summer hanging baskets are pretty and there are seats in the garden. Many of their attractive bedrooms overlook the coast. More reports please.

🍽 Using local produce, the good bar food includes filled lunchtime ciabattas, soup, venison terrine with red onion chutney, home-roasted honey-glazed ham and free-range eggs, beer-battered fish, red lentil and butternut squash tagine with lemon and coriander couscous, fillet of grey mullet with smoked haddock and spinach risotto, confit duck leg with shallot jus and apple chutney, and puddings such as marmalade bread and butter pudding with clotted cream ice-cream and dark chocolate tart; Sunday roasts. *Starters/Snacks: £2.00 to £6.25. Main Courses: £8.95 to £17.50. Puddings: £4.95 to £6.95*

Free house ~ Licensee Louise Treseder ~ Real ale ~ Bar food (12-2.30, 6.30-9(9.30 summer)) ~ Restaurant ~ (01872) 552428 ~ Children welcome ~ Dogs allowed in bar and bedrooms ~ Live music Sat evenings and folk every other Thurs ~ Open 11-11(1am Sat) ~ Bedrooms: £45S(£58B)/£86S

Recommended by Damon Rutland, the Didler, Comus and Sarah Elliott

TRURO

SW8244 MAP 1

Old Ale House 🍺 £

Quay Sreet; TR1 2HD

Eight real ales and good value, wholesome food in particularly well run, bustling town pub

There's always a good mix of customers in this enjoyable and well run town centre pub. They keep on handpump or tapped from the cask eight real ales which change every day but might include Keltek King and Magic, Marstons Pedigree, Otter Ale, St Austell HSD, Sharps Doom Bar, Skinners Kiddlywink and Wells & Youngs Eagle IPA; they hold two beer festivals a year with up to 26 ales. Eleven wines by the glass and quite a few country wines. The dimly lit bar has an engaging diversity of furnishings, some interesting 1920s bric-a-brac, beer mats pinned everywhere, matchbox collections, and newpapers and magazines to read. There's an upstairs room with darts, pool, juke box and table football.

🍽 Tasty wholesome bar food prepared in a spotless kitchen in full view of the bar includes open sandwiches and half bloomers with toppings such as bacon, onions and melted cheese or tuna, mayonnaise and melted cheese, soup, sautéed potatoes with bacon and mushrooms in a creamy garlic sauce, cauliflower and broccoli bake, various sizzling skillets, a pie of the day, lamb and mint hotpot and beef stew. *Starters/Snacks: £2.95. Main Courses: £3.25 to £6.95. Puddings: £1.50 to £2.95*

Enterprise ~ Lease Mark Jones and Beverley Jones ~ Real ale ~ Bar food (12-2.30; not evenings) ~ (01872) 271122 ~ Children allowed away from bar ~ Open 11-11(midnight Sat); 12-10.30 Sun; closed 25 and 26 Dec

Recommended by the Didler, Michael and Alison Sandy, Dr and Mrs M W A Haward, Ted George, George and Beverley Tucker, Ian Phillips, Alan Johnson, Henry Fryer, Barry Collett, Comus and Sarah Elliott

WATERGATE BAY

Beach Hut

SW8464 MAP 1

B3276 coast road N of Newquay; TR8 4AA

Bustling, informal beach bar with cheerful young staff, good mix of customers, decent drinks and popular food

Of course this is not a pub as such, but we include it because it's a bustling, modern bar with an informal and relaxed atmosphere, a good mix of customers of all ages, and a fantastic beach location. To set the scene inside there are surfing photographs on the planked walls, a large surfboard above a sizeable leatherette wall seat by one big table and another above the bar counter. Wicker and cane armchairs with blue or pink cushions around green and orange-painted tables sit on the nicely weathered stripped wooden floor, there's plenty of mushroom and cream paintwork, and an unusual sloping bleached-board ceiling. Big windows and doors open out on to a glass-fronted decking area – where there are some picnic-sets and views across the sand to the sea. There's also a slightly simpler end room. Decent wines by the glass, lots of coffees and teas and hot chocolate served by friendly young staff; as we went to press, they were hoping to start stocking real ales. Piped soft rock music. They also run an extreme sports academy.

🍽 **As well as usefully serving breakfast and other meals all day, the generous helpings of modern food include sandwiches, duck egg on toast, devilled mackerel, mussels with wine and cream, moroccan vegetable tagine, beefburger with cheese and garlic mayo, crab linguine, coq au vin, fish of the day, rib-eye steak, and puddings like caramel and chestnut mess and treacle sponge with proper custard.** *Starters/Snacks: £5.65 to £7.00. Main Courses: £9.75 to £16.90. Puddings: £4.75*

Free house ~ Licensee Mark Williams ~ Bar food (all day from 8.30am) ~ (01637) 860877 ~ Children welcome ~ Dogs allowed in bar ~ Open 8.30am-11pm; 10.30-5 in winter
Recommended by Ryta Lyndley, Alec Lewery, Chris and Val Ramstedt

ZENNOR

Tinners Arms

SW4538 MAP 1

B3306 W of St Ives; TR26 3BY

Good mix of customers, friendly atmosphere, real ales and tasty food; bedrooms

Even when this popular pub is really busy at peak times, the organised landlady and her staff manage to keep things running smoothly and the atmosphere remains friendly and unspoilt. There are low wooden ceilings, cushioned settles, benches and a mix of chairs around wooden tables on the stone floor, antique prints on the stripped plank panelling and a log fire in cool weather. Sharps Own, St Austell Tinners and a guest beer on handpump, two farm ciders and 25 malt whiskies. In good weather, you can sit on benches in the sheltered front courtyard or at tables on a bigger side terrace. The pub was built in 1271 to house the masons who constructed St Senara's church. There are fine nearby coastal walks.

🍽 **As well as tasty lunchtime bar food such as sandwiches, ploughman's, soup, home-cooked ham and egg and a vegetarian dish of the day, there are evening dishes like roasted foie gras with black pudding and apple and vanilla chutney, mushroom pasta with white truffle oil, local rabbit stew, wild halibut with grapefruit, oranges and pak choi, organic lamb shank with garlic and rosemary sauce, daily specials, and puddings like treacle tart and apple pie with clotted cream.** *Starters/Snacks: £4.50 to £10.00. Main Courses: £8.50 to £20.00. Puddings: £5.95 to £8.00*

Free house ~ Licensees Grahame Edwards and Richard Motley ~ Real ale ~ Bar food (12-2.30, 6.30-9) ~ (01736) 796927 ~ Children welcome away from main bar ~ Dogs welcome ~ Open 11.30-11; 12-10.30 Sun ~ Bedrooms: £50/£90S
Recommended by the Didler, Dr Peter Crawshaw, Mr and Mrs Gravener, Andrea Rampley, Donna and Roger, Tracey and Stephen Groves, Dr A McCormick, S J and C C Davidson, Ewan and Moira McCall, Stuart Turner

LUCKY DIP

Besides the fully inspected pubs, you might like to try these Lucky Dips recommended to us and described by readers (if you do, please send us reports: feedback@goodguides.com).

BOLVENTOR [SX1876]

☆ *Jamaica Inn* PL15 7TS [signed just off A30 on Bodmin Moor]: Genuinely 18th-c bar with oak beams, stripped stone, massive log fire and well kept Sharps Doom Bar (easy to ignore the big all-day cafeteria, games machines, souvenir shop and tourist coaches), young enthusiastic staff, reasonably priced bar food, plaque commemorating murdered landlord Joss Merlyn, great Daphne du Maurier connection; pretty secluded garden with play area, 17 bedrooms, moorland setting *(Abi Benson, Peter and Audrey Dowsett, Dr and Mrs M E Wilson, Michael and Alison Sandy)*

BOSCASTLE [SX0990]

☆ *Napoleon* PL35 0BD [High St, top of village]: Good atmosphere in popular low-beamed 16th-c pub, wholesome generous bar food, well kept St Austell ales, decent wines, good coffee, friendly service, log fires, interesting Napoleon prints, slate floors and cosy rooms on different levels inc small evening bistro, traditional games; piped music; children welcome, small covered terrace and large sheltered garden, steep climb up from harbour (splendid views on the way), open all day *(LYM, the Didler, Ted George)*

BOTALLACK [SW3632]

☆ *Queens Arms* TR19 7QG: Friendly old pub with good home-made food inc local seafood, meat sourced within 3 miles, well kept Sharps and Skinners ales, good service, log fire in unusual granite inglenook, dark wood furniture, tin mining and other old local photographs on stripped-stone walls, family extension; tables out in front and pleasant back garden, wonderful clifftop walks nearby, lodge accommodation, open all day *(Richard Stanfield, Stuart Turner)*

BOTUSFLEMING [SX4061]

Rising Sun PL12 6NJ [off A388 nr Saltash]: Convivial low-ceilinged rural local, lively games bar, smaller quieter room with stripped stone, two good coal fires, well kept changing ales; picnic-sets in garden looking over quiet valley to church, has been cl Mon-Thurs lunchtimes, open all day wknds *(the Didler)*

BREAGE [SW6128]

Queens Arms TR13 9PD [3 miles W of Helston just off A394]: L-shaped local with friendly landlord and staff, six well kept ales inc Sharps Doom Bar and Skinners Betty Stogs, farm cider, decent wines by the glass, enjoyable good value food from baguettes with cornish brie and ham to seafood and steaks, good coal fires, plush banquettes, brass-topped tables, daily papers, restaurant, back games area with pool; piped music; dogs welcome, some picnic-sets outside, covered smokers' area, bedrooms, medieval wall paintings in church opposite, open all

day Sun *(David and Julie Glover, BB, Dennis Jenkin)*

BUDE [SS2006]

Brendon Arms EX23 8SD: Popular (particularly in summer) canalside pub, with two big friendly pubby bars, back family room, well kept ales inc St Austell and Sharps, enjoyable bargain food inc good crab sandwiches and interesting specials, nice coffee, hot spicy apple juice, good friendly service; juke box, sports TV, pool and darts; children welcome, dogs in public bar, disabled access, picnic-sets on front grass, heated smokers' shelter, bedrooms and holiday apartments *(Ryta Lyndley, Barry and Anne)*

CALLINGTON [SX3569]

Bulls Head PL17 7AQ [Fore Street]: Sadly we heard in July 2010 that the centenarian landlady at this ancient unspoilt local had died – early reports suggest few immediate changes; relaxed friendly atmosphere, well kept St Austell ales, handsome black timbering and stonework; erratic opening times *(Giles and Annie Francis)*

CALSTOCK [SX4368]

☆ *Tamar* PL18 9QA [Quay]: Cheerful local dating from 17th c just opposite River Tamar with its imposing viaduct; dark stripped stone, flagstones, tiles and bare boards, pool room with woodburner, more modern fairy-lit back dining room, good generous straightforward food at bargain prices, summer cream teas, well kept ales such as Otter and Sharps Doom Bar, good service, darts, some live music; children away from bar and well behaved dogs welcome, nicely furnished terrace, heated smokers' shelter, hilly walk or ferry to Cotehele (NT) *(BB)*

CAMELFORD [SX1083]

Masons Arms PL32 9PB [A39; Market Pl]: Heavy-beamed character stone pub, well kept St Austell ales, good food choice inc local fish *(Helene Grygar)*

CAWSAND [SX4350]

☆ *Cross Keys* PL10 1PF [The Square]: Slate-floored traditional local with lots of matchboxes, banknotes and postcards, some cask tables, steps up to turkey-carpeted dining room with nautical décor, wide range of enjoyable generous food especially seafood (worth booking in season), reasonable prices, changing ales such as Hop Back Summer Lightning and Skinners Best, flexible service; pool, may be piped music, no nearby parking; children and dogs welcome, seats outside, pleasant bedrooms *(Jonathon Bunt)*

CHARLESTOWN [SX0351]

Harbour Inn PL25 3NJ [part of Pier House Hotel]: Glass-fronted warehouse conversion alongside hotel, great spot looking over classic little harbour and its historic sailing ships, up to seven ales inc Sharps Doom Bar, enjoyable pubby food, live music Sat night;

sports TVs, pool; interesting film-set conservation village with shipwreck museum, parking away from pub *(BB, Mrs J King)*

CRACKINGTON HAVEN [SX1496]
☆ **Coombe Barton** EX23 0JG [off A39 Bude—Camelford]: New management at much-extended old inn in beautiful setting overlooking splendid sandy bay, modernised pubby bar with plenty of room for young summer crowds, wide range of simple bar food inc local fish, neat and pleasant young staff, Sharps and St Austell, good wine choice, lots of local pictures, surfboard hanging from plank ceiling, big plain family room, restaurant; darts, pool, fruit machines, piped music, TV; children welcome, dogs allowed in bar, side terrace with plenty of tables, good cliff walks, roomy bedrooms, open all day in season *(Barry and Anne, LYM)*

CREMYLL [SX4553]
☆ **Edgcumbe Arms** PL10 1HX: Super setting by Plymouth foot-ferry, good Tamar views, picnic-sets out by water; attractive layout and décor, with slate floors, big settles, comfortably old-fashioned furnishings inc fireside sofas, old pictures and china, well kept St Austell ales, cheerful staff, reasonably priced food from doorstep sandwiches up, wknd carvery, good family room/games area; pay car park some way off; children in eating area, dogs allowed in one bar (most tables here too low to eat at), bedrooms, open all day *(Gordon Briggs, LYM)*

CRIPPLES EASE [SW5036]
Engine TR20 8NF [B3311 St Ives—Penzance]: Family-friendly former tin-mine counting house set high in superb moorland location, sea views on all sides from nearby hill (very popular on summer evenings), cheerful efficient service even at busy times, decent uncomplicated food from sandwiches up, well kept ales inc Greene King Abbot and Sharps Doom Bar, pool; terrace, good value bedrooms *(the Head family)*

CROWLAS [SW5133]
Star TR20 8DX [A30]: Imposing Victorian roadside local with big open-plan bar, six interesting changing ales inc own range of good Penzance microbrews, sewing-machine tables in raised area, pool, adjacent dining area, no intrusive music; back courtyard tables with brewery views, open all day *(Richard Stanfield, Alan Bowker)*

CROWS NEST [SX2669]
☆ **Crows Nest** PL14 5JQ [signed off B3264 N of Liskeard; OS Sheet 201 map ref 263692]: Old-fashioned 17th-c pub back under the family who made it a popular Main Entry some years ago, friendly service and chatty locals, enjoyable food from chef/landlord, well kept St Austell ales, decent wines by the glass, big log fire, attractive furnishings under bowed beams; children welcome, picnic-sets on terrace by quiet lane, handy for Bodmin Moor walks *(John and Bernadette Elliott, LYM, Henry Fryer)*

CUBERT [SW7857]
☆ **Smugglers Den** TR8 5PY [off A3075 S of Newquay]: Big welcoming open-plan 16th-c thatched pub, good fresh food inc local seafood, well kept Sharps, Skinners and St Austell, good service, neat ranks of tables, dim lighting, stripped stone and heavy beam and plank ceilings, west country pictures and seafaring memorabilia, steps down to further area with enormous inglenook, another step to big side family dining room, well lit pool area, darts; piped music, games machine; dogs welcome, small courtyard and lawn with climbing frame, has been cl winter Mon-Weds lunchtimes *(Dr Peter Crawshaw, the Didler, W N F Boughey, Adrian Johnson, BB)*

DULOE [SX2358]
Olde Plough House PL14 4PN [B3254 N of Looe]: Three linked rooms all with woodburners, dark polished slate floors, a mix of pews and other seats, Fullers, Sharps and Skinners, enjoyable food inc steak cooked on a hot rock, friendly service, small more modern restaurant; piped music; children welcome, dogs in bar, picnic-sets out by road *(Henry Fryer, Anne McCarthy, Sam Ward, LYM)*

EDMONTON [SW9672]
☆ **Quarryman** PL27 7JA [off A39 just W of Wadebridge bypass]: Welcoming three-room beamed bar, part of a small holiday courtyard complex; some good individual cooking besides generous pubby lunchtime food inc good baguettes, salads and fish and chips, good curry night (first Tues of month), attentive staff, Sharps (summer only), Skinners and a couple of guest beers, interesting decorations inc old sporting memorabilia, cribbage and dominoes, no mobiles; well behaved dogs and children welcome, disabled facilities, courtyard with picnic-sets, open all day *(Kelvin and Carol Butcher, the Didler, Robert Kibble, Dr and Mrs M W A Haward, LYM)*

EGLOSHAYLE [SX0071]
☆ **Earl of St Vincent** PL27 6HT [off A389, just outside Wadebridge]: Pretty dining pub with 200 working antique clocks, also golfing memorabilia, art deco ornaments and rich furnishings, good food from sandwiches to steaks, St Austell ales and good cornish cider; piped music; well behaved children allowed lunchtime, lovely garden *(Mr and Mrs Gravener, LYM, the Didler, Andrea Rampley, Dr and Mrs M W A Haward, Kelvin and Carol Butcher)*

FALMOUTH [SW8032]
☆ **Seven Stars** TR11 3QA [The Moor (centre)]: Quirky 17th-c local, unchanging and unsmart (not to everyone's taste), with long-serving and entertaining vicar-landlord, no gimmicks, machines or mobile phones, warm welcome, Bass and Skinners Cornish Knocker tapped from the cask, home-made rolls, chatty regulars, big key-ring collection, quiet back snug; corridor hatch serving roadside courtyard *(the Didler, Gavin Robinson, Joe Green, Henry Fryer, BB)*

Watermans TR11 3AT [Market St]:
Unassuming pub with well priced Sharps and
Skinners ales, picture window overlooking
harbour, bring your own food; side pool
table, back TV; tables out on quay
(Michael and Alison Sandy, the Didler)

FOWEY [SX1251]
Galleon PL23 1AQ [Fore St; from centre
follow Car Ferry signs]: Superb spot by
harbour and estuary, good ale range inc local
microbrews, good generous straightforward
food, reasonable prices, nice choice of
wines, fast friendly service, fresh modern
nautical décor, lots of solid pine, dining
areas off, jazz Sun lunchtime; pool, big
screen TV, evenings can get loud with young
people; children welcome, disabled facilities,
attractive extended waterside terrace and
sheltered courtyard with covered heated
area, estuary-view bedrooms *(Nick Lawless,
Alain and Rose Foote, JPR, BB, Mick and
Moira Brummell)*

☆ *King of Prussia* PL23 1AT [Town Quay]:
Handsome quayside building with good
welcoming service in roomy neat upstairs
bar, bay windows looking over harbour to
Polruan, enjoyable pubby food inc carve your
own Sun roasts, St Austell ales kept well,
sensibly priced wines, side family restaurant;
piped music, pool; seats outside, open all
day in summer, six pleasant bedrooms
(Alan Johnson, LYM, Chris Glasson)

Safe Harbour PL23 1BP [Lostwithiel St]:
Redecorated 19th-c former coaching inn set
away from main tourist area, lounge/dining
area and locals bar, good value locally
sourced home-made food, well kept
St Austell ales, welcoming landlord, old local
prints, upstairs overflow dining room; pool,
darts, games machine; heated side terrace,
seven bedrooms, self-catering apartment,
open all day till midnight *(Nick Lawless, JPR,
David Uren)*

☆ *Ship* PL23 1AZ [Trafalgar Sq]: Bustling local
with friendly staff, wide choice of good
value generous food from sandwiches up inc
fine local seafood, well kept St Austell ales,
coal fire and banquettes in tidy bar with lots
of yachting prints and nauticalia, steps up to
family dining room with big stained-glass
window, pool/darts room; piped music, small
sports TV; dogs allowed, comfortably old-
fashioned bedrooms, some oak-panelled
*(LYM, Nick Lawless, James Morrell,
Peter Martin)*

GOLANT [SX1254]
☆ *Fishermans Arms* PL23 1LN [Fore St
(B3269)]: Bustling partly flagstoned small
waterside local with lovely views across River
Fowey from front bar and terrace, good value
generous home-made food inc good crab
sandwiches and seafood, efficient friendly
service, Sharps Doom Bar and Skinners Betty
Stogs, good wines by the glass, log fire,
interesting pictures; dogs welcome, pleasant
garden, cl Sun afternoon *(B and M Kendall,
Roger and Linda Hargreaves, Charles Meade-
King, the Didler, BB)*

GWEEK [SW7026]
Gweek Inn TR12 6TU [back roads E of
Helston]: Cheerful family chain pub, large
comfortable open-plan bar with low beams,
brasses, lots of motoring trophies
(enthusiast licensees) and woodburner in
big stone fireplace, well kept Greene King
Old Speckled Hen, Sharps Doom Bar and
Skinners Betty Stogs, decent wines, good
reasonably priced standard food inc nice
puddings choice (may try to keep your
credit card while you eat), bright and
roomy bar restaurant, live music Fri;
tables on grass (safe for children),
summer kiosk with all-day snacks, short
walk from seal sanctuary *(Dr and Mrs
M E Wilson)*

GWITHIAN [SW5840]
Red River TR27 5BW [Prosper Hill]: Former
Pendarves Arms refitted in clean-cut
contemporary style, sofa and stools around
pubby tables on stripped boards, pine dado,
neat dining area with pews and wheelback
chairs, several well kept ales, enjoyable
reasonably priced food, welcoming friendly
staff; picnic-sets in small garden across road,
delightful village nr dunes, beach and
coastal path, bedrooms *(anon)*

HARROWBARROW [SX4069]
Cross House PL17 8BQ [off A390 E of
Callington; School Rd – over towards
Metherell]: Substantial stone building,
spreading carpeted bar with some booth
seating, cushioned wall seats and stools
around pub tables, decent pubby bar food,
well kept Sharps and Skinners, friendly
service, good coal fire, darts area,
restaurant; children and dogs welcome,
plenty of picnic-sets on good-sized lawn,
good play area *(BB, Les Last)*

HEAMOOR [SW4631]
Sportsmans Arms TR18 3HH [Carmen Sq]:
Fully refurbished by newish licensees,
friendly chatty local atmosphere,
enjoyable reasonably priced home-made
food (not Mon), well kept Skinners and
guest ales, good house wine, restaurant
with dark wood furniture on red carpet,
woodburner; children and dogs welcome,
some seats out at front, open all day
(Dennis Jenkin)

HELFORD [SW7526]
Shipwrights Arms TR12 6JX [off B3293 SE
of Helston, via Mawgan]: Thatched pub of
great potential by beautiful wooded creek,
at its best at high tide, terraces making the
most of the view, plenty of surrounding
walks, and summer foot ferry from Helford
Passage; nautical décor, winter open fire,
separate dining area; has had Flowers,
Sharps and Skinners ales, decent wines,
friendly staff, bar food inc summer
barbecues and lunchtime buffet platters,
but still up for sale as we go to press –
news please; quite a walk from nearest car
park, has been cl winter Sun and Mon
evenings *(LYM, the Didler, Dr and Mrs
M E Wilson)*

HELFORD PASSAGE [SW7626]

Ferryboat TR11 5LB [signed from B3291]: Reworked as pub/fish restaurant in super position by sandy beach, about a mile's walk from gate at bottom of Glendurgan Garden (NT), slate-floor beamed bar with open fire, oyster bar, dining room, good if not cheap food, competent service, St Austell Tribute; children and dogs welcome, summer ferry to Helford, open all day *(John Marsh, John and Victoria Fairley, LYM)*

HELSTON [SW6527]

☆ *Blue Anchor* TR13 8EL [Coinagehall St]: Many (not all) love this 15th-c no-nonsense, highly individual, thatched local; quaint rooms off corridor, flagstones, stripped stone, low beams and well worn furniture, traditional games, family room, limited bargain lunchtime food (perhaps best time for a visit), ancient back brewhouse still producing distinctive and very strong Spingo IPA, Middle and seasonals like Bragget with honey and herbs; seats out behind, bedrooms, open all day *(LYM, the Didler, Richard Stanfield, Steve and Liz Tilley)*

HOLYWELL [SW7658]

St Pirans TR8 5PP: Great location backing on to dunes and popular with holidaymakers, friendly helpful staff, well kept St Austell Tribute and Proper Job, enjoyable pub food; children welcome, tables on large back terrace *(David and Jill Hunter)*

LANNER [SW7339]

☆ *Fox & Hounds* TR16 6AX [Comford; A393/B3298]: Cosily comfortable rambling low-beamed pub with good choice of fresh food from sandwiches to massive steaks, well kept St Austell ales tapped from the cask, good house wines, friendly service, warm fires, high-backed settles and cottage chairs on flagstones, stripped stone and dark panelling, newspapers and books; pub games, piped music; children welcome in dining room, dogs in bar, disabled facilities, great floral displays in front, picnic-sets in neat back garden with pond and play area, open all day wknds *(Jonathon Bunt, John Marsh, Dennis Jenkin, David Crook, LYM)*

LELANT [SW5436]

☆ *Old Quay House* TR27 6JG [Griggs Quay, Lelant Saltings; A3047/B3301 S of village]: Large modern pub in marvellous spot by bird sanctuary estuary, welcoming and neatly kept with good value food, real ales such as Bass, St Austell Tribute and Sharps Doom Bar, good service, dining area off well divided open-plan bar, children allowed upstairs; garden with views over saltings, decent motel-type bedrooms, open all day summer *(Alan Johnson, Ian Shorthouse)*

LERRYN [SX1356]

☆ *Ship* PL22 0PT [signed off A390 in Lostwithiel; Fore St]: Lovely spot especially when tide's in, Sharps and Skinners, local farm cider, good wines, country wines and whiskies, wide food choice from imaginative menu, sensible prices, huge woodburner,

attractive adults-only dining conservatory (booked quickly evenings and wknds), games room with pool; dogs on leads and children welcome, picnic-sets and pretty play area outside, nr famous stepping-stones and three well signed waterside walks, decent bedrooms in adjoining building *(Nick Lawless, LYM)*

LOOE [SX2553]

Olde Salutation PL13 1AE [Fore St, E Looe]: Good welcoming local bustle in big squarish slightly sloping beamed and tiled bar, good value food from notable crab sandwiches to wholesome specials and Sun roasts, fast friendly service, well kept ales inc Sharps Doom Bar, red leatherette seats and neat tables, blazing fire in nice old-fashioned fireplace, lots of local fishing photographs, side snug with olde-worlde harbour mural, step down to simple family room; may be piped music, forget about parking; open all day, handy for coast path *(BB, Christine and Neil Townend, Gordon Briggs, David Uren)*

LOSTWITHIEL [SX1059]

☆ *Royal Oak* PL22 0AG [Duke St]: Nice town local dating from 13th c under newish licensees, well kept Fullers London Pride, Sharps Doom Bar and Wells & Youngs Bombardier, spacious neat lounge with log-effect gas fire, beamed and flagstoned back public bar, darts and board games, restaurant; piped music (live wknds), games machines, pool; children welcome, dogs in bar, picnic-sets on raised terrace by car park, four bedrooms, open all day and till late wknds *(Andy and Claire Barker, Dave Braisted, Dr and Mrs M W A Haward, LYM)*

LUDGVAN [SW5033]

☆ *White Hart* TR20 8EY [off A30 Penzance—Hayle at Crowlas]: Appealing old-fashioned 19th-c pub under same management as Turks Head in Penzance (see Main Entries), friendly and welcoming, with well kept Sharps, Skinners and a changing guest beer tapped from the cask, standard pub food, small unspoilt beamed rooms with wood and stone floors, nooks and crannies, woodburners, newspapers; interesting church next door *(the Didler, Dave Webster, Sue Holland, David Crook, Richard Stanfield, LYM)*

MARAZION [SW5230]

Fire Engine TR17 0BB [Higher Fore St]: Open-plan, with well kept St Austell ales from central bar, good hearty pub food, friendly staff, interesting local maritime photographs, fantastic St Michael's Mount views from back windows; dogs welcome, suntrap sloping lawn with lower terrace *(Dave Webster, Sue Holland, Eamonn and Natasha Skyrme, Alan Bowker)*

Godolphin Arms TR17 0EN [West End]: Great views across beach and Mounts Bay towards St Michael's Mount, real ales inc Sharps, informal lower bar with pool table, upper lounge bar and dining room, popular Sun carvery, family room with play area; decked terrace, ten brightly painted bedrooms, most with sea view, good breakfast *(Dave Webster, Sue Holland, Norman and Sarah Keeping)*

MARHAMCHURCH [SS2203]

Bullers Arms EX23 0HB: Oak beams and settles in pleasant rambling L-shaped bar, good choice of well prepared food and of well kept local and national beers, decent wine by the glass, obliging staff, darts in flagstoned back part, restaurant; children welcome; tables and play area in sizeable garden, a mile's walk to the sea, bedrooms *(LYM, Andy and Jill Kassube)*

MAWNAN SMITH [SW7728]

☆ *Red Lion* TR11 5EP [W of Falmouth, off former B3291 Penryn—Gweek; The Square]: Old thatched and beamed pub, popular and chatty, with cosy series of dimly lit lived-in rooms, open-view kitchen doing wide choice of good food from interesting menu especially seafood (should book summer evening), quick friendly service, lots of wines by the glass, real ales such as Sharps kept well, good coffee, daily papers, fresh flowers, woodburner, dark woodwork, country pictures, plates and bric-a-brac; piped music, TV; children and dogs welcome, picnic-sets outside, handy for Glendurgan and Trebah Gardens, open all day *(LYM, Stephen and Jean Curtis, Comus and Sarah Elliott, Norman and Sarah Keeping, J B Taylor, Dr and Mrs M E Wilson)*

MENHENIOT [SX2862]

White Hart PL14 3QZ [off A38]: Extended former coaching inn with beamed public and lounge bars, slate and carpeted floors, enjoyable good value uncomplicated food, well kept ales inc a cask-tapped local one, restaurant; some seats outside, reasonably priced neatly modernised bedrooms *(Nigel Clifton)*

METHERELL [SX4069]

Carpenters Arms PL17 8BJ [follow Honicombe sign from St Anns Chapel just W of Gunnislake A390; Lower Metherell]: Heavily beamed local with huge polished flagstones and massive stone walls in cosy bar and brightly lit lounge, enjoyable home-made food, well kept St Austell, Sharps and guests, friendly helpful service; children welcome in the modern carpeted eating areas, picnic-sets on front terrace, bedrooms, handy for Cotehele *(Les Last, LYM)*

MEVAGISSEY [SX0144]

☆ *Fountain* PL26 6QH [Cliff St, down alley by Post Office]: Popular fishermen's pub with new licensees; low beams, slate floor, some stripped stone, good coal fire, old local pictures, St Austell ales, enjoyable food, back locals' bar with glass-topped cellar, upstairs restaurant; pretty frontage with picnic-sets, bedrooms, open all day summer *(Andy and Claire Barker, Ted George, the Didler, Joe Green, R K Phillips, David Uren, BB, Ian Phillips)*

MINIONS [SX2671]

Cheesewring PL14 5LE: Popular well run village pub useful for Bodmin Moor walks, real ales inc Sharps Doom Bar and Special,

good choice of reasonably priced home-made food, lots of brass and ornaments *(Ian Phillips, Jenny and Peter Lowater)*

MOUSEHOLE [SW4626]

☆ *Ship* TR19 6QX [Harbourside]: Busy harbourside local under new management; opened-up dimly lit main bar with black beams, flagstones, open fire, panelling, built-in wooden wall benches and stools around low tables, sailors' fancy ropework, darts, well kept St Austell ales, pubby food inc good local fish; piped music, TV, games machine, upstairs lavatories; children and dogs welcome, lovely village, bedrooms, open all day *(LYM, Paul Goldman, Adrian Johnson, Martin and Anne Muers)*

MYLOR BRIDGE [SW8036]

Lemon Arms TR11 5NA [Lemon Hill]: Popular and friendly traditional village pub improved under latest landlord, good sensibly priced food (best to book), St Austell ales and reasonably priced wines; children and dogs welcome, wheelchair access with help, back terrace, good coastal walks *(Alan Bowker, David Elliott, Chris and Angela Buckell, Mick and Moira Brummell, J D O Carter)*

NEWBRIDGE [SW4231]

Fountain TR20 8QH [A3071 Penzance—St Just]: Stone-built pub with big pine tables and cheery inglenook log fire in attractively old-fashioned beamed and flagstoned core's cosy dining area, friendly efficient staff, above-average reasonably priced pubby food inc good fish, bargain pies (Fri night), well kept local ales, modern extension; tables in pretty front courtyard, bedrooms, camping available *(Jane and Alan Bush)*

NEWLYN [SW4628]

Red Lion TR18 5JP [Fore St]: Small beamed fishermen's local in great spot above harbour, lovely views, nooks and crannies, nautical memorabilia, friendly landlord, well kept Sharps Doom Bar and Skinners Betty Stogs, low-priced food; darts, pool, piped music; dogs allowed *(Giles and Annie Francis)*

Tolcarne TR18 5PR [Tolcarne Pl]: Traditional 17th-c quayside pub, cosy and lived-in with open fire, local fishing photos, wide choice of good value home-made food inc good seafood, friendly staff and locals, well kept Brakspears and Sharps; terrace (harbour wall cuts off view), good parking *(Jane and Alan Bush)*

NEWQUAY [SW8061]

Fort TR7 1HA [Fore St]: Massive recently built pub in magnificent setting high above surfing beach and small harbour, decent standard food all day from sandwiches, hot baguettes and baked potatoes up, open-plan areas well divided by balustrades and surviving fragments of former harbourmaster's house, good solid furnishings from country kitchen to button-back settees, soft lighting and one panelled area, friendly service, St Austell ales, games part with two well lit pool tables, excellent indoor play area; great views from long glass-walled side section and from sizeable garden with terrace and play areas, good bedrooms, open all day *(BB, the Head family)*

Griffin TR7 1SP [Cliff Rd]: Cosy local with enjoyable food from varied menu inc good fish and chips, well kept Skinners Betty Stogs, friendly efficient staff, restaurant; limited parking; tables outside *(Michael Tack)*

Lewinnick Lodge TR7 1NX [Pentire headland, off Pentire Rd]: Modern bar/restaurant built into the bluff above the sea, big picture windows for the terrific views, open uncluttered layout and furnishings, popular if not cheap food (lunch served till 4) inc lots of fish and carvery, decent drinks choice, good service and pleasant relaxed atmosphere even when busy; good outside seating *(Mick and Moira Brummell)*

Red Lion TR7 1HE [North Quay Hill]: Large pub overlooking harbour, good choice of reasonably priced food, well kept ales inc Skinners Betty Stogs, prompt service *(Michael Tack)*

PADSTOW [SW9175]

☆ *Golden Lion* PL28 8AN [Lanadwell St]: Cheerful black-beamed locals' bar, high-raftered back lounge with plush banquettes, well kept ales such as Sharps Doom Bar, reasonably priced simple bar lunches inc good crab sandwiches, evening steaks and fresh seafood, prompt friendly service, coal fire; pool in family area, piped music, games machines, sports TV; nice floral displays at front, terrace tables, bedrooms, open all day *(the Didler, Michael B Griffith, John Saville, Adrian Johnson, BB)*

Old Custom House PL28 8BL [South Quay]: Large bright and airy open-plan seaside bar, comfortable and well divided, with rustic décor and cosy corners, bare boards, raised section, big family area and conservatory, good food choice from baguettes to bargain deals for two, St Austell ales, good friendly service, adjoining fish restaurant, pool; big-screen TV, some live music; good spot by harbour, open all day, attractive sea-view bedrooms *(BB, Ted George)*

Shipwrights PL28 8AF [North Quay; aka the Blue Lobster]: Big open-plan low-ceilinged quayside bar, stripped brick, lots of wood, flagstones, lobster pots and nets, quick popular food, well kept St Austell and Sharps, friendly service, further upstairs eating area; busy with young people in evenings; dogs welcome, a few tables out by water, more in back suntrap garden *(BB, Dave Irving, Jenny Huggins)*

PELYNT [SX2054]

☆ *Jubilee* PL13 2JZ [B3359 NW of Looe]: Popular early 17th-c beamed inn with well kept St Austell ales, good wines by the glass, home-made locally sourced food from good sandwiches up inc Sun roasts, friendly helpful staff, interesting Queen Victoria mementoes (pub renamed 1887 to celebrate her jubilee), some handsome antique

furnishings, log fire in big stone fireplace, separate bar with darts, pool and games machine; children and dogs welcome, disabled facilities, large terrace, 11 comfortable bedrooms, open all day wknds *(LYM, Dennis Jenkin)*

PENDEEN [SW3834]

North TR19 7DN: Small comfortable local with friendly staff, well kept St Austell ales, good curries, interesting photographs, upstairs restaurant; bedrooms *(Tracey and Stephen Groves)*

PENDOGGETT [SX0279]

☆ *Cornish Arms* PL30 3HH [B3314]: Picturesque friendly old coaching inn with traditional oak settles on civilised front bar's handsome polished slate floor, fine prints, above-average food from good sandwiches and fresh fish to splendid steaks and Sun lunch (best to book), also good authentic thai food from resident thai chefs, welcoming service, well kept Bass and Sharps Doom Bar, good wines by the glass, comfortably spaced tables in small dining room, proper back locals' bar with woodburner and games; provision for children, disabled access (staff helpful), terrace with distant sea view, bedrooms, open all day *(Mark Porter, Paul and Jane Meredith, Henry Fryer, LYM, Mrs Teresa Bateman)*

PENTEWAN [SX0147]

Ship PL26 6BX [just off B3273 St Austell—Mevagissey; West End]: Big 17th-c beamed pub opp tiny village's harbour, comfortable and clean with bar, snug and lounge/dining area, lots of dark tables and open fire, up to four St Austell ales, good reasonably priced fresh food inc plenty of fish, curries and popular Sun carvery, helpful staff; piped music, occasional live; children and dogs welcome, views from tables outside, nr good sandy beach and big caravan park, open all day summer, all day wknds winter *(Paul Hobbs, Joe Green, Mrs J King)*

PENZANCE [SW4730]

Admiral Benbow TR18 4AF [Chapel St]: Well run rambling pub, full of life and atmosphere and packed with interesting nautical gear, friendly thoughtful staff, good value above-average food inc local fish, real ales such as Sharps, Skinners and St Austell, cosy corners, fire, downstairs restaurant in captain's cabin style, upper floor with pool, pleasant view from back room; children welcome, open all day summer *(LYM, Clifford Blakemore, Richard Stanfield, Jerry Brown, Tim and Ann Newell)*

Crown TR18 2EP [Victoria Sq]: Small local with neat bar and open fire in snug back room, ales such as Otter, Skinners and Timothy Taylors Landlord, good choice of wines, enjoyable good value food (Fri-Sun lunchtimes, Thurs-Sat evenings) *(Giles and Annie Francis)*

☆ *Dolphin* TR18 4EF [Barbican; Newlyn road, opp harbour after swing-bridge]: Part old-fashioned pub and part bistro, good value food especially fresh fish (landlady's husband is a fisherman), St Austell ales, good wines by the glass, helpful service, roomy bar, great fireplace, dining area a few steps down, cosy family room; big pool room with juke box etc, no obvious nearby parking; pavement picnic-sets, open all day *(LYM, the Didler, Robert W Buckle)*

PERRANARWORTHAL [SW7738]

☆ *Norway* TR3 7NU [A39 Truro—Penryn]: Large pub doing well under enterprising licensees, helpful friendly service, wide choice of generous carefully prepared food using local produce inc vegetarian options, all-day Sun carvery, morning coffee and afternoon tea, good selection of St Austell ales and of wines by glass, unusual sherry menu with accompanying nibbles, half-a-dozen linked areas, beams hung with farm tools, lots of prints and rustic bric-a-brac, old-style wooden seating and big tables on slate flagstones, open fires, Mon night quiz; children well catered for, tables outside, open all day *(BB, Michael and Alison Sandy, Jonathon Bunt, Gene and Tony Freemantle, David Crook)*

PHILLACK [SW5638]

Bucket of Blood TR27 5AE [Churchtown Rd]: Welcoming bustle in traditional low-beamed thick-walled village pub, sturdy stripped pine tables, enjoyable generous fresh food (not Mon or Tues), low prices, well kept St Austell Tinners and HSD, gruesome ghost stories, locals' back snug; tables outside *(Adrian Johnson, Ian Shorthouse, LYM)*

PILLATON [SX3664]

☆ *Weary Friar* PL12 6QS [off Callington—Landrake back road]: Tucked-away welcoming 12th-c pub, good food in bar and restaurant, well kept ales, farm cider, good service, knocked-together carpeted rooms, dark beams, copper and brass, log fires in stone fireplaces; no dogs inside; children welcome, tables outside, church next door (Tues evening bell-ringing), comfortable bedrooms *(LYM, Ted George, Tom Bray)*

POLPERRO [SX2051]

☆ *Crumplehorn Mill* PL13 2RJ [top of village nr main car park]: Converted mill keeping beams, flagstones and some stripped stone, snug lower beamed bar leading to long attractive main room with cosy end eating area; wide choice of good food from snacks to specials, welcoming friendly service, well kept St Austells and Sharps, log fire; children welcome, outside seating, good value bedrooms, self catering *(BB, Peter Salmon, Nigel and Kath Thompson)*

POLRUAN [SX1250]

Russell PL23 1PJ [West St]: No frills fishermen's local, sensibly priced food inc curries and enjoyable Sun lunch, St Austell beers, friendly staff, large bar with interesting old local photographs, log fire; piped radio; children and dogs welcome, pavement tables, open all day Easter-Nov *(Nick Lawless, Ian Phillips)*

PORT ISAAC [SW9980]

☆ *Golden Lion* PL29 3RB [Fore Street]: Bustling local atmosphere in simply furnished old rooms, open fire in back one, window seats and three balcony tables looking down on rocky harbour and lifeboat slip far below, straightforward decent food inc generous baguettes and good fish range, St Austell ales, darts, dominoes, cribbage; piped music, games machine; children in eating areas, dramatic cliff walks, open all day *(LYM, the Didler, Guy Vowles, Ewan and Moira McCall, David Hoult, the Brewers, Barry and Anne)*

Slipway PL29 3RH [Middle St]: Small hotel just across from delightful village's slipway and beach, small unpretentious cellar-like bar with low dark beams, flagstones and some stripped stonework, Sharps ales, decent wines by the glass, nice bar food inc seafood, good restaurant; leave car at top of village unless you enjoy a challenge; children welcome away from bar, crazy-paved heated terrace with awning, bedrooms, open all day in summer *(the Brewers, Tom and Ruth Rees, LYM)*

PORTHLEVEN [SW6225]

Harbour Inn TR13 9JB [Commercial Rd]: Large neatly kept pub/hotel in outstanding harbourside setting, pleasant well organised service, expansive lounge and bar with impressive dining area off, big public bar with panelling and leather seating, up to four local ales, comprehensive wine list, usual fare; quiet piped music; picnic-sets on big quayside terrace, decent bedrooms, some with harbour view, good breakfast *(John and Gloria Isaacs, Tracey and Stephen Groves)*

PORTLOE [SW9339]

☆ *Ship* TR2 5RA: Unspoilt bright L-shaped local, enjoyable generous food inc fresh fish (good crab sandwiches), well kept St Austell ales, good choice of wines, friendly welcoming service, interesting nautical and local memorabilia and photographs, amazing beer bottle collection; piped music; children and dogs welcome, disabled access to main bar, smokers' gazebo, sheltered and attractive streamside picnic-sets over road, pretty fishing village with lovely cove and coast path above, bedrooms, open all day Fri-Sun summer *(Kim Smith, Dr and Mrs M E Wilson, BB, Comus and Sarah Elliott, Chris and Angela Buckell, David Uren)*

PORTSCATHO [SW8735]

Plume of Feathers TR2 5HW [The Square]: Cheerful largely stripped-stone pub in pretty fishing village, well kept St Austell and other ales, Healey's cider, pubby food from sandwiches and huge ploughman's up, bargain fish night Fri, sea-related bric-a-brac in comfortable linked room areas, small side locals' bar (can be very lively evenings), restaurant; very popular with summer visitors, warm local atmosphere out of season; piped music; children, dogs and boots welcome, disabled access, lovely coast walks, open all day summer (other times if busy) *(Chris and Angela Buckell, David Crook, David Uren, LYM)*

SENNEN COVE [SW3526]

☆ *Old Success* TR19 7DG [Off A30 Land's End road]: The star's for the glorious Whitesand Bay view from the recently redone terraced garden or inside this traditional seaside hotel; brightened up unpretentious bar with lifeboat memorabilia, ship's lanterns, black and white photographs, big ship's wheel used as coat stand, darts, well kept St Austell ales, local cider, good reasonably priced bar food, cheerful service even under pressure; piped music, live wknds, TV; children welcome and dogs, 12 refurbished bedrooms, three self-catering flats, popular with surfers, open all day *(Andy and Claire Barker, LYM, Alan Johnson, Robert Kibble, Simon J Barber, Richard Stanfield, Mr and Mrs Gravener, Ewan and Moira McCall, Stuart Turner)*

ST AGNES [SW7250]

St Agnes TR5 0QP: Early 18th-c inn with bar and separate dining room, sensibly priced home-made food from pubby things up inc lunchtime bargains, some live music; children and dogs welcome, tables on outside deck, six bedrooms *(Comus and Sarah Elliott)*

ST BREWARD [SX0977]

☆ *Old Inn* PL30 4PP [off B3266 S of Camelford; Churchtown]: Broad slate flagstones, low oak beams, stripped stonework, two massive granite fireplaces dating from 11th c, welcoming friendly staff, good pubby food inc carvery Sat evening and Sun, well kept Bass and Sharps, lots of wines by the glass, sensibly placed darts, roomy extended restaurant with tables out on deck; piped music, games machine; provision for dogs and children, moorland behind (cattle and sheep wander into the village), open all day Fri-Sun and summer *(Kelvin and Carol Butcher, the Didler, LYM)*

ST DOMINICK [SX4067]

☆ *Who'd Have Thought It* PL12 6TG [off A388 S of Callington]: Large, comfortable and welcoming country pub under mother and daughter (chef) management, wide choice of good food from generous sandwiches to blackboard specials, well kept St Austell ales, decent wines, superb Tamar views especially from conservatory, cosily plush lounge areas with open fires; dogs allowed in public bar, garden tables, handy for Cotehele (NT) *(Ted George, Mayur Shah, Jacquie Jones, LYM)*

ST EWE [SW9746]

Crown PL26 6EY [off B3287]: Tucked-away rose-covered pub with low beams and traditional furnishings, flagstones and carpets, two nice log fires, lots of bric-a-brac, St Austell ales kept well, good house wines, helpful attentive licensees, generous if pricey locally sourced food (less choice off season), large back dining room up steps; piped music; children in eating areas, dogs allowed in bar but not garden, disabled

facilities, handy for Lost Gardens of Heligan, usually open all day wknds *(LYM, Chris and Angela Buckell)*

ST GERMANS [SX3557]

Eliot Arms PL12 5NR [Fore St]: Stone-built slate-roofed pub with reasonably priced food from filled rolls up; picnic-sets out in front walled area with flowers and hanging baskets, seven chintzy bedrooms *(Chris and Angela Buckell, Charles Gysin)*

ST ISSEY [SW9272]

Pickwick PL27 7QQ [Burgois, signed off A389 at St Issey]: Rambling old hillside pub with estuary views, enjoyable changing food (all-day in season) inc local meats and game, well kept cornish ales, decent wines, friendly helpful staff, log fire, Dickensian kitsch and dark oak beams, open bar with family area, restaurant; piped music, pool, machines, no dogs inside; disabled access, picnic-sets in sizeable garden with sea views and adventure play area, bowling green and tennis, caravan site, bedrooms, open all day summer *(Ian Shorthouse)*

ST IVES [SW5140]

☆ *Sloop* TR26 1LP [The Wharf]: Busy low-beamed, panelled and flagstoned harbourside pub with bright St Ives School pictures and attractive portrait drawings in front bar, booth seating in back bar, good value food from sandwiches and interesting baguettes to lots of fresh local fish, quick friendly service even though busy, Greene King and Sharps, good coffee; piped music, TV; children in eating area, a few beach-view seats out on cobbles, open all day (breakfast from 9am), cosy bedrooms, handy for Tate Gallery *(LYM, Alan Johnson, the Didler, Donna and Roger, Robert Kibble, Richard Stanfield, Peter Salmon)*

ST JUST IN PENWITH [SW3731]

Kings Arms TR19 7HF [Market Sq]: Busy unpretentious local with well kept St Austell ales tapped from casks, friendly relaxed service, comfortable elderly furniture on stone floors, old local photographs, good value freshly made bar food from baguettes up; popular live music nights; dogs welcome, tables out in front, good value bedrooms with big breakfast, open all day *(the Didler)*

☆ *Star* TR19 7LL [Fore St]: Relaxed and informal low-beamed two-room local, friendly landlord, five well kept St Austell ales, no food (bring your own lunchtime sandwiches or pasties), dimly lit main bar with dark walls covered in flags and photographs, coal fire, sleepy pub cat, darts and euchre, nostalgic juke box, live celtic music Mon evening, open mike Thurs; tables in attractive back yard with smokers' shelter, open all day *(the Didler, George and Beverley Tucker, Richard Stanfield, LYM)*

ST MAWES [SW8433]

Idle Rocks TR2 5AN [Tredenham Rd (harbour edge)]: Comfortable, old-fashioned waterfront hotel with lovely sea views, Skinners Betty Stogs and decent wines by the glass (at a price), enjoyable lunchtime food in two-tier restaurant looking on to terrace and harbour (more formal in evening but still relaxed), also nice snacks in pleasant small bar area and separate lounge, daily papers, friendly helpful young staff; well behaved dogs (but no small children) allowed on sun terrace over harbour, smallish bedrooms overlooking the water are the best bet *(Dennis Jenkin, BB)*

☆ *Rising Sun* TR2 5DJ [The Square]: Light and airy, with relaxed nicely redone bar on right with end woodburner, seaview bow window opposite, rugs on stripped wood, a few dining tables, sizeable carpeted left-hand bar with dark wood furniture, enjoyable food, well kept St Austell ales, good wines by the glass, friendly staff, wood-floored conservatory; piped music; sunny terrace with picnic-sets just across road from harbour wall, bedrooms *(Michael and Alison Sandy, David Uren, Andy and Claire Barker, George Atkinson, Comus and Sarah Elliott, LYM)*

Victory TR2 5DQ [Victory Hill]: Locals' bare-boards bar on left, carpeted dining area on right with partitions (may be upstairs dining room in season), well kept Otter, Sharps and perhaps Cornish Shag (brewed at sister pub, the Roseland in Philleigh), decent pubby food inc local fish, log fires, welcoming attentive staff, plain wooden seating, board games; piped music; one or two picnic-sets outside, good value bedrooms, open all day *(LYM, MA, R K Phillips, AEB, Barry Collett, Comus and Sarah Elliott, David Uren)*

ST MAWGAN [SW8765]
☆ *Falcon* TR8 4EP [NE of Newquay, off B3276 or A3059]: Attractive old wisteria-clad stone inn, log-fire bar with antique coaching prints and falcon pictures, St Austell ales kept well, enjoyable food, good friendly service, compact stone-floored dining room, darts; children welcome, front cobbled courtyard and peaceful back garden with wishing well (they ask to keep a credit card if you eat outside), pretty village, bedrooms, has been open all day in summer *(D W Stokes, W N F Boughey, Peter Jacobs, David Eberlin, James House, Mayur Shah, LYM)*

ST MERRYN [SW8874]
Cornish Arms PL28 8ND [Churchtown (B3276 towards Padstow)]: Managed by Rick Stein as a traditional local rather than gastropub; enjoyable inexpensive food such as mussels and chips, steak and ale pie and scampi in a basket (can be a wait for a table and food at peak times), friendly staff, well kept St Austell ales, good choice of wines by the glass, log fire, fine slate floor, some 12th-c stonework and RNAS memorabilia; popular with families, dogs welcome, picnic-sets at front and on sunny side terrace under large heated parasols, nice views, open all day summer from breakfast *(LYM, Nigel and Kath Thompson)*

ST NEOT [SX1867]
☆ *London* PL14 6NG [N of A38 Liskeard—Bodmin]: Popular 16th-c beamed country pub on Bodmin Moor, open-plan but well divided, with soft lighting, two log fires and some stripped stone, cheerful efficient staff, good reasonably priced home-made food, good choice of real ales, decent house wines, dining area behind timber divider; piped music; children welcome, picnic-sets on small front terrace below 15th-c church with outstanding medieval stained glass, attractive village in wooded valley, three bedrooms *(BB, Richard Fulbrook)*

ST TUDY [SX0676]
Cornish Arms PL30 3NN [off A391 nr Wadebridge]: Attractive low-beamed 16th-c village local with well kept Bass, St Austell, Sharps and a possible guest, decent home-made food in flagstoned front bar and restaurant, pool room; children welcome *(the Didler)*

STITHIANS [SW7037]
Golden Lion TR16 6NW [Stithians Lake, Menherion]: Welcoming pub with good generous food from open sandwiches up, St Austell ales, friendly efficient staff even at busy times, oak beams and granite walls, candlelit tables, conservatory; large well maintained garden and lakeside terrace, campsite *(Adrian and Dawn Collinge)*

STRATTON [SS2306]
Kings Arms EX23 9BX [Howells Rd (A3072)]: Lively and friendly 17th-c three-room local with well kept Exmoor, Sharps and several guest beers, reasonably priced food from sandwiches up, good service, attractive tiled tables; piped music; children welcome, dogs too (may get a biscuit), tables out by car park *(Dennis Jenkin)*

TREBARWITH [SX0585]
Port William PL34 0HB [Trebarwith Strand]: Lovely seaside setting with glorious views and sunsets, waterside picnic-sets across road and on covered terrace, fishing nets, fish tanks and maritime memorabilia inside, gallery with local artwork, well kept St Austell Tinners and HSD, farm cider, enjoyable food (may be a wait for a table at busy times); pool and other games, piped music; children in eating area, well equipped comfortable bedrooms, open all day *(LYM, Colin McKerrow, G K Smale)*

TREBURLEY [SX3477]
Springer Spaniel PL15 9NS [A388 Callington—Launceston]: Relaxed place with locally sourced food inc sandwiches from choice of interesting breads, well kept Sharps and Skinners, good wine choice, reasonable prices, clean décor with high-backed settle by woodburner, farmhouse chairs and other seats, olde-worlde prints, further cosy room with big solid teak tables, attractive restaurant up some steps; dogs very welcome in bar, children in eating areas, covered terrace *(Jacquie Jones, LYM)*

TREEN [SW3923]
☆ *Logan Rock* TR19 6LG [just off B3315 Penzance—Lands End]: Low-beamed

traditional bar with St Austell ales, enjoyable home-made food from sandwiches up, inglenook fire, small back snug with excellent cricket memorabilia – landlady eminent in county's cricket association, family room; no under-14s in bar, pretty split-level garden behind with covered area, good coast walks, open all day in season (the Didler, John and Gloria Isaacs, Stuart Turner, LYM)

TREGADILLETT [SX2983]

☆ *Eliot Arms* PL15 7EU [Village signposted off A30 at junction with A395, W end of Launceston bypass]: Creeper-covered with series of small rooms, interesting collections inc 72 antique clocks, 400 snuffs, hundreds of horsebrasses, barometers, old prints and shelves of books/china, fine mix of furniture on Delabole slate from high-backed settles and chaise longues to more modern seats, open fires, well kept Courage and Sharps, generous food; piped music, games machine and darts; children and dogs welcome, seats out front and back, lovely hanging baskets and tubs, bedrooms, open all day (the Didler, John and Bernadette Elliott, LYM)

TYWARDREATH [SX0854]

New Inn PL24 2QP [off A3082; Fore St]: Timeless 18th-c local, friendly and relaxed, with Bass tapped from the cask and St Austell ales on handpump, caring friendly landlord, back games/children's room with juke box, open fires; large secluded garden behind, nice village setting, bedrooms, open all day (the Didler, BB)

VERYAN [SW9139]

New Inn TR2 5QA [village signed off A3078]: Comfortably homely one-bar beamed local under new management, enjoyable food using local produce, St Austell ales, friendly attentive service, inglenook woodburner, polished brass and old pictures; piped music, nearby parking unlikely in summer; disabled front access, quiet garden behind the pretty house, comfortable bedrooms, interesting partly thatched village not far from nice beach (the Didler, R K Phillips, Norman and Sarah Keeping, Chris and Angela Buckell, BB)

WIDEMOUTH [SS1902]

☆ *Bay View* EX23 0AW [Village signposted (with Bude Coastal Route) off A39 N of Pounstock; Marine Drive]: Sizeable hotel with wonderful views of Widemouth Bay, several spreading areas with rugs on stripped-wood floors or flagstones, comfortable leather sofas, low chunky tables, log-effect gas fires, relaxed atmosphere, Sharps Doom Bar, Skinners Betty Stogs and a beer named for them, straightforward food (all day Sun), friendly helpful staff, separate restaurant; children and dogs welcome, front

terrace and picnic-sets on grass, play area and maybe bouncy castle, bedrooms (front ones with best views), open all day (the Didler, Paul and Annette Hallett, Jackie and Alan Moody, Ewan and Moira McCall, LYM, Maurice and Gill McMahon)

ZELAH [SW8151]

Hawkins Arms TR4 9HU [A30]: 18th-c beamed stone-built local, enjoyable good value food inc freshly cooked pies, well kept Bays and a guest ale, log fire, copper and brass in bar and dining room; children welcome, pleasant back terrace (Geoff and Marianne Millin, Paul and Dawn Rundle)

ISLES OF SCILLY

ST AGNES [SV8808]

☆ *Turks Head* TR22 0PL [The Quay]: One of the UK's most beautifully placed pubs, idyllic sea and island views from garden terrace, can get very busy on fine days, good food from pasties to popular fresh seafood (best to get there early), friendly licensees and good cheerful service, well kept ales and cider; has been cl winter, open all day other times (Michael Sargent, Bob and Margaret Holder, Nick Hawksley, LYM, Dr and Mrs R E S Tanner)

ST MARY'S [SV9010]

☆ *Atlantic Inn* TR21 0HY [The Strand; next to but independent from Atlantic Hotel]: Spreading and hospitable dark bar with well kept St Austell ales, good range of food, sea-view restaurant, low beams, hanging boat and other nauticalia, mix of locals and tourists – busy evenings, quieter on sunny lunchtimes; darts, pool, games machines, piped and live music; nice raised verandah with wide views over harbour, good bedrooms in adjacent hotel (Michael Sargent, Neil and Anita Christopher, Bob and Margaret Holder, BB)

Bishop & Wolf TR21 0LL [Hugh St/Silver St (A3110)]: Sea/boating décor with secluded corners and gallery above road, lots of woodwork and maritime bric-a-brac, St Austell ales, decent bar food, upstairs restaurant and sports bar; piped music and some live; children welcome, terrace picnic-sets, open all day (Neil and Anita Christopher)

Mermaid TR21 0HY [The Bank]: Splendid picture-window views across town beach and harbour from all-day back restaurant extension doing good local fish, efficient service, unpretentious dimly lit bar with lots of seafaring relics and ceiling flags, stone floor and rough timber, big stove, Ales of Scilly, simple bar food, pool; packed Weds and Fri when the gigs race; cellar bar with boat counter, TV and piped music (may be live wknds) (Neil and Anita Christopher)

The letters and figures after the name of each town are its Ordnance Survey map reference. 'Using the *Guide*' at the beginning of the book explains how it helps you find a pub, in road atlases or on large-scale maps as well as on our own maps.

Cumbria

Stunning scenery and fantastic walks surround many of the pubs and inns in this county and so it's essential that they offer an informal bar, hearty lunchtime food, and a warm fire for often damp and chilly walkers; it helps if dogs are welcome, too. Pubs on top form this year include the White Hart at Bouth (bustling and friendly with six real ales and decent food), the Blacksmiths Arms at Broughton Mills (consistently interesting food and an amiable atmosphere), the Masons Arms at Cartmel Fell (extremely popular for food, real ales and super views), the Punch Bowl in Crosthwaite (the new licensee is settling in well), the Highland Drove in Great Salkeld (well run and friendly with enjoyable food), the Drunken Duck near Hawkshead (at its most pubby at lunchtime), the Watermill at Ings (up to 16 real ales including their own, well liked food and plenty of character), the Sun in Kirkby Lonsdale (a good balance between a pub and restaurant), the Strickland Arms in Levens (handy for Sizergh Castle and with a genuinely friendly welcome), the Three Shires at Little Langdale (in the same family for 28 years now), the Kirkstile Inn at Loweswater (a smashing all-rounder), the Newfield Inn at Seathwaite (a great pub for walkers and climbers), the Farmers Arms at Ulverston (a busy and lively town pub), the Brown Horse at Winster (estate produce for the first-rate food) and the Gate Inn at Yanwath (excellent food and really welcoming staff). Our two new entries are the Mill Inn at Mungrisdale (a bustling pub in a fine setting) and the Church House in Torver (enjoyable food cooked by chef/landlord but with a cheerful bar, too). And although there's some especially good food in many of the above pubs, the Gate Inn at Yanwath continues to shine through. It is our Cumbria Dining Pub 2011.

AMBLESIDE   NY3704   MAP 9

Golden Rule

Smithy Brow; follow Kirkstone Pass signpost from A591 on N side of town; LA22 9AS

Simple town local with cosy, relaxed atmosphere and real ales; no food

This no-frills town local doesn't change at all – which is just how its regular customers like it. The bar area has built-in wall seats around cast-iron-framed tables (one with a local map set into its top), horsebrasses on the black beams, assorted pictures on the walls, a welcoming winter fire and a relaxed atmosphere. Robinsons Cumbria Way, Dizzy Blonde, Double Hop, Hartleys XB, Hatters and Unicorn on handpump. A brass measuring rule hangs above the bar. There's also a back room with TV (not much used), a left-hand room with darts and a games machine, and a further room down a couple of steps on the right with lots of seating. The back yard has benches and a covered heated area, and the window boxes are especially colourful. There's no car park.

🍴 **No food.**

Robinsons ~ Tenant John Lockley ~ Real ale ~ No credit cards ~ (015394) 32257 ~
Children welcome away from bar ~ Dogs welcome ~ Open 11am-midnight

*Recommended by MP, Andy and Jill Kassube, Chris Sale, David and Sue Atkinson, Dr and Mrs A K Clarke,
Chris Johnson, Helen Clarke*

ARMATHWAITE

NY5046   MAP 10

Dukes Head

Off A6 a few miles S of Carlisle; turn right at T junction; CA4 9PB

**Friendly welcome, interesting food in comfortable lounge, real ales and heated outside
area; bedrooms**

This is a genuinely traditional inn in a quiet Eden Valley village and whether you are a
regular or a visitor, you can be sure of a friendly welcome from the knowledgeable
landlord. It's all nicely old-fashioned and the comfortable lounge bar has oak settles and
little armchairs among more upright seats, oak and mahogany tables, antique hunting
and other prints and some brass and copper powder-flasks above the open fire. Black
Sheep Bitter, Jennings Bitter and Lancaster Blonde on handpump, several wines by the
glass, Weston's cider and sometimes home-made lemonade and ginger beer; the separate
public bar has darts, table skittles, board games and TV. There are seats in a heated area
outside with more on the lawn behind; boules.

🍽 **Enjoyable bar food includes sandwiches, soup, hot potted shrimps, a salad of black
pudding, local sausage and chorizo topped with a poached egg and mustard vinaigrette,
vegetable red thai curry, steak, kidney and mushroom in ale pie, venison, pheasant and
rabbit hotpot, daily specials such as salmon and monkfish terrine, tartlet of red pepper,
onion and tomato with a cheese crust and lambs liver and onion gravy, and puddings like
proper sherry trifle and bread and butter pudding; they hold all sorts of themed food
evenings.** *Starters/Snacks: £3.95 to £6.95. Main Courses: £8.95 to £15.95. Puddings: £4.25 to
£4.75.*

Punch ~ Tenant Henry Lynch ~ Real ale ~ Bar food ~ Restaurant ~ (016974) 72226 ~ Children
welcome ~ Dogs allowed in bar and bedrooms ~ Open 11am(11.30 Sun)-11.30pm(12.30 Sat) ~
Bedrooms: £42.50S/£62.50S

*Recommended by Angus Lyon, Paul Boot, Christine and Neil Townend, Archibald Rankin, Roger and Anne Newbury,
Alan Thwaite*

BASSENTHWAITE

NY2332   MAP 9

Sun

Off A591 N of Keswick; CA12 4QP

Bustling old pub with good views, real ales and changing bar food

New licensees have taken over this white-rendered slate house, so we are keeping our
fingers crossed that things won't change too much. The rambling bar has low 17th-c
black oak beams, two good stone fireplaces with big winter log fires, built-in wall seats
and plush stools around heavy wooden tables and areas that stretch usefully back beside
the servery. Jennings Bitter, Cumberland Ale and Golden Host and a guest like Wychwood
Dirty Tackle on handpump. A huddle of white houses looks up to Skiddaw and other high
fells, and you can enjoy the view from the tables in the front yard by the rose bushes and
honeysuckle. The pub is handy for osprey viewing at Dodd Wood and the village is
charming.

🍽 **Bar food now includes sandwiches and filled baked potatoes, chicken liver pâté, black
pudding and bacon stack, cumberland sausage, liver and bacon, slow-braised lamb
shoulder, daily specials like pork steak in peppercorn sauce and tattie pot with red
cabbage, and puddings such as rice pudding and marmalade bread and butter pudding.**
Starters/Snacks: £3.50 to £7.95. Main Courses: £7.95 to £15.20. Puddings: £3.95

Jennings (Marstons) ~ Lease Mike and Susan Arnold ~ Real ale ~ Bar food (12-5, 6-9) ~
(017687) 76439 ~ Children welcome ~ Dogs allowed in bar ~ Open 12-11.30(10.30 Sun)

Recommended by Adrian Johnson, Tina and David Woods-Taylor, G Jennings, Geoff and Linda Payne, Rob and Catherine Dunster, Sylvia and Tony Birbeck

BASSENTHWAITE LAKE   NY1930   MAP 9

Pheasant ★ ⑪ 🍷 🛏

Follow Pheasant Inn sign at N end of dual carriageway stretch of A66 by Bassenthwaite Lake; CA13 9YE

Charming, old-fashioned bar in smart hotel with enjoyable bar food and a fine range of drinks; comfortable bedrooms

They've opened a new bistro in this civilised and well run hotel which will provide an alternative to the lunchtime bar food and more formal restaurant menu. It's the surprisingly pubby and old-fashioned bar here that many of our readers enjoy dropping into for a quiet pint or informal lunch. There are mellow polished walls, cushioned oak settles, rush-seat chairs and library seats, hunting prints and photographs, and Bass, Coniston Bluebird and Cumberland Corby Ale on handpump served by friendly, knowledgeable staff; also, 12 good wines by the glass and over 60 malt whiskies. Several comfortable lounges have log fires, beautiful flower arrangements, fine parquet flooring, antiques and plants. Dogs are allowed in the residents' lounge at lunchtime and they do let them into the bar during the day too, unless people are eating. There are seats in the garden, attractive woodland surroundings and plenty of walks in all directions.

⑪ **Enjoyable if not particularly cheap, the lunchtime bar food includes open sandwiches, ploughman's, good soup with home-made bread, chicken liver or stilton, walnut and apricot pâté, their own potted silloth shrimps, cumberland sausage braised in red wine, poached haddock with wilted spinach, a poached egg and light cheese sauce, shepherd's pie, daily specials and puddings.** *Starters/Snacks: £4.75 to £8.00. Main Courses: £8.25 to £14.50. Puddings: £5.75*

Free house ~ Licensee Matthew Wylie ~ Real ale ~ Bar food (not in evening – restaurant and bistro only then) ~ Restaurant ~ (017687) 76234 ~ Children over 8 only ~ Dogs allowed in bar and bedrooms ~ Open 11.30-2.30, 5.30-10.30(11 Sat); 12-2.30, 6-10.30 Sun ~ Bedrooms: £85B/£160B

Recommended by Louise Gibbons, Stuart Turner, Noel Grundy, Sylvia and Tony Birbeck, John and Sylvia Harrop, Mike and Sue Loseby, Adrian Johnson, Henry Midwinter, Pat and Stewart Gordon, W K Wood

BEETHAM   SD4979   MAP 7

Wheatsheaf 🍷

Village (and inn) signposted just off A6 S of Milnthorpe; LA7 7AL

17th-c inn with handsome timbered cornerpiece, lots of beams, interesting food and quite a choice of drinks

Opposite a pretty 14th-c church, this is a striking old coaching inn in a quiet village. There's an opened-up front lounge bar with lots of exposed beams and joists and the main bar (behind on the right) has an open fire. Thwaites Guzzler and Tirril Queen Jean on handpump, several wines by the glass and quite a few malt whiskies. Two upstairs dining rooms are open only at weekends; quiet piped music. Plenty of surrounding walks.

⑪ **Often interesting, the good bar food includes sandwiches, ploughman's, soup, potted shrimps, mushroom, garlic and stilton pepper pot, gammon with orange, honey and pineapple, sausage and mash, steak and mushroom in ale pie, slow-cooked lamb shoulder with mint, wine and herb gravy, pork tenderloin stuffed with armagnac prunes wrapped in bacon with pan juices and cream, halibut loin with hot buttered garlic prawns with lemon risotto and a scallop cream, and puddings such as rich chocolate pot and crème brûlée with boozy berries.** *Starters/Snacks: £4.95 to £6.95. Main Courses: £7.95 to £15.95. Puddings: £4.95*

Free house ~ Licensees Mr and Mrs Skelton ~ Real ale ~ Bar food (12-9) ~ Restaurant ~ (015395) 62123 ~ Children welcome ~ Open 12-11(10.30 Sun) ~ Bedrooms: £65B/£75B

Recommended by Ray and Winifred Halliday, Karen Eliot, Dennis Jones, Noel Grundy, William and Ann Reid

BOUTH

White Hart 🍺

Village signposted off A590 near Haverthwaite; LA12 8JB

Fine range of real ales, tasty bar food and plenty of bric-a-brac in a cheerful lakeland inn; good surrounding walks; bedrooms

Bustling and friendly, this is a cheerful inn with a thoroughly lakeland feel. The six real ales are quite a draw, too, and might include Black Sheep Bitter, Coniston Bluebird, Jennings Cumberland and three changing guests on handpump; 25 malt whiskies and several wines by the glass. The sloping ceilings and floors show the building's age and there are lots of old local photographs and bric-a-brac, farm tools, stuffed animals, a collection of long-stemmed clay pipes and two woodburning stoves; piped music. There are some seats outside and fine surrounding walks.

🍴 **Using local beef and lamb, the well liked bar food includes sandwiches, soup, garlic mushrooms, chicken korma, five-bean chilli, gammon and egg, steak in Guinness pie, cumberland sausage with rich onion and cranberry gravy, sirloin steak, and daily specials.** *Starters/Snacks: £4.75 to £6.95. Main Courses: £10.75 to £15.95. Puddings: £4.75*

Free house ~ Licensee Nigel Barton ~ Real ale ~ Bar food (12-2, 6-8.45; all day Sun) ~ Restaurant ~ (01229) 861229 ~ Children welcome ~ Dogs welcome ~ Open 12-11(10.30 Sun) ~ Bedrooms: £60S(£50B)/£90S(£70B)

Recommended by Rob and Penny Wakefield, Dr Peter Andrews, Dennis Jones, Alison Ball, Ian Walton, Blaise Vyner

BOWNESS-ON-WINDERMERE

SD4096 MAP 9

Hole in t' Wall 🍺

Lowside; LA23 3DH

Bustling old pub with split-level rooms, country knick-knacks, real ales and traditional food

This is an interesting tavern that never changes and it's Bowness's oldest pub. The two split-level rooms have beams, stripped stone and flagstones, lots of country bric-a-brac and old pictures and there's a splendid log fire under a vast slate mantelpiece (in summer the logs are replaced with silk flowers); the upper room has attractive plasterwork. Robinsons Double Hop, Hartleys XB and Unicorn on handpump and several wines by the glass; friendly staff, juke box and piped music. The small flagstoned front courtyard has sheltered picnic-sets under a large umbrella and outdoor heaters. The pub does get very busy during the tourist season.

🍴 **Decent bar food includes sandwiches, ploughman's, soup, deep-fried breaded camembert, cumberland sausage with onion gravy, beer-battered sole goujons, beef in Guinness pie, lasagne, slow-braised lamb shoulder, a daily changing vegetarian dish, and puddings like sticky toffee pudding and chocolate sponge.** *Starters/Snacks: £4.25 to £6.25. Main Courses: £7.95 to £11.75. Puddings: £3.95*

Robinsons ~ Tenant Susan Burnet ~ Real ale ~ Bar food (12-2.30, 6-8(8.30 in summer); 12-3, 4-7 Fri and Sat; not Sun evening) ~ (015394) 43488 ~ Children welcome ~ Open 11-11; 12-10.30 Sun

Recommended by Dennis Jones

Stars after the name of a pub show exceptional character and appeal. They don't mean extra comfort. And they are nothing to do with food quality, for which there's a separate knife-and-fork symbol. Even quite a basic pub can win stars, if it's individual enough.

BROUGHTON MILLS   SD2190   MAP 9

Blacksmiths Arms

Off A593 N of Broughton-in-Furness; LA20 6AX

Friendly little pub with imaginative food, local beers and open fires; fine surrounding walks

After a day on the fells, this amiable small pub and its warm log fires is just the place to head for. There are four little bars that are simply but attractively decorated with straightforward chairs and tables on ancient slate floors and they keep Dent Aviator, Hawkshead Bitter and Moorhouses Pride of Pendle on handpump, nine wines by the glass and summer farm cider; darts, cards and cribbage. The hanging baskets and tubs of flowers in front of the building are pretty in summer.

🍴 **Consistently good bar food includes lunchtime sandwiches and ploughman's, soup, smoked haddock fishcakes with poached free-range egg, crispy pancetta and pea purée, beef and mushroom pie with braised oxtail sauce and thyme mash, slow-braised lamb shoulder with minted gravy, corn-fed chicken with butter beans, chorizo and a red pesto dressing, bass with samphire and a shrimp, parsley and lemon butter, daily specials such as ham hock and black pudding terrine with home-made piccalilli and spatch-cocked partridge with a warm salad of pancetta, garlic and tomatoes with a pesto dressing, and puddings like apple and cinnamon brûlée with apple crisp and sticky toffee pudding with warm butterscotch sauce.** *Starters/Snacks: £3.95 to £7.95. Main Courses: £9.85 to £16.95. Puddings: £4.45*

Free house ~ Licensees Mike and Sophie Lane ~ Real ale ~ Bar food (12-2, 6-9; not Mon) ~ Restaurant ~ (01229) 716824 ~ Children welcome ~ Dogs welcome ~ Open 12-11(5-11 Mon); 12-10.30 Sun; 12-2.30, 5-11 Tues-Fri in winter; closed Mon lunchtime

Recommended by the Didler, Veronica Gwynn, Tina and David Woods-Taylor, John Luckes, E Ling, Michael Butler

---

CARLETON   NY5329   MAP 9

Cross Keys

Off A66 roundabout at Penrith on A686 to Alston, on right after 0.25 miles, after farmshop; CA11 8TP

Friendly refurbished pub with several connected seating areas, real ales and popular bar food

Although many customers are here to enjoy the tasty bar food, the friendly staff are just as happy if it is only a drink you're after. The beamed main bar has pubby tables and chairs on the light wooden floorboards, modern metal wall lights and pictures on the bare stone walls, and Theakstons Black Bull, Tirril 1823 and a changing guest on handpump. Steps lead down to a small area with high bar stools around a high drinking table and then upstairs to the restaurant – a light, airy room with big windows, large wrought-iron candelabras hanging from the vaulted ceiling, pale solid wooden tables and chairs and doors to a verandah. At the far end of the main bar, there's yet another couple of small connected bar rooms with darts, games machine, pool, juke box and dominoes; TV and piped music. There are fell views from the garden. This is under the same ownership as the Highland Drove in Great Salkeld.

🍴 **Pleasing bar food includes filled baguettes, soup, chicken liver pâté with cumberland sauce, spicy devilled mushrooms, platters to share, home-made burger, beer-battered haddock, wild mushroom and leek risotto, steak in ale pie, honey-roast ham hock with parsnip and dijon mustard mash and cider jus, caramelised duck breast with cherry sauce, and puddings like vanilla panna cotta with sweet star anise syrup and chocolate and caramel cheesecake with chantilly cream.** *Starters/Snacks: £3.95 to £5.95. Main Courses: £7.95 to £17.95. Puddings: £4.95*

Free house ~ Licensee Paul Newton ~ Real ale ~ Bar food (12-2.30, 5.30(6 Sun and in winter)-9(8.30 Sun); not 25 Dec or 1 Jan) ~ Restaurant ~ (01768) 865588 ~ Children welcome ~ Dogs allowed in bar ~ Open 12-3, 5-midnight; midday-1am(midnight Sun) Sat

Recommended by Helen Clarke, Phil Bryant, Michael Doswell

CARTMEL

SD3778 MAP 7

Kings Arms

The Square, off Causeway; LA11 6QB

Timbered pub in an ancient village with seats facing lovely village square

If you arrive at this timbered pub early, you might be lucky enough to bag one of the prized seats outside overlooking the square; there's a fine medieval stone gatehouse nearby. Inside, the neatly kept, rambling bar has small antique prints on the walls, a mixture of seats including old country chairs, settles and wall banquettes, maybe fresh flowers on the tables, and tankards hanging over the bar counter. A friendly atmosphere, quite a mix of customers, Barngates Tag Lag, Bass and Hawkshead Bitter and Red on handpump and several wines by the glass; good service and piped music.

🍴 **Traditional bar food includes lunchtime sandwiches, home-made rump burger with bacon and cheese, beer-battered cod, cumberland sausage with onion gravy, gammon and egg, butternut squash and minted pea risotto, steak in Guinness pie, slow-cooked lamb shoulder, and puddings such as lemon and vanilla pod cheesecake and sticky toffee pudding.** *Starters/Snacks: £4.65 to £7.00. Main Courses: £6.95 to £19.50. Puddings: £5.25*

Enterprise ~ Lease Richard Grimmer ~ Real ale ~ Bar food (12-2.30, 5.30-8.30) ~ Restaurant ~ (01539) 536220 ~ Children welcome ~ Dogs allowed in bar ~ Open 11-11(10.30 Sun)

Recommended by Pat and Stewart Gordon, Pat and Tony Martin, JDM, KM

CARTMEL FELL

SD4189 MAP 9

Masons Arms 🍺

Strawberry Bank, a few miles S of Windermere between A592 and A5074; perhaps the simplest way of finding the pub is to go uphill W from Bowland Bridge (which is signposted off A5074) towards Newby Bridge and keep right then left at the staggered crossroads – it's then on your right, below Gummer's How; OS Sheet 97 map reference 413895; LA11 6NW

Plenty of character in beamed bar, good food, real ales plus many foreign bottled beers, and fine views from terrace

Not easy to find but well worth the effort when you do, this well run pub is a friendly place with good food and drink. It's in a lovely spot with stunning views down over the Winster Valley to the woods below Whitbarrow Scar – rustic benches and tables on the terrace make the most of this. Inside, the main bar has plenty of character, with low black beams in the bowed ceiling and country chairs and plain wooden tables on polished flagstones. A small lounge has oak tables and settles to match its fine Jacobean panelling, there's a plain little room beyond the serving counter with pictures and a fire in an open range, a family room with an old-parlourish atmosphere and an upstairs dining room; piped music and board games. Black Sheep Bitter, Cumbrian Dickie Doodle, Hawkshead Bitter and Lakeland Gold and Thwaites Wainwright on handpump, quite a few foreign bottled beers, several wines by the glass and locally made damson beer and gin. There are comfortable self-catering cottages and apartments behind.

🍴 **Very good bar food includes lunchtime sandwiches and ciabattas, soup, black pudding on a toasted muffin with mushrooms, bacon and a soft poached egg, sticky spare ribs, steak burger with cheese and onion rings, battered haddock with mushy peas, pork and apple sausages with red wine onion gravy, chicken tikka masala, daily specials such as fillet of sea trout with prawn and parsley sauce and wild mushroom and leek risotto, and puddings like clotted cream cheesecake with Drambuie-soaked fruits and chocolate muddie.** *Starters/Snacks: £5.95 to £7.95. Main Courses: £9.95 to £16.95. Puddings: £5.25 to £7.45*

Individual Inns ~ Managers John and Diane Taylor ~ Real ale ~ Bar food (12-2.30, 6-9; all day weekends) ~ Restaurant ~ (015395) 68486 ~ Children welcome ~ Open 11.30-11; 12-10.30 Sun

Recommended by Helen and Brian Edgeley, Ewan and Moira McCall, D M Heath, Tina and David Woods-Taylor, Nick Lawless, Brian Dawes, Bill Adie, G Jennings, Alison Ball, Ian Walton, Pat and Stewart Gordon, Mike Gorton, Anthony Green, Jo Lilley, Simon Calvert, Ann and Tony Bennett-Hughes, Mr and Mrs P R Thomas

CASTERTON
SD6379 MAP 7

Pheasant ♀

A683 about 1 mile N of junction with A65, by Kirkby Lonsdale; OS Sheet 97 map reference 633796; LA6 2RX

Neat beamed rooms in pleasant inn, real ales and well liked food; seats in attractive garden with fell views; bedrooms

Well run by a friendly family, this traditional 18th-c inn has beamed bars that are neatly kept and modernised. There are wheelback chairs and dark red button-back wall banquettes on the patterned carpets, a nicely arched oak-framed fireplace with a coal-effect gas fire, and Dent Aviator, Greene King Old Speckled Hen and Theakstons Best Bitter on handpump. Also, six wines by the glass, 19 malt whiskies, and helpful staff; piped music and board games. There are some tables under cocktail parasols outside by the road, with more in the pleasant garden. The nearby church (built for the girls' school of Brontë fame here) has some attractive pre-Raphaelite stained glass and paintings. More reports please.

🍴 As well as lunchtime sandwiches, the well liked bar food includes soup, smoked mackerel mousse, steak pie, vegetable lasagne, crispy battered haddock, popular roast beef with yorkshire pudding and gravy, breaded chicken suprême with a creamy mushroom sauce, crispy duckling with sage and onion stuffing and apple sauce, daily specials like goose and duck liver pâté, slow-roasted lamb shoulder with mint sauce and whole lemon sole in lemon butter, and puddings such as sherry trifle and sticky toffee pudding with hot toffee sauce. *Starters/Snacks: £4.00 to £8.00. Main Courses: £8.00 to £22.00. Puddings: £4.00 to £5.20*

Free house ~ Licensee the Dixon family ~ Real ale ~ Bar food (12-2, 6-9) ~ Restaurant ~ (015242) 71230 ~ Children welcome ~ Open 12-3, 6-11(10 Sun) ~ Bedrooms: £39B/£90B

Recommended by Ewan and Moira McCall, Pat and Stewart Gordon, Dr and Mrs T E Hothersall, Derek and Sylvia Stephenson

CLIFTON
NY5326 MAP 9

George & Dragon ⑪ ♀ 🛏

A6; near M6 junction 40; CA10 2ER

18th-c former coaching inn with attractive bars and sizeable restaurant, local ales, well chosen wines, enjoyable food and seats outside; bedrooms

This is a friendly old coaching inn done up with great style. There's a relaxed reception room with leather chairs around a low table in front of an open fire, bright rugs on flagstones, a table in a private nook to one side of the reception desk (just right for a group of six) and a comfortable bed for Porter the patterdale terrier. Through some wrought-iron gates is the main bar area with more cheerful rugs on flagstones, assorted wooden farmhouse chairs and tables, grey panelling topped with yellow-painted walls, photographs of the Lowther Estate and of the family with hunting dogs, various sheep and fell pictures and some high bar stools by the panelled bar counter. Hawkshead Bitter, Lancaster Blonde and a guest beer on handpump and 15 wines by the glass from a well chosen list. A further room with another open fire is similarly furnished. The sizeable restaurant to the left of the entrance is made up of four open-plan rooms: plenty of old pews and church chairs around tables set for dining, a woodburning stove and a contemporary open kitchen. Outside, there are tables on the decoratively paved front entrance with more in a high-walled enclosed courtyard, and a herb garden.

🍴 Enjoyable bar food includes sandwiches, soup, mushrooms with thyme on toast with a free-range egg, mussels in white wine and cream, shorthorn beefburger, rare-breed pork sausages with onion gravy, blue cheese risotto, a pie and a pasta dish of the day, venison medallions with a wild mushroom cream, specials like wild boar carpaccio with pear and truffle oil and monkfish with saffron potatoes and cucumber, and puddings such as dark chocolate mousse and rhubarb crumble; when available, they use produce from the estate. *Starters/Snacks: £4.50 to £6.95. Main Courses: £8.95 to £14.95. Puddings: £4.95 to £6.95*

Free house ~ Licensee Paul McKinnon ~ Real ale ~ Bar food (12-2.30, 6-9.30) ~ Restaurant ~ (01768) 865381 ~ Children welcome ~ Dogs allowed in bar and bedrooms ~ Open 12-11 ~ Bedrooms: £66.75S/£89S

Recommended by Michael Doswell, Malcolm and Jo Hart

COCKERMOUTH

NY1230   MAP 9

Bitter End ◖

Kirkgate, by cinema; CA13 9PJ

Own-brewed beers and lots of bottled beers in three interesting bars

Not surprisingly, this charming little pub does get pretty busy at peak times as many customers are keen to sample the eight real ales they keep on handpump. These include their own brews Bitter End Lakeland Amber, Best Gold, Bitter, Blonde, Honey and Pale Ale, and guests such as Jennings Bitter and Cumberland. Quite a few bottled beers from around the world and eight wines by the glass. The cosy main rooms have a different atmosphere in each – from quietly chatty to sporty, with the décor reflecting this, such as unusual pictures of a Cockermouth that even Wordsworth might have recognised, to more up-to-date sporting memorabilia, framed beer mats and various bottles, jugs and books; welcoming log fire and piped music. The public car park round the back is free after 7pm.

🍴 Quite a choice of bar food includes sandwiches, ham hock terrine with apricot chutney, mussels with white wine and cream, beer-battered haddock, tagliatelle with courgettes, lemon and pine nuts, home-made cheeseburger, steak in ale pie, lasagne, cumberland sausage with red onion marmalade and gravy, gammon and egg, fillet of pork with cider sauce, steaks and Sunday roasts. *Starters/Snacks: £3.25 to £6.95. Main Courses: £8.75 to £14.95. Puddings: £4.00*

Own brew ~ Licensee Susan Askey ~ Real ale ~ Bar food (12-2, 6-9) ~ (01900) 828993 ~ Children welcome ~ Open 12-2.30, 6-11; 12-midnight Sat; 12-3, 6-11 Sun

Recommended by Helen Clarke, Mr and Mrs Maurice Thompson, the Didler, Adrian Johnson, Geoff and Linda Payne, Pat and Stewart Gordon, Keith and Rowena Ward

CONISTON

SD3097   MAP 9

Black Bull ◖ 🛏

Yewdale Road (A593); LA21 8DU

Own-brewed beers, Donald Campbell memorabilia, walkers' bar and seats outside; bedrooms

The own-brewed beers here remain quite a draw: Coniston Bluebird Bitter and XB, Old Man Ale, Olivers Light Ale and Special Oatmeal Stout, all on handpump. It's a bustling old inn and the back area has slate flagstones and is liked by walkers and their dogs, while the beamed and carpeted front part has cast-iron-framed tables, comfortable banquettes and stools, an open fire and a relaxed, comfortable feel; there's quite a lot of memorabilia devoted to Donald Campbell's attempts at the water speed records. The residents' lounge contains the 'big toe' of the Old Man of Coniston – a large piece of stone in the wall. The former coachyard has plenty of tables and chairs; parking may not be easy at peak times. More reports please.

🍴 Usefully served all day, the bar food includes sandwiches and toasties, filled baked potatoes, ploughman's, soup, chicken liver pâté, morecambe bay potted shrimps, chilli con carne, beer-battered haddock, gammon and eggs, cumberland sausage, and daily specials such as sweet potato, chickpea and spinach curry and chicken breast stuffed with black pudding and wrapped in bacon with a white wine sauce. *Starters/Snacks: £5.95 to £6.95. Main Courses: £8.50 to £12.95. Puddings: £3.95 to £4.95*

Own brew ~ Licensee Ronald Edward Bradley ~ Real ale ~ Bar food (all day) ~ Restaurant ~ (015394) 41335/41668 ~ Children welcome ~ Dogs allowed in bar and bedrooms ~ Open 8am-11pm ~ Bedrooms: £49.50S/£90S

Recommended by Tony Goff, Mr and Mrs D J Nash, Michael Butler, Angus Lyon

CROSTHWAITE

SD4491 MAP 9

Punch Bowl ⊕ 🍷 🛏

Village signposted off A5074 SE of Windermere; LA8 8HR

Civilised dining pub, fine choice of drinks, impressive food, good wines and real ales, and seats on terrace overlooking the valley; lovely bedrooms

A new licensee has taken over this stylish place and our readers have enjoyed their visits very much – it's a fine all-rounder. The public bar is raftered and hop-hung with a couple of eye-catching rugs on flagstones, bar stools by the slate-topped counter, Barngates Tag Lag and Westmorland Gold, Ulverston Another Fine Mess and guest beers on handpump, 22 wines by the glass and around a dozen malt whiskies; very friendly, helpful staff. This room opens on the right into two linked carpeted and beamed rooms with well spaced country pine furnishings of varying sizes, including a big refectory table. The walls, painted in restrained neutral tones, have an attractive assortment of prints, and there are some copper objects and a dresser with china and glass; winter log fire, woodburning stove, lots of fresh flowers and daily papers. On the left, the wooden-floored restaurant area (also light, airy and attractive) has comfortable high-backed leather dining chairs. Throughout, the pub feels relaxing and nicely uncluttered. There are some tables on a terrace stepped into the hillside, overlooking the lovely Lyth Valley. This is a good place to stay and the bedrooms are well equipped and comfortable.

🍴 **Excellent restaurant-style food includes lunchtime sandwiches, soup, tempura king prawns and salt and pepper calamari with black rice wine and soy dressing, home-smoked saddle of venison, pumpkin, parmesan and sage risotto, braised lamb shoulder with garlic mousseline potatoes and rosemary jus, rustic beef bourguignon, fillet of cod with broccoli and toasted almonds, specials like smoked ham hock terrine, local rose veal with celeriac, puy lentils and madeira jus and T-bone steak with béarnaise or peppercorn sauce, and puddings such as passion-fruit soufflé with dark chocolate sorbet and apple and rhubarb crumble.** *Starters/Snacks: £3.95 to £8.95. Main Courses: £9.95 to £18.95. Puddings: £4.50 to £8.50*

Free house ~ Licensee Chris Meredith ~ Real ale ~ Bar food (all day) ~ Restaurant ~ (015395) 68237 ~ Children welcome ~ Dogs allowed in bar ~ Open 11-11 ~ Bedrooms: £93.75B/£125B

Recommended by Anthony Green, Pat and Graham Williamson, D M Heath, Michael Harrison, David Thornton, Bill Adie, G Jennings, Rob and Catherine Dunster, Karen Eliot

ELTERWATER

NY3204 MAP 9

Britannia ◀

Off B5343; LA22 9HP

Extremely popular inn surrounded by wonderful walks and scenery; six real ales and well liked food; bedrooms

As there are walks of every gradient right from the front door and it's in such wonderful scenery, this pub does get packed at peak times. The atmosphere is old-fashioned and the little front bar has beams and a couple of window seats that look across to Elterwater itself through the trees; the small back bar is traditionally furnished: thick slate walls, winter coal fires, oak benches, settles, windsor chairs and a big old rocking chair. Coniston Bluebird and a beer from Coniston named for the pub, Dent Aviator, Cumbrian Loweswater Gold, Jennings Bitter and Thwaites Wainwright on handpump, and quite a few malt whiskies. The lounge is comfortable and there's a hall and dining room. Plenty of seats outside and summer morris and step garland dancers.

🍴 **All-day bar food includes filled rolls, ploughman's, soup, pâté with port sauce, morecambe bay shrimps, beer-battered fresh haddock, chicken, ham and leek pie, wild and button mushroom stroganoff and cumberland sausage with onion gravy, with evening dishes such as slow-braised lamb shoulder with mint and honey and duck breast with black pudding and red wine and redcurrant jus, and puddings like profiteroles with warm chocolate sauce and sticky toffee pudding with hot toffee sauce.** *Starters/Snacks: £4.50 to £5.90. Main Courses: £8.70 to £12.50. Puddings: £4.80 to £5.40*

Free house ~ Licensee Clare Woodhead ~ Real ale ~ Bar food (all day) ~ Restaurant ~ (015394) 37210 ~ Children welcome ~ Dogs allowed in bar and bedrooms ~ Open 10.30am-11pm ~ Bedrooms: £60S/£90S

Recommended by Noel Grundy, Mr and Mrs Maurice Thompson, Tina and David Woods-Taylor, Ewan and Moira McCall, David and Sue Atkinson, Mr and Mrs J Hilton, Alison Ball, Ian Walton, G Jennings, Mrs Pam Mattinson, J Woodgate, John and Helen Rushton, Michael Doswell, Chris Johnson, Jo Lilley, Simon Calvert

GREAT SALKELD

NY5536 MAP 10

Highland Drove 🍴

B6412, off A686 NE of Penrith; CA11 9NA

Bustling place with a cheerful mix of customers, good food in several dining areas, fair choice of drinks, and fine views from upstairs verandah; bedrooms

'All that a village pub should be' says one of our readers and many others agree with him. It's well run and neatly kept and the friendly staff are sure to make you welcome. The chatty main bar has sandstone flooring, stone walls, cushioned wheelback chairs around a mix of tables and an open fire in a raised stone fireplace. The downstairs eating area has more cushioned dining chairs around wooden tables on the pale wooden floorboards, stone walls and ceiling joists and a two-way fire in a raised stone fireplace that separates this room from the coffee lounge with its comfortable leather chairs and sofas. There's also an upstairs restaurant. Best to book to be sure of a table. Theakstons Black Bull and a couple of guests such as Hydes Over A Barrel and John Smiths on handpump, several wines by the glass and 23 malt whiskies. Piped music, TV, juke box, darts, pool, games machine and dominoes. The lovely views over the Eden Valley and the Pennines are best enjoyed from seats on the upstairs verandah. There are more seats on the back terrace.

🍴 Good food includes lunchtime filled baguettes and ploughman's, soup, scotch egg with sausagemeat and black pudding with a green peppercorn sauce, home-cured bresaola with parmesan mousse and pesto dressing, beer-battered haddock, home-made beefburger, wild mushroom and leek risotto, cumberland sausage with onion gravy, fruity chicken curry, steak in ale pie, honey-roasted ham hock with mustard mash and cider jus, and puddings like chocolate and caramel cheesecake and apple and almond torte with crème anglaise; smashing Sunday roasts. *Starters/Snacks: £2.95 to £7.95. Main Courses: £7.95 to £17.95. Puddings: £4.50*

Free house ~ Licensees Donald and Paul Newton ~ Real ale ~ Bar food (12-2, 6-9; not Mon lunchtime) ~ Restaurant ~ (01768) 898349 ~ Children welcome ~ Dogs allowed in bar ~ Open 12-3, 6-midnight; 12-midnight Sat; closed Mon lunchtime ~ Bedrooms: £40S/£70S

Recommended by Chris Millar, Richard J Holloway, Dr Kevan Tucker, Chris and Jo Parsons, Maurice and Gill McMahon, Dave Braisted, Mike and Lynn Robinson

HAWKSHEAD

NY3501 MAP 9

Drunken Duck 🍴 🍷 🍺 🛏

Barngates; the hamlet is signposted from B5286 Hawkshead—Ambleside, opposite the Outgate Inn; or it may be quicker to take the first right from B5286, after the wooded caravan site; OS Sheet 90 map reference 350013; LA22 0NG

Stylish small bar, several restaurant areas, own-brewed beers and bar meals as well as innovative restaurant choices; lovely bedrooms, stunning views

This civilised inn is a lovely place to stay and the evening food in three restaurant areas is excellent – but during the day there's much more of an informal, almost pubby, feel and it's popular for lunch after a walk; get there early if you want a seat. The small, smart bar has leather bar stools by the slate-topped bar counter, leather club chairs, beams and oak floorboards, photographs, coaching prints and hunting pictures on the walls, and some kentish hop bines. From their Barngates brewery, there might be Cracker, Moth Bag, Red Bull Terrier and Westmorland Gold on handpump as well as 17 wines by the glass from a fine list, a good choice of spirits, and belgian and german draught beers. The bedrooms are beautifully appointed. Outside, wooden tables and benches on grass opposite the building offer spectacular views across the fells, and there are thousands of spring and summer bulbs.

🍴 From the lunch menu (until 4pm), the good bar food includes sandwiches (which you can take away as well), ploughman's, soup, pork, potted duck, boiled duck egg, pickled onion and gherkins, pork, chicken and stuffing pie with air-dried ham and piccalilli, fish of the day with herb butter, confit duck leg with rösti potato, and corn-fed chicken breast with fondant potato and pan-jus; more pricey evening choices such as confit rabbit terrine, venison and duck liver parfait with fig chutney, crab and shrimp tortellini with prawn bisque, gnocchi with wild mushrooms, truffle oil and parmesan, loin of venison with puy lentils, pancetta and sweet potato purée, pied bleu mushrooms and game jus, halibut with chorizo, herb mash and balsamic jus, and puddings like baked chocolate mousse cake with candied fennel and pineapple brûlée, passion fruit, caramelised pineapple and coconut sorbet; an interesting cheeseboard, too. *Starters/Snacks: £3.95 to £7.95. Main Courses: £7.95 to £15.95. Puddings: £5.50 to £7.50*

Own brew ~ Licensee Steph Barton ~ Real ale ~ Bar food (12-4, 6.30-9.30) ~ Restaurant ~ (015394) 36347 ~ Children welcome ~ Dogs allowed in bar ~ Open 11.30-11; 12-10.30 Sun ~ Bedrooms: £90B/£120B

Recommended by Chris Johnson, Brian Dawes, David and Sue Atkinson, Janet and Peter Race, Mike and Sue Loseby, Peter and Eleanor Kenyon, Martin and Pauline Jennings, Simon Rodway, Mr and Mrs Maurice Thompson, Noel Grundy, Tim and Rosemary Wells

HESKET NEWMARKET
NY3438   MAP 10

Old Crown 🍺
Village signposted off B5299 in Caldbeck; CA7 8JG

Straightforward local with own-brewed beers in an attractive village

The own-brewed real ales are still the main strong draw to this unpretentious local. On handpump these might include Hesket Newmarket Blencathra Bitter, Doris's 90th Birthday Ale, Great Cockup Porter, Haystacks Refreshing Ale, Helvellyn Gold, Skiddaw Special Bitter, Old Carrock Strong Ale, Catbells Pale Ale and Sca Fell Blonde. The little bar has a few tables, a winter log fire, bric-a-brac, mountaineering kit and pictures, and a friendly atmosphere; darts, board games, pool and juke box. There's also a dining room and garden room. The pub is in a pretty setting in a remote, attractive village. You can book tours (a minimum of eight people) to look round the brewery: £10 for the tour and a meal. More reports please.

🍴 Bar food includes lunchtime sandwiches, filled baguettes and soup, evening choices such as a meaty or vegetarian curry, cumberland sausage, steak in ale pie, and beer-battered haddock, and puddings like apple crumble and bakewell tart; Sunday roasts. *Starters/Snacks: £3.50 to £4.75. Main Courses: £7.50 to £13.00. Puddings: £4.00*

Own brew ~ Lease Keith Graham ~ Real ale ~ Bar food (12-2, 6.30-9; not Mon-Thurs lunchtimes (but does food Weds and Thurs lunchtimes in school hols) ~ Restaurant ~ (016974) 78288 ~ Children welcome ~ Dogs allowed in bar ~ Open 12-2.30, 5.30-11(10.30 Sun); closed Mon-Thurs lunchtimes (open Weds and Thurs lunchtimes in school hols)

Recommended by Mike and Sue Loseby, Maurice and Gill McMahon, Stephen Colling

INGS
SD4498   MAP 9

Watermill 🍺
Just off A591 E of Windermere; LA8 9PY

Busy, cleverly converted pub with fantastic range of real ales including own brews; well liked food; bedrooms

'I wish this was my local' say so many of our readers about this well run, bustling inn. There's a fantastic choice of real ales served by efficient, friendly staff, enjoyable food usefully served all day, and it's a popular place to stay overnight, too (some bedrooms are bigger than others). The building has plenty of character and is cleverly converted from a wood mill and joiner's shop and the bars have a lively atmosphere, a happy mix of chairs, padded benches and solid oak tables, bar counters made from old church wood, open fires, and interesting photographs and amusing cartoons by a local artist. The spacious lounge bar, in much the same traditional style as the other rooms, has rocking chairs and a big open fire. As well as their own brewed Watermill A Bit'er Ruff and Wruff Night, Collie Wobbles, Dogth Vadar and Isle of Dogs, they keep up to 11 other beers on handpump: Bitter End Bitter, Blackbeck Black Belle, Coniston Bluebird, Cumbrian Grasmoor Dark Ale, Foxfield Sands and Some Like It Stout, Hawkshead Bitter, Moorhouses Black Cat, Theakstons Old Peculier and Wensleydale Falconer. They have a beer festival in May. Also, scrumpy cider, a huge choice of foreign bottled beers and 40 malt whiskies; darts and board games. Seats in the gardens and lots to do nearby. Dogs may get free biscuits and water.

🍴 Using their own reared beef, the good bar food includes lunchtime sandwiches, filled baguettes and filled baked potatoes, soup, garlic mushrooms, pâté with home-made cumberland sauce, various platters, lasagne, mediterranean pasta bake, cumberland sausage with beer and onion gravy, beer-battered haddock, chicken with a creamy mustard and rosemary sauce, daily specials like lamb casserole, spicy pork and fish of the day, and puddings such as apple and cinnamon crumble and hot chocolate fudge cake. *Starters/Snacks: £3.85 to £5.95. Main Courses: £9.75 to £13.95. Puddings: £4.25 to £4.75*

Free house ~ Licensee Brian Coulthwaite ~ Real ale ~ Bar food (12-9) ~ (01539) 821309 ~ Children welcome ~ Dogs allowed in bar and bedrooms ~ Storytelling first Tues of the month ~ Open 11.45-11(10.30 Sun) ~ Bedrooms: £44S/£78S

Recommended by Dennis Jones, Jo Lilley, Simon Calvert, Michael Tack, Mike Ernest, JDM, KM, Paul Boot, J S Burn, Andy and Jill Kassube, Mike and Sue Loseby, the Didler, Margaret and Jeff Graham, John Clancy, Mr and Mrs Maurice Thompson, Martin Smith, Steve Whalley, A N Bance, Alison Ball, Ian Walton, Mike Gorton, Mr and Mrs Ian King, John and Helen Rushton, Chris Johnson, DC, Maurice and Gill McMahon, Joe Green

KESWICK

NY2623   MAP 9

Dog & Gun 🍺

Lake Road; off top end of Market Square; CA12 5BT

Buzzy and unpretentious town pub with popular food and drink

Bustling and friendly, this town pub has a good-natured atmosphere and a cheerful mix of both locals and visitors – and dogs are genuinely welcomed, too. The homely bar has low beams, a partly slate floor (the rest are carpeted or bare boards), some high settles, a fine collection of striking mountain photographs by the local firm G P Abrahams, brass and brewery artefacts and coins (which go to the Mountain Rescue Service) in beams and timbers by the fireplace. Hawkshead Bitter and Lakeland Gold, Keswick Thirst Rescue and Thirst Run, Theakstons Old Peculier and Yates Bitter on handpump.

🍴 As well as their extremely popular goulash, bar food includes sandwiches, filled baked potatoes, ploughman's, chicken liver pâté, sausage and mash, vegetable curry, chicken stuffed with cheese and wrapped in bacon, steak in ale pie, daily specials, and puddings such as sticky toffee pudding or jam roly-poly; no fried food at all. *Starters/Snacks: £3.95 to £4.95. Main Courses: £6.30 to £10.95. Puddings: £4.30 to £5.95*

Orchid ~ Manager Peter Ede ~ Real ale ~ Bar food (all day) ~ (017687) 73463 ~ Children welcome if dining with adults before 9pm ~ Dogs welcome ~ Open 12-11

Recommended by Phil Bryant, Helen Clarke, Mike and Sue Loseby, John Luckes, Bill Adie, Chris and Jo Parsons, Geoff and Linda Payne, Brendon Skinner, Ian and Jane Haslock, Mr and Mrs Maurice Thompson, Michael Tack, Rob and Catherine Dunster

---

'Children welcome' means the pub says it lets children inside without any special restriction. If it allows them in, but to restricted areas such as an eating area or family room, we specify this. Some pubs may impose an evening time limit. We do not mention limits after 9pm as we assume children are home by then.

KIRKBY LONSDALE

SD6178   MAP 7

Sun 🏮 ♟ 🛏
Market Street (B6254); LA6 2AU

Nice contrast between mellow bar and stylish contemporary restaurant, good interesting food and several real ales; comfortable bedrooms

As friendly and efficiently run as ever, this 17th-c inn achieves the pub/restaurant balance perfectly. The attractive rambling bar has two log fires and some interesting seats from pews to armchairs to cosy window seats; also, beams, flagstones and stripped oak boards, nice lighting, and big landscapes and country pictures on the cream walls above its handsome panelled dado. There's also a back lounge with a leather sofa and comfortable chairs. Hawkshead Bitter, Timothy Taylors Landlord and Thwaites Wainwright on handpump, several wines by the glass and 10 malt whiskies; helpful, welcoming staff and piped music. The back dining room is very up to date: comfortable tall-backed seats and tables on woodstrip flooring, a clean-cut cream and red décor with a modicum of stripped stone and attractive plain modern crockery. It's an unusual-looking building with its upper floors supported by three sturdy pillars above the pavement and a modest front door.

🍴 **At lunchtime, the enjoyable bar food includes sandwiches, soup, ham hock terrine with pineapple chutney, mussels in white wine and cream, battered cod with crème fraîche and pea shoots, artichoke, beetroot and tomato tarte tatin, and chicken, bacon and mushroom pie; evening choices such as chicken livers and mushrooms on toasted brioche, braised beef cheeks with steak, oyster and kidney pudding, breast of goosnargh duck and cassoulet and king scallops with haggis, whisky mustard, neeps and tatties, and puddings like chocolate and caramel fondant with vanilla ice-cream and almond and honey crème brûlée with orange florentines; Sunday roasts.** *Starters/Snacks: £4.25 to £7.95. Main Courses: £10.95 to £18.95. Puddings: £4.25*

Free house ~ Licensee Mark Fuller ~ Real ale ~ Bar food ~ Restaurant ~ (015242) 71965 ~ Children welcome ~ Dogs allowed in bar and bedrooms ~ Open 9am-11pm; closed till 3pm Mon ~ Bedrooms: £70B/£100S(£110B)

Recommended by Ray and Winifred Halliday, Pat Crabb, G and P Vago, Stu Mac, Michael Doswell, John and Eileen Mennear, Maurice and Gill McMahon, Dennis Jones

LANGDALE

NY2806   MAP 9

Old Dungeon Ghyll 🍺
B5343; LA22 9JY

Straightforward place in lovely position with real ales and fine walks; bedrooms

At the heart of the Great Langdale Valley and surrounded by fells including the Langdale Pikes flanking the Dungeon Ghyll Force waterfall, this straightforward and friendly local is the perfect place for damp walkers and climbers. The whole feel of the place is basic but cosy and there's no need to remove boots or muddy trousers – you can sit on seats in old cattle stalls by the big warming fire and enjoy Hawkshead Lakeland Gold, Salamander Mudpuppy, Theakstons Old Peculier, Yates Bitter and guest beers on handpump; up to 20 malt whiskies and farm cider. Darts and board games. It may get lively on a Saturday night (there's a popular National Trust campsite opposite).

🍴 **Decent helpings of traditional food include lunchtime sandwiches, filled baked potatoes and ploughman's as well as soup, pizzas, spicy chilli, battered haddock, half a chicken with chips and cumberland sausage with onion gravy.** *Starters/Snacks: £4.00 to £6.00. Main Courses: £8.25 to £11.95. Puddings: £4.75*

Free house ~ Licensee Neil Walmsley ~ Real ale ~ Bar food (12-2, 6-9) ~ Restaurant ~ (015394) 37272 ~ Children welcome ~ Dogs welcome ~ Folk music first Weds evening of the month ~ Open 11-11(10.30 Sun); closed Christmas week ~ Bedrooms: £51/£102(£112S)

Recommended by Dave Irving, Jenny Huggins, Chris Johnson, Simon Daws, the Didler, Ewan and Moira McCall, Tim Maddison, Mike Gorton, John and Helen Rushton

LEVENS

Strickland Arms ♀ ◀

4 miles from M6 junction 36, via A590; just off A590, by Sizergh Castle gates; LA8 8DZ

Friendly, open-plan pub with much enjoyed food, local ales and a fine setting; seats outside

Run by helpful, friendly people this extremely popular dining pub is in a fine spot by the entrance to Sizergh Castle. It's largely open plan with a light and airy modern feel, and the bar on the right has oriental rugs on the flagstones, a log fire, Thwaites Lancaster Bomber and Wainwright and a couple of guests from breweries like Kirkby Lonsdale and Tirril on handpump, 30 malt whiskies and a dozen wines by the glass. On the left are polished boards and another log fire, and throughout there's a nice mix of sturdy country furniture, candles on tables, hunting scenes and other old prints on the walls, heavy fabric for the curtains and some staffordshire china ornaments; it's best to book ahead if you want to eat downstairs but there is a further dining room upstairs. Piped music and board games. The flagstoned front terrace has plenty of seats. The castle, in fact a lovely partly medieval house with beautiful gardens, is open in the afternoon (not Friday or Saturday) from April to October. They have disabled access and facilities. The pub is owned by the National Trust.

〒 Using estate beef and other local produce, the good bar food includes a very good value two-course lunch during the week as well as lunchtime sandwiches and filled baguettes, soup, ham hock and peach terrine with damson chutney, home-potted morecambe bay shrimps, saffron potato, spinach, mushroom and cheese pie, beer-battered fish with mushy peas, beef in ale pie, gammon with pineapple and a free-range egg, lamb hotpot, specials such as pigeon breast with chutney and chargrilled tuna steak with red onion and coriander pesto, and puddings like rich chocolate mousse and raspberry eton mess. *Starters/Snacks: £4.25 to £6.25. Main Courses: £9.95 to £15.95. Puddings: £4.00 to £6.25*

Free house ~ Licensees Kerry Parsons and Martin Ainscough ~ Real ale ~ Bar food (12-2(2.30 Sat), 6-9; all day Sun and bank hols) ~ (015395) 61010 ~ Children welcome ~ Dogs welcome ~ Live music every other month on Sun afternoon ~ Open 11.30-11; 12-10.30 Sun; 11.30-3, 5.30-11 weekdays in winter

Recommended by Andy and Claire Barker, Peter and Josie Fawcett, Andy and Jill Kassube, Margaret and Jeff Graham, Michael Doswell, Pat and Stewart Gordon, Michael Butler, John and Sylvia Harrop, Mike Gorton, Maurice and Gill McMahon, Jo Lilley, Simon Calvert, V and E A Bolton, Dr Kevan Tucker, Dr Peter Andrews, Mr and Mrs P R Thomas, Ray and Winifred Halliday

LITTLE LANGDALE

Three Shires ◀ 🛏

From A593 3 miles W of Ambleside take small road signposted The Langdales, Wrynose Pass; then bear left at first fork; LA22 9NZ

Friendly inn with valley views from seats on terrace, enjoyable food and several local real ales; comfortable bedrooms

There's always a good mix of customers in this popular inn – those dropping in for lunch after walking and many who are staying for a few days. It's the sort of place people tend to return to again and again and has been run by the same friendly family for 28 years now. There are warm winter fires and the comfortably extended back bar has a mix of green lakeland stone and homely red patterned wallpaper (which works rather well), stripped timbers and a beam-and-joist stripped ceiling, antique oak carved settles, country kitchen chairs and stools on its big dark slate flagstones, and lakeland photographs. An arch leads through to a small additional area and there's a front dining room. Coniston Old Man, Ennerdale Copper, Hawkshead Bitter and Jennings Cumberland on handpump, over 50 malt whiskies and a decent wine list; darts and board games. There are lovely views from seats on the terrace over the valley to the partly wooded hills below and more seats on a neat lawn behind the car park, backed by a small oak wood. The award-winning summer hanging baskets are very pretty. The three shires are the historical counties Cumberland, Westmorland and Lancashire, which meet at the top of the nearby Wrynose Pass.

🍴 Well liked bar food at lunchtime includes sandwiches and filled baguettes, ploughman's, soup, cumberland sausages with onion gravy and beef in ale pie, with evening choices such as honey and black pepper glazed duck leg confit with balsamic syrup, grilled fillet of plaice with a cockle and herb butter, goats cheese and butternut squash in rosemary cream sauce with pasta, pork loin marinated in garlic, fennel and thyme with a mushroom and truffle cream sauce, slow-braised venison shoulder with rich red wine gravy, and puddings like steamed honey and thyme sponge with vanilla cream sauce and caramelised lemon tart. *Starters/Snacks: £4.25 to £17.95. Main Courses: £9.95 to £17.95. Puddings: £3.95 to £5.95*

Free house ~ Licensee Ian Stephenson ~ Real ale ~ Bar food (12-2, 6-9) ~ Restaurant ~ (015394) 37215 ~ Children welcome ~ Dogs allowed in bar ~ Open 11-10.30(11 Fri and Sat) ~ Bedrooms: /£99B

Recommended by Ewan and Moira McCall, Peter and Eleanor Kenyon, John and Sue Woodward, Tina and David Woods-Taylor, Mr and Mrs Maurice Thompson, Val Carter, John and Helen Rushton, Barry Collett, Peter Salmon, JDM, KM, Dave Irving, Jenny Huggins

LOWESWATER   NY1421   MAP 9

Kirkstile Inn 🛏

From B5289 follow signs to Loweswater Lake; OS Sheet 89 map reference 140210; CA13 0RU

Popular inn in lovely spot with busy bar, own-brewed beers, good bar food and quite a mix of customers; bedrooms

Our readers very much enjoy staying at this 16th-c inn and it's in a glorious position surrounded by stunning peaks and fells; marvellous walks of all levels and maybe red squirrels in the garden. The atmosphere is friendly and relaxed, there's a good mix of customers and they even brew their own beer served by welcoming staff. The bustling main bar is low-beamed and carpeted with a roaring log fire, comfortably cushioned small settles and pews and partly stripped-stone walls; there's a slate shove-ha'penny board. As well as their own-brewed Loweswater Gold, Grasmoor Dark and Melbreak Bitter they keep a guest like Yates Bitter on handpump; several wines by the glass. The fine view can be enjoyed from picnic-sets on the lawn, from the very attractive covered verandah in front of the building and from the bow windows in one of the rooms off the bar.

🍴 Reliably good bar food includes sandwiches, filled baked potatoes and filled baguettes, ploughman's, soup, smoked haddock parfait with tomato chutney, black pudding and cumberland sausage pattie in herb breadcrumbs with apple sauce, steak in ale pie, vegetable and cashew nut stir fry, slow-roasted lamb shoulder with redcurrant, honey and rosemary sauce, king prawn risotto, and puddings like treacle tart with cinder toffee ice-cream and a cheesecake of the day. *Starters/Snacks: £3.75 to £5.50. Main Courses: £8.50 to £17.95. Puddings: £4.95*

Own brew ~ Licensee Roger Humphreys ~ Real ale ~ Bar food (12-2, 6-9) ~ Restaurant ~ (01900) 85219 ~ Children welcome ~ Dogs allowed in bar and bedrooms ~ Occasional jazz ~ Open 11-11; 12-10.30 Sun ~ Bedrooms: £61.50B/£93B

Recommended by Mr and Mrs Maurice Thompson, Sylvia and Tony Birbeck, Martin Smith, Mike and Sue Loseby, the Didler, JDM, KM, Roger and Kathy Elkin, Val Carter, Geoff and Linda Payne, Simon Watkins, Alison Ball, Ian Walton, Chris Clark, Comus and Sarah Elliott, Maurice and Gill McMahon, Adrian Johnson, Edward Mirzoeff, Dennis Jones, Angus Lyon

MUNGRISDALE   NY3630   MAP 10

Mill Inn

Off A66 Penrith—Keswick, 1 mile W of A5091 Ullswater turn-off; CA11 0XR

Bustling pub in fine setting with marvellous surrounding walks, real ales, home-cooked bar food and seats in garden; bedrooms

This 17th-c lakeland inn is in the lee of the Blencathra fell range and surrounded by stunning scenery, and there are walks of all grades close by; the garden has seats by the little river. Inside, the neatly kept bar has a wooden bar counter with an old millstone built into it, traditional dark wooden furnishings, hunting pictures on the walls, an open log fire in the stone fireplace and Robinsons Cumbria Way, Dizzy Blonde, Hartleys XB and a guest beer on handpump; there's a separate dining room and an upstairs residents' lounge. Darts, winter pool, bar billiards and dominoes.

⑪ Using fell-bred lamb and beef, the bar food includes sandwiches, soup, chicken liver pâté, fish and chips, cumberland sausages with onion gravy, mushroom stroganoff, a curry of the day, a pie of the day, chicken with a mushroom, garlic and stilton cream sauce, slow-braised lamb shoulder with a redcurrant and rosemary jus, and puddings like chocolate truffle torte and bread and butter pudding. *Starters/Snacks: £3.10 to £6.75. Main Courses: £6.95 to £15.00. Puddings: £4.25*

Robinsons ~ Tenant Helen McAleese ~ Real ale ~ Bar food (12-2, 6-9) ~ Restaurant ~ (017687) 79632 ~ Children welcome ~ Dogs allowed in bar and bedrooms ~ Open 11-11 ~ Bedrooms: £47.50S/£75S

Recommended by Robert Wivell, Mike and Sue Loseby, Noel Grundy, Dave Braisted, Geoff and Linda Payne, Comus and Sarah Elliott

NEAR SAWREY

SD3795   MAP 9

Tower Bank Arms ◖

B5285 towards the Windermere ferry; LA22 0LF

Backing on to Beatrix Potter's farm, with well kept real ales and tasty bar food; bedrooms

Many illustrations in the Beatrix Potter books can be traced back to their origins in this village – including the pub which features in *The Tale of Jemima Puddleduck*. It's run by a friendly landlord and the low-beamed main bar has plenty of rustic charm, seats on the rough slate floor, game and fowl pictures, a grandfather clock, a log fire and fresh flowers; there's also a separate restaurant. Barngates Cracker, Hawkshead Bitter and Brodie's Prime, Loweswater Gold and Yates Mad March Hare on handpump (in winter the choice may be smaller); board games. There are pleasant views of the wooded Claife Heights from seats in the garden. It does get pretty crowded during the school holidays – especially in the summer. More reports please.

⑪ As well as lunchtime sandwiches, bar food includes soup, chicken liver pâté, roasted mediterranean vegetable pasta, beef in ale stew, cumberland sausage with onion gravy, salmon with a lemon and dill crust, slow-cooked lamb with a mint and rosemary jus, and puddings such as sticky toffee pudding and meringue with mixed berries. *Starters/Snacks: £3.95 to £6.50. Main Courses: £7.50 to £14.50. Puddings: £4.00 to £4.50*

Free house ~ Licensee Anthony Hutton ~ Real ale ~ Bar food (12-2, 6-9(8 Sun, winter Mon-Thurs and bank hols) ~ Restaurant ~ (015394) 36334 ~ Children welcome ~ Dogs allowed in bar and bedrooms ~ Open 11-11; 12-10.30 Sun; 11.30-2.30, 5.30-10.30 weekdays in winter ~ Bedrooms: £55S/£88S

Recommended by Ann and Tony Bennett-Hughes, Stuart Turner, Martin Smith, Jo Lilley, Simon Calvert, Michael Doswell, Adrian Johnson, Noel Grundy

RAVENSTONEDALE

NY7203   MAP 10

Black Swan ⑪ 🛏

Just off A685 SW of Kirkby Stephen; CA17 4NG

Bustling hotel with thriving bar, several real ales, enjoyable food, and good surrounding walks; bedrooms

In fine walking country at the foot of the Howgill Fells (they have leaflets describing the walks and their lengths), this is a family-run Victorian hotel in a charming peaceful village. It's attractively refurbished but with original period features throughout, and the thriving U-shaped bar has stripped-stone walls, plush bar stools by the bar counter, a comfortable green button-back banquette, various dining chairs and little plush stools around a mix of tables with fresh flowers. Black Sheep Ale and Bitter, John Smiths, and guests like Hesket Newmarket Doris's 90th Birthday Ale and Tirril 1823 on handpump, seven wines by the glass and 30 malt whiskies; piped music, TV, darts, board games and newspapers and magazines to read. Service is genuinely friendly and helpful. There are picnic-sets in the tree-sheltered streamside garden over the road; they also run the village store with outside café seating.

🍴 Using only local suppliers, the good, seasonal changing bar food includes sandwiches, soup, chicken liver pâté wrapped in bacon with red onion marmalade, salad of black pudding, pancetta and chorizo sausage with sweet chilli sauce, beer-battered fresh haddock, lentil and vegetable shepherd's pie topped with goats cheese mash, gammon with egg or pineapple, steak, venison and ale casserole with herb dumplings, specials such as moules marinière or halibut with a casserole of mushrooms, bacon and shallots, and puddings like lime and mint-infused panna cotta with tequila and cheesecake with cherry compote. *Starters/Snacks: £3.95 to £8.95. Main Courses: £7.95 to £15.95. Puddings: £3.95 to £5.50*

Free house ~ Licensees Louise and Alan Dinnes ~ Real ale ~ Bar food (12-2, 6-9, but some sort of food all day) ~ Restaurant ~ (015396) 23204 ~ Children welcome ~ Dogs allowed in bar and bedrooms ~ Live music last Weds of the month ~ Open 8am(8.30am Sun)-midnight(1am Sat) ~ Bedrooms: £47B/£75B

Recommended by Margaret Dickinson, Mrs E Appleby, Noel Thomas, David Heath, Liz Bell, Lesley and Peter Barrett

SEATHWAITE   SD2295   MAP 9
Newfield Inn 🍺
Duddon Valley, near Ulpha (ie not Seathwaite in Borrowdale); LA20 6ED

Climbers' and walkers' cottagey inn with a genuine local feel, real ales and hearty food

Despite its weekend and holiday popularity with walkers and climbers, this cottagey 16th-c inn has a genuinely friendly and relaxed local atmosphere. The slate-floored bar has wooden tables and chairs, some interesting pictures and Jennings Cumberland Ale and Sneck Lifter and a couple of guests like Cumbrian Dickie Doodle and Ennerdale Blonde on handpump; several malt whiskies. There's a comfortable side room and a games room with board games. Tables outside in the nice garden have good hill views. The pub owns and lets the next-door self-catering flats and there's a large area for children to play. This is a quieter corner of the lakes and there are plenty of fine surrounding walks.

🍴 Usefully serving food all day and using only local farms and suppliers, the traditional bar food includes filled rolls, lunchtime snacks like beans on toast and ham, egg and chips, soup, garlic mushrooms, lasagne, steak pie, spicy bean casserole, steaks, daily specials, and puddings like toffee crunch pie and pineapple upside-down pudding. *Starters/Snacks: £4.95 to £6.95. Main Courses: £7.95 to £17.95. Puddings: £2.50 to £4.95*

Free house ~ Licensee Paul Batten ~ Real ale ~ Bar food (all day) ~ Restaurant ~ No credit cards ~ (01229) 716208 ~ Children welcome ~ Dogs allowed in bar ~ Open 11-11; closed evenings 25 and 26 Dec

Recommended by Paul and Jane Walker, John Luckes, E Ling, Alan Hill, Mr and Mrs W W Burke

STAVELEY   SD4797   MAP 9
Eagle & Child 🍺 🛏
Kendal Road; just off A591 Windermere—Kendal; LA8 9LP

Welcoming inn with warming log fires, a good range of local beers and enjoyable food; bedrooms

This little inn is at the foot of the Kentmere Valley and makes an excellent base for walkers and motorists exploring the area. There's a welcoming fire under an impressive mantelbeam, a friendly, bustling atmosphere, and a roughly L-shaped flagstoned main area with plenty of separate parts to sit in, furnished with pews, banquettes, bow window seats and high-backed dining chairs around polished dark tables. Also, police truncheons and walking sticks, some nice photographs and interesting prints, a few farm tools, a delft shelf of bric-a-brac and another log fire. The five real ales on handpump come from breweries such as Dent, Caledonian, Hawkshead, Loweswater and York and they have several wines by the glass, 20 malt whiskies and farm cider; piped music, darts and board games. An upstairs barn-theme dining room (with its own bar for functions and so forth) doubles as a breakfast room. There are picnic-sets under cocktail parasols in a sheltered garden by the River Kent, with more on a good-sized back terrace and a second garden behind.

🍴 Tasty bar food includes sandwiches, soup, chicken liver and port pâté with chutney, deep-fried breaded brie with sweet cumberland sauce, vegetable or meaty lasagne, lamb hotpot, steak in ale pie, chicken wrapped in smoked bacon with a barbecue sauce, gammon with egg and pineapple, fresh fish of the day, and puddings like sticky ginger pudding and vanilla cheesecake. *Starters/Snacks: £3.50 to £5.95. Main Courses: £8.95 to £15.95. Puddings: £4.95 to £5.50*

Free house ~ Licensees Richard and Denise Coleman ~ Real ale ~ Bar food (12-2.30(2.45 weekends), 7-9) ~ Restaurant ~ No credit cards ~ (01539) 821320 ~ Children welcome ~ Dogs allowed in bar ~ Open 11-11 ~ Bedrooms: £45S/£65S

Recommended by Jo Lilley, Simon Calvert, Dennis Jones, Russell and Alison Hunt, the Didler, MLR, Chris Evans, Bob Broadhurst, Ann and Tony Bennett-Hughes, Joe Green

STONETHWAITE
NY2513 MAP 9

Langstrath 🍺 🛏

Off B5289 S of Derwent Water; CA12 5XG

Civilised little place in lovely spot, with tasty bar food and several real ales; bedrooms

New licensees have taken over this civilised little inn so we are keeping our fingers crossed that not too much will change. The neat and simple bar (at its pubbiest at lunchtime) has a welcoming coal and log fire in a big stone fireplace, just a handful of cast-iron-framed tables, plain chairs and cushioned wall seats, and on its textured white walls maybe quite a few walking cartoons and attractive lakeland mountain photographs. Four real ales on handpump from breweries like Black Sheep, Hawkshead, Hesket Newmarket and Jennings and 25 malt whiskies; piped music and board games. The small room on the left (actually the original cottage built around 1590) is a residents' lounge; the restaurant has fine views. Outside, a big sycamore shelters several picnic-sets and there are fine surrounding walks as the pub is in a lovely spot in the heart of Borrowdale and en route for the Cumbrian Way and the Coast to Coast Walk.

🍴 Bar food now includes filled baguettes, soup, potted brown shrimps, black pudding and pancetta salad with a honey and mustard dressing, bean, coriander and chilli cakes with spiced tomato chutney, steak in ale pudding, slow-cooked herdwick lamb with red wine gravy, corn-fed chicken breast filled with spinach and tomatoes, wrapped in dry-cured local ham with a fresh herb sauce, fresh fish of the day, and puddings like sticky toffee pudding with butterscotch sauce and a trio of sorbets with lime syrup. *Starters/Snacks: £4.00 to £7.00. Main Courses: £9.00 to £17.00. Puddings: £4.00 to £6.00*

Free house ~ Licensees Guy and Jacqui Frazer-Hollins ~ Real ale ~ Bar food (12-2, 6-9(8 Sun); not Mon or as below) ~ Restaurant ~ (017687) 77239 ~ Children over 7 ~ Dogs allowed in bedrooms ~ Open 12.30-10.30(10 Sun); closed Mon all year, winter Tues and Weds and part of Dec and Jan ~ Bedrooms: £63S(£65B)/£95S(£100B)

Recommended by Dave Wright, Simon Daws, Simon Watkins, Alison Ball, Ian Walton, Jonathan Lane

TALKIN
NY5457 MAP 10

Blacksmiths Arms 🍷 🛏

Village signposted from B6413 S of Brampton; CA8 1LE

Neatly kept and welcoming, tasty bar food, several real ales and good surrounding walks; bedrooms

Extended from an 18th-c blacksmith's, this is a friendly village inn with welcoming staff. There are several neatly kept carpeted rooms and the bars are a popular place for a drink or meal after enjoying one of the surrounding walks. The warm lounge on the right has a log fire, upholstered banquettes, tables and chairs, and country prints and other pictures on the walls. The restaurant to the left is attractive, there's a long lounge opposite the bar with smaller round tables, and another room up a couple of steps at the back. Black Sheep Bitter, Geltsdale Brampton Bitter and Cold Fell and Yates Bitter on handpump, 20 wines by the glass and 30 malt whiskies; piped music, darts and board games. There are a couple of picnic-sets outside the front door with more in the back garden. More reports please.

🍴 Tasty bar food includes lunchtime sandwiches, toasties and filled baked potatoes, soup, deep-fried brie with cranberry sauce, vegetable curry, steak and kidney pie, beer-battered fresh haddock, sweet and sour chicken, beef stroganoff and specials such as tandoori king prawns, sausages with onion gravy, shoulder of lamb with mint and honey and duck breast in a port and plum sauce. *Starters/Snacks: £3.95 to £7.95. Main Courses: £7.25 to £19.95. Puddings: £3.85 to £5.85*

Free house ~ Licensees Donald and Anne Jackson ~ Real ale ~ Bar food (12-2, 6-9) ~ Restaurant ~ (016977) 3452 ~ Children welcome ~ Open 12-3, 6-midnight ~ Bedrooms: £45S/£65S

Recommended by Alan Thwaite, Dr and Mrs Leach, Maurice and Gill McMahon, Mike and Lynn Robinson, Michael Sargent

THRELKELD

NY3225   MAP 9

Horse & Farrier 🍺

A66 Penrith—Keswick; CA12 4SQ

Well run 17th-c fell-foot dining pub with good food and drinks; bedrooms

There are fine walks straight from the doorstep of this attractive 17th-c inn and stunning views towards the Helvellyn range. The neat, mainly carpeted bar has sturdy farmhouse and other nice tables, seats from comfortably padded ones to pubby chairs and from stools to bigger housekeeper's chairs and wall settles, country pictures on its white walls, one or two stripped beams and some flagstones. Jennings Bitter, Cumberland and Sneck Lifter and a couple of seasonal guests on handpump, several wines by the glass and winter open fires; friendly, efficient service. The partly stripped-stone restaurant is smart and more formal, with quite close-set tables. They have good disabled access and facilities, and a few picnic-sets outside. If you plan to stay, the rooms in the inn itself are the best bet.

🍴 Well liked bar food at lunchtime includes sandwiches, soup, mushroom, cherry tomato and garlic tagliatelle, cumberland sausage on chive mash with pan gravy, steak and kidney pie, battered cod, chilli con carne and a curry of the day, with evening choices like terrine of wild boar and venison, chicken breast stuffed with gruyère and wrapped in smoked bacon with a mushroom, onion and creamy white wine sauce and slow-braised lamb shoulder with redcurrant and mint sauce, and puddings such as banoffi pie and raspberry cheesecake. *Starters/Snacks: £3.50 to £5.95. Main Courses: £7.85 to £17.25. Puddings: £4.25 to £4.65*

Jennings (Marstons) ~ Lease Ian Court ~ Real ale ~ Bar food (12-9) ~ Restaurant ~ (017687) 79688 ~ Children welcome ~ Dogs allowed in bar and bedrooms ~ Open 7.30am-midnight ~ Bedrooms: £50B/£80B

Recommended by Tina and David Woods-Taylor, Mary M Grimshaw, Geoff and Linda Payne, Dominic McGonigal, Maurice and Gill McMahon, Dr Kevan Tucker

---

Please keep sending us reports. We rely on readers for news of new discoveries, and particularly for news of changes – however slight – at the fully described pubs: feedback@goodguides.com, or (no stamp needed) The Good Pub Guide, FREEPOST TN1569, Wadhurst, E Sussex TN5 7BR.

TORVER

Church House 🍴 🍷

A593/A5084 S of Coniston; LA21 8AZ

Rambling coaching inn with cheerful bar, friendly staff, enjoyable food, five real ales and seats in a neat garden with fine views; bedrooms

In a quiet village this rambling 14th-c coaching house is run by a landlord who worked as a chef for David Bowie for many years, so there's quite an emphasis on the particularly good food. But the bar has a cheerful, pubby atmosphere and five real ales: heavy beams, built-in wall seats and stools around plain tables on the slate flooring, a fine log fire in a sizeable stone fireplace, bits and pieces of lakeland bric-a-brac and a bar made from polished wooden barrels where they serve Barngates Tag Lag, Hawkshead Bitter, Loweswater Gold and a couple of changing guests on handpump, several wines by the glass and quite a few malt whiskies; friendly staff. There's also a comfortable lounge and a separate yellow-walled dining room; the jack russell terrier Molly loves catching beer mats. The big garden has plenty of seats and the hill views are splendid (the inn is in the shadow of Coniston Old Man); Coniston Lake is a short walk away. As well as bedrooms they have hard standing for six caravans.

🍴 Using local produce, the highly thought-of food includes sandwiches, soup, moules marinière, crispy confit duck with red wine and parmesan risotto, beer-battered haddock, risotto with a tomato and roasted red pepper sauce, saffron and mozzarella, cumberland sausage with honey mustard mash and red onion and red wine gravy, steak and kidney in ale pudding, beef bourguignon, and puddings such as bitter chocolate tart with glazed poached pear and white chocolate and ginger cream and rhubarb trifle with ginger bread. *Starters/Snacks: £4.25 to £7.95. Main Courses: £11.25 to £18.95. Puddings: £5.65 to £7.95*

Enterprise ~ Lease Mike and Mandy Beaty ~ Real ale ~ Bar food (12-3, 6-9) ~ Restaurant ~ (015394) 41282 ~ Children welcome ~ Dogs allowed in bar and bedrooms ~ Open 12-12; 12-3, 6-midnight Weds and Thurs in winter; closed winter Mon and Tues lunchtimes ~ Bedrooms: £45S/£70S

Recommended by John and Hilary Penny

ULVERSTON

Bay Horse 🍴 🍷 🛏

Canal Foot signposted off A590 and then you wend your way past the huge Glaxo factory; LA12 9EL

Civilised waterside hotel at its most relaxed at lunchtime, with super food, wine and beer; a nice, smart place to stay

This civilised hotel is at its most informal at lunchtime and the bar has a relaxed atmosphere despite its smart furnishings: attractive wooden armchairs, some pale green plush built-in wall banquettes, glossy hardwood traditional tables, blue plates on a delft shelf, a huge stone horse's head, and black beams and props with lots of horsebrasses. Magazines are dotted about, there's an open fire in the handsomely marbled grey slate fireplace and decently reproduced piped music; TV and board games. Jennings Cumberland and Bitter and Houston Blonde Bombshell on handpump, a dozen wines by the glass (champagne, too) from a carefully chosen and interesting wine list and ten malt whiskies. The conservatory restaurant has fine views over Morecambe Bay (as do the bedrooms) and there are some seats out on the terrace. More reports please.

🍴 Good lunchtime bar food includes sandwiches, filled baked potatoes, soup, chicken liver pâté with cranberry and ginger purée, lambs liver with black and white puddings on rich madeira sauce, crab and salmon fishcakes with a fresh herb cream sauce, steak and kidney pie, hazelnut pancakes filled with fresh wild mushrooms and a garlic and chive cream sauce, braised lamb shank with orange, ginger and red wine, and puddings like chocolate praline terrine and sticky toffee pudding with butterscotch sauce. *Starters/Snacks: £4.00 to £8.75. Main Courses: £12.50 to £14.50. Puddings: £5.95*

Free house ~ Licensee Robert Lyons ~ Real ale ~ Bar food (12-2(3 for light meals in winter; till 4 weekends); one evening sitting 7.30-8) ~ Restaurant ~ (01229) 583972 ~ Children must be over 10 in evening restaurant ~ Dogs allowed in bar and bedrooms ~ Open 11-11; 12-10.30 Sun ~ Bedrooms: £80B/£120B

Recommended by John and Sylvia Harrop, Henry Midwinter

Farmers Arms

Market Place; LA12 7BA

Attractively modernised town pub with quickly changing real ales, a dozen wines by the glass and good food

If something's happening in town, this convivial, bustling pub is usually a part of it and they can be busy on Thursday market day. There's a good mix of customers, cheerful and efficient staff and up to half a dozen real ales. The front bar is appealingly modernised but the original fireplace and timbers blend in well with the more contemporary furnishings – mostly wicker chairs on one side and comfortable sofas on the other; the overall effect is rather unusual, but somehow it still feels like a proper village pub. A table by the fire has newspapers, glossy magazines and local information, and a second smaller bar counter leads into a big raftered eating area. On handpump, the real ales come from breweries such as Coniston, Courage, Hawkshead, Stringers, Theakstons and Yates and they have a dozen wines by the glass; piped music. In front is a very attractive terrace with outdoor heaters, plenty of wooden tables looking on to the market cross, and lots of colourful plants in tubs and hanging baskets. They have three cottages to rent.

As well as sandwiches and various nibbles, the enjoyable bar food includes various sharing deli boards, pizzas, burger with cheese, bacon and onion rings, crab cakes with sweet chilli salsa, nachos and sour cream, steak and mushroom in ale pie, moroccan vegetable stew, thai chicken curry, slow-cooked lamb shank with couscous and chickpea stew, specials like lemon sole topped with morecambe bay potted shrimps and stir-fried duck breast strips; also puddings and popular Sunday roasts. *Starters/Snacks: £4.25 to £5.95. Main Courses: £9.99 to £16.95. Puddings: £4.00 to £4.95*

Free house ~ Licensee Roger Chattaway ~ Real ale ~ Bar food (9-3, 5-8.30) ~ Restaurant ~ (01229) 584469 ~ Children in dining room only ~ Open 9am-midnight(1am Sat, 11pm Sun)

Recommended by Dr Peter Andrews, Karen Eliot, Chris Clark

WINSTER

SD4193 MAP 9

Brown Horse 🍴 🍷 🛏

A5074 S of Windermere; LA23 3NR

Welcoming bar, smarter restaurant and informal atmosphere, super food using own estate produce, real ales, good wines and seats outside; bedrooms

There's a chatty, bustling atmosphere in the bar of this thoroughly enjoyable country pub although many of the customers are here for the exceptional food. The proper public bar has cheerful staff, beams and some half-panelling, stools and a mix of wooden chairs around pubby tables (each with a lit candle), a woodburning stove in a little stone fireplace, and high bar chairs by the counter. Bewdley Old School Bitter, Lancaster Amber and Moorhouses Pride of Pendle on handpump, a dozen good wines by the glass and maybe damson gin. The restaurant has a relaxed, informal atmosphere, high-backed leather dining chairs around attractive light and dark wood tables, more candles and fresh flowers. Piped music, TV and board games. There's a front terrace with solid tables and chairs and a side garden with views of the Winster Valley.

The free-range meat and poultry used in the first-rate cooking comes from their own estate and they grow their own fruit, vegetables and salad: sandwiches, soup, shredded crab with sesame wafers and avocado purée, pressed terrine of ham hock with celeriac rémoulade and pickled eggs, beer-battered haddock with pea purée, provençale vegetable tart with parmesan, local pheasant with sauce bourguignon, roast loin of pork with pommes fondantes, 21-day mature dry-cured sirloin steak with café de paris butter, and puddings. *Starters/Snacks: £3.95 to £9.95. Main Courses: £9.95 to £15.50. Puddings: £5.25 to £6.25*

Free house ~ Licensees Karen and Steve Edmondson ~ Real ale ~ Bar food (12-2, 6-9) ~ Restaurant ~ (015394) 43443 ~ Children welcome ~ Dogs allowed in bar ~ Open 12-11(10 Sun) ~ Bedrooms: /£90S

Recommended by Tina and David Woods-Taylor, Peter Webb, Walter and Susan Rinaldi-Butcher, Henry Midwinter, Michael Doswell, Alison Ball, Ian Walton, Malcolm and Pauline Pellatt, Christopher Mobbs, Michael Tack

YANWATH   NY5128   MAP 9

Gate Inn 🍴 ♀

2.25 miles from M6 junction 40; A66 towards Brough, then right on A6, right on B5320, then follow village signpost; CA10 2LF

CUMBRIA DINING PUB OF THE YEAR

Emphasis on imaginative food but with local beers and thoughtful wines, a pubby atmosphere and warm welcome from the helpful staff

'A pub as good as you could wish to find for atmosphere and excellent food' says one of our readers – and many agree with him. It's an immaculately kept 17th-c inn with welcoming, helpful staff and a proper bar of charming antiquity. This cosy bar has country pine and dark wood furniture, lots of brasses on the beams, church candles on all the tables and a good log fire in the attractive stone inglenook. Hesket Newmarket High Pike Dark Amber Bitter, Loweswater Gold and Tirril Old Faithful on handpump, a dozen wines by the glass, quite a few malt whiskies and Weston's cider. Two restaurant areas have oak floors, panelled oak walls and heavy beams; piped music. There are seats on the terrace and in the garden.

🍴 **First-class food at lunchtime includes soup, mussels with chives, cream and white wine, a platter of fish, cheese and meat with chutney and pickles, beer-battered fish with mushy peas, tuscan bean casserole with parsley dumplings and venison burger with fig and elderflower relish; evening choices such as salmon tartare, game and pistachio terrine with apple and ginger chutney, pork belly and toulouse sausage cassoulet, marinated pheasant breast with honeyed parsnip mash, gilthead bream with lemon balm and tiger prawn risotto, with puddings like sticky date pudding with toffee sauce and lemon cheesecake with champagne sorbet.** *Starters/Snacks: £4.50 to £10.95. Main Courses: £8.95 to £18.95. Puddings: £5.50 to £6.95*

Free house ~ Licensee Matt Edwards ~ Real ale ~ Bar food (12-2.30, 6-9) ~ Restaurant ~ (01768) 862386 ~ Children welcome ~ Dogs allowed in bar ~ Open 12-11

Recommended by Michael and Maggie Betton, Tracey and Stephen Groves, Dave Braisted, J S Burn, Richard J Holloway, John and Eleanor Holdsworth, Mr and Mrs Maurice Thompson, Chris and Jo Parsons, Michael Doswell, Neil and Karen Dignan, Maurice and Gill McMahon, Sylvia and Tony Birbeck, Mrs C Farley, Peter and Eleanor Kenyon

LUCKY DIP

Besides the fully inspected pubs, you might like to try these Lucky Dips recommended to us and described by readers (if you do, please send us reports: feedback@goodguides.com).

ALLITHWAITE [SD3876]
Pheasant LA11 7RQ [B5277]: Friendly family-run pub with good value freshly cooked food all day, prompt service, real ales, log fire; children welcome, outside tables on deck with Humphrey Head views, open all day *(Dr Peter Andrews)*
ALSTON [NY7146]
Cumberland CA9 3HX [Townfoot]: Welcoming pub popular with walkers, well kept changing ales, real ciders, enjoyable food; terrace with great views from picnic-sets, quoits, refurbished bedrooms, good breakfast *(Ken Savage, Mr and Mrs Maurice Thompson)*

AMBLESIDE [NY3704]
Queens LA22 9BU [Market Pl]: Roomy hotel bar with dining area, 15 mainly local ales all helpfully described, inexpensive generous food, friendly obliging service; bedrooms *(Chris Johnson, Mr and Mrs Maurice Thompson)*
Unicorn LA22 9DT [North Rd]: Bustling backstreet beamed local with plenty of atmosphere, excellent staff, well kept Robinsons, decent bar food, coal fire; regular live music; dogs welcome in bar, six good value bedrooms (two sharing bath), good breakfast *(Chris Johnson)*
☆ *Wateredge Inn* LA22 0EP [Borrans Rd]: Refurbished after 2009 floods; lovely spot

with sizeable garden running down to edge of Windermere (own moorings), lots of tables here, same splendid view through big windows in much-modernised bar, prompt cheerful staff, ales from Barngates, Theakstons, Tirril and local Watermill, several wines by the glass, wide choice of enjoyable food till 8.30pm, cosy beamed area down steps with fireside sofa; piped music, can get very busy; children welcome, dogs in bar, 22 comfortable bedrooms, open all day *(LYM, Hugh Roberts, Margaret and Jeff Graham, Mr and Mrs D J Nash, Ian and Deborah Carrington, Margaret Dickinson, Chris Johnson)*

APPLEBY [NY6819]

☆ *Royal Oak* CA16 6UN [B6542/Bongate]: Attractive old beamed and timbered coaching inn, popular bar food (all day Sun), well kept ales such as Black Sheep, Hawkshead and Jennings, friendly efficient young staff, log fire in panelled bar, armchair lounge with carved settle, traditional snug, nicely refurbished dining room; piped music; children and dogs welcome, terrace tables, good-sized bedrooms, decent breakfast, open all day *(LYM, Margaret and Peter Staples, Maurice and Gill McMahon)*

ARMATHWAITE [NY5045]

☆ *Fox & Pheasant* CA4 9PY: Friendly licensees and locals in attractive spotless coaching inn, lovely River Eden views, well kept Robinsons ales, decent wines by the glass, sensibly short choice of good fresh reasonably priced food, inglenook log fire in main beamed and flagstoned bar, another in second bar, charming small dining room; picnic-sets outside, comfortable bedrooms *(W M Lien)*

ARNSIDE [SD4578]

Albion LA5 0HA [Promenade]: Extended pub with great estuary and mountain views, Thwaites ales, good staff; pleasant verandah decking *(JDM, KM, Henry Midwinter)*

ASKHAM [NY5123]

Punch Bowl CA10 2PF Sadly, this attractive village-green inn closed as we went to press and Enterprise Inns were looking for new licensees; had been a popular place with plenty of regular customers, local beers and good food; spreading main bar with beams and pubby furnishings, locals' bar, snug lounge and more formal dining room; terrace, bedrooms, was open all day – news please *(LYM)*

BAMPTON [NY5118]

☆ *Mardale* CA10 2RQ [village signposted off A6 in Shap; in Bampton turn left over bridge by Post Office]: Pretty pub in quaint village, several opened-up rooms decorated in contemporary style, chunky modern country tables and chairs on big flagstones, a few rugs, one or two big lakeland prints and some rustic bygones, log fire in raised fireplace, well kept changing ales (mainly cumbrian) inc one brewed for the pub, 40 european bottled beers, several wines by the glass, short choice of food all day inc

bargain lunch (Mon-Thurs), friendly staff; well behaved children allowed, dogs very welcome (pub has its own), good walks from the door, bedrooms, open all day *(Mike and Linda Hudson, LYM, Michael Doswell, Margaret Dickinson, BB, Sian Morris)*

BARDSEA [SD3074]

Bradylls Arms LA12 9QT [Main St]: Simple generous reasonably priced food from good sandwiches up, Black Sheep, Greene King and Jennings, plush seating and some stripped stone, back conservatory restaurant with lovely Morecambe Bay views; garden, very attractive village nr sea *(John and Sylvia Harrop, BB)*

BARROW-IN-FURNESS [SD1969]

Furness Railway LA14 5UB [Abbey Rd]: Comfortable Wetherspoons with good choice of ales, enjoyable food inc deals, friendly staff; disabled access *(Michael Tack)*

BOOT [NY1701]

Boot Inn CA19 1TG [aka Burnmoor; signed just off the Wrynose/Hardknott Pass road]: Comfortable beamed pub with ever-burning fire, Black Sheep, Jennings and a guest ale (summer beer festival), decent wines and malt whiskies, friendly staff, reasonably priced home-made local food from sandwiches up, restaurant and dining conservatory; games room with pool and TV; children and dogs welcome, sheltered front lawn with play area, good walks, lovely surroundings, open all day *(LYM, Adrian Johnson, Mr and Mrs D J Nash)*

☆ *Brook House* CA19 1TG: Converted small Victorian hotel with good views and walks, friendly family service, wide choice of good sensibly priced home-made food inc some interesting dishes and unusual sandwiches, great whisky selection, several well kept mainly cumbrian ales inc Coniston and Yates, decent wines; log fires, small plushly modernised bar, comfortable hunting-theme lounge, peaceful separate restaurant; tables outside, seven good value bedrooms, good breakfast (for nearby campers too), mountain weather reports, excellent drying room, open all day *(the Didler, John and Sylvia Harrop, Alison Ball, Ian Walton, Neil Whitehead, Victoria Anderson, Derek and Sylvia Stephenson)*

Woolpack CA19 1TH [Bleabeck, midway between Boot and Hardknott Pass]: Last pub before the notorious Hardknott Pass; simply refurbished under friendly new owners (previously at the Boot Inn), main walkers' bar with log woodburner, snug and restaurant, up to eight well kept ales inc Woolpackers (still brewed for the pub by previous landlord), enjoyable home-made locally sourced food all day, June beer festival; children and dogs welcome, garden with mountain views, play area, seven bedrooms *(Alan Hill, Neil Whitehead, Victoria Anderson, B and F A Hannam)*

BORROWDALE [NY2617]

Borrowdale Hotel CA12 5UY [B5289, S end of Derwent Water]: A hotel, but enjoyable lunchtime bar food from sandwiches up in conservatory, smart, friendly and roomy bar, well kept Jennings Cumberland, pleasant service, good value restaurant; garden tables, lovely fell-foot scenery, good bedrooms *(Martyn Jones)*

BOTHEL [NY1839]

Greyhound CA7 2HS [A595]: Well kept and very clean, good generous food at reasonable prices, Jennings ales *(Helen Clarke, Steven Lewis)*

BOWLAND BRIDGE [SD4189]

☆ *Hare & Hounds* LA11 6NN [signed from A5074]: Attractive refurbished country pub, welcoming young staff, real ales inc an own-label brew, enjoyable well executed traditional food from doorstep sandwiches up, early-bird deals, good roaring log fire in small bar, areas off with polished flagstones, some stripped stone; children welcome, picnic-sets on front terrace and in spacious side garden, bedrooms; quiet hamlet in lovely scenery *(Stuart Turner, LYM, Michael Doswell)*

BOWNESS-ON-WINDERMERE [SD4096]

Royal Oak LA23 3EG [Brantfell Rd]: Handy for steamer pier, pier interconnecting rooms, lots of bric-a-brac, open fire, well kept ales such as Coniston Bluebird, Everards Tiger, Greene King Abbot and Jennings Cumberland, generous reasonably priced food from baguettes to specials, friendly efficient service; pool, darts and juke box; children welcome, tables out in front, bedrooms *(Dennis Jones, Joe Green)*

BRAITHWAITE [NY2324]

Middle Ruddings CA12 5RY: Friendly family-run hotel, good food in bar or carpeted dining conservatory with Skiddaw views, attentive service, three well kept local ales; children and dogs welcome, garden with terrace picnic-sets, bedrooms *(Mr and Mrs Maurice Thompson, Maurice and Gill McMahon)*

Royal Oak CA12 5SY: Bustling local atmosphere, good choice of enjoyable food (best to book evenings) inc children's helpings, prompt helpful service, four well kept Jennings ales, well worn-in flagstoned bar; piped music, Sky TV; dogs welcome except mealtimes, open all day *(Mike and Eleanor Anderson, Mr and Mrs D J Nash)*

BROUGHTON-IN-FURNESS [SD2187]

Old Kings Head LA20 6HJ [Church St]: Smart but relaxed family-run pub with son cooking enjoyable popular food inc good Sun lunch, friendly obliging service, well kept Beckstones and a guest ale, stone fireplace, chintz and knick-knacks, separate games area; big attractive garden behind with covered heated terrace, comfortable bedrooms *(E Ling, Angus Lyon)*

BUTTERMERE [NY1716]

☆ *Bridge Hotel* CA13 9UZ [just off B5289 SW of Keswick]: Popular with walkers (but no dogs), with lakeside and other walks for all levels nearby; a hotel feel but with traditional comfortable beamed bar, well

kept Black Sheep, Hawkshead, Keswick and Theakstons Old Peculier, enjoyable bar food (not Weds and may close if quiet), more upmarket things in plush dining room; may debit your card with a steep voidable deposit if you eat outside; children welcome, flagstoned terrace, bedrooms, self-catering, open all day *(David and Sue Smith, the Didler, Sylvia and Tony Birbeck, Mike Gorton, LYM, Mr and Mrs Maurice Thompson)*

CALDBECK [NY3239]

☆ *Oddfellows Arms* CA7 8EA [B5299 SE of Wigton]: Split-level pub with nice spacious feel, friendly and lived-in, with particularly well kept Jennings, enjoyable food from lunchtime sandwiches up inc great home-made chips, good choice of wines by the glass, affable landlord, quick pleasant service; fine old photographs and woodburner in bustling comfortable front bar, big back dining room, exemplary lavatories; piped music, games area with darts, pool and TV; children and muddy walkers welcome, open all day Fri-Sun and summer, low-priced bedrooms, nice village *(Helen Clarke, G Jennings, Phil Bryant)*

CARLISLE [NY4056]

Kings Head CA3 8RF [pedestrianised Fisher St]: Heavy beams, lots of old local prints, drawings and black and white photographs, friendly service, bargain pub lunches, good range of mainly cumbrian beers inc Yates, raised dining area; piped music, TV; interesting historical plaque outside, partly covered courtyard, open all day *(the Didler, Eric Larkham, Derek and Sylvia Stephenson)*

CARTMEL [SD3778]

Cavendish Arms LA11 6QA [Cavendish St, off main square]: Open-plan simply furnished low-ceilinged bar with great log fire (not always lit), well kept Jennings Cumberland and Wells & Youngs Bombardier, helpful staff, extensive range of food, linen napkins, restaurant; children welcome, tables out in front and behind by stream, nice village with notable priory church, good walks, ten bedrooms, open all day *(Dennis Jones, Mr and Mrs W W Burke, LYM)*

CASTLE CARROCK [NY5455]

Duke of Cumberland CA8 9LU: Reopened after 12-year closure and given clean simple refurbishment by friendly family owners; upholstered wall benches and mix of pubby furniture on slate floor, small open fire, compact dining area with old farmhouse tables and chairs, local beers such as Geltsdale, enjoyable good value straightforward food; children welcome *(Dr and Mrs D A Blackadder)*

CHAPEL STILE [NY3205]

Wainwrights LA22 9JH [B5343]: White-rendered former farmhouse, good choice of beers, plenty of wines by the glass, enjoyable quickly served food, roomy new-feeling bar welcoming walkers and dogs, slate floor and fire, other spreading carpeted areas with beams, some half-panelling, cushioned settles and mix of dining chairs around wooden tables, old kitchen range; piped music, TV and games machines; children welcome, terrace picnic-sets, fine views, open all day summer *(Ewan and Moira McCall, John Woodward, LYM, John and Helen Rushton, Michael Doswell, Martin Smith)*

CONISTON [SD3098]

☆ *Sun* LA21 8HQ [signed left off A593 at the bridge]: Welcoming 16th-c inn in terrific setting below dramatic fells, interesting Donald Campbell and other lakeland photographs in recently extended old-fashioned bar with beams, flagstones, log fire range, cask seats and old settles; well kept Black Sheep, Coniston Bluebird, Copper Dragon, Hawkshead and four local guests, several wines by the glass, wide choice of enjoyable food all day, big conservatory restaurant off carpeted lounge, more seating in large refurbished upstairs room with suspended rowing boat; well behaved children and dogs welcome, great views from front terrace, big tree-sheltered garden, eight comfortable bedrooms, hearty breakfast, open all day *(Ewan and Moira McCall, Luke Bosman, Mr and Mrs J Hilton, E Ling, Brian Fairey, Mike Gorton, LYM)*

Yewdale LA21 8DU [Yewdale Rd]: Centrally positioned Victorian stone-built inn, enjoyable food all day, well kept Greene King ales, good friendly service; children welcome, some tables out at front, eight bedrooms, good breakfast *(Michael Butler)*

CROOK [SD4695]

☆ *Sun* LA8 8LA [B5284 Kendal—Bowness]: Good bustling atmosphere in low-beamed bar with two dining areas off, generous traditional food (all day wknds), reasonable prices, prompt cheerful service, Fullers London Pride and John Smiths, good value wines, roaring log fire *(Sylvia and Tony Birbeck, G Jennings, LYM)*

DACRE [NY4526]

Horse & Farrier CA11 0HL [between A66 and A592 SW of Penrith]: Popular 18th-c village pub with good local home-made food (not Sun evening) from sandwiches to more unusual things, helpful friendly staff, well kept Jennings, unsmart front room with big old-fashioned range and nice beam-and-plank ceiling, more modern dining extension down steps on the left; darts and dominoes; children and dogs welcome, post office, pretty village, cl Mon lunchtime *(Brian Abbott, Noel Grundy, Natalie Wittering, BB)*

DENT [SD7086]

George & Dragon LA10 5QL [Main St]: Owned by Dent with seven of their beers (inc a real lager) and Weston's cider in comfortable flagstoned bar, open fire, dark panelling, partitioned tables, affable chatty landlord, good generous food inc reasonably priced evening restaurant meals, prompt friendly service; comfortable bedrooms, good breakfast, lovely village *(Brian and Anna Marsden)*

Sun LA10 5QL [Main St]: Old-fashioned local with four well kept changing ales, good value walkers' food from sandwiches up, beamed and flagstoned traditional bar with coal fire and darts; children welcome, open all day in summer, bedrooms *(LYM, Ann and Tony Bennett-Hughes, Brian and Anna Marsden)*

ENNERDALE BRIDGE [NY0615]

Shepherds Arms CA23 3AR [off A5086 E of Egremont]: Welcoming walkers' inn well placed by car-free dale, weather-forecast blackboard and helpful books, lots of pictures, log fire and woodburner, Coniston Bluebird, Jennings, Timothy Taylors Landlord and guests like Hesket Newmarket, good wine choice, reasonably priced home-made food from sandwiches up, panelled dining room and conservatory; may be piped music; children and dogs welcome, bedrooms, open all day (may be winter afternoon break Mon-Thurs) *(LYM, Sylvia and Tony Birbeck, Tina and David Woods-Taylor)*

ESKDALE GREEN [NY1200]

☆ *Bower House* CA19 1TD [0.5 miles W]: Civilised old-fashioned stone-built inn extended around beamed and alcoved core, good fires, efficient friendly staff, well kept local ales, good choice of interesting food in bar and biggish restaurant inc home-made black pudding; nicely tended sheltered garden by cricket field, charming spot with great walks, bedrooms, open all day *(Tina and David Woods-Taylor, David Jackson, LYM)*

FAR SAWREY [SD3795]

☆ *Sawrey Hotel* LA22 0LQ: Comfortable, warm and welcoming stable bar with tables in wooden stalls, harness on rough white walls, even water troughs and mangers; big helpings of good value simple lunchtime bar food, well kept Hawkshead, Jennings and Theakstons, good coffee, pleasant staff, appealingly relaxed and old-fashioned second bar in main hotel, log fires in both, restaurant; seats on nice lawn, beautiful setting, walkers, children and dogs welcome, good bedrooms *(LYM, Dennis Jones, Steve and Sue Griffiths, Noel Grundy)*

FOXFIELD [SD2085]

☆ *Prince of Wales* LA20 6BX [opp station]: Cheery bare-boards pub with half a dozen good changing ales inc bargain beers brewed here and at their associated Tigertops brewery, bottled imports, farm cider, enjoyable home-made food inc lots of unusual pasties, coal fire, pub games inc bar billiards, daily papers and beer-related reading matter; children very welcome, games for them, reasonably priced bedrooms, open all day Fri-Sun, from mid-afternoon wkdys *(BB, the Didler)*

GLENRIDDING [NY3817]

Inn on the Lake CA11 0PE: Hotel in outstanding setting by Ullswater, lounge bar and terrace looking down to lake, separate more pubby Ramblers Bar with lots of wood and exposed stone, good choice of enjoyable reasonably priced food, real ales, smart lake-view restaurant; children and dogs welcome, extensive grounds, 47 bedrooms *(Mr and Mrs D J Nash, Brendon Skinner)*

Travellers Rest CA11 0QQ [back of main car park, top of road]: Friendly unpretentious low-beamed and panelled two-bar pub with big helpings of decent food for hungry walkers (all day in summer, from breakfast on), Jennings Cumberland and Marstons, simple yet comfortable pubby décor; Ullswater views from terrace picnic-sets; open all day Sun and summer *(David and Sue Smith, John and Helen Rushton)*

GOSFORTH [NY0703]

Gosforth Hall CA20 1AZ [off A595 and unclassified road to Wasdale]: Jacobean building with interesting history, beamed carpeted bar (popular with locals) with fine plaster coat of arms above woodburner, lounge/reception area with huge fireplace, ales such as Hawkshead and Yates; restaurant; TV; back garden with boules, nine bedrooms, self-catering lodge *(Mr and Mrs Maurice Thompson)*

GRASMERE [NY3307]

☆ **Tweedies** LA22 9SW [part of Dale Lodge Hotel]: Lively properly pubby atmosphere in big square hotel bar, warm and cosy, with enjoyable food all day from pizzas and lunchtime baguettes to some imaginative dishes and Sun roasts, children's choices too, four or five changing ales (Sept beer festival), farm cider, plenty of wines by the glass, attractively updated traditional décor, sturdy furnishings in adjoining flagstoned family dining room; walkers and dogs welcome, picnic-sets out in large pleasant garden, bedrooms, open all day *(Mr and Mrs Maurice Thompson, Mr and Mrs D J Nash)*

GREYSTOKE [NY4430]

Boot & Shoe CA11 0TP: Cosy two-bar pub by the green in pretty 'Tarzan' village, low ceilings, exposed brickwork and dark wood, good generous reasonably priced food inc popular theme nights, well kept Black Sheep and local microbrews; sports TV; on national cycle route, bedrooms *(Phil Bryant, Maurice and Gill McMahon, Angus Lyon)*

HALE [SD5078]

Kings Arms LA7 7BH [A6 S of Beetham]: Traditional pub doing good generous pubby food (all day wknds) inc good Sun roasts, friendly landlord, real ales, plenty of brass, china and hunting prints, two open fires; restaurant section *(Mr and Mrs Ian King)*

HAVERTHWAITE [SD3284]

Anglers Arms LA12 8AJ [just off A590]: Busy split-level lived-in pub with good choice of real ales, friendly helpful staff, good fairly priced generous fresh food from sandwiches to steaks, sports memorabilia, separate upstairs dining room, lower area with pool; handy for steam railway *(Tony and Maggie Harwood, Dennis Jones)*

HAWKSHEAD [SD3598]

☆ **Queens Head** LA22 0NS [Main St]: Timbered pub in charming village, low-ceilinged bar

with heavy bowed black beams, red plush wall seats and stools around hefty traditional tables, decorative plates on panelled walls, open fire, snug little room off, several eating areas; Robinsons ales and a guest, good wine and whisky choice, bar food and more elaborate evening meals; piped music, TV, darts; children welcome, seats outside, pretty window boxes, bedrooms and two holiday cottages, residents' pass for public car park, open all day *(Martin and Pauline Jennings, LYM, Martin Smith)*

KESWICK [NY2623]

Bank Tavern CA12 5DS [Main St]: Friendly low-beamed L-shaped carpeted bar, spotless and well run, with Jennings and guest ales, simple good value pub food (very popular at lunchtime – pub can get packed wknds), lots of nooks and crannies, log-effect gas fire, children's room; dogs welcome, bedrooms, open all day *(Mr and Mrs Maurice Thompson, Anne Boyd, Ben Williams)*

Pheasant CA12 5PP [Crosthwaite Rd (A66, a mile out)]: Small friendly beamed local with enjoyable food and well kept Jennings ales, good service, log fire, dining room; children welcome if eating, bedrooms, nr ancient church of St Kentigern *(Stephen Fountain)*

LANGDALE [NY2906]

Stickle Barn LA22 9JU [by car park for Stickle Ghyll]: Lovely views from roomy and busy café-style walkers' and climbers' bar (boots welcome), three or four changing ales such as Barngates, decent good value food inc packed lunches, quick friendly service, mountaineering photographs; piped music – live Sat, games machines, TV; big terrace with inner verandah, open all day; bunkhouse accommodation *(Chris Johnson)*

LINDALE [SD4180]

☆ **Royal Oak** LA11 6LX: Roomy open-plan village pub popular for good gently upscale food using local ingredients, wider evening choice, welcoming helpful staff, modestly priced wines, well kept Robinsons ales; blue banquettes and padded chairs in carpeted bar, wood-floored dining areas either side, restrained décor with a few modern prints, clean and tidy *(Dr Peter Andrews, Maurice and Gill McMahon)*

LORTON [NY1526]

☆ **Wheatsheaf** CA13 9UW [B5289 Buttermere—Cockermouth]: Refurbished after recent flood damage, nice local atmosphere in neatly furnished bar with two log fires, affable hard-working landlord, Jennings and regular changing guests, several good value wines, good home-made food (all day Sun) from sandwiches to fresh fish (Thurs, Fri evening), smallish restaurant; children and dogs on a lead welcome, tables behind, campsite, open all day wknds, cl Mon lunchtime and wkdy lunchtimes winter *(Sylvia and Tony Birbeck, Edward Mirzoeff, Geoff and Linda Payne, Pat and Stewart Gordon, BB)*

NETHER WASDALE [NY1204]

Strands CA20 1ET: Welcoming old post house

in lovely spot below the remote high fells around Wast Water, own Strands ales and Jennings, popular good value food, two bars with open fires, beams and bare boards, dining room, games room; children and dogs welcome, garden, 14 bedrooms *(Mr and Mrs Maurice Thompson)*

OUTGATE [SD3599]

☆ *Outgate Inn* LA22 0NQ [B5286 Hawkshead—Ambleside]: Neatly kept country pub with three pleasantly modernised rooms, good value fresh simple food from sandwiches up, well kept Robinsons ales, cheerful log fire, trad jazz Fri evening (very busy then); terrace picnic-sets, three bright comfortable bedrooms, good breakfast, nice walks, open all day summer wknds (restricted hours winter Mon and Tues) *(BB)*

PATTERDALE [NY3915]

Patterdale Hotel CA11 0NN: Large hotel's bar popular with locals, residents and walking parties for its enjoyable generous food, Hesket Newmarket ales, helpful friendly staff; good views, comfortable bedrooms *(Abi Benson, Ben Williams)*

White Lion CA11 0NW: Cheerful flagstoned bar with a ready market of walkers and climbers (can be crowded wknds), well kept ales such as Jennings and Tirril, substantial inexpensive food all day in long narrow room on left, helpful friendly service; dogs welcome, bedrooms *(Mr and Mrs Maurice Thompson)*

PENRUDDOCK [NY4227]

☆ *Herdwick* CA11 0QU [off A66 Penrith—Keswick]: Attractively cottagey and sympathetically renovated 18th-c inn, warm welcoming atmosphere, well kept Jennings and summer guest beers from unusual curved bar, decent wines, friendly efficient service, sensibly priced food from lunchtime sandwiches up, good open fire, stripped stone and white paintwork, nice dining room with upper gallery; games room with pool and darts; children in eating areas, five good value bedrooms *(S D and J L Cooke, Comus and Sarah Elliott, Maurice and Gill McMahon, LYM, Angus Lyon)*

POOLEY BRIDGE [NY4724]

Sun CA10 2NN: Friendly local with bare boards and panelling, small lounge bar, steps past servery to bigger bar, three well kept Jennings ales and guests, good wine choice, enjoyable reasonably priced pub food, restaurant; intermittent piped music; garden tables, play fort, great views, bedrooms; currently up for sale – news please *(Tim and Rosemary Wells, Tony and Maggie Harwood, Peter Thompson)*

ROSTHWAITE [NY2514]

Scafell CA12 5XB [B5289 S of Keswick]: Hotel's big plain slate-floored back bar useful for walkers, weather-forecast board, well kept ales such as Black Sheep and Theakstons, blazing log fire, enjoyable food from sandwiches up, afternoon teas, also appealing cocktail bar/sun lounge and dining room; piped music, pool; children and dogs welcome, tables out overlooking beck,

refurbished bedrooms *(BB, Sylvia and Tony Birbeck, Simon Watkins, Lawrence R Cotter)*

SANDFORD [NY7316]

☆ *Sandford Arms* CA16 6NR [village and pub signposted just off A66 W of Brough]: Neat former 18th-c farmhouse in peaceful village, enjoyable food (all day wknds Apr-Oct) from chef/landlord, L-shaped carpeted main bar with stripped beams and stonework, a collection of Royal Doulton character jugs and some Dickens ware, ales from Black Sheep, Lancaster and Tirril, comfortable raised and balustraded eating area, more formal dining room and second flagstoned bar, log fire; piped music; children and dogs welcome, seats in front garden and covered courtyard, bedrooms, cl Tues *(LYM, Mrs Hazel Rainer)*

SATTERTHWAITE [SD3392]

☆ *Eagles Head* LA12 8LN: Unpretentious and attractive beamed pub in pretty village on edge of Grizedale Forest (beautiful scenery), particularly welcoming and obliging landlord, good fairly priced generous pubby food (not Mon) inc notable filled rolls, wider evening choice, well kept local ales inc Barngates and one brewed for the pub, big log fire, lots of local photographs and maps; children welcome, picnic-sets outside, comfortable bedrooms *(Roger and Kathy Elkin)*

SCALES [NY3426]

White Horse CA12 4SY [A66 W of Penrith]: Traditional lakeland pub, fires in comfortable beamed bar, little snug and another room with butter churns, kettles, marmalade slicer and black range; several beers inc Camerons and perhaps a beer brewed for them (you can try before you buy), straightforward food; piped music; children welcome, garden tables, pretty flowering tubs, lovely setting below Blencathra (leave muddy boots outside), open all day in summer *(Graham and Elizabeth Hargreaves, LYM)*

SHAP [NY5614]

☆ *Greyhound* CA10 3PW [A6, S end]: Good value former coaching inn, quickly served enjoyable food in open-plan bar, more choice in two restaurants, eight well kept ales inc Jennings, good house wines, cheerful bustle and friendly helpful young staff; dogs welcome, popular with Coast-to-Coast walkers, ten comfortable bedrooms, good breakfast *(J S Burn, John Wymer, Andy West)*

SPARK BRIDGE [SD3084]

Royal Oak LA12 8BS [off A5092 N of Ulverston]: Large riverside dining pub dating from 17 c, good home-made food (all day Sun) inc children's menu, relaxed informal atmosphere in beamed and carpeted bar, friendly service, well kept real ales, decent house wines, open fire; well behaved dogs welcome, small garden, three bedrooms, open all day *(BB)*

ST BEES [NX9711]

Queens CA27 0DE [Main St]: Friendly 17th-c two-bar pub, well kept Jennings, good food from sandwiches to specials, beams, log fires and suede-look furnishings, dining area and airy conservatory; garden behind, coast walks, 14 bedrooms, good breakfast (David and Ruth Hollands)

STAVELEY [SD4798]

☆ **Hawkshead Brewery Bar** LA8 9LR [Staveley Mill Yard, Back Lane]: Spacious modern span-roof beer hall, tap for good Hawkshead range, guest beers too and fine choice of other drinks inc bottled beers and local cider, enthusiastic chatty staff, long nicely made bavarian-style tables, groups of leather sofas, new oak boards, view down into brewery or over River Kent, food from adjoining café and bakery, T-shirts etc for sale; brewery tours available, open 12-5 (6 Weds-Sun) (Mr and Mrs Maurice Thompson, Dennis Jones, MLR, the Didler)

TIRRIL [NY5026]

☆ **Queens Head** CA10 2JF [B5320, not far from M6 junction 40]: Attractively old-fashioned linked bars with low beams, black panelling, flagstones, bare boards, high-backed settles and four open fireplaces inc a roomy inglenook, well kept Robinsons, good range of enjoyable fairly priced food, friendly staff, restaurant; piped music and pool in back bar; children welcome in eating areas, bedrooms, attached shop, open all day Fri-Sun (M E and J R Hart, LYM, Tony and Maggie Harwood)

TROUTBECK [NY4103]

Mortal Man LA23 1PL [A592 N of Windermere; Upper Rd]: Reopened and refurbished under new management; beamed and partly panelled bar with cosy room off, log fires, Black Sheep, Cumberland, Timothy Taylors Landlord and a beer brewed for the pub by Hawkshead, several wines by the glass, enjoyable food in bar and picture-window restaurant, friendly service; children and dogs welcome, great views from sunny garden, lovely village, comfortable bedrooms, has been open all day (Dave Traynor, LYM)

☆ **Queens Head** LA23 1PW [A592 N of Windermere]: Interestingly furnished and decorated rambling beamed and flagstoned bar, great log fire in raised stone fireplace, another coal fire, well kept Robinsons ales from counter based on a finely carved Elizabethan four-poster, hops and fresh flowers, enjoyable all-day food (prices edging high), newer dining rooms similarly decorated to main bar; piped music; children

welcome, dogs in bar, seats outside with fine view over Troutbeck valley to Applethwaite moors, bedrooms, open all day (Michael Doswell, LYM, Dr Kevan Tucker, Margaret Dickinson, Dennis Jones, Peter and Josie Fawcett, Mr and Mrs W W Burke, Helen Clarke)

WALTON [NY5264]

Centurian CA8 2DH: Artfully simple and comfortable refurbishment popular with walkers and cyclists, big informal flagstoned bar with large range fire, lunchtime snacks from sandwiches up, more ambitious evening choice of good inventive food using local produce inc sausages from their own rare breed pigs, local Geltsdale, Jennings and Timothy Taylors ales, decent wines; small entrance lounge with daily papers, conservatory restaurant (not always used) overlooking Cold Fell; more great views from large terrace, five bedrooms, cl winter wkdy lunchtimes (David and Sue Smith)

WASDALE HEAD [NY1807]

Wasdale Head Inn CA20 1EX [NE of Wast Water]: Mountain hotel under new management and worth knowing for its stunning fellside setting, good range of local ales (Great Gable beers no longer brewed or sold here), roomy walkers' bar with nice fire, enjoyable home-made food, good choice of wines, striking mountain photographs, traditional games; panelled residents' bar, lounge and restaurant; children welcome, dogs in bar, 12 bedrooms, seven self-catering apartments, open all day (Tim and Rosemary Wells, LYM, David and Sharon Collison, the Didler, Mr and Mrs Maurice Thompson, Simon Daws, Tina and David Woods-Taylor)

WINDERMERE [SD3801]

Langdale Chase LA23 1LW: Victorian country-house hotel doing good bar lunches inc unusual sandwiches in conservatory with stunning Windermere views; extensive lakeside grounds, 37 bedrooms (Margaret and Jeff Graham)

WITHERSLACK [SD4482]

Derby Arms LA11 6RH [just off A590]: Nicely redecorated spacious family pub, heavy curtains, rugs and dark oak, Coniston Bluebird and Thwaites Wainwright, good food from sandwiches through steaks to traditional puddings, evening entertainment; dogs welcome (Ray and Winifred Halliday, Sarah Priday)

Bedroom prices normally include full english breakfast, VAT and any inclusive service charge that we know of. Prices before the '/' are for single rooms, after for two people in double or twin (B includes a private bath, S a private shower). If there is no '/', the prices are only for twin or double rooms (as far as we know there are no singles). If there is no B or S, as far as we know no rooms have private facilities.

Derbyshire

A good clutch of new entries this year includes the Church Inn at Chelmorton (straight in with a Beer Award), the Bulls Head at Denby (a contemporary dining pub), the Ladybower Inn at Ladybower Reservoir (with both Stay and Beer Awards) and the Flying Childers in Stanton in Peak (a super choice of beers). Pubs that are doing well here tend to be in lovely old or interesting buildings and most of them have well kept beer, and in several examples a very enterprising range. Of note are the Bear at Alderwasley with up to eight, the Old Poets Corner in Ashover with ten (the enthusiastic owner also holds beer festivals), the Brunswick in Derby with an impressive 16, about half of which are from their own microbrewery. The starred Olde Gate at Brassington, as ever, deserves a mention for its genuine traditional pubbyness, as does the kindly old landlady at the unspoilt Barley Mow at Kirk Ireton with her five beers traditionally served straight from the cask. Local brewers have a great presence here and an interesting brewer to watch out for is the relatively new Blue Monkey (based in Ilkeston) which has already done well getting its beers into a good number of Derbyshire Main Entries. There's plenty of very reasonably priced food in this county (notably the Old Poets Corner at Ashover) but not huge competition for the County Dining Pub Award. The obvious winner and our Derbyshire Dining Pub 2011 is the Plough at Hathersage – its clever menu ranges from good quality pubby standards to more elaborate special occasion food. Two other pubs that deserve a mention this year are the Red Lion at Litton with its very friendly landlady and the nice and simple White Horse at Wolley Moor with its three local beers.

ALDERWASLEY
SK3153   MAP 7

Bear ★ ♀ ◗

Village signposted with Breanfield off B5035 E of Wirksworth at Malt Shovel; inn 0.5 miles SW of village, on Ambergate—Wirksworth high back road; DE56 2RD

Unspoilt country inn with low-beamed cottagey rooms, good range of real ales and a peaceful garden; bedrooms

A terrific all-rounder and justifiably popular, this happy character-laden tavern has lovely dark low-beamed rooms with warming open fires and a cheerful miscellany of antique furniture including high-backed settles and locally made antique oak chairs with derbyshire motifs. One little room is filled right to its built-in wall seats by a single vast table. Other décor includes staffordshire china ornaments, old paintings and engravings. There's no obvious front door – you get in through the plain back entrance by the car park and as it can get busy you may need to book. Bass, Derby Bluebear, Hartington IPA, Thornbridge Jaipur and Timothy Taylors Landlord are on handpump alongside a guest or two from brewers such as Greene King, and they do several wines by the glass from a decent list, as well as malt whiskies. Well spaced picnic-sets out on the side grass have peaceful country views.

🍴 As well as sandwiches and home-made crusty rolls (afternoons only) the regularly changing menu might include smoked haddock fishcakes with citrus mayonnaise, fried whitebait, steak and potato pie, fried scallops with bacon and mushroom cream sauce, ham, egg and chips, lamb shanks, twice cooked pork belly on red cabbage, root vegetable stew with cheese mash and steaks, with puddings such as profiteroles, apple crumble and bread and butter pudding. *Starters/Snacks: £3.95 to £5.95. Main Courses: £8.95 to £15.95. Puddings: £4.50*

Free house ~ Licensee Pete Buller ~ Real ale ~ Bar food (12-9(9.30 Fri, Sat)) ~ (01629) 822585 ~ Children welcome ~ Dogs allowed in bar ~ Open 12-11(10.30 Sun) ~ Bedrooms: /£75S(£90B)

Recommended by Stephen Shepherd, Richard Cole, P A Rowe, Eric Condliffe, Peter F Marshall, Pam and John Smith, John and Enid Morris, the Didler, Brian and Jean Hepworth, Bruce and Sharon Eden, Ryta Lyndley, Derek and Sylvia Stephenson

ASHOVER

SK3462   MAP 7

Old Poets Corner 🍺 £ 🛏

Butts Road (B6036, off A632 Matlock—Chesterfield); S45 0EW

A fine range of interesting real ales and ciders in simple village pub with enthusiastic owners; hearty, reasonably priced food

They keep an impressive range of ten real ales at this delightfully laid-back and deservedly popular pub. Several are brewed in the pub's own microbrewery and are served alongside guests from mainly local brewers such as Batemans, JHB, Oakham and Phoenix. You can do a brewery tour and they hold regular beer festivals. As well as a terrific choice of eight farm ciders they also stock a good choice of perries, fruit wines, malt whiskies and belgian beers. With a cosy, lived-in feel, the relaxed and informal bar has a mix of chairs and pews with well worn cushions, a pile of board games by a piano, a big mirror above a warming fire, lots of knick-knacks and hops around the counter; piped music. A small room opening off the bar has another fireplace, a stack of newspapers and vintage comics, and a french door leading to a tiny balcony with a couple of tables; simple dining room. The landlord is very keen on music and holds acoustic, folk and blues sessions once or twice a week. Posters around the walls list what's coming up, which might also include weekly quiz nights, occasional poetry evenings and morris dancers. The bedrooms are attractive, and they also have a holiday cottage for up to eight people.

🍴 Good honest bar food, very reasonably priced and served in generous helpings, includes sandwiches and pies (with a few available all day from a fridge by the bar), hot baguettes, battered king prawns, whitebait, a selection of home-made sausages, haddock in beer batter with mushy peas, leek and mushroom crumble and beef stew, and puddings such as spotted dick or bubble mint cheesecake. On Sundays they do a good value lunchtime carvery and serve curries in the evening. *Starters/Snacks: £1.95 to £5.50. Main Courses: £6.95 to £12.95. Puddings: £1.75 to £4.25*

Own brew ~ Licensees Kim and Jackie Beresford ~ Real ale ~ Bar food ~ Restaurant ~ (01246) 590888 ~ Children welcome away from bar until 9pm ~ Dogs allowed in bar and bedrooms ~ Live music Sun and Tues evenings ~ Open 12-11 ~ Bedrooms: /£70S

Recommended by the Didler, Dr Peter Andrews, Keith and Chris O'Neill, Sam Frankland, John and Enid Morris, Andrew and Mary Ransom, John and Susan Miln, John and Sarah Perry, Derek and Sylvia Stephenson, Ryta Lyndley, Ben Williams

BEELEY

SK2667   MAP 7

Devonshire Arms 🍽 🍷 🍺 🛏

B6012, off A6 Matlock—Bakewell; DE4 2NR

Contemporary twist to lovely old interior; local beers, good wine list, interesting carefully sourced food, attractive comfortable bedrooms

Almost more restaurant-with-rooms, this handsome stone-built village inn (converted from cottages back in 1741) makes for a slightly more formal dining experience but does give a nod to pubbyness at lunchtime. Contemporary colours nicely set off attractive traditional interior features: between black beams, flagstones, stripped stone, traditional settles and cheerful log fires, you will find light brightly coloured modern furnishings, prints and floral arrangements. Despite the accent on dining they keep six changing real ales, most likely including Black Sheep, Peak Ales Chatsworth Gold, Theakstons Old Peculier, Thornbridge Jaipur and Whim Hartington, and they've several wines by the glass from a well chosen list and a good range of malt whiskies, as well as local mineral water. The inn stands in an attractive village in the Peak District on the fringes of the Chatsworth Estate and you can walk to Chatsworth house itself from here (though you might not feel comfortable in the pub in walking gear). Note that although dogs are allowed to stay in the comfortable bedrooms they are not allowed in the bar.

🍴 **Not cheap but the imaginative food is cooked to order, so there might be a wait at busy times. The short but well balanced changing menu could include starters such as warm butternut panna cotta with goats cheese, tempura fish assiette, moules marinière, crayfish and prawn cocktail, battered cod, roast bream with capers, pigeon with button mushrooms, confit potatoes with brandy and sultanas, beef fillet medallions with wild mushroom cream, and puddings such as roast plum soup with vanilla ice-cream and chocolate brownie with marshmallow cream; afternoon snack menu.** *Starters/Snacks: £3.95 to £7.95. Main Courses: £6.95 to £16.95. Puddings: £5.95*

Free house ~ Licensee Alan Hill ~ Real ale ~ Bar food (12-9.30) ~ (01629) 733259 ~ Children welcome ~ Dogs allowed in bedrooms ~ Open 12-11.30(10.30 Sun) ~ Bedrooms: £105B/£125B

Recommended by James A Waller, B and M A Langrish, Mike and Sue Loseby, Keith and Chris O'Neill, Marian and Andrew Ruston, Margaret and Jeff Graham, M G Hart, S P Watkin, P A Taylor, Dr and Mrs A K Clarke, Richard Cole, Stephen Shepherd

BRASSINGTON   SK2354   MAP 7

Olde Gate ★

Village signposted off B5056 and B5035 NE of Ashbourne; DE4 4HJ

Lovely old interior, candlelit at night, country garden

This unspoilt listed building (just a few minutes' drive from Carsington Water) is full of attractive old architectural features, from its mullioned windows to a Georgian panelled room. Fine old furnishings include an ancient wall clock, rush-seated old chairs and antique settles, including one lovely ancient black solid oak one. Log fires blaze away, gleaming copper pots sit on a 17th-c kitchen range, pewter mugs hang from a beam, and a side shelf boasts a collection of embossed Doulton stoneware flagons. To the left of a small hatch-served lobby, a cosy beamed room has stripped panelled settles, scrubbed-top tables and a blazing fire under a huge mantelbeam. Brakspear Oxford Gold and Marstons Pedigree are on handpump alongside a guest such as Jennings Golden Host, and they keep a good selection of malt whiskies; crib dominoes and maybe Sunday evening boules in summer and Friday evening bell-ringers. A very inviting garden has a good number of tables looking out to idyllic little silvery-walled pastures and there are some benches in the small front yard.

🍴 **Food here is fairly priced. As well as filled baguettes (not Sunday) the lunchtime menu includes warm goats cheese tartlet with red onion marmalade, gammon, egg and chips, steak and Guinness pie, penne with tomato, mushroom and basil sauce, battered fish and rump steak. The evening menu might add more elaborate dishes such as medallions of monkfish with cream curry sauce, braised oxtail and duck breast with plum and star anise sauce.** *Starters/Snacks: £4.25 to £6.50. Main Courses: £7.50 to £13.95. Puddings: £3.95 to £5.50*

Marstons ~ Lease Peter Scragg ~ Real ale ~ Bar food (12-2(2.30 Sun), 6.30-8.45 Tues-Sat; not Sun evening) ~ (01629) 540448 ~ Children welcome away from main bar area ~ Dogs welcome ~ Open 12-2.30(3.30 Sat, 4 Sun), 6(8.30 Sun in winter)-11(midnight Sat); closed all day Mon (except bank hols), Tues lunchtime

Recommended by Brian and Jacky Wilson, Mike Proctor, Tully, Susan Lang, John and Enid Morris, the Didler, Peter F Marshall, David and Sue Atkinson, David Hunt

Prices of main dishes sometimes now don't include vegetables – if in doubt, ask.

CHELMORTON

Church Inn 🍺

Village signposted off A5270, between A6 and A515 SE of Buxton; keep on up through village towards church; SK17 9SL

SK1170   MAP 7

Cosy and convivial village inn beautifully set in High Peak walking country – good value

In a quiet spot at the end of the road up to the moors, opposite a largely 18th-c church prettily tucked into the woodland, this pub has fine views over the village and the hills beyond from good teak tables on its two-level terrace. The chatty low-ceilinged carpeted bar is traditionally furnished with cushioned built-in benches and simple chairs around polished cast-iron-framed tables – one or two still with their squeaky sewing treadles. Shelves of readable books, Tiffany-style lamps and house plants in the curtained windows, atmospheric Dales' photographs and prints, and a coal-effect stove in the stripped-stone end wall all add a cosy feel, but the greatest boost to the atmosphere is the helpful can-do attitude of the cheerful young licensees. Well kept Adnams, Marstons Bitter and Pedigree and a couple of guests such as Storm Tornado and Thornbridge Jaipur on handpump; darts and pool in a tiled-floor games area on the left; piped music and board games. We have not yet heard from readers staying in the annexe bedrooms, but we'd expect these to appeal strongly to walkers.

🍽 Sensibly priced food runs from sandwiches and cheesy melts through generous hot meat baps with chips to black pudding fritters, chicken goujons, steak and kidney pie, chilli and chicken balti, with daily specials such as beef braised in Guinness with stilton dumplings, rabbit pie with suet crust pastry, battered haddock and mushroom stroganoff. *Starters/Snacks: £3.75 to £5.00. Main Courses: £7.75 to £12.00. Puddings: £4.00*

Free house ~ Licensees Julie and Justin Satur ~ Real ale ~ Bar food (12-2.30, 6.30(7 in winter)-9; 12-9 Fri, Sun) ~ (01298) 85319 ~ Children welcome ~ Dogs allowed in bar ~ Open 12-3.30, 6.30-midnight; 12-midnight Sat, Sun; 12-3, 7-midnight weekdays in winter ~ Bedrooms: /£70S

Recommended by Peter F Marshall, J and E Dakin, Bruce and Sharon Eden, Mr and Mrs A Woolstone, Barry Collett

DENBY

Bulls Head

Denby Common, between A609 and A6007 S of Ripley; DE5 8PW

SK4047   MAP 7

Wide choice of food usefully served all day in clean-cut modern dining pub, pubbier side too; good-sized garden

A fire in 2006 prompted rebuilding in an expansive contemporary style – sweeps of light ceramic floor tiling or pale boards (as well as some carpet), curving wall, stairs up to a mezzanine with glazed balustrade, big abstract artworks on the off-white or dark brown walls. Even this main area is not too modern: there's a mix of familiar pub tables (restained a uniform darkish brown on top) and of seats from simple wooden chairs to high-backed leather dining chairs, even a couple of wing armchairs by the two stoves in a two-way fireplace. And on the right a smaller bar, with some flagstones and a woodburner in a virtual wall of logs, is more conventionally pubby, with a games machine. The neat black-uniformed young staff are friendly and efficient; Bass and Greene King IPA and Abbot on handpump, piped pop music, disabled facilities. There are picnic-sets on a spread of grass behind, with a terrace there, and another in front with modern chrome and wood tables under a big canopy. Handy for Denby Pottery visitor centre.

🍽 The grill-style menu includes cajun chicken strips, garlic mushrooms with cream, black pudding with horseradish dip, filled baguettes, ham, egg and chips, peking duck wrap, sharing platters, spicy white crab cakes, a full range of steaks and toppings, hickory chicken breast, chilli, steak and kidney pie, tuna loin with mediterranean sauce, salmon and rocket lasagne and vegetable enchiladas. *Starters/Snacks: £3.50 to £5.95. Main Courses: £6.95 to £16.95. Puddings: £3.95 to £5.25*

Probably a Pub Company Ltd ~ Manager Simon West ~ Real ale ~ Bar food (11.30-9.30(10 Fri, Sat); 12-9 Sun) ~ Restaurant ~ (01773) 513000 ~ Children welcome ~ Dogs allowed in bar ~ Jazz Mon evenings ~ Open 11.30-11(12 Fri, Sat); 12-10.30 Sun

Recommended by Phil and Jane Hodson, Derek and Sylvia Stephenson

DERBY   SK3635   MAP 7

Brunswick ◨ £

Railway Terrace; close to Derby Midland station; DE1 2RU

One of Britain's oldest railwaymen's pubs, now something of a treasure trove of real ales, with its own microbrewery adjacent

This former railwaymen's hostelry, dating from 1842, offers a total of 16 or so beers on handpump or tapped straight from the cask, with seven or eight of them coming from their own purpose-built microbrewery (some very reasonably priced at just £1.80 a pint). Changing guests might be from brewers such as Banks's, Burton Bridge, Everards, Marstons, RCH and Timothy Taylors. You can do a tour of the brewery for £7.50 which includes a meal and a pint. The welcoming high-ceilinged bar has heavy well padded leather seats, whisky-water jugs above the dado, and a dark blue ceiling and upper wall with squared dark panelling below. Another room is decorated with little old-fashioned prints and swan's neck lamps, and has a high-backed wall settle and a coal fire; behind a curved glazed partition wall, a chatty family parlour narrows to the apex of the triangular building. Informative wall displays tell you about the history and restoration of the building, and there are interesting old train photographs; TV, games machines and darts. There are two outdoor seating areas, including a terrace behind. They'll gladly give dogs a bowl of water.

🍴 **Straightforward and very inexpensive lunchtime bar food includes toasties, home-made soup, chilli and chips, and weekly changing specials such as ostrich burgers, wild boar sausages and chilli cheeseburgers.** *Starters/Snacks: £1.50 to £2.50. Main Courses: £3.00 to £5.50*

Everards ~ Tenant Graham Yates ~ Real ale ~ Bar food (11.30-2.30 Mon-Weds; 11.30-5 Thurs and Sat; 11.30-7 Fri; not Sun) ~ No credit cards ~ (01332) 290677 ~ Children in family parlour ~ Dogs welcome ~ Jazz Thurs evenings ~ Open 11-11; 12-10.30 Sun

Recommended by John and Helen Rushton, Andy Lickfold, Martin Grosberg, the Didler, Brian and Jean Hepworth

EARL STERNDALE   SK0966   MAP 7

Quiet Woman

Village signposted off B5053 S of Buxton; SK17 0BU

Friendly and splendidly unpretentious rural local in lovely Peak District countryside

Rustic, unspoilt and unsophisticated this old-fashioned country pub is a charming portal to an older England. The interior is very simple, with hard seats, plain tables (including a sunken one for dominoes or cards), low beams, quarry tiles, lots of china ornaments and a coal fire. There's a pool table in the family room (where you may be joined by a friendly jack russell eager for a place by the fire), darts, dominoes and skittles. Coach House Greys, Marstons Best and Pedigree, and a guest such as Brains Rev James are on handpump. They also sell gift packs of their own-label bottled beers which are Quiet Woman Old Ale, Quiet Woman Headless and Nipper Ale – the latter named after one of their previous jack russells (you can also buy Nipper or Quiet Woman woollen sweaters and polo shirts). There are picnic-sets out in front, and the budgies, hens, turkeys, ducks and donkeys are great entertainment for children. It's a popular place with walkers, with some very rewarding hikes across the nearby Dove valley towards Longnor and Hollinsclough; they have a caravan for hire in the garden, and you can arrange to stay at the small campsite next door. You can buy free-range eggs, local poetry books and even hay here.

🍴 **Bar food is limited to locally made very tasty pork pies (not always available).** *Starters/Snacks: £1.20 to £2.60*

Free house ~ Licensee Kenneth Mellor ~ Real ale ~ Bar food ~ No credit cards ~ (01298) 83211 ~ Children in pool room ~ Open 12-3(Sat 4, Sun 5), 7-11
Recommended by Dennis Jones, B and M Kendall, Malc Newton, the Didler, Barry Collett

FENNY BENTLEY
Coach & Horses
SK1750 MAP 7
A515 N of Ashbourne; DE6 1LB

Cosy former coaching inn with pretty country furnishings, roaring fires and food all day

The main part of this popular 16th-c coaching inn is quite traditional, with a welcoming atmosphere, a good mix of customers, flagstone floors, black beams hung with horsebrasses and wagon-wheels, hand-made pine furniture that includes flowery-cushioned wall settles, warm winter fires on exposed brick hearths and pewter mugs. There's also a conservatory dining room; quiet piped music, board games. Marstons Pedigree and a couple of guests from brewers such as Hartington and Whim are on handpump, and the landlord is knowledgeable about malt whiskies – he stocks just over two dozen. There are views across fields from tables in the side garden by an elder tree, and modern tables and chairs under cocktail parasols on the front terrace. The pub is within a few minutes' walk of the popular Tissington Trail (which follows a former railway line) and is best joined at the nearby picture-book village of Tissington.

As well as lunchtime and afternoon sandwiches, tasty bar food includes a continental deli board, smoked salmon mousse, fried trout with citrus butter, steak and stilton suet pudding, chicken breast stuffed with beef and sun-dried tomato, sausage with tomato, herb and onion gravy, chicken balti, and quorn, vegetable and mushroom stroganoff. Also specials (featuring fish on Fridays) and Sunday roasts; puddings from the blackboard. Starters/Snacks: £3.85 to £6.75. Main Courses: £8.95 to £15.25. Puddings: £3.75 to £4.75

Free house ~ Licensees John and Matthew Dawson ~ Real ale ~ Bar food (12-9) ~ Restaurant ~ (01335) 350246 ~ Children welcome ~ Open 11-11; 12-10.30 Sun
Recommended by Mike Proctor, John and Enid Morris, Bob and Pauline Fletcher, Jeremy and Ruth Preston-Hoar, the Didler, Bernard Stradling, Jill and Julian Tasker, John and Sharon Hancock

FOOLOW
Bulls Head
SK1976 MAP 7
Village signposted off A623 Baslow—Tideswell; S32 5QR

A nicely located inn by a village green with well kept ales and decent food

At the heart of a very pretty village in the limestone country of the Peak District, this likeable place has a simply furnished flagstoned bar where the old photographs on display feature a good collection of Edwardian naughties. Usually Adnams, Black Sheep, Peak Ales Swift Nick and a guest beer are on handpump and they've just over two dozen malts; piped music. A step or two takes you down into what may once have been a stable with its high ceiling joists, stripped stone and woodburning stove. On the other side, a sedate partly panelled dining room has more polished tables and plates arranged around on delft shelves. The west highland terriers are called Holly and Jack. Picnic-sets at the side have nice views and from here you can follow paths out over rolling pasture enclosed by dry-stone walls. The plague village of Eyam is not far away or you can just stroll round the green and duck pond.

Tasty bar food includes lunchtime snacks such as sandwiches and hot filled baps, as well as soup, thai fishcakes with sweet chilli sauce, stilton-stuffed mushrooms, minted lamb casserole and steak, ale and mushroom pie. The evening menu is slightly more restauranty, with starters such as smoked haddock rarebit, duck and mango salad and main courses like venison medallions in cumberland sauce, or roast bass with fennel. They do a good value OAP two-course lunch menu during the week. Starters/Snacks: £4.95 to £6.00. Main Courses: £7.95 to £13.95. Puddings: £4.50

Free house ~ Licensee Marilyn Bond ~ Real ale ~ Bar food (12-2, 7-9(5-8 Sun)) ~ Restaurant ~ (01433) 630873 ~ Children welcome ~ Dogs allowed in bar and bedrooms ~ Live music Fri evening ~ Open 12-3, 6.30-11; closed Mon except bank hols ~ Bedrooms: £60S/£80S

Recommended by Sam Frankland, Greta and Guy Pratt, Derek and Sylvia Stephenson, Michelle and Graeme Voss, Peter F Marshall, T R and B C Jenkins

HATHERSAGE

SK2380   MAP 7

Plough 🍴 🍷 🛏

Leadmill; B6001 towards Bakewell, OS Sheet 110 map reference 235805; S32 1BA

DERBYSHIRE DINING PUB OF THE YEAR

Comfortable dining pub usefully placed for exploring the Peak District, with good food, beer and wine, waterside garden and bedrooms

This 16th-c inn stands in nine acres of its own land in a lovely spot on the banks of the River Derwent. It has a pretty garden that slopes right down to the water and a lovely suntrap courtyard. Recently freshened up but still fairly traditional, the immaculately kept bar has dark wood tables – with cruets giving away the emphasis on dining here – on smart tartan carpets, a long banquette running almost the length of one wall, decorative plates on terracotta walls and pewter tankards hanging from a dark beam, with a big log fire at one end and a woodburning stove at the other; quiet piped music. They've a good wine list (with a dozen by the glass), 25 malt whiskies, and Black Sheep and a couple of guests from brewers such as Adnams and Timothy Taylor on handpump.

🍴 As well as lunchtime pubby standards such as fish and chips, ploughman's and pie of the day, the changing menu might include starters such as rillette of crab with gazpacho jelly and almond purée, marinated venison with root vegetable salad and crème fraîche, and main courses such as hake with parsley crust, cannon of lamb with black pudding, strozzapreti with potato, green beans and pesto, lamb sweetbreads with minted pea purée and rosemary gravy, roast pigeon with a cassoulet of haricots blancs and rib-eye steak. Food is not cheap, and you are advised to book a table. *Starters/Snacks: £5.00 to £10.00. Main Courses: £10.00 to £17.00. Puddings: £5.00 to £6.75*

Free house ~ Licensees Bob, Cynthia and Elliott Emery ~ Real ale ~ Bar food ~ Restaurant ~ (01433) 650319 ~ Children welcome ~ Open 11-11; 12-10.30 Sun ~ Bedrooms: £70B/£95B

Recommended by Mr and Mrs Roberts, Barry and Anne, James A Waller, Brian and Jacky Wilson, Kathy and Chris Armes, W K Wood, David and Cathrine Whiting, Fred and Lorraine Gill, Marian and Andrew Ruston, P A Rowe, DC, John and Enid Morris, Alun Jones, Rochelle Seifas, Jill and Julian Tasker, Michael and Maggie Betton

Scotsmans Pack 🛏

School Lane, off A6187; S32 1BZ

Cosy inn with decent, good value food

With its relaxed welcoming atmosphere, this friendly place is popular with both drinkers and diners. Perhaps the nicest area is on the left as you enter, with a fireplace and patterned wallpaper that's somewhat obscured by a splendid mass of brasses, stuffed animal heads and the like. Elsewhere there's plenty of dark panelling, lots of hanging tankards, plates on delft shelving and other knick-knacks arranged around the bar, and a good few tables, many with reserved signs (it's worth booking ahead, particularly at weekends). Half a dozen real ales, kept under light blanket pressure, include Jennings Cumberland, Marstons Bitter and Pedigree and guests from brewers such as Black Sheep, Timothy Taylor and Wychwood; piped music, games machine, TV, board games and darts. It's well placed for walkers, is near the churchyard containing the supposed grave of Little John, and has a pleasant terrace adjoining a trout-filled stream.

🍴 Food ranges from pubby standards such as sandwiches, ploughman's, steak and ale pie, fish and chips and rabbit casserole to more elaborate daily specials such as avocado and crab thermidor, spaghetti with smoked salmon flakes, mediterranean vegetable risotto, sautéed queen scallops with roast pumpkin risotto and sweet chilli dressing, pork loin cutlets on apple and sage stuffing with calvados sauce and local steaks; also puddings such as crème brûlée with shortbread and lemon tart with mixed berry compote. *Starters/Snacks: £2.95 to £6.25. Main Courses: £7.00 to £21.50. Puddings: £3.50 to £4.50*

Marstons ~ Lease Nick Beagrie, Steve Bramley and Susan Concannon ~ Real ale ~ Bar food (12-2, 6-9; 12-9 Sat, Sun; 12-9 Fri-Sun in summer) ~ (01433) 650253 ~ Children welcome ~ Open 11(12 Sun)-midnight; 11-3, 5-12 in winter ~ Bedrooms: £45S/£75B

Recommended by Peter F Marshall, David Carr, Barry and Anne, Brian and Jacky Wilson

HAYFIELD

SK0388   MAP 7

Lantern Pike

Glossop Road (A624 N) at Little Hayfield, just N of Hayfield; SK22 2NG

Friendly retreat from the surrounding moors of Kinder Scout, with reasonably priced food and bedrooms

Lying within the bounds of the Peak District National Park, this is a homely place to come down to if you've been walking on the windswept moors or up on Lantern Pike itself. The traditional red plush bar proudly displays photos of the original *Coronation Street* cast, many of whom were regulars here, along with Terry Warren, one of its earlier script writers, and Arthur Lowe of *Dad's Army* fame. It's quite possible that the interior, with its warm fire, brass platters, china and toby jugs, fresh flowers on the tables and counter lined with red plush stools (Timothy Taylors Landlord and a guest, often from local Howard Town on handpump, and several malt whiskies) hasn't changed much since those days; TV and piped music. Tables on a stone-walled terrace look over a big-windowed weaver's house towards Lantern Pike. More reports please.

🍴 Served in generous helpings, bar food includes sandwiches, panini, smoked salmon salad, spicy breadcrumbed chicken wings, pork cutlet with stilton sauce, crab salad, seafood platter, and changing blackboard specials such as haddock fishcake, mediterranean lemon chicken, chilli, vegetable curry and rump steak, and home-made ice-creams. *Starters/Snacks: £3.95 to £6.95. Main Courses: £8.95 to £12.95. Puddings: £3.95*

Enterprise ~ Lease Stella and Tom Cunliffe ~ Real ale ~ Bar food (12-2.30, 5-8.30; 12-8.30 Sun; 5-8 Mon) ~ Restaurant ~ (01663) 747590 ~ Children welcome ~ Dogs allowed in bar and bedrooms ~ Open 12-11(5-11 Mon); 12-3, 5-11 in winter ~ Bedrooms: £40B/£50B

Recommended by Dennis Jones

Royal

Market Street, just off A624 Chapel-en-le-Frith—Buxton; SK22 2EP

Bustling old-fashioned hotel with a good range of real ales

Some nice atmospheric dark panelling hints at the former role of this traditional stone hotel as a vicarage. These days, separate pubby areas work their way round a counter and have several fireplaces, bookshelves, brasses and house plants, newspapers to read, piped music and board games. Friendly staff serve Hydes alongside four guest ales from brewers such as Bollington, Copper Dragon, Hornbeam, Northumberland and Saltaire on handpump, and they hold a beer festival on the first weekend of October. There's a sunny terrace in front by the car park. More reports please.

🍴 The good value, very traditional bar menu includes sandwiches, garlic mushrooms, spinach and mushroom pancake, cod and chips, chicken curry, sirloin steak, hotpot and cheese and onion pie, as well as daily changing fish and vegetarian dishes and a hot pudding. On Mondays to Thursdays there are weekday lunchtime and early evening two-course meal deals, with an additional discount for pensioners. *Starters/Snacks: £2.95 to £3.75. Main Courses: £6.25 to £13.95. Puddings: £2.75 to £2.95*

Free house ~ Licensee David Ash ~ Real ale ~ Bar food (11-2.30, 6-9; 11-9 Sat; 11-7 Sun) ~ Restaurant ~ (01663) 742721 ~ Children welcome ~ Dogs welcome ~ Open 11-11(10.30 Sun) ~ Bedrooms: £50B/£70B

Recommended by the Didler

HOLBROOK   SK3645   MAP 7
Dead Poets 🍺 £
Village signposted off A6 S of Belper; Chapel Street; DE56 0TQ

Reassuringly pubby and unchanged, with an excellent range of real ales and simple cottagey décor

It's a rare thing these days to find a place as simple and unaltered as this atmospheric drinkers' local. Although there's a handful of basic snacks, the nine real ales here are the thing: Bass, Greene King Abbot and Marstons Pedigree are served in jugs from the cellar, alongside six guests on handpump from brewers such as Abbeydale, Blue Monkey, Castle Rock, Derventio, Oakham and Whim. They also serve Old Rosie and Thatcher's farm cider, a dozen whiskies and 20 country wines. Its interior is fairly dim, with black beams in the ochre ceiling, stripped-stone walls and broad flagstones, although there is a lighter conservatory at the back. There are candles on scrubbed tables, a big log fire in the end stone fireplace, high-backed winged settles forming neat cubicles along one wall, and pews and a variety of chairs in other intimate corners and hideaways. A small snug has bottle- and book-lined shelves and a woodburning stove. The décor makes a few nods to the pub's present name (it used to be the Cross Keys) including a photo of W B Yeats and a poem dedicated to the pub by Les Baynton, and there are old prints of Derby dotted around; piped music. Behind is a sort of verandah room with lanterns, heaters and a few plants, and more seats out in the yard.

🍴 **Alongside cobs (nothing else at weekends), bar food is limited to a few good value hearty dishes such as home-made soup and chilli con carne or casserole.** *Starters/Snacks: £2.00 to £4.95*

Everards ~ Tenant William Holmes ~ Real ale ~ Bar food (12-2 only) ~ No credit cards ~ (01332) 780301 ~ Children welcome in conservatory till 8pm ~ Dogs welcome ~ Open 12-2.30, 5-12; 12-midnight Fri, Sat; 12-11 Sun

Recommended by the Didler, Richard Stanfield

HOPE   SK1783   MAP 7
Cheshire Cheese 🍺 🛏
Off A6187, towards Edale; S33 6ZF

Cosy up-and-down old stone pub, with good real ales, in attractive Peak District village; bedrooms

This very popular honey-coloured 16th-c haunt can easily fill to capacity with locals as well as tourists. As there is glorious range of local walks, taking in the summits of Lose Hill and Win Hill, or the cave district of the Castleton area (the village of Hope itself is worth strolling around too, and as parking is limited, it might be worth arriving here on foot). Two very snug oak-beamed rooms are arranged on different levels, each with its own warming fire. Bradfield Blonde and Peak Ales Swift Nick are on handpump alongside a couple of changing guests and they've a dozen malts.

🍴 **As well as lunchtime snacks such as sandwiches and salads, food includes daily changing dishes such as arbroath smokie fishcake, steak and kidney suet pudding, lasagne, roast cod with prawn and dill sauce, and lamb shank in minted gravy; puddings such as home-made crumbles and spotted dick.** *Starters/Snacks: £4.25 to £6.95. Main Courses: £8.95 to £13.95. Puddings: £4.95*

Enterprise ~ Lease Craig Oxley ~ Real ale ~ Bar food (12-2(3 Sat), 6.30-9; 12-7 Sun) ~ (01433) 620381 ~ Children welcome till 9pm if eating ~ Dogs allowed in bar ~ Quiz Weds evening ~ Open 12-4, 6.30-11.30; 12-11.30 Sat; 12-10 Sun; closed Mon ~ Bedrooms: £50S/£75S(£85B)

Recommended by Dave Irving, Jenny Huggins, Peter F Marshall, John Fiander, Peter D La Farge, the Didler

---

We say if we know a pub allows dogs.

INGLEBY

SK3427   MAP 7

John Thompson ◧ £ ⇔

NW of Melbourne; turn off A514 at Swarkestone Bridge or in Stanton by Bridge; can also be reached from Ticknall (or from Repton on B5008); DE73 7HW

Own-brew pub that strikes the right balance between attentive service, roomy comfort and good value lunchtime food

Nicely pubby and beautifully kept, everything ticks along in a perfectly relaxed way here with plenty of readers enthusing about the quality of the beer brewed out back, the tasty good value food, and the friendly staff. Simple but comfortable, the big modernised lounge has ceiling joists, some old oak settles, button-back leather seats, sturdy oak tables, antique prints and paintings and a log-effect gas fire; piped music. A couple of smaller cosier rooms open off; piano, games machine, board games, darts, TV, and pool in the conservatory. They usually serve three of their own beers but may supplement a guest such as Black Sheep or Timothy Taylors Landlord. Surrounded by pretty countryside and near the River Trent, there are lots of tables by flower beds on the neat lawns, or you can sit on the partly covered terrace. Readers enjoy staying in the detached chalet lodges that were recently built in the grounds. The pub takes its name from the licensee's father.

🍽 **The short lunchtime menu includes sandwiches, soup, baked potatoes, salads, mediterranean vegetable risotto and roast beef carvery, with puddings such as fruit crumble and Mrs Thompson's famous bread and butter pudding – a speciality of the pub for the past 40 years.** *Starters/Snacks: £3.00 to £4.75. Main Courses: £6.25 to £7.25. Puddings: £3.00 to £3.25.*

Own brew ~ Licensee Nick Thompson ~ Real ale ~ Bar food (12-2) ~ (01332) 862469 ~ Children welcome in conservatory ~ Dogs allowed in bar ~ Open 11-2.30, 6-11; 11-11 Sat; 12-10.30 Sun; closed Mon lunchtime in winter ~ Bedrooms: /£60S

Recommended by the Didler, Margaret Walster, Pam and John Smith, Audrey McKenzie, Theo, Anne and Jane Gaskin, Richard Stanfield, Mr and Mrs H Franklin, Phil and Jane Hodson, David and Gill Carrington, Simon Donan, Jill and Julian Tasker, Yvonne Brown, Dr and Mrs TE Hothersall, Stephen Shepherd

KIRK IRETON

SK2650   MAP 7

Barley Mow ◧ ⇔

Village signed off B5023 S of Wirksworth; DE6 3JP

Character-laden old inn that focuses on real ale and conversation; bedrooms

This marvellously unaltered Jacobean house, with its very kindly landlady (she's been here over 30 years) and good mix of customers, is a gently relaxing place to sit and quietly chat. An inn since around 1800, it evokes how some grander rural pubs might have looked a century or so ago. The small main bar has a relaxed very pubby feel, with antique settles on the tiled floor or built into the panelling, a roaring coal fire, four slate-topped tables and shuttered mullioned windows. Another room has built-in cushioned pews on oak parquet and a small woodburning stove, and a third room has more pews, a tiled floor, low beams and big landscape prints. In casks behind a modest wooden counter are five well kept, often local, changing real ales mostly from smaller brewers such as Abbeydale, Blue Monkey, Cottage, Storm and Whim; french wines and farm cider too. There's a good-sized garden, a couple of benches out in front and a shop in what used to be the stable. This hilltop village is very pretty and is within walking distance of Carsington Water. Bedrooms are comfortable and readers enjoy the good breakfasts served in the stone-flagged kitchen.

🍽 **Very inexpensive lunchtime filled rolls are the only food; the decent evening meals (no choice) are reserved for those staying here; good breakfasts.** *Starters/Snacks: £1.50*

Free house ~ Licensee Mary Short ~ Real ale ~ No credit cards ~ (01335) 370306 ~ Children welcome away from bar ~ Dogs allowed in bar and bedrooms ~ Open 11-2, 7-11(10.30 Sun) ~ Bedrooms: £35S/£55B

Recommended by the Didler, Pam and John Smith, Steve Kirby, Andrew and Mary Ransom, Eddie Edwards, Tich Critchlow

LADYBOWER RESERVOIR

SK1986 MAP 7

Ladybower Inn 🍺 🛏

A57 Sheffield—Glossop, just E of junction with A6013; S33 0AX

All-day food in comfortable proper pub nestling above reservoir in good walking country; good value bedrooms

The long carpeted bar's series of linked bays gives a comfortable feeling of separate small areas without losing the companionable atmosphere of a good-sized pub – one that has good regional ales on handpump such as Acorn Barnsley, Bradfield Farmers Blonde and Greene King Ruddles County, and a guest such as Thornbridge Hopton; also decent wines by the glass. Furnishings are mainly straightforwardly pubby – wall banquettes, captain's and country kitchen chairs and the like; the most relaxed place to eat is down at the end on the right, with leather-padded traditional dining chairs around heavier tables, Lancaster bomber pictures recalling the Dambusters' practice runs on the reservoir, and a coal-effect fire. There's another fire at the other end, with darts there. Staff are friendly and enthusiastic; unobtrusive piped music; round picnic-sets out in front. Staying in the annexe bedrooms. If you stay you won't be disturbed by traffic noise – but the road is busy, so crossing from the car park opposite needs care.

🍴 As well as sandwiches, the very generous home cooking, using local farm supplies, trout from the reservoir and plenty of seasonal vegetables, might include cullen skink, garlic and thyme sautéed mushrooms on tapenade toast, potted grouse with onion marmalade, ploughman's, lamb and vegetable ragoût with herb dumplings, venison sausages with braised puy lentils and mash, fennel tart with goats cheese and thyme, salmon baked in puff pastry with roquefort and spinach with chive cream sauce, and rump steak. *Starters/Snacks: £3.95 to £6.00. Main Courses: £8.50 to £15.50. Puddings: £4.50*

Free house ~ Licensee Deborah Wilde ~ Real ale ~ Bar food (12-9) ~ (01433) 651241 ~ Children welcome ~ Open 10-midnight(10pm Sun) ~ Bedrooms: £40S/£70S

Recommended by D J and P M Taylor, Mrs J Ekins-Daukes, James A Waller, Fiona Pleasant

Yorkshire Bridge

A6013 N of Bamford; S33 0AZ

Agreeable hotel close to the Upper Derwent Valley Reservoirs, with five real ales and decent bedrooms

The fairly traditional spreading interior of this pleasant hotel makes a useful stopping point in the dramatic Upper Derwent Valley. One area has a plush country-cottage feel with patterened carpets, floral wallpaper and curtains, sturdy cushioned wall settles, staffordshire dogs and toby jugs above a big stone fireplace, china on delft shelves and a panelled dado. Another extensive area, also with a fire, is lighter and more airy with pale wood furniture, good big black and white photographs and lots of polished brass and decorative plates on the walls. The Bridge Room (with yet another fire) has oak tables and chairs, and the Garden Room gives views across a valley to steep larch woods. Peak Ales Bakewell Best and Chatsworth Gold, Kelham Island Pale Rider and Easy Rider, and a guest such as Copper Dragon Scotts 1816 are on handpump and they offer several wines by the glass; piped music; disabled lavatories.

🍴 Straightforward bar food includes lunchtime rolls, baked potatoes, salads, quiche, pot-roasted lamb, steak and kidney pie and a daily changing fish dish. *Starters/Snacks: £3.75 to £5.95. Main Courses: £8.75 to £16.95. Puddings: £4.50*

Free house ~ Licensees Trevelyan and John Illingworth ~ Real ale ~ Bar food (12-2, 6-9(9.30 Fri, Sat); 12-8.30 Sun) ~ (01433) 651361 ~ Children welcome ~ Open 11-11(10.30 Sun) ~ Bedrooms: £65B/£96B

Recommended by Mike and Sue Loseby, Bruce and Sharon Eden, John and Enid Morris, Richard and Julie Hay, N R White

---

The 🍺 symbol shows pubs which keep their beer unusually well, have a particularly good range or brew their own.

LITTON

SK1675 MAP 7

Red Lion 🍺

Village signposted off A623, between B6465 and B6049 junctions; also signposted off B6049; SK17 8QU

Convivial all-rounder with reasonably priced food and unspoilt charm, prettily placed by village green

This is a jolly nice pub that has a happy atmosphere and is well run by a hard-working and ever-cheerful landlady. The two homely linked front rooms are nicely traditional with low beams, some panelling and blazing log fires. There's a bigger back room with good-sized tables and large antique prints on its stripped-stone walls. The small bar counter has Abbeydale Absolution, Oakwell Barnsley and a couple of guests such as Adnams Broadside and Blue Monkey BG Sips, a good choice of decent wines (with a dozen by the glass) and several malt whiskies (all spirits are available as doubles for an extra £1); darts, shove-ha'penny, bagatelle, board games and piped music (evenings only). It does get very full at times, so do book if you want to eat here. Outdoor seating is on the pretty village green, which is covered in daffodils in early spring. A particularly interesting time to visit this Peak District village is during the annual well-dressing carnival (usually the last week in June), when locals create a picture from flower petals, moss and other natural materials.

🍽 **Well liked good value bar food includes sandwiches and filled baguettes, crayfish tail salad, fish and chips, liver and bacon with horseradish mash, steak and kidney pie, spicy vegetable curry, burgers and daily specials such as thai fishcakes with sweet chilli dip, seafood linguine, oxtail casserole, bobotie, baked bass with chilli, ginger, coriander and garlic, and puddings such as apple and berry crumble and spotted dick. Unusually, there's an entire gluten-free menu too; Sunday roast all day.** *Starters/Snacks: £2.60 to £5.95. Main Courses: £6.95 to £10.95. Puddings: £2.75 to £4.60*

Enterprise ~ Lease Suzy Turner ~ Real ale ~ Bar food (12-8(8.30 Thurs-Sun)) ~ (01298) 871458 ~ Children over 6 welcome ~ Dogs allowed in bar ~ Quiz first Mon of the month ~ Open 12-11 (midnight Sat, 10.30 Sun)

Recommended by Maurice and Janet Thorpe, Peter F Marshall, Malcolm and Pauline Pellatt, Greta and Guy Pratt, John and Enid Morris, the Didler, Barry Collett, Michelle and Graeme Voss, Hazel Matthews

SHELDON

SK1768 MAP 7

Cock & Pullet £

Village signposted off A6 just W of Ashford; DE45 1QS

Well run village pub with an appealingly unfussy atmosphere and good value bar food

With its low beams, exposed stonework, flagstones, scrubbed oak tables, pews and open fire, this cosily unpretentious, family-run place looks like it's been a pub for hundreds of years, but surprisingly it was only converted some dozen years ago and is now very much a village local with courteous staff and reasonably priced food and beers. A collection of 30 clocks, various representations of poultry (including some stuffed) and a cheerful assembly of deliberately mismatched furnishings are dotted around the little rooms. A plainer public bar has pool, darts and a TV; piped music. Hartington and Timothy Taylors Landlord are on handpump with one guest such as Theakstons. At the back a pleasant little terrace has tables and a water feature, and as this pretty village is just off the Limestone Way it's a popular all-year-round stop with walkers.

🍽 **Inexpensive bar food typically includes prawn cocktail, sandwiches, fish pie, a curry and vegetarian dish of the day, steak in ale pie, steaks and specials such as turkey, ham and mushroom pie and sausage and mash with onion gravy; Sunday roast.** *Starters/Snacks: £3.00 to £4.95. Main Courses: £6.00 to £11.00. Puddings: £3.50*

Free house ~ Licensees David and Kath Melland ~ Real ale ~ Bar food (12-2.30, 6-9) ~ Restaurant ~ No credit cards ~ (01629) 814292 ~ Children welcome ~ Dogs allowed in bar and bedrooms ~ Open 11(12 Sun)-midnight ~ Bedrooms: /£60B

Recommended by Dr and Mrs A K Clarke, DC, J and E Dakin, A J Liles, Peter F Marshall, Lawrence R Cotter, Dennis Jones

STANTON IN PEAK

SK2364 MAP 7

Flying Childers ◖ £

Village signposted off B5056 Bakewell—Ashbourne; Main Road – which is twisty and steep; DE4 2LW

Top-notch beer and inexpensive simple bar lunches in warm-hearted unspoilt pub – a delight

The friendly landlord here tracks down a changing stream of interesting beers, beside his regular Wells & Youngs Bombardier: on our inspection visit he had Sharps Doom Bar and Storm Red Mist on handpump, and was talking enthusiastically about forthcoming treats from Cottage and Spire. The room to enjoy them best in is the snug little right-hand bar, virtually built for chat, with its dark beam-and-plank ceiling, dark wall settles, a single pew, plain tables, a hot coal and log fire, a few team photographs, and dominoes and cribbage; piped music. There's a bigger similarly plain bar on the right and a couple of picnic-sets out in front. This beautiful steep stone village overlooks a rich green valley and there are good walks all around. Flying Childers was an unbeatable racehorse of the early 18th century.

▥ **Prepared by the landlady – as friendly as her husband – lunchtime bar food includes soup, filled cobs, toasties and casseroles.** *Starters/Snacks: £1.70 to £4.50*

Free house ~ Licensees Stuart and Mandy Redfern ~ Real ale ~ Bar food (lunchtimes only) ~ (01629) 636333 ~ Children welcome in lounge ~ Dogs welcome ~ Acoustic night first Thurs of the month, quiz night fourth Thurs ~ Open 12-3, 7-11; closed Mon, Tues lunchtime
Recommended by the Didler, Dennis Jones, Pete Baker

WOOLLEY MOOR

SK3661 MAP 7

White Horse

Badger Lane, off B6014 Matlock—Clay Cross; DE55 6FG

Dining pub run by young licensee couple, with good food in attractive old stone building in pretty countryside

This smart old inn in a charming rural spot is enjoyed by readers for its thoughtfully prepared food. The interior is uncluttered, with neatly arranged furniture (including a leather sofa on new stone floors or wooden boards), boldly patterned curtains and blinds, little to distract on the cream walls and uniform lamps on window sills. There's a buoyantly chatty feel to the tap room, with three local beers from Bradfield and Peak Ales on handpump from the newly built brick counter; conservatory; piped music. The garden has a boules pitch, picnic-sets and a children's play area with a wooden train, boat, climbing frame and swings. Ogston Reservoir is just a couple of minutes' drive from here.

▥ **Good bar food includes sandwiches and filled baguettes, ploughman's, tempura chicken with oriental dipping sauce, black pudding, smoked bacon and poached egg on toast, battered cod, sausage and mash with red onion gravy, seared scallops with pea purée, sun-dried tomato, goats cheese and olive pansotti, crispy pork belly with spring onion mash and smoked bacon sauce, steak and ale casserole and sirloin steak.** *Starters/Snacks: £4.95 to £5.25. Main Courses: £4.95 to £10.25. Puddings: £4.95*

Free house ~ Licensees David and Melanie Boulby ~ Real ale ~ Bar food (12-1.45(2.30 Sun), 5.30-8.45; not Sun evening) ~ Restaurant ~ (01246) 590319 ~ Children welcome ~ Open 12-3, 5.30-11; 12-3.30 Sun; closed first three weeks of Jan
Recommended by Michael and Margaret Slater, Phil and Jane Hodson, Sam Frankland, Andrew and Mary Ransom, Peter F Marshall, Michael and Maggie Betton

> Post Office address codings confusingly give the impression that a few pubs are in Derbyshire, when they're really in Cheshire (which is where we list them).

LUCKY DIP

Besides the fully inspected pubs, you might like to try these Lucky Dips recommended to us and described by readers (if you do, please send us reports: feedback@goodguides.com).

ASHBOURNE [SK1846]
Green Man Royal Hotel DE6 1GH [St John St]: 17th-c coaching inn with gallows sign spanning road, now tap for Leatherbritches (brewery at back) with their full range kept well and five guests (Aug bank hol beer festival), summer farm ciders, good choice of enjoyable reasonably priced fresh food, cosy traditional oak-panelled bar with leather sofas and open fires, modern bar with sports TVs, pool and music; children and dogs welcome, 18 newly refurbished bedrooms, open all day, till late Fri, Sat *(Pam and John Smith, the Didler)*

ASHFORD IN THE WATER [SK1969]
☆ *Bulls Head* DE45 1QB [Church St]: Comfortable beamed pub dating from 16th c and set well back from road, wide choice of good changing food from lunchtime sandwiches up, friendly efficient service, well kept Robinsons, blazing log fire in turkey-carpeted open-plan bar, daily papers; may be piped music; overshoes for walkers, tables out behind and in front, lovely village *(Peter F Marshall, Bruce and Sharon Eden, BB, P J and R D Greaves, Neil and Brenda Skidmore)*

ASHOVER [SK3463]
Black Swan S45 0AB [Church St]: Popular village pub with well priced food inc good range of sandwiches, beamed open-plan bar with fire, well kept Black Sheep, Greene King Abbot, Thornbridge Wild Swan and guests, prompt cheerful service, dining room; popular with younger people wknds, may be live music; terrace, good local walks *(the Didler)*

BARLOW [SK3474]
Old Pump S18 7TD [B6051 (Hackney Lane)]: Villagey dining pub with long narrow beamed bar and tiny alcove, book-ended by dining room and two comfortably traditional little rooms, two changing ales, enjoyable food inc good value Sun lunch, competent young staff; children welcome, some tables out at front and in sheltered side garden, bedrooms, open all day Sun *(LYM, Peter F Marshall, Jeremy and Ruth Preston-Hoar)*

BASLOW [SK2572]
Wheatsheaf DE45 1SR [Nether End]: Recently redone Marstons pub, good choice of food all day inc specials board, their ales kept well; children's play area, bedrooms *(G Wordsworth)*

BELPER [SK3547]
Cross Keys DE56 1FZ [Market Pl]: Friendly pub with well kept Bass, Batemans (inc a house beer) and one or two guests, straightforward food, coal fire and bar billiards in lounge, pool and TV in bar; regular beer festivals, open all day *(the Didler)*
Thorntree DE56 1FF [Chesterfield Rd (B6013)]: Comfortable unfussy two-bar local

with congenial licensees, well kept Bass, Greene King and three guests *(the Didler, Stephen Shepherd)*

BIRCHOVER [SK2362]
Druid DE4 2BL [off B5056; Main St]: Two-storey dining pub with four spacious areas, good varied food inc some unusual choices, friendly welcoming service, well kept beers such as Marstons Pedigree; children welcome, picnic-sets out in front, good area for walks, open all day Sat, cl Sun evening *(Trevor and Sylvia Millum, Stephen Fountain, Tich Critchlow, Steve and Sue Griffiths, LYM)*
Red Lion DE4 2BN [Main St]: Friendly early 18th-c stone-built two-room pub, recently refurbished by sardinian landlord, good value home-made food with some italian influences, well kept ales (up to five in summer), glass-covered well inside, woodburners; seats outside with nice rural views, good local walks *(S P Watkin, P A Taylor, the Didler)*

BONSALL [SK2758]
☆ *Barley Mow* DE4 2AY [off A5012 W of Cromford; The Dale]: Friendly, basic, one-room beamed stone-built pub, colourful atmosphere and character furnishings, decent straightforward food, well kept ales such as Greene King, Leatherbritches and Whim, coal fire, pictures and bric-a-brac, live music Fri and Sat inc UFO-enthusiast landlord playing his accordion; short walk out to lavatories; nice little front terrace, events such as hen racing and marrow dressing, walks organised from the pub, open all day wknds, cl Mon *(Pete Baker, the Didler, Adrian Johnson, Tony Harrison, Rob Garrett)*

BUXTON [SK1266]
☆ *Bull i' th' Thorn* SK17 9QQ [Ashbourne Rd (A515) 6 miles S of Buxton, nr Flagg and Hurdlow]: Fascinating medieval hall doubling as straightforward roadside dining pub, handsome panelling, old flagstones and big log fire, armour, longcase clocks and all sorts of antique features; good value straightforward food all day, well kept Robinsons, jovial landlord, plain games room and family room; children and dogs welcome, terrace and big lawn, rare breeds farm behind, good walks, bedrooms, big breakfast, open all day from 9.30am, may be cl Mon *(the Didler, Barry Collett)*
☆ *Old Sun* SK17 6HA [High St]: Charming old building with friendly helpful landlady, well kept Marstons-related ales and a guest, good choice of wines by the glass, farm cider, bargain food from good sandwiches and baked potatoes up served till 10pm, several cosy and interesting traditional linked areas, low beams and soft lighting, open fires, bare boards or tiles, stripped wood screens, old local photographs; piped music, TV; children in back bar, open all day *(the Didler, Barry Collett, LYM)*

CALVER [SK2374]

Derwentwater Arms S32 3XQ [in centre bear left from Main St into Folds Head; Low Side]: Largely bright and modern inside, big windows looking down from village-centre knoll, hard-working young licensees, good value food (best to book), Theakstons and guest ales; children and dogs welcome, terraces on slopes below (disabled access), boules, open all day Sun *(Susan Lee, G Wordsworth, BB)*

Eyre Arms S32 3XH [Chesterfield Rd, Calver Sough]: Large Mansfield family dining pub, helpful friendly staff, enjoyable generous food (all day wknds), wide drinks' choice inc three real ales and good coffee, smart beamed lounge with blazing fire, shelves of bottles and plates, lots of copper and brass, family room, fish tank and piano; piped music, fruit machines; outside tables and play area, open all day *(Michael Butler)*

CARSINGTON [SK2553]

Miners Arms DE4 4DE [just N of B5035 Wirksworth—Ashbourne]: Friendly place nr Carsington Reservoir, generously served food inc popular Sun carvery, three or four real ales, decent cider; garden with plenty of room for children, pleasant village, good walking/cycling country *(Malc Newton)*

CASTLETON [SK1582]

☆ *Bulls Head* S33 8WH [Cross St (A6187)]: Imposing building spreading through several attractive linked areas, handsome panelling and pictures, appealing mix of comfortable seating inc sofas and easy chairs, heavy drapes, good reasonably priced food from ciabattas up, helpful friendly service, well kept Robinsons Dragon's Fire and Unicorn, coal fires; fairly unobtrusive piped music, may be live jazz; some roadside picnic-sets, five bedrooms *(Barry and Anne, BB)*

☆ *Castle Hotel* S33 8WG [High St/Castle St]: Roomy and welcoming Vintage Inn with extensive choice of good well priced food all day inc great puddings, good selection of real ales and of wines by the glass, decent coffee, friendly efficient staff even when busy, log fires, stripped-stone walls, beams and some ancient flagstones; piped music; children welcome, heated terrace, comfortable bedrooms, good breakfast, open all day *(LYM, N R White, Mrs J Ekins-Daukes, Bruce and Sharon Eden, R C Vincent)*

☆ *George* S33 8WG [Castle St]: Busy but relaxed, good value food from hearty sandwiches to imaginative main dishes, four well kept ales, two good-sized rooms, one mainly for eating, ancient beams and stripped stone, no music; children and dogs welcome, wide forecourt with lots of flower tubs, good walks, may be cl Mon lunchtime *(Keith and Chris O'Neill, Mike and Lynn Robinson)*

Olde Cheshire Cheese S33 8WJ [How Lane]: 17th-c inn with two linked beamed and carpeted areas, cosy and spotless, with well kept ales such as Acorn, Bradfield and Peak, good range of reasonably priced enjoyable

food all day, good house wine, friendly staff, two gas woodburners, lots of photographs, toby jugs and brassware, back dining room; piped music, TV, and they swipe your credit card before running a tab; children welcome in restaurant, dogs in bar, ten bedrooms, open all day *(BB, Fred and Lorraine Gill, Keith Rochell, Mike and Lynn Robinson)*

☆ *Olde Nags Head* S33 8WH [Cross St (A6187)]: Small solidly built and recently refurbished hotel dating from 17th c, interesting antique oak furniture and coal fire in civilised beamed and flagstoned bar with nice pictures, beers such as Black Sheep and Timothy Taylors, good coffee, helpful staff, good locally sourced food (inc meat from rare breeds) in bars and bistro, good value Sun carvery (second helpings encouraged); attractive village, comfortable bedrooms, open all day till late *(R C Vincent, Fred and Lorraine Gill, Mike and Lynn Robinson, LYM)*

CHAPEL-EN-LE-FRITH [SK0581]

Cross Keys SK23 0QQ [Chapel Milton]: Neatly kept old family pub with good value generous standard food (all day Sun), well kept beers inc Black Sheep, friendly service, smartly decorated small restaurant; children welcome, cl wkdy lunchtimes *(Malcolm and Pauline Pellatt)*

Fallow Deer SK23 0RB [Foresters Way, Bowden Lane]: Comfortable new Marstons dining pub, three of their beers, good value standard food all day inc bargain deals and children's menu, friendly efficient young staff, coal-effect gas fire; terrace tables, fenced play area with CCTV *(Dennis Jones, Guy and Caroline Howard)*

Hanging Gate SK23 9UH [Manchester Rd, Cockyard]: Beamed dining area with alcoves, good value food from extensive menu inc lunchtime and early evening set deals, also OAP and children's menus, real ale, good choice of wine; soft piped music *(Guy and Caroline Howard)*

CHESTERFIELD [SK3871]

Chesterfield Arms S41 7PH: Carefully restored and doing well under beer-enthusiast landlord, ten changing ales inc Everards and Leatherbritches, six real ciders, enjoyable straightforward home-made food (Thurs curry night), open fire, oak panelling and stripped wood floors; back room for beer festivals; open all day *(the Didler)*

Rutland S40 1XL [Stephenson Pl]: Uncomplicated pub next to crooked-spire church, thriving atmosphere, well kept Badger Best, Timothy Taylors Landlord, local Brampton and several other interesting changing ales, Weston's cider, low-priced pub food all day from sandwiches up; friendly polite service even when busy, rugs and assorted wooden furniture on bare boards, old photographs, darts; piped music; children welcome, open all day *(Tony Hobden, Alan Johnson, Keith and Chris O'Neill, the Didler)*

CHINLEY [SK0382]
Old Hall SK23 6EJ [Whitehough]: Impressive 16th-c stone-built inn with well kept Marstons and good changing choice of local ales such as Thornbridge (beer festivals), bottled belgian beers, real ciders in summer; efficient enthusiastic young staff, good choice of well priced home-made food (all day Sun till 7.30pm) from sandwiches up, minstrels' gallery restaurant, some live music; dogs welcome, garden picnic-sets, four good bedrooms, open all day *(Richard and Ruth Dean)*

CHISWORTH [SJ9992]
Hunters SK13 5DL [A626 Glossop—Marple]: Improved under new licensees, well kept Robinsons Mild and Bitter, good value food, log-fire bar, sizeable restaurant, snug/games room; lots of outside tables, superb views, great walking country *(Dennis Jones)*

CODNOR [SK4249]
Poet & Castle DE5 9QY [Alfreton Rd]: Lots of changing ales inc Ashover, Everards and Titanic, farm ciders, simple wholesome food (popular Sun lunch), comfortable low-ceilinged bar/lounge, music nights; open all day *(the Didler)*

COXBENCH [SK3643]
Fox & Hounds DE21 5BA [off B6179 N of Derby; Alfreton Rd]: Friendly village pub nicely set by Trent & Mersey Canal, wide choice of good interesting fresh food (not Sun evening), well kept Marstons Pedigree and Wells & Youngs Bombardier, reasonable prices, long partly flagstoned beamed and panelled bar, attractive raised restaurant area, family room; can get very busy; terrace picnic-sets with canal view, lovely hanging baskets and tubs, open all day, cl Mon *(Brian and Jean Hepworth, Maurice and Janet Thorpe)*

CRICH [SK3454]
Cliff DE4 5DP [Cromford Rd, Town End]: Thriving unpretentious two-room local with well kept Black Sheep, Greene King IPA and local ales, reliable straightforward food, welcoming landlady and friendly regulars, open fire; children welcome, great views and walks, handy for National Tramway Museum *(the Didler)*

DERBY [SK3538]
☆ *Abbey Inn* DE22 1DX [Darley St, Darley Abbey]: A treasure, former abbey gatehouse opp Derwent-side park (pleasant riverside walk from centre), massive 15th-c or older stonework remnants, brick floor, studded oak doors, coal fire in big stone inglenook, stone spiral stair to upper bar (open Sun afternoon) with oak rafters and tapestries, pleasant service, bargain Sam Smiths and lunchtime bar food; the lavatories with their beams, stonework and tiles are worth a look too; piped music; children welcome, open all day wknds *(the Didler, LYM, Kevin Flack)*
Babington Arms DE1 1TA [Babington Lane]: Large well run open-plan Wetherspoons with up to 18 real ales, regulars inc Derby, Falstaff, Greene King Abbot and Marstons

Pedigree, good welcoming service, well priced food, comfortable seating with steps up to relaxed back area; attractive verandah, open all day *(the Didler, Brian and Jean Hepworth)*
Brewery Tap DE1 2ED [aka Royal Standard; Derwent St/Exeter Pl]: Brightly lit comfortably modernised bare boards corner pub (former Royal Standard) now tap for local Derby Brewing Company, five guest ales too and lots of bottled imports, decent good value food all day (till 5pm Sun) from sandwiches up, service can be slow; small upstairs room and roof terrace overlooking the Derwent; open all day, till 1am Fri, Sat *(Malc Newton)*
Falstaff DE23 6UJ [Silver Hill Rd, off Normanton Rd]: Basic unsmart local, aka the Folly, brewing its own good value ales, guest beers too, left-hand bar with games, coal fire in quieter lounge; occasional disco; open all day *(the Didler)*
☆ *Flower Pot* DE1 3DZ [King St]: Extended real ale pub with glazed panel showing its own Headless microbrewery, and great choice of reasonably priced changing beers from small breweries (over 20 at wknds), some cask-tapped; friendly staff, three linked rooms inc comfortable back bar with lots of books, side area with old Derby photographs and brewery memorabilia, good value basic bar food, daily papers, pub games; piped music/juke box, separate concert room – good live bands Thurs-Sat and busy then; disabled access and facilities, tables on small cherry-tree terrace, open all day *(the Didler, Pam and John Smith, Brian and Jean Hepworth)*
Old Silk Mill DE1 3AF [Full St]: Refurbished keeping traditional feel, cosy inside with two open fires, eight changing ales from main bar inc a house beer from Blue Monkey, second hop-adorned bar (open Thurs and Fri evenings, Sat, Sun lunchtime) with usually four cask-tapped beers, friendly service, live music; open all day *(the Didler)*
☆ *Olde Dolphin* DE1 3DL [Queen St]: Quaint 16th-c timber-framed pub just below cathedral, four small dark unpretentious rooms inc appealing snug, big bowed black beams, shiny panelling, opaque leaded windows, lantern lights and coal fires; well kept ales such as Adnams, Bass, Black Sheep, Caledonian Deuchars IPA, Greene King Abbot, Marstons Pedigree and Timothy Taylors Landlord (good July beer festival), bargain simple food all day, good value upstairs steak bar (not always open); no children; sizeable outside area for drinkers/smokers, open all day *(the Didler, LYM, Jeremy King, Brian and Jean Hepworth)*
Rowditch DE22 3LL [Uttoxeter New Rd (A516)]: Popular welcoming local with recently opened microbrewery, well kept Marstons Pedigree and guests too, country wines, attractive small snug on right, coal fire, Sat pianist; no children or dogs; pleasant back garden, cl wkdy lunchtimes *(the Didler)*

☆ **Smithfield** DE1 2BH [Meadow Rd]: Friendly bow-fronted local, well kept changing ales such as Durham, Headless, Oakham, Roosters and Whim, hearty bar lunches, back lounge with traditional settles, old prints, curios and breweriana, coal fires, daily papers; piped music, good games room (children welcome here), quiz and band nights; riverside terrace with wknd barbecues, open all day (the Didler)

☆ **Standing Order** DE1 3GL [Irongate]: Spacious Wetherspoons in grand and lofty-domed former bank, main part with large island bar, booths down each side, handsome plasterwork, pseudo-classical torsos, high portraits of mainly local notables; good range of ales, usual popular food all day, reasonable prices, daily papers, quick service even when very busy; good disabled facilities, open all day (the Didler, Jeremy King, Brian and Jean Hepworth, BB)

Station Inn DE1 2SN [Midland Rd, below station]: Neat simple local with friendly long-serving landlord, particularly well kept Bass (in jugs from cellar), Black Sheep and guests, good food lunchtime and early evening in large back lounge and dining area, long quarry-tiled panelled bar, stained glass; side room with darts, pool and TV; piped music; ornate façade, open all day Fri, cl Sun evening (the Didler)

DRONFIELD [SK3479]

Coach & Horses S18 2GD [Sheffield Rd (B6057)]: Well managed and comfortably refurbished tap for Thornbridge microbrewery's interesting beers, friendly knowledgeable staff, good home-made food using local produce, such as pigeon risotto, decent wines by the glass, pleasant civilised furnishings inc sofas; next to Sheffield FC ground, open all day Fri-Sun (Andy and Jill Kassube, the Didler, Mozzer Cooper, Jonny Major)

EDALE [SK1285]

Old Nags Head S33 7ZD [off A625 E of Chapel-en-le-Frith; Grindsbrook Booth]: Relaxed well used traditional pub at start of Pennine Way, good friendly staff coping well, generous pubby food, well kept local ales, log fire, flagstoned area for booted walkers, airy back family room with board games; can get very busy wknds, TV; front terrace and garden, open all day, cl Mon, Tues lunchtimes out of season (LYM, T G Sunderland, John and Helen Rushton)

EDLASTON [SK1842]

☆ **Shire Horse** DE6 2DQ [off A515 S of Ashbourne, just beside Wyaston]: Rambling timbered pub run by hospitable sisters, blazing fires and gleaming brass in civilised and well furnished long beamed bar with unusual slate-roofed counter and cottagey areas off, good very popular bar food and some interesting recipes for evening conservatory restaurant, reasonable prices; efficient attentive service, Bass, Marstons Pedigree and a guest beer, good choice of wines; piped music; children welcome, tables

out in front and in back garden with terrace, peaceful spot and nice views (M Ross-Thomas, BB)

ELMTON [SK5073]

Elm Tree S80 4LS [off B6417 S of Clowne]: Softly lit and popular country pub with good value unpretentious bar food all day, children's menu, up to seven well kept ales inc Black Sheep and Wells & Youngs, wide choice of wines, quick friendly service, stripped stone and panelling, back barn restaurant (Fri, Sat evenings and for good Sun lunch); children welcome, garden tables, play area (JJW, CMW)

ELTON [SK2260]

☆ **Duke of York** DE4 2BW [village signed off B5056 W of Matlock; Main St]: Unspoilt local kept spotless by very long-serving friendly landlady, bargain Adnams and Marstons, lovely little quarry-tiled back tap room with coal fire in massive fireplace, glazed bar and hatch to flagstoned corridor, nice prints and more fires in the two front rooms – one like private parlour with piano and big table, the other with pool, darts, dominoes, friendly chatty locals; outside lavatories; in charming village, open 8.30pm-midnight and Sun lunchtime (the Didler, Tich Critchlow)

EYAM [SK2276]

Miners Arms S32 5RG [off A632 Chesterfield—Chapel-en-le-Frith; Water Lane]: Three-roomed pub with decent food (not Sun evening) from good sandwiches to some interesting dishes, friendly efficient service, well kept beers such as Caledonian Deuchars IPA, Greene King Old Speckled Hen and Theakstons Best, plush beamed rooms, lots of pictures, lovely open fire, restaurant; darts, TV, piped music; children and dogs welcome, tables outside, decent walks nearby especially below Froggatt Edge, open all day (Dennis Jones, LYM)

FOOLOW [SK2078]

☆ **Barrel** S32 5QD [Bretton, N of village]: Outstanding views from stone-roofed turnpike inn's front terrace, low-beamed knocked-through bar with modern extension, emphasis on good locally sourced food, well kept ales, charming service, lots of brass, stags' heads, log fires; piped music, may be live Weds; children and dogs welcome, courtyard garden, good walking, four bedrooms, good breakfast, open all day wknds (LYM, Peter F Marshall, Keith and Chris O'Neill, Dennis Jones)

FROGGATT EDGE [SK2476]

☆ **Chequers** S32 3ZJ [A625, off A623 N of Bakewell]: Smart well run dining pub with good food (all day wknds), solid country furnishings in civilised and cosily attractive dining bar with woodburner, antique prints and longcase clock, good choice of wines by the glass, well kept changing ales such as Black Sheep and Double Maxims Ward's, friendly staff; unobtrusive piped music; children welcome, peaceful back garden with Froggatt Edge just up through the woods behind, comfortable clean bedrooms (quarry lorries use the road from 6am wkdys), very good breakfast, open all day wknds *(LYM, Stephen Shepherd, P A Rowe, Ian Malone, James A Waller, John and Susan Miln)*

Grouse S11 7TZ [Longshaw, off B6054 NE of Froggatt]: Plush front bar, log fire and wooden benches in back bar, big dining room, decent home cooking with good value smaller helpings and nice sandwiches, well kept Caledonian Deuchars IPA, Banks's and Marstons Pedigree, friendly prompt service, fine views; dogs welcome, verandah and terrace, neat bedrooms, good moorland walking country, open all day *(James A Waller, Michael and Margaret Slater, Barry and Anne, DC)*

GLOSSOP [SK0294]

Globe SK13 8HJ [High St W]: Own microbrews inc a good rich porter, local guest ales, bottled beers and farm cider, bargain food inc nice vegetarian dishes, friendly licensees, comfortable relaxed atmosphere, old fittings and photographs; wknd live music upstairs (busy then), occasional beer festivals; garden, cl lunchtime and Tues, open till early hours *(the Didler, Frank Blanchard)*

Star SK13 7DD [Howard St]: Unpretentious alehouse opp station with six well priced changing beers such as local Howard Town, Pictish, Shaws and Whim, farm cider, friendly helpful staff, no food (you can bring your own), interesting layout inc flagstoned tap room with hatch service, old local photographs; piped music; bedrooms, cl lunchtime Mon-Thurs, open all day Fri-Sun *(Dennis Jones, the Didler)*

GREAT HUCKLOW [SK1777]

Queen Anne SK17 8RF [Main St]: Comfortably refurbished 17th-c stone-built pub, good choice of enjoyable food from baguettes up inc two-course lunchtime deals, takeaway pizzas too, well kept ales such as Copper Dragon, Jennings and Tetleys, low beams, big log fire, gleaming brass and copper, walkers' bar, pub games; french windows to small back terrace and charming garden with picnic-sets and lovely views, two quiet bedrooms, cl Mon, open all day Fri-Sun *(David and Ruth Hollands, the Didler, G Wordsworth, Peter F Marshall)*

GREAT LONGSTONE [SK1971]

☆ *Crispin* DE45 1TZ [Main St]: Spotless comfortably traditional village pub popular for good value pubby food inc set menus and OAP lunches, four well kept Robinsons ales, good wine and whisky choice, welcoming and particularly obliging landlord, buoyant atmosphere, coal-effect fire; faint piped music; picnic-sets out in front with heated canopy, more tables in back garden, good walking area *(Peter F Marshall, James A Waller, BB, John and Jackie Rippon, Derek and Sylvia Stephenson)*

HARDWICK HALL [SK4663]

Hardwick Inn S44 5QJ [quite handy for M1 junction 29; Doe Lea]: Golden stone building dating from 15th c at the south gate of Hardwick Park, several busy linked rooms inc proper bar, open fires, fine range of some 220 malt whiskies and of wines by the glass, well kept Black Sheep, Greene King, Theakstons and Wells & Youngs, generous bar food all day, carvery restaurant, long-serving landlord and helpful staff; unobtrusive piped music; children allowed, pleasant back garden, more tables out in front, open all day *(J Stickland, LYM, Bob and Angela Brooks, Martin and Anne Muers, the Didler, Michael Butler)*

HARTINGTON [SK1260]

Charles Cotton SK17 0AL [Market Pl]: Popular four-square stone-built hotel in attractive village centre, large comfortable carpeted bar, simple dining room off, tearoom too, good straightforward generous home-made food all day, changing real ales such as Greene King IPA, Shepherd Neame Spitfire and Whim Hartington, bottled beers and real cider, good wines, cafetière coffee, friendly helpful service, open fire; nostalgic piped music; dogs welcome in bar, bedrooms, open all day *(the Didler, Richard and Jean Green, David and Sue Atkinson)*

☆ *Devonshire Arms* SK17 0AL [Market Pl]: Traditional two-bar pub in attractive village, popular and welcoming, with well kept Marstons Pedigree, Jennings Cumberland and Wells & Youngs Bombardier, good home-made food (all day wknds), log fires; may be quiet piped classical music; children and dogs welcome, tables out in front facing duck pond, more in small garden, good walks, open all day wknds *(Dennis Jones, John and Joan Calvert, Brian and Anna Marsden, Alan Johnson, Michael Butler, John Wooll, BB, Steve and Sue Griffiths, Jill and Julian Tasker, Mike Proctor)*

Jug & Glass SK17 0BA [A515 Ashbourne—Buxton just N of B5054 junction]: Low-beamed 17th-c moorland inn, enjoyable straightforward food, well kept changing ales such as Church End, coal fire in bar, dining room with woodburner; dogs welcome in part of bar, useful for walkers on High Peak Trail, nine bedrooms, open all day, cl Tues, Weds *(David and Sue Atkinson)*

HASSOP [SK2272]

☆ *Eyre Arms* DE45 1NS [B6001 N of Bakewell]: Neatly kept 17th-c ivy-clad pub, low-beamed log-fire rooms, settles and comfortable plush chairs, lots of copper and brass, grandfather clock, good choice of enjoyable food inc children's menu, Black Sheep, Marstons and Peak ales, several wines by the glass, public bar with teapot collection; piped classical music; fine Peak views from garden with gurgling fountain, good nearby walks, cl Mon evenings Nov-Easter *(Chris Gallagher, DC, LYM, Derek and Sylvia Stephenson)*

HAYFIELD [SK0486]

Sportsman SK22 2LE [Kinder Rd]: Wide choice of enjoyable food in roomy and neatly kept traditional pub, good friendly staff, well kept Thwaites beers, decent wines, lots of malt whiskies, two coal fires; children welcome, lovely location (handy for Kinder Scout walks), bedrooms *(Michelle Griffiths, John and Sylvia Harrop)*

HEAGE [SK3750]
Black Boy DE56 2BN: Smart village pub/restaurant with welcoming licensees, popular food in bar and upstairs dining area inc speciality fish dishes, well kept regularly changing ales, open fire; no dogs; children welcome *(Michael Mellers)*

HEANOR [SK4445]
Queens Head DE75 7NJ [Breach Rd, Marlpool]: Well refurbished after period as a chinese restaurant, nice interior with cosy bar and various snugs/alcoves, tiled floors, open fires and woodburners, passageway with wicker chairs and old barrel tables; up to 16 well kept ales inc Castle Rock, Thornbridge and Oakham, real ciders and perry, good range of wines, daily papers; outside tables; open all day *(Yvonne and Rob Warhurst, the Didler)*

HOGNASTON [SK2350]
☆ *Red Lion* DE6 1PR [off B5035 Ashbourne—Wirksworth]: Traditional 17th-c inn with open-plan beamed bar, three open fires, attractive mix of old tables, old-fashioned settles and other comfortable seats on ancient flagstones, friendly licensees; good home-made food from shortish menu in bar and conservatory restaurant, nice wines by the glass, Marstons Pedigree and three local guests; piped music; boules, handy for Carsington Water, three good bedrooms, big breakfast *(Brian and Anna Marsden, Rob and Catherine Dunster, Cathryn and Richard Hicks, Arthur Pickering, LYM)*

HOLYMOORSIDE [SK3369]
Lamb S42 7EU [Loads Rd, just off Holymoor Rd]: Small spotless village pub, half a dozen particularly well kept ales such as Adnams, Black Sheep, Daleside Blonde, Fullers London Pride and Timothy Taylors Landlord, charming comfortable lounge, coal fire in cosy bar, friendly locals, pub games; tables outside, leafy spot, cl wkdy lunchtimes *(the Didler)*

HORSLEY WOODHOUSE [SK3944]
Old Oak DE7 6AW [Main St (A609 Belper—Ilkeston)]: Busy roadside local linked to nearby Bottle Brook and Leadmill microbreweries, their ales and wknd back bar with another half-dozen well priced guests tapped from the cask, farm cider, good basic snacks; linked beamed rooms, blazing coal fires, chatty friendly atmosphere, occasional live music; children and dogs welcome, hatch to covered courtyard tables (nice views), cl wkdy lunchtimes, open all day wknds *(the Didler, Brian Coleman)*

HULLAND WARD [SK2647]
Black Horse DE6 3EE [Hulland Ward; A517 Ashbourne—Belper]: Welcoming 17th-c pub with good fresh food at sensible prices in low-beamed quarry-tiled bar or back country-view dining room, popular Sun carvery, well kept ales inc Peakstones Rock and Wadworths 6X, good service; well behaved

children and dogs welcome, garden tables, four comfortable bedrooms, nr Carsington Water *(Richard and Jean Green, the Didler)*

IDRIDGEHAY [SK2848]
Black Swan DE56 2SG [B5023 S of Wirksworth]: Attractive bistro-style restaurant/pub with imaginative sensibly priced food, good friendly service, decent wines, atrium dining area with extensive valley views; children welcome, nice garden, cl Sun evening *(LYM, Richard and Jean Green)*

ILKESTON [SK4742]
Good Old Days DE7 5LJ [Station Rd]: Welcoming half-timbered one-room pub with new downstairs family room, well kept interesting small brewery ales, simple food, darts, dominoes and pool; piped music, TV; children and dogs welcome, tables in canalside garden, own moorings, open all day Fri-Sun *(Christie, the Didler)*
Spanish Bar DE7 5QJ [South St]: Busy café-bar with well kept fairly priced changing ales such as Mallards and Whim, bottled belgian beers, friendly efficient service even when busy, log fire, evening overspill room with woodburner; Tues quiz night, popular Sun lunchtime card games with free nibbles; small garden, skittle alley, open all day *(the Didler)*

LEA [SK3257]
Jug & Glass DE4 5GJ: Cosy stone-built village local with friendly licensees, good competitively priced standard food from sandwiches up, Black Sheep, Copper Dragon, Marstons Pedigree and Timothy Taylors Landlord; good walking country, cl Mon lunchtime *(Malcolm and Pauline Pellatt, Paul J Robinshaw)*

LITTLE LONGSTONE [SK1971]
Packhorse DE45 1NN [off A6 NW of Bakewell via Monsal Dale]: Three comfortably refurbished linked beamed rooms, pine tables on flagstones, welcoming enthusiastic landlord, well kept Thornbridge ales, good choice of wines by the glass, popular good value substantial food (Sat breakfast from 8.30), good service, coal fires; hikers welcome (on Monsal Trail), terrace in steep little back garden *(LYM, Dennis Jones, Derek and Sylvia Stephenson)*

LULLINGTON [SK2513]
☆ *Colvile Arms* DE12 8EG [off A444 S of Burton; Main St]: Popular neatly preserved 18th-c village pub with high-backed settles in simple panelled bar, cosy comfortable beamed lounge, pleasant atmosphere, friendly staff, four well kept ales inc Bass, Marstons Pedigree and a Mild, enjoyable good value food; may be piped music; picnic-sets on small sheltered back lawn overlooking bowling green, cl wkdy lunchtimes *(LYM, the Didler)*

MAKENEY [SK3544]
☆ *Holly Bush* DE56 0RX [from A6 heading N after Duffield, take 1st right after crossing River Derwent, then 1st left]: Down-to-earth two-bar village pub (ex farmhouse) with

three blazing coal fires (one in old-fashioned range by snug's curved high-backed settle), flagstones, beams, black panelling and tiled floors, lots of brewing advertisements; half a dozen or so well kept changing ales (some brought from cellar in jugs), real cider, cheap food inc rolls and pork pies, may be local cheeses for sale, games lobby with hatch service (children allowed here), regular beer festivals; picnic-sets outside, dogs welcome, open all day Fri-Sun *(BB, Richard Stanfield, the Didler)*

MATLOCK BATH [SK2958]

Temple DE4 3PG [Temple Walk]: 18th-c hotel with wonderful Derwent Valley views, comfortable bar, dining area and restaurant, usually three well kept changing ales from more or less local small breweries (regular beer festivals), nice wines, good well priced freshly made food; children welcome, tables outside, summer barbecues, bedrooms, open all day wknds *(the Didler)*

MILFORD [SK3545]

William IV DE56 0RR [Milford Bridge]: Friendly and relaxing stone-built riverside pub, long room with low beams, bare boards, quarry tiles, old settles and a blazing coal fire, well kept Bass, Marstons Pedigree, Timothy Taylors Landlord and guests, good filled rolls; cl lunchtime wkdys, open all day wknds *(the Didler)*

MILLERS DALE [SK1473]

☆ *Anglers Rest* SK17 8SN [just down Litton Lane; pub is PH on OS Sheet 119 map ref 142734]: Spotless ivy-clad pub in lovely quiet riverside setting on Monsal Trail, two bars and dining room, log fires, good simple home-made food (not Tues lunchtime, pie night Thurs), well kept Marstons Pedigree and Tetleys, efficient pleasant service, reasonable prices; darts, pool and muddy walkers in public bar; children welcome, wonderful gorge views and riverside walks *(Mr and Mrs R Coleby, Peter F Marshall, the Didler)*

MILLTOWN [SK3562]

Nettle S45 0ES [Fallgate, Littlemoor]: Interesting old beamed pub with coal fire in small traditional bar, linked busier areas behind, well kept Bradfield Farmers Blonde and guests, good value changing bar food, pub games; open all day Sun *(the Didler)*

MONSAL HEAD [SK1871]

☆ *Monsal Head Hotel* DE45 1NL [B6465]: Popular inn in outstanding hilltop location, cosy stables bar with stripped timber horse-stalls, harnesses and brassware, cushioned oak pews on flagstones, big open fire; Peakstones Rock and guest ales, german bottled beers, several wines by the glass, good value bar food from lunchtime sandwiches up (they may ask to keep your credit card while you eat); children (over 3), well behaved dogs and muddy walkers welcome, big garden, stunning Monsal Dale views with its huge viaduct, seven bedrooms, open all day till midnight *(LYM, Ian and Debs, Mike and Sue Loseby, Paul J Robinshaw, Keith and Chris O'Neill, S P Watkin, P A Taylor,*

Peter F Marshall, Derek and Sylvia Stephenson)

MONYASH [SK1566]

☆ *Bulls Head* DE45 1JH [B5055 W of Bakewell]: Unpretentious high-ceilinged local with simple furnishings and log fire, ales such as Bradfield, John Smiths and Peak, straightforward pubby food (all day Sun), dining room, small back bar with pool, darts and board games; may be piped music; children and dogs welcome, gate from garden to village play area, inexpensive bedrooms, open all day wknds *(Mr and Mrs R Shardlow, Malc Newton, LYM, BB)*

NEW MILLS [SJ9886]

Fox SK22 3AY [Brookbottom; OS Sheet 109 map ref 985864]: Tucked-away unmodernised country local, nice for a family summer outing, friendly long-serving landlord, particularly well kept Robinsons, good value basic food (not Tues evening) inc good sandwiches, log fire, darts and pool; children welcome, lots of tables outside, good walking area, open all day Fri-Sun *(David Hoult, John Fiander, Bob Broadhurst, the Didler)*

OAKERTHORPE [SK3856]

Amber DE55 7LL [Furnace]: Charming old-fashioned village local with friendly landlady, straightforward food, well kept Abbeydale, Fullers London Pride, Timothy Taylors Landlord and guests, blazing winter fires, lots of antiques inc a piano, well worn seating; good views from the back terrace, walks *(the Didler)*

OCKBROOK [SK4236]

☆ *Royal Oak* DE72 3SE [off B6096 just outside Spondon; Green Lane]: Quiet 18th-c village local run by same friendly family for half a century, bargain honest food (not Sat, Sun or Tues evenings) from super lunchtime cobs to steaks, Sun lunch and OAP meals, Bass and interesting guest beers, good soft drinks' choice; tiled-floor tap room, turkey-carpeted snug, inner bar with Victorian prints, larger and lighter side room, nice old settle in entrance corridor, open fires, darts and dominoes; children welcome, sheltered cottage garden and cobbled front courtyard, separate play area *(the Didler, BB)*

OVER HADDON [SK2066]

☆ *Lathkil* DE45 1JE [signed from B5055 SW of Bakewell]: Traditional inn with fantastic views over Lathkil Dale; airy beamed bar with open fire and upholstered settles, up to five ales such as Abbeydale, Blue Monkey, Everards, Peak and Whim, buffet-style lunch menu, more elaborate food Fri, Sat evenings, spacious sunny dining room; piped music; can get very busy with day trippers/walkers (muddy boots to be left in lobby); dogs and children welcome, walled garden, bedrooms, open all day except Mon, Weds, Thurs in winter *(Peter F Marshall, John Beeken, the Didler, Hugh Roberts, S P Watkin, P A Taylor, LYM, Roger Thornington)*

PARWICH [SK1854]

Sycamore DE6 1QL [by church]: Chatty old country pub well run by cheerful welcoming young landlady, super log fire in neat comfortable main bar, generous wholesome food lunchtimes and most Weds-Sat evenings, Robinsons beers inc seasonal, lots of old local photographs, hatch-served tap room with games; tables out in front and on grass by car park, quiet village, good walks *(the Didler)*

PENTRICH [SK3852]

☆ *Dog* DE5 3RE [Main Rd (B6016 N of Ripley)]: Extended pub popular for its enjoyable good value all-day food, well kept ales such as Bass, Fun fair Dodgem and Hook Norton from carved church-look bar counter, nice wines by the glass; woodburner, pubby bar furniture, smarter modern dining area beyond part with leather sofas etc; piped pop music may obtrude; extensive garden behind, nice views, good walks *(the Didler, BB, Derek and Sylvia Stephenson)*

RIPLEY [SK3950]

Pear Tree DE5 3HR [Derby Rd (B6179)]: Long open bar with hot coal fires each end, small lounge, old-fashioned and unspoilt, well kept and priced Greene King ales inc a Mild, friendly chatty staff, darts and dominoes; open all day *(the Didler)*

Talbot Taphouse DE5 3LT [Butterley Hill]: Full range of local Amber ales and changing guests kept well by knowledgeable landlord, farm ciders and bottled beers too, long narrow panelled room with new bar counter, comfy chairs, brick fireplace; friendly staff; open all day Fri-Sun, from 5pm Mon-Thurs *(Michael Mellers, the Didler)*

ROWSLEY [SK2565]

Grouse & Claret DE4 2EB [A6 Bakewell—Matlock]: Attractive family dining pub in old stone building, spacious, clean and comfortable, with welcoming landlord and friendly helpful staff, enjoyable low-priced food (all day wknds) from sandwiches up, well kept ales such as Jennings Cumberland, decent wines, open fires, tap room popular with walkers; tables outside, good value bedrooms *(Guy and Caroline Howard, Brian and Jacky Wilson, David Carr)*

☆ *Peacock* DE4 2EB [Bakewell Rd]: Civilised small 17th-c country hotel with comfortable chairs and sofas and a few antiques in spacious uncluttered lounge, interesting stone-floored inner bar, restful colours; enjoyable if not cheap food from lunchtime sandwiches to restaurant meals, Greene King IPA and a local guest beer, good wines, beautifully served coffee; attractive riverside gardens, trout fishing, good bedrooms *(Eleanor Dandy, LYM, Mr and Mrs W W Burke)*

SHARDLOW [SK4330]

Dog & Duck DE72 2GR [London Rd]: Sizeable rambling pub with split-level extension behind, well kept Marstons Pedigree and Wychwood Hobgoblin, tasty bargain food, friendly welcoming service; outside seating *(John Wooll)*

☆ *Malt Shovel* DE72 2HG [3.5 miles from M1 junction 24, via A6 towards Derby; The Wharf]: Busy old-world beamed pub in

18th-c former maltings, interesting odd-angled layout with cosy corners, Marstons-related ales, quick friendly service, bargain food (not Sat evening) from baguettes up, good central open fire, farm tools and bric-a-brac; lots of terrace tables by Trent & Mersey Canal, pretty hanging baskets and boxes *(the Didler, LYM)*

New Inn DE72 2HG [The Wharf]: Popular unpretentious canalside pub, two large rooms with central bar, well kept Ringwood, decent house wine, wide range of good pubby food inc several vegetarian dishes, nice coffee, prompt pleasant service *(Richard and Jean Green)*

Old Crown DE72 2HL [off A50 just W of M1 junction 24; Cavendish Bridge, E of village]: Good value pub with great range of Marstons-related ales and guests all kept well, nice choice of malt whiskies, pubby food (not Fri, Sun evenings) from sandwiches and baguettes up, beams with masses of jugs and mugs, walls covered with other bric-a-brac and breweriana, big inglenook; children and dogs welcome, simple good value bedrooms, good breakfast, open all day *(the Didler, LYM)*

Shakespeare DE72 2GP [London Rd (old A6)]: Pleasant beamed pub with good value pubby lunchtime food, cheerful service, well kept Bass and Marstons Pedigree, evening restaurant (not Sun, Mon); garden *(Brian and Jean Hepworth)*

SMISBY [SK3419]

Smisby Arms LE65 2UA [Nelsons Sq]: Ancient low-beamed village pub with good range of enjoyable reasonably priced mainstream food, friendly efficient service, well kept ales inc house Smisby, decent coffee, bright little dining extension down steps; a few tables out in front *(Richard and Jean Green)*

SOUTH WINGFIELD [SK3755]

Old Yew Tree DE55 7NH [B5035 W of Alfreton; Manor Rd]: Friendly local with obliging staff, good value well prepared pub food, good changing ales, log fire, panelling, kettles and pans hanging from beams; separate restaurant area; children welcome *(John and Susan Miln)*

SPARKLOW [SK1265]

Royal Oak SK17 9QJ [Monyash—Longnor road, just off A515 S of Buxton]: Relaxed country atmosphere in open-plan beamed pub, wide choice of fairly priced local food all day, friendly helpful service, three ales inc Whim Hartington, good wine choice, small bar, split-level lounge/dining room, log fire; children welcome, on Tissington Trail, overnight stabling, barn with bunk bedrooms, campsite *(Ian and Suzy Masser, Mike Proctor, Richard Stanfield)*

SPONDON [SK3935]

☆ *Malt Shovel* DE21 7LH [off A6096 on edge of Derby, via Church Hill into Potter St]: Homely traditional pub with several well kept mainly Marstons-related ales from hatch in tiled corridor, with cosy panelled and quarry-tiled or small turkey-carpeted rooms off, helpful staff, inexpensive bar lunches, old-fashioned décor, huge inglenook, steps down to big games bar with darts and pool; lots of picnic-sets, some under cover, in big well used back garden with good play area, open all day Fri-Sun (the Didler, Pete Baker, BB)

SUTTON CUM DUCKMANTON [SK4371]
Arkwright Arms S44 5JG [A632 Bolsover—Chesterfield]: Friendly mock-Tudor pub with bar, pool room and dining room, all with real fires, good choice of well priced food lunch and evening till 7.30pm (not wknd evenings), up to nine changing ales, a dozen real ciders and two perries (beer/cider festivals on bank hols); games machine; no children in bar, dogs in pool room only, picnic-sets out at front and in side garden with play equipment, open all day (JJW, CMW)

TANSLEY [SK3159]
Royal Oak DE4 5FY [A615 Matlock—Mansfield]: Pleasant village pub with wide choice of enjoyable good value food cooked to order, inc vegetarian options, two dining rooms (one upstairs) with well spaced tables, friendly efficient service; popular and best to book (Emma Morley)

TICKNALL [SK3523]
☆ *Wheel* DE73 7JZ [Main St (A514)]: Stylish contemporary décor in bar and restaurant, enjoyable interesting home-made food (all day wknds), friendly staff, well kept Marstons Pedigree and a guest; children welcome, nice outside area with café tables on raised deck, nr entrance to Calke Abbey (Kay Brough)

TUPTON [SK3966]
Britannia S42 6XP [Ward St, New Tupton]: Tap for Spire brewery (can arrange tours), four of theirs kept well and up to four guest beers, good bottled range, farm cider, chatty licensees, lively bar with sports TV, quieter lounge; open from 4 Mon-Fri, from 3 Sat, all day Sun (the Didler)

WARDLOW [SK1875]
☆ *Three Stags Heads* SK17 8RW [Wardlow Mires; A623/B6465]: Basic no-frills farm pub of great individuality, flagstoned floors (often muddied by boots and dogs in winter), old country furniture, heating from cast-iron kitchen ranges, old photographs, plain-talking landlord and locals in favourite corners, Abbeydale ales inc Black Lurcher (brewed for the pub at a hefty 8% ABV), lots of bottled beers, hearty seasonal food on hardy home-made plates; may be free roast chestnuts, perhaps live folk music; no credit cards; children and dogs welcome, hill views from front terrace, cl lunchtimes, open all day wknds (the Didler, Mike Proctor, Dennis Jones, Steve Sharples, LYM)

WHITTINGTON MOOR [SK3873]
☆ *Derby Tup* S41 8LS [Sheffield Rd; B6057 just S of A61 roundabout]: Spotless no-frills Castle Rock local with up to ten well kept interesting changing ales from long line of gleaming handpumps, farm cider, irish whiskeys, pleasant service, simple furniture, coal fire and lots of standing room as well as two small side rooms (children allowed here); daily papers, good value basic bar lunches; can get very busy wknd evenings, dogs welcome, open all day at least Fri-Sun (the Didler, LYM, Keith and Chris O'Neill, Peter F Marshall)

Red Lion S41 8LX [Sheffield Rd (B6057)]: Simple 19th-c stone-built two-room local tied to Old Mill with their beers, friendly hard-working landlady, thriving atmosphere, old local photographs, low lighting; live music (can be loud), sports TV; open all day (the Didler)

WINDLEY [SK3244]
Puss in Boots DE56 4AQ [S on B5023]: Former mill nicely situated above the Ecclesbourne river in wooded countryside, two character rooms with open fires, low beams and oak panelling, lots of plates and brass, well kept Bass and Marstons Pedigree, popular home-made lunchtime food from good farm ham sandwiches up, well run place with friendly regulars; swings in pleasant garden, good walks (the Didler)

WINSTER [SK2360]
Miners Standard DE4 2DR [Bank Top (B5056 above village)]: Simply furnished 17th-c stone local, relaxed at lunchtime, livelier evenings, well kept ales such as Black Sheep, Flowers IPA and Marstons Pedigree, good value generous pubby food inc huge pies; big woodburner, lead-mining photographs and minerals, lots of brass, backwards clock, ancient well, snug and restaurant; children allowed away from bar, attractive view from garden, campsite next door, interesting stone-built village below, open all day wknds (Dennis Jones, Trevor and Sylvia Millum)

WIRKSWORTH [SK2854]
Royal Oak DE4 4FG [North End]: Small chatty old-fashioned terraced local with proper friendly licensees, well kept changing ales inc Bass, Timothy Taylors Landlord and Whim Hartington, dominoes, may be good filled cobs, old copper kettles, key fobs and other bric-a-brac, interesting old photographs; opens 8pm, cl lunchtime except Sun (the Didler)

YEAVELEY [SK1840]
Yeaveley Arms DE6 2DT [on by-roads S of Ashbourne]: Reopened and refurbished after long closure, comfortable modern open-plan interior with bar, lounge and big airy restaurant, leather sofas and chairs; enjoyable food from pub favourites to more innovative things, good value two-course lunch menu, friendly efficient service, Marstons Pedigree and guests such as Peakstones Rock; no dogs inside; children welcome, seats out at front and on back terrace with smokers' shelter, nr Carsington Water, open all day summer, all day wknds winter (Paul and Margaret Baker)

Devon

Devon is one of the biggest counties for Main Entries in this *Guide* and the pubs here are as diverse as you can imagine. It's also a particularly friendly area and the hard-working landlords and landladies seem to cope with the summer holidaymakers with good-natured cheerfulness and efficiency. We have found some strong new pubs and a couple that are back in these pages after a break. These include the Drewe Arms in Broadhembury (new owners have extended the bar and smartened up the restaurant), the Floating Bridge in Dartmouth (bustling little local right by the River Dart with plenty of outside seating), the Rock at Georgeham (enthusiastic young landlords serve interesting food and five real ales), the Holt in Honiton (a nice surprise to find tapas and the full range of Otter beers), the New Inn at Roborough (tucked away down lanes and run by a keen young couple serving good value food), the Devils Stone Inn at Shebbear (the smartly dressed landlord keeps his pub shipshape), the Sea Trout in Staverton (the bars have been refurbished, a new conservatory added and the bedrooms spruced up), and the Cary Arms near Torquay (informal, friendly bar area in unusual, splendidly placed hotel). Other pubs on top form this year are the Masons Arms in Branscombe (the bustling, chatty bar is most enjoyable and bedrooms are popular), the Coach & Horses in Buckland Brewer (run by the same family for over 20 years and with good, fairly priced food), the Drake Manor in Buckland Monachorum (the long-serving landlady welcomes both locals and visitors), the Merry Harriers in Clayhidon (interesting food and a good choice of drinks), the New Inn at Coleford (a smashing place to stay), the Drewe Arms in Drewsteignton (a fine old pub in a pretty village), the Turf Hotel near Exminster (remote pub not accessible by car with large waterside gardens), the Rock at Haytor Vale (at its most informal at lunchtime), the Elephants Nest at Horndon (cosy old inn on Dartmoor with attractive bedrooms), the Church House in Marldon (busy village pub with interesting food and friendly licensees), the Church House in Rattery (one of the country's oldest pubs), and the Bridge Inn at Topsham (quite unchanging and an unspoilt old gem). The bountiful local produce on land and in the sea help produce some fine meals at many of the pubs listed above but our Devon Dining Pub 2011 is the Merry Harriers in Clayhidon.

AVONWICK

SX6958 MAP 1

Turtley Corn Mill ♀

0.5 miles off A38 roundabout at SW end of South Brent bypass; TQ10 9ES

Careful conversion of tall mill house with interestingly furnished spreading areas, local beers, well liked food, and huge gardens; bedrooms

The interior of this tall, carefully converted mill house with its working waterwheel has been done with a great deal of thought. The spreading series of linked areas have big windows looking out over the grounds, a pleasant array of prints, a history of the mill and some other decorations (framed 78rpm discs, elderly wireless sets, house plants) on pastel walls and a mix of comfortable dining chairs around heavy baluster-leg tables in a variety of sizes. There are bookcases, fat church candles and oriental rugs in one area, dark flagstones by the bar, a strategic woodburning stove dividing one part, a side enclave with a modern pew built in around a really big table, and so on. Dartmoor Jail Ale, St Austell Tribute, Sharps Doom Bar and Summerskills Tamar on handpump, ten wines by the glass, 30 malt whiskies and decent coffee. The extensive garden has plenty of well spaced picnic-sets, a giant chess set and a small lake with interesting ducks. They will keep your credit card if you eat outside. This is under the same ownership as a new Cornwall Main Entry, the Finnygook at Crafthole. More reports please.

🍴 Well presented bar food includes sandwiches, ploughman's, soup, duck liver pâté, beer-battered haddock with minted mushy peas, butternut squash risotto with feta and toasted pumpkin seeds, burger with bacon, cheese and fries, cornish crab salad, chicken breast stuffed with wild mushrooms with a port and parsley sauce, beef in Guinness pie, seafood kebabs with piquant sauce, and puddings like lemon fudge cake with fruit compote and chocolate brownie with chocolate sauce and ice-cream; they also offer a two- and three-course set lunch. *Starters/Snacks: £4.50 to £6.50. Main Courses: £9.95 to £17.95. Puddings: £5.95 to £6.75*

Free house ~ Licensees Lesley and Bruce Brunning ~ Real ale ~ Bar food (12-9.30(9 Sun)) ~ (01364) 646100 ~ Children welcome until 7.30pm (unless staying overnight) ~ Dogs welcome ~ Open 11-11; 12-10.30 Sun ~ Bedrooms: /£89S

Recommended by B J Harding, Henry Pursehouse-Tranter, Lynda and Trevor Smith, Andy and Claire Barker

BANTHAM

SX6643 MAP 1

Sloop 🛏

Off A379/B3197 NW of Kingsbridge; TQ7 3AJ

Friendly old pub close to fine beach and walks, character bar, real ales and tasty bar food; bedrooms

Under new licensees since our last edition, this 14th-c pub is a friendly place with a good mix of both locals and holiday visitors. The black-beamed bar has a bustling atmosphere, country chairs around wooden tables, stripped-stone walls and flagstones, a woodburning stove and easy chairs in a quieter side area. St Austell Dartmoor Best, Tribute and a guest beer on handpump; piped music. There are some seats outside at the back, and the surfing beach and fine cliff walks are only ten minutes away.

🍴 Reasonably priced bar food includes lunchtime sandwiches, ploughman's, mussels in thyme, white wine and cream, garlic mushrooms with blue cheese, burger and chips, vegetarian lasagne, battered fish, local crab salad, lambs liver with onion gravy and bacon, fish pie, beef stroganoff, and puddings like treacle tart and crème brûlée with raspberry and ginger compote. *Starters/Snacks: £4.50 to £6.95. Main Courses: £6.95 to £19.95. Puddings: £4.95*

St Austell ~ Lease N Croft and R Seymour ~ Real ale ~ Bar food (12-2(4 Sun), 6.30-9) ~ Restaurant ~ (01548) 560489 ~ Children welcome away from bar area ~ Dogs welcome ~ Open 11-11; 11-2.30, 6-11 in winter ~ Bedrooms: £41.50B/£82B

Recommended by Lynda and Trevor Smith, Maurice Ricketts, MP, Peter and Margaret Glenister

BEESANDS

SX8140 MAP 1

Cricket

About 3 miles S of A379, from Chillington; in village turn right along foreshore road;
TQ7 2EN

Welcoming small pub by beach, with enjoyable food (especially fish) and beer; bedrooms

The restaurant in this busy little pub has been extended this year and more bedrooms
have been added – five of which have sea views. It's neatly kept and open-plan with dark
traditional pubby furniture (carpeted in the dining areas and with a stripped wooden
floor by the bar), and some nice, well captioned photographs of local fisherpeople, knots
and fishing gear on the walls. Otter Ale and Bitter and St Austell Tribute on handpump,
several wines by the glass and local cider; piped music. The cheerful black labrador is
called Brewster. There are picnic-sets beside the seawall and Start Bay beach is just over
the other side. The pub is popular with South Devon Coastal Path walkers; good
wheelchair access.

🍴 **With quite an emphasis on fresh local fish and shellfish, the well liked bar food
includes lunchtime sandwiches and salads, soup, ham hock terrine and apple chutney,
local mussels with chorizo and tomato sauce, a home-made pie and vegetarian dish of the
day, mackerel with caramelised onions and balsamic, whole plaice with black butter,
popular seafood pancake, diver-caught scallops with chive mash, asparagus and white
truffle oil, duck with sultana sauce, steaks, daily specials, and puddings.** *Starters/Snacks:*
£5.00 to £8.00. Main Courses: £8.00 to £20.00. Puddings: £4.50 to £6.00

Heavitree ~ Tenant Nigel Heath ~ Real ale ~ Bar food (12-2.30, 6-8.30) ~ Restaurant ~
(01548) 580215 ~ Children allowed in bar ~ Dogs allowed in bar ~ Open 11(12 Sun)-11; 11-3,
6-11 in winter ~ Bedrooms: £45S/£65S

Recommended by Roger Wain-Heapy, Mark Sykes, Peter and Margaret Glenister, Adrian and Dawn Collinge,
Richard Tilbrook, Roy Hoing, John and Gina Ollier, Alan Sutton, David Elliott

BRANSCOMBE

SY1888 MAP 1

Fountain Head 🍺

Upper village, above the robust old church; village signposted off A3052 Sidmouth—
Seaton, then from Branscombe Square follow road up hill towards Sidmouth, and after
about a mile turn left after the church; OS Sheet 192 map reference SY188889; EX12 3BG

Old-fashioned stone pub with own-brewed beers and reasonably priced food

Nestling in a little valley with pleasant surrounding walks, this 500-year-old stone pub is
unspoilt and friendly. There's an unchanging, old-fashioned feel – no games machines,
piped music or TV – and the room on the left (formerly a smithy) has forge tools and
horseshoes on the high oak beams; also, a log fire in the original raised firebed with its
tall central chimney, cushioned pews and mate's chairs, and Branscombe Vale Branoc,
Summa That and a guest beer on handpump. Their annual beer festival is held in June
and they have several wines by the glass and local cider. On the right, an irregularly
shaped, more orthodox snug room has another log fire, a white-painted plank ceiling
with an unusual carved ceiling-rose, brown-varnished panelled walls and rugs on its
flagstone-and-lime-ash floor. Local artists' paintings and greeting cards are for sale;
darts. You can sit outside on the front loggia and terrace listening to the little stream
gurgling under the flagstoned path.

🍴 **Reasonably priced bar food includes lunchtime sandwiches and ploughman's, soup, pâté
of the day, fresh local crab, mussels and fish, lasagne, chicken and gammon with honey
and ginger, steaks, and a spit roast, barbecue and live music on some summer Sunday
evenings.** *Starters/Snacks: £4.50 to £5.95. Main Courses: £7.50 to £10.95. Puddings: £4.25*

Free house ~ Licensees Jon Woodley and Teresa Hoare ~ Real ale ~ Bar food ~ Restaurant ~
(01297) 680359 ~ Children welcome away from bar area ~ Dogs welcome ~ Open 11-3, 6-11;
12-3, 6-10.30 Sun

Recommended by the Didler, John and Fiona McIlwain, Revd R P Tickle, John Wymer, Helene Grygar, Phil and
Sally Gorton, Warren Marsh, Richard Stanfield, George Atkinson, Phyl and Jack Street

Masons Arms ♀ ◖ ⛱

Main Street; signed off A3052 Sidmouth—Seaton, then bear left into village; EX12 3DJ

Rambling low-beamed rooms, woodburning stoves, good choice of real ales and wines, bar and more elaborate restaurant food and seats in quiet terrace and garden; bedrooms

Our readers very much enjoy staying overnight at this picturesque 14th-c longhouse and tell us that the bedrooms in the converted cottages are lovely; we're hoping nothing much changes now that the pub is a managed house under St Austell. The rambling main bar remains the heart of the place though and there are plenty of locals and visitors, quite a bit of character and a chatty welcome from the friendly staff. The roaring winter log fire (where spit roasts are held) has a massive hearth, there are comfortable seats and chairs on slate floors and ancient ships' beams. The Old Worthies bar also has a slate floor, a fireplace with a two-sided woodburning stove and woodwork that has been stripped back to the original pine. There's also the original restaurant (warmed by one side of the woodburning stove) and another beamed restaurant above the main bar. Branscombe Vale Branoc and Best Bitter, Otter Amber and Bitter and Teignworthy Springtide on handpump, a dozen wines by the glass and quite a few malt whiskies; darts, shove-ha'penny, cribbage, dominoes and board games. Outside, the quiet flower-filled front terrace has tables with little thatched roofs and extends into a side garden. You may have to leave your credit card behind the bar. It's best to arrive early for a car park space in peak season. Do let us know what you think of the new regime.

🍴 Bar food includes lunchtime sandwiches, filled panini and ploughman's, soup, sesame crusted goats cheese with mango and cumin relish, chicken curry, wild mushroom and spinach pasta with basil pesto, beer-battered haddock, cumin lamb cutlets with roasted garlic jus, fish stew, and puddings like tempura banana fritter with maple syrup and toffee ice-cream and steamed blackcurrant sponge with vanilla custard; the restaurant menu is more elaborate. *Starters/Snacks: £4.50 to £7.50. Main Courses: £10.95 to £16.25. Puddings: £5.25*

St Austell ~ Licensee Paul Couldwell ~ Real ale ~ Bar food ~ Restaurant ~ (01297) 680300 ~ Children allowed in bar with parents but not in restaurant ~ Dogs allowed in bar and bedrooms ~ Open 11-11; 12-10.30 Sun; 11-3, 6-11 weekdays in winter ~ Bedrooms: /£80S(£85B)

Recommended by Barry Steele-Perkins, the Didler, Gavin Robinson, Phyl and Jack Street, Stephen Shepherd, Andrea Rampley, Dr Phil Putwain, David Randall, David and Sue Smith, Nick Wallis, Steve Whalley, David West, Tim and Joan Wright, David and Stella Martin, Malcolm and Sue Scott, Mike Gorton, Richard Stanfield

BROADHEMBURY   ST1004   MAP 1

Drewe Arms ♀

Off A373 Cullompton—Honiton; EX14 3NF

New licensees and quite a few changes in rather smart extended inn; real ales, helpful service, bar and restaurant food

There have been a lot of changes since this ancient thatched pub was taken over by new licensees. The small bar has been extended back into the old kitchen area and a new kitchen has been added, the dining room has been modernised and there's now a terraced eating area in the garden. There are still neatly carved beams in the high ceiling of the bar, handsome stone-mullioned windows (one with a small carved roundabout horse), sofas in front of the roaring winter fire in the big black-painted fireplace and plenty of bric-a-brac. The flagstoned entry has a narrow corridor of a room by the servery where they keep O'Hanlons Original Port Stout and Otter Bitter on handpump, 20 wines by the glass and 17 malt whiskies; newspapers, board games and piped music. You can sit in the lovely garden which has a lawn stretching back under the shadow of chestnut trees towards a church with its singularly melodious hour-bell. More reports on the changes please.

🍴 Bar food now includes sandwiches, soup, parma ham and roasted pears with olive salad, sharing platters, sausages with mustard mash and cider gravy, smoked haddock fishcakes with tartare sauce, red onion and goats cheese tart and beer-battered cod, with more

elaborate restaurant dishes, and puddings like plum and apple crumble and pineapple
fritter with maple syrup and clotted cream. *Starters/Snacks: £5.00 to £7.00. Main Courses:
£8.95 to £14.95. Puddings: £5.25 to £6.50*

Free house ~ Licensees Anthony Russell and Sara Carke ~ Real ale ~ Bar food (12-2.30,
6.30-9.30; 12-3, 6-8 Sun) ~ Restaurant ~ (01404) 841267 ~ Children welcome ~ Dogs allowed
in bar ~ Open 12-3, 6-11(midnight Fri and Sat); 12-10.30 Sun; closed Mon

Recommended by Andrea Rampley, Colin and Louise English

BUCKFAST   SX7467   MAP 1
Abbey Inn

*Just off A38 at A384 junction; take B3380 towards Buckfastleigh, but turn right into
Buckfast Road immediately after bridge; TQ11 0EA*

Right by River Dart with tables on terrace, neat rooms and St Austell beers; bedrooms

Try to arrive at this former quarry house early on a fine day and then you can bag one of
the tables on the terrace overlooking the River Dart. Inside, it's a sizeable, pleasant
place and the bar has partly panelled walls, quite a mix of chairs and tables, local
paintings, and a woodburning stove in an ornate fireplace. The big dining room has more
panelling and river views. St Austell Dartmoor Best, HSD and Tribute on handpump,
several wines by the glass and local cider; helpful, obliging staff and piped music. The
pub is down a steep little drive from the car park. More reports please.

⏲ **Bar food includes sandwiches, soup, pâté, deep-fried camembert with red onion
marmalade, beer-battered fish and chips, roast vegetable lasagne, steak in ale pie, free-
range chicken breast stuffed with cheese and wrapped in bacon with a red wine sauce,
venison casserole with dumplings, and puddings such as apple crumble and chocolate
mousse cake.** *Starters/Snacks: £3.95 to £6.50. Main Courses: £7.95 to £13.95. Puddings: £4.95*

St Austell ~ Tenants Rob Bowrin, J P D'hotman ~ Real ale ~ Bar food ~ Restaurant ~
(01364) 642343 ~ Children welcome ~ Dogs allowed in bar ~ Open 10.30-11 ~
Bedrooms: £55S/£75S

Recommended by Glenda Bennett, George Atkinson, Alison Trowell, Henry Pursehouse-Tranter, Michael Dandy

BUCKLAND BREWER   SS4220   MAP 1
Coach & Horses

Village signposted off A388 S of Monkleigh; OS Sheet 190 map reference 423206; EX39 5LU

**Friendly old village pub with a mix of customers, open fires, tasty bar food and real ales;
good nearby walks**

At any time of year, this ancient thatched pub is an enjoyable place to visit. In fine
weather you can sit at picnic-sets on the front terrace and in the side garden, and in
winter there are warm fires in cosy rooms. The heavily beamed bar (mind your head on
some of them) has comfortable seats (including a handsome antique settle) and a
woodburning stove in the inglenook – there's also a good log fire in the big stone
inglenook of the small lounge. A little back room has darts and pool; the three-legged
cat is called Marmite. Cotleigh Golden Seahawk, Otter Ale and St Austell Tribute on
handpump, Winkleigh cider and friendly staff; skittle alley (that doubles as a function
room), piped music, games machine and occasional TV for sports. The pub is handy for
the RHS garden Rosemoor and there are walks on the nearby moorland and along the
beaches of Westward Ho! This is a pretty village.

⏲ **Reasonably priced popular bar food includes sandwiches, filled baguettes and baked
potatoes, ploughman's, pasties, soup, various curries, daily specials such as butternut
squash and parsnip cakes with stilton sauce, beef and mushroom in ale pie, lamb with
bacon, garlic and basil in red wine, salmon steak in oatmeal with chilli jam, venison in
port with dumplings, and puddings like treacle tart and banoffi pie; Sunday roasts.**
Starters/Snacks: £3.94 to £6.95. Main Courses: £7.95 to £13.95. Puddings: £3.75 to £4.75

Free house ~ Licensees Oliver and Nicola Wolfe ~ Real ale ~ Bar food ~ Restaurant ~
(01237) 451395 ~ Well behaved children welcome ~ Open 12-3, 5.30(6 Sun)-midnight
Recommended by the Didler, John Marsh, Bob and Margaret Holder, Ewan and Moira McCall, Ryta Lyndley

BUCKLAND MONACHORUM   SX4968   MAP 1

Drake Manor 🍺

Off A386 via Crapstone, just S of Yelverton roundabout; PL20 7NA

**Nice little village pub with snug rooms, popular food, quite a choice of drinks and pretty
back garden; bedrooms**

There's a good mix of both locals and visitors in this charming and friendly little pub and
the long-serving landlady offers a warm welcome to all. The heavily beamed public bar on
the left has brocade-cushioned wall seats, prints of the village from 1905 onwards, some
horse tack and a few ship badges on the wall and a really big stone fireplace with a
woodburning stove; a small door leads to a low-beamed cubbyhole. The snug Drakes Bar
has beams hung with tiny cups and big brass keys, a woodburning stove in another stone
fireplace, horsebrasses and stirrups, a fine stripped pine high-backed settle with a hood,
and a mix of other seats around just four tables (the oval one is rather nice). On the
right is a small, beamed dining room with settles and tables on the flagstoned floor.
Shove-ha'penny, darts, euchre and board games. Courage Best, Dartmoor Jail Ale, Otter
Ale and Sharps Doom Bar on handpump, 20 malt whiskies, ten wines by the glass and a
couple of draught ciders. The sheltered back garden – where there are picnic-sets – is
prettily planted and the floral displays in front are delightful all year round. As well as
offering bedrooms, there's also an attractive self-catering apartment.

🍴 Using their own home-reared pork and other local produce, the enjoyable daily specials
might include tuna and mozzarella fishcakes with spicy salsa, steak and kidney pie,
spiced butternut squash, spinach and walnut bake, chicken suprême with asparagus
wrapped in bacon with a white wine and cream sauce, baked ham with pineapple and
cheese, large battered haddock, braised rabbit with apricots and madeira and winter
venison pie; also, lunchtime filled baguettes, ploughman's, pork sausages and minted
lamb burger with goats cheese and red onion marmalade. *Starters/Snacks: £4.40 to £7.95.
Main Courses: £7.95 to £16.50. Puddings: £3.95 to £4.25*

Punch ~ Lease Mandy Robinson ~ Real ale ~ Bar food (12-2, 7-10(9.30 Sun)) ~ Restaurant ~
(01822) 853892 ~ Children in restaurant and area off main bar ~ Dogs allowed in bar ~
Open 11.30-2.30(3 Sat), 6.30-11(11.30 Fri and Sat); 12-11 Sun ~ Bedrooms: /£80B
Recommended by Nick and Meriel Cox, Richard Tilbrook, Martyn Williams, R and S Bentley

CADELEIGH   SS9107   MAP 1

Cadeleigh Arms ♀

*Village signposted off A3072 just W of junction with A396 Tiverton—Exeter in Bickleigh;
EX16 8HP*

**Attractively refurbished and civilised pub in rolling countryside, carefully chosen wines,
popular bar food and relaxed atmosphere**

Much enjoyed by our readers, this is a rather civilised and attractive small pub where you
can be sure of a warm welcome. They do keep Otter Bitter on handpump as well as a
carefully chosen little wine list and farm cider, but many customers are here to enjoy the
popular bar food. To the left of the door, high-backed farmhouse, church and blond wooden
chairs sit around a mix of tables (one is an old barrel) and there's a bay window seat, an
ornamental stove in the stone fireplace and rather striking hound paintings; darts and
board games. This part leads to a flagstoned room with a high-backed settle to one side of
the log fire in its big sandstone fireplace, and similar chairs and tables; newspapers,
magazines and books to read. Down a couple of steps is a light and airy dining room with
country landscapes, pale wooden chairs and tables, and views over the valley; unobtrusive
piped music. There are some picnic-sets on a gravel terrace with more on a sloping lawn.

⑪ Well liked bar food includes sandwiches, soup, good ham hock terrine with celeriac remoulade, baked egg with pesto and sunblush tomatoes, bangers and mash with onion gravy, a tian of mediterranean vegetables with goats cheese, fish pie, liver and bacon, smoked haddock with spinach and saffron risotto and a poached egg, steaks, and puddings like cinnamon panna cotta with roasted plums. *Starters/Snacks: £4.25 to £6.95. Main Courses: £9.95 to £15.95. Puddings: £4.95*

Free house ~ Licensee Jane Dreyer ~ Real ale ~ Bar food (12-2.30, 7-9; not Sun evening or Mon) ~ Restaurant ~ (01884) 855238 ~ Children welcome ~ Dogs allowed in bar ~ Open 12-2(2.30 Sun), 6-11; closed Sun evening, all day Mon; 25 Dec

Recommended by John and Susan Miln, Anthony Barnes, Jane Hudson

CLAYHIDON   ST1817   MAP 1

Merry Harriers ⑪ ♈ 🍺

3 miles from M5 junction 26: head towards Wellington; turn left at first roundabout signposted Ford Street and Hemyock, then after a mile turn left signposted Ford Street; at hilltop T-junction, turn left towards Chard – pub is 1.5 miles on right; EX15 3TR

DEVON DINING PUB OF THE YEAR

Bustling dining pub with imaginative food, several real ales and quite a few wines by the glass; sizeable garden

'As good as it gets for many miles' says one of our readers about this bustling pub – and many agree with him. The hardworking licensees and their well trained staff are sure to make you welcome and there's a good mix of both locals and visitors. Several small linked green-carpeted areas have comfortably cushioned pews and farmhouse chairs, a sofa beside the woodburning stove, candles in bottles, horsey and hunting prints and local wildlife pictures. Two dining areas have a brighter feel with quarry tiles and lightly timbered white walls. Cotleigh Harrier, Otter Head and a guest like Exmoor Gold on handpump, a dozen wines by the glass, two local ciders, 25 malt whiskies and a good range of spirits; skittle alley and solitaire. There are plenty of tables and chairs in the sizeable garden and on the terrace and they have a new wendy house for children; there are good surrounding walks.

⑪ Growing some of the vegetables, keeping their own hens and using seasonal local produce, the interesting bar food might include lunchtime filled baguettes, soup, tempura tiger prawns with sweet chilli sauce, scallops with lemon cream sauce and crispy parma ham, honey-roasted ham with free-range eggs, organic pork and apple sausages with wholegrain mustard mash and onion gravy, wild mushroom and spinach risotto, chicken korma, steak and kidney pie, daily specials such as smoked haddock fishcakes with horseradish mayonnaise and roasted guinea fowl breast on sweet potato mash with caramelised shallots, and puddings like dark chocolate terrine and warm treacle tart with clotted cream; Sunday roasts. *Starters/Snacks: £4.00 to £5.50. Main Courses: £7.00 to £13.00. Puddings: £4.50 to £5.00*

Free house ~ Licensees Peter and Angela Gatling ~ Real ale ~ Bar food (not Sun evening or Mon) ~ Restaurant ~ (01823) 421270 ~ Children welcome ~ Dogs welcome ~ Open 12-3, 6.30-11; 12-4 Sun; closed Sun evening, all day Mon; 25 and 26 Dec

Recommended by John and Gloria Isaacs, John and Verna Aspinall, Gerry and Rosemary Dobson, Bob and Margaret Holder, Jenna Phillips, PLC, Brian Glozier, I H G Busby, Mike Gorton

CLYST HYDON   ST0201   MAP 1

Five Bells

West of the village and just off B3176 not far from M5 junction 28; EX15 2NT

Attractive thatched pub with several distinctive areas, well liked food and drink, and carefully planted cottagey garden

In spring and summer the immaculate cottagey garden in front of this attractive thatched pub is full of thousands of flowers and the big window boxes and hanging baskets are very pretty, too. Up some steps to the side there are plenty of seats on a sizeable flat lawn and pleasant country views. Inside, the bar is divided at one end into different seating areas by brick and timber pillars: china jugs hang from big horsebrass-studded beams, there are many plates lining the shelves, lots of copper and brass and a nice mix of dining chairs around small tables, with some comfortable pink plush banquettes on a little raised area. Past the inglenook fireplace is another big (but narrower) room they call the Long Barn which has a series of prints on the walls, a pine dresser at one end and similar furnishings. Cotleigh Tawny, O'Hanlons Stormstay and Otter Bitter on handpump, local farm cider, a wide range of soft drinks and several wines by the glass; board games and maybe piped music.

📖 Well liked bar food includes sandwiches, soup, chicken, pheasant and cranberry terrine, twice-baked goats cheese soufflé, ratatouille, cream cheese and spinach lasagne, fish pie, a changing curry, steak and kidney pudding, specials such as beer-battered cod, duck breast with orange and Cointreau sauce and beef fillet medallions with pâté-stuffed mushrooms and madeira sauce, and puddings like butterscotch sticky meringue and white chocolate and Drambuie cheesecake. *Starters/Snacks: £4.25 to £6.75. Main Courses: £7.95 to £15.95. Puddings: £4.95 to £5.95*

Free house ~ Licensees Mr and Mrs R Shenton ~ Real ale ~ Bar food (not Mon lunchtime) ~ (01884) 277288 ~ Children welcome away from bar area ~ Live jazz second Weds of the month, folk fourth Fri of the month ~ Open 11.30-3, 6.30-11; 12-3, 6.30-10.30 Sun; closed Mon lunchtime

Recommended by Evelyn and Derek Walter, Bob and Angela Brooks, Mark Sykes, Mr and Mrs Richard Osborne

COCKWOOD

SX9780 MAP 1

Anchor ♀ 🍺

Off, but visible from, A379 Exeter—Torbay; EX6 8RA

Busy dining pub specialising in seafood (other choices available), with six real ales, too

From the tables on the sheltered verandah here you can look across the road to the inlet (which is a pleasant spot to wander around). The fine range of real ales on handpump remains quite a draw: Bass, Exmoor Ale, Otter Ale, Bitter and Head and Timothy Taylors Landlord. They also have a fine wine list with a dozen by the glass, 20 brandies, 20 ports and 130 malt whiskies; lots of liqueur coffees, too. As well as an extension made up of mainly reclaimed timber and decorated with over 300 ship emblems, brass and copper lamps and nautical knick-knacks, there are several small, low-ceilinged, rambling rooms with black panelling and good-sized tables in various alcoves; the snug has a cheerful winter coal fire. Piped music and games machine. There's often a queue to get in, but to cope with the crowds they do two sittings in the restaurant on winter weekends and every evening in summer. More reports please.

📖 A huge range of fish dishes includes 29 different ways of serving River Exe mussels, seven ways of serving local scallops and five ways of serving oysters, as well as crab and brandy soup and various platters to share. Also, non-fishy dishes such as sandwiches, ploughman's, local sausages with onion gravy, pasta with tomato, garlic and herbs, steak and kidney pudding, daily specials, and puddings. *Starters/Snacks: £3.95 to £8.95. Main Courses: £5.95 to £10.95. Puddings: £4.25*

Heavitree ~ Tenants Mr Morgan and Miss Sanders ~ Real ale ~ Bar food (all day) ~ Restaurant ~ (01626) 890203 ~ Children welcome if seated and away from bar ~ Dogs allowed in bar ~ Jazz Weds, other live music Thurs, jam session Sun ~ Open 11-11; 12-10.30 Sun

Recommended by John and Fiona McIlwain, B and M Kendall, Peter and Giff Bennett, Mike and Monnie Jefferies, the Didler

---

'Children welcome' means the pub says it lets children inside without any special restriction. If it allows them in, but to restricted areas such as an eating area or family room, we specify this. Places with separate restaurants often let children use them, hotels usually let them into public areas such as lounges. Some pubs impose an evening time limit – let us know if you find one earlier than 9pm.

COLEFORD

SS7701 MAP 1

New Inn ♀ ⇥

Just off A377 Crediton—Barnstaple; EX17 5BZ

Ancient thatched inn with interestingly furnished areas, well liked food, real ales and welcoming licensees; bedrooms

Our readers continue to enjoy staying overnight at this 800-year-old inn and the breakfasts are especially good. You can expect a warm welcome from the friendly staff and hard-working licensees who continue to make improvements both inside and out. It's a U-shaped building with the servery in the 'angle', and interestingly furnished areas leading off it: ancient and modern settles, cushioned stone wall seats, some character tables – a pheasant worked into the grain of one – and carved dressers and chests; also, paraffin lamps, antique prints on the white walls and landscape plates on one of the beams, with pewter tankards on another. Captain, the chatty parrot, may greet you with a 'hello' or even a 'goodbye'. Otter Ale, Sharps Doom Bar and a guest like Cottage Puffing Billy or Skinners Betty Stogs on handpump, local cider, 20 wines by the glass and several malt whiskies; darts and board games. There are new chairs and tables on decking under the pruned willow tree by the babbling stream and more in a covered dining area.

🍽 **Using local produce where possible, the often inventive bar food includes filled baguettes, soup, scallop and bacon salad with a sweet chilli dressing, chicken liver pâté topped with toasted pine nut butter, oriental duck salad, popular beefburgers topped with stilton, roasted butternut squash and mushroom risotto, gammon and free-range egg, cajun chicken with lime and sour cream, fillets of red mullet, salmon and hake in a vermouth and dill cream sauce and venison and mushroom pie with port and pickled walnuts.** *Starters/Snacks: £4.50 to £6.50. Main Courses: £7.95 to £10.50. Puddings: £3.50 to £5.00*

Free house ~ Licensees Carole and George Cowie ~ Real ale ~ Bar food ~ Restaurant ~ (01363) 84242 ~ Children welcome ~ Dogs allowed in bar ~ Open 12-3, 6-11(10.30 Sun); closed 25 and 26 Dec ~ Bedrooms: £65B/£85B

Recommended by Mrs P Sumner, Andrea Rampley, P and J Shapley, Anthony Barnes, Dr A McCormick, B J Harding, Mike and Mary Carter, Jane Hudson

COMBEINTEIGNHEAD

SX9071 MAP 1

Wild Goose ♀ ◖

Just off unclassified coast road Newton Abbot—Shaldon, up hill in village; TQ12 4RA

Fine choice of real ales and well liked bar food in well run, friendly pub with seats in attractive garden

To find this well run, friendly pub just head for the 14th-c church next door. The back beamed spacious lounge has a mix of wheelbacks and red plush dining chairs, a decent collection of tables, agricultural artefacts on the walls and french windows to the garden with nice country views beyond. The front bar has seats in the window embrasures of the thick walls, flagstones in a small area by the door and some beams and standing timbers; a step down on the right at the end leads to yet another room with dining chairs around the tables and a big old fireplace with an open log fire. Piped music, games machine, darts, TV, bar billiards, shove-ha'penny and board games. A cosy section on the left has an old settee and comfortable well used chairs. Up to seven real ales on handpump might include Skinners Betty Stogs and St Austell Tribute with guests such as Otter Bitter, Palmers Tally Ho, Sharps Doom Bar, Skinners Ginger Tosser and Teignworthy Mad Hatter; they also keep two farm ciders and ten wines by the glass. The sheltered and walled back garden has plenty of seats around outdoor heaters.

🍽 **Well liked bar food using only Devon suppliers includes lunchtime sandwiches, ploughman's, soup, three-egg omelettes and sausage or ham with egg, and blackboard specials such as chicken liver parfait, stuffed mussels, pesto pasta, beef in Guinness pie, fish and chips, smoked chicken with stilton sauce, bass with chilli and lime zest butter, and puddings like chocolate truffle cake and tarte au citron.** *Starters/Snacks: £5.25 to £8.95. Main Courses: £7.25 to £16.50. Puddings: £4.75 to £4.95*

Free house ~ Licensees Jerry and Kate English ~ Real ale ~ Bar food ~ Restaurant ~ (01626) 872241 ~ Children in dining room only ~ Dogs allowed in bar ~ Live music Fri evening ~ Open 11-3, 5.30-11(midnight Sat); 12-3, 7-11 Sun

Recommended by J D O Carter, P and J Shapley, B and M Kendall, John and Fiona McIlwain, Mike and Monnie Jefferies, David Heath, Laurence Smith

CULMSTOCK
ST1013   MAP 1

Culm Valley ♀ ☕

B3391, off A38 E of M5 junction 27; EX15 3JJ

Quirky, friendly dining pub with imaginative food, interesting real ales, lively atmosphere, and outside seats overlooking River Culm

You will get a friendly welcome from the slightly off-beat landlord and his dogs in this rather quirky no-frills pub. It's not to everyone's taste and some do feel that housekeeping could do with a bit of attention – but many of our readers love the place. The atmosphere is lively and informal, there's a good mix of both chatty locals and visitors and the bar has a hotch-potch of modern and unrenovated furnishings, horse racing paintings and various knick-knacks to do with racing on the walls and a big fireplace. Further along is a dining room with a chalkboard menu, a small front conservatory and leading off here, a little oak-floored room with views into the kitchen. A larger back room has paintings by local artists for sale. Board games and a small portable TV for occasional rugby, rowing and racing events; the dogs are called Lady and Spoof. Brewdog Skull Candy, Coastal Handliner, Exeter Avocet, Quercus Origin and Stonehenge Great Bustard are tapped from the cask and the landlord and his brother import wines from smaller french vineyards so you can count on a few of those as well as some unusual french fruit liqueurs, somerset cider brandies, vintage rum, good sherries, madeira and local farm cider. Outside, tables are very attractively positioned overlooking the bridge and the River Culm. The gents' is in an outside yard.

🍴 Under the newish chef the often imaginative food includes lunchtime sandwiches, ploughman's, interesting soups, cracked crab claws, mixed tapas, moules marinière, pea and pesto risotto, indonesian chicken, duck breast with an orange reduction, partridge, parsnip and chestnut pie, shellfish platter, john dory grilled with samphire, and puddings like lemon cheesecake and sticky toffee pudding. *Starters/Snacks: £6.00 to £10.00. Main Courses: £10.00 to £20.00. Puddings: £5.00*

Free house ~ Licensee Richard Hartley ~ Real ale ~ Bar food (not Sun evening) ~ Restaurant ~ No credit cards ~ (01884) 840354 ~ Children allowed away from main bar ~ Dogs welcome ~ Open 12-3, 6-11; 12-11 Fri and Sat; 12-10.30 Sun ~ Bedrooms: £35B/£65B

Recommended by G K Smale, Evelyn and Derek Walter, Adrian Johnson, John and Hilary Penny, Christine and Neil Townend, Jenna Phillips, Dr and Mrs A K Clarke, Andrea Rampley, John Prescott, Gary Marchant, Tony Winckworth, John and Gloria Isaacs, Mike Gorton, John andFiona Merritt, Michael Beale, Adrian and Dawn Collinge

DALWOOD
ST2400   MAP 1

Tuckers Arms

Village signposted off A35 Axminster—Honiton; keep on past village; EX13 7EG

Pretty, thatched inn with friendly, hard-working young licensees, real ales and well liked bar food

Parts of this pretty creamwashed thatched longhouse date back to the 13th c and after the church, it is the oldest building in the parish. The young licensees and their staff are sure to make you welcome whether you are a regular or a visitor and the atmosphere is relaxed and informal. The flagstoned bar has plenty of beams, traditional furnishings, a mixture of dining chairs, window seats and wall settles and a log fire in the inglenook fireplace with lots of horsebrasses above it. The back bar has an enormous collection of miniature bottles and there's also a more formal dining room; lots of copper implements and platters. Branscombe Vale Branoc, Otter Bitter and a changing local guest beer on handpump, several wines by the glass and up to 20 malt whiskies. Piped music and a double skittle alley. In summer, the hanging baskets are pretty and there are seats in the garden.

🍴 Well liked bar food at lunchtime includes filled baguettes and filled baked potatoes, ploughman's, beer-battered fish, home-made burger topped with cheese, sausage and mash, ham and egg and thai crab linguine, with evening dishes like slow-roasted pork belly with a rosemary, garlic and cider cream sauce, lamb rump topped with tomato and chilli chutney, baked chicken breast with a creamy wild mushroom sauce, salmon fillet with pesto dressing, and puddings like a trio of brûlée and white chocolate and treacle tart. *Starters/Snacks: £4.25 to £6.45. Main Courses: £9.95 to £16.95. Puddings: £4.95*

Free house ~ Licensee Tracey Pearson ~ Real ale ~ Bar food ~ Restaurant ~ (01404) 881342 ~ Children in restaurant but must be well behaved ~ Dogs allowed in bar ~ Open 11.30-3, 6.30(6 Sat)-11.30; 12-4, 7-10.30 Sun ~ Bedrooms: £42.50S/£69.50S

Recommended by Marcus Mann, Bob and Margaret Holder, John Luckes, Michelle Gallagher, Shaun Holley, Jane Hudson, Paul Aldred, Neil Kellett

DARTMOUTH
SX8751   MAP 1

Cherub

Higher Street; walk along river front, right into Hauley Road and up steps at end; TQ6 9RB

Ancient timbered building with bustling bar, plenty of atmosphere and good food and drink; can get busy at peak times

This handsome inn is Dartmouth's oldest building (dating from 1380) and is exceptionally pretty in summer, with lots of flowering baskets. Its age shows on the outside with the two heavily timbered upper floors each jutting out further than the one below. Inside, there are many original features. The bustling bar has a lot of atmosphere, tapestried seats under creaky heavy beams (old ships' timbers), leaded lights, a big stone fireplace with a woodburning stove, and Otter Bitter, St Austell Dartmoor Best and Proper Job, Sharps Doom Bar and one or two guest beers on handpump; quite a few malt whiskies and several wines by the glass. Good service. The low-ceilinged restaurant is upstairs; piped music. No children inside.

🍴 A wide choice of well liked bar food includes lunchtime sandwiches, soup, mussels in cider, bacon, tarragon and shallot broth with cream, chicken liver pâté with red onion marmalade, potted crab, mushroom and stilton linguine, bangers and mash, ham and egg, beer-battered cod, steak and kidney pudding, red mullet fillet topped with a chilli, ginger and garlic crumb on creamed leeks and winter pheasant breast with apple, calvados and crème fraîche. *Starters/Snacks: £4.95 to £7.25. Main Courses: £10.95 to £14.95. Puddings: £5.25*

Free house ~ Licensee Dean Singer ~ Real ale ~ Bar food (not Mon or Tues evenings in winter) ~ Restaurant ~ (01803) 832571 ~ Dogs allowed in bar ~ Open 11-11; 12-10.30 Sun; 11-2.30, 5-11 Mon-Thurs in winter

Recommended by the Didler, Dick and Madeleine Brown, Donna and Roger, Andrea Rampley, Christine and Neil Townend, Peter and Heather Elliott, Alan Sutton, Alun and Jennifer Evans, Guy Vowles, Peter and Margaret Glenister, Michael Dandy, Roger Wain-Heapy

Floating Bridge

Opposite Upper Ferry, use Dart Marina Hotel car park; Coombe Road (A379); TQ6 9PQ

Quayside local with seats outside making the most of the position, simple bar, neat dining room, friendly staff, and popular summer roof terrace

Run by a friendly landlady, this quayside local is under the same ownership as the nearby Dart Marina Hotel. It's right by the ferry and the River Dart views can be enjoyed through windows in the bar, from the picnic-sets outside and across the lane by the water, and from the sizeable roof terrace. The simple bar has cushioned, wood-slatted wall seats and wheelback chairs around straightforward pubby tables (each with a little nightlight), some rather fine model boats, black and white photographs of local boating scenes and ship's badges on the walls; St Austell Tribute and Sharps Doom Bar on handpump and quite a few wines by the glass; the piped music was cheerful 1960s while we were there. The dining room on the left is lighter with more wheelback chairs around scrubbed kitchen tables on the bare boards, and photographs of naïve gig rowing and a big old yacht on the white walls above a grey vertical panelled dado. The window boxes are pretty against the white-painted building.

🍴 As well as sandwiches, the tasty bar food includes soup, chicken liver parfait, mushroom pasta, sausage and mash with onion gravy, steak and onion pudding, popular fish and chips, and puddings like hot chocolate brownie with clotted cream and chocolate sauce and pear and almond tart; Sunday roasts. *Starters/Snacks: £5.50 to £7.00. Main Courses: £9.00 to £14.00. Puddings: £5.50 to £6.50*

Enterprise ~ Lease Ann Firmstone ~ Real ale ~ Bar food (12-2.30, 6-9.30) ~ Restaurant ~ (01803) 832354 ~ Children welcome ~ Dogs allowed in bar ~ Open 11am-midnight; 12-11.30 Sun; closed Sun evening, all day Mon and Tues

Recommended by Ian Malone, Richard and Sissel Harris, Michael Dandy

DITTISHAM
SX8654 MAP 1

Ferry Boat
Manor Street; best to park in village – steep but attractive walk down; TQ6 0EX

Cheerful riverside pub with shipping knick-knacks, real ales and friendly staff

There's a lively mix of locals, sailors and visitors in this bustling little pub and the cheerful staff offer a friendly welcome to all. The bar has beams, open log fires, brass gear and a ship's clock, ship's badges over the serving counter, photographs of boats and ships and straightforward pubby furniture; they chalk the tide times up on the wall. To make the most of the fine riverside position, try to bag one of the seats in the big picture window. Otter Ale, St Austell Tribute, Sharps Doom Bar and Youngs on handpump, a dozen wines by the glass and Addlestone's cider; piped music. If you arrive by boat, there are moorings on the adjacent pontoon and there's a bell to summon the ferry across the Greenway Quay. Parking nearby is not easy – best to park by the church. More reports please.

🍴 Pubby bar food includes filled baguettes, soup, mackerel pâté, ham and egg, haddock and chips, chilli con carne, sausage and mash, a curry of the day, popular home-made pies, and puddings. *Starters/Snacks: £4.50 to £5.50. Main Courses: £7.00 to £14.50. Puddings: £4.50*

Punch ~ Lease Ray Benson ~ Real ale ~ Bar food ~ (01803) 722368 ~ Children welcome ~ Dogs welcome ~ Open 11am-midnight; 12-11 Sun

Recommended by Dr Ron Cox, Wendy and Carl Dye, Peter and Margaret Glenister, Henry Pursehouse-Tranter

DREWSTEIGNTON
SX7390 MAP 1

Drewe Arms
Off A30 NW of Moretonhampstead; EX6 6QN

Pretty thatched pub, warmly welcoming, proper basic bar plus dining rooms, well liked food and real ales; bedrooms

This is a pretty thatched pub in a lovely village and our readers enjoy their visits here very much. The unchanging and unspoilt room on the left still has a serving hatch and basic wooden wall benches, stools and tables. And three dining areas – Mabel's Kitchen with its original Rayburn and a history of Aunt Mabel (Britain's longest serving and oldest landlady), the Card Room which has a woodburning stove and the back Dartmoor Room which is ideal for a private party, with lots of prints and pictures on the walls and an array of copper saucepans. Hop Back Summer Lightning, Sharps Doom Bar and Druid Ale (brewed by Otter exclusively for the pub) tapped from casks in the original tap room and local cider; board games. There are seats under umbrellas along the front terrace surrounded by lovely flowering tubs and hanging baskets, with more in the terraced garden. As well as comfortable bedrooms, they have bunk rooms which are ideal for walkers. Castle Drogo is nearby.

🍴 **Tasty bar food includes soup, duck liver, port and cherry pâté, moules marinière, pizzas (you can take them away too), various platters, butternut squash, kidney bean and buffalo cheese pie, sausage and mash with caramelised onion gravy, venison burger with cheese and spicy tomato sauce, steak and kidney pudding, beer-battered cod, king prawns in lemon butter, and puddings.** *Starters/Snacks: £4.00 to £6.25. Main Courses: £7.25 to £16.50. Puddings: £3.95 to £5.95*

Enterprise ~ Lease Fiona Newton ~ Real ale ~ Bar food (all day in summer; 12-2.30, 6-9.30 in winter) ~ Restaurant ~ (01647) 281224 ~ Children welcome ~ Dogs allowed in bar and bedrooms ~ Open 11am-midnight; 11-3, 6-midnight in winter ~ Bedrooms: £60S/£90S(£80B)

Recommended by Di and Mike Gillam, B and M Kendall, Adrian Johnson, Gene and Tony Freemantle, Alison Ball, Ian Walton, Jane Hudson, Tich Critchlow, Ian Herdman, Steve and Liz Tilley, R J Herd, B J Harding, Roy and Lindsey Fentiman, Andrea Rampley

EAST ALLINGTON   SX7648   MAP 1

Fortescue Arms 🍴

Village signposted off A381 Totnes—Kingsbridge, S of A3122 junction; TQ9 7RA

Pretty village pub, good choice of drinks, highly thought-of food cooked by landlord and attractive outside seating; bedrooms

Although they keep Butcombe Bitter, Dartmoor IPA and a guest like Bays Gold on handpump in this pretty village pub, most customers are here to enjoy the often imaginative food; several wines by the glass and Luscombe cider. The main part of the two-room bar has a nice mix of wooden tables and cushioned dining chairs on the black slate floor, an open log fire, a dark green dado under cream walls, church candles and some brewery memorabilia and attractive tartan curtains. The second room is set for eating with similar furniture, a few old photographs and red carpeting; piped music; there's also a stylish contemporary restaurant. The sheltered courtyard has some picnic-sets and there are teak steamer chairs under a pair of small marquees on the terrace.

🍴 **Cooked by the licensee, who's from Austria, the good food includes sandwiches, soup, smoked duck breast with fennel and grape salad and home-made chutney, three-bean chilli, liver and bacon with onion gravy, venison ragoût, chicken curry, pork fillets filled with ham and cheese with a dijon mustard sauce, fillet of beef with roasted peppers and red wine sauce, and puddings like apfelstrudel with crème pâtissière and sticky toffee pudding with butterscotch sauce.** *Starters/Snacks: £4.50 to £8.30. Main Courses: £8.50 to £12.75. Puddings: £5.65*

Free house ~ Licensee Werner Rott ~ Real ale ~ Bar food ~ Restaurant ~ (01548) 521215 ~ Children in own area; must be over 6 in restaurant ~ Dogs allowed in bar and bedrooms ~ Open 12-3, 6-11(10.30 Sun); closed Mon lunchtime ~ Bedrooms: £40S/£60S

Recommended by Mrs L Aquilina, Pauline and Philip Darley, Peter and Heather Elliott, Lynda and Trevor Smith, Roger Wain-Heapy

EXETER   SX9292   MAP 1

Hour Glass 🍺

Melbourne Street, off B3015 Topsham Road (some nearby parking); EX2 4AU

Inventive food in old-fashioned local, friendly service, and good choice of real ales and wines by the glass

You will feel just as comfortable coming to this small old-fashioned back street pub for a drink on your own or meeting up with friends to enjoy the inventive food. There are beams, a mix of pub chairs and tables on the bare boards, dark red walls, an open fire in a small brick fireplace and a relaxed, chatty atmosphere; resident cats, piped music and board games. Branscombe Vale Branoc, Exeter Ferryman and St Austell Proper Job on handpump served from the central island bar and a smashing range of wines by the glass.

🍴 **Good, interesting bar food includes soup, puy lentil and herb salad with goats curd and hazelnut oil, smoked eel with pressed potato terrine and sour plums, cauliflower and chilli risotto with anchovy breadcrumbs, pollack and mussel stew with saffron and fennel, braised lamb shoulder with garlic, rosemary and white beans, chicken with grapes, ricotta and baby gem, and puddings such as chocolate mousse and lemon tart.** *Starters/Snacks: £4.50 to £8.50. Main Courses: £10.00 to £16.50. Puddings: £4.50 to £6.50*

Enterprise ~ Lease J Slade ~ Real ale ~ Bar food (12.30-2.30(3 weekends), 7-9.30(6.30-9 Sun)) ~ Restaurant ~ (01392) 258722 ~ Children welcome away from public bar ~ Dogs welcome ~ Open 12-3, 5-11; 12-11 Fri and Sat; 12-10.30 Sun; closed Mon lunchtime

Recommended by John and Fiona McIlwain, the Didler

Imperial 🍺 £

New North Road (St David's Hill on Crediton—Tiverton road, above St David's station); EX4 4AH

19th-c mansion in own grounds with interesting seating areas and cheap food and drink

The light and airy former orangery here with its unusual lightly mirrored end wall is a smashing place to sit and enjoy one of 14 real ales. There are various different areas (refurbished this year) including a couple of little clubby side bars, a left-hand bar that looks into the orangery, and a fine ex-ballroom filled with elaborate plasterwork and gilding brought here in the 1920s from Haldon House (a Robert Adam stately home that was falling on hard times). The furnishings give Wetherspoons' usual solid well spaced comfort, and the walls are hung with plenty of interesting pictures and other things to look at. Exmoor Stag, Greene King Abbot, IPA and Ruddles, Otter Bright, Ringwood Fortyniner and eight guests on handpump and farm cider. The setting of this fine mansion is impressive: it stands in its own six-acre hillside park and is reached along a sweeping drive; there are plenty of picnic-sets in the grounds and elegant garden furniture in the attractive cobbled courtyard. It's very popular with students.

🍴 **Very reasonably priced bar food includes sandwiches, soup, filled baked potatoes, ploughman's, spicy battered king prawns, meaty or vegetarian burgers (the price also includes a pint), sweet chilli noodles, moroccan meatballs with couscous, mixed grill, and puddings like vanilla cheesecake and profiteroles.** *Starters/Snacks: £2.79 to £3.99. Main Courses: £3.99 to £9.39. Puddings: £1.99 to £3.99*

Wetherspoons ~ Manager Paul Dixey ~ Real ale ~ Bar food (all day) ~ (01392) 434050 ~ Children welcome away from orangery ~ Open 9am-midnight(1am Sat)

Recommended by Tony and Wendy Hobden, B and M Kendall, the Didler, Mike Gorton, Pat and Tony Martin

EXMINSTER
SX9686   MAP 1

Turf Hotel ★

Follow the signs to the Swan's Nest, signposted from A379 S of village, then continue to end of track, by gates; park and walk right along canal towpath – nearly a mile; there's a fine seaview out to the mudflats at low tide; EX6 8EE

Remote but very popular waterside pub with fine choice of drinks, super summer barbecues and lots of space in big garden

You can't reach this extremely popular pub by car – you must either walk (which takes about 20 minutes along the ship canal) or cycle or catch a 60-seater boat which brings people down the Exe estuary from Topsham quay (15-minute trip, adult £4.50, child £2); there's also a canal boat from Countess Wear Swing Bridge every lunchtime. Best to phone the pub for all sailing times. For those arriving in their own boat, there's a large pontoon as well as several moorings. Inside, the end room has a slate floor, pine walls, built-in seats, lots of photographs of the pub, and a woodburning stove; along a corridor (with an eating room to one side) is a simply furnished room with wood-plank seats around tables on the stripped wooden floor. Exeter Avocet and Ferryman, Otter Ale and Bitter and O'Hanlons Yellowhammer on handpump, local cider and juices, ten wines by the glass (and local wine too) and jugs of Pimms. There are plenty of picnic-sets spread around the big garden; the sea and estuary birds are fun to watch at low tide. Although it does get packed in fine weather and there are inevitable queues, the staff remain friendly and efficient both inside the pub and running the outdoor barbecue.

🍴 **Good bar food using organic and local produce includes lunchtime sandwiches and toasties, soup, spanish-style baby squid with aioli dip, home-made burger, pasta with aubergine, tomato and basil topped with mozzarella and parmesan, beer-battered fish, thai chicken curry, king prawns with garlic and pesto, smoked haddock with creamy mash, poached egg and spring greens, and puddings like treacle toffee pudding and crumbles with clotted cream.** *Starters/Snacks: £4.95 to £6.50. Main Courses: £7.50 to £16.95. Puddings: £4.75*

Free house ~ Licensees Clive and Ginny Redfern ~ Real ale ~ Bar food (12-2.30(3 Sat and Sun), 6.30-9(9.30 Fri and Sat); not Sun evening) ~ (01392) 833128 ~ Children welcome ~ Dogs welcome ~ Open 11-11; 11-10.30 Sun; open only weekends in Oct, Nov, Feb, March winter; closed Dec and Jan

Recommended by David Carr, J D O Carter, Mike Gorton, Barry Steele-Perkins, John and Fiona McIlwain, the Didler

GEORGEHAM   SS4639   MAP 1

Rock
Rock Hill, above village; EX33 1JW

Beamed family pub, good food cooked by landlord, up to six real ales on handpump, plenty of room inside and out, and relaxed atmosphere

Although the enjoyable food cooked by the chef/landlord is quite a draw to this beamed pub, they also keep five real ales on handpump: Fullers London Pride, Greene King Abbot, St Austell Tribute, Sharps Doom Bar and Timothy Taylors Landlord. Also, a dozen wines by the glass. The two areas of the sizeable bar are separated by a step. The top pubby part has an open woodburning stove in a stone fireplace, a mix of wooden tables and captain's and farmhouse chairs on the red tiled floor and half-planked walls. The lower bar has panelled wall seats, some nice little built-in settles forming a cosy booth, fresh flowers on the tables, some old local photographs and ancient flat irons and faint piped pop music; board games. Leading off here is the red-carpeted dining room with leather seated high-backed pale wooden dining and other chairs including some chapel ones around various tables (one is a refectory), and some attractive black and white photographs of north devon people; friendly young bar staff. The vine-adorned, light and airy back conservatory/skittle alley is popular with families and there are seats beyond that on the little terrace. They have wheelchair access.

🍴 **Using local produce (and some provided by customers) the interesting bar food includes sandwiches, soup, salt and pepper chilli squid, various deli boards with onion jam and rustic breads, pasta with toppings such as salmon and crayfish with tarragon cream or meatballs in tomato and basil sauce, steak in ale pie, beer-battered cod, home-made venison, cranberry and sage sausages, lamb with asparagus and wild mushrooms, duck breast with mint and pea risotto, foie gras sauce and cinnamon jus, and puddings.** *Starters/Snacks: £3.50 to £9.50. Main Courses: £8.95 to £16.95. Puddings: £3.95 to £8.00*

Punch ~ Lease Daniel Craddock ~ Real ale ~ Bar food (12-2.30, 6-9.30; 12-3, 6-9 Sun) ~ Restaurant ~ (01271) 890322 ~ Children welcome away from public bar ~ Dogs welcome ~ Open 11am-11.30pm; 12-11 Sun

Recommended by Stephen Shepherd, Brian Glozier, Dr and Mrs Stephen Barber, Bob and Margaret Holder, David Eberlin

---

Please tell us if the décor, atmosphere, food or drink at a pub is different from our description. We rely on readers' reports to keep us up to date:
feedback@goodguides.com, or (no stamp needed)
The Good Pub Guide, FREEPOST TN1569, Wadhurst, E Sussex TN5 7BR.

HAYTOR VALE

SX7777 MAP 1

Rock ★ Ⓨ 🛏

Haytor signposted off B3387 just W of Bovey Tracey, on good moorland road to Widecombe; TQ13 9XP

Civilised Dartmoor inn at its most informal at lunchtime; super food, real ales and seats in pretty garden; comfortable bedrooms

---

Many customers come to this civilised and neatly kept inn to stay overnight and enjoy the evening restaurant food but our readers feel just as welcome when they drop in for a drink at lunchtime before or after a walk. Dartmoor Jail Ale, Otter Bright and St Austell Dartmoor Best on handpump and several wines by the glass. The two neatly kept communicating, partly panelled bar rooms have lots of dark wood and red plush, polished antique tables with candles and fresh flowers, old-fashioned prints and decorative plates on the walls, and warming winter log fires (the main fireplace has a fine Stuart fireback). There are seats in the large, pretty garden opposite with tables and chairs on a small terrace next to the pub itself. The bedrooms are comfortable with good facilities (some are up steep stairs), and the breakfasts are smashing. There is a car park at the back.

🍴 **Good lunchtime food includes** soup, ploughman's, ham hock terrine with piccalilli, pork and leek sausages with red wine gravy, fish and chips, wild mushroom risotto, smoked haddock and bacon fishcakes with tarragon mayonnaise and steak in ale pie; evening dishes like local mussels in thai green sauce, scallops with celeriac purée and crispy bacon, wild bass with crushed pink fir apples, glazed beetroot tempura king prawn and vierge dressing, saddle of venison with parsnip purée and port sauce, and puddings such as orange crème brûlée and treacle and walnut tart with clotted cream; they also offer a two- and three-course set menu. *Starters/Snacks: £4.50 to £6.95. Main Courses: £7.25 to £14.95. Puddings: £5.50 to £6.95*

Free house ~ Licensee Christopher Graves ~ Real ale ~ Bar food ~ Restaurant ~ (01364) 661305 ~ Children welcome ~ Open 11(10.30 Sat)-11; 12-11 Sun; closed 25 and 26 Dec ~ Bedrooms: £70B/£76.95S(£95.95B)

Recommended by Mrs Mary Woods, Anthony Barnes, Barry and Anne, Neil and Anita Christopher, Mayur Shah, John and Gloria Isaacs

HOLNE

SX7069 MAP 1

Church House

Signed off B3357 W of Ashburton; TQ13 7SJ

Medieval inn on Dartmoor, plenty of surrounding walks, log fires, real ales and tasty bar food; bedrooms

---

Originally built as a resting place for visiting clergy and worshippers at the church (well worth a visit), this medieval Dartmoor inn has plenty of surrounding walks. The lower bar has stripped pine panelling and an 18th-c curved elm settle and is separated from the lounge bar by a 16th-c heavy oak partition; open log fires, lit candles and fresh flowers in both rooms. Dartmoor IPA and Teignworthy Gun Dog on handpump, farm cider and several good wines by the glass; piped music and board games. Charles Kingsley (of *Water Babies* fame) was born in the village.

🍴 **Under the new licensee the traditional bar food includes** lunchtime sandwiches and filled baguettes, soup, creamy garlic mushrooms, pâté with spicy tomato and caramelised onion chutney, ploughman's, vegetable or beef lasagne, a pie and a curry of the day, scampi, gammon and pineapple, daily specials, and puddings. *Starters/Snacks: £4.95 to £10.95. Main Courses: £6.95 to £11.50. Puddings: £3.95*

Free house ~ Licensee Anthony Walker ~ Real ale ~ Bar food (12-2.15, 6-9; not Sun evening) ~ (01364) 631208 ~ Children welcome ~ Dogs welcome ~ Open 12-11(10.30 Sun); 12-3, 6-11 in winter ~ Bedrooms: £37.50S/£75S

Recommended by John Butcher, Val Offer, P and J Shapley, Bob and Angela Brooks, R K Phillips, Frances Naldrett, Mrs J Ekins-Daukes

HONITON
SY1198   MAP 1

Holt 🍺
High Street, W end; EX14 1LA

Friendly, informal family-run pub with super tapas and other interesting food and fine range of Otter beers

Well run and welcoming, this simple little pub is quite a surprise. For a start they keep the full range of Otter beers on handpump – Ale, Amber, Bitter, Bright and Head – but also offer delicious and interesting tapas from the open kitchen. There's just one room downstairs with chunky pine chairs and tables (a pot of thyme on each one) on the stone floor, a couple of brown leather sofas at one end facing each other across a circular table, a coal-effect woodburner in the brick fireplace with a shelf of books to one side, and shuttered windows, one of which looks down on to a small stream. Upstairs a bigger, brighter room has similar furniture on floorboards and small, very attractive musician prints, much larger contemporary pictures and an old Chamonix travel poster on the pale grey or maroon walls. Funky and cheerful 1970s piped music and friendly staff. It's all very relaxed and informal. The black cat is called Dangermouse.

🍽 **Listing their local growers and producers on a blackboard by the open kitchen, the interesting bar food includes sandwiches, soup, a range of tasty tapas, maple smoked chicken and ham hock terrine with smoked chilli and tomato pickle, salad of slow-cooked pork cheek, grilled black pudding, apple and candied walnuts, white onion tarte tatin with wild mushrooms, fennel, shallots and tarragon, roasted lamb rump with spiced couscous, lamb faggot and dates and guinea fowl suprême with bacon, sweetcorn and parsley and mustard sauce.** *Starters/Snacks: £4.50 to £7.50. Main Courses: £7.50 to £15.50. Puddings: £5.50*

Free house ~ Licensees Joe and Angus McCaig ~ Real ale ~ Bar food ~ Restaurant ~ (01404) 47707 ~ Well behaved children welcome ~ Dogs allowed in bar ~ Music festival four times a year ~ Open 11-3, 5.30-11(midnight Sat); closed Sun and Mon

Recommended by Tim Thornburn, Sophie Clapp, John and Dinah Waters, Paul Milican, Stephen Hunt, Jane Hudson, JHW

HORNDON
SX5280   MAP 1

Elephants Nest 🍺 🛏
If coming from Okehampton on A386, turn left at Mary Tavy Inn, then left after about 0.5 miles; pub signposted beside Mary Tavy Inn, then Horndon signposted; on the Ordnance Survey Outdoor Leisure Map it's named as the New Inn; PL19 9NQ

Isolated old inn surrounded by Dartmoor walks, some interesting original features, real ales and good food; bedrooms

This is a lovely cosy old inn and an enjoyable place to stay overnight in the attractively furnished and well appointed bedrooms. The main bar has lots of beer pump clips on the beams, high bar chairs by the bar counter, Dartmoor Jail Ale, Palmers IPA, Sharps Doom Bar and a guest like Otter Bright on handpump, farm cider and several wines by the glass. There are two other rooms with nice modern dark wood dining chairs around a mix of tables and throughout there are bare stone walls, flagstones and three woodburning stoves. The spreading, attractive garden has plenty of picnic-sets under parasols and from here you look over dry-stone walls to the pastures of Dartmoor's lower slopes and the rougher moorland above.

🍽 **Using very local produce, the good bar food includes lunchtime filled baguettes or wraps (not Sundays), soup, an antipasti plate, hamburger with onion marmalade, lamb curry, popular fish pie, venison with a blackberry and sloe gin glaze, specials such as steak and kidney pudding and scallops with chorizo, and puddings like bread and butter pudding with whisky and marmalade and treacle tart with clotted cream; Sunday roasts.** *Starters/Snacks: £4.95 to £8.95. Main Courses: £8.95 to £19.95. Puddings: £3.30 to £4.95*

There are report forms at the back of the book.

Free house ~ Licensee Hugh Cook ~ Real ale ~ Bar food ~ (01822) 810273 ~ Children welcome away from bar ~ Dogs welcome ~ Open 12-3, 6.30-11(10.30 Sun) ~ Bedrooms: £75B/£85B

Recommended by John and Bernadette Elliott, Andrea Rampley, Viv Jameson, P and J Shapley, Dr and Mrs M W A Haward

KING'S NYMPTON
SS6819   MAP 1

Grove 🍴

Off B3226 SW of South Molton; EX37 9ST

Thatched 17th-c pub in remote village, locals beers, interesting bar food and cheerful licensees

Extremely popular and always busy, this thatched 17th-c pub is run by cheerful and friendly licensees. The low-beamed bar has a winter open fire, lots of bookmarks hanging from the ceiling, simple pubby furnishings on the flagstoned floor, bare stone walls, and Exmoor Ale, O'Hanlons Firefly, Otter Ale and Skinners Betty Stogs on handpump, several wines by the glass and 43 malt whiskies; darts, shove-ha'penny, dominoes and cards. The surrounding countryside is quiet and wooded with twisty valley pastures. They have a self-catering cottage to rent. This is a lovely village and very much off the tourist route.

🍴 Naming their local suppliers and trading with regulars for their own-grown excess vegetables and fruit, the interesting bar food includes sandwiches, ploughman's, chicken liver pâté, goats cheese salad with garlic croûtons and chilli jam, minted lamb burger with melted brie and minted yoghurt, wild rabbit stew, chicken stuffed with brie, asparagus and parma ham, individual beef wellington, skate with brown butter and caper sauce, and puddings like hot chocolate pudding with clotted cream ice-cream and rhubarb burnt cream; Sunday roasts. *Starters/Snacks: £3.75 to £4.50. Main Courses: £6.00 to £19.50. Puddings: £3.75 to £6.00*

Free house ~ Licensees Robert and Deborah Smallbone ~ Real ale ~ Bar food (12-2(4 Sun), 6-9; not Mon lunchtime) ~ Restaurant ~ (01769) 580406 ~ Children welcome but must be seated and supervised ~ Dogs welcome ~ Open 12-3, 6-11; 12-4, 7-10.30 Sun; closed Mon lunchtime (except bank hols)

Recommended by Mark Flynn, Robert and Carole Hewitt

KINGSBRIDGE
SX7344   MAP 1

Dodbrooke Inn 🍺 £

Church Street, Dodbrooke (parking some way off); TQ7 1DB

Chatty, bustling local, genuinely welcoming licensees, good mix of customers and honest food and drink

There's always a mix of locals of all ages in this quaint little local but you'll be made just as welcome if it's your first visit. The atmosphere is comfortably traditional and the bar has plush stools and built-in simple cushioned stall seats around straightforward pub tables (and an interesting barrel one), ceiling joists, some horse harness, old local photographs and china jugs, and a log fire. Bass, Bath Ales Gem Bitter, Dartmoor IPA and Sharps Doom Bar on handpump and local farm cider. There's a simply furnished small dining room as well.

🍴 Honest, good value bar food includes sandwiches, ploughman's, a changing pâté, garlic mushrooms, sausage or scampi basket, home-cooked ham and egg, daily specials such as beer-battered cod in three sizes or rump steak with a pepper, brandy and cream sauce, and puddings like fresh lemon tart or belgian chocolate pudding. *Starters/Snacks: £4.95 to £6.95. Main Courses: £7.50 to £14.95. Puddings: £4.50*

Free house ~ Licensees Michael and Jill Dyson ~ Real ale ~ Bar food (12-1.30, 6.30-8.30(9 Sat)) ~ (01548) 852068 ~ Children welcome if over 5 ~ Open 12-2, 5-11; 12-2.30, 7-10.30 Sun; closed Mon and Tues lunchtimes; evenings 25 and 26 Dec

Recommended by MP

KINGSTON

SX6347 MAP 1

Dolphin

Off B3392 S of Modbury (can also be reached from A379 W of Modbury); TQ7 4QE

Peaceful old pub with walks to the sea, cheerful atmosphere and decent drinks and food

To find this traditional country pub, head for the imposing church nearby. It's a cosy old place with several knocked-through beamed rooms and plenty of cheerful locals. There are cushioned wall settles, wheelback chairs and stools around a mix of wooden tables on the red patterned carpet, amusing drawings and photographs on the stone walls and an open fire as well as a woodburning stove. Courage Best, Otter Ale and Sharps Doom Bar on handpump and summer farm cider. There are some seats and tables outside and nice walks down to the sea from here. The gents' is across the road.

🍴 Pubby bar food includes sandwiches, ploughman's, soup, mushrooms in white wine and garlic, breaded whitebait, steak in ale or fish pies, pork belly slowly cooked in cider, lamb shank with leek mash, a vegetarian dish of the day and rib-eye steak. *Starters/Snacks: £2.95 to £4.95. Main Courses: £5.95 to £14.95. Puddings: £3.95 to £5.95*

Punch ~ Lease Janice Male ~ Real ale ~ Bar food (12-2.30(2 in winter), 6(7 summer Sun)-9; not winter Sun evening) ~ (01548) 810314 ~ Children welcome ~ Dogs allowed in bar ~ Open 12-3, 6-11(10.30 Sun) ~ Bedrooms: £42.50B/£70B

Recommended by Roger Wain-Heapy, Peter and Andrea Jacobs, Jerry Brown, Geoff and Carol Thorp, David Uren, Bob and Angela Brooks, Suzy Miller, Peter and Margaret Glenister

MARLDON

SX8663 MAP 1

Church House 🍴 ♟

Just off A380 NW of Paignton; TQ3 1SL

Spreading bar plus several other rooms in this pleasant inn, well liked drinks and bar food, and seats on three terraces

Our readers very much enjoy their visits to this bustling pub and even when it's pretty busy (as it often is) the staff remain friendly and efficient. The attractively furnished spreading bar has several different areas that radiate off the big semicircular bar counter: unusual windows, some beams, dark pine chairs around solid tables and yellow leather bar chairs. Leading off here is a cosy little candlelit room with just four tables on the bare-boarded floor, a dark wood dado and stone fireplace. There's also a restaurant with a large stone fireplace and at the other end of the building, a similarly interesting room is split into two parts with a stone floor in one bit and a wooden floor in another (which has a big woodburning stove). The old barn holds yet another restaurant with art displays by local artists. Bass, Bays Gold, Otter Ale and St Austell Dartmoor Best on handpump, 15 wines by the glass and several malt whiskies; piped music. There are picnic-sets on three carefully maintained grassy terraces behind the pub.

🍴 Attractively presented food using some of their own-grown vegetables includes sandwiches, soup, a sharing plate of mixed bruschetta with olives, twice-baked cornish smoked cheese and leek soufflé, savoury pancakes filled with pepper stew and tomato sauce, mushroom-stuffed corn-fed chicken suprême with roast garlic sauce, fillet of salmon with pearl barley risotto and crab butter, slow-roasted lamb shoulder with a mint and red wine jus and rib-eye steak with a tarragon, bacon and red onion butter. *Starters/Snacks: £5.50 to £7.00. Main Courses: £9.00 to £20.00. Puddings: £5.50 to £7.00*

Enterprise ~ Lease Julian Cook ~ Real ale ~ Bar food (12-2(2.30 Sun), 6.30-9.30(9 Sun)) ~ Restaurant ~ (01803) 558279 ~ Children welcome ~ Dogs allowed in bar ~ Open 11.30-2.30, 5-11(5.30-11.30 Sat); 12-3, 5.30-10.30 Sun

Recommended by Dr A McCormick, Michael Dandy, Alan Sutton, Peter Salmon, Michael and Joan Johnstone, Mike and Mary Carter, Mike Gorton, Mrs C Farley

Tipping is not normal for bar meals, and not usually expected.

MOLLAND   SS8028   MAP 1

London 🍺

Village signposted off B3227 E of South Molton, down narrow lanes; EX36 3NG

A proper Exmoor inn with customers and their dogs to match, a warm welcome, honest food and real ales; bedrooms

This remains very much a traditional Exmoor pub with plenty of friendly locals and welcoming licensees. The two small linked rooms by the old-fashioned central servery have hardly changed in 50 years and have lots of local stag-hunting pictures, tough carpeting or rugs on flagstones, cushioned benches and plain chairs around rough stripped trestle tables and Exmoor Ale and a changing guest beer on handpump. On the left an attractive beamed room has accounts of the rescued stag which lived a long life at the pub many years ago and on the right, a panelled dining room with a great curved settle by its fireplace has particularly good hunting and gamebird prints, including ones by McPhail and Hester Lloyd. A small hall has stuffed birds and animals. The low-ceilinged lavatories are worth a look with their Victorian mahogany and tiling (and in the gents' a testament to the prodigious thirst of the village cricket team). There are picnic-sets in the cottagey garden. Don't miss the next-door church, with its untouched early 18th-c box pews – and in spring, a carpet of tenby daffodils in the graveyard.

🍴 Fair value honest bar food includes sandwiches, ploughman's, soup, thai fishcakes with sweet chilli sauce, stuffed peppers, chicken with bacon, cheese and barbecue sauce, venison sausages with mustard mash and onion gravy, fish and chips, steaks, a hearty mixed grill, and puddings such as crumble or popular sticky toffee pudding.
Starters/Snacks: £4.25 to £4.50. Main Courses: £5.95 to £12.95. Puddings: £4.25

Free house ~ Licensee Martin Pateman ~ Real ale ~ Bar food (12-2, 6-8.30-ish; not Sun evening) ~ Restaurant ~ (01769) 550269 ~ Children welcome ~ Dogs allowed in bar and bedrooms ~ Open 12-3, 6-11; 12-3 Sun; closed Sun evening ~ Bedrooms: /£75B
Recommended by Tony Winckworth, Dennis and Doreen Haward

NOSS MAYO   SX5447   MAP 1

Ship 🍷 🍺

Off A379 via B3186, E of Plymouth; PL8 1EW

Busy pub, seats overlooking inlet and visiting boats, thick-walled bars with log fires, west country beers, popular food and friendly atmosphere

In fine weather the terrace in front of this well run pub is a huge bonus. You can sit at the octagonal wooden tables under parasols (there are heaters for cooler evenings) and look over the inlet; visiting boats can tie up alongside. Inside, it's attractively furnished and the two thick-walled bars have a happy mix of dining chairs and tables on the wooden floors, log fires, bookcases, dozens of local pictures and charts, newspapers and magazines to read, and a chatty atmosphere; board games. Dartmoor Jail Ale, Palmers Best and St Austell Proper Job and Tribute on handpump, 25 malt whiskies and a dozen wines by the glass. Parking is restricted at high tide. More reports please.

🍴 Good bar food includes filled baguettes, ploughman's, soup, duck liver pâté with red onion marmalade, ham and free-range eggs, sausages and mash with onion gravy, chicken curry, goats cheese and spinach risotto with parmesan biscuits, steak and kidney pie, cod fillet topped with sun-dried tomato tapenade, rump of lamb with redcurrant and mint sauce, and puddings such as dark chocolate torte and apple and plum crumble.
Starters/Snacks: £4.75 to £6.25. Main Courses: £9.50 to £12.50. Puddings: £5.75 to £6.75

Free house ~ Licensees Charlie and Lisa Bullock ~ Real ale ~ Bar food (all day) ~ Restaurant ~ (01752) 872387 ~ Children welcome ~ Dogs allowed in bar ~ Open 11-11; 12-10.30 Sun
Recommended by Roger Wain-Heapy, Suzy Miller, John and Verna Aspinall, Alain and Rose Foote, Michael and Maggie Betton, Hugh Roberts, Roy Hoing, Di and Mike Gillam, Geoff and Carol Thorp, Lynda and Trevor Smith, June and Robin Savage, David Rule

PETER TAVY   SX5177   MAP 1

Peter Tavy Inn ♀

Off A386 near Mary Tavy, N of Tavistock; PL19 9NN

Old stone inn with pretty garden, bustling bar with beams and big log fire, west country beers and fair choice of food

They only serve west country beers in this attractive old stone pub and on handpump these might include Dartmoor Jail Ale, Otter Bright, Palmers Tally Ho and Sharps Doom Bar; also, local cider, 30 malt whiskies and several wines by the glass. The low-beamed bar has a bustling atmosphere and a good mix of customers, high-backed settles on black flagstones, smaller settles in stone-mullioned windows and a fine log fire in the big stone fireplace. There's a snug dining area, with nicely carved wooden dining chairs, hops on beams and plenty of pictures on the partly stone walls, and a restaurant. From the picnic-sets in the pretty garden there are peaceful views of the moor rising above nearby pastures.

🍴 **Well liked lunchtime bar food includes filled baguettes and baked potatoes, soup, an antipasti plate, breaded camembert with cumberland sauce, ham and egg, vegetable crumble, gammon with an apricot and mango glaze, lamb curry and stuffed shoulder of pork with apple sauce, with evening extras like steak and stilton pie, venison steak with a wild mushroom sauce and lemon sole with lemon butter.** *Starters/Snacks: £4.50 to £5.95. Main Courses: £6.95 to £15.95. Puddings: £4.20 to £4.75*

Free house ~ Licensees Chris and Joanne Wordingham ~ Real ale ~ Bar food ~ (01822) 810348 ~ Children welcome ~ Dogs welcome ~ Open 12-3, 6-11(10.30 Sun)

Recommended by Helen and Brian Edgeley, Phil and Jane Villiers, Andrea Rampley, Dr and Mrs M W A Haward, Jacquie Jones

PORTGATE   SX4185   MAP 1

Harris Arms ♀

Turn off A30 E of Launceston at Broadwoodwidger turn-off (with brown Dingle Steam Village sign), and head S; Launceston Road (old A30 between Lewdown and Lifton); EX20 4PZ

Enthusiastic, well travelled licensees in roadside pub with exceptional wine list and popular food

The wine list here is fantastic as both Mr and Mrs Whiteman are qualified award-winning wine-makers. There are around 30 of their favourites by the glass and detailed, helpful notes with each wine; you can buy them to take home, too. The bar has burgundy end walls and cream ones in between, some rather fine photographs, afghan saddle-bag cushions scattered around a mixture of dining chairs and along a red-plush built-in wall banquette and a woodburning stove. On the left, steps lead down to the dining room with elegant beech dining chairs (and more afghan cushions) around stripped wooden tables, and some unusual paintings on the walls. Bays Best and Sharps Doom Bar on handpump, local cider and Luscombe organic soft drinks; there may be a pile of country magazines. There are seats under heaters outside on a decked area, pots of lavender and plenty of picnic-sets in the sloping back garden looking out over the rolling wooded pasture hills. They are growing 24 vines.

🍴 **Seasonal bar food using their own-grown produce and eggs from their own hens includes soup, piri-piri prawns, ham and eggs, fish and chips, slow-cooked pork belly with cider sauce, duck breast, confit duck leg, braised red cabbage and orange sauce, specials like cornish sardines on toast, local sausages with onion gravy, twice-baked goats cheese soufflé with garlic foam and coq au vin, and puddings such as treacle sponge with butterscotch sauce and dark chocolate truffle with mascarpone and pistachio.** *Starters/Snacks: £4.50 to £6.26. Main Courses: £9.25 to £17.95. Puddings: £5.00 to £6.00*

Free house ~ Licensees Andy and Rowena Whiteman ~ Real ale ~ Bar food ~ Restaurant ~ (01566) 783331 ~ Well behaved children welcome ~ Dogs allowed in bar ~ Open 12-3, 6.30-11; 12-3 Sun; closed Sun evening, all day Mon, first week in Nov

Recommended by Mary Goodfellow, Mo and David Trudgill, Valerie and Michael Howard, Mayur Shah, Comus and Sarah Elliott

POSTBRIDGE

Warren House

B3212 0.75 miles NE of Postbridge; PL20 6TA

Straightforward old pub, relaxing for a drink or snack after a Dartmoor hike

In bleak but rather splendid surroundings, this is a popular pub and a valuable refuge after a walk. It's straightforward but friendly and the cosy bar has plenty of atmosphere. There are simple furnishings such as easy chairs and settles under the beamed ochre ceiling, old pictures of the inn on the partly panelled stone walls and dim lighting (fuelled by the pub's own generator); one of the fireplaces is said to have been kept alight almost continuously since 1845. There's also a family room. Butcombe Bitter, Greene King Abbot and Otter Ale on handpump, local farm cider and malt whiskies; piped music, darts and board games. The picnic-sets on both sides of the road have moorland views.

📶 **Decent bar food includes filled baguettes, ploughman's, mushroom stroganoff, rabbit or steak in ale pies, breaded plaice, cajun chicken, local lamb shank with red wine and rosemary gravy, and puddings like sticky toffee pudding with toffee sauce.** *Starters/Snacks: £4.95 to £6.50. Main Courses: £7.75 to £15.00. Puddings: £4.95*

Free house ~ Licensee Peter Parsons ~ Real ale ~ Bar food (all day but more restricted winter Mon and Tues) ~ (01822) 880208 ~ Children in family room ~ Dogs allowed in bar ~ Open 11-11; 12-10.30 Sun; 11-5 Mon and Tues during Nov-Feb
Recommended by Andrea Rampley, Lois Dyer, Mrs Mary Woods

RATTERY

Church House

Village signposted from A385 W of Totnes, and A38 S of Buckfastleigh; TQ10 9LD

One of Britain's oldest pubs with some fine original features and peaceful views

Run by a knowledgeable and welcoming landlord, this charming pub is well worth the narrow winding lanes to get here. It's one of the country's oldest pubs and has some fine original features – notably the spiral stone steps behind a little stone doorway on your left as you come in that date from about 1030. There are massive oak beams and standing timbers in the homely open-plan bar, large fireplaces (one with a little cosy nook partitioned off around it), traditional pubby chairs and tables on the patterned carpet, some window seats, and prints and horsebrasses on the plain white walls. The dining room is separated from this room by heavy curtains and there's a lounge area, too. Dartmoor Jail Ale, Gidleys Valley, Otter Ale and Teignworthy Old Moggie on handpump, several malt whiskies and nine wines by the glass. The garden has picnic-sets on the large hedged-in lawn and peaceful views of the partly wooded surrounding hills.

📶 **Popular bar food includes sandwiches, filled baguettes and baked potatoes, ploughman's, soup, devilled whitebait, sausages with mash and onion gravy, cider and honey-baked ham and egg, a fry up, stilton and vegetable crumble, steak and kidney pie, coconut chicken curry, specials such as scallops in garlic, monkfish with a mushroom and brandy cream sauce and half a roast duck with orange sauce, and puddings like toffee pecan cheesecake and lemon meringue pie.** *Starters/Snacks: £4.95 to £7.50. Main Courses: £7.95 to £15.75. Puddings: £4.95 to £5.50*

Free house ~ Licensee Ray Hardy ~ Real ale ~ Bar food (11.30-2, 6.30-9) ~ Restaurant ~ (01364) 642220 ~ Children welcome ~ Dogs allowed in bar ~ Open 11(12 Sun)-2.30, 6-11(10.30 Sun)
Recommended by Lucien Perring, Paul Goldman, Geoff and Carol Thorp, Maureen Wood, Bob and Angela Brooks, Eryl and Keith Dykes, June and Robin Savage, MP

> Half pints: by law, a pub should not charge more for half a pint than half the price of a full pint, unless it shows that half-pint price on its price list.

ROCKBEARE

SY0195 MAP 1

Jack in the Green ⑪ ♀

Signposted from new A30 bypass E of Exeter; EX5 2EE

Neat dining pub with traditionally furnished bars, real ales, a dozen wines by the glass and interesting food

Although most people come to this well run and sizeable dining pub to enjoy the wide choice of good food those just wanting a drink are quite happy sitting in the bar with a pint. It's been run by the same friendly and enthusiastic licensees for 19 years now and this neatly kept bar has comfortable sofas and low tables and Butcombe Bitter, Otter Ale and Sharps Doom Bar on handpump, a dozen wines by the glass and local cider; piped music. The larger dining side is similarly traditional in style – some of its many old hunting and shooting photographs are well worth a close look and there are button-back leather chesterfields by the big woodburning stove. There are plenty of seats outside in the courtyard.

⑪ Well presented food includes ploughman's, chicken liver parfait, grilled black pudding, dry-cured bacon and poached egg salad, bangers and mash with onion gravy, roast butternut squash ravioli with brown butter and sage, steak and kidney or fish pies, thai green chicken curry, lamb and vegetable hotpot, duck breast with poached rhubarb and juniper, brill fillet with saffron risotto, and puddings like treacle tart with clotted cream and blackcurrant délice; Sunday roasts. *Starters/Snacks: £4.95 to £8.95. Main Courses: £8.95 to £14.50. Puddings: £5.95 to £6.95*

Free house ~ Licensee Paul Parnell ~ Real ale ~ Bar food (all day Sun) ~ Restaurant ~ (01404) 822240 ~ Well behaved children in one bar only ~ Live jazz May-Sept ~ Open 11-3, 5.30(6 Sat)-11; 12-10.30 Sun; closed 25 Dec-6 Jan

Recommended by P Waterman, Dr and Mrs M E Wilson, Cathryn and Richard Hicks, David and Sue Medcalf, Gene and Tony Freemantle, Mrs P Sumner, Andy and Claire Barker, Ron and Sheila Corbett, Mrs Mary Woods, B and M Kendall

SHEBBEAR

SS4309 MAP 1

Devils Stone Inn

Off A3072 or A388 NE of Holsworthy; EX21 5RU

Neatly kept village pub liked by locals with friendly landlord, real ales and fair value food cooked by landlady; bedrooms

Run by a warmly welcoming and smartly dressed landlord, this is a neatly kept village pub just by the actual Devils Stone. The focal point of the bar in cold weather is the open woodburning stove with a couple of brown leather armchairs in front of it facing each other across a small carved table on big flagstones. There's also a long, L-shaped pew with tapestry cushions along one wall, a second pew by an attractive table, and an old photograph of pupils from Shebbear school, country scene prints, and quite a few certificates to do with town twinning on the walls. Along the bar counter are smart cream high-backed leather chairs and back here are a couple of old carver chairs and tables and a few trophies. Sharps Doom Bar and Special and St Austell HSD and Tribute on handpump and winter hot mulled wine. The plain back games room has darts, pool, a juke box and a fruit machine. Across the entrance hall is a dining room with some sturdy dining tables on big dark flagstones and mixed sets of dining chairs. The back garden has picnic-sets on a terrace and on grass. There's a drinking bowl for dogs in the bar.

Real ale to us means beer which has matured naturally in its cask – not pressurised or filtered. We name all real ales stocked. We usually name ales preserved under a light blanket of carbon dioxide too, though purists – pointing out that this stops the natural yeasts developing – would disagree (most people, including us, can't tell the difference!).

🍴 Good value pubby food includes sandwiches and panini, filled baked potatoes, ploughman's, omelettes, burgers, ham or sausages and egg, lasagne, steak in ale pie and chicken in barbecue sauce, with evening dishes like garlic mushrooms, warm stilton and bacon salad, pork hock in cider sauce and half a duck with honey and orange, steaks, and puddings such as cheesecake and sponge pudding. *Starters/Snacks: £3.95 to £4.95. Main Courses: £7.95 to £14.95. Puddings: £3.95*

Free house ~ Licensees Chris and Steve Hurst ~ Real ale ~ Bar food (12-2.30, 6-9) ~ Restaurant ~ (01409) 281210 ~ Well behaved children welcome ~ Dogs allowed in bar and bedrooms ~ Open 12-3, 6-11; 12-11 Fri-Sun ~ Bedrooms: £35S/£70S

Recommended by Ryta Lyndley, Rob Marsh

SHEEPWASH   SS4806 MAP 1

Half Moon 🍷 🛏

Off A3072 Holsworthy—Hatherleigh at Highampton; EX21 5NE

Ancient inn loved by fishermen, friendly staff, real ales and enjoyable food; bedrooms

Fishermen love this friendly 15th-c inn as they have 12 miles of River Torridge and a small tackle shop and rod room with good drying facilities; they can issue rod licences, too. The chatty main bar is simply furnished with solid old furniture and there's a wealth of beams and a large log fireplace fronted by flagstones. Nottingham Legend, St Austell Dartmoor Best and Tribute and Sharps Doom Bar on handpump, several wines by the glass, and a decent choice of malt whiskies. There's an attractive separate dining room; bar billiards. Some of the bedrooms are in a converted stable and are ideal for guests with dogs. This is a tiny Dartmoor village off the beaten track.

🍴 Good, popular bar food includes sandwiches, filled baked potatoes, ploughman's, soup, pear and roquefort salad, moules marinière, battered haddock, chicken with bacon and barbecue sauce, vegetable or prawn and mushroom curry, pork tenderloin with cider and mustard sauce, kidneys in a rich tomato and sherry sauce, whole bass with lemon and dill butter, lamb chianti and half a honey-roast duck with spicy plum, chilli and ginger sauce. *Starters/Snacks: £3.95 to £5.95. Main Courses: £7.95 to £14.95. Puddings: £4.25*

Free house ~ Licensees Chris and Tony Green ~ Real ale ~ Bar food (11.30-2, 6.15(7 Sun)-9) ~ Restaurant ~ (01409) 231376 ~ Well behaved children welcome ~ Dogs allowed in bar and bedrooms ~ Open 11-2.30, 6-11; 12-3, 7-11 Sun ~ Bedrooms: £45B/£90B

Recommended by J V Dadswell, Roy Hoing, Mike and Sue Loseby, Ryta Lyndley

SIDBURY   SY1496 MAP 1

Hare & Hounds 🍺

3 miles N of Sidbury, at Putts Corner; A375 towards Honiton, crossroads with B3174; EX10 0QQ

Large, well run roadside pub with log fires, beams and attractive layout, popular daily carvery, efficient staff and big garden

There's a friendly and good-natured atmosphere in this sizeable roadside pub and although it's the popular daily carvery that draws in the crowds, they have Branscombe Vale Drayman and Otter Ale and Bitter tapped from the cask and locals do drop in for a pint and a chat. There are two log fires (and rather unusual wood-framed leather sofas complete with pouffes), heavy beams and fresh flowers, plenty of tables with red plush-cushioned dining chairs, windows seats and a long bar with well used bar stools. It's mostly carpeted, with bare boards and stripped-stone walls at one end. At the opposite end, on the left, another dining area has french windows leading out to a large marquee providing extra seating. The big garden, giving marvellous views down the Sid valley to the sea at Sidmouth, has picnic-sets and a children's play area. More reports please.

🍴 Using only local produce, the extensive daily carvery has a choice of four meats and enough turnover to keep up a continuous supply of fresh vegetables – every lunchtime and evening and all day Sunday. Also, sandwiches, filled baguettes and baked potatoes, soup, garlic mushrooms, liver and smoked bacon pâté, a curry of the day, vegetarian moussaka, haddock and broccoli bake, various grills, daily specials such as beer-battered cod, squash and mushroom risotto and ham with parsley sauce, and puddings. *Starters/Snacks: £4.25 to £5.95. Main Courses: £7.95 to £14.95. Puddings: £4.50*

Heartstone Inns ~ Managers Graham Cole and Lindsey Chun ~ Real ale ~ Bar food (all day) ~ (01404) 41760 ~ Children welcome ~ Dogs allowed in bar ~ Open 10am-11pm(10.30pm Sun)

Recommended by Dr Phil Putwain

SIDFORD
SY1389 MAP 1

Blue Ball ◧
A3052 just N of Sidmouth; EX10 9QL

Big, popular inn with friendly staff, five real ales, well liked food including breakfasts; neat garden; bedrooms

Run with friendliness and efficiency, this handsome thatched pub has been in the same family since 1912. The central bar covers three main areas: light beams, bar stools and a nice mix of wooden dining chairs around circular tables on the patterned carpet, three log fires, prints, horsebrasses and plenty of bric-a-brac on the walls and Bass, Otter Bitter, St Austell Tribute, Sharps Doom Bar and a changing guest on handpump; attentive service. The public bar has darts and board games; skittle alley and piped music. There are seats on a terrace and in the flower-filled garden and a well designed wooden smokers' gazebo. Coastal walks are only about ten minutes away.

🍴 As well as opening for breakfasts, the well liked bar food includes sandwiches, filled baked potatoes, ploughman's, soup, chicken liver parfait with red onion marmalade, potted crab, ham and eggs, vegetarian lasagne, beer-battered fish of the day, local sausages with onion gravy, steak and kidney pudding, braised venison steak and specials like chinese-style baby back ribs, scallop and pancetta salad, duck breast with butternut squash purée and port and orange jus and fillet of turbot with prawn, dill and white wine sauce. *Starters/Snacks: £4.50 to £6.25. Main Courses: £7.95 to £14.95. Puddings: £3.95 to £4.95*

Punch ~ Lease Roger Newton ~ Real ale ~ Bar food (8-10 for breakfast, 12-2.30, 6-9; 12-3, 5-8.30 Sun) ~ Restaurant ~ (01395) 514062 ~ Children in dining areas only ~ Dogs allowed in bar ~ Open 11-11(midnight Sat); 12-11 Sun ~ Bedrooms: £60B/£95B

Recommended by Mark Flynn, John Wymer, Joan and Michel Hooper-Immins, Dennis Jenkin, George Atkinson, Geoff and Carol Thorp, Sara Fulton, Roger Baker, John and Fiona McIlwain, Steve Whalley, John and Fiona Merritt

SPREYTON
SX6996 MAP 1

Tom Cobley ◧
From A30 Whiddon Down roundabout take former A30 (opposite A382), then first left, turning left at crossroads after 1.1 miles; in village centre turn left; can also be reached from A3124; EX17 5AL

Extraordinary range of real ales in busy village pub; cheerful licensees; bedrooms

It's the fantastic range of up to 22 well kept real ales that remains the draw to this bustling village pub. On handpump or tapped from the cask these might include Bays Devon Dumpling, B & T Black Dragon Mild, Cotleigh Barn Owl, Cottage Broadgauge, Country Life Black Boar, Dartmoor Jail Ale, Otter Ale and Amber, St Austell Proper Job and Tribute, Skinners Betty Stogs, Wizard Lundy Gold and quickly changing guest beers. Local ciders, several wines by the glass and a range of whiskies, too. The comfortable little bar has straightforward pubby furnishings, an open fire in the brick fireplace, sporting trophies, local photographs, country scenes and prints of Tom Cobley (who was born in the village) on the walls; darts. There's a large back restaurant with beamery and piped music. Seats in the tree-shaded garden with more out in front by the quiet street.

🍴 Bar food includes sandwiches, filled baked potatoes, ploughman's, sausages with onion gravy, mushroom and red pepper stroganoff and cottage or steak and mushroom pies, with evening choices like breaded garlic mushrooms, stilton and vegetable crumble, battered cod, pork hock with apple and cider gravy and liver and onions. *Starters/Snacks: £4.00 to £8.00. Main Courses: £7.00 to £16.00. Puddings: £4.25*

Free house ~ Licensees Roger and Carol Cudlip ~ Real ale ~ Bar food (not Mon lunchtime) ~ Restaurant ~ (01647) 231314 ~ Children welcome ~ Dogs allowed in bar ~ Open 12-3, 6-11 (1am Fri and Sat); 12-4, 7-11 Sun; closed Mon lunchtime ~ Bedrooms: £30S/£60(£80S)
Recommended by Dr D J and Mrs S C Walker, Peter Thornton

STAVERTON

SX7964   MAP 1

Sea Trout 🛏

Village signposted from A384 NW of Totnes; TQ9 6PA

Hard-working, enthusiastic licensees in bustling village inn, real ales, enjoyable food and seats in garden; refurbished bedrooms

Doing especially well under the present licensees, this is a partly 15th-c village inn with a friendly, bustling atmosphere. The neatly kept and rambling beamed lounge bar has sea trout and salmon flies and stuffed fish on the walls and elegant armed wheelbacks around a mix of wooden tables on the part-carpeted, part-wooden floor. The locals' bar is simpler with wooden wall and other seats, a stag's head, a gun and horsebrasses on the walls, a large stuffed fish in a cabinet above the woodburning stove and a cheerful mix of locals and visitors. Palmers Best, Copper Ale and 200 on handpump and nine wines by the glass. The panelled restaurant and conservatory are both furnished with smart high-backed fabric dining chairs around more wooden tables. There are seats in the attractive terraced garden and the bedrooms either overlook this or the country lane; lots to do and see nearby. They are kind to dogs with treats and water bowls dotted about the garden.

🍽 Enjoyable bar food includes lunchtime sandwiches and filled baguettes, soup, devilled kidneys, vegetarian curry, thick-cut ham and egg, calves liver and bacon and crispy fried fish and chips, with more elaborate choices such as smoked chicken, apple and walnut salad with raspberry dressing, wild mushroom tortellini with a creamy tarragon sauce, pork tenderloin with ginger and lemon grass noodles topped with an omelette, salmon with prawn colcannon and a red wine jus, and puddings like white chocolate and mixed berry brûlée with a coconut macaroon and banoffi pie. *Starters/Snacks: £4.00 to £7.00. Main Courses: £7.95 to £15.95. Puddings: £4.50 to £5.25*

Palmers ~ Tenants Jason and Samantha Price ~ Real ale ~ Bar food (12-2(2.30 Sat, 3 Sun), 6(7 Sun)-9(9.30 Fri and Sat)) ~ Restaurant ~ (01803) 762274 ~ Children welcome ~ Dogs allowed in bar ~ Open 11-11(11.30 Sat); 11.30-10.30 Sun ~ Bedrooms: £61S/£92S
Recommended by Danny Savage, Bob Duxbury, Alan Sutton

STOKENHAM

SX8042   MAP 1

Church House 🍷

Opposite church, N of A379 towards Torcross; TQ7 2SZ

Refurbished and extended old pub in pretty countryside, well liked food and real ales

Particularly popular on Sunday lunchtimes and with families (there's a children's play area with a wooden tower, a slide, swings and an old wooden dinghy to play in), this is an attractive old pub overlooking a common. Three rambling, low-beamed open-plan original areas have a bustling atmosphere, lots of knick-knacks, quite a mix of seating on the flagstones, Greene King Abbot, Otter Ale and Bitter and a guest like O'Hanlons Firefly on handpump, several bourbons and wines by the glass and local cider. There's also a dining conservatory. The pub was built to cater for the masons who were building the ancient church next door.

🍽 Using local produce, the tasty bar food includes sandwiches, various platters, soup, leek and goats cheese tartlet, sausages (they make their own) with onion gravy, beer-battered fresh cod, chicken with mushroom sauce, steak and kidney pie, game casserole, a fish dish of the day, duck with redcurrant, orange and mint sauce, and puddings like treacle tart and rhubarb and custard panna cotta; best to book for their Sunday roasts. *Starters/Snacks: £3.95 to £6.50. Main Courses: £7.95 to £18.95. Puddings: £4.50 to £5.95*

Heavitree ~ Tenants Richard Smith and Simon Cadman ~ Real ale ~ Bar food (12-2, 6-9) ~ Restaurant ~ (01548) 580253 ~ Children welcome ~ Dogs allowed in bar ~ Jazz Weds evening ~ Open 11(12 Sun)-2.30, 6-11

Recommended by Torquil MacLennan, Richard Fendick, MP, Alistair Stanier, Mrs Mary Woods, B J Harding

TIPTON ST JOHN SY0991 MAP 1

Golden Lion

Pub signed off B3176 Sidmouth—Ottery St Mary; EX10 0AA

A good mix of diners and drinkers in friendly village pub with plenty of seats in attractive garden

Although many customers come to this attractive village pub to eat, a few tables are still reserved for those just wanting a chat and a pint and they keep Bass and Otter Ale and Bitter on handpump and a dozen wines by the glass. The main bar – which is split into two – has a comfortable, relaxed atmosphere, as does the back snug, and throughout the building there are paintings from west country artists, art deco prints, tiffany lamps and hops, copper pots and kettles hanging from the beams; maybe piped music and board games. There's a verandah for dog walkers and smokers, seats on the terracotta-walled terrace with outside heaters and grapevines and more seats on the grass edged by pretty flowering borders; summer Sunday evening jazz out here.

Good bar food at lunchtime includes sandwiches, ploughman's, soup, prawns in garlic butter, home-cooked ham and eggs, moules frites, steak and kidney pudding, battered cod and smoked duck salad with onion marmalade, with evening choices like deep-fried brie, seafood salad, a vegetarian dish of the day, chicken with sherry and cream sauce, pork tenderloin with creamy cider and apple sauce, duck with balsamic and plum sauce, and daily specials like coq au vin and bass. *Starters/Snacks: £4.50 to £6.50. Main Courses: £9.50 to £16.00. Puddings: £4.50 to £5.50*

Heavitree ~ Tenants François and Michelle Teissier ~ Real ale ~ Bar food (not winter Sun evening) ~ (01404) 812881 ~ Children welcome ~ Jazz summer Sun evenings ~ Open 12-3, 6-11; 12-3, 7-10.30 Sun; closed Sun evening Sept-March

Recommended by J D O Carter, Martin Sagar, Norman and Sarah Keeping, Helene Grygar, Roy Fox, Jane Hudson

TOPSHAM SX9688 MAP 1

Bridge Inn ★ ◖

2.5 miles from M5 junction 30: Topsham signposted from exit roundabout; in Topsham follow signpost (A376) Exmouth on the Elmgrove Road, into Bridge Hill; EX3 0QQ

Very special old drinkers' pub with up to eight real ales and in the landlady's family for five generations

'A wonderful rarity', 'a gem' and 'one of the very best unspoilt pubs in the country' are just three comments used by enthusiastic readers about this utterly old-fashioned and unchanging pub. It was a 16th-c maltings, has been run by the same family for over 100 years and has many fine old features. The friendly staff and chatty locals are welcoming to visitors and the relaxed, informal atmosphere is helped by the ban on mobile phones, games machines and piped music. There are small rooms and snugs, a woodburning stove, traditional tables with wooden chairs and benches, a very high-backed settle and the 'bar' is the landlady's front parlour (as a notice on the door politely reminds customers). Up to seven real ales are tapped from the cask: Blue Anchor Spingo Special, Branscombe Vale Branoc and Summa That, Mordue Bunny Hop, Otter Amber, RCH Firebox and Teignworthy Springtide. Organic cider, country wines, non-alcoholic pressés and decent wines by the glass, too. Outside, picnic-sets overlook the weir.

🍴 Simple, tasty bar food includes well filled meaty and vegetarian pasties, sandwiches, a hearty winter soup and ploughman's; pork pies until 8.30pm. *Starters/Snacks: £3.00 to £3.60. Main Courses: £4.50 to £6.90*

Free house ~ Licensee Mrs C Cheffers-Heard ~ Real ale ~ Bar food (lunchtime only) ~ No credit cards ~ (01392) 873862 ~ Children in two rooms ~ Dogs allowed in bar ~ Live folk first Sun lunch of the month, blues first Mon evening of the month ~ Open 12-2, 6-10.30(11 Sat); 12-2, 7-10.30 Sun

Recommended by John and Fiona McIlwain, Barry Steele-Perkins, Dr and Mrs M E Wilson, Andrea Rampley, Phil and Sally Gorton, Julia Mann, John Prescott, Maurice Ricketts, the Didler, Julian Distin

TORBRYAN

SX8266   MAP 1

Old Church House

Most easily reached from A381 Newton Abbot—Totnes via Ipplepen; TQ12 5UR

Ancient inn with original features in neat rooms, friendly service; popular food and beer

Built in 1340 on the site of an ancient cottage, this old pub housed workmen restoring the part-Saxon church with its battlemented Norman tower next door. It's a friendly place and the particularly attractive bar on the right of the door is neatly kept and bustling, with benches built into the fine old panelling as well as a cushioned high-backed settle and leather-backed small seats around its big log fire. On the left, there's a series of comfortable and discreetly lit lounges, one with a splendid deep inglenook Tudor fireplace with a side bread oven; piped music. Skinners Betty Stogs and Cornish Knocker on handpump and 35 malt whiskies; good service. Plenty of nearby walks.

🍴 Generous helpings of lunchtime bar food includes filled baguettes, soup, chicken liver pâté with red onion marmalade, garlic mushrooms, haddock mornay, beef in ale pie, chicken with bacon and a port and stilton cream sauce, various curries, and daily specials like grilled goats cheese with slow-roasted tuscan red peppers, bangers and mash, honey-glazed ham with free-range eggs and fish of the day. *Starters/Snacks: £4.00 to £7.00. Main Courses: £7.00 to £15.00. Puddings: £4.00 to £5.00*

Free house ~ Licensees Kane and Carolynne Clarke ~ Real ale ~ Bar food ~ Restaurant ~ (01803) 812372 ~ Children welcome away from bar ~ Dogs allowed in bar ~ Live music Sun evenings ~ Open 11-11 ~ Bedrooms: £54B/£79B

Recommended by Peter Salmon, J D O Carter

TORCROSS

SX8242   MAP 1

Start Bay

A379 S of Dartmouth; TQ7 2TQ

Fresh local fish dishes in exceptionally popular, straightforward dining pub; seats outside overlooking the beach

To be sure of a table in this popular dining pub, it's best to arrive early or late as it does get packed in between (particularly in season) and queues often form outside even before the doors open. It's the fresh fish and shellfish at fair prices that draws in the crowds and they dress their own cock crabs, shell their hand-picked scallops and take delivery of the fish caught off the beach in front of the pub. The whole place is very much set out for eating, with wheelback chairs around plenty of dark tables, country pictures and some photographs of storms buffeting the pub on the cream walls and a winter coal fire. A small chatty drinking area by the counter has a brass ship's clock and barometer and there's booth seating in a family room with sailing boat pictures. Pool and darts in the winter. Bass and Otter Ale and Bitter on handpump, local cider, juices and local wine, too. They do warn of delays in food service at peak times but the staff remain friendly and efficient. There are seats (highly prized) outside that look over the three-mile pebble beach and the freshwater wildlife lagoon of Slapton Ley is just behind the pub. Dogs are allowed outside food-serving hours.

🍴 Their speciality is fish in light batter: cod or haddock (medium, large or jumbo), plaice, lemon sole and other fish and shellfish as available; also, sandwiches, filled baked potatoes, burgers, vegetable lasagne, gammon and pineapple, steaks, and puddings like summer pudding or treacle sponge. *Starters/Snacks: £4.00 to £6.95. Main Courses: £7.20 to £14.50. Puddings: £4.50*

Heavitree ~ Tenant Stuart Jacob ~ Real ale ~ Bar food (11.30-2.15, 6-9.30(10 in summer); all day on bank hols) ~ (01548) 580553 ~ Children allowed in large family room ~ Open 11.30-11

Recommended by David Heath, Mrs Mary Woods, Mike Gorton, Geoffrey Medcalf, Donna and Roger, Peter and Margaret Glenister, Michael Dandy

TORQUAY
SX9265 MAP 1

Cary Arms ♀ 🛏

Off B3199 Babbacombe Road, via Babbacombe Downs Road; turn steeply down Beach Road near Babbacombe Theatre; TQ1 3LX

Interesting bar in secluded hotel with lovely sea views, plenty of outside seating, enjoyable if not cheap food, real ales and friendly service; sea view bedrooms

---

This is an unusual, higgledy-piggledy place in a secluded bay at the bottom of a tiny, very steep road. The fine sea and cliff views can be enjoyed from picnic-sets on the terraces, from good quality teak chairs and tables on gravel, and from the big windows in the bar; there are steps leading down to the quay below, a charming little raised platform with just one table and a few chairs (you must book in advance for this as it's much prized in good weather), an outside bar, a barbecue and a pizza oven. Inside, the beamed, grotto-effect bar has rough pinky granite walls, various alcoves, rustic, hobbit-style red leather cushioned chairs around carved wooden tables on slate or bare boards, an open woodburning stove with a ship's wheel above it, and some high bar chairs beside the stone bar counter where they serve Bays Gold, Dartmoor Jail Ale, Otter Bitter and St Austell Tribute on handpump, local cider and decent wines by the glass; cheerful young staff. There's also a small, glass-enclosed entrance room with large ship lanterns and cleats; darts and board games. We would expect this to be an enjoyable place to stay and the residents' lounge is very civilised; they also have spa facilities and self-catering cottages. There are six mooring spaces and they can arrange a water taxi for guests arriving by boat.

🍴 Enjoyable food includes sandwiches, pigeon, pork, bacon and cranberry terrine with plum compote, seared scallops with vermouth cream sauce, steak in ale pie, wild mushroom strudel with provençale sauce, beer-battered local fish, dressed crab with crème fraîche and roasted red peppers, suprême of guinea fowl topped with duck liver with a port and raspberry sauce, specials like local sausages with cider and onion sauce and spatchcocked chicken with garlic and herb buttered, and puddings such as boozy fruit trifle and treacle tart with clotted cream; they also offer a meal for dogs: £5 for rice and lamb on our visit. *Starters/Snacks: £5.00 to £7.50. Main Courses: £12.00 to £18.00. Puddings: £5.00*

Free house ~ Licensee Jen Podmore ~ Real ale ~ Bar food (12-3, 6.30-9) ~ (01803) 327110 ~ Children welcome ~ Dogs allowed in bar and bedrooms ~ Monthly jazz ~ Open 12-11 ~ Bedrooms: £150S/£200S

Recommended by Christopher and Victoria Wren, Ben Gooder

If a pub tries to make you leave a credit card behind the bar, be on your guard.
The credit card firms and banks which issue them condemn this practice. After all, the
publican who asks you to do this is in effect saying: 'I don't trust you'. Have you any
more reason to trust his staff? If your card is used fraudulently while you have let
it be kept out of your sight, the card company could say you've been negligent
yourself – and refuse to make good your losses. So say that they can 'swipe'
your card instead, but must hand it back to you. Please let us know if
a pub does try to keep your card.

TOTNES

Steam Packet

St Peters Quay, on W bank (ie not on Steam Packet Quay); TQ9 5EW

Seats outside overlooking quay, interesting layout and décor inside and popular food and drink; bedrooms

In fine weather, the terrace (heated in winter) in front of this busy pub is very popular, with seats and tables under parasols among attractive flower tubs and overlooking the River Dart; there are walks along the river bank. Inside, it's interestingly laid out with bare stone walls and wooden flooring and one end has an open log fire, a squashy leather sofa with lots of cushions against a wall of books, a similar seat built into a small curved brick wall (which breaks up the room) and a TV. The main bar has built-in wall benches and plenty of stools and chairs around traditional pub tables and a further area has a coal fire and dark wood furniture. Bass, Dartmoor Jail Ale, Otter Ale and Sharps Doom Bar on handpump and several wines by the glass. The conservatory restaurant has high-backed leather dining chairs around wooden tables and smart window blinds.

🍽 **Good bar food includes lunchtime sandwiches and filled baguettes, soup, salmon and dill fishcakes with red pepper coulis, pork and leek sausages, nut roast terrine with vegetarian gravy, battered fresh cod, butternut squash, spinach and tomato lasagne, thai green chicken curry, steak and kidney pudding, and specials like seared scallops with bacon lardons, crispy pork and sweet chilli stir fry and dressed crab.** *Starters/Snacks: £4.50 to £6.95. Main Courses: £6.95 to £17.95. Puddings: £4.50 to £6.50*

Buccaneer Holdings ~ Manager Richard Cockburn ~ Real ale ~ Bar food (12-2.30(3 Sat and Sun); 6-9.30(9 Sun)) ~ Restaurant ~ (01803) 863880 ~ Children welcome ~ Dogs allowed in bar ~ Open 11-11; 12-10.30 Sun ~ Bedrooms: £59.50B/£79.50B

Recommended by Henry Pursehouse-Tranter, Marianne and Peter Stevens, Dave Braisted, Peter and Heather Elliott, Bob Duxbury, Mrs P Bishop, George Atkinson, Michael Dandy, Mike Gorton

WIDECOMBE

Rugglestone

Village at end of B3387; pub just S – turn left at church and NT church house, OS Sheet 191 map reference 720765; TQ13 7TF

Unspoilt local near busy tourist village, with just a couple of bars, cheerful customers, friendly staff, four real ales and traditional pub food

In rural surroundings, this is a friendly little local just up the road from the bustling tourist village. The unspoilt bar has only four tables, a few window and wall seats, a one-person pew built into the corner by the nice old stone fireplace and a good mix of both locals and visitors. The rudimentary bar counter dispenses Butcombe Bitter, St Austell Dartmoor Best and a couple of guests like Blackawton Original Bitter and St Austell Tribute tapped from the cask; local farm cider and a decent small wine list. The room on the right is a bit bigger and lighter-feeling with another stone fireplace, beamed ceiling, stripped pine tables and a built-in wall bench and there's also a small dining room. There are seats across the little moorland stream in the field and tables and chairs in the garden. They have a holiday cottage to rent out and they are kind to dogs.

🍽 **Tasty bar food includes filled baguettes, soup, pasty, ploughman's, breaded mushrooms with garlic mayonnaise, ham and eggs, burger with cheese and bacon, steak and stilton pie, beer-battered haddock, spicy meatballs, roasted vegetable lasagne and lambs liver with bacon and onion gravy.** *Starters/Snacks: £4.75 to £6.50. Main Courses: £8.95 to £10.95. Puddings: £4.50*

Free house ~ Licensees Richard Palmer and Vicky Moore ~ Real ale ~ Bar food ~ Restaurant ~ (01364) 621327 ~ Children allowed but must be away from bar area ~ Dogs welcome ~ Open 11.30-3, 6-11.30; 11.30am-midnight Sat; 12-11.30 Sun

Recommended by JHW, Barry and Anne, Les and Norma Haydon, Alan Sutton, Bob and Angela Brooks, Mayur Shah, Helen Rawsthorn, Mike Beasley, the Didler

WINKLEIGH   SS6308   MAP 1

Kings Arms

Village signposted off B3220 Crediton—Torrington; Fore Street; EX19 8HQ

Friendly pub with woodburning stoves in beamed main bar, west country beers and popular food

This thatched village pub is popular locally but there's a welcome for visitors, too. The most character can be found in the cosy beamed main bar with old-fashioned built-in wall settles and benches around scrubbed pine tables on flagstones and a woodburning stove in a cavernous fireplace; another woodburning stove separates the bar from the green or red-painted dining rooms (one has military memorabilia and a mine shaft). Butcombe Bitter, Otter Bitter and Sharps Doom Bar on handpump and local cider; darts and board games. There are seats in the garden.

🍴 Traditional bar food includes **sandwiches and filled baguettes, filled baked potatoes, ploughman's, soup, chicken liver pâté, ham or sausages with eggs and beans, burgers, vegetarian shepherd's pie, fish pie, lambs liver and bacon with onion gravy, and puddings like cheesecake or marmalade bread and butter pudding.** *Starters/Snacks: £2.35 to £7.95. Main Courses: £6.50 to £15.50. Puddings: £2.95 to £4.95*

Enterprise ~ Lease Chris Guy and Julia Franklin ~ Real ale ~ Bar food (all day) ~ Restaurant ~ (01837) 83384 ~ Children welcome ~ Dogs allowed in bar ~ Open 11-11; 12-10.30 Sun

Recommended by Mark Flynn, Peter Thornton, Mrs P Sumner, Geoffrey Medcalf

WOODBURY SALTERTON   SY0189   MAP 1

Diggers Rest

3.5 miles from M5 junction 30: A3052 towards Sidmouth, village signposted on right about 0.5 miles after Clyst St Mary; also signposted from B3179 SE of Exeter; EX5 1PQ

Bustling village pub with real ales, well liked food and lovely views from terraced garden

You can be sure of a warm welcome from the jovial landlord in this thatched village pub and there's a good mix of both drinkers and diners. The main bar has antique furniture, local art on the walls and a cosy seating area by the open fire with its extra large sofa and armchair. The modern extension is light and airy and opens on to the garden which has contemporary garden furniture under canvas parasols on the terrace and lovely countryside views. Exmoor Gold, Otter Bitter and St Austell Tribute on handpump, several wines by the glass and farm cider; piped music. The window boxes and flowering baskets are pretty.

🍴 Enjoyable bar food includes **lunchtime filled baguettes, soup, chicken liver parfait, scallops with a sweet chilli dressing, steak in ale or fish pies, wild mushroom, cashew and spinach stroganoff, butter-roasted chicken with mustard jus, duck breast with rösti potatoes, local belly of pork with crackling and thyme and garlic potatoes, and puddings such as sticky toffee pudding and passion fruit crème brûlée.** *Starters/Snacks: £4.25 to £9.95. Main Courses: £6.95 to £10.75. Puddings: £4.95*

Free house ~ Licensees Philip and Shelley Berryman ~ Real ale ~ Bar food (12-2.15, 6.30-9.15) ~ (01395) 232375 ~ Well behaved children welcome ~ Dogs allowed in bar ~ Open 11-3, 5.30-11; 12-3, 5.30-10.30 Sun

Recommended by Dr and Mrs M E Wilson, John and Susan Miln, Colin and Louise English

---

Several well known guide books make establishments pay for entry, either directly or as a fee for inspection. These fees can run to many hundreds of pounds. We do not. Unlike other guides, we never take payment for entries. We never accept a free meal, free drink, or any other freebie from a pub. We do not accept any sponsorship – let alone from commercial schemes linked to the pub trade. All our entries depend solely on merit.

LUCKY DIP

Besides the fully inspected pubs, you might like to try these Lucky Dips recommended to us and described by readers (if you do, please send us reports: feedback@goodguides.com).

ABBOTSHAM [SS4226]
Thatched Inn EX39 5BA: Extensively refurbished family pub popular at lunchtime for good value pubby food from sandwiches and baked potatoes to fresh fish and Sun roasts, good service, ales such as Country Life and Sharps, several ciders, mix of modern seating and older features (dates from 15th c); garden tables, handy for the Big Sheep *(Andy and Jill Kassube)*

APPLEDORE [SS4630]
☆ *Beaver* EX39 1RY [Irsha St]: Relaxed harbourside pub, good choice of enjoyable well priced food especially fresh local fish, friendly helpful staff, ales such as St Austell Tribute and Sharps, farm cider, decent house wines, great range of whiskies, lovely estuary view from popular raised dining area; pool in smaller games room; children and dogs welcome, disabled access (but no nearby parking), tables on small sheltered water-view terrace *(Andy and Jill Kassube, Peter Thornton)*
Royal George EX39 1RY [Irsha St]: Good beer choice inc local Country Life, thriving narrow bar (dogs allowed) with attractive pictures, well worn-in front room, simple fresh food inc good local fish, decent wines, dining room with superb estuary views; disabled access (but no nearby parking), picnic-sets outside, picturesque street sloping to sea *(Dr D J and Mrs S C Walker)*

ASHBURTON [SX7569]
Exeter Inn TQ13 7DU [West St]: Welcoming pleasantly old-fashioned beamed pub, straightforward low-priced food, real ales, local cider and decent wines, log fire; attractive little suntrap courtyard *(Patricia Wood)*

ASHPRINGTON [SX8157]
☆ *Durant Arms* TQ9 7UP [off A381 S of Totnes]: Still for sale but business as usual as we went to press; more small country hotel than pub, good food from snacks up inc plenty of local fish, St Austell ales and local wines in three comfortable linked and turkey-carpeted areas, one with small corner bar counter; piped music; children welcome in top lounge, flagstoned courtyard, eight comfortable bedrooms *(Gerry and Rosemary Dobson, Rynap, Howard and Lorna Lambert, LYM)*
Watermans Arms TQ9 7EG [Bow Bridge, on Tuckenhay rd]: Busy quarry-tiled heavy-beamed 17th-c pub in great waterside spot, high-backed settles and other sturdy furnishings, stripped stonework, roaring log fires, chatty and helpful landlord, friendly staff, well kept Palmers ales, decent wines, Thatcher's cider, wide choice of enjoyable food inc children's, three eating areas, darts and dominoes; piped music, TV; dogs welcome (pub has two), heated covered dining terrace, close-set tables over road by

creek, 15 comfortable bedrooms, open all day *(LYM, Graeme Roberts, Ian Shorthouse)*

ASHWATER [SX3895]
Village Inn EX21 5EY: Roomy and well decorated slate-floored pub with welcoming licensees, wide choice of good generous food from sandwiches up, fair prices, well kept Dartmoor, Sharps and a guest beer, good wine list, dining room, pool room, no music or machines, venerable grape vine in conservatory; tables on interestingly planted terrace *(John and Bernadette Elliott, Mark Flynn)*

BAMPTON [SS9520]
☆ *Exeter Inn* EX16 9DY [A396 some way S, at B3227 roundabout]: Long low stone-built roadside pub, several updated linked rooms, mainly flagstoned, two log fires and woodburner, large restaurant, good traditional food at sensible prices inc plenty of fresh fish, friendly efficient service, up to four changing ales such as Cotleigh and Exmoor tapped from the cask, decent coffee, daily papers, no piped music; children and dogs welcome, disabled facilities, tables out in front, ten revamped bedrooms, fairly handy for Knightshayes, open all day *(Dennis and Doreen Haward, BB)*
☆ *Quarrymans Rest* EX16 9LN [Briton St]: Big beamed and carpeted lounge, friendly and relaxed, leather sofas by inglenook woodburner, steps up to comfortable stripped-stone dining room with heavy pine tables and leather chairs, good interesting generous up-to-date food (best to book wknds), well kept ales such as Exmoor Fox, Sharps Doom Bar and Wychwood Dirty Tackle, farm ciders, locals' bar with pool in games room, no music; picnic-sets out in front and up in pretty secluded back garden, smokers' shelter, three comfortable bedrooms, good breakfast *(Peter Moffat, Michael Cleeve, BB)*

BARBROOK [SS7248]
Beggars Roost EX35 6LD: Welcoming 17th-c pub adjoining Exmoor Manor Hotel, enjoyable freshly prepared local food inc traditional Sun lunch, good beer and cider choice, log fire, theme nights and live music inc June jazz wknd; children and dogs welcome, garden tables, campsite next door *(Tim Mountain, Helen Farrow)*

BEAFORD [SS5515]
Globe EX19 8LR: Refurbished village coaching inn, enjoyable food, Fullers London Pride and Sharps Doom Bar. friendly staff; children and dogs welcome, disabled access, garden, bedrooms *(Katie Squire)*

BEER [ST2289]
Anchor EX12 3ET [Fore St]: Friendly sea-view dining pub with wide choice of enjoyable food inc good local fish, Greene King and Otter, good value wines, coffee, service can take a while when busy, rambling open-plan

layout with old local photographs, large eating area; sports TV, piped music; children well looked after, lots of tables in attractive clifftop garden over road, delightful seaside village, reasonably priced bedrooms *(George Atkinson, Howard and Margaret Buchanan, Bob and Margaret Holder, Peter and Giff Bennett, LYM)*

☆ *Barrel o' Beer* EX12 3EQ [Fore St]: Friendly family-run pub built around 1900, good fresh upscale food with emphasis on local fish/seafood, home-baked bread, Exe Valley and other ales, log fire, small back dining area; piped music; no under-5s, open all day *(David Hunt, Mr and Mrs A Curry, Suzanne Way, BB)*

☆ *Dolphin* EX12 3EQ [Fore St]: Hotel's friendly open-plan local quite near sea, comfortable old-fashioned décor, oak panelling and interesting nooks, marvellous old distorting mirrors, nautical bric-a-brac and antique boxing prints, huge range of good value food inc fresh local fish, large back restaurant, well kept Cotleigh and Dartmoor ales, decent wine and coffee, good service; piped music; children and dogs welcome, back picnic-sets, bedrooms *(George Atkinson, LYM)*

BELSTONE [SX61293]
Tors EX20 1QZ [a mile off A30]: Small family-run Victorian pub/hotel in peaceful Dartmoor-edge village, changing well kept ales such as Sharps, Otter and Palmers, over 60 malt whiskies, enjoyable food in bar and restaurant; dogs and well behaved children welcome, disabled access, seats out on nearby grassy area, bedrooms, open all day Summer *(Chris and Angela Buckell)*

BICKINGTON [SX8072]
Dartmoor Half Way TQ12 6JW [A383 Ashburton—Newton Abbot]: Old posting inn with bar in three sections, lots of horse tack and pictures, well cooked reasonably priced pubby food, nice staff, well kept real ales, log fires, pleasant environment; space for touring caravans, bedrooms, open all day Fri-Sun *(Neil and Anita Christopher)*

BICKLEIGH [SS9307]
☆ *Fishermans Cot* EX16 8RW: Greatly extended thatched riverside Marstons pub, wide choice of good local food, their ales kept well, reasonable prices, friendly service, lots of round tables on stone and carpet, pillars, plants and some panelled parts, fishing bric-a-brac, raised dining area, charming view over shallow rocky race below 1640 Exe bridge; piped music, can get busy especially wknds; dogs welcome, terrace and waterside lawn, 19 good bedrooms, open all day *(David and Julie Glover, DW T, Adrian and Dawn Collinge, BB)*
Trout EX16 8RJ [A396, N of junction with A3072]: Useful touristy thatched pub with very spacious comfortable bar and dining lounge, real ales, nice coffee, decent pubby food inc good value Sun roasts, cheerful service; children welcome, tables on pretty lawn, well equipped bedrooms, good breakfast *(LYM, Andy West)*

BIDEFORD [SS4526]
Kings Arms EX39 2HW [The Quay]: Cheerful old-fashioned 16th-c local with Victorian harlequin floor tiles in alcovey front bar, friendly staff, local ales such as Jollyboat kept well, decent wines by the glass, nice coffee, reasonably priced food (not Fri or Sat evenings) from filled rolls to steaks, back raised family area; piped music; dogs welcome, pavement tables *(Dave Irving, Jenny Huggins)*
Lacey's Ale & Cider House EX39 2BU [Bridge St]: Series of connecting buildings stepping up hill with bar uppermost, Country Life beers, good value restaurant, clean comfortable female-friendly atmosphere, daily newspapers *(Dave Irving, Jenny Huggins)*

BISHOP'S TAWTON [SS5629]
☆ *Chichester Arms* EX32 0DQ [signed off A377 outside Barnstaple; East St]: Friendly 15th-c cob and thatch pub, well priced good generous food from home-made soup and sandwiches to fresh local fish and seasonal game (all meat from named farms), quick obliging service even when crowded, well kept Exmoor ales, decent wines, heavy low beams, large stone fireplace, restaurant; children welcome, disabled access not good but staff very helpful, picnic-sets on front terrace and in back garden, open all day *(LYM, David Eberlin, Mr and Mrs Barrie, Andy and Jill Kassube)*

BLACK DOG [SS8009]
Black Dog EX17 4QS [off B3042 at Thelbridge]: Popular thatched and beamed village pub with friendly hard-working landlord, enjoyable food inc good Sun carvery *(Mrs P Sumner)*

BLACKAWTON [SX8050]
☆ *Normandy Arms* TQ9 7BN [Signposted off A3122 W of Dartmouth]: New licensees and some refurbishment at this old pub (previously run by highly thought-of chef); drinkers' area with tub leather chairs and sofas by woodburner, up to three local ales, two main dining areas with high-backed leather dining chairs around wooden tables on slate floors, pictures of village and the pub over the years; piped music; children and dogs welcome, benches outside in front and picnic-sets in small garden across lane, pretty village, four redone bedrooms, cl Sun evening *(LYM)*

BRAMPFORD SPEKE [SX9298]
☆ *Lazy Toad* EX5 5DP [off A377 N of Exeter]: Welcoming nicely restored pub, beams and flagstones, settles and log fire, separate eating area, good food from locally sourced ingredients and own smokery, home-grown herbs and soft fruits, good friendly service even when busy, well kept Adnams, St Austell and Warriors, good choice of wines by the glass; dogs welcome (friendly resident cocker called Sam), disabled facilities, courtyard and garden, cl Sun evening, Mon *(R P Sawbridge, Nigel Clifton, John and Bryony Coles, David Hall)*

BRANDIS CORNER [SS4103]
Bickford Arms EX22 7XY [A3072
Hatherleigh—Holsworthy]: Restored 17th-c
beamed village pub, good locally sourced
food cooked to order so may be a wait, Sun
carvery, Skinners ales, farm cider, log fires,
restaurant; well behaved children welcome if
eating, garden, attractive countryside,
comfortable bedrooms, good breakfast
(Roger and Sue Colebrook)
BRAYFORD [SS7235]
☆ *Poltimore Arms* EX36 3HA [Yarde Down;
3 miles towards Simonsbath]: Unspoilt
17th-c two-bar beamed local, so remote it
generates its own electricity, friendly
landlord and cheerful efficient staff, enticing
good value blackboard food from local
produce inc good Sun lunches, ales such as
Adnams, Cotleigh and Greene King tapped
from the cask, good wines by the glass,
basic traditional furnishings, fine
woodburner in inglenook, interesting
ornaments, two attractive restaurant areas;
children welcome, also dogs on leads (pub
has own dogs), picnic-sets in side garden,
has been cl winter lunchtimes *(LYM,
Andrew Scott)*
BRIDESTOWE [SX5287]
Fox & Hounds EX20 4HF [A386
Okehampton—Tavistock]: Welcoming moors-
edge inn under long-serving family
management, old-fashioned and well worn-
in, good value generous food inc steaks and
specials, good range of real ales, two bars,
restaurant, games room and skittle alley;
dogs and children welcome, six bedrooms,
bunkhouse, campsite with play area, open all
day *(BB, Robert Pitman)*
White Hart EX20 4EL [Fore St (old A38, off
A30/A386)]: Partly flagstoned beamed main
bar, some nice old furnishings in lounge,
panelled dining room, tasty food, well kept
beer and decent wines, friendly helpful staff;
informal streamside back garden, peaceful
Dartmoor village, two comfortable bedrooms
(Ellie Weld, David London)
BRIXHAM [SX9256]
Blue Anchor TQ5 8AH [Fore St/King St]:
Welcoming harbourside pub of some
character, well kept Dartmoor Best, Greene
King Abbot and a guest, banquettes and
plenty of nautical hardware, good value
generous food in two small dining rooms
with some interesting old photographs –
one a former chapel down some steps; open
all day *(David Uren, David Carr)*
☆ *Maritime* TQ5 9TH [King Street (up steps
from harbour – nearby parking virtually
non-existent)]: Single bar packed with bric-
a-brac, chamber-pots hanging from beams,
hundreds of key fobs, cigarette cards, pre-
war ensigns, toby jugs, mannequins,
astronomical charts, even a binnacle by the
door, friendly landlady, Bays Best and
St Austell, 78 malts, no food or credit cards,
lively terrier and parrot (mind your fingers);
piped music, small TV, darts and board
games; well behaved children and dogs

allowed, fine views over harbour, nearby
parking difficult, bedrooms *(LYM, the Didler,
Henry Pursehouse-Tranter, David Carr)*
BROADHEMPSTON [SX8066]
Monks Retreat TQ9 6BN [The Square]: Black
beams, massive old walls, lots of copper,
brass and china, cheerful welcoming staff,
well kept Bass, Butcombe and a guest beer,
good changing well priced food using local
produce from lunchtime sandwiches up, steps
to sizeable dining area, huge stone fireplace;
a few picnic-sets out in front, by arch to
attractive churchyard *(John and
Dinah Waters, BB)*
BUDLEIGH SALTERTON [SY0681]
Feathers EX9 6LE [High St]: Long beamed
room with nice bustling atmosphere, decent
well presented food from good sandwiches
up, friendly prompt service, well kept
Branscombe Vale Branoc, O'Hanlons
Yellowhammer and Wells & Youngs
Bombardier, good mix of customers
(George Atkinson)
BURGH ISLAND [SX6444]
Pilchard TQ7 4BG [300 yds across tidal sands
from Bigbury-on-Sea; walk, or summer Sea
Tractor if tide's in – unique bus on stilts]:
Sadly the splendid beamed and flagstoned
upper bar with its lanterns and roaring log
fire is now reserved for guests at the
associated flamboyantly art deco hotel, but
the more utilitarian lower bar is still worth a
visit for the unbeatable setting high above
the sea swarming below this tidal island;
well kept Sharps, Thwaites Lancaster Bomber
and an ale brewed for the pub, local farm
cider, lunchtime baguettes; tables outside,
some down by beach *(Brian Glozier, LYM)*
BUTTERLEIGH [SS9708]
Butterleigh Inn EX15 1PN [off A396 in
Bickleigh]: Friendly small-roomed heavy-
beamed country pub under newish licensees,
enjoyable reasonably priced food inc Sun
carvery, four real ales, good choice of wines,
two big fireplaces, back dining room;
children welcome, picnic-sets in large
garden, four comfortable bedrooms
*(Malcolm Smith, N Scattergood, Dawn and
Ian Robertson, LYM)*
CALIFORNIA CROSS [SX7053]
☆ *California* PL21 0SG [brown sign to pub off
A3121 S of A38 junction]: Neatly modernised
18th-c or older pub with beams, panelling,
stripped-stone and log fire, wide choice of
good sensibly priced food from sandwiches
to steaks in dining bar and family area, good
restaurant menu, popular Sun lunch (best to
book), good friendly service, sofa in small
separate snug, Coach House, Fullers and
Greene King ales, decent wines, local farm
cider; piped music; children and dogs
welcome, attractive garden, back terrace,
open all day *(BB, Helen and Brian Edgeley,
Lucien Perring)*
CHAGFORD [SX7087]
☆ *Ring o' Bells* TQ13 8AH [off A382]:
Welcoming old pub with beamed and
panelled bar, well kept ales, enjoyable

reasonably priced generous food, good friendly service, log fire in big fireplace; dogs and well behaved children welcome, sunny walled garden, nearby moorland walks, four bedrooms, open all day *(Sarah Moore, LYM, A B and C A Bailey)*

CHALLACOMBE [SS6941]

Black Venus EX31 4TT [B3358 Blackmoor Gate—Simonsbath]: Low-beamed 16th-c pub with friendly landlady, two well kept changing ales, Thatcher's farm cider, enjoyable fairly priced food from sandwiches to popular Sun lunch, pews and comfortable chairs, woodburner and big open fire, roomy and attractive dining area; children welcome, garden tables, play area, grand countryside *(Matthew Shackle, Sheila Topham, BB)*

CHERITON BISHOP [SX7792]

☆ ***Old Thatch Inn*** EX6 6JH [off A30]: Old-fashioned thatched pub well geared to holiday traffic and generally very well liked, traditionally furnished lounge and rambling beamed bar separated by big stone fireplace, O'Hanlons, Otter, Sharps and a guest, enjoyable freshly prepared bar food from sandwiches up, friendly service; children and dogs welcome, sheltered garden, pretty tubs and baskets, clean comfortable bedrooms, cl Sun evening *(Mr and Mrs Richard Osborne, R T and J C Moggridge, LYM, John Luckes, Norman and Sarah Keeping, Paul Goldman, Mr S W Buckley, Jane Hudson, Nick Lawless)*

CHITTLEHAMHOLT [SS6420]

☆ ***Exeter Inn*** EX37 9NS [off A377 Barnstaple—Crediton, and B3226 SW of South Molton]: Spotless 16th-c thatched coaching inn with friendly staff and long-serving licensees, wide range of good food (should book wknds) from sandwiches up inc speciality hog pudding, ales such as Otter and Sharps, farm cider, good wine choice, open stove in huge fireplace, beams spotted with hundreds of matchboxes, shelves of old bottles, traditional seating, lounge with comfortable seating; piped music; children and dogs welcome, terrace, bedrooms and self-catering *(Neil and Anita Christopher, LYM)*

CHITTLEHAMPTON [SS6325]

Bell EX37 9QL [signed off B3227 S Molton—Umberleigh]: Cheerful family-run 18th-c village inn, tasty local food from sandwiches to bargain hot dishes, good choice of beers inc local ones, outstanding range of malt whiskies; children and dogs welcome, nice quiet garden, bedrooms *(Roger Fox, Andy and Jill Kassube)*

CHRISTOW [SX8384]

Artichoke EX6 7NF: Pretty thatched local with small comfortable open-plan rooms stepped down hill, low beams, some black panelling, flagstones, reliable food inc fish, game and nice puddings, lovely log fire (another in dining room), Otter tapped from cask, welcoming helpful service; tables on back terrace, pretty village nr Canonteign Waterfalls and Country Park *(BB, Amanda Goodridge, Les Last)*

CHUDLEIGH [SX8679]

Bishop Lacey TQ13 0HY [Fore St, just off A38]: Unpretentious and interesting partly 14th-c low-beamed church house, cheerful obliging landlady and staff, character locals, well kept O'Hanlons, Sharps and changing west country microbrews, farm cider, home-made food inc good curries, log fires, dark décor, two bars, dining room; live bands in next-door offshoot; children welcome, garden tables, good value bedrooms, open all day *(the Didler, Hugh Roberts, Sue and Mike Todd)*

Highwaymans Haunt TQ13 0DE [signed off A38, N of Chudleigh on B3344]: Welcoming old thatched and beamed pub with enjoyable good value locally sourced food (should book wknds), Greene King ales; children welcome, terrace picnic-sets *(Ann and John Jordan)*

CHURCHSTOW [SX7145]

Church House TQ7 3QW [A379 NW of Kingsbridge]: Well cared-for refurbished pub dating from 13th c doing well under friendly licensees, heavy black beams and stripped stone, wide choice of enjoyable home-made food inc popular evening carvery (Weds-Sat), well kept local ales, decent wines, back conservatory with floodlit well; children welcome, tables on big terrace *(LYM, Geoff and Marianne Millin, Michael and Joan Johnstone, Hugh Stafford)*

CLAYHIDON [ST1615]

Half Moon EX15 3TJ: Attractive old village pub with pleasant staff and warm friendly atmosphere, wide choice of good home-made food, well kept Cotleigh and a guest ale, farm cider, good wine list, comfortable bar with good inglenook log fire; children and dogs welcome, picnic-sets in tiered garden over road, valley views *(John and Fiona Merritt, Jerry Brown, BB, Mike Gorton)*

CLOVELLY [SS3225]

New Inn EX39 5TQ [High St (car-free village, visitors charged £5.50 each to enter)]: Friendly 17th-c inn halfway down the steep cobbled street, Arts & Crafts décor, simple easy-going lower bar with flagstones and bric-a-brac (narrow front part has more character than back eating room), well kept Sharps Cornish Coaster and a beer brewed for the pub by local Country Life, good value bar food, upstairs restaurant; great views, small garden, good bedrooms *(Andy and Jill Kassube)*

CLYST ST MARY [SX9791]

Half Moon EX5 1BR [under a mile from M5 junction 30 via A376]: Attractive old pub next to disused multi-arched bridge (Devon's oldest) over Clyst, emphasis on the reasonably priced home-made food using local meat and fish, four ales inc Otter and Fullers, good choice of wines by the glass, friendly attentive staff, red plush seating and plenty of dining tables, pine cladding, log fire; nostalgic juke box, live music Sat night; children welcome in lounge (no under-11s in restaurant), disabled access, six bedrooms, open all day wknds

(George Atkinson, Dr and Mrs M E Wilson, Alain and Rose Foote)

COCKWOOD [SX9780]

☆ *Ship* EX6 8RA [off A379 N of Dawlish]: Comfortable traditional 17th-c pub overlooking estuary and harbour, good value generous food inc good fish dishes and puddings (freshly made by landlady so takes time), Butcombe and Sharps Doom Bar, friendly helpful staff, partitioned beamed bar with big log fire and ancient oven, decorative plates and seafaring memorabilia, small restaurant; piped music; children and dogs welcome, nice steep-sided garden *(Paul Booth, Bob Jones, Dr and Mrs John Fripp)*

COLYFORD [SY2592]

☆ *Wheelwright* EX24 6QQ [Swan Hill Rd (A3052 Sidmouth—Lyme Regis)]: Attractive 17th-c thatched pub, welcoming and civilised, with low beams, log fire, soft lighting, interesting well priced food all day from good lunchtime sandwiches and deli boards to fresh fish and local produce, well kept Badger ales and a guest, lots of bottled beer, nice wines, new back extension; children and dogs welcome, picnic-sets on front terrace *(John Burgess, Roy Fox, A M Falconer, B D Jones, Richard Stanfield)*

COLYTON [SY2494]

Gerrard Arms EX24 6JN [St Andrews Sq]: Friendly unpretentious open-plan local with Bass, Branscombe Vale Branoc and a guest tapped from the cask, good value home-made food, skittle alley; courtyard and garden *(the Didler)*

COMBE MARTIN [SS5846]

Pack o' Cards EX34 0ET [High St]: Unusual 'house of cards' building originally built late 17th c to celebrate card winnings, with four floors, 13 rooms and 52 windows; snug bar area and various side rooms, St Austell ales, inexpensive pub food inc children's choices and good Sun roast; pretty riverside garden with play area, bedrooms *(Michael and Hilary Andrews)*

Royal Marine EX34 0AW [Seaside]: Large open-plan bar area with some window seats overlooking sea, nice mix of customers, Barum and Otter ales, enjoyable food from sandwiches through seafood to good value Sun roasts, friendly helpful service; children welcome, bedrooms *(Michael and Hilary Andrews)*

CORNWORTHY [SX8255]

☆ *Hunters Lodge* TQ9 7ES [off A381 Totnes—Kingsbridge]: Small low-ceilinged two-roomed bar, welcoming chatty staff, enjoyable sensibly priced food cooked by landlady, well kept Sharps Doom Bar, traditional seating around heavy elm tables, cottagey dining room, log fire in big 17th-c fireplace; children and dogs welcome, big lawn with terrace and extensive views, cl Mon lunch *(MP, R K Phillips, LYM)*

COUNTISBURY [SS7449]

Blue Ball EX35 6NE [A39, E of Lynton]: Beautifully set rambling heavy-beamed pub, friendly licensees, good range of generous local food in bar and restaurant, three ales inc one brewed for the pub, decent wines, farm ciders, handsome log fires; piped music; children, dogs and walkers welcome (two pub dogs), views from terrace tables, good nearby cliff walks (pub provides handouts of four circular routes), comfortable bedrooms, open all day *(Mr and Mrs D J Nash, LYM, Philip Kingsbury, Caroline and Gavin Callow)*

CREDITON [SS8300]

Crediton Inn EX17 1EZ [Mill St (follow Tiverton sign)]: Small friendly local with long-serving landlady, well kept Fullers London Pride, Sharps Doom Bar and quickly changing guests (Nov beer festival), cheap well prepared wknd food, back games room; free bookable skittle alley, open all day Mon-Sat, *(the Didler)*

CROYDE [SS4439]

Manor House Inn EX33 1PG [St Marys Rd, off B3231 NW of Braunton]: Friendly family pub with cheerful efficient service, well kept Bass, Wadworths 6X and a house beer, good choice of enjoyable fairly priced food from baguettes and baked potatoes to blackboard specials, restaurant and dining conservatory; piped music, games end; skittle alley, disabled facilities, attractive terraced garden with good big play area *(Neil and Brenda Skidmore)*

Thatched Barn EX33 1LZ [B3231 NW of Braunton; Hobbs Hill]: Lively thatched pub nr great surfing beaches, australian run with cheerful efficient young staff, laid-back feel (can get packed in summer); rambling and roomy, with beams, open fire, settles and good seating, wide choice of enjoyable generous all-day food from sandwiches up, well kept changing local ales, morning coffee, teas, smart restaurant with dressers and lots of china; piped music; children in eating areas, tables on flower-filled suntrap terraces, large gardens shared with neighbouring Billy Budds, good play area, bedrooms simple but clean and comfortable, open all day *(LYM, Alex Tucker, Andy and Jill Kassube, Adrian and Dawn Collinge, Pat and Tony Martin)*

DARTMOUTH [SX8751]

☆ *Royal Castle Hotel* TQ6 9PS [the Quay]: Rambling 17th-c or older hotel behind Regency façade overlooking inner harbour, good well priced lunches from upstairs restaurant, long traditional downstairs bar with dining area for all-day food from sandwiches to good steaks, perhaps winter lunchtime spit-roasts from 17th-c range, more contemporary bar on left (TV, piped music, dogs welcome – no children), cheerful efficient staff, well kept Bays, Dartmoor and Sharps, good choice of wines, live music Thurs; children allowed lunchtime, 25 comfortable bedrooms, open all day *(Mrs Mary Woods, Richard Tilbrook, Gerry and Rosemary Dobson, Peter and Giff Bennett, Alison Ball, Ian Walton, George Atkinson, Michael Dandy, LYM, Mike and Sue Shirley, Susan and Nigel Wilson)*

DODDISCOMBSLEIGH [SX8586]

☆ *Nobody Inn* EX6 7PS [off B3193]: Friendly 16th-c inn with three well kept ales inc Exe Valley, local ciders, great wine and whisky choice, enjoyable bar food, good log fire, beamed lounge with handsomely carved antique settles among other seats, guns and hunting prints by big inglenook, evening restaurant; children and dogs welcome, garden tables, well refurbished bedrooms, open all day (*W K Wood, J D O Carter, Cass Stainton, J L Wedel, Chris and Angela Buckell, Geoff and Carol Thorp, Robert Lorimer, Bob and Angela Brooks, Hugh Roberts, Andrea Rampley, Mike and Monnie Jefferies, Anthony Longden, Adrian and Dawn Collinge, LYM, Gene and Kitty Rankin, Peter Leather*)

DUNSFORD [SX8189]

☆ *Royal Oak* EX6 7DA [signed from Moretonhampstead]: Comfortably worn in village inn, good generous food cooked to order, changing ales inc Dartmoor and Sharps, local cider, friendly landlord, airy lounge with woodburner and view from sunny dining bay, simple dining room, steps down to pool room; piped music, quiz nights; children well looked after, sheltered tiered garden, good value bedrooms in converted barn (*the Didler, Robert Gomme, LYM*)

EAST PRAWLE [SX7836]

Pigs Nose TQ7 2BY [Prawle Green]: Relaxed quirky three-room 16th-c inn with low beams and flagstones, local ales tapped from the cask, farm ciders, open fire, mix of old furniture, lots of interesting bric-a-brac and pictures, jars of wild flowers and candles on tables, darts, small family area with unusual toys, nice dogs, laid-back service; unobtrusive piped music, hall for live bands (friendly landlord was 60s tour manager); tables outside, nice spot on village green (*Tich Critchlow, the Didler, Geoff and Carol Thorp, Simon Foster, Roger Wain-Heapy*)

EXETER [SX9292]

Chaucers EX4 3LR [basement of Tesco Metro, High St]: Large dim-lit modern olde-worlde pub/bistro/wine bar down lots of steps, beamed low ceiling and timber-framed walls, several levels with booths and alcoves, comfortable furnishings, candles in bottles, Marstons-related ales, well priced wines, enjoyable good value food from snacks to specials, quick friendly service; piped music, no children (*Adrian and Dawn Collinge, Michael Dandy*)

Double Locks EX2 6LT [Canal Banks, Alphington, via Marsh Barton Industrial Estate; OS Sheet 192 map ref 933901]: Unsmart and individual, by ship canal, remote yet busy, Wells & Youngs and guest ales, Gray's farm cider in summer, variety of plain home-made bar food all day; piped music, live wknds, service can get swamped; children and dogs welcome, seats out on decking with distant view to city and cathedral (nice towpath walk out – or hire a canoe at the Quay), big play area, camping, open all day (*the Didler, Michael Beale, LYM*)

Fat Pig EX1 1BL [John St]: Refurbished Victorian pub, welcoming and relaxed, with several local ales inc Exeter, good wine choice, imaginative blackboard food, nice fire; tables in heated courtyard (*Elizabeth Saunders, Mike Gorton*)

Great Western EX4 4NU [St Davids Hill]: Regulars enjoying up to a dozen or so well kept changing ales inc some rarities in large commercial hotel's comfortably worn-in plush-seated bar, friendly efficient staff, fresh good value pubby food all day from sandwiches up (kitchen also supplies hotel's restaurant), daily papers; may be piped music, sports TV, pay parking; children welcome, 35 bedrooms, open all day (*Tony and Wendy Hobden, Phil and Sally Gorton, the Didler, BB*)

Old Fire House EX4 4EP [New North Rd]: Compact city-centre pub in Georgian building behind high arched wrought-iron gates, ten changing ales, good choice of wines, bargain food, friendly staff, beams, simple furniture; popular with young people evenings; piped music, live folk and jazz; picnic-sets in small front courtyard (*Dr and Mrs M E Wilson, the Didler*)

Prospect EX2 4AN [The Quay (left bank, nr rowing club)]: Early 19th-c pub in good quayside position, enjoyable substantial bar food all day from baguettes up, well kept Otter, St Austell Tribute and Skinners Betty Stogs, friendly efficient young staff, plenty of comfortable tables inc raised river-view dining area; gentle piped music, live bands Mon and Tues; children welcome, tables out by historic ship-canal basin, open all day (*Dave Irving, Jenny Huggins, Tony and Wendy Hobden*)

Rusty Bike EX4 4LZ [Howell Rd]: Comfortably refurbished back-street pub with bistro-feel (same owners as Fat Pig in John St), pine tables on stripped boards in large open bar, big black and white photographs, adjoining dining area, four changing ales, farm cider, good wine choice, enjoyable blackboard food; piped music, popular with students, limited parking (*Mike Gorton*)

Welcome EX2 8DU [Haven Banks, off Haven Rd (which is first left off A377 heading S after Exe crossing)]: Two-room pub little changed since 1960s (ditto the juke box), gas lighting and flagstones, very friendly old-school landlady, changing ales; a few tables out overlooking basin on Exeter Ship Canal, can be reached on foot via footbridges from The Quay (*the Didler, Phil and Sally Gorton*)

Well House EX1 1HB [Cathedral Yard, attached to Royal Clarence Hotel]: Good position with big windows looking across to cathedral in partly divided open-plan bar, good choice of local ales, quick service, wide range of food, lots of Victorian prints, daily papers, Roman well below (can be viewed when pub not busy); open all day (*the Didler, BB*)

White Hart EX1 1EE [South St]: Peaceful old-fashioned rambling pub in two distinct parts, heavy beams, oak flooring, nice furnishings inc antiques, charming inner cobbled courtyard, a couple of Marstons-related ales kept well, good choice of reasonably priced food inc deals; refunds may be given for car park behind if eating; bedrooms *(Les and Norma Haydon, Joan and Michel Hooper-Immins, Dave Irving, Jenny Huggins, LYM)*

EXMOUTH [SY9980]

Grove EX8 1BJ [Esplanade]: Roomy unpretentious old-fashioned family pub set back from beach, basic traditional furnishings, caricatures and local prints, good value all-day food inc plenty of local fish, quick obliging staff, Wells & Youngs and guest beers, decent house wines, good coffee, attractive fireplace at back, sea views from appealing upstairs dining room and balcony; live music Fri; picnic-sets in big garden (no view) with play area *(Peter Salmon, Mark Flynn, Alain and Rose Foote, Jo Rees, Dr and Mrs M E Wilson, PL, David Hunt)*

EXTON [SX9886]

Puffing Billy EX3 0PR: Well laid out brightly decorated dining pub with inventive competitively priced modern food using local organic supplies, good friendly service, local beers and good wine choice in bar extension; gets busy wknds; picnic-sets outside *(B D Jones, R P Sawbridge)*

FROGMORE [SX7742]

Globe TQ7 2NR [A379 E of Kingsbridge]: Extended and refurbished pub with friendly staff and regulars, well kept Otter, Skinners and South Hams, local farm cider in summer, good wine by the glass, enjoyable well priced food from sandwiches to steak, fine log fire in cosy restaurant, darts; piped music, TV, games machine; dogs welcome, terrace tables, creek and coast walks, eight well appointed modern bedrooms, good breakfast *(Tony and Gill Powell, Dennis Jenkin, LYM)*

GALMPTON [SX8856]

Manor TQ5 0NL [village and pub signed off A3022; Stoke Gabriel Rd]: Large friendly open-plan Edwardian local with well kept ales such as St Austell Dartmoor and Sharps Doom Bar, good choice of food inc local fish, two-part bar and family dining area; tables outside, open all day *(Mrs J King)*

GOODLEIGH [SS5934]

New Inn EX32 7LX: Small village pub with welcoming atmosphere in low-beamed hop-hung bar, chatty locals on bar stools, two well kept changing ales, wide blackboard choice of good reasonably priced food cooked to order, log fire *(Gordon Tong, Ross Balaam)*

HALBERTON [ST0112]

Barge EX16 7AG [High St]: Friendly local with well kept Sharps Doom Bar, enjoyable inexpensive simple food; handy for canal walks *(J D O Carter)*

HARBERTON [SX7758]

☆ *Church House* TQ9 7SF [off A381 S of Totnes]: Ancient partly Norman village pub with unusually long bar, ales such as Butcombe, Courage, Marstons and St Austell, good choice of wines by the glass, farm cider, wide range of enjoyable well priced food, good friendly service, woodburner in big inglenook, medieval latticed glass and oak panelling, attractive 17th- and 18th-c pews and settles, family room; bedrooms *(LYM, Dr Nigel Bowles, David and Pamela White, F A Ashley)*

HATHERLEIGH [SS5404]

☆ *Tally Ho* EX20 3JN [Market St (A386)]: Good generous uncomplicated food (not Sun evening) from lunchtime sandwiches up, good value wines, real ales such as local Clearwater and St Austell, quick friendly service, attractive heavy-beamed and timbered linked rooms, sturdy furnishings, big log fire and woodburner, traditional games, restaurant, busy Tues market day (beer slightly cheaper then); unobtrusive piped music; dogs welcome, tables in nice sheltered garden, three good value pretty bedrooms, open all day *(LYM, Dr J Barrie Jones, the Didler, Ron and Sheila Corbett)*

HEANTON PUNCHARDON [SS5034]

Tarka EX31 4AX: Castle-look Vintage Inn overlooking estuary (lovely sunsets), enjoyable food inc nice specials, good staff particularly helpful with children *(Pat and Tony Martin, Barrie and Mary Crees, John and Fiona McIlwain)*

HOLSWORTHY [SS3403]

Old Market EX22 6AY [Chapel St]: Town-centre pub with well kept ales such as Bays, Sharps and Skinners, good value local food from sandwiches up, Sun carvery, restaurant; dogs welcome, garden, three bedrooms *(Andy and Jill Kassube)*

Rydon Inn EX22 7HU [Rydon (A3072 W)]: Good food in comfortable dining pub, friendly staff, well kept beer, decent coffee; dogs welcome by arrangement in part of bar, disabled access and facilities, fine views from garden and conservatory *(Jean and David Lewis, Ryta Lyndley)*

HONITON [ST1599]

Heathfield EX14 2UG [Walnut Rd]: Popular ancient pub smartly refurbished by Greene King, well run and spacious, with their ales, enjoyable reasonably priced food inc bargain meals, cheerful service; bedrooms *(Bob and Margaret Holder)*

HORNS CROSS [SS3823]

☆ *Hoops* EX39 5DL [A39 Clovelly—Bideford, W of village]: Welcoming picturesque thatched inn with oak settles, stone floors, beams and inglenook fires, good food, generous if not cheap, using local suppliers, service usually good, well kept cask-tapped ales such as local Country Life and one brewed for the pub, local farm cider, good wine choice, daily papers, darts; piped music, TV; well behaved children in eating area till 8pm, dogs in bar, small courtyard, comfortable bedrooms, good breakfast, open all day (John Urquhart, LYM, Andy and Jill Kassube, Trevor Higginbotham, Ryta Lyndley, Paul and Annette Hallett, Annette Tress, Gary Smith)

HORSEBRIDGE [SX4074]

☆ *Royal* PL19 8PJ [off A384 Tavistock—Launceston]: Cheerful dimly lit ancient local with dark half-panelling, log fires, slate floors, scrubbed tables and interesting bric-a-brac, good reasonably priced food inc plenty of fish, friendly landlord and staff, well kept St Austell and Skinners, Rich's farm cider, bar billiards, cribbage, dominoes, café-style side room, no music or machines; no children in evening, picnic-sets on front and side terraces and in big garden, quiet rustic spot by lovely old Tamar bridge (LYM, Giles and Annie Francis, Ted George, Dr Peter Andrews, Les Last, Jacquie Jones)

IDDESLEIGH [SS5608]

☆ *Duke of York* EX19 8BG [B3217 Exbourne—Dolton]: Homely unspoilt rustic local continuing well under new licensees, chatty regulars, roaring log fire, well kept ales and generously served food; children and dogs welcome, little back garden, bedrooms, open all day (LYM, Peter Thornton)

IDE [SX8990]

☆ *Poachers* EX2 9RW [3 miles from M5 junction 31, via A30; High St]: Nice beamed inn in quaint village, good home-made food, Bass, Branscombe Vale Branoc, Otter and guests from ornate curved wooden bar, non-standard mix of old chairs and sofas, big log fire, restaurant; tables in pleasant garden with barbecue, three comfortable bedrooms (the Didler)

IDEFORD [SX8977]

☆ *Royal Oak* TQ13 0AY [2 miles off A380]: Unpretentious 16th-c thatched and flagstoned village local, friendly helpful service, Greene King, Otter and guests, basic pub snacks, navy theme inc interesting Nelson and Churchill memorabilia, panelling, big open fireplace; children and dogs welcome, tables out at front and by car park over road (the Didler)

ILFRACOMBE [SS5247]

George & Dragon EX34 9ED [Fore St]: Oldest pub here and handy for harbour, clean and comfortable with friendly local atmosphere, four well kept ales, decent wines, tasty generous low-priced pub food cooked by amiable landlord, attractive olde-worlde décor with stripped stone, beams, open fireplaces, lots of ornaments, china etc, no mobile phones; piped music, quiz nights, can get busy wknds (JDM, KM, Reg Fowle, Helen Rickwood)

KENTISBEARE [ST0608]

Wyndham Arms EX15 2AA [3.5 miles from M5 junction 28, via A373]: Village pub rescued from closure and refurbished by enthusiastic local volunteers, pleasant staff, enjoyable food, well kept ales inc Otter, big log fire in long beamed main bar, restaurant,

games room, live music; sheltered courtyard (BB, John and Dinah Waters)

KILMINGTON [SY2798]

☆ *Old Inn* EX13 7RB [A35]: Thatched 16th-c pub, beams and flagstones, welcoming licensees, enjoyable good value food using local supplies, well kept Cotleigh and Otter, good choice of wines, small character front bar with traditional games, back lounge with leather armchairs by inglenook log fire, small restaurant; children welcome, skittle alley, beer gardens (LYM, Richard and Sue Fewkes, John Butcher, Val Offer, Nigel Fortnam, Faith Thomas)

KINGSWEAR [SX8851]

Royal Dart TQ6 0AA [The Square]: Victorian building in fine setting by ferry and Dart Valley Railway terminal, South Hams and Teignworthy ales, enjoyable food, bargain prices, chatty staff, unpretentious modernised bar, great view of Dartmouth from balcony, upstairs restaurant, interesting WWII history when naval base; riverside tables (the Didler)

Ship TQ6 0AG [Higher St]: Simple attractive local with kind friendly family service, well kept Adnams and Otter Ale, Bright and Head from horseshoe bar, farm cider, nice wines, coal fire, nautical bric-a-brac and local photographs, ginger cat, honest well sourced food inc good fresh fish (best views from restaurant up steps); big-screen TV; a couple of river-view tables outside, open all day Fri-Sun and summer (the Didler, Richard Tilbrook, Mrs P Bishop, Alun and Jennifer Evans, Tony and Wendy Hobden, BB)

Steam Packet TQ6 0AD [Fore St]: Small friendly traditional local, well kept Bays and guests, pubby food in bar and restaurant; outside tables overlooking steam railway, good views across to Dartmouth, too (the Didler)

KNOWLE [SY0582]

Britannia/Dog & Donkey EX9 6AL [B3178 NW of Budleigh Salterton]: Victorian pub doing well under welcoming licensees, enjoyable good value food, well kept beers, small public bar with log fire, lounge leading to dining room; picnic-sets out on lawn (Peter Thornton)

LAKE [SX5288]

☆ *Bearslake* EX20 4HQ [A386 just S of Sourton]: Rambling low thatched stone pub, leather sofas and high bar chairs on crazy-paved slate floor one end, three more smallish rooms with woodburners, toby jugs, farm tools and traps, stripped stone, well kept Otter and Teignworthy, good range of spirits and whiskies, decent wines, beamed restaurant; children allowed, large sheltered streamside garden, Dartmoor walks, six comfortably olde-worlde bedrooms, generous breakfast (Peter Bunting, Chris and Angela Buckell, BB)

LANDSCOVE [SX7766]

Live & Let Live TQ13 7LZ: Friendly open-plan local, good value home cooking inc bargain winter lunches, ales inc Teignworthy, farm ciders, log fire; decked terrace, more tables in small orchard across lane, cl Mon *(Mr and Mrs Martin Tomlinson, J D O Carter, LYM)*

LIFTON [SX3885]

☆ *Arundell Arms* PL16 0AA [Fore St]: Consistently good interesting lunchtime bar food in substantial country-house fishing hotel, warmly welcoming and individual, with rich décor, nice staff and sophisticated service, good choice of wines by the glass, morning coffee with home-made biscuits, afternoon tea, restaurant; also adjacent Courthouse bar (complete with original cells) doing fairly priced pubby food (not Mon evening), St Austell Tribute and Dartmoor Jail; can arrange fishing tuition – also shooting, deer-stalking and riding; pleasant bedrooms, useful A30 stop *(Mayur Shah, MA)*

LITTLEHEMPSTON [SX8162]

Tally Ho! TQ9 6NF [off A381 NE of Totnes]: Low-beamed 14th-c pub, neat and cosy, with interesting mix of chairs and settles, lots of cheerful bric-a-brac on stripped-stone walls, some panelling, efficient friendly service even when busy, enjoyable food from sandwiches to steaks, Greene King IPA and perhaps a guest, restaurant; piped music; children welcome, flower-filled terrace, bedrooms (main rail line nearby) *(LYM, Geoff and Carol Thorp, Glenda Bennett)*

LOWER ASHTON [SX8484]

Manor Inn EX6 7QL [Ashton signposted off B3193 N of Chudleigh]: Country pub improved under current welcoming licensees, good quality sensibly priced food (not Sun evening or Mon, best to book Fri and Sat evenings), four well kept ales, good choice of wine, open fires in both bars, back restaurant; dogs welcome, disabled access, garden picnic-sets with nice rural outlook *(Alan Bussey, Mike Gorton, LYM)*

LUPPITT [ST1606]

☆ *Luppitt Inn* EX14 4RT [back roads N of Honiton]: Unspoilt basic farmhouse pub, an amazing survivor, with chatty long-serving landlady, tiny room with corner bar and a table, another not much bigger with fireplace, cheap Otter tapped from the cask, intriguing metal puzzles made by neighbour, no food or music, lavatories across the yard; cl lunchtime and Sun evening *(the Didler, Phil and Sally Gorton, John and Fiona McIlwain)*

LUSTLEIGH [SX7881]

☆ *Cleave* TQ13 9TJ [off A382 Bovey Tracey—Moretonhampstead]: Beautifully set country tavern, friendly staff, good food from sandwiches and pub favourites to more enterprising things, real ales such as Otter, relaxed low-ceilinged bars, antique high-backed settles among other seats, log fire; may ask to keep your credit card while you eat; children welcome, sheltered garden, has been open all day in summer *(LYM, Jim Lyon, Alan Sutton, Bob and Angela Brooks)*

LYDFORD [SX5184]

☆ *Castle Inn* EX20 4BH [off A386 Okehampton—Tavistock]: Tudor inn owned

by St Austell, traditional home-made food (all day Thurs-Sun), traditional twin bars, big slate flagstones, bowed low beams, granite walls, four inglenook log fires, notable stained-glass door, restaurant; lovely nearby NT river gorge, open all day *(LYM, Mrs Ann Gray)*

LYMPSTONE [SX9984]

Redwing EX8 5JT [Church Rd]: Reopened after major refurbishment by new local family owners, beams and old exposed brickwork, comfortable seating on oak or black slate floors, pictures for sale by local artists, home-made food with emphasis on local produce, converted loft restaurant; garden with terrace, unspoilt village, shore walks *(BB)*

Swan EX8 5ET [The Strand]: Pleasant olde-worlde décor, split-level dining area with leather sofas by big fire, good value generous food inc good fresh fish and italian specials, ales inc Marstons, friendly staff, games room with pool; small front garden with smokers' area *(the Didler, Jo Rees)*

LYNMOUTH [SS7249]

Village EX35 6EH [Lynmouth St]: Welcoming and neatly kept, interesting good value bar food, St Austell ales, Addlestone's cider, warm stove; beer garden, bedrooms *(Simon Baker)*

LYNTON [SS6548]

Hunters EX31 4PY [pub well signed off A39 W of Lynton]: Superb Heddon Valley position by NT information centre down very steep hill, great walks inc one down to the sea; big spreading bar with plush banquettes and so forth, woodburner, Exmoor and several other ales, wide choice of generous food; piped music; picnic-sets on balconied terrace overlooking attractive pondside garden with peacocks, open all day summer, hours may be restricted when season tails off *(Bob and Margaret Holder, BB)*

MEAVY [SX5467]

☆ *Royal Oak* PL20 6PJ [off B3212 E of Yelverton]: Friendly licensees in heavy-beamed partly 15th-c pub, pews and plush banquettes, smaller locals' bar (dogs allowed here) with flagstones and big open fireplace, well kept Dartmoor, Sharps and guest, enjoyable home-made food from good ploughman's up, teas and coffee; seats outside and on green of pretty Dartmoor-edge village, popular with walkers, open all day summer *(David and Sue Smith, LYM, Steve Whalley, Michael and Joan Johnstone, Peter Thornton)*

MEETH [SS5408]

Bull & Dragon EX20 3EP [A386 Hatherleigh—Torrington]: 16th-c beamed and thatched village pub with large open bar, welcoming landlord and pleasant young staff, well kept Sharps Doom Bar, food from good value sandwiches up; handy for Tarka Trail *(Dave Irving, Jenny Huggins)*

MORETONHAMPSTEAD [SX7586]

White Hart TQ13 8NF [A382 N of Bovey Tracey; The Square]: Smartly refurbished small 17th-c hotel, welcoming helpful service, stripped floor back bar with log fire, well kept Otter and St Austell Tribute, good choice of wines by the glass, good food from sandwiches up, elegant relaxing lounge with open fire, attractive brasserie; children and dogs welcome, courtyard tables, 28 well equipped country-style bedrooms, good breakfast, no private parking (nr public car park), well placed for Dartmoor, open all day *(LYM, David and Katharine Cooke, Ian Malone)*

MORTEHOE [SS4545]
Chichester Arms EX34 7DU [off A361 Ilfracombe—Braunton]: Welcoming former 16th-c vicarage, varied choice of enjoyable local food, quick friendly service, well kept St Austell, Sharps and Wizard, reasonably priced wine, plush and leatherette panelled lounge, comfortable dining room, pubby locals' bar with darts and pool, interesting old local photographs; skittle alley and games machines in summer children's room, tables out in front and in shaded pretty garden, good coast walk *(Andy and Jill Kassube, Chris Reading)*

NEWTON ABBOT [SX8571]
Dartmouth TQ12 2JP [East St]: Genuine friendly old place brewing its own beers, interesting guests and farm ciders too, decent wines, low ceilings, dark woodwork, roaring log fire; children welcome till 7pm, nice outside area, open all day *(the Didler)*
Locomotive TQ12 2JP [East St]: Cheerful traditional town pub, well kept Adnams and guests, linked rooms inc games room with pool; TV, juke box; open all day *(the Didler, David Carr)*
☆ *Olde Cider Bar* TQ12 2LD [East St]: Basic old-fashioned cider house, casks of interesting low-priced farm ciders (helpful long-serving landlord may give tasters), a couple of perries, more in bottles, good country wines from the cask too, baguettes and pasties etc, great atmosphere, dark stools made from cask staves, barrel seats and wall benches, flagstones and bare boards; small back games room with machines; terrace tables, open all day *(David Carr, the Didler)*
Richard Hopkins TQ12 2EH [Queen St]: Big partly divided open-plan Wetherspoons, busy and friendly, with ten beers inc Bays, Exmoor, O'Hanlons and Red Rock, real cider, usual food; covered tables out at front, open all day *(the Didler)*
Two Mile Oak TQ12 6DF [A381 2 miles S, at Denbury/Kingskerswell crossroads]: Appealing beamed coaching inn, log fires, traditional furnishings, black panelling and candlelit alcoves, well kept Bass and Otter tapped from the cask, straightforward bar food inc wkdy lunchtime bargains, decent coffee, cheerful staff; piped music, TV, games machine; children in lounge, dogs in bar, terrace and lawn, open all day *(LYM, the Didler, George Atkinson)*
Wolborough TQ12 1JQ [Wolborough St]: Popular simple town local, compact wood-

floored bar with etched windows, well kept Teignworthy ales and local guests, some tapped from the cask, friendly staff; open all day, cl Mon lunchtime; small terrace *(the Didler)*

NEWTON FERRERS [SX5447]
☆ *Dolphin* PL8 1AE [riverside Road East – follow Harbour dead end signs]: Simply furnished 18th-c pub under new management; L-shaped bar with a few low black beams, slate floors and some white plank panelling, traditional bar food, Badger ales; can get packed in summer, limited parking; children and dogs welcome, terraces over lane looking down on River Yealm and yachts, has been open all day (except Mon-Thurs in winter) *(LYM)*

NEWTON ST CYRES [SX8798]
Beer Engine EX5 5AX [off A377 towards Thorverton]: Friendly former railway hotel brewing four good beers for over 25 years, wide choice of good home-made food inc local fish and popular Sun lunch; children welcome, decked verandah, steps down to garden, open all day *(the Didler, Dr A J and Mrs Tompsett, Gene and Kitty Rankin, LYM)*

NOMANSLAND [SS8313]
Mount Pleasant EX16 8NN [B3137 Tiverton—South Molton]: Informal country local, huge fireplaces in long low-beamed main bar, well kept Cotleigh, St Austell and Sharps, several wines by the glass, Weston's Old Rosie cider, good freshly cooked generous food, good friendly service, nice mix of furniture inc comfy old sofa, candles on tables, country pictures, daily papers, cosy dining room (former smithy), darts in public bar; piped music; well behaved children and dogs welcome, picnic-sets in back garden, open all day *(LYM, Nick Townsend, Adrian and Dawn Collinge)*

NORTH BOVEY [SX7483]
Ring of Bells TQ13 8RB [off A382/B3212 SW of Moretonhampstead]: Bulgy-walled thatched inn dating from 13th c, low beams, flagstones, big log fire, sturdy rustic tables and winding staircases, well run by knowledgeable landlord, Otter, St Austell and a guest, good local food, friendly staff, carpeted dining room and overspill room; children and dogs welcome, garden by lovely tree-covered village green below Dartmoor, good walks, five big clean bedrooms, open all day *(LYM, Peter Thornton)*

OTTERTON [SY0885]
Kings Arms EX9 7HB [Fore St]: Big open-plan pub handy for families from extensive nearby caravan site, enjoyable pubby food from doorstep sandwiches up inc nice fish, Sun carvery, fast friendly service even when busy, Fullers London Pride and Otter, reasonable prices, restaurant; TV, darts, pool and good skittle alley doubling as family room; dogs welcome, beautiful evening view from attractive back garden with play area, bedrooms, charming village, open all day *(J D O Carter, Colbak)*

PAIGNTON [SX8860]
Isaac Merritt TQ3 3AA [Torquay Rd]:
Spacious well run Wetherspoons conversion
of former shopping arcade, particularly good
range of west country ales, food all day,
friendly welcoming service, low prices, cosy
alcoves, comfortable family dining area, air
conditioning; good disabled access
(the Didler, Henry Pursehouse-Tranter)

PARKHAM [SS3821]
Bell EX39 5PL: Cheerful old thatched village
pub, well run and spotless, with large
comfortable family eating areas, good
home-made food inc fresh fish and Aga-
cooked Sun roasts, friendly efficient service,
well kept ales such as Sharps Doom Bar
and Skinners Betty Stogs, decent choice
of wine, nice coffee, lots of nooks and
crannies, log fire *(Andy and Jill Kassube,
Peter Thornton, LYM)*

PARRACOMBE [SS6644]
☆ *Fox & Goose* EX31 4PE [off A39 Blackmoor
Gate—Lynton]: Popular rambling village pub,
hunting and farming memorabilia and
interesting photographs, well kept ales such
as Cotleigh and Exmoor, good choice of
wines by the glass, farm cider, sandwiches
and good unfussy blackboard food inc lots of
fish and nice west country cheeses, friendly
staff, log fire, separate dining room; children
and dogs welcome, small front verandah,
terraced garden leading to garden room
*(LYM, Betsy and Peter Little, V Brogden,
John Pawson, A and H Piper, George Atkinson)*

PLYMOUTH [SX4854]
☆ *China House* PL4 0DW [Sutton Harbour, via
Sutton Rd off Exeter St (A374)]: Attractive
conversion of Plymouth's oldest warehouse,
lovely boaty views, dimly lit and inviting
interior with beams and flagstones, bare
slate and stone walls, two good log fires,
interesting photographs, enjoyable food,
good choice of real ales and wines by the
glass, attentive staff, piped music, no dogs;
good parking and disabled access/facilities,
tables out on waterside balconies, open all
day *(Alain and Rose Foote, Dick and
Madeleine Brown, LYM)*
Dolphin PL1 2LS [Barbican]: Basic
unchanging chatty local, good range of beers
inc cask-tapped Bass, coal fire (not always
lit), Beryl Cook paintings inc one of the
friendly landlord; open all day *(Dr J Barrie
Jones, the Didler)*
Lounge PL1 4QT [Stopford Pl, Stoke]: Old-
fashioned panelled corner local, friendly
landlord and chatty regulars, well kept Bass
and guest ales, popular lunchtime food (not
Mon), busy on match days; open all day Sat,
Sun *(the Didler)*
Thistle Park PL4 0LE [Commercial Rd]:
Welcoming bare-boards pub nr National
Maritime Aquarium, full range of well kept
South Hams ales (used to be brewed on
premises), Thatcher's cider, friendly service,
lunchtime bar food, evening upstairs thai
restaurant, interesting décor, open fire, back
pool room, juke box, live music wknds; no

children; dogs in bar, roof garden, smokers'
shelter, open all day till late *(the Didler)*

PRIXFORD [SS5436]
Ring o' Bells EX31 4DX: Neat and
comfortable with enjoyable locally sourced
fresh food *(John and Fiona McIlwain)*

RINGMORE [SX6545]
Journeys End TQ7 4HL [signed off B3392 at
Pickwick Inn, St Anns Chapel, nr Bigbury;
best to park up opp church]: Ancient village
inn with friendly chatty licensees, character
panelled lounge and other linked rooms,
several well kept changing local ales tapped
from the cask, farm cider, decent wines,
pubby food from sandwiches up, log fires,
bar billiards (for over-16s), family dining
conservatory with board games; pleasant big
terraced garden with boules, attractive
setting nr thatched cottages not far from
sea, bedrooms antique but comfortable and
well equipped *(Suzy Miller, Michael and
Maggie Betton, John Butcher, Val Offer,
Bob and Angela Brooks, the Didler, LYM)*

ROBOROUGH [SS5717]
New Inn EX19 8SY [Leave M4 junction 17,
follow A429 to Cirencester, left to Stanton
St Quinton and Grittleton]: Tucked-away
thatched pub with new licensees as we went
to press – reports please; beamed bar with
upholstered tub chairs in front of brick
fireplace, up a step to tiny back room
leading to dining area, additional room
opposite bar; children and dogs have been
welcome, picnic-sets on sunny front terrace,
has been closed winter lunchtimes Mon and
Tues *(BB)*

SALCOMBE [SX7438]
Ferry Inn TQ8 8JE [off Fore St nr
Portlemouth Ferry]: Splendid location,
breathtaking estuary views from three floors
of stripped-stone bars rising from sheltered
and attractive flagstoned waterside terrace,
inc top one opening off street (this may be
only one open out of season), middle dining
bar, classic seaside pub menu, Palmers and
farm cider, good house wines, friendly young
staff; may be loud piped music, can get
busy, no nearby parking *(B J Harding,
Bob and Angela Brooks, LYM, MP)*
☆ *Fortescue* TQ8 8BZ [Union St, end of
Fore St]: Good proper pub with five linked
nautical-theme rooms, friendly service,
enjoyable promptly served food, well kept
ales such as Bass, Courage and Otter, decent
wines, good woodburner, old local black and
white shipping pictures, small dining room
with games, small dining room; children
welcome, courtyard picnic-sets *(Gerry and
Rosemary Dobson, P M Newsome)*
Kings Arms TQ8 8BU [Fore St]: Imaginative
reasonably priced food in tastefully
redecorated dining room; good smokers' area
outside, separate upper deck with good
harbour views *(B J Harding)*
Victoria TQ8 8BU [Fore St]: Neat and
attractive 19th-c family pub opp harbour car
park, nautical décor, comfortable furnishings
and big open fires, enjoyable reasonably

priced food from open sandwiches up, well kept St Austell ales, decent wines, friendly enthusiastic service, separate family area; busy wknds, piped music; large sheltered tiered garden behind with good play area and chickens, bedrooms *(Roger Wain-Heapy, MP, Richard Fendick, Bob and Angela Brooks, Neil and Anita Christopher)*

SAMPFORD COURTENAY [SS6300]

New Inn EX20 2TB [B3072 Crediton—Holsworthy]: Attractive 16th-c thatched pub under new family management, enjoyable reasonably priced food, local ales tapped from casks, open-plan low-beamed bar, log fires, music and quiz nights; garden with play area, picturesque village *(D P and M A Miles)*

SAMPFORD PEVERELL [ST0314]

☆ *Globe* EX16 7BJ [a mile from M5 junction 27, village signed from Tiverton turn-off; Lower Town]: Spacious comfortable village pub backing on to Grand Western Canal, popular with walkers and locals, enjoyable good value home-made food from sandwiches to massive mixed grill and popular carvery (Fri and Sat evenings, all day Sun, Mon lunch), breakfast (8-11am), coffee and cream teas, seven well kept ales inc Cotleigh, Exmoor and Otter (Nov beer festival), good wine choice, friendly efficient staff, cosy beamed lounge with boothed eating area, back restaurant; big-screen sports TV in bar, piped music; children and dogs welcome, disabled facilities, courtyard and enclosed garden with play equipment, six bedrooms, open all day *(Adrian and Dawn Collinge, Tony Hobden, LYM)*

SANDFORD [SS8202]

☆ *Lamb* EX17 4LW [The Square]: Relaxed homely local with small choice of good reasonably priced interesting food (bar snacks all day – from 9.30 wkdys), well kept O'Hanlons Royal Oak and Palmers Copper, village farm cider, good value wines by the glass, friendly efficient service, cheery regulars, sofas by log fire, fresh flowers, daily papers, books and magazines, skittle alley/cinema – live music here too (last Fri of month); dogs very welcome (they have their own), tables in attractive sheltered garden, three bedrooms, generous breakfast, open all day *(Kate Wheeldon, BB)*

SANDY PARK [SX7189]

☆ *Sandy Park Inn* TQ13 8JW [A382 Whiddon Down—Moretonhampstead]: Friendly little thatched inn, snug bars, beams, varnished built-in wall settles around nice tables, high stools by counter, Otter, St Austell Tribute and guest beers, food from good sandwiches up, small dining room on left, inner private room; children and dogs welcome, big garden with fine views and smokers' shelter, open all day *(LYM, R T and J C Moggridge, Mr and Mrs R A Saunders, Jane Hudson)*

SCORRITON [SX7068]

Tradesmans Arms TQ11 0JB: Open-plan Dartmoor-edge pub with newish owners and friendly staff, good choice of ales, locally

sourced food, wonderful rolling hill views from conservatory and garden *(Geoff and Marianne Millin)*

SHALDON [SX9371]

☆ *Ness House* TQ14 0HP [Ness Drive]: Updated Georgian hotel on Ness headland overlooking Teign estuary, comfortable nautical-theme bar, mixed furniture on bare boards, log fire, Badger ales and decent wines by the glass, young friendly well trained staff, enjoyable if pricey food in narrow beamed restaurant or small conservatory, afternoon tea; no dogs; children welcome, disabled facilities, terrace with lovely views, back garden picnic-sets, nine bedrooms, open all day *(Mrs C Farley, Mr and Mrs Martin Tomlinson, B and M Kendall)*

SIDBURY [SY4097]

Hare & Hounds EX10 0QQ [A375/B3174]: Wide choice of well priced food from sandwiches up inc good daily carvery, friendly efficient service even though busy, Otter and Branscombe ales; no children in bar, marquee extension and seats in garden *(George Atkinson)*

SILVERTON [SS9503]

Lamb EX5 4HZ [Fore St]: Flagstoned local with changing ales inc Exe Valley tapped from the cask, enjoyable pubby food, friendly landlord, separate eating area; handy for Killerton (NT), open all day Thurs-Sun *(the Didler, Nigel and Sue Foster)*

SLAPTON [SX8245]

☆ *Queens Arms* TQ7 2PN: Neatly modernised one-room village local with welcoming landlady, good inexpensive straightforward local food, well kept Dartmoor, Otter and Teignworthy, snug comfortable corners, World War II mementoes, dominoes and draughts; parking needs skill; children and dogs welcome, lots of tables in lovely sun-trap stepped garden *(Donna and Roger, Roger Wain-Heapy, MP, Julian Distin, Simon Foster)*

SOURTON [SX5390]

☆ *Highwayman* EX20 4HN [A386, S of junction with A30]: A fantasy of dimly lit stonework and flagstone-floored burrows and alcoves, all sorts of things to look at, one room a make-believe sailing galleon; local farm cider (perhaps a real ale in summer), organic wines, good proper sandwiches or pasties, friendly chatty service, nostalgic piped music; outside fairy-tale pumpkin house and an old-lady-who-lived-in-the-shoe house – children allowed to look around pub but can't stay inside; period bedrooms with four-posters and half-testers, bunkrooms for walkers/cyclists *(Andrea Rampley, the Didler, LYM)*

SOUTH BRENT [SX6960]

Royal Oak TQ10 9BE [Station Rd]: Popular traditional and modern food, three well kept local ales, good choice of wines by the glass, welcoming helpful service, comfortable open-plan bar with some leather sofas, restaurant; children and dogs welcome, small courtyard, five good new bedrooms *(Dr and Mrs John Fripp)*

SOUTH MOLTON [SS7125]

George EX36 3AB [Broad St]: Refurbished centrally positioned former coaching inn, well kept Jollyboat and St Austell ales in friendly compact bar, enjoyable bar and restaurant food, popular live music wknds; nine comfortable bedrooms *(Mr and Mrs Martin Tomlinson)*

SOUTH POOL [SX7740]

Millbrook TQ7 2RW [off A379 E of Kingsbridge]: Charming little creekside pub with more of a bistro flavour at night, dining area off cheerful compact bar, good food from generous if not cheap lunchtime crab sandwiches up, well kept ales such as Palmers and South Hams tapped from the cask, local farm cider, log fires, no piped music; children welcome, covered seating and heaters for front courtyard and waterside terrace *(LYM, Diana Hunt, Simon Foster, Mrs Mary Woods)*

SOUTH ZEAL [SX6593]

Oxenham Arms EX20 2JT [off A30/A382]: Stately interesting 12th-c building doing well under new management, elegant mullioned windows and Stuart fireplaces in partly panelled and beamed front bar, small beamed inner room with open fire and remarkable old monolith, well kept ales tapped from the cask, quite a few wines by the glass, enjoyable food, contemporary dining room; imposing garden with lovely views, seven bedrooms *(Michael B Griffith, Viv Jameson, Phil and Sally Gorton, Andrea Rampley, LYM)*

ST GILES ON THE HEATH [SX3690]

Pint & Post PL15 9SA [A388]: Pretty 18th-c thatched pub, small bar with a well kept ale such as Skinners Betty Stogs, cheery locals, good pubby food in intimate dining room with woodburner; children welcome *(Giles and Annie Francis)*

☆ **STAPLE CROSS** [ST0320]

☆ *Staplecross Inn* TA21 0NH [Holcombe Rogus—Hockworthy]: Thoroughly Exmoor atmosphere in simply renovated village pub, short choice of well cooked locally sourced food, Butcombe, Otter and a guest beer, three linked rooms with quarry tiles, stripped stone and huge woodburners in capacious fireplaces; opens 4 wkdys, open all day wknds, cl Mon *(BB, John and Fiona McIlwain, Anthony Longden)*

STICKLEPATH [SX6494]

☆ *Devonshire* EX20 2NW [off A30 at Whiddon Down or Okehampton]: Warmly welcoming licensees in old-fashioned 16th-c thatched village local next to foundry museum, low-beamed slate-floor bar with big log fire, longcase clock and easy-going old furnishings, key collection, sofa in small snug, well kept low-priced ales tapped from the cask, farm cider, good value sandwiches and home-made pasties from the Aga, games room, lively folk night (1st Sun of month); dogs welcome, good walks, bedrooms, open all day Fri and Sat *(Edward Leetham, LYM, Neil and Anita Christopher, Phil and Sally Gorton, the Didler, Ross Balaam)*

STOCKLAND [ST2404]

☆ *Kings Arms* EX14 9BS [Village signposted from A30 Honiton—Chard; and also, at every turning, from N end of Honiton High Street]: Thatched pub under new management – reports please; elegant dark-beamed bar divided by medieval oak screen, refectory tables and settles, huge stone fireplace, back flagstoned bar with cushioned benches and stools around heavy wooden tables, Exmoor, Otter and St Austell, cosy restaurant with inglenook and bread oven, skittle alley; front terrace, garden, bedrooms *(Michelle Gallagher, Shaun Holley, Jane Hudson, LYM, Mrs Blethyn Elliott)*

STOKE FLEMING [SX8648]

Green Dragon TQ6 0PX [Church St]: Popular friendly village pub with yachtsman landlord, well worn-in with beams and flagstones, boat pictures, cosy dogs and cats, snug with sofas and armchairs, grandfather clock, open fire, well kept Otter, Addlestone's and Aspall's ciders, good choice of wines by the glass, enjoyable reasonably priced food inc good fish soup; tables out on partly covered heated terrace *(John and Fiona Merritt, LYM, Richard Tilbrook, Guy Vowles, Mr and Mrs G Owens)*

STOKE GABRIEL [SX8457]

☆ *Church House* TQ9 6SD [off A385 just W of junction with A3022; Church Walk]: Friendly early 14th-c pub, lounge bar with fine medieval beam-and-plank ceiling, black oak partition wall, window seats cut into thick butter-coloured walls, huge log fireplace, ancient mummified cat, Bass, Hancocks HB and a guest beer, enjoyable good value homely food (steak and kidney pie a hot tip), little locals' bar; no children, piped music may obtrude, limited parking; dogs welcome in bar, picnic-sets on small front terrace, open all day *(Dr and Mrs M E Wilson, Richard Tilbrook, B J Harding, Mrs P Bishop, LYM)*

STRETE [SX8446]

Kings Arms TQ6 0RW [A379 SW of Dartmouth]: Unusual cross between village local and seafood restaurant, same good generous food in country-kitchen bar and more contemporary restaurant up steps, prompt friendly service, real ales, good wines by the glass; piped music; children and dogs welcome, back terrace and garden with views over Start Bay, open all day, cl Sun evening *(Roger Wain-Heapy, Wendy and Carl Dye, Alan Sutton, Guy Vowles, LYM, Richard and Sissel Harris)*

TALATON [SY0699]

Talaton Inn EX5 2RQ [former B3176 N of Ottery St Mary]: Simply modernised country pub dating from 16th c, roomy and comfortable timbered lounge bar and restaurant, very good inexpensive home-made food, good friendly service, well kept Otter and guests, fresh flowers and candles, large carpeted public bar, skittle alley, pool;

picnic-sets out in front *(Revd R P Tickle, Hamish Paterson, Jane Hudson)*

TAVISTOCK [SX4975]

Trout & Tipple PL19 0JS [A386 (Parkwood Rd) towards Okehampton]: Welcoming pub doing good food inc various trout dishes (nearby trout farm), well kept Dartmoor Jail and three quickly changing guest ales (Feb and Oct beer festivals), farmhouse cider, decent wines, interesting bar décor with fly-fishing theme, lots to look at, nice log fire, former stables dining room, upstairs games room; they ask to keep a credit card while you eat, car park across road; children and dogs welcome, terrace seating, cl Tues lunchtime *(David and Sue Smith, Mrs J King)*

TEIGNMOUTH [SX9372]

☆ *Ship* TQ14 8BY [Queen St]: Upper and lower decks like a ship, good friendly atmosphere, nice mix of locals, families and tourists, good reasonably priced food (all day in summer) especially simply cooked local fish and good Sun lunch, good obliging service, real ales inc Bass and Greene King Abbot, interesting wine list, fresh coffee, gallery restaurant; open all day, fine floral displays, lovely quayside setting, beautiful views *(B and F A Hannam)*

TOPSHAM [SX9688]

Exeter Inn EX3 0DY [High St]: Well run 17th-c local with friendly chatty landlord, well kept Teignworthy Beachcomber and interesting guests, farm ciders, long bar and front area with pool, reasonable prices; big-screen sports TV; bedrooms, open all day *(the Didler)*

☆ *Globe* EX3 0HR [Fore St; 2 miles from M5 junction 30]: Substantial traditional inn dating from 16th c, welcoming chatty landlord, six west country ales in heavy-beamed bow-windowed bar (popular with locals), good interesting home-made food from sandwiches and snacks up, good value house wines, friendly helpful service, log-effect gas fire, compact dining lounge, restaurant, nice relaxed atmosphere; children in eating areas, well priced attractive bedrooms, parking can be tricky, open all day *(Barry Steele-Perkins, LYM, Les and Norma Haydon, the Didler, George Atkinson, Adrian and Dawn Collinge, Alissa Delbarre)*

☆ *Lighter* EX3 0HZ [Fore St]: Big, busy well run pub looking out over quay, quickly served food from good sandwiches and light dishes to fresh fish, Badger ales, nautical décor, panelling and large central log fire, friendly staff, good children's area; games machines, piped music; lots of waterside tables outside – good bird views at half tide, handy for antiques centre *(Barry Steele-Perkins, Dr A J and Mrs Tompsett, Dr and Mrs M E Wilson, J D O Carter, the Didler, BB)*

Route 2 EX3 0JQ [Monmouth Hill]: Former Steam Packet reworked as café/bar and under same ownership as nearby Globe Hotel; local home-made food from breakfast on, several wines by the glass, ales such as Otter and Sharps Doom Bar, local ciders;

children welcome, three upstairs self-catering apartments, cycle hire (and repair), open 8-8, but later for live music (3rd Sat of month) *(LYM)*

TORQUAY [SX9265]

Buccaneer TQ1 3LN [Babbacombe Downs Rd]: Friendly open-plan pub with great sea views, well kept St Austell ales and guests, popular home-made food, darts and pool in games area, quiz nights; open all day *(the Didler)*

Crown & Sceptre TQ1 4QA [Petitor Rd, St Marychurch]: Friendly two-bar local in 18th-c stone-built beamed coaching inn, six or more mainstream and other changing ales, interesting naval memorabilia and chamber-pot collection, friendly long-serving landlord, basic good value lunchtime food (not Sun), snacks any time, live jazz (Tues), folk (Fri); dogs and children welcome, two gardens *(the Didler)*

Hole in the Wall TQ1 2AU [Park Lane, opp clock tower]: Ancient two-bar local nr harbour, good value usual food, several well kept ales inc Bays and Sharps, Blackawton cider, proper old-fashioned landlord and friendly service, smooth cobbled floors, low beams and alcoves, lots of nautical brassware, ship models, old local photographs, chamber-pots, restaurant/function room (band nights); some seats out at front, open all day *(Les and Norma Haydon, the Didler)*

TORRINGTON [SS4919]

☆ *Black Horse* EX38 8HN [High St]: Popular twin-gabled pub dating from 15th c, overhanging upper storeys, beams hung with stirrups, solid furniture, lounge with striking ancient black oak partition wall and a couple of attractive oak seats, back restaurant, generous food inc OAP lunchtime deals and good evening dishes, traditional Sun lunch, friendly service, Courage Best and Directors, John Smiths and two changing guests, darts and shove-ha'penny; piped music; children and dogs welcome, disabled access, three refurbished bedrooms, open all day summer, all day Fri and Sat winter *(Dave Irving, Jenny Huggins, LYM)*

Puffing Billy EX38 8JD [Old Station House, A386 NW]: Popular family pub in former station building on Tarka Trail walk/cycle route, done out in old Southern Railway colours; well kept real ale, decent wines and tasty good value food inc children's dishes, lots of train memorabilia and pictures, own carriage on short piece of track; dogs welcome, garden with pets corner *(Dave Irving, Jenny Huggins)*

TOTNES [SX8060]

Albert TQ9 5AD [Bridgetown]: Two-room roadside pub with low beams, flagstones, panelling and lots of knick-knacks, friendly landlord brewing own Bridgetown ales, good local atmosphere; neat garden *(the Didler)*

Bay Horse TQ9 5SP [Cistern St]: Popular traditional two-bar inn dating from 15th c, friendly landlord, good value home-made food, well kept Dartmoor, Otter, Sharps and guests, regular beer festivals; piped music, live jazz (last Sun of month); garden, nice bedrooms, open all day *(the Didler)*

☆ *Royal Seven Stars* TQ9 5DD [Fore St, The Plains]: Exemplary town-centre bar and coffee bar in well run civilised old hotel, warm and friendly, well kept ales such as Bays Gold, Courage Best, Princetown Jail and Sharps Doom Bar, enjoyable good value food all day from breakfast on, plenty of seating variety, pretty restaurant; heated tables out in front, river across busy main road, bedrooms, open all day *(the Didler, Mr and Mrs Martin Tomlinson, Bob Duxbury, BB, Roger Wain-Heapy)*

Rumour TQ9 5RY [High St]: Spotless up-to-date bar-bistro, well kept Greene King, Skinners and guests, bottled belgian beers, wide-ranging wines by the glass, local fruit juices, enjoyable food from pizzas to some enterprising dishes using local produce, bare-boards dining area with bentwood chairs and informal contemporary décor, good service; open all day *(the Didler)*

TRUSHAM [SX8582]

☆ *Cridford Inn* TQ13 0NR [off B3193 NW of Chudleigh, just N of big ARC works]: Interesting 14th-c pub run by enthusiastic licensees, Norman in parts, with UK's oldest domestic window, lots of stripped-stone, flagstones and stout timbers, inglenook woodburner, smart white leather bar seats, chic white-beamed restaurant, enjoyable food inc lovely puddings, good wine choice, well kept Teignworthy and seasonal ales; children in eating area, nice sunny terrace, letting cottages *(Mike Gorton, Di and Mike Gillam, Richard and Patricia Jefferson, LYM, Barry Steele-Perkins)*

TURNCHAPEL [SX4952]

Boringdon Arms PL9 9TQ [off A379 via Plymstock and Hooe; Boringdon Terr]: Spotless 18th-c pub at foot of cliffs and built back into them, friendly landlord and staff, six well kept mainly local ales, bargain lunchtime food, log fire in massive fireplace, nautical memorabilia; tables outside, bedrooms *(Andy and Carole Pritchard)*

Clovelly Bay PL9 9TB [Boringdon Rd]: Welcoming family-run waterside pub with great views across to Plymouth, good locally sourced food, well kept Sharps Doom Bar and St Austell Tribute, Addlestone's cider, good choice of wines, log fires, friendly community atmosphere; juke box; outside seating, five bedrooms *(John and Gloria Isaacs)*

TWO BRIDGES [SX6175]

Two Bridges Hotel PL20 6SW [B3357/B3212 across Dartmoor]: Rambling 18th-c hotel in protected central Dartmoor hollow, popular with walkers – boots and sticks left in porch, good choice of beers and wines, good food in bar and striking dining room *(D P and M A Miles, LYM)*

UMBERLEIGH [SS6024]

☆ *Rising Sun* EX37 9DU [A377 S of Barnstaple]: Civilised fishing inn with good

food from light dishes to fine steaks, friendly staff, real ales such as St Austell, good wines by the glass, farm cider, relaxed partly divided bar with woodburner, flagstones and lots of stuffed fish and fishing memorabilia, five River Taw salmon and sea trout beats; children and dogs welcome, tables outside, nine good bedrooms, open all day summer *(Mark Lange, Mark Flynn, LYM)*

WEARE GIFFARD [SS4722]

Cyder Press EX39 4QR: Welcoming modernised local in pretty village overlooking River Torridge, friendly licensees, three real ales, decent food inc Sun roasts, darts in public bar, separate dining area; handy for Tarka Trail, beautiful countryside *(Dave Irving, Jenny Huggins)*

WELCOMBE [SS2317]

☆ *Old Smithy* EX39 6HG [signed off A39 S of Hartland]: Cosy thatched pub with good enterprising food, well kept Sharps Doom Bar and two changing guests, good coffee, friendly buoyant atmosphere combining local and the surfing contingent in simple open-plan family bar with old dark wood tables and open fires, live music; children and dogs welcome, plenty of seats in pretty terraced garden, lovely setting by lane leading eventually to attractive rocky cove, open all day summer, normally cl wkdy lunchtime winter *(LYM, Quentin and Carol Williamson, Peter Thornton)*

WEMBWORTHY [SS6609]

☆ *Lymington Arms* EX18 7SA [Lama Cross]: Large early 19th-c beamed dining pub, clean and bright, with wide choice of reliably good food (not Sun evening or Mon) inc some interesting specials, good service from character landlady and friendly staff, well kept Dartmoor IPA and Sharps Doom Bar, Winkleigh farm cider, decent wines, comfortably plush seating and red tablecloths in partly stripped-stone bar, big back evening restaurant (not Sun or Mon); children welcome, picnic-sets outside, pleasant country setting, bedrooms *(Mrs P Sumner, Ron and Sheila Corbett, Mark Flynn, BB)*

WESTON [ST1400]

☆ *Otter* EX14 3NZ [off A373, or A30 at W end of Honiton bypass]: Big busy family pub with heavy low beams, enjoyable food from light dishes to substantial meals and good Sun carvery, OAP specials, cheerful helpful staff, Cotleigh and Otter, good log fire; piped music; children welcome, disabled access, picnic-sets on big lawn leading to River Otter, play area *(Philip Kingsbury, Bob and Margaret Holder, LYM)*

WESTWARD HO! [SS4329]

Village Inn EX39 1HU [Youngaton Rd]: Unassuming centrally positioned local, cosy bar with log fire and old photographs, inexpensive food from baguettes up inc two-course lunchtime bargains, Country Life and Otter ales, conservatory; pool; seats outside, pétanque, nr good beach and cliff walks, bedrooms *(Michael and Hilary Andrews)*

WIDECOMBE [SX7176]

Old Inn TQ13 7TA [B3387 W of Bovey Tracey]: Busy comfortably refurbished dining pub, large eating area and roomy side conservatory with central fire – get there before about 12.30 in summer to miss the coach-loads, enjoyable quickly served standard food, well kept beers; children and dogs welcome, nice garden with water features and pleasant terrace, great walks from this pretty moorland village *(Irene and Derek Flewin, LYM, Dr and Mrs M E Wilson, Chris and Angela Buckell, Mike and Mary Carter)*

WONSON [SX6789]

☆ *Northmore Arms* EX20 2JA [right of A382 on lane signed Throwleigh/Gidleigh over hump-back bridge, then left to Wonson; OS Sheet 191 map ref 674903]: Far from smart and a favourite with those who take to its idiosyncratic style (not everyone does); two simple old-fashioned rooms, log fire and woodburner, low beams and stripped stone, well kept Adnams, Cotleigh and Exe Valley tapped from the cask, good house wines, cheap plain food (all day Mon-Sat), darts and board games; children and dogs welcome, picnic-sets outside, bedrooms, beautiful remote walking country, normally open all day *(LYM, the Didler, Howard and Lorna Lambert)*

WOODLAND [SX7869]

☆ *Rising Sun* TQ13 7JT [village signed off A38 just NE of Ashburton, then pub usually signed, nr Combe Cross]: Surprisingly plush and expansive, with friendly attentive staff, wide choice of good food from open sandwiches to home-made pies and local seafood, well kept Dartmoor Jail and a local guest, good choice of wines by the glass, farm cider, beams and soft lighting, snug corner by log fire, family area, restaurant; children and dogs welcome, picnic-sets and play area in spacious garden, four comfortable good value bedrooms *(Donna and Roger, Barry Cross, LYM, J Hughes)*

LUNDY

LUNDY [SS1344]

☆ *Marisco* EX39 2LY: One of England's most isolated pubs (yet full every night), great setting, steep trudge up from landing stage, galleried interior with lifebelts and shipwreck salvage, two St Austell ales labelled for the island, its spring water on tap, good value house wines, welcoming staff, good basic food (all day from breakfast on) using island produce and lots of fresh seafood, open fire; no music, TV or machines; children welcome, tables outside, souvenir shop; doubles as general store for the island's few residents *(Dave Braisted)*

If a service charge is mentioned prominently on a menu or accommodation terms, you must pay it if service was satisfactory. If service is really bad, you are legally entitled to refuse to pay some or all of the service charge as compensation for not getting the service you might reasonably have expected.

Dorset

A good number of the Main Entries in this lovely county have charmingly traditional interiors and have happily escaped the increasingly ubiquitous trend for a misplaced modern leather sofa wherever it will fit. Indeed you'll find one of the country's most appealing unspoilt pubs here – the Square & Compass at Worth Matravers. Other well-preserved gems include the National Trust-owned Vine at Pamphill and the simple unchanging Digby Tap in Sherborne with its good value food and beer. New Main Entries this year include the handsome Stapleton Arms in Buckhorn Weston, the useful Coventry Arms in Corfe Mullen and the contemporarily styled Olive Branch in Wimborne Minster. The George at Chideock, much improved under its new licensees, finds itself reinstated this year. Pubs doing notably well at the moment take in the Brace of Pheasants at Plush and the Crown at Uploders. Of these, the smart but relaxed Brace of Pheasants with its good fresh local fish is our Dorset Dining Pub of the Year 2011. You'll find plenty of west country beer served at the Main Entries here; look out for the Dorset Brewing Co, Isle of Purbeck and Palmers which represent the Dorset brewers.

BUCKHORN WESTON   ST7524 MAP 2

Stapleton Arms ♀ ◖

Off A30 Shaftesbury—Sherborne via Kington Magna; Church Hill; SP8 5HS

Handsome old building, sizeable, civilised bar and separate dining room, good choice of real ales and wines by the glass, enjoyable food and friendly service; bedrooms

With a pillored entrance and elegant metal tables and chairs on york flagstones and gravel, this is an upmarket dining pub. The large bar is split almost into two by the glazed-in entrance lobby, and there are mulberry or green walls, slate flagstones, candles and bowls of lilies. To the left, two comfortable cushioned sofas face each other across a low wooden table in front of the log fire in its fine old stone fireplace, there's a table of magazines, and by the counter, some high bar stools and a nice little butchers' block table – just right for a quiet pint and a newspaper. To the right, a long L-shaped wall seat has sizeable cushions and there are plenty of farmhouse and pew chairs around wooden tables and a cosy spot with a sofa and leather pouffes. Drinks include Butcombe Bitter, Cheddar Ales Potholer, Moor Revival and a guest such as Church End Goats Milk on handpump, Cheddar Valley cider and decent wines by the glass; home-made pork pies and scotch eggs for sale. Off to the far left, the dark green dining room has church candles in the fireplace and attractive cushioned dining chairs around nice old dark wooden tables on coir carpeting; board games. We haven't heard from anyone who has stayed here but would expect the rooms to be very comfortable.

🍽 The daily changing seasonal menu (with locally sourced meats) includes dishes such as ploughman's, swede and sorrel soup, confit duck leg with spiced tomato chutney, charcuterie board, steamed mussels with chilli, ginger and coconut, griddled pork chop with sweet potato, rhubarb and ginger compote, sausages and mash, fried gurnard with cherry tomato and walnut butter, and puddings such as steamed treacle sponge, tiramisu with amaretto cream and a local cheeseboard. *Starters/Snacks: £4.50 to £8.00. Main Courses: £9.90 to £16.00. Puddings: £5.00 to £6.50*

Free house ~ Licensee Rupert Reeves ~ Real ale ~ Bar food (12-3, 6-10(9.30 Sun)) ~
Restaurant ~ (01963) 370396 ~ Children welcome ~ Dogs allowed in bar ~ Open 11-3, 6-11;
11-11 Sat; 12-10.30 Sun.~ Bedrooms: £72B/£120B

Recommended by Ian Malone, Samantha McGahan, Mark Flynn, Colin and Janet Roe

BURTON BRADSTOCK   SY4889   MAP 1

Three Horseshoes
Mill Street; DT6 4QZ

Cottagey thatched pub with welcoming staff and a full range of Palmers beers

With its traditional carpeted interior and busy atmosphere this old thatched place, just
400 yards away from Chesil Beach and the coastal path, is a useful stop. Its pleasant
low-ceilinged L-shaped bar has a woodburner, an array of pictures and local photos, and
there's a separate restaurant; piped music. Five Palmers beers are on handpump (kept
under light blanket pressure in winter), alongside several wines by the glass. Recently
refurbished, the suntrap back garden has a large partly covered terrace with outdoor
heaters.

🍴 **Generously served bar food features seasonally available local fish and game and
includes lunchtime sandwiches, soup, goats cheese and spinach tart, steak and ale pie,
and specials such as bass on crispy spinach or local wild rabbit; children's menu and
restaurant menu (booking advised at peak times).** *Starters/Snacks: £4.50 to £5.75. Main
Courses: £7.25 to £12.95. Puddings: £1.50 to £4.60*

Palmers ~ Tenant Paul Middlemast ~ Real ale ~ Bar food (12-2, 6-9) ~ Restaurant ~
(01308) 897259 ~ Children welcome ~ Dogs allowed in bar ~ Open 11am(12 Sun)-11pm(midnight Sat)

*Recommended by Michael Dandy, Bob and Margaret Holder, M G Hart, George Atkinson, John and Gloria Isaacs,
Jenny and Peter Lowater, Fred and Lorraine Gill*

CHETNOLE   ST6008   MAP 2

Chetnole Inn 🍺
Village signposted off A37 a few miles S of Yeovil; DT9 6NU

**Attractive, neatly kept country pub, beams and huge flagstones, country décor, real ales,
popular food and seats in back garden with ducks; bedrooms**

The bar at this nicely run beamed inn has a relaxed country kitchen feel with wheelback
chairs and pine tables on huge flagstones, old tools on lemon walls, masses of hops and
a woodburning stove. Friendly staff serve Otter Bitter and Sharps Doom Bar and a guest
such as Butcombe on handpump and 16 malt whiskies. Less traditional and much
frequented by the locals, the neatly kept snug has a couple of leather sofas close to an
open fire, darts, juke box, games machine and board games; skittle alley. The attractive
dining room has more wheelback chairs around pale wooden tables on stripped
floorboards, fresh flowers and linen napkins, and a small open fire. There are picnic-sets
in the delightful back garden (where they keep ducks) and a few out in front.

🍴 **Using their own duck eggs and local produce, the well liked bar food includes
lunchtime sandwiches, a good ploughman's, soup, local carpaccio, crab cakes with sweet
chilli dip, baked apples with goats cheese and walnut and red onion salad, fish pie,
sausage of the day and mash, steak and Guinness pie, butternut risotto, pork belly with
pork jus and caramelised onion mash, sirloin steak, and puddings such as Baileys crème
brûlée, lemon cheesecake and chocolate brownie with chocolate sauce.** *Starters/Snacks:
£4.25 to £7.00. Main Courses: £9.00 to £15.00. Puddings: £5.50 to £6.25*

Free house ~ Licensee Mike Lewin ~ Real ale ~ Bar food (12-2, 6.30(7 Sun)-9) ~ Restaurant ~
(01935) 872337 ~ Dogs allowed in bar ~ Open 12-2.30, 6.30(7 Sun)-11; cl Sun evening and
Mon in winter ~ Bedrooms: £60S/£95S

*Recommended by Paul and Annette Hallett, Eithne Dandy, Michael Dandy, Mrs A A Loukes, M G Hart,
Pat and Roger Davies*

CHIDEOCK

SY4292   MAP 1

George

A35 Bridport—Lyme Regis; DT6 6JD

Comfortably traditional local with well liked food

The warm friendly welcome and cosy low ceilinged carpeted bar at this pleasantly traditional thatched village pub are just what you'd hope for as a break from the busy A35. Warm log fires, brassware and pewter tankards hanging from dark beams, wood pews, long built-in tongue and groove wooden banquettes, tools on the cream walls and high shelves of bottles, plates and mugs lend an unchanged country feel. Stools are propped around a semicircular timbered counter that serves three Palmers beers on handpump; piped music and table skittles. A garden room opens on to a pretty walled garden and terrace with planted oak barrels and seating for a good number of people.

 Tasty bar food might include sandwiches, baguettes, ploughman's, cullen skink, scampi and chips, ham and eggs, thai fishcake, seafood pie, beef stroganoff, bass with pesto, scallops, tagliatelle carbonara, apple pie, sticky toffee pudding and crème brûlée. *Starters/Snacks: £4.95 to £7.95. Main Courses: £8.95 to £25.00. Puddings: £4.95 to £5.95*

Palmers ~ Tenants Paul and Jo Riddiough ~ Real ale ~ Bar food (12-2.15, 6.15-9; 12-2.30, 7-9 Sun) ~ Restaurant ~ (01297) 489419 ~ Children welcome ~ Dogs allowed in bar ~ Live music third Tues of the month ~ Open 11.30-3, 6-11; 11.30-11(11.30-3, 6-11 winter) Sat; 12-10.30(12-3, 7-10.30 winter) Sun; closed Sun evening Nov-March
Recommended by John Burgess, Dennis Jenkin, William Ruxton, Peter Salmon, David and Stella Martin, Bob Clucas

CHURCH KNOWLE

SY9381   MAP 2

New Inn ♀

Village signposted off A351 just N of Corfe Castle; BH20 5NQ

An attractive 16th-c pub with pleasantly furnished rooms and an inviting garden; well positioned for walks

This much enjoyed welcoming stone and partly thatched pub in the Purbecks takes considerable care over its food and wine. You can choose your wine (with help from the staff if you wish) from a tempting display in the walk-in wine cellar and there are several by the glass plus a wine of the month; apple juice from Herefordshire. Three real ales might include Dorset Jurassic, Greene King Old Speckled Hen and St Austell Tribute on handpump. Part of the fun here is the entertaining miscellany of bric-a-brac (including a stuffed hoopoe and a glass case with some interesting memorabilia such as ration books and Horlicks tablets). Two stone-walled areas are linked by an arch, with fireplaces at each end and a brick alcove that used to be the original farmhouse kitchen oven and are furnished with mixed old chairs and tables on red patterned carpets; disabled facilities; TV. You can camp in two fields behind (you must book) and there are fine surrounding walks and views from the good-sized garden.

 Bar food includes lunchtime sandwiches and ploughman's, with starters such as blue vinney soup, fried elvers, fried herring roe on toast, garlic vol-au-vent, main courses such as good steak and kidney pie, grilled sardines, grilled bream stuffed with ginger, lemon and rosemary, roast of the day, lasagne, curry, mediterranean vegetable quiche, steaks, and puddings such as maple and pecan cheesecake, spotted dick, lemon posset with shortbread biscuit and some unusual locally made ice-creams. *Starters/Snacks: £4.85 to £6.50. Main Courses: £8.50 to £14.95. Puddings: £4.95 to £5.50*

Punch ~ Tenants Maurice and Rosemary Estop ~ Real ale ~ Bar food (12-2.15, 6-9.15) ~ Restaurant ~ (01929) 480357 ~ Children welcome ~ Open 11(12 Sun)-3, 6-11
Recommended by Adrian Johnson, Phil and Jane Hodson, R and S Bentley, Mike and Sue Loseby, Adrian and Dawn Collinge, Tony Brace, Barrie and Mary Crees, Robert Watt, James A Waller

---

Post Office address codings confusingly give the impression that some pubs are in Dorset, when they're really in Somerset (which is where we list them).

CORFE MULLEN
SY9798 MAP 2

Coventry Arms
A31 W of Wimborne; Mill Street; BH21 3RH

Interestingly furnished roadside pub open for breakfast with four connected bars and dining rooms, good, popular food, and welcoming staff; seats in streamside garden

Extremely well run by friendly, helpful staff, this popular roadside pub was filling up fast on our early lunchtime visit – they also usefully open for breakfast, too. There are plenty of signs inside the 15th-c heart but the four dining areas and bar have been interestingly furnished and decorated in a shabby-chic style. There's all manner of seating throughout from a high-backed curved settle and a pew with scatter cushions, wooden, cushioned and high-backed black leather dining chairs, library and small bentwood chairs and a cloth-upholstered sofa, and tables of every size and shape on flagstones or parquet flooring. A prized seat is the cushioned settle beside both the bar counter and the fire with a pretty carved table in front of it. Decorations include a stag's head, several stuffed fish, a goose in a glass cabinet, lots of bottles and flagons, cigarette cards, a shelf of guidebooks and a mummified cat found in the roof (traditionally thought to ward off evil spirits). Timothy Taylors Landlord and a guest such as Fullers London Pride are tapped from cooled casks and a good choice of wines are served by the glass. Outside, the terrace has tables and chairs, there are picnic-sets on grass, and ducks on the River Stour.

🍴 As well as sandwiches, bar food includes ham hock and game terrine, fried herring roes with hollandaise sauce, haddock and salmon fishcakes, smoked chicken and bacon salad, cottage pie of local venison, lentil and root vegetable casserole, lamb shank with herb mash, braised pork belly with port gravy, grilled pork loin chop, steaks, and puddings such as blueberry cheesecake and bread and butter pudding; choice of Sunday roasts. *Starters/Snacks: £5.00 to £8.00. Main Courses: £9.00 to £20.00. Puddings: £5.25*

Enterprise ~ Lease John Hugo ~ Real ale ~ Bar food ~ Restaurant ~ (01258) 857284 ~ Children welcome ~ Dogs welcome ~ Open 8-3, 5.30-11; 9am-11pm Sat, Sun
Recommended by Mike and Shelley Woodroffe, Mrs Mary Woods, Mr and Mrs W W Burke

FARNHAM
ST9515 MAP 2

Museum 🍴 ▽ 🛏
Village signposted off A354 Blandford Forum—Salisbury; DT11 8DE

Stylish civilised inn with appealing rooms including a bustling bar, inventive if not cheap food and super bedrooms

Distinctly upmarket, this thatched free house has an excellent choice of wines with several by the glass, Ringwood Best Bitter and Wadworths Henry's along with a guest such as Timothy Taylors Landlord on handpump and around 30 malt whiskies. The little flagstoned bar remains a real focus for locals of all ages and has a lively atmosphere, light beams, a big inglenook fireplace, good comfortably cushioned furnishings and fresh flowers on all the tables; board games. Cheery yellow walls and plentiful windows give the place a bright, fresh feel. To the right, a dining room has a fine antique dresser, while off to the left a cosier room has a very jolly hunting model and a seemingly sleeping stuffed fox curled in a corner. Another room feels rather like a contemporary baronial hall, soars up to a high glass ceiling, with dozens of antlers and a stag's head looking down on a long refectory table and church-style pews. This leads to an outside terrace with more wooden tables. The bedrooms in the main building are very comfortable.

🍴 Lunchtime bar food (no sandwiches but some pubby dishes) might include goats cheese and roast fig with chicory and walnuts, fish and chips, sausage and red onion gravy and burger with seared foie gras, while in the evening (dishes are carefully compiled and interesting if not cheap) you choose from the restaurant menu which might have starters such as leek and potato soup, crab tortellini, seared lyme bay scallops with smoked haddock kedgeree, parsnip foam and crispy shallots, main courses such as slow-roasted gloucester old spot pork belly with cider jus and grain mustard mash, roast tikka

cod loin with coconut purée, spiced yellow peas and onion bhaji, blue cheese hash brown, fried duck breast with wild garlic, pearl barley and port jus, well hung sirloin steak, and a couple of puddings such as rice pudding with poached pear and raspberry jam.
Starters/Snacks: £6.00 to £11.00. Main Courses: £12.00 to £22.00. Puddings: £5.50 to £8.50

Free house ~ Licensee David Sax ~ Real ale ~ Bar food ~ Restaurant (Fri and Sat evening and Sun lunch) ~ (01725) 516261 ~ Children must be over 10 in restaurant ~ Dogs allowed in bar and bedrooms ~ Open 12-3, 6(7 Sun)-11 ~ Bedrooms: £100S(£125B)/£110S(£135B)

Recommended by P Waterman, Cathryn and Richard Hicks, Neil and Karen Dignan, Julia and Richard Tredgett, Mr and Mrs W W Burke, John and Enid Morris

MIDDLEMARSH

ST6607 MAP 2

Hunters Moon
A352 Sherborne—Dorchester; DT9 5QN

Plenty of bric-a-brac in several linked areas, reasonably priced food and a good choice of drinks

The comfortably traditional beamed interior at this former coaching inn is cosily filled with a great variety of tables and chairs on red patterned carpets, an array of ornamentation from horsebrasses up, and softly lit by converted oil lamps. Booths are formed by some attractively cushioned settles, walls comprise exposed brick, stone and some panelling and there are three log fires (one in a capacious inglenook); piped music, children's books and toys and board games. Drinks include Butcombe Bitter and a couple of guests such as Sharps Betty Stoggs and Doom Bar on handpump and farm cider, while all their wines are available by the glass. A neat lawn has circular picnic-sets as well as the more usual ones, and the ensuite bedrooms are in what was formerly a skittle alley and stable block. More up-to-date reports please, particularly on the food.

🍴 Bar food includes lunchtime filled baguettes and bloomers, portland scallops, a wide choice of steaks, pizza, baked potatoes and pasta, pub classics such as scampi, lasagne and slow-roasted lamb shank, battered cod, and daily specials like pheasant or venison. Many main dishes are offered in smaller or larger helpings to suit different appetites. Among the puddings are a cheesecake of the day, dorset apple cake and bakewell tart.
Starters/Snacks: £3.95 to £6.45. Main Courses: £4.95 to £15.45. Puddings: £4.45 to £5.25

Enterprise ~ Lease Dean and Emma Mortimer ~ Real ale ~ Bar food ~ (01963) 210966 ~ Children welcome ~ Dogs welcome ~ Open 10.30-2.30, 6-11(10.30 in winter); 10.30-10.30(11 Sat in summer) weekends Sat; 10.30-10.30 Sun ~ Bedrooms: £60S/£70S

Recommended by Mike and Sue Loseby

MUDEFORD

SZ1792 MAP 2

Ship in Distress
Stanpit; off B3059 at roundabout; BH23 3NA

Wide choice of fish dishes, quirky nautical décor and friendly staff in cheerful cottage

Stashed with all manner of nautical bits and pieces, the interior of this former smugglers' pub is thoroughly good fun and much more enjoyable than the unassuming exterior suggests. There's everything from rope fancywork and brassware through lanterns, oars, ceiling nets and ensigns, to an aquarium, boat models (we particularly like the Mississippi steamboat), and the odd piratical figure; darts, games machine, board games, a big screen TV and piped music. Besides a good few boat pictures, the room on the right has tables with masses of snapshots of locals caught up in various waterside japes under the glass tabletops; Ringwood Best and guests such as Adnams Broadside, Dorset Jurassic and Brains Rev James are served on handpump alongside several wines by the glass. A spreading two-room restaurant area, as cheerful in its way as the bar, has a lobster tank, contemporary works by local artists for sale, and a light-hearted mural sketching out the impression of a window open on a sunny boating scene. There are tables out on the suntrap back terrace and a covered area for smokers.

🍴 Enjoyable fresh local fish and seafood are the thing here, although there are also meat and vegetarian options: reasonably priced bar food includes sandwiches, cottage pie, scampi, a pint of prawns and cod and chips, as well as more expensive à la carte offerings (which you can eat in the bar or in the restaurant) such as fish soup, moules marinière, dover sole, crab and lobster. *Starters/Snacks: £5.95 to £6.95. Main Courses: £6.95 to £10.95. Puddings: £4.50*

Punch ~ Lease Maggie Wheeler ~ Real ale ~ Bar food ~ Restaurant ~ (01202) 485123 ~ Children welcome ~ Dogs allowed in bar ~ Open 11am–midnight(11pm Sun)

Recommended by N R White, Victor Craven, Hans Becker, JDM, KM, I D Barnett, Graham Oddey

NETTLECOMBE   SY5195   MAP 2

Marquis of Lorne 🍺

Off A3066 Bridport—Beaminster, via West Milton; DT6 3SY

Tasty food and beer in well positioned country pub with large, mature garden

The countryside surrounding this homely place is particularly beautiful and Eggardon Hill, one of Dorset's most spectacular Iron Age hill forts with views over the coast and surrounding countryside, is within walking distance. A lovely big mature garden is full of pretty herbaceous borders, with picnic-sets under apple trees and a rustic-style play area. Inside, the traditional bars and dining rooms are named after local hills. The comfortable bustling main bar has a log fire, mahogany panelling and old prints and photographs around its neatly matching chairs and tables; two dining areas lead off, the smaller of which has another log fire. The wooden-floored snug (liked by locals) has board games and table skittles; TV and piped music. Three real ales from Palmers are well kept on handpump and they've a decent wine list with a dozen by the glass.

🍴 In addition to tasty sandwiches, filled baguettes and ploughman's, bar food includes starters such as chicken liver, pork and port pâté, goats cheese tart or local scallops with risotto, parmesan and basil dressing, and main courses like battered cod, roast chicken with stilton sauce, local fish specials and several vegetarian options such as vegetable lasagne; puddings include a crumble or pie of the day and local ice-creams. *Starters/Snacks: £4.80 to £7.50. Main Courses: £8.95 to £16.95. Puddings: £3.95 to £4.80*

Palmers ~ Tenants David and Julie Woodroffe ~ Real ale ~ Bar food (12-2, 6.30-9) ~ Restaurant ~ (01308) 485236 ~ No children under 10 in bedrooms ~ Dogs allowed in bar ~ Open 12-2.30, 6.30-11.30; 12-3, 6.30-11 Sun; 6.30-10.30 in winter ~ Bedrooms: £50B/£90S(£90B)

Recommended by Yana Pocklington, Patricia Owlett, Mr P Avery, Steve Derbyshire, Mike and Lynn Robinson, Ian Malone, Jenny and Peter Lowater, Fred and Lorraine Gill

PAMPHILL   ST9900   MAP 2

Vine 🍺

Off B3082 on NW edge of Wimborne: turn on to Cowgrove Hill at Cowgrove signpost, then turn left up Vine Hill along avenue of trees; BH21 4EE

Charming and unchanging, run by the same family for years

Run by the same family for three generations but actually owned by the National Trust as part of the Kingston Lacy estate, this tiny place is splendidly old-fashioned and will appeal to people who like simpler pubs. Of its two tiny bars one, with a warm coal-effect gas fire, has only three tables, the other just half a dozen or so seats on its lino floor, some of them huddling under the narrow wooden stairs that lead to an upstairs games room; darts and board games. Local photographs (look out for the one of the regular with his giant pumpkin) and notices decorate the painted panelling; quiet piped music. Two real ales served on handpump or from the cask usually feature Fullers London Pride and a guest from a brewer such as Goddards or Otter; local cider and a selection of foreign bottled beers. There are picnic-sets and benches out on a sheltered gravel terrace and more share a fairy-lit, heated verandah with a grapevine. Round the back, a grassy area with tables has a climbing frame; outside lavatories. The National Trust estate includes

Kingston Lacy house and the huge Badbury Rings Iron Age hill fort (itself good for wild flowers), and there are many paths.

🍴 **Lunchtime bar snacks such as good, fresh sandwiches and ploughman's.** *Starters/Snacks: £2.50 to £5.00*

Free house ~ Licensee Mrs Sweatland ~ Real ale ~ Bar food (12-2) ~ No credit cards ~ (01202) 882259 ~ Children welcome away from bar ~ Dogs welcome ~ Open 11(12 Sun)-3, 7-10.30(11 Thurs-Sat)

Recommended by Pete Baker, Theocsbrian, N R White, the Didler, Richard and Anne Ansell, Mr and Mrs P D Titcomb

PLUSH

ST7102   MAP 2

Brace of Pheasants 🍴 🛏

Village signposted from B3143 N of Dorchester at Piddletrenthide; DT2 7RQ
DORSET DINING PUB OF THE YEAR

Fairly smart but relaxed 16th-c thatched pub with friendly service and decent garden; good nearby walks

This rather nice place is tucked away in a pretty village and is very much the centre of village life with plenty of friendly locals (and their dogs) popping in. The cosy beamed bar has good solid tables, windsor chairs, fresh flowers, a huge heavy-beamed inglenook at one end with cosy seating inside, and a good warming log fire at the other. Palmers Copper and Sharps Doom Bar and a local guest such as Yeovil Star Gazer are tapped from the cask; there's a good choice of wines with 18 by the glass and farm cider on draught; friendly service. A decent-sized garden includes a terrace and a lawn sloping up towards a rockery. The pub is well placed for walks in beautifully folded countryside – an attractive bridleway behind goes to the left of the woods and over to Church Hill. The ensuite bedrooms are nicely fitted out and comfortable.

🍴 **Local fish is usually on the enjoyable menu which might include fried local scallops with black pudding and chilli sauce, fried lambs kidneys with mustard cream sauce, warm roast red pepper, goats cheese and thyme tart, liver and bacon, caesar salad, skate wing with lemon and ginger butter and roast cherry tomatoes, garlic and herb marinated venison steak with red wine reduction, and puddings such as vanilla panna cotta with marinated baby figs and apple crumble and ice-cream.** *Starters/Snacks: £4.00 to £8.00. Main Courses: £10.00 to £16.00. Puddings: £5.00 to £6.00*

Free house ~ Licensees Phil and Carol Bennett ~ Real ale ~ Bar food ~ Restaurant ~ (01300) 348357 ~ Children welcome ~ Dogs allowed in bar ~ Open 12-3, 7-11; 12-4 Sun; closed Sun evening and all day Mon ~ Bedrooms: £85B/£95B

Recommended by James A Waller, the Didler, Gerry and Rosemary Dobson, John Sleigh, Dr and Mrs J Temporal, G Vyse, Mike and Sue Loseby, Col and Mrs Patrick Kaye, Mr and Mrs John Clifford, Tom and Rosemary Hall, D and J Ashdown, N R White, Phil Bryant, Colin and Janet Roe

POOLE

SZ0391   MAP 2

Cow 🍷

Station Road, Ashley Cross, Parkstone; beside Parkstone Station; BH14 8UD

Interesting open-plan pub with contemporary décor, good modern food, and fine wines

The pale walls of this airy bistro bar are hung with big modern cow prints done in bright pinks, yellows and blues. Squashy sofas with huge colourful cushions and leather seating cubes are arranged at low tables on stripped wood floors, and an exposed brick chimney has an open fire. Fullers London Pride, Isle of Purbeck IPA, Ringwood Best and Rugby Sidestep are on handpump, and an extensive wine list has a dozen wines by the glass and many remarkable bottles; discreet flat screen TV in one corner, piped music, board games and a good array of newspapers. In the evening you can eat very well in the sizeable bistro where there are more heavy stripped tables on bare boards and plenty of wine bottles lining the window sills. Seats outside are on an enclosed and heated terrace area.

🍴 From a sensibly short menu, good modern lunchtime bar food includes starters such as warm duck rillette with kohlrabi rémoulade, poached egg and honey jus, pear and blue cheese tatin with chicory salad, main courses such as cod and chips with mushy peas, minted lamb casserole, steak and ale pie, bass fillet with shrimp risotto and sorrel cream, and puddings such as dark chocolate truffle torte and coconut crème brûlée with coconut confit. *Starters/Snacks: £5.50 to £10.50. Main Courses: £10.50 to £17.50. Puddings: £6.00 to £6.50*

Free house ~ Licensee David Sax ~ Real ale ~ Bar food (12-2.30, 7-9.30; not Sun evening) ~ Restaurant ~ (01202) 749569 ~ Children allowed until 7.30pm ~ Dogs allowed in bar ~ Open 11-11.30; 12-midnight Sat; 12-10.30 Sun
Recommended by JDM, KM, Mr and Mrs W W Burke

POWERSTOCK
SY5196 MAP 2

Three Horseshoes ♀
Off A3066 Beaminster—Bridport via West Milton; DT6 3TF

Friendly inn in fine countryside with imaginative food and a fair choice of drinks; walks nearby

Taken over by a nicely sincere new landlord since the last edition of the *Guide*, this welcoming village pub has been enjoyed in the past for its tasty food and we're hoping the same will be true under the new owner. It's set very much in deepest Dorset in a village snuggled into back lanes far from any major town, and in fine walking country. The traditional L-shaped bar has good log fires, magazines and newspapers to read, stripped panelling, country furniture including settles, Palmers Copper and IPA on handpump, and several wines by the glass served by friendly staff. There are local paintings for sale in the dining room; piped music and board games. Smart teak seats and tables under large parasols on the back terrace (steps down to it) have a lovely uninterrupted view and there's a big sloping garden. Two of the bedrooms have fine valley views.

🍴 Cooked by the landlord/chef, enterprising food typically includes sandwiches, wild boar and quail scotch egg, crispy pigs cheeks with fried quails eggs and brown shrimps, ham, egg and chips, venison sausages with onion gravy, wild boar pasties, battered cod with chunky tartare, pearl barley risotto with spinach, mushrooms and dorset blue vinney, steak with roasted bone marrow crust and pepper sauce, and puddings such as apple and berry crumble and lemon parfait with ginger biscuit and berries. *Starters/Snacks: £6.00 to £8.00. Main Courses: £10.00 to £20.00. Puddings: £5.00 to £6.00*

Palmers ~ Tenants Karl Bashford and Suzanna Prekopova ~ Real ale ~ Bar food (12-2.30, 6-9.30) ~ (01308) 485328 ~ Children welcome ~ Dogs welcome ~ Open 12-3, 6.30-11 ~ Bedrooms: /£75B
Recommended by G Vyse, Iain Jones, Steve Derbyshire, SRD, George Atkinson

SHERBORNE
ST6316 MAP 2

Digby Tap 🍺 £
Cooks Lane; park in Digby Road and walk round corner; DT9 3NS

Regularly changing ales in simple alehouse, open all day, very inexpensive beer and food

Readers have been delighted at the offer of a pint of beer for just £2 at this chatty tavern in a back street just moments away from Sherborne Abbey. A rather timeless gem, its simple flagstoned bar is full of chatty character and continues beautifully unchanged over the decades. The range of reasonably priced beers include Sharps Cornish Coaster or Otter Bitter and three guests from local brewers such as Cottage, Moles and Yeovil; several wines by the glass and malt whiskies. A little games room has pool and a quiz machine and there's a TV room. There are some seats outside.

🍴 Good value, straightforward lunchtime food includes sandwiches, filled baguettes and baked potatoes, ham, egg and chips, chilli beef and maybe liver and bacon, mixed grill or plaice stuffed with prawns; no puddings. *Starters/Snacks: £1.95 to £5.25*

Free house ~ Licensees Oliver Wilson and Nick Whigham ~ Real ale ~ Bar food (12-1.45, not Sun)
~ No credit cards ~ (01935) 813148 ~ Children welcome ~ Dogs welcome ~ Open 11-11; 12-11 Sun
Recommended by Michael Dandy, Michael B Griffith, Phil and Sally Gorton, Mike and Sue Losebey, Maurice Ricketts

SHROTON

ST8512   MAP 2

Cricketers ♀ ■ 🛏

Off A350 N of Blandford (village also called Iwerne Courtney); follow signs; DT11 8QD

Well run pub with neatly uniformed and friendly staff, well liked food and lots of wines by the glass; walks and nice views nearby

This friendly early 20th-c red brick pub sits right on the Wessex Ridgeway and is overlooked by the formidable Iron Age grassy ramparts of Hambledon Hill which gradually descends down to become the village cricket pitch in front of the pub. The bright divided bar has good quality old furniture, a big stone fireplace, alcoves and cricketing memorabilia and is kept pubby with beers from breweries such as Butcombe, Otter, Piddle and St Austell; new world wine list; good friendly service from the attentive licensee couple and their uniformed staff. The comfortable back restaurant overlooks the garden and has a fresh neutral décor; piped music, TV. The garden is secluded and pretty with big sturdy tables under cocktail parasols, well tended shrubs and a well stocked (and well used) herb garden by the kitchen door. Walkers are welcome if they leave their walking boots outside.

🍴 As well as filled baguettes and ploughman's, the well liked bar food might include home-cured gravadlax, seasonal mussels from Poole Harbour, sharing platters, battered cod, king prawn and scallop stir fry, mediterranean couscous salad, lemon and herb chicken breast with tomato couscous, thai red duck curry and good roast pork belly with cider, apple and cream sauce, and puddings such as cheesecake, sticky toffee pudding and chocolate brownies; children can have half helpings from the main menu. *Starters/Snacks: £4.75 to £6.95. Main Courses: £8.95 to £12.95. Puddings: £4.95*

Heartstone Inns ~ Managers Andrew and Natasha Edwards ~ Real ale ~ Bar food (12-2.30, 6.30-9.30; not Sun evening) ~ Restaurant ~ (01258) 860421 ~ Children welcome ~ Open 12-3, 6-11; 12-11 Sat, Sun; 12-3, 6-11 Sat in winter ~ Bedrooms: £45S/£75S

Recommended by Colin and Janet Roe, Clare West, Stan Edwards, Robert Watt, Bruce and Penny Wilkie, George Atkinson

SYDLING ST NICHOLAS

SY6399   MAP 2

Greyhound 🍴 ♀ 🛏

Off A37 N of Dorchester; High Street; DT2 9PD

Genuinely welcoming staff, attractively presented food, good range of drinks and country décor in beamed rooms

This terrific pub in a classic Dorset village is a great all-rounder. The beamed and flagstoned serving area is airy and appealing with a big bowl of lemons and limes, a backdrop of gleaming bottles and copper pans, and plenty of bar stools, with more opposite arranged along a drinking shelf. On one side a turkey-carpeted area with a warm coal fire in a handsome portland stone fireplace has a comfortable mix of straightforward tables and chairs, and country decorations such as a stuffed fox eyeing a collection of china chickens and a few farm tools. At the other end, a cosy separate dining room with smart white table linen has some books and a glass-covered well set into its floor, and a garden room with succulents and other plants on its sills has simple modern café furniture. Sydling Bitter brewed for the pub by St Austell is on handpump along with Wadworths 6X and a guest such as Ringwood Fortyniner, 14 wines are sold by the glass and they've several malt whiskies; fairly unobtrusive piped music and board games. On Thursdays they now have a cocktail hour, with four different cocktails offered each week. The small front garden has a play area alongside its picnic-sets; bedrooms are in a separate block.

🍴 Accomplished, if not cheap, bar food features meat reared in Dorset and a range of fish including shellfish from Lyme Bay. As well as lunchtime sandwiches, filled baguettes and ploughman's, the menu might include starters such as pigeon breast with puy lentils, crispy pancetta and game sauce, seared scallops with pea shoots and white truffle oil, ham hock, black pudding and foie gras terrine with fig chutney and brioche toast, main courses such as pork belly with parsnip purée and roast apple, duck breast with mushroom risotto and crème fraiche, battered cod, bass fillets with chorizo, cherry tomatoes and basil flamed in sherry on steamed red chard, fish pie, and puddings such as dorset apple cake and poached pears in vanilla and white wine on cappuccino brûlée. *Starters/Snacks: £4.50 to £7.50. Main Courses: £9.95 to £16.95. Puddings: £4.95*

Free house ~ Licensees John Ford, Karen Trimby, Ron Hobson, Cherry Ball ~ Real ale ~ Bar food (12-2(3 Sun), 6.30-9) ~ Restaurant ~ (01300) 341303 ~ Children welcome ~ Dogs allowed in bar ~ Open 11-2.30, 6-11; 12-3 Sun; closed Sun evening ~ Bedrooms: /£70S(£80B)

Recommended by James A Waller, Tom McLean, John and Hilda Burns, John Wymer, Bruce Jamieson, Roy Fox, Dave Hollins, Lois Dyer, Dr A McCormick, M G Hart, T R and B C Jenkins, Ian and Deborah Carrington, Mr and Mrs W W Burke, P Waterman

TARRANT MONKTON   ST9408   MAP 2
Langton Arms 🍴 🛏
Village signposted from A354, then head for church; DT11 8RX

Fresh flowers in light rooms, attractive bistro, good children's play area and comfortable bedrooms

Run by a particularly welcoming couple, this updated 17th-c thatched dining inn is next to the church in a charming village (with a ford that can flow quite fast in wet weather) that makes a useful base for walks or pottering around the area. Hung with loads of old black and white photos, the beamed bar has flagstone floors, a light oak counter with recessed lighting, fresh flowers on the wooden tables, and three (usually local) beers such as Palmers, Piddle and Ringwood on handpump; TV in the public bar. The bistro restaurant is in an attractively reworked barn and the skittle alley doubles as a family room during the day; piped music. Dogs are allowed only in the Carpenters Bar and in the comfortable ensuite bedrooms (in a modern block at the back). In fine weather, you can sit at picnic-sets outside and there's a wood-chip children's play area.

🍴 Using some local ingredients, food includes sandwiches, ploughman's, sharing platters, starters such as fig and parma ham salad, gravadlax and baked avocado with blue cheese, main courses such as venison and boar sausages with apple mash and red wine gravy, thai green chicken curry, steak or game pie, battered haddock, red snapper fillet on wilted spinach with coconut cream, confit pork belly with herb butter stuffing and wrapped in parma ham with cider mustard mash and red wine jus, spinach and ricotta cannelloni, rib-eye steak, and puddings such as treacle tart and apple and mixed berry crumble, and a good west country cheeseboard. *Starters/Snacks: £4.95 to £8.95. Main Courses: £8.95 to £17.95. Puddings: £5.95 to £8.95*

Free house ~ Licensees Barbara and James Cossins ~ Real ale ~ Bar food (12-2.30, 6-9(10 Fri); 12-10(9 Sun) Sat) ~ Restaurant ~ (01258) 830225 ~ Children welcome ~ Dogs allowed in bar and bedrooms ~ Open 11.30-midnight; 12-10.30 Sun ~ Bedrooms: £70B/£90B

Recommended by Robert Watt, James A Waller, Mark Sykes, Leslie and Barbara Owen, Rob and Catherine Dunster, Mr and Mrs P R Thomas, Roy and Jean Russell

UPLODERS   SY5093   MAP 2
Crown
Village signposted off A35 E of Bridport; DT6 4NU

Homely, low-beamed village pub with log fires and inviting atmosphere

Warmed in winter by log fires with year-round friendly caring service and cheery locals, the dark beamed and flagstoned bar at this happy gold stone pub is filled with loads of bric-a-brac, including a shelf of toby jugs, black beams liberally festooned with pewter and china tankards, copper kettles, horsebrasses and Service hats. Until it was recently injured by an enthusiastic local you could also have a go on the lovely old harmonium here – the landlord is hoping to get it fixed; piped music. Sturdy balustrading with standing timber pillars divides the pub into different parts. Palmers IPA and Copper are served on handpump; piped music. There are tables out in an attractive two-tier garden, in quiet village surroundings.

🍽 **Bar food includes sandwiches, creamy garlic mushrooms, crab cocktail, fish pie, rack of lamb, home-made pork and lamb sausages, home-made puddings, and they do fish and chips takeaways.** *Starters/Snacks: £4.90 to £7.50. Main Courses: £6.50 to £19.90. Puddings: £4.90*

Palmers ~ Tenants Ralph and Gail Prince ~ Real ale ~ Bar food (12-2, 6-9) ~ Restaurant ~ (01308) 485356 ~ Dogs welcome ~ Open 12-3, 6-11

Recommended by Malcolm and Kate Dowty, Phyl and Jack Street, David and Ros Hanley, JPR, Mark Flynn, John and Gloria Isaacs, Mrs S Knight

WEST STOUR
ST7822 MAP 2

Ship 🍷 🛏
A30 W of Shaftesbury; SP8 5RP

Civilised and pleasantly updated roadside dining inn, offering a wide range of food

The smallish bar on the left at this well cared-for roadside inn is airy with big sash windows looking beyond the road and car park to a soothing view of rolling pastures, cream décor and a mix of chunky farmhouse furniture on dark boards. The smaller flagstone public bar has a good log fire and low ceilings. On the right, two carpeted dining rooms with stripped pine dado, stone walls and shutters, are furnished in a similar pleasantly informal style, and have some attractive contemporary cow prints; TV, darts, lots of board games and piped music. Welcoming neatly dressed staff serve farm cider in summer, elderflower pressé, organic apple juices, good wines by the glass, and Palmers IPA and a couple of guests from local brewers such as Cheddar Ales and Sharps on handpump. The bedlington terriers are called Douglas and Toby. As there's a sharp nearby bend, keep your fingers crossed that drivers are obeying the 30mph limit when you walk to and from the car park opposite.

🍽 **Served in generous helpings, jolly decent food includes a wide choice of lunchtime baguettes (one reader recommends the good steak, mushroom and onion), ciabattas and panini and perhaps apple and black pudding fritter with horseradish cream, pâté of the day, moules marinière, fish pie, spinach, blue cheese and potato pie, braised blade of beef with red wine, mushroom and bacon sauce, dauphinoise potatoes and roast tomatoes, caramelised duck breast with black cherry, orange and port sauce, steak and Guinness pie, and puddings such as peach parfait with orange sorbet, belgian waffle with chocolate sauce, or lime, ginger and coconut cheesecake.** *Starters/Snacks: £4.50 to £6.95. Main Courses: £8.95 to £17.00. Puddings: £4.50*

Free house ~ Licensee Gavin Griggs ~ Real ale ~ Bar food (12-2.30, 6-9; not Sun evening) ~ Restaurant ~ (01747) 838640 ~ Children welcome ~ Dogs allowed in bar ~ Open 12-3.30, 6-11(1am Fri, midnight Sat); 12-11(7 in winter) Sun; closed Sun evening in winter ~ Bedrooms: £55B/£80B

Recommended by George Atkinson, Paul and Annette Hallett, Nick and Sylvia Pascoe, G Vyse, Colin and Janet Roe, Douglas and Ann Hare, Robert Watt, Steve Jackson, Tracey and Stephen Groves

WIMBORNE MINSTER
SZ0199 MAP 2

Green Man 🍺 £
Victoria Road at junction with West Street (B3082/B3073); BH21 1EN

Cosy and warm-hearted town pub with bargain simple food

It's no surprise that the lavish summer floral displays outside this cheery family-run pub have repeatedly won awards – the riot of colour certainly creates a glowing welcome.

This is a proper community pub – even early in the day quite a few regulars drop in for a chat, and there are photo montages of most of them in their younger days. Copper and brass ornaments brighten up the muted warm tones – soft lighting, dark red walls, maroon plush banquettes and polished dark pub tables in four small linked areas. One of these has a log fire in a biggish brick fireplace, another has a coal-effect gas fire, and they have two darts boards, a silenced games machine, piped music and TV; the Barn houses a pool table in the summer months. Very well kept and served on handpump are Wadworths Henrys, 6X and Bishops Tipple. There's a nice little border terrier called Cooper, and the flower bedecked back terrace has heaters and picnic-sets.

🍴 **Food here is good value. As well as a popular breakfast, they offer a wide choice of sandwiches, filled rolls and baked potatoes and simple pubby dishes such as fish and chips, burgers, steak and ale pudding, cheese and broccoli bake, chilli and chicken curry; good Sunday roasts (booking advised).** *Starters/Snacks: £2.95. Main Courses: £5.95 to £7.50. Puddings: £2.50 to £2.95*

Wadworths ~ Managers Kate and Andrew Kiff ~ Real ale ~ Bar food (10-2) ~ Restaurant ~ (01202) 881021 ~ Children allowed until 7pm ~ Dogs allowed in bar ~ Live music Fri, Sat evenings and monthly Sun evenings ~ Open 10am-midnight

Recommended by Graham and Jane Lynch-Watson, Jenny and Brian Seller, Alan Wright

Olive Branch 🍽

East Borough, just off Hanham Road (B3073, just E of its junction with B3078); has good car park; BH21 1PF

Handsome spacious town house, contemporary décor, good lighting, friendly staff, quite a choice of drinks, and enjoyable bistro-type food

Opened-up inside and extended, this is a handsome old town house with contemporary décor and a relaxed but civilised atmosphere. At the street end of the building is the bar which has some fine Jacobean panelling and attractive plasterwork, squishy sofas and leather stools around low tables beside the log fire, high chunky tables with matching stools and bar chairs, and a butcher's block with daily newspapers. Badger Best, Hopping Hare and Tanglefoot are on handpump alongside a good choice of wines by the glass; friendly, helpful service. The spreading dining room (with plenty of modern grey paintwork) is carefully divided into separate areas by partitions and standing timbers and has heavy trusses in the high-pitched roof, light brown leather or attractively cushioned wooden high-backed dining chairs around a mix of tables on the wood-strip floor, and framed Penguin books on the pale canary walls. There are lots of dog latin mottoes, night lights in contemporary steel containers, church candles and the lighting is good. A cosy side room, just right for a private party, has modern paintings on red or cream walls. The outside terrace has quite a few teak tables and chairs, and parking is easy.

🍴 **Enjoyable bistro food might include starters such as roast squash and feta salad, minestrone and roast chicken tart, main courses such as roast ham hock salad, lamb shank, shepherd's pie, roast monkfish with watercress pesto and pea purée, pea and asparagus pasta, and puddings such as vanilla panna cotta and sticky toffee pudding.** *Starters/Snacks: £5.25 to £9.00. Main Courses: £8.00 to £17.00. Puddings: £4.50*

Badger ~ Managers Adrian Jenkins and Jackie Cosens ~ Real ale ~ Bar food (12-3, 6-10; 12-9 Sun) ~ Restaurant ~ (01202) 884686 ~ Children welcome in restaurant ~ Open 10-11(11.45 Sat); 11-10.30 Sun

Recommended by Dominic Barrington, Joan and Michel Hooper-Immins

---

Bedroom prices normally include full english breakfast, VAT and any inclusive service charge that we know of. Prices before the '/' are for single rooms, after for two people in double or twin (B includes a private bath, S a private shower). If there is no '/', the prices are only for twin or double rooms (as far as we know there are no singles). If there is no B or S, as far as we know no rooms have private facilities.

WORTH MATRAVERS

Square & Compass ★ 🍺

At fork of both roads signposted to village from B3069; BH19 3LF

Unchanging country tavern with masses of character, in the same family for many years; lovely sea views and fine nearby walks

A stalwart of the *Guide* and hugely popular with readers (and other tourists, too, so perhaps pick your time of visit carefully), this splendidly idiosyncratic pub is much as it was around 100 years ago when the Newman family first took it on. There's no bar counter, the Palmers Copper and three guests from local brewers such as Blindmans, Forge and Wessex and up to 13 ciders, including one made on the premises, are tapped from a row of casks and passed to you in a drinking corridor through two serving hatches; several malt whiskies. A couple of basic unspoilt rooms have simple furniture on the flagstones, a woodburning stove and a loyal crowd of friendly locals, darts and shove-ha'penny – a table tennis championship is held here twice a year. From benches out in front there's a fantastic view down over the village rooftops to the sea around St Aldhelm's Head and there may be free-roaming hens, chickens and other birds clucking around your feet. A little museum (free) exhibits local fossils and artefacts, mostly collected by the current friendly landlord and his father. There are wonderful walks from here to some exciting switchback sections of the coast path above St Aldhelm's Head and Chapman's Pool – you will need to park in the public car park 100 yards along the Corfe Castle road (which has a £1 honesty box).

🍴 **Bar food is limited to tasty home-made pasties and pies which are served till stocks run out.** *Starters/Snacks: £3.00*

Free house ~ Licensee Charlie Newman ~ Real ale ~ Bar food (all day) ~ No credit cards ~ (01929) 439229 ~ Children welcome ~ Dogs welcome ~ Occasional live music Fri, Sat ~ Open 12-11; 12-3, 6-11 weekdays in winter

Recommended by Chris Flynn, Wendy Jones, JDM, KM, Graham and Jane Lynch-Watson, Mike and Sue Loseby, Andrea Rampley, Ian Herdman, Mrs Carolyn Dixon, Steve Derbyshire, Richard Stanfield, Ian and Barbara Rankin, S J and C C Davidson, Theocsbrian, N R White, Tich Critchlow, the Didler, Robert Wivell, John and Gloria Isaacs, Adrian Johnson, John and Enid Morris

LUCKY DIP

Besides the fully inspected pubs, you might like to try these Lucky Dips recommended to us and described by readers (if you do, please send us reports: feedback@goodguides.com).

ASKERSWELL [SY5393]
☆ *Spyway* DT2 9EP [off A35 Bridport—Dorchester]: Popular prettily set beamed country pub, enjoyable reasonably priced food from sandwiches to good Sun roasts, charming family service, real ales such as Badger and Otter tapped from the cask, old-fashioned high-backed settles, cushioned wall and window seats, old-world décor, two dining areas with steps between; children welcome away from bar, disabled access, spectacular views from back terrace and large attractive garden, good walks, comfortable bedrooms, good breakfast *(George Atkinson, the Didler, Peter Meister, LYM)*

BEARWOOD [SZ0596]
Bear Cross BH11 9LU [Bear Cross, Magna Rd – A341 roundabout]: Large refurbished pub with nice buzzy atmosphere, contemporary décor with traditional touches, some squashy leather sofas, carpet and bare boards, well cooked fresh food inc daily specials, good

friendly service, Badger ales kept well, restaurant *(Ian Malone)*

BLANDFORD FORUM [ST8806]
Crown DT11 7AJ [West St]: Best Western hotel's refurbished spacious bar, full Badger range from nearby brewery inc seasonal ales, adjacent eating area, good range of bar food from good sandwiches up, genteel restaurant; tables outside, bedrooms *(Colin and Janet Roe)*

BOURNEMOUTH [SZ0891]
Goat & Tricycle BH2 5PF [West Hill Rd]: Interesting two-level rambling Edwardian local (two former pubs knocked together) with Wadworths and guest beers kept well from pillared bar's impressive rank of ten or more handpumps (beer descriptions and tasters provided), farm cider, enjoyable reasonably priced pubby food, friendly staff and pub dog called Jack, coal fire, good lively atmosphere; children welcome, good disabled access, yard with covered bower *(Joan and Michel Hooper-Immins,*

Hans Becker, Steve Jackson, Barbarrick, Alain and Rose Foote)

BOURTON [ST7731]

☆ **White Lion** SP8 5AT [High St, off old A303 E of Wincanton]: Lively 18th-c low-beamed and stripped-stone dining pub with welcoming energetic landlord, appealing place with fine inglenook fire in pubby bar, two cosy rooms off and good-sized restaurant, bar snacks and enjoyable good value main meals, good service, beers such as Butcombe and Sharps Doom Bar, Thatcher's cider, nice wines; picnic-sets on back paved area and raised lawn, two neat bedrooms (Edward Mirzoeff, LYM, Mike and Cherry Fann, Colin and Janet Roe)

BRIDPORT [SY4692]

George DT6 3NQ [South St]: Cheery well worn-in town local, traditional dark décor, assorted furnishings and floor rugs, bargain home-made chip-free pub lunches (not Sun) cooked in view, good crab sandwiches, well kept Palmers, good choice of wines by the glass, efficient service, hot coal fire, hatch-served family room; piped radio, steps up to lavatories; dogs welcome, open all day, from 9am for popular wkdy breakfast or coffee (the Didler, John Wymer, Joan and Michel Hooper-Immins, LYM)

Woodman DT6 3NZ [South St]: Welcoming one-room local, well kept Branscombe Vale and interesting guests, good straightforward home-made food, skittle alley, live music, Sun quiz; attractive garden, open all day (John Wymer, the Didler)

BUCKLAND NEWTON [ST6804]

☆ *Gaggle of Geese* DT2 7BS : 19th-c country pub with relaxed atmosphere, sofas and armchairs next to log fire, books and games, enjoyable locally sourced modern pub food, Sun roasts, Ringwood, St Austell and two west country guest ales, good wine choice, nice coffee, red candlelit dining room with persian rugs and mix of old and new furniture, darts, skittle alley; children and dogs welcome, garden with terrace, orchard and pond, paddock with chickens and goats, charity poultry auction May and Sept, open all day wknds (Pat and Roger Davies, BB)

CATTISTOCK [SY5999]

☆ *Fox & Hounds* DT2 0JH [off A37 N of Dorchester]: Welcoming and attractive 17th-c or older pub, helpful service, enjoyable good value food inc OAP meals, Palmers ales from attractively carved counter, Taunton cider, good value wine choice, flagstones and nicely moulded Jacobean beams, stripped stone, log fire in huge inglenook, minimal décor, table skittles, pleasant side dining room, back public bar with well lit darts and TV, immaculate skittle alley, folk night 2nd Mon of month; piped music; dogs welcome (pigs ears provided at the bar), good local walks, comfortable bedrooms, cl Mon lunchtime, open all day wknds (Roger Thornington, Nic Soden, Lucinda Chapman, Mr and Mrs B Cox, BB)

CERNE ABBAS [ST6601]

☆ *New Inn* DT2 7JF [Long Street]: Handsome Tudor inn under new welcoming landlord, mullioned window seats in carpeted beamed bar, open fire, old photographs and prints, friendly attentive service, tasty sensibly priced food inc some unusual dishes, Palmers ales, good wines by the glass, restaurant; children welcome, tables on coach-yard terrace and attractive sheltered lawn beyond, eight bedrooms, has been open all day wknds and summer (LYM, David and Sue Smith)

CHARMINSTER [SY6793]

Inn For All Seasons DT2 9QZ [North St]: Bar with easy chairs, sofas and log fire, well kept Sharps Doom Bar and another ale, several whiskies, good food from open sandwiches to Sun carvery, cheerful helpful service, bright airy back conservatory-style dining room, fresh flowers; soft piped music; long sloping garden to stream with fields beyond, bedrooms (Simon Collett-Jones, B and K Hypher)

CHEDINGTON [ST4805]

Winyards Gap DT8 3HY [A356 Dorchester—Crewkerne]: Attractive dining pub surrounded by NT land, enjoyable good value food, well kept beers, friendly staff and dog, stylish dining room, skittle alley; children and dogs welcome, spectacular view over Parrett Valley and into Somerset from tables out in front, good walks, open all day wknds (Mr and Mrs N Davies, LYM)

CHICKERELL [SY6480]

Turks Head Inn DT3 4DS [6 East St (separate from the Turks Head Hotel in front, at number 8)]: Stone-built village pub with wide choice of enjoyable well priced food, good service, well kept Courage Directors, Wadworths 6X and a guest, pleasant beamed bar with lots of old local photographs, spacious simply furnished eating area (former skittle alley); children welcome, dogs in bar, wheelchair access, heated front terrace (Phil and Jane Hodson)

CHIDEOCK [SY4191]

☆ *Anchor* DT6 6JU [off A35 from Chideock]: Simple seaside pub in outstanding spot, dramatic sea and cliff views and big front terrace, well kept Palmers ales, good choice of wines by the glass, local farm cider, good value home-made food (all day summer) inc good fresh fish, quick friendly service despite crowds, woodburners, interesting local photographs; can get a bit untidy outside, limited parking but refunds given for beach car park if eating; children and dogs welcome, open all day summer (Richard Stanfield, Richard Mason, LYM, Pamela and Alan Neale, Stephen Shepherd, Lawrence Pearse, Peter Salmon, the Didler, George Atkinson, John and Gloria Isaacs)

Clockhouse DT6 6JW [A35 W of Bridport]: Attractive open-plan thatched village local with friendly landlord, well kept Otter ales, straightforward food inc bargain deals (Lawrence Pearse, BB)

CHRISTCHURCH [SZ1592]

☆ *Olde George* BH23 1DT [Castle St]: Bustling and cheerfully old-fashioned two-bar low-beamed pub dating from 15th c, Dorset

Piddle ales and a guest such as Exmoor Gold, real ciders and nice wine, wide choice of enjoyable sensibly priced food all day using local suppliers, Sun carvery and different evening menu, friendly staff; dogs welcome (they provide food), lots of teak seats and tables in heated character coach-yard, open all day *(Val and Alan Green, Joan and Michel Hooper-Immins, Hans Becker, Hugh Roberts, BB)*

Thomas Tripp BH23 1HX [Wick Lane]: Best known as a music pub, live acts most nights, but also has good beer and some interesting food, lively staff, good atmosphere; attractive terrace *(Hans Becker)*

CORFE CASTLE [SY9682]

Bankes Arms BH20 5ED [East St]: Big busy pub on attractive village square, elongated with various rooms on different levels, flagstones and comfortable traditional décor, subtle lighting, several wines by the glass, well kept ales such as Badger, Gales and Ringwood, good choice of food (some a little pricey, may ask to keep a credit card while you eat), restaurant; piped music; children and dogs welcome, tables on terrace and in nice garden with end play area overlooking steam railway, ten bedrooms (fair walk from car park with bags) *(Joan and Michel Hooper-Immins, Jenny and Brian Seller)*

Castle Inn BH20 5EE [East St]: Neatly refurbished straightforward two-room pub mentioned in Hardy's *Hand of Ethelberta*, enjoyable fairly priced food using local supplies inc popular Fri fish night, Ringwood ales, open fire, beams and flagstones; sizeable garden *(Susan and Jeremy Arthern, Mike and Sue Loseby)*

Fox BH20 5HD [West St]: Old-fashioned take-us-as-you-find-us stone-built local, real ales such as Greene King Abbot and Wadworths 6X tapped from the cask, good log fire in early medieval stone fireplace, glassed-over well in second bar; dogs but not children allowed, informal castle-view garden *(Mike and Sue Loseby, the Didler, LYM)*

☆ *Greyhound* BH20 5EZ [A351; The Square]: Bustling and picturesque old pub in centre of tourist village, three small low-ceilinged panelled rooms, steps and corridors, well kept ales such as Ringwood, Sharps and Thwaites, local cider, enjoyable good value varied menu, friendly helpful staff, traditional games inc Purbeck long board shove-ha'penny, family room; piped music, live Fri; garden with fine views of castle and countryside, pretty courtyard opening on to castle bridge, open all day wknds and summer *(LYM, the Didler, Mike and Sue Loseby, Christine Vallely, L Bond, Nigel Clifton, Tony Brace, Charles Gysin)*

CRANBORNE [SU0513]

Fleur-de-Lys BH21 5PP [Wimborne St (B3078 N of Wimborne)]: Attractive 17th-c inn under newish licensees, long panelled lounge/dining room, flagstones and log fire, Badger ales, restaurant, simple beamed public bar; nice setting on edge of Cranborne Chase, bedrooms *(Stan Edwards, LYM)*

DORCHESTER [SY6990]

☆ *Blue Raddle* DT1 1JN [Church St, nr central short stay car park]: Cheery and welcoming, long carpeted and partly panelled bar, well kept Otter and Sharps, Weston's farm cider, good wines and coffee, good home-made food from sandwiches to wild boar stew, open fire; piped music; disabled access (but one step), cl Mon lunchtime *(the Didler, Gene and Kitty Rankin, Karen Holland, Pam and John Smith, BB, Michael Dandy)*

Tom Browns DT1 1HU [High East St]: Unpretentious Dorset Brewing Company local with friendly L-shaped bare-boards bar, their ales inc Tom Browns Bitter and guests (they plan to reopen back microbrewery), limited choice of bar food, Sun roast, traditional games, vintage juke box and regular live music; well behaved children and dogs welcome, disabled access, big garden down to river, open all day *(Stan Edwards, Joan and Michel Hooper-Immins, BB)*

EAST CHALDON [SY7983]

Sailors Return DT2 8DN [Village signposted from A352 Wareham—Dorchester; from village green, follow Dorchester, Weymouth signpost; note that the village is also known as Chaldon Herring; OS Sheet 194 map reference 790834]: Thatched country pub under newish friendly management; flagstoned bar with much of its original rural-tavern character, newer part with open beams showing roof, good choice of well kept ales inc Ringwood, local cider in summer, enjoyable food inc local game and fish; children and dogs welcome, garden picnic-sets, useful for coast path, open all day in season *(Richard Stanfield, LYM)*

EAST LULWORTH [SY8581]

Weld Arms BH20 5QQ [B3070 SW of Wareham]: Civilised bar with log-fire sofas, well kept Palmers and Ringwood, pleasant service, two dining rooms; children and dogs welcome, picnic-sets out in big garden with play area *(LYM, Richard Stanfield)*

EAST MORDEN [SY9194]

☆ *Cock & Bottle* BH20 7DL [B3075 W of Poole]: Popular dining pub under new licensee but no major changes so far; wide choice of good imaginative food (best to book), Badger ales, several wines by the glass, friendly service, two dining areas with heavy rough beams; children in restaurant area only; garden and adjoining field, pleasant pastoral outlook *(John and Enid Morris, Pamela and Alan Neale, William Ruxton, Neil and Karen Dignan, Peter Veness, Dr and Mrs J Temporal, LYM)*

EAST STOUR [ST8123]

Kings Arms SP8 5NB [B3095, 3 miles W towards Shaftesbury; The Common]: Above-average very good value pubby food inc all-day Sun roasts (best to book), Palmers and guests such as St Austell and Wadworths 6X, decent wines, friendly efficient staff, large bar with light airy dining area; children welcome, big garden, bluebell walks nearby, bedrooms *(Paul Goldman, Robert Watt)*

EVERSHOT [ST5704]

Acorn DT2 0JW [off A37 S of Yeovil]: Upmarket inn (Sow & Acorn in *Tess of the d'Urbevilles*) with two well kept changing ales, good choice of wines by the glass inc champagne, real ciders, restaurant front part with up-to-date décor as well as log fires and oak panelling, bar snacks from good open sandwiches to salads and pubby hot dishes in beamed and flagstoned back bar with darts and pool, skittle alley; piped music; children allowed in eating areas, dogs in bar, terrace with dark oak furniture, ten bedrooms, pretty village, good walks, open all day *(Roger Thornington, Michael Dandy, LYM, Alan Johnson, John Wymer)*

GILLINGHAM [ST8027]

Dolphin SP8 4HB [Peacemarsh (B3082)]: Beamed town pub improved under present tenants, good quality food, well kept Badger beers, restaurant area; garden *(Steve Jackson, BB)*

GUSSAGE ALL SAINTS [SU0010]

☆ *Drovers* BH21 5ET [8 miles N of Wimborne]: Partly thatched pub with good choice of enterprising well cooked food at sensible prices, friendly if sometimes slow service, Ringwood ales and guests kept well, good wines by the glass, log fire and pleasantly simple country furnishings, public bar with piano and darts; well behaved dogs welcome, tables on pretty front lawn with views across the Dorset hills, adjoining farm shop, quiet village *(LYM, Stan Edwards, Robert Watt, Leslie and Barbara Owen, Julia and Richard Tredgett)*

HIGHCLIFFE [SZ2193]

Galleon BH23 5EA [Lymington Rd]: Fresh contemporary refurbishment with leather sofas, light wood floors and open fires, well prepared food from snacks and pub favourites up, local ales inc Ringwood, conservatory opening on to terrace and sunny garden; piped music; children welcome, summer barbecues, open all day till midnight *(David M Cundy)*

HORTON [SU0407]

Drusillas BH21 7JH [Wigbeth]: Picturesque 17th-c beamed pub/restaurant in nice countryside looking out to Horton folly, tablecloths even in the bar, wide choice of good food from snacks up inc lots of fish and decent vegetarian options, well priced wines, Ringwood ales and a guest, good friendly service, log fire, thatched extension; children welcome *(Jennifer Banks, Mr and Mrs W W Burke)*

Horton Inn BH21 5AD [B3078 Wimborne— Cranborne]: Good value food, well kept Ringwood ales, friendly service, plenty of room in long bar and separate restaurant; garden with pleasant terrace, bedrooms *(Mr and Mrs W W Burke, John Wymer)*

HURN [SZ1397]

Avon Causeway BH23 6AS [village signed off A338, then follow Avon, Sopley, Mutchams sign]: Roomy, civilised and comfortable hotel/dining pub under new management, food from sandwiches and pub favourites up,

Wadworths ales, helpful welcoming staff, interesting railway decorations, good disabled access; Pullman-coach restaurant (breakfast served here) by former 1870s station platform; 12 bedrooms, nr Bournemouth Airport, open all day *(Val and Alan Green, LYM)*

IBBERTON [ST7807]

Crown DT11 0EN: Nicely updated traditional village pub, ochre walls, flagstones, toby jugs and open fire, dining area at the back, Butcombe, Palmers and Ringwood, above-average pubby food inc interesting dishes and good value set deals, friendly helpful staff; lovely garden, beautiful spot under Bulbarrow Hill *(M and GR, BB)*

IWERNE MINSTER [ST8614]

Talbot DT11 8QN [Blandford Rd]: Emphasis on good local food inc game and line-caught fish, popular Sun lunch, Badger ales, sensibly priced wines by the glass, friendly service and atmosphere, pleasant log-fire dining room with walnut furniture, interesting local photographs; tables on heated terrace, five comfortable bedrooms, good breakfast *(Joan and Michel Hooper-Immins)*

KINGSTON [SY9579]

Scott Arms BH20 5LH [West St (B3069)]: Newish licensee at this extensively modernised holiday pub rambling through several levels, some sofas and easy chairs, beams, stripped stone, bare boards and log fires, well kept Dorset and Ringwood ales, good choice of enjoyable reasonably priced local food, family dining area; darts, pool, games machine, piped music; large attractive garden with outstanding views of Corfe Castle and the Purbeck hills, wknd barbecues, good walks *(Mike and Sue Loseby, Matthew Shackle, Dr A J and Mrs Tompsett, Paul and Elizabeth Wright, LYM)*

LITTON CHENEY [SY5490]

☆ *White Horse* DT2 9AT: Relaxed and unpretentious, with good value food from sandwiches and traditional dishes to imaginative cooking using good fresh local ingredients, particularly well kept Palmers ales, decent reasonably priced wines by the glass, friendly service, big woodburner, lots of pictures, some pine panelling, stripped stone and flagstones, country kitchen chairs in dining area, table skittles; may be piped jazz; children and dogs welcome, disabled access, good spot on quiet lane into quaint village (small pub car park), picnic-sets on pleasant streamside front lawn *(George Atkinson, BB, David and Julie Glover)*

LYME REGIS [SY3391]

Cobb Arms DT7 3JF [Marine Parade, Monmouth Beach]: Lively welcoming local, spaciously refurbished with well kept Palmers ales, wide range of reasonably priced generous bar food inc local fish and Sun roasts, decent wines, quick service even when busy, good value cream teas, a couple of sofas, interesting ship pictures and marine fish tank, pool, juke box – popular with local young people till late; children and dogs welcome, tables on small back terrace, next to harbour, beach and coastal walk, bedrooms, good breakfast, open all day *(Jim and Frances Gowers)*

☆ *Harbour Inn* DT7 3JF [Marine Parade]: More eating than pubby with friendly efficient service even at busy times, food from lunchtime sandwiches to local fish, good choice of wines by the glass, well kept Otter and St Austell, farm cider, clean-cut modern décor keeping original flagstones and stone walls (lively acoustics), thriving family atmosphere, big paintings for sale, sea views from front windows; piped music; disabled access from street, verandah tables *(Gerry and Rosemary Dobson, Alain and Rose Foote, Mr and Mrs D Hammond)*

☆ *Pilot Boat* DT7 3QA [Bridge St]: Popular modern all-day family food place nr waterfront, neatly cared for by long-serving licensees, friendly service even when busy, good value enjoyable food inc plenty of fish, well kept Palmers ales, good choice of wines by the glass, plenty of tables in cheery nautically themed areas, skittle alley; quiet piped radio; children and dogs welcome, tables out on terrace (watch out for seagulls) *(Stan Edwards, Neil and Brenda Skidmore, Alain and Rose Foote, Joan and Michel Hooper-Immins, Colin Gooch, LYM, Richard Mason)*

☆ *Royal Standard* DT7 3JF [Marine Parade, The Cobb]: Right on broadest part of beach, properly pubby bar with log fire, fine built-in stripped high settles, local photographs and even old-fashioned ring-up tills, quieter eating area with stripped brick and pine, friendly helpful service, three Palmers ales, good choice of wines by the glass, food from massive crab sandwiches up inc local fish, good cream teas; darts, prominent pool table, some live music; may be piped pop, gets very busy in season – long waits then; children welcome, good-sized suntrap courtyard with own servery and wendy house *(David A Hammond, Dave Irving, Jenny Huggins, Gene and Kitty Rankin, BB)*

LYTCHETT MINSTER [SY9593]

Bakers Arms BH16 6JF [Dorchester Rd]: Large, popular partly thatched Vintage Inn, modernised interior with beams, timbers and log fires, enjoyable all-day food inc lunchtime deals and good Sun roasts, changing ales such as Fullers, Ringwood and Sharps; children welcome, garden picnic-sets, open all day *(LYM, Peter Grant)*

☆ *St Peters Finger* BH16 6JE [Dorchester Rd]: Well run two-part beamed Badger roadhouse with cheerful efficient staff, popular sensibly priced food from sandwiches and baguettes up, small helpings available, good beer and wine choice, welcoming end log fire, cottagey mix of furnishings in different sections giving a cosy feel despite its size; good skittle alley, tables on big terrace, part covered and heated *(Leslie and Barbara Owen, Martin and Alison Stainsby)*

MANSTON [ST8116]

☆ *Plough* DT10 1HB [B3091 Shaftesbury—Sturminster Newton, just N]: Good-sized

traditional country pub with well kept Palmers ales, good fairly priced home-made food from sandwiches up, will cater for special diets, prompt friendly service, richly decorated plasterwork, ceilings and bar front, conservatory; garden tables *(David Lamb, Steve Jackson)*

MELPLASH [SY4897]

☆ *Half Moon* DT6 3UD [A3066 Bridport—Beaminster]: Thatched roadside pub laid out sensibly for dining, landlord doing good range of reasonably priced standard food from sandwiches up, OAP lunches, well kept Palmers ales, good choice of wines, cheerful landlady, beams, brasses, glass ornaments and country pictures, log fire; may be unobtrusive piped music; picnic-sets out in front, more in good-sized attractive garden behind, shares car park with cricket club next door *(BB)*

MILTON ABBAS [ST8001]

☆ *Hambro Arms* DT11 0BP [signed off A354 SW of Blandford]: Well managed pub in beautiful late 18th-c thatched landscaped village, two beamed bars and restaurant, good log fire, well kept ales such as Dorset Piddle and Ringwood, good interesting food from sandwiches and panini up, popular Sun carvery, gourmet evenings, prompt friendly service even when busy; darts, pool and TV in back public bar; no dogs, children in restaurant, tables on terrace, comfortable bedrooms, open all day wknds *(Mr and Mrs W W Burke, LYM, N R White)*

MOTCOMBE [ST8426]

Coppleridge SP7 9HW : Good value food from sandwiches to speciality steaks, real ales inc Butcombe, decent wines and welcoming service in former 18th-c farmhouse's bar/lounge and two smallish dining rooms; big airy bedrooms, good-sized grounds *(Colin and Janet Roe)*

MUDEFORD [SZ1891]

☆ *Haven House* BH23 4AB [beyond huge seaside car park at Mudeford Pier]: Popular much-extended pub in great spot on beach with superb views and bird-watching, enjoyable good value pubby food and seafood, well kept ales inc Ringwood, good welcoming service, popular linked family cafeteria (all day in summer); nice in winter with old-fashioned feel in quaint little part-flagstoned core; tables on sheltered back terrace, lovely seaside walks (dogs banned from beach May-Sept) *(David Jackson, Richard and Liz Thorne, LYM)*

NORDEN HEATH [SY94834]

☆ *Halfway* BH20 5DU [A351 Wareham—Corfe Castle]: Cosily laid-out partly thatched pub with friendly staff, Badger beers, good wines by the glass, enjoyable food all day, pitched-ceiling back serving bar where the locals congregate, front rooms with flagstones, log fires, stripped stonework, snug little side area; picnic-tables outside with play area, good nearby walks, open all day *(BB, Richard Stanfield)*

NORTH WOOTTON [ST6514]

Three Elms DT9 5JW [A3030 SE of

Sherborne]: Comfortable early 19th-c open-plan country pub freshened up by current landlord, ales such as Butcombe, St Austell Tribute and Yeovil, good sensibly priced home-made food from lunchtime baguettes up, woodburner; piped music, children and dogs welcome, disabled access, big garden behind with nice country views *(BB, Linda Ashman)*

OSMINGTON [SY7282]
Sunray DT3 6EU [A353 Weymouth—Wareham]: Extended much-improved family-run pub, hearty good value food (all day Sun) from open kitchen, good friendly service, well kept ales such as Dorset Piddle and Ringwood, relaxing atmosphere and light contemporary décor; children welcome, large garden and terrace, play area *(Joan and Michel Hooper-Immins)*

OSMINGTON MILLS [SY7381]
☆ *Smugglers* DT3 6HF [Off A353 NE of Weymouth]: Bustling old family-orientated inn under new management, well extended, with cosy timber divided areas, two open woodburners, old local pictures, Badger ales, all-day food; piped music, discreet games machines; picnic-sets on crazy paving by little stream, thatched summer bar, good play area, useful for coastal path, four bedrooms, open all day *(LYM)*

PIDDLEHINTON [SY7197]
☆ *Thimble* DT2 7TD [High St (B3143)]: Neatly kept partly thatched pub with two handsome fireplaces and deep glazed-over well in attractive low-beamed core, well kept Badger, Palmers and Ringwood, good wines, popular bar food from sandwiches up, pleasant welcoming staff, interesting bottle collection, darts and cribbage; children and dogs welcome, big floodlit garden with summer house, barbecues, stream and little bridge *(LYM, Sarah and Roger Baynton-Williams, Martin Clerk, N R White, Ian and Deborah Carrington)*

PIDDLETRENTHIDE [SY7198]
☆ *European* DT2 7QT [B3143 N of Dorchester]: Refurbished roadside inn under friendly new owners; two opened-up linked beamed rooms, built-in wall seats, terracotta tiled floors, woodburner in sandstone fireplace, good food, well kept Palmers; picnic-sets out at front and back, two bedrooms (nice views), has been cl Sun evening, Mon *(BB, LYM, Mike and Sue Loseby, Cathryn and Richard Hicks)*
☆ *Piddle* DT2 7QF [B3143 N of Dorchester]: Most tables set for the good popular food with emphasis on fish, but also enjoyable sandwiches and ploughman's, comfortable leatherette sofas in refurbished bar, polite helpful staff, Dorset Piddle and Ringwood ales, well chosen wines, children's room, end pool room with sports TV; dogs welcome in bar, informal streamside garden with picnic-sets and play area, good bedrooms *(Dennis Jenkin, Lois Dyer, Phil Bryant, BB)*
Poachers DT2 7QX [B3143 N of Dorchester]: Bright up-to-date décor, comfortable lounge end, Butcombe, Palmers Copper and

Ringwood Fortyniner, good wine, generous food from good ciabattas up, smiling service, three linked beamed dining areas; piped music; dogs welcome, garden with tables on decking and stream at bottom, 21 comfortable good value motel-style bedrooms around residents' heated swimming pool, good breakfast, open all day *(Dennis Jenkin)*

PIMPERNE [ST9009]
☆ *Anvil* DT11 8UQ [well back from A354]: Attractive 16th-c thatched family pub with wide choice of food from generous lunchtime baguettes to substantial main dishes, well kept Isle of Purbeck and Palmers ales, cheerful efficient young staff, bays of plush seating in bright and welcoming bar, neat black-beamed dining areas; fruit machine, piped music; good garden with fish pond and big weeping willow, 12 bedrooms, nice surroundings *(BB, Stan Edwards)*

POOLE [SZ0589]
New Beehive BH13 7JF [Cliff Drive, Canford Cliffs]: Bar/restaurant in former nursing home, Bass, Dorset Piddle and Hook Norton ales, enjoyable reasonably priced food, good service, three dining areas inc conservatory; tables in pleasant garden *(Mr and Mrs W W Burke)*
Rising Sun BH15 1NZ [Dear Hay Lane]: Large recently refurbished pub, comfortable bar area with sofas and armchairs, also high tables and stools, good choice of popular food inc local fish, friendly attentive staff, good wine choice, ales such as Ringwood, daily papers, restaurant; discreet TVs; plenty of tables in attractive garden areas front and back *(anon)*

PORTLAND [SY6872]
George DT5 2AP [Reforne]: Cheery 17th-c stone-built local mentioned by Thomas Hardy, low doorways and beams, flagstones, small rooms, reputed smugglers' tunnels, scrubbed tables carved with names of generations of sailors and quarrymen, interesting prints and mementoes, well kept ales inc Courage and Greene King, Addlestone's cider, basic bargain lunches, family room, newer end bar, events most nights; nice garden, open all day *(Joan and Michel Hooper-Immins, the Didler)*
Royal Portland Arms DT5 1LZ [Fortuneswell]: Friendly stone-built character local, homely and unfussy, with fine range of quickly changing ales (many west country microbrews) tapped from the cask, farm cider, live bands; open all day, till late Fri, Sat *(the Didler)*

PORTLAND BILL [SY6768]
Pulpit DT5 2JT: Extended touristy 1950s pub in great spot nr Pulpit Rock, well run by cheery long-serving landlord, popular food from landlady inc good steak and kidney pie and local fish (nice crab salad), well kept Fullers and Ringwood, picture-window views, dark beams and stripped stone; may be piped music; dogs welcome, disabled access, tiered sea-view terrace, play area, short stroll to lighthouse and cliffs *(Colin Gooch,*

Joan and Michel Hooper-Immins, Terry and
Nickie Williams)

PYMORE [SY4794]

Pymore Inn DT6 5PN [off A3066 N of
Bridport]: Attractive Georgian beamed and
stone-built pub with good atmosphere,
chef/landlord doing enjoyable food inc good
fish choice (most tables laid for eating),
friendly prompt service, St Austell ales,
good choice of wines by the glass, prints on
panelled walls, old settles and woodburner,
small pretty dining room; wheelchair
access, large pleasant garden *(Bob and
Margaret Holder)*

SANDFORD ORCAS [ST6220]

☆ *Mitre* DT9 4RU [off B3148 and B3145 N of
Sherborne]: Thriving tucked-away country
local with welcoming landlord, three well
kept ales, wholesome home-made food from
good soup and sandwiches up, flagstones,
log fires and fresh flowers, small bar and
larger pleasantly homely dining area; pretty
terrace, has been cl Mon lunchtime *(LYM,
David Foord, David Hudd)*

SHAFTESBURY [ST8622]

Grosvenor SP7 8JA [High St]: Former coaching
inn with fine Georgian façade reworked as
stylish boutique hotel, contemporary bar
opening on to central courtyard garden, airy
restaurant, good modern cooking; 16
bedrooms *(Robert Whitaker)*

Half Moon SP7 8BS [Salisbury Rd, Ludwell
(A30 E, by roundabout)]: Comfortable and
pleasantly extended Badger family dining
pub with their usual food inc popular Sun
lunch, well kept beers, quick helpful service,
spotless housekeeping, low ceilings, tiled
and wood floors on different levels, mixed
tables and chairs, old local photographs;
garden with adventure playground
(B and K Hypher, Robert Watt)

Two Brewers SP7 8HE [St James St]:
Refurbished 18th-c pub nicely tucked away
below steep famously photogenic Gold Hill,
well divided open-plan bar, log fire, friendly
attentive staff, good range of ales inc
Ringwood, reasonably priced wines, Stowford
Press cider, good choice of popular well
priced food from baguettes up (children's
helpings available), Sun roasts, back dining
room, skittle alley; dogs welcome in bar,
picnic-sets in attractive garden with lovely
views *(Dr and Mrs M E Wilson, LYM,
John Coatsworth, N R White)*

SHAPWICK [ST9301]

☆ *Anchor* DT11 9LB [off A350 Blandford—
Poole; West St]: Emphasis on good
interesting food freshly made but not
particularly cheap, friendly attentive service,
good wine choice (champagne by the glass),
three ales inc Ringwood, three simply
furnished uncluttered areas, open fires;
children welcome, tables out in front, more
in attractive garden with terrace and play
area behind, handy for Kingston Lacy (NT)
*(BB, Ian Herdman, Richard and Sue Fewkes,
Mr and Mrs W W Burke, Robert Watt)*

SHAVE CROSS [SY4198]

Shave Cross Inn DT6 6HW [On back lane

Bridport—Marshwood, signposted locally;
OS Sheet 193 map reference 415980]: Former
medieval monks' lodging, small character
timbered and flagstoned bar with huge
inglenook, Branscombe Vale Branoc, Dorset
Marshwood Vale and pub's own-label 4Ms,
farm ciders, vintage rums, attractive
restaurant with grandfather clock, expensive
carribean influenced food, service can be
slow, ancient skittle alley with bar billiards,
pool, darts and a juke box; piped music;
children and dogs welcome, sheltered pretty
garden with thatched wishing-well, carp
pool and play area, seven newly built
boutique bedrooms, cl Mon *(Adrian Johnson,
Richard Stanfield, Bob and Angela Brooks,
LYM, the Didler)*

STOBOROUGH [SY9286]

Kings Arms BH20 5AB [B3075 S of Wareham;
Corfe Rd]: Up to four well kept changing
ales, Thatcher's farm cider, good choice of
enjoyable reasonably priced food in bar and
restaurant, live music Sat; children welcome,
disabled access, views over marshes to River
Frome from big terrace tables, open all day
wknds *(Maria Preece, David Lamb,
Robert Wivell)*

STOKE ABBOTT [ST4500]

New Inn DT8 3JW [off B3162 and B3163
2 miles W of Beaminster]: Spotless 17th-c
thatched pub with friendly licensees and
pleasant efficient service, well kept Palmers
ales, good food at sensible prices,
woodburner in big inglenook, beams, brasses
and copper, some handsome panelling,
paintings for sale, flagstoned dining room;
occasional piped music; children welcome,
wheelchair access, two lovely gardens,
unspoilt quiet thatched village, good walks,
bedrooms, cl Sun evening, Mon *(John Wymer,
The Farmers, LYM, Fred and Lorraine Gill)*

STOURTON CAUNDLE [ST7115]

☆ *Trooper* DT10 2JW [village signed off A30
E of Milborne Port]: Pretty stone-built pub in
lovely village setting, friendly staff and
atmosphere, bargain good simple food, well
kept ale, tiny low-ceilinged bar, stripped-
stone dining room, darts, cribbage,
dominoes, shove-ha'penny, skittle alley;
piped music, TV, outside gents'; children
and dogs welcome, a few picnic-sets out
in front, pleasant side garden with small
play area, has been open all day summer
wknds, cl Mon lunchtime *(Dr A McCormick,
LYM)*

STRATTON [SY6593]

Saxon Arms DT2 9WG [off A37 NW of
Dorchester; The Square]: Traditional but
recently built flint-and-thatch local,
open-plan, bright and spacious with light
oak tables and comfortable settles on
flagstones or carpet, open fire, well kept
Otter, Ringwood and Timothy Taylors
Landlord, good value wines, tasty generous
food inc good choice of specials and
lunchtime set deals, large comfortable dining
section on right, traditional games; piped
music; children and dogs welcome, terrace
tables overlooking village green, open all

day wknds (Ian and Deborah Carrington,
M G Hart, LYM, Michael Dandy)

STUDLAND [SZ0382]

☆ *Bankes Arms* BH19 3AU [off B3351, Isle of
Purbeck; Manor Rd]: Very popular spot above
fine beach, outstanding country, sea and
cliff views from huge garden over road with
lots of seating; comfortably basic big bar
with raised drinking area, beams, flagstones
and good log fire, nine well kept changing
ales inc own Isle of Purbeck brews, local
cider, good wines by the glass, wide choice
of food all day from baguettes to local fish
and good crab salad (they ask to keep a
credit card while you eat), darts and pool in
side area; can get very busy with trippers
wknds and in summer, parking in season can
be complicated or expensive if not a NT
member, piped music, machines, sports TV;
children (over 8) and dogs welcome, just off
Coast Path, big comfortable bedrooms
(John and Enid Morris, Richard Stanfield,
Jenny and Brian Seller, Mike and Sue Loseby,
JDM, KM)

STURMINSTER MARSHALL [SY9499]

Black Horse BH21 4AQ [A350]: Welcoming
and clean under newish owners, good
value food from nice sandwiches up, Badger
ales, comfortable long bar (Mr and
Mrs P R Thomas)

Red Lion BH21 4BU [opp church; off A350
Blandford—Poole]: Attractive proper village
pub opp handsome church, welcoming
bustling local atmosphere, wide choice of
enjoyable imaginative home-made food inc
good value wkdy set lunches and Sun roasts,
efficient service, well kept Badger ales, nice
wines, old-fashioned roomy U-shaped bar
with nice log fire, good-sized lived-in dining
room in former skittle alley; piped music;
children and dogs welcome, disabled access,
back garden with wicker furniture and
picnic-sets, open all day Sun (BB,
Ian Herdman, John Branston, Peter Veness)

SWANAGE [SZ0278]

Black Swan BH19 2NE [High St]: Quieter
than pubs closer to the seafront, small
neatly kept bar, welcoming helpful landlady,
good choice of enjoyable food, two well kept
ales inc Ringwood Best, separate dining
room; lovely courtyard garden
(Christine Vallely, JPR)

☆ *Red Lion* BH19 2LY [High St]: Busy two-bar
low-beamed 17th-c local, friendly helpful
landlord, wonderful choice of ciders, ales
such as Flowers, Palmers, Ringwood, Sharps
and Timothy Taylors, good value simple food
inc nice fish; piped music, some live;
children's games in large barn, picnic-sets in
extended garden with partly covered terrace,
comfortable bedrooms in former back coach
house, open all day (Ian and Barbara Rankin,
Alan Wright, N R White, Tich Critchlow,
the Didler)

SYMONDSBURY [SY4493]

☆ *Ilchester Arms* DT6 6HD [signed off A35 just
W of Bridport]: Welcoming part-thatched old
pub with cheery landlord and attentive staff,

enjoyable good value lunchtime food from
sandwiches up, wider evening range inc local
fish, several well kept local ales, Taunton
farm cider, nice wines, cosy rustic open-plan
low-beamed bar with high-backed settle
built in by inglenook, pretty restaurant with
another fire, pub games, skittle alley
doubling as family room (no children in bar);
level entrance (steps from car park),
tables in nice brookside back garden with
play area, peaceful village, good walks
(Malcolm and Kate Dowty, LYM,
George Atkinson, Martin and Sue Radcliffe,
Mr and Mrs D Bartlett, David Crook)

UPWEY [SY6684]

Riverhouse DT3 5QB [B3159, nr A354
junction]: Coal-effect gas fireplace dividing
flagstoned bar side from neat carpeted
dining side, main emphasis on wide range of
quickly served enjoyable food from
lunchtime baguettes up, Courage beers, good
wine choice and coffees; well reproduced
piped music; disabled access, sizeable
garden with play area and water for dogs,
cl Sun evening (Stuart Paulley, BB)

WAREHAM [SY9287]

Duke of Wellington BH20 4NN [East St]:
Small traditional 18th-c beamed pub, half a
dozen mainly local ales kept well, wide choice
of reasonably priced food especially fish,
some original features inc panelling, fire,
copper ornaments, old local photographs;
piped music; back courtyard tables, bedrooms,
open all day (Mike Gorton, Richard Stanfield,
Mrs Joy Griffiths, the Didler)

Kings Arms BH20 4AD [North St (A351, N
end of town)]: Traditional stone and thatch
town local, very well kept ales such as Gales,
Ringwood and Sharps, good value pubby
food, friendly staff, back serving counter and
two bars off flagstoned central corridor,
beams and inglenook, darts; children
welcome, garden behind with picnic-sets
(LYM, Matthew Cull, Richard Stanfield)

Old Granary BH20 4LP [The Quay]: Fine old
brick building with riverside terrace,
emphasis on the enjoyable food but two
small beamed rooms by main door for
drinkers, well kept Badger ales, good wines
by the glass, neat efficient young staff, airy
dining room with leather high-backed chairs
and pews around pale wood tables, brick
walls and new oak standing timbers, two
further rooms with big photographs of the
pub, woodburners, more relaxed atmosphere;
quiet piped jazz; boats for hire over bridge
(Dave Hollins)

Quay Inn BH20 4LP [The Quay]: Comfortable
and roomy 18th-c inn in great spot by the
water, varied menu inc pubby favourites and
cook your own food on a hot stone,
attentive service, well kept Ringwood ales,
reasonably priced wine list, open fires;
children welcome, terrace area and picnic-
sets out on quay, boat trips, bedrooms, open
all day summer, parking nearby can be
difficult (Stan Edwards, John and
Gloria Isaacs)

WAREHAM FOREST [SY9089]

☆ *Silent Woman* BH20 7PA [Wareham—Bere Regis]: Long neatly kept Badger dining pub divided by doorways and standing timbers, enjoyable home-made food, well kept Best, Tanglefoot and a seasonal beer, country wines, pleasant staff, traditional furnishings, farm tools and stripped masonry on left where children allowed; piped music; dogs welcome, wheelchair access, plenty of picnic-sets outside inc a covered area, walks nearby (S Holder, BB, Fiona Avery)

WEST BAY [SY4690]

Bridport Arms DT6 4EN: Large light and airy two-level seaside bar, pleasantly stripped areas around original inglenook flagstoned core, well kept Palmers, quick friendly service, quite a food operation majoring on fish, baguettes and pubby bar lunches too; children welcome, picnic-sets outside, paying public car park, bedrooms in adjoining hotel with own entrance (BB, Michael Clarke)

George DT6 4EY [George St]: Refurbished harbourside inn with two bars and restaurant, masses of shipping pictures, some model ships and nautical hardware, good range of food inc fresh fish/seafood, well kept Palmers ales, good wines, friendly helpful staff; pool; children and dogs welcome, picnic-sets outside, seven bedrooms, open all day (John and Gloria Isaacs, BB)

☆ *West Bay* DT6 4EW [Station Road]: 18th-c harbourside pub under new management, island servery separating fairly simple bareboards front part with coal-effect gas fire from cosier country-kitchen-feel dining area, locally sourced food inc plenty of seafood, Palmers ales, skittle alley; piped music; dogs welcome, disabled facilities, tables in side and back gardens, three bedrooms, open all day Fri-Sun (Peter Meister, LYM)

WEST LULWORTH [SY8280]

Castle Inn BH20 5RN [B3070 SW of Wareham]: Pretty 16th-c thatched inn in lovely spot nr Lulworth Cove, good walks and lots of summer visitors; beamed flagstoned bar concentrating on wide choice of enjoyable generous food, friendly chatty staff, good choice of local ales, farm cider and perry, decent house wines, maze of booth seating divided by ledges, cosy more modern-feeling lounge bar, pleasant restaurant; piped music; children and dogs welcome, front terrace, long attractive garden behind on several levels, boules and barbecues, 12 bedrooms (Richard Stanfield, Dave Hollins, N R White, LYM)

WEST PARLEY [SZ0898]

Curlew BH22 8SQ [Christchurch Rd]: Vintage Inn in early 19th-c farmhouse, mixed furnishings in informal beamed areas around central bar, two log fires, candles on tables, wide choice of enjoyable food inc plenty for vegetarians, three well kept ales inc Ringwood BB, plenty of good value wines, friendly well trained staff; picnic-sets in well tended front garden (David and Sally Frost, Ian Malone, Val and Alan Green)

WEYMOUTH [SY6778]

Boot DT4 8JH [High West St]: Friendly unspoilt local dating from 1600s nr harbour, well worn comfort with beams, bare boards, panelling, hooded stone-mullioned windows and coal fires, cosy gently sloping snug, well kept Ringwood ales and guests from fine brass handpumps, real cider, no food or music; disabled access, pavement tables, open all day (the Didler, Joan and Michel Hooper-Immins)

☆ *Nothe Tavern* DT4 8TZ [Barrack Rd]: Roomy and comfortable early 19th-c pub nr to Nothe Fort, wide range of enjoyable food inc local fresh fish and good value Sun carvery, OAP wkdy deals too, friendly staff coping at busy times, well kept ales such as Courage, Ringwood, Otter and Wadworths, decent wines, good choice of malt whiskies, lots of dark wood, whisky-water jugs on ceiling, interesting prints and photographs, children welcome in restaurant with distant harbour glimpses; may be quiet piped music; more views from terrace (Phil and Jane Hodson, BB)

Ship DT4 8BE [Custom House Quay]: Neatly modern extended waterfront pub with several nautical-theme open-plan levels, three well kept Badger ales from long bar, good choice of wines by the glass, enjoyable good value usual food (only upstairs at night) from sandwiches, baguettes and ciabattas up; unobtrusive piped music; wheelchair access downstairs, some quayside seating and pleasant back terrace (Phil and Jane Hodson, LYM, Gerry and Rosemary Dobson)

Wellington Arms DT4 8PY [St Alban St]: Handsome green and gold 19th-c tiled façade, well restored panelled interior, carpets, banquettes, mirrors and lots of old local photographs, well kept Ringwood ales, bargain pubby food from sandwiches up inc daily roast, friendly landlord and family; children welcome in back dining room, disabled access, open all day from 10 (Phil and Jane Hodson, Joan and Michel Hooper-Immins, the Didler)

WIMBORNE MINSTER [SU0000]

Kings Head BH21 1JG [The Square]: Appealing brasserie/bar in old-established hotel, enjoyable food, well kept Greene King ales, cheery well trained staff, roomy bar areas; comfortable bedrooms (Tim and Rosemary Wells)

WINKTON [SZ1696]

☆ *Fishermans Haunt* BH23 7AS [B3347 N of Christchurch]: Comfortably refurbished big-windowed riverside inn on fringes of New Forest, Fullers/Gales beers, reasonably priced pubby food (all day wknds), two log fires, restaurant views of River Avon; piped music, games machine, Fri quiz; children and dogs welcome, disabled facilities, tables among shrubs in quiet back garden, heaters in covered area, 11 comfortable bedrooms, open all day (LYM, Sara Fulton, Roger Baker, B Targett, Baden and Sandy Waller)

Essex

Essex has an agreeable set of nicely varied pubs, this year enhanced by three pleasing new Main Entries, each with their own special take: the Bulmer Fox at Bulmer Tye is an enjoyable light and airy dining pub, the Elmdon Dial at Elmdon, a good all-rounder, has something gently individual about it and the Crown & Thistle at Great Chesterford is an interesting village pub. Places doing particularly well here this year are the cheery Three Willows at Birchanger and Crown at Little Walden and the pubby Prince of Wales at Stow Maries. For a special meal, the Sun at Dedham with its carefully sourced and prepared meals shines out, and it's our Essex Dining Pub 2011. Quite remarkably, exactly half the Main Entries in this chapter have a beer award. Not particularly because they carry an awesomely vast range of beers as we see in some counties (here you'll find between four and seven) but because they are notably well kept, and, rather delightfully, this is a jolly good county for beer festivals with five of our Main Entries hosting one if not two a year.

ARKESDEN   TL4834   MAP 5

Axe & Compasses ♀
Off B1038; CB11 4EX

Comfortably traditional pub with Greene King beers and decent food

This enjoyable thatched village pub dates back to the 17th c. The oldest part is the traditionally carpeted lounge bar which has low-slung ceilings, polished upholstered oak and elm seats, plush easy chairs, a blazing fire and gleaming brasses. A smaller quirky public bar is uncarpeted, with built-in settles and darts. The atmosphere is relaxed and welcoming with friendly service from the pleasant staff and licensee. You'll find a very good wine list (with 15 wines by the glass) and around two dozen malt whiskies, along with Greene King Abbot, IPA and Old Speckled Hen served under a light blanket pressure on handpump. There are seats out on a side terrace with pretty hanging baskets; parking at the back.

🍴 They grow their own herbs on a farm in the village, and the tasty bar food includes sandwiches, chicken liver pâté, whitebait, crunchy squid with lime and chilli mayonnaise, prawn and smoked mackerel roulade, grilled or battered haddock, good breaded scampi, steak and kidney pie, moussaka and sirloin steak, and there is a more elaborate pricier restaurant menu. *Starters/Snacks: £5.95 to £6.95. Main Courses: £10.95 to £15.95. Puddings: £5.25*

Greene King ~ Managers Themis and Diane Christou ~ Real ale ~ Bar food (12-2, 6.45-9.15) ~ Restaurant ~ (01799) 550272 ~ Children welcome in restaurant ~ Open 12-2.30, 6-11; 12-3, 7-10.30 Sun
Recommended by Philip and Jan Medcalf, Mr and Mrs B Watt

The 🍺 symbol shows pubs which keep their beer unusually well, have a particularly good range or brew their own.

AYTHORPE RODING

Axe & Compasses 🍺

B184 S of Dunmow; CM6 1PP

Friendly roadside stop, nice balance of eating and drinking

The counter at this neatly kept weatherboarded pub has comfortable bar chairs, and leatherette settles, stools and dark country chairs around a few pub tables on pale boards and turkey carpet. The original part on the left has dark old bent beams and wall timbers, with a two-way fireplace marking off a snug little raftered dining area, which has sentimental prints on dark masonry and a big open-faced clock; piped music. Although popular with diners, locals do pop in for a pint of the Nethergate IPA or three or four guests from brewers such as Fullers, Sharps and Suffolk, which are racked behind the bar in temperature-stabilised casks; also up to three Weston's farm ciders on handpump. The small garden behind has stylish modern tables and chairs.

🍴 **Tasty well presented food includes starters such as chicken and brandy liver parfait with spiced chutney, fried scallops with confit pork belly, pea purée and pancetta crisp, fried pigeon breast, moules marinière and main courses such as seared duck breast with orange jus, sesame chicken breast with lime roasted new potatoes and mushroom sauce, steak, Guinness and oyster pie, butternut squash, root vegetable and nut crumble, and puddings such as black cherry chocolate sundae, spotted dick and custard and chocolate and hazelnut brownie with chocolate sauce.** *Starters/Snacks: £4.50 to £8.95. Main Courses: £8.95 to £15.95. Puddings: £5.50 to £5.50*

Free house ~ Licensee David Hunt ~ Real ale ~ Bar food (12-2.30, 6-9.30; 12-8.30 Sun) ~ Restaurant ~ (01279) 876648 ~ Children welcome ~ Dogs allowed in bar ~ Open 11-11(midnight Sat); 12-10.30 Sun

Recommended by BOB, M and GR

BIRCHANGER

Three Willows

Under a mile from M11 junction 8: A120 towards Bishops Stortford, then almost immediately right to Birchanger Village; don't be waylaid earlier by the Birchanger Services signpost; CM23 5QR

Full of cricketing memorabilia, a happy civilised place serving good food

It's worth booking ahead or arriving early at this creamy yellow dining pub which is popular with an older set at lunchtime and a more varied crowd in the evening. With the friendly landlord much in evidence and its cheery warm service, it's a reliable place for a good meal. The spacious cricket-themed carpeted main bar is full of cricketing prints, photographs, cartoons and other memorabilia, and there's a well furnished small lounge bar; Greene King Abbot and IPA and a guest on handpump, and decent house wines. Though children are not welcome inside, there is plenty for them outside including a sturdy climbing frame, swings and a basketball hoop. There are picnic-sets out on a terrace (with heaters) and on the lawn behind (you can hear the motorway and Stansted Airport out here).

🍴 **Besides a wide range of generously served pubby standards such as sandwiches, filled baked potatoes and ploughman's (lunchtime only), steak and ale pie, steaks and vegetable curry, they serve quite a lot of fresh fish dishes – maybe cod, tuna steak, crab salad and lemon sole. Puddings might include raspberry and hazelnut meringue and jaffa puddle pudding.** *Starters/Snacks: £3.95 to £7.95. Main Courses: £8.98 to £14.98. Puddings: £3.90*

Greene King ~ Tenants Paul and David Tucker ~ Real ale ~ Bar food (12-2, 6-9) ~ (01279) 815913 ~ Open 11.30-3, 6-11; 12-3 Sun; closed Sun evening

Recommended by Mrs Margo Finlay, Jörg Kasprowski, Stephen and Jean Curtis, Roy Hoing, Grahame and Myra Williams, Terry and Nickie Williams, J Marques, David and Valerie Mort

BULMER TYE   TL8438 MAP 5

Bulmer Fox

A131 S of Sudbury; CO10 7EB

Well run dining pub, fresh and light, with thriving chatty atmosphere and plenty of individuality

The first time we've seen this in a pub: a stylish mosaic drinking fountain with an elegant tap above a copper basin, for you to fill a glass or jug. Another nice touch, though not unique, is the neat set of order forms on each table, for writing your own food order (they take orders at the bar, too). Several areas, all linked and flowing together, give a good choice of moods, from the main part where the lively and chatty atmosphere is amplified by the bright acoustics of its dark bare boards (look out for one or two 'rugs' painted on them), through a rather quieter side room, to an intimate little central snug with just a couple of tables on its ancient tiles. They have Adnams and Greene King IPA on handpump, and bustling staff give service that's kind and thoughtful as well as efficient. The sheltered back terrace has some of its tables in an arbour.

🍴 **Enjoyable and fairly priced, the food here might include sandwiches, moules marinière, crab, avocado and red pepper mousse, rump burger, roast breast and confit leg of guinea fowl with mushroom jus, grilled bass fillet with smoked salmon and white wine cream, meze platter, fried calves liver and bacon with polenta and roast tomatoes and salsa verde, lamb provençale casserole, risotto stuffed courgettes, and puddings such as white and dark chocolate torte with raspberry compote and sticky toffee pudding. A big plus is that they cook things exactly how you ask – 'rare' really means rare.** *Starters/Snacks: £4.75 to £6.00. Main Courses: £7.25 to £14.50. Puddings: £4.50*

Free house ~ Licensee Henry Ford ~ Real ale ~ Bar food (12-2(3 Sun), 6-9.30) ~ (01787) 312277/ 377505 ~ Children welcome ~ Open 12-3.30, 6-11

Recommended by Mrs Anna Glover, John Prescott

BURNHAM-ON-CROUCH   TQ9495 MAP 5

White Harte

The Quay; CMO 8AS

Lovely waterside position, and with an aptly nautical theme to the décor

It's worth a small detour to sit relaxing on the small jetty by the River Crouch (with its lazy yachts), just across the road from this comfortably old-fashioned hotel. Inside, the relaxed partly carpeted bars are filled with assorted nautical bric-a-brac and hardware – anything from models of Royal Navy ships to a compass set in the hearth. Other traditionally furnished high-ceilinged rooms have sea pictures on brown panelled or stripped brick walls, with cushioned seats around oak tables, and an enormous log fire making it cosy in winter. In summer they open the doors and windows, giving the place a nice airy feel. Charming staff serve Adnams and Crouch Vale from handpump.

🍴 **Bar food includes lunchtime sandwiches, soup, steak and kidney pie, a choice of three local fish such as cod, plaice and skate, and specials such as lasagne, curry and cottage pie.** *Starters/Snacks: £3.60 to £5.80. Main Courses: £7.80 to £10.80. Puddings: £3.60 to £4.80*

Free house ~ Licensee G John Lewis ~ Real ale ~ Bar food ~ Restaurant ~ (01621) 782106 ~ Children welcome ~ Dogs allowed in bar and bedrooms ~ Open 11-11; 12-10.30 Sun ~ Bedrooms: £28(£62B)/£50(£82B)

Recommended by Hazel Morgan, Bernard Patrick, David Jackson

Please keep sending us reports. We rely on readers for news of new discoveries, and particularly for news of changes – however slight – at the fully described pubs: feedback@goodguides.com, or (no stamp needed) The Good Pub Guide, FREEPOST TN1569, Wadhurst, E Sussex TN5 7BR.

CLAVERING

Cricketers

B1038 Newport—Buntingford, Newport end of village; CB11 4QT

Attractively updated dining pub; bedrooms

Combining old-fashioned charm with just a dash of extra sparkle from some new materials and furnishings, the main area of this upmarket dining pub has bays of deep purple button-back banquettes and neat padded leather dining chairs, dark floorboards, very low beams (the padding is a necessity, not a gimmick), and a big open fireplace. Back on the left is more obviously an eating part – two fairly compact carpeted areas, a step between them. The right side is similar but set more formally for dining, and has some big copper and brass pans on its dark beams and timbers. They have well kept Adnams Bitter and Broadside and a guest from a local brewer such as Nethergate on handpump, Aspall's cider, over a dozen wines by the glass, freshly squeezed orange, pear and apple juices and good coffee; piped music. Signed books by son Jamie are on sale. The attractive front terrace has wicker-look seats around teak tables among colourful flowering shrubs.

⌷ As well as sandwiches, seasonal dishes (home-made breads and well hung meat but not cheap) have an italian flavour and might include starters such as vegetable antipasti, spring onion bhajis with mango and lime chutney, carpaccio with truffle oil and parmesan crisps, rump of lamb with balsamic jus, fried gurnard with warm roast pepper, asparagus and rocket salad, steak and ale pie, spinach and goats cheese pancake cannelloni with passata and crispy herb pangritata, and puddings such as treacle tart, apple and cinnamon crème brûlée and baked coffee cheesecake with espresso coffee glaze; good cheeseboard. *Starters/Snacks: £4.95 to £8.95. Main Courses: £13.75 to £20.50. Puddings: £6.00*

Free house ~ Licensee Trevor Oliver ~ Real ale ~ Bar food (12-2, 6.30-9.30) ~ Restaurant ~ (01799) 550442 ~ Children welcome ~ Open 7-11 ~ Bedrooms: £65B/£90B

Recommended by Mrs Margo Finlay, Jörg Kasprowski, David and Valerie Mort, J Marques, Christopher and Elise Way, Peter Rozée, Tina and David Woods-Taylor, Richard Cole, David Glynne-Jones, Mr and Mrs John Taylor, N R White

DEDHAM

Sun 🍴 🍷 🍺 🛏

High Street (B2109); CO7 6DF

ESSEX DINING PUB OF THE YEAR

Popular stylish inn in Constable country, with seasonal italian food and an impressive wine selection

Tremendous attention to detail goes into the running of this lovely old coaching inn, which has a particularly good coaching arch. High carved beams, squared panelling, wall timbers and big log fires in splendid fireplaces are the historic setting for handsome furnishings that include high settles, sofas with sorbet-coloured cushions and other good quality wooden tables and chairs. A charming little window seat in the bar looks across to the church, which is at least glimpsed in several of Constable's paintings. Drinks include an enterprising wine list of more than 70 bin ends (20 by the glass), some interesting soft drinks and Adnams Broadside, Crouch Vale Brewers Gold and a couple of guests from brewers such as Green Jack and Otter. Service is relaxed, friendly and efficient; TV, piped music and board games. On the way out to mature trees and picnic-sets on the quiet back lawn, notice the unusual covered back staircase with what used to be a dovecote on top, and if you have time, beautiful walks into the heart of Constable country lead out of the village, over water meadows towards Flatford Mill. The panelled bedrooms are nicely done with abundant character, and an archway annexe houses their fruit and vegetable shop.

⌷ A few snacks include good sandwiches, ploughman's and omelettes but otherwise the menu here is pretty determinedly italian. Food is not cheap but prices reflect the quality of the ingredients used in a menu which places much emphasis on seasonal game, fish, fruit and vegetables and well documented local suppliers. The daily changing choice might include starters such as antipasti, tuscan bread soup, ricotta and swiss chard ravioli with sage butter sauce, main courses such as courgette risotto, game bird of the day roasted in chianti, tomatoes and rosemary, cod fillet roasted with marjoram and capers, and puddings such as pear and almond tart, panna cotta with grappa and marinated cherries and hazelnut and espresso cake. *Starters/Snacks: £4.95 to £8.75. Main Courses: £6.95 to £8.75. Puddings: £4.50 to £5.50*

Free house ~ Licensee Piers Baker ~ Real ale ~ Bar food (12-2.30(3 Sat, Sun), 6.30-9(10 Fri, Sat)) ~ Restaurant ~ (01206) 323351 ~ Children welcome ~ Dogs allowed in bar ~ Open 11-11 ~ Bedrooms: £70B/£95B

Recommended by Felicity Davies, John and Enid Morris, Jean and Douglas Troup, Marion and Bill Cross, Marcus Mann, Tom and Ruth Rees, Simon Cottrell, Hugh Roberts, Trevor Swindells, Patrick Harrington, Jim and Frances Gowers, Paul Humphreys, N R White, Ryta Lyndley

ELMDON   TL4639   MAP 5

Elmdon Dial

Village signposted off B1039 Royston—Saffron Walden; Heydon Lane; CB11 4NH

Pleasing mix of traditional and contemporary in well run pub with good food and drink; peaceful garden

The partly timbered tap bar, with big oriental rugs on its boards, has plenty to look at, from interesting prints and framed *Flying* covers (the landlord is ex-RAF) to the furniture itself, which besides a leather sofa and some carefully collected chairs includes a beautifully carved early 18th-c pew said to come from Norwich Cathedral. It has a big-screen TV for sports events; bar skittles and board games. The separate lounge bar is rather smarter, and brightly up to date in its cheerful orange and pink décor, leather tub chairs and modern tables; its handsome mantelpiece houses a decanter collection. Adnams, Mighty Oak Oscar Wilde and Timothy Taylors Landlord on handpump are well kept, service is charming and efficient, and it's all very civilised. The back dining room is a modern extension: pitched ceiling, biggish prints on puce walls, stylish high-backed chairs around simple pine tables. Its big end windows look out on a neat terrace with picnic-sets under cocktail parasols, and more on a sizeable lawn with a big weeping willow. It's a restful spot, with birdsong and the chimes of the nearby church's clock (its unusual stained-glass sundial gives the pub its name).

⏚ As well as sandwiches and ploughman's, bar food might include hot chicken liver salad, smoked salmon tagliatelle with cream and dill, mini fillet steak with a mini steak, ale and mushroom pie with red wine sauce, roasted butternut and sweet potato filo parcel with spinach and mozzarella and tomato passata, baked cod on roast mediterranean vegetable mash and hollandaise and home-made burgers; also puddings such as baked alaska and raspberry tart. *Starters/Snacks: £4.00 to £6.00. Main Courses: £9.50 to £16.50. Puddings: £5.00*

Free house ~ Licensee Chris Crane ~ Real ale ~ Bar food (12-2(2.30 Sun), 6-9; not Sun evening) ~ Restaurant ~ (01763) 837386 ~ Children welcome ~ Dogs allowed in bar ~ Open 12-3, 6-11 (midnight Sat); 12-10.30 Sun; closed Mon

Recommended by Mrs Jane Kingsbury, Mrs Margo Finlay, Jörg Kasprowski

GOLDHANGER   TL9008   MAP 5

Chequers ◀

Just off B1026 E of Heybridge; The Square, Church Street; CM9 8AS

Good range of real ales in cheerful village pub, simple furnishings, friendly staff and popular bar food

Tucked in a snug corner next to a lovely old church, this unspoilt old pub was once a courthouse. The particularly nice entrance corridor with its good old red and black tiling and black wall panelling leads to a traditional rambling interior with six separate rooms. On the right, a fairly functional low-ceilinged games room has bar billiards, a games machine and gas-effect woodburner. A tiny snug has a window to the little courtyard (with picnic-sets and umbrellas on paving and a grape vine), a coal-effect gas fire, sofa, pine pew, TV and a delft shelf with various knick-knacks including a bottle collection, and the green carpeted public bar has lots of beer labels stuck to the ceiling and farm implements around a big fireplace. A step takes you up to a big airy lounge bar with a huge sash window overlooking the graveyard, one or two big black beams in the lowish ceiling, some nice old black panelling, a quirky miscellany of tables and chairs, two solid pews and an old upright piano. A glass-fronted bread oven has shelves displaying a few knick-knacks for sale. Off in the far corner, standing timbers lead to a traditional dining room with black beams, some exposed brickwork and dark wood pub furniture. Friendly staff behind the low counter serve an interesting range of half a dozen real ales including Caledonian Deuchars IPA, St Austell Tribute and Wells & Youngs Bitter and three changing guest beers from brewers such as Leeds, Moorhouses and Titanic on handpump. They also host beer festivals here; piped pop music.

🍴 Popular bar food includes lunchtime sandwiches, winter soup, duck and port pâté with cumberland sauce, thai mussels, ham and free-range eggs, jumbo beer-battered cod, asparagus, broccoli, pea and broad bean risotto, 8oz steak burger with bacon and emmenthal, chicken and bacon in a creamy stilton and leek sauce, jamaican jerk steak with crispy prawns, whole bass with fennel and thyme, and puddings like banana and toffee cheesecake and bread and butter pudding. *Starters/Snacks: £3.75 to £6.50. Main Courses: £8.75 to £13.50. Puddings: £4.75*

Punch ~ Lease Philip Glover and Dominic Davies ~ Real ale ~ Bar food (12-3, 6.30-9; not Sun evening or bank hol Mon evening) ~ Restaurant ~ (01621) 788203 ~ Children welcome except in tap room ~ Dogs allowed in bar ~ Open 11-11; 12-10.30 Sun
Recommended by Jean and David Lewis, David Jackson, Colin Smith, Susan and Nigel Wilson

GOSFIELD   TL7829   MAP 5

Kings Head

The Street (A1017 Braintree—Halstead); CO9 1TP

Comfortably contemporary dining pub with proper public bar

Splashes of warm modern colour brighten the ancient interior of this enjoyable old pub. The softly lit beamed main bar, with red panelled dado and ceiling, has neat modern black leather armchairs, bucket chairs and a settee as well as sturdy pale wood dining chairs and tables on its dark boards, and a log fire in a handsome old brick fireplace with big bellows. Black timbers mark off a red carpeted and walled dining area with red furnishings, opening into a carpeted conservatory; piped music. They have Adnams Bitter and Timothy Taylors Landlord and a guest such as Shepherd Neame Spitfire on handpump, a dozen wines by the glass and 57 internationally sourced whiskies; daily papers. The good-sized quite separate public bar, with a purple pool table, darts and TV, has its own partly covered terrace; the main terrace has round picnic-sets.

🍴 Neat black-clad young staff serve very fairly priced food which includes starters such as chicken, pine nut and apricot pâté, mushroom and brie filo parcels with tomato chutney, beef carpaccio, main courses such as lancashire hotpot, duck breast in black bean sauce with stir-fried vegetables and noodles, roast pork belly with green pea stew, chicken, leek and stilton pie, tiger prawns with sweet chilli sauce, skate wing with caper and lemon butter, rump steak, roast pepper stuffed with vegetable couscous with Boursin cheese topping, and puddings such as warm chocolate and nut brownie with chocolate sauce and Baileys and toffee cheesecake with raspberry coulis; Sunday roast. *Starters/Snacks: £4.50 to £7.25. Main Courses: £7.25 to £17.95. Puddings: £5.00*

Enterprise ~ Manager Mark Bloorfield ~ Real ale ~ Bar food (12-2.30, 6-9.30; 12-6 Sun) ~ Restaurant ~ (01787) 474016 ~ Children welcome ~ Dogs allowed in bar ~ Open 12-3, 6-11; 12-midnight Sat; 12-11 Sun
Recommended by R T and J C Moggridge, Nick Gadd, Justin and Emma King

By law, pubs must show a price list of their drinks. Let us know if you are inconvenienced by any breach of this law.

GREAT CHESTERFORD

TL5142   MAP 5

Crown & Thistle

1.5 miles from M11 junction 9A; pub signposted off B184, in High Street; CB10 1PL

Good home cooking and good drinks in an interesting ancient pub, simple and civilised

There's some attractive decorative plasterwork inside as well as outside this substantial village pub, particularly around the early 16th-c inglenook fireplace – which has a good winter log fire. Three changing real ales might include Adnams, Buntingford Twitchell and Fullers London Pride on handpump. Ten decent wines by the glass and good coffee add to the creature comforts, as do the unusual wooden benches – apparently recycled from a station, from those golden railway days when their furniture could be designed more for comfort than to defeat vandals. The low-ceilinged area by the bar counter, which has padded bar stools, is carpeted; a bare-boards room behind, with architectural and country prints, is a little brighter. On the left, a couple of steps take you into a long handsomely proportioned dining room with a photographic mural of the village making up its end wall. Service is helpful and friendly. A suntrap back courtyard has picnic-sets, with more and a toddlers' slide on the side grass.

🍴 **As well as lunchtime sandwiches, bar food might include king prawns in garlic oil, mushroom topped with stilton and cherry tomatoes, beetroot, green bean and artichoke tartlet, ham, egg and chips, lamb curry, steak and kidney pudding, sausage and mash and stuffed peppers with couscous, and puddings such as sticky toffee pudding and fruit crumble; Sunday roasts.** *Starters/Snacks: £3.95 to £6.50. Main Courses: £6.95 to £14.95. Puddings: £4.95*

Free house ~ Licensee Simon Clark ~ Real ale ~ Bar food (12-2(2.30 Sun), 7-9; not Sun evening) ~ (01799) 530278 ~ Children welcome ~ Dogs allowed in bar ~ Open 12-3, 6-1am(7-11 Sun)

Recommended by Mark Gamble, Mrs Margo Finlay, Jörg Kasprowski

HASTINGWOOD

TL4807   MAP 5

Rainbow & Dove £

0.5 miles from M11 junction 7; Hastingwood signposted after Ongar signs at exit roundabout; CM17 9JX

Pleasantly traditional low-beamed pub with good value food; handy for M11

The licensees here must be very proud to have taken over the freehold of this 16th-c cottage from Punch. They've subsequently decorated its three little low-beamed rooms which are now light and airy in pale greens and creams. A woodburning stove, some stripped stone and golfing memorabilia keep it feeling down to earth and homely. Adnams Broadside and a couple of guests such as Everards and Sharps are on handpump alongside ten wines by the glass; piped music, winter darts and occasional jazz nights. Hedged off from the car park, a stretch of grass has covered picnic-sets; dogs welcome lunchtimes only.

🍴 **The reasonably priced pubby food is popular so it's worth getting here early. Traditional meals include lunchtime sandwiches and baguettes as well as ploughman's, gammon and egg, turkey escalope with mushroom sauce, vegetable curry, steak, kidney and ale pie and battered cod, with puddings such as meringue stack and good ice-creams.** *Starters/Snacks: £4.15 to £5.95. Main Courses: £6.75 to £14.95. Puddings: £4.15*

Free house ~ Licensees Andrew Keep and Kathryn Chivrall ~ Real ale ~ Bar food (12-2.30(3 Sun), 7-9.30) ~ (01279) 415419 ~ Children welcome ~ Open 11.30-3, 6-11; 12-4 Sun; closed Sun evening

Recommended by Colin and Janet Roe, John Saville, Jerry Brown, Paul Humphreys, Jeremy King, Gordon and Margaret Ormondroyd, David and Sue Smith, David Greene

---

The details at the end of each Main Entry start by saying whether the pub is a free house, or if it belongs to a brewery or pub group (which we name).

HORNDON-ON-THE-HILL

Bell ♀ 🍺 🛏

M25 junction 30 into A13, then left into B1007 after 7 miles, village signposted from here; SS17 8LD

Very popular historic pub with mostly restauranty food and very good range of drinks

The heavily beamed bar at this beautiful Tudor inn maintains a strongly pubby appearance, though in fact it's the good imaginative food that takes precedence. It's furnished with lovely high-backed antique settles and benches, with rugs on the flagstones and highly polished oak floorboards. Look out for the curious collection of ossified hot cross buns hanging along a beam in the saloon bar. The first was put there some 90 years ago to mark the day (it was a Good Friday) that Jack Turnell became licensee. During the war, privations demanded that they hang a concrete bun. The hanging tradition continues to this day, but now the oldest person in the village (or available on the day) hangs the bun. An impressive range of drinks includes Bass (tapped straight from the cask), Greene King IPA and Crouch Vale Brewers Gold with three guests, and over a hundred well chosen wines (16 by the glass). You do need to get here early or book as tables are often all taken soon after opening time.

🍴 As well as a handful of pubby dishes such as sandwiches, moules marinière, sausage and mash and braised lamb shank with mustard mash, a pricier daily changing menu might include starters such as steamed cockle, shrimp and salmon pancake with shellfish bisque, purple sprouting millefeuilles with stilton and walnut oil, beef carpaccio with roast beetroot, main courses such as aubergine and halloumi lasagne with celeriac purée, basil sauce and ratatouille, monkfish tail wrapped in parma ham with mushy peas, crispy pancetta and velouté sauce, rib-eye steak with blue cheese butter, and puddings such as almond, pistachio and hazelnut profiteroles with hot chocolate sauce and whisky parfait and glazed lemon tart with ginger ice-cream. *Starters/Snacks: £4.95 to £9.00. Main Courses: £8.50 to £9.95. Puddings: £5.50 to £8.10.*

Free house ~ Licensee John Vereker ~ Real ale ~ Bar food (12-2, 6.30-9.45) ~ Restaurant ~ (01375) 642463 ~ Children welcome ~ Dogs allowed in bar and bedrooms ~ Open 11-2.30, 5.30-11; 11-3, 6-11 Sat; 12-4, 7-10.30 Sun ~ Bedrooms: £59B/£68B

Recommended by Sandra Harrold, Stephen Mowatt, John and Enid Morris, Clifford Blakemore, Steve Moore, J V Dadswell, Mrs Margo Finlay, Jörg Kasprowski

LITTLE BRAXTED

Green Man £

Kelvedon Road; village signposted off B1389 by NE end of A12 Witham bypass – keep on patiently; OS Sheet 168 map reference 848133; CM8 3LB

Prettily traditional brick-built pub with a garden and reasonably priced food

This homely place has a thoroughly traditional interior, even boasting a collection of some 200 or more horsebrasses, along with harnesses, mugs hanging from beams, tankards over the bar, a lovely copper urn and plenty of pictures and notices. Patterned carpets, little curtained windows and windsor chairs lend a cottagey atmosphere, and in winter, the traditional little lounge is especially appealing with its warm open fire. The tiled public bar has books, darts, cards, cribbage and dominoes, and friendly staff serve Greene King IPA, Abbot and a guest. Picnic-sets in the pleasant sheltered garden behind are a good place to while away an hour or two. More reports please.

🍴 Good sensibly priced food in generous helpings includes lunchtime sandwiches and warm baguettes, soup, ploughman's, baked potatoes and sausage and mash, and specials such as minted lamb shank in redcurrant gravy, thai chicken curry and steak and kidney pudding, and good home-made puddings. *Starters/Snacks: £2.95 to £6.95. Main Courses: £7.25 to £9.95. Puddings: £3.95 to £4.50.*

Greene King ~ Tenant Matthew Ruffle ~ Real ale ~ Bar food (12-2.30, 6-9; 12-6 Sun) ~ Restaurant ~ (01621) 891659 ~ Children welcome until 8pm ~ Dogs allowed in bar ~ Open 11.30-3, 5-11; 12-7 Sun

Recommended by Mr and Mrs John Taylor, Tina and David Woods-Taylor, Penny Lang

LITTLE WALDEN

TL5441 MAP 5

Crown 🍺

B1052 N of Saffron Walden; CB10 1XA

Bustling 18th-c cottage with a warming log fire and hearty food

Readers make particular mention of the warm and cheery welcome at this homely low-ceilinged local. Décor is traditional, with bookroom-red walls, floral curtains, bare boards and navy carpeting. A higgledy-piggledy mix of chairs ranges from high-backed pews to little cushioned armchairs spaced around a good variety of closely arranged tables, mostly big, some stripped. The small red-tiled room on the right has two little tables. They light a fire in one of the three fireplaces, though not in the unusual walk-through one! Four changing beers are tapped straight from casks racked up behind the bar – normally Adnams Best and Broadside, Greene King Abbot and Woodfordes Wherry; piped light music; disabled access. Tables out on the terrace take in views of surrounding tranquil countryside.

🍴 **The traditional bar food is good value and popular, so you may need to book at weekends: sandwiches, including a delicious hot pork baguette (not Sunday), whitebait, ham, egg and chips, lasagne, cod fillet, scampi and chips, smoked haddock mornay, lamb shank with redcurrant gravy, four cheese ravioli, steaks, and home-made puddings such as steamed fruit pudding and fruit crumble.** *Starters/Snacks: £4.25 to £6.95. Main Courses: £8.25 to £12.95. Puddings: £3.50 to £4.50*

Free house ~ Licensee Colin Hayling ~ Real ale ~ Bar food (not Sun evening) ~ Restaurant ~ (01799) 522475 ~ Children welcome ~ Dogs allowed in bar and bedrooms ~ Trad jazz Weds evening ~ Open 11.30-3, 6-11; 12-10 Sun ~ Bedrooms: £65S/£70S \

Recommended by the Didler, David Jackson, John Wooll, Simon Watkins, R T and J C Moggridge

MARGARETTING TYE

TL6801 MAP 5

White Hart 🍺

From B1002 (just S of A12/A414 junction) follow Maldon Road for 1.3 miles, then turn right immediately after river bridge, into Swan Lane, keeping on for 0.7 miles; The Tye; CM4 9JX

Fine choice of ales tapped from the cask in cheery country pub with good family garden

An impressive range of eight well kept real ales are all tapped straight from the cask at this cream-painted weatherboarded pub. Besides well kept Adnams Best and Broadside and Mighty Oak IPA and Oscar Wilde, they bring on a constant stream of nationwide guest beers from brewers such as Farmers Ales, Nethergate and Red Fox. They do takeaways and have interesting bottled beers, too, and during their popular June and October beer festivals have up to 60 beers a day; winter mulled wine. With walls and wainscoting painted in chalky traditional colours, the open-plan yet cottagey interior has a mix of attractive old chairs and a stuffed deer's head mounted on the chimneybreast above the woodburning stove. A neat carpeted back conservatory is similar in style, and the front lobby has a charity paperback table; darts, quiz machine, skittles, board games and piped music. There are plenty of picnic-sets out on grass and terracing around the pub, with a sturdy play area, a safely fenced duck pond, an aviary with noisy cockatiels (they don't quite drown the larks), and pens of rabbits, guinea-pigs and a pygmy goat. Dogs are very welcome, they even have towels in the porch for a clean-up. We'd love to hear about their new bedrooms.

🍴 **Bar food includes sandwiches, pâté of the day, fried camembert with fruit coulis, king prawn cocktail, baked bass, steak and ale pie, liver and bacon, seasonal game dishes, battered catch of the day, leek, red onion and feta quiche (the chef is vegetarian so the vegetarian dishes here should be good), and puddings such as mixed berry cheesecake and hot chocolate fudge cake and home-made crumbles and pies.** *Starters/Snacks: £4.00 to £10.00. Main Courses: £8.00 to £16.00. Puddings: £4.00 to £5.95*

> It's very helpful if you let us know up-to-date food prices when you report on pubs.

Free house ~ Licensee Elizabeth Haines ~ Real ale ~ Bar food (12-2, 6-9; 12-2.30, 6-9.30 Sat; 12-4.30, 6.30-8.30 Sun; not Mon evening) ~ (01277) 840478 ~ Children welcome away from main bar ~ Dogs allowed in bar ~ Open 11.30-3, 6-midnight; 11.30-midnight Sat; 12-midnight Sun ~ Bedrooms: /£70B
Recommended by David Jackson, Robert Turnham

MILL GREEN
TL6401   MAP 5

Viper 🍽 £

The Common; from Fryerning (which is signposted off NE bound A12 Ingatestone bypass) follow Writtle signposts; CM4 OPT

Delightfully unpretentious with local ales, simple pub food and no modern intrusions

This timeless old local, tucked away in a quiet wooded corner, is charmingly unspoilt. Its cosy little lounge rooms have spindleback and armed country kitchen chairs and tapestried wall seats around neat little old tables, and there's a log fire. Booted walkers (and dogs) are directed towards the fairly basic parquet-floored tap room, which is more simply furnished with shiny wooden traditional wall seats and a coal fire. Beyond, another room has country kitchen chairs and sensibly placed darts, also dominoes and cribbage; the pub cat is Millie and the white west highland terrier is Jimmy. They stock an interesting range of five well kept beers on handpump: Viper (produced for the pub by Nethergate), Mighty Oak Jake the Snake and Oscar Wilde and a couple of quickly changing guests from brewers such as Brentwood and Wibblers; also Old Rosie farm cider. Live bands play during their Easter and August beer festivals. Tables on the lawn overlook a beautifully tended cottage garden ~ a dazzling mass of colour in summer, further enhanced at the front by overflowing hanging baskets and window boxes. Morris men often dance here.

🍴 **Simple but tasty lunchtime bar snacks might include sandwiches, baked potatoes, soup, pâtés, ploughman's, steak and ale pie, sausage and mash, curry and lasagne, and traditional puddings such as jam sponge and chocolate pudding; Sunday roasts. The tasty bread comes from a local baker a mile or so down the road.** *Starters/Snacks: £4.25 to £6.95. Puddings: £3.95*

Free house ~ Licensees Peter White and Donna Torris ~ Real ale ~ Bar food (12-2(3 Sat, Sun); not evenings) ~ No credit cards ~ (01277) 352010 ~ Dogs welcome ~ Open 12-3, 6-11; 12-11(10.30 Sun) Sat
Recommended by Roxanne Chamberlain, the Didler, LM

PELDON
TM0015   MAP 5

Rose 🍽 🍷

B1025 Colchester—Mersea (do not turn left to Peldon village); CO5 7QJ

Friendly dining pub in an appealing building, with good food, thoughtful staff and great wine choice

As this appealing pastel-coloured old inn is run by the Essex wine merchant Lay & Wheeler, they have a very good wine list, with around 19 by the glass, listed with helpful descriptions on a blackboard. Friendly efficient table service throughout places emphasis on the dining aspect and, as it can get very busy, you do need to book. The traditional interior, with standing timbers supporting the heavy low ceilings with their dark bowed 17th-c oak beams, little leaded-light windows and a gothick-arched brick fireplace has creaky close-set tables and some antique mahogany and padded wall banquettes. In contrast, the very spacious airy conservatory dining area (disabled access), with views over the garden, has a modern brightly lit feel. On handpump are Adnams Best and Broadside, Greene King IPA and an interesting guest. The spacious garden has good teak seats, and ducks on a pretty pond; the bedroom over the kitchen can be noisy at night, and the shower is set very low under a sloping ceiling.

🍴 **Much enjoyed, changing bar food (prices remain sensible) might include a club sandwich, starters such crayfish and pineapple salad or seared ducks liver, pancetta and** pine nut bruschetta, main courses such as lemon sole fillet with tiger prawns and cream sauce, baked mackerel on fennel, carrot and orange salad, slow-braised pork belly with apple compote and cider jus and courgette, new potato and rocket frittata with rocket salad, with puddings such as banoffi pie and iced peanut parfait with toffee sauce. *Starters/Snacks: £3.00 to £7.00. Main Courses: £9.00 to £18.00. Puddings: £5.00*

Lay & Wheeler ~ Licensee Dean Cole ~ Real ale ~ Bar food (12-2.15, 6.30-9(9.30 Fri, Sat); 12-9(6 in winter) Sun) ~ Restaurant ~ (01206) 735248 ~ Children welcome away from bar ~ Open 11-11; 12-10.30 Sun; 12-7 Sun in winter ~ Bedrooms: £40S/£60S

Recommended by P and J Shapley, Marcus Mann, Ryta Lyndley, David Jackson, Evelyn and Derek Walter, Gordon Neighbour, John and Enid Morris, Mike and Mary Carter

STAPLEFORD TAWNEY   TL5001   MAP 5

Mole Trap 🍺

Tawney Common, which is a couple of miles away from Stapleford Tawney and is signposted off A113 just N of M25 overpass – keep on; OS Sheet 167 map reference 500013; CM16 7PU

Tucked away but humming with customers, traditionally run with an interesting selection of guest beers

This isolated little country pub is run with considerable old-fashioned individuality and few pretensions. The smallish carpeted bar (mind your head as you go in) has a black dado, beams and joists, brocaded wall seats, library chairs and bentwood elbow chairs around plain pub tables, and steps down through a partly knocked-out timber stud wall to a similar area. There are a few small pictures, 3-D decorative plates, some dried-flower arrangements and (on the sloping ceiling formed by a staircase beyond) some regulars' snapshots, with a few dozen beermats stuck up around the serving bar, and warming fires; quiet piped radio. As well as Fullers London Pride on handpump, they have three constantly changing guests from brewers such as Dark Star, Crouch Vale and Green Jack. The pub fills up quickly at lunchtimes, so it's worth getting here early if you want to eat. Outside are some plastic tables and chairs and a picnic-set, and a happy tribe of resident animals, many rescued, including friendly cats, rabbits, a couple of dogs, hens, geese, sheep, goats and horses. Note that food service stops promptly, sometimes even before the allotted time.

🍴 Besides sandwiches and popular Sunday roasts, tasty food includes ploughman's, lasagne, steak and kidney pie, ham, egg and chips and a vegetarian option like quiche, with traditional home-made puddings such as cherry and apple and lemon meringue pie. *Starters/Snacks: £3.50. Main Courses: £8.95 to £10.50. Puddings: £3.95*

Free house ~ Licensees Mr and Mrs Kirtley ~ Real ale ~ Bar food (not Sun, Mon evenings) ~ No credit cards ~ (01992) 522394 ~ Open 11.30-2.30(3 Sat, 4 Sun), 6-11(10.30 Sun)

Recommended by David Jackson, R T and J C Moggridge, the Didler, Simon and Sally Small, Mrs Ann Gray, P and J Shapley, David and Valerie Mort

STOCK   TQ6999   MAP 5

Hoop 🍺

B1007; from A12 Chelmsford bypass take Galleywood, Billericay turn-off; CM4 9BD

Happy weatherboarded pub with interesting beers and a large garden

This old weatherboarded pub opens all day during the eight days of their beer festival around the late May bank holiday, during which they put on over 200 real ales and 80 ciders and perries. The rest of the time they have Adnams and three guests from brewers such as Brentwood, Purple Moose and Whitstable on handpump. The fairly simple interior feels pubbily functional (just the right down-to-earth setting for the cheery locals and visitors enjoying the happy bustle here) with all its wood fixtures and fittings, including a bare board floor, wooden tables and brocaded wooden settles. Standing timbers and beams in the open-plan bar hint at the building's great age and its original layout as a row of three weavers' cottages. In winter, a warm fire burns in a big brick-walled fireplace. A restaurant up in the timbered eaves (very different in style, with a separate à la carte menu) is light and airy with pale timbers set in white walls and more wood flooring. Prettily bordered with flowers, the large sheltered back garden has picnic-sets and a covered seating area. Parking is limited, so it is worth getting here early.

🍴 **Pubby food includes sandwiches, goats cheese and red onion filo tart, ploughman's, prawn and crayfish cocktail, battered fish and chips, calves liver, bacon and mash, scampi and chips, toad in the hole, ham, beef, mushroom and ale pie and sirloin steak, and puddings such as bread and butter pudding and mixed berry pavolva; they may ask to hold your credit card if you run a tab.** *Starters/Snacks: £4.00 to £6.00. Main Courses: £5.00 to £10.00. Puddings: £4.00 to £6.00*

Free house ~ Licensee Michelle Corrigan ~ Real ale ~ Bar food (12-2(3 Sat, 5 Sun), 6-9; not Sun evening) ~ Restaurant ~ (01277) 841137 ~ Children welcome if eating ~ Dogs allowed in bar ~ Open 11-11; 12-10.30 Sun

Recommended by MJVK, John and Enid Morris, DFL, LM, John Prescott, Edward Mirzoeff

STOW MARIES
TQ8399   MAP 5

Prince of Wales

B1012 between South Woodham Ferrers and Cold Norton Posters; CM3 6SA

Unfussy traditional local with interesting beers and good pubby food

A relaxed pubby atmosphere and the cheery bustle of locals and visitors are characteristic of this little white weatherboarded pub. Few of its characterful little low-ceilinged rooms have space for more than one or two eclectic tables, chairs and wall benches on their Victorian quarry-tiled or oak floors. Years ago this was the village bakery, and on Thursday evenings they fire up the Victorian baker's oven to produce home-made pizzas. There are log fires throughout the winter months and in summer a large terrace leads to a lawn, or there's a conservatory dining area. The licensee was a co-founder of Crouch Vale Brewery so you can be sure that the half a dozen widely sourced guest beers, from brewers such as Crouch Vale, Dark Star, Hop Back, RCH and Titanic, will be well kept. He also stocks bottled and draught belgian beers and fruit beers; board games.

🍴 **Tasty bar food might include ciabattas, garlic prawns, whitebait, ham, egg and chips, fish and chips, pies, liver and bacon, lasagne and rib-eye steak. On some summer Sundays, they barbecue steaks and all sorts of fish from bass to black barracuda.** *Starters/Snacks: £3.45 to £6.25. Main Courses: £6.95 to £15.95. Puddings: £3.95*

Free house ~ Licensee Rob Walster ~ Real ale ~ Bar food (12-2.30, 7(6 Fri, Sat)-9.30, 12-9.30 Sun) ~ (01621) 828971 ~ Children in family room ~ Jazz third Fri of the month ~ Open 11-11(midnight Fri, Sat); 12-10.30 Sun ~ Bedrooms: £45B/£68B

Recommended by John Saville, David Jackman, David Jackson, Peter Meister, Roger and Pauline Pearce, David Warren

WENDENS AMBO
TL5136   MAP 5

Bell 🍺

B1039 just W of village; CB11 4JY

Cheery local with pubby bar food and entertaining play area in the big garden

The cheery landlady at this wonky pink-washed village pub runs a good ship with enthusiasm and pride. The small cottagey low-ceilinged rooms are traditional and pubby, with locals gathered for a pint and a chat with the friendly staff around the little serving counter, brasses on ancient timbers, wheelback chairs around neat tables, comfortably cushioned seats worked into snug alcoves, quite a few pictures on cream walls, and an inviting open fire. Adnams and Woodfordes Wherry are well kept on handpump, along with three changing guests from brewers such as Crouch Vale, Oakham and Wolf and Weston's Old Rosie; during the August bank holiday weekend they bring in dozens of real ales for their beer and music festival. The extensive back garden has a suntrap terrace leading to a big tree-sheltered lawn and a great timber play area that should keep kids entertained for a while; board games and piped music. The landlady's friendly new dog, called Pub Dog, is a deaf old english bull dog.

Ⅱ **Tasty food includes filled baguettes, smoked salmon and capers, curry of the day, sausages and mash, fish and chips, steak, mushroom and ale or fish pie, sirloin steak, goats cheese and red onion marmalade puff pastry tart and changing specials such as roasted mediterranean vegetables and slow-roasted belly of pork; good Sunday lunches.** *Starters/Snacks: £4.50 to £6.50. Main Courses: £7.50 to £12.50. Puddings: £3.50 to £4.50*

Free house ~ Licensee Anne Güney ~ Real ale ~ Bar food (12-2.30(3 Sun), 6.30-9 (not Sun evening and Mon)) ~ Restaurant ~ (01799) 540382 ~ Children welcome ~ Dogs welcome ~ Open 11.30(12 Sun)-midnight; 11.30-3, 5-midnight Mon in winter
Recommended by Eddie Edwards, Roxanne Chamberlain, Jerry Brown

LUCKY DIP

Besides the fully inspected pubs, you might like to try these Lucky Dips recommended to us and described by readers (if you do, please send us reports: feedback@goodguides.com).

ABRIDGE [TQ4696]
Blue Boar RM4 1UA: Small hotel given smart contemporary refurbishment, good value food all day from pub favourites up, restaurant with open kitchen, relaxed atmosphere; terrace, six bedrooms *(Robert Lester)*

BELCHAMP ST PAUL [TL7942]
Half Moon CO10 7DP [Cole Green]: Thatched pub overlooking green, with well kept Adnams, Earl Soham and Greene King, generous good value honest food, friendly service (can be slow at busy times), snug beamed lounge, open fire, cheerful locals' bar, restaurant, Aug beer/music festival; children welcome, tables out in front and in back garden *(LYM, Jeremy King)*

BRIGHTLINGSEA [TM0916]
Rosebud CO7 0EH [Hurst Green]: Good reasonably priced food inc local seafood and game, Adnams, Woodfordes and Wells & Youngs ales, friendly staff *(Fiona Pleasant)*

BURNHAM-ON-CROUCH [TQ9596]
Ship CM0 8AA [High St]: Comfortable Adnams pub with enjoyable generous food (emphasis on fish), well kept beer, reasonable prices, efficient friendly staff, nautical theme; bedrooms *(Chris Harvey, Mrs Margo Finlay, Jörg Kasprowski, Andy Lickfold)*

CASTLE HEDINGHAM [TL7835]
Bell CO9 3EJ [B1058]: Beamed and timbered three-bar pub dating from 15th c, unpretentious and well worn in, with Adnams, Mighty Oak and guests (July beer festival), enjoyable pubby food inc specials; piped and some live music (lunchtime Jazz last Sun of month); dogs welcome, children away from public bar, garden, handy for Hedingham Castle, open all day Fri-Sun *(Ian Wilson, Peter Meister, Peter Thornton, LYM)*

CHAPPEL [TL8928]
Swan CO6 2DD [Wakes Colne; off A1124 Colchester—Halstead]: Oak-beamed dining pub improved under present licensee, enjoyable food inc good value Sun lunch,

well kept Adnams and local ales, inglenook log fire; cobbled courtyard, view of Victorian viaduct from spreading garden by River Colne, open all day wknds *(Jean and Douglas Troup, Colin and Penny Smith, LYM)*

CHATHAM GREEN [TL7115]
☆ *Windmill* CM3 3LE: Generous food, good changing ales and one brewed for them by local Brentwood, reasonably priced wines by the glass, friendly helpful staff, comfortably cushioned chairs and pews around sturdy tables, some rustic bric-a-brac; a few picnic-sets outside, seven bedrooms in stub of former windmill, open all day Fri, Sat, till 7pm Sun *(BB, Roy and Lindsey Fentiman, Mark Morgan, Edith Pateman)*

CHELMSFORD [TL7107]
☆ *Alma* CM1 7RG [Arbour Lane, off B1137]: Upscale pub/restaurant, airy contemporary décor, good food from lunchtime ciabattas, bar dishes and bargain off-season lunches up, friendly service; leather sofas and flagstones in bar with real ales such as Adnams Broadside and Greene King IPA, good choice of wines by the glass, smart dining area with big open fireplace; piped music; pleasant front and back terraces, children welcome in restaurant, open all day *(Mike and Mary Carter, LYM, Mrs Margo Finlay, Jörg Kasprowski)*

☆ *Queens Head* CM2 0AS [Lower Anchor St]: Lively well run Victorian side-street local with very well kept Crouch Vale ales and interesting guests, summer farm cider, good value wines, friendly staff, winter log fires, bargain lunchtime food from doorstep sandwiches up (not Sun); children welcome, colourful courtyard, open all day *(the Didler, Justin and Emma King)*

CHIGWELL [TQ4493]
Olde Kings Head IG7 6QA [High Rd (A113)]: Large handsome 16th-c weatherboarded pub with wide choice of sensibly priced food inc carvery, quick friendly service, good choice of wines by the glass, real ales, some antique furnishings and interesting Dickens'

memorabilia (features in *Barnaby Rudge*), dark low-beamed décor, conservatory, upstairs restaurant; piped music; children welcome, picnic-sets on attractive back terrace *(Robert Lester)*

COGGESHALL [TL8422]

White Hart CO6 1NP [Bridge St]: Civilised inn with lots of low 15th-c beams in cosy neatly kept front bar, antique settles among other comfortable seats, prints and fishing trophies, prompt service even when busy; wide choice of food from sandwiches up, well kept Adnams or Greene King IPA, decent wines and coffee, restaurant; pleasant small courtyard, 18 comfortable bedrooms *(BB, Peter and Jean Hoare)*

COLCHESTER [TM9824]

Hospital Arms CO3 3HA [Crouch St (opp hospital)]: Friendly pub with several small linked areas, wide range of well kept Adnams ales, enjoyable inexpensive pubby food from sandwiches and baguettes up, quick friendly service, home of Colchester RFC; games machines *(Kevin Flack, Pat and Tony Martin)*

Red Lion CO1 1DJ [High St]: Vestiges of Tudor grandeur survive in this comfortable central hotel, good bar food from doorstep sandwiches up, well kept real ales, welcoming friendly staff, restaurant; 24 bedrooms *(Tim Elliot, LYM)*

DANBURY [TL7704]

Cricketers Arms CM3 4ED [Penny Royal Rd]: Cheerful beamed country local overlooking common, good value home-made food, Shepherd Neame beers, woodburner; good walks *(Tina and David Woods-Taylor)*

Griffin CM3 4DH [A414, top of Danbury Hill]: Recently refurbished, spacious and well divided, with wide range of food all day inc Sun carvery, well kept Adnams Broadside and guest beers, 16th-c beams and some older carved woodwork, good log fires, pleasant service; piped music; children welcome, terrace seating, views, open all day *(Gerry Thaxton)*

DEBDEN [TL5533]

Plough CB11 3LE [High St]: Friendly renovated pub in attractive village, several well kept ales inc Black Sheep, restaurant; fair-sized garden behind *(Eddie Edwards)*

DUTON HILL [TL6026]

☆ *Three Horseshoes* CM6 2DX [off B184 Dunmow—Thaxted, 3 miles N of Dunmow]: Popular friendly traditional village local, well kept Mighty Oak and guests, late May bank hol beer festival, central fire, aged armchairs by fireplace in homely left-hand parlour, lots of interesting memorabilia, darts and pool in small public bar, no food; dogs welcome, old enamel signs out at front, pleasant views and pond in garden, cl lunchtime Mon-Weds *(BB, the Didler)*

EDNEY COMMON [TL6504]

Green Man CM1 3QE [Highwood Rd]: Plainly comfortable pub/restaurant with good food, extensive wine list (several by the glass), well kept beer, friendly staff; cl Mon *(Mrs Margo Finlay, Jörg Kasprowski)*

EPPING [TL4602]

Black Lion CM16 4DA [High St]: Unpretentious beamed 17th-c pub, locals' side bar, warming log fire in quieter front bar, four or five ales inc some unusual ones, basic lunchtime food; small back garden *(Owen Patchett)*

EPPING FOREST [TL4501]

Forest Gate CM16 4DZ [Bell Common]: Large friendly open-plan pub dating from 17th c, beams and panelling, good mix of customers, well kept Adnams, Nethergate and guests, enjoyable home-made bar food; tables on front lawn *(the Didler)*

FEERING [TL8720]

☆ *Sun* CO5 9NH [Feering Hill, B1024]: Interesting old pub with 16th-c beams (watch out for the very low one over the inner entrance door), plenty of bric-a-brac, woodburners in huge inglenooks, carved bar counter with half a dozen well kept ales, efficient service, enjoyable home-made food from sandwiches up; daily papers, board games; well behaved children allowed, partly covered paved terrace, attractive garden behind, some wknd barbecues *(LYM, the Didler)*

FINCHINGFIELD [TL6832]

Red Lion CM7 4NN [Church Hill – B1053 just E of B1057 crossroad]: Beams and brasses, Greene King and related ales, enjoyable sensibly priced food, friendly staff, log fire in huge dividing chimneybreast, dining room up a few steps; piped pop; children and dogs welcome, covered terrace tables, attractive garden, nice spot opp churchyard and 15th-c guild hall *(Jeremy King, Mrs Margo Finlay, Jörg Kasprowski)*

FINGRINGHOE [TM0220]

Whalebone CO5 7BG [off A134 just S of Colchester centre, or B1025]: Airy country-chic rooms with cream-painted tables on oak floors, well kept ales such as Brains, good changing food with some interesting choices (freshly cooked so can be a wait), nice coffee, friendly chatty staff; TV, piped music, no children; charming back garden with peaceful valley view, front terrace, open all day wknds *(LYM, Ryta Lyndley)*

FULLER STREET [TL7416]

Square & Compasses CM3 2BB [back road Great Leighs—Hatfield Peverel]: Small refurbished traditional country pub, welcoming and popular, with wide choice of fresh food from sandwiches up, choice of local ales and wines by the glass, big log fire in L-shaped beamed bar, attention to detail such as linen napkins; soft piped music; gentle country views from tables outside *(Barbara Cornell, Michelle Donnelly, LYM, Mrs Margo Finlay, Jörg Kasprowski)*

FYFIELD [TL5706]

☆ *Queens Head* CM5 0RY [corner of B184 and Queen St]: Smart dining pub dating from 15th c, enterprising if not cheap (not Sun evening) from light dishes up inc popular set menu, snug low-beamed L-shaped bar with fresh flowers on sturdy elm tables, button-back banquettes and high-backed chairs, facing fireplaces; three ales inc Crouch Vale, Weston's Old Rosie cider, good choice of wines by the glass inc champagne; piped music, no children; small outside covered area at front, prettily planted back garden with picnic-sets down to sleepy River Roding, open all day wknds *(Howard Dell, LYM, Jeremy King, Mr and Mrs C F Turner, Tina and David Woods-Taylor)*

GOSFIELD [TL7829]

Green Man CO9 1TP [3 miles N of Braintree]: Recently reopened after refurbishment, beams and inglenook, generous food (not Sun evening) with emphasis on fresh seafood, friendly efficient service; garden, open all day Fri-Sun *(Ian Wilson, LYM)*

GREAT STAMBRIDGE [TQ8991]

Royal Oak SS4 2AX [Stambridge Rd]: Pleasant country pub with good food in bar and separate restaurant, well kept Greene King IPA, several wines by the glass, friendly staff; big garden with nice views *(Tina and David Woods-Taylor, Rosanna Luke, Matt Curzon)*

HATFIELD BROAD OAK [TL5416]

Dukes Head CM22 7HH [High St]: Reopened under new young couple and already popular for its enjoyable good value food, friendly service, log fire, conservatory; close to Hatfield Forest, and Stansted Airport *(David Kenny)*

HATFIELD PEVEREL [TL7911]

Duke of Wellington CM3 2EA [The Street]: Welcoming staff, comprehensive menu, well kept Greene King, decent wines, competitive prices *(Charles Gysin)*

HOWE STREET [TL6914]

Green Man CM3 1BG [just off A130 N of Chelmsford]: Spacious heavily beamed and timbered building dating from 14th c, sensibly priced hearty food (all day Sat, Sun carvery till 6pm), Greene King ales, log fire, pub dog called Bailey, live music, pool and darts; garden with decked area and children's playthings, barbecues, adjoining paddock with small river, campsite, open all day Sat, cl Sun evening *(anon)*

HOWLETT END [TL5834]

☆ *White Hart* CB10 2UZ [Thaxted Rd (B184 SE of Saffron Walden)]: Comfortable pub/restaurant, two smartly set modern dining rooms either side of small tiled-floor bar with Greene King IPA and leather armchairs, enjoyable food from generous sandwiches and light dishes up, nice choice of wines, helpful service, friendly retriever; children welcome, terrace and big garden, quiet spot *(Philip and Cheryl Hill, BB)*

KELVEDON HATCH [TQ5798]

Eagle CM15 0AA [Ongar Rd (A128)]: Friendly family local set back from road, low-ceilinged bar area, good choice of food from sandwiches and baguettes to specials and Sun roasts, well kept Adnams and Marstons ales, efficient service; piped music, TV, quiz night Mon; children welcome, covered seating area out at front *(LM)*

LAMARSH [TL8835]

Lion CO8 5EP [take Station Rd off B1508 Sudbury—Colchester; Lamarsh then signed]: Attractive pub dating from 14th c, abundant beams and timbers, big log fire, local pictures, enjoyable sensibly priced food (not Sun evening), well kept ales such as Greene King, Mauldons and Mighty Oak, Aspall's cider, friendly helpful staff; restaurant, games room; nice country views from seats out at front *(Steve and Sue Griffiths, LYM)*

LANGHAM [TM0232]

Shepherd & Dog CO4 5NR [Moor Rd/High St]: Chatty village pub with wide choice of popular sensibly priced food inc curries (cooked by landlord's father), Greene King and Nethergate ales, friendly attentive service, L-shaped bar with spacious areas off; piped music; children and dogs welcome, enclosed side garden, open all day Sun *(N R White, LYM)*

LAYER BRETON [TL9418]

Hare & Hounds CO2 0PN [Crayes Green]: Refurbished traditional beamed pub overlooking common, enthusiastic friendly landlord, good choice of well kept ales such as Woodfordes Wherry, tasty home-made food from shortish menu, well priced wine; live music, quiz nights, fruit machine; close to Abberton Reservoir *(John McLellan)*

LEIGH-ON-SEA [TQ8385]

☆ *Crooked Billet* SS9 2EP [High St]: Homely old pub with waterfront views from big bay windows, packed on busy summer days when service can be frantic but friendly, well kept Adnams, Fullers London Pride and three changing guests inc seasonal ales, enjoyable basic pub food; log fires, beams, panelled dado and bare boards, local fishing pictures and bric-a-brac; piped music, winter jazz Fri nights, no under-21s after 6pm; side garden and terrace, seawall seating over road shared with Osborne's good shellfish stall (plastic glasses for outside), pay-and-display parking by flyover, open all day *(LM, N R White, David Jackson, LYM)*

LITTLE TOTHAM [TL8811]

☆ *Swan* CM9 8LB [School Rd]: Welcoming country local with good changing cask-tapped ales from the area, farm ciders and perry, enjoyable good value straightforward food (not Sun evening, Mon) inc basket meals, low 17th-c beams, log fire, back dining area, tiled games bar with darts; June beer festival; children and dogs welcome, disabled facilities, small terrace and informal front garden, camping, open all day *(Jerry Brown, the Didier, David Jackson, BB, Jean and David Lewis)*

LITTLEY GREEN [TL6917]

Compasses CM3 1BU [off A130 and B1417 SE of Felsted]: Unpretentiously quaint and old-fashioned country pub, isolated but thriving, with Adnams and guest ales tapped from cellar casks, farm cider and perry, good range of whiskies, basic food, roaring log fire; tables in big back garden, benches at front, good walks, open all day Thurs-Sun *(the Didler, Roy and Lindsey Fentiman)*

MATCHING GREEN [TL5310]

Chequers CM17 0PZ [off Downhall Rd]: Victorian pub comprehensively modernised as contemporary upmarket pub/restaurant, not cheap but enjoyable traditional and mediterranean-style food from ciabattas up, friendly staff, well kept Greene King IPA, candles on pine tables, lounge with sofas and woodburner, american-style central bar, cabaret nights; garden, quiet spot with picnic-sets overlooking pretty cricket green, cl Mon *(Mrs Margo Finlay, Jörg Kasprowski, Tina and David Woods-Taylor)*

MATCHING TYE [TL5111]

Fox CM17 0QS [The Green]: Attractive low-beamed 17th-c pub opp peaceful village green, decent range of good quality food, Greene King and Shepherd Neame, good welcoming service, comfortable dark wood furniture, brasses, model vehicles, cricket and transport pictures, restaurant; tables in big garden *(Grahame and Myra Williams)*

MORETON [TL5307]

Nags Head CM5 0LF [signed off B184, at S end of Fyfield or opp Chipping Ongar school]: Cosy welcoming country pub, enjoyable good value freshly made food from nice lunchtime sandwiches up, well kept Greene King ales, three big log fires (not always lit), comfortable mix of tables and medley of salvaged rustic beams and timbers, restaurant; children welcome, picnic-sets on side grass *(Gordon Neighbour, Holly Maslin, Tina and David Woods-Taylor)*

MOUNT BURES [TL9031]

☆ *Thatchers Arms* CO8 5AT: Well run modernised pub with good food (fresh, so may be a wait) using local game and meats, mid-week meal deals, well kept interesting ales (occasional beer festivals), friendly staff and dog; peaceful Stour Valley views at back; dogs welcome, plenty of picnic-sets out behind, cl Mon, open all day wknds *(David and Lesley Elliott, John Prescott, BB, Colin Smith)*

ORSETT [TQ6483]

Dog & Partridge RM16 3HU [A128 S of Bulphan]: Roadside pub with friendly helpful staff and good straightforward food (vegetables from local farm), well kept beer; large garden with duck pond *(Tina and David Woods-Taylor)*

PAGLESHAM [TQ9492]

☆ *Plough & Sail* SS4 2EQ [East End]: Relaxed 17th-c weatherboarded dining pub in pretty spot, generally good food from sandwiches through familiar favourites to interesting specials inc fresh fish, popular Sun lunch, friendly attentive staff but service can suffer when busy; well kept changing ales such as Mighty Oak Maldon Gold, decent house wines, low beams and big log fires, pine tables, lots of brasses and pictures, traditional games; unobtrusive piped music; front picnic-sets and hanging baskets, attractive side garden, open all day Sun *(LM,*

John Roots, Mrs Margo Finlay, Jörg Kasprowski, LYM)*

☆ *Punchbowl* SS4 2DP [Church End]: 16th-c former sailmaker's loft with low beams and stripped brickwork, pews, barrel chairs and lots of brass, lower room laid for dining, beers such as Adnams, Cottage and Nethergate, straightforward fairly priced food inc good OAP menu, prompt friendly service; cribbage and darts; piped music (mostly 60s and 70s); children usually welcome but check first, lovely rural view from sunny front garden *(LYM, Pat and Tony Martin, Mrs Margo Finlay, Jörg Kasprowski)*

PELDON [TL9916]

Plough CO5 7QR [Lower Rd]: Enjoyable blackboard food in small traditional tiled and white-boarded village pub, quick friendly service, Greene King and a guest ale, well spaced stripped pine tables and coastal paintings in restaurant, public bar *(BB, David Jackson)*

PLESHEY [TL6614]

☆ *White Horse* CM3 1HA [The Street]: 15th-c beamed pub refurbished under new management; four bar areas, open fires, big back extension with two dining rooms, traditional home-made blackboard food from huffers up inc meal deals, Adnams and two changing local guests, theme nights; piped music; no dogs; children welcome, tables on terrace and in good-sized garden, pretty village with ruined castle, open all day Sun *(LYM)*

ROYDON [TL4010]

New Inn CM19 5EE [High St]: Village-green pub, carpeted timbered bar with small raised back dining area, framed plates and photographs, separate dining room, well kept Adnams, Courage and Greene King IPA, friendly staff and locals, simple enjoyable good value food (not Sun or Mon evenings) inc OAP deals (Tues-Fri); piped radio, TV; children welcome, back garden with picnic-sets and timber-framed shelter *(LM)*

SAFFRON WALDEN [TL5338]

Eight Bells CB10 1BU [Bridge St; B184 towards Cambridge]: Old pub given contemporary fresh refurbishment, linked rooms inc bare-boards snug with leather chairs by open brick fireplace, back restaurant in handsomely raftered and timbered medieval hall with modern dark wood furniture, some interesting if pricey food, Adnams and Timothy Taylors Landlord, art for sale; soft piped music; garden tables, handy for Audley End, open all day Fri and Sat, cl Sun evening *(LYM, Jeremy King, P and D Carpenter)*

SIBLE HEDINGHAM [TL7535]

Bottle Hall CO9 3LN [Delvin End]: Quietly placed welcoming country pub, enjoyable reasonably priced pubby food, good service; open evenings only *(David Kirkcaldy)*

STEEPLE [TL9302]

Sun & Anchor CM0 7RH [The Street]: Village pub set back from road with cream and brown 50s décor, well kept ales inc local

Wibblers Apprentice from side room by bar, well priced food from good thick-cut sandwiches to generous Sun roasts, friendly efficient staff; disabled facilities, small terrace with plastic furniture, well spaced picnic-sets on big rectangular lawn *(LM)*

☆ **Dolphin** CM77 8EU [A120 E of Braintree, by village turn]: Cheerful heavily beamed and timbered bar, good value straightforward fresh food (all day) cooked to order, Greene King and guest ales tapped from the cask, brasses, antlers and lots of small prints, newspapers, log fire, bright extended eating area on left; piped music; children and dogs welcome, pretty back garden with heated covered area, nice hanging baskets, views over fields *(LYM, the Didler, Jeremy King)*

TENDRING [TM1523]
Cherry Tree CO16 9AP [Crow Lane, E of village centre]: Under new management but same chef, good food inc set deals, well kept ales, decent coffee *(Ryta Lyndley)*

THEYDON BOIS [TQ4599]
Queen Victoria CM16 7ES [Coppice Row (B172)]: Cosy beamed and carpeted traditional lounge, roaring log fire, local pictures, mug collection, two further bars, popular good value food inc children's menu, friendly efficient staff, well kept McMullens ales, decent house wines, restaurant; piped music; dogs welcome, picnic-sets on well laid out front terrace, open all day *(Robert Lester, N R White)*

UPSHIRE [TL4100]
Horseshoes EN9 3SN [Horseshoe Hill, E of Waltham Abbey]: Welcoming well run Victorian pub with small bar area and dining room, popular food (not Sun evening, Mon) inc lots of good fresh fish and generous Sun roasts (must book), well kept McMullens ales, friendly helpful staff; tidy garden overlooking Lea Valley, more tables out in front, good walks, open all day

(Andy Millward, Brian Glozier, Anthony and Marie Lewis)

WALTHAM ABBEY [TQ4199]
Volunteer EN9 3QT [0.5 miles from M25 junction 26; A121 towards Loughton]: Roomy extensively refurbished family pub with reliable reasonably priced food, McMullens ales, prompt friendly service, attractive conservatory, flowers on tables; piped music; some tables on terrace facing road, pretty hanging baskets, nice spot by Epping Forest *(Edward Mirzoeff, BB)*

WICKHAM ST PAUL [TL8336]
☆ **Victory** CO9 2PT [SW of Sudbury; The Green]: Attractive and spacious old dining pub, interesting choice of good fresh food, friendly efficient service, Adnams and Woodfordes Wherry, beams and timbers, leather sofas and armchairs, inglenook woodburner; piped pop music; children welcome, neat garden overlooking village cricket green, open all day, cl Mon *(Mrs J Kendrick, BB)*

WIVENHOE [TM0423]
Flag CO7 9HS [Colchester Rd, upper village]: Notable for its enjoyable OAP bargain lunches, nice wine and coffee too, friendly quick staff *(Ryta Lyndley)*

WOODHAM MORTIMER [TL8104]
Hurdlemakers Arms CM9 6ST [Post Office Rd]: Small quietly placed traditional country local, flagstoned lounge with settles, low ceiling, timbered walls and big open fire, well kept ales, wide choice of enjoyable fresh food from good baguettes and panini up, friendly efficient service; public bar; children welcome, picnic-sets among trees and shrubs *(BB, Tina and David Woods-Taylor)*

WRITTLE [TL6706]
Wheatsheaf CM1 3DU [The Green]: Popular traditional two-room 19th-c local, friendly and chatty, with well kept Adnams, Greene King, Mighty Oak and guests, folk nights 3rd Fri of month; terrace tables, open all day Fri-Sun *(the Didler)*

Gloucestershire

There are some real gems here, both unspoilt and rather smart, and a lot of enthusiasm for both from our many readers. Pubs with a lot of positive support include the Bowl at Almondsbury (handy for the M5 so gets busy at peak times), the Queens Arms in Ashleworth (the south african licensees have much long-standing loyal support), the Boat at Ashleworth Quay (simple old alehouse in the same family for hundreds of years), the Village Pub in Barnsley (new management but all is running smoothly), the Kings Head in Bledington (popular for food and as somewhere to stay), the Horse & Groom at Bourton-on-the-Hill (a proper pubby bar despite being a highly thought-of dining pub), the Bakers Arms in Broad Campden (friendly welcome for all in a traditional local), the Eight Bells in Chipping Campden (a really good atmosphere despite being in a tourist town), the Yew Tree at Clifford's Mesne (the wine shop is going down a storm), the Five Mile House at Duntisbourne Abbots (the father and son team are extremely popular here), the Old Spot in Dursley (nine real ales kept by a knowledgeable and helpful landlord), the Plough at Ford (the many customers like the generous helpings of food and the friendliness), the Hollow Bottom in Guiting Power (lots of racing memorabilia and a bustling happy atmosphere), the Bathurst Arms in North Cerney (smashing food, wine and bedrooms), the Wheatsheaf in Northleach (excellent food and french wines), the Anchor in Oldbury-on-Severn (another very well run all-rounder), the Bell at Sapperton (a super place and firm favourite with all), the Butchers Arms in Sheepscombe (the lively mix of customers much enjoy their visits), the Mount at Stanton (a lovely spot and run by keen young licensees), the Gumstool at Tetbury (a busy characterful bar attached to a smart hotel) and the Farriers Arms in Todenham (a lovely landlady runs this nice unspoilt place). This has to be one of our strongest counties for food with 15 pubs holding one of our Food Awards. Our Gloucestershire Dining Pub 2011 is the Bathurst Arms in North Cerney.

ALMONDSBURY   ST6084 MAP 2
Bowl

1.5 miles from M5 junction 16 (and therefore quite handy for M4 junction 20); from A38 towards Thornbury, turn left signposted Lower Almondsbury, then first right down Sundays Hill, then at bottom right again into Church Road; BS32 4DT

Busy pub, handy for M5, with popular food, fine range of real ales and a pretty setting

Being close to the M5 means this friendly pub does get crowded at peak times but service is quick and efficient and our readers enjoy their visits; best to get there early if you want to eat in the main bar which has the most character. This room is long and beamed with traditional settles, cushioned stools and mate's chairs around elm tables, horsebrasses on stripped bare stone walls and a big winter log fire at one end with a woodburning stove at the other. There's also a restaurant extension. Brains Up and Over and Rev James, Butcombe Bitter and Gold and Fullers Chiswick on handpump; a dozen wines by the glass and farm cider; piped music. There are seats in front of the pub and on the back terrace and the flowering tubs, hanging baskets and window boxes are lovely in summer. This is a pretty setting next to the church. Take a pound for the car park which is refundable at the bar.

🍴 Under the new licensee, the well liked bar food includes filled baguettes, soup, chicken liver, pancetta and black pudding salad, ham hock terrine with sweet mustard pickle, thai mussels with coconut, lemon grass and chilli, chicken and ham pie, deep-fried haddock with home-made tartare sauce, popular burger with smoked cheese, creamy butter bean, leek and mushroom gratin, beef bourguignon with honey-roast parsnips, and puddings like lemon tart with crème fraîche and berry crème brûlée; Sunday roasts. *Starters/Snacks: £3.95 to £6.95. Main Courses: £7.95 to £14.95. Puddings: £3.50 to £4.95*

Brains ~ Manager Kevin Lole ~ Real ale ~ Bar food (12-2.30, 6-9.30 Mon-Thurs; 12-9.30(8 Sun) Fri and Sat) ~ (01454) 612757 ~ Children allowed during food service times ~ Open 12-11 (10.30 Sun) ~ Bedrooms: /£69S

Recommended by Barry and Anne, Stephen Shepherd, Sheila Topham, Andy and Claire Barker, Moira and John Cole, Bob and Angela Brooks, James Morrell, Chris and Martin Taylor, Donna and Roger, David A Hammond, the Brewers, Pat and Tony Martin

ASHLEWORTH   SO8125   MAP 4

Queens Arms

Village signposted off A417 at Hartpury; GL19 4HT

Neatly kept pub with civilised bar, interesting food, thoughtful wines and sunny courtyard

Many of the customers to this low-beamed dining pub have been loyal throughout the 13 years that the friendly south african licensees have been here. It's all very neatly kept and the civilised main bar has a nice mix of farmhouse and brocaded dining chairs around big oak and mahogany tables on the green carpet, and faintly patterned wallpaper and washed red ochre walls; at night it is softly lit by fringed wall lamps and candles. Brains Rev James and guests like Greene King IPA or Timothy Taylors Landlord on handpump, 14 wines by the glass including south african ones, 22 malt whiskies, winter mulled wine and summer home-made lemonade; piped music, board games and (on request) a skittle alley. The little black cat, Bonnie, does still entertain customers with her ping-pong ball, but now that she is 14 she is a bit less active. There are cast-iron chairs and tables in the sunny courtyard; two perfectly clipped mushroom-shaped yews dominate the front of the building.

🍴 First class – if not cheap – bar food might include filled baguettes, crispy whitebait tossed in garlic butter, salmon fishcakes, rabbit casserole, steak and kidney pie, barbecue pork ribs, chicken topped with mozzarella and capers with a creamy masala sauce, greek-style lamb shank, bobotie (a south african dish), monkfish on parmesan and basil risotto topped with tomato beurre blanc, and puddings such as melktert (another south african speciality – a light custard tart with cinnamon) and raspberry crème brûlée. *Starters/Snacks: £4.95 to £8.95. Main Courses: £7.95 to £18.50. Puddings: £4.95 to £5.95*

Free house ~ Licensees Tony and Gill Burreddu ~ Real ale ~ Bar food (not Sun evening) ~ Restaurant ~ (01452) 700395 ~ Well behaved children allowed ~ Open 12-3, 7-11; 12-3 Sun; closed Sun evening; 25 and 26 Dec

Recommended by Bernard Stradling, Kim Merrifield, Dave and Jackie Kenward, Edna Jones

---

Stars after the name of a pub show exceptional quality. One star means most people (after reading the report to see just why the star has been won) would think a special trip worth while. Two stars mean that the pub is really outstanding – for its particular qualities it could hardly be bettered.

ASHLEWORTH QUAY

SO8125   MAP 4

Boat ★ ◀

Ashleworth signposted off A417 N of Gloucester; quay signed from village; GL19 4HZ

Delightful and unchanging Severn-side pub with swiftly changing beers – and in the same family for hundreds of years

The same family have run this quaint unmodernised alehouse since it was originally granted a licence by Charles II. It's a tiny place, kept spotlessly clean, and the little front parlour has a built-in settle by a long scrubbed deal table that faces an old-fashioned open kitchen range with a side bread oven and a couple of elderly fireside chairs; there are rush mats on the scrubbed flagstones, house plants in the window, fresh garden flowers, and old magazines to read; cribbage and dominoes in the front room. Two antique settles face each other in the back room where swiftly changing beers such as Box Steam Funnel Blower, RCH East Street Cream, Pitchfork and Old Slug Porter, Wye Valley Butty Bach and Wye Valley HPA are tapped from the cask, along with the full range of Weston's farm ciders. The front suntrap crazy-paved courtyard is bright with plant tubs in summer and there's a couple of picnic-sets under parasols; more seats and tables under cover at the sides.

🍴 **Lunchtime filled rolls and ploughman's as well as cakes and ice-cream.** *Starters/Snacks: £2.00 to £3.75*

Free house ~ Licensees Ron, Elisabeth and Louise Nicholls ~ Real ale ~ Bar food (lunchtime only; not Mon and Weds) ~ No credit cards ~ (01452) 700272 ~ Children welcome ~ Open 11.30-2.30(3 Sat), 6.30-11; 12-3, 7-11 Sun; evening opening 7pm in winter; closed all day Mon, Weds lunchtime

Recommended by Guy Vowles, the Didler, Theocsbrian, Stuart Doughty

BARNSLEY

SP0705   MAP 4

Village Pub 🍽 🍷 🛏

B4425 Cirencester—Burford; GL7 5EF

Enjoyable modern food in civilised communicating rooms, candles and open fires, good choice of drinks and seats in the back courtyard; bedrooms

Although this smart and civilised place is under new ownership, this year things are running as smoothly as ever. Locals and their dogs still drop in for a drink and a chat and the imaginative food draws in customers from far and wide. The low-ceilinged communicating rooms have flagstones and oak floorboards, oil paintings, plush chairs, stools and window settles around polished candlelit tables, three open fireplaces and country magazines and newspapers to read. Hook Norton Old Hooky and a couple of guest beers on handpump and an extensive wine list with several by the glass. The sheltered back courtyard has good solid wooden furniture under parasols, outdoor heaters and its own outside servery. This is now under the same ownership as Calcot Manor Hotel at Tetbury (their Gumstool bar is also a Main Entry in this chapter).

🍴 **Imaginative food includes snacks like quail scotch eggs and sea trout blinis with crème fraîche, soup, pork and pigeon terrine with pickles, crab with home-made mayonnaise, warmed goats cheese with pear, watercress and walnut praline, aubergine parmigiana, braised lamb hotpot with caper sauce, beer-battered haddock with mushy peas, venison haunch with apple and braised red cabbage, halibut with brown shrimp and lemon, and puddings such as chocolate pot with hazelnut biscuit and treacle tart with clotted cream.** *Starters/Snacks: £5.00 to £10.50. Main Courses: £12.00 to £15.50. Puddings: £6.00*

Free house ~ Licensee Neil Williams ~ Real ale ~ Bar food (12-2.30(3 weekends), 6-9.30(10 Fri and Sat)) ~ (01285) 740421 ~ Children welcome ~ Dogs welcome ~ Open 11-11(10.30 Sun) ~ Bedrooms: /£90B

Recommended by Guy Vowles, Bernard Stradling, Anthony and Pam Stamer, Steve and Liz Tilley, Michael Sargent

BISLEY

SO9006 MAP 4

Bear 🍺

Village signposted off A419 just E of Stroud; GL6 7BD

Friendly 16th-c inn with popular bar food, real ales and garden across a quiet road

There's plenty of character in this elegantly gothic 16th-c inn and a good mix of customers, too. The meandering L-shaped bar has a bustling atmosphere, a long shiny black built-in settle and a smaller but even sturdier oak settle by the front entrance, and brass and copper implements around an enormously wide low stone fireplace (not very high – the ochre ceiling's too low for that); the separate stripped-stone area is used for families. St Austell Tribute, Tetleys and Wells & Youngs Bombardier on handpump. A small front colonnade supports the upper floor of the pub, and the sheltered little flagstoned courtyard made by this has a traditional bench. The garden is across the quiet road and there's quite a collection of stone mounting-blocks.

🍽 **Enjoyable bar food includes filled baguettes, soup, garlic mushrooms, tuna niçoise salad, vegetable moussaka, smoked haddock fishcakes with parsley sauce, moroccan lamb with couscous, steak and kidney pie, stilton chicken, pork loin with ginger and spring onions in coconut sauce, beef stroganoff, and puddings like rhubarb crumble and home-made profiteroles with warm chocolate sauce.** *Starters/Snacks: £4.50 to £5.95. Main Courses: £8.95 to £13.95. Puddings: £3.95*

Punch ~ Lease Colin and Jane Pickford ~ Real ale ~ Bar food ~ Restaurant ~ (01452) 770265 ~ Children welcome but at busy times in family room only ~ Dogs allowed in bar ~ Open 12-3, 6-11(midnight Sat); 12-11 Sun ~ Bedrooms: £50S/£65S

Recommended by Dave Irving, Jenny Huggins, Bernard Stradling, Myra Joyce, Nick and Meriel Cox

BLAISDON

SO7016 MAP 4

Red Hart 🍺

Village signposted off A4136 just SW of junction with A40 W of Gloucester; OS Sheet 162 map reference 703169; GL17 0AH

Bustling and friendly, some interesting bric-a-brac in attractive rooms, popular bar food and several real ales

The exuberant landlord and his attentive staff are sure to make you welcome in this busy village inn. There are always plenty of chatty locals (and maybe Spotty, the jack russell, who is 14 now) and a fair choice of real ales – on handpump these might include Goffs Jouster, Hook Norton Bitter, RCH East Street Cream and Timothy Taylors Landlord. The flagstoned main bar has cushioned wall and window seats, traditional pub tables, a big sailing-ship painting above the log fire and a bustling atmosphere; piped music, table skittles and board games. On the right, there's an attractive beamed restaurant with interesting prints and bric-a-brac, and on the left, you'll find additional dining space for families. There are some picnic-sets in the garden and a children's play area, and at the back of the building is a terrace for summer barbecues. The little church above the village is worth a visit.

🍽 **Well liked bar food includes sandwiches, soup, pork and onion pâté with red onion chutney, deep-fried camembert with cranberry sauce, chicken in a creamy stilton sauce, gammon with egg or pineapple, liver and bacon with red onion gravy, poached salmon with lemon and dill sauce and specials such as goats cheese tart with sun-dried tomatoes, steak and mushroom in ale pie, lamb shank with a red wine and rosemary sauce and slow-roasted pork belly with black pudding and celeriac mash.** *Starters/Snacks: £3.95 to £5.75. Main Courses: £6.50 to £13.95. Puddings: £3.95*

Real ale to us means beer which has matured naturally in its cask – not pressurised or filtered. We name all real ales stocked. We usually name ales preserved under a light blanket of carbon dioxide too, though purists – pointing out that this stops the natural yeasts developing – would disagree (most people, including us, can't tell the difference!).

Free house ~ Licensee Guy Wilkins ~ Real ale ~ Bar food ~ Restaurant ~ (01452) 830477 ~ Well behaved children welcome ~ Dogs allowed in bar ~ Open 12-2.30, 6-11(11.30 Sat); 12-3.30, 7-10.30 Sun

Recommended by Mr and Mrs M J Girdler, Robert Turnham, Reg Fowle, Helen Rickwood, Theocsbrian, David and Gilly Wilkins

BLEDINGTON

SP2422   MAP 4

Kings Head 🍽 🍷 🍺 🛏

B4450; OX7 6XQ

Beams and atmospheric furnishings in civilised old inn, super wines by the glass, real ales and interesting food; bedrooms

This is a rather smart old place in a pretty setting just back from the village green. The main bar is full of ancient beams and other atmospheric furnishings (high-backed wooden settles, gateleg or pedestal tables) and there's a warming log fire in the stone inglenook where there are bellows and a big black kettle; sporting memorabilia of rugby, racing, cricket and hunting. To the left of the bar, a drinking area for locals has built-in wall benches, stools and dining chairs around wooden tables, rugs on bare boards and a woodburning stove. Hook Norton Best and guests from breweries such as Cottage, Purity, Stroud and Wye Valley on handpump, an excellent wine list with ten by the glass, 20 malt whiskies and interesting bottled ciders; board games, darts and TV. There are seats in front of the inn with more in the back courtyard garden. Some of the courtyard bedrooms have been redecorated this year.

🍽 Using meat from the family farm, game from the nearby estates and local vegetables, the interesting bar food might include a small choice of lunchtime sandwiches, baltic cured sea trout with beetroot relish and sour cream, lamb kofta kebabs with bombay potato and cucumber salad, cheese, herb and spinach fritters with sweet pepper marmalade, angus beefburger with fries, chargrilled free-range chicken with chorizo and leek tartiflette, steak in ale or cod and smoked haddock pies, daily specials, and puddings like caramelised rhubarb and custard with rhubarb schnapps and dark chocolate tart with home-made vanilla ice-cream; good breakfasts. *Starters/Snacks: £4.50 to £7.50. Main Courses: £9.50 to £20.00. Puddings: £5.00 to £6.50*

Free house ~ Licensees Nicola and Archie Orr-Ewing ~ Real ale ~ Bar food (12-2(2.30 weekends), 7-9(9.30 Fri and Sat)) ~ Restaurant ~ (01608) 658365 ~ Children welcome ~ Dogs allowed in bar ~ Open 11-3, 6-11; 11-11 Sat; 12-10 Sun; closed 25 and 26 Dec ~ Bedrooms: £60B/£75B

Recommended by Ian Malone, Ann and Colin Hunt, Helene Grygar, Richard Greaves, Guy Vowles, Bernard Stradling, John and Val Shand, Anthony and Pam Stamer, Jamie May, Lesley Dick

BOURTON-ON-THE-HILL

SP1732   MAP 4

Horse & Groom 🍽 🍷 🛏

A44 W of Moreton-in-Marsh; GL56 9AQ

Handsome Georgian inn, fine range of food and drink, and lovely views from seats outside; stylish bedrooms

Our readers have very much enjoyed their visits to this well run honey-coloured stone inn this year. The licensee brothers and their staff are friendly and efficient, the beers are well kept and the food extremely good. But despite quite an emphasis on meals (and it is best to book a table in advance to be sure of a table) there is a proper pubby bar where they don't take bookings and where there are plenty of chatty locals. This light and airy bar has a nice mix of wooden chairs and tables on bare boards, stripped-stone walls, a good log fire, Goffs Jouster and guests like Battledown Tipster and Patriot Missile on handpump, 14 wines including fizz by the glass, local lager and home-made summer cordials. There are plenty of original period features throughout. The large back garden has lots of seats under smart umbrellas and lovely views over the surrounding countryside. It's best to get here early to be sure of a space in the smallish car park. Batsford Arboretum is not far away.

🍴 Using local and home-grown produce, the short choice of interesting modern food includes soup, mackerel and leek fishcakes with mustard cream sauce, warm salad of goats cheese with roasted beetroot, caramelised red onions and watercress, cassoulet of butternut squash with leeks, haricot beans and a parmesan crust, beer-battered hake with minted pea purée and cucumber tartare, pork wellington with a green peppercorn sauce, beef braised with ginger and soy, sautéed noodles and wilted greens, and puddings such as spiced apple flapjack crumble and chocolate fudge brownie with chocolate sauce and vanilla ice-cream. *Starters/Snacks: £4.50 to £7.50. Main Courses: £10.00 to £18.50. Puddings: £4.50 to £6.50*

Free house ~ Licensee Tom Greenstock ~ Real ale ~ Bar food (not Sun evening) ~ (01386) 700413 ~ Children welcome ~ Open 11-2.30(3 Sat), 6-11; 12-3.30 Sun; closed Sun evening ~ Bedrooms: £80B/£110B

Recommended by Roger Braithwaite, Michael Doswell, Derek Thomas, Paul Boot, Bernard Stradling, Richard Tilbrook, Peter J and Avril Hanson, P Waterman, Anthony and Pam Stamer, Mr and Mrs A H Young, Martin and Karen Wake, Mike and Sue Loseby, Bob Butterworth, Dennis and Gill Keen

BOX   SO8500   MAP 4

Halfway House
By Minchinhampton Common; GL6 9AE

Light, airy bars and downstairs restaurant, several real ales and well liked bar food

Although there were quite a few licensee changes over the last couple of years, things seem to have settled down now at this tall 300-year-old house. The open-plan bars are light and airy and ramble around the central serving bar and there are simple sturdy blond wooden chairs around good wooden tables, a built-in wall seat and stripped wooden floors. The bar has yellowy cream walls and ceiling, the dining area is mainly a warm terracotta, there are windows with views to the common and an unusual pitched-roof area. There's also a downstairs restaurant. Butcombe Bitter and Sharps Cornish Coaster and Doom Bar on handpump and decent wines; piped music. There are seats in the landscaped garden.

🍴 Well liked bar food includes sandwiches, soup, chicken liver pâté with onion marmalade, smoked salmon and langoustine cocktail, mozzarella, red onion and tomato tartlet, chicken with chorizo, mushrooms and pesto, asparagus and pea risotto with a poached free-range egg, salmon fillet with niçoise salad and honey and mustard dressing, steaks with a choice of sauces, bass with mussels and a creamy white wine and shallot sauce, and puddings like warm bakewell tart and banoffi pie. *Starters/Snacks: £4.50 to £7.50. Main Courses: £9.50 to £19.50. Puddings: £5.50*

Free house ~ Licensee Niall McInerney ~ Real ale ~ Bar food (12-2(3 Sun), 6.30-9.30) ~ Restaurant ~ (01453) 832631 ~ Children welcome ~ Dogs allowed in bar ~ Open mike night Tues, live band second Fri evening of the month ~ Open 11-3, 5(6 Mon)-11; 11-11 Fri, 12-11 Sat and Sun; closed Mon lunchtime

Recommended by Guy Vowles, Dave Irving, Jenny Huggins, E McCall, T McLean, D Irving

BRIMPSFIELD   SO9413   MAP 4

Golden Heart 🍺

Nettleton Bottom (not shown on road maps, so we list the pub instead under the name of the nearby village); on A417 N of the Brimpsfield turning northbound; GL4 8LA

Nice old-fashioned furnishings in several cosy areas, big log fire, friendly licensees, and seats on a suntrap terrace; bedrooms

As one reader put it 'proper traditional pubs like this are getting hard to find'. There is some genuine old character here and it's especially popular with the friendly locals – just the place for a pint and a chat. The main low-ceilinged bar is divided into five cosily distinct areas; there's a roaring log fire in the huge stone inglenook fireplace in one, well worn and traditional built-in settles and other old-fashioned furnishings throughout, quite a few brass items and typewriters, exposed stone walls and wood panelling; maybe newspapers to read. A comfortable parlour on the right has another decorative fireplace and leads into a further room that opens on to the terrace. Brakspears Bitter, Festival Gold, Marstons Pedigree and Wychwood Hobgoblin on handpump, some rare ciders and several wines by the glass. From the tables and chairs under parasols on the suntrap terrace, there are pleasant views down over a valley; nearby walks. The bedrooms are at the back of the pub and so escape any road noise.

🍴 **Bar food – perhaps not the strongest point here – includes some more ambitious dishes alongside familiar pubby things such as sandwiches, ploughman's, filled baked potatoes, omelettes and chicken curry.** *Starters/Snacks: £5.25 to £5.95. Main Courses: £10.95 to £15.95. Puddings: £4.25*

Free house ~ Licensee Catherine Stevens ~ Real ale ~ Bar food ~ (01242) 870261 ~ Children welcome ~ Dogs welcome ~ Open 11-3, 5.30-11; all day school hols; 11(12 Sun)-11 Sat ~ Bedrooms: £35S/£55S

Recommended by Giles and Annie Francis, Mrs Jane Kingsbury, Colin Moore, Tom and Ruth Rees, Gwyn and Anne Wake, Bob and Angela Brooks, Ken Marshall, Chris Flynn, Wendy Jones, Comus and Sarah Elliott, Neil and Anita Christopher

BROAD CAMPDEN   SP1537   MAP 4

Bakers Arms 🍺

Village signposted from B4081 in Chipping Campden; GL55 6UR

Friendly village pub with five real ales, traditional food and a good mix of customers

There's a warm welcome for all at this bustling, traditional pub and a good mix of both locals and visitors. With some beautiful walks nearby this makes a perfect start or finish and walkers' groups are welcomed in one of the back rooms (best to pre-order your food first). The tiny beamed bar has perhaps the most character and the atmosphere is chatty and relaxed. There's a mix of tables and seats around the walls (which are stripped back to bare stone), an inglenook fireplace at one end, and, from the attractive oak bar counter, Donnington BB, Stanway Stanney Bitter, Tetleys, Wells & Youngs Bombardier and a guest like Purity Gold on handpump; board games. The pictorial rug on the wall which features the pub took 1,000 hours to make; the dining room is beamed with exposed stone walls. There are new seats under parasols on a terraced area, with more by flower tubs on other terraces in the back garden.

🍴 **Popular bar food includes lunchtime sandwiches, filled baguettes and giant yorkshire puddings, ploughman's, soup, ham and sautéed potatoes, lasagne, stilton and vegetable crumble, steak and kidney pudding, cottage pie, chicken curry, daily specials such as lamb shank in mint gravy, salmon fishcakes and pork and apricot casserole, and puddings like treacle tart and spotted dick; Sunday roasts.** *Starters/Snacks: £3.95 to £5.95. Main Courses: £7.50 to £9.95. Puddings: £3.15 to £4.25*

Free house ~ Licensees Ray and Sally Mayo ~ Real ale ~ Bar food (12-9 in summer; 12-2(2.30 Sat), 6-9 and 12-6 Sun in winter) ~ Restaurant ~ No credit cards ~ (01386) 840515 ~ Children welcome away from bar ~ Folk music third Tues evening of the month ~ Open 11.30-11; 12-10.30 Sun; 11.30-2.30, 5.30-11 Mon-Thurs in winter; closed 25 Dec, evenings 26 and 31 Dec

Recommended by Michael Dandy, Di and Mike Gillam, John R Ringrose, Mike Proctor, Martin and Pauline Jennings, Simon Watkins, Paul Humphreys, Guy Vowles

BROADWELL   SP2027   MAP 4

Fox

Off A429 2 miles N of Stow-on-the-Wold; GL56 0UF

Attractive stone pub in pretty village, with friendly staff, real ales, honest food and seats in the sizeable garden

You can be sure of a friendly welcome from the helpful staff in this golden stone pub. It's set above the broad green in a Cotswold village and there are picnic-sets on gravel in the sizeable family-friendly back garden; aunt sally. Inside, the bar has traditional pubby furnishings on flagstones, stripped-stone walls, beams hung with jugs, a log fire and Donnington BB and SBA on handpump; they also have a large number of rums and winter mulled wine. There are two carpeted dining areas, too. Piped music, darts and board games. The pub cat is called Molly.

⑪ **Good honest pubby food includes lunchtime filled baguettes and ploughman's, soup, garlic mushrooms, whitebait, ham and eggs, barbecue pork ribs, lasagne, beer-battered cod, popular lamb shank with red wine and rosemary, a big mixed grill, and puddings like bread and butter pudding and sticky toffee pudding.** *Starters/Snacks: £4.75 to £4.95. Main Courses: £7.95 to £17.95. Puddings: £3.95 to £4.95*

Donnington ~ Managers Michael and Carol East ~ Real ale ~ Bar food (11.30-2, 6.30-9; not Sun evening) ~ Restaurant ~ (01451) 870909 ~ Children welcome ~ Dogs allowed in bar ~ Open 11-2.30(3 Sat), 6-11(11.30 Sat); 12-3, 7-11 Sun

Recommended by John and Sue Woodward

BROCKHAMPTON   SP0322   MAP 4

Craven Arms ♀

Village signposted off A436 Andoversford—Naunton – look out for inn sign at head of lane in village; can also be reached from A40 Andoversford—Cheltenham via Whittington and Syreford; GL54 5XQ

Friendly village pub with well liked bar food, real ales, seats in a big garden and nice surrounding walks

This attractive 17th-c pub is down a long lane in a gentrified hillside village and the large garden has plenty of seats and lovely views; fine surrounding walks. Inside, there are low beams, thick roughly coursed stone walls and some tiled flooring, and though much of it has been opened out to give a sizeable eating area off the smaller bar servery, it's been done well to give a feeling of several communicating rooms. The furniture is mainly pine with some comfortable leather sofas, wall settles and tub chairs, and there are gin traps and various stuffed animal trophies, and a warm log fire. Butcombe Bitter, Otter Bitter, Wye Valley Butty Bach and a guest beer on handpump and several wines by the glass; darts, pool, juke box and board games. The dog is called Max and the cat Polly. The pub was up for sale as we went to press so things may change.

⑪ **Tasty bar food includes filled baguettes, soup, duck and pear pâté with chutney, mussels in white wine, garlic and chilli, ham and egg, sausages with onion gravy, steak in ale pie, fresh battered cod, steaks cooked on grill stones, evening specials like roasted vegetable and cheese bake and duck with cherry brandy sauce, and puddings.** *Starters/Snacks: £3.95 to £5.50. Main Courses: £7.95 to £14.95. Puddings: £4.95*

Free house ~ Licensees Barbara and Bob Price ~ Real ale ~ Bar food (not Sun evening or Mon) ~ Restaurant ~ (01242) 820410 ~ Children welcome ~ Dogs allowed in bar ~ Open 12-3, 6-11; 12-5.30 Sun; closed Sun evening, Mon

Recommended by Rich and Mo Mills, Mrs G Casey, Richard Tilbrook, Neil and Anita Christopher, R Ball, Mari Jo Cruise

CHEDWORTH   SP0512   MAP 4

Seven Tuns ♀

Village signposted off A429 NE of Cirencester; then take second signposted right turn and bear left towards church; GL54 4AE

Bustling, enjoyable little pub with several open fires, lots of wines by the glass, good bar food and plenty of outside seats

Handy for the nearby Roman villa, this is a thoroughly enjoyable little 17th-c pub in a charming village. There's a cheerful, bustling atmosphere and a good mix of customers, and the small snug lounge on the right has comfortable seats and decent tables, sizeable antique prints, tankards hanging from the beam over the serving bar, a partly boarded ceiling, and a good winter log fire in a big stone fireplace. Down a couple of steps, the public bar on the left has an open fire and this leads into a dining room with yet another open fire. Wells & Youngs Bitter and Special and a guest such as Hook Norton Old Hooky on handpump, up to 14 wines by the glass and 19 malt whiskies; darts, skittle alley, board games and piped music. One sunny terrace has a boules pitch and across the road there's another little walled raised terrace with a waterwheel and a stream; plenty of tables and seats. There are nice walks through the valley.

🍴 **Enjoyable bar food includes lunchtime sandwiches and ploughman's, soup, ham hock, apricot and pistachio terrine, king scallops in herb butter, home-cooked ham and eggs, beer-battered hake fillet, cumberland sausages with red wine gravy, risotto of smoked salmon, peas, rocket and parmesan and warm duck salad with beetroot, dark cherries and sherry vinaigrette.** *Starters/Snacks: £5.00 to £7.00. Main Courses: £9.00 to £15.00. Puddings: £5.00 to £7.00*

Youngs ~ Tenant Mr Davenport-Jones ~ Real ale ~ Bar food (12-2.30(3 Sat and Sun), 6.30-9.30(9 Sun)) ~ Restaurant ~ (01285) 720242 ~ Children welcome ~ Dogs welcome ~ Open 12-3, 6-11; all day July and Aug; 12-midnight(10.30 Sun) Sat

Recommended by Jeff and Wendy Williams, E McCall, T McLean, D Irving, Susan Lang, Edward Mirzoeff, Richard Tilbrook, Keith and Sue Ward, Guy Vowles, Richard and Sheila Fitton

CHELTENHAM   SO9624   MAP 4

Royal Oak 🍷 🍺

Off B4348 just N; The Burgage, Prestbury; GL52 3DL

Bustling and friendly with quite a range of bar food, good choice of drinks and seats in the sheltered garden; handy for Cheltenham racecourse

There are always organised events going on at this attractive Cotswold-stone pub from comedy evenings to italian nights, to beer and sausage festivals – all great fun. The congenial low-beamed bar has fresh flowers and polished brasses, a comfortable mix of seating including chapel chairs on the newly restored parquet flooring, some interesting pictures on the ochre walls and a new woodburning stove in the stone fireplace. Malvern Hills Black Pear, Oakham JHB and Timothy Taylors Landlord on handpump and several wines by the glass. Service is efficient and friendly. Dining room tables are nicely spaced so that you don't feel crowded and the skittle alley can also be used as a function room; piped music. There are seats and tables under canopies on the heated terrace and in a sheltered garden. This is the closest pub to Cheltenham racecourse, so it does get busy on race days. More reports please.

🍴 **As well as daily specials, the interesting bar food includes lunchtime ciabattas, duck liver and peppercorn pâté with fig and port reduction, ham, tomato and egg, mixed wild mushroom pancake with garlic cream, tempura battered sprats with lemon grass and coriander dressing, goats cheese galette with roast vine tomato stuffed with ricotta and cumin, slow-roasted pork belly with raisins and thyme and a honey and clove-scented gravy, chicken breast with leek and emmenthal and a red pepper sauce, luxury fish pie, and puddings; Sunday roasts.** *Starters/Snacks: £4.75 to £6.50. Main Courses: £7.50 to £13.95. Puddings: £5.25*

Enterprise ~ Lease Simon and Kate Daws ~ Real ale ~ Bar food (all day Sun) ~ Restaurant ~ (01242) 522344 ~ Children welcome ~ Open 11-11; 12-10.30 Sun; 11-3, 5.30-11 Mon-Thurs in winter

Recommended by Michael Sargent, Andy and Claire Barker, Rob and Catherine Dunster

'Children welcome' means the pub says it lets children inside without any special restriction. If it allows them in, but to restricted areas such as an eating area or family room, we specify this. Some pubs may impose an evening time limit. We do not mention limits after 9pm as we assume children are home by then.

CHIPPING CAMPDEN SP1539 MAP 4

Eight Bells 🍴 🍺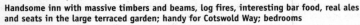

Church Street (which is one way – entrance off B4035); GL55 6JG

Handsome inn with massive timbers and beams, log fires, interesting bar food, real ales and seats in the large terraced garden; handy for Cotswold Way; bedrooms

Despite being in a tourist town, this handsome old inn is a friendly and relaxed place with locals popping in and out for a drink and a chat – and there's a genuine welcome for all. The bars have heavy oak beams, massive timber supports and stripped-stone walls, with cushioned pews, sofas and solid dark wood furniture on the broad flagstones, and log fires in up to three restored stone fireplaces. Inset into the floor of the dining room is a glass panel showing part of the passage from the church by which Roman Catholic priests could escape from the Roundheads. Hook Norton Best, Goffs Jouster, Purity Pure Ubu, and a guest such as Goffs Cheltenham Gold on handpump from the fine oak bar counter, quite a few wines by the glass and Old Rosie cider. Piped music and board games. There's a large terraced garden with plenty of seats, and striking views of the almshouses and church. The pub is handy for the Cotswold Way walk which takes you to Bath.

🍴 **Well presented and very good, the bar food includes lunchtime sandwiches (not Sunday), soup, home-smoked mackerel pâté, spicy lamb koftas with tzatziki and toasted pitta bread, beef and mustard sausages with red wine gravy, sun-dried tomato, pine nut and spinach risotto with a poached egg, beer-battered cod with mint and pea purée, lamb shank on sweet potato mash with an orange zest and redcurrant jus, and puddings like a smashing ice-cream sundae and apple and rhubarb cobbler; they also offer a set two- and three-course lunch menu.** *Starters/Snacks: £4.95 to £7.50. Main Courses: £12.50 to £19.95. Puddings: £5.75*

Free house ~ Licensee Neil Hargreaves ~ Real ale ~ Bar food ~ Restaurant ~ (01386) 840371 ~ Well behaved children welcome but only in dining room after 6pm ~ Dogs allowed in bar ~ Open 12-11(10.30 Sun) ~ Bedrooms: £60S/£85B

Recommended by Martin and Pauline Jennings, Noel Grundy, Eithne Dandy, Hugh Roberts, Les and Judith Haines, Mike Proctor, MDN, George Atkinson, Paul Humphreys, Michael Dandy, Eleanor Dandy, Mike and Sue Loseby, Martin Smith, Rob and Catherine Dunster, Mr Ray J Carter

CLIFFORD'S MESNE SO6922 MAP 4

Yew Tree 🍷 🍺

From A40 W of Huntley turn off at May Hill 1, Clifford's Mesne 2½ signpost, then pub eventually signed up steep narrow lane on left; Clifford's Mesne also signposted off B4216 S of Newent, pub then signed on right; GL18 1JS

Unusual dining pub nicely tucked away on slopes of May Hill; wine bargains

The friendly licensees here have introduced a seating area in their informal wine shop to give more space for customers who just want to come in for a drink – making it a sort of wine bar with nibbles. If you buy a bottle with your meal, they charge just the shop price plus £5. So you end up paying, say, £11 for a wine which in another pub would typically cost £18, or £16 instead of over £30, or even £25 instead of around £60 – the better the wine, the bigger the bargain. We wish that more pubs used this customer-friendly pricing system. The smallish two-room beamed bar has an attractive mix of small settles, a pew and character chairs around interesting tables including antiques, rugs on an unusual stone floor, and a warm woodburning stove. You can eat more formally up a few steps, in a carpeted dining room beyond a sofa by a big log fire. Cotswold Spring Gloucestershire's Glory and Wickwar BOB on handpump, local farm cider and good value winter mulled wine; prompt, genial service; daily papers and unobtrusive piped nostalgic pop music. Teak tables on a side terrace are best placed for the views, with plenty of nearby walks, and there are steps down to a sturdy play area.

🍴 **Using seasonal local produce and home-grown vegetables and herbs, the enjoyable food includes potted stilton with toast, kidneys in a creamy dijon sauce on a garlic croûte, moules marinière, beefcake with rich gravy, wild mushroom and chestnut strudel,** sausages with onion gravy, gloucester old spot loin steak with apricot butter, pheasant and fig pudding, daily specials like rabbit casserole with wild garlic and cider or sea bream on a fennel cassoulet, and puddings; good local cheeses. *Starters/Snacks: £5.00 to £9.00. Main Courses: £8.45 to £15.00. Puddings: £3.50 to £4.50*

Free house ~ Licensees Mr and Mrs Philip Todd ~ Real ale ~ Bar food (12-2, 6-9; 12-4 Sun) ~ Restaurant ~ (01531) 820719 ~ Children welcome ~ Dogs welcome ~ Live music monthly ~ Open 12-2.30, 6-11; 12-5 Sun; closed Sun evening, Mon and Tuesday lunchtime

Recommended by Reg Fowle, Helen Rickwood, TB, K and B Barker, Alastair Stevenson, Bernard Stradling, Mike and Mary Carter, J E Shackleton, Rod Stoneman, Chris and Val Ramstedt, Alistair Stanier, R J Amor

COATES   SO9600   MAP 4

Tunnel House 🍺

Follow Tarlton signs (right then left) from village, pub up rough track on right after railway bridge; OS Sheet 163 map reference 965005; GL7 6PW

Warm welcome for all at this friendly, interestingly decorated pub, lots of character, popular food and drink, and seats in the sizeable garden; guards derelict canal tunnel

There's always a good mix of customers in this lively, friendly pub and it's especially popular with students from the Royal Agricultural College – there are plenty of photos of them on the walls. The rambling rooms have beams, flagstones, a happy mix of furnishings including massive rustic benches and seats built into the sunny windows, lots of enamel advertising signs, racing tickets and air travel labels, a stuffed wild boar's head and stuffed owl, plenty of copper and brass and an upside-down card table complete with cards and drinks fixed to the beams; there's a nice log fire with sofas in front of it. The more conventional dining extension and back conservatory fill up quickly at mealtimes. Hook Norton Bitter, Vale Wychert Ale and a guest beer on handpump, several wines by the glass and two draught ciders; piped music. There are impressive views from tables on the pleasant terrace in front of the eccentric bow-fronted stone house and a big garden sloping down to the derelict entrance tunnel of the old Thames and Severn Canal (which is under slow restoration). Good walks nearby; disabled lavatories.

🍴 Under the new licensee, the good bar food now includes sandwiches and filled baguettes, ploughman's, soup, wild mushroom tartlet with a creamy garlic sauce, chicken and bacon in soy sauce, garlic and ginger on a big mixed salad, spiced falafel burger with tzatziki and feta, beer-battered cod, gloucester old spot sausages with red onion marmalade-laced gravy, seafood tagliatelle, and puddings like coconut and pineapple cheesecake and white and dark chocolate torte with hazelnut brittle and red berry coulis. *Starters/Snacks: £5.00 to £7.00. Main Courses: £7.00 to £12.00. Puddings: £4.00 to £6.00*

Free house ~ Licensee Rupert Longsdon ~ Real ale ~ Bar food (12-9.30) ~ Restaurant ~ (01285) 770280 ~ Children welcome ~ Dogs welcome ~ Open 12-midnight(1am Sat, 11 Sun)

Recommended by Neil and Anita Christopher, Suzy Miller, Donna and Roger, Mike and Lynn Robinson, Stuart Doughty, Richard and Sheila Fitton, Chris and Angela Buckell, John Beeken

COWLEY   SO9714   MAP 4

Green Dragon 🛏

Off A435 S of Cheltenham at Elkstone, Cockleford signpost; OS Sheet 163 map reference 970142; GL53 9NW

Cosy bars with winter fires, good food, real ales and terraces overlooking Cowley Lake; comfortable bedrooms

There are seats on terraces outside this well run country inn that overlook Cowley Lake and the River Churn; plenty of nearby local walks. Inside, this is rather smart and has a good bit of real character, and the two beamed bars have a cosy and genuinely old-fashioned feel with big flagstones and wooden floorboards, candlelit tables and winter log fires in two stone fireplaces. Butcombe Bitter, Courage Directors and Otter Ale on handpump are served by friendly, efficient staff; piped music and a skittle alley. The furniture and the bar itself in the upper Mouse Bar were made by Robert Thompson, and little mice run over the hand-carved chairs, tables and mantelpiece; there's also a larger Lower Bar with a woodburning stove and an upstairs restaurant. The bedrooms are very comfortable and well equipped and the breakfasts are good.

🍴 **Good bar food includes sandwiches, chicken caesar salad, butternut squash with pasta, rosemary and white wine cream sauce, gloucester old spot sausages with rich gravy, haddock fillet in lemon batter, slow-cooked pork belly with red sauerkraut and dijon cream sauce, garlic marinated chicken strips with wild mushrooms and gremolata, steak and kidney pudding and 28-day-aged sirloin steak with peppercorn and brandy sauce.** *Starters/Snacks: £6.25 to £6.95. Main Courses: £10.95 to £18.95. Puddings: £4.95 to £6.25*

Buccaneer Holdings ~ Managers Simon and Nicky Haly ~ Real ale ~ Bar food (12-2.30(3 Sat, 3.30 Sun), 6-10(9 Sun)) ~ Restaurant ~ (01242) 870271 ~ Children welcome ~ Dogs allowed in bar and bedrooms ~ Open 11-11; 12-10.30 Sun ~ Bedrooms: £70B/£95B

Recommended by Nigel and Sue Foster, Giles and Annie Francis, Susan Lang, Mike and Mary Carter, Guy Vowles, E McCall, T McLean, D Irving, Keith and Sue Ward, Dave Irving, Jenny Huggins

DIDMARTON   ST8187   MAP 2

Kings Arms ♀ ⇌

A433 Tetbury road; GL9 1DT

Bustling pub with knocked-through rooms, several local beers, good bar food and pleasant back garden; bedrooms and self-catering cottages

Well run and welcoming, this 17th-c former coaching inn is run by a friendly and efficient landlord. The several knocked-through beamed bar rooms work their way around a big central counter, with deep terracotta walls above a dark green dado in some rooms, yellow and cream paintwork in others, an attractive mix of wooden tables and chairs on bare boards, quarry tiles and carpet, fresh flowers, and a big stone fireplace. There's also a smart restaurant. Three real ales from breweries such as Otter, Timothy Taylors and Uley on handpump and ten wines by the glass; darts and TV (for international sporting events). There are seats out in the pleasant back garden and boules. As well as comfortable bedrooms they have self-catering cottages in a converted barn and stable block. Westonbirt Arboretum is close by.

🍴 **Good bar food includes lunchtime filled ciabattas, smoked salmon and poached egg muffin, seared scallops with chorizo and paprika oil, home-made beefburger with cheese and bacon, macaroni cheese, chicken breast in dijon mustard and tarragon, salmon and smoked haddock fishcakes, beef goulash with sour cream, prawn curry, and puddings such as banoffi pie and chocolate fudge brownie.** *Starters/Snacks: £4.50 to £6.95. Main Courses: £8.95 to £14.95. Puddings: £5.85*

Free house ~ Licensees R A and S A Sadler ~ Real ale ~ Bar food (12-2, 6-9; all day Sun) ~ Restaurant ~ (01454) 238245 ~ Children welcome ~ Dogs allowed in bar ~ Open 11-11; 12-10.30 Sun; closed evenings 25 and 26 Dec and evening 1 Jan ~ Bedrooms: £55S/£75S

Recommended by Andy and Claire Barker, the Brewers, Mark O'Sullivan, Bob and Angela Brooks, John Chambers, Bruce and Sharon Eden, Jamie May, Guy Vowles

DOYNTON   ST7174   MAP 2

Cross House 🍺

Village signposted with Dyrham off A420 Bristol—Chippenham just E of Wick; High Street; BS30 5TF

Friendly staff and customers, honest food, five real ales and lots of wines by the glass; close to Dyrham Park and walking country

The convivial landlord and his efficient, helpful staff are sure to make you welcome in this 18th-c village pub. It's an easy-going and old-fashioned place and the softly lit carpeted bar has some beams and stripped stone, simple pub furniture brightened up with cheerful scatter cushions, a woodburning stove in a big stone fireplace, and a happy mix of customers. Two or three steps take you down to a cottagey candlelit dining room. Bass, Bath Ales Gem Bitter, Courage Best, Sharps Doom Bar and Timothy Taylors Landlord on handpump and around 18 wines by the glass; darts, games machine, TV and piped music. There are picnic-sets out by the road. This is fine walking country and Dyrham Park is quite close.

🍴 Honest bar food at reasonable prices includes good sandwiches, ploughman's, garlic mushrooms, goats cheese and smoked bacon with redcurrant jelly, slow-roasted pork belly and black pudding with a red wine sauce, pies such as steak and kidney, rabbit or fish, lamb shank with barbecue sauce, and puddings such as fruit crumble and pancakes with butterscotch sauce. *Starters/Snacks: £3.60 to £7.25. Main Courses: £9.25 to £12.95. Puddings: £3.50*

Unique (Enterprise) ~ Lease André and Adrian Large ~ Real ale ~ Bar food (12-2, 6.30-9.30 (10 weekends)) ~ Restaurant ~ (0117) 937 2261 ~ Children welcome ~ Dogs allowed in bar ~ Open 11.30-3(3.30 Sat), 6-11; 12-10.30 Sun

Recommended by Andy and Claire Barker, Chris and Angela Buckell, Mr and Mrs P R Thomas, Barry and Anne, Colin and Peggy Wilshire, Dr and Mrs A K Clarke, Stan Edwards

DUNTISBOURNE ABBOTS   SO9709   MAP 4

Five Mile House

Off A417 at Duntisbourne Abbots exit sign; then, coming from Gloucester, pass filling station and keep on parallel to main road for 200 yards; coming from Cirencester, take Duntisbourne Abbots services sign, then immediate right and take underpass below main road, then turn right at T junction; avoid going into Duntisbourne Abbots village; pub is on the old main road; GL7 7JR

A lively landlord and a favourite with many for its good food, beer and atmosphere; plenty of original character, open fires and newspapers; nice views from the garden

This genuinely friendly village pub is the sort of place our readers return to again and again. It's run by a cheerful father and son team who offer a welcome to all their customers – whatever their age. There's plenty of original character and the front room has a companionable bare-boards drinking bar on the right (plenty of convivial banter from the locals), with wall seats around the big table in its bow window and just one other table. On the left is a flagstoned hallway tap room snug formed from two ancient high-backed settles by a stove in a tall carefully exposed old fireplace; newspapers to read. There's a small cellar bar, a back restaurant down steps and a family room on the far side; darts. Donnington BB, Otter Ale and Wye Valley Butty Bach on handpump and an interesting wine list (strong on new world ones); the friendly pub dog is called Sacha, and the gardens have nice country views and a very smart smokers' shelter; the summer marquee has been refurbished this year. The country lane was once Ermine Street, the main Roman road from Wales to London.

🍴 Cooked by the landlord and his team, the very popular bar food includes sandwiches, filled baked potatoes, deep-fried mild goats cheese with chilli jam, battered haddock with mushy peas, gammon with egg and pineapple, lamb shoulder stuffed with mint and redcurrant with a port sauce, specials like field mushrooms with a stilton and pistachio crumb and root vegetable mash and chicken breast stuffed with stilton, wrapped in bacon with a mushroom and brandy cream sauce, and puddings such as bakewell tart and crème brûlée; they have a takeaway menu and hold steak and chip and gourmet evenings. *Starters/Snacks: £5.00 to £6.95. Main Courses: £10.00 to £20.00. Puddings: £5.50*

Free house ~ Licensees Jo and Jon Carrier ~ Real ale ~ Bar food (12-2.30, 6-9; not Sun evening) ~ Restaurant ~ (01285) 821432 ~ Children welcome if well behaved ~ Dogs allowed in bar ~ Open 12-3, 6-11; 12-3, 7-10.30 Sun

Recommended by Mrs P Sumner, Giles and Annie Francis, Bren and Val Speed, Guy Vowles, the Didler, Bernard Stradling, Di and Mike Gillam, Ann and Colin Hunt, Dennis Jenkin, Neil and Anita Christopher, Ewan and Moira McCall, Neil and Karen Dignan, George and Maureen Roby, Nick and Meriel Cox, E McCall, T McLean, D Irving, Dave Irving, Jenny Huggins, Donna and Roger

Post Office address codings confusingly give the impression that some pubs are in Gloucestershire, when they're really in Warwickshire (which is where we list them).

DURSLEY   ST7598   MAP 4

Old Spot ◖ £

Hill Road; by bus station; GL11 4JQ

Unassuming and cheery town pub with nine real ales and regular beer festivals

A favourite with many of our readers, this bustling and very well run town local has a genuinely friendly landlord who keeps an excellent choice of real ales from all over the country. On handpump these might include Batemans GHA, Brains SA Gold, Butcombe Brunel IPA, Miles Tap Bitter, a changing beer from Pub Dog, Uley Old Ric, Wadworths JCB, Wickwar BOB and Wye Valley Butty Bach; they also hold four annual beer festivals a year and stock quite a few malt whiskies, too. There are always plenty of good-humoured locals and the front door opens into a deep pink small room with stools on shiny quarry tiles along its pine-boarded bar counter and old enamel beer advertisements on the walls and ceiling; there's a profusion of porcine paraphernalia. A small room on the left leads off from here and the little dark wood-floored room to the right has a stone fireplace. A step takes you down to a cosy Victorian tiled snug and (to the right) the meeting room. There are seats in the heated and covered garden.

🍴 **Bar food includes sandwiches, filled baked potatoes, ploughman's, haddock and chive fishcakes, cottage or steak in ale pies, home-cooked ham with parsley sauce, cauliflower cheese, pork and apple burger with apple sauce, chicken fajitas, and puddings like white chocolate cheesecake and treacle tart.** *Starters/Snacks: £3.45 to £5.75. Main Courses: £7.25 to £9.75. Puddings: £3.75*

Free house ~ Licensee Steve Herbert ~ Real ale ~ Bar food (12-3; no evening meals) ~ (01453) 542870 ~ Children in family room only (best to book) ~ Dogs welcome ~ Open 11(12 Sun)-11

Recommended by Andy and Claire Barker, Liz Hryniewicz, the Didler, Dr and Mrs A K Clarke, Julian Jewitt, PL, Chris and Angela Buckell, Colin and Peggy Wilshire

EBRINGTON   SP1839   MAP 4

Ebrington Arms

Off B4035 E of Chipping Campden or A429 N of Moreton-in-Marsh; GL55 6NH

17th-c village inn with enthusiastic young licensees, good choice of real ales, wines by the glass and enjoyable food; bedrooms

Run by an enthusiastic and hard-working young couple, this is a 17th-c Cotswold-stone village pub with a good mix of customers. There's plenty of character and charm and the beamed bar has ladder-back chairs around a mix of tables on the flagstoned floor, a fine inglenook fireplace and some seats built into the airy bow window. The beamed dining room is similarly furnished and has some original iron work in its inglenook fireplace. Hook Norton Hooky Bitter, Oakham Inferno, Stroud Organic Ale, Uley Bitter and Wye Valley Butty Bach on handpump and several wines by the glass; darts, a monthly quiz and maybe TV for sports. An arched stone wall shelters a terrace with picnic-table sets under parasols and there are more on the lawn. The inn is handy for Hidcote and Kiftsgate gardens. We have not heard from readers who have stayed here but would imagine it would be most enjoyable.

🍴 **Good, interesting bar food includes sandwiches, soup, ham hock and parsley terrine with piccalilli, seared scallops with celeriac purée, black pudding and crispy bacon, beer-battered pollack with minted pea purée, griddled beefburger with red onion marmalade and horseradish cream, butternut squash, goats cheese and spinach lasagne, steak, ale and mustard casserole with horseradish dumplings, and puddings like pineapple tarte tatin with honeycomb ice-cream and spiced sweet potato cake with caramel sauce.** *Starters/Snacks: £4.50 to £6.50. Main Courses: £10.00 to £17.00. Puddings: £4.75 to £5.75*

Free house ~ Licensees Clare and Jim Alexander ~ Real ale ~ Bar food ~ (01386) 593223 ~ Children welcome ~ Dogs allowed in bar ~ Folk music first Mon of the month ~ Open 12-3, 6-11; 12-11 Sat and Sun ~ Bedrooms: /£100B

Recommended by Keith and Sue Ward, Martin and Pauline Jennings, Eithne Dandy

FORD   SP0829   MAP 4

Plough

B4077 Stow—Alderton; GL54 5RU

16th-c inn opposite racehorse trainer's yard, lots of horse talk, bustling atmosphere, good food and beer; bedrooms

The friendly, efficient staff in this extremely popular inn treat all their customers – regulars or visitors – with the same courtesy. There's a chatty atmosphere and the beamed and stripped-stone bar has racing prints and photos on the walls (many of the customers here are to do with racing as a well known racehorse trainer's yard is opposite), old settles and benches around the big tables on its uneven flagstones, oak tables in a snug alcove and open fires or woodburning stoves (a couple are the real thing). Darts, TV (for the races) and piped music. Donnington BB and SBA on handpump. There are some picnic-sets under parasols and pretty hanging baskets at the front of the stone building and a large back garden with a play fort for children. The Cotswold Farm Park is nearby. The comfortable bedrooms away from the pub are the quietest and there are views of the gallops. It does get pretty packed on race meeting days.

❚❙ Generous helpings of popular bar food includes lunchtime sandwiches and filled baguettes, ploughman's, soup, pâté of the day, glazed goats cheese with roasted peppers, beetroot and sunblush tomatoes, gloucester old spot sausages with rich onion gravy, haddock and salmon fishcake with a free-range poached egg and parsley sauce, steak in ale pie, crispy duck with orange sauce, a vegetarian and fish dish of the day, and puddings. *Starters/Snacks: £4.50 to £6.50. Main Courses: £9.95 to £17.95. Puddings: £4.95*

Donnington ~ Tenant Craig Brown ~ Real ale ~ Bar food (all day Fri-Sun) ~ Restaurant ~ (01386) 584215 ~ Children welcome ~ Dogs allowed in bar ~ Open 10am-midnight ~ Bedrooms: £50S/£70S

Recommended by Keith and Ann Arnold, Helene Grygar, R J Herd, Chris Glasson, Giles and Annie Francis, Michael Sargent, the Didler, DFL, D Goodger, Dr A Y Drummond, Anne and Jeff Peel, Simon Watkins, William Goodhart, Michael Dandy, Chris and Val Ramstedt, Mrs Blethyn Elliott, Gerry and Rosemary Dobson, Brian Glozier, Jeff and Wendy Williams, Peter Sampson, Peter and Audrey Dowsett

FOSSEBRIDGE   SP0711   MAP 4

Fossebridge Inn

A429 Cirencester—Stow-on-the-Wold; GL54 3JS

Handsome old inn with proper bar, good mix of customers, real ales, enjoyable food and seats in four acres of grounds; lovely bedrooms

At the heart of this handsome refurbished Georgian inn is the bustling, friendly bar which always has plenty of locals dropping in for a pint and a chat. This keeps the atmosphere relaxed and informal and the two rooms have beams and arches, stripped-stone walls and fine old flagstones, a happy mix of dining chairs, stools and wooden tables and open log fires; also, copper implements, candles and fresh flowers. Up some stairs on the left is the dining room. Festival Amber and St Austell Proper Job and Tribute on handpump and several wines by the glass. Two other dining rooms are rather grand. Outside, there are picnic-sets under parasols and four acres of lovely lawned, streamside gardens with a lake. Comfortable smart bedrooms and a self-catering cottage. The Roman villa at Chedworth is nearby.

❚❙ First-rate bar food includes lunchtime sandwiches and ploughman's, soup, game terrine with red onion marmalade, oriental filo prawns with sweet chilli dipping sauce, chargrilled burger with bacon, cheese and tomato relish, beer-battered haddock with home-made tartare sauce, sausages with mustard mash and caramelised onion gravy, wild mushroom risotto, steak and kidney pudding, pheasant with bread sauce and game jus, and puddings like chocolate mousse with poached pear and vanilla syrup and blackberry and apple crumble with vanilla custard; Sunday roasts. *Starters/Snacks: £5.25 to £7.00. Main Courses: £10.50 to £18.95. Puddings: £6.00*

We say if we know a pub allows dogs.

Free house ~ Licensee Samantha Jenkins ~ Real ale ~ Bar food (12-3, 6.30-10) ~ Restaurant ~ (01285) 720721 ~ Children welcome ~ Dogs allowed in bar and bedrooms ~ Open 12-midnight ~ Bedrooms: £110B/£120B

Recommended by Dr and Mrs A K Clarke, Guy Vowles, Keith and Sue Ward, Richard Tilbrook

GREAT RISSINGTON   SP1917   MAP 4

Lamb ♀ ⇍

Turn off A40 W of Burford to the Barringtons; keep straight on past Great Barrington until Great Rissington is signed on left; GL54 2LN

Busy inn with civilised bar, well liked bar food, changing real ales and seats in the sheltered garden; bedrooms and good surrounding walks

This is a comfortable inn with a good mix of customers. Most people head for the rather civilised two-roomed bar which has heritage red- and stone-coloured walls, high-backed leather chairs grouped around polished tables, and a woodburning stove in the Cotswold-stone fireplace. Some interesting things to look out for are parts of a propeller, artefacts in display cases and pictures of the Canadian crew from the Wellington bomber that crashed in the garden in October 1943. The restaurant has another woodburning stove and various old agricultural tools on the walls. Brakspears Bitter, Hook Norton Old Hooky and Wychwood Hobgoblin on handpump, quite a few wines by the glass from a comprehensive list and several malt whiskies; piped music. You can sit outside on the front terrace or in the sheltered, well kept hillside garden. There's a local circular walk which takes in part of the idyllic village, church, River Windrush and stunning countryside surrounding the pub. The bedrooms have been refurbished this year.

🍴 Popular bar food includes filled baguettes and baked potatoes, soup, deep-fried whitebait, duck liver and orange pâté with cumberland sauce, beer-battered haddock, goats cheese, olive and tomato tart, scampi, steak and kidney pie, half a shoulder of lamb with a redcurrant and red wine gravy, chargrilled steaks, and puddings. *Starters/Snacks: £4.75 to £6.95. Main Courses: £9.50 to £18.95. Puddings: £4.95*

Free house ~ Licensees Paul and Jacqueline Gabriel ~ Real ale ~ Bar food (12-2.30, 6.30-9 (9.30 Fri and Sat)) ~ Restaurant ~ (01451) 820388 ~ Children welcome ~ Dogs allowed in bar and bedrooms ~ Open 11.30-11.30; 12-11 Sun ~ Bedrooms: £55B/£80B

Recommended by Paul Humphreys, Andrew and Judith Hudson, Roger Fox, George Atkinson, Steve and Sue Griffiths, Helene Grygar, Martin and Pauline Jennings, Guy Vowles

GUITING POWER   SP0924   MAP 4

Hollow Bottom

Village signposted off B4068 SW of Stow-on-the-Wold (still called A436 on many maps); GL54 5UX

Popular old inn with lots of racing memorabilia and a good bustling atmosphere

This is a most enjoyable snug old stone cottage and you will be made just as welcome by the efficient, friendly staff if it is just a drink and a chat you are after rather than a full meal. There's a wide mix of visitors and locals – in particular those involved in racing, and lots of racing memorabilia including racing silks, tunics, photographs, race badges, framed newspaper cuttings and horseshoes; as we went to press, their local horse had just won the Gold Cup and they have dedicated an area in the bar to him. The comfortable beamed bar has plenty of atmosphere and a winter log fire in an unusual pillar-supported stone fireplace, and the public bar has flagstones and stripped-stone masonry, and racing on TV; newspapers to read, darts, board games and piped music. Festival Gold, Donnington SBA and a beer named for the pub on handpump, several wines (including champagne) by the glass and 20 malt whiskies. From the pleasant garden behind the pub there are views towards the peaceful sloping fields; decent nearby walks.

🍴 Tasty bar food includes good filled baguettes and baked potatoes, ploughman's, soup, pâté with cumberland sauce, home-made beefburger, a pie and a roast of the day, ham and free-range eggs, smoked haddock in a cheese and chive sauce, calves liver with grilled bacon and roasted shallots, aberdeen angus steaks, and puddings like banoffi pie and raspberry trifle. *Starters/Snacks: £5.95 to £7.95. Main Courses: £8.95 to £19.95. Puddings: £5.95*

Free house ~ Licensees Hugh Kelly and Charles Pettigrew ~ Real ale ~ Bar food (all day) ~ Restaurant ~ (01451) 850392 ~ Children welcome ~ Dogs allowed in bar ~ Live music first Sun evening of the month ~ Open 9am–midnight ~ Bedrooms: £50B/£75B

Recommended by Susan Lang, Helene Grygar, Michael and Jenny Back, DFL, John Taylor, Keith and Sue Ward, Michael Sargent, John and Val Shand, Guy Vowles

LOWER ODDINGTON
SP2326   MAP 4

Fox 🍽 🍷 🛏

Signposted off A436 between Stow and Chipping Norton; GL56 0UR

Popular dining inn with particularly good food and wines, several real ales and helpful staff

There's no doubt that most customers come to this creeper-covered old place to enjoy the good, interesting food served by neat, uniformed staff – but there is a small pubby part by the bar counter where they keep Greene King Abbot, Hook Norton Bitter and a guest beer on handpump. The simply furnished bar rooms have beams and flagstones, a mix of wooden dining chairs around pine tables, fresh flowers and an inglenook fireplace; there are hunting-scene figures above the mantelpiece, a growing number of hunting pictures, a display cabinet with pewter mugs and stone bottles, and maybe daily newspapers. The elegant red-walled dining room has another open fire and dark wood furniture. Outside, the cottagey garden is pretty and has lots of white tables and chairs under an awning on the heated terrace. A good eight-mile walk starts from here (though a stroll around the pretty village might be less taxing).

🍽 Modern and very good, the food might include soup, chicken liver pâté, moules marinière, courgette and pesto tagliatelle, honey and mustard baked ham with parsley sauce, steak and kidney pie, calves liver with onion and bacon gravy, guinea fowl with wild mushrooms and madeira, lamb rump with celeriac mash and red wine sauce, and puddings like iced mango parfait with fruit coulis and banoffi pie; side dishes are extra. *Starters/Snacks: £5.50 to £7.00. Main Courses: £12.00 to £18.00. Puddings: £5.50*

Free house ~ Licensees James Cathcart and Ian MacKenzie ~ Real ale ~ Bar food ~ Restaurant ~ (01451) 870555 ~ Children welcome ~ Dogs allowed in bar ~ Open 12–3, 6–11 ~ Bedrooms: /£75S(£95B)

Recommended by Peter and Josie Fawcett, Phil and Helen Holt, Jeff and Wendy Williams, Anthony and Pam Stamer, Bernard Stradling, John Taylor, Keith and Sue Ward, Andrea Rampley, William Goodhart, Caroline and Michael Abbey, Rod Stoneman, Chris Glasson, Martin Smith, Susan Lang, Alan Thwaite, MDN, Richard Greaves

NAILSWORTH
ST8499   MAP 4

Egypt Mill 🛏

Just off A46; heading N towards Stroud, first right after roundabout, then left; GL6 0AE

Stylishly converted mill with lovely summer terrace and interesting split-level bar

Certainly this handsome 16th-c building is not a straightforward pub but customers do drop in for a drink and a chat. It's a fine conversion of a three-floor stone-built mill still with working waterwheels and the millstream flowing through; the brick-and-stone-floored split-level bar gives good views of the wheels. There are also big pictures and lots of stripped beams in the comfortable carpeted lounge, along with some hefty yet elegant ironwork from the old mill machinery. Nailsworth Mayor's Bitter and Stroud Life on handpump and several wines by the glass; piped music and TV. It can get quite crowded on fine weekends, but it's spacious enough to feel at its best when busy. In summer, the floodlit terraced garden overlooking the millpond is a pleasant place to relax and there's a little bridge over from the car park. More reports please.

🍴 **Bar food** includes lunchtime sandwiches, soup, pork hock terrine with home-made piccalilli, tempura prawns with soy, sweet chilli and ginger dressing, mushroom and chestnut wellington with a wholegrain mustard sauce, home-made faggots with onion gravy, steak and kidney pudding, slow-cooked moroccan lamb shank, thai king prawn red curry, 21-day-aged steaks, and puddings like white and dark chocolate mousse with blackcurrant compote and sticky date and ginger pudding with butterscotch sauce; Sunday roasts. *Starters/Snacks: £5.00 to £6.95. Main Courses: £8.50 to £14.50. Puddings: £5.50*

Free house ~ Licensees Stephen Webb and Rob Aldridge ~ Real ale ~ Bar food (all day) ~ Restaurant ~ (01453) 833449 ~ Children welcome ~ Open 11-11(midnight Sat); 12-10.30 Sun ~ Bedrooms: £80S/£100S

Recommended by Andy and Claire Barker, Bob and Angela Brooks, David A Hammond, Stan Edwards

Weighbridge

B4014 towards Tetbury; GL6 9AL

Super two-in-one pies served in cosy old-fashioned bar rooms, a fine choice of drinks and a sheltered garden

The genuinely helpful, welcoming staff and fine choice of drinks are much appreciated by our readers at this bustling, well run pub. The relaxed bar has three cosily old-fashioned rooms with stripped-stone walls, antique settles and country chairs, window seats and open fires. The black beamed ceiling of the lounge bar is thickly festooned with black ironware – sheepshears, gin traps, lamps and a large collection of keys, many from the old Longfords Mill opposite the pub. Upstairs is a raftered hayloft with an engaging mix of rustic tables. No noisy games machines or piped music. Uley Old Spot and Wadworths 6X and a couple of guest beers like Palmers 200 and Wychwood Hobgoblin on handpump,14 wines (and champagne and prosecco) by the glass, Weston's cider and several malt whiskies. Behind the building is a sheltered landscaped garden with picnic-sets under umbrellas. Good disabled access and facilities.

🍴 The extremely popular two-in-one pies come in a large bowl – half of which contains the filling of your choice while the other is full of home-made cauliflower cheese (or broccoli mornay or root vegetables) and topped with pastry: salmon in creamy sauce, pulses and root vegetables with spicy tomato sauce, steak and mushroom, turkey and trimmings, pork, bacon and celery in stilton sauce or chicken, ham and leek in a cream and tarragon sauce; you can also have mini versions or straightforward pies. Other dishes include filled baguettes and baked potatoes, omelettes, beef bourguignon, gammon with parsley sauce, mixed bean kiev, and puddings such as tiramisu and chocolate fondant. *Starters/Snacks: £3.45 to £5.95. Main Courses: £8.95 to £14.95. Puddings: £4.65 to £6.65*

Free house ~ Licensee Howard Parker ~ Real ale ~ Bar food (all day) ~ Restaurant ~ (01453) 832520 ~ Children allowed away from the bars until 9pm ~ Dogs welcome ~ Open 12-11(10.30 Sun)

Recommended by Dave Irving, Jenny Huggins, Stuart Doughty, James Morrell, JJW, CMW, John Taylor, Tom and Ruth Rees, Andy and Claire Barker

NORTH CERNEY
SP0208   MAP 4

Bathurst Arms 🍴 ♦ 🛏

A435 Cirencester—Cheltenham; GL7 7BZ
GLOUCESTERSHIRE DINING PUB OF THE YEAR

Bustling inn with beamed bar, open fires, fine wines, real ales and super food; comfortable bedrooms

'An absolute delight' says one reader after his regular visit to this handsome old inn. Reports this year are especially enthusiastic with warm praise for the attentive and friendly landlord and his young staff. There's a lot of genuine character and the original beamed and panelled bar has a fireplace at each end (one quite huge and housing an open woodburner), a good mix of old tables and nicely faded chairs and old-fashioned window seats. There are country tables in an oak-floored room off the bar, as well as winged high-backed settles forming a few booths around other tables; piped music and TV. The restaurant has leather sofas and another woodburning stove. Hook Norton Hooky Bitter and guests like Battledown Premium and Prescott Hill Climb on handpump, there's a wine room where you can choose your own wines or one of the 30 by the glass, and local soft drinks and juices. The pleasant riverside garden has picnic-sets sheltered by trees and shrubs, and plenty of surrounding walks. Cerney House Gardens are worth a visit.

🍴 First-class food includes sandwiches, soup, salt cod brandade with cucumber pickles, cress and home-made onion and thyme bread, goats cheese panna cotta with roasted walnuts and pea salad, beer-battered pollack with home-made tartare sauce, beefburger with cheese, coleslaw and tomato and gherkin relish, open lasagne of spring vegetables with a poached free-range egg, gammon with caramelised pineapple, spring onion mash, poached crayfish tails and chive butter, calves liver with smoked garlic, wholegrain mustard mash and roasted garlic jus, and puddings like caramel brûlée with sesame sugar, salted popcorn and butterscotch ice-cream and dark chocolate mousse with orange purée and frozen vanilla yoghurt; popular Sunday roasts. *Starters/Snacks: £4.95 to £6.95. Main Courses: £9.95 to £16.95. Puddings: £4.95 to £6.95*

Free house ~ Licensee James Walker ~ Real ale ~ Bar food (12-2(2.30 Fri and Sat), 6-9(9.30 Fri and Sat); 12-3, 7-9 Sun) ~ Restaurant ~ (01285) 831281 ~ Children welcome ~ Dogs allowed in bar and bedrooms ~ Open 12-11(10.30 Sun); 12-3, 6-midnight in winter ~ Bedrooms: £62B/£82.50B

Recommended by Stuart Doughty, Michael Doswell, Ken Marshall, E McCall, T McLean, D Irving, R L Borthwick, Howard and Lorna Lambert, Evelyn and Derek Walter, David Skelding, Val Carter, Martin Stafford, R J Herd, Gary Dunstan, Canon Michael Bourdeaux, Guy Vowles, Mr and Mrs M J Girdler, Richard and Sheila Fitton

NORTHLEACH

SP1114   MAP 4

Wheatsheaf 🍴 🍷 🛏

West End; the inn is on your left as you come in following the sign off the A429, just SW of its junction with the A40; GL54 3EZ

Smart coaching inn with excellent contemporary food, real ales, candles and fresh flowers, and a relaxed atmosphere; good bedrooms

You can expect a warm welcome and some excellent food in this handsome 17th-c stone coaching inn. The big-windowed airy linked rooms have high ceilings, contemporary paintwork, lots of pictures, church candles and fresh flowers, an attractive mix of dining chairs and stools around wooden tables, flagstones in the central bar and wooden floors in the airy dining rooms and three open fires. Fullers London Pride, Hook Norton Hooky Bitter and St Austell Tribute on handpump and several wines by the glass from a french list. There are seats in the pretty back garden and they have fishing on the River Coln. This is an attractive Cotswold town with a fine old market square.

🍴 First-rate food using top local ingredients includes nibbles like devilled kidneys or colchester rock oysters, soup, eggs benedict, treacle-cured salmon with pickled cucumber and horseradish, mussels with chilli and garlic, corn-fed chicken breast with chorizo and mushrooms, roast lamb rump with provençale vegetables, cod fillet with capers, roast tomato and olive oil potatoes, steak frites with béarnaise, and puddings such as lemon posset with shortbread and hot chocolate pudding. *Starters/Snacks: £5.00 to £8.00. Main Courses: £10.00 to £17.00. Puddings: £5.00 to £6.00*

Punch ~ Lease Sam and Georgina Pearman ~ Real ale ~ Bar food (12-2.30(3 Sun), 6-9.30(10 Fri and Sat)) ~ Restaurant ~ (01451) 860244 ~ Children welcome ~ Dogs welcome ~ Open 10am-11pm ~ Bedrooms: £60S/£80S(£100B)

Recommended by David and Cathrine Whiting, Mr and Mrs W W Burke, T Harrison, Valerie Worthington, Katharine Cowherd, Chris Glasson, Roger Braithwaite, Charles Gysin

---

We accept no free drinks, meals or payment for inclusion. We take no advertising, and are not sponsored by the brewing industry – or by anyone else.
So all reports are independent.

OLDBURY-ON-SEVERN

ST6092   MAP 2

Anchor ♀ ◖

Village signposted from B4061; BS35 1QA

Bustling and friendly country pub with good food, a fine choice of drinks, pretty garden and hanging baskets

Deservedly popular, this is a particularly well run and friendly pub with a good mix of visitors and chatty locals who are all equally welcomed by the efficient and helpful staff. The neatly kept lounge has an easy-going atmosphere, modern beams and stone, a mix of tables including an attractive oval oak gateleg, cushioned window seats, winged seats against the wall, oil paintings by a local artist and a big winter log fire; the bar has old photographs and farming and fishing bric-a-brac on the walls. Diners can eat in the lounge or bar area or in the dining room at the back of the building (good for larger groups) and the menu is the same in all rooms. Bass, Butcombe Bitter, Otter Bitter and a changing guest on handpump are well priced for the area; 83 malt whiskies and quite a few wines by the glass. In summer, you can eat in the pretty garden and the hanging baskets and window boxes are lovely then; boules. They have wheelchair access and a disabled lavatory. Plenty of walks to the River Severn and along the many footpaths and bridleways, and St Arilda's church nearby is interesting on its odd little knoll with wild flowers among the gravestones (the primroses and daffodils in spring are quite a show).

🍴 Enjoyable and reasonably priced, the bar food includes ciabatta sandwiches, ploughman's, soup, warm goats cheese and chorizo salad with red onions and bell peppers, oak-smoked salmon and tiger prawn cocktail, home-baked ham and free-range eggs, mushroom and aubergine lasagne, smoked haddock and salmon fish pie, lambs liver and bacon casserole, local venison with green peppercorn and brandy sauce, and puddings like lemon and ginger cheesecake and chocolate puddle pudding; they also have a good value two-course set menu (Monday-Friday lunchtimes, Sunday-Thursday evenings). *Starters/Snacks: £3.25 to £5.95. Main Courses: £6.30 to £13.95. Puddings: £4.25 to £4.95*

Free house ~ Licensees Michael Dowdeswell and Mark Sorrell ~ Real ale ~ Bar food (12-2(2.30 Sat, 3 Sun), 6-9) ~ Restaurant ~ (01454) 413331 ~ Children in dining room only ~ Dogs allowed in bar ~ Open 11.30-3, 6-11.30; 11.30am-midnight Sat; 12-11 Sun

Recommended by Colin and Peggy Wilshire, John and Verna Aspinall, James Morrell, Alan and Eve Harding, Tom Evans, Chris and Angela Buckell, Bob and Angela Brooks, Peter Meister, John and Gloria Isaacs, Dr and Mrs C W Thomas

SAPPERTON

SO9403   MAP 4

Bell 🍴 ♀ ◖

Village signposted from A419 Stroud—Cirencester; OS Sheet 163 map reference 948033; GL7 6LE

Super pub with beamed cosy rooms, a really good mix of customers, delicious food, local ales and a very pretty courtyard

As ever, the hard-working licensees of this charming place continue to keep a beady eye on the day-to-day running of their much-loved pub – always striving to keep their many customers happy: a bit of redecoration, menu changes, new garden furniture and extended opening hours are just a few things that have been tweaked. Harry's Bar (named after their sociable springer spaniel who is 12 now) has big cushion-strewn sofas, benches and armchairs where you can read the daily papers with a pint, in front of the woodburning stove – or simply have a pre-dinner drink. The two other cosy rooms have beams, a nice mix of wooden tables and chairs, country prints and modern art on stripped-stone walls, one or two attractive rugs on the flagstones, fresh flowers and open fires. The gents' has schoolboy humour cartoons on the walls. Bath Ales Gem, Otter Bitter, Uley Old Spot and Wickwar Spring Ale on handpump, over 20 wines by the glass and carafes from a large and diverse wine list with very helpful notes, Ashton Press cider, 20 malt whiskies, several armagnacs and cognacs, and local soft drinks. There are tables out on a small front lawn and in a partly covered and very pretty courtyard, for eating outside. Horses have their own tethering rail (and bucket of water).

[!] As well as a lunchtime pub classics such as ploughman's (big enough for two), ham and free-range eggs and bangers and mash with onion gravy, the imaginative food (using seasonal local produce) includes veal bresaola with wild garlic and sweet red pepper mousse, poached smoked haddock potato cake with a poached egg and sweet mustard and dill, home-ground burger with melted cheese and bacon, goats cheese pie, free-range chicken with braised pak choi, ginger and garlic, daily specials like moules marinière, beer-battered pollack and wild bass fillet with sea salt and lemon, and puddings such as baked chocolate and hazelnut cheesecake with praline shortbread and poached pear with polenta cake and spiced sticky red wine; they also offer weekend snacks and cream teas, and their Sunday roasts are very popular (best to book). *Starters/Snacks: £5.25 to £9.50. Main Courses: £10.75 to £19.50. Puddings: £6.95*

Free house ~ Licensees Paul Davidson and Pat LeJeune ~ Real ale ~ Bar food (12-2.15(2.30 Sun), 7-9.30(9 Sun)) ~ (01285) 760298 ~ Children allowed but must be over 10 after 6.30pm~ Dogs welcome ~ Open 11-3, 6.30-11; 11-11 Sat; 12-10.30 Sun; 11-3, 6.30-11 Sat in winter

Recommended by T A R Curran, Richard and Sheila Fitton, Henry Midwinter, James Morrell, Stuart Doughty, E McCall, T McLean, D Irving, Bernard Stradling, Howard G Allen, Martin and Karen Wake, Dr A Y Drummond, Chris and Martin Taylor, Chris Flynn, Wendy Jones, Peter Sampson, Neil Kellett

SHEEPSCOMBE

SO8910   MAP 4

Butchers Arms

Village signed off B4070 NE of Stroud; or A46 N of Painswick (but narrow lanes); GL6 7RH

Bustling country pub, enjoyable bar food, real ales, friendly young licensees and fine views

There's a thriving atmosphere in this bustling country pub and a lively cross-section of customers – all made welcome by the friendly licensees and their staff. The lounge bar has beams, wheelback chairs, cushioned stools and other comfortable seats around simple wooden tables, built-in cushioned seats in the big bay windows, interesting oddments like assorted blow lamps, irons and plates, and a woodburning stove. The restaurant has an open log fire. Butcombe Bitter, Otter Bitter and a guest like Skinners Betty Stogs on handpump, several wines by the glass and Weston's cider; darts, chess, cribbage and draughts. The view over the lovely surrounding steep beechwood valley is terrific and there are seats outside to make the most of it. It is thought that this area was once a royal hunting ground for Henry VIII. Groups of walkers or cyclists can pre-book their food orders.

[!] Using meat from the village where possible and other local produce, the popular bar food includes lunchtime sandwiches and filled baguettes, soup, salmon, cod, lemon and dill fishcakes, duck and chicken liver pâté with plum chutney, popular home-made burger with various toppings, mushroom and thyme risotto, steak, stout and mushroom pie, beer-battered fish and chips and specials such as lambs liver and bacon, local trout with a caper, lemon and chive sauce and gloucester old spot steak topped with blue cheese and apple compote with a port jus; also, Sunday roasts and a weekday pie and a pint deal. *Starters/Snacks: £4.50 to £8.95. Main Courses: £8.75 to £13.95. Puddings: £3.95 to £4.50*

Free house ~ Licensees Mark and Sharon Tallents ~ Real ale ~ Bar food (12-2.30, 6.30-9.30; all day weekends; no food after 6pm Sun in Jan and Feb) ~ Restaurant ~ (01452) 812113 ~ Children welcome ~ Dogs allowed in bar ~ Open 11.30-3, 6.30-11; 11.30-11.30 Sat; 12-10.30 Sun

Recommended by Mr and Mrs P R Thomas, Dr and Mrs A K Clarke, Martin and Pauline Jennings, John and Jennifer Wright, Guy Vowles

---

A very few pubs try to make you leave a credit card at the bar, as a sort of deposit if you order food. They are not entitled to do this. The credit card firms and banks which issue them warn you not to let credit cards out of your sight. If someone behind the counter used your card fraudulently, the card company or bank could in theory hold you liable, because of your negligence in letting a stranger hang on to your card. Suggest instead that if they feel the need for security, they 'swipe' your card and give it back to you. And do name and shame the pub to us.

STANTON   SP0634   MAP 4

Mount 🍴

Village signposted off B4632 SW of Broadway; keep on past village on no-through road up hill, bear left; WR12 7NE

17th-c pub in a lovely spot with fantastic views; keen, friendly young licensees and good food

Our readers have very much enjoyed their visits this year to this well run 17th-c pub – and tend to go back again and again. It's in a lovely spot up a steep lane from the golden-stone village, and you can be sure of a warm welcome from the keen young licensees. The bars have low ceilings, heavy beams and flagstones and there's a big log fire in the inglenook fireplace. The roomy extension has big picture windows overlooking the village. Donnington BB and SBA on handpump and a good choice of wines by the glass; darts and board games, and they keep dog biscuits behind the bar. On a fine day, try to bag one of the seats on the terrace as there are fantastic views over the Vale of Evesham towards the welsh mountains; boules. The pub is on the Cotswold Way National Trail.

🍴 Using carefully chosen local produce the good, popular food includes lunchtime filled baguettes, ploughman's, soup, oysters with shallot and red wine vinegar, various tapas, chicken liver foie gras parfait with red onion marmalade, free-range scrambled eggs with smoked salmon, tomato and chickpea curry, gloucester old spot sausages on cheddar mash with a rich jus, daily specials like brixham crab on vanilla-scented apples, fillet of black bream on a pepper, mussel and garlic stew and free-range chicken breast on creamy leeks with bacon and thyme, and puddings such as sticky toffee pudding and lime and lemon cheesecake; they also have a three-course set menu. *Starters/Snacks: £4.50 to £6.50. Main Courses: £9.95 to £15.00. Puddings: £4.50*

Donnington ~ Tenants Karl and Pip Baston ~ Real ale ~ Bar food (12-2, 6-9) ~ Restaurant ~ (01386) 584316 ~ Children welcome ~ Dogs welcome ~ Open 12-3, 6-11

Recommended by Keith and Sue Ward, Alan Jones, A and M Jones, John and Joyce Farmer, P and J Shapley, Michael Neilan, Richard Tilbrook, Ewan and Moira McCall, Julie and Bill Ryan, P M Newsome, Martin and Pauline Jennings, Tom Holman

TETBURY   ST8494   MAP 4

Gumstool 🍴 🍷 🛏

Part of Calcot Manor Hotel; A4135 W of town, just E of junction with A46; GL8 8YJ

Civilised bar with relaxed atmosphere (part of the very smart Calcot Manor Hotel), super choice of drinks and enjoyable food

Of course, this is not a pub as such and it is attached to the very smart Calcot Manor Hotel, but as a bar/brasserie it does have an informal and relaxed atmosphere and is a highly enjoyable place for a drink or meal. Butcombe Bitter and Gold and Sharps Own on handpump, lots of interesting wines by the glass and quite a few malt whiskies. The stylish layout is well divided to give a feeling of intimacy without losing the overall sense of contented bustle: flagstones, elegant wooden dining chairs and tables, well chosen pictures and drawings on mushroom-coloured walls, and leather armchairs in front of the big log fire; piped music. Westonbirt Arboretum is not far away.

🍴 Prices are reasonable for such a civilised setting and the food is excellent: salmon and prawn terrine with lime mayonnaise, twice-baked smoked cheese soufflé with apple and walnut salad, baked squash with moroccan-spiced couscous and chickpeas, popular fish and chips, sausages with red onion gravy, corn-fed grouse and beef pie, chicken wrapped with pancetta, button mushrooms and onions, daube of beef with roasted vegetables, and puddings like pear and ginger tarte tatin with clotted cream and panna cotta with griotte cherries. *Starters/Snacks: £3.75 to £10.25. Main Courses: £9.25 to £16.90. Puddings: £5.95 to £6.25*

Free house ~ Licensees Paul Sadler and Richard Ball ~ Real ale ~ Bar food (12-2(2.30 Sat, 4 Sun), 5.30-9.30(9 Sun)) ~ Restaurant ~ (01666) 890391 ~ Children welcome ~ Open 11-11; 12-10.30 Sun ~ Bedrooms: £207B/£230B

Recommended by Bernard Stradling, Les and Judith Haines, Clifford Blakemore, Mr and Mrs P R Thomas, Rod Stoneman, Dr and Mrs C W Thomas, Gordon and Margaret Ormondroyd

TODENHAM

SP2436   MAP 4

Farriers Arms ♀

Between A3400 and A429 N of Moreton-in-Marsh; GL56 9PF

Friendly country pub with interesting décor, good bar food and fine views

There's a lovely welcoming atmosphere in this unspoilt old pub created by the friendly and helpful landlady, and her staff. The bar has exposed stone and old plastered walls, hop-hung beams, fine old polished flagstones by the stone bar counter and a woodburning stove in a huge inglenook fireplace. A cosy room off the bar (full of old books and photographs) can seat parties of ten people and the restaurant has been recently refurbished. Hook Norton Hooky Bitter and two regularly changing guest beers on handpump, ten wines by the glass and locally brewed lager; piped music, darts and board games. The pub has fine views over the surrounding countryside from the walled garden and a couple of tables on the terrace overlook the quiet village road and church; aunt sally. Good surrounding walks.

🍴 **Popular food using local produce includes filled baguettes, ploughman's, soup, black pudding topped with rarebit, ham and free-range eggs, home-made lamb burger, steak in ale pie, roast vegetable and goats cheese cannelloni with pesto and parmesan cream, smoked haddock and prawn fishcakes with a smoked cheddar and chive sauce, duck breast with pak choi in garlic and redcurrant sauce, and puddings like white and dark chocolate tart and banoffi pie; Sunday roasts.** *Starters/Snacks: £4.95 to £7.95. Main Courses: £8.95 to £15.95. Puddings: £4.95 to £5.50*

Free house ~ Licensees Nigel and Louise Kirkwood ~ Real ale ~ Bar food (12-2(2.30 Sun), 6-9) ~ Restaurant ~ (01608) 650901 ~ Children welcome ~ Dogs allowed in bar ~ Open 12-3, 6-11; evening opening 6.30 in winter

Recommended by Ian and Nita Cooper, Pat Crabb, Alun and Jennifer Evans, Michael Dandy, Rob and Catherine Dunster, W M Paton

UPPER ODDINGTON

SP2225   MAP 4

Horse & Groom 🍴 ♀

Village signposted from A436 E of Stow-on-the-Wold; GL56 0XH

Pretty 16th-c Cotswold-stone inn with imaginative food, lots of wines by the glass, and local beers and other local drinks; bedrooms

The charming licensees in this well run dining pub offer a warm welcome to all their customers from walkers at lunchtime to those out for a special evening meal. The bar has pale polished flagstones, a handsome antique oak box settle among other more modern seats, some nice armchairs at one end, oak beams in the ochre ceiling, stripped-stone walls and a log fire in the inglenook fireplace. Wickwar BOB and Wye Valley Bitter and Hereford Pale Ale on handpump, 25 wines by the glass (including champagne), local apple juice and pressé, local cider and a locally brewed lager. There are seats and tables under green parasols on the terrace and in the pretty garden.

🍴 **Using top-quality local produce the enjoyable – if not cheap – bar food at lunchtime includes sandwiches and ciabatta rolls (they bake their own bread), ploughman's, baked whole brie with garlic and thyme pesto oil and tomato chutney, home-cooked ham with free-range eggs, toad in the hole with red onion gravy and beer-battered fish of the day, with evening dishes like cornish oysters with shallot and red wine vinegar, gravadlax of beef with celeriac and wholegrain mustard rémoulade, fried polenta, butternut squash and mushrooms with tapenade dressing, slow-braised crispy old spot pork belly with cider and honey shallot mash and juniper-scented greens, duck breast with ginger and rhubarb sauce, and puddings such as glazed lemon tart with raspberry sorbet and coffee crème caramel with coconut sorbet.** *Starters/Snacks: £5.95 to £8.00. Main Courses: £6.95 to £16.50. Puddings: £3.95 to £6.95*

Free house ~ Licensees Simon and Sally Jackson ~ Real ale ~ Bar food ~ Restaurant ~ (01451) 830584 ~ Children welcome ~ Open 12-3, 5.30-11; 12-3, 6-10.30 Sun ~ Bedrooms: £79S/£99S(£105B)

Recommended by T A R Curran, Alun and Jennifer Evans, Phil Bryant, Julie and Bill Ryan, Graham Oddey, Alan Thwaite

WOODCHESTER   SO8302   MAP 4

Ram 🍺

High Street, South Woodchester; off A46 S of Stroud; GL5 5EL

Attractive country pub, up to half a dozen interesting ales, a friendly landlord and lovely views from seats on the terrace

In good weather, the seats on the terrace outside this bustling country pub are a fine place to enjoy the spectacular valley views; there are interesting surrounding walks, too. Inside, the range of real ales kept by the obliging landlord continue to draw in customers. On handpump and constantly changing there might be Butcombe Bitter, Harviestoun Bitter & Twisted, Stroud Budding and Organic and Uley Old Spot. The relaxed L-shaped beamed bar has a nice mix of traditional furnishings (including several cushioned antique panelled settles) on bare boards, stripped stonework and an open fire. They hold various summer events such as open-air theatre, live music and so forth.

🍴 Bar food includes sandwiches, soup, butternut squash and leek gratin, ham and egg, gloucester old spot sausages and mash, steak in ale pie, braised lamb shank with redcurrant rosemary jus, pork loin with mustard mash and cider sauce, and puddings such as raspberry cheesecake and chocolate brownies; at lunchtime (not Sunday) there's a small choice of main courses for £5. *Starters/Snacks: £3.00 to £6.00. Main Courses: £5.00 to £11.50. Puddings: £4.25*

Free house ~ Licensee Tim Mullen ~ Real ale ~ Bar food (12-2.30, 6-9) ~ Restaurant ~ (01453) 873329 ~ Children welcome ~ Dogs welcome ~ Regular live music ~ Open 11-11(10.30 Sun)

Recommended by Dave Irving, Jenny Huggins, Andy and Claire Barker, John Taylor, J R Cason, Dr and Mrs A K Clarke, Dave Braisted, Mr Rene-Cason

LUCKY DIP

Besides the fully inspected pubs, you might like to try these Lucky Dips recommended to us and described by readers (if you do, please send us reports: feedback@goodguides.com).

ALDERTON [SP9933]
Gardeners Arms GL20 8NL [Beckford Rd, off B4077 Tewkesbury—Stow]: Attractive thatched Tudor pub with snug bars and informal restaurant, wide choice of decent home-made food from filled baps and baked potatoes to bistro dishes, fresh fish (inc takeaway fish and chips) and good Sun roast; well kept Greene King and guest beers, above-average wines, hospitable landlady and good service, log fire; may be piped music; dogs and children welcome, tables on sheltered terrace, good-sized well kept garden with boules (*LYM, Pat and Graham Williamson, Theocsbrian, Martin and Pauline Jennings*)
ALDSWORTH [SP1510]
Sherborne Arms GL54 3RB [B4425 Burford—Cirencester]: Family-run pub with good choice of enjoyable food, mainstream ales such as Greene King IPA, farm cider, beams, stripped stone, log fire, smallish bar and big dining area, conservatory, games/function room; piped music; children and dogs

welcome, disabled access, pleasant front garden with smokers' shelter (*Jim and Frances Gowers, BB*)
AMBERLEY [SO8401]
☆ *Black Horse* GL5 5AL [off A46 Stroud—Nailsworth to Amberley; left after Amberley Inn, left at war memorial; Littleworth]: Relaxed local with spectacular valley views from conservatory and terrace, good choice of changing ales, Moles Black Rat cider, decent wines by the glass, enjoyable varied food from baguettes to specials, friendly helpful staff; wood and flagstone floors, high-backed settles, woodburner, cheerful sporting pictures, brasses and bells, large family area, games room, live music; they keep your card in a locked box if running a tab, big TV; children, walkers and wet dogs welcome, plenty of tables outside, barbecue; best to park by war memorial and walk down (*Chris and Angela Buckell, LYM, E McCall, T McLean, D Irving, LM, Guy Vowles, Neil and Anita Christopher, John Coatsworth*)

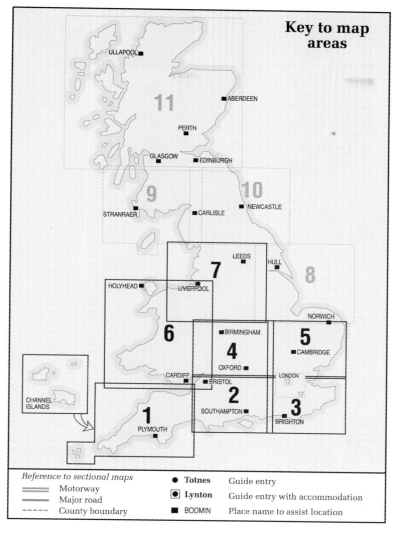

Key to map areas

Reference to sectional maps
- ═══ Motorway
- ─── Major road
- - - - County boundary

- ● Totnes — Guide entry
- ◉ Lynton — Guide entry with accommodation
- ■ BODMIN — Place name to assist location

MAPS IN THIS SECTION

For Maps 8 – 13 see later colour section

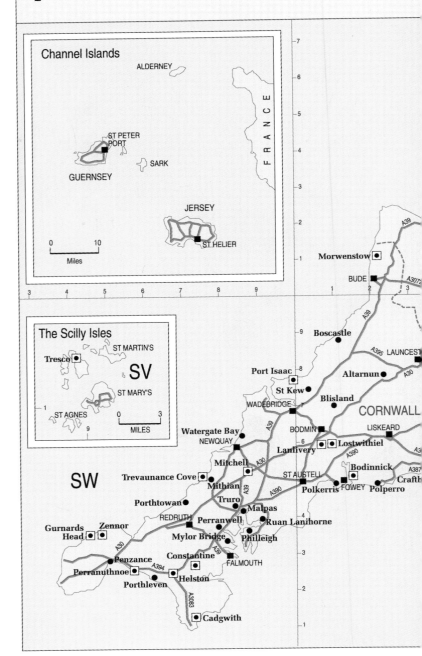

1

Channel Islands

ALDERNEY

FRANCE

ST PETER PORT
GUERNSEY

SARK

JERSEY

ST HELIER

0   10
Miles

7
6
5
4
3
2
1

3   4   5   6   7   8   9

Morwenstow ●

BUDE ■   A3072

A39

The Scilly Isles

ST MARTIN'S

Tresco ●   **SV**

ST MARY'S

ST AGNES

0   3
MILES

9

Boscastle ●

A395   LAUNCEST■

Port Isaac
●

St Kew ●   Altarnun ●

A30

Blisland ●

WADEBRIDGE

CORNWALL

A39

BODMIN ■   LISKEARD ■

6   ● Lostwithiel   A3

Watergate Bay ●   Lanlivery ●   A390

NEWQUAY ■   Bodinnick ●   A387

SW   ST AUSTELL   ● Crafth

Mitchell ●   Polkerris ● ■   Polperro ●

A30   A39   FOWEY

Trevaunance Cove ●

Mithian ●   A390

Truro ●

Porthtowan ●   Malpas ●

REDRUTH   Perranwell ●   Ruan Lanihorne ●

Gurnards   Zennor ●   Mylor Bridge ●   Philleigh ●
Head ●

A30   Penzance ●   Constantine ●

Perranuthnoe ●   A394   FALMOUTH

Porthleven ●   Helston ●

A3083

Cadgwith ●

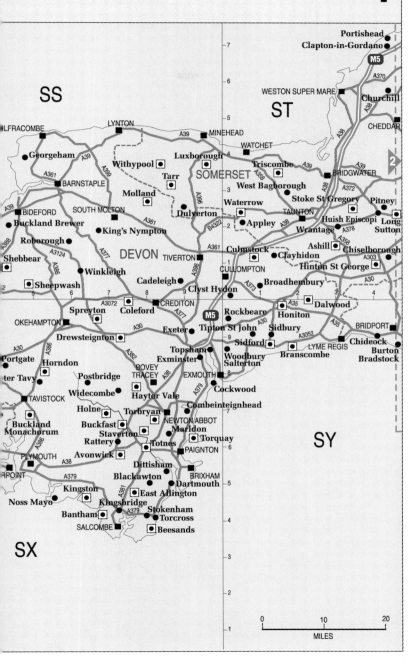

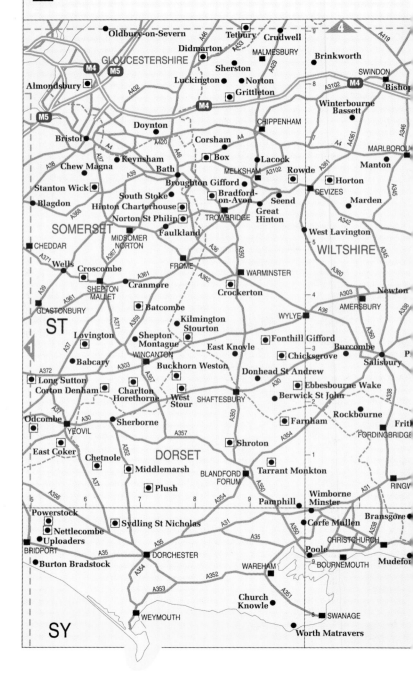

2

Oldbury-on-Severn • Tetbury ■ Crudwell •

Didmarton ■ MALMESBURY

GLOUCESTERSHIRE

Brinkworth •

Sherston • SWINDON

Luckington • • Norton Bishop

Grittleton M4

Almondsbury ■ Winterbourne Bassett •

CHIPPENHAM ■

M5

Doynton • MARLBOROU

Bristol • Corsham A4

Keynsham • Box • Lacock • Manton

Chew Magna • Bath MELKSHAM Rowde •

A39 Broughton Gifford • Horton •

Stanton Wick ■ South Stoke • Bradford- DEVIZES

Blagdon • Hinton Charterhouse ■ on-Avon Seend Marden •

Norton St Philip ■ TROWBRIDGE Great Hinton

CHEDDAR ■ Faulkland • West Lavington •

MIDSOMER NORTON WILTSHIRE

Wells ■ Croscombe • WARMINSTER ■

SHEPTON MALLET Cranmore • Crockerton •

GLASTONBURY

ST Batcombe • WYLYE ■

Kilmington Stourton • AMERSBURY Newton

Lovington • Fonthill Gifford •

Shepton Montague • Chicksgrove • Burcombe •

Babcary • WINCANTON East Knoyle • Salisbury P

Long Sutton ■ Buckhorn Weston • Donhead St Andrew •

Corton Denham • Charlton Horethorne • West Stour Ebbesbourne Wake •

Odcombe ■ SHAFTESBURY ■ Berwick St John

YEOVIL Rockbourne • Frith

East Coker • Sherborne • Farnham • FORDINGBRIDGE

Chetnole • Shroton •

DORSET Middlemarsh • BLANDFORD FORUM Tarrant Monkton • RINGW

Plush • Pamphill • Wimborne Minster •

Powerstock ■ Sydling St Nicholas • Corfe Mullen • Bransgore •

Nettlecombe ■ CHRISTCHURCH

Uploaders ■ Poole ■

BRIDPORT DORCHESTER ■ BOURNEMOUTH Mudefor

Burton Bradstock • WAREHAM ■

Church Knowle •

WEYMOUTH ■ SWANAGE ■

SY Worth Matravers •

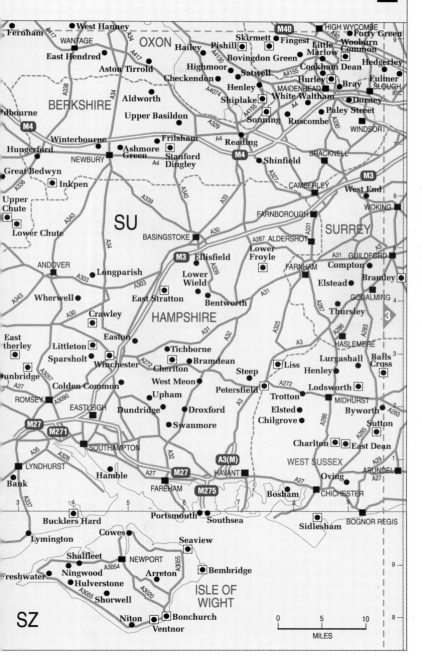

2

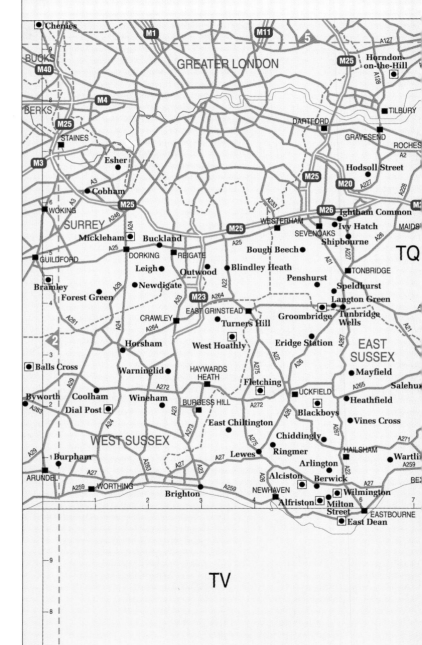

3

Chenies

BUCKS
M40
M1
M11
5

GREATER LONDON

A127

Horndon
on-the-Hill
M25
A128

BERKS
M4

DARTFORD

TILBURY

M25
STAINES

GRAVESEND

ROCHES
A2

Esher

Hodsoll Street

M3

A3
Cobham

M25
M20
A221
A228
M2

M25
WOKING
SURREY
A246
A24

M25
WESTERHAM
Tghtham Common
M26
Ivy Hatch
MAIDS

Mickleham
Buckland

SEVENOAKS
Shipbourne
A26

A25
DORKING
REIGATE
A25
Bough Beech
TONBRIDGE
TQ

GUILDFORD
Leigh
Outwood
Blindley Heath
Penshurst
Speldhurst

Bramley
Forest Green
Newdigate
A22
M23
A264
Langton Green
Groombridge
Tunbridge
Wells

A261
A24
A23
EAST GRINSTEAD
A267

2
CRAWLEY
A264
Turners Hill
Eridge Station
EAST
SUSSEX

Balls Cross
Horsham
West Hoathly
A22
A26

Warninglid
HAYWARDS
HEATH
Mayfield

Byworth
A283
Coolham
Wineham
A272
Fletching
UCKFIELD
A265
Salehur

Dial Post
BURGESS HILL
A272
A28
Blackboys
Heathfield

A29
WEST SUSSEX
A23
A273
East Chiltington
A275
Chiddingly
Vines Cross
A267
A271

Burpham
A283
A27
Lewes
Ringmer
Arlington
HAILSHAM
Wartli
A259

ARUNDEL
A27
A263
A26
Alciston
Berwick
A22
A27
BEX

A259
WORTHING
Brighton
A259
NEWHAVEN
Wilmington
6
EASTBOURNE

Alfriston
Milton
Street
East Dean

1
2
3
4
7

-9

TV

-8

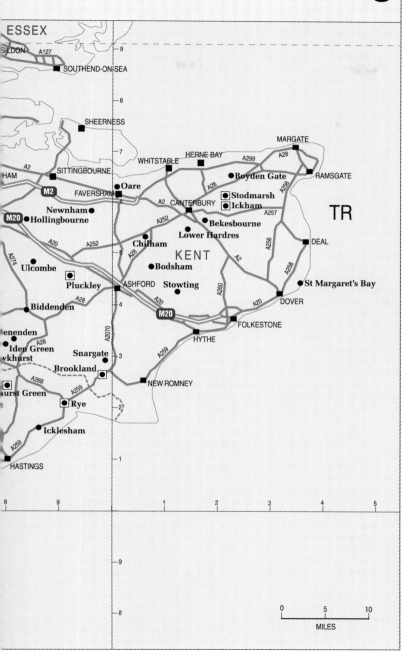

3

ESSEX

BILLDON   A127

■ SOUTHEND-ON-SEA

■ SHEERNESS

MARGATE

WHITSTABLE   HERNE BAY   A299   A28

■ SITTINGBOURNE

HAM   A2

● Boyden Gate   RAMSGATE

M2   FAVERSHAM ● Oare

A28

● Stodmarsh
● Ickham

A2   CANTERBURY

A257

TR

Newnham ●

M20 ● Hollingbourne

A252

A20   A252

Chilham ●

A28

● Bekesbourne
Lower Hardres ●

A256

■ DEAL

A2

A258

KENT

A274

Ulcombe ●

● Bodsham

● St Margaret's Bay

◉ Pluckley

ASHFORD   Stowting ●

A260

DOVER

A28

A20

Biddenden ●

A2070

FOLKESTONE

M20

enenden

● Iden Green
vkhurst

A28

Snargate ●

HYTHE

A259

Brookland ●

◉

urst Green

A268

A259

■ NEW ROMNEY

◉ Rye

● Icklesham

A259

■ HASTINGS

0   5   10
MILES

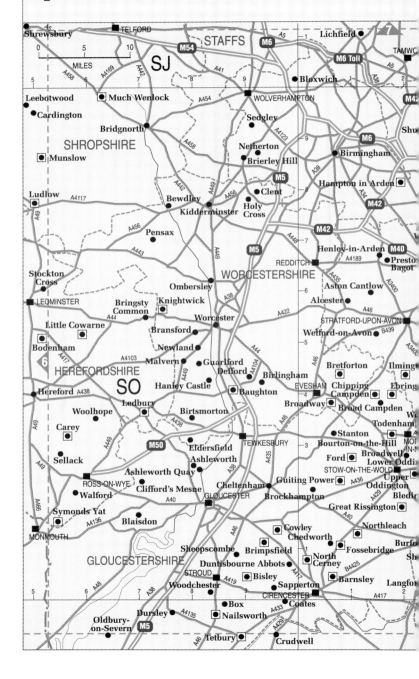

4

Shrewsbury
TELFORD
M54
STAFFS
SJ
M6
A5
Lichfield
TAMW
M6 Toll
A5
A38
Bloxwich
M42

0   5   10
MILES

A4169
A42
A41
9
A454
WOLVERHAMPTON

Leebotwood
Cardington
Much Wenlock
Sedgley
9
M6
Shu
Bridgnorth
SHROPSHIRE
A458
A4123
Netherton
Brierley Hill
Birmingham
Munslow
A442
A449
A456
M5
Clent
Hampton in Arden
M42
Ludlow
A4117
Bewdley
Holy Cross
A38
M42
A49
Kidderminster
A456
Pensax
A443
A449
A448
M42
Henley-in-Arden
M40
Stockton Cross
REDDITCH
WORCESTERSHIRE
A4189
Presto Bagot
LEOMINSTER
Ombersley
A435
Aston Cantlow
A3400
Bringsty Common
Knightwick
A38
6
Alcester
A46
Little Cowarne
Worcester
A422
STRATFORD-UPON-AVON
Bodenham
A44
Bransford
Welford-on-Avon
B439
A3400
A417
Newland
A4103
5
Bretforton
Ilming
HEREFORDSHIRE
Malvern
Guarlford
A44
A46
SO
Defford
A4104
Birlingham
Chipping Campden
Ebring
Hereford
A438
Hanley Castle
EVESHAM
4
Broad Campden
Woolhope
Ledbury
Baughton
Broadway
W
Carey
Birtsmorton
A46
Stanton
Todenham
A438
Bourton-on-the-Hill
MOR
IN-N
Sellack
A449
M50
Eldersfield
TEWKESBURY
3
Ford
Broadwell
A49
Ashleworth
A438
Lower Oddi
Ashleworth Quay
A38
STOW-ON-THE-WOLD
ROSS-ON-WYE
Clifford's Mesne
Cheltenham
Guiting Power
A436
Upper
Walford
GLOUCESTER
Brockhampton
Oddington
A486
Symonds Yat
A40
A429
Bledi
A4136
Blaisdon
Great Rissington
MONMOUTH
A46
Cowley
Northleach
Chedworth
A48
GLOUCESTERSHIRE
Sheepscombe
Brimspield
Fossebridge
Burfo
Duntisbourne Abbots
North Cerney
Sh
STROUD
A419
Bisley
B4425
Woodchester
Sapperton
Barnsley
Langfo
3
CIRENCESTER
1
A417
2
Box
Coates
Dursley
A4135
Nailsworth
A433
A429
M5
Oldbury-on-Severn
A46
Tetbury
Crudwell

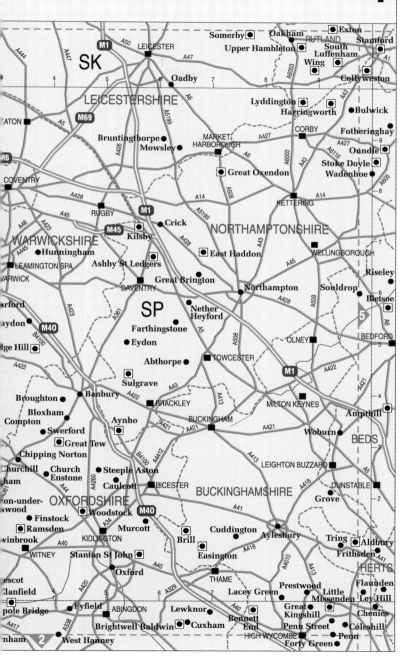

M1 A50 LEICESTER

Somerby ◉ Oakham ◉ Exton ◉ Stamford

SK

Upper Hambleton ◉ RUTLAND

A47

A6003 South Luffenham ◉

Oadby

Wing ◉

LEICESTERSHIRE

A6 Collyweston

M69

Lyddington ◉ A43

Harringworth ● Bulwick ●

Bruntingthorpe ●

A426 Mowsley ●

MARKET HARBOROUGH

CORBY A427 Fotteringhay ●

A6116 Oundle ◉

A43 Stoke Doyle ◉

Wadenhoe ● A605

COVENTRY

◉ Great Oxendon

A428

RUGBY **M1**

A5199 KETTERING A14

M45 Crick ●

Kilsby ●

NORTHAMPTONSHIRE

WARWICKSHIRE

● Hunningham

LEAMINGTON SPA

Ashby St Ledgers ●

◉ East Haddon

A43 WELLINGBOROUGH

Riseley ●

WARWICK

DAVENTRY ● Great Brington

Northampton ● A428 A509 Souldrop ● Bletsoe ●

A6

SP

M40 B4100

Farthingstone ●

● Eydon

● Nether Heyford

A5

A508 OLNEY BEDFORD

A422 Abthorpe ● ■ TOWCESTER

M1 A422

Sulgrave ◉

A43

Broughton ●

Bloxham ● Banbury ■ A422 ■ BRACKLEY A413 MILTON KEYNES

Compton ●

● Swerford Aynho ◉ A421 BUCKINGHAM A421 Woburn ● BEDS

◉ Great Tew

A421 Ampthill ◉

Chipping Norton B4100 A4412

Churchill Church ● Steeple Aston A413 LEIGHTON BUZZARD A5

ham Enstone

A44 A4260 Caulcott ● BICESTER BUCKINGHAMSHIRE A418 DUNSTABLE

on-under-wood OXFORDSHIRE **M40** Grove ●

◉ Woodstock A41

● Finstock Murcott ◉ Cuddington ● Aylesbury Tring ● Aldbury ◉

◉ Ramsden KIDLINGTON Brill ◉ A418 Frithsden ●

winbrook A40 Easington ● HERTS

WITNEY Stanton St John ◉ A4010 A413 Flaunden ●

Oxford ● Prestwood ● Little Ley Hill ●

escot A329 THAME Missenden

lanfield Lacey Green ● Great Chenies ●

ple Bridge ● Fyfield ABINGDON Lewknor ● A40 Kingshill ● Coleshill ●

Brightwell Baldwin ◉ ● Cuxham Bennett Penn Street ● Penn ●

nham **2** West Hanney End HIGH WYCOMBE ■ Forty Green ●

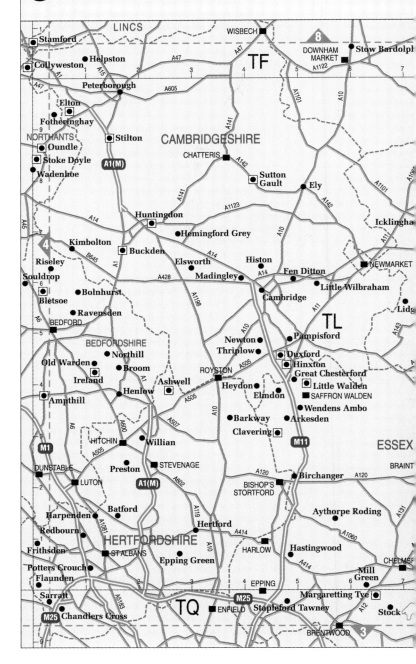

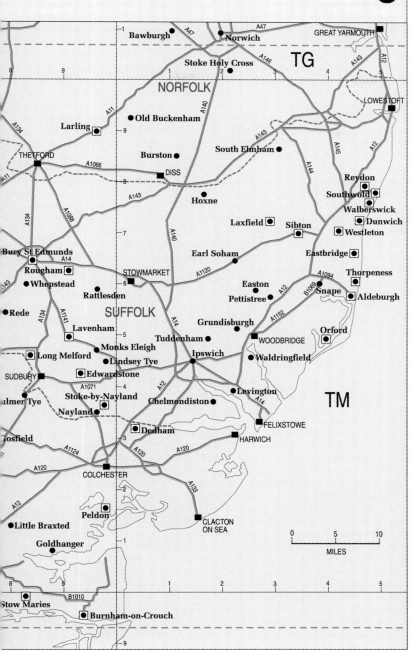

5

Bawburgh ●
A47
Norwich ■
GREAT YARMOUTH ■
A47
A146
TG
A143
A12

Stoke Holy Cross ●
LOWESTOFT ■
A11
NORFOLK
A140
A143
A145
A12

Larling ☐
Old Buckenham ●
A134

THETFORD ■
A1066
A11
Burston ●
South Elmham ●
A144
DISS ■
Reydon ☐
Southwold ☐
A143
Hoxne ●
A134
A1088
Walberswick
A140
Laxfield ☐
Sibton ☐
Dunwich ●
Westleton ☐

Bury St Edmunds ■
Earl Soham ●
Eastbridge ☐
Rougham ☐
A14
STOWMARKET ■
A1120
A1094
Thorpeness ☐
Whepstead ●
Easton ●
A12
Snape ☐
Rattlesden ●
B1069
Aldeburgh ●
Rede ●
SUFFOLK
Pettistree ●
A1141
Lavenham ☐
Grundisburgh ●
A1152
Orford ☐
A14
Tuddenham ●
WOODBRIDGE
A134
Monks Eleigh ●
Long Melford ☐
Lindsey Tye ●
Ipswich ■
Waldringfield ●
Edwardstone ☐
SUDBURY ■
A1071
Levington ●
ulmer Tye
Stoke-by-Nayland ☐
Chelmondiston ●
A14
TM
Nayland ●
FELIXSTOWE ■
osfield
Dedham ☐
HARWICH ■
A1124
A120
A120
A120
COLCHESTER ■
A133
A12
Peldon ☐
CLACTON ON SEA ■
Little Braxted ●
Goldhanger ●

0   5   10
MILES

B1010
Stow Maries ☐
Burnham-on-Crouch ●

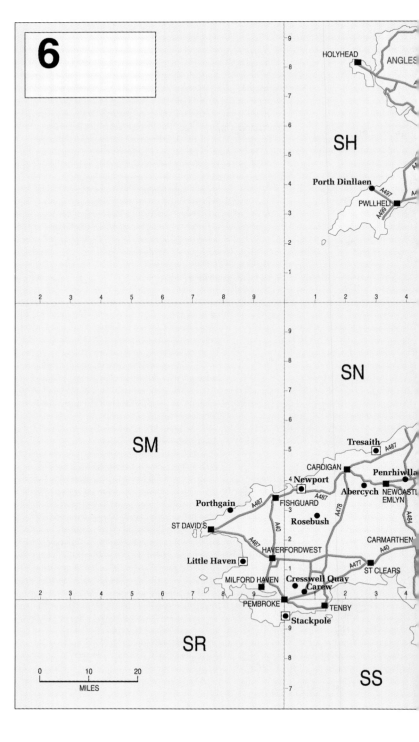

6

HOLYHEAD ■   ANGLES

SH

Porth Dinllaen ●   A497
PWLLHELI ■

SN

SM

Tresaith
●

CARDIGAN ■   Penrhiwlla
4 Newport   Abercych NEWCASTL
● FISHGUARD   A478   EMLYN

Porthgain ●   A487

ST DAVID'S ■   Rosebush ●

A487   HAVERFORDWEST   CARMARTHEN

Little Haven ●   A477
1   ST CLEARS
MILFORD HAVEN ■   Cresswell Quay
Carew   A40

PEMBROKE ■   TENBY ■
Stackpole

SR

SS

0   10   20
MILES

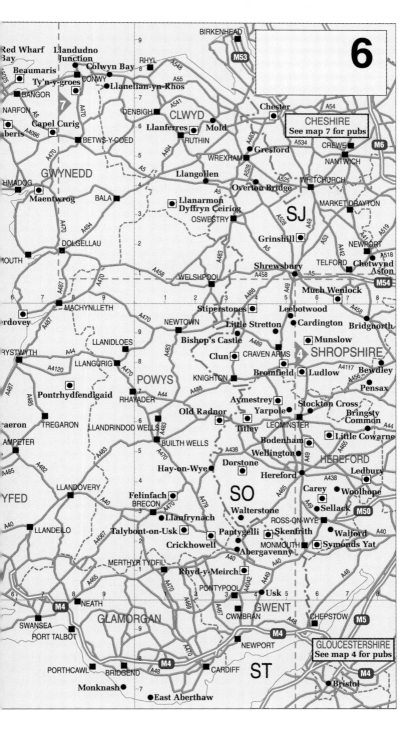

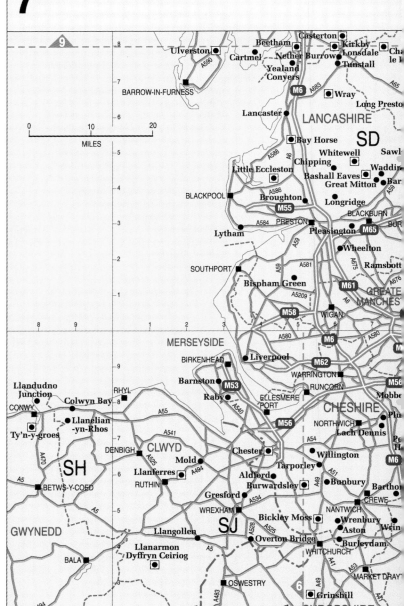

9

Ulverston

Beetham Casterton Kirkby
Cartmel Nether Burrow Lonsdale Cha
Yealand le K
Conyers Tunstall

BARROW-IN-FURNESS

M6 Wray

Lancaster Long Presto

LANCASHIRE

0 10 20
MILES

Bay Horse SD

Whitewell Sawl

Chipping

Little Eccleston Waddi

Bashall Eaves Bar
Great Mitton

BLACKPOOL

Broughton Longridge

BLACKBURN

Lytham PRESTON Pleasington M65 BUR

Wheelton

SOUTHPORT Ramsbott

Bispham Green M61

A5209 GREATE
MANCHES

M58
WIGAN

MERSEYSIDE M6

A580

Liverpool

BIRKENHEAD M62
WARRINGTON
Barnston M53 RUNCORN M56

Llandudno Raby ELLESMERE
Junction RHYL PORT CHESHIRE

CONWY Colwyn Bay Mobbe

Llanelian NORTHWICH Plu
-yn-Rhos
Ty'n-y-groes M56 Lach Dennis Pe
H

SH DENBIGH CLWYD Chester M6

Mold Willington

BETWS-Y-COED Llanferres Tarporley
Aldford Barthon
RUTHIN Burwardsley Bunbury

Gresford CREWE

GWYNEDD WREXHAM NANTWICH

Bickley Moss Wrenbury Wrin

Llangollen SJ Aston
Overton Bridge Burleydam
Llanarmon WHITCHURCH
BALA Dyffryn Ceiriog

MARKET DRAY

OSWESTRY
6 NEWF

Grinshill

SHROPSHIRE
POWYS
Chetwynd Aston TELFORE
DOLGELLAU Shrewsbury

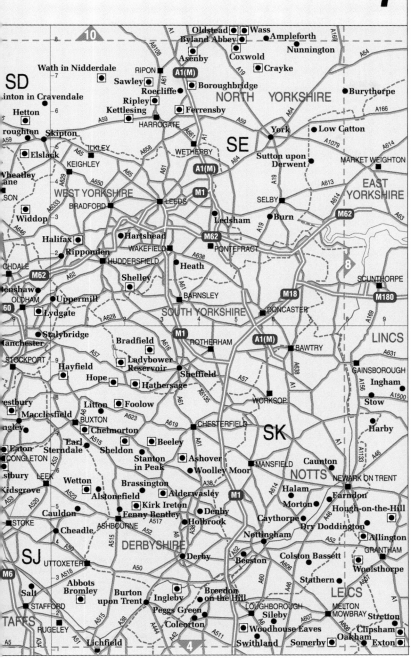

SD

10

Wath in Nidderdale
inton in Cravendale
Hetton
roughton Skipton
A59
Elslack
Wheatley
ane
SON
Widdop

RIPON
Sawley
Ripley
Kettlesing
HARROGATE
ICKLEY
KEIGHLEY
A650
BRADFORD

Oldstead Wass
Byland Abbey
Asenby Coxwold
A1(M)
Boroughbridge
Roecliffe
Ferrensby
WETHERBY
A61
A658
A1(M)
M1
LEEDS

Ampleforth
Nunnington
Crayke

NORTH   YORKSHIRE

York Low Catton
Sutton upon
Derwent

Burythorpe

MARKET WEIGHTON

**EAST
YORKSHIRE**

WEST YORKSHIRE

Halifax
Ripponden
CHDALE
M62
enshaw
OLDHAM
60
Lydgate

Hartshead
WAKEFIELD
HUDDERSFIELD Heath
Shelley
BARNSLEY

Ledsham
M62
PONTEFRACT
A638

Burn
M62

SCUNTHORPE
M180
M18

SOUTH YORKSHIRE

Uppermill

anchester
STOCKPORT
Hayfield
Hope
estbury
Macclesfield
ngley
Eaton Sterndale
CONGLETON
stbury LEEK
Kidsgrove
Cauldon
STOKE
Cheadle

Stalybridge
Bradfield
Ladybower
Reservoir
Hathersage
Litton Foolow
BUXTON
Chelmorton
Earl
Sheldon Beeley
Stanton
in Peak
Brassington
Alstonefield Alderwasley
Kirk Ireton
Wetton
Fenny Bentley
ASHBOURNE
Holbrook

ROTHERHAM
M1
Sheffield

DONCASTER

A1(M)
BAWTRY

LINCS

GAINSBOROUGH
Ingham
Stow
Harby

WORKSOP

SK

CHESTERFIELD

Ashover
Woolley Moor
MANSFIELD Caunton
NOTTS NEWARK ON TRENT
Halam Farndon
Morton Hough-on-the-Hill
Caythorpe Dry Doddington
Denby Nottingham Allington
GRANTHAM

DERBYSHIRE

SJ
UTTOXETER
M6
Salt
STAFFORD
Abbots
Bromley
Burton
upon Trent Ingleby
Peggs Green
Coleorton
RUGELEY
Lichfield

Derby
Beeston
Colston Bassett
Stathern
Woolsthorpe
LEICS

Breedon
on the Hill
LOUGHBOROUGH
Sileby
Woodhouse Eaves
Swithland Somerby

MELTON
MOWBRAY Stretton
Clipsham
Oakham Exton

TAFFS

4

'An invaluable guide' *Sunday Telegraph*

GOOD GUIDE TO

DOG FRIENDLY PUBS, HOTELS AND B&Bs

Edited by Alisdair Aird and Fiona Stapley

4TH EDITION

Over **1,000** places for you and your dog to enjoy

* Over 1,000 places to eat, drink and stay with your dog

* Compiled by the editors of *The Good Pub Guide* with the same commitment to accuracy and independence

* Includes vital information on opening hours, prices and facilities

'[An] invaluable guide...smart and indispensable'
Daily Telegraph

'Essential reading' *Daily Mail*

'A great book for all dog lovers' *Scottish Sunday Post*

From the editors of *The Good Pub Guide* comes the latest edition of the *Good Guide to Dog Friendly Pubs, Hotels and B&Bs* – the definitive guide for dog owners.

AMPNEY CRUCIS [SP0701]

☆ *Crown of Crucis* GL7 5RS [A417 E of Cirencester]: Bustling roadside food pub, good value and plenty of choice, real ales in restored bar, good house wines, efficient service, beams and log fires, split-level restaurant; children welcome, disabled facilities, lots of tables out on grass by car park, quiet modern bedrooms around courtyard, good breakfast, cricket pitch over stream, open all day *(Peter and Audrey Dowsett, Steve Cocking, LYM)*

AMPNEY ST PETER [SP0801]

Red Lion GL7 5SL [A417, E of village]: This unspoilt and unchanging country pub has long been a monument to traditional hospitality under its welcoming veteran landlord – only the third in over a century; just two simple chatty little rooms, Hook Norton and maybe a guest beer from the hatch; only its extremely limited opening hours – as we went to press, Sun lunchtime and weekend evenings – keep it out of the Main Entries *(E McCall, T McLean, D Irving, Dave Irving, Jenny Huggins, Roger Shipperley, the Didler, Mr Ray J Carter, Stephen Funnell, Giles and Annie Francis, Ewan and Moira McCall, Ray Carter, Richard Tilbrook, LYM, Stuart Doughty, Donna and Roger)*

ARLINGHAM [SO7110]

Red Lion GL2 7JH: Beamed roadside pub with friendly obliging landlord and staff, well kept ales inc John Smiths, farm cider, reasonably priced usual food (not Sun evening) inc children's menu and good Sun roasts (local meat); pool room, skittle alley; dogs welcome, picnic-sets out at front and in small courtyard and back garden, pétanque, not far from Severn estuary walks (leaflets available), three bedrooms, open all day wknds, cl Tues lunchtime and Mon *(Neil and Anita Christopher, Dr A Y Drummond)*

AVENING [ST8898]

Bell GL8 8NF [High St]: Two-bar country local under new welcoming management, log fire in carpeted beamed bar, stripped-stone dining room with local prints, enjoyable food, well kept ales *(John and Gloria Isaacs)*

BIBURY [SP1006]

Catherine Wheel GL7 5ND [Arlington; B4425 NE of Cirencester]: Bright and cheerful under new management; open-plan main bar and smaller back rooms, low beams, stripped stone, log fires, enjoyable fresh food, real ales, raftered dining room; picnic-sets out behind, famously beautiful village, handy for country and riverside walks, four bedrooms *(Dominic Brockbank, Jo White, Mo and David Trudgill, LYM)*

BIRDLIP [SO9316]

Air Balloon GL4 8JY [A417/A436 roundabout]: Loftily placed busy chain dining pub, good range of food from all day sandwiches, wraps and baguettes up, friendly helpful service, changing ales such as Hook Norton Old Hooky, good wine and soft drinks' choice, many levels and alcoves inc restaurant and brasserie; pubbier front corner with open fire, beams and stripped stone; unobtrusive piped music; tables, some covered, on heated terrace and in garden with play area, open all day *(Phyl and Jack Street, Caroline and Michael Abbey)*

BISHOP'S NORTON [SO8425]

Red Lion GL2 9LW: Cosy isolated pub on River Severn, especially popular in summer, with Wickwar ales, fair range of snacks inc baps and ploughman's, log fires; riverside garden, views to Malvern Hills, good walks, open all day wknds *(Dr A Y Drummond)*

BISLEY [SO9006]

Stirrup Cup GL6 7BL [Cheltenham Rd]: Long rambling well furnished local with two or three well kept ales such as Wickwar, good modestly priced food from sandwiches to Sunday roasts, decent wines, prompt friendly service; dogs welcome *(Guy Vowles)*

BLOCKLEY [SP1634]

Crown GL56 9EX [High St]: Golden-stone Elizabethan inn with much-modernised linked bar areas, good food, decent wines, friendly staff, restaurant; piped music; children in eating areas, difficult for wheelchairs, tables in terraced coachyard surrounded by beautiful trees and shrubs, bedrooms *(Keith and Sue Ward, LYM)*

Great Western Arms GL56 9DT [Station Rd (B4479)]: Smartly updated dining area, welcoming attentive licensees, well kept Hook Norton ales, good choice of wines, enjoyable simple home-made food, busy public bar (dogs very welcome here – pub has two retrievers); attractive village, lovely valley view *(Elizabeth Charnley)*

BOURTON-ON-THE-WATER [SP1620]

Duke of Wellington GL54 2BY [Sherbourne St]: Welcoming refurbished stone-built inn under new management, relaxed open-plan carpeted bar with leather sofas, enjoyable food here or in more formal back dining room, log fires; garden with riverside picnic-sets, five bedrooms *(Ted George)*

Old Manse GL54 2BX [Victoria St]: River Windrush view from front garden and end of long beamed bar (no under-21s), good choice of enjoyable food from all-day doorstep sandwiches up, friendly young staff, three Greene King ales; mixed furniture on carpet or boards, big log fire, attractive old prints, bookshelves, some stripped stone, pretty restaurant (children allowed here); soft piped music, TV, games machine; 15 good bedrooms, open all day *(BB, Dennis Jones)*

BROCKWEIR [SO5301]

Brockweir Inn NP16 7NG [signed just off A466 Chepstow—Monmouth]: Welcoming country local nr the River Wye, beams and stripped stonework, quarry tiles, sturdy settles, woodburner, snug carpeted alcoves, well kept local ales, enjoyable food, upstairs restaurant, conservatory, public bar; no credit cards; children in eating areas, small garden with interesting covered terrace, bedrooms, has been open all day Sat

(Edward Hutchings, LYM, Dave Irving, Jenny Huggins)

CAMP [SO9111]

☆ **Fostons Ash** GL6 7ES [B4070 Birdlip—Stroud, junction with Calf Way]: Popular open-plan dining pub, light and airy, with good food inc interesting lunchtime sandwiches and imaginative light dishes, lunchtime bargains, real ales such as Goffs Jouster, Greene King Old Speckled Hen and Stroud Organic, decent wines by the glass; neat welcoming staff, daily papers, one end with easy chairs and woodburner; piped music; rustic tables in attractive garden with heated terrace and play area, good walks *(BB, Myra Joyce)*

CERNEY WICK [SU0796]

Crown GL7 5QH: Old village inn with roomy modern lounge bar, comfortable conservatory dining extension, enjoyable inexpensive food, well kept changing local ales, coal-effect gas fires, games in public bar; children welcome, good-sized garden with swings, small motel-style bedroom extension *(Giles and Annie Francis, BB)*

CHARLTON KINGS [SO9619]

Clock Tower GL53 8DY [Cirencester Rd]: Marstons all-day food pub with popular two-for-one deals, well kept ales, decent wines, friendly staff *(John Clancy)*

Royal George GL53 8JH [Horsefair, opp church]: Big 19th-c pub reopened after extensive refurbishment, smart modern décor, good real ale and food choice; children and dogs welcome *(Stuart Doughty)*

CHELTENHAM [SO9421]

Bath Tavern GL53 7JT [Bath Rd]: One-room friendly bay-windowed local, bargain generous pubby food from good crab sandwiches up, well kept Wye Valley and Sharps Doom Bar, good choice of wines by the glass, nice resident dog *(John Clancy, Brian and Maggie Woodford, Prof Kenneth Surin)*

Bayshill GL50 3PP [St Georges Pl]: Welcoming family-run pub in quiet lane off tourist beat, pleasant interior, reasonably priced food lunchtimes and Tues-Fri evenings, ales such as Greene King IPA and Wadworths 6X; beer garden *(D W Stokes)*

Brown Jug GL53 7NB [Bath Rd]: Traditional pub with well cooked reasonably priced food inc Sun roasts (evening Weds and Thurs only), Wadworths and guest ales, darts, skittle alley, live music and comedy nights; sports TV; children welcome, heated beer garden, cl Mon *(John Clancy)*

Jolly Brewmaster GL50 2EZ [Painswick Rd]: Popular lively local with open-plan linked areas around big semi-circular counter, good range of ales such as Archers, Caledonian Deuchars IPA, Donnington SBA and Hook Norton Best, up to eight farm ciders, perhaps a perry; friendly obliging young staff, newspapers, log fires; dogs welcome, coachyard tables *(Grant Langdon, Richard and Ruth Dean, Stuart Doughty)*

Norwood Arms GL53 0AX [Leckhampton Rd]:

Roomy refurbished pub, good choice of enjoyable food inc speciality pies with choice of mash, Greene King ales; garden and terrace *(John Clancy)*

☆ **Plough** GL52 3BG [Mill St, Prestbury]: Thatched village local opp church, comfortable front lounge, service from corner corridor hatch in flagstoned back tap room, grandfather clock and big log fire, personable licensees; well kept Adnams Best and Broadside and Wells & Youngs Bombardier tapped from the cask, Stowford Press cider, basic pub food inc ready-filled rolls; outstanding good-sized flower-filled back garden with immaculate boules pitch *(Stuart Doughty, Rob and Catherine Dunster)*

CHIPPING CAMPDEN [SP1539]

☆ **Kings** GL55 6AW [High St]: Fresh eclectic contemporary décor in bar/brasserie and separate restaurant, cheery helpful service, good food from lunchtime sandwiches and baguettes to pubby dishes and more elaborate meals, Hook Norton and a guest, good choice of wines by the glass, good log fire, daily papers; secluded back garden with picnic-sets and terrace tables, 12 comfortable bedrooms, open all day Sat *(LYM, Eithne Dandy, Michael Dandy, Peter Dandy)*

☆ **Lygon Arms** GL55 6HB [High St]: Appealing low-beamed bar, good value food till late evening from good sandwiches to interesting more pricey dishes, good wine choice, real ales such as Hook Norton and Wadworths 6X, open fires, stripped stone and lots of horse pictures, small back restaurant; children welcome, tables in shady courtyard, comfortable beamed bedrooms, good breakfast, open all day wknds and summer *(Michael Dandy, LYM, Gene and Kitty Rankin)*

☆ **Red Lion** GL55 6AS [Lower High St]: Linked beamed rooms with flagstones, stripped stone and log fires, good value fresh food from sandwiches and baguettes up, friendly service, Greene King ales, decent wine choice, fine range of malt whiskies, roomy eating area and upstairs dining room; may be quiet piped music, big-screen sports TV and pool in games bar; dogs welcome, sheltered back courtyard, five bedrooms *(Michael Dandy, Chris Glasson)*

CIRENCESTER [SP0202]

☆ **Corinium** GL7 2DG [Dollar St/Gloucester St]: Civilised and comfortable, with big log fire, antique coaching prints, good mix of tables, sofas and small armchairs, well kept Bath Ales and Uley Laurie Lee, Thatcher's cider, decent wines, enjoyable bar food from sandwiches up, cheerful prompt service, restaurant; piped music; entrance through charming courtyard with tables, wheelchair access with help, attractive back garden, good bedrooms *(Donna and Roger, BB, E McCall, T McLean, D Irving, Rob and Catherine Dunster)*

Fleece GL7 2NZ [Market Pl]: Civilised comfortable old hotel with good value enterprising food, friendly effective largely hispanic staff, good choice of wines by the glass, well kept Hook Norton and a guest beer, bay window looking up market place to parish church, roomy lounge and restaurant; terrace tables, bedrooms *(BB, Mr and Mrs W W Burke, George Atkinson, Dave Irving, Jenny Huggins)*

CLEARWELL [SO5708]

Lamb GL16 8JU [off B4228; The Cross]: Friendly unpretentious pub with Wye Valley Bitter and three small brewery guests tapped from the cask, high-ceilinged divided bar, old settles in cosy snug, open fires, no food; dogs welcome, children till 8.30pm, small terrace at back with smokers' shelter cl Mon, Tues and lunchtimes Weds, Thurs *(Theocsbrian)*

COLD ASTON [SP1219]

Plough GL54 3BN [aka Aston Blank; off A436 (B4068) or A429 SW of Stow-on-the-Wold]: Attractive little 17th-c pub, well kept Cotswold, Hook Norton and North Cotswold ales, good choice of wines, food from ciabattas up, friendly efficient staff; standing timbers, low black beams and flagstones, inglenook; small side terraces, unspoilt village with plenty of walks, cl Mon *(Anthony and Pam Stamer, P and J Shapley, Di and Mike Gillam, LYM, Helene Grygar)*

COLEFORD [SO5813]

☆ *Dog & Muffler* GL16 7AS [Joyford, best approached from Christchurch five-ways junction B4432/B4428, by church – B4432 towards Broadwell, then follow signpost; also signposted from the Berry Hill Post Office crossroads; beyond the hamlet itself, bear right and keep your eyes skinned for the pub sign, which may be obscured by the hedge; OS Sheet 162 map reference 580134]: Prettily set 17th-c country dining pub, cosy beamed bar with log-effect gas fire in big fireplace, hop bines, beamed and flagstoned back part with bright conservatory restaurant and verandah; cheerful helpful staff; good popular food from sandwiches up inc interesting vegetarian platters, beers such as Brains Rev James and local Freeminers Speculation, decent wine choice; no dogs; children welcome, large terrace with lovely views, attractive garden with segregated play area, nice walks, good value bedrooms *(Mrs P Sumner, Peter Meister, Brian and Jacky Wilson, LYM)*

COMPTON ABDALE [SP0717]

☆ *Puesdown Inn* GL54 4DN [A40 outside village]: Spacious series of stylish bar areas, wide choice of good enterprising food from sandwiches up, neat friendly staff, Fullers and Hook Norton ales, good coffees and wines by the glass; log fire and woodburner, leather or brightly upholstered sofas and armchairs, big art posters and other interesting pictures, bare boards, bright rugs and rafter-effect ceilings, cream and dark red walls, mainly stripped stone in extensive eating areas; well reproduced piped music; nice garden behind, bedrooms *(BB, Rod Stoneman)*

COOMBE HILL [SO8827]

Swan GL19 4BA [A38/A4019]: Light airy dining pub with several rooms, popular generous fresh food from sandwiches up, quick attentive service, Greene King Abbot, Uley Old Spot and a guest, decent house wine, polished boards and panelling, red leather chesterfields; piped music *(Dr A J and Mrs Tompsett, Rod Stoneman)*

CRANHAM [SO8912]

☆ *Black Horse* GL4 8HP [Village signposted off A46 and B4070 N of Stroud]: Down-to-earth 17th-c country local liked by walkers, cosy lounge, main bar with traditional furniture, window seats and log fire, well kept ales such as Butcombe, Hancocks, Hop Back and Sharps, straightforward bar food (not Sun evening – pub open from 8pm then), upstairs dining rooms; well behaved children and dogs welcome (two pub dogs), tables out in front and to the side, closed Mon *(Giles and Annie Francis, LYM)*

EASTLEACH TURVILLE [SP1905]

☆ *Victoria* GL7 3NQ [off A361 S of Burford]: Open-plan low-ceilinged rooms around central servery, attractive seats built in by the log fire, unusual Queen Victoria pictures, Arkells ales, several good value wines by the glass, sensibly priced pub food (not winter Sun evening) from baguettes up; piped music; children and dogs welcome, small pleasant front garden with picnic-sets overlooking picturesque village, good walks *(Michael Cooper, Dr and Mrs M E Wilson, Helene Grygar, Maurice Holt, LYM)*

EDGE [SO8409]

☆ *Edgemoor* GL6 6ND [Gloucester Rd (A4173)]: Tidy, modernised and spacious 19th-c dining place with panoramic valley view across to Painswick from picture windows and pretty terrace, wide choice of enjoyable good value food inc fine home-made puddings, friendly efficient service, well kept local real ales, nice coffee, restaurant; children welcome, good walks nearby, has been cl Sun evening *(Neil and Anita Christopher, LYM, Martin and Pauline Jennings, M W Riddiford)*

ELKSTONE [SO9610]

☆ *Highwayman* GL53 9PL [Beechpike; A417 6 miles N of Cirencester]: Interesting rambling 16th-c building, low beams, stripped stone, log fires, cosy alcoves, bric-a-brac, antique settles, armchairs and sofa among more usual furnishings; good value home-made food, friendly service, full Arkells range, good house wines; family room and big back eating area; disabled access, outside play area *(the Didler, LYM)*

EWEN [SU0097]

☆ *Wild Duck* GL7 6BY [off A429 S of Cirencester]: Unchanging 16th-c inn with stylishly old-fashioned furnishings and pictures in high-beamed log-fire main bar, lounge with handsome Elizabethan fireplace and antique furnishings, some interesting if not cheap food, six real ales inc one brewed for the pub, very good choice of wines by the glass; piped music; children welcome, tables in neatly kept heated courtyard (if you eat here they may ask to keep your credit card behind the bar), garden, 12 bedrooms, open all day *(LYM, Neil and Anita Christopher, Peter and Audrey Dowsett, Dr and Mrs A K Clarke, Stuart and Doreen Ritchie)*

FAIRFORD [SP1501]

☆ *Bull* GL7 4AA [Market Pl]: Sizeable beamed and timbered hotel bar, civilised and popular with locals, comfortably old-fashioned pubby furnishings (nice bow window seats overlooking little market square), aircraft pictures (RAF base nearby) and thespian photographs, coal-effect gas fire; wide choice of good reasonably priced food, Arkells ales, nice little residents' lounge; children welcome, dogs in bar, charming village and church, 22 bedrooms, open all day *(Howard G Allen, Anthony Barnes, Stuart Doughty, LYM, Peter and Audrey Dowsett)*

FOREST OF DEAN [SO6212]

Speech House GL16 7EL [B4226 nearly 1m E of junction with B4234]: Superbly placed hotel in centre of forest (former 17th-c hunting lodge), refurbished interior with oak panelling, huge log fire, all-day bar food from nice sandwiches up, real ales such as Wye Valley, afternoon teas, big conservatory, restaurant; comfortable bedrooms, tables outside *(Mike and Mary Carter, T McLean, D Irving)*

FORTHAMPTON [SO8731]

Lower Lode Inn GL19 4RE: Brick-built 15th-c pub with River Severn moorings and plenty of waterside tables (prone to winter flooding), beams, flagstones, enormous log fire and traditional seating, enjoyable pubby food inc Sun roasts, friendly helpful landlady, five well kept interesting ales; restaurant, back pool room and juke box; children and dogs welcome (lots of summer holiday families), disabled facilities, caravan site, good value bedrooms with good breakfast, open all day *(John Clancy, MLR)*

FRAMPTON MANSELL [SO9202]

☆ *Crown* GL6 8JG [brown sign to pub off A491 Cirencester—Stroud]: Welcoming licensees doing good traditional home-made food at reasonable prices, well kept changing local ales inc Stroud and Uley, two log fires and woodburner, heavy beams, stripped stone and rugs on bare boards, restaurant, efficient charming service; children and dogs welcome (there's a friendly pub dog), disabled access, picnic-sets in sunny front garden, pretty outlook, 12 decent bedrooms, open all day from 12 *(Myra Joyce, LYM, Keith Buckingham)*

FRAMPTON ON SEVERN [SO7408]

Bell GL2 7EP [The Green (B4071), handy for M5 junction 13, via A38)]: Handsome creeper-covered Georgian inn attractively opened up, enjoyable food in extensive all-day family dining area, Bath Gem, Moles and Sharps Doom Bar, some local liqueurs, several wines by glass, log fire, pool; piped

music, games machine, TV; dogs welcome, plenty of seats outside, good play area and kids' farm, village cricket green opposite, open all day *(Ken and Barbara Turner, Karen Eliot, W K Wood, LYM)*

FRANCE LYNCH [SO9003]

Kings Head GL6 8LT [Lynch Rd]: Welcoming old village local in lovely spot, reasonably priced standard food inc Sun roasts, Sharps Doom Bar, Wells & Youngs BB and guest ales, live music Mon night, summer music festival; well behaved children welcome, garden with play area, open all day Sun and bank hols *(Giles and Annie Francis)*

GLASSHOUSE [SO7121]

☆ *Glasshouse Inn* GL17 0NN [off A40 just W of A4136]: Much-extended red-brick beamed pub with appealing old-fashioned and antique furnishings, cavernous black hearth, big flagstoned conservatory, well kept ales inc Butcombe tapped from the cask, Stowford Press cider, reasonably priced wines, decent home-made food from sandwiches to interesting specials; piped music, no under-14s in bars, no bookings except Sun lunch, and they may try to keep your credit card while you eat; good disabled access, neat garden with rustic furniture, interesting topiary and lovely hanging baskets, nearby paths up wooded May Hill,

cl Sun evening *(LYM, the Didler, Chris and Angela Buckell, Mike and Mary Carter)*

GLOUCESTER [SO8318]

Café René GL1 1TP [Southgate St]: Lots of character in friendly place with enjoyable good value food, three well kept ales, good cheerful service *(Alan and Eve Harding, Andy and Claire Barker)*

☆ *Dick Whittingtons House* GL1 2PE [Westgate St]: Grade I-listed early Tudor building with 18th-c façade, probably former guild hall and mansion house; under newish management with welcoming staff, straightforward food (not Sun evening), six changing local ales inc Wickwar, good mix of customers; piped music, some live; children and dogs welcome, attractive courtyard, open all day *(the Didler)*

Fountain GL1 2NW [Westgate St/Berkeley St]: Popular and civilised, with good range of real ales, farm cider, reasonably priced usual food, attractive prints, handsome stone fireplace (pub dates from the 17th c), plush seats and built-in wall benches; good disabled access, pleasant courtyard, handy for cathedral, open all day *(BB, the Didler, Di and Mike Gillam)*

New Inn GL1 1SF [Northgate St]: Actually one of the city's oldest structures, lovely beamed medieval building with galleried courtyard, recently refurbished with three bars (back one is the busiest), well kept Butcombe, Wychwood and up to eight guests inc smaller local breweries, cheap lunchtime food, coffee shop, restaurant, good service; soft piped music, silent fruit machine; 35 good value bedrooms, open all day (till late Thurs-Sat) *(the Didler, Alan and Eve Harding)*

Toby Jug GL2 8DE [Over; A40 a mile W of Gloucester]: Decent Toby Carvery with enjoyable all-day food, obliging staff, Butcombe beer, several tapped wines, open fires; children welcome, outside tables, handy stop-off *(Dr A J and Mrs Tompsett, LYM)*

GREAT BARRINGTON [SP2013]

☆ **Fox** OX18 4TB [off A40 Burford—Northleach; pub towards Little Barrington]: 17th-c inn, with stripped stone, simple country furnishings and low ceiling, Donnington BB and SBA, farm cider and good apple juice, wide choice of quickly served food (all day Sun and summer Sat, not Mon night in winter) from sandwiches through oysters to local meats; big bare-boards river-view dining room with riverbank mural, traditional games, Aug 'Foxstock' folk festival; can get very busy, games machine, TV; children and dogs welcome, heated terraces by the River Windrush (swans and private fishing), informal orchard with pond, four bedrooms, open all day *(LYM, William Goodhart, the Didler, David Glynne-Jones, David Lamb, Martin and Pauline Jennings, Giles and Annie Francis)*

GREET [SP0230]

Harvest Home GL54 5BH [Evesham Rd (B4078 by Winchcombe Station bridge)]: Neatly kept airy country pub with lovely Malvern Hills views, shortish choice of enjoyable well presented food incl healthy children's menu, good range of Timothy Taylors ales and guests, Stowford Press cider, nice wines; friendly atmosphere, beams, log fires and bay window seats, big raftered barn restaurant; sizeable garden, not far from medieval Sudeley Castle and Winchcombe GWR Station *(LYM, Kathryn Birkett, Dr A J and Mrs Tompsett, Jeremy and Ruth Preston-Hoar)*

GUITING POWER [SP0924]

☆ **Farmers Arms** GL54 5TZ [Fosseway (A429)]: Stripped stone, flagstones, cheap Donnington BB and SBA, wide blackboard range of unpretentious food cooked by landlord, prompt friendly service, nice log fire, carpeted back dining area, games area with darts, dominoes, cribbage, pool, skittle alley; piped music, games machine; children welcome, garden with quoits, lovely village, good walks, bedrooms *(LYM, the Didler, Di and Mike Gillam, Jo Rees)*

HAM [ST6898]

Salutation GL13 9QH: Friendly local with good range of ales and simple well cooked food *(Barry Collett)*

HAWKESBURY UPTON [ST7786]

☆ **Beaufort Arms** GL9 1AU [High St]: 17th-c pub in historic village, well kept Butcombe, Wickwar BOB and good guest beers, local farm cider, good soft drinks' choice, friendly landlord and staff, popular no-nonsense food (no starters), thriving local atmosphere; extended uncluttered dining lounge on right,

darts in more spartan stripped-brick bare-boards bar, interesting local and brewery memorabilia, lots of pictures (some for sale), skittle alley; no credit cards; well behaved children welcome, dogs in bar, disabled access throughout and facilities, picnic-sets in smallish enclosed garden, on Cotswold Way, open all day *(Chris and Angela Buckell, M G Hart, Jim and Frances Gowers)*

HINTON DYRHAM [ST7376]

☆ **Bull** SN14 8HG [2.4 miles from M4 junction 18; A46 towards Bath, then first right (opp the Crown)]: 17th-c stone pub in nice setting, main bar with two huge fireplaces, low beams, oak settles and pews on ancient flagstones, horsebrasses, stripped-stone back area and simply furnished restaurant (children allowed here till 7.30pm), standard food (all day Sun), Wadworths and changing guests; piped music; dogs welcome in bar, seats on front balcony and in sizeable sheltered upper garden with play equipment; open all day wknds, cl Mon lunchtime *(Dr and Mrs A K Clarke, Peter Martin, Edward Mirzoeff, Dr and Mrs Michael Smith, Mrs P Sumner, John Wooll, Alistair Stanier, David A Hammond, LYM, Steve and Liz Tilley)*

HORSLEY [ST8497]

☆ **Tipputs** GL6 0QE [Tiltups End; A46 2 miles S of Nailsworth]: Enjoyable food all day from good value lunches to interesting evening meals, cheerful efficient service, Greene King ale, beams, stripped stone, big log fire and abstract art, comfortable leather seats in anteroom to galleried barn restaurant; nice chairs and tables in pretty garden with raised deck, lovely setting, open all day *(Alan and Eve Harding, Tom and Ruth Rees)*

HYDE [SO8801]

☆ **Ragged Cot** GL6 8PE [Burnt Ash; off A419 E of Stroud]: New licensee again for 17th-c Cotswold-stone inn; rambling bar with three connecting rooms, beams, old school chairs around pale wooden tables on stripped wood flooring, cushioned window and wall seats, log fires, real ales such as Otter; seats under parasols in landscaped garden, bedrooms *(LYM)*

KEMPSFORD [SU1596]

George GL7 4EQ [High St]: Nicely refurbished with woodburners in roomy bare-boards dining area, carpeted bar, welcoming landlord, enjoyable good value traditional food, well kept Arkells; children welcome, big back play area *(Stephen Funnell)*

KILKENNY [SP0118]

☆ **Kilkeney Inn** GL54 4LN [A436, 1 mile W of Andoversford]: Neat spacious dining pub (originally six stone cottages) with extended bright beamed bar, stripped-stone walls and white plasterwork, wheelbacks around tables on quarry tiles or carpet, woodburner; mostly good reports on food but some concerns over service, St Austell Tribute and Wells & Youngs Bitter, several wines by the glass, airy conservatory; piped music; well behaved children allowed, attractive Cotswold views from tables on terrace and lawn, bedrooms,

open all day Sun (LYM, Colin Moore,
Dr A J and Mrs Tompsett)

KINETON [SP0926]

Halfway House GL54 5UG [signed from
B4068 and B4077 W of Stow-on-the-Wold]:
Simple 17th-c beamed village pub doing well
under newish welcoming couple, good nicely
presented food from sandwiches up, well
kept Donnington BB and SBA, decent wines,
farm cider, restaurant, log fire; pool; children
welcome, sheltered back garden, good walks,
bedrooms, open all day wknds (LYM, Mr and
Mrs Adam Helliker, John and Helen Rushton,
Michael Dandy)

KINGSCOTE [ST8196]

☆ *Hunters Hall* GL8 8XZ [A4135 Dursley—
Tetbury]: Tudor beams, stripped stone, big
log fires and plenty of character in
individually furnished spotless linked rooms,
some sofas and easy chairs, wide choice of
good sensibly priced food from lunchtime
sandwiches up, well kept Greene King and
Uley ales, friendly attentive service;
flagstoned back bar with darts, pool and TV;
children and dogs welcome, garden with
good play area, bedrooms, open all day
(Brian Goodson, LYM, Nick and Meriel Cox)

LECHLADE [SU2199]

New Inn GL7 3AB [Market Sq (A361)]:
Prompt obliging service, wide choice of good
value generous food from good filled
baguettes up, huge log fire, several changing
real ales, roomy unpretentious front bar,
charming back restaurant; quiet piped music,
end games machine, big-screen sports TV;
play area in big garden down to the Thames,
good walks, 29 comfortable bedrooms
(Peter and Audrey Dowsett)

LEIGHTERTON [ST8290]

Royal Oak GL8 8UN [off A46 S of
Nailsworth]: Chatty and welcoming stone-
built local, opened-up bar with beams, log
fires, stripped-stone or brick walls and
mullioned windows, good value pubby food
from soup and sandwiches to roasts, good
OAP wkdy lunches, well kept changing ales
inc Butcombe, prompt helpful service; piped
music; wheelchair access throughout, nice
garden, quiet village, good walks, quite
handy for Westonbirt Arboretum (Chris and
Angela Buckell)

LITTLE BARRINGTON [SP2012]

☆ *Inn For All Seasons* OX18 4TN [A40, 3 miles
W of Burford]: Handsome old coaching inn
with attractive comfortable lounge bar, low
beams, stripped stone and flagstones, old
prints, log fire; Sharps Doom Bar and
Wadworths 6X, lots of wines by the glass and
malt whiskies, restaurant and conservatory;
piped music; seats in garden, aunt sally,
walks from door (Evelyn and Derek Walter,
Anthony Longden, LYM)

LITTLE WASHBOURNE [SO9933]

Hobnails GL20 8NQ [B4077 Tewkesbury—
Stow-on-the-Wold]: Attractive traditional
front core with 15th-c beams and log fire,
comfortable and extensive eating areas
around this, wide choice of enjoyable food

inc popular good value carvery, friendly
obliging service, several local ales, decent
wines; children welcome, disabled facilities,
terrace tables, play area, bedroom extension
(Dr A J and Mrs Tompsett, LYM)

LITTLETON-UPON-SEVERN [ST5989]

☆ *White Hart* BS35 1NR [3.5 miles from M48
junction 1]: Former farmhouse with three
main rooms, log fires, nice mix of country
furnishings, loveseat in inglenook,
flagstones at front, huge tiles at back, hops
on beams, fine old White Hart Inn Simonds
Ale sign; family room, back snug, Wells &
Youngs ales and guests, bar food (all day
Sun) using some home-grown produce; may
ask to keep a credit card while you eat; dogs
welcome, wheelchair access with help,
picnic-sets on front lawn, cottagey flower
beds, teak seating on brick terrace
by big car park, walks from the door, open
all day (John and Gloria Isaacs, Bob and
Angela Brooks, Chris and Angela Buckell, LYM,
Donna and Roger)

LONGBOROUGH [SP1729]

Coach & Horses GL56 0QU: Small 17th-c
stone-built local, Donnington ales, enjoyable
wholesome food (not Sun evening or Mon-
Weds), friendly staff, leather armchairs on
flagstones, inglenook stove, darts, dominoes
and cribbage; some piped music; well
behaved children and dogs welcome, tables
out at front looking down on stone cross and
village, two bedrooms (Tracey and
Stephen Groves, Roger Fox, Michael Dandy)

MARSHFIELD [ST7773]

☆ *Catherine Wheel* SN14 8LR [High St; signed
off A420 Bristol—Chippenham]: High-
ceilinged stripped-stone front part with
medley of settles, chairs and stripped tables,
charming Georgian dining room with open
fire in impressive fireplace, cottagey beamed
back area warmed by woodburners, friendly
staff and chatty locals, well kept ales such
as Cotswold and Sharps, interesting wines
and other drinks, enjoyable sensibly priced
food (not Sun evening) from pub favourites
up; darts, dominoes, no music or machines;
dogs on leads and children welcome,
wheelchair access with help, flower-decked
back yard, unspoilt village, four bedrooms,
open all day (Ian Phillips, LYM, Donna and
Roger, GSB, B and F A Hannam, Chris and
Angela Buckell, Dr and Mrs A K Clarke)

Lord Nelson SN14 8LP [A420 Bristol—
Chippenham; High St]: Linked beamed rooms
(inc former stables still with runnel down
uneven flagstones), Bath and Courage ales,
Stowford Press cider, generous inexpensive
food quickly served, plain tables and chairs,
open fires, bistro restaurant; games bar with
pool and machines; charming small
courtyard, bedrooms in cottage annexe
(Guy Vowles, Dr and Mrs A K Clarke)

MAYSHILL [ST6882]

☆ *New Inn* BS36 2NT [Badminton Rd (A432
Frampton Cotterell—Yate)]: Good food (all
day Sun) in popular largely 17th-c coaching
inn with two comfortably carpeted bar rooms

leading to restaurant, friendly staff, well kept changing ales such as Bristol Beer Factory and Cotswold Spring, Stowford Press cider, log fire; children and dogs welcome, garden with play area (*Donna and Roger, Jim and Frances Gowers*)

MEYSEY HAMPTON [SU1199]

Masons Arms GL7 5JT [just off A417 Cirencester—Lechlade; High St]: 17th-c village local now owned by Arkells, enjoyable food, good range of beers, longish open-plan beamed bar with big inglenook fire at one end, restaurant; children and dogs have been welcome, tables out on green, pleasant compact bedrooms (*Prof H G Allen, LYM, Ken and Margaret Grinstead, Noel Grundy, Ewan and Moira McCall, Jeff and Sue Evans, E McCall, T McLean, D Irving*)

MICKLETON [SP1543]

☆ *Kings Arms* GL55 6RT [B4632 (ex A46)]: Civilised open-plan family lounge, good well presented food from well filled sandwiches to unusual specials and good value OAP lunches, courteous well trained staff, Greene King, Hook Norton and Wychwood ales, farm cider, several wines by the glass, nice mix of comfortable chairs, soft lighting, interesting homely décor with lots to look at, log fire; small locals' bar with darts, dominoes and cribbage; piped music; unusual tables in courtyard and sizeable garden, attractive village, handy for Kiftsgate and Hidcote (*Paul Humphreys, Brian and Pat Wardrobe, Michael Dandy, Keith and Sue Ward, BB, Martin and Pauline Jennings*)

MISERDEN [SO9308]

Carpenters Arms GL6 7JA [off B4070 NE of Stroud]: Two open-plan bar areas with low beams, stripped-stone walls, bare boards, and two big log fires, well kept Wye Valley ales, enjoyable reasonably priced pub food using home-grown veg, small dining room; garden tables, handy for Miserden Park (*LYM, Giles and Annie Francis, Prof H G Allen*)

MORETON-IN-MARSH [SP2032]

☆ *Redesdale Arms* GL56 0AW [High St]: Relaxed old coaching inn with prettily lit alcoves, sofas and big stone fireplace in solidly furnished comfortable panelled bar on right, darts in flagstoned public bar, log fires, stripped stone; Hook Norton and Wye Valley, decent wines and coffee, enjoyable food, courteous helpful service, spacious back child-friendly brasserie and dining conservatory; piped music, TV, games machine; heated floodlit courtyard decking, 24 comfortable bedrooms beyond, open all day from 8am (*Mr and Mrs W W Burke, BB, Michael Sargent, George Atkinson, Keith and Sue Ward, Michael Dandy, Lawrence R Cotter*)

White Hart Royal GL56 0BA [High St]: Refurbished partly 15th-c inn, cosy beamed quarry-tiled bar with fine inglenook, adjacent smarter panelled room with Georgian feel, separate lounge and restaurant; Hook Norton and North Cotswold ales, good choice of wines, food from interesting sandwiches and wraps up,

cream teas, friendly attentive service from smart staff; courtyard tables, bedrooms (*Michael Dandy, Eithne Dandy, George Atkinson, BB*)

NAILSWORTH [ST8499]

Britannia GL6 0DG [Cossack Sq]: Large open-plan pub (part of the small Food Club chain) in former manor house, popular bistro food (best to book evenings), bargain wkdy lunch menu, takeaway pizzas, friendly service, well kept Greene King IPA and a couple of local beers, good choice of wines by the glass, big log fire; picnic-sets in front garden (*Colin Moore, Tom and Ruth Rees, J R Cason, Dave Irving, Jenny Huggins*)

George GL6 0RF [Newmarket]: Good valley views, attractive central bar with lounge/eating area one side, dining room the other, beams and flagstones, fresh food, up to four ales inc Moles, friendly and comfortable (*the Didler*)

Village Inn GL6 0HH [Bath Rd]: Thriving pub brewing its own good value Nailsworth ales, guest beers and bargain takeaways too, appealingly done series of rambling linked areas with steps down to back area for view of the brewing process; woody décor with panelling, dividers and oak floors, log fire, pub food inc good local pies, brewery tours; dogs welcome, open all day (*Dave Irving, Jenny Huggins, J R Cason, the Didler, Mr Rene-Cason*)

NAUNTON [SP1123]

☆ *Black Horse* GL54 3AD [off B4068 W of Stow]: Friendly stripped-stone proper pub with well kept Donnington BB and SBA, good simple fresh food from huge baguettes to good value Sun roasts (veg may come from local allotments), good service, plain tables, flagstones, black beams and log fire; darts, cribbage, dominoes, dining room; piped music; children and dogs welcome (friendly resident terrier called Molly), some nice seating outside, charming village, fine Cotswold walks, bedrooms (*Richard Tilbrook, Roger Fox, John Taylor, Michael Dandy, LYM*)

NEWENT [SO7225]

George GL18 1PU [Church St]: Well worn-in former coaching inn, friendly locals, three or four well kept changing ales, standard home-made food, open-plan bar with log fire, evening restaurant; children welcome, nice location opp Shambles museum, bedrooms, open all day (*TB, MLR*)

NEWLAND [SO5509]

☆ *Ostrich* GL16 8NP [off B4228 in Coleford; or can be reached from the A466 in Redbrook, by the turn-off at the England-Wales border – keep bearing right]: Relaxed old pub with roomy low-ceilinged bar, creaky floors, miners' lamps on uneven walls, settles and cushioned window seats, candles in bottles, big fireplace, cheery landlady, several well kept changing ales, food can be good; soft piped music; children and dogs welcome, picnic-sets out at front and in walled garden, picturesque village with interesting church, good walks (*Robert Turnham,*

Dave and Jane Stirling, LYM, Peter Dearing, Dave Braisted, Peter J and Avril Hanson)

NIBLEY [ST6982]

Swan BS37 5JF [Badminton Rd]: Light fresh refurbishment by small local pub group, good food inc OAP lunchtime offers (Mon-Weds), Wickwar ales, fireside leather sofas one side, dining tables the other (Donna and Roger)

NORTH NIBLEY [ST7596]

New Inn GL11 6EF [E of village itself; Waterley Bottom]: Former cider house in secluded rural setting popular with walkers, ales such as Cotleigh, Goffs, Wickwar and Wye Valley from antique pumps, five ciders, basic bar food, lounge bar with cushioned windsor chairs and high-backed settles, partly stripped-stone walls, simple cosy public bar with darts, beer and cider festivals; children and dogs welcome, tables on lawn and covered decked area with pool table, bedrooms, open all day wknds, cl Mon lunchtime (LYM)

NORTHLEACH [SP1114]

Sherborne Arms GL54 3EE [Market Pl]: Comfortably traditional refurbishment, good choice of enjoyable food from baguettes up inc good Sun carvery, children's meals, friendly attentive staff, Courage Best, Greene King Old Speckled Hen and Sharps Doom Bar, good wines and coffee; bar on left (popular with locals) stretching back from smallish front area, cosy lounge on right with wing armchairs and sofas around big stone fireplace, large stripped-stone restaurant up steps; piped music, TV and games machine; dogs welcome, some tables in front and in small side courtyard, three bedrooms, open all day (Neil and Anita Christopher, Peter and Audrey Dowsett, BB)

NORTON [SO8524]

Kings Head GL2 9LR [just off A38; Old Tewkesbury Rd]: Recently refurbished linked rooms, some with flagstones and bare boards, mostly modern light wood furniture, a few wall seats and well stuffed sofas, unusual animal sculptures; well kept Butcombe, Greene King and Sharps, interesting wines, wide food choice inc breakfast from 8am and Sun carvery, attentive service; children welcome, disabled access, garden with big play area (Chris and Angela Buckell)

NYMPSFIELD [SO7900]

☆ *Rose & Crown* GL10 3TU [The Cross; signed off B4066 Stroud—Dursley]: Friendly stone-built 17th-c pub with good choice of reasonably priced home-made food (all day Fri-Sun) inc OAP wkdy lunch deals, well kept ales such as Butcombe, Hook Norton and Uley, decent wines, local farm cider, coffees and teas; log fire in bare-boards beamed front bar with pine tables, pews and old settles, large back dining area, regular events; children and dogs welcome, disabled access, picnic-sets in side yard and sheltered lawn with good play area, handy for Cotswold walks and Woodchester (NT), three

adjacent bedrooms, open all day (BB, John and Gloria Isaacs, Keith and Sue Ward)

OAKRIDGE LYNCH [SO9103]

Butchers Arms GL6 7NZ [off Eastcombe—Bisley road E of Stroud]: Sensibly priced standard food (not Sun evening, Mon) in welcoming beamed pub, well kept Wadworths and a guest, rambling partly stripped-stone bar, open fires, dining room, family room with play area, retriever called Gabriel; Weds quiz; picnic-sets on neat lawn overlooking valley, good walks, cl Mon lunchtime, open all day Fri-Sun in summer (LYM, Sue Kinder)

OLD DOWN [ST6187]

☆ *Fox* BS32 4PR [off A38 Bristol—Thornbury; Inner Down]: Fine range of real ales in popular low-beamed village local, good reasonably priced hearty food with some interesting specials (advisable to book), friendly efficient staff, farm cider and good choice of wines by the glass; log fire, carpeted eating area, high-backed settles in family room; children welcome, disabled access, verandah with grapevine, garden play area (Chris and Angela Buckell, Charles and Pauline Stride, John and Gloria Isaacs, John Luckes, David Langford, James Morrell)

OLD SODBURY [ST7581]

☆ *Dog* BS37 6LZ [3 miles from M4 junction 18, via A46 and A432; The Hill (a busy road)]: Welcoming and popular two-level bar with low beams and stripped stone, wide range of enjoyable food cooked to order (so can be a wait), friendly young staff, three well kept changing ales, good wine and soft drinks; choice; games machine, juke box; children welcome, big garden with barbecue and good play area, bedrooms, open all day (Donna and Roger, Roy Hoing, Meg and Colin Hamilton, Tom Evans, JJW, CMW, Rynap, Dr and Mrs A K Clarke, the Brewers, Dave Irving, Jenny Huggins, LYM)

PAINSWICK [SO8609]

Royal Oak GL6 6QG [St Mary's St]: Partly 16th-c three-room local, friendly welcoming landlady, well kept ales such as Stroud, decent wines, enjoyable pub food, appealing nooks and crannies, some attractive old seats, plenty of prints, open fire, small sun lounge; pretty suntrap courtyard (Pete and Jackie Chunn, Bob and Angela Brooks, LYM)

PARKEND [SO6107]

Fountain GL15 4JD [just off B4234]: 18th-c village inn by terminus of restored Lydney—Parkend railway, three well kept ales inc local Freeminer, Stowford Press cider, wines in glass-sized bottles, bargain food inc OAP lunches Tues and Thurs, welcoming helpful staff; real fire, assorted chairs and settles in two linked rooms, old local tools, bric-a-brac and photographs; children and dogs welcome, wheelchair access, side garden, eight bedrooms, bunkhouse (Chris and Angela Buckell, Mike Horgan)

Rising Sun GL15 4HN [off B4431]: Unpretentious friendly foresters' local popular with walkers and cyclists, plainly furnished open-plan bare-boards bar, ales such as Butcombe Gold and Greene King Bonkers Conkers, well cooked low-priced simple food; picnic-sets in big woodside garden with pond *(Peter Meister, Howard G Allen)*

Woodman GL15 4JF [Folly Rd, Whitecroft]: Roomy and relaxed stripped-stone bar, heavy beams, farm and forestry decorations, artwork for sale, smaller back bar and dining room, good choice of enjoyable fresh food, well kept Wadworths 6X and other ales, decent wines, pleasant service; picnic-sets on front terrace facing green, sheltered back courtyard and garden, bedrooms, good Forest of Dean walks *(Neil and Anita Christopher, Mike Horgan, BB)*

PAXFORD [SP1837]

Churchill Arms GL55 6XH [B4479, SE of Chipping Campden]: Smart dining pub, welcoming and friendly under present management, with good shortish choice of enjoyable food, Hook Norton Bitter, Sharps Doom Bar and Wadworths 6X, good blackboard wine list, low ceilings and some timbering, flagstones, log fire, dining extension; children welcome, seats outside, bedrooms, good breakfast *(DRH and KLH, Canon Michael Bourdeaux, Nick Wilson-Holt, Michael Dandy, John and Hilary Penny, LYM)*

PILNING [ST5684]

Plough BS35 4JJ [handy for M5 junction 17 via B4055 and Station Rd; Pilning St]: Thriving local atmosphere under new licensees, flagstones and bare boards, some faux beams, plates, country prints and repro adverts on dark cream/red dado walls, sofas and armchairs in small lounge area, newspapers in public bar; Wadworths ales, good value bar food (something all day), cheerful efficient staff; children welcome, disabled access to main areas, garden with play area overlooking open country *(Chris and Angela Buckell)*

PURTON [SO6904]

Berkeley Arms GL13 9HU [just upstream from Sharpness village, River Severn left bank]: Basic rustic Severn-side local, a short walk from canal bridge, wonderful estuary view, flagstones, high-backed settles, open fire, well kept Uley, long-serving landlady; garden, cl Mon, Tues *(Gerry Dawson)*

QUEDGELEY [SO8014]

Bumble Bee GL2 2AB [Waterwells roundabout, Telford Way]: Rambling Vintage Inn with good value changing food inc lunchtime deals, Butcombe and Timothy Taylors Landlord, plenty of wines by the glass, lots of prints and old photographs, exposed brick, flagstones and carpet, log fire; piped music; children welcome *(Jeremy King)*

QUENINGTON [SP1404]

Keepers Arms GL7 5BL [Church Rd]: Cosy and comfortable village local with stripped stone, low beams and log fires, amiable landlord, value for money food in bar and restaurant, good range of beers; dogs

welcome, picnic-sets outside, bedrooms *(Mo and David Trudgill, David Hill, P and J Shapley, E McCall, T McLean, D Irving)*

REDBROOK [SO5309]

☆ **Boat** NP25 4AJ [car park signed on A466 Chepstow—Monmouth, then 100-yard footbridge over River Wye; or very narrow steep car access from Penallt in Wales]: Beautifully set Wye-side pub with changing well kept beers tapped from casks, ciders and country wines, enjoyable good value simple food from baguettes and baked potatoes up (nothing fried), helpful staff; stripped-stone walls, flagstone floors and roaring woodburner; dogs and children welcome, rough home-built seats in informal tiered suntrap garden with stream spilling down waterfall cliffs into duck pond, open all day *(LYM, Bob and Margaret Holder, Michael Mellers, Michael and Alison Sandy)*

RODBOROUGH [SO8502]

Bear GL5 5DE [Rodborough Common]: Comfortably cosy and pubby, beamed and flagstoned bar in smart hotel, warm welcome, pleasant window seats, good log fire, hops hung around top of golden-stone walls, interesting reproductions, good choice of well kept beer inc local Nailsworth and Stroud, bar and more expensive restaurant food, afternoon teas; service can be slow, and they charge for using a credit card; children welcome, lovely walks, bedrooms *(Dave Irving, Jenny Huggins, E McCall, T McLean, D Irving, BB)*

RUARDEAN [SO6117]

Malt Shovel GL17 9TW: Friendly and relaxed stripped-stone local with sturdy traditional furnishings and good log fire in flagstoned bar, collection of old enamel signs, good choice of real ales, farm cider, enjoyable seasonal food inc good value baguettes, attractive dining room; appealing old-world bedrooms, fine 12th-c church and Horlicks family connections (the drink reputedly invented in shed behind pub) *(Barry and Anne)*

SALFORD HILL [SP2629]

Greedy Goose GL56 0SP [junction A44/A436, nr Chastleton]: Popular country dining pub recently fully refurbished in individual contemporary style, good interesting well presented food (all day wknds) from extensive menu inc pubby things, friendly efficient uniformed staff, Greene King and Hook Norton from small bar area; decking front and back, lovely views, open all day from 9am *(Keith and Sue Ward, P and J Shapley, Eithne Dandy)*

SAPPERTON [SO9303]

Daneway Inn GL7 6LN [Daneway; off A419 Stroud—Cirencester]: Quiet tucked-away local in charming wooded countryside, flagstones and bare boards, woodburner in amazing floor-to-ceiling carved oak dutch fireplace, sporting prints, well kept Wadworths ales, farm ciders, generous simple food from filled baps up, long-serving landlord and friendly staff; small family room, traditional games in inglenook public bar, folk night Tues; no dogs, tricky wheelchair access; terrace tables and lovely sloping lawn, camping possible, good walks by canal under restoration with tunnel to Coates *(Stuart Doughty, Giles and Annie Francis, Chris and Angela Buckell, E McCall, T McLean, D Irving, LYM)*

SHIPTON MOYNE [ST8989]

Cat & Custard Pot GL8 8PN [off B4040 Malmesbury—Bristol; The Street]: Popular and welcoming with good value food from sandwiches to restaurant dishes (booking recommended), good service even when busy, well kept Flowers, Timothy Taylors and Wadworths, Thatcher's cider, well priced wines, several dining areas; beams and bric-a-brac, hunting prints, cosy back snug, chatty locals; dogs welcome, wheelchair access, picturesque village *(Chris and Angela Buckell, Richard Stancomb, Guy Vowles, BB)*

SIDDINGTON [SU0399]

☆ *Greyhound* GL7 6HR [Ashton Rd; village signed from A419 roundabout at Tesco]: Popular village local, two linked rooms with big log fires, enjoyable good value pubby food from sandwiches up, some unusual specials too and thai curry nights (landlady is from there); well kept Wadworths, darts and cribbage, Sun folk evening; piped music; garden tables, open all day *(LYM, E McCall, T McLean, D Irving)*

SLAD [SO8707]

Woolpack GL6 7QA [B4070 Stroud—Birdlip]: Friendly and unpretentiously old-fashioned hillside village local with lovely valley views, several linked rooms with Laurie Lee and other interesting photographs, some of his books for sale, log fire and nice tables, enjoyable pub food (not Sun evening) from sandwiches and baguettes up inc generous Sun roast, children's menu, well kept Uley and guest ales, local farm ciders and perry, decent wines by the glass; good young staff, games and cards; dogs welcome *(Dr A J and Mrs J Tompsett, Dave Irving, Jenny Huggins, Crispin Pemberton, Myra Joyce, Bob and Angela Brooks, Guy Vowles)*

SLIMBRIDGE [SO7204]

Tudor Arms GL2 7BP [Shepherds Patch; off A38 towards Wildfowl & Wetlands Trust]: Welcoming and obliging, with generous food (all day wknds) from baguettes up, half a dozen interesting changing ales, good wines by the glass, farm ciders and perries; linked areas with parquet floor, flagstones or carpet, some leather chairs and settles, comfortable dining room, conservatory, darts, pool and skittle alley; children and dogs welcome, disabled facilities, picnic-sets outside, handy for Wildfowl Trust and canal boat trips, caravan site off car park, 12 refurbished bedrooms, open all day *(Steve and Liz Tilley, Chris and Angela Buckell, Mrs P Sumner)*

SNOWSHILL [SP0933]

Snowshill Arms WR12 7JU: Unpretentious country pub in honeypot village (so no shortage of customers), Donnington ales,

reasonably priced straightforward food from sandwiches up, log fire, stripped stone, neat array of tables, local photographs; skittle alley, charming village views from bow windows and big back garden with little stream and play area, children welcome if eating, handy for Snowshill Manor and Cotswold Way walks *(LYM, Paul Goldman, K H Frostick, Dr A Y Drummond)*

SOMERFORD KEYNES [SU0195]

☆ *Bakers Arms* GL7 6DN: Pretty stone-built country pub, real ales such as Butcombe, Addlestone's cider, good house wine, wide choice of food, two log fires, lots of pine tables in two linked stripped-stone areas with soft lighting, good service even when busy; children and dogs welcome, nice garden with play area and barbecue, lovely village, handy for Cotswold Water Park *(Richard and Sheila Fitton, E McCall, T McLean, D Irving, Stephen Funnell, Jo Rees)*

SOUTHROP [SP2003]

☆ *Swan* GL7 3NU [off A361 Lechlade—Burford]: 17th-c creeper-covered upscale dining pub, efficiently run, with very good cooking from bar meals to enterprising restaurant food, set menus and Sun roasts, good wines, appealing décor, light front rooms with flagstones and log fire, a snug with another fire; children welcome, two tables out in front, more in sheltered back garden, pretty village especially at daffodil time *(LYM, Maurice Holt, Graham Oddey)*

ST BRIAVELS [SO5504]

George GL15 6TA [High St]: Improved Wadworths pub, their beers and wide choice of good sensibly priced food inc OAP deals, spotless rambling linked black-beamed rooms with attractive old-fashioned décor and big stone fireplace, restaurant; can get very busy wknds (booking advised Sun); children and dogs welcome, flagstoned terrace over former moat of neighbouring Norman fortress, four newly refurbished bedrooms *(LYM, Bob and Margaret Holder, Bob and Angela Brooks, Edward Hutchings, David A Hammond)*

STOKE GIFFORD [ST6279]

Beaufort Arms BS34 8PB [North Rd, not far from Bristol Parkway]: Well run Ember Inn, tidy and spacious, with value-conscious food all day, several real ales *(Colin Moore, Simon Lewis)*

STOW-ON-THE-WOLD [SP1729]

Coach & Horses GL56 0QZ [Ganborough (on A424 about 2.5 miles N)]: Beamed and flagstoned country pub, bright and clean, with reasonably priced tasty food inc good local trout, friendly tenants, well kept Donnington ales and farm cider, decent wines by the glass, cheerful log fire, step up to compact dining area with high-backed settles on wood floor; children welcome, skittle alley, big garden *(Ken and Margaret Grinstead, Rolsh Lake, Michael Dandy, LYM)*

Kings Arms GL54 1AF [The Square]: Enjoyable food from good sandwiches to lots of fish, also fixed-price menu and real food for children, helpful staff, good choice of wines by the glass, Greene King ales, good coffee (opens early for this), daily papers; some Mackintosh-style chairs on polished boards, bowed black beams, some panelling and stripped stone, log fire, charming upstairs dining room; piped music; bedrooms, open all day *(Michael Dandy, BB)*

☆ **Queens Head** GL54 1AB [The Square]: Splendidly unpretentious for this upmarket town, well kept low-priced Donnington BB and SBA, good wines by the glass, good value sandwiches and basic pub meals (not Sun) inc proper steak and kidney pudding, cheerful helpful service; bustling and chatty stripped-stone front lounge, heavily beamed and flagstoned back bar with high-backed settles, big log-effect fire, horse prints; quiet piped music; children and dogs welcome, tables in attractive sunny back courtyard, occasional jazz Sun lunchtime, open all day *(LYM, Tom Holman, Mr and Mrs M J Girdler, Mike Buckingham, the Didler, Phil Bryant, Gerry and Rosemary Dobson, Michael Dandy, Ann and Colin Hunt)*

☆ **Talbot** GL54 1BQ [The Square]: Light and airy modern décor, relaxed café-bar feel, food from sandwiches and baguettes up inc some interesting blackboard specials, good friendly service even when busy, Wadworths ales, lots of good value wines by the glass, nice coffee; huge mirror over big log fire, plain tables and chairs on woodblock floor, modern artwork, daily papers, upstairs room; no children inside, may be piped radio, lavatories upstairs; open all day *(Michael Dandy, Dennis Jones, BB)*

White Hart GL54 1AF [The Square]: Welcoming well refurbished boutique-style inn, small pleasant log-fire bar, another behind and a restaurant, varied choice of good food from pub standards to more upmarket dishes, friendly service, Arkells ales, good coffee; back courtyard, five bedrooms *(Mr and Mrs W W Burke, Michael Dandy, Eithne Dandy, Phil Bryant, BB)*

STROUD [SO8504]

Imperial GL5 3AP [opp railway station]: Old-fashioned railway hotel with large high-ceilinged rooms, four ales inc Butcombe and Wells & Youngs, good food inc extensive thai menu; a few seats on terrace, bedrooms *(George Atkinson)*

Lord John GL5 3AB [Russell St]: Airy split-level Wetherspoons in former PO sorting office, tables in alcoves, low-priced food and wide choice of sensibly priced ales inc interesting guest beers; disabled facilities, terrace tables *(E McCall, T McLean, D Irving, Dave Irving, Jenny Huggins)*

SWINEFORD [ST6969]

☆ **Swan** BS30 6LN [A431, right on the Somerset border]: Popular stone-built pub under newish management, well kept Bath Ales, decent ciders, well chosen wines, good nicely presented food (not cheap), big open fire, plain furniture on bare boards or tiles, pastel paintwork and panelled dado; wheelchair access, large garden with play area, open all day *(Martin Sagar, Chris and Angela Buckell, Jim and Frances Gowers)*

TETBURY [ST8893]

Ormond GL8 8AA [Long St]: Bare-boards hotel bar comfortably reworked with open fire, stripped wood and leather furniture, enjoyable well presented food from lunchtime sandwiches up, decent wines, friendly staff, Sharps and Wickwar ales, restaurant; children welcome, courtyard tables with play area, 15 comfortable bedrooms, open all day *(Di and Mike Gillam)*

☆ **Snooty Fox** GL8 8DD [Market Pl]: High-ceilinged stripped-stone hotel lounge, unstuffy with well kept real ales such as Otter, Nailsworth and Wickwar, good house wines, friendly young staff, bar food from sandwiches up; medieval-style chairs and cast-iron tables, elegant fireplace, brass ceiling fans and Ronald Searle pony-club cartoons, nice side room and ante-room, restaurant; unobtrusive piped music, bar can get very busy wknd evenings; children and dogs welcome, comfortable bedrooms *(LYM, Jim and Frances Gowers, Dr and Mrs A K Clarke, A Green)*

☆ **Trouble House** GL8 8SG [A433 towards Cirencester, nr Cherington turn]: Pretty 17th-c pub previously a Main Entry for its good food, now under new management – reports please; Wadworths ales from small saggy-beamed middle room, stripped pine or oak tables with mixed chairs, big log fire; children and dogs have been welcome, picnic-sets in back gravel courtyard *(LYM)*

TEWKESBURY [SO8832]

Bell GL20 5SA [Church St]: Hotel bar interesting for its black oak beams and timbers, 17th-c oak panelling and medieval leaf-and-fruit frescoes; big log fire, tapestries and armchairs, well kept Greene King, decent bar food and house wines, good coffee; children and dogs welcome, garden above Severn-side walk, opp abbey, bedrooms *(J F M and M West, Martin Smith, BB)*

Berkeley Arms GL20 5PA [Church St]: Welcoming medieval timbered pub (most striking part down the side alley); good choice of Wadworths ales and a guest, open fire, pubby lunchtime food (not Mon) inc bargain Sun roasts, separate front public bar, ancient back barn restaurant with armour and shields *(Reg Fowle, Helen Rickwood)*

☆ **Gupshill Manor** GL20 5SG [Gloucester Rd (off A38 S edge of town)]: Quaint old timbered building with Tardis-like series of lounge and dining areas, plenty of easy chairs and sofas, beams and open fires, well priced food (all day Sun) from pubby dishes up inc lunchtime deals, friendly efficient staff; three well kept ales, good choice of wines by the glass, good coffees; piped music; children welcome, disabled access, teak tables on extensive heated terrace, open all day *(BB,*

Robert W Buckle, Alan and Eve Harding)

☆ **Olde Black Bear** GL20 5BJ [High St]: County's oldest pub (early 14th c), well worth a look for its intricately rambling rooms with ancient tiles, heavy timbering and low beams; reasonably priced wines, up to five ales, open fires, well worn furnishings, good value pubby food; they may try to keep your credit card while you eat, piped music; children welcome, terrace and play area in nice riverside garden, open all day *(Dr and Mrs A K Clarke, the Didler, Donna and Roger, Dave Braisted, LYM)*

Royal Hop Pole GL20 5RT [Church St]: Well done Wetherspoons conversion of old inn keeping original features, their usual value-minded all-day food and drink, good service, lovely garden leading down to river, bedrooms *(John Dwane, Chris and Martin Taylor, Reg Fowle, Helen Rickwood)*

TOCKINGTON [ST6086]
Swan BS32 4NJ [Tockington Green]: Roomy Greene King pub with their ales and wide food choice, decent wines, log fire, beams and standing timbers, bric-a-brac on stripped-stone walls; boules in tree-shaded garden, open all day wknds *(Alan Wright)*

TODDINGTON [SP0432]
Pheasant GL54 5DT [A46 Broadway—Winchcombe, junction with A438 and B4077]: Attractive extended stone-built roadside pub with emphasis on good choice of reasonably priced food, friendly helpful staff, real ales such as Stanway, lots of railway prints – handy for nearby preserved Gloucestershire Warwickshire Railway Station; no dogs while food served *(Ewan and Moira McCall, Dr A J and Mrs Tompsett, Giles and Annie Francis)*

TWYNING [SO8737]
Fleet GL20 6FL [off westbound A38 slip road from M50 junction 1]: Family holiday pub in superb setting at end of quiet lane though just off motorway, good river views from roomy high-ceilinged bars, interesting boating-theme décor, enjoyable fresh food inc lunchtime baguettes, service usually good, five real ales; woodburner, airy back restaurant area, tearoom, games room with darts and bar billiards; piped music, games machines, entertainment Fri, Sat; disabled access, picnic-sets in big waterside garden with two floodlit terraces, rockery cascade and safe enclosed children's area, stop on Tewkesbury—Bredon summer boat run, bedrooms, open all day *(LYM, Dr A J and Mrs Tompsett)*

TYTHERINGTON [ST6788]
Swan GL12 8QB [Duck St]: Big two-bar 16th-c family pub with newish local landlord, tankards and hops on low beams, bare stone and cream walls, parquet or carpeted floors, huge fireplace, fresh flowers on old tables; good food choice inc interesting puddings and popular OAP lunches, well kept ales such as Bath Gem, Butcombe and Fullers (taster glasses available), pleasant attentive service;

wheelchair access from car park, sheltered garden *(Chris and Angela Buckell)*

ULEY [ST7998]
Old Crown GL11 5SN [The Green]: Rustic 17th-c pub prettily set by village green just off Cotswold Way, long narrow room with settles and pews on bare boards, step up to partitioned-off lounge area, good range of well kept changing ales and of wines by the glass, home-made pubby food from sandwiches up, quick friendly service, log fire; small games room up spiral stairs; attractive garden behind, four bedrooms *(Guy Vowles)*

WESTBURY-ON-SEVERN [SO7114]
Red Lion GL14 1PA [A48, corner of Bell Lane]: Beamed and half-timbered traditional 17th-c pub on busy road but by quiet church-side lane to river, welcoming obliging licensees, good choice of fairly priced enjoyable food, well kept ales such as Wells & Youngs Bombardier and Wye Valley Butty Bach, decent wine; comfortable carpeted bar with wall seats, velvet curtains, open fire, snug off to the right, dining room to the left with log fire; children and dogs welcome, some seats out front, more in back garden, three comfortable clean bedrooms, handy for Westbury Court Garden (NT) *(BB, Alun and Ann Keen)*

WHITECROFT [SO6005]
Miners Arms GL15 4PE [B4234 N of Lydney]: Friendly unpretentious local with up to five changing ales, farm ciders and perries, generous good value food inc some greek dishes, attentive helpful service; two rooms on either side of bar, slate and parquet floors, pastel walls with old photographs, conservatory, skittle alley; piped music; children and dogs welcome, disabled access, good gardens front and back, one with stream, quoits and boules, good local walks, handy for steam railway, self-catering accommodation, open all day *(Robert Wivell, Theocsbrian, Mike Horgan, Chris and Angela Buckell)*

WHITMINSTER [SO7607]
Fromebridge Mill GL2 7PD [Fromebridge Lane (A38 nr M5 junction 13)]: Comfortable mill-based dining pub with interconnecting rooms, bare brick walls, flagstoned and carpeted floors, some tables overlooking river, reasonably priced food all day inc popular lunchtime carvery (evenings too at wknds), efficient friendly young staff, well kept Greene King ales; no dogs inside; children welcome, wheelchair access, picnic-sets in big garden with play area, pretty waterside setting, footbridge from car park, handy for M5, open all day *(Steve Whalley, Chris and Angela Buckell, Eric Thomas Yarwood)*

WINCHCOMBE [SP0228]
Old Corner Cupboard GL54 5LX [Gloucester St]: Attractive old golden-stone pub improved under new landlord, fairly priced food in nice back dining room, Fullers, Hook Norton and local Stanway ales, good range

of wines; comfortable stripped-stone lounge bar with heavy-beamed Tudor core, traditional hatch-service lobby, small side room with woodburner in massive stone fireplace, traditional games; children welcome, tables in back garden, open all day *(Dr A J and Mrs Tompsett, LYM)*

☆ *White Hart* GL54 5LJ [High St (B4632)]: 16th-c pub/bistro with big windows looking out over village street, mix of chairs and small settles around pine tables, cricket memorabilia, well kept Goffs and Otter, wine shop next to bar (they add corkage if you buy to drink on the premises), wide choice by the glass too, specialist sausage menu plus other enjoyable food, separate restaurant; children welcome, dogs in bar and bedrooms, open all day from 9am (10am Sun) *(LYM, Jack Morley, Susan Lang, Julia and Richard Tredgett, Ellie Weld, David London)*

WINTERBOURNE DOWN [ST6679]
Golden Hart BS36 1AU [just off A432 Bristol—Yate, towards Winterbourne]: Chef & Brewer converted from row of 16th-c cottages, low beamed main bar with series of higher ceilinged linked rooms (inc two further bars), Fullers London Pride, Wadworths 6X and guests, plenty of wines by the glass, usual food, pleasant helpful staff; huge fireplaces, bare boards or carpet, some stone walls and panelling, cushioned wall or window seats, old pictures and photographs, big conservatory; intrusive piped music, machines; children welcome, wheelchair access (two low steps at front), gardens, play area *(Chris and Angela Buckell)*

WITHINGTON [SP0315]
Mill Inn GL54 4BE [off A436 or A40]: Idyllic streamside setting for mossy-roofed old stone inn, beams, flagstones, inglenook log fire, plenty of character with nice nooks and corners, bargain pubby food, friendly helpful service, dining room; piped music, keg beer (but decent wine list); children very

welcome, large pretty garden, splendid walks, three old-fashioned bedrooms, good breakfast *(Gene and Kitty Rankin, LYM, E McCall, T McLean, D Irving, Guy Charrison, Stephen Morris, Dr and Mrs M E Wilson)*

WOODCHESTER [SO8403]
☆ *Old Fleece* GL5 5NB [Rooksmoor; A46, a mile S of Stroud – not to be confused with Fleece at Lightpill a little closer in]: Part of the small Food Club chain, wide choice of interesting fresh food from unusual lunchtime sandwiches up, children's helpings, friendly helpful staff, well kept Bass and Greene King IPA, good wines by the glass; three unpretentious linked rooms, big windows and bare boards, stripped-stone or dark salmon pink walls, large log fire, candles, daily papers; children welcome, two roadside terraces, one heated *(Dave Irving, Jenny Huggins, BB, Tom and Ruth Rees)*

WOODMANCOTE [SO9727]
Apple Tree GL52 9QG [Stockwell Lane]: Interesting choice of good value food in roomy well run family pub, log fires and comfortable sofas, cheerful courteous staff, Greene King ales, decent wines, restaurant; garden with fine views, idyllic hillside spot *(Jo Rees, Rod Stoneman)*

YATE [ST6983]
Cross Keys BS37 7LQ [signed off B4059 Yate bypass at 'the Fox'; North Rd]: Unpretentious two-bar beamed village local, reasonably priced food (not Sun, Mon) from sandwiches up inc good old-fashioned puddings, Bass, Courage Best and guests such as Box Steam and Bristol Beer Factory, cheerful chatty landlord; warming woodburner, stripped stone and panelling, flagstones and carpet, mixed pubby furniture inc pews and old dining tables, brasses and prints, cards; fruit machine and darts in public bar, Weds quiz; disabled access (perhaps a bit tricky for some wheelchairs), open all day Fri-Sun *(Chris and Angela Buckell, Donna and Roger)*

Anyone claiming to arrange or prevent inclusion of a pub in the *Guide* is a fraud. Pubs are included only if recommended by genuine readers and if our own anonymous inspection confirms that they are suitable.

Hampshire

This year, there's a fine crop of new entries as well as pubs back in these pages after a break. These include the Fishers Pond in Colden Common (a well run Vintage Inn near Marwell Zoo), the Northbrook Arms in East Stratton (under the same excellent management as the Yew Tree at Lower Wield), the Fox at Ellisfield (a friendly and simple country pub), the Bugle in Hamble (a busy little pub just up from the quay), the Jolly Drover in Liss (a traditional inn with a cheerful landlord; nice to stay in), the Plough in Longparish (smartly refurbished and with good food) and the Rose & Thistle at Rockbourne (a pretty thatched village pub with nice food and drinks). This is a strong county with good local breweries supported by genuinely friendly pubs. Those doing especially well this year are the Oak at Bank (a welcoming place after a walk), the Sun in Bentworth (the friendly landlady keeps her seven real ales very well), the Three Tuns in Bransgore (bustling and cheerful with interesting food and beer), the Bakers Arms at Droxford (civilised and welcoming with good food and drinks), the Royal Oak at Fritham (a lovely country tavern and deservedly popular), the Yew Tree at Lower Wield (an excellent landlord), the Plough at Sparsholt (a well run dining pub with enjoyable food), the Harrow at Steep (unchanging, unspoilt and a favourite with many of our readers), the Thomas Lord at West Meon (busy and popular with unusual food), the Mayfly at Wherwell (an idyllic spot) and the Black Boy in Winchester (eccentric and fun). This is not a cheap county to eat out in but pubs do make the best of produce local to them. Our Hampshire Dining Pub 2011 is the Bakers Arms in Droxford.

BANK   SU2806   MAP 2

Oak 🍺

Signposted just off A35 SW of Lyndhurst; SO43 7FE

Tucked-away and very busy New Forest pub with well liked food and interesting décor

In summer, this tucked-away pub is quite a find after a long trek in the New Forest – but in winter, too, customers enjoy the roaring log fire and possibly even a winter barbecue with mulled wine. There's always a bustling atmosphere, a warm welcome and real ales such as Butcombe Bitter and Fullers London Pride and Gales HSB and Seafarers on handpump. On either side of the door in the bay windows of the L-shaped bar are built-in red-cushioned seats, and on the right there are two or three little pine-panelled booths with small built-in tables and bench seats. The rest of the bare-boarded bar has some low beams and joists, candles in individual brass holders on a line of stripped old and newer blond tables set against the wall and all manner of bric-a-brac: fishing rods, spears, a boomerang, old ski poles, brass platters, heavy knives and guns. There are cushioned milk churns along the bar counter and little red lanterns among hop bines above the bar; piped music. The pleasant side garden has picnic-sets and long tables and benches by the big yew trees.

🍴 Popular bar food includes doorstep sandwiches (the fresh local crab is good), garlic mushrooms, whole baked camembert with fruit chutney, pasta parcels filled with cheese and pear in a creamy basil sauce, steak in ale pie, maple syrup-roasted ham and free-range eggs, home-made beef and red onion burger, lime and tarragon-marinated chicken breast and lamb chops with couscous and tzatziki. *Starters/Snacks: £5.50 to £8.95. Main Courses: £9.50 to £16.95. Puddings: £4.75*

Fullers ~ Manager Martin Sliva ~ Real ale ~ Bar food (12-2.30, 6-9.30; 12-9 Sun) ~ (023) 8028 2350 ~ Children welcome until 6pm ~ Dogs welcome ~ Open 11.30-11; 12-10.30 Sun; 11.30-3, 6-11 weekdays in winter

Recommended by Mrs Margo Finlay, Jörg Kasprowski, Jennifer Banks, N R White, Terry and Nickie Williams, Laurence Smith, Shiread family, Lois Dyer, Leslie and Barbara Owen, Phyl and Jack Street, Mike and Sue Loseby, Mr and Mrs D Hammond, Peter Meister, Jenny and Brian Seller, Patrick Spence

BENTWORTH

SU6740   MAP 2

Sun 🍺

Sun Hill; from the A339 coming from Alton, the first turning takes you there direct; or in village follow Shalden 2½, Alton 4½ signpost; GU34 5JT

Smashing choice of real ales and welcoming landlady in popular country pub; nearby walks

Always full of happy customers, this charming 17th-c country pub is run by a warmly friendly and experienced landlady – our readers love it. The two little traditional communicating rooms have high-backed antique settles, pews and schoolroom chairs, olde-worlde prints and blacksmith's tools on the walls, and bare boards and scrubbed deal tables on the left; big fireplaces (one with an open fire) make it especially snug in winter. An arch leads to a brick-floored room with another open fire. There's also a fine choice of seven real ales on handpump: Andwell Resolute Bitter, Bowman Wallops Wood, Fullers London Pride, Hogs Back TEA, Otter Amber, Palmers Dorset Gold and Ringwood Fortyniner. There are seats out in front and in the back garden; pleasant nearby walks.

🍴 Generous helpings of good bar food include sandwiches, soup, pâté and toast, scallops in a white wine sauce, cajun chicken, yorkshire puddings filled with pork and leek sausages or roast beef, home-made burger, vegetable curry, steak in ale pie, fillet of bass with sweet chilli and a crayfish sauce, and puddings like apple crumble and banoffi pie. *Starters/Snacks: £4.25 to £7.25. Main Courses: £8.95 to £15.95. Puddings: £3.95*

Free house ~ Licensee Mary Holmes ~ Real ale ~ Bar food ~ (01420) 562338 ~ Children welcome ~ Dogs allowed in bar ~ Open 12-3, 6-11; 12-11 Sun

Recommended by DGH, Martin and Karen Wake, Mr and Mrs H J Langley, Laurence Smith, the Didler, Susan and John Douglas, Phyl and Jack Street, Ann and Colin Hunt, Mrs Jill Rich, Neil and Karen Dignan, Mr and Mrs D Hammond, Mr and Mrs C Prentis

BRAMDEAN

SU6127   MAP 2

Fox

A272 Winchester—Petersfield; SO24 0LP

Civilised dining pub with long-serving owners; no children inside

This pleasant 17th-c weatherboarded pub has now been run by the same licensees for 25 years. The old-fashioned open-plan bar is civilised and grown up (no children inside) with loyal regulars, black beams, tall stools with proper backrests around the L-shaped counter and comfortably cushioned wall pews and wheelback chairs; the fox motif shows in a big painting over the fireplace and on much of the decorative china. Greene King Morlands Original on handpump, decent wine by the glass and piped music. At the back of the building there's a walled-in terraced area and a neatly kept spacious lawn spreading among the fruit trees. Good surrounding walks. Dogs may be allowed in the bar if the pub is not too busy.

🍴 Bar food includes lunchtime sandwiches, deep-fried whitebait, breaded prawns with a sweet chilli dip, steak and kidney pie, chicken with parma ham in a Boursin sauce, battered cod fillet, pork with a mushroom, brandy and cream sauce, confit of duck in orange gravy and fresh halibut with lime and chilli butter. *Starters/Snacks: £4.95 to £8.95. Main Courses: £9.95 to £19.95. Puddings: £4.75 to £5.25*

Greene King ~ Tenants Ian and Jane Inder ~ Real ale ~ Bar food (not Sun evening) ~ (01962) 771363 ~ Open 11-3(3.30 Sat), 6.30(6 Sat)-11; 12-3.30 Sun; closed Sun evening
Recommended by Simon Collett-Jones, R and S Bentley, Mr and Mrs W W Burke, Helen and Brian Edgeley

BRANSGORE   SZ1997   MAP 2

Three Tuns 🍺

Village signposted off A35 and off B3347 N of Christchurch; Ringwood Road, opposite church; BH23 8JH

Interesting food in pretty thatched pub with proper old-fashioned bar and good beers, as well as a civilised main dining area

In the heart of the New Forest, this 17th-c thatched pub is just the place after a walk and there are plenty of cheerful customers being served efficiently by vibrant young staff. The atmosphere is enjoyable and the roomy low-ceilinged and carpeted main area has a fireside 'codgers' corner', as well as a good mix of comfortably cushioned low chairs around a variety of dining tables. On the right is a separate traditional regulars' bar that seems almost taller than it is wide, with an impressive log-effect stove in a stripped brick hearth, some shiny black panelling and individualistic pubby furnishings. Ringwood Best and Fortyniner and Timothy Taylors Landlord and guests like Dorset Weymouth Harbour Master, Exmoor Gold and Otter Bitter on handpump, and a good choice of wines by the glass. There's an attractive and extensive shrub-sheltered terrace with picnic-sets on its brick pavers and beyond that are more tables out on the grass looking over pony paddocks; the summer hanging baskets are lovely.

🍽 **As well as lunchtime sandwiches and ploughman's, the often interesting bar food includes soup, vietnamese-style seafood pancake, popular home-made pasty, tomato and red onion tartlet with goats cheese, truffle risotto with crispy egg, beefburger with cheese and bacon, beer-battered cod, corn-fed chicken with mushrooms and an ale cream sauce, skate with roasted cobnuts and brown butter, and puddings such as rich chocolate tart with clotted cream and tonka bean crème brûlée with cinnamon fig; Sunday roasts.** *Starters/Snacks: £4.95 to £9.95. Main Courses: £7.75 to £18.95. Puddings: £4.00 to £6.95*

Enterprise ~ Lease Nigel Glenister ~ Real ale ~ Bar food (all day weekends) ~ Restaurant ~ (01425) 672232 ~ Children in restaurant but not in lounge bar after 6pm ~ Dogs allowed in bar ~ Open 11.30-11; 12-10.30 Sun; closed evenings 25 and 26 Dec and 1 Jan
Recommended by Phyl and Jack Street, Richard, Anne and Kate Ansell, Laurence Smith, N R White, Terry and Nickie Williams

BUCKLERS HARD   SU4000   MAP 2

Master Builders House 🛏

From M27 junction 2 follow signs to Beaulieu; turn left on to B3056 and then left to Bucklers Hard – the hotel is 2 miles along on the left; SO42 7XB

Sizeable hotel with character bar in lovely spot overlooking the river in charming village; real ales, pubby food, popular outdoor barbecue and seats in waterside garden; bedrooms

This is a lovely and carefully preserved waterside village and the smart and sizeable hotel here has a proper pubby bar with a great deal of character. This two-level, dimly lit room is the original yachtsmen's bar and has a wide mix of customers of all ages. The main part has heavy beams, a warm winter log fire in an old brick fireplace (have a look at the list of all the ship builders dating from the 18th c on a wooden plaque to one side of it), benches and cushioned wall seats around long tables, rugs on the wooden floor and mullioned windows. There are some bar stools on quarry tiles by the counter where they serve Marstons Pedigree and Ringwood Best and Fortyniner on handpump and decent wines by the glass; friendly young staff. Stairs lead down to a lower room with a fireplace at each end (not always lit). Outside there are picnic-sets on the lawn overlooking the river with its boating activity and a front terrace (mainly used by restaurant guests); the outdoor barbecue is extremely popular. A small gate at the bottom leads to a walkway beside the water – idyllic in fine weather.

🍴 **Bar food includes lunchtime sandwiches, soup, moules marinière, rock oysters with a shot of bloody mary or grilled with garlic butter and parmesan, various salads and sharing boards, linguine with spinach, lemon and pine nuts, confit chicken leg, fish and chips with mushy peas, steaks, and puddings like spiced ginger cake with real ale ice-cream and a crème brûlée of the day.** *Starters/Snacks: £5.00 to £7.50. Main Courses: £7.75 to £18.50. Puddings: £6.00*

Free house ~ Licensee Christoph Brooke ~ Real ale ~ Bar food (12-3, 6.30-9.30; afternoon tea all afternoon) ~ Restaurant ~ (01590) 616253 ~ Children welcome ~ Dogs welcome ~ Open 11-11 ~ Bedrooms: £99B/£109B

Recommended by Mrs Ann Gray, Mr and Mrs D Hammond

CHERITON
SU5828 MAP 2

Flower Pots ★ 🍺 £

Pub just off B3046 (main village road) towards Beauworth and Winchester; OS Sheet 185 map reference 581282; SO24 0QQ

Own-brew beers in rustic pub with simple rooms and straightforward food: no children inside

Happily, nothing much changes in this old-fashioned and traditional village local and the same family have owned it for over 40 years. The two straightforward little rooms are rustic and simple, though the one on the left is a favourite – almost like someone's front room, with country pictures on its striped wallpaper, bunches of flowers and some ornaments on the mantelpiece over a small log fire. Behind the servery is disused copper filtering equipment and lots of hanging gin traps, drag-hooks, scaleyards and other ironwork. The neat extended plain public bar (where there's a covered well) is popular locally; board games. Their own-brewed ales (you can tour the brewery by arrangement) include Flowerpots Bitter, Goodens Gold and Perridge Pale that are tapped from casks behind the bar counter. The pretty front and back lawns have some seats and there's a summer marquee; maybe summer morris dancers. The pub is near the site of one of the final battles of the Civil War, and it got its name through once belonging to the retired head gardener of nearby Avington Park. No children inside.

🍴 **Bar food from a fairly short straightforward menu includes sandwiches, toasties and baps, filled baked potatoes, ploughman's, soup and various hotpots (the lamb and apricot is popular). The menu and serving times may be restricted if they're busy.** *Starters/Snacks: £4.00 to £7.00. Main Courses: £7.70 to £11.00*

Own brew ~ Licensees Jo and Patricia Bartlett ~ Real ale ~ Bar food (not Sun evening or bank hol evenings) ~ No credit cards ~ (01962) 771318 ~ Dogs welcome ~ Open 12-2.30, 6-11; 12-3, 7-10.30 Sun ~ Bedrooms: £47.50S/£80S

Recommended by the Didler, Phil and Sally Gorton, Barry Steele-Perkins, Gerald and Gabrielle Culliford, Ann and Colin Hunt, Paul J Robinshaw, Klaus and Elizabeth Leist, Tony and Jill Radnor, N R White, Irene and Derek Flewin

COLDEN COMMON
SU4821 MAP 2

Fishers Pond

Junction B3354/B2177 (Main Road), at Fishers Pond just S; SO50 7HG

Busy well organised family Vintage Inn by big peaceful woodside lake

This big chain pub's position is so appealing (and so handy for Marwell Zoo) that it could be pretty sure of plenty of customers, even without bothering. But thanks to its good hands-on manager keeping a close eye on everything, it thoroughly deserves its popularity. Various different areas and alcoves, separated more by mood and style than by physical division, are well laid out to make the most of the waterside outlook – dark leather built-in wall banquettes here, dining chairs or little tub armchairs there, grey-painted brick or ochre plasterwork, fitted carpet in one place, rugs on aged terracotta in another, log fires, soft lighting and heavy beams or a much brighter modern end section, all giving plenty of choice for anything from a quiet chat to a lively family celebration. Efficient service, well kept ales such as Black Sheep Best, Leeds Best and Sharps Doom Bar on handpump, a good choice of wines by the glass, decent coffee, fruit machine and video game tucked away by the entrance, unobtrusive piped music. A heated and partly covered waterside terrace has solid teak furniture on its flagstones.

🍽 As with all the pubs in this chain, bar food includes sandwiches, soup, duck liver pâté with redcurrant and juniper jelly, cajun chicken skewers, fishcakes with herb mayonnaise, burger with smoked cheddar and bacon, butternut squash and aubergine moussaka, beef, mushroom and Guinness pie, slow-braised lamb shoulder with mint and rosemary, fish mixed grill, steaks, and puddings such as banoffi cheesecake and chocolate brownie with chocolate fudge sauce. *Starters/Snacks: £2.95 to £6.95. Main Courses: £6.95 to £16.25. Puddings: £3.95 to £4.75*

Vintage Inns ~ Manager Sue Odam ~ Real ale ~ Bar food (all day) ~ (023) 8069 2209 ~ Children welcome ~ Open 11.30-11(10 Sun)

Recommended by Joan and Michel Hooper-Immins, Jim Metcalfe, Ann and Colin Hunt, Terry and Nickie Williams

CRAWLEY   SU4234   MAP 2
Fox & Hounds ♀
Village signposted from A272 and B3420 NW of Winchester; SO21 2PR

Attractive building, three roaring winter log fires, several real ales and reasonably priced food; bedrooms

In a village of fine old houses, this solidly constructed mock-Tudor building is one of the most striking in it. Each timbered upper storey successively juts further out, with lots of pegged structural timbers in the neat brickwork and elaborately carved steep gable-ends. Inside, the neat and attractive linked rooms have a civilised atmosphere, a mix of attractive wooden tables and chairs on polished floors, lots of bottles along a delft shelf and three log fires. The traditional little bar has built-in wall seats and Ringwood Best and Fortyniner, Wadworths 6X and Wychwood Hobgoblin on handpump and a dozen wines by the glass; friendly licensees and efficient young staff. There are picnic-sets in the gardens (one of which has some children's play equipment). The bedrooms, in converted outbuildings, are named after the ducks on the village pond.

🍽 Reasonably priced and popular, the bar food includes sandwiches and basket meals, red onion and goats cheese tart, moules marinière, mushroom stroganoff, a curry of the day, cod with a basil and parmesan crust, steak and mushroom in ale pie, chicken with a stilton and mushroom sauce, daily specials such as a pork ribs in barbecue sauce, salmon and dill fishcakes and duck breast in a rich plum sauce, and puddings like white chocolate mousse with dark chocolate chips and fruit crumble with custard. *Starters/Snacks: £4.50 to £4.95. Main Courses: £7.95 to £14.95. Puddings: £4.50*

Enterprise ~ Lease Peter and Kathy Airey ~ Real ale ~ Bar food (12-2(3 Sun), 6.30-9(9.30 Fri and Sat); not Sun evening) ~ Restaurant ~ (01962) 776006 ~ Children welcome ~ Open 11-3, 6-11(midnight Sat); 12-4 Sun; closed Sun evening ~ Bedrooms: /£60B

Recommended by Phyl and Jack Street, Ian Herdman

DROXFORD
SU6018 MAP 2

Bakers Arms 🍽 🍺

A32 5 miles N of Wickham; High Street; SO32 3PA

HAMPSHIRE DINING PUB OF THE YEAR

Attractively opened-up and friendly pub with well kept beers, good, interesting cooking and cosy corners

The friendly licensees here have worked hard to make a success of this bustling pub – which they've certainly achieved in doing; our readers are full of warm enthusiasm. It's attractively laid-out and although the interesting food does play a big part, the central bar is kept as the main focus: Bowman Swift One and Wallops Wood on handpump, Stowford Press cider, and a careful short choice of wines by the glass. Well spaced mixed tables on carpet or neat bare boards spread around the airy L-shaped open-plan bar, with low leather chesterfields and an assortment of comfortably cushioned chairs down one end; a dark panelled dado, dark beams and joists and a modicum of country oddments emphasise the freshness of the crisp white paintwork. There's a good log fire and board games. To one side, with a separate entrance, is the village post office. There are picnic-sets outside.

🍴 Using their own daily-baked bread, the popular food might include sandwiches, soup, lambs kidneys with mustard and onions on toast, pigeon and bacon salad with walnut dressing, leek, blue cheese and sweet potato tart with pumpkin seed and beetroot dressing, chicken breast with lentils, squash and slow-cooked onion, slow-roasted pork belly with garlic roast potatoes and a cider and mustard cream sauce, fillet of gurnard with brown shrimps and preserved lemon, and puddings such as chocolate and fudge brownie and butterscotch ice-cream and crème brûlée. *Starters/Snacks: £5.75 to £6.00. Main Courses: £11.95 to £17.95. Puddings: £5.50*

Free house ~ Licensees Adam and Anna Cordery ~ Real ale ~ Bar food (not Sun evening or Mon) ~ (01489) 877533 ~ Well behaved children welcome ~ Dogs welcome ~ Open 11.45-2.30, 6-11; 12-3 Sun; closed Sun evening and Mon

Recommended by Ann and Colin Hunt, Chris Sale, Jenny Bolton, Phyl and Jack Street, D and J Ashdown, Val and Alan Green

DUNBRIDGE
SU3126 MAP 2

Mill Arms 🍺

Barley Hill, just by station on Portsmouth—Cardiff line; SO51 0LF

Extended coaching house with plenty of space, several real ales, bistro-style food and a pretty garden; bedrooms

While enjoying your meal or drink, you can watch the trains go by as the railway station is opposite. This is a much-extended 18th-c former coaching inn and the high-ceilinged rooms have a friendly, informal atmosphere, scrubbed pine tables and farmhouse chairs on the oak or flagstone floors, several sofas, a couple of log fires and Ringwood Best and guests like Otter Bitter, Sharps Doom Bar and Wickwar BOB on handpump; several wines by the glass and prompt service by smartly dressed staff. There's also a dining area, a dining conservatory and two skittle alleys; piped music. The large, pretty garden has lots of picnic-sets and there are plenty of walks in the surrounding Test Valley countryside. The bedrooms are bright and comfortable.

🍴 Good bistro-style bar food includes sandwiches, soup, chicken and wild mushroom terrine with spiced pear chutney, seared scallops with citrus-cured and home-smoked bass, home-made burgers, home-baked orange and mustard ham with free-range eggs, local sausages with onion gravy, beef wellington with wild mushroom jus, roasted monkfish wrapped in parma ham with a pea and mint risotto, and puddings like sticky toffee pudding and dark chocolate brownie with white chocolate ice-cream; Sunday roasts. *Starters/Snacks: £4.75 to £6.75. Main Courses: £8.95 to £15.95. Puddings: £4.75 to £5.95*

Enterprise ~ Lease Mr I Bentall ~ Real ale ~ Bar food (12-2.30(3.30), 6-9 (9.30 Fri); all day weekends) ~ Restaurant ~ (01794) 340401 ~ Children welcome ~ Dogs allowed in bar

and bedrooms ~ Open 12-2.30, 6-11; 12-11(10.30 Sun) Sat; closed from 4pm Sun in winter ~
Bedrooms: /£70B
Recommended by Phyl and Jack Street, Dave Braisted, Martin and Karen Wake, Ann and Colin Hunt

DUNDRIDGE   SU5718   MAP 2

Hampshire Bowman 🍺

Off B3035 towards Droxford, Swanmore, then right at Bishops W signpost; SO32 1GD

**Friendly country pub with quickly changing real ales, popular food and peaceful garden
with children's play equipment**

There's always quite a mix of customers in this friendly and relaxed country pub – and a
good chatty atmosphere undisturbed by piped music, mobile phones (£1 fine in the
charity box) or games machines. Five real ales are tapped from the cask: Bowman Quiver,
Swift One and Wallops Wood, Palmers 200 and Stonehenge Danish Dynamite, and they
have summer farm cider and eight wines by the glass. There's a smart stable bar that sits
comfortably alongside the cosy unassuming original bar, some colourful paintings, board
games, puzzles and Archie the new pub dog. The attractive lawn has plenty of picnic-sets
and the heated terrace has more seats under a giant parasol from which you can enjoy
the lovely sunsets; children's play equipment and peaceful nearby downland walks.

🍽 Using seasonal local produce and some of their own herbs and vegetables, the well
liked bar food includes sandwiches, filled baguettes and baked potatoes, ploughman's,
soup, pâté of the day, smoked duck breast salad, moules marinière, ham and egg, lambs
liver and bacon, various pies, thai chicken curry, lamb leg steak with sweet pepper sauce
and natural smoked haddock with a poached egg. *Starters/Snacks: £4.50 to £5.50. Main
Courses: £5.95 to £12.95. Puddings: £4.95*

Free house ~ Licensee Heather Seymour ~ Real ale ~ Bar food (all day Fri-Sun) ~
(01489) 892940 ~ Children welcome ~ Dogs welcome ~ Open 12-11(10.30 Sun)
*Recommended by the Didler, Ann and Colin Hunt, Val and Alan Green, Robert Lorimer, Henry Fryer, Stephen and
Jean Curtis, Howard and Margaret Buchanan, Jim and Jill Harris*

EAST STRATTON   SU5339   MAP 2

Northbrook Arms

Brown sign to pub off A33 4 miles S of A303 junction; SO21 3DU

Easy-going camaraderie in nicely placed village pub, good all round

Now in the same good hands as the Yew Tree at Lower Wield, this pleasantly unassuming
place has a relaxed traditional tiled-floor bar on the right, with well kept Andwell Old
Muddler, Bowman Cheap One and Otter Ale on handpump, decent wines by the glass, a
mix of pubby chairs around sturdy stripped-top tables, a collection of regulars' snapshots,
reference books and bric-a-brac on the sills of the big windows, and a log fire. Piped pop
music is not too obtrusive. On the left it's carpeted, and progressively rather more formal,
ending in a proper dining room beyond a little central hall. There are picnic-sets out on
the green across the quiet village road, with more in the good-sized back courtyard –
which has a skittle alley, as well as the gents', on the far side. There are fine walks
nearby. We have not heard from readers who have stayed here, but would think it a
pleasant overnight stop.

🍽 Enjoyable bar food includes sandwiches, soup, fishcakes with parsley sauce, devilled
lambs kidneys, venison sausages with onion gravy, a pie of the day, a proper burger with
stilton and onion marmalade, gammon and free-range eggs, rump of lamb with port and
tarragon sauce, bass with an olive tapenade, and puddings like apricot and white
chocolate bread and butter pudding and crème brûlée. *Starters/Snacks: £4.95 to £6.95. Main
Courses: £9.25 to £15.95. Puddings: £4.95*

We say if we know a pub has piped music.

Free house ~ Licensees Tim Gray, Wendy Nichols, Simon Smith ~ Real ale ~ Bar food (not Sun evening or Mon) ~ Restaurant ~ (01962) 774150 ~ Children welcome ~ Dogs allowed in bar ~ Open 12-3, 6-11; 12-10.30 Sun; closed Mon and winter Sun evening ~ Bedrooms: £50S/£65S

Recommended by Ann and Colin Hunt

EAST TYTHERLEY
SU2927   MAP 2

Star ⓦ🍴

B3084 N of Romsey; turn off by railway crossing opposite Mill Arms, Dundridge; SO51 0LW

Warm welcome for drinkers and diners in pretty pub, inventive food and real ales; comfortable bedrooms

You can be sure of a warm welcome from the friendly, hard-working licensees in this spic-and-span country pub. The bar has comfortable sofas and tub armchairs, pubby dining tables and chairs, bar stools and chairs, an overflowing bookcase to one side of the log fire and rich red walls. The restaurant is attractively set with proper linen napkins and tablecloths. Andwell Gold Mudler and Cottage Iron Duke or Itchen Valley Godfather on handpump, several wines by the glass including fizz, malt whiskies and Thatcher's rose cider; piped music and board games. There are picnic-set sets in front of the building and tables and chairs on the back terrace by a giant chessboard. The bedrooms overlook the cricket pitch and the breakfasts are particularly good; nearby walks.

🍴 **Cooked by the licensees' son, the good, reasonably priced bar food includes sandwiches, soup, chicken liver and wild mushroom parfait with courgette chutney, crab pot with lime, parsnip and cheddar bread and butter pudding, gammon with honey-glazed carrots and parsley sauce, popular salmon, cod and prawn pie with leek mash, maize-fed chicken with roast butternut squash tagine, confit of duck with pickled damsons, and puddings such as warm chocolate brownie with orange curd and cardamom ice-cream and cappuccino crème brûlée; Sunday roasts.** *Starters/Snacks: £4.25 to £5.75. Main Courses: £7.50 to £9.75. Puddings: £5.50*

Free house ~ Licensees Alan and Lesley Newitt ~ Real ale ~ Bar food (not Sun evening or Mon) ~ Restaurant ~ (01794) 340225 ~ Children welcome ~ Dogs allowed in bar and bedrooms ~ Live music Fri evenings ~ Open 11-2.30(3 Sat), 6-10.30; 11-3.30 Sun; closed Sun evening, Mon ~ Bedrooms: £55S/£80S

Recommended by Ann and Colin Hunt, Christopher and Elise Way, T A R Curran, Glenwys and Alan Lawrence

EASTON
SU5132   MAP 2

Chestnut Horse ⓦ🍴 ⚟

3.6 miles from M3 junction 9: A33 towards Kings Worthy, then B3047 towards Itchen Abbas; Easton then signposted on right – bear left in village; SO21 1EG

Cosy dining pub with log fires, fresh flowers and candles, deservedly popular food and friendly staff; Itchen Valley walks nearby

In a quiet and pretty village of thatched cottages, this is a smart 16th-c dining pub. The open-plan interior manages to have a pleasantly rustic and intimate feel with a series of cosily separate areas, and the snug décor takes in candles and fresh flowers on the tables, log fires in cottagey fireplaces and comfortable furnishings. The black beams and joists are hung with all sorts of jugs, mugs and chamber-pots, and there are lots of attractive pictures of wildlife and the local area. Badger K&B, First Gold and Hopping Hare on handpump, several wines by the glass and 30 malt whiskies. There are seats and tables out on a smallish sheltered decked area with colourful flower tubs and baskets, and plenty of nearby walks in the Itchen Valley.

🍴 **As well as lunchtime sandwiches, the good, interesting (if not cheap) food might include soup, seared pigeon breast with vegetable cider jelly, tian of crab and crayfish, venison and chestnut burger with rhubarb relish, beer-battered fresh cod with minted pea purée, roasted vegetable pasta, pork and leek sausages with onion gravy, corn-fed chicken with spiced prawn stuffing and lobster cream sauce, daily specials, and puddings like chocolate tart and crème brûlée; they offer a good value two-course set lunch.**

Starters/Snacks: £5.95 to £7.95. Main Courses: £14.95 to £17.95. Puddings: £6.50 to £7.95

Badger ~ Tenant Karen Wells ~ Real ale ~ Bar food (not Sun evening) ~ Restaurant ~ (01962) 779257 ~ Children welcome ~ Dogs allowed in bar ~ Open 12-3, 5.30-11; 12-11(10 Sun) Sat; 12-6 Sun; closed Sun evening

Recommended by Helen and Brian Edgeley, Ann and Colin Hunt, Gene and Tony Freemantle, Neil and Karen Dignan, Martin and Karen Wake, Jenny and Brian Seller, Pam and John Smith, Phyl and Jack Street

ELLISFIELD   SU6345   MAP 2

Fox

Off A339 or B3046 S of Basingstoke; Green Lane, Upper Common; RG25 2QW

Simple charm and enjoyable food and beer, tucked away in good walking country

On a quiet lane surrounded by snowdrop woods, this friendly place has a mixed collection of stripped tables, country chairs and cushioned wall benching on its bare boards and ancient floor tiles. Spread around three sides of the bar counter, it has open fires in plain brick fireplaces, some stripped masonry, some puce paintwork, and darts at the back. An enterprising changing choice of ales might typically include Andwell Resolute, Ballards Best and Ramsbury, the handpumps sharing counter space with a big bunch of flowers. The informal garden has picnic-sets and plenty of birdsong in spring; neat outdoor gents'.

🍴 **Good bar food cooked by the landlord includes sandwiches, filled baguettes, soup, breaded fishcakes with lime and chilli sauce, cumberland sausage, crayfish and broccoli linguine, slow-cooked pork belly, lamb shank in mint sauce, oriental-style chicken with noodles, and puddings like chocolate brownie and Baileys cheesecake.** *Starters/Snacks: £3.95 to £5.50. Main Courses: £7.95 to £13.50. Puddings: £5.95*

Free house ~ Licensees Tara McKay and Rob Hamilton ~ Real ale ~ Bar food (12-9) ~ Restaurant ~ (01256) 381210 ~ Children welcome ~ Dogs allowed in bar ~ Open 12-11

Recommended by Phyl and Jack Street, Bob Venus, Tony and Jill Radnor

FRITHAM   SU2314   MAP 2

Royal Oak

Village signed from exit roundabout, M27 junction 1; quickest via B3078, then left and straight through village; head for Eyeworth Pond; SO43 7HJ

Rural New Forest spot and part of a working farm; traditional rooms, log fires, up to seven real ales and simple lunchtime food

'Exactly what a pub should be' says one of our readers and that sums up this smashing country tavern. It's always busy whatever the season but is especially popular at weekends with walkers, cyclists and families. Three neatly kept black beamed rooms are straightforward but full of proper traditional character, with prints and pictures involving local characters on the white walls, restored panelling, antique wheelback, spindleback and other old chairs and stools with colourful seats around solid tables on the oak flooring, and two roaring log fires; both the chatty locals and the hard-working staff are genuinely friendly. The back bar has quite a few books. Up to seven real ales are tapped from the cask: Bowmans Swift One and Wallops Wood, Hop Back Summer Lightning, Keystone Cornerstone, Ringwood Best and Stonehenge Eye-Opener. Also, ten wines by the glass (mulled wine in winter) and a September beer festival. Summer barbecues may be put on in the neatly kept big garden which has a marquee for poor weather and a pétanque pitch. The pub is part of a working farm so there are ponies and pigs out on the green and plenty of livestock nearby.

🍴 **The much liked simple lunchtime food is limited to winter soups, ploughman's, pies and quiches, sausages and maybe summer local crab.** *Starters/Snacks: £4.50 to £7.50*

Prices of main dishes sometimes now don't include vegetables – if in doubt, ask.

Free house ~ Licensees Neil and Pauline McCulloch ~ Real ale ~ Bar food (12-2.30(3 weekends); not evenings) ~ No credit cards ~ (023) 8081 2606 ~ Children welcome if well behaved ~ Dogs welcome ~ Open 11-11; 12-10.30 Sun; 11-3, 6-11 weekdays in winter

Recommended by Richard, Anne and Kate Ansell, Peter Meister, the Didler, N R White, Mr and Mrs W W Burke, Simon Watkins, Mr and Mrs D Hammond, Kevin Flack, Robin and Tricia Walker

HAMBLE

SU4806 MAP 2

Bugle

3 miles from M27 junction 8; SO31 4HA

Bustling village pub by Hamble river, beamed and timbered small rooms, real ales, popular food and seats on terrace

At the bottom of the village and just up from the quay (from seats on the terrace you can see the boats on the Hamble), this is a bustling and friendly little 16th-c pub. The flagstoned main bar – divided into two rooms by timbering – has church chairs around one long table by the woodburning stove in its fine brick fireplace, a mix of other chairs and a window seat around other wooden tables, bar stools along the herringbone-brick and timbered bar counter where they keep Bowman Swift One and Ringwood Best on handpump and a good choice of wines by the glass; there's a further tiny room, too. TV and piped music. To the left of the bar is an attractive small beamed dining room with more timbering in red-painted walls, another brick fireplace and old wooden dining chairs and tables on polished floorboards. Upstairs there's a private dining room with some nice sailing photographs and windows overlooking the water. Plenty of chatty customers, both local and visitors, and helpful staff.

Popular bar food includes sandwiches, devilled whitebait with chunky tartare, salt and pepper fresh squid, caesar salad (you can add bacon and chicken), seasonal risotto with local cheese, moules frites, beer-battered fish with minted crushed peas, seared salmon with watercress pesto, good daily specials, and puddings such as sticky toffee pudding and local ice-creams; Sunday roasts. *Starters/Snacks: £4.00 to £7.00. Main Courses: £7.00 to £18.00. Puddings: £5.00 to £7.00*

Free house ~ Licensee Laurent Cescatti ~ Real ale ~ Bar food (12-2.30(3 Fri), 6-9.30(10 Fri); all day weekends) ~ Restaurant ~ (023) 8045 3000 ~ Children welcome ~ Dogs allowed in bar ~ Open 11-11(midnight Fri and Sat); 12-10.30 Sun

Recommended by Gael Pawson, Bob and Angela Brooks, Mrs Mary Woods

LISS

SU7826 MAP 2

Jolly Drover

London Road, Hill Brow; B2070 S of town, near B3006 junction; GU33 7QL

Particularly well run traditional pub, comfortable and friendly, with enjoyable food and good bedrooms

With an old-school landlord of the best sort, service here is cheerful, helpful and friendly, and the traditional layout of the neatly carpeted low-beamed bar includes leather tub chairs and a couple of sofas in front of the inglenook log fire. They have well kept fff Altons Pride, Fullers London Pride and Sharps Doom Bar on handpump, daily papers, and a silenced games machine in one alcove. Several areas, with a gentle décor mainly in muted terracotta or pale ochre, include two back dining areas, one of which opens on to a sheltered terrace with teak furniture, and a lawn with picnic-sets beyond. The german shepherd rescue is called Emma. The bedrooms are in a barn conversion.

Using local organic meat, the enjoyable food includes sandwiches, soup, deep-fried cheeses with redcurrant jelly, home-cooked ham with free-range eggs, cranberry and brie flan, sausages with onion gravy, battered haddock, lamb stew and dumplings, steak in ale pie, hot chicken curry and puddings; they also offer two- and three-course set menus. If you stay in the neat bedrooms, they do good breakfasts. *Starters/Snacks: £4.00 to £6.00. Main Courses: £10.00 to £16.00. Puddings: £5.00*

Enterprise ~ Lease Barry and Anne Coe ~ Real ale ~ Bar food (12-2(2.30 Sun), 7-9.30; not Sun evening) ~ Restaurant ~ (01730) 893137 ~ Children welcome ~ Open 11-2.30(3 Sat), 6-11; 11-4 Sun; closed Sun evening ~ Bedrooms: £70S/£80S

Recommended by Ross Balaam, Philip and Christine Kenny

LITTLETON   SU4532   MAP 2

Running Horse ♀
Village signposted off B3049 just NW of Winchester; Main Road; SO22 6QS

Smart dining pub with bar food plus more elaborate choices in elegant rooms, local real ales, several wines by the glass and nice front and back terraces

With a warm and welcoming atmosphere and enjoyable food, it's not surprising that this smart dining pub is so popular. The bar has some deep leather chairs as well as ochre-cushioned metal and wicker ones around matching modern tables on its polished boards, good colour photographs of Hampshire landscapes and townscapes, a log fire and venetian blinds in the bow windows. The marble and hardwood modern bar counter (with swish leather, wood and brass bar stools) has Andwell Resolute and Bowmans Wallops Wood on handpump and a dozen wines by the glass; there's also a flagstoned back restaurant. Good disabled access and facilities; piped music. There are green metal tables and chairs out on the front and back terraces and picnic-sets on the back grass by a spreading sycamore.

Good, popular bar food includes sandwiches, soup, moules marinière, ham hock terrine, wild mushroom tagliatelle, pork and leek sausages with red onion gravy, home-made burger with a choice of cheese toppings, beer-battered fish, thai-style green curry (vegetable, chicken or monkfish), more elaborate choices such as duck cooked three ways with a light madeira jus and lemon sole with crayfish mousse and crayfish bisque, and puddings like chocolate torte and sticky toffee pudding with butterscotch sauce; they also offer a set two-course weekday lunch. *Starters/Snacks: £3.95 to £6.95. Main Courses: £8.95 to £14.95. Puddings: £5.75*

Free house ~ Licensee Charlie Lechowski ~ Real ale ~ Bar food (12-2, 6-9(9.30 Fri and Sat); 12-8 Sun) ~ Restaurant ~ (01962) 880218 ~ Children welcome ~ Dogs allowed in bar ~ Open 11-11; 12-9.30 Sun ~ Bedrooms: £65B/£85B

Recommended by Dave Braisted, Phyl and Jack Street, Richard Abnett, Karen Eliot, Mrs Ann Adams, Helen and Brian Edgeley, John and Joan Calvert, Michael Doswell

LONGPARISH   SU4244   MAP 2

Plough
B3048, off A303 just E of Andover; SP11 6PB

Bustling, upmarket pub with friendly staff, real ales, attractive bars, popular food and seats in garden

A good break from the A303, this is a welcoming open-plan country pub with a comfortably upmarket feel and friendly staff. The various rooms have flagstones and oak flooring, high-backed wooden or black leather dining chairs around a mix of tables, some beams and standing timbers, contemporary paintwork, wine bottles along shelves and open fireplaces (one with a woodburning stove). Itchen Valley Hampshire Rose, Otter Bitter and Ringwood Best on handpump and several wines by the glass. There are chickens, rabbits and a tortoise in the garden and plenty of seats on decking and under parasols.

> We mention bottled beers and spirits only if there is something unusual
> about them – imported belgian real ales, say, or dozens of malt whiskies;
> so do please let us know about them in your reports.

🍴 Good bar food includes sandwiches, soup, ham hock terrine with spiced apple compote, grilled goats cheese and pepper polenta, beer-battered fish with home-made tartare sauce, sausages with onion gravy, seared salmon fillet with tomato vinaigrette, lamb rump with minted potato dauphinoise, a duo of duck with five-spice jus, daily specials, and puddings like stem ginger cheesecake with raspberry sorbet and glazed coconut custard with a warm macaroon. *Starters/Snacks: £3.95 to £7.95. Main Courses: £7.95 to £18.95. Puddings: £4.95 to £5.50*

Enterprise ~ Lease David Hicks and Kerry Stannard ~ Real ale ~ Bar food (12-2.30(4 winter Sun), 6-9.30; 12-8 summer Sun) ~ Restaurant ~ (01264) 720358 ~ Children welcome ~ Dogs allowed in bar ~ Open 11.30-4, 6-midnight; 12-9 Sun

Recommended by Phyl and Jack Street, Edward Mirzoeff, Neil and Karen Dignan, Michael and Jenny Back

LOWER FROYLE   SU7643   MAP 2

Anchor 🛏️

Village signposted N of A31 W of Bentley; GU34 4NA

Civilised pub, lots to look at, real ales, good wines and interesting bar food; comfortable bedrooms

Many customers do come to this rather civilised 14th-c pub to enjoy the good food but the cheerful, chatty locals at the bar keep things informal and relaxed. There are low beams and standing timbers, flagstones in the bar and wood stripped floors elsewhere, sofas and armchairs dotted here and there, a mix of nice old tables and dining chairs, lit candles in candlesticks, an open fire and high bar chairs at the counter. Throughout there are all sorts of interesting knick-knacks, books, lots of copper, horsebrasses, photographs (several of Charterhouse School) and all manner of pictures and prints; paint colours are fashionable, values are traditional and they keep Bowmans Quiver and Swift One and Triple fff Altons Pride on handpump, nine wines by the glass (including fizz) and interesting pressés. The bedrooms are stylish.

🍴 Under the new licensee, the interesting bar food includes lunchtime sandwiches and 'boards', soup, jellied ham hock and parsley with piccalilli, pickled mackerel with horseradish cream, leek and stilton eccles cake with walnut and pear salad, lamb and harissa burger with avocado purée, sausages with colcannon and onion gravy, steak in ale pie, beer-battered haddock with mushy peas, pork cooked five ways with bacon and cabbage and mustard sauce, skate wing with butter and capers, and puddings like cambridge burnt cream and poached rhubarb and sticky toffee pudding with clotted cream. *Starters/Snacks: £6.00 to £9.50. Main Courses: £11.50 to £18.50. Puddings: £6.00 to £7.50*

Free house ~ Licensee Tracy Levett ~ Real ale ~ Bar food (12-2.30(3 Sat), 6.30-9.30(10 Sat); 12-4, 7-9 Sun) ~ Restaurant ~ (01420) 23261 ~ Children welcome ~ Dogs allowed in bar and bedrooms ~ Open 11-11(10.30 Sun) ~ Bedrooms: £90S/£100S

Recommended by Tony and Jill Radnor, Mark Flynn, Martin and Karen Wake, John Branston, E Ling

LOWER WIELD   SU6339   MAP 2

Yew Tree 🍴 🍷

Turn off A339 NW of Alton at Medstead, Bentworth 1 signpost, then follow village signposts; or off B3046 S of Basingstoke, signposted from Preston Candover; SO24 9RX

Smashing landlord, relaxed atmosphere, super choice of wines and good food in bustling country pub; sizeable garden and nearby walks

Mr Gray is an excellent landlord who really cares about his customers and his pub – our readers enjoy their visits very much. There's a small flagstoned bar area on the left with pictures above its stripped brick dado, a steadily ticking clock and a log fire. Around to the right of the serving counter – which has a couple of stylish wrought-iron bar chairs – it's carpeted, with a few flower pictures; throughout there is a mix of tables, including some quite small ones for two, and miscellaneous chairs. Twelve wines by the glass from a well chosen list which may include summer rosé and Louis Jadot burgundies from a shipper based just along the lane. Bowman Eldorado and a beer from Triple fff named after the pub on handpump. There are solid tables and chunky seats out on the front terrace, picnic-sets in a sizeable side garden, pleasant views and a cricket field across the quiet lane; nearby walks.

🍴 **Enjoyable bar food includes sandwiches, soup, salmon and dill fishcake with dill-infused tartare sauce, gorgonzola and crispy bacon salad, sausages of the week with spring onion mash and onion gravy, roasted pepper with a leek, butternut squash and tomato ragoût, thai green chicken curry, steak and mushroom in ale pudding, belly of pork on a caramelised apple with a calvados and apple sauce, chinese-spiced salmon with oriental noodles, and puddings like chocolate and orange truffle cake and pecan pie with clotted cream.** *Starters/Snacks: £3.95 to £6.95. Main Courses: £7.50 to £17.95. Puddings: £4.50*

Free house ~ Licensee Tim Gray ~ Real ale ~ Bar food (not Mon) ~ (01256) 389224 ~ Children welcome ~ Dogs allowed in bar ~ Open 12-3, 6-11; 12-10.30 Sun; closed Mon; first two weeks in Jan

Recommended by Geoff and Molly Betteridge, Peter Barton, John Oates, Denise Walton, Peter and Andrea Jacobs, Tony and Jill Radnor, Margaret Ball, Darryl and Lindy Hemsley, Phyl and Jack Street, Ian Herdman, R B Gardiner

LYMINGTON   SZ3295   MAP 2

Ship
Quay Road; SO41 3AY

Lively, well run pub overlooking harbour with seats outside on quay; fair value, interesting food and good choice of drinks

Not surprisingly, this well run and lively pub is extremely popular given its prime position overlooking the harbour of this civilised little town. It's all very light and modern, with lots of nautical bits and pieces such as big model yachts, ropework, old ships' timbers and various huge flags. To the left is a room with a raised log fire, comfortably cushioned wall seats and blue gingham and leather sofas, and this runs into the bar where there is plenty of standing room in front of the counter; Adnams Broadside, Fullers London Pride and Hook Norton Old Hooky on handpump, decent house wines (the bottles are stored in an unusual wall rack) and good soft drinks. Past here, a raised area has brightly cushioned wall seats, stools and other seats around all sorts of tables (including a nice glass-topped chest one) and by some french windows is yet another area with a mix of old wooden and fabric dining chairs around tile-topped tables. The restaurant is most attractive and similarly furnished: subtle lighting, church candles, standing timbers, planked walls, mirrors on blue and cream paintwork and driftwood decorations; friendly and efficient young staff. The decked terrace which overlooks the water gets packed in fine weather; there are showers for visiting sailors.

🍴 **Very reasonably priced for the location, the enjoyable bar food includes sandwiches, filled baked potatoes, soup, various platters, crab cakes with a light chilli dressing, chicken terrine and duck rillette with onion marmalade, home-made burger topped with cheese and bacon, beer-battered haddock with spicy ketchup, venison cottage pie with madeira sauce, black olive and onion tart with cumin-roasted vegetables, grilled salmon steak with niçoise salad, and puddings like chocolate and hazelnut brownie and banoffi split sundae.** *Starters/Snacks: £4.50 to £7.25. Main Courses: £8.50 to £17.95. Puddings: £4.50 to £6.50*

Mitchells & Butlers ~ Manager Chris James ~ Real ale ~ Bar food (12(11 Sat)-10) ~ Restaurant ~ (01590) 676903 ~ Children welcome ~ Dogs welcome ~ Open 11-11(midnight Fri and Sat)

Recommended by John Voos

Bedroom prices normally include full english breakfast, VAT and any inclusive service charge that we know of. Prices before the '/' are for single rooms, after for two people in double or twin (B includes a private bath, S a private shower). If there is no '/', the prices are only for twin or double rooms (as far as we know there are no singles).

PETERSFIELD

SU7227 MAP 2

Trooper 🍴 🍺 🛏

From A32 (look for staggered crossroads) take turning to Froxfield and Steep; pub 3 miles down on left in big dip; GU32 1BD

Charming landlord, popular food, decent drinks, and little persian knick-knacks and local artists' work; comfortable bedrooms

With a happy bustling atmosphere and a warm welcome from the charming Mr Matini, this remains a good all-round pub. The bar has a mix of cushioned dining chairs around dark wooden tables, old film star photos and paintings by local artists (for sale) on the walls, little persian knick-knacks here and there, quite a few ogival mirrors, lots of lit candles, fresh flowers and a log fire in the stone fireplace; there's a sun room with lovely downland views, carefully chosen piped music and newspapers and magazines to read. A couple of real ales from local breweries such as Ballards, Bowmans, Itchen Valley and Ringwood on handpump and several wines by the glass. The attractive raftered restaurant has french windows to a paved terrace with views across the open countryside, and there are lots of picnic-sets on an upper lawn. The horse rail in the car park is reserved 'for horses, camels and local livestock'.

🍴 As well as lunchtime sandwiches and filled baguettes, the good, popular bar food includes soup, smoked pigeon breast with beetroot vinaigrette, mussels with coconut milk, shallots, lemon grass, chilli and coriander, toad in the hole with onion gravy, wild mushroom roulade, pork tenderloin with star anise and tarragon, a half shoulder of slow-cooked lamb with honey and mint gravy, fresh fish of the day, butterscotch banana pecan crumble and baked chocolate cheesecake; Tuesday is their good value pie and pudding day. *Starters/Snacks: £5.50 to £7.50. Main Courses: £10.00 to £21.00. Puddings: £5.50*

Free house ~ Licensee Hassan Matini ~ Real ale ~ Bar food (not Sun evening or Mon lunchtime) ~ Restaurant ~ (01730) 827293 ~ Children must be seated and supervised by an adult ~ Dogs allowed in bar ~ Open 12-3, 6-11; 12-3.30 Sun; closed Sun evening, Mon lunchtime, 25 and 26 Dec, 1 Jan ~ Bedrooms: £69B/£89B

Recommended by Martin and Karen Wake, Ann and Colin Hunt, Keith and Chris O'Neill, Henry Fryer, Geoff and Linda Payne, Jenny and Peter Lowater, T A R Curran

PORTSMOUTH

SZ6399 MAP 2

Old Customs House

Vernon Buildings, Gunwharf Quays; follow brown signs to Gunwharf Quays car park – usually quickest to park on lower level, come up escalator, turn left towards waterside then left again; PO1 3TY

Handsome and well converted historic building in a prime waterfront development with real ales and popular bar food

At peak times, this red brick former customs house does get pretty busy but outside these hours it's a very pleasant place for a quiet drink. There are several big-windowed high-ceilinged rooms with bare boards, nautical prints and photographs on pastel walls, coal-effect gas fires, nice unobtrusive lighting and well padded chairs around sturdy tables in varying sizes; the sunny entrance area has leather sofas. Broad stairs take you up to a carpeted more restauranty floor with similar décor. Fullers Discovery, ESB, HSB, London Pride and Seafarers on handpump, a decent range of wines by the glass and good coffees and teas. Staff are efficient, housekeeping is good, the piped music well reproduced, and the games machines silenced. Picnic-sets out in front are just yards from the water. Just around the corner is the graceful Spinnaker Tower (165 metres tall with staggering views from its viewing decks). The bar has disabled access and facilities.

🍴 They usefully serve food all day starting with a proper breakfast; also, sandwiches, soup, various sharing boards, devilled mushrooms, smoked salmon, watercress and pepper tart, beer-battered cod, beefburger with real ale relish, lamb steak with redcurrant salad, half a roast chicken with sea salt and rosemary, crab claw and crayfish salad, and puddings such as toffee and pecan drizzle cake and chocolate torte. *Starters/Snacks: £3.95 to £6.95. Main Courses: £7.25 to £13.95. Puddings: £4.95*

Fullers ~ Manager David Hughes ~ Real ale ~ Bar food (all day from 9am) ~ Restaurant ~
(023) 9283 2333 ~ Children allowed until 8pm but must go to upstairs restaurant after that ~
Open 9am-midnight(1.30am Sat, 11 Sun)

*Recommended by Andy and Claire Barker, Philip and June Caunt, Maureen Wood, Val and Alan Green,
Ann and Colin Hunt*

ROCKBOURNE   SU1118   MAP 2

Rose & Thistle ♀
Signed off B3078 Fordingbridge—Cranborne; SP6 3NL

**Pretty pub in lovely village with friendly staff, informal bars, real ales, good food and
seats in garden**

In a tranquil spot in a pretty village on the edge of the New Forest, this is an attractive
16th-c thatched pub that is doing especially well under its present landlady. There are
homely dining chairs, stools and benches around a mix of old pubby tables in the bar and
two-roomed restaurant, two log fires (one is a big brick inglenook), old engravings and
cricket prints and an informal and relaxed atmosphere. Fullers London Pride, Palmers
Copper Ale, Timothy Taylors Landlord and a guest such as Downton Apple Blossom on
handpump, ten wines by the glass and Orchard Pig and Black Rat cider. There are benches
and tables under the pretty hanging baskets at the front of the building with picnic-sets
under parasols on the grass; good nearby walks.

🍴 Well liked bar food includes sandwiches, ploughman's, soup, creamy garlic mushrooms,
free-range scrambled eggs with smoked salmon and watercress, sausages with wholegrain
mustard mash and onion gravy, tagliatelle with sunblush tomatoes, spinach, feta and pine
nuts, free-range chicken marinated in lemon, thyme and garlic with herb lentils, free-
range pork belly with black pudding stuffing, braised apricots and calvados gravy, and
puddings like rhubarb and ginger crème brûlée and treacle tart. *Starters/Snacks: £6.95 to
£9.25. Main Courses: £8.95 to £16.95. Puddings: £5.95*

Free house ~ Licensee Kerry Dutton ~ Real ale ~ Bar food (12-2.30, 7-9.30; not Sun evening) ~
Restaurant ~ (01725) 518236 ~ Children welcome ~ Dogs allowed in bar ~ Open 11-3, 6-11;
11-11 Sat; 12-10.30(8 in winter) Sun

Recommended by Nick Lawless, Peter Barnwell, Kevin Flack

SOUTHSEA   SZ6499   MAP 2

Wine Vaults ◀
Albert Road, opposite Kings Theatre; PO5 2SF

Bustling pub with new licensee, a fine choice of real ales and reasonably priced food

Although it does get packed at weekends, this bustling place is quieter during the week.
It's the range of eight real ales on handpump that continues to draw in the customers
and these might include Adnams Broadside, Dark Star Hophead and Saison, Fullers
Discovery, ESB, Gales HSB and London Pride and Oakleaf Hole Hearted. There are several
rooms on different floors – all fairly straightforward and chatty – and the main bar has
wood-panelled walls, pubby tables and chairs on the wooden floor and bar stools by the
long plain bar counter; there's a restaurant area away from the hustle and bustle of the
bars. Maybe newspapers to read, piped music and TV for sports events. More reports
please.

> If a service charge is mentioned prominently on a menu or accommodation terms, you
> must pay it if service was satisfactory. If service is really bad, you are legally entitled
> to refuse to pay some or all of the service charge as compensation for not getting
> the service you might reasonably have expected.

🍴 Some sort of food is offered all day and might include wraps and filled baguettes (until 5pm), soup, fishcakes with lemon mayonnaise, home-made burgers, chorizo and olive sausages and mash, steak in ale pie, beer-battered haddock, vegetable lasagne, daily specials like moroccan lamb tagine, thai green chicken curry and balsamic salmon with feta and mediterranean vegetable couscous, and puddings such as apple and rhubarb crumble and chocolate fudge cake. *Starters/Snacks: £3.50 to £4.95. Main Courses: £6.95 to £12.95. Puddings: £4.25*

Fullers ~ Manager Sophie Mannering ~ Real ale ~ Bar food (all day) ~ Restaurant ~ (023) 9286 4712 ~ Children welcome ~ Dogs allowed in bar ~ Open 12-11(12 Fri and Sat; 10.30 Sun)

Recommended by the Didler, Andy West, Ann and Colin Hunt

SPARSHOLT
SU4331 MAP 2

Plough 🍴 🍷

Village signposted off B3049 (Winchester—Stockbridge), a little W of Winchester; SO21 2NW

Neat, well run dining pub with interesting furnishings, an extensive wine list, and popular bar food; garden with children's play fort

---

'A smashing pub that never fails to express' is just one of the enthusiastic reader reports we received this year – and many others agree. It's a particularly well run pub with excellent service and very good food and although the main emphasis is on dining they do keep Wadworths IPA, 6X, JCB and seasonal beers on handpump. The main bar has an interesting mix of wooden tables and chairs with farm tools, scythes and pitchforks attached to the ceiling and the extensive wine list has a fair selection by the glass including champagne and pudding wine. Disabled access and facilities. Outside there are plenty of seats on the terrace and lawn and a children's play fort.

🍴 Enjoyable bar food includes sandwiches, soup, chicken liver parfait with fruit chutney, salmon and crab fishcakes on saffron sauce, wild mushroom, courgette and asparagus tagliatelle, beef and mushroom in ale pie, chicken breast filled with goats cheese mousse on garlic and bacon sauce, fillet of bass with olive mash, sun-dried tomatoes and spinach, and puddings such as sticky toffee pudding and crème brûlée. *Starters/Snacks: £4.95 to £8.95. Main Courses: £11.50 to £18.95. Puddings: £3.95 to £5.75*

Wadworths ~ Tenants Richard and Kathryn Crawford ~ Real ale ~ Bar food ~ (01962) 776353 ~ Children welcome except in main bar area ~ Dogs welcome ~ Open 10-3, 6-11

Recommended by Phyl and Jack Street, John and Joan Calvert, John Michelson, Henry Fryer, Jill and Julian Tasker, David Jackson, Peter and Andrea Jacobs, Mr and Mrs P D Titcomb, Jeff and Wendy Williams

STEEP
SU7525 MAP 2

Harrow 🍺

Take Midhurst exit from Petersfield bypass, at exit roundabout take first left towards Midhurst, then first turning on left opposite garage, and left again at Sheet church; follow over dual carriageway bridge to pub; GU32 2DA

Unchanging, simple place with long-serving landladies, beers tapped from the cask, unfussy food and a big free-flowering garden; no children inside

---

The same family have been running this genuinely unspoilt and unpretentious pub for 81 years now and it is a firm favourite with many of our readers. Everything revolves around village chat and the friendly locals who will probably draw you into light-hearted conversation. There are adverts for logs next to calendars of local views being sold in support of local charities, news of various quirky competitions and no pandering to modern methods – no credit cards, no waitress service, no restaurant, no music and outside lavatories. The cosy public bar has hops and dried flowers hanging from the beams, built-in wall benches on the tiled floor, stripped pine wallboards, a good log fire in the big inglenook, and wild flowers on the scrubbed deal tables; board games. Dark

Star Hophead, Otter Bitter and Palmers Copper are tapped straight from casks behind the counter and they've local wine, and apple and pear juice; staff are polite and friendly, even when under pressure. The big garden is left free-flowering so that goldfinches can collect thistle seeds from the grass but there are some seats on paved areas now. The Petersfield bypass doesn't intrude on this idyll, though you will need to follow the directions above to find the pub. No children inside and dogs must be on leads.

🍴 Good helpings of unfussy bar food include sandwiches, home-made scotch eggs, hearty ham, split pea and vegetable soup, ploughman's, cottage pie, flans and quiches, and puddings such as treacle tart or seasonal fruit pies. *Starters/Snacks: £4.70. Main Courses: £9.00 to £12.50. Puddings: £4.50*

Free house ~ Licensees Claire and Denise McCutcheon ~ Real ale ~ Bar food (not Sun evening; limited Mon evening) ~ No credit cards ~ (01730) 262685 ~ Dogs welcome ~ Open 12-2.30, 6-11; 11-3, 6-11 Sat; 12-3, 7-10.30 Sun; closed winter Sun evenings

Recommended by Phil and Sally Gorton, the Didler, Ian Phillips, David Gunn, Tony and Jill Radnor, Neil and Karen Dignan, W A Evershed, Ann and Colin Hunt, Peter Price

SWANMORE   SU5815   MAP 2

Rising Sun ♀ 🍺

Village signposted off A32 N of Wickham and B2177 S of Bishops Waltham; pub E of village centre, at Hillpound on the Droxford Road; SO32 2PS

Proper country pub (now a free house) with friendly staff, good beers and popular food

Sunday lunchtime is a particularly busy and cheerful time to visit this 17th-c coaching inn; it's quieter during the week. The low-beamed carpeted bar has some easy chairs and a sofa by its good log fire and a few tables with pubby seats. Beyond the fireplace on the right is a pleasant much roomier dining area (with similarly unpretentious furnishings) running back in an L past the bar; one part of this has stripped brick barrel vaulting. Adnams Broadside, Courage Directors, Otter Bright and Ringwood Best on handpump and a dozen wines by the glass; faint piped music. There are picnic-sets out on the side grass with a play area and the Kings Way long-distance path is close by – some readers tell us it's best to head north where there's lovely downland country, fine views and interesting winding lanes.

🍴 Well liked bar food includes lunchtime sandwiches, filled baguettes and baked potatoes, ploughman's, soup, omelettes, vegetable lasagne, home-cooked ham and eggs, fresh beer-battered fish, a pie of the day, lambs liver and bacon, daily specials such as devilled whitebait, cumberland sausage ring, beef bourguingon and baked black cod with banana, and puddings such as raspberry crème brûlée and red cherry cheesecake. Smaller helpings are available as well as a weekday two-course set menu. *Starters/Snacks: £4.20 to £8.20. Main Courses: £7.50 to £21.95. Puddings: £3.95 to £5.75*

Free house ~ Licensees Mark and Sue Watts ~ Real ale ~ Bar food (12-2(2.30 Sun), 6-9(8.30 Sun)) ~ Restaurant ~ (01489) 896663 ~ Children allowed but must be well behaved ~ Dogs allowed in bar ~ Open 11.30-3, 5.30-11; 12-3.30, 5.30-10.30 Sun

Recommended by Phyl and Jack Street, Val and Alan Green, Ann and Colin Hunt, Howard and Margaret Buchanan, Gill and Keith Croxton

TICHBORNE   SU5730   MAP 2

Tichborne Arms

Village signed off B3047; SO24 0NA

Traditional pub in rolling countryside, with real ales and well liked bar food; big garden

There's a good mix of customers in this attractive thatched pub: walkers and their dogs (the Wayfarers Walk and Itchen Way pass close by), locals chatting with a drink over the newspapers and those out for a meal. Bowman Swift One, Cheriton Pots Ale, Otter Amber and Palmers Copper tapped from the cask, several wines by the glass and farm cider; darts, board games and shove-ha'penny. The comfortable square-panelled room on the right has wheelback chairs and settles (one very long), a woodburning stove in the stone fireplace, all sorts of antiques, pictures and stuffed animals and latticed windows. On the left is a larger, livelier, partly panelled room used for eating with a woodburning stove. Pictures and documents on the walls recall the bizarre Tichborne Case, in which a mystery man from Australia claimed fraudulently to be the heir to this estate. The big, neat garden has plenty of picnic-sets and the surrounding countryside is attractively rolling.

① **Tasty bar food includes sandwiches and filled baguettes (not Sundays), filled baked potatoes, ploughman's, soup, creamy garlic mushrooms, smoked trout pâté, baked brie with redcurrant sauce, vegetable and cheese lasagne, luxury fish pie, lambs liver and bacon, daily specials, and puddings like lemon and lime bread and butter pudding and chocolate and strawberry cheesecake.** *Starters/Snacks: £5.95 to £7.95. Main Courses: £9.50 to £16.95. Puddings: £4.95*

Free house ~ Licensee Nicky Roper ~ Real ale ~ Bar food (not Sun evening) ~ (01962) 733760 ~ Children welcome ~ Dogs welcome ~ Open 11.45-3(4 Sat), 6-11.30; 12-4 Sun; closed Sun evening

Recommended by the Didler, Sandiford Durvin, Pete Baker, Conor McGaughey, Tony and Jill Radnor, Martin and Karen Wake, Pam and John Smith

UPHAM

SU5320   MAP 2

Brushmakers Arms

Shoe Lane; village signpost from Winchester—Bishops Waltham downs road, and from B2177; SO32 1JJ

Pleasant old place with extensive displays of brushes, local beers and traditional bar food

Tucked away down a lane, this is an old village local with plenty of regulars and, especially at weekends, walkers and their dogs. The L-shaped bar (divided in two by a central brick chimney with a woodburning stove) has quite a collection of old and new brushes, there are a few beams in the low ceiling and comfortably cushioned settles and chairs around a variety of tables; there's also a little back snug with a games machine and piped music. Fullers London Pride and ESB, Ringwood Best and a changing guest beer on handpump; the pub cats are called Luna and Baxter. The big garden is well stocked with mature shrubs and trees and there are picnic-sets on a sheltered back terrace, with more on a tree-sheltered lawn. It's best to park by the duck pond; good walks nearby.

① **Bar food includes lunchtime sandwiches, soup, omelettes, cheese and bacon potato skins, baked brie with redcurrant sauce, chilli con carne, battered cod, mushroom stroganoff, chicken balti, and puddings.** *Starters/Snacks: £4.95 to £6.95. Main Courses: £8.95 to £16.95. Puddings: £4.95*

Free house ~ Licensee Keith Venton ~ Real ale ~ Bar food (12-2, 6-9(9.30 Fri, Sat)) ~ Restaurant ~ (01489) 860231 ~ Children welcome ~ Dogs allowed in bar ~ Open 11-3, 5.45-11; 12-10.30 Sun

Recommended by Sue Orchard, Tony and Jill Radnor, Ann and Colin Hunt, Val and Alan Green

WEST MEON

SU6424   MAP 2

Thomas Lord 🏮

High Street; GU32 1LN

Friendly, popular pub with interesting décor, imaginative food and local ales

Bustling and friendly, this is a popular village pub that has been individually decorated in a rustic style and is named for the founder of Lord's cricket ground. There's an interesting mix of wooden dining and pubby chairs around lots of different wooden tables (each with a candle on it – lit on a dark day) on the bare boards and an old brown leather sofa by one of the log fires (there are two); also, cricketing prints and memorabilia, various pictures and portraits above the wooden dados and stuffed animals in display cabinets above the bar counter. The back room is lined with books which you can buy for 50p. Bowman Swift One and Wallops Wood, Ringwood Best and Triple fff Altons Pride tapped from the cask, farm ciders, several wines by the glass and quite a few ports and madeiras. The formal garden is most attractive with plenty of seats and tables, an outdoor bar and a wood-fired pizza oven and there's also a chicken run and a neat area for home-grown produce. Good walks to the west of the village.

Ⅱ Using carefully sourced local produce, the often interesting – if not cheap – food includes sandwiches, soup (one of our readers swears he had squirrel), bacon-rolled pigs head with sage rösti and apple purée, brown crab cocktail, pork and apple sausages with cider cream, tasty lamb burger, sprouting lentil and spinach potato cake with a duck egg, beef stew with swede mash and chicken breast with wild garlic and mustard sauce. *Starters/Snacks: £5.00 to £8.00. Main Courses: £11.00 to £18.00. Puddings: £5.00 to £6.00*

Enterprise ~ Lease David Thomas and Richard Taylor ~ Real ale ~ Bar food (12-2(3 Fri-Sun), 7-9(9.30 Fri and Sat); not Mon) ~ (01730) 829244 ~ Children welcome ~ Dogs welcome ~ Open 12-3, 5-11; 12-11 Sat and Sun; closed Mon (except bank hols)

Recommended by Simon Collett-Jones, Val and Alan Green, Darryl and Lindy Hemsley, Phyl and Jack Street, Edward Bradley, Ann and Colin Hunt, Mr and Mrs W W Burke

WHERWELL   SU3839   MAP 2

Mayfly

Testcombe (over by Fullerton, and not in Wherwell itself); A3057 SE of Andover, between B3420 turn-off and Leckford where road crosses River Test; OS Sheet 185 map reference 382390; SO20 6AX

Extremely popular pub with decking and conservatory seats overlooking the River Test, well kept beers and wide range of enjoyable bar food usefully served all day

We've had nothing but warm praise from many of our readers on this well run and extremely popular pub over this last year. The setting is pretty special as it's on an island between the River Test and a smaller river to the back and there are lots of tables on the grass as well as on a decked area overlooking the water – best to get here early if you want to bag one of these. Inside, the spacious, beamed and carpeted bar has fishing pictures and fishing equipment on the cream walls, rustic pub furnishings and a woodburning stove. There's also a conservatory with riverside views; piped music. Adnams Best, Gales HSB, Hop Back Summer Lightning, Palmers Gold and Wadworths 6X on handpump and lots of wines by the glass; good, courteous service. Dogs must be kept on a lead.

Ⅱ Usefully served all day, the popular bar food includes a daily hot and cold buffet (at its largest in summer), as well as soup, salmon and monkfish terrine, sausages and mash with onion gravy, gammon with egg or pineapple, smoked haddock fishcakes, spinach and mascarpone lasagne, somerset chicken, rack of lamb on spring onion mash with a rich minted gravy, duck breast over sweet potato mash with black cherry jus, and puddings such as gooseberry cheesecake and apple and raspberry pie; Sunday roasts. *Starters/Snacks: £5.50 to £6.95. Main Courses: £9.95 to £18.95. Puddings: £5.95*

Free house ~ Licensee Barry Lane ~ Real ale ~ Bar food (11.30-9) ~ (01264) 860283 ~ Children welcome if well behaved ~ Dogs welcome ~ Open 10am-11pm

Recommended by David A Hammond, Terry and Nickie Williams, Betsy and Peter Little, Edward Mirzoeff, Mr and Mrs A Curry, Michael and Jenny Back, Lois Dyer, MJVK, Terry Buckland, George Atkinson, Shirley Mackenzie, David Wyatt

---

'Children welcome' means the pub says it lets children inside without any special restriction. If it allows them in, but to restricted areas such as an eating area or family room, we specify this. Places with separate restaurants often let children use them, hotels usually let them into public areas such as lounges. Some pubs impose an evening time limit – let us know if you find one earlier than 9pm.

WINCHESTER

SU4828 MAP 2

Black Boy ◀

A mile from M3 junction 10 northbound; B3403 towards city then left into Wharf Hill;
rather further and less easy from junction 9, and anyway beware no nearby daytime parking
– 220 metres from car park on B3403 N, or nice longer walk from town via College Street
and College Walk, or via towpath; SO23 9NQ

Busy town pub with several different areas crammed full of interesting knick-knacks;
straightforward lunchtime bar food and local ales

Customers enjoy the splendidly eccentric décor, fascinating array of knick-knacks and nice
old-fashioned feel at this most unusual pub. The several different areas run from a bare-
boards barn room with an open hayloft down to an orange-painted room with big oriental
rugs on red-painted floorboards. There's a stuffed baboon, a stuffed dog, a snake, a
pigeon and other random animals, floor-to-ceiling books in some parts, lots of big clocks,
mobiles made of wine bottles or strings of spectacles, some nice modern nature
photographs in the lavatories and on the brightly stained walls on the way, and plenty of
other things that you'll enjoy tracking down. Furnishings are similarly wide-ranging; two
log fires. The five well kept beers on handpump are more or less local: Flowerpots Bitter,
Hop Back Summer Lightning and Ringwood Best alongside a couple of guests from
breweries such as Bowman, Hampshire, Itchen Valley and Triple fff; decent wines, piped
music, table football and board games. There are a couple of slate tables out in front
with more seats on an attractive secluded terrace.

🍴 **Lunchtime bar food includes sandwiches with chips or soup, a pasta dish, beer-**
battered cod, toad in the hole, caesar salad and shepherd's pie. *Starters/Snacks: £5.50 to*
£6.95. Main Courses: £8.00 to £10.00. Puddings: £4.00 to £5.00

Free house ~ Licensee David Nicholson ~ Real ale ~ Bar food (not Sun evening, Mon or Tues
lunchtime) ~ (01962) 861754 ~ Children must be well behaved and supervised ~ Dogs welcome
~ Open 12-11(midnight Fri and Sat); 12-10.30 Sun
Recommended by Georgina Campbell, Ann and Colin Hunt, Brad W Morley, Chris Sale, Val and Alan Green,
Henry Fryer, MJVK, Phil and Sally Gorton

Willow Tree

Durngate Terrace; no adjacent weekday daytime parking, but Durngate car park is around
corner in North Walls; a mile from M3 junction 9, by Easton Lane into city; SO23 8QX

Snug pub with landlord/chef using much local produce for enjoyable food; nice riverside
garden

A cheerful and friendly chef/landlord runs this bustling Victorian local. The carpeted
lounge bar on the right has a relaxed atmosphere, wall banquettes, low ceilings and soft
lighting; two bays of good sturdy dining tables at the back have quite a few books
around them. The quite separate proper public bar has Greene King Morlands Old Speckled
Hen and Wadworths 6X on handpump, several wines by the glass and malt whiskies; piped
music, TV, games machine, juke box (a rarity nowadays), chess, backgammon and pool.
There's also a more comfortable dining room. A narrow tree-shaded garden, partly paved
and with plenty of heaters, stretches back between two branches of the River Itchen.

🍴 **As well as their bargain weekday lunch offer, the popular lunchtime bar food – cooked**
by the landlord – includes sandwiches, ploughman's, omelettes, beer-battered cod, a
vegetarian dish, calves liver and bacon with onion gravy, bangers and mash and a half
shoulder of lamb; more elaborate evening meals such as duck and pistachio gallantine
with pear chutney, crisp-skinned duck breast with raspberry vinegar and slow-cooked pork
belly with mustard mash, and puddings like eton mess and nutty rhubarb crumble; Sunday
roasts. *Starters/Snacks: £5.00 to £7.50. Main Courses: £10.00 to £17.50. Puddings: £5.00*

Greene King ~ Tenant James Yeoman ~ Real ale ~ Bar food (12-3, 6-10; not Sun evening) ~
Restaurant ~ (01962) 877255 ~ Children welcome ~ Dogs allowed in bar ~ Open 12-11(10 Sun)
Recommended by Ann and Colin Hunt

Wykeham Arms ♀

Kingsgate Street (Kingsgate Arch and College Street are now closed to traffic; there is access via Canon Street); SO23 9PE

Tucked-away pub with much to look at, several real ales and lots of wines by the glass; no children inside

There are three log fires in this tucked-away old pub (under a new licensee again) and all sorts of interesting collections dotted about. The series of bustling rooms radiates from the central bar; there are 19th-c oak desks retired from nearby Winchester College, a redundant pew from the same source, kitchen chairs and candlelit deal tables and big windows with swagged curtains. A snug room at the back, known as the Jameson Room (after the late landlord Graeme Jameson), is decorated with a set of Ronald Searle 'Winespeak' prints and a second one is panelled. Fullers London Pride, Seafarers and Gales HSB and a couple of guest beers like Butcombe Bitter and Fullers Discovery on handpump, lots of wines by the glass; good service. There are tables on a covered back terrace with more on a small courtyard.

🍴 Bar food includes sandwiches, soup, whitebait with caper mayonnaise, charred ox tongue and local beetroot salad with grated horseradish and crème fraîche, potato gnocchi with goats cheese, beer-battered fish of the day, calves liver and bacon with red onion jam, rack of lamb with mint jus and duck leg confit with warmed marinated mushrooms. *Starters/Snacks: £4.00 to £11.00. Main Courses: £7.50 to £12.50. Puddings: £6.25 to £6.95*

Fullers ~ Manager Jon Howard ~ Real ale ~ Bar food (12-3(3.30 Sun), 6-9.30) ~ Restaurant ~ (01962) 853834 ~ Children over 10 allowed in restaurant ~ Dogs allowed in bar ~ Open 11-11(10.30 Sun) ~ Bedrooms: £70B/£119B

Recommended by the Didler, Phil and Sally Gorton, Phyl and Jack Street, Chris Sale, Colin and Janet Roe, Martin and Karen Wake, Val and Alan Green, Chris Glasson, Mrs Mary Woods, John Oates, Denise Walton, Mr and Mrs A Curry, Ann and Colin Hunt, Pam and John Smith

LUCKY DIP

Besides the fully inspected pubs, you might like to try these Lucky Dips recommended to us and described by readers (if you do, please send us reports: feedback@goodguides.com).

ALRESFORD [SU5832]
☆ **Bell** SO24 9AT [West St]: Comfortable Georgian coaching inn with welcoming licensees, spic and span, with good quickly served food from sandwiches up, well kept Itchen Valley Winchester, nice wines, log fire, daily papers, smallish dining room, may be summer jazz on Sun; attractive back courtyard, good bedrooms, open all day *(John Oates, Denise Walton, Leon Wise, Ann and Colin Hunt)*
Swan SO24 9AD [West St]: Long narrow oak-panelled red-carpeted bar in 18th-c hotel (former coaching inn), three real ales inc Fullers London Pride, decent wines, tea and coffee, good choice of popular reasonably priced food inc good Sun carvery, restaurant; 23 bedrooms *(Val and Alan Green, Gordon Neighbour, Ann and Colin Hunt)*
ALTON [SU7139]
Eight Bells GU34 2DA [Church St]: Straightforward old-fashioned local with small well worn low-beamed bar and another room behind, several good changing ales such as Bowmans Swift One, Flowerpots Goodens Gold and Ringwood Best, rolls served most lunchtimes, helpful landlord; limited parking; small back garden with well,

open all day *(Joan and Michel Hooper-Immins)*
Railway Arms GU34 2RB [Anstey Rd]: Tap for Triple fff brewery, popular and convivial, with their full range and guests from small breweries all well kept, snack food, stripped pine interior with railway theme; front terrace with engine sculpture, handy for Watercress Line, open all day *(N R White)*
AMPFIELD [SU4023]
☆ **White Horse** SO51 9BQ [A3090 Winchester—Romsey]: Snug low-beamed front bar with candles and soft lighting, inglenook log fire and comfortable country furnishings, far-spreading beamed dining area behind, well kept Greene King IPA, Wadworths 6X and a guest, good choice of enjoyable food inc all-day snacks, several wines by the glass, efficient friendly service, locals' bar with another inglenook; piped music; children and dogs welcome, high-hedged garden with plenty of picnic-sets, cricket green beyond, good walks in Ampfield Woods, handy for Hillier gardens, open all day *(Phyl and Jack Street, BB, HPS)*
AXFORD [SU6043]
Crown RG25 2DZ [B3046 S of Basingstoke]: Country pub with efficient friendly staff, well kept Fullers London Pride, several wines by

the glass, enjoyable home-made food from sandwiches to good fish and chips and Sun roasts, three linked rooms, small log fire; children welcome, suntrap terrace and sloping shrub-sheltered garden, cl Mon *(Gordon Neighbour, Steve Hagger, LYM)*

BASING [SU6653]

☆ *Millstone* RG24 8AE [Bartons Lane, Old Basing; follow brown signs to Basing House]: Well run busy pub with lots of picnic-sets out by River Loddon looking across to former viaduct through scrubland, enjoyable food, full Wadworths range kept well, Weston's farm cider, good choice of wines by the glass, dark panelling, old prints and etchings, sturdy pub furnishings; may be faint piped jazz; children and dogs welcome, by ruins of Basing House, open all day *(Douglas and Ann Hare, BB)*

BAUGHURST [SU5860]

☆ *Wellington Arms* RG26 5LP [Baughurst Rd]: Charming little country restaurant – well worth a Main Entry and Food Award if it were more of a pub – with attractive simple décor, largely organic fresh ingredients in good food inc their own rare-breed eggs, herbs, salads and fruit, cheerful helpful service, good wines by the glass, Wadworths 6X; picnic-sets in attractive garden *(BB, Neil and Karen Dignan)*

BEAUWORTH [SU5624]

Milbury's SO24 0PB [off A272 Winchester/Petersfield]: Attractive ancient pub with Greene King and other ales, friendly landlord, simple traditional bar food, reasonably priced wines by the glass, log fires in huge fireplaces, beams, panelling and stripped stone, massive 17th-c treadmill for much older incredibly deep well; piped music; children in eating areas, garden with fine downland views, good walks, has been open all day wknds and summer *(Helen and Brian Edgeley, the Didler, LYM, Ann and Colin Hunt)*

BENTLEY [SU8044]

Bull GU10 5JH [A31 Alton—Farnham dual carriageway, east of village]: New licensees for this 15th-c pub; main room with low black beams and partly stripped brick walls, back room with log fire in huge hearth, Courage, Ringwood and Timothy Taylors, straightforward food; children and dogs welcome, side terrace, open all day *(LYM)*

BISHOP'S WALTHAM [SU5517]

Barleycorn SO32 1AJ [Lower Basingwell St]: Buoyant 18th-c two-bar local, enjoyable good value generous pub food, friendly efficient service, well kept Greene King ales and a guest, decent wine, beams and some low ceiling panelling, open fires; children and dogs welcome, large garden with back smokers' area, open all day *(Robert Lorimer, Henry Fryer, Ann and Colin Hunt, Stephen and Jean Curtis, Val and Alan Green)*

☆ *Bunch of Grapes* SO32 1AD [St Peters St – just along from entrance to central car park]: Neat and civilised little pub in quiet medieval street, smartly furnished keeping

individuality and unspoilt feel (run by same family for a century), Courage Best, Goddards and a guest tapped from the cask, high prices, good chatty landlord and regulars, no food; charming back terrace garden with one bar, opening times may vary *(the Didler, Stephen and Jean Curtis, BB, Henry Fryer)*

BISHOPSTOKE [SU4619]

Anglers SO50 6LQ [Riverside]: Comfortable old-fashioned pub with 1950s feel, three real ales inc Ringwood Best in front bar, cheerful staff, all-day pubby food inc bargain Sun carvery in back room; Weds quiz, Fri live music; nice spot across from river, three bedrooms *(Ann and Colin Hunt)*

BLACKNEST [SU7941]

Jolly Farmer GU34 4QD [Binsted Rd]: Bright and airy pub with nice food and relaxed atmosphere, beers such as Fullers London Pride and HSB, friendly helpful staff, log fire one end, family room; tables on sheltered terrace and in garden *(Jeff Watts)*

BOLDRE [SZ3198]

☆ *Red Lion* SO41 8NE [off A337 N of Lymington]: Attractive black-beamed rooms with entertaining collection of bygones, pews and other seats, log fires, attentive friendly staff, well kept Ringwood ales and a guest beer, great choice of wines by the glass, decent coffee, food usually good; children and dogs allowed, tables in nice back garden, open all day *(Glenwys and Alan Lawrence, LYM, Jeff and Wendy Williams, Keith and Margaret Kettell, Phyl and Jack Street, Mr and Mrs W W Burke, Ann and Colin Hunt)*

BRAISHFIELD [SU3725]

Newport Inn SO51 0PL [Newport Lane – from centre follow Michelmersh, Timsbury signpost]: Plain old-fashioned two-bar brick local, unchanging and in same family for 70 years, well kept Fullers/Gales ales, bargain sandwiches or ploughman's, cribbage, piano singsongs Sat night; informal and relaxing tree-shaded garden *(the Didler, Phil and Sally Gorton, BB)*

☆ *Wheatsheaf* SO51 0QE [Village signposted off A3090 on NW edge of Romsey]: Rambling pub with eclectic décor; mix of furniture from rustic to Regency, lots to look at inc Spy caricatures, staffordshire dogs, a fishnet stocking kicking out from the wall and a jokey 'Malteser grader' (a giant copper skimmer); Ringwood Best and guests like Bowmans, Otter and Triple fff, straightforward bar food; piped music; children away from bar and dogs welcome, terrace, boules, woodland walks nearby, close to Hillier gardens *(John and Enid Morris, LYM, Gene and Kitty Rankin, Mrs Margo Finlay, Jörg Kasprowski)*

BRAMBRIDGE [SU4721]

☆ *Dog & Crook* SO50 6HZ [nr M3 junction 12, via B3335]: Cheerful bustling 18th-c pub, traditional home-made food inc plenty of fresh fish, cosy dining room, beamed bar with friendly drinking end, Fullers and

Ringwood ales, lots of wines by the glass, neat efficient staff; piped music, TV, regular events and summer music nights; dogs welcome, garden with heated decking and arbour, Itchen Way walks nearby (Ann and Colin Hunt, Phyl and Jack Street, LYM)

BROOK [SU2713]

☆ **Green Dragon** SO43 7HE [B3078 NW of Cadnam, just off M27 junction 1]: Immaculate old New Forest dining pub dating from 15th c, good welcoming service even when busy, enjoyable fresh food inc plenty of seasonal game and fish as well as sensibly priced pubby favourites, well kept Fullers and Ringwood, daily papers, bright linked areas with stripped pine and other pubby furnishings; attractive small terrace and larger garden, paddocks beyond, picturesque village (PL, Bob and Angela Brooks, R and M Thomas, Howard G Allen, BB)

BROUGHTON [SU3032]

Greyhound SO20 8AA [High St]: Reopened after major refurbishment, good food with italian emphasis, cheerful staff; dogs allowed in bar, disabled facilities, good local walks (John Balfour)

Tally Ho SO20 8AA [High St, opp church; signed off A30 Stockbridge—Salisbury]: Relaxed local atmosphere in open-plan largely tiled square bar, helpful welcoming landlady, good value home-made food from sandwiches up, two well kept Ringwood ales, good house wines, two open fires, hunting prints and other pictures, darts, no piped music; children welcome, charming secluded back garden, good walks; has been cl Tues (Ann and Colin Hunt, BB)

BURGHCLERE [SU4660]

Carpenters Arms RG20 9JY [Harts Lane, off A34]: Small unpretentious pub with well kept Arkells ales (some tapped from the cask), sensibly priced home-made food, helpful staff, good country views from dining extension and terrace picnic-sets, open fire; children and dogs welcome (resident springers), handy for Sandham Memorial Chapel (NT), six comfortable annexe bedrooms, open all day (Mr and Mrs H J Langley, John Quinn, Sean Dunn)

BURLEY [SU2103]

Queens Head BH24 4AB [The Cross; back rd Ringwood—Lymington]: Large pub dating partly from 17th c and probably earlier, several rambling rooms, good friendly atmosphere, some flagstones, beams, timbering and panelling, wide choice of food all day inc deals, well kept ales, nice coffee; pub and New Forest village can get packed in summer; children welcome, open all day (LYM, Dennis and Doreen Haward, Ann and Colin Hunt)

☆ **White Buck** BH24 4AZ [Bisterne Close; 0.7 miles E, OS Sheet 195 map ref 223028]: Long comfortably divided bar in 19th-c mock-Tudor hotel, popular and welcoming, with vast choice of enjoyable generous food, Fullers/Gales and a guest beer, good wines by the glass and coffee, lots of pictures, log

fires each end, courteous attentive staff, pleasant dining room with tables out on decking (should book – but no bookings Sun lunchtime); children and dogs welcome, heated front terrace and spacious lawn, lovely New Forest setting, superb walks towards Burley itself and over Mill Lawn, good quiet bedrooms, open all day (BB, Sara Fulton, Roger Baker, Mrs Joy Griffiths, John and Joan Calvert, Mr and Mrs D Hammond, Gill and Keith Croxton)

BURSLEDON [SU4809]

☆ **Fox & Hounds** SO31 8DE [Hungerford Bottom; 2 miles from M27 junction 8]: Popular rambling 16th-c Chef & Brewer of unusual character, ancient beams, flagstones and big log fires, linked by pleasant family conservatory area to ancient back barn with buoyant rustic atmosphere, lantern-lit side stalls, lots of interesting farm equipment; real ales such as Adnams and Ringwood, lots of wines, good coffee, enjoyable reasonably priced food from sandwiches up, cheerful obliging staff, daily papers; children allowed, tables outside (Phyl and Jack Street, LYM)

☆ **Jolly Sailor** SO31 8DN [off A27 towards Bursledon Station, Lands End Rd; handy for M27 junction 8]: Busy efficiently laid out Badger dining pub in prime spot overlooking yachting inlet, good service, reliable food, their usual ales and good wine choice, log fires; open all day (LYM, the Didler, Gael Pawson)

CADNAM [SU2913]

☆ **Sir John Barleycorn** SO40 2NP [Old Romsey Rd; by M27 junction 1]: Wide choice of good up-to-date food in picturesque low-slung thatched pub extended from cosy beamed and timbered medieval core, good service, Ringwood and a guest such as St Austell Tribute, two log fires, modern décor and stripped wood flooring; dogs and children welcome, suntrap benches in front and out in colourful garden, open all day (Phyl and Jack Street, Bob and Angela Brooks, LYM)

White Hart SO40 2NP [Old Romsey Rd, handy for M27 junction 1]: Big rambling Blubeckers family restaurant pub, enjoyable food all day, Greene King ales, cheerful efficient service, spotless simple modern furnishings on parquet floors, stripped brickwork; piped music; garden tables, play area (Mike Gorton, Mrs Joy Griffiths, LYM)

CANTERTON [SU2613]

Sir Walter Tyrell SO43 7HD [off A31 W of Cadnam, follow Rufus's Stone sign]: Large pretty pub by lovely New Forest clearing often with ponies, hard-working staff coping well with families and big groups, well kept ales inc Ringwood, popular enjoyable food, long divided front bar, long back dining room; big play area, sheltered terrace, adjacent camp site, good base for walks (Howard G Allen)

CHALTON [SU7316]

☆ **Red Lion** PO8 0BG [off A3 Petersfield—Horndean]: Largely extended thatched all-day dining pub with interesting 16th-c core around ancient inglenook fireplace, wide range of food from good sandwiches up, well kept Fullers/Gales ales and lots of country wines, decent coffee, helpful smart staff, well spaced tables; children and dogs allowed, good disabled access and facilities, nice views from neat rows of picnic-sets on rectangular lawn by large car park, good walks, handy for Queen Elizabeth Country Park, open all day (Ann and Colin Hunt, David M Smith, Conor McGaughey, LYM)

CHARLTON DOWN [SU3549]
Hare & Hounds SP11 0JA [Hungerford Lane, off A343 N of Andover]: Comfortable tucked-away country pub, enjoyable food inc fresh fish and vegetarian dishes in recently extended dining area, real ales, log fires, friendly staff; pleasant terrace, good walks, cl Sun evening, Mon (Phyl and Jack Street, BB)

CHARTER ALLEY [SU5957]
White Hart RG26 5QA [White Hart Lane, off A340 N of Basingstoke]: Handsome beamed village pub with Palmers, Triple fff and guests, continental beers, summer farm cider, decent wines inc country ones, food from baps up (not Sun evening), comfortable lounge bar with woodburner in big fireplace, dining area, simple public bar with skittle alley; small garden and water-feature terrace, nine bedrooms, open all day Sun (J V Dadswell)

CHAWTON [SU7037]
☆ *Greyfriar* GU34 1SB [off A31/A32 S of Alton; Winchester Rd]: Popular flower-decked beamed dining pub opp Jane Austen's house, enjoyable if pricey food from good baguettes and sandwiches up, Sun roasts, Fullers ales, decent wines by the glass, good coffees, relaxed atmosphere and quite a few older midweek lunchers, comfortable seating and sturdy pine tables in neat linked areas, open fire in restaurant end; piped music; dogs in bar, children till 9pm, tables on terrace in small garden, good nearby walks, open all day (Patrick Spence, LYM, Ann and Colin Hunt, Maureen and Keith Gimson, Tracey and Stephen Groves)

CHILWORTH [SU4118]
☆ *Chilworth Arms* SO16 7JZ [Chilworth Rd (A27 Southampton—Romsey)]: Stylish modern dining pub with popular italian-influenced food from home-made pizzas to more adventurous things, fixed-price lunch/early evening menu Mon-Thurs, good wine choice, well kept ales, neat efficient young staff, chunky furniture inc quite a lot of leather, log fires, conservatory-style back restaurant, chattier areas too; piped nostalgic music; disabled facilities, large neat garden with terrace, open all day (Phyl and Jack Street, Howard G Allen, BB, Dr and Mrs A K Clarke)

COLDEN COMMON [SU4722]
Rising Sun SO21 1SB [Spring Lane]: Two welcoming bars, one with games area, film star pictures, arched red-carpeted dining

room, sensibly priced straightforward food from sandwiches up, OAP lunch, cheerful service, real ales such as Fullers/Gales and Ringwood Best; quiet piped music; big garden with play area (Phyl and Jack Street)

CRAWLEY [SU4233]
Rack & Manger SO21 2PH [B3049 (former A272), about 5 miles N of Winchester]: Light and airy extended roadside pub under newish management, good interesting food with italian influences, well kept Greene King ales; garden, downland surroundings (Mike Markwick)

CRONDALL [SU7948]
Plume of Feathers GU10 5NT [The Borough]: Attractive smallish 15th-c village pub popular for good range of home-made food from standards to more innovative dishes, friendly helpful staff, well kept Greene King and some unusual guests, good wines by the glass, beams and dark wood, prints on cream walls, log fire in big brick fireplace; children welcome, picturesque village (KC)

CROOKHAM [SU7952]
Exchequer GU51 5SU [Crondall Rd]: Former George & Lobster refurbished by new owner, three local ales tapped from the cask, locally sourced food (not Sun evening) in bar and restaurant, bar games and quiz nights; piped music; nr Basingstoke Canal and popular with walkers, open all day wknds (anon)

DAMERHAM [SU1016]
☆ *Compasses* SP6 3HQ [signed off B3078 in Fordingbridge, or off A354 via Martin; East End]: Appealing old country inn, well kept ales inc Ringwood, good choice of wines by the glass, lots of malt whiskies, good food from sandwiches up, small neat lounge bar divided by log fire from pleasant dining area with booth seating, pale wood tables and kitchen chairs, conservatory, separate bar with pool, friendly locals and dogs; children welcome, long pretty garden by attractive village's cricket ground, high downland walks, nice bedrooms (N R White)

DIBDEN PURLIEU [SU4106]
Heath SO45 4PU [Beaulieu Rd; B3054/A326 roundabout]: Comfortable and welcoming family dining pub, popular and spacious, with bright clean contemporary linked areas, good choice of enjoyable food all day, hardworking friendly young staff, beers such as Ringwood, Shepherd Neame Spitfire and Wadworths 6X (Phyl and Jack Street)

DROXFORD [SU6118]
Hurdles SO32 3QT [Station Rd, Brockbridge]: Smart warmly welcoming dining pub mixing traditional with modern, good interesting food from baguettes up inc good value set menu (Mon-Fri), monthly gourmet evenings, prompt service, several wines by the glass (some quite pricey), Bowmans Wallops Wood, Hop Back Summer Lightning and Ringwood Best, chesterfields by log fire; children and dogs welcome, plenty of garden tables, smokers' shelter, open all day wknds (till 8 Sun) (Phyl and Jack Street, Sally and Tom Matson, Roger and Anne Mallard)

DUMMER [SU5846]

Queen RG25 2AD [under a mile from M3 junction 7; take Dummer slip road]: Comfortable beamed pub well divided with lots of softly lit alcoves, Courage Best, Fullers London Pride, John Smiths and a guest such as Hogs Back TEA, decent choice of wines by the glass, popular food from lunchtime sandwiches and light dishes up, friendly service (can be slow), big log fire, Queen and steeplechase prints, no mobile phones, restaurant allowing children; games machine, well reproduced piped music; picnic-sets under cocktail parasols on terrace and in extended back garden, attractive village with ancient church *(LYM, Mrs Ann Gray)*

DURLEY [SU5116]

Farmers Home S032 2BT [B3354 and B2177; Heathen St/Curdridge Rd]: Helpful long-serving landlord in comfortable beamed pub with two-bay dining area and big restaurant, generous reasonably priced food inc fresh fish and lovely puddings, good service, well kept Fullers/Gales ales and Ringwood Best, decent wine, log fire; children welcome, big garden with good play area, nice walks *(Phyl and Jack Street)*

☆ *Robin Hood* S032 2AA [Durley Street, just off B2177 Bishops Waltham—Winchester – brown signs to pub]: Open-plan beamed pub under same enthusiastic licensees as the Plough at Sparsholt (see Main Entries), friendly welcoming staff, well kept Greene King ales, reliably good food from varied menu, log fire and leather sofas in bare-boards bar, dining area with stone floors and mix of old pine tables and chairs, bookcase door to lavatories; children and dogs welcome, disabled facilities, decked terrace with barbecue, garden with play area and nice country views, open all day Sun *(Phyl and Jack Street, LYM, CES)*

EAST BOLDRE [SU3700]

☆ *Turf Cutters Arms* S042 7WL [Main Rd]: Small dim-lit New Forest country local under welcoming licensees, ponies wandering past, perhaps a regular arriving on horseback, lots of beams and pictures, nicely worn-in furnishings on bare boards and flagstones, log fire, simple local food from sandwiches and basic dishes to quite a lot of game, good choice of well kept ales, several dozen malt whiskies; children welcome, garden tables, good heathland walks *(BB, Phil and Sally Gorton)*

EAST END [SZ3696]

East End Arms S041 5SY [back road Lymington—Beaulieu, parallel to B3054]: Civilised and friendly New Forest country local, stylish and enterprising meals making a nice contrast with the simplicity of its plain bright bar, log fire, well kept Ringwood Best on handpump and other ales tapped from the cask, good choice of wines by the glass, helpful staff, longish neat candlelit dining lounge with nice pictures; tables in small pleasant garden, popular with families *(BB, Dr Martin Owton, Phil and Sally Gorton)*

EAST MEON [SU6822]

☆ *Olde George* GU32 1NH [Church St; signed off A272 W of Petersfield, and off A32 in West Meon]: Relaxing heavy-beamed rustic pub popular for bar and restaurant food from sandwiches up, good service, inglenook log fires, cosy areas around central bar counter, Badger ales, good choice of wines; children welcome, nice back terrace, five comfortable bedrooms (book well ahead), good breakfast, pretty village with fine church, good walks *(Ann and Colin Hunt, LYM, E Clark, W A Eversched)*

EASTON [SU5132]

Cricketers S021 1EJ [off B3047]: Pleasantly smartened-up traditional local, home-made food with some modern touches in bar and smallish restaurant, good friendly service, Marstons-related ales inc Ringwood, good choice of wines by the glass, dark tables and chairs on carpet, bare-boards area with darts, shove-ha'penny and other games; sports TV, piped music (and some live); children and dogs welcome, front terrace with heated smokers' shelter, handy for Itchen Way walks, three bedrooms, open all day summer *(BB, Ann and Colin Hunt, Mrs Margaret Weir)*

EMERY DOWN [SU2808]

☆ *New Forest* S043 7DY [village signed off A35 just W of Lyndhurst]: In one of the best bits of the Forest for walking, well run and popular, with good reasonably priced food (all day wknds) inc local venison, friendly attentive uniformed staff, ales such as Fullers, Ringwood and Shepherd Neame, real cider, good choice of wines by the glass, coffee and tea all day, attractive softly lit separate areas on varying levels, each with its own character, hunting prints, two log fires; piped music; children and dogs welcome, covered heated terrace, small pleasant three-level garden, bedrooms, open all day *(N R White, Martin Gough, Mr and Mrs D Hammond, Stephen Moss, LYM, Mr and Mrs Roberts)*

EMSWORTH [SU7405]

Blue Bell PO10 7EG [South St]: Small timeless quayside pub with memorabilia everywhere, friendly busy atmosphere, good choice of popular no-nonsense food (not Sun eve) inc local fish, should book wknds, Sharps Doom Bar and guest, live music; dogs welcome, terrace, Sun market in adjacent car park, open all day *(Terry and Nickie Williams, Ann and Colin Hunt, Miss A G Drake, Graham Middleton)*

☆ *Coal Exchange* PO10 7EG [Ships Quay, South St]: Cosy cheerful L-shaped Victorian local nr harbour, well kept Fullers range and a guest ale, good value home-made food inc some unusual choices, Tues curry night, log fire each end, low ceilings; dogs welcome, tables outside, handy for Wayfarers Walk and Solent Walk, open all day Fri-Sun *(Ann and Colin Hunt, Tony and Wendy Hobden, Caryn Mackenzie)*

ENBORNE [SU4264]
Craven Arms RG20 0HG [W, towards Hamstead Marshall]: Welcoming roadside country pub with good choice of well kept ales, decent changing food; children welcome, plenty of room in and out, play area and summer barbecues *(Peter and Jean Hoare)*

☆ *Golden Pot* RG27 0NB [B3272]: Small attractive creeper-covered dining pub with very good food from traditional to more imaginative things, small helpings available, carvery Sun lunchtime, three changing ales, good choice of wines by the glass inc champagne, neatly refurbished linked areas, efficient cheerful service; piped music – live Mon; dogs allowed in bar, tables outside amongst colourful flowers, cl Sun evening *(Joan and Tony Walker, Mrs Pam Mattinson, KC, LYM)*

EVERTON [SZ2994]
Crown SO41 0JJ [Old Christchurch Rd; pub signed just off A337 W of Lymington]: Quietly set New Forest-edge restaurant/pub with enjoyable varied food, good service, Ringwood and guest ales, reliable wine choice, two attractive dining rooms off tiled-floor bar, log fires; picnic-sets on front terrace and in garden behind *(Phyl and Jack Street, David Sizer, BB)*

EXTON [SU6120]
☆ *Shoe* SO32 3NT [village signposted from A32 NE of Bishop's Waltham]: New licensees for pleasant country pub on South Downs Way, three linked rooms with log fires, Wadworths 6X, IPA and seasonal guest, traditional food; children and dogs welcome, disabled facilities, seats under parasols at front, more in garden across lane overlooking River Meon *(BB)*

FAIR OAK [SU4919]
Fox SO50 7HB [Winchester Rd (A3051)]: Popular smartly refurbished pub with enjoyable food (all day wknds) inc breakfast and wkdy lunchtime bargains, nice wine, welcoming bright young staff, modern décor in lounge, restaurant, coffee room and conservatory; big garden, path to nearby Bishopstoke woods, open all day *(Phyl and Jack Street)*

Lapstone SO50 7AP [Botley Rd]: Traditional pub atmosphere, well kept ales such as Sharps Doom Bar, good value standard food, friendly staff, live music and quiz nights; children and dogs welcome, nice back garden with play area, open all day Fri-Sat, Sun 12-9, cl Mon *(Ann and Colin Hunt)*

FAREHAM [SU5206]
Sir Joseph Paxton PO14 4PF [Hunts Pond Rd]: Sizable pub on edge of estate, cosy beamed part with larger plainer area off, well kept ales such as St Austell Tribute, straightforward cheap bar food, friendly staff *(Ann and Colin Hunt)*

FARNBOROUGH [SU8756]
☆ *Prince of Wales* GU14 8AL [Rectory Rd, nr stn]: Half a dozen or more good changing ales in friendly Edwardian local, stripped brickwork, open fire and antiquey touches in its three small linked areas, popular lunchtime food (not Sun) from sandwiches to imaginative specials, good friendly service, decent malt whiskies; open all day Sun *(Dr Martin Owton, Thurstan Johnston, Phil and Sally Gorton)*

FARRINGDON [SU7135]
Rose & Crown GU34 3ED [off A32 S of Alton; Crows Lane – follow Church, Selborne, Liss signpost]: Comfortable airy 19th-c pub with attractive L-shaped bar, friendly attentive service, well kept ales inc Adnams, good food (all day Sun) with some interesting choices inc vegetarian, formal back dining room, jazz nights (last Mon of month); well behaved children and dogs welcome, wide views from big back garden, open all day wknds *(BB, Ann and Colin Hunt, Tony and Jill Radnor, Simon Collett-Jones)*

FINCHDEAN [SU7312]
George PO8 0AU: Cosy front bar with larger back eating area, good value food, smart efficient staff, well kept Wells & Youngs ales; dogs allowed in bar, good nearby walks, open all day Sun *(Ann and Colin Hunt, W A Evershed)*

GOSPORT [SZ6100]
Queens PO12 1LG [Queens Rd]: Classic bare-boards local, long-serving landlady keeps Ringwood Fortyniner, Roosters, Wells & Youngs Special and two guests in top condition, beer festivals, quick service, three areas off bar with good log fire in interesting carved fireplace, sensibly placed darts; TV room – children welcome here daytime; cl lunchtimes Mon-Thurs, open all day Sat *(Ann and Colin Hunt)*

HAMBLE [SU4806]
Olde Whyte Harte SO31 4JF [High St; 3 miles from M27 junction 8]: Proper village pub, locally popular, with big inglenook log fire, well integrated flagstoned eating area allowing children, generous fresh food all day, Fullers/Gales ales, good wines by the glass, decent coffee, cheeky graffiti on low dark 16th-c beams, monkeys and yachting memorabilia; piped music; small walled garden, handy for nature reserve, open all day *(LYM, Gael Pawson, Terry and Nickie Williams, Ann and Colin Hunt)*

Victory SO31 4HA [High St]: Enjoyable ample bar food at reasonable prices, cheerful welcoming staff; well kept ales, nautical theme *(Samuel Fancett)*

HAMBLEDON [SU6414]
Vine PO7 4RW [West St]: Welcoming 400-year-old beamed village local, well kept Marstons ales, reasonably priced food, good service, nice mix of furnishings, old sporting/country prints, bric-a-brac; garden with decking, good walks *(LYM, Patrick Spence, Ann and Colin Hunt, Mike Samuels)*

HANNINGTON [SU5455]
Vine RG26 5TX [signposted off A339]: Spacious 19th-c village pub with light bright

décor, comfy leather sofas and woodburner, popular food from standards up using home-grown produce, real ales such as Black Sheep and Fullers London Pride, friendly service, dining conservatory; children and dogs welcome, big garden with terrace, nice spot up on downs, good walks, cl Sun evening and Mon in winter *(Ann and Colin Hunt, N R White)*

HARTLEY WINTNEY [SU7656]
Cricketers RG27 8QB [Cricket Green]: Nice setting opp cricket green, leisurely and relaxed, with a couple of easy chairs, cricket memorabilia, well kept Caledonian Deuchars IPA, Courage Directors and Sharps Doom Bar, enjoyable bar food and good value linked french restaurant, extensive wine list, friendly efficient service; some tables outside *(LM)*

HAYLING ISLAND [SU7098]
Inn on the Beach PO11 0AS [Sea Front, South Hayling]: Largish modern pub on shingle, revamped by new owners but keeping nautical theme, good choice of food, Hogs Back ales, friendly staff, lovely IOW views *(Geoff and Linda Payne)*
Maypole PO11 0PS: Spotless two-bar local well run by hard-working couple, parquet floors and polished panelling, plenty of good seating, well kept Fullers/Gales beers, good choice of generous reasonably priced pub food inc fish on Fri; garden *(Terry and Nickie Williams)*

HIGHCLERE [SU4358]
Yew Tree RG20 9SE [Hollington Cross]: Marco Pierre White's smartly reworked country inn, good food not too expensive in nicely furnished comfortable low-beamed eating areas, relaxed civilised atmosphere, serious wine list, efficient service, stylish contemporary bar, big inglenook log fire, attractive lighting and pictures; picnic-sets under cocktail parasols on pleasant terrace, six good bedrooms *(LYM, Hunter and Christine Wright)*

HILL HEAD [SU5402]
Osborne View PO14 3JR [Hill Head Rd]: Modern extended clifftop Badger dining pub, enjoyable food from baguettes up, their ales kept well, three stepped-back levels and picture windows for stunning IOW views, nautical prints and memorabilia, lots of stripped wood and red carpet, young staff; may be piped music, busy wknds; garden and beach access, nr Titchfield Haven bird reserve, open all day *(Val and Alan Green, Ann and Colin Hunt)*

HILL TOP [SU4003]
Royal Oak SO42 7YR [B3054 Beaulieu—Hythe]: Good-sized pub looking out over New Forest, well kept Adnams, Ringwood and Wadworths, good range of above-average food (all day wknds); pleasant garden behind, handy for Exbury Gardens *(Dr Martin Owton, Phil and Sally Gorton, Phyl and Jack Street)*

HOLBURY [SU4203]
Bridge Tavern SO45 2HD [Ipers Bridge; Rollestone Rd just W, towards Beaulieu]: In

pleasant spot by New Forest, welcoming landlord, well kept Robinsons, cosy locals bar with nice fire, restaurant; streamside garden *(Phil and Sally Gorton)*

HOOK [SU7354]
Crooked Billet RG27 9EH [A30 about a mile towards London]: Comfortably extended and welcoming roadside pub with large dining area, wide choice of enjoyable food inc interesting specials and plenty of fish, swift helpful service, well kept Courage Best and Directors and a quickly changing guest beer, reasonably priced wines, good range of soft drinks, daily papers in area with sofa and log fire; soft piped music; children welcome, attractive smallish garden by stream with trout and ducks *(Mike and Monnie Jefferies)*
Hogget RG27 9JJ [a mile W, A30/A287]: Nicely refurbished and extended with emphasis on dining side, good home-made food from local ingredients inc lunchtime set deals, well kept Marstons-related ales, good wines by the glass, friendly relaxed atmosphere; heated outside area, open all day (from 7.30am Fri for breakfast) *(Peter Mercer, David and Sue Smith, Jennifer Banks)*

HORDLE [SZ2996]
Mill at Gordleton SO41 6DJ [Silver St]: More upmarket restaurant-with-rooms than pub but does have bar, Piddle and Ringwood ales, good wines, friendly helpful staff, good if not cheap food; pretty garden with waterside terraces, seven smart comfortable bedrooms *(N R White)*

HORSEBRIDGE [SU3430]
John o' Gaunt SO20 6PU [off A3057 Romsey—Andover, just SW of Kings Somborne]: Unspoilt traditional pub in River Test village, good value food, friendly service, ales such as Ringwood, Palmers and Timothy Taylors, log fire in simple L-shaped bar, nice prints in small back dining area; can get busy wknds; picnic-sets out in side arbour *(BB, Ann and Colin Hunt)*

HOUGHTON [SU3432]
☆ *Boot* SO20 6LH [Village signposted off A30 in Stockbridge]: Bustling country local with lots of stuffed creatures in cheery log-fire bar, good local Andwell ales, food generous and generally good from interesting baguettes up, nice relaxed service, roomy more decorous lounge/dining room; well behaved children and dogs welcome, long garden with half a dozen picnic-sets down by lovely (unfenced) stretch of River Test, where they have fishing; good walks, and opp Test Way cycle path *(LYM, Robert Watt, Edward Mirzoeff, Ann and Colin Hunt, Martin and Karen Wake)*

HURSLEY [SU4225]
Kings Head SO21 2JW [A3090 Winchester—Romsey]: Substantial welcoming pub doing enjoyable local food, well kept ales such as Greene King and Wells & Youngs; garden tables, six comfortable bedrooms, open all day Fri and Sun *(Chris and Jeanne Downing)*

ITCHEN ABBAS [SU5332]
Trout SO21 1BQ [4 miles from M3 junction 9; B3047]: Restaurant and bar in former coaching inn, efficient italian manager and helpful staff, enjoyable food from baguettes and pubby favourites up, Sun roasts, Greene King ales, good value wines; quiz nights; children welcome, tables and play area in sheltered pretty side garden, three bedrooms *(Tony and Jill Radnor, LYM)*

KEYHAVEN [SZ3091]
☆ *Gun* SO41 0TP: Busy rambling 17th-c pub looking over boatyard and sea to Isle of Wight, low-beamed bar with nautical bric-a-brac and plenty of character (less in family rooms and conservatory), good generous local food inc crab, well kept beers tapped from the cask such as Flowers Original, Ringwood Best, Shepherd Neame Spitfire and Wychwood Hobgoblin, lots of malt whiskies, helpful young staff, bar billiards; piped music; tables out in front and in big back garden with swings and fishpond, can stroll down to small harbour and walk to Hurst Castle *(BB, Norma and David Hardy, N R White, Jenny and Brian Seller)*

KINGS WORTHY [SU4932]
Cart & Horses SO23 7QN [A3090 E of Winchester, just off A33]: Fully revamped adding modern touches to traditional interior, cosy corners, beams and inglenook, interesting range of food, Greene King Old Speckled Hen and a guest, Aspall's cider, good choice of wines by the glass, skittle alley; tables out at front *(LYM)*

KINGSCLERE [SU5160]
Star RG20 4SY [A339 N of Kingsclere]: 19th-c beamed Vintage Inn, central log-fire bar flanked by two simple dining areas, village pub atmosphere, Ringwood ales, good choice of food from pubby dishes up, efficient friendly service even when busy; some picnic-sets on grass at front *(KC)*
Swan RG20 5PP [Swan St]: Old-fashioned 15th-c village inn, lots of beams, welcoming landlord and friendly helpful staff, Theakstons XB and two guests, enjoyable reasonably priced home-made food (not Sun evening); dogs welcome, tables outside, good walks, nine bedrooms *(Ann and Colin Hunt)*

LANGSTONE [SU7104]
Ship PO9 1RD [A3023]: Busy waterside 18th-c former grain store, lovely views to Hayling Island from roomy softly lit nautical bar with upper deck dining room, Fullers ales, good choice of wines by the glass, log fire, wide range of generous reasonably priced food inc local fish and venison; children welcome, plenty of tables on heated terrace by quiet quay, good coast walks, open all day *(Andy West, W A Evershed, Irene and Derek Flewin)*

LINWOOD [SU2110]
High Corner BH24 3QY [signed from A338 via Moyles Court, and from A31; keep on]: Big rambling pub very popular for its splendid New Forest position up a track,

with extensive neatly kept wooded garden and lots for children to do; some character in original upper bar with log fire, big back extensions for the summer crowds, nicely partitioned restaurant, verandah lounge, interesting family rooms, wide choice of generous bar snacks and restaurant-style food, well kept Wadworths; welcomes dogs and horses (stables and paddock available), seven redecorated bedrooms, has been open all day wknds *(Mr and Mrs W W Burke, Dennis and Doreen Haward, LYM)*
Red Shoot BH24 3QT [signed from A338 via Moyles Court, and from A31; go on up heath to junction with Toms Lane]: Nice New Forest setting, big picture-window bar with attractive old tables, mixed chairs and rugs on bare boards, country pictures on puce walls, large back dining area, generous honest good value food, friendly helpful staff, well kept Greene King IPA, Wadworths 6X and two or three ales brewed at the pub inc Muddy Boot (beer festivals Apr and Oct), log fire; children, dogs and muddy boots welcome, some disabled access, sheltered side terrace, open all day wknds and summer – very touristy then (by big campsite and caravan park) *(BB, S Harris)*

LISS [SU7728]
Blue Bell GU33 6JE [Farnham Rd, West Liss]: Pleasant old pub with helpful staff, decent bar snacks, more innovative food in restaurant, good wine list, Wychwood and Ringwood ales, pool room; piped music; garden with terrace *(Michael and Jenny Back)*

LOCKS HEATH [SU5006]
☆ *Jolly Farmer* SO31 9JH [Fleet End Rd, not far from M27 junction 9]: Flower-decked pub with relaxing series of softly lit linked rooms, nice old scrubbed tables and masses of interesting bric-a-brac and prints, wide choice of enjoyable popular food (all day wknds) inc good value two-sitting Sun lunch, interesting long-serving landlord and good friendly service, Fullers/Gales ales, decent wines inc country ones, coal-effect gas fires; two sheltered terraces (one with play area and children's lavatories), nearby walks, five nice bedrooms, good breakfast, open all day *(Phyl and Jack Street, M G Hart, Ann and Colin Hunt, LYM)*

LONG SUTTON [SU7447]
☆ *Four Horseshoes* RG29 1TA [signed off B3349 S of Hook]: Welcoming open-plan black-beamed country local with two log fires, long-serving landlord cooking bargain pubby food, friendly landlady serving good range of changing ales such as Palmers, decent wines and country wine, no piped music or machines, small glazed-in verandah; disabled access, picnic-sets on grass over road, boules and play area, three good value bedrooms (bunk beds available for cyclist/walkers) *(Tony and Jill Radnor, BB)*

LONGPARISH [SU4344]
Cricketers SP11 6PZ: Cheerful homely village pub with good chatty landlady, connecting rooms and cosy corners, woodburner, wide

choice of carefully cooked food from light snacks up, prompt service, good range of real ales; sizeable back garden; cl Mon *(Phyl and Jack Street)*

LONGSTOCK [SU3537]

☆ *Peat Spade* SO20 6DR [off A30 on W edge of Stockbridge]: Airy attractive dining pub with enjoyable food (evenings are more restauranty than pubby), friendly efficient service, Ringwood Best and a guest, several wines by the glass, bistroish décor with fishing/shooting theme, upstairs lounge; no under-10s; dogs welcome in bar, pleasant courtyard tables, plenty of Test Way and water-meadow walks, good fishing by arrangement, nicely furnished if not over-large bedrooms, open all day *(Phyl and Jack Street, LYM)*

LOWER SWANWICK [SU4909]

Ship SO31 7FN [Bridge Rd]: Friendly Fullers pub with their beers, decent wines, reasonably priced pubby food, comfortable panelled lounge, lots of marine memorabilia, separate eating area, good River Hamble views and walks *(Val and Alan Green)*

LYMINGTON [SZ3293]

☆ *Chequers* SO41 8AH [Ridgeway Lane, Lower Woodside – dead end just S of A337 roundabout W of Lymington, by White Hart]: Old beamed pub with enjoyable good value food, real ales such as Ringwood, good wines by the glass, polished boards and quarry tiles, attractive pictures, plain chairs and wall pews, woodburner, traditional games; well behaved children and dogs allowed, tables and summer marquee in neat walled back garden, attractive front terrace, good walks and handy for bird-watching on Pennington Marshes *(Pete Coxon, Nick Horne, Louise McKee, Franklyn Roberts, LYM)*

☆ *Fishermans* SO41 8FD [All Saints Rd, Woodside]: Nice welcoming atmosphere, good choice of traditional and more interesting food inc popular Sun lunch, friendly helpful staff, well kept Fullers and guests, decent wines *(John and Christine Cross, Colin Wood, David Sizer)*

☆ *Kings Head* SO41 3AR [Quay Hill]: In steep cobbled lane of smart small shops, friendly dimly lit old local with Adnams, Fullers/Gales, Greene King and Ringwood ales, several wines by the glass, pleasant helpful staff, good choice of sensibly priced standard food, nicely mixed old-fashioned furnishings in rambling beamed and mainly bare-boarded rooms, log fire, good classic yacht photographs, daily papers; may be piped music, can get very busy; children and dogs welcome, nice little sunny courtyard behind, open all day wknds *(M Ross-Thomas, Alan Wright, Ian Herdman, LYM, Neil Edmundson, N R White, Louise McKee, Stephen Shepherd)*

Wagon & Horses SO41 5SB [Undershore Rd; rd to IOW ferry]: Well run comfortable Wadworths pub, friendly staff, some interesting food, beamed restaurant with

leaded windows, games room; terrace tables, handy for IOW ferry *(Chris Sale, Joan and Michel Hooper-Immins)*

LYNDHURST [SU2908]

Crown SO43 7NF [top end of High St opposite church]: Best Western hotel bar with cheerful log fire and comfortable leather seating, enjoyable food from sandwiches up, good service, Ringwood ales, several wines by the glass, good coffee, lounge overlooking garden, restaurant; piped music; comfortable bedrooms, good breakfast *(George Atkinson, Phyl and Jack Street)*

Fox & Hounds SO43 7BG [High St]: Big busy low-beamed pub, comfortable and much-modernised, with good range of food inc blackboard specials, obliging staff, Ringwood and several other ales, decent wines, exposed brickwork and standing timbers, family room beyond former coach entry, games room; four bedrooms *(John Robertson, Phyl and Jack Street)*

MARCHWOOD [SU3809]

Pilgrim SO40 4WU [Hythe Rd, off A326 at Twiggs Lane]: Popular picturesque thatched pub, good choice of enjoyable sensibly priced food inc Sun lunch, good friendly service, well kept Fullers ales, open fires; bedroom block in former restaurant across road *(Phyl and Jack Street, LYM, Paula Crompton)*

MATTINGLEY [SU7357]

Leather Bottle RG27 8JU [3 miles from M3, junction 5; in Hook, turn right then left on to B3349 Reading Road (former A32)]: Old red-brick Blubeckers pub, decent all-day pubby food, welcoming staff, ales such as Andwell and Fullers, well spaced tables in linked areas, black beams, flagstones and bare boards, inglenook log fire, extension opening on to covered terrace; piped music; dogs welcome in bar, disabled facilities, two garden areas, open all day *(LYM, KC)*

MINLEY MANOR [SU8357]

Crown & Cushion GU17 9UA [A327, just N of M3 junction 4A]: Attractive small traditional pub with enjoyable fairly priced food inc some unusual choices, well kept Shepherd Neame ales, coal-effect gas fire; big separate raftered and flagstoned rustic 'meade hall' behind, very popular wknds (evenings more a young people's meeting place), huge log fire, friendly staff cope well when busy; children in eating area, heated terrace overlooking own cricket pitch *(LYM, Peter Sampson, David and Sue Smith)*

MINSTEAD [SU2810]

Trusty Servant SO43 7FY [just off A31, not far from M27 junction 1]: Attractive 19th-c building in pretty New Forest hamlet with interesting church, wandering cattle and ponies and plenty of easy walks; bright and simple mildly upscale refurbishment, two-room bar and big dining room, welcoming management, good drinks choice, enjoyable food from chunky sandwiches up, big sloping garden, open all day *(Caroline McArthur, Ann and Colin Hunt, Bob and Angela Brooks, Kevin Flack, Phyl and Jack Street, LYM)*

MORTIMER WEST END [SU6364]
Red Lion RG7 2HU [Church Rd; Silchester turn off Mortimer—Aldermaston rd]: Smart dining pub under new management, lots of beams, stripped masonry, timbers and panelling, well presented food from panini up, helpful staff, well kept Badger, good range of wines by the glass, log fire; children and dogs welcome, seats in pleasant garden and on small front terrace, handy for Roman Silchester, open all day (LYM, J V Dadswell)

NEWTOWN [SU6112]
Travellers Rest PO17 6LL [off A32 N of Wickham]: Friendly lived-in country pub gently enlarged but still cosy, one chatty local bar, two further rooms mainly for food, four well kept ales, open fires and traditional furnishings; pretty back garden (Val and Alan Green, LYM)

NORTH WALTHAM [SU5645]
☆ *Fox* RG25 2BE [signed off A30 SW of Basingstoke; handy for M3 junction 7]: Good food from sandwiches to venison and popular Sun roasts (best to book), helpful efficient staff, real ales such as Adnams, Ringwood and St Austell, foxy décor, log fire in long bright dining area; children welcome, lovely garden with farmland views, pleasant village in nice spot (walk to Jane Austen's church at Steventon) (Patrick Spence)

ODIHAM [SU7451]
Water Witch RG29 1AL [Colt Hill – quiet no through rd signed off main st]: Olde-worlde décor in nicely kept Chef & Brewer nr picturesque stretch of Basingstoke Canal, big but cosily divided, wide choice of food, good friendly staff, real ales; disabled access, some picnic-sets outside, big garden with children's facilities (Chris and Jeanne Downing)

OTTERBOURNE [SU4623]
Old Forge SO21 2EE [Main Rd]: Popular bistro-style chain pub, comfortable tables spread through linked rooms, wide choice of food all day inc lovely puddings, friendly young staff, ales such as Everards and Timothy Taylors, good choice of wines by the glass, log fires and rather individual décor (PL, Henry Fryer, Phyl and Jack Street, Jeremy Davis)
Otter SO21 2HW [Boyatt Lane off Winchester Rd]: Unpretentious dining pub with enjoyable food, good staff, real ale; garden tables (M and GR, Mrs Joy Griffiths)

OVINGTON [SU5631]
☆ *Bush* SO24 0RE [off A31 W of Alresford]: Charming spot with streamside garden and pergola dining terrace, appealing low-ceilinged bar high-backed settles, pews and masses of old pictures, blazing fire, well kept Wadworths ales, good choice of wines by the glass, good if pricey food (not Sun evening, and they may try to keep your credit card while you eat); children (perhaps best to book) and dogs welcome, nice walks, open all day summer hols and can get very busy

(Julia and Richard Tredgett, LYM, Phil and Sally Gorton, Henry Fryer, Martin and Karen Wake, John and Enid Morris, Pam and John Smith, Ben Andrews)

OWSLEBURY [SU5123]
Ship SO21 1LT [off B2177 Fishers Pond—Lower Upham; Whites Hill]: 17th-c pub with black oak beams and timbers, central log fire, real ales inc Greene King, chesterfield and log fire in bar, pub games and skittle alley, comfortable dining area and restaurant; plenty of space outside (Mr and Mrs A H Young, LYM)

PARK GATE [SU5108]
Village Inn SO31 1AZ [Botley Rd]: Pleasantly refurbished Ember Inn with three well kept ales, decent food with things to share, good welcoming service, civilised family atmosphere (Keith and Sue Ward)

PETERSFIELD [SU7423]
George GU32 3HH [The Square]: Café-style with lots of metal tables outside, Caledonian Deuchars IPA, Skinners Betty Stogs, sandwiches (Ian Phillips)
Good Intent GU31 4AF [College St]: Neat and tidy proper pub with well kept Fullers/Gales and a guest ale, enjoyable fresh pubby food strong on sausages, friendly licensees, low oak beams and log fires in 16th-c core, well spaced good-sized pine tables with flowers, camera collection, cosy family area; piped music, live Sun; dogs welcome, front terrace, bedrooms (Tony and Wendy Hobden, Val and Alan Green)
Square Brewery GU32 3HJ [The Square]: Friendly neatly kept Fullers pub with four of their ales, small choice of above-average sensibly priced pub food, armchairs one end with TV and games machines, popular with after-work drinkers (Jeremy David, Keith and Chris O'Neill)
White Horse GU32 1DA [up on old downs rd about halfway between Steep and East Tisted, nr Priors Dean – OS Sheet 186 or 197 map ref 715290]: Charming building (aka Pub With No Name) high and isolated on the downs, two well worn-in idiosyncratically old-fashioned rustic parlours (candlelit at night), open fires, cheerful staff, good range of well kept ales, beer festivals, family dining room; tables out by floodlit pond, open all day wknds (Ann and Colin Hunt, the Didler, W A Evershed, LYM)

PLAITFORD [SU2719]
Shoe SO51 6EE [Salisbury Rd (A36)]: Roomy place under new management, welcoming attentive staff, well kept ales such as Hop Back and Ringwood, farm cider, enjoyable food, live music; children very welcome, garden, bedrooms (Stephen Moss)

PORTSMOUTH [SZ6399]
Bridge Tavern PO1 2JJ [East St, Camber Dock]: Flagstones, bare boards and lots of dark wood, comfortable furnishings, good water views, Fullers ales, straightforward food from baguettes up, maritime theme; nice waterside terrace (Ann and Colin Hunt, W A Evershed)

Churchillian PO6 3LS [Portsdown Hill Rd, Widley]: Open-plan extended 1960s dining pub with picture-window views over Portsmouth to IOW, Irving Type 42, Marstons Pedigree, Ringwood Best and Shepherd Neame Spitfire, generous home-made pubby food, friendly bustle; may be piped music and machines; terrace picnic-sets, handy for Fort Widley equestrian centre and nature trail *(Nigel and Sue Foster)*

Fountain PO2 9AA [London Rd, North End]: Unchanging tiled pub with large bar and family room off, nicely polished brass, interesting pictures of local pubs, mirrors each end, unusual ceiling lights, well kept beer inc Gales HSB, no food; seats outside *(Ann and Colin Hunt)*

Pembroke PO1 2NR [Pembroke Rd]: Buoyant atmosphere in well run traditional local, unspoilt under long-serving landlord, Bass and Fullers London Pride, fresh rolls; open all day *(Ann and Colin Hunt)*

Still & West PO1 2JL [Bath Sq, Old Portsmouth]: Great location with super views of narrow harbour mouth and across to Isle of Wight, especially from glazed-in panoramic upper family area and waterfront terrace with lots of picnic-sets; nautical bar with fireside sofas and cosy colour scheme, Fullers ales, good choice of wines by the glass, food all day; piped music may be loud, nearby pay & display; children welcome, handy for Historic Dockyard, open all day *(LYM, Paul Rampton, Julie Harding, Kevin Flack, Andy West, Ann and Colin Hunt, W A Evershed)*

Tap PO2 0BQ [London Rd, North End]: Small smartened-up open-plan pub, several well kept ales, straightforward bargain food *(Ann and Colin Hunt)*

PRESTON CANDOVER [SU6041]
Purefoy Arms RG25 2EJ [B3046]: Recently taken over and reworked as gently upmarket dining pub, imaginative food as well as some traditional things, real ale, good choice of wines by the glass, friendly staff, two bare-boards half-panelled bars, lounge and restaurant, some informal atmosphere; dogs welcome, big garden overlooking fields, nearby snowdrop walks, attractive village, cl Sun evening, Mon *(Ann and Colin Hunt)*

ROMSEY [SU3523]
☆ **Dukes Head** SO51 0HB [A3057 out towards Stockbridge]: Attractive 16th-c dining pub with good landlady and friendly staff, small comfortable linked rooms, big log fire, good range of enjoyable food, Ringwood and guest ales, decent wines by the glass; children welcome, sheltered back terrace and pleasant garden, open all day *(LYM, Phyl and Jack Street, J V Dadswell)*

ROTHERWICK [SU7156]
☆ **Falcon** RG27 9BL [off B3349 N of Hook, not far from M3 junction 5]: Big, bright and simply decorated with jovial helpful portuguese landlord, good food (some a little pricey) inc tapas and more usual pub things (roasts etc only on Sun), Fullers

London Pride and Sharps Doom Bar, good wines (plenty of iberian), efficient service; piped music; children and dogs welcome, tables out in front, sizeable back garden, open all day Sun *(D P and M A Miles, David and Sheila Pearcey, David and Sue Smith, Tracey and Stephen Groves, Sharon Oldham, LYM)*

ROWLAND'S CASTLE [SU7310]
☆ **Castle Inn** PO9 6DA [off B2148/B2149 N of Havant; Finchdean Rd]: Cheerful proper country pub with friendly hands-on tenants, comfortable bar with enormous log fire and good choice of Fullers/Gales ales, nice coffee, neat staff, two appealing little dining rooms on left, attractively priced pubby food with more exotic evening choices; children and dogs welcome, pony paddock by good-sized garden, good disabled facilities, open all day *(LYM, Andy West, Ann and Colin Hunt)*

SETLEY [SU3000]
Filly SO42 7UF [Lymington Rd (A337 Brockenhurst—Lymington)]: Popular roadside pub with wide choice of enjoyable generous home-made food inc Sun carvery, Ringwood ales, decent wines, helpful cheerful service, interesting beamed front bar with inglenook, nice roomy eating areas; children welcome, sheltered tables outside, New Forest walks, open all day *(Ann and Colin Hunt, Colin Wood, LYM)*

SHALDEN [SU]
Golden Pot GU34 4DJ [B3349 Odiham Rd N of Alton]: Refurbished and under new management, emphasis on dining but drinkers welcome, modern airy décor with bare boards and log fires, enjoyable food and friendly service, beers inc Andwell; picnic-sets outside *(N R White)*

SHAWFORD [SU4724]
Bridge Hotel SO21 2BP: Reliable beamed riverside Chef & Brewer family dining pub, promptly served enjoyable food all day, efficient friendly staff, Hogs Back TEA, Palmers Copper and Ringwood Fortyniner, decent wines, several interesting rooms, smart décor, cosy nooks and corners; pleasant terrace, big garden, play area, downland and Itchen Way walks *(John and Joan Calvert, Phyl and Jack Street)*

SHEDFIELD [SU5614]
Old Forge SO32 2HS [Winchester Rd (B2177)]: Friendly, with wide choice of enjoyable good value food inc popular Sun carvery, plenty of seating, coloured walls, black beams and dark oak *(Samuel Fancett)*

Wheatsheaf SO32 2JG [A334 Wickham—Botley]: Busy friendly no-fuss local, Flowerpots ales tapped from the cask, farm cider, short sensible choice of bargain bar lunches (evening food Tues-Thurs); dogs welcome, garden, handy for Wickham Vineyard, open all day *(Jenny and Peter Lowater, Val and Alan Green)*

SILCHESTER [SU6262]
☆ **Calleva Arms** RG7 2PH [The Common]: Friendly pub with good varied food at

sensible prices from sandwiches up, Fullers/Gales and a guest beer, decent wines by the glass, interestingly carved seats in roomy bar, smart dining areas, family conservatory; handy for the Roman site, sizeable attractive garden *(J V Dadswell)*

SMANNELL [SU3849]

Oak SP11 6JJ: Snug brick-and-flint country pub, bare-boards log-fire bar, beams and oak panelling, mix of traditional pine furniture, decent pub food inc Sun roasts, Wadworths ales, raftered garden room; piped music and some live; cl Sun evening, Mon *(Giles and Annie Francis)*

SOBERTON [SU6116]

☆ *White Lion* SO32 3PF [School Hill; signed off A32 S of Droxford]: Georgian-fronted 16th-c village pub, good home-made food (not Sun and Mon evenings) from good value lunchtime bar snacks to wider and rather smarter evening menu, welcoming landlord and friendly staff, well kept Bowmans Swift One and Wallops Wood plus two guests, good house wines, comfortable dining lounge, rambling restaurant and unspoilt little bare-boards low-ceilinged bar with pews and built-in wall seats, golden lab called Jazz; children in eating areas, small sheltered garden with suntrap terrace and covered tables, nice spot by green, good walks nearby, open all day Fri, Sat, till 9pm Sun, Mon *(LYM, Darryl and Lindy Hemsley, Val and Alan Green, Ann and Colin Hunt)*

SOPLEY [SZ1596]

☆ *Woolpack* BH23 7AX [B3347 N of Christchurch]: Pretty thatched dining pub with rambling open-plan low-beamed bar, welcoming helpful staff, good traditional food, real ales such as Ringwood Best and Fortyniner, good choice of wines by the glass, modern dining conservatory; children in eating areas, dogs in certain areas, terrace and charming garden with weeping willows, duck stream and footbridges, open all day *(Sue and Mike Todd, Hans Becker, LYM)*

SOUTHAMPTON [SU4113]

Cowherds SO15 7NN [The Common (off A33)]: Popular Vintage Inn dining pub in nice setting by common, low beams, cosy alcoves and tables in little bay windows, lots of Victorian photographs, carpets, polished boards and flagstones, log fires, above-average pub food inc fresh fish, ales such as Ringwood, good wine choice; tables outside with tie-ups and water for dogs *(Tracey and Stephen Groves)*

☆ *Duke of Wellington* SO14 2AH [Bugle St (or walk along city wall from Bar Gate)]: Ancient timber-framed building on 13th-c foundations, Wadworths and guests kept well, good choice of wines by the glass, good value food (not Sun evening) from vast club sandwiches up, friendly helpful service, bare boards, great log fire; piped music in cheery front bar, staider back area welcoming children; handy for Tudor House Museum, open all day *(Val and Alan Green)*

Guide Dog SO14 6SF [Earls Rd]: Great range of well kept changing ales in friendly and comfortably unpretentious local; quiet piped music, sports TV *(Sam Negus)*

Stile SO17 1TS [University Rd, Highfield]: Friendly open-plan stone-floors-and-wood pub with well kept ales such as Black Sheep and Fullers London Pride, quickly served low-priced pubby food, popular with students *(Dr and Mrs A K Clarke, Tracey and Stephen Groves)*

Wellington Arms SO15 3DE [Park Rd, Fremantle]: Cosy local with friendly landlady, plush banquettes in one bar, small tables and chairs in the other, several changing ales inc some unusual ones, good choice of whiskies, lots of Wellington memorabilia, jazz nights; terrace tables *(Tracey and Stephen Groves)*

SOUTHSEA [SZ6499]

Eldon Arms PO5 4BS [Eldon St/Norfolk St]: Rambling tavern under newish management, Fullers London Pride and four changing guests, Thatcher's cider, simple cheap lunchtime food (not Mon), Sun carvery, flowers on tables, old pictures and advertisements, attractive mirrors, bric-a-brac and shelves of books; piped music, sensibly placed darts, bar billiards, pool, games machine; dogs on leads and children welcome, tables in back garden, open all day *(Ann and Colin Hunt)*

☆ *Hole in the Wall* PO5 3BY [Gt Southsea St]: Small friendly unspoilt local in old part of town, up to six good changing ales inc local Bowman, Irving and Oakleaf, Wheal Maiden alcoholic ginger beer, Thatcher's ciders, evening speciality local sausages and substantial pies, old prints, dark panelling, nicely worn boards, over 700 pump clips on ceiling, daily papers, quiz night Thurs, Oct beer festival; small outside tiled area at front with benches, cl till 4 but open Fri lunchtime *(Mike and Eleanor Anderson, Andy West)*

King Street Tavern PO5 4EH [King St]: Sympathetically refurbished corner pub in attractive conservation area, spectacular Victorian tiled façade, bare boards and original fittings, four well kept Wadworths ales and guests, real ciders, straightforward home-made food, live music; courtyard tables, cl Sat and Mon lunchtimes *(Ann and Colin Hunt)*

Sir Loin of Beef PO4 9NH [Highland Rd, Eastney]: Light and airy corner pub, simple inside, with up to eight frequently changing well kept ales, tasters offered, bottled belgian beers, reasonably priced bar food, helpful friendly staff, buoyant atmosphere, interesting submarine memorabilia, juke box *(Andy West)*

White Horse PO5 3AU [Southsea Terrace]: Bright and airy modern décor, big windows overlooking Solent-edge green, cheerful young staff, well kept Fullers/Gales ales, enjoyable pubby food; big well thought-out garden *(Andy West)*

SOUTHWICK [SU6208]
Golden Lion PO17 6EB [High St; just off B2177 on Portsdown Hill]: Friendly two-bar pub (where Eisenhower and Montgomery came before D-Day) recently refurbished without spoiling character, Suthwyk ales, food (not Sun and Mon evenings or Tues) in bar and restaurant; children and dogs welcome, garden, picturesque estate village with scenic walks, open all day Sat *(Ann and Colin Hunt)*
Red Lion PO17 6EF [High St]: Neatly kept low-beamed village pub, prompt smiling service even though busy, Fullers/Gales and a guest ale, generous food, good value if not cheap, from interesting baguettes up, good choice of wines by the glass; good walks *(Irene and Derek Flewin, Ann and Colin Hunt, W A Evershed)*
STOCKBRIDGE [SU3535]
Three Cups SO20 6HB [High St]: Lovely low-beamed building dating from 1500, more restaurant than pub now, lots of smartly set pine tables but still some high-backed settles, country bric-a-brac and four well kept ales inc Ringwood; food can be very good, amiable service, good wines by the glass; children and dogs welcome, vine-covered verandah and charming cottage garden with streamside terrace, bedrooms, open all day *(LYM, Geoffrey Kemp)*
☆ *White Hart* SO20 6HF [High St; A272/A3057 roundabout]: Thriving divided beamed bar, attractive décor with antique prints, oak pews and other seats, smart friendly staff, reliable generous fresh food from good sandwiches and baguettes up, Fullers/Gales beers, good wines by the glass, decent coffee, comfortable restaurant with blazing log fire (children allowed); dogs in bar, disabled facilities, terrace tables and nice garden, 14 good bedrooms, open all day *(Helen and Brian Edgeley, Dennis Jenkin, Edward Mirzoeff, Phyl and Jack Street, Dr and Mrs A K Clarke, Ann and Colin Hunt, LYM)*
STRATFIELD TURGIS [SU6960]
Wellington Arms RG27 0AS: Handsome small country inn with relaxing armchairs and other individual furnishings in restful and surprisingly pubby tall-windowed two-room bar, part with polished flagstones, part carpeted, open fire, well kept Badger ales, good food and service; garden, comfortable bedrooms *(Jennifer Banks, Richard Endacott)*
SWANMORE [SU5716]
Brickmakers SO32 2PA: Smartly redone under friendly new owners, three real ales inc Bowman, decent lunchtime food from good ciabattas up, separate evening menu, armchairs and log fire; garden with raised deck *(Val and Alan Green)*
SWAY [SZ2898]
Hare & Hounds SO41 6AL [Durns Town, just off B3055 SW of Brockenhurst]: Bright, airy and comfortable New Forest family dining pub, enjoyable generous fresh food, Greene King and Ringwood ales, good coffee, smart friendly staff, low beams, central log fire;

piped music; dogs welcome, picnic-sets and play frame in neatly kept garden, open all day Sat *(B R Merritt, Phyl and Jack Street, LYM)*
TIMSBURY [SU3325]
☆ *Bear & Ragged Staff* SO51 0LB [A3057 towards Stockbridge; pub marked on OS Sheet 185 map ref 334254]: Reliable roadside dining pub with wide blackboard choice of popular food all day, friendly efficient service, lots of wines by the glass, Greene King IPA, log fire, good-sized beamed interior; children in eating area, tables in extended garden with play area, handy for Mottisfont, good walks *(J V Dadswell, Andrew Shore, LYM)*
Malthouse SO51 0NG [A3057 N of village]: Spacious roadside family pub, very popular in good weather for its secluded lawn and terrace and big well equipped play area; fireside leather sofas in pleasant lounge area, real ales such as Gales, Ringwood and Wadworths from central bar, conservatory-style dining areas, wide choice of decent food inc good value carvery, fast friendly service; dogs welcome, nr fine Norman church, pleasant paths to Michelmersh, handy for Mottisfont Abbey (NT) *(Chris Turner, Phyl and Jack Street)*
TITCHFIELD [SU5406]
☆ *Fishermans Rest* PO15 5RA [Mill Lane, off A27 at Titchfield Abbey]: Airy open-plan pub/restaurant with wide choice of good value fresh food, informal tables throughout, good service, well kept Greene King ales and Ringwood Best, two log fires, daily papers, trouty décor; fine riverside position opp Titchfield Abbey, tables out behind overlooking water, open all day *(Peter Meister, Ann and Colin Hunt, LYM)*
☆ *Titchfield Mill* PO15 5RF [A27, junction with Mill Lane]: Open airy Vintage Inn family dining pub in neatly kept converted River Meon watermill, olde-worlde room off main bar, smarter dining room, upstairs gallery, stripped beams and interesting old machinery, efficient friendly staff, good value wines by the glass, Ringwood Best and guests, freshly squeezed orange juice; piped music; sunny terrace by mill stream with two waterwheels (food not served here), open all day *(Gael Pawson, Ann and Colin Hunt)*
Wheatsheaf PO14 4AD [East St; off A27 nr Fareham]: Welcoming and unspoilt with well kept Flowerpots and guests, shortish choice of popular food, long bow-windowed front bar, side snug, back dining room, log fires; piped music; terrace *(Val and Alan Green)*
TOTFORD [SU5737]
Woolpack SO24 9TJ [B3046 Basingstoke—Alresford]: Handy roadside pub, clean comfortable and friendly, with good locally sourced home-made food, real ales inc a good house beer, nice italian coffee, efficient service, open fire in stripped-brick bar, large dining room; pool; tables out by small pond, lovely setting in good walking

country, bedrooms *(Janet Whittaker, Caroline Mackenzie)*

TURGIS GREEN [SU6959]

Cricketers RG27 0AH [Bottle Lane]: Welcoming dining pub in charming early 19th-c building, particularly good lunches and popular theme nights, good wine choice, local real ale; children welcome *(George Williams, Peter Sampson)*

TWYFORD [SU4824]

☆ ***Bugle*** SO21 1QT [B3355/Park Lane]: Nicely done modern pub with contemporary furniture, lots of leather, carpet or dark flagstones, good enterprising food, well kept ales such as Bowmans Swift One and Upham Ale and Goodens Gold, woodburner, highly coloured landscape photographs; piped pop music; attractive verandah seating area, good walks nearby, open all day *(Val and Alan Green, B J Harding, Phyl and Jack Street, BB, Tony and Wendy Hobden)*

Phoenix SO21 1RF [High St (B3335)]: Cheerful open-plan local with lots of prints, bric-a-brac and big end inglenook log fire, friendly long-serving landlord (here throughout the *Guide*'s life) and attentive staff, Greene King ales, good coffee, good value wines, raised dining area, pool, side skittle alley; unobtrusive piped music; children allowed at one end lunchtime, garden with smokers' area *(Ann and Colin Hunt)*

UPPER CLATFORD [SU3543]

Crook & Shears SP11 7QL [off A343 S of Andover, via Foundry Rd]: Cosy 17th-c thatched pub, several homely olde-worlde seating areas, bare boards and panelling, good changing ale range, decent food from doorstep sandwiches up, open fires and woodburner, small dining room, back skittle alley with own bar; pleasant secluded garden behind *(the Didler)*

WALHAMPTON [SZ3396]

Walhampton Arms SO41 5RE [B3054 NE of Lymington; aka Walhampton Inn]: Large comfortable Georgian-style family roadhouse with emphasis on restaur, food inc reliable carvery (not Mon) in raftered former stables and two adjoining areas, pleasant lounge, Ringwood ales, cheerful helpful staff; attractive courtyard, good walks, open all day *(Phyl and Jack Street)*

WELL [SU7646]

Chequers RG29 1TL [off A287 via Crondall, or A31 via Froyle and Lower Froyle]: Appealing low-beamed and panelled country pub, enjoyable food inc popular Sun lunch, good friendly service, well kept Badger, decent wines by the glass, roaring log fire, 18th-c country-life prints and old sepia photographs, pews, brocaded stools and a few GWR carriage lamps; picnic-sets on vine-covered terrace and in spacious back garden *(LYM, Trish Bellamy, Sally Garside)*

WEST END [SU4514]

White Swan SO18 3HW [Mansbridge Rd]: Pleasantly refurbished family food pub in nice spot, Itchen Valley and Wells & Youngs

ales, busy carvery restaurant, conservatory; attractive terrace by River Itchen (so liable to flooding) *(Phyl and Jack Street)*

WHERWELL [SU3840]

White Lion SP11 7JF [B3420]: Early 17th-c multi-level beamed village pub under newish friendly management, Harveys, Hogs Back, Ringwood Best and Shepherd Neame Spitfire, several wines by the glass, enjoyable generous food from baguettes to Sun roasts, open fire, dining rooms either side of bar; piped music; dogs on leads and well behaved children welcome, new furniture in redone courtyard garden, Test Way walks, three bedrooms, open all day *(B J Harding, Phyl and Jack Street, Stephen Pacey, LYM)*

WICKHAM [SU5711]

Greens PO17 5JQ [The Square]: Civilised dining place with pubby feel, efficient friendly staff, enjoyable food from typical bar lunches to imaginative specials, Bowmans Swift One and another ale, extensive wine list, several balustraded areas on different levels; pleasant lawn overlooking water meadows, cl Sun evening and Mon *(Darryl and Lindy Hemsley, Mrs Joy Griffiths, Phyl and Jack Street)*

Kings Head PO17 5JN [The Square]: Refurbished open-plan bar, big windows and open fires, sofa and armchairs, Fullers/Gales ales, food from sandwiches up inc tapas, back dining area up some steps; piped music; tables out on square and in back garden (former coach yard) *(BB, Val and Alan Green, Ann and Colin Hunt)*

WINCHESTER [SU4829]

Bakers Arms SO23 9JX [down passage off High St]: Busy old town pub with cheap usual food, quick friendly service, real ales such as Fullers and Shepherd Neame Spitfire; TV; pretty wrought-iron and glass canopy over passageway tables *(Dave Braisted, Val and Alan Green)*

Bell SO23 9RE [St Cross Rd (B3335 off M3 junction 11)]: Old two-bar whitewashed pub handy for St Cross Hospital (ancient monument, not a hospital), short choice of good value fresh food inc nice sandwiches, helpful staff, well kept Greene King ales and usually a guest, decent wines by the glass, polished boards and half-panelling, leather sofas, plush modern chairs and pine tables, cricket memorabilia; quiet piped music; nice walled garden with swing and slide, lovely water-meadows walk from centre, open all day *(Val and Alan Green)*

☆ ***Eclipse*** SO23 9EX [The Square, between High St and cathedral]: Chatty licensees in picturesque unspoilt 14th-c local with massive beams and timbers in its two small cheerful rooms, chilled ales inc Fullers London Pride and Ringwood, decent choice of wines by the glass, good value lunchtime food from ciabattas to popular Sun roasts, open fire, oak settles, friendly burmese cat; children in back area, seats outside, very handy for cathedral *(Ann and Colin Hunt, LYM, Val and Alan Green)*

Old Gaol House SO23 8RZ [Jewry St]: Traditional Wetherspoons attracting good mix of customers, ten real ales, decent sensibly priced food all day, nice coffee, walls of books; children welcome *(Ann and Colin Hunt, Val and Alan Green)*

☆ **Old Vine** SO23 9HA [Great Minster St]: Lively big-windowed town bar with well kept ales such as Bowmans Swift One, Flowerpots, Ringwood Best and Timothy Taylors Landlord, neat efficient staff, high beams, worn oak boards, smarter and larger dining side with good up-to-date food choice; faint piped music; by cathedral, with sheltered terrace, partly covered and heated, charming bedrooms, open all day *(Ann and Colin Hunt, Pat and Roger Davies, Simon Rodway, BB, Alastair and Rebecca Lockwood)*

Queen SO23 9PG [Kingsgate Rd]: Roomy recently refurbished two-bar pub in attractive setting opp College cricket ground, enjoyable standard food, well kept Greene King ales, decent wines, friendly competent staff, low ceilings, panelling, central fireplace, dining room; disabled facilities, front terrace, big garden, open all day *(Kathy Heathcote)*

Royal Oak SO23 9AU [Royal Oak Passage, off upper end of pedestrian part of High St opp St Thomas St]: Notable for the intriguing cellar bar (not always open) whose massive 12th-c beams and Saxon wall give it some claim to be the country's oldest drinking spot, otherwise standard pub with Greene King ales and decent food; piped music, games machines, can get packed Fri and Sat nights *(Ann and Colin Hunt, the Didler, Tony Brace, LYM)*

WOLVERTON [SU5658]

George & Dragon RG26 5ST [Towns End; just N of A339 Newbury—Basingstoke]: Low-beamed pub in remote rolling country, linked cosy areas, wide choice of enjoyable unpretentious food, long-serving licensees and attentive service, good beer range inc a house ale, decent wines, log fire, pleasant dining area, skittle alley; children welcome, big garden with small terrace, separate bedroom block, good breakfast *(Miss A Hawkes, Ian Herdman, J V Dadswell)*

If a pub tries to make you leave a credit card behind the bar, be on your guard. The credit card firms and banks which issue them condemn this practice. After all, the publican who asks you to do this is in effect saying: 'I don't trust you'. Have you any more reason to trust his staff? If your card is used fraudulently while you have let it be kept out of your sight, the card company could say you've been negligent yourself – and refuse to make good your losses. So say that they can 'swipe' your card instead, but must hand it back to you. Please let us know if a pub does try to keep your card.

Herefordshire

Once again the Stagg at Titley triumphs as one of the great food pubs, where they take great care with ingredients and preparation; the wines are impressive too, and readers like staying here. It's our Herefordshire Dining Pub 2011. The Mill Race at Walford is another very civilised dining venue, run by pleasant staff and with a contemporary look to its décor, as is the Cottage of Content at Carey, with good food and a very enjoyable rural setting. In Ledbury, the Feathers is doing well as a hotel bar with food. The Whittalls continue to give customers a very warm welcome at the Three Horseshoes at Little Cowarne, with its pretty garden, choice of local cider and perry, and local ingredients used in the food, and there's also a splendid choice of cider and perry at the friendly Crown in Woolhope and a huge range of beers at the Victory in Hereford. For its wonderful location in the Wye gorge, the Saracens Head at Symonds Yat is hard to beat, while in the unspoilt Golden Valley at Dorstone, the Pandy is evocatively ancient (they've recently added bedrooms). Among the simpler places, the Carpenters Arms at Walterstone is splendidly unchanged and very genuine.

AYMESTREY   SO4265   MAP 6

Riverside Inn
A4110, at N end of village, W of Leominster; HR6 9ST

Lovely spot with a terrace making the most of the view; cosy rooms and open fires

The position of this half-timbered inn is very special, by an ancient stone bridge over the River Lugg, which is overlooked by picnic-sets in the tree-sheltered garden. Within the rambling beamed bar are several cosy areas with décor drawn from a pleasant mix of periods and styles. Fine antique oak tables and chairs mix with stripped-pine country kitchen tables, fresh flowers, hops strung from a ceiling wagon-wheel, horse tack, nice pictures and warm winter log fires; fairly quiet piped pop music. The landlord clearly enjoys chatting to his customers, and service is efficient and friendly. Hobsons and Wye Valley Hereford Pale Ale plus a guest such as Wye Valley Butty Bach on handpump, local draft ciders and bottled Brook Farm cider (pressed in the next village), and more than 20 malt whiskies. Fly-fishing is available for residents.

🍴 **Using local rare-breed meat and venison from local shoots, and growing much of their own fruit and vegetables, enjoyable lunchtime bar food includes filled baguettes, soup, shin of beef and oxtail casserole, and rib-eye steak. The more expensive evening menu features items such as fillet steak or tenderloin of organic rare-breed pork stuffed with apricots, prunes and pistachios; puddings could include lemon cheesecake with limoncello coulis.** *Starters/Snacks: £3.95 to £6.25. Main Courses: £8.95 to £20.00. Puddings: £5.75*

Free house ~ Licensees Richard and Liz Gresko ~ Real ale ~ Bar food ~ Restaurant ~ (01568) 708440 ~ Children welcome ~ Dogs allowed in bar and bedrooms ~ Open 11-3, 6-11; 12-3 Sun; closed lunchtime Mon, Sun evening and Mon evening in winter ~ Bedrooms: £45B/£70B

Recommended by Brian Brooks, Jayne Richards, John Morris, D R Grossmark, Mr and Mrs M Stratton, Jane Hudson, Paul J Robinshaw, Stanley and Annie Matthews, Jeff and Wendy Williams

BODENHAM   SO5454   MAP 4

Englands Gate

On A417 at Bodenham turn-off, about 6 miles S of Leominster; HR1 3HU

Some fine original features in this comfortable 16th-c inn; pleasant garden

The half-timbered construction of this black and white coaching inn is as evident inside as out. It has heavy brown beams and joists in low ochre ceilings around a vast central stone chimneypiece, well worn flagstones, sturdy timber props, one or two steps, and lantern-style lighting. One corner has a high-backed settle with scatter cushions, a cosy partly stripped-stone room has a long stripped table (just right for a party of eight) and a lighter upper area with flowers on its tables has winged settles painted a soft eau de nil. Hobsons, Wye Valley Butty Bach and Hereford Pale Ale and a guest from brewers such as Brains Rev James are on handpump, and the pub holds a beer and sausage festival in July; piped pop music, board games and TV. There are tables with sun umbrellas out in the garden and on the terrace. New this year are seven ensuite bedrooms in a converted coach house next door; dogs are allowed in some bedrooms for an additional fee of £20 per night. More up-to-date reports please.

📶 **Bar food might include filled baguettes, meatballs in spicy tomato sauce with linguine, ploughman's, deep-fried brie in beer batter or spicy creole prawns with chilli and lime yoghurt, and more expensive dinner items such as mixed grill, steak or roasted breast of duck.** *Starters/Snacks: £4.75 to £5.95. Main Courses: £6.95 to £19.95*

Free house ~ Licensee Evelyn McNeil ~ Real ale ~ Bar food (12-2.30, 6-9.30; 12-3 Sun) ~ (01568) 797286 ~ Children welcome until 9pm ~ Dogs allowed in bar and some bedrooms ~ Open 12-11(midnight Sat, 10 Sun) ~ Bedrooms:/79B
Recommended by Roger and Anne Newbury, Dr A J and Mrs Tompsett, Reg Fowle, Helen Rickwood, R T and J C Moggridge

BRINGSTY COMMON   SO6954   MAP 4

Live & Let Live 🍺

Off A44 Knightwick—Bromyard 1.5 miles W of Whitbourne turn; take track southwards at black cat inn sign, bearing right at fork; WR6 5UW

Restored country tavern surrounded by rolling partly wooded common; good drinks

You really do feel miles from anywhere here, at this nicely unprecious old timbered cottage with its massive chimney, on a high, ancient-feeling common offering plenty of good walking opportunities. The cosy bar has non-matching scrubbed or polished old tables on its flagstones, a very high-backed traditional winged settle by the log fire in the cavernous stone fireplace, and a variety of seats from comfortably cushioned little chairs to a long stripped pew. Earthenware jugs hang from the low stripped beams, with more bygones on the mantelshelf. The landlady is usually behind the hop-hung bar counter (with old casks built into its facing) serving the well kept Wye Valley Butty Bach and a couple of local guests from brewers such as Hobsons and Ludlow from handpump, Robertson's and Oliver's ciders, and local apple juice. A pair of cottagey dining rooms are tucked in upstairs under the steep rafters. Outside, a glass-topped well and big wooden hogshead have been pressed into service as tables for the flagstoned terrace. Picnic-sets give long peaceful views from the grassy former orchard, which blends into the common.

📶 **The traditional bar food is not a highlight here.** *Starters/Snacks: £4.50 to £10.00. Main Courses: £10.00 to £20.00. Puddings: £4.95 to £6.75*

If you know a pub's ever open all day, please tell us.

Free house ~ Licensee Sue Dovey ~ Real ale ~ Bar food ~ Restaurant ~ No credit cards ~ (01886) 821462 ~ Children welcome until 9.30pm ~ Dogs welcome ~ Open 12-11(10.30 Sun); Closed 2.30-6.30 Tues-Fri in winter; closed Mon (except bank hols)

Recommended by Reg Fowle, Helen Rickwood, Chris Flynn, Wendy Jones, the Didler, Mike and Mary Carter, Dave Braisted, Chris Evans, Noel Grundy

CAREY

SO5631   MAP 4

Cottage of Content

Village signposted from good back road betweeen Ross-on-Wye and Hereford E of A49, through Hoarwithy; HR2 6NG

Country furnishings in a friendly rustic cottage, seats on terraces and tasty food

You can make the most of the tranquil position of this nicely tucked-away medieval cottage by bagging one of the picnic-sets, either on the flower-filled front terrace or in the rural-feeling garden at the back. Originally three labourers' cottages with its own integral cider and ale parlour, the building has kept much of its old character, with a multitude of beams and country furnishings such as stripped pine kitchen chairs, long pews by one big table and various old-fashioned tables on flagstones or bare boards. Hobsons Best and Wye Valley Butty Bach are on handpump, and the friendly landlady serves a local cider during the summer months; piped music.

🍴 **Enjoyable bar food includes starters such as twice-baked goats cheese soufflé with basil cream or locally smoked salmon on beetroot and preserved lemon salad, and main courses such as rib-eye steak with stilton and mushroom pudding, and whole roasted sea bream; Sunday roast.** *Starters/Snacks: £5.25 to £8.95. Main Courses: £8.95 to £17.25. Puddings: £5.50*

Free house ~ Licensees Richard and Helen Moore ~ Real ale ~ Bar food ~ (01432) 840242 ~ Children welcome ~ Dogs allowed in bar ~ Live music first Weds of the month ~ Open 12-2, 6.30-10.30(11 Sat); closed Sun evening and Mon (except lunchtime bank hols) ~ Bedrooms: £50(£60B)/£60(£70B)

Recommended by Mike and Mary Carter, Reg Fowle, Helen Rickwood, the Didler, C R Cann, Mrs A S Crisp, Neil and Anita Christopher, Phil Bryant

DORSTONE

SO3141   MAP 6

Pandy

Pub signed off B4348 E of Hay-on-Wye; HR3 6AN

Ancient timbered inn by village green, with flagstones, vast open fireplace; play area

A couple of steps away from the little triangular green, in this quiet spot in the Golden Valley, this whitewashed building dates in part from the 12th century. Its neatly kept homely rooms are comfortably traditional with low heavy hop-strung beams in the ochre ceilings, stout timbers, upright chairs on broad worn flagstones and in various alcoves, upholstered stools ranged along the counter (and locals to occupy them) and a vast open fireplace stacked with logs. They keep Wye Valley Butty Bach and a guest such as Hancocks HB on handpump alongside decent wines, just under two dozen malt and irish whiskies, and a summer farm cider; board games, quoits, cribbage and piped music. The handsome red setter is called Apache, and the neat side garden has picnic-sets and a play area. As we went to press, they were about to open four bedrooms (one with facilities for the disabled) in a new annexe built of spruce logs. More reports please.

🍴 **Bar food includes filled baguettes, scampi, fish pie, pizza, steaks, specials such as moroccan lamb with couscous or salmon aioli, and puddings such as caribbean bread and butter pudding and chocolate torte.** *Starters/Snacks: £4.75 to £5.95. Main Courses: £8.95 to £16.95. Puddings: £4.75*

Free house ~ Licensees Bill and Magdalena Gannon ~ Real ale ~ Bar food (12-3, 6-9; not Mon lunchtime) ~ Restaurant ~ (01981) 550273 ~ Children welcome ~ Dogs allowed in bar ~ Open 12-3, 6-11; 12-11 Sat; 12-3, 6.30-10.30 Sun; closed Mon lunchtime (except summer and bank hols) ~ Bedrooms: /£85S

Recommended by Guy Vowles, R T and J C Moggridge, the Didler

HEREFORD

SO5139   MAP 6

Victory 🍺 £

St Owen Street, opposite fire station; HR1 2QD

Home of Spinning Dog beers and a good range of ciders; unremarkable from outside but humorous nautical décor within

It's worth the diversion from the city centre to this place, especially for its range of drinks. Service is friendly and informal, and if they're not too busy they'll show you around the Spinning Dog brewery. They keep six of their own beers, the cheapest at only £2 a pint, as well as three farm ciders and a perry; juke box, piped music, darts, games machine, TV, skittle alley, table skittles, cribbage, quoits, board games and a back pool table. The counter re-creates a miniature galleon complete with cannon poking out of its top, and down a companionway the long back room is amusingly decked out as the inside of a man o' war with dark wood, rigging and netting everywhere, benches along sides that curve towards a front fo'c'sle, stanchions and ropes forming an upper crow's nest, and appropriate lamps. The garden has a pagoda, climbing plants and some seats. We'd love to get more reports on this remarkable pub.

🍽 **Tuesday night is curry and quiz night; they also do Sunday roasts; as we went to press they told us they may serve food in the future on other days.** *Starters/Snacks: £2.95. Main Courses: £6.95. Puddings: £2.95*

Own brew ~ Licensee James Kenyon ~ Real ale ~ Bar food (12-4 Sun) ~ No credit cards ~ (01432) 342125 ~ Children welcome ~ Dogs welcome ~ Live band Sat ~ Open 3(1pm Fri)-12; 11am-12am Sat; 10.30am-11pm Sun

Recommended by Reg Fowle, Helen Rickwood, Ann and Colin Hunt

LEDBURY

SO7137   MAP 4

Feathers 🍽 🍷 🛏

High Street (A417); HR8 1DS

Handsome timbered hotel with chatty relaxed bar, more decorous lounges, good food, friendly staff and comfortable bedrooms

Well run by polite, friendly staff and one of several striking half-timbered buildings in an appealing old market town, this elegant hotel dates from 1521. The beamed interior has restored brickwork, seats around oak tables on oak flooring, hop bines, some country antiques, 19th-c caricatures and fancy fowl prints on the stripped brick chimneybreast (lovely winter fire), copper jam pots and fresh flowers on the tables – some very snug and cosy, in side bays. The Top Bar attracts a convivial mix of chatty drinkers and informal diners, while the lounge is a civilised place for afternoon teas, with high-sided armchairs and sofas in front of a big log fire, and newspapers to read. Fullers London Pride and a guest such as Greene King Old Speckled Hen are on handpump, with several wines by the glass and 30 malt whiskies. In summer, the sheltered back terrace has abundant pots and hanging baskets.

🍽 **The menu might include soup, spiced, crusted and seared carpaccio of tuna or saffron risotto with clams and mussels, main courses such as lamb, cumin and coriander burgers, fish and shellfish ragoût, fillet of beef or loin of pork, and puddings such as blackcurrant posset or sticky toffee pudding.** *Starters/Snacks: £5.95 to £12.00. Main Courses: £14.95 to £21.00. Puddings: £5.95*

Free house ~ Licensee David Elliston ~ Real ale ~ Bar food (12-2, 7-9.30(10 Fri, Sat); 12-2.30, 7-9.30 Sun) ~ Restaurant ~ (01531) 635266 ~ Children welcome ~ Dogs allowed in bar and bedrooms ~ Open 10-11(10.30 Sun) ~ Bedrooms: £89.50B/£130B

Recommended by T A R Curran, Dave Braisted, Reg Fowle, Helen Rickwood, Phil Bryant, Dave and Jenny Hughes, P J and R D Greaves, Chris and Val Ramstedt, Pete Coxon, Tracey and Stephen Groves, David Howe

LITTLE COWARNE

SO6050   MAP 4

Three Horseshoes ♀

Pub signposted off A465 SW of Bromyard; towards Ullingswick; HR7 4RQ

Long-serving licensees and friendly staff in a bustling country pub with well liked food and home-grown summer salad; bedrooms

Norman and Janet Whittall have now been running this warmly welcoming and beautifully placed modern brick country tavern for over 20 years. They have a local Oliver's real cider and perry, in addition to Greene King Old Speckled Hen, Ruddles Best and Wye Valley Bitter on handpump, and a dozen wines by the glass. The quarry-tiled L-shaped middle bar has leather-seated bar stools, upholstered settles and dark brown kitchen chairs around sturdy old tables, old local photographs above the corner log fire, and hop-draped black beams in the dark peach ceiling. Opening off one side is a skylit sun room with wicker armchairs around more old tables and at the other end there's a games room with darts, pool, juke box, games machine and cribbage; obliging service and disabled access. A popular Sunday lunchtime carvery is offered in the roomy and attractive, stripped-stone raftered restaurant extension. The delightful rural position here makes the terrace or lawn in the particularly lovely garden a distinct lure at warmer times of the year.

🍴 Cooked by their son Philip and using their own-grown produce, game from local shoots and carefully sought out local suppliers, enjoyable food might include tomato and red lentil soup, salmon fishcake with lime and ginger, and main courses like steak and ale pie, vietnamese lamb stew and rice, steak, fillet of bass with roasted peppers, or tomato and goats cheese tart. Arrive early for a table on Thursday, as their pensioners' lunch is very popular. *Starters/Snacks: £4.50 to £6.00. Main Courses: £9.00 to £16.00. Puddings: £3.95 to £4.25*

Free house ~ Licensees Norman and Janet Whittall ~ Real ale ~ Bar food ~ Restaurant ~ (01885) 400276 ~ Children welcome until 9pm ~ Open 11-3(3.30 Sat), 6.30-11(12.30 Sat); 12-4, 7-10.30 Sun; closed Sun evening in winter ~ Bedrooms: £40S/£70S

Recommended by Tim and Joan Wright, MLR, Denys Gueroult, Ann and Colin Hunt, Noel Grundy, Alan and Eve Harding, Reg Fowle, Helen Rickwood, John Robertson, Jeff and Wendy Williams, Ian and Jane Irving, Anthony Barnes, Stuart Turner

SELLACK

SO5526   MAP 4

Lough Pool ★ ♀

Back road Hoarwithy—Ross-on-Wye; HR9 6LX

Character-laden cottage with individual furnishings in beamed bars, a good choice of food and drinks, and lots of seats outside in the pretty garden

In front of this appealing black and white cottage, picnic-sets occupy an area of lawn that makes a most inviting place for sitting in the sun. The beamed central room has rustic chairs and cushioned window seats around wooden tables on the mainly flagstoned floor, sporting prints, bunches of dried flowers and fresh hop bines, and a log fire at one end with a woodburner at the other. Leading off are other rooms, gently brightened up with attractive individual furnishings and antique bottles, and nice touches such as the dresser with patterned plates and an array of old bottles and flagons. Books and newspapers are left out for customers, and there are crayons and paper for children. Wye Valley Bitter and Butty Bach and a guest such as Sharps Doom Bar are on handpump, with around 20 malt whiskies, local farm ciders, perries and apple juices, and several wines by the glass from a thoughtful wine list. More reports please.

🍽 They offer a pubby bar menu as well as their more elaborate restaurant-style menu. Using home-grown herbs and rare-breed meat from nearby farms, food (from both menus) might include lunchtime open sandwiches, platters, bouillabaisse, liver and bacon with onion gravy, steak and ale pie, crab linguine, herefordshire beef suet pudding, pappardelle pasta with wild mushroom and rocket, breast of duck, steak, fresh fish, puddings such as apple crumble and crème anglaise, and pistachio cheesecake with stewed apple crème fraîche, and a british and local cheeseboard; Sunday roasts. *Starters/Snacks: £4.95 to £6.25. Main Courses: £8.95 to £16.25. Puddings: £4.50 to £7.50*

Free house ~ Licensees David and Janice Birch ~ Real ale ~ Bar food (12-2.30, 7-9.30) ~ Restaurant ~ (01989) 730236 ~ Children welcome ~ Dogs allowed in bar ~ Open 11.30-3, 6.30-11; closed Mon and Sun evening (except bank hols)

Recommended by Duncan Cloud, Bernard Stradling, Ann and John Jordan, Mrs B Barker, Mike and Mary Carter

STOCKTON CROSS   SO5161   MAP 4

Stockton Cross Inn
Kimbolton; A4112, off A49 just N of Leominster; HR6 0HD

Cosy half-timbered pub with local ales and tasty food, huge log fire, and seats in a pretty garden

This spotlessly kept half-timbered coaching inn makes a pleasant stop if you are visiting nearby Berrington Hall, and its log fire in the main bar makes it particularly welcoming on a chilly day. It's attractively furnished and heavily beamed, with a handsome antique settle and old leather chairs and brocaded stools, and at the far end is a woodburning stove with heavy cast-iron-framed tables and sturdy dining chairs, and up a step, a small area has more tables. Old-time prints, a couple of épées on one beam and lots of copper and brass complete the traditional picture; piped music, board games. Served by efficient staff are Wye Valley Butty Bach and Hereford Pale Ale and a guest on handpump, Robinson's Flagon cider (made six miles away) and several wines by the glass. There are tables out in the pretty garden. More up-to-date reports please.

🍽 Reasonably priced bar food typically includes sandwiches, sausage and mash, rump steak, black pudding and welsh rarebit salad, fried red snapper with fennel purée, fried lambs liver and bacon with onion gravy, goats cheese and pepper filo parcels, and puddings such as dark chocolate and orange tart. *Starters/Snacks: £3.95 to £7.95. Main Courses: £8.95 to £14.75. Puddings: £4.50 to £6.95*

Free house ~ Licensee Mike Betley ~ Real ale ~ Bar food ~ (01568) 612509 ~ Children welcome if well behaved ~ Open mike night second Weds of the month ~ Open 12-3, 7-11; 12-3 Sun; closed Sun evening and Mon (except bank hols)

Recommended by Alan and Eve Harding, Reg Fowle, Helen Rickwood, D R Grossmark, Mrs B Barker

SYMONDS YAT   SO5616   MAP 4

Saracens Head 🛏

Symonds Yat E, by ferry, ie over on the Gloucestershire bank; HR9 6JL

Lovely riverside spot with a fine range of drinks in this friendly inn; waterside terraces, comfortable bedrooms and plenty of walks nearby

The position here is quite something, at the epicentre of the most scenic stretch of the Wye gorge, far below the celebrated Symonds Yat viewpoint. Picnic-sets out on the waterside terrace look across the river. Inside it is warm and relaxed with cheerful staff who make you feel at home. The busy, basic flagstoned public bar has Theakstons Old Peculier, Wye Valley Butty Bach and Hereford Pale Ale plus a couple of guests such as Butcombe Bitter and Greene King Old Speckled Hen on handpump, and several wines by the glass; pool, games machine, TV and piped music. There's also a cosy lounge and a modernised bare-boards dining room. As well as bedrooms in the main building (no under-7s), there are two contemporary ones in the boathouse annexe. It's well worth approaching this spot on foot: an entertaining riverside walk crosses the Wye a little downstream by an entertainingly bouncy wire bridge at the Biblins and recrosses at the pub by the long-extant hand-hauled chain ferry that one of the pub staff operates.

🍴 As well as lunchtime sandwiches, baguettes and ploughman's, food typically includes **moules marinière, beefburger, pie of the day, sausage and mash, slow-braised lamb shank, hot peppered smoked salmon, and three local cheeses served on a slate.** *Starters/Snacks: £5.95 to £8.95. Main Courses: £9.95 to £18.95. Puddings: £5.50*

Free house ~ Licensees P K and C J Rollinson ~ Real ale ~ Bar food (12-2.30, 6.30-9) ~ Restaurant ~ (01600) 890435 ~ Children welcome ~ Dogs allowed in bar ~ Open 11-11(10.30 Sun) ~ Bedrooms: £55B/£79B

Recommended by Reg Fowle, Helen Rickwood, Michael Mellers, David Heath, Marcus Mann, Barry and Anne, Mike Horgan

TITLEY
S03359 MAP 6

Stagg 🍴 ☿ 🛏
B4355 N of Kington; HR5 3RL
HEREFORDSHIRE DINING PUB OF THE YEAR

Terrific food using tip-top ingredients served in extensive dining rooms, a fine choice of drinks, two-acre garden, comfortable bedrooms

Justly celebrated as one of Britain's top food pubs and earning consistent praise from readers, this is also a splendid place to stay. The little bar is comfortably hospitable with a civilised atmosphere and a great collection of 200 jugs attached to the ceiling. Hobsons and a guest such as Ludlow are on handpump, and they've several wines by the glass (including champagne and pudding wines) from a carefully chosen 100-bin wine list, local potato vodka, Robinson's Flagon draught cider and other local bottled ciders and perries, malt whiskies, apple juice and pressés. The accommodation is in bedrooms above the pub as well as in the additional rooms within a Georgian vicarage four minutes' walk away, and the breakfasts are wonderful, too. The two-acre garden has seats on the terrace and a croquet lawn.

🍴 Particularly good food, prepared using their own-grown vegetables, pigs and free-range chickens, includes a bar snack menu (not Saturday evenings or Sunday lunch) that might have open sandwiches, devilled lambs kidneys, scallops on creamed leeks or faggots with mash. A more elaborate menu might have starters like pigeon with black pudding and parsnip salad, pork rillettes and foie gras terrine, followed by rump steak, venison haunch with slow-cooked shoulder and roasted root vegetables, or monkfish on mussel risotto, and puddings such as lemon tart or spiced rhubarb jelly; three-course Sunday lunches are £16.90, with children's portions available. The british cheeseboard is stupendous, with 22 different ones, mostly from Herefordshire and Wales. Even the potato and parsnip crisps, chorizo and black pudding are home made. *Starters/Snacks: £4.90 to £5.90. Main Courses: £8.90 to £18.90. Puddings: £5.90*

Free house ~ Licensees Steve and Nicola Reynolds ~ Real ale ~ Bar food (12-2, 6.30-9) ~ Restaurant ~ (01544) 230221 ~ Children welcome ~ Dogs allowed in bar and bedrooms ~ Open 12-3, 6.30-11; closed Sun evening, Mon, first two weeks Nov and two weeks in Jan-Feb ~ Bedrooms: £70B/£85B

Recommended by Chris Flynn, Wendy Jones, Alan and Jill Bull, Reg Fowle, Helen Rickwood, Theo, Anne and Jane Gaskin, Norman and Sarah Keeping, Andy Witcomb, Di and Mike Gillam, Richard Cole, Dr Kevan Tucker, M G Hart, P J and R D Greaves, Rod Stoneman, Dr and Mrs Michael Smith, David Heath

> Post Office address codings confusingly give the impression that a few pubs are
> in Herefordshire, when they're really in Gloucestershire or even Wales
> (which is where we list them).

WALFORD
SO5820   MAP 4

Mill Race ♀
B4234 Ross-on-Wye—Lydney; HR9 5QS

Contemporary furnishings in uncluttered rooms, food with emphasis on good quality ingredients, attentive staff, terrace tables, nearby walks

Run by friendly staff, this airy, stylish place puts the accent on its carefully sourced food, and makes a great effort to hit all the right notes. The décor is fresh and contemporary, with a row of strikingly tall arched windows. There are comfortable leather armchairs and sofas on flagstones, as well as smaller chairs around broad pedestal tables. The granite-topped modern bar counter has Wye Valley ale and a guest such as St Georges on handpump, local Gwatkin's cider and apple juice, several malt whiskies and reasonably priced wines by the glass; opposite are a couple of tall, nicely clean-cut tables with matching chairs. The walls are mainly cream or dark pink with photographs of the local countryside, and good unobtrusive lighting. One wall stripped back to the stonework has a woodburning stove, also open to the comfortable and compact dining area on the other side; piped music. There are tables out on the terrace and leaflets available at the pub detailing pleasant walks of an hour or so. As we went to press, the owners were planning to add extra seating and planting around the terrace, and were about to start building a farm shop at the front of the pub.

🍴 The pub owns a 1,000-acre farm and woodland close by, which supplies them with game, rabbits, poultry, beef, fruit and vegetables – other ingredients come from rigorously sourced local (where possible) suppliers. The menu is not over-elaborate, relying instead on the quality of the produce. Maybe baguettes, starters like local goats cheese and red onion tart, and main courses such as pie of the day or prawn and scallop risotto at lunchtime, while the evening menu might include starters such as whitebait or local pigeon and pickled beetroot, and main courses such as steamed mussels or pork loin with parsnip purée. Puddings might feature vanilla cheesecake with berry compote or wild berry and apple crumble. *Starters/Snacks: £4.50 to £10.00. Main Courses: £8.95 to £16.50. Puddings: £5.00*

Free house ~ Licensee Jane Thompson ~ Real ale ~ Bar food (12-2(2.30 Sat, Sun), 6-9.30(9 Sun)) ~ (01989) 562891 ~ Children welcome ~ Open 11-3, 5-11; 11-11 Sat; 12-10.30 Sun
Recommended by Neil Kellett, Reg Fowle, Helen Rickwood, Bernard Stradling, Mike and Mary Carter, Guy Vowles

WALTERSTONE
SO3424   MAP 6

Carpenters Arms
Village signposted off A465 E of Abergavenny, beside Old Pandy Inn; follow village signs, and keep eyes skinned for sign to pub, off to right, by lane-side barn; HR2 0DX

Unchanging country tavern in the same family for many years

'Take a trip back in time: service is wonderfully old-fashioned, and the landlady Vera is nice and chatty' remarked one reader who loved the quiet out-of-the-way position of this cottagey place. Vera has been here some seventy years and took over from her mother, and for her it's a labour of love, with every customer welcomed as special. Thankfully, little has changed over the years: its traditional rooms, with Breconshire Golden Valley and Wadworths 6X tapped from the cask, have ancient settles against stripped-stone walls, some pieces of carpet on broad polished flagstones, a roaring log fire in a gleaming black range (complete with pot-iron, hot-water tap, bread oven and salt cupboard), and pewter mugs hanging from beams. The snug main dining room has mahogany tables and oak corner cupboards and maybe a big vase of flowers on the dresser. Another little dining area has old oak tables and church pews on flagstones. The refurbished outside lavatories are cold but in character.

🍴 Straightforward food such as sandwiches and rolls, soup, gammon, steaks, lamb cutlet with redcurrant and rosemary sauce, a vegetarian choice, daily specials, Sunday roasts, and puddings (made by the landlady's daughter) such as treacle tart and bread and butter pudding. *Starters/Snacks: £4.50 to £12.50. Main Courses: £7.50 to £20.00. Puddings: £4.00*

Free house ~ Licensee Vera Watkins ~ Real ale ~ Bar food ~ Restaurant ~ No credit cards ~ (01873) 890353 ~ Open 12-11

Recommended by MLR, Reg Fowle, Helen Rickwood, Nick and Sandra Blaney, Stuart and Doreen Ritchie, Howard Deacon, Maurice and Gill McMahon

WELLINGTON

S04948 MAP 6

Wellington 🍺

Village signposted off A49 N of Hereford; pub at far end; HR4 8AT

Welcoming pub with good food and beer, and a warm log fire

The interior of this Victorian red-brick pub has been imaginatively reworked to generate a comfortably civilised atmosphere, while at the back a pleasant garden has tables. The bar has big high-backed dark wooden settles, an open brick fireplace with a log fire in winter and fresh flowers in summer, historical photographs of the village, and antique farm and garden tools around the walls; the charming candlelit restaurant is in the former stables and includes a conservatory. Hobsons Best, Wye Valley Butty Bach and Hereford Pale Ale, and a guest such as Greene King Abbot are on handpump, and they hold a beer festival in July. Good attentive service; board games and piped music. More up-to-date reports please.

🍴 Good bar food includes sandwiches, ham, egg and chips, beer-battered fish, and sausage and mash. The restaurant menu (not cheap) might have parma ham and porcini mushrooom lasagne or oak-smoked salmon with celeriac rémoulade as starters, and main courses such as roasted saddle of venison with beetroot and goats cheese dauphinoise, duck breast with braised puy lentils and roasted pimento peppers, or wild mushroom and ricotta tortellini; puddings could feature baked lemon and vanilla cheesecake or cinnamon, orange and clotted cream rice pudding with pistachio praline. *Starters/Snacks: £4.50 to £8.00. Main Courses: £11.00 to £18.00. Puddings: £4.25 to £5.25*

Free house ~ Licensees Ross and Philippa Williams ~ Real ale ~ Bar food ~ Restaurant ~ (01432) 830367 ~ Children welcome ~ Dogs allowed in bar ~ Open 12-3, 6-11; closed Sun evening, Mon lunchtime

Recommended by Chris Flynn, Wendy Jones, Alan and Eve Harding, Reg Fowle, Helen Rickwood, J E Shackleton, Denys Gueroult

WOOLHOPE

S06135 MAP 4

Crown

Village signposted off B4224 in Fownhope; HR1 4QP

Cheery local with fine range of local ciders and perries, and tasty food

The enthusiastic landlord keeps an impressive range of 18 local ciders and perries here, all from within 15 miles of this tucked-away village local, including a cider and a perry on draught alongside Wye Valley Bitter and a rapidly changing guest such as Moorlands Original or St Austell Tribute; regular beer and cider festivals. The bar is straightforwardly traditional, with cream walls, some standing timbers, patterned carpets, dark wood pubby furniture, built-in banquettes, cottagey curtained windows and a couple of woodburners; piped music, darts and TV for sports events. There are terrific views from the lovely big garden, which also has darts, quoits and cushions in the particularly comfortable smoking shelter, and the garden bar is open in the cricket season; disabled access.

🍴 Well liked food includes lunchtime baguettes, soup, twice-baked hop soufflé with cream and mushroom sauce, local game terrine with pear chutney, slow-braised pork belly with caramelised apple, chilli, roasted butternut squash with peppers and gorgonzola, beef and ale pie, and a specials' board featuring fish; children's portions are available. *Starters/Snacks: £4.25 to £5.95. Main Courses: £7.50 to £12.95. Puddings: £4.50 to £5.00*

Free house ~ Licensees Matt and Annalisa Slocombe ~ Real ale ~ Bar food (12-2(3.30 Sun),

6.30-9(10 Sat)) ~ Restaurant ~ (01432) 860468 ~ Children welcome ~ Open 12-2.30, 6.30-11;
12-midnight Sat; 12-11 Sun

*Recommended by Noel Grundy, Reg Fowle, Helen Rickwood, R T and J C Moggridge, Richard Wyld, Caroline and
Michael Abbey, Dr and Mrs Michael Smith, Dave and Jenny Hughes*

YARPOLE   SO4664   MAP 6

Bell 🍴

Just off B4361 N of Leominster; HR6 OBD

A comfortable old black and white pub, with a pleasant dining area and extensive gardens

New licensees have taken over this pub so we are keeping our fingers crossed that things
will remain as enjoyable. Years ago this ancient timbered building was extended into a
former cider mill and now comprises a basic tap room, a comfortable beamed lounge bar
with a log fire and a large, strikingly high-raftered restaurant featuring a cider press and
mill wheel. A mix of traditional furniture, some modern art on the walls and even brass
taps embedded into the stone counter, keep it all comfortably relaxed; piped music.
Hook Norton Old Hooky, Timothy Taylors Landlord and a guest such as Shepherd Neame
Spitfire are on handpump and they've a short but interesting wine list. There are picnic-
sets under green parasols in the lovely flower-filled garden and the pub is very handy for
Croft Castle. More reports please.

🍴 Available in the bar or in the restaurant, food typically includes starters such as
pressed ham terrine or butternut squash risotto (also available as a main course), and
main courses such as fish pie, poussin with cauliflower and asparagus purée and rack of
lamb with spring vegetable broth; puddings too. *Starters/Snacks: £4.50 to £6.50. Main
Courses: £8.50 to £17.95. Puddings: £3.00 to £5.00*

Enterprise ~ Lease Campbell Tierney ~ Real ale ~ Bar food (12-2.30, 6.30-9.30) ~ Restaurant ~
(01568) 780359 ~ Children welcome ~ Dogs allowed in bar ~ Open 12-3, 6.30-11(midnight Sat);
closed Sun evening, Mon

*Recommended by Reg Fowle, Helen Rickwood, Michael Butler, Alan and Eve Harding, J E Shackleton, M G Hart,
P J and R D Greaves, Dave Braisted*

LUCKY DIP

Besides the fully inspected pubs, you might like to try these Lucky Dips recommended to us and
described by readers (if you do, please send us reports: feedback@goodguides.com).

ASTON CREWS [SO6723]
☆ *Penny Farthing* HR9 7LW: Roomy and
civilised partly 15th-c pub, well kept Black
Sheep, good choice of reasonably priced
food and wines, good friendly service, log
fires; easy chairs, lots of beams and country
bric-a-brac feature well in bar with skeleton;
newspapers, two restaurant areas, one with
a pretty valley and Forest of Dean views;
tables in charming garden, bedrooms
(Reg Fowle, Helen Rickwood, Julian Cox, BB)
BRIMFIELD [SO5267]
Roebuck Inn SY8 4NE [Village signposted
just off A49 Shrewsbury—Leominster]: What
was a smart dining pub with bistro-style
food cooked by french chef/patron is now up
for sale and the brewery are looking for new
licensees; impressive inglenook fireplace in
front lounge, open fire and pubby feel in
middle bar, and bistro dining room with
contemporary furnishings; terrace
*(J E Shackleton, Peter Holmes, LYM, Mr and
Mrs A H Young)*

COLWALL [SO7542]
Colwall Park WR13 6QG [Walwyn Rd (B4218
W of Malvern)]: Unpretentiously comfortable
hotel bar with friendly pubby atmosphere,
well kept ales inc Hobsons and Wye Valley,
local cider, nice wines by the glass, good
food from shortish menu inc generous
sandwiches (home-baked bread); dogs
allowed; terrace tables, bedrooms *(Roger and
Diana Morgan, Iain Nesbitt)*
☆ *Wellington* WR13 6HW [A449 Malvern—
Ledbury]: Welcoming enthusiastic landlord,
wide choice of generous food from good
standards to more imaginative dishes, set
price lunch wkdys, well kept ales such as
Goffs, good wines by the glass, neat two-
level bar and bright dining area, nice fire;
children welcome *(Bob Adey, J E Shackleton,
Mrs B H Adams, Barry Standham)*
CRASWALL [SO2736]
☆ *Bulls Head* HR2 OPN [Hay-on-Wye—
Llanfihangel Crucorney Golden Valley road]:
Remote stone-built country pub purposefully

keeping original low-beamed flagstoned bar with its peeling wallpaper and crumbling plaster, log fire in old cast-iron stove, hatch servery for Wye Valley ales and farm ciders tapped from the cask; contrasting smart spacious dining area up steps, cheap but good-sized enclosed garden with play area, peaceful walking country; cl Mon, Tues except July and Aug *(MLR, David Edwards, LYM)*

EARDISLAND [SO4258]

Cross HR6 9BW [A44]: Friendly two-room local in lovely village, quick service, good value honest food (not Tues), Hobsons and Wye Valley ales; events inc Thurs quiz night; TV; dogs welcome, open all day *(LYM, Michael Butler)*

EARDISLEY [SO3149]

Tram HR3 6PG: Old beamed community-active village local with enjoyable home cooking from chef/landlord, two beers such as Wye Valley Butty Bach and Timothy Taylors Landlord, one bar with woodburner, another served by hatch, with log fire and pool, resident cats; dogs welcome, smokers' annexe, garden with boules *(Reg Fowle, Helen Rickwood, Alistair Stanier, MLR, C E Clarke)*

FOWNHOPE [SO5734]

New Inn HR1 4PE: Welcoming clean pub popular at lunchtime for enjoyable food from sandwiches up, friendly local atmosphere and attentive staff, well kept ales such as Hobsons, Woods and Wye Valley, small dining area; picturesque village with unusual church and nice views *(Alastair Cowan)*

GARWAY [SO4622]

Garway Moon HR2 8RQ: Attractive good sized local in pretty location, friendly service, simple food, well kept beer; log fire *(anon)*

GORSLEY [SO6726]

Roadmaker HR9 7SW [B4221, just off M50 junction 3]: 19th-c village pub now run by group of retired Gurkha soldiers, tasty pub food from baguettes up, also good nepalese curries (wkdy takeaways), well kept Brains Rev James and Butcombe, large carpeted lounge bar with central log fire, evening restaurant (also Sun lunch), courteous service; no dogs; terrace with water feature, open all day *(Reg Fowle, Helen Rickwood, Neil and Anita Christopher, Joe Green)*

HAMPTON BISHOP [SO5538]

Bunch of Carrots HR1 4JR: Spaciously refurbished beamed country pub by River Wye (fishing available), good cheerful service, consistently good carvery and wide choice of other popular well priced food in bars and restaurant (booking advised wknds especially in summer), well kept real ales, local farm cider, lovely log fires; children and dogs welcome, garden with play area, open all day *(Ken Marshall, J S Hurst)*

HAREWOOD END [SO5227]

Harewood End Inn HR2 8JT [A49 Hereford—Ross-on-Wye]: Attractive and comfortable

panelled dining lounge with wide choice of enjoyable well priced food inc good vegetarian options, helpful friendly staff, well kept ales such as Brains Rev James and Flowers, sensibly priced wines; nice garden and walks, bedrooms *(Dr and Mrs Michael Smith, Tony and Gill Powell)*

HEREFORD [SO5139]

Barrels HR1 2JQ [St Owen St]: Two-bar local with excellent low-priced Wye Valley ales from barrel-built counter (beer festival end Aug), several farm ciders, no food, friendly efficient staff; side pool room with games, juke box and big-screen sports TV, lots of modern stained glass; piped blues and rock, some live jazz; picnic-sets out on partly decked and covered area behind, open all day *(MLR, Reg Fowle, Helen Rickwood, Derek and Sylvia Stephenson, the Didler, Dr and Mrs Michael Smith, BB)*

Lichfield Vaults HR1 2LR [Church St]: Comfortable and roomy half-timbered traditional pub in picturesque pedestrianised street nr cathedral; charming greek landlord and friendly staff, refurbished front and back bars with chunky olde-worlde décor, beams and dark panelling, wood and quarry-tiled floors, some exposed brickwork, inglenook fireplace; ales such as Adnams and Theakstons from long bar, food from sandwiches to greek platters and good value Sun lunch; picnic-sets in pleasant back courtyard, open all day *(Reg Fowle, Helen Rickwood, Phil Bryant)*

Stagecoach HR4 0BX [West St]: 16th-c black and white building, comfortable unpretentious lounge with dark oak panelling, Wye Valley ales with a guest such as Hobsons, friendly attentive service, bargain food, low-beamed upstairs restaurant; games machines and TV in bar; open all day *(Jestyn Phillips, Reg Fowle, Helen Rickwood, Alan and Eve Harding)*

HOARWITHY [SO5429]

New Harp HR2 6QH [off A49 Hereford—Ross-on-Wye]: Contemporary rustic décor in open-plan dining pub, good local food (some quite expensive) from chef/landlord, friendly helpful service, well kept changing ales, woodburner, flagstones and some stripped masonry; piped music; children and dogs welcome, pretty tree-sheltered garden with stream, picnic-sets and decked area, unusual italianate Victorian church, open all day wknds *(LYM, Mary Lawrence, GSB, S P Watkin, P A Taylor, Alistair Stanier)*

KENTCHURCH [SO4125]

Bridge Inn HR2 0BY [B4347 Pontrilas—Grosmont]: Ancient attractively refurbished rustic pub under newish ownership, big log fire, decent home-made food inc set deals, changing ales such as Otter, small pretty back restaurant overlooking River Monnow (two miles of trout fishing), playful collie called Freddie; waterside tables, bedrooms, handy for Herefordshire Trail *(Reg Fowle, Helen Rickwood)*

KINGSLAND [SO4461]
Corner HR6 9RY [B4360 NW of Leominster]:
Good reasonably priced food at this
welcoming 16th-c black and white inn, well
kept Hobsons and a guest beer, good wine
choice, friendly service, timbered bar,
restaurant in converted hay loft; good value
bedrooms *(Jayne Richards, Reg Fowle,
Helen Rickwood, Alan and Eve Harding)*

KINGTON [SO3056]
☆ ***Olde Tavern*** HR5 3BX [Victoria Rd, just off
A44 opp B4355 – follow sign to Town Centre,
Hospital, Cattle Market; pub on right opp
Elizabeth Rd, no inn sign but 'Estd 1767'
notice]: Gloriously old-fashioned with hatch-
served side room opening off small plain
parlour and public bar, plenty of dark brown
woodwork, big windows, settles and other
antique furniture on bare floors, gas fire,
old local pictures, china, pewter and curios;
well kept mainly local beers (they no longer
brew Dunn Plowman ales), Weston's cider,
beer festivals, no food – may do rolls and
chocolate bars, friendly atmosphere;
children and dogs welcome, little yard at
back, outside gents', cl wkdy lunchtimes
*(BB, the Didler, MLR, Mike and
Eleanor Anderson)*
Oxford Arms HR5 3DR [Duke St]:
Woodburners in main bar on left and dining
area on right, smaller lounge with sofas and
armchairs, two well kept local ales, good
value food; cl lunchtime Mon, Tues *(MLR,
Alan and Eve Harding)*
Royal Oak HR5 3BE [Church Rd]: Cheerful
two-bar pub with good value generous pubby
food, well kept Hook Norton and Wye Valley,
friendly efficient service, old theatre posters
and musical instruments in restaurant;
garden with terrace, neat simple bedrooms,
cl Mon lunchtime *(MLR)*

LEDBURY [SO7137]
☆ ***Prince of Wales*** HR8 1DL [Church Lane;
narrow passage from Town Hall]: Friendly
busy local, charmingly old-fashioned, tucked
nicely down narrow cobbled alley, well kept
ales such as Hobsons, Spinning Dog and one
brewed for the pub, Weston's cider, foreign
bottled beers; bargain simple home-made
food from sandwiches up, pleasant attentive
staff, low-beamed front bars, long back
room; a couple of tables in flower-filled yard
*(TB, Phil Bryant, Derek and Sylvia Stephenson,
Jim and Frances Gowers)*
Talbot HR8 2DX [New St]: 16th-c beamed
pub reopened and doing well after 2009 fire,
enjoyable food, good choice of real ales and
of wines by the glass, friendly service,
reasonable prices; bedrooms *(Dave and
Jenny Hughes, BB)*

LEINTWARDINE [SO4073]
Sun SY7 0LP [Rosemary Lane, just off
A4113]: Recently reopened with few changes
following death of long-serving landlady;
bare benches by coal fire in red-tiled front
parlour, well kept Hobsons tapped from the
cask, small settee and a couple of chairs by
the sitting room's gas fire, no food; plans for

a garden room *(Margaret Dickinson,
Brian and Jacky Wilson, Giles and
Annie Francis, BB)*

LEOMINSTER [SO4959]
Bell HR6 8AE [Etnam St]: Old pub under
enthusiastic new couple, opened-up interior
with beams, bare boards and big log fire;
Malvern Hills, Wye Valley and guest ales from
central servery, lunchtime food only from
sandwiches up, good mix of customers;
tables in sheltered back courtyard, open all
day *(MLR)*

LETTON [SO3346]
Swan HR3 6DH [A438 NW of Hereford]:
Friendly atmosphere and accommodating
service, good value home-made food inc
bargain Sun lunch, two well kept local ales,
large opened-up beamed bar, occasional quiz
nights; well appointed bedrooms, good
garden *(MLR, Reg Fowle, Helen Rickwood)*

LONGTOWN [SO3228]
Crown HR2 0LT: Welcoming place in nice
scenic spot, well kept Wye Valley Butty
Bach, food from sandwiches up, woodburner
in main bar, neat dining room, large back
room with darts and pool; garden, good
walks *(MLR)*

LUGWARDINE [SO5441]
☆ ***Crown & Anchor*** HR1 4AB [just off A438 E of
Hereford; Cotts Lane]: Cottagey timbered
pub with enjoyable food inc plenty of
lunchtime sandwiches and splendid smoked
ham and eggs, well kept Butcombe, Timothy
Taylors Landlord and guest beers, several
wines by the glass; various smallish rooms,
some interesting furnishings, fresh flowers,
big log fires, daily papers, no piped music or
machines; children welcome, pretty garden,
open all day *(Dr A J and Mrs Tompsett,
Denys Gueroult, Rochelle Seifas, LYM)*

MADLEY [SO4138]
Red Lion HR2 9PH: Welcoming traditional
beamed pub, well kept ales, log fire in
comfortable dining area, flagstoned public
bar, interesting bric-a-brac, back pool table;
friendly labrador called Charlie *(Reg Fowle,
Helen Rickwood, Peter Clark)*

MUCH BIRCH [SO4931]
Pilgrim HR2 8HJ: Substantially extended
hotel; lounge bar with comfortable sofas
and armchairs leading to dining room and
conservatory, well kept Wye Valley Bitter,
good value simple lunches inc Fri OAP
bargains and wider restaurant menu;
beautiful grounds, terrace tables with
sweeping view of Black Mountains,
20 bedrooms *(MLR, Alistair Stanier)*

MUCH DEWCHURCH [SO4831]
Black Swan HR2 8DJ [B4348 Ross-on-Wye—
Hay]: Roomy and attractive beamed and
timbered pub, partly 14th-c, with warm local
atmosphere and log fires in cosy well worn
bar and lounge with eating area, well kept
Hook Norton ales, decent wines, basic
inexpensive food; pool room with darts, TV,
juke box, no credit cards; dogs welcome
*(Bob and Margaret Holder, Alistair Stanier,
Anne Helne)*

MUCH MARCLE [SO6634]
Royal Oak HR8 2ND [off A449 Ross-on-Wye—Ledbury]: Superb rural spot with magnificent views, pleasant lounge with open fire, enjoyable reasonably priced food, efficient friendly service, well kept Wye Valley, large back dining area; garden *(Alan and Eve Harding)*

ORLETON [SO4967]
☆ *Boot* SY8 4HN [off B4362 W of Woofferton]: Popular pub under newish landlord, beams, timbering, even some 16th-c wattle and daub, inglenook fireplace in charming cosy traditional bar, steps up to further bar area, good-sized two-room dining part, enjoyable interesting food, friendly service, local ales and ciders; seats in garden under huge ash tree, barbecue, fenced-in play area *(LYM, J Martin, Dr P Brown, Alistair Stanier)*

PEMBRIDGE [SO3958]
New Inn HR6 9DZ [Market Sq (A44)]: Timeless ancient inn overlooking small black and white town's church, unpretentious three-room bar with antique settles, beams, worn flagstones and substantial log fire, one room with sofas, pine furniture and books; several well kept ales (usually a local brew), farm cider, generous plain food, friendly service, traditional games, quiet little family dining room; simple bedrooms *(Allan Westbury, MLR, Alistair Stanier, David Heath, LYM)*

ROSS-ON-WYE [SO5924]
☆ *Kings Head* HR9 5HL [High St]: Comfortable, warm and friendly hotel bar with beams and panelling, log-effect fire, lots of old pictures and some cosy armchairs, good generous sensibly priced food, swift friendly service, Cottage and Wye Valley ales; front restaurant and back dining conservatory; dogs welcome, 15 bedrooms, good breakfast, open all day *(Sally and Tom Matson, George Atkinson, Mrs P Sumner, Pete Coxon)*
Mail Rooms HR9 5BS [Gloucester Rd]: Modern Wetherspoons, their usual food using local ingredients, attractively priced beers (inc some interesting local ones) and wines, good coffee, pleasant attentive service; silenced TV; children in family area till 7pm, nice back terrace, open all day *(George Atkinson)*

SHOBDON [SO4061]
☆ *Bateman Arms* HR6 9LX: Striking 18th-c inn with enjoyable generous bargain food freshly made from local suppliers (so can take a while; not Mon), Sun roasts, well kept Wye Valley Butty Bach and guest beers, good wines by the glass; cheerful service, log fire in comfortable beamed bar with relaxed local feel, well decorated restaurant; nine bedrooms, good walks, open all day *(Ann and Colin Hunt, Alan and Eve Harding, Alistair Stanier)*

ST OWEN'S CROSS [SO5424]
☆ *New Inn* HR2 8LQ [junction A4137 and B4521, W of Ross-on-Wye]: New licensees for half-timbered 16th-c dining pub; huge inglenook fireplaces, dark beams and timbers,

nooks and crannies, old pews and mix of tables and chairs, Marstons, Wychwood and a guest, several malt whiskies and wines by the glass, no reports since new licensees took over; food all day inc thai dishes in bar and restaurant; piped music; children welcome, dogs in bar, spacious sheltered garden with play things, views to Black Mountains, open all day *(Rodney and Norma Stubington, Dr and Mrs Michael Smith, Canon Michael Bourdeaux, Alan and Eve Harding, Theocsbrian, LYM, Robert Turnham)*

STAPLOW [SO6941]
Oak HR8 1NP: Friendly and busy roadside village pub, chunky oak furniture and restored beams, Marstons-related ales, open kitchen doing pubby food from good choice of sandwiches up *(Dave and Jenny Hughes)*

STAUNTON-ON-WYE [SO3645]
New Inn HR4 7LR: Compact 16th-c two-bar village pub, pleasantly relaxed and old-fashioned, with well kept Wye Valley, good value generous home-made food lunchtimes and Fri, Sat evenings, friendly landlord and regulars, cosy alcoves; nice garden with quoits and boules, cl Mon *(MLR, Reg Fowle, Helen Rickwood)*

STIFFORDS BRIDGE [SO7348]
Red Lion WR13 5NN [A4103 3 miles W of Great Malvern]: Refurbished beamed roadside pub, wide choice of generous good value food, Greene King and some interesting guest ales, farm ciders; children and dogs welcome, tables in well kept garden *(Denis Kavanagh, Tim and Joan Wright)*

SUTTON ST NICHOLAS [SO5345]
Golden Cross HR1 3AZ: Doing well under hard-working landlord, well presented locally sourced food inc meal deals, weekly changing ales (perhaps locals such as Golden Valley or Mayfields); good service, clean décor, some breweriana, live music Fri; pretty village *(Reg Fowle, Helen Rickwood)*

SYMONDS YAT [SO5516]
Wye Knot HR9 6BJ [B4164]: Clean and welcoming, bar divided by central woodburner, Theakstons and Wye Valley ales from pine-clad counter, decent reasonably priced food, helpful friendly staff, separate dining room; Sun quiz night, beer festivals; children welcome, terrace, three bedrooms *(Reg Fowle, Helen Rickwood)*

TILLINGTON [SO4645]
☆ *Bell* HR4 8LE: Popular family-run pub with warmly welcoming landlord, proper home cooking (so can be a wait) in bar and compact restaurant from baguettes and other lunchtime snacks up, good value Sun carvery (must book); well kept Wye Valley and guests, neat attentive service, daily papers, comfortable pine furniture with banquettes in lounge extension; children and dogs welcome, steps up to good big garden with play area *(Reg Fowle, Helen Rickwood, Alan and Eve Harding, Alistair Stanier)*

ULLINGSWICK [SO5949]
Three Crowns HR1 3JQ [village off A465 S of Bromyard (and just S of Stoke Lacy) and

signposted off A417 N of A465 roundabout –
keep straight on through village and past
turn-off to church; pub at Bleak Acre,
towards Little Cowarne]: Attractive dining
pub with old timbered rooms and open fires,
smallish low-beamed hop-strewn bar,
traditional settles, old wooden tables and
more usual seats, candles and proper
napkins on tables; well kept Wye Valley and
a guest such as Hobsons, several wines by
the glass, food can be good, service
sometimes slow; children welcome, dogs
in bar, tables on attractively planted lawn,
nice views, bedrooms *(LYM, Chris Flynn,
Wendy Jones)*

☆ **WHITNEY-ON-WYE** [SO2447]
Rhydspence HR3 6EU [A438 Hereford—
Brecon]: Splendid half-timbered inn on the
border with Wales, rambling rooms with
heavy beams and timbers, attractive old-
fashioned furnishings, log fire in fine big
stone fireplace in central bar; Bass and
Robinsons, tasty bar food and grills,
enjoyable Sun lunch, restaurant; children
welcome, but no dogs inside, garden with
Wye Valley views, comfortable bedrooms
*(Alistair Stanier, LYM, Rodney and
Norma Stubington)*

WINFORTON [SO2946]
Sun HR3 6EA [A438]: Friendly unpretentious
pub with enjoyable home-made food (not Sun
evening) all sourced locally, Wye Valley Butty
Bach, local ciders, country-style beamed areas
either side of central servery, stripped-stone
and woodburners; piped music; children and
dogs welcome, garden tables, cl Mon *(Mr and
Mrs J P Syner, MLR, LYM)*

WOOLHOPE [SO6135]
Butchers Arms HR1 4RF [off B4224 in
Fownhope]: Tucked-away 14th-century low-
beamed pub reopened under new chef/owner
(a popular previous Main Entry), locally
sourced food well liked by some readers,
wide choice of wines by the glass inc
champagne, well kept ales, good service,
open fires; garden with stream, good walks,
cl Sun evening, Mon *(LYM, Dr and
Mrs Michael Smith, Tansy Spinks,
Nick Rampley, John and Jennifer Spinks)*

WORMELOW TUMP [SO4930]
Tump HR2 8EJ: Ancient timbered low-
ceilinged pub with more modern bar area,
Brains Dark and Flowers IPA, well presented
food inc good value Sun lunch, interesting
locals *(Reg Fowle, Helen Rickwood,
Alistair Stanier)*

'Children welcome' means the pub says it lets children inside without any special
restriction. If it allows them in, but to restricted areas such as an eating area or family
room, we specify this. Places with separate restaurants often let children use them,
hotels usually let them into public areas such as lounges. Some pubs impose an
evening time limit – let us know if you find one earlier than 9pm.

Hertfordshire

Recently, this county has been slightly thin on the ground as far as Main Entries are concerned, so we're delighted with our three new finds here: the ultra-modern reworked Clarendon at Chandlers Cross with its fairly elaborate food, the smartly updated Cricketers at Redbourn with a surprisingly good range of real ales and the Kings Arms at Tring, with its proper landlord, great beers and Bargain Award for its cheerful spicy menu. Old-timers that are still going particularly strong are the cheery family-friendly Cock at Sarratt and the Holly Bush at Potters Crouch, with its lovely staff. For a good meal out, both the Alford Arms in Frithsden (which has a proper pubby bar, too) and the Fox at Willian offer a real treat, but it's the Fox, with its very carefully prepared imaginative food, that is our Hertfordshire Dining Pub 2011. As Hertfordshire is just on the edge of London, at nearly half our Main Entries, you'll find Fullers beers; brewing since 1845, they claim to be London's only remaining traditional family brewer – head for the unpretentious White Horse in Hertford to take in the full range.

ALDBURY   SP9612   MAP 4

Greyhound

Stocks Road; village signposted from A4251 Tring—Berkhamsted, and from B4506; HP23 5RT

Spacious yet cosy old dining pub with traditional furnishings, popular food and courtyard

The tasty food at this handsome virginia creeper-covered inn does draw a crowd, but the friendly staff cope well and meals are served promptly. Three or four beers on handpump are usually Badger First Gold, King & Barnes Sussex and Tanglefoot and possibly a Badger guest. The beamed interior shows some signs of considerable age (around the copper-hooded inglenook, for example) towards the front, and is fairly traditionally furnished. It becomes more contemporary as you work your way through to leather chairs, a sofa and coffee table, then wicker chairs at big new tables in the airy oak-floored restaurant in an area at the back which overlooks a suntrap gravel courtyard. In winter the lovely warm fire and subtle lighting make it all feel really cosy. Benches at the front face a picturesque village green complete with whipping post and stocks, and a duck pond lively with wildfowl.

As well as toasted panini, dishes might include smoked haddock chowder, salt and pepper crispy squid with soy, chilli and sesame dip, warm vegetable quiche, smoked eel and carrot salad with horseradish cream, steak, ale and mushroom pie, butternut and pine nut risotto, pork fillet with celeriac and apple rémoulade and whisky and prune jus, a huge mixed grill and rib-eye steak; Sunday roast. *Starters/Snacks: £4.95 to £8.25. Main Courses: £10.45 to £14.95. Puddings: £4.55 to £6.45*

Badger ~ Tenant Tim O'Gorman ~ Real ale ~ Bar food (12-2.30, 7-9; 12-9 Sat; 12-8 Sun) ~ Restaurant ~ (01442) 851228 ~ Children welcome ~ Dogs allowed in bar ~ Open 11-11; 12-10.30 Sun ~ Bedrooms: £65S/£75B

Recommended by Roy Hoing, Peter and Giff Bennett, N R White, Mrs P Sumner

Valiant Trooper ◀

Trooper Road (towards Aldbury Common); off B4506 N of Berkhamsted; HP23 5RW

Cheery traditional all-rounder with appealing interior, six real ales, generous helpings of pubby food, and a garden

This very pleasant old country pub tends to feel a little more down to earth than the Greyhound. The first of a series of lovely unspoilt old rooms is beamed and tiled in red and black, with built-in wall benches, a pew and small dining chairs around attractive country tables, and an inglenook fireplace. Further in, the middle bar has spindleback chairs around tables on a wooden floor and some exposed brickwork. The far room has nice country kitchen chairs around individually chosen tables, and a woodburning stove, and the back barn has been converted to house a restaurant; dominoes, cribbage and bridge on Monday evenings. They keep a jolly decent range of half a dozen well kept beers on handpump: Brakspears, Fullers London Pride, local Tring Trooper Ale and three guests such as Adnams, Hook Norton and Sharps Doom Bar alongside local Millwhite's cider. The enclosed garden has a wooden adventure playground and the pub is well placed for walks through the glorious beechwoods of the National Trust's Ashridge Estate.

〖¶〗 **Quickly served bar food includes sandwiches, burgers, nachos, fish and chips, mushroom lasagne, scampi and chips, rabbit in thyme gravy, hake topped with prawn and herb sauce, chicken and prawn stir fry and rib-eye steak.** *Starters/Snacks: £5.00 to £9.00. Main Courses: £8.50 to £9.50. Puddings: £4.00 to £4.75*

Free house ~ Licensee Beth Parmar ~ Real ale ~ Bar food (12-3, 6.30-9; 12-9 Sat; 12-4 Sun; not Mon) ~ Restaurant ~ (01442) 851203 ~ Children in restaurant ~ Dogs allowed in bar ~ Open 12-11(10.30 Sun)
Recommended by Peter and Giff Bennett, Gordon Neighbour, Peter Martin, Kevin Thomas, Nina Randall, Steve and Sue Griffiths, Tim Maddison

ASHWELL   TL2739   MAP 5

Three Tuns

Off A505 NE of Baldock; High Street; SG7 5NL

Comfortable gently old-fashioned hotel bars, generous helpings of tasty food and a substantial garden

Converted to an inn in 1806, this well run hotel and pub was built in the reign of Queen Anne. Wood panelling, dark green walls, relaxing chairs, big family tables, lots of pictures, stuffed pheasants and fish, piped light classical music and antiques lend an air of Victorian opulence to the cosy lounge. The public bar is more modern, with leather sofas on reclaimed oak flooring, and cribbage, dominoes, games machine and TV. They stock a good choice of wines as well as Greene King IPA, St Edmunds and a guest on handpump. A big terrace has metal tables and chairs, while a large garden has picnic-sets and boules under the shade of apple trees. The charming village is full of pleasant corners and is popular with walkers as the landscape around rolls enough to be rewarding.

〖¶〗 **Changing bar food might include filled baguettes, chicken liver pâté, herring fillets in a sweet-cure marinade, devilled whitebait, lamb brochette with mint couscous, vegetable lasagne, chicken and coconut curry, steak and kidney pie, spanish pork casserole and sword fish with melon salsa, puddings such as caramelised brandy banana and Tia Maria cheesecake; Sunday roast.** *Starters/Snacks: £4.95 to £6.95. Main Courses: £6.95 to £15.95. Puddings: £4.95 to £5.75*

Greene King ~ Lease Bill Pennell ~ Real ale ~ Bar food (12-2.30, 6.30-9.30; 12-9.30 Sat, Sun) ~ Restaurant ~ (01462) 742107 ~ Children welcome ~ Dogs allowed in bar and bedrooms ~ Open 11-11.30(12.30 Sat, 11.30 Sun) ~ Bedrooms: £39(£53B)/£59(£69S)(£79B)
Recommended by Eithne Dandy, Mike and Lynn Robinson, Gordon Neighbour

We list pubs that serve food all day on at least some days at the end of the book.

BARKWAY

TL3834 MAP 5

Tally Ho ♀ ◀

London Road (B1368, which parallels A10 S of Royston); SG8 8EX

Quirky little local with great range of drinks

Feeling rather like a comfy living room, the cottagey little bar at this friendly local has an inviting old sofa, cosy armchairs in the big end bow window, horsebrasses and a warm log fire. There's another fire through in the dining area angling back on the left – very old-world, with fresh flowers and silver candelabra, and old-fashioned prints on brown ply panelling. At the last count, the extraordinary range of drinks here included 48 wines by the glass, 136 malt whiskies, over 200 different spirits, Aspall's farm cider, and Buntingford Highwayman and a couple of guests from brewers such as Nethergate and Rebellion, which look as if they are tapped from big casks behind the bar, but in fact are gently pumped. Beyond the car park a garden has well spaced picnic-sets, a weeping willow and fruit trees.

🍴 **Bar food might include potato and celery soup, smoked salmon with rocket and crème fraîche, fish pie, chicken kiev, steak and mushroom pudding, chicken breast with mushroom sauce, home-made haggis and sirloin steak, and puddings such as apple and cinnamon crumble, crème brûlée and baked chocolate fondant with banana ice-cream.** *Starters/Snacks: £4.95 to £7.95. Main Courses: £6.95 to £16.25. Puddings: £4.95 to £5.95*

Free house ~ Licensees Paul and Roz Danter ~ Real ale ~ Bar food (12-2, 6.30-9) ~ Restaurant ~ (01763) 848389 ~ Children welcome ~ Dogs allowed in bar ~ Open 11.30-11; 12-4 Sun; closed Sun evening

Recommended by M R D Foot, R T and J C Moggridge

BATFORD

TL1415 MAP 5

Gibraltar Castle

Lower Luton Road; B653, S of B652 junction; AL5 5AH

Pleasantly traditional pub with interesting militaria displays, some emphasis on food (booking advised); pretty terrace

The interior of this neatly kept welcoming pub is decked out with an impressive collection of military memorabilia – everything from rifles to swords, medals, uniforms and bullets (with plenty of captions to read). Otherwise quite traditional, the long carpeted low-beamed bar (with Fullers London Pride and ESB and a guest such as Jennings Cumberland on handpump) has a pleasant old fireplace, comfortably cushioned wall benches and a couple of snugly intimate window alcoves, one with a fine old clock. Pictures depict the pub's namesake and various moments in Gibraltar's history; several board games are piled on top of the piano, and they've piped music. In one area the low beams give way to soaring rafters. Outside, there are tables on a front terrace overlooking a nature reserve, on a pretty little decked area with lots of flowers at the back and in a tree-lined garden to one side of this – all are appealing places to while away a pleasant summer's day.

🍴 **Bar food includes a good range of lunchtime sandwiches, ploughman's, tomato and puff pastry tart, duck and port pâté with rhubarb chutney, risotto of the day, fish and chips, steak and kidney pudding, chicken pie and daily specials such as fried sailfish with beetroot and dill sauce and lamb wellington stuffed with goats cheese and wrapped with parma ham with red wine jus.** *Starters/Snacks: £5.95 to £7.95. Main Courses: £7.95 to £17.95. Puddings: £4.95 to £9.95*

Fullers ~ Tenant Hamish Miller ~ Real ale ~ Bar food (12-2.30(6 Sun), 6-9; not Sun evening) ~ (01582) 460005 ~ Children welcome ~ Dogs welcome ~ Open 11.30-11(12 Fri, Sat); 12-10.30 Sun

Recommended by David and Ruth Shillitoe

CHANDLERS CROSS
TQ0698 MAP 5

Clarendon

3 miles from M25 junction 20; A41 towards Watford, right at first traffic lights signposted Sarratt, then keep on into Redhall Lane; WD3 4LU

Good food in stylish new up-market pub/restaurant

Completely remodelled after a two-year closure, this is now an ultra-modern bar and restaurant. Big colourful contemporary artworks on bare brick or sage-green walls, soft lighting, a long and high dark wood bar counter with tall comfortable swivelling chrome and leather chairs that wouldn't be out of place in a Mayfair hotel, the gleaming stainless-steel kitchen that opens into an end dining area with black-topped tables on conical orange pedestals – clearly, a great deal of money has been spent here. There's an open fire in a side area with dark leather chesterfields, they have plenty of cheerful and well drilled young staff, and Tring Ridgeway and Fannie Ebbs on handpump as well as a good choice of wines by the glass; piped pop music, usually unobtrusive. Outside, a substantial brick-built smokers' shelter has its own open fire; a neatly landscaped terrace has square-cut metal benches and tables.

🍴 Though you can also eat from the menu of the grander upstairs restaurant, they don't really go in for pubby meals here. Dishes from both menus might include pea soup with smoked trout and crème fraîche, foie gras and chicken liver parfait with lentils and beans and walnut and raisin toast, rump of lamb with tomato, garlic and rosemary, grilled plaice and prawns with a pea, spring onion and garlic sauce, macaroni and cauliflower gratin with cocoa beans and tomato compote, and puddings such as home-made vanilla yoghurt with blueberry compote and nut crumble, almond cake with buttermilk sorbet and glazed poached pear, and eton mess. *Starters/Snacks: £5.50 to £8.50. Main Courses: £12.50 to £23.50. Puddings: £5.00 to £8.00*

Free house ~ Licensee David Cowham ~ Real ale ~ Bar food (12-5, 6-10; 10-11.30am (breakfast), 12-4, 6-9 Sun) ~ Restaurant ~ (01923) 270009 ~ Children welcome ~ Open 11-midnight; 10-10 Sun
Recommended by C Galloway, Peter and Giff Bennett

EPPING GREEN
TL2906 MAP 5

Beehive

Off B158 SW of Hertford, via Little Berkhamsted; back road towards Newgate Street and Cheshunt; SG13 8NB

Cheerful bustling country pub, popular for its good value food

Now a free house, this popular pub is well liked for its generous helpings of good value food and relaxed atmosphere. The pleasantly traditional bar is cosily chatty with a low ceiling, wheelback chairs and brocaded benches around tables on a patterned carpet. During the winter months, a woodburning stove in a panelled corner keeps it cosy and warm. Adnams, Greene King IPA and a guest are on handpump alongside a good range of wines by the glass; service is prompt and pleasant; piped music. Between the low, tiled, weatherboarded building and quiet country road is a neat lawn and new decked area with plenty of tables to take in the summer sunshine; good nearby woodland walks.

🍴 Fresh fish is delivered daily from Billingsgate, and main courses might include baked cod with bacon, mushroom and thyme sauce, mushroom and ale pie, and snacks such as sandwiches, baked potatoes, ploughman's, crab and mango salad, smoked haddock and spring onion fishcake, with puddings such as vanilla and rosemary crème brûlée or white chocolate and blueberry sponge pudding. *Starters/Snacks: £3.95 to £7.95. Main Courses: £5.95 to £15.95. Puddings: £4.00 to £5.00*

Post Office address codings confusingly give the impression that some pubs are in Hertfordshire, when they're really in Bedfordshire, Buckinghamshire or Cambridgeshire (which is where we list them).

Free house ~ Licensee Martin Squirrell ~ Real ale ~ Bar food (12-2.30(4 Sun), 6-9.30(8.30 Sun)) ~ Restaurant ~ (01707) 875959 ~ Children welcome ~ Open 11.30-3, 5.30-11; 12-10.30 Sun
Recommended by David Jackson, Mike and Lynn Robinson, Jestyn Phillips, J Marques, Gordon Neighbour

FLAUNDEN
TL0101   MAP 5

Bricklayers Arms 🍴 ♀

4 miles from M25 junction 18; village signposted off A41 – from village centre follow Boxmoor, Bovingdon road and turn right at Belsize, Watford signpost into Hogpits Bottom; HP3 0PH

Cosy country restaurant with fairly elaborate food and very good wine list

It's worth bearing in mind that the emphasis at this low brick-and-tiled virginia creeper-covered dining pub is very much on the upmarket intricately presented food (with prices to match) and its calmly civilised atmosphere – it's not the place for a quick cheap lunch. Stubs of knocked-through oak-timbered wall keep some feeling of intimacy in a series of areas that were originally separate rooms. The well refurbished low-beamed bar is snug and comfortable, with roaring winter log fires and pink plush cushions on dark brown wooden wall seats. The extensive wine list includes about 20 by the glass, and they've Fullers London Pride, Greene King IPA and a guest or two from brewers such as Tring and Rebellion on handpump. This is a lovely peaceful spot in summer, when the beautifully kept old-fashioned garden with its foxgloves against sheltering hedges comes into its own. Just up the Belsize road there's a path on the left which goes through delightful woods to a forested area around Hollow Hedge.

🍴 Some of the herbs and vegetables come from the pub's garden, and they smoke their own meat and fish. Food, which can be very good, might include crispy duck salad with beansprouts and black bean dressing, a selection of their own smoked fish, steak, kidney and ale pie, fried calves liver with port jus and bacon lardons, pea, butternut and herb risotto, pork knuckle on red cabbage and cider vinegar with bramley apple jus, well hung beef fillet with brandy cream sauce, and puddings such as lemon tart with grapefruit and orange sorbet and hot apple tart; Sunday roasts. *Starters/Snacks: £5.95 to £8.95. Main Courses: £9.95 to £22.50. Puddings: £4.50 to £6.95*

Free house ~ Licensee Alvin Michaels ~ Real ale ~ Bar food (12-2.30(3.30 Sun); 6.30-9.30 (8.30 Sun)) ~ Restaurant ~ (01442) 833322 ~ Children welcome ~ Dogs allowed in bar ~ Open 12-11.30(12.30 Sat, 10.30 Sun)
Recommended by Eleanor Dandy, Rob Harris, Peter and Giff Bennett, Chris Woodhead, John and Victoria Fairley, G K Smale

FRITHSDEN
TL0109   MAP 5

Alford Arms 🍴 ♀

From Berkhamsted take unmarked road towards Potten End, pass Potten End turn on right, then take next left towards Ashridge College; HP1 3DD

Thriving dining pub with chic interior, good food from imaginative menu and a thoughtful wine list

Though most people are here for a meal, there's still a good pubby feel in one area where you might find a few locals (and perhaps a jack russell perched on a stool) chatting at the bar. Usually, though, it's full to the brim with cheerful diners. You do need to book and readers tell us service can slow down just a little when it's very busy. The fashionably elegant but understated interior has simple prints on pale cream walls, with blocks picked out in rich Victorian green or dark red, and an appealing mix of good antique furniture (from Georgian chairs to old commode stands) on bare boards and patterned quarry tiles. It's all pulled together by luxurious, opulently patterned curtains; darts and piped jazz. All the wines on their list are european, with most of them available by the glass, and they've Brakspears, Flowers Original, Rebellion IPA and a guest such as Sharps Doom Bar on handpump. The pub stands by a village green and is surrounded by lovely

National Trust woodland. There are plenty of tables outside.

🍴 The seasonally changing menu might include herb-crusted local rabbit croquette with spiced cauliflower dip, devilled crispy chicken livers with turnip fritter and chive crème fraîche dressing, seared scallops on white pudding with apple and parsnip purée, local venison and smoked pancetta meatballs, chicken and black pudding suet pudding, fried bream with beetroot purée, salsify, pickled cucumber and chervil dressing, and rib-eye steak; and puddings such as lemon and thyme posset with crème fraîche ice-cream and steamed apple pudding with maple syrup and marsala ice-cream. *Starters/Snacks: £3.75 to £8.75. Main Courses: £11.50 to £17.50. Puddings: £4.50 to £6.75*

Salisbury Pubs ~ Lease Darren Johnston ~ Real ale ~ Bar food (12-2.30(3 Sat, 4 Sun), 6.30(7 Sun)-9.30(10 Sat)) ~ Restaurant ~ (01442) 864480 ~ Children welcome ~ Dogs allowed in bar ~ Open 11-11; 12-10.30 Sun

Recommended by Peter and Giff Bennett, Michael J Boniface, Kevin Thomas, Nina Randall, John Picken, J Marques, John Faircloth, David Restarick

HARPENDEN   TL1312   MAP 5

White Horse

Redbourn Lane, Hatching Green (B487 just W of A1081 roundabout); AL5 2JP

Smart up-to-date dining pub with civilised bar side

There are striking modern decorative touches throughout this refurbished restaurant. On the right, a cosy roomful of dark red leather armchairs has an odd lighting unit masquerading as a wall of old books (rather droll unless you view stripping leather-bound books of their spines as mutilation). It looks past a rack of wine bottles into the main back dining area: long, pale grey button-back banquettes and matching chairs, maroon walls, pale floorboards. The artworks throughout are for sale. The smallish front bar, with modern brown leather seating contrasting with traditional white-painted plank panelling, has Adnams and a guest such as Black Sheep on handpump as well as a good range of wines by the glass and an imposing row of keg beer founts. The piped music is fairly unobtrusive, service by neat staff is prompt and helpful, and they do good coffee and have the daily papers. An extensive newish stone terrace has plenty of teak tables.

🍴 The menu includes some very surprising combinations – we'd love to hear what you think: apple, ricotta and vanilla tortellini with hazelnut butter, sweetcorn, chicken and mushroom risotto, mussels with Guinness cream, roast john dory with lobster foam, grilled pork chop with vanilla mash, apple and bacon salsa and cider cream, chicken breast with hay-infused chips and walnut mayonnaise, and puddings such as smoked chocolate mousse with brioche ice-cream and hazelnut dressing. *Starters/Snacks: £6.00 to £7.50. Main Courses: £6.50 to £18.50. Puddings: £4.00 to £6.50*

Free house ~ Licensees Harwood Warrington and Giovanni Pilla ~ Real ale ~ Bar food (12-3, 6-10; 12-7 Sun) ~ Restaurant ~ (01582) 469290 ~ Children welcome ~ Dogs allowed in bar ~ Open 12-11(midnight Sat, 10pm Sun)

Recommended by Michael Dandy

HERTFORD   TL3212   MAP 5

White Horse 🍺 £

Castle Street; SG14 1HH

Up to nine real ales at this traditional town-centre local

A terrific range of about eight Fullers beers and possibly a guest such as Adnams (with more during their May and August bank holiday beer festivals) are on handpump at this chattily unpretentious little pub; also a dozen country wines. Tucked away in a side road, parts of the timber-framed building date from the 14th century and you can still see Tudor brickwork in the three quietly cosy upstairs family rooms. Its two downstairs rooms are small and homely, the one on the left being more basic, with bare boards, some brewery memorabilia and a few rather well worn tables, stools and chairs. A warming open fire separates it from the more comfortable beamed right-hand bar, which has a winged leather armchair, some old local photographs and a red-tiled floor; bar billiards. Two simple benches out on the pavement face the castle, and there are tables and chairs on a back terrace with hanging baskets and window boxes.

🍽 **Very inexpensive pubby food includes sandwiches, baguettes, ploughman's, chilli, lasagne, sausages, Sunday roast, and, on summer Thursday evenings, maybe sirloin steak and chicken.** *Starters/Snacks: £3.25 to £6.95*

Fullers ~ Lease Matthew Clark ~ Real ale ~ Bar food (12-2(1-3 Sun)) ~ (01992) 501950 ~ Children welcome ~ Dogs welcome ~ Open 12-11(midnight Fri, Sat, 10.30 Sun)
Recommended by LM, Pat and Tony Martin

POTTERS CROUCH   TL1105   MAP 5

Holly Bush 🍺 £

2.25 miles from M25 junction 21A: A405 towards St Albans, then first left, then after a mile turn left (ie away from Chiswell Green), then at T junction turn right into Blunts Lane; can also be reached fairly quickly, with a good map, from M1 exits 6 and 8 (and even M10); AL2 3NN

Lovingly kept cottage with gleaming furniture, fresh flowers and china, well kept Fullers beers, good value food, and an attractive garden

The licensees and staff are genuinely happy looking after their customers at this immaculately kept wisteria-swamped white pub. Service is calm, friendly and sincere, even when they're busy. Thoughtfully positioned fixtures create the illusion that there are lots of different rooms – some of which have the feel of a smart country house. In the evening, neatly placed candles cast glimmering light over darkly varnished tables, all sporting fresh flowers. There are quite a few antique dressers (several filled with plates), a number of comfortably cushioned settles, a fox's mask, some antlers, a fine old clock with a lovely chime, daily papers and, on the right as you go in, a big fireplace. The long, stepped bar has particularly well kept Fullers Chiswick, ESB, London Pride and a Fullers seasonal beer on handpump. Behind the pub, the fenced-off garden has a nice lawn, handsome trees and sturdy picnic-sets – it's a very pleasant place to sit in summer. Though the pub seems to stand alone on a quiet little road, it's only a few minutes' drive from the centre of St Albans (or a pleasant 45-minute walk).

🍽 **Food here offers impressive value for money, so no wonder it's so popular. The lunchtime menu is still very pubby – sandwiches, baked potatoes, ploughman's, burgers and platters, with fuller evening dishes (still good value) such as salmon en croûte, lamb chop with onion and rosemary sauce, sausage and mash, beef and ale hotpot with puff pastry lid, and puddings such as sticky toffee pudding and lemon bakewell tart.** *Starters/Snacks: £3.70 to £9.70. Main Courses: £8.50 to £12.50. Puddings: £3.90 to £5.90*

Fullers ~ Tenants Ray and Karen Taylor ~ Real ale ~ Bar food (12-2(2.30 Sun), 6-9; not Sun-Tues evenings) ~ (01727) 851792 ~ Open 12-2.30, 6-11; 12-3, 7-10 Sun
Recommended by Peter and Giff Bennett, J Marques, Tina and David Woods-Taylor, Paul Humphreys

PRESTON   TL1824   MAP 5

Red Lion 🍺

Village signposted off B656 S of Hitchin; The Green; SG4 7UD

Homely village local with changing beers and neatly kept colourful garden

Welcoming to locals and visitors alike, the cheery main room on the left at this nice old village-owned inn is pubbily simple with sturdy well varnished pub furnishings including padded country-kitchen chairs and cast-iron-framed tables on a patterned carpet, a log fire in a brick fireplace and foxhunting prints. The somewhat smaller room on the right has steeplechasing prints, some varnished plank panelling, and brocaded bar stools on flagstones around the servery; dominoes. They keep very good beer, with Fullers London

Pride and Wells & Youngs alongside three regularly changing guests from brewers such as Mauldons. They also tap farm cider from the cask, have several wines by the glass (including an english house wine), a perry and mulled wine in winter. A few picnic-sets out on the front grass face across to lime trees on a peaceful village green. At the back, a pergola-covered terrace gives way to many more picnic-sets (with some shade from a tall ash tree) and a neatly kept colourful herbaceous border in a good-sized sheltered garden beyond.

🍴 Reasonably priced bar food might include sandwiches and ploughman's, fish pie, chilli, chicken curry, ham, egg and chips, grilled plaice with caper butter, steaks, and chocolate fudge cake. *Starters/Snacks: £3.75 to £5.30. Main Courses: £6.75 to £9.50. Puddings: £3.75*

Free house ~ Licensee Raymond Lamb ~ Real ale ~ Bar food (not Tues) ~ (01462) 459585 ~ Children welcome ~ Dogs welcome ~ Open 12-2.30(3.30 Sat), 5.30-11; 12-3.30, 7-10.30 Sun
Recommended by Ross Balaam, Martin Wilson, Andy Lickfold

REDBOURN
TL1011   MAP 5

Cricketers 🍺

3.2 miles from M1 junction 9; A5183 towards St Albans, bear right on to B487, first right into Chequer Lane, then third right into East Common; AL3 7ND

Good food and beer in a nicely placed pub, with recent attractive updating

They rightly pride themselves on their fine range of five rapidly changing well kept ales on handpump here, with Greene King IPA as the house beer. On our early summer inspection visit they had Buntingford None of the Above, Burton Bridge, Tring Mansion and Westgate Morris Mayhem, as well as local Millwhite's Rum Cask cider. But don't get the idea that this is some beery real ale dive: the snugly odd-shaped front bar is a civilised place, with leather tub armchairs, plush banquettes and some leather cube stools on its pale carpet, and leads back into an attractive and comfortably modern dining room, also gaining from its oddly wiggly shape. They have a good choice of wines by the glass and do decent coffees. Staff are friendly and helpful; well reproduced piped music. An upper restaurant overlooks the cricket pitch and common, which has gentle interesting walks (map board by the next-door local museum). There are picnic-sets out on the side grass and sheltered bench seating by the front door.

🍴 Bar food might include starters such as ham hock terrine with caramelised onion and toasted brioche, crayfish and herb risotto and black pudding, bacon and new potato salad, main courses such as confit pork belly with spiced apple chutney and red wine glaze, seared calves liver with smoked bacon and red onion jus, tarragon and parmesan frittata with ratatouille salad, pancetta wrapped rabbit saddle with prune stuffing and colcannon mash, fried bream, courgette and leek with dill and roast garlic butter and rib-eye steak; puddings such as white chocolate and cherry cheesecake and treacle tart with clotted cream. *Starters/Snacks: £3.50 to £6.00. Main Courses: £9.50 to £15.00. Puddings: £4.50*

Free house ~ Licensees Colin Baxter and Andy Stuart ~ Real ale ~ Bar food (12-3, 6-9 (10 Fri, Sat); 12-5 Sun; not Sun evening) ~ Restaurant ~ (01582) 620612 ~ Children welcome ~ Dogs allowed in bar ~ Open 12-11(11.30 Thurs, 12 Fri, Sat); 12-10.30 Sun
Recommended by David M Smith, Alex Balance, John Picken

SARRATT
TQ0498   MAP 5

Cock

Church End: a very pretty approach is via North Hill, a lane N off A404, just under a mile W of A405; WD3 6HH

Plush pub popular with older dining set at lunchtime and families outside during summer weekends; Badger beers

A latched front door opens into the homely carpeted snug with a cluster of bar stools, vaulted ceiling and original bread oven at this cheery family-friendly pub. Through an archway, the partly oak-panelled cream-walled lounge has a lovely log fire in an inglenook, pretty Liberty-style curtains, pink plush chairs at dark oak tables, lots of interesting artefacts, and several namesake pictures of cockerels. Badger Best, Sussex, Tanglefoot and a seasonal Badger guest on handpump; piped music. The restaurant is in a nicely converted barn. In summer, children play happily on the bouncy castle and play area, leaving parents to take in the open country views from picnic-sets on the pretty, sheltered lawn and terrace. There are more picnic-sets in front that look out across a quiet lane towards the churchyard.

🍽 **At lunchtimes and during the early evenings you're likely to find an older set making the most of the good value OAP meals on offer here. Pubby dishes include sandwiches, ploughman's, whitebait, cheese and broccoli tagliatelle, chicken caesar salad, battered cod, steak and ale pie and rib-eye steak.** *Starters/Snacks: £5.25 to £6.95. Main Courses: £9.50 to £16.95. Puddings: £5.25*

Badger ~ Tenants Brian and Marion Eccles ~ Real ale ~ Bar food (12-2.30, 6-9; 12-7 Sun; not Mon, Sun evenings) ~ Restaurant ~ (01923) 282908 ~ Children welcome ~ Dogs allowed in bar ~ Jazz on Sun at 3.30pm ~ Open 12-11(11.30 Sat, 9 Sun)

Recommended by Peter and Judy Frost, David Jackson, Susan and John Douglas, Roy Hoing, Barry and Anne, Tracey and Stephen Groves, Peter and Giff Bennett, LM, N R White, D J and P M Taylor

TRING

SP9211   MAP 4

Kings Arms 🍺 £

King Street, by junction with Queen Street (which is off B4635 Western Road – continuation of High Street); HP23 6BE

Cheerful backstreet pub with wide appeal, good changing beers and good value food

This is thoroughly traditional, in the way we all fondly imagine pubs used to be years ago – though very few actually were! The atmosphere is chatty and relaxed, and staff really seem to care here. As well as Wadworths 6X, four quickly changing ales might be from favourite brewers Oakham, Sharps, Tring and Vale, but you might find anything here – on our inspection visit, there was Castle Rock Screech Owl, Houston Blonde Bombshell, Marston Moor Merrie Maker and Sharps Cornish Coaster, and they have Weston's cider and a good choice of wines by the glass. Kept spic and span, the bar gives the intimate feel of two or three separate areas, with a mix of cushioned pews and bentwood chairs and stools around the cast-iron-framed tables on its carpet; old brewery advertisements are framed on the green walls, one corner has old pine panelling, and there are two little fireplaces. An attractive side wagon yard has heaters for the good mix of tables and —— picnic-sets.

🍽 **If you drop in at lunchtime even for just a drink you'll be strongly tempted to eat, as we were, by the delicious aromas – the good value menu runs to some exotic spicy things as well as more straightforward hot sandwiches and light dishes: bruschetta, home-made burgers, prawn, sweet potato and coriander cakes, nachos, chilli, hot sausage sandwich, smoked haddock and chorizo quesadillas and pork and paprika meatballs.** *Starters/Snacks: £4.00 to £6.20. Main Courses: £7.80 to £9.80. Puddings: £2.00 to £4.00*

Free house ~ Licensee John Francis ~ Real ale ~ Bar food (12-2.15(2.30 Fri, Sat, 3 Sun), 7-9.30(9 Fri)) ~ (01442) 823318 ~ Well behaved children welcome till 8.30pm ~ Dogs allowed in bar ~ Open 12-2.30(3 Fri), 7-11.30; 11.30-3, 7-11.30 Sat; 12-4, 7-11 Sun

Recommended by Tracey and Stephen Groves, David M Smith

Robin Hood 🍺

Brook Street (B486); HP23 5ED

Really welcoming pub with good beer and popular pubby food

This carefully run pub is pleasingly traditional with a homely atmosphere and genial service in its several immaculately kept smallish linked areas. The main bar has banquettes and standard pub chairs on spotless bare boards or carpets and, early in the evening, regulars pop in to occupy the stools lined along the counter. Later on, couples arrive for the tasty food. Beers include five very well kept Fullers brews and a guest. Towards the back, you'll find a conservatory with a vaulted ceiling and woodburner. The licensees' two little yorkshire terriers are called Buddy and Sugar; piped music. There are tables out on the small pleasant back terrace.

🍴 **Enjoyably pubby food includes filled baguettes, baked potatoes, thai spiced fishcakes, fish and chips, scampi, chilli and steak and kidney pudding, vegetable curry, and puddings such as crème brûlée and ice-cream. They do sausage specials on Tuesday and Thursday nights and Sunday roast.** *Starters/Snacks: £3.95 to £5.95. Main Courses: £7.95 to £13.95. Puddings: £3.95*

Fullers ~ Tenants Terry Johnson and Stewart Canham ~ Real ale ~ Bar food (12-2.15, 6-9.15; not Sun evening) ~ (01442) 824912 ~ Children welcome ~ Dogs welcome ~ Quiz night first Weds and third Sun of the month ~ Open 11.30-3, 5.30-11(11.30 Fri); 12-4, 6-11.30 Sat; 12-4, 7-11 Sun

Recommended by Tracey and Stephen Groves, John Branston

WILLIAN   TL2230   MAP 5

Fox

A mile from A1(M) junction 9; A6141 W towards Letchworth then first left; SG6 2AE
HERTFORDSHIRE DINING PUB OF THE YEAR

Civilised (not cheap) dining pub with well prepared food, especially imaginative dishes, and a nice range of drinks

Doing rather well at the moment, this thoughtfully managed dining pub has a fresh clean-cut feel. Contemporary styling takes in comfortable light wood chairs and tables on stripped boards or big ceramic tiles, with modern pictures on white or pastel walls. Carefully lit, with boxy contemporary bar stools running along its pale blue frontage, the modern counter serves Adnams, Brancaster Best, Fullers London Pride, Woodfordes Wherry, and a guest from a brewer such as Buntingford, from handpumps, a good wine list with just over a dozen by the glass and a nice range of spirits. Pleasantly attentive young staff seem to really enjoy their work; well reproduced piped music and relatively unobtrusive TV. A side terrace has smart tables under cocktail parasols, and there are picnic-sets in the good-sized garden behind, below the handsome tower of the 14th-c All Saints church.

🍴 **As well as sandwiches, the well executed changing menu includes a good cross-section of dishes, with starters such as leek and potato soup with blue cheese en croûte, salmon and dill terrine, a dozen brancaster staithe oysters; main courses such as seared local tenderloin of pork and honey-glazed pork belly with apple crumble, battered cod fillet with pea purée, beef and pork burger with caramelised Guinness onions, roast brill with cardamom shallot and cream cheese sauce, roast butternut squash and mangetout risotto with beetroot crisps, cajun spiced cod fillet with turmeric and coriander cream; and puddings such as lychee panna cotta with roast nut crunch and red grape sorbet and chocolate truffle brioche with glazed orange and cardamom and pistachio ice-cream, and a british cheese platter; they add service automatically.** *Starters/Snacks: £4.90 to £9.50. Main Courses: £8.95 to £18.50. Puddings: £5.25 to £5.50*

Free house ~ Licensee Cliff Nye ~ Real ale ~ Bar food (12-2(3 Sun), 6.45-9.15; not Sun evening) ~ Restaurant ~ (01462) 480233 ~ Children welcome ~ Dogs allowed in bar ~ Open 12-11(midnight Fri, Sat, 10.30 Sun)

Recommended by Jill and Julian Tasker, Allan Finlay, David and Ruth Shillitoe, A and H Piper, Mr and Mrs T B Staples, D M Jack, J Marques

---

Real ale to us means beer which has matured naturally in its cask – not pressurised or filtered. We name all real ales stocked. We usually name ales preserved under a light blanket of carbon dioxide too, though purists – pointing out that this stops the natural yeasts developing – would disagree (most people, including us, can't tell the difference!).

LUCKY DIP

Besides the fully inspected pubs, you might like to try these Lucky Dips recommended to us and described by readers (if you do, please send us reports: feedback@goodguides.com).

ALDENHAM [TQ1498]
Round Bush WD25 8BG [Roundbush Lane]: Friendly village pub with plenty of atmosphere, well cooked generous food, ales such as Black Sheep and St Austell in good condition, efficient service; big garden (*Jack and Sandra Clarfelt*)

ASHWELL [TL2639]
Rose & Crown SG7 5NP [High St]: Friendly traditional local, Greene King ales and a seasonal guest, enjoyable food (not Sun evening) from changing menu, L-shaped bar with 16th-c beams and lovely log fire, candlelit restaurant; children welcome, big garden with play area and pétanque, open all day wknds (*Andrew Marrison, Johny Fletcher*)

AYOT GREEN [TL2213]
Waggoners AL6 9AA [off B197 S of Welwyn]: Refurbished former 17th-c coaching inn doing well under french owners; food in cosy low-beamed bar, more upmarket french cooking in comfortable good-sized restaurant extension, friendly attentive staff, good wine list, real ales; attractive and spacious suntrap back garden with sheltered terrace (some A1(M) noise), wooded walks nearby (*Leon Warner, Mrs Ann Adams, BB, J Marques*)

BALDOCK [TL2433]
Cock SG7 6BG [High St]: Proper welcoming local with huge blazing fire, Greene King ales and guests (*Peter Mahaffey*)

BELSIZE [TL0300]
Plough WD3 4NP: Small friendly local, central bar and barn-like beamed lounge with open fire, Tring beers, enjoyable good value home-made food; picnic-sets in nice garden, good walks (*Andrew Scarr, Roy Hoing*)

BENINGTON [TL3022]
Lordship Arms SG2 7BX [Whempstead Rd]: Comfortable and welcoming one-bar pub, well kept Black Sheep, Crouch Vale, Timothy Taylors and five guests, Aspall's cider, reasonably priced simple lunchtime food inc landlady's good Sun lunch (must book), curry night Weds (no booking); telephone memorabilia, classic car meets (2nd Tues of month from 6pm May-Sept); garden (*Steve Nye*)

BERKHAMSTED [SP9907]
Old Mill HP4 2NB [A4251, Hemel end]: Huge rambling dining pub, attractive layout, very wide choice of enjoyable food (usually something available all day), three well kept ales, friendly efficient staff, two good fires; tables outside, some overlooking unspectacular stretch of Grand Union Canal (*Kevin Thomas, Nina Randall, BB, Ross Balaam*)

BISHOP'S STORTFORD [TL4821]
Half Moon CM23 2LD [North St]: Well kept changing real ales, Weston's farm cider and lots of country wines, helpful friendly staff, good lunchtime food, lovely old building with bare-boards rooms of different sizes

and levels, décor tastefully in keeping; piped and live music; open all day (*Nic Courtman*)

BRAGBURY END [TL2621]
Chequers SG2 8TH: Well looked after Vintage Inn dating from 1774, low-beamed rooms off central bar, ales such as Adnams, Fullers London Pride and Wells & Youngs Bombardier, good choice of wines by the glass, decent food all day at reasonable prices; quick friendly service, inglenook log fire; piped music; tables in front garden (*Anthony and Marie Lewis*)

CHIPPERFIELD [TL0400]
Cart & Horses WD4 9BA [Commonwood, just S]: Smallish pub popular for its enjoyable reasonably priced food inc good steak and kidney pudding, well kept Greene King Abbot (*Ross Balaam*)

Two Brewers WD4 9BS [The Common]: Recent refurbishment at this attractive 18th-c country hotel housing popular bay-windowed Chef & Brewer, roomy linked areas, two log fires, pretty décor; all-day food from sandwiches up inc set price offers, good choice of wines by the glass, well kept Adnams, Fullers and Wells & Youngs, pleasant staff; provision for children, disabled facilities, terrace seating, 20 comfortably redone bedrooms, lovely spot on common and handy for M25, open all day (*Peter and Judy Frost, David Gurr, Steve and Sue Griffiths, LYM*)

CHISWELL GREEN [TL1304]
Three Hammers AL2 3EA [just S of St Albans; Watford Rd]: Good Ember Inn with enjoyable low-priced food, up to six ales, decent wines, friendly helpful staff, several areas on different levels around central bar, lots of beams (some quite low), comfortable sofas and armchairs by fireplace, photographs of old St Albans; no children inside; garden tables (*KC, John and Joyce Snell, Jack and Sandra Clarfelt*)

CHORLEYWOOD [TQ0395]
☆ *Black Horse* WD3 5EG [Dog Kennel Lane, the Common]: Warm welcome to all, inc children, walkers and dogs, good value pubby food from good sandwiches up, OAP lunch some days, well kept Adnams, St Austell Proper Job, Wadworths 6X and Wells & Youngs Bitter, decent wines (and tea and coffee); good cheery service even when busy, low dark beams and two log fires in thoroughly traditional rambling bar, daily papers; big-screen TV; picnic-sets overlooking common, open all day (*Peter and Giff Bennett, Roy Hoing, LM, BB, Peter and Judy Frost*)

☆ *Gate* WD3 5SQ [Rickmansworth Rd]: Open-plan family dining pub with clean-cut and attractive contemporary décor, wide range of good up-to-date food inc sharing plates, well kept Adnams and Timothy Taylors Landlord, Aspall's cider, good choice of wines by the glass, genial largely antipodean staff coping well when busy; piped music; plenty of garden tables, handy for M25 junction 18 (Michael Dandy, John Branston, Tom Evans, Brian Glozier, Peter and Giff Bennett, LYM)

☆ **Land of Liberty Peace & Plenty** WD3 5BS [Long Lane, Heronsgate, just off M25 junction 17]: Well kept local Red Squirrel, Tring and interesting guest beers, Millwhite's and Weston's ciders and perry, belgian bottled beers, decent coffee, enjoyable lunches with some imaginative dishes, all-day snacks, good service; simple traditional layout, darts, skittles and board games; TV, no children inside; dogs welcome, covered back decking, more picnic-sets in garden behind, open all day (N R White, Stan Edwards, BB)

COLEMAN GREEN [TL1912]

John Bunyan AL4 8ES: Quietly set beamed country local with well kept McMullens ales, good range of reasonably priced unpretentious home-made food, efficient friendly service; warm log fire, simple furnishings, masses of decorative plates, mugs, jugs and other china; big garden fronting green, play area and terrace, good walks (Tim Hayward)

COLNEY HEATH [TL2007]

☆ **Plough** AL4 0SE [Sleapshyde; handy for A1(M) junction 3; A414 towards St Albans, doubling back at first roundabout then turning off left]: Cosily refurbished 18th-c low-beamed thatched local, chatty atmosphere, good value generous home-made standard food from sandwiches up (lunchtime Mon-Sat, and Fri, Sat evening); well kept Fullers London Pride and Greene King IPA and Abbot, friendly efficient staff, big log fire, small brighter back dining area; white iron tables on pretty front terrace, picnic-sets on sheltered back terrace and lawn overlooking open fields (Stan Edwards, John Picken, BB)

COTTERED [TL3229]

☆ **Bull** SG9 9QP [A507 W of Buntingford]: Friendly well run dining pub with airy low-beamed front lounge, good furniture on stripped wood, log fire, good if not cheap food from sandwiches up (may add 10% service charge), Greene King ales, decent wines; unobtrusive piped music; no prams, no under-7s Mon-Sat, big garden with tables under majestic old trees, open all day Sun (Lois Dyer, J Marques, Jack and Sandra Clarfelt, Simon Watkins, Paul Marston, Gordon Neighbour, R T and J C Moggridge, LYM)

FURNEUX PELHAM [TL4327]

Brewery Tap SG9 0LL [Bealey Croft End]: Generous and enjoyable home-made food, well kept Greene King IPA and Abbot, cheerful staff, pleasant dining room; piped music, pool; children welcome, back garden room and terrace overlooking neat attractive garden (Simon Watkins)

GOSMORE [TL1827]

Bull SG4 7QG [High St]: Welcoming pub with fresh décor and open fire, Greene King and Wells & Youngs, home-made food

inc bargain lunch deals (John Baxter)

GRAVELEY [TL2327]

Waggon & Horses SG4 7LE [High St (B197), a mile from A1(M) junction 8]: Attractive former coaching inn with good generous fairly priced food from sandwiches up, well kept Adnams, Flowers and Wells London Pride, good wine choice; friendly staff, comfortable beamed and timbered lounge, big open fire; secluded streamside back garden with terrace, duck pond over road (Jerry Brown)

GREAT OFFLEY [TL1427]

☆ **Green Man** SG5 3AR [signed off A505 Luton—Hitchin; High St]: Roomy and comfortably olde-worlde Chef & Brewer with very wide choice of enjoyable generous food, well organised friendly staff, Marstons Pedigree, Theakstons Bitter and Old Peculier and Wells & Youngs Bombardier, good choice of wines by the glass, good coffee; blazing log fires, large flagstoned conservatory; may be unobtrusive piped classical music; children welcome, peaceful country views from picnic-sets in back garden with pleasant terrace, striking inn sign, open all day (LYM, Cliff Fine)

HARPENDEN [TL1415]

Amble AL5 4UL [Station Rd]: Comfortably reworked with mix of contemporary décor and familiar fittings, Black Sheep, Timothy Taylors Landlord, good coffees, home-made food inc tapas nights; open all day and from 10am Sat for breakfast (Niamh O'Connor, Matt Eddleston)

Engineer AL5 1DJ [St Johns Rd]: Two-bar pub in residential area, Adnams, Black Sheep, Fullers London Pride and Shepherd Neame Spitfire, good choice of wines by the glass, good value bar food from sandwiches up; welcoming helpful staff; conservatory restaurant with different menu inc Sun roasts; piped music, games, TV; pleasant garden with terrace and small fish pond (Michael Dandy, Eleanor Dandy)

Fox AL5 3QE [Luton Rd, Kinsbourne Green; 2.2 miles from M1 junction 10; A1081 towards town]: Contemporary dining pub, tiled floor, usual leather armchairs and sofas, lots of modern dining tables in alcoves; enjoyably up-to-date pubby food, friendly helpful service, interesting wines by the glass, well kept Adnams and Timothy Taylors Landlord, open fire; piped music; terrace tables (Eithne Dandy, Clifford Blakemore)

Plough & Harrow AL5 1PR [on roundabout, junction of Southdown Rd and Walkers Rd]: Large open-plan pub with wide choice of good value usual food inc huge Sun lunches, real ales such as Greene King IPA and Shepherd Neame Spitfire, decent wines, cheery service; piped music, TVs and games; good garden with big play area (Stuart Paulley)

HATFIELD [TL2308]

Horse & Groom AL9 5AT [Park St, Old Hatfield]: Friendly old-fashioned town local with good value lunchtime food (not Sun) from sandwiches up, bargain meal-and-a-pint night Tues, four well kept ales inc Greene King; dark beams and dado, roaring fires each end, lots of old local photographs, darts and dominoes, quiz night every other Thurs; a few tables out behind, handy for Hatfield House (anon)

HEMEL HEMPSTEAD [TL0411]

☆ *Crown & Sceptre* HP2 6EY [Bridens Camp; leaving on A4146, right at Flamstead/Markyate sign opp Red Lion]: Neatly refurbished rambling pub, welcoming and relaxed, with six well kept ales inc Black Sheep, Greene King and St Austell, good home-made pubby food at low prices, friendly efficient staff, log fires; children and dogs welcome, garden and heated front picnic-sets, open all day summer wknds (Mr and Mrs Graham Wood, LYM, Ross Balaam, Dennis Jones)

Marchmont Arms HP1 3AT [by roundabout on new northerly route of A4147]: 18th-c pub/brasserie, wide choice of interesting modern food (all day Sun), good wines, two real ales, friendly professional staff, stylish contemporary décor, log fires; children welcome, nice garden, open all day (Val and Alan Green)

White Lion HP3 9SB [London Rd]: Small dimly lit town pub, friendly locals, well kept Fullers ales, Thurs poker night; back courtyard (David Gurr)

HERTFORD [TL3212]

Six Templars SG14 1PS [The Wash]: Reliable Wetherspoons next to castle; modern, roomy and good value (Martin and Alison Stainsby)

HEXTON [TL1030]

Raven SG5 3JB [signed off B655]: Part of attractive mock-Tudor estate village, very popular for wide range of good value food from baguettes up, children's meals, friendly efficient service, ales such as Everards, Greene King and Potton, good choice of wines by the glass; open fire, plenty of dining tables in four linked areas, paintings (some for sale); piped music; big garden with heated terrace, barbecue and play area (Michael Dandy)

HIGH WYCH [TL4714]

Hand & Crown CM21 0AY [signed off A1184 Harlow—Sawbridgeworth]: Nice interior with some interesting features inc huge central fireplace dividing off restaurant area, wide choice of good fairly priced food, well kept Adnams and Greene King, plenty of whiskies, quick friendly service; piped music may obtrude (Grahame and Myra Williams, BB)

Rising Sun CM21 0HZ: Cosy old-fashioned local, serving hatch to carpeted lounge with log fire, central area with well kept Courage, Mighty Oak and guests tapped from the cask, friendly landlord and locals, bar food (not Sun evening, Mon); bare-boards games room (children allowed) with darts and woodburner; no mobile phones; small garden (the Didler)

HUNTON BRIDGE [TL0800]

Waterside Tavern WD4 8RE [just off A41 nr Kings Langley; Bridge Rd]: Refurbished early 18th-c pub/restaurant on several levels inc a gallery, compact bar with comfortable seating area, good range of food freshly made pizzas, Fullers London Pride, helpful friendly service; big canalside garden excellent for children, open all day Sun (David Eagles)

ICKLEFORD [TL1831]

Plume of Feathers SG5 3YD [Upper Green]: Old beamed pub with seven ales inc Adnams, Batemans, Black Sheep and Fullers, friendly staff and regulars, well appointed dining area; nice quiet spot overlooking green (Jerry Brown)

KNEBWORTH [TL2320]

Lytton Arms SG3 6QB [Park Lane, Old Knebworth]: Lutyens-designed pub with spotless big-windowed rooms around large central servery, wide choice of changing ales and ciders, beer festivals, good range of wines inc champagne by the glass; food from sandwiches and baked potatoes up, good log fire, daily papers, conservatory; children and dogs welcome, picnic-sets on front terrace, back garden with covered terrace and summer barbecues, nice surroundings, open all day (Conor McGaughey, Stan Edwards, Mike and Jennifer Marsh, LYM)

LITTLE GADDESDEN [SP9913]

Bridgewater Arms HP4 1PD [Nettleden Rd, off B4506]: Pleasant well cared for 19th-c stone dining pub, reasonably priced food inc enjoyable set lunches, Greene King IPA and Abbot, good wine choice inc rosé by the glass, good coffee, friendly attentive service; daily papers, carpeted bar with log fire, smart high-ceilinged restaurant, games in small bare-boards public area; garden tables, good walks from the door (Mike and Jennifer Marsh, John and Penelope Massey Stewart, LYM)

LITTLE HADHAM [TL4322]

Nags Head SG11 2AX [Hadham Ford, towards Much Hadham]: Popular 16th-c country dining pub with small linked heavily black-beamed rooms, reasonably priced food from snacks up, small bar with three Greene King beers and decent wines; restaurant down a couple of steps; children in eating areas, tables in pleasant garden (LYM, Gordon Neighbour)

MUCH HADHAM [TL4219]

☆ *Bull* SG10 6BU [High St]: Neatly kept dining pub with good home-made food changing daily, good choice of wines by the glass inc champagne, well kept Hancocks HB, cheerful efficient service even when busy; inglenook log fire in unspoilt bar, attractive pastel décor in roomy civilised dining lounge and back dining room; children welcome, good-sized garden (Ross Balaam, Simon Watkins, Steve and Sue Griffiths, LYM)

NORTHAW [TL2702]

Sun EN6 4NL [B156]: Civilised nicely refurbished pub dating from 16th c, opp the church; painted panelling and some exposed brickwork, central open fire, curved bar counter with stained-glass gantry, snug with another fireplace, wide choice of locally sourced food all day inc mid-week sandwiches and Sun roasts, good service, real ales; two dining rooms with mix of old furniture on brick and bare boards; terrace hanging baskets and circular picnic-sets under umbrellas, more tables in garden, cl Sun evening, Mon *(Charles Gysin)*

Two Brewers EN6 4NW [Northaw Rd W (B156)]: Several traditional snug areas, nice dining room and garden with view of ancient parish church, three well kept ales inc Wells & Youngs Bombardier, enjoyable generous food, friendly efficient staff *(Ross Balaam)*

NUTHAMPSTEAD [TL4134]

☆ *Woodman* SG8 8NB [off B1368 S of Barkway]: Tucked-away thatched and weatherboarded village pub, welcoming and well run, with comfortable unspoilt core, worn tiled floor, nice inglenook log fire, another fire opposite and 17th-c low beams and timbers, plainer extension; enjoyable home-made traditional food (not Sun evening), home-baked bread, well kept McMullens, efficient friendly service; interesting USAF memorabilia and memorial outside (nearby World War II airfield); benches out overlooking tranquil lane, comfortable bedrooms, open all day Sat *(Mike and Lynn Robinson, BB, Marion and Bill Cross, Simon Watkins, John Walker, M R D Foot, Steve Nye)*

RADLETT [TL1600]

Cat & Fiddle WD7 7JR [Cobden Hill; A5183, opp Tabard RUFC]: Welcoming 18th-c inn, three small rooms with fires, five well kept ales, good value enjoyable food; children welcome, picnic-sets in small tree-sheltered garden with barbecue and play area *(Nigel Barrow)*

Red Lion WD7 7NP [Watling St]: Pleasant rambling hotel dating from 18th c, lots of prints in neatly modernised carpeted bar, well kept Wells & Youngs ales, bar food inc all-day sandwiches, large restaurant; front terrace, 13 comfortable bedrooms, good breakfast *(Mike and Lynn Robinson)*

REDBOURN [TL1111]

Chequers AL3 7AD [St Albans Rd (A5183), nr M1 junction 9]: Small rebuilt Chef & Brewer family dining pub with thatch, flagstones, open fires and dark wood; wide choice of usual good value food, Adnams, Fullers London Pride and Greene King Old Speckled Hen, good choice of wines by the glass, friendly helpful service; piped music, games; large back terrace and small pleasant garden *(Michael Dandy, Dennis and Doreen Haward)*

REED [TL3636]

☆ *Cabinet* SG8 8AH [off A10; High St]: 16th-c weatherboarded pub-restaurant, good food from upscale pricey things to cheaper set lunch deals and bar meals, Fullers London Pride and two guests in compact bar with inglenook log fire, fine choice of wines by

the glass, brick-floor snug with darts, smart dining room, ghost called Stan; children and dogs welcome, charming big garden with pond, open all day wknds, cl Mon *(M R D Foot, LYM)*

RICKMANSWORTH [TQ0594]

Feathers WD3 1DJ [Church St]: Revitalised pub quietly set off the high street, civilised and smart, with beams, panelling and low lighting, Adnams, Fullers London Pride and interesting guests, food (all day wknds) from sandwiches up inc lunchtime deals, staff cope well when busy; children till 5pm, picnic-sets out at back, open all day *(Tracey and Stephen Groves)*

SARRATT [TQ0499]

Cricketers WD3 6AS [The Green]: Big bustling beamed dining pub in attractive spot overlooking large green, recently refurbished (cricket theme), good variety of enjoyable food, several changing ales, good wine choice, enthusiastic young staff; tables out by pond, open all day *(Peter and Giff Bennett)*

ST ALBANS [TL1407]

Cock AL1 3NF [St Peters St/Hatfield Rd]: Comfortably modernised beamed town pub with interesting history – said to have once had a floor of human bones (now wood and stone); real ales, good choice of interesting food inc lunch and evening set deals, two-way open fire, daily papers, restaurant with light wood tables and leather chairs; sports TV; heated garden *(LYM)*

Farmers Boy AL1 1PQ [London Rd]: Tastefully refurbished bay-windowed pub with its own Alehouse brews, continental bottled beers, log fire, back open kitchen doing bar lunches; Sky TV; suntrap terrace behind, open all day *(the Didler, Stephen and Jean Curtis)*

Farriers Arms AL3 4PT [Lower Dagnall St]: Plain, friendly, two-bar backstreet local, McMullens inc Mild and guest beers, bar food wkdys, lots of old pictures of the pub; (Campaign for Real Ale started here in the early 1970s) *(the Didler, P Dawn)*

Hare & Hounds AL1 1RL [Sopwell Lane]: Traditional pub with real ales such as Timothy Taylors Landlord, Sharps Doom Bar and Woodfordes Wherry, enjoyable good value local food inc good Sun lunch, sofa by nice open fire; sports TV; seats outside *(P Dawn, Nick Rowe)*

Lower Red Lion AL3 4RX [Fishpool St]: Hospitable beamed local dating from 17th c (right-hand bar has the most character), up to eight or so well kept changing ales inc local Alehouse (regular beer festivals), imported beers, enjoyable inexpensive lunchtime food inc sandwiches, speciality sausages and popular Sun roast; red plush seats and carpet, board games; no nearby parking; tables in good-sized back garden, bedrooms (some sharing bath), open all day Fri-Sun *(Phil Bryant, the Didler, P Dawn)*

☆ *Plough* AL4 0RW [Tyttenhanger Green, off A414 E]: Village pub with well kept Fullers and five changing guest beers, friendly efficient staff, bargain straightforward lunchtime food, good log fire, interesting old beer bottles and mats, longcase clock, back conservatory; big garden with play area *(LYM, the Didler)*

☆ *Six Bells* AL3 4SH [St Michaels St]: Well kept rambling pub popular for its good fresh generous food from lunchtime ciabattas to interesting specials, cheerful attentive service even when busy, several well kept ales from Fullers, Greene King and Timothy Taylors; low beams and timbers, log fire, quieter panelled dining room; children welcome, occasional barbecues in small back garden, handy for Verulamium Museum, open all day *(LYM, David and Ruth Shillitoe, Maria Thomas, Mrs M G Uglow, Mike and Jennifer Marsh)*

White Lion AL1 1RN [Sopwell Lane]: Good atmosphere in small friendly front bar and roomy linked lounge areas, enjoyable proper cooking (not Sun evening or Mon) inc interesting dishes, well kept ales such as Adnams and Wells & Youngs; darts and other games; big back garden, play area *(the Didler)*

STANDON [TL3922]
Star SG11 1LB [High St]: Friendly pub with enjoyable good value pubby food, good service, well kept Greene King ales; children welcome, garden tables *(Ross Balaam, Vanessa Clay)*

STAPLEFORD [TL3017]
Woodhall Arms SG14 3NW [High Rd]: Well kept Greene King, Wells & Youngs and guest ales, good bar food (not Sat evening), Sun roasts, separate spacious restaurant; ten comfortable bedrooms, good breakfast *(Mike and Lynn Robinson)*

THERFIELD [TL3337]
☆ *Fox & Duck* SG9 9PN [signed off A10 S of Royston; The Green]: Open-plan bow-windowed pub with country chairs and big stripped-top dark tables on stone flooring, good choice of enjoyable well priced food inc enterprising sandwiches and locally grown veg, Greene King IPA, decent wines and coffee; friendly helpful staff, good-sized carpeted back restaurant, darts in smaller boarded area on left (TV and games machine); bedrooms, garden with good play equipment, more picnic-sets out on front green, quiet village, pleasant walks nearby *(Joan Sweeney, Simon Watkins, BB)*

WADESMILL [TL3517]
Sow & Pigs SG12 0ST [Cambridge Rd, Thundridge (A10 N of Ware)]: Cheerful refurbished dining pub, enjoyable generous food from sandwiches up, friendly staff, changing real ales, good house wines, nice coffee with home-made shortbread; spacious beamed dining room off central bar with pig ornaments, log fire; no dogs, children in

eating areas, tables outside, open all day *(Chris Smith, LYM, J Marques)*

WARESIDE [TL3915]
Chequers SG12 7QY: Proper old-fashioned country local with down-to-earth landlady, well kept Greene King and Timothy Taylors Landlord, good straightforward home-made food at reasonable prices, friendly staff, log fire; children, dogs and walkers welcome *(Ross Balaam, Gordon Neighbour, Mrs Margo Finlay, Jörg Kasprowski)*

WATER END [TL0410]
Red Lion HP1 3BD [Leighton Buzzard Rd (A4146)]: Large Chef & Brewer extended from 18th-c core with beams and timbers, their usual food from sandwiches and baked potatoes up, friendly service, real ales such as Courage and Batemans from attractive carved bar, wide choice of wines by the glass; garden and terrace tables (some traffic noise) *(David Gurr)*

WATFORD [TQ1293]
Partridge WD19 5TP [St Georges Drive, Carpenters Park]: Modern family-friendly local in shopping area, well cooked food, real ale, live music; no credit cards *(Stan Edwards)*

WHEATHAMPSTEAD [TL1716]
Cross Keys AL4 8LA [off B651 at Gustard Wood 1.5 miles N]: 17th-c pub attractively placed in rolling wooded countryside, enjoyable food in bar and beamed restaurant, inglenook woodburner, model car collection; good garden, three comfortable bedrooms, good breakfast *(Mike and Lynn Robinson, LYM)*

☆ *Wicked Lady* AL4 8EL [Nomansland Common; B651 0.5 miles S]: Unpretentious chain dining pub with clean contemporary décor, wide range of good well presented food inc some unusual dishes, well kept Timothy Taylors Landlord, good choice of wines by the glass, reasonable prices; friendly attentive young staff, various rooms and alcoves, plenty of tables, low beams, log fires and lots of stainless steel, conservatory; garden with nice terrace *(Michael Dandy, Giles Barr, Eleanor Dandy, LYM, Eithne Dandy, Andy Lickfold, John and Joyce Snell)*

WIGGINTON [SP9310]
Greyhound HP23 6EH [just S of Tring]: Friendly Rothschild estate pub in quiet village, reasonably priced standard pub food, real ales; garden, good Ridgeway walks *(Roy Hoing)*

WILLIAN [TL2230]
Three Horseshoes SG6 2AE [Baldock Lane]: Welcoming traditional village pub under newish licensees, enjoyable home-made pubby food, well kept Greene King ales, log fires; handy for A1(M), open all day, cl Mon lunchtime *(LYM, Louise James, Steve Nye)*

For those of you who use Sat-Nav devices, we include a postcode for every entry in the *Guide*.

Isle of Wight

Like the island itself, the cheery pubs here continue largely unchanged over the years and, on the whole, readers comment on them with warmth; we had no need to drop any Main Entries from this chapter this year. Doing particularly well at the moment are the easy-going Folly at Cowes and Sun at Hulverstone, the atmospheric old Buddle at Niton (with half a dozen real ales it has more than any other Main Entry here), the Seaview Hotel (which now has its own farm) and the welcoming New Inn at Shalfleet (a great all-rounder). Although readers have enjoyed eating at all the pubs on the Island we didn't feel that any particular one shone out enough to be Isle of Wight Dining Pub of the Year – so fingers crossed for next year. It's good to see that virtually all the Main Entries on the Island carry a beer from the local brewer Goddards. The other Island brewer to look out for is Yates – not to be confused with the Yates of Cumbria.

ARRETON
SZ5386   MAP 2

White Lion
A3056 Newport—Sandown; PO30 3AA

Pleasantly pubby local with basic food

The neatly kept beamed lounge at this welcoming white-painted village house is comfortably old-fashioned, with dark pink walls or stripped brick above a stained pine dado, gleaming brass and horse tack and lots of cushioned wheelback chairs on the patterned red carpet. The piped music tends to be very quiet, and the public bar has a games machine, darts and board games; Bass and Timothy Taylors Landlord are on handpump. There's also a restaurant, family room and stable room. The pleasant garden has a small play area; more reports please.

🍴 **Straightforward but tasty food, served in generous helpings, includes sandwiches, ploughman's, whitebait, nachos, sausage and mash, burgers, vegetable curry, lasagne, steaks, and daily specials such as duck in plum sauce and fajitas.** *Starters/Snacks: £4.25 to £6.25. Main Courses: £6.50 to £13.95. Puddings: £4.75*

Enterprise ~ Lease Chris and Kate Cole ~ Real ale ~ Bar food (12-9) ~ (01983) 528479 ~ Children welcome ~ Dogs welcome ~ Open 11-11; 12-10.30 Sun

Recommended by Andy and Yvonne Cunningham, Simon Collett-Jones

---

BEMBRIDGE
SZ6587   MAP 2

Crab & Lobster 🛏
Foreland Fields Road, off Howgate Road (which is off B3395 via Hillway Road); PO35 5TR

Prime clifftop location with great views; pleasant bedrooms

It's well worth stopping at this seaside pub (perched on low cliffs within yards of the shore) to take in the terrific Solent views from the waterside terrace – though bear in mind that in summer lots of people may have the same idea; the dining area and some of the bedrooms share the same views. Inside it's roomier than you might expect and is done out in an almost parlourish style, with lots of yachting memorabilia, old local photographs and a blazing winter fire; darts, dominoes and cribbage. Goddards Fuggle-Dee-Dum, Greene King IPA and Sharpes Doom Bar are on handpump, with a dozen wines by the glass, about 16 malt whiskies and good coffee.

🍴 **Bar food includes filled baguettes, steak sandwich, ploughman's, chicken caesar salad, curries, lasagne, steaks and quite a few seafood dishes such as crab cakes, seafood tagliatelle, a mixed seafood grill and whole lobster; they may keep your credit card if you run a tab.** *Starters/Snacks: £2.25 to £8.50. Main Courses: £6.95 to £16.95. Puddings: £3.75 to £7.95*

Enterprise ~ Lease Caroline and Ian Quekett ~ Real ale ~ Bar food (12-2.30, 6-9(9.30 Fri, Sat) with limited menu 2.30-5.30 weekends and holidays) ~ (01983) 872244 ~ Children welcome ~ Dogs allowed in bar ~ Open 11-11; 12-10.30 Sun ~ Bedrooms: £50S(£55B)/£85S(£90B)

Recommended by Mrs Maricar Jagger, Guy Consterdine, Thomas Moore, George Atkinson, Simon Collett-Jones, Paul Humphreys, Tony and Maggie Harwood, Evelyn and Derek Walter, Felicity Davies, Mr and Mrs H J Langley

BONCHURCH
SZ5778 MAP 2

Bonchurch Inn

Bonchurch Shute; from A3055 E of Ventnor turn down to Old Bonchurch opposite Leconfield Hotel; PO38 1NU

Unusual italian-owned establishment rambling around central courtyard; italian influence in menu and wines

There is something rather unique about this distinctively run place. A delightful paved and cobbled courtyard (feeling slightly continental with its tables, fountain and pergola) awaits when you round the corner off the road. The bar, restaurant, family room and kitchens are spread around this sheltered little square, and the entire set-up is snuggled below a steep, rocky slope. The unusual layout derives from its Victorian origins as the stables for the nearby manor house. The furniture-packed bar has a good chatty local atmosphere and conjures up sea voyages, with its floor of narrow-planked ship's decking and old-fashioned steamer-style seats. A separate entrance leads to the fairly basic family room, which can feel a little cut off from the congenial atmosphere of the public bar. Drinks include Courage Directors and Best tapped from the cask and a handful of italian and french wines by the glass; piped music, darts, shove-ha'penny, dominoes and cribbage. The pub owns a holiday flat for up to six people.

🍴 **Tasty bar food includes italian dishes such as lasagne, tagliatelle carbonara, seafood risotto or spaghetti, as well as traditional dishes such as sandwiches, a good crab cocktail, grilled plaice, battered squid, chicken chasseur and steak.** *Starters/Snacks: £5.00 to £7.50. Main Courses: £8.00 to £16.00. Puddings: £4.00 to £6.00*

Free house ~ Licensees Ulisse and Gillian Besozzi ~ Real ale ~ Bar food (12-2, 6.30-8.45) ~ Restaurant ~ (01983) 852611 ~ Children in family room ~ Dogs welcome ~ Open 12-3, 6(6.30 Sun and in winter)-11; 7-10.30 Sun evening in winter ~ Bedrooms: /£120B

Recommended by J L and J A Johnston, Geoff and Linda Payne

COWES
SZ5092 MAP 2

Folly

Folly Lane – which is signposted off A3021 just S of Whippingham; PO32 6NB

Glorious water views from popular place with cheery family holiday atmosphere, moorings and good range of food served from breakfast on

Big windows in the bar and seats on a covered waterside terrace enjoy entertaining views of all the nautical activity on the wide Medina estuary beside this happy-go-lucky pub. It's popular with sailors, locals and families and is the sort of place where a late night dance on the tables is not unheard of. Staff are hands-on and cope well even when it gets busy. Rumour has it that this splendidly positioned building originated from a french sea-going barge that beached here during a smuggling run in the early 1700s. Whether or not that's true, the laid-back timbered interior certainly gives the sense of a ship's below decks. Straightforward but atmospheric furnishings include simple wooden tables and chairs, and stools at the bar; Greene King Old Speckled Hen, Goddards and possibly a guest on handpump; pool, TV, games machine and piped music. If you're using the river, they have moorings, a water taxi, showers and long-term parking on a field, and they keep an eye on weather forecasts and warnings. Watch out for the ruts and speed humps along the lane if you come by car.

Ⓜ **Breakfast is served first thing, followed by the lunchtime and (more substantial) evening menus. Dishes are generously served and sensibly priced and include sandwiches, ploughman's, chicken tikka wrap, sharing boards, butternut squash, lentil and coconut curry, fish and chips, beef and ale pie, sirloin steak, and daily specials such as slow-cooked beef ribs, and puddings such as lemon tart and ice-cream sundae.** *Starters/Snacks: £2.95 to £4.45. Main Courses: £7.45 to £10.95. Puddings: £3.75 to £5.25*

Greene King ~ Managers Andy and Cheryl Greenwood ~ Real ale ~ Bar food (12-9) ~ (01983) 297171 ~ Children welcome ~ Dogs welcome ~ Live music Sat evening, Thurs from May and Fri in July, Aug ~ Open 11-11(11.30 Sat, 10.30 Sun)

Recommended by B and M Kendall, Quentin and Carol Williamson, George Atkinson, Simon Collett-Jones

FRESHWATER   SZ3487   MAP 2

Red Lion ♀

Church Place; from A3055 at E end of village by Freshwater Garage mini-roundabout follow Yarmouth signpost, then take first real right turn signed to Parish Church; PO40 9BP

Good mix of locals and visiting diners, decent food and composed atmosphere

A gently grown-up atmosphere predominates here, and although food is quite a draw, chatting locals, occupying stools along the counter, keep up a pubby atmosphere. No young children are allowed inside, and do be careful as they fine ringing mobile phones (money to the RNLI). The not over-done but comfortably furnished open-plan bar has fires, low grey sofas and sturdy country-kitchen style furnishings on mainly flagstoned floors and bare boards. The well executed paintings (between photographs and china platters) are by the licensee's brother and are worth a look. Flowers Original, Goddards, Shepherd Neame Spitfire and Wadworths 6X are kept under light blanket pressure. There are tables on a carefully tended grass and gravel area at the back (some under cover), and beside the kitchen's herb garden, and a couple of picnic-sets in a quiet square at the front have pleasant views of the church. The pub is virtually on the Freshwater Way footpath that connects Yarmouth with the southern coast at Freshwater Bay.

Ⓜ **Food is listed on blackboards behind the bar and includes a sensible cross-section of dishes. As well as lunchtime filled baguettes and ploughman's, it might include crab and avocado cocktail, fried brie with cranberry sauce, herring roes on toast, whitebait, sausage and mash, fish pie, steak and ale pie, kedgeree, mushroom stroganoff and sirloin steak with stilton sauce. They also do takeaways.** *Starters/Snacks: £5.50 to £7.50. Main Courses: £7.95 to £15.50. Puddings: £5.00*

Enterprise ~ Lease Michael Mence ~ Real ale ~ Bar food (12-2, 6.30-9) ~ (01983) 754925 ~ Children over 10 ~ Dogs welcome ~ Open 11.30-3, 5.30-11; 11.30-4, 6-11 Sat; 12-3, 7-10.30 Sun

Recommended by Stuart Paulley, Paul Humphreys, Geoff and Linda Payne, Mrs Mary Woods, B and M Kendall

HULVERSTONE

Sun 🍺

B3399; PO30 4EH

Lovely thatched building with terrific coastal views, down-to-earth old-world appeal and four quickly changing real ales

---

Thatched and whitewashed, this rustically pretty country pub is unpretentiously traditional and full of friendly chatter. The cheerily pubby low-ceilinged bar has a blazing fire at one end (with horsebrasses and ironwork hung around the fireplace), a nice mix of old furniture on flagstones and floorboards, and lots of old lifeboat pictures on brick and stone walls; piped music, darts and board games. Leading off from one end is the traditionally decorated more recently constructed dining area, with large windows making the most of the view. Friendly helpful staff serve four quickly changing real ales from brewers such Adnams, Goddards, Ringwood and Timothy Taylor. Staff are helpful and friendly. The building is in a captivating setting, with views from its charmingly secluded split level cottagey garden (which has a terrace and several picnic-sets) down to a wild stretch of coast, and it's well positioned for splendid walks along the cliffs and up Mottistone Down to the prehistoric Long Stone.

🍽 Pork, lamb and beef are sourced from the adjacent farm for bar food which includes sandwiches, ploughman's, grilled black pudding with cranberry sauce, cajun spiced potato wedges, rare breed pork and beef sausages with onion gravy, pie of the day, chicken breast topped with bacon and blue cheese, aberdeen angus burger, cod and chips with mushy peas and bass with creamy mussels and steaks. *Starters/Snacks: £4.75 to £6.25. Main Courses: £8.25 to £13.50. Puddings: £4.25*

Enterprise ~ Lease Mark and Leslie Blanchard ~ Real ale ~ Bar food (12-9) ~ (01983) 741124 ~ Children welcome away from bar area ~ Dogs allowed in bar ~ Live music Sat evening ~ Open 11-11; 12-10.30 Sun

Recommended by Mrs Mary Woods, B and M Kendall, Liz and Brian Barnard, Stuart Paulley, Simon Watkins, Paul Humphreys, Peter Meister

NINGWOOD

Horse & Groom

A3054 Newport—Yarmouth, a mile W of Shalfleet; PO30 4NW

Spacious family dining pub with enjoyable all-day food, excellent play area and crazy golf

---

Children and families will find plenty to keep them occupied at this relaxed and welcoming pub. There are ample tables in the garden, which has a terrific play area, a bouncy castle, crazy golf, tyre trails and more. The roomy interior has a good pubby feel and is thoughtfully arranged with comfortable leather sofas grouped around low tables and a nice mix of sturdy tables and chairs, well spaced for a relaxing meal. Walls are pale pink, which works nicely with the old flagstone flooring. Greene King IPA, Goddards Special and Ringwood Best are kept under light blanket pressure; staff are friendly and helpful; piped music, games machine.

🍽 Good value food includes sandwiches, burgers, ploughman's, whitebait, fie pie, chicken korma, roast vegetable lasagne, grilled fish of the day and steaks. They've a thoughtful children's menu and do a very good value Sunday carvery. *Starters/Snacks: £3.95 to £5.95. Main Courses: £7.95 to £12.95. Puddings: £2.95 to £4.95*

Enterprise ~ Lease Pete Tigwell and Martin Bullock ~ Real ale ~ Bar food (12-9) ~ (01983) 760672 ~ Children welcome away from bar area ~ Dogs allowed in bar ~ Open 11-11; 12-10.30 Sun

Recommended by BOB

NITON

SZ5075 MAP 2

Buddle ◗

St Catherines Road, Undercliff; off A3055 just S of village, towards St Catherines Point; PO38 2NE

Distinctive stone pub with imaginative menu and half a dozen real ales; nice clifftop garden

There's something charmingly timeless about the heavily black beamed bar at this characterful old pub, with its big flagstones, old-fashioned captain's chairs arranged around solid wooden tables and walls hung with pewter mugs – it's not hard to imagine smugglers huddled up by the broad stone fireplace with its massive black oak mantelbeam. Six real ales on handpump might include Adnams Best, Fullers London Pride, Goddards Fuggle-Dee-Dum, Ringwood Fortyniner and Yates Buddle; piped music, darts and bar billiards. The pub is situated on a southerly cliff near St Catherines Lighthouse and there are great views from the well cared-for garden, with its tables spread over the sloping lawn and stone terraces. It's surrounded by National Trust land, there's a good walk to the nearby lighthouse and it's handy for the coast path. Tea rooms along one side of the lawn keep it nice and sheltered.

🍴 **The licensees try to source ingredients locally and they tell us that all their meat is Island reared. Tasty dishes might include chicken breast in beer batter, spinach, ricotta and red onion quiche, scallops and smoked bacon salad with lemon grass, pork loin in creamy wholegrain mustard and honey sauce and sirloin steak.** *Starters/Snacks: £4.25 to £6.50. Main Courses: £7.95 to £14.95. Puddings: £4.25*

Enterprise ~ Lease John and Fiona Page ~ Real ale ~ Bar food (12-2.30, 6-9) ~ (01983) 730243 ~ Children allowed in Old Barn ~ Dogs welcome ~ Open 11-11(12 Sat); 12-10.30 Sun
Recommended by David Glynne-Jones, Geoff and Linda Payne

SEAVIEW

SZ6291 MAP 2

Seaview Hotel ♀ 🛏

High Street; off B3330 Ryde—Bembridge; PO34 5EX

Small relaxed hotel with informal bar, good wine list and lovely bedrooms

You can take your choice of atmosphere at this gently civilised 200-year-old hotel. Tucked away at the back, you'll find the simple pubby bar which is relaxing and down-to-earth with traditional wood furnishings on bare boards, lots of seafaring paraphernalia around softly lit ochre walls and a log fire. At the front, the comfortable more refined bar has good soft furnishings, is modelled on a naval wardroom and is home to one of the most extensive private collections of naval pictures, photographs and artefacts to be found on the Island. Drinks include Goddards, Yates Undercliff Experience and a guest such as Green King IPA on handpump, a good selection of malt whiskies, a farm cider (in summer) and a good wine list (including a couple from local vineyards); piped music, TV, darts and board games. Tables on little terraces either side of the path to the front door take in glimpses of the sea and coast, and some of the comfortable bedrooms also have a sea view. If you run a tab, they may ask to keep your credit card behind the bar.

🍴 **Deer, cattle and chickens are reared on the pub's own farm which also produces seasonal herbs and vegetables, all of which are used in the good, well presented and generously served bar food here: sandwiches and baguettes, hot crab ramekin, mussels and chips, smoked trout salad, battered haddock and chips, cheesy mash fish pie, cottage pie and venison sausages with mustard mash and onion gravy. There is a much more elaborate restaurant menu.** *Starters/Snacks: £2.95 to £7.95. Main Courses: £8.95 to £13.95. Puddings: £5.75 to £7.50*

Free house ~ Licensee Andrew Morgan ~ Real ale ~ Bar food (12-2.30, 6.30-9.30) ~ Restaurant ~ (01983) 612711 ~ Children welcome ~ Dogs allowed in bar and bedrooms ~ Open 10.30-11 (10.30 Sun) ~ Bedrooms: £155B/£165B
Recommended by David Glynne-Jones, George Atkinson, Paul Humphreys, Franklyn Roberts, B and M Kendall

SHALFLEET

SZ4089 MAP 2

New Inn ♀

A3054 Newport—Yarmouth; PO30 4NS

Cheerful pub with seafood specialities, good beers and wines, too

Readers very much enjoy the happy atmosphere, great seafood and well kept beer at this rambling 18th-c former fisherman's haunt. As it's popular, you will need to book, and there may be double sittings in summer. The partly panelled flagstoned public bar has yachting photographs and pictures, a boarded ceiling, scrubbed pine tables and a log fire in the big stone hearth. The beamed and carpeted lounge bar has boating pictures and a coal fire, and the snug and gallery have slate floors, bric-a-brac and more scrubbed pine tables. Goddards Fuggle-Dee-Dum and Special, Ringwood and a guest such as Greene King IPA are kept under a light blanket pressure, and they stock around 70 wines; piped music.

🍴 Their famous crab sandwich, seafood platter and crab and lobster salads are served alongside a good choice of fish dishes, such as thai marinated sole filled with pak choi and sautéed prawns, and pubbier options such as sandwiches, baguettes, ploughman's, sausage and mash, steak and ale pie, gnocchi with mushroom, parsley and walnut cream sauce and various steaks. *Starters/Snacks: £5.00 to £9.00. Main Courses: £7.00 to £15.00. Puddings: £4.00 to £6.00.*

Enterprise ~ Lease Mr Bullock and Mr McDonald ~ Real ale ~ Bar food (12-2.30, 6-9.30) ~ (01983) 531314 ~ Children welcome ~ Dogs welcome ~ Open 12-11(10.30 Sun)

Recommended by Terry and Nickie Williams, Rochelle Seifas, Gareth James, David Glynne-Jones, Mike Tucker, George Atkinson, Paul Humphreys, David Hoult

SHORWELL

SZ4582 MAP 2

Crown

B3323 SW of Newport; PO30 3JZ

Popular pub with pretty streamside garden and play area

The appealing tree-sheltered garden with its sweet little stream, broadening into a small trout-filled pool is quite a draw at this pretty inland pub. It has a decent children's play area within easy view of closely spaced picnic-sets and white garden chairs and tables set out on the grass. Inside, four pleasant opened-up rooms, spread around a central bar, with either carpet, tiles or flagstones, and chatty regulars lending some local character. The beamed knocked-through lounge has blue and white china in an attractive carved dresser, old country prints on stripped-stone walls and a winter log fire with a fancy tile-work surround. Black pews form bays around tables in a stripped-stone room off to the left with another log fire; piped music and board games. Four real ales are usually Goddards Special, Ringwood Best and Fortyniner and Sharps Doom Bar, all on handpump.

🍴 Bar food includes prawn cocktail, pâté of the day, sausage and mash, spaghetti bolognese and pie of the day, with eight or so daily specials such as grilled trout with bean and chorizo salad and roast peppers with goats cheese. *Starters/Snacks: £4.25 to £5.95. Main Courses: £8.50 to £12.00. Puddings: £3.50 to £4.95*

Enterprise ~ Lease Nigel and Pam Wynn ~ Real ale ~ Bar food (12-9) ~ (01983) 740293 ~ Children welcome ~ Dogs welcome ~ Open 10.30-11

Recommended by Mr and Mrs H J Langley, Chris Bell, Quentin and Carol Williamson, Terry and Nickie Williams

---

Bedroom prices normally include full english breakfast, VAT and any inclusive service charge that we know of. Prices before the '/' are for single rooms, after for two people in double or twin (B includes a private bath, S a private shower). If there is no '/', the prices are only for twin or double rooms (as far as we know there are no singles). If there is no B or S, as far as we know no rooms have private facilities.

VENTNOR   SZ5677   MAP 2

Spyglass ◀

Esplanade, SW end; road down is very steep and twisty, and parking nearby can be difficult – best to use the pay-and-display (free in winter) about 100 yards up the road; PO38 1JX

Interesting waterside pub with appealing seafaring bric-a-brac, four well kept beers and enjoyable food

No matter what the season, this cheery bubbling place seems to brim with customers enjoying themselves. They have live music most nights and on Sunday lunchtime, and you will definitely be able to hear the piped music here. The snug quarry-tiled old interior is charmingly done out with a fascinating jumble of seafaring memorabilia (anything from ships' wheels to stuffed seagulls). Ringwood Best and Fortyniner are well kept alongside a couple of guests such as Goddards Special and Wychwood Hobgoblin; games machine. It's in a super position, perched on the wall just above the beach and tables outside on a terrace have lovely views over the sea. There are strolls westwards from here along the coast towards the Botanic Garden, as well as heftier hikes up on to St Boniface Down and towards the eerie shell of Appuldurcombe House.

🍴 Generous helpings of tasty bar food might include sandwiches, ploughman's, salads, baked potatoes, scampi, calamari, a pint of prawns, roast chicken, macaroni cheese, steaks and burgers; they may ask to hold your credit card if you run a tab. *Starters/Snacks: £4.50 to £6.50. Main Courses: £6.95 to £13.95. Puddings: £4.25 to £5.50*

Free house ~ Licensees Neil and Stephanie Gibbs ~ Real ale ~ Bar food (12-9.30) ~ (01983) 855338 ~ Children welcome ~ Dogs allowed in bar ~ Live music Sun lunchtime and most nights ~ Open 10.30am-11pm ~ Bedrooms: /£75B

Recommended by Penny and Peter Keevil, Dennis and Doreen Haward, George Atkinson, Tony and Maggie Harwood

---

LUCKY DIP

Besides the fully inspected pubs, you might like to try these Lucky Dips recommended to us and described by readers (if you do, please send us reports: feedback@goodguides.com).

BEMBRIDGE [SZ6488]
Pilot Boat PO35 5NN [Station Rd/Kings Rd]: Small harbourside pub reworked in style of a ship, good food from sandwiches to local seafood, decent choice of ales; tables out overlooking water or in pleasant courtyard behind, well placed for coast walks, open all day *(Mrs Maricar Jagger, Andy and Yvonne Cunningham, William Goodhart)*
BINSTEAD [SZ5792]
Fleming Arms PO33 3RD: Welcoming with wide choice of good reasonably priced food, Ringwood Best and Flowers; dogs allowed in bar area, garden *(Keith Widdowson)*
CALBOURNE [SZ4286]
Sun PO30 4JA [Sun Hill]: Family-friendly old roadside pub with enjoyable sensibly priced food, quick friendly service even when busy, varying real ales, cosy no-frills bar, plain lower-level extension, extensive views across Brighstone Forest *(Tony and Maggie Harwood)*
CARISBROOKE [SZ4687]
☆ ***Blacksmiths Arms*** PO30 5SS [B3401 1.5 miles W]: Quiet hillside pub with friendly landlord and staff, good fresh food especially fish, decent wines and cider, scrubbed tables in neat beamed and flagstoned front bars, superb Solent views from airy bare-boards family dining extension; children, dogs and walkers welcome, terrace tables and smallish

back garden with play area, open all day *(LYM, Penny and Peter Keevil)*
CHALE [SZ4877]
☆ ***Clarendon (Wight Mouse)*** PO38 2HA [off A3055/B3399]: Big efficient family dining pub rambling around with flagstones here, carpet there, modern-look woody extension around attractive traditional core with log fire, Badger ales from long bar, well priced standard food from good baguettes up, fast friendly service, plenty to keep children occupied; extensive outdoor seating and bar, play area, great views out over cliffs, good value bedrooms in adjoining hotel *(Simon Watkins, P Mitch, Paul Humphreys, LYM)*
FRESHWATER [SZ3285]
Highdown PO39 0HY [Highdown Lane, SW off Moons Hill]: Welcoming straightforward roadside inn, log-fire bar with stripped-wood floor, refurbished restaurant, popular food inc local fish, seasonal game and plenty of vegetarian options; children welcome, garden with terrace and play area, four updated bedrooms *(B and M Kendall, Mark Flynn)*
GODSHILL [SZ5281]
Taverners PO38 3HZ [High St]: Welcoming 17th-c pub with newish landlord/chef, spacious bar and two front dining areas,

beams, bare boards and slate floors, woodburner, good seasonal food with emphasis on fresh local produce, children's menu and Sun roasts, friendly service, well kept Fullers London Pride, a house beer from Yates and a guest ale; dogs welcome, garden with terrace and play area, open all day, cl Sun evening exc bank/school summer hols *(C and R Bromage, George Atkinson)*

GURNARD [SZ4796]

Woodvale PO31 8LE [Princes Esplanade]: Large 1930s inn with picture-window Solent views, charming staff, Marstons Pedigree, Ringwood Fortyniner, Yates, and Youngs, good generous all-day food (clearly marked if gluten-free), billiards, live music Fri and Sat evenings; outside seating, bedrooms *(Quentin and Carol Williamson)*

ROOKLEY [SZ5183]

☆ *Chequers* PO38 3NZ [S of village, Chequers Inn Rd/Niton Rd]: Well equipped family pub with enjoyable usual food all day from sandwiches up, puddings cabinet, well kept ales such as Goddards, close-set tables in unpretentious dining lounge with log fire, friendly service, good children's games in plain and roomy family area, flagstoned locals' bar with pool, darts and TV, mother-and-baby room; children and dogs welcome, large fenced play area, downland views, handy for Godshill, open all day *(LYM, C and R Bromage)*

SANDOWN [SZ5984]

Old Comical PO36 8ES: Old pub with L-shaped lounge and back room, friendly staff, well kept beer, settles, old books

and lots of RAF memorabilia, games room, juke box, regular live music *(Tony and Maggie Harwood)*

SHANKLIN [SZ5881]

☆ *Fishermans Cottage* PO37 6BN [bottom of Shanklin Chine]: Thatched shoreside cottage in terrific setting surrounded by beached boats, tucked into the cliffs, steep walk down beautiful chine, lovely seaside walk to Luccombe; flagstones and some stripped stone, repro furniture, nets slung from low beams, old local pictures and bric-a-brac, good value food from sandwiches to specials, convivial atmosphere, helpful staff, well kept ales inc Goddards, frequent entertainment; piped music; children welcome, disabled access, terrace tables, open all day summer when fine, cl winter *(Martin Gough, BB, Colin Gooch)*

Steamer PO37 6BS [Esplanade]: Nautical-theme bar, fun for holiday families, with good range of real ales, enjoyable fresh food inc local seafood, cheery staff, live music most wknds; fine sea views from covered floodlit terrace, eight bedrooms, open all day *(John and Judy Selby)*

YARMOUTH [SZ3589]

Kings Head PO41 0PB [Quay St]: Cosy low-ceilinged traditional pub opp car ferry, rather dark and quaint, with well kept real ales, good food from sandwiches to well prepared local fish, friendly staff, plush seats, log fires; piped music; good for families, dogs welcome, courtyard seats, bedrooms *(Tony and Maggie Harwood, Franklyn Roberts)*

A very few pubs try to make you leave a credit card at the bar, as a sort of deposit if you order food. They are not entitled to do this. The credit card firms and banks which issue them warn you not to let credit cards out of your sight. If someone behind the counter used your card fraudulently, the card company or bank could in theory hold you liable, because of your negligence in letting a stranger hang on to your card. Suggest instead that if they feel the need for security, they 'swipe' your card and give it back to you. And do name and shame the pub to us.

Kent

All-rounders here that we know are doing particularly well include the Green Man at Hodsoll Street (friendly, family-run and by the village green), the Windmill at Hollingbourne (with a large, child-friendly garden), the unpretentious Woodcock at Iden Green, the Plough at Ivy Hatch (well refurbished and with a landscaped garden), the Hare at Langton Green (with a good choice of drinks), the stylishly roomy Granville at Lower Hardres, the George & Dragon at Speldhurst (in a very fine half-timbered building; good choice of wines), the Tiger at Stowting (much liked on all counts, including its choice of drinks – five real ales, local cider and apple juice) and the Pepper Box at Ulcombe (cosily cottagey within, and with a delightful garden). For food we'd particularly single out the Timber Batts at Bodsham, where its french owners bring their own country's wine and food (but also have traditional pubby favourites), the Three Chimneys at Biddenden (much liked for food and local cider), the smart Chaser at Shipbourne (with a very good range of wines by the glass; log fires and efficient staff) and the idiosyncratic Red Lion at Stodmarsh. The cosy, open-plan Bottle House at Penshurst is enjoyed for its seasonal dishes and friendly service and is our Kent Dining Pub of the Year for 2011. At the simpler end of the scale, the Gate Inn at Boyden Gate is nicely unchanged, with the landlord now having served 35 years here, the Shipwrights Arms at Oare has masses of character and a good choice of local ales, and the marvellously unspoilt Red Lion at Snargate has now been in the same family for exactly 100 years.

BEKESBOURNE   TR1856   MAP 3

Unicorn

Coming from Patrixbourne on A2, turn left up Bekesbourne Hill after passing railway line (and station); coming from Littlebourne on A257, pass Howletts Zoo – Bekesbourne Hill is then first turning on right; turning into pub car park is at bottom end of the little terrace of houses on the left (the pub is the far end of this terrace); CT4 5ED

Small, friendly pub, simply furnished bars, local beer and pubby food

They make a point of serving only Kentish beers here, such as Ramsgate Gadds No. 5, Shepherd Neame Early Bird and Westerham Brewery Grasshopper, all on handpump, alongside Biddenden cider. There are just a few scrubbed old pine tables and wooden pubby chairs on worn floorboards, a nice old leather sofa beside the open fire, a canary ceiling and walls above a dark green dado, minimal décor and a handful of bar stools against the neat counter; piped music and board games. A side terrace is prettily planted and there's a garden with benches and bat and trap in summer. Parking in front is tricky but there's a large car park at the back reached from the small track at the end of the adjacent terrace of cottages. Note that dogs are not allowed at food times. More reports please.

🍴 Bar food includes lunchtime ciabattas and ploughman's, soup, ham hock and apple terrine, curried cauliflower fritters with minted yoghurt dip, chicken with barbecue sauce, cheese and bacon, ham and eggs, beer-battered cod, minted couscous with roasted vegetables, a changing pie, and puddings like lemon tart and chocolate tiramisu. *Starters/Snacks: £3.95 to £6.00. Main Courses: £6.95 to £13.95. Puddings: £4.25*

Free house ~ Licensee Martin Short ~ Real ale ~ Bar food (12-2, 7-9; 12-5 Sun; not Sun evening and limited menu Mon) ~ (01227) 830210 ~ Well behaved children welcome ~ Folk or acoustic music every Sun ~ Open 12-3, 6-11; 12-11 Sat; 12-10.30 Sun; closed Mon in winter
Recommended by BOB

BENENDEN
TQ8032   MAP 3

Bull 🍴 ☕
The Street; by village green; TN17 4DE

Attractive and friendly old inn with relaxed and informal atmosphere, enjoyable home-made food, four local real ales

A roaring fire burns in the brick inglenook in the main bar of this 17th-c inn, with cushioned seats built into the bay window, a mix of spindleback, rush-seated dining chairs and brocaded stools around a few tables on the stripped wooden floor. It has a small unobtrusive flat-screen TV, big church candles on pewter dishes on each table and historic local photographs. Dark Star Hophead, Harveys Best, Larkins Traditional and a guest such as Rother Valley Hoppers Ale on handpump from the carved wooden bar counter topped by a mass of hops; english wine and Biddenden cider; you can take beer and cider away with you in two-pint hoppers. Good coffees. There's also a little two-sided woodburning stove and piped jazz. Through an open doorway, and down a couple of steps, is a bigger room with similar dining chairs and a mix of cushioned settles on dark terracotta tiles, hops on the white-painted beams, old photographs of the pub on the green wallpapered walls, a cupboard of darts trophies (and a darts board), cribbage and board games. The atmosphere is relaxed and informal and the friendly, hands-on landlord and landlady and chatty staff give quick, efficient service. To the right of the entrance is the dining room with burgundy patterned and brocaded dining chairs, built-in cushioned seats, a mix of tables, another woodburning stove and a cream corner cupboard with decorative plates. In front of the pub by the road are some picnic-sets. More reports please.

🍴 With daily delivered fresh fish and meat bought only from local farmers, the enjoyable food includes sandwiches and filled baguettes, ploughman's, soup, burgers with cheese or bacon toppings, home-cooked ham and eggs, a chilli, a proper fish pie, and daily specials like wild rabbit casserole, scallops with bacon lardons and garlic butter and slow-cooked pork belly with cider cream, with puddings such as berry cheesecake or warm chocolate nut brownies; Thursday curry night, fish and chips on Friday and popular Sunday roasts; over-60s menu. *Starters/Snacks: £4.25 to £6.95. Main Courses: £8.95 to £14.95. Puddings: £3.95 to £4.25*

Free house ~ Licensees Mark and Lucy Barron-Reid ~ Real ale ~ Bar food (12-2.15, 7-9.15; two sittings Sun at 12.15 and 2.30; not Sun evening) ~ Restaurant ~ (01580) 240054 ~ Children welcome ~ Dogs allowed in bar ~ Monthly Thursday music club, live music most Sun afternoons ~ Open 12-11(midnight Sat); closed Mon lunchtime
Recommended by Mrs J Ekins-Daukes, Conor McGaughey

'Children welcome' means the pub says it lets children inside without any special restriction. If it allows them in, but to restricted areas such as an eating area or family room, we specify this. Some pubs may impose an evening time limit. We do not mention limits after 9pm as we assume children are home by then.

BIDDENDEN   TQ8238 MAP 3

Three Chimneys ⚊ ♟

A262, 1 mile W of village; TN27 8LW

Pubby beamed rooms of considerable individuality, log fires, imaginative food and pretty garden

Nestling into the ground with its tiny windows and entrance, this appealing old cottage is a fine all-rounder with particularly efficient, friendly staff and a civilised and relaxed atmosphere. As well as a modern conservatory, there's a series of low-beamed, very traditional little rooms with plain wooden furniture and old settles on flagstones and coir matting, some harness and sporting prints on the stripped brick walls and good log fires. Adnams Best and a couple of guests tapped straight from casks racked behind the counter, several wines by the glass, local Biddenden cider and apple juice and several malt whiskies. The simple public bar has darts, dominoes and cribbage; dogs must be on a lead inside the building. French windows in the candlelit bare-boards restaurant open on to the garden where there are seats. Sissinghurst Gardens are nearby.

🍴 Excellent – if not cheap – food changes daily according to which ingredients are sourced; the menu typically includes soup, ploughman's, deep-fried breadcrumbed brie with fruity cumberland sauce, baked field mushroom topped with caramelised onions and goats cheese, a changing tart like warm thai crab or broccoli, stilton and bacon, potted brown shrimps, local pork and sage sausages with a port and red onion gravy, sunblush tomato couscous with balsamic roasted vegetables, goats cheese and a tomato sauce, local lamb rump with roast sweet potatoes, butternut squash, aubergine purée and a tomato and pancetta ragoût, guinea fowl with braised spring greens and parmesan new potatoes, grilled salmon with creamed leaks and white bean stew, duck leg confit with dauphinoise potatoes and braised red cabbage, puddings like dark chocolate and brandy parfait and sticky toffee pudding. *Starters/Snacks: £3.95 to £8.95. Main Courses: £11.95 to £18.95. Puddings: £5.50 to £6.50*

Free house ~ Licensee Craig Smith ~ Real ale ~ Bar food (6.30-9.30; 12-2.30, 6.30-9.30 Sat) ~ Restaurant ~ (01580) 291472 ~ Children welcome in eating areas ~ Dogs welcome ~ Open 11.30-3(3.30 Sat), 5.30-11; 12-3.30, 6-10.30 Sun

Recommended by Peter Meister, Tracey and Stephen Groves, Anthony Longden, Steve and Nina Bullen, Pat and Tony Martin, the Didler, Tina and David Woods-Taylor, Liz Hryniewicz, Cathryn and Richard Hicks, Robert Kibble, A and H Piper, Jill and Julian Tasker, John and Enid Morris, Colin and Louise English, Dr Kevan Tucker

BODSHAM   TR1045 MAP 3

Timber Batts ⚊ ♟

Following Bodsham, Wye sign off B2068 keep right at unsigned fork after about 1.5 miles; TN25 5JQ

Lovely french food (bar snacks, too) and charming french owner in cottagey old country pub, good real ales, enjoyable wines and fine views

'What a superb find; we had a truly memorable lunch lasting over two hours and provided by the genial Monsieur Gross' enthused one reader of this accomplished dining pub within a 15th-c former farmhouse. The little heavy-beamed cottagey area to the right of the door has a couple of comfortable armchairs and two wicker chairs each with a small table, an open fire in the brick fireplace with photographs of the pub above it, some hunting horns and a few high bar chairs; down a little step is more of a drinking part with a mix of cushioned dining chairs, a wall settle, two long tables and several bar stools. There are various froggy cushions and knick-knacks on the window sills (the pub is known locally as Froggies at the Timber Batts). Adnams Bitter and Woodfordes Wherry and a guest such as Adnams Explorer are on handpump; very good french wines by the glass (some from Mr Gross's cousin's vineyard). To the left of the entrance is the large but informally rustic beamed restaurant with a happy mix of attractive stripped pine tables and pews and all sorts of dark tables and dining chairs on the carpet, wine labels in a glass frame and wine box tops on the walls, a nice stripped pine cupboard in one corner, and a brick fireplace. From straightforward seats and tables in the back hilltop garden there are lovely views over the wide-spreading valley.

🍴 As well as pubby choices such as filled baguettes, croque monsieur, omelettes, ham and eggs, moules marinière and frites, and sausage and mash, the delicious french food using top local produce (cooked by the landlord's son) might include interesting soup, calamari with garlic butter, goats cheese salad, duck foie gras terrine, roasted rack of local lamb with herbs, fillet of beef with roquefort sauce, whitstable rock oysters, duck leg confit, pheasant poached in cider, wild halibut in cider cream sauce, and puddings such as crème brûlée and lemon posset; lovely french cheeses. They list their suppliers on their menu and offer a three-course lunch menu. *Starters/Snacks: £5.50 to £7.50. Main Courses: £8.50 to £15.00. Puddings: £6.50*

Free house ~ Licensee Joel Gross ~ Real ale ~ Bar food (12-2.30, 7-9.30; not Sun evening) ~ Restaurant ~ (01233) 750237 ~ Children welcome ~ Dogs welcome ~ Open 12-3, 6.30-11
Recommended by Derek Thomas, Hunter and Christine Wright, Dr Kevan Tucker, Bruce Eccles, N R White, Jill and Julian Tasker, John and Enid Morris, Alan Cowell

BOUGH BEECH
Wheatsheaf ♀ ☕

TQ4846   MAP 3

B2027, S of reservoir; TN8 7NU

Former hunting lodge with lots to look at, fine range of local drinks, popular food and plenty of seats in appealing garden

A nicely relaxed and unhurried spot for a meal or a drink, this ancient ivy-clad building is believed to originate as a medieval royal hunting lodge and has masses of interesting things and historical details to look at. Its neat central bar and long front bar (which has an attractive old settle carved with wheatsheaves) have unusually high ceilings with lofty oak timbers, a screen of standing timbers and a revealed king post; dominoes and board games. Divided from the central bar by two more rows of standing timbers – one formerly an outside wall to the building – are the snug and another bar. Other similarly aged features include a piece of 1607 graffiti, 'Foxy Holamby', thought to have been a whimsical local squire. On the walls and above the massive stone fireplaces there are quite a few horns and heads as well as african masks, a sword from Fiji, crocodiles, stuffed birds, swordfish spears and a matapee. Thoughtful touches include piles of smart magazines, board games, tasty nibbles and winter chestnuts to roast. Westerham Brewery Grasshopper and a guest such as Harveys Best on handpump, a decent wine list, several malt whiskies, summer Pimms and winter mulled wine. Outside is appealing too, with plenty of seats, flowerbeds and fruit trees in the sheltered side and back gardens and there's a heated smokers' gazebo. Shrubs help divide the garden into various areas, so it doesn't feel too crowded even when it's full.

🍴 Tasty bar food includes items such as filo-wrapped prawns with sweet chilli dip, grilled goats cheese on ciabatta with caramelised red onion and pesto, spiced pork casserole, sausages and mash, crispy duck with plum sauce, poached smoked haddock or vegetable curry, with puddings like spotted dick and blueberry and lemon cheesecake. *Starters/Snacks: £4.95 to £7.95. Main Courses: £8.95 to £15.95. Puddings: £4.25 to £4.75*

Enterprise ~ Lease Liz and David Currie ~ Real ale ~ Bar food ~ (01732) 700254 ~ Children welcome ~ Dogs welcome ~ Live music first Weds of the month ~ Open 11-11
Recommended by John Branston, Pat and Tony Martin, Colin and Louise English, Jeremy and Jane Morrison, DFL, David and Sue Atkinson, Mrs B Forster, Bob and Margaret Holder, D P and M A Miles, Mrs J Ekins-Daukes, B J Harding, Andrea Rampley

If a service charge is mentioned prominently on a menu or accommodation terms, you must pay it if service was satisfactory. If service is really bad, you are legally entitled to refuse to pay some or all of the service charge as compensation for not getting the service you might reasonably have expected.

BOYDEN GATE

TR2265   MAP 3

Gate Inn 🍺 £

Off A299 Herne Bay—Ramsgate – follow Chislet, Upstreet signpost opposite Roman Gallery; Chislet also signposted off A28 Canterbury—Margate at Upstreet – after turning right into Chislet main street keep right on to Boyden; the pub gives its address as Marshside, though Boyden Gate seems more usual on maps; CT3 4EB

Long-serving landlord in unchanging pub, well kept beers, simple food, and tame ducks and geese to feed

The landlord has been at this delightfully unpretentious rustic pub by the marshes for 35 years, and little has changed in that time. The comfortably worn and traditional interior is properly pubby with an inglenook log fire serving both the well worn quarry-tiled rooms, flowery-cushioned pews around tables of considerable character, hop bines hanging from the beams and attractively etched windows. Shepherd Neame Master Brew, Spitfire and a couple of seasonal ales are tapped from the cask and you can also get interesting bottled beers and several wines by the glass; board games. Seats in its sheltered garden are bounded by two streams, with tame ducks and geese; the pub sells bags of duck food for 10p.

🍴 **Bar food includes lots of different sandwiches, winter soup, a big choice of baked potatoes and burgers, ploughman's, home-made vegetable flan, sausage hotpot and gammon and egg.** *Starters/Snacks: £2.00 to £4.60. Main Courses: £4.95 to £7.25. Puddings: £2.50 to £3.00*

Shepherd Neame ~ Tenant Chris Smith ~ Real ale ~ Bar food (11.45-1.45, 6-8.45; 12-1.45, 7-8.30 Sun) ~ No credit cards ~ (01227) 860498 ~ Children welcome ~ Dogs welcome ~ Open 11-2.30, 6-11; 12-4.30, 7-10.30 Sun

Recommended by John Wooll, Kevin Thorpe, N R White, E D Bailey, Bruce Eccles

BROOKLAND

TQ9825   MAP 3

Royal Oak 🍽

Just off A259 Rye—New Romney; High Street; TN29 9QR

Lovely old building with carefully modernised rooms, comfortable atmosphere, good bar food and seats in garden; bedrooms

'Hooray, hooray, hooray! And thank you again *Good Pub Guide* – a treasure! From the moment we arrived we were made to feel welcome' was one of several very positive comments from readers about this thoughtfully modernised, spotless 17th-c inn on Romney Marsh. It's a skilful blend of old features along with warm terracotta paintwork, knocked-through walls, standing timbers and lovely big windows. The bar is light and airy with leather upholstered chairs around oak tables and one nice old pew spread over a floor surface that runs from flagstones into oak boards then bricks; piped music and a woodburning stove. Locals pop in to sit on the high bar chairs by the granite-topped counter for a chat and a pint of Adnams Best and Harveys Best and a guest like Sharps Doom Bar on handpump; 17 wines by the glass. The informative and friendly landlord knows a lot about the local area – so do ask him if you get a chance. His equestrian interests are manifest in a lovely set of racing watercolours and a couple of signed photographs on the lime white wall panelling in the bar, and in a rather special set of Cecil Aldin prints displayed in the beamed restaurant (with its well spaced tables and big inglenook fireplace). French windows from here open on to a terrace with metal chairs and there are picnic-sets in the narrow garden which is laid out around a terrace; quaint views of the ancient church and graveyard next door.

🍴 **Using local suppliers and producers which they list on their menu, the well presented and very good bar food features sandwiches, ploughman's, chargrilled beefburger, cod and chips, and more expensive items on a changing menu that might include starters like soup, fried pigeon breasts marinated in juniper and thyme or thai fish cakes, with main courses such as fillet steak, chump of romney marsh lamb or almond and garlic croustade; puddings board and children's dishes. They do a spit roast in the inglenook on Wednesday evenings.** *Starters/Snacks: £5.50 to £9.50. Main Courses: £12.50 to £5.95. Puddings: £7.50*

Enterprise ~ Lease David Rhys Jones ~ Real ale ~ Bar food (12-2(2.30 Sat, Sun), 6.30-9(9.30 Fri, Sat); not Sun evening) ~ Restaurant ~ (01797) 344215 ~ No children under 12 in evening restaurant ~ Dogs allowed in bar and bedrooms ~ Open 12-3, 6-11; closed Sun and Mon evenings ~ Bedrooms: /£75(£95B)

Recommended by Colin and Louise English, Sue Fincham, Sara Fulton, Roger Baker, V Brogden, Peter Meister, E D Bailey

Woolpack

On A259 from Rye, about 1 mile before Brookland, take the first right turn signposted Midley where the main road bends sharp left, just after the expanse of Walland Marsh; OS Sheet 189 map reference 977244; TN29 9TJ

15th-c pub with simple furnishings, massive inglenook fireplace, big helpings of tasty food and large garden

This crooked early 15th-c cottage has stacks of atmosphere evoking its days as a smugglers' haunt. Its ancient entrance lobby has an uneven brick floor and black-painted pine-panelled walls, and to the right, the simple quarry-tiled main bar has basic cushioned plank seats in the massive inglenook fireplace, a painted wood-effect bar counter hung with lots of water jugs and the low-beamed ceiling includes some very early ships' timbers (maybe 12th c) thought to be from local shipwrecks; a long elm table has shove-ha'penny carved into one end and there are other old and newer wall benches, chairs at mixed tables with flowers and candles and photographs of locals on the walls. The two pub cats, Liquorice and Charlie Girl, are often toasting themselves around the log fire. To the left of the lobby is a sparsely furnished little room and an open-plan family room; piped music. Shepherd Neame Master Brew, Spitfire and two seasonal brews on handpump. In summer, the award-winning hanging baskets are really quite a sight and there are plenty of picnic-sets under parasols in the attractive garden with its barbecue area; it's all nicely lit up in the evenings. More up-to-date reports please.

Reasonably priced, the pubby food includes sandwiches and baguettes, filled baked potatoes, ploughman's, soup, steak pie, stilton and vegetable bake, battered cod, generous moules marinière, mixed grill, and puddings like apple and cinnamon crumble and bitter chocolate and orange sponge pudding. *Starters/Snacks: £4.00 to £6.00. Main Courses: £5.00 to £18.00. Puddings: £4.00 to £5.00*

Shepherd Neame ~ Tenant Barry Morgan ~ Real ale ~ Bar food (12-2.30, 6-9; all day weekends and during school holidays) ~ (01797) 344321 ~ Children in family room ~ Dogs welcome ~ Open 11-3, 6-11 (all day during school holidays); 11-11 Sat; 12-10.30 Sun

Recommended by Peter Meister, Conrad Freezer, Colin and Louise English, Pat and Tony Martin

CHILHAM
TR0653 MAP 3

White Horse

The Square; CT4 8BY

Popular old pub on lovely village square with fresh modern décor in several areas, local beers and good organic bar food

The village square here looks ready-made for a film set, with the welcoming 15th-c pub near the church at one end, the castle entrance on the far side, and a perfect composition of half-timbered and brick-built cottages lining much of the rest. Handsomely carved ceiling beams bear witness to the pub's antiquity, as does a massive fireplace with the Lancastrian rose carved at the end of its mantelbeam – a relic of the Wars of the Roses, uncovered only in 1966, during refurbishments. There's a central bar and three separate but connected seating areas: white paintwork, bright modern paintings, chunky light oak seating and tables on pale wooden flooring and more traditional pubby furniture on quarry tiles, a log fire, horsebrasses, a couple of stained-glass panels; piped music and TV. Two or three from Flowers, Fullers London Pride, Harveys Best, Sharps Doom Bar and Shepherd Neame Master Brew are on handpump; several wines by the glass as well as local cider. The grand park of nearby Chilham Castle makes a good outing. More reports please.

🍴 Using organic local produce, the good, popular bar food includes sandwiches using their home-made bread, ploughman's, soup, pâté with fig relish, tasty fish pie, free-range chicken in mushroom sauce, battered cod or haddock, a changing vegetarian dish, pork belly with apple sauce, and puddings like fruit crumble or chocolate mousse; good Sunday roast and they may serve home-made cakes and coffee all day. *Starters/Snacks: £3.95 to £5.95. Main Courses: £7.95 to £14.95. Puddings: £4.95*

Enterprise ~ Lease Lisa Smart ~ Real ale ~ Bar food (12-2.30, 6.30-9.30; 12-4 Sun; not Sun evening) ~ (01227) 730355 ~ Children welcome ~ Dogs allowed in bar ~ Open 12-11(10.30 Sun)

Recommended by Alan Cowell

GROOMBRIDGE   TQ5337   MAP 3

Crown
B2110; TN3 9QH

Charming village pub with quite a bit of bric-a-brac in snug, low-beamed rooms, local beers, and well liked bar food

This typically Wealden tile-hung tavern is the end of a horseshoe-shaped row of cottages, grouped around a lovely steep green with views to the village below. Its snug left-hand room has old tables on worn flagstones and a sizeable brick inglenook with a big winter log fire. The other low-beamed rooms have roughly plastered walls, some squared panelling and timbering, and a quite a bit of bric-a-brac, from old teapots and pewter tankards to antique bottles. Walls are decorated with small topographical, game and sporting prints and there's a circular large-scale map with the pub at its centre. The end dining room has fairly close-spaced tables with a variety of good solid chairs, and a log-effect gas fire in a big fireplace. Harveys Best, Larkins Best and a guest on handpump and several wines by the glass. There's a back car park, pub garden and picnic-sets out in front on wonky but sunny brick terrace that overlooks the green. A public footpath across the road beside the small chapel leads through a field to Groombridge Place Gardens, and Harrison's Rocks and High Rocks nearby are fascinating outcrops considered prime terrain by rock-climbers.

🍴 Pubby bar food at lunchtime includes filled baguettes, ploughman's, soup, cumberland sausage with onion gravy, beer-battered haddock, home-cooked ham and eggs, popular home-made steak burgers with cheese and bacon, steak in ale pie, chicken pasta with bacon, avocado and tomato and grilled smoked haddock with dauphinoise potatoes. *Starters/Snacks: £4.50 to £5.50. Main Courses: £8.90 to £10.90. Puddings: £4.50*

Free house ~ Licensee Peter Kilshaw ~ Real ale ~ Bar food (12-2.30(3 Sat, Sun), 6.30-9(9.30 Sat); not Sun evening) ~ Restaurant ~ (01892) 864742 ~ Children welcome ~ Dogs allowed in bar ~ Open 11-3, 6-11; 11-11 summer Fri and Sat; 12-10.30 Sun; 12-5.30 Sun in winter; closed winter Sun evening ~ Bedrooms: £40/£45(£60S)

Recommended by Nigel and Jean Eames, N R White, B J Harding, Ann and Colin Hunt, Mrs B Forster, R and S Bentley

HAWKHURST   TQ7531   MAP 3

Great House ♀
Gills Green; pub signed just off A229 N; TN18 5EJ

Emphasis on good bistro-style food, drinkers' area too, several wines by the glass, attractive furnishings and plenty of space

From the back of this airy, white-weatherboarded pub the orangery looks out over the back terrace and its seating to a very attractive garden. Now very much a stylish dining venue, it does still have locals still popping in for a pint and a chat, with high-backed bar chairs by the counter, and just inside the main door are a couple of heavy-beamed small drinking areas with sofas, armchairs and bright scatter cushions; Harveys Best and a seasonal brew are on handpump, and they do good wines by the glass. There are some dark wooden slatted dining tables and smart clothed dining chairs on the slate floor, gilt-framed pictures on the red or green walls and a small brick fireplace. Stairs lead down to a light and airy dining room with big picture windows, carved built-in seating with more colourful cushions and high-backed leather dining chairs around various wooden tables; Farrow & Ball paintwork and plenty of modern art. The atmosphere throughout is relaxed and chatty and the french staff are friendly; piped music and TV. More reports please.

🍴 **Bistro-style food includes sandwiches and toasted panini, mediterranean fish soup, cheese or fish platters, sausages and mash, fish pie, beer-battered haddock and chunky chips, baked fillet of salmon, moroccan-style lamb stew with aromatic couscous, slow-cooked local lamb shank, locally reared 28-day matured limousin beef rib-eye with gratin dauphinois, and puddings like cassis tart and apple and rhubarb crumble with honeycomb ice-cream.** Starters/Snacks: £4.50 to £9.95. Main Courses: £9.95 to £22.00. Puddings: £4.95 to £5.96.

Free house ~ Licensees Martial and Natasha Chaussy ~ Real ale ~ Bar food (12-3, 6-9.45; all day weekends) ~ Restaurant ~ (01580) 753119 ~ Children welcome ~ Dogs allowed in bar ~ Open 11.30-11; closed Mon during Jan and Feb

Recommended by Elizabeth Stowe, Colin and Stephanie McFie, Peter Veness, BOB

HODSOLL STREET

TQ6263 MAP 3

Green Man

Hodsoll Street and pub signed off A227 S of Meopham; turn right in village; TN15 7LE

Bustling village pub, friendly atmosphere, lots of food specials, real ales and seats in garden

By the green in a delightful village, this very friendly place is nicely hidden away and well worth knowing about. Its big airy carpeted rooms work their way around a central bar with Greene King Old Speckled Hen, Harveys Best, Timothy Taylors Landlord and a changing guest such as Black Sheep on handpump; decent wines. There are traditional neat tables and chairs spaced tidily around the place, interesting old local photographs and antique plates on the walls and a warm winter log fire; piped music. There may be summer morris dancers; the nearby North Downs have plenty of walks. In summer, the pretty hanging baskets at the front of this little pub are very pretty, and there are seats on the well tended lawn and a children's climbing frame.

🍴 **As well as a popular two-course weekday lunch, the well liked bar food includes sandwiches, soup, deep-fried breaded brie with cranberry sauce, mushroom provençale on toasted brioche, beer-battered cod, cherry tomato and stilton risotto, lamb shank, steak and kidney wrapped in filo pastry, trout stuffed with thai prawns, lamb shank with red wine jus, pork fillet stuffed with black pudding and wrapped in bacon, a mixed grill, puddings; they also have a steak and ribs night on Tuesdays, a fish evening on Wednesdays and a curry night on Thursdays.** Starters/Snacks: £4.50 to £6.00. Main Courses: £8.50 to £16.00. Puddings: £4.50

Enterprise ~ Lease John, Jean and David Haywood ~ Real ale ~ Bar food (12-2(3 Sun), 6.30-9.30; 12-8.30 Sun) ~ (01732) 823575 ~ Children welcome ~ Dogs welcome ~ Live music second Thurs of the month ~ Open 11-2.30, 6-11; 11-11 Fri and Sat; 12-10.30 Sun

Recommended by Jeremy Hancock, Dr Jennifer Sansom, Gwyn Jones, Jan and Rod Poulter, D P and M A Miles, Arthur S Maxted, E D Bailey

HOLLINGBOURNE

TQ8354 MAP 3

Windmill

A mile from M20 junction 8: A20 towards Ashford (away from Maidstone), then left into B2163 – Eyhorne Street village; ME17 1TR

Small pubby core with several real ales but mainly set for dining; sunny little garden

'We liked the pubby atmosphere and prompt, friendly service' remarked one reader about this old coaching inn just off the M20. There are several small or smallish mainly carpeted areas with heavy low black beams that link together around the central island serving bar – sometimes partly separated by glazed or stained-glass panels. There's a pleasantly old-world feel, a good log fire in the huge inglenook fireplace, solid pub tables with padded country or library chairs, soft lighting, black timbers in ochre walls and shelves of books. The pubbiest part can be found tucked away up steps towards the back with bar stools and Fullers London Pride, Harveys Best and Shepherd Neame Master Brew on handpump and several wines by the glass; piped music. A neatly kept, spacious sunny little garden has picnic-sets under cocktail parasols and a play area.

⏚ **At lunchtime, bar food includes sandwiches, filled baked potatoes and baguettes, ploughman's, deep-fried potato skins with garlic and chive mayonnaise, liver and bacon with onion gravy, steaks, chicken coated in cajun spices, mixed grill, wok-tossed vegetables with pasta, various home-made burgers, a pie of the day, and daily specials such as lemon sole or chicken and smoked applewood cheddar pasta bake; they also offer a good value two-course set menu from Monday to Thursday.** *Starters/Snacks: £4.25 to £8.95. Main Courses: £7.95 to £24.95. Puddings: £3.50 to £5.95*

Enterprise ~ Lease Lee and Jan Atkinson ~ Real ale ~ Bar food (12-2.30, 6-10; 12-10 Sat(9 Sun)) ~ Restaurant ~ (01622) 880280 ~ Children must remain seated in bar ~ Dogs welcome ~ Open 12-3, 5-11; 12-11 Sat; 12-10.30 Sun

Recommended by Dr Kevan Tucker, Michael Doswell, Roger and Pauline Pearce, Charles and Pauline Stride, N R White

ICKHAM   TR2258   MAP 3

Duke William
Off A257 E of Canterbury; The Street; CT3 1QP

Friendly, relaxed family-owned village pub with light, airy bar and back dining conservatory, real ales and good wines, newspapers to read and WIFI internet access, enjoyable bar food and plenty of seats outside; bedrooms

At the back of this informal village pub, doors lead from the conservatory to a big terrace with a covered area to one side, plenty of wooden and metal tables and chairs and a lawn with picnic-table sets and some swings and a slide; there's also a designated smokers' area, too. The big spreading bar has huge new oak beams and stripped joists, a fine mix of seats from settles to high-backed cushioned dining chairs, dark wheelback and bentwood chairs around all sorts of wooden tables on the stripped wooden floor, a log fire with a couple of settles and a low barrel table in front of it, a central bar counter with high stools and brass coat hooks, and a snug little area with one long table, black leather high-backed dining chairs, a flat-screen TV and computer that drinkers may use; daily papers, quiet piped music, cheerful modern paintings and large hop bines. Harveys, Shepherd Neame Master Brew and a guest such as Skinners IPA on handpump and decent wines; Happy Hour is 4-6pm. Staff are chatty and attentive. A low-ceilinged dining room leads off to the left with dark wood chairs, tables and more cushioned settles, with paintings and mirrors on the walls. At the back of the pub, there's a light dining conservatory with all manner of interesting paintings, prints and heraldry on the walls and similar furniture on the stone floor. Although we have not heard from readers, this would be very pleasant place to stay. More reports please.

⏚ **Tasty bar food includes filled baguettes, starters like soup, chicken liver pâté, whitebait, field mushroom topped with goats cheese and prawns, with main courses such as steak and ale pie, calves liver and bacon, slow-roasted belly of pork with cider and apple sauce, chicken with tarragon and mushrooms, and puddings like treacle sponge and chocolate orange fondant; there's also a good value two-course lunch menu and Sunday roasts (booking advised).** *Starters/Snacks: £4.50 to £6.50. Main Courses: £8.00 to £16.00. Puddings: £4.50 to £5.50*

We mention bottled beers and spirits only if there is something unusual about them – imported belgian real ales, say, or dozens of malt whiskies; so do please let us know about them in your reports.

Free house ~ Licensee Louise White ~ Real ale ~ Bar food (12-3, 6-9) ~ Restaurant ~
(01227) 721308 ~ Well behaved children welcome ~ Dogs allowed in bar ~ Open 10.30am-11pm
~ Bedrooms: /£65S

Recommended by Prof and Mrs J Fletcher

IDEN GREEN   TQ8031   MAP 3

Woodcock

*Village signposted off A268 E of Hawkhurst and B2086 at W edge of Benenden; in village
centre follow Standen Street signpost, then fork left down Woodcock Lane (this is not the
Iden Green near Goudhurst); TN17 4HT*

**Simple country local with friendly staff, chatty regulars, an informal atmosphere, well
liked food and pretty garden**

This friendly little local is in a quiet spot by woodland on a tiny Wealden lane. The low-
ceilinged bar has an open woodburning stove in a fine old inglenook fireplace with a
comfortable squashy sofa and low table in front of it, stripped brick walls hung with
horse tackle, horsebrasses and various copper and brass items, a couple of big standing
timbers, a second sofa and cushioned settle to one side of the bar and some high bar
chairs. The chatty regulars tend to congregate around the high bar stools enjoying the
Greene King Abbot, IPA, Morlands Original and XX Mild on handpump served by friendly
staff. A couple of steps lead up to the two rooms of the panelled dining area which has
old photographs and hunting prints on the walls and pine tables and chairs. There are
seats in the pretty back garden and a car park just along the lane from the pub.

🍴 **Well liked bar food includes lunchtime filled baguettes, ploughman's, soup, home-made
burgers, tasty sausages with bubble and squeak, ham and egg, leek in caerphilly cheese
pie, and puddings like chocolate and orange cheesecake and sticky toffee pudding with
toffee sauce and caramel ice-cream.** *Starters/Snacks: £5.00 to £8.00. Main Courses: £6.00 to
£22.00. Puddings: £6.00*

Greene King ~ Lease Andrew Hemmings ~ Real ale ~ Bar food (12.30-2.30(3 Sun), 6-9;
(not Sun evening) ~ (01580) 240009 ~ Children welcome ~ Dogs allowed in bar ~ Open 12-11;
closed all day Mon except bank holidays

Recommended by Steve Coates, V Brogden

IGHTHAM COMMON   TQ5855   MAP 3

Harrow 🍴 🍷

Signposted off A25 just W of Ightham; pub sign may be hard to spot; TN15 9EB

**Emphasis on good food in friendly, smart dining pub, fresh flowers and candles; pretty
back terrace**

This comfortable and genial dining pub, handily placed for Ightham Mote, has tables and
chairs out on a pretty little pergola-enclosed back terrace. And while most customers are
here to enjoy the particularly good food, there's a tiny bar inside the door and a larger
bar area to the right. Both these two rooms are attractively decorated with fresh flowers
and candles on tables, smart dining chairs on the herringbone-patterned wood floor with
a winter fire. The bigger room is painted a cheerful sunny yellow above the wood-
panelled dado, there's a charming little antiquated conservatory and a more formal dining
room; piped music. Gravesend Shrimpers and Loddon Hoppit on handpump, several wines
by the glass and a warm welcome from the amiable landlord and his attentive staff.

🍴 **Good, popular food includes bar dishes like pork sausages with onion gravy, home-
baked ham and eggs, risotto verde, thai-style prawn curry, cajun chicken, as well as
more elaborate dishes such as salmon and chive fishcake with citrus cream sauce, goats
cheese and caramelised red onion tart with grape salad, duck suprême with dauphinoise
potatoes and plum tarte tatin, king scallops wrapped in pancetta with a garlic and herb
dressing and seasonal game like venison or pheasant; Sunday roasts.** *Starters/Snacks: £5.50
to £13.50. Main Courses: £8.50 to £18.50. Puddings: £5.75*

Free house ~ Licensees John Elton and Claire Butler ~ Real ale ~ Bar food (12-2, 6-9) ~ Restaurant ~ (01732) 885912 ~ Children welcome but not in dining room on Sat evening ~ Open 12-3, 6-11; 12-4 Sun; closed Sun evening and all day Mon

Recommended by Derek Thomas, David and Sharon Collison, B and M Kendall, Susan Wilson, Andrea Rampley, Nick and Carolyn Carter

IVY HATCH   TQ5854   MAP 3

Plough ♀

Village signposted off A227 N of Tonbridge; High Cross Road; TN15 0NL

Refurbished old pub, real ales and wines by the glass, interesting british and european bar food cooked by the landlord; seats in newly landscaped garden

This nicely refurbished tile-hung pub is in the midst of some very rewarding walking territory, through orchards and woodlands and along the greensand escarpment around One Tree Hill, and Ightham Mote is close by. There's a light wooden floor throughout, leather chesterfields grouped around an open fire, quite a mix of cushioned dining chairs around wooden tables, some large plants dotted about and high bar chairs by the wooden-topped bar counter where they keep Harveys Best and a seasonal ale plus a seasonal guest from Westerham Brewery on handpump; quite a few wines by the glass, and local fruit juice. There's also a conservatory; piped music and board games. Seats in the landscaped garden are surrounded by cob trees.

🍴 Using seasonal local produce, home-grown herbs, cobnuts (which go into rustic autumnal salads) and cress, the good bar food cooked by the landlord includes items such as sandwiches, ploughman's, home-made steak burger, baked ham with hand-cut chips and own free-range eggs, steamed mussels, chicken livers with black pudding and bacon and watercress and sage vinaigrette, fried grey mullet fillet with confit garlic aioli, rib-eye steak and fried calves liver with streaky bacon and mash with sage butter, and puddings like apple and almond crumble and pear and frangipane tart; Sunday roasts. Their home-made chutneys and eggs from their own chickens may be on sale. *Starters/Snacks: £4.85 to £7.50. Main Courses: £7.95 to £19.45. Puddings: £4.75 to £6.75*

Free house ~ Licensee Miles Medes ~ Real ale ~ Bar food (12-2.45, 6-9; all day Sat (sandwiches only 3-6); 12-6 Sun) ~ Restaurant ~ (01732) 810100 ~ Children welcome ~ Open 12-11; 10am-11pm Sat; 10am-10.30pm Sun; closed 3-6 Mon-Fri and after 6.30 Sun in winter

Recommended by Bob and Margaret Holder, Mr and Mrs J M Sennett

LANGTON GREEN   TQ5439   MAP 3

Hare 🍴 ♀

A264 W of Tunbridge Wells; TN3 0JA

Interestingly decorated Edwardian pub with a fine choice of drinks and popular food

Part of the much-liked Brunning and Price chain of pubs, this roomy mock-Tudor former hotel dates from 1901. Inside it is high-ceilinged and the rooms have been knocked through, with plenty of light flooding through large windows; the front bar tends to be where drinkers gather. Décor, more or less in period with the building, runs from dark-painted dados below light walls, 1930s oak furniture and turkish-style carpets on stained wooden floors to old romantic pastels and a huge collection of chamber-pots hanging from beams. Interesting old books, pictures and two huge mahogany mirror-backed display cabinets crowd the walls of the big room at the back, which has lots of large tables (one big enough for at least a dozen) on a light brown carpet; board games. Greene King IPA, Abbot, Morland Original and Ruddles, alongside a couple of guests on handpump, over 70 whiskies, up to 20 wines by the glass and a fine choice of vodkas and other spirits. French windows open on to a big terrace with picnic-sets and pleasant views of the tree-ringed village green. Parking is limited.

Pubs close to motorway junctions are listed at the back of the book.

🏠 Regularly changing bar food could feature sandwiches, ploughman's, home-cooked ham and eggs, braised shoulder of lamb, steak and venison suet pudding, crab linguine with ginger and coriander, smoked haddock and dill fishcakes, local sausages and mash, chicken and ham pie topped with mash, and puddings like chocolate brownie and mango and passion fruit panna cotta. *Starters/Snacks: £4.70 to £8.50. Main Courses: £8.95 to £16.95. Puddings: £4.95 to £5.25*

Brunning & Price ~ Lease Rob Broadbent ~ Real ale ~ Bar food (12-9.30(10 Fri, Sat; 9 Sun)) ~ (01892) 862419 ~ Well behaved children welcome if eating; no changing facilities ~ Dogs allowed in bar ~ Open 11.30-11(midnight Fri and Sat); 12-10.30 Sun

Recommended by Gerry and Rosemary Dobson, B J Harding, Vernon Rowe, Ian Phillips, John Branston

LOWER HARDRES
TR1453   MAP 3
Granville ♀
B2068 S of Canterbury; Faussett Hill, Street End; CT4 7AL

Surprisingly modern décor in several connected rooms, a fine choice of wines, good service and deservedly popular food (booking required at busy times); cosy little shady garden

The unassuming exterior of this dining pub belies what lies within – a spacious, airy interior with contemporary furnishings in several linked areas. It has comfortable squashy sofas, a mix of pale and dark tables with cushioned dining chairs, and – through shelves of large coloured church candles – a glimpse of the chefs hard at work in the kitchen. The appealing décor includes interesting modern photographs and animal linocuts on pale yellow walls above a dark red dado, a couple of large modern candelabra-type ceiling lights, one area with the floor attractively patterned in wood and tiles and an unusual central fire with a large conical hood; daily papers, piped music and board games. The proper public bar has settles, farmhouse chairs, a woodburning stove, Shepherd Neame Master Brew and a seasonal beer on handpump and good wines from a long blackboard list. French windows lead to the garden with rustic-style picnic-sets under a large spreading tree and there are some more traditional picnic-sets on a small sunny terraced area.

🍴 Well liked and consistently good bar food (booking strongly advisable) could include soup, squash risotto, steamed mussels, roast pork belly, roast leg of lamb and cod with tartare sauce, with puddings like flourless chocolate cake with raspberry sorbet and cream and tiramisu. *Starters/Snacks: £4.95 to £7.95. Main Courses: £9.95 to £17.95. Puddings: £5.50 to £7.50*

Shepherd Neame ~ Tenant Gabrielle Harris ~ Real ale ~ Bar food (12-2(2.30 Sun), 7-9; not Sun evening or Mon) ~ (01227) 700402 ~ Children welcome ~ Dogs welcome ~ Open 12-3, 5.30-11; 12-10.30 Sun

Recommended by Dr Kevan Tucker, R Goodenough, Barry and Patricia Wooding

NEWNHAM
TQ9557   MAP 3
George
The Street; village signposted from A2 just W of Ospringe, outside Faversham; ME9 0LL

Old-world village pub with open-plan rooms, a fair choice of drinks and food, and seats in spacious garden; pleasant walks nearby

This village pub is very usefully located for walks in this remote-feeling part of the North Downs. There's a series of spreading open-plan rooms with stripped, polished floorboards, stripped brickwork, gas-type chandeliers, candles and lamps on handsome tables and attractively upholstered mahogany settles. Blazing fires, hop-strung beams and Shepherd Neame Master Brew and a seasonal beer on handpump and several wines by the glass; piped music. The spacious sheltered garden has some picnic-sets.

🍴 Bar food includes lunchtime sandwiches, filled baguettes and baked potatoes, ploughman's, ham and eggs, bangers and mash, vegetable curry, steak and kidney pudding, daily specials, and puddings such as banoffi pie; Sunday lunch. *Starters/Snacks: £4.00 to £6.00. Main Courses: £10.00 to £16.00. Puddings: £4.00 to £6.00*

Shepherd Neame ~ Tenants Chris and Marie Annand ~ Real ale ~ Bar food (12-2.30, 7-9.30; Sunday lunch 12-6) ~ Restaurant ~ (01795) 890237 ~ Children welcome ~ Open 11-3, 6.30-11; 12-10.30 Sun
Recommended by Keith and Chris O'Neill, Tony and Jill Radnor, Kevin Thorpe

OARE

TR0163   MAP 3

Shipwrights Arms

S shore of Oare Creek, E of village; coming from Faversham on the Oare road, turn right into Ham Road opposite Davington School; or off A2 on B2045, go into Oare village, then turn right towards Faversham, and then left into Ham Road opposite Davington School; OS Sheet 178 map reference 016635; ME13 7TU

Remote pub in marshland with lots of surrounding bird life and up to five real ales in simple little bars

This beautifully placed, characterful waterside tavern serves beer brewed in Kent and tapped from the cask, with five ales from Goachers, Hopdaemon and Whitstable, plus a summer guest. The three simple little bars are dark and separated by standing timbers and wood partitions or narrow door arches. A medley of seats runs from tapestry-cushioned stools and chairs to black wood-panelled built-in settles forming little booths, and there are pewter tankards over the bar counter, boating jumble and pictures, pottery boating figures, flags or boating pennants on the ceilings, several brick fireplaces and a good woodburning stove; piped local radio. Look out for the electronic wind gauge above the main door which takes its reading from the chimney. There are seats in the large garden and the path along Oare Creek leads to the Swale estuary.

🍴 **Basic bar food such as sandwiches, ploughman's, sausage and mash, liver and bacon and fish pie.** *Starters/Snacks: £3.50 to £6.95. Main Courses: £7.95 to £10.95. Puddings: £2.95 to £4.50*

Free house ~ Licensees Derek and Ruth Cole ~ Real ale ~ Bar food (12-2.30, 7-9; not Sun evening or Mon) ~ Restaurant ~ (01795) 590088 ~ Children welcome away from bar area ~ Dogs allowed in bar ~ Open 11-3(4 Sat), 6-11; 12-4, 6-10.30 Sun; closed Mon
Recommended by N R White, the Didler, Kevin Flack, Rob and Kirstin, Andrea Rampley, Colin Moore, Colin and Louise English, Conor McGaughey, Colin McKerrow, Tony Brace, Pete Baker, Bruce Eccles

PENSHURST

TQ5142   MAP 3

Bottle House 🍴 ⏰

Coldharbour Lane; leaving Penshurst SW on B2188 turn right at Smarts Hill signpost, then bear right towards Chiddingstone and Cowden; keep straight on; TN11 8ET
KENT DINING PUB OF THE YEAR

Low beamed, connected bars in country pub, friendly service, chatty atmosphere, real ales and decent wines, popular bar food and sunny terrace; nearby walks

A firm favourite among many readers for its consistently excellent food, this chatty, bustling old pub has plenty of cosy nooks, with standing timbers separating the open-plan rooms into intimate areas. There are beams and joists (one or two of the especially low ones are leather padded), an attractive mix of old wheelback and dining chairs around all sorts of wooden tables, photographs of the pub and local scenes on the walls (some of which are stripped stone), an old brick floor by the copper-topped wooden bar counter with dark wooden boarding elsewhere; the fireplace houses a woodburning stove and most of the tables are set with fresh flowers. Harveys Best and Larkins Traditional on handpump, local apple juice and a good choice of wines; friendly, helpful young service and piped music. The sunny, brick-paved terrace has green-painted picnic-sets under parasols and some olive trees in white pots; parking is limited. Good surrounding walks in this attractive area of rolling country.

🍴 **From a monthly changing seasonal menu featuring local produce, and a daily changing specials board, popular bar food might include ploughman's, starters like soup, duck and** foie gras parfait with red onion marmalade and fillet of beef carpaccio, main courses such as rack of lamb, steak and ale pie, confit duck leg with thyme potato cake and port sauce, red mullet with egg noodles and soy, ginger and honey dressing, or sunblush tomato and basil tart topped with goats cheese, and puddings like warm pecan pie or chocolate fondant. *Starters/Snacks: £2.50 to £8.95. Main Courses: £9.95 to £17.95. Puddings: £4.95 to £5.50*

Free house ~ Licensee Paul Hammond ~ Real ale ~ Bar food (12-10(9 Sun and bank hols)) ~ Restaurant ~ (01892) 870306 ~ Children welcome ~ Dogs allowed in bar ~ Open 11-11(10.30 Sun)

Recommended by Tina and David Woods-Taylor, Jamie May, LM, Bob and Margaret Holder, R and S Bentley, Ann and Colin Hunt, Gerry and Rosemary Dobson, Steve Coates, Simon and Helen Barnes, N R White

PLUCKLEY

TQ9243 MAP 3

Dering Arms ♀ 🛏

Pluckley Station, which is signposted from B2077; or follow Station Road (left turn off Smarden Road in centre of Pluckley) for about 1.3 miles S, through Pluckley Thorne; TN27 0RR

Fine fish dishes plus other good food in handsome building, stylish main bar, carefully chosen wines and roaring log fire; comfortable bedrooms

Originally a hunting lodge when built in the 1840s and embellished with many dutch gables, this eye-catching brick building is one of several in the village built by the Dering Estate. And while much emphasis is also placed on the fish and seafood, the bar is characterful and comfortable and they do keep a beer named for the pub from Goachers on handpump, a good wine list of 120 wines, 40 malt whiskies and occasional local cider. High-ceilinged and stylishly plain, this main bar has a solid country feel with a variety of wooden furniture on the flagstone floors, a roaring log fire in the great fireplace, country prints and some fishing rods. The smaller half-panelled back bar has similar dark wood furnishings, and an extension to this area has a woodburning stove, comfortable armchairs, sofas and a grand piano; board games. Classic car meetings (the long-serving landlord has a couple of classics) are held here on the second Sunday of the month. Readers very much enjoy staying overnight here – and the breakfasts are excellent.

🍴 In the bar, dishes include soup, fried herring roes with crispy smoked bacon, garlic king prawns, a pie of the day, salmon fillet with Pernod and lemon butter sauce, confit of duck, rib-eye steak and seafood platter (24 hours' notice); daily specials such as various fish dishes, grilled lobster, lamb steak and casseroled guinea fowl, with puddings like tiramisu or fresh fruit salad. *Starters/Snacks: £3.95 to £7.95. Main Courses: £12.50 to £24.95. Puddings: £4.65 to £5.95*

Free house ~ Licensee James Buss ~ Real ale ~ Bar food (not Sun evening or Mon) ~ Restaurant ~ (01233) 840371 ~ Children welcome ~ Dogs allowed in bar ~ Open 11.30-3.30, 6-11; 12-3.30 Sun; closed Sun evening, all Mon, 25-28 Dec, 1 Jan ~ Bedrooms: £40(£65S)/£50(£75S)

Recommended by Sara Fulton, Roger Baker, Philip and Cheryl Hill, Patrick Noble, John Prescott, Colin and Louise English, Derek Thomas, Joan and Alec Lawrence, Bruce Eccles

SHIPBOURNE

TQ5952 MAP 3

Chaser ◉ ♀

Stumble Hill (A227 N of Tonbridge); TN11 9PE

Comfortable, civilised country pub, log fires, good, popular food, quite a few wines by the glass; covered and heated outside terrace

Run by obliging staff and in a rural location and warmed by log fires, this smartly updated country pub ticks over very nicely indeed, though it does get very busy at peak times, when booking is necessary. Most customers are here to enjoy the food but there's a good range of drinks, with Greene King IPA and Abbot and a couple of guest beers like Greene King Old Speckled Hen on handpump, a huge number of wines by the glass, 40 malt whiskies and a fair choice of brandies and liqueurs; piped music and board games. There are several open-plan areas that meander into each other, all converging on a large central island bar counter: stripped wooden floors, frame-to-frame pictures on deepest red and cream walls, stripped pine wainscoting, an eclectic mix of solid old wood tables (with candles) and chairs, shelves of books and open fires. A striking school chapel-like restaurant right at the back has dark wood panelling and a high timber-vaulted ceiling. French windows open on to a covered and heated central courtyard with teak furniture and big green parasols, and a side garden is nicely enclosed by hedges and shrubs, with the pretty church rising behind (well worth a visit). There's a small car park or you can park in the lane opposite by a delightful green; farmers' market on Thursday morning.

🍴 Using carefully chosen local produce, the enjoyable food from a daily changing menu and specials board typically includes sandwiches, ploughman's, soup, starters like whitebait, halloumi and mediterranean vegetable kebab or smoked salmon and prawn roulade, sausages and mash, steak burger topped with tomato and gouda cheese, fish pie, spinach, rocket and smoked applewood cheddar risotto, shoulder of lamb, dressed crab and sirloin steak, and puddings; they serve breakfast on Thursday, Saturday and Sunday. *Starters/Snacks: £4.00 to £7.00. Main Courses: £8.00 to £16.00. Puddings: £4.95 to £6.50*

Whiting & Hammond ~ Manager Darren Somerton ~ Real ale ~ Bar food (12-9.30(9 Sun)) ~ (01732) 810360 ~ Children welcome but must be well behaved ~ Dogs allowed in bar ~ Open 11(12 Sun)-11(midnight Fri, Sat)

Recommended by Derek Thomas, Bob and Margaret Holder, Martin and Pauline Jennings, Neil Hardwick, Gordon and Margaret Ormondroyd, Tina and David Woods-Taylor, Christian Mole, Tony Brace, N R White, David and Sally Cullen, Gene and Kitty Rankin

SNARGATE   TQ9928   MAP 3

Red Lion ★ 🍺

B2080 Appledore—Brenzett; TN29 9UQ

Unchanging, simple pub, good chatty atmosphere and straightforward furnishings; no food

The year 2011 marks the centenary of the same family running this tremendously evocative pub on the Romney Marsh, where nothing much has altered since 1890. The three little rooms have a timeless, old-fashioned charm as well as their original cream tongue and groove wall panelling, heavy beams in a sagging ceiling, dark pine Victorian farmhouse chairs on bare boards, lots of old photographs and other memorabilia and there's a coal fire; outdoor lavatories, of course. Lighting is dim but candles are lit at night. One small room, with a frosted glass wall through to the bar and a sash window looking out to a cottage garden, has only two dark pine pews beside two long tables, a couple more farmhouse chairs and an old piano stacked with books. Toad in the hole, darts, shove-ha'penny, cribbage, dominoes, nine men's morris and table skittles. Four or five ales feature Goachers and changing guests tapped straight from casks on a low rack behind an unusual shop-like marble-topped counter (little marks it out as a bar other than a few glasses on two small shelves, some crisps and half a dozen spirits bottles); you can also get farm cider from Kent – Double Vision cider from nearby Staplehurst and, in summer, East Stour; country wines.

🍴 **No food.**

Free house ~ Licensee Mrs Jemison ~ Real ale ~ No credit cards ~ (01797) 344648 ~ Children in family room only ~ Dogs allowed in bar ~ Open 12-3, 7-11(10.30 Sun)

Recommended by the Didler, Simon Rodway, Colin and Louise English, Andrea Rampley, Tim Maddison, Peter Meister

---

Stars after the name of a pub show exceptional character and appeal. They don't mean extra comfort. And they are nothing to do with food quality, for which there's a separate knife-and-fork symbol. Even quite a basic pub can win stars, if it's individual enough.

SPELDHURST TQ5541 MAP 3

George & Dragon ♀

Village signposted from A264 W of Tunbridge Wells; TN3 0NN

Fine old pub, beams, flagstones and huge fireplaces, local beers, good food and attractive outside seating areas

Based around a medieval manorial hall, this half-timbered building conjures up quite a sense of antiquity with its ancient beams and with a winter log fire burning in a huge sandstone fireplace in the main room. The entrance hall (where there is a water bowl for thirsty dogs) is rather splendid – though we're still not sure about the chandelier. On the right, the half-panelled room is set for dining with a mix of old wheelback and other dining chairs and a cushioned wall pew around several tables, a few little pictures on the walls, horsebrasses on one huge beam and a sizeable bar counter with Harveys Best, Larkins Traditional Ale and an ale from Westerham Brewery on handpump, 16 wines by the glass and local organic fruit juice; friendly, efficient staff. A doorway leads through to another dining room with similar furnishings and another big inglenook. To the left of the main door is a room more used for those wanting a drink and a chat (though people do eat in here, too), with a woodburning stove in a small fireplace, high-winged cushioned settles and various wooden tables and dining chairs on the stripped wooden floor; piped music. There's also an upstairs restaurant. In front of the pub are teak tables, chairs and benches on a nicely planted gravel terrace, while at the back there's a covered area with big church candles on more wooden tables and a lower terrace with seats around a 300-year-old olive tree; more attractive planting here and some modern sculpturing.

🍴 Enjoyable – if not cheap – bar food at lunchtime includes sandwiches, ploughman's, soup, smoked salmon terrine, seared pigeon breasts with smoked bacon and puy lentils, beer-battered fish and chips, venison and root vegetable pie, slow-braised lamb shank, sea bream fillet with brown shrimp butter, slow-roasted pork belly with apple compote, rump steak; puddings. They may add a 12.5% service charge to all bills. *Starters/Snacks: £5.50 to £12.50. Main Courses: £10.50 to £18.50. Puddings: £5.50*

Free house ~ Licensee Julian Leefe-Griffiths ~ Real ale ~ Bar food (12-2.30(4 Sun), 7(6.30 Sat)-9.30; not Sun evening) ~ Restaurant ~ (01892) 863125 ~ Children welcome ~ Dogs allowed in bar ~ Open 11-11(10.30 Sun)

Recommended by Andrea Rampley, Simon and Helen Barnes, Derek Thomas

ST MARGARET'S BAY TR3744 MAP 3

Coastguard ♀ ◧

Off A256 NE of Dover; keep on down through the village to the bottom of the bay, pub off on right; CT15 6DY

Terrific views, some nautical décor, fine range of drinks and well liked food

In the bay beneath the white cliffs of Dover, this terrifically positioned pub is usefully placed for some of the finest coastal walking in the county. Inside, the warm, carpeted, wood-clad bar has some shipping memorabilia, a rapidly changing range of interesting ales such as Adnams Gunhill, Gadds No. 5 and Surrey Hills Shere Drop on handpump, 45 malt whiskies, Weston's cider and a carefully chosen wine list including those from Kent vineyards; good service even when busy. The restaurant has wooden dining chairs and tables on a wood-strip floor and more fine views; piped music. Tables out on the prettily planted balcony from where you can look across the Straits of Dover; there are more seats down by the beach below the National Trust cliffs.

🍴 Well presented bar food typically includes sandwiches, soup, pork and game terrine, scallops seared with garlic butter, moroccan-spiced roast vegetable frittata with slow-roasted tomatoes, gratin of broccoli with mushrooms and leeks, beer-battered cod, local sirloin steak, and puddings such as dark chocolate stout cake with beer-marinated cherries and steamed stem ginger pudding. *Starters/Snacks: £5.00 to £9.00. Main Courses: £10.50 to £28.00. Puddings: £5.00 to £9.00*

Free house ~ Licensee Nigel Wydymus ~ Real ale ~ Bar food (12.30-2.45, 6.30-8.45) ~
Restaurant ~ (01304) 853176 ~ Children allowed away from bar ~ Dogs allowed in bar ~
Open 10.30am-11pm
Recommended by Andrew York, Christopher Turner, David Jackman

STODMARSH
TR2160   MAP 3

Red Lion 🍴 🛏

High Street; off A257 just E of Canterbury; CT3 4BA

**Super country pub with very cheerful landlord, lots to look at, super choice of food and
drink and pretty garden with roaming ducks and chickens**

A stroll away from the rich bird life in Stodmarsh National Nature Reserve, this cheerfully
quirky country pub is much enjoyed by readers as a place to drink, eat or stay. The
idiosyncratic bar rooms wrap themselves around the big island bar and have lots of
interesting things to look at: a life-size Tintin and Snowy, a tiger's head, hops, wine
bottles (some empty and some full) crammed along mantelpieces and along one side of
the bar, all manner of paintings and pictures, copper kettles and old cooking implements,
well used cookery books, big stone bottles and milk churns, trugs and baskets, old tennis
racquets and straw hats; one part has a collection of brass instruments, sheet music
all over the walls, some jazz records and a couple of little stall areas have hop sacks
draped over the partitioning. There are green-painted, cushioned mate's chairs around a
mix of nice pine tables, lit candles in unusual metal candleholders, a big log fire and
fresh flowers; piped jazz, and bat and trap. The conservatory adds dining space. Greene
King IPA and Harveys Best are tapped straight from the cask, and they've a good wine
list with several by the glass, excellent summer Pimms, winter mulled wine and cider.
Picnic-sets are under umbrellas in the back garden, with pretty flowerbeds and roaming
ducks and chickens. The two cats are called Jack and Daniel. Please note that the
bedrooms don't have their own bathrooms.

🍴 Extremely good, interesting food using top quality local meat and seasonal produce
includes six starters like asparagus spears, cornish spider crab with oak-smoked salmon
and melba toast and smoked free-range chicken pancetta, nine main courses such as
chargrilled fillet steak with cream peppercorn sauce, roasted duck breast with mixed bean
cassoulet, bouillabaisse with crab and prawns from Hythe and usually three vegetarian
dishes; traditional puddings include treacle sponge and apple and rhubarb crumble.
Starters/Snacks: £5.00 to £7.00. Main Courses: £12.95 to £19.95. Puddings: £4.95

Free house ~ Licensee Robert Whigham ~ Real ale ~ Bar food (12.30-2.30, 7-9.30) ~ Restaurant
~ (01227) 721339 ~ Children welcome ~ Dogs allowed in bar ~ Open 11-11 ~ Bedrooms: £45/£70
Recommended by N R White, Andy Towse, David and Ruth Shillitoe

STOWTING
TR1241   MAP 3

Tiger 🍴

*3.7 miles from M20 junction 11; B2068 N, then left at Stowting signpost, straight across
crossroads, then fork left after 0.25 miles and pub is on right; coming from N, follow
Brabourne, Wye, Ashford signpost to right at fork, then turn left towards Posting and
Lyminge at T junction; TN25 6BA*

**Peaceful pub with friendly staff, interesting traditional furnishings, well liked food,
several real ales and open fires; good walking country**

On warmer days this 17th-c inn is a pleasant place to sit out on the front terrace for a
meal or a drink, and there's an outside smokers' shelter with an environmentally friendly
heater and stools made from tractor seats. Inside it's traditionally furnished with a happy
mix of wooden tables and chairs and built-in cushioned wall seats on wooden floorboards
and with woodburning stoves at each end of the bar. There's an array of books meant to
be read rather than left for decoration, board games, candles in bottles, brewery
memorabilia and paintings, lots of hops and some faded rugs on the stone floor towards

the back of the pub. Fullers London Pride, Harveys Best and Shepherd Neame Master Brew and a couple of guests like Goachers and Old Dairy Brewery Red Top on handpump, lots of malt whiskies, several wines by the glass, local Biddenden cider and local fruit juice. Plenty of nearby walks along the Wye Downs or North Downs Way.

🍴 Enjoyable bar food from a daily changing menu, using seasonal kentish produce, includes items such as sandwiches, grilled asparagus spears with soft free-range eggs and organic hollandaise sauce, crab meat and brown shrimp with fresh mango and sweet red chilli salsa, terrine of free-range chicken, root vegetable and ham hock, slow-roasted pork belly, seared wild bass fillet and parmesan soufflé with chestnut mushroom white wine cream, and puddings like gypsy tart, rhubarb and ginger crumble. *Starters/Snacks: £3.00 to £10.00. Main Courses: £9.95 to £20.00. Puddings: £5.50 to £7.50*

Free house ~ Licensees Emma Oliver and Benn Jarvis ~ Real ale ~ Bar food (12(4 Mon)-9(9.30 Fri, Sat, 8 Sun)) ~ Restaurant ~ (01303) 862130 ~ Children welcome if well behaved ~ Dogs allowed in bar ~ Jazz every second Mon evening ~ Open 12(4 Mon)-midnight; 12-11 Sat; 12-10.30 Sun; closed Mon lunchtime, Tues

Recommended by Brian and Anna Marsden, Jill and Julian Tasker, Paul Goldman, N R White

TUNBRIDGE WELLS   TQ5839   MAP 3

Sankeys

Mount Ephraim (A26 just N of junction with A267); TN4 8AA

Pubby street-level bar, informal downstairs brasserie, real ales and good wines, chatty atmosphere and super fish dishes

In two very distinct parts, this efficiently run place has a fine reputation for fish dining in its downstairs brasserie, but exudes a much pubbier atmosphere in its paraphernalia-filled upper bar. At street level the bar is light and airy, decorated with a unique collection of rare enamel signs, antique brewery mirrors and old prints, framed cigarette cards and lots of old wine bottles and soda siphons. It's comfortably laid out with leather sofas and pews around all sorts of tables on bare wooden boards, and they keep a couple of beers from Goachers and Westerham Brewery on handpump, fruit beers and exotic brews and several wines by the glass from a good list; big flat screen TV for sports (not football) and piped music. Downstairs is a brasserie with big mirrors on the stripped brick walls, pews or chairs around sturdy tables, a chatty, informal atmosphere and there's an oyster bar and fresh fish display. French windows open on to an inviting sun-trap decked garden with wicker and chrome chairs and wooden tables. More reports please.

🍴 Very good value pubby food at lunchtime in the upstairs bar includes filled baguettes, filled baked potatoes, smoked haddock mornay with spinach and topped with a poached egg, fish cakes, rib-eye steak and a sharing seafood plate. Downstairs, the emphasis is on fish: oysters, pickled cockles, fresh anchovies, potted shrimps, local lemon sole, plaice, john dory, black bream, lobster and huge cornish cock crabs. Sunday roasts and summer barbecues. *Starters/Snacks: £2.00 to £6.00. Main Courses: £4.00 to £13.95. Puddings: £4.00 to £4.95*

Free house ~ Licensee Matthew Sankey ~ Real ale ~ Bar food (12-3(5 Sat, 4 Sun), 6-10; not Sun evening) ~ Restaurant ~ (01892) 511422 ~ Children welcome only until 6pm in bar but any time in restaurant ~ Dogs allowed in bar ~ Live bands second Sun of the month and bank hols ~ Open 12-12(2am Fri and Sat)

Recommended by Bob and Margaret Holder, Conor McGaughey, BOB, Pat and Tony Martin

ULCOMBE   TQ8550   MAP 3

Pepper Box

Fairbourne Heath; signposted from A20 in Harrietsham, or follow Ulcombe signpost from A20, then turn left at crossroads with sign to pub, then right at next minor crossroads; ME17 1LP

Friendly country pub with homely bar, lovely log fire, well liked food, fair choice of drinks and seats in pretty garden

An inviting place to arrive at whatever the weather, this rural pub is very well run by friendly licensees. The homely bar has standing timbers and a few low beams (some hung with hops), copper kettles and pans on window sills and two leather sofas by the splendid inglenook fireplace (nice horsebrasses on the bressumer beam) with its lovely log fire. A side area, more functionally furnished for eating, extends into the opened-up beamed dining room with a range in another inglenook and more horsebrasses. Shepherd Neame Invicta, Master Brew and a seasonal beer on handpump, local apple juice and several wines by the glass; piped music. The two cats are called Murphy and Jim. There's a hop-covered terrace and a garden with shrubs, with delightful views of the Weald. The name of the pub refers to the pepperbox pistol – an early type of revolver with numerous barrels; the village church is worth a look. The Greensand Way footpath runs close by.

🍴 As well as lunchtime sandwiches and filled baguettes and ploughman's, the well liked bar food could include soup, tiger prawns, breaded camembert with rhubarb chutney, confit leg and roasted breast of duck with dauphinoise potatoes, peppered lamb fillet with pickled beetroot, watercress and minted salad, steak, cod and chips, fish specials and portabella mushrooms stuffed with goats cheese and basil. *Starters/Snacks: £4.00 to £7.50. Main Courses: £7.50 to £9.50. Puddings: £4.50 to £5.00*

Shepherd Neame ~ Tenant Sarah Pemble ~ Real ale ~ Bar food (12-2.15, 7-9.45; 12-3 Sun; not Sun evening) ~ Restaurant ~ (01622) 842558 ~ Well behaved children allowed lunchtime only and must be over 3 ~ Dogs allowed in bar ~ Open 11-3, 6-midnight; 11am-midnight Sat; 12-5 Sun; closed Sun evening

Recommended by Philip and Cheryl Hill, Michael Tack, Nick Lawless, N R White, Donna and Roger, Tina and David Woods-Taylor

LUCKY DIP

Besides the fully inspected pubs, you might like to try these Lucky Dips recommended to us and described by readers (if you do, please send us reports: feedback@goodguides.com).

ADDINGTON [TQ6559]
Angel ME19 5BB [just off M20 junction 4; Addington Green]: 14th-c pub in classic village-green setting, olde-worlde décor with candles in bottles on scrubbed deal tables and big fireplaces, enjoyable fairly priced up-to-date food, fair choice of beers, lots of wines by the glass, good friendly service, stables restaurant *(A N Bance)*
APPLEDORE [TQ9529]
Black Lion TN26 2BU [The Street]: Compact 1930s village pub with bustling atmosphere, very welcoming helpful staff, good generous food all day from simple sandwiches to imaginative dishes, lamb from Romney Marsh and local fish, three or four well kept changing ales, Biddenden farm cider, log fire, partitioned back eating area; piped music; tables out on green, attractive village, good Military Canal walks *(Colin and Louise English, Alec and Joan Laurence)*
Railway Hotel TN26 2DF [Station Rd (B2080 E)]: Friendly refurbished Victorian hotel with rail memorabilia and open fire in big front

bar, Badger K&B and good value food, daily papers, pool, darts, big back children's room with toys and TV, restaurant; good disabled access and facilities, garden tables, 12 bedrooms in small motel wing *(Peter and Jean Hoare)*
BEARSTED [TQ7956]
Bell ME14 4PA [Ware St; by railway bridge, W of centre]: Friendly and spacious with well kept Greene King ales and a guest, good range of competitively priced food; can get busy; big garden, heated terrace *(Michael Tack, Patrick Noble)*
Oak on the Green ME14 4EJ [The Street]: Two hop-festooned bar areas with bare boards and half-panelling, bustling and friendly, with wide choice of home-made food all day inc children's menu, well kept regularly changing ales, restaurant; disabled access, seats out at front under big umbrellas, open all day *(Michael Tack)*
BRASTED [TQ4654]
Stanhope Arms TN16 1HZ [Church Rd]: Greene King pub in shadow of church,

unfussy good value home-made food, well kept ales, plain cosy bar, dining room; garden with smokers' facility, may be cl Mon *(Gwyn Jones, LYM)*

BRENCHLEY [TQ6841]

Halfway House TN12 7AX [Horsmonden Rd]: Attractive olde-worlde mix of rustic and traditional furnishings on bare boards, two log fires, particularly friendly landlord and efficient staff, enjoyable home-made food inc good fish and popular Sun roasts, good changing ales tapped from the cask, two tranquil eating areas; dogs welcome, picnic-sets and play area in big garden, bedrooms *(Jamie May)*

BROADSTAIRS [TR3866]

Brown Jug CT10 2EW [Ramsgate Rd]: Long-serving landlady in basic and unchanging old-style two-bar local, well kept Greene King and guests, some tapped from the cask, board and quiz games; lunchtime opening hours may vary, open all day wknds *(the Didler)*

Neptunes Hall CT10 1ET [Harbour St]: Chatty early 19th-c two-bar Shepherd Neame local, attractive bow windows, original shelving and panelling, carpeted back lounge with open fire, lunchtime snacks (not Sun or during winter), friendly landlord, military photographs; occasional live folk (daily during Aug folk festival); children and dogs welcome, covered heated terrace, open all day *(the Didler)*

CANTERBURY [TR1558]

New Inn CT1 1NP [Havelock St]: Relaxed Victorian terraced local tidied up by present landlord, changing ales such as Greene King and Harveys, simple food, modern back conservatory; nearby parking difficult *(Peter Dean)*

☆ *Parrot* CT1 2AG [Church Lane – the one off St Radigund St, 100 yds E of St Radigunds car park]: Sympathetically updated Youngs pub with their ales and guests, heavy beams, wood and flagstone floors, stripped masonry, dark panelling, big open fire, good value bar food with more extensive traditional menu in upstairs vaulted restaurant, decent wine choice, friendly efficient staff; nicely laid out courtyard with central wood-burning barbecue, open all day *(Pete Coxon, Paul Goldman, Duncan Smart, Bruce M Drew, Norman Fox)*

Phoenix CT1 3DB [Old Dover Rd]: Two friendly linked rooms in olde-worlde beamed tavern with central woodburner and lots of prints, up to eight changing ales inc Wells & Youngs Bombardier (beer festivals), cheap hearty all-day pub food, newspapers; piped music, sports TV; disabled access, picnic-sets on back terrace, smokers' shelter, open all day *(Tony Hobden, Kevin Thorpe)*

Three Tuns CT1 2UD [Watling St, opp St Margaret St]: Old corner pub refurbished and reopened under new management, friendly service, standard food (not Sun evening), Caledonian Deuchars IPA, Wells & Youngs Bombardier and a guest; sports TV,

pool; terrace, children till 7pm, open all day *(N R White)*

Unicorn CT2 8BS [St Dunstans St]: Friendly and popular early 17th-c pub, four well kept ales inc Caledonian Deuchars IPA and Shepherd Neame Master Brew, imaginative good value food (till 6.45 Sat and not Sun) inc meal deals, warm fire, bar billiards, Sun quiz night; garden *(Prof and Mrs J Fletcher)*

CAPEL [TQ6444]

Dovecote TN12 6SU [Alders Rd; SE of Tonbridge]: Cosy beamed pub with some stripped brickwork and open fire, pitched-ceiling dining end, enjoyable food (not Sun evening, Mon) from sandwiches to Sun roasts, up to six ales tapped from the cask inc Gales and Harveys, farm ciders, friendly staff; lots of picnic-sets in back garden with terrace and play area, nice country surroundings, open all day Sun *(Patrick Noble, N R White)*

CAPEL-LE-FERNE [TR2439]

Valiant Sailor CT18 7JJ [New Dover Rd (B2011)]: Friendly pleasantly refurbished roadside pub, three or four ales inc well kept Fullers London Pride, good value food, good service, newspapers; pool and darts; handy for cliff walks and Battle of Britain memorial, open all day *(Brian and Anna Marsden)*

CHIDDINGSTONE [TQ5045]

Castle Inn TN8 7AH [off B2027 Tonbridge—Edenbridge]: New management at this rambling old pub in pretty NT village, handsome beamed bar, settles and sturdy wall benches, attractive mullioned window seat, woodburners, brick-floor snug, Harveys Best and local Larkins inc winter Porter (brewed in village), Stowford Press cider, good choice of wines, food from landlord/chef (reports please), friendly staff; children and dogs welcome, tables out in front and in nice secluded garden, circular walks from village, open all day *(LYM)*

CHIDDINGSTONE CAUSEWAY [TQ5146]

Little Brown Jug TN11 8JJ [B2027]: Open-plan Whiting & Hammond pub with comfortable bar and big dining extension, good food at sensible prices from sandwiches to full meals, well kept Greene King ales, good wine list, friendly efficient service, roaring fire; attractive garden with play area, beer and music festivals, open all day wknds *(R and S Bentley, Martin Stafford, Robert Gomme, Gerry and Rosemary Dobson)*

CHILLENDEN [TR2653]

☆ *Griffins Head* CT3 1PS: Attractive beamed, timbered and flagstoned 14th-c pub with two bar rooms and back flagstoned dining room, gently upscale local atmosphere, big log fire, full range of Shepherd Neame ales, good choice of home-made food; pleasant garden surrounded by wild roses, super Sun barbecues, attractive countryside *(Philip and Cheryl Hill)*

CHIPSTEAD [TQ5056]

☆ *George & Dragon* TN13 2RW [nr M25 junction 5]: Attractive country dining pub now under same owners as the George and Dragon at Speldhurst; heavy black beams and standing timbers, grey-green panelling, old tables and chapel chairs on bare boards, log fires, good changing food all day using organic local produce, Westerham ales inc Georges Marvellous Medicine brewed for the pub, good choice of wines by the glass, good service, upstairs restaurant; piped music; children and dogs welcome, terrace and garden with veg/herbs, play area, open all day (LYM, Sophie Broster, Derek Thomas)

COBHAM [TQ6768]

Leather Bottle DA12 3BZ [handy for M2 junction 1]: Old beamed and timbered pub, much modernised, with interesting woodwork and lots of Dickens memorabilia, Courage Best and a guest such as Sharps, friendly young staff, bar food and restaurant; disabled access, picnic-sets on big back lawn with play area and fishpond, pretty village, five bedrooms, open all day (N R White, LYM)

COWDEN [TQ4640]

Fountain TN8 7JG [off A264 and B2026; High St]: Good sensibly priced blackboard food in attractive tile-hung beamed village pub, steep steps up to unpretentious dark-panelled corner bar, well kept Harveys, decent wines, old photographs on cream walls, good log fire, mix of tables in adjoining room, woodburner in small back dining room with one big table; piped music; walkers and dogs welcome, picnic-sets on small terrace and lawn, pretty village (LM, Gwyn Jones, BB)

☆ *Queens Arms* TN8 5NP [Cowden Pound; junction B2026 with Markbeech rd]: Friendly two-room country pub like something from the 1930s, with splendid landlady, well kept Adnams, coal fire, darts; dogs welcome, occasional folk music or morris dancers; may be cl wkdy lunchtimes but normally opens 10am (the Didler)

CROCKHAM HILL [TQ4450]

Royal Oak TN8 6RD [Main Rd]: Cosy two-bar village pub, well run and friendly, with good value home-made pub lunches from sandwiches up, well kept Westerham ales, daily papers, comfortable high-backed seats, cartoons by local artist, no music or machines; dogs and walkers welcome, small garden, handy for walks and Chartwell (N R White, Gwyn Jones)

DARTFORD [TQ5473]

Malt Shovel DA1 1LP [Darenth Rd]: Two-bar 17th-c pub under newish management, Wells & Youngs and a guest ale, decent food, dining room, crib nights (Quentin and Carol Williamson)

DEAL [TR3751]

Berry CT14 7EQ [Canada Rd]: Small no frills local opp old Royal Marine barracks, welcoming enthusiastic landlord, L-shaped carpeted bar, well kept Harveys Best and four changing microbrews (tasting notes on slates, beer festivals), farm cider and perry, no food, coal fire, newspapers, quiz and darts teams, pool, live music Thurs; small

vine-covered terrace, open all day wknds, cl Tues-Thurs lunchtimes (Kevin Thorpe, Dr Kevan Tucker)

☆ *Bohemian* CT14 6HY [Beach St]: Airy and chatty modern-fronted café-bar opp pier, at least four real ales, continental beers, perry and several wines by the glass, enjoyable food inc wknd brunch, friendly helpful staff, L-shaped bar with chunky pine furniture and big squashy built-in leather sofa, polished wood floor, decorative fireplace, a few photographs and contemporary paintings, magazines, good seafront views from upstairs restaurant with well presented modern food; TV in area off, piped music; wheelchair access, heated back decking, open all day (BB, Guy Vowles, N R White, Mr and Mrs P R Thomas, Dr Kevan Tucker)

Deal Hoy CT14 6DU [Duke St]: Corner local in Victorian terrace, comfortable front bar with sofas and beer adverts, back bar with pastel paintings, old books, sheet music and LPs, Shepherd Neame ales, live music; outside area with decking and palms, open all day (till 8 Sun) (Kevin Thorpe)

☆ *Kings Head* CT14 7AH [Beach St]: Handsome three-storey Georgian inn just across from promenade and sea, good landlord and atmosphere, interesting maritime décor and cricket memorabilia in comfortable dimly lit areas around central servery, flame-effect gas fires, Shepherd Neame ales and a guest such as Marstons Pedigree, usual food from cheap sandwiches up, darts; piped music, TV, popular with young locals wknd evenings; good front terrace area, good value bedrooms, open all day (LYM, N R White, DM)

Prince Albert CT14 6LW [Middle St]: Little Victorian corner pub in conservation area, ornate interior with plenty of bric-a-brac, three changing ales, food (not Mon or Tues) inc popular Sun carvery in back dining area, live folk music; small garden behind, bedrooms, cl lunchtimes exc Sun (Kevin Thorpe, Dr Kevan Tucker)

Royal CT14 6JD [Beach St]: Seafront hotel dating from early 18th c, comfortable with plenty of casual drinkers, Shepherd Neame, decent bar food; seaview deck, 18 bedrooms (MDN)

Ship CT14 6JZ [Middle St]: Dim-lit local in historic maritime quarter, five well kept changing ales inc Ramsgate Gadds, friendly landlord, lots of dark woodwork, stripped brick and local ship and wreck pictures, piano and woodburner in side bar; dogs welcome, small pretty walled garden, open all day (N R White, Dr Kevan Tucker, Mr and Mrs P R Thomas)

DOVER [TR3241]

Blakes CT16 1PJ [Castle St]: Small flagstoned cellar bar down steep steps, brick and flint walls, fire, Harveys Best and three interesting changing ales, farm ciders and perries, over 50 malt whiskies, good choice of wines by the glass, good lunchtime bar food (not Sun) inc good value doorstep sandwiches and home-smoked fish/cheese, part-panelled upstairs restaurant, chatty licensees, daily papers; well behaved children welcome, suntrap back terrace, bedrooms, open all day, cl Sun *(Kevin Thorpe)*

Three Cups CT17 0RX [Crabble Hill (A256)]: Welcoming bistro-style open-plan pub, friendly staff, good value food from open kitchen, Marstons Pedigree, blackboard wines, daily papers, comfortable settees, some high stools and bar tables, modern sunken fireplace, local panoramas, back pool table; piped music, TV; big garden with tables on decking, open all day *(Darren Croucher, Robin Pescott)*

DUNKS GREEN [TQ6152]

☆ **Kentish Rifleman** TN11 9RU [Dunks Green Rd]: Tudor pub restored in modern rustic style, friendly helpful staff, well kept ales such as Greene King and Westerham, reasonably priced wholesome food (not Sun evening), cosy log fire, rifles on low beams, enlarged dining room, small public bar; service charge levied; children and dogs welcome, tables in pretty garden with well, good walks, open all day wknds *(BB, N R White, Simon and Sally Small, Mark Sowery, Nigel and Jean Eames, Bob and Margaret Holder, Conor McGaughey, Robert Gomme, Tina and David Woods-Taylor, B and M Kendall)*

DUNTON GREEN [TQ5156]

Bullfinch TN13 2DR [London Rd, Riverhead]: Smart open-plan modern décor with mix of sofas, armchairs and banquettes, snacks and slightly upmarket traditional food, pleasant efficient staff, well kept McMullens ales, good wine choice, daily papers; large garden with heated terrace, open all day wknds *(Revd R P Tickle, Derek Thomas)*

EAST FARLEIGH [TQ7452]

Horseshoes ME15 0PR [Dean St]: Popular 15th-c pub next to riding stables, log fires and low beams, several cosy areas, Harveys Best, Timothy Taylors Landlord, good choice of enjoyable fresh food inc Sun roasts, pleasant efficient staff; children welcome, disabled facilities, terrace and large lawn *(Michael Tack)*

EDENBRIDGE [TQ4445]

Old Eden TN8 5AX [High St]: Dim-lit 15th-c pub, old bricks and beams, low doors, open fires, blackboard food from sandwiches to fresh fish, home-baked bread and pies, three Westerham ales and Stowford Press cider; large games room with pool, machines and TV; back garden, open all day *(John Robertson)*

EYNSFORD [TQ5365]

Malt Shovel DA4 0ER [Station Rd]: Traditional dark-panelled pub with black beams and copper kettles, well kept interesting changing ales, good choice of wine by the glass, friendly attentive staff, wide range of pub food inc plenty of daily specials, popular Sun lunch, restaurant; car park across busy road; children welcome, handy for castles and Roman villa *(N R White)*

FAVERSHAM [TR0161]

Anchor ME13 7BP [Abbey St]: Friendly two-bar pub with good food from baguettes up, well kept Shepherd Neame ales, simple bare-boards bar with log fire, ancient beams, dark panelling, low lighting, frosted windows, boat pictures and models, restaurant; piped radio; dogs welcome, tables in pretty enclosed garden with bat and trap, attractive 17th-c street nr historic quay, open all day *(Quentin and Carol Williamson, the Didler)*

Bear ME13 7AG [Market Pl]: Late Victorian (back part from 16th c), locals' front bar, snug hung with chamber pots and back dining lounge all off side corridor, friendly service, relaxed atmosphere, four well kept Shepherd Neame ales, basic good value lunchtime home cooking; couple of pavement tables, lively musical following, open all day Fri-Sun *(the Didler, John Wooll, Gwyn and Anne Wake)*

Elephant ME13 8JN [The Mall]: Well run dim-lit traditional town pub, friendly and chatty, with five well kept changing local ales, belgian beers, Weston's cider, no food (you can bring your own), central log fire; live music, juke box, games machine; children and dogs welcome, suntrap back garden with pets corner, boat and fishpond, open from 3pm wkdys, all day wknds *(N R White, the Didler, Conor McGaughey, James Pearson, Kevin Flack, BB)*

FINGLESHAM [TR3353]

☆ **Crown** CT14 0NA [just off A258 Sandwich—Deal; The Street]: Popular neatly kept low-beamed country local dating from 16th c, good value generous home-made food from usual pub dishes to interesting specials, warmly friendly helpful service, well kept ales inc Ramsgate, Biddenden cider, daily papers, softly lit carpeted split-level bar with stripped stone and inglenook log fire, two other attractive dining rooms; lovely big garden with play area, bat and trap, field for caravans, open all day Fri-Sun *(N R White)*

FOLKESTONE [TR2235]

Chambers CT20 2BE [Sandgate Rd]: Spacious well converted cellar bar, relaxed and friendly, with well kept Hopdaemon, Ramsgate and changing guests, bottled imports, enjoyable tex-mex influenced food, frequent live music, adjoining coffee bar; tables outside *(Andrew York, Bruce Bird)*

FORDWICH [TR1859]

Fordwich Arms CT2 0DB [off A28 in Sturry]: Handsome 1930s pub with smart green settees and attractive log fire, good food (not Sun evening) inc two-course lunches offers, real ales such as Flowers Original, Shepherd Neame and two from Wadworths; piped music may obtrude; spacious terrace and garden by River Stour, ancient town hall opp worth visiting, open all day *(Tony and Wendy Hobden, LYM, Tony Hobden)*

GOODNESTONE [TR2554]

Fitzwalter Arms CT3 1PJ [The Street; NB this is in East Kent NOT the other

Goodnestone]: Old beamed dimly lit village local with two small rustic bars, Shepherd Neame ales, enjoyable food, friendly chatty service, dining area, log fires *(N R White)*

GOUDHURST [TQ7037]

☆ *Green Cross* TN17 1HA [Station Rd (A262 W)]: Good interesting restaurantry food, especially fish and seafood, well kept Harveys Best, good wines and own sloe gin, smart and roomy back restaurant, contrasting simple two-room bar with good fire and TV, friendly efficient service; no dogs; terrace tables, light and airy good value bedrooms *(BB, David S Allen)*

☆ *Star & Eagle* TN17 1AL [High St]: Striking medieval building, now small hotel, with settles and Jacobean-style seats in heavily beamed open-plan areas, intriguing smuggling-days history, log fires, good choice of food but prices high, well kept Adnams, Harveys and Westerham from fairly modern bar with lovely views, friendly helpful staff, restaurant; children welcome, tables outside with same views, attractive village, ten up-to-date character bedrooms, good breakfast, open all day *(LYM, Robert Kibble, N R White)*

GRAVESEND [TQ6473]

Crown & Thistle DA12 2BJ [The Terrace]: Chatty old-fashioned little local with interesting changing beers, brewery pictures, bar nibbles, may be filled rolls (you can bring in food), occasional live music; no children; handy for historic riverside, open all day *(the Didler)*

HARBLEDOWN [TR1358]

Old Coach & Horses CT2 9AB [Church Hill]: Airy yet cosy modern two-room split-level bistro/bar with interesting enjoyable food, helpful friendly service, real ales, good wines by the glass; great views from garden, peaceful setting, cl Sun evening *(Andy Towse, Tudor Rowe, Charlotte Whigham)*

HERNE [TR1865]

☆ *Butchers Arms* CT6 7HL [Herne St (A291)]: Tiny pub with half a dozen well kept changing ales tapped from the cask inc Dark Star and Harveys, interesting bottled beers, chatty former motorcycle-racing landlord, just a couple of benches and butcher's-block tables (seat about ten), growing bric-a-brac collection, some wines but no food (you can bring your own) beyond fierce pickles and other nibbles, chess, no music or TV; dogs welcome, disabled access, tables out under awning, cl Sun and Mon, short lunchtime opening and closes 9.30pm *(Paul Narramore, Kevin Thorpe)*

HOLLINGBOURNE [TQ8455]

Dirty Habit ME17 1UW [B2163, off A20]: Dim-lit ancient beamed pub under same management as the Great House in Hawkhurst (see Main Entries), good sensibly priced upscale food using local ingredients, efficient staff, well kept Fullers London Pride, Harveys Best and Shepherd Neame Master Brew, nooks, crannies and uneven floors, big fireplace, back dining room;

peaceful spot on North Downs Way *(Brian and Anna Marsden, Mr and Mrs William Hargraves, LYM)*

Park Gate Inn ME17 1PG [Ashford Rd (A20, nr M20 junction 8 and Leeds Castle)]: Popular well run Vintage Inn divided into cosy areas with beams and flagstones, part just for drinkers, friendly efficient staff, wide range of food from sandwiches to specials, good choice of wines by the glass, well kept Harveys Best and Shepherd Neame Spitfire; children welcome, picnic-sets in neat garden, open all day *(Michael Tack)*

HORTON KIRBY [TQ5668]

Bull DA4 9DF [Lombard St]: Unpretentious one-pub village corner pub, great selection of real ales inc Dark Star, enthusiastic knowledgeable landlord doing a monthly Brewery Showcase, farm ciders, enjoyable food from landlady (not Mon or evenings Tues-Sat), friendly chatty atmosphere; big garden with country views, open all day (from 4pm Mon) *(N R White)*

HYTHE [TR1534]

Red Lion CT21 5AU: Welcoming 17th-c hotel, smartly renovated, with comfortable fireside chairs and spacious dining areas, well kept ales inc Ramsgate Gadds No.3 and Whitstable Native, enjoyable food; quiet piped music; lawned garden and gravel terrace, bedrooms *(Bruce Bird)*

IDE HILL [TQ4851]

Cock TN14 6JN [off B2042 SW of Sevenoaks]: Pretty village-green local dating from 15th c, chatty and friendly with long-serving landlord, two bars with steps between, Greene King ales, enjoyable traditional food inc game (not Sun or Mon evenings, snacks Sun lunchtime), good inglenook log fire; well behaved children and dogs welcome, picnic-sets out at front, handy for Chartwell and nearby walks *(LYM, N R White, Heather and Dick Martin)*

IDEN GREEN [TQ7437]

Peacock TN17 2PB [A262 E of Goudhurst]: Tudor, with blazing inglenook log fire in low-beamed main bar, quarry tiles and old sepia photographs, well priced enjoyable pubby food (all day Sat, not Sun evening) from sandwiches up, very helpful service, well kept Shepherd Neame ales, pastel dining room with cork-studded walls, public bar; TV; well behaved dogs welcome, no muddy boots, good-sized garden, cl Sun evening *(BB, Nigel and Jean Eames, Conrad Freezer)*

IGHTHAM [TQ5956]

☆ *George & Dragon* TN15 9HH [A227]: Picturesque and very popular timbered dining pub, early 16th-c but much modernised, good reasonably priced food from generous snacks (all day till 6.30, not Sun) up, plenty of friendly smartly dressed staff, well kept Shepherd Neame ales, decent wines, sofas among other furnishings in long sociable main bar, heavy-beamed end room, woodburner and open fires, restaurant; children and dogs welcome, back terrace, handy for Ightham Mote (NT), good walks, open all day *(Bob and Margaret Holder, LYM, Steve and Nina Bullen, Brian Goodson, Colin and Janet Roe, Gavin Markwick, Gordon and Margaret Ormondroyd, Derek Thomas)*

IGHTHAM COMMON [TQ5955]
Old House TN15 9EE [Redwell, S of village; OS Sheet 188 map ref 591559]: Basic two-room country local tucked down narrow lane, no inn sign, bare bricks and beams, huge inglenook, interesting changing ales, some tapped from the cask, retired cash register and small TV in side room, darts; no food, cl wkdy lunchtimes, opens 7pm (even later Tues) *(the Didler, BB)*

KILNDOWN [TQ7035]
☆ *Globe & Rainbow* TN17 2SG [signed off A21 S of Lamberhurst]: Welcoming well cared for pub with small cheerful bar, good Harveys and Fullers London Pride, decent wines, simple bare-boards dining room with good sensibly priced fresh local food; piped music; country views from decking out by cricket pitch *(Alec and Joan Laurence, John Baxter, BB)*

KINGSDOWN [TR3748]
Kings Head CT14 8BJ [Upper St]: Chatty tucked-away local with Fullers London Pride, Greene King IPA and a guest beer, wknd bar lunches, friendly staff, four small split-level rooms, black timbers, faded cream walls, pubby decorations and open fires, darts; piped music, games machine; children and dogs welcome, garden with skittle alley, open all day Sun, cl wkdy lunchtimes *(N R White)*

LAMBERHURST [TQ6735]
Brown Trout TN3 8HA [B2169, off A21 nr entrance to Scotney Castle]: Extended old pub reopened after major refurbishment by new owners, well prepared and nicely presented food with option for smaller helpings, good service, beams and log fire; garden *(Kevin Horner, BB)*
☆ *Elephants Head* TN3 8LJ [Furnace Lane, Hook Green; B2169 towards T Wells]: 15th-c timber-framed pub, mullioned windows, heavy beams, brick or oak flooring, big inglenook, plush-cushioned pews, friendly staff, well priced popular food inc good Sun carvery, Harveys ale; darts and games machine in small side area; children welcome, picnic-sets by front green and in big back garden with peaceful view, terrace and good play area, nr Bayham Abbey and Owl House *(Peter Meister, Nigel and Jean Eames, B J Harding, Klaus and Elizabeth Leist, Don Mitchell, LYM)*
Swan TN3 8EU [Lamberhurst Down]: Pretty dining pub by green (and vineyards), comfortable contemporary wine bar feel, some sofas, flagstones or bare boards, modern art on mushroom walls, log fires, good wines by the glass inc local ones, well kept Harveys and Westerham ales, decent food inc local trout, good service; children

welcome, back terrace *(Hugh Bower, BB)*

LOOSE [TQ7552]
Chequers ME15 0BL [Old Loose Hill]: Rambling 17th-c riverside dining pub, beamed, partly panelled and neatly kept, good fresh lunches inc enjoyable Sun roasts, four well kept ales inc Harveys Best and Timothy Taylors Landlord, nice atmosphere, friendly attentive service, flame-effect fire; small walled garden, good walks *(Pam and John Smith)*

LUDDESDOWN [TQ6667]
☆ *Cock* DA13 0XB [Henley St, N of village – OS Sheet 177 map reference 664672; off A227 in Meopham, or A228 in Cuxton]: Early 18th-c country pub, friendly long-serving no-nonsense landlord, at least six ales inc Adnams, Goachers, Harveys and Shepherd Neame, sensibly priced all-day pubby food (not Sun evening) from wide choice of sandwiches up, rugs on polished boards in pleasant bay-windowed lounge bar, quarry-tiled locals' bar, woodburners, pews and other miscellaneous furnishings, aircraft pictures, masses of beer mats and bric-a-brac inc stuffed animals, model cars and beer can collections, bar billiards and darts, back dining conservatory; no children in bar or part-covered heated back terrace; dogs welcome, big secure garden, good walks, open all day *(LYM, N R White, A N Bance, Kevin Thorpe)*

MAIDSTONE [TQ7655]
Rifle Volunteers ME14 1EU [Wyatt St/Church St]: Relaxed unspoilt backstreet pub tied to local Goachers, three of their ales inc Mild, good value simple home-made food, friendly long-serving landlord, two gas fires, darts; tables outside *(the Didler)*

MARSH GREEN [TQ4344]
Wheatsheaf TN8 5QL [Marsh Green Rd (B2028 SW of Edenbridge)]: Harveys and several other well kept changing ales, Biddenden cider, good value fresh food from lunchtime sandwiches up, friendly helpful staff, simple linked bare-boards areas with old photographs and wooden partitions, roomy conservatory; TV; garden and small terrace, good walks nearby, open all day *(Gavin Robinson, R and S Bentley, N R White, B and M Kendall, Mrs Sheena Killick)*

MINSTER [TR9474]
Playa ME12 2NL [The Leas]: Wide Thames Estuary views, welcoming landlord, Shepherd Neame ales, enjoyable good value home-made food in bar and restaurant, live music most wknds; tables outside *(Colin Moore, Steve Coates)*

NEW ROMNEY [TR0624]
Ship TN28 8BN [High St (A259)]: Tudor smugglers' pub with three airy up-to-date areas around L-shaped bar, Shepherd Neame ales, friendly staff, enjoyable reasonably priced food, attractive restaurant, darts, bar billiards; disabled facilities, covered terrace and lawn, seven bedrooms *(Peter and Jean Hoare)*

NEWENDEN [TQ8327]
White Hart TN18 5PN [Rye Rd (A268)]:
Friendly 16th-c local, long low-beamed bar
with big stone fireplace, well kept Harveys
and guests, dining area with decent good
value food; back games area, sports TV,
piped music; children welcome, large garden,
boules, nr river (boat trips to Bodiam Castle)
(V Brogden, BB)

NORTHBOURNE [TR3352]
Hare & Hounds CT14 0LG [off A256 or
A258 nr Dover; The Street]: Chatty village
pub with good choice of ales inc well kept
Harveys, generous popular food (lamb from
nearby farm), friendly efficient service,
spacious modernised brick and wood interior,
log fires; dogs welcome, terrace tables
(N R White)

OARE [TR0063]
Three Mariners ME13 0QA [Church Rd]:
Comfortable simply restored old pub with log
fire and well spaced tables, good quality
food inc wkdy lunch deals, freshly prepared
and worth the wait, well kept Shepherd
Neame ales, good choice of wines by the
glass; attractive garden overlooking
Faversham Creek, open all day wknds,
cl Mon (operates then as mid-morning
post office) *(Warren Marsh, Alistair Jones,
Hilary Jones)*

OLD ROMNEY [TR0325]
Rose & Crown TN29 9SQ [A259 opp church]:
Simple friendly village pub with good value
standard food, Courage, Greene King, Rother
Valley and guest ales, Biddenden cider, old
local photographs, dining conservatory;
children welcome, pretty garden with boules,
chalet bedrooms, open all day *(Julia and
Richard Tredgett)*

OTFORD [TQ5259]
Bull TN14 5PG [High St]: Attractively laid
out 15th-c Chef & Brewer, wide food choice
from sandwiches up all day, good Sun lunch,
friendly attentive staff, four well kept ales,
decent wines, several quietly spacious rooms,
two huge log fires, panelling, soft lighting
and candles; nice garden, good walks nearby
(B J Harding, Conor McGaughey)
Crown TN14 5PQ [High St, pond end]: 16th-c
two-bar local opp village pond, pleasantly
chatty lounge with sofas, well kept Harveys
Best, Westerham and guest ales, cheerful
staff, locally sourced food inc good Sun
roasts, darts, frequent interesting events;
sports TV; back garden, walkers and dogs
welcome *(N R White, Brian and
Anna Marsden)*

PENSHURST [TQ5243]
Leicester Arms TN11 8BT [High St]: Country
hotel feel with comfortable old bars and
meadowland-view dining room up steps, well
kept Fullers London Pride and Greene King
Old Speckled Hen, decent reasonably priced
food, friendly polite service; lavatories down
steps (disabled one in car park opposite);
children and dogs welcome, pretty back
garden, seven bedrooms, open all day
(Peter Meister, Ann and Colin Hunt)

☆ *Rock* TN8 7BS [Hoath Corner, Chiddingstone
Hoath, on back road Chiddingstone—
Cowden; OS Sheet 188 map reference
497431]: Tiny cottage under new young
couple so far keeping rural local atmosphere;
beams, undulating brick floor, simple
furnishings, woodburner in fine brick
inglenook, large stuffed bull's head for ring
the bull, up a step to smaller room with long
wooden settle by nice table, Larkins ales,
simple food; dogs welcome, picnic-sets in
front and on back lawn *(Tina and
David Woods-Taylor, LYM)*
Spotted Dog TN11 8EP [Smarts Hill, off
B2188 S]: Quaint old weatherboarded pub
spruced up under new family, heavy low
beams and timbers, attractive moulded
panelling, rugs and tiles, antique settles,
inglenook log fire, Harveys, Larkins and two
guests, local cider, mostly traditional food
(all day wknds) inc wkdy lunch deals, smart
staff; children and dogs welcome, tiered
back terrace (they may ask to keep your
credit card while you eat here), open all day
(LYM)

PLAXTOL [TQ6054]
☆ *Golding Hop* TN15 0PT [Sheet Hill (0.5 miles
S of Ightham, between A25 and A227)]:
Secluded traditional country local, simple
dim-lit two-level bar with hands-on landlord
who can be very welcoming, cask-tapped
Adnams, and guests kept well, local farm
ciders (sometimes their own), short choice
of basic good value bar food (not Mon or
Tues evenings), old photographs of the pub,
woodburners, bar billiards; portable TV for
big sports events; no children inside; suntrap
streamside lawn and well fenced play area
over lane, good walks, open all day Sat
*(the Didler, B and M Kendall, N R White,
Bob and Margaret Holder, Conor McGaughey,
LYM)*

PLUCKLEY [TQ9144]
☆ *Mundy Bois* TN27 0ST [Mundy Bois – spelled
Monday Boys on some maps – off Smarden
Road SW of village centre]: Creeper-clad and
tile-hung local, informal main bar, massive
inglenook, Shepherd Neame and a beer from
Hopdaemon, pubby food plus restaurant
choices inc good Romney Marsh lamb,
sensible prices, small snug bar with sofas by
log fire, board games, darts, pool; piped
music, juke box, TV, games machine; children
and dogs welcome, pretty garden and terrace
with views, play area, cl Sun evening, Mon,
Tues *(LYM, Philip and Cheryl Hill)*

RAMSGATE [TR3764]
Artillery Arms CT11 9JS [West Cliff Rd]:
Chatty open-plan corner local, five well kept
changing ales inc interesting microbrews and
usually Ramsgate Gadds, farm cider, cheap
rolls all day, daily papers, fire at top end,
old aircraft seats, artillery prints and
interesting listed windows depicting
Napoleonic scenes; juke box (free Sun) can
be loud, TV; good wheelchair access,
children and dogs welcome, open all day
(Kevin Thorpe)

RINGLESTONE [TQ8755]
Ringlestone Inn ME17 1NX [Ringlestone Rd, signed Doddington off B2163 NE of Hollingbourne]: Former monks' hospice, an inn by 1615, furnished to match the antiquity of its worn brick floor, stripped masonry, sturdy beams and inglenook log fire, Shepherd Neame ales, farm cider, country wines and liqueurs, enjoyable if pricey food; can get very busy in summer; children and well behaved dogs welcome, big attractive garden with play area, open all day wknds, cl Tues evening *(LYM, Patrick Noble)*

ROCHESTER [TQ7468]
Coopers Arms ME1 1TL [St Margarets St]: Jettied Tudor building behind cathedral, cosily unpretentious and quaint inside, bustling local atmosphere, friendly staff, two comfortable bars, generous cheap wkdy bar lunches, well kept Courage Best and Directors; tables in attractive courtyard *(B J Harding)*
Man of Kent ME1 1YN [John St]: Small basic backstreet corner pub with impressive range of local ales inc Goachers, Hopdaemon and Ramsgate, also local farm ciders, draught and bottled continental beers, friendly knowledgeable staff, no-frills interior with log fire and resident dog called Dude, live music; decked back garden, open all day *(Patrick Noble)*

ROLVENDEN [TQ8431]
Bull TN17 4PB [Regent St]: Good home-made food inc game (they shoot their own) and popular Sun lunch, Harveys Best, friendly landlord, refurbished split-level bar with dark leather chairs on wood floor, pale walls and grey panelling, restaurant on right, labrador called Milo; sports TV; children welcome, big garden behind *(BB)*

SANDWICH [TR3358]
Bell CT13 9EF [Upper Strand St]: Comfortable nicely refurbished Edwardian hotel opp river, enjoyable bar food, well kept Greene King IPA, restaurant; children welcome, 34 bedrooms *(MDN)*
Fleur de Lis CT13 9BZ [Delf St]: Popular 18th-c former coaching inn with comfortable split-level lounge end, open fire, food (all day wknds) from sandwiches up, real ales, friendly staff, TV and games end, panelled back restaurant; piped music; 12 bedrooms, open all day *(N R White)*
George & Dragon CT13 9EJ [Fisher St]: Civilised open-plan 15th-c beamed pub keeping feel of small original rooms, enjoyable good value food from open-view kitchen inc popular Sun lunch, friendly obliging staff, well kept ales such as Adnams, Harveys and Shepherd Neame, good choice of wines by the glass; children and dogs welcome, pretty back terrace *(Barry and Sue Pladdys, MDN, Denise Small)*

SARRE [TR2564]
Crown CT7 0LF [Ramsgate Rd (A253) off A28]: Carefully restored historic 15th-c pub (Grade I listed), welcoming staff, locally sourced food in two beamed and carpeted bars or restaurant, well kept Shepherd Neame, decent house wines, own cherry brandy, log fires; pleasant side garden, 12 bedrooms, open all day *(N R White)*

SEASALTER [TR0864]
☆ *Sportsman* CT5 4BP [Faversham Rd, off B2040]: Restauranty dining pub just inside sea wall and rather unprepossessing from outside; good imaginative contemporary cooking with plenty of seafood (not Sun evening or Mon, best to book and not cheap), home-baked breads, good wine choice inc english, well kept Shepherd Neame ales, friendly staff; two plain linked rooms and long conservatory, wooden floor, pine tables, wheelback and basket-weave dining chairs, big film star photographs; children welcome, open all day Sun *(Prof and Mrs J Fletcher, LYM, Colin and Stephanie McFie, Colin McKerrow, V Brogden)*

SELLING [TR0455]
☆ *Rose & Crown* ME13 9RY [Signposted from exit roundabout of M2 junction 7; follow Perry Wood signs]: Tucked-away 16th-c country pub, hops strung from beams, two inglenook log fires, friendly service, well kept Adnams and Harveys, several ciders, food from sandwiches up; piped music; children welcome, dogs on leads in bar, cottagey back garden with play area, closed Sun evening *(Colin and Louise English, the Didler, Andrew Clarke, LYM, N R White, Stephen Corfield)*
☆ *White Lion* ME13 9RQ [off A251 S of Faversham (or exit roundabout, M2 junction 7); The Street]: Comfortable 17th-c pub with well kept Shepherd Neame ales from unusual semicircular bar counter, decent wines, friendly helpful staff, wide blackboard choice of good home-made food, hop-hung main bar with paintings for sale, log fire with working spit, another fire in small lower lounge with comfortable settees, back restaurant; quiz nights; children welcome, picnic-sets in attractive garden, colourful hanging baskets *(LYM, Mike Trainer, John Roots, C and R Bromage)*

SEVENOAKS [TQ5555]
☆ *Bucks Head* TN15 0JJ [Godden Green, just E]: Relaxed flower-decked pub with welcoming thoughtful service, some good value blackboard food from sandwiches up, roast on Sun, well kept Shepherd Neame and a guest, log fires in splendid inglenooks, neatly kept bar and restaurant area; children and dogs welcome, front terrace overlooking informal green and duck pond, back lawn with mature trees, bird fountain, pergola and views over quiet country behind Knole *(Simon and Sally Small, Gwyn Jones)*
Kings Head TN13 2QA [Bessels Green; A25 W, just off A21]: Popular village-green local, friendly polite young staff, fires, generous reasonably priced food, nice cider, restaurant; dogs welcome, spacious garden (traffic noise) *(John Branston)*

White Hart TN13 1SG [Tonbridge Rd (A225 S, past Knole)]: Attractively revamped 17th-c coaching inn recently taken over by Brunning & Price, good choice of popular food all day, changing ales, extensive wine list, good friendly service; children and dogs welcome, disabled facilities, pleasant garden with well established shrubs *(Derek Thomas)*

SOUTHFLEET [TQ5970]

Wheatsheaf DA13 9PH [High Cross Rd, Westwood; from A2, keep straight on through Southfleet itself, past the Ship]: Thatched Tudor country pub, unpretentious and welcoming, with heavy-beams, high-backed settles, soft lighting and inglenook log fire, well kept ales, popular food; can get very busy wknds; children welcome, tables in good-sized garden with pond, handy for Bluewater *(BB, N R White)*

STALISFIELD GREEN [TQ9552]

Plough ME13 0HY [off A252 in Charing]: 15th-c hall house on village green high on N Downs, good local ales such as Hopdaemon, bottled belgian beers, enjoyable country cooking using local produce, friendly licensees (and cats), beams and log fires, large old-fashioned tables and chairs in dining areas each side of bar; unobtrusive piped music, some live; big pleasant garden, good view and walks *(Joan and Alec Lawrence, Annette Tress, Gary Smith)*

STAPLEHURST [TQ7846]

☆ *Lord Raglan* TN12 0DE [About 1.5 miles from town centre towards Maidstone, turn right off A229 into Chart Hill Road opposite Chart Cars; OS Sheet 188 map reference 785472]: Well run country pub, cosy chatty area around narrow bar counter, hop-covered low beams, big winter log fire, mixed comfortably worn dark wood furniture, usually good food from sandwiches up, Goachers, Harveys and a guest, farm cider and perry, good wine list; children and dogs welcome, reasonable wheelchair access, high-hedged terrace, picnic-sets in side orchard, closed Sun *(Alec and Joan Laurence, Joan and Alec Lawrence, LYM)*

STONE IN OXNEY [TQ9327]

Crown TN30 7JN [off B2082 Iden—Tenterden]: Smart country pub with friendly newish landlord, well kept Shepherd Neame and a guest like Larkins tapped from the cask, enjoyable well priced food inc nice herby burgers, light airy open feel with lots of wood and big inglenook *(Peter Meister, LYM)*

☆ *Ferry* TN30 7JY: Attractive 17th-c smugglers' haunt, good popular local food inc fish (scallops from Rye the hot tip), friendly landlord and efficient staff, changing guest ales and a beer brewed for them by Westerham, small place bar with woodburner and inglenook, bare boards, steps up to pleasant dining area, games room; suntrap front courtyard, big back garden, lovely setting by marshes *(Colin and Louise English,*

Alec and Joan Laurence, Peter Meister, Julia and Richard Tredgett)

TENTERDEN [TQ8833]

☆ *White Lion* TN30 6BD [High St]: 16th-c behind Georgian façade, beams and timbers, masses of pictures, china and books, cheerful helpful young staff, wide choice of popular good value food, Marstons and related beers, sensibly priced wines, big log fire, relaxed and friendly even when crowded with young people at night, cosy area off bar, softly lit back panelled restaurant; piped music, games machines; dogs welcome, heated terrace overlooking street, 15 charming beamed bedrooms, good breakfast, open all day *(Donna and Roger, J A Snell)*

THURNHAM [TQ8057]

☆ *Black Horse* ME14 3LD [not far from M20 junction 7; off A249 at Detling]: Large olde-worlde dining pub with enjoyable food all day, children's menu, well kept changing ales such as Sharps Doom Bar and Westerham Grasshopper, farm ciders and country wines, friendly efficient uniformed service, bare boards and log fires; dogs and walkers welcome, pleasant garden with partly covered back terrace, nice views, by Pilgrims Way, comfortable modern bedroom block, good breakfast *(Tom and Jill Jones, Brian and Anna Marsden, Peter Meister)*

TONBRIDGE [TQ5946]

Ivy House TN9 1BW [High St]: Smallish place nr Tonbridge School recently refurbished as bar/restaurant, some interesting food (all day wknds) from open kitchen inc good value set lunch, beams and panelled walls, modern light wood tables and leather chairs on bare boards, compact bar area with open fire, well kept Harveys; outside tables *(Gavin Markwick)*

Vauxhall Inn TN11 0NA [Vauxhall Lane/Pembury Rd]: Spacious old Chef & Brewer with wide choice of food inc fish and game, good value fixed-price menu (Mon-Thurs), Fullers London Pride and two changing guests, good wine range, tea and coffee; disabled parking and facilities, bedrooms in adjacent Premier Inn, open all day *(Martin and Alison Stainsby)*

TOYS HILL [TQ4752]

☆ *Fox & Hounds* TN16 1QG [Off A25 in Brasted, via Brasted Chart and The Chart]: Traditional country pub with plain tables and chairs on dark boards, leather sofa and easy chair by log fire, hunting prints, plates, old photographs, pewter mugs and copper jugs, modern carpeted dining extension with big windows overlooking tree-sheltered garden, enjoyable home-made food (not Sun evening) inc some interesting choices, well kept Greene King ales, several wines by the glass, traditional games, no mobile phones; piped music; children and dogs welcome, roadside verandah used by smokers, good local walks and views, handy for Chartwell and Emmetts Garden, open all day summer, cl Mon evening (and from 8pm Sun in winter) *(LYM, Tina and David Woods-Taylor, N R White, Cathryn and Richard Hicks, LM)*

TROTTISCLIFFE [TQ6460]

George ME19 5DR [Taylors Lane]: Well preserved old pub, popular enjoyable food, friendly service, well kept Greene King and Shepherd Neame ales; garden, open all day Fri-Sun *(Patrick Noble)*

TUDELEY [TQ6145]

Poacher TN11 0PH [Hartlake Rd]: Smart modern bar and restaurant, light and airy, with wide range of enjoyable food inc daily specials, ales such as Sharps Doom Bar, friendly staff; terrace tables *(Nigel and Jean Eames)*

TUNBRIDGE WELLS [TQ5837]

Bull TN2 5LH [Frant Rd]: Friendly refurbished pub with two linked areas, neatly set dining part with well spaced pine tables and chunky chairs on stripped wood, similar bar area, corner black sofa, well kept Shepherd Neame ales, decent wine and food, daily papers; TV, piped pop, pool; dogs allowed *(Tony and Wendy Hobden, Steve Halsall, BB)*

Opera House TN1 1RT [Mount Pleasant Rd]: Large Wetherspoons restoration of 1900s opera house (still do one or two operas a year), original circle, boxes, stage lighting and ornate ceiling; real ales inc more or less local guests, usual cheap Wetherspoons food; can get crowded wknd evenings, no dogs; children welcome, open all day *(E Clark, Ann and Colin Hunt, Ben Williams)*

UNDER RIVER [TQ5552]

✗ *White Rock* TN15 0SB [SE of Sevenoaks, off B245]: Welcoming village pub, attractive and relaxed, with good food (all day Sun, best to book) from pubby things up, coffee and cakes between times, well kept Westerham Grasshopper, beams, bare boards and stripped brickwork in cosy original part with adjacent dining area, public bar in modern extension; quiet piped music; children welcome, nice front garden, back terrace and large lawn, pretty churchyard and walks nearby, open all day *(Tina and David Woods-Taylor, B J Harding, DFL, Katharine Cowherd, Mrs P Sumner, E D Bailey)*

WEALD [TQ5250]

Windmill TN14 6PN [Windmill Rd]: Village pub revamped by irish landlady, well kept Greene King ales, food inc Sun roasts and themed nights, two open fires, monthly live bands; children welcome, garden *(Wayne Saich, Christopher Jones, Chris Nash)*

WEST MALLING [TQ6857]

Lobster Pot ME19 6JU [Swan St]: Popular traditional corner pub with six well kept changing ales, farm cider, chatty local atmosphere, friendly service, open fire; open all day wknds *(Ben Lord, N R White)*

WEST PECKHAM [TQ6452]

Swan on the Green ME18 5JW [Off A26/B2016 W of Maidstone]: Own-brewed Swan ales and Biddenden cider in relaxed open-plan beamed bar, modern artwork and stripped brickwork, mixed furnishings, generally popular if not cheap food (not Sun

and Mon evenings, may close other times out of season); piped classical music; children and dogs welcome, charming village green (great for a summer drink), interesting part-Saxon church, open all day summer wknds *(Tina and David Woods-Taylor, Bob and Margaret Holder, Derek Thomas, N R White, LYM, Mrs J Ekins-Daukes)*

WESTBERE [TR1862]

Old Yew Tree CT2 0HH [just off A18 Canterbury—Margate]: Heavily beamed early 14th-c pub in pretty village, simply furnished, good quality interesting food, Shepherd Neame Bitter and guests, friendly helpful staff; picnic-sets in garden behind *(Pat and Alan Hardwick)*

WHITSTABLE [TR1066]

Old Neptune CT5 1EJ [Marine Terr]: Great view over Swale Estuary from picturesque seafront pub, unpretentious olde-worlde feel inside, enjoyable lunchtime food, real ales, wknd live music; dogs and children welcome, picnic-sets on beach (plastic glasses out here) *(Keith and Chris O'Neill, N R White, Gwyn and Anne Wake, Andrea Rampley)*

Pearsons CT5 1BT [Sea Wall]: Smartly refurbished 18th-c food pub, bright and airy with lots of stripped pine, popular well presented fresh fish and seafood, Ramsgate Gadds ales, upstairs restaurant with sea view, downstairs bar with limited seating; children welcome in eating areas, open all day wknds, just above shingle beach *(LYM, Mary McSweeney, N R White)*

WINGHAM [TR2457]

☆ *Dog* CT3 1BB [Canterbury Rd]: Pub/restaurant in Grade II* listed medieval building, log fires, uneven walls, heavy beams, old brickwork and panelling, leather sofas and armchairs on wood floors, conservatory restaurant, enjoyable food inc good value set lunch, well kept Courage, Ramsgate and Shepherd Neame, good wines by the glass *(Gavin Markwick)*

WITTERSHAM [TQ8927]

Swan TN30 7PH [Swan St]: Friendly village local dating from 17th c, well kept Harveys, Goachers and changing guests tapped from the cask (beer festivals), bargain food from nice sandwiches up, good service, back lounge with open fire, china and pictures, public bar with darts and pool; TV; garden picnic-sets, open all day *(Peter Meister, Dick and Heather Martin)*

WROTHAM [TQ6159]

Bull TN15 7RF [1.7 miles from M20 junction 2 – Wrotham signed]: Welcoming carefully restored 14th-c inn with emphasis on popular locally sourced food, extensive eating areas around beamed bar, well kept Dark Star ales, good wine list, efficient service, separate restaurant, log fires; children allowed, 11 comfortable bedrooms, pretty village, open all day Sun *(LYM, Brian and Anna Marsden, N R White)*

Moat TN15 7RR [London Rd]: Well refurbished Badger family dining pub in Tudor-style building with flagstones and

stripped beams and masonry, good value
food, their usual ales kept well, friendly
staff; children welcome, garden tables, great
playground, open all day (Gordon and
Margaret Ormondroyd)
WYE [TR0446]
Tickled Trout TN25 5EB [signed off A28 NE
of Ashford]: Popular summer family pub with
lots of picnic-sets on lawn by River Stour,
friendly staff, spacious modern
conservatory/restaurant, rustic-style bar with
beams and stripped brickwork, stained glass
and partitions, enjoyable if pricey food
promptly served from baguettes up,
interesting changing real ales, good log fire;

children welcome (LYM, Brian and
Anna Marsden)
YALDING [TQ6950]
☆ *Walnut Tree* ME18 6JB [B2010 SW of
Maidstone]: Nice country pub, warm and
friendly, with pleasant two-level brick-floor
bar, lots of old beams, inglenook and
another fire, country furniture, interesting
pictures, friendly efficient staff, good well
priced food all day from sandwiches and
tapas up, good-sized restaurant, well kept
Harveys Best, Timothy Taylors Landlord and
guests; piped music – occasional live; some
tables on front terrace, bedrooms, attractive
village (Steve and Claire Harvey)

Lancashire
(with Greater Manchester and Merseyside)

New this year is the Red Pump at Bashall Eaves, a friendly country inn with local meats on offer and pleasant rural views, and the attractively refurbished, gently upmarket Cartford at Little Eccleston returns to the Main Entries. Among the more beer-oriented pubs, three outstanding ones are in character-laden Victorian buildings – the Philharmonic Dining Rooms in Liverpool, the Marble Arch in Manchester and the far less grand but delightfully individual Station Buffet on the platform at Stalybridge Station. At the bustling Taps in Lytham the cheapest real ale bitter goes for just £1.80 a pint, while the cheerful community pub the Church Inn at Uppermill has a fine range of own brews, in addition to very good value food and the pub's remarkable array of animals outside; the thatched Wheatsheaf at Raby gains a Beer Award for its fine choice of nine changing ales. For malt whiskies, the most impressive choice is at the Fishermans Retreat, Ramsbottom, where they stock in excess of 500 types. We have had strong reports for some of our more food-oriented Main Entries. The trio of pubs run by the same owners – the Three Fishes at Great Mitton, the Highwayman at Nether Burrow and the Clog & Billycock at Pleasington – all succeed admirably in providing locally sourced food, while the Eagle & Child at Bispham Green also has enjoyable food and a good range of ales, and the Inn at Wray (in Wray) has some particularly good value meal deals. The Bay Horse (in Bay Horse) is another fine restaurant tavern, not cheap but with good food. The Highwayman at Nether Burrow is our Lancashire Dining Pub of the Year 2011. The Lower Buck at Waddington is a pleasant all-rounder and readers enjoy staying and dining at the Inn at Whitewell (in Whitewell), wonderfully placed in the Forest of Bowland.

BARNSTON

SJ2783   MAP 7

Fox & Hounds 🍺 £

3 miles from M53 junction 3: A552 towards Woodchurch, then left on A551; CH61 1BW

Tidy pub with unusual collections, reasonably priced lunchtime food and good range of drinks including interesting guest beers

Open all day, this spotless and efficiently run little pub offers a cheerful welcome. The drinks' selection features six real ales, with Theakstons Best and Old Peculier alongside interesting guests from brewers such as Brimstage, Coach House, Cottage and Wem on handpump; in addition there are more than 60 whiskies and several wines by the glass. The main part of the roomy carpeted bay-windowed lounge bar has blue plush pleated built-in banquettes and plush-cushioned captain's chairs around solid tables, and plenty of old local prints below a delft shelf of china, with a collection of police and other headgear. Tucked away opposite the serving counter is a charming old quarry-tiled corner with an antique kitchen range, copper kettles, built-in pine kitchen cupboards and lots of earthenware or enamelled food bins. With its own entrance at the other end of the pub, a small locals' bar is worth a peek for its highly traditional layout and collection of hundreds of horsebrasses and metal ashtrays up on its delft shelf; darts and TV. Next to it is a snug where children are allowed. There are some picnic-sets under cocktail parasols out in the yard behind, with a profusion of colourful baskets and tubs.

🍴 **Good value traditional food includes toasted ciabattas, open sandwiches, soup, filled baked potatoes, quiche and various platters. Main courses include lamb shank, steak pie, fish of the day, sausage and mash and Sunday roasts.** *Starters/Snacks: £2.00 to £4.95. Main Courses: £5.50 to £13.95. Puddings: £2.95 to £4.95*

Free house ~ Licensee Ralph Leech ~ Real ale ~ Bar food (12-2(2.30 Sun); not evenings) ~ (0151) 648 1323 ~ Children in snug ~ Dogs allowed in bar ~ Open 11-11(10.30 Sun)
Recommended by Alan and Eve Harding, Paul Boot, Tony Nolan, John and Helen Rushton, Maurice and Gill McMahon

BARROW   SD7337   MAP 7

Eagle ⊕ 🍷 ◁

Village signposted off A59; Clitheroe Road (A671 N of Whalley); BB7 9AQ

Stylishly redesigned pub with splendid food, relying on fresh local ingredients; appealing modern furnishings and a good buzzy atmosphere

With a good mix of customers, this stylishly transformed dining venue has won a national award for its justly celebrated sausages. You'd be forgiven for thinking the building is new: there's a carved wooden eagle as you walk in, past glass cases showing off champagne bottles and some of the landlord's awards, then on the right is the bar, its light leather chairs and sofas and big low tables giving a nice blend of the individual and comfortably modern. To the left is the brasserie-style dining room, with a busy open kitchen and a glass cabinet displaying their 35-day dry-aged steaks; an area at the back has chandeliers and big mirrors. Blackboards on the walls stress the provenance of fresh, local ingredients. At the back is a clubby and elegantly panelled piano bar, with its own bar counter and a pianist three evenings a week. Polite, uniformed young staff serve five real ales including Caledonian Deuchars IPA, Courage Directors, Theakstons Best and guests from breweries such as Bowland and Moorhouses; good, changing wine list. A few tables outside overlook the enormous car park.

🍴 **Very good food includes outstandingly good sausages made on the premises using organic local pork or beef (try the Connoisseur: pork with apple poached in calvados and cider, and a hint of honey, thyme and blueberries), as well as soup, lobster linguine in tomato and cream sauce, grilled scallops with black pudding beignets, braised local lamb shank with port and rosemary jus, fish pie, beef, mushroom and oxtail pie, steaks, daily specials, local cheeses, and puddings like chocolate orange fondant.** *Starters/Snacks: £4.95 to £7.55. Main Courses: £9.95 to £19.95. Puddings: £5.50 to £6.50*

Free house ~ Licensee Kevin Berkins ~ Bar food (12-2.30, 6-9.30 (10 Fri, Sat); 12-8 Sun) ~ Restaurant ~ (01254) 825285 ~ Children welcome ~ Open 12-12(1am Sat, 11.30 Sun)
Recommended by Steve Whalley, John and Eleanor Holdsworth

BASHALL EAVES   SD6943   MAP 7

Red Pump

NW of Clitheroe, off B6478 or B6243; BB7 3DA

Cosy bar, good food in more up-to-date dining rooms; regional beers in beautifully placed country inn; bedrooms

In lovely country where the River Hodder carves a course beneath Longridge Fell just south of the moors of the Forest of Bowland, this 18th-c inn has splendid views, and residents can fish in the nearby river. As well as two pleasantly up-to-date dining rooms, there's a traditional, cosy central bar with bookshelves, cushioned settles and a log fire; board games. The choice of regional ales on handpump features Black Sheep, Moorhouses Witches Cauldron and a guest such as Tirril Old Faithful; 11 wines by the glass and a good range of malt whiskies. The three pleasant bedrooms have good views.

🍴 **Using locally sourced meat, game from local shoots and herbs from their own garden, much-liked food includes starters such as smoked local goats cheese and red onion tart, seared pigeon breast and venison ravioli, main courses such as slow-roasted pendle belly pork, sausage and champ, steak, mixed vegetables with herbed pancakes and a duo of sauces and a rabbit fest dish featuring slow-cooked confit leg of rabbit, rabbit haggis and fried loin of rabbit wrapped in bacon, and puddings; children's menu; good value Sunday lunch.** *Starters/Snacks: £3.95 to £6.50. Main Courses: £8.95 to £14.95. Puddings: £3.95 to £6.75*

Free house ~ Licensees Jonathan and Martina Myerscough ~ Real ale ~ Bar food (12-2(2.30 Sat), 6-9; 12-7 Sun) ~ Restaurant ~ (01254) 826227 ~ Children welcome in bar if dining, but not in restaurant after 8pm or at weekends ~ Open 12-2(2.30 Sat), 6-11; 12-7 Sun; closed Sun evening, Mon, some Tues and late Feb ~ Bedrooms: £65S/£95B

Recommended by Steve Whalley, Margaret Dickinson, Rob Bowran, Roger Thornington

BAY HORSE

SD4952 MAP 7

Bay Horse 🍴 �🍷

1.2 miles from M6 junction 33: A6 southwards, then off on left; LA2 0HR

Comfortably stylish pub with emphasis on innovative food; good range of drinks; garden

With innovative use made of local produce, this civilised country dining pub is a popular spot for a special meal out. A beamed red-walled bar is cosily pubby, attractively decorated as it is with cushioned wall banquettes in bays, gentle lighting, including table lamps on window sills and fresh flowers on the counter, with a good log fire; piped music. Its restaurant area has red décor, a log fire, candle-flame-effect lights and nice tables, including one or two good-sized ones in intimate self-contained corners. As well as a decent, fairly priced wine list (15 wines by the glass), 15 malt whiskies, freshly squeezed orange juice and pressed apple juices, helpful efficient staff serve Black Sheep and Hawkshead beers from handpumps. The pub is in a peaceful location (though the railway is not far off) and there are tables out in the garden behind.

🍴 **A good deal of effort goes into the food, with thoughtful use of carefully sourced ingredients and lovely presentation. Though not cheap, helpings are generous. As well as imaginative lunchtime sandwiches, lunch and evening menus might include starters such as cured salmon with pickled samphire, duck salad with walnuts and beetroot and pressing of pork sausage, black pudding and lancashire cheese, main courses like fillet of aged cumbrian beef, sausages and mash, braised pork belly and vegetable lancashire cheese pie, and puddings such as apple and pear crumble and lemon posset with shortbread.** *Starters/Snacks: £4.25 to £16.95. Main Courses: £11.00 to £22.00. Puddings: £4.75 to £5.25*

Mitchells ~ Tenant Craig Wilkinson ~ Real ale ~ Bar food (12-1.45(3 Sun), 6.30-9) ~ Restaurant ~ (01524) 791204 ~ Children welcome ~ Open 12-3, 6.30-11(midnight Sat); 12-4.30, 8-11 Sun; closed Mon ~ Bedrooms: /£89B

Recommended by Karen Eliot, Martin Stafford, Chris Stevenson, Rory and Jackie Hudson, Adrian Johnson, Dave Braisted, Dr Kevan Tucker, Mr and Mrs J E Fisher, Steve Whalley, Mrs P M Hibbert, Dr and Mrs A K Clarke, Rob and Catherine Dunster

BISPHAM GREEN

SD4813 MAP 7

Eagle & Child 🍴 �🍷

Maltkiln Lane (Parbold—Croston road, off B5246); L40 3SG

Well liked pub with antiques in stylishly simple interior, interesting range of beers, appealing rustic garden

Getting terrific reports this year for food, beer and atmosphere, this country pub has a spacious slightly rustic garden, a well tended but unconventional bowling green and, beyond, a wild area that is home to crested newts and moorhens. Inside, it is largely open-plan and discerningly furnished with a lovely mix of small old oak chairs, an attractive oak coffer, several handsomely carved antique oak settles (the finest apparently made partly from a 16th-c wedding bed-head), old hunting prints and engravings and low hop-draped beams. There are red walls and coir matting up a step and oriental rugs on ancient flagstones in front of the fine old stone fireplace and counter. Friendly young staff serve an interesting range of beers with Thwaites Original alongside guests such as Coniston Bluebird, Phoenix Arizona, Prospect Silver Tally, Slaters Top Totty and Southport Golden Sands. They also keep Saxon farm cider, decent wines and around 25 malt whiskies. They hold a popular beer festival over the first May bank holiday weekend. A handsome side barn houses a deli; the pub's dogs are called Betty and Doris.

🍴 There's quite an emphasis on the well cooked food (you need to book). The bar menu includes several imaginative sandwiches, steamed mussels with white wine and garlic, chargrilled chicken caesar salad, rump steak, steak and ale pie, crayfish and lemon risotto, while a more expensive menu has items such as langoustines, black forest dry-cured ham with olive, pine nut and herb salad, rib-eye steak with bordelaise sauce, moroccan-style roast lamb rump with couscous and fried fillets of bass with prawns, saffron and white wine butter sauce. *Starters/Snacks: £5.50 to £8.00. Main Courses: £9.50 to £13.50. Puddings: £4.50*

Free house ~ Licensee David Anderson ~ Real ale ~ Bar food (12-2, 5.30-8.30(9 Fri, Sat); 12-8.30 Sun) ~ (01257) 462297 ~ Children welcome ~ Dogs welcome ~ Open 12-3, 5.30-11; 12-11 Sat; 12-10.30 Sun

Recommended by Margaret Dickinson, Jeremy King, Deirdre Holding, Peter Heaton, Mike Tucker, Adrian and Dawn Collinge, Dr Clive Elphick, Yvonne and Mike Meadley, John and Helen Rushton, Ann and Tony Bennett-Hughes, Maurice and Gill McMahon, Michael Butler, W K Wood

BROUGHTON
SD4838 MAP 7

Plough at Eaves

A6 N through Broughton, first left into Station Lane just under a mile after traffic lights, then bear left after another 1.5 miles; PR4 0BJ

Cosy old place in a peaceful backwater; good value traditional food

Well tucked away from the pressures of the modern world, this pleasantly unpretentious old country tavern has a spacious garden around the side and at the back, with a well equipped children's play area. The two homely low-beamed lattice-windowed bars are traditionally furnished with a mix of wooden chairs, tables and upholstered seats. There are three aged guns over a log-burning stove, and a row of Royal Doulton figurines above an open log fire in the restaurant bar, which extends into a conservatory. Thwaites Original, Lancaster Bomber and Wainwright on handpump, quiet piped music and games machine. Seats on the front terrace make the ideal vantage point from which to watch the world go by. More reports please.

🍴 Bar food includes sandwiches, scallops and prawns in cheese sauce, streaky bacon with black pudding and poached egg, steak and kidney pie, fish and chips, steaks, and home-made puddings including fresh fruit pavlova and chocolate fudge cake. *Starters/Snacks: £4.25 to £7.95. Main Courses: £7.50 to £15.00. Puddings: £4.25*

Thwaites ~ Tenants Doreen and Mike Dawson ~ Real ale ~ Bar food (12-2.15(3.15 Sat), 6-9 (9.15 Sat); 12-8 Sun) ~ Restaurant ~ (01772) 690233 ~ Children welcome ~ Open 12-3, 5.30-11.30; 12-1am Sat; 12-10.30 Sun; closed Mon (except bank hols)

Recommended by Keith and Rowena Ward, Dr and Mrs A K Clarke

'Children welcome' means the pub says it lets children inside without any special restriction. If it allows them in, but to restricted areas such as an eating area or family room, we specify this. Places with separate restaurants often let children use them, hotels usually let them into public areas such as lounges. Some pubs impose an evening time limit – let us know if you find one earlier than 9pm.

CHIPPING

SD6141   MAP 7

Dog & Partridge

Hesketh Lane; crossroads Chipping—Longridge with Inglewhite—Clitheroe; PR3 2TH

Comfortable old-fashioned dining pub in grand countryside, with traditional food

In attractively varied country between the high moors of the Forest of Bowland and the abrupt rise of Longridge Fell, this much-altered pub dates in parts to 1515. The main lounge has small armchairs around fairly close-set low tables, beams, exposed stone walls, a good winter log fire and multicoloured lanterns. Friendly helpful staff serve Tetleys Bitter and Mild and a weekly changing guest such as Black Sheep Bitter on handpump. Smart casual dress is preferred in the stable restaurant. More reports please.

🍴 **Tasty bar food includes sandwiches, prawn cocktail, leek and mushroom crumble, steak and kidney pie, roast duckling with apple sauce and stuffing, pork chops and grilled sirloin steak, with home-made puddings such as fruit pie and sherry trifle.** *Starters/Snacks: £3.30 to £5.50. Main Courses: £7.20 to £14.75. Puddings: £4.00 to £4.30*

Free house ~ Licensee Peter Barr ~ Real ale ~ Bar food (12-1.45; 7-9; 12-8.30 Sun) ~ Restaurant (7(6.30 Sat)-9 Mon-Sat; 12-8.30 Sun) ~ (01995) 61201 ~ Children welcome ~ Open 11.45-3, 6.45-11; 11.45-10.30 Sun; closed Mon
Recommended by Tim and Rosemary Wells, Bob Broadhurst

DENSHAW

SD9711   MAP 7

Rams Head

2 miles from M62 junction 2; A672 towards Oldham, pub N of village; OL3 5UN

Roaring fires and tasty food in an inviting old-world moorland pub with delicatessen and tea room

The sweeping moorland views are one reason to venture out to this dining-oriented pub, 1,200 feet above sea level and high above the Tame Valley; it's a useful objective for walkers. The cosily traditional interior has beam-and-plank ceilings and good log fires, and is furnished with oak settles and benches built into the panelling of its four thick-walled little rooms. Up to three real ales – Black Sheep and Timothy Taylors Bitter and Landlord – are on handpump; piped music. You can buy locally sourced meat and other produce and have a coffee in their rather nice little adjacent deli. Perhaps not ideal for younger children. More reports please.

🍴 **Tasty bar food features seasonal game and plenty of seafood: soup, game terrine, seafood or olive platters, fillets of bass with fennel and crayfish cream sauce, slow-braised lamb shank on parsnip mash or moroccan couscous, mussels, steak, game hotpot, duo of ribble valley suckling pig, and puddings like bread and butter pudding.** *Starters/Snacks: £4.95 to £7.95. Main Courses: £8.95 to £12.95. Puddings: £3.95 to £5.95*

Free house ~ Licensee Geoff Haigh ~ Real ale ~ Bar food (12-2, 6-10; 12-8.30 Sun) ~ Restaurant ~ (01457) 874802 ~ Children welcome if well behaved, not Sat evening ~ Open 12-2.30, 6-11; 12-10.30 Sun; closed Mon (except bank hols)
Recommended by Gordon and Margaret Ormondroyd, Dr Kevan Tucker, Jill and Julian Tasker

GREAT MITTON

SD7139   MAP 7

Three Fishes 🍴 🍷 🍺

Mitton Road (B6246, off A59 NW of Whalley); BB7 9PQ

Stylish modern revamp, tremendous attention to detail, excellent regional food with a contemporary twist, interesting drinks

Deservedly popular as an excellent all-rounder, this imaginatively converted and well laid-out pub copes very well even at the busier times, with friendly staff serving well presented regional cuisine. Despite its size, it has plenty of intimate corners; the areas closest to the bar are elegantly traditional with a couple of big stone fireplaces, rugs on polished floors, upholstered stools and a good chatty feel. Then there's a series of individually furnished and painted rooms with exposed stone walls, careful spotlighting and wooden slatted blinds, ending with another impressive fireplace; facilities for the disabled. The long bar counter (with elaborate floral displays) serves Thwaites Double Century, Original and Wainwright and a guest from a brewery like Hawkshead, a dozen wines by the glass and unusual soft drinks such as locally made sarsaparilla and dandelion and burdock. Overlooking the Ribble Valley, the garden and terrace have tables and perhaps their own summer menu. You write your name on a blackboard when you arrive and they find you when a table becomes free – the system works surprisingly well. This pub is under the same ownership as two other Main Entries – the Highwayman at Nether Burrow and Clog & Billycock at Pleasington, just outside Blackburn.

🍴 You order your meal at various food points dotted around, and the emphasis is on traditional lancastrian dishes with a modern twist. Products are carefully sourced from small local suppliers, many of whom are immortalised in black and white photographs on the walls, and located on a map on the back of the menu. Most dish descriptions indicate the origins of the main ingredient – the beef, particularly, is exclusive to here. As well as imaginative lunchtime sandwiches, there might be starters such as smoked mackerel pâté with capers and warm toasted crumpets, lancashire smokehouse beech and juniper smoked salmon, treacle-baked cumbrian ribs, main courses such as braised skirt of ribble valley beef and potato pie, sirloin steak, curd cheese and onion pie with short-crust pastry, and puddings such as apple crumble with vanilla custard, jam roly-poly or double chocolate mousse; children's menu. You may need to order side dishes with some main courses. They serve a limited snack menu in the afternoon. *Starters/Snacks: £3.50 to £7.50. Main Courses: £9.50 to £19.60. Puddings: £5.00 to £5.50*

Free house ~ Licensee Andy Morris ~ Real ale ~ Bar food (12-2, 6-9, 12-8.30 Sun and bank hols; lighter meals 2-5.30 Mon-Sat) ~ (01254) 826888 ~ Children welcome ~ Dogs welcome ~ Open 12-11(10.30 Sun)

Recommended by W K Wood, Cedric Robertshaw, Steve Whalley, Maurice and Gill McMahon, Jo Lilley, Simon Calvert, Ken Richards, Peter and Josie Fawcett, Margaret Dickinson, Pauline and Derek Hodgkiss

LANCASTER   SD4761   MAP 7

Borough 🍺

Dalton Square; LA1 1PP

Enterprising city-centre pub with chattily civilised atmosphere, excellent range of beers and drinks and meticulously sourced local food

This erstwhile mayor's house and working men's club has been stylishly rejuvenated into a welcoming place for a drink or a meal. Relaxed and civilised, the front areas with their chandeliers and dark leather sofas and armchairs still have something of the look of a private members' club; there are carefully chosen antique tables and lamps, as well as panelled stained glass, old prints and photographs, chunky candles, high stools and elbow tables. Behind here is the bar, where friendly staff serve seven well kept local ales such as Bowland Hen Harrier, Hawkshead Bitter, Lancaster Amber and Thwaites Original and Wainwright alongside three guests – from 12-4pm one beer sells for just £2 a pint; also a wider than usual range of bottled beers, a good choice of wines and malt whiskies, and a pile of fresh oranges ready for juicing. Beyond the bar area is a big dining room with tables in the middle and booths along one side; on the other side is the deli counter offering tasty local snacks all day and a little shop selling jams and other local produce. The lovely tree-sheltered garden, with wooden tables, opens off at the back. The statue of Queen Victoria in the square outside is among several notable gifts to the city by one of its most famous sons, Lord Ashton. More reports please.

Post Office address codings confusingly give the impression that some pubs are in Lancashire, when they're really in Cumbria or Yorkshire (which is where we list them).

🍴 With a real emphasis on independent local suppliers, the menu includes soup, sandwiches, ploughman's, black pudding with sliced new potatoes, morecambe bay potted shrimps, mussels in white wine and garlic cream sauce, fried pigeon breast on parsnip purée, lancashire hotpot, rump or sirloin steak, fish pie, and puddings like apple and berry crumble or fruit salad; also deli boards as nibbles or to share, and two-course 'school dinners' daily except Sunday 12-6.30pm for £6.95. *Starters/Snacks: £2.95 to £6.95. Main Courses: £8.95 to £21.95. Puddings: £2.95 to £5.95*

Free house ~ Licensees Hannah and Martin Horner ~ Real ale ~ Bar food (12-9(9.30 Fri, Sat)) ~ Restaurant ~ (01524) 64170 ~ Children welcome ~ Dogs allowed in bar ~ Comedy last Sun of the month, poker night Monday ~ Open 11am-11.30pm(12.30 Fri, Sat)

Recommended by Karen Eliot, Mike Horgan, Jo Lilley, Simon Calvert

LITTLE ECCLESTON
SD4240 MAP 7
Cartford
Cartford Lane, off A586 Garstang—Blackpool, by toll bridge; PR3 0YP

Prettily placed 17th-c coaching inn on riverbank, attractively refurbished

The setting here is very appealing: tables in the garden look out over the River Wyre (crossed by its toll bridge), the Trough of Bowland and Beacon Fell. Inside, the unusual four-level layout has been given a very sympathetic, fresh makeover that combines traditional and contemporary elements, with pinks and reds, and light wooden floors and banquettes alongside oak beams and a log fire; piped music, TV and board games. A Bowland ale, Hawkshead Lakeland Gold, Moorhouse Pride of Pendle and Theakston Old Peculier are on handpump alongside speciality bottled beers and Weston's cider; several wines by the glass; friendly service from french owners. It has seven individually furnished ensuite rooms; we would welcome comments from readers who stay here.

🍴 Bar food might include sandwiches, various platters such as local antipasti, seafood or organic crudités, starters like black pudding melt, tiger prawns in mild thai green curry, main courses like oxtail and beef in real ale suet pudding with red wine jus, fish pie, fish and chips and lamb hotpot, vegetarian pie, steaks, and puddings like bread and butter pudding and chocolate fondant with mascarpone. *Starters/Snacks: £3.35 to £7.25. Main Courses: £8.95 to £21.50. Puddings: £4.95 to £5.95*

Free house ~ Licensees Patrick and Julie Beaume ~ Real ale ~ Bar food (12-2, 5.30(5 Mon)-9(10 Sat, 8.30 Sun)) ~ Restaurant ~ (01995) 670166 ~ No children under 12 in bedrooms ~ Open 12-11(midnight Sat, 10 Sun); closed till 5pm Mon (except bank hols) ~ Bedrooms: £65S(£50B)/£90S

Recommended by Peter and Josie Fawcett, Alison Playfoot, Donna and Roger

LIVERPOOL
SJ3589 MAP 7
Philharmonic Dining Rooms ★ 🍴 £
36 Hope Street; corner of Hardman Street; L1 9BX

Beautifully preserved Victorian pub with superb period interior, ten real ales and sensibly priced food

Worth a visit for the architecture alone, this spectacularly ornate Victorian former club positively drips with period details. The centrepiece is a mosaic-faced serving counter, from which heavily carved and polished mahogany partitions radiate under the intricate plasterwork high ceiling. The echoing main hall boasts stained glass including contemporary portraits of Boer War heroes Baden-Powell and Lord Roberts, rich panelling, a huge mosaic floor, and copper panels of musicians in an alcove above the fireplace. More stained glass in one of the little lounges declares 'Music is the universal language of mankind' and backs this up with illustrations of musical instruments. Two side rooms are called Brahms and Liszt, and there are two plushly comfortable sitting rooms. This is no museum piece, however, and it can be very busy here, with ten handpumps as testament to a high turnover. As well as Cains Finest Bitter and Jennings Cumberland, up to eight changing guest ales might be from brewers such as Caledonian Deuchars and Sharps, with usually an array of seasonal brews and several malt whiskies; quiz machine, fruit machine and piped music. Don't miss the original 1890s Adamant gents' lavatory (all pink marble and mosaics); ladies are allowed a look if they ask first.

Reasonably priced food (available in the bar or in the table-service grand lounge dining room) includes soup, sandwiches, ploughman's, a range of pies (including steak in ale), sausage and mash, fish and chips, a sharing platter, and puddings. *Starters/Snacks: £2.50 to £4.95. Main Courses: £5.45 to £9.95. Puddings: £3.50 to £3.75*

Mitchells & Butlers ~ Manager Nicola Hamilton-Coburn ~ Real ale ~ Bar food (10-10) ~ Restaurant ~ (0151) 707 2837 ~ Children welcome until 7pm ~ Open 10am-midnight

Recommended by the Didler, Ben Williams, Tony and Wendy Hobden, Eric Larkham, Rob and Catherine Dunster, Andy Lickfold

LONGRIDGE   SD6038   MAP 7

Derby Arms ♀

Chipping Road, Thornley; 1.5 miles N of Longridge on back road to Chipping; PR3 2NB

Welcoming, traditional country pub with hunting and fishing paraphernalia (and menu to match) and a very decent wine list

You get the feeling that a lot of thought goes into the running of this convivial old stone-built country pub, where the charming family and staff are ever willing to get things right. Among hunting and fishing bric-a-brac in its main bar, old photographs commemorate notable catches and there's some nicely mounted bait above the comfortable red plush seats, together with a stuffed pheasant that seems to be flying in through the wall. To the right a smaller room has sporting trophies and mementoes, and a regimental tie collection; piped music and darts. The gents' has dozens of riddles on the wall – you can buy a sheet of them in the bar and the money goes to charity. Along with a good range of wines, including several by the glass and half bottles (they're particularly strong on south african), you'll find Black Sheep and Marstons Pedigree on handpump. A few tables out in front, and another two behind the car park, have fine views across to the Forest of Bowland, and there's a boules piste. They put on lots of themed evenings – such as jazz, folk and cabaret.

You order your meal at the bar and will be shown to your table when it's ready. They do lots of seasonal game such as pheasant, hare, rabbit, partridge, woodcock, rabbit and mallard, and offer several fresh fish dishes such as potted shrimps, mussels, fresh dressed crab, oysters and monkfish. Other enjoyable food might include sandwiches, ploughman's, roast belly pork on bubble and squeak potato cake with apple and cider sauce, or rump steak; the two- or three-course table d'hôte menu is good value; puddings such as home-baked fruit pies, sherry trifle and bread and butter pudding. *Starters/Snacks: £3.00 to £6.00. Main Courses: £7.00 to £14.00. Puddings: £3.50 to £4.75*

Punch ~ Lease Will and Carole Walne ~ Real ale ~ Bar food (12-2.15, 6-9.15(10 Sat); 12-9.15 Sun) ~ Restaurant ~ (01772) 782623 ~ Children welcome away from main bar ~ Open 12-4, 6-12; 12-12 Sat; 12-11.30 Sun

Recommended by Margaret Dickinson, Maurice and Gill McMahon, Andy and Jill Kassube

LYDGATE   SD9704   MAP 7

White Hart ⑪ ♀ ⇥

Stockport Road; Lydgate not marked on some maps, so not to be confused with the one near Todmorden; take A669 Oldham—Saddleworth and after almost 2.5 miles turn right at brow of hill to A6050, Stockport Road; OL4 4JJ

Smart up-to-date dining pub (drinkers welcome too) with excellent food (not cheap), five beers, good wine list, garden and comfortable bedrooms

Although an elegant dining venue with bedrooms, this scenically placed stone-built inn overlooking the moors often has a good few locals clustered round the bar, or in the two simpler rooms at the end. The modern refurbishment successfully blends new with old: beams and exposed stonework alternate with deep red or purple walls, punctuated with a mix of modern paintings, black and white photos, and stylised local scenes; most rooms have a fireplace and fresh flowers. The warmly elegant brasserie is the biggest of the main rooms and service from the smartly dressed staff is good. The very extensive wine list includes around 16 by the glass, and beers are Lees Bitter, Timothy Taylors Golden Best and Landlord with a couple of changing guests from brewers such as Phoenix and Pictish on handpump; piped music, TV in front lounge and newspapers. The pub is located just outside the eastern fringes of Oldham, on the moors of the Pennines and a few miles from the border of the Peak District National Park – picnic-sets on the lawn behind make the most of the position. More reports please.

🍴 **The thoughtfully prepared meals are pricier than in most pubs around here, but the quality is consistently high. Served throughout the building, the menu typically includes sandwiches, potted shrimps, fried scallops with grilled chorizo, pea purée and fried leeks, battered haddock with marrowfat peas, braised beef cheek with haggis mash, fried bass with smoked bacon and king prawn risotto, honey-roast duck breast with mango and chilli, parsnip and blue cheese risotto, and puddings such as bakewell tart or glazed lemon tart with honey ice-cream and red wine sauce.** *Starters/Snacks: £5.00 to £7.00. Main Courses: £13.00 to £24.00. Puddings: £4.50*

Free house ~ Licensee Charles Brierley ~ Real ale ~ Bar food (12-2.30, 6-9.30; 1-7.30 Sun) ~ Restaurant ~ (01457) 872566 ~ Children welcome ~ Dogs allowed in bar ~ Open 12-midnight ~ Bedrooms: £95B/£127.50B

Recommended by Brian and Anna Marsden, P J and R D Greaves, David and Cathrine Whiting

LYTHAM   SD3627   MAP 7

Taps 🍺 £

A584 S of Blackpool; Henry Street – in centre, one street in from West Beach; FY8 5LE

Thriving seaside pub with down-to-earth atmosphere, spirited landlord, eight real ales and straightforward lunchtime snacks; open all day

In this bustling town pub you can see the fine range of beers on offer through a view-in cellar: there is an impressive choice of six ever-changing guest beers kept alongside Greene King IPA and Taps Best, which is brewed for the pub by Titanic on handpump and sells for just £1.80 a pint; also country wines and a farm cider. The landlord is a rugby fan, with an expanding collection of rugby memorabilia and old photographs and portraits of rugby stars on the walls, so it rather goes without saying that beer is important here (and perhaps explains why there are seat belts on the bar and headrests in the gents'). With a good mix of customers, the Victorian-style bare-boarded bar has a sociable unassuming feel, plenty of stained-glass decoration in the windows, depictions of fish and gulls reflecting the pub's proximity to the beach (it's a couple of minutes' walk away), captain's chairs in bays around the sides, open fires, and a coal-effect gas fire between two built-in bookcases at one end; shove-ha'penny, dominoes, quiz machine and fruit machine. There are a few seats and a heated canopied area outside. Parking is difficult near the pub so it's probably best to park at the West Beach car park on the seafront (free on Sunday) and walk.

🍴 **A handful of cheap bar snacks includes sandwiches, soup, hot roast sandwich, filled baked potatoes, burgers, chilli and curry.** *Starters/Snacks: £2.25 to £4.45. Puddings: £1.95 to £2.75*

Greene King ~ Manager Ian Rigg ~ Real ale ~ Bar food (12-2, not Sun) ~ No credit cards ~ (01253) 736226 ~ Children welcome away from bar till 7pm ~ Open 11-11(midnight Fri, Sat)

Recommended by Ken Richards, Steve Whalley, G Jennings, the Didler

---

We mention bottled beers and spirits only if there is something unusual about them – imported belgian real ales, say, or dozens of malt whiskies; so do please let us know about them in your reports.

MANCHESTER

SJ8397 MAP 7

Britons Protection 🍺 £

Great Bridgewater Street, corner of Lower Mosley Street; M1 5LE

Lively city pub with a maze of unspoilt rooms, huge range of whiskies, five real ales and inexpensive lunchtime snacks; garden

Often busy with concert-goers and musicians from the Bridgewater Hall next door, this likeably unpretentious and rambling place has a terrific range of around 235 malt whiskies and bourbons (said to be the largest collection in the city), as well as Jennings Cumberland, Robinsons Unicorn, Tetleys and a changing guests such as Farriers on handpump and good wines. One of the most notable features here are the tiled battle murals depicting the Peterloo Massacre of 1819, which took place a few hundred yards away. The first of a series of unspoilt little rooms, the plush little front bar has a fine chequered tile floor, some glossy brown and russet wall tiles, solid woodwork and elaborate plastering. There are two cosy inner lounges, both served by hatch, with attractive brass and etched-glass wall lamps, a mirror above the coal-effect gas fire in the simple art nouveau fireplace and, again, good solidly comfortable furnishings. As something of a tribute to Manchester's notorious climate, the massive bar counter has a pair of heating pipes as its footrail. There are tables out in the garden behind. It can get very busy at lunchtime and weekends, while in the evenings they sometimes host poetry readings, storytelling, silent film shows and acoustic gigs; note they may close early on match days. No children.

🍽 **Straightforward bar food includes soup, various pies and home-made daily specials such as steak with mushroom sauce, hotpot, lasagne or minted lamb chop.** *Starters/Snacks: £2.95. Main Courses: £4.50 to £5.95*

Punch ~ Lease Peter Barnett ~ Real ale ~ Bar food (11-2) ~ (0161) 236 5895 ~ Open 11am (11.30 Sat, 12 Sun)-midnight

Recommended by the Didler, Neil Whitehead, Victoria Anderson, John Fiander, Simon Greenwood, Dr and Mrs A K Clarke, Jeremy King, Dr Kevan Tucker

Dukes 92

Castle Street, below the bottom end of Deansgate; M3 4LZ

Waterside conversion with spacious interior, great range of cheeses and pizzas all day

This imaginatively converted stable block is named after the Duke's Lock, the 92nd and final one on the Rochdale Canal, which runs directly outside at a point where fine Victorian warehouses line the canal basin. Old and modern furnishings, including comfortable chaises-longues and deep armchairs, throughout the ground floor are well spaced and contrast with boldly bare whitewashed walls. Its stylish gallery bar, accessed by an elegant spiral staircase, overlooks the canal. The handsome granite-topped counter serves three real ales, two usually from Moorhouses, as well as decent wines and a wide choice of spirits; piped music. Tables outside on a big terrace enjoy good waterside views.

🍽 **The menu is short but includes an excellent range of over three dozen cheeses and pâtés with generous helpings of granary bread; also sandwiches, soup and salads. From mid-afternoon onwards they serve pizzas only. Puddings include warm chocolate toffee brownie and ice-cream sundae; the restaurant has a grill menu with burgers and steaks.** *Starters/Snacks: £2.95 to £6.50. Main Courses: £6.50 to £13.95. Puddings: £4.50*

Free house ~ Licensee James Ramsbottom ~ Real ale ~ Bar food (12-10.30(11 weekends)) ~ Restaurant ~ (0161) 839 8646 ~ Children welcome till 8.30pm ~ Open 11.30-11(midnight Thurs, 1 Fri, Sat); 12-11 Sun

Recommended by Ben Williams, Mrs Hazel Rainer, Jeremy King, Andy and Jill Kassube

> Bedroom prices are for high summer. Even then you may get reductions for more than one night, or (outside tourist areas) weekends. Winter special rates are common, and many inns cut bedroom prices if you have a full evening meal.

Marble Arch 🍺

Rochdale Road (A664), Ancoats; corner of Gould Street, just E of Victoria Station; M4 4HY

Cheery town pub with noteworthy Victorian interior, ten real ales including own brews, very reasonably priced food and a small garden

This friendly city own-brew pub is well worth seeking out for its classic Victorian interior as well as for its beer. It features a magnificently restored lightly barrel-vaulted high ceiling and extensive marble and tiling. A frieze advertising various spirits, the chimney-breast above the carved wooden mantelpiece and sloping mosaic floor particularly stand out. Furniture is a cheerful mix of rustic tables and chairs, including a long communal table and a display cabinet with pump clips; chess and backgammon are kept behind the bar. From windows in the back room, which is set aside for those eating, you can look out over the brewery (tours by arrangement) where they produce their distinctive Ginger Marble, Lagonda IPA, Manchester Bitter, Pint and seasonal brews as well as Phoenix passion-fruit beer. They also have two guest ales from brewers such as Abbeydale and Pictish and a farm cider; piped music, juke box, and the Laurel and Hardy Preservation Society meet here on the third Wednesday of the month and show old films; small garden.

🍴 **In addition to sandwiches, freshly cooked food from a changing menu might include black pudding cake, burgers, fish and chips, lamb loin and grilled rib-eye steak.** *Starters/Snacks: £5.00 to £6.00. Main Courses: £7.00 to £10.00. Puddings: £4.00 to £5.00*

Own brew ~ Licensee Jan Rogers ~ Real ale ~ Bar food (12-9(8 Sun)) ~ (0161) 832 5914 ~ Children welcome ~ Open 12-11(midnight Fri, Sat; 10.30 Sun)

Recommended by the Didler, Chris Johnson, Neil Whitehead, Victoria Anderson, Jeremy King, Joe Green, Andy and Jill Kassube, John and Helen Rushton

NETHER BURROW   SD6175 MAP 7

Highwayman 🍴 🍷

A683 S of Kirkby Lonsdale; LA6 2RJ

LANCASHIRE DINING PUB OF THE YEAR

Substantial and skilfully refurbished old stone house with country interior serving carefully sourced and prepared food; lovely gardens

Run by the same team who have the Three Fishes at Great Mitton and the Clog & Billycock at Pleasington, the owners here take great pride in promoting local suppliers at this most inviting and efficiently run pub. Black and white wall prints (and placemats) show the characterful local farmers and producers who supply the ingredients, and a map on the menu shows 'regional food heroes'. Although large, its stylishly simple flagstoned 17th-c interior is nicely divided into intimate corners, with a couple of big log fires and informal wooden furnishings. Local Thwaites Lancaster Bomber, Double Century and Wainwright are served on handpump, alongside good wines by the glass, just over a dozen whiskies and a particularly good range of soft drinks. Service is busy, welcoming and efficient. French windows open to a big terrace and lovely gardens. They don't take bookings at the weekend (except for groups of six or more), but write your name on a blackboard when you arrive, and they will find you when a table becomes free.

🍴 **Tweaked to bring them up to date, traditional lancastrian recipes are prepared using carefully sourced products. As well as bar nibbles and imaginative sandwiches, ploughman's and platters of local seafood and cured meats, starters might include smoked cod fishcake with poached free-range egg, deep-fried parsnip fritters with cumin dip, goosnargh duck liver pâté with orange marmalade relish, with main courses such as battered haddock with marrowfat peas, braised ox cheek pudding, cheese and onion pie, lamb hotpot with pickled red cabbage, dry-cured gammon steak with poached egg, and puddings such as burnt english custard, stewed rhubarb and jam roly-poly pudding; they do just snacks in the afternoon; Sunday roasts.** *Starters/Snacks: £3.50 to £7.50. Main Courses: £9.50 to £21.00. Puddings: £3.50 to £5.50*

Thwaites ~ Lease Andy Morris and Craig Bancroft ~ Real ale ~ Bar food (12-2, 6-9, 12-8.30 Sun and bank hols; lighter meals 2-5.30 Mon-Sat) ~ (01254) 826888 ~ Children welcome ~ Dogs allowed in bar ~ Open 12-11(10.30 Sun)

Recommended by Dr Kevan Tucker, Jo Lilley, Simon Calvert, Steve Whalley, Karen Eliot, Noel Thomas, Paul and Penny Dawson, Maurice and Gill McMahon, Margaret Dickinson, Dr Peter Andrews, G Jennings, Ray and Winifred Halliday

PLEASINGTON   SD6528   MAP 7

Clog & Billycock 🍴 ☐

Village signposted off A677 Preston New Road on W edge of Blackburn; Billinge End Road; BB2 6QB

Excellent, well sourced local food in appealingly modernised stone-built village pub; very busy, but service is efficient and unhurried

Enjoying a rapidly spreading reputation for its food under the guidance of chef Nigel Haworth, this skilfully refurbished village pub is the third in the admirable local group of Ribble Valley Inns. Named after the preferred attire of a former landlord, the building has been extended on both sides and completely redesigned; light and airy, with flagstoned floors and pale grey walls, in places it has the feel of an upmarket barn conversion, though there's a cosier room opening off, with high-backed settles and a fireplace at the end. The whole pub is packed with light wooden tables, and although you may find them all full on arrival, such is the size of the place that you probably won't have to wait long in the little bar area for one to become free. Service is efficient and the staff are polite and helpful, and the sheer volume of satisfied customers ensures a very good, chatty atmosphere. Well kept Thwaites Bomber, Nutty Black and Wainwright, a very good choice of wines and a wide range of other drinks too. There are some tables outside, beside a small garden.

🍴 **What's not made on the premises won't have travelled far, and the menu identifies most of their suppliers, some of whom can also be seen in photographs. Particularly good food includes well filled sandwiches, deep-fried parsnip fritters with cumin dip, lancashire cheese on toast with sweet-cured bacon, warm morecambe bay shrimps with butter and a toasted muffin, various platters such as home-cured rare-breed meats, very good steaks, fish pie, an excellent hotpot with pickled red cabbage, seasonal specials, local cheeses and organic ice-creams, and puddings such as rhubarb and ginger sponge. There's a snack menu during the afternoon.** *Starters/Snacks: £4.50 to £8.50. Main Courses: £7.50 to £19.50. Puddings: £4.50 to £5.00*

Thwaites ~ Lease Andy Morris and Craig Bancroft ~ Bar food (12-2, 6-9, 12-8.30 Sun and bank hols; lighter meals 2-5.30 Mon-Sat) ~ Restaurant ~ No credit cards ~ (01254) 201163 ~ Children welcome ~ Dogs allowed in bar ~ Open 12-11(10.30 Sun)

Recommended by GLD, W K Wood, Steve Whalley, Ray and Winifred Halliday, Margaret Dickinson, RJH, Karen Eliot, Jim and Maggie Cowell

RABY   SJ3179   MAP 7

Wheatsheaf 🍺

From A540 heading S from Heswall, turn left into Upper Raby Road, village in about a mile; The Green, Raby Mere Road; CH63 4JH

Cottagey village pub, decent lunchtime bar food; nine real ales

A fine array of thoughtfully sourced nine changing ales – from brewers such as local Brimstage, Greene King, St Austell, Tetleys, Thwaites and Wells & Youngs – are available at this very pretty thatched black and white pub in the Wirral. Its nicely chatty rambling rooms are simply furnished, with an old wall clock and homely black kitchen shelves in the cosy central bar, and a nice snug formed by antique settles built in around its fine old fireplace. A second, more spacious room, has upholstered wall seats, small hunting prints on cream walls and a smaller coal fire. The spacious restaurant (Tuesdays to Saturday evening) is in a converted cowshed that leads into a larger conservatory; piped music is played in these areas only. There are picnic-sets on the terrace and in the pleasant garden behind, with more seats out front.

🍴 **Reasonably priced pubby lunchtime food is home-made and as well as a wide range of sandwiches and toasties includes baked potatoes, ploughman's, omelettes, steak and ale** pie, fish and chips, braised knuckle of lamb; three-course Sunday lunch; in the evening à la carte restaurant food is available in the adjacent Cowshed Restaurant. *Starters/Snacks: £3.50 to £12.95. Main Courses: £6.95 to £17.95. Puddings: £3.95*

Free house ~ Licensee Alan Philip Davies ~ Real ale ~ Bar food (12-2(2.30 Sun), 6-9(9.30 Fri, Sat); not Mon or Sun evenings) ~ Restaurant (evenings 6-9.30, Tues-Sat) ~ (0151) 336 3416 ~ Children welcome ~ Dogs allowed in bar ~ Open 11.30-11(midnight Fri, Sat); 12-10.30 Sun

Recommended by Paul Boot, Alan and Eve Harding, MLR, Clive Watkin, Maurice and Gill McMahon, Roger and Anne Newbury

RAMSBOTTOM
SD8017 MAP 7

Fishermans Retreat ◀

Twine Valley Park/Fishery signposted off A56 N of Bury at Shuttleworth; Bye Road; BL0 0HH

Good views from this friendly remote-feeling pub with hundreds of whiskies, all for sale by the bottle in new shop; trout and some meats on menu come from their own land

In the peaceful Twine Valley on the edge of the Pennines, this pub dates from 1992, soon after the family had purchased the valley's farmland, fishing lodges and derelict mills. It has an incredible range of malt whiskies, currently numbering over 500. Almost half are ranked on shelves above the bar counter, each new one added as the collection grew, but all are available in the whisky shop in a corner of the main room; this also sells wines and half the fun is looking at the price stickers on some of the rarer or vintage bottles. The owners do occasional tutored whisky tastings. The bar has something of the feel of a mountain lodge, with its bare stone walls and beamed ceilings, though the wallpaper around the fireplace adds a more civilised touch. A similar dining room opens off. Four well kept beers such as Black Sheep, Timothy Taylors Landlord and changing beers such as Copper Dragon Golden Pippin and Moorhouse Blond Witch, plus a good wine list, with the emphasis on new world ones; particularly friendly staff. There are a few picnic-sets outside and lovely views of the valley. Over the next year they plan a few changes, adding a new dining room so the main room can become a lounge for drinkers. You can arrange coarse fishing on the lakes. More reports please.

🍴 From the surrounding estate and its trout lakes, they get much of the the fish, beef (all dry-aged on the premises), venison and vegetables used in their food, which typically includes sandwiches, soup, black pudding and fresh queen scallops with smoked bacon and mature lancashire cheese sauce, hot smoked mackerel with lemon and caper butter, slow-roasted topside of pre-aged beef, mince and onion pie, peppers stuffed with roasted vegetables and feta cheese, rainbow trout fillet fried with bacon and crushed almonds, fish pie, steaks, and puddings like bakewell tart or whinberry crumble. *Starters/Snacks: £4.00 to £7.50. Main Courses: £9.00 to £23.00. Puddings: £3.50 to £6.00*

Free house ~ Licensee Hervey Magnall ~ Real ale ~ Bar food (12-9(9.30 Sat)) ~ (01706) 825314 ~ Children welcome ~ Open 12-11; closed Mon

Recommended by John and Helen Rushton, Steve Whalley

SAWLEY
SD7746 MAP 7

Spread Eagle

Village signposted just off A59 NE of Clitheroe; BB7 4NH

Nicely refurbished pub with imaginative food and riverside restaurant

This sensitively updated pub is beautifully set by the River Ribble close to the substantial ruins of a 12th-c Cistercian abbey. The fresh clean interior has a pleasing mix of nice old and quirky modern furniture – anything from an old settle and pine tables to new low chairs upholstered in animal-print fabric, all set off well by the grey rustic stone tiled floor. Low ceilings, cosy sectioning, a warming fire and cottagey windows keep it all feeling intimate. The dining areas are more formal, with modern stripes, and, as a bit of a quip on the decorative trend for walls of unread books, a bookshelf mural – much easier to keep dust free; piped music. Real ales include Theakstons, Thwaites Wainwright,

Timothy Taylors Landlord and a guest such as Hawkshead on handpump. The pub is handy for exhilarating walks in the Forest of Bowland; there are two smoking porches.

🍴 **Good food includes tempting sandwiches, starters such as soup, fried scallops with black pudding and italian ham, corned beef hash cake with a poached egg, mediterranean sharing platters, main courses such as fish pie, rib-eye steak, haddock and chips, and puddings like warm chocolate brownie and a taster plate of four puddings.** *Starters/Snacks: £4.25 to £7.25. Main Courses: £10.95 to £16.95. Puddings: £3.50 to £5.95*

Free house ~ Licensee Kate Peill ~ Real ale ~ Bar food (12-2, 6-9.30; 12-7.30 Sun) ~ Restaurant ~ (01200) 441202 ~ Children welcome ~ Singer Fri nights ~ Open 11-11; 12-10.30 Sun
Recommended by G Dobson, Mrs Sheila Stothard, Steve Whalley, R L Borthwick, Dr Kevan Tucker, Christopher Mobbs

STALYBRIDGE
SJ9598   MAP 7

Station Buffet 🍺 £
The Station, Rassbottom Street; SK15 1RF

Classic Victorian station buffet bar with eight quickly changing beers and a few cheap basic meals

A miraculous railway-age survival, this unpretentious Victorian platform bar has an impressive range of eight beers on handpump. These include Boddingtons and Timothy Taylors, and six quickly rotating guests from brewers such as All Gates, Bank Top, Howard Town and Phoenix, alongside belgian and other foreign bottled beers and a farm cider; board games, cards, newspapers and magazines. Busy with happy customers, the bar has a welcoming fire below an etched-glass mirror, period advertisements and photographs of the station and other railway memorabilia on cosy wood-panelled and red walls, and there's a newly rebuilt conservatory. An extension along the platform leads into what was the ladies' waiting room and part of the station master's quarters, featuring original ornate ceilings and Victorian-style wallpaper. Picnic-sets outside are on sunny Platform One by the Manchester to Huddersfield line.

🍴 **They do cheap old-fashioned snacks such as tasty black peas and sandwiches, and three or four daily specials such as home-made meat and potato pie and mushy peas, bacon casserole and all-day breakfast; freshly made coffee and tea by the pot.** *Starters/Snacks: £0.70 to £1.20. Main Courses: £3.50 to £6.50. Puddings: £1.20 to £1.50*

Free house ~ Licensees John Hesketh and Sylvia Wood ~ Real ale ~ Bar food (12-9) ~ No credit cards ~ (0161) 303 0007 ~ Children till 8pm ~ Dogs welcome ~ Open 11-11; 12-10.30 Sun
Recommended by Brian and Anna Marsden, Dennis Jones, Mike Horgan, John Fiander, the Didler, Chris Flynn, Wendy Jones, Bob Broadhurst, Tony and Maggie Harwood

TUNSTALL
SD6073   MAP 7

Lunesdale Arms 🍴 ♈
A683 S of Kirkby Lonsdale; LA6 2QN

Light and airy civilised pub with an emphasis on good imaginative food; separate area with traditional games

The opened-up interior of this bustling dining pub has bare boards and a lively acoustic that give it a distinctly cheery buzz. A white-walled area has a good mix of stripped solid dining tables and blue sofas facing each other across a low table (with daily papers) by a woodburning stove in a solid stone fireplace. Another area has pews and armchairs (some of the big unframed oil paintings are for sale) and to one end, an airy games section with pool, table football, board games and TV. A snugger little flagstoned back part has another woodburning stove. Besides Black Sheep and a local guest on handpump, they have several wines by the glass and 20 malts; piped music. The church in this Lune Valley village has Brontë associations.

🍴 **They place considerable emphasis on the tasty food, with a constantly changing menu that might include lunchtime sandwiches, soup, sharing platter with prosciutto and dips,** steak and Guinness pie, cumberland sausage and mash, chicken and ham hock pie, lancashire cheese rarebit with home-made apricot and ginger chutney, rib-eye steak, salmon fishcakes, and puddings such as seville orange sponge and chocolate tart; Sunday lunch. *Starters/Snacks: £4.95 to £6.00. Main Courses: £6.00 to £12.95. Puddings: £4.95*

Free house ~ Licensee Emma Gillibrand ~ Real ale ~ Bar food ~ (01524) 274203 ~ Children welcome ~ Dogs allowed in bar ~ Open 11-3, 6-midnight; 11-3.30, 6-1am Sat; 12-3.30, 6-11 Sun; closed Mon (except bank hols)

Recommended by Mr and Mrs D Mackenzie, Malcolm and Pauline Pellatt, Jo Lilley, Simon Calvert, Ann and Tony Bennett-Hughes

UPPERMILL
SD0006   MAP 7

Church Inn 🍺 £

From the main street (A607), look out for the sign for Saddleworth Church, and turn off up this steep narrow lane – keep on up!; OL3 6LW

Lively, good value community pub with own brews from a big range, lots of pets, and good food; children very welcome

Look out of the window at one end of the bar and you might be face to face with one of the alpacas they've recently added to the burgeoning menagerie of animals at this enjoyably quirky pub, high up on the moors, and with fine views down the valley: the pub also has rabbits, chickens, dogs, ducks, geese, horses, 14 peacocks in the adjacent field and some cats resident in an adjacent barn – they were planning to add wallabies and chipmunks as we went to press. The big unspoilt L-shaped main bar has high beams and some stripped stone. Comfortable furnishings include settles and pews as well as a good individual mix of chairs, lots of attractive prints and staffordshire and other china on a high delft shelf, jugs, brasses and so forth; TV (only when there's sport on) and unobtrusive piped music; the conservatory opens on to a terrace. The horse-collar on the wall is worn by the winner of their annual gurning (face-pulling) championship which is held during the lively traditional Rush Cart Festival, which is usually over the August bank holiday. Local bellringers arrive on Wednesdays to practise with a set of handbells that are kept here, while anyone is invited to join the morris dancers who meet here on Thursdays. When the spring water levels aren't high enough for brewing, they bring in guest beers such as Black Sheep and Hydes Jekylls Gold. At other times you might find up to 11 of their own-brew Saddleworth beers, starting at just £1.70 a pint. Some of the seasonal ones (look out for Rubens, Ayrtons, Robins and Indya) are named after the licensee's children, only appearing around their birthdays; dark lager on tap too. Children and dogs are made to feel very welcome.

🍽 **Very reasonably priced bar food includes soup, sandwiches, steak and ale pudding, jumbo cod, a range of pies, mixed grill, and puddings such as jam roly-poly or hot chocolate fudge cake and ice-creams.** *Starters/Snacks: £2.20 to £5.25. Main Courses: £5.85 to £12.25. Puddings: £2.75*

Own brew ~ Licensee Julian Taylor ~ Real ale ~ Bar food (12-2.30, 5.30-9; 12-9 Sat, Sun and bank hols) ~ (01457) 820902 ~ Children welcome ~ Dogs welcome ~ Open 12-12(11 Sun)

Recommended by Dr Kevan Tucker, John Fiander, Ben Williams, the Didler

WADDINGTON
SD7243   MAP 7

Lower Buck

Edisford Road; BB7 3HU

Chatty, welcoming village pub with reasonably priced, tasty food; five real ales

Picnic-sets in a cobbled area in front of this pretty, 18th-c village pub makes a lovely spot for sitting out, and there's more seating in the sunny back garden. Inside it's nicely old-fashioned, with several little cream-painted rooms, each with coal fires; darts and pool; two dining rooms. The friendly landlord keeps a range of five ales, usually Bowland Hen Harrier, Moorhouses Premier and Timothy Taylors Landlord alongside a couple of guests like Bowland Gold and Sawley Tempted, over a dozen malts and several wines by the glass. It's handily placed for walks in the Ribble Valley.

Ⓜ Using meat reared at a farm in nearby Longridge and vegetables grown in Longridge too, the reasonably priced tasty food includes lunchtime sandwiches and ploughman's, morecambe bay shrimps, short-crust pastry pies, fish pie, hotpot, sirloin steak, and specials such as broccoli and stilton soup, duck breast terrine, steak and kidney pudding, poached salmon fillet stuffed with brie and wrapped in parma ham on a bed of tomato sauce, and puddings such as strawberry and raspberry mousse. *Starters/Snacks: £3.95 to £9.75. Main Courses: £9.50 to £15.95. Puddings: £3.95*

Free house ~ Licensee Andrew Warburton ~ Real ale ~ Bar food (12-2.30, 6-9; 12-9 Sat, Sun and bank hols) ~ Restaurant ~ (01200) 423342 ~ Children welcome ~ Dogs welcome ~ Open 11(12 Sun)-11(midnight Sat)

Recommended by Donna and Roger, John and Eleanor Holdsworth, Steve Whalley

WHEATLEY LANE   SD8338   MAP 7

Old Sparrow Hawk

Wheatley Lane Road; towards E end of village road which runs N of and parallel to A6068; one way of reaching it is to follow Fence, Newchurch 1¼ signpost, then turn off at Barrowford ¾ signpost; BB12 9QG

Comfortably civilised pub, with well prepared food and five real ales

Pendle Hill rises near this black and white pub (under a new licensee this year), and heavy wood tables out on a spacious and attractive front terrace (pretty flower beds and a water feature) have good views to the moors beyond Nelson and Colne. Attractively laid out in several distinct areas, some with carpet and some with red tiles, it's nicely characterful with dark oak panelling and timbers, stripped stonework, lots of snug corners including a nice area with a fire, interesting furnishings including a sofa under a domed stained-glass skylight; daily papers. The cushioned leatherette bar counter (cheerful with fresh flowers) carries Bass, Greene King IPA, Thwaites Original, a couple of guests such as Bank Top Flat Cap and Mild on handpump, draught Fransizkaner wheat beer and good wines by the glass. TV, piped music and board games.

Ⓜ Good fresh bar food includes sandwiches, ploughman's, soup, potted duck liver parfait, warm black pudding with poached duck egg, beer-battered haddock with hand-cut chips, steak and ale pie, locally reared rib-eye steak, corn-fed chicken breast stuffed with wild mushrooms, slow-cooked pork belly, and puddings like earl-grey scented crème brûlée or chocolate cake with pistachio ice-cream; Sunday roasts. *Starters/Snacks: £4.25 to £6.75. Main Courses: £10.25 to £16.95. Puddings: £3.95 to £5.50*

Mitchells & Butlers ~ Lease Amanda Bailey ~ Real ale ~ Bar food (12-2.30, 5-9; 12-9.30 Sat; 12-8 Sun) ~ Restaurant ~ (01282) 603034 ~ Children welcome until 8pm ~ Open 12-11(midnight Sat, 10.30 Sun)

Recommended by Dr Kevan Tucker, Pauline and Derek Hodgkiss, Dr and Mrs T E Hothersall, Donna and Roger, Steve Whalley, Ann and Tony Bennett-Hughes

WHEELTON   SD6021   MAP 7

Dressers Arms 🍺

2.1 miles from M61 junction 8; Briers Brow, off A674 Blackburn road from Wheelton bypass (towards Brinscall); 3.6 miles from M65 junction 3, also via A674; PR6 8HD

Good choice of beer at this traditional pub in a converted cottage row

With eight real ales on offer, this is a pleasant place to enjoy a drink and is popular with walkers. The choice features beers from breweries like Black Sheep, Copper Dragon, Robinsons, Slaters and Tetleys; also 16 malt whiskies and some well chosen wines, with several by the glass. The snug low-beamed rooms are traditionally furnished with dark wood benches and red plush furnishings on patterned carpets, with a handsome old woodburning stove in the flagstoned main bar; newspapers, magazines, piped music, juke box, pool table, games machine and TV. There are lots of picnic-sets under a large umbrella with lighting and heaters on a terrace in front of the pub.

🍴 **Under a new chef, pubby bar food includes sandwiches, steak pudding, liver and onions, fish and chips, sirloin steak and fish specials; Sunday carvery.** *Starters/Snacks: £3.95 to £6.50. Main Courses: £6.95 to £12.00. Puddings: £4.25*

Own brew ~ Licensees Steve and Trudie Turner ~ Real ale ~ Bar food (12-2.30, 5-9; all day Sat, Sun and bank hols) ~ Restaurant ~ (01254) 830041 ~ Children allowed in bar until 9.30pm ~ Dogs allowed in bar ~ Open 10am-12.30am(1am Sat)

Recommended by W K Wood, Charles and Pauline Stride, Michael Butler, Mr and Mrs Barrie, Donna and Roger, Peter Heaton, Maurice and Gill McMahon, Ben Williams, Jo Lilley, Simon Calvert, Dr Kevan Tucker

WHITEWELL
SD6546   MAP 7

Inn at Whitewell ★ ♇ ⇌

Most easily reached by B6246 from Whalley; road through Dunsop Bridge from B6478 is also good; BB7 3AT

Elegant manor house hotel with smartly pubby atmosphere, good bar food and luxury bedrooms

A stylish place to stay, dine or enjoy a drink, this ancient, upmarket inn is much enjoyed for its super setting deep among the hills and moors that rise to the high points of the Forest of Bowland. Handsome old wood furnishings, including antique settles, oak gateleg tables and sonorous clocks, stand out well against powder-blue walls that are neatly hung with big attractive prints. The pubby main bar has roaring log fires in attractive stone fireplaces and heavy curtains on sturdy wooden rails; one area has a selection of newspapers and magazines, local maps and guide books; there's a piano for anyone who wants to play and even an art gallery; board games. Early evening sees a cheerful bustle which later settles to a more tranquil and relaxing atmosphere. Drinks include a good wine list of around 230 wines with 18 by the glass (there is a good wine shop in the reception area), organic ginger beer, lemonade and fruit juices and three real ales on handpump that might be from Bowland, Copper Dragon and Moorhouses. Staff are courteous and friendly. The building is nicely positioned with delightful views from the riverside bar and adjacent terrace. They own several miles of trout, salmon and sea-trout fishing on the Hodder, and can arrange shooting and make up a picnic hamper.

🍴 **Besides lunchtime sandwiches, well presented bar food might include soup, smoked salmon, belly pork, fish pie, grilled norfolk kipper, crispy confit of goosnargh duck legs with black olive potato cake, lancashire hotpot, and puddings; they also have a separate dining room menu.** *Starters/Snacks: £4.50 to £9.00. Main Courses: £9.20 to £17.90. Puddings: £5.10*

Free house ~ Licensee Charles Bowman ~ Real ale ~ Bar food (12-2, 7.30-9.30) ~ Restaurant ~ (01200) 448222 ~ Children welcome ~ Dogs allowed in bar and bedrooms ~ Open 10-midnight ~ Bedrooms: £83B/£113B

Recommended by Steve Whalley, Noel Grundy, GLD, Noel Thomas, Mark Sowery, Dr Clive Elphick, Yvonne and Mike Meadley, Donna and Roger, David Heath, John and Helen Rushton, John and Sylvia Harrop, Jo Lilley, Simon Calvert

WRAY
SD6067   MAP 7

Inn at Wray

2 miles E of Hornby off A683 Kirkby Lonsdale—Lancaster; LA2 8QN

Comfortable and civilised family-run dining pub with good, interesting food

In a quietly attractive village in the Lune Valley, this dining pub has impressed readers for its friendly welcome. Thoughtfully updated, it's fresh and airy with cream walls and some light exposed stone. As you go in, a snug room, feeling just like a little sitting room, has comfortable soft leather sofas and easy chairs and a low table (with magazines) in front of a coal fire. A short corridor opens into further rooms, with oriental rugs on polished boards or flagstones, logs stacked by a big fire in one, a big woodburning stove in another and quite a few carefully placed pictures – one lot more a collection of grand frames, really. A larger end room has rather more imposing tables and a cabinet of home-made preserves, cordials and country wines. Two elegant upstairs carpeted dining rooms have comfortably upholstered chairs around smart tables and a wall of books; welcoming and obliging service; piped music. They have Thwaites Wainwrights and a beer brewed for them by Tirril on handpump, and do good coffee.

🍴 As well as a couple of particularly good value meal deals (notably on Tuesdays and Wednesdays, when you can get starters and puddings for 1p when you order a main course from a special menu), enjoyable food includes sandwiches, soup, confit of duck, devilled whitebait, three-cheese soufflé, pot-roasted beef with yorkshire pudding, goosnargh chicken breast with fresh basil pesto, chargrilled tuna steak, wild mushroom and spinach pancakes, and puddings. Starters/Snacks: £3.50 to £7.95. Main Courses: £8.95 to £13.95. Puddings: £4.90

Free house ~ Licensee Phillip Montgomery ~ Real ale ~ Bar food ~ Restaurant ~ (01524) 221722 ~ Children welcome ~ Dogs allowed in bar ~ Open 12-3, 6-11; 12-11 Sat; 12-10.30 Sun; closed Mon ~ Bedrooms: £45B/£65B

Recommended by Karen Eliot, Paul Boot, Chris and Meredith Owen, Dr Kevan Tucker, Maurice and Gill McMahon

YEALAND CONYERS   SD5074   MAP 7

New Inn

3 miles from M6 junction 35; village signposted off A6; LA5 9SJ

Good generous food all day and a warm welcome at this village pub near the M6

This ivy-covered 17th-c village pub is usefully positioned for walks through Leighton Moss RSPB reserve and up Warton Crag. At its side a sheltered lawn has picnic-sets among colourful roses and flowering shrubs. The cosy beamed bar is traditionally furnished with sets of plush upholstered stools grouped around intimately set round tables on patterned carpet, and there's a log fire in the big stone fireplace. On the right, two communicating blue-themed dining rooms have closely set tables with dark wood pub chairs on navy carpet, navy tablecloths and blue spriggy wallpaper; piped music. Robinsons Hartleys XB and another of their beers are served on handpump alongside around 30 malt whiskies; very friendly service.

🍴 Hearty helpings of bar food include sandwiches, baguettes and baked potatoes (all with interesting fillings), goats cheese salad, cumberland sausage and mash, spicy bean tortilla, salmon fillet, scampi, battered haddock and chips (Fridays), beef in beer, and a good choice of puddings such as treacle tart and sticky toffee pudding with butterscotch sauce; children's menu. Starters/Snacks: £4.50 to £6.95. Main Courses: £5.95 to £11.50. Puddings: £4.85 to £6.50

Robinsons ~ Tenants Bill Tully and Charlotte Pinder ~ Real ale ~ Bar food (11.30(12 Sun)-9.30) ~ Restaurant ~ (01524) 732938 ~ Children welcome ~ Dogs allowed in bar ~ Open 11.30-11; 12-10.30 Sun

Recommended by Canon George Farran, Dr Kevan Tucker, Dennis Jones, Dr and Mrs A K Clarke, Dr D J and Mrs S C Walker

LUCKY DIP

Besides the fully inspected pubs, you might like to try these Lucky Dips recommended to us and described by readers (if you do, please send us reports: feedback@goodguides.com).

ADLINGTON [SD6114]
Bay Horse PR6 9ER [Babylon Lane, Heath Charnock]: Country pub popular with walkers, good well priced food, great choice of beers, log fires in cosy bar; children welcome, extensive crown bowling green behind, bedrooms, open all day (Yvonne and Mike Meadley)

ALTRINCHAM [SJ7689]
Railway Inn WA14 5NT [153 Manchester Rd (A56), Broadheath]: Early Victorian, with lounge, bar, games room (darts and dominoes), snug and dining room, church pews, well kept bargain Holts Bitter and Mild, friendly landlady and locals; back terrace, open all day (the Didler)

APPLEY BRIDGE [SD5210]
Dicconson Arms WN6 9DY [B5375 (Appley
Lane N)/A5209, handy for M6 junction 27]:
Well run and civilised, with good nicely
presented food (all day Sun), friendly
attentive service, two well kept ales in
uncluttered bar area with clubby chairs,
dining room beyond, pine floors,
woodburner; some seats outside
(Jeremy King, Mr and Mrs I Templeton)

ARKHOLME [SD5872]
Bay Horse LA6 1AS [B6254 Carnforth—
Kirkby Lonsdale]: Neatly kept and homely old
three-room country pub, one or two well
kept changing ales, friendly landlord and
prompt service, enjoyable home-made food
inc children's; lovely inglenook, pictures of
long-lost London pubs; disabled access,
bowling green, handy for Lune Valley walks,
cl Mon *(MLR, Tony and Maggie Harwood)*

BARLEY [SD8240]
Pendle BB12 9JX: Friendly 1930s pub in
shadow of Pendle Hill, three cosy rooms, two
open fires, well kept local ales, simple
substantial pub food (all day wknds),
conservatory; garden, lovely village, good
walking country, bedrooms *(Len Beattie)*

BARTON [SD5137]
Sparling PR3 5AA [A6 N of Broughton]:
Popular contemporary gastropub with some
imaginative food inc set deals, roomy bar
with comfortable settees and other seats,
plenty of tables in linked areas off, wood
and flagstoned floors; real ales, good choice
of wines by the glass, bright young staff;
children welcome, handy for M6
(Margaret Dickinson)

BELMONT [SD6715]
☆ *Black Dog* BL7 8AB [Church St (A675)]:
Nicely set Holts pub with their usual good
value food (all day Fri-Sun, not Tues
evening); bargain beers, friendly prompt
staff, cheery small-roomed traditional core,
coal fires, picture-window extension;
children welcome, seats outside with
moorland views above village, attractive
partly covered smokers' area, good walks,
decent well priced bedrooms (breakfast from
9am), open all day *(Len Beattie,
Peter Dearing, Peter Heaton, Simon Le Fort,
Yvonne and Mike Meadley, the Didler,
Norma and Noel Thomas, LYM)*

BIRKENHEAD [SJ3289]
Stork CH41 6JN [Price St]: Early Victorian,
four well restored civilised rooms around
island bar, polished mosaic floor, old
photographs, several well kept changing
ales, bargain basic food wkdy lunchtime and
early evening, tiled façade; open all day
(the Didler, Pete Baker)

BLACKSTONE EDGE [SD9617]
☆ *White House* OL15 0LG [A58 Ripponden—
Littleborough, just W of B6138]: Beautifully
placed moorland dining pub with remote
views, emphasis on good value hearty food
from sandwiches up (all day Sun), prompt
friendly service, well kept Theakstons Best
and changing regional guests, belgian

bottled beers; cheerful atmosphere, carpeted
main bar with hot fire, other areas off, most
tables used for food; children welcome
*(Andy and Jill Kassube, Gordon and
Margaret Ormondroyd, LYM)*

BOLTON [SD7109]
Howcroft BL1 2JU [Pool St]: Friendly local
serving as tap for good Bank Top ales, also
guest beers, enjoyable good value pubby
lunches, lots of small screened-off rooms
around central servery with fine glass and
woodwork inc cosy snug with coal fire;
bright and airy front room, conservatory, pub
games; crown bowling green, open all day
(the Didler)
Sweet Green BL3 6DD [Crook St]: Friendly
and well run with four small rooms off
central bar, attractive tiled fireplace, three
regular and eight changing ales, bar food inc
sandwiches, pub games; seats outside, open
all day *(Franklin McKinstry)*
Wilton Arms BL1 7BT [Belmont Rd, Horrocks
Fold]: Friendly low-beamed roadside pub,
good choice of enjoyable well priced fresh
food, well kept ales, open fires; garden
overlooking valley, Pennine walks, open all
day *(W K Wood)*

BOLTON BY BOWLAND [SD7849]
Coach & Horses BB7 4NW [Main St]:
Refurbished stone-built beamed
pub/restaurant with bar and two dining
areas, good interesting food from open
sandwiches up at reasonable prices,
changing ales inc Bowland, Copper Dragon
and Moorhouses, good choice of wines,
friendly welcoming staff, log fires; children
welcome, tables out at back, lovely
streamside village with interesting church,
bedrooms *(BB, Neil and Jacqui Victor-Corrie,
Mr and Mrs P Eastwood)*

BRINDLE [SD5924]
☆ *Cavendish Arms* PR6 8NG [3 miles from
M6 junction 29, by A6 and B5256 (Sandy
Lane)]: Refurbished traditional village pub
dating from 15th c, welcoming and popular,
with good inexpensive home-made food from
sandwiches up inc all-day Sun roasts, Banks's
and three changing guest ales; beams, cosy
snugs with open fires, stained-glass
windows, carpets throughout; children
welcome, dogs in tap room, heated canopied
terrace with water feature, more tables in
side garden, good walks, open all day
*(Dave Braisted, Yvonne and Mike Meadley,
Donna and Roger, LYM)*

BURY [SD7912]
Brown Cow BL8 1DA [Woodhill Rd, Burrs
Country Park]: Roomy open-plan bar, quiet,
simple and very out of the way, with
reasonably priced pubby food and two
real ales; garden with play area, steam
East Lancs Railway runs by garden *(TB,
Marlene and Jim Godfrey)*
Trackside BL9 0EY [East Lancs Railway
Station, Bolton St]: Welcoming busy station
bar by steam East Lancs Railway, bright, airy
and clean with nine changing ales, bottled
imports, farm cider, good choice of bargain

wkdy lunches (not Mon, Tues, from breakfast time till 4pm wknds), fine display of beer labels on ceiling; children welcome till 7.30pm, pavement tables, open all day *(the Didler, TB)*

CARNFORTH [SD5173]

Longlands LA6 1JH [Tewitfield, about 2 miles N; A6070, off A6]: Bustling family-run village inn with good local beer range, friendly helpful staff, good interesting food in bar and restaurant (worth booking); live music Mon; bedrooms, self-catering cottages *(MLR, Tony and Maggie Harwood, Alan and Eve Harding)*

CHORLTON CUM HARDY [SJ8193]

Horse & Jockey M21 9HS: Refurbished low-beamed pub with mock-Tudor façade, half a dozen ales from smaller breweries served by knowledgeable chatty staff (own microbrewery planned), all-day bar food, more restauranty things in high-ceilinged evening/wknd dining room (part of former Victorian brewery); good mix of customers from mothers with prams to the local history society; dogs allowed in tap room, picnic-sets on front terrace looking across to green, open all day *(Pete Yearsley)*

CONDER GREEN [SD4556]

Stork LA2 0AN [just off A588]: Fine spot where River Conder joins the Lune estuary among bleak marshes, two blazing log fires in rambling dark-panelled rooms, good reasonably priced food with south african influences, friendly efficient staff, real ales such as Black Sheep; children welcome, handy for Glasson Dock, bedrooms, open all day *(Tony and Maggie Harwood, LYM)*

CROSBY [SJ3100]

Crows Nest L23 7XY [Victoria Rd, Great Crosby]: Unspoilt characterful roadside local with cosy bar, snug and Victorian-style lounge, all neatly looked after by welcoming landlady, well kept Cains, Theakstons and guests; tables outside, open all day *(the Didler)*

CROSTON [SD4818]

Grapes PR26 9RA [Town Rd]: Popular chatty village pub with well kept Holts ales and guests, good freshly prepared food inc blackboard specials, three small pubby rooms and restaurant; seats outside *(Yvonne and Mike Meadley)*

DALTON [SD4907]

Beacon WN8 7RR [Beacon Lane]: Refurbished pub opp Beacon Country Park, well kept Jennings, Marstons and guest ales, interesting food all day; children welcome, dogs in bar, garden with play area *(George Cowie, Frances Gosnell)*

DENTON [SJ9395]

Lowes Arms M34 3FF [Hyde Rd (A57)]: For now no longer brewing its own LAB ales but serving good local Hornbeam and Phoenix, jovial landlord and efficient staff, good bargain food inc vegetarian; separate large games room with juke box; tables outside, smoking shelter, open all day wknds *(Dennis Jones)*

ECCLES [SJ7798]

Albert Edward M30 0LS [Church St]: Cheery roadside local with three rooms, flagstones and old tiles, fire, bargain Sam Smiths; small back terrace, open all day *(the Didler)*

Lamb M30 0BP [Regent St (A57)]: Full-blooded Edwardian three-room local, splendid etched windows, fine woodwork and furnishings, extravagantly tiled stairway, trophies in display case, bargain Holts and lunchtime sandwiches; full-size snooker table in original billiards room, friendly atmosphere; open all day *(the Didler)*

Royal Oak M30 0EN [Barton Lane]: Large old-fashioned Edwardian corner pub, several busy rooms off corridor, handsome tilework, mosaic floors and fittings, well kept cheap Holts, good licensees, pool; children allowed daytime in back lounge (may be organ singalongs), open all day, Sun from 7pm *(the Didler)*

Stanley Arms M30 0QN [Eliza Ann St/ Liverpool Rd (A57), Patricroft]: Lively unspoilt mid-Victorian corner local with bargain Holts, popular front bar, hatch serving lobby and corridor to small back rooms, one with cast-iron range, lunchtime cobs, friendly licensees; open all day *(the Didler)*

White Lion M30 0ND [Liverpool Rd, Patricroft, a mile from M63 junction 2]: Welcoming Edwardian traditional local, clean, tidy and popular with older people; great value Holts, games in lively public bar, other rooms off tiled side drinking corridor inc one with piano *(the Didler)*

ECCLESTON [SD5117]

☆ *Original Farmers Arms* PR7 5QS [Towngate (B5250, off A581 Chorley—Southport)]: Long low-beamed pub/restaurant, wide choice of enjoyable food all day inc bargain specials and popular Sun roasts; cheery décor, good changing choice of real ales, several wines by the glass, efficient smart staff; piped music and machines, parking can be tight when busy; children welcome, comfortable good value bedrooms some with own bathroom, open all day *(Paul and June Holmes, Jeremy King, BB)*

EUXTON [SD5518]

Euxton Mills PR7 6JD [A49 S, 3 miles from M6 junction 28]: Neatly kept roomy pub with good choice of bargain food, friendly service, well kept ales such as Jennings *(Yvonne and Mike Meadley)*

FLEETWOOD [SD3348]

☆ *North Euston* FY7 6BN [Esplanade, nr tram terminus]: Big architecturally interesting Victorian railway hotel dominating the seafront, extensive pubby bar giving great sea and hill views; friendly helpful staff, good changing real ale choice such as Greene King, Timothy Taylors and Theakstons, enjoyable lunchtime food from sandwiches up, lots of separate-seeming areas inc large family room, café-bar and two restaurants; live music Fri-Sun; seats outside, comfortable bedrooms, open all day (Sun afternoon break) *(Margaret Dickinson, BB)*

FORTON [SD4950]

New Holly PR3 0BL [Lancaster Rd (A6)]: Smart spotless family-friendly pub, wide choice of good generous sensibly priced food using local supplies, Thwaites ales, brisk friendly service; tables out under cover, lovely hanging baskets, play area, bedrooms *(Margaret Dickinson, Mrs Nikki Mellor)*

GALGATE [SD4855]

Plough LA2 0LQ [A6 S of Lancaster, handy for M6 junction 33]: 17th-c former coaching inn nr Lancaster Canal, beams and brasses, log fire, decent all-day food, real ales, dining room; children welcome, picnic-sets and hanging baskets in nice flower-filled garden, open all day *(Tony and Maggie Harwood)*

GARSTANG [SD4945]

☆ *Th'Owd Tithebarn* PR3 1PA [off Church St]: Large barn with flagstoned terrace overlooking Lancaster Canal marina, Victorian country life theme with long refectory table, old kitchen range, masses of farm tools, stuffed animals and birds, flagstones and high rafters; generous simple food all day from filled baguettes up, Black Sheep and York ales, good value wines by the glass, quieter parlour welcoming children; piped music; open all day summer *(Dr Kevan Tucker, LYM, Abi Benson)*

GOOSNARGH [SD5738]

☆ *Horns* PR3 2FJ [pub signed off B5269, towards Chipping]: Plush early 18th-c inn with relaxed atmosphere, neatly kept rooms with patterned carpets and log fires, popular food from pub standards up, Bowland ales, a dozen wines by the glass, good choice of malts, friendly service; piped music; children welcome, garden, caravan park, six clean chintzy bedrooms (some with road noise), not far from M6 *(LYM, Donna and Roger, Mark Sheard, W K Wood)*

☆ *Stags Head* PR3 2AU [Whittingham Lane (B5269)]: Lots of separate mainly old-world areas rambling around a central servery, plenty of nice features inc proper old-fashioned radiators, open fire too; good value interesting home-made food from local produce (even make their own pork scratchings), children's helpings, good service, well kept changing ales, popular restaurant; piped music, and live music Fri nights; tables out in pleasant pergola with lawn *(Margaret Dickinson, BB)*

GREAT HARWOOD [SD7331]

Victoria BB6 7EP [St Johns St]: Splendid beer range with Bowland Gold and eight changing guests, friendly landlady and regulars, unspoilt traditional Edwardian layout with five rooms off central bar, one with darts, one with pool, two quiet snugs, some handsome tiling; tables out behind, opens 4.30pm (3 Fri, all day wknds), cl wkdy lunchtimes *(the Didler)*

GRINDLETON [SD7545]

Duke of York BB7 4QR [off A59 via Chatburn; Brow Top]: Smartly refurbished

dining pub in attractive Ribble Valley countryside, good imaginative well presented food from chef/proprietor inc set deals, good wines, efficient friendly service; various areas inc one with open fire, Black Sheep and Thwaites; picnic-sets on raised decking, garden, cl Mon *(John and Sylvia Harrop, John and Helen Rushton, John and Eleanor Holdsworth)*

HAWKSHAW [SD7515]

☆ *Red Lion* BL8 4JS [Ramsbottom Rd]: Roomy, comfortable and attractive pub/hotel, friendly welcome and efficient cheerful service, good generous fresh local food in cosy bar and separate well run restaurant, good changing ales; comfortable if rather creaky bedrooms, quiet spot by River Irwell, open for food all day wknds *(W K Wood, John and Sylvia Harrop)*

Waggon & Horses BL8 4JL [Bolton Rd]: Short choice of good well priced home-made food using fresh local ingredients (worth booking Fri, Sat evenings) in bar and small restaurant, good service *(Yvonne and Mike Meadley, Rachel and Ross Gavin, Norma and Noel Thomas)*

HESKIN GREEN [SD5315]

☆ *Farmers Arms* PR7 5NP [Wood Lane (B5250, N of M6 junction 27)]: Family-run country pub, popular and cheerful, with wide choice of good value home cooking inc vegetarian in two-level dining area, helpful staff, real ales inc John Smiths; heavy black beams, sparkling brasses, china and stuffed animals, public bar with darts; piped music and some live, Sky TV; picnic-sets in big colourful garden, play area, more tables front and side, comfortable bedrooms, open all day wknds *(BB, Margaret Dickinson)*

HEST BANK [SD4766]

☆ *Hest Bank Inn* LA2 6DN [Hest Bank Lane; off A6 just N of Lancaster]: Good fresh food in picturesque three-bar coaching inn, nice setting close to Morecambe Bay (so gets very wide range of customers in the easy-going bar areas), five well kept ales, decent wines, friendly helpful young staff, separate attractive refurbished restaurant area with pleasant conservatory; children welcome, plenty of tables out by Lancaster Canal, open all day *(Tony and Maggie Harwood, BB)*

HEYSHAM [SD4161]

Royal LA3 2RN [Main St]: Four changing ales, well priced wines and decent food inc early evening bargains in charming early 16th-c low-beamed two-bar pub; no dogs at meal times; tables out in front, good-sized sheltered garden, pretty fishing village with great views from interesting church *(Tony and Maggie Harwood, Abi Benson)*

HYDE [SJ9495]

Cheshire Ring SK14 2BJ [Manchester Rd (A57, between M67 junctions 2 and 3)]: Welcoming pub tied to Beartown brewery, their good value ales kept well, guest beers and imports on tap, farm ciders and perries, good house wines, bargain home-made curries Thurs; piped and live music; open all day wknds, from 4pm Mon and Tues, 1pm Weds-Fri *(Dennis Jones, the Didler)*

Joshua Bradley SK14 5EZ [Stockport Rd, Gee Cross]: Former mansion handsomely converted to pub/restaurant keeping panelling, moulded ceilings and imposing fireplaces; good range of well priced pubby food, Hydes ales, friendly efficient staff; heated terrace, play area *(Dennis Jones)*

Sportsman SK14 2NN [Mottram Rd]: Bright cheerful Victorian local, Pennine ales and several changing guests (frequent beer festivals), welcoming licensees, bargain bar food, cuban restaurant, open fires; pub games, full-size snooker table upstairs; children and dogs welcome *(Dennis Jones, the Didler)*

IRBY [SJ2586]

Irby Mill CH49 3NT [Mill Lane, off Greasby Rd]: Converted miller's cottage (original windmill demolished 1898) gaining popularity under new management, eight well kept ales, good choice of wines by the glass, decent reasonably priced food all day (till 6pm Sun); two low-beamed flagstoned rooms and comfortable carpeted lounge, coal-effect gas fire, interesting old photographs and history; tables on terraces and side grass, open all day *(David Duff, Tony Tollitt, BB)*

LANCASTER [SD4761]

Ring o' Bells LA1 1RE [King St]: Clean, warm and friendly with enjoyable competitively priced home-made food, well kept ales such as Coniston Bluebird, good choice of other drinks; big garden, summer barbecues *(Natalie Hughes, Tony and Maggie Harwood)*

Robert Gillow LA1 1HP: Small newly opened pub with traditional feel, friendly staff and customers, nice reasonably priced food inc all-day snacks, several well kept beers, cocktails, good coffee, pleasant upstairs restaurant; regular live jazz, folk and blues, Tues quiz night; piped music; open all day from 9am and till late Fri, Sat *(George and Carolyn Hill)*

☆ **Sun** LA1 1ET [Church St]: Both traditional and comfortably contemporary, good range of customers, four well kept Lancaster ales and guests, plenty of continental beers, good choice of wines by the glass, some unusual teas and coffees, bar food (till 7pm Fri, Sat evenings); beamed bar with panelling, chunky modern tables, several fireplaces (the biggest filled with a huge cask), conservatory; piped music, TV; children welcome away from bar, terrace, comfortable bedrooms, open all day *(John Ashford, Jo Lilley, Simon Calvert, Karen Eliot, Paul Boot, Tony and Maggie Harwood, Rob and Catherine Dunster, Andy and Jill Kassube, LYM, Joe Green, Stephen H Johnston, Ray and Winifred Halliday, David Kirkcaldy)*

Wagon & Horses LA1 1RD [St Georges Quay]: Well refurbished old quayside pub, good

choice of enjoyable food (all day Sun) inc deals, Robinsons ales, woodburner; Sky TV; heated covered courtyard, newly done bedrooms, parking may be difficult, open all day *(Tony and Maggie Harwood)*

LEIGH [SJ6599]

Waterside WN7 4DB [Twist Lane]: Civilised pub in tall converted 19th-c warehouses by Bridgewater Canal, handy for indoor and outdoor markets, wide choice of enjoyable bargain food all day inc OAP and other deals, Greene King ales, good friendly service, chatty lunchtime atmosphere; live music or disco Thurs-Sat; children welcome, disabled access and facilities, plenty of waterside tables, ducks and swans, open all day *(Ben Williams)*

LIVERPOOL [SJ3489]

☆ **Baltic Fleet** L1 8DQ [Wapping, nr Albert Dock]: Unpretentious triangular pub with easy convivial local atmosphere, wide range of interesting beers inc own good Wapping brews, good choice of wines by the glass, enjoyable straightforward well priced food (not Sat lunchtime); bare boards, big arched windows, simple mix of furnishings, nautical paraphernalia, newspapers, upstairs lounge; piped music, TV; children welcome in eating areas, dogs in bar, back terrace, open all day *(LYM, Pete Baker, Tony and Wendy Hobden, Eric Larkham, Rob and Catherine Dunster, the Didler)*

Belvedere L7 7EB [Sugnall St]: Unspoilt Victorian pub with friendly chatty bar, original fittings inc etched glass, coal fires, well kept Copper Dragon and guests, good pizzas; darts and other games; open all day *(Pete Baker, the Didler)*

☆ **Brewery Tap** L8 5XJ [Stanhope St]: Victorian pub with full Cains range at reasonable prices, guest beers, friendly efficient staff, good value food wkdy lunchtimes; nicely understated décor, wooden floors, plush raised side snug, interesting old prints and breweriana, handsome bar, gas fire, daily papers; sports TV, no dogs; children till 8pm, disabled access, brewery tours, open all day *(the Didler, Eric Larkham)*

Central Commercial L1 1JP [opp Central Station]: Classic Victorian pub with mahogany woodwork, engraved glass and mirrors, marble pillars and elaborately moulded domed ceiling; Thwaites Original and a guest; piped music *(the Didler, LYM)*

Crown L1 1JQ [Lime St]: Well preserved art nouveau showpiece with fine tiled fireplace and copper bar front, dark leather banquettes, splendid ceiling in airy corner bar, smaller back room with another good fireplace, impressive staircase sweeping up under cupola to handsome area with ornate windows; generous bargain food, well priced Cains and guest beers *(the Didler, Tony and Wendy Hobden, Brian and Janet Ainscough)*

☆ **Dispensary** L1 2SP [Renshaw St]: Small chatty central pub with well kept Cains ales and guests, bottled imports, friendly staff, no food; polished panelling, marvellous etched windows, bare boards, comfortable raised back bar, Victorian medical artefacts; sports TVs; open all day *(Tony and Wendy Hobden, Eric Larkham, Maurice and Gill McMahon, the Didler, John and Helen Rushton)*

☆ *Doctor Duncan* L1 1HF [St Johns Lane]: Friendly Victorian pub with several rooms inc impressive back area with pillared and vaulted tiled ceiling; full Cains range and guest beers well kept, belgian beers on tap, enjoyable good value food, pleasant helpful service, daily papers; may be piped music; can get lively in evenings, busy wknds; family room, open all day *(Giles and Annie Francis, Eric Larkham, the Didler)*

Everyman Bistro L1 9BH [Hope St, below Everyman Theatre]: Popular low-ceilinged tiled-floor clattery basement with long wooden tables, four well kept ales such as Brimstage and George Wrights, side room with good value fresh food; open all day, cl Sun *(the Didler)*

Fly in the Loaf L1 9AS [Hardman St]: Former bakery with smart gleaming bar serving Okells (from Isle of Man) and up to six ales from smaller brewers, foreign beers too, popular home-made food; one long room, small raised front area with sofas and high stools; sports TV, upstairs lavatories, open all day, till midnight wknds *(Eric Larkham, Martin Grosberg)*

Globe L1 1HW [Cases St, opp Central Station]: Chatty traditional little local in busy shopping area (can get packed), friendly staff, well kept ales such as Black Sheep, Cains and Caledonian Deuchars IPA, lunchtime filled cobs; sloping floor, quieter cosy back room, prints of old Liverpool; 60s piped music; open all day *(the Didler)*

Lion L2 2BP [Moorfields, off Tithebarn St]: Beautifully preserved ornate Victorian tavern, great changing beer choice, over 80 malt whiskies, friendly landlord interested in pub's history, lunchtime food inc splendid cheese and pie specialities; sparkling etched glass and serving hatches in central bar, unusual wallpaper and matching curtains, big mirrors, panelling and tilework, two small back lounges, one with fine glass dome, coal fire; silent fruit machine; open all day *(the Didler, Jeremy King)*

Monro L1 5AG [Duke St]: Stylishly refurbished gastropub, popular comfortable and well run, with good choice of interesting food inc vegetarian menu and lunchtime/ early evening deals; Marstons and guests from small bar, fast friendly service; open all day *(the Didler)*

Peter Kavanaghs L8 7LY [Egerton St, off Catherine St]: Shuttered Victorian pub with interesting décor in several small rooms inc old-world murals, stained glass and lots of bric-a-brac (bicycle hanging from ceiling); piano, wooden settles and real fires, well kept Cains, Greene King, Wychwood and guests, friendly licensees happy to show you

around inc cellars, popular with locals and students; open all day *(the Didler, Eric Larkham, Pete Baker)*

Richmond L1 1EB [Williamson St]: Popular small corner pub in pedestrianised area, nice old interior and fittings inc an original Bass mirror, Bass, Cains, Timothy Taylors Landlord and changing guests, over 50 malts; sports TV; tables out at front, open all day from 10am *(the Didler)*

Roscoe Head L1 2SX [Roscoe St]: Unassuming old local with cosy bar and two other spotless unspoilt little rooms, friendly long-serving landlady, well kept Jennings, Marstons, Tetleys and guests from smaller brewers, inexpensive home-made lunches, interesting memorabilia, traditional games inc cribbage; Tues quiz; open all day *(the Didler, Eric Larkham, Pete Baker)*

Ship & Mitre L2 2JH [Dale St]: Friendly local with fine art deco exterior and ship-like interior, popular with university people, up to 12 changing unusual ales (many beer festivals), over 70 bottled continentals, farm ciders, good value basic food (all day Fri-Sun); upstairs function room with original 1930s décor; well behaved children till 7pm, dogs welcome, open all day *(the Didler, Martin Grosberg, Eric Larkham)*

Swan L1 4DQ [Wood St]: Neon sign for this busy unsmart three-floor pub, bare boards and dim lighting, well kept Hydes and guests, bottled belgian beers, Weston's farm cider, good value cobs and wkdy lunches, friendly staff; loud juke box draws younger crowd, open all day *(the Didler)*

☆ *Thomas Rigbys* L2 2EZ [Dale St]: Spacious beamed and panelled Victorian pub with mosaic flooring, old tiles and etched glass, great range of beers inc Okells and imports; impressively long bar, steps up to main area, table service, reasonably priced hearty home-made food all day till 7pm; disabled access, outside seating, open all day *(the Didler, John and Helen Rushton)*

Volunteer L22 8QR [East St]: Classic friendly old local with superb etched glass and wood panelling, busy bar, comfortable lounge (table service here), well kept Black Sheep, Tetleys and guests, newspapers; open all day *(the Didler)*

White Star L2 6PT [Rainford Gdns, off Matthew St]: Lively traditional local dating from 18th c, cosy bar, lots of woodwork, boxing photographs, White Star shipping line and Beatles' memorabilia (they used to rehearse in back room); well kept ales inc Bass, Bowland and Caledonian Deuchars IPA, basic lunchtime food, friendly staff; sports TVs; open all day *(Pete Baker, the Didler)*

LONGRIDGE [SD6137]

Corporation Arms PR3 2YJ [Lower Rd (B6243)]: Comfortably refurbished 18th-c pub next to reservoir, wide range of largely traditional food all day, small helpings available, three or four changing ales such as Bowland and Brysons, lots of malt whiskies, nice atmosphere in three small linked rooms and restaurant; good bed and breakfast, open all day *(Andy and Jill Kassube)*

LOW MOOR [SD7241]

Edisford Bridge Hotel BB7 3LJ [B6243 W]: Lovely spot above River Ribble, enjoyable food inc bargain lunch, friendly staff, well kept Jennings ales, several quiet rooms with separate dining area; pleasantly shady garden behind *(KC, Caroline and Gavin Callow)*

LYDIATE [SD3604]

Scotch Piper L31 4HD [Southport Rd; A4157]: Medieval thatched pub, well worn-in, with heavy low beams, flagstones, thick stone walls and dogs sprawled in front of roaring fires, Banks's and a guest from tiny counter in main room, corridor to middle room with darts and back snug, no food; bikers' night Weds, outside lavatories; big garden, open all day wknds *(the Didler)*

MANCHESTER [SJ8498]

Angel M4 4BR [Angel St, off Rochdale Rd]: Good value food from standards to upscale dishes inc game and fish, monthly gourmet evenings, good wine choice, Facers Angel (brewed for the pub) and three changing guests, bottled beers, farm ciders; smaller upstairs dining room, art exhibitions; children and dogs welcome, disabled facilities, tables out in small back area, open all day *(Chris Johnson, Jeremy King, the Didler)*

☆ *Ape & Apple* M2 6HQ [John Dalton St]: Big no-frills open-plan pub, well kept bargain Holts, hearty bar food (Weds curry night), comfortable seats in bare-boards bar with lots of old prints and posters, armchairs in upstairs lounge, friendly atmosphere; piped music, TV area, games machines, Thurs quiz night; unusual brick cube garden, bedrooms, open all day, cl 9pm Sun *(the Didler, Dr and Mrs A K Clarke)*

Bank M2 3FF [Mosley St]: Converted neo-classical bank (originally built as a library in 1802), good range of changing ales, good value food all day inc interesting sausage menu, friendly helpful staff *(Dr and Mrs A K Clarke)*

Bar Fringe M4 5JN [Swan St]: Long bare-boards bar specialising in continental beers, also five changing ales from small local breweries and farm cider; friendly staff, basic snacks till 4pm (no food wknds), daily papers, shelves of empty beer bottles, cartoons, posters, motorcycle hung above door, rock juke box; no children or dogs; tables out behind, open all day, till 12.30 Sat, Sun *(Jeremy King, Chris Johnson, the Didler)*

☆ *Bridge* M3 3BW [Bridge St]: Relaxed dining pub with decent food in bar and back restaurant, changing ales such as Thwaites Lancaster Bomber, pleasant staff; long narrow panelled room with two fine tiled and ironwork fireplaces, leather sofas, upstairs room with small roof terrace; piped music; children welcome till 7pm, back terrace (dogs allowed here), open all day *(Jeremy King)*

Castle M4 1LE [Oldham St, about 200 yards from Piccadilly, on right]: Refurbished 17th-c pub well run by former *Coronation Street* actor, simple traditional front bar, small snug, full Robinsons range from fine bank of handpumps; games in back room, nice tilework outside, live music; open all day *(the Didler)*

Circus M1 4GX [Portland St]: Compact traditional two-room pub with particularly well kept Tetleys from minute corridor bar (or may be table service), friendly landlord, celebrity photographs and football memorabilia, leatherette banquettes in panelled back room; often looks closed but normally open all day (may have to knock); can get very busy *(the Didler, Neil Whitehead, Victoria Anderson)*

City Arms M2 4BQ [Kennedy St, off St Peters Sq]: Tetleys and five quickly changing guests (guess the mystery ale competition on Fri), belgian bottled beers, occasional beer festivals, busy for bargain bar lunches, quick friendly service; coal fires, bare boards and banquettes, prints, panelling and masses of pump clips, handsome tiled façade and corridor; piped music, TV, games machine; wheelchair access but steps down to back lounge, open all day *(the Didler, Dennis Jones)*

Coach & Horses M45 6TB [Old Bury Rd, Whitefield; A665 nr Besses o' the Barn Station]: Thriving early 19th-c Holts pub, several separate rooms, bargain ales, table service, darts, cards; open all day *(the Didler)*

Crescent M5 4PF [Crescent (A6) – opp Salford University]: Three areas off central servery with eight changing ales (regular beer festivals), many continental bottled beers and real cider, friendly licensees and young staff, buoyant local atmosphere (popular with uni); low-priced home-made food inc good breakfast and Weds curry night, bare boards and open fire, plenty of character; pool room, juke box; small enclosed terrace, open all day *(the Didler, Martin Grosberg, Ben Williams)*

Crown & Kettle M4 5EE [Oldham Rd/Great Ancoats St]: Busy three-room refurbished Victorian pub, Greenfield and changing guests (beer festivals), belgian beers, several farm ciders, good choice of malts, popular bar food inc good value Sun roasts; bare boards and carpet, some panelling and exposed brick, decorative windows, ornate high ceilings with remarkably intricate plasterwork, area with bookcases, coal fire; sports TV; open all day *(the Didler, Chris Johnson, BB, Jeremy King)*

Dutton M3 1EU [Park St, Strangeways]: Welcoming old-fashioned corner local nr prison, three unusually shaped cosy rooms, Hydes from central servery, lots of bric-a-brac; open all day *(the Didler)*

Egerton Arms M3 5FP [Gore St, Salford; A6 by station]: Well cared-for characterful local with chandeliers, art nouveau lamps, attractive prints and dark varnished tables, well kept low-priced Holts and guests, friendly service; small room with pool and TV; piped music, silent fruit machines; open all day *(the Didler, Jeremy King)*

Font M1 5NP [New Wakefield St]: Modern open-plan café-style bar by railway viaduct, good home-cooked food, well kept changing ales (usually have Bazens), lots of foreign bottled beers, reasonable prices, downstairs bar; loud music evenings when popular with students, monthly live bands; open all day *(the Didler)*

Grey Horse M1 4QX [Portland St, nr Piccadilly]: Small traditional one-bar Hydes local, their Bitter and Mild kept well, some unusual malt whiskies, friendly licensees, panelled servery with colourful gantry, lots of prints, photographs and plates; piped 60s/70s music, small TV, net curtains; can bring good sandwiches from next door, open all day *(the Didler, Dr and Mrs A K Clarke)*

Hare & Hounds M4 4AA [Shudehill, behind Arndale]: Old-fashioned 18th-c local with long narrow bar linking front snug and comfortable back lounge, notable tilework, panelling and stained glass, cheap Holts beer, friendly staff; loud piped music, TV; open all day *(Joe Green, Jeremy King, the Didler)*

Jolly Angler M1 2JW [Ducie St]: Plain one-room backstreet local, down to earth and friendly, with well kept Hydes ales, coal or peat fire, informal folk nights Thurs, Sat; darts, pool and sports TV; open all day Sat *(Jeremy King, the Didler, BB)*

Kings Arms M3 6AN [Bloom St, Salford]: Plain tables, bare boards and flagstones contrasting with opulent maroon/purple décor and stained glass, changing ales, good value lunchtime food (till 6.30pm, not Sat); juke box, music, poetry or theatre nights upstairs; open all day (cl Sun evening) *(the Didler)*

Knott Fringe M3 4LY [Deansgate]: Friendly modern glass-fronted café-bar under railway arch by Castlefield heritage site; Marble organic ales and guests, lots of continental imports, good value all-day food with emphasis on greek dishes, upstairs smokers' balcony overlooking Rochdale Canal; open all day *(Dennis Jones, the Didler, Chris Johnson, Dr and Mrs A K Clarke)*

Lass o' Gowrie M1 7DB [36 Charles St; off Oxford St at BBC]: Unspoilt tiled Victorian sidestreet local, welcoming big-windowed long bar with cosy room off, stripped brickwork, nine well kept ales inc Greene King, Wadworths and a good house beer (Betty's Bitter) brewed by Outstanding; bargain food (good home-made pies), friendly service; terrace overlooking river, open all day *(the Didler, LYM)*

Mark Addy M3 5EJ [Stanley St, off New Bailey St, Salford]: Unusual converted waiting rooms for boat passengers, barrel-vaulted red sandstone bays with wide glassed-in brick arches, cast-iron pillars and flagstones, views over river; now a full range of food inc signature cheese and pâté board, four real ales, lots of wines by the glass, fast friendly service; piped music, sports TV facing bar; flower-filled waterside courtyard *(Dennis Jones, LYM)*

☆ **Mr Thomas Chop House** M2 7AR [Cross St]: Good generous home-made lunchtime food inc some unusual choices, friendly staff coping well when busy, ales inc Bass, Boddingtons and Lees, good wines by the glass; attractive Victorian décor, basic front bar with bare boards, panelling, original gas lamp fittings and stools at wall and window shelves, back green-tiled eating area with two rows of tables, period features inc wrought-iron gates for wine racks; open all day *(Jeremy King, the Didler)*

New Oxford M3 6DB [Bexley Sq, Salford]: Up to 15 well kept changing beers and a house ale brewed by Northern (regular beer festivals), good range of imported beers, farm ciders, friendly staff; light and airy café-style feel in small front bar and back room, coal fire, good value basic food till 6pm; nice terrace, open all day *(the Didler, Ben Williams)*

Paramount M1 4BH [Oxford St]: Well run Wetherspoons with their usual good prices and good value food, particularly friendly service, bargain beer festivals *(Ben Williams)*

☆ **Peveril of the Peak** M1 5JQ [Great Bridgewater St]: Vivid art nouveau green external tilework, interesting pictures, lots of mahogany, mirrors and stained or frosted glass, log fire, very welcoming family service; changing mainstream ales from central servery, cheap basic lunchtime food (not Sun), three sturdily furnished bare-boards rooms, busy lunchtime but friendly and homely evenings; TV; children welcome, pavement tables, cl wknd lunchtimes, open all day Fri *(Jeremy King, the Didler, Dr Kevan Tucker, Neil Whitehead, Victoria Anderson, LYM)*

Plough M18 7FB [Hyde Rd (A57), Gorton]: Classic tiling, windows and gantry in unspoilt old Robinsons local, wooden benches in large public bar, two quieter back lounges, small pool room, lots of pub games; TV; open all day *(the Didler)*

☆ **Rain Bar** M1 5JG [Great Bridgewater St]: Bare boards and lots of woodwork in former umbrella works, well kept Lees ales, plenty of wines by the glass, generous good value pubby food all day, friendly efficient staff, relaxed atmosphere, nooks and corners, coal fire in small snug, large upstairs bar/function room; Weds quiz, piped music may be loud, can be busy with young crowd evenings; good back terrace overlooking spruced-up Rochdale Canal, handy for Bridgewater Hall, open all day *(the Didler, Jeremy King, Dr and Mrs A K Clarke)*

Rising Sun M2 5HX [Queen St, off Deansgate]: Long, pleasantly traditional 18th-c pub, clean and well run, with five good changing ales, bargain food inc curry choice and good fish and chips (seating can be cramped), polite staff, old pictures; sports TV *(Jeremy King, Barrie Sneyd)*

Royal Oak M20 6WF [Wilmslow Rd, Didsbury]: Suburban pub with very well kept Marstons Bitter and Pedigree and usually a Jennings ale, huge cheese (and pâté) ploughman's, interesting old music hall posters; tables outside, open all day *(LYM, Barbarrick)*

Salutation M15 6ED [Higher Chatham St]: Traditional Victorian pub with broad mix of customers, two or three well kept ales inc Black Sheep, friendly staff, cheap food (usually one choice such as curry/stew); covered outside tables on narrow terrace, bedrooms, open all day *(Peter Owen)*

☆ **Sinclairs** M3 1SW [Cathedral Gates, off Exchange Sq]: Charming low-beamed and timbered 16th-c Sam Smiths pub (rebuilt here in redevelopment), all-day food inc fresh oysters, no real ale (keg beers), brisk friendly service, bustling atmosphere, quieter upstairs bar with snugs and Jacobean fireplace; tables out in Shambles Sq (plastic glasses), open all day *(the Didler, John and Helen Rushton, LYM, Ben Williams)*

Smithfield M4 5JZ [Swan St]: Clean bright refurbishment by welcoming new owners, one long room with eight interesting ales inc Phoenix and a house beer brewed by Facers, plenty of bottled beers too, enjoyable food; bedrooms in nearby building, open all day *(Chris Johnson, the Didler, BB)*

Unicorn M4 1PW [Church St]: Friendly and relaxed four-room pub, well kept Bass and Copper Dragon from island bar, oak panelling, lovely snug; open all day, Sun till 7pm *(the Didler)*

MARPLE [SJ9389]

Hare & Hounds SK6 7EJ [Dooley Lane (A627 W)]: Popular old pub above River Goyt, modern layout and décor, some imaginative food inc good meze, well kept Hydes ales from stainless-steel servery, good service; sports TV, no dogs; well behaved children welcome, open all day *(Dennis Jones)*

Ring o' Bells SK6 7AY [Church Lane; by Macclesfield Canal, Bridge 2]: Popular Robinsons local with new landlady, canal and other local memorabilia in four linked rooms, decent food, darts and quiz nights *(David Hoult)*

MARPLE BRIDGE [SJ9889]

Hare & Hounds SK6 5LW [Mill Brow]: Classic, comfortable stone-built country pub in lovely spot, smallish and can get crowded, good interesting local food (not Mon, Tues) from short menu, well kept Robinsons, log fires; garden behind *(David Hoult, E A McClelland)*

MAWDESLEY [SD5016]

Robin Hood L40 2RG [Blue Stone Lane (Croston—Eccleston road, N of village – keep going)]: Spotless open-plan dining pub with button-back wall banquettes, reproduction Victorian prints, decorative plates, stained-glass seat dividers, some stripped stone; generous home cooking (all

day wknds) from sandwiches up, children's menu, OAP bargain lunches, friendly staff coping well with the bustle, well kept Boddingtons, Timothy Taylors and four interesting guests, decent wines; children's room, small pretty upstairs restaurant; may be piped music, games machine; neat side terrace, good fenced play area, open all day *(Tony and Maggie Harwood, Yvonne and Mike Meadley)*

MELLOR [SJ9888]

☆ **Devonshire Arms** SK6 5PP [this is the Mellor nr Marple, S of Manchester; heading out of Marple on the A626 towards Glossop, Mellor is the next road after the B6102, signposted off on the right at Marple Bridge; Longhurst Lane]: Cheerful, unpretentious and cosy, front bar with old leather-seated settles and open fire, two small back rooms with Victorian fireplaces, Robinsons ales, summer sangria, wide choice of generous pubby food (all day wknds); jazz 2nd Tues of month; children welcome, delightful garden with waterfall tumbling into fish pond crossed by japanese bridge, play area on small tree-sheltered lawn, boules *(LYM, David Hoult, John Fiander, Dr and Mrs A K Clarke)*

☆ **Millstone** BB2 7JR [the one up nr Blackburn; Mellor Lane]: Restauranty stone-built village dining pub, smart and well run, panelled bar with comfortable lounge one side, modern dining extension the other, good food from all-day bar meals to enterprising cooking and popular substantial Sun lunch, obliging friendly staff, well kept Thwaites, good choice of wines by the glass; big log fire, mementoes of former landlord and England cricketer Big Jim Smith; good bedrooms and breakfast, open all day *(BB, Andy and Jill Kassube, GLD)*

MORECAMBE [SD4264]

Midland Grand Plaza LA4 4BZ [Marine Rd W]: Classic art deco hotel in splendid seafront position, brought bang up to date with comfortable if unorthodox contemporary furnishings in spacious seaview Rotunda Bar; rather pricey but enjoyable food from tapas to restaurant meals, helpful staff; children welcome, 44 comfortably redone bedrooms, open all day *(Margaret Dickinson, BB, Mr and Mrs John Taylor)*

Palatine LA4 5BZ [The Crescent]: Comfortably refurbished seafront pub, enjoyable reasonably priced wholesome food, four Lancaster ales and guests, friendly helpful staff; leather armchairs and some high tables with stools, upstairs sea-view dining room *(Pat and Tony Martin)*

Shrimp LA4 5TP [Lancaster Rd, Torrisholme]: Well run chain pub on large roundabout, good value carvery, Thwaites ales, good choice of wines by the glass, friendly efficient service, pleasant bar area, lots of framed celebrity pictures *(Jeremy King)*

NEWTON [SD6950]

Parkers Arms BB7 3DY [B6478 7 miles N of Clitheroe]: Welcoming licensees, locally sourced food (suppliers listed) in bar and restaurant (which has lovely views), good lunchtime sandwiches, beers from Bowland and Copper Dragon, decent range of wines, log fires; children welcome, garden, bedrooms, lovely spot *(LYM, Len Beattie, Norma and Noel Thomas, R L Borthwick)*

RADCLIFFE [SD7608]
Sparking Clog M26 3WY [Radcliffe Moor Rd]: Bright and clean with welcoming friendly staff, wide choice of good value enjoyable food, three Marstons ales *(Ben Williams)*

RILEY GREEN [SD6225]
☆ *Royal Oak* PR5 0SL [A675/A6061]: Cosy low-beamed three-room former coaching inn, good generous home cooking inc notable steaks, four well kept Thwaites ales from long back bar, friendly efficient service; ancient stripped stone, open fires, seats from high-backed settles to red plush armchairs on carpet, lots of nooks and crannies, soft lighting, impressive woodwork, fresh flowers, interesting model steam engines and plenty of bric-a-brac; two comfortable dining rooms; can be packed Fri night and wknds; tables outside, short walk from Leeds & Liverpool Canal, footpath to Hoghton Tower, open all day Sun *(Norma and Noel Thomas, Eric Ruff, Yvonne and Mike Meadley, Margaret Dickinson, John and Eleanor Holdsworth, Charles and Pauline Stride, BB)*

RIMINGTON [SD8045]
Black Bull BB7 4DS [Rimington Lane]: Reopened as french-themed inn/restaurant; bar and two dining areas (one quite smart), good french country cooking, attentive service, well kept ales such as Black Sheep and Thwaites, good choice of wines by the glass, decent coffee; bedrooms planned *(LYM, Yvonne and Mike Meadley, Peter and Liz Smalley, Margaret Dickinson)*

RINGLEY [SD7605]
Horseshoe M26 1FT [Fold Rd, Stonelough; right off A667 at sign for Kidd's Garden Centre]: Good imaginative food, wider choice evenings, friendly landlord, well kept Thwaites, three areas off main bar, open fire, interesting local pictures; well behaved children lunchtime, pleasant back garden *(Peter Johnston)*

ROCHDALE [SD8913]
Baum OL12 0NU [Toad Lane]: Old-fashioned charm, great choice of changing ales, lots of bottled beers, food from tapas and good sandwiches to home-made casseroles etc; bare boards, old advertisements, conservatory; garden tables, handy for Co-op Museum, open all day *(Andy and Jill Kassube, Ken and Lynda Taylor)*

ROMILEY [SJ9390]
Duke of York SK6 3AN [Stockport Rd]: Old-fashioned pub with good friendly atmosphere, six well kept ales, reasonably priced food from bar snacks up, lots of woodwork, bar opening into two smaller rooms, one up steps with hatch service; back vaults bar, upstairs restaurant *(Dennis Jones)*

SALTERFORTH [SD8845]
Fanny Grey BB18 5SL [B6251 Barnoldswick—Foulridge]: Recently improved moorland pub with great views across to the Dales, good food using locally reared meat, Copper Dragon and Tetleys, big central log fire; children welcome, garden, good walks, open all day *(Dr Kevan Tucker)*

SLAIDBURN [SD7152]
☆ *Hark to Bounty* BB7 3EP [B6478 N of Clitheroe]: Attractive old stone-built pub with linked rooms, wide choice of fresh food (lots of tables) inc light dishes and old-fashioned puddings, friendly hard-working young staff, four real ales, decent wines and whiskies; comfortable chairs by open fire, games room one end, restaurant the other; pleasant back garden, charming Forest of Bowland village, good walks, bedrooms, open all day *(Neil Whitehead, Victoria Anderson, LYM, John and Sylvia Harrop, Yvonne and Mike Meadley, Norma and Noel Thomas)*

SLYNE [SD4765]
Keys LA2 6AU [A6 N of Lancaster]: Sizeable pub given contemporary refurbishment, good drinks' choice inc regional ales, interesting menu, restaurant; children welcome, suntrap terrace *(Tony and Maggie Harwood)*
Slyne Lodge LA2 6AZ [Main Rd]: Popular well run inn with interesting décor, enjoyable good value pubby food (all day wknds) in bar and restaurant, well kept Jennings ales, friendly helpful staff; open fire, conservatory; Sky TV in side bar; children welcome, terrace tables, ten reasonably priced bedrooms in former stables *(Tony and Maggie Harwood)*

SOUTHPORT [SD3317]
Scarisbrick PR8 1NZ [Lord St]: Relaxed hotel bar in medieval baronial style, comfortable armchairs, well priced real ales inc house Flag & Turret from central counter, adjoining café and bistro bar welcoming children, bargain food from filled baps up, quick friendly service; open all day *(BB, Tony and Wendy Hobden, George Atkinson)*
Sir Henry Segrave PR8 1RH [Lord St]: Well placed comfortable Wetherspoons, good choice of food all day, well kept cheap beer, efficient service even when busy; open from 7am till late *(George Atkinson)*

STANDISH [SD5711]
☆ *Crown* WN1 2XF [not far from M6 junction 27; Platt Lane]: Refurbished traditional country pub with open fire in comfortable panelled bar, impressive range of well kept ales (even a daily beers' list) inc local Mayflower and Prospect, several bottled continentals; good food inc grills priced and chosen by weight from chiller, early-bird deals and Sun roasts, airy dining extension and pleasant conservatory; children allowed away from bar, comfortable clean bedrooms *(Stuart Parkinson, Andy Witcomb, LYM, Peter Johnston)*

STOCKPORT [SJ8990]
☆ *Arden Arms* SK1 2LX [Millgate St, behind Asda]: Welcoming Victorian pub with good

reasonably priced lunchtime food, well kept Robinsons, cheerful efficient service, well preserved traditional horseshoe bar, tiny old-fashioned snug (accessed through servery), longcase clocks, well restored tiling and panelling, two coal fires; tables in sheltered courtyard, open all day *(Dennis Jones, the Didler, G D K Fraser)*

Armoury SK3 8BD [Shaw Heath]: Friendly traditional local with small bar and comfortable old-fashioned lounge, well kept Robinsons ales, perhaps Old Tom tapped from cask in winter, family room upstairs; TV; open all day *(the Didler, G D K Fraser)*

Blossoms SK2 6NU [Buxton Rd (A6)]: Bustling main-road Victorian local, Robinsons ales inc Old Tom from bar-top cask, nice home-made pies wkdy lunchtimes, three rooms off corridor inc attractive back lounge with handsome fireplace, pool room; open all day *(the Didler)*

Crown SK4 1AR [Heaton Lane, Heaton Norris]: Partly open-plan Victorian pub popular for its 16 well kept changing ales, also bottled beers and real cider, three cosy lounge areas off bar, spotless stylish décor, wholesome bargain lunches; darts; frequent live music; tables in cobbled courtyard, huge viaduct above *(Dennis Jones, Chris Morris, the Didler, G D K Fraser)*

Navigation SK4 1TY [Manchester Rd (B6167, former A626)]: Friendly pub refurbished under new licensees, Beartown ales and a guest, farm ciders, good pies; open all day *(the Didler)*

Nursery SK4 2NA [Green Lane, Heaton Norris; off A6]: Popular 1930s pub on narrow cobbled lane (E end of N part of Green Lane); enjoyable straightforward lunchtime food from kitchen servery on right, friendly efficient service, well kept Hydes, big bays of banquettes in panelled stained-glass front lounge, brocaded wall banquettes in back one; children welcome if eating, immaculate bowling green behind, open all day wknds *(the Didler, BB)*

Queens Head SK1 1JT [Little Underbank (can be reached by steps from St Petersgate)]: Splendid Victorian restoration, long and narrow, with charming separate snug and back dining area, rare brass cordials' fountain, double bank of spirits' taps and old spirit lamps, old posters and adverts; reasonably priced lunchtime snacks, bargain Sam Smiths, daily papers, good friendly bustle, bench seating and bare boards; famous tiny gents' upstairs; open all day, till 7pm Sun *(the Didler)*

Railway SK1 2BZ [Avenue St (just off M63 junction 13, via A560)]: Bright and airy L-shaped bar with full Pennine range and changing guest ales, lots of foreign beers, farm cider, home-made bar lunches (not Sun), bargain prices, friendly staff; old Stockport prints and memorabilia, bar billiards, tables out behind; open all day *(the Didler, Dennis Jones)*

☆ *Red Bull* SK1 3AY [Middle Hillgate]: Steps up to friendly well run local, impressive beamed and flagstoned bar with dark panelling, substantial settles and seats, open fires, lots of pictures, mirrors and brassware, traditional island servery with well kept Robinsons ales, good value home-cooked bar lunches (not Sun); has recently expanded into adjoining building, open all day except Sun afternoon *(the Didler, LYM)*

Swan With Two Necks SK1 1RY [Princes St]: Traditional local with comfortable panelled bar, back skylit lounge and drinking corridor, bargain pub lunches from sandwiches up, teas with home-made scones, Robinsons ales; open all day *(the Didler)*

STRINES [SJ9686]

Sportsmans Arms SK6 7GE [B6101Marple—New Mills]: Pleasant roadside local with panoramic Goyt Valley view from picture-window lounge bar, good ever-changing ale range, enjoyable well priced straightforward food, small separate bar; tables out on side decking, heated smokers' shelter, open all day wknds *(David Hoult)*

TATHAM [SD6169]

Tatham Bridge Inn LA2 8NL [B6480, off A683 Lancaster—Kirkby Lonsdale]: Welcoming old pub with cosy low-beamed bar, well kept ales inc Black Sheep, good range of enjoyable food from sandwiches up, dining room along corridor (best to book wknds); bedrooms *(Nigel Long)*

TOCKHOLES [SD6622]

Victoria BB3 0NL [Golden Soney]: Good value bar food in cosy and friendly, comfortably modernised moorland pub with snug alcoves, partly stripped-stone walls, woodburner, well kept ales; children welcome *(LYM, Peter Johnston)*

TREALES [SD4432]

Derby Arms PR4 3SD: Recently refurbished well run pub, good food in bar areas and sizeable restaurant, well kept Robinsons ales *(Maurice and Gill McMahon)*

TYLDESLEY [SD6902]

Mort Arms M29 8DG [Elliott St]: Bargain Holts ales in two-room 1930s pub, etched glass and polished panelling, comfortable lounge with old local photographs, friendly landlord and regulars; darts and dominoes; open all day *(the Didler)*

WADDINGTON [SD7243]

Waddington Arms BB7 3HP [Clitheroe Rd]: Tall stone coaching inn with enjoyable reasonably priced food (all day wknds) using fresh local produce from sandwiches up, cheerful staff, five well kept ales, decent wines; stripped-pine tables on flagstones and bare boards, woodburner in big 17th-c inglenook, small dining room with motor-racing prints, modern décor; children welcome, pleasant back garden, six good value bedrooms (church bells) *(Steve Whalley, Philip and Helen Temperley)*

WALLASEY [SJ3094]

Queens Royal CH45 2JT [Marine Promenade]: Welcoming seafront hotel with good choice of food inc seafood, carvery (Fri-Sun) and pre-theatre menu, well kept ales such as Brimstage and Weetwood *(Ian Lovatt, Mr and Mrs R Ogle)*

WEST BRADFORD [SD7444]
Three Millstones BB7 4SX [Waddington Rd]: Attractive old dining pub with good food inc set deals in four comfortable linked areas, compact bar with ales such as Black Sheep and Moorhouses, good coffee, friendly efficient service, open fire *(John and Eleanor Holdsworth)*

WEST KIRBY [SJ2186]
White Lion CH48 4EE [Grange Rd (A540)]: Interesting 17th-c sandstone building; friendly proper pub with several small beamed areas on different levels, four mainstream beers, good value simple bar lunches inc lots of sandwiches, coal stove; no children even in attractive secluded back garden up steep stone steps, open all day *(MLR, Clive Watkin)*

WHALLEY [SD7336]
Swan BB7 9SN [King St]: Refurbished 17th-c coaching inn in great countryside, long light-wood bar, local Bowland and other beers, enjoyable well priced food, good service; disabled access, bedrooms *(Yvonne and Mike Meadley)*

WISWELL [SD7437]
☆ *Freemasons Arms* BB7 9DF [Vicarage Fold; just NE of Whalley]: Tucked-away civilised pub/restaurant, plenty of character with period furniture, old paintings and prints, rugs on flagstone floors, open fires; very good upmarket food (must book wknd evenings), cheaper early evening set menu, well kept changing local ales such as Bowland and Moorhouses, remarkable choice of wines, friendly efficient service; smallish bar with linked dining rooms, upstairs gun room for pre- or post-dinner drinks; children welcome, dogs in some areas, front terrace,

parking can be tricky, lovely village *(Margaret Dickinson, Nick White, Steve Whalley)*

WORSLEY [SD7500]
Barton Arms M28 2ED [Stablefold; just off Barton Rd (B5211), handy for M60 junction 13)]: Bright clean Ember Inn, popular and friendly, with good value food, Black Sheep, Caledonian Deuchars IPA and Timothy Taylors Landlord; children welcome *(Tony and Wendy Hobden, Ben Williams)*

WREA GREEN [SD3931]
Villa PR4 2PE [Moss Side Lane (B5259)]: Lots of small seating areas in smart hotel's welcoming panelled bar, well kept Copper Dragon, Jennings and guests, enjoyable food, log fire, daily papers; Fri jazz; disabled facilities, good-sized garden, bedrooms, open all day *(the Didler, Ken Richards)*

WRIGHTINGTON [SD5011]
Rigbye Arms WN6 9QB [3 miles from M6 junction 27; off A5209 via Robin Hood Lane and left into High Moor Lane]: 17th-c inn in attractive moorland setting, welcoming and relaxed, with good value generous food (all day Sun) inc some interesting specials, friendly prompt service even when busy, well kept ales such as Black Sheep and Timothy Taylors Landlord, decent wines, several carpeted rooms, open fires; garden, bowling green, open all day Sun *(John and Sylvia Harrop, Margaret Dickinson, Yvonne and Mike Meadley, Mrs Dorothy King)*

WRIGHTINGTON BAR [SD5313]
☆ *Mulberry Tree* WN6 9SE [B5250, N of M6 junction 27]: Light, airy and well maintained restaurant/pub, very good (if pricey) imaginatively served food, cheaper bar menu, good wines, polite attentive staff; plenty of tables in different areas *(Margaret and Jeff Graham, Tony and Maggie Harwood)*

Please tell us if any Lucky Dips deserve to be upgraded to a Main Entry – and why: feedback@goodguides.com, or (no stamp needed) The Good Pub Guide, FREEPOST TN1569, Wadhurst, E Sussex TN5 7BR.

Leicestershire and Rutland

Although not one of our largest counties, this is a strong area for really good pub food with nearly half our Main Entries holding one of our Food Awards. From this healthy batch of dining pubs a few really stand out: the Joiners Arms at Bruntingthorpe (first-class food and almost a restaurant now), the Olive Branch in Clipsham (a top-class all-rounder), the Old White Hart in Lyddington (the landlord cooks the enjoyable food) and the Kings Arms at Wing (they have their own smokehouse and the food is genuinely interesting). Other pubs doing especially well this year include the Cow & Plough at Oadby (amazing breweriana), the Grainstore in Oakham (their own-brew beers are exceptional) and the New Inn at Peggs Green (a quirky place with friendly irish licensees). We're pleased with our new entries, too, this year which are the George in Coleorton (an enjoyable little pub with honest food), the Marquess of Exeter at Lyddington (the chef/patron has refurbished and rejuvenated the attractive bars), the White Swan at Sileby (lots of eccentric objects to look at and good, homely food), the Coach House at South Luffenham (a popular place to stay with cosy bars) and the Finches Arms in Upper Hambleton (just by Rutland Water with a warm welcome and newly updated bedrooms). For that special meal out, once again our Leicestershire and Rutland Dining Pub of the year is the Olive Branch in Clipsham.

BREEDON ON THE HILL
SK4022   MAP 7
Three Horse Shoes 🍽
Main Street (A453); DE73 1AN

Comfortable pub with friendly licensees and popular food

Opposite the village lock-up, this 18th-c pub places much emphasis on the popular, often interesting, food. The building has been restored to reveal its attractive structure and there are heavy worn flagstones, a log fire, pubby tables, a dark wood counter and green walls and ceilings that give a stylishly simple and timeless feel to the clean-cut central bar. Marstons Pedigree on handpump, 30 malt whiskies and decent house wines. Beyond here, a further eating room has maroon walls, dark pews and cherry-stained tables. The two-room dining area on the right has a comfortably civilised chatty feel with big quite close-set antique tables on seagrass matting and colourful modern country prints and antique engravings on canary walls. Even at lunchtime there are lighted candles in elegant modern holders.

> Tipping is not normal for bar meals, and not usually expected.

🍴 Enjoyable – if not cheap – food includes sandwiches, ploughman's, rabbit terrine with cumberland sauce, mussels in white wine and cream, venison burger with stilton dressing, beer-battered fish, sausages with mash and onion gravy, roast vegetable casserole, beef and mushroom pudding, chicken breast with beetroot sauce, duck breast with whisky, salmon with sweet potato curry, and puddings like treacle tart and lemon cheesecake; they also offer a brunch menu. *Starters/Snacks: £4.50 to £6.95. Main Courses: £10.95 to £17.50. Puddings: £4.95*

Free house ~ Licensees Ian Davison, Jennie Ison, Stuart Marson ~ Real ale ~ Bar food ~ Restaurant ~ (01332) 695129 ~ Dogs allowed in bar ~ Open 11.30-2.30, 5.30-11; 12-3 Sun; closed Sun evening; 25 and 26 Dec, 1 Jan

Recommended by Steve Cocking, Theocsbrian, Dr and Mrs A K Clarke, Michael Doswell, Derek and Sylvia Stephenson, Mrs Terry Dodd

BRUNTINGTHORPE
SP6089   MAP 4

Joiners Arms 🍴 ♇

Off A5199 S of Leicester: Church Walk/Cross Street; LE17 5QH

Good contemporary cooking in civilised and attractive dining pub – which has kept a proper bar, too

There's an area to the left by the small, light oak bar counter that's set aside for drinkers but there's no doubt that this is an enjoyable dining place rather than a straightforward pub. There's a long black-cushioned pew with a linenfold centre, various dining chairs around five tables on the wood-effect floor and a coal and wood fire. The rest of the two-beamed rooms are set for eating with a mix of elegant dining chairs (antique cushioned and farmhouse ones), candles on the tables, terracotta tiles, and a big bowl of lilies. It's all very civilised and relaxed with sparkling glass and gleaming cutlery; service is friendly and efficient. Greene King IPA on handpump and 19 good wines (and champagne) by the glass; piped middle-of-the-road music. In front of the pub are a couple of picnic-sets.

🍴 First-class and imaginative, the food might include soup, wild mushroom feuilletée, ham hock terrine with a poached egg and pineapple relish, dolcelatte and watercress risotto, lambs kidneys with chorizo and butterbean cassoulet, cod with garlic mash and chive beurre blanc, medallions of beef fillet with wild mushroom and madeira sauce, confit duck with truffle mash and red wine jus, and puddings such as chocolate fondant with caramel and hazelnut ice-cream and lemon brûlée with shortbread biscuits; they also offer a Tuesday three-course set supper. *Starters/Snacks: £5.00 to £7.50. Main Courses: £7.00 to £12.00. Puddings: £5.00 to £6.00*

Free house ~ Licensee Stephen Fitzpatrick ~ Real ale ~ Bar food (not Sun evening or Mon) ~ Restaurant ~ (0116) 247 8258 ~ Children welcome ~ Open 12-2.30, 6-11; 12-3 Sun; closed Sun evening and all day Mon

Recommended by Jeff and Wendy Williams

CLIPSHAM
SK9716   MAP 8

Olive Branch ★ 🍴 ♇ 🍷 🛏

Take B668/Stretton exit off A1 N of Stamford; Clipsham signposted E from exit roundabout; LE15 7SH

LEICESTERSHIRE AND RUTLAND DINING PUB OF THE YEAR

A special place for an exceptional meal in comfortable surroundings, fine choice of drinks and luxury bedrooms

'I've never known this place anything other than excellent in all respects' says one of our readers and adds that he was looking forward to his next visit. The staff are welcoming (and this welcome extends to your dog, too), the food is first class, the range of drinks exceptional and the bedrooms lovely. The various small but charmingly attractive rooms have a relaxed country cottage atmosphere, with dark joists and beams, rustic furniture, an interesting mix of pictures (some by local artists), candles on tables, and a cosy log fire in the stone inglenook fireplace. Many of the books were bought at antiques fairs by one of the partners, so it's worth asking if it's for sale, if you see something you like; piped music. A carefully chosen range of drinks includes Grainstore Olive Ale and a guest beer on handpump, an enticing wine list (with a dozen by the glass), a fine choice of malt whiskies, armagnacs and cognacs, and quite a few different british and continental bottled beers. Outside, there are tables, chairs and big plant pots on a pretty little terrace, with more on the neat lawn, sheltered in the L of its two low buildings. The bedrooms are in Beech House just opposite and the breakfasts are delicious.

🍽 **Extremely highly thought-of (if not cheap) food might include sandwiches, soup, a smashing tapas board, salmon terrine with pickled fennel and Pernod dressing, sausages with mustard mash and onion gravy, crab and saffron risotto, fish and chips with minted peas, braised lamb shoulder with a herb crust and ratatouille, honey-roasted duck breast with turnip gratin and glazed beetroot, and puddings like rhubarb trifle with ginger chantilly and rhubarb sorbet and sticky toffee pudding; they also offer a two- and three-course set lunch.** Starters/Snacks: £5.15 to £12.50. Main Courses: £11.75 to £22.50. Puddings: £5.50 to £7.95

Free house ~ Licensees Sean Hope and Ben Jones ~ Real ale ~ Bar food (12-2(3 Sun), 7-9.30(9 Sun); 12-2, 2.30-5.30, 7-9.30 Sat) ~ Restaurant ~ (01780) 410355 ~ Children welcome ~ Dogs allowed in bar and bedrooms ~ Open 12-3, 6-11; 12-11(10.30 Sun) Sat ~ Bedrooms: £110S(£130B)/£130S(£160B)

Recommended by Derek and Sylvia Stephenson, Jeff and Wendy Williams, Ian and Helen Stafford, Michael Sargent, W N F Boughey, DFL, Mike and Sue Loseby, Roy Bromell, Peter and Josie Fawcett, D M Jack, Jill and Julian Tasker, Graeme Manson, Barry Collett, Bruce and Sharon Eden, Howard and Margaret Buchanan, Michael Doswell, B and F A Hannam

COLEORTON
SK4117 MAP 7

George
Loughborough Road (A512 E); LE67 8HF

Usefully placed and attractively traditional civilised proper pub with big garden

The carpeted bar on the right is nicely laid out to give a comfortable feel of varied and fairly small separate areas: dark leather sofa and tub chairs by a woodburning stove in front, scatter-cushioned pew and mixed chairs below shelves of books in one corner, other mixed seating elsewhere. This room has lots of local photographs on its ochre or dove-grey walls, black beams and joists, and a dark-panelled dado. A bigger room on the left, broadly similar and again with plenty to look at, has another woodburning stove, and more of a dining-room feel. Long-serving mature staff make sure of a warm and friendly atmosphere; Greene King Abbot and Old Speckled Hen and Marstons Pedigree on handpump. The pub dogs are border collies. The spreading garden behind has sturdy wooden furniture among sizeable trees, and a play area.

🍽 **Honest pub food using local produce includes lunchtime filled panini, soup, chicken liver pâté with caramelised onions, ham with parsley sauce, smoked salmon omelette, beer-battered fish and chips, vegetable pie, chicken fillet with mozzarella and n mustard wrapped in bacon with a tomato sauce, lambs liver and bacon and chinese-spiced pork with plums.** Starters/Snacks: £3.95 to £5.95. Main Courses: £9.25 to £18.95. Puddings: £4.75

Free house ~ Licensee Mark and Jan Wilkinson ~ Real ale ~ Bar food (all day Mon-Sat; 12-3 Sun; not Sun evening) ~ (01530) 834639 ~ Well behaved children allowed away from bar areas ~ Dogs allowed in bar ~ Open 12-11(4 Sun); closed Sun evening

Recommended by Ian and Jane Irving, Comus and Sarah Elliott, Paul J Robinshaw, Dave and Jenny Hughes

Post Office address codings confusingly give the impression that some pubs are in Leicestershire, when they're really in Cambridgeshire (which is where we list them).

EXTON   SK9211   MAP 7

Fox & Hounds 🍴 🛏

Signposted off A606 Stamford—Oakham; LE15 8AP

Well run, friendly inn with comfortable lounge bar, real ales, popular food cooked by the landlord and quiet garden; bedrooms

---

Handy for Rutland Water and the gardens at Barnsdale, this is a handsome old coaching inn in a restful village with friendly, helpful licensees. The comfortable high-ceilinged lounge bar is traditionally civilised with some dark red plush easy chairs and wheelback seats around lots of pine tables, maps and hunting prints on the walls, fresh flowers and a winter log fire in a large stone fireplace. Grainstore Ten Fifty, Greene King IPA and a changing guest beer on handpump and several wines by the glass; TV and piped music. The lovely sheltered walled garden has seats among large rose beds overlooking pretty paddocks. The spotlessly clean bedrooms are charming and the breakfasts very good.

🍴 **Cooked by the landlord, the enjoyable bar food includes lunchtime filled panini, soup, mozzarella, tomato and basil, home-made duck spring rolls, spinach and goats cheese tart, sausage and mash, calves liver with bacon and red onion gravy, chicken with stilton and bacon in a white wine sauce, rack of lamb with roast new potatoes, summer crab, smoked salmon and avocado salad, halibut with chargrilled vegetables, and puddings like lemon tart and summer pudding.** *Starters/Snacks: £4.50 to £5.75. Main Courses: £8.95 to £15.75. Puddings: £4.75*

Free house ~ Licensees Valter and Sandra Floris ~ Real ale ~ Bar food (not Sun evening or Mon) ~ Restaurant ~ (01572) 812403 ~ Children welcome ~ Dogs allowed in bar and bedrooms ~ Open 11-3, 6-11; 11-11 summer Sat; 11-4 Sun; closed Sun evening and Mon ~ Bedrooms: £40(£45B)/£60(£70B)

Recommended by Richard and Jean Green, Margaret and Peter Staples, Leslie and Barbara Owen, Susan and Nigel Brookes, Roy Bromell, Mark Farrington, Barry Collett, Trevor and Sylvia Millum, Colin McKerrow

LYDDINGTON   SP8797   MAP 4

Marquess of Exeter 🍴

Main Street; LE15 9LT

Newly refurbished stone inn with contemporary décor, real ales, excellent food cooked by the landlord and seats outside

---

Recently refurbished with a contemporary touch, this handsome stone inn is a welcoming place under its new chef/patron. The beamed bars have stripped-stone walls with others painted pale grey or yellow, all manner of attractive dining chairs, leather sofas and tub chairs and wooden wall settles around a mix of tables on the wood-strip or flagstone floors, pine chests and old barrels, fresh flowers and several open fires (one has heraldic shields above it). Marstons Pedigree and a guest like Brakspears Bitter on handpump and several wines by the glass. The L-shaped restaurant has plenty of space. There are seats out on the terrace and on the lawns. The pub is named after the Burghley family, who have long owned this charming village. We would expect this to be a nice place to stay but have had no feedback as yet.

🍴 **Excellent food (you must book ahead to be sure of a table) includes sandwiches, soup, grilled squid and red pepper and chilli salsa, chicken liver parfait with fig chutney, butternut squash and gorgonzola risotto, beer-battered cod, grilled breast of lemon and garlic chicken with minty chilli peas, steak with café de paris butter, slow-roasted shoulder of lamb for two, and puddings like hot chocolate and beetroot cake with vanilla ice-cream and warm rice pudding with brandied poached fruits; they also offer a two- and three-course set lunch.** *Starters/Snacks: £5.15 to £12.50. Main Courses: £10.50 to £13.25. Puddings: £4.75 to £6.50*

Marstons ~ Lease Brian Baker ~ Real ale ~ Bar food (12-2.30, 6.30-10; all day Sun; not Mon) ~ Restaurant ~ (01572) 822477 ~ Children welcome but must be supervised by parents ~ Dogs allowed in bar and bedrooms ~ Open 12-11(10.30 Sun) ~ Bedrooms: £67.50B/£87.50B

Recommended by Roy Bromell, Mike and Margaret Banks, Jeff and Wendy Williams, Mike and Sue Loseby

Old White Hart 🍽️ 🛏️

Village signposted off A6003 N of Corby; LE15 9LR

Well run, popular inn with welcoming staff, roaring fires and very good food; pretty garden

Much enjoyed by a great many of our readers, this is a fine old pub run by a very friendly, helpful couple who have now been here 13 years. The softly lit front bar has a glass-shielded log fire, low ceilings and heavy bowed beams, a relaxed local atmosphere and just four close-set tables. This room opens into an attractive restaurant, and on the other side is another tiled-floor room with rugs, lots of fine hunting prints, cushioned wall seats and mate's chairs and a woodburning stove. Greene King IPA and Abbot and Timothy Taylors Landlord on handpump alongside several wines (and champagne and fizz) by the glass; board games. The pretty walled garden (with eight floodlit boules pitches) is very pleasant with seats under outdoor heaters; if you sit out here on Thursday evening you may hear the church bell-ringers. The pub is handy for Bede House and there are good nearby walks.

🍽️ Mr East is a butcher who makes his own sausages and cured meats, and the very good food might include filled panini, soup, goose liver parfait with red onion marmalade, crab thermidor, sausages with sweet potato mash and gravy, lamb pie with redcurrant jus, seafood pie, a fresh fish and vegetarian dish of the day, and puddings like pear and butterscotch crumble with vanilla sauce and lemon tart with star anise and cinnamon berries; they also have an early bird menu. *Starters/Snacks: £3.75 to £6.95. Main Courses: £7.95 to £16.95. Puddings: £5.95 to £6.50*

Free house ~ Licensees Stuart and Holly East ~ Real ale ~ Bar food (not winter Sun evening) ~ Restaurant ~ (01572) 821703 ~ Children welcome ~ Open 12-3, 6-11; 12-3.30, 7-10.30 Sun ~ Bedrooms: £60B/£85B

Recommended by Jeff and Wendy Williams, Susan and Neil McLean, Brian and Janet Ainscough, R L Borthwick, Mike and Sue Loseby, Roy Bromell, John Robertson, Rochelle Seifas, Anthony Barnes, Leslie and Barbara Owen, Ian and Helen Stafford, Ryta Lyndley, Adrian Johnson, John Wooll

MOWSLEY
SP6488 MAP 4

Staff of Life 🍽️ 🍷

Village signposted off A5199 S of Leicester; Main Street; LE17 6NT

Neat, high-gabled pub popular for a good meal out; seats in back garden

This is a well run little village pub with friendly staff and good, popular bar food. The roomy bar is spotlessly kept and quite traditional with a panelled ceiling, high-backed settles on flagstones, warming fire, wicker chairs on shiny wood floors and stools lined up along the unusual circular counter. Banks's Bitter and a guest like Brakspears Oxford Gold on handpump and up to 20 wines (and champagne and fizz) in three different-sized glasses; piped music. There are some seats out in front of the building with more on a delightful little deck shaded by leafy foliage.

🍽️ At lunchtime, the well liked bar food might include sandwiches, sausages or faggots with onion gravy, beer-battered fish and meatballs in rich tomato sauce with pasta, with evening choices like pork, pistachio and apricot terrine with apple and fig chutney, baked whole camembert to share with red onion marmalade, vegetable tarte tatin with pesto dressing, shin of beef with port jus and wholegrain mustard sauce, chicken with celeriac purée and a cider cream sauce, and puddings such as chocolate brownies with chocolate sauce and vanilla panna cotta with balsamic berries. *Starters/Snacks: £5.00 to £8.50. Main Courses: £8.50 to £20.00. Puddings: £5.50 to £6.75*

Free house ~ Licensee Spencer Farrell ~ Real ale ~ Bar food (12-2.30(3.30 Sun), 6-9.30; not Sun evening, Mon or Tues lunchtime) ~ Restaurant ~ (0116) 240 2359 ~ No children in bar area or on back terrace after 7pm ~ Open 12-3, 6-11; 12-10.30 Sun; closed Mon lunchtime (except bank hols) and Tues lunchtime

Recommended by P Tailyour, Michael Sargent, George Atkinson, Duncan Cloud, Leslie and Barbara Owen, Michael Butler, Rob and Catherine Dunster

OADBY   SK6202   MAP 4

Cow & Plough 🍺

Gartree Road (B667 N of centre); LE2 2FB

Fantastic collection of brewery memorabilia, seven real ales and good bar food

As well as a fine range of real ales, this bustling pub has an extraordinary collection of breweriana. It's an unusual place that opened as a pub about 20 years ago and is converted from an old farm and dairy buildings. There are a few original cosily individual rooms and an extensive long, light, flagstoned front extension. Two of the original dark back rooms, known as the Vaults, contain an extraordinary collection of brewery memorabilia – almost every piece has a story behind it: enamel signs and mirrors advertising long-forgotten brews, an aged brass cash register, and furnishings and fittings salvaged from pubs and even churches (there's some splendid stained glass behind the counter). One section has descriptions of all Leicester's pubs. The long front extension has plenty of plants and fresh flowers, a piano, beams liberally covered with hops, and a real mix of traditionally pubby tables and chairs, with lots of green leatherette sofas, and small round cast-iron tables. The conservatory, too, has a fine collection of brewery and pub signs and the like and a very eclectic mix of chairs and tables. On handpump there are seven real ales: four from local Steamin' Billy brewery and guests such as Fullers London Pride, Holdens Mild and Thornbridge Brock; also, a dozen country wines, several wines by the glass and up to six ciders. TV, darts, board games and piped music. There are picnic-sets outside in the old yard.

🍴 Bar food includes lunchtime sandwiches and wraps, filled baked potatoes, soup, nachos, pizzas and good burgers with evening choices like home-made chicken liver parfait with onion marmalade, fishcake with lemon hollandaise, thai-style beef stir fry, a risotto of the day, chicken with roast garlic mash and lamb with rosemary mash and a ginger and apricot jus; Sunday carvery. *Starters/Snacks: £3.95 to £4.95. Main Courses: £5.50 to £8.50. Puddings: £4.50*

Free house ~ Licensee Barry Lount ~ Real ale ~ Bar food (12-2.30, 6-9; 12-5 Sun) ~ Restaurant ~ (0116) 272 0852 ~ Children welcome ~ Dogs welcome ~ Open 12-11
Recommended by Duncan Cloud, Barry Collett, the Didler

OAKHAM   SK8509   MAP 4

Grainstore 🍺 £

Station Road, off A606; LE15 6RE

Super own-brewed beers in a converted railway grain warehouse, friendly staff, cheerful customers and pubby food

Depending on the time of day, this interesting place will either be very lively or a bit more relaxed. It's always friendly, however, whatever time it is and most customers are here to try the own-brewed beers – the staff will happily let you taste a sample or two. The beer is brewed above the down-to-earth bar and as they use the traditional tower method, during work hours you'll hear noises of the brewery workings filtering down from the floors above. There are ten beers and they are served traditionally at the left end of the bar counter and through swan necks with sparklers on the right. This was once a three-storey Victorian grain warehouse and the décor is plain and functional with wide well worn bare floorboards, bare ceiling boards above massive joists supported by red metal pillars, a long brick-built bar counter with cast-iron bar stools, tall cask tables and simple elm chairs; games machine, darts, board games, giant Jenga and bottle-walking. In summer they pull back the huge glass doors opening the bar up to a terrace with picnic-sets, often stacked with barrels. You can tour the brewery by arrangement, they do take-aways, and hold a real ale festival with over 80 real ales and lots of live music during the August bank holiday weekend; disabled access.

🍴 Wholesome unfussy food includes panini, baked potatoes, mussels prepared in three ways, good sharing platters, burgers, sausage and mash and chicken curry. *Starters/Snacks: £2.95 to £5.95. Main Courses: £5.95 to £8.95. Puddings: £3.95*

Own brew ~ Licensee Peter Atkinson ~ Real ale ~ Bar food (11-3; not Sun) ~ (01572) 770065 ~
Children welcome till 8pm ~ Dogs welcome ~ Live music first Sun and third Thurs of the month
~ Open 11-11(midnight Fri, Sat)

*Recommended by Mike and Sue Loseby, Dr and Mrs T E Hothersall, Tony and Maggie Harwood, Barry Collett,
the Didler, Andy Lickfold, Ian and Helen Stafford, Derek and Sylvia Stephenson*

PEGGS GREEN
SK4117   MAP 7

New Inn £

*Signposted off A512 Ashby—Shepshed at roundabout, then turn immediately left down
Zion Hill towards Newbold; pub is 100 yards down on the right, with car park on opposite
side of road; LE67 8JE*

**Intriguing bric-a-brac in an unspoilt pub, a friendly welcome, good value food and drinks;
cottagey garden**

With friendly Irish licensees and chatty locals, it would be hard not to feel welcomed in
this unspoilt little pub. The two cosy tiled front rooms are each filled with a diverting
collection of old bric-a-brac which covers almost every inch of the walls and ceilings.
The little room on the left, a bit like an old kitchen parlour (they call it the Cabin), has
china on the mantelpiece, lots of prints and photographs, and little collections of this
and that, three old cast-iron tables, wooden stools and a small stripped kitchen table.
The room to the right has nice stripped panelling and more appealing bric-a-brac. The
small back Best room, with a stripped wooden floor, has a touching display of old local
photographs including some colliery ones. Bass, Marstons Pedigree and Theakstons Best
on handpump; board games. There are plenty of seats in front of the pub, with more in
the peaceful back garden. They tell us they don't mind dogs or children but we would
firmly suggest you phone beforehand.

🍴 **Unbelievably cheap food includes filled rolls and baked potatoes, soup, ham and eggs,
corned beef hash, sausages in onion gravy and a few daily specials. When they are not
serving food you can order local take-aways and have it delivered to the pub and on
summer evenings and Sunday lunchtimes you can bring your own picnic and they will
provide rugs.** *Starters/Snacks: £1.95 to £3.25. Main Courses: £4.25 to £5.25. Puddings: £1.95*

Enterprise ~ Lease Maria Christina Kell ~ Real ale ~ Bar food (12-2, Mon, Fri and Sat, 6-8 Mon;
filled rolls might be available at other times) ~ No credit cards ~ (01530) 222293 ~
Open 12-2.30, 5.30-11; 12-3, 6.30-11 Sat; 12-3, 7-10.30 Sun; closed Tues-Thurs lunchtimes

Recommended by Paul J Robinshaw, Philip Bishop, the Didler, Duncan Cloud

SILEBY
SK6015   MAP 7

White Swan

*Off A6 or A607 N of Leicester; in centre turn into King Street (opposite church), then after
mini-roundabout turn right at Post Office signpost into Swan Street; LE12 7NW*

**Exemplary town local, a boon to its chatty regulars, its good honest home cooking luring
others from further afield**

Packed with bric-a-brac from bizarre hats to decorative plates and lots of prints, this
solidly built red-brick pub has all the touches that marked the best of between-wars
estate pub design, such as its deco tiled lobby, the polychrome tiled fireplaces, the shiny
red anaglypta ceiling, the comfortable layout of linked but separate areas including a
small restaurant (now lined with books). It quickly draws you in with its bright and
cheerful feeling of genuine welcome, and this, with its food and the can-do attitude of
its helpful staff, is what sets it above the thousands of other good locals. They have well
kept Fullers London Pride, Lees Ansells and Marstons Pedigree on handpump, and good
value house wines. The elderly boxer is called Leo – and likes balloons.

🍴 **Very popular, homely bar food includes filled rolls (they bake their own bread), soup,
parma ham, goats cheese and walnut salad, a roast and a pie of the day, a home-made**

vegetarian flan, sausages and onion gravy, chicken parmesan, salmon pasta, gressingham duck breast with a whisky and marmalade glaze, and puddings like apple crumble and white chocolate and stem ginger cheesecake; they offer OAP lunches, Tuesday and Wednesday evening curries and good Sunday roasts. *Starters/Snacks: £3.50 to £4.75. Main Courses: £7.99 to £13.99. Puddings: £2.50 to £3.99*

Free house ~ Licensee Theresa Miller ~ Real ale ~ Bar food (12-1.30, 7-8.30; not Sat lunch, Sun evening or Mon) ~ (01509) 814832 ~ Children welcome ~ Open 12-2, 7-11; 7-11 Sat; 12-3 Sun; closed Sat lunchtime, Sun evening and Mon; 1-7 Jan

Recommended by Jim Farmer, GNI

SOMERBY

SK7710 MAP 7

Stilton Cheese 🐷

High Street; off A606 Oakham—Melton Mowbray, via Cold Overton, or Leesthorpe and Pickwell; can also be reached direct from Oakham via Knossington; LE14 2QB

Established place with chatty staff, local real ales, fair-priced bar food and seats on a terrace

Tasty, reasonably priced bar food and five real ales remain quite a draw at this solidly built ironstone pub. The traditional and comfortable hop-strung beamed bar/lounge has dark red patterned carpets, upholstered banquettes, dark wood pubby tables and chairs, country prints on its stripped-stone walls, copper pots hung from beams and, quite rare these days, a stuffed badger; shove-ha'penny, cribbage and dominoes. Grainstore Ten Fifty, Marstons Pedigree and Tetleys Bitter and a couple of guests from breweries such as Newby Wyke and Oakham on handpump; farm cider, lots of wines by the glass and over 30 malt whiskies. There are seats on the terrace.

🍽 Reasonably priced bar food includes pubby staples such as sandwiches, ploughman's, soup, battered cod, lasagne, sausages and mash and macaroni cheese, as well as specials like duck liver and raisin pâté, grilled fresh sardines with garlic butter, chicken and bacon burgers topped with stilton, wild boar and apple sausages, changing pies and suet puddings, pork fillet in sage and cider sauce and game pie, and puddings like Tia Maria crème caramel and black cherry cheesecake. *Starters/Snacks: £3.50 to £5.50. Main Courses: £8.25 to £13.95. Puddings: £3.95*

Free house ~ Licensees Carol and Jeff Evans ~ Real ale ~ Bar food (12-2, 6(7 Sun)-9) ~ Restaurant ~ (01664) 454394 ~ Children welcome ~ Dogs allowed in bedrooms ~ Open 12-3, 6(7 Sun)-11 ~ Bedrooms: £30/£40

Recommended by Philip and Susan Philcox, Mike and Margaret Banks, Richard Tingle, Phil and Jane Hodson, Duncan Cloud, Ken and Barbara Turner

SOUTH LUFFENHAM

SK9401 MAP 4

Coach House 🛏

Stamford Road (A6121); LE15 8NT

Good food and comfortable simple bedrooms in friendly and nicely reworked old inn

Bright scatter cushions on the little dark brown pews, fat candles on each of the mixed stripped tables, and a good log fire liven up the dark-flagstoned main bar, its thick walls either stripped stone or with terracotta-coloured plaster. On the left a separate little red-walled snug has been carefully fitted out with neat built-in wooden seating – very cosy. Welcoming staff serve Adnams, Greene King IPA and Timothy Taylors Landlord from handpump, and a good choice of wines by the glass; there may be piped radio. A smarter and more modern-feeling back dining room, light and airy with its floor-to-ceiling windows, has comfortable brown suede seating. There are tables and chairs out on the small back deck.

If we know a pub has an outdoor play area for children, we mention it.

🍴 Using some home-grown produce, the good bar food includes sandwiches, soup, salmon fishcakes with chilli chutney, sausages and onion gravy, butternut squash and pea risotto, popular beef in ale casserole, nice lamb stew, whole plaice and Sunday roasts. *Starters/Snacks: £5.00 to £8.00. Main Courses: £9.00 to £17.00. Puddings: £5.00 to £6.95*

Free house ~ Licensee Charles Thomas ~ Real ale ~ Bar food (not Sun evening or Mon lunchtime) ~ Restaurant ~ (01780) 720166 ~ Children welcome ~ Dogs allowed in bar ~ Open 12-2, 5-11; 11-11 Sat; 12-5 Sun; closed Sun evening and Mon lunchtime ~ Bedrooms: £50S/£70S

Recommended by Marcus Mann

STATHERN   SK7731 MAP 7

Red Lion ♀ 🍺

Off A52 W of Grantham via the brown-signed Belvoir road (keep on towards Harby – Stathern signposted on left); or off A606 Nottingham—Melton Mowbray via Long Clawson and Harby; LE14 4HS

Fine range of drinks and popular food in civilised dining pub with open fires and good garden with a play area; own shop, too

Surrounded by the lovely Vale of Belvoir, this rather civilised dining pub is decorated in a charming rustic style. The yellow room on the right, with its collection of wooden spoons and lambing chairs, has a simple country-pub feel. The lounge bar has sofas, an open fire and a big table with books, newspapers and magazines. It leads off the smaller, more traditional flagstoned bar with terracotta walls, another fireplace with a pile of logs beside it, and lots of beams and hops. A little room with tables set for eating leads to the long, narrow main dining room, and out to a nicely arranged suntrap with good hardwood furnishings spread over its lawn and terrace. The atmosphere throughout is relaxed and informal; piped music. Red Lion Ale (from Grainstore) and a couple of guests such as Brewsters Decadence and Fullers London Pride on handpump, draught belgian and continental bottled beers, several ciders, and a varied wine list (several by the glass). There's an unusually big play area behind the car park with swings, climbing frames and so on. This is under the same ownership as the Olive Branch in Clipsham. More reports please.

🍴 As well as a popular two- and three-course set lunch, the often imaginative food includes sandwiches, soup, filo basket filled with a fricassée of wild mushrooms, pigeon breast with pearl barley risotto and roasted root vegetables, sausages with mustard mash and onion gravy, fish and chips with mushy peas, confit duck leg with chorizo mash and beetroot salsa, lamb chump with mixed bean cassoulet, and puddings such as vanilla panna cotta with rhubarb sorbet and hot chocolate fondant with passion-fruit marshmallow and passion-fruit ice-cream. *Starters/Snacks: £4.25 to £6.50. Main Courses: £9.95 to £17.50. Puddings: £4.95 to £6.25*

Free house ~ Licensees Sean Hope and Ben Jones ~ Real ale ~ Bar food (12-2(3 Sun), 6-9) ~ Restaurant ~ (01949) 860868 ~ Children welcome ~ Dogs allowed in bar ~ Open 12-3, 6-11; 12-11 Sat; 12-7 Sun; closed Sun evening

Recommended by Leslie and Barbara Owen, David Glynne-Jones, Roy Bromell, Jeff and Wendy Williams

STRETTON   SK9415 MAP 8

Jackson Stops

Rookery Lane; a mile or less off A1, at B668 (Oakham) exit; follow village sign, turning off Clipsham Road into Manor Road, pub on left; LE15 7RA

New owners and some refurbishment in former farmhouse; handy for the A1

New owners have recently refurbished this former farmhouse but without changing the original character of the place. The paintwork is now mainly french grey and white throughout and there are nightlight candles in little glass containers on all the tables.

The black-beamed country bar down on the left has some wall timbering, a couple of bar stools, a cushioned wall pew and an elderly settle on the worn tile and brick floor and a coal fire in one corner. Grainstore Triple B and a changing local guest on handpump and several wines by the glass. The smarter main room on the right is light and airy with a nice mix of ancient and modern tables on dark blue carpeting and another coal fire in a stone corner fireplace. Right, along past the bar is the dining room with stripped-stone walls, a tiled floor and an old open cooking range and there's a second smaller dining room, too; piped music.

🍴 **Lunchtime bar food includes filled baguettes and ciabattas, soup, home-made burgers, honey-and-mustard-roasted ham and eggs and mozzarella and olive pasta bake, with more elaborate evening choices such as smoked salmon with horseradish cream, chicken breast stuffed with mozzarella and pesto, wrapped in parma ham and served with a sun-dried tomato dressing, calves liver with crispy bacon and dill mash and bass with a leek and saffron sauce, and puddings like white chocolate panna cotta with amaretto plums and almond praline and raspberry crème brûlée.** *Starters/Snacks: £4.95 to £6.95. Main Courses: £10.25 to £18.95. Puddings: £5.00*

Free house ~ Licensees Linda Ramsden and Max Enterkin ~ Real ale ~ Bar food (12-2.30(3 Sun), 7-9.30) ~ Restaurant ~ (01780) 410237 ~ Children welcome ~ Dogs allowed in bar ~ Open 12-3, 6-midnight; 12-5 Sun; closed Sun evening and Mon

Recommended by Gordon and Margaret Ormondroyd, Leslie and Barbara Owen, Roxanne Chamberlain, Derek and Sylvia Stephenson, John and Eleanor Holdsworth, John Wooll, Alison Ball, Ian Walton, Ken and Lynda Taylor, John Prescott, Maurice and Janet Thorpe, W M Paton, Michael Doswell

SWITHLAND
SK5512 MAP 7

Griffin 🍺

Main Street; between A6 and B5330, between Loughborough and Leicester; LE12 8TJ

A good mix of cheerful customers, well liked food and six real ales in a bustling pub

In a small, tucked-away village, this attractive stone-built pub is a friendly and popular place. The beamed communicating rooms have some panelling and a nice mix of wooden tables, chairs and bar stools. Everards Beacon, Original and Tiger plus three guests such as Adnams Bitter, Everards Flourish and Greene King Abbot on handpump, several malt whiskies and wines by the glass from a good list; piped music and skittle alley. There are seats in the tidy streamside garden, overlooking open fields. The pub is handy for Bradgate Country Park and there are walks in Swithland Woods.

🍴 **Well liked bar food includes filled baguettes, ploughman's, soup, chicken liver pâté with home-made chutney, ham and eggs, mushroom risotto, steak and mushroom in ale pie, pork tenderloin with an apple and brandy cream sauce, lambs liver with bacon and onion gravy and monkfish medallions with mussels and a creamy wine sauce.** *Starters/Snacks: £3.95 to £7.50. Main Courses: £6.95 to £18.00. Puddings: £4.00 to £6.00*

Everards ~ Tenant John Cooledge ~ Real ale ~ Bar food (some sort of food all day; not Mon) ~ Restaurant ~ (01509) 890535 ~ Children welcome ~ Open 10am-11pm

Recommended by David Jackson, Pam and John Smith, Duncan Cloud, Michael Butler

UPPER HAMBLETON
SK8907 MAP 4

Finchs Arms 🛏

Off A606; Oakham Road; LE15 8TL

Welcoming inn with log fires, real ales, good food, attentive staff and fine waterside views; comfortable bedrooms

From the suntrap hillside terrace behind this 17th-c stone inn there are outstanding views over Rutland Water; good surroundings walks. Inside, the beamed and flagstoned bar has a good, bustling atmosphere, nice old wooden tables, chairs and settles and Black Sheep Best, Grainstore Nip and Tetleys Bitter on handpump and several wines by the glass; there are three log fires. The elegant restaurant has views of the water, some decorative bay trees and wicker and chrome dining chairs on the stripped wooden floor. Our readers enjoy staying in the newly refurbished bedrooms here.

🍴 **Using seasonal local game and other local produce, the popular bar food includes sandwiches, soup, grilled goats cheese with warm mulled figs, chicken liver parfait, smoked haddock risotto with a poached egg, wild mushroom and parmesan pasta, grilled cod with chorizo and basil mash, venison with creamed celeriac and sweet potatoes, and puddings such as lemon tart with blackcurrant sorbet and plum tarte tatin with vanilla ice-cream.** *Starters/Snacks: £4.50 to £6.50. Main Courses: £9.50 to £12.00. Puddings: £5.00 to £6.50*

Free house ~ Licensees Celia and Colin Crawford ~ Real ale ~ Bar food ~ Restaurant ~ (01572) 756575 ~ Children welcome ~ Open 11-11; 12-10.30 Sun ~ Bedrooms: £75B/£95B

Recommended by Maurice and Janet Thorpe, John Robertson, Michael Doswell, Marcus Mann, Pat and Stewart Gordon, Clive Watkin, Ryta Lyndley, R L Borthwick

WING   SK8902   MAP 4

Kings Arms 🍴 ☐ 🛏

Village signposted off A6003 S of Oakham; Top Street; LE15 8SE

Nicely kept old pub, big log fires, super choice of wines by the glass and good modern cooking

There's a fine choice of drinks in this civilised 17th-c inn though most customers are here to enjoy the excellent modern food. The neatly kept and attractive bar has various nooks and crannies, nice old low beams and stripped stone, two large log fires (one in a copper-canopied central hearth) and flagstoned or wood-strip floors. Friendly, helpful staff serve over 20 wines by the glass, as well as Grainstore Cooking, Marstons Pedigree and Shepherd Neame Spitfire on handpump, several grappas and malt whiskies and Sheppey's cider; board games. There are seats out in front, and more in the sunny yew-sheltered garden; the car park has plenty of space. There's a medieval turf maze up the road, and we are told that the pub is just a couple of miles away from one of England's two osprey hot-spots.

🍴 **They have their own smokehouse producing everything from charcuterie to smoked nuts to smoked eel, cook with some unusual ingredients such as squirrel and bake their own bread and biscuits: sandwiches, soup, beef or venison bresaola, home-made black pudding in light batter, maple smoked honey and cider ham with free-range eggs, shepherd's pie, top quality burger with smoked bacon, grilled cheese, their own ketchup and chilli jam, muntjac saddle with dauphinoise potatoes, a trio of rabbit, cod loin with leek and sun-dried tomato risotto and dill aioli, and puddings like chocolate fondant with white chocolate kirsch centre, pistachio ice-cream and griottine cherries and apple crumble with rum custard and cinnamon yoghurt ice-cream.** *Starters/Snacks: £5.50 to £7.50. Main Courses: £9.00 to £16.00. Puddings: £6.50 to £7.00*

Free house ~ Licensee David Goss ~ Real ale ~ Bar food (12-2(2.30 Sat), 6.30-8.30(9 Fri, Sat)) ~ Restaurant ~ (01572) 737634 ~ Well behaved children welcome but must be over 12 in evening ~ Dogs allowed in bar ~ Open 12-3, 6.30-11; 12-3 Sun; closed Sun evening, Mon lunchtime (all day winter Mon) and winter Tues lunchtime ~ Bedrooms: £62.50S/£85S

Recommended by Gary Kelly, Phil and Jane Hodson, Mike and Sue Loseby, D Goodger, Bruce and Sharon Eden, Michael Sargent

---

Several well known guide books make establishments pay for entry, either directly or as a fee for inspection. These fees can run to many hundreds of pounds. We do not. Unlike other guides, we never take payment for entries. We never accept a free meal, free drink, or any other freebie from a pub. All our entries depend solely on merit. And we are the only guide in which virtually all the Main Entries have been gained by a unique two-stage sifting process: first, a build-up of favourable reports from our thousands of reader-reporters; then anonymous vetting by one of our senior editorial staff.

WOODHOUSE EAVES

SK5313 MAP 7

Wheatsheaf 🛏

Brand Hill; turn right into Main Street, off B591 S of Loughborough; LE12 8SS

Bustling and friendly country pub, interesting things to look at, good bistro-type food and a fair choice of drinks; well equipped bedrooms

The open-plan interior of this rather smart country is full of interesting motor-racing, family RAF and flying memorabilia, and a cosy dining area called The Mess even has an RAF Hurricane propeller. The beamed bar areas are traditionally furnished and have wooden pews, log fires and daily papers to read. The atmosphere is cheerful and chatty and the service helpful and welcoming, even when pushed. Adnams Broadside, Greene King IPA, Marstons Pedigree and Timothy Taylors Landlord on handpump and several wines including champagne by the glass from a thoughtfully compiled list. The floodlit, heated terrace has plenty of seating.

🍴 Interesting bar food includes sandwiches and filled baguettes and ciabattas, soup, chicken liver pâté with redcurrant jelly, chinese bang-bang chicken, mushroom ravioli in a basil cream sauce, fish and chips, pork and leek sausages with leek mash and mustard sauce and daily specials like chargrilled lamb chops with apricot and mint sauce, duck breast, with a Cointreau and orange sauce and medallions of beef with a creamy brandy and wild mushroom sauce. *Starters/Snacks: £4.00 to £6.25. Main Courses: £10.50 to £21.00. Puddings: £5.25*

Free house ~ Licensees Richard and Bridget Dimblebee ~ Real ale ~ Bar food (12-2(2.30 Sat, 3 Sun), 6.30-9.15; best to check for Sun evening) ~ Restaurant ~ (01509) 890320 ~ Children welcome ~ Dogs allowed in bar ~ Open 11.30-3, 6-11; 11.30-11 Sat; 12-5, 6-10.30 Sun ~ Bedrooms: £60S/£80B

Recommended by the Didler, George and Linda Ozols, DF, NF, John Saville

LUCKY DIP

Besides the fully inspected pubs, you might like to try these Lucky Dips recommended to us and described by readers (if you do, please send us reports: feedback@goodguides.com).

ABY [TF4177]
Railway Tavern LN13 0DR: Friendly well run village pub, nice home-made food in open bar, good service, well kept Batemans and Everards, coal fire, railway memorabilia, games room *(Derek and Sylvia Stephenson)*

BARKBY [SK6309]
Malt Shovel LE7 3QG [Main St]: Old village pub with enjoyable good value food inc bargain steak night Mon, half a dozen real ales, good choice of wines by the glass, charming service, U-shaped open-plan bar, small dining room (was the local jail); garden with partly covered heated terrace *(Phil and Jane Hodson)*

BARROWDEN [SK9400]
☆ *Exeter Arms* LE15 8EQ [Main St, just off A47 Uppingham—Peterborough]: Former coaching inn popular with locals, open-plan bar with beams, stripped stone and open fire, own-brewed ales plus a couple of guests from long central counter, pubby food and specials; collection of pump clips, beer mats and brewery posters, darts; piped music; children and dogs welcome, picnic-sets on narrow front terrace with lovely views over village green and Welland Valley, big informal garden behind with boules, red kites in nearby Fineshades woods and nice

walks, bedrooms, cl Sun evening, Mon lunchtime *(Duncan Cloud, Barry Collett, the Didler, LYM)*

BELTON [SK4420]
Queens Head LE12 9TP [4.4 miles from M1 junction 23: after about 2.6 miles turn right off A512 Ashby Road; Long Street/B5324; can return to M1 junction 23A via A42]: New licensee for this former alehouse; minimalist décor with modern brown leather bucket seats and cushioned sofas on bare boards, unusual contemporary gas fire, Belvoir Dark Horse from cushioned bar counter, two-room dining area with fire; service charge added; verandah, picnic-sets on side lawn, bedrooms, has been open all day *(LYM)*

BOTCHESTON [SK4804]
Greyhound LE9 9FF [Main St, off B5380 E of Desford]: Beamed village pub with enjoyable fresh generous food from lunchtime bargains to unusual dishes (should book), pine tables in two light and airy dining rooms, three well kept changing ales, friendly service; children welcome, garden with play area *(Duncan Cloud)*

BRANSTON [SK8129]
☆ *Wheel* NG32 1RU [Main St]: Refurbished beamed 18th-c village pub with stylishly simple décor, friendly attentive landlady and

staff, chef/landlord doing proper country food, some quite out of the ordinary, changing ales such as Adnams and Batemans from central servery, log fires; attractive garden, next to church, splendid countryside nr Belvoir castle, cl Mon *(BB, Mike and Jan Beckett, David Russell, Phil and Jane Hodson)*

BRAUNSTON [SK8306]

Blue Ball LE15 8QS [off A606 in Oakham; Cedar St]: Pretty thatched and beamed dining pub, enjoyable local food from sandwiches and other bar snacks up, good service, well kept Marstons-related ales, decent wines, log fire, candles, flowers and country pine in quiet linked rooms inc small conservatory; children welcome, tables outside, attractive village *(R L Borthwick, LYM)*

Old Plough LE15 8QT [off A606 in Oakham; Church St]: Black-beamed village local under new management, comfortably opened up, log fire, back dining conservatory; tables in small sheltered garden, has been open all day *(LYM)*

BURROUGH ON THE HILL [SK7510]

Grants LE14 2JQ [off B6047 S of Melton Mowbray; Main St]: Cosy newly decorated old pub (former Stag & Hounds), Parrish ales brewed next door by landlord, bargain food inc Sun carvery, open fires; garden, good walk to nearby Iron Age fort *(LYM, Patrick Cleere)*

BURTON OVERY [SP6797]

☆ *Bell* LE8 9DL [Main St]: Interesting choice of consistently good food from lunchtime sandwiches up in L-shaped open-plan bar and dining room, good log fire, comfortable settees, ales inc Adnams Best and Timothy Taylors Landlord; children welcome, nice garden, lovely village, open all day wknds *(R L Borthwick)*

CALDECOTT [SP8693]

Plough LE16 8RS [Main St]: Welcoming pub in attractive ironstone village, carpeted bar with banquettes and small tables leading to spacious eating area, Thwaites and a guest such as Langton, wide range of enjoyable inexpensive food *(Barry Collett)*

CASTLE DONINGTON [SK4427]

Jolly Potters DE74 2NH [Hillside]: Genuine unspoilt town local, basic and friendly, with pews on flagstones, good coal fire, hanging mugs and jugs, well kept Bass, Fullers, Marstons Pedigree and guest beers; open all day *(the Didler)*

☆ *Nags Head* DE74 2PS [Diseworth Rd/Hill Top; A453, S end]: Low-beamed bistro pub with wide choice of reasonably priced food (all day wknds, at least in summer), Banks's and related beers, good range of wines by the glass, large airy dining area with open-view kitchen, quarry-tiled bar opening into smaller back dining room; may be piped music *(Brian and Jean Hepworth, LYM)*

COLEORTON [SK4016]

Angel LE67 8GB [The Moor]: Friendly modernised old pub, good range of enjoyable home-made food, well kept beers, hospitable attentive staff, beams and coal fires; tables outside *(Gill and Keith Croxton)*

COPT OAK [SK4812]

Copt Oak LE67 9QB [Whitwick Rd, handy for M1 junction 22]: Comfortable family dining pub with good views over Charnwood Forest, wide choice of food (all day Sun) inc deals, quick friendly service, Brakspears and Marstons Pedigree, woodburner; piped music, can be very busy wknds *(Duncan Cloud, David and Gill Carrington)*

COTTESMORE [SK9013]

☆ *Sun* LE15 7DH [B668 NE of Oakham]: 17th-c thatched stone-built village pub with good atmosphere and pleasant staff, good choice of wines by the glass, Adnams Best, Everards Tiger and guest, good coffee, wide choice of good reasonably priced bar food from lunchtime sandwiches up, stripped pine on flagstones, inglenook fire, lots of pictures and ornaments, carpeted back restaurant; piped music; dogs and children welcome, terrace tables, open all day wknds *(Jeremy Hancock, Richard and Jean Green, LYM, Michael and Maggie Betton)*

EAST LANGTON [SP7292]

Bell LE16 7TW [off B6047; Main St]: Appealing creeper-clad beamed country inn buzzing with locals and families, well kept Brewsters, Greene King and local Langton, nice wine, good interesting food inc popular Sun carvery, good service, long low-ceilinged stripped-stone bar, spacious restaurant, modern pine furniture, log fires; picnic-sets on sloping front lawn, bedrooms *(Rona Murdoch, LYM, Duncan Cloud, R L Borthwick)*

EMPINGHAM [SK9908]

☆ *White Horse* LE15 8PS [Main Street; A606 Stamford—Oakham]: Sizeable old stone pub handy for Rutland Water; bustling open-plan carpeted lounge bar, big log fire, Adnams, Oakham and Timothy Taylors Landlord, good choice of wines by the glass, wide range of fresh pubby food and more elaborate specials, cheerful service; TV, piped music; children welcome, rustic tables out among flower tubs, bedrooms, open all day *(Duncan Cloud, John Robertson, Leslie and Barbara Owen, Clive Watkin, David and Ruth Hollands, Barry Collett, Dave and Jenny Hughes, LYM, Phil and Jane Hodson)*

FOXTON [SP6989]

☆ *Foxton Locks* LE16 7RA [Foxton Locks, off A6 3 miles NW of Market Harborough (park by bridge 60/62 and walk)]: Large busy comfortably reworked L-shaped bar, good choice of enjoyable well priced food inc winter fixed-price menu, converted boathouse does snacks, quick friendly service, half a dozen well kept ales such as Caledonian Deuchars IPA, Fullers London Pride and Theakstons; children welcome, large raised terrace and covered decking, steps down to fenced waterside lawn – nice setting at foot of long flight of canal locks, good walks *(Gerry and Rosemary Dobson, Duncan Cloud,*

Margaret and Peter Staples, Martin Smith, John Wooll)

GREAT BOWDEN [SP7488]

Red Lion LE16 7HB [off A6 N of Market Harborough; Main St]: Attractive bar with two fireplaces, ales such as Greene King and Jennings, well chosen wines, enjoyable regularly changing home-made food, friendly helpful staff, cosy dining room; piped music; children and dogs welcome, tables in big garden, bedrooms, open all day wknds (Gary Marsden, LYM)

GREETHAM [SK9214]

Plough LE15 7NJ [B668 Stretton—Cottesmore]: Friendly popular village local tied to Grainstore, their beers kept well, enjoyable and interesting home-made food from baguettes up inc good cheese selection, coal-effect gas fire dividing cosy lounge from eating area, pub games; tables out behind (with quoits), handy for Rutland Water, open all day Fri-Sun (Pierre Richterich)

Wheatsheaf LE15 7NP [B668 Stretton—Cottesmore]: Linked L-shaped rooms, popular well prepared food from good sandwiches (home-made bread) up, nice home-made ice-cream too, friendly welcoming service, well kept ales such as Greene King and Oldershaws, good choice of wines, blazing open stove; soft piped music, games room with darts, pool and big-screen sports TV; children welcome, wheelchair access, front lawn, terrace by pretty stream with duck house, annexe bedrooms, open all day Fri/Sat, cl Mon (Michael and Jenny Back, Bruce and Sharon Eden, Barry Collett, Pat and Graham Williamson, BB)

GUMLEY [SP6890]

Bell LE16 7RU [NW of Market Harborough; Main St]: Neatly kept beamed village pub under new licensees; wide choice of good value food (not Sun or Mon evenings) inc bargain OAP lunches, Black Sheep, Fullers, Greene King and Timothy Taylors, traditional country décor, lots of hunting prints, small fire, darts, cribbage and dominoes, separate dining room, border collie called Bailey; no mobile phones, muddy boots or children under 10; pretty terrace garden with pond and aviary (not for children or dogs), open all day, cl Sun evening (LYM)

HATHERN [SK5021]

Dew Drop LE12 5HY [Loughborough Rd (A6)]: Traditional two-room beamed local, welcoming landlord, well kept Greene King and guests, lots of malts, coal fire, good lunchtime cobs, darts and dominoes; tables outside (the Didler)

HEMINGTON [SK4527]

☆ **Jolly Sailor** DE74 2RB [Main St]: Cheerful and welcoming picturesque three-room village pub, generous sensibly priced fresh food inc popular Sun lunch (best to book), six well kept ales, Weston's Old Rosie cider, decent wines by the glass, good range of soft drinks, warm log fire, big country pictures, bric-a-brac on heavy beams and

shelves, table skittles, daily papers, restaurant; children welcome, picnic-sets out in front, open all day wknds (MP, the Didler)

HOBY [SK6717]

☆ **Blue Bell** LE14 3DT [Main St]: Attractive rebuilt thatched pub run by present licensees, good range of enjoyable realistically priced food (all day wknds – best to book), small helpings available, Sun roasts, good welcoming uniformed service, up to six well kept ales, good choice of wines by the glass and of teas/coffees, open-plan and airy with beams, comfortable traditional furniture, old local photographs, skittle alley, darts; piped music; children and dogs welcome, valley view garden with picnic-sets and boules, open all day (Phil and Jane Hodson, R L Borthwick)

HUNGARTON [SK6907]

Black Boy LE7 9JR [Main St]: Large partly divided open-plan bar, good well priced food cooked to order (wknd booking advised), changing ales such as Batemans, Greene King Abbot and Wells & Youngs Bombardier, friendly service, minimal decoration, open fire; cl Sun evening (R L Borthwick)

ILLSTON ON THE HILL [SP7099]

☆ **Fox & Goose** LE7 9EG [Main St, off B6047 Market Harborough—Melton]: Individualistic two-bar local, plain, comfortable and convivial, with interesting pictures and assorted oddments, well kept Everards and guest ales, quick service, good coal fire, no food; cl Mon lunchtime (LYM, the Didler)

KEGWORTH [SK4826]

☆ **Cap & Stocking** DE74 2FF [handy for M1 junction 24, via A6; Borough St]: Nicely old-fashioned unchanging three-room pub, brown paint, etched glass, coal fires, big cases of stuffed birds and locally caught fish, Bass (from the jug) and well kept guests such as Jennings and Wells & Youngs, home-made food (not Weds evening) from fresh sandwiches to bargain Sun lunch, dominoes, back room opening to secluded garden with decking; piped music, no credit cards; children welcome (the Didler, LYM)

Red Lion DE74 2DA [a mile from M1 junction 24, via A6 towards Loughborough; High St]: Half a dozen or more good changing ales and good range of whiskies and vodkas in four brightly lit traditional rooms around small servery, limited choice of good wholesome food (not Sun), assorted furnishings, coal and flame-effect fires, delft shelf of beer bottles, daily papers, darts and cards, family room; small back yard, garden with play area, well equipped bedrooms, open all day (the Didler, BB)

KIBWORTH BEAUCHAMP [SP6894]

Coach & Horses LE8 0NN [A6 S of Leicester]: Snug 16th-c carpeted local with mugs on beams and candlelit restaurant, wide choice of home-made food inc good value OAP lunches and all-day Sun roasts, well kept Bass, Fullers London Pride, Greene King IPA and Wadworths 6X, regular events; piped music, TVs; children welcome, dogs in bar, disabled access, some outside seating at front and on side terrace, open all day wknds, cl Mon lunchtime *(Mike and Margaret Banks, Duncan Cloud, BB)*

KILBY [SP6295]

Dog & Gun LE18 3TD [Main St, off A5199 S of Leicester]: Welcoming much-extended cleanly kept pub, locally popular for wide choice of good straightforward food from baguettes up inc bargain set lunches, helpful service, Fullers London Pride and Greene King IPA and Abbot, good wine choice, coal fire, attractive side restaurant with grandfather clock, afternoon teas; disabled access and parking, colourful back garden with terrace and pergola, open all day *(Veronica Brown, Michael and Jenny Back, Duncan Cloud)*

KNIPTON [SK8231]

Manners Arms NG32 1RH [signed off A607 Grantham—Melton Mowbray; Croxton Rd]: Handsome Georgian hunting lodge beautifully renovated by Duke and Duchess of Rutland as upscale country inn, hunting prints and furniture from Belvoir Castle, log fire, well kept Belvoir and other ales, good choice of wines by the glass, enjoyable food, sizeable restaurant with attractive conservatory, sumptuous lounge; piped music; terrace with ornamental pool, lovely views over pretty village, ten comfortable individually furnished bedrooms, open all day *(Phil and Jane Hodson, S J and C C Davidson, BB)*

KNOSSINGTON [SK8008]

Fox & Hounds LE15 8LY [off A606 W of Oakham; Somerby Rd]: Handsome 18th-c ivy-covered village pub, simply modernised knocked-through beamed bar with log fire, lots of hunting prints, comfortable end dining area, Fullers, Greene King and guest such as Adnams, good choice of wines, food from pubby favourites up inc Sun roasts; piped music; children and dogs welcome, big back garden, open all day wknds, cl Mon (but open evening in summer) *(Phil and Jane Hodson, LYM)*

LEICESTER [SK5804]

Ale Wagon LE1 1RE [Rutland St/Charles St]: Basic 1930s two-room local with great beer choice inc own Hoskins ales, Weston's cider and perry, coal fire, events such as comedy nights; juke box, sports TV; handy for station, open all day (Sun afternoon break) *(the Didler)*

Black Horse LE3 5LT [Braunstone Gate/Foxon St]: Unspoilt two-room Victorian corner local, well kept Everards ales and up to five guests, farm cider, traditional layout (with outside lavatories), darts and dominoes, character back lounge, frequent live acoustic music; popular with students; open all day Sat *(the Didler)*

Criterion LE1 5JN [Millstone Lane]: Modern building with dark wood and burgundy décor in carpeted main room, Oakham ales and up to ten guests at wknds, 100 bottled beers, decent wines by the glass, good value stone-

baked pizzas, tapas and more traditional pub food (not Sun evening, Mon), relaxed room on left with games, old-fashioned juke box, music, comedy and quiz nights; wheelchair access (small front step), picnic-sets outside, open all day *(the Didler, John Martin)*

☆ *Globe* LE1 5EU [Silver St]: Lots of woodwork in cheerfully well worn partitioned areas off central bar, mirrors and wrought-iron gas lamps, charming more peaceful upstairs dining room, five Everards ales and four guest beers, friendly staff, bargain food 12-7 from snacks up inc a good vegetarian choice; piped music (not in snug), very popular with young people wknd evenings; children welcome, open all day *(Val and Alan Green, the Didler, LYM)*

Rutland & Derby Arms LE1 5JN [Millstone Lane]: Smartly renovated old pub with clean-cut modern bar/brasserie décor, friendly staff, interesting well priced food using local organic meat inc bargain two-course Sun lunch, home-baked sourdough bread, Everards and guest ales, wide choice of lagers, spirits and juices; well reproduced piped music; terrace tables at back *(Jeremy King)*

Shakespeares Head LE1 5SH [Southgates]: Welcoming chatty local with good low-priced Oakwell Barnsley and Old Tom Mild, well filled cobs Fri and Sat, popular Sun roasts; basic bar, lounge popular with older regulars; open all day *(the Didler)*

☆ *Swan & Rushes* LE1 5WR [Oxford St/Infirmary Sq]: Well kept Batemans, Oakham and fine range of guest and bottled beers, farm cider, welcoming staff and thriving atmosphere in two rooms with big oak tables, enjoyable home-made lunchtime food (not Sun), fish and chips Fri evening, live music Sat; open all day Fri-Sun *(the Didler)*

LOUGHBOROUGH [SK5320]

Albion LE11 1QA [canal bank, about 0.2 miles from Loughborough Wharf]: Welcoming chatty local by Grand Union Canal, four unusual ales inc local Wicked Hathern, cheap straightforward home-made food, cosy carpeted bar, coal fire, darts; children welcome, canalside seating, back terrace *(the Didler, Clive and Fran Dutson, Michael and Hilary Andrews)*

☆ *Swan in the Rushes* LE11 5BE [The Rushes (A6)]: Bare-boards town local with good value Castle Rock and interesting changing ales, foreign bottled beers, farm cider, good value chip-free food (not Sat and Sun evenings), good service, daily papers, traditional games, open fire, three smallish high-ceilinged rooms; good juke box, music nights; children in eating areas, tables outside, four bedrooms, open all day *(the Didler, Andy Lickfold, LYM)*

Tap & Mallet LE11 1EU [Nottingham Rd]: Basic friendly pub with well kept Jennings, Marstons and five changing guests inc microbrews, foreign beers, farm cider and perry, nice cobs, coal fire, pool, juke box; walled back garden with play area and pets corner, open all day *(the Didler)*

MANTON [SK8704]

Horse & Jockey LE15 8SU [St Marys Rd]: Welcoming recently refurbished early 19th-c pub, well kept Grainstore ales, promptly served inexpensive food from baguettes up all day at least wknds, big coal fire; picnic-sets outside, on Rutland Water cycle route (bike racks provided), four bedrooms *(R L Borthwick, Comus and Sarah Elliott)*

MARKET HARBOROUGH [SP7387]

Angel LE16 7AF [High St]: Popular former coaching inn with good range of reasonably priced food in bar and restaurant, friendly uniformed staff, well kept Marstons and a guest, good coffee, daily papers; discreet sports TV; 24 bedrooms *(P Tailyour, Michael Dandy, Gerry and Rosemary Dobson)*

Sugar Loaf LE16 7NJ [High St]: Popular Wetherspoons, smaller than many, with half a dozen sensibly priced real ales, good value food all day; children allowed, frequent beer festivals, open all day *(Gerry and Rosemary Dobson)*

☆ *Three Swans* LE16 7NJ [High St]: Comfortable banquettes and plush-cushioned library chairs in traditional bay-windowed front bar of Best Western conference hotel, local ales such as Grainstore and Langton, good spread of pubby food from sandwiches up inc set deals, decent wines, good friendly service, flame-effect fires (one in grand coaching-era inglenook), flagstoned back area, corridor to popular conservatory bistro (evenings Mon-Sat), formal upstairs restaurant; piped music; attractive suntrap courtyard, useful parking, good bedrooms *(Gerry and Rosemary Dobson, George Atkinson, Michael Dandy, BB)*

MARKET OVERTON [SK8816]

Black Bull LE15 7PW [off B668 in Cottesmore]: Attractive thatched and low-beamed stone-built pub in pretty village well placed for Rutland Water, friendly enthusiastic landlord and energetic staff, good interesting home-made food in long red-carpeted bar and two separate dining areas, four well kept ales inc Theakstons and Wells & Youngs, banquettes and sofas, newspapers; some piped music; children welcome, tables out in front by small carp pool *(BB, Barry Collett)*

MEDBOURNE [SP7992]

☆ *Nevill Arms* LE16 8EE [B664 Market Harborough—Uppingham]: Handsome stone-built Victorian inn nicely located by stream and footbridge, wide range of good bar and restaurant food inc Sun roasts, pleasant helpful staff, well kept ales such as Fullers London Pride and Greene King IPA, beams and mullioned windows, log fires, modern artwork, stylish back restaurant; no dogs; back terrace with stable-conversion café (8am-4pm), streamside picnic-sets, 11 refurbished bedrooms, good breakfast, open all day *(John Wooll, Mike and*

Sue Loseby, Duncan Cloud, Barry Collett, Nigel and Sue Foster, Richard and Jean Green, Rona Murdoch, LYM)

NEWTON BURGOLAND [SK3709]

☆ *Belper Arms* LE67 2SE [off B4116 S of Ashby]: Ancient rambling pub said to date from 13th c, roomy lounge with low-beamed areas off, changing floor levels, stripped brick, some good antique furniture and plenty to look at inc framed story of pub's ghost, nice log fire; Greene King and Theakstons ales, Weston's cider, many wines by the glass, several malt whiskies, enjoyable reasonably priced food, cheerful helpful service, restaurant; some piped music; children and dogs welcome, big garden with terrace, open all day *(Duncan Cloud, Richard and Jean Green, Alan Thwaite, the Didler)*

NORTH KILWORTH [SP6183]

White Lion LE17 6EP [4.5 miles from M1 junction 20; A4304 towards Market Harborough]: Comfortable village pub recently reopened and extensively refurbished, enjoyable basic home-made food, good choice of wine *(Jill Mordaunt)*

OAKHAM [SK8508]

Wheatsheaf LE15 6QS [Northgate]: Attractive 17th-c local nr church, friendly helpful staff, well kept Adnams, Everards and guests, good lunchtime pub food, open fires, plenty of bric-a-brac, cheerful bar, comfortable quieter lounge and conservatory (children welcome here); pretty suntrap back courtyard with entertaining installation *(Barry Collett)*

OLD DALBY [SK6723]

☆ *Crown* LE14 3LF [Debdale Hill]: Creeper-clad with intimate farmhouse rooms up and down steps, black beams, antique oak settles among other seats, rustic prints, open fires, several well kept ales inc Belvoir and Castle Rock from expanded bar area, plenty of wines by the glass, good up-to-date fresh local food (not Sun evening, Mon) from bar menu or more expensive evening one, good service, extended dining room opening on to terrace; children and dogs welcome, disabled facilities, attractive garden with boules, cl Mon lunchtime *(Phil and Jane Hodson, MP, Comus and Sarah Elliott, Adrian Johnson, the Didler, LYM)*

REDMILE [SK7935]

☆ *Windmill* NG13 0GA [off A52 Grantham—Nottingham; Main St]: Snug low-beamed bar with low sofas, easy chairs and log fire in capacious hearth, comfortable roomier dining areas with woodburners, wide choice of good generous home-made food from baguettes to game from local Belvoir Estate, meal deals and Sun roasts too, well kept Adnams and Shepherd Neame Spitfire, Aspall's cider, good wines by the glass inc champagne, local cordials, neat and friendly young staff; children welcome, sizeable well furnished front courtyard, cl Sun evening, Mon *(Maurice and Janet Thorpe, Phil and Jane Hodson, BB)*

SADDINGTON [SP6591]
Queens Head LE8 0QH [S of Leicester between A5199 (ex A50) and A6; Main St]: Welcoming pub with well kept Everards and guest ales, decent wines, attentive staff, daily papers, lots of knick-knacks, steps from area to area; children welcome, country and reservoir views from dining conservatory and tables in long sloping garden *(Duncan Cloud, LYM)*

SHAWELL [SP5480]
White Swan LE17 6AG [Main St; village signed down declassified rd (former A427) off A5/A426 roundabout – turn right in village; not far from M6 junction 1]: Attractive recently refurbished 17th-c pub, beams, panelling and open fire, Brakspears ales, friendly helpful landlord, good value pubby food (all day summer), restaurant; tables out in front, bedrooms, open all day *(Gerry and Rosemary Dobson, R W Allen, Ryan Rogers)*

SHEARSBY [SP6290]
Chandlers Arms LE17 6PL [Fenny Lane, off A50 Leicester—Northampton]: Comfortable old creeper-clad village pub, four well kept ales inc Black Sheep, good soft drinks range, good choice of food inc some lunchtime bargains, wall seats and wheelback chairs, resident terrier; piped music, Weds quiz night, pool; tables in secluded raised garden, nice hanging baskets, attractive village *(JJW, CMW, BB)*

SIBSON [SK3500]
Cock CV13 6LB [A444 N of Nuneaton; Twycross Rd]: Ancient picturesque black and white timbered and thatched building with Dick Turpin connection, Bass and Hook Norton, a dozen wines by the glass, decent if pricey food, cheerful quick service, low doorways, heavy black beams and genuine latticed windows, immense inglenook; piped music, games machine; children welcome, tables in courtyard and small garden, handy for Bosworth Field *(Joan and Tony Walker, LYM, Martin Smith)*

SOUTH CROXTON [SK6810]
Golden Fleece LE7 3RL [Main St]: Large recently refurbished pub, clean minimalist feel with comfortable modern furniture, friendly helpful staff, good food cooked with flair inc cheaper wkdy lunchtime/early evening set menu, Sun carvery, real ales, good house wine, log fire, restaurant; lovely area *(O K Smyth, Phil and Jane Hodson)*

SPROXTON [SK8524]
Crown LE14 4QB [Coston Rd]: Friendly enthusiastic landlord, enjoyable reasonably priced food running up to partridge or lobster, well kept Greene King, good wines and coffee, light and airy bar with open fire, two dining rooms; tables in lovely sunny courtyard, attractive village, nice walks *(Phil and Jane Hodson, Howard and Margaret Buchanan)*

SWINFORD [SP5779]
Chequers LE17 6BL [handy for M1/M6/A14 interchange; High St, opp church]: Long pub

with bare boards bar and carpeted dining areas, Adnams, Ansells and a guest ale such as Morrissey Fox Blonde, wide ranging menu, some pine panelling and old local photographs, traditional games inc table skittles; garden with terrace and play area, St George's day worm charming championship *(George Atkinson)*

THORPE LANGTON [SP7492]
☆ *Bakers Arms* LE16 7TS [off B6047 N of Market Harborough]: Civilised restaurant with bar rather than pub, very good regularly changing imaginative food in cottagey beamed linked areas (must book), stylishly simple country décor, well kept local Langton ale, good choice of wines by the glass, friendly efficient staff; no under-12s; garden picnic-sets, cl wkdy lunchtimes, Sun evening and Mon *(LYM, Duncan Cloud, Gerry and Rosemary Dobson, John and Sylvia Harrop, R L Borthwick, Jeff and Wendy Williams)*

THORPE SATCHVILLE [SK7311]
Fox LE14 2DQ [Main St (B6047)]: 1930s pub/restaurant with french chef/landlord doing good food from interesting snacks to full french meals, affordable wines and some unusual beers, good service, carpeted front bars and more formal back restaurant with open fire; tables out at front and in garden behind, cl all day Sun, Mon lunchtime *(R V Peel)*

WHITWICK [SK4316]
Three Horseshoes LE67 5GN [Leicester Rd]: Unpretentious unchanging two-room local with tiny snug; long quarry-tiled bar with old wooden benches and open fires, well kept Bass and Marstons Pedigree, piano, darts, dominoes and cards, newspapers, no food (but fish and chips shop below); outdoor lavatories, no proper pub sign so easy to miss *(the Didler)*

WOODHOUSE EAVES [SK5214]
Curzon Arms LE12 8QZ [Maplewell Rd]: Welcoming pub under new management, enjoyable food from good sandwiches up, Adnams Bitter, Jennings Cocker Hoop and Sharps Doom Bar, interesting collection of wall clocks, carpeted dining room; children and dogs welcome, good-sized front lawn and terrace *(R L Borthwick)*
Old Bulls Head LE12 8RZ [Main St]: Large open-plan dining pub on two levels, good choice of interesting food inc enjoyable Sun lunch, well kept Marstons Pedigree and Timothy Taylors Landlord, reasonable prices, friendly welcoming staff, beamery, books and bric-a-brac, games area; pleasant outside space *(Mrs Joy Griffiths, Hunter and Christine Wright)*

WYMESWOLD [SK6023]
Three Crowns LE12 6TZ [Far St (A6006)]: Snug chatty 18th-c local in attractive village, good friendly staff, four real ales such as Adnams, Bass and Belvoir, good soft drinks choice, reasonably priced pubby food, pleasant character furnishings in beamed bar and lounge, lots of atmosphere; picnic-sets

out on decking (the Didler, Comus and Sarah Elliott)

WYMONDHAM [SK8518]

☆ *Berkeley Arms* LE14 2AG [Main St]: Sofas and chunky tables and chairs in beamed tiled-floor bar, comfortable smarter dining areas, welcoming young licensees, enjoyable home-made pubby food, more imaginative dishes Thurs-Sat, traditional Sun lunch, well kept Greene King IPA, Marstons Pedigree and guests; piped music, games machine; children welcome (and dogs – not in evening), tables out at front and in large garden with decked smokers' shelter, nearby windmill and craft workshops, cl Sun evening and Mon lunchtime (Ken Marshall, BB)

If a pub tries to make you leave a credit card behind the bar, be on your guard. The credit card firms and banks which issue them condemn this practice. After all, the publican who asks you to do this is in effect saying: 'I don't trust you'. Have you any more reason to trust his staff? If your card is used fraudulently while you have let it be kept out of your sight, the card company could say you've been negligent yourself – and refuse to make good your losses. So say that they can 'swipe' your card instead, but must hand it back to you. Please let us know if a pub does try to keep your card.

Lincolnshire

The competition for Dining Pub of the Year in Lincolnshire has been a two-horse race for too long, with the George of Stamford winning every year since 2003. It's still on top form and a fabulous place to visit, but this year, its main competitor for the Award, the civilised but lively Wig & Mitre in Lincoln seems to just pip the post as the readers' favourite and is our Lincolnshire Dining Pub 2011. Completely different, but well worth a visit while you're in Lincoln, the chatty Victoria, with its eight real ales, is doing well at the moment. Other pubs that deserve special mention this year are the Welby Arms at Allington (a great place to break from the A1) and the Cross Keys at Stow (a well liked reliable dining pub). New as a Main Entry this year, the Queens Head at Kirkby la Thorpe is the sort of good dining pub where they go that extra mile – maybe home-made breads and the like. There are some great brewers in this county – Tom Woods, Batemans, Oldershaw and Highwood to name but a few, and while some of the Main Entries here might stock one or two of their beers, it seems rather a shame that they don't make more of this regional strength – let's hope we see more of their beers in these pubs next year.

ALLINGTON   SK8540   MAP 7

Welby Arms ♀ 🍺 🛏

The Green; off A1 at N end of Grantham bypass; NG32 2EA

Friendly inn near A1, with popular food, six real ales and seats outside; pleasant bedrooms

It's such good news that this really rather nice pub is so close to the A1. It's a jolly well run and welcoming oasis, with helpful, friendly staff, a bustling atmosphere (that doesn't seem to disturb the two cats), good value meals and a great range of drinks. The large traditionally furnished bar is divided by a stone archway and has black beams and joists, log fires (one in an attractive arched brick fireplace), red velvet curtains and comfortable burgundy button-back wall banquettes and stools. They keep a fine choice of six real ales on handpump: Bass, Jennings Cumberland, John Smiths and Timothy Taylors Landlord and a couple of guests such as Caledonian Deuchars IPA and Morlands Old Speckled Hen; also, 20 malt whiskies and 22 wines by the glass; piped music and board games. The civilised back dining lounge (where they prefer you to eat) looks out on to tables in a sheltered walled courtyard with pretty summer hanging baskets, and there are more picnic-sets out on the front lawn.

🍽 **Popular bar food might include hot and cold filled baguettes, ploughman's, ham, egg and chips, chicken burger and chilli, whitebait, mediterranean vegetable and mushroom lasagne, steak and mushroom pie, battered haddock and steak.** *Starters/Snacks: £3.95 to £7.50. Main Courses: £4.95 to £8.95. Puddings: £3.95*

> Post Office address codings confusingly give the impression that a few pubs are in Lincolnshire, when they're really in Cambridgeshire (which is where we list them).

Enterprise ~ Lease Matt Rose ~ Real ale ~ Bar food (12-2, 6-9; 12-8.30 Sun) ~ Restaurant ~ (01400) 281361 ~ Children welcome ~ Open 12-3, 6-11; 12-10.30 Sun ~ Bedrooms: £48S/£70S
Recommended by Gordon and Margaret Ormondroyd, Michael and Jenny Back, Jill and Julian Tasker, John R Ringrose, John and Angie Millar, Janet and Peter Race, D Goodger, Maurice and Janet Thorpe, E Ling, Mrs P Bishop, MJVK, Blaise Vyner, John Robertson, W M Paton

BARNOLDBY LE BECK

TA2303   MAP 8

Ship ♀

Village signposted off A18 Louth—Grimsby; DN37 0BG

Very good fish menu (and other choices) at this tranquil plush dining pub

With its rather charming collection of Edwardian and Victorian bric-a-brac this calming place is just a little bit different. The neatly kept bar (it's quite firmly run) houses stand-up telephones, violins, a horn gramophone, bowler and top hats, old racquets, crops, hockey sticks and a lace dress. Heavy dark-ringed drapes swathe the windows, with plants in ornate china bowls on the sills. Furnishings include comfortable dark green plush wall benches with lots of pretty propped-up cushions, and heavily stuffed green plush Victorian-looking chairs on a green fleur de lys carpet; piped music. Most customers are here to enjoy the first-class fish dishes, but drinkers do pop in too – they have Black Sheep and Timothy Taylors Landlord on handpump, a good wine list and up to a dozen malt whiskies. A fenced-off sunny area behind has hanging baskets and a few picnic-sets under pink parasols.

⑪ Using top quality fish (some of which comes from their own boats), good food includes **pâté with redcurrant jelly, mushroom rarebit with a herb crust, seared scallops with pancetta and pesto, garlic and chilli king prawns, smoked salmon with lemon and dill mayonnaise, fried skate with caper butter, herb crusted halibut, fried bass fillets with mediterranean vegetables, spicy beef strips, chicken breast stuffed with tomato and basil and wrapped in serrano ham with balsamic reduction, puddings such as bakewell tart with custard and white chocolate brûlée with raspberry ripple, and a good local cheeseboard.** *Starters/Snacks: £4.50 to £7.95. Main Courses: £8.50 to £20.00. Puddings: £5.50 to £6.50*

Inn Business ~ Manager Michele Hancock ~ Real ale ~ Bar food (12-2, 6.30-9) ~ Restaurant ~ (01472) 822308 ~ Children welcome ~ Open 12-3, 6-11(12 Sat)
Recommended by Alistair and Kay Butler, Dr and Mrs J Temporal, Michael and Maggie Betton, Newbury family, P Pywell

BELCHFORD

TF2975   MAP 8

Blue Bell ⑪♀

Village signposted off A153 Horncastle—Louth (and can be reached by the good Bluestone Heath Road off A16, just under 1.5 miles N of the A1104 roundabout); Main Road; LN9 6LQ

Emphasis on imaginative modern food at a cottagey 18th-c dining pub

Most customers at this smart restauranty place have booked a table to enjoy the first-class food, though they do keep Black Sheep and Greene King IPA on handpump (several wines by the glass). The cosy comfortable bar has a relaxing pastel décor, and some armchairs and sofas as well as more upright chairs around good solid tables. Service is pleasant and attentive. The neat terraced garden behind has picnic-sets, and this is a good base for Wolds walks and the Viking Way; hikers must remove their boots; more reports please.

⑪ They do have some good value pubby lunchtime dishes like filled ciabatta rolls, beef, mushroom and Guinness pie, sausage and mash with shallot red wine jus, gammon and egg and breaded scampi, but most emphasis is on the more inventive (and pricier) choices such as pea, ham and mint soup, smoked haddock and leek risotto with poached egg, thai fishcakes with cucumber and green pepper relish, smoked chicken breast with bean and pepper chilli and crème fraîche, saddle of wild venison on pumpkin, sage and smoked bacon risotto with red wine jus, baked bass stuffed with ginger, chilli, coriander and soy, twice-baked stilton soufflé with waldorf salad, puddings such as warm pecan pie and local ice-creams, and a local cheeseboard. *Starters/Snacks: £4.25 to £9.95. Main Courses: £5.95 to £18.95. Puddings: £3.95 to £5.25*

Free house ~ Licensees Darren and Shona Jackson ~ Real ale ~ Bar food (12-2, 6.30-9) ~ Restaurant ~ (01507) 533602 ~ Children welcome ~ Open 11.30-2.30, 6.30-11; 12-4 Sun; closed Sun evening, Mon and second and third weeks in Jan
Recommended by Malcolm Brown

BILLINGBOROUGH   TF1134   MAP 8

Fortescue Arms

B1177, off A52 Grantham—Boston; NG34 0QB

Low-beamed country pub, bric-a-brac, several real ales, traditional food and pretty gardens

The several turkey-carpeted rooms at this traditional rural pub have lots of ancient stonework, exposed brickwork, wood panelling and beams, bay-window seats and a big see-through fireplace. Décor and bric-a-brac are what you'd expect in a pub of this type – everything from Victorian prints to fresh flowers and pot plants, brass and copper, a stuffed badger and pheasant, and various quiz books. Attractive dining rooms at each end have flagstones and another open fire. Unusually, a long red and black tiled corridor runs right the way along behind the serving bar, effectively turning it into an island. Here you'll find Adnams, Everards Tiger, Greene King Abbot and Timothy Taylors Landlord on handpump; piped music. There are picnic-sets on a lawn under apple trees on one side, and on the other a sheltered courtyard with flowers planted in tubs and a manger; more reports please.

🍽 **Bar food includes sandwiches and filled baguettes, ploughman's, soup, crispy whitebait, several pies, chicken breast in white wine and mushroom sauce, battered cod, a vegetarian dish and steaks; Sunday roasts.** *Starters/Snacks: £3.95 to £6.95. Main Courses: £7.95 to £18.95. Puddings: £3.95 to £5.95*

Charnwood Pub Company ~ Managers Terry and Nicola Williams ~ Real ale ~ Bar food (12-2, 6-9; 12-9.30 Sun) ~ Restaurant ~ (01529) 240228 ~ Children welcome ~ Open 12-3, 5.30-11; 12-11 Sat, Sun
Recommended by BOB

DRY DODDINGTON   SK8546   MAP 8

Wheatsheaf

1.5 miles off A1 N of Grantham; Main Street; NG23 5HU

Happy bustling pub with good food cooked by chef/patron; handy for A1

You can be sure of a genuinely warm and friendly welcome at this 16th-c colourwashed village inn. It's well run by an enthusiastic young couple – the landlord is the chef. The front bar is basically two rooms, with a woodburning stove, a variety of settles and chairs, and tables in the windows facing across to the green and the lovely 14th-c church with its crooked tower. The serving bar on the right has Greene King Abbot, Timothy Taylors Landlord, Tom Woods Best and a guest such as Milestone Rich Ruby on handpump, and a nice choice of 11 wines by the glass. A slight slope takes you down to the comfortable thickly carpeted and extended dining room with its relaxing red and cream décor; piped music. Once a cow byre, this part is even more ancient than the rest of the building, perhaps dating from the 13th c. The front terrace has neat dark green tables under cocktail parasols, among tubs of flowers; disabled access at the side.

🍽 **Using their own-grown vegetables and herbs and supporting small local rare-breed producers, good food includes filled ciabattas, ploughman's, smoked salmon and scrambled egg, omelettes, black pudding and poached egg salad, chicken with brie and bacon sauce, roast aubergine pasta, pork loin with cider gravy, whole plaice with caper** and nut-brown butter, and puddings such as vanilla panna cotta with home-grown rhubarb and strawberry compote and chocolate torte with toffee ice-cream. *Starters/Snacks: £4.25 to £9.95. Main Courses: £9.95 to £14.95. Puddings: £3.95 to £4.95*

Free house ~ Licensees Dan Bland and Kate Feetham ~ Real ale ~ Bar food (12-2(2.30 Sat, 3 Sun), 6-9(9.30 Sat); 5-7 Sun) ~ Restaurant ~ (01400) 281458 ~ Children welcome ~ Dogs allowed in bar ~ Open 12-2.30, 5-11; 12-11(10.30 Sun) Sat; closed Mon, Tues lunchtime

Recommended by Michael and Jenny Back, Beryl and Bill Farmer, Tom and Ruth Rees, Maurice and Janet Thorpe, William and Ann Reid, A Wadkin

HOUGH-ON-THE-HILL

SK9246   MAP 8

Brownlow Arms

High Road; NG32 2AZ

Refined country house with beamed bar, real ales, imaginative food and a graceful terrace; bedrooms

Do check the limited opening times at this terribly smart, upmarket old stone inn, which most people visit for a sophisticated dining experience (you will probably need to book), though they do keep Marstons Bitter and Pedigree and Timothy Taylors Landlord on handpump. The beamed bar is comfortable and welcoming with plenty of panelling, some exposed brickwork, local prints and scenes, a large mirror, and a pile of logs beside the big fireplace. Seating is on elegant stylishly mismatched upholstered armchairs, and the carefully arranged furnishings give the impression of several separate and surprisingly cosy areas; piped easy listening, several wines by the glass and a good choice of malt whiskies served by friendly, impeccably polite staff. The well equipped bedrooms are attractive and breakfasts are hearty.

🍴 **First-class (though not cheap) food might include chicken liver parfait with spiced fruit chutney, cheese soufflé with ham and local cheese, guinea fowl with black pudding and apple compote, baked mushroom stuffed with goats cheese with sweet and sour onions and pesto dressing, bass with fennel purée and saffron potatoes, rack of lamb with dauphinoise potatoes and rosemary jus, and puddings such as panna cotta with rhubarb and treacle tart.** *Starters/Snacks: £4.95 to £8.95. Main Courses: £11.50 to £23.50. Puddings: £6.95*

Free house ~ Licensee Paul L Willoughby ~ Real ale ~ Bar food (6.30-9.30, 12-2.30 Sun) ~ Restaurant ~ (01400) 250234 ~ Children allowed if over 12 ~ Open 6-11; 12-3.30 Sun; closed Mon, Sun evening ~ Bedrooms: £65B/£96B

Recommended by Mr and Mrs B Watt

INGHAM

SK9483   MAP 8

Inn on the Green 🍴

The Green; LN1 2XT

Nicely modernised place popular for good, thoughtfully prepared food; chatty atmosphere

This friendly dining pub, with most tables occupied by people eating, has a good, chatty atmosphere and the feel of a proper pub (particularly in the locals' bar) despite its emphasis on the popular food. Its beamed and timbered dining room is spread over two floors with lots of exposed brickwork, a mix of brasses and copper, local prints, bric-a-brac and a warm winter fire. The brick bar counter has home-made jams, marmalade and chutney for sale alongside Black Sheep, a couple of guests such as Batemans XXXB and half a dozen or so wines by the glass. Opposite is a comfortably laid-back area with two red leather sofas; piped music; good service; more reports please.

🍴 **Using some home-grown produce, good food might include sandwiches, venison, wood pigeon and black pudding terrine with apple chutney, salt cod cakes with tomato provençale, seared halibut with saffron and mussel sauce, rabbit and mustard stew, braised duck leg with green lentils and spicy sausage and bacon, chicken breast with mushroom**

stuffing baked in pastry, escalope of free-range pork with wild mushroom sauce, and puddings such as lavender rice pudding and baked lemon cheesecake with orange sorbet. *Starters/Snacks: £3.95 to £6.50. Main Courses: £6.95 to £15.00. Puddings: £3.60 to £4.95*

Free house ~ Licensees Andrew Cafferkey and Sarah Sharpe ~ Real ale ~ Bar food (12-2(4.45 Sun), 6.30-9(9.30 Fri, Sat); not Tues lunchtime, Sun evening) ~ Restaurant ~ (01522) 730354 ~ Children welcome if eating ~ Open 11.30-3, 6-11; 12-10.30 Sun; closed Mon

Recommended by Alistair and Kay Butler

KIRKBY LA THORPE
TF0945 MAP 8

Queens Head

Village and pub signposted off A17, just E of Sleaford, then turn right into Boston Road cul-de-sac; NG34 9NW

Reliable dining pub very popular for its enjoyable food and good service

You can choose almost any degree of formality (and fresh air) in this extensive place, from the teak tables and chairs of a lantern-lit back arbour with a glazed canopy, through a sizeable carpeted bar with button-back banquettes and sofas as well as dining chairs around its shiny dark tables, to a light and airy conservatory with informal dining tables, or – beyond heavily swagged curtains – a smartly linen-set beamed restaurant area. It's all very well organised, with plenty of neat dark-waistcoated staff, open wood-burning stoves, huge flower arrangements, thoughtful lighting, nice decorative touches such as the big prints and five handsome longcase clocks (making it very lively here at midday), and easy disabled access; piped music. Two Batemans beers are on handpump and in summer they serve home-made lemonade.

🍴 The tempting home-made made breads here, used in a good range of sandwiches and served alongside quite a few dishes, are particularly tempting. You can eat from the bar or restaurant menu (the full choice does make rather extensive reading) with dishes such as game terrine with walnut bread, smoked mackerel and crayfish with sun-dried tomato bread, mushrooms in pastry, steak and ale pie, local pigeon breasts with orange braised red cabbage and port jus, battered coley fillet with mushy peas, plenty of salads, lasagne, three-nut, parsnip and sweet potatoes cakes, puddings such as apple and hazelnut crumble with cinnamon ice-cream, ginger pudding with butterscotch sauce and toffee ice-cream, lemon and ginger cheesecake with passion-fruit sorbet, and a good local cheeseboard; popular weekday early evening meal deals. *Starters/Snacks: £5.95 to £7.95. Main Courses: £7.95 to £18.95. Puddings: £5.45 to £7.95*

Free house ~ Licensee John Clark ~ Real ale ~ Bar food (12-2.30, 6-9.30(10 Sat); 12-8.30 Sun) ~ Restaurant ~ (01529) 305743 ~ Younger children till 7pm only ~ Open 12-3, 6-11; 12-10.30 Sun

Recommended by Maurice and Janet Thorpe, Mr and Mrs J Brown

LINCOLN
SK9771 MAP 8

Victoria 🍺 £

Union Road; LN1 3BJ

Simple and popular real ale pub with eight beers and very good value lunchtime food

As well as Batemans XB, Castle Rock Harvest Pale and Timothy Taylors Landlord, five guests on handpump at this friendly old-fashioned backstreet local might be from brewers such as Batemans, Oldershaw and Ossett; also foreign draught and bottled beers, farm cider and perry and good value soft drinks. They hold beer festivals at the end of June, during the August bank holiday and at Halloween. Just the place for a chat and a pint, the simply furnished little tiled front lounge is manned by friendly staff, has a coal fire and pictures of Queen Victoria, and attracts a nicely mixed clientele. Being a proper town pub, it gets especially busy at lunchtime and later on in the evening. There's a small conservatory and heated terraced area with lots of tables and chairs, with good views of the castle.

🍴 Basic lunchtime food, from a short menu, includes filled cobs, baked potatoes, pies and sausage and mash; Sunday roast. *Starters/Snacks: £1.50 to £3.95. Main Courses: £5.95 to £6.95*

Batemans ~ Tenant Neil Renshaw ~ Real ale ~ Bar food (12-2.30; not evenings) ~ (01522) 541000 ~ Children welcome ~ Dogs welcome ~ Open 11am-midnight(1am Fri, Sat); 12-midnight Sun

Recommended by Chris Johnson, the Didler, Ryta Lyndley, Adam Jackson, P Dawn

Wig & Mitre ★ 🍴 🍷

Steep Hill; just below the cathedral; LN2 1LU

LINCOLNSHIRE DINING PUB OF THE YEAR

Very popular multi-faceted town bar with imaginative (though not cheap) food all day and a chatty bustling atmosphere

Service at this civilised and relaxed café-style dining pub is impeccable and very friendly. Full of character and with plenty of attractive period architectural features, it spreads over a couple of floors. The big-windowed beamed downstairs bar has exposed stone walls, pews and gothic furniture on oak floorboards, and comfortable sofas in a carpeted back area. Upstairs, the calmer dining room is light and airy, with views of the castle walls and cathedral, shelves of old books and an open fire. Walls are hung with antique prints and caricatures of lawyers and clerics, and there are plenty of newspapers and periodicals lying about – even templates to tempt you to a game of noughts and crosses. They have nearly three dozen wines by the glass (from a good list), lots of liqueurs and spirits and well kept Batemans XB, Black Sheep and possibly a guest such as Wells & Youngs London Gold on handpump. It can get busy at peak times, so it's useful to know that you can pop in and get something to eat at almost any time of day.

🍴 As well as a full breakfast and a sandwich menu, the seasonal dishes might include pea and ham soup with truffle oil, smoked duck breast with celeriac rémoulade and pickled mushrooms, red onion tart with goats cheese, watercress and dried tomatoes, sausage and mash, chicken thigh stuffed with tarragon mousse, pork collar with english mustard mash, caramelised onions and cider apple brandy sauce, mushroom, red onion, spinach and goats cheese tart, and puddings such as raspberry jam steamed sponge with custard and apple crème brûlée with cinnamon shortbread. *Starters/Snacks: £4.95 to £7.50. Main Courses: £10.50 to £15.95. Puddings: £4.95*

Free house ~ Licensee Toby Hope ~ Real ale ~ Bar food (8am-10pm) ~ Restaurant ~ (01522) 535190 ~ Children welcome ~ Dogs welcome ~ Open 8am-midnight

Recommended by Adrian Johnson, Phil and Jane Hodson, Keith and Chris O'Neill, Mr and Mrs A H Young, Dave Braisted, Adam Jackson, Chris Flynn, Wendy Jones, Ryta Lyndley

STAMFORD   TF0306   MAP 8

George of Stamford ★ 🍴 🍷 🛏

High Street, St Martins (B1081 S of centre, not the quite different central pedestrianised High Street); PE9 2LB

Handsome coaching inn, beautifully relaxed and civilised, with very good food and wines, and a lovely courtyard and garden; bedrooms

Generating plenty of enthusiastic reader reports, this carefully preserved and rather grand old coaching inn is an exceptional place on all counts. Very civilised but not in the least stuffy, its various lovely areas are furnished with all manner of seats from leather, cane and antique wicker to soft settees and easy chairs – there's a room to suit all occasions. The central lounge is particularly striking with sturdy timbers, broad flagstones, heavy beams and massive stonework, and the York Bar is surprisingly pubby with a relaxed, local feel. There's an oak-panelled restaurant (jacket or tie required) and a less formal Garden Restaurant which has well spaced furniture on herringbone glazed bricks around a central tropical grove. The staff are professional and friendly, with waiter drinks' service in the charming cobbled courtyard at the back: comfortable chairs and tables among attractive plant tubs and colourful hanging baskets on the ancient stone buildings. A fine range of drinks includes Adnams Broadside, Grainstore Triple B and Greene King Ruddles County on handpump, an excellent choice of wines (many of which are italian, with about 17 by the glass), freshly squeezed orange juice and malt whiskies. The immaculately kept walled garden is beautifully planted and there's a sunken lawn where croquet is often played.

🍴 **Quality as high as this does come at a price. The simplest option is the York Bar snacks which include sandwiches and toasties, ploughman's, soup, chicken liver pâté with cumberland sauce and sausages and mash. In the restaurants there might be gruyère fritters with thai jelly, chicken liver parfait with orange and redcurrant sauce, lasagne, dressed cromer crab, chicken breast with steamed bacon and mushroom pudding, rack of lamb with garlic and herb crust and redcurrant and rosemary jus, fried bream with courgette rösti, confit tomato and parsley oil, bass with parmesan crust, charred vegetable gateau and basil pesto, pudding and cheese trolleys. Their morning coffee and afternoon teas are popular.** *Starters/Snacks: £5.90 to £11.40. Main Courses: £7.85 to £19.95. Puddings: £6.70*

Free house ~ Licensees Chris Pitman and Ivo Vannocci ~ Real ale ~ Bar food (12-11) ~ Restaurant ~ (01780) 750750 ~ Children over 10 in restaurant ~ Dogs allowed in bar and bedrooms ~ Open 11(12 Sun)-11 ~ Bedrooms: £95B/£140B

Recommended by Gerry and Rosemary Dobson, John Wooll, Ryta Lyndley, Michael Dandy, Michael Sargent, Colin and Louise English, W N F Boughey, Roy Hoing, Mike and Sue Loseby, Mrs P Bishop, Marcus Mann, Ian Phillips, Clive Watkin, J Woodgate, the Didler, John and Sylvia Harrop, Andy Lickfold, Eithne Dandy, Roy Bromell, Edward Mirzoeff

STOW   SK8881   MAP 8

Cross Keys

Stow Park Road; B1241 NW of Lincoln; LN1 2DD

Dependable dining pub with traditional décor

Many customers visit this reliable extended dining pub to enjoy the good food and most tend to head for the cosy, popular bar. This is carpeted and fairly traditional with a big woodburner, dark wheelback chairs and tables, dark wood panelling, country prints on cream walls and decorative china on a delft shelf; piped music. Further in, you'll find a couple of neatly laid dining areas. Fairly priced drinks include Batemans XB, Theakstons Best and two or three guests from brewers such as Black Sheep and Roosters on handpump. Well worth a visit, nearby Stow Minster is notable for its fantastic Saxon arches and among, other things, its Viking ship graffiti.

🍴 **Bar food runs from traditional dishes up to more imaginative ones and might include sandwiches, twiced-baked cheese soufflé with red onion marmalade, duck and port pâté with plum and apple chutney, sausages on parsley mash with gravy, pasta with mediterranean vegetables in a tomato sauce, lambs liver with bacon and onion sauce, lamb cutlets with a redcurrant and rosemary gravy, breast of gressingham duck with an orange and Grand Marnier sauce, and puddings like vanilla panna cotta with caramelised oranges and sticky toffee pudding with butterscotch sauce.** *Starters/Snacks: £3.50 to £6.50. Main Courses: £7.25 to £17.95. Puddings: £4.75*

Free house ~ Licensees Richard and Helen Davies ~ Real ale ~ Bar food ~ Restaurant ~ (01427) 788314 ~ Children welcome ~ Open 12-2, 6-10; 12-8.30 Sun; closed Mon lunchtime

Recommended by Dr and Mrs J Temporal, Janet and Peter Race, Alistair and Kay Butler

---

Cribbage is a card game using a block of wood with holes for matchsticks
or special pins to score with; regulars in cribbage pubs are usually
happy to teach strangers how to play.

WOOLSTHORPE

SK8334 MAP 8

Chequers 🍴 🍷

The one near Belvoir, signposted off A52 or A607 W of Grantham; NG32 1LU

Interesting food at this comfortably relaxed inn, with good drinks and appealing castle views from outside tables

This 17th-c coaching inn is run with great care by friendly licensees and service here is cheery and welcoming. Emphasis does tend to be on the food, so it is worth booking. The heavy-beamed main bar has two big tables (one a massive oak construction), a comfortable mix of seating including some handsome leather chairs and leather banquettes, and a huge boar's head above a good log fire in the big brick fireplace. Among cartoons on the wall are some of the illustrated claret bottle labels from the series commissioned from famous artists, initiated by the late Baron Philippe de Rothschild. The lounge on the right has a deep red colour scheme, leather sofas and a big plasma TV, and on the left, there are more leather seats in a dining area in what was once the village bakery. A corridor leads off to the light and airy main restaurant, with contemporary pictures and another bar; piped music and board games. Everards Tiger and Wells & Youngs on handpump, over 30 wines by the glass, 50 malt whiskies, and local fruit pressé. There are good quality teak tables, chairs and benches outside and, beyond these, some picnic-sets on the edge of the pub's cricket field, with views of Belvoir Castle. If you stay here, please do let us know how you find the recently refurbished bedrooms.

🍴 **Good, often interesting bar food might include sandwiches, braised lamb and pearl barley broth, king prawn and fried ginger risotto, crispy lamb sweetbreads with port syrup, steak and kidney suet crust pie, battered haddock, sausage and mash, fried bass with garlic and herb butter, red thai vegetable curry, grilled rib-eye steak with peppercorn sauce, and puddings such as prune and almond tart with clotted cream ice-cream and orange and cardamom rice pudding, and an english cheeseboard; they offer an early-bird deal and a three-course set menu option.** *Starters/Snacks: £4.50 to £10.50. Main Courses: £10.00 to £17.50. Puddings: £5.50 to £6.50*

Free house ~ Licensee Justin Chad ~ Real ale ~ Bar food (12-2.30(4 Sun), 6-9.30(8.30 Sun)) ~ Restaurant ~ (01476) 870701 ~ Children welcome ~ Dogs allowed in bar and bedrooms ~ Open 12-3, 5.30-11; 12-11.30 Sat(10.30 Sun) ~ Bedrooms: £50B/£70S

Recommended by Felicity Davies, Bob and Angela Brooks, Gordon and Margaret Ormonroyd, Ellie Weld, David London, Peter and Josie Fawcett, D Goodger, Richard and Jean Green, Michael and Maggie Betton

---

LUCKY DIP

Besides the fully inspected pubs, you might like to try these Lucky Dips recommended to us and described by readers (if you do, please send us reports: feedback@goodguides.com).

ALFORD [TF4575]
☆ *Half Moon* LN13 9DG [West St (A1004)]: Well run pub/hotel with four real ales such as Everards Tiger, Fullers London Pride and Greene King IPA, very wide food choice from sandwiches and baked potatoes to particularly good fish dishes; long-serving licensees and competent helpful staff, spacious L-shaped bar, attractive dining room, decorous lounge; children welcome (adaptable menu for them), nice fairy-lit back garden with barbecue, up-to-date bedrooms *(Derek and Sylvia Stephenson, BB)*

BRANDY WHARF [TF0196]
☆ *Cider Centre* DN21 4RU [B1205 SE of Scunthorpe (off A15 about 16 miles N of Lincoln)]: Up to 15 draught ciders, many more in bottles etc, also country wines and meads; plain take-us-as-you-find-us bright main bar and dimmer lounge with lots of cider memorabilia and jokey bric-a-brac, reasonably priced straightforward food (all day Sun); piped music; children in eating area, simple glazed verandah, tables in meadows or by river with moorings and slipway, play area, open all day wknds, may be cl Mon *(the Didler, LYM)*

CASTLE BYTHAM [SK9818]
☆ *Castle Inn* NG33 4RZ [off A1 Stamford—Grantham, or B1176]: Comfortable black-beamed 17th-c village pub with landlady cooking enjoyable food from good value snacks up, friendly obliging staff, beers such as Adnams Bitter, Fullers London Pride and Newby Wyke Bear Island, occasional beer festivals, real cider, good hot drinks; mixed wooden furniture, huge blazing fire; children and dogs welcome, disabled access, tables

on back terrace, cl Mon-Sat lunchtimes but may open for advance group bookings *(Michael and Jenny Back, LYM)*

CAYTHORPE [SK9348]

Red Lion NG32 3DN [signed just off A607 N of Grantham; High St]: Enjoyable home-made food inc good Sun lunch, well kept Adnams and Everards, good sensibly priced wine, freshly updated bare-boards bar with light wood counter, black beams and open fire, carpeted restaurant; back terrace by car park *(Maurice and Janet Thorpe, BB)*

CLEETHORPES [TA3009]

No 2 Refreshment Room DN35 8AX [Station Approach]: Comfortably refurbished carpeted platform bar, friendly staff, well kept Greene King, Worthingtons and guests, no food; Thurs quiz; tables out under heaters, open all day from 9am *(the Didler, P Dawn)*

☆ *Willys* DN35 8RQ [High Cliffe Rd; south promenade]: Open-plan bistro-style seafront pub with panoramic Humber views, café tables, tiled floor and painted brick walls; visibly brews its own good ales, changing guests and belgian beers also available, good home-made bargain bar lunches (evening food Mon, Tues and Thurs), friendly fast service; nice mix of customers from young and trendy to weather-beaten fishermen; quiet juke box; a few tables out on the promanade, open all day *(the Didler, Pat and Tony Martin, P Dawn, Chris Johnson)*

COLSTERWORTH [SK9324]

White Lion NG33 5NE [High St]: Comfortably refurbished and welcoming, sofas in bar, large dining area with fresh flowers on pine tables, above-average good value pubby food all day; friendly helpful staff, well kept Adnams, Batemans and a changing guest; Sky TV, pool and darts; children welcome, garden picnic-sets *(Karen Sharman)*

CONINGSBY [TF2458]

☆ *Lea Gate Inn* LN4 4RS [Leagate Road (B1192 southwards, off A153 E)]: Heavy-beamed 16th-c fenland pub with three cosy linked rooms, medley of furnishings inc great high-backed settles around the biggest of the three log fires, dim lighting, ancient oak panelling, attractive dining room, even a priest hole; food (all day Sun) from sandwiches up, Adnams, Batemans and Wells & Youngs Bombardier; children welcome, dogs in bar, pleasant garden, site of old gallows at front, eight motel bedrooms, open all day Sun *(Anthony Barnes, LYM, the Didler)*

EWERBY [TF1247]

Finch Hatton Arms NG34 9PH [Main St]: Former 1875 hunting lodge with mock-Tudor carpeted interior, lots of beams and timbers, farming tools, brass and plates; enjoyable food (not Sun evening) inc blackboard choice and OAP wkdy lunch, takeaways, helpful service, real ales, Weston's Old Rosie cider, lots of wines and soft drinks; coal fire, two bars and two dining rooms; piped music; eight bedrooms *(BB, JJW, CMW)*

GAINSBOROUGH [SK8189]

Eight Jolly Brewers DN21 2DW [Ship Court, Silver St]: Small comfortable real ale pub with up to eight inc regulars Abbeydale, Castle Rock and Glentworth, low prices, also farm cider and country wines, simple lunchtime food (not Sun); friendly staff and locals, beams, bare bricks and brewery posters, quieter areas upstairs; live folk music; terrace, open all day wknds *(the Didler)*

GRANTHAM [SK9136]

☆ *Blue Pig* NG31 6RQ [Vine St]: Cosy three-bar Tudor pub with enjoyable home-made pubby food inc OAP bargains, well kept Caledonian Deuchars IPA, Timothy Taylors Landlord and changing guests, good choice of wines, quick cheerful service; low beams, panelling, stripped stone and flagstones, open fire, daily papers, lots of pig ornaments, prints and bric-a-brac; piped music, juke box, games machines, no children or dogs; tables out behind, open all day *(the Didler, Ian and Nita Cooper, BB)*

Lord Harrowby NG31 9AB [Dudley Rd, S of centre]: Friendly 60s-feel local, lots of RAF pictures and memorabilia in pleasant lounge, well kept Tom Woods and guests, games-oriented public bar; cl wkdy lunchtimes, open all day wknds *(the Didler)*

GREAT CASTERTON [SK9909]

Plough PE9 4AA [Main St]: Unassuming pub in village nr A1, interesting nicely presented food (not Sun evening), using carefully sourced ingredients, real ales and good choice of wines by the glass; good service, comfortable bow-windowed bar and neatly refurbished dining room; picnic-sets out on sheltered lawn with weeping willow, cl Mon *(Marlene and Jim Godfrey)*

GRIMSTHORPE [TF0423]

Black Horse PE10 0LY [A151 W of Bourne]: Extensive, handsome grey-stone coaching inn, light and airy long narrowish bar, eclectic mix of furniture, open fires; Batemans and guests, enjoyable food inc wknd carvery and wkdy two-course set lunch deal, friendly local atmosphere; children welcome lunchtime only; garden, three bedrooms, cl Sun evening, Mon *(LYM, J and N Savory)*

HEIGHINGTON [TF0369]

Butcher & Beast LN4 1JS [High St]: Welcoming Batemans pub with their ales and three local guests, enjoyable hearty bar food, two small cosy front rooms, dining area; garden down to stream, pretty village *(Chris Johnson)*

HEMINGBY [TF2374]

Coach & Horses LN9 5QF [off A158/B1225 N of Horncastle]: Unpretentious beamed village local, long and low, with pews and sewing-machine tables, good value food inc bargain Sun lunch, well kept Batemans and Riverside, good service, central fireplace *(Derek and Sylvia Stephenson)*

KIRKBY ON BAIN [TF2462]

Ebrington Arms LN10 6YT [Main St]: Popular, good value food inc cheap Sun lunch, five or more well kept changing ales such as Black Sheep, prompt friendly service; low 16th-c beams, two open fires, nicely set-out dining areas each side, copper-topped tables, banquettes, jet fighter and racing car pictures, daily papers; games area with darts, back restaurant, beer festivals Easter and Aug bank hols; may be piped music; wheelchair access, tables out in front, swings on side lawn, campsite behind, open all day *(Alistair and Kay Butler, W M Lien)*

LEADENHAM [SK9452]
Willoughby Arms LN5 0PP [High St; A17 Newark—Sleaford]: Stripped stone and beams, good food, well kept beer, low prices; handy for Viking Way walks, bedrooms *(Tully, David Toulson)*

LINCOLN [SK9769]
Golden Eagle LN5 8BD [High St]: Popular two-bar traditional Castle Rock pub with their ales and up to seven changing guests (regular beer festivals), bargain lunchtime rolls, cheery back bar; pub games, open mike night every other Tues; tables in good sized garden behind, nr football ground, open all day *(the Didler)*
Morning Star LN2 4AW [Greetwell Gate]: Friendly traditional local handy for the cathedral, enjoyable good value lunches, well kept reasonably priced ales, helpful service; coal fire, aircraft paintings, two bar areas and comfortable snug; some live music; nice covered outside area, open all day *(the Didler)*
Strugglers LN1 3BG [Westgate]: Cosily worn-in beer lovers' haunt, well kept ales such as Bass, Black Sheep Best, Greene King Abbot, Northumberland Premium, Oldershaw Caskade, Rudgate Ruby Mild and Timothy Taylors Landlord, bargain pub lunches (from 10.30am, not Sun); coal-effect fire in back snug, some live music; no children inside; dogs welcome after 3pm, steps down to back courtyard with heated back canopy, open all day (till 1am Thurs-Sat) *(Peter and Josie Fawcett, BB, the Didler)*
Widows Cullen LN2 1LU [Steep Hill]: Ancient revamped building on two floors, cheap Sam Smiths beers and bar food, chatty mix of customers, good service *(David Toulson, Chris Johnson)*

LITTLE BYTHAM [TF0117]
Willoughby Arms NG33 4RA [Station Rd, S of village]: Former 19th-c private railway station, well kept Batemans XB, Newby Wyke, Ufford White Hart and four interesting guests inc a porter (regular beer festivals), Weston's farm cider, decent reasonably priced food from baguettes up, friendly helpful staff; daily papers, leather sofa and armchairs on bare boards, coal fire, back dining extension, cellar bar; piped and some live music; children and dogs welcome, good disabled access, picnic-sets in sizeable garden with splendid country views, three bedrooms, good breakfast, open all day *(Mike Markwick, S J and C C Davidson, the Didler, Richard and Jean Green, BB)*

LONG BENNINGTON [SK8344]
☆ *Reindeer* NG23 5DJ [just off A1 N of Grantham – S end of village, opp school]: Thriving atmosphere in attractively traditional low-beamed pub with popular long-serving landlady; good home-made food from sandwiches up in bar and more formal dining lounge, cut-price small helpings, well kept ales such as John Smiths, Timothy Taylors Landlord and Wells & Youngs Bombardier, good wines, friendly service, coal-effect stove in inglenook; piped music not too obtrusive; picnic-sets under cocktail parasols in small front courtyard *(BB, Jerry Brown, Maurice and Janet Thorpe)*

LUDFORD [TF1989]
Black Horse LN8 6AJ [A631 Market Rasen—Louth]: Welcoming old-fashioned pub doing good, imaginative, locally sourced food; local ales too *(Newbury family)*

NAVENBY [SK9857]
Kings Head LN5 0EE [A607 S of Lincoln]: Friendly roadside pub under popular management, comfortable lounge bar, busy dining area, enjoyable food inc bargain set lunch deals, well kept Everards Tiger, Greene King IPA and John Smiths; small pretty garden *(Maurice and Janet Thorpe, BB)*

NORTON DISNEY [SK8859]
Green Man LN6 9JU [Main St, off A46 Newark—Lincoln]: Old village pub given clean modern refurbishment, food from traditional to more imaginative things using local produce, three well kept ales inc Black Sheep, restaurant; tables out behind *(Jerry Brown)*

OASBY [TF0039]
Houblon Arms NG32 3NB: Large and rambling, with lots of low beams, panelling and stonework, well kept Batemans and a guest ale, good interesting food, welcoming landlady and friendly service; four comfortable bedrooms *(Alun and Jennifer Evans)*

SCOTTER [SE8800]
☆ *White Swan* DN21 3UD [The Green]: Comfortable well kept dining pub, enjoyable well prepared generous food inc bargain set lunches and early evening deals (Mon-Sat), welcoming cheerful staff, Black Sheep, John Smiths, Websters and interesting changing guest beers; several levels inc snug panelled area by fireplace, big-windowed raftered restaurant looking over lawn with picnic-sets to duck-filled River Eau (best to book wknds); piped music, steps up to entrance; children welcome, 14 comfortable bedrooms in modern extension, open all day Fri-Sun *(BB, Alistair and Kay Butler)*

SKENDLEBY [TF4369]
Blacksmiths Arms PE23 4QE [off A158 about 10 miles NW of Skegness]: Nice straightforward food inc good bargain Sun lunch in back restaurant extension; also an old-fashioned two-room bar, cosy and quaint, with view of the cellar; deep 17th-c well, Batemans XB and Highwood Tom Woods

kept well, friendly staff, open fire *(Derek and Sylvia Stephenson)*

SNITTERBY [SK9894]

Royal Oak DN21 4TP [High St]: Refurbished pub in delightful village setting by ford, friendly enthusiastic landlord, good choice of well kept ales inc several local ones (microbrewery planned), enjoyable simple home-made food from short good value menu; relaxed atmosphere with newspapers and open fire; dogs welcome, picnic-sets outside *(Adam Jackson)*

SOUTH ORMSBY [TF3675]

☆ *Massingberd Arms* LN11 8QS [off A16 S of Louth]: Small brick-built village local with unusual arched windows, welcoming landlord, good range of changing ales, short choice of good fresh food inc game and good Sun lunch, restaurant; no credit cards; pleasant garden, good Wolds walks, open all day Weds-Sun, cl Mon lunchtime *(the Didler)*

SOUTH RAUCEBY [TF0245]

Bustard NG34 8QG [Main St]: Much-modernised beamed stone-built pub with good bar food inc some unusual dishes, well kept ales, welcoming staff; comfortable plush seating, log fire, pictures of bustards and other birds, small dining area; children welcome, attractive sheltered garden *(BB, Sarah Flynn)*

STAMFORD [TF0207]

☆ *Crown* PE9 2AG [All Saints Pl]: Substantial, well modernised stone-built hotel with emphasis on good seasonal country cooking, using local produce from good sandwiches up, friendly helpful staff, well kept Adnams, Fullers and Ufford ales, decent wines, whiskies and coffee; spacious main bar, long leather-cushioned bar counter, substantial pillars, step up to more traditional flagstoned area with stripped stone and lots of leather sofas and armchairs, civilised dining room; back courtyard, 26 comfortable bedrooms, good breakfast, open all day *(Gerry and Rosemary Dobson, BB, Michael Dandy, John Branston, Eithne Dandy)*

Tobie Norris PE9 2BE [St Pauls St]: Great period atmosphere in carefully run flagstoned pub with lots of nooks and crannies, well kept Adnams, Ufford and three guest beers, good choice of food (not Fri-Sun evenings) inc nice pizzas; open all day *(Sarah Flynn, Peter and Pam Watkins, David Carr)*

SURFLEET SEAS END [TF2729]

☆ *Ship* PE11 4DH [Reservoir Rd; off A16 N of Spalding]: Immaculately rebuilt pub just below seawall, woodburner, chesterfields and handsomely made seating in good-sized civilised bar with old scrubbed tables in open bays, enjoyable reasonably priced food inc OAP and early-bird deals, changing well kept ales such as Batemans XB, Marstons Pedigree and Slaters Wee Sleekit; tables on front terrace, boating-view benching and picnic-sets up on embankment across lane, good value bedrooms *(Margaret and Peter Staples, BB)*

TATTERSHALL THORPE [TF2159]

Blue Bell LN4 4PE [Thorpe Rd; B1192 Coningsby—Woodhall Spa]: Attractive very low-beamed pub said to date from 13th c and used by the Dambusters; RAF memorabilia and appropriate real ales such as Tom Woods Bomber County, well priced pubby bar food, log fires, small dining room; garden tables, bedrooms *(the Didler)*

TEALBY [TF1590]

Olde Barn LN8 3YB [Cow Lane (B1203)]: Recently refurbished village dining pub in extended former barn, enjoyable food inc lunchtime set deals (Tues-Sat), well kept ales such as Black Sheep; children welcome, big back garden with terrace, handy for Viking Way, cl Sun evening, Mon *(Ann Carrodus, Michael and Maggie Betton)*

THEDDLETHORPE ALL SAINTS [TF4787]

☆ *Kings Head* LN12 1PB [off A1031 N of Maplethorpe; Mill Rd]: Remote 15th-c thatched pub doing well under current good licensees, small low-beamed front bar with easy chairs by open fire, neatly furnished main bar with plush wall banquettes, sturdy rustic furniture in dining room, carpets throughout; well above average fresh local food inc plenty of fish, lunchtime deals, Batemans XB and a guest; pretty side garden, open all day, cl Mon *(Robert Vevers)*

THREEKINGHAM [TF0836]

Three Kings NG34 0AU [just off A52, 12 miles E of Grantham; Saltersway]: Big entrance hall (former coaching inn), beamed and dark panelled bar with coal fire, pubby furniture inc banquettes, compact dining room, good choice of home-made food from baguettes up, Bass, Timothy Taylors Landlord, and a guest; terrace with covered smokers' area, cl Mon *(Maurice and Janet Thorpe)*

WAINFLEET [TF5058]

☆ *Batemans Brewery* PE24 4JE [Mill Lane, off A52 via B1195]: Circular bar in brewery's ivy-covered windmill tower with Batemans ales in top condition, czech and belgian beers on tap, ground-floor dining area with unpretentious lunchtime food such as local sausages and pork pies; plenty of old pub games (more outside), lots of brewery memorabilia and plenty for families to enjoy; entertaining brewery tours and shop, tables out on terrace and grass, open 11.30-3.30pm *(the Didler)*

WELBY [SK9738]

Crown & Anchor NG32 3LP [Main St]: Attractive refurbished village pub, friendly local atmosphere in spacious bar, enjoyable food here and in small dining room, must book Satevening; Everards and Shepherd Neame Spitfire *(PL)*

WESTON [TF2925]

☆ *Chequers* PE12 6RA [High Rd, just off A151]: Sizeable carpeted dining pub with good inventive food using local produce, nice wines, cool uncluttered décor, small contemporary bar with leather armchairs,

Adnams and Greene King IPA, good coffee; may be piped nostalgic music; disabled access, garden with heated covered terrace and play area, cl Sun evening, Mon and Tues (BB)

WOODHALL SPA [TF1962]

☆ *Abbey Lodge* LN10 6UH [B1192 towards Coningsby]: Welcoming family-run roadside inn with enjoyable reasonably priced food from sandwiches up, affable staff, nice pubby feel mixing eating and drinking sides well; bustling discreetly decorated bar with good choice of beers and wines, Victorian and older furnishings, World War II RAF pictures, Marstons Pedigree; children over 10 in restaurant, may be piped music; cl Sun *(John Robertson, John Branston, Mr and Mrs B B Wiles, LYM)*

Please tell us if the décor, atmosphere, food or drink at a pub is different from our description. We rely on readers' reports to keep us up to date: feedback@goodguides.com, or (no stamp needed) The Good Pub Guide, FREEPOST TN1569, Wadhurst, E Sussex TN5 7BR.

Norfolk

Food plays a strong part in pubs here with first-class produce in the leading role – rare-breed pork and beef, game from large estates and, of course, delicious fish and seafood. About one-third of the Main Entries holds one of our Food Awards and many more are pretty close to achieving one. Local beer is important in this county, too, and the breweries are well supported with 12 pubs gaining one of our Beer Awards. Breweries to look out for are Beestons, Elmtree, Front Street, Humpty Dumpty, Woodfordes, Wolf and Yetmans – with others just over the border such as Adnams, Cliff Quay and Mauldons (Suffolk) and Elgoods (Cambridgeshire). Pubs on top form this year include the Kings Head in Bawburgh (very well run and always busy), the White Horse in Blakeney (interesting food using local ingredients), the Jolly Sailors (own-brew beers and bustling atmosphere) and White Horse (a smashing all-rounder) both in Brancaster Staithe, the Hoste Arms in Burnham Market (despite being more of a hotel there's a proper pubby bar), the Crown in East Rudham (one of the Flying Kiwi Inns and thoroughly enjoyable), the Kings Head in Letheringsett (civilised country house and part of the same little group), the Fat Cat in Norwich (an extraordinary choice of beers), the Rose & Crown in Snettisham (very well run and with a fine mix of customers), the Three Horseshoes in Warham (old-fashioned and unchanging) and the Fur & Feather at Woodbastwick (the brewery tap for Woodfordes Brewery). Four new entries here are the Ostrich at Castle Acre, the Swan in Ingham, the King William IV at Sedgeford and the Wildebeest Arms at Stoke Holy Cross. For top-notch food, our Norfolk Dining Pub 2011 is the Kings Head in Letheringsett.

AYLSHAM   TG1926   MAP 8

Black Boys ♀ ◖ ⇦
Market Place, just off B1145; NR11 6EH

Fair value food in nicely updated traditional market-place inn with a warm-hearted bar

From the outside, this small hotel has quite an imposing Georgian façade but it's been appealingly brought up to date inside and the atmosphere is informal and friendly. There are high dark beams in the ochre ceiling, some walls stripped back to the warm red brickwork with a dark-panelled dado, neat wood flooring and comfortably old-fashioned chairs or built-in wall seats around good well spaced solid tables. There's also an adjoining dining area. Adnams Best and Broadside, Fullers London Pride and Greene King IPA on handpump and eight decent wines by the glass; helpful young staff jolly things along. Neat modern tables and chairs out in front face the market place. The five bedrooms (there's a £5 charge for dogs if they stay) are attractively furnished.

🍴 With some fair priced snacks and light meals, the tasty bar food includes sandwiches, filled baked potatoes, ploughman's, soup, potted brown shrimps, sausages with onion gravy, ham and eggs, omelettes, cromer crab salad, steak and kidney pudding, oriental chicken stir fry with noodles, wild mushroom risotto, beer-battered cod, barbecue pork ribs, venison and mushroom stroganoff, and puddings like treacle tart with clotted cream ice-cream and baked chocolate cheesecake with raspberry sorbet. *Starters/Snacks: £4.25 to £8.95. Main Courses: £7.95 to £16.95. Puddings: £4.95 to £5.50*

Unique (Enterprise) ~ Lease Matthew Miller ~ Real ale ~ Bar food (all day Sun) ~ Restaurant ~ (01263) 732122 ~ Children welcome ~ Dogs allowed in bar and bedrooms ~ Open 11(12 Sun)-11 ~ Bedrooms: £55B/£65B

Recommended by John Wooll, Ian and Nita Cooper, Lawrence Pearse, John Cook

BAWBURGH   TG1508   MAP 5

Kings Head 🍴 ⏏

Pub signposted down Harts Lane off B1108, which leads off A47 just W of Norwich; NR9 3LS

Bustling old pub, small rooms with plenty of atmosphere, cheerful service, wide choice of interesting bar food and several real ales

With a decent range of real ales, enjoyable food and pleasant, informed staff, it's not surprising that this 17th-c pub is so popular. There are leather sofas and seats, a variety of nice old wooden tables and wooden or leather dining chairs on stripped wooden floors, low beams and some standing timbers, a warming log fire in a large knocked-through canopied fireplace, and a couple of woodburning stoves in the restaurant areas. To be sure of a table at peak times, you must book in advance. Adnams Bitter and Broadside, Woodfordes Wherry and a guest such as Fullers London Pride on handpump, 16 wines by the glass and several malt whiskies; piped music. There are seats outside in the garden and a little green opposite.

🍴 Listing their suppliers on the menu, the interesting food might include bar nibbles, sandwiches, soup, potato, wild garlic and rosemary rösti with a poached duck egg and wild garlic pesto, sausages of the week with cinnamon merlot onions and rich beef bone gravy, smoked haddock kedgeree, popular cheese-stuffed burger with beetroot and horseradish chutney and home-made ketchup, specials such as curried cauliflower fritters with spiced lentils and raita and local rabbit with skinny fried and roasted pepper and chilli sauce, and puddings like jaffa cake tart with crème fraîche and cranachan parfait with whisky and ginger jelly and a flapjack. *Starters/Snacks: £3.50 to £6.95. Main Courses: £7.95 to £16.95. Puddings: £5.50*

Free house ~ Licensee Anton Wimmer ~ Real ale ~ Bar food (12-2, 5.30-9; 12-4 Sun; not winter Mon) ~ Restaurant ~ (01603) 744977 ~ Children welcome ~ Dogs allowed in bar ~ Open 11-11; 12-10.30 Sun

Recommended by John Robertson, Ian and Nita Cooper, Tina and David Woods-Taylor, John Cook, David and Cathrine Whiting

BINHAM   TF9839   MAP 8

Chequers 🍺

B1388 SW of Blakeney; NR21 0AL

Friendly, hard-working licensees and own-brewed beers in cheerful local

The own-brewed beers here are well kept and very good and the friendly licensees work hard to create a cheerful and relaxed atmosphere. On handpump these Front Street ales include Binham Cheer, Callum's Ale and Unity Strong, they keep a guest such as Clarks Rams Revenge, have around 30 belgian bottled beers and decent house wines, too. The long low-beamed building has splendid coal fires at each end, sturdy plush seats and some nice old local prints. There are picnic-sets out in front and on the grass behind the building. This is an interesting village with a huge priory church.

🍽 **Bar food** includes lunchtime sandwiches and filled baguettes, soup, ham and egg, sausages and mash, chicken breast with a creamy mushroom sauce, steak in ale pie, lasagne, and puddings. *Starters/Snacks: £4.75 to £5.90. Main Courses: £7.50 to £12.80. Puddings: £3.25 to £4.95*

Own brew ~ Licensees Mr and Mrs Chroscicki ~ Real ale ~ Bar food (12-2, 6(7 Sun)-9) ~ (01328) 830297 ~ Children welcome ~ Open 11.30-2.30, 6-11(11.30 Sat); 12-2.30, 7-11 Sun
Recommended by Mike Proctor, Chris Johnson, R C Vincent, Steve Nye, Tracey and Stephen Groves

BLAKENEY   TG0243   MAP 8

White Horse 🍽 ♀
Off A149 W of Sheringham; High Street; NR25 7AL

Cheerful small hotel with popular dining conservatory, enjoyable food and drinks and helpful staff; bedrooms

The main bar here is really relaxing and friendly (especially out of season) and there's a good mix of customers of all ages. It's a former coaching inn just a stroll from the small tidal harbour and although many customers come to enjoy the popular food, those just wanting a drink and a chat do pop in. Adnams Bitter and Broadside, Woodfordes Wherry and Yetmans on handpump and a huge choice of 36 wines by the glass. The informal long main bar is cream-coloured above a pale green dado (two end walls have tartan wallpaper) and has high-backed suede dining and other chairs around light oak tables on the green-patterned carpet, contemporary window blinds and watercolours by a local artist (for sale). There's also an airy conservatory and smarter restaurant. The suntrap courtyard and pleasant paved garden both have plenty of tables. This area is a haven for bird-watchers and sailors.

🍽 **They support local farmers, producers and fishermen, butcher their own meat, bake their own bread and make their own pickles:** sandwiches and filled ciabattas, ploughman's, soup, smoked prawns with chilli mayonnaise, pork rillettes with spiced chutney, moules marinière, smoked haddock and crayfish kedgeree with a soft boiled egg, aubergine parmigiana with pumpkin purée, roast tomatoes and toasted almonds, ballottine of guinea fowl stuffed with their own black pudding, parsnip purée and herb gnocchi, red mullet with mussel, bacon and tomato stew and aioli, and puddings such as pumpkin tart with clotted cream and ginger bread with caramel sauce and vanilla ice-cream. *Starters/Snacks: £3.95 to £7.50. Main Courses: £10.95 to £17.25. Puddings: £5.25*

Free house ~ Licensee Dan Goff ~ Real ale ~ Bar food (12-2.15, 6-9(9.30 Fri and Sat)) ~ Restaurant ~ (01263) 740574 ~ Children allowed away from bar ~ Dogs allowed in bar ~ Open 11-11 ~ Bedrooms: /£140S(£70B)
Recommended by Malcolm and Jane Levitt, MDN, David Carr, Tracey and Stephen Groves, Brian and Anna Marsden

BRANCASTER STAITHE   TF7944   MAP 8

Jolly Sailors 🍺
Main Road (A149); PE31 8BJ

Bustling pub with own-brewed beers, traditional food, friendly staff and plenty of seats in sizeable garden; great for bird-watching nearby

With their own-brewed beers (the brewery is nearby rather than on site) and a genuinely friendly welcome, it's not surprising that our readers enjoy this little village pub so much. The main bar has a mix of wheelback, cushioned captain's and other dark wooden dining chairs around pubby tables on red quarry tiles, a log fire in the brick fireplace, stripped-stone walls, pot plants and Brancaster Best plus Adnams Broadside and Regatta and Woodfordes Wherry on handpump and a dozen wines by the glass; there's a serving hatch to the outside terraced seating area. Two further snug areas have local books, board games and views to the harbour; darts. The dining lounge has old-fashioned comfortable furnishings, easy chairs by the open fire and scrub-top tables, and a further room, facing the garden, has pool and TV. Plenty of seats outside in the enclosed garden and a children's playground. This is prime bird-watching territory and the pub is set on the edge of thousands of acres of National Trust dunes and salt flats; walkers are welcome.

🍴 As well as pizzas (you can take them away as well), bar food includes filled baguettes, ploughman's, soup, popular local mussels, fish and chips, tagliatelle with mushroom and parmesan sauce, gammon and egg, game pie, pork curry, and puddings like crème caramel and toffee and bourbon pancake with vanilla ice-cream. *Starters/Snacks: £3.95 to £4.95. Main Courses: £5.95 to £10.95. Puddings: £3.95 to £4.95*

Free house ~ Licensees Cliff and James Nye ~ Real ale ~ Bar food (all day summer and winter weekends; 12-2.30, 6-9 Mon-Fri in winter) ~ Restaurant ~ (01485) 210314 ~ Children welcome ~ Dogs allowed in bar ~ Open 12-11(10.30 Sun); 12-midnight (Fri and Sat; 12-3, 6-11 Mon-Thurs in winter

Recommended by Mrs Carolyn Dixon, Tracey and Stephen Groves, Michael Dandy, Henry Pursehouse-Tranter, John and Victoria Fairley, Terry and Elizabeth Tyrrell, Gwyn and Anne Wake

White Horse 🍴 ♈ 🛏

A149 E of Hunstanton; PE31 8BY

Bustling bar, big airy dining conservatory looking over tidal bird marshes, real ales and good food; comfortable bedrooms

If staying at this well run and extremely popular place, try to book a room with a sea view and its own little terrace; the coast path runs along the bottom of the garden. This is not a straightforward pub but it does have a busy and informal front bar with plenty of locals dropping in, Adnams Bitter and Explorer, Brancaster Best and Woodfordes Wherry on handpump, 14 wines by the glass and a dozen malt whiskies; good photographs on the walls, bar billiards, occasional piped music and TV. A little further in is an area with cushioned wicker armchairs and sofas, local landscapes for sale, and a table with daily papers. This leads into the airy conservatory restaurant with big picture windows looking across the wide tidal marshes to Scolt Head island; there are well spaced furnishings in unvarnished country-style wood and some light-hearted seasidey decorations. Service is first rate and there's a really good mix of customers. As well as seats on the sun deck with lovely views, there are plenty of tables under cover on the heated terrace beside the bar. Lots to do and see nearby.

🍴 Making the most of the local fish and seafood, the fair-value bar food includes sandwiches, soup, mussels and oysters, salmon fishcakes with pomegranate, cucumber and fennel salad, local sausages with onion gravy, fresh pasta with wild mushrooms, blue cheese and toasted hazelnut gremolata, steak burger with smoked bacon and cheese, seafood platter, beer-battered cod and slow-roasted pork belly with cider sauce with puddings like chocolate brownie with chocolate sauce and lemon tart; the restaurant main courses are more expensive. *Starters/Snacks: £5.25 to £6.95. Main Courses: £7.25 to £11.50. Puddings: £3.95 to £4.95*

Free house ~ Licensees Cliff Nye and Kevin Nobes ~ Real ale ~ Bar food (all day in bar and on outside terrace; 12-2, 6.30-9 restaurant) ~ Restaurant ~ (01485) 210262 ~ Children welcome ~ Dogs allowed in bar and bedrooms ~ Open 12-11(10.30 Sun) ~ Bedrooms: £95B/£130B

Recommended by Brian and Anna Marsden, George and Beverley Tucker, Dennis and Gill Keen, Mrs J Andrews, JJW, CMW, P Waterman, Mike and Sue Loseby, Michael Dandy, John Ainscough, Peter and Josie Fawcett, Henry Pursehouse-Tranter, Jenny and Brian Seller, John Wooll, Malcolm and Jo Hart, Tracey and Stephen Groves, A Kirk, R L Borthwick, M R D Foot, John and Victoria Fairley, Jeff and Wendy Williams, Brian and Janet Ainscough, Roger and Kath

> Bedroom prices normally include full english breakfast, VAT and any inclusive service charge that we know of. Prices before the '/' are for single rooms, after for two people in double or twin (B includes a private bath, S a private shower). If there is no '/', the prices are only for twin or double rooms (as far as we know there are no singles). If there is no B or S, as far as we know no rooms have private facilities.

BURNHAM MARKET

Hoste Arms 🍴 ☐ 🛏

The Green (B1155); PE31 8HD

Civilised and stylish with first-class food and drinks, a proper bar plus several lounge areas and dining rooms and a lovely garden; elaborately decorated bedrooms

Although much emphasis is placed on the thriving restaurant and hotel side of this civilised and smart old coaching inn, there's a proper front bar with all the atmosphere of a village pub. This room is panelled and has a log fire, a series of watercolours showing scenes from local walks, a nice mix of chatty customers and Greene King Abbot and Woodfordes Nelsons Revenge and Wherry on handpump. The extensive and carefully chosen wine list has helpful notes and around 18 (including champagne and fizz) by the glass; lots of whiskies and liqueurs. There's a conservatory with leather armchairs and sofas, a lounge for afternoon tea and several restaurants (for which it's best to book to be sure of a table). The lovely walled garden has plenty of seats and a big awning covers the moroccan-style dining area.

🍴 Food is imaginative and highly thought-of: lunchtime sandwiches, soup, tempura black pudding with crispy shallots, a poached egg and devilled sauce, smoked chicken, mango, pawpaw and coconut salad with peanut dressing, local mussels with white wine and cream, beer-battered cod with minted crushed peas, wild mushroom, spinach and mascarpone risotto, steak burger with crispy bacon and cheese, chicken stir fry with asian vegetables and noodles, braised ox cheeks with horseradish mash and crispy pancetta, a fish dish of the days, and puddings such as banoffi tart with toffee ice-cream and honeycomb and mixed berry cheesecake with lemon curd. *Starters/Snacks: £5.15 to £8.95. Main Courses: £12.25 to £19.95. Puddings: £6.95*

Free house ~ Licensee Emma Tagg ~ Real ale ~ Bar food ~ Restaurant ~ (01328) 738777 ~ Children welcome ~ Dogs allowed in bar and bedrooms ~ Open 11-11(10.30 Sun) ~ Bedrooms: £112S/£137B

Recommended by Peter and Giff Bennett, Fred and Lorraine Gill, Malcolm and Jane Levitt, Simon Rodway, Roy Hoing, Pete Coxon, Mike and Sue Loseby, Derek and Sylvia Stephenson, Mike Proctor, Alistair and Kay Butler, Michael Dandy, Mr and Mrs W W Burke, Walter and Susan Rinaldi-Butcher, David Carr, George and Linda Ozols, Derek Thomas, John and Victoria Fairley, Keith and Sue Ward, George Atkinson, David Cosham

BURSTON

Crown 🍺

Village signposted off A140 N of Scole; Mill Road; IP22 5TW

Friendly, relaxed village pub usefully open all day with a warm welcome, real ales and well liked bar food

As this village pub is open all day there's a nice flow of customers dropping in for a drink and a chat – all of whom are welcomed by the friendly, cheerful staff. Regulars tend to gather in an area by the bar counter with its high bar chairs where they serve Adnams Bitter, Greene King Abbot and guests from local breweries such as Cliff Quay and Elmtree on handpump. In cold weather, the best places to sit in this heavy-beamed, quarry-tiled room is on the comfortably cushioned sofas in front of the big log fire in its huge brick fireplace and there are also some stools by the low chunky wooden table and newspapers and magazines to read. The public bar on the left has a nice long table and panelled settle on an old brick floor in one alcove, another sofa, straightforward tables and chairs on the carpet by the pool table, darts and juke box, and up a step, more tables and chairs. Both of these cream-painted rooms are hung with cheerful naïve local character paintings. The simple beamed dining room, just off the main bar, has pine tables and chairs on the big modern quarry tiles and logs piled up in another big brick fireplace. Outside, there's a smokers' shelter, a couple of picnic-sets in front of the old brick building and more seats in a hedged-off area with a barbecue. They hold all sorts of events: beer and music festivals, quiz and live music evenings, specialist food events and so forth.

🍽 Using local produce, the well liked bar food includes sandwiches, filled baguettes and pittas, soup, pork and pigeon terrine with medlar jelly, mussels in white wine and cream, aubergine and tomato parmigiana, ham and egg, steak and mushroom in Guinness pie, beer-battered hake, chicken suprême with a wild mushroom risotto and gorgonzola sauce and bass with red pepper, anchovies and saffron potatoes. *Starters/Snacks: £5.00 to £9.00. Main Courses: £9.00 to £15.50. Puddings: £4.50 to £5.00*

Free house ~ Licensees Bev and Steve Kembery and Jonathan Piers-Hall ~ Real ale ~ Bar food (12-2(4 Sun), 6.30-9; not Sun evening) ~ Restaurant ~ (01379) 741257 ~ Children welcome ~ Dogs allowed in bar ~ Live music Thurs evening and every other Sun at 5pm ~ Open 12-1(10.30 Sun)

Recommended by Sue Austin

CASTLE ACRE

TF8115   MAP 8

Ostrich

Stocks Green; PE32 2AE

Friendly old village pub with original features, fine old fireplaces, real ales and tasty food

Doing well under its present landlady, this 16th-c village inn is prettily placed overlooking a tree-lined green. Wandering around the various rooms you can still see some of the original masonry, beams and trusses in the lofty ceilings, although the place was largely rebuilt in the 18th century. The L-shaped low-ceilinged front bar (on two levels) has a woodburning stove in a huge old fireplace, lots of wheelback chairs and cushioned pews around pubby tables on the wood-strip floor and gold patterned wallpaper; a step leads up to an area in front of the bar counter where there are similar seats and tables and a log fire in a brick fireplace. Greene King IPA, Abbot and Old Speckled Hen and a guest beer on handpump, a dozen wines (including fizz) by the glass and several malt whiskies. There's a separate dining room with another brick fireplace. The sheltered garden has picnic-sets under parasols. There are some remains of a Norman castle in the village as well as a Cluniac monastery.

🍽 Bar food includes lunchtime sandwiches and panini, soup, duck pâté with sweet cherries, beer-battered fish, toad in the hole with onion gravy, roasted vegetable lasagne, gammon and egg with honey and mustard sauce, chicken schnitzel, fish or venison stews and rib-eye steak. *Starters/Snacks: £4.95 to £6.95. Main Courses: £9.95 to £16.95. Puddings: £4.95 to £7.95*

Greene King ~ Tenant Tiffany Turner ~ Real ale ~ Bar food (12-3, 6-9; 12-3 Sun; not Sun evening) ~ (01760) 755398 ~ Children welcome ~ Dogs allowed in bar ~ Open 10am-11pm; 10-12.30am (11.30 Sun) Sat ~ Bedrooms: /£75B

Recommended by Dr and Mrs R G J Telfer, Tom and Sally Millest, Brian Glozier, Debby Horsman, Charles Gysin, John Baxter

CLEY NEXT THE SEA

TG0443   MAP 8

George ♀ 🛏

Off A149 W of Sheringham; High Street; NR25 7RN

Pubby bar and two dining rooms in sizeable inn, real ales and super choice of wines and bar and restaurant food; bedrooms

Although there are two dining rooms here, if it's just a quiet drink that you want head for the little public bar. As well as Adnams Broadside, Woodfordes Wherry and Yetmans on handpump and 30 wines by the glass, there are photographs of Norfolk wherries and other local scenes on the cream walls, a long leather settle and sturdy dark wooden chairs by a couple of green-topped tables on the carpet, a huge candle in a big glass jar on one window sill, a table of newspapers and a stained-glass window showing St George and the dragon. The dining rooms are similarly furnished with pale wooden cushioned dining chairs around a mix of tables; the end room has prints of Leonardo drawings on the fleur-de-lys wallpaper, brown blinds on the windows, an ornamental woodburning stove in the end room with nightlights along the mantelbeam and some rather nice old-fashioned glass wall lamps. There are seats in the garden across the little road and nearby walks. Some of the bedrooms overlook the salt flats (which are fantastic for bird lovers).

🍴 **Tasty bar food includes sandwiches, ploughman's, soup, local oysters, crab tian with thai mayonnaise, locally smoked prosciutto with caramelised pears and walnuts, tomato, basil and mozzarella tart, pork sausages with crispy onions and red wine sauce, beer-battered haddock, corn-fed chicken on roasted mediterranean vegetables with a tomato coulis and charmoula-spiced lamb cutlets on herb couscous.** *Starters/Snacks: £3.95 to £6.25. Main Courses: £8.95 to £15.95. Puddings: £5.25 to £6.25*

Free house ~ Licensee Daniel Goff ~ Real ale ~ Bar food ~ Restaurant ~ (01263) 740652 ~ Children welcome ~ Dogs allowed in bar and bedrooms ~ Live music monthly in winter ~ Open 10am-11pm ~ Bedrooms: /£80S

Recommended by John and Victoria Fairley, Tracey and Stephen Groves, Nigel Long

COLKIRK   TF9226   MAP 8

Crown ♀

Village signposted off B1146 S of Fakenham, and off A1065; Crown Road; NR21 7AA

Neatly kept, bustling local with cheerful landlord, splendid wines, popular tasty food and a pleasant garden

Our readers very much enjoy this cottagey little local and the friendly staff are sure to make you welcome whether you are a regular or a visitor. If it's just a chat and a drink you want, head for the bar on the right – those eating head for the left-hand room. Both rooms are comfortable and cosy and kept spotless with solid country furniture on the rugs and flooring tiles, interesting things to look at and open fires. Greene King IPA and Abbot and a guest beer on handpump and a splendid range of wines, many by the glass; quick service even when busy. There's also a separate dining room. Outside, the suntrap terrace and pleasant garden have plenty of picnic-sets.

🍴 **Popular bar food includes lunchtime sandwiches and filled baguettes, soup, a changing pâté, coconut prawns with a chilli dip, leek and stilton flan, chicken in a creamy mushroom and brandy sauce, fresh battered haddock and chips, salmon and halibut in a white wine sauce, steak in ale pie, and puddings like lemon and lime cheesecake and bread and butter pudding.** *Starters/Snacks: £4.50 to £5.95. Main Courses: £8.95 to £17.95. Puddings: £5.25*

Greene King ~ Tenant Roger Savell ~ Real ale ~ Bar food (12-1.45(2 Sun), 6-8.30(8 Sun)) ~ Restaurant ~ (01328) 862172 ~ Children welcome ~ Dogs allowed in bar ~ Open 11-2.30, 6-10.30(11 Sat, 10 Sun)

Recommended by Tracey and Stephen Groves, Mr and Mrs T B Staples, R A P Cross, D M Jack, Gillian Grist

EAST RUDHAM   TF8228   MAP 8

Crown 🍴 ♀ 🛏

A148 W of Fakenham; The Green; PE31 8RD

Stylish and contemporary open-plan seating areas, cosy back sitting room and further dining room, civilised and friendly atmosphere, real ales and first-class modern food; bedrooms

Friendly and rather civilised, this spotlessly kept beamed pub is extremely popular with our readers. The contemporary open-plan bar has several distinct seating areas with brown leather and wood dining chairs around a mix of tables (including a huge round one), a log fire in a modern brick fireplace (with a grandfather clock and bookshelves on either side) and rugs on the stripped floorboards. High bar chairs beside the handsomely slate-topped counter are popular and they keep their own-brewed Kiwi Ale and Adnams Bitter and Broadside on handpump and several wines by the glass. The other end of the room is slightly more informal with a mix of leather-seated dining chairs around all sorts of tables, a couple of built-in wall seats, another bookshelf beside a second fireplace and 1950s and 1960s actor prints in Shakespearean costume on the walls. There's also more of a pubby part with planked and cushioned white-painted built-in seats and nice photographs on the pink walls and a cosy lower area to the back of the building with comfortable leather sofas and armchairs and a flatscreen TV; newspapers to read. Upstairs is yet another dining room with a high-pitched ceiling. There are neat picnicsets under parasols on the front gravel. This pub is in the same little Flying Kiwi Inns group as the Kings Head at Letheringsett and the Crown, Wells-next-the-Sea.

🍴 **Attractively presented and very good – if not cheap – the modern bar food might include** lunchtime sandwiches and ploughman's, appetisers such as quail eggs with curried mayonnaise, soup, an antipasti slate, braised ham hock terrine with piccalilli, courgette, sun-dried tomato and spinach pasta with pesto, chicken with herb risotto and shallot jus, slow-cooked pork belly with cider syrup, moroccan lamb with spiced couscous, bass fillet with basil gnocchi and tapenade, and puddings like chocolate and cherry torte with cherry coulis and green tea and iced yoghurt parfait with roast rhubarb; they also offer breakfasts and morning coffee. *Starters/Snacks: £4.95 to £7.95. Main Courses: £10.95 to £18.95. Puddings: £5.95 to £7.95*

Free house ~ Licensee Chris Coubrough ~ Real ale ~ Bar food (12-2.30, 6.30-9.30; they offer breakfast from 8am) ~ (01485) 528530 ~ Children welcome ~ Dogs allowed in bar and bedrooms ~ Open 8am-11pm(10.30 Sun) ~ Bedrooms: /£90B

Recommended by R C Vincent, Tracey and Stephen Groves, Christopher and Elise Way, Anthony Barnes, John Wooll, George and Linda Ozols, David and Sue Atkinson, R L Borthwick, Mr and Mrs Roberts, Jeff and Wendy Williams

EDGEFIELD

TG0934 MAP 8

Pigs 🍴 ☐ ◖

Norwich Road; B1149 S of Holt; NR24 2RL

New licensee for well run pub, five real ales tapped from the cask, interesting and often unusual food and seats outside; new bedrooms

A new licensee has taken over this popular pub and has opened up the bedrooms. It's a friendly place with good, interesting food and several real ales tapped from the cask in the carpeted bar which might include Adnams Bitter and Broadside, Woodfordes Wherry and guests from Wolf and Yetman. They also have continental beers on tap, a good range of wines by the glass and coffee. A games area has bar billiards and board games and there's a proper children's playroom, too. On the left, arches open through to a simply furnished area with a mix of random dining chairs and built-in pews around the plain tables on broad stripped-pine boards. On the right, a light and airy dining extension is similar in style, with some tables in stalls formed by low brick stub walls and single standing timbers; the kitchen is in open view. Outside, a big covered terrace has sturdy rustic tables and benches on flagstones, and there's an adventure play area; boules. Wheelchair access is easy.

🍴 **Using carefully sourced local produce, the interesting bar food includes** sandwiches (the all-day breakfast on toast is popular), their own version of tapas such as potted rabbit, smoked sprats, rare-breed crispy pigs ears and so forth, a house salad, rosemaryroasted chicken breast with lemon and thyme mash, beer-battered haddock, slow-cooked pork with smoky bacon beans, apple chutney and black pudding, game suet pudding, and puddings like milk jelly with poached quince and lardy cake with rum and raisin icecream; there's a Sunday pudding club. *Starters/Snacks: £5.00 to £5.95. Main Courses: £9.95 to £17.50. Puddings: £5.00 to £5.95*

Free house ~ Licensee Tim Abbott ~ Real ale ~ Bar food (12-2.30(3 Sat), 6-9; 12-9 Sun) ~ Restaurant ~ (01263) 587634 ~ Children welcome ~ Dogs allowed in bar ~ Open 11-3, 6-11; 12-10.30 Sun ~ Bedrooms: /£130B

Recommended by Derek Field, Charles Gysin, Ian and Nita Cooper, Dr and Mrs R G J Telfer, Tracey and Stephen Groves, Amanda Stark, David Carr, Muriel and John Hobbs, Annette Tress, Roy Hoing, Roger and Lesley Everett, Sheila Topham, Bill and Marian de Bass, Philip and Susan Philcox

ERPINGHAM   TG1732   MAP 8

Saracens Head 🛏

At Wolterton – not shown on many maps; Erpingham signed off A140 N of Aylsham; keep on through Calthorpe, then where road bends right take the straight-ahead turn-off signposted Wolterton; NR11 7LZ

New licensees for this remote and rather civilised inn, some gentle changes to bars and dining room and seats in smartened-up courtyard; bedrooms

Friendly new licensees have taken over this rather civilised inn and have made some gentle changes to lighten the place up a bit – while keeping the informal and relaxed atmosphere. The two-room bar has been redecorated but remains simple and stylish with high ceilings, light terracotta walls and cream and gold curtains at its tall windows – all lending a feeling of space, though it's not actually large. There's a mix of seats from built-in wall settles to wicker fireside chairs as well as log fires and flowers, and the windows look out on to a charming old-fashioned gravel stableyard with new chairs, benches and tables. A pretty six-table parlour (now olive green) on the right has another big log fire. Woodfordes Wherry on handpump, several wines by the glass and local soft drinks. The bedrooms have all been renovated and breakfasts are good. More reports on the changes, please.

🍴 **Bar food now includes soup, chicken caesar salad, cherry tomato, courgette, red onion and pesto puff pastry tart, line-caught cod with roasted fennel, chicken with a blue cheese topping, slow-cooked pork belly, confit duck leg with plum and cassis sauce, and puddings such as caramel crème brûlée and rhubarb and raspberry crumble.** *Starters/Snacks: £4.75 to £8.50. Main Courses: £8.95 to £17.00. Puddings: £5.50*

Free house ~ Licensees Tim and Janie Elwes ~ Real ale ~ Bar food (not Mon, not Tues lunchtime) ~ (01263) 768909 ~ Children welcome but must be well behaved ~ Dogs allowed in bar and bedrooms ~ Open 11.30-11; 12-10 Sun; closed Mon all day and Tues lunchtime ~ Bedrooms: £60B/£90B

Recommended by Pete Devonish, Ian McIntyre, Mike and Shelley Woodroffe, Philip and Susan Philcox, R C Vincent, John and Victoria Fairley, MDN

GREAT MASSINGHAM   TF7922   MAP 8

Dabbling Duck 🍺

Off A148 King's Lynn—Fakenham; Abbey Road; PE32 2HN

Unassuming from the outside but with a friendly atmosphere, traditional furnishings, warm coal fires, several real ales and interesting food

There's a relaxed, friendly atmosphere in this unassuming-looking pub and a good mix of both locals and visitors. The bar to the right of the door is nicely informal with a very high-backed settle, some comfortable armchairs and a leather and brass-button settle facing each other across a pine table in front of a coal fire in the huge raised fireplace. Further in, there are some beams and standing timbers, an attractive mix of wooden dining chairs and tables, reproduction prints of 18th- and 19th-c cartoons on pale grey walls, rugs on the stripped wooden floor and another fireplace with shelves of books to one side. At the back of the pub is a room just right for a private group and to the left there's more of a drinking bar with library chairs and leather easy chairs on bare boards, darts, another coal fire, and country prints above a tall grey dado. Adnams Broadside, Beestons Worth the Wait, Greene King IPA, Woodfordes Wherry and a guest such as Elgoods Golden Newt on handpump from a bar counter made of great slabs of polished tree trunk; daily papers on a rod and a pile of interesting old journals. There are tables and chairs on a front terrace looking over the sizeable village green with its big duck ponds.

Post Office address codings confusingly give the impression that a few pubs are in Norfolk, when they're really in Cambridgeshire or Suffolk (which is where we list them).

🍽 From a seasonally changing menu, the often elaborate bar food includes sandwiches, soup, smoked salmon with chargrilled citrus and vodka chicory with a beetroot and honey dressing, baked goats cheese en croûte with a sherry and rhubarb vinaigrette and a pear and pecan salad, chicken with wild mushrooms, chestnuts, spinach, sunblush tomatoes and a wholegrain mustard sauce, clams with linguine in a garlic and lime cream, and pub classics like beer-battered fish and home-made burger; Sunday roasts. *Starters/Snacks: £5.25 to £6.75. Main Courses: £6.95 to £15.65. Puddings: £5.25 to £6.25*

Free house ~ Licensee Dominic Symington ~ Real ale ~ Bar food (12-2.30(3 Sun), 6.30-9; not Sun evening) ~ Restaurant ~ (01485) 520827 ~ Children welcome ~ Dogs allowed in bar and bedrooms ~ Open 12-11(10.30 Sun) ~ Bedrooms: /£80B

Recommended by Tracey and Stephen Groves, Pete Devonish, Ian McIntyre, Derek and Sylvia Stephenson, Christopher and Elise Way, Graham and Carol Uren, DC, Gillian Grist, John Cook, R C Vincent

HUNWORTH

TG0735 MAP 8

Hunny Bell

Signed off B roads S of Holt; NR24 2AA

Friendly village pub with neat bar and airy dining room, four real ales, interesting bar food and seats overlooking the green

The neatly kept bar in this welcoming and carefully furnished 18th-c pub has ceiling joists, a nice mix of cushioned dining chairs around wooden tables on the stone-tiled floor, a woodburning stove and high bar stools by the oak bar counter. There's also a cosy snug with homely armchairs, pouffes and housekeeper's chairs on old floor tiles, and throughout, there are some original stripped-brick walls. The high-raftered dining room has a red colour theme and another woodburning stove. Adnams Bitter, Greene King Abbot, Woodfordes Wherry and a guest beer from Fullers or Wolf on handpump; board games. Picnic-sets on the terrace look across the lane to the village green; there are more seats among fruit trees in the garden. It's in the same small local group as the Wildebeest Arms at Stoke Holy Cross.

🍽 Good bar food includes lunchtime sandwiches, soup, chicken liver parfait with onion marmalade, cromer crab and avocado purée tian with smoked mackerel and tiger prawns, honey-roast ham and free-range eggs, baked field mushroom with creamy leeks and goats cheese herb crust and lyonnaise potatoes, Guinness-battered cod, rosemary roast chump of lamb with red pepper jus, sirloin of beef with a herb crust, onion confit and garlic mayonnaise, and puddings like vanilla crème brûlée with pear sorbet and hazelnut madeleine and Snickers frozen peanut parfait with dark chocolate glaze and peanut brittle. *Starters/Snacks: £4.95 to £7.75. Main Courses: £6.95 to £17.75. Puddings: £5.50 to £5.95*

Animal Inns ~ Manager Henry Watt ~ Real ale ~ Bar food (12-2(3 Sun), 6-9.30(6.30-8.30 Sun)) ~ Restaurant ~ (01263) 712300 ~ Children welcome ~ Dogs allowed in bar ~ Open 11.30-3, 5.30-midnight; 12-4, 6.30-10.30 Sun

Recommended by Derek Field, Bill and Marian de Bass, Pete Devonish, Ian McIntyre, Charles Gysin, Philip and Susan Philcox, Tracey and Stephen Groves, Keith and Jenny Grant

INGHAM

TG3926 MAP 8

Swan 🍺 🛏

Off A149 SE of North Walsham; signposted from Stalham; NR12 9AB

Nicely placed and warmly welcoming ancient thatched pub tied to Woodfordes, their good beers, enjoyable food; comfortable bedrooms

Dwarfed by the soaring flint tower of the church beside it, this quietly set 14th-c country pub is in easy reach of both the Broads and the coast. Inside, stripped flint and ancient masonry abound, and the rustic atmosphere is underlined by low beams, hefty standing timbers, dim lighting, a few farm tools, and the two big woodburning stoves either side of the massive chimneybreast. This divides the main area into two more intimate spaces – the further side, with parquet rather than bare boards, has a rather quieter atmosphere than the cheery part by the bar, as does a small brick-floored area up by the back entrance, with leather sofas by a plexiglass table. Particularly well kept Woodfordes Wherry, Mardlers Mild, Sundew, Nelsons Revenge and Admirals Reserve on handpump, decent wines by the glass; charming efficient staff. A sheltered sunny back terrace has picnic-sets, some under cocktail parasols, with more round the side. The simple, comfortable bedrooms are in converted stabling.

🍽 **The chef/landlord bakes his own bread and makes his own ice-creams and the food may include soup, cheddar and haddock soufflé, tuna with sauce vierge, confit onion and charred mediterranean vegetable tart, lunchtime fish and chips, ballottine of chicken with parma ham and mascarpone, herby rump of lamb with basil jus, grilled bass with samphire, and puddings like hot chocolate fondant with burnt honey ice-cream and crème brûlée; good breakfasts.** *Starters/Snacks: £5.25 to £8.50. Main Courses: £12.95 to £19.50. Puddings: £5.25*

Woodfordes ~ Manager Daniel Smith ~ Real ale ~ Bar food (12-2, 7-9; 12-3 Sun; best to check for Sun evening and Mon (may be closed) ~ (01692) 581099 ~ Children welcome ~ Open 12-3.30, 6.30-11 ~ Bedrooms: /£70B

Recommended by Peter Sutton, Richard Ball, Roy Hoing

LARLING   TL9889   MAP 5

Angel 🍺 🛏

From A11 Thetford—Attleborough, take B1111 turn-off and follow pub signs; NR16 2QU

Good-natured chatty atmosphere in busy pub, several real ales and tasty bar food; bedrooms

The same friendly family have run this bustling pub since 1913 and they still have the original visitors' books with guests from 1897 to 1909. The comfortable 1930s-style lounge on the right has a good mix of customers, cushioned wheelback chairs, a nice long cushioned and panelled corner settle, some good solid tables for eating and squared panelling; also, a collection of whisky-water jugs on the delft shelf over the big brick fireplace, a woodburning stove, a couple of copper kettles and some hunting prints. Adnams Bitter and four guest beers on handpump, 100 malt whiskies and ten wines by the glass. They hold an August beer festival with over 70 real ales and ciders, live music and barbecues. The quarry-tiled black-beamed public bar has a good local feel with darts, juke box (a rarity nowadays), board games and piped music. A neat grass area behind the car park has picnic-sets around a big fairy-lit apple tree and there's a safely fenced play area. They also have a four-acre meadow and offer caravan and camping sites from March to October. Peter Beale's old-fashioned rose nursery is nearby as is St George's, England's only whisky distillery.

🍽 **Generous helpings of well liked bar food include sandwiches, filled baked potatoes, ploughman's, soup, creamy mushroom pot, whitebait, ham or sausages and egg, omelettes, sweet pepper lasagne, chicken and mushroom stroganoff, prawn thai red curry, mixed grill, and specials like beer-battered fresh cod and steak and kidney pie.** *Starters/Snacks: £3.95 to £7.95. Main Courses: £7.95 to £17.50. Puddings: £4.75 to £5.95*

Free house ~ Licensee Andrew Stammers ~ Real ale ~ Bar food (all day) ~ Restaurant ~ (01953) 717963 ~ Children welcome ~ Open 10am-midnight ~ Bedrooms: £45B/£80S

Recommended by Stuart and Alison Ballantyne, Roy Hoing, Michael Mellers, Rita Scarratt, Adrian Johnson, R T and J C Moggridge, Andy and Claire Barker

---

Real ale to us means beer which has matured naturally in its cask – not pressurised or filtered. We name all real ales stocked. We usually name ales preserved under a light blanket of carbon dioxide too, though purists – pointing out that this stops the natural yeasts developing – would disagree (most people, including us, can't tell the difference!).

LETHERINGSETT   TG0638   MAP 8

Kings Head 🍴 🍷
A148 (Holt Road) W of Holt; NR25 7AR

NORFOLK DINING PUB OF THE YEAR

Several comfortably contemporary areas in neat country house, friendly chatty young staff, real ales and good wines by the glass, bistro-type food and plenty of outside seating

---

Although this looks more like a small country house than a straightforward pub, the carefully furnished rooms have real character and interest. It's all very civilised but informal with equal emphasis on both drinks and food – and plenty of space to enjoy both. To the right of the main door, a small room has dining chairs around scrubbed wooden tables, bookshelves beside a black fireplace, a flatscreen TV and apple-green paintwork. The main bar, to the left, has some high wooden bar chairs by the counter, their own-brewed Kiwi Ale, Adnams Best and a couple of guest beers on handpump, quite a choice of wines by the glass and good coffee; it's comfortable, with daily papers, big black leather armchairs and sofas and various stools and dining chairs, reproduction hunting and coaching prints on the mushroom paintwork, rugs on the quarry-tiled floor and an open fire in an ornate black fireplace. The partly skylit dining room has built-in white-painted planked wall seating with maroon cushions and a mix of dining chairs around wooden tables, rugs on stripped floorboards, and a few farm tools and cabinets of taps and spiles on the cream-painted flint and cob walls. A back area under a partly pitched ceiling with painted rafters has more comfortable leather sofas and armchairs in front of another big flatscreen TV; Scrabble and piped music. Outside, there are lots of picnic-sets under parasols on the front gravel with many more on a grass side lawn (where there's also a play fort under tenting). This is in the same Flying Kiwi Inns group as the Crowns at East Rudham and Wells-next-the-Sea.

🍴 **Good bistro-style food includes** lunchtime filled baguettes and ploughman's, soup, a deli slate, ham hock and parsley terrine with piccalilli, beer-battered local haddock, roasted squash and garlic risotto, slow-cooked pork belly with creamed celeriac mash, crackling and red wine jus, rack of lamb with garlic potatoes and rosemary pesto, baked black bream fillets with pancetta salad, pickled beetroot and tarragon mayonnaise, and puddings such as steamed orange and ginger pudding with vanilla anglaise and warm chocolate brownie with white chocolate ice-cream. *Starters/Snacks: £4.95 to £7.50. Main Courses: £11.50 to £18.95. Puddings: £4.95 to £7.25*

Free house ~ Licensee Chris Coubrough ~ Real ale ~ Bar food (12-2.30, 6.30-9.30; all day summer Sun) ~ (01263) 712691 ~ Children welcome ~ Dogs allowed in bar ~ Open 11-11
Recommended by Pete Devonish, Ian McIntyre, Charles Gysin, R C Vincent, David Carr, Derek Field, Tracey and Stephen Groves

MORSTON   TG0043   MAP 8

Anchor
A149 Salthouse—Stiffkey; The Street; NR25 7AA

Quite a choice of rooms filled with bric-a-brac and prints, real ales and all-day food

---

New licensees again for this bustling pub and it's now usefully open all day. On the right, there are three traditional rooms with pubby seating and tables on original wooden floors, coal fires, local 1950s beach photographs and lots of prints and bric-a-brac. Greene King IPA, local Winters Golden and Woodfordes Wherry on handpump and several wines by the glass. The contemporary airy extension on the left has groups of deep leather sofas around low tables, grey-painted country dining furniture, fresh flowers and fish pictures. There are tables and benches out in front of the building. You can book seal-spotting trips from here and the surrounding area is wonderful for bird-watching and walking.

🍴 As well as serving breakfasts from 9am (to non-residents, too) bar food now includes sandwiches, filled baked potatoes, ploughman's, soup, salmon and spring onion fishcakes, ham and egg, bangers and mash, lasagne, steak and mushroom pie, spinach and wild mushroom linguine, lots of seasonal daily-fresh fish, and puddings such as key lime cheesecake and sticky toffee pudding. *Starters/Snacks: £4.25 to £6.25. Main Courses: £8.95 to £14.95. Puddings: £5.25*

Free house ~ Licensees Jim and Jane Temple ~ Real ale ~ Bar food (9am-9pm) ~ Restaurant ~ (01263) 741392 ~ Children welcome ~ Dogs allowed in bar ~ Open 9am-11pm
Recommended by George Atkinson, Derek and Sylvia Stephenson, Charles Gysin, Terry Devine, Derek Field, Adrian Johnson, Brian and Anna Marsden

NORTH CREAKE   TF8538   MAP 8

Jolly Farmers
Burnham Road; NR21 9JW

Friendly village local with three cosy rooms, open fires and woodburners, well liked food and several real ales

Cheerful licensees run this yellow-painted pub and whether you are a regular or a visitor, you are sure to get a friendly welcome. There are three cosy and relaxed rooms and the main bar has a large open fire in a brick fireplace, a mix of pine farmhouse and high-backed leather dining chairs around scrubbed pine tables on the quarry-tiled floor and pale yellow walls. Beside the wooden bar counter are some high bar chairs and they keep Woodfordes Nelsons Revenge and Wherry and a couple of guests like Greene King IPA and Abbot tapped from the cask and several wines by the glass; piped music. There's also a cabinet of model cars. A smaller bar has pews and a woodburning stove and the red-walled dining room has similar furniture to the bar and another woodburning stove. There are seats outside on the terrace and in the garden. This is a charming flintstone village. More reports please.

🍴 Cooked by the landlady, the tasty bar food includes sandwiches, ploughman's, soup, warm salad of pigeon and bacon, mushroom, brie and hazelnut en croûte, lasagne, honey-roast ham and egg, liver and bacon with root vegetable mash, and specials such as moules marinière, slow-cooked pork belly with a wild mushroom sauce and local crab salad. *Starters/Snacks: £4.00 to £7.75. Main Courses: £8.00 to £15.00. Puddings: £4.50 to £5.50*

Free house ~ Licensees Adrian and Heather Sanders ~ Real ale ~ Bar food (not Mon or Tues) ~ (01328) 738188 ~ Children welcome ~ Dogs allowed in bar ~ Open 12-2.30, 7(5 Fri)-11; 12-3, 7-10.30 Sun; closed Mon and Tues
Recommended by Charles A Hey, R L Borthwick, John Wooll

NORWICH   TG2309   MAP 5

Adam & Eve £
Bishopgate; follow Palace Street from Tombland, N of cathedral; NR3 1RZ

Ancient place with a good mix of customers, real ales and fair value food, and seats by fantastic array of hanging baskets and tubs

In fine weather you can sit outside this old pub at one of the many picnic-sets and admire the award-winning colourful tubs and hanging baskets. But this is a cosy place in winter, too, and there's a lot of history to the building. It is thought to date back to at least 1249 (when it was used by workmen building the cathedral) and even has a Saxon well beneath the lower bar floor, though the striking dutch gables were added in the 14th and 15th centuries. The little old-fashioned bars have antique high-backed settles, cushioned benches built into partly panelled walls and tiled or parquet floors. Adnams Bitter, Theakstons Old Peculier, Wells & Youngs Bombardier and a guest such as Mauldons Mole Trap on handpump, over 50 malt whiskies, quite a few wines by the glass and Aspall's cider; piped music and board games. Ghost Walks start from here from May-October (the pub offers a 'spooky meal' plus the walk for £10).

🍴 Decent, good value pubby food includes sandwiches and filled baguettes, filled baked potatoes, ploughman's, soup, chilli con carne, sausages and mash with bacon and onion gravy, cheese and vegetable bake, beer-battered fresh cod, steak and mushroom pie, and specials like vegetarian cannelloni, chicken in a mushroom and madeira sauce and rack of ribs with chips. *Starters/Snacks: £3.95 to £5.95. Main Courses: £6.95 to £11.95. Puddings: £4.45*

Unique (Enterprise) ~ Lease Rita McCluskey ~ Real ale ~ Bar food (12-7; 12-5 Sun; not evenings) ~ (01603) 667423 ~ Children in snug until 7pm ~ Open 11-11; 12-10.30 Sun; closed 25 and 26 Dec, 1 Jan

Recommended by Andy and Claire Barker, the Didler, Lawrence Pearse, Colin and Ruth Munro, David Carr, Barry Collett, N R White, Ralph Holland

Eagle

Newmarket Road (A11, between A140 and A147 ring roads); NR2 2HN

Well run pub with plenty of differing seating areas for both drinking and dining, real ales, lots of coffees, wines by the glass and quite a choice of fairly priced food

They usefully open here at 8.30 in the morning offering breakfasts and pastries with coffee – very handy for customers driving in the city. It's a sizeable place that spreads around both downstairs and upstairs, giving plenty of different seating areas. It's been refurbished this year to give a much more contemporary look: comfortable sofas and armchairs by the open fire in its ornate fireplace, white-painted chairs around pine tables on tiled or stripped-wood flooring, cream paintwork above a red dado and more sofas and straightforward pubby seating in a cosy end room. There's also a low-ceilinged dining room and a spiral staircase in the bar leading to another dining room with high-backed brown leather chairs around various tables on the new light wood floor. Wolf Coyote Bitter and a house beer from Bass called Eagles Nest on handpump and decent wines; games machine. A 'conservatory' with chrome and bentwood chairs and wooden tables leads on to a sunny terrace with picnic-sets and a smart barbecue, and there are more seats on grass. More reports please.

🍴 As well as the early morning breakfasts, the popular bar food includes sandwiches, soup, croque monsieur, ham with a duck egg, beer-battered cod on pea purée, beefburger on toasted ciabatta, crab mornay, blue cheese, spinach and herb tart, corn-fed chicken with chorizo and a red wine jus, pork tenderloin wrapped with sage and parma ham with a creamy vermouth sauce, and puddings; Sunday roasts. *Starters/Snacks: £4.75 to £5.95. Main Courses: £6.95 to £13.95. Puddings: £4.95*

Free house ~ Licensee Nigel Booty ~ Real ale ~ Bar food (12-2.15(3 weekends), 6-9(9.30 weekends)) ~ Restaurant ~ (01603) 624173 ~ Children welcome ~ Dogs allowed in bar ~ Open 8.30am-11.30pm; 10am-11pm Sun

Recommended by David Carr

Fat Cat 🏴

West End Street; NR2 4NA

A place of pilgrimage for beer lovers, and open all day

A visit to this enthusiastically run and extremely popular little pub is a bit like coming to a private beer festival with everyone talking to each other and trying a half of this and a half of that. As well as their own beers (brewed at their sister pub, The Cidershed) Fat Cat Bitter, Honey Ale, Marmalade Cat, Stout Cat, Wild Cat and Top Cat, the fantastic choice (on handpump or tapped from the cask in a stillroom behind the bar – big windows reveal all) might include Adnams Best and Broadside, Bass, Crouch Vale Brewers Gold, Dales Golden Daffodil, Derby Double Mash, Elmtree Night Light, Fullers ESB, Green Jack Albion Mild and Mahseer, Hopback Summer Lightning, Humpty Dumpty Golden Gorse, Iceni Fine Soft Day, Invictus Dark Ale, Kelham Island Pale Rider, Oakham Bishops Farewell, Oldershaw Old Boy, Phoenix Arizona, Shepherd Neame Spitfire, Spectrum Light Fantastic, Timothy Taylors Landlord and Woodfordes Wherry. You'll also find imported draught beers and lagers, over 50 bottled beers from around the world and ciders and perries. There's a lively bustling atmosphere at busy times, with maybe tranquil lulls in the middle of the afternoon and a good mix of cheerful customers. The no-nonsense furnishings include plain scrubbed pine tables and simple solid seats, lots of brewery memorabilia, bric-a-brac and stained glass. There are tables outside.

🍴 **Bar food consists of rolls and good pies at lunchtime (not Sunday).**

Free house ~ Licensee Colin Keatley ~ Real ale ~ Bar food (filled rolls available until sold out; not Sun) ~ No credit cards ~ (01603) 624364 ~ Children allowed until 6pm ~ Open 12-11; 11-midnight Sat
Recommended by Mick Hitchman, the Didler, David Carr, Ralph Holland

OLD BUCKENHAM   TM0691   MAP 5

Gamekeeper
B1077 S of Attleborough; The Green; NR17 1RE

Pretty pub with nicely refurbished bars, friendly service, interesting food, real ales and seats on the terrace

This is a most enjoyable and pretty 16th-c pub with a very attractive interior and a warm welcome from the helpful, friendly staff. The civilised beamed bar, with two main areas, has leather armchairs and a sofa in front of the big open woodburning stove in the capacious inglenook fireplace, a pleasant variety of nice old wooden seats and tables on the fine old flagstones or wooden flooring and local watercolours on the walls; there's an unusual interior bow window. Adnams Bitter, Timothy Taylors Landlord and Woodfordes Wherry on handpump, quite a few wines by the glass and several malt whiskies. Besides the comfortable main back dining area, there's a small separate room used for private dining. The back terrace has seats and tables and there are picnic-sets on the grass beyond.

🍴 Generous helpings of interesting bar food includes sandwiches, soup, rabbit, sage and chilli samosa with soured cream, a charcuterie platter to share, local mussels with white wine and cream, burger with bacon and cheese, butternut squash and blue cheese risotto with a nut crumble topping, cod with szechuan ratatouille and a lemon and potato cake, slow-cooked pork belly with a creamy mustard sauce and a duo of duck with puy lentils and chorizo. *Starters/Snacks: £4.75 to £6.90. Main Courses: £8.95 to £18.95. Puddings: £4.75 to £6.00*

Enterprise ~ Lease David Francis ~ Real ale ~ Bar food (not Sun evening) ~ Restaurant ~ (01953) 860397 ~ Children allowed away from bar ~ Dogs allowed in bar ~ Open 11.30-3, 6-11; 12-5 Sun; closed Sun evening
Recommended by David and Cathrine Whiting, Sheila Topham, Julia Mann, Michael Mellers, Nicola Eaton, Noreen Collin, John Cook

RINGSTEAD   TF7040   MAP 8

Gin Trap 🍴 ⅄
Village signposted off A149 near Hunstanton; OS Sheet 132 map reference 707403; PE36 5JU

Attractive coaching inn with friendly licensees, interesting bar food and real ales; bedrooms

With an art gallery next door and a plant nursery nearby, this attractive white-painted 17th-c coaching inn is well placed for a drink or meal. There are two areas to choose from. The original part is the well worn bar with beams, a woodburning stove, captain's chairs and cast-iron-framed tables, Adnams Bitter and Woodfordes Wherry on handpump and nine wines by the glass; piped music and board games. Many diners tend to head for the light and airy conservatory that overlooks the garden where there are seats and tables. In front of the building, a handsome spreading chestnut tree shelters the car park. The Peddar's Way is close by.

🍴 Using local fish, meat and game, the well liked – if not cheap – bar food includes sandwiches, soup, ham hock terrine with pear and walnut chutney, sage gnocchi with butternut squash, pine nuts and tomato confit, beer-battered haddock with tartare sauce, chicken breast with cauliflower purée and madeira and thyme gravy, pot-roasted lamb shoulder with pearl barley and vegetable broth, and puddings like dark chocolate tart with mild chocolate sorbet and banana and rum parfait with banana bread sandwich. *Starters/Snacks: £5.00 to £8.50. Main Courses: £9.00 to £14.50. Puddings: £6.00 to £6.50*

Free house ~ Licensees Cindy Cook and Steve Knowles ~ Real ale ~ Bar food (12-2(2.30 weekends), 6.30-9(6.30-9.30 Fri and Sat)) ~ Restaurant ~ (01485) 525264 ~ Children welcome (not in bedrooms) ~ Dogs allowed in bar and bedrooms ~ Open 11.30-11; 11.30-2.30, 6-11 in winter ~ Bedrooms: £60S(£70B)/£100S(£120B)

Recommended by Brian and Anna Marsden, John Wooll, Pete Devonish, Ian McIntyre, Roy Hoing, Tracey and Stephen Groves, Michael Dandy, M V Burke, Mrs Margo Finlay, Jörg Kasprowski, Jeff and Wendy Williams, Ryta Lyndley, Andy and Claire Barker, Mrs Carolyn Dixon

SEDGEFORD

TF7036   MAP 8

King William IV ♀ 🛏

B1454, off A149 Kings Lynn—Hunstanton; PE36 5LU

Extended and refurbished inn with enthusiastic owners, plenty of space inside, a wide choice of bar food, five real ales, several wines by the glass and attractive covered outdoor dining area; bedrooms

Mr and Mrs Skerritt have worked hard since taking over this bustling inn by extending the existing building, refurbishing throughout and opening up letting bedrooms. There's a relaxed, homely bar and several intimate dining areas decorated with paintings of the north Norfolk coast, high-backed dark leather dining chairs around a mix of pine tables on the slate tiles and log fires; Adnams Bitter, Greene King Abbot and Old Speckled Hen, Woodfordes Wherry and a changing guest beer on handpump and nine good wines by the glass; friendly obliging staff. As well as seats on the terrace and picnic-sets under parasols on the grass, there's an attractive covered dining area surrounded by flowering tubs. The bedrooms are well equipped and comfortable and our readers tell us the breakfasts are rather special.

🍴 A good choice of bar food using local produce might include lunchtime filled baps and baguettes, ploughman's, soup, coquille st jacques, sautéed lambs kidneys, wild mushroom tagliatelle, steak in ale pie, fresh battered cod, venison with a whisky and pepper sauce, parmesan-crusted bass with pesto sauce, duck breast in a red wine and berry sauce, and puddings such as apple, mascarpone and cinnamon puff with butterscotch sauce and fruits of the forest cheesecake. *Starters/Snacks: £4.35 to £10.95. Main Courses: £8.75 to £16.95. Puddings: £4.50 to £6.15*

Free house ~ Licensee Nick Skerritt ~ Real ale ~ Bar food (not Mon lunchtime) ~ Restaurant ~ (01485) 571765 ~ Children allowed but not after 6.30pm ~ Dogs allowed in bar and bedrooms ~ Open 11.30-11(6-11 Mon); 12-10.30 Sun; closed Mon lunchtime (except bank hols) ~ Bedrooms: £55B/£95B

Recommended by George Atkinson, Tracey and Stephen Groves, Carolyn Browse, Stuart and Joan Bloomer, Amanda Stark

Several well known guide books make establishments pay for entry, either directly or as a fee for inspection. These fees can run to many hundreds of pounds. We do not. Unlike other guides, we never take payment for entries. We never accept a free meal, free drink, or any other freebie from a pub. We do not accept any sponsorship – let alone from commercial schemes linked to the pub trade. All our entries depend solely on merit.

SNETTISHAM   TF6834   MAP 8

Rose & Crown 🍽 🍷 🛏

Village signposted from A149 King's Lynn—Hunstanton just N of Sandringham; coming in on the B1440 from the roundabout just N of village, take first left turn into Old Church Road; PE31 7LX

Constantly improving old pub, log fires and interesting furnishings, thoughtful food, fine range of drinks and stylish seating on heated terrace; well equipped, popular bedrooms

There's something for everyone in this well run and pretty white cottage and the wide mix of customers creates a cheerful and relaxed atmosphere. The smallest of the three bars is a pale grey colour with coir flooring and old prints of King's Lynn and Sandringham. Each of the other two bars has a separate character: an old-fashioned beamed front bar with black settles on its tiled floor and a big log fire, and a back bar with another large log fire and the landlord's sporting trophies and old sports equipment (which are being slowly edged out to make way for the pub cricket team photos). There's also the Garden Room with inviting wicker-based wooden chairs, careful lighting and a quote by Dr Johnson in old-fashioned rolling script on a huge wall board, and a residents' lounge (liked by non-residents, too) with squashy armchairs and sofas, rugs on the floor, newspapers, magazines, jigsaws and board games. Adnams Bitter, Fullers London Pride, Greene King IPA and Woodfordes Wherry on handpump, a dozen wines by the glass, organic fruit juices and farm cider. In the garden, there are stylish café-style blue chairs and tables under cream parasols on the terrace, outdoor heaters and colourful herbaceous borders. Two of the comfortable bedrooms are downstairs and there are disabled lavatories and wheelchair ramps. The Bank House in King's Lynn (see our Lucky Dip section) is under the same management.

🍽 Using allotment herbs and salads, local game, meat and fish and other carefully sourced produce, the enjoyable bar food includes lunchtime sandwiches, soup, mini thai fishcakes with crispy prawn wontons, an antipasti plate, bangers and mash with onion gravy, burgers with prime meat, bacon and cheese or moroccan-spiced vegetables, gammon and egg, line-caught cod and smoked haddock, duck egg omelette, specials like seafood paella and gressingham duck breast with braised red cabbage, and puddings such as ginger savarin with bramley apple compote and sweetened mascarpone and crème caramel with exotic fruits. *Starters/Snacks: £4.95 to £7.95. Main Courses: £9.75 to £16.95. Puddings: £5.75*

Free house ~ Licensee Anthony Goodrich ~ Real ale ~ Bar food (12-2(2.30 weekends and school holidays), 6.30-9(9.30 Fri and Sat) ~ Restaurant ~ (01485) 541382 ~ Children welcome ~ Dogs welcome ~ Open 11-11; 12-10.30 Sun ~ Bedrooms: £75B/£95B

Recommended by DF, NF, John Wooll, John Robertson, Barry and Patricia Wooding, Pete Coxon, John Saville, Michael Dandy, Eithne Dandy, Tracey and Stephen Groves, R L Borthwick, Jeff and Wendy Williams

STIFFKEY   TF9643   MAP 8

Red Lion

A149 Wells—Blakeney; NR23 1AJ

Traditional pub with bustling atmosphere, attractive layout, tasty food and real ales; bedrooms

In an unspoilt village, this bustling and traditional pub is run by a friendly landlord. The oldest parts of the unpretentious bars have a few beams, aged flooring tiles or bare floorboards and big open fires. There's also a mix of pews, small settles and a couple of stripped high-backed settles, a nice old long deal table among quite a few others, Greene King Old Speckled Hen, Woodfordes Nelsons Revenge and Wherry and a guest beer on handpump, and 25 malt whiskies; a good mix of customers; board games. A back gravel terrace has proper tables and seats, with more on grass further up beyond; there are some pleasant walks nearby. The bedrooms are eco-friendly.

Every entry includes a postcode for use in Sat-Nav devices.

🍴 Bar food includes sandwiches, ploughman's, soup, blanchbait with lemon chive mayonnaise, local mussels, vegetable curry, lasagne, honey and mustard ham with eggs, lamb stew and dumplings, fish pie, and puddings such as chocolate mousse and fruit crumble; Sunday roast beef. *Starters/Snacks: £4.00 to £7.00. Main Courses: £8.95 to £18.95. Puddings: £4.00 to £6.00*

Free house ~ Licensee Stephen Franklin ~ Real ale ~ Bar food (12-2.30, 6-9; all day Sun) ~ (01328) 830552 ~ Children welcome ~ Dogs welcome ~ Open 11-11 ~ Bedrooms: £80B/£100B

Recommended by Mrs Carolyn Dixon, Derek Field, Mike and Shelley Woodroffe, the Didler, Pete Devonish, Ian McIntyre, Mike Proctor, Chris Johnson, A Kirk, Roy Hoing, Gwyn and Anne Wake

STOKE HOLY CROSS
Wildebeest Arms 🍴 ♀

TG2302   MAP 5

Village signposted off A140 S of Norwich; turn left in village; NR14 8QJ

Stylish restaurant pub with good enterprising food, thriving relaxed atmosphere, attractive terrace

Decidedly more restaurant than pub, this well run place is so popular locally that it's worth booking at weekends. Though all the inside tables are set for diners, you can indeed drop in for a drink – there are several bar stools by the sleek semicircular bar, and a few casual chairs as well as the outside tables. The long room was well refurbished in 2009, to an understated african theme with carefully placed carvings and hangings on the dark sandy walls. On the polished boards, unusual dark leather chairs are grouped around striking tables consisting of heavy slabs of well grained wood on elegant wrought-iron supports. The atmosphere is a cheerful blend of expectation and contentment, depending on what stage of their meal people are at; the neatly dressed staff are helpful and efficient. They have a fine range of wines by the glass, including champagne, and Woodfordes Wherry on handpump. The subtly lit front terrace is a great asset, well sheltered from the road by tall woven willow hurdles, with comfortable wicker armchairs or cushioned benches around glass-topped tables, most under big heated canvas parasols. It's in the same small local group as the Hunny Bell at Hunworth.

🍴 The hallmarks of the deft and rewarding cooking here are its frequent use of unusual – even daring – combinations of ingredients, and its strong visual appeal: soup, chorizo, watermelon and rocket salad with a lemon mustard dressing, crab and saffron tortellini with a crisp crab cake, crab bisque and fennel foam, wild mushroom and parmesan risotto, chicken with puy lentils, mushroom duxelles, roasted celeriac and red wine jus, dijon and herb-crusted lamb rump with wild mushrooms and red wine reduction, hake fillet with confit fennel, samphire and fish velouté, and puddings like sticky prunes with earl grey tea and crème fraîche ice-cream and bread and butter pudding; they also offer a two- and three-course set lunch menu. *Starters/Snacks: £4.95 to £9.95. Main Courses: £12.95 to £22.95. Puddings: £4.95 to £7.50*

Animal Inns ~ Manager Henry Watt ~ Real ale ~ Bar food ~ Restaurant ~ (01508) 492497 ~ Children welcome ~ Open 12-3.30, 6.30-midnight; 12-4, 7-11 Sun

Recommended by R Goodenough, Nicola Eaton

STOW BARDOLPH
Hare Arms ♀

TF6205   MAP 5

Just off A10 N of Downham Market; PE34 3HT

Long-serving licensees in this bustling village pub, real ales, good mix of customers, tasty bar food and a big back garden

You are likely to be greeted by peacocks when visiting this friendly village pub – they wander around the car park and garden and sit on the roof; quite a few chickens pecking about, too. The neatly kept bar has some interesting bric-a-brac such as old advertising signs and golf clubs suspended from the ceiling, fresh flowers, dark pubby furniture and comfortable built-in wall seats, a good log fire and a cheerful, bustling atmosphere; there's also a well planted conservatory where families are allowed. From the central bar they serve Greene King IPA, Abbot, Old Speckled Hen, Ruddles County and a guest beer on handpump, quite a few wines by the glass and several malt whiskies. There are plenty of seats in the large garden behind, with more in the pretty front garden. Church Farm Rare Breeds Centre is a five-minute walk away and is open all year.

🍽 Using their own eggs and other local produce, the well liked bar food includes lunchtime sandwiches, filled baked potatoes and ploughman's, local sprats with horseradish dip, salads with satay chicken or chilli squid rings, puff pastry filled with camembert, pesto, roasted cherry tomatoes and toasted pine nuts, sausages with spring onion mash and red onion gravy, a curry of the day, gammon with pineapple, steak in a creamy brandy sauce with pastry lid, daily specials, and puddings; they also offer two- and three-course set menus (Monday to Thursday) and Sunday roasts. *Starters/Snacks: £4.25 to £8.00. Main Courses: £8.50 to £18.00. Puddings: £4.25 to £4.75*

Greene King ~ Lease David and Trish McManus ~ Real ale ~ Bar food (12-2, 6.30-10; all day Sun) ~ Restaurant ~ (01366) 382229 ~ Children in small conservatory ~ Open 11-2.30, 6-11; 12-10.30 Sun; closed 25 and 26 Dec

Recommended by George Atkinson, John Wooll, Mark, Amanda, Luke and Jake Sheard, Mike Proctor, Moira and John Cole, Ian Phillips, John Saville, Tracey and Stephen Groves

SWANTON MORLEY   TG0217   MAP 8

Darbys 🍺

B1147 NE of Dereham; NR20 4NY

Unspoilt country local with six real ales, plenty of farming knick-knacks, tasty bar food and children's play area

There's a good range of local real ales in this friendly pub – and plenty of cheery regulars to enjoy them. The long bare-boarded country-style bar has a comfortable lived-in feel with big stripped-pine tables and chairs, lots of gin traps and farming memorabilia, a good log fire (with the original bread oven alongside) and tractor seats with folded sacks lining the long, attractive serving counter. Adnams Bitter and Broadside, Beeston Afternoon Delight, Woodfordes Wherry and two guests such as Buffys Norwich Terrier and Grain Oak on handpump, several wines by the glass and quite a few coffees; good, efficient service. A step up through a little doorway by the fireplace takes you through to the attractive dining room with neat, dark tables and chairs on the wooden floor; the children's room has a toy box and a glassed-over well, floodlit from inside. Piped music, TV and board games. There are picnic-sets and a children's play area in the back garden. Plenty to do locally (B&B is available in carefully converted farm buildings a few minutes away) as the family also own the adjoining 720-acre estate.

🍽 Tasty bar food includes filled rolls and baked potatoes, soup, duck and orange pâté, vegetable pasta bake, burgers such as lamb and mint or pork and apple, quite a few salads, omelettes, ham and egg, beer-battered haddock, chicken in a white wine and leek sauce, good steak and kidney pudding, rare breed steaks, and puddings. *Starters/Snacks: £3.95 to £6.25. Main Courses: £7.50 to £17.75. Puddings: £4.75*

Free house ~ Licensees John Carrick and Louise Battle ~ Real ale ~ Bar food (12-2.15, 6-9.45; all day weekends) ~ Restaurant ~ (01362) 637647 ~ Children welcome ~ Dogs allowed in bar ~ Open 11.30-3, 6-11; 11.30-11 (summer Fri) Sat; 12-10.30 Sun ~ Bedrooms: £35S(£40B)/£60(£70S)(£75B)

Recommended by John Cook, S T W Norton, R C Vincent, Margaret and Peter Staples

---

Bedroom prices normally include full english breakfast, VAT and any inclusive service charge that we know of. Prices before the '/' are for single rooms, after for two people in double or twin (B includes a private bath, S a private shower). If there is no '/', the prices are only for twin or double rooms (as far as we know there are no singles).

THORNHAM

Lifeboat

Turn off A149 by Kings Head, then take first left turn; PE36 6LT

Good mix of customers and lots of character in traditional inn, real ales and super surrounding walks; bedrooms

The main bar in this well placed inn has low settles, window seats, pews, carved oak tables and rugs on the tiles, and masses of guns, swords, black metal mattocks, reed-slashers and other antique farm tools; lighting is by antique paraffin lamps suspended among an array of traps and yokes on the great oak-beamed ceiling. A couple of little rooms lead off here. Up some steps from the conservatory is a sunny terrace with picnic-sets and further back is a children's playground with a fort and slide. Adnams Bitter, Greene King IPA and Abbot, Woodfordes Wherry and a guest beer on handpump. The inn faces half a mile of coastal sea flats and there are lots of surrounding walks. More reports please.

🍴 **Bar food includes filled baguettes, ploughman's, soup, whitebait with tartare sauce, vegetarian lasagne, burger with bacon, cheese and onion marmalade, beer-battered fish and chips, barbecue pork ribs, rump of lamb with minted gravy, and puddings.** *Starters/Snacks: £4.00 to £6.95. Main Courses: £9.95 to £19.95. Puddings: £4.70*

Maypole Group ~ Manager Tristan McEwen ~ Real ale ~ Bar food (12-2.30, 6.30-9.30) ~ Restaurant ~ (01485) 512236 ~ Children welcome ~ Dogs allowed in bar and bedrooms ~ Open 10am-11pm(10.30 Sun) ~ Bedrooms: £76B/£114B

Recommended by Rev David Maher, Derek and Sylvia Stephenson, David and Ruth Hollands, Bruce and Sharon Eden, George Atkinson, Gwyn and Anne Wake, the Didler, Mike and Sue Loseby, John Saville, Mike Proctor, Michael Dandy, David and Sue Atkinson, John and Victoria Fairley, JJW, CMW, J K Parry, Derek Field, Allan Westbury, Roger and Kath, Brian and Anna Marsden

WARHAM

TF9441   MAP 8

Three Horseshoes ★

Warham All Saints; village signposted from A149 Wells-next-the-Sea—Blakeney, and from B1105 S of Wells; NR23 1NL

Old-fashioned pub with gas lighting in simple rooms, interesting furnishings and pubby food; gramophone museum

'A lovely step into the past' is how one of our readers described this unspoilt and old-fashioned pub. The simple interior with its gas lighting looks little changed since the 1920s and parts of the building date back to the 1720s. There are stripped deal or mahogany tables (one marked for shove-ha'penny) on a stone floor, red leatherette settles built around the partly panelled walls of the public bar, royalist photographs and open fires in Victorian fireplaces. An antique American Mills one-arm bandit is still in working order (it takes 5p pieces but might not pay out!), there's a big longcase clock with a clear piping strike and a twister on the ceiling to point out who gets the next round; darts and board games. Humpty Dumpty Bad Egg and Woodfordes Sundew and Wherry on handpump, local cider and extremely good and very popular home-made lemonade; friendly service. One of the outbuildings houses a wind-up gramophone museum – opened on request. There's a courtyard garden with flower tubs and a well, and a garden.

🍴 **Generous helpings of proper pubby food include sandwiches, smashing soups, beans on toast, filled baked potatoes, home-cooked gammon, suet-topped pies, rabbit, pigeon or pheasant casseroles, and puddings like spotted dick or syrup sponge.** *Starters/Snacks: £4.80 to £6.00. Main Courses: £7.20 to £12.50. Puddings: £3.20*

Free house ~ Licensee Iain Salmon ~ Real ale ~ Bar food (12-2, 6-8(8.30 summer)) ~ No credit cards ~ (01328) 710547 ~ Children welcome away from bar area but not allowed in bedrooms ~ Dogs welcome ~ Open 12-2.30(3 Sat and Sun), 6-11; closed 25 and 26 Dec ~ Bedrooms: £28/£56(£60S)

Recommended by Tracey and Stephen Groves, John Wooll, the Didler, Henry Pursehouse-Tranter, David Carr, Muriel and John Hobbs, Chris Johnson, Barry Collett, David and Sue Atkinson, Steve Nye, Roy Hoing, Brian and Anna Marsden

WELLS-NEXT-THE-SEA

TF9143   MAP 8

Crown ⊕ ♟ ⇔

The Buttlands; NR23 1EX

Smart coaching inn with a friendly informal bar, local ales, good modern food and stylish orangery; bedrooms

This rather smart old coaching inn is in the same small Flying Kiwi Inns group as the Crown at East Rudham and the Kings Head at Letheringsett, also Main Entries in this county. There's a good mix of both drinkers and diners in the friendly, relaxed bar and a bustling, cheerful atmosphere. As well as beams and the odd standing timber, the contemporary décor includes burnt-orange walls hung with local photographs, grey-painted planked wall seats with orange cushions and high-backed dark brown leather dining chairs around wooden-topped tables on the stripped-wood floor and newspapers to read in front of the open fire. Their own-brewed Kiwi Ale and guests like Adnams Bitter and Woodfordes Wherry on handpump, quite a few wines by the glass and several whiskies and brandies; helpful staff and piped music. There's a stylish dining orangery and a more formal, rather smart restaurant, too.

🍴 Well presented bar food includes **filled baguettes** (you may have to ask for them), **soup, various appetisers, devilled lambs kidneys, pear, stilton and walnut salad, kipper and whisky pâté, beetroot, rosemary and pine nut risotto, thai fish and watermelon curry, chicken breast with a mushroom and tarragon sauce, confit duck leg on ginger and vegetable lentils,** and puddings like **peanut butter parfait with chocolate chip cookie and dark chocolate sauce and lemon and almond tart with butterscotch sauce; Sunday roasts.** *Starters/Snacks: £3.95 to £9.95. Main Courses: £10.95 to £21.95. Puddings: £4.95 to £6.55*

Free house ~ Licensees Chris and Jo Coubrough ~ Real ale ~ Bar food (12-2.30, 6.30-9.30) ~ Restaurant ~ (01328) 710209 ~ Children welcome ~ Dogs allowed in bar and bedrooms ~ Open 11-11 ~ Bedrooms: £120B/£140B

Recommended by David Carr, N R White, Bruce and Sharon Eden, Steve and Liz Tilley, John Cook, John and Gloria Isaacs, DF, NF, R C Vincent

Globe

The Buttlands; NR23 1EU

Attractive contemporary layout, good food and drink, and nice back courtyard; bedrooms

Even when this handsome Georgian inn is very busy, the atmosphere remains friendly and informal and service copes well. There's plenty of space and the opened-up rooms have a relaxed contemporary feel and spread spaciously back from the front bar with its comfortable sofas and armchairs. Three big bow windows look over to a green lined by tall lime trees, there are tables on oak boards, walls in grey and cream hung with drawings on driftwood of quirky fish and shellfish and well judged modern lighting. Adnams Bitter and Broadside, and Woodfordes Wherry on handpump, a thoughtful choice of wines, and nice coffee; piped music, board games and TV. An attractive heated back courtyard has colourful hanging baskets and dark green cast-iron furniture on pale flagstones among terracotta tubs with box balls. The quay is a short walk away.

🍴 Enjoyable bar food includes **lunchtime sandwiches, soup, chicken liver parfait with chutney, fishcake with a fresh herb sauce, ham and free-range eggs, beefburger with blue cheese, beer-battered haddock, fresh crab or lobster,** daily specials like **wild mushroom and spinach risotto and sausages with bubble and squeak and red wine jus,** and puddings such as **vanilla panna cotta with berry compote and chocolate brownie with ice-cream.** *Starters/Snacks: £4.95 to £6.95. Main Courses: £8.95 to £15.95. Puddings: £4.95*

Free house ~ Licensee Viscount Coke ~ Real ale ~ Bar food (12-2.30, 6.30-9) ~ Restaurant ~ (01328) 710206 ~ Children welcome ~ Dogs welcome ~ Jazz every second Sun evening ~ Open 11-11(10.30 Sun) ~ Bedrooms: /£125B

Recommended by Tracey and Stephen Groves, Bruce and Sharon Eden, George Atkinson, David Carr, Brian and Anna Marsden, DF, NF, Henry Pursehouse-Tranter, Mike and Shelley Woodroffe, Gwyn and Anne Wake

WEST BECKHAM

TG1439   MAP 8

Wheatsheaf

Off A148 Holt—Cromer; Church Road; NR25 6NX

Traditional pub with new landlords, several real ales, country cooking and seats in the garden

New licensees have taken over this brick-built pub and redecorated the bars without making any major changes. These bars are mostly set for dining with beams, standing timbers, cottagey doors and a couple of roaring winter log fires, and the furnishings are pleasantly traditional with plenty of dark wooden wheelback chairs, settles and comfortably cushioned wall seats around pubby tables. Greene King IPA and Old Speckled Hen and Woodfordes Wherry on handpump and quite a few wines by the glass. The charming, ramshackle garden has a covered terrace and seats both here and on the grass.

Bar food now includes filled baguettes, soup, whitebait, various tapas, lamb and Guinness casserole, steak in ale or fish pies, vegetarian or meaty lasagne, daily specials like beer-battered pollack and chicken in a honey, lemon and wholegrain mustard marinade, and puddings like vanilla crème brûlée and marmalade bread and butter pudding. *Starters/Snacks: £4.95 to £6.45. Main Courses: £8.75 to £13.75. Puddings: £5.25*

Free house ~ Licensees Gillian and Bernard Fletcher ~ Real ale ~ Bar food (not Sun evening) ~ Restaurant ~ (01263) 822110 ~ Children welcome ~ Dogs allowed in bar ~ Open 12-2.30, 6.30-11; 12-3.30 Sun; closed Sun evening

Recommended by George Atkinson, Derek Field, Fred and Lorraine Gill, Philip and Susan Philcox, Allan Westbury, D and M T Ayres-Regan, Terry Mizen

WIVETON

TG0442   MAP 8

Bell 🍴 🛏

Blakeney Road; NR25 7TL

Busy, open-plan dining pub, drinkers welcomed too, local beers, fine food and seats outside; bedrooms

There's no doubt that most customers are here to enjoy the good modern bar food but they do keep some tables for those just wanting a chat and a drink. It's a friendly and mainly open-plan dining pub with some fine old beams, an attractive mix of dining chairs around wooden tables on the stripped wooden floor, a log fire and prints on the yellow walls. The sizeable conservatory has smart beige dining chairs around wooden tables on the coir flooring and throughout, the atmosphere is chatty and relaxed. Wolf Straw Dog, Woodfordes Wherry and Yetmans Red on handpump, and several wines by the glass. Outside, there are picnic-sets on grass in front of the building looking across to the church, and at the back, stylish wicker tables and chairs on several decked areas are set among decorative box hedging. The bedrooms are comfortable and they also have a self-catering cottage to let. More reports please.

Enjoyable bar food includes soup, various lunchtime bruschettas, duck liver parfait with pear chutney, crab cakes with lime and coriander mayonnaise, white bean and root vegetable cassoulet with cheddar mash, calves liver and bacon with red onion sauce, beer-battered haddock with minted mushy peas, chicken korma, roast lamb chump with creamed leeks and tomato fondue, slow-roasted pork belly with apple and cider jus and 28-day-aged rib-eye steak. *Starters/Snacks: £4.95 to £6.45. Main Courses: £8.95 to £17.95. Puddings: £4.95*

Free house ~ Licensee Berni Morritt ~ Real ale ~ Bar food (12-2.15, 6-9.15) ~ Restaurant ~ (01263) 740101 ~ Children welcome ~ Dogs allowed in bar ~ Open 12-11(10.30 Sun) ~ Bedrooms: /£95S

Recommended by Robert Watt, Pete Devonish, Ian McIntyre, Simon Rodway, George Cowie, Frances Gosnell, Mark, Amanda, Luke and Jake Sheard

WOODBASTWICK

TG3214   MAP 8

Fur & Feather 🍺

Off B1140 E of Norwich; NR13 6HQ

Full range of first-class beers from next-door Woodfordes brewery, friendly service and popular bar food

Our readers really enjoy their visits to this thatched cottagey pub – 'a real winner' is how one describes it. The Woodfordes brewery is right next door, so their beers are in tip-top condition, tapped from the cask by friendly, efficient staff and include Admirals Reserve, Headcracker, Mardlers, Nelsons Revenge, Norfolk Nip, Norfolk Nog, Sundew and Wherry. You can also visit the brewery shop. Ten wines by the glass and around a dozen malt whiskies. The style and atmosphere are not what you'd expect of a brewery tap as it's set out more like a comfortable and roomy dining pub; piped music. There are seats and tables out in a pleasant garden. This is a lovely estate village.

🍴 **Good, popular bar food includes sandwiches and panini, filled baked potatoes, soup, honey-roast ham and egg, butternut squash and wild mushroom risotto, burgers with various toppings, local sausages with beer and onion gravy, crispy onions and bacon snaps, slow-cooked pork belly with wholegrain mustard mash, crackling and red wine sauce, lamb curry, fish pie and steamed steak and kidney pudding; they also serve breakfast from 9am.** *Starters/Snacks: £4.75 to £5.75. Main Courses: £9.50 to £16.95. Puddings: £5.25 to £5.75*

Woodfordes ~ Tenant Tim Ridley ~ Real ale ~ Bar food (all day) ~ Restaurant ~ (01603) 720003 ~ Children welcome but must be well behaved ~ Open 10am-11pm(10.30 Sun and winter Mon-Thurs)

Recommended by Malcolm and Kate Dowty, the Didler, Roy Hoing, Mike Proctor, JDM, KM, Fred and Lorraine Gill, Shiread Family, R C Vincent, John and Victoria Fairley, Tracey and Stephen Groves, Ralph Holland, Andy and Claire Barker, John Cook, David and Cathrine Whiting

---

LUCKY DIP

Besides the fully inspected pubs, you might like to try these Lucky Dips recommended to us and described by readers (if you do, please send us reports: feedback@goodguides.com).

ACLE [TG4111]
Bridge Inn NR13 3AS [N on A1064]: Big riverside pub geared to holiday traffic, two rooms off central bar, good log fire, well kept Adnams and Woodfordes, Aspall's cider, enjoyable reasonably priced food from doorstep sandwiches up inc good vegetarian choice and nice puddings such as toffee lumpy bumpy, circular vaulted-ceilinged restaurant, several interconnecting rooms comfortably furnished with a variety of settles, chairs and tables; large garden with crazy golf and play area, moorings *(John Branston, Michael Butler)*
BANNINGHAM [TG2129]
Crown NR11 7DY [Colby Rd]: Welcoming 17th-c beamed pub, good choice of enjoyable sensibly priced food, well kept Adnams and Greene King, decent wines; garden jazz festival Aug, open all day wknds *(E Clark)*

BLAKENEY [TG0243]
☆ *Kings Arms* NR25 7NQ [West Gate St]: A stroll from the harbour, friendly and chatty, with good choice of popular food all day, Greene King Old Speckled Hen, Marstons Pedigree and Theakstons Best, three simple linked low-ceilinged rooms and airy garden room, some mementoes of the licensees' theatrical careers, darts, board games; games machine; big garden, children and dogs welcome, bedrooms, open all day *(LYM, Brian and Anna Marsden, Ian Phillips, Henry Pursehouse-Tranter, Gwyn and Anne Wake, Mr and Mrs R Thurston)*
BLICKLING [TG1728]
☆ *Buckinghamshire Arms* NR11 6NF [B1354 NW of Aylsham]: Handsome well run Jacobean inn much visited for its enviable spot by gates to Blickling Hall (NT), small and appealing proper unpretentious bar,

lounge set for eating with woodburner, smarter more formal dining room with another woodburner, enjoyable fairly priced food, ales such as Adnams, Fullers, Wolf and Woodfordes kept well, good choice of wines by the glass, cheery keen young staff; children welcome, lots of lawn tables, lovely walks nearby, bedrooms *(Sandra Brame, LYM, Mike Proctor, Dr and Mrs R G J Telfer, Christopher and Elise Way, JDM, KM, Mr and Mrs W W Burke, Margaret and Peter Staples, George and Beverley Tucker, Chris Goode, Jenny and Brian Seller, Tracey and Stephen Groves, Terry Mizen)*

BROOKE [TM2899]

Kings Head NR15 1AB [Norwich Rd (B1332)]: Reopened under new management, enjoyable well priced food from traditional things up inc bargain specials, real ales, good choice of wines by the glass, good service, light and airy bar with log fire, eating area up a step, small back room; children welcome, picnic-sets in sheltered garden, open all day from 9am (does breakfast wknds) *(BB, John Lunniss)*

BURNHAM OVERY STAITHE [TF8444]

Hero PE31 8JE [A149]: Modernised spacious pub welcoming locals and walkers alike, wide choice of interesting up-to-date food from good baguettes up, well priced wines by the glass, Adnams and Woodfordes, good coffee, comfortable contemporary pastel décor, woodburner, two dining areas; children welcome, tables in garden *(Bruce and Sharon Eden, James Stretton, David and Sue Medcalf)*

BURNHAM THORPE [TF8541]

☆ *Lord Nelson* PE31 8HL [off B1155 or B1355, nr Burnham Market]: 17th-c pub with interesting Nelson memorabilia, antique high-backed settles in little low-lit bar with snug off, well kept Greene King Abbot, Woodfordes Wherry and three guests tapped from the cask, lots of wines by the glass, rum-based recipes (Nelsons Blood and Lady Hamiltons Nip), two dining rooms, one with flagstones and open fire, friendly helpful staff; children and dogs welcome, tree-shaded picnic-sets in big garden with play area and pétanque, barbecues, open all day summer, cl Mon evening (except school/bank hols) *(David Gunn, the Didler, LYM, Mike Proctor, Ian Phillips, Henry Pursehouse-Tranter, Walter and Susan Rinaldi-Butcher, David Carr, Tracey and Stephen Groves, Allan Westbury)*

CASTLE RISING [TF6624]

Black Horse PE31 6AG: All-day dining pub with plenty of tables in two front areas and back dining room, friendly efficient staff, real ales such as Adnams, Greene King and Woodfordes, decent choice of wines by the glass; piped music, no dogs; children particularly welcome, close-set tables out under parasols, by church and almshouses in unspoilt pretty village *(Tracey and Stephen Groves, John Wooll, JDM, KM)*

CATFIELD [TG3821]

Crown NR29 5AA [The Street]: Archetypal village inn, immaculate and tasteful, with good choice of real ales and ciders, warmly welcoming landlady, enjoyable food from italian chef/landlord; bedrooms, not far from Hickling Broad, cl Mon (except bank hols when cl Tues) *(Roy Hoing, Heather Weaver)*

CAWSTON [TG1422]

Ratcatchers NR10 4HA [off B1145; Eastgate, S of village]: Beamed dining pub with old chairs and fine mix of walnut, beech, elm and oak tables, quieter candlelit dining room on right, enjoyable food, Adnams Bitter and Broadside and a beer from Woodfordes, quite a few malt whiskies, conservatory; piped music, no dogs; children welcome, heated terrace, open all day Sun *(LYM, Roy Hoing, A Kirk)*

CLEY NEXT THE SEA [TG0443]

☆ *Three Swallows* NR25 7TT [Holt Rd off A149]: Unpretentious old-fashioned local with banquettes, pine tables and log fire, steps up to small family eating area, second log fire in stripped pine dining room on left, good choice of enjoyable reasonably priced food (all day wknds) from sandwiches up, well kept Adnams and Greene King from unusual richly carved bar, decent wines, old photographs, dominoes, cribbage; children and dogs welcome, disabled access, picnic-sets out at front facing green, big garden with surprisingly grandiose fountain, budgerigars and friendly goat called Sadie; handy for the salt marshes, four simple annexe bedrooms, open all day *(Barry Collett, Derek Field, Roy Hoing, David Carr, DF, NF, Michael Tack, LYM)*

COCKLEY CLEY [TF7904]

Twenty Churchwardens PE37 8AN [off A1065 S of Swaffham]: Friendly pub in converted former school next to church, three linked beamed rooms, good open fire, popular bar food inc home-made pies, well kept Adnams; no credit cards; tiny unspoilt village *(Ron Westrup, Rita Scarratt)*

COLTISHALL [TG2719]

☆ *Kings Head* NR12 7EA [Wroxham Rd (B1354)]: Welcoming reliable dining pub close to river, good imaginative food especially fish, generous bar snacks and good value lunch deals, friendly helpful service, well kept Adnams, nice wines by the glass, open fire, fishing nets and stuffed fish inc monster pike (personable chef/landlord a keen fisherman); piped music; reasonably priced bedrooms, decent breakfast, moorings nearby *(Alun Jones, BB, David and Ruth Shillitoe, Roger and Lesley Everett)*

COLTON [TG1009]

Ugly Bug NR9 5DG [well signed once off A47]: Comfortable country pub with plenty of beamery, plush banquettes and some old enamel signs in extensive carpeted bar, enthusiastic friendly staff, enjoyable food inc changing blackboard choice in bar and restaurant, ales from Humpty Dumpty and Theakstons, good value wines, jazz nights;

terrace and big garden with koi carp lake, eight bedrooms, cl Tues lunchtime *(BB, Julia and Richard Tredgett)*

CROMER [TG2242]

Red Lion NR27 9HD [off A149; Tucker St/ Brook St]: Pubby dim-lit carpeted bar in substantial Victorian hotel with elevated sea views, stripped flint and William Morris wallpaper, old bottles and chamber-pots, lifeboat pictures, well kept Adnams, Woodfordes Wherry and two guests, friendly efficient staff, pleasant old-fashioned atmosphere, enjoyable standard food (all day Sun), restaurant, conservatory; piped music, no dogs; children welcome, disabled facilities, back courtyard tables, 12 comfortable bedrooms, open all day *(Fred and Lorraine Gill, Lawrence Pearse, Denys Gueroult, JDM, KM)*

DERSINGHAM [TF6930]

Feathers PE31 6LN [B1440 towards Sandringham; Manor Rd]: Solid Jacobean sandstone inn improved under present owners, relaxed modernised dark-panelled bar, well kept Adnams, Bass and a guest, decent pubby food (good gourmet burgers), friendly service, log fires, back eating room, more contemporary restaurant, converted barn with pool, darts and machines (live music here Sat fortnightly); piped music; children and dogs welcome, large garden with play area, attractive secluded adults' garden with pond, six comfortable well furnished bedrooms, open all day *(LYM, Tracey and Stephen Groves, John Wooll)*

DRAYTON [TG1813]

Cock NR8 6AE [Drayton High Rd]: Popular and pleasantly refurbished, good value food inc bargain Sun lunch, good choice of Marstons-related ales, friendly efficient staff *(R C Vincent)*

EAST BARSHAM [TF9133]

White Horse NR21 0LH [B1105 3 miles N of Fakenham]: Extended pub with big log fire in long beamed main bar, steps to other areas, well kept Adnams, decent wine, good coffee, pleasant swift service, enjoyable straightforward food inc curry nights and OAP lunches, two small attractive dining rooms; piped music, darts; children welcome, well priced bedrooms *(R C Vincent)*

EAST RUSTON [TG3428]

Butchers Arms NR12 9JG [back rd Honing— Happisburgh, N of Stalham]: Comfortable village local, friendly and well run, generous food, real ales, two dining rooms; attractive garden, handy for Old Vicarage garden *(Roy Hoing)*

GELDESTON [TM3990]

☆ *Locks* NR34 0HW [off A143/A146 NW of Beccles; off Station Rd S of village, obscurely signed down long rough track]: Remote candlelit pub at navigable head of River Waveney, ancient tiled-floor core with beams and big log fire, Green Jack and guest ales tapped from casks, enjoyable food, large extension for summer crowds, wknd music nights; riverside garden, open all day wknds

and summer; in winter cl Mon, Tues and Weds-Fri lunchtimes *(LYM, the Didler, Robert Lorimer)*

GREAT RYBURGH [TF9627]

Blue Boar NR21 0DX [Station Rd]: Friendly rambling 18th-c beamed inn, good value locally sourced food in bar and airy dining room, real ales, inglenook log fire; garden with enclosed play area, nice setting opp church, pleasant local walks, bedrooms *(Julia and Richard Tredgett)*

GREAT YARMOUTH [TG5206]

Red Herring NR30 3HQ [Havelock Rd]: Friendly open-plan alehouse, well kept local Blackfriars and guests, farm cider, old local photographs, rock collection, games area with pool; open all day wknds *(the Didler)*

St Johns Head NR30 1JB [North Quay]: Friendly traditional pub, real ales inc bargain Elgoods, pool, juke box; open all day *(the Didler)*

HARLESTON [TM2483]

J D Young IP20 9AD [Market Pl]: Refurbished hotel/pub, convivial bar with three real ales, comfortable library-feel dining room with lights on well spaced tables, open fire, enjoyable good value food all day from 7am, friendly efficient staff; bedrooms *(Martin and Pauline Jennings)*

Swan IP20 9AS [The Thoroughfare (narrow main street on one-way circuit, look out for narrow coach entry)]: Unpretentious 16th-c coaching inn, friendly chatty locals, well kept Adnams and guests like Brandon, reasonably priced wine, decent good value food, cheerful service, two linked lounge rooms, ancient timbers, log fire in big inglenook, separate public bar; farmers' market in car park (3rd Sat of month), bedrooms *(KC, Dr D J and Mrs S C Walker)*

HEYDON [TG1127]

Earle Arms NR11 6AD [off B1149]: Nice pub in delightfully unspoilt estate village, well kept Adnams and Woodfordes Wherry, enjoyable food using local fish and meat, racing prints and good log fire in old-fashioned bar, more formal dining room; children welcome, dogs on leads in bar, picnic-sets in small cottagey back garden *(Andrew Rudalevige, Sheila Topham, LYM)*

HICKLING [TG4123]

Greyhound NR12 0YA [The Green]: Small busy pub with enjoyable food inc nice crab salad and good Sun roasts in bar and neat restaurant, well kept ales, friendly long-serving landlord; well behaved children welcome, pretty garden with terrace tables, bedroom annexe *(Roy Hoing, Rosemary Willett)*

HILLINGTON [TF7125]

Ffolkes Arms PE31 6BJ [Lynn Rd (A148)]: Roomy 18th-c food-orientated pub, comfortably modernised, with extensive traditional menu, sensible prices, well kept Adnams, friendly attentive staff; children welcome, big garden behind with play area, handy for Sandringham, reasonably priced bedroom block *(George Atkinson)*

HOLKHAM [TF8943]

☆ *Victoria* NR23 1RG [A149 nr Holkham Hall]:
Upmarket but informal small hotel (owned by
Holkham Estate), eclectic mix of furnishings
inc deep low sofas, lighted candles in heavy
sticks, big log fire, well kept Adnams Bitter,
Woodfordes Wherry and a guest, nice wines,
decent coffees, friendly service, good if not
cheap local seasonal food, anglo-indian
décor in linked dining rooms (best to book);
piped music; children welcome, dogs in bar,
sheltered courtyard with retractable awning,
walks to nature-reserve salt marshes and sea,
ten stylish bedrooms, open all day (Fred and
Lorraine Gill, Tracey and Stephen Groves,
Mike and Sue Loseby, Michael Dandy,
George Atkinson, LYM)

HOLME NEXT THE SEA [TF7043]

White Horse PE36 6LH [Kirkgate St]:
Attractive, cosy and rambling with warm log
fire, good choice of enjoyable well priced
food inc local fish and Sun roasts, helpful
efficient service, well kept real ales, decent
wine, small restaurant, two friendly pub dogs
and cat; children welcome, big garden with
marquee (John Wooll)

HOLT [TG0738]

Feathers NR25 6BW [Market Pl]:
Unpretentious town hotel with popular locals
bar comfortably extended around original
panelled area with open fire, attractive
entrance/reception area with antiques, quick
friendly service, Greene King ales, decent
wines, good choice of enjoyable food, nice
coffee, dining room; piped music, busy on
Sat market day; dogs welcome, 15 bedrooms
(David Carr, BB)

☆ *Kings Head* NR25 6BN [High St/Bull St]:
Cheerful reworked two-bar pub (same owners
as nearby Pigs at Edgefield – see Main
Entries), enjoyable fresh food all day from
baguettes up, prompt friendly service, good
choice of beers inc Adnams, Buffys,
Woodfordes and Yetmans, fair choice of
wines, open fires, some leather easy chairs,
pleasant dining conservatory; children
welcome, back terrace with heated smokers'
shelter, good-sized garden, four stylish
bedrooms (John Wooll, Derek Field,
David Carr, Charles Gysin, Gerry and
Rosemary Dobson, BB)

HORSTEAD [TG2619]

☆ *Recruiting Sergeant* NR12 7EE [B1150 just S
of Coltishall]: Large, friendly and pleasantly
refurbished, with good value generous food
from fresh baguettes up inc good fish
choice, splendid service even though busy,
real ales inc one brewed for the pub,
impressive choice of reasonably priced wines
by the glass, big open fire, brasses and
muskets, music-free smaller room; children
welcome (R C Vincent, Alun Jones)

ITTERINGHAM [TG1430]

Walpole Arms NR11 7AR [Village signposted
off B1354 NW of Aylsham]: 18th-c brick pub
close to Blickling Hall with sizeable open-
plan beamed bar, stripped-brick walls, mix of
dining tables, quietly chatty atmosphere;

Adnams Bitter and Broadside, Woodfordes
Wherry and a guest on handpump, several
wines by the glass, light and airy dining
room with beamery, ambitious food, two-
acre landscaped garden with seats and tables
on a vine-covered terrace; children welcome,
dogs allowed in bar, open all day, cl Sun
evening (Pete Devonish, Ian McIntyre,
R C Vincent, LYM)

KING'S LYNN [TF6119]

☆ *Bank House* PE30 1RD [Kings Staithe Sq]:
Attractive and civilised big-windowed
bar/brasserie under same management as
Rose & Crown at Snettisham (see Main
Entries), contemporary conversion of
handsome Georgian building in splendid
quiet quayside spot, Fullers London Pride
and Greene King Abbot, decent food from
sandwiches to steaks inc light dishes all
day, may be wkdy lunch deals too, daily
papers, sofas, armchairs and pastel colours;
11 good bedrooms, open all day (BB,
John Wooll)

Bradleys PE30 5DT [South Quay]: Stylishly
simple bar/restaurant with good sensibly
priced food, good choice of wines by the
glass, Adnams, more expensive upstairs
restaurant with river views, ornate mirrors,
elegant curtains and plenty of flowers,
pleasant helpful service; quayside tables and
small courtyard garden, open all day
(John Wooll, Mrs Hazel Rainer)

Crown & Mitre PE30 1LJ [Ferry St]: Old-
fashioned riverside pub full of Naval and
nautical memorabilia, well kept Highwood
Tom Wood and five changing guests, own
brews still planned by no-nonsense landlord,
home-made pubby food from doorstep
sandwiches up, river-view back conservatory;
well behaved children and dogs welcome,
quayside tables, barbecue (R C Vincent,
John Wooll)

Dukes Head PE30 1JS [Tuesday Market Pl]:
Imposing early 18th-c hotel with small cosy
bar on left, popular dining room on right,
good value tasty food from baguettes to
daily roast, bargain lunchtime deals,
Adnams, cheerful attentive service, local
pictures, back lounge and formal restaurant;
bedrooms (John Wooll, Pete Coxon,
George Atkinson)

Lattice House PE30 1EG [corner Market Lane,
off Tuesday Market Pl]: Old beamed and
raftered no-frills Wetherspoons, good choice
of ales, well priced food, friendly attentive
staff; children welcome, open all day
(R C Vincent)

LESSINGHAM [TG3928]

Star NR12 0DN [School Rd]: Under new local
ownership, small and welcoming, with low
ceilings and inglenook woodburner,
enjoyable unpretentious food, real ales, side
restaurant; dogs welcome, two good value
bedrooms in back block (Kay Wheat)

LODDON [TM3698]

Kings Head NR14 6EZ [Bridge St]: Enjoyable
reasonably priced food from sandwiches up,
bargain children's meals Mon-Thurs, several

real ales, helpful staff, restaurant
(D and D G Humpherson)

MIDDLETON [TF6516]

Crown PE32 1RH [A47 Kings Lynn—
Norwich]: Modernised dining pub with wide
choice of good fairly priced food, Nethergate
and Woodfordes ales, compact pine panelled
bar, dining room in two parts, low lighting;
farm shop in car park *(George Atkinson,
Tracey and Stephen Groves)*

MUNDFORD [TL8093]

Crown IP26 5HQ [off A1065 Thetford—
Swaffham; Crown Rd]: Unassuming olde-
worlde pub, warmly welcoming, with heavy
beams and huge fireplace, interesting local
memorabilia, good range of real ales, dozens
of malt whiskies, enjoyable down-to-earth
food at sensible prices, spiral iron stairs to
large restaurant, games, TV and juke box in
red-tiled locals' bar; children and dogs
welcome, back terrace and garden with
wishing well, bedrooms (own bathrooms),
open all day *(LYM, Gillian Grist)*

NEWTON [TF8315]

George & Dragon PE32 2BX [A1065 4 miles
N of Swaffham]: Useful roadside pub with
several small dining areas, enjoyable good
value home-made food inc nice sandwiches
and unusual vegetarian options, beer kept
well by knowledgeable landlady; pleasant
garden with play area, great views to Castle
Acre Priory *(Sarah Williams, M R D Foot)*

NORTH WOOTTON [TF6424]

House on the Green PE30 3RE [Ling Common
Rd]: Improved under new licensees, tidy and
roomy, with tasty pub food and helpful
service; children welcome, lots of tables out
on back terrace and lawn, play area
(R C Vincent)

NORTHREPPS [TG2439]

Foundry Arms NR27 0AA [Church St]:
Refurbished under newish welcoming
licensees, well kept Adnams and Woodfordes,
decent choice of wines, traditional pub food
(not Mon), reasonable prices; children and
dogs welcome, garden picnic-sets, open all
day Fri-Sun *(Karen Bell, Conrad Freezer)*

NORWICH [TG2108]

Alexandra NR2 3BB [Stafford St]: Friendly
two-bar local with well kept Chalk Hill and
guest ales, cheap home-made food inc good
cobs, open fire, pool, classic juke box; open
all day *(the Didler, Ralph Holland)*

Cidershed NR3 4LF [Lawson Rd]: Own
Burnard cider in converted 1970s village
hall, also home to Fat Cat brewery with their
beers and guests, no food apart from rolls,
interesting layout, secondhand books, lots of
live music inc Sun afternoon blues/jazz;
children and dogs welcome, seats out at
front and behind, open all day *(the Didler,
David Carr)*

Coach & Horses NR1 1BA [Thorpe Rd]:
Light and airy tap for Chalk Hill brewery,
friendly staff, generous home-made food
12-9 (8 Sun), also breakfast, bare-boards
L-shaped bar with open fire, dark wood,
posters and prints, pleasant back dining

area; sports TV; disabled access possible
(not to lavatories), front terrace, open all
day *(the Didler, David Carr)*

Duke of Wellington NR3 1EG [Waterloo Rd]:
Friendly rambling local with 14 well kept
changing ales (Aug beer festival), foreign
bottled beers, real fire, traditional games;
nice back terrace, open all day *(the Didler,
Ralph Holland)*

☆ *Kings Arms* NR1 3HQ [Hall Rd]: Busy
Batemans local with several changing guest
beers, good whisky and wine choice, friendly
atmosphere, may be lunchtime food (can
bring your own – plates, cutlery provided),
airy garden room; unobtrusive sports TV;
vines in courtyard, open all day *(the Didler)*

Kings Head NR3 1JE [Magdalen St]: Lots of
well kept changing regional ales and a local
farm cider, good choice of imported beers,
handsome Victorian-style décor, friendly
atmosphere; open all day *(the Didler,
David Carr, Ralph Holland)*

Ribs of Beef NR3 1HY [Wensum St, S side of
Fye Bridge]: Well used welcoming old pub,
good range of real ales inc local brews, farm
cider, good wine choice, deep leather settees
and small tables upstairs, attractive smaller
downstairs room with river view and some
local river paintings, generous cheap food
(till 5pm Sat, Sun), quick cheerful service;
tables out on narrow waterside walkway
(John Wooll, the Didler, David Carr)

Rushcutters NR7 0HE [Yarmouth Rd, Thorpe
St Andrew]: Wonderful riverside location on
Norwich outskirts, good-sized interior with
lots of seating areas, beams and log fire,
wide choice of usual food inc nice fish, well
kept Adnams and Woodfordes, friendly
efficient service; plenty of garden tables
down to river with swans, open all day
(Lawrence Pearse)

Trafford Arms NR1 3RL [Grove Rd, off
A11/A140 Ipswich rd]: Large estate-type
local with great choice of well kept ales,
decent freshly made food (not Sun evening),
pool; open all day *(the Didler, Ralph Holland)*

Unthank Arms NR2 2DR: Relaxed Victorian
corner pub, spaciously refurbished, with
good interesting sensibly priced food (all
day Sun), good choice of wines by the glass,
real ales, open fires, upstairs dining room
and lounge, friendly service; children
welcome, garden behind with covered area,
open all day *(Robert Watt)*

White Lion NR3 3AQ [Tap & Spile by 1995]:
Small traditional pub with well kept Milton
ales, belgian bottled beers, enjoyable
generous home-made food (all day Fri and
Sat), reasonable prices, pub games inc bar
billiards *(Steve Nye)*

Wig & Pen NR3 1RN [St Martins Palace
Plain]: Friendly and relaxed beamed bar opp
cathedral close, lawyer and judge prints,
roaring stove, prompt generous food,
Adnams, Buffys and guests, good value
wines; piped music, sports TV; tables out at
front, open all day, cl Sun evening *(the
Didler, Bruce Graham, David Carr, N R White)*

OLD HUNSTANTON [TF6842]
☆ *Ancient Mariner* PE36 6JJ [part of L'Estrange Arms Hotel, Golf Course Rd]: Converted barns and stables of adjacent Victorian hotel, popular with locals and holidaymakers, low beams, timbers, bare bricks, flagstones and maritime bric-a-brac, several areas inc conservatory and upstairs family gallery, generous food from good sandwiches up, well kept Adnams and guest ales, good coffee and wines by the glass, friendly efficient young staff, open fires, papers and magazines; piped music, big-screen sports TV; terrace and long sea-view garden down to dunes, play area, 36 bedrooms in hotel, open all day Fri-Sun and summer *(JJW, CMW, BB, Tracey and Stephen Groves, RS, ES, George Atkinson, Ralph Holland)*

ROYDON [TF7022]
Three Horseshoes PE32 1AQ [the one nr Kings Lynn; Lynn Rd]: Two-bar country pub with pleasant décor in bar and restaurant, decent choice of enjoyable good value food, friendly helpful landlady, Greene King and other ales; tables outside *(John Wooll)*

SALTHOUSE [TG0743]
☆ *Dun Cow* NR25 7XA [A149 Blakeney—Sheringham; Purdy St]: Airy pub overlooking salt marshes, generous unpretentious food all day from good fresh crab sandwiches to local fish, fast friendly service even when busy, well kept Adnams and Woodfordes Wherry, decent wines, open fires, high 18th-c rafters and cob walls in big main bar, family bar and games room with pool; piped radio, blues nights; coast views from attractive walled front garden, sheltered courtyard with figs and apples, separate family garden with play area, good walks and bird-watching, bedrooms and self-catering, nice smokery next door *(Roy Hoing, John Saville, David Carr, Derek Field, BB, Derek and Sylvia Stephenson)*

SCULTHORPE [TF8930]
Hourglass NR21 9QD [The Street]: Long open room combining light modern style with beams and bare boards, good choice of enjoyable well presented food, Wells & Youngs Bombardier and Woodfordes Wherry, pleasant attentive service *(George Atkinson, John Wooll)*
☆ *Sculthorpe Mill* NR21 9QG [inn signed off A148 W of Fakenham, opp village]: Welcoming dining pub in rebuilt 18th-c mill, appealing riverside setting, seats out under weeping willows and in attractive garden behind; light, airy and relaxed with leather sofas and sturdy tables in bar/dining area, good reliable well priced food from sandwiches up, may have excellent fresh crab, prompt friendly service, well kept Greene King ales, nice house wines, upstairs restaurant; piped music; six comfortable bedrooms, good breakfast, open all day wknds and summer *(Mark, Amanda, Luke and Jake Sheard, Roy Hoing, John Wooll, Mark Sheard, LYM)*

SHERINGHAM [TG1543]
Lobster NR26 8JP [High St]: Almost on seafront, seafaring décor in friendly panelled bar with old sewing-machine treadle tables and warm fire, usually a wide range of well kept changing ales (bank hols beer festivals), farm ciders, bottled belgians, nice well priced wines by the glass, good value quickly served generous bar meals (helpful with special diets), restaurant with seafood inc fresh lobster (get there early) and good crab, games in public bar inc pool; dogs on leads, two courtyards, heated marquee, open all day *(Brian and Anna Marsden, Alistair and Kay Butler, Fred and Lorraine Gill, David Carr, N R White)*

SMALLBURGH [TG3324]
☆ *Crown* NR12 9AD: 15th-c thatched and beamed village inn with friendly proper landlord, old-fashioned pub atmosphere, well kept Adnams and Black Sheep, good choice of wines by the glass, enjoyable straightforward home-made food in bar and upstairs dining room, prompt service, daily papers, darts; no dogs or children inside; picnic-sets in sheltered and pretty back garden, bedrooms, cl Mon lunchtime, Sun evening *(Philip and Susan Philcox, BB)*

SOUTH CREAKE [TF8635]
☆ *Ostrich* NR21 9PB [B1355 Burnham Market—Fakenham]: Well kept ales inc Adnams and Woodfordes Wherry in airily redecorated welcoming village pub, polished boards, local paintings and shelves of books, plenty of tables for the popular food from sandwiches to ostrich fillet, helpful young staff, woodburner; children and dogs welcome, stylish back terrace, bedrooms, open all day wknds *(Tony Middis, John Wooll, Mike Proctor, Anthony Barnes, LYM)*

SOUTH WALSHAM [TG3613]
Ship NR13 6DQ [B1140]: Welcoming refurbished village pub, good fresh food (all day Sun) from sandwiches through traditional to imaginative things, may be special offers, well kept Adnams and Woodfordes, stripped bricks and beams, restaurant; children welcome, tables on front elevated terrace and on tiered back one, open all day wknds *(Nigel Williams)*

SOUTHREPPS [TG2536]
☆ *Vernon Arms* NR11 8NP [Church St]: Popular old-fashioned village pub, welcoming and relaxed, with enjoyable food running up to steaks and well priced crab and lobster specials (may need to book), friendly young staff, real ales such as Adnams, Black Sheep, Timothy Taylors and Wells & Youngs, good choice of wines and malt whiskies, log fire; children, dogs and muddy walkers welcome *(Trevor and Sheila Sharman, Conrad Freezer, Judith Salter)*

SPOONER ROW [TM0997]
Three Boars NR18 9LL [just off A11 SW of Wymondham]: Olde-worlde two-bar pub in tiny village, well kept Adnams, good range of wines, enjoyable food from light lunchtime choices to more expensive things, friendly

service, amazing collection of food/wine books *(Evelyn and Derek Walter, Noreen Collin)*

SPORLE [TF8411]

Squirrels Drey PE32 2DR [The Street]: Log fire in comfortable lounge, big antique round table in bar, good food inc local crab and game, Adnams, Greene King and guests, Aspall's cider, good friendly service, refurbished restaurant, conservatory; children and dogs welcome, garden with play area, cl Mon *(Martin Hickey)*

TERRINGTON ST JOHN [TF5314]

Woolpack PE14 7RR [off A47 W of King's Lynn]: Cheery local under new management, red plush banquettes, wheelbacks, dark pub tables, large back dining room, Black Sheep, Woodfordes and Tom Woods, good value enjoyable home-made food, friendly helpful service; picnic-sets on grass, good disabled access, open all day Fri-Sun *(Bruce and Sharon Eden, Michael and Jenny Back, LYM)*

THORNHAM [TF7343]

Orange Tree PE36 6NJ [Church St]: Neatly updated beamed dining pub, bright and smart, with enjoyable contemporary food (all afternoon Sun) inc local seafood, very good choice of wines by the glass, Adnams and Woodfordes, friendly staff, long thin bare-boards bar with rustic furniture, back carpeted dining area up a level; good-sized garden with play area, six courtyard bedrooms *(Meriel Packman, Tracey and Stephen Groves)*

WALSINGHAM [TF9336]

Bull NR22 6BP [Common Place/Shire Hall Plain]: Unpretentious pub in pilgrimage village, darkly ancient bar's walls covered with clerical visiting cards, well kept ales such as Adnams, welcoming landlord and good-humoured staff, food (not Oct-Mar) from lunchtime sandwiches up, log fire, pool room; picnic-sets in courtyard and on attractive flowery terrace by village square *(John and Gloria Isaacs, David Carr)*

WEASENHAM ST PETER [TF8522]

Fox & Hounds PE32 2TD [A1065 Fakenham—Swaffham; The Green]: Welcoming 18th-c beamed local with bar and two dining areas, cheery chatty landlord, three Tom Woods ales, good honest home-made food at reasonable prices (inc breakfast), lots of military prints; children welcome, nice garden and terrace *(D and M T Ayres-Regan, George Atkinson)*

WELLS-NEXT-THE-SEA [TF9143]

Edinburgh NR23 1AE [Station Rd/Church St]: Traditional pub near main shopping area doing good affordable home-made pubby food, well kept Bass, Woodfordes and a guest ale, open fire, local photographs for sale, sizeable restaurant (check winter opening times); piped music and occasional live, sports TV, no credit cards (bank next door); children and dogs welcome, disabled access, courtyard with heated smokers' shelter, three bedrooms, open all day *(Mike and Shelley Woodroffe)*

WEST ACRE [TF7815]

Stag PE32 1TR [Low Rd]: Good choice of well kept changing ales in appealing local's unpretentious small bar, cheerful staff, good value limited food, neat dining room; attractive spot in quiet village, cl Mon *(BB, Rita Scarratt)*

WEST RUNTON [TG1842]

Village Inn NR27 9QP [Water Lane]: Roomy comfortable flint pub with enjoyable fresh homely food inc good Sun roast, decent wines, ales such as Adnams, Greene King, Woodfordes and Wolf, helpful staff, restaurant; large attractive garden, pleasant village with good beach and nice circular walk to East Runton *(Nigel Tate, Jenny and Brian Seller)*

WEYBOURNE [TG1143]

☆ *Ship* NR25 7SZ [A149 W of Sheringham; The Street]: Popular village pub with six local ales such as Buffys, Grain, Humpty Dumpty and Winters, big straightforward bar with pubby furniture and woodburner, two dining rooms, reasonably priced food; piped music can be loud; well behaved children welcome, dogs in bar, nice garden and pretty hanging baskets, handy for Muckleburgh Military Vehicle Museum, open all day in summer *(Derek Field, LYM)*

WIGHTON [TF9439]

☆ *Carpenters Arms* NR23 1PF [High St – off main rd, past church]: Unusual décor with mix of brightly painted tables and chairs on wood floor, bric-a-brac on shelves, vintage Holkham pottery, assorted artwork, leather sofas, and a mulberry dining room; warm welcome, good generous local food (not Mon lunchtime in winter) from pub favourites to more individual dishes, charming service, well kept Adnams, Woodfordes and a local beer bottled for them; picnic-sets in informal back garden, open all day wknds and bank hols *(BB, Tracey and Stephen Groves, Mike and Shelley Woodroffe)*

WINTERTON-ON-SEA [TG4919]

☆ *Fishermans Return* NR29 4BN [off B1159; The Lane]: Bustling unpretentious two-bar local with well kept Adnams, Woodfordes and guests, good wine and cider choice, food can be good, long-serving licensees, coal fire, family room and dining room, darts and pool; piped music/juke box; children and dogs welcome, pretty front terrace, nearby sandy beach, three bedrooms, open all day wknds *(LYM, Sandra Brame, Mike Proctor, Peter Sutton, Lawrence R Cotter)*

WRETHAM [TL9290]

Dog & Partridge IP24 1QS [Watton Rd; A1057]: Small country local, Adnams and a guest like Cliff Quay, Aspall's cider, enjoyable pubby food from baguettes up; dogs welcome, garden *(David and Gill Carrington)*

WROXHAM [TG2814]

☆ *Green Man* NR13 6NQ [Rackheath; A1151 towards Norwich]: Warm and comfortable, with easy chairs, plush banquettes and other seats in open-plan bar, log fires, interesting World War II memorabilia (nearby air base), popular generous pubby food (two small dining areas can get crowded), reasonable prices, Greene King and Woodfordes ales; children in eating areas, bowling green *(LYM, Fiona Florence)*

WYMONDHAM [TG1001]

☆ *Green Dragon* NR18 0PH [Church Street]: Picturesque heavily timbered 14th-c inn, simple beamed and timbered back bar, log fire under Tudor mantelpiece, interesting pictures, bigger dining area (children allowed), friendly helpful staff, four well kept ales inc Adnams; children and dogs welcome, modest bedrooms, nr glorious 12th-c abbey church *(LYM, the Didler, Mr and Mrs W W Burke)*

A very few pubs try to make you leave a credit card at the bar, as a sort of deposit if you order food. They are not entitled to do this. The credit card firms and banks which issue them warn you not to let credit cards out of your sight. If someone behind the counter used your card fraudulently, the card company or bank could in theory hold you liable, because of your negligence in letting a stranger hang on to your card. Suggest instead that if they feel the need for security, they 'swipe' your card and give it back to you. And do name and shame the pub to us.

Northamptonshire

We were delighted when reader reports and subsequent inspections unearthed four terrific new Main Entries here – and they form a nice cross-section, too. The properly pubby New Inn at Abthorpe is run by a local farmer who serves his own meat on the rather good menu, the Collyweston Slater at Collyweston is a modern dining pub with more elaborate food, while the Shuckburgh Arms at Stoke Doyle is a nicely reworked dining pub, also with imaginative food. On another tack altogether, the Malt Shovel in Northampton offers an astonishing dozen or so real ales, and its very cheap lunchtime snacks, we're pleased to say, earn it a Bargain Award. Old hands that are doing well here include the exceptionally welcoming Cartwright at Aynho, the charming Kings Arms at Farthingstone, the lovely ancient Althorp Coaching Inn at Great Brington with its eight real ales, and the George at Kilsby, a jolly nice pub with a new Bargain Award this year. The civilised Falcon at Fotheringhay continues on its well run course as a terrific place for a special meal, with its thoughtfully prepared imaginative food, and is our Northamptonshire Dining Pub of the Year for 2011.

ABTHORPE   SP6446   MAP 4

New Inn
Signed from A43 at first roundabout S of A5; Silver Street; NN12 8QR

Friendly traditional local with tasty food

A cheery farming family run this quietly tucked-away partly thatched country local. You can stay in a converted barn on their farm in Slapton (just a short walk across the fields) and they supply some of the meat used in the restaurant. It's the sort of laid-back place that has children running happily in the big garden, and locals popping into the traditional but fairly basic rambling bar for a pint. Here you'll find four good Hook Norton beers on handpump and Stowford Press cider, beams, stripped stone and an inglenook log fire. Entertainments include darts, table skittles, a juke box and TV; piped music.

🍽 **Using their own meat and home-grown herbs, pubby lunchtime dishes might include sandwiches, liver and bacon, sausage and mash, chicken caesar salad and vegetable pasta, with evening dishes such as tomato, basil and fried chorizo salad with goats cheese crust, roast sardines with chilli sauce, roast vegetable risotto, roast pork belly with black pudding and mustard gravy, home-made burgers, chicken and chickpea curry, 8oz steak, and puddings such as lemon posset, brandy sultana brûlée and chocolate coffee pot.** *Starters/Snacks: £3.95 to £5.25. Main Courses: £6.25 to £8.95. Puddings: £4.50*

Hook Norton ~ Tenant Rob Smith ~ Real ale ~ Bar food (12-2, 6-9; not Mon, Tues) ~ Restaurant ~ (01327) 857306 ~ Children welcome ~ Dogs allowed in bar ~ Open 12-2.30, 6-11(12 Weds-Fri); 12-11.30 Sun; closed Mon, Tues lunchtime

Recommended by Christopher Hayle, Alan Sutton, Peter and Pam Watkins, George Atkinson

ASHBY ST LEDGERS

SP5768   MAP 4

Olde Coach House 🛏

4 miles from M1 junction 18; A5 S to Kilsby, then A361 S towards Daventry; village also signed off A5 N of Weedon; Main Street; CV23 8UN

Carefully modernised farmhouse with lots of different areas, real ales and good wines, friendly staff and plenty of outside seating; bedrooms

We rather like the minimalist contemporary refurbishments which have cleverly retained some of the original character, especially in the lower parts, at this handsome creeper-clad stone inn. Several dining areas, all very relaxed, take in paintwork that ranges from white and light beige to purple, and flooring that includes stripped wooden boards, original red-and-white tiles and beige carpeting. All manner of pale wooden tables are surrounded by a mix of church chairs, smart high-backed leather dining chairs and armchairs, with comfortable squashy leather sofas and stools in front of the log fire. There are hunting pictures, large mirrors, an original old stove and oven, champagne bottles along a gantry and fresh flowers. It's well run by a friendly young landlady and her personable staff, and is a popular place for both a drink and a meal. Wells & Youngs Bitter and Bombardier and a changing guest such as Everards Tiger are on handpump, with about a dozen good wines by the glass; TV, piped music. There are picnic-sets in the back garden among shrubs and trees, modern tables and chairs out in front under the pretty hanging baskets, a dining courtyard and you can play boules here. The church nearby is interesting.

🍴 **Bar food includes sandwiches, duck pâté with kumquat jam, smoked pigeon breast with herb croûte, sharing platters (meaty, vegetarian, fishy and so forth), stone-baked pizzas, beer-battered fish, steak and coriander burger, pie of the day, roast pork belly with sage mash and creamy cider jus, mushroom and shallot pie, steaks, and puddings such as apple and pear crumble, chocolate brownie and lemon tart with raspberry sorbet; Monday evening is curry night, and there is a very good value lunchtime set menu (not Saturday or Sunday).** *Starters/Snacks: £4.00 to £8.95. Main Courses: £8.50 to £13.95. Puddings: £5.00 to £5.50*

Mercury Inns ~ Manager Anni Kitz ~ Real ale ~ Bar food (12-2.30, 6-9.30; 12-8 Sun) ~ Restaurant ~ (01788) 890349 ~ Children welcome ~ Dogs allowed in bar ~ Open 12-3, 5.30-11; 12-11(10.30 Sun) Sat ~ Bedrooms: £65B/£65B

Recommended by Rob and Catherine Dunster, P M Newsome, George Atkinson, Mary McSweeney, Michael and Jenny Back

AYNHO

SP5133   MAP 4

Cartwright 🛏

Croughton Road (B4100); OX17 3BE

Well run modernised inn with tasty food and civilised bar

This carefully refurbished stone 16th-c coaching inn is spacious and neatly modernised. Its linked areas have well chosen artwork on cream and maroon-painted or exposed stone walls, smartly contemporary furniture on wood or tiled floors, and leather sofas by a big log fire in the bar. Notably friendly attentive uniformed staff greet you warmly on arrival, and they have daily papers and a nice shortlist of wines by the glass, as well as Adnams and Black Sheep from handpumps on the corner counter; piped music, TV. Outside, there are a few tables in a pretty corner of the former coachyard. In the pleasant village, look out for the apricot trees planted against some older houses, with the same against the front of the pub. Readers enjoy staying here and compliment the good breakfasts.

> If we know a Main Entry pub does sandwiches, we always say so. If they're not mentioned, you'll have to assume you can't get one.

🍴 As well as good sandwiches, particularly good bar food might include scallops with potato purée, spinach and smoked bacon cream, twice-baked mushroom and chestnut soufflé with stilton cream, cullen skink with a poached egg, butternut and gorgonzola risotto, battered cod, confit duck with three-bean cassoulet and five-spice jus, puddings such as dark chocolate brûlée with orange shortbread, iced prune and armagnac parfait with spiced syrup, and a good cheeseboard. *Starters/Snacks: £5.45 to £9.00. Main Courses: £9.45 to £17.45. Puddings: £7.45 to £7.75*

Free house ~ Licensee Caroline Parkes ~ Real ale ~ Bar food (12-2 (2.30 Sun), 7-9.30(9 Sun)) ~ Restaurant ~ (01869) 811885 ~ Children welcome ~ Open 9-11 ~ Bedrooms: £90B/£99B

Recommended by Michael Dandy, Stuart Turner, Eithne Dandy, George Atkinson, David and Anne, Andy and Jill Kassube, Susan and John Douglas, E A and D C T Frewer

Great Western Arms

Just off B4031 W, towards Deddington; Aynho Wharf, Station Road; OX17 3BP

Attractive civilised old pub with interesting railway memorabilia, well liked food and moorings

The cosy series of linked rooms at this enjoyable place is rambling enough to give each an intimate feel. Golden stripped-stone walling blends attractively with warm cream and deep red plasterwork and works well with the fine furnishings that include fine solid country tables and regional chairs on broad flagstones. A homely log fire warms cosy seats in two of the areas. There are candles and fresh flowers throughout as well as daily papers and glossy magazines, and readers enjoy the extensive GWR collection which includes lots of steam locomotive photographs; the dining area on the right is rather elegant. Two or three Hook Norton beers on handpump, with good wines by the glass; service is welcoming and attentive; piped music, pool and skittle alley. Opening out of the main bar, the former stable courtyard behind has white cast-iron tables and chairs, and there are moorings on the Oxford Canal and a marina nearby. They leave continental breakfasts in the comfortable bedrooms.

🍴 Bar food might include prawn cocktail, pigeon breast wrapped in prosciutto with pepper sauce, venison terrine with cumberland sauce, ham, egg and chips, venison, mushroom and cranberry casserole, sausage and mash, venison burger, chicken curry with mango chutney, steak and ale pie, rabbit braised in cider and grain mustard, breaded scampi and T-bone steak, with puddings listed on the blackboard. *Starters/Snacks: £4.50 to £6.75. Main Courses: £8.75 to £20.00. Puddings: £4.50 to £5.50*

Hook Norton ~ Tenants René Klein and Ali Saul ~ Real ale ~ Bar food (12-9) ~ Restaurant ~ (01869) 338288 ~ Children welcome ~ Dogs allowed in bar ~ Open 11-11 ~ Bedrooms: £65B/£75B

Recommended by Gerry and Rosemary Dobson, Stuart Turner, George Atkinson, Phil and Jane Hodson, Robert Watt, Eithne Dandy, Michael Dandy, Jean and Douglas Troup, David and Lin Short, Sir Nigel Foulkes

BULWICK   SP9694   MAP 4

Queens Head

Just off A43 Kettering—Duddington; NN17 3DY

New licensees at ancient pub with interesting beers

New licensees were taking over this lovely 600-year-old stone cottage row just as we went to press. The place was being tidied up a bit but we're sure that the timeless beamed bar with its stone floors and fire in a stone hearth at one end will still have the feel of a traditional village pub – do let us know what you think if you visit. We hope at least that the bellringers will continue to pop in after their Wednesday practice, and the darts and dominoes teams will remain active; also shove-ha'penny, dominoes and piped music. Four or five constantly changing beers are served from a stone bar counter and might be from brewers such as Brewsters, Nethergate and Oakham. The garden terrace, with its new decking, is a really lovely spot, with the summer sounds of swallows and martins, sheep in the adjacent field and bells ringing in the nearby church.

🍴 As we went to press the menu was unfinalised but we know the chef's work from his days at the Olive Branch in Clipsham so we feel positive about the changes. He intends to include traditional pub dishes with a gentle imaginative twist and perhaps a modest french influence and he plans to make good use of the stone-bake oven outside. *Starters/Snacks: £6.00 to £10.00. Main Courses: £12.00 to £15.00. Puddings: £5.95*

Free house ~ Licensees Jonathan Allen and Jane Bowles ~ Real ale ~ Bar food (12-2.30, 6-9.30; not Sun evening) ~ Restaurant ~ (01780) 450272 ~ Children welcome ~ Dogs allowed in bar ~ Open 12-3.30, 6-11; closed Mon

Recommended by Michael and Jenny Back, Peter Martin, Jeff and Wendy Williams, Mike and Sue Loseby, John Robertson, D Goodger, Phil and Jane Hodson, Anthony Barnes

COLLYWESTON
SK9902   MAP 4

Collyweston Slater
A43; The Drove; PE9 3PQ

Good roomy modern main-road dining pub usefully doing at least some food all day; comfortable bedrooms

This handsome stone building, with teak tables on its flagstoned terrace and massive local roof slates, looks so traditional that the inside comes as a slight surprise. It's L-shaped, with brown leather easy chairs and sofas in the central angle, a smart modern two-part formal dining room (with a log fire) as the left leg, and on the right two or three more informal areas stretching back to a raised end section up a few steps. This part has contrasting light and dark leather tub chairs as well as dining chairs around sturdy pub tables, and a raised stove in one dividing wall. Throughout there are fresh flowers, some beams and stripped stone, and a mix of dark flagstones, dark boards and fitted carpet. Neat, friendly and efficient young staff, Everards Beacon, Tiger and Original on handpump, a good choice of wines by the glass, daily papers; the piped music is fairly unobtrusive and you can play pétanque in the garden. Though the road is quite busy all night, the bedrooms are well sound-insulated.

🍴 Served with proper linen napkins, the freshly made food runs from sandwiches (through the afternoon) and pubby favourites with an understated modern twist such as good burgers with excellent chunky chips to more elaborate dishes like chicken liver parfait with sour plum chutney and toasted brioche, beef carpaccio with horseradish panna cotta and truffle cream, smoked salmon terrine with poached oysters and cucumber sorbet, main courses such as bass with mussel risotto, pea shoots and creamed leeks with crab, rump of lamb with aubergine caviar, carrot tart, sweetbreads and lamb kidney, and puddings such as custard panna cotta with apple jelly, apple crisp, sherbert and apple sorbet, plum crumble with vanilla ice-cream and plum custard, and a cheeseboard with quince jelly and fig roll. *Starters/Snacks: £5.95 to £7.95. Main Courses: £7.95 to £10.95. Puddings: £5.95 to £6.95*

Everards ~ Lease Dameon Clarke ~ Real ale ~ Bar food (11.30-3 (4 Sun), 6-9.30; not Sun evening) ~ Restaurant ~ (01780) 444288 ~ Children welcome ~ Open 11.30-11 ~ Bedrooms: £75S/£85S

Recommended by Jan and Alan Summers, Jeff and Wendy Williams, Phil and Jane Hodson

CRICK
SP5872   MAP 4

Red Lion
1 mile from M1 junction 18; in centre of village off A428; NN6 7TX

Nicely worn-in friendly coaching inn off M1 with straightforward lunchtime food and pricier more detailed evening menu

Handy if you want a break from the motorway, the traditional low-ceilinged bar at this old stone thatched pub has lots of comfortable seating, some rare old horsebrasses, pictures of the pub in the days before it was surrounded by industrial estates and a tiny log stove in a big inglenook. Four well kept beers on handpump include Wells & Youngs Bombardier, Greene King Old Speckled Hen, Caledonian Deuchars IPA and a guest such as Robinsons Dizzy Blonde. There are a few picnic-sets under parasols on a terrace by the car park, and in summer you can eat out in the old coachyard which is sheltered by a perspex roof and decorated with lots of pretty hanging baskets.

🍽 Bar food includes sandwiches and ploughman's, chicken and mushroom or steak pie, leek and smoky bacon bake and plaice and vegetable pancake rolls. Prices go up a little in the evening when they offer a wider range of dishes that might include stuffed salmon fillet, lamb shank, half a roast duck and sirloin steak; puddings such as lemon meringue pie; bargain-price Sunday roast. *Starters/Snacks: £2.50 to £4.75. Main Courses: £7.00 to £14.00. Puddings: £2.10 to £3.00*

Wellington ~ Lease Tom and Paul Marks ~ Real ale ~ Bar food (12-2, 6.30-9; not Sun evening) ~ (01788) 822342 ~ Children under 12 lunchtimes only ~ Dogs allowed in bar ~ Open 11-2.30, 6.15-11; 12-3, 7-10.30 Sun

Recommended by Paul Humphreys, Michael Dandy, J K Parry, Gerry and Rosemary Dobson, Dr D J and Mrs S C Walker, Margaret and Peter Staples, Edward Mirzoeff, George Atkinson, Ted George, I J and S A Bufton, Michael Butler, Simon and Mandy King

EAST HADDON   SP6668   MAP 4

Red Lion

High Street; village signposted off A428 (turn right in village) and off A50 N of Northampton; NN6 8BU

Appealing old hotel with pleasant grounds and good food

This elegantly substantial golden stone inn is attractively decorated for a comfortable but slightly smarter dining experience. A small amount of carefully chosen and arranged bric-a-brac is set off against walls painted in warm pastel shades and floors that are from reclaimed wood and stone. Drinks include Wells & Youngs Bombardier and Eagle, Youngs and a guest such as Potbelly Pigs Do Fly, and ten wines by the glass; piped music. French windows open to a walled side garden which is pretty with lilac, fruit trees, roses and neat flowerbeds and leads back to the bigger lawn, which has well spaced picnic-sets. A small side terrace has more tables under parasols, and a big copper beech shades the gravel car park.

🍽 Attractively presented bar food includes starters such as coarse pork terrine, minted pea soup and devilled whitebait, main courses such as braised pork belly and crackling, smoked haddock fishcakes with curried mayonnaise, home-made burger, cod and chips, tomato and caramelised onion tart, chicken breast with chorizo and herb risotto, and puddings such as rice pudding with cognac-marinated sultanas and Baileys crème brûlée. *Starters/Snacks: £3.95 to £6.95. Main Courses: £9.95 to £17.50. Puddings: £4.95*

Charles Wells ~ Lease Nick Bonner ~ Real ale ~ Bar food (during opening hours; stops 10pm Sat) ~ Restaurant ~ (01604) 770223 ~ Children welcome ~ Open 12-2.30, 5.30-11; 12-7 Sun; closed Sun evening ~ Bedrooms: £60S/£75S

Recommended by JJW, CMW, John and Susan Miln, Ryta Lyndley, R W Allen, Michael Dandy

EYDON   SP5450   MAP 7

Royal Oak

Lime Avenue; village signed off A361 Daventry—Banbury, and from B4525; NN11 3PG

Enjoyable low-beamed old place with good food including tapas

With some lovely period features, such as its fine flagstone floors and leaded windows, this attractive 300-year-old ironstone inn is a fascinating building with an interesting layout. The cosy snug on the right has cushioned wooden benches built into alcoves, seats in a bow window, some cottagey pictures and an open fire in an inglenook fireplace. The bar counter (with stools) runs down a long central flagstoned corridor room and links three other small characterful rooms. An attractive covered terrace with hardwood furniture is a lovely place for a meal outside. Friendy staff serve Fullers London Pride, Hook Norton Hooky and a guest such as Tetleys by handpump; piped music, board games, and table skittles in an old stable.

🍽 **The new licensee has introduced a proper full tapas menu which complements starters such as mushroom and ale soup and fried goats cheese with red onion compote, main courses such as roast lamb rump, vegetable provençale, bass with shellfish dressing, penne with pine nuts, tomatoes, rocket and mozzarella, and puddings such as coffee crème brûlée with mocha biscotti and glazed lemon tart with spiced berry compote.** *Starters/Snacks: £3.75 to £6.00. Main Courses: £12.00 to £16.00. Puddings: £4.50*

Free house ~ Licensee John Crossan ~ Real ale ~ Bar food (12-2.30, 7-9.30; takeaway only Mon evening) ~ Restaurant ~ (01327) 263167 ~ Children welcome ~ Dogs allowed in bar ~ Open 12-3, 6-11(7-10.30 Sun); closed Mon lunchtime

Recommended by George Atkinson, Kevin Thomas, Nina Randall, J V Dadswell, Christopher Hayle, Rob and Catherine Dunster, Malcolm and Pauline Pellatt

FARTHINGSTONE
SP6155   MAP 4

Kings Arms 🍺

Off A5 SE of Daventry; village signposted from Litchborough on former B4525 (now declassified); NN12 8EZ

Individual place with cosy traditional interior and lovely gardens

We agree with the reader who describes the garden at this quirky gargoyle-embellished 18th-c stone country pub as a 'must see'. With a surprise around every corner, it's laid out in such a way that you feel tucked away in your own little nook, and the tranquil terrace is charmingly decorated with hanging baskets, flower and herb pots and plant-filled painted tractor tyres. Inside, the timelessly intimate flagstoned bar has a huge log fire, comfortable homely sofas and armchairs near the entrance, whisky-water jugs hanging from oak beams, and lots of pictures and decorative plates on the walls. A games room at the far end has darts, dominoes, cribbage, table skittles and board games. Drinks include Hoggleys Northamptonshire, St Austell Tribute, a guest such as Black Sheep, a short but decent wine list and quite a few country wines. Look out for the interesting newspaper-influenced décor in the outside gents'. This is a picturesque village and there are good walks near here including the Knightley Way. It's worth ringing ahead to check the opening and food serving times and do note that they don't take credit cards.

🍽 **Food is carefully prepared and they grow their own salad vegetables and herbs. As well as sandwiches and baguettes, dishes might include smoked duck and black pudding salad, salmon fishcakes with dill and mustard sauce, pork in ginger, tomato and garlic sauce, sticky chicken thighs and yorkshire pudding filled with spicy sausage and bean casserole. They have a short list of carefully sourced produce on sale including cornish fish and british cheeses.** *Starters/Snacks: £3.50 to £5.95. Main Courses: £5.95 to £9.50. Puddings: £4.25 to £5.25*

Free house ~ Licensees Paul and Denise Egerton ~ Real ale ~ Bar food (12-2 Sat, Sun only) ~ No credit cards ~ (01327) 361604 ~ Children welcome ~ Dogs welcome ~ Open 7-11.30; 6.30-midnight Fri; 12-4, 7-midnight Sat; 12-4, 9-11 Sun; closed Mon and weekday lunchtimes

Recommended by Adrian Johnson, Anne Edmonds

'Children welcome' means the pub says it lets children inside without any special restriction. If it allows them in, but to restricted areas such as an eating area or family room, we specify this. Places with separate restaurants often let children use them, hotels usually let them into public areas such as lounges. Some pubs impose an evening time limit – let us know if you find one earlier than 9pm.

FOTHERINGHAY   TL0593   MAP 5

Falcon ⑪ ♀

Village signposted off A605 on Peterborough side of Oundle; PE8 5HZ
NORTHAMPTONSHIRE DINING PUB OF THE YEAR

Upmarket dining pub, good range of drinks and food from snacks up, and attractive garden

Still maintaining the high standards we know it for, this civilised pub is popular for its good inventive food, and they now do a snackier bar menu and two- and three-course meal deals. It's neatly kept and sedately furnished with cushioned slatback arm and bucket chairs, good winter log fires in stone fireplaces, and fresh flower arrangements. Surprisingly, given the emphasis on dining here, it does have a thriving little locals' tap bar and a darts team. The very good range of drinks includes three changing beers from brewers such as Digfield and Greene King IPA on handpump, good wines (20 by the glass), Weston's organic cider, organic cordials and fresh orange juice. There's a pretty conservatory restaurant, and if the weather is nice the attractively planted garden is particularly enjoyable. The vast church behind is worth a visit, and the ruins of Fotheringhay Castle, where Mary Queen of Scots was executed, is not far away.

⑪ As well as imaginative sandwiches, thoughtful bar food might include butternut squash soup, sautéed king prawns with tomato and red onion salsa, thai-style crab salad, sautéed scallops with pea and mint purée, pancetta, pea shoots and tomato and chive beurre blanc, sausage and mash, salmon fishcakes, grilled lemon sole with caper and parsley butter, rump of lamb with salsa verde, sirloin steak with stilton dauphinoise and red wine jus, and puddings such as chocolate and honeycomb semifreddo with warm chocolate cake and bakewell tart with plum ripple ice-cream, and a good cheeseboard.
Starters/Snacks: £4.50 to £6.95. Main Courses: £8.95 to £17.95. Puddings: £4.50 to £6.25

Free house ~ Licensee Sally Facer ~ Real ale ~ Bar food (12.15-2.15(3 Sun), 6.15-9.15(8.30 Sun))
~ Restaurant ~ (01832) 226254 ~ Children welcome ~ Dogs allowed in bar ~ Open 12-11(10.30 Sun)
Recommended by Ian and Nita Cooper, O K Smyth, M L and B S Rantzen, Jan and Alan Summers

GREAT BRINGTON   SP6664   MAP 4

Althorp Coaching Inn ◀

Off A428 NW of Northampton, near Althorp Hall; until recently known as the Fox & Hounds; NN7 4JA

Friendly golden stone thatched pub with great choice of real ales, tasty food and sheltered garden

Cheery staff at this lovely old coaching inn serve a splendid range of around eight real ales including Fullers London Pride, Greene King IPA and Abbot, with thoughtfully sourced and often local guests from brewers such as Abbeydale, Goffs, Quartz and Saltaire. Also ten wines by the glass and a decent range of malt whiskies. The ancient bar has all the traditional features you'd wish for, from a dog or two sprawled out by the fire, to old beams, saggy joists and an attractive mix of country chairs and tables (maybe with fresh flowers) on its broad flagstones and bare boards. Also plenty of snug alcoves, nooks and crannies, some stripped pine shutters and panelling, two fine log fires and an eclectic medley of bric-a-brac from farming implements to an old clocking-in machine and country pictures; piped music and board games. The extended dining area has been altered to allow views of the 30 or so casks racked in the cellar, one of the old coaching bars is now used for pub games, and an old garden cottage, adjoining the lovely little paved courtyard (also accessible by the old coaching entrance) with sheltered tables and tubs of flowers, has been improved for dining; more seating in the side garden.

⑪ Food here is popular so it's advisable to book. The new menu includes sandwiches and baguettes, greek salad, whisky-marinated smoked salmon, grilled sardines with garlic ciabatta, penne with chicken breast and smoked bacon and white wine, grilled salmon with honey and mustard dressing, beef or vegetable lasagne, grilled cod and moroccan lamb, puddings such as warm chocolate brownie, summer fruit pudding, and a cheeseboard. *Starters/Snacks: £5.25 to £5.95. Main Courses: £9.25 to £12.95. Puddings: £4.50 to £7.25*

Free house ~ Licensee Michael Krempels ~ Real ale ~ Bar food (12-3, 6.30-9.30; 12-6, 6-8 Sun) ~ Restaurant ~ (01604) 770651 ~ Children welcome ~ Dogs allowed in bar ~ Live music Tues evening ~ Open 11-11.30; 12-10.30 Sun

Recommended by Gerry and Rosemary Dobson, Tim and Ann Newell, George Atkinson, John and Susan Miln, JJW, CMW, Alan Sutton

GREAT OXENDON   SP7383   MAP 4

George 🍷 🛏

A508 S of Market Harborough; LE16 8NA

Elegant 16th-c pub with emphasis on dining (you may need to book); garden and comfortable bedrooms

Don't be deterred by the rather gaunt exterior of this well run place; inside it's cosy and convivial. The bar rather suggests the intimate feel of a gentleman's club, with its dark walls, dark brown panelled dado and patterned wallpaper, green leatherette bucket chairs around little tables and big log fire (not to mention the stylish naughty pictures in the gents' lavatories). The entrance lobby has easy chairs and a former inn sign, and the turkey-carpeted conservatory overlooks a big well tended shrub-sheltered garden; piped easy-listening music. Friendly efficient staff serve Adnams, Timothy Taylors Landlord and a guest such as Langton Caudle on handpump, a dozen or so wines by the glass and around ten malts.

🍴 As well as sandwiches, good bar food might include gruyère fritters with cranberry sauce, salmon, sweet potato and red pepper cake with tartare sauce, home-made burger, pie of the day, duck breast with Cointreau, steaks, and vanilla bread and butter pudding and warm chocolate fondant with coffee ice-cream. They do a good value curry on Monday evening and a good value weekday set menu; two- and three-course Sunday lunch. *Starters/Snacks: £4.50 to £7.25. Main Courses: £10.95 to £19.95. Puddings: £5.45 to £5.95*

Free house ~ Licensee David Dudley ~ Real ale ~ Bar food (12-2, 6-9.30) ~ Restaurant ~ (01858) 465205 ~ Children welcome ~ Dogs allowed in bedrooms ~ Open 12-3, 5.30-11; closed Sun evening and bank hol evenings ~ Bedrooms: £57.50B/£65.50B

Recommended by Gerry and Rosemary Dobson, Dave Braisted, Jeff and Wendy Williams, R T and J C Moggridge, O K Smyth, MDN, Rob and Catherine Dunster, Nigel and Sue Foster, Mr J V Nelson, Dennis Jones, Tom and Jill Jones

HARRINGWORTH   SP9197   MAP 4

White Swan

Seaton Road; village SE of Uppingham, signposted from A6003, A47 and A43; NN17 3AF

Handsome country pub with good food and local real ales; bedrooms

The fairly traditional exposed stone bar at this eye-catching 16th-c former coaching inn has a rather nice hand-crafted oak counter with mirrors set in its base that are surmounted by attractive carved swans, and behind there's an enticing row of sweets in old-fashioned jars, along with scales and paper bags. Friendly staff serve Adnams and a couple of thoughtfully sourced guests such as Hobbleys Kislingbury and Potbelly Pigs Do Fly from handpump, local apple juice and farm cider, and they have a summer cocktail board. There are plush stools arranged along the counter, dark wheelbacks at dark tables, pictures of World War II aircraft at nearby Spanhoe Airfield and old village photographs on the walls. An open fire divides the bar and two cosy dining areas which have solid country pine tables, attractive window seats and high cushioned settles; piped music, darts and board games. There are tables out on a partly covered terrace. The building itself has a Cotswoldy look with its pretty hanging baskets on limestone walls and imposing central gable, and it's not far from the majestic 82-arch Victorian railway viaduct spanning the River Welland.

🍴 Attractively presented well prepared bar food might include thai fishcake with spicy tomato and coriander sauce, warm wood pigeon, black pudding, bacon and chard salad, fresh fish of the day, pesto and mozzarella baked aubergine with tomato and basil sauce, smoked haddock with a grain mustard sauce and poached egg, roast duck breast with port sauce, battered haddock and sausage and mash, and puddings such as warm cherry and almond tart with clotted cream and chocolate marquise with white chocolate ice-cream and honeycomb caramel sauce. *Starters/Snacks: £5.50 to £7.95. Main Courses: £7.95 to £14.95. Puddings: £5.25 to £5.50*

Free house ~ Licensees Adam and Gina Longden ~ Real ale ~ Bar food (till 3 Sun) ~ Restaurant ~ (01572) 747543 ~ Children welcome ~ Open 12-2.30(3.30 Sun), 6-11; closed Sun evening, Mon lunchtime ~ Bedrooms: £45S/£70S

Recommended by John Wooll, Brigette Lepora, Mrs K Hooker

KILSBY   SP5671   MAP 4

George £

2.5 miles from M1 junction 18: A428 towards Daventry, left on to A5 – look out for pub off on right at roundabout; CV23 8YE

Handy for M1; warm welcome, good local atmosphere, proper public bar, old-fashioned décor and tasty wholesome food

The friendly hardworking landlady at this relaxing pub offers the sort of welcome that makes visitors feel like locals, and she keeps a good balance between the popular dining aspect and the traditional public bar. The high-ceilinged wood panelled lounge on the right, with plush banquettes, a coal-effect gas stove and a big bay window, opens to the left into a smarter but relaxed attractive area with solidly comfortable furnishings. The long brightly decorated but simple back public bar (dogs welcome in here) has a TV, darts, and that rarity these days, a free-play pool table. Adnams, Greene King Old Speckled Hen, Fullers London Pride and a guest such as Jennings Cumberland are on handpump, and they've a splendid range of malt whiskies, served in generous measures. There are picnic-sets out in the back garden.

🍴 The new Bargain Award here is for the handful of pubby dishes they offer at lunchtime such as fish and chips, faggots and spring onion mash with mushy peas, ploughman's and pasta of the day. As well as sandwiches, other dishes might include filled baguettes, fried brie with cranberry sauce, sausage, egg and chips, daily specials such as roast pork hock with mustard sauce, beef and ale shortcrust pastry pie, arbroath smokie fishcakes, pancakes filled with feta and spinach and steaks. Monday is pie and a pint night and Thursday is burger night; Sunday roast. *Starters/Snacks: £4.90 to £5.90. Main Courses: £4.90 to £11.90. Puddings: £2.90 to £4.90*

Punch ~ Lease Maggie Chandler ~ Real ale ~ Bar food (12-2(4 Sun), 6-9) ~ Restaurant ~ (01788) 822229 ~ Children welcome if dining with an adult ~ Dogs allowed in bar ~ Open 11.30-3, 5.30(6 Sat)-11; 12-5, 6-11 Sun ~ Bedrooms: £38/£56

Recommended by Ted George, Rob and Catherine Dunster, R T and J C Moggridge, David and Sue Atkinson, Michael Butler, Michael Dandy

---

NETHER HEYFORD

SP6658   MAP 4

Olde Sun 🍺 £

1.75 miles from M1 junction 16: village signposted left off A45 westbound – Middle Street; NN7 3LL

Unpretentious place handy for M1 with diverting bric-a-brac, reasonably priced food and garden with play area

All nature of bric-a-brac hangs from the ceiling and is packed into nooks and crannies in the several small linked rooms that make up this tucked-away 18th-c golden stone pub. There's brassware (one fireplace is a grotto of large brass animals), colourful relief plates, 1930s cigarette cards, railway memorabilia and advertising signs, World War II posters and rope fancywork. The nice old cash till on one of the two counters where they serve the well kept Banks's, Greene King Ruddles, Marstons Pedigree and a guest such as Thwaites Original, is wishfully stuck at one and a ha'penny. Furnishings are mostly properly pubby, with the odd easy chair. There are beams and low ceilings (one painted with a fine sunburst), partly glazed dividing panels, steps between some areas, rugs on parquet, red tiles or flagstones, a big inglenook log fire – and up on the left a room with full-sized hood skittles, a games machine, darts, Sky TV, cribbage and dominoes; piped music. The enjoyable collections continue into the garden, where there are blue-painted grain kibblers and other antiquated hand-operated farm machines, some with plants in their hoppers, beside a fairy-lit front terrace with picnic-sets.

🍴 **A short choice of snacky meals includes tasty sandwiches, scampi and chips, potato baked with tuna, onions and cream cheese, cottage pie, chilli, curry, coq au vin and steak.** *Starters/Snacks: £3.75 to £6.45. Main Courses: £5.95 to £15.95. Puddings: £3.25*

Free house ~ Licensees P Yates and A Ford ~ Real ale ~ Bar food ~ Restaurant ~ (01327) 340164 ~ Children welcome ~ Dogs welcome ~ Open 12-2.30, 5-11; 12-11 Sat, Sun
Recommended by Ian and Helen Stafford, Dr D J and Mrs S C Walker, R T and J C Moggridge, David and Sue Atkinson

NORTHAMPTON

SP7559   MAP 4

Malt Shovel 🍺 £

Bridge Street (approach road from M1 junction 15); best parking in Morrisons central car park, far end – passage past Europcar straight to back entrance; NN1 1QF

Friendly and well run real ale pub with bargain pub lunches and over a dozen beers

The heart of this pub is the long bar counter with its formidable battery of handpumps serving half a dozen or more well kept and interesting quickly changing guest beers, as well as its regular Frog Island Natterjack, Fullers London Pride and the brewer-landlord's three Great Oakley house beers including Wots Occurring and Harpers. They have belgian bottled beers and a good choice of other drinks including Rich's farm cider, plenty of old breweriana including some from what is now the Carlsberg Brewery opposite, and quite a few unusual things to look at including some high-mounted ancient beer engines. Staff are cheery and helpful; darts, daily papers, good coal fire, disabled facilities; may be piped music (the good Wednesday night blues bands attract enthusiastic audiences). The secluded back yard has picnic-sets, a smokers' shelter and occasional barbecues.

🍴 **Bargain lunchtime food includes baguettes, wraps, baked potatoes, ploughman's, mediterranean pasta bake and a few specials such as steak and kidney pudding, liver and bacon casserole and seafood salad, with puddings such as blackberry and apple crumble and tiramisu.** *Starters/Snacks: £1.50 to £4.95. Main Courses: £5.75 to £5.95. Puddings: £3.75 to £3.99*

Free house ~ Licensee Mike Evans ~ Real ale ~ Bar food (12-2, not Sun) ~ (01604) 234212 ~ Dogs allowed in bar ~ Open 11.30-3, 5-11; 12-3, 7-10.30 Sun
Recommended by G Jennings, Bruce Bird, the Didler, George Atkinson, D and K, JJW, CMW, Maria Scotland, Joanna Oldham

OUNDLE

TL0388 MAP 5

Ship 🕮

West Street; PE8 4EF

Bustling down-to-earth town pub with interesting beers and good value pubby food

None of the cheery chatter and bustle at this proper enjoyable local seems to disturb Midnight, the sleepy black and white pub cat, though we suspect he might disappear on the odd occasion that there's a live band here. The heavily beamed lounge bar (watch your head if you're tall) is made up of three cosy areas that lead off the central corridor. Up by the street there's a mix of leather and other seats, with sturdy tables and a warming log fire in a stone inglenook, and down one end a charming little panelled snug has button-back leather seats built in around its walls. The wood-floored public side has a TV, games machine and board games and you can play poker here on Wednesdays; piped music. Friendly staff serve Brewsters Hophead, Elgoods Black Dog, Oakham Bishops Farewell and a guest, and they've a good range of malt whiskies. The wooden tables and chairs out on the series of small sunny covered terraces are lit at night.

🍴 **Enjoyable bar food served in generous helpings might include soup, vegetarian or beef lasagne, haddock, chicken breast with mushroom sauce, pork curry and 9oz sirloin; Sunday roast.** *Starters/Snacks: £3.50 to £6.00. Main Courses: £8.00 to £12.50. Puddings: £4.50*

Free house ~ Licensees Andrew and Robert Langridge ~ Real ale ~ Bar food (12-3, 6-9; 12-9 Sat, Sun) ~ (01832) 273918 ~ Children welcome ~ Dogs allowed in bar and bedrooms ~ Folk second Mon of the month, live band Sat monthly ~ Open 11-11.30(11.45 Sat); 12-11.30 Sun ~ Bedrooms: £30(£35S)/£60(£70B)

Recommended by the Didler, John Robertson, Barry Collett, Ryta Lyndley

STOKE DOYLE

TL0286 MAP 5

Shuckburgh Arms

Village signposted (down Stoke Hill) from SW edge of Oundle; PE8 5TG

Good atmosphere and enjoyable food in attractively reworked 17th-c pub, nicely set in quiet hamlet

A couple of low black beams in the age-bowed ceiling, the big inglenook with its black stove, friendly service, and Digfield Barnwell (from a nearby farm) and Timothy Taylors Landlord on handpump all preserve traditional values in this well run pub. The appealing reworking by the newish licensees has brought neat bar chairs by the granite-top bar counter, a couple of high tables with stylish matching deco seats, and plenty of pale tables with elegant yet comfortable modern chairs. The décor in the four rooms gently confirms the understated smartness, with dark-grained wood flooring here, beige carpet there, pastel sage and dusky pink walls, and a few pictures. They have decent wines by the glass; faint piped music. The garden has a decked area and play frame. We haven't yet heard from readers staying in the separate bedroom block, but would expect this to be a good place to stay.

🍴 **Bar food includes thai cod, salmon and prawn fishcake, whitebait, baked chorizo and black pudding with beetroot and rocket salad, steak burger, lamb tagine, coq au vin, baked goats cheese and caramelised red onion bruschetta, rosemary and honey-glazed duck breast with redcurrant and orange port jus and sirloin steak, with puddings such as lemon posset with poached rhubarb and gingernut crumble and dark chocolate parfait with praline and cappuccino ice-cream.** *Starters/Snacks: £4.50 to £6.75. Main Courses: £11.50 to £18.75. Puddings: £4.95*

Free house ~ Licensees Don and Fran Harding ~ Real ale ~ (01832) 272339 ~ Children welcome ~ Dogs allowed in bedrooms ~ Open 12-3, 6-11; closed Sun evening ~ Bedrooms: £35S/£50S(£60B)

Recommended by Robin M Corlett

We say if we know a pub allows dogs.

SULGRAVE

SP5545 MAP 4

Star

E of Banbury, signposted off B4525; Manor Road; OX17 2SA

Pleasant country pub with decent food and nice gardens

It's unlikely that the new licensees will change much at this lovely old creeper-covered farmhouse. A restful calm gently permeates the little bar which is quietly furnished with small pews, cushioned window seats and wall benches, kitchen chairs and cast-iron tables. Framed newspaper front pages record historic events such as Kennedy's assassination and the death of Churchill. There are polished flagstones in an area by the big inglenook fireplace, with red carpet elsewhere. Three Hook Norton beers are served from handpumps on the tiny counter. Quite appropriately, given its close proximity to Silverstone, the new landlord is displaying his collection of motor racing memorabilia in the dining room. In summer, you can eat outside under a vine-covered trellis, and there are benches at the front and in the back garden. The building dates from the 17th century and is just a short walk from Sulgrave Manor, the ancestral home of George Washington.

🍴 Bar food includes some very reasonably priced pubby dishes such as sausage and mash, pie of the day and lasagne, with more elaborate dishes such as chicken liver pâté with toasted brioche and plum sauce, grilled asparagus with a crumbed and deep-fried egg and parma ham, fried duck on rösti potatoes with cassis jus, mushroom risotto with salad in a tortilla basket, and puddings such as chocolate baked cheesecake and lemon tart with lemon sorbet. *Starters/Snacks: £4.50 to £5.75. Main Courses: £7.50 to £15.75. Puddings: £4.95*

Hook Norton ~ Tenants Barry and Gillie Andrews ~ Real ale ~ Bar food (12-2.30, 6-9.30) ~ Restaurant ~ (01295) 760389 ~ Children welcome ~ Dogs allowed in bar ~ Open 12-3, 6-11; 11-11 Sat, Sun ~ Bedrooms: £49S/£79B

Recommended by Malcolm and Pauline Pellatt, Howard and Margaret Buchanan, David and Diane Young, Roger Noyes, Dennis and Doreen Haward, G Jennings, P M Newsome

WADENHOE

TL0183 MAP 5

Kings Head

Church Street; village signposted (in small print) off A605 S of Oundle; PE8 5ST

Country pub in idyllic riverside spot; decent range of beers, pubby food

In summer, you can relax at picnic-sets among willows and aspens on grass leading down to the River Nene, in the idyllically sited garden belonging to this cheery stone-built 16th-c inn – you can even arrive by boat and moor here. Inside, there's an uncluttered simplicity (maybe too much so for some) to the very welcoming partly stripped-stone main bar, which has pleasant old worn quarry-tiles, solid pale pine furniture with a couple of cushioned wall seats, and a leather-upholstered chair by the woodburning stove in the fine inglenook. The bare-boarded public bar has similar furnishings and another fire; steps lead up to a games room with darts, dominoes and table skittles, and there's more of the pale pine furniture in an attractive little beamed dining room. Four changing real ales are likely to be from local brewers Digfield and Potbelly served alongside a dozen wines by the glass.

🍴 Food tends to be fairly pubby at lunchtime with sandwiches, baked potatoes, burgers, sausage and mash, chicken and mushroom and vegetable pie and fish and chips. The more elaborate evening menu changes every two months or so but might have dishes such as seared scallops with pork belly, country pâté with onion jam, spinach, mushroom and stilton wellington with rocket and roast onion salad and garlic sauce, fried bass on samphire with clam butter, and puddings such as treacle tart and chocolate brownies with home-made vanilla ice-cream. *Starters/Snacks: £4.95 to £5.95. Main Courses: £6.95 to £12.95. Puddings: £4.95*

Free house ~ Licensee Peter Hall ~ Real ale ~ Bar food (12-2.15(3 Sun), 6-9) ~ Restaurant ~ (01832) 720024 ~ Children welcome ~ Dogs allowed in bar ~ Open 11-3, 5.30-11, 11-11 Fri, Sat; 12-6 Sun; closed Sun evening

Recommended by Michael Tack, Ryta Lyndley, Ian Phillips, George Atkinson, Howard and Margaret Buchanan

LUCKY DIP

Besides the fully inspected pubs, you might like to try these Lucky Dips recommended to us and described by readers (if you do, please send us reports: feedback@goodguides.com).

APETHORPE [TL0295]

☆ *Kings Head* PE8 5DG [Kings Cliffe Rd]: Roomy and attractive stone-built pub in conservation village, comfortable and welcoming lounge with log fire, cosy bar, well kept Fullers, Timothy Taylors and a guest ale, good coffee, friendly efficient service, arch to big dining area with wide choice of good fairly priced fresh food inc fish, separate bar food menu, theme nights and live music; children welcome, picnic-sets in charming sheltered courtyard, cl Mon *(Colin Dean, Mrs M G Uglow, Joan and Tony Walker, M B Manser)*

ASHTON [TL0588]

Chequered Skipper PE8 5LD [the one NE of Oundle, signed from A427/A605 island]: Handsomely rebuilt thatched pub on chestnut-tree green of elegant estate village, helpful and friendly young staff, changing ales such as Brewsters, Nethergate and Oakham, enjoyable reasonably priced food (not Mon) from snacks to restauranty main courses, light and airy open-plan layout with dining areas either side *(George Atkinson)*

Old Crown NN7 2JN [the one off A508 S of M1 junction 15]: Beamed and stone-built 18th-c dining pub under newish management, good sensibly priced bistro-style food, Courage Directors and Wells & Youngs ales, decent wines, inglenook woodburner; children welcome, picnic-sets out on lawn *(Viv Jameson)*

BADBY [SP5659]

Maltsters NN11 3AF [The Green]: Stone-built pub refurbished under new management, long beamed carpeted room with fire each end, pine tables and chairs, good choice of enjoyable well priced food from lunchtime ciabattas up, Black Sheep, Greene King and Wells & Youngs ales, friendly service; nice garden with terrace, well placed for walks on nearby Knightley Way, bedrooms, open all day *(George Atkinson, Laurence Smith)*

☆ *Windmill* NN11 3AN [village signposted off A361 Daventry—Banbury]: Sadly the long-serving licensees who made this homely thatched pub a popular Main Entry have left – news please *(Michael Butler, Sara Fulton, Roger Baker, Dennis and Doreen Haward, Richard Morris, LYM)*

BRAFIELD-ON-THE-GREEN [SP8258]

☆ *Red Lion* NN7 1BP [A428 5 miles from Northampton towards Bedford]: Smart comfortably modern bistro-style McManus dining pub set well back from the road, good traditional and upscale food in two main rooms, small drinking area with a couple of settees, good choice of wines by the glass, changing ales such as Great Oakley and Hoggleys, friendly attentive staff; picnic-sets front and back, open all day wknds *(Eithne Dandy, Michael Dandy, Jeremy King)*

BRAUNSTON [SP5466]

Boathouse NN11 7HB [A45 at canal junction]: Large family pub in pleasant waterside spot, good choice of straightforward food inc deals, Marstons ales, friendly attentive staff; seats by canal, play area, moorings *(George Atkinson)*

BRAYBROOKE [SP7684]

Swan LE16 8LH [Griffin Rd]: Nicely kept thatched pub with good drinks choice inc Everards ales, good value generous food (all day Sat), friendly service, fireside sofas, soft lighting, exposed brickwork, stone-ceilinged alcoves, restaurant; quiet piped music, silent fruit machine; children very welcome, dogs too, disabled facilities, attractive hedged garden with covered terrace, open all day wknds *(Jeremy King)*

BUCKBY WHARF [SP6066]

☆ *New Inn* NN6 7PW [A5 N of Weedon]: Good range of tasty quickly served pubby food from good baguettes to popular 'Desperate Dan Pie', friendly staff, well kept Frog Island, Hook Norton and guests, good short choice of wines, several rooms radiating from central servery inc small dining room with nice fire, games area with table skittles; TVs, games machine; children welcome, dogs outside only, pleasant terrace with heated smokers' area, by busy Grand Union Canal lock, popular with boaters, open all day *(LYM, Brian and Anna Marsden, George Atkinson, John Saville)*

BUGBROOKE [SP6756]

Wharf Inn NN7 3QB [The Wharf; off A5 S of Weedon]: Super spot by Grand Union Canal, plenty of tables on big lawn with moorings, large water-view restaurant, bar/lounge with small informal raised eating area either side, lots of stripped brickwork, good food using local organic produce inc Sun roasts, good cheerful service, well kept local Frog Island and other beers, lots of wines by the glass, woodburner; piped music; children welcome, dogs in garden only, disabled facilities, heated smokers' shelter, open all day *(Mary McSweeney, Gerry and Rosemary Dobson, George Atkinson, BB)*

CHAPEL BRAMPTON [SP7366]

☆ *Brampton Halt* NN6 8BA [Pitsford Rd, off A5199 N of Northampton]: Well laid-out pub on Northampton & Lamport Railway (which is open wknds), large restaurant, railway memorabilia and train theme throughout, wide choice of enjoyable generous food (smaller helpings available) from sandwiches up inc Sun roasts, beers such as Adnams, Fullers London Pride and Sharps Doom Bar, good wine choice, cheerful efficient service even when busy, games and TV in bar; piped music; children welcome, lots of tables in garden with awnings and heaters, summer barbecues, pretty views over small lake, Nene Valley Way walks *(LYM, Eithne Dandy, Revd R P Tickle, George Atkinson)*

CHELVESTON [SP9969]
Star & Garter NN9 6AJ [The Green]: Small
pub with friendly welcome, enjoyable food,
Courage Directors and Wells & Youngs,
decent wine by the glass, compact restaurant
(Les Scott-Maynard)

CLIPSTON [SP7181]
Old Red Lion LE16 9RS [The Green]:
Unpretentious little village-green pub with
locals bar and log-fire lounge, well kept
Wells & Youngs ales and a guest from central
servery, decent home-made bar food inc
sandwiches and snacks, small back dining
room; children welcome (Gerry and
Rosemary Dobson)

COSGROVE [SP7942]
Barley Mow MK19 7JD [The Stocks]: Old
village pub by Grand Union Canal, well kept
Everards range and perhaps a guest ale, good
value pubby food with blackboard specials,
cheerful service, lounge/dining area with
dark furniture, small public bar, pool, table
football and skittles; children welcome, tables
on terrace and on lawn down to canal, open
all day (Gerry and Rosemary Dobson)

DENFORD [SP9976]
Cock Inn NN14 4EQ [High St, S of
Thrapston]: Refurbished and reopened as
dining pub, good freshly cooked food (not
Sun evening, Mon, Tues) inc lunchtime
bargains, up to five well kept changing ales,
good coffee, cosy L-shaped bar with log fire,
bare boards, beams and plank ceiling,
woodburner in long restaurant; piped music
– monthly live; children and dogs welcome,
picnic-sets in front and back gardens, River
Nene walks, cl Mon and Tues lunchtimes,
otherwise open all day (Ryta Lyndley)

DUDDINGTON [SK9800]
Royal Oak PE9 3QE [A43 just S of A47]:
Attractive stone-built refurbished hotel;
modern bar area with leather sofas and
chairs on stone floor, log fire, wood
panelling, flowers on top of brick bar, three
changing real ales; restaurant with stone
walls, oak floor and oak furniture, enjoyable
home-made food inc OAP bargain lunches
(Mon-Fri) and two-course evening deals
(Mon-Thurs), roasts all day Sun; piped music,
no dogs; children welcome, disabled
facilities, picnic-sets out at front, five good
bedrooms, pleasant village, open all day
wknds (Marcus Mann, Carolyn Browse)

FARTHINGHOE [SP5339]
Fox NN13 5PH [just off A422 Brackley—
Banbury; Baker St]: Nicely refurbished old
village pub, beams, some stripped stone,
slate and bare wood floors, open fire,
enjoyable locally sourced food (not Sun
evening), Wells & Youngs ales and guests;
piped music; children welcome, picnic-sets
in pleasant garden, summer barbecues, four
bedrooms in adjoining barn, open all day
(David and Lexi Young)

GEDDINGTON [SP8982]
Star NN14 1AD [just off A43 Kettering—
Corby]: Old pub with leather chairs and log
fire, good choice of enjoyable food in bar

and restaurant inc hearty pies some
enterprising dishes, changing real ales,
tables outside, pleasant village with
Eleanor Cross and packhorse bridge,
handy for Broughton House (Howard and
Margaret Buchanan)

GREAT DODDINGTON [SP8864]
Stags Head NN29 7TQ [High St (B573 S of
Wellingborough)]: Old stone-built local with
pleasant bar and split-level lounge/dining
room, ales inc Wadworths 6X, nice wines
and good soft drinks choice, good value
hearty pub food from reasonably priced
sandwiches up, smart cheery service, also
separate barn restaurant extension, public bar
with pool and games; piped music; picnic-sets
out in front and in garden (Mike and
Margaret Banks)

GREAT HOUGHTON [SP7959]
Old Cherry Tree NN4 7AT [Cherry Tree
Lane; No Through Road off A428 just before
White Hart]: Thatched village pub with low
beams, open fires, stripped stone and
panelling, enjoyable fresh food from
lunchtime baguettes up, wider evening
choice, prompt friendly service, well kept
Wells & Youngs and occasional guest ales,
good wine choice, steps up to restaurant;
quiet piped music; garden tables (Gerry and
Rosemary Dobson)

GREENS NORTON [SP6649]
Butchers Arms NN12 8BA [High St]:
Comfortable welcoming village pub, four well
kept changing ales, enjoyable food from
sandwiches up, separate bar and games room
with darts and pool; piped music, some live;
children and dogs allowed, disabled access,
picnic-sets and play area, pretty village nr
Grafton Way walks (David Smith, Mark Semke,
Ken Savage)

HACKLETON [SP8054]
White Hart NN7 2AD [B526 SE of
Northampton]: Comfortably traditional
18th-c country pub, wide choice of
enjoyable generous food from sandwiches up
inc early evening bargains, good friendly
staff, Fullers London Pride, Greene King IPA
and a guest, decent choice of other drinks,
good coffee, dining area up steps with
flame-effect fire, stripped stone, beamery
and brickwork, illuminated well, brasses and
artefacts, split-level flagstoned bar with log
fire, pool and hood skittles; curry/quiz night
Tues; quiet piped music; children (not in bar
after 5pm) and dogs welcome, disabled
access, garden with picnic-sets and goal
posts, open all day (JJW, CMW, Gerry and
Rosemary Dobson)

HARDINGSTONE [SP7657]
Crown NN4 6BZ [High St]: Two-bar pub with
two or three real ales, chinese food (takeaways too), games room with pool and darts;
piped music; children welcome, picnic-sets
in sizeable garden with play area (BOB)

HARLESTONE [SP7064]
Fox & Hounds NN7 4EW [A428, Lower
Harlestone]: Contemporary M&B dining pub
refurbishment with pale wood furnishings

and flooring, light and airy décor, good choice of enjoyable food inc popular Sun lunch, waiter service throughout, ales such as Fullers London Pride, good choice of wines by the glass, decent coffee; children welcome, tables in nice garden, handy for Althorp and Harlestone Firs walks, open all day *(Sarah and John Webb, Eithne Dandy, JJW, CMW)*

HARRINGTON [SP7780]

Tollemache Arms NN6 9NU [High St; off A508 S of Market Harborough]: Pretty thatched Tudor pub in lovely quiet ironstone village, very low ceilings in compact bar with log fire and in pleasant partly stripped-stone dining room, good food such as game hotpot, up to four well kept ales inc Elgoods, Grainstore and Great Oakley, friendly attentive staff; children welcome, nice back garden with country views *(George Atkinson, BB)*

KETTERING [SP8778]

Alexandra Arms NN16 0BU [Victoria St]: Friendly real ale pub, with up to 14 changing quickly, hundreds each year, also Julian Church ales brewed in cellar, may be sandwiches, games bar with hood skittles; back terrace, open all day (from 2pm wkdys) *(the Didler)*

KISLINGBURY [SP6959]

☆ *Cromwell Cottage* NN7 4AG [High St]: Sizeable low-ceilinged M&B family dining pub, informal lounge seating, open fire, separate smart bistro dining area with candles at tables, wide choice of enjoyable food inc fixed-price choices and specials, well kept Adnams, Black Sheep and Wells & Youngs Bombardier, cheerful efficient staff *(Gerry and Rosemary Dobson, E A and D C T Frewer, George Atkinson, Roger Braithwaite)*

Olde Red Lion NN7 4AQ [High St, off A45 W of Northampton]: Roomy renovated 19th-c stone-fronted pub, good freshly cooked bar and restaurant food, well kept Timothy Taylors ales and a guest, beams, woodburners and open fire, events inc summer beer festival; piped music and some live, no dogs; children welcome, disabled access, suntrap back terrace with marquee, barbecues, two bedrooms, cl Sun to Tues lunchtime *(Robin M Corlett, Tracey Lamb)*

LITTLE BRINGTON [SP6663]

☆ *Saracens Head* NN7 4HS [4.5 miles from M1 junction 16, first right off A45 to Daventry; also signed off A428; Main St]: Friendly old pub with enjoyable reasonably priced food from interesting baguettes and wraps up, well kept real ales such as Batemans, Greene King and Timothy Taylors, roomy U-shaped lounge with good log fire, flagstones, chesterfields and lots of old prints, book-lined dining room; plenty of tables in neat back garden, handy for Althorp House and Holdenby House *(Gerry and Rosemary Dobson, Geoffrey Hughes, Rob and Catherine Dunster, George Atkinson, BB)*

LOWICK [SP9780]

Snooty Fox NN14 3BH [off A6116 Corby—Raunds]: Spacious and attractively reworked 16th-c stone-built pub under newish management; leather sofas and chairs, beams and stripped stonework, log fire in huge fireplace, good food from open kitchen, well kept ales, nice coffee, good friendly service, board games; piped music; dogs and children welcome, picnic-sets on front grass, play area, open all day *(Ryta Lyndley, Mrs Joyce Smith, LYM)*

MAIDWELL [SP7477]

☆ *Stags Head* NN6 9JA [Harborough Rd (A508 N of Northampton)]: Well run and comfortable dining pub with log fire in pubby part by bar, extensive eating areas, enjoyable pubby food very popular lunchtime with older people, helpful friendly staff and cheery locals, well kept ales such as Black Sheep Best, St Austell Tinners, Tetleys and Youngs, good choice of other drinks; slightly muffled piped music; disabled facilities, picnic-sets on back terrace (dogs on leads allowed here), good-sized sheltered sloping garden beyond, bedrooms, not far from splendid Palladian Kelmarsh Hall and park *(Mr and Mrs D J Nash, Gerry and Rosemary Dobson, R L Borthwick, George Atkinson, Michael Tack, John Saul, BB, Jeff and Wendy Williams)*

MEARS ASHBY [SP8686]

Griffins Head NN6 0DX [Wilby Rd]: Pleasant little village pub, ales such as Everards Sunchaser, Fullers London Pride and St Austell Tribute, enjoyable food from sandwiches and snacks up inc OAP specials, attentive friendly staff, front lounge with hunting prints and log fire in huge fireplace, cosy dining area, basic back bar with juke box; children welcome, neat flower-filled garden with view over fields to church, open all day *(George Atkinson)*

NASSINGTON [TL0696]

Queens Head PE8 6QB [Station Rd]: Very smartly refurbished, stylish bar/bistro and separate restaurant, wide choice of enjoyable good value food using local ingredients, pleasant helpful uniformed staff, nice choice of wines by the glass, changing real ales, good coffee; pretty garden by River Nene, delightful village, nine chalet bedrooms *(Phil and Jane Hodson)*

NEWNHAM [SP5759]

Romer Arms NN11 3HB [The Green]: Pine panelling, mix of flagstones, quarry tiles and carpet, log fire, light and airy back dining conservatory, cheerful obliging licensees, good generous home cooking (not Sun evening) inc bargain deals, Adnams, Wells & Youngs and the occasional guest, good soft drinks choice, public bar with darts and pool; piped music; enclosed back garden looking over fields, small attractive village *(George Atkinson)*

NORTHAMPTON [SP7759]

Britannia NN4 7AA [3.75 miles from M1 junction 15; Old Bedford Rd (off A428)]: Big modernised Chef & Brewer with massive beams, mix of flagstones and carpet, 18th-c 'kitchen', well kept changing ales, good choice of wines by the glass, food all day from sandwiches up (card swiped for tab), conservatory; piped music, no dogs; children welcome, tables by River Nene, open all day *(JJW, CMW, LYM, Michael Dandy)*

OLD [SP7873]

White Horse NN6 9QX [Walgrave Rd, N of Northampton between A43 and A508]: Refurbished Marstons pub under new management, good food inc set menus, friendly service; garden overlooking 13th-c church *(Alan Sutton)*

OUNDLE [TL0388]

Talbot PE8 4EA [New St]: Handsome former merchant's house, now a hotel, incorporating material salvaged in the 17th c; various rooms inc comfortable atmospheric bar, good value food, restaurant, attentive service; courtyard seats, 40 bedrooms *(George Atkinson)*

RAVENSTHORPE [SP6670]

☆ *Chequers* NN6 8ER [Chequers Lane]: Cosy good-natured local with cheerful friendly young landlord, well kept ales such as Elgoods, Fullers London Pride, Greene King IPA and Jennings Straw, generous sensibly priced food from baguettes to popular Sun lunch and fish take-aways, banquettes, cushioned pews and polished sturdy tables, coal-effect fire, games tables; quiet piped music, TV; children welcome, partly covered side terrace, covered play area, open all day Sat *(Rob and Catherine Dunster, George Atkinson, BB, JJW, CMW)*

RUSHDEN [SP9566]

Station Bar NN10 0AW [Station Approach]: Not a pub, part of station HQ of Rushden Historical Transport Society (non-members can sign in), restored in 1940s/60s style, with Fullers, Oakham and guests, tea and coffee, friendly staff, filled rolls (perhaps some hot dishes), gas lighting, enamel signs, old-fangled furnishings; authentic waiting room with piano, also museum and summer steam-ups; open all day Sat, cl wkdy lunchtimes *(the Didler)*

SIBBERTOFT [SP6782]

☆ *Red Lion* LE16 9UD [Village signposted off A4303 or A508 SW of Market Harborough; Welland Rise]: Simple village inn with friendly licensees, unpretentious bar with suede dining chairs around modern pine tables, leatherette wall banquettes, pastel-painted half-panelling, big gilt mirror over fireplace, ales from Black Sheep, Timothy Taylors and Wells & Youngs, over 200 wines (20 or so by the glass), food can be good, back dining room with contemporary high-backed chairs around light wood tables, woodburner; children welcome, big garden with covered terrace, self-catering studio flats, cl Sun evening, Mon, Tues lunchtime *(Gerry and Rosemary Dobson, Rob and Catherine Dunster, LYM)*

SLIPTON [SP9579]

☆ *Samuel Pepys* NN14 3AR [off A6116 at first roundabout N of A14 junction, towards Twywell and Slipton]: Smartly reworked old stone pub under new licensees, long gently modern bar with heavy low beams and log fire, great central pillar, area with squashy leather seats around low tables, up to five ales, some tapped from the cask, interesting reasonably priced wines, enjoyable food from sandwiches up, friendly service, dining room extending into roomy conservatory with country views; piped music; children welcome, dogs in bar, wheelchair access, well laid-out sheltered garden inc heated terrace, open all day wknds *(Michael and Jenny Back, Dr and Mrs Michael Smith, LYM)*

STOKE BRUERNE [SP7449]

Boat NN12 7SB [3.5 miles from M1 junction 15 – A508 towards Stony Stratford then signed on right; Bridge Rd]: Old-world flagstoned bar in picturesque canalside spot by beautifully restored lock (plus more modern central-pillared back bar and bistro without the views), Marstons and related ales, usual food from baguettes up, attentive service, extension with all-day tearooms and comfortable upstairs restaurant; piped music, can get busy in summer especially wknds; welcomes dogs and children (local school in for lunch from 12), disabled facilities, tables out by towpath opp British Waterways Museum and shop, boat trips, bar open all day summer Sats *(George Atkinson, Brian and Anna Marsden, Gerry and Rosemary Dobson, LYM)*

Navigation NN12 7SD: Large canalside Marstons pub, several levels and cosy corners, sturdy wood furniture, good Jennings Sneck Lifter and Wychwood Hobgoblin, quite a few wines by the glass, wide choice of good well priced pubby food, busy young staff, separate family room, pub games; piped music (outside too); plenty of tables out overlooking water, big play area, open all day *(Brian and Anna Marsden, John Cook, Rob and Catherine Dunster)*

SUDBOROUGH [SP9682]

Vane Arms NN14 3BX [off A6116; Main St]: Traditional thatched village pub doing well under new landlord, low beams, stripped stonework, cosy plush lounge, inglenook fires, enjoyable fairly priced food, well kept Everards and guests, friendly staff, upstairs restaurant, skittles; bedrooms in purpose-built block, pretty village, may be cl Mon *(Ian Phillips, LYM)*

THORNBY [SP6675]

Red Lion NN6 8SJ [Welford Rd; A5199 Northampton—Leicester]: Friendly old country pub with half a dozen well kept ales inc Greene King IPA and various microbrews, good well priced food (not Sun evenings, Mon lunchtime), front bar, log fire, beamed dining area; children and dogs welcome, open all day wknds when can be busy *(Andrew O Brien, Gerry and Rosemary Dobson, LYM)*

THORPE MANDEVILLE [SP5344]

☆ *Three Conies* OX17 2EX [off B4525 E of Banbury]: Attractive welcoming 17th-c pub with wide choice of food from good value sandwiches up, Weds curry night, well kept Hook Norton ales inc a bargain beer brewed for the pub (even cheaper Fri afternoon), beamed bare-boards bar with some stripped stone, mix of old dining tables, three good log fires, large dining room; piped music; children and dogs welcome, disabled facilities, tables out in front and behind on decking and lawn, open all day *(LYM, Nigel and Sue Foster, Richard and Audrey Chase)*

THORPE WATERVILLE [TL0281]

Fox NN14 3ED [A605 Thrapston—Oundle]: Extended and redecorated stone-built pub, emphasis on chef/landlord's enjoyable food inc Sun roasts, well kept Wells & Youngs ales from central bar, several wines by the glass, nice fire, light modern dining area; piped music; children welcome, small garden with play area, open all day *(Grahame Sherwin, George Atkinson)*

TITCHMARSH [TL0279]

Wheatsheaf NN14 3DH [signed from A14 and A605, just E of Thrapston; North St]: Smartly refurbished village pub popular for its good generous food inc local steaks, relaxed friendly atmosphere, well kept real ales, lots of stripped stone, open fires, restaurant, darts and skittles; garden *(LYM, Iain Akhurst, Howard and Margaret Buchanan)*

TOWCESTER [SP6948]

Saracens Head NN12 6BX [Watling St W]: Substantially modernised coaching inn with interesting *Pickwick Papers* connections (especially in the kitchen Dickens described, now a meeting room), open fire in long comfortable three-level lounge with dining area, Greene King ales, good choice of pub food inc bargain deals, neat staff, games bar; piped music, TV; children welcome, small back courtyard with smokers' shelter, 21 well equipped bedrooms, good breakfast, open from 7am *(LYM, Dr and Mrs Michael Smith, George Atkinson, Derek and Sylvia Stephenson, Alan and Eve Harding)*

TURWESTON [SP6037]

Stratton Arms NN13 5JX [pub itself just inside Bucks]: Friendly chatty village local, five well kept ales, good choice of other drinks, reasonably priced food (not Sun evening or Mon), low ceilings, log fires; TV, games machine; children and dogs welcome, good-sized garden by Great Ouse, barbecues and play area *(Michael Tack)*

WALGRAVE [SP8072]

Royal Oak NN6 9PN [Zion Hill, off A43 Northampton—Kettering]: Welcoming old stone-built local, up to five well kept changing ales, decent wines, wide choice of enjoyable good value food (not Sun evening) inc some unusual dishes and lunchtime deals, friendly efficient service, long three-part carpeted beamed bar, small lounge, restaurant extension behind; children

welcome, small garden, play area, open all day Sun *(Gerry and Sharon Dobson, J V Dadswell, Barry Collett)*

WEEDON [SP6359]

Crossroads NN7 4PX [3 miles from M1 junction 16; A45 towards Daventry; High St, on A5 junction]: Refurbished spacious Chef & Brewer with beamed bar and dining area, lots of nooks and crannies, log fires, friendly attentive staff, beers such as Lees and Wells & Youngs, decent all-day food inc set deals, good coffee; piped music; children welcome, disabled facilities, tables on terrace and in attractive gardens down to river (no food outside), comfortable Premier Lodge bedroom block, open all day *(George Atkinson, LYM)*

WELFORD [SP6480]

Wharf Inn NN6 6JQ [pub just over Leics border]: Castellated Georgian folly in delightful setting by two Grand Union Canal marinas, Banks's, Marstons Pedigree and three changing guest beers in cheery unpretentious bar, enjoyable good value straightforward food inc daily specials, pleasant dining section, good service; children welcome, big waterside garden *(Gerry and Rosemary Dobson)*

WELLINGBOROUGH [SP9069]

Locomotive NN8 4AL [Finedon Rd (A5128)]: Traditional two-bar local with up to six interesting changing ales, nice lunchtime baguettes, friendly landlord and regulars, lots of train memorabilia inc toy locomotive running above bar, log fire, daily papers, piano, games room with pool, darts, pin table and hood skittles; may be quiet piped music; dogs welcome, picnic-sets in small front garden, open all day (Sun afternoon break) *(the Didler, Ian and Helen Stafford)*

WELTON [SP5866]

☆ *White Horse* NN11 2JP [off A361/B4036 N of Daventry; behind church, High St]: Neat simple beamed village pub on different levels, decent reasonably priced food, Adnams and interesting guests, nice house wines, cheerful attentive staff, big open fire, separate games bar with darts and skittles, small dining room; children and dogs welcome attractively lit garden with terrace, barbecue and play area *(Andy Fell)*

YARDLEY HASTINGS [SP8656]

☆ *Red Lion* NN7 1ER [High St, just off A428 Bedford—Northampton]: Pretty thatched pub, friendly and relaxed, with good choice of enjoyable seasonal food (not Sun evening, Mon), well kept Wells & Youngs and one or two guest beers, nice wines, good range of soft drinks, prompt cheerful service, linked rooms with beams and stripped stone, lots of pictures, old photographs, plates and interesting brass/copper, small annexe with hood skittles; quiet piped music, games machine, TV; children and dogs welcome, nicely planted sloping garden, cl Mon lunchtime, open all day wknds *(Bruce and Sharon Eden, Jeremy King, Gerry and Rosemary Dobson, JJW, CMW, Mike and*

Margaret Banks, Jim Lyon, BB, George Atkinson)
Rose & Crown NN7 1EX [just off A428
Bedford—Northampton]: Spacious recently
reopened 18th-c pub in pretty village,
flagstones, beams, stripped stonework and
quiet corners, step up to big comfortable
family dining room, flowers on tables, wide
choice of enjoyable if pricey food inc
popular Sun lunch, five real ales, decent
range of wines and soft drinks, newspapers;
piped music; dogs welcome, picnic-sets in
small courtyard and good-sized garden, open
from 5pm Mon-Thurs, all day Fri and Sat,
cl Sun evening *(JJW, CMW)*

'Children welcome' means the pub says it lets children inside without any special
restriction. If it allows them in, but to restricted areas such as an eating area or family
room, we specify this. Some pubs may impose an evening time limit. We do not
mention limits after 9pm as we assume children are home by then.

Northumbria
(County Durham, Northumberland and Tyneside)

Real ales play a strong part in pubs here and half our Main Entries hold one of our Beer Awards. Local breweries to watch out for are Allendale, Big Lamp, Hadrian & Border, Hexhamshire, High House Farm, Jarrow, Mordue, Northumberland and Wylam, with Cumbrian ones like Cumberland, Derwent and Geltsdale, and from Durham, Consett Ale Works, Durham and Hill Island. Pubs doing particularly well this year are the Barrasford Arms at Barrasford (interesting food cooked by the landlord), the Errington Arms in Corbridge (a well run place near Hadrian's Wall), the Victoria in Durham (an unspoilt Victorian tavern and great for a drink), the Morritt Arms at Greta Bridge (a super pubby bar in a smart hotel), the Feathers at Hedley on the Hill (very carefully sourced and imaginative food), the Rose & Crown at Romaldkirk (a popular all-rounder), Battlesteads at Wark (five local beers and nice to stay at) and the Anglers Arms in Weldon Bridge (another sizeable hotel with a bustling bar and friendly welcome). A couple of new entries are the County at Aycliffe (smart contemporary décor, interesting food and new bedrooms) and the Coach at Lesbury (an enjoyable inn with friendly staff, a modern makeover and good food and drink). Making use of wonderful fresh fish and seafood, local game and fine lamb and beef, our Northumbria Dining Pub 2011 is the Feathers at Hedley on the Hill.

ANICK
NY9565   MAP 10

Rat 🍺

Village signposted NE of A69/A695 Hexham junction; NE46 4LN

Views over North Tyne Valley from terrace and garden, refurbished bar and lounge, lots of interesting knick-knacks, half a dozen mainly local real ales and interesting bar food

The hard-working and enthusiastic licensees in this relaxed country pub have been making some careful changes this year. They've redecorated both the bar (which now has new seating) and lounge, added new windows to the conservatory (which has pleasant valley views) and invested heavily in the charming garden – though it still has a dovecote and statues, pretty flower beds and seats on the terrace overlooking the North Tyne Valley. The character throughout has not changed and the cosy, traditional bar has a coal fire in the blackened kitchen range, lots of cottagey knick-knacks from antique floral chamber-pots hanging from the beams to china and glassware on a delft shelf and little curtained windows that allow a soft and gentle light; piped music, daily papers and magazines. The half a dozen changing and well kept real ales on handpump are mainly local: Allendale Best Bitter, Bass, Cumberland Corby Ale, Geltsdale Cold Fell, High House Farm Auld Hemp and Wylam Gold Tankard. They also keep ten wines (including champagne) by the glass, a local gin and farm cider. Parking is limited, but you can also park around the village green.

🍴 Using carefully sourced local meat, game birds and rabbit and seasonal local vegetables and fruit (and they hope to start their own kitchen garden), the good, interesting bar food includes sandwiches, soup, game terrine with fig chutney, pear, celery, pine nuts and blue cheese salad, sausages with leek potato cake and onion gravy, pan haggerty of parsnips and mushrooms topped with cheese, very popular roast rib of beef with béarnaise sauce (for two people and best ordered in advance), coley with creamed samphire, lemon and capers, and puddings like seasonal fruit crumble with vanilla custard and apple and ginger sponge with jersey cream ice-cream; Sunday roasts (must book in advance). *Starters/Snacks: £3.95 to £7.95. Main Courses: £9.50 to £21.00. Puddings: £4.95*

Free house ~ Licensees Phil Mason and Karen Errington ~ Real ale ~ Bar food (12-2(3 Sun), 6-9; not Sun evening or Mon (except bank hols 12-6; summer Mon lunchtime sandwiches)) ~ Restaurant ~ (01434) 602814 ~ Children welcome ~ Open 12-11 (12-3, 6-11 Mon and winter Tues-Fri); 12-10.30 Sun

Recommended by Chris Clark, W K Wood, GNI, Eric Larkham, Pat and Stewart Gordon, Comus and Sarah Elliott, Michael Doswell

AYCLIFFE   NZ2822   MAP 10

County 🍽 🍷 🍺

Off A1(M) junction 59, by A167; DL5 6LX

Friendly, well run pub with contemporary décor in several rooms, four real ales, good wines and popular, interesting food; new bedrooms

Overlooking the pretty village green, this is a popular pub with genuinely friendly staff, enjoyable food and several real ales. It's more or less open-plan throughout with bold paintwork (blue, green and yellow), lots of modern art and careful lighting. The wooden-floored bar has attractive solid pine dining chairs and cushioned settles around a mix of pine tables, some high bar chairs by the counter, Black Sheep Best, Theakstons Best and a couple of guest beers on handpump and several wines by the glass. The carpeted lounge has a woodburning stove in a brick fireplace with candles in brass candlesticks on either side, a second fireplace with nightlights, similar furniture to the bar and painted ceiling joists. The wooden-floored restaurant is minimalist with high-backed black leather dining chairs and dark window blinds. You can sit outside at a few tables or on the green. They've recently opened bedrooms and we'd love to hear from readers who've stayed here.

🍴 Good, interesting bar food includes sandwiches, soup, duck and green peppercorn terrine with tomato chutney, breaded goats cheese with chive risotto, beer-battered cod with mushy peas, suprême of chicken wrapped in bacon with a rich forestière sauce, steak and kidney pie, red snapper on shrimp mash with lemon and caper butter, duck breast with celeriac purée and blood orange jus, and puddings like dark chocolate tart with white chocolate ice-cream and warm treacle and stem ginger tart with golden syrup and Cointreau ice-cream. *Starters/Snacks: £4.25 to £6.95. Main Courses: £8.95 to £21.95. Puddings: £3.50 to £5.00*

Free house ~ Licensee Colette Farrell ~ Real ale ~ Bar food (12-2(2.30 Sun), 6-9) ~ Restaurant ~ (01325) 312273 ~ Children welcome ~ Open 11.45-3(4 Sun), 5.45-midnight; 11.45-midnight Sun ~ Bedrooms: £49S/£69S(£89B)

Recommended by Michael Butler, Mary Goodfellow, MJVK, Alan Thwaite, S Bloomfield

---

We checked prices with the pubs as we went to press in summer 2010.
They should hold until around spring 2011.

BARRASFORD   NY9173 MAP 10

Barrasford Arms

Village signposted off A6079 N of Hexham; NE48 4AA

Friendly proper pub with good country cooking, real ales, a bustling bar and plenty of nearby walks; bedrooms

Mr Binks's food is as deft as ever and our readers thoroughly enjoy their meals in this bustling sandstone inn. But the traditional bar plays a big part here too and has a genuinely local atmosphere as well as a good log fire, old local photographs and some country bric-a-brac from horsebrasses to antlers. Cumberland Corby Ale, Hadrian & Border Gladiator and Wylam Golden Tankard on handpump and good value wines by the glass. One nice dining room, carefully decorated in greys and creams and dominated by a great stone chimneybreast hung with guns and copper pans, has wheelback chairs around half a dozen neat tables; a second, perhaps rather more restrained, has more comfortably upholstered dining chairs; piped music, TV. They have well equipped bunkhouse accommodation as well as 11 proper bedrooms. The pub is on the edge of a small North Tyne village quite close to Hadrian's Wall, with lovely valley views and looks across to impressive medieval Haughton Castle (not open to the public); there may be sheep in the pasture just behind.

🍴 Cooked by the landlord and his team using carefully sourced local meats, game and fish, the enjoyable food includes sandwiches, soup, crispy corn-fed duck, potato and watercress salad with a sweet and sour sauce, chicken liver pâté with pear chutney, roast butternut squash and sage risotto, pot-roasted chicken with a leek, parsley and mushroom broth, slow-cooked lamb shank with rosemary and garlic, escalope of organic salmon with pasta and a dill fish cream, and puddings like warm bitter chocolate tart with white chocolate ice-cream and chocolate sauce and vanilla crème brûlée with a shortbread biscuit; good cheeses and popular Sunday roasts. *Starters/Snacks: £4.50 to £6.00. Main Courses: £8.00 to £14.50. Puddings: £4.50 to £5.00*

Free house ~ Licensee Tony Binks ~ Real ale ~ Bar food (12-2(3 Sun), 7-9) ~ Restaurant ~ (01434) 681237 ~ Children welcome ~ Open 12-2.30, 6-midnight; 12-1am Sat; 12-11.30 Sun; closed Mon lunchtime ~ Bedrooms: £65B/£85B

Recommended by Peter Logan, Bruce and Sharon Eden, W K Wood

BLANCHLAND   NY9650 MAP 10

Lord Crewe Arms 🛏

B6306 S of Hexham; DH8 9SP

Ancient, historic building with some unusual features, real ales, straightforward bar food and a more elaborate restaurant menu; bedrooms

A new licensee has taken over this comfortable hotel set high up on the moors. The most informal part is the ancient-feeling bar that is housed in an unusual long and narrow, stone barrel-vaulted crypt, its curving walls being up to eight feet thick in some places. Plush stools are lined along the bar counter on ancient flagstones and next to a narrow drinks' shelf down the opposite wall, and they keep Black Sheep Best, Theakstons Best and a guest from Hadrian & Border on handpump and several wines by the glass; flatscreen TV. Upstairs, the Derwent Room has low beams, old settles and sepia photographs on its walls and the Hilyard Room has a massive 13th-c fireplace once used as a hiding place by the Jacobite Tom Forster (part of the family who had owned the building before it was sold in 1704 to the formidable Lord Crewe, Bishop of Durham). Built by the Premonstratensians around 1235 as the abbot's lodging for their adjacent monastery, the building is immersed in history, with a lovely walled garden that was formerly the cloisters. It's a most appealing place to stay.

Unlike other guides, entry in this *Guide* is free. All our entries depend solely on merit.

🍴 Bar food includes sandwiches, ploughman's, soup, salads such as ham hock and egg and chicken caesar, potted crab and shrimp toast, sausage and black pudding fritters, spinach and ricotta filo bake, burgers, cumberland sausages, battered fish and chips, lasagne, and puddings like custard tart and chocolate brownie; the restaurant menu is more elaborate. *Starters/Snacks: £3.50 to £6.65. Main Courses: £7.50 to £17.00. Puddings: £4.50*

Free house ~ Licensee Neil Brown ~ Real ale ~ Bar food (all day) ~ Restaurant ~ (01434) 675251 ~ Children welcome ~ Dogs welcome ~ Open 11-11; 12-10.30 Sun ~ Bedrooms: £50B/£90B

Recommended by Dr A McCormick, Comus and Sarah Elliott

CARTERWAY HEADS   NZ0452   MAP 10

Manor House Inn 🍺

A68 just N of B6278, near Derwent Reservoir; DH8 9LX

Handy after a walk, with simple bar and more comfortable lounge, bar food and five real ales; bedrooms

This slate-roofed and simple stone inn is a useful place if you've been walking around the nearby Derwent Valley and Reservoir. The straightforward locals' bar has an original boarded ceiling, pine tables, chairs and stools, old oak pews and a mahogany counter. The comfortable lounge bar (warmed by a woodburning stove) and restaurant both have picture windows that make the most of the lovely setting. Copper Dragon Golden Pippin, Greene King Old Speckled Hen and Ruddles County, Timothy Taylors Landlord and a guest beer on handpump and around 70 malt whiskies; TV, darts, board games and piped music. There are rustic tables in the garden. More reports please.

🍴 Usefully served all day, the bar food includes sandwiches and wraps, soup, chicken liver pâté with onion marmalade, pasta of the day, chicken caesar salad, free-range omelette, cumberland sausage with onion gravy, beer-battered haddock with pea purée, vegetarian crêpe, slow-roasted pork belly on creamed bacon and cabbage with a rich jus and steaks. *Starters/Snacks: £3.00 to £7.95. Main Courses: £7.95 to £13.95. Puddings: £3.95 to £4.95*

Free house ~ Licensees Neil and Emma Oxley ~ Real ale ~ Bar food (all day) ~ Restaurant ~ (01207) 255268 ~ Children welcome ~ Dogs allowed in bar and bedrooms ~ Open 11-11; 12-10.30 Sun ~ Bedrooms: £45S/£65S

Recommended by Comus and Sarah Elliott, Mr and Mrs Barrie, Eric Larkham, Michael Doswell

CORBRIDGE   NY9964   MAP 10

Angel 🍺 🛏

Main Street; NE45 5LA

Enterprising food and a fine drinks' range in crisply modernised coaching inn; comfortable bedrooms

There's a fine choice of real ales in this imposing white coaching inn and some interesting food, too. The sizeable main bar is functional in a briskly modern style – light and airy with just a few prints on its pastel walls, plain light wood tables and chairs, overhead spotlighting and a big-screen TV. The carpeted lounge bar has quite a modern feel, too, with its strongly patterned wallpaper and some tall metal-framed café-bar seats as well as its more homely leather bucket armchairs. The best sense of the building's age is in a separate lounge, with button-back wing armchairs, sofa, oak panelling and big stone fireplace; and look out for the fine 17th-c arched doorway in the left-hand porch. A smart raftered restaurant has local artwork and some stripped masonry; piped music. Hadrian & Border Centurion Best and Tyneside Blonde, Mordue IPA and Workie Ticket, Timothy Taylors Landlord and Wylam Gold Tankard on handpump, a dozen wines by the glass, 30 malt whiskies and Weston's cider; daily papers. You can sit out in front on the cobbles below a wall sundial; the building is nicely set at the end of a broad street, facing the handsome bridge over the River Tyne.

🏠 Well liked bar food includes sandwiches, soup, scallops on black pudding and chorizo, seared pigeon breast with a rocket and raspberry salad with raspberry coulis and pepper dressing, mushroom and pea risotto, lambs liver with bacon and champ, battered cod and chips with mushy peas, venison burger with honey and five spice, roast duck breast on asian salad, and puddings such as warm gooseberry cake and white chocolate and ginger cheesecake with chantilly cream. *Starters/Snacks: £4.50 to £7.95. Main Courses: £9.95 to £17.95. Puddings: £5.50*

Free house ~ Licensee John Gibson ~ Real ale ~ (01434) 632119 ~ Children welcome ~ Open 11-11(midnight Sat); 12-10.30 Sun ~ Bedrooms: £70S/£105B

Recommended by Andy and Jill Kassube, Michael Doswell, Eric Larkham, Mike and Lynn Robinson, Pete Coxon, Sue Milliken

Errington Arms
About 3 miles N of town; B6318, on A68 roundabout; NE45 5QB

Relaxed and friendly 18th-c stone-built inn with enjoyable food and local beer

Our readers really enjoy their visits to this 18th-c roadside inn and you are sure of a warm welcome from the friendly, helpful staff. There's a good mix of walkers and diners and its location right beside Hadrian's Wall ensures that there are always plenty of customers. The bars have exposed oak beams, a nice mix of candlelit tables on the light wooden floor, some pine planking and stripped stonework, burgundy paintwork, ornamental plaques, a large heavy mirror and a log fire; there's a modicum of bric-a-brac, on window sills and so forth. Cumberland Corby Ale and Wylam Northern Kite on handpump and several wines by the glass; piped music. Out on the front terrace are some sturdy metal and teak tables under canvas parasols.

🏠 Nicely presented, popular bar food includes sandwiches, soup, chicken liver parfait, smoked haddock gratin, crispy king prawns with garlic butter and parmesan, thai vegetable curry, lambs liver with bacon and cabbage, 'pig on a plate' (pork belly, pork loin, black pudding and sausage in cider) and grilled lemon sole with caramelised apples and fennel with a tarragon cream sauce; they also offer a good value two-course set meal (Tuesdays-Thursdays). *Starters/Snacks: £3.50 to £7.95. Main Courses: £7.95 to £14.95. Puddings: £2.95 to £4.50*

Punch ~ Lease Nicholas Shotton ~ Real ale ~ Bar food (11-3(4 Sun), 6-9; not Sun evening or Mon) ~ (01434) 672250 ~ Children welcome ~ Dogs allowed in bedrooms ~ Swing night monthly on various Thurs ~ Open 11-3, 6-11; 12-4 Sun; closed Sun evening, Mon ~ Bedrooms: £35S/£70S

Recommended by Alan Thwaite, GSB, David and Sue Smith, Comus and Sarah Elliott, David and Katharine Cooke, Andy and Jill Kassube, Mike and Lynn Robinson

COTHERSTONE
NZ0119   MAP 10

Fox & Hounds 🛏
B6277 – incidentally a good quiet route to Scotland, through interesting scenery; DL12 9PF

Bustling 18th-c inn with cheerful beamed bar, homely bar food and quite a few wines by the glass; bedrooms

This is a popular place to stay and makes an excellent focal point to routes along the dramatic wooded Tees Valley from Barnard Castle. It's a bustling country inn with a simple but cheery beamed bar which has a partly wooden floor (elsewhere it's carpeted), a good winter log fire, thickly cushioned wall seats and local photographs and country pictures on the walls in its various alcoves and recesses. Black Sheep Best and a guest such as York Guzzler on handpump alongside several malt whiskies from smaller distilleries; efficient service from the friendly staff. Don't be surprised by the unusual lavatory attendant – an african grey parrot called Reva. Seats outside on a terrace and quoits.

There are report forms at the back of the book.

🍴 Well liked bar food includes sandwiches, soup, creamy garlic mushrooms, beer-battered haddock with minted mushy peas, french-style vegetable stew with a cheese crust, black pudding and steak in ale pie, pheasant in rich gravy, salmon fillet with a lemon and chive hollandaise, chicken filled with cheese, wrapped in bacon with a creamy leek sauce, and puddings like sticky toffee pudding and lemon meringue ice-cream sundae. *Starters/Snacks: £4.30 to £6.50. Main Courses: £8.00 to £9.20. Puddings: £4.50*

Free house ~ Licensees Nichola and Ian Swinburn ~ Real ale ~ Bar food ~ Restaurant ~ (01833) 650241 ~ Children welcome if dining ~ Dogs allowed in bedrooms ~ Open 12-3, 6-11(10.30 Sun); closed 25 and 26 Dec ~ Bedrooms: £47.50B/£75B

Recommended by Mike Wignall, Vicky Sherwood, R Hayworth, GNI, Guy Morgan, Chris and Jo Parsons, Ian Herdman, S G N Bennett, Jerry Brown, John Urquhart

DIPTONMILL
NY9261   MAP 10

Dipton Mill Inn 🍷 🍺 £

Just S of Hexham; off B6306 at Slaley, Blanchland and Dye House, Whitley Chapel signposts (and HGV route sign); not to be confused with the Dipton in Durham; NE46 1YA

Own-brew beers, good value bar food and a garden with terrace and aviary

Tucked away in a little hamlet by steep hills in a peaceful wooded valley, this little two-roomed pub is not easy to find, but it's worth making the effort if you like real ale. All five of the own-brews from the family-owned Hexhamshire Brewery are well kept here on handpump: Devils Elbow, Devils Water, Old Humbug, Shire Bitter and Whapweasel; also a dozen wines by the glass, over 20 malt whiskies and Weston's Old Rosie cider. The neatly kept snug bar has dark ply panelling, low ceilings, red furnishings, a dark red carpet and newspapers to read by two welcoming open fires. In fine weather it's pleasant to sit out on the sunken crazy-paved terrace by the restored mill stream, or in the attractively planted garden with its aviary. There's a nice walk through the woods along the little valley and Hexham racecourse is not far away.

🍴 Good value, homely bar food includes sandwiches, ploughman's, soup, vegetable casserole, popular mince and dumplings, chicken in sherry sauce, steak and kidney pie, lambs liver and sausage, salmon salad, and puddings like syrup sponge and custard and chocolate rum truffle torte. *Starters/Snacks: £2.50 to £3.75. Main Courses: £7.00 to £8.00. Puddings: £2.25 to £3.00*

Own brew ~ Licensee Geoff Brooker ~ Real ale ~ Bar food (12-2, 6.30-8.30; not Sun evening) ~ No credit cards ~ (01434) 606577 ~ Children welcome ~ Open 12-2.30, 6-11; 12-3 Sun; closed Sun evening

Recommended by the Didler, Eric Larkham, Mike and Lynn Robinson

DURHAM
NZ2742   MAP 10

Victoria 🍺

Hallgarth Street (A177, near Dunelm House); DH1 3AS

Unchanging and neatly kept Victorian pub with royal memorabilia, cheerful locals and well kept regional ales; bedrooms

'If only all the city and town pubs were like this' says one reader wistfully, after his visit to this 19th-c tavern. There's a good mix of locals and students and the unspoilt and unchanging layout consists of three little rooms leading off a central bar with typical Victorian décor: mahogany, etched and cut glass and mirrors, colourful William Morris wallpaper over a high panelled dado, some maroon plush seats in little booths, leatherette wall seats and long narrow drinkers' tables. There are also some handsome iron and tile fireplaces for the coal fires, a piano, photographs and articles showing a very proper pride in the pub, lots of period prints and engravings of Queen Victoria and staffordshire figurines of her and the Prince Consort. Consett Ale Works Red Dust, Big Lamp Bitter, Durham Definitive, Hill Island Juniper and Wylam Gold

Tankard on handpump, over 40 irish whiskies and cheap house wines; dominoes.
🍴 **No food.**

Free house ~ Licensee Michael Webster ~ Real ale ~ No credit cards ~ (0191) 386 5269 ~ Children welcome ~ Dogs welcome ~ Open 11.45-3, 6-11; 12-2, 7-10.30 Sun ~ Bedrooms: £48B/£65B

Recommended by Jeff Edwards, Mark Walker, Stephen Locke, Chris Sale, the Didler, J A Ellis, Comus and Sarah Elliott, Eric Larkham, Mike and Lynn Robinson

GREAT WHITTINGTON

NZ0070   MAP 10

Queens Head 🍺

Village signposted off A68 and B6018 just N of Corbridge; NE19 2HP

Relaxed and civilised inn with log fires and outside seating

This is a handsome old golden-stone pub with picnic-sets under parasols on the little front lawn. Inside, there's a mix of stripped stone and grey/green paintwork, soft lighting and dark leather chairs around sturdy tables, one or two good pictures and a large clock; Caledonian Deuchars IPA, Hadrian & Border Tyneside Blonde and Jennings Tom Fool on handpump, several wines by the glass and quite a few malt whiskies. There's a rather nice hunting mural above the old fireplace in the long narrow bar with high stools on bare boards by the counter and along the opposite wall. The emphasis tends to be on the laid dining areas with their modern furnishings on bright tartan carpeting.

🍴 Under the new licensee, bar food includes lunchtime sandwiches, soup, tempura prawns, salmon and dill fishcakes, duck leg spring rolls, liver and bacon with onion gravy, vegetable lasagne, gammon and egg, beer-battered fish, rack of lamb with a spiced aubergine, tomato and basil sauce, and puddings such as banoffi pie and passion-fruit cheesecake. *Starters/Snacks: £4.25 to £6.50. Main Courses: £8.50 to £16.95. Puddings: £4.95*

Free house ~ Licensee Claire Murray ~ Real ale ~ Bar food (12-2.30, 6-9; 12-9.30 Fri, Sat; 12-6 Sun) ~ Restaurant ~ (01434) 672267 ~ Children welcome ~ Dogs allowed in bar ~ Open 12-3, 5.30-11; 12-midnight(11 Sun) Sat

Recommended by GSB, Michael Doswell, Jenny and Dave Hughes

GRETA BRIDGE

NZ0813   MAP 10

Morritt Arms 🍽 🍷 🛏

Hotel signposted off A66 W of Scotch Corner; DL12 9SE

Country house hotel with nice pubby bar, extraordinary mural, interesting food and an attractive garden with play area; nice bedrooms

Although much emphasis is placed on the thriving hotel side in this striking 17th-c former coaching inn, they manage to keep a friendly, pubby bar at its heart. Big windsor armchairs and sturdy oak settles cluster around traditional cast-iron-framed tables, large windows look out on the extensive lawn and there are warm open fires. Around the bar runs a remarkable mural painted in 1946 by J T Y Gilroy – better known for his old Guinness advertisements – of Dickensian characters. Black Sheep Best and Timothy Taylors Landlord on handpump and 17 wines by the glass from an extensive list; knowledgeable, helpful staff. The attractively laid-out garden has some seats with teak tables in a pretty side area looking along to the graceful old bridge by the stately gates to Rokeby Park; there's also a play area for children.

People named as recommenders after the Main Entries have told us that the pub should be included. But they have not written the report – we have, after anonymous on-the-spot inspection.

⊞ Good modern bar food includes sandwiches, soup, pressed ham and parsley terrine with home-made pease pudding and cumberland sauce, sunblush tomato risotto with goats cheese, pesto and spring onion salad, free-range chicken suprême with pepper sauce, seared bass fillet with a dill beurre blanc, daily specials like sausages with leek mash and onion gravy and beef stroganoff with mushrooms and a creamy brandy sauce, and puddings such as iced sticky toffee terrine with butterscotch sauce and a deep-fried wonton and baked chocolate and orange cheesecake with marmalade ice-cream and orange crisp. *Starters/Snacks: £4.50 to £7.00. Main Courses: £12.00 to £22.00. Puddings: £6.00 to £7.00*

Free house ~ Licensees Peter Phillips and Barbara Johnson ~ Real ale ~ Bar food (12-3, 6-9.30 (afternoon teas 3-6)) ~ Restaurant ~ (01833) 627232 ~ Children welcome ~ Dogs allowed in bar and bedrooms ~ Open 11-11(10.30 Sun) ~ Bedrooms: £80S(£85B)/£100S(£110B)

Recommended by S G N Bennett, Maurice Ricketts, Comus and Sarah Elliott, Jerry Brown, Barry Collett, Pat and Stewart Gordon

HALTWHISTLE
NY7166   MAP 10
Milecastle Inn
Military Road; B6318 NE – OS Sheet 86 map reference 715660; NE49 9NN

Close to Hadrian's Wall and some wild scenery, with cosy little rooms warmed by winter log fires; fine views and a walled garden

Handy for some of the most celebrated sites of Hadrian's Wall and liked by walkers, this is a useful place and open all day. The snug little rooms of the beamed bar are decorated with brasses, horsey and local landscape prints and attractive fresh flowers, and have two winter log fires; at lunchtime the small comfortable restaurant is used as an overflow. Big Lamp Prince Bishop and a couple of guests on handpump and several malt whiskies. There are tables and benches in the pleasantly sheltered big walled garden with a dovecote and rather stunning views; two self-catering cottages and a large car park. More reports please.

⊞ Straightforward bar food includes sandwiches, soup, deep-fried breaded mushrooms with garlic mayonnaise, omelettes, battered fish, vegetable pasta bake, various pies, steaks, daily specials, and puddings. *Starters/Snacks: £3.75 to £6.95. Main Courses: £8.75 to £16.25. Puddings: £4.50*

Free house ~ Licensees Clare and Kevin Hind ~ Real ale ~ Bar food (12-8.45; 12-2.30, 6-8.30 in winter) ~ Restaurant ~ (01434) 321372 ~ Children welcome if eating ~ Open 12-11(10 Sun); 12-3, 6-10 in winter; closed Sun evenings Jan and Feb

Recommended by Bruce and Sharon Eden, Sheena W Makin, Maurice and Gill McMahon, Mr and Mrs John Taylor, Dr Kevan Tucker, Sylvia and Tony Birbeck

HAYDON BRIDGE
NY8364   MAP 10
General Havelock
A69 Corbridge—Haltwhistle; NE47 6ER

Bustling and chatty riverside dining pub with local beers and interesting food

Just a short and very pretty stroll downstream from Haydon Bridge itself, this old stone terrace house has fine South Tyne river views from both the terrace and stripped-stone barn dining room. The attractively lit L-shaped bar is imaginatively decorated in shades of green, and is at its best in the back part with a stripped pine chest of drawers topped with bric-a-brac, colourful cushions on long pine benches and a sturdy stripped settle, interestingly shaped mahogany-topped tables and good wildlife photographs. They stock a couple of local beers such as Geltsdale Cold Fell and High House Farm Nel's Best on handpump, ten wines by the glass and a choice of apple juices; board games and boules.

⊞ Cooked by the landlord (who makes his own bread and ice-cream) and using local produce, the well liked bar food includes lunchtime baguettes, soup, smoked haddock risotto with a poached egg, twice-baked stilton soufflé, beef and wild mushrooms in ale stew, corn-fed chicken with bacon, mushrooms and chicken livers on bubble and squeak, lamb shank in red wine and redcurrant jelly, a fish of the day, and puddings such as chocolate, rum and raisin crème brûlée and rhubarb compote with rhubarb ice-cream with a crumble topping; Sunday roasts. *Starters/Snacks: £4.00 to £5.75. Main Courses: £8.50 to £10.00. Puddings: £4.00 to £4.75*

Free house ~ Licensees Gary and Joanna Thompson ~ Real ale ~ Bar food (12-2(4 Sun), 7-9; not Sun evening or Mon) ~ Restaurant ~ (01434) 684376 ~ Children allowed in lounge area ~ Dogs allowed in bar ~ Open 12-3, 7-midnight; 12-5 Sun; closed Sun evening, Mon

Recommended by Chris Clark, Comus and Sarah Elliott, Bruce and Sharon Eden, James Thompson, Mrs L Wells, Andy and Jill Kassube, Helen and Brian Edgeley

HEDLEY ON THE HILL
NZ0759 MAP 10

Feathers

Village signposted from New Ridley, which is signposted from B6309 N of Consett; OS Sheet 88 map reference 078592; NE43 7SW

NORTHUMBRIA DINING PUB OF THE YEAR

Interesting beers from small breweries, imaginative food and a friendly welcome in this quaint tavern

You can be sure of a warm welcome from the friendly staff in this comfortable hilltop tavern. The three neat beamed bars have a proper pubby atmosphere, open fires, stripped stonework, solid furniture, including settles, and old black and white photographs of local places and farm and country workers. Four local ales such as Hadrian & Border Gladiator, Mordue Workie Ticket, Northumberland Pit Pony and Wylam Gold Tankard on handpump, farm ciders, 28 wines by the glass, 34 malt whiskies and several bourbons. They hold a beer and food festival at Easter with over two dozen real ales (and a barrel race on Easter Monday). Darts and dominoes. Picnic-sets in front are a nice place to sit and watch the world drift by.

Cooked by the landlord using home-butchered game from local shoots, beef from rare breeds and home-baked bread (and listing their carefully chosen suppliers on the daily changing menu), the imaginative food might include ploughman's, soup, a home-made charcuterie board with pickles, home-made black pudding with a poached free-range egg and devilled gravy, seared local rabbit loin with chickpeas and chorizo in a spicy tomato sauce, root vegetable casserole with blue cheese fritters, old spot pork with cabbage and bacon, real ale gravy and apple sauce, grilled red sea bream and bass with an anchovy and basil dressing, and puddings like sticky date pudding with butterscotch sauce and dark chocolate brownie with chocolate sauce and jersey cream ice-cream. *Starters/Snacks: £5.00 to £6.50. Main Courses: £7.00 to £12.00. Puddings: £4.00 to £5.00*

Free house ~ Licensees Rhian Cradock and Helen Greer ~ Real ale ~ Bar food (12-2(2.30 Sun), 6-8.30; not Sun evening or Mon lunchtime or first two weeks in Jan) ~ (01661) 843607 ~ Children welcome ~ Open 12-11(10.30 Sun); closed Mon lunchtime (opens 6pm) and all lunchtimes first two weeks in Jan

Recommended by Denis Newton, Andy and Jill Kassube, Mike and Lynn Robinson, David and Cathrine Whiting, Eric Larkham, James Thompson, John Coatsworth, Lawrence Pearse, Alan Thwaite, W K Wood

LESBURY
NU2311 MAP 10

Coach
B1339; NE66 3PP

Well run stone inn with enjoyable food and local ales, and attractively refurbished bars

At the heart of a pretty village and handy for Alnwick Castle Gardens, this atmospheric stone pub has been carefully refurbished. It manages to combine the pubby side with the very good food, and there's a warm welcome for all. The paintwork throughout is cream, sage green and soft grey and the bar has high, dark leather stools by the wooden counter, and a row of pubby tables and stools along one wall on the tartan carpet. Black Sheep Best and Mordue Workie Ticket on handpump; piped music and TV. Leading off to the left is a small area with comfortable sofas and armchairs around low tables and to the other side is a little dining room with high-backed cane and leather dining chairs around light wooden tables; yet another seating area has a woodburning stove in a small brick fireplace and tub-like wicker and leather chairs. The neat terrace has rustic furniture under parasols (there are more seats in front, too) and lovely flowering tubs and baskets among lavender beds.

🍴 Generous helpings of good-bar food include substantial sandwiches and wraps, soup, moules marinière, kipper pâté, omelettes, fresh pasta with roasted mediterranean vegetables and goats cheese, maple-glazed gammon on bubble and squeak topped with an egg, chicken curry, fresh salmon and broccoli fishcakes with home-made tartare sauce, beef and leek pudding, gressingham duck breast with mango and chilli sauce, and puddings such as lime mousse with raspberries and bread and butter pudding. *Starters/Snacks: £3.50 to £8.50. Main Courses: £8.60 to £16.40. Puddings: £5.25*

Punch ~ Tenant Susan Packard ~ Real ale ~ Bar food (12-8.30(7 Sun)) ~ Restaurant ~ (01665) 830865 ~ Children allowed but no small children after 7.30pm ~ Open 11-11; 12-10.30 Sun; closed Sun evening Oct-Mar

Recommended by Michael Doswell, P A Rowe, Dr Peter D Smart, Comus and Sarah Elliott

NEW YORK
NZ3269 MAP 10

Shiremoor Farm

Middle Engine Lane; at W end of New York A191 bypass, turn S into Norham Road, then first right (pub signed); NE29 8DZ

Large dining pub with interesting furnishings and décor, popular food all day, decent drinks and a covered, heated terrace

Even though this large dining pub is always incredibly busy, the efficient and friendly staff manage to stay on top of things. The building is a spacious transformation of derelict agricultural buildings, with the conical rafters of the former gin-gan showing in one area. Gentle lighting in several well divided, spacious areas cleverly picks up the surface modelling of the pale stone and beam ends. It's furnished with a mix of interesting and comfortable furniture, a big kilim on broad flagstones, warmly colourful farmhouse paintwork on the bar counter and several other tables, a few farm tools and evocative country pictures. Black Sheep Ale, Mordue Workie Ticket and Timothy Taylors Landlord on handpump, together with decent wines by the glass. There are seats outside on the covered, heated terrace.

🍴 The blackboard menus change constantly and as well as sandwiches, there might be soup, duck and port pâté with tomato chutney, baked tilapia with a parmesan crust, toasted pistachios and chilli jam, hot and spicy pork sausages with leek mash and onion gravy, stir-fried vietnamese king prawns, braised lamb shank with rosemary and redcurrant jelly, and puddings like black cherry and kirsch trifle and marshmallow and caramel chocolate tart; good Sunday roasts. *Starters/Snacks: £2.95 to £5.95. Main Courses: £6.95 to £11.95. Puddings: £3.50 to £4.95*

Free house ~ Licensee C W Kerridge ~ Real ale ~ Bar food (12-10) ~ (0191) 257 6302 ~ Children welcome ~ Open 11-11

Recommended by Mike and Lynn Robinson, Lawrence Pearse, Sheena W Makin, Michael Doswell

---

The letters and figures after the name of each town are its Ordnance Survey map reference. 'Using the *Guide*' at the beginning of the book explains how it helps you find a pub, in road atlases or on large-scale maps as well as on our own maps.

NEWBURN

Keelman ◖ £ ⇌

Grange Road: follow Riverside Country Park brown signs off A6085 (the riverside road off A1 on Newcastle's west fringes); NE15 8ND

Impressive range of own-brewed beers in a converted pumping station, easy-going atmosphere, excellent service and straightforward food; bedroom block

The big draw to this neatly kept and sizeable pub is the splendid array of beers from their own Big Lamp Brewery. The impressive row of eight handpumps usually dispenses the full range, obviously kept in tip-top condition and very reasonably priced. If you're confused about which one to go for, the neatly dressed staff will happily let you sample a couple first: Big Lamp Bitter, Blackout, Embers, Premium, Prince Bishop Ale, Summerhill Stout and Sunny Daze. There's a relaxed atmosphere and a good mix of customers in the high-ceilinged bar, which is light and airy with lofty arched windows and well spaced tables and chairs. There are more tables in an upper gallery and the modern all-glass conservatory dining area (pleasant at sunset) contrasts stylishly with the original old building; piped music. You'll find plenty of picnic-sets, tables and benches out on the spacious terraces, among flower tubs and beds of shrubs, and there's a good play area. Bedroom prices are for room only.

⑪ Reasonably priced, straightforward food includes sandwiches, soup, pâté with cumberland sauce, filled yorkshire puddings, spaghetti bolognese, brie, courgette and almond crumble, chicken, bacon and leeks with a rosemary and thyme dumpling, beef in ale pie, salmon fishcakes and mixed grill; Sunday roasts. *Starters/Snacks: £2.95 to £5.95. Main Courses: £5.95 to £11.75. Puddings: £3.40 to £3.95*

Own brew ~ Licensee George Story ~ Real ale ~ Bar food (12-9) ~ Restaurant ~ (0191) 267 0772 ~ Children welcome ~ Open 11-11; 12-10.30 Sun ~ Bedrooms: £44.50S/£59.50S

Recommended by Paul and Ursula Randall, Mike and Lynn Robinson, Gerry and Rosemary Dobson, Joe Green, David and Sue Smith, Mr and Mrs Barrie, Eric Larkham, GSB

NEWCASTLE UPON TYNE

Crown Posada ◖

The Side; off Dean Street, between and below the two high central bridges (A6125 and A6127); NE1 3JE

Busy city-centre pub with grand architecture, lots of locals in the long narrow bar, tip-top beers and a warm welcome

This is the city's oldest pub and has not changed for decades. It's architecturally fascinating and certainly worth a special visit to see the elaborate coffered ceiling, stained glass in the counter screens and the line of gilt mirrors each with a tulip lamp on a curly brass mount matching the great ceiling candelabra. It's a long narrow room, making quite a bottleneck by the serving counter where they keep Hadrian & Border Gladiator, Jarrow Bitter and guests like Cumberland Corby Ale, Durham Definitive and Wylam Golden Tankard on handpump. A long soft green built-in leather wall seat is flanked by narrow tables, thick low-level heating pipes make a popular footrest when the east wind brings the rain off the North Sea and an old record player in a wooden cabinet provides mellow background music when the place is quiet. During the week, regulars sit reading papers in the front snug, but at weekends it is often packed. It's only a few minutes' stroll to the castle.

⑪ Lunchtime sandwiches only.

Sir John Fitzgerald ~ Licensee Derek Raisbeck ~ Real ale ~ (0191) 232 1269 ~ Open 11-11; 12-midnight Sat; 7-10.30 Sun; closed Sun lunchtime

Recommended by Chris Sale, Joe Green, the Didler, Mike and Eleanor Anderson, Eric Larkham, James Thompson, Myke and Nicky Crombleholme, Mike and Lynn Robinson, Andy and Jill Kassube

NEWTON ON THE MOOR

NU1705 MAP 10

Cook & Barker Arms 🛏

Village signposted from A1 Alnwick—Felton; NE65 9JY

A nicely traditional country pub with a chatty bar, four real ales, an extensive wine list and well liked bar food; comfortable bedrooms

The bar in this neatly kept stone-built inn has a friendly, bustling atmosphere and, even when things are pretty busy, the efficient staff cope well. There are beams, stripped stone and partly panelled walls, brocade-seated settles around oak-topped tables, horsebrasses, a highly polished oak servery and lovely coal fires. The restaurant has oak-topped tables with comfortable leather chairs and french windows opening on to the terrace; TV. Black Sheep Best, Everards Tiger, Timothy Taylors Landlord and a guest such as Hadrian & Border Secret Kingdom on handpump, an extensive wine list and quite a few malt whiskies. Surprisingly quiet given its proximity to the A1, it has an inviting garden and the bedrooms are comfortable.

🍴 **The licensees own a farm which supplies their beef, lamb and pork and the bar food can be very good: sandwiches, soup, chicken liver parfait, mussels with white wine, cream and garlic, gammon and free-range eggs, lambs liver, bacon, sausage and black pudding, chicken with leeks, bacon and stilton sauce, stir-fried beef with noodles and plum and ginger sauce and bass on a crab and dill tagliatelle; the restaurant menu is more elaborate.** *Starters/Snacks: £4.00 to £8.00. Main Courses: £7.00 to £15.00. Puddings: £4.95*

Free house ~ Licensee Phil Farmer ~ Real ale ~ Bar food (12-2, 6-9; light snacks 2-5) ~ Restaurant (12-2, 7-9) ~ (01665) 575234 ~ Children welcome ~ Dogs allowed in bedrooms ~ Open 11-11; 12-10.30 Sun ~ Bedrooms: £65B/£85B

Recommended by Michael Doswell, Joyce and Maurice Cottrell, Comus and Sarah Elliott, Tony Baldwin, Rory and Jackie Hudson, J A Snell, Roy and Jean Russell, Bruce and Sharon Eden, John and Angie Millar, P A Rowe, Jenny and Peter Lowater, John and Sylvia Harrop, Sheena W Makin, Derek Thomas, MJVK, Mr and Mrs John Taylor, Jill and Julian Tasker, Sue Milliken

NEWTON-BY-THE-SEA

NU2424 MAP 10

Ship 🍺

Village signposted off B1339 N of Alnwick; Low Newton – paid parking 200 metres up road on right, just before village (none in village); NE66 3EL

In a charming square of fishermen's cottages close to the beach, good simple food and a fine spread of drinks; best to check winter opening times

This is the perfect place to relax close to the sea after enjoying one of the surrounding walks. It's a row of converted fishermen's cottages that looks across the sloping village green to the sandy beach; it can get pretty busy at peak times and it's best to book in advance then. Inside, the plainly furnished but cosy bare-boards bar on the right has nautical charts on its dark pink walls and another simple room on the left has beams, hop bines, some bright modern pictures on stripped-stone walls and a woodburning stove in the stone fireplace; darts, dominoes. They started brewing here a couple of years ago and on handpump you might find Dolly Daydream, Sandcastles at Dawn, Sea Coal, Sea Dog, Sea Wheat and Ship Hop. Out in the corner of the square are some tables among pots of flowers, with picnic-sets over on the grass. No nearby parking, but there's a car park up the hill.

🍴 **At lunchtime, the tasty bar food includes sandwiches (the crab is popular), stotties, toasted ciabattas and ploughman's, with more elaborate evening choices such as a vegetarian moroccan tagine, hand-picked crab salad, venison with a red wine sauce, bass fillets with olive mash, roasted cherry tomatoes and a fennel and chilli salad, steaks, and puddings like apple crumble and chocolate brownie.** *Starters/Snacks: £3.50 to £5.95. Main Courses: £8.00 to £16.50. Puddings: £3.00 to £5.50*

Free house ~ Licensee Christine Forsyth ~ Real ale ~ Bar food (12-2.30, 7-8 (check in winter)) ~ No credit cards ~ (01665) 576262 ~ Children welcome ~ Dogs welcome ~ Live folk/blues/jazz; phone for details ~ Open 11-11; 12-10.30 Sun; phone for opening hours in winter

Recommended by Comus and Sarah Elliott, Danny and Gillian O'Sullivan, Roger Fox, Mike and Sue Loseby, the Didler, Penny and Peter Keevil, James Thompson, Andy and Jill Kassube, Graham Oddey, GSB

ROMALDKIRK   NY9922   MAP 10

Rose & Crown ★ ⑪ � 🍷 ⇐

Just off B6277; DL12 9EB

A civilised base for the area, with accomplished cooking, attentive service and a fine choice of drinks; lovely bedrooms

This handsome 18th-c coaching inn is a lovely place to stay overnight and you can then make the best of the excellent food served by the first-class staff. The cosily traditional beamed bar has lots of brass and copper, old-fashioned seats facing a warming log fire, a Jacobean oak settle, a grandfather clock, old farm tools and gin traps and black and white pictures of Romaldkirk on the walls. Allendale Best, Black Sheep Best and Theakstons Best on handpump alongside 14 wines by the glass, organic fruit juices and pressed vegetable juices. The smart, newly refurbished brasserie-style Crown Room (bar food is served in here too) has large cartoons of french waiters, big old wine bottles and high-backed dining chairs. The hall has farm tools, wine maps and other interesting prints, along with a photograph (taken by a customer) of the Hale Bopp comet over the interesting old village church. There's also an oak-panelled restaurant. Tables outside look out over the village green with its original stocks and water pump. The extraordinary Bowes Museum and High Force waterfall are close by. The owners also provide their own in-house guide to days out and about in the area and a *Walking in Teesdale* book. '

🍴 As well as making their own jams, chutneys and marmalade (which you can buy to take away) and using only seasonal local produce (they list their suppliers on the menu), the imaginative bar food includes filled baguettes, ploughman's, soup, smoked pink trout mousse, chicken liver pâté with port and orange sauce, eggs benedict, leek, bacon and black pudding risotto with a poached egg, salmon fishcakes with a chive cream sauce, steak, kidney and mushroom in ale pie, pigeon with pancetta, puy lentils and madeira, smoked chicken carbonara, and puddings such as fresh lime cheesecake and fat vanilla meringue with hokey pokey ice-cream and toffee sauce; **Sunday roasts** *Starters/Snacks: £4.50 to £6.75. Main Courses: £8.50 to £16.50. Puddings: £5.25*

Free house ~ Licensees Christopher and Alison Davy ~ Real ale ~ Bar food (12-1.45, 6.30-9.30) ~ Restaurant ~ (01833) 650213 ~ Children welcome but must be over 6 in restaurant ~ Dogs allowed in bar and bedrooms ~ Open 11(12 Sun)-11; closed 24-26 Dec ~ Bedrooms: £92B/£140S(£160B)

Recommended by Rodney and Norma Stubington, Malcolm Wood, Jill and Julian Tasker, Mike and Sue Loseby, Roxanne Chamberlain, John Coatsworth, Lesley and Peter Barrett

SEAHOUSES   NU2232   MAP 10

Olde Ship ★ 🍺 ⇐

Just off B1340, towards harbour; NE68 7RD

Lots of atmosphere and maritime memorabilia in this bustling little hotel; views across harbour to Farne Islands; bedrooms

This year, the friendly family who own this homely little hotel celebrate their centenary here – quite a landmark. The bar is popular with locals and gently lit by stained-glass sea picture windows, lantern lights and a winter open fire, and remains a tribute to the sea and seafarers with a rich assemblage of nautical bits and pieces. Even the floor is scrubbed ship's decking and, if it's working, an anemometer takes wind speed readings from the top of the chimney. Besides lots of other shiny brass fittings, ship's instruments and equipment, and a knotted anchor made by local fishermen, there are sea pictures and model ships, including fine ones of the North Sunderland Lifeboat, and Seahouses' lifeboat, the *Grace Darling*. There's also a model of the *Forfarshire*, the paddle steamer that local heroine Grace Darling went to rescue in 1838 (you can read more of the story in the pub), and even the ship's nameboard. The battlemented side terrace (you'll find fishing memorabilia out here too) and one window in the sun lounge look out across the harbour to the Farne Islands, and as dusk falls you can watch the Longstones lighthouse shine across the fading evening sky. Black Sheep Best, Courage Directors, Greene King Old Speckled Hen and Ruddles County and Hadrian & Border Farne Island Pale on handpump, a good wine list and quite a few malt whiskies; piped music and TV. It's not really suitable for children though there is a little family room, and along with walkers, they are welcome on the terrace. You can book boat trips to the Farne Islands Bird Sanctuary at the harbour, and there are bracing coastal walks, particularly to Bamburgh, Grace Darling's birthplace.

🍴 **Bar food might include sandwiches, ploughman's, soup, chopped grapefruit and celery topped with prawns and seafood sauce, chicken and mushroom casserole, vegetable lasagne, scampi, grilled lemon sole, and puddings like apricot crumble and tiramisu.** *Starters/Snacks: £5.00 to £5.50. Main Courses: £8.00 to £12.00. Puddings: £4.00 to £5.75*

Free house ~ Licensees Judith Glen and David Swan ~ Real ale ~ Bar food (no evening food mid-Dec to mid-Jan) ~ Restaurant ~ (01665) 720200 ~ Children only allowed in family room and must be over 10 to stay overnight ~ Open 11(12 Sun)-11 ~ Bedrooms: £58S/£116B

Recommended by Comus and Sarah Elliott, Mr and Mrs A Hetherington, Dave Irving, Jenny Huggins, Derek and Sylvia Stephenson, Mike and Lynn Robinson, R Hayworth, Colin and Louise English, Mike and Sue Loseby, the Didler, Emma Harris, George Cowie, Frances Gosnell, John and Angie Millar, Andy and Jill Kassube, Dave and Shirley Shaw, Malcolm Wood, Tracey and Stephen Groves, Mike and Shelley Woodroffe

STANNERSBURN   NY7286 MAP 10

Pheasant 🛏

Kielder Water road signposted off B6320 in Bellingham; NE48 1DD

Warmly friendly village local close to Kielder Water, with quite a mix of customers and homely bar food; streamside garden; bedrooms

As well as converting the cottage next door into extra bedrooms, the friendly licensees here hope to extend the dining room as well. The low-beamed comfortably traditional lounge has ranks of old local photographs on stripped stone and panelling, red patterned carpets and upholstered stools ranged along the counter. A separate public bar is similar but simpler and opens into a further cosy seating area with beams and panelling; piped music. Black Isle Red Kite, Timothy Taylors Landlord and Wylam Rocket on handpump and 42 malt whiskies; courteous staff. The pub is in a restful valley amid quiet forests, not far from Kielder Water, with picnic-sets in its streamside garden and a pony paddock behind. More reports please.

🍴 **Good bar food includes lunchtime sandwiches, soup, farmhouse pâté, cider-baked gammon with cumberland sauce, spinach and ricotta cheese cannelloni, lasagne, grilled fresh salmon with hot pepper marmalade and crème fraîche, steak and kidney pie, fresh dressed crab salad, and puddings like fruit crumbles and bakewell tart with ice-cream; Sunday roasts.** *Starters/Snacks: £3.95 to £5.95. Main Courses: £8.95 to £9.95. Puddings: £3.95 to £4.95*

Free house ~ Licensees Walter and Robin Kershaw ~ Real ale ~ Bar food ~ Restaurant ~ (01434) 240382 ~ Children welcome ~ Dogs allowed in bedrooms ~ Open 11.30(12 Sun)-3, 6.30-midnight; 12-2, 7-11 Weds-Sun in winter; closed Mon and Tues Nov-Mar; 25-27 Dec ~ Bedrooms: £55S/£90S

Recommended by Dave Braisted, Sylvia and Tony Birbeck, Mr and Mrs D J Nash

---

Real ale may be served from handpumps, electric pumps (not just the on-off switches used for keg beer) or – common in Scotland – tall taps called founts (pronounced 'fonts') where a separate pump pushes the beer up under air pressure.

STANNINGTON

NZ2179   MAP 10

Ridley Arms

Village signposted just off A1 S of Morpeth; NE61 6EL

Comfortably airy, with several differing linked rooms; good choice of real ales

Tucked away on the edge of the village and with a new licensee, this is an extended and attractive 18th-c stone building. It's been arranged into several separate areas, each with a slightly different mood and style from the next. The front is a proper bar area with darts and a fruit machine and stools along the counter. The beamed dining areas lead back from here, with a second bar counter, comfortable bucket armchairs around shiny dark wood tables on polished boards or carpet, portraits and cartoons on cream, panelled or stripped-stone walls, careful lighting and some horsey statuettes. Black Sheep, Caledonian Deuchars IPA, Derwent England Dream and Jarrow River Catcher on handpump and several wines by the glass; piped music. There are picnic-sets in front by the road and tables on a terrace behind; good disabled access.

🍴 Well liked bar food includes sandwiches, soup, black pudding and chorizo crostini with a soft boiled egg and sage dressing, leek and gruyère soufflé with tomato and basil chutney, beef in ale casserole with herb dumplings, trio of local sausages with real ale gravy, red pepper, feta and courgette lasagne, deep-fried haddock with mushy peas, harissa-marinated chicken with herb couscous and minted yoghurt, and puddings like banana toffee brownie and rum ice-cream and strawberry and vanilla cheesecake. *Starters/Snacks: £3.95 to £5.95. Main Courses: £8.95 to £14.50. Puddings: £3.95 to £4.50*

Sir John Fitzgerald ~ Manager Barry Dixon ~ Real ale ~ Bar food (12-9.30(6 Sun); not Sun evening) ~ (01670) 789216 ~ Children welcome ~ Open 11.30-11(10.30 Sun)

Recommended by Derek and Sylvia Stephenson, Comus and Sarah Elliott, Dr Peter D Smart, Michael Doswell, Eric Larkham, GSB, Mike and Lynn Robinson

WARK

NY8676   MAP 10

Battlesteads 🍺 🛏️

B6320 N of Hexham; NE48 3LS

Good local ales, fair value interesting food and a relaxed atmosphere; comfortable bedrooms

Reports from our readers on this bustling stone hotel have been especially warm recently and the interesting food, real ales and comfortable bedrooms all come in for enthusiastic praise. The nicely restored carpeted bar has a woodburning stove with traditional oak surround, low beams, comfortable seats including some low leather sofas, and old *Punch* country life cartoons on the terracotta walls above its dark dado. This leads through to the restaurant and spacious conservatory. There's a relaxed unhurried atmosphere and five good changing local ales such as Black Sheep Best, Consett Ale Works Red Dust, Hadrian & Border Secret Kingdom, High House Farm Nel's Best and Jarrow Rivet Catcher from handpumps on the heavily carved dark oak bar counter; good coffee, cheerful service and piped music. There are tables on a terrace in the walled garden. Disabled access to some of the ground-floor bedrooms.

🍴 Using home-grown vegetables and other local produce, the good value bar food includes lunchtime sandwiches, soup, ham hock and chicken terrine with pickled baby turnip, salad of hot smoked salmon and fresh crab with rhubarb, red pepper, pink peppercorn and absinthe dressing, wild mushroom and ricotta risotto with wild garlic butter, braised local lamb shank with leek, rosemary and mead jus, daily specials like grilled fresh sardines and mixed game casserole, and puddings such as chocolate marble truffle torte with warm chocolate sauce and whisky and marmalade bread and butter pudding. *Starters/Snacks: £3.75 to £6.25. Main Courses: £8.50 to £22.50. Puddings: £5.75*

Free house ~ Licensees Richard and Dee Slade ~ Real ale ~ Bar food (12-3, 6.30-9.30) ~ Restaurant ~ (01434) 230209 ~ Children welcome ~ Dogs allowed in bar ~ Open 11-11; closed Feb ~ Bedrooms: £60S/£95B

Recommended by David Heath, S D and J L Cooke, David and Christine Merritt, Kay and Mark Denison, Helen and Brian Edgeley, R L Borthwick, Matt and Vicky Wharton

WELDON BRIDGE

NZ1398 MAP 10

Anglers Arms 🛏

B6344, just off A697; village signposted with Rothbury off A1 N of Morpeth; NE65 8AX

Large helpings of food in appealing bar or converted railway dining car, real ales and a friendly welcome; fishing on the River Coquet and comfortable bedrooms

You can be sure of a warm welcome in this sizeable place and although emphasis is placed on the comfortable bedrooms and enjoyable food, there is a traditional turkey-carpeted bar tucked into its heart. This bustling bar is divided into two parts: cream walls on the right and oak panelling and some shiny black beams hung with copper pans on the left, with Courage Directors, Greene King Old Speckled Hen, Jennings Cumberland and Timothy Taylors Landlord on handpump; around 30 malt whiskies and decent wines. There's also a grandfather clock and sofa by the coal fire, staffordshire cats and other antique ornaments on its mantelpiece, old fishing and other country prints, a profusion of fishing memorabilia and some taxidermy. Some of the tables are lower than you'd expect for eating, but their chairs have short legs to match – different and rather engaging; piped music. The restaurant is in a former railway dining car with crisp white linen and a red carpet. There are tables in the attractive garden with a good play area that includes an assault course. The pub is beside a bridge over the River Coquet and they have rights to fishing along a mile of the riverbank.

🍴 As well as sandwiches and ploughman's, the genenerously served bar food includes chicken liver pâté with cumberland sauce, scallops with black pudding and a honey and soy dressing, vegetable stroganoff, steak in ale pie, sausages with bacon and onion bubble and squeak, battered cod and chips, chicken stuffed with stilton and leeks and wrapped in bacon with a wild mushroom sauce, an oriental sizzling platter, and puddings. *Starters/Snacks: £5.95 to £7.95. Main Courses: £8.95 to £16.95. Puddings: £5.95*

Enterprise ~ Lease John Young ~ Real ale ~ Bar food (12-9.30(9 Sun)) ~ Restaurant ~ (01665) 570271 ~ Children welcome ~ Dogs allowed in bedrooms ~ Open 11-11; 12-10.30 Sun ~ Bedrooms: £47.50S/£80S

Recommended by Pat and Stewart Gordon, Michael Butler, Jenny and Peter Lowater, Dennis Jones, Ann and Tony Bennett-Hughes

LUCKY DIP

Besides the fully inspected pubs, you might like to try these Lucky Dips recommended to us and described by readers (if you do, please send us reports: feedback@goodguides.com).

ALLENDALE [NY8355]
Golden Lion NE47 9BD [Market Pl]: 18th-c two-room village inn with fairly priced enjoyable food, several mainly local well kept ales, good choice of other drinks inc reasonably priced wines, chatty Yorkshire landlord; games area with pool and darts, upstairs restaurant, occasional live music; children and dogs welcome (pub dogs), bedrooms *(JJW, CMW, Mike and Lynn Robinson, Comus and Sarah Elliott)*
Kings Head NE47 9BD [Market Pl (B6295)]: Early 18th-c former coaching inn refurbished and opened up, four real ales, good selection of wines and soft drinks, enjoyable food, nice log fire, newspapers; children welcome, bedrooms, open all day *(JJW, CMW, Comus and Sarah Elliott)*

ALNMOUTH [NU2410]
☆ *Red Lion* NE66 2RJ [Northumberland St]: Former 18th-c coaching inn, relaxed and unpretentious, with good pubby food from baguettes to local fish, cheerful efficient staff, well kept Black Sheep and local guests such as Wylam, mainly new world wines by the glass; attractive bistro-style dining room, log fire in cosy panelled locals' bar; dogs welcome, neat garden by alley with raised deck looking over Aln estuary, comfortable bedrooms, open all day (Sun till 8pm) *(Pete Devonish, Ian McIntyre, Comus and Sarah Elliott, Celia Minoughan, Michael Doswell, Ann and Tony Bennett-Hughes, Mr and Mrs D J Nash)*
ALNWICK [NU1813]
Blackmores NE66 1PN [Bondgate Without]: Light and airy reworking of Victorian stone

building into smart contemporary pub/boutique hotel, ales such as Black Sheep and Caledonian Deuchars IPA in lively front bar, several wines by the glass, good food all day from snacky things up in bar, bistro or upstairs restaurant; terrace, 13 bedrooms *(Comus and Sarah Elliott, GSB, Jenny and Peter Lowater, Michael Doswell)*

John Bull NE66 1UY [Howick St]: Popular chatty drinkers' pub, essentially the front room of an early 19th-c terraced house, four changing ales, real cider, bottled belgian beers and over 100 malt whiskies; cl wkdy lunchtime *(the Didler)*

Oaks NE66 2PN [South Rd (A1068, off A1)]: Welcoming small hotel with good mix of customers, neat lounge bar with period furniture and fittings in linked rooms, well kept Jennings and Wychwood, huge helpings of enjoyable food in bar and charming dining room, carvery; pleasant attentive staff, civilised atmosphere; 12 bedrooms *(D W Stokes)*

BAMBURGH [NU1834]
Castle NE69 7BW [Front St]: Clean comfortably old-fashioned pub with friendly landlord, well kept ales such as Black Sheep and Mordue Workie Ticket, winter mulled wine, standard food all day inc good craster kippers, open fires; big courtyard, garden *(Lawrence Pearse, Comus and Sarah Elliott)*

Mizen Head NE69 7BS [Lucker Rd]: Newly refurbished family-run hotel, light airy bar, open fire, tasty locally sourced food; children and dogs welcome, nice bedrooms *(Penny and Peter Keevil)*

BARDON MILL [NY7566]
Twice Brewed NE47 7AN [Military Rd (B6318 NE of Hexham)]: Large busy inn well placed for fell-walkers and major Hadrian's Wall sites, six ales inc local microbrews and two for the pub by Yates, 50 rums, 20 malts, reasonably priced wines; good value hearty pub food from baguettes up, quick friendly staff, local photographs and art for sale; quiet piped music, no dogs; children welcome, picnic-sets in back garden, 14 bedrooms, open all day *(Dave Braisted, Pete Coxon, Dave Irving, Jenny Huggins)*

BARNINGHAM [NZ0810]
Milbank Arms DL11 7DW: Cosy little one-room village local, simple and unspoilt with welcoming landlord (in same family for 70 years), no kitchen *(C Elliott)*

BEADNELL [NU2229]
Beadnell Towers NE67 5AU: Large welcoming off-season haven with above-average food, Black Sheep, Hadrian & Border and Mordue ales, reasonably priced wines by the glass, good service; can get more touristy in summer; good bedrooms *(DHV, Comus and Sarah Elliott)*

Craster Arms NE67 5AX [The Wynding]: Popular pubby food, Black Sheep, friendly efficient service, roomy old building with modern fittings; children welcome, nice front garden, open all day *(Danny Savage, DHV)*

BEAMISH [NZ2153]
☆ *Beamish Mary* DH9 0QH [off A693 signed 'No Place and Cooperative Villas', S of museum]: Friendly down-to-earth former pit village inn doing well under present licensee, eight well kept mainly local ales (May beer festival), farm cider, good home-made pubby food at bargain prices; coal fires, two bars with 1960s-feel mix of furnishings, bric-a-brac, 1920s/30s memorabilia and Aga with pots and pans; regular live music in converted stables; sports TV; children allowed until evening, bedrooms *(Peter and Judith Smith)*

Black Horse DH9 0RW [Red Row (off Beamishburn Rd NW, nr A6076); OS Sheet 88 map ref 205541]: Late 17th-c country pub reworked as a stylish dining place, contemporary/rustic interior in heritage colours with beams, flagstones and some exposed stonework, good well presented food using own produce inc good value set lunch, nice wines, well kept Hawkshead Lakeland Gold and Wells & Youngs Bombardier, friendly attentive staff; cosy fire-warmed front room extending to light spacious dining area with central bar, another dining room upstairs; children welcome, restful views from big paved terrace, picnic-sets on grass, cl 2-3.30pm wkdys *(Michael Doswell)*

Shepherd & Shepherdess DH9 0RS: Useful for its position near outstanding open-air heritage museum, welcoming helpful service, good range of reasonably priced fresh food generously served inc vegetarian and children's choices, well kept ales such as Black Sheep and Wells & Youngs Bombardier, decent wines; open L-shaped carpeted bar with low beams and open fires; piped music (turned down on request); outside tables and big play area, open all day *(LYM, Mr and Mrs Maurice Thompson, Alan Thwaite)*

BELFORD [NU1033]
Blue Bell NE70 7NE [off A1 S of Berwick; Market Pl]: Substantial old coaching inn (hotel rather than pub) with decent food from sandwiches up in pubby bar, Black Sheep, good choice of wines and whiskies, sensible prices, friendly service, two restaurant areas; piped music; children welcome, big garden, pleasant bedrooms *(Comus and Sarah Elliott, LYM)*

BELSAY [NZ1277]
Highlander NE20 0DN [A696 S of village]: Roomy country dining pub, enjoyable food from lunchtime baguettes up, quick friendly service, Black Sheep and Caledonian Deuchars IPA; good log fires, comfortable raised side area with nice plain wood tables and high-backed banquettes, plenty of nooks and corners for character, plainer locals' bar; unobtrusive piped music; open all day *(Guy and Caroline Howard)*

BERWICK-UPON-TWEED [NT9952]
☆ *Foxtons* TD15 1AB [Hide Hill]: More chatty and comfortable two-level wine bar than pub, with wide choice of good imaginative

food, prompt friendly service, good range of wines, whiskies and coffees, real ales such as Caledonian and Timothy Taylors, lively side bistro; busy, so worth booking evenings, open all day, cl Sun *(John and Sylvia Harrop)*

Pilot TD15 1LZ [Low Greens]: Small, welcoming, beamed and panelled backstreet local, old nautical photographs and knick-knacks, comfortable back lounge, well kept Caledonian Deuchars IPA and regional guests; summer lunchtime food; darts and quoits, fiddle music Thurs; children and dogs welcome, garden tables, two bedrooms, open all day *(the Didler)*

BIRTLEY [NZ2856]

Mill House DH3 1RE [Blackfell, via A1231 slip road off southbound A1]: Extensively refurbished dining pub with enjoyable food all day inc bargain two-course lunches, oyster bar and tapas too, compact bar area, changing real ales, nice wines by the glass; dining room with olde-barn décor, alcoved eating areas and conservatory, friendly staff *(Dave and Jenny Hughes)*

Moulders Arms DH3 2LW [Peareth Terrace]: Friendly pleasantly refurbished pub by church in old part of village, comfortable lounge with raised back area and wide views from front, three real ales, good value food from sandwiches up, large public bar; garden *(Mr and Mrs Maurice Thompson)*

BOURNMOOR [NZ3051]

Dun Cow DH4 6DY [Primrose Hill (A1052)]: Traditional country pub with comfortable bar and restaurant, friendly landlord, efficient young staff, food all day, two changing ales; piped music, TV; children welcome, garden with smokers' marquee *(Mark Walker, Mike and Lynn Robinson)*

CASTLE EDEN [NZ4237]

Castle Eden Inn TS27 4SD [B1281 S of Peterlee]: Refurbished under newish licensees, enjoyable fairly priced local food, Black Sheep, Caledonian Deuchars IPA and Timothy Taylors Landlord *(Andy Maher)*

CATTON [NY8257]

Crown NE47 9QS: Cosy traditional local owned by Allendale Brewery, their full range kept well, farm cider, reasonably priced malt whiskies, fresh honest home-made food (landlord bakes his own bread), cafetière coffee; log fire, warmly friendly atmosphere, dominoes and board games, stripped stone and local art, dining extension; children and dogs welcome, small garden, lovely walks *(Michael Doswell, Marcus Byron)*

CONSETT [NZ1050]

Company Row DH8 5AB [Front St]: Large Wetherspoons with their usual low-priced food and drink – a useful find for lunch (may get more lively evenings); sunny tables outside *(Dave Irving, Jenny Huggins, Mike and Lynn Robinson)*

Grey Horse DH8 6NE [Sherburn Terrace]: Well run two-bar beamed 19th-c pub brewing its own Consett ales in former back stables, dozens of malt whiskies, occasional beer festivals; very friendly licensees, two coal

fires, pool; pavement tables, open all day *(Mike and Lynn Robinson)*

CORBRIDGE [NY9863]

Dyvels NE45 5AY [Station Rd]: Refurbished stone inn with good value traditional food from sandwiches up, well kept ales such as Black Sheep, Caledonian Deuchars IPA and Hadrian & Border; children welcome, picnic-sets on side terrace and lawn, bedrooms, open all day *(Andy and Jill Kassube)*

Wheatsheaf NE45 5HE [Watling St/St Helens St]: Big stone-built village hotel doing well under present management, enjoyable popular food inc bargain carvery (all day Sun), well kept Timothy Taylors Landlord and Wylam, pleasant Victorian décor in panelled lounge and big conservatory restaurant with distant hill views; piped music, Tues quiz; children and dogs welcome, terrace tables, six renovated bedrooms, open all day *(Andy and Jill Kassube, LYM)*

COTHERSTONE [NZ0119]

Red Lion DL12 9QE: Traditional beamed 18th-c village local with serving hatch, Jennings Cumberland, Caledonian Deuchars IPA and a local guest, two log fires, snug, no food; children, walking boots and dogs welcome, garden tables, cl wkdy lunchtimes *(Mr and Mrs Maurice Thompson)*

CRAMLINGTON [NZ2373]

☆ *Snowy Owl* NE23 8AU [just off A1/A19 junction via A1068; Blagdon Lane]: Large Vintage Inn, relaxed and comfortable, with reasonable prices, good choice of food all day inc popular Sun lunch, friendly efficient young staff, beers such as Black Sheep, Jennings Cumberland and Timothy Taylors Landlord, nice wines; beams, flagstones, stripped stone and terracotta paintwork, soft lighting and an interesting mix of furnishings and decorations, daily papers; may be piped music; disabled access, bedrooms in adjoining Innkeepers Lodge, open all day *(Dr Peter D Smart, Guy and Caroline Howard, Colin and Louise English)*

CRASTER [NU2519]

☆ *Jolly Fisherman* NE66 3TR [off B1339, NE of Alnwick]: Simple local in great spot, long a favourite for its lovely sea and coastal views from picture window and grass behind, and for its good value crab sandwiches, crab soup and locally smoked seafood (good chips, too); this makes up for the take-us-as-you-find-us style, which can verge on scruffiness (not to everyone's taste); well kept ales such as Black Sheep or Mordue, good cider, games area with pool; children and dogs welcome, open all day in summer *(John and Sylvia Harrop, the Didler, C A Hall, Penny and Peter Keevil, Christine and Malcolm Ingram, Ann and Tony Bennett-Hughes, LYM, Michael Doswell)*

DARLINGTON [NZ2814]

Number Twenty 2 DL3 7RG [Coniscliffe Rd]: Long bistro-feel Victorian pub with high ceiling, bare boards and exposed brickwork, up to 22 beers on handpump inc own Village ales (brewed by Hambleton), draught continental beers, simple lunchtime food in compact panelled back room, good friendly service; open all day, cl Sun *(Mark Brittain)*

DUNSTAN [NU2419]

Cottage NE66 3SZ [off B1339 Alnmouth—Embleton]: Comfortable single-storey pub with low beams, dark wood and some stripped brickwork, banquettes and dimpled copper tables, enjoyable bar food inc interesting specials, well kept ales such as Black Sheep, Hadrian & Border, Mordue and Wylam, friendly efficient staff, restaurant, leafy conservatory; children welcome, terrace tables and attractive garden with play area, ten bedrooms, open all day wknds *(LYM, Marlene and Jim Godfrey, Andy and Jill Kassube, Comus and Sarah Elliott)*

DURHAM [NZ2642]

Colpitts DH1 4EG [Colpitts Terrace/Hawthorn Terrace]: Comfortable traditional two-bar pub with friendly licensees, cheap well kept Sam Smiths, open fires, back pool room; seats in yard, open all day *(the Didler)*

Court Inn DH1 3AW [Court Lane]: Comfortable town pub with good hearty home-made food all day from sandwiches to steaks and late-evening bargains, real ales such as Bass, Marstons Pedigree and Mordue; extensive stripped brick eating area, no mobile phones; bustling in term-time with students and teachers, piped pop music; seats outside, open all day *(BB, Eric Larkham, Mike and Lynn Robinson, David and Laraine Webster, Mark Walker)*

☆ *Dun Cow* DH1 3HN [Old Elvet]: Unchanging backstreet pub in pretty 16th-c black and white timbered cottage, cheerful licensees, tiny chatty front bar with wall benches, corridor to long narrow back lounge with banquettes, machines etc (can be packed with students); particularly well kept Camerons and other ales such as Black Sheep and Caledonian Deuchars IPA, good value basic lunchtime snacks, decent coffee; piped music; children welcome, open all day Mon-Sat, Sun too in summer *(LYM, Chris Sale, the Didler, Eric Larkham, Dave Irving, Jenny Huggins, Danny and Gillian O'Sullivan)*

Market Tavern DH1 3NJ [Market Pl]: Lively old-fashioned bare-boards pub with two or three well kept ales and good value fresh bar lunches *(Mike and Lynn Robinson, Eric Larkham, Comus and Sarah Elliott)*

Shakespeare DH1 3NU [Saddler St]: Unchanging pub with signed actor photographs in busy basic front bar, charming panelled snug and neatly refurbished back room, well kept Caledonian Deuchars IPA, Fullers London Pride and two guests, simple cheap bar snacks, friendly staff; pub and board games; children (till 6pm) and dogs welcome, convenient for castle, cathedral and river, open all day *(LYM, the Didler)*

EBCHESTER [NZ1054]

☆ *Derwent Walk* DH8 0SX [Ebchester Hill (B6309 outside)]: Interesting pub by Gateshead—Consett walk of same name;

reliable good value home-made food from unusual hot sandwiches up inc signature cobblers, great choice of wines by the glass at reasonable prices, good friendly staff, full Jennings range kept well, nice log fire and appealing old photographs, conservatory with fine Derwent Valley views; walkers welcome, pleasant heated terrace *(Andy and Jill Kassube, Mike and Lynn Robinson)*

EGLINGHAM [NU1019]

Tankerville Arms NE66 2TX [B6346 Alnwick—Wooler]: Traditional pub with contemporary touches, cosy friendly atmosphere, beams, bare boards, some stripped stone, banquettes, warm fires; Black Sheep, good wines, interesting changing menu, raftered split-level restaurant; children welcome, nice views from garden, three bedrooms, attractive village *(Colin and Louise English, Comus and Sarah Elliott, Mary Goodfellow, LYM)*

ELLINGHAM [NU1625]

Pack Horse NE67 5HA [signed off A1 N of Alnwick]: Compact stone-built country local with light and airy dining room, feature fireplace in beamed bar, small comfortable lounge; enclosed garden, good value bedrooms, peaceful village *(Comus and Sarah Elliott)*

ELWICK [NZ4532]

McOrville TS27 3EF [0.25 miles off A19 W of Hartlepool]: Open-plan dining pub with good blackboard food, Black Sheep and a changing ale, carved panelling, slippers provided for walkers *(JHBS)*

EMBLETON [NU2322]

Dunstanburgh Castle Hotel NE66 3UN: Comfortable hotel in attractive spot near magnificent coastline, enjoyable bar and restaurant food inc game and fresh fish, pleasant young staff, beers such as Black Sheep and Theakstons, well priced wines, two relaxing lounges for coffee; bedrooms *(John and Sylvia Harrop, Mr and Mrs D J Nash)*

Greys NE66 3UY: Carpeted main front bar with pubby furniture, more lived-in part with old photographs and cuttings, large back dining area, good value home-made food from sandwiches to local fish, up to five well kept ales inc Black Sheep and Hadrian & Border, afternoon teas; small walled back garden, raised decking with village views *(Andy and Jill Kassube)*

Sportsman NE66 3XF: Large plain bar/bistro in pub/hotel with nearby beach and stunning views to Dunstanburgh Castle, impressive food using prime local produce inc fish and game, small interesting wine list, real ales such as Mordue Workie Ticket and Timothy Taylors Landlord, friendly cheerful service; frequent wknd live music; dogs welcome, heated terrace, coastal view bedrooms, may cl in winter *(Mr and Mrs D J Nash)*

FELTON [NU1800]

☆ *Northumberland Arms* NE65 9EE [West Thirston; B6345, off A1 N of Morpeth]: Attractive old inn with beams, stripped

THE GOOD PUB GUIDE

The Good Pub Guide
FREEPOST TN1569
WADHURST
E. SUSSEX
TN5 7BR

Please use this card to tell us which pubs *you* think should or should not be included in the next edition of *The Good Pub Guide*. Just fill it in and return it to us – no stamp or envelope needed. Don't forget you can also use the report forms at the end of the *Guide*

ALISDAIR AIRD

In returning this form I confirm my agreement that the information I provide may be used by The Random House Group Ltd, its assignees and/or licensees in any media or medium whatsoever.

YOUR NAME AND ADDRESS (BLOCK CAPITALS PLEASE)

☐ *Please tick this box if you would like extra report forms*

REPORT ON
(pub's name)

Pub's address

☐ **YES Main Entry**   ☐ **YES Lucky Dip**   ☐ **NO don't include**

Please tick one of these boxes to show your verdict, and give reasons and descriptive comments, prices etc

☐ Deserves FOOD award   ☐ Deserves PLACE-TO-STAY award

REPORT ON .
(pub's name)

Pub's address

☐ **YES Main Entry**   ☐ **YES Lucky Dip**   ☐ **NO don't include**

Please tick one of these boxes to show your verdict, and give reasons and descriptive comments, prices etc

☐ Deserves FOOD award   ☐ Deserves PLACE-TO-STAY award

stone and good coal fires in roomy and comfortable open-plan bar, nice mix of furnishings inc big settees, elegant small restaurant, conservatory pool room; good sensibly priced food, well kept Bass and Black Sheep, good coffee and wines, friendly service and atmosphere; piped music; dogs welcome, steps down to bench by River Coquet, five bedrooms, open all day *(Mr and Mrs D J Nash, Comus and Sarah Elliott, BB)*

GLANTON [NU0614]

Queens Head NE66 4AP [Front St]: Village pub with red carpeted bar and dining room, above-average local food, Hadrian & Border Tyneside Blonde *(M and GR)*

HALTWHISTLE [NY7064]

Black Bull NE49 0BL [just off Market Sq, behind minute restaurant]: Cosy low-beamed pub in cobbled street, log fires, stripped stone and some flagstones, enjoyable food inc blackboard specials, well kept real ales, corridor to small dining room; limited disabled access, dogs welcome in flagstoned part, garden *(Mrs L Wells)*

HART [NZ4634]

White Hart TS27 3AW [just off A179 W of Hartlepool; Front St]: Interesting nautical-theme pub with old ship's figurehead outside, fires in both bars, food from landlady-chef, two changing real ales; open all day (cl Mon afternoon) *(JHBS)*

HARTLEPOOL [NZ5032]

Causeway TS24 7QT [Stockton Rd, Stranton]: Friendly red-brick Victorian local with panelled bare-boards bar and two carpeted snugs, well kept local Camerons and Marstons-related ales, enjoyable lunchtime food (not Sun), low prices, open fires; live music three nights a week; open all day *(John and Eileen Mennear)*

Tall Ships TS26 0BF [Middle Warren Local Centre, Mulberry Rise]: Newly built Ember Inn (opened Jan 08) in lofty position with good views of Hartlepool Bay; five changing ales (try before you buy), good value food all day inc early-bird deals, quiz nights (Tues, Thurs); outside picnic-sets, open all day *(JHBS)*

HAWTHORN [NZ4145]

Stapylton Arms SR7 8SD [off B1432 S of A19 Murton exit]: Chatty, carpeted bar with old local photographs, a well kept ale such as Black Sheep, enjoyable food made by landlady from sandwiches to steaks and Sun roasts, friendly family service; dogs on leads, may be open all day on busy wknds, nice wooded walk to sea (joins Durham Coastal Path) *(JHBS)*

HIGH HESLEDEN [NZ4538]

Ship TS27 4QD [off A19 via B1281]: Half a dozen good value changing ales from the region, log fire, sailing ship models inc big one hanging with lanterns from boarded ceiling, landlady cooks enjoyable bar food and some interesting restaurant dishes; yacht and shipping views from car park, six bedrooms in new block, cl Mon *(JHBS)*

HOLY ISLAND [NU1241]

Crown & Anchor TD15 2RX [causeway passable only at low tide, check times (01289) 330733]: Comfortably unpretentious pub/restaurant, enjoyable food from shortish menu inc good fish and chips, Wells & Youngs Bombardier and Caledonian Deuchars IPA, welcoming helpful staff, compact bar, roomy modern back dining room; dogs welcome, enclosed garden with picnic-sets, bedrooms *(Mr and Mrs D J Nash, Dr A McCormick, John and Sylvia Harrop, Dave Irving, Jenny Huggins)*

Manor House TD15 2RX: Neat hotel bar with welcoming attentive staff, well kept local and national beers from corner servery, good, generous, sensibly priced food inc OAP deals, afternoon teas, old-fashioned dining room; nice garden, bedrooms *(Piotr Chodzko-Zajko)*

HORSLEY [NZ0965]

Lion & Lamb NE15 0NS [B6528, just off A69 Newcastle—Hexham]: Main bar with scrubbed tables, stripped stone, flagstones and panelling, lounge with big sofas; four changing ales inc a local beer, small smart restaurant, good quality fresh food, attentive service; under-21s with parent/guardian only, Tyne views from attractive garden with roomy terrace, good adventure play area, open all day *(GSB)*

HURWORTH-ON-TEES [NZ2814]

Bay Horse DL2 2AQ [Church Row]: Welcoming dining pub with good choice of enjoyable food inc fixed-price lunch menu, three real ales, big public bar; charming village by River Tees *(Peter Thompson)*

JARROW [NZ3363]

Robin Hood NE32 5UB [Primrose Hill]: Popular and friendly local, Jarrow beers from adjoining brewery and a guest ale, several rooms, restaurant *(Mr and Mrs Maurice Thompson, Eric Larkham)*

LANGDON BECK [NY8531]

Langdon Beck Hotel DL12 0XP [B6277 Middleton—Alston]: Isolated unpretentious inn with two cosy bars and spacious lounge, well placed for walks and Pennine Way; Black Sheep, Jarrow and a guest ale (late May beer festival), good choice of generous food inc local teasdale beef and lamb, decent coffee, helpful friendly staff; garden, wonderful fell views, bedrooms, open all day, cl Mon winter *(Mr and Mrs Maurice Thompson, Roxanne Chamberlain)*

LANGLEY ON TYNE [NY8160]

Carts Bog Inn NE47 5NW [A686 S, junction B6305]: Isolated moorside pub recently reopened after refurbishment, heavy beams and stripped-stone walls, old photographs, lovely open fire, good range of reasonably priced food from sandwiches up, well kept Allendale, Mordue and Wylam, friendly efficient young staff; games room with pool and darts; picnic-sets in big garden with views, quoits *(LYM, Dennis Jones)*

LUCKER [NU1530]

☆ *Apple* NE70 7JH [off A1 N of Morpeth]: Refurbished old stone building, sensibly priced pubby dishes and specials, Allendale and Hadrian & Border ales, good value wines, woodburner in comfortable bar's big fireplace, roomy big-windowed side dining area (Comus and Sarah Elliott, LYM)

MELDON [NZ1185]
Dyke Neuk Inn NE61 3SL [B6343 W of Morpeth, 2 miles E of Hartburn]: Comfortably refurbished country pub, enjoyable food in beamed bar, fast friendly service, well kept ales, separate restaurant, lots of pictures; pleasant good-sized garden (Chris Gooch)

MILFIELD [NT9333]
Red Lion NE71 6JD [Main Rd (A697 Wooler—Cornhill)]: Welcoming 17th-c former coaching inn with good sensibly priced food from chef/landlord, organic wine, good service (John and Liz Stillard, Comus and Sarah Elliott)

NETHERTON [NT9807]
Star NE65 7HD [off B6341 at Thropton, or A697 via Whittingham]: Simple unchanging village local under charming long-serving landlady (licence has been in her family since 1917); welcoming regulars, Camerons Strongarm tapped from cellar casks and served from hatch in small entrance lobby, large high-ceilinged room with wall benches, many original features; no food, music, children or dogs; cl lunchtime, open from 7pm, cl Mon, Thurs (the Didler, Eric Larkham)

NEWBIGGIN-BY-THE-SEA [NZ3188]
Queens Head NE64 6AT [High St]: Friendly chatty landlord, John Smiths and guest ales at low prices, several high-ceilinged rooms, thriving local atmosphere, dominoes; dogs welcome (not in sitting room), open all day from 9.45am (the Didler)

NEWCASTLE UPON TYNE [NZ2464]
☆ *Bacchus* NE1 6BX [High Bridge E, between Pilgrim St and Grey St]: Smart, spacious and comfortable, with ocean-liner look, good ship and shipbuilding photographs, good modern lunchtime food from interesting doorstep sandwiches and panini through unusual light dishes to more substantial things, keen prices; half a dozen changing ales, plenty of bottled imports, perhaps farm cider, decent coffee, relaxed atmosphere; open all day (usually just evening on Sun) (Eric Larkham, Michael Doswell, Mike and Lynn Robinson)
Bodega NE1 4AG [Westgate Rd]: Majestic Edwardian drinking hall next to Tyne Theatre, interesting ales such as Big Lamp Prince Bishop, Captain Cook Black Porter, Durham Magus, Mordue Geordie Pride (sold here as No 9) and Outlaw Wrangler, farm cider; friendly service, basic lunchtime food, colourful walls and ceiling, bare boards, snug front cubicles, spacious back area with two magnificent stained-glass cupolas; piped music, machines, big-screen TV, very busy Newcastle United match days; open all day (the Didler, Eric Larkham, Jeremy King)
☆ *Bridge Hotel* NE1 1RQ [Castle Sq, next to high-level bridge]: Big cheery well divided high-ceilinged bar around servery with replica slatted snob screens, well kept changing ales such as Black Sheep, Keelburn, Lees and Mordue, farm cider; friendly staff, bargain generous lunchtime food (not Sat), Sun afternoon teas, magnificent fireplace, great river and bridge views from raised back area; sports TV, piped music, games machines, live music upstairs inc long-standing Mon folk club; flagstoned back terrace overlooking part of old town wall, open all day (Andy and Jill Kassube, the Didler, Eric Larkham, James Thompson, Andy Lickfold, LYM)
Centurion NE1 5HL [Central Station, Neville St]: Glorious high-ceilinged Victorian décor with tilework and columns in former first-class waiting room, well restored with comfortable leather seats giving club-like feel, Black Sheep and local ales such as Allendale and Jarrow, farm cider, friendly staff; piped music, unobtrusive sports TV; useful deli next door (Chris Sale, Mike and Eleanor Anderson, Eric Larkham, Mike and Lynn Robinson, Andy and Jill Kassube)
☆ *Cluny* NE1 2PQ [Lime St]: Trendy bar/café in interesting 19th-c mill/warehouse, striking setting below Metro bridge; good value home-made food all day from massive sandwiches up, cheerful staff, up to eight well kept ales inc Banks's and Big Lamp, exotic beers and rums, settees in comfortable raised area with daily papers and local art magazines, back gallery with artwork from studios in same complex; piped music, good live music nightly; children welcome till 7pm, picnic-sets out on green, open all day (cl Mon afternoon) (Mike and Lynn Robinson, LYM, Andy and Jill Kassube, Alex and Claire Pearse, Eric Larkham, James Thompson)
Cooperage NE1 3RF [The Close, Quayside]: Ancient building in good waterfront setting, four real ales, great whisky choice, stripped-stone bar, beamed lounge; disabled facilities (LYM, the Didler)
Cumberland Arms NE6 1LD [Byker Buildings]: Friendly unspoilt traditional local, seven particularly well kept mainly local ales (straight from the cask if you wish) inc a house beer from Wylam, eight farm ciders, beer/cider festivals, good value pubby food all day, obliging staff; live music or other events most nights (regular ukulele band); tables out overlooking Ouseburn Valley, four new bedrooms, cl Mon lunchtime otherwise open all day (Mike and Lynn Robinson, Eric Larkham, the Didler)
Free Trade NE6 1AP [St Lawrence Rd, off Walker Rd (A186)]: Splendidly basic proper pub with outstanding views upriver from big windows, terrace tables and seats on grass; real ales such as High House Farm, Jarrow and Mordue, good sandwiches, warmly friendly atmosphere, real fire, original Formica tables; steps down to back room and lavatories; open all day (Eric Larkham, Andy and Jill Kassube)
Newcastle Arms NE1 5SE [St Andrews St]:

Open-plan pub on fringe of Chinatown, Caledonian Deuchars IPA and five quickly changing guests inc a porter or stout, farm ciders and perries, beer festivals; friendly staff, interesting old local photographs; piped music, big-screen sports TV, can get very busy especially on match days; open all day *(Eric Larkham)*

Waterline NE1 3DH [Quayside, by New Law Courts]: Stylish Tyne warehouse conversion by Millennium Bridge, lots of beams and pillars, nooks and crannies, maritime bric-a-brac, welcoming efficient staff, well kept Caledonian Deuchars IPA and Courage Directors; enjoyable good value food all day inc freshly made pizzas from open kitchen, bargain house wine, open fires, games room; children welcome, good views from terrace *(Michael Doswell, Myke and Nicky Crombleholme, Dave Irving, Jenny Huggins)*

PIERCEBRIDGE [NZ2115]

George DL2 3SW [B6275 just S of village, over bridge]: Old, recently refurbished riverside pub/hotel, bar food from good sandwiches up, Captain Cook ale, river-view dining room; children welcome, decked terrace and attractive garden with bridge to small island (not easy for disabled people), 36 bedrooms, open all day *(LYM, Marlene and Jim Godfrey, Mr and Mrs John Taylor)*

PONTELAND [NZ1771]

Badger NE20 9BT [Street Houses; A696 SE, by garden centre]: Well done Vintage Inn, five well kept beers such as Black Sheep and Timothy Taylors, good range of wines by the glass, standard food all day, prompt friendly service; good log fire, relaxing rooms and alcoves, old furnishings and olde-worlde décor; loud piped music; children welcome, open all day *(Gerry and Rosemary Dobson, Dr Peter D Smart, BB)*

RENNINGTON [NU2118]

☆ *Horseshoes* NE66 3RS [B1340]: Comfortable flagstoned pub with nice local feel (may be horses in car park), well kept ales such as Hadrian & Border and John Smiths, good value generous food inc two-course lunch deals, good local fish and meat, decent wines by the glass; friendly efficient unrushed service, simple neat bar with woodburner, spotless compact restaurant; children welcome, tables outside, attractive quiet village near coast, cl Mon *(Grahame Sherwin, Guy and Caroline Howard, Mike and Lynn Robinson, Comus and Sarah Elliott)*

☆ *Masons Arms* NE66 3RX [Stamford Cott; B1340 N]: Comfortably carpeted beamed bar with neat pubby furniture, well kept ales such as Hadrian & Border, Northumberland and Theakstons, good malt whisky range, enjoyable straightforward food, smiling relaxed service, woodburner between bar and family room; tables on lavender-edged roadside terrace, more picnic-sets behind, 17 comfortable bedrooms in former stables block *(LYM, George Cowie, Frances Gosnell, Michael Butler, the Dutchman, Ann and*

Tony Bennett-Hughes, Guy and Caroline Howard, Comus and Sarah Elliott, Roy and Jean Russell, J M Renshaw)*

RIDSDALE [NY9084]

Gun NE48 2TF [on A68]: Long carpeted lounge/eating area, big picture window with lovely moor view, open fire, Wylam and another ale, food from sandwiches and snacks to Sun carvery, friendly licensees; pool room; three good value bedrooms *(Pat and Stewart Gordon)*

ROMALDKIRK [NY9922]

Kirk DL12 9ED: Village green local doubling as part-time PO, friendly newish landlord, Timothy Taylors Landlord and Yard of Ale, food Weds-Sun inc Sun roasts, cosy log-fire bar, 18th-c stonework, darts; may be piped music; picnic-sets out at front, popular with walkers and cyclists, attractive moorland village *(Mr and Mrs Maurice Thompson)*

ROOKHOPE [NY9342]

Rookhope Inn DL13 2BG [off A689 W of Stanhope]: Friendly old inn on Coast-to-Coast bike route, real ales such as Black Sheep and Timothy Taylors Landlord, enjoyable home-made food from fresh sandwiches to good Sun roasts, black beams and open fires, small dining room; sports TV; seats outside, spectacular views, five bedrooms *(Andy and Jill Kassube)*

ROTHBURY [NU0501]

☆ *Newcastle Hotel* NE65 7UT: Small solid Victorian pub/hotel at end of green, comfortable lounge with dining area, second bar, friendly service, good reasonably priced food inc seasonal game, high teas Apr-Oct, Caledonian Deuchars IPA and Greene King ales, upstairs dining room; good value bedrooms, pretty village with river walks, handy for Cragside (NT), open all day *(Mike and Lynn Robinson, Dave Irving, Jenny Huggins)*

RUNNING WATERS [NZ3240]

Three Horseshoes DH1 2SR: Homely old country inn with good low-priced food, friendly staff, views over Durham; dogs welcome in bar, garden tables, beautiful peaceful surroundings, six comfortable bedrooms, good breakfast *(Jerry Brown)*

SEAHOUSES [NU2131]

Lodge NE68 7UA [Main St]: Refurbished family-friendly pub, woodburner in carpeted bar with cushioned stools and wall banquettes, large fish tank looking through to dining room with pine furniture on light wood floor; piped music, TV, pool; terrace garden, chalet-style bedrooms behind, bunkhouse *(the Dutchman)*

SEATON [NZ3950]

Seaton Lane Inn SR7 0LP [Seaton Lane]: Contemporary roadside bar/restaurant/hotel, popular with locals, good choice of enjoyable food from sandwiches and pub favourites up inc two-course set menu, well kept Mordue, Theakstons and Wells & Youngs ales; lounge and restaurant on split levels, attentive staff; 18 bedrooms *(Mr and Mrs Maurice Thompson, Barry Moses)*

SEATON CAREW [NZ5130]
Schooner TS25 1EZ [Warrior Drive]: Newish two-level bar with good value generous food all day, steak nights (Mon and Weds) and Sun carvery; central coal-effect gas fire, seafaring prints and theme, conservatory; pool, Sky TV for sports; children welcome, garden with play area *(Jeremy King)*

SEATON SLUICE [NZ3477]
Kings Arms NE26 4RD [West Terrace]: Friendly pub in pleasant seaside location, good range of beers and enjoyable pub food (especially the fish) *(John and Gloria Isaacs)*

SEDGEFIELD [NZ3528]
Dun Cow TS21 3AT [Front St]: Popular refurbished village inn with low-beamed bar, back tap room and dining room, above-average food, cheerful efficient staff, well kept ales such as Black Sheep and Camerons; children welcome, good value comfortable bedrooms, good breakfast *(John and Sylvia Harrop)*

SLALEY [NY9658]
☆ *Travellers Rest* NE46 1TT [B6306 S of Hexham (and N of village)]: Attractive and busy stone-built country pub, spaciously opened up, with farmhouse-style décor, beams, flagstones and polished wood floors, huge fireplace, comfortable high-backed settles forming discrete areas, attentive staff, popular generous food from simple low-priced hot dishes (12-5pm) to wider but still relatively cheap mealtime choice (not Sun evening) in bar and appealingly up-to-date dining room, good children's menu; basic sandwiches, friendly staff, real ales such as Allendale, Black Sheep and Wylam, limited wines by the glass; dogs welcome, tables outside with well equipped adventure play area on grass behind, three good value bedrooms, open all day *(Mr and Mrs Maurice Thompson)*

SOUTH SHIELDS [NZ3567]
Alum Ale House NE33 1JR [Ferry St (B1344)]: Relaxed 18th-c pub handy for ferry, big bars with good choice of real ales (beer festivals), hot drinks, good value basic lunchtime bar food; coal fire in old inglenook range, polished boards, pictures and newspaper cuttings; piped music and some live, games machines; children welcome, open all day *(the Didler, Pam and John Smith, Eric Larkham)*
Maltings NE33 4PG [Claypath Rd]: Former dairy now home to Jarrow brewery, their full range and guest ales from upstairs bar (showpiece staircase); open all day, no food Fri-Sun evenings *(Eric Larkham)*

STAMFORDHAM [NZ0772]
Bay Horse NE18 0PB [off B6309]: Refurbished beamed and stone-built pub at end of the green in an attractive village, good value generous food (not Sun evening, Mon) from sandwiches through steaks to homely puddings, OAP bargain lunch Tues and Thurs, well kept ales such as Caledonian Deuchars IPA, Consett, High House Farm and Wylam; good coffee, bare-boards bar area with leather

sofas and woodburner, restaurant, steps down to games room with pool, darts and TV; six bedrooms *(Michael Doswell)*

STOCKTON-ON-TEES [NZ4419]
Sun TS18 1SU [Knowles St]: Popular town local noted for its Bass, good prices, quick service, darts; open all day *(the Didler)*

SUNDERLAND [NZ3956]
Fitzgeralds SR1 3PZ [Green Terrace]: Bustling split-level city pub popular with locals and students (especially on match days); up to ten real ales inc several from local Darwin, helpful staff, friendly atmosphere, generous cheap bar lunches; children welcome lunchtime *(Mike and Lynn Robinson, Mr and Mrs Maurice Thompson)*
Rosedene SR2 9BT [Queen Alexandra Rd]: Former Georgian mansion, large main room and central bar area, popular food (not Sun evening), four mainly Greene King ales, restaurant, conservatory; Mon quiz night *(Mr and Mrs Maurice Thompson)*

THROPTON [NU0302]
Cross Keys NE65 7HX [B6341]: Attractive little village pub, enjoyable reasonably priced blackboard food with emphasis on fish, Black Sheep, good wine and soft drinks' choice; open fires in small cosy beamed bar with rooms off inc snug with high-backed settles, games room with darts and pool, back dining area; games machine, sports TV; children and dogs welcome, steeply terraced garden looking over village to hills, open all day at least in summer *(LYM, JJW, CMW, Mr and Mrs D J Nash)*
☆ *Three Wheat Heads* NE65 7LR [B6341]: 300-year-old village inn with welcoming licensees, good generous all-day food from extensive menu inc daily roasts, well kept Black Sheep and Theakstons, good coal fires (one in fine tall stone fireplace), darts and pool in public bar, dining room with lovely views; quiet piped music; children and dogs welcome, garden with play area, chickens and ducks, good value comfortable bedrooms, good breakfast, handy for Cragside (NT), open all day *(LYM, JJW, CMW, Sheena W Makin, Dave Irving, Jenny Huggins)*

WARENFORD [NU1429]
White Swan NE70 7HY [off A1, 3 or 4 miles S of Belford]: Simply decorated bar with a changing real ale, enjoyable imaginative food at reasonable prices in cosy restaurant, efficient helpful service, warm fires *(LYM, Mr J V Nelson)*

WARKWORTH [NU2406]
Masons Arms NE65 0UR [Dial Pl]: Welcoming village pub in shadow of castle, newish management doing enjoyable food inc daily specials and Sun carvery, local beers, friendly staff, Tues quiz night; dogs and children welcome, disabled facilities, back flagstoned courtyard, appealing village not far from sea, open all day *(Guy and Caroline Howard, Clive Flynn)*
Warkworth House NE65 0XB [Bridge St]: Hotel combining proper friendly pubby bar with bistro and restaurant, all with

enjoyable generous reasonably priced food, welcoming helpful staff, comfortable sofas, two changing real ales, good range of spirits and of good value wines by the glass, proper coffee; darts and bar billiards; dogs welcome, good bedrooms, open all day *(Kevin and Rose Lemin)*

WASHINGTON [NZ3054]

Courtyard NE38 8AB [Arts Centre, Biddick Lane, Fatfield]: Popular with locals, walkers and cyclists, modernish open-plan stone and beamed bar with up to six changing ales, Black Rat cider and Hereford perry, bottled belgian beers, good value food inc bargain Sun lunch, friendly helpful staff; beer festivals (Easter and August bank hol), live folk music Mon; benches in large courtyard, open all day *(Mr and Mrs Maurice Thompson, Kevin Thorpe)*

WEST BOLDON [NZ3561]

Black Horse NE36 0QQ [Rectory Bank, just off A184]: Mix of old and modern furnishings from pews and Victorian tables to comfortable sofas, lots of bric-a-brac, contemporary photographs and artworks; good choice of tasty food, real ales such as Bass, John Smiths, Tetleys and Timothy Taylors Landlord, restaurant; some monumental outside seating *(Mike and Lynn Robinson)*

WHITLEY BAY [NZ3473]

Briardene NE26 1UE [The Links]: Smart brightly decorated two-room pub, fine seaview spot, up to eight interesting changing ales, good value pubby food from sandwiches up, friendly efficient staff; seats outside, open all day *(Mike and Lynn Robinson, Eric Larkham)*

WOLSINGHAM [NZ0737]

Bay Horse DL13 3EX [Uppertown]: Welcoming landlord and helpful staff, three

local ales, imaginative good value food, traditional bar, smart dining room; seven good affordable bedrooms *(Jerry Brown)*

WOLVISTON [NZ4525]

Ship TS22 5JX [High St]: Gabled red-brick Victorian pub in centre of bypassed village, open-plan multi-level carpeted bar, bargain food, changing real ales from northern breweries; quiz nights; garden *(JHBS)*

WOOLER [NT9928]

Tankerville Arms NE71 6AD [A697 N]: Pleasant hotel bar in modernised early 17th-c coaching inn, relaxed and friendly, with reasonably priced food inc local meat and fish, ales such as Hadrian & Border, good wines by the glass, small restaurant and larger airy one overlooking nice garden; 16 bedrooms, good local walks *(Comus and Sarah Elliott)*

WYLAM [NZ1164]

☆ *Boathouse* NE41 8HR [Station Rd, handy for Newcastle—Carlisle railway line; across Tyne from village (and Stephenson's birthplace)]: Thriving convivial pub with splendid ale range inc local Wylam, keen prices, good choice of malt whiskies, bargain wknd lunches, polite helpful young staff; open stove in bright low-beamed bar, dining room; children and dogs welcome, seats outside, close to station and river, open all day *(the Didler, Mr and Mrs Maurice Thompson, Eric Larkham, Comus and Sarah Elliott)*

YARM [NZ4213]

Black Bull TS15 9AE [High St]: Old refurbished coaching inn, bar on left off flagstoned corridor, three ales inc Bass and Black Sheep, decent well priced pub food, lower bar area with access to riverside terrace and garden; can get crowded wknds *(Mike and Eleanor Anderson)*

Nottinghamshire

Just under two-thirds of the pubs in this county have a Beer Award, with Nottingham as something of a mecca for real ale, accounting for most of them. Of these, the two that stand out are the cheery Lincolnshire Poacher with its tremendous range of drinks, including 11 real ales, and the welcoming Vat & Fiddle with its ten real ales, most of which are from the next door Castle Rock Brewery. The other bonus in the city is the remarkably good value food – all but one of the Main Entries here has a Bargain Award. Further afield, the unspoilt Victoria at Beeston is worth seeking out for its fantastic range of beers and interesting location by the rail tracks. If you're looking for terrific food, the Caunton at Caunton Beck is a very civilised place for a special meal, as is the beautifully refurbished Full Moon at Morton which was new in the *Guide* last year. For its genuinely local ingredients and thoughtful cooking, it is our Nottinghamshire Dining Pub 2011. Two new Main Entries this year are the Bottle & Glass at Harby, which offers a notably fine wine list and good country cooking, and the stylish Boathouse at Farndon – modern interior and imaginative food.

BEESTON
SK5336   MAP 7

Victoria ♀ ◧
Dovecote Lane, backing on to railway station; NG9 1JG

Genuine down-to-earth all-rounder with impressive choice of drinks (including up to 15 real ales) and enjoyable, fairly priced food

The chatty lounge and bar at this cheery Victorian railway inn are adjacent to the railway station. A covered heated area outside has tables overlooking the platform and trains pass just a few feet away. With a genuinely pubby feel, the three fairly simple rooms have kept their original long narrow layout and are nicely unpretentious, with unfussy décor and simple solid traditional furnishings, stripped woodwork and floorboards (woodblock in some rooms), fires and stained-glass windows; newspapers, dominoes, cribbage and board games. Getting through up to 500 widely sourced beers a year, the superb choice of around a dozen guest ales could be from brewers such as Blackfriars, Blue Monkey, Brampton, Caythorpe, Full Mash, Holdens, Oldershaws, Ossett and Thwaites, all very well kept alongside Castle Rock Harvest Pale and Everards Tiger. The quite extraordinary range of drinks continues with continental draught beers, two farm ciders, over 120 malt whiskies, 20 irish whiskeys, about 30 wines by the glass and a very good range of soft drinks including Belvoir fruit pressés. A nice varied crowd gathers here, but even at busy times service is helpful and efficient. A great time to visit is during their two-week beer and music festival at the end of July, or during the smaller ones in January, at Easter and in October; no mobile phones; limited parking.

> Post Office address codings confusingly give the impression that a few pubs are in Nottinghamshire, when they're really in Derbyshire (which is where we list them).

🍴 The good value menu, of which about half is vegetarian, might include wild boar liver pâté with tequila and cranberry, smoked trout fillets with dill mayonnaise, beef braised in Fullers, chicken arrabiata, monkfish and prawns sautéed with thai spices, cottage pie, sausage and mash, red pepper and ricotta tart, butternut and baby broad bean risotto, and puddings such as treacle sponge and belgian chocolate cheesecake. *Starters/Snacks: £3.95 to £5.50. Main Courses: £7.95 to £15.50. Puddings: £3.95 to £4.25*

Free house ~ Licensees Neil Kelso and Graham Smith ~ Real ale ~ Bar food (12-8.45 Sun-Tues; 12-9.30 Weds-Sat) ~ (0115) 925 4049 ~ Children welcome away from counter till 8pm ~ Dogs allowed in bar ~ Live music Sun, Mon evening Oct-May ~ Open 10.30(12 Sun)-11

Recommended by MP, Dr and Mrs A K Clarke, the Didler, David Eberlin, John Read, Maurice Ricketts, Andy Lickfold, M C and S Jeanes

CAUNTON
SK7459   MAP 7

Caunton Beck 🍴 ♀
Newark Road; NG23 6AE

Civilised dining pub with very good (if not cheap) food all day from breakfasts first thing, good wine list, nice terrace

Surprisingly, given its aged appearance, this lovely inn is almost new, but it seems older because it was reconstructed using original timbers and reclaimed oak, around the skeleton of the old Hole Arms. Scrubbed pine tables, clever lighting, an open fire, country-kitchen chairs, low beams and rag-finished paintwork in its spacious interior create a comfortably relaxed atmosphere. A determination to offer kind accommodating service is a fundamental goal here, and the warm flexible hospitality does indeed contribute to making this a memorable place. Over two dozen of the wines on the very good wine list are available by the glass, and they've beers from brewers such as Batemans, Black Sheep and Marstons on handpump; espresso coffee, daily papers and magazines. With lots of summer flowers and plants, the terrace is very pleasant.

🍴 Food service begins first thing with hearty english breakfasts (served until midday; 11.30am weekends and bank holidays), and continues with delicious sandwiches and a fairly elaborate seasonally changing menu and specials list later on: twice-baked haddock and leek soufflé, seared lambs kidneys with tarragon mustard café au lait, potato and spinach gnocchi with colston bassett stilon, roast salmon with dill hollandaise, rump of beef with café de paris butter, puddings such as lemon and raspberry tart, dark chocolate and hazelnut cream, and a good cheeseboard. *Starters/Snacks: £4.75 to £7.50. Main Courses: £12.50 to £15.50. Puddings: £4.95*

Free house ~ Licensee Julie Allwood ~ Real ale ~ Bar food (8am-10pm) ~ Restaurant ~ (01636) 636793 ~ Children welcome ~ Dogs allowed in bar ~ Open 8am-11pm

Recommended by R Y and A M Ball, Blaise Vyner, Dave and Pauline, Keith and Chris O'Neill, Philip Bishop, James Stretton, Jeremy King, Ian and Nita Cooper, Mark, Amanda, Luke and Jake Sheard, Gordon and Margaret Ormondroyd

CAYTHORPE
SK6845   MAP 7

Black Horse 🍺
Turn off A6097 0.25 miles SE of roundabout junction with A612, NE of Nottingham; into Gunthorpe Road, then right into Caythorpe Road and keep on; NG14 7ED

Quaintly old-fashioned little pub brewing its own beer, simple interior and homely enjoyable food; no children or credit cards

The good value meals at this timeless 300-year-old country local attract an older group of regulars at lunchtime, so you will need to book. The uncluttered carpeted bar has just five tables, brocaded wall banquettes and settles, a few bar stools (for the cheerful evening drinkers), a warm woodburning stove, decorative plates on a delft shelf and a few horsebrasses on the ceiling joists. Off the front corridor is a partly panelled inner room with a wall bench running right the way around three unusual long copper-topped tables, and quite a few old local photographs; darts and dominoes. Down on the left, an end room has just one huge round table. They brew two tasty Caythorpe beers in outbuildings here, one of which will be well kept alongside Adams or Batemans, Greene King Abbot and Caythorpe Dover Beck and possibly a weekend guest such as Exmoor Gold. There are some plastic tables outside, and the River Trent is fairly close for waterside walks.

🍴 **Simple freshly cooked traditional food from a shortish menu includes parsnip soup, ploughman's, prawn cocktail, rollmops, good fried cod, haddock or plaice with parsley sauce, beef in mushroom sauce, fillet steak, and puddings such as baked plums with baked egg custard or golden sponge with custard.** *Starters/Snacks: £2.75 to £6.00. Main Courses: £6.50 to £18.00. Puddings: £2.75 to £4.50*

Own brew ~ Licensee Sharron Andrews ~ Real ale ~ Bar food (12-2, 7-8.30; not Mon, Sun, Sat evening and third Tuesday of the month) ~ No credit cards ~ (0115) 966 3520 ~ Dogs allowed in bar ~ Open 12-2.30, 6.30(6 Sat)-11; 12-5, 8-11.30 Sun; closed Mon except bank hols

Recommended by the Didler, P Dawn, Rob and Chris Warner

COLSTON BASSETT   SK6933   MAP 7

Martins Arms ♛ 🍺

Village signposted off A46 E of Nottingham; School Lane, near market cross in village centre; NG12 3FD

Smart dining pub with imaginative food (if pricey), good range of drinks including seven real ales and lovely grounds

Serious food and fine dining are an option at this lovely country pub with its comfortably civilised atmosphere. The elegant restaurant is smartly decorated with period fabrics and colourings, and neatly uniformed staff, antique furnishings, hunting prints and warm log fires in Jacobean fireplaces all set the tone of the place. On the other hand, they do offer a short snacky bar menu in the little tap room which has its own corner bar with half a dozen or so well kept real ales on handpump, including Bass, Greene King IPA, Marstons Pedigree, Timothy Taylors Landlord and three guests from brewers such as Black Sheep, Elgoods and Woodfordes Wherry; also Belvoir organic ginger beer, a good range of malt whiskies and cognacs and an interesting wine list; cribbage, dominoes and board games. The sizeable lawned garden (which has summer croquet) backs on to estate parkland. You might be asked to leave your credit card behind the bar if you want to eat out here. They've converted the stables into an antiques shop and readers recommend visiting the church opposite and Colston Bassett Dairy, which sells its own stilton, is just outside the village.

🍴 **Using carefully sourced ingredients, including organic vegetables, and served with home-made bread, chutneys and so forth, the not cheap but very good food includes imaginatively filled sandwiches, ploughman's, starters such as ham hock terrine with pineapple chutney, sautéed chicken liver with mushroom and amaretto on toasted brioche, tempura scallops with sweet chilli sauce, main courses such as potato cake with cheddar, mushroom, red pepper and pea risotto, roast monkfish wrapped in parma ham, partridge and pear casserole, chicken and leek pie with sweet-corn fritter, fillet steak with colston bassett stilton and port sauce, and puddings such as lemon meringue tart and date and walnut pudding with vanilla ice-cream.** *Starters/Snacks: £5.00 to £6.95. Main Courses: £11.95 to £18.95. Puddings: £6.00*

Free house ~ Licensees Lynne Strafford Bryan and Salvatore Inguanta ~ Real ale ~ Bar food (12-2(2.30 Sun), 6-9.30; not Sun evenings) ~ Restaurant ~ (01949) 81361 ~ Children welcome in dining room and snug ~ Open 12-3(3.30 summer Sat), 6-11; 12-5(4 in winter), 7-10.30 Sun

Recommended by the Didler, Harry Whinney

> The 🍺 symbol shows pubs which keep their beer unusually well, have a
> particularly good range or brew their own.

FARNDON   SK7652   MAP 7

Boathouse

Just off A46 SW of Newark; turn off to village, keeping on towards river – pub in North End, just past Britannia; NG24 3SX

Big-windowed contemporary bar-restaurant overlooking River Trent

The emphasis here is decidedly on the food side, but they do have Caythorpe Bitter and Marstons Pedigree on handpump as well as a good choice of wines by the glass – and on Sunday live acoustic music nights they do free tapas for drinkers. There is a proper bar counter (stylish, made of small black blocks coursed like a Cotswolds stone wall, with a pale wood top), with smart chrome and ply bar chairs here and around two tall steel-pedestal tables. The main area, with rows of polished pedestal dining tables and comfortable cloth-upholstered seating, is indeed reminiscent of a made-over boathouse, with high ceiling trusses supporting bare ventilation or heating ducts, and little decoration. A second dining area is broadly similar, though with some dark leather chairs, too. The young staff, casually neat in their aprons, are efficient; well reproduced piped pop music. In good but cool weather they supply blankets for the wicker chairs around teak tables on the terrace.

🍴 **The fact that some dishes come on slate platters gives an immediate idea of the style of food here: home-made breads, creamy mushrooms with truffle oil and parmesan on toast, seared king scallops with warm chorizo, coriander and potato salad and roast pepper coulis, rosemary, thyme and lamb sausages with salsa verde, battered haddock with minted marrowfat peas, thai fish and noodles, roast duck breast with sweet potato cake, plum, orange and ginger dressing and crispy leeks, goats cheese and red pepper risotto with beetroot and chive salsa, home-made burgers, steaks, and puddings such as chocolate and amaretto parfait and summer pudding.** *Starters/Snacks: £4.50 to £9.00. Main Courses: £9.00 to £17.00. Puddings: £4.00 to £7.00*

Free house ~ Licensee Nathan Barton ~ Real ale ~ Bar food (12-2.30(3 Fri), 6-9.30) ~ (01636) 676578 ~ Children welcome ~ Open 11am(10am Sat)-midnight; 10am-11pm Sun

Recommended by Michael and Maggie Betton, G Musson

HALAM   SK6754   MAP 7

Waggon & Horses

Off A612 in Southwell centre, via Halam Road; NG22 8AE

Civilised dining pub with inventive seasonally changing menu

Immaculately kept, the open-plan interior of this old low-ceilinged but much altered place has a congenial dining atmosphere and is neatly divided into intimate sections naturally formed by the layout of the original 17th-c building. Various floral pictures (some painted by the staff) hang on calming pale green walls, and sturdy high-back pine dining chairs are set around a mix of solid mainly stripped tables on wood and tiled floors. Kind obliging staff serve two Thwaites beers on handpump; piped music. Out past a grandfather clock in the lobby are a few roadside picnic-sets by pretty window boxes.

🍴 **Imaginative food might include black pudding and stilton salad, scallop and bacon salad, halibut with lemon and herb butter, fried liver with onions and bacon, pumpkin and shallot risotto, blade of beef with leeks and stilton, and puddings such as cranberry and almond sponge, blueberry and vanilla cheesecake; good value two and three-course menu (lunchtime and 6pm to 7pm Tuesday-Friday).** *Starters/Snacks: £5.00 to £10.00. Main Courses: £10.00 to £24.00. Puddings: £5.00 to £6.00*

Thwaites ~ Tenant Roy Wood ~ Real ale ~ Bar food (11.45-2, 5.45-8) ~ (01636) 813109 ~ No children under 10 Fri, Sat evenings ~ Open 11.45-3, 5.45-10(11 Sat); 11.45-3 Sun; closed Sun evening, Mon (except bank hols)

Recommended by Michael and Maggie Betton, Rob and Catherine Dunster, Derek and Sylvia Stephenson, Colin Fisher, Patrick Stevens

HARBY

SK8870   MAP 7

Bottle & Glass ♀

Village signposted off A57 W of Lincoln; entering village turn left at Swinethorpe, Eagle signpost, into High Street; NG23 7EB

Good food all day in civilised country dining pub

The layout here echoes its days as a village local, with its pair of bay-windowed front bars. But it's a faint echo: the big vineyard map of the Côte de Beaune on the end wall of the left-hand bar is a truer guide to the pub's heart and soul than the log fire, dark flagstones and attractively pubby furnishings in the front part – lots of bright cushions on the built-in wall benches and the little arts-and-crafts chairs. Red walls and big prints feature here and in the right-hand bar – broadly similar, with polished floorboards, stripped pews and a high shelf of paperbacks. Besides a splendid range of wines by the glass, they have Black Sheep and a guest such as Titanic Black Ice on handpump, and service is good. Beyond a small area with squashy sofas and armchairs is a long rather more formal restaurant. A back terrace has modern black wrought-iron furniture, and there are picnic-sets on the grass beyond. The pub is in the same family as the Caunton Beck in Caunton.

🍴 **The bar blackboard aims squarely at honest country food such as ham hock terrine, sausage and mash, chicken and mushroom pie, salmon fillet and rack of lamb – not cheap but good value, with two-course and three-course deals, and puddings such as charred pineapple frangipane with coconut foam. Soups and deluxe sandwiches are good and come with enterprising breads.** *Starters/Snacks: £4.50 to £6.25. Main Courses: £9.95 to £14.95. Puddings: £4.95*

Free house ~ Licensee Michael Hope ~ Real ale ~ Bar food (11-10) ~ Restaurant ~ (01522) 703438 ~ Dogs allowed in bar ~ Open 11-11
Recommended by Peter and Eleanor Kenyon, David and Ruth Hollands, Adam Jackson

MORTON

SK7251   MAP 7

Full Moon 🍴

Pub and village signposted off Bleasby—Fiskerton back road, SE of Southwell; NG25 0UT

NOTTINGHAMSHIRE DINING PUB OF THE YEAR

Five real ales and good food at stylish village local with play area in nice garden

This last year has seen warm praise from readers for this attractive old pub. A new Main Entry in the 2010 edition, it has built well on the reputation its enthusiastic licensees gained at their previous pub. They have brought the Full Moon smartly and comfortably up to date with an interesting colour scheme in cream, greens and browns, and an eclectic mix of reclaimed furnishings – all simple and clean. Smart grey slate runs the length of the long counter, which was constructed from good reclaimed pitch pine: Bass and Blue Monkey are on handpump alongside three guests from brewers such as Nottingham, Theakstons and Wells & Youngs; TV, piped music and board games. Lots of effort has gone into the garden which comprises a peaceful shady back terrace with picnic-sets, a sizeable lawn and some sturdy play equipment.

🍴 **The menu is fairly short but a lot of care goes into the purchase of ingredients, most of which do genuinely come from local suppliers: starters such as terrine of the day, potted crab with parmesan toast and salad, black pudding and bacon topped with poached egg and mustard dressing, main courses such as battered haddock with minted pea purée, beef and roast vegetable pie with red cabbage, home-made burgers with sour dough buns, chicken breast stuffed with mushroom duxelles with pesto and onion cream, cream of mushroom and thyme linguine, fried duck breast with blackcurrant and cinnamon and lyonnaise potatoes, and puddings such as chocolate brownie with chocolate sauce, lemon tart and profiteroles with strawberries and chocolate sauce.** *Starters/Snacks: £4.75 to £7.50. Main Courses: £10.00 to £17.50. Puddings: £4.00 to £6.50*

We say if we know a pub has piped music.

Free house ~ Licensees Will and Rebecca White ~ Real ale ~ Bar food (10-2.30, 6-9.30; 9.30-7 Sun) ~ Restaurant ~ (01636) 830251 ~ Children welcome ~ Dogs allowed in bar ~ Open 10-3, 5.30-11.30; 10-midnight Sat; 9.30am-10.30pm Sun

Recommended by the Didler, David Glynne-Jones, MP, Derek and Sylvia Stephenson, Dr and Mrs A K Clarke, Pete Yearsley, Prof Kenneth Surin

NOTTINGHAM

SK5739 MAP 7

Bell 🍺

Angel Row, off Market Square; NG1 6HL

Up to a dozen real ales from remarkable cellars in historic yet thriving place with regular live music and simple food

Deceptively large and masked by a late Georgian frontage, the interior of the two 500-year-old timber-framed buildings that form this pub show many considerable signs of their venerable age. With quite a café feel in summer, the front Tudor bar (to the left and right of the corridor) is perhaps the brightest with french windows opening to tables on the pavement, and bright blue walls with glass panels protecting patches of 300-year-old wallpaper. The room with the most aged feel is the larger very pubby low-beamed Elizabethan Bar, with its half-panelled walls, maple parquet floor and comfortable high-backed armchairs. Upstairs, at the back of the heavily panelled Belfry (usually open only at lunchtime), you can see the rafters of the 15th-c crown post roof, and look down on the busy street below; TV, silent fruit machine and piped music. The labyrinthine cellars (tours by appointment) go about ten metres into the sandstone rock, and the efforts of the hardworking Carmelite monks from the attached friary who are said to have dug them are still much appreciated, as the cellars now house the well kept beers that are served here – usually Greene King Abbot, IPA and Old Speckled Hen and guests from brewers such as local Nottingham and Oakham. The friendly welcoming staff and landlord also serve ten wines by the glass, quite a few malt whiskies and a farm cider.

🍴 **Reasonably priced straightforward bar food includes soup, lamb kofta kebab, burgers, ploughman's, paella, beef pie and battered cod.** *Starters/Snacks: £3.29 to £7.95. Main Courses: £5.55 to £9.99. Puddings: £1.99 to £3.99*

Greene King ~ Manager Craig A Sharp-Weir ~ Real ale ~ Bar food (12-9pm) ~ Restaurant ~ (0115) 947 5241 ~ Children welcome in Belfry and Elizabethan Bar till 6pm if dining ~ Live music Sun lunchtime and Mon, Tues and late Sat evenings ~ Open 10am-11.30pm; 10am-1am Sat; 11am-11.30pm Sun

Recommended by Jeremy King, Barry Collett, the Didler

Keans Head 🍷 🍺 £

St Marys Gate; NG1 1QA

Bustling central pub, usefully serving good value food all day, wide choice of drinks, with smiling service and informal chatty atmosphere

The single room that comprises this cheery Tynemill pub (in the attractive Lace Market area) has something of a continental bar. It's fairly functional, but inviting nevertheless, with simple wooden café furnishings on the wood-boarded floor, some exposed brickwork and red tiling, a low sofa by big windows overlooking the street, stools along the wood boarded bar and a small fireplace. Friendly staff serve Castle Rock Harvest Pale, Preservation and Screech Owl and three guests from brewers such as Batemans, Oldershaw and Titanic from handpumps, draught belgian beers, interesting bottled beers and soft drinks, about 20 wines by the glass, 39 malt whiskies and lots of teas and coffees; daily newspapers and piped music. St Mary's Church next door is worth a look.

🍴 **An interesting mix of tasty traditional english and italian food might include home-made focaccia, antipasti, whitebait, pork pie, sandwiches, ploughman's, pizzas, pie of the day, potato and aubergine curry, sausage of the day and mash, wild rabbit fricassée with potato dauphinoise, steamed hake with samphire, pine nuts, spinach and linguine.** *Starters/Snacks: £3.50 to £5.50. Main Courses: £5.50 to £9.95. Puddings: £3.25 to £4.95*

Castle Rock ~ Manager Charlotte Blomeley ~ Real ale ~ Bar food (12-9(5 Sun, Mon); not Sun, Mon evenings) ~ (0115) 947 4052 ~ Children welcome till 7pm ~ Open 11.30am-11pm (12.30pm Fri, Sat); 12-10.30 Sun
Recommended by Jeremy King, the Didler, P Dawn

Lincolnshire Poacher 🍺 £

Mansfield Road; up hill from Victoria Centre; NG1 3FR

Chatty down-to-earth pub with great range of drinks (including a dozen real ales), good value food and outdoor seating

It's the tremendous range of beers and cheery relaxed atmosphere that make this such an enjoyable pub – it can get very busy in the evening with a younger crowd. The traditional big wood-floored front bar is fairly simple with wall settles, plain wooden tables and breweriana. It opens on to a plain but lively room on the left with a corridor that takes you down to the chatty panelled back snug, with newspapers, cribbage, dominoes, cards and backgammon. A conservatory overlooks tables on a large heated area behind. The impressive range of drinks includes Batemans XB, Castle Rock Harvest Pale and Screech Owl, alongside well kept guests from a good variety of brewers such as Abbeydale, Black Sheep, Leeds, Newby Wyke and Woodfordes. Other drinks include seven continental draught beers, around 20 belgian bottled beers, good farm cider, around 70 malt whiskies and nicely priced soft drinks.

🍴 **Good value tasty bar food from a changing blackboard menu might include celery and roasted red pepper soup, sausage and mash, goulash, spaghetti carbonara, burger and sautéed potatoes, butternut and chickpea madras and halloumi and courgette salad.**
Starters/Snacks: £2.50 to £5.00. Main Courses: £4.50 to £8.00. Puddings: £2.00 to £3.50

Castle Rock ~ Manager Karen Williams ~ Real ale ~ Bar food (12-9) ~ (0115) 941 1584 ~ Children welcome till 8pm ~ Dogs welcome ~ Live music Sun evening ~ Open 11-11(midnight Thurs); 10am-midnight Sat; 12am-11pm Sun
Recommended by John Robertson, Bruce Bird, Jeremy King, the Didler, MP, Derek and Sylvia Stephenson, Geoff and Kaye Newton, David Hunt

Olde Trip to Jerusalem ★ 🍺 £

Brewhouse Yard; from inner ring road follow The North, A6005 Long Eaton signpost until you are in Castle Boulevard, then almost at once turn right into Castle Road; pub is up on the left; NG1 6AD

Unusual pub partly built into sandstone caves, good range of real ales, reasonably priced pubby food

With the building seemingly clinging to a sandstone cliff face, some of the rambling rooms at this famous place are actually burrowed into the rock itself, making it rather unlike any other pub you are likely to visit. The siting of the current (largely 17th-c) building is attributed to the days when a brewhouse was established here to supply the needs of the castle on the cliff top. Carved into the rock, the downstairs bar has leatherette-cushioned settles built into dark panelling, tables on flagstones and snug banquettes built into low-ceilinged rocky alcoves. The pub's name refers to the 12th-c crusaders who used to meet nearby on their way to the Holy Land – pub collectors of today still make their own crusades here, and no doubt enjoy the pub's little tourist shop with its panelled walls soaring up into a dark rock cleft. Staff cope efficiently with the busy mix of tourists, chatting locals and students. As well as half a dozen beers from the Greene King stable (kept in top condition on handpump), you'll find a changing guest, probably from Nottingham Brewery. They've ring the bull, seats in a snug courtyard and you'll need to book if you want to do their cellar tour.

🍴 **Straightforward bar food includes breakfasts, sandwiches, burgers, fish and chips, roast beef in giant yorkshire pudding, sausage and mash, beef and ale pie and steaks.**
Starters/Snacks: £3.49 to £4.49. Main Courses: £6.95 to £10.49. Puddings: £2.49 to £4.49

Prices of main dishes sometimes now don't include vegetables – if in doubt, ask.

Greene King ~ Manager Rosie St John-Lowther ~ Real ale ~ Bar food (11-8) ~ (0115) 9473171 ~ Children welcome till 7pm ~ Open 11-11(midnight Fri, Sat)

Recommended by the Didler, Ross Balaam, John Fiander, Jeremy King, Bob and Angela Brooks, Barry Collett, P Dawn

Vat & Fiddle 🍺 £

Queens Bridge Road, alongside Sheriffs Way (near multi-storey car park); NG2 1NB

Eleven real ales at very welcoming down-to-earth pub next to Castle Rock Brewery

The fairly functional but well loved open-plan interior at this plain little brick pub has a strong unspoilt 1930s feel, with cream and navy walls and ceiling, varnished pine tables and bentwood stools and chairs on parquet and terrazzo flooring, patterned blue curtains, some brewery memorabilia, and Kipper the landlady's cat. An interesting display of photographs depicts nearby demolished pubs, and there are magazines and newspapers, TV, darts and board games. Steady and unchanging, it's the personalised chatty atmosphere that marks it out from other Nottingham entries. As well as half a dozen Castle Rock beers, they serve several interesting guests from brewers such as Batemans, Daleside and Newby Wyke. They also have around 60 malt whiskies, a couple of changing farm ciders, a good range of continental bottled beers and good value soft drinks; occasional beer festivals. There are picnic-sets in front by the road.

🍴 Two or three wholesome lunchtime specials, such as chilli or curry are served at lunchtime, and rolls are available until they run out of stock. *Starters/Snacks: £2.95. Main Courses: £5.25 to £6.95*

Castle Rock ~ Manager Sarah Houghton ~ Real ale ~ Bar food (12-2.30 Mon-Fri; cobs all day) ~ No credit cards ~ (0115) 985 0611 ~ Children welcome ~ Dogs allowed in bar ~ Open 11-11 (midnight Fri, Sat); 12-11 Sun

Recommended by the Didler, Bruce Bird

LUCKY DIP

Besides the fully inspected pubs, you might like to try these Lucky Dips recommended to us and described by readers (if you do, please send us reports: feedback@goodguides.com).

AWSWORTH [SK4844]
Gate NG16 2RN [Main St, via A6096 off A610 Nuthall—Eastwood bypass]: Friendly old traditional local nr site of once-famous railway viaduct (photographs in passage), well kept Greene King ales, coal fire in quiet comfortable lounge, cosy bar with TV, small pool room, skittle alley; tables out in front, open all day *(the Didler)*
BAGTHORPE [SK4751]
Dixies Arms NG16 5HF [2 miles from M1 junction 27; A608 towards Eastwood right on B600 via Sandhill Rd, left into School Rd; Lower Bagthorpe]: Reliably well kept ales such as Greene King Abbot and Theakstons Best in friendly unspoilt 18th-c beamed and tiled-floor local, good fire in small part-panelled parlour's fine fireplace, entrance bar with tiny snug, longer narrow room with toby jugs, darts and dominoes, busy wknds with live music and Sun quiz; good big garden with play area and football pitch, own pigeon, gun and morris dancing clubs, open all day *(the Didler)*
BEESTON [SK5236]
Crown NG9 1FY [Church St]: Bought and sensitively refurbished by Everards, real ale enthusiast landlord serving up to ten (some

keenly priced), also real ciders and good choice of bottled beers, lunchtime food plus all-day basic snacks; front snug and bar with new quarry-tiled floor, carpeted parlour with padded wall seats, Victorian décor and new polished bar in lounge, beams, panelling, bric-a-brac, old red telephone box; terrace tables, open all day *(the Didler, MP)*
BINGHAM [SK7039]
☆ *Horse & Plough* NG13 8AF [off A52; Long Acre]: Low beams, flagstones and stripped brick, prints and old brewery memorabilia, comfortable open-plan seating inc pews, well kept Caledonian Deuchars IPA, Fullers London Pride, Wells & Youngs Bombardier and three guest beers (tasters offered), good wine choice, good value home-made wkdy bar food, popular upstairs grill room (then Tues-Sat evenings and Sun lunch) with polished boards, hand-painted murals and open kitchen; piped music; children and dogs welcome, disabled facilities, open all day *(MP, the Didler, BB)*
BUNNY [SK5829]
☆ *Rancliffe Arms* NG11 6QT [Loughborough Rd (A60 S of Nottingham)]: Substantial early 18th-c former coaching inn reworked with emphasis on linked dining areas, upscale

food from enterprising sandwich range to adventurous dishes, popular carvery Mon evening and Weds, chunky country chairs around mixed tables on flagstones or carpet, friendly efficient service, sofas and armchairs in comfortable log-fire bar with Marstons and other changing ales; children welcome, smart canopied modern decking outside, open all day wknds *(John and Sylvia Harrop, Phil and Jane Hodson, Gerry and Rosemary Dobson, BB, Alistair and Kay Butler)*

CAR COLSTON [SK7242]

Royal Oak NG13 8JE [The Green, off Tenman Lane (off A46 not far from A6097 junction)]: Helpful licensees doing good home-made food (not Sun evening) in biggish 19th-c pub opp one of England's largest village greens, well kept Marstons-related ales, decent choice of wines by the glass, woodburner in lounge bar with tables set for eating, public bar with unusual barrel-vaulted brick ceiling; children welcome, picnic-sets on spacious back lawn, open all day wknds, cl Mon lunchtime *(Richard and Jean Green, MP, David Glynne-Jones, Phil and Jane Hodson, Alan Bowker, Sarah Greenway)*

CARLTON-ON-TRENT [SK7964]

Great Northern NG23 6NT [Ossington Rd; village signed just off A1 N of Newark!]: Large busy local next to main railway line, very frequent trains and lots of railway memorabilia; friendly atmosphere, usual food with good skillet dishes and fresh fish Fri, well kept Greene King ales, dark wood furniture, big games room, family room; tables out overlooking trains *(Phil and Jane Hodson)*

COTGRAVE [SK6435]

Rose & Crown NG12 3HQ [Main Rd, off A46 SE of Nottingham]: Friendly and comfortable village pub, good value generous food all day inc midwk and early evening bargains, more elaborate evening/wknd dishes, young helpful staff, three or four changing ales, good wine and soft drinks choice, log fires, newspapers, back eating area with fresh flowers and candles; piped music; children welcome, garden picnic-sets *(John and Sylvia Harrop, JJW, CMW, Richard Butler, Marie Kroon)*

CUCKNEY [SK5671]

Greendale Oak NG20 9NQ [High Croft]: Newish licensees doing enjoyable usual food (not Sun evening) inc lunchtime bargains, well kept Wells & Youngs Bombardier and two guests, good service, roomy L-shaped bar with banquettes, chamber-pots, Davy lamps, coins and banknotes on beams, separate restaurant; no dogs; children welcome, garden with picnic-sets, play area and chickens, five refurbished bedrooms, open all day Fri-Sun *(Derek and Sylvia Stephenson)*

EASTWOOD [SK4846]

Foresters Arms NG16 2DN [Main St, Newthorpe]: Friendly cosy local with well kept Greene King ales, darts, dominoes and table skittles, open fire, old local photographs, lounge with wknd organ singalong; TV; nice garden *(the Didler)*

ELKESLEY [SK6875]

☆ *Robin Hood* DN22 8AJ [just off A1 Newark—Blyth; High St]: Neat dining pub with good food inc midwk deals, friendly competent staff, Black Sheep, Marstons Pedigree and Wells & Youngs Bitter, dark furnishings on patterned carpets, yellow walls, pool and board games; piped music, TV; children and dogs welcome, picnic-sets and play area, cl Sun evening, Mon lunchtime *(Patrick Stevens, Derek and Sylvia Stephenson, Rita and Keith Pollard)*

GRANBY [SK7436]

☆ *Marquis of Granby* NG13 9PN [off A52 E of Nottingham; Dragon St]: Popular, stylish and friendly 18th-c pub in attractive Vale of Belvoir village, tap for Brewsters with their ales and interesting guests from chunky yew bar counter, decent home-made food – Fri evening (fish and chips) to Sun lunchtime, two small comfortable rooms with broad flagstones, some low beams and striking wallpaper, open fire; children and dogs welcome, open from 4pm Mon-Fri, all day wknds *(the Didler, BB)*

HICKLING [SK6929]

Plough LE14 3AH [Main St]: Interesting old pub doing well under newish licensees, two levels and several rooms extended around old cottage inc cosy snug, open fires, four well kept ales, good choice of wines and soft drinks, fair range of reasonably priced food (not Sun evening, Mon), children's menu, friendly service (can be slow when busy); soft piped music, live Thurs night; informal garden with slide by locally navigable Grantham Canal basin, towpath walks, open all day Fri-Sun, cl Mon lunchtime *(JJW, CMW)*

HOVERINGHAM [SK6946]

☆ *Reindeer* NG14 7GR [Main St]: Friendly beamed pub with intimate bar and busy restaurant (best to book), Castle Rock, Caythorpe and two changing guest ales, good wines by the glass, good home-made food from pubby things to enterprising dishes, lunchtime set deals and vegan choices too, daily papers, open fires; children welcome, seats outside, open all day wknds, cl Mon and Tues lunchtimes *(the Didler, Graham and Jan Pigott)*

KIMBERLEY [SK4944]

☆ *Nelson & Railway* NG16 2NR [Station Rd; handy for M1 junction 26 via A610]: Comfortable beamed Victorian pub with well kept Greene King ales and guests, mix of Edwardian-looking furniture, brewery prints (was tap for defunct H&H brewery) and railway signs, dining extension, traditional games inc alley and table skittles; piped music, games machine; children and dogs allowed, tables and swings in good-sized front cottagey garden, good value bedrooms, open all day *(the Didler, LYM)*

Stag NG16 2NB [Nottingham Rd]: Friendly 16th-c traditional local kept spotless by devoted landlady, two cosy rooms, small central counter and corridor, low beams, dark panelling and settles, good range of ales inc Adnams, Black Sheep, Marstons and Timothy Taylors (May beer festival), no food, vintage working penny slot machines and Shipstones brewery photographs; attractive back garden with play area, opens 5pm (1.30 Sat, 12 Sun) *(the Didler)*

LAMBLEY [SK6345]
Woodlark NG4 4QB [Church St]: Welcoming and interestingly laid-out village local, neatly furnished bare-brick beamed bar, careful extension into next house giving comfortable lounge/dining area, popular good value freshly made food, downstairs steak bar (wknd evenings), up to seven well kept ales inc Black Sheep, Castle Rock and Copper Dragon, open fire; children welcome, tables on side terrace, open all day Fri, short afternoon break Sat and Sun *(BB, the Didler)*

LANGAR [SK7234]
Unicorns Head NG13 9HE [Main St]: Comfortable heavily beamed dining pub with newish licensees, good choice of well priced food (all day wknds, lunchtime deals wkdys), attentive service, three Everards ales; piped music, Weds quiz night; children welcome, courtyard picnic-sets, open all day wknds *(JJW, CMW)*

LAXTON [SK7266]
☆ *Dovecote* NG22 0NU [off A6075 E of Ollerton]: Village pub with three traditionally furnished dining areas, good food (may need to book evenings), well kept changing beers such as Black Sheep, Fullers and Springhead, farm cider, friendly landlord and good staff, pool room with darts and dominoes; piped music – live last Fri; children welcome, dogs in bar, small front terrace and sloping garden with church views, bedrooms, camping, open all day Sun *(Keith and Chris O'Neill, LYM, Terry Devine, Jenny and Peter Lowater)*

LINBY [SK5351]
Horse & Groom NG15 8AE [Main St]: Picturesque three-room village pub with welcoming enthusiastic landlord, Greene King, Theakstons, Wells & Youngs and changing guests, friendly staff, enjoyable well presented food (not Sun-Thurs evenings) from shortish menu, inglenook log fire, conservatory, no mobile phones; quiet piped music, big-screen TV, games machine in lobby; tables outside, big play area, attractive village nr Newstead Abbey, open all day *(M Mossman, the Didler, P Dawn)*

LONG EATON [SK4833]
Hole in the Wall NG10 1JX [6 Regent St]: Two-room 19th-c backstreet local with original serving hatch, good choice of well kept ales such as Acorn, Nottingham, Oakham and Ufford, breweriana; decked area outside, open all day *(Neil Rowe)*

LOWDHAM [SK6646]
Worlds End NG14 7AT [Plough Lane]: Small village pub with good choice of reasonably

priced food most of the day (not Sun evening) inc popular OAP wkdy lunches and other deals, friendly service can be slow when busy, three real ales, log fire in pubby beamed bar, restaurant; piped music; children welcome, garden with picnic-sets (some covered), lots of flower tubs and baskets, open all day *(M Mossman, JJW, CMW)*

MANSFIELD [SK5561]
Il Rosso NG18 4AF: Refurbished dining pub (former Plough) with accent on enjoyable italian-leaning food, well kept beer inc Adnams, good service *(Derek and Sylvia Stephenson)*
Nell Gwynne NG18 5EX [Sutton Rd (A38 W of centre)]: Former gentlemen's club, chatty and welcoming with locals of all ages, two changing beers, no food, log-effect gas fire, old colliery plates and mementoes of old Mansfield pubs, games room; sports TV, piped music; open all day wknds and from 2pm Mon-Fri *(the Didler)*
Railway Inn NG18 1EF [Station St; best approached by viaduct from nr Market Place]: Friendly traditional local with long-serving landlady, ales such as Batemans XB, good bottled beer choice, bargain home-made lunchtime food (also midwk evenings), bright front bar and cosier back room; small courtyard garden, handy for Robin Hood Line station, open all day, cl Sun evening *(the Didler)*

MANSFIELD WOODHOUSE [SK5463]
Greyhound NG19 8BD [High St]: Friendly 17th-c village local with well kept mainstream ales, cosy lounge, darts, dominoes and pool in busy bar, no food; regular beer festivals, open all day *(the Didler)*

MAPLEBECK [SK7160]
☆ *Beehive* NG22 0BS [signed down pretty country lanes from A616 Newark—Ollerton and from A617 Newark—Mansfield]: Relaxing beamed country tavern in nice spot, chatty landlady, tiny front bar, slightly bigger side room, traditional furnishings and antiques, coal or log fire, well kept Maypole and guests, no food; tables on small terrace with flower tubs and grassy bank running down to stream, summer barbecues, play area, may be cl winter wkdy lunchtimes, very busy wknds and bank hols *(LYM, the Didler)*

NEWARK [SK7953]
Castle & Falcon NG24 1TW [London Rd]: Well kept John Smiths and two interesting guests, friendly landlord, comfortable back lounge and family conservatory, lively games bar with darts, dominoes, pool and TV, skittle alley; small terrace, evening opening 7pm, cl lunchtime Mon-Thurs *(the Didler)*
☆ *Fox & Crown* NG24 1JY [Appleton Gate]: Convivial bare-boards open-plan Castle Rock pub with their keenly priced ales and several interesting guests from central servery, Stowford Press cider, dozens of whiskies, vodkas and other spirits, good tea, coffee and decent wines by the glass, friendly obliging staff, bargain simple food from

filled rolls and baked potatoes up, several side areas; piped pop music; children welcome, good wheelchair access, open all day *(Phil and Jane Hodson, the Didler, Derek and Sylvia Stephenson, N R White, Mrs Hazel Rainer, BB)*

NEWSTEAD [SK5252]
Station Hotel NG15 0BZ [Station Rd]: Basic down-to-earth red-brick village local opp Robin Hood Line station, unmodernised character rooms off central bar, well kept bargain Oakwell ales, no food except for Thurs curry night, chatty welcoming landlady, fine railway photographs, pub games; juke box, TV *(the Didler, Pete Baker, P Dawn)*

NORTH MUSKHAM [SK7958]
Muskham Ferry NG23 6HB [Ferry Lane, handy for A1 (which has small sign to pub)]: Traditional well furnished panelled pub in splendid location on River Trent, relaxing views from bar/restaurant, fairly priced food inc children's meals and Sun roast, three well kept real ales, good wine and soft drinks choice, friendly chatty staff; piped radio, games machine, pool; dogs welcome, waterside terrace, moorings, open all day *(JJW, CMW, Phil and Jane Hodson, LYM)*

NOTTINGHAM [SK5843]
Bread & Bitter NG3 5JL [Woodthorpe Drive]: In former suburban bakery still showing ovens, three bright and airy bare-boarded rooms, Castle Rock and great choice of other beers, farm cider, decent wine choice, good value home-made food all day, defunct brewery memorabilia; open all day from 9am *(the Didler)*

Broadway Cinema Café/Bar NG1 3AL [Broad St]: Reasonably priced imaginative food inc vegetarian, well kept local ales and continental lagers, helpful staff, good mix of customers *(MP)*

☆ *Canal House* NG1 7EH [Canal St]: Converted wharf building, bridge over indoors canal spur complete with narrowboat, lots of bare brick and varnished wood, huge joists on steel beams, long bar with good choice of house wines, well kept Castle Rock and changing guests, lively efficient staff, sensibly priced pubby food (not Sun evening), lots of standing room; good upstairs restaurant and second bar, masses of tables out on attractive waterside terrace; piped music (live Sun), busy with young people at night; open all day *(the Didler, Jeremy King, BB, Mrs Hazel Rainer)*

Cock & Hoop NG1 1HF [High Pavement]: Tiny carpeted front bar with fireside armchairs and flagstoned cellar bar attached to decent hotel, characterful décor, interesting food (all day Sun – inc good roasts), well kept ales such as Blue Monkey, Cumberland and Nottingham, attentive friendly service; piped music; children and dogs welcome, disabled facilities, smart bedrooms (ones by the street can be noisy wknds), open all day *(the Didler, George Atkinson, Simon J Barber, LYM)*

☆ *Fellows Morton & Clayton* NG1 7EH [Canal St (part of inner ring road)]: Former canal warehouse under new management, own good beers (finished by Nottingham) plus Black Sheep, Fullers, Mallards and Timothy Taylors, good value all-day pubby food (not Sun evening), softly lit bustling downstairs bar with red plush alcove seats, shiny wood floors and lots of exposed brickwork, two raised areas, photographs of old Nottingham, daily papers, restaurant; piped music – live Fri, games machines, several big TVs, no dogs; well behaved children in eating areas, large canal-view deck, open all day, till late Fri and Sat *(the Didler, R T and J C Moggridge, Martin Grosberg, Jeremy King, LYM)*

Gladstone NG5 2AW [Loscoe Rd, Carrington]: Welcoming backstreet local with well kept ales inc Castle Rock, Courage Directors, Fullers London Pride, Greene King Abbot and Timothy Taylors Landlord, good range of malt whiskies, comfortable lounge with reading matter, basic bar with old sports equipment and darts; piped music, big-screen sports TV; upstairs folk club Weds, quiz Thurs; tables in yard with lots of hanging baskets, cl wkdy lunchtimes, open all day wknds (from 3pm Fri) *(the Didler)*

Horse & Groom NG7 7EA [Radford Rd, New Basford]: Nine good changing ales in well run unpretentious open-plan local by former Shipstones brewery, still with their name and other memorabilia, good value fresh straightforward food from sandwiches to Sun lunch, daily papers, nice snug; live music and regular beer festivals in stable block behind, open all day *(the Didler)*

Johnson Arms NG7 2NZ [Abbey St]: Good choice of beers inc Adnams, Black Sheep and Castle Rock (beer festivals), decent cheap pubby food (not Sun evening); free juke box, live music (first Sat of month), Tues quiz night; picnic-sets in garden with pétanque, open all day *(David and Sue Atkinson)*

King William IV NG2 4PB [Manvers St/ Eyre St, Sneinton]: Two-room refurbished Victorian corner pub, plenty of character, with Kelham Island, Newby Wyke, Oakham and several other well kept changing ales from circular bar, Weston's Old Rosie cider, good fresh cobs, friendly staff, fine tankard collection, pool upstairs, irish music Thurs; silenced sports TV; heated smokers' shelter, handy for cricket, football and rugby grounds, open all day *(P Dawn, the Didler)*

Larwood & Voce NG2 6AJ [Fox Rd, West Bridgford]: Well run open-plan dining pub mixing modern and traditional, good locally sourced home-made food all day from lunchtime bar meals to more extensive and imaginative evening menu, good choice of wines by the glass inc champagne, nice cocktails, three real ales, cheerful staff; sports TV, on the edge of the cricket ground and handy for Notts Forest FC, open all day, from 9am wknds for breakfast *(David Glynne-Jones, P Dawn)*

☆ *Lion* NG7 7FQ [Lower Mosley St, New Basford]: Ten ales inc regulars Batemans and Mallards from one of city's deepest cellars (glass viewing panel – can be visited at quiet times), farm ciders, ten wines by the glass, good value home-made food all day inc doorstep sandwiches, children's helpings and summer barbecues; well fabricated feel of separate areas, bare bricks and polished dark oak boards, coal or log fires, daily papers, wknd live music inc Sun lunchtime jazz; terrace and smokers' shelter, open all day *(the Didler)*

News House NG1 7HB [Canal St]: Friendly two-room Castle Rock pub with their ales and half a dozen or more changing guests, belgian and czech imports on tap, farm cider, good wine and hot drinks choice, decent fresh lunchtime food inc good value Sun lunch, mix of bare boards and carpet, local newspaper/radio memorabilia, bar billiards, darts; big-screen sports TV; tables out at front, attractive blue exterior tiling, open all day *(the Didler)*

Pitcher & Piano NG1 1HN [High Pavement]: Remarkable lofty-roofed well converted church with enjoyable food, decent wines, well kept Marstons, some live music; open all day *(Katrin Schmidt)*

☆ *Plough* NG7 3EN [St Peters St, Radford]: Friendly 19th-c local brewing its own good value Nottingham ales, also guest beers and farm cider, two coal fires, traditional games, decent cheap food inc fresh cobs and popular Sun lunch, Thurs quiz; sports TV; open all day Fri-Sun *(the Didler)*

Roebuck NG1 6FH [St James St]: Light airy Wetherspoons conversion of interesting building, brick columns separating bar from main part, well spaced tables, extensive choice of well kept ales (occasional beer festivals), ciders and perry, good wine choice, usual food, friendly staff; muted TV; disabled facilities, open all day *(Jeremy King)*

Salutation NG1 7AA [Hounds Gate/ Maid Marion Way]: Proper pub, low beams, flagstones, ochre walls and cosy corners inc two small quiet rooms in ancient lower back part, plusher modern front lounge, half a dozen real ales, quickly served food till 7pm, helpful staff; piped music; open all day *(P Dawn, BB, Barry Collett)*

Sir John Borlase Warren NG7 3GD [Ilkeston Rd/Canning Circus (A52 towards Derby)]: Roadside pub with four comfortable linked rooms, interesting Victorian decorations, enjoyable good value food all day, friendly staff, Everards, Greene King, Timothy Taylors and guests, artwork for sale, mix of customers inc students; children welcome (not Fri or Sat evenings), tables in nicely lit back garden, open all day *(the Didler, BB, P Dawn)*

Vale NG5 3GG [Mansfield Rd]: Half a dozen changing ales in friendly 1930s local with original layout, panelling and woodwork, low-priced food, Sun quiz night; open all day *(the Didler)*

ORSTON [SK7741]
Durham Ox NG13 9NS [Church St]: Comfortable open-plan split-level village pub opp church, four well kept mainstream ales and a guest, short choice of well presented food, old local photographs, small dining room with coal fire; piped music and some live; children and dogs welcome, tables out at front and in big back garden with four heated summer houses, hitching rails for horses and ferrets, pleasant countryside, open all day wknds; all profits go to a charity (www.oliversarmy.org) *(the Didler, David Glynne-Jones, David and Sue Atkinson)*

RADCLIFFE ON TRENT [SK6439]
Royal Oak NG12 2FD [Main Rd]: Revamped and opened up by small local Mole Face chain, wide choice of enjoyable food from open kitchen inc breakfast (10am-noon), sandwiches (home-baked bread) and bar/restaurant meals, good friendly service, plenty of wines by the glass inc champagne, real ales such as Caledonian Deuchars IPA, Marstons Pedigree and Wells & Youngs Bombardier; children welcome, open all day from 10am *(David Glynne-Jones)*

REMPSTONE [SK5724]
White Lion LE12 6RH [Main St]: Friendly comfortably old-fashioned village pub, well kept Adnams and Marstons Pedigree, standard pub food, no music or machines; some seats out behind *(Comus and Sarah Elliott)*

RUDDINGTON [SK5733]
Three Crowns NG11 6LB [Easthorpe St]: Open-plan village pub with well kept Fullers, Nottingham and guest ales, lunchtime bar food, interesting evening menu (not Sun or Mon) in refurbished back restaurant, Sun carvery, local art for sale; open all day wknds, cl Mon lunchtime *(the Didler)*

White Horse NG11 6HD [Church St]: Cheerful 1930s local with half a dozen ales inc Black Sheep and Wells & Youngs Bombardier (beer festivals), enjoyable home-made food, comfortable lounge, old photographs, bar with games inc pool; TV; heated back terrace, nice garden, open all day *(the Didler)*

SELSTON [SK4553]
☆ *Horse & Jockey* NG16 6FB [handy for M1 junctions 27/28; Church Lane]: Dating from 17th c, intelligently renovated with interesting 18th/19th-c survivals and good carving, different levels, low heavy beams, dark flagstones, individual furnishings, good log fire in cast-iron range, friendly staff, mainstream ales such as Timothy Taylors Landlord with unusual guests like Wild Walkers Old Bighead, real cider, home-made wkdy lunchtime food, games area with darts and pool; dogs welcome, terrace with very smart smokers' shelter, pleasant rolling country *(the Didler, BB, Derek and Sylvia Stephenson)*

SOUTH LEVERTON [SK7881]
Plough DN22 0BT [Town St]: Tiny village local doubling as morning post office, basic

trestle tables, benches and pews, log fire, helpful welcoming staff, Greene King and changing guests, traditional games; nice garden, open all day (from 2pm wkdys) *(the Didler)*

SOUTHWELL [SK7053]

Hearty Goodfellow NG25 0HQ [Church St (A612)]: Refurbished traditional open-plan pub doing well under friendly landlord, good value lunchtime food from snacks up, Everards Tiger and five changing guests, good range of house wines, lots of polished wood, two brick fireplaces; children and dogs welcome, nice tree-shaded garden beyond car park, handy for Southwell Workhouse (NT) and Minster *(Paul J Robinshaw, Malcolm and Pauline Pellatt, the Didler)*

Saracens Head NG25 0HE [Market Place]: Interesting old hotel's cosy beamed character bar, enjoyable food from good sandwiches up, well kept Greene King ales, friendly service, restaurant; children in eating areas, coach yard tables, bedrooms *(LYM, Gerry and Rosemary Dobson)*

TEVERSAL [SK4761]

Carnarvon Arms NG17 3JA [Fackley Rd (B6014)]: Spacious refurbishment with contemporary touches, wide range of enjoyable food, well kept Greene King ales, friendly well trained staff, airy dining room; handy for Hardwick Hall *(Malcolm Wood, Derek and Sylvia Stephenson)*

THURGARTON [SK6949]

Red Lion NG14 7GP [Southwell Rd (A612)]: Cheery 16th-c pub with redecorated split-level beamed bars and restaurant, Black Sheep, Marstons and Springhead from dark panelled bar, food (all day wknds and bank hols), comfortable banquettes and other seating, lots of nooks and crannies, grandfather clock, open fires, big windows to attractive good-sized two-level back garden with well spaced tables (dogs on leads allowed here); games machine, steepish walk back up to car park; children welcome *(JJW, CMW, BB)*

UNDERWOOD [SK4751]

☆ *Red Lion* NG16 5HD [off A608/B600, nr M1 junction 27; Church Lane, almost in Bagthorpe]: Welcoming 17th-c split-level beamed village pub, reliable sensibly priced food inc set-lunch deals (Mon-Fri), other bargains and good fresh fish (best to book), Caledonian Deuchars IPA, Marstons Pedigree and interesting guests, good soft drinks choice, pleasant service, open-plan quarry-tiled bar with dining area, some cushioned settles, open fire; piped music, games machine in lobby; no dogs; children till 7pm away from bar, good play area in big woodside garden with terrace and barbecues, good nearby walks, open all day Fri-Sun

(Derek and Sylvia Stephenson, David Chapman, BB, JJW, CMW)

WATNALL CHAWORTH [SK5046]

☆ *Queens Head* NG16 1HT [3 miles from M1 junction 26: A610 towards Nottingham, left on B600, then keep right; Main Rd]: Good value pubby food inc good fish and chips in tastefully extended 17th-c roadside pub, well kept Adnams, Everards, Greene King, Wells & Youngs and changing guests, efficient staff, beams and stripped pine, coal fire, intimate snug, dining area; piped music; picnic-sets on attractive back lawn with big play area, open all day *(the Didler)*

Royal Oak NG16 1HS [Main Rd; B600 N of Kimberley]: Friendly beamed village local with interesting plates and pictures, Greene King and changing guests, good fresh cobs, woodburner, back games and pool rooms, comfortable upstairs lounge open Fri-Sun, some live music and beer festivals; sports TV; tables outside, open all day *(the Didler)*

WEST BRIDGFORD [SK5837]

☆ *Stratford Haven* NG2 6BA [Stratford Rd, Trent Bridge]: Good Castle Rock pub, bare-boards front bar leading to linked areas inc airy skylit back part with relaxed local atmosphere, their well kept ales plus Batemans, Everards and six changing guests (monthly brewery nights), exotic bottled beers, farm ciders, ample whiskies and wines, good value home-made food all day, good friendly service, daily papers, some live music (nothing loud); dogs welcome, handy for cricket ground and Nottingham Forest FC, tables outside, open all day *(the Didler, MP, BB)*

WEST LEAKE [SK5126]

☆ *Star* LE12 5RQ [Melton Lane, off A6006]: Comfortable oak-panelled lounge with good central log fire, pewter mugs, china, pictures, attractive table lamps and side eating area, character beamed and quarry-tiled country bar with traditional games, good value home-made food (not Sun evening) from substantial baps to cheap steaks, several well kept ales inc Theakstons Mild, good coffee, jovial landlord, helpful service; children in eating area, picnic-sets on front terrace (quiet spot) and in garden with play area, bedrooms, open all day *(LYM, David Hunt)*

WYSALL [SK6027]

Plough NG12 5QQ [Keyworth Rd; off A60 at Costock, or A6006 at Wymeswold]: Attractive 17th-c beamed village local popular for sensibly short choice of good value generous food, cheerful staff, changing real ales, rooms either side of bar with nice mix of furnishings, soft lighting, big log fire; french doors to pretty terrace with flower tubs and baskets *(M Mossman)*

Oxfordshire

Although this is not a particularly cheap county when it comes to drinking or eating out (plenty of smart dining places for that special meal), there are some delightful little country – and town – taverns, if it's just an informal drink and light lunch that you want: the Olde Reindeer in Banbury (good value lunchtime food and six real ales), the Saye & Sele Arms in Broughton (the landlord cooks the popular food), the Black Horse in Checkendon (old-fashioned and in the same family for 105 years), the Chequers in Chipping Norton (chatty and cheerful with five real ales), the Rising Sun at Highmoor (popular with walkers), the Olde Leathern Bottel at Lewknor (honest food and handy for the M40), three Oxford pubs – the Bear (new to us this year and a charming little pub), the Rose & Crown (long-serving licensees and well liked food and beer) and the Turf Tavern (a dozen ales, good food and lots of atmosphere), the Rose & Crown in Shilton (a busy village pub and good mix of customers) and the Red Lion in Steeple Aston. As mentioned, there are a lot of first-class dining pubs offering exceptional food and out of a long list, those on really top form this year are the Half Moon at Cuxham (exceptional food cooked by a young landlord using his own produce), the White Hart in Fyfield (lovely old building with super food cooked by the licensee, also using home-grown ingredients), the Plough in Kingham (a restaurant-with-rooms with creative food – bar snacks, too – and a proper drinkers' bar), the Nut Tree in Murcott (own-reared animals and home-grown produce used in the imaginative food), the Royal Oak in Ramsden (a thoroughly good all-rounder with much enjoyed food and the Lamb at Satwell (interesting meals in a friendly, well run inn). It wasn't an easy decision to make, given the competition, but our Oxfordshire Dining Pub 2011 is the Plough in Kingham. New Main Entries and very much worth checking out are the Lord Nelson in Brightwell Baldwin (a lot of character and good food and drinks), the Bear in Oxford (mentioned above), the Crown at Pishill (an attractive 15th-c inn with log fires and comfortable bedrooms), the Lamb at Shipton-under-Wychwood (the mother and son team are doing a fantastic job) and the Talk House at Stanton St John (an upmarket inn in a pretty village).

'Children welcome' means the pub says it lets children inside without any special restriction. If it allows them in, but to restricted areas such as an eating area or family room, we specify this. Places with separate restaurants often let children use them, hotels usually let them into public areas such as lounges. Some pubs impose an evening time limit – let us know if you find one earlier than 9pm.

ALVESCOT
SP2704 MAP 4

Plough
B4020 Carterton—Clanfield, SW of Witney; OX18 2PU

Neatly kept bar with bric-a-brac and aircraft prints, Wadworths ales, pubby food and colourful hanging baskets

Some ornamental pheasants are to join the chickens and japanese quail in the gardens here and there are picnic-sets on the back terrace among the particularly colourful hanging baskets; there's also a children's play area and aunt sally. Inside, you'll get a friendly welcome and the neatly kept bar has lots to look at: aircraft prints and a large poster of Concorde's last flight as well as plenty of cottagey pictures, china ornaments and house plants, a big antique case of stuffed birds of prey, sundry bric-a-brac and a woodburning stove. Comfortable seating includes cream, red and green cushioned dark wooden chairs around dark wooden tables, some cushioned settles and, of course, the bar stools bagged by chatty regulars in the early evening. Wadworths IPA and 6X on handpump. There's a proper public bar with TV, darts, board games and piped music; skittle alley and a large collection of keys in the entrance hall. The pub cats are called Dino, Bo and Patch.

🍴 Bar food includes ham and eggs, lasagne, sausages with gravy in a giant yorkshire pudding, venison, chestnut and Guinness casserole, italian chicken, breaded seafood platter, liver and bacon, and puddings like tiramisu and fruit crumbles; afternoon teas. *Starters/Snacks: £4.95 to £6.00. Main Courses: £8.95 to £15.50. Puddings: £3.95 to £4.50*

Wadworths ~ Tenant Kevin Robert Keeling ~ Real ale ~ Bar food (all day) ~ (01993) 842281 ~ Children welcome ~ Open 12-midnight(10.30 Sun)
Recommended by David Lamb, Peter and Audrey Dowsett, KN-R, Tina and David Woods-Taylor

ASTON TIRROLD
SU5586 MAP 2

Chequers
Village signposted off A417 Streatley—Wantage; Fullers Road; OX11 9EN

Atmosphere and food of a rustic french restaurant in pubby surroundings, nice french wines, restrained décor and stylish service; charming cottagey garden

Although this formally calls itself the Sweet Olive at the Chequers and is almost more of a rustic french restaurant than a village pub, it does have a relaxed pubby feel and Brakspears Bitter and Fullers London Pride on handpump. The sturdy stools by the bar counter do get used in the chatty main room and there's also grass matting over the quarry tiles, six or seven sturdy stripped tables with mate's chairs and cushioned high-backed settles against the walls, a small fireplace and plain white walls. There are two or three wine cartoons and wine box-ends panelling the back of the servery, a nice range of french wines by the glass and good coffees; attentive service. A second rather smaller room, set more formally as a restaurant, has a similarly restrained décor of pale grey dado, white-panelled ceiling and red and black flooring tiles; piped music. A small cottagey garden, well sheltered by flowering shrubs, angles around the pub, with picnic-sets under cocktail parasols; aunt sally. More reports please.

🍴 Good, enjoyable food includes filled baguettes, soup, crispy duck salad, home-made gravadlax with caesar salad, slow-cooked moroccan lamb, chicken with fresh pasta and a wild mushroom sauce, scallops with lime butter and risotto, venison with a port wine sauce, oxtail in puff pastry with red burgundy sauce, and puddings such as dark chocolate mousse with espresso ice-cream and vanilla sauce and treacle sponge and custard. *Starters/Snacks: £4.50 to £7.95. Main Courses: £9.95 to £17.50. Puddings: £5.95*

Enterprise ~ Lease Olivier Bouet and Stephane Brun ~ Real ale ~ Bar food (not Sun evening, Weds and note when closed) ~ Restaurant ~ (01235) 851272 ~ Children welcome ~ Dogs allowed in bar ~ Open 12-3, 6-midnight; closed Sun evening, Weds, all Feb and two weeks in July
Recommended by J V Dadswell, Neil and Karen Dignan, Dr and Mrs P Reid

BANBURY

SP4540   MAP 4

Olde Reindeer 🍺 £

Parsons Street, off Market Place; OX16 5NA

Plenty of shoppers and regulars in this interesting town pub, fine real ales, simple food and roaring log fires

With friendly, chatty staff and plenty of customers keen to enjoy the real ales and fair value lunchtime food, this unpretentious town pub has a good bustling atmosphere. The welcoming front bar has heavy 16th-c beams, very broad polished oak floorboards, a magnificent carved overmantel for one of the two roaring log fires and traditional solid furnishings. It's worth looking at the handsomely proportioned Globe Room used by Cromwell as his base during the Civil War. Quite a sight, it still has some very fine carved 17th-c dark oak panelling. Fullers London Pride, Hook Norton Bitter, Old Hooky and Hooky Gold and a couple of changing guests on handpump, country wines, several whiskies and winter mulled wine; piped music. The little back courtyard has tables and benches under parasols, aunt sally and pretty flowering baskets.

🍴 **Straightforward lunchtime bar food in generous helpings might include sandwiches, soup, omelettes, good filled baked potatoes, all day breakfast, popular bubble and squeak and daily specials; they also offer an OAP two-course weekday menu.** *Starters/Snacks: £2.50 to £3.75. Main Courses: £4.95 to £7.95. Puddings: £2.90 to £3.45*

Hook Norton ~ Tenants Tony and Dot Puddifoot ~ Real ale ~ Bar food (11-2.30; not evenings) ~ Restaurant ~ (01295) 264031 ~ Children allowed in own area with parents ~ Dogs allowed in bar ~ Open 11-11; 12-3 Sun; closed Sun evening

Recommended by Ann and Colin Hunt, Chris Bell, the Didler, Mick and Cathy Couchman, Andy Lickfold, George Atkinson, Ted George

BLOXHAM

SP4235   MAP 4

Joiners Arms

Off A361; Old Bridge Road; OX15 4LY

Interestingly furnished rooms on several levels, a good mix of customers and attractive seating areas outside

As we went to press, a new licensee had taken over this golden stone inn and had plans for various refurbishments. The several rambling and appealing rooms have plenty of exposed stone, careful spotlighting, white-painted dining chairs around pale tables on the wooden flooring, open fires and a relaxed and friendly atmosphere. Courage Best and Theakstons Best on handpump and several wines by the glass. A big room just off the bar has rafters in the high ceiling and an exposed well in the floor. Outside, there are pretty window boxes and plenty of seats under parasols on the various levels – the most popular is down some steps by a stream where there are picnic-sets and a play house. More reports please.

🍴 **Bar food includes lunchtime filled baguettes, soup, smoked salmon pâté, fresh sardines, a burger with bacon, cheese and gherkins, steak and mushroom in ale or fish pies, lamb, apricot and mint sausages, goats cheese, spinach and mushroom filo tartlet, beer-battered fresh haddock, pork loin with grain mustard and honey sauce and steaks.** *Starters/Snacks: £3.95 to £5.95. Main Courses: £6.00 to £14.95. Puddings: £4.00*

Free house ~ Licensee Mark Page ~ Real ale ~ Bar food (12-2.30, 6-9; all day Sun) ~ Restaurant ~ (01295) 720223 ~ Children welcome ~ Dogs allowed in bar ~ Open 10am(12 Sun)-midnight

Recommended by BOB, Mr and Mrs John Taylor

Post Office address codings confusingly give the impression that some pubs are in Oxfordshire, when they're really in Berkshire, Buckinghamshire, Gloucestershire or Warwickshire (which is where we list them).

BRIGHTWELL BALDWIN   SU6594   MAP 4

Lord Nelson ⊕♔ ♀
Off B480 Chalgrove—Watlington, or B4009 Benson—Watlington; OX49 5NP

Attractive inn with several different character bars, real ales, good wines by the glass and enjoyable food; bedrooms

Prettily placed on a quiet lane opposite the church, this is a 300-year-old inn with 18th-c gable ends and an attractive arched verandah. Most people are here to enjoy the good food but they do keep Black Sheep Best and Brakspears Bitter on handpump, 14 wines by the glass (including champagne) and a few malt whiskies. There are wheelback and other dining chairs around a mix of dark tables, candles and fresh flowers, wine bottles on window sills, horsebrasses on standing timbers, lots of paintings on the white or red walls and a big brick inglenook fireplace. One cosy room has cushions on comfortable sofas, little lamps on dark furniture, ornate mirrors and portraits in gilt frames; piped music. There are seats on the back terrace with more in the willow-draped garden.

🍴 **Enjoyable bar food using local produce includes sandwiches, ploughman's, soup, coarse pâté with home-made chutney, scallops, pancetta and black pudding with roasted beetroot, asparagus, mint and lemon risotto, omelettes, free-range pork chop with apple and sage, slow-roasted duck with spiced plum sauce, chargrilled calves liver with red wine sauce, bass with rosemary and lyonnaise potatoes, and puddings; they also offer a two-course set lunch and supper.** *Starters/Snacks: £5.95 to £7.95. Main Courses: £12.50 to £22.00. Puddings: £5.50*

Free house ~ Licensees Roger and Carole Shippey ~ Real ale ~ Bar food (12-2.30, 6-10) ~ Restaurant ~ (01491) 612497 ~ Children welcome ~ Dogs allowed in bar ~ Open 12-3, 6-11; 12-10.30 Sun ~ Bedrooms: £70B/£90B

Recommended by Hugh Roberts, Neil and Karen Dignan, D and M T Ayres-Regan, Roy Hoing

BROUGHTON   SP4238   MAP 4

Saye & Sele Arms ◀
B4035 SW of Banbury; OX15 5ED

Smartly furnished and enjoyable 16th-c house with four real ales, attentive service, good food cooked by the landlord and seats on the terrace and lawn

This year, a new pergola has been erected in the garden here; there's a new tiled smoking shelter and a sizeable new herb garden; the hanging baskets around the pleasant terrace are pretty and there are picnic-sets and other tables and chairs on lawn; aunt sally. Inside, the sizeable bar room is split into three distinct areas: a dining room at one end with over 200 colourful water jugs hanging from the beams and neatly folded napkins on the tables, then a tiled area beside the bar counter with cushioned window seats, a few brasses and dark wooden furnishings and finally, a carpeted room with red walls and a big fireplace. Adnams Best and guests such as Brains Rev James, Sharps Doom Bar and Vale Best on handpump and nine wines by the glasss; friendly, helpful service. The pub is handy for Broughton Castle.

🍴 **As well as lunchtime sandwiches, the popular bar food cooked by the landlord might include soup, chicken liver pâté with spicy chutney, smoked salmon, lime and spinach roulade, well liked proper pies, fig, tomato, red onion and goats cheese tart, jumbo sausages with onion gravy, loin of lamb on minted mash with a redcurrant, garlic and rosemary sauce, specials such as fresh salmon and prawns in a creamy cheese and mustard sauce, grilled pork loin with fresh pineapple, tomato and parmesan, and puddings like souffléd bread and butter pudding and white and dark chocolate délice; Sunday roasts and regular themed food evenings.** *Starters/Snacks: £4.35 to £7.50. Main Courses: £5.10 to £17.95. Puddings: £5.25*

Free house ~ Licensees Danny and Liz McGeehan ~ Real ale ~ Bar food (12-2(3 Sun), 7-9.30; not Sun evening) ~ Restaurant ~ (01295) 263348 ~ Children allowed if dining with an adult ~ Open 11.30-2.30(3 Sat), 7-11; 12-5 Sun; closed Sun evening

Recommended by Ann and Colin Hunt, Carolyn Drew, Rob and Catherine Dunster, Kevin Thomas, Nina Randall, Jane Hudson, Clive and Fran Dutson

BURFORD

SP2512   MAP 4

Highway 🛏

High Street (A361); OX18 4RG

Comfortable old inn overlooking this honeypot village's main street, a good choice of wines and well liked bar food; bedrooms

The main feature in the bar of this 15th-c inn is the pair of big windows each made up of several dozen panes of old float glass – and a long cushioned window seat; these windows overlook the High Street. There are all sorts of other interesting touches, too, such as the stag candlesticks for the rather close-set tables on the well worn floorboards, the neat modern dark leather chairs, the Cecil Aldin hunting prints, the careful balance of ancient stripped stone with filigree black and pale blue wallpaper and the nice old station clock above the big log fire in the attractively simple stone fireplace. A small corner counter has Hook Norton Best and a guest from Vale or Wye Valley on handpump and up to 20 wines (including champagne) by the glass; piped music and board games. On the right a second bar room, with another big window seat, is carpeted but otherwise similar in style; there's also a cellar restaurant. A few front picnic-sets stand above the pavement. The pub springer spaniels are called Cassie and Oscar.

🍽 Using their own herbs and allotment produce and local game and fish, the tasty bar food includes sandwiches, pressed pigs cheek with piccalilli, soup, risotto of the day, a trio of free-range sausages with pomegranate mash and red onion marmalade, chicken breast with wild mushroom and tarragon sauce, rack of lamb with mint jus, venison casserole with herb dumplings, and puddings such as warm chocolate nemesis and lemon tart and crème fraîche. *Starters/Snacks: £3.50 to £8.50. Main Courses: £10.50 to £18.95. Puddings: £5.50 to £7.50.*

Free house ~ Licensees Scott and Tally Nelson ~ Real ale ~ Bar food (12-2.30(3 Sun), 6.30-9(9.30 Fri and Sat)) ~ (01993) 823661 ~ Children welcome ~ Dogs allowed in bar and bedrooms ~ Open 12-11; closed first two weeks in Jan ~ Bedrooms: £79B/£89B

Recommended by Ben and Laurie Braddick, Steve and Liz Tilley, Graham Oddey

Lamb 🍷 🍴 🛏

Village signposted off A40 W of Oxford; Sheep Street (B4425, off A361); OX18 4LR

Proper pubby bar in civilised inn, real ales and an extensive wine list, traditional bar food and more elaborate restaurant menu and pretty gardens; bedrooms

Many customers come to this civilised 15th-c inn to stay overnight or to dine but the heart of the place is still in the cosy bar where there's a genuine mix of both hotel guests and locals and an informal, friendly atmosphere. Also, high-backed settles and old chairs on flagstones in front of the log fire, Hook Norton Best and Wadworths 6X on handpump and an extensive wine list with a dozen by the glass; board games. The roomy beamed main lounge is charmingly traditional, with distinguished old seats including a chintzy high-winged settle, ancient cushioned wooden armchairs and seats built into its stone-mullioned windows, bunches of flowers on polished oak and elm tables, rugs on the wide flagstones and polished oak floorboards and a winter log fire under its fine mantelpiece; plenty of antiques and other decorations including a grandfather clock. A pretty terrace with teak furniture leads down to small neatly kept lawns surrounded by flowers, shrubs and small trees, and the garden itself is a real suntrap, enclosed as it is by the warm stone of the surrounding buildings.

> If you stay overnight in an inn or hotel, they are allowed to serve you an alcoholic drink at any hour of the day or night.

🍴 Bar food includes open sandwiches, ploughman's, sharing deli boards (charcuterie, fish or antipasti), chicken liver pâté with redcurrant jelly, red onion and goats cheese tart, bangers and mash with red wine thyme gravy, beer-battered fish and chips, smoked haddock risotto with a poached egg, mixed grill, daily specials, and puddings like chocolate mousse with kirsch cherries and chantilly cream and rhubarb crumble with crème anglaise; the restaurant menu is more elaborate. *Starters/Snacks: £4.50 to £7.95. Main Courses: £11.95 to £16.95. Puddings: £5.95 to £7.95*

Free house ~ Licensee Paul Heaver ~ Real ale ~ Bar food (12-2.30(3 Sun), 6.30-9.30(9 Sun)) ~ Restaurant ~ (01993) 823155 ~ Children welcome ~ Dogs allowed in bar and bedrooms ~ Open 11-11 ~ Bedrooms: £115B/£145B
Recommended by the Didler, Steve and Liz Tilley, MDN, David and Sue Smith, Eithne Dandy, Michael Dandy

CAULCOTT   SP5024   MAP 4

Horse & Groom
Lower Heyford Road (B4030); OX25 4ND

Bustling and friendly with obliging licensee, enjoyable bar food and changing beers

This is a thatched 16th-c cottage run by a friendly chef/patron. It's not a huge place: an L-shaped red-carpeted room angles around the servery, with plush-cushioned settles, chairs and stools around a few dark tables at the low-ceilinged bar end and a blazing fire in the big inglenook, with brassware under its long bressumer beam; shove-ha'penny and board games. The far end, up a shallow step, is set for dining with lots of decorative jugs hanging on black joists and some decorative plates; also, attractive watercolours and original drawings. The friendly staffordshire bull terrier is called Minnie. Hook Norton Bitter and three changing guests such as Black Sheep Golden Sheep, Exmoor Ale and Skinners Betty Stogs on handpump and decent house wines. There's a small side sun lounge and picnic-sets under cocktail parasols on a neat lawn.

🍴 As well as 12 different types of speciality sausages, the lunchtime bar food includes filled baguettes and baked potatoes, ploughman's, soup, king prawns in garlic and white wine, free-range omelette, ham and egg and burgers, with evening choices like red thai vegetable curry, gressingham duck breast with orange sauce, creamy fish and seafood pie, tenderloin of gloucester old spot with mustard and cognac sauce, and puddings such as sticky toffee pudding with butterscotch sauce. *Starters/Snacks: £4.95 to £5.95. Main Courses: £6.95 to £9.95. Puddings: £4.50 to £5.50*

Free house ~ Licensee Jerome Prigent ~ Real ale ~ Bar food (not Sun evening or Mon) ~ (01869) 343257 ~ Children must be over 7 ~ Open 12-3, 6-11; 12-3, 7-10.30 Sun
Recommended by Mr and Mrs W W Burke, Karen Eliot, Jane Hudson, Roger and Anne Newbury, David Lamb

CHECKENDON   SU6684   MAP 2

Black Horse
Village signposted off A4074 Reading—Wallingford; coming from that direction, go straight through village towards Stoke Row, then turn left (the second left turn after the village church); OS Sheet 175 map reference 666841; RG8 OTE

Simple place liked by walkers and cyclists for a pint and a snack

The same friendly family have now run this charmingly old-fashioned country tavern for 105 years now. It's tucked into woodland well away from the main village and is much loved by walkers. The back still room where Hook Norton Hooky Bitter and West Berkshire Good Old Boy and Old Father Thames are tapped from the cask has a relaxed, unchanging feel and the room with the bar counter has some tent pegs ranged above the fireplace, a reminder that they used to be made here. A homely side room has some splendidly unfashionable 1950s-look armchairs and there's another room beyond that. There are seats out on a verandah and in the garden.

🍴 They offer only filled rolls and pickled eggs.

Free house ~ Licensees Margaret and Martin Morgan ~ Real ale ~ No credit cards ~ (01491) 680418
~ Children allowed but must be very well behaved ~ Open 12-2(2.30 Sat), 7-11; 12-3, 7-10.30 Sun
Recommended by Torrens Lyster, Richard Greaves, the Didler

CHIPPING NORTON

SP3127   MAP 4

Chequers ★ ♀ ◖
Goddards Lane; OX7 5NP

Busy, friendly town pub open all day with several real ales, popular bar food, cheerful mix of customers and simple bars

Hidden away in a quiet part of town, this is a well run pub much enjoyed by our readers for its relaxed, cheerful atmosphere and good range of beers. There's a mix of both locals and visitors and the three softly lit beamed rooms have no frills, but are clean and comfortable with low ochre ceilings, lots of character and a blazing log fire. Efficient staff serve Fullers Chiswick, London Pride, ESB and two guest beers on handpump, and they have good house wines, many available by the glass. The conservatory restaurant is light and airy and used for more formal dining. The town's theatre is next door.

🍴 **Popular bar food includes sandwiches, soup, chicken liver pâté, ham and egg, pasta with chicken, sage and onion butter, cheese and chive risotto, beer-battered fish and chips, pork and leek sausages, steak in ale pie, red thai chicken curry, steaks, and puddings like Baileys crème brûlée and lemon curd syllabub.** *Starters/Snacks: £3.95 to £5.50. Main Courses: £6.95 to £12.00. Puddings: £3.95 to £4.50*

Fullers ~ Lease John Cooper ~ Real ale ~ Bar food (12-2.30, 6-9.30; 12-4 Sun; not Sun, Mon or Tues evenings) ~ Restaurant ~ (01608) 644717 ~ Children allowed in public bar ~ Dogs allowed in bar ~ Live music every other month ~ Open 11-11(midnight Fri and Sat)
Recommended by Richard Greaves, Chris Glasson, the Didler, Richard Tilbrook, Helene Grygar, Stuart Turner, Derek and Sylvia Stephenson, MP, Barry Collett, Ann and Colin Hunt, Guy Vowles

CHURCH ENSTONE

SP3725   MAP 4

Crown
Mill Lane; from A44 take B4030 turn-off at Enstone; OX7 4NN

Friendly country pub with helpful licensees, enjoyable food cooked by the landlord and well kept real ales

Many customers come to this attractive old pub to enjoy the popular food cooked by the friendly hands-on licensee and most tables are booked in advance – in both the bar and restaurant. The smart and uncluttered congenial bar has beams, wheelback chairs and built-in cushioned wall seats around heavy wooden tables, country pictures on the stone walls and a good log fire in the large stone fireplace with horsebrasses along its bressumer beam; the atmosphere is cheerful and relaxed and they keep Box Steam Dark & Handsome, Fullers London Pride and Hook Norton Hooky Bitter on handpump and several decent wines by the glass. There's also a beamed, red-walled, carpeted dining room and an airy slate-floored conservatory, both with farmhouse chairs and tables. On the front terrace are some white metal tables and chairs overlooking the quiet lane with picnic-sets in the sheltered back garden.

🍴 **Using seasonal local produce, the good bar food includes sandwiches, venison terrine, king scallop and bacon salad, steak in ale pie, beer-battered cod, pasta with wild mushrooms, pesto and cream, guinea fowl with smoked bacon, chipolata and mustard sauce, sirloin steak with blue cheese and garlic butter, specials like devilled kidneys and john dory with creamy leeks, and puddings such as warm chocolate pudding with chocolate sauce and blackberry and almond tart with vanilla ice-cream; Sunday roasts.** *Starters/Snacks: £4.75 to £8.50. Main Courses: £8.50 to £14.95. Puddings: £4.75*

Free house ~ Licensees Tony and Caroline Warburton ~ Real ale ~ Bar food (not Sun evening) ~ Restaurant ~ (01608) 677262 ~ Children welcome ~ Dogs allowed in bar ~ Open 12-3, 6-11; 12-4 Sun; closed Sun evening, 26 Dec, 1 Jan

Recommended by Helene Grygar, Phil and Jane Hodson, Derek and Sylvia Stephenson, Barry Collett, Andy and Jill Kassube, Richard Greaves, Stuart Turner, Chris Glasson

CHURCHILL
SP2824 MAP 4

Chequers

B4450 Chipping Norton—Stow-on-the-Wold (and village signposted off A361 Chipping Norton—Burford); Church Road; OX7 6NJ

Exceptionally welcoming licensees in a busy village pub with plenty of space, well kept real ales and popular food

However busy it is – particularly at weekends – you can be sure of a genuinely warm welcome from the exceptional landlady here. Mrs Golding has a remarkable memory and will remember your name after just one visit, even if it was some months earlier. Furnished in a country house style and with a relaxed, friendly atmosphere, the front bar has a light flagstoned floor, a couple of old timbers, modern oak furnishings, some exposed stone walls around a big inglenook (with a good winter log fire) and country prints on the walls; newspapers are laid out on a table. At the back, there's a big extension that's a bit like a church with soaring rafters and upstairs is a cosy but easily missed area mainly laid out for eating. Hook Norton Hooky Bitter and a changing guest such as Adnams Best, Fullers London Pride, Greene King Abbot or Timothy Taylors Landlord on handpump and a good wine list. The pub's exterior is Cotswold stone at its most golden and the village church opposite is impressive.

🍽 **Popular bar food includes sandwiches and hot panini, soup, chicken liver parfait and red onion marmalade, wild mushroom and pancetta risotto, steak and kidney pie, venison steak sizzler with a cranberry and whisky reduction, rib-eye steak with garlic butter, daily specials such as lambs liver and mash, guinea fowl wrapped in bacon and mozzarella, and puddings like white chocolate cheesecake with a red berry compote and sherry and orange trifle; Sunday roasts.** *Starters/Snacks: £5.00 to £6.50. Main Courses: £7.50 to £19.50. Puddings: £5.00 to £6.00*

Free house ~ Licensees Peter and Assumpta Golding ~ Real ale ~ Bar food (12-2(3 Sun), 7-9.30(9 Sun) ~ Restaurant ~ (01608) 659393 ~ Children welcome ~ Open 11-11

Recommended by Stuart Turner, Jean and Douglas Troup, Ann and Colin Hunt, Bernard Stradling, P and J Shapley, Di and Mike Gillam, Martin and Pauline Jennings, Henry Midwinter, Myra Joyce, Barry Collett, George and Maureen Roby, Tom Evans, Graham Oddey, Richard Greaves

CLANFIELD
SP2802 MAP 4

Clanfield Tavern 🍴 ⏣

Bampton Road (A4095 S of Witney); OX18 2RG

Pleasantly extended ancient pub with bistro-style food and good choice of drinks

They do keep several real ales in this busy 17th-c pub though much emphasis is placed on the interesting bistro-style food. It's been largely opened up inside but keeps the feel of several separate areas rambling under heavy beams around a central stairwell enclosed in very broad old bare boards. Mainly carpeted, it's not over-cluttered with furniture: a built-in high-backed settle by the log fire in one big fireplace under a heavy black mantelbeam, some other nice old cushioned settles, mixed more or less pubby chairs, a table of newspapers and magazines and a snug flagstoned area behind the bar with a couple of sofas by a big glass-fronted woodburning stove. Banks's Bitter and a couple of guests like Jennings Golden Host and Ringwood Fortyniner on handpump from the smallish serving bar and a good choice of wines by the glass. On the left, this part has ancient pale polished flagstones, an attractive bow-window seat and darts. For a meal, perhaps the best place is the attractive conservatory through on the right with neat comfortably modern furnishings and good blinds. Tiny windows peep from the heavy stone-slabbed roof and there are picnic-sets on a flower-bordered small lawn that look across to the village green and stream.

🍴 Using local beef and lamb and other carefully sourced ingredients as well as their own herbs and vegetables, the interesting food includes sandwiches, soup with home-made bread, sautéed duck hearts with wild mushrooms and a soft-boiled duck egg, rabbit terrine with apple and cider chutney, home-smoked salmon with capers, a burger with bacon and cheese and triple-cooked chips, caramelised cauliflower and goats cheese risotto, beer-battered pollack with mushy peas, and puddings like dark chocolate torte and banana mousse and cambridge burnt cream; they offer a good value two-course weekday lunch, take-away fish or burgers and chips, Thursday evening rare-breed steaks, and Sunday roasts. *Starters/Snacks: £4.50 to £6.50. Main Courses: £9.50 to £22.95. Puddings: £4.95 to £5.50*

Real Food Pub Company ~ Lease Tom Gee ~ Real ale ~ Bar food (12-2.30(3 weekends), 6-9(9.30 Sat); not Mon) ~ Restaurant ~ (01367) 810223 ~ Children welcome ~ Dogs allowed in bar ~ Open 12-3, 6-11; 12-12(10.30 Sun) Sat; closed Mon
Recommended by William Goodhart, Graham Oddey

CUXHAM
SU6695   MAP 4

Half Moon 🍴

4 miles from M40 junction 6; S on B4009, then right on to B480 at Watlington; OX49 5NF

Lovely 17th-c country pub with relaxed atmosphere and delicious food cooked by friendly landlord

There's no doubt that most emphasis in this lovely 17th-c country pub is on the well presented food skilfully cooked by the young chef/patron. But there's a small red and black tiled bar with a brick fireplace and Brakspears Bitter on handpump, and the atmosphere is friendly and informal. The two main eating areas have old beams, an attractive mix of Edwardian tables, dining chairs and cushioned settles, a modicum of antique lamps, pewter tankards, stone bottles, mirrors and wall prints, several wines by the glass and home-made ginger beer and lemonade. There are wooden slatted chairs and tables in the good-sized garden and pretty window boxes. This is a sleepy village surrounded by fine countryside.

🍴 Using home-grown vegetables, home-reared gloucester old spot pigs, their own free-range eggs, locally shot game and other local and organic produce, the excellent food might include soup, home-smoked salmon, mussels with wine, cream and garlic, potted crab, duck hearts on toast, pigeon pâté with apple chutney, butternut squash risotto with red peppers and parmesan, organic mutton burger with chilli and mint, home-made sausages and mash with onion gravy, venison scotch pie with baked beans, muntjac three ways with root purée, pork belly with scallops, lentils, apples and green sauce, fish stew with rouille, and puddings like lemon curd cheesecake with raspberry sorbet and sticky toffee pudding with clotted cream. *Starters/Snacks: £4.95 to £7.50. Main Courses: £9.50 to £18.50. Puddings: £5.50 to £7.00*

Brakspears ~ Tenants Andrew Hill and Eilidh Ferguson ~ Real ale ~ Bar food (12-2(3 weekends), 6-9(9.30 Sat); not Sun evening or Mon) ~ (01491) 614151 ~ Children only allowed after 7pm if eating ~ Dogs welcome ~ Open 12-3, 6-11; 12-11 Sat; 12-10.30 Sun; closed Sun evening and all day Mon
Recommended by LM, Karen Eliot, I H G Busby, Bernard Stradling, Tina and David Woods-Taylor

EAST HENDRED
SU4588   MAP 2

Eyston Arms 🍴

Village signposted off A417 E of Wantage; High Street; OX12 8JY

Attractive bar areas with low beams, flagstones, log fires and candles, imaginative food and helpful service

In an attractive village at the foot of the Downs, this is a pleasant dining pub – though locals do pop in for a drink and a chat. There's a friendly welcome from the cheerful staff and several separate-seeming areas with contemporary paintwork and modern country-style furnishings: low ceilings and beams, stripped timbers, the odd standing timber, an inglenook fireplace, nice tables and chairs on the flagstones and carpet, some cushioned wall seats, a piano and a relaxed atmosphere. Even on a sunny day the candles may be lit; good wines and piped music. Fullers London Pride and Wadworths 6X on handpump and several wines by the glass. Picnic-sets outside overlook the pretty lane and there are seats in the back courtyard garden.

🍴 **Imaginative bar food includes lunchtime sandwiches, breast of pigeon salad with hazelnut vinaigrette, carpaccio of beef with bean sprouts, radish, spring onions and green chilli dressing, an antipasti plate for two, pasta with chilli king prawns and smoked salmon, vegetable 'squeak' cakes topped with a fried egg, spinach and red pepper coulis, lamb rump with rosemary parmentier potatoes, onion purée and red wine and juniper reduction, crispy confit duck leg on a cassoulet of toulouse sausage, haricot beans and spinach, steaks with café de paris butter or béarnaise sauce, and puddings such as lemon and blueberry drizzle cake with crème fraîche and rhubarb and vanilla panna cotta with a ginger biscuit.** Starters/Snacks: £5.00 to £9.00. Main Courses: £11.00 to £24.00. Puddings: £6.00

Free house ~ Licensees George Dailey and Daisy Barton ~ Real ale ~ Bar food (12-5 Sun; not Sun evening) ~ (01235) 833320 ~ Children must be well behaved – no babies ~ Dogs allowed in bar ~ Open 12-3, 6-11; 11-6 Sun; closed Sun evening

Recommended by Henry Midwinter, Michael Doswell, JJW, CMW, Robert Lorimer, William Goodhart, Jane Hudson, Bruce and Sharon Eden

FERNHAM   SU2991   MAP 4

Woodman 🍺

A420 SW of Oxford, then left into B4508 after about 11 miles; village a further 6 miles on; SN7 7NX

Good choice of real ales and interesting bar food in a charming old-world country pub

This is a first-class pub and our readers thoroughly enjoy their visits here. You can be sure of a warm welcome from the helpful and attentive staff, the real ales change constantly and the food is particularly good. The heavily beamed main rooms have the most character and are full of an amazing assortment of old objects like clay pipes, milkmaids' yokes, leather tack, coach horns, an old screw press, some original oil paintings and good black and white photographs of horses. Comfortable seating includes cushioned benches, pews and windsor chairs, and the candlelit tables are simply made from old casks; big wood fire. There are also some comfortable newer areas and a large room for Sunday lunches. Tapped from the cask, the real ales might include Oakham JHB, Timothy Taylors Landlord and Wadworths 6X and St George & the Dragon. Several wines by the glass and winter mulled wine; piped music and TV. There are seats outside on the terrace. Disabled lavatories.

🍴 **Very popular bar food includes filled baguettes and panini, ploughman's, soup, chicken liver pâté with apricot and ginger chutney, mixed seafood tian with lemon dressing, steak and mushroom in ale pie, home-cooked honey-roast ham with free-range eggs, beer-battered cod with minty mushy peas, vegetable filo tart with sunblush tomato and fennel salad, a curry or sausages of the day and slow-roasted pork belly with caramelised apple, black pudding mash and wholegrain mustard jus; Sunday roasts.** Starters/Snacks: £3.95 to £6.95. Main Courses: £9.95 to £17.95. Puddings: £5.85

Free house ~ Licensee Steven Whiting ~ Real ale ~ Bar food ~ Restaurant ~ (01367) 820643 ~ Children welcome ~ Dogs welcome ~ Open 11-11; 12-10.30 Sun

Recommended by Phyl and Jack Street, Tony and Tracy Constance, William Goodhart, Lesley and Peter Barrett

Real ale to us means beer which has matured naturally in its cask – not pressurised or filtered. We name all real ales stocked. We usually name ales preserved under a light blanket of carbon dioxide too, though purists – pointing out that this stops the natural yeasts developing – would disagree (most people, including us, can't tell the difference!).

FINSTOCK

SP3616   MAP 4

Plough 🍴 ♈ 🍺

Just off B4022 N of Witney; High Street; OX7 3BY

Good food in village pub, decent choice of drinks, open fire and seats outside

This thatched village pub is nicely split up by partitions and alcoves. The long low-beamed rambling bar is comfortable and relaxed with leather sofas by the massive stone inglenook fireplace and some unusual horsebrasses and historical documents to do with the pub on the walls. The roomy, low-beamed dining room has candles and fresh flowers on the stripped-pine tables. Adnams Broadside and Butts Organic Jester with a guest like Cotswold Spring Codrington Codger on handpump, several wines by the glass, 20 malt whiskies and traditional cider; pub billiards, board games and piped music. The pub cats are called Rufus and Pushka. Outside, the neatly kept garden has tables and chairs, and aunt sally. There are popular local walks among woodland and along the River Evenlode but if your walking party wish to eat, you must book in advance. More reports please.

🍴 Even when not on a walk, it's essential to book a table in advance to enjoy the good bar food cooked by one of the landlords using some home-grown produce: sandwiches, soup, chicken liver parfait with fig chutney, potted brown shrimps, baked root vegetables with apricots and goats cheese, beer-battered fish and chips, pasta with sausage, chilli, fennel and lemon, chicken suprême with wild mushroom sauce, roast fillet of venison with red wine and juniper sauce, rib-eye steak with herb butter, and puddings like lemon and blueberry posset and warm chocolate puddle cake. *Starters/Snacks: £5.00 to £8.00. Main Courses: £10.00 to £17.00. Puddings: £5.00 to £6.00*

Free house ~ Licensees Joe McCorry and Martin Range ~ Real ale ~ Bar food (not Sun evening or Mon (except bank hols)) ~ Restaurant ~ (01993) 868333 ~ Children at discretion of licensees ~ Dogs allowed in bar ~ Open 12-2.30, 6-11; 12-11 Sat; 12-6(4 in winter) Sun; closed Sun evening, Mon (except bank hols), maybe two weeks in Feb

Recommended by Guy Vowles, Jon Carpenter, Mr and Mrs J C Cetti, George and Linda Ozols, D R Ellis

FYFIELD

SU4298   MAP 4

White Hart 🍴 ♈ 🍺

In village, off A420 8 miles SW of Oxford; OX13 5LW

Impressive place with grand main hall, minstrel's gallery and interesting side rooms, imaginative modern food, fine choice of drinks and seats outside

Full of history and with a civilised and friendly atmosphere, this well run place is much enjoyed by our readers. There's plenty to look at as the bustling main restaurant is a grand hall with soaring eaves, beams, huge stone-flanked window embrasures and flagstoned floors; it's overlooked by a minstrel's gallery on one side and several other charming and characterful side rooms on the other. In contrast, the side bar is cosy with a large inglenook fireplace at its centre and a low-beamed ceiling; throughout, there are fresh flowers and evening candles. Hook Norton Hooky, Loddon Hullabaloo, Rebellion Zebedee and Sharps Doom Bar on handpump, around 16 wines by the glass (including champagne), several malt whiskies and home-made summer elderflower pressé; they hold beer festivals on May and August bank holiday weekends. Piped music and board games. There are elegant metal seats around tables under smart umbrellas on the spacious heated terrace and lovely gardens that include their own kitchen garden. Plenty to see nearby and the Thames-side walks are well worth taking.

🍴 Using their own herbs, vegetables and fruit, and cooked by the licensee, the excellent – if not cheap – food (it's essential to book a table in advance) includes soup, chicken and duck liver parfait with apricot chutney, home-cured gravadlax with marinated cucumber salad, various sharing boards (antipasti, fish and vegetarian), salmon and caper fishcakes with chive beurre blanc, potato and rosemary ravioli with wild mushrooms, slow-cooked lamb breast with sweetbreads and carrot and cumin purée, 28-day-aged rib-eye steak with dijon and tarragon butter, and puddings such as rich chocolate cake with pistachio ice-cream and spiced roast pineapple sabayon with saffron ice-cream; they also offer a two- and three-course set lunch and **Sunday roasts.** *Starters/Snacks: £5.50 to £7.00. Main Courses: £13.00 to £19.00. Puddings: £6.00*

Free house ~ Licensee Mark Chandler ~ Real ale ~ Bar food (12-2.30(4 Sun), 7-9.30; not Sun evening and Mon) ~ Restaurant ~ (01865) 390585 ~ Children welcome but must be well behaved ~ Open 12-3, 5.30-11; 12-11(10.30 Sun) Sat; closed Mon (except bank hols)

Recommended by Bruce and Sharon Eden, Andy and Claire Barker, Helene Grygar, Rochelle Seifas, David and Sue Atkinson, Graham and Toni Sanders, David and Jill Wyatt, I J and S A Bufton, GSB, Tony and Tracy Constance, Henry Midwinter

GREAT TEW   SP3929   MAP 4
Falkland Arms
Off B4022 about 5 miles E of Chipping Norton; The Green; OX7 4DB

Idyllic golden-stone cottage in lovely village, with plenty of character in the unspoilt bar and a fine choice of ales

New licensees have taken over this lovely untouched thatched pub; it's just one of the fine golden-stone buildings in this idyllic village. The unspoilt and partly panelled bar has high-backed settles and a diversity of stools around plain stripped tables on flagstones and bare boards, one-, two- and three-handled mugs hanging from the beam-and-board ceiling, dim converted oil lamps, shutters for the stone-mullioned latticed windows, and an open fire in the fine inglenook fireplace. Wadworths IPA, 6X and a seasonal ale plus guests such as Isle of Purbeck Fossil Fuel, Mauldons Moletrap Bitter and Vale Edgars Golden Ale and Gravitas on handpump. The counter is decorated with tobacco jars and different varieties of snuff which you can buy and you'll also find 30 malt whiskies, country wines and Weston's farm cider; darts and board games. You have to go out into the lane and then back in again to use the lavatories. There are tables out in front of the pub and picnic-sets under cocktail parasols in the garden behind. Dogs must be on a lead. Small good value bedrooms (no under-16s).

Bar food includes lunchtime filled baguettes and ploughman's, soup, chicken liver pot with apple chutney, a charcuterie or smoked fish plate to share, roasted vegetable and spiced potato crumble, sausages with red onion gravy, spiced lamb burger with salsa, steak in Guinness pie, chicken breast in a rich tomato sauce, and puddings like lemon posset and crème brûlée. *Starters/Snacks: £4.95 to £6.50. Main Courses: £8.95 to £16.95. Puddings: £4.95*

Wadworths ~ Managers Ben Coombes and Ami Smith ~ Real ale ~ Bar food (12-2.30(4 weekends), 6-9) ~ Restaurant ~ (01608) 683653 ~ Children allowed in restaurant lunchtimes only ~ Dogs allowed in bar ~ Live folk Sun evening ~ Open 11.30-11; 12-10.30 Sun ~ Bedrooms: £50S/£85S(£115B)

Recommended by Richard Greaves, MDN, the Didler, Tich Critchlow, George Atkinson, Andy and Jill Kassube, Ann and Colin Hunt

HAILEY   SU6485   MAP 2
King William IV
The Hailey near Ipsden, off A4074 or A4130 SE of Wallingford; OX10 6AD

Attractive old pub, wonderful views from seats in the garden, friendly staff, well liked food and real ales

In fine weather, it's best to get here early as the many seats on the terrace and in the large garden get quickly snapped up by customers keen to enjoy the wide-ranging views across peaceful rolling pastures – with maybe red kites patrolling overhead. Inside, the beamed bar has some good, sturdy furniture on the tiles in front of the big winter log fire and there are three other cosy seating areas that open off here. Brakspears Bitter and a seasonal guest are tapped from the cask, there's an interesting wine list and farm cider; good, friendly service. The pub is popular with walkers and horse riders (and you can tether your horse in the car park); the Ridgeway National Trail is nearby.

🍴 Enjoyable bar food includes lunchtime filled baguettes (not Sunday), soup, chicken liver pâté, local sausages with chips, spinach, mushroom and cream cheese filo parcel with provençale sauce, a pie of the day, goan fish curry, an african chicken dish with spices, almonds, apricots and yoghurt, popular lamb kleftiko (with honey, garlic, mead and oregano), and puddings such as pear and ginger sponge and walnut and treacle tart. Sunday roasts and maybe summer barbecues. *Starters/Snacks: £5.00 to £6.50. Main Courses: £8.95 to £13.00. Puddings: £4.75*

Brakspears ~ Tenant Neal Frankel ~ Real ale ~ Bar food (12-1.45(2 Sun), 6.30-9.30(9 Sun)) ~ (01491) 681845 ~ Childen allowed in two rooms off bar area ~ Dogs welcome ~ Open 11.30-2.30, 6-11; 12-3, 6(6.30 in winter)-10.30 Sun

Recommended by Richard and Sissel Harris, the Didler, Steve and Linda Langdon, Mr Ray J Carter, Richard Endacott, Ray Carter

HIGHMOOR   SU6984   MAP 2
Rising Sun
Witheridge Hill, signposted off B481; OS Sheet 175 map reference 697841; RG9 5PF

Thoughtfully run and pretty pub with a mix of diners and drinkers

In a little village in the heart of the Chilterns, this is a pretty black and cream pub which is very popular at lunchtime with walkers. You can be sure of a warm welcome from the friendly, chatty licensees and their pleasant staff and the two front rooms are for those just wanting a drink – the rest of the place is laid out for dining. On the right by the bar, there are wooden tables and chairs and a sofa on the stripped wooden floors, cream and terracotta walls and an open fire in the big brick inglenook fireplace. The main area spreading back from here has shiny bare boards and a swathe of carpeting with well spaced tables and attractive pictures on the walls. Brakspears Bitter and Oxford Gold and a guest beer on handpump, and Weston's cider; piped music and board games. There are seats and tables in the pleasant back garden; boules.

🍴 Well liked bar food using home-grown herbs (which they also sell) includes sandwiches, wraps and rarebits, ploughman's, soup, chicken livers on toasted brioche with tarragon butter, crab pâté, butternut squash, okra and aubergine curry with apple and sultana chutney, chicken and mushroom pie, honey and five spice chinese-style ribs, pork and leek sausages, pigeon, smoked bacon and cannellini bean stew, smoked haddock fillet with colcannon mash and mustard cream sauce, venison medallions with haggis and a port and raisin sauce, and puddings such as lemon meringue pie and mango cheesecake. *Starters/Snacks: £5.95 to £7.50. Main Courses: £8.95 to £14.50. Puddings: £4.95*

Brakspears ~ Tenant Judith Bishop ~ Real ale ~ Bar food (12-2(3 Sun), 6.30-9; not Sun evening) ~ Restaurant ~ (01491) 640856 ~ Children allowed under strict supervision in dining areas only ~ Dogs allowed in bar ~ Open 12-2.30, 5.30-11; 12-11 Sat; 12-7 Sun; closed Sun evening

Recommended by Torrens Lyster, Paul Humphreys, Martin and Karen Wake, John Roots, Roy and Jean Russell, Bob and Margaret Holder, David and Sue Smith

KINGHAM   SP2624   MAP 4
Plough
Village signposted off B4450 E of Bledington; or turn S off A436 at staggered crossroads a mile SW of A44 junction – or take signed Daylesford turn off A436 and keep on; The Green; OX7 6YD

OXFORDSHIRE DINING PUB OF THE YEAR

Friendly dining pub combining an informal pub atmosphere with upmarket food; bedrooms

Inventive food and friendly staff continue to draw contented customers into this bustling restaurant-with-rooms. But despite the emphasis on dining, there's a properly pubby bar with some nice old high-backed settles as well as brightly cushioned chapel chairs on its broad dark boards, candles on its stripped tables, a big log fire at one end, a woodburning stove at the other (by an unusual cricket table) and cheerful farmyard animal and country prints. There's a piano in one corner and a snug separate one-table area opposite the servery which has Hook Norton Hooky Bitter and Purity Mad Goose on handpump and good wines by the glass. The fairly spacious and raftered two-part dining room is up a few steps. If you stay, the breakfast is good. The heated smokers' shelter is at the back of the building.

Ⓜ️ **Extremely good food includes bar snacks such as snails and mushrooms on toast, home-made sausage roll with home-made ketchup, hand-raised pork pie with pickle, minted local lamb burger with fried quail eggs and crisp lemon sole with lemon mayonnaise, as well as more imaginative (and pricey) dishes like oysters with shallot vinegar, pressed ham hock with hodge podge pudding, apple and celeriac, smoked eel sausage, potato pancake and watercress and horseradish, spring vegetable and sea kale stew with tomatoes and potato dumplings, trout, shallot and potato terrine with leeks, cornish fish pie, sirloin of beef with braised beef-stuffed cabbage, morels and wild garlic, and puddings such as stout and honey tart with home-made Guinness ice-cream and cheltenham pudding with lemon curd and lemon and raisin ice-cream; interesting local cheeses.** *Starters/Snacks: £2.80 to £8.00. Main Courses: £12.00 to £24.00. Puddings: £4.00*

Free house ~ Licensees Emily Watkins and Miles Lampson ~ Real ale ~ Bar food (all day) ~ Restaurant ~ (01608) 658327 ~ Small children allowed in bar only ~ Dogs allowed in bar ~ Open 12-11(10.30 Sun) ~ Bedrooms: /£85S(£110B)

Recommended by Graham Oddey, Richard Greaves, Fred Beckett, J Harvey, Bernard Stradling, Keith and Sue Ward, Guy Vowles, Myra Joyce, Richard Tilbrook, Anthony and Pam Stamer, George Atkinson, Mr and Mrs W W Burke

LANGFORD
SP2402   MAP 4

Bell

Village signposted off A361 N of Lechlade, then pub signed; GL7 3LF

Civilised pub with beams, flagstones, a good log fire, well chosen wines and beer, and enjoyable bar food

Although this is a busy little dining pub with smashing food, it has an informal country atmosphere and welcoming, friendly licensees. The simple low-key furnishings and décor add to the appeal: the main bar has just six sanded and sealed mixed tables on grass matting, a variety of chairs, three nice cushioned window seats, an attractive carved oak settle, polished broad flagstones by a big stone inglenook fireplace with a good log fire, low beams and butter-coloured walls with two or three antique engravings. A second even smaller room on the right is similar in character; daily papers on a little corner table. Hook Norton Hooky Bitter, Marstons Pedigree and St Austell Tribute on handpump, farm cider and a dozen wines by the glass. The bearded collie is called Madison. There are two or three picnic-sets out in the small garden with a play house; aunt sally. This is a quiet and charming village.

Ⓜ️ **As well as delicious fish dishes such as hake, crab and leek risotto with lobster sauce, seared king scallops with chorizo, rocket and parmesan and bass with herby potatoes and a tomato and basil sauce, the interesting food might include sandwiches, soup, bresaola with balsamic juice, mushrooms and leeks in a stilton and port sauce, pork and herb sausages with wholegrain mustard mash and onion gravy, thai green chicken curry, steak and mushroom pie, gammon and eggs, duck breast with braised red cabbage and apple and red wine jus, slow-roasted pork belly with a red wine jus, and puddings like rhubarb crumble and tarte tatin with italian toffee ice-cream.** *Starters/Snacks: £4.50 to £8.95. Main Courses: £8.95 to £15.95. Puddings: £4.95*

Free house ~ Licensees Paul and Jackie Wynne ~ Real ale ~ Bar food (not Sun evening or Mon) ~ Restaurant ~ (01367) 860249 ~ Children welcome but no-under 5s after 7pm ~ Dogs welcome ~ Open 12-3, 7-11(midnight Fri, 11.30 Sat); 12-3.30 Sun; closed Sun evening, all day Mon

Recommended by KN-R, L James, P and J Shapley, Grahame and Myra Williams, Henry Midwinter, Phil and Jane Hodson, Mrs Jean Lewis, Graham Oddey, George Atkinson

---

Prices of main dishes sometimes now don't include vegetables – if in doubt, ask.

LEWKNOR   SU7197   MAP 4

Olde Leathern Bottel

Under a mile from M40 junction 6; just off B4009 towards Watlington; OX49 5TH

Unchanging bustling country local with decent food and beer, and seats in sizeable garden

As this well run and genuinely friendly pub is handy for the M40, it can get pretty busy at lunchtimes and weekends. The two bar rooms have heavy beams and low ceilings, rustic furnishings, open fires and an understated décor of old beer taps and the like; best to arrive early to be sure of a table. The family room is separated only by standing timbers, so you won't feel segregated from the rest of the pub. Brakspears Bitter, Marstons Pedigree and Wychwood Hobgoblin on handpump and all their wines are available by the glass. The attractive sizeable garden is splendid and there are plenty of picnic-sets under parasols and a children's play area; boules and an outside dartboard, too. The pub is handy for walks on the Chiltern escarpment.

🍽 **Well cooked, honest bar food includes lunchtime filled baguettes, soup, chicken liver parfait, battered fish and chips, ham and free-range eggs, vegetarian lasagne, scampi, beef curry and puddings like crème brûlée and sherry trifle.** *Starters/Snacks: £4.95 to £7.95. Main Courses: £7.95 to £16.95. Puddings: £4.95*

Brakspears ~ Tenant L S Gordon ~ Real ale ~ Bar food ~ (01844) 351482 ~ Children welcome ~ Dogs welcome ~ Open 11-2.30(3 Sat), 5.30(6 Sat and in winter)-11; 12-3, 7-10.30 Sun

Recommended by Ross Balaam, Tracey and Stephen Groves, Chris Glasson, Roger and Anne Newbury, Tina and David Woods-Taylor, Paul Humphreys, D and M T Ayres-Regan, Andy and Jill Kassube, Dr Kevan Tucker, Ian Herdman, Torrens Lyster, David and Lexi Young

MURCOTT   SP5815   MAP 4

Nut Tree 🍽 🍷

Off B4027 NE of Oxford, via Islip and Charlton-on-Otmoor; OX5 2RE

Imaginative food (using their own produce), good wines and ales in friendly village pub

As we went to press we heard that there will be some changes here. The bar is to be relocated to where it originally was, a new dining room is to be added (and the kitchen refurbished) and the gardens will be landscaped. The licensees are determined that these changes will not detract from their pub trade and that they will remain a proper local. There will still be a couple of woodburning stoves. Hook Norton Hooky Bitter and a couple of guests from Fullers and Vale on handpump and several wines (including champagne) by the glass from a carefully chosen list. There are seats outside in the garden and pretty hanging baskets and tubs; aunt sally. On a wall in front of the pub is an unusual collection of gargoyles, each loosely modelled on a local character. There are ducks on the village pond. More reports please.

🍽 **Using their own gloucester old spot pigs and growing their own salads and vegetables, the interesting food (at a price) includes sandwiches, ploughman's, soup, smoked salmon and scrambled eggs on toast, parfait of chicken livers with caramelised apple chutney, salad of fresh cornish crab, smoked and fresh salmon fishcake with tomato butter sauce, roast chump of lamb with confit garlic, haunch of venison with butternut squash purée and bourguignon garnish, and puddings such as hot passion-fruit soufflé and warm chocolate fondant with sea salt caramel and peanut butter ice-cream; they also offer a two- and three-course weekday set menu.** *Starters/Snacks: £7.50 to £12.00. Main Courses: £15.50 to £25.00. Puddings: £6.00 to £7.50*

Free house ~ Licensees Mike and Imogen North ~ Real ale ~ Bar food (12-2.30(3 Sun), 7-9(6.30-8 summer Sun)) ~ Restaurant ~ (01865) 331253 ~ Children welcome ~ Dogs allowed in bar ~ Open 12-11(10.30 Sun); closed winter Sun evenings, all day Mon

Recommended by Mike Buckingham, George and Beverley Tucker, Peter Sampson

OXFORD   SP5106   MAP 4

Bear 🍺

Alfred Street/Wheatsheaf Alley; OX1 4EH

Charming little pub just off the High Street with friendly staff, two cosy rooms, six real ales and well liked bar food

This is a delightful little pub and the oldest in the city. Under its present licensee, we've had warm praise from our readers for the friendly, interested staff serving well kept real ales, the decent food and bustling, chatty atmosphere. There are two charming little low-ceilinged, beamed and partly panelled ancient rooms, not over-smart and often packed with students, with two winter coal fires, thousands of vintage ties on walls and up to six real ales from handpump on the fine pewter bar counter: Fullers Chiswick, ESB, Gales HSB and London Pride and a couple of guest beers. There are seats under parasols in the back terraced garden where they hold summer barbecues.

🍽 **Bar food includes sandwiches, nibbles like olives and hummus with local bread, a proper ploughman's, various burgers including a vegetarian one, fish and chips, garlic tiger prawns, sausage and mash, game pie, and puddings such as chocolate fudge cake and treacle sponge.** *Starters/Snacks: £2.95 to £5.00. Main Courses: £7.00 to £9.75. Puddings: £4.50*

Fullers ~ Manager Stuart Scott ~ Real ale ~ Bar food (all day) ~ (01865) 728164 ~ Children allowed in back room ~ Open 11-11

Recommended by Paul Humphreys, Michael Dandy, Andrea Rampley, Gordon Stevenson, Tim Williams, Pippa Manley, the Didler

Rose & Crown

North Parade Avenue; very narrow, so best to park in a nearby street; OX2 6LX

Long-serving licensees in this lively friendly local, a good mix of customers, fine choice of drinks and proper home cooking

Slightly out of the city centre and with a good mix of undergraduates and more mature customers, this rather straightforward local is now a free house. It is still run, as it has been for 27 years, by the sharp-witted Mr Hall and his wife who welcome all well behaved customers (though not children or dogs). The front door opens into a passage by the bar counter and the panelled back room, with traditional pub furnishings, is slightly bigger with reference books for crossword buffs; no mobile phones, piped music or noisy games machines, but they do have board games. Adnams Bitter, Hook Norton Old Hooky and a couple of guest beers on handpump, around 30 malt whiskies and a large choice of wines. The pleasant walled and heated back yard can be covered with a huge awning; at the far end is a 12-seater dining/meeting room. The lavatories are pretty basic.

🍽 **Traditional but enjoyable food includes interesting sandwiches and baguettes, filled baked potatoes, ploughman's, pitta bread and dips, omelettes, sausage and mash, all-day breakfast, a hot dish of the day such as honeyed chicken or beef stew with herb dumplings, and puddings like cheesecake or apple pie; popular Sunday roasts.** *Starters/Snacks: £2.45 to £7.95. Main Courses: £6.50 to £13.95. Puddings: £1.95 to £4.75*

Free house ~ Licensees Andrew and Debbie Hall ~ Real ale ~ Bar food (12-2.15(3.15 Sun), 6-9) ~ No credit cards ~ (01865) 510551 ~ Open 10-midnight (closed 2.30-5 in Aug and early Sept)

Recommended by Chris Glasson, the Didler, Robert Lorimer, Tony and Jill Radnor, Torrens Lyster

---

Bedroom prices normally include full english breakfast, VAT and any inclusive service charge that we know of. Prices before the '/' are for single rooms, after for two people in double or twin (B includes a private bath, S a private shower).

Turf Tavern

Tavern Bath Place; via St Helen's Passage, between Holywell Street and New College Lane; OX1 3SU

Interesting character pub hidden away behind high walls, with a dozen ales, regular beer festivals, nice food and knowledgeable staff

Buried in its hidden courtyard and secluded from the modern bustle of the city, this extremely popular pub is run by helpful, knowledgeable staff and there's always a good mix of customers of all ages. The two dark-beamed and low-ceilinged small bars fill up quickly, though many prefer (whatever the time of year) to sit outside in the three attractive walled-in flagstoned or gravelled courtyards (one has its own bar); in winter, they have coal braziers so you can roast chestnuts or toast marshmallows and there are canopies with lights and heaters. Up to a dozen constantly changing real ales on handpump: Greene King IPA, Abbot, Morlands Old Speckled Hen and Ruddles Best and a couple from the White Horse Brewery including one named for the pub and maybe Beartown Bear Ass, Bushy's Old Bushy Tail, Everards Beacon, Nottingham Rock Ale Bitter, Stonehenge Danish Dynamite and West Berkshire Good Old Boy. They hold a spring and summer beer festival, keep Weston's Old Rosie cider and offer winter mulled wine.

🍴 Reasonably priced bar food includes sandwiches, filled baked potatoes, soup, burgers with all sorts of toppings, crayfish, smoked salmon, king prawn and pea risotto, ham and eggs, sausages with cheddar mash and red onion gravy, all-day breakfast, peppered mushroom suet pudding, chicken with bacon, cheese and barbecue sauce, and puddings like apple pie with cornish clotted cream ice-cream and vanilla and mascarpone cheesecake with a chilli, toffee, lime and ginger sauce. *Starters/Snacks: £3.45 to £4.95. Main Courses: £6.95 to £8.75. Puddings: £2.95 to £4.45*

Greene King ~ Manager Stella Berry ~ Real ale ~ Bar food (12-7.30) ~ (01865) 243235 ~ Children welcome ~ Dogs welcome ~ Open 11-11(10.30 Sun)

Recommended by LM, Rob and Catherine Dunster, Andy and Claire Barker, Roger Shipperley, the Didler, Martin Grosberg, Michael Dandy, Colin and Louise English, Andrea Rampley, G Jennings, MP, David and Sue Smith, Clive and Fran Dutson, Donna and Roger, Ann and ColinHunt, Alan Thwaite, Philip and June Caunt, Dick and Madeleine Brown

PISHILL

SU7190 MAP 2

Crown

B480 Nettlebed—Watlington; RG9 6HH

Fine old inn with attractive beamed bars, winter fires, real ales, several wines by the glass and good bar food; bedrooms

In winter, this mainly 15th-c red brick and flint pub is most appealing with its three roaring log fires – but in summer, it's just as enjoyable as there are plenty of picnic-sets under blue parasols in the pretty garden and lots of nearby walks. The partly panelled walls in the beamed bars are hung with old local photographs and maps, there are nice old chairs around a mix of wooden tables, candles everywhere, Brakspears Bitter, Loddon Hullabaloo and Rebellion IPA on handpump and nine wines by the glass. The knocked-through back area has standing oak timbers. The fine thatched barn they use for parties and functions is some 500 years old. You can stay in the self-contained cottage.

🍴 Good, attractively presented bar food includes sandwiches, ploughman's, soup, warm salad of smoked bacon and black pudding, deep-fried whitebait, seafood salad, goats cheese and onion marmalade tart, beer-battered haddock, steak in ale pudding, chicken breast stuffed with brie and wrapped in bacon with a honey and mustard sauce, and puddings like crème brûlée and sticky toffee pudding. *Starters/Snacks: £6.00 to £7.50. Main Courses: £9.00 to £18.00. Puddings: £5.00 to £6.00*

Free house ~ Licensee Lucas Wood ~ Real ale ~ Bar food (12-2.30(3 Sun), 7-9.30(9 Sun)) ~ (01491) 638364 ~ Dogs allowed in bar ~ Open 11.30-3, 6-11; 12-3.30, 7-10 Sun ~ Bedrooms: /£90B

Recommended by Susan and John Douglas, Paul Humphreys, Penny and Peter Keevil, the Didler

RAMSDEN   SP3515   MAP 4

Royal Oak 🍽 ♟ 🍺

Village signposted off B4022 Witney—Charlbury; OX7 3AU

Chatty, unpretentious pub with friendly licensees, 26 wines by the glass, good food and a heated back terrace; bedrooms

One of our readers enjoyed this pub so much that he moved to the village to be closer to it! We've had nothing but warm praise this year for the friendly, long-serving staff, the interesting beers and good food; it's a nice place to stay, too. The atmosphere is unpretentious and easy-going and the basic furnishings are comfortable, with fresh flowers, bookcases with old and new copies of *Country Life* and, when the weather gets cold, a cheerful log fire; no piped music or games machines. Butts Barbus Barbus, Hook Norton Hooky Bitter, Wye Valley HPA and guests like Warwickshire Rugby Ball Stitcher and Wickwar Cotswold Way on handpump, a fine choice of 26 wines by the glass from a carefully chosen list and three farm ciders. There are tables and chairs out in front and on the heated terrace behind the restaurant (folding back doors give easy access). The bedrooms are in separate cottages.

🍴 Using as much seasonal local produce as possible, the popular – if not particularly cheap – bar food includes lunchtime sandwiches, soup, chicken liver parfait with raisins and cognac, moules marinière, baked butternut squash filled with ratatouille and a herb crust, chargrilled home-made burgers, steak and kidney pudding, crab and smoked salmon fishcakes with a tomato and pepper sauce, a pie of the week, half a lamb shoulder with rosemary and garlic jus and a sri lankan curry. *Starters/Snacks: £4.95 to £8.50. Main Courses: £8.95 to £16.50. Puddings: £5.50*

Free house ~ Licensee Jon Oldham ~ Real ale ~ Bar food (12-2, 7-10) ~ Restaurant ~ (01993) 868213 ~ Children in restaurant with parents ~ Dogs allowed in bar ~ Open 11.30-3, 6.30-11; 12-3, 7-11 Sun ~ Bedrooms: £45S/£65S

Recommended by Tracey and Stephen Groves, Michael Doswell, Nigel Epsley, JJW, CMW, Dennis and Doreen Haward, Malcolm and Jo Hart, Roy Harding, Jane Hudson, Chris Glasson, Garry and Hannah Mortimer, Richard and Laura Holmes, Phil and Jane Hodson

SATWELL   SU7083   MAP 2

Lamb 🍽

2 miles S of Nettlebed; follow Shepherds Green signpost; RG9 4QZ

16th-c country pub with sizeable gardens, cosy bar and dining room, real ales, wines by the glass and good bar food

Well run and friendly, this 16th-c pub is popular for its good food and welcoming staff. It was originally two cottages and at its heart is the low-beamed bar with a log fire in the original inglenook fireplace, nice pubby furniture on the floor tiles, lots of old photographs of nearby Henley and various agricultural and other antique knick-knacks on the walls. Black Sheep Best, Loddon Leaping Lamb and Timothy Taylors Landlord on handpump, ten wines by the glass and several malt whiskies; piped music. The dining room next to the bar is a cosy place for a meal. Outside, there's a large garden with a woodland area, seats on a sizeable lawn and chickens; boules and summer barbecues. As the pub is on the edge of the Chilterns, there are plenty of surrounding walks.

🍴 Enjoyable bar food includes lunchtime sandwiches, smoked chicken pâté with onion marmalade, moules marinière, a lunchtime brunch, gratin of aubergine, goats cheese and morel mushrooms, popular fish and chips cooked in beef dripping, calves liver with bacon and mash, pork chop with wild mushrooms and apple chutney, lamb shank with herbed mash and rosemary jus, and puddings like apple tarte tatin with vanilla ice-cream and orange tart with burnt honey and lemon crème fraîche. *Starters/Snacks: £4.95 to £6.95. Main Courses: £9.50 to £12.75. Puddings: £4.95 to £6.25*

Free house ~ Licensees Chris and Emma Smith ~ Real ale ~ Bar food (12-2.30, 7-9.30; all day weekends) ~ Restaurant ~ (01491) 628482 ~ Children welcome ~ Dogs allowed in bar ~ Open 12-3, 6-11; 12-11(10.30 Sun) Sat

Recommended by BOB, Susan and John Douglas

SHILTON   SP2608   MAP 4

Rose & Crown

Just off B4020 SE of Burford; OX18 4AB

Simple and appealing little village pub, with a relaxed civilised atmosphere, real ales and a fair choice of bar food

This is a popular and pretty 17th-c stone-built pub in a nice village with a good mix of both locals and visitors – and it remains as simple and as unspoilt (in a subtly upmarket way) as ever. The small front bar has proper wooden beams and timbers, exposed stone walls, and a log fire in a big fireplace, with half a dozen or so tables on the red tiled floor, and a few locals at the planked counter. This opens into a similar, bigger room used mainly for eating, with flowers on the tables, and another fireplace. Brakspear Oxford Gold, Hook Norton Old Hooky and Wells & Youngs Bitter on handpump and nine wines by the glass; big cafetières of coffee. At the side, an attractive garden has picnic-sets.

🍴 Bar food, using local game and meat, includes lunchtime ciabattas, soup, smoked duck breast with an orange-dressed salad, pressed pigs head with apple and black pudding purée, faggots with peas and mash, ham and egg, smoked haddock, salmon and prawn fish or steak and mushroom in ale pies, fettuccine provençale, pork and duck cassoulet, slow-roasted and pressed lamb shoulder, and puddings like almond, prune and armagnac tart and steamed chocolate pudding with chocolate sauce. *Starters/Snacks: £4.50 to £6.50. Main Courses: £7.00 to £15.50. Puddings: £4.50 to £5.00*

Free house ~ Licensee Martin Coldicott ~ Bar food (12-2.45, 7-9; not winter Sun evening) ~ (01993) 842280 ~ Well behaved children welcome ~ Dogs allowed in bar ~ Open 11.30-3, 6-11; 11.30-11 Fri and Sat; 12-10 Sun

Recommended by Helene Grygar, Ian and Nita Cooper, Jean and Douglas Troup, William Goodhart, Anthony Barnes, Martin and Karen Wake, David Lamb, Richard Wyld, J L Wedel

SHIPLAKE   SU7779   MAP 2

Baskerville 🍽 ♟

Station Road, Lower Shiplake (off A4155 just S of Henley); RG9 3NY

Emphasis on imaginative food though a proper public bar, too; real ales, several wines by the glass, interesting sporting memorabilia and a pretty garden

Behind the rather plain 1930s exterior, this is a pub of real quality with imaginative food served by friendly staff – though the licensees are keen that locals do still drop in for a drink and a chat. There are some bar chairs around the light, modern bar counter, a few beams, pale wooden dining chairs and tables on the light wood floors, plush red banquettes around the windows and a couple of log fires in brick fireplaces. A fair amount of sporting memorabilia and pictures, especially old rowing photos (the pub is very close to Henley) and signed rugby shirts and photographs (the pub runs its own rugby club), plus some maps of the Thames are hung on the red walls, and there are flowers and large house plants dotted about. It all feels quite homely, but in a smart way, with some chintzy touches such as a shelf of china cow jugs. Fullers London Pride, Loddon Hoppit and Timothy Taylors Landlord on handpump, 30 malt whiskies and a dozen wines by the glass. There's a separate dining room and a small room for private family or business groups. The pretty garden has a proper covered barbecue area, smart teak furniture under huge parasols and some rather fun statues made out of box. There's a timber play frame for children.

🍴 Using local, organic produce, the good bar food includes breakfast (from 9.30-11.30), snacks like scotch or pork pies and pasties, open sandwiches, soup, mussels with blue cheese, bacon and cider, ham hock terrine with home-made piccalilli, a hand-made burger, venison, pork and port sausages with a rich onion gravy, smoked mackerel on horseradish mash with creamed leeks and a free-range poached egg, steak and kidney in ale pie, beer-battered haddock, lamb hotpot, red tilapia fillet with lemon braised fennel and a herby salsa, and puddings such as double chocolate brownie and orange and vanilla crème brûlée; they also offer two- and three-course set menus; Sunday roasts. *Starters/Snacks: £5.50 to £10.00. Main Courses: £13.50 to £20.00. Puddings: £6.50*

Free house ~ Licensee Allan Hannah ~ Real ale ~ Bar food (12-2, 7-9.30(10 Fri and Sat);
12-4 Sun; not Sun evening) ~ Restaurant ~ (0118) 940 3332 ~ Children welcome but not in
restaurant after 8pm Fri and Sat ~ Dogs allowed in bar and bedrooms ~ Open 11.30-2.30, 6-11;
12-4, 7-10.30 Sun; closed 26 Dec, 1 Jan ~ Bedrooms: £75S/£85S

Recommended by Joe Green, Paul Humphreys, Neil and Karen Dignan, MP

SHIPTON-UNDER-WYCHWOOD   SP2717   MAP 4

Lamb 🍴 🍷 🛏

Off A361 to Burford; High Street; OX7 6DQ

**Handsome stone inn with friendly licensees, attractive bars, popular food and good choice
of drinks; bedrooms**

Doing particularly well under its present mother and son team, this friendly pub is handy
for many of the Cotswold attractions. The beamed bar has a fine oak-panelled settle, a
nice mix of solid old farmhouse-style and captain's chairs on the wood-block floor,
church candles on polished tables, cushioned bar stools, partly stripped-stone walls and
an open log fire. Clarks Westgate Flankers Tackle, Greene King IPA and Hook Norton Old
Hooky on handpump and 20 good wines and champagne by the glass. The pub dogs are
called Sky and Izzy. The garden area has been extended and there are contemporary black
chairs and tables plus teak furniture on the terrace. We have not heard from readers who
have stayed here but would imagine it to be most enjoyable.

🍴 **Popular bar food using fresh local produce includes sandwiches, soup, a deli board,
home-cured prosciutto, potted duck and orange pâté with kumquat syrup, spicy lime
scallops, beef cobbler, beer-battered cod, lamb tagine with apricots and prunes, baked
butternut squash with wild mushrooms and stilton sauce, lemon and ginger chicken with
stir-fried vegetables, honey-roasted gressingham duck breast, and puddings like rich
chocolate pudding with chocolate sauce and lemon tart.** *Starters/Snacks: £4.85 to £8.95.
Main Courses: £7.00 to £17.50. Puddings: £5.50 to £7.95*

Greene King ~ Lease Tracey and Paul Hunt ~ Real ale ~ Bar food (12-2.30, 6.30-9.30) ~
Restaurant ~ (01993) 830465 ~ Children welcome ~ Dogs allowed in bar and bedrooms ~
Open 11.30-11 ~ Bedrooms: £75S/£95B

Recommended by Guy Vowles, Lawrence R Cotter

STANTON ST JOHN   SP5709   MAP 4

Star

*Pub signposted off B4027, in Middle Lane; village is signposted off A40 heading E of Oxford
(heading W, you have to go to the Oxford ring-road roundabout and take the unclassified
road signposted to Stanton St John, Forest Hill, etc); OX33 1EX*

**Nice old village pub with interesting rooms, friendly landlord, Wadworths beers and
generously served bar food**

Tucked away at the end of the village, this is a quietly civilised and relaxed old pub. It's
appealingly arranged over two levels and the oldest parts are two characterful little low-
beamed rooms, one with ancient brick flooring tiles and the other with quite close-set
tables. Up some stairs is an attractive extension on a level with the car park with old-
fashioned dining chairs, an interesting mix of dark oak and elm tables, rugs on
flagstones, bookshelves on each side of an attractive inglenook fireplace (a fine fire in
winter), shelves of good pewter and a portrait in oils on the terracotta-coloured walls.
Wadworths IPA and 6X on handpump and several wines by the glass. There's a family
room and conservatory, too; piped music, darts and board games. The walled garden has
seats among the flowerbeds and there's some children's play equipment.

🍴 **Bar food includes sandwiches, ploughman's, filled baked potatoes, aberdeen angus
cheeseburger, beef in ale pie, vegetarian cannelloni, smoked haddock fishcakes, gammon
with egg and pineapple, chicken in stilton and wine and lamb shank in redcurrant and
rosemary.** *Starters/Snacks: £4.95 to £6.95. Main Courses: £9.95 to £13.50. Puddings: £4.95*

Wadworths ~ Tenant Michael Urwin ~ Real ale ~ Bar food (12-2.30(3 Sun), 7-9) ~ (01865) 351277 ~ Children welcome ~ Dogs welcome ~ Open 12-3, 6.30-11; 12-3, 7-10.30 Sun

Recommended by John Robertson, Dennis and Doreen Haward, Tina and David Woods-Taylor, David Lamb, Peter Sampson

Talk House ♀ 🛏

Middle Road/Wheatley Road (B4027 just outside village); OX33 1EX

Attractive thatched dining pub, inventive seasonal modern pub food in several separate areas and sheltered courtyard; comfortable bedrooms

The thatched part, at the front on the left, dates from about 1550, giving a splendid dining area with steeply pitched rafters soaring above stripped-stone walls, a mix of old dining chairs around big stripped tables and large rugs on flagstones. Most of the rest of the building has been well converted more recently, keeping a similar style – fat candles on stripped tables, massive beams, flagstones or stoneware tiles, log fires below low mantelbeams, a relaxed and leisured feel. At the front on the right are dark leather button-back sofas and leather-cushioned easy chairs, with two more dining areas at the back. They have three well kept Fullers ales on handpump, a good range of enjoyable wines by the glass, daily papers and smiling helpful staff. An inner courtyard has comfortable teak tables and chairs, with a few picnic-sets on a side lawn. The snug ground-floor bedrooms are behind here.

🍴 The versatile menu, using food from named local farms, runs from good value nibbles such as tomato crostini, aioli, mini-sausages and spiced kalamari, through small or large helpings of various pasta dishes and platters such as smoked duck pie or a warm salad of black pudding, pancetta and potato, to main dishes such as slow-cooked belly pork with white bean salad; they do a good value two- or three-course set menu. If you stay, breakfasts are good. *Starters/Snacks: £2.75 to £8.00. Main Courses: £10.00 to £17.00. Puddings: £5.00 to £6.50.*

Fullers ~ Manager John McKay ~ Real ale ~ Bar food (12-3, 6-9; all day Sat, Sun and bank hols) ~ Restaurant ~ (01865) 351648 ~ Children welcome ~ Dogs allowed in bar ~ Live jazz first Weds of the month ~ Open 10am-midnight(1.30am Fri and Sat); 10am-11pm Sun ~ Bedrooms: /£65S

Recommended by Miss A G Drake

STEEPLE ASTON   SP4725   MAP 4

Red Lion £

Off A4260 12 miles N of Oxford; OX25 4RY

Friendly village pub with beamed bar, nice straightforward food, local beers and a suntrap terrace

With a warm welcome from the friendly, hard-working licensees and good-value enjoyable food, it's not surprising our readers like this little village pub so much. The neatly kept, comfortable and partly panelled bar is chatty and relaxed with beams, an antique settle and other good furnishings. Hook Norton Hooky Bitter and Red Pride and a seasonal guest beer on handpump and several wines by the glass; good service. There's a back conservatory-style dining extension, too. The suntrap front terrace has lovely flowers and shrubs.

🍴 As well as their popular and very good value 'pub classic' dishes like ham and eggs, lambs liver and bacon and fishcakes, other fair-value bar food includes sandwiches, home-made scotch eggs, a sharing deli plate, creamy garlic mushrooms, smoked salmon and pea risotto, cajun chicken, blue cheese and spinach pancakes, battered fish and chips, steak and mushroom in ale pie and sirloin steak with garlic butter; Sunday roasts. *Starters/Snacks: £2.95 to £4.95. Main Courses: £5.50 to £9.95. Puddings: £3.95 to £4.45*

Hook Norton ~ Tenants Melvin and Sarah Phipps ~ Real ale ~ Bar food (12-2.30, 6-9; 12-3.30 Sun (not Sun evening)) ~ Restaurant ~ (01869) 340225 ~ Well behaved children welcome lunchtime and until 7pm ~ Dogs allowed in bar ~ Open 12-3, 5.30-11; 12-5 Sat; closed Sun evening

Recommended by Gill and Keith Croxton, Brian Glozier, Ron and Sheila Corbett, Stephen Shepherd, Chris Bell, George and Beverley Tucker, Dale Mason

SWERFORD   SP3830   MAP 4

Masons Arms 🍴 🍷

A361 Banbury—Chipping Norton; OX7 4AP

**Attractive dining pub with chef/landlord, real ales and 20 wines by the glass, a civilised
and relaxed atmosphere and country views from outside tables**

The relaxed, friendly atmosphere and real ales on handpump in this attractive dining pub
prevent it from becoming an out-and-out restaurant – but most customers are here to
enjoy the modern food cooked by the chef/patron. The dining extension is light and airy
and the bar has pale wooden floors with rugs, a carefully illuminated stone fireplace,
thoughtful spotlighting, and beige and red armchairs around big round tables in pale
wood. Doors open on to a small terrace with a couple of stylish tables, while steps lead
down into a cream-painted room with chunky tables and contemporary pictures. Round
the other side of the bar is another roomy dining room with great views by day, candles
at night and a civilised feel. Hook Norton Hooky Bitter and Theakstons Best, 20 wines by
the glass and a few malt whiskies. Behind is a neat square lawn with picnic-sets and
views over the Oxfordshire countryside.

🍽 **As well as pubby choices such as sandwiches, ploughman's, sharing boards, caesar
salad, vegetarian pasta, home-baked ham and eggs and chicken korma, the interesting
food might include soup, smoked haddock and cream cheese pâté, polenta-coated risotto
balls with tomato and onion stew, 18-hour slow-roasted shoulder of gloucester old spot
pork with chorizo and olive mash, tea-soaked sultanas and rich gravy, slow-cooked shin of
beef with dauphinoise potatoes and red wine jus, gurnard with a minestrone of
vegetables, daily specials, and puddings like bakewell tart with raspberry compote and
chocolate brownie with mint chocolate chip ice-cream.** *Starters/Snacks: £4.50 to £10.00.
Main Courses: £8.00 to £14.00. Puddings: £5.95*

Free house ~ Licensee Bill Leadbeater ~ Real ale ~ Bar food (12-2(3 Sun), 7-9; not Sun evening)
~ Restaurant ~ (01608) 683212 ~ Children welcome ~ Open 10-3, 6-11; 11-4, 6-10.30 Sun

Recommended by Helene Grygar, Michael Dandy, Paul and Suzanne Martin

---

SWINBROOK   SP2812   MAP 4

Swan 🍷 🛏

Back road a mile N of A40, 2 miles E of Burford; OX18 4DY

**Civilised 17th-c pub with handsome oak garden room, smart bars, local beers and
contemporary food; bedrooms**

Owned by the Dowager Duchess of Devonshire (the last of the Mitford sisters who grew up
in the village), this civilised 17th-c pub has lots of interesting old Mitford family
photographs blown up on the walls. There's a little bar with simple antique furnishings,
settles and benches, an open fire, and (in an alcove) a stuffed swan; locals do still drop
in here for a pint and a chat. The small dining room to the right of the entrance opens
into this room and there are two green oak garden rooms with high-backed beige and
green dining chairs around pale wood tables and views over the garden and orchard.
Hook Norton Hooky Bitter and a couple of guests from breweries like Vale and Wadworths
on handpump, several wines by the glass, Weston's organic cider and local juices. This is
a lovely spot by a bridge over the River Windrush and seats by the fuchsia hedge make
the best of the view. The bedrooms are in a smartly converted stone barn beside the pub.
More reports please.

🍽 **Using beef from the family farm and other local produce, the bar food includes
lunchtime sandwiches, duck liver pâté with red onion marmalade, ginger potted prawns,
parsnip risotto with blue cheese and basil and almond pesto, confit goose leg with ginger,
lime and sultana dressing and a potato blini, spiced fillet of bream with coconut and
turmeric sauce and coriander chutney, and puddings like rhubarb and hazelnut macaroon
crumble and ginger pudding with walnut and prune ice-cream with hot spiced treacle.**
Starters/Snacks: £5.00 to £7.50. Main Courses: £10.00 to £20.00. Puddings: £5.00 to £6.50

Free house ~ Licensees Archie and Nicola Orr-Ewing ~ Real ale ~ Bar food (12-2(3 weekends), 7-9(9.30 Fri and Sat) ~ (01993) 823339 ~ Children welcome ~ Dogs allowed in bar ~ Live music bank hols ~ Open 11.30-11; 12-10 Sat ~ Bedrooms: £70B/£120B

Recommended by Mrs Margaret Weir, Derek Thomas, Graham Oddey, Mr and Mrs John Taylor, Anthony and Pam Stamer, Susan and John Douglas, Di and Mike Gillam, David Glynne-Jones, Richard Tilbrook, MDN, Brian Glozier, Henry Midwinter, Myra Joyce, Malcolm and Jo Hart, Bruce and Sharon Eden, Bernard Stradling, Mrs Blethyn Elliott, John and Enid Morris, Richard Wyld, Jeff and Wendy Williams, Richard Greaves, Ann and Colin Hunt, Andy and Claire Barker, Guy Vowles

TADPOLE BRIDGE   SP3200   MAP 4

Trout ♀ ⇋

Back road Bampton—Buckland, 4 miles NE of Faringdon; SN7 8RF

Busy country inn with River Thames moorings, fine choice of drinks, popular modern food and a lovely summer garden; bedrooms

'Well worth those extra miles to get there' says one of our readers after another enjoyable visit to this comfortable and civilised pub. It's in a lovely peaceful spot by the Thames and there are six moorings for visiting boats – you can also hire punts with champagne hampers. Inside, the L-shaped bar has attractive pink and cream checked chairs around a mix of nice wooden tables, some rugs on the flagstones, green paintwork behind a modern wooden bar counter, fresh flowers, two woodburning stoves and a large stuffed trout. The airy restaurant is appealingly candlelit in the evenings. Ramsbury Bitter, Wells & Youngs Bitter and guests from Arkells, Hook Norton, White Horse, Wickwar and Wychwood on handpump, 14 wines by the glass from a wide-ranging and carefully chosen list, some fine sherries and several malt whiskies. There are good quality teak chairs and tables under blue parasols in the lovely garden. The bedrooms were being refurbished as we went to press.

As well as lunchtime filled baguettes (not Sunday), the popular bar food includes chicken liver parfait with sauternes jelly, cornish crab, smoked salmon and crayfish with mustard crème fraîche, beer-battered haddock, steamed beef in ale pudding, wellington of spinach and gruyère cheese with pepper sauce, venison and chestnut pie, confit duck leg with black pudding mash and red onion gravy and saddle of rabbit with smoked lardons and port jus. *Starters/Snacks: £4.95 to £8.95. Main Courses: £9.95 to £18.95. Puddings: £5.95 to £6.95*

Free house ~ Licensees Gareth and Helen Pugh ~ Real ale ~ Bar food (not winter Sun evening) ~ Restaurant ~ (01367) 870382 ~ Children welcome ~ Dogs welcome ~ Open 11.30-3, 6-11; 11.30-11 Sat; 11.30-3(4 Sun), 6-11 Sat in winter; closed winter Sun evening ~ Bedrooms: £80B/£120B

Recommended by Jenny Clarke, Andy and Claire Barker, Mary Rayner, William Goodhart, Mr and Mrs J C Cetti, Suzy Miller, Bob and Angela Brooks, Charles Gysin, Martin Cawley, Bruce and Sharon Eden, Bob and Margaret Holder, Graham Oddey, Henry Midwinter

WEST HANNEY   SU4092   MAP 2

Plough

Just off A338 N of Wantage; Church Street; OX12 0LN

Thatched village pub with good choice of drinks, decent food and plenty of seats outside

Built as farm cottages in 1525 for an estate belonging to Henry VIII, this pretty and neatly thatched village pub (now a free house) has a friendly, relaxed atmosphere and plenty of loyal locals. The comfortable simply furnished bar has horsebrasses on beams, some bar stools, wheelback chairs around wooden tables, a log fire in the stone fireplace and lots of photographs of the pub on the walls. Three pub cats and some house plants add to the warm, informal feel. Brakspears Bitter, Timothy Taylors Landlord and three changing guest beers on handpump, several wines by the glass and two farm ciders; separate dining room. There are seats and tables on the back terrace overlooking the walled garden with plenty of picnic-sets on the grass; aunt sally and a trampoline. Good walks start with a village path right by the pub. More reports please.

🍴 Using local farm produce, the popular bar food includes sandwiches and filled baguettes, ploughman's, soup, thai fishcakes with a chilli dip, venison pâté, ham and eggs, aberdeen angus burgers, toad in the hole with onion gravy, lamb shank in red wine and rosemary, chicken breast stuffed with brie and daily fresh fish; they also offer a two-course set menu. *Starters/Snacks: £3.95 to £6.95. Main Courses: £6.95 to £12.95. Puddings: £4.50*

Free house ~ Licensee Trevor Cooper ~ Real ale ~ Bar food (12-2(3 Sun), 6-9) ~ Restaurant ~ (01235) 868674 ~ Children welcome ~ Dogs welcome ~ Live music Whit Mon and Aug bank hol beer festivals ~ Open 12-3, 6-11; 12-11 Sun and summer Sat

Recommended by David Lamb, D R Williams, Bob and Angela Brooks

WOODSTOCK
SP4416   MAP 4

Kings Arms 🛏️
Market Street/Park Lane (A44); OX20 1SU

Stylish hotel in centre of attractive town, well liked food, enjoyable atmosphere and a wide choice of drinks; comfortable bedrooms

The simple and unfussy bar in this stylish town-centre hotel has an informal, relaxed atmosphere and quite a mix of customers. Also, brown leather furnishings on the stripped wooden floor, smart blinds and black and white photographs throughout and at the front, an old wooden settle and interesting little woodburner. There's a marble bar counter, and, in the room leading to the brasserie-style dining room, an unusual stained-glass structure used for newspapers and magazines; the restaurant is attractive, with its hanging lights and fine old fireplace. Brakspears Bitter and Oxford Gold on handpump, good coffees, ten wines by the glass and 20 malt whiskies; piped music. Comfortable bedrooms and good breakfasts (available from 7.30-noon for non-residents, too). There are seats and tables on the street outside.

🍴 As well as filled rolls, bar food includes soup, goats cheese and celeriac soufflé, crayfish cocktail, baked nut loaf with chestnut mushroom and braised celery cream sauce, honey and mustard baked ham with free-range eggs, calves liver and bacon, slow-roasted pork belly with fennel compote, herb-crusted salmon steak with mussel and caper sauce, and puddings such as apple brûlée with stem ginger ice-cream and caramel snap with coffee hazelnut mousse and chocolate brownie. *Starters/Snacks: £4.75 to £7.75. Main Courses: £8.50 to £19.75. Puddings: £4.75 to £7.75*

Free house ~ Licensees David and Sara Sykes ~ Real ale ~ Bar food ~ Restaurant ~ (01993) 813636 ~ Children welcome in bar and restaurant but no under-12s in bedrooms ~ Dogs allowed in bar ~ Open 11-11 ~ Bedrooms: £75S/£140S

Recommended by Rob and Catherine Dunster, Mr and Mrs John Taylor, Derek and Sylvia Stephenson, Michael Dandy, Dave and Jenny Hughes, Martin and Pauline Jennings, John and Sharon Hancock, Pippa Manley, Paul Goldman

LUCKY DIP

Besides the fully inspected pubs, you might like to try these Lucky Dips recommended to us and described by readers (if you do, please send us reports: feedback@goodguides.com).

ABINGDON [SU5098]
Spread Eagle OX14 1PL [Northcourt Rd]: Doing well under present licensees, popular food (booking advised evenings) includes cook your own meat/fish on a hot rock, Greene King Morland, nice pubby atmosphere *(Tina and David Woods-Taylor)*
ADDERBURY [SP4735]
☆ *Red Lion* OX17 3NG [The Green; off A4260 S of Banbury]: Attractive and congenial, with good choice of enjoyable well priced food (all day wknds), helpful friendly staff,

Greene King ales and a guest, good wine range and coffee, three linked bar rooms, big inglenook log fire, panelling, high stripped beams and stonework, old books and Victorian/Edwardian pictures, daily papers, games area on left; piped music; children in eating area, picnic-sets out on roadside terrace, 12 character bedrooms, good breakfast, open all day summer *(Ian Herdman, George Atkinson, LYM)*
ASCOTT UNDER WYCHWOOD [SP2918]
☆ *Swan* OX7 6AY [Shipton Rd]: Fresh

contemporary refurbishment with good reasonably priced food from ciabattas to more adventurous things in bar and restaurant, well kept Brakspears, Hook Norton and Wadworths 6X, good choice of wines, friendly helpful service from smart staff, beams and some stripped stone, woodburner; disabled access, terrace tables, good bedrooms *(Helene Grygar, William Goodhart, Alun and Jennifer Evans, Miss Sue Callard, J C Burgis, Richard Greaves)*

BARNARD GATE [SP4010]

☆ *Boot* OX29 6XE [off A40 E of Witney]: Welcoming and attractive stone-tiled dining pub with enjoyable food from sandwiches up, well kept Wells & Youngs ales, decent wines, stout standing timbers and stub walls with latticed glass, huge log fire, solid country tables and chairs on bare boards, masses of celebrity footwear, piano; children welcome, tables out in front, open all day wknds *(Pete and Jackie Chunn, LYM)*

BECKLEY [SP5611]

☆ *Abingdon Arms* OX3 9UU [signed off B4027; High St]: Old dining pub under newish management in unspoilt village, comfortably modernised simple lounge, smaller public bar with antique carved settles, open fires, well kept Brakspears and guests, fair range of wines, good choice of enjoyable home-made food inc two-course deals (Mon-Thurs) and Sun roasts, good service; piped music and some live; children and dogs welcome, big garden dropping away from floodlit terrace to trees, summer house, superb views over RSPB Otmoor reserve – good walks, open all day wknds *(Canon Michael Bourdeaux, Colin McKerrow, LYM)*

BEGBROKE [SP4713]

Royal Sun OX5 1RZ [A44 Oxford—Woodstock]: Busy much refurbished open-plan stripped-stone pub with emphasis on prompt good value food from baguettes to Sun carvery, well kept Hook Norton, good friendly service; may be piped music; tables on terrace and in small streamside garden *(Alan and Eve Harding)*

BINFIELD HEATH [SU7479]

☆ *Bottle & Glass* RG9 4JT [off A4155 at Shiplake; between village and Harpsden]: Chocolate-box thatched black and white timbered Tudor cottage, emphasis on good value interesting food from sandwiches up, bleached pine tables, low beams and flagstones, black squared panelling, pastel shades, fine fireplace, well kept Brakspears and Wychwood, good choice of wines by the glass, friendly service, shove-ha'penny, dominoes; no children or dogs inside; lovely big garden with tables under little thatched roofs *(Susan and John Douglas, the Didler, LYM)*

BOARS HILL [SP4901]

Fox OX1 5DR [between A34 and B4017; Fox Lane]: Spacious comfortable Chef & Brewer in pretty wooded countryside, interesting rambling rooms on different levels, huge log fireplaces, prompt service, enjoyable all-day

food, decent wines by the glass, two well kept ales; may be soft piped classical music or jazz; children welcome, pleasant raised verandah, charming big sloping garden with fish pond, open all day *(William Goodhart, JJW, CMW)*

BRIGHTWELL [SU5890]

Red Lion OX10 0RT [signed off A4130 2 miles W of Wallingford]: Welcoming and locally popular for its well kept changing ales such as Appleford Power Station and enjoyable home-made food, two-part bar with snug seating by log fire, unobtrusive dining extension; dogs welcome, tables outside, peaceful village *(Anne Worsnop, Stephen Rudge)*

BUCKLAND [SU3497]

☆ *Lamb* SN7 8QN [off A420 NE of Faringdon]: Smart 18th-c stone-built dining pub with popular food (not Mon) from lunchtime special deals to grander and more expensive evening menus, several ales inc local ones, good choice of wines by the glass, lamb motif everywhere, formal restaurant; piped music; children welcome, pleasant tree-shaded garden, good walks nearby, comfortable bedrooms, cl Sun evening and over Christmas/New Year *(Henry Midwinter, Helene Grygar, the Didler, Graham and Toni Sanders, LYM)*

BUCKNELL [SP5525]

☆ *Trigger Pond* OX27 7NE [handy for M40 junction 10; Bicester Rd]: Neatly kept and welcoming stone-built beamed pub opp the pond, wide choice of good sensibly priced food from baguettes up (must book Sun lunch), fast friendly service, Wadworths ales inc seasonal, good value wines, small bar with dining areas either side, inglenook woodburner; colourful terrace and garden *(Bruce Braithwaite, Mr and Mrs R Green, George Atkinson, David Lamb, Guy Vowles)*

BURFORD [SP2512]

☆ *Angel* OX18 4SN [Witney St]: Long heavy-beamed dining pub in attractive ancient building, warmly welcoming with good reasonably priced brasserie food, good range of drinks; big secluded garden, three comfortable bedrooms *(KN-R, David Glynne-Jones, Leslie and Barbara Owen, LYM)*

Cotswold Arms OX18 4QF [High St]: Enjoyable good value pubby food from snacks up in cosy bar, more choice in larger back dining area, White Horse ales, welcoming helpful staff, beautiful stonework, two flame-effect stoves; children welcome, tables in front and back gardens *(Michael Dandy, Peter Thompson)*

Cotswold Gateway OX18 4HX [The Hill]: Busy hotel's traditional carpeted bar, welcoming and relaxed, with Brakspears, Wadworths and Wells & Youngs, several wines by the glass, enjoyable bar food from baguettes up, friendly efficient staff, more formal restaurant; piped music; comfortable bedrooms *(Keith and Sue Ward, Michael Dandy)*

Golden Pheasant OX18 4QA [High St]: Small early 18th-c hotel's flagstoned split-level bar, civilised yet relaxed and pubby, settees, armchairs, well spaced tables and woodburner, enjoyable food from baguettes to steaks, well kept Greene King ales, good house wines, friendly helpful service, back dining room down steps; children welcome, pleasant back terrace, bedrooms, open all day *(Michael Dandy, Tim and Joan Wright, BB)*

Mermaid OX18 4QF [High St]: Handsome jettied Tudor dining pub with beams, flagstones, panelling and stripped stone, good log fire, well kept Greene King ales, lots of wines by the glass, winter mulled wine, enjoyable promptly served food at sensible prices, bay seating around row of close-set tables on the left, further airy back dining room and upstairs restaurant; piped music, games machine; children in eating areas, picnic-sets under cocktail parasols outside, open all day *(Michael Dandy, LYM)*

☆ *Royal Oak* OX18 4SN [Witney St]: Relaxed homely 17th-c stripped-stone local, an oasis in this smart village, with long-serving friendly landlord, Wadworths ales and an occasional guest from central servery, simple generous good value food using local produce from filled rolls up, good service, over 1,000 beer mugs, steins and jugs hanging from beams, antlers over big log fire (underfloor heating too), light wood tables, chairs and benches on flagstones, more in carpeted back room with bar billiards; well behaved children and dogs welcome, terrace tables, sensibly priced bedrooms by garden behind, good breakfast, open all day Sat, cl Tues lunchtime *(Mr and Mrs W W Burke, Michael Dandy, Mrs S Sturgis)*

CASSINGTON [SP4510]

Chequers OX29 4DG: Smartly refurbished by new licensees, good food choice, back conservatory; bedrooms *(Mary McSweeney)*

CHARLBURY [SP3519]

Bull OX7 3RR [Sheep St]: Comfortable beamed stripped-stone bistro-style dining pub, restaurant on left with inglenook log fire, another in dining bar on right with rattan chairs, interesting food from sandwiches up, a house bitter brewed by Goffs and two guests, good choice of wines by the glass; no dogs; children welcome, attractive sunny back terrace, four bedrooms, cl Sun evening, Mon *(BB, C A Murphy)*

CHIPPING NORTON [SP3127]

Fox OX7 5DD [Market Pl]: Well placed unpretentious pub with lots of pictures and open fire in quiet lounge, well kept Hook Norton, good coffee, simple inexpensive bar food, welcoming helpful landlord, upstairs dining room; children and dogs welcome, good value bedrooms, hearty breakfast *(Chris Glasson, MP, LYM)*

CHISLEHAMPTON [SU5998]

☆ *Coach & Horses* OX44 7UX [B480 Oxford—Watlington, opp B4015 to Abingdon]: Extended 16th-c coaching inn, two homely and civilised beamed bars, big log fire, sizeable restaurant with polished oak tables and wall banquettes, good choice of well

prepared sensibly priced food (not Sun evening), friendly attentive service, well kept ales inc Fullers London Pride; piped music; neat terraced gardens overlooking fields by River Thame, some tables out in front, good bedrooms in courtyard block, open all day, cl 3.30-7 Sun *(Roy Hoing, Andrea Rampley, BB)*

CHRISTMAS COMMON [SU7193]

Fox & Hounds OX49 5HL [off B480/B481]: Upmarket Chilterns pub in lovely countryside, emphasis on airy and spacious front barn restaurant and conservatory with interesting food from open kitchen, well kept Brakspears and a guest, proper coffee, two compact beamed rooms simply but comfortably furnished, bow windows, red and black tiles and big inglenook, snug little back room; children and dogs welcome (there's a friendly pub dog), rustic benches and tables outside, open all day wknds *(the Didler, Susan and John Douglas, LYM)*

CLIFTON [SP4931]

☆ *Duke of Cumberlands Head* OX15 0PE [B4031 Deddington—Aynho]: Warmly welcoming thatch and stone pub with big low-beamed lounge, good log fire in vast fireplace and simple furnishings; some emphasis on food from good reasonably priced bar snacks up, friendly service, well kept Hook Norton and guests, good wine and whisky choice, cosy stripped-stone dining room, live music (classical/jazz) Sat night; children and dogs welcome, garden with barbecue, ten mins' walk from canal, six bedrooms *(Chris Glasson, Simon and Mandy King, Roy Hoing, Mrs Pat Parkin-Moore, Maurice Ricketts, Mr and Mrs A Woolstone, LYM)*

CLIFTON HAMPDEN [SU5495]

☆ *Barley Mow* OX14 3EH [towards Long Wittenham, S of A415]: Interesting and welcoming thatched Chef & Brewer dining pub, plenty of atmosphere with very low ancient beams, some appropriate furniture and nice dark corners, oak-panelled family room, real ales and good choice of wines by the glass, efficient friendly young staff, log fire, decent food all day from sandwiches up, restaurant; piped music; no dogs inside, tables on pleasant terrace and in well tended waterside garden, short stroll from Thames; open all day *(LYM, Chris Evans)*

COLESHILL [SU2393]

☆ *Radnor Arms* SN6 7PR [B4019 Faringdon—Highworth; village signposted off A417 in Faringdon and A361 in Highworth]: Pub and village owned by NT, bar with cushioned settles, plush carver chairs and woodburner, back alcove with more tables, steps down to main dining area, once a blacksmith's forge with lofty beamed ceiling, log fire, dozens of tools and blacksmith's gear on walls, Brakspears and Loddon Hoppit tapped from cask, local cider, summer home-made lemonade, shortish choice of bar food inc baguettes, pleasant service; children and dogs welcome, cl Sun evening, Mon *(Anne Morris,*

Tony and Tracy Constance, Graham Oddey, Andy and Claire Barker, LYM)

CRAWLEY [SP3412]

☆ *Lamb* OX29 9TW [Steep Hill; just NW of Witney]: Refurbished 18th-c stone-built dining pub, simple beamed bar with polished boards and lovely fireplace, steps to candlelit dining room, good food from sandwiches and pubby dishes to more enterprising things, good choice of wines by the glass, well kept Brakspears, helpful friendly service; piped music; children welcome, dogs in bar, views from tables on back terrace and lawn, pretty village, good walks – on Palladian Way, cl Sun evening (BB, Ian Phillips)

CROPREDY [SP4646]

Brasenose OX17 1PW [Station Rd]: Welcoming family-run village inn nr Oxford Canal, good choice of enjoyable pub food at pine tables in attractive dining room, well kept Adnams and Hook Norton, long bar with woodburner (dogs welcome here); comfortable bedrooms, decent breakfast, self-service laundry useful for boaters, has been open all day Fri-Sun (BB, Chris Glasson, John Buckeridge)

Red Lion OX17 1PB [off A423 N of Banbury]: Popular rambling 15th-c thatch-and-stone pub charmingly placed opp pretty village's churchyard, good food and service, Hook Norton, Timothy Taylors and Woodfordes, low beams, inglenook log fire, high-backed settles, brass, plates and pictures, unusual dining room murals, games room; piped music, limited parking; children allowed in dining part, picnic-sets on part-covered terrace, nr Oxford Canal (Bridge 152) (Chris Bell, LYM, George Atkinson, Clive and Fran Dutson)

CROWELL [SU7499]

Shepherds Crook OX39 4RR [B4009, 2 miles from M40 junction 6]: Unpretentious beamed bar with stripped brick and flagstones, open fire, high-raftered dining area, enjoyable food with emphasis on fish (particularly good value Weds evening, fish and chips Fri), interesting well kept ales; children and dogs welcome, tables out on green, decent walks (Torrens Lyster, Tracey and Stephen Groves, D and M T Ayres-Regan, LYM)

CUDDESDON [SP5902]

☆ *Bat & Ball* OX44 9HJ [S of Wheatley; High St]: Cheerful pub full of cricket memorabilia, low beams, some flagstones, informal mix of furnishings, well kept ales such as Marstons Pedigree and Wychwood, decent wines, enjoyable pub food, big back dining area; may be piped music; children welcome, pleasant back terrace, decent bedrooms (some small), open all day (LYM)

CUMNOR [SP4503]

☆ *Bear & Ragged Staff* OX2 9QH [signed from A420; Appleton Rd]: Extensive restaurant/pub dating from 16th c, clean contemporary décor in linked rooms with wood floors, leather-backed dining chairs and mix of tables, low lighting, enjoyable

food from shared charcuterie and meze plates to pub standards and up, wkdy lunch deals, good friendly service, flagstoned bar with log fire, changing beers and good wine choice, leather sofas and armchairs in airy garden room; children welcome, decked terrace, fenced play area, open all day (LYM, Bruce and Sharon Eden, Joan and Tony Walker, Bob and Angela Brooks)

CURBRIDGE [SP3208]

Lord Kitchener OX29 7PD [Lew Rd (A4095 towards Bampton)]: Bustling local atmosphere, welcoming efficient staff, extensive good value menu inc two-for-one lunch deals (not Sun) in neat, light and roomy dining extension, old local photographs, big log fire, real ales; piped music; small garden with play area, open all day (David Lamb)

DEDDINGTON [SP4631]

☆ *Crown & Tuns* OX15 0SP [New St]: Bistro-style conversion of 16th-c coaching inn, different levels with alcoves, low beams, flagstone and wood floors, log fires, good food inc speciality home-made pies in big earthenware dishes and Sun roasts, helpful friendly service, well kept Greene King and Hook Norton, good choice of wines and coffees; children till 7.30pm, walled garden, open all day Sun (food till 5pm), cl Mon lunchtime (Richard Hodges, JJW, CMW, Michael Dandy, Mr and Mrs A Woolstone)

☆ *Deddington Arms* OX15 0SH [off A4260 (B4031) Banbury—Oxford; Horse Fair]: Beamed and timbered hotel with emphasis on sizeable contemporary back dining room doing very good food, comfortable bar with mullioned windows, flagstones and log fire, good food here too, Adnams, Black Sheep and a guest, good choice of wines by the glass, attentive friendly service; unobtrusive piped music; attractive village with lots of antiques shops and good farmers' market 4th Sat of month, nice walks, comfortable chalet bedrooms around courtyard, good breakfast, open all day (LYM, George Atkinson, Phyl and Jack Street, Michael Dandy, Paul Humphreys)

☆ *Unicorn* OX15 0SE [Market Pl]: Cheerful 17th-c inn run by helpful mother and daughter, good sensibly priced generous food (not Sun evening) inc plenty of fish in L-shaped bar and beamed dining areas off, well kept Hook Norton and Wells & Youngs, good choice of wines by the glass, proper coffee, daily papers, inglenook fireplace, pub games; piped music; dogs welcome in bar, cobbled courtyard leading to long walled back garden, open all day (from 9am for good farmers' market 4th Sat of month), good bedrooms and breakfast (BB, MP, Michael Dandy)

DORCHESTER [SU5794]

George OX10 7HH [just off A4074 Maidenhead—Oxford; High St]: Handsome timbered hotel in lovely village, roaring log fire and charming furnishings in smart beamed bar, enjoyable food inc OAP deals,

Brakspears, cheerful efficient service; piped music; children welcome, bedrooms, open all day *(LYM, Jonnie Supper, John and Helen Rushton)*

White Hart OX10 7HN [now bypassed by A4074]: Former 16th-c coaching inn, well kept Adnams and Black Sheep, enjoyable food inc cheaper set menu choices, good friendly service, impressive raftered dining room; 28 bedrooms, charming village *(Ian Malone)*

DUNS TEW [SP4528]

White Horse OX25 6JS [off A4260 N of Kidlington]: 16th-c beamed pub with stripped brick and stonework, rugs on flagstones, oak timbers and panelling, inglenook woodburners, candlelit stripped tables, well kept Greene King ales, decent wine list, food from lunchtime baguettes up (more evening choice), two dining rooms; disabled access, terrace tables, bedrooms in former stables, attractive village *(Stephen Funnell, LYM)*

EAST HANNEY [SU4193]

Black Horse OX12 0JE [Main St]: Comfortable open-plan proper village pub, ales such as Adnams, Batemans and Fullers, good value home-made food inc speciality pies, friendly staff; tables outside *(Helene Grygar, BB)*

EAST HENDRED [SU4588]

Plough OX12 8JW [off A417 E of Wantage; Orchard Lane]: Big beamed village pub with friendly staff, wide blackboard range of enjoyable food from good sandwiches and baguettes up, well kept Greene King related ales, lofty-raftered main room, interesting farming and wartime memorabilia, public bar; piped music, big-screen sports TV; pleasant back garden with good play area, attractive village *(Brian and Anna Marsden, BB)*

EATON [SP4403]

Eight Bells OX13 5PR [signed off B4017 SW of Oxford]: Cosy unpretentious old pub, good traditional food at reasonable prices from generous sandwiches to popular Sun roasts, friendly helpful service, up to four real ales (occasional beer festivals), relaxed atmosphere in two small low-beamed bars with open fires, lounge/dining area; well behaved dogs welcome, pleasant garden, nice walks, open all day Sun, cl Mon *(LYM, Louise Wheeler)*

EYNSHAM [SP4309]

Newlands OX29 4LD [Newland St]: Unpretentiously comfortable beamed and flagstoned bar, good choice of enjoyable fresh food, quick friendly service, real ales, decent wine, nice coffee, big inglenook log fire, stripped early 18th-c pine panelling, pretty restaurant on left; very busy and bustling wknds, may be piped music *(Michael Smedley)*

Queens Head OX29 4HH [Queen St]: Improved old two-bar village pub with good friendly service, enjoyable reasonably priced local food, well kept ales inc regular guests; nice outside eating area *(André and Jack Anker)*

FIFIELD [SP2318]

Merrymouth OX7 6HR [A424 Burford—Stow]: Simple but comfortable stone inn dating to 13th c, L-shaped bar, bay-window seats, flagstones, low beams, some walls stripped back to old masonry, warm stove, quite dark in some areas, good generous food inc blackboard fish choice, three well kept ales inc Hook Norton, cheery landlord and friendly staff: piped music; children and dogs welcome, tables on terrace and in back garden, nine stable-block bedrooms *(LYM, Stuart Turner, Noel Grundy, P M Newsome, Stanley and Annie Matthews)*

FILKINS [SP2304]

Five Alls GL7 3JQ [signed off A361 Lechlade—Burford]: Big 18th-c Cotswold-stone pub doing well under young energetic team, very good sensibly priced home-made food, good service, well kept Brakspears, beams, flagstones, stripped stone and log fire, settees, armchairs and rugs on polished boards, good-sized eating areas; quiz night 2nd Sun of month, piped music, TV; well behaved children and dogs welcome, tables on front and back terraces, neat lawns, aunt sally, five refurbished bedrooms, nice village, cl Mon lunchtime, open all day wknds *(BB, Graham Oddey, Mr and Mrs O P Davies, Peter and Marion Gray)*

FRILFORD [SU4497]

Dog House OX13 6QJ [Faringdon Rd]: Comfortable hotel with beamed open-plan log-fire bar, restaurant and conservatory, good value traditional food from sandwiches up, Greene King ales, good service; children welcome, garden with heated terrace, 20 bedrooms *(anon)*

FRITWELL [SP5229]

Kings Head OX27 7QF [quite handy for M40 junction 10; East St]: Village pub under newish management, good welcome, food in bar and dining room inc good Sun roast; children and dogs welcome *(Stephen Vause)*

FULBROOK [SP2512]

Carpenters Arms OX18 4BH [Fulbrook Hill]: Simple stylish décor in long 17th-c Cotswold-stone pub, skilfully cooked food from diverse menu inc good fresh fish, competent personable young staff, bare-boards half-panelled bar with country furniture, other cosy rooms and conservatory; children welcome, disabled access and facilities, attractive terrace tables in garden behind, cl Sun evening and Mon *(Mike Moss)*

Masons Arms OX18 4BU [Shipton Rd]: Spotless village pub, very friendly, with enjoyable good value food cooked by landlady, well kept Hook Norton and Wadworths 6X, farm cider, good range of malts, nice log fire open to both rooms off bar, stripped stone and tiled floor, lots of plants, pleasant window seats, small dining room; children and dogs welcome, open wknds only *(Caroline and Michael Abbey, Mike and Mary Clark)*

GODSTOW [SP4809]

☆ **Trout** OX2 8PN [off A40/A44 roundabout via Wolvercote]: Pretty 17th-c M&B dining pub in lovely riverside location (gets packed in fine weather), usually very good bistro-style food all day, four beamed linked rooms with contemporary furnishings, flagstones and bare boards, log fires in three huge hearths, Adnams and Timothy Taylors Landlord, several wines by the glass; piped music; children welcome till 7pm, plenty of terrace seats under big parasols (dogs allowed here), footbridge to island (may be closed), abbey ruins opposite, open all day (LYM, Glenn and Evette Booth, John and Elisabeth Cox, Michael and Maggie Betton, Susan and John Douglas, Robert Lorimer, A R Mascall, Ros Lawler, Tina and David Woods-Taylor, Andrea Rampley, Martin and Pauline Jennings, John Wenzel, Richard and Sissel Harris, Mrs M E Mills, Phil and Jane Hodson)

GORING [SU5980]

☆ **Catherine Wheel** RG8 9HB [Station Rd]: Smart and well run with nice informal atmosphere in two neat and cosily traditional bar areas, especially the more individual lower room with its low beams and big inglenook log fireplace; enjoyable home-made food inc game and some unusual choices, Brakspears, Hook Norton and Wychwood ales, Stowford Press cider, good value wine, good coffee; back restaurant (children welcome here), notable doors to lavatories; nice courtyard and garden behind, handy for Thames Path, attractive village, open all day (Michael and Deborah Ethier, the Didler, BB, Phil Bryant)

☆ **Miller of Mansfield** RG8 9AW [High St]: Contemporary dark green décor, lots of easy chairs, log fires and modern art in three linked areas of large bow-windowed bar, good if not cheap bar food all day (helpings can be meagre), well kept Marlow Rebellion and West Berkshire Good Old Boy, friendly helpful young staff, large smart and airy back restaurant; well reproduced piped music; children welcome, good tables under big canopy on heated side terrace, 15 stylish bedrooms, open all day (Michael and Deborah Ethier, David and Sue Smith, Gavin Robinson, BB)

HAILEY [SP3414]

Bird in Hand OX29 9XP [Whiteoak Green; B4022 Witney—Charlbury]: Extended 17th-c stone inn, interesting food from shortish menu, quick friendly service, well kept ales such as Ramsbury, beams and timbers, some stripped stone, comfortable armchairs on polished boards, large log fire, cosy corners in attractive carpeted restaurant, lovely Cotswold views; parasol-shaded terrace tables, bedrooms, open all day (Helene Grygar, Nigel and Sue Foster, BB)

☆ **Lamb & Flag** OX29 9UB [B4022 1 mile N of Witney; Middletown]: Rambling stone-built 17th-c village pub with plenty of character, beams and some ancient flagstones, inglenook woodburner, friendly attentive staff, affordable freshly made food inc popular Sun lunch, well kept Greene King ales, good choice of wines by the glass, decent coffee, bright lighting, darts; big well kept family-friendly garden (BB, David and Sue Smith)

HANWELL [SP4343]

Moon & Sixpence OX17 1HN [Main St]: Dining pub with wide choice of good food from pub favourites up in comfortable bar and dining area (often fully booked), good value set lunch, friendly efficient staff, Hook Norton, decent wines by the glass; small terrace, pretty location (Graham and Nicky Westwood)

HARWELL [SU4988]

☆ **Kingswell** OX11 0LZ [A417; Reading Rd]: Substantial hotel with dependably good imaginative bar food as well as restaurant meals, plenty of choice, helpful staff; comfortable bedrooms (Henry Midwinter)

HEADINGTON [SP5407]

☆ **Black Boy** OX3 9HT [Old High St]: Stylish refurbishment with two bars, dining area and restaurant, good reasonably priced food, inventive without being pretentious, well kept ales inc a weekly guest, good coffee and tea, charming landlady, Thurs jazz nights; children welcome (kids' cooking class Sun morning), nice garden, cl Sun evening and Mon (Jill Cripps, Tim Venn)

HENLEY [SU7682]

☆ **Anchor** RG9 1AH [Friday St]: Old-fashioned, homely and individualistic, two nicely lived-in front rooms, hearty food (not Sun or Mon evenings) from lunchtime up inc sandwiches up, proper traditional puddings, well kept Brakspears, good range of malt whiskies and new world wines by the glass, simple back dining room; well behaved children welcome, charming back terrace, open all day (the Didler, LYM)

HIGHMOOR [SU7084]

☆ **Dog & Duck** RG9 5DL [B481]: Appealing unspoilt 17th-c country pub under newish management, enjoyable food from good baguettes up, also good vegetarian options, Brakspears ales, friendly staff, log fires in small cosily furnished beamed bar and not much larger flagstoned dining room with old prints and pictures, family room off; children and dogs welcome, attractive long garden with some play equipment and small sheep paddock, surrounding walks (Paul Humphreys, the Didler, LYM)

HOOK NORTON [SP3533]

Pear Tree OX15 5NU [Scotland End]: Take-us-as-you-find-us village pub with engaging landlord and character locals, full Hook Norton range kept well from nearby brewery, country wines, bar food (not Sun evening) from doorstep sandwiches to enjoyable bargain Sun roast, knocked-together bar area with country-kitchen furniture, good log fire, daily papers; occasional live music Tues, TV; children and dogs welcome, attractive garden with play area, bedrooms, open all day (K H Frostick, LYM,

Ann and Colin Hunt, Steve Nye, Giles and Annie Francis)

☆ **Sun** OX15 5NH [High Street]: Beamed bar, huge log fire and flagstones, cosy carpeted back room leading into attractive dining room, enjoyable local food from bar snacks to restaurant meals, well kept Hook Norton ales, several wines by the glass, darts and dominoes; children and dogs welcome, disabled facilities, tables out in front and on back terrace, well equipped bedrooms, good breakfast *(Roger M Hancock, Sir Nigel Foulkes, LYM)*

KELMSCOTT [SU2499]

Plough GL7 3HG [NW of Faringdon, off B4449 between A417 and A4095]: Reopened under original owner after long closure due to floods; refurbished interior with ancient flagstones, stripped stone and log fire, wide choice of food (more restauranty evenings), beers such as local Halfpenny, Wye Valley and Wychwood, farm cider; children, dogs and booted walkers welcome, tables out in covered area and garden, lovely spot nr upper Thames (good moorings a few mins' walk away), eight redone bedrooms, open all day wknds *(LYM)*

KINGSTON LISLE [SU3287]

☆ *Blowing Stone* OX12 9QL [signed off B4507 W of Wantage]: Doing well under former licensees and chef from the White Horse at Woolstone; good fresh local food from snacks up, well kept real ales, light and airy contemporary feel in bar, dining areas and big sunny conservatory, log fire; children and dogs welcome, tables out in lovely garden, handy for Uffington Castle hill fort and the downs, popular with horseracing community *(LYM, Michael Sissons)*

KIRTLINGTON [SP4919]

☆ *Oxford Arms* OX5 3HA [Troy Lane]: Oak-beamed 19th-c pub popular for its hearty well prepared food using good local ingredients, genial hands-on landlord/chef and charming young staff, good reasonably priced wines by the large glass, Hook Norton Best and two other ales from central bar with small standing area, leather settees and log fire one end, separate dining room; well behaved children and dogs on leads welcome, disabled access, small sunny back garden with big heated umbrellas, cl Sun evening *(Oxana Mishina)*

LONG HANBOROUGH [SP4214]

☆ *George & Dragon* OX29 8JX [Main Rd (A4095 Bladon—Witney)]: Comfortable and clean single-storey L-shaped thatched pub, good generous food (best to book wknds) from extensive menu inc vegetarian and gluten-free choices, friendly efficient staff, well kept Courage, Brakspears, Fullers London Pride and Wells & Youngs Bombardier, Weston's cider, good range of wines, modern dining extension to 18th-c or older core (originally a low-beamed farm building), wood floors and stone walls; soft piped music; children welcome *(Alan Thwaite, P M Newsome, Peter and Audrey Dowsett, Helene Grygar)*

LONG WITTENHAM [SU5493]

Plough OX14 4QH [High St]: Friendly chatty local with low beams, inglenook fires and lots of brass, well kept ales inc Butcombe, good value wines by the glass, wide choice of generous well priced food (all day wknds), good friendly service, dining room, games in public bar; dogs welcome, Thames moorings at bottom of nice spacious garden with aunt sally, bedrooms *(David Lamb, Canon Michael Bourdeaux)*

LONGWORTH [SU3899]

☆ *Blue Boar* OX13 5ET [Tucks Lane]: Pretty 17th-c thatched stone pub, three small low-beamed rooms, well worn-in, log fires, one by fine old settle, brasses, hops and assorted knick-knacks, main eating area plus restaurant extension, Brakspears, Fullers London Pride and Timothy Taylors Landlord, good choice of other drinks, enjoyable food, friendly staff; piped music; children and dogs welcome, tables in front and on back terrace, short walk from Thames, open all day *(LYM, Tina and David Woods-Taylor)*

Lamb & Flag OX13 5HN [off W end of A420 Kingston Bagpuize bypass]: Spacious pub refurbished under father and son licensees, wide choice of fair value food (all day Sun) inc good authentic thai dishes, Greene King ales; children welcome, open all day *(David Lamb, Philip Kingsbury)*

LOWER HEYFORD [SP4824]

☆ *Bell* OX25 5NY [Market Sq]: Charming creeper-clad building in small thatched village square, good range of generous enjoyable fresh food from baguettes to specials, well kept interesting beers, good coffees, cheerful helpful staff, uncluttered pleasantly refurbished rooms around central beamed bar; children welcome, disabled facilities, nice leafy walled garden with aunt sally, nearby Oxford Canal walks *(Edward Mirzoeff, BB)*

MAIDENSGROVE [SU7288]

Five Horseshoes RG9 6EX [off B480 and B481, W of village]: 16th-c dining pub with lovely views from common high in the Chilterns, rambling bar with low ceiling and log fire, enjoyable food inc salmon smoked by new landlord and local game, friendly attentive service, Brakspears, good choice of wines by the glass, airy conservatory restaurant; children and dogs welcome, plenty of tables outside, good walks, open all day summer wknds, cl Mon evening *(Henry Midwinter, Philip Kingsbury, LYM)*

MIDDLE ASSENDON [SU7385]

Rainbow RG9 6AU [B480]: Well run country pub, pretty and cottagey, with unspoilt low-beamed cosy bar and simple L-shaped carpeted dining room, tasty food home-made by landlady, well kept Brakspears, good choice of wines by the glass, friendly landlord and dog; picnic-sets on front lawn, peaceful setting, may be red kites overhead *(Susan and John Douglas, Ross Balaam, Phil Bryant)*

MIDDLE BARTON [SP4425]
Carpenters Arms OX7 7DA [North St]:
Thatched village local with welcoming
landlady, tasty reasonably priced generous
food, good range of ales, open-plan bar with
fire, restaurant; bedrooms *(J Harvey)*
MINSTER LOVELL [SP3111]
New Inn OX29 0RZ [Burford Rd]: Handsomely
reworked and extended restauranty pub with
enjoyable food (not Sun evening) from
lunchtime sandwiches and light dishes to
major meals, good choice of wines by the
glass, Hook Norton and Wadworths 6X, open
fire, tremendous views over pretty Windrush
valley; children welcome, tables on big heated
terrace, lovely setting *(Justin Kyriacou)*
White Hart OX29 0RA [B4047 Witney—
Burford, opposite B4477 village turn-off]:
16th-c former coaching inn, roomy and
simple, with well updated period furniture
and fittings, well kept Brakspears, Fullers
London Pride and own Old Ruin, reasonably
priced food from sandwiches and grilled
panini to gourmet burgers and good Sun
roasts (best to book), friendly efficient
service, good log fire, restaurant; juke box in
bar; back garden with tree-shaded tables,
heated smokers' shelter, open all day *(CP)*
OXFORD [SP5007]
Anchor OX2 6TT [Hayfield Rd]: Chef/landlord
at this 1930s pub continues to produce good
quality interesting food using local supplies,
friendly efficient service, good value house
wine, well kept beers such as Vale Pale and
Wadworths 6X, period furnishings, log fire,
separate dining area; nr Bridge 240
(Aristotle) on Oxford Canal *(David Gunn,
Clive and Fran Dutson)*
Chequers OX1 4DH [off High St]: Narrow
16th-c courtyard pub with several areas on
three floors, interesting architectural
features, panelling and stained glass, up to
six rotating ales inc Lancaster Blonde, good
choice of well priced pubby food (sausage
specialities), quick friendly service, games
room with balcony; walled garden
(George Atkinson)
Dewdrop OX2 7DX [Banbury Rd,
Summertown]: Friendly place with long-
serving landlord, decent food inc curries and
more traditional things, well kept ales, good
choice of wines, some refurbishment; tables
out at front and back *(Robert Lorimer)*
☆ *Eagle & Child* OX1 3LU [St Giles]: Two
charmingly old-fashioned panelled front
rooms, well kept Brakspears, Hook Norton
and interesting guests, quick friendly
service, stripped-brick back dining extension
and conservatory, Tolkien and CS Lewis
connections; piped music, games machine;
children allowed in back till 8pm, open all
day *(BB, Michael Dandy, the Didler, Tim and
Ann Newell, G Jennings, LYM, Susan and
Nigel Brookes, MP, Clive and Fran Dutson,
Donna and Roger)*
Far From the Madding Crowd OX1 2BY
[Friars Entry]: Busy open-plan free house, six
good changing ales, quarterly beer festivals,

straightforward food all day *(the Didler)*
Gardeners Arms OX2 6JE [1st left after
Horse & Jockey going N up Woodstock Rd]:
Relaxed atmosphere in chatty open-plan
panelled bar, good home-made vegetarian
food at appealing prices (appealing flavours
too, even for carnivores), friendly staff,
several well kept changing ales such as Hook
Norton, farm cider; children welcome in back
room, tables outside, cl Sun evening, Mon
and Tues lunchtimes *(LYM, MP)*
Harcourt Arms OX2 6DG [Cranham Terrace]:
Individual 1930s corner local with proper
landlord, character bare-boards interior,
subtle lighting, modern art, two log fires,
Fullers ales inc London Porter, good value
snacks, board games, eclectic piped music
(even mongolian nose flute), good mix of
customers *(MP, the Didler, Andrew Barron)*
Head of the River OX1 4LB [Folly Bridge;
between St Aldates and Christchurch
Meadow]: Civilised well renovated pub by
river, boats for hire and nearby walks;
spacious split-level downstairs bar with
dividing brick arches, flagstones and bare
boards, Fullers range inc Gales HSB, good
choice of wines by the glass, popular pubby
food from sandwiches up inc some
contemporary dishes, good service, daily
papers; piped music, games machines; tables
on stepped heated waterside terrace,
bedrooms *(LM, Michael Dandy)*
Isis Farmhouse OX4 4EL [off Donnington
Bridge Rd; no car access]: Charming
waterside spot for early 19th-c former
farmhouse (accessible only to walkers),
relaxed and informal under newish private
owners (was brewery-owned), short choice of
food, local Appleford ales, lots of mainly
nautical bric-a-brac hanging from high
ceiling and covering the walls, traditional
games; bowling alley, picnic-sets out on
heated terrace and in garden, aunt sally by
arrangement, short walk to Iffley Lock and
nearby lavishly decorated early Norman
church, open all day *(LYM, Tim and
Ann Newell)*
☆ *Kings Arms* OX1 3SP [Holywell St]: From
early 17th c, convivial, relaxed and popular
with students, quick helpful service, well
kept Wells & Youngs ales and four guests
such as Bath Gem and St Austell Tribute,
fine choice of wines by the glass, eating
area with counter servery doing enjoyable
good value food all day from sandwiches up,
cosy comfortably worn-in partly panelled
side and back rooms, interesting pictures
and posters, daily papers; a few tables
outside, open all day from 10.30am
*(LYM, Roger Shipperley, Alan Thwaite,
Paul Humphreys, Michael Dandy, the Didler,
Colin and Louise English, Andrea Rampley,
Tim and Ann Newell)*
Lamb & Flag OX1 3JS [St Giles/Banbury Rd]:
Old pub owned by nearby college, modern
airy front room with light wood panelling and
big windows over street, more atmosphere in
back rooms with stripped stonework and low

boarded ceilings, a beer by Palmers for the pub (L&F Gold), Shepherd Neame Spitfire, Skinners Betty Stogs and guests, some lunchtime food inc sandwiches *(Michael Dandy, the Didler, Roger Shipperley)*

Magdalen Arms OX4 1SJ [Iffley Rd]: Bustling revamped pub in same vein as Anchor & Hope in S London (management formerly there – see Lucky Dips); french posters on brown/maroon walls, closely placed scrubbed tables and mixed chairs, simple modern british cooking (can be good) in large bar or curtained-off restaurant, friendly service (sometimes slow), several ales inc Fullers and Theakstons; children and dogs welcome, seats out at front, cl Sun evening, Mon *(Pippa, Mr and Mrs A Woolstone)*

Old Bookbinders OX2 6BT [Victor St]: Dark and mellow local tucked away in Jericho area, friendly and unpretentious, with old fittings and lots of interesting bric-a-brac, Greene King and good choice of guest ales (beer festivals), enjoyable simple food, reasonable prices, darts and shove ha'penny, concealed bookcase door to lavatories; cl lunchtimes, open all day Fri-Sun *(the Didler)*

Oxford Retreat OX1 2EW [Hythe Bridge St]: Modernised waterside pub with well kept Fullers London Pride, good choice of wines by the glass and cocktails, enjoyable well served food from pubby things up, restaurant with chunky tables and leather chairs overlooking river, attentive staff, log fire; sports TV; garden with decking, open all day and till 3am Fri and Sat *(Pippa Manley)*

Royal Oak OX2 6HT [Woodstock Rd, opp Radcliffe Infirmary]: Maze of little rooms meandering around central bar, low beams and bare boards, simple furnishings, wide and interesting range of beers on tap and in bottle inc belgian imports, basic pubby lunchtime food inc good ploughman's and good value Sun roasts, friendly helpful young staff, daily papers, open fire, prints and bric-a-brac, games room with darts, pool etc; eclectic piped music; smallish garden and raised terrace with picnic-sets, open all day *(Michael Sargent, A Hawkes, J D Franklin)*

☆ ***Watermans Arms*** OX2 0BE [South St, Osney (off A420 Botley Rd via Bridge St)]: Nicely relaxed old-fashioned riverside local tucked away nr Osney Lock, welcoming landlord, Greene King ales, good generous home cooking; tables outside, open all day *(Robert Lorimer)*

☆ ***White Horse*** OX1 3BB [Broad St]: Bustling and studenty, squeezed between bits of Blackwells bookshop, small narrow bar with snug one-table raised back alcove, low beams and timbers, ochre ceiling, beautiful view of the Clarendon building and Sheldonian, good choice of ales inc Brakspears, St Austell, Timothy Taylors and White Horse, friendly staff, good value simple lunchtime food (the few tables reserved for this); open all day *(Roger Shipperley, Michael Dandy, the Didler,*

Andrea Rampley, Terry and Nickie Williams, Ann and Colin Hunt, BB)

READING [SU6980]

Reformation RG4 9BP [Horsepond Rd]: Friendly black-beamed village local, good value home-made food from nice lunchtime baguettes up, Brakspears ales, some country bric-a-brac, piano, open fires, conservatory; events like tractor runs and log-splitting competitions; children very welcome, garden with play area, open all day Sun till 8pm *(Paul Humphreys)*

ROTHERFIELD GREYS [SU7282]

☆ ***Maltsters Arms*** RG9 4QD: Quietly set country local with friendly helpful staff, well kept Brakspears ales and Wychwood Hobgoblin, nice home-made food from panini to good Sun roasts (best to book wknds), decent wines by the glass, cafetière coffee, lots of cricket memorabilia, dining room with open fire; soft piped music; terrace with heated smokers' area, garden picnic-sets, not far from Greys Court (NT), lovely country views and walks *(Howard Dell, R K Phillips, Paul Humphreys, DHV, Roy Hoing, Roy and Jean Russell, Sharon Oldham, Ross Balaam, Tony and Gill Powell)*

ROTHERFIELD PEPPARD [SU7081]

Unicorn RG9 5LX [Colmore Lane]: Friendly straightforward country pub with a warm welcome, good unfussy food inc particularly nice ham and good value open sandwiches, well kept Brakspears and Hook Norton, roaring log fire *(Barry and Anne)*

SHENINGTON [SP3742]

☆ ***Bell*** OX15 6NQ [off A422 NW of Banbury]: Good wholesome home cooking in hospitable 17th-c two-room pub, good sandwiches as well, well kept Hook Norton Best, good wine choice, fair prices, friendly informal service and long-serving licensees, relaxed atmosphere, heavy beams, some flagstones, stripped stone and pine panelling, coal fire, amiable dogs, cribbage, dominoes; children in eating areas, tables out in front, small attractive back garden, charming quiet village, good walks, simple comfortable bedrooms, generous breakfast, cl Mon (and perhaps other wkdy) lunchtimes *(Susan and Peter Ferris-Williams, LYM, Sir Nigel Foulkes, Ed Tyley, Roy Davenport, Graham and Nicky Westwood)*

SHIPTON-UNDER-WYCHWOOD [SP2717]

☆ ***Shaven Crown*** OX7 6BA [High St (A361)]: Ancient building with magnificent lofty medieval rafters and imposing double stairway in hotel part's hall, separate more down-to-earth back bar with booth seating, lovely log fires, enjoyable good value food from sandwiches up, Archers, Hook Norton and Wychwood Hobgoblin, several wines by the glass, restaurant; piped music; children and dogs welcome, peaceful courtyard with outside heaters, bowling green *(Chris Glasson, George Atkinson, LYM)*

SHRIVENHAM [SU2488]

☆ ***Prince of Wales*** SN6 8AF [High St; off A420 or B4000 NE of Swindon]: Warmly friendly 17th-c stone-built local with thriving atmosphere, hearty food (not Sun evening) from enterprising sandwiches to Sun roasts, well kept Wadworths, good soft drinks choice, spotless low-beamed lounge, pictures and brasses, log fire and candles, small dining area, side bar with darts, board games and machines; may be quiet piped music, no dogs; children welcome, picnic-sets and heaters in secluded back garden *(Matt Brown, Helene Grygar)*

SOULDERN [SP5231]

Fox OX27 7JW [off B4100; Fox Lane]: Pretty pub under newish management, good choice of enjoyable fairly priced food inc the Fox Sandwich (roast beef between two yorkshire puddings), well kept Hook Norton and two guests (beer festivals), good choice of wines by the glass, comfortable open-plan beamed layout, big log fire, settles and chairs around oak tables, quiz nights; delightful village, garden and terrace tables, aunt sally, four bedrooms *(Marc Ballmann, David Lamb)*

SOUTH NEWINGTON [SP4033]

Duck on the Pond OX15 4JE: Dining pub with tidy modern-rustic décor in small flagstoned bar and linked carpeted eating areas up a step, food from wraps, melts and other light dishes to steak and family Sun lunch, changing ales such as Purity and Wye Valley, range of coffees, neat friendly young staff, woodburner; piped music; spacious grounds with tables on deck and lawn, aunt sally, pond with waterfowl, walk to River Swere, open all day wknds *(BB, George Atkinson)*

SOUTH STOKE [SU5983]

Perch & Pike RG8 0JS [off B4009 2 miles N of Goring]: Relaxing brick and flint pub just a field away from the Thames, cottagey low-beamed bar with open fire, well kept beer, enjoyable home-made food, sizeable timbered restaurant extension where children allowed; may be piped music; tables on terrace and flower-bordered lawn, four bedrooms *(LYM, Tim Maddison, D and M T Ayres-Regan)*

SPARSHOLT [SU3487]

Star OX12 9PL [Watery Lane]: Change of management at this compact 16th-c country pub, blackboard food from new chef, usually three real ales, quick friendly service, log fire; may be piped music; back garden, pretty village – snowdrops fill churchyard in spring *(David Lamb)*

STEVENTON [SU4691]

North Star OX13 6SG [Stocks Lane, The Causeway, central westward turn off B4017]: Traditional village pub through yew tree gateway, tiled entrance corridor, main area with ancient high-backed settles around central table, well kept Greene King ales from side tap room, hatch service to another room with plain seating, a couple of tables and good coal fire, simple lunchtime food, friendly staff; piped music, sports TV; tables on side grass *(Helene Grygar, the Didler, LYM)*

STOKE LYNE [SP5628]

Peyton Arms OX27 8SD [from minor road off B4110 N of Bicester fork left into village]: Beautifully situated and largely unspoilt stone-built pub, character landlord (Mick the Hat) and loyal regulars, very well kept Hook Norton from casks behind small corner bar in front snug, filled rolls, tiled floor, inglenook fire, memorabilia, games room with darts and pool; no children or dogs in bar; pleasant garden with aunt sally, open all day Sat, cl Sun evening and Mon *(the Didler, Torrens Lyster, Roger Shipperley)*

STOKE ROW [SU6884]

☆ *Cherry Tree* RG9 5QA [off B481 at Highmoor]: Contemporary upscale pub restaurant with particularly good food, Sun lunch till 5pm, attentive staff, well kept Brakspears ales, good choice of wines by the glass, minimalist décor and solid country furniture in four linked rooms with stripped wood, heavy low beams and some flagstones; TV in bar; seats in attractive garden, nearby walks, five good bedrooms in converted barn, open all day but cl Sun evening *(Roy and Jean Russell, Bob and Margaret Holder, Richard Endacott, BB)*

☆ *Crooked Billet* RG9 5PU [Nottwood Lane, off B491 N of Reading – OS Sheet 175 map ref 684844]: Very nice place, but restaurant not pub (you can't have just a drink); charming rustic pub layout though, with heavy beams, flagstones, antique pubby furnishings and great inglenook log fire, crimsonly Victorian dining room; wide choice of well cooked interesting food using local produce (you can have just a starter), cheaper set lunches Mon-Sat, helpful friendly staff, Brakspears tapped from cask (no counter), good wines, relaxed homely atmosphere – like a french country restaurant; children truly welcome, occasional live music, big garden by Chilterns beechwoods, open all day wknds *(LYM, Bruce and Sharon Eden, Roy and Jean Russell)*

STONESFIELD [SP3917]

White Horse OX29 8EA [The Ridings; between Charbury and Woodstock]: Tastefully refurbished by friendly new owners, smallish comfortable lounge bar and restaurant, well presented fresh local food from standard to more imaginative dishes, two interesting ales, cheerful efficient staff, open fire, newspapers, monthly jazz/blues; garden picnic-sets, good local walks, open all day Sat, cl Sun evening and Mon *(Mrs Theresa Austin, MC and H Cannons, Guy Vowles, Cara Pullen, Julia Sinclair and Malcolm Hastings)*

TETSWORTH [SP6801]

Red Lion OX9 7AS [A40, between M40 junctions 6 and 7]: Neat attractive pub overlooking big village green, several spacious areas around central bar counter with pale wood floors, well kept Flowers and a guest such as Rebellion, good choice of food with some caribbean influences, restaurant; children and dogs welcome, terrace tables, open all day *(LYM, Chris and Jo Parsons)*

THAME [SP7105]

Cross Keys OX9 3HP [Park St/East St]: One-bar local improved under newish landlord, six ales inc own Thame beers such as Mrs Tipples Ghost and Mr Splodges Mild *(Roger Shipperley, Tim and Ann Newell)*

James Figg OX9 2BL [Cornmarket]: Former coaching inn reopened after major refurbishment, clean and well furnished, portrait of James Figg (local 18th-c boxer) above open fire, four ales inc Vale and Wells & Youngs Bombardier, Addlestone's cider, straightforward locally sourced food, good service, converted stables with own bar for music/functions; busier and noisier in evenings; children and dogs welcome *(Tim and Ann Newell)*

Six Bells OX9 2AD [High St]: Well run and popular with open-plan log-fire bar, cosier back rooms, friendly relaxed atmosphere, interestingly varied food inc bargain market-day set lunch (Tues), four Fullers ales; children and dogs welcome, large terrace *(Tim and Ann Newell)*

TOWERSEY [SP7304]

Three Horseshoes OX9 3QY [Chinnor Rd]: Friendly unpretentious country local with well kept ales such as Jennings and Shepherd Neame, decent pubby food from baguettes up, old-fashioned furnishings in two flagstoned low-beamed bars, good log fire, darts, small restaurant; children allowed lunchtime, biggish garden with fruit trees and play area *(LYM, Jestyn Phillips)*

UPTON [SU5186]

George & Dragon OX11 9JJ [A417 Harwell—Blewbury]: Welcoming little pub with enjoyable reasonably priced uncomplicated food, Greene King Morland, small end dining area; big garden *(Julia and Richard Tredgett)*

WANTAGE [SU3987]

King Alfreds Head OX12 8AH [Market Pl]: Pub/bistro with interestingly refurbished linked areas, good well priced food, real ale, efficient friendly staff; unusual garden and barn area *(R K Phillips, Susan Robson)*

Lamb OX12 9AB [Mill St, past square and Bell; down hill then bend to left]: Popular comfortable pub with low beams, log fire and cosy corners, well kept Fullers London Pride and Greene King, wide choice of good generous food; children welcome, disabled facilities, garden tables *(LYM)*

☆ *Royal Oak* OX12 8DF [Newbury St]: Popular two-bar local with 12 well kept ales inc Pitstop, Wadworths and West Berkshire (two originally brewed for the pub), good choice of ciders and perries, friendly knowledgeable landlord, lots of pump clips, old ship photographs, darts; bedrooms, cl wkdy lunchtimes *(BB, the Didler)*

Shoulder of Mutton OX12 8AX [Wallingford St]: Friendly chatty local, coal fire in bar, passage to lounge and tiny snug, well kept Butts and guest ales, traditional old furnishings; tables on back terrace,

lovely hanging baskets, open all day *(the Didler)*

WESTCOTT BARTON [SP4325]

Fox OX7 7BL [Enstone Rd; B4030 off A44 NW of Woodstock]: Spacious stone-built village pub, low beams and flagstones, pews and high-backed settles, up to five well kept changing ales, log fire, food in bar and small restaurant; piped music, steps down to lavatories; children and dogs welcome, pleasant garden with play area and peaceful view, open all day Sun *(LYM)*

WESTON-ON-THE-GREEN [SP5318]

Chequers OX25 3QH [handy for M40 junction 9, via A34; Northampton Rd (B430)]: Extended thatched pub, homely and welcoming, with three areas off large semicircular raftered bar, popular food from small but interesting menu inc sandwiches, ales such as Batemans and Fullers, good wines by the glass; tables under parasols in attractive garden *(Val and Alan Green)*

WITNEY [SP3509]

Angel OX28 6AL [Market Sq]: Wide choice of bargain food from good sandwiches up in unpretentious lived-in 17th-c town local, real ales such as Courage Best, Hook Norton and Wells & Youngs Bombardier, quick friendly service even when packed, daily papers, hot coal fire; piped music, big-screen sports TV, pool room; lovely hanging baskets, smokers' shelter, parking nearby can be difficult *(Peter and Audrey Dowsett)*

Fleece OX28 4AZ [Church Green]: Smart and civilised town pub on green, popular for its wide choice of good food inc early-bird deals, prompt friendly service, Greene King ales, leather armchairs on wood floors, daily papers; piped music; children welcome, tables out at front *(David and Sue Smith, Nigel and Sue Foster)*

☆ *Three Horseshoes* OX28 6BS [Corn St; junction with Holloway Rd]: Welcoming attentive service in attractive 16th-c modernised stone-built pub, wide choice of good home-made food from pubby lunchtime things to more imaginative restaurary dishes, Greene King ales and a guest beer, decent house wines, heavy beams, flagstones, log fires, well polished comfortable old furniture, separate dining room; back terrace *(LYM, Nigel and Sue Foster)*

WOLVERCOTE [SP4909]

Plough OX2 8AH [First Turn/Wolvercote Green]: Comfortably well worn-in pubby linked areas, friendly helpful service, bustling atmosphere, armchairs and Victorian-style carpeted bays in main lounge, well kept Greene King ales, farm cider, decent wines, good value usual food in flagstoned former stables dining room and library (children allowed here), traditional snug, woodburner; picnic-sets on front terrace looking over rough meadow to canal and woods *(BB, Tony and Jill Radnor)*

Red Lion OX2 8PG [Godstow Rd]: Big plush dining extension with coal-effect fires, enjoyable food from pubby things up, several real ales, friendly atmosphere, original bar with lots of photographs, prints and memorabilia; piped music; children welcome, lots of garden tables, play area *(Ros Lawler)*

WOODSTOCK [SP4416]

☆ *Bear* OX20 1SZ [Park St]: Small heavy-beamed bar at front of ancient hotel, cosy alcoves, casual mix of antique oak, mahogany and leather furniture, paintings and sporting trophies, blazing inglenook log fire, good fresh sandwiches and hot bar lunches (not cheap), quick friendly service, good choice of wines by the glass and of whisky, may be a real ale, restaurant; no dogs; tables in back courtyard, good bedrooms, open all day *(BB, Derek and Sylvia Stephenson)*

Star OX20 1TA [Market Pl]: Big welcoming beamed pub, Wells & Youngs ales, good choice of wines by the glass, enjoyable food, refurbished interior, open fires; pavement tables and more in back courtyard, good-sized bedrooms *(BB, Robert Pattison)*

Woodstock Arms OX20 1SX [Market St]: 16th-c heavy-beamed stripped-stone pub, lively and stylishly modernised, with prompt welcoming service by helpful young staff, enjoyable food from varied menu, well kept Greene King IPA and Old Speckled Hen, good wine choice, daily papers, log-effect gas fire in splendid stone fireplace, long narrow bar, end eating area; piped music; dogs welcome, tables out in attractive yard, bedrooms, open all day *(Chris Glasson, Michael Dandy)*

WOOLSTONE [SU2987]

White Horse SN7 7QL [off B4507]: Appealing old partly thatched pub under newish management, Victorian gables, plush furnishings, spacious beamed and part-panelled bar, two big open fires, Arkells ales, food from baguettes up, service friendly but may suffer when busy, restaurant; plenty of seats in front and back gardens, secluded interesting village handy for White Horse and Ridgeway, bedrooms, open all day *(LYM, Martin and Karen Wake)*

WROXTON [SP4141]

North Arms OX15 6PY [Mills Lane; off A422 at hotel, pub at back of village]: Prettily thatched stone pub with good fresh well prepared food from generous snacks up, well kept Greene King, good cider, friendly atmosphere, log fire in huge inglenook, nice wooden furnishings, character restaurant; attractive quiet garden in peaceful part of lovely village, walks in abbey gardens opposite (now the grounds of a US college) during term time *(Penny and Peter Keevil, LYM)*

YARNTON [SP4812]

Turnpike OX5 1PJ [A44 N of Oxford]: Large Vintage Inn pub/restaurant with good atmosphere in spacious low-ceilinged bar areas, prompt friendly service, reliable usual food all day, three real ales, log fire *(Dave and Jenny Hughes)*

If a service charge is mentioned prominently on a menu or accommodation terms, you must pay it if service was satisfactory. If service is really bad, you are legally entitled to refuse to pay some or all of the service charge as compensation for not getting the service you might reasonably have expected.

Shropshire

This county has a lovely range of pubs with somewhere to appeal to most tastes and we've been very pleased to find that they're virtually all on particularly good form. Both the Brunning & Price pubs here, with their good complement of Awards, tick most boxes. They have a terrific range of real ales and wines and serve good, interesting food and although the Armoury in Shrewsbury was very much a candidate, it's the Fox at Chetwynd Aston that is our Shropshire Dining Pub of the Year 2011. With a new Food Award this year, the other place in the county for a good meal is the cosy Crown at Munslow. For great real ales head to Bishop's Castle where the well liked Six Bells and Three Tuns (both with a good cheery local atmosphere) serve their own-brew beers. Readers love the buoyantly characterful Church Inn at Ludlow with its eight beers and the good value straightforward George & Dragon at Much Wenlock. Great news is that there are three new Bargain Awards here, one goes to the friendly Stiperstones Inn at Stiperstones and the other two to our new Main Entries, the villagey White Horse at Clun (which also has a Beer Award for their seven local ales) and the traditional Old Castle at Bridgnorth.

BISHOP'S CASTLE   SO3288   MAP 6
Six Bells ◀
Church Street; SY9 5AA

Deservedly popular own-brew pub

On market day (Friday) locals and farmers gather in the public bar while ladies lunch in the lounge bar at this well liked town pub, with the warm welcome (and particularly friendly service), good value fresh food and superb beers accounting for its popularity. The no-frills bar is really quite small, with an assortment of well worn furniture and old local photographs and prints. The second, bigger room has bare boards, some stripped stone, a roaring woodburner in the inglenook, benches around plain tables, and lots of board games (you may find people absorbed in Scrabble or bridge). The excellent beers here are brewed by the landlord himself and include Big Nevs (most people's favourite), Cloud Nine, Goldings Best and a seasonal brew; there is also a wide range of country wines and farm cider in summer. You can arrange a tour of the brewery, and they have a beer festival on the second full weekend in July.

🍴 **Good value tasty bar food includes lunchtime soup, sandwiches, ploughman's and quiche, and in the evening there's sausages and mash, a fish dish, a couple of vegetarian options such as cheese and leek sausage and pork tenderloin with mustard and cider sauce; indulgent puddings such as sherry trifle. Booking is advised for Friday and Saturday evenings.** *Starters/Snacks: £3.75 to £6.00. Main Courses: £6.50 to £10.00. Puddings: £4.00*

> Post Office address codings confusingly give the impression that some pubs are in Shropshire, when they're really in Cheshire (which is where we list them).

Own brew ~ Licensee Neville Richards ~ Real ale ~ Bar food (12-1.45, 6.30-8.45; not Sun evening or Mon) ~ No credit cards ~ (01588) 630144 ~ Children welcome ~ Dogs allowed in bar ~ Open 12-2.30, 5-11; 12-11 Sat; 12-3.30, 7-11 Sun; closed Mon lunchtime

Recommended by the Didler, David M Smith, William Goodhart, Brian and Anna Marsden, Mike and Lynn Robinson

Three Tuns 🍺

Salop Street; SY9 5BW

Unpretentious own-brew pub scoring well for food as well as beer from its unique four-storey Victorian brewhouse

It's said that there has been a brewery here since 1642, though the current John Roberts brewhouse (across the yard from the pub) is Victorian. The four beers brewed here (one is named 1642) are served in the pub from old-fashioned handpumps, you can buy carry-out kegs and the brewery sells beer by the barrel. The modernised dining room (it's worth booking) is done out in smart oak and glass, while the stone-flagged public, lounge and snug bars remain characterfully ungimmicky with a lively bustling atmosphere. Staff are cheery and the pub is genuinely part of the local community – you might chance upon the film club, live jazz, morris dancers, a brass band playing in the garden or the local rugby club enjoying a drink, and in July they hold a popular annual beer festival. There are newspapers to read and a good range of board games; ten wines by the glass.

🍽 Tasty and served in generous helpings, and making a good attempt at using only local produce, bar food includes sandwiches, starters such as piri-piri chicken salad, smoked venison, whisky and cranberry pâté with apple and ale chutney, main courses such as beer battered fish and chips with mushy peas, lentil and vegetable curry, grilled bass with tarragon sauce, beef goulash and dumplings, well hung steak, puddings such as spiced orange cheesecake with passion-fruit and mango sorbet and chocolate tart with panna cotta and raspberry ice-cream, and a regional cheese plate. *Starters/Snacks: £4.10 to £6.95. Main Courses: £9.25 to £13.60. Puddings: £4.70 to £5.20*

Scottish Courage ~ Lease Tim Curtis-Evans ~ Real ale ~ Bar food (12-3, 7-9; not Sun evening) ~ (01588) 638797 ~ Children welcome ~ Dogs allowed in bar ~ Live music most Fri or Sat evenings ~ Open 12-11(10.30 Sun)

Recommended by Leigh and Gillian Mellor, David and Doreen Beattie, MLR, the Didler, Ann and Colin Hunt, Dr D J and Mrs S C Walker, Brian and Anna Marsden, Mike and Lynn Robinson, Alistair Stanier, Denise Dowd, Marek Theis

BRIDGNORTH   SO7192   MAP 6

Old Castle £

West Castle Street; WV16 4AB

Traditional pub, relaxed and friendly, with well kept ales, an up-to-date attitude to food, and a good-sized suntrap terrace

Do walk up the street to see the castle ruin, best seen before rather than after a drink: its 20-metre (70-ft) Norman tower tilts at such an extraordinary angle that it makes the leaning tower of Pisa look a model of rectitude. The low-beamed open-plan bar is properly pubby, with tiles and bare boards, cushioned wall banquettes and settles around cast-iron-framed tables, and bar stools by the counter which serves well kept Greene King IPA, Hobsons Best and a guest such as Everards Sunchaser on handpump, as well as a couple of farm ciders and decent wines by the glass. A back conservatory extension has darts and pool; piped music, games machines, big-screen TV for sports events, smokers' shelter. A big plus here is the sunny back terrace, with shrub borders, big pots of flowers and some playthings; the decking at the far end gives a high view over the west side of town.

🍽 Good value bar food includes sandwiches, baguettes and baked potatoes, chicken dippers, salads, crusted cod, chilli, lasagne, parsnip and sweet potato bake, thai vegetable curry, moroccan chicken, steaks, and puddings such as chocolate marmalade pudding and apple and blackberry flapjack. *Starters/Snacks: £3.60 to £5.80. Main Courses: £6.50 to £6.85. Puddings: £3.95*

Punch ~ Lease Bryn Charles Masterman and Kerry Senior ~ Real ale ~ Bar food (12-3, 6.30-8.30;
not Sun evening) ~ (01746) 711420 ~ Children welcome ~ Dogs allowed in bar ~ Open 11.30-11
Recommended by Mike and Mary Clark, Robert W Buckle

BROMFIELD   SO4877 MAP 6

Clive ♀ 🛏

A49 2 miles NW of Ludlow; SY8 2JR

Sophisticated minimalist dining pub with similarly stylish bedrooms

This elegant dining pub takes its name from Clive of India, who once lived here. Its crisp
Georgian brick exterior gels well with a refreshing minimalist look inside. The focus is on
the dining room, with its modern light wood tables. A door leads through into the bar,
sparse but neat and welcoming, with round glass tables and metal chairs running down
to a sleek bar counter with fresh flowers, newspapers and spotlights. Then it's down a
step to the Clive Arms Bar, where traditional features like the huge brick fireplace (with
woodburning stove), exposed stonework and soaring beams and rafters are appealingly
juxtaposed with well worn sofas and new glass tables; piped jazz. The good wine list
includes several by the glass, and Hobsons Best and a guest such as Ludlow Gold are on
handpump; they also have a range of coffees and teas. An attractive secluded terrace has
tables under cocktail parasols and a fish pond. They have 15 stylishly modern, good-sized
bedrooms, and breakfast is excellent.

🍴 Besides interestingly filled baguettes and sandwiches, good bar food might include
cornish crab cakes, pea, pancetta and mint risotto, chicken, anchovy and smoked bacon
salad, fish of the day, fried duck breast with truffled lyonnaise potatoes, braised endive
and beetroot salad, veal braised with vegetables, thyme and girolle mushrooms, baked
goats cheese in filo pastry with walnut and apple salad, sirloin steak, and puddings such
as lemon posset, chocolate cup with shortbread biscuit and iced blackcurrant parfait with
apple purée; possibly two-course lunch menu. *Starters/Snacks: £5.25 to £7.50. Main Courses:
£10.50 to £13.95. Puddings: £5.95*

Free house ~ Licensees Paul and Barbara Brooks ~ Real ale ~ Bar food (12-3, 6.30-10; 12-10 Sat;
12-9.30 Sun) ~ Restaurant ~ (01584) 856565 ~ Children welcome ~ Open 11-11; 12-10.30 Sun
~ Bedrooms: £75B/£100B
*Recommended by Alan and Eve Harding, Mike and Mary Carter, Gerry and Rosemary Dobson, Maurice and
Gill McMahon, Rod Stoneman, David Heath*

CARDINGTON   SO5095 MAP 4

Royal Oak

*Village signposted off B4371 Church Stretton—Much Wenlock, pub behind church; also
reached via narrow lanes from A49; SY6 7JZ*

Wonderful rural position, heaps of character inside, too

'A bit frayed around the edges but worth it for the character and atmosphere' is what one
reader cheerfully wrote to us about this beautifully sited rural place. Reputedly Shropshire's
oldest continually licensed pub, it dates from the 15th c and one can imagine that little
has changed inside since then. Its rambling low-beamed bar has a roaring winter log fire,
cauldron, black kettle and pewter jugs in its vast inglenook fireplace, the old standing
timbers of a knocked-through wall, and red and green tapestry seats solidly capped in elm;
darts, shove-ha'penny and dominoes. A comfortable dining area has exposed old beams and
studwork. Hobsons Best and two or three guests such as Charles Wells Bombardier and
Cottage Goldrush are on handpump. This is glorious country for walks, like the one to the
summit of Caer Caradoc a couple of miles to the west (ask for directions at the pub), and
the front courtyard makes the most of the setting. Dogs are only allowed in the bar when
food isn't being served. If you run a tab, they may ask to keep your credit card.

🍴 Bar food includes lunchtime baguettes and ploughman's, and from the menu and
specials' board, starters such as garlic mushrooms crostini with creamy white sauce and

melted cheese, fried black pudding on wholegrain mustard, main courses such as steak and mushroom pie, battered cod, grilled bass with red pepper sauce, chicken tikka masala, lamb shank in mint gravy, grilled trout with almonds, tasty fidget pie (gammon and apples) and mushroom stroganoff, steaks, and puddings such as apple pie and chocolate and clotted cream cheesecake. *Starters/Snacks: £3.95 to £9.50. Main Courses: £7.50 to £19.95. Puddings: £2.95 to £4.25*

Free house ~ Licensees Steve Oldham and Eira Williams ~ Real ale ~ Bar food (12-2, 6.30-9 Tues-Sat; 12-2.30, 7-9 Sun) ~ Restaurant ~ (01694) 771266 ~ Children welcome ~ Open 12-2.30, 6.30-11(midnight Fri); 12-3.30, 7-midnight Sun; closed Mon (except bank hol lunchtimes)

Recommended by Brian Brooks, Edward Leetham, MDN, Brian and Anna Marsden, R T and J C Moggridge, Maurice and Gill McMahon, David Edwards, Roger and Anne Newbury, John Dwane, David Heath, Graeme Moisey

CHETWYND ASTON
SJ7517   MAP 7

Fox

Village signposted off A41 and A518 just S of Newport; TF10 9LQ

SHROPSHIRE DINING PUB OF THE YEAR

Civilised dining pub with generous food and a fine array of drinks served by ever-attentive staff

This voluminous 1920s building was handsomely done up by Brunning & Price a few years ago – its style will be familiar to anyone who has tried their other pubs. A series of linked semi-separate areas, one with a broad arched ceiling, has plenty of tables in all shapes and sizes, some quite elegant, and a vaguely matching diversity of comfortable chairs, all laid out in a way that's fine for eating but serves equally well for just drinking and chatting. There are masses of attractive prints, three open fires and a few oriental rugs on polished parquet, boards or attractive floor tiling; big windows and careful lighting help towards the relaxed and effortless atmosphere; board games. The handsome bar counter, with a decent complement of bar stools, serves an excellent changing range of about 23 wines by the glass, 50 malt whiskies, Brunning & Price Original (brewed for them by Phoenix), Salopian Oracle, Woods Shropshire Lad, and three guests from brewers such as Holdens and Weetwood are well kept on handpump. Although they do provide highchairs, pushchairs and baby buggies are not allowed; good disabled access. The spreading garden is quite lovely, with a sunny terrace, picnic-sets tucked into the shade of mature trees and extensive views across quiet country fields.

As well as sandwiches, well liked food, served in generous helpings from a changing menu, might include starters such as minestrone soup, tempura bass fillet with sweet and sour coleslaw, fried pigeon breast with cranberry, apple and red cabbage salad and charcuterie for two, main courses such as gnocchi with fennel and pea pesto and summer vegetables, tandoori cod loin with lemon and coriander pilau rice and cucumber raita, battered haddock, chips and mushy peas, chicken and asparagus pie, braised shoulder of lamb with minted gravy, and puddings such as eton mess, black forest knickerbocker glory and warm chocolate brownie with chocolate fudge sauce and hazelnut ice-cream. *Starters/Snacks: £4.50 to £6.25. Main Courses: £6.95 to £13.50. Puddings: £5.25 to £6.50*

Brunning & Price ~ Manager Samantha Forrest ~ Real ale ~ Bar food (12-10(9.30 Sun and bank hols)) ~ (01952) 815940 ~ Children welcome till 7pm; no pushchairs ~ Dogs allowed in bar ~ Open 12-11(10.30 Sun)

Recommended by Michael Beale, J S Burn, Suzy Miller, Henry Pursehouse-Tranter, Bruce and Sharon Eden, Paul and Margaret Baker, Chris Smith

---

Bedroom prices are for high summer. Even then you may get reductions for more than one night, or (outside tourist areas) weekends. Winter special rates are common, and many inns cut bedroom prices if you have a full evening meal.

CLUN

SO3080   MAP 6

White Horse ◖ £

The Square; SY7 8JA

Cheery village local with seven real ales and good value traditional food

It's not often these days that we include a main entry with the full complement of pub entertainments, but you'll find a TV, games machine, darts, pool, juke box and board games in the games room at the back of this refurbished 18th-c village pub. The heart of the pub, however, is the cheery low-beamed front bar, where drinkers and eaters mingle in a friendly atmosphere, warmed in winter by a cosy inglenook woodburning stove. From the bar, a door leads into a separate little dining room where you will see a rare plank and muntin screen. Attentive staff serve up to seven, usually local, well kept changing ales from brewers such as Hobsons, Salopian, Stonehouse, Three Tuns and Wye Valley, as well as Weston's farm cider and a good range of bottled beers; small garden.

🍴 **Traditional, good value pubby food served in generous helpings includes sandwiches, stilton and port pâté, stuffed mushrooms, smoked salmon with prawns and horseradish cream, ploughman's and salads, chilli, gammon steak, lamb cutlets, cod and chips, suet pudding of the day, steaks and mixed grill.** *Starters/Snacks: £4.00 to £10.00. Main Courses: £5.00 to £15.00. Puddings: £3.95*

Free house ~ Licensee Jack Limond ~ Real ale ~ Bar food (12-2, 6.30-8.30) ~ (01588) 640305 ~ Children welcome ~ Dogs allowed in bar and bedrooms ~ Open 12-12 ~ Bedrooms: £32.50S/£55S

Recommended by Alan and Eve Harding, A N Bance, MLR, Ann and Colin Hunt, Dr D J and Mrs S C Walker, Malcolm and Jo Hart

GRINSHILL

SJ5223   MAP 7

Inn at Grinshill ♀ ⇔

Off A49 N of Shrewsbury; SY4 3BL

Looks after its customers admirably: a civilised place to stay or dine

The smartly comfortable 19th-c bar at this elegantly refurbished early Georgian country inn has an open log fire, while the spacious contemporary main restaurant has a view straight into the kitchen and doors into the back garden, which is laid out with tables and chairs; TV, piped music and board games. Real ales include Caledonian Deuchars IPA, Ruddles County, Theakstons XB and a guest such as local Rowton on handpump, and they have about eight wines by the glass. Though not at all high, the nearby hill of Grinshill has an astonishingly far-ranging view.

🍴 **Since they last appeared in the *Guide*, the licensees here have introduced a more reasonably priced traditional pubby menu with dishes such as sharing boards, chicken liver pâté with cumberland sauce, pasta and pie of the day, sausage and mash, fried calves liver with streaky bacon and rosemary jus, smoked haddock and salmon fishcakes and chinese-style chicken; there's a more elaborate, pricier restaurant menu.** *Starters/Snacks: £2.75 to £5.50. Main Courses: £9.95 to £11.50. Puddings: £4.95 to £5.50*

Free house ~ Licensees Kevin and Victoria Brazier ~ Real ale ~ Bar food (12-2.30(3 Sun), 6.30-9.30) ~ Restaurant ~ (01939) 220410 ~ Children welcome ~ Open 11-3, 6-11; 12-4 Sun; closed Sun evening and Mon ~ Bedrooms: £60S(£80B)/£90S(£120B)

Recommended by Alan and Eve Harding, Noel Grundy, Martin Stafford, J S Burn, Steve Whalley, Dr Kevan Tucker, Stuart King

---

'Children welcome' means the pubs says it lets children inside without any special restriction; some may impose an evening time limit earlier than 9pm – please tell us if you find this.

LEEBOTWOOD

SO4798 MAP 6

Pound

A49 Church Stretton—Shrewsbury; SY6 6ND

Upmarket dining pub in an ancient cruck-framed building

New to the *Guide* last year, this thatched pub, which is thought to be the oldest building in the village, dates from 1458 and at one time served as a hostelry for drovers on their way to market. Inside it's been thoroughly smartened up with stylishly modern and minimalist fixtures and wooden furnishings. Pleasant staff serve Fullers London Pride and a guest such as Salopian Shropshire Gold on handpump, plus several wines by the glass; background music. More tables are on a flagstoned terrace outside; more reports please.

🍴 **Bar food (there may be a wait at busy times) includes chicken liver parfait with balsamic onion relish, crayfish and orange cocktail with caperberries and wild rocket, potted pork with apricot and caper relish and horseradish butter, sausage and cheddar mash with onion gravy, chilli and coriander burger with cheese and bacon, parmesan and herb risotto with asparagus, duck breast with butternut squash purée and smoked cider butter sauce, well hung sirloin steak, and puddings such as rhubarb crumble with warm spices, iced peanut butter parfait with toasted figs and raspberry syrup.** *Starters/Snacks: £4.95 to £6.50. Main Courses: £9.95 to £14.95. Puddings: £5.50 to £5.75*

Enterprise ~ Lease John and Debbie Williams ~ Real ale ~ Bar food (12-2.30, 6.30-9; 12-9 Sat, Sun) ~ Restaurant ~ (01694) 751477 ~ Open 12-11
Recommended by David Heath, Alan and Eve Harding, DHV, Neil and Anita Christopher

LITTLE STRETTON

SO4492 MAP 6

Ragleth

Village signposted off A49 S of Church Stretton; Ludlow Road; SY6 6RB

Prettily placed and attractively renovated, with fine hill walks nearby

This opened-up 17th-c brick-built dining pub is located beneath the steep slopes of the Long Mynd, and is a particularly inviting place on a fine summer's day, with tables on a lawn shaded by a tulip tree looking across to a thatched and timbered church; and there's a good play area. Inside, the bay-windowed front bar is light and airy with fresh plaster and an eclectic mix of light wood old tables and chairs. Some of the original wall brick-and-timber work has been exposed and there's a cheery atmosphere with locals and their dogs, visitors, and a warming winter fire. The heavily beamed brick-and-tile-floored public bar has a huge inglenook; TV, darts, board games and piped music. Attentive owners and staff serve Hobsons Best, Wye Valley Butty Bach and a guest such as Greene King Old Speckled Hen on handpump.

🍴 **Good reasonably priced bar food might include baguettes, soup, ploughman's, a choice of fresh fish specials, crispy half duckling with orange and Grand Marnier sauce, lamb cutlets with rosemary and redcurrant gravy, roasted mediterranean vegetable lasagne, and steak and ale pie; Sunday roasts.** *Starters/Snacks: £4.00 to £5.50. Main Courses: £8.00 to £12.00. Puddings: £1.95 to £3.95*

Free house ~ Licensees Chris and Wendy Davis ~ Real ale ~ Bar food (12-2.15, 6.30-9.15) ~ Restaurant ~ (01694) 722711 ~ Children welcome ~ Dogs allowed in bar ~ Open 12-3, 6-midnight; 12-midnight Sat, 11 Sun); 12-4, 6-11 Sat, Sun in winter
Recommended by Dan Bones, Richard Carter, MDN, Gerry and Rosemary Dobson, Dave Braisted, George and Maureen Roby

LUDLOW   SO5174   MAP 4

Church Inn

Church Street, behind Butter Cross; SY8 1AW

Characterful town-centre inn with an impressive range of real ales

Handily situated just up the road from the castle, this lively pub has good views of the
church and surrounding countryside from its civilised upstairs lounge bar: vaulted
ceilings, display cases of glass, china and old bottles, and musical instruments on the
walls. Bustling with cheery customers, the ground floor is divided into three areas that
are appealingly decorated, with hops hanging from the heavy beams, comfortable
banquettes in cosy alcoves off the island counter (part of it is a pulpit), and pews and
stripped stonework from the church. There are displays of old photographic equipment,
plants on window sills and church prints in the side room, a long central area with a fine
stone fireplace (good winter fires) leads to lavatories, and the more basic side bar has
old black and white photos of the town; daily papers and piped music. Coming mostly
from brewers of the region, eight real ales on handpump are likely to include a choice
from Hobsons, Ludlow, Mayfield, Weetwood and Wye Valley; they also serve several malt
whiskies and mulled cider. The bedrooms are simple but comfortable, breakfasts are good,
and one reader told us their dog was welcomed with dogs treats and a bowl of water. The
landlord (a former mayor of Ludlow) is also the owner of the Charlton Arms, down the hill
on Ludford Bridge.

Straightforward but wholesome tasty food includes sandwiches, ludlow sausage
baguette, scampi and chips, sausage and mash, cod in beer batter, sirloin steak,
shropshire pork pies, and a changing choice of vegetarian dishes such as quiche.
Starters/Snacks: £3.95 to £6.95. Main Courses: £7.95 to £11.45. Puddings: £4.95

Free house ~ Licensee Graham Willson-Lloyd ~ Real ale ~ Bar food (12-2.30, 6.30-9(8.30 Sun))
~ (01584) 872174 ~ Children welcome away from bar ~ Dogs welcome ~ Guitarist second Weds
of the month ~ Open 11(12 Sun)-midnight(1am Fri, Sat) ~ Bedrooms: £40B/£70B

*Recommended by Joe Green, Ann and Colin Hunt, Dr D J and Mrs S C Walker, Gerry and Rosemary Dobson,
Alan and Eve Harding, Stuart Doughty, P J and R D Greaves, Mr and Mrs A H Young, Chris Flynn, Wendy Jones,
P Dawn, Pete Coxon, MLR, Mike and Lynn Robinson, Andy Lickfold, Peter Martin*

MUCH WENLOCK   SO6299   MAP 4

George & Dragon £

High Street (A458); TF13 6AA

**Bustling, snugly atmospheric, plenty to look at, reasonably priced food, good beer
selection and usefully open all day**

Readers enjoy this cosy old place for a straightforward but good value bar meal – their
Sunday lunch is particularly reasonable. Tidied up a little since the last edition, it's filled
with a thoroughly engaging collection of all sorts of pub paraphernalia. You'll find old
brewery and cigarette advertisements, bottle labels, beer trays and George-and-the-Dragon
pictures, as well as around 500 jugs hanging from the beams. The front door takes you
straight into a beamed and quarry-tiled room with wooden chairs and tables and antique
settles all the way around the walls, and there are a couple of attractive Victorian
fireplaces (with coal-effect gas fires). At the back is a timbered dining room. Five real ales
on handpump feature Greene King Abbot, St Austell Tribute and two or three guests from
brewers such as Wadworths and Shepherd Neame; they also have a very wide selection of
wines by the glass; piped music, dominoes, cards, board games and daily papers.

Available in the restaurant or bar, good value lunchtime food includes filled baguettes,
sandwiches, ploughman's, faggots and peas, pie of the day, vegetable lasagne, ham, egg
and chips, battered cod, daily specials such as lamb braised with rosemary, garlic and
tomato and beef wellington, with a few additional evening dishes such as stilton and
walnut pâté and duck breast with black cherry and port sauce. They have various special
offers including pie and a pint on Tuesday, and two meals for £10 on Thursday.
Starters/Snacks: £3.95 to £5.95. Main Courses: £5.95 to £8.95. Puddings: £3.95 to £4.50

Punch ~ Lease James Scott ~ Real ale ~ Bar food (12-2.30, 6-9 (not Weds or Sun evenings)) ~
Restaurant ~ (01952) 727312 ~ Children welcome ~ Dogs allowed in bar ~ Open 12-11(1am Fri,
Sat)

*Recommended by Chris Glasson, Les and Sandra Brown, Ann and Colin Hunt, Alistair Stanier, Reg Fowle,
Helen Rickwood*

Talbot 🛏

High Street (A458); TF13 6AA

Ancient building with friendly welcome, tasty food, pretty courtyard and bedrooms

A charming coaching arch takes you into the courtyard (with green metal and wood
garden furniture and pretty flower tubs) of this unspoilt medieval inn which is on a
characterful street in the centre of this little town. Its several cosily neat traditional
areas (good for both drinkers and diners) are welcoming and friendly, and have low
ceilings and comfortable red tapestry button-back wall banquettes around their tables.
Walls are decorated with local pictures and cottagey plates, and there are art deco-style
lamps and gleaming brasses. Bass and a guest, usually from Wye Valley, are served on
handpump, they've several malt whiskies and nine wines by the glass; quiet piped music,
TV. Bedrooms are characterful and readers say they are good value.

🍴 **The fairly priced lunchtime menu has sandwiches and baked potatoes. Other dishes
might include stilton and walnut pâté, coquilles st jacques, liver and onions, lamb and
leek pie, chilli, steaks, giant yorkshire pudding, smoked haddock and pasta bake, and
pheasant wrapped in bacon with a creamy whisky sauce. There are daily specials and a
more elaborate evening menu; good Sunday roasts.** *Starters/Snacks: £4.95 to £5.50. Main
Courses: £8.95 to £9.50. Puddings: £4.25*

Free house ~ Licensees Mark and Maggie Tennant ~ Real ale ~ Bar food (12-2.30(2 Sun),
6-9 (8.30 Sun)) ~ Restaurant ~ (01952) 727077 ~ Children welcome ~ Open 11am-midnight ~
Bedrooms: £40B/£80B

*Recommended by the Head family, Ann and Colin Hunt, David and Lin Short, Andrew and Mary Ransom, Alan and
Eve Harding, Pete Yearsley*

MUNSLOW   SO5287   MAP 4

Crown 🍴

B4368 Much Wenlock—Craven Arms; SY7 9ET

Cosy, ancient village inn with local ales, cider, good wines and imaginative food

The rather imposing exterior of this comfortable inn hints at its origins as a court house.
(Its pretty back façade shows more evidence of its Tudor origins.) Full of nooks and
crannies, it's much cosier inside than you would expect, and often quite busy. The split-
level lounge bar has a pleasantly old-fashioned mix of furnishings on its broad
flagstones, a collection of old bottles, country pictures and a bread oven by its good log
fire. There are more seats in a traditional snug with its own fire and the eating area has
tables around a central oven chimney, stripped-stone walls, and more beams and
flagstones; piped music. Three beers on handpump are usually offerings from Holdens,
Ludlow and Three Tuns, alongside a local farm cider, several malt whiskies and a good
wine list. Look out for Jenna the boxer, who usually makes her rounds at the end of the
evening.

🍴 **The imaginative food is produced with thought – they display a list of their local
suppliers up on the bar wall; as it's all cooked from fresh, don't expect your meal to
arrive instantly. As well as lunchtime sandwiches, the changing menu might include
kedgeree, sage and parmesan risotto cakes with onion marmalade and port wine syrup,
battered cod with caper and chive butter, roast pork belly on sweet and sour cabbage with
balsamic and rosemary jus, braised shoulder of lamb with smoked onion purée and
tarragon and port wine sauce, puddings such as chocolate and orange tart with vanilla
poached pear and vanilla crème brûlée with caramelised pineapple and brandy snap, and
an impressive selection of cheeses.** *Starters/Snacks: £4.95 to £6.95. Main Courses: £8.95 to
£16.95. Puddings: £5.50*

Free house ~ Licensees Richard and Jane Arnold ~ Real ale ~ Bar food (12-2, 6.45-8.45) ~
Restaurant ~ (01584) 841205 ~ Children welcome ~ Open 12-3.30, 6.45-11; closed Sun evening,
Mon ~ Bedrooms: £55B/£85S(£90B)

Recommended by Denise Dowd, Marek Theis, Michael and Margaret Slater, Les and Sandra Brown, Ann and Colin Hunt, Gerry and Rosemary Dobson, Alan and Eve Harding, Maurice and Gill McMahon, Patricia Walker

SHREWSBURY   SJ4812   MAP 6

Armoury
Victoria Quay, Victoria Avenue; SY1 1HH

**Vibrant atmosphere in interestingly converted riverside warehouse, enthusiastic young
staff, good food all day, excellent drinks' selection**

With amazingly long runs of big arched windows giving views across the broad river, the
spacious open-plan interior at this former warehouse is light and fresh, but the eclectic
décor, furniture layout and lively bustle give a personal feel. Mixed wood tables and
chairs are grouped on expanses of stripped wood floors, a display of floor-to-ceiling
books dominates two huge walls, there's a grand stone fireplace at one end and masses
of old prints mounted edge to edge on the stripped brick walls. Colonial-style fans whirr
away on the ceilings, which are supported by occasional green-painted columns, and
there are small wall-mounted glass cabinets displaying smoking pipes. The long bar
counter has a terrific choice of drinks, with up to eight real ales from brewers such as
Adnams, Phoenix, Purple Moose, Salopian and Woods on handpump, a great wine list
(with 20 by the glass), around 50 malt whiskies, a dozen different gins, lots of rums and
vodkas, a variety of brandies and some unusual liqueurs. The massive uniform red brick
exteriors are interspersed with hanging baskets and smart coach lights at the front; there
may be queues at the weekend. The pub doesn't have its own parking, but there are
plenty of places nearby.

Ⓜ **Superbly cooked bar food, from an interesting daily changing menu, could include
sandwiches, ploughman's, warm pigeon breast, bacon and beetroot salad with port and
cinnamon dressing, fried goats cheese with pickled berries and ginger biscuit, grilled bass
fillet with rocket, fennel and orange salad, steak burger with bacon and cheese, chinese-
style roast pork belly with pak choi, oyster mushrooms and sesame vegetables, steak and
ale pie, mixed winter squash risotto with beetroot, apple and rocket salad and king
prawn, grilled squid and chickpea salad with chilli and lime dressing, and puddings such
as dark chocolate torte with cherry compote and peanut butter flapjack with banana ice-
cream and butterscotch sauce.** *Starters/Snacks: £4.50 to £6.35. Main Courses: £6.85 to £16.60.
Puddings: £4.40 to £5.25*

Brunning & Price ~ Manager John Astle-Rowe ~ Real ale ~ Bar food (12-10(9.30 Sun)) ~
(01743) 340525 ~ Children welcome ~ Dogs allowed in bar ~ Open 12-11(10.30 Sun)

Recommended by Ian and Helen Stafford, Michael Beale, Denise Dowd, Marek Theis, Tony and Wendy Hobden, Henry Pursehouse-Tranter, Jacquie Jones, Owen Davies, Ann and Colin Hunt, Brian Brooks, Rochelle Seifas, George and Maureen Roby, Andy and Jill Kassube, Joe Green, P Dawn

STIPERSTONES   SJ3600   MAP 6

Stiperstones Inn £
Village signposted off A488 S of Minsterley; OS Sheet 126 map reference 364005; SY5 0LZ

**Welcoming, simple country inn run by caring owners offering good value food in fine
walking country**

There are some stunning hikes on the Long Mynd or up the dramatic quartzite ridge of
the Stiperstones near here, and the friendly landlady, Lara, is always happy to give
advice; the industrial archaeology of the abandoned lead mines at nearby Snailbeach is
also fascinating. Great for a refreshing revitaliser after your walk (do book if you are
planning to eat), this cosy traditional place has warming open fires, besides which
Skittles, the pub's tortoiseshell cat, usually presides. The small modernised lounge has
comfortable leatherette wall banquettes and lots of brassware on ply-panelled walls. The

plainer public bar has darts, board games, TV, games machine and mancala. Two reasonably priced guest beers which might be Hobsons Town Crier and Three Tuns XXX are on handpump; piped music. They have two inexpensive bedrooms and we would welcome reports from readers who stay here.

¶ Served all day, the good value bar menu is traditionally pubby and includes sandwiches, ploughman's and baked potatoes, starters such as garlic mushrooms and breaded brie wedges, and main courses such as steak and ale pie, lamb shank in red wine and rosemary sauce, salmon and dill fishcakes, two curries, chilli, spinach and ricotta cannelloni, battered haddock and steaks, with puddings such as apple and blackberry crumble and whinberry pie – the whinberries are picked on a local hill. *Starters/Snacks: £3.25 to £3.50. Main Courses: £5.95 to £14.95. Puddings: £3.95*

Free house ~ Licensees Lara Sproson and Phil Jones ~ Real ale ~ Bar food (12-9) ~ (01743) 791327 ~ Children welcome ~ Dogs allowed in bar and bedrooms ~ Open 11.30am-midnight(2am Fri, Sat) ~ Bedrooms: £35S/£60S

Recommended by DM, Dr and Mrs A K Clarke, Tracy Collins

LUCKY DIP

Besides the fully inspected pubs, you might like to try these Lucky Dips recommended to us and described by readers (if you do, please send us reports: feedback@goodguides.com).

ALL STRETTON [SO4595]
Yew Tree SY6 6HG [Shrewsbury Rd (B4370)]: Appealing old pub, warm and welcoming, with enjoyable well priced food (not Mon evening) inc home-made pies, Bass, Hobsons Best and a changing guest such as Wye Valley; good log fire, lots of interesting watercolours, lounge bar and lively nicely worn-in public bar with darts; no credit cards; well behaved children and dogs welcome (pub dogs and cats), small village handy for Long Mynd *(A N Bance, Paul Walmsley)*

ASTON MUNSLOW [SO5187]
Swan SY7 9ER: Ancient pub with several rambling linked areas in varying styles, good value lunch deals, well kept Hobsons, fairly priced wines, log fires; garden with shady areas *(Ann and Colin Hunt)*

ATCHAM [SJ5409]
☆ *Mytton & Mermaid* SY5 6QG: Comfortable 18th-c hotel rather than pub, but with really nice friendly atmosphere, big log fire and sofas in relaxed bar, good interesting food here (all day Sun) or in large bustling restaurant, efficient young staff, well kept real ales such as Salopian Shropshire Gold, good wine choice; limited parking; children welcome, pleasant Severn-view bedrooms – more in courtyard, nice setting opp entrance to Attingham Park (NT) *(Tony and Wendy Hobden, Clifford Blakemore, Brian Brooks, Canon George Farran, Pete Yearsley)*

BASCHURCH [SJ4221]
New Inn SY4 2EF [Church Rd]: Welcoming pub with good fresh home-made food in bar and restaurant, three well kept ales inc Salopian Shropshire Gold, good choice of wines by the glass, decent coffee; terrace, open all day wknds *(J S Burn, Noel Grundy)*

BISHOP'S CASTLE [SO3288]
Boars Head SY9 5AE [Church St]: Comfortable, beamed and stripped-stone bar with well made wall benches around pleasant tables, big log fire, welcoming efficient young staff, well kept ales such as Adnams, Theakstons and Weetwood, enjoyable good value pubby food (all day in summer); four good roomy high-raftered bedrooms in converted barn *(Alan and Eve Harding)*

☆ *Castle Hotel* SY9 5BN [Market Sq, just off B4385]: Imposing 18th-c panelled coaching inn with three neatly kept bar areas, fire in each, enjoyable food inc more extensive evening choice, well kept Hobsons and Six Bells, decent wines and malt whiskies; bar billiards and other games; dogs welcome, disabled access, tables in front and in back garden with nice views, seven bedrooms, good breakfast, cl bank hol Mon *(the Didler, LYM, Leigh and Gillian Mellor, Mike and Lynn Robinson, Di and Mike Gillam, Ann and Colin Hunt, Brian and Anna Marsden, Denise Dowd, Marek Theis)*

BRATTON [SJ6314]
Gate TF5 0BX: Doing well under friendly newish landlady, enjoyable food, up to four usually local ales *(Nick Jenkins)*

BRIDGES [SO3996]
☆ *Horseshoe* SY5 0ST [nr Ratlinghope]: Simple, down to earth yet comfortable, with light oak beams, woodburners and lots of rustic bygones; three local ales, small dining room, enjoyable bar food (not Sun evening) inc Weds bargain supper, friendly helpful staff, good local atmosphere; piped and live music, no credit cards; children and dogs welcome, tables out by the little River Onny, bedrooms, open all day (may cl Sun evening) *(Gavin Robinson)*

BRIDGNORTH [SO6890]
☆ *Down* WV16 6UA [The Down; Ludlow Rd 3 miles S]: Roadside country dining pub overlooking rolling countryside, good value food inc popular carvery, efficient service even when busy, several mainly local ales inc

Down & Out brewed for them by Three Tuns; piped music; nine comfortable newish bedrooms *(Alan and Eve Harding, BB)*

Jewel of the Severn WV16 4DS [High St]: Relatively new Wetherspoons, relaxing modern décor, good service; sports TV; children welcome, disabled facilities, open all day till late *(Ann and Colin Hunt, Henry Pursehouse-Tranter, Dave Braisted)*

Kings Head WV16 4QN [Whitburn St]: Well restored 17th-c timbered coaching inn with high-raftered back stable bar, food here from 5pm (all day wknds) or in all-day restaurant with separate menu; Hobsons, Wye Valley and several changing guests, log fires, beams and flagstones, pretty leaded windows; children and dogs welcome, courtyard picnic-sets *(the Didler, John Oates, Denise Walton)*

☆ *Railwaymans Arms* WV16 5DT [Severn Valley Station, Hollybush Rd (off A458 towards Stourbridge)]: Bathams, Hobsons and other good value local ales kept well in chatty old-fashioned converted waiting-room at Severn Valley steam railway terminus, bustling on summer days; with coal fire, old station signs and train nameplates, superb mirror over fireplace, may be simple summer snacks, annual beer festival; awkward disabled access; children welcome, tables out on platform – the train to Kidderminster (station bar there too) has an all-day bar and bookable Sun lunches; pub open all day wknds *(Colin Moore, the Didler, Dr Kevan Tucker, Ian and Helen Stafford, Barbarrick, Alistair Stanier, Henry Pursehouse-Tranter, LYM)*

Swan WV16 4DX [High St]: Old half-timbered town-centre pub with opened-up interior, relaxed atmosphere, well kept beers inc Woods; piped music; open all day *(Ann and Colin Hunt)*

BROCKTON [SO5793]

☆ *Feathers* TF13 6JR [B4378]: Stylish restauranty country dining pub with good interesting food inc lunchtime and early evening deals, home-baked bread, good friendly service even when busy, well kept changing ales such as Three Tuns and Woods; comfortable seats in attractively decorated beamed rooms and delightful conservatory; children allowed, has been cl wkdy lunchtimes and Mon *(Alan and Eve Harding, LYM)*

BURLTON [SJ4526]

☆ *Burlton Inn* SY4 5TB [A528 Shrewsbury—Ellesmere, nr B4397 junction]: Attractively refurbished old pub with friendly landlord, wide choice of enjoyable food at well spaced tables, Robinsons ales; sporting prints, log fires, comfortable snug, restaurant with garden dining room; children welcome, disabled facilities, garden with pleasant terrace, comfortable clean bedrooms, good breakfast *(LYM, J S Burn, John and Gina Ollier)*

BURWARTON [SO6185]

☆ *Boyne Arms* WV16 6QH [B4364 Bridgnorth—Ludlow]: Handsome Georgian coaching inn

with enjoyable generous food (not Mon evening) inc lunchtime/early evening set deals, Hobsons and other more or less local well kept ales, decent coffee; cheerful atmosphere, restaurant, separate bar with pool and other games; large garden with good timber adventure playground *(Alan and Eve Harding, BB)*

CHURCH STRETTON [SO4593]

Bucks Head SY6 6BX [High St]: Modernised old town pub with several good-sized areas inc a restaurant, four well kept Marstons ales, decent good value pubby food, friendly attentive staff, black beams and timbers, mixed dark-wood tables and chairs; four bedrooms, open all day *(Ann and Colin Hunt, Gerry and Rosemary Dobson)*

CLEE HILL [SO5975]

Kremlin SY8 3NB [track up hill off A4117 Bewdley—Cleobury, by Victoria Inn]: Shropshire's highest pub (former quarrymaster's house), enjoyable straightforward good value food inc Sun roasts, friendly service, real ales and farm cider; splendid view south from garden and terrace, play area, bedrooms, cl Mon till 4.30pm otherwise open all day *(David Elliott, Joe Green)*

COALBROOKDALE [SJ6604]

☆ *Coalbrookdale Inn* TF8 7DX [Wellington Rd, opp Museum of Iron]: Handsome dark brick 18th-c pub with half a dozen quickly changing ales from square counter in simple convivial tiled-floor bar, good sensibly priced food cooked to order here or in quieter dining room, farm ciders, country wines; good log fire, local pictures, piano, naughty beach murals in lavatories; long flight of steps to entrance; dogs welcome, a few tables outside, good bedrooms *(Ann Harrison, the Didler, BB)*

CORFTON [SO4985]

☆ *Sun* SY7 9DF [B4368 Much Wenlock—Craven Arms]: Lived-in unchanging three-room country local, own good Corvedale ales (inc an unfined beer) and a guest, long-serving jolly landlord (if not busy in back brewery); decent pubby food from generous baguettes to bargain Sun lunch, lots of breweriana, quarry-tiled public bar with darts and pool, quieter carpeted lounge, dining room with covered well; tourist information; piped music; children welcome, dogs in bar, good wheelchair access throughout and disabled lavatories, tables on terrace and in large garden with good play area *(BB, Dr D J and Mrs S C Walker, MLR)*

CRAVEN ARMS [SO4382]

Craven Arms SY7 9QJ [Shrewsbury Rd]: Enjoyable low-priced food inc carvery, bargain OAP mid-week lunch, cheerful attentive service, three well kept ales inc Salopian Shropshire Gold *(A N Bance, Alan and Eve Harding, Dr and Mrs A K Clarke, Joe Green)*

CRESSAGE [SJ5704]

☆ *Riverside* SY5 6AF [A458 NW, nr Cound]: Spacious pub/hotel, neat, light and airy, with enjoyable well presented food inc lunchtime baguettes, efficient cheerful staff, a house ale brewed by Coors and a guest; lovely Severn views from roomy conservatory, bar with central woodburner (dogs welcome here); big terraced garden with wandering rare-breed chickens, seven comfortable bedrooms, good breakfast (own free-range eggs), open all day wknds in summer *(Nigel Espley, Pete Yearsley, LYM)*

CROSS HOUSES [SJ5307]

Bell SY5 6JJ: Traditional cheery two-bar local, good value straightforward home-made food, well kept local Salopian ales; attractive side beer garden, back campsite, bedrooms *(BOB)*

DORRINGTON [SJ4703]

Bridge Inn SY5 7ED [A49 N]: Busy attractively refurbished streamside dining pub, well prepared food inc good value set deals, Sun roasts, roomy bar/dining area with wood floor, conservatory restaurant; piped jazz, no dogs; children welcome, garden tables, open all day *(P J and R D Greaves)*

ELLESMERE [SJ3934]

☆ *Black Lion* SY12 0EG [Scotland St; back car park on A495]: Good, simple, substantial food at bargain prices (pay at bar in advance), friendly helpful staff, two well kept Marstons ales; relaxed beamed bar with interesting décor and some unusual features such as the traditional wood-and-glass screen along its tiled entrance corridor, comfortable roomy dining room; piped music; bedrooms, handy car park, not far from canal wharf *(BB, Alan and Eve Harding, Tony and Wendy Hobden)*

GRINDLEY BROOK [SJ5242]

Horse & Jockey SY13 4QJ [A41]: Under new enthusiastic licensee, enjoyable good value food all day from baguettes to Sun lunch, friendly service, four well kept ales inc Stonehouse and Three Tuns, tea and coffee; handy for Sandstone Trail and Llangollen Canal, open all day *(Alan and Eve Harding, Tony and Wendy Hobden)*

HOPTON WAFERS [SO6376]

☆ *Crown* DY14 0NB [A4117]: Attractive 16th-c creeper-covered inn, light décor and comfortable furnishings, beams and big inglenook, enjoyable sensibly priced food (all day Sun), home-baked bread, well kept ales inc Hobsons and Woods, good choice of wines; relaxed atmosphere and cheerful efficient staff; children and dogs welcome, inviting garden with terraces, duck pond and stream, bedrooms, open all day *(Roger and Linda Norman, Alan and Eve Harding, LYM)*

IRONBRIDGE [SJ6703]

Golden Ball TF8 7BA [Newbridge Rd/Wesley Rd, off Madeley Hill]: Interesting partly Elizabethan pub at the top of the town, good views and atmosphere, five well kept changing ales, good generous fairly priced food in low-beamed bar or neat back restaurant, friendly efficient staff, open fire; children welcome, sheltered garden tables

with more out in front, pleasant terraced walk down to river, four comfortable bedrooms, open all day wknds *(Alan and Eve Harding)*

☆ *Malthouse* TF8 7NH [The Wharfage (bottom road alongside Severn)]: Converted 18th-c malthouse wonderfully located in historic gorge, spacious bar with iron pillars supporting heavy pine beams, lounge/dining area, up to three well kept changing ales such as Brains Rev James and Fullers London Pride, good reasonably priced food all day inc tapas; live music Fri, Sat; children and dogs welcome, terrace tables, 12 bedrooms inc separate cottage, open all day *(LYM, Ross Balaam, Dr Kevan Tucker, Gerry and Rosemary Dobson)*

LEINTWARDINE [SO4175]

☆ *Jolly Frog* SY7 0LX [Toddings; A4113 out towards Ludlow]: Restauranty pub/bistro with welcoming cheerful atmosphere, frequently changing menus with emphasis on good fresh fish, not cheap but lunchtime and early evening better value set meals, imaginative cooking without being fussy or pretentious, also pizza oven and home-baked bread; good wine list and coffees, well kept Ludlow Gold, mix of table sizes (highchairs for small children), log fire; good views from tables out on decking *(Alan and Eve Harding)*

LLANYMYNECH [SJ2721]

Bradford Arms SY22 6EJ: Enthusiastic ex-RAF landlord serving three real ales (also available in tasters), enjoyable home-made food at bargain prices; small garden, pick-up service for Offa's Dyke walkers, drying room *(Pete Yearsley)*

LONGVILLE [SO5393]

☆ *Longville Arms* TF13 6DT [B4371 Church Stretton—Much Wenlock]: Two neat and spacious bars with beams, stripped stone and some oak panelling, welcoming landlord and good service, real ales inc Woods, good generous food in bar and large comfortable restaurant; games room with darts and pool; children welcome and dogs (may get a biscuit), disabled facilities, terraced side garden with good play area, lovely countryside, bedrooms, open all day wknds *(David Edwards, Alistair Stanier, LYM, David and Doreen Beattie)*

LUDLOW [SO5174]

Charlton Arms SY8 1PJ [Ludford Bridge]: Refurbished former coaching inn in great spot overlooking River Teme and the town, two bars, lounge and restaurant, good food, cheerful efficient service, well kept ales inc local Ludlow Gold; waterside garden and terrace, ten bedrooms (may be traffic noise), open all day *(Andy Lickfold, Joe Green)*

Old Bull Ring Tavern SY8 1AB [Bull Ring]: Striking timbered building run well by a friendly family, home-made food (so can take a while) inc great pies and roasts, good sandwiches too, real ales, decent coffee, upstairs restaurant; children welcome, terrace tables *(David and Ruth Hollands, Joe Green, Ann and Colin Hunt)*

Queens SY8 1RU [Lower Galdeford]: Family-run pub with enjoyable food concentrating heavily on fresh local produce, long bar, pine tables in dining area, friendly pub dog *(Joe Green)*

Rose & Crown SY8 1AP [off Church St, behind Buttercross]: Small unpretentious pub with 13th-c origins, bargain food all day, ales such as Banks's and Greene King; courtyard seats at front and on terrace behind, pretty spot, bedrooms, open all day *(Dave Braisted)*

Squirrel SY8 1LS [Foldgate Lane; off Sheet Rd off A49]: Busy modern pub with cheerful efficient service, wide choice of good value generous food from light dishes up, well kept Marstons-related ales, proper dining room; terrace tables, play area, next to Travelodge *(Alan and Eve Harding, J S Hurst)*

Unicorn SY8 1DU [Corve St, bottom end]: Small 17th-c coaching inn with restored low-beamed and partly panelled bar, good food using local produce, well kept ales such as Three Tuns, good service; children and dogs welcome, terrace among willows by river, open all day wknds *(H L Dennis, LYM)*

Wheatsheaf SY8 1PQ [Lower Broad St]: Traditional 17th-c beamed pub spectacularly built into medieval town gate, good value generous pubby food, Sun carvery, efficient cheerful staff, well kept Marstons and related ales; attractive comfortable bedrooms *(Alan and Eve Harding, Joe Green)*

MADELEY [SJ69034]

All Nations TF7 5DP [Coalport Rd]: Simple unspoilt 18th-c pub up steps from road, good value Worfield Dableys, Coalport Dodger, Mild and a seasonal ale from back brewery, guest beers too, bargain hefty filled rolls and pork pies; coal fires each end, old photographs; picnic-sets on heated terrace, handy for Blists Hill, open all day Fri-Sun *(MLR)*

MAESBURY MARSH [SJ3125]

☆ *Navigation* SY10 8JB: Warehouse conversion in great location on restored stretch of Montgomery Canal; three well kept changing ales and farm cider in characterful bar area with beams, stripped brickwork and choir stalls complete with misericords, sofas by roaring fire, good food from pubby things to more enterprising dishes, early-bird deals (6-7pm wkdy evenings), friendly helpful service; children and dogs welcome, waterside terrace, cl Sun evening to Tues lunchtime *(Pete Yearsley, Nigel Hemsted)*

MARTON [SJ2802]

☆ *Sun* SY21 8JP [B4386 NE of Chirbury]: Family-run village pub with welcoming efficient service, father and son team doing good bar food and more adventurous dishes in contemporary restaurant, good Sun lunch; well kept Marstons and Hobsons, nice choice of wines; cl Sun evening to Tues lunchtime *(Alan and Eve Harding, Pete Yearsley)*

MUCH WENLOCK [SO6299]

Gaskell Arms TF13 6AQ [High St (A458)]: 17th-c coaching inn with comfortable old-fashioned lounge divided by brass-canopied log fire, enjoyable straightforward bar food at fair prices, friendly attentive service, three well kept ales such as Stonehouse, Woods and Wye Valley; brasses and prints, civilised beamed restaurant, locals' public bar; subdued piped music; no dogs; well behaved children allowed, disabled facilities, roomy neat back garden with terrace, 14 bedrooms, open all day *(Alan and Eve Harding, Ann and Colin Hunt, Dr and Mrs A K Clarke)*

Raven TF13 6EN [Barrow St]: Small friendly family-run hotel (former 17th-c coaching inn), bar with dining room off, good well priced food here and in more upmarket restaurant, two ales inc one brewed for them by Woods; interesting 1894 Olympic Games memorabilia; no dogs; children welcome, bedrooms around courtyard and in forge annexe, open all day *(Pete Yearsley)*

NESSCLIFFE [SJ3819]

Old Three Pigeons SY4 1DB [off A5 Shrewsbury—Oswestry (now bypassed)]: 16th-c pub with quaint and appealing dining area, good reasonably priced food, well kept ales such as Salopian and Stonehouse, good choice of wines by the glass, warm log fires, two bar areas; children welcome, some tables outside, opp Kynaston Cave, good cliff walks *(Peter Holmes, LYM)*

NEWCASTLE [SO2482]

☆ *Crown* SY7 8QL [B4368 Clun—Newtown]: Pretty village pub continuing well under new management, warm and friendly, settees and woodburner in smart stripped-stone lounge with two dining areas, well kept ales, good choice of reasonably priced food; rustic locals' bar and games room; piped music; tables outside, charming bedrooms above bar, attractive views and walks *(A N Bance, LYM)*

NORBURY [SO3692]

☆ *Sun* SY9 5DX [off A488 or A489 NE of Bishop's Castle]: Civilised dining pub in sleepy village beneath southern flank of Norbury Hill; tiled-floor bar with settees and Victorian tables and chairs, cushioned stone wall seats, mysterious farming implements, woodburner, charming dining lounge with fresh flowers and candles, leather wing chairs and a chesterfield, dark oak dresser, log fire; enjoyable if not cheap food, friendly service, Wye Valley Bitter and usually a guest, decent wines; soft piped music; children welcome lunchtime/early evening, dogs in bar, pretty little rustic garden with pond, prime hill-walking country (not far from the Stiperstones), six bedrooms, good breakfast, cl wkdy lunchtime, Sun evening and Mon *(LYM, Richard Belcher, Mike Scott)*

NORTHWOOD [SJ4633]

Horse & Jockey SY4 5NN: Low-beamed country local with simple décor, well kept Adnams and a guest, decent food in bar and separate dining room inc deals, nice fire; games area with pool and darts; live music, quiz nights; children and dogs welcome *(Tony and Wendy Hobden)*

NORTON [SJ7200]

☆ *Hundred House* TF11 9EE [A442 Telford—Bridgnorth]: Neatly kept pubby hotel bar with appealing gothic décor, Highgate and three guests, good wine choice, very good food in bar and two tucked-away dining areas inc Sun set lunch deals; woodburners and working Coalbrookdale ranges in handsome old fireplaces, prompt pleasant service, spotless quirky ladies'; occasional piped music; lovely garden with herbs (they sell seeds for charity), ten comfortable individual bedrooms, open all day *(Jill Sparrow, Jenny Jackson, Stuart Doughty, LYM)*

PICKLESCOTT [SO4399]

Bottle & Glass SY6 6NR [off A49 N of Church Stretton]: Remote unspoilt 16th-c country pub with new licensee, quarry-tiled bar and lounge/dining areas, log fires, well kept Hobsons, enjoyable food, friendly chatty service; picnic-sets out in front *(LYM, Bob Broadhurst, Mike Tucker, Mr and Mrs D Hammond)*

PORTH-Y-WAEN [SJ2623]

Lime Kiln SY10 8LX [A495, between village and junction with A483, S of Oswestry]: Simple friendly pub with pews and big pine tables, well kept Banks's, Marstons and a guest ale, enjoyable bar food inc notable gammon steak; picnic-sets in side garden, open all day wknds *(Rev W R Fillery, LYM)*

QUEENS HEAD [SJ3326]

☆ *Queens Head* SY11 4EB [just off A5 SE of Oswestry, towards Nesscliffe]: Emphasis on wide choice of generous good value food all day from speciality sandwiches and other snacks to lots of fish and steaks, well kept Theakstons and two guest beers, decent wines by the glass, pleasant helpful staff; two well refurbished dining areas with hot coal fires, nice roomy conservatory overlooking restored section of Montgomery Canal; picnic-sets with parasols in suntrap waterside garden, country walks, open all day *(Lionel Townsend, Bruce and Sharon Eden, Tony and Wendy Hobden)*

SHIFNAL [SJ7407]

Odfellows TF11 9AU [Market Pl]: Friendly bistro-style pub with wide range of interesting sensibly priced food (lunchtime bargains) in four linked rooms, well kept ales such as Holdens, Salopian and Wye Valley, good wine choice, foreign lagers, large unusual conservatory; tables outside, seven bedrooms, open all day *(Pete Yearsley)*

White Hart TF11 8BH [High St]: Half a dozen or more interesting changing ales in chatty 17th-c timbered pub, quaint and old-fashioned with separate bar and lounge; enjoyable home-made lunchtime food (not Sun), good choice of wines by the glass, welcoming staff; couple of steep steps at front door, open all day *(the Didler)*

SHREWSBURY [SJ4912]

Admiral Benbow SY1 1NF [Swan Hill]: Great choice of mainly local ales, bottled belgian beers, also real ciders and perry; no children;

open all day wknds *(the Didler)*

Coach & Horses SY1 1NF [Swan Hill/Cross Hill]: Friendly old-fashioned Victorian local, panelled throughout, with main bar, cosy little side room and back dining room, enjoyable fresh food inc daily roast and some imaginative dishes, Salopian Shropshire Gold, Wye Valley and three guest ales, real cider, relaxed atmosphere, prompt helpful service even when busy; interesting Guinness prints; quiz night first Mon of month; piped music – live Sun; children allowed in dining room, dogs in bar, disabled facilities, smokers' roof terrace, open all day *(the Didler, Alan and Eve Harding, Tony and Wendy Hobden, Joe Green)*

Cromwells SY1 1EN [Dogpole]: Warm, cosy and friendly, with good fresh food from baguettes to inventive puddings in smallish dim-lit bar and attractive panelled restaurant; well kept ales inc Stonehouse and Woods, good house wines, attentive friendly service; piped music; raised garden and attractive heated terrace behind, six nice bedrooms, good breakfast, open all day Sat *(Alan and Eve Harding, John and Sylvia Harrop)*

Golden Cross SY1 1LP [Princess St]: Attractive partly Tudor town-centre hotel with restaurant and quiet bar, welcoming attentive service, short choice of good interesting food cooked to order (so allow time) inc mid-week lunch deals, good range of wines by the glass, well kept ales such as Hobsons and Salopian; five good value bedrooms *(Alan and Eve Harding, Clifford Blakemore)*

Kings Head SY1 1PP [Mardol]: Ancient jettied timbered pub with opened-up low-beamed interior, brass, bric-a-brac and pictures of old Shrewsbury, interesting medieval painting uncovered on chimney-breast, enjoyable bargain food, one or two well kept changing ales, friendly landlord; piped radio, darts; open all day *(Ann and Colin Hunt, Alan and Eve Harding)*

Loggerheads SY1 1UG [Church St]: Chatty old-fashioned local, panelled back room with flagstones, scrubbed-top tables, high-backed settles and coal fire, three other rooms with lots of prints, flagstones and bare boards; quaint linking corridor and hatch service of Banks's Bitter and Mild and other Marstons-related ales, enjoyable bargain lunchtime food (not Sun), friendly service; darts, dominoes, poetry society, occasional live music; open all day *(the Didler, Alan and Eve Harding, Joe Green)*

Old Bucks Head SY3 8JR [Frankwell]: Quietly placed old inn with traditional bar and restaurant, cheerful staff, enjoyable pubby food inc bargain Sun lunch, well kept local Salopian; pleasant raised terrace garden, ten good value bedrooms, open all day Sat *(Robert W Buckle, Alan and Eve Harding)*

Old Post Office SY1 1SZ [off Milk St almost opp the Wheatsheaf, nr St Julians Craft

Centre]: Friendly half-timbered split-level town pub, enjoyable good value pubby food in bar and restaurant, well kept Marstons-related ales, open fires; piped and live music, comedy club last Sun of month; tables in heated courtyard, six bedrooms *(Alan and Eve Harding)*

☆ **Three Fishes** SY1 1UR [Fish St]: Well run timbered and heavily beamed 16th-c pub in quiet cobbled street, small tables around three sides of central bar, flagstones, old pictures, six or so changing beers from mainstream and smaller breweries like Stonehouse, good value wines; fairly priced food inc blackboard specials ordered from separate servery, good friendly service even if busy, no mobiles; open all day Fri, Sat *(LYM, John and Helen Rushton, Mark Sykes, George Atkinson, Pam Adsley, the Didler, Martin Grosberg, Tony and Wendy Hobden)*

Wheatsheaf SY1 1ST [High St]: Comfortable open-plan beamed lounge, enjoyable low-priced home-made food, five well kept ales such as Banks's Hobsons and Ringwood, several wines by the glass, cheerful efficient staff; open all day *(Alan and Eve Harding)*

White Horse SY2 6JJ [Wenlock Rd]: Modernised family-friendly pub with all-day bargain food, cheerful service, well kept Greene King ales, nice house wine; disabled facilities, open all day *(Alan and Eve Harding)*

STOTTESDON [SO6782]

☆ **Fighting Cocks** DY14 8TZ [High St]: Welcoming old half-timbered family-run pub in unspoilt countryside, good substantial home cooking using local produce inc own pork, well kept local ales; log fire, low ceiling, live music Mon; small shop behind; nice views from garden tables, good walks, may be cl wkdy lunchtime *(Carol Ashton)*

TELFORD [SJ6910]

Crown TF2 6EA [Market St, Oakengates (off A442, handy for M54 junction 5)]: Bright 19th-c local (list of licensees to 1835), Hobsons BB and many changing guests, May and Oct beer festivals with up to 60 ales, lots of foreign bottled beers, a real cider or perry, helpful knowledgeable staff; no food (can bring your own), bustling bare-boards front bar with woodburner, small sky-lit side room, quarry-tiled back room; live music Weds, Thurs, mid-Sept folk festival; suntrap courtyard, handy for station, open all day *(the Didler)*

Station Hotel TF2 6DU: Popular roadside pub with chatty landlord, well kept Hobsons, Salopian and interesting guests, real cider and perry, large baps usually available; historical pictures of the town, open fire; open all day from 10am, cl Sun 4-7pm *(the Didler)*

UCKINGTON [SJ5709]

Horseshoe Inn SY4 4UL [B5061 E of Atcham]: Large low-beamed pub refurbished and improved under current owners, enjoyable reasonably priced food (all day Sat, not Sun evening), real ales such as Hobsons and Three Tuns, inglenook

woodburner; picnic-sets outside, open all day *(S J and C C Davidson)*

UPTON MAGNA [SJ5512]

Corbet Arms SY4 4TZ: Welcoming and friendly with above-average food from landlord/chef inc good value Sun lunch, well kept Marstons and a guest such as Stonehouse; big L-shaped carpeted dining lounge, black beams and panelling, fireside sofas, interesting old signage, darts in smaller public bar; great view to the Wrekin from attractive garden, handy for Haughmond Hill walks and Attingham Park (NT), neat bedrooms *(Alan and Eve Harding, Robert W Buckle)*

WELLINGTON [SJ6511]

Cock TF1 2DL [Holyhead Rd (B5061 – former A5)]: Former 18th-c coaching inn popular for its friendly real ale bar, Hobsons and six well kept quickly changing beers usually from small breweries, separate belgian beer bar, real cider, big fireplace; cl lunchtime Mon-Weds, open all day Thurs-Sat *(D Weston)*

Old Orleton TF1 2HA [Holyhead Rd (B5061, off M54 Junction 7)]: Sympathetically modernised old coaching inn with restaurant and bar, good upmarket food, two well kept Hobsons beers, Weston's farm cider, good service; nice view of the Wrekin, bedrooms *(Paul J Robinshaw, D Weston)*

Wickets TF1 2EB [Holyhead Rd (B5061)]: Light modern refurbishment but keeping some interesting memorabilia dating from World War I; good value well cooked food from snacks up (best to book evenings), three real ales, good seating in tiled bar, dining room *(John Morgan)*

WENLOCK EDGE [SO5696]

Wenlock Edge Inn TF13 6DJ [B4371 Much Wenlock—Church Stretton]: Renovated stone-built country pub in lovely spot, public bar, lounge and more modern dining extension, enjoyable home-made food all day from baguettes up, Adnams, Greene King and Hobsons, good wines by the glass, decent coffee; friendly staff, open fire and inglenook woodburner; children welcome in eating areas, dogs in bar, terrace tables front and back, lots of walks, five bedrooms, open all day *(LYM, Bruce and Sharon Eden, Alistair Stanier)*

WHITCHURCH [SJ5441]

Old Town Hall Vaults SY13 1QU [St Marys St]: Simple cosy 18th-c local (birthplace of composer Sir Edward German), L-shaped front bar with secluded snug behind, seven real ales, good value straightforward food *(Tony and Wendy Hobden)*

☆ **Willey Moor Lock** SY13 4HF [Tarporley Rd; signed off A49 just under 2m N]: Large opened-up family-run pub in picturesque spot by Llangollen Canal, low beams, countless teapots, two log fires, cheerful chatty atmosphere, half a dozen changing ales from small breweries, around 30 malt whiskies; enjoyable good value quickly served pub food from sandwiches up; piped music, games machine, several dogs and cats, various 'rule' notices; children welcome away from bar, terrace tables, secure garden with big play area *(Donna Davies, LYM, Alan and Eve Harding, MLR)*

WHITTINGTON [SJ3532]

Narrowboat SY11 4NU [Welsh Frankton, A495 Ellesmere—Oswestry]: Spacious and welcoming waterside pub with chandlery, water and overnight mooring; simple bar with good range of reasonably priced food (can also be eaten in restaurant part, which predominates), Evan Evans Cwrw and Wells & Youngs Bombardier; tables out on grass by lively Llangollen Canal *(Tony and Wendy Hobden)*

WOORE [SJ7342]

Coopers Arms CW3 9SD [Nantwich Rd]: Good value dining pub with special wkdy offers before 6pm, well served pub food with plenty of choice inc good fish, changing real ales, carpeted lounge bar with stone fireplace; TV and darts in public bar; children welcome *(Brian and Jacky Wilson)*

YORTON [SJ5023]

Railway SY4 3EP: Run by same family for over 70 years, friendly and chatty mother and daughter, unchanging atmosphere; plain tiled bar with hot coal fire, old settles and a modicum of railway memorabilia, big back lounge (not always open) with fishing trophies, well kept Salopian, Woods and guests, farm ciders, may be sandwiches on request; darts and dominoes; seats out in yard *(the Didler)*

A very few pubs try to make you leave a credit card at the bar, as a sort of deposit if you order food. They are not entitled to do this. The credit card firms and banks which issue them warn you not to let credit cards out of your sight. If someone behind the counter used your card fraudulently, the card company or bank could in theory hold you liable, because of your negligence in letting a stranger hang on to your card. Suggest instead that if they feel the need for security, they 'swipe' your card and give it back to you. And do name and shame the pub to us.

Somerset

We have a good clutch of new Main Entries this year, with the Garricks Head in Bath (open all day and by the Theatre Royal), the Kings Arms at Charlton Horethorne (civilised and food-oriented, with good bedrooms), the Pony & Trap at Chew Magna (a fine dining pub in a peaceful setting and nicely transformed under new owners), the Lock-Keeper at Keynsham (a good all-rounder with a lovely riverside setting), the Devonshire Arms at Long Sutton (returning to the Main Entries, a former hunting lodge given a fresh, contemporary look and with attractive areas outside), the Masons Arms at Odcombe (a very well run local with own-brew beers), the Rising Sun at West Bagborough (a good all-rounder beneath the Quantocks), the Royal Oak at Withypool (returning as a Main Entry, and back in fine form) and the Canal Inn at Wrantage (where new owners are getting things right). Other pubs doing especially well at the moment are the Red Lion at Babcary (a chatty all-rounder with enjoyable food), the Star at Bath (nicely unassuming and untouched, with well kept ales), the Highbury Vaults in Bristol (very good value food, eight real ales; an unpretentious university hang-out), the Crown at Churchill (much liked for its unmodernised, cottagey character, terrific range of real ales and reasonably priced food), the marvellously unchanged and genuine Black Horse at Clapton-in-Gordano, the Strode Arms at Cranmore (where the food is much enjoyed), the very welcoming George at Croscombe (with up to eight real ales), Woods in Dulverton (an exceptional wine list, excellent food and a friendly, informal atmosphere), the smart and restaurant Pilgrims at Lovington, the evocatively historic George at Norton St Philip, the Halfway House at Pitney (a nicely gimmick-free village local, with a fine choice of real ales and ciders), the Montague Inn at Shepton Montague (with impressive food and wine), the characterful and rurally placed Pack Horse at South Stoke, the Carpenters Arms at Stanton Wick (quiet rural location and lovely accommodation), the Rose & Crown at Stoke St Gregory (rebuilt after a fire; super food and good wine selection) and the City Arms in Wells (with a good choice of ales and ciders). The Woods in Dulverton is our Somerset Dining Pub of the Year for the second year running.

APPLEY   ST0721   MAP 1

Globe

Hamlet signposted from the network of back roads between A361 and A38, W of B3187 and W of Milverton and Wellington; OS Sheet 181 map reference 072215; TA21 0HJ

Unspoilt, small-roomed country pub, tasty food, real ales and seats in the garden

Full of character, this 500-year-old pub is a nicely unspoilt place for a drink, and the food is reasonably priced. The simple beamed front room has a built-in settle and bare wood tables on the brick floor and another room has a GWR bench and 1930s railway posters; there's a further room with easy chairs and other more traditional ones, open fires, a growing collection of musical posters and instruments, and art deco items and *Titanic* pictures; skittle alley. A brick entry corridor leads to a serving hatch with Cotleigh Harriers and Sharps Doom Bar on handpump. There are seats outside in the garden; the path opposite leads eventually to the River Tone.

🍴 **Bar food includes lunchtime filled baguettes, soup, salmon and pollack fishcake, a choice of burgers, four-cheese and bacon or mushroom pasta bake, venison pie, sausages and mash, rump steak, salmon with steamed mussels, and puddings.** *Starters/Snacks: £4.25 to £6.50. Main Courses: £6.95 to £15.95. Puddings: £4.95*

Free house ~ Licensee LeBurn Maddox ~ Real ale ~ Bar food (not Mon (except bank hols)) ~ Restaurant ~ (01823) 672327 ~ Children welcome ~ Open 12-3, 7-11(12 Sat, 10.30 Sun); closed Mon except bank hols

Recommended by John and Fiona McIlwain, the Didler, Bob and Margaret Holder, Kay Wheat, S G N Bennett, John Prescott

ASHILL
ST3116 MAP 1

Square & Compass

Windmill Hill; off A358 between Ilminster and Taunton; up Wood Road for 1 mile behind Stewley Cross service station; OS Sheet 193 map reference 310166; TA19 9NX

Friendly simple pub with local ales, tasty food and good regular live music in a separate sound-proofed barn

They now have eight ensuite double rooms in a separate building at this tucked-away pub overlooking the Blackdown Hills. This is a traditional pub with sweeping views over the rolling pastures around Neroche Forest and a nice mix of chatty customers. The little bar has upholstered window seats that take in the fine view, heavy hand-made furniture, beams, an open winter fire – and perhaps the pub cat, Lilly. Butcombe Bitter, St Austell Tinners and a guest like St Austell Tribute on handpump and good house wines by the glass. The piped music is often classical. There's a garden with picnic-sets, a large glass-covered walled terrace and good regular live music in their sound-proofed barn. More reports please.

🍴 **The generously served bar food includes sandwiches, filled baguettes and baked potatoes, ploughman's, soup, whitebait, mediterranean goats cheese tart, steak and ale pie, sausages and mash, beef curry, steaks, spinach and ricotta cannelloni, fish and chips, specials like turkey and ham pie or salmon and mackerel fishcakes, and puddings such as banoffi pie or chocolate fudge cake; children's meals.** *Starters/Snacks: £3.95 to £6.00. Main Courses: £5.95 to £15.00. Puddings: £4.50*

Free house ~ Licensees Chris, Janet and Beth Slow ~ Real ale ~ Bar food ~ (01823) 480467 ~ Children welcome ~ Dogs welcome ~ Monthly live music in separate barn ~ Open 12-3, 6.30-11 ~ Bedrooms: £60B/£80B

Recommended by Dr A McCormick, Alain and Rose Foote, Roy Hoing, John and Fiona McIlwain

BABCARY
ST5628 MAP 2

Red Lion 🍴 ⛉

Off A37 S of Shepton Mallett; 2 miles or so N of roundabout where A37 meets A303 and A372; TA11 7ED

Relaxed, friendly thatched pub with interesting food, local beers and comfortable rambling rooms

Well liked for its unhurried, chatty atmosphere this friendly thatched pub is a fine all-rounder. Several distinct areas work their way around the carefully refurbished bar. To the left of the entrance is a longish room with dark pink walls, a squashy leather sofa and two housekeeper's chairs around a low table by the woodburning stove and a few well spaced tables and captain's chairs (including a big one in a bay window with built-in seats). There are elegant rustic wall lights, some clay pipes in a cabinet and local papers to read; board games and gardening magazines, too. Leading off here, with lovely dark flagstones, is a more dimly lit public bar area with a panelled dado, a high-backed old settle and other more straightforward chairs; table skittles and piped music. The good-sized smart dining room has a large stone lion's head on a plinth above the open fire (with a huge stack of logs to one side), a big rug on polished boards and properly set tables. Otter Bright, Teignworthy Reel Ale and a guest such as Tom Woods Shepherds Delight on handpump, fruit smoothies, around ten wines by the glass and a few malt whiskies. There's a long informal garden with picnic-sets and a play area with a slide for children. The pub is handy for the A303 and for shopping at Clark's Village at Street.

🍴 Much liked bar food includes sandwiches, soup, smoked haddock and pea risotto, warm bacon and chicken liver salad, haddock and chips, mushroom and spinach korma with jasmine rice, honey-glazed pork belly, whole baked bass, steak, rabbit and pancetta polenta pastry pie, and puddings such as chocolate brownie or apple crumble. *Starters/Snacks: £3.95 to £6.95. Main Courses: £7.50 to £18.00. Puddings: £4.25 to £5.95*

Free house ~ Licensee Charles Garrard ~ Real ale ~ Bar food (12-2.30, 7-9.30; 12-3 Sun) ~ Restaurant ~ (01458) 223230 ~ Children welcome ~ Dogs allowed in bar ~ Live entertainment first Fri of the month and some Sun nights ~ Open 12-3, 6-midnight; 12-10.30 Sun

Recommended by D P and M A Miles, Martin Hatcher, Guy Consterdine, Bob and Margaret Holder, Rod and Chris Pring, Bob and Angela Brooks, Jan and Alan Summers, Paul and Annette Hallett, Steve Whalley, Terry Buckland

BATCOMBE   ST6839 MAP 2

Three Horseshoes
Village signposted off A359 Bruton—Frome; BA4 6HE

Attractive dining pub with smart rooms and quite a choice of drinks; bedrooms

New owners have taken over this 17th-c dining pub, and we trust it will continue its winning ways. The long, rather narrow main room is smartly traditional: beams, local pictures on the lightly ragged dark pink walls, built-in cushioned window seats, solid chairs around a nice mix of old tables and a woodburning stove at one end with a big open fire at the other. At the back on the left, the Gallery Bar has lightly coloured walls, tiled floors and modern pictures for sale and there's also a pretty stripped-stone dining room (no mobile phones); best to book to be sure of a table, especially at weekends. Butcombe Bitter, Cheddar Ales Potholer and a guest like Moor Revival on handpump, ten wines by the glass and local apple juices and ciders. The pub is on a quiet village lane by the church, which has a striking tower. Reports on the new regime please.

🍴 Food might feature starters like soup, seared scallops with curried cauliflower purée, main courses such as cumberland sausage and mash, honey-roasted belly pork with sweet potato mash and cider gravy, thai green prawn curry and risotto of spinach, sweet potato and goats cheese, and puddings like rhubarb crumble and white chocolate and strawberry cheesecake. *Starters/Snacks: £4.50 to £6.00. Main Courses: £9.00 to £16.00. Puddings: £4.50 to £6.50*

Free house ~ Licensee Kav Javvi ~ Real ale ~ Bar food (12-2, 6-9.30(9 Sun)) ~ Restaurant ~ (01749) 850359 ~ Children welcome ~ Dogs allowed in bar ~ Open 11-3, 6-11; 11-11 Sat; 12-10.30 Sun ~ Bedrooms: £60B/£75B

Recommended by Col and Mrs Patrick Kaye, Caroline Battersby, Neil and Karen Dignan, Mr and Mrs A H Young, Keith Bayliss, Mr and Mrs M Charge

BATH

Garricks Head ♀

St Johns Place/Westgate, beside Theatre Royal; BA1 1ET

Civilised pub next to Theatre Royal, good choice of beers, wines and cocktails, relaxed bar and dining room, pre-theatre meals, and usefully open all day

Next door to the Theatre Royal (and they offer pre-show set meals), this is a civilised and relaxed little golden-stone pub. The high-windowed bar has a couple of gingham-covered wooden armchairs beside the gas-effect coal fire with church candles on the mantelpiece and some fine silver meat domes on the wall above, wheelback and other dining chairs around a mix of wooden tables on the bare-boarded floor, a big black squishy sofa and some more gingham armchairs at the far end, and a couple of sizeable brass chandeliers. Palmers Best and a couple of guests like Bristol Beer Factory Exhibition and Otter Bitter on handpump, a good choice of wines by the glass, proper cocktails, and a decent range of whiskies and other spirits. Service is friendly and there may be quiet piped jazz music. To the left of the main door is the dining room with similar furnishings but smartly set up for eating. There are some chairs and a couple of tables outside on the street.

🍴 **Good bar food includes sandwiches, soup, smoked salmon, marinated ruby beetroot and goats cheese salad, beer-battered hake and chips, roasted chicken breast, chargrilled beefbuger or lamb, chilli and mint burger, and puddings.** *Starters/Snacks: £4.50 to £10.00. Main Courses: £10.00 to £18.00. Puddings: £5.00 to £7.50*

Free house ~ Licensee Charles Digney ~ Real ale ~ Bar food (12-3, 5.30-10) ~ Restaurant ~ (01225) 318368 ~ Children welcome ~ Dogs allowed in bar ~ Open 12-11(12.30 Sat, 10.30 Sun)
Recommended by Jeremy King, Dr and Mrs A K Clarke, Edward Mirzoeff, George Atkinson, Michael Dandy, Mr and Mrs W W Burke

Old Green Tree ◖

Green Street; BA1 2JZ

Fine choice of six real ales, enjoyable traditional food, lots of cheerful customers

One reader found this atmospheric tavern something of a throwback to a town pub half a century ago. It's laid-back and cosy rather than particularly smart and the three small oak-panelled and low wood-and-plaster ceilinged rooms include a comfortable lounge on the left as you go in, its walls decorated with wartime aircraft pictures in winter and local artists' work during spring and summer, and a back bar; the big skylight lightens things up attractively. No music or machines; chess, cribbage, dominoes, backgammon, shut the box, Jenga. Green Tree Bitter (brewed for them by Blindmans Brewery), plus Butcombe Bitter and RCH Pitchfork, with guests such as Cottage Concorde, Exmoor Gold and Wickwar Station Porter on handpump, a dozen wines by the glass from a nice little list with helpful notes, and 35 malt whiskies. The gents' is basic and down steep steps. No children. It can get packed, so to get a table you must arrive before midday.

🍴 **Generous helpings of popular lunchtime bar food includes soup and sandwiches, ploughman's, a changing pâté, bangers and mash with beer and onion gravy, summer salads such as smoked duck and poached apple and smoked trout with asparagus, and winter beef in ale pie and pork and cider casserole; no starters or puddings.** *Main Courses: £6.50 to £10.00*

Free house ~ Licensees Nick Luke and Tim Bethune ~ Real ale ~ Bar food (12-3; not evenings, not Sun) ~ No credit cards ~ Open 11-11.30; 12-10.30 Sun; closed Sun lunch during summer
Recommended by Colin and Peggy Wilshire, the Didler, Malcolm Ward, Terry and Nickie Williams, Alan Thwaite, Rob and Catherine Dunster, N R White, Michael Dandy, Roger Wain-Heapy, Dr and Mrs A K Clarke, JJW, CMW, Barry Collett

Star 🍺

Vineyards; The Paragon (A4), junction with Guinea Lane; BA1 5NA

Quietly chatty and unchanging old town local, brewery tap for Abbey Ales; filled rolls only

A real step back in time awaits as you enter this chatty local, its atmosphere not spoilt by noisy fruit machines or music. It's the brewery tap for Abbey Ales and keeps Bellringer plus Bass (tapped from the cask), and three guests such as Abbey Resurrection, Hook Norton 303AD and Wychwood Hobgoblin on handpump; alcoholic ginger beer, Hells Bells cider (also made by Abbey Ales) and a wide selection of malt whiskies. The four (well, more like three and a half) small linked rooms are served from a single bar, separated by panelling with glass inserts. They are furnished with traditional leatherette wall benches and the like – even one hard bench that the regulars call Death Row – and the lighting's dim and not rudely interrupted by too much daylight; shove-ha'penny, darts and board games. It does get particularly busy at weekends.

🍴 **Filled rolls only, though they have bar nibbles on Thursday evenings.** *Starters/Snacks: £2.10*

Punch ~ Tenants Paul Waters and Alan Morgan ~ Real ale ~ (01225) 425072 ~ Children welcome ~ Dogs welcome ~ Live folk Fri nights ~ Open 12-2.30, 5.30-midnight(1am Fri); noon-1am Sat; 12-midnight Sun
Recommended by Roger Wain-Heapy, Michael Cooper, Dr and Mrs A K Clarke, Phil and Sally Gorton, the Didler, N R White

BLAGDON   ST5058   MAP 2

New Inn

Off A368; Park Lane/Church Street; BS40 7SB

Lovely view over Blagdon Lake from nicely set pub; comfortable old furnishings in bustling bar, real ales and traditional food

From the tables outside you can enjoy a drink or a meal here looking towards the very lake where they get their trout. Inside are two log fires in inglenook fireplaces, heavy beams hung with horsebrasses and a few tankards, some comfortable antique settles and mate's chairs among more modern furnishings, old prints and photographs and Wadworths IPA, 6X and JCB on handpump; several wines by the glass. There's a plainer side bar, too; cheerful, helpful service. Wheelchair access (best from the front) but no disabled facilities.

🍴 **Tasty and reasonably priced bar food includes sandwiches, baguettes and toasties, filled baked potatoes, ploughman's, soup, deep-fried somerset brie, crab cakes, steak, fresh trout from Blagdon Lake, vegetable risotto, beef in ale, and puddings like bakewell tart and lemon sponge pudding.** *Starters/Snacks: £3.50 to £5.00. Main Courses: £5.50 to £13.95. Puddings: £3.50 to £4.50*

Wadworths ~ Manager Roger Owen ~ Real ale ~ Bar food ~ (01761) 462475 ~ Children allowed if over 10 ~ Dogs welcome ~ Open 11-3, 6-11; 12-3, 6.30-10.30 Sun
Recommended by Chris and Angela Buckell, Dr and Mrs A K Clarke

BRISTOL   ST5773   MAP 2

Albion

Boyce's Avenue, Clifton; BS8 4AA

Dining pub close to boutiquey shops, with modern food and a good choice of drinks

This attractively refurbished old coaching inn is very much at the hub of things in Clifton village. By the main door there's a flagstoned area with a big old pine table and a couple of candlesticks, a dresser filled with jars of pickles and an open kitchen. Further in, the L-shaped bar has high chairs by the counter with its extravagant flower arrangement, chapel chairs around good oak tables on the stripped wooden floor, brown leather armchairs in front of the coal-effect gas fire with its neat log stacks on either side of the brick fireplace and some cushioned wall seats; up a step is an end room with a rather fine and very long high-backed new settle right the way across one wall, similar tables and chairs and unusual silvery peony-type wallpaper (elsewhere, the sage green half-panelled walls are hung with portraits). Bath Ales Gem Bitter, Butcombe Bitter, Exmoor Ale and Wickwar BOB on handpump, good wines by the glass, a couple of farm ciders, 25 malt whiskies and winter hot cider; piped music, board games. The covered and heated front terrace has plenty of picnic-sets and other seats under fairy lights and there are church candles in hurricane lanterns. More up to date reports please.

🍽 Interesting – though not cheap – modern cooking might include soup, mussels, whitebait, dry-aged single rib of aberdeen angus with ox cheek, wild salmon with sorrel and crab, tagliatelle with pickled girolles and baked ricotta, and puddings like chocolate fondant with pistachio ice-cream or lemon sorbet with vodka. *Starters/Snacks: £3.50 to £13.00. Main Courses: £16.50 to £23.25. Puddings: £5.00 to £7.00*

Enterprise ~ Lease James Phillips ~ Real ale ~ Bar food (12-3, 6-10; not Sun evening or Mon) ~ Restaurant ~ (0117) 973 3522 ~ Children welcome until 9pm ~ Dogs allowed in bar ~ Open 12-midnight(11 Sun); 5-midnight Mon; closed Mon lunchtime, 25 and 26 Dec

Recommended by Bob and Margaret Holder, Jeremy King, Steve and Liz Tilley, Comus and Sarah Elliott, Donna and Roger

Highbury Vaults 🍺 £

St Michael's Hill, Cotham; BS2 8DE

Cheerful town pub with eight real ales, good value tasty bar food and friendly atmosphere

This thoroughly unpretentious local near the university is well worth seeking out for its range of beers, with Bath Ales Gem Bitter, Brains SA, St Austell Tribute, Wells & Youngs Bitter and London Gold, and three guests from breweries such as Bristol Beer Factory and Teignworthy on handpump and several malt whiskies. The little front bar, with the corridor beside it, leads through to a long series of small rooms – wooden floors, green and cream paintwork and old-fashioned furniture and prints, including lots of period royal family engravings and lithographs in the front room. There's now a model railway running on a shelf the full length of the pub, including tunnels through the walls. The attractive back terrace has tables built into a partly covered flowery arbour. In early Georgian days, this was used as the gaol where condemned men ate their last meal – the bars can still be seen on some windows.

🍽 Good value and well liked bar food includes filled rolls, ploughman's, soup, sausage or a pie and mash, various curries, chilli con carne and winter casseroles. *Starters/Snacks: £3.65. Main Courses: £5.00 to £6.95. Puddings: £3.40*

Youngs ~ Manager Bradd Francis ~ Real ale ~ Bar food (12-2(2.30 Sat, 4 Sun), 5.30-8.30; not Sat or Sun evenings) ~ No credit cards ~ (0117) 973 3203 ~ Children welcome until 9pm ~ Dogs allowed in bar ~ Open 12-12(11 Sun); closed evening 25 Dec, lunchtimes 26 Dec and 1 Jan

Recommended by Chris and Angela Buckell, the Didler, Donna and Roger

CHARLTON HORETHORNE   ST6623   MAP 2

Kings Arms 🛏

B3145 Wincanton—Sherborne; DT9 4NL

Imposing and rather smart but with a good mix of drinkers and diners, relaxed bars and more formal restaurant, good choice of ales and wines, and enjoyable food; comfortable bedrooms

After extensive reworking, this formerly closed village pub with its imposing frontage was reopened in spring 2009 by licensees who have made a great success of their previous pubs. It's now an upmarket bar and restaurant with plenty of cheerful drinkers and diners mixing easily – and both made just as welcome by the friendly, helpful staff. The main bar has all manner of local modern art (all for sale) on the dark mulberry or cream walls, nice old carved wooden dining chairs and pine pews around a mix of tables on the slate floor, and a woodburning stove; leading off here is a cosy room with sofas, newspapers on low tables and quite a few trophies. Butcombe and three guests from brewers such as Keystone, St Georges and Wadworths on handpump are served from the rather fine granite bar counter; also several wines by the glass. To the left of the main door is an informal dining room with Jacobean-style chairs and tables on the pale wooden floor and more local artwork. The back restaurant (you have to walk past the open kitchen which is quite fun to peek into) is smart with decorative wood and glass mirrors, wicker or black leather high-backed dining chairs around chunky polished pale wooden tables on the coir carpeting, and handsome striped curtains. At the back of the building, the attractive courtyard has plenty of chrome and wicker chairs around teak tables under green parasols and there is a good smokers' shelter overlooking the croquet lawn. The bedrooms are well equipped and very comfortable.

🍴 **Tasty food could include starters like sweetcorn fritters with avocado guacamole, terrine of ham hock or baked smoked haddock with spinach and leek gratin, main courses such as butternut squash risotto, rib-eye steak, fish pie or veal and chorizo sausages with sage mash, and puddings like bakewell tart and carrot cake with beetroot ice-cream; children's menu.** *Starters/Snacks: £5.00 to £7.00. Main Courses: £13.00 to £17.00. Puddings: £6.00*

Free house ~ Licensee Tony Lethbridge ~ Real ale ~ Bar food (12-2.30, 7-10) ~ Restaurant ~ (01963) 220281 ~ Children welcome ~ Dogs allowed in bar ~ Open 9am-11pm ~ Bedrooms: /£95S

Recommended by the Gravelles, Charles Gysin, Mark Flynn, Edward Mirzoeff, John Branston, Neville and Anne Morley

CHEW MAGNA   ST5861   MAP 2

Pony & Trap

From B3130 in village, follow Bishop Sutton, Bath signpost; Knowle Hill, New Town; BS40 8TQ

Tucked-away country dining pub with fine views behind, cosy little rooms, well kept beer and good food

Modern wood and metal tables on the terrace behind and picnic-sets on the grass make the most of this delightfully rural pub's setting near Chew Valley Lake; chickens potter about in a run down below. Inside, the parquet-floored front bar has a mix of small chairs, cushioned wall seats and built-in benches, little pictures and high shelves of earthenware flagons; church candles and fresh flowers brighten it up, and a snug area on the left has an old range, some dark plank panelling and a housekeeper's chair tucked into one comfortable corner. The lighter two-level back dining area has rush-seated chairs around stripped-top white tables on slate flagstones, roses in small vases and picture windows with rolling pasture views. Butcombe, Courage Best and Otter on handpump, several wines by the glass and Ashton Press cider. There's a front smokers' shelter with a heater. Good nearby walks.

🍴 **Imaginative food could feature sandwiches, ploughman's, sweet potato and cumin soup, pressed pork and venison terrine, beef carpaccio, rib-eye steak, chorizo sausage and borlotti bean stew with chargrilled pigeon breast and coriander, trio of pork, seared duck breast on braised red cabbage with green peppercorn sauce, fillet of salmon on vine tomato and red pepper tapenade tart, and puddings.** *Starters/Snacks: £4.50 to £10.95. Main Courses: £8.50 to £15.95. Puddings: £4.25*

Free house ~ Licensee Josh Eggleton ~ Real ale ~ Bar food (12-2.30, 7-9.30; 12-5.30 Sun) ~ Restaurant ~ (01275) 332627 ~ Children welcome ~ Dogs allowed in bar ~ Open 11-3, 7-midnight; 11-6.30 Sun

Recommended by John Urquhart, Stephen and Jean Curtis, John and Gloria Isaacs, Dr and Mrs A K Clarke, Michael Doswell, Martin Hatcher

It's very helpful if you let us know up-to-date food prices when you report on pubs.

CHISELBOROUGH

ST4614   MAP 1

Cat Head

Leave A303 on A356 towards Crewkerne; take the third left turn (at 1.4 miles), signposted Chiselborough, then after another 0.2 miles turn left; Cat Street; TA14 6TT

Village local handy for the A303, neat attractive bars in an old sandstone building, pretty garden

The garden is a special feature here, full of colourful blooms, and you can also sit out on the terrace. The traditional flagstoned rooms have light wooden tables and chairs, some high-backed cushioned settles, flowers and plants, a woodburning stove in a fine fireplace and curtains around the small mullioned windows. Butcombe Bitter and Sharps Doom Bar on handpump, and carefully chosen wines; piped music, darts and a skittle alley. New licensees took over here just before we went to press, and we'd be interested to get feedback from readers.

🍴 **As well as a lunchtime menu with sandwiches, ploughman's, sausage and mash, steak and kidney pudding and fish pie, evening fare includes items like soup, prawn and mint risotto, chicken breast stuffed with tomato coulis and blue cheese, sirloin steak and fillet of bass.** *Starters/Snacks: £4.50 to £10.00. Main Courses: £8.50 to £11.00. Puddings: £5.25 to £5.50*

Enterprise ~ Lease Beverley Jones ~ Real ale ~ Bar food (12-2.30, 6-9) ~ (01935) 881231 ~ Children welcome ~ Dogs allowed in bar ~ Open 12-3, 6.30-11; closed Sun evening

Recommended by Bob and Margaret Holder, Dr and Mrs M E Wilson, Richard O'Neill, Kate and Ian Hodge, Guy Consterdine, Stephen Colling, Ian Scott-Thompson, Maurice Ricketts, Sheila Topham, John and Fiona McIlwain, George and Gill Rowley

CHURCHILL

ST4459   MAP 1

Crown 🍺 £

The Batch; in village, turn off A368 into Skinners Lane at Nelson Arms, then bear right; BS25 5PP

Unspoilt and unchanging small cottage with friendly customers and staff, super range of real ales and homely lunchtime food

Open all day, this untouched, distinctly laid-back pub is well placed for some of the best walking in the Mendips. Little changes here and the small and rather local-feeling stone-floored and cross-beamed room on the right has a wooden window seat, an unusually sturdy settle, built-in wall benches and chatty, friendly customers; the left-hand room has a slate floor and some steps past the big log fire in a big stone fireplace lead to more sitting space. No noise from music or games (except perhaps dominoes) and a fine range of up to ten real ales tapped from the cask: Bass, Bath Ales Gem Bitter, Butcombe Bitter, Cotleigh Batch, Palmers IPA, RCH Hewish IPA, Old Slug Porter and PG Steam and St Austell Tribute and Black Prince. Several wines by the glass and local ciders. Outside lavatories are basic. There are garden tables at the front, a smallish back lawn and hill views; the Mendip morris men come in summer. There's no pub sign outside but no one ever seems to have a problem finding it.

🍴 **Using beef from the field next door, the straightforward and reasonably priced lunchtime bar food includes sandwiches (the rare roast beef is popular), good soup, filled baked potatoes, ploughman's, cauliflower cheese, chilli con carne, tasty beef casserole, and puddings like treacle pudding and apple crumble.** *Starters/Snacks: £4.45 to £5.25. Main Courses: £5.65 to £8.25. Puddings: £3.90*

Free house ~ Licensee Tim Rogers ~ Real ale ~ Bar food (12-2.30; not evenings) ~ No credit cards ~ (01934) 852995 ~ Children welcome away from bar ~ Dogs welcome ~ Open 11-11(midnight Fri and Sat); 12-10.30 Sun

Recommended by Tom Evans, Roger Wain-Heapy, Ellie Weld, David London, Col and Mrs Patrick Kaye, the Didler, Barry and Anne, Bob and Margaret Holder, John and Gloria Isaacs, Adrian Johnson, MLR, Simon and Mandy King, Michael Doswell, Michael Beale

CLAPTON-IN-GORDANO

ST4773   MAP 1

Black Horse 🍺 £

4 miles from M5 junction 19; A369 towards Portishead, then B3124 towards Clevedon; in north Weston-in-Gordano, opposite school, turn left signposted Clapton, then in village take second right, maybe signed Clevedon, Clapton Wick; BS20 7RH

Nicely old-fashioned pub with lots of cheerful customers, friendly service, real ales and cider, and straightforward pub food; pretty garden

One reader has been coming to this unspoilt local for more than 60 years, and notes that it has hardly changed in that time. The partly flagstoned and partly red-tiled main room has winged settles and built-in wall benches around narrow, dark wooden tables, window seats, a big log fire with stirrups and bits on the mantelbeam, and amusing cartoons and photographs of the pub. A window in an inner snug is still barred from the days when this room was the petty-sessions gaol; high-backed settles – one a marvellous carved and canopied creature, another with an art nouveau copper insert reading 'East, West, Hame's Best' – lots of mugs hanging from its black beams, and plenty of little prints and photographs. There's also a simply furnished room which is the only place families are allowed; darts, board games and piped music. Burtonwood Websters Green Label, Butcombe Bitter, Courage Best, Wadworths 6X and a couple of guests like Exmoor Gold and Wickwar BOB on handpump or tapped from the cask, several wines by the glass, farm ciders and efficient service. There are some old rustic tables and benches in the garden, with more to one side of the car park, and the summer flowers are really quite a sight. Paths from the pub lead up Naish Hill or along to Cadbury Camp.

🍴 Straightforward lunchtime bar food includes filled baguettes and baps, ploughman's and a few hot dishes like soup, lamb stew, chicken and chorizo in spicy tomato sauce and cauliflower and broccoli cheese. *Starters/Snacks: £3.75 to £5.45. Main Courses: £6.50 to £7.50*

Enterprise ~ Lease Nicholas Evans ~ Real ale ~ Bar food (not evenings, not Sun) ~ (01275) 842105 ~ Children in very plain family room only ~ Dogs welcome ~ Live music Mon evening ~ Open 11-11; 12-10.30 Sun

Recommended by Donna and Roger, the Didler, Roy Hoing, Bob and Margaret Holder, Tom Evans, Dr D J and Mrs S C Walker, Barry and Anne, Chris and Angela Buckell, Dr and Mrs A K Clarke

CORTON DENHAM

ST6322   MAP 2

Queens Arms 🛏

Village signposted off B3145 N of Sherborne; DT9 4LR

Civilised stone inn, super choice of drinks, interesting food and a sunny garden

In very pleasant country by the Dorset border, this informally smart village inn has a fine choice of drinks. Highgate Dark Mild and Moor Revival with guests such as Abbeydale Riot, Adnams Extra and Harveys Best are on handpump, alongside a big range of local ciders and apple juice, 60 malt whiskies, 30 wines by the glass and a host of unusual bottled beers from Belgium, Germany, USA and elsewhere. The plain high-beamed bar has a woodburning stove in the inglenook at one end, with rugs on flagstones in front of the raised fireplace at the other end, some old pews, barrel seats and a sofa, church candles and maybe a big bowl of flowers; a little room off here has just one big table – nice for a party of eight or so. On the left, the comfortable dining room (dark pink with crisp white paintwork) has good oak tables and a log fire. A south-facing back terrace has teak tables and chairs under parasols (or heaters if it's cool), with colourful flower tubs. The village lane has some parking nearby, though not a great deal. More up to date reports please.

🍴 Using their own pigs and chickens, the food at lunchtime might include sandwiches, ploughman's, soup, sausage and mash with red onion marmalade, home-made beefburger, grilled aubergine parcels on three-bean cassoulet, battered whiting with tartare sauce; also, often inventive evening choices like braised leek and quail egg tart with hollandaise sauce, pork belly stuffed with apricot, spiced fish stew, and puddings like triple chocolate cheesecake and steamed syrup pudding. *Starters/Snacks: £5.50 to £9.20. Main Courses: £9.70 to £6.50. Puddings: £5.50 to £5.90*

Free house ~ Licensees Rupert and Victoria Reeves ~ Real ale ~ Bar food (12-3, 6-10; 12-4, 6-9.30 Sun) ~ Restaurant ~ (01963) 220317 ~ Children welcome ~ Dogs allowed in bar ~ Open 11-3, 6-11; 11-11 Sat; 12-10.30 Sun ~ Bedrooms: £70S(£80B)/£100B

Recommended by Barry Steele-Perkins, Samantha McGahan, Mark Flynn, Charles Gysin, David Hudd, Philip and Jan Medcalf

CRANMORE
ST6643   MAP 2

Strode Arms 🍴 ⛾

West Cranmore; signposted with pub off A361 Frome—Shepton Mallet; BA4 4QJ

Much liked food and a wide choice of drinks in this pretty country pub with attractive, comfortable bars; seats on front terrace and in back garden

This handsome old place originated as a farmhouse, built around 1400, and though we are getting good reports for the food here, the rambling bar is a perfect place to just sit and have a drink. The rooms have charming country furnishings, fresh flowers and pot plants, a grandfather clock on the flagstones, remarkable old locomotive engineering drawings and big black and white steam train murals in a central lobby; there are newspapers to read and lovely log fires in handsome fireplaces. Wadworths 6X, IPA and a seasonal beer on handpump, around eight wines by the glass from an interesting list, several malt whiskies and quite a few liqueurs and ports. In summer, the building is an attractive sight with its neat stonework, cartwheels on the walls, pretty tubs and hanging baskets, and seats under umbrellas on the front terrace; there are more seats in the back garden. The East Somerset Light Railway is nearby and there may be a vintage sports car meeting on the first Tuesday of each month.

🍴 **Often very enjoyable food at fair prices includes filled baguettes, ploughman's, soup, warm scottish smoked salmon and cream cheese tart, paella, huntingdon fidget pie, medallions of pork tenderloin with black pudding and cider cream sauce, fried bass fillet with garlic butter king prawns and risotto of butternut squash and sweet potato, roasted guinea fowl breast, sirloin steak, mushroom, cashew nut and banana curry, and puddings like lemon posset.** *Starters/Snacks: £3.95 to £5.95. Main Courses: £7.95 to £14.95. Puddings: £4.50*

Wadworths ~ Tenants Tim and Ann-Marie Gould ~ Real ale ~ Bar food (12-2, 6-9; not Sun evening) ~ Restaurant ~ (01749) 880450 ~ Children welcome lunchtimes and early evening ~ Dogs welcome ~ Open 11.30-3, 6-11; 12-3, 7-10.30 Sun

Recommended by David and Diane Young, Ted George, Neil and Karen Dignan, M G Hart, Mrs Ann Gray, Bob and Margaret Holder, Sylvia and Tony Birbeck

CROSCOMBE
ST5844   MAP 2

George 🍺

Long Street (A371 Wells—Shepton Mallet); BA5 3QH

Carefully renovated old coaching inn, warmly welcoming, informative canadian landlord, bar food cooked by landlady, good local beers, attractive garden; bedrooms

Readers are unanimous in praise of this super-friendly inn where the owners have recently remodelled the bar to allow four real ales to be served from the cask. One area has canadian timber reclaimed from the local church. The main bar has some stripped stone, dark wooden tables and chairs and more comfortable seats, winter log fires in inglenook fireplaces and the family grandfather clock. The attractive dining room has more stripped stone, local artwork and photographs on the burgundy walls and high-backed cushioned dining chairs around a mix of tables. Up to eight real ales (four tapped from the cask, the rest on handpump) feature King George the Thirst (brewed exclusively for them by Blindmans), Butcombe Bitter, St Austell Proper Job and up to five guest beers from breweries such as Abbey Ales, Arbor Ales, Cheddar and Moor, three local ciders and ten wines by the glass. Darts, cribbage, dominoes, board games, a skittle alley, shut the box and a canadian wooden table game called crokinole; occasional piped music and separate TV room. The friendly pub dog is called Tessa. The attractive, sizeable garden has seats on the heated and covered terrace; children's area.

🍽 **Cooked by the landlady, the popular food includes sandwiches, filled baked potatoes, ploughman's, soup, chicken liver pâté, smoked haddock fishcake, various curries, cheese and vegetable pie, steak in ale pie, lemon sole, rack of lamb, local organic steaks, and puddings like apple and blackberry crumble, home-made ice-cream and chocolate and rich chocolate cheesecake; children's menu. Five-curry buffet on the last Thursday of the month; Sunday roasts.** *Starters/Snacks: £2.75 to £7.85. Main Courses: £5.85 to £17.95. Puddings: £4.65 to £5.95*

Free house ~ Licensees Peter and Veryan Graham ~ Real ale ~ Bar food (12-2, 6-9) ~ Restaurant ~ Children welcome ~ Dogs allowed in bar ~ Live jazz monthly ~ Open 12-2.30, 6-11 ~ Bedrooms: £35S/£70S

Recommended by Richard and Mary Bailey, Sylvia and Tony Birbeck, R E Spain, Terry Buckland, Maureen Wood, Phyl and Jack Street, Peter Dearing, Bruce Eccles, Richard and Judy Winn

DULVERTON   SS9127   MAP 1

Woods ★

Bank Square; TA22 9BU
SOMERSET DINING PUB OF THE YEAR

Smartly informal place with exceptional wines and enjoyable food

This is a popular place among many readers for a civilised meal, although it's perhaps rather too restauranty for some. The wine list is extraordinarily good: you can order any of the 400 or so that they keep on this list by the glass and the landlord also has an unlisted collection of about 500 well aged, new world wines which he will happily chat about. Inside, it's comfortably relaxed with a good mix of drinkers and diners and very Exmoor – plenty of good sporting prints on the salmon pink walls, some antlers, other hunting trophies, stuffed birds and a couple of salmon rods. There are bare boards on the left by the bar counter, which has St Austell Dartmoor Best, HSD and Tribute tapped from the cask, a farm cider, many sherries and some unusual spirits; attentive, helpful staff and daily papers to read. Its tables partly separated by stable-style timbering and masonry dividers, the bit on the right is carpeted and has a woodburning stove in the big fireplace set into its end wall, which has varnished plank panelling; there may be unobjectionable piped music. Big windows keep you in touch with what's going on out in the quiet town centre (or you can sit out on the pavement at a couple of metal tables). A small suntrap back courtyard has a few picnic-sets.

🍽 **Using their own-bred pigs, the excellent food might include filled baguettes, ploughman's, soup, salmon fishcake on herb salad, cheeseburger in ciabatta bread, steak and ale pie, confit leg of organic corn-fed chicken on puy lentils with madeira sauce, grilled bream, buttered linguine in wild mushroom cream sauce, and puddings like apple tarte tatin or hot chocolate mousse with clotted cream ice-cream.** *Starters/Snacks: £6.50 to £8.50. Main Courses: £8.00 to £16.50. Puddings: £5.50 to £6.50*

Free house ~ Licensee Patrick Groves ~ Real ale ~ Bar food ~ Restaurant ~ (01398) 324007 ~ Children welcome ~ Dogs welcome ~ Open 11-3, 6-11.30(1am Sat); 12-3, 7-11.30 Sun

Recommended by Tony and Tracy Constance, Annette Tress, Gary Smith, Sheila Topham, Millie and Mick Dunk, Dennis and Gill Keen, Richard, Anne and Kate Ansell, Lynda and Trevor Smith, Bob and Margaret Holder, Mr and Mrs B Cox

EAST COKER

Helyar Arms ♀ 🛏

Village signposted off A37 or A30 SW of Yeovil; Moor Lane; BA22 9JR

Neat village pub, comfortable big bar, well liked bar food and a fair range of drinks; attractive bedrooms

Well run by friendly staff, this spotless village tavern is a pleasant spot for a drink or a meal. There's a heavy beamed, spacious and comfortable turkey-carpeted bar carefully laid out to give a degree of intimacy to its various candlelit tables, soft lighting, a couple of high-backed settles and squashy leather sofas in front of a warm log fire. Also, lots of hunting and other country pictures, brass and copper ware and daily papers to read. Steps lead up to a good-sized back high-raftered dining room with well spaced tables. Butcombe Bitter, St Austell Tribute and Wychwood Hobgoblin on handpump and several wines by the glass; piped music, TV and skittle alley. There are a few picnic-sets out on a neat lawn and the village has plenty of charm.

🍴 Bar food cooked by the landlord includes sandwiches, ploughman's, soup, deep-fried somerset brie with red pepper lyonnaise, lasagne, beer-battered cod, mixed grill, slow-cooked belly of pork, rack of lamb, steaks, and puddings like apple and blackberry crumble; pie day on Wednesday, curry night on Thursday and two-course deals on Tuesday and Friday. *Starters/Snacks: £4.50 to £9.00. Main Courses: £8.50 to £18.00. Puddings: £4.50 to £8.00*

Punch ~ Lease Mathieu Eke ~ Real ale ~ Bar food (12-2.30, 6.30-9.30(9 Sun)) ~ Restaurant ~ (01935) 862332 ~ Children welcome ~ Dogs welcome ~ Open 11-3, 6-11.30; 11am-11.30pm Sat; 12-10.30 Sun ~ Bedrooms: £65S/£89S

Recommended by Theo, Anne and Jane Gaskin, Mr and Mrs P R Thomas, Malcolm and Sue Scott, M G Hart, S G N Bennett

FAULKLAND

Tuckers Grave ★ £

A366 E of village; BA3 5XF

Unspoilt and unchanging little cider house with friendly locals and charming licensees

This absolutely tiny, simple cider house has a very special atmosphere of a type that is getting increasingly hard to find: 'my favourite pub in the world, and thankfully nothing has changed' remarked one reader. The flagstoned entrance opens into a teeny unspoilt room with casks of Bass and Butcombe Bitter on tap and Thatcher's Cheddar Valley cider in an alcove on the left. Two old cream-painted high-backed settles face each other across a single table on the right and a side room has shove-ha'penny. There are winter fires and maybe newspapers to read; also a skittle alley and lots of tables and chairs on an attractive back lawn with good views.

🍴 There may be lunchtime sandwiches.

Free house ~ Licensees Ivan and Glenda Swift ~ Real ale ~ No credit cards ~ (01373) 834230 ~ Children in separate little room ~ Open 11.30-3, 6-11; 12-3, 7-10.30 Sun; closed Mon lunchtime (except bank hols)

Recommended by Donna and Roger, Ian Phillips, the Didler, Ewan and Moira McCall, Pam and John Smith, E McCall, T McLean, D Irving

HINTON CHARTERHOUSE
ST7758   MAP 2

Rose & Crown

B3110 about 4 miles S of Bath; BA2 7SN

18th-c village pub with friendly young licensees, well kept ales and traditional bar food

In front of this stone-built 18th-c pub are picnic-sets under parasols in the terraced garden and some pretty window boxes. The partly divided bar has panelling, blue plush cushioned wall seats and bar stools, a mix of wooden chairs and tables on the spreading carpet, candles in bottles and an ornate carved stone fireplace; there's a second small brick fireplace on the other side. Butcombe Bitter, Fullers London Pride and a guest like Batemans Hooker on handpump; TV and piped music. The long dining room, with steps down to a lower area, has an unusual beamed ceiling, and you may well encounter the dog called Tia Maria. More reports please.

🍴 **Tasty, straightforward bar food includes sandwiches, soup, pâté with apple and tomato chutney, whitebait with dill and tartare sauce, steaks from a local farm, steak in ale pie, ham and free-range eggs, haddock and chips, cauliflower, broccoli and stilton bake, and liver and bacon with onion gravy.** *Starters/Snacks: £4.95 to £6.95. Main Courses: £7.95 to £12.95. Puddings: £4.25 to £5.25*

Butcombe ~ Manager Tom Watson ~ Real ale ~ Bar food (12-2, 6-9.30(9 Mon); 12-2.30, 6-8.30 Sun) ~ Restaurant ~ (01225) 722153 ~ Children welcome ~ Dogs allowed in bar ~ Open 11-3, 5-midnight; 11-midnight Sat, Sun ~ Bedrooms: £50S/£70B

Recommended by Dr and Mrs M E Wilson, Meg and Colin Hamilton

HINTON ST GEORGE
ST4212   MAP 1

Lord Poulett Arms

Off A30 W of Crewkerne and off Merriott road (declassified – former A356, off B3165) N of Crewkerne; TA17 8SE

Thatched 17th-c stone inn with charming antiques-filled rooms, well presented food, good choice of drinks and a pretty garden; bedrooms

In a handsome village of golden hamstone, this substantial, civilised and relaxed place is appealing both inside and out, with a good mix of customers. It has several attractive cosy linked areas: rugs on bare boards or flagstones, open fires (one in an inglenook and one in a raised fireplace that separates two rooms), walls of honey-coloured stone or painted in bold Farrow & Ball colours, hops on beams, antique brass candelabra, fresh flowers and candles, and some lovely old farmhouse, windsor and ladderback chairs around fine oak or elm tables. Branscombe Branoc and Otter Ale on handpump, 14 wines by the glass, jugs of Pimms, cider and home-made mulled wine. The cat is called Honey. Outside, under a wisteria-clad pergola, there are white metalwork tables and chairs in a mediterranean-style lavender-edged gravelled area and picnic-sets in a wild flower meadow; boules. The bedrooms have baths and you may have to ask for a shower attachment. This is a charming and peaceful village; nearby walks.

🍴 **To be sure of a table, it's best to book in advance (note they only do bar snacks in the afternoon). Using home-grown vegetables and local organic produce (some maybe from the allotment they've recently taken over), the well presented bar food includes lunchtime sandwiches, soup, rhubarb and roasted beetroot salad, beefburger, fish and chips, sausages and chive mash, steaks, garlic and rosemary marinated roast chicken suprême, sticky lamb, apricot and chickpea tajine, and puddings like banoffi eton mess and champagne rhubarb, stem ginger and treacle tart with blood orange and rich chocolate brownie; children's menu.** *Starters/Snacks: £2.00 to £6.00. Main Courses: £6.00 to £12.00. Puddings: £3.50*

We include some hotels with a good bar that offers facilities comparable to those of a pub.

Free house ~ Licensees Steve Hill and Michelle Paynton ~ Real ale ~ Bar food (12-9.15) ~ Restaurant ~ (01460) 73149 ~ Children welcome ~ Dogs allowed in bar ~ Open 12-11; closed 25 Dec, 26 Dec, 1 Jan ~ Bedrooms: £60B/£85B

Recommended by Dr and Mrs M E Wilson, Michael Doswell, George and Gill Rowley, Martin and Karen Wake, Jonathon Bunt, Theo, Anne and Jane Gaskin, Cathryn and Richard Hicks, Guy Consterdine, Bob and Margaret Holder, Mr and Mrs W W Burke, Clare West, Stephen Colling, Dr A McCormick, Adrian Stear, John and Fiona McIlwain, Heidi Montgomery

HUISH EPISCOPI

ST4326 MAP 1

Rose & Crown £

Off A372 E of Langport; TA10 9QT

In the same family for over 140 years and a real throwback; local ciders and beers, simple food and friendly welcome

The friendly, knowledgeable owner at this pub makes a point of stocking local drinks in the central flagstoned still room, with casks of Teignworthy Reel Ale and a couple of guests such as Glastonbury Mystery Tor and Palmers 200; local Burrow Hill farm cider and cider brandy and Gamer's pear cider; there's no bar as such. This servery is the only thoroughfare between the casual little front parlours, with their unusual pointed-arch windows and genuinely friendly locals; good helpful service. Shove-ha'penny, dominoes, board games, bagatelle and cribbage, and a much more orthodox big back extension family room has pool, games machine and a juke box; skittle alley and popular quiz nights. There are tables in a garden and a second enclosed garden has a children's play area; you can camp (free by arrangement to pub customers) on the adjoining paddock. Summer morris men, fine nearby walks and the site of the Battle of Langport (1645) is close by.

⑪ Using some home-grown fruit and vegetables and free-range eggs, the simple, inexpensive food includes generously filled sandwiches, filled baked potatoes, ploughman's, pork, apple and cider cobbler, steak in ale pie, stilton and broccoli tart, and puddings such as chocolate torte with chocolate sauce. *Starters/Snacks: £2.90 to £5.80. Main Courses: £5.95 to £7.60. Puddings: £3.75*

Free house ~ Licensee Stephen Pittard ~ Real ale ~ Bar food (12-2, 5.30-7.30; not Sun evenings) ~ No credit cards ~ (01458) 250494 ~ Children welcome ~ Dogs welcome ~ Singers' night third Sat of the month outside summer, plus occasional live bands ~ Open 11.30-3, 5.30-11; 11.30-11.30 Fri and Sat; 12-10.30 Sun

Recommended by the Didler, Andrea Rampley, Anthony and Vivienne Irons

KEYNSHAM

ST6669 MAP 2

Lock-Keeper ♀

Keynsham Road (A4175 NE of town); BS31 2DD

Friendly riverside Youngs pub with plenty of room out by the water; snugly old-fashioned inside

Under a couple of giant parasols, good teak chairs and tables on a big heated and decked terrace make the most of this bustling and popular pub's position by the fast-flowing river. Steps lead down to waterside grass with plenty of picnic-sets, an outside bar and barbecue; there's a pétanque pitch by the car park. Inside, locals congregate in the simple left-hand bar, with a big painted settle, cushioned wall benches, a trophy cabinet and old local photographs. Two more little rooms have all manner of cushioned dining chairs, more photographs and rustic waterside prints, and a decorative woodburning stove; bare floorboards throughout and a relaxed, worn-in feel. Wells & Youngs Bitter and Special and a guest such as Bath Gem on handpump, a good choice of wines and quite a choice of coffees, and cheerful, friendly young staff. The light modern conservatory is quite different in style but with similar furnishings.

ⓘ Reasonably priced bar food includes lunchtime sandwiches and toasted ciabattas, ploughman's, soup, fishcakes, steak and ale pie, fish and chips, rib-eye steak, specials, and puddings. *Starters/Snacks: £3.50 to £5.95. Main Courses: £7.95 to £15.95. Puddings: £4.50 to £6.00*

Youngs ~ Managers Samir and Azenora Hadzigrahic ~ Real ale ~ Bar food (12-3, 6-9(9.30 Fri, Sat); 12-8 Sun) ~ (0117) 986 2383 ~ Children welcome but no highchairs provided ~ Dogs allowed in bar ~ Live music some Fri and Sat nights ~ Open 11-11(midnight Fri, Sat); 12-11 Sun
Recommended by Dr and Mrs A K Clarke, Chris and Angela Buckell

LONG SUTTON   ST4625 MAP 1

Devonshire Arms

B3165 Somerton—Martock, just off A372 E of Langport; TA10 9LP

Handsome gabled inn, stylish and smart for a drink or a meal, real ales and good choice of wines by the glass, plenty of room both inside and out, and well thought-of food; bedrooms

This tall gabled stone inn (a former hunting lodge) is a smart and civilised place for a drink or meal – and there's plenty of space to do either. The simple and pubby back bar has modern shiny metal and leather bar stools, rush-seated high-back chairs around dark tables on the flagstones, Moor Revival and a guest like Oakham JHB on handpump or tapped from the cask from the curved pale wooden bar counter; local cider brandy and quite a few wines by the glass. The stylish main bar with its maroon or mushroom painted walls is more comfortable with squashy leather sofas facing each other across a modern glass-topped log table beside the open fire in its big, elegant stone fireplace (with a rather fine gilt-edged mirror above it); and there's a long, cushioned, wall bench with lots of scatter cushions, chunky black tables, attractive window blinds, and church candles in tall glass and metal containers. The elegant dining room has dark brown wicker dining chairs around solid pale wooden tables on the broad stripped floorboards, big antique prints on cream walls and a few massive orchids. Outside in front are teak seats and tables looking across the lane to a small green, and at the back of the building, there's an enclosed courtyard with box hedge roundels, a waterball feature and more teak furniture, and even further back, a carefully made series of neat, raised terraces. Although we have not heard from people who have stayed there, we would expect this to be a lovely place to stay.

ⓘ Featuring local suppliers listed on a blackboard, food might include lunchtime sandwiches and ploughman's, wood pigeon and baby spinach salad with roasted hazelnuts, duck liver pâté with mushrooms, steamed mussels in cider, lambs liver with mash, fried pollack, veal burger with local cheddar and hand-cut chips, quantock duck confit with spring onion and puy lentils, fried fillet of bream, and puddings like lemon mousse and dark chocolate fondant. *Starters/Snacks: £4.95 to £8.95. Main Courses: £9.50 to £14.50. Puddings: £5.50 to £6.40*

Free house ~ Real ale ~ Bar food ~ Restaurant ~ (01458) 241271 ~ Pianist weekly evenings ~ Open 12-3, 6-11; closed 25 and 26 Dec, 1 Jan ~ Bedrooms: £70B/£80S(£90B)
Recommended by Steve and Hilary Nelson, Roderick Braithwaite, Edward Mirzoeff, Fergus Dowding, G K Smale

LOVINGTON   ST5831 MAP 2

Pilgrims 🍴 🍷

B3153 Castle Cary—Keinton Mandeville; BA7 7PT

Civilised, relaxed dining pub with particularly good food cooked by landlord, local beer and cider; decked terrace; bedrooms

An excellent place for a special meal, this smart place is decidedly more restaurant than pub, but has a pubby corner by the corner counter. Cottage Champflower on handpump from the nearby brewery, 16 wines by the glass, local cider and apple juice, cider brandy and a rack of daily papers. A cosy little dark green inner area has sunny modern country and city prints, a couple of shelves of books and china, a cushioned pew and some settees by the big fireplace. With flagstones throughout, this runs into the compact eating area, with candles on tables and some stripped stone. There's also a separate, more formal carpeted dining room. The landlady's service is efficient and friendly. The enclosed garden has tables, chairs and umbrellas on a decked terrace. The car park exit has its own traffic lights – on your way out, line your car up carefully or you may wait for ever for them to change.

🍴 Using organic vegetables from local farms and naming their local suppliers, the rewarding bar food (not cheap) typically includes spiced parsnip soup, teriyaki beef, mushroom tart, mussels in cider, monkfish and scallops with smoked bacon and black rice, slow-roasted duck leg on puy lentils, breast of free-range chicken stuffed with goats cheese, beer-battered or roasted cod, veal escalopes with parma ham, a selection of somerset cheeses, and puddings like chocolate torte or rhubarb and custard. *Starters/Snacks: £4.00 to £9.00. Main Courses: £9.00 to £23.00. Puddings: £5.00 to £8.00*

Free house ~ Licensees Sally and Jools Mitchison ~ Real ale ~ Bar food (not Sun evening, Mon, Tues lunchtime) ~ Restaurant ~ (01963) 240597 ~ Children welcome but not in accommodation ~ Dogs allowed in bar ~ Open 12-3, 7-11; closed Sun evening, Mon, Tues lunchtime ~ Bedrooms: /£80B

Recommended by Paul and Annette Hallett, Edward Mirzoeff

LUXBOROUGH   SS9837   MAP 1

Royal Oak 🍴 🛏

Kingsbridge; S of Dunster on minor roads into Brendon Hills – OS Sheet 181 map reference 983378; TA23 0SH

Smashing place in wonderful countryside, interesting bar food, local beers and ciders, and attentive, friendly staff; bedrooms

Very well run by caring, friendly licensees and with a really good mix of visitors and chatty locals, this beautifully placed inn in the Brendon Hills continues to earn praise. The compact bar, which has the most character and a relaxed, cheerful atmosphere, has lovely old flagstones, several rather fine settles (one with a very high back and one still with its book rest), scrubbed kitchen tables, lots of beer mats on beams, a cart horse saddle and a huge brick fireplace with a warm log fire; a simpler back room has an ancient cobbled floor, some quarry tiles and a stone fireplace. One room just off the bar is set for dining, with attractive old pine furniture and horse and hunting prints, and there are two dining rooms as well. One is green painted and a larger end one has stuffed fish in glass cabinets, fish paintings and fishing rods on the dark red walls, leather and brass-tack dining chairs and more formal ones around quite a mix of old tables, with turkey rugs on the black slate floor. Exmoor Ale and Gold and a couple of guests such as Cottage Iron Duke and Quantock Sunraker on handpump, 14 wines by the glass and Cheddar Valley and Rich's farmhouse cider; darts and board games. There are some seats out in the charming back courtyard and memorable nearby walks in the wonderful surrounding countryside: the Coleridge Way is popular. We would like to hear from readers who stay here.

🍴 Using lamb and duck eggs from Luxborough and Exmoor beef, the enjoyable bar food includes items such as crab filo parcel, goats cheese and sun-dried tomato tart, chicken liver parfait, grilled line-caught swordfish steak with tomato and chilli salsa, sticky chilli-glazed belly of pork, fillet of spring lamb, daily specials (including plenty of fish dishes), and puddings. *Starters/Snacks: £4.95 to £7.25. Main Courses: £6.95 to £16.50. Puddings: £3.95 to £4.95*

Free house ~ Licensees James and Sian Waller ~ Real ale ~ Bar food ~ Restaurant ~ (01984) 640319 ~ Children must be over 10 in evening and in bedrooms ~ Dogs allowed in bar and bedrooms ~ Open 12-2.30, 6-11 (all day during summer school hols); 12-11 Sat and Sun ~ Bedrooms: £55B/£90S(£65B)

Recommended by Dennis and Gill Keen, Helene Grygar, S G N Bennett, Richard Cole, the Didler, Henry Beltran, Barry and Anne, Bob and Margaret Holder, Ewan and Moira McCall, M G Hart, Adrian Johnson, R O'Connell, Lynda and Trevor Smith

NORTON ST PHILIP   ST7755 MAP 2

George 🛏

A366; BA2 7LH

Wonderful ancient building full of history and interest with well liked food, real ales, wines by the glass and characterful bedrooms

Worth a stopover on anyone's tour of historic Somerset, this spectacular medieval building is said to be Britain's longest continually licensed premises, and one reader remarked it is like going back 200 years the moment you enter. It originates from about 700 years ago when it housed merchants buying wool and cloth from the rich sheep-farming Hinton Priory at the great August cloth market. The central Norton Room, which was the original bar, has really heavy beams, an oak-panelled settle and solid dining chairs on the narrow strip wooden floor, a variety of 18th-c pictures, an open fire in the handsome stone fireplace and a low wooden bar counter. Four Wadworths ales – perhaps 6X, Henry's, St George and the Dragon and Horizon – on handpump, and 25 wines by the glass. As you enter the building, there's a room on the right with high dark beams, squared dark half-panelling, a broad carved stone fireplace with an old iron fireback and pewter plates on the mantelpiece, a big mullioned window with leaded lights and a round oak 17th-c table reputed to have been used by the Duke of Monmouth who stayed here before the Battle of Sedgemoor – after their defeat, his men were imprisoned in what is now the Monmouth Bar. The Charterhouse Bar is mostly used by those enjoying a drink before a meal: a wonderful pitched ceiling with trusses and timbering, heraldic shields and standards, jousting lances and swords on the walls, a fine old stone fireplace, high-backed cushioned heraldic-fabric dining chairs on the big rug over the wood plank floor and an oak dresser with some pewter. The dining room (a restored barn with original oak ceiling beams, a pleasant if haphazard mix of early 19th-c portraits and hunting prints and the same mix of vaguely old-looking furnishings) has a good relaxing, chatty atmosphere; piped music. The bedrooms are very atmospheric and comfortable – some reached by an external Norman stone stair-turret and some across the cobbled and flagstoned courtyard and up into a fine half-timbered upper gallery (where there's a lovely 18th-c carved oak settle); note there's a £10 charge for dogs. A stroll over the meadow behind the pub (past the picnic-sets on the narrow grass pub garden) leads you to an attractive churchyard around the medieval church whose bells struck Pepys (here on 12 June 1668) as 'mighty tuneable'.

🍽 **Well liked bar food includes sandwiches or wraps, soup, duck liver and orange pâté, deep-fried calamari, caramelised onion, red pepper and goats cheese tartlet, greek-style lamb, chicken masala, steak and ale pie, leek and mushroom bake, and puddings such as lime-backed cheesecake; there's a more elaborate restaurant menu with items like pork tenderloin medallions with brandy and mushroom cream sauce or duo of grilled bass fillets with parma ham and pine nuts.** *Starters/Snacks: £4.95 to £6.95. Main Courses: £8.20 to £10.50. Puddings: £5.50 to £6.50*

Wadworths ~ Manager Becks Rossiter ~ Real ale ~ Bar food (12-2.30, 6-9(9.30 Fri); 12-9.30 Sat; 12-8.30 Sun) ~ Restaurant ~ (01373) 834224 ~ Children welcome ~ Dogs allowed in bar and bedrooms ~ Open 11.30(12 Sun)-11 ~ Bedrooms: £65B/£130B

Recommended by Roger Wain-Heapy, Mr and Mrs W W Burke, Donna and Roger, the Didler, Dr and Mrs M E Wilson, Mr and Mrs A H Young, John and Joan Nash, Ian Phillips, Bruce and Sharon Eden, Paul Humphreys

ODCOMBE   ST5015 MAP 2

Masons Arms 🍺 🛏

Off A3088 or A30 just W of Yeovil; Lower Odcombe; BA22 8TX

Well run and pretty village pub with plenty of customers, friendly staff, own-brew beers, and well liked food; good bedrooms.

There's a genuinely cheerful atmosphere in this well run and pretty thatched cottage and a good mix of customers. The homely little bar has joists and a couple of standing timbers, a mix of cushioned dining chairs around all sorts of tables (each with a little glass oil lamp, lit at night) on the cream and blue patterned carpet, there are a couple of tub chairs and a table in the former inglenook fireplace, and horsebrasses on the stone walls. Up a step is a similar area and steps down lead to a dining room with a squashy brown sofa and a couple of cushioned dining chairs in front of the woodburning stove, and some black and white local photographs and country prints on the sandstone walls. Friendly, chatty staff serve their own brewed beer – Odcombe No 1, Spring and Roly Poly on handpump – and they also make their own sloe and elderflower cordials and summer fruit brandy. The garden has a good, thatched smokers' shelter and picnic-sets on some grass, and at the bottom there's a vegetable patch, some chickens and rabbits, and a campsite. The bedrooms are well equipped and comfortable and the breakfasts are hearty.

🍴 Popular bar food includes ciabattas and baguettes, fishcakes, game casserole, deep fried goats cheese, sausage and mash and corned beef hash, as well as an à la carte menu with items like crispy duck pancakes with hoi sin sauce, scallops with black pudding and pea purée, free-range pork loin with dauphinoise potatoes and mushroom sauce, saffron risotto with chargrilled vegetables, halibut with parma ham, and puddings like chocolate bread and butter pudding or apricot cheesecake. *Starters/Snacks: £5.00 to £9.50. Main Courses: £7.25 to £16.00. Puddings: £4.00 to £4.75*

Free house ~ Licensees Drew Read and Paula Tennyson ~ Real ale ~ Bar food (12-2, 6.30-9.30) ~ (01935) 862591 ~ No children under 12 in bar after 9pm ~ Dogs welcome ~ Open 12-3, 6-midnight ~ Bedrooms: £55S/£85B

Recommended by John Cunningham, Joyce and Maurice Cottrell

PITNEY
ST4527   MAP 1

Halfway House 🍺

Just off B3153 W of Somerton; TA10 9AB

Up to ten real ales, local ciders and continental bottled beers in bustling friendly local; good simple food

With no music or machines and run by friendly licensees, this is a good, honest village local that prides itself on its excellent range of beers and ciders. Tapped from the cask and changing regularly, they have up to ten well kept real ales including Adnams Broadside, Butcombe Bitter, Hop Back Summer Lightning, Otter Bright (or Hop Back Crop Circle), RCH Pitchfork and Teignworthy Reel Ale, plus various guests, as well as up to six local ciders and around 20 or so continental bottled beers; several wines by the glass and 15 malt whiskies, too. A good mix of people are usually found chatting at communal tables in the three old-fashioned rooms, all with roaring log fires, and there's a homely feel underlined by a profusion of books, maps and newspapers; cribbage, dominoes and board games. There are tables outside.

🍴 As well as lunchtime sandwiches, the simple generous food includes filled baked potatoes, soup, sandwiches, ploughman's, sausage and mash, ham and egg, curries with all the trimmings, and specials like casseroles and caesar salad; they also have their own garden smokery. *Starters/Snacks: £3.50 to £5.95. Main Courses: £4.50 to £11.50. Puddings: £3.50*

Free house ~ Licensees Julian Lichfield and Caroline Lacy ~ Real ale ~ Bar food (12-2.30, 7.30-9) ~ (01458) 252513 ~ Children welcome ~ Dogs welcome ~ Open 11.30-3, 5.30-11(midnight Sat); 12-3.30, 7-11 Sun

Recommended by the Didler, Andrea Rampley, Brian and Bett Cox, MLR, Bob and Margaret Holder, Patrick and Daphne Darley

---

Real ale to us means beer which has matured naturally in its cask – not pressurised or filtered. We name all real ales stocked. We usually name ales preserved under a light blanket of carbon dioxide too, though purists – pointing out that this stops the natural yeasts developing – would disagree (most people, including us, can't tell the difference!).

PORTISHEAD   ST4576   MAP 1

Windmill

3.7 miles from M5 junction 19; A369 into town, then follow Sea Front sign off left and into Nore Road; BS20 6JZ

Sweeping views from large and efficient family dining pub with quite a few real ales and decent food; substantially altered since last year

Now dramatically remodelled, this dining pub makes the most of the terrific panorama over the Bristol Channel and into South Wales, with a new curving glass frontage rising two storeys, while the adjacent windmill itself is untouched. The inside has been completely re-styled with new kitchens and new furnishings to give a more contemporary feel to the place. The lower floor is retained as a family area and the middle floor as the bar. They have six real ales on handpump such as Bass, Butcombe Bitter and Gold, Courage Best and two quickly changing guests from local breweries, and several wines by the glass. Out on the seaward side are picnic-sets on three tiers of lantern-lit terrace and substantial decking areas; disabled access, including a lift.

🍴 The menu includes such items as **sandwiches, filled baked potatoes, soup, beer-battered tiger prawns with hoi sin sauce, chargrilled pork loin, slow-roasted lamb shank, haddock and chips, sausage and mash, shepherd's pie, smoked fish lasagne, szechuan vegetables with steamed rice, and puddings like cheesecake of the day and banoffi pie.** *Starters/Snacks: £1.75 to £6.95. Main Courses: £7.95 to £13.95. Puddings: £1.95 to £4.50*

Free house ~ Licensee J S Churchill ~ Real ale ~ Bar food (all day) ~ (01275) 843677 ~ Children in family area ~ Dogs allowed in bar ~ Open 11-11(10.30 Sun)

Recommended by Tom Evans, Steve and Claire Harvey, Irene and Derek Flewin, Ryta Lyndley, Chris and Angela Buckell, John and Fiona McIlwain

SHEPTON MONTAGUE   ST6731   MAP 2

Montague Inn 🍴 ♉

Village signposted just off A359 Bruton—Castle Cary; BA9 8JW

Good views from restaurant extension in a busy country pub, friendly licensees

This bustling dining pub is going great guns, both for its interesting drinks and as a place to enjoy a meal in civilised surroundings. There's a good welcome from the friendly, knowledgeable landlord and a warm atmosphere, and the rooms are simply but tastefully furnished with stripped wooden tables and kitchen chairs; there's a log fire in the attractive inglenook fireplace. The recent restaurant extension is bright and spacious with french windows opening on to the terrace where there are smart teak seats and tables; steps lead down to the garden. Bath Ales Gem and Stout, Wadworths Strong in the Arm and a guest from a local brewery tapped from the cask, local ciders, a decent selection of malts, a good range of wines (including english ones) with 20 by the glass, and home-made lemonade.

🍴 Using **carefully sourced, very local and seasonal produce, the good, enjoyable bar food includes lots of fish and game specials, lunchtime choices such as open sandwiches, ploughman's, soup, lambs liver with herb mash, frittata of roast vegetables and goats cheese, with evening dishes like terrine of chicken, pork and duck, beef teriyaki with udon noodles, confit of free-range duckling, thai vegetable and coconut curry, sirloin steak, and puddings like tarte tatin with berry compote and clotted cream and white peach parfait and thyme-poached apricots with lemon shortbread.** *Starters/Snacks: £4.95 to £8.50. Main Courses: £6.95 to £18.95. Puddings: £5.50*

Free house ~ Licensee Sean O'Callaghan ~ Real ale ~ Bar food (12-2(3 Sun), 7-9; not Sun evening) ~ Restaurant ~ (01749) 813213 ~ Children welcome ~ Dogs allowed in bar ~ Live jazz summer Sun lunchtimes ~ Open 12-3, 6-11(11.30 Sat); 12-3 Sun; closed Sun evening

Recommended by Edward Mirzoeff, G Vyse, Richard Wyld

SOUTH STOKE

ST7461   MAP 2

Pack Horse

Off B3110, S edge of Bath; BA2 7DU

Fine old pub with plenty of history, friendly, helpful staff, a pubby local feel, lots of farm ciders and enjoyable food

Well placed for some fine walking along the traces of a long-defunct canal in the deep valley just to the south, this former priory has an inviting garden with seats, roses and a boules pitch. The central alleyway that runs right through the middle of the pub used to be the route along which the dead were carried to the church cemetery; it stops along the way at a central space by the serving bar with its Butcombe Bitter, Sharps Doom Bar and guest ale such as Adnams Explorer on handpump and fine choice of four local farm ciders. Service is friendly and helpful. The ancient main room has a good local atmosphere and plenty of regulars dropping in, a log fire in the handsome stone inglenook, antique oak settles (two well carved) and cushioned captain's chairs on the quarry-tiled floor, some royalty pictures, a chiming wall-clock, a heavy black beam-and-plank ceiling and rough black shutters for the stone-mullioned windows (put up in World War I). There's another bar down to the left which also has an open fireplace; a couple of shove-ha'penny slates are set into two tables; piped music.

🍴 **The enjoyable food features lunchtime sandwiches, ploughman's, various salads, haddock and chips, fishcakes, ham with egg and bubble and squeak, and an evening menu that might feature soup, goats cheese wrapped in parma ham, stuffed portabella mushrooms, crab cakes, creamy mushroom pancakes with couscous and thyme-roasted tomatoes, pork escalope with caramelised apple mash, rib-eye steak, and puddings like clementine mess or pear and cinnamon fool.** *Starters/Snacks: £4.50 to £5.50. Main Courses: £9.00 to £14.00. Puddings: £5.00*

Punch ~ Lease Stephen Peart ~ Real ale ~ Bar food (12-2(3 Sun), 6.30-9; not Mon) ~ (01225) 832060 ~ Children welcome ~ Dogs allowed in bar ~ Open 12-3, 6-11; 12-11 Sat; 12-10 Sun; closed Mon lunchtime

Recommended by Guy Vowles, Colin McKerrow, Donna and Roger

STANTON WICK

ST6162   MAP 2

Carpenters Arms

Village signposted off A368, just W of junction with A37 S of Bristol; BS39 4BX

Bustling warm-hearted dining pub in country setting with interesting bar food, friendly staff and good drinks

Run by competent and relaxed bar staff and warmed by log fires, this attractive little stone dining pub is often full of happily chatting customers. The Coopers Parlour on the right has one or two beams, seats around heavy tables, tartan carpet and attractive curtains and plants in the windows; on the angle between here and the bar area, there's a fat woodburning stove in an opened-through corner fireplace. The bar has wood-backed wall settles with cushions, stripped-stone walls and a big log fire in an inglenook. There's also a snug inner room (lightened by mirrors in arched 'windows') and a restaurant with leather sofas and easy chairs in a comfortable lounge area. Butcombe Bitter, Otter Bitter and Sharps Doom Bar on handpump, ten wines by the glass and several malt whiskies; TV in the snug. This is a lovely rural setting and there are picnic-sets on the front terrace, pretty flower beds and attractive hanging baskets and tubs. This is on a very quiet lane and only ten minutes' drive to the Chew Valley – the perfect place to walk off lunch. The refurbished bedrooms are comfortable and attractively done in boutique style.

If you report on a pub that's not a Main Entry, please tell us any lunchtimes or evenings when it doesn't serve bar food.

🍴 Enjoyable and generously served bar food includes sandwiches and light lunchtime classics such as scampi, risotto with red peppers, spinach and brie, honey-roasted ham with free-range egg and chips, as well as soup, fishcake with lime and coriander mayonnaise, steamed mussels, duck and port pâté, steaks, haddock and chips, thai chicken curry, confit of duck with potato dauphinoise and roasted root vegetables, roasted red pepper, aubergine, courgette and goats cheese bake, and puddings like lemon and lime cheesecake or treacle tart. *Starters/Snacks: £4.95 to £8.95. Main Courses: £11.95 to £19.95. Puddings: £4.95 to £6.50*

Free house ~ Licensee Simon Pledge ~ Real ale ~ Bar food (12-2, 6-9.30(10 Fri and Sat); 12-9 Sun) ~ Restaurant ~ (01761) 490202 ~ Children welcome ~ Dogs allowed in bar ~ Open 11-11; 12-10.30 Sun ~ Bedrooms: £72.50B/£105B

Recommended by JCW, Michael Doswell, Bob and Angela Brooks, Ian Malone, M G Hart

STOKE ST GREGORY   ST3527   MAP 1

Rose & Crown 🍴 ☍ ⊨

Woodhill; follow North Curry signpost off A378 by junction with A358 – keep on to Stoke, bearing right in centre, passing church and follow lane for 0.5 miles; TA3 6EW

Friendly, family-run, comprehensively rebuilt after a dreadful fire, good choice of drinks and very good food; bedrooms

The welcoming family who have been here for many years have been at great pains to get things right since reopening after a huge fire, although one or two readers feel the building has inevitably lost a little of its character. More or less open-plan, there's a bar area with wooden stools by a curved brick and pale wood-topped counter and this leads into a long, airy dining room with all manner of light and dark wooden dining chairs and pews around a mix of tables under a high-raftered ceiling. There are two other beamed dining rooms with similar furnishings, photographs on the walls of the fire damage, the village and so forth, and one room has a woodburning stove and another has an 18th-c glass-covered well in one corner. Throughout, there are flagstoned or wooden floors. Exmoor Ale, Otter Ale and a guest like Butcombe Bitter on handpump, Wood's Traditional farmhouse cider and several wines by the glass. There are seats outside on the sheltered front terrace. They have three ensuite bedrooms, two of which can connect to make a family room.

🍴 Particularly good bar food at lunchtime includes sandwiches and ciabattas, ploughman's, soup, mussels in creamy cider sauce with home-made chips, haddock and chips, sausages and mash, steak and kidney pie, stilton and mushroom vol-au-vent, with evening choices such as seared scallops on black pudding with apple purée, fillet or sirloin steak, tandoori chicken, roasted lamb rump with redcurrant sauce, vegetable stroganoff, and puddings like raspberry and clotted cream pavlova or apple and gooseberry crumble. They make their own sausages and salami. *Starters/Snacks: £4.75 to £6.50. Main Courses: £8.50 to £11.95. Puddings: £4.50 to £4.85*

Free house ~ Licensees Stephen, Sally, Richard and Leonie Browning ~ Real ale ~ Bar food ~ Restaurant ~ (01823) 490296 ~ Children welcome ~ Open 11-3, 6-11(12 Sat); 12-3, 6-10.30 Sun ~ Bedrooms: £55B/£85B

Recommended by Bob and Margaret Holder, Edward Delling-Williams, Mike and Mary Carter

TARR   SS8632   MAP 1

Tarr Farm ⊨

Tarr Steps – rather narrow road off B3223 N of Dulverton, very little nearby parking (paying car park quarter-mile up road); OS Sheet 181 map reference 868322 – as the inn is on the E bank, don't be tempted to approach by car from the W unless you can cope with a deep ford; TA22 9PY

Lovely Exmoor setting and lots to do nearby, decent range of drinks, well liked food and seats outside; bedrooms

The position here is quite idyllic, just above the wooded River Barle at the point it is spanned by the celebrated medieval clapper bridge known as Tarr Steps; and the bedrooms are very comfortable. The recently refurbished pub part consists of a line of compact and unpretentious rooms, also with good views, slabby rustic tables, stall seating, soft furnishings, wall seats and leather chairs, three woodburning stoves, walls clad with oak and antique pine, nice game bird pictures and a pair of stuffed pheasants. The serving bar up a step or two has Exmoor Ale and Gold on handpump, eight wines by the glass and a good choice of other drinks. The residents' end has a smart little evening restaurant (you can eat from this menu in the bar) and a pleasant log-fire lounge with dark leather armchairs and sofas. Slate-topped stone tables outside make the most of the setting.

🍴 Using local suppliers, free-range eggs, poultry and pork, bar food could include lunchtime sandwiches and ciabattas, ploughman's, potted venison, soused red mullet, minted lamb shoulder chops, roast chicken breast wrapped in parma ham, a fish special, tagliatelle in tomato, butter bean and basil pesto sauce, with puddings like chocolate cheesecake and lemon mousse; cream teas; two-course lunch for £10 on weekdays except bank holidays. *Starters/Snacks: £4.50 to £8.95. Main Courses: £7.50 to £13.00. Puddings: £3.50 to £5.50*

Free house ~ Licensees Richard Benn and Judy Carless ~ Real ale ~ Bar food (12-3, 6.30-9.30) ~ Restaurant ~ (01643) 851507 ~ Children in accommodation must be over 10 ~ Dogs welcome ~ Open 11-11; closed 1-10 Feb ~ Bedrooms: £90B/£150B

Recommended by Helene Grygar, Richard Cole, Sheila Topham, Dominic McGonigal, Adrian Johnson, John and Jackie Chalcraft, Dr A McCormick, Lynda and Trevor Smith

TRISCOMBE   ST1535   MAP 1
Blue Ball

Village signposted off A358 Crowcombe—Bagborough; turn off opposite sign to youth hostel; OS Sheet 181 map reference 155355; TA4 3HE

Fine old building, enjoyable food and drink, and seats on decking making the most of the views; bedrooms

This lovely old place beneath the Quantock Hills has recently been taken over as a free house and just reopened after refurbishment as we went to press, and we hope it continues its winning ways. On the first floor of the original stables, it's a smart place, sloping down gently on three levels, each with its own fire, and cleverly divided into seating by hand-cut beech partitions. Cotleigh Tawny and two guests from breweries such as Otter or Sharps on handpump, several wines by the glass and local farm cider; piped music. The decking at the top of the woodside, terraced garden makes the most of the views. There is a chair lift to the bar/restaurant area for the disabled. Reports on the new regime please.

🍴 From a changing menu, food could include lunchtime sandwiches, soup, scallops and king prawns, carpaccio of beef, turbot with crab risotto, duck with plum sauce, red onion and tomato tarte tatin, and puddings like passion-fruit crème brûlée. *Starters/Snacks: £4.50 to £8.95. Main Courses: £10.95 to £17.95. Puddings: £5.25*

Free house ~ Licensee Peter Alcroft ~ Real ale ~ Bar food ~ (01984) 618242 ~ Children welcome ~ Dogs allowed in bar ~ Open 12-2.30, 6.30-11; closed Sun evening, Mon ~ Bedrooms: £45B/£75B

Recommended by Dr and Mrs A K Clarke, Neil and Anita Christopher, Martin Hatcher, Mike and Mary Carter, Helene Grygar

WATERROW   STO525   MAP 1
Rock ♀ 🛏

A361 Wiveliscombe—Bampton; TA4 2AX

Welcoming family-run inn, local ales, good food and a nice mix of customers; bedrooms

This friendly 15th-c black and white inn lies not far from the southern fringes of Exmoor National Park, and it's not unknown for red deer to wander within yards of the front door. The bar area has a dark brown leather sofa and low table with newspapers and books in front of the stone fireplace with its log fire, and big blackboard menus. There's a mix of dining chairs and wooden tables on the partly wood and partly red carpeted floor, a few high-backed bar chairs, hunting paintings and photographs, a couple of built-in cushioned window seats; real ales brewed by Cotleigh, Exmoor and a guest on handpump, several wines by the glass and Sheppy's farm cider. A back room has a popular pool table; darts and piped music. Up some steps from the bar is the heavily beamed restaurant. The welsh collie is called Meg. There are a few seats under umbrellas by the road. More reports please.

🍴 Using local produce and beef from their own farm, the good bar food might include lunchtime sandwiches, soup, thai crab cakes, grilled goats cheese and red onion crostini, chargrilled rib-eye steak, calves liver with mash and bacon, roasted barbary duck breast, fish pie, sausages and mash, haddock and chips, and puddings like baked lemon cheesecake or bread and butter pudding. *Starters/Snacks: £4.50 to £6.75. Main Courses: £9.95 to £16.95. Puddings: £4.50 to £6.50*

Free house ~ Licensees Matt Harvey and Joanna Oldman ~ Real ale ~ Bar food (12-2.30, 6-9.30) ~ Restaurant ~ (01984) 623293 ~ Children welcome ~ Dogs allowed in bar and bedrooms ~ Open 12-3, 6-11 ~ Bedrooms: £50B/£75B

Recommended by David and Julie Glover, Dr A McCormick

WELLS   ST5445   MAP 2

City Arms 🍺

High Street; BA5 2AG

Busy town-centre pub with seven real ales, fine choice of ciders, and food served all day from 9am

We've had lots of reports enthusing about the superb range of drinks here, and the friendliness of the staff. There are always customers dropping in and out, and the main bar has leather sofas around low tables, leather chairs around large, heavy tables with carved legs, a gas-effect log fire and plenty of prints and paintings on the cream walls. The upstairs restaurant has a vaulted ceiling, red walls and chandeliers, and there's also a first-floor terrace in the cobbled courtyard. Board games and piped music. On handpump, the real ales might include Butcombe Bitter, Cheddar Ales Gorge Best Bitter, Glastonbury Hedgemonkey, Sharps Doom Bar, three guest ales and four ciders. The building was originally a jail and you can still see a couple of small, barred windows, a solitary cell and chains and locks in the courtyard.

🍴 As well as the breakfasts (served from 9am), bar food includes sandwiches, soup, chicken liver pâté, smoked haddock and spinach bake with a cheesy mash topping, steak in ale pie, beer-battered cod, lemon chicken stir fry, vegetarian risotto with broad beans, peas and mint, and puddings like warm chocolate brownie with fudge sauce and glazed lemon tart *Starters/Snacks: £2.50 to £4.95. Main Courses: £6.50 to £13.95. Puddings: £3.95 to £5.25*

Free house ~ Licensee Penelope Lee ~ Real ale ~ Bar food (all day till 10pm; they also serve breakfast from 9am) ~ Restaurant ~ (01749) 673916 ~ Children welcome ~ Dogs welcome ~ Open 9am(10am Sun)-11.30pm (midnight Sat)

Recommended by David Lamb, Sylvia and Tony Birbeck, Steve and Liz Tilley, Joe Green, Jim and Frances Gowers, Bruce Ashmore, Bob and Angela Brooks, Terry Buckland, Richard and Judy Winn

Fountain

St Thomas Street; BA5 2UU

Friendly and attractive small pub in town centre, with plenty of room, bustling atmosphere

A relaxing spot for a drink and placed just behind the cathedral, this gets a good mix of visitors and locals. It's run by friendly people and you can be sure of a warm welcome despite the many customers popping in and out. There's a big, comfortable bar with a bustling atmosphere, some interesting bric-a-brac, Butcombe Bitter and Sharps Doom Bar on handpump and several wines by the glass; unobtrusive piped music and board games. There's a popular upstairs restaurant, too. Now prettily painted yellow with blue shutters and adorned with window boxes, the pub was built in the 18th c to house builders working on the nearby cathedral; some parts are thought to be even older. More reports please.

🍴 Traditional bar food includes sandwiches, soup, steak and sausages and mash. *Starters/Snacks: £4.50 to £7.50. Main Courses: £8.95 to £14.50. Puddings: £4.50 to £6.95*

Punch ~ Tenants Adrian and Sarah Lawrence ~ Real ale ~ Bar food ~ Restaurant ~ (01749) 672317 ~ Children welcome ~ Open 12-2, 6(7 Sun)-11

Recommended by R K Phillips, Terry Buckland, Dr and Mrs A K Clarke, Nick Patton, Sylvia and Tony Birbeck

WEST BAGBOROUGH

ST1733 MAP 1

Rising Sun
Village signposted off A358 NW of Taunton; TA4 3EF

Charming and civilised village pub, welcoming staff, candles and fresh flowers, individual furnishings, real ales and good wines by the glass, and highly thought of food

On our early evening visit, this welcoming pub in a tiny village below the Quantocks was lit up with candles throughout – one on each table and big church ones in ornate candlesticks on the mantelpiece above the fine stone fireplace where a log fire was burning. The little bar to the right of the massive main door has settles (one rather well made) and some carved dining chairs around polished tables on the flagstones, a wall seat with brocaded cushions by another table, an old-fashioned child's desk with daily papers, handsome heavy-draped curtains and, by the counter where they serve Butcombe Bitter, Exmoor Ale and St Austell Proper Job on handpump, some black leather bar chairs. Pretty fresh flowers and some quirky ornaments are dotted about. The smart and cosy left-hand dining room has an attractive mix of Chippendale and other dining chairs around just a few dark wooden tables, and there's also a most attractive back snug room with a coal-effect gas fire, big modern photographs on the walls and just four tables and chairs. Upstairs – which is just right for a private party – has trusses in the high-pitched ceiling, leather and brass seats around a couple of big refectory tables, an oriental rug on the wooden floor and big prints of cathedral cities. It's all very civilised but informal. Outside are a few teak seats by the lane.

🍴 Good bar food could include filled rolls, ploughman's, whitebait, carpaccio of beef, rainbow trout, wild mushroom risotto, warm chicken and bacon salad, sirloin steak, and puddings. *Starters/Snacks: £4.95 to £10.95. Main Courses: £8.95 to £19.95. Puddings: £5.25 to £5.50*

Free house ~ Licensees Jon and Christine Brinkman ~ Real ale ~ Bar food ~ Restaurant ~ (01823) 432575 ~ Children welcome ~ Dogs allowed in bar ~ Open 11-3, 6-11; 12-3, 7-10.30 Sun; closed Sun evening and Mon in winter

Recommended by Michael Cleeve, Bob and Margaret Holder, Patrick and Daphne Darley

WITHYPOOL

SS8435 MAP 1

Royal Oak 🛏
Village signposted off B3233; TA24 7QP

Warm welcome from friendly licensees at this prettily placed country inn, a roaring open fire and good bar food

In a particularly enchanting corner of Exmoor, this nicely old-fashioned country village inn is run by very welcoming licensees, and R D Blackmore stayed here while writing *Lorna Doone*. There's a fine raised log fireplace in the lounge, as well as comfortably cushioned wall seating and slat-backed chairs, sporting trophies and paintings and various copper and brass ornaments on its walls. The locals' bar has some old oak tables and plenty of character. Exmoor Ale and Gold on handpump and several wines by the glass. There are wooden benches on the terrace and, just up the road, some grand views from Winsford Hill; the River Barle runs through the village itself, with pretty bridleways following it through a wooded combe.

🍴 Enjoyable food (not cheap) includes lunchtime sandwiches, soup, chicken liver parfait, grilled goats cheese with greek salad, rump steak, steak and ale pie, belly pork with cider cream sauce, lambs liver with crispy bacon and onion gravy, specials like duck breast with fondant potatoes and plum sauce, and puddings like apple pie and warm lemon tart with clotted cream. *Starters/Snacks: £4.50 to £6.75. Main Courses: £9.95 to £14.95. Puddings: £5.25*

Free house ~ Lease Richard Benn ~ Real ale ~ Bar food (12-2, 6.30-9; 12-2.30, 7-9 Sun) ~ Restaurant ~ (01643) 831506 ~ Children in eating area of bar and restaurant ~ Dogs welcome ~ Open 11(12 Sun)-11 ~ Bedrooms: £65B/£110B

Recommended by Bob and Margaret Holder, Sheila Topham, David Treherne Pollock, J L Wedel, Andrew Scott, John Pawson, Lynda and Trevor Smith, John and Fiona McIlwain, Martin Hatcher

WRANTAGE   ST3022   MAP 1
Canal Inn
4 miles from M5 junction 25; A358E, then left on to A378; TA3 6DF

Friendly roadside pub with flowers and candles, attractive bars and more formal dining room, chatty staff, real ales, and good, home-made food

With bowls of lilies, lighted church candles and a warm log fire in its solid pine frame, this friendly roadside pub was just the ticket on our bitterly cold evening visit. The two rooms of the bar are separated by stable-style partitioning: a green suede sofa, green leather dining chairs and some homely plush stools around granite or wood-topped tables on the flagstones, and Exmoor Ale, Moor Revival and Otter Bright on handpump. The adjoining room has wrought-iron and other dining chairs around heavy wooden tables, and the pink walls are hung with small sporting prints (for sale) and a picture of a pair of African Grey parrots; helpful, chatty service and faint piped pop music. The more formal back dining room is heavily beamed and has slightly gothic red plush chairs around a mix of tables. Outside, there's a nicely done smokers' shelter and picnic-sets in the fenced-off garden.

🍴 Well liked food might include starters like asparagus wrapped in parma ham with a hollandaise sauce, smoked salmon and prawn fishcake with beetroot crème fraîche, main courses like chicken wrapped in bacon stuffed with sausage, rump steak, fresh fish, porcini mushroom, spinach and mozzarella risotto balls, and puddings such as white chocolate and raspberry panna cotta and sticky toffee pudding. *Starters/Snacks: £4.50 to £6.50. Main Courses: £7.25 to £14.95. Puddings: £4.95 to £6.00*

Free house ~ Licensee Emma Purvis ~ Real ale ~ Bar food (12-3(3.30 Sat), 6.30(6 Sat, Sun)-9.30) ~ Restaurant ~ (01823) 480210 ~ Children welcome ~ Dogs allowed in bar ~ Occasional live music ~ Open 12-3, 5-11; 12-11 Sat; 12-10.30 Sun

Recommended by Bob and Margaret Holder

LUCKY DIP

Besides the fully inspected pubs, you might like to try these Lucky Dips recommended to us and described by readers (if you do, please send us reports: feedback@goodguides.com).

ASHCOTT [ST4336]
Ashcott Inn TA7 9QQ [A39 W of Glastonbury]: Stripped-stone, beamed bar with big inglenook, friendly efficient landlord, usual food inc popular good value Sun lunch, ales such as Butcombe and Otter; piped music; skittle alley, terrace and garden tables, open all day summer *(Maureen Wood, LYM)*
☆ *Ring o' Bells* TA7 9PZ [High St; pub well signed off A39 W of Street]: Friendly neatly kept local with wide choice of good value fresh food from sandwiches and pubby things to imaginative specials, three quickly changing mainly local ales, Wilkins's farm

cider; steps up and down making snug comfortable areas, decent wines, helpful service, inglenook woodburner; skittle alley, some live folk music; attractive back garden with play area and shaded terrace *(Chris and Angela Buckell, Joe Green, Sarah Butcher, Frank Willy, Ian and Nita Cooper, BB)*
AXBRIDGE [ST4354]
☆ *Lamb* BS26 2AP [The Square; off A371 Cheddar—Winscombe]: Big rambling carpeted pub with heavy 15th-c beams and timbers, stone and roughcast walls, large stone fireplaces, old settles, unusual bar front with old bottles set in plaster, Butcombe and guest ales, well chosen wines,

wide choice of good food inc vegetarian and children's, OAP lunch deals (Tues, Thurs), friendly service; board games, table skittles, skittle alley; they may try to keep your credit card while you eat; dogs allowed, pretty and sheltered small back garden, medieval King John's Hunting Lodge opposite (NT), open all day Thurs-Sun *(Mel de Wit, Chris and Angela Buckell, M G Hart, LYM)*

BARTON ST DAVID [ST5432]

Barton Inn TA11 6BZ [Main St]: Unpretentious, well lived-in and locally well loved brick pub, open-plan bar with bare boards and quarry tiles, old pews and battered tables, rough pine panelling, well kept constantly changing cask-tapped ales, real ciders, simple food such as pizzas and baguettes (no menu), lots of pictures, posters and bric-a-brac; big screen TV for rugby; wet dogs and muddy walkers welcome, wheelchair accessible (friendly locals may also lend a hand), pub sign in mirror writing, events such as frog racing and worm charming *(Chris and Angela Buckell, the Didler)*

BATH [ST7564]

☆ *Coeur de Lion* BA1 5AR [Northumberland Pl; off High St by W H Smith]: Tiny stained-glass fronted single-room pub, perhaps Bath's prettiest, simple, cosy and jolly, with candles and log-effect gas fire; well kept Abbey ales and guests, good well priced food from huge baps to roasts (vegetarian options too), good Christmas mulled wine; may be piped music, stairs to lavatories; tables out in charming flower-filled flagstoned pedestrian alley, open all day *(LYM, Barry Collett, Roger Wain-Heapy, Michael Dandy, Dr and Mrs A K Clarke, the Didler, Michael and Alison Sandy, Dr and Mrs M E Wilson)*

Crystal Palace BA1 1NW [Abbey Green]: Spacious two-room pub with something of a wine-bar feel, dark panelling and tiled floors, freshly prepared straightforward food (not Sun evening) inc lunchtime snacks, speedy friendly service, well kept Marstons-related ales, log fire, family room and conservatory; piped music; sheltered heated courtyard with lovely hanging baskets *(Dr and Mrs A K Clarke, Alan Thwaite, Michael Dandy, LYM)*

☆ *Hop Pole* BA1 3AR [Albion Buildings, Upper Bristol Rd]: Bustling family-friendly Bath Ales pub with guest beers, decent wines by the glass, enjoyable food (not Sun evening, Mon lunchtime) from sandwiches to full meals in bar and former skittle alley restaurant; traditional settles and other pub furniture on bare boards in four tastefully reworked linked areas, lots of black woodwork, ochre walls, some bric-a-brac, board games, daily papers; Mon quiz night, piped music, discreet sports TV; wheelchair accessible, attractive two-level back courtyard with boules, fairy-lit vine arbour and summer houses with heaters, opp

Victoria Park with its great play area, open all day *(Jeremy King, Dr and Mrs A K Clarke, the Didler, Chris and Angela Buckell, GSB, BB, Colin and Peggy Wilshire, Roger Wain-Heapy)*

Pig & Fiddle BA1 5BR [Saracen St]: Lively, not smart, with good sensibly priced ales such as Abbey, Bath and Butcombe, pleasant staff, two big open fires, clocks on different time zones, bare boards and bright paintwork, steps up to darker bustling servery and little dining area; games area and several TVs; lots of students at night, piped trendy music then; picnic-sets on big heated front terrace, open all day *(Dr and Mrs A K Clarke, the Didler, BB)*

Raven BA1 1HE [Queen St]: Small buoyant city-centre local, two ales for the pub from Blindmans and local guests, a changing farm cider, limited food inc good pies, quick friendly service; open fire, bare boards and some stripped stone, newspapers, upstairs area; live acoustic music; open all day *(the Didler, Andy Lickfold, Colin Campbell, Ian Phillips, Michael Dandy, Dr and Mrs A K Clarke)*

Salamander BA1 2JL [John St]: Busy city local tied to Bath Ales, their full range and guests kept well, good choice of wines by the glass, bare boards, black woodwork and dark ochre walls, popular food inc some unusual choices, friendly young staff; two rooms downstairs, open-kitchen upstairs restaurant, daily papers, Sun quiz; piped music, no dogs; children till 8pm, open all day *(BB, the Didler, Alan Thwaite, Steve Jackson, Michael Dandy, N R White, Dr and Mrs A K Clarke)*

Saracens Head BA1 5LP [Broad St]: Centrally placed beamed coaching inn with enjoyable unfussy food at sensible prices, well kept ales, efficient service even at busy times; children in dining area *(Barry and Anne)*

Wagon & Horses BA1 7DD [London Rd W]: Roomy pub under new management, popular for bargain OAP lunch and other deals, pleasant roomy décor, Avon Valley views *(Meg and Colin Hamilton)*

BAYFORD [ST7228]

Unicorn BA9 9NL: Proper pub doing well under current friendly landlord, good locally sourced food at fair prices, good mix of well kept changing ales, farm ciders; beams and flagstones, cosy snug beyond fireplace, end restaurant area; four bedrooms, open all day *(Edward Mirzoeff)*

BECKINGTON [ST8051]

☆ *Woolpack* BA11 6SP [Warminster Rd, off A36 bypass]: Well refurbished civilised old inn with charming helpful staff, enjoyable home-made food from sandwiches up, Greene King ales, decent wines, farm cider; big log fire and chunky candlelit tables in flagstoned bar, attractive smarter oak-panelled dining room (separate menu), conservatory; can get very busy Sat night and service may slow; children and dogs welcome, 11 appealing period bedrooms, open all day *(Norman and Sarah Keeping, Peter and Jean Hoare, LYM)*

BINEGAR [ST6149]

Horse & Jockey BA3 4UH: Popular and welcoming with three long rooms, friendly helpful staff, substantial bar food especially pizzas, ales inc Butcombe and Otter, local Thatcher's farm cider; skittle alley *(Anne Morris, Paul Humphreys)*

BISHOP'S WOOD [ST2512]

☆ *Candlelight* TA20 3RS [off A303/B3170 S of Taunton]: Reopened after renovation by former team from the Farmers at West Hatch; roomy yet cosy dining pub with beams and log fires, enjoyable varied home-made food from sandwiches up using local produce, well kept beers such as Bass, Exmoor and Otter, good service; children and dogs welcome, disabled access, nice side garden and back terrace by fish pond *(Patrick and Daphne Darley, Bob and Margaret Holder)*

BLAGDON HILL [ST2118]

Lamb & Flag TA3 7SL [4 miles S of Taunton]: Atmospheric country pub with 17th-c beams, mixed traditional furniture, unusual orange and green colour scheme, woodburner in double-sided fireplace, four well kept ales, short choice of good value food (not Mon lunchtime), small helpings available; games room/skittle alley, some live music; children and dogs welcome, picnic-sets in nice garden with Taunton Vale views, open all day *(Stuart McLoughlin)*

BLEADON [ST3457]

☆ *Queens Arms* BS24 0NF [just off A370 S of Weston; Celtic Way]: Popular 16th-c village pub with informal chatty atmosphere in carefully divided areas, candles on sturdy tables flanked by winged settles, solid fuel stove, old hunting prints; generous reasonably priced food (not Sun evening) from lunchtime baguettes to steaks, friendly service, well kept Butcombe and guests tapped from the cask, local cider, several wines by the glass; flagstoned restaurant and stripped-stone back bar with woodburner, darts, clean lavatories (mind the steps); children (away from bar) and dogs welcome, picnic-sets on pretty heated terrace, open all day *(LYM, Comus and Sarah Elliott, Dr and Mrs A K Clarke, Dennis Jenkin, M Mossman, Tom Evans, Ian and Nita Cooper, Michael Doswell, KC)*

BLUE ANCHOR [ST0243]

Smugglers TA24 6JS [end of B3191, off A39 E of Minehead]: Mellow building in spectacular clifftop setting, well run hotel bars inc airy flagstoned dining room, civilised upper restaurant, small beamed and flagstoned cellar, good range of enjoyable food, real ales inc Otter, pleasant staff, log fires; piped music; children welcome (dogs too, if bar not busy), big sheltered garden, comfortable pretty bedrooms, site for touring caravans *(Mr and Mrs D J Nash)*

BRADFORD-ON-TONE [ST1722]

☆ *White Horse* TA4 1HF [fairly nr M5 junction 26, off A38 towards Taunton]: 17th-c stone-built local in centre of quiet village, good reasonably priced food in bar and dining

room, friendly competent staff, well kept Cotleigh, Exmoor and Otter, decent wines; sofas by open fire, skittle alley; piped music; back garden with arbour and boules, unusual glass pub sign, handy for M5 *(Giles and Annie Francis, Shirley and Bob Gibbs, BB)*

Worlds End TA4 1ET [S of village, towards Silver St; on A38 NE of Wellington]: Neat spacious roadside pub, imaginative good value food inc vegetarian options, friendly efficient service *(Heather Coulson, Neil Cross)*

BRENDON HILLS [ST0334]

☆ *Raleghs Cross* TA23 0LN [junction B3190/B3224]: Busy family-friendly upland inn with helpful friendly staff, well kept Cotleigh, Exmoor and a guest, local cider, good interesting food inc fresh fish and popular carvery, rows of plush banquettes in big bar, back restaurant; no dogs; children in restaurant and family room, big garden with play area, views to Wales on clear days, good walking country, 17 comfortable bedrooms, open all day summer *(John Saville, Bob and Angela Brooks, George Stephenson, LYM)*

BRISTOL [ST5672]

☆ *Adam & Eve* BS8 4ND [Hope Chapel Hill, Hotwells]: Quietly tucked-away pub, refurbished under newish management, dark bare boards and clean cheerful décor, several real ales inc well kept Bath Gem, cider and perry, belgian beers, good organic wines and juices, inexpensive creative food changing daily, interesting recipes and organic ingredients; friendly staff, relaxed country-pub atmosphere, log fire, pleasant nooks and corners, café chairs and wall settles, worthwhile photographs and pictures; not much parking nearby *(Mark O'Sullivan, BB)*

☆ *Bag o' Nails* BS1 5UW [St Georges Rd, by B4466/A4 Hotwells roundabout]: No-frills place popular for its half a dozen or more well kept changing ales and bottled beers, friendly staff and locals, good cobs; piped music; beer festivals, open all day Fri-Sun *(the Didler, WW, Simon and Amanda Southwold)*

Bay Horse BS1 2LJ: Open-plan panelled lounge with raised area, emphasis on eating but fine for just a drink, straightforward food from baguettes to steaks inc meal deals, ales such as St Austell Tribute and Wychwood Hobgoblin *(Donna and Roger)*

Colston Yard BS1 5BD [Upper Maudlin St/Colston St]: Former Smiles Brewery Tap reopened as a Butcombe pub, very popular, with their full range and guests kept well, interesting bottled beers, good choice of wines and spirits; enjoyable food from lunchtime sandwiches to grills and evening restaurant menu, two floors in minimalist pastel style; disabled facilities *(Chris and Angela Buckell)*

Commercial Rooms BS1 1HT [Corn St]: Spacious Wetherspoons conversion (former merchants' club) with lofty stained-glass domed ceiling, gas lighting, comfortable quieter back room with ornate balcony; wide changing choice of real ales inc local ones, friendly helpful landlord, nice chatty bustle (busiest wknd evenings), usual food all day, cheap prices; ladies' with chesterfields and open fire; no dogs; children welcome, side wheelchair access and disabled facilities, good location, open all day from 9am and till late Fri-Sun *(Simon and Amanda Southwell, the Didler, Dr and Mrs A K Clarke, Chris and Angela Buckell)*

Cornubia BS1 6EN [Temple St]: 18th-c backstreet real ale pub with good Hidden ales and several recherché guest beers, interesting bottled beers, farm cider and perry, limited wkdy pubby food till 7.30pm (Sun till 6pm), friendly service, small woody seating areas; can be crowded evenings, not for wheelchairs; picnic-sets on cobbles outside *(Luke Daniels, Susan and Nigel Brookes, the Didler, John and Gloria Isaacs)*

Coronation Tap BS8 4AX [Sion Pl, Clifton; off Portland St]: Friendly bustling old-fashioned cider house, fat casks of interesting farm ciders along with own strong Exhibition (served in half-pint glasses only), real ales too, good live music *(Chris and Angela Buckell, LYM)*

Cottage BS1 6XG [Baltic Wharf, Cumberland Rd]: Converted, stone-built, panelled harbour master's office nr Maritime Heritage Centre, comfortable, roomy and civilised with fine views of Georgian landmarks and Clifton suspension bridge, enjoyable generous pub food from sandwiches up at reasonable prices, well kept Butcombe ales and a guest, nice wines, good friendly service; piped music; portable wheelchair ramps, waterside terrace tables, access through sailing club, on foot along waterfront, or by round-harbour ferry, neighbouring camp/caravan site, open all day *(Colin and Peggy Wilshire, Chris and Angela Buckell)*

Eldon House BS8 1BT [Lower Clifton Hill]: Recently extended and refurbished with some contemporary touches, polished wood floors, mixed wooden tables and chairs, round stone-walled room with glazed roof, snug with original stained glass and half-door servery; decent good value food (all day Fri, Sat, not Sun evening) inc set menus, well kept Bath ales and two guests, several wines by the glass; eclectic piped music, board games Mon night, Tues quiz; children till 8pm, pavement seats, open all day Fri-Sun *(Chris and Angela Buckell)*

Grain Barge BS8 4RU [Hotwell Rd]: Floating 100-ft barge tied to Bristol Beer Factory, their full range, good well priced freshly made food inc ale sausages/pies and beer-battered fish; picnic-sets on top deck, sofas and tables with metal chairs on wood floor below; live music Fri night, open all day *(the Didler, WW, Donna and Roger)*

Graze Bar & Chophouse BS1 4JZ [Queen Sq]: New stylish big-windowed Bath Ales pub, their beers kept well, imaginative good value food all day from open kitchen, cheerful efficient staff; modern light wood tables, benches and chairs, cow wallpaper and bull's head over green-tiled bar, comfortable raised seating areas, suspended modern lighting; wheelchair access through side door, open all day and from 9am wknds *(Chris and Angela Buckell)*

Hatchet BS1 5NA [Frogmore St]: Tucked-away old pub with plenty of character, simple reasonably priced bar lunches inc substantial sandwiches, well kept Butcombe, friendly young staff, beamed rooms with alcohol-related epigrams on walls; popular with local workers *(John Wooll, Stan Edwards, Dr and Mrs A K Clarke)*

Hillgrove Porter Stores BS2 8LT [Hillgrove St N]: Friendly unfussy local with basic interior inc comfortable lounge, well kept Cheddar, Goffs and five changing guests (prices reduced on Mon), good choice of wines by the glass, welcoming landlady, Sun quiz night; not for wheelchairs; back terrace, open 4-midnight *(the Didler)*

☆ **Hope & Anchor** BS8 1DR [Jacobs Wells Rd, Clifton]: Friendly recently refurbished 18th-c pub, half a dozen changing ales such as Cheddar, Otter and Wickwar from central bar, nice wines, tables of various sizes on bare boards, darker back area, sensibly priced hearty food all day – very popular lunchtime, friendly staff; soft piped music, occasionally live, can get crowded late evening; children welcome, disabled access, barbecues in good-sized tiered back garden with interesting niches *(Jeremy King, the Didler, Simon and Amanda Southwell, Dr and Mrs A K Clarke)*

Horseshoe BS15 4PA [Siston Common; off A4175]: Large open-plan family-friendly food pub with good value simple menu and specials, Sharps Doom Bar, helpful staff *(M G Hart)*

Inn on the Green BS7 0PA [Filton Rd, Horfield]: Civilised real ale pub with changing choice of up to a dozen or more, five farm ciders, tasters offered, short choice of well priced food (not Sun evening, Mon) inc Sat evening deals, friendly service; bare boards and quarry tiles, some half-panelling, pubby furniture inc pews and settles, more seating in former skittle alley; occasional live music, beer festivals; wheelchair access throughout, tables out front and back *(Chris and Angela Buckell, Jeremy King)*

☆ **Kensington Arms** BS6 6NP [Stanley Rd]: Smart dining pub in discreet shades of grey and cream, nice relaxed atmosphere with cheerful helpful young staff, good food from light pub lunches to bigger pricier evening dishes, well kept Greene King ales, good if not cheap wine choice, interesting rums etc, flowers and lit candles; may be piped music; disabled facilities and access (not to dining room/upstairs dining room), well behaved children and dogs welcome, heated terrace *(Susan and Nigel Brookes, Susanna Wadeson)*

☆ **Kings Head** BS1 6DE [Victoria St]: Friendly relaxed 17th-c pub with big front window and splendid mirrored bar back, corridor to cosy panelled back snug with serving hatch, well kept Bath Gem, Wadworths 6X and

Sharps Doom Bar; toby jugs on joists, old-fashioned local prints and photographs, interesting gas pressure gauge, reasonably priced wholesome food wkdy lunchtimes (get there early for a seat); 60s piped music, no credit cards; pavement tables, cl Sat lunchtime, open all day Weds-Fri *(Jeremy King, G Russell, Susan and Nigel Brookes, the Didler, WW, BB)*

Merchants Arms BS8 4PZ [Merchants Rd, Hotwells]: Tiny two-room pub close to historic dockside, welcoming landlord and friendly locals, well kept Bath ales and a guest, limited food; popular Thurs quiz; sports TV; wheelchair access with help (narrow door and steps) *(Simon and Amanda Southwell, Dr and Mrs A K Clarke, Chris and Angela Buckell, John and Gloria Isaacs)*

Nova Scotia BS1 6XJ [Baltic Wharf, Cumberland Basin]: Unreconstructed old local on S side of Floating Harbour, views to Clifton and Avon Gorge; Bass, Courage Best and guest beers, real ciders, bargain hearty food from good doorstep sandwiches to Sun roasts; pubby seats in four linked areas, snob screen, mahogany and mirrors, nautical charts as wallpaper, characterful locals; wheelchair access (easiest through snug), plenty of tables out by water, bedrooms sharing bathroom *(Chris and Angela Buckell, Stan Edwards)*

Old Fish Market BS1 1QZ [Baldwin St]: Imposing building well converted, good mural showing it in 1790s, lots of dark wood inc handsome counter, parquet floor, relaxed friendly atmosphere, good value mainly thai food all day, well kept Fullers ales and Butcombe as a guest, good coffee, daily papers; quiet piped music, big-screen sports TVs, games machines; open all day *(Simon and Amanda Southwell, Dr and Mrs A K Clarke, Donna and Roger, Jeremy King)*

Orchard BS1 6XT [Hanover Pl]: Friendly unpretentious one-room local with half a dozen well kept ales, real ciders (perhaps a winter mulled one), cheap pubby food; Tues quiz; tables out in front, handy for SS *Great Britain (Chris Evans, Tony and Wendy Hobden, Simon Lewis)*

Portcullis BS8 4LE [Wellington Terrace]: Compact two-storey pub in Georgian building with spectacular views, well kept local Cheddar Potholer and Matthews Brassknocker and several changing guest beers, farm ciders, fine range of wines by the glass and spirits, friendly service, basic cheap bar food (not Mon) inc well filled rolls; flame-effect gas fire, dark wood and usual pubby furniture, jack russell called Daisy, cards, Thurs quiz night; wheelchair access with difficulty and help *(Chris and Angela Buckell, Donna and Roger)*

Rose of Denmark BS8 4QL [Dowry Pl]: Friendly pubby atmosphere and genuine welcome, good value home-made food inc all-day breakfast from 7.30am, well kept ales tapped from the cask, open fires, restaurant *(Matthew Mahiri, John and Gloria Isaacs)*

☆ **Royal Oak** BS8 4JG [The Mall, Clifton]: Simple traditional open-plan pub with well kept ales such as Butcombe, Fullers London Pride and Sharps Doom Bar, real ciders and perry, short choice of bargain lunchtime food from soup and sandwiches to roasts, friendly welcoming service; beams and bare boards, stripped stone and painted brick walls, Aga in front bar, open fire and settles in upper back part, rugby memorabilia, newspapers, darts; quiet piped music and occasionally live, TV; tricky wheelchair access, smokers' area out at back, cl Sun evening otherwise open all day *(Georgina Chambers, Ian Phillips, Chris and Angela Buckell, Jeremy King, Georgina Wolfe, B and K Hypher)*

Royal Oak BS7 8TN [Gloucester Rd]: Red-brick corner pub reopened after major refit (was the John Cabot), light airy bar, flagstones or bare boards, modern prints on pale cream walls, blue-green woodwork, comfortable lounge area with sofas, armchairs and woodburner; cheerful helpful staff, Butcombe, Sharps Doom Bar and Timothy Taylors Landlord, Thatcher's cider, decent wine list, home-made food (not Sun evening) from shortish menu, broad mix of customers; piped music; children welcome, wheelchair accessible (not to raised dining area), compact garden with terrace, play area and fenced kitchen garden, open all day *(Chris and Angela Buckell)*

Seven Stars BS1 6JG [Thomas Lane]: Unpretentious one-room real ale pub nr harbour (and associated with Thomas Clarkson and slave trade abolition), much enjoyed by students and local office workers, up to eight ales inc Absolution brewed for them by Sharps, occasional farm cider and perry festivals, interesting malts and bourbons, dark wood, bare boards, old local prints and photographs, can bring in take-aways; juke box, pool, games machines; disabled access, but narrow alley with uneven cobbles and cast-iron kerbs *(Chris and Angela Buckell)*

Three Tuns BS1 5UR [St Georges Rd]: Reopened and tidied up under new owners, extended bar area with mix of pubby furniture on bare boards, a couple of armchairs in alcoves, well kept Timothy Taylors Landlord and several regularly changing guests, Thatcher's cider, lunchtime rolls, cheerful chatty staff; very busy wknds when live music; nr cathedral *(Chris and Angela Buckell)*

Wellington BS7 8UR [Gloucester Rd, Horfield (A38)]: Lively and roomy 1920s pub refitted in traditional style by Bath Ales, their beers and guests kept well by friendly knowledgeable staff, good choice of bottled beers, eclectic wine list, enjoyable fresh traditional food inc generous Sun roasts; large horseshoe bar, sofas and low tables in extended lounge with dining area overlooking sunny terrace; very busy on home match days for Bristol RFC or Rovers; children welcome, dogs outside only, disabled facilities, refurbished bedrooms, open all day (Chris and Angela Buckell)

Zero Degrees BS1 5BA [Colston St]: Converted Victorian tramshed, its austere stone exterior giving way to big contemporary industrial-style bar popular with young people, lots of chrome and modern art; own low-priced beers brewed behind glass walls, up-to-date food from open kitchen inc wood-fired pizzas and mussel dishes, cheerful helpful staff, upper gallery; loud piped music; good disabled facilities, rooftop Bristol views from terrace tables, open all day (Chris and Angela Buckell)

BUCKLAND DINHAM [ST7551]

☆ **Bell** BA11 2QT [High St (A362 Frome—Radstock)]: 16th-c pub with friendly helpful licensees, great atmosphere and interesting décor in narrow beamed main bar, pine furnishings inc booth settles, woodburner in huge inglenook; enjoyable food inc local speciality sausages and pies, Butcombe, Fullers London Pride, Wychwood Hobgoblin and guests, three farm ciders, quite a few malt whiskies, two-level dining room (a remote control helicopter directs you to your table), antiques for sale; cribbage and dominoes, beer/cider festivals; piped and some live music, cinema in attached barn; children and dogs welcome, pet weddings, walled garden with side terraces, campsite, cl Mon, Tues lunchtimes (LYM, Alan Bulley)

BURROW BRIDGE [ST3530]

King Alfred TA7 0RB: Proper old-fashioned friendly local, enjoyable unpretentious fresh food (all meat from Somerset) inc popular Sun lunch, reasonable prices, pleasant efficient service, four well kept ales and local cider; games, some live music (Alison Clewes, Bob and Margaret Holder, Jim Winkworth, J S Hurst)

CHARLTON ADAM [ST5328]

Fox & Hounds TA11 7AU [Broadway Rd, just off A37, about 3 miles N of Ilchester]: Big friendly and neatly refurbished pub with prompt pleasant service, enjoyable home-made food, well kept beers (David and Stella Martin)

CHEDDAR [ST4553]

Gardeners Arms BS27 3LE [Silver St]: Tucked away in the old part and originally four farmworkers' cottages, relaxed and cheerful, with generous food from pubby things up, well kept Sharps Doom Bar and a guest such as Butcombe, Thatcher's cider; attractive two-room beamed dining area, interesting old local photographs, woodburner; no credit cards; well behaved children and dogs welcome (menus for both), playthings in quiet back garden, parking for motorcaravans, open all day wknds (K Botten, S Longman, John Marsh, Nick Miskell, LYM)

CHEW MAGNA [ST5763]

☆ **Bear & Swan** BS40 8SL [B3130 (South Parade)]: Open-plan Fullers pub with their ales and a guest, good choice of wines, good food inc nice puddings, mix of pine tables, pews and big log fire, L-shaped dining room with stripped stone, bare boards and woodburner; TV, small car park (street parking not easy); children and dogs welcome, old-fashioned bedrooms – make your own breakfast (Chris and Angela Buckell, Comus and Sarah Elliott, Andrea Rampley, LYM, D R Grossmark, Dr and Mrs A K Clarke, Steve and Liz Tilley)

Pelican BS40 8SL [S Parade]: Recently refurbished village pub, pastel grey/green shades, wood flooring, candles on chunky tables, leather sofas by log fire, Butcombe and Teignworthy ales, enjoyable food from daily changing menu, friendly staff; dogs welcome, courtyard tables (Ros Ham)

CHILCOMPTON [ST6451]

Somerset Wagon BA3 4JW [B3139; Broadway]: Cosy and friendly with well kept Wadworths ales, enjoyable reasonably priced food inc speciality ribs, pleasant olde-worlde areas off central bar, lots of settles, newspapers, log fire; small front garden (Ian Phillips)

CLEVEDON [ST4071]

☆ **Old Inn** BS21 6AE [Walton Rd (B3124 on outskirts)]: Friendly mix of regulars and visitors in neatly extended beamed pub, good solid furniture on carpets, good value generous pubby food all day from baguettes up, well kept changing ales such as Cotswold Spring, Cottage and Otter, half a dozen wines by the glass; piped music, silent TV; children welcome, bedrooms (Tom Evans, Chris and Angela Buckell, Robin and Tricia Walker)

CLUTTON HILL [ST6360]

Hunters Rest BS39 5QL [off A39 Bristol—Wells]: Extended rambling 18th-c pub with mix of stone and plaster walls, black beams and joists, Butcombe, Matthews, Otter and a guest beer, farm ciders, wide choice of enjoyable bar food from interestingly filled home-baked rolls and pastries (oggies) to hearty home cooking; family room, log fires, restaurant, no piped music; disabled facilities, big garden with play area and view to Mendips, five bedrooms (Chris and Jeanne Downing)

COMBE FLOREY [ST1531]

☆ **Farmers Arms** TA4 3HZ [off A358 Taunton—Williton, just N of main village turn-off]: Neatly kept thatched and beamed dining pub, popular and can get packed lunchtime, welcoming polite staff, wide choice of good reasonably priced food using prime local produce, well kept ales such as Cotleigh and Exmoor, local farm cider, comfortable drinking area with log fire; children welcome, plenty of tables in attractive garden, by summer steam line (Bob and Margaret Holder, Christine and Neil Townend, W N Murphy, BB)

COMBE HAY [ST7359]
☆ *Wheatsheaf* BA2 7EG [off A367 or B3110 S of Bath]: Good upscale food from short changing menu (not cheap), lunchtime set meals, Butcombe beers, local farm cider, good if pricey wine choice, quick friendly service; plush fireside sofas, big fresh and airy dining area with trendy light modern furnishings (a radical change for this 1576 pub); tables in attractive terraced garden overlooking church and steep valley, dovecotes built into the walls, plenty of good nearby walks, comfortable bedrooms in outbuildings, cl Mon (*LYM, Dr and Mrs A K Clarke, Mr and Mrs A H Young, Ian Phillips*)

COMPTON MARTIN [ST5457]
Ring o' Bells BS40 6JE [A368 Bath—Weston]: Popular country pub in attractive spot, traditional front part with rugs on flagstones, inglenook seats by log fire, up step to spacious carpeted back part, stripped stone, Butcombe ales and guests, reasonably priced wine, tasty pub food with some south african influences (licensees are from there); cheerful helpful young staff, newspapers; well behaved children and dogs welcome, charming big garden with play area, open all day wknds (*LYM, George and Gill Rowley, Bob and Angela Brooks, C and R Bromage, Stuart Paulley, Chris and Angela Buckell, James Morrell*)

CONGRESBURY [ST4563]
☆ *White Hart* BS49 5AR [Wrington Rd, off A370 Bristol—Weston]: Clean and comfortable country pub, L-shaped main bar, heavy black beams in bowed ceiling, big stone inglenooks each end, country kitchen furniture, two areas off, big conservatory; well kept Badger beers, specialist gins, short choice of enjoyable pub food, friendly service, music; picnic-sets on back terrace and in big garden, nice walks (*LYM, Tom Evans, Richard Fendick, Bob and Margaret Holder, Hugh Roberts, Bob and Angela Brooks*)

COSSINGTON [ST3640]
Red Tile TA7 8LN [Middle Rd]: Attractive pub with enjoyable food, good service, changing ales such as Butcombe, Cheddar and Sharps, cosy fire; children and dogs welcome, garden tables under walnut tree, adventure play area (*J B Taylor*)

COTFORD ST LUKE []
Chapel TA4 1HX [Graham Way]: Century-old chapel converted to bar and restaurant, mosaic tiled floors, oak panelling, reclaimed staircase to galleried area, impressive wood-vaulted ceiling; good beer and wine choice, enjoyable generous food; open all day Sun (*Scott Brown, Geoff May*)

CREWKERNE [ST4409]
Oscars TA18 7LE [Market Sq]: Friendly low-beamed pub/wine bar, changing ales such as Cotleigh Harrier, real cider, carvings on beams, embossed wallpaper; some outside seating at back (*Dave Braisted*)

CROWCOMBE [ST1336]
☆ *Carew Arms* TA4 4AD [just off A358 Taunton—Minehead]: Interesting well worn-in 17th-c beamed inn, hunting trophies and inglenook woodburner in small old-fashioned front bar, well kept Exe Valley, Exmoor and Otter ales, farm cider, pubby food inc Fri takeaway fish and chips and Sun roast, friendly efficient service; traditional games and skittle alley, dining room allowing children; dogs welcome, informal garden with good playthings, six bedrooms, open all day summer wknds (*LYM, the Didler, Ewan and Moira McCall, Jane and Alan Bush*)

DINNINGTON [ST4013]
Dinnington Docks TA17 8SX [aka Rose & Crown; Fosse Way]: Good cheery atmosphere in large old-fashioned country local, unspoilt and unfussy, with good choice of inexpensive genuine home cooking, Butcombe and guest ales, Burrow Hill farm cider, log fire, friendly attentive staff; memorabilia to bolster the myth that there was once a railway line and dock here, sofas in family room, skittle alley; large garden behind (*Roger Hardisty, Dr and Mrs M E Wilson, Maurice Ricketts*)

DULVERTON [SS9127]
Bridge Inn TA22 9HJ [Bridge St]: Unpretentious local with Lorna Doone connections, enjoyable home-made food from local suppliers, three well kept ales inc Exmoor and Otter, Addlestone's cider, decent wine choice and 30 malt whiskies, log fire; folk night 3rd Sat of month; children welcome and dogs (resident one called Molly), riverside terrace, open all day Fri-Sun, cl Mon evening (*JJW, CMW, Peter Dearing*)
Lion TA22 9BU [Bank Sq]: Old-fashioned two-bar country-town hotel, big log fire, cheerful staff, Exmoor real ale, decent wines and coffee, sensibly priced pub food; dogs welcome and children away from main serving bar, 14 bedrooms, pleasant setting (*George Atkinson, Roger and Ann King*)

DUNDRY [ST5566]
Dundry Inn BS41 8LH [Church Rd off A38 SW of Bristol]: Comfortable roomy village pub with outstanding views over Bristol, good value usual food inc Sun carvery, friendly staff, well kept Butcombe, pictures for sale; garden bar, bedrooms, handy for airport (*M G Hart*)

DUNSTER [SS9943]
☆ *Luttrell Arms* TA24 6SG [High St; A396]: Small hotel in 15th-c timber-framed abbey building, well used high-beamed back bar hung with bottles, clogs and horseshoes, stag's head and rifles on walls above old settles and more modern furniture, big log fires; enjoyable bar food inc substantial sandwiches with home-baked bread, small helpings available, friendly attentive staff, well kept ales inc Exmoor, good wines in three glass sizes; dogs welcome in bar; ancient glazed partition dividing off small galleried and flagstoned courtyard, upstairs

access to quiet attractive garden with Civil War cannon emplacements and great views, comfortable if pricey bedrooms (may have to stay two nights wknds) *(BB, Dr and Mrs A K Clarke, Kay Wheat)*

☆ **Stags Head** TA24 6SN [West St (A396)]: Friendly helpful staff and lively atmosphere in unassuming 15th-c roadside inn, good value food, Exmoor and a guest such as O'Hanlons Yellow Hammer, candles, beams, timbers and inglenook log fire; steps up to small back dining room; games chest; dogs welcome, comfortable simple bedrooms, good breakfast *(Pam and John Smith, S P Watkin, P A Taylor, BB)*

EAST HARPTREE [ST5655]

Waldegrave Arms BS40 6BD [Church Lane]: Welcoming stone-floored 17th-c pub keeping local feel although largely set out for chef/landlord's good food (cheaper lunchtime menu), cheerful young staff, Bath and Box Steam ales; log fires in small beamed bar and larger dining area, eclectic mix of furniture and plenty of things to look at; children and dogs welcome, picnic-sets in attractive sheltered garden, delightful village, open all day Mon *(John and Gloria Isaacs, Jane and Alan Bush, Warren Marsh, C and R Bromage, Catherine Dyer)*

EAST LAMBROOK [ST4218]

☆ *Rose & Crown* TA13 5HF: Neatly kept stone-built dining pub spreading extensively from compact 17th-c core with inglenook log fire, efficient friendly staff and relaxed atmosphere, good generous inexpensive food freshly made using local supplies inc very popular wkdy OAP lunches, full Palmers range kept well, farm cider, decent wines by the glass; restaurant extension with old glass-covered well; picnic-sets on neat lawn, opp East Lambrook Manor Garden *(JDM, KM, BB, Guy Consterdine, Colin and Janet Roe, Cliff Sparkes, Mr and Mrs B Cox)*

ENMORE [ST2434]

Tynte Arms TA5 2DP: Open-plan low-beamed pub with wide choice of good generous food inc lots of fish, home-made puddings and good value set menus, friendly service, west country ales from long bar; plenty of dining tables, chesterfields and settles, end inglenook, china collection; no dogs; car park over road, good walking country *(Bob and Margaret Holder)*

EVERCREECH [ST6538]

Bell BA4 6HY [Bruton Rd (B3081)]: Stone-built pub with enjoyable home-made food and well kept ales inc Butcombe, clean high-ceilinged linked rooms, open fires, skittle alley; disabled facilities, courtyard and open-view garden, quiet village handy for Bath & West Showground, three bedrooms *(Abigail Carlton)*

EXEBRIDGE [SS9324]

Anchor TA22 9AZ [B3222 S of Dulverton; pub itself actually over the river, in Devon]: Comfortable child-friendly pub in idyllic Exmoor-edge spot, some attractive furnishings, oak panelling and pictures,

adventurous good value food, good friendly service, well kept Greene King ales, local farm cider, above-average wines; woodburner, family eating area and restaurant; smaller back games bar, skittle alley; dogs welcome, nice big riverside garden with plenty of tables and play area, fishing rights, opp Exe Valley trout smokery, six comfortable bedrooms, good breakfast, open all day at least in summer *(David and Julie Glover, LYM)*

FAILAND [ST5171]

Failand Inn BS8 3TU [B3128 Bristol—Clevedon]: Refurbished welcoming old coaching inn with wide choice of popular family food, Butcombe and Courage, good wines by the glass, comfortable dining extension; piped music; children and dogs welcome, garden with decking and heated smokers' shelter, open all day *(Tom Evans)*

FIVEHEAD [ST3522]

Crown TA3 6PQ [nr church]: Interesting 16th-c village pub, traditional décor in two small rooms, one with woodburner, attentive friendly landlord, good choice of reasonably priced food, small helpings for children and others, local real ales; dogs welcome *(J V Dadswell)*

FRESHFORD [ST7960]

Inn at Freshford BA2 7WG [off A36 or B3108]: Refit and new management for roomy, beamed, stone-built dining pub tied to Box Steam, their ales and guests kept well, real ciders, decent wines by the glass, good choice of malts, food from lunchtime sandwiches up, more evening choice, helpful attentive service; wheelchair access from car park, pretty hillside garden, attractive spot nr river *(Chris and Angela Buckell, LYM)*

FROME [ST7748]

George BA11 1AF [Market Pl]: Large welcoming Georgian coaching, Wadworths ales, fairly priced pubby food, newspapers *(Ian Phillips)*

GLASTONBURY [ST5039]

☆ *Who'd A Thought It* BA6 9JJ [Northload St]: High-backed curved settle, coal fire, pine panelling, stripped brick, beams and flagstones, nicely quirky oddments, well kept Palmers ales, good choice of wines by the glass, good value food from toasties to good steaks, daily papers; children and dogs welcome, pleasant garden, comfortable bedrooms, open all day *(LYM, Joe Green, Anthony and Vivienne Irons, Bob and Angela Brooks)*

HALLATROW [ST6357]

☆ *Old Station* BS39 6EN [A39 S of Bristol]: Good food and well kept ales such as Bass and Butcombe in idiosyncratic bar packed with cluttered railway, musical and other bric-a-brac, also italian evening dishes in Flying Scotsman railcar restaurant (can look in during daytime); piped music; children in eating areas, garden with well equipped play area, five bedrooms (may not serve breakfast) *(Stuart Paulley, Ken Marshall, John and Fiona McIlwain, LYM)*

HARDWAY [ST7234]
☆ *Bull* BA10 0LN [off B3081 Bruton—
Wincanton at brown sign for Stourhead and
King Alfred's Tower; Hardway]: Charming
beamed 17th-c country dining pub popular
locally, especially with older people wkdy
lunchtimes, good food (not Sun evening) in
comfortable bar and characterful dining
rooms, good informal service, well kept
Butcombe and Otter, farm cider, nice wines
by the glass, log fire; unobtrusive piped
music; tables and barbecues in garden
behind, more in large garden over road,
bedrooms *(Colin and Janet Roe, SRD)*

HOLCOMBE [ST6649]
☆ *Holcombe Inn* BA3 5EB [off A367; Stratton
Rd]: Extensively modernised quietly placed
country pub, good food, Otter and a guest
ale, local cider, several wines by the glass;
pleasant layout with several linked areas inc
pubby tables on flagstones, sofas, easy
chairs, panelling and carpet elsewhere,
woodburners, good-sized dining area; piped
music; children, dogs and walkers welcome,
picnic-sets outside, peaceful farmland views,
bedrooms, cl Sun evening *(LYM, S G N Bennett,
Terry Buckland, Ian Phillips)*

HOLFORD [ST1541]
Plough TA5 1RY [A39]: Friendly unassuming
beamed village pub, Butcombe, Otter and
Palmers, decent wines by the glass, good
value food from doorstep sandwiches up, log
fire in snug; no dogs inside; attractive
garden, wonderful Quantocks walks
(Peter Wiser)

HUNTWORTH [ST3134]
Boat & Anchor TA7 0AQ [just off M5
junction 24, signed off exit roundabout,
then turn right towards narrow swing
bridge]: Nicely situated with roomy eating
areas inc conservatory (not always open),
pub food from baguettes to steaks, Sun
carvery, young friendly staff, well kept
Butcombe and Otter, nice house wines;
inscrutable parrot called Drew; children
welcome, lovely garden by Bridgwater &
Taunton Canal, eight bedrooms *(Bob and
Margaret Holder, Richard Fendick)*

ILCHESTER [ST5222]
Ilchester Arms BA22 8LN [Church St]:
Friendly hotel with three well kept real ales
in small peaceful pine-panelled bar on right,
restaurant on two levels with wide choice of
good reasonably priced mediterranean-
leaning food inc light lunches, efficient
smiling service; comfortable bedrooms
*(Bob and Margaret Holder, Tim and
Rosemary Wells, Ian Malone)*

KELSTON [ST7067]
Old Crown BA1 9AQ [Bitton Rd; A431 W of
Bath]: Four small traditional rooms with
beams and polished flagstones, carved
settles and cask tables, logs burning in
ancient open range, two more coal-effect
fires, Bath, Butcombe, Fullers and Wadworths
(some cask-tapped), Thatcher's cider, good
choice of wines by the glass and whiskies,
friendly helpful staff; enjoyable food from

new chef in bar (not Sun or Mon evenings)
and small restaurant (not Sun); dogs
welcome on leads, children in eating areas,
wheelchair-accessible with help, picnic-sets
under apple trees in sunny sheltered back
garden, bedrooms in converted outbuildings,
open all day wknds *(LYM, Chris and
Angela Buckell, Dr and Mrs A K Clarke,
Ian and Rose Lock)*

KEYNSHAM [ST6568]
Brassmills BS31 2UG [Avon Mill Lane]:
Large, comfortable and popular Vintage Inn
in former brass foundry, wide food range,
well kept changing ales, plenty of wines by
the glass, relaxed atmosphere, open fire;
pleasant terrace and garden overlooking
River Chew, open all day *(Jim and
Frances Gowers, Dr and Mrs A K Clarke)*

KILVE [ST1442]
☆ *Hood Arms* TA5 1EA [A39 E of Williton]:
Welcoming neatly kept beamed 18th-c
country pub, good food from bar snacks up
inc popular Sun lunch, well kept Otter,
Palmers and guest ales, smart staff; cosy
plush lounge, warm woodburner in bar,
restaurant, skittle alley; children and dogs
welcome, nice back garden with tables on
sheltered terrace, play area, 12 bedrooms –
two in back lodge *(Bob and Margaret Holder,
John and Helen Rushton, LYM)*

KINGSTON ST MARY [ST2229]
Swan TA2 8HW: Cosy 17th-c roadside pub
reopened under new tenants, clean and tidy,
with long knocked-through bar, new
furniture on carpets, flowers on tables,
reasonably priced home-made food (not Sun
evening), well kept Exmoor, Fullers London
Pride, Sharps Doom Bar and Wadworths 6X,
traditional cider, good choice of wines, big
log fire; children and dogs welcome, disabled
access, garden with play area, *(Chris and
Angela Buckell)*

LANSDOWN [ST7268]
Blathwayt Arms BA1 9BT: Interesting old
hilltop building with enjoyable food inc
some unusual dishes and good Sun roast,
well kept ales, decent wines, good service;
children welcome, racecourse view from
garden, open all day *(Dr and Mrs A K Clarke,
Meg and Colin Hamilton)*

LITTON [ST5954]
☆ *Kings Arms* BA3 4PW [B3114, NW of
Chewton Mendip]: Attractive, partly 15th-c,
character pub reopened after fresh up-to-
date refurbishment, good food from
ciabattas to home-made pizzas and pub
staples up, Sun carvery, well kept Greene
King ales and a guest, wide choice of wines
by the glass inc champagne, good service;
children welcome, picnic-sets on sloping
lawn, open all day *(LYM, Gordon Stevenson,
John Roobottom)*

LOWER LANGFORD [ST4660]
Langford Inn BS40 5BL [off B3133/A38]:
Roomy beamed family dining pub, popular
good value food all day, Sun roasts, well
kept ales inc Butcombe, decent wines,
cheerful service; piped music, Thurs quiz

night; picnic-sets in courtyard and side garden, seven barn-conversion bedrooms *(Hugh Roberts, Bob and Margaret Holder)*

MARK [ST3747]

Pack Horse TA9 4NF [B3139 Wedmore—Highbridge; Church St]: Attractive 16th-c village pub run by welcoming greek cypriot family, very popular wknds for its wide food choice inc good Sun roast, fresh Brixham fish and delicious puddings; Butcombe and Fullers London Pride, good friendly service; next to church *(MP)*

MELLS [ST7249]

☆ *Talbot* BA11 3PN [W of Frome, off A362 or A361]: Interesting old inn, austere public bar in carefully restored tithe barn, farm tools on stone walls, big mural behind counter, attractive dining room in main building, sporting and riding pictures, solid dining tables and chairs; Butcombe tapped from cask, helpful pleasant staff, darts; piped music, TV; children and dogs welcome, nice cobbled courtyard, comfortable bedrooms *(Roger Wain-Heapy, Dr and Mrs M E Wilson, Meg and Colin Hamilton, LYM)*

MERRIOTT [ST4412]

Kings Head TA16 5PR [Church St]: Old village pub under new ownership, interesting good value food, three real ales, inglenook log fire, skittle alley, live music wknds; garden, bedrooms *(Bob and Margaret Holder)*

MIDFORD [ST7660]

☆ *Hope & Anchor* BA2 7DD [Bath Rd (B3110)]: Open-plan roadside pub, wide choice of good generous home-made food from traditional to more imaginative dishes, civilised bar, heavy-beamed and flagstoned restaurant end, and new back conservatory; six well kept changing ales such as Butcombe, Hidden and Wadworths, good house wines, proper coffee, relaxed atmosphere, log fire; children welcome, tables on sheltered back terrace with upper tier beyond, pleasant walks on disused Somerset & Dorset rail track, open all day *(M G Hart, Roger Wain-Heapy, John and Gloria Isaacs, Geoffrey Kemp, Dr and Mrs M E Wilson, Ian and Helen Stafford, BB)*

MIDSOMER NORTON [ST6654]

White Hart BA3 2HQ [The Island]: Well worn chatty Victorian local with several rooms, Bass, Butcombe and a guest tapped from the cask, two farm ciders, local coal-mining memorabilia, bargain simple lunchtime food, cheerful helpful staff; no credit cards; dogs welcome, open all day *(the Didler)*

MILBORNE PORT [ST6718]

Queens Head DT9 5DQ [A30 E of Sherborne]: Enjoyable generous low-priced food inc plenty of sandwiches, well kept Butcombe, good wines by the glass, good coffee, quick friendly service; neat beamed lounge, restaurant and conservatory, games in public bar, skittle alley; provision for children and quiet dogs, reasonable disabled access, tables in sheltered courtyard and garden with play area, three cosy good value bedrooms *(LYM, Ron and Sheila Corbett, Dennis Jenkin)*

MILVERTON [ST1225]

Globe TA4 1JX [Fore St]: Smartly reworked pub/restaurant, good food from interesting lunchtime baguettes/ciabattas up, well kept Exmoor ale, friendly polite staff *(Bob and Margaret Holder, Giles and Annie Francis)*

MINEHEAD [SS9646]

Queens Head TA24 5NR [Holloway St]: Attractive bay-windowed stone building, mainly open-plan, up to eight well kept ales inc Exmoor from central bar, alcove seating, raised family dining area on left, pleasant décor with old local photographs, enjoyable usual food, good friendly service; back pool room; may be piped music, nearby parking difficult; disabled access *(Chris and Angela Buckell)*

MONKSILVER [ST0737]

Notley Arms TA4 4JB [B3188]: Sadly closed at beginning of 2010; has been friendly village pub on edge of Exmoor National Park with beamed and L-shaped bar, country furnishings, paintings on ochre walls, woodburners, tack room with appropriate décor, real ales, several ciders; neat garden with swift clear stream at bottom *(LYM)*

MONTACUTE [ST4916]

Phelips Arms TA15 6XB [The Borough; off A3088 W of Yeovil]: Welcoming obliging licensees in airy open-plan bar, well kept Palmers, good choice of wines by the glass, farm cider, nice fireplace and old-fashioned décor, restaurant; children welcome, skittle alley, attractive walled garden behind, pretty square next to Montacute House, bedrooms *(Tom and Rosemary Hall, BB)*

MOORLINCH [ST3936]

Ring o' Bells TA7 9BT [signed off A39]: Fine old building, carpeted throughout, with black beams, stone and rough plaster walls, modern furniture, grandfather clock, woodburners and open fires; same chef/landlord doing good value hearty food inc good Sun roasts, well kept Flowers and changing guests, local ciders, helpful staff; sports TV in public bar, pool, skittle alley; children welcome, wheelchair access from back *(Joe Green, Chris and Angela Buckell)*

MUDFORD [ST5719]

Half Moon BA21 5TF [A359 N of Yeovil]: Restored, characterful, roadside pub with wide choice of enjoyable generous food all day, well kept changing ales tapped from the cask such as RCH Pitchfork, Weston's cider, welcoming service; linked rooms, some with original lathe and plaster walls, beams and flagstones, lots of farming and nautical bric-a-brac, big fireplace; no dogs; children welcome, disabled access and parking, tables in courtyard, six annexe bedrooms, open all day *(Col and Mrs Patrick Kaye)*

NAILSEA [ST4469]

Blue Flame BS48 4DE [West End]: Small well worn 19th-c farmers' local, two rooms with mixed furnishings, well kept Fullers London Pride, RCH and guests from casks behind bar, Thatcher's cider, fresh rolls, coal fire, pub games; plain-speaking landlord, outside lavatories inc roofless gents', limited parking (may be filled with Land Rovers and tractors); children's room, sizeable informal garden, open all day summer *(the Didler)*

Moorend Spout BS48 4BB [Union St]: Low-priced straightforward food (not Sun evening) inc mid-week two-course bargains in neatly kept early 18th-c beamed local, friendly helpful family service, well kept Butcombe and Greene King; may be piped music; terrace and sheltered lawn *(Steve and Claire Harvey)*

Ring O'Bells BS48 4NQ [St Marys Grove]: Well kept Bass, Courage and a guest ale, real ciders, bar food inc good lunchtime sandwiches; folk nights, skittle alley, sports TV; children and dogs welcome, garden with floodlit boules pitch and play area, open all day *(Steve and Liz Tilley)*

NETHER STOWEY [ST1939]

Rose & Crown TA5 1LJ [St Mary St]: Friendly former 16th-c coaching inn, good value straightforward home-made food, three well kept ales (maybe Nether Underestimate A Blonde from nearby Stowey Brewery), Thatcher's farm cider, decent wine; interesting old local photographs and memorabilia, open fire, back bar with pool, darts and TV, restaurant; games machine; dogs and children welcome, tables in walled garden with play area, bedrooms, open all day *(Stephen Colling)*

NORTH BREWHAM [ST7236]

☆ *Old Red Lion* BA10 0JL [off A359 Frome—Bruton]: Flagstoned low-beamed former farmhouse with good blackboard food, ales such as Butcombe, Fullers and Greene King, log fire, friendly efficient service, spacious bar, comfortable dining room; handy for King Alfred's Monument, bedrooms *(Mrs R M Hill)*

NORTH CURRY [ST3125]

☆ *Bird in Hand* TA3 6LT [Queens Sq; off A378 (or A358) E of Taunton]: Friendly village pub, cosy main bar with old pews, settles, benches and yew tables on flagstones, some original beams and timbers, locally woven willow work, cricket memorabilia, inglenook log fire; Otter and two guests, Parson's cider, decent wines by the glass, good bar food inc seasonal game; piped music; children and dogs welcome, open all day Sun *(Richard Benthall, Michelle and Graeme Voss, Bob and Margaret Holder, PLC, Gillian Hunter, LYM)*

NORTH PETHERTON [ST2933]

Swan TA6 6QA [Fore St]: Friendly pub under new management, decent food, well kept Sharps Doom Bar, good service *(Jim and Frances Gowers)*

NORTON FITZWARREN [ST2026]

Cross Keys TA2 6NR [A358 roundabout NW of Taunton]: Comfortably extended and refurbished 19th-c stone-built beamed pub, good value food all day, changing ales such as Cottage, Otter, Timothy Taylors Landlord and Wells & Youngs Bombardier, decent wines by the glass, friendly cheerful staff; stone-tiled bar and carpeted dining area

with some plank panelling, log fire in big hearth, skittle alley; children welcome, riverside garden, open all day *(Ian Phillips, Andrew Bosi)*

NORTON ST PHILIP [ST7755]

☆ *Fleur de Lys* BA2 7LG [High St]: Chatty local in 13th-c thatched stone cottages, friendly landlord and helpful staff, well kept Wadworths beers, sensibly priced wine, good value home-made food from baguettes up; log fire in huge fireplace, steps and pillars giving cosy feel of separate rooms in beamed and flagstoned areas around central servery; children and dogs welcome, skittle alley *(Paul Humphreys, the Didler, Dr and Mrs M E Wilson, R K Phillips, Pam and John Smith, John Coatsworth, BB)*

NORTON SUB HAMDON [ST4715]

Lord Nelson TA14 6SP [off A356 S of Martock]: Popular old corner pub in picturesque village, enthusiastic helpful licensees and staff, decent well priced food, well kept beers, beams, flagstones and log fires, restaurant; live music and quiz nights; some tables outside *(Stephen Colling)*

OAKE [ST1526]

☆ *Royal Oak* TA4 1DS [Hillcommon, N; B3227]: Neat village pub with several separate-seeming areas around central servery, little tiled fireplace and big woodburner, brasses on beams and walls, well kept ales such as Cotleigh, Exe Valley, Exmoor and Sharps, some tapped from the cask, good food and service, long dining areas; skittle alley; piped music; children welcome, pleasant sheltered garden, open all day wknds (food all day then) *(Theo, Anne and Jane Gaskin, LYM, Michelle and Graeme Voss, FJS and DS)*

OAKHILL [ST6347]

Oakhill Inn BA3 5HU [A367 Shepton Mallet—Radstock]: Dining pub with sofas and easy chairs among candlelit tables around bar, friendly atmosphere and welcoming staff, decent if not particularly cheap food inc some interesting choices, ales such as Butcombe, dining extension in former skittle alley, rugs on bare boards, wall of clocks, log fires; nice views from garden, five bedrooms, open all day wknds *(Ian Phillips, Michael Doswell)*

OVER STRATTON [ST4315]

☆ *Royal Oak* TA13 5LQ [off A303 via Ilminster turn at South Petherton roundabout]: Relaxed thatched family dining pub, friendly enthusiastic licensees, well priced enjoyable food, well kept Badger; attractive line of linked rooms, flagstones and thick stone walls, prettily stencilled beams, scrubbed kitchen tables, pews, settles etc, log fires and rustic décor; charity library; tables outside *(LYM, Bob and Margaret Holder, Kate and Ian Hodge)*

PORLOCK [SS8846]

☆ *Ship* TA24 8QD [High St]: Picturesque old family pub, thatch, beams, flagstones and big inglenook log fires, quick friendly staff, enjoyable food from sandwiches up, well kept ales such as Cotleigh, Exmoor and St

Austell, back dining room, small locals' front bar with games; children welcome, attractive split-level sunny garden with decking, play area, nearby nature trail to Dunkery Beacon, five bedrooms, open all day *(JJW, CMW, MLR, LYM)*

PORLOCK WEIR [SS8846]

☆ *Ship* TA24 8QD: Unpretentious thatched bar in wonderful spot by peaceful harbour (so can get packed), long and narrow with dark low beams, flagstones and stripped stone, simple pub furniture, woodburner; four well priced ales inc Cotleigh, Exmoor and Otter, real ciders and a perry, good whisky and soft drinks' choice, friendly prompt staff, bargain simple food from thick sandwiches up; games rooms across small back yard, tearoom; piped music, big-screen TV, little free parking on pay & display opp; children and dogs welcome, sturdy picnic-sets out at front and side, good coast walks, three decent bedrooms *(Mr and Mrs D J Nash, Dr and Mrs M E Wilson, John Saville, Barry and Anne, Peter Dearing, BB)*

PORTBURY [ST4975]

☆ *Priory* BS20 7TN [Station Rd, 0.5 miles from A369 (just S of M5 junction 19)]: Spreading Vintage Inn dining pub/hotel, lots of linked beamed areas, appealing mix of comfortable furnishings in alcoves, log fire, friendly prompt staff, well kept ales such as Butcombe, Leeds Best and Sharps Doom Bar, good range of wines by the glass, interesting fresh fruit juices, wide choice of enjoyable well priced food all day till 10pm inc good fish specials; no under-21s; piped nostalgic music; pleasant front and back garden tables, bedrooms, open all day *(Roger Braithwaite, Steve and Liz Tilley, BB)*

PORTISHEAD [ST4676]

Poacher BS20 6AJ [High St]: Large pub popular for wide range of freshly made low-priced food, up to five well kept ales such as Adnams, Butcombe, Exmoor and Sharps; a proper part for village beer-drinkers, with big fireplace, friendly staff; quiz nights, cl Sun evening *(Tom Evans)*

Royal BS20 7HG [Pier Rd (NE end of town, nr sea)]: 1830s former hotel popular in summer for superb location overlooking Severn estuary and bridges, light and spacious with linked Victorian parlours off tiled entrance, well kept Butcombe, Cheddar Potholer, Exmoor Gold, Sharps Doom Bar and guests, decent wines, enjoyable food inc children's helpings and wider evening choice, friendly staff; piped music; dogs welcome, wheelchair ramp from car park, large terrace, open all day, cl Sun evening *(Chris and Angela Buckell, Tom Evans, Mr and Mrs P R Thomas)*

PRIDDY [ST5450]

☆ *Hunters Lodge* BA5 3AR [from Wells on A39 pass hill with TV mast on left, then next left]: Welcoming and unchanging farmers', walkers' and potholers' pub above Ice Age cavern, in same family for generations; well kept beers such as Blindmans and Cheddar

tapped from casks behind bar, Wilkins's farm cider, simple cheap food, log fires in huge fireplaces, low beams, flagstones and panelling, old lead-mining photographs; perhaps live folk music; no mobiles or credit cards; children and dogs in family room, wheelchair access, garden picnic-sets, bedrooms *(the Didler, Chris and Angela Buckell, MLR, LYM)*

New Inn BA5 3BB [off B3135; The Green]: Low-beamed, stripped-stone, 15th-c pub under welcoming newish owners, well kept Bath, Cheddar and Exmoor ales, six ciders, big helpings of good value home-made food inc all-day breakfast and Sun carvery in bar; lounge and spacious conservatory, modern wood furniture, wall and window seats, log fires, beer and folk festivals; children welcome, wheelchair-accessible with help, tables out facing quiet village green, bedrooms (some ensuite) *(John and Gloria Isaacs, Chris and Angela Buckell, Nigel Cant)*

☆ *Queen Victoria* BA5 3BA [village signed off B3135; Pelting Drove]: Characterful stone-built country local in lovely position, friendly staff and regulars, three good log fires (one open on two sides), well kept Butcombe and guests tapped from casks, local ciders, several wines by the glass, nice coffee, good value pubby food from baguettes up; beams, stripped stone and flagstones, some dark panelling, mixed furniture inc pews, interesting bric-a-brac; some live folk music; well behaved children and dogs welcome, new disabled facilities, garden with play area and car park over road, great walks, open all day Fri-Sun *(M Mossman, Chris and Angela Buckell, Tom Evans, Terry Buckland)*

PURITON [ST3141]

Puriton Inn TA7 8AF [just off M5 junction 23; Puriton Hill]: Character pub well screened from motorway, dark, clean and tidy, with ample straightforward food, well kept Butcombe, Flowers and Wadworths, warmly welcoming service even when busy; pool; good disabled access, front terrace and back garden with play area *(B and F A Hannam)*

RIDGEHILL [ST5363]

Crown BS40 8AY [Crown Hill/Regis Lane; off B3130 2 miles S of Winford]: Deep in the country, large dining pub with several beamed rooms, welcoming attentive service, log fire in delightful old fireplace; lovely valley views from window tables and terrace *(Tom Evans)*

RODE [ST8053]

Bell BA11 6PW [Frome Rd (A361)]: Sister pub to the Castle in Bradford-on-Avon (see Wilts Main Entries); reopened after extensive refurbishment inc many quirky touches, bare boards or flagstones, oak-panelling, log fires, old club portraits on green flock or fish-printed wallpaper, various stuffed animals, mishmash of furniture inc scrub-top painted pine tables, chapel chairs and old rescued leather sofas/armchairs, 1930s standard lamps; six mainly local beers inc Flatcapper brewed for the pub by Three Castles, food all day; big terrace and lawned garden (BOB)

Mill BA11 6AG [NW off Rode Hill]: Popular family pub in beautifully set former watermill, smart restaurant layout and up-to-date décor, good quality food inc early evening deals, good choice of real ales and of wines by the glass, children's room with impressive games; live music Fri (may be loud); garden and decks overlooking River Frome, big play area (Mr and Mrs A Curry)

ROWBERROW [ST4458]

☆ *Swan* BS25 1QL [off A38 S of A368 junction]: Neat and spacious dining pub opp pond, olde-worlde beamery and so forth, good log fires, friendly atmosphere especially in nicely unsophisticated old bar part, wide range of good food (small helpings available), prompt pleasant service; well kept Butcombe ales and a guest like Blindmans Golden Spring, decent choice of wines by the glass, Thatcher's cider, perry; children welcome, good-sized garden over road (LYM, George and Gill Rowley, Tom Evans, Bob and Angela Brooks, John and Fiona McIlwain)

RUISHTON [ST2524]

Blackbrook TA3 5LU [just off M5 junction 25]: Busy refurbished chain dining pub, a useful stop, good choice of food in various roomy areas inc a carvery, OAP deals too, ales such as Fullers London Pride and Sharps Doom Bar, quick friendly service; unobtrusive piped music, sports TV; children welcome, disabled facilities, picnic-sets in good-sized garden (dogs allowed here only), play area, open all day (Richard Fendick, Dr and Mrs A K Clarke)

RUMWELL [ST1923]

Rumwell Inn TA4 1EL [A38 Taunton—Wellington, just past Stonegallows]: Roomy roadside pub with welcoming landlord and friendly staff, comfortable and clean with old beams and cosy corners; well priced enjoyable food from good lunchtime sandwiches up, changing well kept ales, roaring log fire, family room; tables in nice garden, handy for Sheppy's Cider, cl Sun evening (Bob and Margaret Holder, Meg and Colin Hamilton, John Gould, Peter Salmon)

SALTFORD [ST6968]

☆ *Jolly Sailor* BS31 3ER [off A4 Bath—Keynsham; Mead Lane]: Great spot by lock and weir on River Avon, with dozens of picnic-sets, garden heaters and own island between lock and pub; enjoyable generous standard food all day, cheerful efficient service, well kept changing ales such as Butcombe and Sharps Doom Bar, good value wines by the glass, flagstones, low beams, log fires, daily papers, conservatory dining room; piped pop music; children allowed if eating, disabled facilities, open all day (Chris and Angela Buckell, BB)

SHEPTON BEAUCHAMP [ST4017]

Duke of York TA19 0LW: Welcoming well run

free house with good range of generous reasonably priced food inc good specials and fresh fish, well kept ales such as Butcombe, Otter and Teignworthy; skittle alley, darts; garden (Anthony and Vivienne Irons)

SIMONSBATH [SS7739]

☆ *Exmoor Forest Inn* TA24 7SH [B3223/B3358]: Beautifully placed inn under friendly new owners, circular tables by the bar counter, larger area with cushioned settles, upholstered stools and mate's chairs around mix of dark tables, hunting trophies, antlers and horse tack, woodburner; enjoyable local food inc game, ales such as Cotleigh, Dartmoor, Exmoor and a guest, real cider, good choice of wines by the glass and malt whiskies, residents' lounge, airy dining room; children and clean dogs (towels provided) welcome, seats in front garden, fine walks along River Barle, own trout and salmon fishing, ten comfortable bedrooms, open all day in full season (LYM, George Atkinson, Millie and Mick Dunk, Dave Braisted, Melvyn Owen, Steve and Liz Tilley, Sheila Topham, Lynda and Trevor Smith)

SOMERTON [ST4828]

Unicorn TA11 7PR [West St]: Old inn with three interconnecting rooms, one with fine inglenook and bread oven, wide choice of sensibly priced home-made food, several well kept ales, good wine choice, restaurant; courtyard picnic-sets, six bedrooms (Ben Champion, Warren Marsh)

STAPLE FITZPAINE [ST2618]

☆ *Greyhound* TA3 5SP [off A358 or B3170 S of Taunton]: Light rambling country pub with wide range of good food (best to book evenings), changing ales, good wines by the glass, welcoming atmosphere and attentive staff; flagstones, inglenooks, pleasant mix of settles and chairs, log fires throughout, olde-worlde pictures, farm tools and so forth; children and dogs welcome, comfortable bedrooms, good breakfast (A H Latham, Bob and Margaret Holder, LYM, Roy and Jean Russell)

STOGUMBER [ST0937]

White Horse TA4 3TA [off A358 at Crowcombe]: Friendly old village pub with well kept Cotleigh, Greene King and Marstons, enjoyable food from sandwiches to Sun roasts, long neat bar, old village photographs with more recent ones for comparison, good log fires; games room and skittle alley; children welcome, nice quiet back terrace, bedrooms, open all day wknds and summer (LYM, Jennifer Banks)

STOKE ST MARY [ST2622]

Half Moon TA3 5BY [from M5 junction 25 take A358 towards Ilminster, 1st right, right in Henlade]: Much-modernised village pub very popular lunchtime for wide choice of hearty good value food inc daily carvery, pleasant staff but service can be slow, Boddingtons, Butcombe, Fullers London Pride and Greene King Abbot, nice coffee, quite a few malt whiskies; thriving local atmosphere

in several comfortable open-plan areas inc restaurant; children welcome, well tended garden (LYM, Bob and Margaret Holder)
STOKE SUB HAMDON [ST4717]
Prince of Wales TA14 6RW [Ham Hill]: On top of Ham Hill with superb views, changing real ales tapped from the cask, good value enjoyable food, friendly staff; children, dogs and muddy boots welcome, open all day from 8.30am (Dilys Marsland)
TAUNTON [ST2525]
☆ *Hankridge Arms* TA1 2LR [Hankridge Way, Deane Gate (nr Sainsbury); just off M5 junction 25 – A358 towards city, then right at roundabout, right at next roundabout]: Well appointed Badger dining pub based on 16th-c former farm, splendid contrast to the modern shopping complex around it, different-sized linked areas, well kept ales, generous enjoyable food from interesting soups and sandwiches through pubby things to restaurant dishes, quick friendly young staff, decent wines, big log fire; piped music; dogs welcome, plenty of tables in pleasant outside area (Dr and Mrs A K Clarke, John Gould, Andy West)
Plough TA1 1PB [Station Rd]: Small, homely and welcoming with four well kept local ales and eight racked ciders; simple food all day inc unusual pies, bare boards, panelling, candles on tables, cosy nooks, open fire, friendly pub dog (others welcome); open all day till late (Jules Akel, John and Fiona McIlwain, Andrew Bosi)
Vivary Arms TA1 3JR [Wilton St; across Vivary Park from centre]: Pretty low-beamed 18th-c local (Taunton's oldest), good value fresh food in snug plush lounge and small dining room, friendly helpful young staff, relaxed atmosphere; well kept ales inc Butcombe, decent wines, interesting collection of drink-related items; lovely hanging baskets and flowers (Bob and Margaret Holder, Robert W Buckle, John Gould)
THURLOXTON [ST2729]
Maypole TA2 8RF [A38 Taunton—Bridgwater, between M5 junctions 24 and 25]: Spacious but cosy beamed pub with several traditional areas, welcoming staff, wide choice of tasty home-made food inc good Sun carvery, real ales, log fire; may be piped music, skittle alley; enclosed garden with play area, peaceful village (Heather Coulson, Neil Cross)
TIMBERSCOMBE [SS9542]
Lion TA24 7TP [Church St]: Refurbished Exmoor-edge former coaching inn dating from 15th c; thriving village-pub atmosphere in comfortable flagstoned main bar with rooms off, enjoyable pub food from good fresh ciabattas up, friendly service, well kept Exmoor tapped from the cask, nice wine, good log fire; dogs welcome, bedrooms (Dennis Jenkin)
TIMSBURY [ST6758]
Seven Stars BA2 0JJ [North Rd]: Bright and cheerful stone-built village pub popular for its good value well cooked food, Butcombe

and other local ales in good condition, several small eating areas off locals' bar; good wheelchair facilities, garden with adventure playground (LYM, Dean Brownhill)
TINTINHULL [ST5019]
Crown & Victoria BA22 8PZ [Farm St, village signed off A303]: Roomy, light and airy main bar, good fire, attractive choice of enjoyable fairly priced food cooked to order, Sun roasts, well kept Butcombe and Wadworths, good choice of wines, good friendly service, pleasant conservatory; disabled facilities, big garden with play area, bedrooms, handy for Tintinhull House (NT) (David and Sue Smith, Andy Flowers, LYM)
TRUDOXHILL [ST7443]
☆ *White Hart* BA11 5DP [off A361 SW of Frome]: Enjoyable home-made food inc good individual pies, real ales such as St Austell Tribute, Sharps Doom Bar and a locally brewed house beer, beams and stripped stone, two log fires; children welcome, picnic-sets in sheltered side garden, barbecues, nice village, open all day wknds (Hugh Roberts, LYM)
UPTON [ST0129]
☆ *Lowtrow Cross Inn* TA4 2DB: Well run by cheery landlord and staff, good fresh home-made food, nice relaxed mix of locals and diners; characterful low-beamed bar with log fire, bare boards and flagstones, two carpeted country-kitchen dining areas, one with enormous inglenook, plenty of atmosphere, well kept ales such as Cotleigh Tawny and Exmoor Fox; no dogs; children welcome, attractive surroundings, bedrooms (BB, Mrs Joyce Ansell, Richard, Anne and Kate Ansell)
VOBSTER [ST7049]
☆ *Vobster Inn* BA3 5RJ [Lower Vobster]: Roomy old stone-built dining pub, good reasonably priced food from spanish chef/landlord inc good local cheese plate, some spanish dishes and fresh fish daily from Cornwall, good service, Butcombe and a Blindmans seasonal ale, good wines by the glass; three comfortable open-plan areas with antique furniture inc plenty of room for just a drink; dogs allowed in bar, side lawn with colourful bantams, peaceful views, boules, adventure playground behind, bedrooms (Sue Cane, Bob and Angela Brooks, BB, Edward Mirzoeff, Sylvia and Tony Birbeck)
WANSTROW [ST7141]
☆ *Pub* BA4 4SZ [Station Rd (A359 Nunney—Bruton)]: Proper old-fashioned local, attractive, individual and civilised, with friendly owners, bargain genuine home cooking by landlady, five or six well kept changing ales inc local Blindmans, interesting wines by the glass, comfortable traditional furniture on flagstones, settles snugged around log fire, case of interesting books in dining room, games room, skittle alley; outside lavatories; tables in charming little floral courtyard, cl Mon lunchtime (Mick White, BB)

618 • SOMERSET

WELLOW [ST7358]
☆ **Fox & Badger** BA2 8QG [signed off A367
SW of Bath]: Opened-up village pub,
flagstones one end, bare boards the other,
some snug corners, woodburner in massive
hearth, decent choice of ales and local
Thatcher's cider, wide range of enjoyable bar
food from doorstep sandwiches up; children
and dogs welcome, picnic-sets in covered
courtyard, open all day Fri-Sun (Dr and
Mrs M E Wilson, LYM, S G N Bennett,
Maureen Wood, Paul Humphreys)

WELLS [ST5445]
Crown BA5 2RF [Market Pl]: Former 15th-c
coaching inn overlooked by cathedral,
various bustling areas with light wood
flooring, plenty of matching chairs and
cushioned wall benches, Butcombe and
Sharps Doom Bar, food in bar and bistro;
piped music, TV and games machine; no
dogs; children until 8pm, small heated
courtyard, 15 bedrooms, open all day
(Steve and Liz Tilley, LYM, Dave Braisted,
Anthony Barnes, Brian and Anna Marsden)
Globe BA5 2PY [Priest Row]: Popular,
unassuming local with welcoming lived-in
rooms either side of ancient flagstoned
corridor, open fire, well kept ales such as
Butcombe and Shepherd Neame Spitfire,
food from nice sandwiches up inc good
Sun lunch, friendly competent service;
big-screen TV, games area (Pete Devonish,
Ian McIntyre,
Mr and Mrs C Evans, BB, Sue and Mike Todd)
Kings Head BA5 2SG [High St]: Interesting
old narrow-fronted building, beams and
galleries at various levels in high-ceilinged
back hall house, flagstoned front bar with
log fire and comfortable furniture inc
unusual swivel bar stools; enjoyable
lunchtime pubby food from sandwiches up,
Moor, Cheddar and occasional guest beers,
Thatcher's cider, cheerful attentive staff;
may be loud live music some evenings;
dogs welcome on leads (in courtyard with
own bar at food times), wheelchair access
with help (Terry Buckland, Chris and
Angela Buckell)

WEST BUCKLAND [ST1621]
Blackbird TA21 9HX [A38 N of village,
3 miles E of Wellington and handy for
M5 junction 26]: Partly 16th-c roadside inn
with enjoyable good value food inc Sun
roasts, well kept ales such as Cotleigh and
Exmoor, friendly service, large restaurant,
open fires; pleasant garden, bedrooms
(John Gould)

WEST MONKTON [ST2628]
☆ **Monkton** TA2 8NP: Comfortable dining pub
very popular for its good low-priced fresh
food inc set deals (best to book), linked
areas inc smallish bar serving well kept local
beers; wheelchair access from car park, lots
of tables in streamside meadow, peaceful
spot, cl Sun evening, Mon (Sue Daly,
Heather Pitch, Patrick and Daphne Darley,
Chris and Angela Buckell, Bob and
Margaret Holder)

WEST PENNARD [ST5438]
Lion BA6 8NH [A361 E of Glastonbury;
Newtown]: Traditional stone-built village
inn, bar and dining areas off small
flagstoned black-beamed core, enjoyable
food, Butcombe and Greene King, inglenook
woodburner and open fires; piped music;
children welcome, tables on big forecourt,
seven bedrooms in converted side barn, open
all day (BB, Comus and Sarah Elliott)

WESTON-SUPER-MARE [ST3062]
Captains Table BS23 2EF [Birnbeck Road]:
Unpretentious local atmosphere, wide choice
of good food in bar and sea-view restaurant
inc fresh fish/seafood, good service, real ales;
disabled access, terrace (Andrew O'Brien)
Woolpack BS22 7XE [St Georges, just off M5
junction 21]: Opened-up and extended
17th-c coaching inn with full Butcombe
range and a guest ale kept well, decent
wines, enjoyable pubby food inc carvery,
friendly local atmosphere; pleasant window
seats and library-theme area, small attractive
restaurant, conservatory, skittle alley; no
dogs; children welcome, disabled access,
terrace areas with rustic furniture (Chris and
Angela Buckell, Bob and Angela Brooks,
Rod Dykeman)

WHEDDON CROSS [SS9238]
Rest & Be Thankful TA24 7DR [A396/B3224,
S of Minehead]: Good choice of reasonably
priced uncomplicated food from sandwiches
up inc Sun carvery, Butcombe, Exmoor and
guest ales, three real ciders, good friendly
service; comfortably refurbished modern
twin-room bar with back-to-back log fires,
wooden tables and chairs, leather sofas and
a huge jug collection hanging from beams,
restaurant; flagstoned games area with darts
and pool, skittle alley; juke box or piped
music; children and clean dogs welcome,
tables out in back courtyard adjoining
Exmoor public car park (with disabled
lavatory), good walks, five comfortable
bedrooms, nice breakfast (LYM,
Sheila Topham, John and Helen Rushton)

WINDWHISTLE HILL [ST3809]
Windwhistle TA20 4DQ [A30 Chard—
Crewkerne]: Extended roadside pub, beamed
open-plan bar with log fires and lots of
copper/brass, airy high-ceilinged family
room (good carvery here Sun), food from
open sandwiches and warm baguettes to
hearty pub dishes, real ales, restaurant; no
dogs inside; picnic-sets in garden with
adjoining paddocks, lovely views
(Eamonn and Natasha Skyrme)

WINFORD [ST5365]
Prince of Waterloo BS40 8AR [B3130]:
Rambling 16th-c stone pub, large front bar
with dining area, slightly smaller back
bar/restaurant, lowish black beams, some
painted stonework, old cartoons and prints,
horse tack, pews and pubby furniture on
carpet or flagstones, window seats; Bass,
Butcombe and Courage, enjoyable well
presented pub food inc vegetarian options,
cheerful helpful staff; dogs welcome away

from diners, wheelchair access to bars but steps between them, bedrooms in adjacent house, handy for Bristol Airport *(Chris and Angela Buckell)*

WINSCOMBE [ST4257]

☆ *Woodborough* BS25 1HD [Sandford Rd]: Big beamed 1930s village dining pub, smart, comfortable and busy, with wide choice of good generous local food, helpful friendly staff, good wine choice, large public bar, skittle alley; disabled access, bedrooms *(George and Gill Rowley, Michelle Cottis, Jim and Frances Gowers)*

WINSFORD [SS9034]

☆ *Royal Oak* TA24 7JE [off A396 about 10 miles S of Dunster]: Prettily placed thatched and beamed, refurbished Exmoor inn, wide choice of good locally sourced food, friendly staff, well kept Exmoor ales, Thatcher's cider, good wines by the glass; lounge bar with big stone fireplace and large bay-window seat looking across towards village green and foot and packhorse bridges over River Winn, more eating space in second bar, several comfortable lounges; children and dogs welcome, good bedrooms *(LYM, Rod and Chris Pring, John Saville, Johnn and Jennifer Wright)*

WITHAM FRIARY [ST7440]

☆ *Seymour Arms* BA11 5HF [signed from B3092 S of Frome]: Well worn-in unchanging flagstoned country tavern, same friendly licensees since 1952, two simple rooms off 19th-c hatch-service lobby, one with darts, the other with central table skittles; well kept Butcombe, guest ales and Rich's local cider tapped from backroom casks, low prices, open fires, panelled benches; cards and dominoes, no food; good-sized attractive garden by main rail line, open all day wknds *(the Didler, SRD)*

WOOKEY [ST5245]

☆ *Burcott* BA5 1NJ [B3139 W of Wells]: Unspoilt beamed roadside pub with two simply furnished old-fashioned front bar rooms, flagstones, lantern wall lights, woodburner; three changing ales such as Hop Back, Otter and RCH, several wines by the glass, food (not Sun, Mon evenings, or Mon lunchtime in winter) from substantial sandwiches up in bar and restaurant; small games room with built-in wall seats; soft piped music, no dogs; well behaved children allowed in restaurant, front window boxes and tubs, picnic-sets in sizeable garden with Mendip Hill views, four self-catering units in

converted stables *(Jenny and Brian Seller, Phil and Sally Gorton, LYM, M G Hart)*

WOOKEY HOLE [ST5347]

Wookey Hole Inn BA5 1BP: Usefully placed open-plan family pub with unusual trendy décor, welcoming and relaxed, with three eating areas and bar, wood floors and good log fire, four changing local ales, several belgian beers, ciders and perry, good generous innovative food (10% service charge added) using lots of local ingredients; tables with paper cloths for drawing on (crayons provided), efficient friendly staff, may be jazz Sun lunchtime; pleasant garden with various sculptures, five individually styled bedrooms with japanese beds *(Terry Buckland, Rosie Inge)*

WOOLVERTON [ST7954]

Red Lion BA2 7QS [set back from A36 N of village]: Roomy refurbished pub, beams, panelling and lots of stripped wood, candles and log-effect fire, well kept Wadworths, decent wines by the glass, enjoyable good value food all day from baguettes up inc children's meals, friendly staff; locals' bar with fire (dogs allowed here); piped music; open all day, plenty of tables outside, play area *(LYM, Dr and Mrs M E Wilson, James Morrell)*

WRAXALL [ST4971]

☆ *Old Barn* BS48 1LQ [just off Bristol Rd (B3130)]: Idiosyncratic gabled barn conversion: scrubbed tables, school benches and soft sofas under oak rafters, stripped boards and flagstones, welcoming atmosphere and friendly service, well kept Butcombe, Fullers, St Austell, Sharps and a guest tapped from the cask (plans for their own brews too), farm ciders, good wines by the glass, may not be food; unusual board games; occasional piped music and sports TV; children and dogs welcome, nice garden with terrace barbecue (bring your own meat), smokers' shelter, open all day *(Steve and Liz Tilley, the Didler)*

WRINGTON [ST4762]

Plough BS40 5QA [2.5 miles off A370 Bristol—Weston, from bottom of Rhodiate Hill]: Large pub refurbished under new licensees, Wells & Youngs and a guest like Butcombe, decent choice of wines, enjoyable home-made food, beams and stripped stone, open fires; children and dogs welcome, wheelchair access, terrace and garden picnic-sets, boules, open all day *(BB, Jane Undery)*

Staffordshire

A terrific addition to the Staffordshire Main Entries this year is the cheerfully unspoilt Coopers Tavern at Burton upon Trent which takes great pride in its pedigree historic associations with Bass. And, of course, while in Burton upon Trent the straightforward Burton Bridge Inn with its range of Burton Bridge ales is not to be missed either. Staffordshire and particularly Burton upon Trent (its water is excellent for beer-making) has a fine brewing history and there are plenty of local brewers. As well as Burton Bridge, other breweries to look out for are Peakstones, Titanic and Tower and for sheer choice, the simple but friendly Blue Bell in Kidsgrove gets through an astonishing 300 different brews a year. Other pubs in this county that are doing well include the peaceful George at Alstonefield with its embracing welcome, the lovely old Holly Bush at Salt with its generous food served all day and the Hand & Trumpet at Wrinehill which is sadly the only pub in the county with a Food Award. It is genuinely in a different league when it comes to a special meal out and, as such, the Hand & Trumpet at Wrinehill is our Staffordshire Dining Pub of the Year 2011.

ABBOTS BROMLEY   SK0824   MAP 7

Goats Head
Market Place; WS15 3BP

Well run old-world pub with good food; attractive location

On Wakes Monday, which is the Monday between 6 and 12 September inclusive, the ancient Horn Dance is performed at various locations throughout this unspoilt village, including outside this charming old black and white timbered pub. It's a friendly place with a real village feel and is well liked for its good hospitable atmosphere and fairly priced tasty food. The opened-up cream-painted interior is unpretentious but comfortable, with attractive oak floors, a warming coal fire in a big inglenook and furnishings that take in the odd traditional oak settle; piped music, juke box and TV. Served by attentive staff, the Black Sheep, Marstons Pedigree, Timothy Taylors Landlord and a guest such as Charles Wells Bombardier or St Austell Tribute are well kept on handpump, and you can have any of the wines on their good wine list by the glass; there's a beer and music festival on the last bank holiday Sunday in May. Picnic-sets and teak tables out on a neat sheltered lawn look up to the church tower behind.

🍴 Generously served enjoyable bar food is all home made, and the chips here are good: sandwiches, thai-style fishcakes, fried goats cheese with chutney, garlic king prawns, lasagne, steak and ale pie, roast leg of lamb with mint and onion gravy, chicken breast with creamy leek and stilton sauce, faggots with mushy peas and vegetable fajitas, and daily specials such as pork belly with black pudding, fish and chips, and puddings such as apricot crumble. *Starters/Snacks: £4.95 to £6.95. Main Courses: £7.95 to £15.95. Puddings: £4.95 to £6.50*

Punch ~ Lease Dawn Skelton and Edward and Selina Smith ~ Real ale ~ Bar food (12-2.30(3 Sat), 6-9(9.30 Fri, Sat); 12-4.30 Sun; not Sun evening) ~ Restaurant ~ (01283) 840254 ~ Children welcome ~ Dogs allowed in bar ~ Open 12-11.30pm(12.30am Sat, 11pm Sun) ~ Bedrooms: /£40

Recommended by Dr and Mrs J Temporal, Richard and Jean Green, DC, David Austin, Susan and Nigel Brookes, Helene Grygar, Henry Pursehouse-Tranter

ALSTONEFIELD
SK1355   MAP 7

George ♀
Village signposted from A515 Ashbourne-Buxton; DE6 2FX

Nice old pub with decent food; a Peak District classic

This super stone-built pub is run by a very friendly landlady, who clearly puts her customers first. One reader told us their dog was given a warm welcome, too. A good variety of customers, including plenty of walkers, enjoy soaking up the charming atmosphere in the unchanging straightforward low-beamed bar with its collection of old Peak District photographs and pictures, warming coal fire and copper-topped counter with well kept Burtons Bitter, Marstons Pedigree and a guest such as Brakspear Oxford Gold on handpump, a dozen wines by the glass and organic soft drinks; dominoes. The neatened up dining room has a woodburning stove. The pub is in a peaceful Peak District farming hamlet and you can sit out by the green, beneath its old inn sign, and watch the world go by, or out in the big sheltered stableyard behind the pub.

🍴 The menu is quite short but well balanced and fairly priced. As well as lunchtime sandwiches, there might be ham hock and parsley terrine, seared scallops with tomato consommé, mushroom baked with brie and pancetta on a toasted muffin with thyme, chicken breast with roast tomatoes, lentils and creamed mushrooms, fried salmon fillet with spinach and minted pea purée, home-made burger on a sourdough bun, steak, mushroom and Guinness pie, and puddings such as lemon posset with lemon sorbet, warm bitter chocolate sponge pudding with vanilla bean and praline ice-cream, and a british cheeseboard. *Starters/Snacks: £4.00 to £7.00. Main Courses: £9.00 to £22.00. Puddings: £5.00 to £7.00*

Marstons ~ Tenant Emily Hammond ~ Real ale ~ Bar food (12-2.30, 7-9(6.30-8 Sun)) ~ Restaurant ~ (01335) 310205 ~ Children welcome ~ Dogs allowed in bar ~ Open 11.30-3, 6-11; 11.30-11 Sat; 12-9.30 Sun

Recommended by Michelle Sullivan, Paul J Robinshaw, Mike Proctor, Henry Pursehouse-Tranter, Peter J and Avril Hanson, Richard and Jean Green, Bernard Stradling, the Didler, David and Sue Atkinson, Jill and Julian Tasker, Ken and Barbara Turner, Verity Kemp, Richard Mills, Hector and Eileen Tierney, Sheila Blackhurst

BURTON UPON TRENT
SK2523   MAP 7

Burton Bridge Inn ◧ £
Bridge Street (A50); DE14 1SY

Straightforward cheery tap for the Burton Bridge Brewery; lunchtime snacks only

The superbly kept beers served at this genuinely friendly down-to-earth local are brewed by Burton Bridge Brewery who are housed just across the long old-fashioned blue-brick yard at the back. You'll probably find half a dozen on handpump from the range that includes Bitter, Festival, Golden Delicious, Gold Medal, Porter, Sovereign Gold and XL, alongside around 20 whiskies and over a dozen country wines. On Sundays they may add a guest beer such as Castle Rock Harvest Pale. The simple little front area leads into an adjacent bar with wooden pews, and plain walls hung with notices, awards and brewery memorabilia. Separated from the bar by the serving counter, the little oak-beamed lounge is snugly oak panelled and has a flame-effect fire and a mix of furnishings; skittle alley. The panelled upstairs dining room is open only at lunchtime.

🍴 Simple but hearty bar snacks take in sandwiches, ploughman's, chilli, faggots and ham, egg and chips; no puddings. *Starters/Snacks: £2.45 to £3.45. Main Courses: £4.75 to £5.75*

Own brew ~ Licensee Carl Stout ~ Real ale ~ Bar food (12-2; not Sun) ~ No credit cards ~ (01283) 536596 ~ Children welcome ~ Dogs allowed in bar ~ Open 11.30-2.30, 5-11; 11.30-11.30 Fri, Sat; 12-3, 7-11 Sun

Recommended by the Didler, Theo, Anne and Jane Gaskin, Barbarrick, Edward Leetham, P Dawn

Post Office address codings confusingly give the impression that some pubs are in Staffordshire, when they're really in Cheshire or Derbyshire (which is where we list them).

Coopers Tavern 🍺

Cross Street; DE14 1EG

Characterful unspoilt real ale pub of local historic importance

Once the tap for Bass Brewery across the road, the walls of this old-fashioned back street pub display some glorious examples of Bass brewing ephemera, including mirrors and glazed adverts. No frills but still homely and warm with a coal fire, an old-fashioned front parlour with a pleasant jumble of furniture leads through to the back bar which doubles as the cellar. Here Bass, Castle Rock and between four and seven changing guests from brewers such as Hopback, Sarah Hughes, Thornbridge and Tower, a cider and a perry are racked and drawn straight from the cask by the friendly landlady. Raised up behind the barrels, a cushioned semicircular bench gives you the feeling that you are sitting right among them.

🍴 **Food is limited to pork pies; maybe Sunday roasts too.** *Starters/Snacks: £1.25*

Joules ~ Tenant Mary Bagley ~ Real ale ~ Bar food ~ (01283) 532551 ~ Open 12-2.30, 5(6 Mon, Tues)-11; 12-midnight Fri, Sat; 12-11 Sun; closed Mon and Tues lunchtimes

Recommended by Barbarrick, Edward Leetham

CAULDON   SK0749   MAP 7

Yew Tree ★★ £

Village signposted from A523 and A52 about 8 miles W of Ashbourne; ST10 3EJ

Treasure-trove of fascinating antiques and dusty bric-a-brac; very eccentric

'It is a pub you either love or hate', and 'definitely not for the faint hearted' are the words of two readers about this uniquely idiosyncratic place – we love it. It's not spic and span (far from it) and in the past has been affectionately described as a junk shop with a bar. Over the years, the characterful landlord has amassed a museum's worth of curiosities. The most impressive pieces are perhaps the working polyphons and symphonions – 19th-c developments of the musical box, often taller than a person, each with quite a repertoire of tunes and elaborate sound-effects. But there are also two pairs of Queen Victoria's stockings, ancient guns and pistols, several penny-farthings, an old sit-and-stride boneshaker, a rocking horse, swordfish blades, a little 800 BC greek vase, and even a fine marquetry cabinet crammed with notable early staffordshire pottery. Soggily sprung sofas mingle with 18th-c settles, plenty of little wooden tables and a four-person oak church choir seat with carved heads which came from St Mary's church in Stafford; above the bar is an odd iron dog-carrier. As well as all this, there's an expanding choir of fine tuneful longcase clocks in the gallery just above the entrance, a collection of six pianolas (one of which is played most nights) with an excellent repertoire of piano rolls, a working vintage valve radio set, a crank-handle telephone, a sinuous medieval wind instrument made of leather, and a Jacobean four-poster which was once owned by Josiah Wedgwood and still has his original wig hook on the headboard. Clearly, it would be almost an overwhelming task to keep all that sprucely clean. The drinks here are very reasonably priced (so no wonder it's popular with locals), and you'll find well kept Bass, Burton Bridge and Rudgate Ruby Mild on handpump or tapped from the cask, along with about a dozen interesting malt whiskies; piped music (probably Radio 2), darts, shove-ha'penny, table skittles, dominoes and cribbage. When you arrive, don't be put off by the plain exterior, or the fact that the pub is tucked unpromisingly between enormous cement works and quarries and almost hidden by a towering yew tree.

🍴 **Simple good value tasty snacks include pork, meat and potato, chicken and mushroom and steak pies, hot big filled baps and sandwiches, quiche, smoked mackerel or ham salad, and home-made puddings.** *Starters/Snacks: £0.80 to £1.90. Puddings: £1.60 to £1.80*

Free house ~ Licensee Alan East ~ Real ale ~ Bar food (12-2.30, 6(7 Sun)-9) ~ No credit cards ~ (01538) 308348 ~ Children in polyphon room ~ Dogs welcome ~ Folk music first Tues of the month ~ Open 10-2.30(3 Sat), 6-midnight; 12-3, 7-midnight Sun

Recommended by Helene Grygar, Mike Proctor, S J and C C Davidson, John Dwane, Mike Horgan, the Didler, Jill and Julian Tasker, David Austin, Thomas Lane

CHEADLE

Queens at Freehay

1 mile SE of Cheadle; take Rakeway Road off A522 (via Park Avenue or Mills Road), then after 1 mile turn into Counslow Road; ST10 1RF

Nice dining pub with a couple of local beers and decent garden

This agreeable dining pub with its pleasant welcoming staff is an enjoyable place to go for a meal. The comfortable lounge bar is attractively decorated with small country pictures and pretty curtains with matching cushions. It opens through an arch into a light and airy dining area, with neatly spaced tables; swift attentive service. Burton Bridge and Peakstones Rock Abbey are on handpump; piped music. The 18th-c origins of the building are most apparent from the simple but attractive little back garden.

🍽 **Food is mainly familiar, but all cooked carefully with good flavours and nicely presented. Besides lunchtime sandwiches and ploughman's, bar food includes hoisin duck in a tortilla wrap, duck and orange pâté, local black pudding with crispy bacon and cheddar, beef and Guinness pie, battered cod and chips, moroccan lamb tagine, sweet and sour pork and sirloin steak, with blackboard specials such as half a roast duckling and roast monkfish, and puddings such as apple pie and lemon or bakewell tart.** *Starters/Snacks: £3.50 to £5.95. Main Courses: £8.95 to £14.95. Puddings: £4.95 to £5.95*

Free house ~ Licensee Adrian Rock ~ Real ale ~ Bar food (12-2, 6-9.30; 12-2.30, 6.30-9.30 Sun) ~ Restaurant ~ (01538) 722383 ~ Well supervised children welcome ~ Open 12-3, 6-11; 12-3.30, 6.30-10.30 Sun

Recommended by Meg and Colin Hamilton, Mr and Mrs M Plant

KIDSGROVE

Blue Bell 🍺

25 Hardings Wood; off A50 NW edge of town; ST7 1EG

Astonishing tally of thoughtfully sourced real ales on six constantly changing pumps at little beer pub

In the last 12 years an astounding 3,000 or so brews have passed through the six handpumps at this simple but friendly place. The constantly changing range is carefully selected from smaller often unusual brewers such as Acorn, Burton Bridge, Castle Rock, Crouch Vale, Oakham, RCH and Whim. These are topped off with around 30 belgian, czech and german bottled beers, up to three draught farm ciders and a perry. If you arrive here by car, you need to keep your eyes skinned to spot this understated cream-painted place. Converted from two cottages, it can look more like a house. Its four small, carpeted rooms are unfussy and straightforward, with blue upholstered benches, basic pub furniture, a gas-effect coal fire and maybe soft piped music. There are tables in front and more on a little back lawn. Note the reduced opening hours.

🍽 **Food is limited to weekend filled rolls.**

Free house ~ Licensees Dave and Kay Washbrook ~ Real ale ~ Bar food (filled rolls weekends only) ~ No credit cards ~ (01782) 774052 ~ Well behaved children welcome ~ Dogs welcome ~ Open 7.30-11; 1-4, 7.30-11 Sat; 12-10.30 Sun; closed lunchtimes and Mon except bank hol evenings

Recommended by the Didler, Mike Proctor, R T and J C Moggridge, Martin Grosberg

> Stars after the name of a pub show exceptional quality. One star means most people (after reading the report to see just why the star has been won) would think a special trip worth while. Two stars mean that the pub is really outstanding – for its particular qualities it could hardly be bettered.

LICHFIELD
SK0705   MAP 4

Boat

3.8 miles from M6 toll junction T6 (pay again when you rejoin it); head E on A5, turning right at first roundabout into B4155, keeping straight ahead into Barrack Lane at first crossroads, then left on to A461 Walsall Road; leaving pub, keep straight on to rejoin A5 at Muckley Corner roundabout; WS14 0BU

Efficiently run dining pub, handy break for imaginative meal off M6 toll

This neatly kept and thoughtfully run place offers more than just a handy break from the motorway. Views straight into the kitchen and the huge floor-to-ceiling food blackboards that greet you as you enter are indicative of the emphasis on the carefully prepared food here. Well lit by a big skylight, this first section has a cheery café atmosphere with bright plastic flooring, striking photoprints, leather club chairs and sofas around coffee tables and potted palms. The comfortable dining areas are more conventional and calmly relaxing, with sturdy modern pale pine furniture on russet pink carpets and prints on white walls and the windows on the left have views of the disused canal. The solid light wood bar counter has three, often locally sourced, changing real ales, from brewers such as Backyard Brewhouse, Cotleigh and Oakham on handpump, and around ten wines by the glass. Service is friendly and obliging; faint piped music. A landscaped area outside is paved with a central raised decking area; good wheelchair access throughout.

🍴 **As well as lunchtime sandwiches, attractively presented good bar food from a fairly extensive menu (the chef tells us they are careful with their sourcing) might include king prawns in garlic and white wine, fried pigeon breast with bubble and squeak potato cake, seared scallops with crispy parma ham, fried duck breast with plum and ginger, wild mushroom risotto, pork tenderloin with fresh herbs wrapped in puff pastry, swordfish with cajun rice and caramelised banana, fish and chips, and puddings such as chocolate mousse with shortbread biscuits, plum and almond tart and toffee and banana crumble.** *Starters/Snacks: £3.50 to £7.50. Main Courses: £5.95 to £20.00. Puddings: £3.75 to £4.25*

Free house ~ Licensee Ann Holden ~ Real ale ~ Bar food (12-2.15, 6-9.30; 12-8.15 Sun) ~ (01543) 361692 ~ Dogs allowed in bar ~ Open 12-3, 6-11; 12-11 Sun

Recommended by John and Helen Rushton, Colin Fisher, David Green, Pat and Tony Martin, S P Watkin, P A Taylor, Bren and Val Speed, Paul J Robinshaw, Michael Beale

Queens Head 🍺 £

Queen Street; public car park just round corner in Swan Road, off A51 roundabout; WS13 6QD

Bargain lunchtime hot dishes, cheese platter all day and good range of real ales at friendly place

Cheery with friendly conversation, the single long room in this handsome Victorian red brick building, done up rather like an old-fashioned alehouse, has a mix of comfortable aged furniture on bare boards, big sash windows, some stripped brick and Lichfield and other pictures on ochre walls above a panelled dado. The atmosphere is comfortably relaxed and grown-up, and staff are kind and helpful; terrestrial TV for sports events, darts and board games. As well as Bathams, Marstons Pedigree and Timothy Taylors Landlord, three guests might be from brewers such as Blythe, Brakspear and Ringwood beers; also 25 malt whiskies; small garden. They may allow children in on request but don't count on it.

🍴 **As well as a cheese platter (on offer all day) from a splendid choice of 15 cheeses, really good value bar food might include venison burger, steak, kidney and ale pie, goat curry, quorn tagine with couscous, and puddings such as white chocolate and ginger cheesecake and Mars Bar mousse; Sunday roast and curry night Tuesdays.** *Starters/Snacks: £2.95 to £4.95. Main Courses: £4.95 to £6.95. Puddings: £2.00*

Marstons ~ Tenant Stuart Harvey ~ Real ale ~ Bar food (12-2.15(3 Sun), 6-9 Tues; cheese platter 12-9.30) ~ No credit cards ~ (01543) 410932 ~ Dogs welcome ~ Open 12-11(11.30 Fri, Sat)

Recommended by R T and J C Moggridge, John Branston, the Didler, Paul J Robinshaw

SALT   SJ9527   MAP 7

Holly Bush

Village signposted off A51 S of Stone (and A518 NE of Stafford); ST18 0BX

Delightful medieval pub popular for generous mainly traditional all-day food

This charming white-painted 14th-c house with its lovely deep thatch and flower-bedecked walls has a picture book exterior. Inside, it's just as attractive with several cosy areas spreading off from the standing-room serving section, with high-backed cushioned pews, old tables and more conventional seats. The oldest part has a heavy-beamed and planked ceiling (some of the beams are attractively carved), a woodburning stove and a salt cupboard built into the big inglenook, with other nice old-fashioned touches such as an ancient pair of riding boots on the mantelpiece. A modern back extension, with beams, stripped brickwork and a small coal fire, blends in well. Adnams, Marstons Pedigree and a guest are on handpump, alongside a dozen wines by the glass. The back of the pub is beautifully tended, with rustic picnic-sets on a big lawn. They operate a type of locker system for credit cards, which they will ask to keep if you run a tab.

🍴 As well as lunchtime sandwiches, generously served bar food might include **staffordshire oatcake stuffed with spiced black pudding with herby tomato sauce, pears stuffed with blue cheese, home-smoked trout with horseradish sauce, braised venison with chestnuts, rabbit casserole with herb dumplings, steak and kidney pudding, braised lamb and apples, scampi, steaks, traditional puddings such as apple crumble and bread and butter pudding, and an english cheeseboard; they've a wood-fired pizza oven in the beer garden.** *Starters/Snacks: £2.95 to £4.25. Main Courses: £7.95 to £15.95. Puddings: £3.45 to £4.95*

Admiral Taverns ~ Licensees Geoffrey and Joseph Holland ~ Real ale ~ Bar food (12-9.30(9 Sun)) ~ (01889) 508234 ~ Children welcome ~ Open 12-11(10.30 Sun)

Recommended by Henry Pursehouse-Tranter, Susan and Nigel Brookes, Brian and Anna Marsden, Chris and Jo Parsons, S J and C C Davidson, Mike Horgan, Adrian Johnson, Brian and Jacky Wilson

WETTON   SK1055   MAP 7

Olde Royal Oak

Village signposted off Hulme End—Alstonefield road, between B5054 and A515; DE6 2AF

Friendly traditional pub in lovely location; good value straightforward food

Warm and cosy with open fires and delightfully welcoming licensees, this aged stone-built village pub is a popular stop for walkers (Wetton Mill and the Manifold Valley are nearby): they leave covers for muddy boots at both doors. With a croft for caravans and tents behind, it's just the sort of low-key place you'd hope to find tucked in at the heart of this lovely National Trust countryside. The traditional bar has white ceiling boards above its black beams, small dining chairs around rustic tables, an oak corner cupboard and a coal fire in the stone fireplace. It extends into a more modern-feeling area, which in turn leads to a carpeted sun lounge that looks over the small garden; piped music, darts, TV, shove-ha'penny, cribbage and dominoes. You can choose from more than 30 whiskies, and two real ales on handpump might include Blue Monkey, Wells & Youngs Bombardier or Titanic. So far, rumours that this place might change hands have come to nothing.

🍴 Reasonably priced pubby food includes **filled baps, leek and potato soup, breaded mushrooms, spicy chicken dippers, battered cod, parsnip, sweet potato and chestnut bake, gammon with pineapple and egg, vegetable curry and steaks, and puddings such as treacle sponge or caramel apple pie.** *Starters/Snacks: £3.50 to £4.95. Main Courses: £5.95 to £12.75. Puddings: £3.75*

Free house ~ Licensees Brian and Janet Morley ~ Real ale ~ Bar food ~ (01335) 310287 ~ Children welcome ~ Dogs welcome ~ Open 12-2.30(3 Sat, Sun), 7-11; closed Mon, Tues ~ Bedrooms: /£40S

Recommended by Paul J Robinshaw, Mike Proctor, Rob and Chris Warner, A J Liles, the Didler, Rob and Catherine Dunster

WRINEHILL

SJ7547   MAP 7

Hand & Trumpet ⓦ ⓨ ◀

A531 Newcastle—Nantwich; CW3 9BJ

STAFFORDSHIRE DINING PUB OF THE YEAR

Big attractive dining pub with good food all day, professional service, nice range of real ales and wines; pleasant garden

Airy and stylish yet still managing an intimate feel, this sturdy building is a handsome conversion in the Brunning & Price mould. Linked open-plan areas working their way around the counter have a mix of dining chairs and sturdy tables on polished tiles or stripped oak boards and several big oriental rugs that soften the acoustics and appearance. There are lots of nicely lit prints on cream walls between mainly dark dado and deep red ceilings. It's all brightened up with good natural light from bow windows and in one area a big skylight. At its heart is a solidly built counter with half a dozen handpumps dispensing well kept Caledonian Deuchars IPA, Phoenix B&P Original, Salopian Oracle and guests from brewers such as Gertie Sweet Traditional, Titanic and Wincle. They also keep a fine range of about nine wines by the glass and about 74 whiskies. French windows open on to a spacious balustraded deck with teak tables and chairs looking down to ducks swimming on a big pond in the sizeable garden which has plenty of trees. Service is relaxed and friendly; good disabled access and facilities; board games.

🍴 Food is well prepared, and the menu ranges from good takes on traditional dishes to more imaginative ones. As well as interesting sandwiches, starters might include cream of mushroom, rosemary and garlic soup, chilli and garlic squid with pineapple, mango, coriander and lime salad, coarse chicken liver, bacon, apricot and pistachio terrine, warm crab linguine with ginger, red chilli and coriander, rump steak sandwich with mustard butter, onion jam and tomato chutney, fried scallops with minted pea and broad bean pûrée, roast tomatoes and fennel salad, basil and lemon roast chicken with wild garlic and spring onion potato cake and red pepper dressing, battered haddock with mushy peas, black bream and stir-fried vegetables and noodles, bass, salmon and hake casserole with tomato, lobster and dill sauce, and puddings such as white chocolate and mango cheesecake with passion fruit and mango compote and toffee and chocolate sundae with chocolate nut brownie. *Starters/Snacks: £4.50 to £9.95. Main Courses: £9.75 to £16.25. Puddings: £4.70 to £5.25*

Brunning & Price ~ Manager John Unsworth ~ Real ale ~ Bar food (12-10(9.30 Sun)) ~ (01270) 820048 ~ Children welcome ~ Dogs allowed in bar ~ Open 11.30-11(10.30 Sun)

Recommended by David S Allen, Henry Pursehouse-Tranter, Paul Boot, Paul and Margaret Baker, Dr and Mrs A K Clarke

LUCKY DIP

Besides the fully inspected pubs, you might like to try these Lucky Dips recommended to us and described by readers (if you do, please send us reports: feedback@goodguides.com).

ALREWAS [SK1715]
☆ *George & Dragon* DE13 7AE [off A38; Main St]: Three welcoming low-beamed linked rooms, generous honest food inc bargain two-course lunch, three well kept Marstons-related ales, efficient attentive staff; piped music; children welcome in eating area, pleasant partly covered garden with good play area, popular with canal users, opens 5pm wkdys *(Mrs Hazel Rainer, Paul J Robinshaw, John and Helen Rushton, Martin Smith, LYM)*
William IV DE13 7AN [William IV Rd, off Main St]: Large 19th-c open-plan pub, well kept Marstons Pedigree, good food inc wkdy two-for-one lunchtime bargains, friendly service, lounge with raised eating area;

children welcome, garden tables, short walk from Grand Trunk Canal *(Paul J Robinshaw)*
ALTON [SK0742]
Bulls Head ST10 4AQ [High St]: 17th-c beamed inn doing enjoyable good value food in small inglenook bar and slate-floor restaurant, well kept Marstons and a guest ale, friendly staff and locals; piped music; children welcome, good walks, seven bedrooms *(John Dwane, Paul J Robinshaw)*
AMINGTON [SK2304]
Pretty Pigs B79 0ED [Shuttington Rd]: Popular old inn based on former small manor house, cheap ales such as Bass and Greene King, good value food inc carvery (restaurant up a couple of steps); tables outside *(John and Helen Rushton)*

ARMITAGE [SK0716]
Plum Pudding WS15 4AZ [Rugeley Rd
(A513)]: Canalside pub and italian
restaurant, good food in bar and dining room,
Black Sheep, friendly staff; no dogs; children
welcome, tables on waterside terrace and
narrow canal bank, moorings, open all day
Sun *(Susan and Nigel Brookes, BB)*
BARTON-UNDER-NEEDWOOD [SK1818]
Shoulder of Mutton DE13 8AA [Main St]:
Village pub with low beams and panelling,
pleasant staff, well kept Bass and guest
beers, good range of bar meals and snacks,
open fire, pool in public bar, live music Fri;
seats out at front and on terrace, four
bedrooms, open all day *(Simon Le Fort)*
Waterfront DE13 8DZ [Barton Marina, Barton
Turns]: Huge pub, new but cleverly done so
that it looks long-established, part of marina
complex, wide choice of enjoyable food inc
pubby favourites (light dishes all day), six or
more real ales, good service, thriving
atmosphere; children welcome until early
evening, open all day *(David M Smith,
John and Helen Rushton)*
BLITHBURY [SK0819]
Bull & Spectacles WS15 3HY [Uttoxeter Rd
(B5014 S of Abbots Bromley)]: 17th-c pub
with obliging friendly service, wide choice of
homely food inc popular bargain lunchtime
Hot Table – half a dozen or so generous
main dishes with help-yourself veg and some
puddings *(David Green)*
BLYTHE BRIDGE [SJ9640]
Black Cock ST11 9NT [Uttoxeter Rd (A521)]:
Roadside local with friendly landlord, tables
set for the enjoyable home-made food,
several well kept real ales, good wine choice,
1950s and Beatles memorabilia *(the Didler)*
BURSLEM [SJ8649]
Leopard ST6 3AA [Market Pl]: Traditional old
city-centre pub, three rooms inc snug,
enjoyable home-made food, half a dozen
good local ales, well priced wines
(Susan and Nigel Brookes)
BURTON UPON TRENT [SK2424]
Derby Inn DE14 1RU [Derby Rd]: Well worn-
in idiosyncratic local with particularly good
Marstons Pedigree, friendly long-serving
landlord (still talking of retirement – but go
while you can), brewery glasses collection in
cosy panelled lounge, lots of steam railway
memorabilia in long narrow bar, local
produce for sale; outside lavatories, sports
TV; dogs welcome, open all day Fri and Sat
(the Didler)
Elms DE15 9AE [Stapenhill Rd (A444)]: Well
kept Bass, Tower and changing guests in
small character bar with wall benches, larger
lounge, friendly staff; open all day wknds
(the Didler)
Old Cottage Tavern DE14 2EG
[Rangemoor St/Byrkley St]: No longer owned
by local Burton Old Cottage but still serving
their ales and guests, good value food, two
bars, snug and compact back restaurant,
games room, upstairs skittle alley; bedrooms,
open all day *(the Didler)*

BUTTERTON [SK0756]
Black Lion ST13 7SP [off B5053]: Nicely
placed traditional 18th-c low-beamed stone-
built inn, logs blazing in inner room's
kitchen range, good-humoured efficient
service, enjoyable food from filled rolls up,
several well kept ales, reasonable prices,
traditional games and pool room; piped
music; children in eating areas, terrace
tables, tidy bedrooms, cl Mon and Tues
lunchtimes *(the Didler, LYM)*
CANNOCK [SJ9610]
Shoal Hill WS11 1RF [Sandy Lane]: In nice
rural setting and popular with walkers,
spacious modern interior, good range of
fairly priced food from baguettes to specials,
OAP and children's menus, friendly helpful
staff, Thwaites ales, good choice of wines by
the glass, large light restaurant; open all day
Fri-Sun *(Nigel Espley)*
CHEDDLETON [SJ9751]
☆ *Boat* ST13 7EQ [Basford Bridge Lane, off
A520]: Cheerful canalside local handy for
Churnet Valley steam railway, flint mill and
country park; neat long bar, low plank
ceilings, well kept Marstons-related and
other ales, friendly staff and locals, good
value generous simple food from sandwiches
and filled oatcakes up, interesting pictures,
attractive dining room with polished floor,
black-leaded range and brass fittings;
children welcome, dogs allowed in part of
bar, fairy-lit heated terrace overlooking
Cauldon Canal *(Helene Grygar, P Dawn, LYM)*
CODSALL [SJ8603]
Codsall Station WV8 1BY [Chapel Lane/
Station Rd]: Comfortable welcoming pub in
simply restored vintage waiting room and
ticket office of working station, Holdens
beers inc one brewed for the pub, good
value plentiful basic food (not Sun, Mon)
from sandwiches up, lots of railway
memorabilia, conservatory; terrace, open all
day Fri-Sun *(the Didler)*
CONSALL [SK0049]
☆ *Black Lion* ST9 0AJ [Consall Forge, OS Sheet
118 map ref 000491; best approach from
Nature Park, off A522, using car park
0.5 miles past Nature Centre]: Traditional
take-us-as-you-find-us local tucked away in
rustic old-fashioned canalside settlement by
restored steam railway station, generous
helpings of enjoyable unpretentious food
made by landlord (may be only sandwiches
midweek), wide range of well kept ales, good
coal fire; piped music, can get very busy wknd
lunchtimes; good walking area *(Bob and
Laura Brock, LYM, S J and C C Davidson,
the Didler, Clive and Fran Dutson, P Dawn,
Edward Leetham)*
DENSTONE [SK0940]
Tavern ST14 5HR [College Rd]: Welcoming
village pub, comfortable lounge with
antiques, good imaginative food (not Sun
evening) from shortish menu, pleasant
service, well kept Marstons ales, good choice
of wines by the glass, dining conservatory
(John Dwane, M Ross-Thomas)

ENVILLE [SO08286]

☆ **Cat** DY7 5HA [A458 W of Stourbridge (Bridgnorth Rd)]: Ancient beamed pub on Staffordshire Way, two appealingly old-fashioned log-fire rooms on one side of servery, plush banquettes on the other, local Enville ales and interesting guests, well priced generous bar food inc sandwiches and mix-and-match range of sausage, mash and gravies, restaurant; children in family room and main lounge, dogs in bar, pretty courtyard sheltered by massive estate wall, cl Sun evening, Mon *(the Didler, Lynda and Trevor Smith, Guy Vowles, LYM, Henry Pursehouse-Tranter, John Robertson)*

FORTON [SJ7521]

Swan TF10 8BY [A519 Newport—Eccleshall]: Former estate manager's house; large open room with mirrors and small wooden bar, separate section with library and sofas, restaurant opening into modern conservatory, enjoyable reasonably priced food from sandwiches up inc bargain carvery (wkdy lunchtimes, all day Sun), four ales inc Marstons, good friendly service; piped music, no dogs; children welcome, shop selling wine and local produce, handy for Shropshire Union Canal walks, ten bedrooms (four in converted barn), open all day *(Henry Pursehouse-Tranter)*

FRADLEY [SK1414]

☆ **White Swan** DE13 7DN [Fradley Junction]: Perfect canalside location at Trent & Mersey and Coventry junction, bargain food from baguettes to Sun carvery, well kept Black Sheep, Greene King Abbot, Marstons Pedigree and a guest like Hydes, cheery traditional public bar with woodburner, quieter plusher lounge and lower vaulted back bar (where children allowed), cribbage, dominoes; waterside tables, open all day *(LYM, Mrs Hazel Rainer, David M Smith)*

GAILEY [SJ9010]

Spread Eagle ST19 5PN [A5/A449]: Spacious refurbished Marstons pub, variety of separate areas inc relaxing sofas and family part with toys, good service, lunchtime and afternoon bargains inc carvery; good disabled access and facilities, big terrace, lawn with play area *(Henry Pursehouse-Tranter, Pat Crabb, Neil and Brenda Skidmore)*

GNOSALL [SJ8220]

Boat ST20 0DA [Gnosall Heath, by Shrops Union Canal Bridge 34]: Small canalside pub under friendly hard-working family, first-floor bar with curved window seat overlooking barges, good wholesome food inc popular Sun lunch, homely local atmosphere, open fire; children welcome, tables out by canal, moorings *(Charles and Pauline Stride)*

Navigation ST20 0EQ [Newport Rd]: Relaxed two-bar pub with dining conservatory and terrace overlooking Shropshire Union Canal, good friendly service, popular reasonably priced traditional food and specials, well kept Banks's ales *(the Head family)*

HANLEY [SJ8847]

Coachmakers Arms ST1 3EA [Lichfield St]: Chatty traditional town local under threat of demolition; four small rooms and drinking corridor, half a dozen or more good changing ales, farm cider, darts, cards and dominoes, original seating and local tilework, open fire, live jazz and country music some Weds; children welcome, open all day, till 1am Fri and Sat *(the Didler)*

HAUGHTON [SJ8620]

Bell ST18 9EX [A518 Stafford—Newport]: Good value food inc popular set lunch deals, Marstons ales, good friendly service even when busy; cl Mon *(John and Helen Rushton)*

HIGH OFFLEY [SJ7725]

Anchor ST20 0NG [off A519 Eccleshall—Newport; towards High Lea, by Shropshire Union Canal, Bridge 42; Peggs Lane]: Real boaters' pub on Shropshire Union Canal, little changed in the century or more this family have run it, two small simple front rooms, Marstons Pedigree and Wadworths 6X in jugs from cellar, Weston's farm cider, may be lunchtime toasties, owners' sitting room behind bar, occasional wknd singalongs; outbuilding with small shop and semi-open lavatories, lovely garden with great hanging baskets and notable topiary anchor, caravan/campsite, cl Mon-Thurs winter *(the Didler)*

HIMLEY [SO8990]

☆ **Crooked House** DY3 4DA [signed down rather grim lane from B4176 Gornalwood—Himley, OS Sheet 139 map ref 896908]: Extraordinary sight, building thrown wildly out of kilter (mining subsidence), slopes so weird things look as if they roll up not down them; otherwise a basic well worn low-priced pub with Marstons-related ales, farm cider, cheery staff, enjoyable straightforward food (all day in summer), Mon pie night, some local antiques in level more modern extension, conservatory; children in eating areas, big outside terrace, open all day wknds and summer *(Dave Braisted, the Didler, LYM)*

HOAR CROSS [SK1323]

☆ **Meynell Ingram Arms** DE13 8RB [Abbots Bromley Road, off A515 Yoxall—Sudbury]: Good interesting food (not Sun evening) from sandwiches to restaurant meals in comfortably extended country dining pub, friendly staff, well kept Blythe and Marstons Pedigree, several neat redecorated little rooms rambling around central counter, log fire, some beams and brasses, hunting pictures and bespectacled fox's head, dining room with coal-effect fire; children and dogs welcome, tables on front grass and in courtyard behind, open all day *(R J Herd, Michelle and Graeme Voss, LYM, Susan and Nigel Brookes, S J and C C Davidson, R T and J C Moggridge)*

HOPWAS [SK1704]

☆ **Tame Otter** B78 3AT [Hints Rd (A51 Tamworth—Lichfield)]: Welcoming 19th-c Vintage Inn by Birmingham & Fazeley Canal (moorings), beams and cosy corners, three fires, nice mixed furnishings, old photographs and canalia, enjoyable fairly priced food all day, efficient staff, well kept Banks's, Bass and Marstons Pedigree, good choice of wines; large garden *(Martin Smith, E Clark, David Green)*

LEEK [SJ9856]

Den Engel ST13 5HG [Stanley St]: Relaxed belgian-style bar in high-ceilinged former bank, over 100 belgian beers inc lots on tap, three dozen genevers, three or four changing real ales, enjoyable food in upstairs restaurant, good if not speedy service; piped classical music, can get packed wknds; dogs welcome, tables on back terrace, cl lunchtimes, open all day wknds *(the Didler, S J and C C Davidson)*

☆ *Wilkes Head* ST13 5DS [St Edward St]: Convivial three-room local dating from 18th c (still has back coaching stables), tied to Whim with their ales and interesting guests, good choice of whiskies, farm cider, friendly chatty landlord, welcoming regulars and dogs, filled rolls, pub games, gas fire, lots of pump clips; juke box in back room, Mon music night; children allowed in one room (but not really a family pub), fair disabled access, tables outside, open all day except Mon lunchtime *(the Didler)*

LICHFIELD [SK1108]

Duke of Wellington WS14 9BJ [Birmingham Rd]: Busy open-plan real ale pub, well kept Fullers London Pride, Marstons Pedigree and up to six changing guests, friendly staff, good mix of customers, log fire, pool and darts; nice garden, open all day Thurs-Sun *(the Didler)*

Hedgehog WS13 8JB [Stafford Rd (A51)]: Family-friendly Vintage Inn in sizeable 17th-c building, lots of well spaced tables and plenty of nooks and corners, enjoyable good value food all day inc lunchtime deals and Sun roasts, well kept ales such as Banks's, Bass, Everards and Marstons Pedigree; picnic-sets in big garden, bedrooms, open all day *(Martin Smith, R C Vincent, Roger and Linda Norman)*

Horse & Jockey WS14 9JE [Tamworth Rd (A51 Lichfield—Tamworth)]: Dining pub with friendly helpful service, enjoyable generous food from home-made pies to fresh fish, four linked softly lit rooms with some panelling, settles, sepia photographs, books, plates and so forth, Black Sheep, Marstons, Timothy Taylors and guests *(David Green)*

LITTLE BRIDGEFORD [SJ8727]

Worston Mill ST18 9QA [Worston Lane; nr M6 junction 14; turn right off A5013 at Little Bridgeford]: Useful sensibly priced dining pub in attractive 1814 watermill, ales such as Greene King and Marstons, friendly service, conservatory; children welcome, attractive grounds with adventure playground and nature trail (lakes, islands etc); open all day *(LYM, J D O Carter, Alan and Eve Harding)*

MILWICH [SJ9533]

Red Lion ST15 8RU [Dayhills; B5027 towards Stone]: Unpretentious bar at end of working farmhouse, old settles, tiled floor, inglenook log or coal fire, Bass, Worthington and a guest tapped from the cask, friendly welcome, darts, dominoes and cribbage; lavatories in converted cowshed; open all day Sun *(the Didler)*

ONECOTE [SK0455]

Jervis Arms ST13 7RU [B5053]: Busy country pub, black-beamed main bar with inglenook woodburner, well kept Titanic, Wadworths 6X and three or four changing guests, good value food, separate dining and family rooms; attractive streamside garden, open all day Sun *(Helene Grygar, LYM, the Didler)*

PENKRIDGE [SJ9214]

Littleton Arms ST19 5AL [St Michaels Sq/ A449 – M6 detour between junctions 12 and 13]: Busy M&B dining pub/hotel (former coaching inn) with contemporary layout, varied choice of enjoyable good value food inc lunchtime deals, several wines by the glass, ales such as Salopian Oracle, Wells & Youngs Bombardier and Wye Valley HPA, friendly young staff; piped music; children welcome, ten bedrooms, open all day *(Jeremy King, Stuart Paulley, Nigel Epsley, Alan and Eve Harding)*

☆ *Star* ST19 5DJ [Market Pl]: Charming busy open-plan local with big helpings of bargain food, well kept Marstons-related ales, efficient cheery service, lots of low black beams and button-back red plush, open fires; no credit cards, piped music, sports TV; open all day, terrace tables *(Dave Irving, Jenny Huggins, Alan and Eve Harding, BB)*

RANTON [SJ8422]

☆ *Hand & Cleaver* ST18 9JZ [Butt Lane, Ranton Green]: Tastefully extended country pub with landlord doing good well priced food from sandwiches to some enterprising cooking, friendly attentive service, good wines by the glass, four changing well kept ales, log fires, lots of exposed beams and timber, piano, darts, restaurant; children and dogs welcome, cl Mon *(Henry Pursehouse-Tranter, Richard Clarke)*

Yew Tree ST18 9JT: Dining pub revitalised under new owners, food from pub standards up using local produce inc Sun carvery, well kept Greene King ales, restaurant; gardens either side, bedrooms, open all day Sun, cl Mon *(Paul and Margaret Baker)*

RUGELEY [SK0220]

Wolseley Arms ST17 0XS [Wolseley Bridge, A51/A513 NW]: Modernised Vintage Inn with farmhouse-style interior, wide choice of food all day inc lunchtime set deals, changing ales such as Bass, Marstons and Timothy Taylors; children welcome, disabled access, handy for Shugborough Hall and Cannock Chase, open all day *(Henry Pursehouse-Tranter)*

SHEBDON [SJ7426]

Wharf ST20 0PY [signed off A519 N of Newport; Adbaston Rd, nr Harper Adams agricultural college]: Proper old-fashioned pub below Shropshire Union Canal embankment (magnificent aqueduct nearby), good reasonably priced food, real ales and farm cider; children welcome, big garden, cl wkdy lunchtimes *(Charles and Pauline Stride)*

SHEEN [SK1160]
Staffordshire Knot SK17 0ET [off B5054 at Hulme End]: Welcoming 17th-c stone-built village pub, flagstones and two side fires, enjoyable food inc good Sun roasts, well kept Marstons Pedigree, friendly helpful staff *(Phil Clasper)*

SLITTING MILL [SK0217]
Horns WS15 2UW [Slitting Mill Rd]: Two large comfortably furnished rooms, one with bar and pool, the other set for dining, good choice of food (not Mon) inc bargain bar menu, Adnams, Greene King and John Smiths; garden, on edge of Cannock Chase *(Dave Braisted, David Green)*

STAFFORD [SJ9321]
Radford Bank ST17 4PG [Radford Bank (A34)]: Very child-friendly Innkeepers Fayre with bargain all-day carvery in large downstairs lounge – easy wheelchair access; nice outdoor seating area and play area, canal walks nearby *(Henry Pursehouse-Tranter)*
Shire Horse ST16 1GZ [1 mile from M6 junction 14 via A34 – junction A34/A513]: New Chef & Brewer built to look old, small secluded areas and open fires, bric-a-brac, welcoming staff and good atmosphere, wide choice of enjoyable all-day food inc lunchtime set deals (Mon-Thurs), three changing ales; parking fee refunded against food/drink; children welcome, disabled facilities, outside tables by road, bedrooms in next door Premier Inn, open all day *(Martin Grosberg, Alan and Eve Harding, Henry Pursehouse-Tranter)*
Vine ST16 2JU [Salter St]: Large traditional hotel with comfortable well divided bar, wide all-day food choice inc restaurant bargains for two, well kept low-priced Banks's, good service; children welcome, good disabled access, 27 bedrooms *(Henry Pursehouse-Tranter)*

STONE [SJ9033]
Swan ST15 8QW [Stafford St (A520)]: Immaculate converted warehouse by Trent & Mersey Canal, up to ten well kept ales inc interesting local brews (summer beer festival), good cider and wine choice too, log fires, buoyant atmosphere, good friendly service, bar lunches (not Sun or Mon); frequent live music nights; terrace tables, open all day *(Andrew Blagbrough)*

STOURTON [SO8485]
☆ *Fox* DY7 5BL [1.2 miles W along A458 from junction with A449]: Roadside pub in same family for over 30 years, cosy series of rooms, sturdy varnished tables, pews and settles on carpet or bare boards, open woodburners, dining areas inc smart conservatory with neat bentwood furniture,

food from sizeable baguettes up, Bathams Best and perhaps a guest; piped music; children welcome, picnic-sets on terrace and big stretch of sloping grass, handy for Kinver Country Park walks and Staffordshire Way, bedrooms, open all day *(LYM, Theo, Anne and Jane Gaskin, M G Hart)*

STOWE [SK0027]
Cock ST18 0LF [off A518 Stafford—Uttoxeter]: Nicely laid out bistro-style conversion of old village pub, good food inc bargain set lunches, friendly efficient service *(Susan and Nigel Brookes, Leslie and Barbara Owen)*

SWINSCOE [SK1348]
Dog & Partridge DE6 2HS [A52 3 miles W of Ashbourne; Town End Lane]: 17th-c stone-built beamed coaching inn set down from road, superb views from dining room's conservatory extension, wide choice of reasonably priced food, good service, Greene King ales, lots of bric-a-brac; children and dogs welcome, garden with play area *(Dennis Jones, Bernard Stradling)*

SWYNNERTON [SJ8535]
Fitzherbert Arms ST15 0RA [off A51 Stone—Nantwich]: Olde-worlde beamed country pub with above-average good value food in bar and restaurant, three well kept ales, friendly helpful staff, lovely log fire; comfortable bedrooms, nice village setting *(Susan and Nigel Brookes, R T and J C Moggridge, Stuart Paulley)*

TAMWORTH [SK2004]
Globe B79 7AT [Lower Gungate]: Edwardian town-centre pub, interesting selection of beers, inexpensive home-made food, cheerful service; piped music; good reasonably priced bedrooms *(John and Sylvia Harrop)*

TEAN [SK0138]
Dog & Partridge ST10 4LN [Uttoxeter Rd]: Good generous food, reasonably priced and well served, in pleasant conservatory restaurant, good range of ales and wines, nice countryside *(Meg and Colin Hamilton)*

TRYSULL [SO8594]
Bell WV5 7JB [Bell Rd]: Extended village local, softly lit lounge with lots of table lamps, big grandfather clock, inglenook fire and good chatty atmosphere, cosy bar with brasses and locomotive number-plates, Bathams and guests, interesting bar food from sandwiches up at fair prices, evening restaurant Weds-Sat, friendly service; open all day wknds *(the Didler)*

WESTON [SJ9727]
Saracens Head ST18 0HT [Stafford Rd]: Simple pub doing enjoyable home-made food at attractive prices, friendly staff, a couple of well kept ales, decent wine, large conservatory; unobtrusive piped music; not far from Trent & Mersey Canal *(Michael Edwards)*

WHITMORE [SJ8040]
Mainwaring Arms ST5 5HR [3 miles from M6 junction 15 – A53 towards Mkt Drayton]: Popular old place of great character, with good value simple local food, real ales such as Bass and Marstons Pedigree, wide range of

foreign bottled beers and ciders, quick
friendly service, rambling linked rooms with
beams, stripped stone, four open fires,
antique settles among more modern seats;
children in eating area, seats outside, open
all day Fri and Sat *(Vicky Ashworth)*
YOXALL [SK1420]
Foresters DE13 8PH [Wood Lane]: Welcoming
three-room refurbished dining pub, good
freshly cooked food from lunchtime panini
up with more elaborate pricey evening
dishes (booking advised), decent sensibly
priced wine list, friendly proficient service,

small bar area with Marstons Pedigree and
Thatcher's cider; children welcome, outside
seating, cl Sun evening, Mon
(Edward Leetham, Leo and Barbara Lionet)
Golden Cup DE13 8NQ [Main St (A515)]: Well
furnished friendly village inn dating from
early 18th c, good service, reasonably priced
home-made food from sandwiches up, well
kept Marstons and Timothy Taylors Landlord,
lounge bar, games in public bar; waterside
garden, good reasonably priced bedrooms,
open all day wknds *(Paul and June Holmes,
John and Helen Rushton)*

Please tell us if any Lucky Dips deserve to be upgraded to a Main Entry –
and why: feedback@goodguides.com, or (no stamp needed)
The Good Pub Guide, FREEPOST TN1569, Wadhurst, E Sussex TN5 7BR.

Suffolk

New Main Entries this year are the Greyhound at Pettistree and the White Horse at Whepstead, both ticking all the boxes for enjoyable food and drink served by welcoming staff. Doing particularly well among the town pubs are the Cross Keys in Aldeburgh (super seafront position), the Fat Cat in Ipswich (with a tremendous range of 22 real ales, as well as local cider and lager, making it very much a drinkers' haunt), and the civilised and reliable Crown and the ever-popular Lord Nelson, both in Southwold. More rural places that our readers especially enjoy include the Ship on the coast at Dunwich, the Dog at Grundisburgh (earning a Beer Award this year, and with interesting food too), the half-timbered Swan at Hoxne (with good food and beer, and a lovely streamside garden), the Angel at Lavenham (good drinks and bedrooms, and a prime location in a marvellously preserved old village), the nicely unchanging Kings Head at Laxfield, the pleasantly pubby Kings Head at Orford, the friendly Brewers Arms at Rattlesden, the Golden Key at Snape (with plenty of enthusiastic reports for the outstanding food as well as for the welcoming owners, this is our Suffolk Dining Pub of the Year 2011), the Plough & Sail also at Snape (much liked for its food), the St Peters Brewery at South Elmham (lots of character, with own-brew beers served in a stunning manor house), the Crown at Stoke-by-Nayland (earning a Stay Award, and a very good all-rounder, with excellent food) and the Dolphin at Thorpeness (a pleasant all-rounder on the coast).

ALDEBURGH   TM4656   MAP 5

Cross Keys

Crabbe Street; IP15 5BN

Seats outside 16th-c pub near beach, chatty atmosphere, friendly licensee and local beer

The position on the seafront makes this a favourite spot in summer. Inside, there's a cheery bustling atmosphere helped along by the obliging licensee and his staff. The low-ceilinged interconnecting bars have two inglenook fireplaces, antique and other pubby furniture, the landlord's collection of oils and Victorian watercolours, and paintings by local artists on the walls. Adnams Bitter, Broadside and Explorer on handpump, Aspall's cider, decent wines by the glass and several malt whiskies; piped music and games machine. The bedrooms are attractively refurbished. The terrace behind is sheltered by two walls and has views across the promenade and shingle to the sea.

Simple bar food could include sandwiches, ploughman's, popular local cod and chips, oysters, fish pie, steak and kidney pie, moules and chips, and puddings such as treacle sponge. *Starters/Snacks: £3.90 to £5.95. Main Courses: £3.95 to £11.50. Puddings: £3.50*

Adnams ~ Tenants Mike and Janet Clement ~ Real ale ~ Bar food (12-2(2.30 Sat, Sun), 7-9; not Sun evening) ~ (01728) 452637 ~ Children welcome ~ Dogs welcome ~ Open 11(12 Sun)-midnight ~ Bedrooms: £55B/£89.50S(£85B)

Recommended by Simon Rodway, Charles and Pauline Stride, S T W Norton, Barry Collett, Dr D J and Mrs S C Walker

BURY ST EDMUNDS

TL8564   MAP 5

Nutshell

The Traverse, central pedestrian link off Abbeygate Street; IP33 1BJ

Tiny, simple local with lots of interest on the walls and a couple of real ales

Described by one reader as 'a delightful half pub', this friendly place is quite a curio and is as small as its name suggests. Its timeless interior contains a short wooden bench along its shop-front corner windows, one cut-down sewing-machine table, an elbow rest running along its rather battered counter, and Greene King IPA and Abbot on handpump. A mummified cat, found walled up here, hangs from the dark brown ceiling (and also seems to have a companion rat), along with stacks of other bric-a-brac, from bits of a skeleton through vintage bank notes, cigarette packets and military and other badges to spears and a great metal halberd; piped music, chess and dominoes. The stairs up to the lavatories are very steep and narrow; more reports please.

🍴 **No food.**

Greene King ~ Tenant Jack Burton ~ Real ale ~ No credit cards ~ (01284) 764867 ~ Children welcome till 7pm ~ Dogs welcome ~ Open 11-11; 12-10.30 Sun
Recommended by the Didler, Danny Savage

Old Cannon 🍺 🛏

Cannon Street, just off A134/A1101 roundabout at N end of town; IP33 1JR

Busy own-brew town pub with local drinks and good bar food

Half a dozen interesting real ales and a good range of other drinks make this yellow-brick pub well worth seeking out. The bar is dominated by two huge gleaming stainless-steel brewing vessels, and has views up to a steel balustraded open-plan malt floor above the counter where they serve the pub's own Gunner's Daughter and Old Cannon Best alongside seasonal ales and a guest or two on handpump. A row of chunky old bar stools line the ochre-painted counter (which also serves Aspall's cider and apple juice, a local lager, continental beers and a dozen wines by the glass) with its steel handrail, and into the room, a mix of old and new chairs and tables and upholstered banquettes stand on a well worn bare-boards floor; piped music. Behind, through the old side coach arch, is a good-sized cobbled courtyard neatly set with rather stylish metal tables and chairs, and planters and hanging baskets. The refurbished bedrooms are in what was the old brewhouse across the courtyard. Dogs allowed on Sunday and Monday evenings only; August bank holiday beer festival. More reports please.

🍴 **Uncomplicated but particularly tasty bar food** includes items like lunchtime baguettes, orford smoked trout with cucumber and dill mayonnaise, beer-battered lowestoft cod, tamarind-glazed roast gressingham duck breast, lamb cutlets with sage and caper crust, and sausages with onion gravy and beer-batter pudding; thai banquet first Tuesday of the month. *Starters/Snacks: £4.25 to £5.50. Main Courses: £8.75 to £14.95. Puddings: £2.25 to £5.25*

Free house ~ Licensee Clare Curtis ~ Real ale ~ Bar food (12-2(3 Sun), 6-9; not Sun, Mon evenings) ~ Restaurant ~ (01284) 768769 ~ Children welcome weekend lunchtimes ~ Dogs allowed in bar ~ Live entertainment one Mon of the month ~ Open 12-3, 5-11; 12-11 Sat; 12-10.30 Sun; 12-3, 5-11 Sat and 12-4, 7-10.30 Sun in winter ~ Bedrooms: £69S/£85S
Recommended by M and GR, Mike and Shelley Woodroffe, Jeremy King, John Saville

---

'Children welcome' means the pub says it lets children inside without any special restriction. If it allows them in, but to restricted areas such as an eating area or family room, we specify this. Places with separate restaurants often let children use them, hotels usually let them into public areas such as lounges. Some pubs impose an evening time limit – let us know if you find one earlier than 9pm.

CHELMONDISTON   TM2037   MAP 5

Butt & Oyster

Pin Mill – signposted from B1456 SE of Ipswich; IP9 1JW

Chatty old riverside pub with pleasant views, decent food and drink, and seats on the terrace

Named for the flounders and oysters which used to be caught here, this unpretentious old bargemen's pub has a terrific riverside position with views of all the comings and goings of craft on the River Orwell. Window seats inside share the same pleasing view as the terrace. The half-panelled timeless little smoke room is pleasantly worn and unfussy and has model sailing ships around the walls and high-backed and other old-fashioned settles on the tiled floor. Adnams Best, Broadside, Explorer and a couple of seasonal brews are on handpump or tapped from the cask, and several wines by the glass and local cider; board games. The annual Thames Barge Race (end June/beginning July) is fun.

⏹ **Tasty bar food includes sandwiches, soup, baked goats cheese on a salad of olives and tomatoes, smoked trout pâté, steak, various sharing platters, beer-battered cod, home-cooked ham and eggs, burgers with various toppings, chargrilled chicken breast marinated in pesto, vegetarian thai green coconut curry, and steaks; children's menu.** *Starters/Snacks: £4.50 to £6.50. Main Courses: £10.25 to £16.95. Puddings: £4.95*

Adnams ~ Lease Steve Lomas ~ Real ale ~ Bar food (12-9.30) ~ Restaurant ~ (01473) 780764 ~ Children welcome ~ Dogs allowed in bar ~ Folk Sun evenings monthly ~ Open 11(12 Sun)-11

Recommended by JDM, KM, Simon Rodway, the Didler, Pat and Tony Martin, N R White, Peter Meister

DUNWICH   TM4770   MAP 5

Ship

St James Street; IP17 3DT

Pleasantly traditional pub in a coastal village, local ales and cider

Just a stone's throw from the sea in what is left of a charming village (coastal erosion having put paid to much of it over the centuries), this old brick pub is usefully placed for some of the best coastal walks in Suffolk. The traditionally furnished main bar has benches, pews, captain's chairs and wooden tables on its tiled floor, a woodburning stove (left open in cold weather) and lots of sea prints. From the handsomely panelled bar counter, you can get Adnams Bitter and three guests such as Brandon Rusty Bucket, Greenjack Excelsior and Humpty Dumpty Reedcutter served from antique handpumps, Aspall's cider, ten wines by the glass and several malts; dominoes and cribbage. A simple conservatory looks on to a back terrace, and the large garden is very pleasant, with its well spaced picnic-sets, two large anchors and enormous fig tree, and they may have Shakespeare performances in August. The RSPB reserve at Minsmere and nearby Dunwich Museum are certainly worth visiting.

⏹ **Using meat and vegetables from local farms, bar food includes soup, ploughman's, cod and chips, pie of the day, wholetail scampi, roasted vegetable tart, sausages and mash, and puddings.** *Starters/Snacks: £4.25 to £8.50. Main Courses: £7.50 to £16.00. Puddings: £4.25 to £5.50*

Free house ~ Licensee Matt Goodwin ~ Real ale ~ Bar food (12-3, 6-9) ~ Restaurant (evening only) ~ (01728) 648219 ~ Children welcome away from bar ~ Dogs allowed in bar and bedrooms ~ Open 11(12 Sun)-11 ~ Bedrooms: /£95B

Recommended by Mrs S Bezant, Tim Maddison, M and GR, Trevor Swindells, RS, ES, Colin and Ruth Munro, Charles and Pauline Stride, Revd R P Tickle, MJVK, Edward Mirzoeff, Giles and Annie Francis

EARL SOHAM
TM2263   MAP 5

Victoria 🍺 £
A1120 Yoxford—Stowmarket; IP13 7RL

Nice beers from brewery across the road in this friendly, informal local

There's an easy-going atmosphere in this simply furnished place. The outstanding attraction is the beer on handpump, brewed across the road in the Earl Soham brewery, with Albert Ale, Victoria Bitter and a couple of seasonal brews; also Aspall's cider. Fairly basic and definitely well worn, the bar is sparsely furnished with kitchen chairs and pews, plank-topped trestle sewing-machine tables and other simple scrubbed pine country tables, and there's stripped panelling, tiled or board floors, an interesting range of pictures of Queen Victoria and her reign, and open fires; shove-ha'penny, chess and cards. There are seats on a raised back lawn, with more out in front. The pub is quite close to a wild fritillary meadow at Framlingham, and a working windmill at Saxtead.

🍴 **Straightforward bar food includes sandwiches, ploughman's, soup, beef casserole, specials, and puddings.** *Starters/Snacks: £4.75 to £6.50. Main Courses: £6.50 to £9.95. Puddings: £4.50*

Own brew ~ Licensee Paul Hooper ~ Real ale ~ Bar food (12-2, 9.45) ~ (01728) 685758 ~ Children welcome ~ Dogs welcome ~ Open 11.30-3, 6-11; 12-3, 7-10.30 Sun

Recommended by Charles and Pauline Stride, Ian and Nita Cooper, Mike and Sue Loseby, Derek and Sylvia Stephenson, WAH, John Saville, Tim Maddison

EASTBRIDGE
TM4566   MAP 5

Eels Foot 🛏
Off B1122 N of Leiston; IP16 4SN

Country local with hospitable atmosphere, fair value food, and Thursday evening folk sessions; bedrooms

Readers have enjoyed popping in to this nicely pubby place for one of the regular informal folk jamming nights, or after an afternoon's walking or bird-watching at nearby Minsmere RSPB reserve. The upper and lower parts of the bar have light modern furnishings on stripped wood floors, a warming fire, and Adnams Bitter, Broadside and Gun Hill on handpump, several wines by the glass, malts and Aspall's cider; darts in a side area, board games, cribbage and a neat back dining room. There are seats on the terrace and benches out in the lovely big back garden. This is a popular spot with bird-watchers, cyclists and walkers and the fresh water marshes bordering the inn offer plenty of opportunity for watching the abundance of birds and butterflies; a footpath leads you directly to the sea. The bedrooms (one with wheelchair access) in the newish building are comfortable and attractive.

🍴 **Good value bar food includes baguettes, whitebait, beer-battered cod, steak in ale pie, smoked haddock and spring onion fishcakes, three-cheese cannelloni, and puddings such as treacle tart and white chocolate and berry pudding.** *Starters/Snacks: £4.95 to £6.25. Main Courses: £7.95 to £13.95. Puddings: £4.50*

Adnams ~ Tenant Corinne Webber ~ Real ale ~ Bar food (12-2.30, 7-9 (6.30-8 Thurs)) ~ Restaurant ~ (01728) 830154 ~ No children in bar after 9.30pm ~ Dogs allowed in bar ~ Live music Thurs evening and last Sun of the month ~ Open 11.30-11(10.30 Sun) ~ Bedrooms: £70B/£90B

Recommended by Danny Savage, Charles and Pauline Stride, Revd R P Tickle, Lois Dyer, Roy Hoing

> Post Office address codings confusingly give the impression that some pubs are in Suffolk, when they're really in Cambridgeshire, Essex or Norfolk (which is where we list them).

EASTON   TM2858   MAP 5

White Horse ♀

N of Wickham Market on back road to Earl Soham and Framlingham; IP13 0ED

Lovely old pub with sensibly short choice of jolly good food, good wines and local beers

This pretty pink-rendered 16th-c inn has tables in a rustic garden where you can enjoy a game of croquet. Inside, it has two neat and smartly simple rooms, unspoilt and traditional, with country kitchen chairs, good small settles, cushioned stripped pews and stools, and open fires; board games and piped music. You can have any wine from the carefully chosen list of about 30 by the glass, and they've Adnams Bitter and a local guest such as Woodfordes Wherry on handpump. There are darts in the separate games room, table tennis in the barn. They plan to have bedrooms available in 2011. Note that opening hours may be limited on some major holidays. More reports please.

🍽 Using thoughtfully sourced local products (they've recently begun growing vegetables and rearing livestock on their own smallholding) and with a high standard set in the kitchen, the seasonally changing menu, which tends to be imaginative, also takes on traditional dishes: maybe soup, venison carpaccio, locally shot pigeon breast with puy lentils and rocket leaves, smoked trout and smoked salmon salad, lambs liver with dry-cured suffolk bacon, cod in beer batter, home-cooked suffolk ham with double free-range eggs from the garden, game pie, and puddings such as chocolate brownie with honeycomb ice-cream and blackberry cheesecake. *Starters/Snacks: £5.00 to £9.00. Main Courses: £8.00 to £17.00. Puddings: £4.00 to £7.00*

Punch ~ Lease Tim Wood ~ Real ale ~ Bar food (12-2, 6.30-9) ~ Restaurant ~ (01728) 746456 ~ Children welcome ~ Dogs welcome ~ Open 12-2.30, 6-11; closed Tues in winter
Recommended by Ian Phillips, David Blackburn

EDWARDSTONE   TL9542   MAP 5

White Horse ◀

Village signposted off A1071 in Boxford; pub at Mill Green, just E; CO10 5PX

Own-brew pub, traditional furnishings in simple rooms, hearty food, self-catering and a campsite

Eight real ales at this unpretentious local feature several from their own Mill Green brewery on the site. Their own-brew Green Goose, Mawkin Mild, Livelys Fair and White Horse Bitter are on handpump and tapped straight from the barrel, alongside seasonal brews and guests from breweries like Adnams and Crouch Vale; also local farm cider and organic fruit juices. There are several varying-sized bar rooms as well as a tiny little room with just one table and lots of beer mats on the walls. The floors are bare boards throughout, the cream walls above a pink dado are hung with rustic prints and photographs, there's a mix of second-hand tables and chairs including an old steamer bench and panelled settle, a piano, and woodburning stove as well as a fireplace. Piped music, darts, bar billiards, ring the bull, quoits, dominoes, cards and board games. There are some sturdy teak tables and seats on an end terrace, an attractive smokers' shelter with green panelled seating, and some makeshift picnic-sets on a grassy area. The self-catering 'cottages' are rather scandinavian in style, and there's a campsite with a shower block. More reports please.

🍽 Hearty pub food, using beef, lamb and vegetables from local farms and free-range eggs, features soup, ploughman's, salads, venison pie, fish and chips, curries, various burgers, sausage and mash, apple and almond sponge and dark chocolate pots. *Starters/Snacks: £3.25 to £4.25. Main Courses: £4.95 to £12.95. Puddings: £4.25 to £4.50*

Own brew ~ Licensee Amy Mitchell ~ Real ale ~ Bar food (12-3, 5-9; not Sun evening and Mon except bank hols) ~ (01787) 211211 ~ Children welcome until 8pm ~ Dogs welcome ~ Open mike night Weds, live band last Sat of the month ~ Open 12-3(not Mon), 5-11; 12-12 Fri-Sun; cl Mon-Thurs lunchtime in winter ~ Bedrooms: /£80B
Recommended by MDN, Giles and Annie Francis, John Prescott

GRUNDISBURGH

Dog ⟨🍴⟩ ♀ ☕▮

Off A12 via B1079 from Woodbridge bypass; The Green – village signposted; IP13 6TA

Civilised, friendly pub run by two brothers; enjoyable food, excellent choice of drinks and a log fire; garden with play area

This thoroughly convivial all-rounder near the village green has continued to generate enthusiastic feedback from readers. Nicely villagey, the public bar on the left has oak settles and dark wooden carvers around a mix of tables on the tiles, and an open log fire. The softly lit and relaxing carpeted lounge bar has comfortable seating around dark oak tables, antique engravings on raspberry walls and unusual flowers in the windows; it links with a similar bare-boards dining room, with some attractive antique oak settles; TV and darts. The impressive array of ten real ales includes Adnams, Earl Soham and guests from brewers like Cliff Quay, Nethergate and Woodfordes on handpump, half a dozen wines by the glass, ciders, local lager and good espresso coffee. There are quite a few picnic-sets out in front by flowering tubs and the fenced back garden has a play area. The jack russell is called Poppy.

🍴 They cure a lot of their own produce and the seasonal ingredients they use are carefully sourced, with game coming from local estates and meat from local farms. The particularly enjoyable bar food might include lunchtime sandwiches and baguettes, soup, potato gnocchi tossed with mascarpone and fresh herbs, fried tiger prawns, fried marinated chicken breast, sausages and mash, various pies, roast saddle of rabbit wrapped in bacon with rösti potatoes and gravy, roast fillet of bass, and puddings such as chocolate mocha tart and spotted dick and custard. *Starters/Snacks: £1.75 to £4.95. Main Courses: £4.95 to £12.00. Puddings: £2.75 to £4.50*

Punch ~ Lease Charles and James Rogers ~ Real ale ~ Bar food (12-2, 5.30-9) ~ Restaurant ~ (01473) 735267 ~ Children welcome away from bar ~ Dogs allowed in bar ~ Open 12-3, 5.30-11; 12-11 Fri and Sat; 12-10.30 Sun; closed Mon

Recommended by MDN, Mrs J Ekins-Daukes, Charles and Pauline Stride, Tom Gondris, Jeremy King, S T W Norton, Christopher Sims

HOXNE

Swan ♀

Off B1118, signed off A140 S of Diss; Low Street; IP21 5AS

Friendly, relaxed old pub with good choice of drinks, bar food and seats in large garden

In fine weather it is very inviting to sit out under parasols on two sheltered terraces here, or in the spacious garden which extends to a stream; there may be a boules match in progress. Laden with historic atmosphere, the timber-framed 15th-c building contains a relaxed pubby bar with two solid oak counters, broad oak floorboards and a deep-set inglenook fireplace. Adnams Best and Broadside, Woodfordes Wherry and a guest such as Timothy Taylors Landlord or Sharps Doom Bar are on handpump or tapped from the cask, alongside wines by the glass and Aspall's cider; they hold beer festivals in May and November. Nearby, the tree to which King Edmund was tied to at his execution is said to form part of a screen in the neighbouring church.

🍴 Well presented bar food might feature filled sandwiches and baguettes, soup, creamy garlic mushrooms, meat or vegetarian lasagne, slow-roasted belly pork with black pudding and cider gravy, fish and chips, rib-eye steak, buttered gnocchi with spinach and pesto cream sauce, and puddings such as treacle and apple tart. *Starters/Snacks: £2.50 to £6.50. Main Courses: £7.95 to £15.95. Puddings: £5.00*

Enterprise ~ Lease Jo-Anne and David Rye ~ Real ale ~ Bar food ~ Restaurant ~ (01379) 668275 ~ Children welcome ~ Dogs allowed in bar ~ Open 12-3, 6-11; 12-10.30 Sun

Recommended by Evelyn and Derek Walter, Tina and David Woods-Taylor, Jeremy King

---

If we know a pub does summer barbecues, we say so.

ICKLINGHAM   TL7872   MAP 5

Red Lion

A1101 Mildenhall—Bury St Edmunds; IP28 6PS

16th-c thatched pub with a relaxed atmosphere, good food and usually local beers

Full of character, this friendly old place has a pleasant chatty atmosphere and plenty of
signs of its age throughout. From behind the counter, Fudge, the pub dog, offers a cheery
meet-and-greet service while the helpful landlord serves three guests from brewers such
as Earl Soham, Humpty Dumpty and Woodfordes on handpump, several wines by the glass
and lots of country wines. The most striking part is the beamed bar with its cavernous
inglenook fireplace, attractive furnishings including a nice mixture of wooden chairs and
oriental rugs on the wood floor; board games, cribbage, darts and piped music. The
carpeted dining area, behind a knocked-through fireplace, has wooden tables and chairs.
There are picnic-sets with colourful parasols on a lawn in front (the pub is well set back
from the road). West Stow Country Park and the Anglo-Saxon Village are close by.

📶 **Bar food might include soup, ploughman's, locally smoked pigeon, beer-battered
haddock with minted mushy peas and chunky chips, pork and ale sausages with cheese,
mushroom and chive risotto, goan chicken and prawn curry, burgers with various toppings,
and puddings such as almond tart with clotted cream ice-cream and buttermilk pudding
with lemon and vanilla.** *Starters/Snacks: £4.50 to £6.50. Main Courses: £9.95 to £11.95.
Puddings: £4.50 to £6.50*

Free house ~ Licensees Ed Lockwood and Aileen Towns ~ Real ale ~ Bar food (12-2.30,
6-9(6.30-8.30 winter)) ~ Restaurant ~ (01638) 711698 ~ Children welcome if well behaved ~
Dogs allowed in bar ~ Open 12-2.30(3 Sat, Sun), 6-11; closed Sun evening, Mon (except bank
hols)

*Recommended by Russell Sawyer, Mrs D M Bailey, N R White, Tim and Rosemary Wells, Jeremy King,
Sheila Topham, Nick and Ginny Law, D M Picton*

IPSWICH   TM1844   MAP 5

Fat Cat 🍺

Spring Road, opposite junction with Nelson Road (best bet for parking up there); IP4 5NL

Fantastic range of changing real ales in a well run town pub; garden

Not many pubs in the country have such a staggering selection of real ales as this
thoroughly likeable place – 22 at the last count. With just Adnams on handpump, the
rest are tapped straight from the cask in the tap room. Coming from far and wide they
might be from brewers such as Crouch Vale, Dark Star, Elgoods, Fat Cat, Fullers, Green
Jack, Hop Back, Oakham, Skinners, St Peters, RCH and Woodfordes – the list is pretty
much endless. They also stock quite a few belgian bottled beers, Aspall's cider, local lager
and fruit wines. The bare-boarded bars have a mix of café and bar stools, unpadded wall
benches and cushioned seats around cast-iron and wooden pub tables, and lots of enamel
brewery signs and posters on canary-yellow walls. Often to be seen perched on a pub
stool, the pub cat is called Dave, and the sausage dog is called Stanley. There's also a
spacious back conservatory, and several picnic-sets on the terrace and lawn. Very little
nearby parking.

📶 **They don't have a kitchen but keep a supply of scotch eggs, pasties, pies and
sometimes filled baguettes in the fridge, and are quite happy for you to bring in
takeaways (not Fri, Sat).** *Starters/Snacks: £2.60 to £2.90*

Free house ~ Licensees John and Ann Keatley ~ Real ale ~ Bar food ~ (01473) 726524 ~
Open 12-11(midnight Fri); 11am-1am Sat

Recommended by Danny Savage, the Didler, N R White

> Food details, prices, timing etc refer to bar food (if that's separate and different
> from any restaurant there).

LAVENHAM

TL9149 MAP 5

Angel ♀ ◧ 🛏

Market Place; CO10 9QZ

Handsome old inn with a good range of drinks, sizeable back garden and comfortable bedrooms

Thought to be Lavenham's oldest inn, this Tudor building has picnic-sets out front making the most of the setting in the former market square of this delightful small town. The light and airy long bar area has plenty of polished dark tables, a big inglenook log fire under a heavy mantelbeam, and some attractive 16th-c ceiling plasterwork (even more elaborate pargeting in the residents' sitting room upstairs). Round towards the back, on the right of the central servery, is a further dining area with heavy, stripped-pine country furnishings. They have shelves of books and lots of board games. Adnams Bitter, Greene King IPA and Nethergate Maypole and a guest like Adnams Irish Stout on handpump, several malts and a dozen wines by the glass. There are tables under parasols in a sizeable sheltered back garden; it's worth asking if they've time to show you the interesting Tudor cellar. This makes a very pleasant base to stay.

🍴 **Ambitious bar food from a seasonal menu and specials' board could include lunchtime sandwiches, baked tartlet of leeks, wild mushroom and gruyère cheese, steak in ale pie, venison and redcurrant casserole, fried calves liver with bubble and squeak, confit of duck with braised red cabbage and dauphinoise potatoes, sweet potato and goats cheese strudel, and puddings like blackberry and apple charlotte or lemon and lime parfait.** *Starters/Snacks: £4.50 to £6.50. Main Courses: £8.50 to £14.95. Puddings: £4.95 to £6.75*

Maypole Group ~ Manager James Haggar ~ Real ale ~ Bar food (12-2.15, 6.45-9.15) ~ Restaurant ~ (01787) 247388 ~ Children welcome ~ Dogs welcome ~ Open 11am-11.30pm; 12-10.30 Sun ~ Bedrooms: £85B/£105B

Recommended by MDN, Michael Doswell, Mrs Carolyn Dixon, DFL, the Didler, Simon and Mandy King, J R and P D Holt, Jeff and Wendy Williams, Tina and David Woods-Taylor, Tom and Jill Jones, Mrs Margo Finlay, Jörg Kasprowski, N R White, John Saville, B R and M F Arnold

LAXFIELD

TM2972 MAP 5

Kings Head ★ ◧

Gorams Mill Lane, behind church; IP13 8DW

Evocatively unspoilt thatched pub with helpful staff, well liked bar food and several real ales; bedrooms and self-contained flat

Described by one reader as 'refreshingly old-fashioned' this character-laden pub has no bar; instead, the helpful staff potter in and out of a cellar tap room (don't be shy to wander in here too) to pour pints of Adnams Bitter, Broadside, Explorer, Extra, Gunhill, Lighthouse and three others such as Everards Tiger straight from the cask. People are intrigued by the chequer-tiled front room, with its striking high-backed square settle that works its way right round the room and is accessed by one corner and takes in an open fire and accommodates one substantial table. It's all dimly lit by a single overhead bulb. Two other equally unspoilt rooms – the card and tap rooms – have pews, old seats, scrubbed deal tables and some interesting wall prints; board games. Outside, the garden has an immaculately mown lawn, colourful herbaceous borders, an arbour covered by a grape and hop vine, a small pavilion for cooler evenings, and plenty of benches and tables; boules.

🍴 **Bar food includes sandwiches, soup and dishes like prawns or mushrooms in garlic butter, steak and ale pie, smoked kippers, lasagne, lamb shank, sausages and mash, and puddings such as sherry trifle and sticky toffee pudding.** *Starters/Snacks: £4.00 to £4.95. Main Courses: £7.50 to £13.95. Puddings: £4.50 to £5.00*

Adnams ~ Tenant Bob Wilson ~ Real ale ~ Bar food (not Sun evening) ~ Restaurant ~ (01986) 798395 ~ Children welcome ~ Dogs welcome ~ Open 12-11(10.30 Sun); closed 3-6(7 Sun) in winter ~ Bedrooms: /£60S

Recommended by John M Murphy, Tim Maddison, Charles and Pauline Stride, Ian and Nita Cooper, the Didler, Simon and Mandy King, S T W Norton, Dr D J and Mrs S C Walker, Stephen and Jean Curtis

LEVINGTON

TM2339 MAP 5

Ship

Gun Hill; from A14/A12 Bucklesham roundabout take A1156 exit, then first sharp left into Felixstowe Road, then after nearly a mile turn right into Bridge Road at Levington signpost, bearing left into Church Lane; IP10 0LQ

Plenty of nautical trappings and character, in a lovely rural position

With new licensees this year, this popular place can be busy at lunchtime, when it's best to book if you plan to eat. Its theme tends towards the nautical, with lots of ship prints and photographs of sailing barges, a marine compass under the serving counter in the middle room and a fishing net slung overhead. Along with benches built into the walls, there are comfortably upholstered small settles (some of them grouped round tables as booths) and a big black round stove. The flagstoned dining room has more nautical bric-a-brac and beams taken from an old barn. Tapped straight from the barrel or under light blanket pressure, Adnams Bitter and Broadside and a guest such as Adnams Oyster are served alongside 11 wines by the glass and Aspall's cider. Surrounded by lovely countryside (with good nearby walks), the pub is attractively placed by a little lime-washed church and has views (if a little obscured) over the River Orwell estuary. More up-to-date reports please.

🍴 **The menu might feature soup, stilton and leek tart, dressed crab salad, butternut squash and sage risotto, mussels in white wine and garlic cream, fish pie, wild boar and apple sausages with caramelised onions and madeira jus, steak in ale pie, and puddings such as treacle tart with toffee ice-cream and lemmon posset.** *Starters/Snacks: £4.95 to £7.95. Main Courses: £9.50 to £16.95. Puddings: £5.75 to £6.95*

Adnams ~ Tenants Adrian and Susan Searing ~ Real ale ~ Bar food (12-2, 6-9.30; 12-3, 6.30-9.30 Sun) ~ Restaurant ~ (01473) 659573 ~ Dogs allowed in bar ~ Open 11.30-3, 6-11; 11.30-11 Sat; 12-10.30 Sun

Recommended by Tony and Shirley Albert, Ian and Nita Cooper, Mrs Carolyn Dixon, J F M and M West, Rosemary Smith

LIDGATE

TL7257 MAP 5

Star ♀

B1063 SE of Newmarket; CB8 9PP

Snug old pink-washed pub, attentive service, spanish and english food, a warm welcome, and seats out in front and in the back garden

There's an enjoyable blend of english and iberian influences here, thanks to the efforts of the chatty spanish landlady. Nicely pubby, the main room has handsomely moulded heavy beams, a good big log fire, candles in iron candelabra on polished oak or stripped-pine tables, and some antique catalan plates over the bar; darts and piped jazz. Besides a second similar room on the right, there's a cosy little dining room on the left. Greene King IPA, Abbot and Ruddles County on handpump, Aspall's cider and decent house wines. There are some tables out on the raised lawn in front and in a pretty little rustic back garden.

🍴 **Usually enjoyable food (but with main course prices that are pretty high for a pub) includes dishes such as gazpacho, boquerones (fresh anchovies floured and fried), catalan salad, smoked salmon and avocado, grilled squid, spanish roast lamb, tiger prawns and cod in garlic mousseline.** *Starters/Snacks: £5.00 to £6.90. Main Courses: £15.95 to £17.95. Puddings: £6.00*

Greene King ~ Lease Maria Teresa Axon ~ Real ale ~ Bar food (12-2.30, 7-10; not Sun evening) ~ Restaurant ~ (01638) 500275 ~ Children welcome ~ Dogs allowed in bar ~ Open 12-3, 6-11; closed Mon

Recommended by Brian and Elizabeth Tora, Tony and Shirley Albert, Mrs Margo Finlay, Jörg Kasprowski, R T and J C Moggridge, M and GR

We list pubs that serve food all day on at least some days at the end of the book.

LINDSEY TYE

TL9846   MAP 5

Red Rose

Village signposted off A1141 NW of Hadleigh; IP7 6PP

Carefully kept 15th-c pub, with a couple of neat bars, enjoyable food, real ales and plenty of outside seating

This friendly, character-laden old place (now known as the Lindsey Rose) has a happy buzz of diners at peak times, as well as those chatting over a drink. There are low beams and some standing timbers, a mix of wooden tables and chairs, red-painted walls, a few pieces of corn dolly work, and dried teasels in glass jugs on the window sills. In front of a splendid log fire in its old brick fireplace are a couple of comfortable red leather squashy sofas, a low table and some brass measuring jugs. A second room is furnished exactly the same and has a second big brick fireplace, but is much simpler in feel, and perhaps quieter; piped music. Adnams Bitter and a couple of Mauldons guests on handpump, a dozen wines by the glass, and friendly, hard-working staff. It has a neat gravelled car park, flowering tubs and a few picnic-sets in front, and more picnic-sets at the back – where there's also a children's play area and a football pitch.

🍴 As well as filled baguettes and nibbles like venison salami and pesto bread, the popular home-made food includes chicken liver parfait, fish of the day, 8oz red poll beefburger, classic chicken kiev, fish and chips, four-cheese lasagne, and puddings like bakewell tart and rhubarb crumble. *Starters/Snacks: £4.50 to £6.50. Main Courses: £9.50 to £16.00. Puddings: £5.50 to £7.00*

Free house ~ Licensee Peter Miller ~ Real ale ~ Bar food (12-2.30, 6.30-9.30; 12-2.30, 7-9 Sun) ~ (01449) 741424 ~ Children welcome ~ Dogs welcome ~ Live jazz once a month on Sun ~ Open 11-3, 5.30-11; 11-11 Sun

Recommended by Mrs Carolyn Dixon, Pat and Tony Martin, David and Gill Carrington, Mrs Margo Finlay, Jörg Kasprowski

LONG MELFORD

TL8646   MAP 5

Black Lion 🍴 ☐ 🛏

Church Walk; CO10 9DN

Well appointed hotel with relaxed and comfortable bar, modern bar food, attentive uniformed staff and lovely bedrooms

In a strikingly handsome village street that is a real pleasure to stroll along, this well run hotel makes a civilised spot for a meal or a drink. Adnams Bitter and Broadside are on handpump alongside Aspall's cider, freshly squeezed apple juice from a local orchard, a good selection of whiskies and 17 wines by the glass. One side of the oak serving counter is decorated in ochre and has bar stools, deeply cushioned sofas, leather wing armchairs and antique fireside settles, while the other side, decorated in shades of terracotta, has leather dining chairs around handsome tables set for the good modern food; open fires in both rooms. Big windows with swagged-back curtains have a pleasant outlook over the village green and there are large portraits including some of racehorses. Service by neatly uniformed staff is friendly and efficient; piped music. There are seats and tables under terracotta parasols on the terrace and more in the appealing Victorian walled garden.

🍴 Eclectic, attractively presented – if not cheap – food might include soup, scallops with saffron risotto and prosciutto ham, chargrilled lambs kidneys with toasted brioche, pressed ham hock with fried quail egg and chervil salad, slow-roasted gloucestershire old spot pork belly, rump steak and beer-battered haddock, with puddings like egg custard tart with poached rhubarb and peach melba. *Starters/Snacks: £5.25 to £8.50. Main Courses: £11.95 to £18.50. Puddings: £5.95*

Ravenwood Group ~ Licensee Craig Jarvis ~ Real ale ~ Bar food (12-2, 7-9.30(10 Sat, Sun)) ~ Restaurant ~ (01787) 312356 ~ Children welcome ~ Dogs allowed in bar and bedrooms ~ Open 11-11; 12-10.30 Sun ~ Bedrooms: £99.50B/£153B

Recommended by Andy Lickfold, John and Enid Morris, Mrs Margo Finlay, Jörg Kasprowski

MONKS ELEIGH   TL9647   MAP 5

Swan ⑪ ♀
B1115 Sudbury—Stowmarket; IP7 7AU

A relaxing place to enjoy restauranty food; real ales, good wines and friendly efficient service

With quietly efficient service, this is a gently upmarket dining pub, and although the accent is firmly on the food it has its pubby side, too. The long pleasantly bright room has modern high-backed leather-seated wooden dining chairs around light wooden tables on the pale oak flooring, and red walls hung with Jack Vetriano prints and framed UK special edition stamps; there's an open fire in a little brick fireplace in the high-ceilinged end room. There are fresh flowers on top of the cream-painted, wooden-topped bar counter and some narrow ceiling beams. Adnams and a guest from a brewery such as Nethergate on handpump, and a good choice of wines by the glass. The little village post office is in the pub car park.

⑪ As well as a good value set lunch, the imaginative food includes starters such as parsnip soup, grilled pigeon breast with crispy smoked bacon and walnut salad, pancakes filled with spinach and ricotta, main courses such as spicy moroccan chicken breast on rice with mango chutney and garnished with cucumber and mint yoghurt, italian-style sweet and sour duck leg on buttered baby spinach, fillet of monkfish wrapped in parma ham and sage leaves on vegetable paella, with puddings such as chocolate loaf with red berry sauce and date sticky toffee pudding. *Starters/Snacks: £4.75 to £7.50. Main Courses: £8.75 to £19.50. Puddings: £5.50 to £7.50*

Free house ~ Licensee Carol Robson ~ Real ale ~ Bar food ~ Restaurant ~ (01449) 741391 ~ Children welcome ~ Open 12-3, 7-11; closed Mon in winter; closed Sun evening and two weeks in school hols (best to ring)

Recommended by Mrs Carolyn Dixon, Jeremy King, MDN, Mr and Mrs C Prentis

NAYLAND   TL9734   MAP 5

Anchor ⑪ ♀
Court Street; just off A134 – turn off S of signposted B1087 main village turn; CO6 4JL

Friendly well run pub with interesting food using home farm and smokehouse produce, wines from own vineyard, and a riverside terrace

With food very much produced next door, from the adjoining farm and smokehouse, this enjoyable dining pub attracts a good mix of locals and visitors. The bare-boards bar has interesting old photographs of pipe-smoking customers and village characters on its pale yellow walls, farmhouse chairs around a mix of tables, and coal and log fires at each end. Another room behind has similar furniture and an open fire, and leads into a small carpeted sun room. Up some quite steep stairs is the stylish restaurant. Adnams Bitter and Greene King IPA are on handpump alongside several wines by the glass, some from their own vineyard; piped music. This is a lovely spot in summer, when you can sit out on the back terrace and look across to the peaceful River Stour and its quacking ducks. Their adjacent farmland is worked by suffolk punch horses – visitors are welcome to watch these magnificent animals or try their hands at the reins.

⑪ Dishes tend to be simple, relying on the good produce for flavour. From their Heritage Farm next door they produce the free-range eggs, vegetables, lamb, pork and beef used here, and they have their own smokehouse. As well as lunchtime home-baked bread sandwiches, the imaginative food might include starters such as herb soup with cheese and croûtons, smoked duck salad, roasts (including haunch of venison, leg of goat and braised leg of mutton), beer-battered cod with fat chips, a smoked platter of fish, meat and cheeses, sausages and mash, vegetable frittata, and puddings like rhubarb pavlova and bread and butter pudding. To be sure of a table, you must book. *Starters/Snacks: £4.50 to £6.50. Main Courses: £6.50 to £16.50. Puddings: £4.50 to £6.50*

Free house ~ Licensee Daniel Bunting ~ Real ale ~ Bar food (12-2(2.30 Sat), 6.30-9(9.30 Sat);
12-3, 5-8.30 Sun) ~ (01206) 262313 ~ Children welcome ~ Open 11-11(10.30 Sun); 11-3,
5-11 weekdays in winter

Recommended by Christopher Sims, Mr Ray J Carter, MDN, David and Sue Medcalf, Paul Humphreys, Ian Wilson, Jane and Alan Bush

ORFORD

TM4249   MAP 5

Jolly Sailor

Quay Street; IP12 2NU

Lovely old pub with views from the garden, plenty of boating memorabilia; camping and bedrooms

This happy, traditional place is not that changed under its newish licensees. It's filled
with boating pictures and shipping charts, and the Thames Room (in the previous
landlord's sitting room) celebrates that river. Built mainly from wrecked ships' timbers,
the several snug rooms have lots of exposed brickwork, and are served from counters and
hatches in an old-fashioned central cubicle. There's an unusual spiral staircase in the
corner of the flagstoned main bar – which also has horsebrasses, local photographs, two
cushioned pews and a long antique stripped deal table, and an open woodburning stove
in the big brick fireplace (with nice horsebrasses above it). Four Adnams beers are on
handpump. Several picnic-sets on grass at the back have views over the marshes, there's
a play tower and camping in the orchard. The refurbished bedrooms look promising. More
reports please.

🍴 **The bar menu includes lunchtime sandwiches, soup, various fish dishes such as beer-
battered cod or crab cakes, rack of lamb, cumberland sausage and mash, and lemon, basil
and parmesan linguine; children's menu.** *Starters/Snacks: £4.65 to £7.25. Main Courses: £8.25
to £14.00. Puddings: £4.00 to £7.00*

Adnams ~ Tenant Gordon Williams ~ Real ale ~ Bar food (12-3, 6-9; 12-9.30 Sat, Sun) ~
(01394) 450243 ~ Children welcome ~ Dogs welcome ~ Open 11-3, 5.30-11; 11-11 Sat, Sun ~
Bedrooms: /£85B

Recommended by Simon Rodway, Mrs M E Mills, Neil Powell, Tony Middis, Hilary Morris

Kings Head 🛏

Front Street; IP12 2LW

Nicely pubby local with tasty food and Adnams beers

Liked both for its food and authentic atmosphere, this has very much the character of a
traditional harbourside pub. In addition to Adnams Bitter, Broadside and Explorer are
several wines by the glass and local farm cider. The main bar is fairly straightforward but
snug, with heavy low beams and traditional furniture on red carpets. There are nice old
stripped-brick walls and rugs on the ancient bare boards in the candlelit dining room;
piped music, board games, magazines and cards.

🍴 **Well liked bar food might include half a pint of prawns, coarse country pâté,
charcuterie, halloumi and aubergine salad, smoked haddock fishcakes, sausage and mash,
battered cod and chips, game and fish pies, vegetable and goats cheese quiche, and
puddings such as white chocolate panna cotta and american cheesecake with apricot sauce.**
Starters/Snacks: £4.95 to £7.50. Main Courses: £8.50 to £15.00. Puddings: £2.95 to £6.50

Adnams ~ Lease Adrian Searing ~ Real ale ~ Bar food (12-2.30(3 Sun), 6.30-9) ~ Restaurant ~
(01394) 450271 ~ Children welcome ~ Dogs welcome ~ Open 11.30-3, 6-11; 11.30-11.30 Sat;
12-10.30 Sun ~ Bedrooms: £65S/£75S

Recommended by Martin and Alison Stainsby, Derek and Sylvia Stephenson, Trevor Swindells, Dr Peter Andrews, Barry Collett

---

If you have to cancel a reservation for a bedroom or restaurant, please telephone or
write to warn them. You may lose your deposit if you've paid one.

PETTISTREE   TM2954   MAP 5

Greyhound

*Brown sign to pub off B1438 S of Wickham Market, 0.5 miles N of A12; The Street;
IP13 0HP*

Neat and polished, with good imaginative food, decent drinks and service

Just taken over by new owners as we went to press, this has just two smallish rooms – so
is worth booking if you want to be sure of a table. Nothing jars here, with polished dark
tables on the green carpet, matching padding for the chairs and heavy settles, pale sage
dado, rather low dark-brown beams and open fires. They have Crouch Vale Brewers Gold,
Earl Soham Victoria, Woodfordes Wherry and a guest beer on handpump, and several
wines by the glass. The well kept side garden has picnic-sets under cocktail parasols, with
more in the front gravel car park.

🍴 **Food available in the bar or restaurant might include lunchtime sandwiches, soup, puff
pastry tartlet with leeks, mushroom and suffolk blue cheese, rib-eye steak, fried fillet of
bream with crayfish tails and herb dressing, risotto of leeks and shallots with roasted
goats cheese, and puddings like eton mess or strawberry and vanilla panna cotta.**
Starters/Snacks: £4.95 to £5.50. Main Courses: £10.95 to £16.95. Puddings: £4.50 to £5.25

Free house ~ Licensee Karen Cousins ~ Real ale ~ Bar food (12-2, 6(7 Sun)-9) ~ Restaurant ~
(01728) 746451 ~ Children in restaurant ~ Open 12-2.30, 6-11; 12-3, 7-10.30 Sun
*Recommended by Mr and Mrs A Curry, Simon Cottrell, Charles and Pauline Stride, Mrs Hilarie Taylor, Justin and
Emma King*

RATTLESDEN   TL9758   MAP 5

Brewers Arms

Off B1115 via Buxhall or A45 via Woolpit, W of Stowmarket; Lower Road; IP30 0RJ

Friendly staff and interesting, generously served food at a traditional village pub

There's a particularly warm welcome here at this 16th-c village local. Recently
refurbished, this solidly built village local does well for its knowledgeably, helpful service
and well prepared food. There's a mix of pubby seating and more comfortable chairs, and
a beamed lounge bar on the left winds back through standing timbers to the main eating
area – a partly flint-walled room with a magnificent old bread oven. French windows
open on to the garden. Greene King IPA and XX Mild and a guest beer such as Greene
King Hare Raiser are on handpump.

🍴 **Served in generous portions, the good range of interesting bar food includes some
inventive sandwiches and filled baguettes (like fish fingers and minted pea mayonnaise),
starters such as soup, stilton and port rarebit and prawn and crab salad; main courses
such as beer-battered haddock, chilli, steamed steak pudding, marinated shank of lamb,
nut loaf, and specials like monkfish and tiger prawn thermidor; and puddings including
apple pie and coffee mousse with almond praline.** *Starters/Snacks: £5.50 to £6.95. Main
Courses: £11.95 to £16.95. Puddings: £5.50*

Greene King ~ Tenants Jeff and Nina Chamberlain ~ Real ale ~ Bar food (not Sun evening or
Mon) ~ Restaurant ~ (01449) 736377 ~ Children welcome ~ Dogs allowed in bar ~ Open 12-3,
6.30-11(midnight Sat); 12-3.30, 9-midnight Sun; closed Mon
Recommended by J F M and M West, Ian Herdman, Bob and Margaret Holder

---

'Children welcome' means the pub says it lets children inside without any special
restriction. If it allows them in, but to restricted areas such as an eating area or family
room, we specify this. Some pubs may impose an evening time limit. We do not
mention limits after 9pm as we assume children are home by then.

REDE

Plough ♀

Village signposted off A143 Bury St Edmunds—Haverhill; IP29 4BE

Promptly served, well liked food in a 16th-c pub, several wines by the glass and friendly service

In a well tucked-away village, this pretty thatched pub has some idyllic spots outside, at picnic-sets in the sheltered cottagey garden or at the front near the village green. Its pretty bar is traditional with low beams, comfortable seating and a solid-fuel stove in its brick fireplace. Any three of Fullers London Pride, Ringwood Best, Timothy Taylors Landlord and Black Sheep are on handpump, with quite a few wines by the glass; piped music.

🍴 **This is a popular place for a meal, especially at weekends (best to book ahead to be sure of a table). Big blackboards list a quickly changing range of food that is served in generous helpings. The menu might include game paella, crab linguine with chilli, black pudding fritters, calves liver with crispy pancetta, bass with butter bean and bacon sauce, and puddings like white chocolate and raspberry cheesecake.** *Starters/Snacks: £3.95 to £6.95. Main Courses: £10.50 to £21.95. Puddings: £4.95*

Admiral Taverns ~ Tenant Brian Desborough ~ Real ale ~ Bar food (not Sun evening) ~ Restaurant ~ (01284) 789208 ~ Children welcome until 8pm ~ Open 11-3, 6.30-midnight; 12-3, 7-10.30 Sun

Recommended by Marianne and Peter Stevens, Peter and Jean Hoare, Simon Watkins, Adele Summers, Alan Black

REYDON

Randolph 🛏

Wangford Road (B1126 just NW of Southwold); IP18 6PZ

Light and airy, relaxed bar, Adnams beers, bedrooms

There's a fresh, contemporary look to the stylish interior here. The bar tends to have a mixture of drinkers and diners, with modern high-backed black leather dining chairs on parquet flooring around a mix of pale chunky wooden tables (each set with a nightlight in a little blue glass-holder), a few prints of the pub from 1910 and photographs of Southwold beach, and blinds for the big windows; there's also a couple of comfortable armchairs, and a sofa by one table, just inside the door. Adnams Bitter and Broadside on handpump and Aspall's cider. Staff are friendly and efficient. The dining room, just across the way, has rush-seated, high-backed dining chairs around similar tables to those in the bar, red carpeting and a pretty little Victorian fireplace (filled with candles rather than logs); piped music, TV, games machine, darts and board games. Dogs are allowed in the little back bar only. There are picnic-sets on a decked area and on grass, and wheelchair access. The bedrooms are good value, with good breakfasts. More reports please.

🍴 **The nicely varied menu includes food such as soup, mussels in leek and cider cream sauce, pressed game terrine, chargrilled steaks, steamed venison suet pudding, battered cod with hand-cut chips, fried halibut wrapped in smoked bacon, tuscan vegetable and white bean stew topped with goats cheese, and puddings like dark chocolate cappuccino mousse.** *Starters/Snacks: £4.50 to £6.00. Main Courses: £9.50 to £14.95. Puddings: £4.95 to £5.50*

Adnams ~ Lease David and Donna Smith ~ Real ale ~ Bar food ~ Restaurant ~ (01502) 723603 ~ Children welcome ~ Open 11-11 ~ Bedrooms: £65B/£100B

Recommended by Tracey and Stephen Groves

ROUGHAM

TL9063   MAP 5

Ravenwood Hall 🍽 ㅜ ⇦

Just off A14 E of Bury St Edmunds; IP30 9JA

Civilised all-day bar in comfortable country house hotel with lovely grounds, fine wines and imaginative food; peaceful A14 break

The all-day bar makes this thoughtfully run hotel useful to know about. Comprising two fairly compact rooms, the bar area has tall ceilings, gently patterned wallpaper and heavily draped curtains for big windows overlooking a sweeping lawn with a stately cedar. The part by the back serving counter is set for food, its nice furnishings including well upholstered settles and dining chairs, sporting prints and a log fire. Adnams Bitter and Broadside on handpump, Aspall's cider, 17 wines by the glass and 25 malts; neat unobtrusive staff give good service. The other end of the bar, the lounge area, has horse pictures, several sofas and armchairs with lots of plump cushions, one or two attractively moulded beams, and a good-sized fragment of early Tudor wall decoration above its big inglenook log fire; piped music. They have a more formal quite separate restaurant. Outside, teak tables and chairs (some under a summer house) stand around a swimming pool; big enclosures by the car park hold geese and pygmy goats; croquet.

🍽 Bar food can be good and they may use their own smoked meats and fish and home-made preserves: sandwiches, pressed foie gras with smoked duck and peppered madeira jelly, goats cheese mousse with carpaccio of beetroot and candied celery, main courses like roasted rump of lamb with goats cheese fondue and sweet potato dauphinoise, fried red mullet, spring wild garlic risotto, sirloin steak, beer-battered haddock with hand-made chips, and puddings like rhubarb poached in vanilla. *Starters/Snacks: £6.50 to £10.25. Main Courses: £11.95 to £19.95. Puddings: £5.50 to £8.95*

Free house ~ Licensee Craig Jarvis ~ Real ale ~ Bar food (12-2, 7-9.30(10 Fri and Sat)) ~ Restaurant ~ (01359) 270345 ~ Children welcome ~ Dogs welcome ~ Open 9am-midnight ~ Bedrooms: £102B/£173B

Recommended by J F M and M West, Rob and Catherine Dunster, Keith and Margaret Kettell, Derek Field

SIBTON

TM3570   MAP 5

White Horse ⇦

Halesworth Road; IP17 2JJ

Friendly, nicely old-fashioned bar, good mix of customers, real ales and enjoyable food; bedrooms

In a tiny hamlet, this charmingly traditional 16th-c inn run by an enthusiastic and friendly husband and wife team has become a dining venue, but it's very much the sort of place to drop into just for a drink too. The comfortable bar has horsebrasses and tack on the walls, old settles and pews and a large inglenook fireplace with a roaring log fire. Adnams Bitter, Greene King Abbot and a guest such as Brandon Rusty Bucket on handpump, several wines by the glass and Aspall's cider are served from the old oak-panelled counter, and there's a viewing panel showing the working cellar and its Roman floor. Steps take you up past an ancient partly knocked-through timbered wall into a carpeted gallery, and there's a smart dining room too. The big garden has plenty of seats, and the comfortable bedrooms are in a converted outbuilding; excellent breakfasts.

🍽 They put thought into sourcing ingredients for the enjoyable bar food, with meat from local farms and game from local shoots, and they smoke their own products. At lunchtime the menu sensibly includes pubby dishes such as sandwiches and rolls with warm fillings, ploughman's, pork and garlic sausages with creamy mash, venison burger and beer-battered cod with hand-cut chips. In the evening there might be soup, chicken liver pâté, seared breast of peppered local woodpigeon, roasted lamb rump with rösti potato, roasted free-range chicken breast, sirloin steak with hand-cut chips, tomato and vegetable puff pastry roll, and puddings such as bakewell tart, orange steam pudding and east anglian cheeses. *Starters/Snacks: £4.25 to £6.00. Main Courses: £8.25 to £17.00. Puddings: £5.00*

Free house ~ Licensees Neil and Gill Mason ~ Real ale ~ Bar food (till 2.30 Sun) ~ Restaurant ~ (01728) 660337 ~ Children welcome if well behaved ~ Dogs allowed in bar ~ Quiz every Mon (not bank hols) ~ Open 12-2.30(3.30 Sun), 6.30(6 Sat)-11(10.30 Sun); closed Mon lunchtime ~ Bedrooms: £65S/£90B

Recommended by Mr and Mrs B Watt, Keith and Susan Moore, Stephen Sheldrake, Philip Bishop, Bruce and Sharon Eden, S T W Norton, Ian and Nita Cooper

SNAPE

TM4058   MAP 5

Golden Key 🍴 ♀
Priory Lane; IP17 1SA

New landlord in neat pub with cottagey rooms

As we went to press we heard that the enthusiastic landlord was leaving this popular pub and going to the Harbour Inn in Southwold. Obviously things will be very different under the new regime but, as many of the staff are staying on, we hope the change-over won't be too dramatic. The traditional low-beamed lounge bar has an old-fashioned settle curving around a couple of venerable stripped tables on the chequer-board tiled floor, a winter open fire, a mix of pubby tables and chairs, fresh flowers, and local art and horsebrasses on the walls; this leads through to a cottagey little dining room with older-style stripped-pine furniture and there's also a low-ceilinged larger dining room, too. Adnams Bitter, Broadside and Explorer are on handpump with 14 wines by the glass and good coffee. Outside are two terraces (one for the morning and a suntrap evening one), both with contemporary wood and steel tables and chairs under large green parasols, and plenty of hanging baskets. Reports on the new regime, please.

🍴 Enjoyable bar food has included ploughman's, chicken liver pâté with beetroot chutney, whitebait with tartare sauce, potted shrimps, beefburger with cheese and bacon, slow-roasted pork with bubble and squeak and confit duck leg with potato, bacon and cream. *Starters/Snacks: £4.50 to £8.50. Main Courses: £9.50 to £16.00. Puddings: £4.00 to £5.50*

Adnams ~ Real ale ~ Bar food (12-2, 6.30(7 Sun)-9) ~ Restaurant ~ (01728) 688510 ~ Children welcome ~ Dogs allowed in bar ~ Open 12-3(4 Sat, Sun), 6(7 Sun)-11

Recommended by BB

Plough & Sail
The Maltings, Snape Bridge (B1069 S); IP17 1SR

Nicely placed dining pub extended airily around an older bar, real ales, food all day weekends, handy for the Maltings, seats outside

Part of the Snape Maltings that now also house the famous concert hall of that name, this pink-washed pub is a successful blend of traditional and modern. It has a light café feel to most of its partly open-plan interior – perhaps it's the wicker and café-style furnishings. The older heart has a woodburning stove, some high bar chairs by the serving counter and rustic pine dining chairs and tables on terracotta tiling. Another cosy little room has comfortable blue sofas and low coffee tables. Most diners head for the simply furnished bar hall and spacious airy dining room with blue-cushioned dining chairs around straightforward tables on the light, woodstrip flooring and high ceilings with A-frame beams; motifs illustrating the history of the Maltings decorate the walls. Another restaurant upstairs has similar furnishings; piped music and darts. Adnams Best and Broadside and a guest like Woodfordes Wherry on handpump, and several wines by the glass. The flower-filled terrace has plenty of teak chairs and tables, and there are some picnic-sets in front of the building. The shops and other buildings in the attractive complex are interesting to wander through.

🍴 Much liked bar food includes sandwiches, filled baguettes and baked potatoes, ploughman's, garlic mushrooms in herb cream on garlic ciabatta, soup, thai salmon fishcakes, smoked fish platter, steak and ale suet pudding, cod and chips, roasted pork loin steak, and puddings such as apple crumble and chocolate soufflé cake. *Starters/Snacks: £3.95 to £9.95. Main Courses: £8.95 to £14.95. Puddings: £4.75*

Deben Inns ~ Lease Steve and Louise Lomas ~ Real ale ~ Bar food (12-2.30, 6-9.30;
12-9.30 weekends) ~ Restaurant ~ (01728) 688413 ~ Children welcome ~ Dogs allowed in bar ~
Open 11(12 Sun)-11

*Recommended by Louise Gibbons, RS, ES, Tracey and Stephen Groves, Adrian and Dawn Collinge, Mr and
Mrs A Curry*

SOUTH ELMHAM   TM3385   MAP 5

St Peters Brewery
St Peter South Elmham; off B1062 SW of Bungay; NR35 1NQ

**Lovely manor dating back to the 13th c, with some fine original features, own-brew beers
and inventive food**

It's worth venturing out here as much to admire the architecture of this striking building
as to enjoy the beers brewed on the premises, with three changing brews on handpump
from St Peters Brewery; also Aspall's cider and bottled beers from the brewery. This fine
manor house dates back to the late 13th c, but was much extended in 1539 using
materials from the then recently dissolved Flixton Priory. It's simply but beautifully
furnished with antique tapestries and furnishings that are completely in keeping with the
building. As well as the bar there's a particularly dramatic high-ceilinged dining hall with
elaborate woodwork, a big flagstoned floor, an imposing chandelier, and candles and
fresh flowers on crisp white-clothed dining tables with smart dining chairs. A couple
more appealing old rooms are reached up some steepish stairs. The brewery buildings are
laid out around a courtyard and the three beers on handpump here are made using water
from a 100-metre (300-ft) bore hole. Others are available from the shop. Outside, tables
overlook the original moat.

🍴 The pubby lunchtime menu includes grilled sardines, goats cheese and tomato tart,
scallops with grilled black pudding, eggs benedict with ham or smoked salmon, pork chop
with cider cream sauce and black pudding, marinated rump of lamb shank, roasted pepper
and artichoke frittata and steak in ale pie. The evening menu is a little more elaborate
with fried frogs legs served with smoked garlic and herb butter, wild boar and pork
terrine with onion compote, bass fillet with hollandaise sauce, venison haunch medallions
on creamed leek mashed potato with red wine and redcurrant sauce, and puddings such as
eton mess and treacle sponge; Sunday roast. *Starters/Snacks: £5.95 to £7.95. Main Courses:
£8.95 to £12.50. Puddings: £5.95*

Own brew ~ Licensee Sam Goodbourn ~ Real ale ~ Bar food (12-2(4 Sun), 7-9) ~ Restaurant ~
(01986) 782288 ~ Children welcome ~ Open 12-3, 6-10; 12-10 Sat; 12-3 Sun; closed Sun
evening, Mon (except bank hols)

*Recommended by Mrs Jane Kingsbury, Mike and Sue Loseby, the Didler, Simon Cottrell, MDN, Jenny Clarke,
John Saville*

SOUTHWOLD   TM5076   MAP 5

Crown
High Street; IP18 6DP

**Civilised and smart old hotel with relaxed bars, a fine choice of drinks, papers to read,
imaginative food and seats outside; bedrooms**

Run by courteous staff, this comfortable hotel gets consistently strong reports as a place
to stay or drink, and for its extremely good, imaginative food. The cosy smaller back oak-
panelled locals' bar, with its pubby atmosphere and red leatherette wall benches on the
red carpet, is reserved for drinkers. Three or four Adnams beers are on handpump
alongside a splendid wine list, with a monthly-changing choice of 20 interesting varieties
by the glass or bottle. The elegant beamed front bar has a relaxed, informal atmosphere,
with polite knowledgeable service, a stripped curved high-backed settle and other dark
varnished settles, kitchen chairs and some bar stools, and a carefully restored and rather
fine carved wooden fireplace; maybe newspapers to read. The tables out in a sunny
sheltered corner are very pleasant, and the bedrooms are comfortable, light and airy.

🍴 Tables are available on a first-come first-served basis so you do need to arrive early. Using local, organic produce, the interesting bar food (not cheap) includes items such as soup, grilled goats cheese, citrus-cured gravadlax with grapefruit salad, mediterranean calamari, chorizo and olive stew, vegetarian sharing platters, cod fillet, chicken with garden pea risotto, spring lamb neck and liver with pease pudding and pea and mint dressing, rib-eye steak, and puddings such as rhubarb and champagne jelly, warm pistachio and olive oil cake, and local cheeses. *Starters/Snacks: £4.50 to £6.95. Main Courses: £12.50 to £18.50. Puddings: £5.25 to £7.95*

Adnams ~ Manager Francis Guildea ~ Real ale ~ Bar food (12-2.30(2 winter), 6(6.30 winter)-9;12-2.30, 5.30-9.30 Sat, 12-3(2.30 winter), 6(6.30 winter)-9 Sun ~ (01502) 722275 ~ Children welcome ~ Dogs allowed in bar ~ Open 11-11; 12-10.30 Sun ~ Bedrooms: £95B/£145B
Recommended by Tina and David Woods-Taylor, Tony and Shirley Albert, David Rule, Mike and Sue Loseby, MJVK, Stephen Funnell

Lord Nelson 🍺

East Street, off High Street (A1095); IP18 6EJ

Bow-windowed town pub with same family running it for over 20 years, excellent service, home-made pubby food and a good choice of drinks; seats outside

A few steps away from the seafront, this cheerful town pub deservedly attracts plenty of locals and visitors alike, but even at its liveliest the good-natured service remains friendly and attentive. The partly panelled traditional bar and its two small side rooms are kept spotless, with good lighting, a small but extremely hot coal fire, light wood furniture on the tiled floor, lamps in nice nooks and corners and some interesting Nelson memorabilia, including attractive nautical prints and a fine model of HMS *Victory*. They serve all the seasonal range of Adnams beers alongside Aspall's cider, and several good wines by the glass; daily papers and board games. There are seats out in front with a sidelong view down to the sea and more in a sheltered (and heated) back garden, with the brewery in sight (and often the appetising fragrance of brewing in progress). Disabled access is not perfect but is possible.

🍴 Well liked bar food includes sandwiches, ploughman's, soup, spicy chicken wings with sour cream, stuffed roasted red pepper with goats cheese, thai green curry, steak, cod or haddock and chips, and daily specials. *Starters/Snacks: £4.50 to £7.50. Main Courses: £7.95 to £10.50. Puddings: £4.95*

Adnams ~ Tenants David and Gemma Sanchez ~ Real ale ~ Bar food ~ (01502) 722079 ~ Children welcome in side rooms ~ Dogs welcome ~ Open 10.30am-11pm; 12-10.30 Sun
Recommended by Derek Field, Terry Mizen, Simon Rodway, Ian and Nita Cooper, Mike and Sue Loseby, Robert Lorimer, Pat and Tony Martin, Tracey and Stephen Groves, Stephen Funnell, Michael Dandy, Charles and Pauline Stride, S T W Norton, Dr D J and Mrs S C Walker, the Didler, Rob and Catherine Dunster, Tim Maddison

STOKE-BY-NAYLAND

TL9836   MAP 5

Crown ★ 🍽 🍷 🛏

Park Street (B1068); CO6 4SE
SUFFOLK DINING PUB OF THE YEAR

Smart dining pub with attractive modern furnishings, bistro-style food, fantastic wine choice and comfortable bedrooms

Receiving a Stay Award this year, this civilised inn has very comfortable accommodation as well as well presented, bistro-style food and a good selection of drinks. Most of the place is open to the three-sided bar servery, but there are two or three cosy tucked-away areas too. The main part, with a big woodburning stove, has quite a few closely spaced tables in a variety of shapes, styles and sizes; elsewhere, several smaller areas have just three or four tables each. Seating varies from deep armchairs and sofas to elegant dining chairs and comfortable high-backed woven rush seats – and there are plenty of bar stools. There are cheerful wildlife and landscape paintings on the pale walls, quite a few attractive table lamps, low ceilings (some with a good deal of stripped old beams), and floors varying from old tiles through broad boards or dark new flagstones to beige carpet; daily papers. Adnams, Brewers Gold, Woodfordes Wherry and a guest such as Crouch Vale Sovereign are on on handpump and as well as several malts they offer a fantastic choice of 37 wines by the glass from a list of around 200 kept in an unusual glass-walled wine 'cellar' in one corner. A sheltered back terrace, with cushioned teak chairs and tables under big canvas parasols, looks out over a neat lawn to a landscaped shrubbery and there are many more picnic-sets out on the front terrace. Disabled access is good and the car park is big.

🍴 **Imaginative modern food, using carefully sourced local produce and recommended matching wines shown against each menu item, might include soup, beer-battered skate with caper and saffron mayonnaise, goats cheese and honey toast with broad beans, battered haddock with thick-cut chips, new season rump of lamb, beef and kidney pudding, warm salad of woodpigeon, fresh fish as available, and puddings like rhubarb and ginger trifle, peanut butter parfait and saffron-poached pear with home-made earl grey ice-cream.** *Starters/Snacks: £4.50 to £7.95. Main Courses: £8.95 to £18.95. Puddings: £3.20 to £9.25*

Free house ~ Licensee Richard Sunderland ~ Real ale ~ Bar food (12-3, 6-9; 12-9 Sun) ~ Restaurant ~ (01206) 262001 ~ Children welcome ~ Dogs allowed in bar ~ Open 11-11; 12-10.30 Sun ~ Bedrooms: £80S(£90B)/£110S(£135B)

Recommended by MDN, Mrs Carolyn Dixon, Mrs Margo Finlay, Jörg Kasprowski, Bruce and Sharon Eden, Jeremy King, Marcus Mann, John and Enid Morris, John Prescott

THORPENESS
TM4759   MAP 5

Dolphin
Just off B1353; village signposted from Aldeburgh; IP16 4NB

Neatly kept, light and airy extended pub in an interesting village, with enjoyable food and plenty of outside seating; bedrooms

This light and airy pub makes an excellent objective for walks from Aldeburgh, along the coast or along the disused railway line. The main bar is a light airy room with an almost scandinavian feel: little candles in glass vases on each of the well spaced, pale wooden tables and a nice mix of old chairs on broad modern quarry tiles, a built-in cushioned seat in the sizeable bay window, a winter log fire in its brick fireplace, and fresh flowers on the wooden bar counter where they keep Adnams Bitter and two guests such as Brandon Rusty Bucket and Green Jack Trawler Boys on handpump, 18 wines by the glass, and several malt whiskies and bourbons; darts and piped music. The public bar to the left of the door is more traditional with a mix of pubby furniture on the stripped wooden floor, some built-in cushioned wall seats with open 'windows' to the bar, and some fine old photographs of long-ago sporting teams, villagers and local scenes on the bottle-green planked walls; there's also a small area with a few high bar stools. The sizeable dining room has lots of windows hung with cheerful curtains, wide strips of coir matting on light wooden flooring, similar wooden furniture, and seaside prints. French windows lead on to a terrace with teak tables and chairs, and beyond that, there are picnic-sets on an extensive stretch of grass; you can hire electric bikes from here. The pub also runs the village stores; the village itself is a fascinating early 20th-c curio, built as a small-scale upmarket holiday resort.

🍴 **Using vegetables from local allotments and fish from whatever the local fishermen catch, bar food might include lunchtime sandwiches, roast pumpkin soup with sage croûtons, confit guinea fowl terrine with grape and apple chutney, grilled sardines with tomato salsa, grilled lamb chops with niçoise salad and poached egg, chicken caesar salad, marinated grilled vegetable tart, grilled salmon with avocado salsa, and puddings such as baked lemon cheesecake with fig compote, pear and almond tart and chocolate pot with crème fraîche.** *Starters/Snacks: £4.50 to £7.25. Main Courses: £8.00 to £17.00. Puddings: £4.50 to £7.50*

Free house ~ Licensee David James ~ Real ale ~ Bar food (12-2.30(4 Sun), 6.30-9.30; not Sun evening) ~ Restaurant ~ (01728) 454994 ~ Children welcome ~ Dogs allowed in bar and bedrooms ~ Open 11-midnight(11 Sun); 11-3.30, 6-11 in winter ~ Bedrooms: £55B/£85B

Recommended by Trevor Swindells, Bruce and Sharon Eden, Miss K Hunt, Mr M Smith, Rob and Catherine Dunster, Paul Humphreys, Charles and Pauline Stride

TUDDENHAM

TM1948 MAP 5

Fountain ♀

Village signposted off B1077 N of Ipswich; The Street; IP6 9BT

Neatly renovated dining pub with well regarded contemporary cooking and plenty of outside seating

In an appealing village on the outskirts of Ipswich, this brick-built dining pub is a very popular lunchtime spot. Its several linked, almost café-style, rooms have heavy beams and timbering, stripped wooden floors, a mix of wooden dining chairs around a medley of light wood tables, an open fire and a few prints (including some Giles' ones; he spent some time here after World War II) on the white walls – décor is minimal. The bar area has Adnams on handpump and several wines by the glass; piped music. Outside on the covered and heated terrace are wicker and metal chairs and wooden tables, and there are more tables under huge parasols out on a sizeable lawn.

🍴 As well as a two- and three-course set menu, bar food might include grilled halloumi cheese with caramelised walnuts and roast pepper salad, duck and spring onion samosa, cromer crab and sweetcorn fritters with red pepper pineapple salsa, lamb burger, goats cheese with sunblush tomato and basil roulade, roasted pork chop in cider and mustard sauce, grilled salmon fillet, and puddings such as apple crumble and bread and butter pudding. *Starters/Snacks: £5.75 to £8.95. Main Courses: £8.95 to £15.75. Puddings: £4.95*

Free house ~ Licensees Charles Lewis and Scott Davidson ~ Real ale ~ Bar food (12-2(4 Sun), 6-9(9.30 Sat); not Sun evening) ~ Restaurant ~ (01473) 785377 ~ No children under 10 in bar after 6.30pm ~ Open 12-2.30, 6-11; 12-4 Sun; closed Sun evening, first week Jan

Recommended by J F M and M West, Charles and Pauline Stride, MDN, Christopher Sims

WALBERSWICK

TM4974 MAP 5

Anchor ♀

Village signposted off A12; The Street (B1387); IP18 6UA

Relaxed, informal dining in this well run and attractively furnished 1920s pub, fine range of wines, helpful service

There's a good mix of locals and visitors in this light and airy dining pub. With big windows, the bar is simply furnished with heavy stripped tables on original oak flooring, sturdy built-in wall seats cushioned in green leather and nicely framed black and white photographs of local fishermen and their boats on the colourwashed panelling. Log fires in the chimneybreast divide this room into two snug halves. They have loads of bottled beers from all over the world, 25 interesting wines by the glass, Adnams Bitter, Broadside and a guest such as Adnams Explorer on handpump and good coffee; particularly good service, daily papers and board games. Quite an extensive dining area, stretching back from a more modern-feeling small lounge on the left, is furnished much like the bar – though perhaps a bit more minimalist – and looks out on a good-sized sheltered and nicely planted garden. A garden bar serves the flagstoned terrace that overlooks the beach and village allotments, and the pub is right by the coast path. There's a pleasant walk across to Southwold and in summer there may be a pedestrian ferry. We're sure this will be a jolly nice place to stay once the bedrooms are refurbished.

🍴 Using local producers (and vegetables from their allotment), the good modern food might include fish soup, twice-baked cheddar soufflé, mussels in white wine cream, battered cod with hand-cut chips, suffolk ham with bubble and squeak and free-range egg, duck confit, rib-eye steak with anchovy and caper butter and hand-cut chips, and puddings such as hot chocolate pudding, and apple, almond and toffee cake with butterscotch sauce. *Starters/Snacks: £4.75 to £10.95. Main Courses: £12.95 to £18.95. Puddings: £4.75*

Adnams ~ Lease Mark and Sophie Dorber ~ Real ale ~ Bar food (12-3, 6-9) ~ Restaurant ~ (01502) 722112 ~ Young children welcome but not in bar ~ Dogs allowed in bar ~ Open 11-11 ~ Bedrooms: £85B/£110B

652 • SUFFOLK

Recommended by Simon Rodway, David Rule, Mike and Sue Loseby, Simon and Mandy King, Tom and Ruth Rees, Robert Lorimer, John Ainscough, Miss K Hunt, Mr M Smith, Hugo Jeune, John and Enid Morris, Michael Dandy, George Wallace, Tracey and Stephen Groves, Jeff and Wendy Williams

WALDRINGFIELD   TM2844   MAP 5

Maybush
Off A12 S of Martlesham; The Quay, Cliff Road; IP12 4QL

Busy pub with tables outside by the riverbank; nautical décor and a fair choice of drinks and bar food

A good supply of tables outside make the most of the terrific location by the estuarine River Deben, with its abundant bird life. The knocked-through spacious bar is divided into separate areas by fireplaces or steps. There's a hint at a nautical theme, with an elaborate ship's model in a glass case, and a few more in a light, high-ceilinged extension, as well as lots of old lanterns, pistols and aerial photographs on buttermilk walls; piped music, cards, dominoes and an original Twister board. Adnams Best, Broadside and Gun Hill are on handpump, with a fair choice of wines by the glass. There are river cruises available nearby but you have to pre-book.

🍽 **Popular uncomplicated food includes sandwiches, ploughman's, soup, whitebait, spinach and ricotta cannelloni, battered cod and chips, fish pie, various burgers, rump steak, lasagne, and puddings such as apple pie and lemon meringue pie.** *Starters/Snacks: £3.95 to £7.95. Main Courses: £8.95 to £15.95. Puddings: £4.95*

Adnams ~ Lease Steve and Louise Lomas ~ Real ale ~ Bar food (12-9.30) ~ Restaurant ~ (01473) 736215 ~ Children welcome ~ Dogs allowed in bar ~ Open 11(12 Sun)-11
Recommended by Mrs Carolyn Dixon, Miss K Hunt, Mr M Smith, Jim and Frances Gowers, David Blackburn

WESTLETON   TM4469   MAP 5

Crown
B1125 Blythburgh—Leiston; IP17 3AD

Lovely old coaching inn with a cosy chatty bar, plenty of dining areas, carefully chosen drinks and interesting food; comfortable and stylish bedrooms

Much enjoyed as a place to stay, this comfortable old inn has spotless bedrooms and is well positioned for exploring the coast. Although the emphasis here is on the carefully cooked food, locals do pop into the attractive little bar – with a lovely log fire and plenty of original features – for the Adnams Bitter and a guest on handpump; also a thoughtfully chosen wine list; piped music and board games. There's also a parlour, a dining room and conservatory. The charming terraced gardens have plenty of well spaced tables.

🍽 **With quite a modern twist, the often very enjoyable food (not cheap) might include lunchtime sandwiches, starters such as beetroot and goats cheese tartlet, seared scallops with braised pork belly, main courses such as fried breast of guinea fowl, beef and wild mushroom suet pudding, haddock and chips, baked baby leek and parmesan loaf, and puddings like caramelised pineapple and star anise tarte tatin or chocolate mousse with hazelnut praline and coffee bean sauce.** *Starters/Snacks: £4.50 to £11.50. Main Courses: £13.50 to £20.00. Puddings: £5.95 to £8.00*

Free house ~ Licensee Chris Ling ~ Real ale ~ Bar food (12-2.30, 7-9.30) ~ Restaurant ~ (01728) 648777 ~ Children welcome ~ Dogs allowed in bar and bedrooms ~ Open 11-11(10.30 Sun) ~ Bedrooms: £115B/£140B
Recommended by Tony Middis, Michael and Ann Cole, Simon and Mandy King, M V Burke, George and Beverley Tucker, John and Enid Morris, Keith and Margaret Kettell, George Wallace, John and Sharon Hancock, Brian and Elizabeth Torr, K Almond, Edward Mirzoeff

> Real ale to us means beer which has matured naturally in its cask –
> not pressurised or filtered.

WHEPSTEAD

TL8258   MAP 5

White Horse 🍽 ☘

Off B1066 S of Bury; Rede Road; IP29 4SS

Imaginative food and relaxed civilised atmosphere in charmingly reworked country pub

This is a triumph for the Kingshotts, even better than their former pub, the Beehive at Horringer (which under them was for many years a mainstay of our Suffolk section). Service is as friendly and efficient as ever. The well kept Adnams Bitter and Broadside, with a guest such as Old Cannon Gunner's Daughter, come from handpumps on a gleaming copper bar counter; they have a good choice of wines by the glass and of other drinks such as local lager. The dark-beamed bar has a winter log fire in its big 17th-c fireplace (a cluster of lighted church candles in summer). Linked rooms off give more choice of where to sit, mainly at sturdy, country-kitchen tables on beige carpet or antique floor tiles, with some attractively cushioned traditional wall seats. Landscape paintings (for sale) and old prints decorate walls painted in soft canary or sage; the bookshelves have books that are actually worth reading. The resident westie is called Skye. A neat sheltered back terrace is brightened up by colourful oilcloth tablecloths, and at the picnic-sets out on the grass, birdsong emphasises what a peaceful spot this is.

🍽 Making the most of a newly kitted-out kitchen, and with an emphasis on very locally sourced ingredients, the enjoyable and very well presented food here features starters such as creamy fish soup, seared breast of pigeon or buffalo mozzarella on herb salad, main courses like smoked haddock florentine, braised pork cooked with dates and juniper berries, chicken and cashews in curried coconut sauce, beef or venison burger, puddings like ginger crème brûlée or lemon meringue pie. From Monday to Thursday, for under £10, they serve a regional dish of the week showcasing local producers' such as lamb and coriander patties with warm potato salad and minted yoghurt dressing. *Starters/Snacks: £2.95 to £6.95. Main Courses: £8.95 to £14.95. Puddings: £4.95*

Free house ~ Licensees Gary and Di Kingshott ~ Bar food ~ (01284) 735760 ~ Children welcome ~ Dogs welcome ~ Open 11.30-3, 7-11; closed Sun evening

Recommended by Dr G and Mrs J Kelvin, Adele Summers, Alan Black, Geoffrey Baber, John Saville, Marianne and Peter Stevens

LUCKY DIP

Besides the fully inspected pubs, you might like to try these Lucky Dips recommended to us and described by readers (if you do, please send us reports: feedback@goodguides.com).

ALDEBURGH [TM4656]
White Hart IP15 5AJ [High St]: Friendly beamed and panelled Victorian local with four real ales inc Adnams, pubby food from bargain lunchtime sandwiches up, log fire, heavy stripped tables; folk nights; open all day *(Ben Williams)*
ALDRINGHAM [TM4461]
Parrot & Punchbowl IP16 4PY [B1122/B1353 S of Leiston]: Attractive and welcoming beamed country pub, good fairly priced food inc local fish, good wine choice, well kept Adnams and Greene King IPA, decent coffee, two-level restaurant; children welcome; nice sheltered garden, also family garden with adventure play area *(BB, Sam and Viv Sargent)*
BILDESTON [TL9949]
Crown IP7 7EB [B1115 SW of Stowmarket]: Good upmarket food (not cheap) in this picturesque and impressively refurbished 15th-c timbered country inn, smart beamed main bar with leather armchairs and inglenook log fire, more intimate back area

with contemporary art; ales such as Greene King and Mauldons, good choice of wines by the glass, dining room; children welcome, disabled access and parking, tables laid for dining in attractive central courtyard, more in large beautifully kept garden with decking, quiet comfortable bedrooms *(G Warboys, Simon and Mandy King, Jeremy King, LYM)*
Kings Head IP7 7ED [High St]: Old beamed village pub brewing its own beers (brewery tours), good value home-made food from baguettes up, wood floor bar with inglenook woodburner, darts; garden with terrace and play equipment, open all day wknds, cl Mon, Tues and Weds-Fri lunchtimes *(David and Gill Carrington)*
BLAXHALL [TM3656]
Ship IP12 2DY [off B1069 S of Snape; can be reached from A12 via Little Glemham]: Popular low-beamed 18th-c pub, enjoyable traditional home-made food in bar and restauarant, well kept Adnams Bitter, Timothy Taylors Landlord, Woodfordes Wherry

and three guests; some live music; children in eating areas, dogs in bar, eight chalet bedrooms, attractive country setting; open all day Sun *(LYM)*

BLYFORD [TM4276]

Queens Head IP19 9JY [B1123 Blythburgh—Halesworth]: 15th-c thatched pub doing well under newish licensees, enjoyable food using home-grown produce, well kept Adnams ales, very low beams, some antique settles, huge fireplace; tables outside *(Mark Sheard, Kirsten Corrigan, LYM)*

BLYTHBURGH [TM4575]

White Hart IP19 9LQ [A12]: Open-plan roadside family dining pub, a former courthouse dating to the 16th c, with fine ancient beams, woodwork and staircase, full Adnams range kept well, Aspall's cider and good choice of wines, good coffee, food from huge sandwiches up, friendly service, inglenook log fire; children in eating areas, back terrace and spacious lawns looking down on tidal bird marshes, magnificent church over the road, four bedrooms, open all day *(Charles and Pauline Stride, Bruce and Sharon Eden, Barry Collett, LYM)*

BOXFORD [TL9640]

☆ *Fleece* CO10 5DX [Broad St]: Partly 15th-c pub doing well under current owners, good home-made food, well kept Adnams, cosy panelled bar, airy lounge bar with wonderful medieval fireplace; children welcome, stable area behind with chickens and rabbits, play area *(LYM, Giles and Annie Francis)*

White Hart CO10 5DX [Broad St]: Contemporary dining pub with light modern furniture and décor in low-beamed old building, enjoyable fairly priced food from sandwiches up, friendly helpful service, Greene King and a guest ale *(Jeremy King, MDN)*

BRAMFIELD [TM3973]

☆ *Queens Head* IP19 9HT [The Street; A144 S of Halesworth]: High-raftered redecorated lounge with scrubbed pine tables, impressive fireplace and some old farm tools, side room with comfortable fireside seats, well kept Adnams, Aspall's cider, several wines by the glass, seasonal home-made elderflower cordial, reasonably priced food (emphasis on local organic, home-made bread and ice-creams; monthly live music (Fri); children (away from bar) and dogs welcome, cheerful blue-painted picnic-sets in pretty garden with dome-shaped willow bower, nice church next door *(LYM, Tina and David Woods-Taylor, J F M and M West, Simon Rodway, R L Borthwick, M and GR, S T W Norton)*

BRANDESTON [TM2460]

Queens Head IP13 7AD [The Street, towards Earl Soham]: Unpretentiously attractive open-plan country pub, good food (not Sun evening) inc some interesting dishes, particularly good vegetarian choice and nice puddings, well kept Adnams, good wines by the glass; friendly relaxed atmosphere with two open fires, leather banquettes and old pews, light and airy restaurant section;

piped music; children and dogs welcome, disabled facilities, big neat garden with good play area, campsite *(LYM, D Filby, Paul Humphreys)*

BRENT ELEIGH [TL9348]

☆ *Cock* CO10 9PB [A1141 SE of Lavenham]: Timeless thatched country pub with friendly locals, Adnams, Greene King Abbot and a guest, organic farm cider, some simple food, cosy ochre-walled snug and second small room, antique flooring tiles, lovely coal fire, old photographs of village (church well worth a look); darts and toad in the hole; well behaved children and dogs welcome, picnic-sets up on side grass with summer hatch service, attractive inn sign, one bedroom, open all day Fri-Sun *(Mrs Carolyn Dixon, the Didler, BB)*

BROCKLEY GREEN [TL7247]

☆ *Plough* CO10 8DT: Friendly neatly kept knocked-through bar, beams, timbers and stripped brick, scrubbed tables and open fire; good food from lunchtime sandwiches to some enterprising dishes and nice puddings, cheerful efficient staff, Greene King IPA, Woodfordes Wherry and a guest, good choice of wines by the glass and malt whiskies, restaurant; children and dogs welcome, extensive attractive grounds with good tables and terrace, peaceful country views, refurbished bedrooms *(Marianne and Peter Stevens, LYM, A Black)*

BUNGAY [TM3389]

Castles NR35 1AF [Earsham St]: Pleasantly informal dining pub doing good food, black-beamed front restaurant area, open fire, friendly efficient staff, Greene King IPA, small pubby back bar with french windows to pretty garden, afternoon teas; nice spot in front of castle, four comfortable bedrooms *(David and Sally Cullen)*

BURY ST EDMUNDS [TL8564]

Fox IP33 1XX [Eastgate St]: Attractive ancient beamed pub with informal bustling atmosphere, enjoyable locally sourced food inc fresh Lowestoft fish, well kept Greene King ales; bedrooms behind *(M and GR)*

☆ *Rose & Crown* IP33 1NP [Whiting St]: Cheerful black-beamed town local with affable helpful landlord, bargain simple lunchtime home cooking (not Sun), particularly well kept Greene King ales inc Mild, pleasant lounge with lots of piggy pictures and bric-a-brac; good games-oriented public bar, rare separate off-sales counter; pretty back courtyard, open all day wkdys *(Julia Mann, Tom and Jill Jones)*

BUTLEY [TM3650]

Oyster IP12 3NZ [B1084 E of Woodbridge]: Old beamed country pub now under same enthusiastic management as the Golden Key at Snape, fresh local food, well kept Adnams, good wine by the glass; stripped-pine tables and pews, good coal fire, live music; children welcome *(LYM)*

BUXHALL [TM9957]

☆ *Crown* IP14 3DW [off B1115 W of Stowmarket; Mill Rd]: Warm welcome from enthusiastic landlord, cosy low-beamed inglenook bar with leather chairs and pews, airy dining room, well kept Greene King ales, good choice of wines by the glass, enjoyable food; children and dogs welcome, plenty of tables on heated terrace, pretty enclosed garden, nice country views, cl Sun evening, Mon (*Dr G and Mrs J Kelvin, Jeremy King, LYM*)

CAMPSEA ASHE [TM3356]

Dog & Duck IP13 0PT [Station Rd]: Attractive clean family-friendly pub, good range of enjoyable food, welcoming helpful licensees and staff, Adnams and Woodfordes Wherry tapped from the cask, pleasant dining room; tables out in front, nice garden with good play area, five bedrooms with own bathrooms (*anon*)

CAVENDISH [TL8046]

☆ **Bull** CO10 8AX [A1092 Long Melford—Clare]: Spotless old pub with heavy beams, timbers and fine fireplaces, Adnams ales and good choice of food, reasonable prices, attentive service; children in eating areas; garden tables, car park (useful in this honeypot village) (*Mr and Mrs T B Staples, LYM*)

☆ **George** CO10 8BA [The Green]: Attractively laid out as more restaurant than pub, good interesting food from snacks up inc lunchtime set deals, nice atmosphere and friendly efficient service, beamed and bow-windowed front part, further good-sized eating area; well priced wines, good coffees and teas; tables out in garden behind, lovely village, bedrooms (*Hunter and Christine Wright, BB, Sarah Flynn, Penny Lang, Marianne and Peter Stevens*)

CHILLESFORD [TM3852]

☆ **Froize** IP12 3PU [B1084 E of Woodbridge]: Restaurant rather than pub (open only when they serve food, ie not Mon, nor Sun-Weds evenings), reliably good cooking in pleasant bar and restaurant, warmly welcoming service, good value two-course buffet-style or carvery lunch, wide choice of more elaborate evening meals, local fish, pork, game and venison, original puddings; good wines by the glass, well kept Adnams; may be cl Feb for hols (*Tim Elliot, LYM*)

COTTON [TM0667]

☆ **Trowel & Hammer** IP14 4QL [off B1113 N of Stowmarket; Mill Rd]: Spreading linked areas, lots of beamery and timber baulks, plenty of wheelbacks and one or two older chairs and settles around a mix of tables, red carpets, big log fire, Adnams, Courage and Greene King, fairly priced food (all day Sun) can be good; pool room; piped music, maybe live Sat; games machine, sports TV; well behaved children welcome, colourful back garden with swimming pool, open all day (*LYM, Ian and Nita Cooper, Jeremy King, M Walker*)

CRETINGHAM [TM2260]

☆ **Bell** IP13 7BJ [The Street]: Small attractive pub doing well under present licensees, good value pubby food with spanish specials, several well kept ales, neat leather armchairs

in bare-boards bar, sofa and dining tables in quarry-tiled second room, fine old fireplace, beams and timbers; nice garden with boules, two tidy bedrooms (*LYM, S T W Norton*)

DENNINGTON [TM2867]

☆ **Queens Head** IP13 8AB [A1120; The Square]: Well refurbished beamed and timbered Tudor pub prettily placed by church, L-shaped main bar, Adnams and maybe a guest, local cider, enjoyable food (best to book wknds) inc some unusual choices and creative children's menu, friendly service; piped music; children in family room, side lawn by noble lime trees, pond at back with ducks and carp, backs on to Dennington Park with swings and so forth (*LYM, Eamonn and Natasha Skyrme, Simon Cottrell, MDN, Ian and Nita Cooper*)

EAST BERGHOLT [TM0734]

☆ **Kings Head** CO7 6TL [Burnt Oak, towards Flatford Mill]: Enjoyable food inc unusual dishes in popular well laid-out dining pub, friendly obliging staff, well kept Adnams and Greene King, decent wines and coffee; beamed lounge with comfortable sofas in softly lit part by servery, Constable prints and books, two-room restaurant; quiet piped music; side garden and small back terrace (*Bruce and Sharon Eden, BB*)

ELVEDEN [TL8179]

Elveden Inn IP24 3TP [just off A11]: Old-fashioned dimly lit pub filled with interesting bric-a-brac, friendly landlord, well kept ales such as Greene King Old Speckled Hen; garden tables, near Center Parc (*Giles and Annie Francis*)

FELIXSTOWE FERRY [TM3237]

Ferry Boat IP11 9RZ: Much modernised 17th-c pub tucked between golf links and dunes nr harbour, Martello tower and summer rowing-boat ferry; good value generous food from snacks to fresh fish, Adnams and Greene King, good log fire; piped music, busy summer wknds, and they may try to keep your credit card while you eat; dogs welcome, tables out in front, on green opposite and in fenced garden, good coast walks (*David Blackburn, WAH, LYM*)

Victoria IP11 9RZ: Child-friendly extended Victorian riverside pub, good value no-nonsense food inc local fish, cheerful efficient staff, well kept Adnams and Greene King ales, tempting liqueur coffees, good log fire in snug, upstairs sea-view dining area, buzzy atmosphere; dogs welcome, disabled access, picnic-sets on heated terrace (*Ryta Lyndley*)

FORWARD GREEN [TM0959]

☆ **Shepherd & Dog** IP14 5HN [A1120 E of Stowmarket]: Smart dining pub with attractive pastel décor, comfortable dining tables and some sofas, good interesting food in contemporary bar and restaurant, well kept Greene King IPA and Fullers London Pride, good wines by the glass and coffee; disabled access, terrace tables, cl Sun evening, Mon (*BB, Ian and Nita Cooper, Conrad Freezer*)

FRAMLINGHAM [TM2863]

Castle Inn IP13 9BP [Castle St]: Small and smartly decorated next to the castle, decent food (not evenings) from interesting snacks to specials, cream teas and good coffee too; three Adnams beers, Aspall's cider, good service even when busy, juke box; children and dogs welcome, front picnic-sets overlooking duck pond, more in pretty back courtyard, open all day *(Paul Humphreys, Ian Phillips)*

Station Hotel IP13 9EE [Station Rd (B1116 S)]: Simple high-ceilinged big-windowed bar with scrubbed tables on stripped boards, four well kept Earl Soham ales and a guest, good choice of house wines, reasonably priced food (can be good), friendly service; relaxed atmosphere, plenty of train pictures, back snug with tiled floor; children welcome, picnic-sets in pleasant good-sized garden *(BB, Colin and Ruth Munro, J F M and M West)*

FRAMSDEN [TM1959]

Dobermann IP14 6HG [signed off B1077]: Charmingly restored tucked-away thatched local festooned with summer flowers, friendly welcome; two neatly kept low-beamed linked rooms with central open fire, sofa and armchairs among other seats, good freshly made bar food, well kept Adnams and a guest beer, efficient service; no under-14s, small sheltered garden, boules, one bedroom, cl Mon *(LYM, J F M and M West)*

FRESSINGFIELD [TM2677]

☆ *Fox & Goose* IP21 5PB [B1116 N of Framlingham; Church St]: Dining pub in beautifully timbered 16th-c building next to church, very good well priced food with emphasis on local produce in bistro-style area with log fire or in more formal upstairs restaurant, friendly attentive service; Adnams and a guest tapped from the cask in small bar area, good wines by the glass; gentle piped music; children welcome, downstairs disabled facilities, seats out by duck pond, cl Mon *(John and Enid Morris, Dr Ian S Morley, Paul Humphreys, LYM)*

Swan IP21 5PE [B1116 Harleston—Framlingham]: Welcoming village pub with helpful landlady, well kept Adnams and Timothy Taylors Landlord, good food and house wines, linked areas with more formal restaurant extension; children welcome *(Paul Humphreys)*

GREAT BARTON [TL8967]

Bunbury Arms IP31 2NX [Ixworth Rd]: Much-extended 19th-c pub, light and roomy open-plan L-shaped bar, dining area with daily carvery and other enjoyable food inc children's, well kept Greene King ales, friendly uniformed staff; open all day Sun *(Trevor Swindells)*

GREAT FINBOROUGH [TM0157]

Chestnut Horse IP14 3AT [The Green]: Unpretentious old village local, enjoyable pub food, well kept Greene King IPA, decent wines by the glass, some live music; annual Race of the Bogmen (Easter Mon); children welcome *(J F M and M West)*

GREAT GLEMHAM [TM3461]

Crown IP17 2DA [Between A12 Wickham Market—Saxmundham and B1119 Saxmundham—Framlingham]: Under new management; big entrance hall with sofas on rush matting, open-plan beamed lounge with wooden pews and captain's chairs around stripped and waxed kitchen tables, log fires in two big fireplaces, Adnams Bitter and three guests from old brass handpumps, bar food; children and dogs welcome, disabled access, garden tables, smokers' shelter, cl Mon *(LYM)*

HALESWORTH [TM3877]

☆ *Angel* IP19 8AH [thoroughfare (now pedestrianised)]: Civilised, comfortable and substantial, with lounge bar looking out on pedestrianised street from tall windows, more tables in roofed-in galleried coachyard with Act of Parliament clock; well kept Adnams and Everards, nice wines, busy espresso machine, good log fire, friendly efficient staff, sandwiches and baps all day, cheap traditional bar dishes and pizzas, good italian restaurant; piped music, small bar with machines (dogs allowed here); children welcome (but no babies/toddlers after 7pm), seven well equipped bedrooms, good breakfast, car park – useful here, open all day *(Keith and Susan Moore, BB, Robert Lorimer, Dr D J and Mrs S C Walker)*

White Hart IP19 8AH [thoroughfare]: Roomy well restored open-plan pub, enjoyable good value food inc fresh fish, well kept Adnams and guests, good friendly service *(Dr D J and Mrs S C Walker)*

HARKSTEAD [TM1834]

Bakers Arms IP9 1BT: Small village pub renovated and reopened under new management, ales such as Elgoods and Woodfordes, generous good value food from fairly standard menu and daily specials; dogs welcome in garden *(Tony and Shirley Albert)*

HARTEST [TL8352]

☆ *Crown* IP29 4DH [B1066 S of Bury St Edmunds]: Pink-washed old pub by church behind pretty village green, friendly helpful staff, good choice of enjoyable food inc reasonably priced mid-week lunches, well kept Greene King, smart minimalist décor with quality tables and chairs on tiled floor, good log fire in impressive fireplace; two dining rooms and conservatory; piped music; children and dogs welcome, tables on big back lawn and in sheltered side courtyard, good play area *(John Saville, LYM)*

HASKETON [TM2450]

Turks Head IP13 6JG [Low Rd off Top Rd]: Small unpretentious country pub taken over and run by the villagers, welcoming and efficient, with well kept local beers, enjoyable pub food from short menu (not Mon, Tues); children and dogs welcome, pleasant garden with lots of tables *(J F M and M West)*

HAUGHLEY [TM0262]

Kings Arms IP14 3NT [off A45/B1113 N of Stowmarket; Old St]: Decent good value pub food in 16th-c timbered pub with airy 1950s back part refurbished to match, well kept Greene King ales and a guest, busy public bar with games and TV, log fire; piped music and some live; tables in colourful back garden, nice village, open all day wknds *(BB, Jeremy King)*

HENLEY [TM1552]

Cross Keys IP6 0QP [Main Rd]: Busy unpretentious country local, good value food all day, well kept beer, local cider, enthusiastic community-spirited landlord; quiz and live music nights; children welcome *(J F M and M West)*

HOLBROOK [TM1636]

Compasses IP9 2QR [Ipswich Rd]: Renovated roomy place with good standard food inc children's and OAPs', Adnams and Greene King, decent wine, good service, big log fire, restaurant area; quiz night first Fri of month (basket meals only then); seats out at front under cover, back garden with play area, cl Tues evening *(Colin McKerrow, Charles and Pauline Stride)*

HUNTINGFIELD [TM3473]

Huntingfield Arms IP19 0PU [The Street]: Handsome late 18th-c building by green, friendly licensees, enjoyable inexpensive food inc home-smoked fish, well kept Adnams and a guest, light wood tables and chairs, beams and stripped brickwork, blazing woodburner in front room; pleasant back games area with pool, restaurant; limited parking; tables outside, cl Sun evening *(Robert Lorimer, S T W Norton, John M Murphy)*

ICKLINGHAM [TL7772]

Plough IP28 6PL [The Street]: Cosy bar area with settles, adjacent good-sized restaurant with wide choice of enjoyable blackboard food, six ales inc Greene King IPA and Hook Norton, good choice of wines by the glass inc champagne; no mobile phones; children welcome at lunchtime, big garden, six bedrooms *(Tony Middis, Simon Watkins, M and GR)*

IPSWICH [TM1644]

Dove Street IP4 2LA [76 St Helens St]: Over 20 well kept quickly changing ales, farm ciders, bottled beers and whiskies, cheap hot drinks, friendly staff, bargain basic food; regular beer festivals; dogs welcome *(Joanna Oldham)*

Greyhound IP1 3SE [Henley Rd/Anglesea Rd]: Comfortable Victorian décor, well kept Adnams and guests, good substantial home cooking inc plenty for vegetarians, quick service by well trained young staff; outside lavatories; children welcome, quiet back terrace, open all day Fri-Sun *(the Didler)*

KERSEY [TM0044]

Bell IP7 6DY [signed off A1141 N of Hadleigh; The Street]: Tudor pub in notably picturesque village, quick friendly service, good value pubby food from sandwiches up, Adnams Broadside, Black Sheep and Greene King IPA, decent house wines; modernised low-beamed log-fire bar with dining area, restaurant; children allowed, sheltered back

terrace with fairy-lit side canopy, open all day *(LYM, Jeremy King)*

KESGRAVE [TM2346]

Kesgrave Hall IP5 2PU [Hall Rd]: Refurbished country hotel with Greene King ales in comfortably contemporary bare-boards bar, popular imaginative food all day in open-kitchen bistro (no booking – so best to arrive early), good service; children and dogs welcome, attractive heated terrace with huge retractable awning, 23 stylish bedrooms *(J F M and M West)*

LONG MELFORD [TL8645]

☆ *Bull* CO10 9JG [Hall St (B1064)]: Medieval small hotel, beautifully carved beams in old-fashioned timbered front lounge, antique furnishings, log fire in huge fireplace, more spacious back bar with sporting prints; well kept Greene King ales, wide range of good reasonably priced food, cheerful helpful staff, daily papers, restaurant; children welcome, tables in attractive courtyard, comfortable bedrooms, open all day Sat, Sun *(Ian Herdman, R C Vincent, LYM)*

Crown CO10 9JL [Hall St]: Friendly partly 17th-c pub, good choice of fresh traditional and more contemporary food using local ingredients, real ales such as Adnams and Nethergate from central servery with unusual bar chairs, big log fire, some stripped brickwork and nicely placed furnishings, restaurant; attractive terrace with big awnings, 11 well equipped bedrooms *(Ian Wilson, LYM, Angela Cole)*

LOWESTOFT [TM5492]

Harbour NR33 0AG [Royal Plain]: Seaward-facing modernised open-plan pub, several ales such as Harviestoun Bitter & Twisted and Hop Back Summer Lightning from central bar, wide choice of good value food from sandwiches and ciabattas up inc children's and OAP meals, special deals too; open all day *(Tony and Wendy Hobden)*

MARTLESHAM [TM2446]

☆ *Black Tiles* IP12 4SP [off A12 Woodbridge—Ipswich; Black Tiles Lane]: Spotless and spacious family dining pub, comfortable contemporary bistro-style restaurant with garden room (children allowed here), big woodburner in appealing bar, wide choice of good generous home-made food using local produce served quickly by smart helpful staff; daily roast, Adnams and a guest beer, good choice of wines by the glass; attractive garden (some road noise) with wicker chairs on heated terrace, play area, open all day *(Danny Savage, Jeremy King, LYM)*

MELTON [TM2850]

Wilford Bridge IP12 2PA [Wilford Bridge Rd]: Light, roomy and well organised, with reliable good value food all day inc local fish in two spacious carpeted bars and restaurant, Adnams and smaller brewery ales such as Brandons, good wines by the glass, prompt friendly service; terrace picnic-sets, nearby river walks, handy for Sutton Hoo, open all day *(Gordon Neighbour, Mrs K Brenchley, Mrs K M Andrews)*

MIDDLETON [TM4267]
Bell IP17 3NN [off B1125 Leiston—
Westleton; The Street]: Recent refurbishment
for this traditional part-thatched and
beamed pub, friendly atmosphere, good
reasonably priced food, Adnams ales tapped
from casks behind bar, restaurant, open
fires; garden picnic-sets, pretty setting nr
church, handy for RSPB Minsmere and coast
(BB, Charles and Pauline Stride)

NEWBOURNE [TM2743]
☆ *Fox* IP12 4NY [off A12 at roundabout
1.7 miles N of A14 junction; The Street]:
Pink-washed 16th-c pub, low-beamed bar
with slabby elm and other dark tables on tiled
floor, stuffed fox in inglenook, comfortable
carpeted dining room with modern artwork
and antique mirrors, Adnams, Greene King and
two guests, decent wines by the glass,
generously served food (all day wknds) inc
good value Sun roasts; piped music; children
welcome, dogs in bar, attractive grounds with
rose garden and pond, open all day *(BB,
Charles and Pauline Stride, Miss K Hunt,
Mr M Smith, LYM, M and GR, Peter Meister)*

NORTON [TL9565]
Dog IP31 3LP [Ixworth Rd (A1088)]: 17th-c
pub popular for its enjoyable generous food,
well kept Greene King ales, decent wines,
restaurant; children welcome, garden
(J F M and M West)

ORFORD [TM4249]
Crown & Castle IP12 2LJ: Hotel/restaurant
rather than pub, enjoyable food from pubby
standards up (evening food more upscale
and expensive), small smartly minimalist bar
(used largely for pre-meal drinks – well kept
Greene King and good wines by the glass);
tables outside, residents' garden, 18 good
bedrooms *(Don More, M and GR, Derek and
Sylvia Stephenson)*

POLSTEAD [TL9938]
Cock CO6 5AL [signed off B1068 and A1071
E of Sudbury, then pub signed; Polstead
Green]: Beamed and timbered local with
unassuming bar, woodburner and open fire,
well kept Adnams, Greene King IPA and a
guest, good choice of wines and malt
whiskies, nice coffee, good home-made food
from fresh lunchtime baguettes up, smarter
light and airy barn restaurant; piped music;
disabled facilities, children and dogs
welcome, picnic-sets out overlooking
attractive village's quiet green, side play
area, cl Mon *(BB, Martin and Alison Stainsby,
John Prescott, David and Gill Carrington,
Tom and Jill Jones, Hazel Morgan,
Bernard Patrick)*

RAMSHOLT [TM3041]
☆ *Ramsholt Arms* IP12 3AB [signed off B1083;
Dock Rd]: Lovely isolated spot overlooking
River Deben, welcoming open-plan nautical
bar busy on summer wknds and handy for
bird walks and Sutton Hoo; wide choice of
quickly served food inc good value seafood
and game, you can have a pudding only, two
sittings for Sun lunch; Adnams and a guest,
decent wines by the glass, winter mulled

wine, good log fire; dogs (pub has two) and
children welcome, plenty of tables outside
with summer afternoon terrace bar (not
Sun), roomy bedrooms with stunning view,
open all day *(LYM, Tim Elliot, Tom Gondris,
Mr and Mrs M J Girdler)*

RINGSFIELD [TM4187]
Horseshoes NR34 8LR [Cromwell Rd off
A145]: Simple well cared for local with
comfortable L-shaped bar, lots of ornaments
and equestrian/cricketing pictures, three
ales inc Greene King Old Speckled Hen,
enjoyable food from good sandwiches and
baguette up, Sun roasts; very reasonable
prices, polite thoughtful service
(John Robertson)

SAXTEAD GREEN [TM2564]
Old Mill House IP13 9QE [B1119; The
Green]: Roomy dining pub across the green
from windmill; beamed carpeted bar, neat
country-look flagstoned restaurant
extension, wooden tables and chairs, wide
choice of generous good value fresh food inc
daily carvery, good friendly service, well kept
Adnams, decent wines; discreet piped music;
children very welcome, attractive and
sizeable garden with terrace and good play
area *(Ian and Nita Cooper, LYM, Eamonn and
Natasha Skyrme)*

SHOTLEY GATE [TM2433]
Bristol Arms IP9 1PU [end of B1456; Bristol
Hill]: Superb estuary views from dining room
and picnic-sets outside, good food and
service, well kept beers *(Marcus Mann)*

SHOTTISHAM [TM3244]
Sorrel Horse IP12 3HD [Hollesley Rd]:
Charming two-bar thatched Tudor local,
attentive helpful landlord, Greene King and
guests tapped from the cask, limited home-
made food from cobs up, good log fire in
tiled-floor bar with games area, attractive
dining room; tables out on green, open all
day wknds *(the Didler)*

SNAPE [TM3958]
Crown IP17 1SL [Bridge Rd (B1069)]: Small
beamed 15th-c pub with brick floors,
inglenook log fire and fine double Suffolk
settle, Adnams ales, enjoyable fresh food
using local ingredients inc own veg and
meat (reared behind the pub); folk night last
Thurs of month, darts; children and dogs
welcome, garden *(Simon Rodway, Tom and
Ruth Rees, WAH, Christopher Sims, Jean and
Douglas Troup, LYM, Brian and Elizabeth Torr,
George Cowie, Frances Gosnell)*

SOMERLEYTON [TM4797]
Dukes Head NR32 5QR [Slugs Lane (B1074)]:
Nicely positioned red-brick pub (part of the
Somerleyton Hall estate), stripped-stone bar,
Adnams ales, enjoyable seasonal food from
estate's own farm, friendly young staff,
family dining extension; tables out on grass,
country views, a stiff walk up from River
Waveney, open all day *(Rosemary Willett)*

SOUTH COVE [TM4982]
Five Bells NR34 7JF [B1127 Southwold—
Wrentham]: Friendly, well run and spacious
creeper-covered pub with stripped pine,

three well kept Adnams ales, local Aspall's farm cider, good pubby blackboard food in bar, side room with settles or back restaurant, good service; tables out in front, play area, caravan site in back paddock, bedrooms *(Andrew and Ruth Triggs, RS, ES)*

SOUTHWOLD [TM4975]

☆ *Harbour Inn* IP18 6TA [Blackshore, by the boats; from A1095, turn right at the Kings Head, and keep on past the golf course and water tower]: New licensees taking over as we went to press; waterside pub by Blyth estuary, lots of nautical character, seafaring bric-a-brac, tiny low-beamed tiled and panelled front bar with antique settles, cushioned wooden benches built into stripped panelling, Adnams and maybe a seasonal guest; tables outside, has been open all day *(LYM)*

☆ *Red Lion* IP18 6ET [South Green]: Good atmosphere, warm friendly service, enjoyable reasonably priced pubby food from sandwiches up, well kept Adnams, big windows looking over the green towards the sea, pale panelling, ship pictures, lots of brassware and copper; pub games, separate back dining room; children and dogs welcome, lots of tables outside, right by the Adnams retail shop *(BB, Ian and Nita Cooper, Charles and Pauline Stride, Mike and Sue Loseby)*

Sole Bay IP18 6JN [East Green]: Bright and airy café-inn nr Adnams Brewery, their full range and good wine choice, cheerful and efficient smartly dressed staff, good simple food from doorstep sandwiches up, conservatory; side terrace, moments from the sea and lighthouse *(MDN, Michael Dandy, LYM)*

☆ *Swan* IP18 6EG [Market Pl]: Relaxed, comfortable back bar in smart Adnams-owned hotel, their full range and bottled beers, fine wines and malt whiskies, good bar lunches (not cheap, but worth it), competent staff, coffee and teas in luxurious chintzy front lounge, restaurant; garden, 42 bedrooms inc separate block where (by arrangement) dogs can stay too, good breakfast *(LYM, MDN, Michael Dandy)*

STOKE-BY-NAYLAND [TL9836]

☆ *Angel* CO6 4SA [B1068 Sudbury—East Bergholt]: Handsomely beamed dining pub, stripped brickwork and timbers, a mix of pubby furnishings, big log fire, well kept Adnams and guests, nice choice of wines by the glass, good home-made food; high-ceilinged restaurant with gilt clocks and mirrors; piped and some live music, quiz nights; children welcome, sheltered terrace, comfortable bedrooms, good breakfast, open all day *(Tom and Jill Jones, Brian and Elizabeth Tora, Hazel Morgan, Bernard Patrick, N R White, Steve and Sue Griffiths, John and Enid Morris, LYM)*

STONHAM ASPAL [TM1359]

Ten Bells IP14 6AF [The Street]: Extensively modernised early 17th-c timbered village pub with inglenook in extended beamed

main bar, small lounge bar with dining area beyond, enjoyable home-made food (all day Sun, not Weds) inc specials, well kept ales such as Woodfordes Wherry and Wells & Youngs Bombardier, cheerful relaxed atmosphere; TV, pool; disabled facilities, terrace and garden tables, open all day wknds, shuts 9.30pm Mon *(Jeremy King)*

STRADBROKE [TM2373]

White Hart IP21 5HT [Church St]: Friendly refurbished old local under new owners, enjoyable pubby food, well kept Adnams, two open fires; lovely view of church *(Karl Blair)*

STUTTON [TM1434]

Gardeners Arms IP9 2TG [Manningtree Rd, Upper St (B1080)]: Well kept Adnams and guests in cottagey village pub, friendly helpful landlord, enjoyable, fresh straightforward food inc OAP meals and good value Sun lunch, lots of bric-a-brac, dining room; children and dogs welcome, back terrace, open all day *(N R White)*

SUDBURY [TL8741]

Brewery Tap CO10 2TP [East St]: Tap for Mauldons brewery, their full range and guests kept well, bare boards and scrubbed tables, some food *(John Prescott)*

SWILLAND [TM1852]

☆ *Moon & Mushroom* IP6 9LR [off B1078]: Cheerfully old-fashioned local, ales such as Adnams, Buffys, Crouch Vale, Nethergate and Woodfordes from racked casks behind long counter, old tables and chairs on quarry tiles, log fires; decent choice of home-made food inc game; children and dogs welcome, heated terrace with grapevines and roses, cl Sun evening, Mon *(the Didler, Jeremy King, LYM)*

THORNHAM MAGNA [TM1070]

Four Horseshoes IP23 8HD [off A140 S of Diss; Wickham Rd]: Extensive thatched dining pub dating back to 12th-c, dim-lit, rambling, well divided bar, Greene King ales, good choice of wines and whiskies, home-made food (usually all day wknds) inc good value Sun carvery; very low heavy black beams, plush banquettes, country pictures and brass, big log fireplaces, inside well; piped music; children and dogs welcome, disabled access, handy for Thornham Walks and interesting thatched church, picnic-sets on big sheltered lawn, seven comfortable bedrooms, good breakfast, open all day *(LYM, Ian and Nita Cooper, Jeremy King)*

THURSTON [TL9165]

Fox & Hounds IP31 3QT [Barton Rd]: Quite an imposing building, welcoming inside, with well kept Adnams Bitter, Greene King IPA and guests such as Woodfordes Nelson's Revenge, pubby furnishings in neatly kept carpeted lounge, lots of pump clips, ceiling fans, reasonably priced usual food (not Sun evening or Mon); bare-boards public bar with pool, darts and machines; piped music; dogs welcome, picnic-sets in garden and on small covered side terrace, pretty village, two bedrooms, open all day Fri-Sun *(Jeremy King)*

WALBERSWICK [TM4974]

☆ **Bell** IP18 6TN [just off B1387]: Fine setting nr beach, plenty of original features, 400-year-old brick floors, uneven flagstones, wonky steps and oak beams, traditional main bar with high-backed settles and woodburner, second bar with large open fire; up to seven Adnams beers, enjoyable food from crayfish sandwiches up; darts and board games; piped music; children and dogs welcome, tables on sheltered lawn, comfortable bedrooms overlooking sea or river *(LYM, Simon Rodway, Mike and Sue Loseby, the Didler, MJVK, Colin and Ruth Munro, George Wallace)*

WESTLETON [TM4469]

☆ **White Horse** IP17 3AH [Darsham Rd, off B1125 Blythburgh—Leiston]: Homely comfort and friendly staff in traditional pub with generous straightforward food inc good sandwiches, OAP bargain lunch, well kept Adnams, unassuming high-ceilinged bar with bric-a-brac and central fire, steps down to attractive Victorian back dining room; children in eating area, picnic-sets in cottagey back garden with climbing frame, more out by village duck pond, bedrooms, good breakfast *(Stephen and Jean Curtis, S T W Norton)*

WINGFIELD [TM2276]

☆ **De La Pole Arms** IP21 5RA [off B1118 N of Stradbroke; Church Rd]: Timbered 16th-c pub with friendly staff, enjoyable country cooking using prime local ingredients, well kept Adnams and local guests, Aspall's cider, several wines by the glass; bare boards, flagstones and quarry tiles, leather easy chairs and solid country dining furniture, old maps, log fires in big inglenooks; unobtrusive piped music; children and dogs welcome, good disabled access, lovely back garden, cl Sun evening *(A Black, Paul Humphreys, LYM)*

WOODBRIDGE [TM2749]

Olde Bell & Steelyard IP12 1DZ [New St, off Market Sq]: Ancient and unpretentious with friendly helpful licensees, two smallish beamed bars and compact dining room, Greene King ales and guests from canopied servery, real ciders, food from good value bar snacks to short varied choice of substantial main dishes; traditional games inc bar billiards, live music; dogs welcome (two residents and a cat), back terrace, steelyard still overhanging street, open till late Fri, Sat *(Rob and Catherine Dunster, Dr D J and Mrs S C Walker)*

WOOLPIT [TL9762]

Swan IP30 9QN [The Street]: Old coaching inn pleasantly situated in village square, heavy beams and painted panelling, mixed tables and chairs on carpet, log fire, well presented local food, Adnams ales from slate-top bar; walled garden behind, four bedrooms in converted stables *(D and J Ashdown, LYM)*

Please tell us if any Lucky Dips deserve to be upgraded to a Main Entry – and why: feedback@goodguides.com, or (no stamp needed) The Good Pub Guide, FREEPOST TN1569, Wadhurst, E Sussex TN5 7BR.

Surrey

Despite its proximity to so many urban areas, Surrey does still have some delightful country enclaves. Fortunately, it's in these that a good many of our Main Entries are to be found – some, such as the Three Horseshoes in Thursley, with great walks right from their doorstep. One place with a particularly rural feel is the lovely old starred Parrot at Forest Green; the owners have their own farm and there's a farm shop attached to the pub. You'll also find quite a sizeable farm shop at the Jolly Farmers in Buckland – good food and carefully sourced ingredients, too. These days, there's better food to be had in Surrey – surprisingly this hasn't always been the case. Of the best, the Running Horses at Mickleham offers a terrific menu that you choose from in their smarter restaurant or more relaxed bar, and the Inn at West End which is run with loving passion and offers dishes skilfully prepared from carefully sourced ingredients. Of these, the Inn at West End, with its particularly caring service, is our Surrey Dining Pub of the Year 2011. Other pubs that merit special mention are the grown-up Seven Stars at Leigh which is a great all-rounder, and for beer fans, the Surrey Oaks at Newdigate is run by a landlord who's totally into real ale and hosts 'meet the brewer evenings' and a couple of beer festivals each year.

BLINDLEY HEATH

TQ3645   MAP 3

Red Barn ♀

Tandridge Lane, just off B2029, which is off A22; RH7 6LL

Splendidly converted spacious farmhouse and barn with plenty of character, food all day starting with breakfast

This 300-year-old farmhouse isn't quite as traditional inside as it at first appears. The chief glory of the place is the huge raftered barn at the far end, dramatically converted into a comfortably upscale dining room and lounge area with a central woodburning stove. There are plenty of contemporary twists around the numerous scrubbed beams and timbers from funky round modern lights (and a large model plane) hanging from the soaring rafters to a wall that is dominated by shelves of books stretching high above the window and a wall of antlers. There are cosier areas on either side, each with its own character and an eclectic mix of modern furnishings includes everything from leather or wicker chairs to cow-print pouffes. Efficient, smartly dressed staff take your order at the table, but this is very much a pub, with bar billiards and a pile of board games in the adjacent bar, along with sofas by another sizeable fireplace; piped music. A lighter farmhouse-style room they call the pantry has big wooden tables and a red cooking range; it's where they serve breakfast. Two real ales might be from Adnams, Harveys or Sharps, and there's a good wine list. A big farmer's market is held here the first Saturday morning of each month and they may also have summer barbecues and various food promotions and events. Out on the lawn, you'll find solid granite tables.

🍴 Not cheap, but worth it, the well presented bar food relies on fresh local ingredients, and from a daily changing menu might include sandwiches, ploughman's, battered haddock, penne with somerset blue and rocket, potted salmon and prawns with lemon and toast, suckling pig and black pudding terrine with home-made piccalilli, marinated beetroot, tomato and goats cheese salad, mushroom and pea risotto, lamb rump with bubble and squeak and roast cod, and puddings such as chocolate brownie with berry compote and cinnamon ice-cream and sticky toffee pudding with ginger ice-cream. *Starters/Snacks: £4.95 to £5.95. Main Courses: £9.50 to £18.50. Puddings: £5.00 to £6.50*

Geronimo Inns ~ Manager Alan McTeir ~ Real ale ~ Bar food (12-3, 6-9.30(10 Fri, Sat); 12-8 Sun) ~ (01342) 830820 ~ Children welcome ~ Dogs allowed in bar ~ Open 7am-11pm
Recommended by Derek Thomas, John Branston, Colin and Louise English

BRAMLEY   TQ0044 MAP 3
Jolly Farmer 🍺
High Street; GU5 0HB

Relaxed village inn near Surrey hills with great selection of beers

The traditional interior of this family-owned free house is filled with a miscellany of homely wooden tables and chairs, with various collections of plates, enamel advertising signs, sewing machines, antique bottles, prints and old tools filling the walls and surfaces. Timbered semi-partitions, a mixture of brick and timbering and an open fireplace give it a snug cosy feel; piped music, TV (which can be loud), dominoes and board games. Friendly staff serve Hogsback HBB and a Sharps seasonal beer on handpump alongside six guests (they can go through up to 20 different local real ales a week), typically from brewers such as Great Newsome, Idle, King, Milestone and Oakham, three changing belgian draught beers and 18 wines by the glass. There are tables out by the car park and the village is handy for Winkworth Arboretum and walks up St Martha's Hill.

🍽 As well as lunchtime sandwiches, bar food includes whitebait, grilled halloumi with mediterranean vegetables, ploughman's, home-made burger, fried cod fillet with citrus and saffron butter, pie of the day, daily specials such as fried tiger prawns in garlic, fried duck breast with port and redcurrant sauce, mushroom risotto, grilled bass with creamy dill sauce, and puddings such as eton mess and lemon posset with ginger tuile. One reader told us that food service stopped well before the advertised time so do check with them before you go. *Starters/Snacks: £3.50 to £6.50. Main Courses: £5.50 to £18.00. Puddings: £4.50 to £6.00*

Free house ~ Licensees Steve and Chris Hardstone ~ Real ale ~ Bar food (12-2.30, 7-9.30) ~ Restaurant ~ (01483) 893355 ~ Children welcome ~ Dogs allowed in bar and bedrooms ~ Live music some summer Tues evenings ~ Open 11-11; 12-11 Sun ~ Bedrooms: £60S(£65B)/£70S(£75B)
Recommended by M and GR, Phil and Sally Gorton, Brian and Anna Marsden, Revd R P Tickle, LM, Dr and Mrs A K Clarke, Mr and Mrs Gordon Turner

BUCKLAND   TQ2250 MAP 3
Jolly Farmers 🍴
Reigate Road (A25 W of Reigate); RH3 7BG

Wide range of local produce in part-pub, part-restaurant and part-deli; a good place to eat, or shop, but atmospheric too

This unusual place is all about good, meticulously sourced local produce, both on the menu and in the well stocked farm shop at the back. Most people are here to eat, but the flagstoned bar with its smart, brown leather sofas and armchairs has a comfortably relaxed feel and you'll be made equally welcome if you just drop in for a drink. On the wall is a big regional map with drawing pins marking their suppliers, and hops, beams and timbers keep things traditional. A small brick fireplace separates the bar from the small wooden-floored dining room. Friendly young staff serve Harveys Sussex and a guest such as Dark Star Hophead, a few local wines pop up on the wine list and they make various home-made cordials and lemonade. The shop stretches across three little rooms and stocks plenty of fresh vegetables, deli meats, cheeses, cakes, chocolates and their own range of produce; they do a weekly food market with stalls outside (Saturdays, 9am-3pm) and organise several food festivals and events throughout the year. There are tables out on a back terrace overlooking the car park. The owners run the Wise Old Owl at Kingsfold in Sussex along similar lines.

🍴 You can get something to eat pretty much all day starting with pastries and coffees from 9am with full breakfast at weekends. Later, there are dishes such as grilled smoked haddock with free-range egg, warm potato salad and honey mustard dressing, grilled chicken wings with toasted fennel seed marinade and spicy mayonnaise, goats cheese crème brûlée, ploughman's, seafood platter, steak and kidney pudding, seared swordfish with warm asparagus niçoise salad, battered fish and chips, roast stuffed aubergine with tomato couscous, roast pork fillet with crispy bacon, pineapple and coriander salsa and chilli jelly, butternut squash and sweet potato gratin and well hung rib-eye steak. They do afternoon teas, and the children's menu is above average. *Starters/Snacks: £3.75 to £6.95. Main Courses: £8.95 to £18.95. Puddings: £4.75 to £5.75*

Mitchells & Butlers ~ Lease Jon and Paula Briscoe ~ Real ale ~ Bar food (12-3, 5.30-9.30; breakfast 9.15-11.15am Sat, Sun; 12-9.30 Sat; 12-8.30 Sun) ~ Restaurant ~ (01737) 221355 ~ Children welcome ~ Open 9.15-11.30(10.30 Sun)

Recommended by Cathryn and Richard Hicks, Derek and Maggie Washington, Derek Thomas, LM, John Branston, Colin and Louise English, C and R Bromage

COBHAM   TQ1058   MAP 3

Cricketers

Downside Common; 3.75 miles from M25 junction 10; A3 towards Cobham, first right on to A245, right at Downside signpost into Downside Bridge Road, follow road into its right fork – away from Cobham Park – at second turn after bridge, then eventually turn into the pub's own lane, immediately before Common crossroads; KT11 3NX

In relaxing village green location; lots of character, low beams and pretty garden

Most people visit this unchanging old place to enjoy the idyllic terrace views across the village green and the lovely traditional interior. Crooked standing timbers give structure to the comfortable open-plan layout with its very low heavy oak beams (some have crash-pads on them) and a blazing log fire. In places you can see the wide oak ceiling boards and ancient plastering laths. Furnishings are quite simple, and there are horsebrasses and big brass platters on the walls. Fullers London Pride and Greene King IPA and Old Speckled Hen are on handpump alongside a guest such as Surrey Hills Shere Drop and they stock a good choice of wines including several by the glass; piped music. It's worth arriving early (particularly on Sunday) to be sure of a table. You may have to queue for food and service can slow down when they get busy; they may retain your credit card. The delightful neatly kept garden is well stocked with standard roses, magnolias, dahlias, bedding plants, urns and hanging baskets. Readers tell us the ladies' lavatories could do with a tidy up.

🍴 Bar food (including weekday sandwiches) which was once a strong point here seems not to be pleasing readers at the moment. The menu includes traditional dishes and there is a more elaborate restaurant; Sunday roast. *Starters/Snacks: £5.50 to £7.95. Main Courses: £8.95 to £15.95. Puddings: £4.75*

Enterprise ~ Tenant Mustafa Ozcan ~ Real ale ~ Bar food (12-3, 6.30-9.30; 12-8 Sun) ~ Restaurant ~ (01932) 862105 ~ Children welcome ~ Dogs allowed in bar ~ Open 11-11; 12-10.30 Sun

Recommended by LM, Conor McGaughey, C and R Bromage, Ian Wilson, DGH, Ian Phillips

---

Post Office address codings confusingly give the impression that some pubs are in Surrey when they're really in Hampshire or London (which is where we list them). And there's further confusion from the way the Post Office still talks about Middlesex – which disappeared in local government reorganisation nearly 50 years ago.

COMPTON   SU9646   MAP 2

Withies

Withies Lane; pub signposted from B3000; GU3 1JA

Gently upmarket with attractive pubby bar and pretty garden

Charmingly civilised in a gently old-fashioned way, the cosy low-beamed bar at this
sympathetically altered 16th-c tavern has a lively chatty atmosphere that saves it from
being too sedate, and even when it's busy, the delightful bow-tied staff are helpful and
efficient. Pleasing interior features include some fine 17th-c carved panels between its
windows and a splendid art nouveau settle among old sewing-machine tables, and even on
cool summer days logs burn in its massive inglenook; Adnams, Greene King IPA and Hogs
Back TEA are on handpump. A mass of flowers borders the neat front lawn, and weeping
willows shade the immaculate garden behind, which has plenty of dining tables under an
arbour of creeper-hung trellises, with more on a crazy-paved terrace and others under old
apple trees. The pub is situated on the edge of Loseley Park and close to the extraordinary
Watts Gallery (closed till spring 2011) housing works by the Victorian artist GF Watts.

🍴 **Quickly served tasty food (not cheap) includes good sandwiches (even hot salt beef),
filled baked potatoes, fisherman's broth, oysters, fried sardines, ploughman's, cumberland
sausage and mash, plenty of salads, fish and chips, steak, kidney and mushroom pie,
suckling pig, lobster and steaks.** *Starters/Snacks: £5.00. Main Courses: £12.00. Puddings:
£6.00*

Free house ~ Licensees Brian and Hugh Thomas ~ Real ale ~ Bar food (12-3, 6-10) ~ Restaurant
~ (01483) 421158 ~ Children welcome ~ Open 11-3, 6-11; 12-3 Sun; closed Sun evening
*Recommended by Jeremy and Jane Morrison, Gerry and Rosemary Dobson, Helen and Brian Edgeley,
Andrea Rampley, B and M Kendall, Ellie Weld, David London, LM*

ELSTEAD   SU9044   MAP 2

Mill at Elstead

*Farnham Road (B3001 just W of village, which is itself between Farnham and Milford);
GU8 6LE*

Fascinating building, big attractive waterside garden, Fullers beers, bar food

This largely 18th-c four-storey watermill is in a rather special setting above the prettily
banked River Wey. There are plenty of picnic-sets dotted around by the water, with its
lovely millpond, swans and weeping willows – the entire scene is well floodlit at night.
Inside, big windows throughout the sensitively converted building make the most of the
charming surroundings; you'll see the great internal waterwheel and the hear the gentle
rush of the stream turning below your feet. A series of rambling linked bar areas on the
spacious ground floor, and a restaurant upstairs, change in mood from one part to the
next: brown leather armchairs and antique engravings by a longcase clock; neat modern
tables and dining chairs on dark woodstrip flooring; big country tables and rustic prints
on broad ceramic tiles; dark boards and beams, iron pillars and stripped masonry; a log
fire in a huge inglenook. Service is commendably helpful, friendly and personal. They
have four Fullers beers on handpump, and a good range of wines by the glass; piped
music, board games; dogs allowed in the bar only.

🍴 **Bar food includes smoked salmon and spinach roulade, goats cheese crostini with red
onion chutney, mushroom and spinach tagliatelle with creamy white wine sauce, sausages
with mustard mash and red onion gravy, salmon steak with lemon and tarragon sauce,
rabbit stew with herb dumplings, well hung steak, and specials such as beef, ale and
bacon pie and cod loin wrapped in parma ham on spring onion and bacon mash with lime
and vanilla sauce; Sunday carvery.** *Starters/Snacks: £3.95 to £5.95. Main Courses: £8.95 to
£15.95. Puddings: £4.50 to £6.50*

Fullers ~ Managers Kate and Richard Williams ~ Real ale ~ Bar food (12-9(9.30 Fri, Sat, 8 Sun))
~ Restaurant ~ (01252) 703333 ~ Children welcome ~ Dogs allowed in bar ~ Open 11-11;
11.30-10.30 Sun
Recommended by Peter Dandy, Ian Wilson, Ian Herdman, Simon and Sally Small, N R White

ESHER

TQ1566   MAP 3

Marneys ♀ £

Alma Road (one-way only), Weston Green; heading N on A309 from A307 roundabout, after Lamb & Star pub turn left into Lime Tree Avenue (signposted to All Saints Parish Church), then left at T junction into Chestnut Avenue; KT10 8JN

Cottagey little pub with good value food and attractive garden

Hens, ducks and other ornaments fill the shelves in the little low-beamed black and white plank-panelled bar at this cottagey pub. On the left, past a little cast-iron woodburning stove, a dining area (somewhat roomier but still small) has big pine tables, pews and pale country kitchen chairs, attractive goose pictures and small blue-curtained windows. Courage Best, Fullers London Pride and Hogs Back TEA are on handpump; piped music and perhaps horseracing on the unobtrusive corner TV. The front terrace has dark blue cast-iron tables and chairs under matching parasols, with table lighting and views over the rural-feeling wooded common and duck pond, and the pleasantly planted sheltered garden has a decked area, bar, black picnic-sets and tables under green and blue canvas parasols; more reports please.

🍴 **Very reasonably priced changing bar food might include goats cheese tart, whitebait, fried camembert and redcurrant jelly, warm chicken and bacon salad, chicken curry, steak and ale pie, smoked salmon salad, fresh fish, home-made burgers and steaks, and puddings such as warm chocolate fudge cake.** *Starters/Snacks: £4.95. Main Courses: £7.00 to £13.00. Puddings: £4.95*

Free house ~ Licensee Thomas Duxberry ~ Real ale ~ Bar food (12-2.30(3 Sun), 7-9) ~ (020) 8398 4444 ~ Children welcome ~ Dogs welcome ~ Open 11-11.30; 12-11 Sun

Recommended by John Sleigh, Shirley Mackenzie, LM, David and Ruth Shillitoe, Ian Wilson, C and R Bromage, Michael Dandy, Norma and Noel Thomas

FOREST GREEN

TQ1241   MAP 3

Parrot ★

B2127 just W of junction with B2126, SW of Dorking; RH5 5RZ

Beamed pub with produce from the owners' farm on the menu and in attached shop, good range of drinks and lovely garden

The owners of this appealing old place have their own farm not far away at Coldharbour and you can buy their own meat, as well as cheese, cured and smoked hams, pies, bread and preserves in the pub's farm shop. The pub itself retains all the charm of a genuinely aged village pub, with a lively atmosphere, fine profusion of heavy beams, timbers, flagstones and nooks and crannies hidden away behind the inglenook fireplace. A beer from Dorking, Ringwood Best and Wells & Youngs are served alongside a couple of guests such as Hogs Back TEA and Ringwood Old Thumper on handpump as well as freshly squeezed orange juice, local farm apple juice and 16 wines by the glass; newspapers. There are tables out in several attractive gardens, one with apple trees and rose beds. The pub is in a splendid position with views over fields and the village cricket pitch.

🍴 **With the pork, beef and lamb coming from their own farm, the frequently changing menu might include generous helpings of seared scallops with chilli and tagliatelle, home-cured black pudding with oxtail and apple purée, chicken breast with smoked bacon and leek cream, home-made burger, mutton, sweet pepper and spinach curry, herb baked brill with caper butter, vegetable and stilton pie, and puddings such as chocolate and banana sundae mousse cake, hot plums with whisky and prune parfait and pear and gingerbread and butter pudding with ginger ice-cream.** *Starters/Snacks: £4.50 to £8.00. Main Courses: £8.00 to £16.00. Puddings: £4.50 to £7.50*

Free house ~ Licensee Charles Gotto ~ Real ale ~ Bar food (12-3(5 Sun), 6-10; not Sun evening) ~ Restaurant ~ (01306) 621339 ~ Dogs allowed in bar ~ Open 11-11(midnight Sat); 12-10.30 Sun

Recommended by Simon and Mandy King, Norma and Noel Thomas, Colin and Louise English, Richard and Sissel Harris, N R White, Christopher and Elise Way, Tom and Ruth Rees, D M Jack, C and R Bromage, LM, John Branston, Sheila Topham, Conor McGaughey, Shirley Mackenzie, John and Joan Nash, Gordon Stevenson, Derek Thomas

LEIGH   TQ2147   MAP 3

Seven Stars ♀
Dawes Green, S of A25 Dorking—Reigate; RH2 8NP

Popular welcoming dining pub with enjoyable food and good wines

To many of our readers this tile-hung 17th-c tavern is their ideal pub. Its welcoming, beautifully kept, serves well kept beer and tasty food and has a particularly grown-up atmosphere, with just the murmur of contented chatter to greet you as you're offered a table. The comfortable saloon bar has a 1633 inglenook fireback showing a royal coat of arms, and there's a plainer public bar. The sympathetically done restaurant extension at the side incorporates 17th-c floor timbers imported from a granary. Greene King Old Speckled Hen, Fullers London Pride and Wells & Youngs Bitter are served from handpump, alongside decent wines with about a dozen by the glass. Outside, there's plenty of room in the beer garden at the front, on the terrace and in the side garden.

💷 The nicely varied menu includes lunchtime ciabattas, game pâté, home cured queen scallops with black pudding, crispy whitebait with caper and lemon mayonnaise, ham hock casserole with dumplings, sausage and mash, beer-battered cod, porcini ravioli with creamy mushroom and parmesan sauce, rib-eye steak, and puddings such as crumble of the day, banoffi pie and lemon and lime fool. They do two sittings for Sunday lunch and it's advisable to book at all times. *Starters/Snacks: £5.95 to £6.95. Main Courses: £9.95 to £16.50. Puddings: £5.25 to £5.50*

Punch ~ Lease David and Rebecca Pellen ~ Real ale ~ Bar food (12-2.30(4 Sun), 6-9(6.30-9.30 Fri, Sat); not Sun evening) ~ Restaurant ~ (01306) 611254 ~ Dogs allowed in bar ~ Open 12-11(8 Sun)

Recommended by Norma and Noel Thomas, Donna and Roger, Ron and Sheila Corbett, Mike and Sue Shirley, Michael and Margaret Cross, Tony and Jill Radnor, Ian and Barbara Rankin, J R Osborne, Mr and Mrs Price, Nick Lawless, Neil Powell

MICKLEHAM   TQ1753   MAP 3

Running Horses 🍴 ♀ 🛏
Old London Road (B2209); RH5 6DU

Upmarket pub with elegant restaurant and comfortable bar, and sandwiches through to very imaginative smart dining

Liked equally as a local drinking haunt, walkers' stop and graceful dining destination, this rather nice place is an accomplished all-rounder with a smart yet unpretentious atmosphere. The calming bar is neatly kept and spaciously open-plan, with hunting pictures, racing cartoons and Hogarth prints, lots of race tickets hanging from a beam, fresh flowers or a fire in an inglenook at one end and some cushioned wall settles and other dining chairs around straightforward pubby tables and bar stools. Fullers London Pride, Chiswick and HSB and Wells & Youngs Bitter and a guest such as Dark Star Best are on handpump alongside good wines by the glass, from a serious wine list; piped music. The extensive restaurant is quite open to the bar and although set out quite formally with crisp white cloths and candles on each table, it shares the relaxing atmosphere of the bar. A terrace in front with picnic-sets by lovely flowering tubs and hanging baskets takes in a peaceful view of the old church with its strange stubby steeple. You may be asked to leave your credit card if you run a tab, and it's best to get here early, both to secure parking in the narrow lane (though you can park on the main road), and for a table. A notice by the door asks walkers to remove or cover their boots.

💷 There is a tempting choice of food (not the cheapest you will come across) running from traditional pubby meals such as well filled lunchtime chunky sandwiches, moules marinière, sausage and mash, venison and beef burger, tapas selection, steak, Guinness and mushroom pudding, lamb shank braised with balsamic and burgundy, to a more elaborate restaurant menu (available in the bar too): carpaccio of tuna with crab and smoked salmon roulade and gazpacho dressing, tomato and basil risotto with asparagus and parmesan tuile, and puddings such as orange cake with raspberry and blackberry compote and crème brûlée with pear crust. *Starters/Snacks: £5.75 to £8.95. Main Courses: £10.50 to £18.95. Puddings: £5.95 to £6.25*

Free house ~ Licensees Steve and Josie Slayford ~ Real ale ~ Bar food (12-2.30(3 Sat, Sun), 7-9.30; 6.30-9 Sun) ~ Restaurant ~ (01372) 372279 ~ Children over 10 welcome ~ Dogs allowed in bar ~ Open 11.30-11; 12-10.30 Sun ~ Bedrooms: £95S(£110B)/£110S(£135B)

Recommended by Fiona Smith, John and Joyce Snell, Mike Gorton, Mr Ray J Carter, Conor McGaughey, Sheila Topham, Brian and Anna Marsden, Tony and Jill Radnor, LM, Gordon Stevenson

NEWDIGATE
TQ2043   MAP 3

Surrey Oaks 🍺

Off A24 S of Dorking, via Beare Green; Parkgate Road; RH5 5DZ

Interesting real ales at traditional village pub with traditional food and enjoyable garden for children

The friendly landlord at this former wheelwright's cottage has a passionate interest in real ale, and keeps three quickly rotating guests from smaller brewers such as Dark Star, Loweswater and Ossett, alongside well kept Harveys Best and Surrey Hills Ranmore alongside german and belgian bottled beers, several wines by the glass, a couple of farm ciders and a farm perry. He holds beer festivals over the May Spring and August bank holiday weekends, and meet the brewer evenings. The pubby interior has a cheery atmosphere (with flowers on the tables) and is interestingly divided into four areas. In the older part locals gather by an open fire in a snug little beamed room. A standing area with unusually large flagstones has a woodburning stove in an inglenook fireplace, rustic tables are dotted around the light and airy main lounge to the left, and there's pool in the separate games room; TV, games and fruit machines, skittle alley and piped classical music. The garden is pleasingly complicated, with a terrace, a rockery with pools and a waterfall, a diverting play area and two boules pitches.

🍽 **Under the new chef (do let us know what you think) reasonably priced bar food might include soft herring roes on toast, black pudding topped with poached egg, crab cakes with chilli dip, steak and ale pie, lambs liver, bacon and mash, grilled plaice with parsley butter, pork medallions in pepper sauce, vegetarian stuffed peppers, steak, and puddings such as raspberry crème brûlée and eton mess; Sunday roast. If you wish to run a tab in the garden they may retain your credit card in a card safe.** *Starters/Snacks: £4.00 to £7.50. Main Courses: £7.50 to £9.00. Puddings: £3.50*

Admiral Taverns ~ Lease Ken Proctor ~ Real ale ~ Bar food (12-2(2.30 Sun), 6.30-9; not Sun, Mon evenings) ~ Restaurant ~ (01306) 631200 ~ Children welcome in bar till 8.30, restaurant till 9.30 ~ Dogs welcome ~ Open 11.30-2.30, 5.30-11; 11.30-3, 6-11 Sat; 12am-10pm Sun

Recommended by C and R Bromage, the Didler, Donna and Roger, Pam and John Smith, Peter Dandy, Colin and Louise English, Malcolm and Pauline Pellatt

OUTWOOD
TQ3246   MAP 3

Bell

Outwood Common, just E of village; off A23 S of Redhill; RH1 5PN

Enjoyable pub with Fullers beers, tasty food and nice garden

The softly lit smartly rustic beamed bar at this attractive extended 17th-c country dining pub is warm and cosy with oak and elm tables and chairs (some in Jacobean style), low beams and a vast stone inglenook fireplace. If you want to eat, it's best to book in advance, especially in the evening when drinking-only space is limited, too. Fullers London Pride, ESB and Seafarers are on handpump with good wines by the glass and a large range of liqueurs; piped music. In summer, the well-managed garden has a play area and is a peaceful place to sit among flowers and shrubs on the sheltered lawn and look past its bordering pine trees to the fine view over rolling fields, dotted with oak trees and woods.

🍽 **Generously served enjoyable food might include sausage and mash, fish and chips, prawn fajitas, and puddings such as panna cotta.** *Starters/Snacks: £4.95 to £7.95. Main Courses: £6.95 to £18.95. Puddings: £3.85 to £6.50*

Fullers ~ Managers Jason and Sian Smith ~ Real ale ~ Bar food (12-3, 6-9.30; 12-9 Sun) ~ Restaurant ~ (01342) 842989 ~ Children welcome ~ Dogs welcome ~ Open 12-11(10.30 Sun)

Recommended by Terry Buckland, C and R Bromage, Phil Bryant, John Atkins

THURSLEY
SU9039 MAP 2

Three Horseshoes
Dye House Road, just off A3 SW of Godalming; GU8 6QD

Civilised country village pub with broad range of good food

This pretty tile-hung village pub is an appealing combination of gently upmarket country local and attractive restaurant. It's owned by a consortium of villagers who rescued it from closure. The convivial beamed front bar has Hogs Back TEA and a guest such as Surrey Hills Shere Drop on handpump, a farm cider and perry, a winter log fire and warmly welcoming service; piped music. The attractive two-acre garden has picnic-sets and a big play fort, smart comfortable chairs around terrace tables and pleasant views over the village green. It's well placed for bracing heathland walks over Thursley Common and lucky doggies visiting here get a biscuit or even a doggy bag – do tell us what's in it if you get one!

🍴 Breads, ice-creams, parsnip crisps and so forth are made in house here. As well as the burger and pizza menus, tasty bar food (one or two readers feel it's not cheap) might include tempura crab, beetroot cured salmon with blinis, braised oxtail with port and red wine, steak and kidney pie, wild boar stew with leek dumplings, roast cod with brown shrimp butter and salsa verde, pea and broad bean ravioli with roast squash and sage beurre noisette, puddings such as treacle tart and summer pudding and good coffee; Sunday roast. *Starters/Snacks: £4.50 to £9.50. Main Courses: £9.50. Puddings: £4.50 to £5.50*

Free house ~ Licensees David Alders and Sandra Proni ~ Real ale ~ Bar food (12.30-2.15(3 Sun), 7-9; 12-3 Sun; not Sun evening) ~ Restaurant ~ (01252) 703268 ~ Children welcome ~ Dogs allowed in bar ~ Open 12-3, 5.30-11; 12-11 Sat; 12-10.30 Sun

Recommended by Hunter and Christine Wright, DGH, LM, Michael B Griffith, Ian Herdman, Conor McGaughey, Tony and Jill Radnor, Simon and Sally Small

WEST END
SU9461 MAP 2

Inn at West End 🍴 ☒
Just under 2.5 miles from M3 junction 3; A322 S, on right; GU24 9PW
SURREY DINING PUB OF THE YEAR

Enjoyable fresh-feeling dining pub, with prompt friendly service; excellent food, good wines and terrace

The charming licensee at this enjoyably relaxed place is completely immersed in its day to day running and his fabulously high standards are echoed by his delightfully attentive staff. Polished to a shine and well organised, the pub is open-plan, with bare boards, attractive modern prints on canary-yellow walls above a red dado, and a line of dining tables with crisp white linen over pale yellow tablecloths on the left. The bar counter – Fullers London Pride and a guest such as Exmoor Ale on handpump and 30 malts – straight ahead as you come in, is quite a focus, with chatting regulars perched on the comfortable bar stools. The area on the right has a pleasant relaxed atmosphere, with blue-cushioned wall benches and dining chairs around solid pale wood tables, broadsheet daily papers, magazines and a row of reference books on the brick chimneybreast above an open fire. This opens into a garden room, which in turn leads to a grape and clematis pergola-covered terrace and very pleasant garden; boules. The landlord is also a wine merchant, so the thoughtfully created food is well complemented by the knowledgeably chosen wines (with around 20 by the glass – sensibly in a good range of sizes), several sherries and dessert wines that lean particularly towards Spain and Portugal. He holds wine tastings and can supply by the case.

⑪ **Skilfully prepared using carefully sourced ingredients (some of the herbs and vegetables are grown here, they pluck their own game and use organic meat), the not cheap but very good bar food might include a smoked fish platter, game terrine, fried chicken livers with black pudding and croûtons, chicken caesar salad, kedgeree, cumberland sausage and mash, vegetable cottage pie, well hung sirloin steak, roast chicken breast with garlic and herb sauce, and puddings such as crème brûlée with cranberry shortbread, south african vinegar pudding and toffee, banana, apple and pecan crumble pie with toffee sauce.** *Starters/Snacks: £6.95 to £9.95. Main Courses: £7.95 to £13.95. Puddings: £5.95 to £6.75*

Enterprise ~ Lease Gerry and Ann Price ~ Real ale ~ Bar food (12-2.30, 6-9.30; 12-3, 6-9 Sun) ~ Restaurant ~ (01276) 858652 ~ Children over 5 welcome if seated and dining ~ Dogs allowed in bar ~ Open 12-3, 5-11; 12-11 Sat; 12-10.30 Sun

Recommended by Mr and Mrs G M Pearson, Ian Herdman, Robin Paterson, Bernard Stradling, David M Smith, Edward Mirzoeff, Sheila Topham, Ellie Weld, David London, David and Cathrine Whiting, Bruce M Drew, Guy Vowles, Ian Phillips, Sylvia and Tony Birbeck

LUCKY DIP

Besides the fully inspected pubs, you might like to try these Lucky Dips recommended to us and described by readers (if you do, please send us reports: feedback@goodguides.com).

ABINGER COMMON [TQ1146]
Abinger Hatch RH5 6HZ [off A25 W of Dorking, towards Abinger Hammer]: Modernised dining pub in beautiful woodland spot, popular food (not Sun evening) from light dishes up, Fullers London Pride and Ringwood Best and Fortyniner, sociable landlord and good service, heavy beams and flagstones, log fires, pews forming booths around oak tables in carpeted side area, plenty of space (very busy/noisy wknds); piped music, plain family extension; dogs welcome, some disabled access, tables in nice garden, nr pretty church and pond, summer barbecues, open all day (*C and R Bromage, Franklyn Roberts, CP, LYM*)

ALFOLD [TQ0435]
Alford Barn GU6 8JE [Horsham Rd]: Beautifully preserved 16th-c building with bar and restauarant, good food and service, meal deals, beams and rafters, mixed furniture on flagstones or carpet, log fires; garden with play area, cl Sun evening, Mon (*Shirley Mackenzie*)

ASH VALE [SU8952]
Swan GU12 5HA [Hutton Rd, off Ash Vale Rd (B3411) via Heathvale Bridge Rd]: Welcoming three-room Chef & Brewer on the workaday Basingstoke Canal, huge choice of generous well priced food all day (can take a while when very busy), good sandwiches, Courage, Fullers London Pride, Wadworths 6X and a guest, good value wines by the glass, cheerful staff, large log fire; piped music; children welcome, attractive garden, neat heated terraces and window boxes, open all day (*E Stein, Phil Bryant*)

BANSTEAD [TQ2659]
Mint SM7 3DS [Park Rd, off High St towards Kingswood]: Rambling Vintage Inn, low beams and flagstones, dimly lit cosy areas, friendly helpful staff, good value generous food inc lunch deals, real ales and good choice of wines by the glass; children welcome (*Jenny and Brian Seller, Trisha Nicholls, C and R Bromage, Mrs G R Sharman*)
Woolpack SM7 2NZ [High St]: Well run and busy open-plan dining pub, well kept changing ales such as Sharps Doom Bar, pleasant service; open all day (*C and R Bromage*)

BATTS CORNER [SU8140]
Blue Bell GU10 4EX: Light fresh décor in friendly country pub with enjoyable home-made food, well kept Triple fff Moondance, a beer brewed by them for the pub and Hogs Back TEA, decent wines by the glass, roaring log fire, restaurant; children, dogs and muddy boots welcome, big garden with rolling views and play area, handy for Alice Holt Forest, open all day, cl Sun evening (*N R White, BB*)

BETCHWORTH [TQ1950]
Arkle Manor RH3 7HB [Reigate Rd]: Smart M&B dining pub with enjoyable upscale food, attractive rambling layout with easy chairs and so forth, real ales, good choice of wines by the glass, good service (*C and R Bromage*)
☆ *Dolphin* RH3 7DW [off A25 W of Reigate; The Street]: 16th-c village pub on Greensand Way, plain tables on ancient flagstones in neat front bar, smaller bar, panelled restaurant/bar with blazing fire and chiming grandfather clock, nice old local photographs, enjoyable good value blackboard food, well kept Wells & Youngs ales inc perhaps a seasonal guest; children and dogs welcome, small front courtyard, wknd summer barbecues in back garden, picturesque village (fine pre-Raphaelite pulpit in church), open all day (*LYM, the Didler, Geoffrey Kemp, J R Osborne, LM*)

BLETCHINGLEY [TQ3250]
Prince Albert RH1 4LR [Outwood Lane]: Cosy old-fashioned village pub, Fullers ales, good wines by the glass, good value pubby food

(not Sun evening), linked beamed rooms, panelling and simple furnishings; children welcome, terrace tables, pretty garden, open all day Fri-Sun *(LYM, Conor McGaughey, Quentin and Carol Williamson)*
Red Lion RH1 4NU [Castle St (A25), Redhill side]: Old beamed village dining pub with fresh modern décor, good mainly traditional food all day, friendly staff, well kept Greene King ales, good choice of wines by the glass, monthly quiz and some live music; no children after 6pm, outside covered area, secret garden, open all day *(John Atkins)*

BROCKHAM [TQ1949]
Royal Oak RH3 7JS [Brockham Green]: Nice spot opp fine church on charming village green below North Downs, refurbished bare-boards bar and back dining area, well kept ales such as Ringwood, enjoyable standard food, good friendly service; children welcome, garden *(Conor McGaughey, LM)*

BYFLEET [TQ0661]
Plough KT14 7QT [High Rd]: Small pub with good range of changing ales, usually simple food from sandwiches to three or four bargain hot dishes lunchtime and Weds evening, friendly service, two log fires, rustic furnishings, farm tools, brass and copper, dominoes, more modern back area, no mobiles; terrace and small shady back garden *(Ian Phillips, B and K Hypher)*

CAPEL [TQ1740]
Crown RH5 5JY [signed off A24 at Beare Green roundabout; The Street]: Welcoming pleasantly rustic 17th-c village pub by interesting church, cosy and comfortable beamed small-roomed areas, well kept Wells & Youngs ales and a guest such as Purity, friendly staff and regulars, enjoyable pubby food inc hearty rabbit pie, lounge and public bars, games room, back dining room; they may ask to keep a credit card while you eat; dogs welcome, big garden, open all day wknds *(Barry Moses, Phil Bryant)*

CATERHAM [TQ3254]
Harrow CR3 6AJ [Stanstead Rd, Whitehill]: Refurbished 16th-c pub high up in open country by North Downs Way, beamed L-shaped bar and back dining area, several real ales (sometimes straight from the cask), enjoyable food, good local atmosphere and friendly service; piped music; children and dogs welcome, tables in garden, popular with walkers and cyclists *(N R White)*

CHARLWOOD [TQ2441]
Half Moon RH6 0DS [The Street]: Old pub next to churchyard, good-sized L-shaped bar with pubby furniture and a couple of sofas, front part open to original upstairs windows, good food from baguettes to substantial specials, friendly service, well kept ales such as Harveys and St Austell, formal back dining room; piped music; tables out at front and in nice courtyard area, attractive village handy for Gatwick *(John Michelson, Phil Bryant, BB)*

CHERTSEY [TQ0466]
Crown KT16 8AP [London St (B375)]: Extended Youngs pub/hotel, mixed furnishings in spreading high-ceilinged bar, decent wines by the glass, Wells & Youngs ales and Hogs Back TEA, enjoyable food all day from sandwiches up, Sun roasts, restaurant; big-screen sports TV each end, games machines; children and dogs welcome, garden bar with conservatory, tables in courtyard and garden with pond, wknd barbecues, 49 bedrooms *(Gerry and Rosemary Dobson, Ian Phillips)*
Golden Grove KT16 9EN [Ruxbury Rd, St Anns Hill (nr Lyne)]: Low beam and plank ceiling, bare boards, stripped wood and coal-effect gas fire giving this busy local a snug welcoming feel, bargain straightforward home-made food from sandwiches up (not Sat-Mon evenings) in pine-tabled eating area, Fullers London Pride and Greene King IPA, happy hour till 7pm, cheerful service; piped music, machines; children welcome, big pretty sloping garden with picnic-sets under grape-laden vine, play area, tree-shaded pond *(Hunter and Christine Wright)*
Kingfisher KT16 8LF [Chertsey Bridge Rd (Shepperton side of river)]: Big Vintage Inn particularly liked by older people for its delightful spot by Thames lock, repro period décor and furnishings in spreading series of small intimate areas, Fullers London Pride and Sharps Doom Bar, good value house wines, reasonably priced straightforward food, friendly attentive staff, good log fires, daily papers, large-scale map for walkers, interesting old pictures; soft piped music; families welcome if eating (no other under-21s), roadside garden, open all day *(Ian Phillips)*

CHIDDINGFOLD [SU9635]
Crown GU8 4TX [The Green (A283)]: Popular picturesque medieval inn with fine carving, Elizabethan plaster ceilings, massive beams, lovely inglenook log fire and panelled restaurant, enjoyable sensibly priced traditional food, smart attentive young staff, good choice of well kept ales inc Langham, Sharps and Triple fff; verandah tables, attractive village-green surroundings, comfortable bedrooms *(LYM, Phil Bryant, Phil and Sally Gorton)*

CHIPSTEAD [TQ2757]
Ramblers Rest CR5 3NP [Outwood Lane (B2032)]: Rambling M&B country dining pub with contemporary furnishings and cocktail bar décor in partly 14th-c building, panelling, flagstones, low beams and log fires, enjoyable up-to-date and more traditional food inc popular Sun lunch, real ales, good value wines by the glass, young friendly staff, daily papers; children welcome, large pleasant garden with terrace, attractive views, good walks, open all day *(BB, N R White, Maureen and Keith Gimson, John Branston)*
Well House CR5 3SQ [Chipstead signed with Mugswell off A217, N of M25 junction 8]: Partly 14th-c, cottagey and comfortable with

log fires in all three rooms, well kept ales such as Adnams, Cottage, Dorking, Fullers, Pilgrim and Surrey Hills, food from baguettes up (not Sun evening), bric-a-brac above bar, pewter tankards hanging from ceiling, conservatory; dogs allowed (they have cats), large attractive hillside garden with well reputed to be mentioned in Domesday Book, delightful setting *(LYM, Conor McGaughey, LM, Peter Dandy)*

CHOBHAM [SU9761]

Sun GU24 8AF [High St, off A319]: Congenial low-beamed timbered pub with Courage, Fullers, Hogs Back and perhaps an unusual guest, pizzas and other bargain food, friendly staff, daily papers, woodburner, shining brasses *(LYM, Ian Phillips)*

CHURT [SU8538]

Crossways GU10 2JE: Two compact down-to-earth bar areas, busy in evenings, great changing beer range at reasonable prices, good well priced home-made pub lunches (not Sun) inc nice pies, evening food Weds only (mainly fish and chips), cheerful young staff; garden, open all day Fri and Sat *(Tony and Jill Radnor, R B Gardiner)*

CLAYGATE [TQ1663]

Griffin KT10 0HW [Common Rd]: Properly old-fashioned Victorian village local with well kept ales inc Fullers London Pride, some interesting dishes as well as usual pub food freshly cooked *(Gordon Stevenson)*

COBHAM [TQ1059]

Old Bear KT11 3DX [Riverhill]: Large recently refurbished old low-beamed pub opp the Mole, long bare-boards bar with windsor chairs and inglenook log fire, well kept Flowers and Wychwood, enjoyable if pricey food from traditional things up in bar and parquet-floored restaurant; terrace tables, open all day wknds *(Geoffrey Kemp)*

☆ *Plough* KT11 3LT [3.2 miles from M25 junction 10; right off A3 on A245; in Cobham, right into Downside Bridge Rd; Plough Lane]: New licensee at civilised and welcoming low-beamed country local with traditional interior, log fire in an ancient stone fireplace, restaurant with pews, bare boards and white table linen, Brakespears, Courage Best and a guest or two, generously served bar food (not Sun evening); children welcome, dogs allowed in bar, disabled facilities, terrace with picnic-sets sheltered by high garden wall, open all day *(BB, Shirley Mackenzie, LYM)*

COMPTON [SU9546]

Harrow GU3 1EG [B3000 towards Godalming off A3]: Roadside pub refurbished by newish licensees, split level log-fire bar, beamed dining area, modern furniture inc high-back leather dining chairs, candles on tables, carpets throughout, emphasis on good home-made food (not Sun evening) from lunchtime sandwiches up, Adnams, Greene King and Ringwood ales, friendly attentive service from smart staff; terrace picnic-sets at back, open all day *(Phil Bryant, LYM)*

CRANLEIGH [TQ0539]

Richard Onslow GU6 8AU [High St]: Recently taken over and reworked by Peach gastropub chain, large dining area to the right, smaller more traditional L-shaped bar to the left with open fire, good range of food all day inc cheaper two-course set menu (Mon-Sat before 7pm), breakfast 9-11am, smart friendly staff, Wells & Youngs Bombardier and two local guests, good choice of wines by the glass inc champagne; children welcome, café-style tables out in front, open all day *(Phil Bryant)*

DORKING [TQ1649]

☆ *Kings Arms* RH4 1BU [West St]: Rambling 16th-c pub in antiques area, timbers and low beams, nice lived-in furniture in olde-worlde part-panelled lounge, bargain home-made food from sandwiches to roasts and a good pie of the day, interesting guest ales, friendly efficient service, warm relaxed atmosphere, old-fashioned back dining area; piped music; open all day *(Conor McGaughey)*

EASHING [SU9543]

☆ *Stag* GU7 2QG [Lower Eashing, just off A3 southbound]: Attractive beamed pub dating partly from 15th c, comfortably rambling areas with log fires, enjoyable food inc some interesting dishes, Hogs Back TEA and guests such as Fullers London Pride and Shepherd Neame Spitfire, friendly helpful young staff, daily papers; piped music; dogs welcome, pleasant streamside garden with terrace, bedrooms, open all day wknds (sister pub to Duke of Cambridge in Tilford and Queens Head at E Clandon) *(LM, Simon and Sally Small, Conor McGaughey, Peter Price, LYM)*

EAST CLANDON [TQ0551]

☆ *Queens Head* GU4 7RY [just off A246 Guildford—Leatherhead; The Street]: Rambling dining pub in same small group as Duke of Cambridge at Tilford and Stag in Eashing, enjoyable food from light dishes up inc set deals (Mon-Thurs), good friendly service, well kept ales such as Shepherd Neame Spitfire and Surrey Hills Shere Drop from fine old elm bar counter, comfortable linked rooms, big inglenook log-effect fire; children welcome, picnic-sets on pretty front terrace and in quiet side garden, handy for two NT properties, open all day Sat and till 9pm Sun *(LYM, Geoffrey Kemp, Ian Phillips)*

ELLENS GREEN [TQ0936]

Wheatsheaf RH12 3AS [B2128 N of Rudgwick]: Family-run dining pub with good home-made food from lunchtime sandwiches up, Badger ales, good choice of wines by the glass, tiled floor bar with large fireplace, dining areas either side; some seats in front, more on back terrace, open all day *(Shirley Mackenzie)*

ENGLEFIELD GREEN [SU9872]

☆ *Fox & Hounds* TW20 0XU [Bishopsgate Rd, off A328 N of Egham]: Neat old local handy for Windsor Park, extensive interior with pubby tables and chairs in bare-boards bar opening to carpeted J-shaped dining area with exposed brick and café chairs, conservatory, three log fires, Brakspears, Hogs Back TEA and a guest, enjoyable bar food all day (not Sun evening); piped music and some live jazz; children welcome, dogs in bar, picnic-sets on terrace, decking and front lawn, open all day *(Ian Phillips, Martin and Karen Wake, Jeremy Hebblethwaite, LYM, Chris Glasson, Evelyn and Derek Walter)*

Happy Man TW20 0QS [Harvest Rd]: Friendly and unpretentious two-bar late Victorian backstreet local, good value pubby food, well kept changing ales such as Church End and Hop Back, farm cider, good service, darts area, quiz nights; popular with students in term time; open all day *(Chris Pluthero, Dr Martin Owton, Ian Phillips, Andy and Jill Kassube)*

Sun TW20 0UF [Wick Lane, Bishopsgate]: Well used beamed local, Courage Best, Greene King Abbot and Shepherd Neame Spitfire kept well, good blackboard wine choice, generous inexpensive pubby food from sandwiches up, friendly service, small wooden tables with banquettes and low stools, lots of pub bric-a-brac inc interesting beer bottle collection, colourful photographs, open fire, conservatory; soft piped music; children welcome, biscuit and water for dogs, a few tables out at front, quiet garden with aviary, handy for Savill Garden and Windsor Park *(LM)*

EPSOM [TQ2158]
Derby Arms KT18 5LE [Downs Rd, Epsom Downs]: Reworked M&B dining pub, good range of wines by the glass, two real ales, log fires; nice tables outside, good views – opp racecourse grandstand *(John Branston)*

Olde Kings Head KT17 4QB [Church St]: Welcoming 17th-c weatherboarded pub, well cared-for traditional bar with open fire, dark woodwork, old prints, upholstered wall benches, lowish tables and stools, patterned carpets, Fullers, Harveys and Wells & Youngs, good value standard food; piped radio *(Phil Bryant)*

Rubbing House KT18 5LJ [Langley Vale Rd (on Epsom racecourse)]: Restauranty dining pub with attractive modern décor, good value food promptly served even when busy, Fullers London Pride and Greene King IPA, serious wine list, fantastic racecourse views, upper balcony; tables outside *(Mrs G R Sharman, Maureen and Keith Gimson, DWAJ, Ian Wilson)*

ESHER [TQ1364]
Bear KT10 9RQ [High St]: Thriving Youngs pub with their full range kept well, good choice of wines by the glass, friendly service, popular reasonably priced food in bar and dining end, two landmark life-size bears behind roof parapet; big-screen sports TV; outside seating with awnings, bedrooms, open all day *(Tom and Ruth Rees, Michael Dandy)*

☆ *Prince of Wales* KT10 8LA [West End Lane; off A244 towards Hersham, by Princess Alice Hospice]: Particularly well run rambling Chef

& Brewer dining pub, wide choice of reasonably priced food from warm baguettes up, well kept Adnams, Fullers and Wells & Youngs ales, good wine choice, friendly efficient staff, quiet corners, turkey carpets, old furniture, prints and photographs, some rugby memorabilia, daily papers; piped music; children welcome, disabled access, big shady garden with good decking, lovely village setting by green and duck pond *(Ron and Sheila Corbett, LM, Ian Phillips, Richard and Sheila Fitton)*

FARNHAM [SU8445]
Fox GU10 3PH [Frensham Rd, Lower Bourne]: Greene King roadside pub with their ales and guests, enthusiastic landlord and attentive prompt staff, wide choice of food (all day Sun) from standard to more adventurous dishes, deep crimson décor with heavy curtains, wood cladding and exposed brick, pubby furniture on bare boards or carpet, collection of Frith photographs and old pub signs, raised back areas; picnic-sets and small adventure playground outside, open all day *(Phil Bryant)*

FICKLESHOLE [TQ3960]
White Bear CR6 9PH [Featherbed Lane/Fairchildes Lane; off A2022 Purley Rd just S of A212 roundabout]: 16th-c country dining pub popular for its good value food (all day Fri and Sat, best to book wknds), lots of small rooms, beams, flagstones and open fires, friendly prompt service, four well kept changing ales; children welcome, picnic-sets on front terrace with stone bear, sizeable back garden, open all day *(LYM, Conor McGaughey, J M and R J Hope, John Branston)*

GODSTONE [TQ3551]
Bell RH9 8DX [under a mile from M25 junction 6, via B2236]: Good choice of enjoyable up-to-date and more traditional food in refurbished open-plan M&B family dining pub, comfortably modern furnishings and lighting in handsome old building, separate bar with Timothy Taylors Landlord, three open fires; back terrace and garden *(LYM, David and Diane Young, N R White)*

GRAYSWOOD [SU9134]
Wheatsheaf GU27 2DE [Grayswood Rd (A286 NE of Haslemere)]: Welcoming dining pub, light and airy décor, enjoyable food in bar and restaurant, well kept ales, friendly helpful service; front verandah, side terrace, conference/bedroom extension *(Wendy Chandler)*

GUILDFORD [SU9949]
Boatman GU1 3XJ [Shalford Rd, Millbrook; across car park from Yvonne Arnaud Theatre, beyond boat yard]: Big popular riverside pub under newish ownership, bright contemporary décor with boating theme, large split-level bar dropping down to back dining conservatory with suspended rowing boat, second more formal dining area, enjoyable pubby food all day inc children's menu, well kept Hogs Back TEA and Otter Bitter from stillage behind bar, 15 wines by

the glass, friendly helpful service, newspapers; big garden with moorings and terrace by River Wey, good walks, open all day *(Phil Bryant)*

Keystone GU2 4BL [Portsmouth Rd]: Good choice of food (not Fri-Sun evenings) inc deals, Black Sheep, Wadworths 6X and two guests, friendly helpful young staff, bistro atmosphere with simple décor and furnishings inc a couple of settles and leather sofas; tables on heated back terrace (dogs allowed here only), open all day, cl Sun evening *(John and Joan Nash)*

Three Pigeons GU1 3AJ [High St]: Now a Nicholsons pub, with good beer range priced lower than the high local average, pleasant panelled décor, winding stair to two-level upper bar, nice view of passing High St life *(Phil and Sally Gorton)*

White House GU2 4AJ [High St]: Waterside pub with friendly young staff, Fullers and Gales beers, all-day food from sandwiches up, large bar with side sun lounge, upstairs rooms and small roof terrace; children welcome, a few picnic-sets by River Wey, pretty setting, open all day *(Ian Phillips)*

HASCOMBE [TQ0039]

White Horse GU8 4JA [B2130 S of Godalming]: 16th-c origins with beams and small-windowed alcoves, ales from Harveys, Ringwood, Triple fff and Wychwood, interesting wines by the glass, pubby food (prices edging a little high) from sandwiches up, friendly young staff, bar on right with scrubbed tables and pews on wood floor, carpeted lounge on left with dining areas off, woodburner, resident dogs; small front terrace, spacious sloping back lawn, pretty village with good walks, handy for Winkworth Arboretum (NT), has been open all day wknds *(Martin and Karen Wake, Terry Buckland, Mr and Mrs A H Young, Colin and Louise English, LYM)*

HEADLEY [TQ2054]

Cock KT18 6LE [Church Lane]: Good value up-to-date food from lunchtime doorstep sandwiches up, well kept ales inc Adnams and Harveys, choice of coffees, pleasant young staff, contemporary décor (pub actually dates from 15th c) with several light and airy dining areas; dogs welcome, tables outside – attractive setting, good woodland walks *(Maureen and Keith Gimson, David and Sue Atkinson)*

HOLMBURY ST MARY [TQ1144]

☆ *Kings Head* RH5 6NP: Friendly bare-boards pub in walking country, good fresh food using local supplies, helpful young licensees, well kept ales such as Kings and Surrey Hills, good wines by the glass, two-way log fire (not always lit midweek), small traditional back restaurant (fish recommended), public bar with darts, TV and games machine; pretty spot with seats out facing green, more in big sloping back garden, open all day at least wknds and summer *(Barry Steele-Perkins, Franklyn Roberts)*

HORSELL [SU9859]

Cricketers GU21 4XB [Horsell Birch]: Warm friendly country local, good sensibly priced food inc Sun carvery, Courage Best, Fullers London Pride and Greene King Old Speckled Hen, cheerful efficient service even when busy, log fire, quietly comfortable end sections, extended back eating area, carpet and shiny boards; children well catered for, picnic-sets out in front and in big well kept garden, wide views over Horsell Common *(Guy Consterdine, Ian Phillips)*

Plough GU21 4JL [off South Rd; Cheapside]: Small friendly local overlooking wooded heath, relaxed atmosphere, well kept changing ales inc Black Sheep, Brains, Jennings, Shepherd Neame and Thwaites, good choice of wines by the glass and of malt whiskies, good value fresh food (all day Sat, not Sun evening) inc various pies, quiet dining area one side of L, games machines and TV the other; children and dogs welcome (and hay for visiting horses), garden tables, play area, open all day *(Ian Phillips)*

☆ *Red Lion* GU21 4SS [High St]: Large and very popular with good generous pubby and more sophisticated food inc all-day snacks, Adnams, Courage and Fullers, good wines and other drinks, friendly attentive service even when busy, split-level bar with contemporary décor, bare boards and fire, picture-filled barn restaurant (children allowed), daily papers; ivy-clad passage to garden and comfortable tree-sheltered terrace, good walks, open all day *(Frances Naldrett, Ian Phillips, BB, Gill and Keith Croxton, Michael Hasslacher)*

HORSELL COMMON [TQ0160]

☆ *Bleak House* GU21 5NL [Chertsey Rd, The Anthonys; A320 Woking—Ottershaw]: Smart restauranty pub aka Sands at Bleak House, grey split sandstone for floor and face of bar counter, cool décor with black tables, sofas and stools, good if not cheap food, Hogs Back TEA, Surrey Hills Shere Drop and a guest, fresh juices, friendly attentive uniformed staff; lively acoustics; smokers' marquee in pleasant back garden merging into woods with good shortish walks to sandpits which inspired H G Wells's *War of the Worlds*, bedrooms *(Ian Phillips, Phil Bryant)*

IRONS BOTTOM [TQ2546]

Three Horseshoes RH2 8PT [Sidlow Bridge, off A217]: Welcoming recently renovated local, enjoyable good value home-made food, well kept ales such as Fullers London Pride, Harveys and Surrey Hills, darts; tables outside, summer barbecues *(C and R Bromage)*

KNAPHILL [SU9557]

Hunters Lodge GU21 2RP [Bagshot Rd]: Vintage Inn with comfortable linked beamed rooms, good log fires, assorted tables and chairs, reasonably priced standard food inc enjoyable Sun roasts and some more upmarket dishes, good choice of wines by the glass, Fullers London Pride and Timothy Taylors Landlord, daily papers; disabled facilities, tables in pleasant well established garden *(Mike Hand, Phil Bryant)*

LALEHAM [TQ0568]

Three Horseshoes TW18 1SE [Shepperton Rd (B376)]: Light and airy beamed and flagstoned bar with contemporary décor, comfortable sofas, daily papers, log fire, two restaurant areas and conservatory, good popular food (all day wknds), well kept Harveys Best, Hop Back Summer Lightning and Sharps Doom Bar, lots of wines by the glass, friendly staff; piped music; children welcome in restaurant till 8pm, smart outside seating areas, nr pleasant stretch of the Thames, open all day *(LYM, Adrian Porter, Ron and Sheila Corbett, Susan and Neil McLean)*

LIMPSFIELD [TQ4053]

Bull RH8 0DR [High St]: Friendly village local dating from 16th c, limited choice of well cooked food all day inc breakfast, good choice of modestly priced wines, Adnams and Marstons Pedigree, good service, darts; sports TVs, juke box; children welcome, terrace tables *(Simon Good)*

LINGFIELD [TQ3844]

☆ **Hare & Hounds** RH7 6BZ [turn off B2029 N at the Crowhurst/Edenbridge signpost]: Smallish open-plan bar, bare boards and flagstones, mixed seating inc button-back leather chesterfield, dining area, good wide-ranging food from french landlord, friendly service, Greene King IPA and a guest such as Fullers London Pride; children and dogs welcome, tables in pleasant split-level garden with decking, good walking country near Haxted Mill – leave boots in porch, open all day, cl Sun evening *(Tony and Shirley Albert, LYM, Simon and Helen Barnes, Steven and Yvonne Parker, Derek Thomas, Melanie Alcock, Cathryn and Richard Hicks)*

Old Cage RH7 6AU [Plaistow St]: Part weatherboarded late 16th-c beamed pub, bar areas on different levels, one with fine inglenook, Greene King, Harveys and Sharps, hearty no-nonsense bargain food (they may ask to keep a credit card while you eat), flagstones and bare boards, old pubby furniture and some unusual pews, sofas, brass, old photographs and enamel signs; sports TV; covered area outside *(Phil Bryant)*

MARTYRS GREEN [TQ0857]

Black Swan KT11 1NG [handy for M25 junction 10; off A3 S-bound, but return N of junction]: Chunky seating and spacious contemporary restauranty décor (utterly changed from its days as the 'Slaughtered Lamb' in *An American Werewolf in London*), good food, grand choice of wines and champagnes, several real ales inc Sharps Doom Bar and Surrey Hills Shere Drop, log fire and under-floor heating; children welcome, stylish black slate furniture out on extensively landscaped terrace, open all day *(John and Verna Aspinall, G Pincus, Susan and John Douglas, Shirley Mackenzie, Harry Hersom)*

MERSHAM [TQ3051]

Inn on the Pond RH1 4EU [Nutfield Marsh Rd, off A25 W of Godstone]: Dining pub doing enjoyable interesting food (all day Sun) inc children's meals, good cheerful service, well kept ales from Hogs Back, Kings and Sharps, Stowford Press cider, good choice of wines by the glass inc champagne, comfortable casually contemporary dining room, back conservatory; sheltered terrace behind, views over pond and nearby cricket ground to North Downs *(BB, Fleur Perkie, John Branston, Peter Eyles, Richard Abnett)*

MOGADOR [TQ2453]

Sportsman KT20 7ES [from M25 up A217 past 2nd roundabout, then Mogador signed; edge of Banstead Heath]: Nicely refurbished and extended low-ceilinged pub on Walton Heath (originally 16th-c royal hunting lodge), well kept ales such as Everards Tiger and Sharps Doom Bar, enjoyable food from ciabattas to steaks, prompt helpful service, log fire, flagstoned bar with carpeted raised area, restaurant; picnic-sets out on common and on back lawn, more seats on front verandah, popular with walkers and riders *(N R White, Phil Bryant, Mrs P Sumner, Graham Hill)*

NEWDIGATE [TQ1942]

Six Bells RH5 5DH [Village St]: Good atmosphere in refurbished pub, popular good value food from blackboards in pleasant eating section, well kept ales and decent wines, friendly service; children and dogs welcome, plenty of tables in nice garden with play area, lovely outlook over wooden-towered church *(Jill Brewster, Tony and Jill Radnor)*

OCKLEY [TQ1439]

☆ **Kings Arms** RH5 5TS [Stane St (A29)]: Attractive 17th-c country inn reworked as more restaurant than pub though keeping proper bar, well kept Kings and Sharps Doom Bar, good choice of wines by the glass, enjoyable food from new chef, good service, comfortable olde-worlde décor inc lots of antique prints, good inglenook log fire, heavy beams and timbers, low lighting, live jazz/blues nights; children welcome, immaculate big back garden, good bedrooms *(LYM, Shirley Mackenzie, Gordon Stevenson)*

OTTERSHAW [TQ0263]

☆ **Castle** KT16 0LW [Brox Rd, off A320 not far from M25 junction 11]: Friendly two-bar early Victorian local with log fires, country paraphernalia on black ceiling joists and walls, six well kept ales inc Adnams, Fullers, Harveys and Timothy Taylors, Addlestone's cider, lunchtime and evening bar food (not Sun evening); TV, piped music; children welcome in conservatory till 7pm, dogs in bar, tables on terrace and grass, open all day wknds *(JMM, Ian Phillips, Guy Charrison, LYM)*

OXTED [TQ4048]

Royal Oak RH8 0RR [Caterfield Lane, Staffhurst Wood, S of town]: Cheerful and comfortable traditional bar, good ale range, good value house wines, enjoyable generous mainly local food inc imaginative dishes, back dining room with lovely country views *(William Ruxton, John Branston)*

PIRBRIGHT [SU9454]

Royal Oak GU24 0DQ [Aldershot Rd; A324S of village]: Welcoming old Tudor pub, well kept Greene King, Hogs Back TEA and perhaps guest ales, good range of wines by the glass, sensibly priced pubby food, three log fires, heavily beamed and timbered rambling side areas, ancient stripped brickwork, family room; soft piped music; disabled facilities, extensive colourful gardens, good walks, open all day *(KC, Ian Phillips, LYM)*

White Hart GU24 0LP [The Green]: Dining pub with smart modern décor, sturdy pale wood furniture on black and white tartan carpet, some original flagstones, sofas by log fires in restored fireplaces, enjoyable interesting food, well kept Greene King, Hogs Back and Wells & Youngs, daily papers, relaxed friendly atmosphere; soft piped music; children welcome, good tables and chairs in pleasant fenced front garden, play area behind *(David and Sue Smith, Ian Phillips)*

PUTTENHAM [SU9347]

Good Intent GU3 1AR [signed off B3000 just S of A31 junction; The Street/Seale Lane]: Well worn-in convivial beamed village local under new management (new czech landlady worked for previous owners), well kept changing ales, hearty helpings of enjoyable reasonably priced traditional food, log fire in cosy front bar with alcove seating, newspapers, old photographs of the pub, simple dining area; small sunny garden, good walks *(Brian and Anna Marsden, David and Sue Smith, BB)*

PYRFORD LOCK [TQ0559]

☆ *Anchor* GU23 6QW [3 miles from M25 junction 10 – S on A3, then take Wisley slip rd and go on past RHS garden]: Light and airy Badger family dining pub (can get very busy), food all day (small helpings available), lunchtime sandwiches too, good value wines, cheerful efficient service, daily papers, simple tables on bare boards, quieter more comfortable panelled back area, narrow-boat memorabilia, pleasant conservatory; dogs allowed in part, splendid terrace in lovely spot by bridge and locks on River Wey Navigation (handy for RHS Wisley), fenced-off play area, open all day *(Ian Phillips, C and R Bromage, LYM, Kevin Flack, John Saville, Peter Rozée, Gordon Stevenson, Mrs G R Sharman, Sue and Mike Todd)*

REIGATE [TQ2349]

Black Horse RH2 9JZ [West St (A25)]: Popular and welcoming with emphasis on the enjoyable food (some quite pricey), well kept ales such as Adnams and Wells & Youngs, sofas in relaxing bar area, attractive good-sized modern dining extension; nice spot by heathland *(C and R Bromage, Paul Lucas, Elaine Burtenshaw)*

Yew Tree RH2 9PJ [0.5 miles from M25 junction 8; Reigate Hill (A217)]: Comfortable oak-panelled parquet-floored pub, enjoyable food, well kept ales inc Fullers and Wells & Youngs, cheerful staff, open fire; dogs welcome, split-level paved garden behind *(Susan Davis)*

REIGATE HEATH [TQ2349]

Skimmington Castle RH2 8RL [off A25 Reigate—Dorking via Flanchford Rd and Bonny's Rd]: Nicely located small country pub revamped under present management, emphasis on enjoyable home-made food, ales such as Adnams and Greene King, panelled beamed rooms with big log fireplace; children and dogs welcome *(Ian and Nita Cooper, Conor McGaughey, John Michelson, Gaynor Lawson, Phil Bryant, LYM)*

RIPLEY [TQ0455]

Jovial Sailor GU23 6EZ [Portsmouth Rd]: Large popular Chef & Brewer, decent good value food, cheerful helpful staff, three well kept changing ales, good wine choice, reconstructed well divided interior with standing timbers, beams, stripped brickwork and log fires, country bric-a-brac, daily papers; piped music; good-sized garden, handy for Wisley *(Sue and Mike Todd)*

Seven Stars GU23 6DL [Newark Lane (B367)]: Neat family-run traditional 1930s pub popular at lunchtimes for enjoyable food from sandwiches to plenty of seafood, lots of blackboards, Fullers London Pride, Greene King and Shepherd Neame Spitfire, good wines and coffee, open fire; quiet piped music; picnic-sets in large tidy garden, river and canalside walks *(Phil Bryant, Ian Phillips, Barrie and Mary Crees, Kevin Flack)*

ROWLEDGE [SU8243]

Cherry Tree GU10 4AB [Cherry Tree Rd; off A325 just S of Farnham]: Friendly well looked-after family-run pub, good choice of enjoyable unfussy food inc home-made pies, several well kept ales, refurbished dining room, open fires; children and dogs welcome, tables in nicely maintained garden, handy for Birdworld and Alice Holt Forest *(BOB)*

Hare & Hounds GU10 4AA [The Square]: Well run by father and son team, good generous food inc great choice of fresh fish, welcoming atmosphere, Greene King ales, smallish eating area; attractive garden *(Graham and Toni Sanders)*

SEND [TQ0156]

New Inn GU23 7EN [Send Rd, Cartbridge]: Well placed old pub by Wey Navigation canal, long bar decorated to suit, Adnams, Fullers London Pride, Greene King Abbot and a couple of unusual guests, friendly landlord, good value food from toasted sandwiches up, log-effect gas fires; large waterside garden with moorings and smokers' shelter *(Ian Phillips, Phil Bryant)*

SEND MARSH [TQ0455]

☆ *Saddlers Arms* GU23 6JQ [Send Marsh Rd]: Genial and attentive licensees in unpretentious low-beamed local, homely and warm, with Courage Best, Fullers London Pride, Greene King IPA and Shepherd Neame Spitfire, good value generous home-made food (all day Sun) from sandwiches to pizzas and pubby favourites, open fire, toby jugs, brassware etc, no music or TV; picnic-sets out front and back *(Shirley Mackenzie, Ian Phillips)*

SHACKLEFORD [SU9345]

Cyder House GU8 6AN [Peper Harow Lane]: Smart comfortably refurbished pub doing well under friendly helpful licensees, Badger ales, decent house wines, good if pricey food all day (till 4pm Sun and Mon) from sandwiches and bar snacks to interesting specials and Sun roasts, children's helpings, morning coffee and afternoon tea, mix of furniture inc leather sofas in light and airy linked areas around central servery, wood floors, log fire; well behaved dogs welcome, terrace seating and lawn, play area, nice leafy village setting, good walks, open all day, till 7pm Sun and Mon *(Mr N McGill, Martin and Karen Wake, David and Sue Smith, BB)*

SHALFORD [SU9946]

Parrot GU4 8DW [Broadford Rd]: Big warmly welcoming pub with wide range of enjoyable fairly priced food from good snacks up, Fullers London Pride, Hogs Back TEA and Surrey Hills Shere Drop, quick service from friendly staff, rows of neat pine dining tables, some easy chairs around low tables, pleasant conservatory; children welcome till 8pm, attractive garden, five bedrooms, handy for Losely Park *(C and R Bromage, Kevin Flack, John and Heather Wright)*

Queen Victoria GU4 8BY [Station Row]: No-nonsense tile-hung bay-windowed local popular with walkers, Fullers London Pride, Greene King and Surrey Hills Shere Drop, enjoyable reasonably priced bar lunches, friendly helpful staff, good log fire, games room; piped music, TV and fruit machine in bar; sheltered garden with picnic-sets, bedrooms *(Tony and Wendy Hobden)*

SHAMLEY GREEN [TQ0343]

Bricklayers Arms GU5 0UA [south side of green]: Welcoming deceptively large red-brick village pub, U-shaped layout with good balance of traditional and modern décor, five well kept ales such as Arundel, Exmoor, Fullers, Hogs Back and Surrey Hills, wide range of reasonably priced pubby food inc good specials, bare boards, carpets and flagstones, exposed brick and stripped wood, sofas by central log fire, old local photographs, live music; pool, TV, games machine; children welcome, couple of picnic-sets out in front, more at back, aviary *(Ian Scott-Thompson, Phil Bryant)*

☆ *Red Lion* GU5 0UB [The Green]: Welcoming dining pub with smart décor, dark polished furniture, rows of books, open fires, local cricketing photographs, good food all day from well filled sandwiches with chips to steaks, children's helpings and unusual

puddings, good landlady and service, well kept Adnams Broadside and Wells & Youngs, farm cider, good choice of wines, cafetière coffee, restaurant; open all day, children welcome, sturdy tables in nice garden by village green, another behind with heated covered terrace *(LYM, Shirley Mackenzie, JJW, CMW)*

SHEPPERTON [TQ0765]

Thames Court TW17 9LJ [Shepperton Lock, Ferry Lane; turn left off B375 towards Chertsey, about 90 metres from Square]: Huge Vintage Inn dining pub well placed by Thames, good choice of wines by the glass, ales such as Brakspears Oxford Gold, Fullers London Pride and Sharps Doom Bar, usual well priced food all day from sandwiches to good Sun roasts, galleried central atrium with attractive panelled areas up and down stairs, two good log fires, daily papers; can get very busy summer wknds but copes well; children welcome, large attractive tree-shaded terrace with heaters, open all day *(Phil Bryant, Ian Phillips, Mayur Shah)*

SHERE [TQ0747]

White Horse GU5 9HF [signed off A25 3 miles E of Guildford; Middle St]: Splendid Chef & Brewer with uneven floors, massive beams and timbers, Tudor stonework, oak wall seats and two log fires, one in a huge inglenook, several rooms off small bar; enjoyable good value food all day from sandwiches up (in restaurant only wknds), beers such as Fullers London Pride, Hogs Back TEA and Wells & Youngs Best, lots of sensibly priced wines by the glass; children and dogs welcome, seats out at front and in big garden behind, beautiful film-set village, open all day *(LYM, Ian Phillips, Mrs G R Sharman)*

William Bray GU5 9HS [Shere Lane]: Major refurbishment by new owners, emphasis on good well presented locally sourced food, ales such as Hogs Back, Sharps and Surrey Hills, good choice of wines, attentive service; very busy wknds; dogs welcome, shiny metal tables on front terrace, pretty landscaped garden *(Martin Stafford, J D Derry, N R White, Ian Phillips)*

SOUTH GODSTONE [TQ3549]

Fox & Hounds RH9 8LY [Tilburstow Hill Rd/Harts Lane, off A22]: Pleasant old tile-hung country pub with woodburner in low-beamed bar, welcoming staff, enjoyable good value food from pubby staples to good seafood, nice puddings, well kept Greene King ales from tiny bar counter, restaurant with inglenook; open all day *(John Branston, Conor McGaughey, LYM)*

SUNBURY [TQ1068]

Flower Pot TW16 6AA [Thames St, handy for M3 junction 1, via Green St off exit roundabout]: Popular 18th-c inn across road from Thames, refurbished and under new tenants, enjoyable food (chef has remained), friendly service (can be slow when busy), Marstons-related ales; seven bedrooms *(Gerry and Rosemary Dobson)*

SUTTON GREEN [TQ0054]

Olive Tree GU4 7QD [Sutton Green Rd]: Big rambling modern dining pub with good honest fresh food (not Sun or Mon evenings), cheaper bar menu inc sandwiches, well kept Fullers London Pride, Harveys and Timothy Taylors Landlord, good choice of wines by the glass, pleasant helpful staff, bare boards and open fire, relaxing back dining room with minimalist décor; picnic-sets out at front *(JMM, LM, Paddy and Annabelle Cribb)*

TADWORTH [TQ2354]

Blue Anchor KT20 5SL [Dorking Rd (B2032)]: Renovated flagstoned pub in nice woodland setting, enjoyable varied food, good helpful staff, decent choice of well kept ales and wines, log fires *(John Ecklin)*

Dukes Head KT20 5SL [Dorking Rd (B2032 opp Common and woods)]: Roomy and comfortably refurbished, popular for its enjoyable well priced food all day (not Sun evening) from good sandwiches up, five well kept ales inc a local microbrew, good choice of wines by the glass, helpful jolly staff, two big inglenook log fires; plenty of garden tables, open all day *(Jenny and Brian Seller, C and R Bromage, John Branston)*

THAMES DITTON [TQ1567]

Albany KT7 0QY [Queens Rd, signed off Summer Rd]: M&B bar-with-restaurant in lovely Thames-side position, upscale food, good choice of wines by the glass, beers inc Fullers London Pride and Timothy Taylors Landlord, log fire, daily papers, river pictures; nice balconies, river-view terrace and lawn, moorings, open all day *(Ian Phillips, Gordon Stevenson, Tom and Ruth Rees)*

Ewe KT7 0JW [Hampton Court Way]: Recently refurbished in contemporary style, bar with leather sofas, restaurant, small conservatory overlooking terrace, enjoyable food, Wadworths 6X, friendly service; children welcome *(Michael Dandy)*

Ferry KT7 0XY [Portsmouth Rd]: Bistro-style dining pub under new chef/landlord, good food and wine, friendly service, stripped-wood floor and burgundy leather seating, real ales from brick-faced bar; some tables out at front *(Tom and Ruth Rees, Lauren Bennett)*

☆ *Olde Swan* KT7 0QQ [Summer Rd]: Large riverside pub (one of very few listed Grade I) under new ownership, enjoyable reasonably priced food, Greene King and a guest beer, cosy Victorian-style décor, log fires, one long bar with three good-sized areas inc civilised black-panelled upper bar overlooking quiet Thames backwater, restaurant; provision for children and dogs, moorings and plenty of waterside tables, open all day *(Tom and Ruth Rees, BB)*

TILFORD [SU8743]

Barley Mow GU10 2BU [The Green, off B3001 SE of Farnham; also signed off A287]: Opposite pretty cricket green, with woodburner in snug little low-ceilinged traditional bar, nice scrubbed tables in two small rooms set for food on left, interesting cricketing prints and old photographs, well kept ales such as Courage Best, Greene King Abbot, Hook Norton and Sharps Doom Bar, imaginative wine list, pubby food, wknd afternoon teas; darts and table skittles, no children except in back coach house; narrow front terrace, picnic-sets in back garden fenced off from Wey tributary, open all day Sun and summer Sats *(Phil Bryant, LM, BB)*

Duke of Cambridge GU10 2DD [Tilford Rd]: Civilised pub in same small local group as Stag at Eashing and Queens Head at E Clandon, enjoyable food from standards to more imaginative things inc good fish, children's menu, good choice of wines, Hogs Back TEA and Surrey Hills Shere Drop, efficient helpful service; garden picnic-sets and good play area, open all day wknds *(Canon George Farran)*

WALTON ON THE HILL [TQ2255]

Blue Ball KT20 7UE [not far from M25 junction 8; Deans Lane, off B2220 by pond]: Facing common nr duck pond, cosily refurbished, with good choice of fairly priced home-made food, good atmosphere, friendly uniformed staff, several real ales, decent wines, restaurant (open all day Sun) overlooking big garden; good walking area *(Pam Adsley, C and R Bromage)*

Chequers KT20 7SF [Chequers Lane]: Mock-Tudor Youngs pub with several rooms rambling around central servery, friendly helpful service, well kept ales, bar food and more expensive restaurant, log fires; terrace and neat sheltered garden *(C and R Bromage, LYM, Sarah Howes)*

WALTON-ON-THAMES [TQ1065]

Ashley Park KT12 1JP [Station Approach/Ashley Park Rd]: Comfortable well run Ember Inn, good reasonably priced food, well kept ales, competent service, good atmosphere; open all day, bedrooms in adjoining Innkeepers Lodge *(Ron and Sheila Corbett)*

Swan KT12 2PF [Manor Rd, off A3050]: Riverside Youngs pub with several smartly refurbished linked rooms, decent good value food from sandwiches up, well kept ales, good wine choice, prompt friendly service, attractive restaurant; dogs welcome, new terracing in large garden leading down to Thames, moorings, riverside walks *(Tom and Ruth Rees, Ian Phillips)*

Weir KT12 2JB [Towpath, Waterside Drive off Sunbury Lane]: Edwardian pub in nice Thames-side spot with big terrace overlooking river and weir (and steel walkway), decent choice of food all day (till 7pm Sun) from snacks up, Fullers and Greene King ales, traditional décor, river pictures, newspapers; dogs and children welcome, lovely towpath walks, six bedrooms *(Ian Phillips)*

WARLINGHAM [TQ3955]

☆ *Botley Hill Farmhouse* CR6 9QH [S on Limpsfield Rd (B269)]: Busy pub dating back to 16th c with standard food inc popular Sun roasts, well kept Greene King and Kings ales, good choice of wines by the glass, hard-working friendly staff, low-ceilinged linked rooms up and down steps, soft lighting, spreading carpet, quite close-set tables, big log fireplace in one attractive flagstoned room; wknd entertainment in marquee inc loud live music; children and dogs welcome, disabled access, side and back terraces with plastic furniture, neat garden with play area, ducks and aviary *(N R White, BB, LM)*

WEST CLANDON [TQ0451]

☆ *Bulls Head* GU4 7ST [A247 SE of Woking]: Comfortable, spotless and unchanging, based on 1540s timbered hall house, popular especially with older people at lunchtime for good value hearty food from sandwiches up inc home-made proper pies (no food Sun evening), small lantern-lit beamed front bar with open fire and some stripped brick, old local prints and bric-a-brac, simple raised back inglenook dining area, friendly helpful staff, Surrey Hills Shere Drop, good coffee, no piped music, games room with darts and pool; no credit cards; children and dogs on leads welcome, disabled access, good play area in neat garden, handy for Clandon Park, good walks *(DWAJ, David Lowe, Phil Bryant, Ian Phillips)*

☆ *Onslow Arms* GU4 7TE [A247 SE of Woking]: Popular partly 17th-c country pub with beams, flagstones, dark nooks and corners, warm seats by inglenook log fires, welcoming staff, reasonably priced bar food (not Sun evening) from baguettes up, separate french restaurant doing very good two-course lunch deals, Courage Best and Directors, Greene King Old Speckled Hen and Ringwood Fortyniner, decent wines; piped music; children welcome (and dogs in bar), great well lit garden, helicopter pad, open all day *(LYM, Geoffrey Kemp)*

WEST HORSLEY [TQ0853]

☆ *Barley Mow* KT24 6HR [off A246 Leatherhead—Guildford at Bell & Colvill garage roundabout; The Street]: Welcoming tree-shaded traditional pub, low beams, mix of flagstones, bare boards and carpet, leather sofas, two log fires, well kept ales such as Fullers London Pride, Greene King IPA and Shepherd Neame Spitfire, decent wines, good value food (not Sun evening) inc nice lunchtime sandwiches, daily papers, vintage and classic car pictures (may be an AC Cobra or Jaguar XK outside), comfortable softly lit barn-like dining room; unobtrusive piped music, TV; dogs and children welcome, picnic-sets in good-sized garden, open all day *(David and Sue Smith, John and Joan Nash, Dr and Mrs A K Clarke, LYM, Ian Phillips, David Lowe, Brian Dawes, David M Smith, Franklyn Roberts, David Jackman, John Branston, Mr and Mrs A Sawder, BOB, William Ruxton)*

King William IV KT24 6BG [The Street]: Comfortable and welcoming early 19th-c pub with very low-beamed open-plan rambling bar, good food from sandwiches up here and

in conservatory restaurant, decent choice of wines by the glass, well kept Courage Best and Directors and Surrey Hills Shere Drop, good coffee, log fire, board games; piped music may intrude; children and dogs welcome, good disabled access, small garden with decking and lovely hanging baskets *(Dr and Mrs A K Clarke, Shirley Mackenzie, Ian Phillips, John Branston, Gillian and Tory Moorby)*

WESTHUMBLE [TQ1751]

Stepping Stones RH5 6BS [just off A24 below Box Hill]: Deceptively large dining pub, comfortable with clean uncluttered décor and open fire, enjoyable well priced lunchtime food inc good Sun roasts, more elaborate evening menu, good friendly service even when busy, circular bar with Fullers London Pride, Greene King Old Speckled Hen, Ringwood Best and a guest (drinks brought to table), no music; children and walkers welcome, garden with terrace, summer barbecue and play area *(Norma and Noel Thomas, DWAJ, Conor McGaughey, Brian and Anna Marsden, Derek and Maggie Washington)*

WEYBRIDGE [TQ0763]

Hand & Spear KT13 8TX [Old Heath Rd/Station Rd]: Big well refurbished Youngs pub (former Edwardian station hotel) with several different areas, enjoyable generous food inc some unusual choices such as rabbit and butterbean casserole, Wells & Youngs ales and a guest, friendly staff, lively atmosphere; good seating outside *(Ian Phillips, Phil Bryant)*

Jolly Farmer KT13 9BN [Princes Rd]: Attractive and civilised small low-beamed local opp picturesque cricket ground, friendly efficient service, good value pubby food from sandwiches up, ales such as Gales, Ringwood, St Austell and Sharps, good choice of wines by the glass, daily papers, toby jugs and interesting old photographs; smart front terrace, nice back garden *(Ian Phillips, Phil Bryant)*

Minnow KT13 8NG [Thames St/Walton Lane]: Welcoming M&B dining pub popular with all ages, contemporary pastel décor and unusual decorative panels, chunky tables and chairs, some sofas and armchairs, helpful staff, enjoyable fresh food inc pizzas, pasta and traditional dishes, good range of real ales such as Timothy Taylors Landlord, good wines by the glass, open fire in raised hearth; big front garden with heaters and awning *(Phil Bryant, Ian Phillips)*

Oatlands Chaser KT13 9RW [Oatlands Chase]: Big attractively modernised building in quiet residential road, rambling bar with stylish modern décor, pastels and unusual wallpaper, glazed panels, flagstones and painted boards, feature central fireplace, carefully mismatched furnishings mainly laid out for the wide range of good all-day food inc bargain set menu, Sun roasts and proper children's meals, good service, Greene King, Hogs Back and Wells & Youngs, good wine choice, newspapers; disabled access, lots of tables out at front (some under trees), 19 immaculate bedrooms, open all day *(Minda and Stanley Alexander, Ian Phillips, BB)*

☆ *Old Crown* KT13 8LP [Thames St]: Comfortably old-fashioned three-bar pub dating from 16th c, good value traditional food (not Sun-Tues evenings) from sandwiches to fresh fish, well kept Courage, Everards, Jennings and Wells & Youngs, good choice of wines by the glass, friendly efficient service, family lounge and conservatory, coal-effect gas fire; may be sports TV in back bar with Lions RFC photographs, silent fruit machine; children welcome, secluded terrace, steps down to suntrap garden overlooking Wey/Thames confluence, mooring for small boats *(Minda and Stanley Alexander, DWAJ, JMM, Jeremy King, Ian Phillips, LM)*

WINDLESHAM [SU9464]

☆ *Brickmakers* GU20 6HT [Chertsey Rd (B386, W of B383 roundabout)]: Smart bistro-feel dining pub with enjoyable fresh seasonal food from good interesting ciabattas up, flagstones, pastel colours and different areas, one room with sofas and low tables, beers such as Courage Best and Fullers London Pride, good choice of wines by the glass, nice coffee, friendly service, log fire, conservatory; may be quiet piped classical music; well behaved children allowed, attractive courtyard with flower-filled pergola, heater, boules and barbecues *(Ian Phillips)*

☆ *Half Moon* GU20 6BN [Church Rd]: Enjoyable if not cheap much-extended pub mainly laid for pubby food from sandwiches up, well kept ales such as Fullers London Pride, Hogs Back TEA, Ringwood Fortyniner, Timothy Taylors Landlord and Theakstons Old Peculier, Weston's farm cider, decent wines, plenty of children's drinks, cheerful enthusiastic young staff, log fires, World War II pictures, modern furnishings, attractive barn restaurant out along covered flagstoned walkway; piped music, silenced games machine; huge tidy garden with two terraces and play area *(Gordon Stevenson, Guy Consterdine, Ian Phillips)*

WOKING [TQ9958]

Bridge Barn GU21 6NL [Bridge Barn Lane; right off Goldsworth Rd towards St Johns]: Pleasant much-extended Beefeater by Basingstoke Canal (lots of waterside tables), interesting layout – restaurant up in barn rafters, nooks and crannies in flagstoned bars below, their usual food inc bargains, Fullers London Pride and Shepherd Neame Spitfire, log fire; disabled facilities, well

fenced play area, comfortable Premier Inn bedroom block *(Ian Phillips)*

Inn at Maybury GU22 8AB [Maybury Hill/Old Woking Rd (B382)]: Popular refurbished Victorian dining pub, wide food range, pizza oven and rotisserie, good wine choice, Hogs Back TEA and Timothy Taylors Landlord, log fire, conservatory; piped music, no dogs; children welcome, disabled facilities, plenty of outside tables, open all day *(Ian Phillips)*

Sovereigns GU22 7QQ [Guildford Rd/Victoria Rd]: Large Ember Inn (former station hotel) with their usual food all day, eight well kept changing ales inc mainstream and some unusual choices (each described and tasters offered), daily papers, nice layout of comfortable linked rooms; open all day *(Phil Bryant)*

Wetherspoons GU21 5AJ [Chertsey Rd]: Large and busy with shoppers yet with lots of cosy areas and side snugs, good range of food all day, half a dozen or more interesting well kept real ales, good choice of coffees, bargain prices, friendly helpful staff, daily papers, old local pictures, no music; open all day from 9am *(Ian Phillips, Tony and Wendy Hobden)*

WOOD STREET [SU9550]

White Hart GU3 3DZ [White Hart Lane; off A323 just W of Guildford]: Smartly redone 17th-c country dining pub, good if not cheap food from open kitchen, decent choice of wines by the glass; a couple of picnic-sets out at front, peaceful spot tucked away off green *(Martin and Karen Wake)*

WORPLESDON [SU9854]

☆ *Jolly Farmer* GU3 3RN [Burdenshott Road, off A320 Guildford—Woking, not in village]: Old village pub with dark-beamed log-fire bar, Fullers ales, stripped-brick dining extension with rugs on bare boards, generous traditional food (not cheap and they ask to swipe your credit card if running a tab); piped music; children and dogs welcome, garden tables under cocktail parasols, grape vines and fruit trees, pleasant woodland setting, open all day *(LYM, Mrs Ann Gray, Gerry and Rosemary Dobson)*

WRECCLESHAM [SU8344]

Sandrock GU10 4NS [Sandrock Hill Road]: Popular real ale pub, two minimalist front bars with chunky furniture on bare boards, helpfully described ales from Arundel, Bowman, Exmoor, Hop Back, Otter, Timothy Taylors and Triple fff (annual beer festival), friendly staff, good ample locally sourced pubby food (not Sun evening), open fires; children and dogs welcome, pleasant heated terrace, open all day *(Janet Whittaker, Phil Bryant)*

We mention bottled beers and spirits only if there is something unusual about them – imported belgian real ales, say, or dozens of malt whiskies; so do please let us know about them in your reports.

Sussex

Sussex has a fine choice of pubs that combine real country charm with enjoyable food and drink. And there are several unspoilt, cottagey taverns, too. We've also discovered quite a few new entries that we're pleased with: the George & Dragon at Burpham (a popular dining pub), the Crown at Dial Post (an extended village pub with interesting food cooked by the landlord), the Tiger in East Dean (a lovely refurbished pub with new bedrooms), the Star near Heathfield (plenty of real character and a lovely garden), the Duke of Cumberland Arms at Henley (two little rooms and a big pretty garden), Noahs Ark at Lurgashall (enthusiastic young licensees have rejuvenated the place) and the Sussex Ox at Milton Street (carefully extended and refurbished and with stunning views). Pubs to look out for that are doing especially well this year are the George in Alfriston (a very well run village pub), the Basketmakers Arms in Brighton (exceptionally good value bar food and fine range of beers), the Star & Garter at East Dean (a smashing all-rounder and with super food), the Huntsman at Eridge Station (particularly well run and with interesting bar food), the Griffin in Fletching (exceedingly popular for its food and bedrooms), the Black Jug in Horsham (a bustling town pub), the Lewes Arms in Lewes (the food prices here would be hard to beat for value), the Halfway Bridge Inn at Lodsworth (a dining pub but with a proper chatty bar), the Red Lion at Turners Hill (a cheerful and happy local), the Half Moon in Warninglid (it's the marvellous food that draws in the customers) and the Cat at West Hoathly (the new licensees are really making their mark). There are ten pubs in this county that hold one of our Food Awards and all of them are worth a special trip. However, for that sense of occasion – plus, of course, exceptional food – our Sussex Dining Pub 2011 is the Jolly Sportsman at East Chiltington.

ALCISTON   TQ5005   MAP 3

Rose Cottage

Village signposted off A27 Polegate—Lewes; BN26 6UW

Old-fashioned cottage with cosy fires and country bric-a-brac, a good little wine list and local beers; bedrooms

Many customers head for this traditional little pub after a bracing walk on the South Downs. The winter log fires are welcoming, there are half a dozen tables with cushioned pews and quite a forest of harness, traps, a thatcher's blade and lots of other black ironware; more bric-a-brac on the shelves above the stripped pine dado or in the etched-glass windows and maybe Jasper the parrot (only at lunchtimes – he gets too noisy in the evenings). There's a lunchtime overflow into the restaurant area as they don't take bookings in the bar then. Dark Star Hophead and Harveys Best on handpump and several wines by the glass from a good little list. Piped music, darts and board games. There are heaters outside for cooler evenings and the small paddock in the garden has ducks and chickens; boules. Nearby fishing and shooting. The charming small village (and local church) are certainly worth a look. They take self-catering bedroom bookings for a minimum of two nights.

🍴 **Popular bar food includes lunchtime ploughman's, soup, coarse pâté, cheese-topped grilled garlic mussels, various salads, honey-roast ham with poached eggs, local pork sausages with onion gravy, vegetarian risotto, free-range cajun chicken, fish pie, gressingham duck with cherry brandy sauce and guinea fowl with a pork and thyme stuffing and sloe gin sauce. They will add a 10% service charge for meals served in the restaurant.** *Starters/Snacks: £3.25 to £6.30. Main Courses: £6.50 to £17.95. Puddings: £3.50 to £4.95*

Free house ~ Licensee Ian Lewis ~ Real ale ~ Bar food ~ Restaurant ~ (01323) 870377 ~ Children allowed if over 10 ~ Dogs allowed in bar ~ Open 11.30-3, 6.30-11; 12-3, 6.30-10.30 Sun ~ Bedrooms: /£60S

Recommended by Ian and Barbara Rankin, Mark Farrington, Jenny and Peter Lowater, Paul Lloyd, David Cosham, Bruce Bird, the Didler, Andrea Rampley, PL, Ian and Nita Cooper, Ron and Sheila Corbett, MP, Peter and Giff Bennett

ALFRISTON   TQ5203   MAP 3

George
High Street; BN26 5SY

Venerable inn in lovely village with comfortable, heavily beamed bars, good wines and several real ales; fine nearby walks; bedrooms

---

This is a well run and ancient village inn – and deservedly popular. The busy long bar has massive hop-hung low beams, appropriately soft lighting and a log fire (or summer flower arrangement) in a huge stone inglenook fireplace that dominates the room, with lots of copper and brass around it. There are settles and chairs around sturdy stripped tables, Greene King IPA and Abbot and a guest like Hardys & Hansons Old Trip on handpump, decent wines including champagne by the glass, board games and piped music; good service. The lounge has comfortable sofas, standing timbers and rugs on the wooden floor and the restaurant is cosy and candlelit. There are seats in the spacious flint-walled garden and two long-distance paths, the South Downs Way and Vanguard Way, cross here; Cuckmere Haven is close by.

🍴 **Using local produce, the enjoyable bar food includes lunchtime sandwiches (served with a small soup or fries) and toasties, rarebits, sausages with onion gravy and ham and eggs but there are more substantial choices too, such as chicken and pork terrine with red onion compote, tiger prawn and avocado with wasabi dressing, rustic sharing boards, a risotto of the day, chicken stuffed with gorgonzola and spinach wrapped in prosciutto, marinated rump of lamb with a herb and garlic sauce, and puddings like a crumble of the day and molten chocolate cake with black cherry.** *Starters/Snacks: £4.00 to £7.50. Main Courses: £7.95 to £16.95. Puddings: £5.50*

Greene King ~ Lease Roland and Cate Couch ~ Real ale ~ Bar food (all day) ~ Restaurant ~ (01323) 870319 ~ Children welcome ~ Dogs allowed in bar and bedrooms ~ Open 11-11 (midnight Sat) ~ Bedrooms: £60S/£90B

Recommended by Paul Humphreys, Peter and Giff Bennett, Tina and David Woods-Taylor, Phil Bryant, Andy West, Tracey and Stephen Groves, Ian and Nita Cooper, Eddie Edwards, Jean and Douglas Troup, Mark Farrington, Ann and Colin Hunt

ARLINGTON   TQ5507   MAP 3

Old Oak
Caneheath, off A22 or A27 NW of Polegate; BN26 6SJ

Comfortable beamed rooms in pleasant country pub, traditional bar food, real ales and quiet garden

---

The seats in the quiet garden of this former set of almshouses are a pleasant place to relax with a drink after a walk in the nearby Abbot's Wood nature reserve. The L-shaped bar is open-plan with heavy beams, well spaced tables and comfortable seating, log fires and Harveys Best and a changing guest such as Sharps Doom Bar tapped from the cask; several malt whiskies, piped music and toad in the hole (a Sussex pub game involving tossing a coin into a hole). More reports please.

⑪ Traditional bar food includes filled baguettes and baked potatoes, soup, ploughman's, pâté, home-baked honey and mustard ham with eggs, venison and mushroom casserole, grilled plaice, steak in ale pie, a vegetarian dish, and puddings. *Starters/Snacks: £3.95 to £5.95. Main Courses: £6.95 to £11.95. Puddings: £3.95*

Free house ~ Licensees Mr J Boots and Mr B Slattery ~ Real ale ~ Bar food (12-2.30, 6-9; all day weekends) ~ Restaurant ~ (01323) 482072 ~ Children welcome ~ Dogs allowed in bar ~ Open 11-11

Recommended by Jenny and Peter Lowater, David and Candy Owens, Tina and David Woods-Taylor

BALLS CROSS   SU9826   MAP 2

Stag ◀

Village signposted off A283 at N edge of Petworth, brown sign to pub there too; GU28 9JP

Popular little local with a friendly landlord, well kept beer, nice traditional food and seats in sizeable garden

Thankfully little changes at this cheery 17th-c country pub and the chatty landlord and his friendly staff will give you a genuine welcome. The tiny flagstoned bar has a winter log fire in a huge inglenook fireplace, just a couple of tables, a window seat and a few chairs and leather-seated bar stools. On the right, a second room with a rug on its bare boards has space for just a single table. Beyond is an appealing old-fashioned dining room with quite a few horsey pictures. There are yellowing cream walls and low shiny ochre ceilings throughout, with soft lighting from little fringed wall lamps and fishing rods and country knick-knacks hanging from the ceilings. On the left, a separate carpeted room with a couple of big Victorian prints has bar skittles, darts and board games. Badger K&B, First Gold and Hopping Hare on handpump, decent wines by the glass, summer cider and some nice malt whiskies. The good-sized back garden, divided by a shrubbery, has plenty of seats and a couple of canvas awnings and there are picnic-sets under parasols at the front; the hitching rail does get used. The veteran gents' (and ladies') are outside.

⑪ Bar food includes sandwiches and filled baguettes, ploughman's, game pâté, home-made fish fingers with home-made tartare sauce, sausage and chips, home-baked ham and eggs, home-made burger with bacon and cheese, seared salmon with balsamic salad, chicken, pasta and parmesan bake with pesto and daily specials like venison casserole and steak and kidney pudding. *Starters/Snacks: £5.75 to £7.00. Main Courses: £6.75 to £15.75. Puddings: £4.50*

Badger ~ Tenant Hamish Barrie Hiddleston ~ Real ale ~ Bar food (not Sun evening) ~ Restaurant ~ (01403) 820241 ~ Well behaved children welcome away from main bar ~ Dogs welcome ~ Open 11-3, 6-11; 12-3.30, 7-10.30 Sun ~ Bedrooms: £35/£60

Recommended by Tony and Wendy Hobden, Gerry and Rosemary Dobson, Michael B Griffith, the Didler, John Robertson, R B Gardiner

BERWICK   TQ5105   MAP 3

Cricketers Arms

Lower Road, S of A27; BN26 6SP

Charming small pub with pretty garden, welcoming little bars, nice staff, traditional food (all day weekends and summer weekdays) and local beer

The cottagey front garden here is delightful and in fine weather you can sit at picnic-sets among the small brick paths and mature flowering shrubs and plants; there are more seats behind the pub. Inside, the unpretentious three small rooms are all similarly furnished with simple benches against the half-panelled walls, a pleasant mix of old country tables and chairs, a few bar stools and some country prints; quarry tiles on the floors (nice worn ones in the middle room), two log fires in little brick fireplaces, a huge black supporting beam in each of the low ochre ceilings, and (in the end room) some attractive cricketing pastels; some of the beams are hung with cricket bats. Harveys Best and two seasonal ales tapped from the cask and up to a dozen wines by the glass; cribbage, dominoes and an old Sussex coin game called toad in the hole. The wall paintings in the nearby church done by the Bloomsbury Group during World War II are worth a look, and the pub is very well placed for walks on and beneath the South Downs.

🍴 Popular bar food includes **chicken liver and mushroom terrine, various platters, fresh dressed summer crab salad, chargrilled chicken with pesto, ham and egg, local sausages, a changing vegetarian tart, daily specials. and puddings.** *Starters/Snacks: £5.50 to £6.95. Main Courses: £8.95 to £15.95. Puddings: £5.25*

Harveys ~ Lease Peter Brown ~ Real ale ~ Bar food (12-2.15, 6-9; all day weekends and summer weekdays) ~ (01323) 870469 ~ Children in family room only ~ Dogs welcome ~ Open 11-11; 12-10.30 Sun; 11-3, 6-10.30 weekdays in winter

Recommended by Pierre Richterich, Alan Cowell, M G Hart, the Didler, Andrea Rampley, Nick Lawless, Tony and Shirley Albert, Conor McGaughey, Peter and Giff Bennett, Jenny and Peter Lowater

BLACKBOYS   TQ5220   MAP 3

Blackboys Inn

B2192, S edge of village; TN22 5LG

Weatherboarded old pub with a bustling locals' bar, nice dining rooms, good choice of drinks and food and plenty of seats in the attractive garden; bedrooms

The seating areas in front of this attractive 14th-c pub have been much improved recently and there are plenty of contemporary tables and chairs on a terrace, with more under cover beside the sizeable pond; up a step, a side lawn has yet more seats and a pretty gazebo. Inside, the beamed locals' bar to the left has a good, chatty atmosphere and lots of bric-a-brac and to the right, the main bar has beams and timbers, more bric-a-brac and old photographs on the red walls, dark wooden furniture on the parquet flooring and a winter log fire in the brick fireplace with china plates and an ornate clock on the mantelpiece. The restaurant is similarly furnished. Harveys Best, Hadlow and a couple of seasonal guests on handpump and 15 wines by the glass; piped music, darts and board games. The Vanguard Way passes the pub, the Wealdway goes close by and there's the Woodland Trust opposite.

🍴 Growing some of their own produce and using local fish and game, the bar food includes **soup, ploughman's, burgers, ham or sausage and egg, chilli con carne, tiger prawns, chorizo, tomato and basil with pasta, vegetable and pea shoot risotto, lamb shank with red wine jus, lemon sole with parsley and lemon, chicken with provençale vegetables, chargrilled steaks, and puddings like bakewell tart and chocolate pot.** *Starters/Snacks: £4.50 to £7.50. Main Courses: £7.50 to £10.50. Puddings: £5.95*

Harveys ~ Tenant Paul James ~ Real ale ~ Bar food (12-2.30(3 Fri), 6-9.30(10 Fri); all day weekends) ~ Restaurant ~ (01825) 890283 ~ Children welcome ~ Dogs allowed in bar ~ Open 11.30am-midnight(1am Fri and Sat); 12-11 Sun; midday opening in winter ~ Bedrooms: /£75S(£85B)

Recommended by the Didler, Dr Martin Owton, John Atkins, Alec and Joan Laurence, Michael and Ann Cole, B J Harding

BOSHAM   SU8003   MAP 2

Anchor Bleu

High Street; PO18 8LS

Waterside inn overlooking Chichester Harbour and usefully open all day in summer, several real ales in snug old bars and well liked food (lots of summer fish dishes)

At high tide on a fine day this is an idyllic spot. You can sit on the back terrace (the water comes right up to the windows of the pub) and look out over the ducks and boats on this sheltered inlet of Chichester Harbour. A massive wheel-operated bulkhead door wards off high tides (cars parked on the seaward side are often submerged). Inside, two nicely simple bars have some beams in the low shiny ochre ceilings, worn flagstones and exposed timbered brickwork, lots of nautical bric-a-brac and robust, simple furniture. Hogs Back TEA, Hop Back Summer Lightning (in summer) or Ringwood Fortyniner (in winter), Sharps Cornish Coaster and a guest or two like Otter Ale or Sharps Doom Bar on handpump and several wines by the glass. As King Canute had a palace here, this may be the spot where he showed his courtiers that however much they flattered him as all-powerful, he couldn't turn the tide back. The church a few yards up the lane figures in the Bayeux Tapestry and the village and shore are worth exploring. They may keep your bank card in a locked cupboard behind the bar.

🍴 **Popular bar food includes lunchtime filled baguettes, ploughman's, soup, duck and orange pâté, natural whitebait, chicken, bacon and asparagus or fresh seafood pies, good curries, gammon and pineapple, summer crab and prawn salad, winter game pudding, whole plaice with herb butter, and puddings such as french crêpes with maple syrup and pear and amaretti crumble; maybe afternoon tea and cakes.** *Starters/Snacks: £4.95 to £6.95. Main Courses: £7.95 to £14.00. Puddings: £3.95 to £4.95*

Enterprise ~ Lease Kate Walford ~ Real ale ~ Bar food (12-2.30(3.30 Sat, 4 Sun)) 7-9.30(10 Sat)) ~ Restaurant ~ (01243) 573956 ~ Children welcome ~ Dogs allowed in bar ~ Open 11-11; 12-10.30 Sun; 11.30-3, 6-10.30 weekdays in winter

Recommended by B and M Kendall, Neil Hardwick, Nick Lawless, Mr and Mrs P D Titcomb, Ann and Colin Hunt, Terry and Nickie Williams, Val and Alan Green, Maureen and Keith Gimson, John Beeken, Chris Glasson

BRIGHTON   TQ3104   MAP 3

Basketmakers Arms 🍺 £

Gloucester Road – the E end, near Cheltenham Place; off Marlborough Place (A23) via Gloucester Street; BN1 4AD

Bustling backstreet pub with friendly landlord, plenty of chatty customers, great drinks range and reasonably priced, enjoyable food

Popular for its fine choice of ales and good value bar food, this street-corner local is always full of cheerful customers. The eight real ales on handpump include Butcombe Bitter, Fullers London Pride, Discovery, ESB, HSB, London Porter and Seafarers and a changing weekly guest. They also have good wines by the glass, at least 100 malt whiskies and quite a range of vodkas, gins and rums. The two small low-ceilinged rooms have brocaded wall benches and stools on the stripped wood floor, lots of interesting old tins all over the walls, cigarette cards on one beam with whisky labels on another and beermats, some old advertisements, photographs and posters. The staff are friendly and helpful; piped music. There are three metal tables out on the pavement. Dogs must be on a lead.

🍴 **Using local fish and carefully sourced meat, the good value, enjoyable bar food includes lots of sandwiches, ploughman's, filled baked potatoes, lamb, beef and vegetarian burgers, mexican beef or vegetarian chilli, daily and seasonal specials such as stir-fried scallops with sesame vegetables and noodles, mackerel fillets with roast fennel and a citrus salad, steak in ale pie and beef in Guinness stew with herby dumplings, and puddings like sticky toffee pudding and chocolate brownie; popular Sunday roasts.** *Starters/Snacks: £2.95 to £4.95. Main Courses: £5.95 to £8.95. Puddings: £3.75*

Gales (Fullers) ~ Lease P Dowd ~ Real ale ~ Bar food (12-8.30(7 Fri, 6 Sat and Sun)) ~ (01273) 689006 ~ Children welcome until 8pm ~ Dogs allowed in bar ~ Open 11-11(midnight Fri and Sat); 12-11 Sun

Recommended by Alec Lewery, Mark Sykes, the Didler, Conor McGaughey, Jeremy King, S T W Norton, Ian Phillips

---

The letters and figures after the name of each town are its Ordnance Survey map reference. 'Using the *Guide*' at the beginning of the book explains how it helps you find a pub, in road atlases or on large-scale maps as well as on our own maps.

Greys 🍴 ♈

Southover Street, off A270 Lewes Road opposite The Level (public park); BN2 9UA

A good mix of drinkers and diners in friendly, bustling and interesting local, thoughtful choice of drinks and popular food; live music Monday evenings

This year there's a new heated terrace here with seats and tables under parasols. It's an interesting place and certainly not a standard local, with basic furnishings like simple wall seats and stools around mixed pub tables on bare boards and flagstones, magnolia walls and some wood panelling around a flame-effect stove below a big metal canopy; piped music. The serving bar is on the right with regular customers on the bar stools and at nearby tables: Harveys Best and Timothy Taylors Landlord on handpump, a carefully chosen wine list and several bottled belgian beers. The five or six tables on the left, each with a little vase of flowers and lighted tea lamp, are the food bit – one corner table is snuggled in by a high-backed settle and another at the back is tucked into a quiet corner. The stair wall is papered with posters and flyers from bands, singers and poets who have performed here. The house wines, from Burgundy, are excellent value. There's not much daytime parking on this steep lane or the nearby streets. No children inside. Do note the opening hours. More reports please.

🍴 **Using carefully chosen and sourced local ingredients, the good, popular food includes nibbles like pigs ear goujons with sweet chilli, soup, rabbit pâté with home-made apple bread, deep-fried roasted pumpkin risotto balls with red pepper chutney, beer-battered fish with mushy peas, root vegetable and bean stew with herb dumplings, seasonal game, rib-eye steak with peppercorn sauce, and puddings like ginger beer jelly with poached pear and crumble clusters and sticky toffee pudding with home-made vanilla ice-cream.** *Starters/Snacks: £2.75 to £5.00. Main Courses: £10.00 to £14.50. Puddings: £3.00 to £5.00*

Enterprise ~ Lease Chris Taylor and Gill Perkins ~ Real ale ~ Bar food (6-9(12-4.30 Sun); not Mon or Fri) ~ (01273) 680734 ~ Dogs allowed in bar ~ Live music Mon evening (tickets only) ~ Open 4-11(11.30 Thurs, 12.30am Fri); midday-12.30am Sat; midday-11pm Sun

Recommended by Ian Phillips

BURPHAM   TQ0308   MAP 3

George & Dragon 🍴

Off A27 near Warningcamp; BN18 9RR

Interesting food and real ales in bustling dining pub

Particularly at weekends, there's a good mix of customers in this popular 17th-c dining pub. The front part is a restaurant with tables set for dining on the wooden floor, and there's a small area where drinkers can enjoy Arundel ASB and Pickled Mouse and Sharps Doom Bar on handpump; efficient, friendly service. There are some picnic-sets in front. The lane to reach the pub is long and winding and it's set at the end of the hilltop village between the partly Norman church (which has some unusual decoration) and cricket ground; just a short walk away are splendid views down to Arundel Castle and the river.

🍴 **Very good, interesting bar food includes lunchtime sandwiches and filled baguettes, ploughman's, soup, welsh rarebit, a charcuterie or meze plate, crayfish and trout fishcakes with crayfish bisque, caesar or greek salads, pork and leek sausages with cider and port jus, corn-fed chicken stuffed with wild mushrooms and a thyme jus, lamb rump with juniper and rosemary, halibut with a bourguignon sauce, and puddings like brownies with chocolate sauce and cherry kirsch parfait; Sunday roasts.** *Starters/Snacks: £5.00 to £7.00. Main Courses: £10.00 to £20.00. Puddings: £5.50*

Free house ~ Licensees Sarah and Michael Cheney ~ Real ale ~ Bar food (12-2(3 weekends), 6.30-9) ~ Restaurant ~ (01903) 883131 ~ Children welcome ~ Dogs allowed in bar ~ Open 12-3.30(4.30 weekends), 6-11

Recommended by Fiona Wynn, Pete Stroud, Cathryn and Richard Hicks, Karen Eliot, CP, Guy Vowles, Di and Mike Gillam, M G Hart, Martin and Karen Wake

Black Horse ◧
Off A283; GU28 OHL

Enjoyable country pub with open fires, newspapers to read, several real ales, tasty food and nice garden

---

There's a quietly chatty atmosphere and a good mix of customers in this popular country pub. The simply furnished though smart bar has pews and scrubbed wooden tables on its bare floorboards, pictures and old photographs on the walls and newspapers to read; large open fires, too. The back dining room has lots of nooks and crannies, there's a spiral staircase to a heavily beamed function room and stairs up to a games room with pool, darts and board games; lovely views of the downs. Flowerpots Bitter, Fullers London Pride and two guests like Dark Star Hophead and Langham Best on handpump. The garden is particularly attractive and has tables on a steep series of grassy terraces sheltered by banks of flowering shrubs that look across a drowsy valley to woodland.

🍽 **As well lunchtime bar food like filled baguettes, filled baked potatoes, ploughman's, burgers and various pasta dishes, there might be smoked duck breast with an apricot and rocket salad, king scallops with crispy bacon and an aged balsamic reduction, a pie of the day, beer-battered fish, lamb rump with a rosemary, redcurrant and mint sauce, guinea fowl with a tarragon and wild mushroom sauce, daily specials, and puddings like raspberry and vanilla crème brûlée and sticky toffee and banana pudding with butterscotch sauce.** *Starters/Snacks: £4.95 to £8.95. Main Courses: £8.95 to £12.50. Puddings: £3.50 to £5.00*

Free house ~ Licensee Jeff Paddock ~ Real ale ~ Bar food (12-3, 6-9; not winter Sun evening) ~ Restaurant ~ (01798) 342424 ~ Children welcome away from bar ~ Dogs allowed in bar ~ Open 11.30-11.30; 12-11 Sun

Recommended by Mr Ray J Carter, Martin and Karen Wake, the Didler, Bruce Bird, Kevin Flack, M G Hart

Fox Goes Free
Village signposted off A286 Chichester—Midhurst in Singleton, also from Chichester—Petworth via East Dean; PO18 OHU

Comfortable old pub with well organised staff, popular food and drink and big garden; nice surrounding walks; bedrooms

---

Usefully open all day, this is an enjoyable and friendly old pub and handy for nearby Goodwood. The bar has a bustling atmosphere and is the first of the dark and cosy series of separate rooms: old irish settles, tables and chapel chairs and an open fire. Standing timbers divide a larger beamed bar which has a huge brick fireplace with a woodburning stove and old local photographs on the walls. A dining area with hunting prints looks over the garden. The family extension is a clever conversion from horse boxes and the stables where the 1926 Goodwood winner was housed; darts, games machine and piped music. Ballards Best, a beer named for the pub and a guest such as Harveys Best on handpump and several wines by the glass; friendly, helpful staff. You can sit at one of the picnic-sets under the apple trees in the attractive back garden with the downs as a backdrop and there are rustic benches and tables on the gravelled front terrace, too. The pub is handy for the Weald and Downland Open Air Museum and West Dean Gardens; good surrounding walks include up to the prehistoric earthworks on the Trundle.

🍽 **Bar food includes lunchtime filled baguettes (not Sunday), soup, chicken liver parfait with apple chutney, honey-roast ham and egg, chilli con carne, wild mushroom risotto, steak and kidney pie, chicken breast wrapped in bacon with creamed leeks, braised lamb shank with minted mash, whole lemon sole with garlic butter and herbs, rump steak with peppercorn sauce, and puddings such as chocolate brownies with chocolate sauce and raspberry crème brulée.** *Starters/Snacks: £4.95 to £7.50. Main Courses: £9.50 to £17.00. Puddings: £5.50 to £7.50*

Free house ~ Licensee David Coxon ~ Real ale ~ Bar food (12-2.30, 6.30-10; all day weekends) ~ Restaurant ~ (01243) 811461 ~ Children welcome ~ Dogs allowed in bar ~ Live music Weds evenings ~ Open 11-11(11.30 Sat); 12-10.30 Sun ~ Bedrooms: £60S/£85S

Recommended by Ann and Colin Hunt, J Stickland, Nick Lawless, Bernard Stradling, Helen and Brian Edgeley

CHIDDINGLY
TQ5414   MAP 3

Six Bells ★ £

Village signed off A22 Uckfield—Hailsham; BN8 6HE

Lively, unpretentious village local with good weekend live music, extremely good value bar food and friendly long-serving licensees

Nothing much changes here – which is just how this cheerful village pub's many loyal customers like it. The bars have a shabby charm, lots of fusty artefacts and interesting bric-a-brac collected over the years by the landlord, solid old wood pews and antique seats, plenty of local pictures and posters and log fires. A sensitive extension provides some much-needed family space; board games. Courage Directors, Harveys Best and a guest beer on handpump. Outside at the back, there are some tables beyond a big raised goldfish pond and a boules pitch; the church opposite has an interesting Jefferay monument. Popular weekend live music and Vintage and Kit car meetings outside the pub every month. This is a pleasant area for walks. Note that dogs are allowed in one bar only.

🍴 **Exceptionally good value and well liked, the bar food includes sandwiches, french onion soup, filled baked potatoes, ploughman's, meaty or vegetarian lasagne, chilli con carne, chicken curry, barbecue spare ribs, ham hock, and puddings like banoffi pie and Malteser crunch.** *Starters/Snacks: £2.50. Main Courses: £4.40 to £7.95. Puddings: £3.00 to £3.60*

Free house ~ Licensees Paul Newman and Emma Bannister ~ Real ale ~ Bar food (12-2.15, 6-9; all day Fri-Sun) ~ (01825) 872227 ~ Children allowed away from main bar ~ Dogs allowed in bar ~ Live music Fri-Sun evenings and Sun lunchtime ~ Open 11-3, 6-11; 11am-midnight Sat; 12-10.30 Sun

Recommended by Miriam Warner, Mrs Mary Woods, John Beeken, Mike Horgan, Jenny and Peter Lowater

CHILGROVE
SU8116   MAP 2

Royal Oak

Off B2141 Petersfield—Chichester, signed Hooksway down steep single track; PO18 9JZ

Unchanging and peaceful country pub with welcoming landlord and big pretty garden

Walkers and locals are fond of this traditional country pub and it's been run for many years by the same licensees. The two simple, cosy bars have plain country-kitchen tables and chairs, huge log fires and Exmoor Beast, Gales HSB, Sharps Doom Bar and a guest beer on handpump. There's also a cottagey dining room with a woodburning stove and a plainer family room; piped music, cribbage, dominoes and shut the box. Outside, the big pretty garden has plenty of picnic-sets under parasols. The South Downs Way is close by.

🍴 **Bar food includes filled rolls and baked potatoes, ploughman's, soup, steak and kidney pie, chicken curry, lamb shank with red wine and rosemary gravy, gammon and egg and mixed grill.** *Starters/Snacks: £4.95. Main Courses: £8.95 to £13.95. Puddings: £4.50*

Free house ~ Licensee Dave Jeffery ~ Real ale ~ Bar food ~ Restaurant ~ (01243) 535257 ~ Children in family room ~ Dogs allowed in bar ~ Live music second and last Fri evening of the month ~ Open 11.30-2.30, 6-11; 12-3 Sun; closed Sun evening and Mon; may close mid-Oct-mid-Nov

Recommended by N R White, Ann and Colin Hunt, J A Snell, LM

Though we don't usually mention it in the text, most pubs will now make
coffee or tea – always worth asking.

COOLHAM
TQ1423   MAP 3

George & Dragon

Dragons Green, Dragons Lane; pub signed just off A272, about 1.5 miles E of village; RH13 8GE

Pleasant little country cottage with beamed bars and decent food and drink

A new licensee has taken over this tile-hung cottage but luckily has not made any major changes. The chatty, cosy bar has heavily timbered walls, a partly woodblock and partly polished-tile floor, unusually low and massive black beams (see if you can decide whether the date cut into one is 1677 or 1577), simple chairs and rustic stools and a big inglenook fireplace with an early 17th-c grate. There's also a smaller back bar and restaurant. Badger Best, Tanglefoot and a seasonal ale on handpump and piped music. There are plenty of picnic-sets in the lovely orchard garden with its pretty flowers and shrubs. More reports please.

🍴 **Bar food now includes filled baguettes, ploughman's, soup, duck and orange pâté, baked brie with cranberry sauce, steak in ale pie, minted lamb steaks, hickory chicken, sausages with onion gravy, and puddings like a cheesecake of the day and chocolate fudge cake.** *Starters/Snacks: £4.95 to £5.25. Main Courses: £9.95 to £12.95. Puddings: £4.45*

Badger ~ Tenant Marlene Oliver ~ Real ale ~ Bar food ~ Restaurant ~ (01403) 741320 ~ Children welcome ~ Dogs allowed in bar ~ Live music last Sun of the month ~ Open 11.30-3, 6-11; 11.30-11(8 Sun) Sat

Recommended by Philip and Cheryl Hill, David Cosham, Ian Phillips, Colin and Louise English

DIAL POST
TQ1519   MAP 3

Crown

Worthing Road (off A24 S of Horsham); RH13 8NH

Village pub with good food cooked by landlord, real ales, and bar and two dining rooms; bedrooms

This extended village pub is popular for its interesting food cooked by the landlord – though the bar is a friendly and relaxing place if you just want a drink and a chat. It's a beamed room with a couple of standing timbers, brown squashy sofas and pine tables and chairs on the stone floor, a small woodburning stove in the brick fireplace, and Dark Star Best and Harveys Best and Old on handpump from the attractive herringbone brick counter; maybe unobtrusive piped pop music. The pub dog is called Chops. The straightforwardly furnished dining conservatory, facing the village green, is light and airy; board games and shove-ha' penny. To the right of the bar, the restaurant (with more beams) has an ornamental woodburner in a brick fireplace, a few photographs on the walls, chunky pine tables and chairs and a couple of cushioned pews on the patterned carpet, and a shelf of books; steps lead down to a further dining room. The bedrooms are in the converted stables and there are picnic-sets on grass behind the pub.

🍴 **Good popular food using carefully sourced produce and cooked by the landlord includes sandwiches, ploughman's, various tapas, devilled whitebait with spicy aioli and lime, crab on toast, beer-battered fish, pork and herb sausages, home honey-roasted ham with a free-range egg, steakburger with spicy relish and coleslaw, crispy belly of local pork, daily specials, and puddings such as cheesecake and sticky toffee pudding with caramel sauce; they also offer an early bird two-course set menu.** *Starters/Snacks: £5.00 to £8.00. Main Courses: £7.00 to £13.00. Puddings: £4.00 to £6.00*

Free house ~ Licensees James and Penny Middleton-Burn ~ Real ale ~ Bar food (12-2.15(2.30 Sun), 6(5.30 Fri)-9.30; not Sun evening) ~ Restaurant ~ (01403) 710902 ~ Children welcome but must be dining after 7pm ~ Dogs allowed in bar and bedrooms ~ Open 10.30-3.30, 6(5.30 Fri)-11.30; 12-4 Sun; closed Sun evening and bank hol Mon evenings ~ Bedrooms: £50S/£60S

Recommended by Martin Stafford

If we know a pub has an outdoor play area for children, we mention it.

EAST CHILTINGTON

TQ3715   MAP 3

Jolly Sportsman ⊕⊕ ⊊

2 miles N of B2116; Chapel Lane – follow sign to 13th-c church; BN7 3BA

SUSSEX DINING PUB OF THE YEAR

Excellent modern food in civilised, rather smart place, small bar for drinkers,
contemporary furnishings, fine wine list and huge range of malt whiskies; nice garden

There's no doubt that most customers are here to enjoy the first-class imaginative food
but there's a little bar with a roaring winter fire, a mix of furniture on the stripped wood
floors and Dark Star Hophead and a guest like Triple fff Altons Pride or Dark Star Old
tapped from the cask. They also have a remarkably good wine list with around a dozen by
the glass, over 100 malt whiskies, an extensive list of cognacs, armagnacs and grappa
and quite a choice of bottled belgian beers. The larger restaurant is smart but informal
with contemporary light wood furniture and modern landscapes on coffee-coloured walls.
There are rustic tables and benches under gnarled trees in a pretty cottagey front garden
with more on the terrace and the front bricked area, and the large back lawn with a
children's play area looks out towards the downs; good walks and cycle rides nearby. More
reports please.

⊕ Highly thought-of and using seasonal, carefully sourced produce, the accomplished – if
not cheap – food might include soup, chilli cuttlefish with cucumber relish, warm duck
rillettes with lentil salad, wild garlic and sorrel soufflé with a spring vegetable fricassée,
chicken wrapped in serrano ham with a warm, pea, parmesan and spinach salad, rump of
lamb with a ratatouille-stuffed courgette and red wine sauce, cider-braised pork belly
with black pudding mash, lobster thermidor (or cold with mayonnaise), and puddings
such as chocolate and pistachio praline tart with pistachio ice-cream and apricot, walnut,
ginger and toffee pudding; they also offer good value two- and three-course set menus
(not Sunday). *Starters/Snacks: £4.90 to £9.50. Main Courses: £9.85 to £19.50. Puddings: £4.90
to £7.50*

Free house ~ Licensee Bruce Wass ~ Real ale ~ Bar food (12-3, 7-9.30(10 Fri); all day
weekends) ~ Restaurant ~ (01273) 890400 ~ Children welcome ~ Dogs welcome ~
Open 12-11(10.30 Sun); 12-3, 6-11 weekdays in winter

Recommended by Laurence Smith, Susan and John Douglas, Nick Lawless, John Redfern

EAST DEAN

SU9012   MAP 2

Star & Garter ⊕⊕ ⊊

*Village signposted with Charlton off A286 in Singleton; also signposted off A285; note that
there are two East Deans in Sussex (this one is N of Chichester) – OS Sheet 197 map
reference 904129; PO18 0JG*

Attractively furnished bar and restaurant in light and airy well run pub, relaxed
atmosphere and enjoyable food and drink; bedrooms

Reports from our readers on this well run dining pub have been especially warm and
enthusiastic this year. There's always a good mix of customers which keeps things lively
and the squarish interior has stripped wooden panelling, exposed brickwork and solid oak
floors. Furnishings range from sturdy, individual, mainly stripped and scrubbed tables in
various sizes and an interesting mix of seats from country kitchen chairs through chunky
modern dining chairs to cushioned pews and some 17th-c and 18th-c carved oak settles.
The high ceilings, big sash windows and uncluttered walls give a light and airy feel. The
bar counter, with a few bar stools, is on the left, with Arundel Castle, Sussex Gold and a
guest beer tapped from the cask, 11 wines by the glass and a few malt whiskies; tables
in this area are usually left unlaid while those to the right of the front door and further
on are set for diners. Newspapers to read, board games, darts and piped music; dogs must
be on a lead. The sheltered terrace behind has teak tables and chairs with big canvas
parasols and heaters, and a gazebo for smokers; steps go up to a walled lawn with picnic-
sets. A gate provides level access from the road to the terrace and into the pub for those
who might not manage the front steps. The South Downs Way is close by.

⛏ Most people are here for the fresh seafood which might include selsey crab and lobster, line-caught bass, local mackerel, cod, mussels, scallops and fine platters. There are non-fishy choices, too, such as lunchtime filled baguettes and ploughman's, soup, a tapas plate, duck liver and Cointreau pâté, pigeon breast with bacon and pan juice vinaigrette, tian of goats cheese, aubergine and beef tomato, home-cooked honey-roast ham with free-range eggs, roast rump of lamb with a rich port and redcurrant jus, chicken breast with tarragon sauce, and puddings such as white chocolate panna cotta and prune and armagnac tart; they also offer a two- and three-course set weekday lunch. *Starters/Snacks: £4.50 to £8.50. Main Courses: £7.50 to £18.50. Puddings: £6.00*

Free house ~ Licensee Oliver Ligertwood ~ Real ale ~ Bar food (12-2.30, 6.30-10; all day weekends) ~ Restaurant ~ (01243) 811318 ~ Children welcome ~ Dogs allowed in bar ~ Open 11-3, 6-11; 11am-midnight Sat; 12-10.30 Sun ~ Bedrooms: £70S(£90B)/£90S(£110B)

Recommended by Martin and Karen Wake, Mrs Mary Woods, Nick Lawless, Maureen and Keith Gimson, Henry Midwinter, Christopher Turner, Terry and Nickie Williams, Karen Eliot, Miss A E Dare, M G Hart, Paul and Annette Hallett

Tiger ♀

off A259 Eastbourne—Seaford; BN20 0DA

Charming old pub by cottage-lined village green, two little bars and new dining room, and informal and friendly atmosphere; new bedrooms

Five new bedrooms have been opened and this long, low building has been recently extended – but it's all been done without spoiling what remains a lovely pub. The focal point of the little beamed main bar is the open woodburning stove in its brick inglenook surrounded by polished horsebrasses and there are just a few rustic tables with benches, simple wooden chairs, a window seat and a long cushioned wall bench. The walls are hung with fish prints and a stuffed tiger's head, there are a couple of hunting horns above the long bar counter, Harveys Best and Old and their own-brewed Beachy Head Legless Rambler, Original and Birling Burner on handpump and several wines by the glass. Down a step on the right is a second small room with an exceptionally fine high-backed curved settle and a couple of other old settles, nice old chairs and wooden tables on the coir carpeting, and an ancient map of Eastbourne and Beachy Head and photographs of the pub on the walls. The new dining room to the left of the main bar has a cream woodburner and hunting prints. With such a premium on space, it does pay to get here early if you want a seat. There are picnic-sets on the terrace among the window boxes and flowering climbers or you can sit on the delightful cottage-lined village green. The South Downs Way is close by so the pub is naturally popular with walkers, and the lane leads on down to a fine stretch of coast culminating in Beachy Head.

⛏ Good, popular bar food includes open sandwiches and filled baps, ploughman's, chicken liver and pistachio pâté with an apple, rosemary and onion compote, salmon and smoked haddock fishcake with lemon and dill crème fraîche, home-made burgers with bacon and cheese, sausages of the day with red onion gravy, salads like chicken caesar and swordfish niçoise, wild mushroom and truffle-stuffed pork loin with caramelised apple and celeriac mash, sea bream on a sundried tomato, asparagus and lemon risotto, and puddings like banoffi cheesecake with caramel sauce and a chocolate trio. *Starters/Snacks: £2.95 to £5.00. Main Courses: £6.00 to £18.00. Puddings: £4.50 to £6.95*

Free house ~ Licensee Jo Staveley ~ Real ale ~ Bar food (12-3, 6-9.30 (they offer snacks in the afternoon)) ~ (01323) 423209 ~ Children welcome ~ Dogs allowed in bar ~ Open 10am-11pm (10.30pm Sun) ~ Bedrooms: /£90S

Recommended by Andrea Rampley, LM, Kevin Thorpe

Real ale to us means beer which has matured naturally in its cask – not pressurised or filtered. We name all real ales stocked. We usually name ales preserved under a light blanket of carbon dioxide too, though purists – pointing out that this stops the natural yeasts developing – would disagree (most people, including us, can't tell the difference!).

ELSTED   SU8119   MAP 2

Three Horseshoes

Village signposted from B2141 Chichester—Petersfield; also reached easily from A272 about 2 miles W of Midhurst, turning left heading W; GU29 0JY

Bustling country pub with congenial beamed rooms, a good choice of drinks and fine views from flower-filled garden

In summer, the garden of this pretty tiled white house is lovely and there are plenty of tables and chairs among the flowers and wonderful views of the South Downs; lots of surrounding walks. Inside, the cosy bars have log fires and candlelight, ancient beams and flooring, antique furnishings, fresh flowers and attractive prints and photographs; it's best to book to be sure of a table. Racked on a stillage behind the bar counter, the four real ales include Ballards Best, Bowman Wallops Wood, Youngs Bitter and a guest such as Flowerpots Bitter or Hop Back Summer Lightning; summer cider.

Bar food includes ploughman's, potted shrimps on toast, smoked duck, roasted pepper and bacon salad, pork and herb sausages, steak and kidney in Guinness pie, venison fillet with a port and redcurrant sauce, lamb with apples and apricots, seasonal crab and lobster, and puddings such as lemon posset or chocolate rocky roads. *Starters/Snacks: £7.00 to £10.00. Main Courses: £10.00 to £15.00. Puddings: £5.50*

Free house ~ Licensee Sue Beavis ~ Real ale ~ Bar food ~ Restaurant ~ (01730) 825746 ~ Well-behaved children allowed ~ Dogs allowed in bar ~ Open 11-2.30, 6-11; 12-3, 7-10.30 Sun

Recommended by Paul and Annette Hallett, Mrs Mary Woods, Tony and Jill Radnor, M G Hart, Mrs K Hooker, Patrick Spence, Michael B Griffith, John Beeken, Mrs M Grimwood, Karen Eliot, Henry Midwinter, D and J Ashdown, R B Gardiner, DGH

ERIDGE STATION   TQ5434   MAP 3

Huntsman

No-gimmicks homely pub with friendly staff, interesting bar food (lots of seasonal game), excellent wines, well kept ales and seats in the sizeable garden

This is a well run and enjoyable country local with helpful, friendly staff and a good range of popular food and drink. The two opened-up rooms have dark wooden dining chairs and a nice mix of matching tables on the wooden floorboards and plenty of amusing pictures of hunting scenes on the walls. The quietly friendly landlord has considerable wine expertise (they offer a fantastic choice of over two dozen wines by the glass) and they also keep Badger First Gold and guests from Gribble Ale on handpump, farm cider and several malt whiskies. There are picnic-sets and outdoor heaters on the decking, an outside bar and more seating on the lawn among weeping willows and other trees. The pub is virtually alone here apart from the station itself – which on weekdays is responsible for filling the hamlet's roadside verges with commuters' cars (plenty of space at weekends, though). They also run the Gribble Inn at Oving – another Sussex Main Entry.

Growing some of their own salad and herbs and using other local produce, the interesting bar food includes sandwiches, soup, game terrine with chutney, pigeon with celeriac purée and roasted figs, mutton and mint pie, smoked haddock and spring onion fishcakes, goats cheese, cranberry marmalade and spinach tart, pork and leek sausages with cheddar mash and onion gravy, rabbit, cider and mustard casserole, bass with lemon and sorrel, and puddings like whisky and sultana bread and butter pudding and chocolate truffle torte. *Starters/Snacks: £4.95 to £7.25. Main Courses: £8.95 to £16.95. Puddings: £5.00*

Badger ~ Tenants Simon Wood and Nicola Tester ~ Real ale ~ Bar food (12-2(2.30 Sat), 6-9; not Sun evening or Mon (except bank hols)) ~ (01892) 864258 ~ Children welcome ~ Dogs welcome ~ Open 11.30-2.30, 5.30-11; 11.30-11 Sat; 12-10.30 Sun; closed Mon lunchtime

Recommended by BOB, Simon and Sally Small, Heather and Dick Martin, G Stapely, Mr Clifton, Miss A L Tester, Mrs J Ekins-Daukes, Derek Thomas

EWHURST GREEN
TQ7924 MAP 3

White Dog

Turn off A21 to Bodiam at S end of Hurst Green, cross B2244, pass Bodiam Castle, cross river then bear left uphill at Ewhurst Green sign; TN32 5TD

Comfortable pub with a nice little bar, several real ales and decent food

Handy for Bodiam Castle, this is an attractive, partly 17th-c pub with a mix of locals and visitors. The bar on the left has a proper pubby feel with a fine inglenook fireplace, hop-draped beams, wood-panelled walls, farm implements and horsebrasses, just a few tables with high-backed, rush-seated dining chairs and red plush-topped bar stools by the curved wooden counter on the old brick or flagstoned floor. There's also a high-backed cushioned settle by the counter and Fullers London Pride, Harveys Best and a guest beer from Rother Valley on handpump and several wines by the glass. To the right of the door is the busy but fairly plain dining room with more big flagstones, the same tables and chairs as the bar, fresh flowers, black joists and hops, paintings by local artists for sale, and again, one high-backed settle by the bar; piped music. There's also a games room with darts, pool and a games machine. There are plenty of picnic-sets in the back garden looking over to Bodiam Castle.

🍽 **Bar food includes filled baguettes, soup, tempura prawns with dipping sauce, stuffed shoulder of lamb, tomato and mozzarella tart, steak in ale pie, beer-battered cod, free-range chicken breast with lemon and thyme sauce and 28-day hung beef with garlic butter, and puddings such as vanilla panna cotta with black cherries and chocolate brownies; Sunday roasts.** *Starters/Snacks: £5.25 to £6.95. Main Courses: £8.95 to £11.95. Puddings: £5.75*

Free house ~ Licensee Mrs Danni Page ~ Real ale ~ Bar food (12-2.30(3 Sun), 6.30-10; not Sun or Mon evenings) ~ Restaurant ~ (01580) 830264 ~ Children welcome ~ Dogs allowed in bar ~ Open 12-11(11.30 Sat); 12-6 Sun; closed Sun evening ~ Bedrooms: /£75B

Recommended by R and S Bentley, Philip and Cheryl Hill, Dr Martin Owton, Leslie and Barbara Owen, V Brogden

FLETCHING
TQ4223 MAP 3

Griffin 🍽 🍷 🛏

Village signposted off A272 W of Uckfield; TN22 3SS

Busy, gently upmarket inn with a fine wine list, bistro-style bar food, real ales and big garden with far-reaching views; bedrooms

Civilised and very well run, this bustling inn is extremely popular – especially at weekends – and it's best to book a table in advance then. The beamed and quaintly panelled bar rooms have blazing log fires, old photographs and hunting prints, straightforward close-set furniture including some captain's chairs and china on a delft shelf. There's a small bare-boarded serving area off to one side and a snug separate bar with sofas and TV. Harveys Best, Kings Horsham Best and a couple of guest beers such as Dark Star Original and Hepworth Iron Horse on handpump and a fine wine list with 20 (including champagne and sweet wine) by the glass. The very spacious two-acre back garden has plenty of seats on the sandstone terrace and on the grass and lovely views of rolling countryside. This is a handy place for Glyndebourne.

🍽 **Using carefully sourced local produce, the highly thought-of – if not cheap – food includes filled ciabattas, soup, salt and pepper squid, chicken liver and foie gras parfait with peach and date chutney, linguine with clams, chilli, garlic, parsley and white wine, braised wild boar sausages with champ mash and sweet chicory, courgette, spinach, taleggio cheese and parmesan risotto, chicken breast with smoked paprika and lemon, slow-roasted pork belly with salsa verde and caramelised vegetables, skate wing with cockle vinaigrette, and puddings such as chocolate and pecan tart with mascarpone and candied orange and lemon polenta cake with lemon syrup; maybe summer Sunday barbecues.** *Starters/Snacks: £6.00 to £9.50. Main Courses: £10.00 to £19.00. Puddings: £6.00 to £6.50*

Free house ~ Licensees J Pullan and M Spanek ~ Real ale ~ Bar food (12-2.30(3 weekends), 7-9.30) ~ Restaurant ~ (01825) 722890 ~ Children welcome ~ Dogs allowed in bar ~ Piano in bar Fri evening and Sun lunchtime ~ Open 12-midnight (1am Sat, 11 Sun) ~ Bedrooms: £80B/£85S(£95B)

Recommended by Henny Davison, Harriet Kininmonth, Andy and Claire Barker, Kevin Malia, Tina and David Woods-Taylor, C A Turner, Lucilla Lunn, Hugh Roberts, Charles Kingsley Evans, Ann and Colin Hunt, Sheila Topham, Michael Pelham, Mrs Mary Woods, Laurence Smith

HEATHFIELD
TQ5920   MAP 3

Star ◀

Old Heathfield, off A265/B2096 E; Church Street; TN21 9AH

Pleasant old pub with bustling, friendly atmosphere, good mix of locals and visitors, well liked food and decent choice of drinks; pretty garden

This is a smashing country pub of real character with a good mix of both locals and visitors. The bar has ancient heavy beams, built-in wall settles and window seats, panelling and a roaring winter log fire; a doorway leads to a similarly decorated room more set up for eating with wooden tables and chairs (one table has high-backed white leather dining chairs) and a woodburning stove. There's also an upstairs dining room. Harveys Best, Shepherd Neame Spitfire and Wells & Youngs Bitter on handpump and several wines by the glass; piped music. The garden is very prettily planted, there's rustic furniture under smart umbrellas and lovely views of rolling oak-lined sheep pastures. Turner thought it fine enough to paint.

🍴 Chalked up on boards, the well liked food might include ploughman's, soup, tiger prawns with ginger, chilli and garlic, flaked fresh mackerel with horseradish cream and beetroot salad, field mushroom stuffed with goats cheese and caramelised onion, wild boar sausages with onion gravy, smoked haddock and smoked salmon fishcakes with spring onion salad, knuckle of gammon with a white onion and parsley sauce, irish stew, and puddings like chocolate squidgy meringue and fresh apricot fool. *Starters/Snacks: £4.95 to £7.95. Main Courses: £7.95 to £15.95. Puddings: £3.95 to £5.65*

Free house ~ Licensees Mike and Sue Chappell ~ Real ale ~ Bar food (12-2.30(3 Sun), 7-9.30 (9 Sun)) ~ Restaurant ~ (01435) 863570 ~ Children in eating area of bar ~ Dogs allowed in bar ~ Open 11.30-11; 12-10.30 Sun

Recommended by Mike and Eleanor Anderson, Laurence Smith

HENLEY
SU8925   MAP 2

Duke of Cumberland Arms ◀

Off A286 S of Fernhurst; GU27 3HQ

Charming country pub with two character rooms, local beers and enjoyable food

In fine weather, this wisteria-covered 15th-c stone-built pub is a lovely place to be as there are beautiful hill views from gnarled seats and picnic-sets in the charming big sloping garden and trout in the many ponds. Inside, the two small rooms each have a bright log fire as well as big scrubbed pine or oak tables on brick or flagstoned floors, low ceilings, white-painted wall boards and rustic decorations. As we went to press, a new kitchen was being added and there will be a new restaurant and terrace where the old Cedar Room used to be. Harveys Best and Langham Best and Hip Hop are tapped from the cask and they have several wines by the glass.

🍴 Good, interesting bar food includes filled baguettes, soup, irish oysters with red wine and shallot vinegar, free-range ham and egg, a proper burger, crab salad with horseradish potato salad, corn-fed chicken with pesto mozzarella and avocado dressing, beer-battered haddock, confit pork belly with apple glaze, slow-cooked lamb shank with minted jus, and puddings. *Starters/Snacks: £5.90 to £7.00. Main Courses: £9.95 to £15.95. Puddings: £6.50*

Free house ~ Licensee Robert Delow ~ Real ale ~ Bar food (not Sun evening) ~ Restaurant ~ (01428) 652280 ~ Well behaved children welcome ~ Dogs welcome ~ Open 12-11(10.30 Sun)

Recommended by Terry and Nickie Williams, Michael B Griffith, the Didler, Henry Midwinter, Christopher and Elise Wray, Bruce Bird

HORSHAM   TQ1730   MAP 3

Black Jug ♀
North Street; RH12 1RJ

Bustling town pub with wide choice of drinks, efficient staff and good bar food

---

Friendly, knowledgeable staff manage to keep the mixed crowd of office workers, couples and theatre-goers happy and contented in this well run town pub. The one large open-plan, turn-of-the-century room has a large central bar, a nice collection of sizeable dark wood tables and comfortable chairs on the stripped wood floor, board games and interesting old prints and photographs above a dark wood panelled dado on the cream walls. A spacious conservatory has similar furniture and lots of hanging baskets. A wide range of drinks features an impressive array of wines (with 30 by the glass), five real ales on handpump – Harveys Best and four guests such as Caledonian Deuchars IPA and Flying Dutchman, Sharps Doom Bar, Thwaites Wainwright and over 70 malt whiskies. The pretty flower-filled back terrace has plenty of garden furniture. The small car park is for staff and deliveries only but you can park next door in the council car park.

⏹ **Interesting bar food includes sandwiches, ploughman's, soup, duck liver pâté with rhubarb purée, seared scallops with minted pea and broad bean purée, warm pigeon, pear and roasted hazelnut salad, crab linguine with chilli, ginger and coriander, beer-battered haddock, popular burger with bacon and cheese, roasted aubergine, goats cheese and red pepper lasagne, slow-roasted chinese-spice pork belly with pak choi, braised rabbit, bacon and vegetable broth with tarragon dumplings, and puddings like chocolate tiramisu and bakewell tart with clotted cream.** *Starters/Snacks: £4.50 to £7.95. Main Courses: £9.75 to £16.95. Puddings: £4.50 to £5.50*

Brunning & Price ~ Tenant Alastair Craig ~ Real ale ~ Bar food (12-10(9.30 Sun)) ~ (01403) 253526 ~ Children in restaurant ~ Dogs allowed in bar ~ Open 11.30-11; 12-10.30 Sun
Recommended by Derek and Maggie Washington, Mike and Eleanor Anderson, Dr and Mrs A K Clarke

ICKLESHAM   TQ8716   MAP 3

Queens Head ♀ ◧
Just off A259 Rye—Hastings; TN36 4BL

Friendly, well run country pub with a good range of beers, pubby food and seats in the garden with fine views

---

There's always a wide mix of customers in this popular country pub who are all made welcome by the courteous and efficient staff. The open-plan areas work round a very big serving counter which stands under a vaulted beamed roof, the high beamed walls and ceiling of the easy-going bar are lined with shelves of bottles and covered with farming implements and animal traps, and there are well used pub tables and old pews on the brown patterned carpet. Other areas have big inglenook fireplaces and the back room has some old bikes hanging from the ceiling and is decorated with old bicycle and motorbike prints; piped jazz or blues and darts. Greene King IPA and Abbot, Harveys Best, Ringwood Fortyniner and a couple of guests like Dark Star Hophead and Whitstable IPA on handpump, along with Biddenden cider and several wines by the glass. The peaceful garden has boules, a children's play area and picnic-sets that make the most of the sweeping view of the Brede valley. This is well placed for walks to Winchelsea.

⏹ **Usefully served all day at weekends, the straightforward bar food includes sandwiches, filled baked potatoes, ploughman's, soup, chicken liver pâté, deep-fried brie with cranberry sauce, peppers stuffed with feta, cashews and couscous, steak and kidney pie, all day breakfast, a curry of the day and various grills.** *Starters/Snacks: £4.95 to £6.50. Main Courses: £8.50 to £14.95. Puddings: £3.75 to £4.25*

Free house ~ Licensee Ian Mitchell ~ Real ale ~ Bar food (12-2.30, 6-9.30; all day weekends) ~ (01424) 814552 ~ Well behaved children away from bar but must leave by 8.30pm ~ Dogs allowed in bar ~ Live music 4-6pm Sun ~ Open 11-11; 12-10.30 Sun

Recommended by Peter Meister, Simon Rodway, V Brogden, Robert Kibble, Tom and Jill Jones, N R White, Colin and Louise English, Lorry Spooner, Bruce Bird

LEWES   TQ4110   MAP 3

Lewes Arms 🍺 £

Castle Ditch Lane/Mount Place – tucked behind castle ruins; BN7 1YH

Cheerful little local, several real ales, good, interesting bar food and friendly staff

There's plenty of no-nonsense character in this well run and unpretentious little back street local – and a welcome from the friendly staff for all their customers. The tiny front bar on the right has stools along the nicely curved counter and bench window seats. Two other simple rooms are hung with information and photographs to do with the famously noisy Lewes bonfire night and have straightforward tables and chairs ranging from high-backed settles to cushioned wheelbacks and other dining seats; stripped wooden floors throughout, a couple of Victorian fireplaces (with a decorative woodburner in one), beer mats pinned over doorways and a cheerful, chatty atmosphere. Everards Beacon, Fullers ESB and London Pride, Gales HSB and Seafarers and Harveys Best on handpump, over 30 malt whiskies and several wines by the glass. At the top of some stairs, a door leads to an attractive small back terrace on two levels with picnic-sets under umbrellas, outdoor heaters and a barbecue. The same people run another of our Sussex Main Entries, the Basketmakers Arms in Brighton.

🍴 Generous helpings of really good, fair-value bar food using locally sourced organic and free-range produce includes lunchtime sandwiches, ploughman's, soup, mackerel pâté, a meze plate, meaty or vegetarian burgers, mexican chilli dishes, popular daily specials such as chicken, chorizo, chickpea and spinach stew, smoked haddock and king prawn kedgeree, aubergine, spinach and potato curry with raita, spaghetti with fresh mixed seafood, and puddings like treacle and butterscotch sponge and chocolate brownie. *Starters/Snacks: £3.95 to £6.95. Main Courses: £5.95 to £8.95. Puddings: £4.25*

Fullers ~ Tenants Abigail Mawer and Peter Dowd ~ Real ale ~ Bar food (12-3, 5.30-8.30; 12-9 Sat and 12-5 Sun; not bank hol Mon evenings) ~ (01273) 473152 ~ Children welcome but not in front bar ~ Dogs welcome ~ Poetry evening third Thurs in the month and live monthly folk ~ Open 11-11(midnight Fri and Sat); 12-11 Sun

Recommended by the Didler, Conor McGaughey, Ann and Colin Hunt, John Beeken, Mike and Eleanor Anderson

LODSWORTH   SU9321   MAP 2

Halfway Bridge Inn 🍽 🍷 🛏

Just before village, on A272 Midhurst—Petworth; GU28 9BP

Restauranty coaching inn with contemporary décor in several dining areas, log fires, local real ales and modern food; lovely bedrooms

Although this smart country inn is clearly set up for dining, there are plenty of locals who congregate at the bar for a drink and a chat. The three or four bar rooms have plenty of intimate little corners and are carefully furnished with good oak chairs and an individual mix of tables; one of the log fires is a well polished kitchen range. The inter-connecting restaurant rooms have beams, wooden floors and a cosy atmosphere. Langham Halfway to Heaven, Skinners Betty Stogs and a guest like Sharps Doom Bar on handpump and 14 wines by the glass; piped music. At the back there are seats on a small terrace. The bedrooms in the former stable yard are extremely stylish and comfortable.

🍴 As well as lunchtime sandwiches and filled baguettes, the enjoyable – if not cheap – food might include soup, pigeon breast with a mushroom soufflé and a black pepper cream, seared scallops and belly of pork with a mixed spice fruit compote, vegetable and lentil lasagne, steak, stilton and ale pie, seared calves liver with bacon, caramelised onion and sage jus, smoked haddock with a poached egg, spinach and a mixed cheese sauce, pork medallions with a peach and apple sauce, and puddings such as Baileys and cinnamon-flavoured crème brûlée and strawberry and pink grapefruit parfait with a honey tuile and strawberry coulis. *Starters/Snacks: £4.95 to £9.95. Main Courses: £12.95 to £18.75. Puddings: £4.95 to £6.50*

We say if we know a pub has piped music.

Free house ~ Licensee Paul Carter ~ Real ale ~ Bar food (12-2.30, 6.30-9.15) ~ Restaurant ~ (01798) 861281 ~ Children welcome ~ Dogs allowed in bar ~ Open 11-11; 12-10.30 Sun ~ Bedrooms: £85B/£120B

Recommended by Colin McKerrow, Tracey and Stephen Groves, Ian Wilson, M G Hart, Colin and Janet Roe

Hollist Arms
Off A272 Midhurst—Petworth; GU28 9BZ

Friendly and civilised village pub with local beers, good choice of wines, well liked bar food and seats outside

As this 200-year-old village pub is usefully open all day, it's just the place to head for after enjoying one of the nearby walks – and you're sure to get a warm welcome from the cheerful landlord and his team. A small snug room on the right has two tables by an open fire – just right for a cosy drink. The public bar area on the left has bar stools against the pale wooden counter, wooden stools around a few tables and a comfortable built-in window seat. Kings Horsham Best, Langhams Hip Hop and Shepherd Neame Spitfire on handpump and a good choice of wines. The L-shaped dining room has a couple of big squidgy sofas facing each other in front of the inglenook fireplace and plenty of elegant spoked dining chairs and wheelbacks around tables on the wood-strip floor; the red walls are completely covered with genuinely interesting prints and paintings. Up some steps, the pretty and cottagey back garden has picnic-sets on the terrace or you can sit on a seat beneath the huge horse chestnut tree on the green. More reports please.

[¶] **Bar food includes lunchtime ciabattas, soup, chicken liver pâté with spiced apple chutney, deep-fried goats cheese with quince jelly, prawn melt on toast, macaroni cheese, home-made burgers, smoked haddock and spinach pie, beef bourguignon, slow-cooked lamb shank with moroccan spices, dates and apricots, and daily specials like turkey and bacon lasagne and bass with lemon, garlic and rosemary.** *Starters/Snacks: £3.50 to £6.50. Main Courses: £8.50 to £21.00. Puddings: £5.50*

Free house ~ Licensees George and Juliet Bristow ~ Real ale ~ Bar food (12-2.30, 7-9(9.30 Fri and Sat); 12-3, 6.30-8.30 Sun) ~ Restaurant ~ (01798) 861310 ~ Children welcome ~ Dogs welcome ~ Open 11-11(midnight Sat); 12-10.30 Sun

Recommended by M G Hart, Michael B Griffith, Mrs Romey Heaton, Martin and Karen Wake, Glen and Nola Armstrong

LURGASHALL   SU9327   MAP 2

Noahs Ark
Off A283 N of Petworth; GU28 9ET

Charming old pub overlooking the village green with keen young licensees, real ales and enjoyable food

Picnic-sets outside this tile-hung 16th-c pub look over the village green and cricket pitch – it's a lovely spot. Inside, the enthusiastic young licensees have gently refurbished the bars and dining room keeping plenty of charm and character. The simple, traditional bar, bustling with chatting locals and their dogs at the weekend, has leather-topped bar stools by the counter where they serve Greene King IPA and Abbot and a changing guest beer on handpump, several wines by the glass and farm cider, and there are beams, a mix of wooden chairs and tables on the parquet flooring and an inglenook fireplace. The dining room is spacious and airy with church candles and fresh flowers on light wood dining chairs and tables and a smart but relaxed feel; a couple of comfortable sofas face each other in front of an open woodburning stove. The pub border terrier is called Gillie and visiting dogs are very welcome – there are even dog biscuits behind the bar. There are more picnic-sets in a large side garden.

[¶] **Enjoyable bar food includes sandwiches, soup, baby crab cakes on creamy apple salsa with sweet chilli sauce, a plate of serrano ham, chargrilled chorizo, mozzarella balls and leaves, beer-battered haddock, sausages and mash with caramelised onion gravy, chicken caesar salad, pea and mint risotto with parmesan and truffle oil and roast salmon fillet with local asparagus and hollandaise sauce.** *Starters/Snacks: £4.95 to £7.15. Main Courses: £8.95 to £17.95. Puddings: £4.50 to £5.50*

Greene King ~ Tenants Henry Coghlan and Amy Whitmore ~ Real ale ~ Bar food (12-2.30, 7-9.30; 12-3.30 Sun; not Sun evening) ~ Restaurant ~ (01428) 707346 ~ Children allowed but not in bar after 7pm ~ Dogs allowed in bar ~ Open 11-11(11.30 Sat); 12-9 Sun; 11-3.30, 5.30-11 in winter

Recommended by BOB

MAYFIELD

TQ5927   MAP 3

Rose & Crown

Fletching Street; TN20 6TE

Pretty weatherboarded cottage with unspoilt bars, relaxed atmosphere, local beers and popular bar food

Both locals and visitors are warmly welcomed at this pretty 16th-c weatherboarded pub and there's a genuinely relaxed and friendly atmosphere. Several bars wander round the little central servery but the two cosy small front rooms have the most character: low ceiling boards with coins embedded in the glossy paintwork, bench seats built into the partly panelled walls, pewter tankards hanging above the bar and along a beam and a mix of simple dining chairs around wooden tables on the stripped floorboards. There are candles in the first brick fireplace, a big log fire in the inglenook, Harveys Best and a changing guest on handpump and ten wines by the glass. Down some steps to the left is a larger carpeted room with a couple of big comfortable cushioned sofas, similar tables and chairs, a woodburning stove, several mirrors and steps at the other end of the room that lead up to a less-used back area. Bob the pub chocolate labrador welcomes other well behaved dogs; they hold a Tuesday evening quiz night. There are picnic-sets under parasols on the front terrace.

🍴 **Good bar food includes filled ciabattas, hummus with lemon and pine nuts and red pepper and celery crudités, goats cheese and red onion tart, burgers topped with cheese and bacon or mushroom and stilton, risotto with leeks and gorgonzola, chicken and leek pie, fishcakes with aioli, wild boar and apple sausages with red onion gravy, and puddings like chocolate pot and apple and blackberry crumble; Sunday roasts.** *Starters/Snacks: £4.00 to £5.50. Main Courses: £7.50 to £11.00. Puddings: £4.50*

Free house ~ Licensees Christine Currer and Elizabeth Maltman ~ Real ale ~ Bar food (12-9(9.30 Fri and Sat; 8 Sun)) ~ (01435) 872200 ~ Children welcome ~ Dogs welcome ~ Open 11-11(midnight Sat); 12-10.30 Sun

Recommended by Ingrid and Peter Terry, N R White

MILTON STREET

TQ5304   MAP 3

Sussex Ox

Off A27 just under a mile E of Alfriston roundabout; BN26 5RL

Extended country pub, magnificent downs views and plenty of outside seating, cosy little bar, two dining rooms, real ales and good wines by the glass

On a sunny day, the teak tables and chairs on decking at the back of this carefully extended country pub are much prized – and the downs views are magnificent. There are also some picnic-sets in the garden below and more under parasols at the front of the building. Inside, the two rooms of the bar are just the place for a chat and a pint or a light meal: a couple of high tables (little oil lamps on each) and chairs on the bare boards, bar chairs by the counter where they keep Dark Star Ox Head and Golden Gate and Harveys Best on handpump, champagne and a fine choice of wines by the glass, and lots of local photographs on the walls; friendly, helpful staff. Standing timbers separate a lower, brick-floored room where there's a woodburning stove in the brick fireplace and farmhouse chairs around sturdy pine tables; darts. Leading off here is a dining room, similarly furnished, with hops and more local photographs, and there's also a two-roomed front dining room on two levels with high-backed, rush-seated wooden dining chairs, a mix of tables, and an ornamental woodburning stove. The atmosphere is relaxed and informal and there tends to be a good mix of customers – locals, walkers and families with their children and dogs. Weekend lunchtimes are particularly popular and you would need to book a table in advance.

🍽 **Bistro-style bar food includes sandwiches, ploughman's, soup, nibbles like grilled artichoke hearts and rice-stuffed vine leaves, deep-fried local squid with lemon mayonnaise, sautéed chicken livers, lemon and mint burger, free-range chicken and ham hock pie, beer-battered hake, mixed bean and parmesan risotto, citrus-braised lamb shank with mustard mash, guinea fowl breast with crispy bacon and madeira sauce, and puddings like honey and vanilla panna cotta and chocolate fridge cake with clotted cream.** *Starters/Snacks: £5.50 to £7.50. Main Courses: £8.75 to £11.00. Puddings: £5.00*

Free house ~ Licensee David and Suzanne Pritchard ~ Real ale ~ Bar food (12-2(3 Sun), 6-9; not winter Sun evening) ~ Restaurant ~ (01323) 870840 ~ Children in garden room only ~ Dogs allowed in bar ~ Open 11.30-3, 6-11; 12-3, 6-10.30 Sun; 12-5 Sun in winter; closed winter Sun evening and between Christmas and New Year

Recommended by Peter Meister, Helen Greatorex, Jeremy Christey, Laurence Smith

OVING   SU9005   MAP 2

Gribble Inn 🍺

Between A27 and A259 just E of Chichester, then should be signposted just off village road; OS Sheet 197 map reference 900050; PO20 2BP

Own-brewed beers in bustling 16th-c thatched pub with beamed and timbered linked rooms, well liked bar food and pretty garden

The friendly new licensees continue to brew the fine range of their own beers here, as well as keeping a guest from Badger on handpump: Gribble Ale, Fuzzy Duck, Pigs Ear, Mocha Mole, Plucking Pheasant, Reg's Tipple, Sussex Quad Hopper and Badger First Gold. They hold a beer festival over the August bank holiday. The chatty bar has lots of heavy beams and timbering, old country-kitchen furnishings and pews, and the linked rooms have a cottagey feel and huge winter log fires. Board games and a skittle alley with its own bar. There are seats outside under a covered area and more chairs and tables in the pretty recently tidied-up garden with apple and pear trees.

🍽 **Bar food (using their own ale in several dishes) includes lunchtime sandwiches, pigeon breast with celeriac purée and crispy bacon, ham hock terrine with ale chutney, cider-steamed mussels, steak in ale pie, pork and ale sausages, beer-battered cod, chicken breast filled with spinach and camembert wrapped in bacon and rump of local lamb with minted potatoes.** *Starters/Snacks: £4.50 to £9.00. Main Courses: £6.95 to £18.95. Puddings: £4.95*

Badger ~ Licensees Simon Wood and Nicola Tester ~ Real ale ~ Bar food (12-3, 6-9; 12-3 Sun; not Sun evening) ~ Restaurant ~ (01243) 786893 ~ Children in family room ~ Dogs allowed in bar ~ Jazz first Tues of the month ~ Open 11-3, 5.30-11; 11-11 Sat; 12-10.30 Sun

Recommended by Sue and Mike Todd, Paul Rampton, Julie Harding, David H T Dimock, Val and Alan Green, the Didler, Ian and Barbara Rankin, Guy Vowles, Susan and John Douglas, Rob and Penny Wakefield, Phil and Jane Villiers, John Beeken

RINGMER   TQ4313   MAP 3

Cock

Uckfield Road – blocked-off section of road off A26 N of village turn-off; BN8 5RX

16th-c country pub with a wide choice of popular bar food, real ales in character bar and plenty of seats in the garden

The heart of this 16th-c weatherboarded pub is the cosy and unspoilt bar and it's here that those wanting a chat and a pint tend to aim for. There are heavy beams, a log fire in the inglenook fireplace (lit from October to April), traditional pubby furniture on flagstones and Fullers London Pride, Harveys Best and a guest like Dark Star Hophead or Sharps Doom Bar on handpump, nine wines by the glass, a dozen malt whiskies and

Weston's summer cider; piped music. There are three dining areas. Outside on the terrace and in the garden, there are lots of picnic-sets with views across open fields to the South Downs – pretty sunsets; visiting dogs are offered a bowl of water and a chew and their own dogs are called Fred and Tally.

⑪ **A wide choice of bar food includes sandwiches, ploughman's, soup, chicken liver pâté, deep-fried camembert with cranberry sauce, tiger prawns in garlic butter, pork sausages with chips and beans, steak in ale pie, liver and bacon with onion gravy, mixed nut roast with red wine sauce, salmon fillet with creamy watercress sauce, daily specials like moules marinière, tagliatelle with spinach and mushroom sauce, skate wing with capers and venison loin with redcurrant sauce, and puddings like pineapple upside-down cake and crème brûlée; Sunday roasts.** *Starters/Snacks: £4.50 to £5.95. Main Courses: £6.95 to £17.50. Puddings: £3.95 to £4.95*

Free house ~ Licensees Ian, Val and Matt Ridley ~ Real ale ~ Bar food (12-2.15(2.30 Sat), 6-9.30; all day Sun) ~ Restaurant ~ (01273) 812040 ~ Well behaved children welcome away from bar ~ Dogs allowed in bar ~ Open 11-3, 6-11.30; 11am-11.30pm Sun

Recommended by Dominic Lucas, M G Hart, Tracey and Stephen Groves, Tony and Shirley Albert, Tina and David Woods-Taylor

RYE
TQ9220   MAP 3

Mermaid ♀ 🛏
Mermaid Street; TN31 7EY

Lovely old timbered inn on famous cobbled street with civilised, antiques-filled bar, a good wine list, short choice of decent bar food and smart restaurant; bedrooms

One reader suggests that to get the complete experience of this beautiful and civilised half-timbered inn you should park down by the river and walk up the cobbled street. A sign outside says 'rebuilt in 1420' – in fact, the cellars are two or three centuries older than that. The little bar is where those in search of a light lunch and a drink tend to head: quite a mix of quaint, closely set furnishings such as Victorian gothic carved oak chairs, older but plainer oak seats and a massive deeply polished bressumer beam across one wall for the huge inglenook fireplace. Three antique but not ancient wall paintings show old english scenes. Fullers London Pride, Greene King Old Speckled Hen and Harveys Best on handpump, several malt whiskies and 15 wines by the glass from a good list; piped music in the bar only, playing cards and board games on request. Seats on a small back terrace overlook the car park where – at bank holiday weekends – there may be morris dancers.

⑪ **The short bar menu includes sandwiches, baked whole camembert with cranberry sauce, confit of crispy duck salad with a red and green chilli dressing, fresh salmon and pea fishcakes with mint yoghurt and a cucumber and dill salad, free-range chicken goujons caramelised with lemon and black pepper, steak and kidney pudding and minute steak with a blue cheese salad; the smart restaurant offers fixed-price lunches and dinners from a richly traditional menu.** *Starters/Snacks: £7.00 to £9.75. Main Courses: £9.75 to £11.25. Puddings: £6.95*

Free house ~ Licensees Robert Pinwill and Mrs J Blincow ~ Real ale ~ Bar food (12-3, 6-9) ~ Restaurant ~ (01797) 223065 ~ Children welcome ~ Open 12-11 ~ Bedrooms: £85B/£180B

Recommended by Lorry Spooner, Colin and Louise English, DFL, the Didler, Terry Buckland

Ship
The Strand, at the foot of Mermaid Street; TN31 7DB

Informal and prettily set old inn with a relaxed atmosphere, straightforward furnishings, local ales and inventive food

It's the inventive food and good choice of drinks that customers enjoy in this easy-going 16th-c pub. There are beams and timbers, a mixed bag of rather secondhand-feeling furnishings – a cosy group of overstuffed leather armchairs and sofa, random stripped or Formica-topped tables and various café chairs – suit it nicely, as do the utilitarian bulkhead wall lamps. The ground floor is all opened up, from the sunny big-windowed front part to a snugger part at the back, with a log fire in the stripped brick fireplace below a stuffed boar's head, and a feeling of separate areas is enhanced by the varied flooring: composition, stripped boards, flagstones, a bit of carpet in the armchair corner. Harveys Best and a couple of local guest beers on handpump, local farm cider and perry and lots of wines by the glass; piped music and board games. Out by the quiet lane are picnic-sets and one or two cheerful oilcloth-covered tables. More reports please.

🍴 Using carefully sourced local ingredients, the interesting bar food includes soup, potted crab with toasted potato and thyme bread, an antipasti plate of smoked venison, duck, babaganoush (a middle-eastern dish of mashed aubergine with seasonings) and slow-roasted tomatoes, eggs benedict, mussels with cream, white wine and shallots, spinach, feta and dill filo pie, pork and black bean stew with chorizo and smoked chilli and breaded cod with chunky fries. *Starters/Snacks: £5.50 to £8.00. Main Courses: £10.00 to £18.50. Puddings: £5.25 to £6.50*

Enterprise ~ Lease Karen Northcote ~ Real ale ~ Bar food (12-3(3.30 weekends), 6.30-10; they serve breakfast from 8.30am) ~ (01797) 222233 ~ Children welcome ~ Dogs welcome ~ Open 10am-11pm; 12-10.30 Sun ~ Bedrooms: /£90B

Recommended by BB

Ypres Castle 🍺

Gun Garden; steps up from A259, or down past Ypres Tower; TN31 7HH

Traditional pub with several real ales, varied bar food and seats in sheltered garden

In a quiet corner of this historic town and perched above the river, this bustling pub is usefully open all day. The bars have various old tables and chairs, and somehow, the informal almost scruffy feel adds to its character. There are comfortable seats by the winter log fire, local artwork, quite a mix of customers and a restaurant area; piped music. Fullers ESB, Harveys Best, Larkins Best and Timothy Taylors Landlord on handpump. The sheltered garden is a pleasant place to sit; boules.

🍴 Bar food includes lunchtime sandwiches and filled baguettes, ploughman's, chicken liver pâté, an antipasti plate, fishcakes on wilted spinach, cider-cooked ham and free-range eggs, sunblush tomato and spring onion risotto, lasagne, lamb cutlets with roasted garlic mash, free-range chicken with white wine sauce, a mixed seafood platter (for two) and daily specials. *Starters/Snacks: £5.00 to £7.00. Main Courses: £8.00 to £18.00. Puddings: £4.00 to £6.00*

Free house ~ Licensee Ian Fenn ~ Real ale ~ Bar food (12-3, 6-9; all day Sat; not Sun evening) ~ Restaurant ~ (01797) 223248 ~ Children welcome at lunchtime ~ Dogs allowed in bar ~ Open 11-10 (midnight Fri, 11 Sat); 11-8(6 in winter) Sun

Recommended by Sue and Mike Todd, Mike and Eleanor Anderson, Robert Kibble, Miss Sue Callard, Colin and Louise English

SALEHURST   TQ7424   MAP 3

Salehurst Halt

Village signposted from Robertsbridge bypass on A21 Tunbridge Wells—Battle; Church Lane; TN32 5PH

Relaxed little local in quiet hamlet, chatty atmosphere, real ales, well liked bar food and seats in pretty back garden

This is a well run and popular little pub with a relaxed and unpretentious feel and quite a mix of customers of all ages. To the right of the door, there's a small stone-floored area with a couple of tables, a piano, settle, TV and an open fire. To the left, there's a nice long scrubbed pine table with a couple of sofas, a mix of more ordinary pubby tables and wheelback and mates' chairs on the wood-strip floor and maybe piped music; board games. Dark Star Stout and Harveys Best on handpump, several malt whiskies and decent wines by the glass. The back terrace has metal chairs and tiled tables and there are more seats in the landscaped garden with views out over the Rother valley.

⑪ Bar food usually includes filled baguettes, soup, ploughman's, popular burgers, a large tasty fishcake with tartare sauce, local beer-battered cod, ham and eggs, steak in ale or chicken and tarragon pies, good curries, and puddings like prune and chocolate torte and foraged fruit crumble; Sunday roasts. *Starters/Snacks: £4.80 to £6.00. Main Courses: £7.00 to £13.00. Puddings: £4.50*

Free house ~ Licensee Andrew Augarde ~ Real ale ~ Bar food (not Mon) ~ (01580) 880620 ~ Children welcome ~ Dogs welcome ~ Live music second Sun of the month at 5pm ~ Open 12-3, 6-11; 12-11 (10 Sun) Sat; closed Mon

Recommended by Geoff and Linda Payne, Tony and Wendy Hobden, N R White

SIDLESHAM   SZ8697   MAP 2

Crab & Lobster ⑪ ☐ ⇐

Mill Lane; off B2145 S of Chichester; PO20 7NB

Smart dining pub with stylish furnishings, real ales, a fine choice of wines by the glass, first-class food and seats overlooking the bird reserve; lovely bedrooms

This upmarket place is really a restaurant-with-rooms rather than a pub but it does still welcome walkers and bird-watchers (Pagham Harbour bird reserve is close by) who just want a drink and maybe a light meal. There's a flagstoned bar with comfortable bucket seats around a mix of wooden tables, some bar stools by the light wooden-topped bar counter, a log fire, Harveys Best and Sharps Doom Bar on handpump and 17 wines by the glass including prosecco and champagne. The stylish, upmarket restaurant has fabric dining chairs around tables set for eating and walls painted in pale pastel colours. Good lighting, piped music and friendly, helpful staff. The bedrooms are smart and comfortable and there's also a self-catering cottage. On the back terrace, seats and tables overlook the tranquil marshes.

⑪ The imaginative – if rather pricey – food here specialises in fresh local fish and shellfish but there's plenty of non-fishy dishes, too: lunchtime open sandwiches, clam and red mullet chowder, ham hock terrine with a home-made miniature brioche loaf and quince jelly, beer-battered fresh cod with home-made tartare sauce, baked gratin of swede, celeriac and potato topped with goats cheese and a red pepper sauce, seasonal crab and lobster, slow-roasted old spot pork belly in a pear and cider cream sauce, steak and kidney pudding, daily specials, and puddings such as warm chocolate fondant with white mint and chocolate ice-cream and rhubarb and apple crumble with orange sorbet. *Starters/Snacks: £5.75 to £12.50. Main Courses: £14.50 to £19.50. Puddings: £6.25*

Free house ~ Licensee Sam Bakose ~ Real ale ~ Bar food (12-2.30, 6-9.30; all day at weekends) ~ (01243) 641233 ~ Children welcome ~ Open 11-11 ~ Bedrooms: £85S(£80B)/£150S(£130B)

Recommended by DHV, Peter D La Farge, Peggy and Alec Ward, Susan and John Douglas, Richard Tilbrook, Mr and Mrs P D Titcomb, Tim Gray

SUTTON   SU9715   MAP 2

White Horse ⇐

The Street; RH20 1PS

Opened-up country inn, contemporary décor, real ales, good wines by the glass and modern food; smart bedrooms

Walkers are fond of this quietly set pub as there are walks in lovely surrounding countryside right from the door and packed lunches are available (on request). The bar has a couple of little open brick fireplaces at each end, nightlight candles on mantelpieces, cushioned high bar chairs, Harveys Best and a guest such as Sharps Doom Bar on handpump, good wines by the glass and friendly service. The wooden-topped island servery separates the bar from the two-room barrel-vaulted dining areas (coir carpeting here) and throughout, the minimalist décor is a contemporary clotted cream colour, with modern hardwood chairs and tables on stripped wood and a few small photographs; there's another little log fire, church candles and fresh flowers. Outside, stairs from the back go up to a couple of big wooden tables by the sizeable air vent and more steps lead up to a lawned area with plenty of picnic-sets; there are more seats out in front. Bignor Roman villa is close by.

🍽 **Popular bar food includes lunchtime sandwiches, soup, pork and duck liver terrine with plum chutney, grilled sardines with rosemary and garlic, several platters and salads, cheddar and chive soufflé with cheese sauce, pork and sage sausages with shallot gravy, chicken stuffed with Boursin cheese with parma ham and a pesto sauce, daily specials like red onion and goats cheese tartlet and halibut fillet with citrus butter, and puddings such as brioche and chocolate chip butter pudding and crème brûlée with a clotted cream shortbread biscuit.** *Starters/Snacks: £5.00 to £7.00. Main Courses: £9.50 to £16.50. Puddings: £5.00*

Enterprise ~ Lease Nick Georgiou ~ Real ale ~ Bar food (not Sun or Mon evenings) ~ Restaurant ~ (01798) 869221 ~ Children welcome ~ Dogs allowed in bar ~ Open 11-3, 6-11; 11-4 Sun; closed Sun and Mon evenings ~ Bedrooms: £65S/£85B

Recommended by LM, Guy Vowles, Cathy Robinson, Ed Coombe, A N Bance, Nick Lawless

TROTTON   SU8322   MAP 2

Keepers Arms 🍽 ♈

A272 Midhurst—Petersfield; pub tucked up above road, on S side; GU31 5ER

Pretty cottage with comfortable furnishings on polished wooden boards, open fires, real ales, contemporary food and seats on sunny terrace

On a hillside just above the River Rother, this is a pretty tile-hung cottage with plenty of character. The beamed L-shaped bar has timbered walls and some standing timbers, comfortable sofas and winged-back old leather armchairs around the big log fire and simple rustic tables on the oak flooring. Elsewhere, there are a couple of unusual adult high chairs at an oak refectory table, two huge Georgian leather high-backed chairs around another table and, in the dining room, elegant oak tables, comfortable dining chairs and a woodburning stove; there's another cosy little dining room with bench seating around all four walls and a large central table. Ballards Best, Dark Star Hophead and Otter Bitter on handpump and several wines from a comprehensive list. There are tables and seats on the south-facing terrace.

🍽 **Tasty, popular bar food includes soup, chargrilled mackerel fillet with a horseradish and crème fraîche potato salad and watercress pesto, duck confit leg and breast with lentil and beetroot salad, wild mushroom lasagne, indonesian peanut chicken, beer-battered cod, cumin-roasted lamb with ratatouille and aubergine caviar and scottish sirloin steak with a red onion salad.** *Starters/Snacks: £5.00 to £8.00. Main Courses: £12.00 to £18.00. Puddings: £5.00 to £6.00*

Free house ~ Licensee Nick Troth ~ Real ale ~ Bar food ~ Restaurant ~ (01730) 813724 ~ Children welcome but no babies or toddlers in evening ~ Dogs allowed in bar ~ Open 12-3 (3.30 Sat), 6-11; 12-3.30, 7-10 Sun; closed winter Sun evenings in Jan and Feb

Recommended by Paul Humphreys, Angus Wilson, John Branston

TURNERS HILL   TQ3435   MAP 3

Red Lion 🍺

Lion Lane, just off B2028; RH10 4NU

Bustling country local, warmly welcoming with good value home cooking

One of our readers has been happily visiting this pretty tiled cottage for over 40 years and still heartily recommends it. It's properly old-fashioned and unpretentious with plenty of bar stools for the regulars in the snugly curtained parquet-floored bar: plush-cushioned wall benches, high black beams, a small fire and lots of homely memorabilia. A few steps lead up to a carpeted area with a roaring log fire in the big brick inglenook, cushioned pews and built-in settles forming booths. Cheerfully served by the landlord or his long-serving lunchtime barmaid, there might be Harveys Best, Dark Mild and a

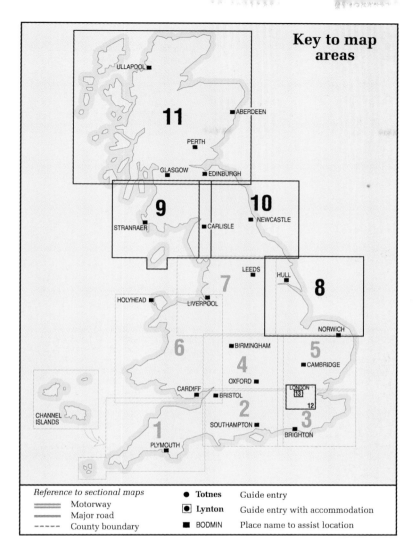

Key to map areas

ULLAPOOL ■

■ ABERDEEN

11

PERTH ■

GLASGOW ■   ■ EDINBURGH

9   **10**

STRANRAER ■   ■ CARLISLE   ■ NEWCASTLE

LEEDS ■   HULL ■   **8**

7

HOLYHEAD ■   LIVERPOOL ■   NORWICH ■

6   ■ BIRMINGHAM   **5**

4   ■ CAMBRIDGE

OXFORD ■

CARDIFF ■   ■ BRISTOL   LONDON 13

CHANNEL ISLANDS   **2**   12

1   SOUTHAMPTON ■   **3**

BRIGHTON ■

PLYMOUTH ■

	Reference to sectional maps	● Totnes	Guide entry
	Motorway	◉ Lynton	Guide entry with accommodation
	Major road	■ BODMIN	Place name to assist location
	County boundary		

MAPS IN THIS SECTION

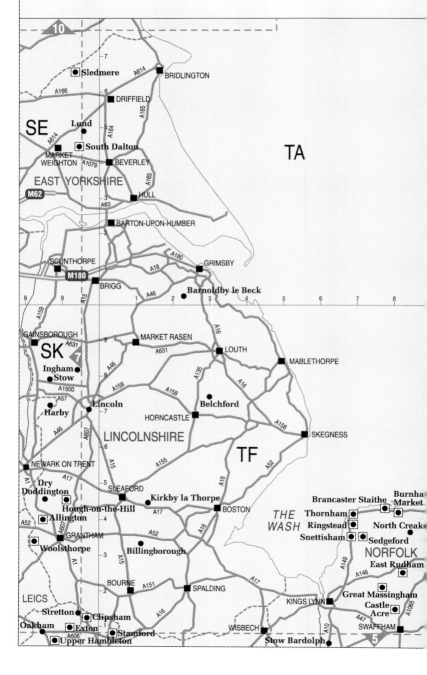

Sledmere
BRIDLINGTON
A614
A166
DRIFFIELD
A165
SE
Lund
A164
South Dalton
MARKET WEIGHTON
A1079
BEVERLEY
EAST YORKSHIRE
A614
TA
M62
A165
A63
HULL
BARTON-UPON-HUMBER
SCUNTHORPE
A180
GRIMSBY
M180
A18
BRIGG
A46
Barnoldby le Beck
A15
A159
GAINSBOROUGH
A631
SK
MARKET RASEN
A16
A631
LOUTH
A46
MABLETHORPE
Ingham
Stow
A1500
A158
A135
A16
A57
Harby
Lincoln
A158
Belchford
HORNCASTLE
A46
A607
LINCOLNSHIRE
A15
TF
A158
SKEGNESS
A155
A16
A52
NEWARK ON TRENT
A1
A17
SLEAFORD
Dry Doddington
A607
Kirkby la Thorpe
BOSTON
THE WASH
Brancaster Staithe
Burnham Market
Hough-on-the-Hill
A17
Thornham
Allington
A52
GRANTHAM
A52
A16
Ringstead
North Creak
Woolsthorpe
A15
Billingborough
Snettisham
Sedgeford
NORFOLK
A151
BOURNE
SPALDING
East Rudham
A17
A149
A148
Great Massingham
LEICS
Stretton
Clipsham
A16
KINGS LYNN
Castle Acre
A1065
Oakham
Exton
Stamford
A606
Upper Hambleton
WISBECH
A10
A47
SWAFFHAM
Stow Bardolph

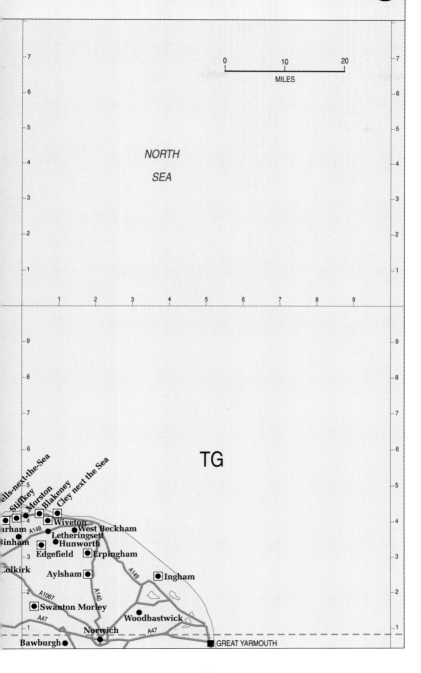

8

0   10   20
MILES

NORTH
SEA

7
6
5
4
3
2
1

1   2   3   4   5   6   7   8   9

9
8
7
6
5
4
3
2
1

TG

ells-next-the-Sea
Stiffkey
Morston
Blakeney
Cley next the Sea
Wiveton
West Beckham
arham
A148
Letheringsett
inham
Hunworth
Edgefield
Erpingham
Colkirk
Aylsham
Ingham
A149
A1067
A140
Swanton Morley
A47
Woodbastwick
Norwich
A47
Bawburgh
GREAT YARMOUTH

GIGHA

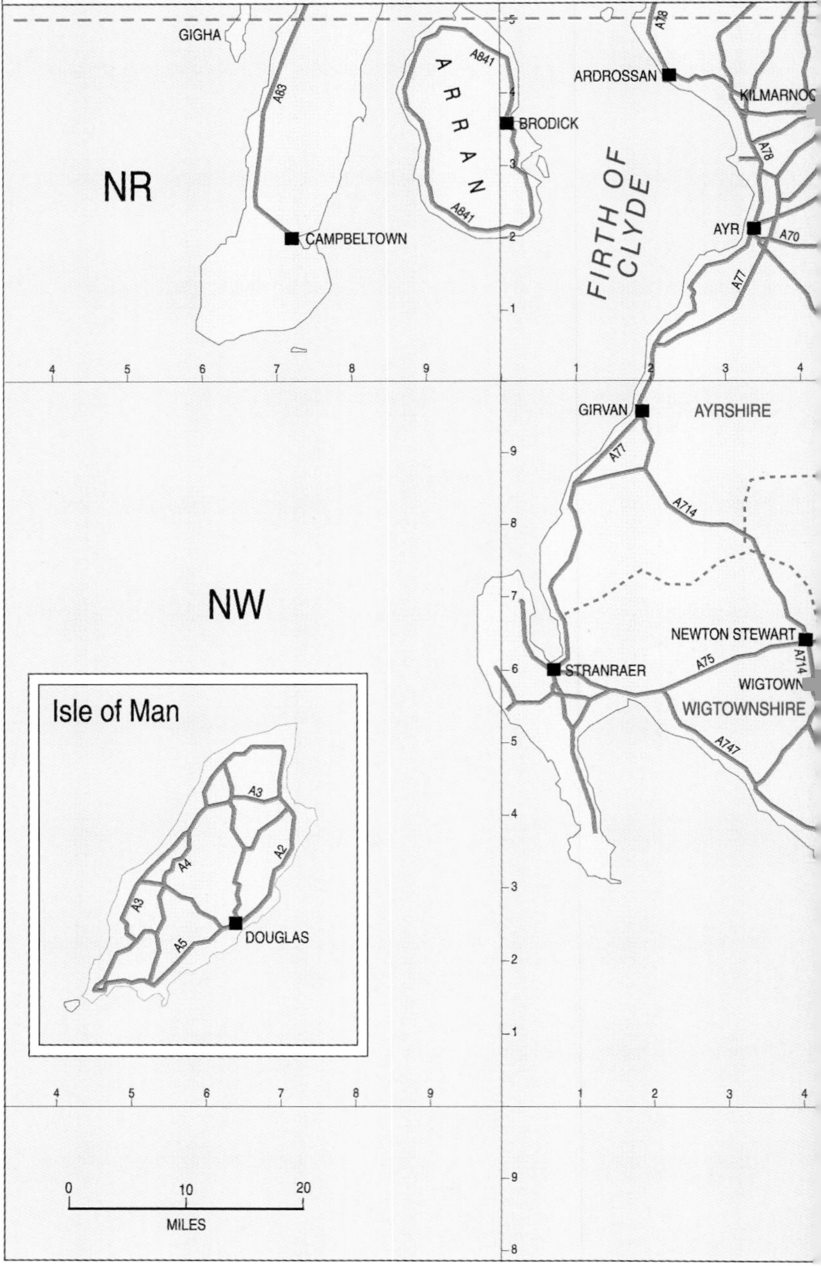

A83

A841

A R R A N

ARDROSSAN

KILMARNOC

NR

BRODICK

FIRTH OF CLYDE

A78

CAMPBELTOWN

A841

AYR

A70

A77

GIRVAN

AYRSHIRE

NW

A77

A714

NEWTON STEWART

A714

STRANRAER

A75

WIGTOWN

WIGTOWNSHIRE

A747

Isle of Man

A3

A4

A2

A3

A5

DOUGLAS

0   10   20

MILES

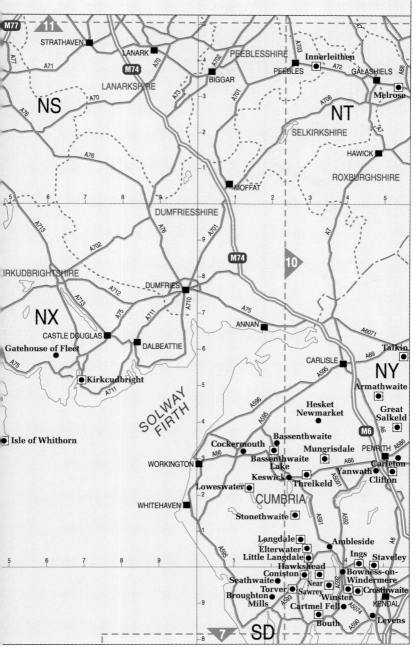

M77
11
STRATHAVEN
A71
A77
LANARK
M74
A70
A73
BIGGAR
NS
LANARKSHIRE
A70
A73
A76
A702
A701
PEEBLESSHIRE
A703
Innerleithen
PEEBLES
A72
GALASHIELS
A68
Melrose
NT
A708
SELKIRKSHIRE
A7
MOFFAT
HAWICK
ROXBURGHSHIRE
A76
A76
A701
DUMFRIESSHIRE
A76
A713
A702
M74
10
IRKUDBRIGHTSHIRE
A702
A712
DUMFRIES
A75
A7
NX
A713
A75
A711
A710
ANNAN
A75
A6071
Talkin
CASTLE DOUGLAS
DALBEATTIE
A75
A711
CARLISLE
A595
A69
NY
Gatehouse of Fleet
Kirkcudbright
Armathwaite
A596
Great
Salkeld
A6
SOLWAY
FIRTH
Hesket
Newmarket
A595
M6
A66
Cockermouth
Bassenthwaite
Mungrisdale
PENRITH
A686
Isle of Whithorn
A66
Bassenthwaite
Lake
A66
Carleton
WORKINGTON
Keswick
A591
Yanwath
A6
Threlkeld
Clifton
Loweswater
CUMBRIA
A591
A592
WHITEHAVEN
Stonethwaite
A595
Langdale
Ambleside
A6
Elterwater
Ings
Staveley
Little Langdale
Hawkshead
Bowness-on-
Coniston
Near
Windermere
Seathwaite
Sawrey
Crosthwaite
Torver
Winster
Broughton
Cartmel Fell
KENDAL
Mills
A590
A593
Bouth
A5074
Levens
7
SD
A590

10

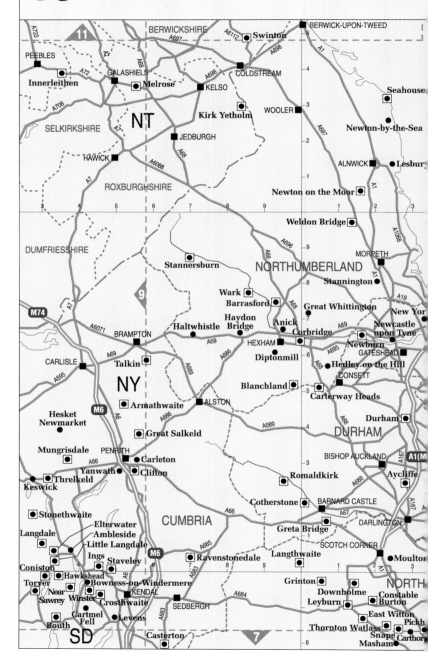

PEEBLES

Innerleithen

GALASHIELS

Melrose

KELSO

COLDSTREAM

BERWICK-UPON-TWEED

BERWICKSHIRE

Swinton

Kirk Yetholm

WOOLER

Seahouse

Newton-by-the-Sea

ALNWICK

Lesbur

SELKIRKSHIRE

NT

JEDBURGH

HAWICK

ROXBURGHSHIRE

Newton on the Moor

Weldon Bridge

DUMFRIESSHIRE

Stannersburn

NORTHUMBERLAND

MORPETH

Stannington

Wark

Barrasford

Haydon Bridge

Haltwhistle

Anick

Corbridge

Great Whittington

New Yor

Newcastle upon Tyne

BRAMPTON

HEXHAM

Newburn

GATESHEAD

CARLISLE

Talkin

NY

Diptonmill

Hedley on the Hill

CONSETT

Blanchland

Carterway Heads

Armathwaite

ALSTON

Durham

Hesket Newmarket

Great Salkeld

DURHAM

Mungrisdale

PENRITH

Carleton

BISHOP AUCKLAND

Aycliffe

Yanwath

Clifton

Threlkeld

Keswick

Romaldkirk

BARNARD CASTLE

DARLINGTON

Stonethwaite

Cotherstone

Langdale

Elterwater
Ambleside
Little Langdale

Ings

CUMBRIA

Greta Bridge

SCOTCH CORNER

Staveley

Coniston

Hawkshead

Ravenstonedale

Langthwaite

Moulton

Torver

Near
Sawrey

Bowness-on-Windermere

Winster

KENDAL

Grinton

NORTH

Crosthwaite

Downholme

Constable
Burton

Bouth

Cartmel
Fell

Levels

SEDBERGH

Leyburn

East Wilton

Pickh

SD

Casterton

Thornton Watlass

Snape

Carthor

Masham

10

NU

N O R T H

S E A

0   10   20

MILES

SOUTH SHIELDS

SUNDERLAND   NZ

HARTLEPOOL

MIDDLESBROUGH A174

A171

Whitby

Beck Hole   Robin Hood's Bay

A172   Osmotherley

ORKSHIRE   Blakey Ridge

SE   Fadmoor   Cropton

Appleton-le-Moors   Levisham

Kirkbymoorside   Sinnington

ndhutton   THIRSK   A170   Pickering

ldstead   Wass   Harome   A169

Ampleforth

TA

SCARBOROUGH

A170   A165

8

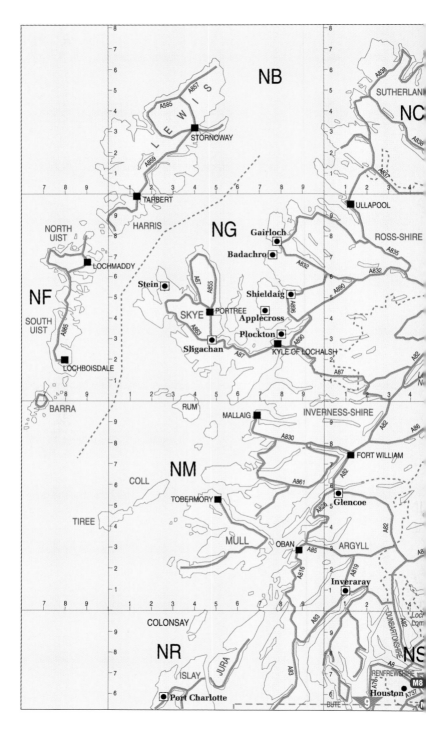

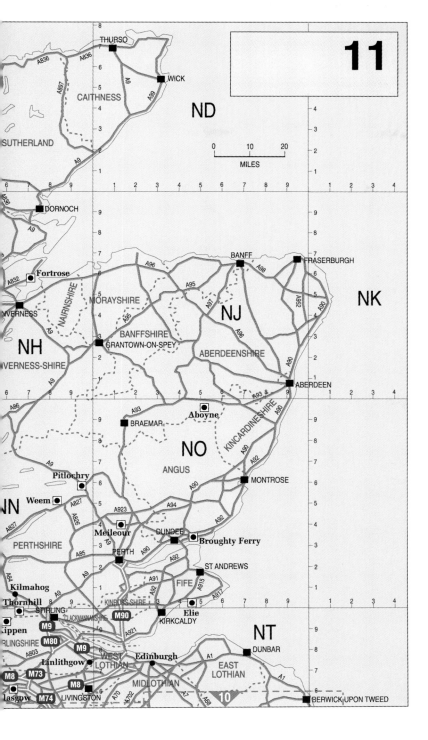

11

0   10   20
MILES

ND

NK

NJ

NH

NO

NT

THURSO
WICK
CAITHNESS
A836
A836
A897
A9
A99

SUTHERLAND
A9

DORNOCH

Fortrose
A832
INVERNESS
NAIRNSHIRE
MORAYSHIRE
A96
A95
BANFF
FRASERBURGH
A98
A952
A90
A97
A95
A9
A96
GRANTOWN-ON-SPEY
BANFFSHIRE
ABERDEENSHIRE
A90
ABERDEEN
INVERNESS-SHIRE
A86
A9
A93
KINCARDINESHIRE

Aboyne
BRAEMAR
A93
NO
ANGUS
A90
A92
MONTROSE
A9
Pitlochry
A90
Weem
A827
A826
A94
A92
A923
Meileour
DUNDEE
Broughty Ferry
PERTHSHIRE
A85
A9
PERTH
A90
A92
ST ANDREWS
A91
FIFE
A915
A84
Kilmahog
Thornhill
A917
STIRLING
KINROSS-SHIRE
Elie
CLACKMANNANSHIRE
M90
ippen
M9
KIRKCALDY
STIRLINGSHIRE
M80
A921
M9
DUNBAR
M8
M73
Linlithgow
WEST LOTHIAN
Edinburgh
A1
A803
lasgow
M74
M8
LIVINGSTON
MIDLOTHIAN
A70
A702
A7
A68
EAST LOTHIAN
A1
BERWICK UPON TWEED

10

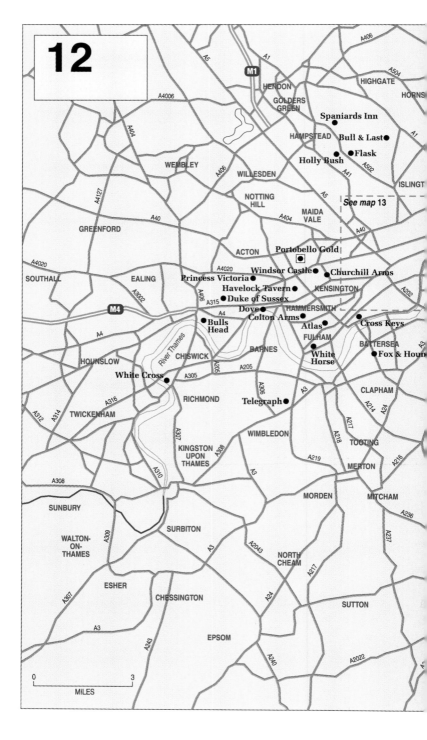

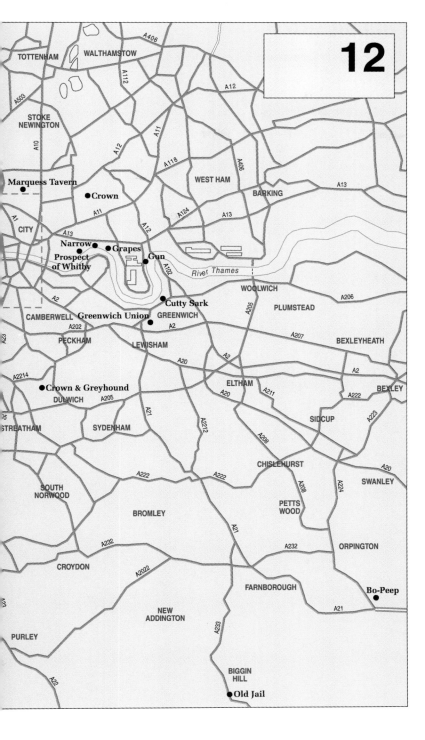

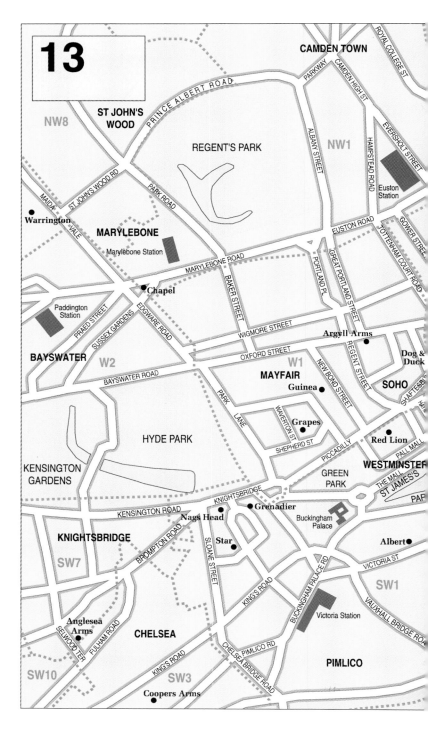

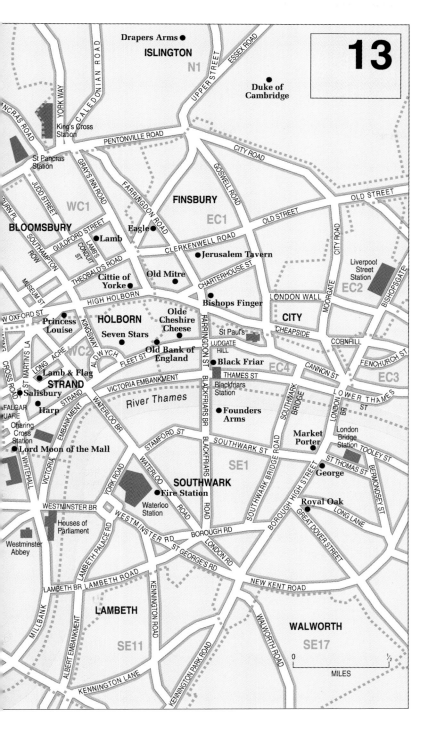

NEW – *THE GOOD PUB GUIDE* iPHONE APP

All of the knowledge and authority of *The Good Pub Guide* is now available on your iPhone!

Use the new *Good Pub Guide* iPhone application to search the 5,000 pubs recommended by the *Guide* – as well as details of over 40,000 other pubs across the country.

The iPhone's GPS capability means a single click will show you the good pubs nearest to you, highlighting those we recommend, with their position identified on clear maps. Simply read the *Good Pub Guide* reviews and head for your preferred selection!

Want to research where the best pubs are for your holiday, a weekend away or just for a Sunday afternoon? The app also allows you to search via place name, postcode or region, and lists the best pubs in the area.

Download the *Good Pub Guide* iPhone app via iTunes for only £5.99 or go to **www.thegoodpubguide.co.uk/iphone** for more details.

Also, look out for a new iPad application in the very near future...

HOW YOU CAN GET INVOLVED IN
THE GOOD PUB GUIDE WEBSITE

www.thegoodpubguide.co.uk

All pub and food reviews in this *Guide* appear on the site. However, we also want you to have your say. Register to tell us what you think about your favourite pubs – and your comments will help readers decide which pubs might suit them. Tell us if a pub is good for beer, food, accommodation, local walks or just has a cracking atmosphere. If other visitors to the website agree, it might be enough for the pub to become a *Good Pub Guide* recommendation next year!

We want licensees to get involved too – and the site allows them to add details about their own pubs for FREE, including recent photos, latest updates on facilities, guest ales, quiz nights, BBQs, beer festivals and any other pub events. So if you're a licensee, please sign up and add your pub details!

You can also register to receive our regular newsletter to get pub news and access to special offers, competitions and more.

LINK WITH US
As well as leaving comments on the website, look for us on Twitter (**twitter.com/goodpubguide**), Facebook and on your mobile phone as we open up more ways for you to be involved with *The Good Pub Guide*.

THE GOOD PUB GUIDE SAT NAV EDITION

In conjunction with Garmin, *The Good Pub Guide* is now available for your Sat Nav. Available as an SD card or download, it integrates quickly and easily into your Garmin Sat Nav and gives you access to over 5,000 pubs recommended in the 2011 *Guide*.

Search for Main Entry or Lucky Dip pubs (or both!) and have the Sat Nav direct you straight to the pub door. The perfect solution for finding your way to those hidden gems across the country.

For more details on this, and how you can buy it, go to
www.garmin.co.uk

seasonal guest on handpump and several wines by the glass; daily newspapers, piped music, a games machine, darts and cribbage. The pub is quietly set on a slope overlooking the village and has picnic-sets up on the side grass.

🍴 **Keenly priced, the generous home cooking might include sandwiches, soup, ploughman's, filled baked potatoes, local sausages and specials such as steak in ale pie, cod, pheasant casserole or haddock and prawns in a creamy cheese sauce.** *Starters/Snacks: £3.75 to £5.95. Main Courses: £6.50 to £9.50. Puddings: £2.50 to £3.75*

Harveys ~ Tenant Ashley Whitby ~ Real ale ~ Bar food (12-2.30) ~ (01342) 715416 ~ Children welcome away from bar ~ Dogs welcome ~ Live music in summer ~ Open 11-11; 12-10 (8 in winter) Sun

Recommended by N R White, Terry Buckland, John Branston, Mike Gorton, Colin and Louise English

VINES CROSS
TQ5917 MAP 3

Brewers Arms

Vines Cross Road of B2203 then left at T junction; 1 mile E of Horam; TN21 9EN

Bustling pub run by a chef/patron with interesting bar food, real ales and decent wines

This is a busy little pub with an enthusiastic landlord who holds live band and opera evenings. The sizeable public bar has some stools by the bar counter, quite a mix of dining chairs, benches and settles around wooden tables on the stripped floorboards and an informal atmosphere. The other three connecting rooms are similarly furnished; one has an open fire, another with red walls has one large table (just right for a large group of friends) and an end room has a woodburning stove in a brick fireplace. Church candles, lots of wall prints and helpful staff. Greene King Morlands Original and Old Speckled Hen and a guest beer on handpump and several wines by the glass. There are a few picnic-sets in front of the pub and pretty flower tubs. More reports please.

🍴 **When the landlord is cooking, the bar food is very good: sandwiches, soup, queen scallops, red onion tarte tatin, deep-fried squid, roast butternut squash risotto, king prawns with aioli, local sausages with champ potato, grilled lemon sole with brown nut butter, slow-cooked pork belly with mustard mash, calves liver with peppercorn jus and grilled rib-eye steak with triple-cooked chips.** *Starters/Snacks: £5.00 to £8.00. Main Courses: £9.00 to £17.00. Puddings: £4.95 to £6.50*

Greene King ~ Lease Tim Early ~ Real ale ~ Bar food (12-2.30(3.30 Sun), 6.30-9.30; not Sun evening) ~ (01435) 812288 ~ Children welcome ~ Dogs allowed in bar ~ Comedy evening last Mon of the month ~ Open 12-3, 6-11; 12-11(10 Sun) Sat; 12-3, 6-11 weekends in winter

Recommended by Mrs J Ekins-Daukes, Lesley Cooper

WARNINGLID
TQ2425 MAP 3

Half Moon 🍽

B2115 off A23 S of Handcross, or off B2110 Handcross—Lower Beeding – village is signposted; The Street; RH17 5TR

Good modern cooking in simply furnished pub with an informal chatty atmosphere, real ales, decent wines and seats in sizeable garden

This busy village pub remains a magnet locally for those who enjoy good food and drink. It's an 18th-c brick and stone building and has a good mix of customers – all of whom are welcomed by the friendly staff. The lively locals' bar has straightforward pubby furniture on the bare boards and a small victorian fireplace and a room just off here (the former kitchen) has oak beams and flagstones. A couple of steps lead down to the main bar which, again, is pretty unpretentious, with an informal chatty feel, plank panelling and bare brick, old photographs of the village and built-in cushioned wall settles and a mix of tables (all with candles and fresh flowers) on bare boards; there's another step down to a smaller carpeted area with big paintings. Harveys Best and changing guests like Dark Star Hophead and Over the Moon and Greene King Old Speckled Hen on handpump, several decent wines by the glass and a few malt whiskies. There are quite a few picnic-sets outside on the lawn in the sheltered, sizeable garden, which has a most spectacular avenue of trees, with uplighters that glow at night. No children inside.

🍴 Attractively presented and extremely popular, the carefully sourced bar food might include sandwiches, soup, moules marinière, oriental pork balls with sweet potato purée and star anise dressing, goats cheese ravioli with a lemon and chervil vinaigrette, home-cooked ham and egg, beef in ale suet pudding, fresh pasta with squash, toasted chilli, tomato and cheese with basil pesto, beer-battered fresh cod, calves liver and smoked bacon with jus and wilted spinach, and puddings like hazelnut brittle parfait with bitter chocolate purée and coffee foam and lemon meringue pie with raspberry coulis. *Starters/Snacks: £5.50 to £7.50. Main Courses: £9.00 to £15.00. Puddings: £6.00 to £6.50*

Free house ~ Licensees John Lea and James Amico ~ Real ale ~ Bar food (not Sun evening) ~ Restaurant ~ (01444) 461227 ~ Dogs allowed in bar ~ Open 11.30-2.30, 5.30-11; 11.30-11 Sat; 12-10.30 Sun

Recommended by Terry Buckland, Susan and Neil McLean, N R White, Brian Dawes, Pat and John Carter, Ian Wilson, Martin and Karen Wake, Andy and Claire Barker

WARTLING
TQ6509   MAP 3
Lamb ♀
Village signposted with Herstmonceux Castle off A271 Herstmonceux—Battle; BN27 1RY

Friendly country pub, comfortable seating areas, cosy little bar, changing real ales, popular bar food and seats on pretty back terrace

With three log fires, this friendly family-owned pub is just the place to head for in winter. There's a little entrance bar with a couple of tables and this leads through to the beamed and timbered snug (mind your head on the low entrance beam) with comfortable leather sofas and some wooden chairs and tables. Harveys Best and Sharps Doom Bar on handpump and ten wines by the glass. The golden retriever is called Freddie. There's a separate restaurant with the same menu as the bar. Up some steps at the back of the building, there are seats on a pretty, flower-filled terrace. More reports please.

🍴 As well as daily specials, the well liked bar food includes toasties, ploughman's, soup, chicken and mushroom pâté, toasted muffin with a poached egg and smoked salmon with a light curry cream, a pie of the day with thyme pastry, home-made burger with various toppings, free-range chicken with a chestnut, wild mushroom and marsala cream sauce, seafood platter, and puddings such as orange and Cointreau cheesecake and chocolate and hazelnut crème brûlée. *Starters/Snacks: £4.25 to £8.95. Main Courses: £8.95 to £17.95. Puddings: £4.95*

Free house ~ Licensees Robert and Alison Farncombe ~ Real ale ~ Bar food (12-2.15, 7-9; 12-2.30 Sun; not Sun evening or Mon) ~ Restaurant ~ (01323) 832116 ~ Children welcome away from bar ~ Dogs allowed in bar ~ Open 11-3, 6-11; 12-3 Sun; closed Sun evening and Mon

Recommended by M G Hart, Mr and Mrs R A Saunders, John Atkins, Mrs Mary Woods, C and R Bromage

WEST HOATHLY
TQ3632   MAP 3
Cat 🛏
Village signposted from A22 and B2028 S of East Grinstead; North Lane; RH19 4PP

Popular 16th-c inn with old-fashioned bar, airy dining rooms, real ales, good food and seats outside; lovely bedrooms

New licensees have taken over this bustling 16th-c tile-hung inn and reports from readers are warmly enthusiastic. There's a lovely old bar with beams, proper pubby tables and chairs on the old wooden floor, a fine log fire in the inglenook fireplace, Dark Star Hophead and Harveys Best and Old on handpump and several wines by the glass; look out for a glass cover over the 75-foot deep well. The dining rooms are light and airy with a nice mix of wooden dining chairs and tables on the pale wood-strip flooring and throughout there are hops, china platters, brass and copper ornaments and a gently upmarket atmosphere. The contemporary-style garden room has glass doors that open on to a terrace with teak furniture. This is a comfortable and enjoyable place to stay (some of the rooms overlook the church) and the breakfasts are very good. The Bluebell Railway is nearby.

⊞ **Cooked by the landlord, the enjoyable food includes lunchtime sandwiches and ploughman's, soup, locally smoked ham and egg, goats cheese, caramelised onion, spinach and roast tomato tart, minted lamb pudding, steak and mushroom in ale pie, beer-battered fish and chips, daily specials such as braised ham hock terrine with home-made piccalilli, cheeseburger with fries and calves liver and bacon with a red wine sauce, and puddings like lemon and lime cheesecake with passion-fruit jelly and champagne sorbet and bread and butter pudding with custard; Sunday roasts.** *Starters/Snacks: £6.00 to £7.50. Main Courses: £9.00 to £18.00. Puddings: £5.50*

Free house ~ Licensees Ian Huxley and Andrew Russell ~ Real ale ~ Bar food (12-2(3 Sun), 6-9(9.30 Fri and Sat); not Sun evening) ~ (01342) 810369 ~ Children welcome if over 7 ~ Dogs allowed in bar ~ Open 12-3, 6-11; 12-4 Sun; closed Sun evening, Mon ~ Bedrooms: £75B/£100B

Recommended by JMM, Terry Buckland, John Branston, Peter Meister, Nick Lawless, Roger and Diana Morgan

WILMINGTON
TQ5404 MAP 3

Giants Rest
Just off A27; BN26 5SQ

Busy country pub with friendly welcome from cheerful landlord, informal atmosphere, tasty bar food and real ales; bedrooms

This busy Victorian pub is surrounded by fine walks up on the South Downs and the village is famous for the huge chalk-carved figure of the Long Man of Wilmington. At weekends when the pub is open all day, there are plenty of walkers crowding in for a drink or a meal – it's best to book a table then. The long wood-floored bar and adjacent open areas have simple chairs and tables, lots of wooden puzzles and board games, an open fire and a nice informal atmosphere. Harveys Best, Hop Back Summer Lightning and Timothy Taylors Landlord on handpump; piped music. There are plenty of seats in the front garden.

⊞ **Quite a choice of bar food might include ploughman's, filled baked potatoes, soup, baked field mushroom with pesto, tomato and goats cheese, hake, coriander and ginger fishcakes, sausages with bubble and squeak, sweet potato, spinach and peanut stew, rabbit and bacon pie, cajun-style chicken and tiger prawns, daily specials, and puddings like chocolate crêpes with chantilly cream and Grand Marnier oranges and passion fruit.** *Starters/Snacks: £4.00 to £8.50. Main Courses: £9.50 to £13.50. Puddings: £3.50*

Free house ~ Licensees Adrian and Rebecca Hillman ~ Real ale ~ Bar food (12-2, 6-9; all day Sat, Sun and bank hols) ~ (01323) 870207 ~ Children welcome ~ Dogs welcome ~ Open 11-3, 6-11; 11-11 Sat ~ Bedrooms: /£60

Recommended by Jean and Douglas Troup, Evelyn and Derek Walter, John Beeken, Laurence Smith, Ian and Barbara Rankin, Jenny and Peter Lowater

WINEHAM
TQ2320 MAP 3

Royal Oak
Village signposted from A272 and B2116; BN5 9AY

Splendidly old-fashioned local with interesting bric-a-brac in simple rooms, attentive staff, real ales and well liked food

Always busy with cheerful regulars and their dogs, this is an old-fashioned and unchanging local. As well as a blazing log fire in an enormous inglenook fireplace with its cast-iron Royal Oak fireback, there's a collection of cigarette boxes, a stuffed stoat and crocodile and some jugs and ancient corkscrews on the very low beams above the serving counter. Other bits of bric-a-brac too, views of quiet countryside from the back parlour and a bearded collie called Bella. Harveys Best and a couple of guests such as Dark Star Hophead and Sussex Extra Stout tapped from the cask in a still room and 20 wines by the glass. There are some picnic-sets outside – picturesque if you are facing the pub.

🍽 **Honest bar food includes good value sandwiches, ploughman's, soup, soft herring roes on toast, wild mushroom and goats cheese risotto, king prawns with tomato, saffron and fennel linguine, cottage pie, local sausages with cider and onion gravy, and puddings like treacle tart and banoffi pie.** *Starters/Snacks: £4.95 to £7.25. Main Courses: £7.95 to £16.95. Puddings: £4.95 to £6.75*

Punch ~ Tenants Sharon and Michael Bailey ~ Real ale ~ Bar food (12-2.30(3 Sun), 7-9.30; not Sun evening) ~ (01444) 881252 ~ Children welcome away from bar area ~ Dogs welcome ~ Open 11-2.30(3.30 Sat), 5.30(6 Sat)-11; 12-4, 7-10.30 Sun

Recommended by Terry Buckland, Neil Hardwick, the Didler, David and Pam Wilcox, Conor McGaughey, Donna and Roger, Ian Phillips

LUCKY DIP

Besides the fully inspected pubs, you might like to try these Lucky Dips recommended to us and described by readers (if you do, please send us reports: feedback@goodguides.com).

ALFRISTON [TQ5203]
☆ *Olde Smugglers* BN26 5UE [Waterloo Sq]: Charming 14th-c pub, low beams and panelling, brick floor, huge inglenook, masses of bric-a-brac and smuggling mementos, welcoming licensees, wide range of good value bar food from sandwiches up, well kept Dark Star, Harveys and a guest like Sharps Doom Bar, real cider, good choice of wines by the glass; can get crowded – lovely village draws many visitors; children in eating area and conservatory, dogs welcome, tables on well planted back suntrap terrace *(LYM, N R White, Pam Adsley, Bruce Bird, MP, John Beeken, Eddie Edwards, Ann and Colin Hunt)*
Star BN26 5TA [High St]: Fascinating fine painted medieval carvings outside, heavy-beamed old-fashioned bar (busy lunchtime, quiet evenings) with some interesting features inc medieval sanctuary post, antique furnishings and big log fire in Tudor fireplace, easy chairs in comfortable lounge, more space behind for eating; some 35 good modern bedrooms in up-to-date part behind, open all day summer *(the Didler, Tina and David Woods-Taylor, LYM)*
AMBERLEY [TQ0211]
Bridge BN18 9LR [B2139]: Popular open-plan dining pub, comfortable and relaxed even when busy, with welcoming staff, pleasant bar and separate two-room dining area, decent range of reasonably priced food from good sandwiches up, well kept ales inc Harveys; children and dogs welcome, seats out in front, more tables in side garden, open all day *(N R White, LYM)*
☆ *Sportsmans* BN18 9NR [Crossgates; Rackham Rd, off B2139]: Warmly welcoming licensees and friendly efficient young staff, good fairly priced food inc popular Sun roasts, well kept Dark Star, Harveys and guests, three bars inc brick-floored one with darts, great views

over Amberley Wild Brooks from pretty back conservatory restaurant and tables outside; dogs welcome, good walks, neat up-to-date bedrooms *(LYM, Bruce Bird, N R White, LM)*
ANGMERING [TQ0604]
Lamb BN16 4EQ [The Square]: Village pub doing enjoyable reasonably priced blackboard food (not Sun evening), up to four ales inc Wells & Youngs Best, friendly landlord, big fireplace; back terrace *(Tony and Wendy Hobden)*
☆ *Spotted Cow* BN16 4AW [High St]: Good interesting sensibly priced food (very popular wkdy lunchtimes with older people) from sandwiches up, friendly and enthusiastic chef/landlord, good friendly service, well kept ales such as Black Sheep, Fullers, Greene King and Harveys, good wines by the glass, smallish bar on left, long dining extension with large conservatory on right, two log fires, smuggling history, sporting caricatures, no piped music; children welcome, disabled access, big garden with boules and play area, lovely walk to Highdown hill fort, open all day Sun (afternoon jazz sometimes then) *(Tony and Wendy Hobden, CP, Pam Adsley, Terry Buckland, Mike and Sue Shirley)*
ANSTY [TQ2923]
Ansty Cross Inn RH17 5AG [Cuckfield Rd (A272)]: Extended pub with young friendly staff, local ales such as Harveys, good choice of wines by the glass, enjoyable food (not Sun evening) from doorstep sandwiches up, inglenook log fire, restaurant *(Neil Hardwick, Tony and Wendy Hobden)*
APULDRAM [SU8401]
Crouchers PO20 7EH [Birdham Rd (A269)]: Converted farmhouse and outbuildings, large bar, good reliable food, pleasant staff, restaurant; bedrooms *(Miss A E Dare)*
ARDINGLY [TQ3430]
☆ *Gardeners Arms* RH17 6TJ [B2028 2 miles N]: Reliable reasonably priced pub food in

olde-worlde linked rooms, Badger beers, pleasant efficient service, daily papers, standing timbers and inglenooks, scrubbed pine on flagstones and broad boards, old local photographs, mural in back part; children and dogs welcome, disabled facilities, attractive wooden furniture on pretty terrace, lots of picnic-sets in side garden, opp S of England Show ground and handy for Borde Hill and Wakehurst Place, open all day *(Susan and John Douglas, Colin and Louise English, LM, BB)*

ARLINGTON [TQ5407]

Yew Tree BN26 6RX [off A22 nr Hailsham, or A27 W of Polegate]: Neatly modernised Victorian village pub popular for its wide range of generous home-made food (you can ask for smaller helpings), Harveys Best and decent wines, log fires, prompt friendly service even when busy, darts in thriving bare-boards bar, plush lounge, comfortable conservatory; children welcome, good big garden with play area, paddock with farm animals, good walks *(BB, MP, John Beeken, Pam Adsley)*

ARUNDEL [TQ0208]

☆ *Black Rabbit* BN18 9PB [Mill Rd; Offham; keep on and don't give up!]: Nicely refurbished busy riverside pub well organised for families, lovely spot nr wildfowl reserve with timeless views of water meadows and castle; long bar with eating areas either end, enjoyable fairly priced pub food all day from nice baguettes up, well kept Badger ales, several decent wines by the glass, good friendly young staff, log fires; piped music; dogs welcome, covered tables and pretty hanging baskets out at front, terrace across road overlooking river, play area, good walks, open all day *(John Beeken, LM, Colin McKerrow, N R White, David H T Dimock, Gene and Kitty Rankin, LYM)*

☆ *Swan* BN18 9AG [High St]: Smart but comfortably relaxed open-plan L-shaped bar with attractive woodwork and matching fittings, friendly efficient young staff, well kept Fullers ales, good tea and coffee, good value enjoyable food from baguettes up, sporting bric-a-brac and old photographs, beaten brass former inn sign on wall, fire, restaurant, live jazz (3rd Sun from 5pm); 15 good bedrooms, open all day *(LYM, Tony and Wendy Hobden, B and M Kendall, Jude Wright)*

BEPTON [SU8620]

Country Inn GU29 0LR [Severals Rd]: Old-fashioned friendly country local, well kept Ballards Midhurst, Black Sheep, Fullers London Pride and Wells & Youngs Bitter, good value food, log fire, heavy beams and stripped brickwork, darts-playing regulars; tables out at front and in big garden with shady trees and play area, quiet spot *(John Beeken, Tony and Wendy Hobden)*

BEXHILL [TQ7208]

Denbigh TN39 4JE [Little Common Rd (A259 towards Polegate)]: Friendly local with enjoyable freshly prepared food, well

kept Harveys Best, decent wine, cheery efficient service; enclosed side garden *(MP)*

BILLINGSHURST [TQ0830]

☆ *Blue Ship* RH14 9BS [The Haven; hamlet signposted off A29 just N of junction with A264, then follow signpost left towards Garlands and Okehurst]: Unspoilt pub in quiet country spot with good friendly landlord, beamed and brick-floored front bar, scrubbed tables and wall benches, blazing inglenook log fire, Badger ales served from hatch, good value home-made traditional food (not Sun or Mon evenings), two small carpeted back rooms, darts, bar billiards, shove-ha'penny, cribbage, dominoes, no mobile phones; children and dogs welcome, seats by trees or tangle of clematis around front door, local produce for sale *(the Didler, C and R Bromage, LYM)*

Limeburners RH14 9JA [Lordings Rd, Newbridge (B2133/A272 W)]: converted from a row of cottages; Fullers; sympathetic refurbishment, opening up the bars; open fire; outside it's had a fresh coat of paint and there's a pleasant front garden area *(Terry and Nickie Williams)*

BODLE STREET GREEN [TQ6514]

White Horse BN27 4RE [off A271 at Windmill Hill]: Roomy country pub with friendly landlord, enjoyable homely food at varnished tables, well kept Harveys, open fires; some tables outside *(R and S Bentley, BB)*

BOGNOR REGIS [SZ9298]

Navigator PO21 2QA [Marine Drive W]: Good value pubby food in picture-window seafront dining area, Greene King, good staff, lively local atmosphere in carpeted bar; comfortable bedrooms, some with sea view *(Terry and Nickie Williams, David H T Dimock)*

Ship PO21 3AP [Aldwick St]: Popular under newish management, enjoyable food, good range of ales and wines, pleasant staff, pool and TV in separate bar; dogs welcome *(David H T Dimock)*

BOLNEY [TQ2622]

Eight Bells RH17 5QW [The Street]: Wide food choice from ciabattas and light dishes up inc bargain OAP lunch Tues and Weds, well kept Harveys and an ale brewed for the pub, local wines from Bookers vineyard, good log fire, dining extension, exemplary lavatories; tables on outside decking with neatly lit steps *(Michael and Margaret Cross, Tony and Wendy Hobden)*

BRIGHTON [TQ3104]

Colonnade BN1 1UF [New Rd, off North St; by Theatre Royal]: Small richly restored Edwardian bar, with red plush banquettes, velvet swags, shining brass and mahogany, gleaming mirrors, interesting pre-war playbills and lots of signed theatrical photographs, well kept Fullers London Pride and Harveys Best, lots of lagers, bar snacks, daily papers; tiny front terrace overlooking Pavilion gardens *(Val and Alan Green, Ian Phillips, BB)*

☆ *Evening Star* BN1 3PB [Surrey St]: Popular chatty pub with up to four good Dark Star ales (originally brewed here), lots of changing guest beers inc continentals (in bottles too), farm ciders and perries, country wines, good lunchtime baguettes (rolls Sun), friendly staff coping well when busy, simple pale wood furniture on bare boards, nice mix of customers; unobtrusive piped music, some live; pavement tables, open all day *(the Didler, N R White, Ian Phillips, BB)*

Foragers BN3 3YU [3 Stirling Place, Hove]: Relaxed Victorian pub doing some unusual food (not Sun evening) inc game and locally foraged produce, interesting wines and spirits, comedy night (last Tues of month), DJ nights Fri and Sat; picnic-sets out at front, garden behind *(Tim Loryman)*

George BN1 4EQ [Trafalgar St]: Three linked rooms (front ones are best) off main bar, mix of furnishings on stripped floor, several big mirrors and nice etchings, good mix of customers, well kept beers such as Harveys and Shepherd Neame, lots of wines by the glass, freshly squeezed fruit juice, inexpensive popular organic and vegetarian/vegan food all day, helpful staff, daily papers, juke box; children welcome, small heated back courtyard *(Jo Connelly, Jeremy King)*

Lord Nelson BN1 4ED [Trafalgar St]: Two-room backstreet local with well kept Harveys, cider and perry, good value food inc pizzas and pasta, log fire, back conservatory; open all day *(the Didler)*

Sussex Cricketer BN3 3AF [Eaton Rd, Hove, by cricket ground]: Ember Inn with welcoming layout and comfortable sofas, enjoyable reasonably priced standard food all day from baguettes up inc two-for-one deals, eight real ales, decent wines by the glass, friendly efficient service *(Tony and Wendy Hobden)*

BUCKS GREEN [TQ0733]

Fox RH12 3JP [Guildford Rd (A281 W of Rudgwick)]: Ancient open-plan inglenook bar with good-sized restaurant specialising in good generous fish, takeaways available too, Badger beers, decent wines by the glass, welcoming efficient service, darts; garden with play area *(Brian and Anna Marsden)*

BURWASH [TQ6724]

Bell TN19 7EH [High St (A265)]: Pretty tile-hung pub with friendly local atmosphere, interesting farming bric-a-brac and good log fire, Harveys and a guest, decent house wines, good choice of sensibly priced blackboard food inc fish, cosy dining room, traditional pub games; piped music, TV; children and dogs welcome, disabled access, roadside picnic-sets facing Norman church, charming village, open all day *(Richard Mason, Hugh Bower, LYM)*

Rose & Crown TN19 7ER [inn sign on A265]: Welcoming low-beamed timbered local tucked away down lane in pretty village, enjoyable food, well kept Harveys, decent wines, inglenook log fire in bar, pleasant restaurant area with woodburner, good service, glass covered well; tables out in small quiet garden, bedrooms *(BB, John Atkins)*

BURWASH WEALD [TQ6523]

Wheel TN19 7LA [A265 Burwash—Heathfield]: Tidy open-plan pub with comfortable sofas and good inglenook log fire, well kept Harveys and other ales, good choice of decent food, dining room leading out to garden; tables on sunny front terrace too, lovely walks in valley opposite *(BB, Conrad Freezer)*

CATSFIELD [TQ7213]

White Hart TN33 9DJ [B2204, off A269; The Green]: Welcoming and friendly white weatherboarded pub, good home cooking at reasonable prices, well kept Harveys, warm log fire, raftered dining room with assorted tables; some seats out at front, fenced side garden, good walks *(Roger and Pauline Pearce)*

CHICHESTER [SU8605]

Bell PO19 6AT [Broyle Rd opp Festival Theatre]: Friendly and comfortable country-pub feel, good interesting changing real ales and wines, generous reasonably priced food from separate counter inc good vegetarian choices, early evening meals for theatre-goers, efficient service even when busy, bric-a-brac on high beams, theatre posters, daily papers, darts and cribbage; Sun quiz night, piped music in bar, games machines; children and dogs welcome, disabled access, pleasant partly covered heated back terrace, cl Sun till 7pm *(Val and Alan Green, N R White, Tony and Wendy Hobden, Bruce Bird, Chris Glasson)*

Fountain PO19 1ES [Southgate]: Attractive two-room front bar, small dining room behind incorporating part of Roman wall, wide choice of enjoyable pubby food, friendly helpful staff, Badger beers, live music; children and dogs welcome, courtyard tables, open all day *(Alec Summers)*

Old Cross PO19 1LP [North St]: Refurbished open-plan pub in partly 16th-c building, bargain pubby food inc pre theatre wkdy evening deals, friendly helpful staff, Ringwood Best and Wells & Youngs Bombardier, log fires *(Alec Summers, Ann and Colin Hunt, Irene and Derek Flewin)*

Wests PO19 1QU [West St]: Former church nicely converted into Marstons pub, multi-level seating around big central bar, decent good value food inc children's menu and deals, good choice of wines by the glass, friendly prompt staff; piped music; opp cathedral, open all day *(Mayur Shah)*

CHIDHAM [SU7804]

☆ **Old House At Home** PO18 8SU [off A259 at Barleycorn pub in Nutbourne; Cot Lane]: Gently updated neat cottagey pub, good friendly service from smart staff, good food especially local fish, four real ales, decent wines, log fire, low beams and timbering; children in eating areas, tables outside, remote unspoilt farm-hamlet location, nearby walks by Chichester Harbour, open all day wknds *(Tony and Wendy Hobden, LYM, Joan and Tony Walker, Ann and Colin Hunt)*

CHILGROVE [SU8214]
Fish House PO18 9HX [B2141 Petersfield—
Chichester]: Upmarket fish restaurant/hotel
but welcoming drinkers; light and airy
beamed bar with old irish marble-topped
counter, antique french fireplace and chunky
teak furniture on oak boards, Black Sheep,
Harveys and Timothy Taylors Landlord,
expensive bar and restaurant food, oyster
bar, large fish tank with view through to
kitchen; piped music; children and dogs
welcome, disabled facilities, terrace tables
and garden, 15 luxury bedrooms, open all
day *(Miss A E Dare, LYM)*
CLAPHAM [TQ1105]
Coach & Horses BN13 3UA [Arundel Rd
(A27 Worthing—Arundel)]: Informally smart
18th-c coaching inn, well cooked good value
food, nice wines by the glass, Courage and
Harveys Best; piped music, pool; children
welcome, tables on sundeck, play area
(Tony and Wendy Hobden)
CLAYTON [TQ2914]
☆ *Jack & Jill* BN6 9PD [Brighton Rd (A273)]:
Friendly unsmart three-room country pub
doing good interesting food among more
pubby choices, nice local cheeseboard, well
kept Harviestoun Bitter & Twisted and
Shepherd Neame Bishops Finger, good wine,
plush wall seats and dark pubby furniture,
flowers on tables, rural memorabilia, log fire
in brick fireplace; children and dogs welcome,
picnic-sets in big back garden with play area,
landmark twin windmills nearby, bedrooms
*(Fr Robert Marsh, Mary M Grimshaw,
Terry and Nickie Williams, Edward Pearce, BB,
Martin Gillard)*
COCKING CAUSEWAY [SU8819]
Greyhound GU29 9QH [A286 Cocking—
Midhurst]: Pretty tile-hung 18th-c pub with
enjoyable home-made food (should book
wknds), four ales such as Ballards Nyewood
Gold, Hop Back Summer Lightning, Skinners
Betty Stogs and Wychwood Hobgoblin,
friendly prompt service, cosy olde-worlde
beamed and panelled bar with log fire, pine
furniture in big new dining conservatory;
grassed area at front, big garden with play
area behind *(Tony and Wendy Hobden,
Aimie O'Donnell, John Beeken)*
COLDWALTHAM [TQ0216]
Labouring Man RH20 1LF [pub signed down
lane off A29 about 2 miles S of Pulborough]:
Refurbished but retaining village pub
atmosphere, welcoming landlord and staff,
enjoyable food from snacks up (gluten-free
diets catered for), three well kept ales such
as Ringwood, Harveys and Sharps, log fires;
quiet piped music; children and dogs
welcome, five comfortable downs-view
bedrooms, cl Mon lunchtimes
(Tony and Wendy Hobden, Bruce Bird)
COLEMANS HATCH [TQ4533]
☆ *Hatch* TN7 4EJ [signed off B2026, or off
B2110 opp church]: Quaint and attractive
little weatherboarded Ashdown Forest pub
dating from 1430, big log fire in quickly
filling beamed bar, small back dining room

with another fire, very wide choice of good
generous home-made food, well kept Harveys,
Larkins and one or two guest beers, friendly
quick young staff, good mix of customers inc
families and dogs; not much parking so get
there early; picnic-sets on front terrace and in
beautifully kept big garden, open all day Sun
and summer Sat *(the Didler, Vernon Rowe,
LYM, Terry Buckland)*
COOKSBRIDGE [TQ4014]
Rainbow BN8 4SS [junction A275 with
Cooksbridge and Newick rd]: Attractive
18th-c flint dining pub, good interesting if
not cheap food from sandwiches and snacks
up, also set deals, efficient friendly service,
good choice of wines, well kept Harveys
Best, small bar well used by locals, stylish
restaurant, log fires; children welcome,
tables out under parasols, summer
barbecues, open all day wknds *(anon)*
COUSLEY WOOD [TQ6533]
☆ *Old Vine* TN5 6ER [B2100 Wadhurst—
Lamberhurst]: Uncluttered bare-boards linked
rooms, open timbering and heavy beams,
pine and dark wooden cushioned dining
chairs around a mix of pale wooden tables, a
few settles, large fireplace with winter log
fire, good lighting, well kept Harveys from
attractive bar counter with Farrow & Ball
paintwork, good food and wine, friendly if
not always prompt service, white carpeted
restaurant; dogs welcome, seats on terrace
(BB, Don Mitchell)
COWBEECH [TQ6114]
☆ *Merrie Harriers* BN27 4JQ [off A271]: White
clapboarded village local under new
ownership, beamed public bar with
inglenook log fire, high-backed settle and
mixed tables and chairs, old local
photographs, carpeted lounge, well kept
Harveys Best and a guest, good food from
nice bar snacks up, friendly service, brick-
walled back restaurant; a few picnic-sets out
in front, rustic seats in terraced garden with
country views *(LYM, Laurence Smith,
Peter Meister)*
COWFOLD [TQ2122]
Coach House RH13 8BT [Horsham Rd]:
Smart, comfortable and welcoming, with
enjoyable food inc some lunchtime and early
evening bargains, Harveys Best and Sharps
Doom Bar, good coffee and service,
attractive traditional main bar, settees by
log fire, roomy neatly laid restaurant area,
locals' bar (no children) with darts and pool;
dogs welcome, lovely garden with terrace
and play area, 13 bedrooms (nine in
converted stables), open all day from
7.30am *(David H T Dimock, Ann and
Colin Hunt, Tony and Wendy Hobden)*
CRAWLEY DOWN [TQ3437]
Dukes Head RH10 4HH [A264/A2028]:
Smartly refurbished with large lounge bar
and three differently styled dining areas,
log fires, good choice of food all day inc
fixed-price menu; seats out at the front,
handy for Gatwick *(Mrs Margo Finlay,
Jörg Kasprowski)*

CROWBOROUGH [TQ5130]
Blue Anchor TN6 1BB [Beacon Rd (A26)]:
Shepherd Neame pub improved under friendly
newish landlord, their ales kept well,
enjoyable home-made food at fair prices;
garden with play area *(Peter Meister)*

CUCKFIELD [TQ3025]
Rose & Crown RH17 5BS [London Rd]:
Tile-hung and festooned with summer
flowers, central bar flanked by open plan
rooms, low 17th-c beams and panelling,
simple furnishings, open fire, good choice of
enjoyable generous home-made food from
sandwiches and baked potatoes up, cheerful
chatty staff, Badger ales and a guest such as
Harveys, good range of wines by the glass;
dogs allowed – but ask, tables out in front
and in garden behind, open all day
(Terry Buckland)

DALLINGTON [TQ6619]
☆ *Swan* TN21 9LB [Woods Corner, B2096 E]:
Popular local with cheerful chatty
atmosphere, well kept Harveys, decent wines
by the glass, enjoyable pubby food inc deals,
takeaway fish and chips (Tues), efficient
service, bare-boards bar divided by standing
timbers, woodburner, mixed furniture inc
cushioned settle and high-backed pew,
candles in bottles and fresh flowers, simple
back restaurant with far-reaching views to
the coast; piped music; steps down to
lavatories and smallish back garden *(BB,
N R White, Mike and Eleanor Anderson)*

DANEHILL [TQ4128]
☆ *Coach & Horses* RH17 7JF [off A275, via
School Lane towards Chelwood Common]:
Well run dining pub in attractive
countryside, good restauranty food (not Sun
evening) served with style, well kept
Harveys, good wines by the glass, little
hatch-served public bar with small
woodburner and simple furniture on polished
boards, main bar with big Victorian prints,
attractive old tables and fine brick floor,
dining extension, home-made chutneys and
jams for sale; may try to keep your credit
card while you eat outside; children and
dogs welcome (nice pub dog), lovely views
from big attractive garden with terrace
under huge maple *(Alan Cowell,
Mr and Mrs R A Bradbrook, LYM)*

DELL QUAY [SU8302]
Crown & Anchor PO20 7EE [off A286 S of
Chichester – look out for small sign]:
Modernised 19th/20th-c beamed pub in
splendid spot overlooking Chichester Harbour
– best at high tide and quiet times, can be
packed on sunny days when staff may
struggle; comfortable bow-windowed lounge
bar, panelled public bar (dogs welcome), two
log fires, lots of wines by the glass, four
Wells & Youngs ales, food all day; terrace,
nice walks *(Kevin Flack, J Stickland, Terry and
Nickie Williams, Ann and Colin Hunt, BB)*

DENTON [TQ4502]
☆ *Flying Fish* BN9 0QB [Denton Rd]: Attractive
17th-c flint village pub by South Downs Way,
floor tiles throughout, simple main bar, tiny

end room with facing sofas, nice middle
room with little log fire by built-in wall
seats, long cushioned pews and mixed dining
chairs, modern paintings, high-ceilinged end
dining room, Shepherd Neame ales, decent
wines by the glass, friendly service, fish and
game and more pubby food cooked by french
chef/landlord, reasonable prices; picnic-sets
in front and on long back decking looking up
to sloping garden, good bedrooms *(BB,
John Beeken, the Didler)*

DITCHLING [TQ3215]
☆ *Bull* BN6 8TA [High St (B2112)]: Handsome
rambling old building, beams, old wooden
furniture on bare boards, fire, well kept
Harveys, Timothy Taylors Landlord and two
guests, home-made food from sandwiches up
inc good Sun roasts, nicely furnished dining
rooms with mellow décor and candles, snug
area with chesterfields; piped music – live
folk last Sun of month; children welcome,
dogs in bar, disabled access, attractive big
garden and suntrap terrace, barbecue, four
nice bedrooms, good breakfast, open all day
(LYM, Nick Lawless, Andy and Claire Barker)
White Horse BN6 8TS [West St]: Chatty local
atmosphere, well kept Harveys and guests,
enjoyable fairly priced bar food, quick
friendly service, log fire and chunky tables in
L-shaped panelled bar; outside gents';
children welcome, back terrace *(N R White,
Nick Lawless, P J and R D Greaves)*

DUNCTON [SU9517]
☆ *Cricketers* GU28 0LB [set back from A285]:
Popular refurbished country pub, well kept
Kings, Skinners Betty Stogs and a local
guest, decent wines by the glass, good
home-made food using local ingredients
(some prices edging a little high), friendly
service, beams and big inglenook, cricketing
memorabilia, traditional games; children and
dogs welcome, disabled facilities, lovely
garden behind with terrace, open all day
*(Bruce Bird, LYM, David Cosham, Sally and
Tom Matson, J A Snell, John Beeken,
Derek and Maggie Washington)*

EARTHAM [SU9309]
☆ *George* PO18 0LT [signed off A285
Chichester—Petworth, from Fontwell off
A27, from Slindon off A29]: Well kept pub
with wide range of good value blackboard
food, friendly helpful staff, local real ales,
well listed wines, log fire in comfortable
lounge, flagstoned public bar (dogs allowed
on leads) with old farm tools and
photographs, smart restaurant; piped music;
children welcome in eating areas, easy
disabled access, large garden, attractive
surroundings and lovely walks, open all day
summer wknds *(Ann and Colin Hunt, LYM)*

EAST ASHLING [SU8207]
☆ *Horse & Groom* PO18 9AX [B2178]: Busy
country pub with well kept Harveys, Hop
Back Summer Lightning and Wells & Youngs
Bitter, good choice of wines by the glass,
bar food from sandwiches up, reasonable
prices and helpful service, unchanging front
drinkers' bar with old pale flagstones and

inglenook woodburner, carpeted area with scrubbed trestle tables, fresh and airy extension with solid pale country-kitchen furniture on neat bare boards; children and dogs in some parts, garden with picnic-sets under umbrellas, bedrooms, cl Sun evening *(LYM, Tracey and Stephen Groves, Ann and Colin Hunt, Martin and Karen Wake, Nick Lawless)*

EAST GRINSTEAD [TQ3936]

☆ *Old Mill* RH19 4AT [Dunnings Rd, S towards Saint Hill]: Interesting 16th-c mill cottage over stream reworked as spacious informal Whiting & Hammond dining pub; lots of panelling, old photographs and pictures, carpeted main dining area with mix of old tables (each with church candle), steps down to ancient very low-ceilinged part with fine timbers and inglenook woodburner, sizeable bar with long curved counter and bright plush stools, library dining area off, enjoyable hearty fresh food (all day), good choice of wines by the glass, Harveys ales inc seasonal, friendly efficient service; piped music; children welcome, picnic-sets in front garden, covered decking next to working waterwheel, handy for Standen (NT) *(LYM, BB, Phil Bryant)*

EAST HOATHLY [TQ5216]

☆ *Kings Head* BN8 6DR [High St/Mill Lane]: Well kept 1648 ales (brewed here) and Harveys Best in long comfortably worn-in open-plan bar, some dark panelling and stripped brick, upholstered settles, old local photographs, log-fire, wide choice of enjoyable sensibly priced hearty food, friendly helpful service, daily papers, restaurant; TV; garden up steps behind *(John Beeken)*

EAST LAVANT [SU8608]

☆ *Royal Oak* PO18 0AX [Pook Lane, off A286]: Restauranty dining pub in pretty Georgian house, really good imaginative food, home-baked breads, good wine list, friendly helpful service, low beams and crooked timbers, stripped brickwork, scrubbed tables and church candles, log fires, small drinking area with wall seats and sofas, ales such as Sharps and Skinners tapped from cask; no children or dogs; tables on flagstoned front terrace with far views, six comfortable bedrooms, self-catering cottages, open all day *(Paul and Annette Hallett, Michael B Griffith, LYM, Bernard Stradling, Miss A E Dare, R and M Thomas)*

EASTBOURNE [TQ5900]

Hurst Arms BN21 1TW [Willingdon Rd]: Popular three-room local with well kept Harveys, friendly chatty staff, darts and pool; big-screen TV, juke box; front terrace and nice back garden, open all day *(the Didler)*

☆ *Lamb* BN21 1HH [High St]: Ancient pub with two main heavily beamed traditional bars off central servery, antique furnishings (but not too smart), good inglenook log fire, well kept Harveys ales, good choice of wines, enjoyable home-made food, upstairs dining

room (Sun lunch), events such as live opera; by ornate church away from seafront, open all day *(Marcus and Lienna Gomm, the Didler, John Atkins)*

Marine BN22 7NE [Seaside]: Comfortable pub nr seafront run by long-serving licensees, panelled bar, lounge with sofas and tub chairs, three real ales, good choice of wines and brandies, pubby food from sandwiches up, back conservatory; children welcome *(John Atkins)*

Pilot BN20 7RW [Holywell Rd, Meads; just off front below approach from Beachy Head]: Friendly lived-in local with enjoyable pub food inc fresh fish, prompt attentive service, well kept Harveys Best and Wells & Youngs Bombardier, good ship and aeroplane photographs, log fire in side bar; piped and occasional live music, TV, games machine, Tues quiz night; steeply terraced garden behind, open all day *(Christopher Turner)*

EASTERGATE [SU9405]

Wilkes Head PO20 3UT [just off A29 Fontwell—Bognor; Church Lane]: Small friendly two-bar local with dining extension, flagstones and inglenook log fire, reasonably priced generous food from sandwiches up, four ales inc Adnams and Hop Back Summer Lightning, pleasant service, darts; tables in big garden with covered smokers' area, open all day wknds *(Tony and Wendy Hobden)*

ELSTED [SU8320]

☆ *Elsted Inn* GU29 0JT [Elsted Marsh]: Popular refurbished country pub, attractive and quietly civilised, with enjoyable fresh food (not Mon), good choice of wines by the glass, real ales such as Ballards and Otter, welcoming helpful staff, log fires, nice country furniture, dining area at back, live music Sun night; dogs welcome, plenty of seating in lovely enclosed downs-view garden with big terrace, four comfortable bedrooms, good breakfast, open all day wknds *(LYM, A N Bance, Mrs Mary Woods, Tony and Wendy Hobden, R Goodenough)*

FERRING [TQ0903]

Henty Arms BN12 6QY [Ferring Lane]: Well kept changing ales, generous attractively priced food even Sun evening, neat friendly staff, log fire, opened-up lounge/dining area, separate bar with games and TV; garden tables *(Tony and Wendy Hobden)*

FISHBOURNE [SU8304]

☆ *Bulls Head* PO19 3JP [Fishbourne Rd (A259 Chichester—Emsworth)]: Comfortable well run 17th-c village pub with popular good value food (not Sun evening), well kept Fullers/Gales beers, neat attentive staff, beams, exposed brick, brassware and good log fire, daily papers; children welcome, terrace picnic-sets and pretty window boxes, four bedrooms *(David H T Dimock, Terry and Nickie Williams, John Beeken)*

FITTLEWORTH [TQ0118]

☆ *Swan* RH20 1EL [Lower St (B2138, off A283 W of Pulborough)]: New licensees off to a good start as this pretty tile-hung inn, comfortable beamed main bar, windsor chairs and bar stools on wood and carpeted floor, big inglenook log fire, Fullers, Harveys and a guest, enjoyable food in bar and separate panelled dining room; children and dogs welcome, big back lawn with plenty of tables, good nearby walks, 15 bedrooms *(LYM, Bruce Bird)*

FLETCHING [TQ4223]

Rose & Crown TN22 3ST [High St]: Well run 16th-c beamed village pub, inglenook log fire and comfortable wall banquettes in carpeted bar, wide range of enjoyable fairly priced home-made food from baguettes up, small restaurant, good attentive service, Harveys and guest ales, dogs welcome, tables in pretty garden, three bedrooms, open all day *(Michael and Ann Cole, C and R Bromage, Linda Parker, Paul Humphreys)*

FRANT [TQ5935]

George TN3 9DU [High St, off A267]: Tucked down charming quiet lane by ancient church and cottages, enjoyable traditional bar food and wider wknd evening dining, cheerful service, convivial low-ceilinged bar with several rooms rambling round servery, big inglenook, well kept Harveys, lots of wines by the glass, pleasant dining room; children and dogs welcome, play area, smokers' shelter and picnic-sets in pretty walled garden *(N R White, BB)*

FRIDAY STREET [TV6203]

Farm at Friday Street BN23 8AP [B2104, Langney]: Extended Whiting & Hammond pub in residential area with olde worlde rustic theme throughout; lots of open-plan areas with brick standing pillars and beamery, leather sofas and pouffes, big log fire in brick fireplace, extensive eating areas up and down stairs, all manner of wooden dining chairs and tables on bare boards (some rugs) and pale flagstones, church candles and plants, library area, hundreds of prints and photographs on walls, wide choice of popular food from open kitchen, Adnams and Harveys, bright, efficient and friendly staff, plenty of local customers of all ages especially at weekends; piped music; picnic-sets on grass by car park, open all day *(anon)*

FUNTINGTON [SU7908]

Fox & Hounds PO18 9LL: Welcoming beamed family pub with wide choice of enjoyable food inc popular Sun carvery (best to book wknds), cottagey dining rooms, comfortable and attractive dining extension, good service, well kept Badger ales, reasonably priced wines, nice coffee, huge log fire, no music; garden behind, pair of inn signs – one a pack of hounds, the other a family of foxes *(Terry and Nickie Williams, Ann and Colin Hunt)*

GATWICK [TQ2539]

Flight Tavern RH11 0QA [Charlwood Rd]: Roomy former Aero Club, lots of Spitfire and other memorabilia, enjoyable well priced pubby food, good drinks choice, conservatory dining area; children welcome, good for plane-spotting – runway 300 metres away beyond trees *(Justin and Emma King)*

GLYNDE [TQ4508]

☆ *Trevor Arms* BN8 6SS: Continuing well under new licensees, impressive dining room with mix of high-backed settles, pews and cushioned dining chairs around mixed tables, carpeted middle room with Glyndebourne pictures leading to snug bar with small fireplace and fine downland views; enjoyable reasonably priced filling food inc home-made pies, OAP wkdy lunch deals, good service, well kept Harveys ales, locals' bar with parquet flooring, panelled dado, old photographs of the pub, darts and toad in the hole; big garden with rows of picnic-sets and downs backdrop, popular with walkers, railway station next door, open all day *(Alec and Marie Lewery, John Beeken, Alec and Joan Laurence, BB)*

GRAFFHAM [SU9217]

White Horse GU28 0NT: Spotless local just outside village, good reasonably priced home-made food (best to book wknds), several well kept changing ales (June beer festival), good choice of wines by the glass, welcoming friendly licensees, log fires, small dining room and conservatory restaurant with South Downs views; terrace, lovely big garden, good local walks, open all day Sun in summer *(Terry and Nickie Williams, Richard Diplock)*

GUN HILL [TQ5614]

☆ *Gun* TN21 0JU [off A22 NW of Hailsham, or off A267]: Big welcoming country dining pub, several refurbished rambling areas either side of large central bar, beams and log fires, locally sourced food from sandwiches and panini up, Harveys, good wines, efficient friendly service, locals' shop in former coach house; children welcome, hay for visiting horses, large garden with play area, right on Wealden Way *(LYM, Hunter and Christine Wright, Laurence Smith, Mike Horgan)*

HALNAKER [SU9008]

☆ *Anglesey Arms* PO18 0NQ [A285 Chichester—Petworth]: Bare boards, settles and log fire, ales such as Bass, Black Sheep, Hepworths and Wells & Youngs, decent wines, good varied if not cheap food inc local organic produce and Selsey fish, friendly accommodating licensees, simple but smart L-shaped dining room (children allowed) with woodburners, stripped pine and some flagstones, traditional games; tables in big tree-lined garden, good nearby walks *(DHV, LYM, M G Hart)*

HAMMERPOT [TQ0605]

☆ *Woodmans Arms* BN16 4EU: Pretty thatched pub comfortably rebuilt after 2004 fire, beams and timbers, enjoyable pubby food from sandwiches and baked potatoes up, Fullers and a guest beer, Sun bar nibbles, neat polite staff, log fire in big fireplace; piped music; tables outside, open all day Fri, Sat and summer Sun, may be closed Sun evening *(Jo Connelly, LYM, Tony and Wendy Hobden)*

HARTFIELD [TQ4735]

Anchor TN7 4AG [Church St]: Popular 15th-c local, heavy beams and flagstones, two woodburners (one in inglenook), little country pictures and houseplants, comfortable dining area, well kept Harveys, Kings and Larkins, own pickled eggs and onions, darts and shove-ha'penny in lower room; piped music; children and dogs welcome, disabled facilities, front verandah, big garden, two bedrooms, open all day *(LYM, the Didler, Colin McKerrow)*

HASTINGS [TQ8209]

First In Last Out TN34 3EY [High St, Old Town]: Congenial and chatty beer-drinkers' local brewing its own good value FILO beers, a guest ale too, monthly beer and music festivals, farm cider, central raised log fire, good simple bar lunches (not Sun or Mon), open-plan bar with dark wood booths and posts, character cat presiding in central armchair, no machines or piped music; gents' down a few steps, parking nearby difficult; small covered back terrace, open all day *(MP, Tony Harper, P Dawn, Arthur Pickering)*

HERMITAGE [SU7505]

☆ *Sussex Brewery* PO10 8AU [A259 just W of Emsworth]: Bustling, welcoming and interesting, with small boards-and-sawdust bar, good fire in huge brick fireplace, simple furniture, little flagstoned snug, six real ales and several wines by the glass, good value hearty food inc wide choice of speciality sausages (even vegetarian ones), small upstairs restaurant; children and dogs welcome, picnic-sets in small back courtyard, open all day *(LYM, Ann and Colin Hunt, Gael Pawson, Catherine Woodman, Graham Middleton)*

HILL BROW [SU7826]

Jolly Drover GU33 7QL [B2070]: Comfortably refurbished dining pub, wide choice of enjoyable food inc pubby staples, changing real ales, friendly helpful staff, leather sofas and big log fire in bar, restaurant; well behaved children welcome, tables on heated terrace and lawn, six bedrooms *(Neil and Pippa King)*

HUNSTON [SU8601]

Spotted Cow PO20 1PD [B2145 S of Chichester]: Flagstoned pub with friendly staff and locals, wide choice of enjoyable food, chilled Fullers/Gales beers, big fires, up-to-date décor, small front bar, roomier side lounge with armchairs, sofas and low tables as ante-room for airy high-ceilinged restaurant; may be piped music; good disabled access, children welcome to eat, big pretty garden, handy for towpath walkers *(David H T Dimock, Ann and Colin Hunt)*

HURSTPIERPOINT [TQ2816]

☆ *New Inn* BN6 9RQ [High St]: Popular 16th-c beamed pub under same management as the Bull in Ditchling, nicely refurbished, with well kept ales inc Harveys, good wines by the glass, enjoyable food with plenty for vegetarians, good friendly young staff,

contrasting linked areas inc oak-panelled dim-lit back part with bric-a-brac and open fire and smart apple-green dining room; sports TV; children and dogs welcome, garden tables, open all day *(LYM, Terry Buckland)*

ICKLESHAM [TQ8716]

☆ *Robin Hood* TN36 4BD [Main Rd]: Friendly no-frills beamed pub with enthusiastic landlord and cheerful attentive staff, great local atmosphere, good value unpretentious home-made food inc blackboard specials, six well kept changing ales (many from small breweries), hops overhead, lots of copper bric-a-brac, log fire, games area with pool, back dining extension; big garden with Brede valley views *(Tom and Jill Jones, Bruce Bird)*

ISFIELD [TQ4417]

Laughing Fish TN22 5XB: Opened-up Victorian local, jovial landlord and friendly staff, good value home-made pubby food (not Sun evening), Greene King and related ales, extensive wine list, open fire, traditional games, events inc entertaining beer race Easter bank hol Mon; children and dogs welcome, disabled access, small pleasantly shaded walled garden with enclosed play area, right by Lavender Line, open all day *(BB, Tony and Wendy Hobden, John Beeken)*

KINGSFOLD [TQ1635]

Wise Old Owl RH12 3SA [Dorking Rd (A24 Dorking—Horsham, nr A29 junction)]: Nicely rambling olde-worlde reworking of 1930s pub, standing timbers dividing seating areas, Dark Star and Kings from long planked counter, good choice of wines by the glass, enjoyable food from sandwiches up inc popular Sun lunch, cream teas, good service, contemporary restaurant with high-backed wicker chairs and mixed tables on coir or wood flooring, some modern art, church candles and fresh flowers, log fires, deli/farm shop; piped music, sports TV, games machines in bar alcove, upstairs lavatories; children welcome, picnic-tables on fenced-off gravel areas, open all day from 9.30am *(Ian Phillips, BB)*

KINGSTON [TQ3908]

☆ *Juggs* BN7 3NT [village signed off A27 by roundabout W of Lewes]: Popular rose-covered village pub, heavy 15th-c beams and very low front door, lots of neatly stripped masonry, sturdy wooden furniture on bare boards and stone slabs, smaller eating areas inc family room, wide choice of enjoyable bar food inc plenty of fish and good vegetarian options, well kept Shepherd Neame, good coffee and wine list, friendly helpful staff, log fires; piped music; children and dogs welcome, disabled facilities, nice covered area outside with heaters, lots of hanging baskets, play area, good walks, open all day *(Tina and David Woods-Taylor, PL, John Beeken, Ann and Colin Hunt, Evelyn and Derek Walter, Mr and Mrs John Taylor, LYM)*

KIRDFORD [TQ0126]
☆ *Half Moon* RH14 0LT [opp church, off A272 Petworth—Billingshurst]: 17th-c tile-hung upmarket bar/restaurant, picturesque and charmingly set, with enjoyable food at linen-set tables in immaculate roomy and rambling low-beamed dining area, good wines by the glass, kind professional service, Fullers London Pride from curved counter in attractive partly quarry-tiled bar with log fire; tables in pretty back garden and out in front *(LYM, Christopher and Elise Way)*

LEWES [TQ4210]
Dorset BN7 2RD [Malling St]: Comfortably refurbished, light and airy, with large mellow area around central bar, smaller snug, lots of bare wood, welcoming competent staff, varied choice of good fairly priced food from good seafood platter to lovely home-made puddings, well kept Harveys, smart restaurant; large terrace, six bedrooms *(Ann and Colin Hunt, BB)*

Gardeners Arms BN7 2AN [Cliffe High St]: Warmly welcoming unpretentious small local opp brewery, light and airy with well kept Harveys and interesting changing ales, farm ciders, some lunchtime food inc good pies, plain scrubbed tables on bare boards around three narrow sides of bar, daily papers and magazines, bar nibbles, toad in the hole played here; open all day *(Pete Baker, BB, the Didler, Mike and Eleanor Anderson, Guy Vowles)*

John Harvey BN7 2AN [Bear Yard, just off Cliffe High St]: No-nonsense tap for nearby Harveys brewery, all their beers inc seasonal kept perfectly, some tapped from the cask, decent value food from huge lunchtime sandwiches, baked potatoes and ciabattas up, friendly efficient young staff, basic dark flagstoned bar with one great vat halved to make two towering 'snugs' for several people, lighter room on left; piped music and machines; a few tables outside, open all day, breakfast from 10am *(Ian Thurman, Ann and Colin Hunt, N R White, the Didler, Gene and Kitty Rankin, Ben Williams, BB)*

Pelham Arms BN7 1XL [High St]: Much improved and very popular under newish owners, good food (booking advised), friendly staff, three Badger ales, character rambling interior, some live music; small courtyard *(BB)*

Snowdrop BN7 2BU [South St]: Tucked under the cliffs and much improved by new owners, narrowboat theme with brightly painted bar front and colourful jugs, lanterns etc hanging from planked ceiling, well kept Dark Star, Harveys and Rectory, hearty helpings of good value changing local food such as venison and rabbit pie, live jazz; dogs very welcome (even a menu for them), small garden and terrace, open all day *(John Beeken, Ann and Colin Hunt, LYM)*

LICKFOLD [SU9226]
Lickfold Inn GU28 9EY [NE of Midhurst, between A286 and A283]: Uncluttered old building with Tudor beams and huge inglenook, bar and back dining room,

restaurant upstairs, enjoyable all-day food from pub favourites up, friendly efficient service, good choice of wines by the glass, Hogs Back TEA and a beer from Langham, quiz night (1st Thurs of month); children and dogs welcome, disabled facilities, terrace and garden seating, open all day (owned by Radio 2 DJ Chris Evans – 50% of profits go to local hospice) *(Jocelyn Barker, LYM)*

LINDFIELD [TQ3425]
Stand Up RH16 2HN [High St]: Beamed early 19th-c pub tied to Dark Star, their ales and guests kept well, farm ciders and perry, some food inc home-made pasties and ploughman's, opened-up interior with cushioned seats in big bay windows, beer and cider festivals, live music; tables in yard behind, open all day *(the Didler, Bruce Bird)*

LITTLEWORTH [TQ1921]
Windmill RH13 8EJ [pub sign on B2135; village signed off A272 southbound, W of Cowfold]: Small spotless local, most hospitable, with log fires in panelled flagstoned public bar and compact cosy beamed lounge/eating area, enjoyable sensibly priced home-made food (takeaway fish and chips Fri night), well kept Badger ales, bric-a-brac large and small inside and out, darts, dominoes, cards and bar billiards, books etc sold for charity; children welcome, peaceful attractive side garden *(Bruce Bird)*

LOWFIELD HEATH [TQ2539]
Flight RH11 0QA [Charlwood Rd]: Pictures and models of aircraft, friendly helpful staff, well kept beers, nice range of food inc home-made cakes and scones; caters well for children in conservatory with view of planes taking off from Gatwick, plenty of tables outside too *(R C Vincent)*

LYMINSTER [TQ0204]
Six Bells BN17 7PS [Lyminster Rd, Wick]: Small well kept former 18th-c flint coaching inn, friendly welcoming service, enjoyable elegantly presented food from sandwiches and baguettes up, traditional Sun lunch, good house wine, well kept Fullers London Pride and Greene King Abbot in small central part between bar dining area and restaurant with inglenook; terrace and garden seating *(Allison and Graham Thackery)*

MAPLEHURST [TQ1924]
White Horse RH13 6LL [Park Lane]: Friendly long-serving licensees in peaceful beamed country local, four seating areas inc homely cosy corners and sun lounge with church furniture and plants, log fire, well kept Harveys, Weltons and interesting guests, local farm cider, decent wines, bargain coffee, good basic pub food, lots of traditional games, no music or machines; children welcome, pleasant outlook from back garden with play area, beautiful wisteria in front, car enthusiasts' evenings *(Bruce Bird)*

MID LAVANT [SU8508]
Earl of March PO18 0BQ [A286]: Refurbished and extended with emphasis on eating but a

few seats for drinkers in flagstoned log-fire bar serving Harveys, Hop Back and other ales; good if pricey food, much sourced locally, in plush dining area and conservatory with seafood bar, polite efficient staff; nice view up to Goodwood from neatly kept garden with good furniture, local walks *(Tony Brace, Tracey and Stephen Groves, Miss A E Dare, Terry and Nickie Williams)*

MIDHURST [SU8820]

Royal Oak GU29 0EP [West Lavington; A286 towards Chichester]: Sizeable pub reopened and refurbished keeping old-world country feel, fine inglenook log fire, several real ales, enjoyable home-made food, friendly staff; dogs and children welcome, garden *(LYM)*

Wheatsheaf GU29 9BX [Wool Lane/A272]: Dating from 16th c with cosy low-beamed and timbered bars, good range of enjoyable reasonably priced food, well kept local ales *(Michael B Griffith, Geoff and Linda Payne)*

MILLAND [SU8328]

Rising Sun GU30 7NA [Iping Rd junction with main rd through village]: Light and cheery main bar with Fullers/Gales beers, enjoyable food from bar snacks to fresh fish, friendly attentive staff, some live music; children welcome (popular with families at wknds), large neat garden with heated terrace, good walking area, open all day wknds *(Michael B Griffith, Robin Ricketts, BB)*

NEWICK [TQ4121]

Royal Oak BN8 4JU [Church Rd]: White weatherboarded pub on lovely village green, neat and comfortable, with enjoyable good value food, Fullers London Pride and Harveys Best, friendly service; children welcome, tables out in front, open all day wknds *(Michael Hazell-Smith)*

NUTBOURNE [SU7805]

Barleycorn PO18 8RS [A259 W of Chichester]: Refurbished open-plan pub under keen young licensees, smart welcoming staff, good reasonably priced local food all-day inc Sun carvery, well kept Ringwood Best, Sharps Doom Bar and Timothy Taylors Landlord; tables outside *(Tony and Jill Radnor, Ann and Colin Hunt)*

Rising Sun RH20 2HE [off A283 E of Pulborough; The Street]: Unspoilt creeper-covered village pub dating partly from 16th c, beams, bare boards and scrubbed tables, friendly helpful licensees (same family ownership for 30 years), well kept Fullers London Pride and guests such as Flowers, Harveys and Ringwood, good range of bar food and blackboard specials, big log fire, daily papers, enamel signs and 1920s fashion and dance posters, cosy snug, attractive back family room, some live music; dogs welcome, garden with small back terrace under apple tree, smokers' shelter, listed outside lavatory *(John Beeken, Sarah Hutchinson)*

OFFHAM [TQ3912]

☆ *Blacksmiths Arms* BN7 3QD [A275 N of Lewes]: Civilised and comfortable open-plan

dining pub with chef/owner doing wide choice of good food inc bargain two-course specials and nice vegetarian choices, well kept Harveys Best and a seasonal beer, good friendly uniformed staff, huge end inglenook; french windows to terrace with picnic-sets, four bedrooms *(Mrs Pat Tribe, Ann and Colin Hunt, LYM)*

Chalk Pit BN7 3QF [Offham Rd (A275 N of Lewes)]: Former late 18th-c chalk pit office building on three levels, well kept Harveys and a guest ale, decent wines by the glass, good choice of popular home-made food inc OAP bargains, attentive friendly staff, neat restaurant extension, skittle alley, toad in the hole played Mon nights; children welcome, garden with terrace seating, smokers' shelter with pool table, three bedrooms, open all day Fri-Sun (usually food all day then, too) *(John Beeken, Ann and Colin Hunt, PL, Phil Bryant)*

PAGHAM [SZ8998]

Lamb PO21 4NJ [Pagham Rd]: Rambling flower-decked pub with generous enjoyable food, Fullers, Greene King and Wells & Youngs, prompt service even when busy, lots of beams, timbers and paintings, restaurant; unobtrusive piped music; garden tables *(Terry and Nickie Williams)*

PARTRIDGE GREEN [TQ1819]

Green Man RH13 8JT [Jolesfield (B2135 N)]: Tile-hung Victorian pub updated under hard-working new licensees, open-plan with light contemporary feel, good sensibly priced home-made food, helpful service, good choice of wines by the glass inc champagne, well kept Dark Star and Harveys; attractive garden behind *(David Cosham, Terry Buckland)*

Partridge RH13 8JS [Church Rd]: Spacious renovated village pub, warm welcome, well kept Fullers London Pride, fresh pubby food from sandwiches up, darts and pool; games machine; terrace, dog-free garden with play area *(Colin Gooch, Richard English)*

PATCHING [TQ0705]

Fox BN13 3UJ [Arundel Rd; signed off A27 eastbound just W of Worthing]: Generous good value home-made food inc good puddings and vegetarian options, popular Sun roasts (best to book), good prompt service even at busy times, well kept Harveys Best and two local guests, good wine choice, large dining area off roomy panelled bar, hunting pictures; quiet piped music; children and dogs welcome, disabled access, nice tree-shaded garden with play area *(Tony and Wendy Hobden, Mrs Pat Tribe)*

PETT [TQ8613]

Two Sawyers TN35 4HB [Pett Rd; off A259]: Family run with meandering low-beamed rooms inc bare-boards bar with stripped tables, tiny snug, passage sloping down to restaurant allowing children, enjoyable food freshly made so can take a while, early-bird bargains, friendly prompt service, well kept Harveys with guests like Dark Star and Ringwood, local farm cider and perry, wide range of wines; piped music; dogs allowed in bar, suntrap front brick courtyard, back garden with shady trees and well spaced tables, three bedrooms, open all day *(Peter Meister, LYM, David Nicholls, Paul Bantock)*

PETWORTH [SU9719]

☆ *Badgers* GU28 0JF [Station Rd (A285 1.5 miles S)]: Smart restauranty dining pub with good up-to-date rather upmarket food served generously at well spaced tables mixing old mahogany and waxed stripped pine, charming wrought-iron lamps, log fires, friendly staff, Badger Best and K&B (there's a fireside drinking area with sofas), good range of wines; over-5s in eating area of bar, stylish tables and seats on terrace by water lily pool, bedrooms, cl winter Sun evenings *(LYM, Paddy and Annabelle Cribb, Kevin Flack)*

Grove GU28 0HY [Grove Lane]: 17th-c stone pub with two-room bar, small sofas either side of open fire, Wells & Youngs Best tapped from the cask, extensive wine list, bar food inc sandwiches and a sausage menu, separate menu in conservatory restaurant; dogs welcome in bar, tables in large garden, cl Sun evening, Mon *(Tony and Wendy Hobden)*

☆ *Welldiggers Arms* GU28 0HG [Low Heath; A283 E]: Unassuming L-shaped bar, low beams, pictures askew on shiny ochre walls, long rustic settles with tables to match, some stripped tables laid for eating, side room, no music or machines, enjoyable food, Wells & Youngs, decent wines, friendly landlord; children (in family area) and dogs welcome, plenty of tables on attractive lawns and terrace, nice views, cl Mon, also evenings Tues, Weds, Sun *(LYM, Gerry and Rosemary Dobson, Christopher and Elise Way, Mrs Blethyn Elliott)*

PEVENSEY [TQ6504]

Moorings BN24 6AP [The Parade]: Popular dining pub right on the beach, modern refurbishment, good choice of food, conservatory *(Pam Adsley)*

PYECOMBE [TQ2912]

Plough BN45 7FN [London Rd (A23)]: Smartly refurbished extended pub with huge helpings of largely Italian food in back conservatory restaurant, Sun roasts too, good short wine choice, real ales such as Fullers London Pride, Greene King Old Speckled Hen and Harveys Best in small front bar which still attracts locals, friendly efficient staff all in black; children welcome, tiered garden, summer barbecues, handy for South Downs Way walks, open all day *(Tony and Wendy Hobden)*

RINGMER [TQ4415]

Old Ship BN8 5RP [Uckfield Rd (A26 Lewes—Uckfield, outside village S of Isfield turn-off)]: Sizeable low-beamed roadside pub with emphasis on dining, wide choice of enjoyable home-made food all day from sandwiches and baked potatoes to steaks and fresh fish, children's menu, friendly service, Harveys Best, Biddenden cider,

nautical pictures and memorabilia; dogs welcome, good-sized attractive garden with play area, open all day *(Tony and Wendy Hobden, Nigel and Jean Eames)*

RIPE [TQ5110]

Lamb BN8 6AS [signed off A22 Uckfield—Hailsham, or off A27 Lewes—Polegate via Chalvington; Church Lane]: Partly panelled rooms around central servery, well kept Shepherd Neame, hearty good value food, open fires, small dining room set out as farmyard stalls, pool in back room; piped music; picnic-sets in pleasant sheltered back garden *(BB, John Beeken)*

ROBERTSBRIDGE [TQ7323]

☆ *George* TN32 5AW [High St]: Attractive contemporary dining pub, armchairs and sofa by inglenook log fire on right, friendly helpful licensees, Adnams, Harveys, Hop Back and Timothy Taylors Landlord, good wines by the glass, enjoyable fairly priced enterprising food, bustling, chatty atmosphere; piped music – live lunchtime last Sun of month; children welcome and dogs (they have one), back courtyard *(Simon Tayler, David and Sally Cullen, BB)*

RODMELL [TQ4105]

Abergavenny Arms BN7 3EZ [back rd Lewes—Newhaven]: Recently reopened beamed and raftered ex-barn, open-plan with wood and tiled floors, large log fire, enjoyable pubby food, Dark Star Hophead and Harveys Best; large two-level back terrace, good walks, handy for Virginia Woolf's Monk's House *(John Beeken)*

ROGATE [SU8023]

☆ *White Horse* GU31 5EA [East St; A272 Midhurst—Petersfield]: Rambling heavy-beamed local in front of village cricket field, civilised and friendly, with Harveys full range kept particularly well, relaxed atmosphere, flagstones, stripped stone, timbers and big log fire, attractive candlelit sunken dining area, good range of enjoyable reasonably priced food (not Sun evening), friendly helpful staff, traditional games (and quite a collection of trophy cups), no music or machines; quiz and folk nights; some tables on back terrace, open all day Sun *(LYM, Michael B Griffith, Gary and Karen Turner, D and J Ashdown)*

ROTHERFIELD [TQ5529]

Kings Arms TN6 3LJ [High St]: Old timber-framed 18th-c village pub, main area set for the enjoyable reasonably priced food, friendly service, real ales, low lighting and traditional décor, lounge bar with sofas and fireplace, public bar, pool; dogs welcome, some tables out at front, good-sized garden behind with small terrace *(Peter Meister, N R White)*

ROWHOOK [TQ1234]

☆ *Chequers* RH12 3PY [off A29 NW of Horsham]: Attractive welcoming 16th-c pub, relaxing beamed and flagstoned front bar with portraits and inglenook fire, step up to low-beamed lounge, well kept Fullers London

Pride, Harveys and guests such as Weltons, decent wines by the glass, good coffee, good food from ciabattas up, separate restaurant; piped music; children and dogs welcome, tables out on front terraces and in pretty garden behind with good play area, attractive surroundings *(LYM, Steve and Hilary Nelson, Ian Phillips, Ian and Rose Lock, Barry Steele-Perkins)*

RUDGWICK [TQ0934]
Kings Head RH12 3EB [off A281; Church St (B2128)]: 13th-c pub by fine old church in pretty village, well kept Fullers, Shepherd Neame and Harveys, good italian cooking inc lots of seafood, reasonable prices; flower-decked seating area at front *(John Beeken)*

RUNCTON [SU8802]
Walnut Tree PO20 1QB [Vinnetrow Rd, towards N Mundham]: Attractive building with friendly efficient staff, good food choice especially puddings, good wine list, local beers, bare boards, timbers and open fires, character touches, two steps up to spacious raftered dining room; good sized garden with terrace open all day *(R and M Thomas)*

RUSPER [TQ1836]
☆ *Royal Oak* RH12 4QA [Friday St, towards Warnham – back rd N of Horsham, E of A24 (OS Sheet 187 map ref 185369)]: Old-fashioned and well worn-in tile-hung pub in very rural spot on Sussex Border Path, small carpeted top bar with leather sofas and armchairs, log fire, steps down to long beamed main bar with plush wall seats, pine tables and chairs and homely knick-knacks, well kept Surrey Hills Ranmore and six changing guests, farm ciders and perries, short choice of enjoyable home-made lunchtime food (evenings and Sun lunch by prearrangement), local farm produce for sale, plain games/family room with darts; a few picnic-sets on grass by road and in streamside garden beyond car park, roaming chickens, open all day Sat, till 9pm Sun *(Kevin Thorpe, Martin Stafford, the Didler, Bruce Bird, Conor McGaughey, BB, Tony and Wendy Hobden)*

RYE [TQ9220]
George TN31 7JT [High St]: Sizeable hotel with lively up-to-date feel in bar and adjoining dining area, beams, bare boards, log fire, leather sofa and armchairs, Adnams, Greene King Old Speckled Hen and Harveys Best, a couple of continental beers on tap, enjoyable interesting food, pleasant service; soft piped jazz; good bedrooms *(Colin and Louise English, John Atkins)*
Globe TN31 7NX [Military Rd]: Small weatherboarded open-plan dining pub, light airy refurbishment, with good locally sourced seasonal food at sensible prices, friendly staff helpful with special diets, ales such as Harveys, light wood dining furniture on polished wood floor, pastel blue panelling, leather sofas, newspapers, woodburner, nice relaxed atmosphere; garden tables, cl Sun evening, Mon *(Colin and Louise English)*

RYE HARBOUR [TQ9419]
☆ *Inkerman Arms* TN31 7TQ [Rye Harbour Rd]: Friendly plain pub nr nature reserve, stools around the bar but otherwise mainly tables for the wide choice of good food inc local scallops Nov-Apr and lots of low-priced fresh fish, fine home-made pies and old-fashioned puddings, well kept Greene King IPA, Harveys Best and perhaps a guest; tables out in small sheltered back area, cl Mon evening and winter Mon lunchtime *(Conrad Freezer)*

SELHAM [SU9320]
☆ *Three Moles* GU28 0PN [village signed off A272 Petworth—Midhurst]: Small, quiet and relaxing pub recently smartened up, steep steps up to bar with well kept ales such as Bowmans Swift One and Skinners Betty Stogs, farm cider, tasty lunchtime bar food from short menu, blazing coal fires, church furniture; garden tables, tucked away in woodland village with tiny late Saxon church, nice walks, open all day wknds, cl Thurs *(Tony and Wendy Hobden, Bruce Bird)*

SELMESTON [TQ5006]
Barley Mow BN26 6UE [A27 Eastbourne—Lewes]: Open-plan pub with wide choice of reasonably priced food all day inc children's, well kept Harveys, good range of wines, eating areas on both sides of central bar area; soft piped music; large garden with decking and play area, open all day *(Alec and Marie Lewery, Alec Lewery, BB)*

SELSFIELD COMMON [TQ3433]
White Hart RH19 4RA [B2028 N of Haywards Heath, nr West Hoathly]: Welcoming cosy bar with well kept Harveys and enjoyable bar food, wider choice in big timbered Sussex barn restaurant, friendly service, lounge with sofas, live music Fri; garden, handy for Wakehurst Place *(M Vingoe, Charles Grint, C and R Bromage, LYM)*

SHOREHAM-BY-SEA [TQ2105]
Red Lion BN43 5TE [Upper Shoreham Rd]: Modest dim-lit low-beamed and timbered 16th-c pub with settles in snug alcoves, wide choice of good value pubby food, half a dozen well kept changing ales such as Arundel and Hepworths (Easter beer festival), farm cider, decent wines, friendly efficient staff, log fire in unusual fireplace, another open fire in dining room, further bar with covered terrace; pretty sheltered garden behind, old bridge and lovely Norman church opp, good downs views and walks *(Bruce Bird, Jestyn Phillips, Tim Loryman, Tracey and Stephen Groves)*

SINGLETON [SU8713]
☆ *Partridge* PO18 0EY [just off A286 Midhurst—Chichester]: Pretty black and cream dining pub now under same ownership as Earl of March at Lavant – reports please, polished boards and flagstones, some small rooms with red settles, spacious back bar extension, log fires, Fullers London Pride, Harveys Best and Hop Back Summer Lightning, good fairly priced standard food, prompt attentive service; piped music;

children and dogs allowed, terrace and nice big walled garden with new tables, handy for Weald & Downland Open Air Museum, open all day wknds and bank hols *(G Dobson, Nick Lawless, LYM)*

SLAUGHAM [TQ2528]

Chequers RH17 6AQ [off A23 S of Handcross]: Smartly refurbished village pub now under same owners as nearby Cowdray Arms at Balcombe – reports please: leather sofas, polished boards and soft lighting, food from pub favourites to more adventurous things, set lunch deals, ales such as Harveys, open fire, modern back extension; sloping garden with country views, lakeside walks, six bedrooms, open all day *(BB)*

SLINFOLD [TQ1131]

Red Lyon RH13 0RR [The Street]: Attractive village pub with well kept ales such as Badger K&B, Fullers and Kings, fresh food from open sandwiches to full restaurant meals; may ask to keep a credit card while you eat; children and dogs welcome, big garden with large heated umbrellas on terrace, play area, regular summer events, four bedrooms *(Ian Phillips, Bob Kane, C and R Bromage, Helen Markham)*

SOMPTING [TQ1605]

Gardeners Arms BN15 0AR [West St]: Smartened up by friendly new licensees, just off main coast rd (the famous Saxon church is unfortunately on the far side of the dual carriageway), good choice of tasty food at reasonable prices (the railway-carriage restaurant is not currently in use), well kept Bass, Harveys and a guest ale; smokers' terrace *(Bruce Bird)*

SOUTH HARTING [SU7819]

White Hart GU31 5QB [B2146 SE of Petersfield]: 16th-c beamed pub under welcoming new management; well spaced tables on polished wood, lounge bar with lower level bar area, Otter Bitter, Sharps Doom Bar and Skinners Betty Stogs, traditional food from lunchtime baguettes up, restaurant with inglenook woodburner; piped music; children, dogs and walkers welcome, good walled garden with spectacular downs views, handy for Uppark, open all day *(Ann and Colin Hunt)*

SOUTHWATER [TQ1528]

Bax Castle RH13 0LA [Two Mile Ash, a mile or so NW]: Popular early 19th-c flagstoned country pub pleasantly extended with former barn restaurant, big log fire in back room, Ringwood, Banks's and Wychwood ales, good value generous home-made food inc good Sun lunch (best to book); some piped music; children and dogs welcome, picnic-sets on two pleasant lawns, play area, nr Downs Link Way on former rail track *(Ian Phillips, Tony and Wendy Hobden)*

STAPLEFIELD [TQ2728]

Jolly Tanners RH17 6EF [Handcross Rd, just off A23]: Neatly kept split-level local by cricket green, welcoming landlord and pub dogs, two good log fires, padded settles, lots

of china, brasses and old photographs, well kept Fullers London Pride, Harveys and guests (always a mild), three real ciders, beer festivals, pubby food, chatty atmosphere; piped music, jazz Sun evening, quiz Thurs; children welcome and dogs (may be a treat), attractive suntrap garden with plenty of space for kids, quite handy for Nymans (NT) *(Sheila Topham, Mike and Eleanor Anderson)*

Victory RH17 6EU [Warninglid Rd]: Nicely placed shuttered dining pub overlooking cricket green (and Brighton veteran car run, first wknd in Nov), friendly licensees, wide choice of enjoyable food inc good fish and seafood, well kept ales such as Harveys Best from zinc-topped counter, local cider and decent wines, rustic décor, beams, old prints and woodburner; children welcome, delightful garden with play area *(N R White, Mr and Mrs P A King)*

STEDHAM [SU8522]

Hamilton Arms GU29 0NZ [School Lane (off A272)]: Proper english local but decorated with thai artefacts and run by friendly thai family, basic pub food as well as good interesting thai bar snacks and restaurant dishes (cl Mon), reasonably priced wines, four or more well kept ales such as Ballards, Fullers London Pride and Gales, back pool room; unobtrusive piped music, muted TV; pretty hanging baskets, tables out by green and quiet lane, village shop in car park, good walks nearby *(Graham and Toni Sanders, Jo Connelly, John Beeken)*

STEYNING [TQ1711]

Chequer BN44 3RE [High St]: Rambling low-beamed Tudor coaching inn, six well kept ales inc Dark Star, Gales, Harveys and Timothy Taylors, good choice of wines, enjoyable well priced usual food (not Sun evening) from sandwiches up inc breakfast from 10am, log fire, antique snooker table, large painting featuring locals, some live music; smokers' shelter, bedrooms, open all day *(Bruce Bird, Greta and Christopher Wells, Richard Wilkie, Jude Wright)*

STOPHAM [TQ0318]

☆ *White Hart* RH20 1DS [off A283 E of village, W of Pulborough]: Fine old pub by medieval River Arun bridge, gently smartened up, with heavy beams, timbers and panelling, log fire and sofas in one of its three snug rooms, well kept ales such as Arundel Gold, Hammerpot Woodcote and Kings Horsham, good generous food (all day wknds) from baguettes and pizzas up, some interesting bric-a-brac, Thurs quiz night; children welcome, waterside tables, some under cover, open all day *(N R White, Tony and Wendy Hobden, Bruce Bird, LYM, Colin McKerrow)*

STOUGHTON [SU8011]

Hare & Hounds PO18 9JQ [signed off B2146 Petersfield—Emsworth]: Airy pine-clad country dining pub with simple contemporary décor, good reasonably priced food inc good Sun roast (till 4pm), four well kept ales inc Harveys, real cider, delightful helpful staff, big open fires, public bar with darts; children in eating areas, tables on pretty front terrace and in back garden, lovely setting nr Saxon church, good local walks *(LYM, Rodney and Mary Milne-Day, Martin and Karen Wake)*

THAKEHAM [TQ1017]

White Lion RH20 3EP [off B2139 N of Storrington; The Street]: Tile-hung 16th-c two-bar village local, good robust home-made food (not Sun-Weds evenings) from open kitchen, friendly informal service, real ales such as Arundel, Fullers and Harveys, good choice of wines by the glass, heavy beams, panelling, bare boards and traditional furnishings inc settles, pleasant dining room with inglenook woodburner, fresh flowers; dogs welcome, sunny terrace tables, more on small lawn, wendy house and rabbits, small pretty village, open all day *(Terry Buckland, Tony and Wendy Hobden, BB)*

TICEHURST [TQ6831]

Bull TN5 7HH [Three Legged Cross; off B2099 towards Wadhurst]: Attractive 14th-c pub with two big log fires in very heavy-beamed old-fashioned simple two-room bar, well kept Harveys, contemporary furnishings and flooring in light and airy dining extension; charming front garden (busy in summer), bigger back one with play area *(Leslie and Barbara Owen, BB)*

TILLINGTON [SU9621]

Horse Guards GU28 9AF [off A272 Midhurst—Petworth]: Prettily set dining pub converted from three cottages, some traditional dishes as well as fancier pricier things, home-baked bread, Harveys and a guest, good choice of wines by the glass, log fire and country furniture in neat low-beamed front bar, lovely views from bow window, simple pine tables in dining room with fire, own and local produce for sale; children welcome, terrace tables and sheltered garden behind, attractive ancient church opposite, three neat bedrooms, good breakfast *(LYM, Richard Tilbrook, M G Hart)*

TURNERS HILL [TQ3435]

Crown RH10 4PT [East St]: Comfortable low-beamed bar, steps down to attractive dining area with pitched rafters, popular reasonably priced pubby food, Harveys Best and Wells & Youngs Bombardier, helpful efficient service, log fire; soft piped music; children welcome, tables out in front, sheltered back garden with pleasant valley views, two bedrooms *(BB, Sue and Mike Todd)*

UPPER DICKER [TQ5409]

Plough BN27 3QJ [Coldharbour Rd]: Much-extended old pub doing enjoyable food at fair prices (all day wknds) inc huge ploughman's, well kept Shepherd Neame ales, welcoming friendly service, armchairs and sofas, woodburners, restaurant; public bar with darts and big-screen TV; children welcome, dogs in bar, garden tables *(Tony and Shirley Albert, Fr Robert Marsh)*

WALDERTON [SU7910]

Barley Mow PO18 9ED [Stoughton rd, just off B2146 Chichester—Petersfield]: Smartly kept country pub with good value generous food from lunchtime sandwiches up inc Sun carvery, well kept ales such as Arundel, Harveys and Ringwood, good wine choice, friendly efficient service even on busy wknds, two log fires and rustic bric-a-brac in U-shaped bar with roomy dining areas, live jazz suppers (3rd Tues of month), skittle alley; children welcome, big pleasant streamside back garden, good walks, handy for Stansted House *(Ann and Colin Hunt)*

WALDRON [TQ5419]

Star TN21 0RA [Blackboys—Horam side road]: Big inglenook log fire in candlelit beamed and panelled bar, padded window seat and nice mix of furniture inc small settle on bare boards and quarry tiles, old prints and photographs, snug off to left, Harveys ales and a guest such as 1648 or Bass, reliable food from good lunchtime sandwiches up, friendly prompt service, separate back dining room; picnic-sets in pleasant garden, a couple more at front overlooking pretty village *(Mike and Eleanor Anderson, Phil and Sally Gorton, PL, BB)*

WEST ITCHENOR [SU7901]

Ship PO20 7AH [The Street]: Large panelled pub in good spot nr Chichester Harbour, tables outside, good long walk to W Wittering or foot ferry to Bosham Hoe; traditional bar one end and two carpeted dining areas, good choice of food from snacks up, efficient friendly service, ales from Arundel, Ballards, Fullers and Kings, two log fires, pine tables and chairs, a seat made from an old boat, some marine bric-a-brac and pictures; children welcome, open all day *(Tony and Wendy Hobden)*

WINCHELSEA [TQ9017]

Bridge TN36 4JT [The Strand (A259)]: Enjoyable food inc fresh local fish in bar and dining lounge, welcoming relaxed atmosphere, well kept beers *(Mark Sykes)*

WITHYHAM [TQ4935]

☆ *Dorset Arms* TN7 4BD [B2110]: Pleasantly unpretentious 16th-c pub handy for Forest Way walks, friendly service, well kept Harveys, decent wines inc local ones, good fresh food from filled rolls to seasonal game, reasonable prices, good log fire in Tudor fireplace, sturdy tables and simple country seats on wide oak boards, darts, dominoes, shove-ha'penny, cribbage, pretty restaurant; piped music; dogs welcome, white tables on brick terrace by small green, cl Mon *(LYM, the Didler, Peter Meister)*

WOODGATE [SU9304]

Prince of Wales PO20 3ST [Lidsey Rd; A29]: Traditional flint building with modern extension, enjoyable food inc various deals, efficient service, decent wine choice, Greene King IPA and Abbot, restaurant, live music Fri evening; outside seats and play area *(Tony and Wendy Hobden)*

WORTHING [TQ1404]
Cricketers BN14 9DE [Broadwater St W,
Broadwater Green (A24)]: Extended panelled
local with welcoming staff, well kept
Harveys, Ringwood and interesting guests
(beer festivals), enjoyable well priced food
inc Sun roasts, friendly staff, old
photographs, prints and copper knick-knacks,
steps down to small lounge with dining room
beyond, log fires; children welcome, good-
sized garden with covered smokers' area
(Bruce Bird)
George & Dragon BN14 7NN [High St, Old
Tarring]: Extended 17th-c pub improved
under newish landlord, four split-level
carpeted areas, good choice of enjoyable
low-priced food (not Fri-Mon evenings), six
well kept ales inc Courage Directors, Harveys
Best and Hop Back Summer Lightning,
tankards hanging from beams, brass platters
and old photographs on panelled walls,
live music some wknds (jazz 1st Tues of
month), Weds quiz; games machine, darts;
children and dogs welcome, tables in
walled back garden, open all day
(Tony and Wendy Hobden, Bruce Bird)
North Star BN13 1QY [Littlehampton Rd
(A259)]: Comfortable Ember Inn, sensibly
priced food inc speciality burgers noon to
8pm, Fullers London Pride, Harveys and

unusual guests, good choice of wines
by the glass, friendly service
(Tony and Wendy Hobden)
Old House At Home BN14 9AD [Broadwater
St E]: Panelled lounge with friendly staff,
well kept ales such as Harveys and Shepherd
Neame, good choice of enjoyable food, open
fires, bric-a-brac and old photographs,
conservatory; children welcome, terrace
tables *(Tim Loryman)*
Selden Arms BN11 2DB [Lyndhurst Rd,
between Waitrose and hospital]: Friendly
chatty local with welcoming long-serving
licensees, well kept Dark Star Hophead and
several changing guests, belgian beers and
farm cider, bargain lunchtime food (not Sun)
inc doorstep sandwiches, log fire, lots of old
pub photographs, occasional live music; dogs
welcome, open all day *(Tony and
Wendy Hobden, Bruce Bird, N R White)*
Swan BN11 1DN [High St]: Villagey
atmosphere with good mix of customers
in big open-plan pub, reasonably priced
pubby lunchtime food and specials,
several well kept ales inc Harveys and Hop
Back, old-fashioned interior with beams
and some stained glass, regular
entertainment from folk nights to quizzes;
handy for hospital *(Bruce Bird, Tony and
Wendy Hobden)*

Warwickshire
(with Birmingham and West Midlands)

With exactly one in two Main Entries here carrying a Beer Award, this is a fantastic county for real ale lovers. Even more than that, this area, which takes in the great West Midlands conurbations and the small villages of Warwickshire and the North Cotswolds, is something of a haven for traditional unspoilt pubs – and as is so often the case, it's these traditional pubs that seem to carry terrific ranges of real ale and even brew their own beers. In this chapter you'll find the basic but very special Turf at Bloxwich (in the same family for some 140 years), the Case is Altered at Five Ways (licensed for some 300 years), the down-to-earth Vine at Brierley Hill (tap for Bathams), the character-laden Old Swan at Netherton (four own-brew beers), the Beacon at Sedgley (a lovely time warp, and it's here in a Victorian tower brewery that the very good Sarah Hughes ales originate), the unpretentious Griffin at Shustoke (the landlord not only produces three beers but stocks another seven guests on top), and finally, in a slightly different niche from the above, the Old Joint Stock in Birmingham (impressive Victorian interior and showcase for the full range of Fullers beers). Only three Food Awards in this area suggest there is catching up to be done here, and there were just two competitors for the County Dining Pub Award: the stylish Crabmill at Preston Bagot, with its imaginative menu, ten wines by the glass and fantastic service, and the equally fabulous Bell at Welford-on-Avon. The Crabmill at Preston Bagot just snatched the Award and is our Warwickshire Dining Pub 2011. Two other pubs here that deserve a mention for doing particularly well at the moment are the nicely run and uniquely decorated Red Lion at Hunningham and the Kings Head at Aston Cantlow – a jolly good all-rounder.

Holly Bush ◀

Henley Street (continuation of High Street towards B4089; not much nearby parking); B49 5QX

Neatly smartened-up traditional tavern with timeless appeal and unusual real ales

Several small or smallish rooms at this relaxed 17th-c pub have a variety of unpretentious furniture on bare boards or flagstones, an abundance of coal or log fires, some stripped masonry and dark board panelling and antique prints, mainly black and white. The chatty heart of the place is at the back on the left, with a few big Victorian lithographs, a warm woodburning stove in a capacious fireplace and two long wall pews, each with a couple of plain tables, facing each other across age-pocked broad bare boards. Here, the serving counter has a splendid changing array of about eight well kept ales: Black Sheep Best, Purity Mad Goose and Pure Gold, Uley Bitter, alongside guests such as Goffs Jouster, Greene King Abbot and St Austell Tribute. They have farm cider and dozens of whiskies. The hard-working landlady is helped by friendly staff. This main room has a window on to the central corridor, which broadens to include a couple of soft pale leather sofas before exiting to a pretty little garden with a sheltered side terrace; piped music. There is good disabled access.

🍴 **Food runs from pubby dishes such as sandwiches, wraps, ploughman's and a tapas menu, to a more imaginative restaurant menu (you can eat from this in the bar) with dishes such as fried chicken livers in cognac and cream, fried tiger prawns with lemon and lime risotto, honey glazed gressingham duck breast with orange and port sauce, pork belly with apple mash, fillet steak with mushroom compote and pepper sauce, baked mushroom, spinach, hazelnut and blue cheese wellington, and puddings such as apple and cinnamon crumble with custard and chocolate, brandy and cherry terrine.** *Starters/Snacks: £3.95 to £8.95. Main Courses: £6.95 to £15.00. Puddings: £4.75 to £5.75*

Free house ~ Licensee Teej Deffley ~ Real ale ~ Bar food (12-2.30(4 Sun), 7-9.30; not Sun evening) ~ Restaurant ~ (01789) 762482 ~ Children welcome ~ Dogs allowed in bar ~ Open 12-11.30(midnight Sat)

Recommended by Di and Mike Gillam, Alan and Eve Harding

ASTON CANTLOW   SP1360   MAP 4

Kings Head ♀
Village signposted just off A3400 NW of Stratford; B95 6HY

Gently civilised Tudor pub with nice old interior, pubby and imaginative food, and a pleasant garden

'Just what a village pub should be, with drinkers, sandwich-eaters and diners all equally welcome' is one reader's comment to us on this well run creeper-swathed pub. The beautifully kept bar on the right is charmingly old, with flagstones, low beams and old-fashioned settles around its massive inglenook log fireplace. A chatty quarry-tiled main room has attractive window seats and big country oak tables – it's all the perfect setting for a civilised meal out. A good range of drinks includes Greene King Abbot, M&B Brew XI and a guest such as Purity Pure Gold on handpump, several wines by the glass from a very decent list and a local cider; piped music. A big chestnut tree graces the lovely garden, and the pub looks really pretty in summer with its colourful hanging baskets and wisteria.

🍴 **As well as a pubby bar menu with dishes such as sandwiches (on a separate board), battered fish of the day, sausage and mash, lamb curry, steak and vegetable pie and home-made burger, a more elaborate menu might include asian-style crab and prawn cake with thai green curry sauce, goats cheese and spinach frittata, home-cured gravadlax with broad bean salsa, moroccan mezze, duck breast with sea salt and pepper crust, baked cod with seafood and chorizo paella, salmon and dill fishcakes with pak choi and chilli sauce, pepper stuffed with vegetable couscous topped with mozzarella, and rib-eye steak with horseradish béarnaise.** *Starters/Snacks: £4.25 to £7.95. Main Courses: £10.00 to £16.75. Puddings: £5.50 to £6.50*

Enterprise ~ Lease Peter and Louise Sadler ~ Real ale ~ Bar food (12-2.30, 6.30-9.30; 12-3 Sun, not Sun evening) ~ Restaurant ~ (01789) 488242 ~ Children welcome ~ Dogs allowed in bar ~ Open 12-3, 6-11; 12-11 Sat; 12-8.30(7.30 in winter) Sun

Recommended by Dr and Mrs S G Barber, Di and Mike Gillam, Peter Sampson, John and Caroline Shaw, Anthony and Pam Stamer, Martin and Pauline Jennings, D W Stokes, Howard and Margaret Buchanan, Mike and Mary Carter

---

'Children welcome' means the pub says it lets children inside without any special restriction. If it allows them in, but to restricted areas such as an eating area or family room, we specify this. Some pubs may impose an evening time limit. We do not mention limits after 9pm as we assume children are home by then.

BARFORD   SP2660   MAP 4

Granville

1.7 miles from M40 junction 15; A429 S (Wellesbourne Road); CV35 8DS

Civilised, attractive respite from the motorway, for fireside comfort or a good meal (all day Sat)

Doing well under its fairly new licensee, this pleasing pub has a gently up-to-date feel with its sage-green paintwork, berber-pattern hangings on the end walls and contemporary lighting. Soft leather deco sofas nestle by the fire in the angle of the L-shaped main bar. You can eat here, at newish pale wood tables and chairs on pale boards or simple more mixed tables and chairs in a carpeted section, or you can head through to a more formally laid raftered and stripped-brick restaurant. They have Hook Norton Hooky and Purity Mad Gold and UBU on handpump, and decent wines by the glass; service is efficient; piped music. A floodlit back terrace has teak tables and chairs under huge retractable awnings, and the grass beyond rises artfully to a hedge of pampas grass and the like, which neatly closes the view; more reports please.

⏣ **Good bar food runs from lunchtime doorstep sandwiches to starters such as duck liver, brandy and orange pâté with red onion marmalade, crispy spring rolls with hoi sin sauce, cucumber noodles and spring onion and sweet chilli dip, sautéed mushrooms with garlic cream sauce. Main courses include sausages and mash, battered fish with mushy peas, pie of the day, lamb shank with redcurrant jus, mushroom stroganoff, rib-eye steak, and they do puddings such as profiteroles with warm chocolate orange sauce, cheesecake of the week and school pudding of the day; british cheeses.** *Starters/Snacks: £4.95 to £5.95. Main Courses: £8.95 to £15.95. Puddings: £4.95 to £5.95*

Enterprise ~ Lease Val Kersey ~ Real ale ~ Bar food (12-2.30, 5.30-9; 12-10(5 Sun) Sat; not Sun evening) ~ Restaurant ~ (01926) 624236 ~ Children welcome ~ Dogs allowed in bar ~ Live band Sun monthly ~ Open 12-3, 5.30-11; 12-11.30(11 Sun) Fri and Sat

Recommended by Philippa Wilsom, David S Allen

BIRMINGHAM   SP0686   MAP 4

Old Joint Stock 🍺

Temple Row West; B2 5NY

Big bustling Fullers pie-and-ale pub with impressive Victorian façade and interior, and a small back terrace

This well run city-centre pub (opposite the cathedral) used to be the City Library and has a most impressive interior. Chandeliers hang from the soaring pink and gilt ceiling, gently illuminated busts line the top of the ornately plastered walls, and there's a splendid, if well worn, cupola above the centre of the room. Big portraits and smart long curtains create an air of unexpected elegance. Around the walls are plenty of tables and chairs, some in cosy corners, with more on a big dining balcony that overlooks the bar and is reached by a grand staircase. A separate room, with panelling and a fireplace, has a more intimate, clubby feel. It does get busy, particularly with local office workers, but effortlessly absorbs what seems like huge numbers of people. As far as we know, this impressive establishment is the northernmost venue to be owned by London-based brewer Fullers and they keep the full range of Fullers beers on handpump alongside a local guest, a dozen wines by the glass and a decent range of malt whiskies that are served from a handsome dark wood island bar counter; helpful friendly service, daily papers, games machine, piped music and board games. Most nights sees something on in the smart purpose-built little theatre on the first floor, and a small back terrace has some cast-iron tables and chairs and wall-mounted heaters.

⏣ **The very reasonably priced pubby menu includes sandwiches, whitebait, ploughman's, a great choice of pies, fish and chips, sausage and mash, beef casserole, roast sweet potato, spinach and leeks in creamy goats cheese and tarragon sauce, a pie tasting plate, chilli beef nachos, and puddings such as rhubarb crumble; british cheese plate.** *Starters/Snacks: £4.25 to £5.25. Main Courses: £8.25 to £15.00. Puddings: £4.25 to £5.70*

Fullers ~ Manager Paul Bancroft ~ Real ale ~ Bar food (12-10(4 Sun)) ~ Restaurant ~ (0121) 200 1892 ~ Children welcome away from main bar ~ Jazz in the bar monthly; theatre ~ Open 11-11; 12-5 Sun; closed Sun evening

Recommended by Dr and Mrs A K Clarke, Colin Gooch, D J and P M Taylor, the Didler, Ian and Nita Cooper, Steve and Liz Tilley, Henry Pursehouse-Tranter, Ian and Helen Stafford, R T and J C Moggridge

BLOXWICH   SJ9902   MAP 4

Turf 🍺

Wolverhampton Road, off A34 just S of A4124, N fringes of Walsall; aka Tinky's; WS3 2EZ

Simple eccentric family-run pub, utterly uncontrived, with five good beers

This basic but very special place, tucked away in a side street and blending in with the other Victorian terraced houses, has been in the same family for nearly 140 years, remaining virtually unchanged in all that time. Once through the front door it still doesn't immediately look like a pub, but more like the hall of a 1930s home. The public bar is through a door on the right, and, reminiscent of a waiting room, it has wooden slatted benches running around the walls, with a big heating pipe clearly visible underneath; there's a superb tiled floor, three small tables, William Morris curtains and wallpaper, and a simple fireplace. What's particularly nice is that even though the unspoilt rooms are Grade II listed, it's far more than just a museum piece but is alive and chatty with friendly locals happy to tell you the history of the place. The friendly landladies serve Oakham JHB, Otter Bright, RCH Pitchfork and Olde Swan Bumble Hole and a changing Mild. There's hatch service out to the hall, on the other side of the old smoking room, which is slightly more comfortable, with unusual padded wall settles with armrests. There's also a tiny back parlour with chairs around a tiled fireplace. The pub's basic charms won't appeal to those who like their creature comforts: the no-frills lavatories are outside, at the end of a simple but pleasant garden. The landladies are not keen on filling in our paperwork, so do please check opening times before you visit.

🍴 **No food.**

Free house ~ Licensees Doris and Zena Hiscott-Wilkes ~ Real ale ~ No credit cards ~ (01922) 407745 ~ Open 1-2.30, 7-11(10.30 Sun)

Recommended by the Didler, Dr and Mrs A K Clarke

BRIERLEY HILL   SO9286   MAP 4

Vine 🍺 £

B4172 between A461 and (nearer) A4100; straight after the turn into Delph Road; DY5 2TN

Incredibly good value, friendly classic down-to-earth Bathams tap; tables in back yard and lunchtime snacks

Known locally as the Bull & Bladder (a reference to the good stained-glass bulls' heads and the very rough representation of bunches of grapes in the front bow windows), this Black Country pub offers a true taste of the West Midlands, with its traditional food, good beer and down-to-earth no-nonsense welcome. Often bustling with chatty locals, the interior meanders through a series of rooms, each different in character. The traditional little front bar has wall benches and simple leatherette-topped oak stools, the comfortable extended snug on the left has solidly built red plush seats, and the tartan decorated larger back bar has brass chandeliers, darts, dominoes and a big-screen TV. A couple of tables and games machines stand in a corridor. Some of the memorabilia you'll see, including one huge pair of horns over a mantelpiece, relates to the Royal Ancient Order of Buffalos, who meet in a room here. The very cheap Bitter and Mild (with perhaps Delph Strong in winter) are kept in top condition and come from the next-door Bathams brewery. There are tables in a back yard and the car park is opposite.

🍴 **A couple of simple but wholesome fresh lunchtime snacks (sandwiches, baguettes, cottage pie, steak and mushroom pie and faggots, chips and peas) are tremendously good value.** *Starters/Snacks: £1.00 to £2.50*

Bathams ~ Manager Melvyn Wood ~ Real ale ~ Bar food (12-3 Mon-Fri) ~ No credit cards ~ (01384) 78293 ~ Children welcome ~ Dogs welcome ~ Open 12-11(10.30 Sun)
Recommended by Theo, Anne and Jane Gaskin, the Didler, Andy and Jill Kassube, MLR, Barbarrick, P Dawn

EDGE HILL
SP3747   MAP 4
Castle
Off A422; OX15 6DJ

Curious gothic folly above historic battlefield, full of interest; open all day

Doing much better under its new licensee, this crenellated octagonal tower (also known as the Round Tower or Radway Tower) is a folly that was built in 1749 by a gothic revival enthusiast to mark the spot where Charles I raised his standard at the start of the Battle of Edge Hill. It's said that after closing time you can hear ghostly battle sounds – a phantom cavalry officer has even been seen galloping by in search of his severed hand, and if you look down from the big attractive garden and terrace, you may be able to convince yourself that you can glimpse the battlefield, down beyond the trees; the views are outstanding when the leaves are gone in winter. The museum-like (and fairly well worn) interior has arched doorways and the walls of the lounge bar, which has the same eight sides as the rest of the main tower, are decorated with maps, swords, pistols, photographs of re-enactments and a collection of Civil War memorabilia. Hook Norton beers are on handpump alongside around 25 malt whiskies; piped music, TV, darts and board games. Upton House is nearby on the A422 and Compton Wynyates, one of the most beautiful houses in this part of England, is not far beyond.

🍽 **Reader's comments rather suggest that the standard of cooking has improved. Dishes might include lunchtime soup, sandwiches and ploughman's, as well as sausage and egg, cottage pie, battered cod, steak in ale pie and rack of pork ribs in barbecue sauce.** *Starters/Snacks: £3.50 to £4.95. Main Courses: £6.50 to £10.50. Puddings: £3.75 to £4.25*

Hook Norton ~ Tenant Tom Douglas ~ Real ale ~ Bar food (12-2.30, 6.30-9) ~ (01295) 670255 ~ Children welcome ~ Dogs allowed in bar ~ Open 11.30-11 ~ Bedrooms: £70S(£70B)/£80S(£80B)
Recommended by George Atkinson, Susan and John Douglas, Pam and John Smith, Jocasta Blockley, Phil and Sally Gorton

FIVE WAYS
SP2270   MAP 4
Case is Altered 🍺
Follow Rowington signposts at junction roundabout off A4177/A4141 N of Warwick, then right into Case Lane; CV35 7JD

Unspoilt convivial local serving well kept beers, including a couple of interesting guests

Real ale drinkers love the peaceful atmosphere at this unspoilt white-painted brick cottage. It's been licensed for over three centuries, and these days the friendly landlady keeps four changing beers that might include Church End Goat's Milk, Greene King IPA, Warwickshire Darling Buds and Wye Valley Butty Bach, all served by a rare type of handpump mounted on the casks that are stilled behind the counter. A door at the back of the building leads into a modest old-fashioned little room with a tiled floor, and an antique bar billiards table protected by an ancient leather cover (it takes pre-decimal sixpences). From here, the simple little main bar has a fine old poster showing the old Lucas Blackwell & Arkwright brewery (now flats) and a clock with its hours spelling out Thornleys Ale – another defunct brewery. There are just a few sturdy old-fashioned tables, with a couple of stout leather-covered settles facing each other over the spotless tiles. Behind a wrought-iron gate is a little brick-paved courtyard with a stone table. Full disabled access.

🍽 **No food.**

Free house ~ Licensee Jackie Willacy ~ Real ale ~ No credit cards ~ (01926) 484206 ~
Open 12-2.30, 6-11; 12-2.15, 7-10.30 Sun

Recommended by Martin Smith, the Didler, Phil and Sally Gorton

GAYDON   SP3654   MAP 4
Malt Shovel 🍺

*Under a mile from M40 junction 12; B4451 into village, then over roundabout and across
B4100; Church Road; CV35 0ET*

**In a quiet village just off the M40; nice mix of pubby bar and smarter restaurant, tasty
food and five real ales**

A jolly decent all-rounder, this spotlessly kept pub with its friendly welcome is a very
handy stop if you are on the M40. Mahogany-varnished boards through to bright
carpeting link the entrance with the bar counter on the right and the blazing log fire on
the left. The central area has a high-pitched ceiling, milk churns and earthenware
containers in a loft above the bar. A few stools are lined up along the counter where five
real ales might include Fullers London Pride, Greene King Abbot, Hook Norton, Everards
Tiger, Wadworths 6X and possibly a guest such as Wye Valley Bitter; most of their dozen
or so wines are available by the glass. Three steps take you up to a snug little space with
some comfortable sofas overlooked by a big stained-glass window and reproductions of
classic posters. At the other end is a busy dining area with flowers on the mix of kitchen,
pub and dining tables; piped music, darts and games machine. They will keep your credit
card if you run a tab outside. The springer spaniel is called Rosie, and the jack russell is
Mollie.

🍴 Enjoyable food, cooked by the chef/landlord, includes good lunchtime sandwiches and
panini's, ploughman's, smoked haddock and spring onion fishcake, salads, duck with
orange, lemon and honey, gammon, egg and chips, beef casserole with horseradish,
battered fish, steaks, sticky toffee pudding and banana and mascarpone cheesecake.
Starters/Snacks: £3.95 to £6.95. Main Courses: £5.95 to £15.95. Puddings: £3.75 to £4.95

Enterprise ~ Lease Richard and Debi Morisot ~ Real ale ~ Bar food (12-2, 6.30-9) ~ Restaurant
~ (01926) 641221 ~ Children welcome ~ Dogs allowed in bar ~ Open 11-3, 5-11, 11-11 Fri, Sat;
12-10.30 Sun

*Recommended by Nigel and Sue Foster, John and Elisabeth Cox, Paul Humphreys, Catherine Dyer, John and
Helen Rushton, Susan and John Douglas, Rory and Jackie Hudson, Pam and John Smith, Tina and David Woods-
Taylor, John and Judy Selby, Paul Goldman, D J and P M Taylor*

GREAT WOLFORD   SP2434   MAP 4
Fox & Hounds 🍽

Village signposted on right on A3400 3 miles S of Shipston-on-Stour; CV36 5NQ

Thoughtfully prepared food at a lovely old country inn

A delightfully timeless atmosphere fills the unpretentious aged bar at this unspoilt
16th-c stone inn. A roaring log fire warms from a fine old inglenook fireplace complete
with aged bread oven. Hops are strung from low beams, a collection of china mugs are
hung from the low ceiling, an appealing collection of tall pews, old chairs and candlelit
tables are spread on spotless flagstones, and the walls are covered with a motley
assortment of antique hunting prints, vintage photographs, and so forth. Soft lighting,
chatty locals and friendly staff enhance its cosy feel. An old-fashioned little tap room
serves Hook Norton Hooky, Purity Pure UBU and a guest from a brewer such as Cottage on
handpump. The terrace has solid wood furniture and a well.

🍴 The chef here is careful about sourcing ingredients and cooks virtually everything from
fresh (including the breads). He likes to combine unusual ingredients and flavours tend
to be decisive: roast garlic and potato soup, sea trout fillet with rhubarb and orange and
samphire butter, fried duck breast with strawberries and balsamic, loin of lamb with
smoked aubergine, black pudding and olive dressing, wild turbot fillet with broad beans,

pancetta and chive cream, fillet steak with oxtail risotto and mushroom cream, and puddings such as lemon and raspberry tart with lemon and yoghurt ice-cream and orange and olive oil cake with clotted cream. *Starters/Snacks: £6.00 to £12.00. Main Courses: £12.00 to £22.00. Puddings: £5.50 to £7.50*

Free house ~ Licensee Gillian Tarbox ~ Real ale ~ Bar food (12-2, 6.30-9, not Sun evening and two weeks in Jan) ~ (01608) 674220 ~ Children welcome ~ Dogs welcome ~ Open 12-2.30, 6-11.30; 12-10.30 Sun; closed Mon ~ Bedrooms: £50B/£80B

Recommended by M Mossman, Chris Glasson, Michael Doswell, David Gunn, Dennis and Gill Keen

HAMPTON IN ARDEN   SP2080   MAP 4
White Lion
High Street; handy for M42 junction 6; B92 0AA

Useful village local; bedrooms

A friendly accommodating welcome awaits at this former farmhouse which is traditional and tidy, with a mix of pubby furniture trimly laid out in the carpeted bar, neatly curtained little windows, low-beamed ceilings and some local memorabilia on the fresh cream walls. Adnams, Black Sheep, Everards, M&B Brew XI and a guest such as Dartmoor Bitter are served on handpump from the timber-planked bar; piped music, TV and board games. It's in an attractive village, oppposite a church mentioned in the Domesday Book, and is handy for the NEC.

⑪ Pubby bar food includes sandwiches, baguettes, chicken caesar salad, fish and chips, sausage and mash, vegetable risotto, sirloin steak, summer pudding and lemon tart. *Starters/Snacks: £4.25 to £9.95. Main Courses: £9.95 to £15.95. Puddings: £4.95*

Punch ~ Tenant John Thorne ~ Real ale ~ Bar food (12-2.30, 6.30-9) ~ Restaurant ~ (01675) 442833 ~ Open 12-11 ~ Bedrooms: £54S/£64S

Recommended by Malcolm and Kate Dowty, Paul Humphreys, Lawrence R Cotter

HENLEY-IN-ARDEN   SP1566   MAP 4
Blue Bell
High Street (A3400, 3.3 miles from M40 junction 16 – exit south-bound only, joining north-bound only); B95 5AT

Friendly and attractive contemporary update of impressive beamed and timbered building

Although the emphasis here is on the quite trendy dining (tables can be filled with diners), there are stools along the counter and readers have popped in for a drink, with one even telling us his two border terriers were made very welcome. The individuality of this ancient building – its handsome coach entry tilted drunkenly over the ages – has been echoed in the personal way that the interior has been brought into the 21st c. Inside, the rambling layout keeps low beams, some wall timbers, dark slate flagstones and a big fireplace, adding a dark red leather settee and armchair here, a couple of dark mulberry-coloured tables there, lots of scatter cushions along one bow-window seat, dark basket-weave high-backed chairs by further mixed dining tables elsewhere – it all adds up to a stylish yet relaxed place. They have well kept changing ales such as Church End Goat's Milk, Highgate Davenports IPA and Purity UBU on handpump, over 20 good wines by the glass, home-made lemonade in summer and mulled wine in winter, and cocktails. Service is interested, friendly and efficient; daily papers; there may be pop piped music. There are tables out on decking behind.

⑪ Virtually everything on the nicely varied menu is prepared here, from breads to ice-cream. As well as a good range of sandwiches and a ploughman's there might be jerusalem artichoke soup with parmesan croûte, goats cheese and roast tomato tatin with red onion marmalade, king scallops st jacques, steak and kidney pie, roast squash, spinach and ricotta cannelloni, roast bass with crab and ginger cream, roast pork belly with port jus, well hung steaks with mushroom gratin and horseradish rösti, and puddings such as limoncello crème brûlée with orange shortbread and sticky toffee pudding with stem ginger caramel sauce. They do a full afternoon tea with a three-tier cake stand, no less. *Starters/Snacks: £4.95 to £7.95. Main Courses: £10.95 to £25.95. Puddings: £5.50 to £6.50*

Free house ~ Licensees Duncan and Leigh Taylor ~ Real ale ~ Bar food (12-9.30(3.30 Sun); not Sun evening; cakes only afternoons) ~ Restaurant ~ (01564) 793049 ~ Children welcome if eating ~ Dogs welcome ~ Open 11(5 Mon)-11; 12-10.30 Sun

Recommended by Martin Smith, R T and J C Moggridge, Sophie Leatharvey

HUNNINGHAM   SP3768   MAP 4

Red Lion ♀

Village signposted off B4453 Leamington—Rugby just E of Weston, and off B4455 Fosse Way 2.5 miles SW of A423 junction; CV33 9DY

Informal, airy and civilised, with good individual food; fine riverside spot

Born near the village, and the son of a local vicar, the landlord at this spacious pub previously worked for Brunning & Price, and has brought many of that group's virtues here, from the general atmosphere and staff attitudes (cheerful and helpful) to the open cleverly sectioned layout, the mix of seating from varnished chapel chairs to a variety of dining chairs, various mainly stripped tables, the rugs on bare boards or even the chunkily old-fashioned radiators and pleasing lighting. He's an avid collector of vintage comic books and perhaps the most striking thing here is the dazzling collection of 320 brightly coloured comics framed and crammed on the white walls; good coal fires, piped music and board games. Drinks include an enterprising changing choice of about 30 wines by the glass, a good range of spirits including 40 single malts, Greene King IPA and a couple of guests such as Holdens Golden Glow and Hook Norton Old Hooky on handpump, and home-made elderflower cordial. One reader was rather delighted to see shire horses crossing the charming 14th-c bridge over the gurgling River Leam, as he sat at one of the teak tables outside on the terrace by the lawn, in the company of cheery families and energetic cyclists. Tables inside have views of the garden and bridge. The landlord tells us he recently purchased a 1948 Massey Ferguson tractor which he plans to install at the bottom of the garden and convert into a safe children's climbing frame – do let us know what you think if you see it; no prams or pushchairs inside.

🍴 Mutton and pork are sourced from local farmers, but the licensee is honest about the viability of sourcing all ingredients locally and genuinely does his best. Food is good, fresh, generous and individual. As well as sandwiches it might include cream of broccoli soup with toasted almonds, goats cheese pâté with red peppers, jasmine tea-cured salmon with lemon crème fraîche mousse, antipasti, minute steak on home-made toast with fried onions and mushrooms, roast pork belly with apple, leek and black pudding mash, fried duck breast and braised leg with spinach and vanilla mash, veal and ham pie with peas and smoked mash, battered cod with mushy peas, rib-eye steak, and puddings such as white chocolate and coffee cheesecake with espresso syrup, poached pear and praline fool and local ice-creams; good Sunday roast. *Starters/Snacks: £4.50 to £5.75. Main Courses: £7.95 to £16.95. Puddings: £4.95 to £8.50*

Greene King ~ Lease Sam Cornwall-Jones ~ Real ale ~ Bar food (12-10(9.30 Sun)) ~ (01926) 632715 ~ Children welcome ~ Dogs welcome ~ Open 12-11(10.30 Sun)

Recommended by Clive and Fran Dutson, Terry Buckland, Ian and Nita Cooper

ILMINGTON   SP2143   MAP 4

Howard Arms

Village signposted with Wimpstone off A3400 S of Stratford; CV36 4LT

Lovely mellow-toned interior; attractive bedrooms

In new hands again, this golden-stone inn is light, airy and gently traditional, with a cosy log fire in a huge stone inglenook, a few good prints on warm golden walls, broad polished flagstones, and a nice mix of furniture from hardwood pews to old church seats;

piped music. Drinks include lots of wines by the glass and Purity Pure Gold and a couple of guests such as Goffs Tournament and Hook Norton on handpump. The garden is particularly charming with fruit trees sheltering the lawn, a colourful herbaceous border and a handful of tables on a neat york-stone terrace. Readers very much enjoy staying in the comfortable bedrooms – the breakfasts are particularly good. The pub is nicely set beside the village green, and there are lovely walks on the nearby hills and pleasant strolls around the village outskirts.

🍽 Bar food might include **twice-baked red leicester cheese soufflé, crispy whitebait with smoked paprika and garlic mayonnaise, steaks, fried salmon on pak choi with garlic prawns, battered fish with minted peas, calves liver with smoked bacon and red wine butter and truffle oil mash, risotto with ceps, truffle oil and parmesan, puddings such as glazed lemon tart with honeycomb ice-cream and lemon syrup, crème brûlée with liquorice jelly and banoffi pie.** *Starters/Snacks: £4.00 to £8.00. Main Courses: £6.00 to £12.00. Puddings: £4.00 to £5.00*

Free house ~ Licensee Tim Churchman ~ Real ale ~ Bar food ~ Restaurant ~ (01608) 682226 ~ Children welcome ~ Dogs allowed in bar ~ Open 11-11; 12-10.30 Sun ~ Bedrooms: £90B/£135B

Recommended by Eithne Dandy, Michael Dandy, Leslie and Barbara Owen, Andrew and Judith Hudson, Bernard Stradling, Andrea Rampley, Mike and Mary Carter, George and Linda Ozols, Karen Eliot, Clive and Fran Dutson, Anthony and Pam Stamer, Mary McSweeney, John and Hilary Penny, Prof H G Allen, David S Allen, Chris Glasson

LONG COMPTON
SP2832   MAP 4

Red Lion
A3400 S of Shipston-on-Stour; CV36 5JS

Traditional character and contemporary touches in comfortably refurbished coaching inn; bedrooms

Smartened up by its new owners since it was last in the *Guide*, this attractive former coaching inn has been well refurbished to give a contemporary twist to its original features. The roomy lounge bar is beamed, with brown panelling and stripped stone and, although airy, it has some nice rambling corners with old-fashioned built-in settles among pleasantly assorted and comfortable seats and leather armchairs and tables on flagstones and carpets, and a warming woodburning stove. Well kept Hook Norton and a guest such as Caledonian 80/- on handpump. The simple public bar has pool, a fruit machine, juke box and TV; piped music. There are tables out in the big back garden, with a play area.

🍽 Bar food includes **sandwiches, seared squid with chorizo and garlic chilli dressing, mushroom with confit onion bruschetta and stilton rarebit, steak and ale pie, twice-baked wensleydale soufflé with apple, celery and walnut salad, grilled marlin loin with mango, chilli and spring onion salsa, grilled pork medallions with bramley apple, redcurrants and port jus, and puddings such as glazed lemon tart with raspberry sorbet, vanilla panna cotta with summer berries and brandy-snap tuile, and an english cheeseboard; good set-price lunch in bar.** *Starters/Snacks: £4.95 to £6.95. Main Courses: £11.95 to £18.95. Puddings: £5.50 to £5.95*

Free house ~ Licensee Lisa Phipps ~ Real ale ~ Bar food (12-2.30, 6-9; 12-9.30(9 Sun) Fri, Sat) ~ Restaurant ~ (01608) 684221 ~ Children welcome ~ Dogs welcome ~ Open 10-3, 6-11; 10-11 Sun ~ Bedrooms: £55B/£99B

Recommended by Chris Glasson, Eithne Dandy

NETHERTON

S09488   MAP 4

Old Swan ◖ £

Halesowen Road (A459 just S of centre); DY2 9PY

Traditional, unspoilt, friendly local serving own-brew beers and bar food

The front public bar at this character-laden place (known locally at Ma Pardow's) is deliciously unspoilt, with a big swan centrepiece in its lovely patterned enamel ceiling, mirrors engraved with a swan design behind the bar, an old-fashioned cylinder stove with its chimney angling away to the wall, and traditional furnishings. The unchanged multi-roomed layout also includes a cosy back snug which is fitted out very much in keeping with the rest of the building, using recycled bricks and woodwork, and even matching etched window panels and there's a more modern lounge. The four beers they brew here are Bumblehole, Dark Swan, Entire and Olde Swan Original, and they do a couple of seasonal ones as well; back car park.

🍴 Lunchtime bar food is pubby and straightforward: soup of the day, baked potatoes, ploughman's, faggots, scampi and fish and chips. The longer evening menu might include **goats cheese salad, pork belly with creamy cider sauce, chicken curry, surf and turf and steaks. Traditional home-made puddings include cheesecake, profiteroles and crème brûlée; pork sandwiches only on Sunday evening.** *Starters/Snacks: £2.95 to £4.95. Main Courses: £7.30 to £14.50. Puddings: £3.25 to £4.45*

Punch ~ Tenant Tim Newey ~ Real ale ~ Bar food (12-2, 6-9; not Sun evening) ~ Restaurant ~ (01384) 253075 ~ Dogs allowed in bar ~ Open 11-11; 12-4, 7-10.30 Sun
Recommended by the Didler

PRESTON BAGOT

SP1765   MAP 4

Crabmill 🍴 ☺

A4189 Henley-in-Arden—Warwick; B95 5EE

WARWICKSHIRE DINING PUB OF THE YEAR

Mill conversion with comfortable décor, relaxed atmosphere and smart bar food

Readers have enjoyed this rambling old cider mill hugely over the last year, sending us particular praise for the accommodating friendly service which stays right on track even when it gets busy. This is a lovely old building that has been attractively decorated with contemporary furnishings and pleasing colour combinations. The smart two-level lounge area has comfortable settees and easy chairs, low tables, big table lamps and one or two rugs on bare boards. The elegant and roomy low-beamed dining area has caramel leather banquettes and chairs at pine tables, and a beamed and flagstoned bar area has some stripped-pine country tables and chairs, snug corners and a gleaming metal bar serving Greene King Abbot and IPA and Purity Pure Ubu on handpump, with ten wines by the glass from a mostly new world list. Piped music is well chosen and well reproduced. There are lots of tables (some of them under cover) out in a large, attractive, decked garden. Booking is advised, especially Sunday lunchtime when it's popular with families.

🍴 As well as their lunchtime snack menu which includes **interestingly filled pitta, bagels and wraps and a couple of good value dishes such as bolognese with linguine, the imaginative menu might include good salt and pepper squid with lime mayonnaise and spiced tomato pickle, seared beef with rocket, radish and parmesan salad, bass fillets with sweet potato, spinach curry and mint yoghurt, grilled rib-eye, seared duck breast with spiced confit onions, harissa and tomato pesto and spinach, goats cheese and crème fraîche tagliatelle.** *Starters/Snacks: £4.00 to £8.50. Main Courses: £9.95 to £17.95. Puddings: £5.25 to £5.95*

People named as recommenders after the Main Entries have told us that the pub should be included. But they have not written the report – we have, after anonymous on-the-spot inspection.

Free house ~ Licensee Sally Coll ~ Real ale ~ Bar food (12-5, 6.30-9.30; 12.30-4 Sun; not Sun evening) ~ Restaurant ~ (01926) 843342 ~ Children welcome ~ Dogs allowed in bar ~ Open 11-11; 12-6 Sun; closed Sun evening

Recommended by Roger and Anne Newbury, Dr A B Clayton, Andy and Claire Barker, Martin and Pauline Jennings, P and J Shapley, Mike and Mary Carter, Martin Smith, KC, Brendon Skinner, Simon and Mandy King, Dr and Mrs D Scott, Dick Vardy, Keith and Sue Ward, Dr and Mrs A K Clarke, John and Helen Rushton

SEDGLEY   SO9293   MAP 4

Beacon ★ 🍺

Bilston Street (no pub sign on our visit, but by Beacon Lane); A463, off A4123 Wolverhampton—Dudley; DY3 1JE

Good, unusual own-brew beers and interesting guests at a beautifully preserved down-to-earth Victorian pub

Named after a former landlady, the well kept Sarah Hughes beers brewed in the traditional Victorian tower brewery (you can arrange a look round) at the back of this plain-looking old brick pub are Dark Ruby, Pale Amber and Surprise Bitter. They also keep a couple of unusual guests from brewers such as Castle Rock and Elland. The front door (it's worth walking round from the car park for a full appreciation of the building) opens into a simple quarry-tiled drinking corridor where you may find a couple of cheery locals leaning up the stair wall, chatting to the barman propped in the doorway of his little central serving booth. Go through the door into the little snug on your left and you can easily imagine a 19th-c traveller tucked up on one of the wall settles, next to the imposing green-tiled marble fireplace with its big misty mirror, the door closed for privacy and warmth, and a drink handed through the glazed hatch. The dark woodwork, turkey carpet, velvet and net curtains, heavy mahogany tables, old piano and little landscape prints all seem unchanged since those times. A timelessly sparse tap room on the right has a black kettle and embroidered mantel over a blackened range, and a nice old stripped wooden wall bench. The corridor that runs round the serving booth, past the stairs and into a big well proportioned dark-panelled old smoking room, with sturdy red leather wall settles down the length of each side, gilt-based cast-iron tables, a big blue carpet on the lino and big dramatic old sea prints. The conservatory is densely filled with plants and has no seats. A children's play area in the garden has a slide, climbing frame and roundabout.

🍴 They serve cheese and onion and ham cobs.

Own brew ~ Licensee John Hughes ~ Real ale ~ No credit cards ~ (01902) 883380 ~ Children allowed in family room ~ Open 12-2.30, 5.30-11; 12-3, 6-11 Sat; 12-3, 7-10.30 Sun

Recommended by the Didler

SHUSTOKE   SP2290   MAP 4

Griffin 🍺 £

5 miles from M6 junction 4; A446 towards Tamworth, then right on to B4114 and go straight through Coleshill; pub is at Church End, a mile E of village; B46 2LB

Ten real ales including own-brew beers, and simple good value lunchtime snacks at this unpretentious country local; garden and play area

The chatty landlord brews Griffin 'Ere It Is, Black Magic Women and Gorgeous George in the barn next door to this genuinely friendly country local, and they are served alongside seven changing guests from brewers such as Hook Norton, RCH, Theakstons and Wadworths; also lots of english wines, farm cider and mulled wine in winter. Usually busy with a cheery crowd, the low-beamed L-shaped bar has log fires in two stone fireplaces (one's a big inglenook), fairly simple décor from cushioned café seats (some quite closely spaced) and sturdily elm-topped sewing trestles, to one nice old-fashioned settle, beer mats on the ceiling and a games machine. Outside, there are old-fashioned seats and tables on the back grass with distant Birmingham views, a play area and a large terrace with plants in raised beds.

🍴 Straightforward bar food in substantial helpings includes sandwiches, ploughman's, cheese and broccoli bake, gammon, scampi, steak and ale pie, mixed grill and 10oz sirloin steak. *Starters/Snacks: £3.50 to £4.50. Main Courses: £5.50 to £7.50*

Own brew ~ Licensee Michael Pugh ~ Real ale ~ Bar food (12-2 Mon-Sat) ~ No credit cards ~ (01675) 481205 ~ Children in conservatory ~ Dogs welcome ~ Open 12-2.30(3 Sun), 7-11(10.30 Sun)

Recommended by Michael Beale, Clive and Fran Dutson, M S and M Imhoff, Dr D J and Mrs S C Walker, Peter Cole

WELFORD-ON-AVON   SP1452 MAP 4

Bell

Off B439 W of Stratford; High Street; CV37 8EB

Enjoyably civilised pub with appealing ancient interior, good food and great range of drinks including five real ales; terrace

Staff at this delightful 17th-c place are knowledgeable, organised and kind and, as a result, readers have thoroughly enjoyed their visits here; most people come to dine and booking is advised. The attractive interior (full of signs of the building's great age) is divided into five comfortable areas, each with its own character, from the cosy terracotta-painted bar to a light and airy gallery room with its antique wood panelling, solid oak floor and contemporary Lloyd Loom chairs. Flagstone floors, stripped or well polished antique or period-style furniture, and three good fires (one in an inglenook), add warmth and cosiness. Hobsons and Purity Pure Gold, two or three guests such as Charles Wells Bombardier, Hook Norton Hooky and Purity Ubu are on handpump, and they've a dozen or so wines including champagne and local ones by the glass; piped music. In summer, the creeper-covered exterior is hung with lots of colourful baskets, and there are tables and chairs on a vine-covered dining terrace. This riverside village has an appealing church and pretty thatched black and white cottages.

🍴 The menu includes a good choice of sandwiches, fried brie with ginger and apricot compote, crispy whitebait, battered haddock, salads, breaded garlic chicken stuffed with smoked cheddar on spinach and sweet potato mash, sausage and mash, beef and tomato casserole, minty lamb curry, and daily specials such as smoked salmon pâté with chervil, cheese and spring onion quiche, grilled bream with salsa verde, steak and ale pie and moroccan chicken with apricot and date couscous, and puddings such as vanilla crème brûlée with caraway shortbread and sticky toffee pudding; **Sunday roast** *Starters/Snacks: £4.95 to £6.95. Main Courses: £10.25 to £17.95. Puddings: £5.50*

Laurel (Enterprise) ~ Lease Colin and Teresa Ombler ~ Real ale ~ Bar food (11.45-2.30(3 Fri, Sat), 6-9.30(10 Fri, Sat); 11.45-9.30 Sun) ~ Restaurant ~ (01789) 750353 ~ Children welcome ~ Open 11.30-3, 6-11; 11.30-11.30 Sat; 11.45-10.30 Sun

Recommended by Keith and Sue Ward, George Bell, Chris and Jeanne Downing, Mr and Mrs A Curry, Leslie and Barbara Owen, Allan Westbury, John and Sharon Hancock, Eithne Dandy, Rod Stoneman, Prof H G Allen, John Saville, Mrs L Mills, Martin and Pauline Jennings, Mike and Mary Carter, Lyn Ellwood

LUCKY DIP

Besides the fully inspected pubs, you might like to try these Lucky Dips recommended to us and described by readers (if you do, please send us reports: feedback@goodguides.com).

ALDERMINSTER [SP2348]
☆ *Bell* CV37 8NY [A3400 Oxford—Stratford]: Refurbished open-plan Georgian dining pub, now part of the Alscot Estate, contemporary styling mixing well with low beams, flagstone/polished wood floors and open fires, small bar with Alscot Ale (brewed for them by Warwickshire) and a guest such as Hook Norton, good range of wines by the glass, enjoyable interesting if not cheap food using some estate-sourced ingredients, pleasant service, restaurant and

conservatory with Stour Valley views; children and dogs welcome, courtyard tables, garden, four redone bedrooms, open all day Fri-Sun *(Moira and John Cole, K H Frostick, David Gunn, Eithne Dandy, LYM)*
ANSLEY [SP3091]
Lord Nelson CV10 9PQ [Birmingham Rd]: Enjoyable reasonably priced food in ample space inc unusual galleon-style restaurant, good beers from neighbouring Tunnel microbrewery (tours available), great staff;

terrace tables, open all day wknds
(Martin Smith)

ARDENS GRAFTON [SP1153]

☆ *Golden Cross* B50 4LG [off A46 or B439 W of
Stratford, OS Sheet 150 map ref 114538;
Wixford Rd]: 18th-c stone-built open-plan
dining pub, attractive and welcoming, with
wide choice of good generous affordable
food from sandwiches to game, set lunch
deals too, pleasant welcoming service (can
be slow when busy), well kept Wells &
Youngs and guests such as Courage, Purity
and St Austell, decent wines; comfortable
light wood furniture on flagstones, log fire,
nice décor and good lighting; piped music;
wheelchair access, attractive garden with
big heated umbrellas on terrace, nice
views *(George Atkinson, Martin and
Pauline Jennings, Stanley and
Annie Matthews)*

ARMSCOTE [SP2444]

☆ *Fox & Goose* CV37 8DD [off A3400
Stratford—Shipston]: Former blacksmith's
forge with locals' bar and woodburner in
dining area, Black Sheep, Butcombe, Hook
Norton and a guest, food all day Fri-Sun;
piped music, TV; children and dogs welcome,
vine-covered deck overlooking lawn, brightly
painted bedrooms named after *Cluedo*
characters, open from 9am, all day Fri-Sun
*(Keith and Sue Ward, Anthony and
Pam Stamer, LYM, Stuart Doughty)*

AVON DASSETT [SP4049]

Avon CV47 2AS [off B4100 Banbury—
Warwick]: Double-fronted mellow-stone pub
with pleasant décor and relaxing
atmosphere, chatty friendly staff, enjoyable
food (all day Sun till 8pm) from pub staples
to more imaginative dishes inc good value
set lunch, changing ales, several wines by
the glass; live music Fri; children, dogs and
muddy walkers welcome – bar's flagstones
cope well, tables out in front, small side
garden, attractive village by country park,
open all day wknds *(Anthony and
Marie Lewis, Guy Vowles)*

BAGINTON [SP3375]

☆ *Old Mill* CV8 3AH [Mill Hill]: Popular olde-
worlde Chef & Brewer watermill conversion
nr airport, Midland Air Museum and Lunt
Roman fort; heavy beams, timbers and
candlelight, slate and wood floors, warm
rustic-theme bar, leather seating by open
fire, linked dining areas, good wine
selection, well kept Courage, Greene King
and Wells & Youngs Bombardier, good choice
of food all day inc fixed-price menu
(Mon-Thurs), friendly uniformed staff;
children welcome, lovely terraced gardens
down to River Sowe, disabled facilities,
26 refurbished bedrooms *(Martin and
Alison Stainsby, LYM, Susan and
John Douglas, Duncan Cloud)*

BARSTON [SP2078]

☆ *Bulls Head* B92 0JU [from M42 junction 5,
A4141 towards Warwick, first left, then
signed down Barston Lane]: Unassuming and
unspoilt partly Tudor village pub, friendly

landlord and efficient service, well kept
Adnams, Hook Norton and two guests,
enjoyable traditional food from sandwiches
to good fresh fish and Sun lunch; log fires,
comfortable lounge with pictures and plates,
oak-beamed bar with a little Buddy Holly
memorabilia, separate dining room; children
and dogs allowed, good-sized secluded
garden alongside, hay barn, open all day Fri-
Sun *(R T and J C Moggridge, Martin Smith,
Clive and Fran Dutson)*

BILSTON [SO9496]

Trumpet WV14 0EP [High St]: Friendly
Holdens pub, their ales and guests kept well,
good free nightly jazz; trumpets and other
instruments hanging from ceiling, lots of
musical memorabilia and photographs, back
conservatory *(the Didler)*

BIRMINGHAM [SP0788]

☆ *Bartons Arms* B6 4UP [High St, Aston
(A34)]: Magnificent Edwardian landmark, a
trouble-free oasis in rather a daunting area,
impressive linked richly decorated rooms
from the palatial to the snug, original
tilework murals, stained glass and mahogany,
decorative fireplaces, sweeping stairs to
handsome rooms upstairs; several well kept
ales inc Oakham from ornate island bar with
snob screens in one section, interesting
imported bottled beers and frequent mini-
beer festivals, good choice of well priced
thai food (not Mon), good young staff; open
all day *(BB, the Didler, Steve Jennings)*

Old Contemptibles B3 2HB [Edmund St]:
Spacious Edwardian pub with lofty ceiling
and lots of woodwork, decent choice of real
ales, friendly young staff, well priced food
inc good range of sausages, popular
lunchtime with office workers; upstairs
lavatories; handy central location
(Jack Matthew, LYM)

Prince of Wales B1 2NP [Cambridge St]:
Traditional pub surviving behind the rep
theatre and symphony hall amidst the
concrete newcomers, L-shaped bar with
friendly mix of customers; half a dozen or
more well kept beers such as Everards,
Timothy Taylors and Wells & Youngs, bargain
straightforward lunchtime food inc good
baguettes, fast friendly service; may be
piped music; popular with Grand Union Canal
users in summer *(Chris Evans)*

☆ *Wellington* B2 5SN [Bennetts Hill]: Superb
range of changing beers mostly from small
breweries (always one from Black Country
Ales), also farm ciders, in roomy old-
fashioned high-ceilinged pub, experienced
landlord and friendly staff, can get very
busy; no food, but plates and cutlery if you
bring your own – on cheese nights people
bring different ones that are pooled; tables
out behind, open all day *(Roger Shipperley,
Dr and Mrs A K Clarke, Richard Tingle,
the Didler, Martin Grosberg, Jack Matthew)*

BRETFORD [SP4277]

Queens Head CV23 0JY [A428 Coventry—
Rugby]: Extended 19th-c beamed dining pub
popular for its wide choice of reasonably

priced food (all day Sun), OAP lunchtime deals Mon-Sat, fast service, four real ales inc Theakstons; film star photographs, live music Weds night; garden with big play area *(Peter and Audrey Dowsett)*

CHURCHOVER [SP5180]

Haywaggon CV23 0EP [handy for M6 junction 1, off A426; The Green]: Good italian food from neapolitan landlord as well as pubbier staples (must book Sun lunch), well kept Purity UBU, good coffee, relaxed atmosphere and friendly staff; two snug eating areas, lots of beams, standing timbers, brasses, nooks and crannies; may be piped music; tables outside with play area, on edge of quiet village, beautiful views over Swift Valley *(R L Borthwick, BB, Rob and Catherine Dunster, John Wooll)*

CLAVERDON [SP2064]

☆ *Red Lion* CV35 8PE [Station Rd; B4095 towards Warwick]: Beamed Tudor dining pub doing enjoyable food (all day Sun) from pub favourites up, friendly attentive service, decent wines and well kept Purity Mad Goose; log fires, linked rooms inc back dining area with country views over sheltered back heated deck and gardens; open all day *(Roger Braithwaite, Clive and Fran Dutson, BB)*

COVENTRY [SP3279]

Old Windmill CV1 3BA [Spon St]: Timber-framed 15th-c pub under new management, lots of tiny old rooms, exposed beams in uneven ceilings, carved oak seats on flagstones, inglenook woodburner, half a dozen real ales, often farm cider, pubby lunchtime bar food (Tues evening curry); popular with students and busy at wknds; piped music, games machines and juke box, darts, no credit cards; open all day, cl Mon lunchtime *(the Didler, LYM)*

Town Wall CV1 4AH [Bond St, among car parks behind Belgrade Theatre]: Busy Victorian city-centre local with five real ales inc Adnams, farm cider, nice hot drinks' choice, good generous lunchtime doorstep sandwiches, filled rolls and cheap hot dishes; unspoilt basic front bar and tiny snug, engraved windows and open fires, bigger back lounge with actor/playwright photographs and pictures of old Coventry, open fires; big-screen sports TV; open all day *(BB, Alan Johnson, Clive and Fran Dutson, Donna and Roger)*

DUDLEY [SO9487]

Park DY2 9PN [George St/Chapel St]: Tap for adjacent Holdens brewery, their beers kept well, decent simple lunchtime food, low prices, friendly service, conservatory, small games room; sports TV; open all day *(the Didler, Colin Fisher)*

DUNCHURCH [SP4871]

Dun Cow CV22 6NJ [a mile from M45 junction 1: A45/A426]: Handsomely beamed Vintage Inn with massive log fires and other traditional features, friendly efficient staff, popular reasonably priced food all day inc specials, good range of wines by the glass,

well kept Bass, Everards, Marstons and guests from small counter; piped music; children welcome, tables in attractive former coachyard and on sheltered side lawn, bedrooms in adjacent Innkeepers Lodge, open all day *(Revd R P Tickle, P M Newsome, George Atkinson, LYM)*

EARLSWOOD [SP1174]

Red Lion B94 6AQ [Lady Lane (past the Lakes)]: Imposing twin-gabled black and white Georgian pub, good value traditional food all day (busy wknds) inc good Sun roast, prompt friendly service; several small but high-ceilinged rooms each with its own character, sturdy tables and chairs, some wall settles, back room with open fire, chandeliers and bigger tables; disabled access *(Martin Smith, Tim Venn)*

EASENHALL [SP4679]

☆ *Golden Lion* CV23 0JA [Main St]: Spotless bar in 16th-c part of busy comfortable hotel, low beams, dark panelling, settles and inglenook log fire, beers such as Purity and Wells & Youngs Bombardier, enjoyable food inc Sun carvery, friendly attentive service; piped music; children welcome, disabled access, tables out at side and on spacious lawn, 20 well equipped bedrooms, decent breakfast, attractive value, open all day *(Rob and Catherine Dunster, Alan Johnson, Simon Cottrell, WW, LYM, John Wooll, Dr and Mrs C W Thomas)*

ETTINGTON [SP2748]

Chequers CV37 7SR [Banbury Rd (A422)]: Nicely refurbished and doing well under newish management, popular locally for its enterprising well presented food, ales such as Black Sheep, Hook Norton and Skinners, good wines, efficient friendly service; log fire in drinkers' area at front, steps up to dining part with painted tables and matching upholstered chairs; big back garden with raised section *(LYM, Paul Booth, Clive and Fran Dutson, Dennis Jones)*

FARNBOROUGH [SP4349]

☆ *Inn at Farnborough* OX17 1DZ [off A423 N of Banbury]: Upmarket dining pub with wide choice of enjoyable food from pubby things to pricier more restaurnty dishes, early evening meal deals Fri, Greene King ales, good choice of wines by the glass; modern minimalist décor blending attractively with flagstones and mullioned windows; garden picnic-sets, cl Mon lunchtime *(LYM, Anthony and Marie Lewis)*

FENNY COMPTON [SP4352]

Wharf Inn CV47 2FE [A423 Banbury—Southam, nr Fenny Compton]: Open-plan pub by Bridge 136 on South Oxford Canal, good layout with small central flagstoned bar, well kept Greene King IPA, fairly straightforward food from breakfast on; piped music, games machine; children welcome, disabled facilities, waterside garden, moorings (gas and laundry for boaters), open all day *(JHBS, Clive and Fran Dutson, LYM)*

FLECKNOE [SP5163]
Old Olive Bush CV23 8AT [off A425 W of
Daventry]: Characterful unspoilt Edwardian
pub in quiet photogenic village, friendly
atmosphere, limited choice of enjoyable
traditional food inc Sun lunch cooked by
landlady, well kept changing ales such as
Church End and Greene King, decent wine;
open fire in bar, steps up to back area with
skittles, dining room with etched-glass
windows and fire; attractive garden behind
(Geoff and Teresa Salt, Clive and Fran Dutson)
FRANKTON [SP4270]
Friendly CV23 9NY [just over a mile S of
B4453 Leamington Spa—Rugby; Main St]:
Old low-ceilinged village dining pub doing
well under its two newish landladies, good
reasonably priced food, two neat well
furnished rooms, open fire, friendly
atmosphere *(Ted George)*
HALESOWEN [SO9683]
Hawne Tavern B63 3UG [Attwood St]:
Banks's, Bathams and Bobs plus six
interesting guests from side street local's
rough-cut central servery, bar with
cushioned pews, darts, pool and juke box in
games area, lounge with leatherette-backed
wall banquettes; good value baguettes (not
Sat lunchtime, Sun), friendly staff; small
terrace, cl till 4.30pm wkdys, open all day
wknds *(the Didler)*
Waggon & Horses B63 3TU [Stourbridge Rd]:
Plenty of real beers inc Bathams and up
to seven or so guests from small brewers in
chatty bare-boards bar and more spacious
lounge, belgian brews, real ciders and
country wine, good snacks, low prices;
brewery memorabilia, lots of character; TV,
Tues music night, very busy wknds; open all
day *(the Didler, Jayne Fisentzides)*
HALFORD [SP2645]
☆ *Halford Bridge* CV36 5BN [Fosse Way
(A429)]: Cotswold-stone inn with solid
modern furniture in roomy civilised lounge
bar, inglenook woodburner, tasty food (not
Sun evening) from good lunchtime
sandwiches and pubby favourites up, well
kept Hook Norton and a guest, good choice
of wines by the glass, friendly helpful staff,
restaurant; attractive inner courtyard with
modern sculpture/water feature,
11 bedrooms, open all day *(Peter and
Jean Hoare, John and Sharon Hancock)*
HAMPTON LUCY [SP2557]
Boars Head CV35 8BE [Church St, E of
Stratford]: Roomy two-bar local next to
lovely church, changing real ales, good value
pubby food inc lunchtime baguettes, friendly
service, low beams and log fire; soft piped
music; secluded back garden, pretty village
nr Charlcote House *(Teresa and
Rodney Marshall)*
HARBURY [SP3959]
Great Western CV47 2ST [Deppers Bridge;
4 miles N of M40 junction 12; B4451]:
Roomy spotless pub under new licensees –
though the model train still clatters round
overhead; enjoyable food from varied menu

inc interesting sharing boards, Black Country
and Ossett ales; terrace tables, good value
bedrooms *(Simon Le Fort, Joan and
Tony Walker, Susan and John Douglas)*
HATTON [SP2467]
Waterman CV35 7JJ [A4177, by Grand Union
Canal]: Above Hatton flight of 21 locks
'Stairway to Heaven'; refurbished former
18th-c coaching inn with far views from
sunny balcony and huge garden; linked
rooms, log fire, good range of food all day
from sandwiches and pub favourites to some
unusual dishes, Sun roasts, local ales, great
choice of wines by the glass, friendly
efficient staff; children welcome, barbecues,
good walks nearby, moorings *(Ian and
Nita Cooper, Martin Smith)*
HILLMORTON [SP5273]
Paddox CV22 5EY [Hillmorton Rd]: Cheerful,
welcoming and recently refurbished, three
bar areas served from wrap-around counter,
well kept Greene King ales, decent wine,
tasty good value pub food, woodburner; quiz
and karaoke nights, darts *(Rob and
Catherine Dunster)*
KENILWORTH [SP2872]
Clarendon Arms CV8 1NB [Castle Hill]: Busy
pub opp castle, good value generous food in
several rooms off long bare-boards bustling
bar, largish peaceful upstairs dining room;
good friendly staff, several real ales inc
locals such as Purity; daytime car park fee
deducted from bill; metal tables on small
raised terrace, open all day wknds
(Alan Johnson, Alun Jones)
Royal Oak CV8 2EZ [New St]: Popular,
friendly roadside pub, well kept Adnams,
Black Sheep, Fullers, Timothy Taylors and
guests, games room; Sky TV; terrace, open
all day wknds *(the Didler)*
Virgin & Castle CV8 1LY [High St]: Maze of
intimate rooms off inner servery, small snugs
by entrance corridor, flagstones, heavy
beams, lots of woodwork inc booth seating,
coal fire; quick friendly service, well kept
Everards and guests, good coffee, reasonably
priced bar food from generous sandwiches
up; games bar upstairs, restaurant; children
in eating areas, disabled facilities, tables in
sheltered garden, open all day *(LYM,
Nigel and Sue Foster, Donna and Roger,
the Didler)*
KNOWLE [SP1876]
Black Boy B93 0EB [off A4177 about
1.5 miles S]: Much-extended open-plan
canalside pub, isolated but popular, with
wide choice of good food, well kept ales,
reasonable prices, attentive staff; fruit
machine; outside seating *(Anthony and
Pam Stamer)*
Herons Nest B93 0EE [A4110 (Warwick Rd)
about a mile S]: Popular beamed Vintage Inn
dining pub, updated but keeping character,
sensibly priced traditional food all day
(service can be slow), plenty of good value
wines by the glass, real ales; open fires,
interesting décor, some flagstones and high-
backed settles, big dining room overlooking

Grand Union Canal; lots of tables out by water, moorings, Innkeepers Lodge bedrooms, open all day *(Martin Smith, John Robertson)*

LAPWORTH [SP1871]

☆ *Boot* B94 6JU [Old Warwick Rd (B4439, by Grand Union Canal)]: Popular upmarket dining pub, good contemporary brasserie menu from panini and interesting light dishes up, efficient friendly service by smart young staff, upscale wines (big glasses), Wadworths 6X; cosy fires, charming raftered upstairs dining room; children and good-natured dogs welcome, beautifully done waterside garden, pleasant walks, open all day *(Martin Smith, R L Borthwick, Mike and Mary Carter, Leslie and Barbara Owen, Patti Mickelson)*

Navigation B94 6NA [Old Warwick Rd (B4439 SE)]: Two-bar beamed and flagstoned local by Grand Union Canal, warm coal fire and some bright canal ware, modern back dining room, wide range of generous food from good sandwiches up, well kept ales such as Holdens, St Austell Tribute and Timothy Taylors Landlord; children welcome, hatch service to waterside terrace, open all day *(Martin Smith, Gerry and Rosemary Dobson, Clive and Fran Dutson, LYM)*

LEAMINGTON SPA [SP3165]

Benjamin Satchwell CV32 4AQ [The Parade]: Well laid out Wetherspoons, tidy and airy, with their usual food all day, quick friendly service, low-priced beers inc local ones, two levels, some cosy seating, back family area, nice relaxed atmosphere; disabled facilities, cheerful hanging baskets at front, open all day *(George Atkinson)*

LITTLE COMPTON [SP2530]

☆ *Red Lion* GL56 ORT [off A44 Moreton-in-Marsh—Chipping Norton]: Low-beamed 16th-c Cotswold-stone inn smartened up under welcoming new licensees, enjoyable good value food from pubby things up, Donnington ales, good choice of wines by the glass, snug alcoves, inglenook woodburner; darts and pool in public bar; well behaved children and dogs welcome, pretty side garden with aunt sally, two nice bedrooms *(LYM, P and J Shapley, Michael Dandy)*

LONG ITCHINGTON [SP4165]

☆ *Buck & Bell* CV47 9PH [The Green]: Brick-built country dining pub with impressive interior, light linked rooms on different levels inc galleried area up spiral staircase, slate floors and stripped brick, woodburners; good up-to-date food with separate menus for light and full meals (some quite pricey), four well kept ales inc Church End, ample wine choice, charming uniformed staff; piped music; children and dogs welcome, picnic-sets in front, open all day *(Martin Smith, Rob and Catherine Dunster, George Atkinson, Nigel and Sue Foster)*

LONG MARSTON [SP1548]

Masons Arms CV37 8RG: Down-to-earth village local much improved under new

management, well kept beer and good straightforward food *(Mark Sykes, Prof H G Allen)*

LOWER BRAILES [SP3139]

George OX15 5HN [B4035 Shipston—Banbury]: Handsome old stone-built inn with cheery and roomy flagstoned front bar, inglenook log fire and dark oak tables, panelled oak-beamed back bar with soft lighting; well kept Hook Norton ales, enjoyable imaginative food (not Sun evening, Mon lunchtime), country-style flagstoned restaurant; live music Fri, Sat; children and dogs welcome, aunt sally in sizeable neatly kept sheltered garden with terrace and covered area, lovely village, good walks, five comfortable bedrooms, open all day wknds *(JHBS, Richard Eden, LYM)*

LOWER GORNAL [SO9291]

Black Bear DY3 2AE [Deepdale Lane]: Simple split-level local based on former 18th-c farmhouse, Kinver ales and microbrewery guests, good choice of whiskies, friendly staff, coal fire; open all day wknds *(the Didler)*

Fountain DY3 2PE [Temple St]: Lively two-room local with helpful friendly landlord and staff, nine changing ales (beer festivals), two farm ciders, country wines and imported beers, enjoyable inexpensive food all day (not Sun evening), back dining area; pigs-and-pen skittles; piped music; open all day *(the Didler)*

Old Bulls Head DY3 2NU [Redhall Rd]: Busy Victorian local with own Black Country ales from back microbrewery and two guest beers, well filled cobs, open fire, games room, some live music; open all day wknds, from 4pm wkdys *(the Didler)*

LYE [SO9284]

Windsor Castle DY9 7DG [Stourbridge Rd]: Contemporary minimalist décor and furnishings, nine good value Sadlers ales brewed here (tours available), guest beers too, friendly helpful staff, good range of enjoyable cheap food inc some imaginative dishes often using their beer (snacks all day, no evening meals Sun); bright lighting and lively acoustics, some brewing memorabilia; open all day *(Dr Kevan Tucker)*

MERIDEN [SP2482]

Bulls Head CV7 7NN [Main Rd]: All-day M&B dining pub dating from the 15th c, modernised interior with log fires, beams, bare boards and flagstones, lots of nooks and crannies, three well kept ales, good choice of wines by the glass, efficient service; disabled facilities, courtyard, 13 Innkeepers Lodge bedrooms *(anon)*

MONKS KIRBY [SP4682]

☆ *Bell* CV23 0QY [just off B4027 W of Pailton]: Hospitable long-serving spanish landlord and his sweet dogs enlivening this dimly lit pub, dark beams, timber dividers, flagstones and cobbles, wide choice of good if not cheap spanish food inc starters doubling as tapas and notable zarzuela fish stew; fine range of spanish wines and of brandies and malt whiskies, relaxed informal service, well kept Greene King ales; appropriate piped music; children and dogs welcome, streamside back terrace with country view, may be cl Mon *(LYM, Jill and Julian Tasker, Susan and John Douglas)*

NAPTON [SP4661]

Napton Bridge Inn CV47 8NQ [Southam Rd (A425), Oxford Canal Napton Bottom Lock]: Big family-run canalside pub with pine panelling, open fires (not always lit) and simple furnishings in three smallish rooms, decent good value food (lots of offers), changing real ales, friendly hard-working staff, restaurant overlooking water; piped music, no dogs; children welcome, back garden, moorings *(George Atkinson, Bob and Laura Brock)*

NEWBOLD ON STOUR [SP2446]

White Hart CV37 8TS [A3400 S of Stratford]: Welcoming dining pub in same family for many years, proper pubby atmosphere, with good varied home-made food inc popular Sun lunch (no food Sun evening), Adnams and Timothy Taylors Landlord, long airy beamed bar, good log fire in large stone fireplace, big bay windows, roomy back bar, separate dining room; ring the bull; children and dogs welcome, picnic-sets out at front and on back lawned area, open all day wknds *(LYM, K H Frostick)*

NEWTON REGIS [SK2707]

Queens Head B79 0NF [Main Rd]: Pleasant two-room beamed local in attractive duck-pond village, well kept ales such as Davenports Busy Fool and Greene King IPA, several wines, good value enjoyable bar food inc specials' board, friendly staff; pool; tables out in front and in small suntrap garden, handy for M42 junction 11 *(Clive and Fran Dutson)*

NUNEATON [SP3790]

Attleborough Arms CV11 4PL [Highfield Rd, Attleborough]: Large fairly recently rebuilt pub, attractively open, modern and comfortable, with wide choice of enjoyable low-priced food, good range of beers and wines, helpful attentive service; good disabled access *(David Green)*

OFFCHURCH [SP3665]

☆ *Stag* CV33 9AQ [N off Welsh Rd, off A425 at Radford Semele]: Recently refurbished 16th-c thatched village pub under enthusiastic licensees, good well presented imaginative food at reasonable prices, Caledonian Deuchars IPA and Purity ales, good wine choice, low beams, oak floors and log fires, two dining areas, friendly efficient young staff; garden with unusual black furniture on terrace, open all day *(John Smart, Joan and Tony Walker)*

OLD HILL [SO9686]

Waterfall B64 6RG [Waterfall Lane]: Friendly unpretentious two-room local, well kept Bathams, Holdens and guests, good value plain home-made food, tankards and jugs hanging from boarded ceiling; piped music; children welcome, back garden with play

area, open all day Fri-Sun *(the Didler, Dave Braisted)*

OLDBURY [SO9989]

Waggon & Horses B69 3AD [Church St, nr Savacentre]: Copper ceiling, original etched windows, open fire and Black Country memorabilia in busy town pub with Enville and two or three guest ales, wide choice of good value lunchtime food (not wknds) from sandwiches up inc vegetarian, decent wines; friendly efficient service even if busy, ornate Victorian tiles in corridor to lively comfortable back lounge with tie collection, side room with high-backed settles and big old tables, bookable upstairs bistro Weds-Fri night; open all day *(the Didler)*

OXHILL [SP3149]

☆ *Peacock* CV35 0QU [off A422 Stratford—Banbury]: Popular pleasantly upgraded stone-built country pub, good varied food inc two-course deals (Tues-Thurs lunchtime, Mon-Thurs evenings), friendly young staff, well kept ales such as Timothy Taylors and Wye Valley and a house beer brewed by Wadworths, good selection of wines by the glass, cosy charterful bar and dining room; children welcome, nice garden and views, pretty village, open all day Fri-Sun, cl Mon lunchtime *(K H Frostick, Clive and Fran Dutson, Roger Braithwaite, David and Catharine Boston, Mr and Mrs J L Connington, Roger M Hancock, Dennis and Doreen Haward)*

PRIORS MARSTON [SP4857]

Holly Bush CV47 7RW [off A361 S of Daventry; Holly Bush Lane]: Beams, flagstones and lots of stripped stone in rambling linked rooms, clean and smart under newish management with above-average well presented food, good young staff, real ales, log fire and woodburners; children welcome, sheltered garden, ten bedrooms *(LYM, Dennis and Doreen Haward)*

RATLEY [SP3847]

☆ *Rose & Crown* OX15 6DS [off A422 NW of Banbury]: Ancient golden-stone beamed village pub, cosy and charming, with five well kept ales, enjoyable good value straightforward food from sandwiches up, friendly welcoming staff; daily papers, woodburners in flagstoned area on left and in right carpeted part with wall seats, small back restaurant; dogs and children welcome, tables in gravel garden, nr lovely church in sleepy village *(E A and D C T Frewer, George Atkinson, Pam and John Smith, BB)*

RUGBY [SP5074]

Raglan Arms CV22 6AD [Dunchurch Rd]: Comfortable three-room pub with notable choice of well kept ales, no food, simple décor *(Ted George)*

SALFORD PRIORS [SP0751]

Bell WR11 8UU [Evesham Rd (B439)]: Smartly refurbished roadside pub, comfortable chairs and sofas in bar, separate dining room, enjoyable home-made food inc bargain set menus, real ales and decent wines, friendly service; outside eating and drinking areas *(Caroline and Michael Abbey)*

SEDGLEY [SO9194]
Mount Pleasant DY3 1RH [High St]: Busy mock-Tudor pub nr town centre, comfortable friendly front bar with fire, cosy split-level back lounge, Enville and seven changing guest beers; opens 6pm *(the Didler)*

SHIPSTON-ON-STOUR [SP2540]
☆ **Black Horse** CV36 4BT [Station Rd (off A3400)]: Cheerfully run 16th-c thatched pub, low-beamed bars off central entrance passage, good honest english cooking (not Sun evening), ales such as Copper Dragon, Purity and Sharps, Hogan's cider, good inglenook log fire; darts, dominoes and cribbage, small dining room; back garden with terrace and aunt sally, heated smokers' area, open all day Sun *(JHBS)*
George CV36 4AJ [High St]: Splendid early Georgian façade, bistro-style inside with several linked areas inc one with deep leather armchairs and log fire, enjoyable mildly upmarket blackboard food, good friendly service, Black Sheep, Fullers and Hook Norton from central marble-topped counter, good choice of wines; newspapers; 16 well modernised bedrooms, open all day *(Michael Dandy)*

SHOTTERY [SP1755]
Bell CV37 9HF: Greene King pub with their ales kept well, friendly staff, good choice of pubby food at reasonable prices, may be winter mulled wine *(Martin and Pauline Jennings)*

SOLIHULL [SP1780]
Boat B91 2TJ [Hampton Lane, Catherine de Barnes (B4102), handy for M42 junctions 5 and 6)]: Large comfortable Chef & Brewer by Grand Union Canal, enjoyable reasonably priced food all day, good friendly service, three changing ales; children very welcome, garden (dogs allowed here), good disabled access, open all day *(Martin Smith, Henry Pursehouse-Tranter)*

STOCKTON [SP4363]
Crown CV47 8JZ [High St]: Friendly village pub with well kept Ansells and two local guests, popular straightforward food inc bargain lunchtime set menu (Tues-Sat), restaurant in ancient barn, log fires; pétanque pitch *(Bob and Laura Brock)*

STRATFORD-UPON-AVON [SP2054]
Dirty Duck CV37 6BA [Waterside]: Bustling 16th-c Greene King Wayside Inn nr Memorial Theatre, their ales, good choice of wines, well presented fairly priced food all day, lots of signed RSC photographs, open fire, modern conservatory restaurant (best to book wknds); children allowed in dining area, attractive small terrace looking over riverside public gardens which tend to act as summer overflow, open all day *(LYM, Bob and Angela Brooks, Michael Dandy, Peter Dandy)*
Encore CV37 6AB [Bridge St]: Well refurbished town-centre dining pub in rambling old building with steps between various modernised areas, wood and stone floors, mix of mostly contemporary furniture, log fire; upstairs restaurant overlooking river, good choice of food inc fixed-price menu, well kept Purity and Timothy Taylors, good coffee; open all day *(Eithne Dandy, Peter Dandy, Dennis Jones)*
☆ **Garrick** CV37 6AU [High St]: Bustling ancient pub with heavy beams and timbers, odd-shaped rooms and simple furnishings on bare boards, good-natured efficient staff, enjoyable food from sandwiches and light dishes up all day, well kept Greene King ales, decent wines by the glass; small air-conditioned back restaurant; piped music, TV, games machine; children welcome, open all day *(Rob and Catherine Dunster, LYM, Chris and Jeanne Downing, Richard Endacott, Bob and Angela Brooks, Michael Dandy, Eithne Dandy, Dennis Jones)*
Golden Bee CV37 6EE [Sheep St]: Spacious airy Wetherspoons with good range of interesting low-priced ales, enjoyable straightforward food all day, quick service, family eating areas; TV *(Dennis Jones)*
Old Thatch CV37 6LE [Rother St/Greenhill St]: Cosy welcoming pub on corner of market square, three well kept ales inc Wye Valley, nice wines, popular fairly priced food, log fire, rustic décor, slate or wooden floors, country kitchen furniture; covered tables outside *(Val and Alan Green, Ted George)*
Pen & Parchment CV37 6YY [Bridgefoot, by canal basin]: Wayside Inn comfortably restored after 2007 floods; well divided, with bare boards, flagstones and carpet, big open fire in old fireplace, prompt helpful service even when busy, good wine choice, Black Sheep and Greene King, good value food all day from standards up; children welcome, disabled facilities, good-sized terrace, canal basin views (busy road), open all day *(D W Stokes)*

STRETTON-ON-FOSSE [SP2238]
☆ **Plough** GL56 9QX [just off A429]: Popular unpretentious 17th-c village local, central servery separating small bar and snug candlelit dining area, enjoyable food from pubby things up inc Sun spit roasts in winter, friendly fast service, Ansells, Hook Norton and interesting guests; stripped brick/stone walls and some flagstones, low oak beams, inglenook log fire, dominoes and cribbage; no dogs; children welcome, a few tables outside, smokers' shelter, cl Sun evening *(K H Frostick, Michael Dandy, BB)*

SUTTON COLDFIELD [SP1296]
Three Tuns B72 1XS [High St]: Cleverly refurbished to incorporate former coach entry as link between two cosy bars, old-world atmosphere (pity about the TVs), well kept Thwaites ales, popular locally; back courtyard *(Clifford Blakemore)*

TANWORTH-IN-ARDEN [SP1170]
☆ **Bell** B94 5AL [The Green]: Smartly comfortable contemporary bar-style décor, good food from light lunchtime dishes to full meals, good choice of wines by the glass, well kept Greene King IPA and Timothy Taylors Landlord, friendly staff; children in eating areas, outlook on pretty village's

green and lovely 14th-c church, back terrace with alloy planters, nine stylish modern bedrooms – good base for walks, also has a post office *(Martin Smith, LYM, Cedric Robertshaw)*

TIPTON [SO9792]

Rising Sun DY4 7NH [Horseley Rd (B4517, off A461)]: Friendly Victorian pub with great choice of well kept ales, farm ciders, enjoyable home-made lunchtime food, back lounge with coal fires, alcoves and original bare boards and tiles; tables outside, open all day *(the Didler)*

TREDINGTON [SP2543]

White Lion CV36 4NS [A3400]: Comfortably modernised stone-built pub, welcoming helpful landlord, enjoyable food from short blackboard menu, ales such as Bass and Greene King IPA, low beams, rugs on quarry tiles, log fire *(K H Frostick, Clive and Fran Dutson)*

UPPER BRAILES [SP3039]

Gate OX15 5AX: Attractively old-fashioned low-beamed village pub, welcoming landlord, wife cooks enjoyable well priced country food inc fresh fish and good Sun roasts; well kept Hook Norton and guests, coal fire, sizeable half-panelled carpeted bar, smaller lounge, alsatian called Shade; piped music in restaurant; dogs and well behaved children welcome, tables in extensive back garden with play area, aunt sally, pretty hillside spot, lovely walks, cl Sun evening, Mon lunchtime *(R J Herd, Clive and Fran Dutson, K H Frostick)*

UPPER GORNAL [SO9292]

☆ *Britannia* DY3 1UX [Kent St (A459)]: Popular old-fashioned 19th-c local with friendly chatty atmosphere, particularly well kept Bathams Best and Mild (bargain prices); tiled floors, coal fires in front bar and time-trapped little back room with its wonderful handpumps, some bar snacks inc good local pork pies; sports TV; nice flower-filled back yard, open all day *(the Didler)*

Jolly Crispin DY3 1UL [Clarence St (A459)]: Friendly well run 18th-c local, Titanic Crispy Nail and eight interesting quickly changing guests, real ciders (cider/perry festivals); compact front bar, wall seats and mixed tables/chairs on tiled floor, beer bottle collection in larger back room, fresh baps, open fires; no children; dogs welcome, beer garden, open all day Fri-Sun, cl lunchtime Mon-Thurs *(the Didler)*

WALSALL [SP0198]

Arbor Lights WS1 1SY [Lichfield St]: Relaxed modern open-plan brasserie-style bar and restaurant, wide choice of wines, ales such as Adnams Broadside and Black Sheep Bitter, meal deals *(Jeremy King)*

Black Country Arms WS1 1QW [High St]: Old restored town pub on three floors with plenty of varnished wood, engraved glass and newly carpeted floors, up to 16 real ales, Moles and Thatcher's ciders, decent pub food; piped music, no dogs; small side terrace, open all day *(Bob Westwood)*

WARWICK [SP2766]

Cape of Good Hope CV34 5DP [Lower Cape]: Traditional unsmart two-room pub on Grand Union Canal by Cape Top Lock, friendly atmosphere, half a dozen well kept ales inc one brewed for them by Church End, satisfying pub food, darts; hatch service for waterside seats *(Martin Smith, Clive and Fran Dutson)*

Old Fourpenny Shop CV34 6HJ [Crompton St, nr racecourse]: Cosy and comfortable split-level pub with up to five well kept changing beers, welcoming licensees, good value food in bar and heavily beamed restaurant, cheerful service; no piped music; pleasant reasonably priced bedrooms *(Pam and John Smith, Ian and Nita Cooper)*

☆ *Rose & Crown* CV34 4SH [Market Pl]: Up-to-date uncluttered refurbishment, bustling and friendly, with big leather sofas and low tables by open fire, dining area with large modern photographs, good choice of sensibly priced interesting food all day, well kept Black Sheep, Purity and Wells & Youngs, plenty of fancy keg dispensers, good wines and coffee, cheerful efficient service; newspapers; piped music; tables out under parasols, comfortable good-sized bedrooms *(Alan Johnson, Revd R P Tickle, Ian and Nita Cooper, Michael Dandy, LYM)*

☆ *Saxon Mill* CV34 5YN [Guy's Cliffe, A429 just N]: Well run M&B dining pub in charmingly set converted mill, mill race and turning wheel behind glass, smart contemporary chairs and tables on polished boards and flagstones, cosy corners with leather armchairs and big rugs, beams and log fire; smiling service, enjoyable good value food in bar and (best to book) upstairs family restaurant, good choice of wines by the glass; shame about the piped music; tables out on terraces by broad willow-flanked river, more over bridge, delightful views across to Grade I ruins of Guy's Cliffe House, open all day *(Adrian Johnson, LYM)*

☆ *Tudor House* CV34 6AW [West St]: Heavily timbered and jettied Tudor inn opp the castle car park, lots of black wood, tiles and parquet floor, leaded lights, lofty pitched ceiling, massive stone fireplace, galleried landing, solid furnishings and Tudoresque décor inc armour; Greene King ales, decent wine, pubby food; tables in front and on back terrace, bedrooms *(Colin Moore, Michael Dandy, BB)*

☆ *Zetland Arms* CV34 4AB [Church St]: Cosy town pub with good sensibly priced traditional food (not wknd evenings) inc nice sandwiches and set menu deals, friendly quick service even when busy, Adnams, Black Sheep and Marstons, decent wines; small panelled front bar with toby jug collection, comfortable larger L-shaped back eating area with small conservatory, pictures of old Warwick; sports TV; children welcome, sheltered garden, bedrooms sharing bathroom *(LYM, Alan Johnson, Dennis Jones)*

WHICHFORD [SP3134]

Norman Knight CV36 5PE: Traditional beamed and flagstoned pub sympathetically extended by newish owners, own good Patriot beers from new microbrewery and changing guests, real ciders and perry, enjoyable food (not Sun evening), friendly helpful service; some live music, classic car/bike meetings 3rd Thurs monthly in summer; dogs and children welcome, tables out by attractive village green, aunt sally, small back campsite, cl Sun evening, Mon in winter *(Clive and Fran Dutson)*

WOLLASTON [SO8884]

Unicorn DY8 3NX [Bridgnorth Rd (A458)]: Friendly traditional local with well kept low-priced Bathams ales, unpretentious L-shaped bar and unspoilt back parlour, lots of brasses and knick-knacks, good lunchtime cobs and hot snacks; tables outside, open all day (Sun afternoon break) *(the Didler)*

WOLVERHAMPTON [SO9298]

☆ *Great Western* WV10 0DG [Corn Hill/Sun St, behind railway station]: Cheerful pub hidden away by a cobbled lane down from the mainline station to GWR low-level one; well kept Bathams, Holdens and guests, real cider, bargain home-made food, interesting railway memorabilia, traditional front bar, other rooms inc neat dining conservatory; Sky TV; yard with barbecues, open all day (may be Sun afternoon break) *(BB, the Didler, Martin Grosberg, Andy Lickfold, Barbarrick, P Dawn, Robert Garner)*

Royal Tiger WV11 1ST [Wednesfield, High St]: Modern Wetherspoons with good atmosphere, friendly locals, good service, wide choice of beers inc Banks's, spacious dining area with comfortable high-backed settles; children welcome, good disabled facilities, terrace out by canal *(Henry Pursehouse-Tranter)*

If a service charge is mentioned prominently on a menu or accommodation terms, you must pay it if service was satisfactory. If service is really bad, you are legally entitled to refuse to pay some or all of the service charge as compensation for not getting the service you might reasonably have expected.

Wiltshire

We've a fine clutch of new entries here this year which include the Royal Oak at Bishopstone (straight in with Food and Wine Awards), the Castle in Bradford-on-Avon (an imposing building and a great all-rounder), the Fox at Broughton Gifford (they keep their own animals and grow their own produce for the interesting food – again, straight in with a Food Award), the Ship in Burcombe (a relaxed country dining pub but with three real ales, too), the Beckford Arms at Fonthill Gifford (back in these pages after a break, but shut for a few months as we go to press – to repair bad fire damage) and the Triple Crown at Marden (lots of horse-racing photographs and an appealing layout). Other pubs in this big county for a particularly good meal out include the Compasses at Chicksgrove (a smashing all-rounder with genuinely friendly staff), the Potting Shed at Crudwell (exciting and interesting food and a lovely atmosphere), the Forester at Donhead St Andrew (an appealing bar as well as a food emphasis), the Linnet at Great Hinton (a proper dining pub with efficient staff), the Malet Arms at Newton Tony (an unpretentious place with a lovely landlord and delicious food), the Vine Tree at Norton (lots of special food events in a civilised pub), the George & Dragon at Rowde (proper character in a 16th-c pub with food emphasis), the Bridge Inn at West Lavington (french influences and a french chef) and the White Horse in Winterbourne Bassett (deservedly busy for its popular meals). Our Wiltshire Dining Pub 2011 is the Potting Shed in Crudwell. But despite all the emphasis on the food (often using home-reared animals and home-grown produce), there are plenty of wonderful unpretentious pubs here and those that deserve special mention are the Quarrymans Arms at Box (loved by our readers for its informal atmosphere and warm welcome), the Two Pigs at Corsham (very eccentric and individual), the Horseshoe in Ebbesbourne Wake (a delightful pub run by second-generation licensees) and the Red Lion in Kilmington (an unchanging local with long-serving landlords).

ALDBOURNE
SU2675 MAP 2

Blue Boar

The Green (off B4192 in centre); SN8 2EN

Bags of character in chatty, low-beamed, traditional pub

There's always a band of chatty locals in this unspoilt and easy-going pub who are happy to include visitors in their cheerful banter. The left-hand bar is homely, with pubby seats around heavily rustic tables on the bare boards or flagstones, lots of low black beams in the ochre ceiling, a boar's head above the bigger of the two fireplaces, a stuffed pine marten over one table; darts, board games and a corner cupboard of village trophies. Lots of unusual bottled beers line the rail above the dark pine dado. Wadworths IPA and 6X and a couple of guest beers on handpump (they may hold beer festivals during April and October) and 20 malt whiskies. A separate bare-boards dining bar on the right, stretching back further, has more table space and is rather more modern in style (though with the same pubby atmosphere). There are picnic-sets and a couple of tall hogshead tables under big green canvas parasols in front of the pub that face the village green.

⏽ Decent pubby food includes sandwiches and filled baguettes, ploughman's, filled baked potatoes, soup, pâté and toast, home-cooked ham and egg, vegetable lasagne, chicken and mushroom pie, battered haddock, chilli con carne, minted lamb shank, and puddings like banana split and chocolate fudge cake. *Starters/Snacks: £3.95 to £8.25. Main Courses: £8.25 to £14.95. Puddings: £4.75 to £6.75*

Wadworths ~ Tenants Jez and Mandy Hill ~ Real ale ~ Bar food (12-2, 6.30-9.30) ~ Restaurant ~ (01672) 540237 ~ Children welcome ~ Dogs allowed in bar ~ Open 11.30-3, 5.30-11; 11.30am-midnight Fri and Sat; 12-11 Sun

Recommended by Dr and Mrs M E Wilson, Richard Tilbrook, Mary Rayner

BERWICK ST JOHN
ST9422   MAP 2

Talbot

Village signposted from A30 E of Shaftesbury; SP7 0HA

Unspoilt and friendly pub in an attractive village, with simple furnishings and tasty, reasonably priced food

---

You can be sure of a warm welcome from the friendly hands-on licensees in this unspoilt village pub. The heavily beamed bar has plenty of character, a huge inglenook fireplace with a good iron fireback and bread ovens, and it's simply furnished with solid wall and window seats, spindleback chairs and a high-backed built-in settle at one end. Ringwood Best, Wadworths 6X and a guest like Ringwood Fortyniner on handpump; darts. There are seats outside and the pub is well placed for choice walks southwards through the deep countryside of Cranborne Chase and towards Tollard Royal.

⏽ Good, reasonably priced bar food includes sandwiches, hot filled baguettes, ploughman's, soup, garlic mushrooms, chilli beef nachos topped with cheese and sour cream, ham and egg, lasagne, beer-battered cod, and daily specials like steak in ale pie, belly of pork with crackling and sage gravy and chicken breast with a mushroom and tarragon sauce. *Starters/Snacks: £5.00 to £7.00. Main Courses: £6.50 to £15.50. Puddings: £4.00 to £4.50*

Free house ~ Licensees Pete and Marilyn Hawkins ~ Real ale ~ Bar food (not Sun evening or Mon) ~ Restaurant ~ (01747) 828222 ~ Children welcome ~ Dogs welcome ~ Open 12-2.30, 6.30-11; 12-4 Sun; closed Sun evening, Mon

Recommended by D and J Ashdown, JDM, KM, Ian Herdman, Colin and Janet Roe, Bruce and Sharon Eden

BISHOPSTONE
SU2483   MAP 2

Royal Oak ⏽ ♟

The one near Swindon; at first exit roundabout from A419 N of M4 junction 15, follow Wanborough sign, then keep on to Bishopstone; keep eyes skinned for small sign to pub, then turn right into Cues Lane; SN6 8PP

Good organic food in a lively and friendly, informal dining pub

---

Mrs Browning, part-owner for the last few years, is a prominent local organic farmer who has been a pillar of the Soil Association for many years, and her farm shop is just behind the pub. Pictures (for sale) of farm animals and fowls adorn the dark green or cream walls, and they are strong on organic wines, as well as their Arkells 2B, 3B and Moonlight on handpump, perhaps home-made elderflower cordial (and their own pork scratchings), and a decent range of whiskies. Though most people are here to eat, there's a thoroughly pubby atmosphere, with a cheerful buzz of conversation, particularly over on the left, where there's a log fire, and a chatty little maze of dark pews at the back. Apart from a comfortable old cloth-covered red sofa, furnishings are mainly scrubbed wood on bare boards or parquet. There are charity shelves and window sills of paperbacks, and board games (Monday is Scrabble night). Outside, picnic-sets are dotted through a bit of a copse, with more on the grass by a barbecue beyond, and smarter modern tables on the front decking. There are cheap serviceable bedrooms in a couple of cabins out behind; the bedroom listed price assumes you also want supper here – if you don't the price is more expensive. It's a pretty village, round a big pond.

🍴 **Much of the food comes from Mrs Browning's farm, with locals trading more, and Liz the chef specialises in slow cooking, making the most of things like ham hocks, lamb shanks and succulent pork bellies (her breakfasts are rather special, too, as are her puddings). The menu changes twice a day and might include sandwiches, sticky ribs with chilli jam, potted crab with sour dough toast, beef (or mushroom) burger with aioli and triple cooked chips, grilled mackerel with horseradish sauce, pork tenderloin in a white wine and creamy mustard sauce, and puddings such as white chocolate and hazelnut brownie and lemon posset.** *Starters/Snacks: £6.50 to £7.00. Main Courses: £8.50 to £21.50. Puddings: £6.00*

Arkells ~ Tenants Tim Finney and Helen Browning ~ Real ale ~ Bar food (12(12.30 Sun)-2.30(3 Sat and Sun), 6.30-9.30(8.30 Sun)) ~ (01793) 790481 ~ Children welcome ~ Dogs welcome ~ Open 12-3, 6-11; 12-midnight(10pm Sun) Sat ~ Bedrooms: £25S/£50S

Recommended by Tony and Tracy Constance, Michael Snelgrove

BOX

ST8369   MAP 2

Quarrymans Arms

Box Hill; coming from Bath on A4 turn right into Bargates 50 yards before railway bridge, then at T-junction turn left up Quarry Hill, turning left again near the top at grassy triangle; from Corsham, turn left after Rudloe Park Hotel into Beech Road, then third left on to Barnetts Hill, and finally right at the top of the hill; OS Sheet 173 map reference 834694; SN13 8HN

Cheerful and unpretentious, with great views, real ales and good value food

Our readers love this pub – for its informal and relaxed atmosphere, genuinely helpful and friendly staff, changing real ales and popular bar food. It's comfortable rather than overly smart (some parts have an air of mild untidiness) and one modernised room with an open fire is entirely set aside for drinking. There's plenty of mining-related photographs and memorabilia dotted around – this was once the local of the Bath-stone miners and the welcoming licensees run interesting guided trips down the mine itself. As well as Butcombe Bitter, Moles Best and Paddys Tarmac Tipple, Wadworths 6X and York Guzzler on handpump, they have 60 malt whiskies and 11 wines by the glass; board games and quiz and poker evenings. An attractive outside terrace has picnic-sets and sweeping views. The pub is ideally placed for cavers, potholers and walkers.

🍴 **Reasonably priced and enjoyable, the bar food includes sandwiches, baked potatoes, soup, creamy garlic mushrooms, moules marinière, spanish omelette, all-day breakfasts, seafood pancakes, pasta with a spicy tomato sauce, chicken wrapped in parma ham with a cream and wine sauce, pork dijonnaise, swordfish steak with wild garlic and a lemon and caper butter, venison pie, and puddings such as chocolate terrine and banoffi pie.** *Starters/Snacks: £2.95 to £8.95. Main Courses: £6.25 to £14.95. Puddings: £4.95 to £5.50*

Free house ~ Licensees John and Ginny Arundel ~ Real ale ~ Bar food (12-3, 6-9) ~ Restaurant ~ (01225) 743569 ~ Children welcome ~ Dogs allowed in bar ~ Open 11-11 ~ Bedrooms: £35B/£65B

Recommended by Ian Herdman, Dr and Mrs A K Clarke, Stephen Turpin, Gordon Tong, Richard and Madeleine Wagner, Guy Vowles

---

Please keep sending us reports. We rely on readers for news of new discoveries, and particularly for news of changes – however slight – at the fully described pubs: feedback@goodguides.com, or (no stamp needed) The Good Pub Guide, FREEPOST TN1569, Wadhurst, E Sussex TN5 7BR.

BRADFORD-ON-AVON

ST8261 MAP 2

Castle ★

Mount Pleasant, by junction with A363, N edge of town; extremely limited pub parking, spaces in nearby streets; BA15 1SJ

Handsome building well reworked in relaxed contemporary style, enjoyable food all day, good drinks, charming service, comfortable bedrooms

This imposing square-cut 18th-c stone building, facing the church in an unfashionable part of town, is a great all-rounder, with well kept more or less local ales on handpump such as Bristol Red, Keystone Gold Spice, Three Castles Barbury Castle, and their own-label Flatcappers beers (also from Three Castles), a fine blackboard range of wines by the glass, coffee served properly (hot milk if you want), friendly and efficient young staff, good bedrooms, and a splendid and highly individual atmosphere. The bar, dominated by its long panelled mahogany serving counter, has a good log fire, restful lighting including church candles, anything from armchairs and chapel chairs to a heavy green leather settle on its polished dark flagstones, plenty of daily papers, and unobtrusive piped music; board games. Lightly ragged ochre walls have *Vanity Fair* cartoons above a high brown dado, and a couple of boarded-floor rooms on the right, with a rather darker décor, are similarly comfortable and relaxed. Beside a lawn, the front terrace has unusual long tables and benches – and sweeping views over the town.

Ⓜ **Rewarding bar food includes sandwiches, soup, chicken livers with smoked bacon, rosemary and red wine sauce, tapas-like dishes such as sticky lemon chicken fillet skewers, cheddar and spring onion potatoes or mini fishcakes with tartare sauce, home-made beefburger with red onion marmalade, vegetarian shepherd's pie, gammon with a duck egg, creamy fish pie, braised beef with celeriac and potato purée, and puddings like winter berry trifle and marmalade bread and butter pudding with custard.** *Starters/Snacks: £4.75 to £6.25. Main Courses: £7.95 to £18.95. Puddings: £4.50 to £6.75*

Free house ~ Licensee Victoria Hill ~ Real ale ~ Bar food (9am-10pm(9.30pm Sun)) ~ (01225) 865657 ~ Children welcome ~ Open 9am-11pm; 10-10.30 Sun ~ Bedrooms: /£90S(£110B)
Recommended by Dr and Mrs M E Wilson, Susan and Nigel Wilson, Michael Doswell, David Eberlin, Ian Phillips, Howard and Elaine Lee, Dr and Mrs A K Clarke

BRINKWORTH

SU0184 MAP 2

Three Crowns ⑪ ♀

The Street; B4042 Wootton Bassett—Malmesbury; SN15 5AF

Much emphasis on the food, but this is still a pub with four good beers and a carefully chosen wine list

Although the food takes centre stage here, this busy dining pub does still have some proper pubbiness. The bar part of the building is the most traditional with big landscape prints and other pictures, some horsebrasses on dark beams, a log fire, a dresser with a collection of old bottles, big tapestry-upholstered pews, a stripped deal table and a couple more made from gigantic forge bellows. Sensibly placed darts, games machine, board games and piped music. Abbey Ales Bellringer, Fullers London Pride, Greene King IPA and Wadworths 6X on handpump, 20 wines by the glass from a carefully chosen, extensive list and around 20 malt whiskies. Most people choose to eat in the conservatory or the light and airy garden room. There's a terrace with outdoor heating to the side of the conservatory and a smoking shelter. The garden stretches around the side and back, with well spaced tables and a climbing frame, and looks over a side lane to the church and on to rolling prosperous farmland.

Ⓜ **Bar food is at its most informal at lunchtime when there might be ploughman's, soup, fishcakes, bangers and mash, liver and bacon, a home-made burger, pies like steak and kidney or veal and mushroom and various salads and curries; there's also a much more elaborate (and expensive) menu with dishes such as crispy half duck with a cherry wine, redcurrant jelly and cream sauce, marinated kangaroo, venison and ostrich with a sauce of sun-dried tomatoes, wild mushrooms and button shallots flamed with brandy and fresh tuna in puff pastry with brie and prawns and a creamy madeira sauce, and puddings like**

hot chocolate sponge and banoffi pie. *Starters/Snacks: £6.95 to £9.00. Main Courses: £10.00 to £25.00. Puddings: £6.95*

Enterprise ~ Lease Anthony Windle ~ Real ale ~ Bar food (12-2, 6-9.30; 12-9 Sun) ~ Restaurant ~ (01666) 510366 ~ Well behaved children welcome and by arrangement after 6.30pm ~ Dogs allowed in bar ~ Open 10am-11.30pm; 12-10.30 Sun

Recommended by Dr and Mrs J Temporal, Ian Herdman, Mr and Mrs P R Thomas, John Saville, Richard and Madeleine Wagner

BROUGHTON GIFFORD   ST8763   MAP 2

Fox

Village signposted off A365 to B3107 W of Melksham; The Street; SN12 8PN

Comfortably stylish new look, newish licensees doing some enterprising food inc good Sun roasts, and a nice garden

With big bird and plant prints, attractive table lamps and even the beams painted white, this civilised pub's fresh light décor contrasts nicely with its broad dark flagstones. You can sink into sofas or armchairs by a table of daily papers and another with magazines and board games, take one of the padded stools by the pink-painted bar counter, or go for the mix of gently old-fashioned dining chairs around the unmatched stripped dining tables, which have candles in brass sticks. Each area runs into the next, with much the same chatty relaxed atmosphere throughout. Real ales such as Bath Gem and Sharps Winter Ale on handpump, a log fire in the stone fireplace, friendly service. The terrace behind has picnic-sets and leads out on to a good-sized sheltered lawn.

They raise their own pigs and sheep (the sheep are not on site), keep their own chickens and ducks, and grow a lot of their own vegetables and fruit – all of which go into the interesting food here; they also have enterprising and delicious bar nibbles such as home-made pork pies on the counter all afternoon, and a menu that includes lunchtime sandwiches, soup, pressed ham terrine with quince chutney, warm buttered brown shrimps on toast, a proper burger with triple-cooked chips, wild mushroom risotto with mixed herbs and a poached egg, rib-eye steak with green peppercorn sauce, wild bass with celeriac purée, spiced aubergine and coriander ragoût and a saffron and herb sauce, and puddings such as chocolate tart and raspberry torte; they keep a fine cheeseboard and offer a choice of good Sunday roasts. *Starters/Snacks: £5.95 to £9.50. Main Courses: £11.50 to £18.50. Puddings: £6.00 to £7.95*

Free house ~ Licensee Derek Geneen ~ Real ale ~ Bar food (12-2.30(3.30 Sun), 7-9; not Mon or Tues) ~ Restaurant ~ (01225) 782949 ~ Children welcome ~ Dogs welcome ~ Live music in summer ~ Open 12(5pm Tues)-midnight(11pm Sun); closed Mon, Tues lunchtime

Recommended by Philip and Jan Medcalf

BURCOMBE   SU0631   MAP 2

Ship

Brown sign to pub off A30 W of Salisbury, then turn right into Burcombe Lane; SP2 0EJ

Good relaxed country dining pub with wide food choice and a pretty waterside garden

Even down by the entrance, with its log fire, low beams, leather-cushioned wall and window seats and dark slate tiles, most people seem to be here for the food. That's certainly the case up a couple of steps past the bar counter, in a spreading area of pale wood dining chairs around bleached tables on neat, dark brown, woodstrip flooring – and many more dark beams, one carrying a rather splendid chandelier. On the walls, partly stripped brick up here, are small modern pictures. They have Butcombe, Ringwood Best and Wadworths 6X on handpump, a very good choice of wines by the glass and a decent whisky range; young staff, unobtrusive piped music. Big church candles on all the tables are lit even in daytime, and on still summer nights they light them on the picnic-sets in the peaceful and pretty informal garden behind, which slopes down to two big weeping willows by the safely fenced-off little River Nadder.

🛈 They have separate boards for pubby food such as ham and cheese melt, sausage and onion ciabatta, ploughman's or burgers (served on wooden platters), and for more elaborate and pricier dishes such as lightly grilled oysters, crab spring rolls, battered herring roe with piquant mustard sauce, asparagus, spinach, courgette and parmesan torte, confit wild rabbit with a grain mustard cream sauce, chicken caesar salad, home-made fishcakes with herbed fries and bass fillet with pea and mint risotto and fennel confit – but whatever you choose, you can eat in any part of the pub and it's all well prepared and attractively served. *Starters/Snacks: £5.95 to £7.95. Main Courses: £8.95 to £11.95. Puddings: £5.75 to £7.50*

Arkells ~ Lease Neill Kefford ~ Real ale ~ Bar food (12-2.30, 6.30(7 Sun)-9) ~ Restaurant ~ (01722) 743182 ~ Children welcome ~ Dogs allowed in bar ~ Open 11-3, 6-11; 12-3, 6.30-10.30 Sun
Recommended by Ken Marshall, David Hunt

CHICKSGROVE   ST9729   MAP 2

Compasses ★ 🍴 🍷 🛏

From A30 5.5 miles W of B3089 junction, take lane on N side signposted Sutton Mandeville, Sutton Row, then first left fork (small signs point the way to the pub, in Lower Chicksgrove; look out for the car park); can also be reached off B3089 W of Dinton, passing the glorious spire of Teffont Evias church; SP3 6NB

An excellent all-rounder with enjoyable food, a genuine welcome, four real ales and seats in the quiet garden; comfortable, popular bedrooms

This is an ancient thatched house that remains peaceful and unchanging, and our readers enjoy their visits here very much. The bar has old bottles and jugs hanging from beams above the roughly timbered counter, farm tools and traps on the partly stripped-stone walls, and high-backed wooden settles forming snug booths around tables on the mainly flagstoned floor. Helpful and friendly young staff serve Butcombe Bitter, Hidden Quest, Keystone Solar Brew and Stonehenge Spire Ale on handpump, eight wines by the glass and several malt whiskies. The quiet garden, terraces and flagstoned farm courtyard are very pleasant places to sit, and there are lovely surrounding walks and plenty to do in the area.

🛈 Splendid bar food using carefully sourced ingredients might include lunchtime sandwiches, ploughman's, ham and eggs, pork and apple sausages with onion gravy, smoked salmon with scrambled eggs, steak in ale pie, mushroom and chestnut-stuffed chicken breast with blue cheese mash and madeira sauce, calves liver, bacon and bean casserole, whole baked sea bream with tomato-roasted potatoes, venison steak with bombay potatoes, tomato and masala sauce, and puddings like chocolate and almond tart with bitter orange sauce and baked lemon meringue alaska. *Starters/Snacks: £5.00 to £9.00. Main Courses: £8.00 to £16.00. Puddings: £5.50*

Free house ~ Licensee Alan Stoneham ~ Real ale ~ Bar food ~ (01722) 714318 ~ Children welcome ~ Dogs welcome ~ Open 12-3, 6-11; 12-3, 7-10.30 Sun ~ Bedrooms: £65B/£85S

Recommended by Bruce and Sharon Eden, Helen and Brian Edgeley, Russell Sunderland, Colin and Janet Roe, Steve Whalley, Ross Balaam, Philip and Jan Medcalf, Ian Herdman, John Branston, Peter and Jan Humphreys, Geoffrey Kemp, S G N Bennett, Simon Lindsey, Rosemary Rogers

CORSHAM   ST8670   MAP 2

Two Pigs 🍺

A4, Pickwick; SN13 0HY

Wonderfully eccentric pub for fans of beer and music, open evenings only (except Sun) and at its best on Monday nights

The cheerfully eccentric feel in this friendly little beer lovers' pub owes much to the individualistic landlord and it's at its most lively on Monday evenings. There's a zany collection of bric-a-brac in the narrow and dimly lit flagstoned bar, including enamel advertising signs on the wood-clad walls, pig-theme ornaments and old radios. There's usually a good mix of customers around the long dark wood tables and benches, and piped blues. Stonehenge Pigswill and a couple of guests like Cotswold Spring Codger and Hop Back Summer Lightning on handpump. A covered yard outside is called the Sty. Do note their opening times – the pub is closed every lunchtime, except on Sunday. No under-21s. More reports please.

🍴 **No food.**

Free house ~ Licensees Dickie and Ann Doyle ~ Real ale ~ No credit cards ~ (01249) 712515 ~ Live blues/rock Mon evening ~ Open 7-11; 12-2.30, 7-10.30 Sun; closed lunchtimes Mon-Sat

Recommended by Mr and Mrs P R Thomas, Dr and Mrs A K Clarke

CROCKERTON   ST8642   MAP 2

Bath Arms
Just off A350 Warminster—Blandford; BA12 8AJ

Attractively modernised dining pub with pretty gardens, relaxed atmosphere, real ales and food cooked by the landlord; bedrooms

As this attractive pub is close to Longleat it does get especially busy during school holidays. It's a friendly place with a relaxed atmosphere and the long, stylishly modernised two-roomed bar has lots of well spaced tables on the parquet floor, beams in the whitewashed ceiling and brasses. There's a restaurant at one end and a log fire in a stone fireplace at the other. Sharps Cornish Coaster, Wessex Crockerton Classic and Potters Ale on handpump and quite a few wines by the glass; piped music. There are plenty of inviting places to sit outside too, with various garden areas featuring plenty of picnic-sets.

🍴 **Cooked by the landlord, the popular food includes filled baguettes, soup, baked mushroom welsh rarebit, scallops with minted carrots and spiced sultanas, cumberland sausage and champ, breaded ling and chips, shepherd's pie, chicken breast with artichoke and mushroom duxelles, sticky beef with braised red cabbage, grilled salmon with fennel and rocket, and puddings like bitter chocolate fondant with white chocolate ice-cream and mixed berry pavlova.** *Starters/Snacks: £5.50 to £6.95. Main Courses: £9.95 to £15.00. Puddings: £4.95*

Wellington ~ Licensee Dean Carr ~ Real ale ~ Bar food (12-2, 6.30-9(9.30 Sat)) ~ Restaurant ~ (01985) 212262 ~ Children welcome ~ Dogs allowed in bar ~ Open 11-3, 6-11; 11-11 Sat and Sun; closed 3-6 Sat and Sun in winter ~ Bedrooms: /£80S

Recommended by Edward Mirzoeff, John Redfern, Andy and Claire Barker, Paul Goldman, Richard and Sally Beardsley, Douglas and Ann Hare, Gordon Tong, Bruce and Sharon Eden, Wyndham Hamilton

CRUDWELL   ST9592   MAP 4

Potting Shed ★
A429 N of Malmesbury; The Street; SN16 9EW
WILTSHIRE DINING PUB OF THE YEAR

Appealing variation on the traditional country-tavern theme, good beers, wines and country cooking

Since this especially enjoyable pub became a new entry in last year's *Guide*, we've had nothing but warm praise from our readers. It is very much a proper country pub rather than just another pub/restaurant, with cheerful and interested young staff and a fine range of drinks such as Bath Ales Gem Bitter, Butcombe Bitter and Timothy Taylors Landlord on handpump, as well as an excellent range of over two dozen wines by the glass, home-made seasonal cocktails using local or home-grown fruit, good coffees and winter mulled wine; also, log fires, one in a big worn stone fireplace, and very mixed plain tables and chairs on pale flagstones in the low-beamed rooms that ramble around the bar; visiting dogs may meet Barney and Rubbles (the owners') and be offered biscuits. There are well worn easy chairs in one corner, and a couple of blacktop daily papers. Four steps take you up into a high-raftered further area, with coir carpeting, and there's one separate smaller room ideal for a lunch or dinner party. The rustic decorations are not overdone and quite fun: a garden-fork door handle, garden-tool beer pumps, rather witty big black and white photographs. Well chosen piped music and board games. They have summer barbecues on fine Saturdays; there are sturdy teak seats around cask tables as well as picnic-sets out on the side grass among weeping willows.

🍴 Using their own-grown fruit and vegetables and produce from the villagers to whom they've loaned allotments, the exciting and interesting food might include sandwiches, soup, home tea-smoked duck with gooseberry and apple tart and pistachio dressing, terrine of red mullet with roasted sweet peppers and potatoes with aged balsamic, wild rabbit fettuccine with chasseur sauce, jerusalem artichoke and ginger risotto with pickled ginger and lemon and parsley dressing, baby squid risotto with roasted scallops and chickpea salsa, roast poussin with bramley apple fondant, herb crust, cauliflower and cashel blue gratin and calvados jus, daily specials, and puddings such as double-layer peanut butter and chocolate brownie with banana smoothie and lemon meringue panna cotta with lemon curd and toasted nuts. *Starters/Snacks: £4.95 to £7.00. Main Courses: £7.95 to £15.95. Puddings: £5.50*

Enterprise ~ Lease Jonathan Barry, Julian Muggridge and Laura Sheffield ~ Real ale ~ Bar food (12-2.30(3 Sun), 7-9.30(9 Sun)) ~ (01666) 577833 ~ Children welcome ~ Dogs welcome ~ Open 11am-midnight(1am Sat, 11pm Sun)

Recommended by Peter and Audrey Dowsett, Richard Tilbrook, Mr and Mrs P R Thomas, MJVK, David Gunn, Guy Vowles, E McCall, T McLean, D Irving, Jules Vaux, Michael Doswell

DONHEAD ST ANDREW   ST9124   MAP 2

Forester 🍴 ♀

Village signposted off A30 E of Shaftesbury, just E of Ludwell; Lower Street; SP7 9EE

Attractive old thatched pub in a charming village, real ales, popular food and fine views from the very pleasant big terrace

Although many customers are here to dine, this 14th-c pub has an appealing bar with a welcoming atmosphere. Also, stripped tables on wooden floors, a log fire in its big inglenook fireplace and usually a few locals chatting around the servery: Butcombe Bitter, Otter Bitter and a guest beer on handpump and 15 wines (including champagne) by the glass. Off here is an alcove with a sofa and table and magazines to read. The comfortable main dining room has country-kitchen tables in varying sizes and there's also a second smaller and cosier dining room. Outside, seats on a good-sized terrace have fine country views. The neighbouring cottage used to be the pub's coach house. You can walk up White Sheet Hill and past the old and 'new' Wardour castles. More reports please.

🍴 Good bar food (using cornish fish) includes lunchtime sandwiches, soup, eggs benedict, fresh calamari fritti with aioli, fresh crab spaghetti with chilli, parsley and garlic, a proper burger with cheese and smoked bacon, free-range chicken breast with creamed leeks, confit duck leg with fig gravy, organic brisket with red wine gravy, bass fillet with sauce vierge, and puddings such as hazelnut and apricot tart with muscat syrup and dark chocolate marquise with crème fraîche sorbet; they also offer a set two- and three-course fish lunch (Tuesday-Friday). *Starters/Snacks: £5.00 to £8.00. Main Courses: £10.00 to £18.50. Puddings: £4.50 to £7.50*

Free house ~ Licensee Chris Matthew ~ Real ale ~ Bar food (12-3, 7-9) ~ Restaurant ~ (01747) 828038 ~ Children welcome ~ Dogs welcome ~ Open 12-3, 6.30-11; 12-4 Sun; closed Sun evenings

Recommended by Roger Wain-Heapy, Colin and Janet Roe, Samantha McGahan, Russell Sunderland

> Stars after the name of a pub show exceptional character and appeal. They don't mean extra comfort. And they are nothing to do with food quality, for which there's a separate knife-and-fork symbol. Even quite a basic pub can win stars, if it's individual enough.

EAST KNOYLE

ST8731   MAP 2

Fox & Hounds ♀

Village signposted off A350 S of A303; The Green (named on some road atlases), a mile NW at OS Sheet 183 map reference 872313; or follow signpost off B3089, about 0.5 miles E of A303 junction near Little Chef; SP3 6BN

Beautiful thatched village pub with splendid views, welcoming service, good beers and popular food

'As good as ever' say several of our readers about this pleasantly rambling country pub. It's in a lovely spot by the village green and there are marvellous views of the Blackmore Vale. The three linked areas are on different areas around the central horseshoe-shaped servery and there are big log fires, plentiful oak woodwork and flagstones, comfortably padded dining chairs around big scrubbed tables with vases of flowers, and a couple of leather settees; the furnishings are all very individual and uncluttered. The atmosphere is welcoming and relaxed, and the staff cheerful and efficient. There's also a small light-painted conservatory restaurant. Hop Back Summer Lightning, Palmers Copper Ale and a guest from maybe Butcombe or Everards handpump, quite a few wines by the glass and farm cider. Piped music, board games and a skittle alley. The nearby woods are good for a stroll, and the Wiltshire Cycle Way passes through the village.

🍴 Consistently good food includes ploughman's, soup, king prawns with a sweet chilli dip, pâté of the day, beer-battered fish, pizzas from their clay oven, thai green chicken curry, onion, ricotta and parmesan tart, beef and mushroom casserole, beer-battered fish of the day, lamb chump on mash and bacon with a rosemary and mint jus, venison haunch steak with a port and redcurrant sauce, and puddings like chocolate lumpy bumpy and blackberry and apple crumble. *Starters/Snacks: £4.00 to £6.50. Main Courses: £8.50 to £15.50. Puddings: £4.50*

Free house ~ Licensee Murray Seator ~ Real ale ~ Bar food (12-2.30, 6.15-9.30) ~ (01747) 830573 ~ Children welcome ~ Dogs welcome ~ Open 11.30-3, 5.30-11

Recommended by G Vyse, Martin and Karen Wake, Bruce and Sharon Eden, Edward Mirzoeff, R I Turner, Paul Goldman, Helen and Brian Edgeley, Michael Doswell, Roger Wain-Heapy

EBBESBOURNE WAKE

ST9924   MAP 2

Horseshoe ★ 🍺 🛏

On A354 S of Salisbury, right at signpost at Coombe Bissett; village is around 8 miles further on; SP5 5JF

Restful, unspoilt country pub with a good welcome, beers tapped from the cask, tasty traditional bar food, and views from the pretty garden

Tucked away in a pretty little village, this is a charming country pub with long-serving and friendly licensees (the second generation in the family to run it). There's a great deal of atmosphere and character in the neatly kept, comfortably furnished bar – as well as fresh home-grown flowers on the tables, lanterns, a large collection of farm tools and other bric-a-brac crowded along its beams, and an open fire. Bowman Swift One, Otter Bitter, Palmers Copper Ale and a couple of guests like Bowman Wallops Wood and a beer from a new brewery near the pub, 6D Handley, tapped from the cask, and local farm cider. A conservatory extension seats nine people; best to book a table in the small restaurant as it fills up quickly. There are pleasant views over the steep sleepy valley of the River Ebble from seats in the pretty little garden and a goat and a chicken in a paddock; good nearby walks. Morris dancers may call some evenings in summer.

🍴 Well liked traditional bar food includes lunchtime sandwiches, ploughman's, soup, trout pâté, ham and eggs, sausage and chips, steak and kidney or wild boar and apricot pies, lamb cutlets with a mint and port sauce, and puddings like lemon roulade and sticky toffee pudding. *Starters/Snacks: £6.95 to £7.25. Main Courses: £10.25 to £17.00. Puddings: £4.75 to £5.25*

Free house ~ Licensees Tony and Pat Bath ~ Real ale ~ Bar food (not Sun evening or Mon) ~
Restaurant ~ (01722) 780474 ~ Children welcome but not in main bar ~ Dogs allowed in bar ~
Open 12-3, 6.30-11; 12-4 Sun; closed Sun evening and Mon lunchtime ~ Bedrooms: /£75B

Recommended by David Kirkcaldy, the Didler, G Vyse, Robert Watt, Tom and Rosemary Hall, Chris Wall,
Ian Herdman, Col and Mrs Patrick Kaye, Richard, Anne and Kate Ansell, Dr and Mrs M E Wilson

FONTHILL GIFFORD

ST9231   MAP 2

Beckford Arms ⓨ ♀ ⇤

Off B3089 W at Fonthill Bishop; SP3 6PX

**Elegant 18th-c coaching inn on the edge of lovely rolling parkland, newly refurbished bar
and restaurant, first-class food and real ales; bedrooms**

As we went to press, we heard that this civilised old coaching inn had suffered a dreadful
fire and would be closed for some months while major rebuilding takes place; we are
hoping it will have reopened by the time this edition is published. Obviously, it's best to
phone ahead to make sure things are up and running again. The main bar has a huge
fireplace, bar stools beside the counter, various old wooden dining chairs and tables on
the parquet flooring and Butcombe Bitter, Keystone Large One and Milestone Lions Pride
on handpump, up to 20 wines by the glass, a fair range of spirits, a fine Saturday
lunchtime bloody mary and bellini made using locally grown grapes; staff are cheerful and
helpful. The elegant sitting room has comfortable sofas facing each other across a low
table of newspapers, a nice built-in window seat and other chairs and tables, and an
open fire in the stone fireplace with candles in brass candlesticks and fresh flowers on
the mantelpiece. There's also a separate restaurant and charming private dining room.
Much of the artwork on the walls is by local artists; the pub dog is called Elsa. On Sunday
and Monday nights they show a free movie in the sitting room. The mature rambling
garden has seats on the brick terrace, hammocks under trees and boules. The inn is on
the edge of a fine parkland estate, with a lake and sweeping vistas. The bedrooms are
stylish and the breakfasts, with home-made jams, are enjoyable.

🍴 **Growing some of their own produce and supporting local growers, the good bistro-style
food includes sandwiches, soup, duck and foie gras galantine with port and armagnac-
soaked prunes, ham and egg, cheese and bacon burger, fish and chips with pea purée and
tartare sauce, twice-baked goats cheese soufflé with field mushrooms and curly kale,
rabbit with creamed polenta, rosemary and olives, skate wing with roast fennel, tomato,
lemon and parsley, confit pork belly with black pudding, puy lentils and apple purée, and
puddings like hot chocolate pudding with pistachio ice-cream and apple, pear and rhubarb
crumble.** *Starters/Snacks: £4.50 to £6.50. Main Courses: £8.50 to £16.00. Puddings: £5.00*

Free house ~ Licensees Dan Brod and Charlie Luxton ~ Real ale ~ Bar food (12-2.30(3.30 Sat
and Sun), 6.30-9) ~ Restaurant ~ (01747) 870385 ~ Children welcome ~ Dogs allowed in bar ~
Open 11-11(10.30 Sun) ~ Bedrooms: £70S/£90B

Recommended by Colin and Janet Roe, Mr and Mrs A Curry, Susan Buchanan, Ian Herdman, Michael Doswell,
Andrea Rampley

GREAT BEDWYN

SU2764   MAP 2

Three Tuns

Village signposted off A338 S of Hungerford, or off A4 W of Hungerford via Little Bedwyn;
High Street; SN8 3NU

**Thriving village pub with local real ales, helpful staff, nicely presented bar food and
eclectic décor**

Very popular locally, though you will be warmly welcomed as a visitor by the friendly
staff, this is a bustling village pub. The traditional décor in the beamed, bare-boards
front bar is lifted out of the ordinary by some quirky touches and almost every inch of
the walls and ceiling is covered by either the usual brasses, jugs, hops and agricultural
implements, or more unusual collections such as ribbons from sailors' hats, showbiz
photos and yellowing cuttings about the royal family. Ramsbury Gold, White Horse Village

Idiot and a couple of changing guests – one named after the pub on handpump; the cellar was once the village morgue. There's an inglenook fireplace and lighted candles in the evenings. In front of the whitewashed building there are quite a few plants, while behind is a raised garden with a heated smoking area. It does get pretty packed at weekends.

Using some of their own-grown produce, the bar food includes soup, rillettes, scallops with bacon, basil and sweet pepper oil, cod fillet with home-made tartare sauce, a popular cassoulet, slow-cooked lamb shoulder with redcurrant and red wine jus, daily specials like smoked haddock florentine with quail eggs and pheasant breast with an apple and walnut stuffing and cider sauce, and puddings such as mango sorbet and a trio of puddings. *Starters/Snacks: £4.95 to £7.95. Main Courses: £8.95 to £18.95. Puddings: £4.95 to £5.95*

Free house ~ Licensees Amanda and Jason Gard ~ Real ale ~ Bar food ~ Restaurant ~ (01672) 870280 ~ Children welcome ~ Dogs allowed in bar ~ Open 12-3, 6-11; 12-6 Sun; closed Sun evening

Recommended by Mr and Mrs Ian Campbell, Alvin and Yvonne Andrews, Paul Boot, Phil Bryant

GREAT HINTON   ST9059 MAP 2
Linnet

3.5 miles E of Trowbridge, village signposted off A361 opposite Lamb at Semington; BA14 6BU

Attractive dining pub, very much a place to come for a good meal rather than just a drink

There's no doubt that most customers in this brick dining pub are here to enjoy the first-class food served by the courteous and efficient staff. The comfortable bar to the right of the door has Wadworths 6X on electric pump, ten wines by the glass and around two dozen malt whiskies; there are bookshelves in a snug end part of the room. The restaurant is candlelit at night; piped music. In summer, the window boxes and flowering tubs, with seats dotted among them, are quite a sight.

Making everything from scratch, the interesting food includes lunchtime sandwiches, soup, pigeon breast on stilton waldorf salad, salmon fishcakes with pesto mayonnaise, cider and thyme gammon steak with free-range egg and their own ketchup, beer-battered cod fillet and triple cooked chips, mutton shepherd's pie, pork tenderloin filled with prunes and spinach wrapped in smoked bacon on a wild mushroom sauce, and puddings like bitter chocolate and orange tart with Cointreau syrup and honey and vanilla cheesecakes with raspberries soaked in whisky; they also offer a £5 lunch dish of the day and a two- and three-course set lunch. *Starters/Snacks: £5.50 to £7.95. Main Courses: £8.25 to £20.95. Puddings: £5.75 to £7.95*

Wadworths ~ Tenant Jonathan Furby ~ Real ale ~ Bar food ~ Restaurant ~ (01380) 870354 ~ Children welcome ~ Dogs allowed in bar ~ Open 11-2.30(3 Sun), 6-11; closed Mon

Recommended by Dr and Mrs J Temporal, Dennis and Gill Keen, Martin Clifton, Michael Doswell, Stan and Dot Garner

GRITTLETON   ST8680 MAP 2
Neeld Arms

Leave M4 junction 17, follow A429 to Cirencester and immediately left, signed Stanton St Quinton and Grittleton; SN14 6AP

Bustling village pub with popular food and beer and friendly staff; comfortable bedrooms

There's always a jolly atmosphere in this 17th-c stone inn and a good mix of both drinkers and diners – it's very much the centre of village life. Largely open-plan and recently refurbished, there's a pleasant mix of seats ranging from bar stools, a traditional settle, window seats and pale wooden dining chairs around a mix of tables. The little brick fireplace houses a woodburning stove, there's an inglenook fireplace on the right, Cotswold-stone walls; and Butcombe Bitter, Wadworths IPA and 6X and Wickwar Coopers

WPA on handpump served from the blue-painted panelled and oak-topped bar counter; dominoes and cribbage. The back dining area has yet another inglenook with a big woodburning stove and even back here, you still feel thoroughly part of the action. There's an outdoor terrace, with a pergola.

🍴 **Good bar food includes sandwiches, soup, chicken liver pâté, mussels with garlic and cream, local sausages and mash, goats cheese, tomato and basil tart, a changing pie, pork medallions with apple and calvados sauce, calves liver with black pudding, bass with butter and parsley sauce, and puddings like lemon tart with mango and passion-fruit sorbet and amaretto trifle; they also hold popular monthly themed events with special menus.** *Starters/Snacks: £4.50 to £7.50. Main Courses: £8.95 to £13.95. Puddings: £4.95*

Free house ~ Licensees Charlie and Boo West ~ Real ale ~ Bar food ~ (01249) 782470 ~ Children welcome ~ Dogs welcome ~ Open 12-3(3.30 Sat), 5.30-11.30(midnight Sat); 12-4, 7-11 Sun ~ Bedrooms: £50B/£80B

Recommended by Sara Fulton, Roger Baker, Dr and Mrs A K Clarke, Ian Malone, W J Taylor, MJVK, John and Enid Morris, Richard Stancomb, Matthew Shackle

HORTON
SU0363 MAP 2

Bridge Inn

Signposted off A361 Beckhampton road just inside the Devizes limit; Horton Road; SN10 2JS

Well run and distinctive canalside pub with good traditional pub food, six real ales and a pleasant garden with aviary

It's lovely to walk from Devizes along the Kennet & Avon Canal to this friendly former flour mill and bakery; it's also handy for walks on the downs. Inside, on the red walls above a high-panelled dado, are black and white photos of bargee families and their barges among other old photographs and country pictures. In the carpeted area on the left, all the sturdy pale pine tables may be set for food, and there's a log fire at the front; to the right of the bar is a pubbier part with similar country-kitchen furniture on reconstituted flagstones and some stripped brickwork. Wadworths IPA and 6X on handpump with up to four guest beers from Wadworths tapped from the cask, and quite a few wines by the glass. Disabled lavatories, piped music and TV. There are moorings for boats by the safely fenced garden which features an aviary and fantail doves as well as picnic-sets and there's one of the original grinding wheels set into the terrace.

🍴 **Traditional bar food includes sandwiches, ploughman's, soup, pâté and toast, beefburger with cheese, ham or sausage and eggs, all-day breakfast, jumbo battered cod, steak in ale pie, liver, onion crispy bacon, vegetable pot, and puddings such as chocolate fudge cake and knickerbocker glory.** *Starters/Snacks: £4.25 to £5.75. Main Courses: £8.95 to £15.95. Puddings: £4.50*

Wadworths ~ Tenant Adrian Softley ~ Real ale ~ Bar food (12-2(2.30 Sat), 6-8.30; not Sun evening or Mon) ~ Restaurant ~ (01380) 860273 ~ Well behaved children welcome ~ Dogs allowed in bar ~ Open 12-3, 6-11; 12-3, 7-10.30 Sun; closed Mon (except bank hols) ~ Bedrooms: /£59B

Recommended by M R Phillips, Dr and Mrs M E Wilson, Elen Matthews, P and J Shapley, Mr and Mrs A H Young, Sheila and Robert Robinson

KILMINGTON
ST7835 MAP 2

Red Lion £

B3092 Mere—Frome, 2.5 miles S of Maiden Bradley; 3 miles from A303 Mere turn-off; BA12 6RP

Atmospheric, no-nonsense country inn owned by the National Trust, with good value traditional lunches and an attractive garden

Mr and Mrs Gibbs run this unchanging 15th-c local with professionalism and friendliness – and 'long may it go on' say several of our readers. The snug, low-ceilinged bar has a good convivial atmosphere, pleasant furnishings such as a curved high-backed settle and red leatherette wall and window seats on the flagstones, photographs of locals pinned up on the black beams and a couple of big fireplaces (one with a fine old iron fireback) with winter log fires. A newer big-windowed eating area is decorated with brasses, a large leather horse collar and hanging plates. Darts, shove-ha'penny and board games. Butcombe Bitter, Butts Jester and a guest like Keystone Large One on handpump, several wines by the glass and Thatcher's cider; helpful service. There are picnic-sets in the big attractive garden (look out for Kim the labrador). A gate gives on to the lane which leads to White Sheet Hill, where there's riding, hang-gliding and radio-controlled gliders, and Stourhead Gardens are only a mile away. Though dogs are generally welcome, they're not allowed at lunchtime. There's a smokers' shelter in a corner of the car park.

🍴 **Served only at lunchtime, the well liked, unpretentious bar food might include sandwiches and toasties, ploughman's, soup, hot pasties, filled baked potatoes, vegetable lasagne, game pie, daily specials like ham, egg and beans, chicken casserole and cottage pie, and puddings such as apple strudel.** *Starters/Snacks: £3.00 to £4.80. Main Courses: £6.95 to £9.45. Puddings: £4.60*

Free house ~ Licensee Chris Gibbs ~ Real ale ~ Bar food (12-1.50; not evenings) ~ No credit cards ~ (01985) 844263 ~ Children welcome ~ Dogs allowed in bar ~ Open 11-2.30, 6.30-11; 12-3, 7-11 Sun

Recommended by Edward Mirzoeff, Michael Doswell, Joan and Michel Hooper-Immins, Andrea Rampley, Steve Jackson, SRD, Chris and Angela Buckell

LACOCK   ST9168   MAP 2

George

West Street; village signposted off A350 S of Chippenham; SN15 2LH

Unspoilt and homely, with plenty of character and an attractive back garden in summer

In a much-loved village owned by the National Trust this is an unspoilt rambling inn right in the centre of it. There's a cheerful welcoming atmosphere and lots of little informal areas to enjoy a drink and a chat. The low-beamed bar has upright timbers in the place of knocked-through walls making cosy corners, armchairs and windsor chairs around close-set tables, seats in the stone-mullioned windows and flagstones just by the counter; quiet piped music. The treadwheel set into the outer breast of the original great central fireplace is a talking point – worked by a dog, it was used to turn a spit for roasting. The walls are covered with things to look at, including a little exhibition on William Henry Fox Talbot together with a collection of vintage cameras, pictures for sale, a copy of an 1840 photo of Lacock by Fox Talbot and souvenirs from the filming in the village of the TV series *Cranford*, and for a Harry Potter film. Wadworths IPA, 6X and St George and the Dragon on handpump. Outside, there are picnic-sets with umbrellas in the attractive courtyard, which has a pillory and a well; extensive lawn beyond with children's play area.

🍴 **Tasty bar food includes sandwiches, filled baguettes, filled baked potatoes, soup, pigeon breast and black pudding salad, rabbit or steak in ale pie, cajun salmon, goats cheese and red onion tart, mixed grill, steaks cooked on hot stones, and puddings like bread and butter pudding and apple and raspberry crumble.** *Starters/Snacks: £3.95 to £6.95. Main Courses: £6.95 to £16.50. Puddings: £4.75*

Wadworths ~ Tenant John Glass ~ Real ale ~ Bar food (12-2, 6-9) ~ Restaurant ~ (01249) 730263 ~ Children welcome ~ Dogs allowed in bar ~ Open 9am-11pm(10.30 Sun); 9am-3, 5-11 Mon-Thurs in winter

Recommended by Blaise Vyner, Ian Herdman, Chris and Jeanne Downing, Bob and Angela Brooks, PL, D and J Ashdown, Donna and Roger, Maureen Wood, Richard and Sheila Fitton, Bryan and Mary Blaxall, Dr and Mrs J Temporal, Adrian Johnson

---

The letters and figures after the name of each town are its Ordnance Survey map reference. 'Using the *Guide*' at the beginning of the book explains how it helps you find a pub, in road atlases or on large-scale maps as well as on our own maps.

Rising Sun 🍺

*Bewley Common, Bowden Hill – out towards Sandy Lane, up hill past Abbey; OS Sheet
173 map reference 935679; SN15 2PP*

Unassuming stone pub with welcoming atmosphere and great views from garden

Apart from some refurbishment, this busy, unpretentious pub happily doesn't change too
much and our readers enjoy their visits here very much. There are three welcoming little
rooms knocked together to form one simply furnished area with a mix of wooden chairs
and tables on stone floors, country pictures and open fires. Moles Best Bitter, Elmo's Fire
and Molecatcher and a guest such as Fullers London Pride on handpump, Black Rat cider
and several wines by the glass. The conservatory shares the same fantastic views as the
big two-level terrace (where there are plenty of modern steel and wood tables and chairs)
– on a clear day you can see up to 25 miles over the Avon Valley; the sunsets can be
stunning.

🍽 Generous helpings of well liked bar food include soup, chicken liver pâté, battered cod
and chips, ham and egg, local sausages with gravy, chicken breast stuffed with brie and
wrapped in bacon, slow-roasted belly of pork on spring onion mash and cider gravy, fillet
of bass with lemon butter, and puddings like apple crumble and chocolate brownie with
honeycomb ice-cream. *Starters/Snacks: £4.00 to £5.50. Main Courses: £8.95 to £15.95.
Puddings: £3.50 to £4.50*

Moles ~ Manager Louise Hall ~ Real ale ~ Bar food (12-2(4 Sun), 6-9; all day Sat and Sun in
July and Aug; no food Sun evening in winter) ~ Restaurant ~ (01249) 730363 ~ Children
welcome ~ Dogs welcome ~ Live entertainment every Weds evening ~ Open 12-3, 6-11;
12-11 Sat; 12-5 Sun; closed 3-6 Sat and Sun in winter
Recommended by P Waterman, Chris and Angela Buckell, Ian Herdman, David A Hammond, George Atkinson

LOWER CHUTE   SU3153   MAP 2

Hatchet

The Chutes well signposted via Appleshaw off A342, 2.5 miles W of Andover; SP11 9DX

Unchanged, neatly kept, 13th-c thatched country pub, with a restful atmosphere

There's so much going for this rural pub. It's an attractive place in a pretty hamlet, the
convivial landlord and his friendly staff are sure to make you welcome and the curry
nights are not to be missed. The very low-beamed bar has a splendid 17th-c fireback in
the huge fireplace (and a roaring winter log fire), a mix of captain's chairs and cushioned
wheelbacks around oak tables, and a peaceful local feel. Timothy Taylors Landlord, Otter
Bitter and a guest like Stonehenge Pigswill on handpump and several wines by the glass;
piped music and board games. There are seats out on a terrace by the front car park or
on the side grass – as well as a smokers' hut and a children's sandpit. If you stay in the
comfortable bedrooms, you'll get a hearty breakfast.

🍽 Thursday night is curry night and other bar food includes lunchtime filled baguettes,
ploughman's, soup, creamy garlic mushrooms, ham and egg, meaty or vegetarian lasagne,
liver and bacon, steak in ale pie, and daily specials. *Starters/Snacks: £5.50 to £6.95. Main
Courses: £8.50 to £14.95. Puddings: £3.95*

Free house ~ Licensee Jeremy McKay ~ Real ale ~ Bar food (12-2.15, 6.30-9.45; 12-3; not Sun
evening) ~ Restaurant ~ (01264) 730229 ~ Children welcome ~ Dogs allowed in bar and
bedrooms ~ Live music first Sun evening of the month ~ Open 11.30-3, 6-11; 12-3, 7-10.30
Sun ~ Bedrooms: £50S/£60S
Recommended by Mr and Mrs H J Langley, Henry Midwinter, Ian Herdman, John Coatsworth

---

'Children welcome' means the pub says it lets children inside without any special
restriction. If it allows them in, but to restricted areas such as an eating area or family
room, we specify this. Some pubs may impose an evening time limit. We do not
mention limits after 9pm as we assume children are home by then.

LUCKINGTON   ST8384 MAP 2

Old Royal Ship
Off B4040 SW of Malmesbury; SN14 6PA

Friendly pub by the village green, with a fair choice of drinks and decent bar food

Especially busy during the Badminton horse trials, this pleasantly opened-up pub is a likeable old place. There's effectively one long bar divided into three areas and the central servery has Bass, Wadworths 6X and a couple of guest beers like Itchen Valley King Arthur and Wickwar Coopers WPA on handpump, a farm cider and a dozen wines by the glass. On the right are neat tables, spindleback chairs and small cushioned settles on dark bare boards, with a small open fireplace and some stripped masonry. Skittle alley, games machine, darts, TV and piped music. The garden beyond the car park has boules, a play area with a big wooden climbing frame and plenty of seats on the terrace or grass. More reports please.

🍴 Bar food includes sandwiches, filled baked potatoes, salmon, lime and coriander fishcakes, burgers, ham and eggs, scampi and chips, chicken breast in a white wine and stilton sauce, steaks and daily specials. *Starters/Snacks: £3.25 to £6.25. Main Courses: £6.25 to £19.95. Puddings: £4.75*

Free house ~ Licensee Helen Johnson-Greening ~ Real ale ~ Bar food (12-2.15, 6(7 Sun)-9.15) ~ Restaurant ~ (01666) 840222 ~ Children welcome ~ Open 11.30-2.30, 6-11; 11.30-11 Sat; 12-4, 7-10.30 Sun
Recommended by Richard Stancomb, Chris and Angela Buckell, John and Gloria Isaacs

MANTON   SU1768 MAP 2

Outside Chance ♀
Village (and pub) signposted off A4 just W of Marlborough; High Street; SN8 4HW

Popular dining pub, civilised and traditional, nicely reworked with interesting sporting theme

Although this is a smart dining pub it still has a local flavour and they are just as happy to welcome drinkers and walkers. It has three small linked rooms, with a thriving loudly chatty atmosphere, flagstones or bare boards, hops on beams, and mainly plain pub furnishings such as chapel chairs and a long-cushioned pew; one room has a more cosseted feel, with panelling and a comfortable banquette. The décor celebrates unlikely winners, such as 100-1 Grand National winners like Coughoo or Fuinavon, Mr Spooner's Only Dreams (a 100-1 winner at Leicester in 2007), or the odd-gaited little Seabiscuit who cheered many thousands of Americans with his dogged pursuit of victory during the Depression years. The lighting is soft (nightlights on tables), the pub is usually full of fresh flowers and there's a splendid log fire in the big main fireplace; piped music and board games. Wadworths IPA and 6X and a guest such as Bishops Tipple on handpump, quite a few good wines by the glass, nicely served coffees, and the neatly dressed young staff are friendly and helpful. A suntrap side terrace has contemporary metal-framed granite-topped tables and the good-sized garden has sturdy rustic tables and benches under ash trees. The garden opens into the local playing fields with a children's play area.

🍴 Good bar food includes cajun crumbed squid with sweet chilli sauce, chicken caesar salad, eggs benedict, fresh and wild mushroom gnocchi in a madeira and parmesan cream sauce with truffle oil, grilled sole with a brown shrimp and chive butter sauce, roast rump of lamb with a port and mint jus, venison steak with herby roast potatoes and a peppercorn sauce, and puddings like summer berries in sparkling rosé wine jelly and sticky date pudding with caramel sauce. *Starters/Snacks: £5.95 to £7.50. Main Courses: £8.95 to £14.95. Puddings: £5.00 to £6.00*

Wadworths ~ Lease Hannah Lampard ~ Real ale ~ Bar food (12-2.30, 7-9(9.30 Fri, Sat)) ~ (01672) 512352 ~ Children welcome ~ Dogs welcome ~ Bridge Mon evening ~ Open 12-3, 5.30-11; 12-11 Sat and Sun
Recommended by Suzy Miller, Guy Vowles, Andrew Tollington, Ian Herdman, Sheila and Robert Robinson, Mr and Mrs A Curry

MARDEN
SU0857 MAP 2

Triple Crown
Village signposted off A342 SE of Devizes; SN10 3RH

New name and smart new look for civilised country pub with a big waterside garden

Until very recently this was the Millstream, and from a neat sheltered back terrace, clipped lawns with sturdy tables and benches sweep down to a tree-lined stream. The new name is supported by loads of photographs throughout the pub of the various triple sporting victors which carry the title – most famously, winners of the 2000 Guineas, the Epsom Derby and the St Leger, or in the US the Kentucky Derby, the Preakness and the Belmont. An appealing layout of linked cosy areas includes good log fires, hops on beams, red-cushioned dark pews and small padded dining chairs around sturdy oak and other good tables (all with lit tea lamps), one bit with big leather bean bags and children's colouring books and so forth, and another rather more formal dining area with rugs on large pale stone tiles. They have a good choice of wines by the glass and of bar nibbles, Wadworths IPA, 6X and a guest beer from a rather ecclesiastical-looking bar counter, and efficient friendly mature staff; there may be piped pop music.

🍴 **Bar food includes sandwiches, soup, grilled squid with chilli and lemon, ham and egg, home-made burger with relish, beer-battered haddock, leek and gruyère tart, braised lamb shoulder, whole cracked crab with home-made mayonnaise, and puddings such as passionfruit posset with a shortbread biscuit and sticky toffee pudding with butterscotch sauce.** *Starters/Snacks: £4.50 to £6.95. Main Courses: £8.50 to £15.95. Puddings: £5.00*

Wadworths ~ Manager Ben Davenport ~ Real ale ~ Bar food (12-2.30(4 Sun), 7-9) ~ Restaurant ~ (01380) 848308 ~ Children welcome ~ Dogs welcome ~ Open 12-3, 5.30-11; 12-11 Sat and Sun

Recommended by Mr and Mrs A H Young, Michael Doswell

NEWTON TONY
SU2140 MAP 2

Malet Arms 🍴
Village signposted off A338 Swindon—Salisbury; SP4 0HF

Smashing village pub with no pretensions, a good choice of local beers and good home-made food

This year, the enthusiastic and friendly landlord is keeping a couple of pigs and using local venison (he runs the deer management on a local estate) in their cooking; and they also now have a goat called Archie (to keep the nettles down – he is not going into the pot). It's an unpretentious and thoroughly welcoming pub with a lot of character and our readers enjoy their visits here very much. The two low-beamed interconnecting rooms have nice furnishings including a mix of different-sized tables with high-winged wall settles, carved pews, chapel and carver chairs, and lots of pictures, mainly from imperial days. The main front windows are said to have come from the stern of a ship, and there's a log and coal fire in a huge fireplace. At the back is a homely dining room. They keep four real ales on handpump from breweries such as Andwell, Itchen Valley, Ramsbury and Stonehenge, a couple of draught lagers like Veltins and Kaltenberg, have 15 malt whiskies, 11 wines by the glass and Weston's Old Rosie cider. The small front terrace has old-fashioned garden seats and some picnic-sets on the grass, and there are more tables in the back garden, along with a wendy house. There's also a little aviary and a horse paddock behind. Getting to the pub takes you through a ford and it may be best to use an alternative route in winter, as it can be quite deep.

🍴 **Chalked up on a blackboard and using their own-baked bread, the very good, changing range of carefully sourced food might include tasty soup, chicken liver pâté, cheddar wontons with real ale chutney, smoked halibut with a lime dressing, popular burgers with blue cheese and bacon, creamy mixed pepper risotto, star anise confit duck leg with asian slaw and sesame noodles, crispy roast pork belly with apple sauce, saddle of venison en croûte with a redcurrant and port sauce, whole lemon sole with sea salt, and puddings such as Mars Bar cheesecake and mixed berry eton mess.** *Starters/Snacks: £5.95 to £6.25. Main Courses: £8.95 to £14.50. Puddings: £4.75*

Free house ~ Licensee Noel Cardew ~ Real ale ~ Bar food (12-2.30, 6.30-10 (7-9.30 Sun)) ~ Restaurant ~ (01980) 629279 ~ Children allowed but not in bar area ~ Dogs allowed in bar ~ Open 11-3, 6-11; 12-3, 7-10.30 Sun; closed 25 and 26 Dec, 1 Jan

Recommended by Nigel and Sue Foster, Pat and Tony Martin, Mark Flynn, Dr and Mrs M E Wilson, N R White, P Waterman, John Prescott, B and M Kendall, Bren and Val Speed, Lois Dyer, Paul Goldman, Andrea Rampley

NORTON   ST8884   MAP 2

Vine Tree 🍴 ♆

4 miles from M4 junction 17; A429 towards Malmesbury, then left at Hullavington, Sherston signpost, then follow Norton signposts; in village turn right at Foxley signpost, which takes you into Honey Lane; SN16 0JP

Civilised dining pub, beams and candlelight, big choice of seasonal food, fine choice of drinks and a sizeable garden

Never people to rest on their laurels, the enthusiastic licensees here have introduced all sorts of interesting events over the last year such as jazz and blues, seafood extravaganzas, hog roasts, lamb assados, quizine evenings and so forth; not surprisingly this makes the place very popular locally. Three neatly kept little rooms open into each other, with aged beams, some old settles and unvarnished wooden tables on the flagstone floors, big cream church altar candles, a woodburning stove at one end of the restaurant and a large open fireplace in the central bar and limited edition and sporting prints; look out for Clementine, the friendly and docile black labrador. It's best to book to be sure of a table at weekends. Butcombe Bitter and St Austell Tinners and a guest like Bath Ales Gem on handpump, 40 wines by the glass including sparkling wines and champagne (and they have their own wine shop, too), and quite a choice of malt whiskies and armagnacs. There are picnic-sets and a children's play area in a two-acre garden plus a pretty suntrap terrace with teak furniture under big cream umbrellas, and an attractive smoking shelter.

🍴 From a big menu, the bar food might include soup, a charcuterie platter, devilled lambs kidneys, a tian of oak-smoked salmon and king prawns, pigeon and black pudding sausage with swede mash and wine gravy, beer-battered whiting with minted pea purée, organic home-made chicken kiev, steak, kidney and Guinness pie, chump of lamb with ratatouille, calves liver with white onion gravy, toulouse cassoulet, and puddings like dark chocolate fondant with white chocolate middle and Baileys crème brûlée. *Starters/Snacks: £4.95 to £9.95. Main Courses: £8.95 to £19.95. Puddings: £4.95 to £7.50*

Free house ~ Licensees Charles Walker and Tiggi Wood ~ Real ale ~ Bar food (12-2.30(3.15 Sun), 7-9.30(10 Fri and Sat)) ~ Restaurant ~ (01666) 837654 ~ Well behaved children welcome ~ Dogs allowed in bar ~ Live jazz and blues on terrace some days in summer ~ Open 11.45-3-ish(4 Sat), 6-midnight; may open all day Sun

Recommended by Richard and Sheila Fitton, Di and Mike Gillam, Neil and Karen Dignan, Mr and Mrs A H Young, Peter and Audrey Dowsett, Rod Stoneman, Michael Doswell, Richard Stancomb, the Brewers, Dr and Mrs J Temporal

PITTON   SU2131   MAP 2

Silver Plough ♆ 🛏

Village signposted from A30 E of Salisbury (follow brown tourist signs); SP5 1DU

Bustling country dining pub with popular bar food, good drinks and nearby walks; bedrooms

Many of our readers enjoy staying overnight at this busy and friendly village pub and the breakfasts are very good. The comfortable front bar has plenty to look at, as the black beams are strung with hundreds of antique boot-warmers and stretchers, pewter and china tankards, copper kettles, toby jugs, earthenware and glass rolling pins, painted clogs, glass net-floats, coach horns and so forth. Seats include half a dozen cushioned antique oak settles (one elaborately carved, beside a very fine reproduction of an Elizabethan oak table) and the timbered white walls are hung with Thorburn and other game bird prints, and a big naval battle glass-painting. The back bar is simpler, but still has a big winged high-backed settle, cased antique guns, substantial pictures and – like the front room – flowers on its tables. There's a skittle alley next to the snug bar; piped music. Badger Gold, K&B, Tanglefoot and a seasonal guest on handpump and 10 wines by the glass. A quiet lawn has picnic-sets and other tables under cocktail parasols and on the terrace is a heated area for smokers. The pub is served by a good network of woodland and downland paths, including the Clarendon Way.

🍽 **Tasty bar food served in ample helpings includes filled baguettes and baked potatoes, soup, chicken liver pâté, tuna niçoise, mushroom stroganoff, lasagne, steak and kidney pie, chicken breast filled with brie, wrapped in bacon on a dijon mustard sauce, calves liver and pancetta on mustard mash with a port and redcurrant sauce, half a honey-roast duck with cranberry and orange sauce, and puddings; Sunday roasts. Please note, they stop serving food at 2pm prompt.** *Starters/Snacks: £4.50 to £7.50. Main Courses: £6.95 to £11.50. Puddings: £2.95 to £5.95*

Badger ~ Tenants Hughen and Joyce Riley ~ Real ale ~ Bar food (12-2, 6-9) ~ Restaurant ~ (01722) 712266 ~ Children allowed in snug ~ Dogs allowed in bar ~ Open 11-3, 6-midnight; 12-3.30, 6.30-midnight Sun ~ Bedrooms: /£50S

Recommended by Ian Herdman, Phyl and Jack Street, JDM, KM, Glenwys and Alan Lawrence, George Atkinson, Helen and Brian Edgeley, Edward Mirzoeff

ROWDE
ST9762   MAP 2

George & Dragon 🍽 🍷 🛏
A342 Devizes—Chippenham; SN10 2PN

Gently upmarket inn with good, varied food and a nice atmosphere; smart modern bedrooms

This 16th-c former coaching inn has plenty of character and quite an emphasis on dining. The two low-ceilinged rooms have lots of beams, large open fireplaces, wooden dining chairs around candlelit tables, antique rugs and walls covered with old pictures and portraits; the atmosphere is pleasantly chatty. Butcombe Bitter, Fullers London Pride and a guest named for the pub on handpump and several wines by the glass; board games and piped music. The inn is not far from the Kennet & Avon Canal and has a pretty back garden with tables and chairs; occasional summer barbecues.

🍽 **Good, if not cheap, bar food includes soup, creamy potted crab, baked fig with goats cheese and prosciutto, wild mushroom risotto with black truffle oil, chilli beefburger with aioli, beer-battered cod fillet with home-made tartare sauce, chicken breast with herb stuffing and red wine jus, roasted rack of lamb with minted pea and broad bean purée, whole cracked cornish crab with lemon mayonnaise, and puddings like lemon posset with lemon shortbread biscuit and chocolate and coffee roulade; they also offer two- and three-course set menus.** *Starters/Snacks: £4.50 to £9.50. Main Courses: £8.50 to £19.50. Puddings: £6.00*

Free house ~ Licensees Philip and Michelle Hale, Christopher Day ~ Real ale ~ Bar food (12-3, 7-10; 12-4, 6.30-10 Sat; 12-4 Sun; not Sun evening) ~ Restaurant ~ (01380) 723053 ~ Children welcome ~ Dogs allowed in bar ~ Open 12-3, 7-11; 12-4, 6.30-11 Sat; 12-4 Sun; closed Sun evening ~ Bedrooms: £55/£70(£85S)

Recommended by Suzy Miller, Betsy and Peter Little, Peter and Jan Humphreys

SALISBURY
SU1429   MAP 2

Haunch of Venison
Minster Street, opposite Market Cross; SP1 1TB

Ancient pub oozing history, with tiny beamed rooms, unique fittings and a famous mummified hand; fine atmosphere and real ales

This is just the place for a lingering drink as it has so much character and atmosphere and dates back to 1320 when it was used by craftsmen working on the cathedral spire. The two tiny downstairs rooms are quite spit-and-sawdust in spirit, with massive beams in the white ceiling, stout oak benches built into the timbered walls, black and white floor tiles, and an open fire. A tiny snug (popular with locals, but historically said to be where the ladies drank) opens off the entrance lobby. Courage Best, Greene King IPA, Hop Back Summer Lightning and a guest from Hop Back on handpump from a unique pewter bar counter, and there's a rare set of antique taps for gravity-fed spirits and liqueurs. They've also up to 100 malt whiskies and ten wines by the glass. Halfway up the stairs is a panelled room they call the House of Lords, which has a small-paned window looking down on to the main bar, and a splendid fireplace that dates back to the building's early years; behind glass in a small wall slit is the smoke-preserved mummified hand of an 18th-c card sharp still clutching his cards.

🍴 Bar food – not the strong point here – includes filled baguettes, soup, lasagne, cold sausage platter, vegetarian gnocchi, steak and kidney pudding, slow-cooked lamb shoulder and haunch of venison with port gravy. *Starters/Snacks: £4.50 to £5.50. Main Courses: £8.00 to £16.20. Puddings: £5.50*

Scottish Courage ~ Lease Anthony Leroy and Justyna Miller ~ Real ale ~ Bar food (12-2.30, 6-9(10 Fri and Sat)) ~ Restaurant ~ (01722) 411313 ~ Children welcome ~ Dogs allowed in bar ~ Open 11-11; 12-10.30 Sun
Recommended by Ann and Colin Hunt, Stephen Shepherd, the Didler, Pete Coxon, Maureen Wood

SEEND   ST9361   MAP 2

Barge

Seend Cleeve; signposted off A361 Devizes—Trowbridge, between Seend village and signpost to Seend Head; SN12 6QB

Busy canalside pub with boat-watching from the nice garden, decent beer and wide choice of wines by the glass

On warm days you can watch the boating activity on the Kennet & Avon Canal from the garden of this busy pub. Inside, the bar has a medley of eye-catching seats which includes milk churns, unusual high-backed chairs (made from old boat parts), a seat made from an upturned canoe and the occasional small oak settle among the rugs on the parquet floor; there's a well stocked aquarium and a pretty Victorian fireplace; piped music. Wadworths IPA, Horizon, 6X and a seasonal beer on handpump kept under light blanket pressure and 30 wines by the glass. More reports please.

🍴 Bar food includes filled baguettes, thai-style crab cake with chilli sauce, vegetarian cannelloni, ham and duck eggs, sausages with onion gravy, rabbit and bacon pie, slow-roasted pork belly with apple sauce and cider jus, and puddings like fruit crumble and sticky toffee pudding. *Starters/Snacks: £3.75 to £8.75. Main Courses: £8.95 to £15.50. Puddings: £3.75 to £5.75*

Wadworths ~ Managers Paul and Sarah Haynes ~ Real ale ~ Bar food (12-3, 6-10 (cold food between 3 and 5)) ~ Restaurant ~ (01380) 828230 ~ Children welcome ~ Dogs allowed in bar ~ Open 11-11
Recommended by Barry Collett, Mr and Mrs A Curry

SHERSTON   ST8585   MAP 2

Rattlebone ♀

Church Street; B4040 Malmesbury—Chipping Sodbury; SN16 0LR

Village pub with lots of atmosphere in rambling rooms, good bar food and real ales, and friendly staff

This bustling old pub is named after its ghost – the Saxon warrior John Rattlebone, and there's certainly a lot of character and atmosphere in the bars. The public bar has a good mix of locals and visitors and the rambling rooms have beams, standing timbers and flagstones, pews, settles and country-kitchen chairs around a mix of tables, armchairs and sofas, and roaring fires. Butcombe Bitter, St Austell Tribute and Wells & Youngs Bitter on handpump and 14 wines by the glass. Piped music, board games, TV and games machine. Outside, there's a skittle alley, two boules pitches, often in use by one of the many pub teams, a boules festival in July and mangold hurling (cattle turnip throwing). The two pretty gardens include an extended terrace where they hold barbecues and spit roasts. They have wheelchair access.

Ⅲ **Good bar food includes sandwiches, ploughman's, soup, smoked salmon fettuccine, ham and free-range eggs, spinach, ricotta and roast pepper lasagne, sausages with onion gravy, lamb curry, fresh cod fillet with a saffron and mussel velouté, breast of duck with roast butternut squash and a chilli, sesame and spring onion dressing, and puddings such as panna cotta with poached plums and creamy bread and butter pudding.** *Starters/Snacks: £4.25 to £9.00. Main Courses: £7.95 to £17.95. Puddings: £4.95 to £5.50*

Youngs ~ Tenant Jason Read ~ Real ale ~ Bar food (12-2.30, 6-9.30; 12-3, 5.30-8 Sun) ~ Restaurant ~ (01666) 840871 ~ Children welcome (in bar until 7pm unless eating) ~ Dogs allowed in bar ~ Open 12-3, 5-11(midnight Fri); 12-midnight(11 Sun) Sat

Recommended by Tom and Ruth Rees, Bob and Angela Brooks, John and Gloria Isaacs, Chris and Angela Buckell

STOURTON   ST7733   MAP 2

Spread Eagle 🛏

Church Lawn; follow Stourhead brown signs off B3092, N of junction with A303 just W of Mere; BA12 6QE

Comfortable country inn next to famous gardens; some food all day in summer; busy, at lunchtimes, quieter later on; bedrooms

As this fine Georgian brick inn is so handy for the A303 it can get extremely busy, so it's best to book a table in advance if you are planning to eat. The interior has an old-fashioned, rather civilised feel with antique panel-back settles, a mix of new and old solid tables and chairs, handsome fireplaces with good winter log fires, smoky old sporting prints, prints of Stourhead and standard lamps or brass swan's-neck wall lamps; piped music. One room by the entrance has armchairs, a longcase clock and a corner china cupboard. Butcombe Bitter and Blond, Wessex Kilmington Best and a guest such as Otter Ale on handpump and several wines by the glass. There are benches in the courtyard behind. The inn is at the entrance to the magnificent Stourhead estate and if you stay overnight, you can wander freely around the famous National Trust gardens outside their normal opening times.

Ⅲ **Good bar food includes lunchtime sandwiches, ploughman's, soup, mussels in a creamy white wine and cider sauce, ham and free-range eggs, shepherd's pie, wild mushroom and asparagus stroganoff, scallop, tiger prawn and salmon brochette, mixed grill, and puddings such as chocolate chip brownie and treacle tart; they serve cream teas through the afternoon.** *Starters/Snacks: £4.95 to £7.25. Main Courses: £9.95 to £16.95. Puddings: £3.50 to £4.95*

Free house ~ Licensee Andrew Wilson ~ Real ale ~ Bar food (12-2.30(3 Sat, Sun), 7-9) ~ Restaurant (evening) ~ (01747) 840587 ~ Children welcome ~ Open 10am-11pm; 10am-10.30pm Sun ~ Bedrooms: £80B/£110B

Recommended by Edward Mirzoeff, Dr and Mrs J Temporal, Andrea Rampley, Michael Doswell, Sheila Topham, Colin and Janet Roe

UPPER CHUTE   SU2953   MAP 2

Cross Keys ♀ 🍺 🛏

Tucked-away village N of Andover, best reached off A343 via Tangley, or off A342 in Weyhill via Clanville; SP11 9ER

Peacefully set, proper country pub, welcoming and relaxed, with enjoyable food and good beer and wines

Run by an enthusiastic and hard-working landlord, this is an hospitable and enjoyable pub – and several of our readers have enjoyed staying here recently, too. It's open-plan with a relaxed, unstuffy atmosphere, early 18th-c beams, some sofas, a cushioned pew built around the window and a good log fire in the big hearth on the left; pubby tables and a couple of leather armchairs by the woodburning stove on the right, darts sensibly placed in an alcove, and shut the box, board games, TV for special events and piped music. Arkells Moonlight Ale, Fullers London Pride and Seafarers and Hop Back Crop Circle on handpump and nine good wines by the glass; service is helpful and the charming staffordshire bull terriers are called Pepper, Pudding and Mouse. There are far-ranging rural views over wooded hills from picnic-sets on the grass and south-facing terrace and a children's play fort. If you're exploring the area on horseback, you can use one of the two stables at the back of the pub.

🍴 **Deliberately unpretentious and popular, it's the proper pies that most customers enjoy so much: steak in ale or steak and stilton, minted lamb, chicken, ham and leek, rabbit and venison or leek and potato, and so forth. They also offer filled baguettes, soup, lamb cutlets, a vegetarian dish, rib-eye steaks, puddings and Sunday roasts.** *Starters/Snacks: £4.25 to £5.95. Main Courses: £7.95 to £15.95. Puddings: £3.95 to £5.00*

Free house ~ Licensees George and Sonia Humphrey ~ Real ale ~ Bar food (12-2(2.30 Sat and Sun), 6-9; not Sun evening) ~ Restaurant ~ (01264) 730295 ~ Children welcome ~ Dogs allowed in bar and bedrooms ~ Open 12-2.30, 6-11; 12-midnight(11 Sun) Sat ~ Bedrooms: £60S/£70S

Recommended by Dave Braisted, Kelly Newton, Martin Hatcher, Phyl and Jack Street, Don Faskle, Derek Goldrei, John and Enid Morris, David and Ruth Hollands, George Atkinson

WEST LAVINGTON   SU0052   MAP 2

Bridge Inn 🍴

A360 S of Devizes; Church Street; SN10 4LD

Friendly village pub with good bar food, real ales and a light, comfortable bar

Always deservedly busy – it's best to book a table if you wish to eat – this is a quietly civilised and friendly pub. The comfortable spacious bar mixes contemporary features such as spotlights in the ceiling with firmly traditional fixtures like the enormous brick inglenook that may be filled with big logs and candles; at the opposite end is a smaller modern fireplace, in an area set mostly for eating. Pictures on the cream-painted or exposed brick walls are for sale, as are local jams, and there are plenty of fresh flowers on the tables and bar; timbers and the occasional step divide the various areas. Wadworths IPA and two guests like Plain Ales Innocence and Sharps Doom Bar on handpump, 11 wines by the glass and several malt whiskies; piped music in the evenings. A raised lawn at the back makes a pleasant place to spend a summer's afternoon, with several tables under a big tree; boules.

🍴 **Extremely good food, with a french leaning, includes lunchtime filled baguettes, ploughman's, fish soup, seared tiger prawns in sweet chilli marinade, snails with garlic and herb butter, a charcuterie plate, baked goats cheese and sunblush tomatoes in puff pastry with ratatouille, corn-fed chicken breast stuffed with garlic butter, wrapped in prosciutto with a red pepper coulis, a cassoulet, seared red mullet on spring onion risotto, and puddings like a trio of crème brûlée and baked alaska.** *Starters/Snacks: £4.50 to £6.50. Main Courses: £8.95 to £19.75. Puddings: £5.25 to £6.25*

Enterprise ~ Lease Cyrille and Paula Portier ~ Real ale ~ Bar food (not Sun evening or Mon) ~ Restaurant ~ (01380) 813213 ~ Children welcome ~ Open 12-3, 6.30-11; 12-5 Sun; closed Sun evening and Mon; two weeks Feb

Recommended by Mr and Mrs A Curry, George Atkinson, Dr and Mrs A K Clarke, Mr and Mrs P R Thomas, Robert Kibble

---

Bedroom prices normally include full english breakfast, VAT and any inclusive service charge that we know of. Prices before the '/' are for single rooms, after for two people in double or twin (B includes a private bath, S a private shower). If there is no '/', the prices are only for twin or double rooms (as far as we know there are no singles).

WINTERBOURNE BASSETT

SU1075   MAP 2

White Horse ⑨⑪

Off A4361 S of Swindon; SN4 9QB

Neat dining pub with wide choice of enjoyable food, thoughtful choice of drinks and a sizeable garden

'The perfect place for a quiet meal or chatty pint' says one of our readers about this well run dining pub. It's deservedly popular and always busy, so it might be as well to book a table in advance to be sure of a seat. The licensees are helpful and friendly, and the neat big-windowed bar is attractively extended with traditional tables and chairs on the waxed wooden floors, old prints and paintings on the walls, plants dotted about and a little brick fireplace. There's a comfortable dining room and warm conservatory, too. Wadworths IPA, 6X and Bishops Tipple on handpump, up to a dozen wines by the glass and maybe winter mulled wine and summer Pimms by the jug; piped music, darts and board games. There are tables outside on a good-sized lawn and lovely hanging baskets.

⑪ Making their own bread and ice-creams, they offer a wide choice of well liked bar food including lunchtime filled baguettes, ploughman's, soup, spicy prawn pil pil, stilton and asparagus tartlet, lunchtime sausages with onion gravy and battered cod, chicken in mushroom sauce, pork and bacon casserole, cumberland beef, baked salmon with a tarragon and orange sauce, and puddings such as lime and mint cheesecake and steamed sponges; Sunday roasts; they offer a very good value two-course lunch. *Starters/Snacks: £3.95 to £6.25. Main Courses: £5.95 to £18.95. Puddings: £4.95*

Wadworths ~ Tenants Chris and Kathy Stone ~ Real ale ~ Bar food (12-2, 6(7 Sun)-9) ~ Restaurant ~ (01793) 731257 ~ Children welcome ~ Open 11.30-3, 6-11; 12-3, 7-11 Sun

Recommended by Jan and Roger Ferris, Tony Baldwin, Michael Doswell, Bruce and Sharon Eden, Anne Morris, Tim and Rosemary Wells

---

LUCKY DIP

Besides the fully inspected pubs, you might like to try these Lucky Dips recommended to us and described by readers (if you do, please send us reports: feedback@goodguides.com).

ALVEDISTON [ST9723]
Crown SP5 5JY [off A30 W of Salisbury]: 15th-c thatched inn refurbished under new licensees – reports please; three cosy very low-beamed partly panelled rooms, two inglenook fireplaces; pretty views from attractive garden, bedrooms, open all day Fri, Sat, till 8.30pm Sun (all wk July/Aug) *(LYM)*
AMESBURY [SU1541]
☆ *Antrobus Arms* SP4 7EU [Church St]: Touch of the old days in handsome hotel, decorous and relaxed, with good food, friendly helpful staff, changing ales such as Hop Back GFB and Summer Lightning, Sharps Doom Bar and Wadworths 6X; log fire in dark red high-ceilinged bar, communicating lounge overlooking attractive walled garden, two dining rooms; children and dogs welcome, 17 attractive bedrooms, open all day *(BB, Stephen Corfield)*
ASHTON KEYNES [SU0493]
Horse & Jockey SN6 6NZ [Gosditch]: Friendly and popular low-ceilinged local, well kept ales such as Brakspears and Wadworths 6X, good choice of above-average food (best to book), eating area off small bar and opening into enclosed garden; tables in front garden too, children and dogs welcome, useful for

Thames Path *(Tina and David Woods-Taylor)*
AXFORD [SU2470]
☆ *Red Lion* SN8 2HA [off A4 E of Marlborough]: Pretty beamed and panelled pub with big inglenook, comfortable sofas, cask seats and other solid chairs, popular food from pub staples to pricier fish etc, friendly staff, well kept real ale and good choice of wines by the glass, picture-window restaurant; valley views from nice terrace, children welcome, cl Sun evening *(Mr and Mrs A Curry, Ian Herdman, Bernard Stradling, Henry Midwinter, LYM, Mrs Mary Woods)*
BADBURY [SU1980]
☆ *Bakers Arms* SN4 0EU [a mile from M4 junction 15, off A346 S]: Proper unassuming village local, a relaxing motorway escape, friendly licensees, good value pubby food (not Sun evening) inc doorstep sandwiches, Arkells ales, generous coffee, warm fire, three small old-fashioned rooms; pool and darts area; TV, silenced games machine, piped music, no under-10s; picnic-sets in garden with heated smokers' area *(Ellie Weld, David London, Bill and Sally Leckey, Peter Hayman, Neil Kellett, Edward Mirzoeff, LYM)*
☆ *Plough* SN4 0EP [A346 (Marlborough Rd) just S of M4 junction 15]: Popular good value

pub food all day inc Sun roasts, friendly helpful staff, well kept Arkells and Donnington SBA, decent wines, coffee from 10am, large rambling bar area (dogs welcome); light and airy dining room (children allowed), daily papers, big Mucha prints; piped pop music may obtrude; tree-shaded garden with terrace and good play area (trunk road noise), open all day *(Pat Crabb, BB, JJW, CMW)*

BARFORD ST MARTIN [SU0531]

☆ *Barford Inn* SP3 4AB [B3098 W of Salisbury (Grovely Rd), just off A30]: Friendly 16th-c coaching inn, dark panelled front bar with big log fire, other interlinking rooms, old utensils and farming tools, beamed bare-brick restaurant; wide choice of generous food, OAP lunch deals, takeaways, brisk unfussy service, well kept Badger ales, lots of wines by the glass; children and dogs welcome, disabled access (not bar) and facilities, terrace tables, more in back garden, charming comfortable bedrooms, good walks, open all day (has been cl Sun afternoon) *(LYM, Chris and Angela Buckell, Edward Mirzoeff, S J and C C Davidson)*

BECKHAMPTON [SU0868]

☆ *Waggon & Horses* SN8 1QJ [A4 Marlborough—Calne]: Handsome stone-and-thatch coaching inn, old-fashioned settles and comfortably cushioned wall benches in open-plan beamed bar, dining area, generous unfussy fair-priced food (not Sun evening), prompt friendly service, well kept Wadworths and a guest; pool and pub games; unobtrusive piped music; children in restaurant, pleasant raised garden with good play area, bedrooms, handy for Avebury, open all day *(LYM, Dave Braisted, Sheila and Robert Robinson)*

BERWICK ST JAMES [SU0739]

☆ *Boot* SP3 4TN [High St (B3083)]: Welcoming flint and stone pub not far from Stonehenge; with friendly efficient staff, well kept Wadworths, huge log fire in inglenook one end, sporting prints over small brick fireplace at the other, lighted candles, small back dining room with collection of celebrity boots, food can be good; children welcome, sheltered side lawn *(Gerry and Rosemary Dobson, Mark Davies, Howard and Margaret Buchanan, Dennis Parnham, Jerry Brown, Terry and Nickie Williams, LYM, K H Frostick, Malcolm and Jane Levitt)*

BIDDESTONE [ST8673]

Biddestone Arms SN14 7DG [off A420 W of Chippenham; The Green]: Welcoming spacious pub mostly set out for its enjoyable food from standards to blackboard specials, good choice of ales inc Wadworths and Wychwood, games in compact public bar, nice fire; children and dogs welcome, pretty garden with well spaced tables, attractive village with lovely pond *(Simone Jones, Michael Doswell, BB)*

White Horse SN14 7DG [The Green]: Popular 16th-c local overlooking duck pond in picturesque village, wide choice of sensibly

priced hearty pub food (all day Sun) inc interesting specials like venison and quail pie, well kept Butcombe, Bath Gem Courage Best and Wadworths 6X, quick cheerful service; lounge and dining area, small hatch-served bar with shove-ha'penny, board games and table skittles; children and dogs welcome, tables in good garden with play area and guinea-pigs, open all day *(Michael Doswell)*

BISHOPS CANNINGS [SU0364]

Crown SN10 2JZ [Chandlers Lane; off A361 NE of Devizes]: Friendly and relaxed two-bar local with wide choice of good value generous food inc good Sun lunch, Wadworths ales, decent wines; good mix of customers, popular quiz Thurs; dogs welcome, tables in nice garden behind, next to handsome old church in pretty village, walk to Kennet & Avon Canal *(Elen Matthews)*

BRADFORD-ON-AVON [ST8260]

Barge BA15 2EA [Frome Rd]: Large open-plan modernised pub set down from canal, ales such as Brewsters, Fullers and Moles, generous food, friendly service, stripped stone and flagstones, solid furniture, log fire; children welcome, garden with smokers' pavilion, steps up to canalside picnic-sets, moorings *(Dr and Mrs M E Wilson, Ian Phillips)*

Cross Guns BA15 2HB [Avoncliff, 2 miles W; OS Sheet 173 map ref 805600]: Congenial bustle on summer days with swarms of people in floodlit partly concreted areas steeply terraced above the bridges, aqueducts and river; appealingly quaint at quieter times, with stripped-stone low-beamed bar, 16th-c inglenook, well kept ales inc Box Steam range, lots of malt whiskies and country wines, enjoyable food, good friendly service, upstairs river-view restaurant; children welcome, open all day *(LYM, Jim and Frances Gowers, Alan Bulley, Roger Wain-Heapy, Dr and Mrs M E Wilson)*

Dandy Lion BA15 1LL [Market St]: More continental café/bar than typical local, stripped wood floor and panelling, modern furniture, steps to snug bare-boarded back room, restaurant upstairs, Wadworths ales, several wines by glass, enjoyable food, friendly service; children away from bar area and dogs welcome *(Dr and Mrs M E Wilson, Ian Phillips, Peter Harrison, John Robertson, LYM)*

BREMHILL [ST9772]

☆ *Dumb Post* SN11 9LJ [off A4/A3102 just NW of Calne]: The long-serving licensees at this quirky unspoilt place were about to retire as we went to press - news please; mismatched no-frills décor with odds and ends hanging from beams, guns and stuffed animal heads on walls, working model waterwheel; perhaps Oscar the parrot, homely armchairs and plush banquettes, big woodburner in brick fireplace and log fire at other end, fine country views from big windows; Wadworths 6X and a changing guest, simple hearty bar food, narrow bar with toby jugs, tap room with pool and darts; piped music, no credit cards; children welcome, dogs in bar, couple of picnic-sets outside and some wooden play equipment, has been cl Mon-Weds lunchtimes *(LYM)*

BROKENBOROUGH [ST9189]

Rose & Crown SN16 0HZ: Open-plan modernised bar with beams and some bare stone walls, lower back part mainly for eating, good choice of enjoyable hearty food – much locally sourced, friendly owners and staff; well kept Uley ales, good choice of wines by the glass; children welcome, cl Mon *(Stephen Funnell, Eddy Fulford, Jim Pearce, David and Jane Hide)*

BROMHAM [ST9665]

Greyhound SN15 2HA [off A342; High St]: Welcoming old beamed pub with light modern décor, comfortable sofas and log fires, walk-across well in back bar, wide choice of good value food, well kept Wadworths, good wine choice; upstairs skittle alley for extra dining space; big enclosed garden (dogs allowed here) with decking and boules *(Mr and Mrs P R Thomas)*

BROUGHTON GIFFORD [ST8764]

Bell on the Common SN12 8LX [The Common]: Imposing rose-draped stone-built local on village common, friendly long-serving landlord, lounge with well kept Wadworths from handpumps on back wall, big coal fire; enjoyable good value homely food, dining room full of copper and country prints, rustic bar with local photographs, small pool room with darts; live irish music (last Sun of month); children welcome, dogs in public bar, charming flower-filled crazy-paved garden, boules, bowls club next door, open all day Fri-Sun *(MRSM, Dr and Mrs M E Wilson, Dr and Mrs A K Clarke, Michael Doswell)*

CASTLE COMBE [ST8477]

☆ *Castle Inn* SN14 7HN [off A420]: Handsome inn in remarkably preserved Cotswold village, beamed bar with big inglenook, padded bar stools and fine old settle, hunting and vintage motor-racing pictures; Butcombe Bitter and a guest, decent wines by the glass, bar and more elaborate food, afternoon teas, two snug and comfortable olde-worlde sitting rooms, formal dining rooms and big upstairs eating room opening on to charming little roof terrace; no dogs; children welcome, tables out at front looking down idyllic main street, fascinating medieval church clock, 11 bedrooms, limited parking, open all day *(John and Enid Morris, John Saville, LYM)*

☆ *Salutation* SN14 7LH [The Gibb; B4039 Acton Turville—Chippenham, nr Nettleton]: Friendly old pub with low beams, stripped stone, log fire in huge handsome fireplace, traditional settles and turkey carpet; prompt service, well kept ales such as Greene King IPA, Wickwar Cotswold Way and Wychwood Hobgoblin, good choice of wines, nice food from big baguettes up, separate raftered,

thatched and timbered barn restaurant, no piped music; children welcome, pretty garden with pergola, open all day Tues and Fri-Sun *(Nigel and Sue Foster, David Treherne Pollock, BB, MRSM)*

CASTLE EATON [SU1495]

Red Lion SN6 6JZ [The Street]: Thames-side dining pub with cosy linked rooms inc sizeable pleasant conservatory, usual pubby food, well kept ales inc one named for the pub, log fire, settees and hunting prints; darts in pool room; children welcome, shrubby riverside garden with boules and outdoor chess, popular with Thames Path walkers, pretty village with unusual church, open all day Fri-Sun *(LYM, Neil and Anita Christopher)*

CHILMARK [ST9732]

Black Dog SP3 5AH [B3089 Salisbury—Hindon]: 15th-c beamed village pub with several cosy linked areas, inglenook woodburner, Wadworths ales, enjoyable food; good-sized roadside garden *(Nigel and Kath Thompson, LYM)*

CHIRTON [SU0757]

☆ *Wiltshire Yeoman* SN10 3QN [Andover Rd (A342 SE of Devizes)]: Chef/landlord doing some imaginative cooking inc good seafood and two-course lunches deals, neat and friendly young staff, well kept Wadworths IPA and 6X, Stowford Press cider, good value wines; proper bar with log fire and well lit games room (pool, darts, games machine), separate carpeted dining room; unobtrusive piped pop music, some live; garden with heated shelter, cl Mon, no food Sun evening *(Philip and Christine Kenny, KC, BB, M and GR, Michael Doswell, Mr and Mrs A Curry)*

CLYFFE PYPARD [SU0776]

Goddard Arms SN4 7PY: Cheery 16th-c local with log fire and raised dining area in split-level main bar, small sitting room with another fire and two old armchairs, down-to-earth chatty and welcoming licensees, ales such as Brakspears, Cottage and Great Western, farm cider, enjoyable, good value basic food; artwork for sale, pool room with darts, cribbage etc; sports TV, no credit cards; picnic-sets in back courtyard, bedrooms, also Youth Hostel accommodation in former skittle alley, tiny pretty thatched village in lovely countryside, open all day wknds *(Dave Braisted, BB)*

CODFORD [ST9639]

George BA12 0NG [just off A36 W of A303 intersection; High St]: Old inn with knocked-through L-shaped bar, stripped brickwork, well spaced tables, big house plants, contemporary art and lighting, log fire; good Timothy Taylors Landlord and Yeovil Star Gazer, Thatcher's cider, enjoyable food from standard to more adventurous things; piped music; well behaved children welcome, disabled access, narrow front terrace, many more tables out behind, bedrooms, has been cl Sun evening and Tues *(Chris and Angela Buckell, Chris and Jeanne Downing, LYM)*

COMPTON BASSETT [SU0372]
White Horse SN11 8RG: Enjoyable food in bar and popular restaurant, cheerful attentive service, Wadworths and guest beers, woodburner; children welcome, garden, good walks *(Helen Carby, Alvin and Yvonne Andrews, Mr and Mrs Ian Campbell)*

CORSHAM [ST8770]
Flemish Weaver SN13 0EZ [High St]: Town pub in attractive 17th-c building under new management, three main areas mostly set for good value popular food, courteous if not fast service, ales such as Bath and Bellringer; children and dogs welcome, tables in back courtyard, may be cl Sun evening *(Dr and Mrs M E Wilson, LYM, Dr and Mrs A K Clarke, Philip and Jan Medcalf, BB)*
Hare & Hounds SN13 0HY [Pickwick (A4 E)]: Refurbished local with well kept changing ales such as Bass, Caledonian Deuchars IPA, Fullers London Pride and Marstons Pedigree, annual beer festival; usual food, friendly efficient service, log-fire; open all day Fri-Sun *(Dr and Mrs A K Clarke)*

CORSLEY HEATH [ST8145]
Royal Oak BA12 7PR [A362 Frome—Warminster]: Proper pub, very popular lunchtime for good modestly priced pubby food, friendly landlady and attentive staff, well kept Wadworths and a guest beer; roomy beamed and panelled bar (no dogs), good fire, pleasant big back family extension with pool, restaurant; dogs welcome in small side bar, disabled facilities, terrace and big garden with valley views, good walks, handy for Longleat *(Terry Buckland, Alan Punchard)*

CORTON [ST9340]
☆ *Dove* BA12 0SZ [off A36 at Upton Lovell, SE of Warminster]: Cheerful helpful landlord and good service, enterprising range of good food from baguettes to fresh fish and steaks, three well kept ales such as Butcombe, Hop Back and Shepherd Neame, good wines by the glass; pleasant partly flagstoned main bar with central log fire and good pictures, conservatory; children welcome, tables on neat back lawn (lovely valley), comfortable wheelchair-friendly bedrooms, good fishing available *(LYM, Edward Mirzoeff)*

CRICKLADE [SU1093]
Red Lion SN6 6DD [off A419 Swindon—Cirencester; High St]: 16th-c former coaching inn, large bar with interesting bric-a-brac and log fire, well kept Moles, Wadworths 6X and seven quickly changing guests, 50 bottled beers, farm cider, good food (not Mon, Sun evening) in bar or restaurant (separate menu), friendly helpful staff, piped music – live on bank hols; children and dogs welcome, big garden with well and fish pond, five bedrooms, open all day *(E McCall, T McLean, D Irving, Paul Boot, Stephen Funnell, Neil and Anita Christopher, Ewan and Moira McCall, Yvonne Simmons, Robert W Buckle)*

CRUDWELL [ST9492]
Wheatsheaf SN16 9ET: Small family-run pub with recently refurbished L-shaped bar, three

well kept Marstons ales, good house wines, enjoyable fairly priced food from sandwiches up inc vegetarian choices and takeaway pizzas, friendly efficient service; children welcome, doubles as village PO, cl Tues lunchtime *(KC)*

DERRY HILL [ST9570]
☆ *Lansdowne Arms* SN11 9NS [A342 Chippenham—Calne]: Stately stone-built pub opp one of Bowood's grand gatehouses, roomy, airy and civilised, with good pub food (can take a while), well kept Wadworths ales, good value wines by the glass, cheerful service; relaxed period flavour, hearty log fire; children welcome, neat side garden and good play area, fine views *(David Crook, Dr and Mrs M E Wilson, David and Sheila Pearcey, Donna and Roger, BB)*

DEVIZES [SU0061]
☆ *Bear* SN10 1HS [Market Pl]: Comfortable ancient coaching inn with carpeted big main bar, log fires, black winged wall settles and upholstered bucket armchairs, steps up to room named after portrait painter Thomas Lawrence, with oak-panelled walls and big open fireplace; three Wadworths ales, up to 15 wines by glass, several malt whiskies, a few bar snacks but mainly restaurant food; popular with an older crowd; wheelchair access, mediterranean-style courtyard, bedrooms *(the Didler, LYM)*
☆ *Hourglass* SN10 2RH [Horton Ave; follow boat brown sign off A361 roundabout, N edge of town]: Modern pub featuring sturdy beams, broad bare boards, cream and terracotta décor, wall of windows looking across canalside terrace to fields beyond; enjoyable enterprising food at reasonable prices, well kept Marstons-related ales, good coffees and wine list, cheerful efficient young staff, daily papers and magazines, unobtrusive piped music *(Dave Pritchard, Mr and Mrs A Curry, Robert Kibble, BB)*

EAST CHISENBURY [SU1352]
☆ *Red Lion* SN9 6AQ: Pretty thatched pub with welcoming newish licensees doing really good enterprising food (not Sun evening, booking advised) inc good value fixed-price wkdy lunch, children's helpings, good service, well kept local Stonehenge and Three Castles, good wine choice; bare boards or flagstones, mixed tables and chairs, large fireplace with woodburner, area with black leather sofa and armchairs, daily papers, dining room; soft piped music; dogs welcome, play area on lawn, open all day wknds, cl Mon *(LYM, Alan and Audrey Moulds, Rochelle Seifas, Antony Willman, Nick Hall)*

EASTON ROYAL [SU1961]
Bruce Arms SN9 5LR [Easton Rd]: Chatty 19th-c local with benches by two long scrubbed antique pine tables on bar's brick floor, homely carpeted and curtained parlour with easy chairs, old pictures, flowers and piano, well kept Wadworths and a guest, real cider, fresh cobs; darts, extension with pool and TV; camping field, open all day Sun *(the Didler)*

FORD [ST8474]

☆ *White Hart* SN14 8RP [off A420 Chippenham—Bristol]: Attractive 16th-c stone-built Marstons country inn, their ales and a guest such as Otter, wide choice of enjoyable food (especially puddings) all day, lovely home-baked bread, smart friendly staff; heavy black beams and good log fire in ancient fireplace, separate dining room, nice relaxed atmosphere; dogs welcome, attractive stream-side grounds, comfortable bedrooms (some in annexe), good breakfast *(Mary Rayner, Dr and Mrs A K Clarke, Andrew Parry, Dr D Jeary, Ian Malone, LYM)*

FOVANT [SU0028]

Pembroke Arms SP3 5JH [A30 W of Salisbury]: Recently refurbished small stone-built pub nr the giant regimental badges cut into the downs; Brakspears ales, decent wine, enjoyable reasonably priced food from sandwiches up, log fire; TV; dogs welcome, picnic-sets in tiered side garden, bedrooms *(BB, Michael Dandy, Dennis Jenkin)*

GREAT WISHFORD [SU0735]

Royal Oak SP2 0PD [off A36 NW of Salisbury]: Two-bar pub with friendly licensees, enjoyable food, well kept Butcombe, Otter and Ringwood, beams, dark panelling, pastel walls, bare boards and log fires; step up to carpeted restaurant (cl Tues); piped music; children and dogs welcome, disabled access, pretty village *(Chris and Angela Buckell, Harry Miller, LYM)*

HAMPTWORTH [SU2419]

Cuckoo SP5 2DU: Unspoilt 18th-c thatched New Forest pub, friendly mix of customers from famers to families in four compact rooms, well kept Hop Back, Ringwood and guests tapped from the cask (Sept beer festival), real cider, pasties and ploughman's, open fire; big garden (adults area with view of golf course), open all day wknds *(the Didler, Joan and Michel Hooper-Immins)*

HEDDINGTON [ST9966]

☆ *Ivy* SN11 0PL [off A3102 S of Calne]: Picturesque thatched 15th-c village local, good inglenook log fire in old-fashioned L-shaped bar, heavy low beams, timbered walls, assorted furnishings on parquet floor, brass and copper; well kept cask-tapped Wadworths ales, popular freshly made food (not Mon or evenings Sun, Tues, Weds), friendly service, back family eating room; sensibly placed darts, piano; may be piped music; disabled access, front garden, open all day wknds *(LYM, the Didler)*

HEYTESBURY [ST9242]

Angel BA12 0ED [just off A36 E of Warminster; High St]: In quiet village just below Salisbury Plain, enjoyable standard food from good sandwiches up, friendly staff and nice pubby atmosphere, Greene King ales, log fire *(Edward Mirzoeff, LYM)*

HINDON [ST9032]

Angel SP3 6DJ [B3089 Wilton—Mere]: Smartened-up dining pub with big log fire, flagstones and other coaching-inn survivals,

sensibly priced food from pub favourites to more unusual dishes, good service, nice choice of wines, ales such as Bass, Ringwood and Sharps; children welcome, dogs in bar, courtyard tables, seven comfortable bedrooms, open all day in summer *(Bruce and Sharon Eden, Jill Bickerton, Ian Scott-Thompson, Mike Mingars, David Zackeim, Helen and Brian Edgeley, LYM)*

Lamb SP3 6DP [B3089 Wilton—Mere]: Smart, attractive old hotel with long roomy log fire bar, two flagstoned lower sections with a very long polished table, high-backed pews and settles, up steps – a third, bigger area; well kept Wells & Youngs and two guests, several wines by the glass and over 100 malt whiskies, enjoyable home-made bar food, polite friendly service; can get very busy; children and dogs welcome, tables on roadside terrace and in garden across road with boules, 19 bedrooms, good breakfast, open all day from 7.30am *(Louise Gibbons, Bruce and Sharon Eden, Edward Mirzoeff, John Coatsworth, J Harvey, LYM, Mike Gorton)*

HOLT [ST8561]

☆ *Toll Gate* BA14 6PX [Ham Green; B3107 W of Melksham]: Appealing individual décor and furnishings and thriving atmosphere in comfortable bar, friendly attentive service, interesting well kept changing ales, farm cider, popular imaginative food from good lunchtime sandwiches and reasonably priced light meals up, daily papers; log fire, another in more sedate high-raftered former chapel restaurant up steps; piped music; no under-12s, dogs welcome, pretty back terrace, compact bedrooms, cl Sun evening, Mon *(Philip and Jan Medcalf, Mr and Mrs A H Young, Michael Doswell, Dr and Mrs M E Wilson, LYM)*

HORNINGSHAM [ST8041]

Bath Arms BA12 7LY [by entrance to Longleat House]: Handsome old stone-built inn stylishly opened up as welcoming dining pub with several linked areas inc a proper bar, good fresh food inc delicious puddings, well kept Wessex ales and local cider, good wine choice, charming staff; blazing log fire, daily papers, side restaurant and conservatory; can get very busy; attractive garden with neat terraces, 15 bedrooms, on sloping green of pretty village *(Michael Doswell, Ian Herdman, BB)*

KINGTON LANGLEY [ST9277]

☆ *Hit or Miss* SN15 5NS [off A350 S; Days Lane]: Welcoming cottagey pub useful for M4 junction 17; cosy lounge bar with low beams and cricket memorabilia, log-fire restaurant, enjoyable food from nice baguettes to good fresh fish, helpful service, Timothy Taylors Landlord and local guests; darts; children and dogs welcome, tables out in front *(LYM, I H G Busby, Michael Doswell)*

KINGTON ST MICHAEL [ST9077]

Jolly Huntsman SN14 6JB [handy for M4 junction 17]: Roomy welcoming stone-built pub, six ales inc Greene King, popular home-made food from pub standards to unusual things like bison steaks; lighted candles on scrubbed tables, comfortable settees, good log fire, pleasant décor; seven well equipped bedrooms in separate block (Mr and Mrs Graham Prevost, Mrs E Appleby, Michael Doswell)

LACOCK [ST9168]

☆ *Red Lion* SN15 2LQ [High St]: Busy NT-owned Georgian inn, sizeable bar with log fire, heavy tables and oriental rugs on flagstones, cosy snug with leather armchairs, well kept Wadworths ales, good choice of food (all day wknds), friendly service; piped music; children and dogs welcome, seats outside, bedrooms, open all day (LYM, Jim and Frances Gowers, Susan and Nigel Brookes, Ellie Weld, David London)

LIDDINGTON [SU2081]

Village Inn SN4 0HE [handy for M4 junction 15, via A419 and B4192; Bell Lane]: Comfortable, warm and welcoming, enjoyable good value food inc wkdy OAP bargains and Sun roasts, well kept Arkells ales; linked bar areas, stripped-stone and raftered back dining extension, conservatory, log fire in splendid fireplace; no under-8s; disabled facilities, terrace tables (KC)

MAIDEN BRADLEY [ST8038]

☆ *Somerset Arms* BA12 7HW [Church St]: Elegantly refurbished relaxed Georgian pub, bare boards and grey/green panelling, bar with log fire and traditional cast-iron tables, adjoining lounge with sofas, magazines and unusual bookshelf wallpaper, interesting seasonal food (not Sun evening, Mon) inc good Stourhead estate steaks, sandwiches and snacks too, well kept Wadworths ales, restaurant; Tues folk night; nice garden, five boutique-style bedrooms (Lucia Golding, Richard Wyld, Edward Mirzoeff)

MALMESBURY [ST9387]

☆ *Old Bell* SN16 0BW: Not a pub, but this impressive Grade I-listed 13th-c small hotel facing the Norman abbey has a snug little bar (priced to reflect the place's standing) with suitable chairs and settles, log fires, good service, good choice of wines by the glass, Courage Directors, bistro and restaurant; attractively old-fashioned garden courtyard providing well for children, bedrooms, good breakfast (Susan and Nigel Brookes, LYM)

Smoking Dog SN16 9AT [High St]: Twin-fronted local with two cosy flagstoned front bars, good choice of wines by the glass, well kept ales inc Brains, log fire, cheerful staff; children and dogs welcome, small quiet colourful garden up steep steps, bedrooms, open all day (LYM, Les and Judith Haines, Ian and Helen Stafford)

MARLBOROUGH [SU1869]

Castle & Ball SN8 1LZ [High St]: Georgian coaching inn with nicely worn-in lounge bar, unusually wide choice of decent food inc good speciality pies, quieter and slightly simpler eating area, Greene King ales, good range of well listed wines by the glass, young enthusiastic staff; seats out under projecting colonnade, good value bedrooms (Michael Sargent, Pete Coxon, Peter Dandy, Comus and Sarah Elliott)

Lamb SN8 1NE [The Parade]: Well worn-in old-fashioned 17th-c coaching inn with further stable-block eating area, enjoyable good value up-to-date food, well kept Wadworths, good choice of wines; amiable landlord and good service; pretty courtyard, six comfortable clean bedrooms (Tony Baldwin, Frank Blanchard)

Wellington Arms SN8 1HQ [High St]: Cosy and neat with enjoyable good value food in eating area down steps, well kept ales such as Wadworths 6X, nice wines, friendly staff and locals; tables in attractive back courtyard, bedrooms (BB, Mr and Mrs Draper)

MARSTON MEYSEY [SU1297]

☆ *Old Spotted Cow* SN6 6LQ [off A419 Swindon—Cirencester]: Civilised country pub with interesting, well priced food inc lunchtime sandwiches, three or four well kept ales (taster glasses available) from proper bar, good value wines, welcoming staff; two open fires, light wood furniture and cosy sofas, rugs on bare boards and parquet, plants and cow pictures on stripped-stone walls; children and dogs welcome, spacious garden with play area, open all day wknds, cl Mon (Stephen Funnell, E McCall, T McLean, D Irving, Richard and Sheila Fitton)

MINETY [SU0390]

Vale of the White Horse SN16 9QY [Station Rd (B4040)]: Friendly two-bar pub with enjoyable food inc a daily bargain dish, small helpings available, prompt service, well kept ales inc Cotswold Spring Old English Rose and Hancocks, good range of wines by the glass; attractive décor, some stripped brick and stone; children welcome, heated balcony tables overlooking pond below, bedrooms (Guy Vowles, E McCall, T McLean, D Irving)

MONKTON FARLEIGH [SU8065]

Kings Arms BA15 2QH [signed off A363 Bradford—Bath]: Imposing 17th-c stone building with sofas, open fire and dining tables in one bar, huge inglenook and more dining tables in L-shaped beamed lounge; good if not cheap food (all day wknds) using local supplies, efficient friendly service, well kept changing ales, good wine and whisky choice; piped music; front partly flagstoned courtyard, well tended two-level back garden, lovely village, three new bedrooms (Mr and Mrs A H Young, John and Gloria Isaacs, Philip and Jan Medcalf, Dr and Mrs M E Wilson)

NUNTON [SU1526]

☆ *Radnor Arms* SP5 4HS [off A338 S of Salisbury]: Pretty ivy-clad village pub very popular for its good value food inc fish and local game (wknd booking essential), friendly staff (helpful with wheelchairs), well kept Badger ales; three pleasantly decorated and furnished linked rooms inc cheerfully busy yet relaxing bar and quieter restaurant, log fires; attractive garden good for children (Val and Alan Green)

OAKSEY [ST9993]

☆ *Wheatsheaf* SN16 9TB [off A429 SW of Cirencester; Wheatsheaf Lane]: Emphasis on good imaginative food (not Sun evening) from father and son team; some recent refurbishment but keeping relaxed village pub atmosphere, stripped stone, low beams and log fires (a centuries-old coffin lid above one), comfortably modern back dining area; Butcombe, Sharps and a guest, 14 wines by the glass inc champagne, pleasant helpful staff; piped music; children and dogs welcome, quiet front terrace and garden, open all day Sun, cl Mon lunchtime (*Richard and Sheila Fitton, Paul A Moore, Dr and Mrs A K Clarke, KC, Peter and Audrey Dowsett, LYM*)

PEWSEY [SU1660]

Coopers Arms SN9 5BL [Ball Rd]: Welcoming 17th-c thatched pub, Fullers London Pride, Wadworths 6X and two guests, new restaurant (cl Mon) doing interesting, freshly prepared food; live music Fri night; bedrooms inc self-catering cottages (*Alan and Audrey Moulds*)

POULSHOT [ST9760]

☆ *Raven* SN10 1RW [off A361]: Friendly half-timbered pub across from village green, well kept Wadworths tapped from cask, wide range of home-made pubby food, two cosy black-beamed rooms, comfortable banquettes, open fire, obliging service; children and dogs welcome, garden picnic-sets, cl Mon (*LYM, Mrs Blethyn Elliott*)

RAMSBURY [SU2771]

Crown & Anchor SN8 2PT [Crowood Lane/Whittonditch Rd]: Friendly and relaxed beamed village pub, popular for good value carefully done simple food, well kept Bass, Tetleys and usually a guest beer, good house wine, helpful service, open fires; pool in public bar; no piped music, children welcome, hanging baskets, small garden with terrace (*Anne Morris*)

SALISBURY [SU1429]

Cloisters SP1 2DH [Catherine St/Ivy St]: Rambling olde worlde city pub with low beams and bare boards, friendly buoyant atmosphere, good value food inc generous Sun roasts, Ringwood, Hop Back Summer Lightning and Sharps Doom Bar, helpful staff; open all day (*Ann and Colin Hunt*)

☆ *New Inn* SP1 2PH [New St]: Good choice of well cooked/presented food from snacks up, Badger ales, decent house wines, cheerful staff coping well when busy, inglenook log fire, massive beams and timbers, quiet cosy alcoves, children's area; walled garden with striking view of nearby cathedral spire, open all day summer wknds (*Edward Mirzoeff, Alan and Eve Harding, Tony and Wendy Hobden, LYM*)

☆ *Old Mill* SP2 8EU [Town Path, West Harnham]: Charming 17th-c pub/hotel in tranquil setting, unpretentious beamed bars with prized window tables, decent good value food from sandwiches up, real ales, good wines and malt whiskies, attractive restaurant showing mill race; children welcome, small floodlit garden by duck-filled mill pond, delightful stroll across water meadows from cathedral (classic view of it from bridge beyond garden), bedrooms (*Pete Coxon, Ian and Helen Stafford, LYM*)

Red Lion SP1 2AN [Milford St]: Attractive and historic Best Western hotel with mix of old-fashioned seats and modern banquettes in popular two-roomed panelled bar opening into other spacious and interesting areas; well kept Bass and Ringwood, smart efficient service, food from sandwiches up; children in eating areas, loggia courtyard seats, comfortable bedrooms (*LYM, Colin and Janet Roe*)

Village SP2 7EF: Unpretentious corner pub, popular and friendly, with good choice of interesting changing ales, railway memorabilia; open all day (*the Didler*)

Wyndham Arms SP1 3AS [Estcourt Rd]: Modern corner local, popular and friendly, with full Hop Back range (brewery was based here) and a Downton ale, bottled beers and country wines, simple bar food; small front room where children welcome, longer main bar, board games; open all day wknds, cl lunchtime other days (*Andy and Jill Kassube, N R White, the Didler*)

SEEND [ST9562]

Three Magpies SN12 6RN [Sells Green – A365 towards Melksham]: Unpretentious partly 18th-c pub popular for its good value straightforward home-made food inc children's choices and Sun roasts; two warm fires, welcoming efficient service, well kept Wadworths ales, decent choice of wines by the glass; dogs allowed in bar, big garden with play area, campsite, open all day Fri-Sun (*Paul Dickinson*)

SEMINGTON [ST9259]

☆ *Lamb* BA14 6LL [The Strand; A361 Devizes—Trowbridge]: Ivy-covered pub refurbished this year, new tables and chairs on wood-strip floor in bar, traditional dining room, open fire, beers from Bath, Butcombe and Moles, decent bar food, efficient friendly staff; piped music; pleasant, colourfully planted walled garden with tables under parasols and views to the Bowood Estate. (*LYM*)

Somerset Arms BA14 6JR [off A350 bypass 2 miles S of Melksham]: 16th-c coaching inn refurbished by enthusiastic new management, heavy-beamed long bar opening into comfortable seating area with sofas and armchairs by open fire, restaurant, enjoyable food (not Sun evening) from baguettes to more ambitious things, pleasant service, four well kept ales inc Bath and Sharps, real ciders, coffees and teas; newspapers; children welcome, small garden behind, newly done bedrooms, short walk from Kennet & Avon Canal, open all day (*Stephen Turpin, Dr A J and Mrs Tompsett*)

SHALBOURNE [SU3162]

Plough SN8 3QF [off A338]: Low-beamed village pub on the green, good choice of fairly priced enjoyable blackboard food, Butcombe and Wadworths, friendly helpful landlady; neat tiled-floor bar with sofa and armchairs in snug; disabled access, small garden with play area *(Bruce and Jo Shawyer, Michael and Jenny Back, Tighe Reeves)*

SHAW [ST8765]
Golden Fleece SN12 8HB [Folly Lane (A365 towards Atworth)]: Attractive former coaching inn with good local atmosphere, bright and clean low-ceilinged L-shaped bar and long sympathetic front dining extension; good food inc bargain lunches – popular with older people – good welcoming service, well kept ales such as Bass, Fullers London Pride and Moles, farm cider, flame-effect fires; garden tables *(Dr and Mrs A K Clarke, Jean and Douglas Troup)*

SHERSTON [ST8586]
Carpenters Arms SN16 0LS [Easton (B4040)]: Small interconnecting rooms with low beams and stripped-stone walls, log fire, well kept Bath and Otter ales, decent good value wines, popular reasonably priced food, fish specials (Thurs, Fri); settles and leather sofas, modern conservatory dining area with flowers on tables; disabled access, tables in pleasant garden with boules *(Chris and Angela Buckell)*

STOCKTON [ST9738]
Carriers BA12 0SQ [just off A36 Salisbury—Warminster, or follow Wylye sign off A303, then turn right]: Thatched village pub with enjoyable well presented food (not Sun, Mon evenings), Ringwood and guests kept well, good wines and coffee, friendly service; open-plan carpeted interior with modern pubby furniture, soft lighting and huge log fire; children and dogs welcome (large resident dog called Bailey), disabled access (not to bedrooms) and facilities, roadside seats, back garden, quiet Wylye Valley village, cl Mon in winter *(Chris and Angela Buckell, BB)*

SUTTON VENY [ST8941]
Woolpack BA12 7AW [High St]: Small village pub reopened after long closure and nicely refurbished by landlord/chef, good mainstream food using local ingredients (best to book), sensibly priced wines by the glass; compact side restaurant, friendly busy atmosphere *(Edward Mirzoeff, Mrs Blethyn Elliott)*

TISBURY [ST9429]
Boot SP3 6PS [High St]: Ancient unpretentious village local with welcoming landlord, well kept changing ales tapped from the cask, good value pubby food, notable fireplace; tables in back garden, cl Sun evening *(Tony and Wendy Hobden)*

TOLLARD ROYAL [ST9317]
King John SP5 5PS [B3081 Shaftesbury—Sixpenny Handley]: Busy refurbished red-brick Victorian dining pub, interesting food in stylish open-plan country-style interior with old pine tables on terracotta and coir floors, black and white hunting photographs

and old etchings, logs stacked by woodburner; Ringwood and two changing guests from long oak counter with wine bottles racked behind, charming helpful service; children and clean dogs welcome, solid tables out in front under cream parasols, picnic-sets in terraced garden, eight comfortable bedrooms, good walks *(Samantha McGahan, Colin and Janet Roe, Robert Whitaker)*

UPAVON [SU1355]
Ship SN9 6EA [High St]: Enjoyable home-made food inc good steak and kidney pie and local game, friendly helpful staff, welcoming locals, four changing ales, two farm ciders, decent range of wines and whiskies; interesting nautical memorabilia, some gentle live music; parking can be tricky; dogs welcome (may get a treat after Sun lunch) *(Martin Gough, Antony Willman)*

UPPER SEAGRY [ST9480]
New Inn SN15 5HA: Popular place doing decent food from baguettes up, well kept Moles, friendly staff and locals, open fire *(MJVK, Steve and Liz Tilley)*

UPPER WOODFORD [SU1236]
☆ *Bridge Inn* SP4 6NU: Now sister pub to the Ship at Burcombe (see Main Entries), enjoyable if not cheap food from light lunches up, friendly young staff, real ales, good choice of wines by the glass; fresh contemporary décor with old and new furniture on wood or stone floors, painted half-panelling, windows into kitchen; children welcome, attractive riverside garden across the road *(BB, John Chambers)*

UPTON SCUDAMORE [ST8647]
☆ *Angel* BA12 0AG [off A350 N of Warminster]: Stylish contemporary dining pub in former 16th-c coaching inn, newly refurbished airy upper part, a few steps down to bar area with sofas and armchairs by open fire and mixed traditional pine furniture, good choice of food from pub favourites to more unusual things, pleasant helpful service, well kept Butcombe, Wadworths 6X and a guest, good value house wines; artwork for sale; piped music; children welcome, dogs on leads in bar, sheltered flagstoned back terrace, ten bedrooms in house across the car park *(LYM, Ken and Sylvia Jones, B and F A Hannam, Michael Doswell)*

WARMINSTER [ST8745]
Organ BA12 9AQ [49 High St]: Sympathetic restoration of former 18th-c inn (shut in 1913), front bar, snug and traditional games room; delightful owners and chatty locals, four unusual beers inc one brewed for the pub, real cider, good cheap lunchtime cheeseboard, skittle alley; no music or under-21s; open 4-12am, all day Sat *(Edward Mirzoeff)*

WESTWOOD [ST8159]
New Inn BA15 2AE [off B3109 S of Bradford-on-Avon]: Traditional country pub with friendly landlord and good staff, several linked rooms, beams and stripped stone, scrubbed tables on slate floor, imaginative

good value food in bar and spacious restaurant, well kept Wadworths, buzzy atmosphere; a few tables out behind, lovely hanging baskets, walks nearby, pretty village, cl Mon *(Philip and Jan Medcalf, BB)*

WHITLEY [ST8866]

Pear Tree SN12 8QX [off B3353 S of Corsham]: Under new team things have not been so consistent at this lovely old former farmhouse, but we are hoping things will settle down – reports please; charming front bar with pubby feel, dining chairs around solid tables, little fireplace on left and fine old stripped-stone one on right, window seats and shutters, big back candlelit restaurant with quirky farmyard theme at one end and airy garden room opening on to terrace; Fullers London Pride, Otter and Sharps Doom Bar, several wines by the glass, food is imaginative and can be very good; children welcome, dogs in bar, neat garden, bedrooms, open all day *(Steven Sherwood, LYM, Michael Doswell)*

WILTON [SU0931]

Bear SP2 0DF [West St]: Cosy traditional pub under newish licensees, cheerful atmosphere, well kept Badger ales, decent cider, good value standard food inc Sun roasts, log fire; pretty back garden *(David Hunt)*

Swan SN8 3SS [the village S of Great Bedwyn]: Light and airy 1930s pub, enjoyable food inc fresh fish (not Sun evening), good service, reasonably priced wines, two Ramsbury ales and a local guest, farm ciders; stripped-pine tables, high-backed settles, pews and a woodburner; children and dogs welcome, disabled access, front garden with picnic-sets, picturesque village with windmill, open all day wknds *(James and Hilary Arnold-Baker, Andrew Gardner, Chris Gooch, David Whiteley)*

WINGFIELD [ST8256]

☆ *Poplars* BA14 9LN [B3109 S of Bradford-on-Avon (Shop Lane)]: Attractive country pub with beams and log fires, very popular for its good interesting sensibly priced food, especially with older people at lunchtime; Wadworths ales, friendly fast service even when busy, warm atmosphere, light and airy family dining extension; nice garden, own cricket pitch *(MRSM, Dr and Mrs M E Wilson, Mr and Mrs A Curry, LYM)*

WINSLEY [ST7960]

☆ *Seven Stars* BA15 2LQ [off B3108 bypass

W of Bradford-on-Avon (pub just over Wilts border)]: Roomy low-beamed linked areas refurbished as a dining pub, good food all home-made from the bread to the ice-cream, Sharps Doom Bar and Bath Ales Gem, cheerful young staff; cool light pastel décor, stripped stone, flagstones and carpet; piped music; picnic-sets on neat terrace, adjacent bowling green, attractive village *(Jane Fuller, BB, Dr and Mrs M E Wilson, John and Angela Main)*

WOOTTON BASSETT [SU0682]

Five Bells SN4 7BD [Wood St]: Friendly town local with great atmosphere, well kept Fullers London Pride and four changing guests, farm cider, imaginative food a cut above usual pub style inc good value substantial sandwiches and special menus/theme nights; board games, darts; TV; shaded courtyard, open all day Fri-Sun *(dt and Sue, BB)*

WOOTTON RIVERS [SU1963]

Royal Oak SN8 4NQ [off A346, A345 or B3087]: 16th-c beamed and thatched pub, good food from lunchtime sandwiches up, ales such as Ramsbury and Wadworths 6X (not always in perfect condition), good choice of wines by the glass, comfortable L-shaped dining lounge with woodburner, timbered bar with small games area; children and dogs welcome, tables out in yard, pleasant village, bedrooms in adjoining house *(John and Gloria Isaacs, LYM, John and Hazel Sarkanen)*

WORTON [ST9757]

Rose & Crown SN10 5SE [village signposted off A360 at Potterne]: Refurbished and now under the same ownership as the Bridge Inn at West Lavington (see Main Entries); good interesting freshly prepared food, attentive polite service, Ringwood, Wadworths 6X and a guest; skittle alley; piped music, no dogs; children welcome, side garden, cl Sun evening, Mon *(Mrs Blethyn Elliott)*

YATTON KEYNELL [ST8676]

Bell SN14 7BG [B4039 NW of Chippenham]: Opened-up beamed village pub popular for good value hearty food, friendly staff, well kept Bath Gem and Sharps Doom Bar, decent wines, dining area with sturdy modern tables and high-backed chairs; well spaced picnic-sets in good-sized fenced garden *(Michael Doswell)*

Worcestershire

Rather charmingly, the family running the Three Kings in Hanley Castle will be celebrating their centenary as licensees at this free house throughout 2011. They are planning several special events and we think it will be a particularly rewarding time to visit this lovely unspoilt country local – this year we had an especially successful inspection trip there. This edition sees the addition of no fewer than five delightful new Main Entries, all with something different to offer. The Swan in Birlingham is a fine old-fashioned place, the Plough & Harrow at Guarlford is a smarter dining pub, the Swan at Newland is a welcoming all-rounder, the Cross Keys at Ombersley is comfortably relaxed and the Marwood at Worcester is enjoyably quirky with interesting decorations. We are delighted that there's such a wide variety of places from the sophisticated to the simple and unspoilt – not to mention a couple of really rather individual places. Doing particularly well at the moment are the Fleece at Bretforton which is owned by the National Trust and, despite the crowds, still manages to feel genuinely unspoilt, the bustling Nags Head at Malvern with 14 real ales and a great deal of character, and the homely Bell at Pensax, which is worth heading to for its good value tasty pubby meals. For a special occasion, the restauranty Fountain at Clent gains a Food Award, the nicely original Butchers Arms in Eldersfield maintains its high standards, and the charming Bell & Cross at Holy Cross with its nicely switched-on staff and delicious seasonal food is our Worcestershire Dining Pub 2011.

BAUGHTON

SO8742   MAP 4

Jockey

4 miles from M50 junction 1; A38 northwards, then right on to A4104 Upton—Pershore; WR8 9DQ

Thoughtfully run dining pub with an appealing layout

The open-plan interior of this local dining pub is nicely divided by stripped brick half walls, some with open timbering to the ceiling. There's a mix of good-sized tables, a few horse-racing pictures on butter-coloured walls and a cream Rayburn in one brick inglenook. Readers enjoy the home-from-home atmosphere and friendly welcome; piped music. Drinks include Courage Directors, Brains Rev James and a changing guest from a brewer such as Wye Valley, and they've farm cider and a rewarding choice of wines, with ten by the glass. There are picnic-sets out in front, with a pleasing array of flowers.

🍴 As well as lunchtime sandwiches, baguettes and baked potatoes (not Sundays), bar food includes starters such as whitebait or king prawns in garlic butter, main courses such as poached salmon fillet with oyster mushroom white wine sauce, steak and kidney pie, sirloin or rib-eye steak, and specials such as mushroom stroganoff, poached salmon in tarragon sauce and venison steak in port and cranberry sauce; weekday lunchtime special offer. *Starters/Snacks: £4.25 to £7.95. Main Courses: £8.95 to £16.95. Puddings: £3.95 to £4.95*

Free house ~ Licensee Colin Clarke ~ Real ale ~ Bar food (12-2(2.30 Sat, Sun), 6(7 Sun)-9) ~
(01684) 592153 ~ Children welcome ~ Open 11.30-3, 6-11; 11.30-11 Fri, Sat; 12-10.30 Sun ~
Bedrooms: £45B/£70B

*Recommended by R T and J C Moggridge, Bernard Stradling, Philip and Jan Medcalf, Chris Evans,
Andy and Claire Barker*

BEWDLEY   SO7875   MAP 4

Little Pack Horse

*High Street; no nearby parking – best to park in main car park, cross A4117 Cleobury road,
and keep walking on down narrowing High Street; DY12 2DH*

Friendly town pub full of interesting paraphernalia; decent food

The 450-year-old unassuming aspect of this pub is very much like the other houses in
this tucked-away historic street, with not much pavement outside and definitely no
parking (see directions above). As a result, the cosily traditional interior is rather a
lovely surprise – cheerfully chatty and warmed by a woodburning stove, with reclaimed
oak panelling and floorboards, and an eye-catching array of old advertisements, photos
and other memorabilia. Alongside Bewdley Worcestershire Way, they keep a couple of
guests from brewers such as Shepherd Neame and St Austell, a selection of bottled ciders,
perry and just under two dozen wines; piped music and TV. An area outside has heaters;
more reports please.

🍴 **Bar food includes sandwiches, smoked mackerel pâté, vegetable tempura, ploughman's,
lasagne, lancashire cheese and thyme sausages with cheddar and chive mash, greek salad,
several pies and steaks. They do a cob and a pint offer.** *Starters/Snacks: £1.80 to £7.95.
Main Courses: £7.95 to £15.00. Puddings: £4.00 to £5.90*

Punch ~ Lease Mark Payne ~ Real ale ~ Bar food (12-3(4 Sat, Sun), 6-9.15; 5.30-9.30 Sat;
5.30-8.15 Sun) ~ Restaurant ~ (01299) 403762 ~ Children welcome away from bar ~
Dogs allowed in bar ~ Open 12-3, 6-11; 12-midnight Sat; 12-10.30 Sun

Recommended by Alan and Eve Harding

BIRLINGHAM   SO9343   MAP 4

Swan 🍺

*Off A4104 S of Pershore, via B4080 Eckington road; then turn off at sign to Birlingham
with integral 'The Swan Inn' brown sign (not the 'Birlingham (village only)' road), then left
into Church Street; WR10 3AQ*

Tucked-away charmer, interesting beers, enjoyable food and good-sized country garden

Newly thatched and covered with roses, this pretty black and white timbered cottage is
just as nice inside: a black-beamed quarry-tiled bar with old-fashioned copper-topped
tables, darts, a woodburning stove in its big stone fireplace and a snug inner carpeted
bit by the smallish counter. This serves Cheddar Valley ciders as well as well kept
changing ales such as Slaters Queen Bee, Three Tuns Solstice and Wye Valley Bitter and
HPA from handpump. The back dining extension is simple but comfortable, with creepers
growing overhead. Service is quick and polite. The garden behind has two parts divided
by shrubs, with a variety of tables and chairs under parasols; we liked the cutlery-holding
mini watering cans – and the birdsong. There's a small smokers' shelter out in front.

🍴 **Bar food might include hot smoked duck and beetroot salad, smoked salmon, prawn
and crayfish salad, gammon steak with pineapple, beef, mushroom and ale pie, sausage
and mash, mushroom stroganoff, baked bream with king prawns, lemon and dill, and
puddings such as rhubarb crumble and strawberry cheesecake; Sunday roasts.**
Starters/Snacks: £3.95 to £5.25. Main Courses: £6.95 to £12.95. Puddings: £4.23

Free house ~ Licensees Imogen and Nicholas Carson ~ Real ale ~ Bar food ~ Restaurant ~
(01386) 750485 ~ Children welcome ~ Dogs welcome ~ Open 12-3, 6.30-11

Recommended by Caroline and Michael Abbey, Jo Rees, Theocsbrian, Chris Evans, Phyllis McCombie

BIRTSMORTON

S07936 MAP 4

Farmers Arms 🍺 £

Birts Street, off B4208 W; WR13 6AP

Unspoilt unrushed half-timbered village local with plenty of character

Little changes from year to year at this black and white timbered rural pub. It's pubbily straightforward but characterful, with friendly staff and chatty locals gathered at the bar for the Hook Norton and two or three changing guests from brewers such as Sharps, St Georges and Timothy Taylors on handpump, and is home to the local cribbage and darts teams – you can also play shove-ha'penny or dominoes. The gently old-fashioned big flagstone room on the right rambles away under very low dark beams, with some standing timbers, a big inglenook and flowery-panelled cushioned settles, as well as spindleback chairs. A lower-beamed room on the left seems even cosier, and in both comfortably worn rooms, white walls are broken up by black timbering. You'll find seats and swings out on the lovely big lawn with views over the Malvern Hills – the pub is surrounded by plenty of walks.

🍽 **Inexpensive simple bar food typically includes sandwiches, ploughman's, chilli, steak and kidney pie, cauliflower cheese, gammon steak, mixed grill, and puddings such as spotted dick with custard and treacle tart.** *Starters/Snacks: £2.80 to £4.75. Main Courses: £5.50 to £12.50 (mixed grill). Puddings: £3.10*

Free house ~ Licensees Jill and Julie Moore ~ Real ale ~ Bar food (12-2, 6-9.30(7-9 Sun)) ~ (01684) 833308 ~ Children welcome ~ Dogs welcome ~ Open 11-4, 6-midnight; 12-4, 7-midnight Sun

Recommended by Mike and Mary Carter, the Didler, Ian and Nita Cooper, R T and J C Moggridge, Caroline and Michael Abbey, Reg Fowle, Helen Rickwood

BRANSFORD

S08052 MAP 4

Bear & Ragged Staff 🍷

Off A4103 SW of Worcester; Station Road; WR6 5JH

Cheerfully run dining pub with pleasant places to sit both inside and outside

With its friendly attentive service and well prepared food, this pub is a good bet for a meal out. In fine weather, the garden and terrace are enjoyable places to sit, with a pleasant backdrop of rolling country. Inside, the interconnecting rooms give fine views too, and in winter you'll find an open fire; piped music. They've a good range of wines to choose from, with about ten by the glass, lots of malt whiskies, quite a few brandies and liqueurs, and Fullers London Pride and Hobsons Twisted Spire on handpump. For more formal dining, there are proper tablecloths and linen napkins on the tables in the restaurant though it's the same menu throughout the building; good disabled access and facilities.

🍽 **Bar food includes lunchtime sandwiches (not Sunday), starters such as beetroot cured salmon with courgette carpaccio, chicken liver parfait with redcurrant and quince sauce, main courses such as three-cheese and red onion cheesecake, battered haddock, curry of the day, roast duck breast with port and cranberry sauce, poached sole fillet with white wine, button onion and broad bean velouté, and puddings such as chocolate and orange terrine with whisky crème fraîche and eton mess. They have a nice little vegetable patch that supplies some of their greens, and they make most of their own bread.** *Starters/Snacks: £1.95 to £6.75. Main Courses: £10.00 to £12.50. Puddings: £5.00 to £5.50*

Free house ~ Licensee Lynda Williams ~ Real ale ~ Bar food (12-2, 6.30-9; not Sun evening) ~ Restaurant ~ (01886) 833399 ~ Children welcome ~ Dogs allowed in bar ~ Open 11.30-2.30, 6-11; 12-6(2.30 in winter) Sun

Recommended by Mike and Mary Carter, Dr and Mrs Michael Smith, Mrs J May, Alan and Eve Harding, Jeff and Wendy Williams

We say if we know a pub allows dogs.

BRETFORTON

SP0943 MAP 4

Fleece ◀

B4035 E of Evesham: turn S off this road into village; pub is in centre square by church; there's a sizeable car park at one side of the church; WR11 7JE

Marvellously unspoilt medieval pub owned by the National Trust

Before becoming a pub in 1848, this lovely old farmhouse was owned by the same family for nearly 500 years and many of the furnishings, such as the great oak dresser that holds a priceless 48-piece set of Stuart pewter, are heirlooms passed down generations of the family. Its little dark rooms have massive beams, exposed timbers and marks scored on the worn and crazed flagstones to keep out demons. There are two fine grandfather clocks, ancient kitchen chairs, curved high-backed settles, a rocking chair and a rack of heavy pointed iron shafts (probably for spit roasting) in one of the huge inglenook fireplaces, and two more log fires. Plenty of oddities include a great cheese-press and set of cheese moulds, and a rare dough-proving table; a leaflet details the more bizarre items, and photographs report the terrible fire that struck this place several years ago; shove ha'penny. Four or five real ales on handpump are from brewers such as Cannon Royall, Hook Norton, Purity, Uley and Woods, alongside two farm ciders (one made by the landlord), local apple juices, german wheat beer and fruit wines, and ten wines by the glass; darts and various board games. As part of the Vale of Evesham Asparagus Festival, they hold an asparagus auction at the end of May and host the village fête on August bank holiday Monday; there's sometimes morris dancing and the village silver band plays here regularly, too. The lawn (with its fruit trees) around the beautifully restored thatched and timbered barn is a lovely place to sit, so there are more picnic-sets and a stone pump-trough in the front courtyard. If you can, try to visit mid-week as this museum-like place and its contents are pretty famous these days and can draw a weekend crowd; they may want to swipe your credit card if you run a tab while sitting outside.

🍽 **Bar food includes sandwiches, baked camembert with cranberry jelly, chicken liver and bacon pâté, sausages or faggots and chive mash, chicken curry, pork, cider and winter vegetable casserole, fish and chips, beefburger, cheesecake and chocolate torte.** *Starters/Snacks: £4.95 to £6.95. Main Courses: £6.95 to £15.00. Puddings: £4.25 to £5.50*

Free house ~ Licensee Nigel Smith ~ Real ale ~ Bar food (12-2.30(4 Sun), 6.30-9(9.30 Sun)) ~ (01386) 831173 ~ Children welcome ~ Dogs allowed in bar ~ Morris dancing and folk session Thurs evening ~ Open 11-11; 12-10.30 Sun; 11-3, 6-11 Mon-Thurs in winter ~ Bedrooms: /£97.50S

Recommended by Jean and Douglas Troup, Peter and Audrey Dowsett, Mike Proctor, Dennis and Doreen Haward, Andy Lickfold, Lawrence Pearse, John Wooll, Michael Dandy, Paul J Robinshaw, Roger and Ann King, Mr and Mrs W W Burke, Mike and Mary Carter

BROADWAY

SP0937 MAP 4

Crown & Trumpet ◀

Church Street; WR12 7AE

Unreconstructed honest local with good real ale and decent food

The relaxed beamed and timbered bar at this cheerfully bustling down-to-earth pub has antique dark high-backed settles, large solid tables and a blazing log fire. Seasonal beers (one for each season) are brewed for the pub by the local Stanway Brewery and served on handpump alongside Marstons Pedigree and Stroud Tom Long, local cider, hot toddies and mulled wine. The pub hosts regular live music and has a range of pub games, including darts, shove-ha'penny, cribbage, dominoes, ring-the-bull and Evesham quoits; they've also a fruit machine, darts, TV and piped music. The hardwood tables and chairs outside among flowers on a slightly raised front terrace are popular with walkers – even in adverse weather.

🍽 **Bar food includes panini, whitebait, pies, vegetable lasagne, sausage and mash, battered haddock, steak and kidney pie, chilli, rib-eye steak, and puddings such as chocolate sponge and treacle tart; Sunday roasts.** *Starters/Snacks: £3.45 to £5.95. Main Courses: £6.95 to £12.95. Puddings: £2.95 to £3.95*

Laurel (Enterprise) ~ Lease Andrew Scott ~ Real ale ~ Bar food (12-2.30(4.30 Sat, Sun), 6(5.45 Sat, Sun)-9.30) ~ (01386) 853202 ~ Children welcome ~ Dogs allowed in bar and bedrooms ~ Live music Sat evening, jazz or blues Thurs except first Thurs of the month ~ Open 11-3(2.30 winter), 5-11; 11-midnight Fri, Sat; 11-11pm Sun ~ Bedrooms: £48S/£65S(£70B)

Recommended by Tracey and Stephen Groves, Guy Vowles

CLENT   SO9279   MAP 4

Fountain

Off A491 at Holy Cross/Clent exit roundabout, via Violet Lane, then turn right at T-junction; Adams Hill/Odnall Lane; DY9 9PU

Restauranty pub often packed to overflowing

Attentive uniformed staff and good food draws the crowd to eat at this lively dining pub (booking is advised), though there may be space for drinkers to stand at the counter. The long carpeted dining bar (three knocked-together areas) has teak chairs and pedestal tables, with some comfortably cushioned brocaded wall seats. There are nicely framed local photographs on the ragged pinkish walls above a dark panelled dado, pretty wall lights and candles on the tables (flowers in summer). Three changing real ales might be from brewers such as Burton Bridge, Marstons and Wychwood, and most of their 36 wines are served by the glass; also a choice of speciality teas and good coffees, and freshly squeezed orange juice; piped music and alley skittles. There are tables out on a deck.

🍴 **As well as an impressive range of lunchtime butties (anything from chicken and garlic mayonnaise to chips and cheese), meals are served in generous helpings and the daily changing menu might include tiger prawns with garlic butter, chicken liver pâté, lamb pot roast, duck à l'orange, veal saltimbocca, chocolate brownies and chocolate orange torte. Some of the salad and other vegetables are grown in their own garden.** *Starters/Snacks: £2.50 to £10.95. Main Courses: £11.50 to £21.95. Puddings: £5.95 to £6.25*

Marstons ~ Lease Richard and Jacque Macey ~ Real ale ~ Bar food (12-2(6 Sun), 6-9(9.30 Fri, Sat); not Sun evening) ~ (01562) 883286 ~ Children welcome till 8pm ~ Open 11-11; 12-9 Sun

Recommended by Gill and Keith Croxton, David and Sally Cullen, Dr Kevan Tucker, Lynda and Trevor Smith

DEFFORD   SO9042   MAP 4

Monkey House

A4104 towards Upton – immediately after passing Oak public house on right, there's a small group of cottages, of which this is the last; WR8 9BW

Astonishingly unspoilt time-warp survival with farm cider and a menagerie of animals

You will have to keep your eyes peeled to find this adorable little black and white cider house, its thatch slung low and ponderous, as it's not well signed. Its name is said to come from a story about a drunken customer who some years ago fell into brambles and swore that he was attacked by monkeys – the landlady may be able to tell you about it as the place has been in the same family for some 150 years. Drinks are limited to Westons Medium or Special Dry cider and a perry tapped from barrels, poured by jug into pottery mugs (some locals have their own) and then served from a hatch beside the door. In the summer you could find yourself sharing the garden with the hens and cockerels that wander in from an adjacent collection of caravans and sheds; there's also a pony called Mandy, and Marie and Jana are the rottweilers. A small spartan side outbuilding has a couple of plain tables, a settle and an open fire. Please note the limited opening times below.

🍴 **No food but you can bring your own.**

Free house ~ Licensee Gill Collins ~ No credit cards ~ (01386) 750234 ~ Children welcome ~ Open 6-10 Weds, Thurs; 11-2.30 Fri; 6-10 Sat; 12-3 Sun; closed Mon, Tues and Fri, Sun evenings

Recommended by the Didler

ELDERSFIELD   SO8131   MAP 4

Butchers Arms ⓨ ◧

Village signposted from B4211; Lime Street (coming from A417, go past the Eldersfield turn and take the next one), OS Sheet 150 map reference 815314; also signposted from B4208 N of Staunton; GL19 4NX

Booking required for good interesting cooking of prime ingredients in unspoilt country local's compact dining room

The interior of this pretty little cottage has been kept stylishly simple and unspoilt. With farm cider and two well kept changing ales such as Dorothy Goodbody and Wye Valley Bitter tapped from the cask (and a short but well chosen choice of wines), the little local's bar has one or two high bar chairs, plain but individual wooden chairs and tables on bare oak boards, a big warming woodburner in quite a cavernous fireplace, black beams, cream paintwork and a traditional quoits board. The little dining room, also simple, has just three tables and seats only 12. Picnic-sets in the good-sized sheltered tree-shaded garden look out on to pasture grazed by the steers that belong to the welcoming young couple who run this place; more reports please.

🍴 Using first-class ingredients from named local farms, including rare-breed meats, line-caught fresh fish and all sorts of freshly gathered wild mushrooms (something of a speciality here), James Winter keeps the choice short and seasonal, and changes it daily. The results are full of flavour and interest. Starters might include mussels with cider, leeks and chervil, braised squid with tomato, chilli and fennel, roast pork with baby root vegetables and beetroot relish, lamb with fried kidneys, lentils, bacon and salsa verde, and puddings such as dark chocolate torte with lime cream and marmalade pudding with Drambuie custard. You must reserve a table to eat at lunchtimes and it's advised in the evening. Don't leave it late as they do get booked up. *Starters/Snacks: £7.00 to £9.50. Main Courses: £16.50 to £21.00. Puddings: £6.00 to £7.50*

Free house ~ Licensees James and Elizabeth Winter ~ Real ale ~ Bar food (12-1, 7-8.45; not Tues lunchtime, Sun evening) ~ Restaurant ~ (01452) 840381 ~ Children over 10 welcome lunchtimes ~ Open 12-2.30, 7-11(10.30 Sun); closed Mon; one week early Jan, one week end Aug

Recommended by John and Mary Ling, John Holroyd, Catherine Myers

GUARLFORD   SO8245   MAP 4

Plough & Harrow ⓨ

B4211 W of Malvern; Rhydd Road, E of village; WR13 6NY

Smart and civilised country dining pub with enjoyable food and nice garden

This feels nicely up to date, with its warm ragged pinkish-buff paintwork, modern prints giving spots of colour and scatter cushions perking up the bar's grey-upholstered wall benches; there's a comfortable and airy two-level bare-boards restaurant a step or two down past an inner sanctum of red sofas. The beige-carpeted bar is fresh and light despite its low beams and joists, and has broadsheet daily papers to read, a good choice of wines by the glass and well kept Wadworths IPA and 6X on handpump; neat staff are helpful and efficient. The well hedged garden behind has flowering shrubs and border plants, and besides round picnic-sets under cocktail parasols has one or two well padded steamer loungers and a splendidly comfortable swing seat.

🍴 Using some of their own veg, bar food might include prawn cocktail with avocado, mushrooms on toast, kipper pâté, fried veal kidneys with mustard cream sauce, black pudding risotto topped with seared roast wood pigeon, sausage and champ with braised red cabbage, pie or stew of the day, puff pastry case filled with roast pepper and fennel on warm broccoli and tomato salad, roast saddle of venison with game jus, and puddings such as ginger cake and custard with white chocolate ice-cream and banana and passion-fruit pavlova. *Starters/Snacks: £4.50 to £7.95. Main Courses: £9.95 to £19.95. Puddings: £6.00*

Wadworths ~ Lease Juliet Tyndall and Mike Weir ~ Real ale ~ (01684) 310453 ~ Children welcome ~ Open 11.30-3, 6-11.30; 12-4 Sun; closed Sun evening, Mon

Recommended by J E Shackleton, Chris Flynn, Wendy Jones

HANLEY CASTLE

SO8342   MAP 4

Three Kings 🍺 £

Church End, off B4211 N of Upton upon Severn; WR8 OBL

Timeless hospitable gem with five real ales and simple snacks

The characterful family that own this genuinely unspoilt friendly country local will be celebrating their centenary year here in 2011. They are planning special events to take place throughout the year. It's the cheerful welcome, rather than the housekeeping, that counts in the eyes of readers who have had a great time here, so we've certainly no quibbles with their happy relaxed approach. A homely little tiled-floor tap room on the right is separated from the entrance corridor by the monumental built-in settle which faces its equally vast inglenook fireplace. A hatch serves very well kept Butcombe Bitter, Hobsons and three guests on handpump from smaller brewers such as All Gates, Beowulf and Cannon Royall, with around 50 malt whiskies and farm cider. On the left, another room has darts, dominoes and cribbage. A separate entrance leads to the timbered lounge with another inglenook fireplace and a neatly blacked kitchen range, little leatherette armchairs and spindleback chairs around its tables, and another antique winged and high-backed settle. Bow windows in the three main rooms and old-fashioned wood-and-iron seats on the front terrace look across to the great cedar which shades the tiny green.

🍴 **Food is limited to sandwiches, toasties and ploughman's.** *Starters/Snacks: £1.00 to £3.00*

Free house ~ Licensee Sue Roberts ~ Real ale ~ Bar food (12-2; not Sun or evenings) ~ No credit cards ~ (01684) 592686 ~ Children welcome ~ Dogs welcome ~ Jam sessions Fri lunchtime, Sun evening and some Sat evenings ~ Open 12-3, 7-11
Recommended by Chris Evans, the Didler, David and Gill Carrington, P Dawn, Michael Beale

HOLY CROSS

SO9278   MAP 4

Bell & Cross ★ 🍴 🍷

4 miles from M5 junction 4: A491 towards Stourbridge, then follow Clent signpost off on left; DY9 9QL

WORCESTERSHIRE DINING PUB OF THE YEAR

Super food, staff with a can-do attitude, delightful old interior and pretty garden

Successful as a dining pub yet still extremely welcoming if you're just popping in for a drink, this charming place is arranged in a classic unspoilt early 19th-c layout with five quaint little rooms and a kitchen opening off a central corridor with a black-and-white tiled floor. Rooms offer a choice of carpet, bare boards, lino or nice old quarry tiles, a variety of moods from snug and chatty to bright and airy, and an individual décor in each – theatrical engravings on red walls here, nice sporting prints on pale green walls there, racing and gundog pictures above the black panelled dado in another room. Two of the rooms have small serving bars, with Kinver Edge, Enville, Wye Valley HPA and a guest such as Timothy Taylors Landlord on hand or electric pump, around 50 wines (with about a dozen by the glass) and a variety of coffees; daily papers, coal fires in most rooms with regulars sometimes playing cards in one of the front two. Service is friendly and attentive, with everything geared to ensure that you have a most enjoyable visit; piped music. A spacious lawn has modern picnic-sets, and you get pleasant views from the garden terrace.

🍴 **As well as lunchtime sandwiches, panini and ploughman's, delicious dishes from a changing seasonal menu might include onion and apple soup with cheddar doughnuts, warm tandoori salmon with cucumber salad and yoghurt dressing, piri piri chicken breast with coriander potato wedges, beer-battered fish and chips, beef pie, grilled bass fillet with caesar salad, smoked haddock with asparagus, sweet pea and saffron risotto, oven-dried tomatoes and chervil cream, vegetable moussaka with spring onion salsa and toasted pitta bread, sirloin steak with blue cheese sauce, and puddings such as coconut pavlova with mango syrup and new york lemon curd cheesecake with honeycomb crisp.** *Starters/Snacks: £3.45 to £7.25. Main Courses: £9.25 to £15.95. Puddings: £5.25 to £5.50*

Enterprise ~ Lease Roger and Jo Narbett ~ Real ale ~ Bar food (12-2, 6.30-9(9.30 Fri, Sat)) ~ (01562) 730319 ~ Children welcome away from the bar ~ Dogs allowed in bar ~ Open 12-3 (3.30 Sat), 6-11; 12-10.30 Sun

Recommended by Heather McQuillan, David and Doreen Beattie, Paul Boot, John and Hilary Penny, Susan and John Douglas, Clifford Blakemore, John and Gloria Isaacs, Philip and Jan Medcalf, Dr D J and Mrs S C Walker, Stephen H Johnston, Peter Martin, Tom and Jill Jones, Joan E Hilditch, Dr and Mrs A K Clarke, Gordon and Margaret Ormondroyd

KIDDERMINSTER   SO8376   MAP 4

King & Castle £

Railway Station, Comberton Hill; DY10 1QX

Traditional railway refreshment room within earshot of steam trains, and with one of the cheapest pints around

With its direct access on to the Severn Valley Railway terminus platform, you can sit outside with your drink and watch passionate train enthusiasts go lovingly about their work as the steam trains shunt in and out. Inside, the neatly re-created Edwardian refreshment room is lively and sometimes noisily good-humoured, with a good mix of customers, including locals in for a pint with their dogs. Furnishings are solid and in character, and there's the railway memorabilia and photographs you'd expect. Bathams, Wyre Piddle Royal Piddle (just £1.90 a pint) and two or three guests from brewers such as Abbeydale are on handpump, and they've several malt whiskies. The cheerful landlady and friendly staff cope well with the bank holiday and railway gala day crowds, though you'll be lucky to find a seat here. You can use a Rover ticket to shuttle between here and the Railwaymans Arms in Bridgnorth (see Shropshire Lucky Dips) and there's a little museum just a few metres away.

⑪ You order the reasonably priced straightforward food in the adjacent dining room and you can either eat it there or in the pub: toasted sandwiches, soup, ploughman's, a proper breakfast, hamburger and chips, vegetable or chicken kiev, cottage pie, chicken tikka masala and battered cod; they also do children's meals and sometimes Sunday lunch. *Starters/Snacks: £2.75 to £5.95. Puddings: £2.25*

Free house ~ Licensee Rosemary Hyde ~ Real ale ~ Bar food (9-3) ~ (01562) 747505 ~ Children welcome if seated ~ Dogs welcome ~ Open 11-11; 12-10.30 Sun
Recommended by Colin Moore, Andy Lickfold, Joe Green, P Dawn, Ian Shorthouse

KNIGHTWICK   SO7355   MAP 4

Talbot ♀ 🍺 🛏

Knightsford Bridge; B4197 just off A44 Worcester—Bromyard; WR6 5PH

Interesting old coaching inn with good beer from its own brewery, and riverside garden

The enthusiastic licensees who run this rambling 15th-c country hotel have been here for over 25 years and have adapted to these times by growing some of their own veg, preparing their own breads, pickles and jams and also rear their own pigs. The heavily beamed and extended traditional lounge bar can be lively with locals warming up by the good log fire and drinking the This, That, T'other and the seasonal ale that are brewed in the pub's own Teme Valley microbrewery using locally grown hops. These are served alongside Hobsons Bitter, over two dozen wines by the glass and a number of malt whiskies. A variety of traditional seats runs from small carved or leatherette armchairs to the winged settles by the windows, and a vast stove squats in the big central stone hearth. The bar opens on to a terrace and arbour with summer roses and clematis. The well furnished back public bar has pool on a raised side area, a games machine and juke box; cribbage. In contrast, the dining room is a sedate place for a quiet (if not cheap) meal. Across the lane, a lovely lawn has tables by the River Teme (they serve out here, too), or you can sit out in front on old-fashioned seats. A farmers' market takes place here on the second Sunday of the month; dogs may be allowed to stay in the bedrooms by prior arrangement.

[¶] **Bar food (not cheap) might include ploughman's, salmon gravadlax, ham hock terrine and chutney, chicken caesar salad, rabbit casserole with ginger and cider, roast butternut squash and turnip risotto, chicken and leek pie, fish and chips, sirloin steak, and puddings such as citrus tart and white chocolate cheesecake. There is a more elaborate restaurant menu.** *Starters/Snacks: £5.00 to £6.50. Main Courses: £8.50 to £16.00. Puddings: £6.00*

Own brew ~ Licensee Annie Clift ~ Real ale ~ Bar food (12-2, 6.30-9) ~ Restaurant ~ (01886) 821235 ~ Children welcome ~ Dogs allowed in bar and bedrooms ~ Open 7.30am-11pm ~ Bedrooms: £55S/£90B

Recommended by Colin and Peggy Wilshire, Simon Rodway, Jim and Frances Gowers, Gordon Tong, Guy Vowles, Dave Braisted, David Heath, Patrick and Daphne Darley

MALVERN   SO7845   MAP 4

Nags Head ◖

Bottom end of Bank Street, steep turn down off A449; WR14 2JG

Remarkable range of real ales, delightfully eclectic layout and décor and warmly welcoming atmosphere

The superb range of well kept beer and tasty bar food attracts a good mix of jolly customers, including plenty of locals and readers who also love the splendid individuality and easy-going chatty mood at this terrifically enjoyable little pub. If you feel confused by the astonishing range of 14 beers, the cheery staff will happily help you with a taster. House beers are Banks's, Bathams, St Georges Charger, Friar Tuck and Dragon Blood, Sharps Doom Bar and Woods Shropshire Lad and they've seven changing guests (last year they got through over 1,000) from brewers spread far and wide. They also keep belgian beers, two farm ciders and just over a dozen malt whiskies. A series of snug individually decorated rooms, with one or two steps between, gives plenty of options on where to sit. Each is charactefully filled with all sorts of chairs including leather armchairs, pews sometimes arranged as booths, a mix of tables with sturdy ones stained different colours, bare boards here, flagstones there, carpet elsewhere, and plenty of interesting pictures and homely touches such as house plants, shelves of well thumbed books and broadsheet newspapers and there's a coal fire opposite the central servery; shove-ha'penny, cribbage and dominoes. Outside are picnic-sets and rustic tables and benches on the front terrace (with heaters and umbrellas) and in the garden.

[¶] **Tasty lunchtime bar food, served in generous helpings, includes good sandwiches, soup, ham, egg and chips, game pie and fish and chips. In the evenings, meals are served in the barn extension dining room only.** *Starters/Snacks: £3.50 to £4.50. Main Courses: £6.95 to £8.70. Puddings: £3.75 to £5.00*

Free house ~ Licensee Clare Willets ~ Real ale ~ Bar food (12-2, 6.30-8.30) ~ Restaurant ~ (01684) 574373 ~ Children welcome ~ Dogs welcome ~ Open 11-11.15(11.30 Fri, Sat); 12-11 Sun

Recommended by Michael Beale, Beryl and David Sowter, Nigel and Sue Foster, Chris Glasson, Barry Collett, David and Gill Carrington, Chris Flynn, Wendy Jones, P Dawn, Clifford Blakemore, Mrs B Barker, Giles and Annie Francis

NEWLAND   SO7948   MAP 4

Swan ◖

Worcester Road (set well back from A449 just NW of Malvern); WR13 5AY

Attractive and interesting old creeper-clad pub, good all round

Owned by an experienced hand (the landlord owns the Nags Head in Malvern as well), you get the immediate impression here that you're in a pub where everything has been really carefully thought out for the pleasure of its customers. It starts with the warmth of the welcome from the efficient young staff, then as you acclimatise to the dim lighting of the dark-beamed bar and look around, plenty of nice touches catch your eye. There's quite an overhead forest of whisky-water jugs, beakers and tankards, the wall has one or two tapestries, and several of the comfortable and clearly individually chosen seats are worth a close look for their carving. The end counter (also carved) has well kept St Georges Dragons Blood, Friar Tuck and Sharps Doom Bar and Wychwood Hobgoblin on handpump with three or so guests from brewers such as Hobsons and Teme Valley straight from the cask. On the right is a broadly similar red-carpeted dining room, and beyond it an ultra-modern glass cube of a garden room. The garden itself is as individual as the pub, with a cluster of huge casks topped with flowers, even a piano doing flower-tub duty, and a set of stocks on the pretty front terrace; there's a bit of traffic noise.

🍴 **Pubby lunchtime food includes sandwiches, ploughman's, baked potatoes, chilli and pies, while in the evening more elaborate dishes might include crispy pancetta, black pudding and poached egg, poached pear, stilton and walnut salad, garlic king prawns with scallops and fried noodles, pesto hake roulade, with puddings such as treacle tart and chocolate biscuit cake.** *Starters/Snacks: £4.50 to £6.90. Main Courses: £8.00 to £17.00. Puddings: £3.90 to £5.50*

Free house ~ Licensee Nick Taylor ~ Real ale ~ Bar food (12-2.30, 6.30-9; 12-3, 7-9 Sun) ~ Restaurant ~ (01886) 832224 ~ Children welcome ~ Dogs welcome ~ Open 12-11
Recommended by Chris Evans, Denys Gueroult

OMBERSLEY   SO8463   MAP 4

Cross Keys
Just off A449; Main Road (A4133, Kidderminster end); WR9 0DS

Enjoyable food cheerfully served in comfortably relaxed bar and smarter restaurant

This proper pub has a good easy-going atmosphere in the carpeted bar, archways opening into several separate areas – perhaps the nicest on the left, with attractive Bob Lofthouse animal etchings, a big antique print of draught horses advertising Talbots mineral waters, and some horse tack on dark-varnished country panelling. The hops strung from beams and joists suggest that they're serious about their beers – well kept Hook Norton Hooky, Timothy Taylors Landlord and Theakstons Mild on handpump; and they have good value wines by the glass, and good coffee. For extreme comfort, head to the back, where one gently lit room is filled with softly upholstered sofas and armchairs. Beyond is a comfortable back dining conservatory, looking out on a terrace with alloy furniture under a big heated canopy. Service is friendly and efficient; there may be unobtrusive piped pop music.

🍴 **The generous menu includes nourishing country dishes such as chicken and leek or steak and kidney pies, salmon and spinach fishcakes and steaks, and an enterprising range of changing specials such as smoked duck breast with figs, lemon chicken caesar salad, pasta carbonara, hot chicken salad, spring onion and salmon fishcakes, lots of fresh fish from swordfish to sea trout, beef wellington, and puddings such as iced hazelnut nougat biscuits, lemon posset with shortbread and summer pudding. At lunchtime (not Sunday), they also do baguettes and very good omelettes.** *Starters/Snacks: £4.50 to £6.95. Main Courses: £10.95 to £17.50. Puddings: £5.25*

Enterprise ~ Lease Valerie James ~ Real ale ~ Bar food (12-2.30, 6-9(9.30 Fri, Sat; 8.30 Sun)) ~ Restaurant ~ (01905) 620588 ~ Children welcome if seated and not in bar ~ Open 12-3, 6-11; 12-10.30 Sun
Recommended by Dave Braisted

Kings Arms
Main Road (A4133); WR9 0EW

Inviting Tudor building with tasty food and attractive courtyard

The charming aged interior at this rambling black and white timbered inn (said to date from about the 1400s) is dimly lit and cosy with various wood-floored nooks and crannies, three splendid fireplaces with good log fires, fresh flowers throughout and lots of rustic bric-a-brac. King Charles is said to have stopped here after fleeing the Battle of

Worcester in 1651 and one room has his coat of arms moulded into its decorated plaster ceiling as a trophy of the visit. Marstons Best and Pedigree a guest or two such as Wychwood Hobgoblin are on handpump, and they've darts and board games. A tree-sheltered courtyard has tables under cocktail parasols and colourful hanging baskets and tubs in summer, and there's another terrace.

🍴 **As well as lunchtime sandwiches, fairly priced food might include roast butternut and cumin soup, mushrooms on toasted brioche with poached egg, parmesan and truffle cream, seared calves liver with grilled pancetta and baby onion jus, roast halibut with dill and lemon dressing, scampi, mustard and beer-battered fish and chips, rib-eye steak, and puddings such as pistachio crème brûlée and coconut panna cotta.** *Starters/Snacks: £3.35 to £6.10. Main Courses: £7.95 to £17.95. Puddings: £5.10*

Banks's (Marstons) ~ Lease Caroline Cassell ~ Real ale ~ Bar food (12-2.30(3 Sun), 6-9.30 (5-8 Sun)) ~ (01905) 620142 ~ Children welcome ~ Dogs allowed in bar ~ Quiz Sun evening ~ Open 12-11(midnight Sat, 10.30 Sun)
Recommended by Adele Summers, Alan Black, Bruce and Sharon Eden, Eric Thomas Yarwood

PENSAX   SO7368   MAP 4

Bell 🍺 £

B4202 Abberley—Clows Top, SE of the Snead Common part of the village; WR6 6AE

Admirably welcoming all-rounder, good fire and reasonably priced tasty food

Picnic-sets in the back garden of this homely roadside mock-Tudor pub look out over rolling fields and copses to the Wyre Forest; you get the same views from some tables inside. Enjoyably down-to-earth, it has a proper country pub atmosphere and extends a genuinely friendly welcome. Beer is an important feature here with the landlord turning over a good range of guests (often local). Alongside Hobsons Best and Twisted Spire and Timothy Taylors, they might be from brewers such as Cannon Royall, Enville and JBH. He also keeps farm cider, a perry and local fruit juices, and hosts a beer festival over the last weekend in June. The L-shaped main bar has a restrained traditional décor with hanging hops, long cushioned pews on its bare boards, good solid pub tables and a woodburning stove; board games. Beyond a small area on the left, with a couple more tables, is a more airy dining room, with french windows opening on to a wooden deck.

🍴 **Besides sandwiches, a short choice of good value tasty bar food might include game or steak and ale pie, sausage and mash and pasta bake, liver and bacon, game pie, battered cod and chips, faggots and pork chop with black pudding; Sunday roast and children's menu.** *Starters/Snacks: £4.95 to £5.95. Main Courses: £6.95 to £14.95. Puddings: £3.95 to £4.95*

Free house ~ Licensees John and Trudy Greaves ~ Real ale ~ Bar food (12-2(3 Sun), 6-9; not Sun evening) ~ (01299) 896677 ~ Children welcome away from bar area ~ Dogs allowed in bar ~ Open 12-2.30, 5-11; 12-11(10.30 Sun) weekends; 12-2.30, 5-11 Sat in winter; closed Mon lunchtime except bank hols
Recommended by M G Hart, Gordon Tong, the Didler, Alistair Stanier, Dave Braisted, Lynda and Trevor Smith

WORCESTER   SO8455   MAP 4

Marwood 🍷

The Tything (A38); some nearby parking; WR1 1JL

Quirky, civilised and relaxed little bar with enjoyable food and some good drinks

So discreet that it's easy to walk straight past, the short frontage of this old building opens into a long narrow series of small linked areas, increasingly intimate the deeper you penetrate. The bar counter itself, about halfway along, does good coffees and wines by the glass; also well kept Greene King IPA, a Malvern Hills house beer and Priessnitz, and a seasonal ale such as St Georges Lazy Days. The mood, lifted by well reproduced piped music (and the odd chandelier), is relaxed and shabby-smart: much-cushioned simple benches or mixed dining chairs, stripped or cast-iron-framed tables, dark flagstones and broad old boards, a few italian deco posters. Service is friendly, and they have open fires in winter. A rather neater room upstairs, bookable, looks across to the Law Courts. A sheltered flagstoned yard behind has rattan tables and chairs.

🍴 Good value bar food, changing seasonally, includes plenty of appetisers such as char-grilled vegetables or small brochettes, starters and light dishes such as seared scallops, salmon, mackerel, salami or crispy pork tartines, good burgers, wild mushroom and spinach risotto, roast salmon with chive crème fraîche, some serious meat (their steaks are well dry-aged), and puddings such as knickerbocker glory, mango vodka and raspberry terrine and crème fraîche sorbet with toasted brioche. *Starters/Snacks: £4.00 to £8.00. Main Courses: £10.00 to £18.00. Puddings: £6.00*

Free house ~ Licensee Ben Coates ~ Real ale ~ Bar food (10-3, 6-10; 12-4 Sun, not Sun evening) ~ Restaurant ~ (01905) 330460 ~ Children welcome in bar till 7.30pm ~ Dogs welcome ~ Open 12-11(midnight Sat)

Recommended by Dr and Mrs James Harris

LUCKY DIP

Besides the fully inspected pubs, you might like to try these Lucky Dips recommended to us and described by readers (if you do, please send us reports: feedback@goodguides.com).

ABBERLEY [SO7567]
Manor Arms WR6 6BN: Good value comfortable country inn nicely tucked away in quiet village backwater opp fine Norman church, façade emblazoned with coats of arms, warm welcome, quick friendly service, six ales inc Wye Valley HPA, enjoyable food from baguettes up, lunchtime bargains, two bars and restaurant, interesting toby jug collection; ten bedrooms (*Brian and Jacky Wilson, Chris Evans*)
ASTLEY [SO8167]
Hampstall DY13 0RY [E of B4196, S of Stourport]: Comfortable Severnside pub, bargain food inc nice fish and chips, well kept beer; terrace tables (*Chris Evans*)
BADSEY [SP0743]
☆ *Round of Gras* WR11 7XQ [B4035 (Bretforton Rd) 2 miles E of Evesham]: Popular for substantial well priced food inc Weds and Sun carvery, seasonal asparagus feasts, comfortable carpeted open-plan bar with log fire, lots of polished wood and panelling, welcoming staff, good ale range, Weston's farm cider, raised restaurant section, games area with darts, pool and TV; children welcome, fair-sized tree-shaded garden with pets corner, open all day (*BB, Trevor and Sheila Sharman*)
BARNARDS GREEN [SO7945]
Blue Bell WR14 3QP [junction B4211 to Rhydd Green with B4208 to Malvern Show Ground]: Comfortable panelled dining pub in pleasant setting, wide choice of enjoyable reasonably priced standard food inc bargains, Marstons-related ales; disabled facilities, nice garden (*Chris Evans, LYM*)
BASTONFORD [SO8150]
Halfway House WR2 4SL [A449 Worcester—Malvern]: Spacious and bright restaurany roadside pub, enjoyable food inc steaks and fresh fish, bargain lunchtime deals too, well kept local ales, woodburner; children welcome, side garden, two new bedrooms, cl Mon (*Chris Evans, BB*)

BECKFORD [SO9835]
Beckford Hotel GL20 7AN [A435]: Reopened under new owners, beams, log fires and some stripped stone, well kept ales such as Fullers ESB, good range of wines by the glass, enjoyable reasonably priced food, smart dining room, friendly helpful staff; wheelchair access, large garden, eight comfortable bedrooms (*Brian Simms*)
BELBROUGHTON [SO9177]
☆ *Queens* DY9 0DU [Queens Hill (B4188 E of Kidderminster)]: 18th-c pub by Belne Brook, several linked areas with nice mix of comfortable seating, 19th-c oak and other tables in varying sizes, popular food inc interesting puddings, good range of well kept ales inc Marstons Pedigree, plenty of wines by the glass, friendly efficient staff, fresh flowers; children welcome, picnic-sets on small roadside terrace, pleasant village (*Clifford Blakemore, Eric Thomas Yarwood*)
Talbot DY9 9TG [off A491]: Thriving village pub with light wood floors and furniture to match, Jennings Cocker Hoop and guests, all-day food in bar and restaurant; garden (*Guy Vowles*)
BERROW GREEN [SO7458]
☆ *Admiral Rodney* WR6 6PL [B4197, off A44 W of Worcester]: Light and roomy high-beamed dining pub, big stripped kitchen tables and two woodburners, good generous pubby food inc wknd fish, friendly staff, well kept Wye Valley and two guests at sensible prices, good choice of wines by the glass, charming end restaurant in rebuilt barn, folk music 3rd Weds of month; surcharge on some credit cards; well behaved children and dogs welcome, disabled facilities, tables outside with pretty view and heated covered terrace, good walks, three good bedrooms, cl Mon lunchtime, open all day wknds (*Robert Roxburgh, Noel Grundy, Eric Thomas Yarwood, LYM*)

BEWDLEY [SO7875]

Mug House DY12 2EE [Severn Side N]:
Pleasantly renovated 18th-c pub in charming
spot by River Severn, friendly helpful service,
enjoyable traditional food, good local ales
inc Wye Valley, log fire, restaurant;
disabled access, terrace tables, bedrooms,
open all day *(Henry Pursehouse-Tranter,
John Coatsworth)*

BREDON [SO9236]

☆ *Fox & Hounds* GL20 7LA [4.5 miles from M5
junction 9; A438 to Northway, left at B4079,
in Bredon follow sign to church]: Cottagey
16th-c thatched pub with open-plan
carpeted bar, low beams, stone pillars and
stripped timbers, central woodburner,
traditional furnishings inc upholstered
settles, a variety of wheelback, tub and
kitchen chairs around handsome mahogany
and cast-iron-frame tables, elegant wall
lamps, smaller side bar, friendly staff,
Banks's Bitter, Greene King Old Speckled
Hen and a guest like Butcombe, several
wines by the glass, food from sandwiches
to specials; piped music; children welcome,
dogs in bar, outside picnic-sets (some under
cover), handy M5 break *(GSB, Dennis and
Doreen Haward, Jo Rees, R J Herd,
Dr J Benbow, Dave and Jackie Kenward, LYM)*

BOURNHEATH [SO9474]

☆ *Gate* B61 9JR [handy for M5 junction 4 via
A491 and B4091; Dodford Rd]: Neatly
comfortable tiled-floor country dining pub
with wide choice of good value food inc tex-
mex and other american specialities, house
Gate Bitter and Brakspears, good choice of
wines by the glass, friendly prompt staff,
conservatory; sheltered garden, open all day
Sun *(Ian Shorthouse, Dave Braisted, BB)*

BROAD HEATH [SO6765]

Fox WR15 8QS [B4204]: Comfortable 16th-c
black and white timbered pub, Joseph Herbert
Smith ales (brewed next door) and guests,
real cider and perry, pubby food, open fire,
games room, Aug bank hol beer festival,
some live music; nice garden with country
views, open all day wknds *(the Didler)*

BROADWAS-ON-TEME [SO7555]

Royal Oak WR6 5NE: Red-brick roadside pub
with relaxed lounge bar and dining area,
unusual lofty-raftered medieval-style dining
hall, and separate public bar with pool, well
kept Jennings and Marstons ales, decent
wines by the glass, food (all day wknds)
from generous lunchtime sandwiches up inc
OAP wkdy deals and Sun carvery, good
service; children welcome, terrace picnic-
sets, open all day wknds *(Jane and
Alan Bush)*

BROUGHTON HACKETT [SO9254]

March Hare WR7 4BE [A422 Worcester—
Alcester]: Popular spacious Marstons pub
doing enjoyable fairly priced food inc
carvery, well kept Banks's, good coffee,
country décor, glass-covered floodlit well;
garden with play area, good walks
nearby *(BB, Chris Evans, Martin and
Pauline Jennings)*

CALLOW END [SO8349]

Old Bush WR2 4TE [Upton Rd]: Attractive
local with good range of Marstons-related
ales, decent wines, good value standard bar
food from sandwiches up, attentive friendly
staff, cosy small areas around central bar,
restaurant; children and dogs welcome,
garden with play area
(Dave and Jenny Hughes, Chris Glasson)

CAUNSALL [SO8480]

Anchor DY11 5YL [off A449]: Traditional
unchanging two-room pub (in same family
since 1927), friendly atmosphere, well kept
Enville, Hobsons, Wye Valley and three
guests, good filled cobs, efficient service;
tables outside, nr canal *(the Didler)*

CHADDESLEY CORBETT [SO8973]

Swan DY10 4SD [off A448 Bromsgrove—
Kidderminster]: Basic unsmart old local,
lively and friendly, with good value generous
food (not Sun-Weds evenings), well kept
Bathams Bitter and Mild, roaring
woodburner; piped music may be loud,
some live music; children allowed, good-
sized garden with play area, open all day
Fri-Sun *(Dave Braisted, Ian Shorthouse,
the Didler)*

CHILDSWICKHAM [SP0738]

☆ *Childswickham Inn* WR12 7HP [off A44 NW
of Broadway]: Good restauranty dining pub
with big rugs on boards or terracotta tiles,
contemporary artwork on part-timbered walls,
woodburner, good food from pubby things to
more pricey brasserie food, friendly attentive
staff, locals' lounge bar with leather sofas
and armchairs (dogs allowed here), good
choice of wines, beers such as Brakspears,
Hook Norton and Greene King; piped music,
TV; children welcome, disabled facilities,
garden with decked area, barbecue, cl Sun
evening, Mon *(Chris Glasson, Dr and Mrs
A K Clarke, Alan and Eve Harding, Dr A J and
Mrs Tompsett, Michael Dandy, LYM)*

CLEEVE PRIOR [SP0849]

Kings Arms WR11 8LQ [Bidford Rd (B4085)]:
Tucked-away 16th-c beamed village pub, well
run and comfortable, with good interesting
food at reasonable prices, friendly helpful
staff, well kept Purity and a guest beer, good
wine choice, dining room set with linen
napkins; children welcome, tables outside
*(Joanne Robinson, Elisabeth M Hughes,
Stanley and Annie Matthews)*

CLOWS TOP [SO7171]

Colliers Arms DY14 9HA [A456 Bewdley—
Tenbury]: Family-run roadside dining pub,
roomy and comfortable, with log-fire bar,
lounge areas and restaurant, good well
prepared food inc fixed-price menu and
specials using local produce (some from own
kitchen garden), pleasant efficient staff, well
kept changing ales, good wine list inc some
interesting english ones; garden and terrace,
nice countryside, cl Sun evening *(Mr and
Mrs John Clifford, Eric Thomas Yarwood)*

CROPTHORNE [SO9944]

New Inn WR10 3NE [Main Rd (B4084 former
A44 Evesham—Pershore)]: Comfortable

village pub with good home-made food (all day wknds) using local produce, friendly service, well kept ales such as Adnams and Black Sheep; piped music; children welcome, large garden, open all day wknds *(Amanda Smith, Norman Lewis, Trevor and Sheila Sharman, Matt)*

CROWLE [SO9256]

Old Chequers WR7 4AA [Crowle Green, not far from M5 junction 6]: Civilised dining pub mixing traditional and contemporary décor; oak beams and log fires, leather sofas, modern tables and chairs in bar and restaurant, friendly prompt service, good choice of enjoyable home-made food (not Sun evening) inc fixed-price deals, baby grand, occasional live jazz on Sun; children welcome, disabled access, picnic-sets in garden behind, open all day *(LYM, Mike and Mary Carter, P G Wooler)*

CUTNALL GREEN [SO8868]

Chequers WR9 0PJ [Kidderminster Rd]: Comfortable and stylish beamed country dining pub with good food from pubby lunchtime snacks and sandwiches to some imaginative dishes, good wine choice, well kept if pricey beer, good service; can get very busy evenings; dogs welcome in bar *(Eric Thomas Yarwood, David and Doreen Beattie)*

DODFORD [SO9372]

Dodford Inn B61 9BG [Whinfield Rd]: Welcoming unpretentious walkers' pub in quiet spot overlooking wooded valley, traditional décor and simple furnishings, interesting well kept changing ales, good honest bar food, central fire; children and dogs welcome, disabled facilities, garden with terrace, camping *(Tim and Joan Wright)*

DRAKES BROUGHTON [SO9248]

☆ *Plough & Harrow* WR10 2AG [A44 NW of Pershore]: Dining pub with good fairly priced food and well kept changing ales, friendly courteous staff, good-sized restaurant area, comfortable and attractive rambling lounge, log fire; children welcome, good disabled access, pleasant terrace, good beer garden with play area, open all day *(Eric Thomas Yarwood)*

EVESHAM [SP0344]

Evesham Hotel WR11 6DA [Coopers Lane]: Idiosyncratic hotel's busy bar with amazing range of malt whiskies and spirits, good if quirky wine list, interesting menu inc good value lunchtime buffet (no tips or service charge), remarkable lavatories; children welcome, indoor swimming pool, 40 bedrooms *(Edward Pearce, Denys Gueroult)*

Old Red Horse WR11 4RE [Vine St]: Rambling pub in beautiful black and white timbered building with inner courtyard, well kept ales, enjoyable food inc deals, good cheerful service, log fire; two bedrooms, open all day *(Alan and Eve Harding)*

FORHILL [SP0575]

☆ *Peacock* B38 0EH [handy for M42 junctions 2 and 3; pub at junction Lea End Lane and

Icknield St]: Attractive, quietly placed and well run Chef & Brewer with wide range of generous enjoyable food all day inc fixed price menu, plenty of tables in comfortably fitted knocked-through beamed rooms, woodburner in big inglenook, Greene King, Highgates, Hobsons, Wells & Youngs and guest ales, friendly prompt helpful service; piped music; children and dogs welcome, disabled facilities, picnic-sets on back terrace and front grass, other heated covered areas, open all day *(Dennis and Gill Keen, LYM, Susan and John Douglas)*

GREAT WITLEY [SO7566]

☆ *Hundred House* WR6 6HS [Worcester Rd]: Handsome much-modernised hotel (former Georgian coaching inn and magistrates' court), friendly service, well kept Banks's and a guest like Malvern Hills, good house wines, wide choice of enjoyable generous food inc good value Sun lunch, bright sunny rooms, nice views from bay windows, pleasant restaurant; no dogs; 27 bedrooms, handy for ruined Witley Court and remarkable church *(Tony and Wendy Hobden, Alan and Eve Harding, Dave Braisted, Eric Thomas Yarwood)*

HAGLEY [SO9180]

Lyttleton Arms DY9 9LJ [Park Rd right off A456]: Civilised place with comfortable contemporary décor, good choice of interesting food all day inc fixed-price wkdy menu (till 6pm), efficient young staff, wide range of wines by the glass; garden, open all day *(Jayne Fisentzides)*

HALLOW [SO8258]

Crown WR2 6LB [Main Rd]: Large oak-beamed pub with enjoyable good value food, three well kept ales inc Hobsons, friendly staff *(Alan and Eve Harding)*

HANLEY SWAN [SO8142]

Swan WR8 0EA [B4209 Malvern—Upton]: Attractive contemporary rustic décor and furnishings blending well with old low beams, bare boards and log fire, extended back part set for dining, enjoyable food inc good steaks and Sun carvery, friendly service, well kept Adnams, St Austell Tribute and Shepherd Neame Spitfire, good wines by the glass, lively atmosphere; piped and some live music; children welcome, disabled facilities, good-sized side lawn with play area, nice spot facing green and big duck pond, five comfortable bedrooms (one over kitchen can be noisy) *(Mark Clare, Sara Fulton, Roger Baker, Reg Fowle, Helen Rickwood, David and Gill Carrington, P Dawn, LYM, Chris Evans)*

INKBERROW [SP0157]

Bulls Head WR7 4DY [A422 Worcester—Alcester]: Handsome Georgian inn refurbished under new licensees, enjoyable reasonably priced food, efficient friendly staff, steps between levels, heavily beamed, timbered and partly flagstoned part with big fireplace; garden behind with terrace *(Mike and Mary Carter, BB)*

KEMPSEY [SO8649]

Huntsman WR5 3QB [signed off A38 in Kempsey itself]: Out-of-the-way 18th-c pub, plain and simply furnished, with well kept Bathams, Greene King and Wye Valley, inexpensive home-made food, restaurant, skittle alley with bar; dogs and children welcome, garden *(LYM, the Didler)*

☆ *Walter de Cantelupe* WR5 3NA [3.7 miles from M5 junction 7: A44 towards Worcester, left on to A4440, then left on to A38 at roundabout; Main Rd]: Traditional carpeted bar with inglenook and pleasant mix of well worn furniture, ales such as Blue Bear, Cannon Royall and Timothy Taylors Landlord, summer farm cider and locally pressed apple juice, bar food can be good (till 10pm Fri, Sat), table skittles; piped music, sports TV; children in dining area till 8.15pm, dogs in bar and bedrooms, pretty suntrap walled garden, handy M5 break, cl Mon *(Phil and Jane Hodson, Chris Evans, Brian and Janet Ainscough, Andy and Jill Kassube, Comus and Sarah Elliott, Ian and Nita Cooper, Denys Gueroult, R T and J C Moggridge, Donna and Roger, G Wordsworth, David and Katharine Cooke, Martin and Pauline Jennings, M G Hart, P Dawn, LYM, Mike and Mary Carter, John Hooley)*

KINNERSLEY [SO8743]

☆ *Royal Oak* WR8 9JR [off A38 S of Worcester]: Well run pub with chef/landlord doing enterprising reasonably priced food, log fire in comfortable carpeted bar, old hunting prints, well kept ales such as Wye Valley Butty Bach, Weston's perry, interesting wines, good coffee, picture-window restaurant; piped pop music may obtrude; disabled access with help, side terrace, three bedrooms in refurbished back block, handy for Croome Park NT *(Mr and Mrs M J Girdler, Mr and Mrs J Berrisford, Chris and Angela Buckell, Guy Vowles, Tim and Joan Wright, BB, Mrs Helen Thomson, Ann Carver)*

LEIGH SINTON [SO7850]

Royal Oak WR13 5DZ [Malvern Rd, junction with A4103 SW of Worcester]: Good inexpensive pubby food, well kept Marstons-related ales, carpeted beamed bar and smallish restaurant, log fire; garden behind with seats in sheltered alcoves *(Chris Evans, Denys Gueroult, Alan Bowker)*

LONGDON [SO8434]

☆ *Hunters Inn* GL20 6AR [B4211 S, towards Tewkesbury]: Beams, flagstones, timbers, some stripped brick and log fires, owned and run by local farming family, big helpings of locally sourced food (all day wknds) inc fresh fish and popular Sun lunch, real ales such as Malvern Hills, Wells & Youngs Bombardier and one brewed for the pub, good choice of wines by the glass, friendly competent service, raftered dining area with linen tablecloths, good views; children welcome, extensive well tended garden, bedrooms, open all day wknds till 1am

(Dr A J and Mrs Tompsett, Lynne Dare, LYM)

MALVERN [SO7640]

☆ *Malvern Hills Hotel* WR13 6DW [opp British Camp car park, Wynds Point; junction A449/B4232 S]: Big comfortable dark-panelled lounge bar, very popular wknds, enjoyable bar food, friendly service, well kept changing ales such as Wye Valley and local Malvern Hills, quite a few malt whiskies, good coffee, open fire, downstairs pool room, smart more expensive restaurant, well reproduced piped music; they may try to keep your credit card while you eat; dogs welcome, great views from terrace, bedrooms small but comfortable, open all day *(Dr and Mrs Michael Smith, Martin and Pauline Jennings, BB, Stanley and Annie Matthews)*

Unicorn WR14 4PZ [Belle Vue Terrace]: Former 16th-c posting inn, four real ales, bargain simple food, pleasant efficient young staff; piped music *(D W Stokes, David and Gill Carrington)*

Wyche WR14 4EQ [Wyche Rd]: Comfortable pub nr top of Malvern Hills with splendid view, up to five ales inc Hobsons and Malvern Hills, pubby food inc bargain specials, live music (last Weds of month); children and dogs welcome, four bedrooms, open all day *(Alistair Stanier)*

MARTLEY [SO7759]

Masons Arms WR6 6YA [B4204 E]: Unusually good thai food as well as standard dishes, bargain lunch and OAP deals, charming attentive service, four real ales, good coffee, decent wines, comfortable bar and dining lounge, separate raftered restaurant, live music Weds; garden with country views and play area *(Denys Gueroult, Chris Evans)*

NORTON [SO8850]

Retreat WR5 2PT [Woodbury Lane]: Pleasant Marstons pub, good value meals inc light dishes, well kept beer *(Chris Evans, Dave Braisted)*

OMBERSLEY [SO8463]

☆ *Crown & Sandys* WR9 0EW [A4133]: Big popular open-plan inn with wide choice of good food from lunchtime sandwiches to imaginative specials, early evening discount (not Sun), several wines by the glass inc champagne, real ales, good friendly uniformed staff, airy modern décor mixing with 17th-c beams and inglenook, various dining areas inc conservatory; piped music; children welcome, terrace with fountain, sizeable garden, seven bedrooms *(Lesley Rackley, Eric Thomas Yarwood, LYM)*

PEOPLETON [SO9350]

Crown WR10 2EE: Refurbished cosy village pub, beamed bar with big inglenook fireplace, well laid-out dining area, good food (must book) from sandwiches up inc set deals, Fullers and Hook Norton ales, good wines by the glass, friendly prompt service; flower-filled back garden *(Anne McCarthy, Sam Ward, Martin and Pauline Jennings)*

PERSHORE [SO9545]

Angel WR10 1AF [High St]: Former coaching inn's comfortably old-fashioned panelled lounge, wide choice of enjoyable generous bar food, two well kept ales, prompt friendly service; decent bedrooms *(Chris Evans, Guy Vowles)*

☆ *Brandy Cask* WR10 1AJ [Bridge St]: Plain high-ceilinged bow-windowed bar, own good ales from courtyard brewery and guests (Aug beer festival), quick friendly helpful service, coal fire, reasonably priced food from sandwiches to steaks, quaintly decorated dining room; well behaved children allowed, terrace, vine arbour and koi pond in long attractive garden down to river (watch the kids) *(BB, the Didler, Guy Vowles)*

POUND GREEN [SO7578]

New Inn DY12 3LF [B4194 NW of Bewdley]: Attractive pub rambling out from beamed central core, quiet nooks and corners, friendly efficient young staff, good reasonably priced food in bar and well laid-out dining room, Timothy Taylors Landlord and two local ales kept well; live music nights, darts, dominoes, pool, fruit machine; pleasant front garden, picturesque area handy for Arley steam railway station, bedrooms *(Steve Jennings)*

POWICK [SO8151]

Three Nuns WR2 4SB [Colletts Green Rd]: Quietly placed little 19th-c village local, very generous reasonably priced food from landlord/chef, well kept Jennings *(Chris Evans)*

SHATTERFORD [SO7981]

☆ *Bellmans Cross* DY12 1RN [Bridgnorth Rd (A442)]: Welcoming french-mood dining pub with good well presented interesting food from sandwiches up inc good Sun lunch, smart tasteful restaurant with kitchen view, french chefs and bar staff, pleasant deft service, neat timber-effect bar with Bass, Greene King Old Speckled Hen and a guest beer, good choice of wines by the glass inc champagne; teas and coffees; picnic-sets outside, handy for Severn Woods walks, open all day wknds *(BB, Theo, Anne and Jane Gaskin, Richard Clarke, Robert Roxburgh)*

SHENSTONE [SO8673]

Hare & Hounds DY10 4BU [A450]: Friendly old roadside pub, well kept Banks's, Enville and a guest, decent generous home-made food (not Sun evening) inc bargain two-course lunches, takeaway fish and chips, beams and log fires; children and dogs welcome, side terrace and back garden with summer bouncy castle, open all day Fri-Sun, cl Mon lunchtime winter *(Dave Braisted)*

Plough DY10 4DL: Secluded two-bar country local in pleasant surroundings, chatty and comfortable, with well kept Bathams, bar snacks inc nice pork pies, open fire *(anon)*

SHRAWLEY [SO7966]

New Inn WR6 6TE [B4196 Holt Heath—Stourport]: Attractive 19th-c pub in quiet village, enjoyable reasonably priced food,

well kept ales inc Theakstons, 1930s replica posters, restaurant; good garden *(Chris Evans, Dave Braisted)*

STOKE PRIOR [SO9565]

☆ *Country Girl* B60 4AY [B4091 S towards Hanbury; Sharpway Gate]: Attractive country pub with imaginative fairly priced food inc good fresh fish, friendly staff, well kept ales, inglenook log fire in beamed lounge, relaxed rustic eating area with some stripped brick and pitched rafters, separate more formal dining room; nice terrace, walks on Dodderhill Common *(BB, Mrs B H Adams, Dave Braisted, Malcolm Everett)*

STOKE WHARF [SO9468]

Navigation B60 4LB [Hanbury Rd (B4091), by Worcester & Birmingham Canal]: Friendly and comfortable, popular for good value food and well kept changing ales *(Phyllis McCombie, Dave Braisted)*

STOKE WORKS [SO9365]

Bowling Green B60 4BH [a mile from M5 Junction 5, via Stoke Lane; handy for Worcester & Birmingham Canal]: Attractive and comfortable, with bargain traditional food, Banks's Bitter and Mild, friendly atmosphere, polished fireplace, big garden with neat bowling green *(Dave Braisted)*

STONEHALL COMMON [SO8849]

Inn at Stonehall WR5 3QG [S of Norton, via Hatfield]: Revamped Victorian country dining pub doing good food from bar snacks to pricier upscale dishes, clean contemporary décor with muted colours, painted panelling and wood floors, sofas by log fire, real ale, careful attentive service; disabled access, big garden with covered dining area, views to Bredon Hills, cl Sun evening, Mon (except bank hols) *(Frank Willy, BB)*

TENBURY WELLS [SO5968]

☆ *Pembroke House* WR15 8EQ [Cross St]: Striking timbered building, oldest in town, combining pubby beamed bar with upmarket dining side, popular with older people lunchtime (not Mon) for good fair-priced food, more elaborate evening meals (not Sun or Mon), friendly efficient staff, Hobsons and a guest ale such as Foxy Lady, woodburner, games area with pool; piped music; smokers' shelter, pleasant garden, open all day wknds *(Denys Gueroult, BB, David Elliott)*

Ship WR15 8AE [Teme St]: Good food from sandwiches up in bright dining room or small L-shaped bar with lots of dark wood inc fine Elizabethan beams, well kept ales such as Hobsons, decent wines; piped music; picnic-sets in coachyard and on neat sheltered back lawn, three comfortable bedrooms *(Stan K, BB)*

UPHAMPTON [SO8464]

Fruiterers Arms WR9 0JW [off A449 N of Ombersley]: Homely country local (looks like a private house), good value Cannon Royall ales (brewed at back of pub) and guests, farm cider, simple rustic Jacobean panelled bar and lounge with comfortable armchairs, beamery, log fire, lots of photographs and memorabilia, filled rolls (Fri-Sun), pool room; garden, some seats out in front *(Dave Braisted, the Didler)*

UPTON SNODSBURY [SO9454]

Oak WR7 4NW [A422 Worcester—Stratford]: Civilised modern refurbishment inc leather seats in flagstoned bar with ceiling wine bottle feature, enjoyable home-made food inc speciality pies from shortish menu (12-7 Sun), well kept real ale, enthusiastic licensees and friendly attentive staff; sturdy terrace tables, lawn picnic-sets, handy for Spetchley Park gardens, four bedrooms *(Mike and Mary Carter, Chris Evans, Caroline and Michael Abbey, Guy Vowles)*

UPTON UPON SEVERN [SO8540]

White Lion WR8 0HJ [High St]: Family-run hotel's pleasant relaxed bar, well kept Greene King and other ales, friendly helpful staff, comfortable bucket chairs, sofas and old prints, good food in bar and brasserie; covered courtyard, 13 bedrooms *(Theocsbrian, BB)*

WELLAND [SO8039]

Anchor WR13 6LN [Drake St (A4104 just over 0.5 miles E of B4208 crossroads)]: Refurbished 17th-c country pub, wood floors, leather sofas and open fires, well kept ales and up to 16 wines by the glass from brick-fronted servery, spreading dining area with fine views, reasonably priced blackboard food; may be piped music; children welcome, nice garden, camping field, bedrooms, cl Sun evening *(Chris Evans, LYM)*

WEST MALVERN [SO7645]

☆ *Brewers Arms* WR14 4BQ [The Dingle]: Attractive little two-bar beamed country local down steep path, Malvern Hills, Marstons, Wye Valley and up to five guests (Oct beer festival), good value food (all day Fri-Sun, breakfast from 9am Sun) inc bargain OAP wkdy lunches, neat airy dining room, Sun night cheese club, amiable pub cat; walkers and dogs welcome, glorious view from small garden, smokers' folly *(Paul Kloss,*

David and Gill Carrington, Roger and Diana Morgan, Dave Braisted)

WILLERSEY [SP1039]

New Inn WR12 7PJ [Main St]: Friendly and attractive old stone-built local in lovely village, generous good value pub food all day from sandwiches up, prompt service, well kept Donnington ales, ancient flagstones, darts and raised end area in traditional main bar with woodburner, pool in separate public bar, skittle alley; piped music, TV; tables outside, good local walks, open all day *(Martin and Pauline Jennings, Roger Fox, Michael Dandy)*

WORCESTER [SO8456]

Alma WR3 7HT [Droitwich Rd (A38)]: Good value hearty food inc OAP deals, well kept ales such as Batemans and St Austell *(Chris Evans)*

Eagle Vaults WR1 2LZ [Friar St]: Open-plan Victorian pub with panelling, etched windows and other original features, cheery licensees, enjoyable bargain food from good deli rolls up, Marstons-related ales; piped music may obtrude; pavement tables *(Phil Bryant, P Dawn)*

Farriers Arms WR1 2HN [Fish St]: Relaxed and welcoming, rambling though pleasant lounge and basic public bar, inexpensive unpretentious food, good cheerful service, well kept ales and good house wines; very handy for cathedral *(LYM, Robert Ager, P Dawn)*

Maple Leaf WR2 4XA [Canada Way, Lower Wick]: Generous home-made food at bargain prices, well kept Banks's, friendly staff, spotless *(Chris Evans)*

Oak Apple WR5 2NL [Spetchley Rd]: Well kept Banks's, enjoyable food from huge baguettes to steaks, low prices *(Chris Evans)*

Postal Order WR1 1DN [Foregate St]: Popular Wetherspoons with good range of well kept beer, Weston's cider and their usual food at reasonable prices *(the Didler, P Dawn, Chris Evans)*

Post Office address codings confusingly give the impression that some pubs are in Worcestershire, when they're really in Gloucestershire, Herefordshire, Shropshire or Warwickshire (which is where we list them).

Yorkshire

It comes as no surprise to those who live in this huge county but for visitors, the first thing that strikes them about pubs here is the genuinely friendly welcome they receive from the landlords and landladies and their staff. And this makes no difference whether it's a simple little tavern, a civilised dining pub or a smart hotel bar – it's just a given trait. Over a third of the Main Entries here hold one of our Beer Awards and the average price of a pint in Yorkshire is certainly more reasonable than it is in many other counties throughout the country. Breweries that crop up regularly include Black Sheep, Copper Dragon, Cropton, Dark Horse, Hambleton, Kelham Island, North Yorkshire, Roosters, Rudgate, Saltaire, Sheffield, John Smiths, Tetleys (famous as a Yorkshire beer for nearly 200 years, though brewing is likely to move from Leeds to Wolverhampton during 2011), Theakstons, Timothy Taylor, Wentworth, Wold Top and York. To mention all the pubs that are on top form at the moment here would result in a very long list so we've picked just a few that our readers have really enjoyed over the last year: the Birch Hall at Beck Hole (an unusual sweet-shop-cum-pub in wonderful surroundings), the Bay Horse in Burythorpe (very good food and a friendly atmosphere), the Durham Ox at Crayke (a fantastic all-rounder), the Blue Lion at East Witton (inventive food, nice to stay in and with an informal bar), the Tempest Arms in Elslack (deservedly busy for its beers and generous food), the Black Sheep Brewery in Masham (a bar/bistro and brewery tours, too), the Nags Head in Pickhill (another excellent all-rounder), the Laurel in Robin Hood's Bay (quite unchanging and in a delightful coastal village), the Fat Cat in Sheffield (an amazing choice of changing beers and cheap food), the St Vincent Arms at Sutton upon Derwent (smashing beers and enjoyable bar food) and the Maltings in York (interesting beers, quirky décor and cheap lunchtime food). Food has always been a strong point in Yorkshire with fish from the east and west coasts, top quality beef and sheep and plentiful game from estates and moors. Again, to avoid a huge list we've only picked out a few places that our readers have rated especially highly for that special meal out – and that they also feel do still have some pubbiness: the Abbey Inn at Byland Abbey (back in these pages after a break), the Blue Lion at East Witton, the Tempest Arms at Elslack, the Star in Harome (exceptional food and bedrooms and a relaxing little bar), the Black Swan at Oldstead (a new entry that we think will do very well), the White Swan in Pickering (a smart hotel but with a buzzy little bar), the Nags Head in Pickhill, the Pipe & Glass at South Dalton (lovely food cooked by the young landlord and four ales, too) and the St Vincent Arms at Sutton upon Derwent. Our Yorkshire Dining Pub 2011 is the Pipe & Glass at South Dalton.

The knife-and-fork symbol 🍴 distinguishes pubs where the food is of exceptional quality.

AMPLEFORTH   SE5878   MAP 10

White Swan

Off A170 W of Helmsley; East End; YO62 4DA

**Quite a choice of seating areas in attractive pub, attentive service, enjoyable food and real
ales; seats on back terrace**

Our readers enjoy this well run and neat golden-stone pub. There's a good atmosphere,
quite a range of popular food and a warm welcome, too. It's a civilised place with a
beamed lounge, cream-coloured décor, sporting prints and mix of tables and chairs on
the slate flooring. The more conventional beamed front bar, liked by locals, has a blazing
log fire, red-patterned wall seating and plenty of stools, some standing timbers and a
comfortable end seating area with big soft red cushions. Black Sheep Best, John Smiths
Bitter and a guest beer on handpump and good wines by the glass. The restaurant area is
more formal with plush furnishings and crisp, white linen-covered tables; piped music,
TV, darts and dominoes. There are seats and tables on the large, attractive back terrace
and the pub is just a couple of miles from Ampleforth Abbey.

🍴 **The well liked bar food includes lunchtime sandwiches and toasties, soup, chicken liver
pâté with chutney, marinated fresh seafood salad, steak in ale pie, battered haddock and
mushy peas, mushrooms in a creamy brandy sauce with pasta, gammon and egg, chicken
in a leek and bacon sauce, salmon suprême with a herb and parmesan crust and tiger
prawn sauce, pork fillet with bacon, apple and blue cheese and half a gressingham
duckling with orange sauce.** *Starters/Snacks: £4.95 to £8.95. Main Courses: £9.25 to £17.75.
Puddings: £4.95 to £6.25*

Free house ~ Licensees Mr and Mrs R Thompson ~ Real ale ~ Bar food ~ Restaurant ~
(01439) 788239 ~ Children welcome ~ Open 12-3, 6-midnight; midday-1am(midnight Sun) Sat

*Recommended by Dr and Mrs Jackson, WW, Dr and Mrs R G J Telfer, John and Eleanor Holdsworth, Walter and
Susan Rinaldi-Butcher, Janet and Peter Race, Margaret Dickinson*

APPLETON-LE-MOORS   SE7388   MAP 10

Moors 🛏

Village N of A170 just under 1.5 miles E of Kirkby Moorside; YO62 6TF

**Neatly kept inn with beams and knick-knacks, real ales and well liked bar food; plenty of
surrounding walks; bedrooms**

The new licensees at this little stone-built pub now keep the place open all day with
food usefully served all day on Sundays. There are black beams and joists in the white
paintwork, a nice built-in high-backed stripped settle next to an old kitchen fireplace,
plenty of other seating and some sparse decorations such as a few copper pans and
earthenware mugs in a little alcove, a couple of plates and one or two pieces of country
ironwork; plenty of standing space. Black Sheep Best and Timothy Taylors Landlord on
handpump and quite a few wines by the glass; piped music, darts and board games. There
are tables in the lovely walled garden with quiet country views and walks straight from
here to Rosedale Abbey or Hartoft End, as well as paths to Hutton-le-Hole, Cropton and
Sinnington.

🍴 **Tasty bar food now includes sandwiches, soup, haddock goujons with sweet chilli sauce,
crispy belly pork strip with apple fondant and black pudding, toad in the hole with gravy,
twice-baked olive and sage soufflé, gammon and eggs, barbecue chicken, steak and
kidney pudding, duck breast with black cherry sauce, slow-braised lamb shank with mint
gravy, and puddings such as orange and Cointreau cheesecake and chocolate brownie with
caramel sauce.** *Starters/Snacks: £4.00 to £6.00. Main Courses: £9.00 to £16.00. Puddings:
£4.00 to £5.00*

Free house ~ Licensee Simon Morrisey ~ Real ale ~ Bar food (12-2.30, 5-9; all day Sun) ~
Restaurant ~ (01751) 417435 ~ Children welcome ~ Dogs welcome ~ Open 11-11 ~
Bedrooms: £45B/£70B

Recommended by Greta and Christopher Wells, Ann and Tony Bennett-Hughes, BOB, Blaise Vyner, I D Barnett

ASENBY   SE3975 MAP 7

Crab & Lobster ⑪ 🍷 🛏

Village signposted off A168 – handy for A1; YO7 3QL

Interesting furnishings and décor in rambling bar, ambitious and enjoyable restaurant-y food, good drinks choice and seats on the attractive terrace; smart bedrooms

The hotel and restaurant side of this handsome and civilised place do play a major part but the rambling L-shaped bar still attracts customers dropping in for a drink and a chat and they keep Copper Dragon Golden Pippin and Theakstons Best on handpump and quite a few wines by the glass; service is efficient rather than friendly. The bustling bar has an interesting jumble of seats from antique high-backed and other settles through sofas and wing armchairs heaped with cushions, to tall and rather theatrical corner seats; the tables are almost as much of a mix, and the walls and available surfaces are quite a jungle of bric-a-brac including lots of race tickets, with standard and table lamps and candles keeping even the lighting pleasantly informal. There's also a cosy main restaurant and a dining pavilion with big tropical plants, nautical bits and pieces and Edwardian sofas; piped music. The gardens have bamboo and palm trees lining the paths, there's a gazebo at the end of the walkways and seats on a mediterranean-style terrace. The opulent bedrooms (based on famous hotels around the world) are in the surrounding house which has seven acres of mature gardens, and a 180-metre golf hole with full practice facilities.

🍽 **Excellent – though certainly not cheap – food includes a lunchtime fish club sandwich (not Sunday), fishcakes of codling, haddock and oak-roast salmon with a poached egg, barbecue spare ribs, pressed terrine of local venison, rabbit and duck with pear and apricot chutney, beer-battered fresh haddock, twice-baked cheese soufflé with orange-braised carrot and pine nut salad, free-range chicken breast in air-dried ham and cheese with fresh pasta and chicken velouté, seafood curry, roast loin of lamb with shoulder confit, shepherd's pie and apple and mint jelly, and puddings such as banoffi cheesecake with caramelised bananas and cinnamon ice-cream and blackcurrant treacle tart with orange ice-cream.** *Starters/Snacks: £5.00 to £11.50. Main Courses: £11.00 to £19.00. Puddings: £5.00 to £7.00*

Vimac Leisure ~ Licensee Mark Spenceley ~ Real ale ~ Bar food (12-2.30, 7(6.30 Sat)-9) ~ Restaurant ~ (01845) 577286 ~ Well behaved children allowed ~ Live jazz Sun lunchtime ~ Open 11am-midnight ~ Bedrooms: £90B/£150B

Recommended by Mike and Lynn Robinson, Pete Coxon, Janet and Peter Race, Jon Clarke, Comus and Sarah Elliott, Dr D Jeary, Dr and Mrs R G J Telfer, Paul Humphreys

BECK HOLE   NZ8202 MAP 10

Birch Hall

Signed off A169 SW of Whitby, from top of Sleights Moor; YO22 5LE

Extraordinary pub-cum-village-shop in lovely valley with friendly landlady, real ales and simple snacks, seats outside and marvellous surrounding walks

'Unique and wonderful' and 'what a fantastic little place' are just two of the comments from enthusiastic readers about this tiny pub-cum-village-shop in stunning surroundings. It's quite unchanging and there are two rooms, with the shop selling postcards, sweeties and ice-creams in between and with a hatch service to both sides. Furnishings are simple – built-in cushioned wall seats and wooden tables (spot the one with 136 pennies, all heads up, embedded in the top) and chairs on the flagstones or composition flooring, and there are some strange items such as french breakfast cereal boxes, a tube of Macleans toothpaste priced 1/3d and a model railway train running around a shelf just above head height. Well kept Durham Magus, Wentworth Oatmeal Stout and a beer from North Yorkshire named for the pub (called Beckwater) on handpump; several malt whiskies. Service could not be more friendly and helpful; dominoes and quoits. Outside, an ancient oil painting of the view up the steeply wooded river valley hangs on the pub wall, there are benches out in front and steps up to a little steeply terraced side garden. They have a self-catering cottage attached to the pub. It's in a lovely steep valley and surrounded by marvellous walks – one of which is along the disused railway line from Goathland – part of the path from Beck Hole to Grosmont is surfaced with mussel shells.

🍴 Bar snacks such as locally made pies, butties and home-made scones and cakes that include their lovely beer cake. *Starters/Snacks: £1.90 to £2.70*

Free house ~ Licensee Glenys Crampton ~ Real ale ~ Bar food (available during all opening hours) ~ No credit cards ~ (01947) 896245 ~ Children in small family room ~ Dogs welcome ~ Open 11-11; 11-3, 7.30-11 Weds-Sun in winter; closed winter Mon evening, all day Tues Nov-March

Recommended by Fred and Lorraine Gill, Stephen Corfield, the Didler, Comus and Sarah Elliott, Dr and Mrs Jackson

BLAKEY RIDGE   SE6799   MAP 10

Lion 🍺 🛏

From A171 Guisborough—Whitby follow Castleton, Hutton le Hole signposts; from A170 Kirkby Moorside—Pickering follow Keldholm, Hutton le Hole, Castleton signposts; OS Sheet 100 map reference 679996; YO62 7LQ

Extended pub in fine scenery and open all day; bedrooms

This extended old pub is at the highest point of the North York Moors National Park and the views are stunning; there are also lots of surrounding hikes – and the Coast to Coast Footpath is nearby – so the inn is popular with walkers. The beamed and rambling bars have warm open fires, a few big high-backed rustic settles around cast-iron-framed tables, lots of small dining chairs, a nice leather sofa, and stone walls hung with some old engravings and photographs of the pub under snow (it can easily get cut off in winter). There are up to seven real ales on handpump: Copper Dragon Golden Pippin, Greene King Morlands Old Speckled Hen and Theakstons Best, Old Peculier, Black Bull and XB; piped music and games machine. If you are thinking of staying, you must book well in advance. This is a regular stop-off for coach parties.

🍴 Usefully served all day, the generous helpings of traditional bar food includes lunchtime sandwiches and filled baked potatoes as well as soup, giant yorkshire pudding with gravy, deep-fried brie with cranberry sauce, home-cooked ham and egg, pizza and chips, stilton and vegetable crumble, well like steak and mushroom pie, beef curry, battered cod, steaks, and puddings like chocolate fudge cake and banana split.
Starters/Snacks: £3.45 to £4.45. Main Courses: £9.95 to £15.75. Puddings: £2.25 to £3.95

Free house ~ Licensee Barry Crossland ~ Real ale ~ Bar food (12-10) ~ Restaurant ~ (01751) 417320 ~ Children welcome ~ Dogs allowed in bar ~ Open 10am-11pm(midnight Sat) ~ Bedrooms: £20(£42.50B)/£74B

Recommended by Dr J Barrie Jones, WW, WAH

BOROUGHBRIDGE   SE3966   MAP 7

Black Bull ♀

St James Square; B6265, just off A1(M); YO51 9AR

Bustling town pub with real ales, several wines by the glass and traditional bar food; bedrooms

This attractive old town pub has been looking after travellers between England and Scotland for centuries and it's still somewhere cheerful locals drop in regularly for a pint and a chat. There are lots of separate drinking and eating areas and the main bar area has a big stone fireplace and comfortable seats and is served through an old-fashioned hatch; there's also a cosy snug with traditional wall settles, a tap room, lounge bar and restaurant. John Smiths, Timothy Taylors Landlord and a guest from Cottage on handpump, ten wines by the glass and 19 malt whiskies; dominoes. The two borzoi dogs are called Spot and Sadie and the two cats Kia and Mershka. The hanging baskets are lovely. More reports please.

🍴 Bar food includes sandwiches, soup, chicken liver pâté with cumberland sauce, sausages with onion gravy, beef curry, a pie of the day, lamb shank in port and honey gravy, steaks, daily specials like beefburgers, mushroom ragoût and bass with king scallops in a spicy tomato and herb sauce, and puddings such as jam sponge and lemon tart. *Starters/Snacks: £3.75 to £6.95. Main Courses: £6.95 to £16.95. Puddings: £3.95 to £4.75*

Free house ~ Licensees Anthony and Jillian Burgess ~ Real ale ~ Bar food (12-2(2.30 Sun), 6-9(9.30 Fri and Sat)) ~ Restaurant ~ (01423) 322413 ~ Children welcome ~ Dogs welcome ~ Folk music Sun lunchtime ~ Open 11-11(midnight Sat); 12-11 Sun ~ Bedrooms: £42S/£65S

Recommended by Michael Doswell, Comus and Sarah Elliott, the Didler, Janet and Peter Race, Bob Broadhurst, Ian and Nita Cooper, Mike and Lynn Robinson

BRADFIELD

SK2290 MAP 7

Strines Inn 🛏️

From A57 heading E of junction with A6013 (Ladybower Reservoir) take first left turn (signposted with Bradfield) then bear left; with a map can also be reached more circuitously from Strines signpost on A616 at head of Underbank Reservoir, W of Stocksbridge; S6 6JE

Surrounded by fine scenery with quite a mix of customers and traditional beer and bar food; bedrooms

Useful for such an isolated position, this traditional old pub is liked by walkers – it's surrounded by superb scenery on the edge of the High Peak National Park and there are fine views, plenty of picnic-sets and peacocks, geese and chickens. Inside, the main bar has black beams liberally decked with copper kettles and so forth, quite a menagerie of stuffed animals, homely red-plush-cushioned traditional wooden wall benches and small chairs and a coal fire in the rather grand stone fireplace. Two other rooms to the right and left are similarly furnished. Jennings Cocker Hoop, Marstons Pedigree and a guest beer on handpump and several wines by the glass; piped music. The bedrooms have four-poster beds and a dining table as the good breakfasts are served in your room – the front room overlooks the reservoir.

🍽 **Fair value bar food includes sandwiches, ploughman's, soup, filled baked potatoes, burgers, filled giant yorkshire pudding, macaroni cheese, a pie of the day, liver and onions, a big mixed grill, and puddings such as treacle sponge and chocolate fudge cake.** *Starters/Snacks: £3.20 to £4.60. Main Courses: £5.30 to £12.95. Puddings: £3.60 to £3.95*

Free house ~ Licensee Bruce Howarth ~ Real ale ~ Bar food (12-2.30, 5.30-8.30 winter weekdays; all day summer and winter weekends) ~ (0114) 285 1247 ~ Children welcome ~ Dogs welcome ~ Open 10.30am-11pm; 10.30-3, 5.30-11 weekdays in winter ~ Bedrooms: £60B/£80B

Recommended by the Didler, Giles and Annie Francis, Neil Whitehead, Victoria Anderson, Brian and Anna Marsden

BROUGHTON

SD9450 MAP 7

Bull

A59; BD23 3AE

Handsome, carefully refurbished inn making good use of pale oak and contemporary paintwork, good choice of drinks and enjoyable food

After a walk through the nearby Hall Estate (3,000 acres of rolling countryside and parkland), this handsome stone inn is just the place to head for as they usefully serve some kind of food all day. It's been carefully refurbished and given a modern twist and they've sensibly kept the various rooms separate: lots of pale oak, handsome flagstones, exposed stone walls, built-in wall seats and a mix of dining chairs around polished tables, contemporary paintwork hung with photographs of local suppliers and open log fires. The four real ales come from breweries such as Copper Dragon, Dark Horse, Saltaire and Thwaites on handpump and they keep a dozen wines, including champagne, by the glass and several malt whiskies. The solid wooden benches and tables on the terrace overlook the grounds of Broughton Hall.

🍴 Using carefully sourced local produce from named suppliers, the nicely presented food might include sandwiches, ploughman's, soup, queenie scallops with a garlic and herb crust, deep-fried haddock, toad in the hole with onion gravy, rabbit fried in breadcrumbs with sweet onion fritters, mutton pudding, salmon fillet with watercress sauce, rose veal escalope with nut brown butter, capers and a fried egg, duck pie, 28-day-aged steaks with a choice of sauces, and puddings such as jam roly-poly with real custard; good Sunday roasts. *Starters/Snacks: £3.50 to £6.50. Main Courses: £8.50 to £21.00. Puddings: £3.50 to £5.50*

Free house ~ Licensee Leanne Richardson ~ Real ale ~ Bar food (all day) ~ (01756) 792065 ~ Children welcome ~ Dogs allowed in bar ~ Open 12-11(8.30 Sun)

Recommended by Steve Whalley, John and Eleanor Holdsworth, Karen Eliot, Stu Mac, Keith Moss, Claire Hall, G Jennings

BURN   SE5928   MAP 7

Wheatsheaf 🍺 £

A19 Selby—Doncaster; Main Road; YO8 8LJ

Plenty to look at and a friendly welcome, half a dozen real ales and good value straightforward food

You can be sure of a warm welcome from the friendly and chatty licensees at this mock-Tudor roadside pub – and some very good value bar food, too; it's best to book to be sure of a table, especially at weekends. There really is masses to see: gleaming copper kettles, black dagging shears, polished buffalo horns and the like around its good log and coal fire (and a drying rack with bunches of herbs above it), decorative mugs above one bow-window seat and cases of model vans and lorries on the cream walls. The highly polished pub tables in the partly divided, open-plan bar have comfortable seats around them and they keep John Smiths and Timothy Taylors Best and guests such as Brown Cow Celestial Light, Great Heck Dave, Marston Moor Brick Dust and Saltaire Blonde on handpump at reasonable prices and 20 malt whiskies. A pool table is out of the way on the left; cribbage, dominoes, games machine, TV and maybe unobtrusive piped music. A small garden behind has picnic-sets on a heated terrace.

🍴 Straightforward bar food at very fair prices includes sandwiches, filled baked potatoes, ploughman's, burgers, lasagne, steak in ale pie, gammon with egg or pineapple, chicken with bacon, cheese and barbecue sauce, giant yorkshire pudding with sausages and gravy, salmon, dill and lemon fishcakes, and puddings like chocolate lumpy bumpy and treacle sponge; popular Sunday roasts. *Starters/Snacks: £1.75 to £3.95. Main Courses: £5.95 to £7.95. Puddings: £2.95*

Free house ~ Licensee Andrew Howdall ~ Real ale ~ Bar food (12-2 daily, 6.30-8.30 Thurs, Fri and Sat; no food Sun-Weds evenings) ~ (01757) 270614 ~ Children welcome ~ Dogs welcome ~ Open 12-midnight

Recommended by Hugh Stafford, Rob and Catherine Dunster, Terry and Nickie Williams, Lawrence R Cotter, Barbarrick, Lesley and Peter Barrett, Pat and Tony Martin, G Dobson

BURYTHORPE   SE7964   MAP 7

Bay Horse 🍽 🍷

Off A64 8.5 miles NE of York ring road, via Kirkham and Westow; 5 miles S of Malton, by Welham Road; YO17 9LJ

Civilised dining pub with warm welcome for both locals and visitors, contemporary décor in comfortable stylish rooms, real ales, good wines and enjoyable modern cooking

Since this became a Main Entry last year, we've had a lot of warm praise from our readers who are delighted to have discovered it. It's a charming dining pub with a warm welcome from the genuinely friendly staff for both locals and visitors and the linked rooms are cosy, relaxed and civilised: up-to-date paintwork, stripped floorboards, a mix of chunky pine tables and elegant high-backed black or wooden dining chairs and shelves of books. The end dining room has several attractive and amusing farmyard animal paintings, the main bar has a couple of nice old carved antique pews with interesting cushions and some ancient hunting prints, and there's a tiny end room with a sofa and open log fire and yet another red-walled room with rugs on flagstones. Tetleys, Theakstons Black Bull and Timothy Taylors Landlord on handpump and 11 good wines by the glass. On the outside terrace are some good contemporary tables and seats under parasols. The nearby Burythorpe House hotel, a former gentleman's residence, is under the same ownership.

🍴 **Imaginative and very good, the bar food includes sandwiches, ploughman's, soup, goats cheese terrine with hazelnuts, caramelised apple and toasted brioche, pheasant breast satay with peanut sauce, ham and egg, fish and chips with mushy peas, burger with bacon, cheese and guacamole, spinach and brie filo parcel with sorrel cream sauce, roasted salmon fillet with fennel, asparagus and cherry tomato salad, duck breast with red onion marmalade, parsley mash and juniper berry sauce, and puddings such as plum crumble with crème anglaise and tia maria crème brûlée.** *Starters/Snacks: £3.95 to £4.25. Main Courses: £6.95 to £8.95. Puddings: £4.50*

Free house ~ Licensee Dawn Pickering ~ Real ale ~ Bar food (12-2.30(3 Sun), 6.30-9; not Mon) ~ Restaurant ~ (01653) 658302 ~ Children welcome ~ Dogs allowed in bar ~ Open 12-3, 6-11.30; 12-11.30 Sun; closed Mon except bank hols

Recommended by Pat and Graham Williamson, Andy and Jill Kassube, Christopher Turner, Marlene and Jim Godfrey

BYLAND ABBEY   SE5478   MAP 7

Abbey Inn 🍴 ☐ 🛏
off A170 Thirsk—Helmsley; YO61 4BD

Carefully refurbished inn opposite magnificent abbey ruins, friendly informal atmosphere, very good choice of drinks, excellent food and seats in big garden; lovely bedrooms

This former Victorian farmhouse overlooks the hauntingly beautiful abbey ruins opposite, which was at one time the largest ecclesiastical building in Europe; two of the comfortable bedrooms enjoy this amazing view. There's been considerable refurbishment in the various rooms under the present licensees: flagstones and rugs or stripped wooden flooring, a happy mix of carved light oak and dark wooden dining chairs around all sorts of tables (lots of Mouseman furniture, too), red-painted or exposed stone walls, evocative photographs and paintings, lots of candles and plants and an open woodburning stove. Copper Dragon Best Bitter and Timothy Taylors Golden Best on handpump, 20 wines by the glass (plus eight pudding ones) and home-made flavoured gins and vodkas; friendly, efficient staff and piped music. There are plenty of solid garden seats and tables under parasols on the terrace and a sizeable garden. They also have a shop selling local produce and delicacies from the kitchen.

🍴 **Using the best seasonal produce and home-grown herbs and vegetables, the excellent food includes sandwiches, snacks like pork pie with home-made chutney, ploughman's, soup, beetroot salmon gravadlax with horseradish and dill cream, rare breed sausages with wholegrain mustard mash and braised shallots, blue cheese soufflé with a celery and red wine poached pear and spiced red wine reduction, chicken breast stuffed with truffle-infused mushrooms, seared foie gras, madeira sauce and truffle mash, hake with garlic and herb butter, seared scallop, caviar and a mini fish pie, and puddings such as banana panna cotta with toffee sauce and caramel crisp and cappuccino tiramisu with chocolate fudge; they also offer full afternoon teas.** *Starters/Snacks: £5.00 to £7.00. Main Courses: £10.00 to £18.00. Puddings: £4.00 to £6.50*

Free house ~ Licensees Melanie Drew and David Robbins ~ Real ale ~ Bar food (all day; not Tues) ~ Restaurant ~ (01347) 868204 ~ Children welcome ~ Open 12-10; 12-4 Sun; closed Tues and maybe winter Mon; two weeks in Jan ~ Bedrooms: /£95B

Recommended by Sue and Gerry, Mrs Sheila Stothard, M and GR, Dr Ian S Morley, Andy and Jill Kassube

Real ale to us means beer which has matured naturally in its cask – not pressurised or filtered. We name all real ales stocked. We usually name ales preserved under a light blanket of carbon dioxide too, though purists – pointing out that this stops the natural yeasts developing – would disagree (most people, including us, can't tell the difference!).

CARTHORPE   SE3083   MAP 10

Fox & Hounds ⏚ ⏛

Village signposted from A1 N of Ripon, via B6285; DL8 2LG

Emphasis on ambitious food in friendly dining pub but drinkers welcome, too; real ales and extensive wine list

As this busy and neatly kept dining pub is so handy for the A1, it might be best to reserve a table if you plan to eat. It's a family-run place with long-serving licensees and has plenty of local customers – though visitors are made welcome, too. The cosy L-shaped bar has quite a few mistily evocative Victorian photographs of Whitby, a couple of nice seats by the larger of its two log fires, plush button-back built-in wall banquettes and chairs, plates on stripped beams and some limed panelling; piped light classical music. There's some theatrical memorabilia in the corridors and an attractive high-raftered restaurant with lots of neatly black-painted farm and smithy tools. Black Sheep Best and Worthingtons on handpump; helpful service.

⏚ **Reliably good and well presented, the restauranty food includes lunchtime sandwiches, soup, smoked haddock with chive butter sauce, duck filo parcels with plum sauce, chicken breast filled with cheese in a creamy sauce, vegetable curry, braised lamb shank with onion gravy, poached halibut with a light mustard sauce, half a gressingham duckling with orange sauce and parsley and thyme stuffing, and puddings such as warm chocolate, pear and almond tart and mango and passion-fruit semifreddo; Sunday roasts.** *Starters/Snacks: £4.25 to £7.95. Main Courses: £10.95 to £21.95. Puddings: £3.95*

Free house ~ Licensees Vince and Helen Taylor ~ Real ale ~ Bar food (not Mon) ~ Restaurant ~ (01845) 567433 ~ Children welcome ~ Open 12-3, 7-11.30; closed Mon and first week in Jan

Recommended by P A Rowe, Michael Doswell, Gerry and Rosemary Dobson, Jon Clarke, Peter and Eleanor Kenyon, Walter and Susan Rinaldi-Butcher, Alan Thwaite, Jill and Julian Tasker, Blaise Vyner

---

CHAPEL LE DALE   SD7477   MAP 7

Hill Inn ⏚

B5655 Ingleton—Hawes, 3 miles N of Ingleton; LA6 3AR

Friendly inn with fine surrounding walks, appealing food cooked by the family and a fair choice of real ales; comfortable bedrooms

With a warm welcome from the licensees, this former farmhouse is rather a haven for weary (often damp) walkers; there are wonderful remote surrounding walks and fantastic views to Ingleborough and Whernside from the bedrooms. There's a relaxed and chatty atmosphere, beams and log fires, straightforward seats and tables on the stripped wooden floors, nice pictures on the walls and stripped-stone recesses. Black Sheep Best, Dent Aviator and Golden Fleece and Theakstons Best on handpump and several wines by the glass. There's a dining room and a well worn-in sun lounge. More reports please.

⏚ **Cooked by the family, the enjoyable food includes lunchtime sandwiches, soup, fishcakes with sweet chilli sauce, home-cooked ham with parsley sauce, cumberland sausages with onion gravy, beetroot and mascarpone risotto topped with cheese, chicken breast with lemon and herbs wrapped in bacon on pasta, lamb shank with mint sauce and redcurrant jelly, bass fillets with a soy, ginger and garlic sauce, beef bourguignon, and puddings such as lemon tart with home-made lemon and mascarpone ice-cream and warm chocolate pudding with white chocolate sauce.** *Starters/Snacks: £4.00 to £6.95. Main Courses: £9.50 to £15.75. Puddings: £5.95*

Free house ~ Licensee Sabena Martin ~ Real ale ~ Bar food (12-2.30(3 Sun), 6.30(6 Sat)-8.45; not Mon except bank hols) ~ Restaurant ~ (015242) 41256 ~ Children welcome ~ Dogs allowed in bar ~ Open 12-3.30, 6.30-11; may stay open longer if busy; 12-11 Sat; 12-4, 6.30-11 Sun; closed Mon (except bank hols) ~ Bedrooms: /£75S

Recommended by Brian and Anna Marsden, John and Sylvia Harrop, Gordon and Margaret Ormondroyd

CONSTABLE BURTON

SE1690 MAP 10

Wyvill Arms 🍴 ♀ 🍺

A684 E of Leyburn; DL8 5LH

Well run and friendly dining pub with imaginative food, a dozen wines by the glass, real ales and efficient helpful service; bedrooms

Our readers very much enjoy their visits to this spotlessly kept and very efficiently run dining pub and you can be sure of a warm welcome from the friendly landlord. There's a small bar area with a mix of seating, a finely worked plaster ceiling with the Wyvill family's coat of arms and an elaborate stone fireplace. The second bar has a lower ceiling with fans, leather seating, old oak tables, various alcoves and – new this year – a model train on a railway track running around the room; the reception area includes a huge leather sofa which can seat up to eight people, another carved stone fireplace and an old leaded church stained-glass window partition. Both rooms are hung with pictures of local scenes. John Smiths and Theakstons Best on handpump, a dozen wines by the glass and some rare malt whiskies; board games. There are several large wooden benches under large white parasols for outdoor dining and picnic-sets by the well. Constable Burton Gardens are opposite and worth a visit.

🍽 Using home-grown herbs and vegetables and game (including wild boar and pigeon) from the estate across the road, the first-class food includes lunchtime sandwiches, soup, pigeon breast on mesclun salad with smoked duck and balsamic dressing, home-grown asparagus with gruyère cheese, terrine of smoked ham, wensleydale cheese and duck mousse with pear and apple chutney, wild boar sausages with horseradish mash and onion gravy, home-made tagliatelle with smoked pine nuts, tomatoes and a pesto sauce, suckling pig on coarse-grain mustard mash with apple froth, monkfish wrapped in parma ham on spicy risotto with a coconut sauce, rib of beef with cheesy mash, venison on roast vegetable purée with a cranberry and cassis jus, and puddings like three-way brûlée and double lemon tart. *Starters/Snacks: £4.50 to £8.50. Main Courses: £6.50 to £9.45. Puddings: £5.95*

Free house ~ Licensee Nigel Stevens ~ Real ale ~ Bar food (12-2.30, 6-9) ~ Restaurant ~ (01677) 450581 ~ Children welcome ~ Dogs allowed in bar and bedrooms ~ Open 11-3, 5.30-11; 12-3, 5.30-10.30 Sun ~ Bedrooms: £60B/£75B

Recommended by David and Cathrine Whiting, John and Eleanor Holdsworth, Noel Thomas, Janet and Peter Race, Walter and Susan Rinaldi-Butcher

COXWOLD

SE5377 MAP 7

Fauconberg Arms 🍴 ♀ 🛏

Off A170 Thirsk—Helmsley, via Kilburn or Wass; easily found off A19, too; YO61 4AD

Friendly family-run and nicely updated 17th-c inn, enjoyable generous food, a good range of drinks and seats in back garden; comfortable bedrooms

This is a lovely place to stay (and the breakfasts are especially good) and as we went to press four new bedrooms were about to be added to this friendly family-run inn. The heavily beamed and flagstoned bar has log fires in both linked areas – one in an unusual arched fireplace in a broad low inglenook – muted contemporary colours, some attractive oak chairs by local craftsmen alongside more usual pub furnishings, nicely chosen old local photographs and other pictures and copper implements and china. Hambleton Bitter and Stud and Wold Top Bitter and Centenery Way Mild on handpump, a thoughtful choice of wines by the glass and 28 malt whiskies. The pub dogs – Peggy, Bramble and Phoebe – welcome other four-legged friends, if well behaved. The candlelit dining room is quietly elegant with a gently upmarket yet relaxed atmosphere. The garden behind the inn has seats and tables on the terrace and views across the fields to Byland Abbey; picnic-sets and teak benches out on the front cobbles look along this charming village's broad tree-lined verges, bright with flower tubs.

🍽 Using seasonal local produce and game, the excellent bar food includes lunchtime sandwiches, soup, seared pigeon breast with quince jelly, walnut, apple and blue wensleydale salad, home-roasted honey-glazed ham and eggs, beer-battered cod with home-made chips and minted pea purée, smashing omelettes with different cheese toppings, pork and apple or vegetarian burgers in a home-made bun with cheese, bacon or spicy peppers, corn-fed free-range chicken with rustic sausage and chips, venison with celeriac chips in a rich game gravy, and puddings such as popular bakewell tart and sticky toffee pudding with toffee sauce; the home-made ice-creams are pretty special. *Starters/Snacks: £4.90 to £8.50. Main Courses: £8.95 to £16.50. Puddings: £4.95*

Free house ~ Licensee Simon Rheinberg ~ Real ale ~ Bar food (12-2.30(4 Sun), 6-9.30) ~ Restaurant ~ (01347) 868214 ~ Children welcome ~ Dogs allowed in bar and bedrooms ~ Open 11-3, 6-11(midnight Fri); 11-midnight Sat; 12-11 Sun; closed Tues ~ Bedrooms: £75B/£95S

Recommended by Dr and Mrs R G J Telfer, Brian and Jacky Wilson, Alan McDougall, Pete Coxon, Tony and Glenys Dyer, Peter Hacker, Phil and Susan Turner

CRAYKE   SE5670   MAP 7

Durham Ox 🍽 ♀ 🛏
Off B1363 at Brandsby, towards Easingwold; West Way; YO61 4TE

Friendly, well run inn, interesting décor in old-fashioned, relaxing rooms, fine drinks and excellent food; lovely views and comfortable bedrooms

This busy inn seems to have the best of all worlds. With universally friendly and helpful staff, it's a lovely place to stay for a few days, has excellent food and a proper pubby bar liked by locals. The old-fashioned lounge bar has an enormous inglenook fireplace, pictures and photographs on the dark red walls, interesting satirical carvings in the panelling (Victorian copies of medieval pew ends), polished copper and brass, and venerable tables, antique seats and settles on the flagstones. In the bottom bar is a framed illustrated account of the local history (some of it gruesome) dating back to the 12th c, and a large framed print of the original famous Durham Ox which weighed 171 stone. Black Sheep Best, Theakstons Best and Timothy Taylors Landlord on handpump, ten wines by the glass and a dozen malt whiskies; piped music. There are seats on the terrace and in the covered courtyard, and fantastic views over the Vale of York on three sides; on the fourth side there's a charming view up the hill to the medieval church. The comfortable bedrooms are in converted farm buildings and the breakfasts are good. The tale is that this is the hill up which the Grand Old Duke of York marched his men.

🍽 **Excellent bar food** might include sandwiches and toasties, ham hock terrine with piccalilli, crispy goats cheese fritters with poached pears and walnut dressing, eggs benedict, sausages with champ mash and shallot gravy, beer-battered haddock with mushy peas, cottage pie with home-made spicy beans, half a rotisserie chicken piri piri with aioli, popular rib-eye steak with skinny fries and béarnaise sauce, local venison with berry sauce, daily specials like porobello mushroom and wild garlic risotto and steamed black bream with pak choi, coriander, ginger and lemon grass, and puddings such as chocolate brownie sundae with hot chocolate sauce and marmalade bread and butter pudding with vanilla egg custard. *Starters/Snacks: £5.95 to £6.95. Main Courses: £9.95 to £18.95. Puddings: £4.50 to £5.95*

Free house ~ Licensee Michael Ibbotson ~ Real ale ~ Bar food (12-2.30(3 Sun), 6-9(8.30 Sun)) ~ Restaurant ~ (01347) 821506 ~ Children welcome but must be well behaved ~ Dogs allowed in bedrooms ~ Open 12-11 ~ Bedrooms: £80B/£100B

Recommended by G Dobson, John and Eleanor Holdsworth, Comus and Sarah Elliott, Karen Eliot, Christopher Turner, Pete Coxon, Peter and Anne Hollindale, Richard and Mary Bailey, Dr and Mrs Jackson, Mrs Sheila Stothard

---

Bedroom prices normally include full english breakfast, VAT and any inclusive service charge that we know of. Prices before the '/' are for single rooms, after for two people in double or twin (B includes a private bath, S a private shower). If there is no '/', the prices are only for twin or double rooms (as far as we know there are no singles). If there is no B or S, as far as we know no rooms have private facilities.

CROPTON

SE7588   MAP 10

New Inn 🍺

Village signposted off A170 W of Pickering; YO18 8HH

Genuinely warm welcome in modernised village pub with own-brew beers, traditional furnishings and brewery tours; bedrooms

The own-brewed beers in this comfortable modernised village inn are quite a draw – and you can take some home with you, too: Cropton Balmy Mild, Endeavour, Honey Gold, Monkmans Slaughter, Two Pints, Uncle Sam's and Yorkshire Moors Bitter. They also keep several malt whiskies and half a dozen wines by the glass. The traditional village bar has wooden panelling, plush seating, lots of brass and a small fire. A local artist has designed historical posters all around the downstairs conservatory that doubles as a visitor centre during busy times. The elegant restaurant has locally made furniture and paintings by local artists. Piped music, TV, games machine, darts, pool, a juke box and board games. There's a neat terrace, a garden with a pond and a brewery shop. Brewery Tours (not Sunday or Monday), 11am and 2pm, are £4.95 per person.

🍽 **Generous helpings of bar food includes lunchtime sandwiches and filled ciabatta rolls, ploughman's, soup, deep-fried brie and mushrooms with chervil sauce, steak in ale pie, broccoli and blue cheese flan, beer-battered cod, sausage ring with yorkshire pudding and onion gravy, slow-braised leg of lamb with garlic jelly and mint jus, and puddings like apple and rhubarb crumble and lemon cheesecake; Sunday roasts.** *Starters/Snacks: £3.95 to £5.50. Main Courses: £8.50 to £13.95. Puddings: £3.95 to £5.25*

Own brew ~ Licensee Philip Lee ~ Real ale ~ Bar food (12-2(2.30 Sun), 6-9(8.30) ~ Restaurant ~ (01751) 417330 ~ Children welcome ~ Dogs allowed in bar and bedrooms ~ Open 11-11.30 (midnight Sat) ~ Bedrooms: £45B/£80B

Recommended by Michael Butler, Mrs Angela Graham, P Dawn, Roger Shipperley, Brian and Anna Marsden

DOWNHOLME

SE1197   MAP 10

Bolton Arms

Village signposted just off A6108 Leyburn—Richmond; DL11 6AE

Enjoyable food in unusual village's cosy country pub, lovely views; bedrooms

Like the village itself, the Ministry of Defence owns this little stone-built pub which makes it one of the last pubs in Britain owned by the state. It's surrounded by MoD land – a largely unspoilt swathe of Swaledale and there are super views over it from the red-walled back conservatory dining room. This is simple, quiet and attractive, up a few steps from the bar. If you eat, they take your order down there and then call you through when it's ready. The friendly and softly lit black-beamed and carpeted bar has two smallish linked areas off the servery, Black Sheep Best and Theakstons Best on handpump from a small stone counter and good wines by the glass at fair prices. There are comfortable plush wall banquettes, a log fire in one neat fireplace, quite a lot of gleaming brass, a few small country pictures and drinks advertisements on pinkish rough-plastered walls. Service is friendly and efficient; piped music and board games. The neat garden, on the same level as the dining room (and up steps from the front), shares its view; there are also some lower picnic-sets and benches. The two bedrooms, sharing a bathroom, are good value.

🍽 **Cooked by the landlord, the popular bar food includes sandwiches, soup, garlic mushrooms with cheese, bacon and a creamy sauce, baked goats cheese on a pear and watercress salad, steak and mushroom pie, gammon and egg, spinach and ricotta pancakes, lambs liver and bacon, chicken breast stuffed with leeks, wrapped in bacon with a wensleydale cheese sauce, kleftiko (a cypriot lamb dish) and a spicy thai stir fry with beef, chicken or king prawns.** *Starters/Snacks: £3.95 to £6.50. Main Courses: £8.95 to £20.50. Puddings: £4.75 to £5.50*

Free house ~ Licensees Steve and Nicola Ross ~ Real ale ~ Bar food (not Tuesday lunchtime) ~ Restaurant ~ (01748) 823716 ~ Children welcome ~ Open 11-3, 6-midnight; closed Tues lunchtime ~ Bedrooms: £45B/£60S

Recommended by John and Sylvia Harrop

EAST WITTON

SE1486   MAP 10

Blue Lion 🍴 🍷 🛏

A6108 Leyburn—Ripon; DL8 4SN

Civilised dining pub with interesting rooms, daily papers and real ales, delicious food and courteous service; comfortable bedrooms

As well as being an enjoyable place to stay, this smart and civilised dining pub offers first-class food and a proper bar with a relaxed and unstuffy atmosphere where drinkers and their dogs mingle quite happily with customers waiting to eat. This big squarish room has high-backed antique settles and old windsor chairs on the turkey rugs and flagstones, ham-hooks in the high ceiling decorated with dried wheat, teazles and so forth, a delft shelf filled with appropriate bric-a-brac, several prints, sporting caricatures and other pictures, a log fire and daily papers. Black Sheep Best and Riggwelter, and Theakstons Best on handpump and an impressive wine list with quite a few (plus champagne) by the glass; courteous, attentive service. Picnic-sets on the gravel outside look beyond the stone houses on the far side of the village green to Witton Fell and there's a big, pretty back garden.

🍴 **Inventive and extremely good – if not cheap – the highly thought-of food might include sandwiches, soup, slow-braised pigs cheek with black pudding, red wine sauce and apple and parsnip purée, soft shell crab deep-fried with chilli, ginger and a fennel salad, home-made tagliatelle with pancetta, wild mushrooms, cream and truffle oil, smoked haddock topped with a poached egg, leek and mushroom sauce and gruyère cheese, beef and onion suet pudding, slow-braised masala mutton with cumin sweet potato, daily specials, and puddings such as iced liquorice terrine with caramel sauce and sticky toffee pudding with banana ice-cream and butterscotch sauce.** *Starters/Snacks: £5.25 to £10.95. Main Courses: £10.95 to £21.95. Puddings: £5.25 to £6.95*

Free house ~ Licensee Paul Klein ~ Real ale ~ Bar food ~ Restaurant ~ (01969) 624273 ~ Children welcome ~ Dogs allowed in bar and bedrooms ~ Open 11-11 ~ Bedrooms: £67.50S/£89S(£99B)

Recommended by Alistair and Kay Butler, Peter and Giff Bennett, the Didler, Jon Clarke, David and Sue Atkinson, Mike and Shelley Woodroffe, Brian and Janet Ainscough, Pat and Stewart Gordon, Edward Mirzoeff, Lynda and Trevor Smith, Terry Mizen

ELSLACK

SD9249   MAP 7

Tempest Arms 🍴 🍷 🛏

Just off A56 Earby—Skipton; BD23 3AY

Friendly inn with three log fires in stylish rooms, several real ales, good food and tables outside; bedrooms

Always deservedly busy, this 18th-c stone inn has a really good mix of customers – all warmly welcomed by the genuinely friendly licensees and their staff. It's stylish but understated with plenty of pubby character, cushioned armchairs, built-in wall seats with comfortable cushions, stools and lots of tables and three log fires – one greets you at the entrance and divides the bar and restaurant. There's quite a bit of exposed stonework, amusing prints on the cream walls and maybe Molly the friendly back labrador. Dark Horse Hetton Pale Ale, Moorhouses Premier Bitter, Theakstons Best, Thwaites Wainwright and Timothy Taylors Landlord on handpump, 16 wines by the glass and 25 malt whiskies. There are tables outside largely screened from the road by a raised bank. The comfortable bedrooms are in a newish purpose-built extension.

🍴 **Generous helpings of good, enjoyable food include lunchtime sandwiches, soup, devilled kidneys and crispy bacon on fried bread, chicken liver pâté with tomato chutney, black pudding and spam fritter with a light curry dip, toad in the hole with onion gravy, portabello mushroom and goats cheeseburger with beetroot salsa, lasagne, steak and kidney pudding, slow-cooked lamb in redcurrant and mint gravy, duck breast with pancetta, shallots and red wine jus, and daily specials like seafood pancake and tiger prawn curry with garlic naan bread and dips.** *Starters/Snacks: £3.75 to £6.75. Main Courses: £8.95 to £12.95. Puddings: £2.95 to £4.95*

Free house ~ Licensees Martin and Veronica Clarkson ~ Real ale ~ Bar food (12-2.30, 6-9(9.30 Fri and Sat); 12-7.30 Sun) ~ Restaurant ~ (01282) 842450 ~ Children welcome ~ Dogs allowed in bar and bedrooms ~ Open 11-11; 12-10.30 Sun ~ Bedrooms: £62.50B/£79.95B

Recommended by Christopher Mobbs, David Heath, Margaret Dickinson, Andy Witcomb, Brian and Janet Ainscough, John and Eleanor Holdsworth

FADMOOR
SE6789   MAP 10

Plough 🍴 🍷
Village signposted off A170 in or just W of Kirkbymoorside; YO62 7HY

Well run and enjoyable dining pub with a friendly welcome, civilised little rooms, particularly good food and fine wines

This is a popular dining pub by the village green and surrounded by lovely open country. The elegantly simple little rooms have cushioned settles and a range of armed wheelbacks and other wooden dining chairs on seagrass floors (some fine rugs, too), horse tack attached to beams, all sorts of prints and pictures on the yellow walls and lots of wine bottles on display. Black Sheep Best and Great Newsome Sleck Dust on handpump and an extensive wine list; piped music. There are seats on the terrace. They also have a quiet little caravan site for Caravan Club registered members.

🍴 It's best to book a table in advance to enjoy the interesting bar food: sandwiches, soup, black pudding and blue stilton wellington with apple and cider chutney, creamy garlic and herb mushrooms topped with cheese, crispy battered fresh haddock, chicken breast stuffed with brie, wrapped in bacon with a spring onion and white wine cream sauce, braised lamb shank with caramelised red onion mash and rosemary-scented gravy, bass fillets topped with king prawns with lemon and dill risotto, daily specials, and puddings like caramelised white chocolate and Malibu crème brûlée with coconut ice-cream and fruit crumble with vanilla custard; they also offer a good value two-course lunch (not Sunday). *Starters/Snacks: £5.00 to £7.95. Main Courses: £8.95 to £17.95. Puddings: £5.50*

Holf Leisure Ltd ~ Licensee Neil Nicholson ~ Real ale ~ Bar food (12-2(3.30 Sun), 6.30-9; not Sun evening, Mon or Tues) ~ Restaurant ~ (01751) 431515 ~ Children welcome ~ Open 12-3, 6.30-11; 12-4 Sun; closed Sun evening, Mon (except bank hols), Tues and 25 Dec

Recommended by John Hume, Marlene and Jim Godfrey, Stanley and Annie Matthews, Stephen Woad

FERRENSBY
SE3660   MAP 7

General Tarleton 🍴 🍷 🛏️
A655 N of Knaresborough; HG5 0PZ

Civilised coaching inn with interesting restauranty food, lots of wines by the glass, friendly service and relaxed atmosphere; comfortable bedrooms

This smart and civilised place is now edging towards becoming more of a restaurant rather than a pub but they do keep Black Sheep Best and Timothy Taylors Landlord on handpump, ten wines by the glass from a fine list and quite a few coffees. The beamed bar area has brick pillars dividing up the several different areas to create the occasional cosy alcove, some exposed stonework and neatly framed pictures of staff on the cream walls. Dark brown leather chairs are grouped around wooden tables, there's a big open fire, a relaxed atmosphere and a door that leads out to a pleasant tree-lined garden – seats here as well as in a covered courtyard. The bedrooms are comfortable and the breakfasts excellent.

🍴 Well presented and beautifully cooked, the popular food includes soup, parfait of chicken livers and potted pork with cumberland jelly, whitby crab spring rolls with mango and coriander salsa, roast butternut squash, spinach and ricotta cannelloni with carrot and lemon grass broth, a trio of chicken with shallot purée and chicken jus, seafood thermidor, slow-braised short rib of beef with crushed root vegetables, specials like beef and kidney hotpot and wild bass fillet with chervil risotto and chargrilled tiger prawns, and puddings such as dark chocolate tart with hazelnut praline and passion fruit and

orange and cardamom bakewell with crème anglaise. *Starters/Snacks: £4.95 to £9.00. Main Courses: £11.25 to £19.50. Puddings: £4.95 to £6.95*

Free house ~ Licensee John Topham ~ Real ale ~ Bar food (12-2, 6-9.15) ~ Restaurant ~ (01423) 340284 ~ Children welcome ~ Open 12-3, 6-11 ~ Bedrooms: £85B/£129B

Recommended by Dr and Mrs J Temporal, Ian and Jane Haslock, Tony and Tracy Constance, Keith and Sue Ward, Jon Clarke, G Jennings, David Thornton, Janet and Peter Race, Blaise Vyner, Roy and Jean Russell, Michael Doswell, Roger Noyes, Hunter and Christine Wright

GRINTON   SE0498   MAP 10

Bridge Inn 🍺 🛏
B6270 W of Richmond; DL11 6HH

Bustling pub with welcoming landlord, comfortable bars, log fires, a fine choice of drinks and good food; neat bedrooms

The friendly landlord of this popular former coaching inn is sure to make you welcome and the atmosphere is cheerful and relaxed. There are bow window seats and a pair of stripped traditional settles among more usual pub seats, all well cushioned, a good log fire, Jennings Cumberland and Cocker Hoop, and guests such as Brakspears Oxford Gold and Ringwood Best on handpump, nice wines by the glass and 25 malt whiskies. On the right, a few steps take you down into a refurbished room with darts, a well lit pool table and ring the bull. On the left, past leather armchairs and a sofa by a second log fire (and a glass chess set) is an extensive two-part dining room. The décor is in mint green and shades of brown, with a modicum of fishing memorabilia. The bedrooms are neat and simple, and breakfasts are good. There are picnic-sets outside and the inn is right opposite a lovely church known as the Cathedral of the Dales.

🍴 They now have their own smokehouse, grow their own herbs and rear their own pigs: filled baguettes, soup, black pudding spring rolls with spiced plum dipping sauce, devilled whitebait, cumberland sausage with onion gravy, vegetable cottage or steak in ale pies, cod in cider and dill batter, sage and garlic-roasted belly of pork on smoked bacon, tomato, onion and wine lentils, free-range chicken filled with cheese, wrapped in bacon with a cranberry and white wine sauce, lamb shank on parsnip mash with a rosemary and wine jus, and puddings like caramel cheesecake and ginger sponge with sticky toffee sauce. *Starters/Snacks: £4.95 to £5.50. Main Courses: £8.25 to £18.95. Puddings: £4.75*

Jennings (Marstons) ~ Lease Andrew Atkin ~ Real ale ~ Bar food (all day) ~ Restaurant ~ (01748) 884224 ~ Children welcome ~ Dogs allowed in bar and bedrooms ~ Informal live music Thurs evenings ~ Open 12-midnight(1am Sat) ~ Bedrooms: £50B/£80B

Recommended by Ann and Tony Bennett-Hughes, Lynda and Trevor Smith, Blaise Vyner, Peter Dearing, David Thornton

HALIFAX   SE1027   MAP 7

Shibden Mill 🍴 🍷 🍺
Off A58 into Kell Lane at Stump Cross Inn, near A6036 junction; keep on, pub signposted from Kell Lane on left; HX3 7UL

Tucked-away restored mill with cosy rambling bar, five real ales and inventive bar food

Tucked into a leafy enclave with a stream rushing noisily past the car park, this is a hidden-away country inn. The rambling bar has cosy side areas with banquettes heaped with cushions and rugs, there are well spaced nice old tables and chairs and the candles in elegant iron holders give a feeling of real intimacy; also, old hunting prints, country landscapes and so forth and a couple of big log fires. Theakstons XB, a beer named after the pub and brewed for them by Moorhouses and a couple of guests like Black Sheep, Copper Dragon Golden Pippin and Thwaites Original on handpump and a dozen wines by the glass (and two champagnes as well). There's an upstairs restaurant; piped music. There are plenty of seats and tables on an attractive heated terrace, and the building is prettily floodlit at night. More reports please.

🍽 The imaginative bar food includes sandwiches, ploughman's, soup, crab and coriander croquettes, rabbit and black pudding pie, watercress and wild garlic risotto with a poached duck egg, spatchcock chicken tikka with mango relish and mint yoghurt, free-range bacon chip with spiced pineapple chutney and a fried egg, duo of lamb with cumin and thyme sauce and milt oil, rose veal with lightly smoked mash and a grain mustard and caper berry velouté, and puddings like twice-baked chocolate brownies with battenburg ice-cream and amaretto and marzipan cheesecake with prunes and a coffee chocolate shot. *Starters/Snacks: £4.50 to £9.95. Main Courses: £11.25 to £17.95. Puddings: £5.25 to £7.25*

Free house ~ Licensee Glen Pearson ~ Real ale ~ Bar food (12-2, 6-9.30; 12-7.30 Sun) ~ Restaurant ~ (01422) 365840 ~ Children welcome ~ Dogs welcome ~ Open 12-2.30, 6-11; 12-11 Sun and Sat ~ Bedrooms: £75B/£90B

Recommended by Cathy Robinson, Ed Coombe, Clive Flynn, Michael Butler, Brian and Ruth Young, Gordon and Margaret Ormondroyd

HAROME   SE6482   MAP 10

Star ★ 🍽 🍷 🍺 🛏

Village signposted S of A170, E of Helmsley; YO62 5JE

Ambitious modern cooking in pretty thatched pub, proper bar with real ales and fine wines, smart restaurant and cocktail bar and seats on terrace and in garden; stylish bedrooms

This pretty thatched 14th-c inn is just right for a special occasion – it's a fine place to stay overnight and the highly thought-of cooking is exceptional. And although of course the emphasis is mainly on the food, the bar still has a proper pubby atmosphere, a dark bowed beam-and-plank ceiling, plenty of bric-a-brac and interesting furniture (this was the first pub that 'Mousey' Thompson ever populated with his famous dark wood furniture); there's also a fine log fire, a well polished tiled kitchen range and daily papers and magazines. They don't take bar reservations so you must arrive early to be sure of a seat; the busy coffee loft is in the eaves and snacks are served in the popular cocktail bar. Black Sheep and Wold Top Gold on handpump, 18 wines by the glass, home-made fruit liqueurs and all manner of coffees and teas with home-made chocolates; piped music. There are some seats and tables on a sheltered front terrace with more in the garden. You may have to book the stylish bedrooms and suites a long way ahead. The Pheasant Hotel nearby is under the same ownership, as is the Corner Shop opposite the inn and Pern's delicatessen in Helmsley.

🍽 Inventive and elaborate, the expensive food (using produce from their own kitchen garden) might include lunchtime sandwiches and ploughman's, soup, terrine of ham knuckle with spiced pineapple pickle, fried quail egg and grain mustard vinaigrette, white crab meat with tomato and basil salad, herb mayonnaise and bloody mary dressing, sorrel risotto with blue cheese and roast hazelnut pesto, belly pork with warm black pudding and apple salad, a duck egg and devilled sauce, lamb with goats cheese, asparagus and lavender vinaigrette, bass fillet with garlic roast snails, burgundy-style sauce and truffle shavings, and puddings such as baked ginger parkin with rhubarb ripple ice-cream and spiced syrup and chocolate and stout pudding with black treacle ice-cream. *Starters/Snacks: £5.00 to £14.00. Main Courses: £16.00 to £26.00. Puddings: £5.00 to £11.00*

Free house ~ Licensees Andrew and Jacquie Pern ~ Real ale ~ Bar food (11.30-2, 6-9.30; 12-6 Sun; not Mon lunchtime) ~ Restaurant ~ (01439) 770397 ~ Children welcome ~ Open 11.30-3, 6-11; 12-11 Sun; closed Mon lunchtime ~ Bedrooms: /£140S(£180B)

Recommended by Ian and Jane Haslock, P R Stevens, Andy and Jill Kassube, Richard Cole, David Robertson, Noel Thomas, Christine Vallely, David Thornton, Pat and Stewart Gordon, Walter and Susan Rinaldi-Butcher, Michael and Lynne Gittins, Peter and Josie Fawcett

---

Stars after the name of a pub show exceptional quality. One star means most people (after reading the report to see just why the star has been won) would think a special trip worth while. Two stars mean that the pub is really outstanding – for its particular qualities it could hardly be bettered.

HARTSHEAD

SE1822   MAP 7

Gray Ox 🍴 ♟

3.5 miles from M62 junction 25; A644 towards Dewsbury, left on to A62, next left on to B6119, then first left on to Fall Lane; pub on right; WF15 8AL

Appealing modern cooking in attractive dining pub, cosy beamed bars, real ales, several wines by the glass and fine views

Bustling and friendly, this is an attractive stone-built dining pub that's handy for the M62. It is at its most pubby at lunchtime and the bars have beams and flagstones, a cosy décor, bentwood chairs, stripped-pine tables and roaring log fires. Comfortable carpeted dining areas with bold paintwork and leather dining chairs around polished tables lead off. Jennings Cumberland and Cocker Hoop with a guest like Sneck Lifter on handpump and several wines by the glass; piped music. There are picnic-sets outside, and fine views through the latticed pub windows across the Calder Valley to the distant outskirts of Huddersfield – the lights are pretty at night.

🍴 Good, enjoyable food includes lunchtime sandwiches, soup, smoked salmon and scrambled egg on toasted brioche, pigeon breast with black budding and broccoli sauce, fresh crab and spring onion risotto, beer-battered haddock, cumberland sausage with mustard mash and red onion marmalade, chicken breast cooked in cider with lyonnaise potatoes, venison faggots with sage and onion rösti with confit baby vegetables and spinach and roast rump of lamb with braised lamb shoulder in panko crumble and seared lambs kidneys; they also offer set menus (not weekends). *Starters/Snacks: £3.95 to £6.95. Main Courses: £9.95 to £16.95. Puddings: £5.00*

Banks's (Marstons) ~ Lease Bernadette McCarron ~ Real ale ~ Bar food (12-2, 6-9; all day weekends) ~ Restaurant ~ (01274) 872845 ~ Children welcome ~ Open 12-3, 6-midnight; 12-midnight Sun
Recommended by John Saville, Gordon and Margaret Ormondroyd, Dr Kevan Tucker, DC, Pat and Tony Martin, R T and J C Moggridge

HEATH

SE3520   MAP 7

Kings Arms 🍺

Village signposted from A655 Wakefield—Normanton – or, more directly, turn off to the left opposite Horse & Groom; WF1 5SL

Old-fashioned gaslit pub in interesting location with dark-panelled original bar, up to seven real ales and standard bar food; seats outside

A bit of a surprise being so close to industrial Wakefield, this is an old-fashioned pub that fits in well with its setting – the village green opposite is surrounded by 19th-c stone merchants' houses. The original bar has gas lighting which adds a lot to the atmosphere, a fire burning in the old black range (with a long row of smoothing irons on the mantelpiece), plain elm stools, oak settles built into the walls and dark panelling. A more comfortable extension has carefully preserved the original style, down to good wood-pegged oak panelling (two embossed with royal arms) and a high shelf of plates; there are also two other small flagstoned rooms and a conservatory that opens on to the garden. Clarks Classic Blonde, Tetleys, Timothy Taylors Landlord and guest beers such as Black Sheep, Ringwood Fortyniner, Timothy Taylors Ram Tam and Wadworths 6X on handpump. There are some sunny benches facing the green, picnic-sets on a side lawn and a nice walled garden; more reports please.

🍴 Straightforward bar food includes sandwiches, soup, deep-fried camembert with cumberland sauce, a stew of the day with dumplings, beef in ale pie, beer-battered haddock, beefburger with cheese, bacon and onion rings and lambs liver with crispy parma ham and red wine and onion gravy. *Starters/Snacks: £3.95 to £6.95. Main Courses: £6.95 to £16.95. Puddings: £3.95 to £5.95*

Clarks ~ Manager Andrew Shepherd ~ Real ale ~ Bar food (12-2(2.30 Sat), 6-9(9.30 Sat); 12-5 Sun) ~ Restaurant ~ (01924) 377527 ~ Children allowed away from main lounge ~ Dogs allowed in bar ~ Open 12-11(midnight Sat); 12-3, 5-11 weekdays in winter
Recommended by Dr and Mrs A K Clarke, the Didler, Helen Beaumont, Michael Butler

HETTON

SD9658   MAP 7

Angel 🍽 ♈ 🛏

Just off B6265 Skipton—Grassington; BD23 6LT

Busy dining pub with rambling timbered rooms, lots of wines by the glass, real ales, imaginative food and seats on the heated terrace; smart bedrooms

'One of our favourite places' and 'as wonderful as ever' are just two of the enthusiastic comments from readers this year about this well run and neatly kept dining pub. The three timbered and panelled rooms ramble around, though perhaps the one with the most pubby atmosphere (and where you can feel comfortable just popping in for a drink) is the main bar with its Victorian farmhouse range in the big stone fireplace. There are lots of cosy nooks and alcoves, comfortable country-kitchen and smart dining chairs, button-back plush seats and window seats, all manner of wooden or tableclothed tables, Ronald Searle wine-snob cartoons, older engravings and photographs and log fires. Black Sheep, Dark Horse Hetton Pale Ale and Timothy Taylors Landlord on handpump, around 20 wines by the glass (including champagne) from a carefully chosen list and quite a few malt whiskies. Outside in front of the building, there are smart wooden tables and chairs on two covered terraces.

🍽 Using carefully sourced, top quality produce and meat bought direct from farms, the hugely popular and imaginative bar food might include sandwiches, lavender-scented poached salmon with beetroot compote and chive crème fraîche, duck terrine with confit baby onions and orange marmalade, courgette and wild mushroom wellington with rosemary velouté, rare breed suckling pig with apple and cider mash, roasted artichokes and pork liquor, fish pie, chicken breast with wild garlic cream and broccoli crumble, pasta with rabbit loin, oyster mushrooms, pine nuts, mustard and crème fraîche, beef and oxtail pudding, and puddings such as roasted plum crumble with star anise ice-cream and hazelnut praline parfait with white chocolate ice-cream. *Starters/Snacks: £2.95 to £7.25. Main Courses: £11.25 to £18.95. Puddings: £5.95 to £7.25*

Free house ~ Licensee Bruce Elsworth ~ Real ale ~ Bar food (12-2.15, 6-9.15(10 Sat); all day Sun) ~ Restaurant ~ (01756) 730263 ~ Children welcome ~ Dogs allowed in bedrooms ~ Open 12-3, 6-11(9 Sun); closed Jan ~ Bedrooms: £125B/£140B

Recommended by George and Linda Ozols, Margaret and Jeff Graham, Ian Malone, James Stretton, Karen Eliot, WAH, Janet and Peter Race, B and M Kendall, Dr and Mrs Michael Smith, Peter and Giff Bennett, Pierre Richterich

KETTLESING

SE2257   MAP 7

Queens Head 🍺

Village signposted off A59 W of Harrogate; HG3 2LB

Lots to look at in friendly stone pub with open fires, chatty atmosphere, real ales and decent food; bedrooms

The landlord and landlady of this quietly placed and pleasant stone pub are a great team and very friendly and informative. The L-shaped, carpeted main bar is decorated with Victorian song sheet covers, lithographs of Queen Victoria, little heraldic shields and a delft shelf of blue and white china. There are also lots of quite close-set elm and other tables around its walls, with cushioned country seats, coal or log fires at each end and maybe unobtrusive piped radio. A smaller bar on the left, with built-in red banquettes, has cricketing prints and cigarette cards, coins and banknotes, and in the lobby there's a life-size portrait of Elizabeth I. Black Sheep, Roosters Yankee and Theakstons Old Peculier on handpump; good service. There are seats in the neatly kept suntrap back garden and benches in front by the lane.

🍽 Popular bar food includes sandwiches, soup, filled yorkshire puddings, home-made burgers, omelettes, battered haddock, gammon and egg, daily specials such as salmon fillet in white wine and parsley sauce, and homely puddings like apple and sultana crumble and banoffi pie; they also do a good value three-course meal. *Starters/Snacks: £3.50 to £6.95. Main Courses: £6.95 to £19.95. Puddings: £3.95*

Free house ~ Licensees Louise and Glen Garbutt ~ Real ale ~ Bar food (11-2, 6-9; all day Sun) ~ (01423) 770263 ~ Children welcome ~ Open 11-2.30, 6-11; 12-10.30 Sun ~ Bedrooms: £74.75S/£86.25S

Recommended by Margaret and Peter Staples, Peter Hacker, Adrian and Dawn Collinge, Simon Le Fort, B and M Kendall, Yana Pocklington, Patricia Owlett

KIRKBYMOORSIDE
SE6986 MAP 10

George & Dragon
Market Place; YO62 6AA

17th-c coaching inn with convivial front bar, snug and bistro, good wines, real ales and decent bar food; comfortable bedrooms

This pretty little town has its market day on Wednesdays, so lunchtime then is a good time to visit this 17th-c coaching inn. The convivial front bar has beams and panelling, smart tub seats around a mix of wooden tables on the part-carpet and part-solid-oak flooring and a roaring log fire in a rather fine fireplace. Copper Dragon Best, Greene King Abbot, North Yorkshire Fools Gold, Shepherd Neame Bishops Finger and Tetleys on handpump from the hand-made ash counter and several malt whiskies; piped music. There's also a snug, a bistro and a smart separate restaurant. Outside on both the front and back terraces, there are plenty of seats and a giant parasol with outdoor heaters under it; more reports please.

As well as teas throughout the afternoon and an early bird menu, the bar food includes lunchtime filled baguettes and ploughman's, soup, garlic and blue cheese mushrooms, duck liver pâté, battered haddock, pasta of the day, steak in ale pie, chicken breast in a creamy tarragon sauce, duck breast with orange sauce, venison steak with a berry sauce, and puddings. *Starters/Snacks: £4.50 to £6.25. Main Courses: £8.00 to £15.50. Puddings: £5.00*

Free house ~ Licensees David and Alison Nicholas ~ Real ale ~ Bar food (12-2(3 Sun), 6(6.30 Sat)-9; also teas all afternoon) ~ Restaurant ~ (01751) 433334 ~ Children welcome ~ Dogs allowed in bedrooms ~ Open 10.30am-11pm; 12-11 Sun ~ Bedrooms: £60B/£90B

Recommended by D and M T Ayres-Regan, Margaret Dickinson

LANGTHWAITE
NY9902 MAP 10

Charles Bathurst
Arkengarthdale, a mile N towards Tan Hill; DL11 6EN

Friendly country inn with bustling atmosphere, a good mix of customers, thoughtful wine list, decent real ales and interesting bar food; comfortable bedrooms and lots of walks

Surrounded by fantastic scenery, this well run inn has plenty of customers – both local and visiting. And while there's a strong emphasis on the good food, the long bar does still have a pubby feel and light pine scrubbed tables, country chairs and benches on stripped floors, plenty of snug alcoves and a roaring fire. The island bar counter has bar stools, Black Sheep Best and Riggwelter, Theakstons Best and Timothy Taylors Landlord on handpump and ten wines by the glass from a sensibly laid-out list with helpful notes. Piped music, darts, pool, TV, dominoes, board games and quoits. There's also a wooden floored dining room with views of Scar House (a shooting lodge owned by the Duke of Norfolk), Robert 'the Mouseman' Thompson tables and chairs, and an open truss ceiling; there are other dining areas as well. The bedrooms are smart and comfortable (the ones not above the dining area are the quietest). There are lovely surrounding walks straight from the front door and fine views over Langthwaite village and Arkengarthdale. It does get busy if they are holding a conference or party.

As well as holding a monthly Tuesday fish evening and offering an early bird menu (the third Friday of the month), the popular bar food includes sandwiches, soup, indian-spiced rabbit spring rolls with soy sauce, marinated squid with spicy salsa, goats cheese panna cotta with beetroot carpaccio, fried salmon with salmon lasagne and crab sauce, pork in ale casserole with leek mash, rump of lamb with ratatouille, black olives and lamb jus, guinea fowl breast with madeira jus, and puddings such as white chocolate and amaretto crème brûlée and sticky toffee pudding with caramel sauce. *Starters/Snacks: £4.25 to £6.95. Main Courses: £9.95 to £19.95. Puddings: £4.95 to £5.75*

Free house ~ Licensees Charles and Stacy Cody ~ Real ale ~ Bar food ~ Restaurant ~ (01748) 884567 ~ Children welcome ~ Open 11am-midnight ~ Bedrooms: /£105B

Recommended by Mike and Lynn Robinson, Brian and Janet Ainscough, Bruce and Sharon Eden, Pat and Stewart Gordon, John and Sylvia Harrop, Alison and Pete, Helen Clarke, Mary Goodfellow

LEDSHAM   SE4529   MAP 7

Chequers ◀

1.5 miles from A1(M) junction 42: follow Leeds signs, then Ledsham signposted; Claypit Lane; LS25 5LP

Friendly village pub, handy for the A1, with hands-on landlord, log fires in several beamed rooms, real ales and well liked bar food; pretty back terrace

In a lovely village and handy for the A1, this particularly well run 16th-c stone inn is run by a friendly hands-on landlord. There are several small, individually decorated rooms with low beams, lots of cosy alcoves, toby jugs and all sorts of knick-knacks on the walls and ceilings, and log fires. From the old-fashioned little central panelled-in servery, they keep Brown Cow Captain Oates Dark Oat Mild, John Smiths, Theakstons Best, Timothy Taylors Landlord and a changing guest on handpump; good, attentive service. A sheltered two-level terrace behind the house has tables among roses and the hanging baskets and flowers are very pretty. RSPB Fairburn Ings reserve is close by.

🍴 **Bar food includes sandwiches, chicken liver pâté, pork, leek and apple sausages with onion gravy, butternut squash, pine nuts and parmesan, steak and mushroom pie, corn-fed chicken breast with dijon mustard sauce, whole plaice with caper, dill and tomato butter, daily specials like gammon steak with a duck egg and sweetcorn rösti, monkfish with smoked bacon and pesto, and puddings such as raspberry cheesecake and double chocolate brownie.** *Starters/Snacks: £5.25 to £8.65. Main Courses: £9.45 to £18.95*

Free house ~ Licensee Chris Wraith ~ Real ale ~ Bar food (12-9 Mon-Sat; not Sun) ~ Restaurant ~ (01977) 683135 ~ Well behaved children allowed ~ Dogs allowed in bar ~ Open 11-11; closed Sun

Recommended by Dr and Mrs A K Clarke, Colin and Louise English, Stephen Shepherd, the Didler, Christine Vallely, MJVK, Neil Whitehead, Victoria Anderson, Pat and Stewart Gordon, Sam and Christine Kilburn, Terry and Nickie Williams, Andy and Jill Kassube

LEVISHAM   SE8390   MAP 10

Horseshoe

Off A169 N of Pickering; YO18 7NL

Friendly village pub with neat rooms, real ales, enjoyable food and seats on village green; bedrooms

A focal point for a delightful, unspoilt village and doing particularly well under its jovial and friendly licensees (who are brothers), this neatly kept traditional pub has seats on the attractive green and is surrounded by fine walks. Inside, there are beams, smart blue banquettes, wheelback and captain's chairs around a variety of tables on the polished wooden floors, vibrant landscapes by a local artist on the walls and a log fire in the stone fireplace; an adjoining snug has a woodburning stove, comfortable leather sofas and old photographs of the pub and the village. Black Sheep and a guest such as Cropton Yorkshire Moors Bitter on handpump and home-made elderflower cordial and sloe and damson gin; board games. There are more seats in the back garden and two of the comfortable bedrooms have fine views.

🍴 **Cooked by one of the landlords using their own eggs (chicken and geese) and other local produce, the attractively presented and enjoyable bar food includes sandwiches, soup, black pudding wrapped in bacon with apple sauce, creamy garlic mushrooms,** mushroom or beef stroganoff, fresh haddock with home-made chips, duck breast on sweet potato mash with a red wine and port sauce, daily specials such as sausage and chickpea casserole, tenderloin of venison with celeriac mash and red wine sauce, and puddings like raspberry and almond tart and ginger and treacle sponge. *Starters/Snacks: £4.25 to £6.50. Main Courses: £9.25 to £15.95. Puddings: £3.95 to £4.50*

Free house ~ Licensees Toby and Charles Wood ~ Real ale ~ Bar food (12-2, 6-8.30) ~ Restaurant ~ (01751) 460240 ~ Children welcome but not ideal for overnight stays ~ Dogs allowed in bar and bedrooms ~ Open 11-11 ~ Bedrooms: £40/£80S
Recommended by Paul Humphreys, Ann and Tony Bennett-Hughes, Andy Lickfold, Nick Dalby

LEYBURN   SE1190   MAP 10

Sandpiper 🍽 🍷
Just off Market Place; DL8 5AT

Emphasis on appealing food though cosy bar for drinkers in 17th-c cottage, real ales and amazing choice of whiskies; bedrooms

Despite there being quite an emphasis on the interesting food in this 17th-c stone cottage, the small cosy bar is liked by locals for a drink and a chat which keeps the atmosphere relaxed and informal. This little bar has a couple of black beams in the low ceiling, wooden or cushioned built-in wall seats around a few tables, and the back room up three steps has attractive Dales photographs; get here early to be sure of a seat. Down by the nice linenfold panelled bar counter there are stuffed sandpipers, more photographs and a woodburning stove in the stone fireplace; to the left is the attractive restaurant with dark wooden tables and chairs on floorboards and fresh flowers. Black Sheep Best and Special and Copper Dragon Freddie Truman on handpump, up to 100 malt whiskies and a decent wine list with several by the glass; piped music. In good weather, you can enjoy a drink on the front terrace among the lovely hanging baskets and flowering climbers.

🍴 Cooked by the chef/patron, the popular food includes lunchtime sandwiches, soup, ham hock and rabbit terrine with piccalilli, haddock and spring onion fishcakes with a parsley and chive sauce, beer-battered fish, pork schnitzel with a free-range egg, grilled vegetable millefeuilles with halloumi and tomato dressing, a pie of the day, pressed lamb with wild garlic and creamed leeks, venison with a liquorice sauce, and puddings like warm chocolate tart with orange and Cointreau ice-cream and vanilla and star anise crème brûlée with coconut macaroons; Sunday roasts. *Starters/Snacks: £5.00 to £8.50. Main Courses: £8.50 to £17.95. Puddings: £5.50*

Free house ~ Licensee Jonathan Harrison ~ Real ale ~ Bar food (12-2.30, 6.30-9(9.30 Fri and Sat); not Mon or winter Tues) ~ Restaurant ~ (01969) 622206 ~ Children welcome ~ Dogs allowed in bar and bedrooms ~ Open 11.30-3, 6.30-11(10.30 Sun); closed Mon and winter Tues ~ Bedrooms: £65S(£70B)/£75S(£80B)
Recommended by Alun Jones, David and Cathrine Whiting, Gordon Briggs, Blaise Vyner

LINTON IN CRAVEN   SD9962   MAP 7

Fountaine
Just off B6265 Skipton—Grassington; BD23 5HJ

Neatly kept pub in charming village, attractive furnishings, open fires, five real ales, decent wines and well liked bar food; seats on the terrace

In a pretty hamlet, this is a civilised and neatly kept pub and, as it tends to be pretty busy at peak times, it's best to arrive early because parking can be difficult. There are beams and white-painted joists in the low ceilings, log fires (one in a beautifully carved heavy wooden fireplace), attractive built-in cushioned wall benches and stools around a mix of copper-topped tables, little wall lamps and quite a few prints on the pale walls. As well as a beer named for the pub, there might be Dark Horse Hetton Pale Ale, John Smiths, Tetleys and a changing guest on handpump and several wines by the glass; piped music, darts and board games. Outside on the terrace, there are teak benches and tables under green parasols and pretty hanging baskets; fine surrounding walks in the lovely Dales countryside.

🍴 Popular bar food includes sandwiches and wraps, ploughman's, soup, thai-style mussels, catalan prawns, a duo of pâté (chicken liver and cream cheese and herb) with onion marmalade, mixed vegetable curry, toad in the hole, gammon and egg, beer-battered haddock, crispy pork belly with ginger beer and apples, slow-cooked lamb shoulder in mint and redcurrant, and puddings like white chocolate cheesecake and chocolate fudge brownie; they also offer morning coffee and nibbles. *Starters/Snacks: £4.50 to £5.95. Main Courses: £8.50 to £16.25. Puddings: £2.75 to £4.95*

Individual Inns ~ Manager Christopher Gregson ~ Real ale ~ Bar food (12-9) ~ Restaurant ~ (01756) 752210 ~ Children welcome ~ Dogs allowed in bar ~ Open 11-11; 12-10.30 Sun
Recommended by WW, John and Helen Rushton, Lynda and Trevor Smith, Margaret and Peter Staples, Jeremy King, Jon Sudlow, Gordon and Margaret Ormondroyd

LONG PRESTON   SD8358   MAP 7

Maypole 🍺 🛏

A65 Settle—Skipton; BD23 4PH

A good base for walkers with friendly staff, a bustling atmosphere, well liked pubby food and a fair choice of real ales

Mr Palmer has been the longest-serving licensee in this pleasant inn for over 300 years and there's a list of landlords dating back to 1695 on the butter-coloured walls of the bar. This carpeted two-room bar also has good solid pub furnishings – heavy carved wall settles and the like and cast-iron-framed pub tables with unusual inset leather tops and plenty of sporting prints and local photographs. There's a separate dining room. Moorhouses Premier Bitter, Timothy Taylors Landlord and a couple of guests like Bowland Pheasant Plucker and Moorhouses Pendle Witches Brew on handpump, ten wines by the glass, Weston's cider and several malt whiskies. The left-hand tap room has darts, dominoes and TV for important sporting events. On a back terrace, there are a couple of picnic-sets under an ornamental cherry tree, with more tables under umbrellas on another terrace (which has outdoor heaters). This makes a good base for walking in the Dales. More reports please.

🍴 Tasty bar food includes sandwiches, ploughman's, soup, deep-fried brie with redcurrant jelly, salmon and tuna fishcakes with lemon and chilli mayonnaise, ham and eggs, battered haddock, thai green vegetable curry, sausages with onion gravy, steak in ale pie, local trout with tarragon and lemon butter, braised shank of lamb with mint and daily specials; they also offer a good value two- and three-course menu on Monday-Thursday lunchtimes. *Starters/Snacks: £3.95 to £6.50. Main Courses: £8.50 to £13.75. Puddings: £3.25 to £4.50*

Enterprise ~ Lease Robert Palmer ~ Real ale ~ Bar food (all day) ~ Restaurant ~ (01729) 840219 ~ Children welcome ~ Dogs allowed in bar and bedrooms ~ Quiz night first Weds of the month (9pm) ~ Open 12-11.30(11 Sun) ~ Bedrooms: £39S/£70B
Recommended by Richard Blackwell, Dudley and Moira Cockroft, Mr and Mrs Ian King

LOW CATTON   SE7053   MAP 7

Gold Cup

Village signposted with High Catton off A166 in Stamford Bridge or A1079 at Kexby Bridge; YO41 1EA

Friendly, pleasant pub with attractive bars, real ales, decent food, seats in garden and ponies in paddock

Run by a helpful and informative landlord, this spacious white-rendered house is a good place for a break after a walk. The beamed bars have a country feel with coach lights on the rustic-looking walls, smart tables and chairs on the stripped wooden floors, an open fire at one end opposite the woodburning stove and quite a few pictures. The restaurant has solid wooden pews and tables (said to be made from a single oak tree) and pleasant views of the surrounding fields. John Smiths and Theakstons Best on handpump; piped music and pool. The garden has a grassed area for children and the back paddock houses Candy the horse and Polly the shetland pony. They have fishing rights on the adjoining River Derwent.

🍴 Using local and home-grown produce, the reasonably priced bar food includes sandwiches, soup, chorizo and field mushrooms on a garlic croûte, leek and wensleydale potato cakes with spicy relish, home-cooked ham with a honey and mustard sauce, breaded cod goujons, popular cajun chicken, slow-braised venison steak in red wine, rack of lamb with a raspberry and mint glaze, half a crispy roast duckling with cherry and brandy sauce and steaks; Sunday roasts. *Starters/Snacks: £4.25 to £6.25. Main Courses: £6.80 to £16.75. Puddings: £3.50 to £4.50*

Free house ~ Licensees Pat and Ray Hales ~ Real ale ~ Bar food (12-2, 6-9; all day weekends; not Mon lunchtime) ~ Restaurant ~ (01759) 371354 ~ Children welcome ~ Dogs allowed in bar ~ Open 12-2.30, 6-11; 12-11(10.30 Sun) Sat; closed Mon lunchtime
Recommended by Gordon and Margaret Ormondroyd, Pat and Graham Williamson

LUND   SE9748   MAP 8

Wellington 🍴 ☐
Off B1248 SW of Driffield; YO25 9TE

Busy, smart pub with plenty of space in several rooms, real ales and helpfully noted wine list and interesting changing food

As there are several real ales and interesting bar food, this neatly kept pub has a good mix of customers. The cosy Farmers Bar has beams, a quirky fireplace, well polished wooden banquettes and square tables and gold-framed pictures and corner lamps on the walls. Off to one side is a plainer, no less smart, flagstoned room with a wine theme. At the other end of the bar, a york-stoned walkway leads to a room with a display of the village's Britain in Bloom awards. There's also a restaurant and a bistro dining area with another open log fire. The main bar in the evening is a haven for drinkers only: Black Sheep, John Smiths and Timothy Taylors Landlord with a guest like Black Sheep Golden Sheep Ale on handpump, a good wine list with a helpfully labelled choice by the glass and 25 malt whiskies. Piped music, board games and TV. There are some benches in a small, pretty back courtyard. More reports please.

🍴 Inventive bar food includes sandwiches, soup, wild rabbit terrine with a grain mustard and cider dressing, pork belly with a chilli and teriyaki sauce, king scallop, black pudding and chorizo salad, sausage with onion gravy, chicken, bacon and leek lasagne, beer-battered haddock, wild mushroom risotto with peconiro and white truffle oil, slow-braised pigs cheek with chorizo and pepper casserole with braising juice, king prawn and mixed fish thai curry, and puddings such as coffee brûlée with walnut tuile and chocolate and chilli pot with cognac ice-cream and merlot jelly. *Starters/Snacks: £4.25 to £8.95. Main Courses: £11.95 to £15.95. Puddings: £4.95 to £6.95*

Free house ~ Licensees Russell Jeffery and Sarah Jeffery ~ Real ale ~ Bar food (not Mon lunchtime) ~ Restaurant (Tues-Sat evenings) ~ (01377) 217294 ~ Children welcome ~ Open 12-3, 6.30-11; 12-11 Sun; closed Mon lunch
Recommended by Roger and Ann King, Dr Ian S Morley

MASHAM   SE2281   MAP 10

Black Sheep Brewery 🍺
Crosshills; HG4 4EN

Lively place with friendly staff, quite a mix of customers, unusual décor in big warehouse room, well kept beers (brewery tours and shop) and popular food

With a bustling atmosphere and a wide range of customers, this is an extremely popular and different place – it's more of a bistro than a pub but, of course, the beers are very well kept. A huge upper warehouse room has a bar serving Black Sheep Best, Ale, Golden

Sheep Ale and Riggwelter on handpump, several wines by the glass and a fair choice of soft drinks. Most of the good-sized tables have cheery american-cloth patterned tablecloths and brightly cushioned green café chairs but there are some modern pubbier tables near the bar. There's a good deal of bare woodwork, with some rough stonework painted cream and green-painted steel girders and pillars. This big area is partly divided up by free-standing partitions and some big plants; piped music and friendly service. Interesting brewery tours and a shop selling beers and more or less beer-related items from pub games and T-shirts to pottery and fudge. A glass wall lets you see into the brewing exhibition centre. Picnic-sets out on the grass.

🍴 **Reasonably priced and enjoyable bar food includes sandwiches and filled baguettes, filled baked potatoes, soup, chicken liver pâté with sweet onion marmalade, omelettes, salads like hot crispy duck, black pudding and bacon with raspberry dressing, roasted mediterranean vegetable lasagne, steak in ale pie, pork and beer sausages on mustard mash with onion gravy, fish pie, chicken pot, and puddings like crème brûlée and apple pie; Sunday roasts.** *Starters/Snacks: £5.95 to £7.95. Main Courses: £8.95 to £10.95. Puddings: £5.00*

Free house ~ Licensee Paul Theakston ~ Real ale ~ Bar food ~ (01765) 680100 ~ Children welcome ~ Open 10.30-4.30 Mon-Weds and Sun; 10.30-11 Thurs, Fri and Sat

Recommended by Paul and Ursula Randall, Mr and Mrs Maurice Thompson, WW, Janet and Peter Race, John and Eleanor Holdsworth, Ian and Helen Stafford

MOULTON

NZ2303   MAP 10

Black Bull 🍴 🍷

Just E of A1, 1 mile E of Scotch Corner; DL10 6QJ

Character bar with interesting furnishings in civilised dining pub, good bar food, more elaborate restaurant menu (strong on fish and shellfish) and smart dining areas (one is a Pullman dining car)

Although this is a civilised dining pub, it does have a bar with a lot of proper character: an antique panelled oak settle and an old elm housekeeper's chair, built-in red cushioned black settles and pews around cast-iron tables, silver-plated turkish coffee pots and copper cooking utensils hanging from black beams, fresh flowers and a huge winter log fire. In the evening you can also eat in the polished brick-tiled conservatory with bentwood cane chairs or in the Brighton Belle dining car. Eight wines, including champagne by the glass and 50 malt whiskies. There are some seats outside in the central court. The pub is handy for the A1.

🍴 **Very good lunchtime bar food includes sandwiches and toasties, soup, potted rabbit terrine with hazelnut salad, baked queenie scallops with smoked bacon and cheese, hot and crunchy rock oysters, bangers and mash with onion gravy, potato gnocchi with tomato sauce and cheese, mushroom and spinach stroganoff, feuilleté of smoked haddock with white wine and prawn sauce, fish pie, and puddings such as rhubarb crème brûlée and sticky toffee pudding with toffee sauce; they also offer plenty of fish and shellfish dishes, two- and three-course set weekday menus and Sunday roasts.** *Starters/Snacks: £5.00 to £8.25. Main Courses: £7.00 to £24.00. Puddings: £5.95 to £7.50*

Free house ~ Licensee Mr Barker ~ Bar food (12-2.30(2 Sat), 6.30-9.30(10 Fri and Sat); 12-4 Sun; not Sun evening) ~ Restaurant (evening) ~ (01325) 377289 ~ Children over 12 welcome ~ Open 12-2.30(2 Sat, 4 Sun), 6-11; closed Sun evening

Recommended by Jill and Julian Tasker, GNI, Pat and Stewart Gordon, Chris Flynn, Wendy Jones

---

Several well known guide books make establishments pay for entry, either directly or as a fee for inspection. These fees can run to many hundreds of pounds. We do not. Unlike other guides, we never take payment for entries. We never accept a free meal, free drink, or any other freebie from a pub. We do not accept any sponsorship – let alone from commercial schemes linked to the pub trade.
All our entries depend solely on merit.

NUNNINGTON   SE6679   MAP 7

Royal Oak

Church Street; at back of village, which is signposted from A170 and B1257; YO62 5US

Friendly staff and good food in reliable, neat pub, lots to look at in beamed bar, winter open fires and real ales

With friendly, helpful staff and enjoyable bar food, this is a well run and attractive little pub. The neatly kept bar has high black beams strung with earthenware flagons, copper jugs and lots of antique keys, one of the walls is stripped back to the bare stone to display a fine collection of antique farm tools and there are open fires; carefully chosen furniture such as kitchen and country dining chairs and a long pew around the sturdy tables on the turkey carpet. The new dining area is linked to the bar by a double-sided wood-burning stove. Black Sheep Best and Wold Top Wolds Way on handpump and several wines by the glass; piped music. The terraced garden has been landscaped. Nunnington Hall (National Trust) is nearby.

🍽 **Popular bar food includes sandwiches, warm black pudding salad, field mushrooms with garlic butter and stilton pâté, whitebait with lemon dressing, spinach and ricotta cannelloni, steak pie, pork fillet in a cream, cider and apple sauce, fisherman's pot, Indonesian-style chicken curry, half a crispy duckling with orange sauce, specials like game terrine and smoked haddock fillet on caper potato cake with a poached egg, and puddings.** *Starters/Snacks: £5.50 to £7.50. Main Courses: £10.95 to £17.95. Puddings: £5.50*

Free house ~ Licensee Anita Hilton ~ Real ale ~ Bar food (not Mon) ~ (01439) 748271 ~ Children welcome ~ Dogs welcome ~ Open 11.45-2.30, 6.30-11; 12-2.30, 7-10.30 Sun; closed Mon (except bank hols)

Recommended by Mary Goodfellow, Maggie Horton, Neil Whitehead, Victoria Anderson, Nick Dalby, Andy and Jill Kassube

OLDSTEAD   SE5380   MAP 7

Black Swan 🍽 🍷 🛏

Main Street; YO61 4BL

16th-c restaurant-with-rooms in remote countryside with first-class food, real ales, several wines by the glass and friendly staff; comfortable bedrooms

In glorious National Park countryside, this is a 16th-c restaurant-with-rooms run by a family who have farmed in the village for generations. Of course, much emphasis is placed on the excellent food but they do have a beamed and flagstoned bar with furniture by 'Mousey' Thompson, window seats with soft cushions and pretty valley views, an open log fire, Black Sheep Best and Copper Dragon Best on handpump, 13 wines by the glass and several malt whiskies; courteous, attentive staff. The back dining rooms are comfortable and attractive. There are picnic-sets outside under parasols. The well equipped ground floor bedrooms have their own terrace; smashing breakfasts. Plenty of fine surrounding walks. Please note that the bedroom price includes dinner for two.

🍽 **Beautifully presented, inventive food includes sandwiches, ploughman's, soup, parmesan and basil risotto with confit tomatoes and black olives, free-range chicken terrine with pea mousse, quails egg and crispy bacon, beer-battered haddock with home-made tartare sauce, slow-cooked old spot pork belly with roast apples, bacon and cider foam, loin of lamb with pressed shoulder and parmesan gnocchi, line-caught wild sea trout with crab-crushed potatoes, samphire and sauce vierge, and puddings such as Valrhona chocolate fondant with peanut butter ice-cream and salted caramel and apple and cinnamon spring rolls with rhubarb panna cotta.** *Starters/Snacks: £6.25 to £6.95. Main Courses: £8.95 to £19.95. Puddings: £6.00 to £8.00*

Free house ~ Licensee Anne Banks ~ Real ale ~ Bar food (12-2(2.30 Sun), 6-9; not Mon-Weds lunchtimes) ~ Restaurant ~ (01347) 868387 ~ Children welcome but must be over 10 in bedrooms ~ Open 12-3, 6-10.30(11 Sat); closed Mon-Weds lunchtimes; two weeks in Jan ~ Bedrooms: /£200S

Recommended by Walter and Susan Rinaldi-Butcher, Jill and Julian Tasker, Dr Ian S Morley

OSMOTHERLEY

SE4597 MAP 10

Golden Lion 🍴 🍺

The Green, West End; off A19 N of Thirsk; DL6 3AA

Welcoming, busy pub with simply furnished rooms, lots of malt whiskies, real ales, interesting bar food and fine surrounding walks

There's an enjoyably bustling atmosphere in this attractive old stone pub and to be sure of a table, it's best to book one beforehand. The roomy beamed bar on the left is simply furnished with old pews and just a few decorations on its white walls, candles on tables, Timothy Taylors Best and Landlord and guests such as Salamander Golden, York Guzzler and Yorkshire Dales Butter Tubs on handpump and 46 malt whiskies. On the right, there's a similarly unpretentious and well worn-in eating area as well as a separate dining room, mainly open at weekends, and a covered courtyard; piped music. Benches out in front look across the village green to the market cross, and there are seats on the terrace. As the inn is the start of the 44-mile Lyke Wakes Walk on the Cleveland Way and quite handy for the Coast to Coast Walk, it's naturally popular with walkers.

🍴 **Interesting bar food includes soup, smoked haddock and sunblush tomato risotto, smoked chicken, avocado and olive salad, salmon fishcakes, charcoal-grilled poussin with rosemary and garlic, calves liver with onions and mash, steak and kidney pudding, venison fillet with red wine jus, and puddings such as apple and walnut cake and chocolate pudding with berries and ginger ice-cream.** *Starters/Snacks: £4.95 to £7.95. Main Courses: £7.95 to £16.00. Puddings: £4.95*

Free house ~ Licensee Christie Connelly ~ Real ale ~ Bar food (12-2.30, 6-9) ~ (01609) 883526 ~ Children welcome ~ Dogs allowed in bar ~ Open 12-11; closed Mon and Tues lunchtimes; open bank hol Mon ~ Bedrooms: £65S/£90S

Recommended by Mr and Mrs Maurice Thompson, Louise Gibbons, David and Sue Smith, Janet and Peter Race, Brian Brooks, Blaise Vyner, Tony and Rosemary Swainson

PICKERING

SE7984 MAP 10

White Swan 🍴 🍷 🛏

Market Place, just off A170; YO18 7AA

Relaxed little bar in civilised coaching inn, several smart lounges, attractive restaurant, real ales, an excellent wine list and first-class food; luxurious bedrooms

Of course, this is not a traditional pub – it's a smart old coaching inn with lovely bedrooms and excellent food and our readers enjoy their visits here very much. But at its heart is a small bar with a friendly welcome and a relaxed atmosphere, wood panelling, sofas and just four tables, a log fire and Black Sheep Best and Timothy Taylors Landlord on handpump, 11 wines by the glass from an extensive list that includes fine old st emilions and pudding wines, and 20 malt whiskies. Opposite, a bare-boards room with a few more tables has another fire in a handsome art nouveau iron fireplace, a big bow window and decorative plates on its plum-coloured walls. The restaurant has flagstones, yet another open fire, comfortable settles and gothic screens, and the residents' lounge is in a converted beamed barn. The old coach entry to the car park is very narrow.

🍴 **At lunchtime, you can enjoy the excellent food in both the bar and restaurant but in the evening you may eat only in the restaurant: filled baguettes, ploughman's, soup, potted whitby crab with celeriac coleslaw, home-smoked venison with berry dressing, spinach and parmesan risotto with roast beetroot, tamworth pork sausages with thyme mash and caramelised onions and lamb hotpot; more elaborate evening dishes like seared king scallops with shallot chutney, capers and crisp smoked bacon and turbot with cockle and shrimp butter, and puddings such as crème caramel with rum-soaked raisins and rich chocolate cake with boozy cherries; Sunday roasts.** *Starters/Snacks: £4.95 to £11.25. Main Courses: £10.95 to £18.95. Puddings: £6.95*

Free house ~ Licensees Marion and Victor Buchanan ~ Real ale ~ Bar food ~ Restaurant ~ (01751) 472288 ~ Children welcome ~ Dogs allowed in bar and bedrooms ~ Open 10am-11pm; 11am-10.30pm Sun ~ Bedrooms: £115B/£150B

Recommended by Peter Burton, P Dawn, Marian and Andrew Ruston, Janet and Peter Race, G D Affleck

PICKHILL   SE3483   MAP 10

Nags Head 🍴 ♀ 🛏

Take the Masham turn-off from A1 both N and S, and village signposted off B6267 in Ainderby Quernhow; YO7 4JG

Busy dining pub with excellent food, a fine choice of carefully chosen drinks, a tap room, smarter lounge and friendly service; comfortable bedrooms

This well run place has it all. There's a genuinely friendly welcome from the knowledgeable landlord and his chatty staff, the food is extremely good, there are four real ales, and it's an excellent place to stay overnight; just the place to take a break from the A1. Most of the tables are laid for eating so if it's just a drink you're after, head for the bustling tap room on the left: beams hung with jugs, coach horns, ale-yards and so forth, and masses of ties hanging as a frieze from a rail around the red ceiling. The smarter lounge bar has deep green plush banquettes on the matching carpet, pictures for sale on its neat cream walls and an open fire. There's also a library-themed restaurant. Black Sheep Best and Golden Sheep Ale, Theakstons Black Bull, and a guest such as Hambleton White Boar on handpump, a good choice of malt whiskies, vintage armagnacs and a carefully chosen wine list with several by the glass. One table is inset with a chessboard; darts, TV and piped music. There's a front verandah, a boules and quoits pitch and a nine-hole putting green.

🍴 Extremely good bar food includes lunchtime choices like eggs benedict, smoked salmon and scrambled egg, pizzas, cottage pie and vegetarian pasta as well as soup, goats cheese ravioli with wild mushrooms and a tomato and herb sauce, pigeon breast with smoked bacon and prune sauce, corn-fed chicken with pea and parma ham risotto, rack and shoulder of lamb with truffle mash and a beetroot salad, rare-breed pork with black pudding and spiced puy lentils, and puddings like carpaccio of pineapple with cinnamon ice-cream and nougat and dark chocolate ganache with peanut ice-cream and cherries in kirsch. *Starters/Snacks: £4.25 to £8.95. Main Courses: £9.50 to £20.00. Puddings: £3.95 to £5.95*

Free house ~ Licensee Edward Boynton ~ Real ale ~ Bar food (12-2, 6-9.30; all day weekends) ~ Restaurant ~ (01845) 567391 ~ Well-behaved children welcome until 7.30pm (after that in dining room only) ~ Dogs allowed in bedrooms ~ Open 11-11(10.30 Sun) ~ Bedrooms: £55B/£80B

Recommended by Melvyn Dyson, J K Parry, Jon Clarke, Ian Malone, J F M and M West, Jill and Julian Tasker, Roger and Lesley Everett

RIPLEY   SE2860   MAP 7

Boars Head ♀ 🍺 🛏

Off A61 Harrogate—Ripon; HG3 3AY

Smart hotel with friendly bar/bistro, several real ales, an excellent wine list, good food and helpful service; comfortable bedrooms

Much emphasis is, of course, placed on the hotel and restaurant side here but they do have a bar/bistro where they keep Black Sheep, Daleside Pride of England, Hambleton White Boar and Theakston Best on handpump, 20 wines by the glass and several malt whiskies – the atmosphere is relaxed and informal. There are green checked tablecloths (most of the tables are arranged to form individual booths), warm yellow walls with jolly little drawings of cricketers or huntsmen running along the bottom, a boar's head (part of the family coat of arms), an interesting religious carving and a couple of cricket bats; efficient staff even when very busy. Some of the furnishings in the hotel came from the attic of next door Ripley Castle, where the Ingilbys have lived for over 650 years. A pleasant little garden has plenty of tables. The bedrooms were being refurbished as we went to press.

🍴 Using a lot of their own produce grown in the kitchen garden within Ripley Castle, the good bar food includes lunchtime sandwiches and baked potatoes, soup, chicken and duck terrine with chutney, mushroom stroganoff, old spot gammon steak with a free-range egg, barnsley chop with rosemary mash and onion gravy, baked cod with chorizo, spatchcock chicken marinated in chilli, rosemary and lemon, and puddings such as apple and blackberry crumble with vanilla anglaise and sticky toffee pudding with butterscotch sauce. *Starters/Snacks: £4.50 to £7.00. Main Courses: £9.95 to £17.00. Puddings: £4.50 to £6.00*

Free house ~ Licensee Sir Thomas Ingilby ~ Real ale ~ Bar food ~ Restaurant ~ (01423) 771888 ~ Children welcome ~ Dogs welcome ~ Open 11-11; 12-10 Sun ~ Bedrooms: £105B/£125B

Recommended by Dr and Mrs J Temporal, John Saul, the Didler, Adrian and Dawn Collinge, Jeremy King, Susan and Nigel Brookes, Ian and Joan Blackwell

RIPPONDEN
SE0419   MAP 7

Old Bridge ♀ ◀

From A58, best approach is Elland Road (opposite Golden Lion), park opposite the church in pub's car park and walk back over ancient hump-back bridge; HX6 4DF

Pleasant old pub by medieval bridge with relaxed communicating rooms, half a dozen real ales, quite a few wines by the glass, lots of whiskies and well liked food

If you're not finding it easy to locate this 14th-c pub (and there's no traditional pub sign outside) – head for the church. There are three communicating rooms, each on a slightly different level and all with a relaxed, friendly atmosphere. Oak settles are built into the window recesses of the thick stone walls, and there are antique oak tables, rush-seated chairs, a few well chosen pictures and prints and a big woodburning stove. The fine range of real ales on handpump might be Timothy Taylors Best, Golden Best and Landlord and three changing guests like Bridestones Pennine Gold, Copper Dragon Black Gold and Goose Eye Golden Goose; also, quite a few foreign bottled beers, a dozen wines by the glass and 30 malt whiskies. The medieval pack-horse bridge over the little River Ryburn is lovely and the pub has a garden overlooking the water. More reports please.

🍴 On weekday lunchtimes, bar food only includes sandwiches and soup or the popular help-yourself carvery and salad buffet; at weekends and in the evening (but not Saturday or Sunday evening), there might be an award-winning pork pie with mushy peas, black pudding and home-smoked chicken croquette, king scallops on carrot and ginger purée with a pea shoot salad, steak in ale pie, corn-fed chicken kiev, seafood pancakes with a creamy dill sauce, duck breast with hash brown of braised duck leg and a red wine sauce, and puddings. *Starters/Snacks: £3.50 to £6.50. Main Courses: £8.00 to £12.50. Puddings: £4.00*

Free house ~ Licensees Tim and Lindsay Eaton Walker ~ Real ale ~ Bar food (12-2(2.30 Sat), 6.30-9.30; not Sat or Sun evenings) ~ (01422) 822595 ~ Children must be seated away from bar and leave before 8pm ~ Open 12-3, 5.30-11; 12-11(10.30 Sun) Fri and Sat

Recommended by G Dobson

ROBIN HOOD'S BAY
NZ9505   MAP 10

Laurel

Village signposted off A171 S of Whitby; YO22 4SE

Unspoilt little pub in pretty fishing village, neat friendly bar and real ales

Quite unchanging and unspoilt, this little local has a charming landlord and is at the heart of one of the prettiest and most unspoilt fishing villages on the north-east coast. The beamed and welcoming main bar is neatly kept and decorated with old local photographs, Victorian prints and brasses, and lager bottles from all over the world. There's an open fire and Adnams Best and Theakstons Best and Old Peculier on handpump; darts, board games and piped music. In summer, the hanging baskets and window boxes are lovely. They have a self-contained apartment for two people.

🍴 You can buy sandwiches from the Old Bakery Tearooms and eat them in the pub.

Free house ~ Licensee Brian Catling ~ Real ale ~ No credit cards ~ (01947) 880400 ~ Children in snug bar only ~ Dogs welcome ~ Open 12-11(10.30 Sun); opening time 2pm Mon-Thurs in winter

Recommended by Brian and Anna Marsden, the Didler

Tipping is not normal for bar meals, and not usually expected.

ROECLIFFE

SE3765 MAP 7

Crown ⓦ ♟ ⇌

Off A168 just W of Boroughbridge; handy for A1(M) junction 48; YO51 9LY

Smartly updated and attractively placed pub with a civilised bar, good enterprising food and fine choice of drinks; new bedrooms

The country-style bedrooms in this well run inn are now open and are proving very popular. It's a busy place and run with a great deal of enthusiasm by the Mainey family who offer all their customers a genuinely warm welcome. The bar has a contemporary colour scheme of dark reds and near-whites with attractive prints carefully grouped and lit; one area has chunky pine tables on flagstones and another part, with a log fire, has dark tables on plaid carpet. Greene King IPA, Shepherd Neame Spitfire, Theakstons Best and Timothy Taylors Landlord on handpump, 20 wines by the glass and home-made lemonade; neat, helpful staff. For meals, you have a choice between a small candlelit olive-green bistro with nice tables, a longcase clock and one or two paintings and a more formal restaurant; at weekends, it's wise to book ahead. The pub faces the village green.

🍽 Using only small local suppliers and game from local estates, smoking their own fish and baking fresh daily bread, the excellent contemporary bar food includes lunchtime sandwiches, soup (the crab one is delicious), a platter of their home-cured fish, sweet soy belly pork on asian vegetables with ginger and lime, bangers with a butter bean cassoulet, a little yorkshire pudding filled with spiced leeks over celeriac and potato dauphinoise, corn-fed chicken breast with roasted peppers and a chorizo cream sauce, steak and kidney in ale pie, sea bream fillet with a chive beurre blanc, and puddings such as coconut panna cotta with fresh banana ice-cream and fresh mango syrup and double chocolate brownie with warm chocolate sauce and amaretti ice-cream; smashing Sunday roasts. *Starters/Snacks: £4.50 to £7.95. Main Courses: £9.95 to £15.95. Puddings: £5.95 to £6.95*

Free house ~ Licensee Karl Mainey ~ Real ale ~ Bar food (12-2.30, 6-9.30; 12-7 Sun) ~ Restaurant ~ (01423) 322300 ~ Children welcome ~ Dogs allowed in bar ~ Open 12-3, 5-11; 12-11 Sun and Sat ~ Bedrooms: £110B/£120B

Recommended by WW, Keith and Sue Ward, Les and Sandra Brown, Michael and Maggie Betton, Peter and Josie Fawcett, Hunter and Christine Wright

SANDHUTTON

SE3882 MAP 10

Kings Arms ⬛

A167, 1 mile N of A61 Thirsk—Ripon; YO7 4RW

Good chef/landlord in cheerful and appealing pub with friendly service and comfortable furnishings; bedrooms

What comes across very strongly in this charmingly refurbished village-edge pub is the desire to look after customers – and send them away happy with their visit. An unusual idea is that in the evening you choose your fresh meat or fish from a glass-fronted counter and discuss any individual cooking requirements with the chefs; our readers have really enjoyed this. The bustling bar has an unusual circular woodburner in one corner, a high central table with four equally high stools, high-backed brown leather-seated dining chairs around light pine tables, a couple of cushioned wicker armchairs, some attractive modern bar stools and photographs of the pub in years gone by. A shelf has some odd knick-knacks such as fish jaws and a bubble-gum machine, there are various pub games and a flatscreen TV. Black Sheep Best, Hambleton Stud and White Boar and John Smiths on handpump, several wines by the glass and efficient, friendly service. The two connecting dining rooms have similar furnishings to the bar (though there's also a nice big table with smart high-backed dining chairs), arty flower photographs on the cream walls and a shelf above the small woodburning stove with more knick-knacks and some candles. There's no car park so parking is slightly haphazard. There are plans to add more bedrooms and open a village shop.

🍽 Cooked by the chef/patron, the good, interesting bar food includes sandwiches, soup, black pudding with dry-cured bacon, apple and madeira sauce, freshly battered scampi, roasted mediterranean vegetable lasagne, chicken suprême filled with feta cheese and olives, monkfish wrapped in pancetta, venison fillet on wild mushrooms with blackberries and blueberries, a giant fishcake with chilli sauce, pork tenderloin with ham and stilton with a sage and cream sauce, and puddings like gooseberry crème brûlée and dark chocolate and macadamia nut cake with a rich chocolate sauce. *Starters/Snacks: £3.00 to £5.95. Main Courses: £7.00 to £17.00. Puddings: £3.95 to £7.95*

Free house ~ Licensees Raymond and Alexander Boynton ~ Real ale ~ Bar food (12-2.30, 5.30-9; 12-5 Sun; not Sun evening) ~ Restaurant ~ (01845) 587887 ~ Children welcome ~ Open 12-11 ~ Bedrooms: £35S/£60S

Recommended by Richard Cole, Michael Doswell, John and Eleanor Holdsworth

SAWLEY   SE2467   MAP 7

Sawley Arms ♀

Village signposted off B6265 W of Ripon; HG4 3EQ

Old-fashioned dining pub with good restauranty food, decent house wines and comfortable furnishings in small carpeted rooms; pretty garden

Now run by Mrs Hawes's son and daughter-in-law, this is a spotlessly kept dining pub with good restaurant-style food. It's ultra-civilised in a decorous sort of way, though locals do pop in for a chat and a drink (mainly in the evening). The small turkey-carpeted rooms have log fires and comfortable furniture ranging from small softly cushioned armed dining chairs and sofas, to the wing armchairs down a couple of steps in a side snug; maybe daily papers and magazines to read; quiet piped music. There's also a conservatory; good house wines. In fine weather you can sit in the pretty garden where the flowering tubs and baskets are lovely; they have two stone cottages in the grounds for rent. Fountains Abbey (the most extensive of the great monastic remains – floodlit on late summer Friday and Saturday evenings, with a choir on the Saturday) – is not far away.

⑪ As well as early bird offers and a new 'take and bake' menu (you can also take home their chutneys, relishes and so forth), the good food includes sandwiches, soup with croûtons, duck liver and orange pâté, deep-fried brie with cranberry, apple and ginger chutney, popular pies (local game, vegetarian, chicken, leek and mushroom and steak in red wine), lamb shank with rosemary, sweet potato dauphinoise and madeira gravy, plaice mornay, pork, apricot and sage cassoulet, and puddings like butterscotch pudding with butterscotch sauce and apple pie. *Starters/Snacks: £2.95 to £7.95. Main Courses: £9.95 to £14.75. Puddings: £2.95 to £5.75*

Free house ~ Licensee Mrs June Hawes ~ Bar food (12-2.30, 6.30-9.30) ~ Restaurant ~ (01765) 620642 ~ Well behaved children in conservatory but phone beforehand ~ Open 11.30-3, 6-11; closed Mon evenings in winter ~ Bedrooms: /£50B

Recommended by Ian and Joan Blackwell, Janet and Peter Race, Alan Thwaite, Ian and Nita Cooper

SHEFFIELD   SK3687   MAP 7

Fat Cat ◖ £

23 Alma Street; S3 8SA

Super own-brewed beers and guest ales in friendly, bustling town local, plenty of bottled beers, too, and remarkably cheap tasty food; brewery visits

With incredibly cheap food and a fantastic range of up to ten real ales, it's not surprising that this well run and friendly town local is always deservedly busy. As well as their own-brewed Kelham Island Best Bitter, Pale Rider and Easy Rider, there's Timothy Taylors Landlord and guests from breweries such as East Coast, Hydes, Sheffield, Rudgate, Wold Top, Yorkshire Dales and so forth all well kept on handpump. Also, draught and bottled belgian beers, Weston's cider and country wines. The two small downstairs rooms have brewery-related prints on the walls, coal fires, simple wooden tables and cushioned seats and jugs, bottles and some advertising mirrors; cards and dominoes and maybe the pub cat wandering around. The upstairs room has a TV for sport. The Brewery Visitor Centre (you can book brewery trips on (0114) 249 4804) has framed beer mats, pump clips and prints on the walls. There are picnic-sets in a fairylit back courtyard.

🍴 **Mainly vegetarian and often gluten free, the extremely cheap bar food includes sandwiches, winter soup, ploughman's, nutty mushroom or steak pies, roasted stuffed peppers, leek, cider and butterbean casserole, spicy mince and rice, cheese quiche, vegetable moussaka, and puddings such as rhubarb crumble and spotted dick; Monday evening chicken and vegetable curries and Sunday roast.** *Starters/Snacks: £3.00. Main Courses: £4.50 to £5.00. Puddings: £1.75*

Own brew ~ Licensee Duncan Shaw ~ Real ale ~ Bar food (12-3, 6-8; not Sun evening) ~ (0114) 249 4801 ~ Children welcome away from main bar ~ Dogs allowed in bar ~ Open 12-11 (midnight Sat)

Recommended by Giles and Annie Francis, the Didler, Marian and Andrew Ruston, John and Sharon Hancock, DC, Ian and Helen Stafford, Ian and Debs, David Carr

Kelham Island Tavern 🍺 £

Kelham Island; S3 8RY

Busy little local with ten changing real ales, basic but decent pub food, a friendly welcome and pretty back garden

There's always a good mix of customers in this busy backstreet local keen to enjoy the fantastic range of real ales here – and the friendly welcome. It's like a permanent beer festival with up to 13 well kept interesting ales on handpump (there's always a mild and a stout or porter) served by well organised and knowledgeable staff – and they try to stick to yorkshire breweries such as Acorn, Black Sheep, Bradfield, Kelham Island, Roosters, Rudgate, Sheffield, Thwaites, Wold Top and Yorkshire Dales; proper ciders, too. Furnishings are pubby and traditional, there's some nice artwork on the yellow walls and maybe Puss Cat the ginger pub cat. The flower-filled and unusual back courtyard garden has plenty of seats and tables and a woodburning stove for chilly evenings. Their front window boxes regularly win awards.

🍴 **Cheap, well liked bar food includes filled cobs, ploughman's, filled baked potatoes, soup, pâté and toast, pies such as steak or fish, three vegetarian dishes, and puddings such as treacle sponge.** *Starters/Snacks: £1.60 to £3.00. Main Courses: £5.00 to £6.00. Puddings: £2.50*

Free house ~ Licensee Trevor Wraith ~ Real ale ~ Bar food (12-3; not Sun) ~ (0114) 272 2482 ~ Children welcome ~ Dogs allowed in bar ~ Live folk Sun evenings ~ Open 12-11.30(midnight Fri and Sat)

Recommended by Simon Wigglesworth-Baker, Bruce Bird

New Barrack 🍺 £

601 Penistone Road, Hillsborough; S6 2GA

Lively and friendly pub with 11 real ales and a fine range of other drinks, good value food and lots going on

There's always something happening at this popular, lively pub. Every weekday evening there's a different theme from chess club to games night to general knowledge quiz competitions and at the weekend, there's live music and comedy acts; it's even busier on match days. The comfortable front lounge has upholstered seats, old pine floors and a log fire, the tap room has another log fire and darts, and the back room can be used for small functions. TV, dominoes, cards, cribbage and daily papers to read. As well as Castle Rock Black Gold, Harvest Pale, Preservation Fine Ale and Screech Owl, they have around seven guest beers such as Acorn Barnsley Bitter, Batemans GHA Pale Ale and a seasonal beer, Bradfield Farmers Bitter and Farmers Brown Cow, Hook Norton Hooky Gold and Oakham JHB – all on handpump; also, real cider, a range of bottled belgian beers and 28 malt whiskies. The small walled back garden has won awards. Local parking is tricky.

🍴 **Tasty bar food includes sandwiches and filled baguettes, all day breakfast, pie and peas, pizzas, sausage and mash, mixed grill, and their very popular beer-battered cod.** *Starters/Snacks: £1.99 to £2.99. Main Courses: £3.50 to £10.99. Puddings: £1.50 to £3.50*

Castle Rock ~ Managers Kevin and Stephanie Woods ~ Real ale ~ Bar food (11-3, 5-9 (Fri and Sat light suppers till midnight); 12-4, 7-9 Sun) ~ (0114) 234 9148 ~ Children welcome until 9pm ~ Dogs welcome ~ Live music Fri and Sat and comedy night first Sun evening of the month ~ Open 11-11(midnight Fri and Sat); 12-11 Sun

Recommended by David Carr, the Didler, JJW, CMW

SHELLEY   SE2112   MAP 7

Three Acres 🍴 � 🛏

Roydhouse (not signposted); from B6116 heading for Skelmanthorpe, turn left in Shelley (signposted Flockton, Elmley, Elmley Moor) and go up lane for 2 miles towards radio mast; HD8 8LR

Delicious food and friendly service in busy, smart dining pub, several real ales; a fine choice of other drinks and relaxed atmosphere; good bedrooms and lovely views

There's no doubt that this civilised former coaching inn places firm emphasis on the hotel and dining side – which is excellent and much enjoyed by our readers – but locals do still drop in for a pint and a chat and they keep Black Sheep Best, Tetleys and Timothy Taylors Landlord on handpump, up to 40 whiskies and a fantastic (if not cheap) choice of wines with at least 17 by the glass; attentive staff. The roomy lounge bar has a relaxed, informal atmosphere, tankards hanging from the main beam, high bar chairs and stools, button-back leather sofas, old prints and so forth. To be sure of a table you must book quite a way ahead – try to get a place with a view across to Emley Moor; piped music. There are also more formal dining rooms.

🍽 Generous helpings of good, interesting – if pricey – food might include lunchtime sandwiches and ploughman's, soup, pork and venison chorizo with celeriac rémoulade and a roast garlic and red pepper salsa, smoked salmon scotch egg with anchovy toast soldiers and curried mayonnaise, beer-battered fresh haddock with home-made tartare sauce, minced rib-eye burger with bacon, cheese and sweet tomato chutney, mushroom, wild garlic, mascarpone and parmesan risotto, ox cheek and kidney pudding, half a free-range chicken with dry-cured bacon, black pudding and star anise and onion gravy, raised mutton pie with parsley sauce, and puddings such as vanilla panna cotta with mixed berry compote and rhubarb and free-range duck egg custard tart; Sunday roasts. *Starters/Snacks: £5.95 to £10.95. Main Courses: £14.95 to £21.75. Puddings: £7.95*

Free house ~ Licensees Neil Truelove and Brian Orme ~ Real ale ~ Bar food (12-2, 6.30-9.30) ~ Restaurant ~ (01484) 602606 ~ Children welcome ~ Open 12-3, 6-11(10.30 Sun) ~ Bedrooms: £80B/£120B

Recommended by Andy and Jill Kassube, Gordon and Margaret Ormondroyd

SINNINGTON   SE7485   MAP 10

Fox & Hounds 🍴 ♥ 🛏

Just off A170 W of Pickering; YO62 6SQ

Carefully run coaching inn with fine choice of drinks, imaginative food and comfortable bar; bedrooms

After a stroll through the pretty village, this neatly kept coaching inn is just the place for a drink or a meal. The carpeted bar has various pictures and old artefacts, a woodburning stove and comfortable wall seats and carver chairs around the tables. The curved corner bar counter has Black Sheep and Copper Dragon Best Bitter on handpump, several wines by the glass and some rare malt whiskies. There's also a lounge and separate restaurant. The cartoons in the gents' are worth a peek; piped music. In front of the building are some picnic-sets, with more in the garden, and the quiet bedrooms are popular with our readers.

🍽 Well presented and especially good, the bar food might include lunchtime sandwiches, soup, seared scallops with black pudding, roast apple and leeks and scrumpy vinaigrette, twice-baked blue cheese soufflé, beer-battered fresh haddock with home-made tartare sauce, pork and sage medallions with pickled walnuts, prunes and crispy crackling, calves liver with a bacon and red wine sauce, a trio of guinea fowl with a different sauce for each, and puddings like dark chocolate panna cotta and treacle tart with orange anglaise and ginger ice-cream. *Starters/Snacks: £4.95 to £8.95. Main Courses: £9.95 to £16.95. Puddings: £5.25 to £6.25*

Free house ~ Licensees Andrew and Catherine Stephens ~ Real ale ~ Bar food ~ Restaurant (evening) ~ (01751) 431577 ~ Children welcome away from public bar ~ Dogs allowed in bar and bedrooms ~ Open 12-2, 6-11; 6.30 evening opening in winter ~ Bedrooms: £69S(£79B)/£100S(£110B)

Recommended by Mr and Mrs D Hammond, Janet and Peter Race, Pat and Stewart Gordon, Martin Cawley, Mrs Romey Heaton, Marian and Andrew Ruston, M S Catling, Leslie and Barbara Owen, Martin Clerk, Pat and Tony Hinkins

SKIPTON   SD9851   MAP 7

Narrow Boat 🍺 £
Victoria Street; pub signed down alley off Coach Street; BD23 1JE

Extended pub near canal with eight real ales, proper home cooking and a good mix of customers

'I wish I lived a bit nearer' says one of our readers wistfully about this lively extended pub. It's a friendly place with a great atmosphere, a good mix of both locals and visitors and a fine choice of up to eight real ales on handpump: Black Sheep, Copper Dragon Golden Pippin and Timothy Taylors Landlord with guests such as Ilkley Gold, Kelham Island Best Bitter, Naylors Pinnacle Bitter, Riverhead Butterley Bitter and Salamander Stout. Draught german and belgian beers, a continental beer menu, farm cider and perry. The bar has old brewery posters and nice mirrors decorated with framed beer advertisements on the walls, church pews, dining chairs and stools around wooden tables, and an upstairs gallery area with an interesting canal mural. The pub is down a cobbled alley with picnic-sets under a front colonnade; the Leeds & Liverpool Canal is nearby.

🍴 **Reasonably priced and well liked, the bar food** includes lunchtime sandwiches and ploughman's, soup, pork pie with mint sauce and peas, ham hock terrine with piccalilli, ham and egg, a burger with cheese and horseradish mayonnaise, a pie of the day, sausage and mash, butternut squash risotto with blue cheese, fish, chips and mushy peas, and puddings. *Starters/Snacks: £3.50 to £4.95. Main Courses: £6.95 to £11.95. Puddings: £3.95 to £4.95*

Market Town Taverns ~ Manager Tim Hughes ~ Real ale ~ Bar food (12-2.30, 5.30-9; 12-4 Sun; not Sun evening) ~ (01756) 797922 ~ Children welcome if dining ~ Dogs welcome ~ Folk club Mon evenings ~ Open 12-11

Recommended by Dr Kevan Tucker, Jo Lilley, Simon Calvert, Mrs Hazel Rainer, the Didler, Dennis Jones, Steve Nye, Alan and Eve Harding, Charles and Pauline Stride

SLEDMERE   SE9364   MAP 8

Triton
B1252/B1253 junction, NW of Great Driffield; YO25 3XQ

Handsome inn in fine countryside with an open-plan interior, traditional furnishings and values, fine range of drinks (50 gins) and enjoyable food; bedrooms

By the walls of Sledmere House and using produce and game from the estate grounds, this neatly kept 18th-c inn has a genuinely friendly landlord. It's open-plan with a determinedly old-fashioned atmosphere, dark wooden farmhouse furniture and some bar stools by the counter on the red patterned carpet, 15 clocks ranging from a grandfather to a cuckoo, lots of willow pattern plates, all manner of paintings and pictures of the area and an open fire. They don't take bookings except in the restaurant area and there's a happy mix of drinkers and diners. John Smiths, Tetleys, Timothy Taylors Landlord and Wold Top Bitter on handpump, a dozen wines by the glass and over 50 different gins.

🍴 Honest bar food includes sandwiches, filled baked potatoes, ploughman's, soup, garlic and chilli prawns, chicken liver pâté with plum and apple chutney, gammon with egg or pineapple, chicken breast in a creamy white wine and mushroom sauce, steak in ale pie, thai fish curry, half a roast duckling with orange and apricot sauce, and puddings such as chocolate amaretti torte and raspberry cheesecake; popular Sunday roasts. *Starters/Snacks: £3.95 to £6.95. Main Courses: £8.95 to £14.95. Puddings: £4.95*

Free house ~ Licensee Lance Moxon ~ Real ale ~ Bar food (12-2, 6-9; 12-7.30 Sun) ~ Restaurant ~ (01377) 236078 ~ Children welcome until 8pm ~ Open 12-3, 6-11; 12-9 Sun; closed Mon lunchtime in winter ~ Bedrooms: £45S/£70S

Recommended by David S Allen, WW, Mrs R Mehlman

SNAPE

SE2684   MAP 10

Castle Arms

Off B6268 Masham—Bedale; DL8 2TB

Hospitable pub, handy for the A1, with friendly service, flagstoned rooms, open fires and fair choice of drinks and food; bedrooms

This is an enjoyable and immaculately kept pub a little off the beaten track in a very pretty village – but also handy for the A1. It's homely inside and the flagstoned bar has an open fire, straightforward pubby tables and chairs, a few bar stools, lots of horsebrasses along beams and a relaxed, happy atmosphere. The dining room (also flagstoned) has candlesticks along the mantelpiece above another open fire and plenty of dark tables and chairs. Banks's Bitter, Jennings Bitter and Marstons Pedigree on handpump and several malt whiskies; friendly, welcoming service. There are picnic-sets at the front with more in the courtyard. The pub is surrounded by fine walks on the Yorkshire Dales and the North York Moors and close to Thorp Perrow Arboretum.

🍴 Popular bar food includes sandwiches, soup, pheasant, duck and chicken liver terrine with pear and red onion chutney, mussels in a rich tomato sauce, mediterranean vegetable tartlet, beer-battered fresh haddock, pork tenderloin strips in a coconut curry sauce, game hotpot, roasted monkfish on saffron mash with crispy pancetta and a scallop and Pernod sauce, and puddings such as peanut brittle cheesecake and black forest trifle with kirsch-soaked cherries and doughnut in a belgian chocolate custard. *Starters/Snacks: £4.00 to £6.95. Main Courses: £5.95 to £16.95. Puddings: £4.00 to £4.95*

Marstons ~ Lease Sandra Haxby ~ Real ale ~ Bar food ~ Restaurant ~ (01677) 470270 ~ Children welcome ~ Dogs allowed in bar and bedrooms ~ Open 12-3, 6(7 Sun)-11 ~ Bedrooms: £65S/£85S

Recommended by Michael Doswell, Janet and Peter Race, WW

SOUTH DALTON

SE9645   MAP 8

Pipe & Glass 🍴 🍷

West End; brown sign to pub off B1248 NW of Beverley; HU17 7PN
YORKSHIRE DINING PUB OF THE YEAR

Attractive dining pub with a proper bar area, real ales, interesting modern cooking, good service, garden and front terrace; new bedrooms

Two new luxury suites with their own terrace and views over Dalton Park have been opened up here and there's also a new extension with disabled and baby-changing facilities. Most customers come to this attractive whitewashed dining pub to enjoy the excellent food cooked by the young landlord but there's a proper bar area, too. This bar area – where they don't take bookings – is beamed and bow-windowed with a log fire, some old prints, plush stools and traditional pubby chairs around a mix of tables and even high-backed settles. Beyond that, all is airy and comfortably contemporary, angling around past some soft modern dark leather chesterfields into a light restaurant area overlooking the park, with high-backed stylish dining chairs around well spaced country tables on bare boards. The decorations – a row of serious cookery books and framed big-name restaurant menus – show how high the licensee aims. Black Sheep with guest beers from breweries like Copper Dragon and Wold Top on handpump, ten wines by the glass, over 50 malt whiskies and Old Rosie cider. Service is friendly and prompt by bright and attentive young staff; piped music. There are tables out on the garden's peaceful lawn beside the park and picnic-sets on the front terrace; people say the yew tree is some 500 years old. The village is charming and its elegant Victorian church spire, 62 metres (204 ft) tall, is visible for miles around.

Inventive and extremely good, the food cooked by the young chef/patron might include lunchtime sandwiches and ploughman's, soup, honey-smoked duck breast with a mini confit duck scotch egg and blood orange dressing, crispy rabbit rissoles with cockle and caper vinaigrette, sorrel and air-dried ham, old spot pork chop with black pudding forcemeat, butternut squash purée and sage, fish pie with cheddar crumb, brown shrimp and fennel salad, specials like fillet of wild turbot with braised oxtail, sea perslane, curly kale colcannon and monkfish cheek fritter, and puddings such as ginger burnt cream with rhubarb compote and a trio of apple puddings – crumble, sponge and sorbet. Starters/Snacks: £4.25 to £9.95. Main Courses: £9.95 to £21.95. Puddings: £4.95 to £9.95

Free house ~ Licensees Kate and James Mackenzie ~ Real ale ~ Bar food (12-2, 6-9.30; 12-4 Sun; not Sun evening or Mon (except bank hols)) ~ Restaurant ~ (01430) 810246 ~ Children welcome ~ Open 12-11(10.30 Sun); closed Mon (except bank hols) and two weeks in Jan ~ Bedrooms: /£150B
Recommended by Richard Cole, Marlene and Jim Godfrey

SUTTON UPON DERWENT   SE7047 MAP 7

St Vincent Arms

B1228 SE of York; YO41 4BN

Consistently cheerful, with eight real ales plus other drinks, well liked bar food and more elaborate evening choices and friendly service

Drawing customers in from far and wide, this cheerful, friendly pub offers eight real ales and enjoyable bar food. There's a bustling parlour-style front bar with panelling, traditional high-backed settles, a cushioned bow-window seat, windsor chairs and a gas-effect coal fire; another lounge and separate dining room open off here; to be sure of a table, it's best to book in advance. Fullers London Pride, ESB and a seasonal ale, Old Mill Bitter, Timothy Taylors Landlord and Golden Best, York Yorkshire Terrier and Wells & Youngs Bombardier on handpump, 14 wines and two champagnes by the glass and several malt whiskies. There are seats in the garden. The pub is named after the admiral who was granted the village and lands by the nation as thanks for his successful commands – and for coping with Nelson's infatuation with Lady Hamilton. Handy for the Yorkshire Air Museum.

Always of a high standard, the popular bar food includes lunchtime sandwiches and filled ciabattas, soup, cornish crab mayonnaise, pork, apricot and black pudding terrine with home-made piccalilli, battered haddock with mushy peas, vegetable stir fry, lamb curry, steak and mushroom in ale pie, beef stroganoff, specials such as toulouse sausages on bubble and squeak mash and a white onion sauce, guinea fowl breast wrapped in parma ham with a madeira, mushroom and cream sauce, and puddings like baked lemon cheesecake. Starters/Snacks: £5.00 to £7.00. Main Courses: £9.50 to £20.00. Puddings: £4.00 to £4.95

Free house ~ Licensee Simon Hopwood ~ Real ale ~ Bar food ~ Restaurant ~ (01904) 608349 ~ Children welcome ~ Dogs allowed in bar ~ Open 11.30-3, 6-11; 12-3, 6.30-10.30 Sun
Recommended by Derek and Sylvia Stephenson, Andy and Jill Kassube, G Dobson, Stanley and Annie Matthews, David and Ruth Hollands, Pierre Richterich

---

'Children welcome' means the pub says it lets children inside without any special restriction. If it allows them in, but to restricted areas such as an eating area or family room, we specify this. Some pubs may impose an evening time limit. We do not mention limits after 9pm as we assume children are home by then.

THORNTON WATLASS

SE2385   MAP 10

Buck 🍺 🛏️

Village signposted off B6268 Bedale—Masham; HG4 4AH

Friendly village pub with five real ales, traditional bars, well liked food and popular Sunday jazz

The long-serving licensees have now been at this honest village pub for 24 years and it remains very much the heart of the local community – though there's always a warm welcome for visitors, too. The pleasantly traditional bar on the right has upholstered old-fashioned wall settles on the carpet, a fine mahogany bar counter, a high shelf packed with ancient bottles, several mounted fox masks and brushes and a brick fireplace. The Long Room (which overlooks the cricket green) has large prints of old Thornton Watlass cricket teams, signed bats, cricket balls and so forth. Black Sheep, Consett Ale Works Steel Town Bitter, Durham Magus, Hambleton Stud and Wold Top Bitter on handpump, a few wines by the glass and over 40 interesting malt whiskies; darts, cribbage and dominoes. The sheltered garden has an equipped children's play area and summer barbecues and they have their own cricket team; quoits. More reports please.

🍴 **Well liked bar food includes sandwiches, soup, scallops with garlic butter and gruyère, wensleydale cheese and red onion marmalade galette, a charcuterie board, omelettes, spinach and ricotta pasta, gammon with egg or pineapple, steak in ale pie, battered fish and chips, lambs liver and smoked bacon with caramelised onion gravy, daily specials such as chicken curry and grilled rib-eye steak with brandy and pepper sauce, and puddings.** *Starters/Snacks: £4.25 to £8.00. Main Courses: £8.95 to £16.00. Puddings: £4.95*

Free house ~ Licensees Michael and Margaret Fox ~ Real ale ~ Bar food (12-2(3 Sun), 6.30-9.15) ~ Restaurant ~ (01677) 422461 ~ Children welcome ~ Dogs allowed in bedrooms ~ Jazz Sun lunchtimes ~ Open 11-11 ~ Bedrooms: £55(£65S)/£80(£90B)

Recommended by Mr and Mrs Barrie, Terry Mizen

WASS

SE5579   MAP 7

Wombwell Arms 🛏️

Back road W of Ampleforth; or follow brown tourist-attraction sign for Byland Abbey off A170 Thirsk—Helmsley; YO61 4BE

Consistently enjoyable village pub, friendly, bustling atmosphere, good mix of locals and visitors, tasty bar food and real ales; bedrooms

With well kept beers and a warm welcome, this bustling village pub is popular with both locals and visitors. The two bars are cosy and neatly kept with plenty of simple character and log fires and the walls of the Poacher's Bar are hung with brewery memorabilia. Theakstons Best and Old Peculier and Timothy Taylors Landlord on handpump, nine wines by the glass (quite a few from Mrs Walker's South Africa) and several malt whiskies; darts. The two restaurants are incorporated into a 17th-c former granary and there are seats outside. They hope to open their microbrewery soon.

🍴 **As well as sandwiches and filled ciabattas, the bar food includes ploughman's, soup, crab and ginger cakes with sweet chilli sauce, pork and apple sausages with mash and gravy, steak in ale pie, bobotie (a south african fruit curry), game casserole, king prawn and scallop risotto, specials like gilt head bream with tomato salsa and gammon with caramelised pineapple and a fried egg, and puddings such as orange and lemon custard tart with lime sorbet and triple chocolate delight.** *Starters/Snacks: £4.25 to £7.50. Main Courses: £9.45 to £18.95. Puddings: £4.95 to £5.25*

Free house ~ Licensees Ian and Eunice Walker ~ Real ale ~ Bar food (12-2(2.30 Sat, 3 Sun), 6.30-9(9.30 Fri and Sat); 12-3, 6.30-8.30) ~ Restaurant ~ (01347) 868280 ~ Children welcome ~ Dogs allowed in bar ~ Open 12-3, 6-11; 12-11 Sat; 12-4, 6-10.30 Sun ~ Bedrooms: £50S/£70S

Recommended by WW, Pat and Graham Williamson, Janet and Peter Race, Val Carter, Edward Leetham, Margaret Dickinson, Pat and Tony Martin

WATH IN NIDDERDALE

SE1467 MAP 7

Sportsmans Arms ⑪ ♀ ⇔

Nidderdale road off B6265 in Pateley Bridge; village and pub signposted over hump-back bridge on right after a couple of miles; HG3 5PP

Beautifully placed restaurant-with-rooms plus welcoming bar, real ales and super choice of other drinks, and imaginative food; comfortable bedrooms

The charming and friendly Mr Carter has now been running this civilised restaurant-with-rooms for over 30 years – and his enthusiasm has not waned. Of course, much emphasis is placed on the hotel side and the fantastic food but there's a welcoming bar with an open fire and Black Sheep and Timothy Taylors Best Bitter on handpump – and locals do still pop in for a pint and a chat. There's a very sensible and extensive wine list with five by the glass (including champagne), over 40 malt whiskies, several russian vodkas and Thatcher's cider; maybe quiet piped music. Benches and tables outside and seats in the pretty garden; croquet. As well as their own fishing on the River Nidd, this is an ideal spot for walkers, hikers and ornithologists, and there are plenty of country houses, gardens and cities to explore. More reports please.

🍽 Using butchers who breed their own animals, trout from the next village, game shot under a mile away and fish and shellfish delivered six times a week, the first-class food might include lunchtime sandwiches, pigeon breast on wild mushroom risotto, goats cheese with caramelised red onions, roasted peppers and walnut oil, beef sausages on a butterbean and red onion sauce, noisettes of lamb on crushed aubergines with whole garlic and cherry tomato jus, smoked haddock with an egg (from their own hens) and seed mustard sauce, line-caught bass on spinach with mango salsa, and puddings like elderflower and vanilla panna cotta with local rhubarb and very popular winter berry pudding (like summer pudding); they have a lobster festival in June. *Starters/Snacks: £4.50 to £9.50. Main Courses: £9.50 to £17.80. Puddings: £3.50 to £7.50*

Free house ~ Licensee Ray Carter ~ Real ale ~ Bar food ~ Restaurant ~ (01423) 711306 ~ Children welcome ~ Dogs allowed in bar ~ Open 12-2.30, 6.30-11 ~ Bedrooms: £70B/£120B

Recommended by Lynda and Trevor Smith, Peter and Josie Fawcett, Janet and Peter Race, Hugh Stafford, Richard Cole, Jill and Julian Tasker, Stephen Woad, Keith Moss, Malcolm and Pauline Pellatt

WHITBY

NZ9011 MAP 10

Duke of York

124 Church Street, Harbour East Side; YO22 4DE

Fine harbourside position, window seats and bedrooms enjoy the view, several real ales and standard bar food

This busy pub is a good place to fortify yourself before trying the famous 199 steps that lead up to the nearby abbey. Try to arrive before the lunchtime crowds so you can bag a table by the window and enjoy the view over the harbour entrance and the western cliff. The comfortable beamed lounge bar has fishing memorabilia (including the pennant numbers of local trawlers chalked on the beams) and Black Sheep, Caledonian Deuchars IPA, Copper Dragon Golden Pippin, Courage Directors and Shepherd Neame Spitfire on handpump; decent wines by the glass and quite a few malt whiskies, piped music, TV and games machine. All the bedrooms (bar one) overlook the water. There's no nearby parking.

🍽 Straightforward bar food includes sandwiches, chilli con carne, steak in ale or fish pies, large local cod or haddock in batter and seasonal crab and lobster salads. *Starters/Snacks: £2.00 to £5.95. Main Courses: £6.50 to £8.95. Puddings: £3.50*

Enterprise ~ Lease Lawrence Bradley ~ Real ale ~ Bar food (all day) ~ (01947) 600324 ~ Children welcome ~ Open 11-11(midnight Sat); 12-11 Sun ~ Bedrooms: /£60B

Recommended by David Carr, the Didler, Pete Coxon, Gwyn and Anne Wake, P Dawn

---

You can send reports directly to us at feedback@goodguides.com

WIDDOP   SD9531 MAP 7

Pack Horse 🍺 £

The Ridge; from A646 on W side of Hebden Bridge, turn off at Heptonstall signpost (as it's a sharp turn, coming out of Hebden Bridge road signs direct you around a turning circle), then follow Slack and Widdop signposts; can also be reached from Nelson and Colne, on high, pretty road; OS Sheet 103 map reference 952317; HX7 7AT

Friendly pub high up on the moors and liked by walkers for generous, tasty food, five real ales and lots of malt whiskies; bedrooms

This isolated, traditional inn is a popular place with walkers on the Pennine Way, Pennine Bridleway and Mary Townley Loop (but leave boots and backpacks in the porch). The bar has welcoming winter fires, window seats cut into the partly panelled stripped-stone walls that take in the moorland view, sturdy furnishings and horsey mementoes. Black Sheep, Copper Dragon Golden Pippin, Thwaites Bitter and a guest such as Cottage Western Glory or Thwaites Lancaster Bomber on handpump, around 130 single malt whiskies and some irish ones as well and ten wines by the glass. The friendly golden retrievers are called Padge and Purdey and the alsatian, Holly. There are seats outside and pretty summer hanging baskets and, as well as comfortable bedrooms and hearty breakfasts, they also offer a smart self-catering apartment. Service for food and beer stops promptly.

🍴 **Honest food at sensible prices includes sandwiches, ploughman's, soup, pâté, garlic mushrooms, large burgers, steak and kidney pie, lasagne, vegetable bake, gammon and eggs, and daily specials; maybe Sunday cream teas.** *Starters/Snacks: £4.95 to £6.95. Main Courses: £6.50 to £13.50. Puddings: £3.50 to £4.95*

Free house ~ Licensee Andrew Hollinrake ~ Real ale ~ Bar food (all day Sun; not Mon or weekday lunchtimes Oct-Easter) ~ (01422) 842803 ~ Children in eating area of bar until 8pm ~ Dogs allowed in bar ~ Open 12-3, 7-11; 12-10.30 Sun; closed Mon and weekday lunchtimes Oct-Easter ~ Bedrooms: £43S/£48S(£69B)

Recommended by Simon Le Fort, Ian and Nita Cooper, Geoff Boswell

YORK   SE5951 MAP 7

Maltings 🍺 £

Tanners Moat/Wellington Row, below Lendal Bridge; YO1 6HU

Bustling, friendly city pub with cheerful landlord, interesting real ales and other drinks plus good value standard food

If you fancy a break from looking at this lovely city and are after some decent, cheap food and a pint of interesting beer, this lively pub, tucked away by the riverside, is just the place to head for. The tricksy décor is entirely contrived and strong on salvaged, somewhat quirky junk: old doors for the bar front and much of the ceiling, a marvellous collection of railway signs and amusing notices, an old chocolate dispensing machine, cigarette and tobacco advertisements alongside cough and chest remedies, what looks like a suburban front door for the entrance to the ladies', partly stripped orange brick walls and even a lavatory pan in one corner. As well as Black Sheep Bitter, the jovial landlord keeps six guest ales on handpump including one each from Roosters and York and four that change daily. He also has four or five continental beers on tap, lots of bottled beers, 13 ciders and 14 country wines – and more irish whiskeys than you normally see. Get there early to be sure of a seat; games machine. The day's papers are framed in the gents'. Nearby parking is difficult; the pub is very handy for the Rail Museum and the station. Please note that dogs are allowed in only after food service.

🍴 **Straightforward bar food in generous helpings might include sandwiches, filled baked potatoes, good chips with cheese, chilli or curry, meaty or vegetarian burgers, battered haddock and beef in ale pie.** *Starters/Snacks: £3.00 to £3.95. Main Courses: £4.25 to £5.50*

You can send reports directly to us at feedback@goodguides.com

Free house ~ Licensee Shaun Collinge ~ Real ale ~ Bar food (12-2 weekdays, 12-4 weekends; not evenings) ~ No credit cards ~ (01904) 655387 ~ Children allowed only during meal times ~ Dogs allowed in bar ~ Open 11-11.30; 12-10.30 Sun

Recommended by Pat and Graham Williamson, Mark Walker, WW, Donna and Roger, the Didler, Martin Grosberg, Pete Coxon, Andy Lickfold, Peter F Marshall, Dennis Jones, Eric Larkham, Tim and Ann Newell, Andy and Jill Kassube, E McCall, T McLean, D Irving, David Carr

LUCKY DIP

Besides the fully inspected pubs, you might like to try these Lucky Dips recommended to us and described by readers (if you do, please send us reports: feedback@goodguides.com).

ABERFORD [SE4337]
Swan LS25 3AA [best to use A642 junction to leave A1; Main St N]: Busy dining pub (may have to wait for a table), vast choice of good generous food from sandwiches to bargain carvery, lots of black timber, prints, pistols, cutlasses and stuffed animals, well kept Black Sheep and Tetleys, generous glasses of wine, good friendly uniformed service, upstairs evening restaurant; children welcome, tables outside *(G Dobson, Gordon and Margaret Ormondroyd, Pete Coxon, Marlene and Jim Godfrey)*
ACKLAM [SE7861]
Half Moon YO17 9RG: Well run popular old village pub, good range of enjoyable home-made pubby food, well kept local beers, friendly staff; tiny Wolds village, good views from the front *(Andrew and Deborah Cullen, Christopher Turner)*
ADDINGHAM [SE0749]
Craven Heifer LS29 0PL [Main St]: Smartly modernised with bar and lofty beamed lounge, popular well cooked pubby food, prompt service, four well kept ales inc Timothy Taylors Landlord; a few tables out in front *(John and Eleanor Holdsworth, Gordon and Margaret Ormondroyd)*
☆ *Fleece* LS29 0LY [Main St]: Comfortable two-level pub, nice farmhouse-style eating area with good value home-made food from hearty sandwiches (home-baked bread) to sophisticated blackboard meals using good local ingredients (some from own back allotment), popular all-day Sun roasts, quick friendly service, well kept yorkshire ales, good choice of wines by the glass, low ceilings, flagstones and log fire, plain tap room with darts and dominoes, quiz nights Tues, trad jazz Weds; very busy wknds; children and dogs welcome, lots of picnic-sets on front terrace, open all day *(John and Sylvia Harrop, Gordon and Margaret Ormondroyd, Jeremy King, Tina and David Woods-Taylor)*
ALDBOROUGH [SE4166]
Ship YO51 9ER [off B6265 just S of Boroughbridge, close to A1]: Attractive 14th-c beamed village dining pub, enjoyable food from young chef, good service, Greene King, John Smiths and Theakstons, some old-fashioned seats around cast-iron framed tables, lots of copper and brass, inglenook fire, restaurant; a few picnic-sets outside,

handy for Roman remains and museum, bedrooms, open all day Sun, cl Mon lunchtime *(LYM, Susan Davey)*
ALLERTHORPE [SE7847]
Plough YO42 4RW [Main St]: Airy two-room lounge bar, popular and cheerful, with wide daily-changing choice of good sensibly priced food inc local game and nice puddings, well kept ales such as Black Sheep, Greene King IPA and Wells & Youngs Bombardier, decent house wines, well served coffee, snug alcoves, hunting prints, World War II RAF and RCAF photographs, open fires, restaurant, games extension with pool; piped music; tables out in pleasant garden, handy for Burnby Hall, open all day wknds *(Greta and Christopher Wells, Michael Butler, LYM)*
APPLETREEWICK [SE0560]
☆ *Craven Arms* BD23 6DA [off B6160 Burnsall—Bolton Abbey]: Creeper-covered 17th-c beamed pub with comfortably down-to-earth settles and rugs on flagstones, oak panelling, fire in old range, good friendly service, up to eight well kept ales, good choice of wines by the glass, home-made food from baguettes up, small dining room and splendid thatched and raftered barn extension with gallery; dogs and walking boots welcome (plenty of surrounding walks), nice country views from front picnic-sets, more seats in back garden *(LYM, WW, John and Eleanor Holdsworth, Pat and Tony Martin)*
ARNCLIFFE [SD9371]
☆ *Falcon* BD23 5QE [off B6160 N of Grassington]: Basic no frills country tavern in same family for generations, lovely setting on moorland village green, coal fire in small bar with elderly furnishings, well kept Timothy Taylors Landlord tapped from cask to stoneware jugs in central hatch-style servery, low-priced simple lunchtime and early evening food from old family kitchen, cheerful service, attractive watercolours, sepia photographs and humorous sporting prints, back sunroom (children allowed at lunchtime) overlooking pleasant garden; no credit cards; miles of trout fishing, good walks, two plain bedrooms (not all year), good breakfast and evening meal, cl winter Thurs evenings *(Michael B Griffith, the Didler, Neil Whitehead, Victoria Anderson, WW, B and M Kendall, LYM)*

ASKRIGG [SD9491]

☆ *Kings Arms* DL8 3HQ [signed from A684 Leyburn—Sedbergh in Bainbridge]: Great log fire in former coaching inn's flagstoned high-ceilinged main bar, traditional furnishings and décor, well kept ales such as Black Sheep, John Smiths and Theakstons, decent wines by the glass, good choice of malts, enjoyable food from sandwiches up, friendly staff, restaurant with fire, barrel-vaulted former beer cellar; piped music; children and dogs welcome, pleasant courtyard, bedrooms run separately as part of Holiday Property Bond complex behind (LYM, Lynda and Trevor Smith, Eric Ruff, Gordon and Margaret Ormondroyd, Stuart Brown)

ASKWITH [SD1648]

Black Horse LS21 2JQ [off A65]: Biggish stone-built open-plan family pub in lovely spot (superb Wharfedale views from dining conservatory and good terrace), well kept Timothy Taylors Landlord, wide choice of enjoyable if not cheap pubby food inc lovely bread and butter pudding, good service, woodburner (not always lit) (Gordon and Margaret Ormondroyd)

AYSGARTH [SE0088]

George & Dragon DL8 3AD [just off A684]: Welcoming 17th-c posting inn with emphasis on good varied food from sandwiches up, two big dining areas, small beamed and panelled bar with log fire, well kept Black Sheep Bitter, Theakstons Best, Yorkshire Dales and a beer brewed for the pub, be piped music; children welcome, nice paved garden, lovely scenery, handy for Aysgarth Falls, seven bedrooms, open all day (Mr and Mrs Maurice Thompson, Keith Moss, LYM)

BAILDON [SE1538]

Junction BD17 6AB [Baildon Rd]: Wedge-shaped traditional local with three linked rooms, friendly atmosphere, well kept Dark Star and changing microbrews, home-made wkdy lunchtime food, live music and singalongs Sun evening, pool; open all day (Ros Lawler, the Didler)

BARDSEY [SE3642]

☆ *Bingley Arms* LS17 9DR [Church Lane]: Redecorated ancient pub with enjoyable fresh food, welcoming efficient service, well kept Black Sheep, John Smiths and Tetleys, good wines by the glass, spacious lounge divided into separate areas, huge fireplace, smaller public bar, upstairs brasserie; children welcome, attractive terraced garden, lovely Saxon church nearby (Danny Savage, John and Eleanor Holdsworth, LYM)

BARMBY ON THE MARSH [SE6828]

Kings Head DN14 7HT [High St]: Early 19th-c village pub refurbished under newish family management, enjoyable locally sourced home-made food inc some interesting choices, four real ales, good service; children welcome, disabled facilities, open all day wknds, cl Mon and Tues lunchtimes (Ross Gibbins)

BEDALE [SE2688]

Old Black Swan DL8 1ED [Market Pl]: Attractive façade, welcoming efficient staff, bargain bar lunches, good choice of ales inc Theakstons, log fire, darts, pool; sports TV; children welcome, disabled facilities, small back terrace, Tues market, open all day (Janet and Peter Race)

BEVERLEY [TA0339]

Dog & Duck HU17 8BH [Ladygate]: Cheerful popular two-bar local handy for playhouse and Sat market, good home-made lunchtime food using local produce from sandwiches to bargain Sun lunch, OAP deals too, well kept Caledonian Deuchars IPA, Copper Dragon, John Smiths and guests, good value wines, several malts, helpful friendly staff, coal fires; piped music, games machine; cheap basic courtyard bedrooms up iron stairs (the Didler)

Tiger HU17 8JG [Lairgate]: Simple interesting local with four small rooms, enjoyable bargain food (not Sun evening, Mon) inc good curries, well kept Adnams and Black Sheep, folk nights, darts; comfortable terrace, smokers' shelter, open all day, till late Fri and Sat (the Didler, D W Stokes, Marlene and Jim Godfrey)

BILTON [SE4750]

☆ *Chequers* YO26 7NN [pub signed just off B1224]: Well kept Black Sheep and two guests such as Brains Rev James and Wells & Youngs Bitter, interesting wines, lots of whiskies, sensibly priced fresh food, pleasant staff, nicely refurbished linked bar areas, leather sofa and armchairs by warm woodburner, part-panelled dining room; piped music may obtrude; outside heated seating shelter, small garden, three bedrooms (Grahame Sherwin, Pete Coxon, BB)

BINGLEY [SE1039]

☆ *Brown Cow* BD16 2QX [Ireland Bridge; B6429 just W of junction with A650]: Genuine and unpretentious, open-plan but snugly divided, with good coal fires, easy chairs, toby jugs, lots of pictures, panelling, good range of beers inc very well kept Timothy Taylors, good reasonably priced food from sandwiches to steaks, restaurant, friendly staff; may be piped music; children welcome, tables on sheltered terrace, pleasant spot by river (James Stretton, LYM)

BRADFORD [SE1533]

Fighting Cock BD7 1JE [Preston St (off B6145)]: Busy bare-boards alehouse by industrial estate, great choice of well kept changing ales, foreign draught and bottled beers, farm ciders, lively atmosphere, all-day doorstep sandwiches and good simple lunchtime hot dishes (not Sun), may be free bread and dripping on the bar, low prices, coal fires; open all day (the Didler, Martin Grosberg, Barbarrick)

Haigys BD8 7QU [Lumb Lane]: Friendly, lively and distinctive local with cosy lounge area, well kept Tetleys and four guests, revolving pool table, music area; open all day wknds, may be closed wkdy lunchtimes (the Didler)

New Beehive BD1 3AA [Westgate]: Robustly old-fashioned Edwardian inn with several rooms inc good pool room, wide range of changing ales, gas lighting, candles and coal fires; basement music nights; nice back courtyard, bedrooms, open all day (till 2am Fri and Sat) *(the Didler)*

Stansfield Arms BD10 0NP [Apperley Lane, Apperley Bridge; off A658 NE]: Smartly refurbished roomy pub popular for its reasonably priced good early bird deals, well kept Black Sheep, Copper Dragon and Timothy Taylors Landlord, cheerful attentive staff, beams, stripped stone and dark panelling, restaurant; can get very busy; tables out on front decking, pleasant setting *(Gordon and Margaret Ormondroyd, Peter and Eleanor Kenyon, John and Eleanor Holdsworth, George and Linda Ozols)*

BRAMHAM [SE4242]

Swan LS23 6QA [just off A1 2 miles N of A64]: Civilised three-room country local with engaging long-serving landlady and good mix of customers, well kept Black Sheep, Caledonian Deuchars IPA and John Smiths *(Les and Sandra Brown)*

BREARTON [SE3260]

☆ **Malt Shovel** HG3 3BX [Village signposted off A61 N of Harrogate]: Popular 16th-c beamed and candlelit dining pub, cosy bar, wood or slate floors, modern conservatory with lemon trees and piano, good imaginative food (not Sun evening) from swiss chef/landlord inc own-smoked fish and meats, also cheaper bistro and thai menus, regular opera/dinner evenings (licensees are trained singers), attentive friendly service, well kept Black Sheep and guest ales, several good wines by the glass; no dogs; children welcome, garden tables, cl Sun evening from 9pm, Mon, Tues *(David S Allen, Gordon and Margaret Ormondroyd, Peter Hacker, Margaret Dickinson, LYM)*

BRIGHOUSE [SE1421]

Globe HD6 3EL [Rastrick Common]: Welcoming local with good value generous home-made food inc good Sun lunch, well kept Black Sheep, Camerons, Greene King and Tetleys, friendly helpful staff, pleasant restaurant; cl Mon *(Gordon and Margaret Ormondroyd)*

Old Ship HD6 1JN [Bethel St]: Heavily timbered pub doing well under present landlord, well kept ales inc Black Sheep, Durham and Roosters (beer festivals), generous well priced lunchtime food using local suppliers *(Andy and Jill Kassube)*

BUCKDEN [SD9477]

Buck BD23 5JA [B6160]: Large creeper-covered stone-built pub/hotel with Black Sheep ales and guests in modernised and extended open-plan bar, log fire and flagstones in original core, good food and wine, airy restaurant, courteous staff; very busy summer and wknds; terrace with good surrounding moorland views, popular walking spot, 14 bedrooms, open all day *(Dudley and Moira Cockroft, Rob and*

Catherine Dunster, Lawrence R Cotter, Lois Dyer, LYM)

BURLEY WOODHEAD [SE1544]

Hermit LS29 7AS: Beamed three-bar roadside pub, oak panelling and comfortable built-in seats, splendid Wharfedale views from small back bar, friendly landlord, well kept Theakstons, good value wholesome food, restaurant; good walks nearby *(Michael Butler)*

BURNSALL [SE0361]

Red Lion BD23 6BU [B6160 S of Grassington]: 16th-c inn in lovely spot by River Wharfe, looking across village green to Burnsall Fell, tables out on front cobbles and on big back terrace; attractively panelled sturdily furnished front dining rooms with log fire, more basic back public bar, several real ales, good wine choice, imaginative bar food (all day wknds), conservatory; children welcome, tables outside, comfortable bedrooms (dogs allowed in some and in bar), open all day, fishing permits, open all day *(Robert Wivell, LYM)*

CALDER GROVE [SE3017]

British Oak WF4 3DL [A639 towards Denby Dale from M1 junction 39]: Popular for good value quickly served food and well kept ales such as Marstons and Tetleys *(Dave Braisted)*

CALDWELL [NZ1613]

Brownlow Arms DL11 7QH: Small appealing pub with enjoyable food from traditional dishes up inc popular Sun lunch, friendly uniformed staff; isolated village, good walks *(BB)*

CARLTON [NZ5004]

Blackwell Ox TS9 7DJ [just off A172 SW of Stokesley]: Three linked rooms off big central bar, thai landlady and helpful friendly staff, well kept beers, standard pub and thai food inc wkdy lunchtime deals, blazing log fire, lots of dark wood; children welcome, garden with play area, bedrooms, picturesque village location, handy for coast-to-coast and Cleveland Way walkers *(WW)*

☆ **Foresters Arms** DL8 4BB [off A684 W of Leyburn]: Friendly place with good food (not Mon) inc local game and venison, Black Sheep, Daleside Blonde, John Smiths and Wensleydale, decent wines by the glass, log fire, low beams and flagstones, restaurant; children and dogs welcome, disabled access, picnic-sets out at front among tubs of flowers, pretty village in heart of Yorkshire Dales National Park, three comfortable bedrooms, lovely views, *(LYM, Terry Mizen, the Didler, Mr and Mrs Maurice Thompson)*

CARLTON HUSTHWAITE [SE4976]

Carlton Bore YO7 2BW: Cosy modernised dining pub with enjoyable fairly priced food, well kept real ale, cheerful service, speedy even when full *(Peter Thompson)*

CATTAL [SE4455]

Victoria YO26 8EB [Station Rd]: Renovated Victorian themed pub, good restaurant food (best to book), efficient friendly service, ales inc local Rudgate, good value wines;

cl lunchtime (not Sun) and all day Mon *(Malcolm and Pauline Pellatt)*

CAWOOD [SE5737]

Ferry YO8 3TL [King St (B1222 NW of Selby), by Ouse swing bridge]: Interesting 16th-c inn with several comfortable areas, well kept ales such as Timothy Taylors Landlord, log fire in massive inglenook, low beams, stripped brickwork, bare boards; flagstone terrace and lawn by River Ouse swing bridge, bedrooms *(Greta and Christopher Wells)*

CAWTHORNE [SE2808]

Spencer Arms S75 4HL [off A635 W of Barnsley]: Low-beamed stone-built dining pub in attractive village by Cannon Hall, enjoyable standard food, well kept Black Sheep and Timothy Taylors Landlord, lots of cosy alcoves, contemporary restaurant (entrance from car park leads through it), friendly helpful staff; outside tables *(Derek and Sylvia Stephenson, Michael Butler, Gordon and Margaret Ormondroyd)*

CHAPEL HADDLESEY [SE5826]

Jug YO8 8QQ [quite handy for M62 junction 34; off A19 towards Selby]: Small two-roomed village local with newish ownership, enjoyable reasonably priced home-made food inc children's, three changing ales, carpets and comfortable banquettes; TV; garden with play equipment *(Matthew Teft)*

CLAPHAM [SD7469]

New Inn LA2 8HH [off A65 N of Settle]: Welcoming riverside inn in famously pretty village, log fires, cartoons and landlady's tapestries in small comfortable lounge, changing well kept ales such as Moorhouses, obliging staff, good honest food, nice coffee, public bar with pool in games area, restaurant; dogs welcome, tables outside, handy for walk to Ingleborough Cavern and more adventurous hikes, 20 comfortable bedrooms *(Greta and Christopher Wells, Susan and Nigel Brookes)*

CLIFTON [SE1622]

☆ *Black Horse* HD6 4HJ [Westgate/Coalpit Lane; signed off Brighouse rd from M62 junction 25]: Friendly 17th-c inn/restaurant, pleasant décor, front dining rooms with good generous food from lunchtime snacks up, can be pricey but good value set meals, back bar area with beam and plank ceiling and open fire, well kept Timothy Taylors Landlord and a house beer brewed by Brass Monkey, decent wines, english setter called Arthur; nice courtyard area, 21 comfortable bedrooms, pleasant village, open all day *(Michael Butler, BB)*

COLEY [SE1226]

Brown Horse HX3 7SD [Lane Ends, Denholme Gate Rd (A644 Brighouse—Keighley, a mile N of Hipperholme)]: Attractive and comfortable, with tables set close for good value traditional food from sandwiches up, Greene King, Timothy Taylors and Tetleys, decent house wines, good service, open fires in three bustling rooms, lots of bric-a-brac on ceilings and walls,

restaurant, small light back conservatory overlooking garden; open all day *(John and Eleanor Holdsworth, Gordon and Margaret Ormondroyd)*

COLTON [SE5444]

☆ *Old Sun* LS24 8EP [off A64 York—Tadcaster]: 18th-c beamed dining pub doing well under newish licensees good interesting food (till 7pm Sun, not Mon lunchtime), also traditional pub dishes and set deals, good wine list with ten by the glass, Black Sheep and Cropton ales, several linked low-ceilinged rooms, log fires, cookery demonstrations, deli; front terrace and decking, new bedrooms in separate building *(BB)*

CONEYTHORPE [SE3958]

☆ *Tiger* HG5 0RY [E of Knaresborough]: Pretty dining pub on green of charming village, friendly efficient staff, enjoyable wholesome home-made food sensibly priced inc Sun carvery, well kept local ales, straightforward open-plan décor in linked areas around bar and adjoining dining room *(Mrs Sheila Stothard, WW)*

CONONLEY [SD9846]

New Inn BD20 8NR [Main St/Station Rd]: Compact busy village pub with good value generous home-made food, five well kept Timothy Taylors ales, good service, pig pictures, games room *(Dudley and Moira Cockroft)*

CRAY [SD9479]

☆ *White Lion* BD23 5JB [B6160 N of Kettlewell]: Highest Wharfedale pub in lovely countryside and popular with walkers; welcoming licensees, simple bar with open fire and flagstones, enjoyable food inc filled yorkshire puddings and good local trout, Copper Dragon, John Smiths and Timothy Taylors Landlord, back room, ring the bull; children and dogs welcome, picnic-sets above quiet steep lane or you can sit on flat limestone slabs in shallow stream opposite, bedrooms *(the Didler, David Jackson, LYM, Walter and Susan Rinaldi-Butcher, Terry Mizen, Richard Blackwell)*

CRIGGLESTONE [SE3217]

Red Kite WF4 3BB [Denby Dale Rd, Durkar (A636, by M1 junction 39)]: Vintage Inn dining pub done like a Georgian house adjoining a cottage row, good service, their usual good value food and wide range of wines by the glass, well kept ales such as Black Sheep, Marstons Pedigree and Timothy Taylors Landlord, log fire, pleasant décor, newspapers; disabled facilities, lots of tables outside, bedrooms in adjacent Holiday Inn Express *(Derek and Sylvia Stephenson, Michael Butler, Stuart Paulley)*

DARLEY [SE1959]

Wellington HG3 2QQ [B6451 S of Pateley Bridge]: Comfortable stone-built country inn under newish licensees, enjoyable generous food, good service, heavily panelled bar and large dining area, real ales, log fires; lovely Nidderdale views, 12 bedrooms *(Mrs R A Cartwright)*

DEWSBURY [SE2622]
Huntsman WF12 7SW [Walker Cottages, Chidswell Lane, Shaw Cross – pub signed]: Cosy low-beamed converted cottages alongside urban-fringe farm, lots of agricultural bric-a-brac, blazing log fire, small front extension, friendly locals, well kept Chidswell (brewed for them), Timothy Taylors Landlord and two guests, decent home-made food (not lunchtimes Sun and Mon or evenings except Thurs and Fri) *(Michael Butler, the Didler)*
Leggers WF12 9BD [Robinsons Boat Yard, Savile Town Wharf, Mill St E (SE of B6409)]: Good value basic hayloft conversion by Calder & Hebble Navigation marina, low-beamed upstairs bar, well kept Everards Tiger and five guests, bottled belgian beers, farm cider and perry, straightforward food, real fire, friendly staff, daily papers, brewery and pub memorabilia, pool; picnic-sets outside, boat trips, open all day *(the Didler, Eric Ruff)*
Shepherds Boy WF13 2RP [Huddersfield Rd, Ravensthorpe]: Four-room pub with interesting ales and good range of foreign lagers, bottled beers and wines, bargain generous basic lunchtime food; open all day *(the Didler)*
☆ *West Riding Licensed Refreshment Rooms* WF13 1HF [Station, Wellington Rd]: Convivial three-room early Victorian station bar, eight well kept changing ales such as Acorn, Anglo Dutch, Fernandes and Timothy Taylors, foreign bottled beers and farm ciders, bargain generous lunchtime food on scrubbed tables, popular pie night Tues, curry night Weds and steak night Thurs, good wknd breakfast too, friendly staff, daily papers, coal fire, lots of steam memorabilia inc paintings by local artists, impressive juke box, jazz nights; children in two end rooms, disabled access, open all day *(the Didler, Joe Green, Andy Lickfold, Andy and Jill Kassube, Tony and Maggie Harwood)*

DONCASTER [SE5702]
Corner Pin DN1 3AH [St Sepulchre Gate W, Cleveland St]: Plushly refurbished beamed lounge with old local pub prints, welsh dresser and china, John Smiths and interesting guests kept well, good value traditional food from fine hot sandwiches to Sun roasts, friendly landlady, cheery bar with darts, games machine and TV; open all day *(the Didler)*
Hare & Tortoise DN4 7PB [Parrots Corner, Bawtry Rd, Bessacarr (A638)]: Civilised Vintage Inn all-day dining pub, varying-sized antique tables in several small rooms off bar, log fire, friendly attentive young staff, good choice of enjoyable well priced pub, beers and wines by the glass *(Stephen Woad, Alistair and Kay Butler)*
Plough DN1 1SF [W Laith Gate, by Frenchgate shopping centre]: Small old-fashioned local with friendly long-serving licensees and chatty regulars, Acorn Barnsley Bitter, Bass and guests, bustling front room with darts, dominoes and sports TV, old town

maps, quieter back lounge; tiny central courtyard, open all day (Sun afternoon break) *(Tim Mountain, the Didler)*
Sun DN5 8RN [York Rd (A638)]: Marstons pub with good value food and friendly service; events inc twice weekly quiz *(R C Vincent)*
Tut 'n' Shive DN1 1SF [W Laith Gate]: Well kept ales such as Black Sheep, Batemans, Brewsters and Greene King, farm cider, bargain food all day, small raised carpeted area, eccentric décor (even old doors pressed into service as wall/ceiling coverings), flagstones lots of pump clips, dim lighting; good juke box, pinball, games machines, big-screen sports TV, music nights; open all day *(the Didler)*

DORE [SK3081]
Dore Moor Inn S17 3AB [A625 Sheffield—Castleton]: Extended well cared-for Vintage Inn (built 1816) on edge of Peak District, wide choice of reasonably priced food, good range of wines by the glass, ales such as Black Sheep, Marstons Pedigree and Timothy Taylors Landlord, pleasant young staff, comfortably appointed with superb central log fires; tables outside, views over Sheffield *(Jo Rees)*

DUNNINGTON [SE6751]
Windmill YO19 5LP [Hull Rd (A1079)]: Welcoming dining pub, large and fairly modern, with popular generously served home-made food, swift friendly service, good range of beers, back dining conservatory, quieter small raised dining area; ten bedrooms, open all day Sun *(Martin Peterson, Clive Gibson)*

EASINGWOLD [SE5270]
☆ *George* YO61 3AD [Market Pl]: Neat, bright and airy market town hotel popular with older people, pleasant bustle though quiet corners even when busy, helpful cheerful service, Black Sheep, Daleside and Moorhouses, food in bar and restaurant, warm log fires, interesting bric-a-brac; good value pleasant bedrooms, good breakfast *(Derek and Sylvia Stephenson, Pete Coxon, Alistair and Kay Butler)*

EAST WITTON [SE1487]
☆ *Cover Bridge Inn* DL8 4SQ [A6108 out towards Middleham]: Cosy 16th-c flagstoned country local with friendly accommodating landlord and staff, good choice of well kept Yorkshire ales, enjoyable generous pub food, sensible prices, small restaurant, roaring fires; children and dogs welcome, riverside garden, three bedrooms, open all day *(WW, the Didler, Mr and Mrs Maurice Thompson, Simon Le Fort, Jon Forster, LYM)*

EGTON BRIDGE [NZ8005]
Horseshoe YO21 1XE [village signposted from A171 W of Whitby]: Attractively placed inn with open fire (not always lit), old oak tables, high-backed built-in winged settles, wall seats and spindleback chairs, a big stuffed trout (caught nearby in 1913), Black Sheep, John Smiths and three guests, standard bar food; piped music; children

welcome, dogs in bar, seats on quiet terrace in attractive mature garden, bedrooms, open all day wknds *(Brian and Sue Wharton, Pat and Stewart Gordon, LYM)*

Postgate YO21 1UX [signed off A171 W of Whitby]: Moorland village pub doing good fairly priced food, friendly staff, well kept Black Sheep and a guest, traditional quarry-tiled panelled bar with beams, panelled dado and coal fire in antique range, elegant restaurant; children and dogs welcome, garden picnic-sets, three nice bedrooms *(LYM, P Dawn, Dr and Mrs R G J Telfer)*

EMBSAY [SE0053]

Elm Tree BD23 6RB [Elm Tree Sq]: Good value open-plan beamed village pub, hearty popular food from tasty sandwiches up, good range of well kept ales inc Black Sheep, Goose Eye and Wells & Youngs, friendly young staff, settles and old-fashioned prints, log-effect gas fire, dining room, games area; busy at wknds especially in evenings; comfortable bedrooms, handy for steam railway *(Dudley and Moira Cockroft)*

FARNDALE EAST [SE6697]

Feversham Arms YO62 7LF [Church Houses, next to Farndale Nature Reserve]: In lovely daffodil valley (very busy then), unspoilt flagstoned bar with brasses around old kitchen range, well kept Black Sheep and Tetleys, good choice of home-made pubby food from sandwiches up, good friendly service, beamed stripped-stone restaurant; children and dogs welcome, small back garden, three bedrooms, self-catering cottage *(WAH)*

FELIXKIRK [SE4684]

☆ *Carpenters Arms* YO7 2DP [Village signposted off A170 E of Thirsk]: As we went to press, the friendly mother and daughter team left what was a busy dining pub in picturesque small moors-edge village; beamed bistro bar has had carpenter's tools, knick-knacks and built-in wall seats, more formal restaurant; food has been good and inventive – reports please *(LYM)*

FILEY [TA1180]

Bonhommes YO14 9JH [The Crescent]: Friendly bar with several well kept ales; open all day till late *(Mary Small)*

FINGHALL [SE1889]

☆ *Queens Head* DL8 5ND [off A684 E of Leyburn]: Welcoming comfortable dining pub, log fires either end of tidy low-beamed bar, settles making stalls around big tables, Black Sheep, Greene King, John Smiths and Theakstons, wide choice of good food from traditional things up, much-extended back Wensleydale-view dining room; children and dogs welcome, disabled facilities, back garden with decking sharing view, three bedrooms *(Mr and Mrs Williams, Sandra Taylor, Karen Sharman, office, BB, Blaise Vyner)*

FLAXTON [SE6762]

Blacksmiths Arms YO60 7RJ [off A64]: Small welcoming traditional pub on attractive village green, enjoyable home-made food,

well kept Copper Dragon and Theakstons, two cosy bars and dining room; three nice bedrooms *(David and Ruth Hollands)*

FLOCKTON [SE2314]

Sun WF4 4DW [off A642 Wakefield—Huddersfield at Blacksmiths Arms]: Revitalised beamed pub with open fires in bar and dining area, popular reasonably priced food, real ales, prompt efficient service; children welcome, garden tables with lovely views *(Michael Butler)*

GARSDALE HEAD [SD7992]

Moorcock LA10 5PU [junction A684/B6259; marked on many maps, nr Garsdale station on Settle—Carlisle line]: Isolated stone-built inn with welcoming landlord, good value enjoyable food all day from sandwiches up, Black Sheep, Copper Dragon and Tetleys, good choice of wines by the glass, decent coffee, informal eclectic décor, log fire in small flagstoned bar, cosy corners in lounge bar, occasional live music; tables outside with views of viaduct and Settle—Carlisle railway, bedrooms, open all day *(Paul Petto, Sue and Stuart Palmer, Peter Salmon)*

GIGGLESWICK [SD8164]

☆ *Black Horse* BD24 0BE [Church St]: Very hospitable father-and-son landlords in prettily set 17th-c village pub, spotless cosy bar with horsey bric-a-brac and gleaming brasses, coal-effect fire, good choice of reasonably priced hearty food inc sandwiches and nice home-made puddings, well kept Timothy Taylors, Tetleys and guests, intimate dining room, good service, piano (often played); heated back terrace, smokers' shelter, three good value comfortable bedrooms, good breakfast, self-catering cottage *(the Didler, D W Stokes, Michael Butler)*

Craven Arms BD24 0EB [just off A65, opp station]: Former Old Station returned to its original name and given contemporary revamp, well presented locally sourced food inc meat from licensee's organic farm, ales such as Black Sheep, Copper Dragon and Tetleys, restaurant; suntrap garden, seven bedrooms, cl Mon *(Peter and Liz Smalley)*

GILLAMOOR [SE6890]

☆ *Royal Oak* YO62 7HX [off A170 in Kirkbymoorside]: Stone-built 18th-c dining pub with interesting food at fair prices, friendly staff, ales such as Black Sheep and Copper Dragon, reasonably priced wines, roomy bar with heavy dark beams, log fires in two tall stone fireplaces (one with old kitchen range), overspill dining room (dogs allowed here); children welcome, eight comfortable modern bedrooms, good breakfast, attractive village handy for Barnsdale Moor walks *(WW, Stanley and Annie Matthews, WAH, BB)*

GILLING EAST [SE6176]

☆ *Fairfax Arms* YO62 4JH [Main St (B1363)]: Attractive refurbished stone-built country inn under same management as the good White Swan at Ampleforth, traditional food with some upmarket twists, Black Sheep and

Tetleys, good wine choice, beams and log fire, restaurant; piped music; children welcome, dogs outside only, disabled access, streamside front lawn, pleasant village with castle and miniature steam railway, 11 good bedrooms, open all day wknds *(WW)*

GILLING WEST [NZ1805]

White Swan DL10 5JG [High St (B6274 just N of Richmond)]: 17th-c country inn with well kept Black Sheep and John Smiths, enjoyable home-made food inc good curries in open plan bar and dining room (bargain suppers Mon and Tues), pleasant accommodating staff, good local atmosphere, log fire, darts; tables in quirkily decorated yard, attractive village, four bedrooms *(Mr and Mrs Maurice Thompson, Jill and Julian Tasker)*

GOATHLAND [NZ8200]

Mallyan Spout Hotel YO22 5AN [opp church]: More hotel than pub with three spacious lounges and traditional bar, good open fires, fine views, enjoyable bar lunches, well kept Black Sheep, good malt whiskies and wines, friendly helpful staff, smart restaurant; well behaved children in eating areas, handy for namesake waterfall, comfortable bedrooms, good buffet breakfast, usually open all day *(LYM, Pete Coxon, Ian Malone)*

GRANTLEY [SE2369]

Grantley Arms HG4 3PJ [off B6265 W of Ripon]: Attractive popular stone-built pub in quiet Dales village, beams and big open fire, good interesting food inc cheaper set menus, well kept ales and decent wines, restaurant; soft piped music *(Janet and Peter Race, John and Eleanor Holdsworth)*

GRASSINGTON [SE0064]

☆ *Devonshire* BD23 5AD [The Square]: Small handsome reliably run hotel, good window seats and tables outside overlooking sloping village square, decent food from sandwiches up, real ales, interesting pictures and ornaments, beams and open fires, pleasant family room, big restaurant; comfortable bedrooms, open all day Sun *(LYM, Janet and Peter Race)*

Foresters Arms BD23 5AA [Main St]: Comfortable opened-up old coaching inn with friendly efficient staff, good well priced food, good choice of ales inc Black Sheep and Tetleys, log fires, dining room off on right; pool and sports TV on left; children welcome, outside tables, 14 affordable bedrooms, open all day *(Dudley and Moira Cockroft, the Didler, Linda Carter)*

GREAT OUSEBURN [SE4461]

Crown YO26 9RF [off B6265 SE of Boroughbridge]: Nicely refurbished by newish owners, good choice of well kept ales, enjoyable food from pubby to more restauranty dishes, back dining extension; garden with terrace tables, open all day wknds, cl Mon lunchtime, Tues *(LYM)*

GUISELEY [SE1941]

Coopers LS20 8AH [Otley Rd]: Light and modern Market Town Taverns café bar with good food from lunchtime sandwiches through pastas and pies to evening paella and steaks, eight real ales inc Black Sheep and Timothy Taylors Landlord, jazz and blues nights in upstairs function/dining room, open all day *(the Didler)*

GUNNERSIDE [SD9598]

Kings Head DL11 6LD [B6270 Swaledale rd]: Small recently refurbished two-room local in pretty riverside Dales village, enjoyable food inc good sandwiches and vegetarian choices, four well kept local ales, cafetière coffee, helpful service, log fire, flagstones and carpet, old village photographs; children, dogs and muddy boots welcome, some tables out by bridge, good walks nearby, open all day wknds *(Peter Dearing, Bruce and Sharon Eden, Mr and Mrs Maurice Thompson)*

HAMPSTHWAITE [SE2558]

Joiners Arms HG3 2EU [about 5 miles W of Harrogate; High St]: Yorkshire ales, decent wines and popular food inc Sun roast, good service, big fireplace, decorative plates on lounge beams, public bar and barrel-vaulted snug, spacious and airy back dining extension with dozens of sauceboats on beams and corner chest of joiner's tools; unobtrusive piped music; tables out in front and pleasant back garden, attractive village *(Pierre Richterich, Ian and Nita Cooper)*

HARDROW [SD8691]

☆ *Green Dragon* DL8 3LZ: Friendly traditional Dales pub full of character, stripped stone, antique settles on flagstones, lots of bric-a-brac, low-beamed snug with log fire in old iron range, another in big main bar, four well kept ales inc one brewed for the pub by Yorkshire Dales, enjoyable generous food, small neat restaurant, annual brass band competition, access (for a small fee) to Britain's highest single-drop waterfall; children and dogs welcome, bedrooms *(LYM, Tony and Maggie Harwood, Danny Savage, Ewan and Moira McCall, Mr and Mrs Maurice Thompson)*

HARROGATE [SE3155]

Coach & Horses HG1 1BJ [West Park]: Very friendly bustling pub with speciality pies and other enjoyable reasonably priced food, several good Yorkshire ales, obliging service, booth seating; open all day *(the Didler, D W Stokes, Eric Larkham, Pete Coxon)*

☆ *Hales* HG1 2RS [Crescent Rd]: Classic Victorian décor in welcoming gas-lit 18th-c local close to Pump Rooms, leather seats in alcoves, stuffed birds, comfortable saloon and tiny snug, Bass, Daleside and guest beers, simple good value lunchtime bar food inc Sun roast *(Eric Larkham, Greta and Christopher Wells)*

☆ *Old Bell* HG1 2SZ [Royal Parade]: Thriving Market Town Taverns pub with eight mainly Yorkshire beers from handsome counter, lots of bottled continentals, impressive choice of wines by the glass, friendly helpful staff, good lunchtime snacks inc sandwiches (interesting choice of breads), more elaborate evening meals upstairs, newspapers, panelling, old sweet shop ads and breweriana, no music or machines; no children; open all day *(Pat and Tony Martin, Pam and John Smith, the Didler, Eric Larkham)*

Swan on the Stray HG1 4AA: Former Black Swan newly refurbished by Market Town Taverns, enjoyable reasonably priced food from shortish menu and a few specials, Copper Dragon and Daleside Blonde, continental beers, Thatcher's cider, daily papers *(Brian and Janet Ainscough)*

Winter Gardens HG1 2RR [Royal Baths, Crescent Rd]: Interesting Wetherspoons transformation of former ballroom in landmark building, well kept ales, generous usual good value food, many original features, comfortable sofas in lofty hall, upper gallery; very busy late evening; attractive terrace, open all day *(Tim and Ann Newell)*

HARTHILL [SK4980]

Beehive S26 7YH [Union St]: Two-bar village pub opp attractive church, chef/landlord doing wide range of enjoyable well priced generous food (not Mon) inc proper pies and Sun lunch, friendly service (can be slow when busy), three well kept ales inc Timothy Taylors Landlord, good wine and soft drinks choice, fresh flowers, games room with pool; piped music; children welcome if eating, picnic-sets in attractive garden, walks nearby, cl Mon lunchtime *(JJW, CMW, Rebecca Walker, Derek and Sylvia Stephenson, Mrs Hazel Rainer, Peter Hacker)*

HEBDEN [SE0263]

Clarendon BD23 5DE: Pleasant and reliable country pub in nice location, Black Sheep, Timothy Taylors Landlord and an ale brewed for the pub by Moorhouses, enjoyable food from sandwiches up, efficient obliging service, bar, snug and dining area; three bedrooms, close to good walks *(D W Stokes)*

HEBDEN BRIDGE [SE0027]

Hare & Hounds HX7 8TN [Billy Lane/Lands End Lane, Wadsworth – above E end of town]: Friendly traditional pub with good choice of bargain pubby food, Timothy Taylors ales, roaring fire, local artwork for sale; tables on terrace with lovely views, plenty of good walks (not to mention the one up from the town), five bedrooms, open all day wknds *(Len Beattie)*

☆ **White Lion** HX7 8EX [Bridge Gate]: Solid stone-built inn with welcoming comfortable bar and country-furnished bare-boards back area with coal fire, sound reasonably priced home cooking all day (just lunchtime Sun), fish specialities, well kept Timothy Taylors Landlord and a guest beer, good service; disabled facilities, attractive secluded riverside garden, ten comfortable bedrooms *(Roy and Lindsey Fentiman, John Fiander, Martin Smith, Ian and Nita Cooper)*

HECKMONDWIKE [SE2123]

New Charnwood WF16 0EH [Westgate]: Attractive town pub establishing reputation for good home-made food from lunchtime sandwiches and pub staples up (they even

do a Timothy Taylors Landlord ice-cream), very popular Sun lunch (best to book), well kept yorkshire ales such as Abbeydale, Fernandes and Ossett, cheerful service *(Andy and Jill Kassube, Stuart Paulley)*

HELWITH BRIDGE [SD8169]

Helwith Bridge Inn BD24 0EH [off B6479 N of Stainforth]: Warm and cosy unpretentious village local, up to eight real ales in flagstoned bar, decent cheap pub food, railway and hiking pictures, friendly regulars and walkers; basic bunkhouse, by Settle—Carlisle railway *(Dr Kevan Tucker)*

HEPWORTH [SE1606]

Butchers Arms HD9 1TE [off A616 SE of Holmfirth; Towngate]: Refurbished dark-beamed country dining pub with very good enterprising food (not cheap) from Le Manoir trained chef, efficient pleasant service, traditional flagstone/bare-boards interior enhanced with contemporary décor, large log fire; outside decked seating area, open all day *(David and Cathrine Whiting, John and Eleanor Holdsworth)*

HIPPERHOLME [SE1224]

Cock of the North HX3 8EF [Brighouse Rd (A644)]: Portakabin-like tap for Halifax Steam, contrasting dark-panelled interior with glass door through to brewery, up to nine of their interesting ales, no food but usually speciality breads and other snacks on counter *(Pat and Tony Martin)*

HOLMFIRTH [SD1408]

Nook HD9 2DN [Victoria Sq; aka Rose & Crown]: Basic 18th-c stone pub brewing its own good ales alongside Timothy Taylors and other guests, home-made pubby food all day and adjoining tapas bar, low beams, flagstones and big open fire, some live music; heated streamside terrace, open all day *(the Didler)*

Old Bridge HD9 7DA [Market Walk]: Roomy and comfortable modernised beamed bar in small hotel, ales such as Black Sheep, Elland and Timothy Taylors, extensive wine list, wide choice of usual food all day from sandwiches up, good cheerful service; riverside tables outside, bedrooms, open all day *(Steve Jennings, Christopher Viner)*

HOLYWELL GREEN [SE0919]

Rock HX4 9BS [handy for M62 J24]: Smart and comfortable, with good atmosphere and open fire in cosy bar areas, popular food (all day Sun) inc good value lunchtime set menu, Timothy Taylors Landlord, conservatory, restaurant; children welcome, nicely decorated bedrooms *(Gordon and Margaret Ormondroyd)*

HORBURY [SE2918]

Boons WF4 6LP [Queen St]: Lively, chatty and comfortably unpretentious flagstoned local, Clarks, John Smiths, Timothy Taylors Landlord and up to four quickly changing guests, no food, Rugby League memorabilia, warm fire, back tap room with pool; TV, no children; courtyard tables, open all day Fri-Sun *(Michael Butler, the Didler)*

Bulls Head WF4 5AR [Southfield Lane]: Large

well divided pub deservedly popular for food, smart attentive staff, Black Sheep and Tetleys, lots of wines by the glass, panelling and wood floors, relaxing linked rooms inc library, snug and more formal restaurant; front picnic-sets *(Michael Butler, Malcolm and Wendy Butler)*

HORNSEA [TA2047]
Victoria HU18 1AN [Market Pl]: Stripped pine in bar, pleasant dining room, reliable pubby food (also breakfast and tea), up to four well kept ales, friendly helpful staff, live acoustic music *(Fred and Lorraine Gill)*

HORSFORTH [SE2438]
Town Street Tavern LS18 4RJ [Town St]: Market Town Taverns pub with eight well kept ales inc Abbeydale, Black Sheep, Copper Dragon, Leeds and Timothy Taylors, lots of continental bottled beers, good generous food in small bare-boards bar and (Tues-Sat) in upstairs evening bistro, good service; small terrace, open all day *(Brian and Janet Ainscough, Andy and Jill Kassube)*

HOVINGHAM [SE6675]
Malt Shovel YO62 4LF [Main St (B1257 NW of Castle Howard)]: Attractive and comfortably unpretentious, with friendly staff, enjoyable sensibly priced home-made food using own veg, well kept Black Sheep and Tetleys, good coffee, cosy dining room; children welcome, appealing village setting *(Andy and Jill Kassube, WW)*

HUBBERHOLME [SD9278]
☆ *George* BD23 5JE: Small beautifully placed ancient Dales inn with River Wharfe fishing rights, heavy beams, flagstones and stripped stone, quick simple enjoyable food, well kept Black Sheep and Copper Dragon, friendly landlord, good log fire, perpetual candle on bar; may charge for water, no dogs, outside lavatories; children allowed in dining area, terrace, seven bedrooms, cl Mon *(LYM, Peter Dearing, David and Sue Atkinson, W M Lien)*

HUDDERSFIELD [SE1416]
Albert HD1 2QF [Victoria Lane]: Well preserved high Victorian pub with Black Sheep and a possible guest ale, handsome mahogany, marble, mirrors, etched glass and chandeliers, traditional red leather wall seats, steps up to compact lounge and dining room; bedrooms *(the Didler)*
Cherry Tree HD1 1BA [John William St]: Busy open-plan split-level Wetherspoons, good choice of mainly yorkshire beers, farm cider, decent food in back dining room, good views, more seating downstairs *(the Didler)*
☆ *Head of Steam* HD1 1JF [Station, St Georges Sq]: Railway memorabilia, model trains, cars, buses and planes for sale, friendly staff, long bar with up to eight changing ales, lots of bottled beers, farm ciders and perry, fruit wines, black leather easy chairs and sofas, hot coal fire, good value enjoyable back buffet, some live jazz and blues nights; unobtrusive piped music, can be very busy; open all day *(Tony and Maggie Harwood, Brian and Anna Marsden, the Didler,*

David Hoult, Andy Lickfold, Chris Flynn, Wendy Jones)
High Park HD2 1PX [Bradley Rd, Bradley]: Neatly kept modern dining pub, attractively done and keeping plenty of room for drinking and chatting, Greene King ales, wide choice of good value pub food inc OAP and other deals, quick friendly service; children welcome, disabled facilities, outside seating, open all day *(Gordon and Margaret Ormondroyd)*
Kings Head HD1 1JF [St Georges Sq]: Handsome Victorian station building housing friendly well run pub, large open-plan room with original tiled floor, two smaller rooms off, Dark Star, Pictish, Timothy Taylors Landlord and six guests, good cobs and pork pies, live afternoon/evening music (Sun, Thurs); disabled access via platform 1, open all day *(the Didler, Andy Lickfold, Chris Flynn, Wendy Jones)*
Nags Head HD2 2EA [New Hey Rd, Ainley Top; handy for M62 junction 24, by A643]: Comfortably refurbished and quite popular, good choice of food at fair prices inc OAP deals, well kept Courage Directors and three other beers, friendly chatty staff; bedrooms, open all day *(Gordon and Margaret Ormondroyd)*
Slubbers Arms HD1 6HW [Halifax Old Rd]: V-shaped traditional three-room character pub, well kept Timothy Taylors and a guest like Copper Dragon, good range of soft drinks, snacks and light meals all day, fast friendly staff, black and white photographs and old wartime posters *(Jeremy King)*
Sportsman HD1 5AY [St Johns Road]: Refurbished and revitalised by owners of the West Riding Licensed Refreshment Rooms at Dewsbury, up to eight mainly local ales, regular beer festivals, good value lunchtime bar snacks; handy for the station, open all day *(Andy and Jill Kassube, the Didler)*
Star HD1 3PJ [Albert St, Lockwood]: Unpretentious friendly local with seven competitively priced changing ales particularly well kept by enthusiastic landlady, continental beers, farm cider, beer festivals in back marquee (food then), bric-a-brac and customers' paintings; cl Mon, and lunchtimes Tues-Thurs, open all day wknds *(the Didler, John R Ringrose)*
White Cross HD2 1XD [Bradley Rd, Colne Bridge (A62/A6107)]: Six particularly well kept changing ales and nicely cooked bargain food in small simple two-room pub, friendly service, popular Feb beer festival; open all day *(the Didler, Bill Pringle)*

HULL [TA0929]
Hop & Vine HU1 3TG [Albion St]: Small pub with three real ales, bottled belgians, farm ciders and perry, friendly licensees, good sandwiches and bargain basic specials all day; open all day, cl Sun lunchtime, Mon *(the Didler)*
☆ *Minerva* HU1 1XE [Pier St/Nelson St]: Nice old-fashioned pub reopened under new local ownership; at heart of restored waterfront

and marina, with seats in front to watch passing boats, several rambling rooms, tiny snug and back room, coal fires, real ales and pubby food, darts, live folk nights; has been open all day *(LYM, Pat and Tony Martin)*

☆ *Olde White Harte* HU1 1JG [passage off Silver St]: Ancient pub with Civil War history under newish management, carved heavy beams, attractive stained glass, two big inglenooks with frieze of delft tiles, Caledonian Deuchars IPA, Theakstons Old Peculier and guests from copper-topped counter, 80 or so malt whiskies, bargain pubby food; children welcome in upstairs restaurant, dogs in bar, heated courtyard, open all day *(the Didler, LYM)*

Wellington HU2 9AB [Russell St]: Smartly kept 19th-c bar with Tetleys and half a dozen or so guests, impressive cabinets of bottled imports, Weston's and guest ciders, friendly staff, interesting memorabilia; back terrace, open all day Fri-Sun, cl lunchtime Mon-Thurs *(the Didler)*

Whalebone HU2 0PA [Wincolmlee]: Friendly local brewing its own ales, good guest beers and farm ciders, bar food, old-fashioned décor; open all day *(the Didler)*

ILKLEY [SE1147]

Bar t'at LS29 9DZ [Cunliffe Rd]: Extended Market Towns Tavern pub, eight mainly yorkshire ales kept well, good wine and bottled beer choice, lively lunchtime bistro atmosphere with good sandwiches and bargain hot dishes, more elaborate evening food (candlelit cellar dining area may open then), quick polite service, daily papers, conservatory; dogs welcome, heated back terrace, open all day *(WW, the Didler, N R White)*

Ilkley Moor Vaults LS29 9HD [Stockeld Rd/ Stourton Rd, off A65 Leeds—Skipton]: Atmospheric flagstoned pub with log fires in both upstairs and downstairs bars, good food from old-fashioned staples to more exotic dishes, home-baked bread, well kept ales inc Timothy Taylors Landlord, decent wines by the glass; children welcome, open all day wknds, cl Mon *(James Stretton, Neil Whitehead, Victoria Anderson)*

Riverside LS29 0BE [Nesfield Rd]: Family-run hotel in good position by River Wharfe, cosy with nice open fire, well kept Copper Dragon, Sam Smiths and Tetleys, good home-cooking till early evening; 13 bedrooms, open all day from 10am *(the Didler)*

Wheatley Arms LS29 8PP [Wheatley Lane, Ben Rhydding]: Nice Ilkley Moor location and now part of the small Individual Inns group, stylish refurbishment with lounge areas and garden room, inglenooks, locals' bar, good food (very popular wknds), efficient service; outside tables, good bedrooms *(Mrs R A Cartwright, John and Eleanor Holdsworth)*

KEIGHLEY [SE0641]

Boltmakers Arms BD21 5HX [East Parade]: Small open-plan split-level character local, friendly and bustling, with full Timothy

Taylors range and a guest kept well, keen prices, limited food, nice brewing pictures, coal fire; sports TV; short walk from Worth Valley Railway, open all day *(the Didler, Bruce Bird, Neil Whitehead, Victoria Anderson)*

Brown Cow BD21 2LQ [Cross Leeds St]: Popular and friendly extensively refurbished local, good licensee keeping Timothy Taylors ales and guests in top condition; open from 4pm Mon-Sat, all day Sun *(the Didler, Bruce Bird)*

Globe BD21 4QR [Parkwood St]: Friendly landlord at this comfortable local by Worth Valley steam railway track, Timothy Taylors ales, pubby food Fri-Sun lunchtimes, coal fire, darts, games room with pool and Sky TV; karaoke, Sun quiz; tables out behind, cl till 4pm Mon-Thurs, open all day Fri-Sun *(the Didler)*

KETTLEWELL [SD9672]

☆ *Racehorses* BD23 5QZ [B6160 N of Skipton]: Comfortable, civilised and friendly two-bar pub with dining area, generous good value food from substantial lunchtime rolls through pub favourites to local game, popular early evening bargains Sun-Thurs, well kept Timothy Taylors and Tetleys, good log fire; children welcome, dogs in bars, front and back terrace seating, well placed for Wharfedale walks, parking can be difficult, 13 good bedrooms, open all day *(BB, Bruce and Sharon Eden, Lois Dyer)*

KIRKBY FLEETHAM [SE2894]

☆ *Black Horse* DL7 0SH [Lumley Lane]: Nicely refurbished old village pub with some contemporary touches but keeping pubby atmosphere, enjoyable food inc good value Sun lunch, well kept Black Sheep, John Smiths, Theakstons and a guest, good choice of wines by the glass, restaurant, darts; children welcome, tables in garden, quoits, three good bedrooms *(Richard Cole, Bill Adie, Jane Taylor and David Dutton)*

KIRKBY OVERBLOW [SE3249]

Shoulder of Mutton HG3 1HD [Main St]: Three linked areas with rugs on bare boards or flagstones, two fires, well kept local ales, several wines by the glass, good fresh well presented pub food, friendly attentive service, upstairs restaurant; garden behind, shop *(Martin and Anne Muers)*

KIRKBYMOORSIDE [SE6986]

Kings Head YO62 6AT [High Market Pl]: Comfortable 16th-c inn with enjoyable home-made food using local produce, good value wkdy early evening set menu, friendly service, well kept Jennings ales, good choice of reasonably priced wines, carpeted bar with stone walls, steps down to lounge/dining area with wood floor and open fire, beamed restaurant with dark wood furniture on rugs, conservatory; children welcome, terrace and walled garden, barbecue, comfortable good value bedrooms *(Andy and Jill Kassube, Stuart and Joan Bloomer)*

KIRKHAM [SE7365]

Stone Trough YO60 7JS [Kirkham Abbey]: Beamed country pub under newish management, several cosy log-fire rooms, well kept Timothy Taylors Landlord and Theakstons Old Peculier, friendly helpful staff, restaurant; children welcome, seats outside, lovely valley views, good walks, Kirkham Abbey and Castle Howard nearby, has been open all day Sun, cl Mon (LYM, Jan Everton, D W Stokes, Steve Cocking, Celia Denton)

KNARESBOROUGH [SE3556]

☆ *Blind Jacks* HG5 8AL [Market Pl]: Friendly individualistic multi-floor tavern in 18th-c building, low beams, simple attractive furnishings, brewery posters etc, particularly well kept Black Sheep, Timothy Taylors (inc their great Dark Mild) and other changing ales, foreign bottled beers, farm cider, friendly helpful staff, limited food (cheese and pâté), bubbly atmosphere downstairs, quieter up; well behaved children allowed away from bar, open all day wknds, cl Mon till 5.30pm; Beer Ritz two doors away sells all sorts of rare bottled beers (Pam and John Smith, the Didler, Joe Green, Ros Lawler, Tim and Ann Newell, B and M Kendall, LYM)

LANGTHWAITE [NZ0002]

☆ *Red Lion* DL11 6RE [just off Reeth—Brough Arkengarthdale rd]: A favourite proper pub dating from 17th c, homely and relaxing, in beguiling Dales village with ancient bridge; friendly and welcoming with character landlady, good cheap lunchtime sandwiches, pasties and sausage rolls, well kept Black Sheep ales, Thatcher's farm cider, country wines, tea and coffee, well behaved children allowed lunchtime in low-ceilinged side snug; the ladies' is a genuine bathroom; seats outside, good walks inc organised circular ones from the pub – maps and guides for sale (Mr and Mrs Maurice Thompson, LYM)

LASTINGHAM [SE7290]

☆ *Blacksmiths Arms* YO62 6TL [off A170 W of Pickering]: Popular old-fashioned beamed pub opposite beautiful Saxon church in attractive village, log fire in open range, traditional furnishings, Theakstons and other regional ales, several wines by the glass, good food inc impressive seafood platter, friendly prompt service, darts, board games; piped music – live 2nd Sun of month; children and walkers welcome, seats in back garden, nice bedrooms, open all day summer (P Dawn, Brian Brooks, Dr and Mrs R G J Telfer, Blaise Vyner, Paul Humphreys, LYM, Brian and Anna Marsden)

LEALHOLM [NZ7607]

Board YO21 2AJ [off A171 W of Whitby]: In wonderful moorland village spot by wide pool of River Esk, old-fashioned stripped-stone bars, big log fire, welcoming licensees and chatty friendly staff, four changing ales, real ciders, over 60 malts, bar snacks (own pickled eggs) and good seasonal food in restaurant inc home-reared meats; some live music, darts; children, dogs and muddy boots welcome, secluded riverside garden

with decking, five bedrooms, self-catering cottage, open all day Sat, may be closed wkdy winter lunchtimes (James Goodwill, Liz Partridge, Ian and Anne Read)

LEAVENING [SE7863]

Jolly Farmers YO17 9SA [Main St]: Bustling welcoming village local, good choice of changing ales, enjoyable good value pubby food with lots of fresh veg, friendly licensees, front bar with eating area behind, separate dining room (Christopher Turner)

LEEDS [SE3033]

Brewery Tap LS1 5DL [New Station St]: Tied to Leeds Brewery, their ales and guest beers kept well, good value food, neat friendly efficient staff; unobtrusive piped music; open all day (Bruce Bird, the Didler)

Cross Keys LS11 5WD [Water Lane]: Designer bar with flagstone floors, stripped brick, original tiling, metal and timbers, good choice of yorkshire ales and imported bottled beers, friendly knowledgeable staff, enjoyable good value interesting food, good Sun roasts, upstairs room; children welcome, tables under big canvas parasols in sheltered courtyard, barbecues, open all day (the Didler, Stu Mac)

Duck & Drake LS2 7DR [Kirkgate, between indoor market and parish church]: Lived-in two-room local with good choice of interesting reasonably priced ales from central servery, farm cider, pleasant hard-working staff, good coal fires, bare boards, beer posters and mirrors, Yorkshire Doubles dartboard; piped music, big-screen TV, games machine; open all day (the Didler, Jeremy King)

☆ *Grove* LS11 5PL [Back Row, Holbeck]: Unspoilt 1930s-feel local overshadowed by towering office blocks, friendly long-serving landlord, tables and stools in main bar with marble floor, panelling and original fireplace, large back room (some live music here) and snug off drinking corridor, good choice of well kept ales inc Caledonian Deuchars IPA, Weston's cider, good live acoustic music; open all day (Mike and Eleanor Anderson, the Didler, Barrie Pepper)

Midnight Bell LS11 5QN [Water Lane]: Friendly tap for Leeds Brewery, their full range and guests, enjoyable home-made food, flagstones and light contemporary décor; waterside tables outside (the Didler)

Mr Foleys LS1 5RG [159 The Headrow]: In former insurance firm's HQ and named after founder, four York ales and several others from local brewers, beer and cider festivals, generous pub food all day from sandwiches up, mixed furnishings on several levels inc some leather sofas, balcony; TV (John Branston, Tony and Wendy Hobden)

Mustard Pot LS7 3QY [Stainbeck Lane, Chapel Allerton]: Friendly management in relaxed easy-going dining pub, straightforward food (all day Sat, till 8pm Sun) inc sandwiches and early evening deals (not Sun), a changing real ale such as Marstons or Wychwood, decent wines by the glass, comfortable banquettes and leather chesterfields, pastel paintwork; unobtrusive piped music; pleasant front garden, summer barbecues, open all day *(anon)*

North Bar LS1 6NU [24 New Briggate]: Extensive range of beers from all over the world inc well kept yorkshire ales such as Outlaw Wild Mule, regular beer festivals, friendly enthusiastic staff, interesting pies, local artwork *(Bruce Bird)*

Palace LS2 7DJ [Kirkgate]: Pleasantly uncityfied, with stripped boards and polished panelling, unusual lighting from electric candelabra to mock street lamps, lots of old prints, friendly helpful staff, good value lunchtime food till 7pm from sandwiches up inc popular Sun roasts in dining area, fine changing choice of ales, may be bargain wine offers; games end with pool, TV, good piped music; tables out in front and in small heated back courtyard, open all day *(the Didler, Joe Green)*

Templar LS2 7NU [Templar St]: Tiled pub with fine panelling, stained glass and some unusual booths, well kept Tetleys and guest beers, popular with older locals; open all day *(the Didler)*

☆ *Victoria* LS1 3DL [Gt George St]: Opulent early Victorian pub with grand cut and etched mirrors, impressive globe lamps extending from majestic bar, carved beams, leather-seat booths with working snob-screens, smaller rooms off, changing ales such as Cottage, Leeds, Timothy Taylors and Tetleys, friendly efficient service even when busy, reasonably priced food 12-6 from sandwiches and light dishes up in separate room with serving hatch; open all day *(the Didler, Neil Whitehead, Victoria Anderson)*

☆ *Whitelocks* LS1 6HB [Turks Head Yard, off Briggate]: Classic Victorian pub (unspoilt but some signs of wear) with long narrow old-fashioned bar, tiled counter, grand mirrors, mahogany and glass screens, heavy copper-topped tables and green leather, well kept Caledonian Deuchars IPA, John Smiths, Theakstons Best and Old Peculier and fine range of guests, good generous all-day food (not Sun evening), friendly hard-working young staff; crowded at lunchtime; children in restaurant and top bar, tables in narrow courtyard, open all day *(Neil Whitehead, Victoria Anderson, Andy Lickfold, the Didler, Joe Green, Eric Ruff, Greta and Christopher Wells, Dr Kevan Tucker, Bruce Bird, Michael Butler, LYM, N R White)*

LEYBURN [SE1190]

Black Swan DL8 5AS [Market Pl]: Attractive old creeper-clad hotel with chatty locals in cheerful open-plan bar, entertaining landlord, good service, decent range of food inc popular Sun carvery, well kept Black Sheep and other ales, good wines by the glass; no credit cards; children and dogs welcome, good disabled access, tables on cobbled terrace, seven bedrooms, open all

day *(Dorothy and Brian Rutter, the Didler, Andy Lickfold, Michael Tack, Colin Smith)*

Golden Lion DL8 5AS [Market Pl]: Comfortable panelled and bay-windowed hotel bar, two light and airy rooms with log-effect gas fire in eating area, varied good value generous food, well kept Black Sheep, decent coffee, friendly efficient service, paintings for sale, evening restaurant; very busy on Fri market day; dogs allowed, tables out in front, good value bedrooms, open all day *(BB, Michael Tack, Gordon Briggs)*

LINTHWAITE [SE1014]

☆ *Sair* HD7 5SG [Lane Top, Hoyle Ing, off A62]: Old-fashioned four-room pub brewing its own good value Linfit beers, pews and chairs on rough flagstones or wood floors, log-burning ranges, dominoes, cribbage and shove-ha'penny, vintage rock juke box; no food or credit cards; dogs welcome, children till 8pm, plenty of tables out in front with fine Colne Valley views, restored Huddersfield Narrow Canal nearby, open all day wknds, from 5pm wkdys *(John R Ringrose, the Didler, John Fiander, LYM)*

LINTON [SE3846]

☆ *Windmill* LS22 4HT [off A661 W of Wetherby]: Welcoming upmarket pub on different levels, beams, stripped stone, antique settles around copper-topped tables, log fires, enjoyable food inc lunchtime bargains, more expensive evening menu (not Sun), John Smiths, Theakstons Best and guests, several wines by the glass, friendly service, restaurant; piped music; children and dogs welcome, sunny back terrace and sheltered garden with pear tree raised from seed brought back from Napoleonic Wars, open all day wknds *(Ray and Winifred Halliday, LYM, S D and J L Cooke, R L Borthwick, Jeremy King, Greta and Christopher Wells, Dr A J and Mrs Tompsett)*

LOCKTON [SE8488]

☆ *Fox & Rabbit* YO18 7NQ [A169 N of Pickering]: Attractive neatly kept roadside pub with warm inviting atmosphere, good choice of generous well presented food (sandwiches too), quick cheerful service, well kept ales inc Black Sheep, plush banquettes, fresh flowers, brasses, hunting prints and old local photographs, big log fire, busy locals' bar with pool, good views from comfortable restaurant; tables outside and in sun lounge, nice spot on moors edge *(Pamela Thorne, A and N Hooper, LYM)*

LOW BRADFIELD [SK2691]

☆ *Plough* S6 6HW [New Rd]: Attractively refurbished popular pub, very good value home-made food (not Mon or Tues evenings), well kept local Bradfield and guest beers, cheery efficient service, inglenook log fire, restaurant; children welcome, picnic-sets in attractive garden, lovely scenery and local walks *(Peter F Marshall)*

LOW ROW [SD9898]

☆ *Punch Bowl* DL11 6PF [B6270 Reeth—Muker]: Under same ownership as Charles

Bathurst at Langthwaite (see Main Entries), fresh, light and almost scandinavian in style, with friendly helpful staff, good interesting food (menu on huge mirror), popular Sun carvery (best to book), several good wines by the glass, well kept Black Sheep, log fire, leather armchairs, sturdy tables and chairs; no dogs allowed inside; children welcome, great Swaledale views from terrace, 11 comfortable bedrooms, good breakfast, open all day in summer *(Alison and Pete, John and Verna Aspinall, Bruce and Sharon Eden, Mrs Ruth Lewis, Robin M Corlett, Walter and Susan Rinaldi-Butcher, Mrs Sheila Stothard, Mike and Lynn Robinson)*

MANFIELD [NZ2213]
Crown DL2 2RF [Vicars Lane]: Welcoming old-fashioned village local, up to six interesting ales, enjoyable simple home-made food, traditional clean décor, pool; garden *(Mr and Mrs Maurice Thompson, Julian Pigg, Dan Connolly)*

MARSDEN [SE0412]
Great Western HD7 6NL [Standedge]: Welcoming pub high on moors opp small reservoir; clean, with warm friendly atmosphere, popular generous lunchtime food from baguettes up inc bargain OAP meals, changing ales *(John and Eleanor Holdsworth)*
Tunnel End HD7 6NF [Reddisher Rd (off A62 via Peel St)]: Pleasant setting overlooking mouth of restored Standedge Canal Tunnel – at three miles under the Pennines, the UK's longest; welcoming friendly staff, well kept ales such as Black Sheep and Timothy Taylors Landlord, simple generous well made food from sandwiches to Sun roasts, reasonable prices, four good-sized but homely rooms, hot log fire in back room, pub cat, quiz nights; children welcome *(Roger Fox)*

MASHAM [SE2280]
Kings Head HG4 4EF [Market Pl]: Handsome stone inn, two much-modernised linked rooms with imposing fireplace and clock, well kept Theakstons ales and up to 20 wines by the glass, enjoyable bar food (all day wknds when can get busy), friendly service, restaurant; piped music, games machine, TV; children in eating areas, good bedrooms in back courtyard area (some for disabled), open all day *(LYM, Peter and Anne Hollindale)*
White Bear HG4 4EN [Wellgarth, Crosshills; signed off A6108 opp turn into town]: Comfortably refurbished stone-built beamed pub, small public bar with well kept local ales and darts, comfortable larger lounge with coal fire, fairly priced food (not Sun evening) from sandwiches up, decent wines by the glass, new restaurant extension; piped music; children and dogs welcome, terrace tables, 14 bedrooms, open all day *(BB, the Didler, Adrian and Dawn Collinge, Clive Gibson)*

MELMERBY [SE3376]
George & Dragon HG4 5HA: Extensively

refurbished and improved, good dining facilities *(Janet and Peter Race)*

MENSTON [SE1744]
Fox LS29 6EB [Bradford Rd (A65/A6038)]: Contemporary M&B dining pub in former coaching inn, enjoyable fairly priced food, friendly staff, Black Sheep, Timothy Taylors Landlord and guest such as Adnams, big fireplace, flagstones and polished boards in one part; piped music; two terraces looking beyond car park to cricket field *(D M Jack)*

MIDDLEHAM [SE1287]
White Swan DL8 4PE [Market Place]: Extended coaching inn opposite cobbled market town square, beamed and flagstoned entrance bar with built-in window pew and pubby furniture, open woodburner, Black Sheep, John Smiths, Theakstons and a guest, several wines by the glass and malt whiskies, decent bistro-style food, modern spacious dining room, large fireplace and small area with contemporary leather seats and sofa, more dining space in back room; children welcome, piped music; comfortable bedrooms *(LYM)*

MIDDLESMOOR [SE0974]
Crown HG3 5ST [top of Nidderdale rd from Pateley Bridge]: Remote inn with beautiful view over stone-built hamlet high in Upper Nidderdale, warmly welcoming former gamekeeper landlord, well kept Black Sheep, rich local atmosphere, blazing log fires in cosy spotless rooms full of photographs, bric-a-brac and awards, usual food, homely dining room; small garden, good value simple bedrooms, good breakfast *(WW, Simon Le Fort)*

MILL BANK [SE0321]
Millbank HX6 3DY [Mill Bank Road, off A58 SW of Sowerby Bridge]: Cottagey dining pub but with contemporary makeover inside; minimalist décor, tap room, bar and restaurant, oak-floor conservatory, local photos for sale, Tetleys, Timothy Taylors Landlord and a guest, 20 wines by the glass inc champagne, several gins, modern food cooked by landlord; interesting garden sculptures, walks nearby, good views *(LYM)*

MILLINGTON [SE8351]
Gait YO42 1TX [aka Gate]: Friendly 16th-c beamed village pub, good straightforward food, happy staff, well kept ales, nice mix of old and newer furnishings, big inglenook fire; children welcome, garden picnic-sets, appealing village in good Wolds walking country, cl Mon-Thurs lunchtimes, open all day Sun *(LYM, Christopher Turner)*

MIRFIELD [SE2017]
Hare & Hounds WF14 8EE [Liley Lane (B6118 2m S)]: Popular smartly refurbished Vintage Inn dining pub, decent good value food all day, Black Sheep, Marstons Pedigree and Timothy Taylors Landlord kept well, cheerful helpful staff; tables outside with good Pennine views, open all day *(Gordon and Margaret Ormondroyd)*
Yorkshire Puddin' WF14 9JJ: Modernised and extended with emphasis on low-priced food

inc bargain OAP menu and Sun carvery, real ales; Tues quiz; children welcome, terrace picnic-sets, open all day *(John and Eleanor Holdsworth)*

MOORSHOLM [NZ6912]

Jolly Sailor TS12 3LN [A171 nearly a mile E]: Good food all day, well kept Black Sheep, good service, cosy little booths in long beams-and-stripped-stone bar; children welcome, tables looking out to the surrounding moors, open all day *(LYM, Cheryl Wright, WAH)*

MUKER [SD9097]

☆ *Farmers Arms* DL11 6QG [B6270 W of Reeth]: Small unpretentious walkers' pub in beautiful valley village, warm fire, friendly staff and locals, well kept Black Sheep, John Smiths and Theakstons, wines, teas and coffees, enjoyable straightforward good value food inc lunchtime baps, simple modern pine furniture, flagstones and panelling, darts and dominoes; children welcome, hill views from terrace tables, River Swale across road, self-catering flat *(Edward Mirzoeff, LYM, the Didler, Lawrence Pearse, Mr and Mrs Maurice Thompson)*

MYTHOLMROYD [SE0125]

Shoulder of Mutton HX7 5DZ [New Rd, just across river bridge (B6138)]: Comfortable friendly local, emphasis on popular low-priced home cooking (not Tues) inc carvery, fish and good range of puddings, OAP lunches and children's helpings, efficient service, family dining areas and cosy child- and food-free areas, well kept ales inc Marstons Pedigree, toby jugs and other china; streamside terrace *(Ian and Nita Cooper, John and Helen Rushton)*

NEWTON UPON DERWENT [SE7249]

Half Moon YO41 4DB: Well kept changing ales, good nicely presented fresh food (not Sun-Tues) from sandwiches up, reasonably priced wine *(C A Hall)*

NORLAND [SE0521]

Moorcock HX6 3RP: Refurbished L-shaped bar and restaurant, wide choice of enjoyable generous food, children's helpings too, Timothy Taylors and Thwaites, pleasant hard-working staff *(Pat and Tony Martin)*

NORTH GRIMSTON [SE8467]

Middleton Arms YO17 8AX: Comfortable, with enjoyable good value simple food from sandwiches up, well kept Wold Top ales, homely dining area; garden tables, nice Wolds-edge spot *(WW)*

NORTHALLERTON [SE3794]

Tithe Bar DL6 1DP [Friarage St]: Market Town Tavern with half a dozen mainly yorkshire ales changing quickly, plenty of continental beers, friendly staff, tasty food lunchtime and early evening, three traditional bar areas with tables and chairs, settle and armchairs, bare boards and brewery posters, upstairs evening brasserie; open all day *(Pete Coxon, Mr and Mrs Maurice Thompson)*

NORWOOD GREEN [SE1326]

☆ *Old White Beare* HX3 8QG [signed off A641 in Wyke, or off A58 Halifax—Leeds just W of Wyke; Village St]: Nicely renovated and extended old pub named after ship whose timbers it incorporates, well kept Copper Dragon and Timothy Taylors, traditional good value home-made food all day inc sandwiches and set deals, friendly service, bar with steps up to dining area, small character snug, imposing galleried flagstoned barn restaurant; children and dogs welcome, front terrace, back garden, Calderdale Way and Brontë Way pass the door, open all day *(Gordon and Margaret Ormondroyd, Michael Butler, John and Eleanor Holdsworth)*

OSSETT [SE2719]

☆ *Brewers Pride* WF5 8ND [Low Mill Rd/Healey Lane (long cul-de-sac by railway sidings, off B6128)]: Friendly basic local with Bobs Brewing Co's White Lion (brewed at the back of the pub), Rudgate Ruby Mild and several guests such as Ossett, cosy front rooms and flagstoned bar, open fires, brewery memorabilia, good well priced food (not Sun), new dining extension, small games room, live music 3rd Sun of month; well behaved children welcome, big back garden, nr Calder & Hebble Canal, open all day *(the Didler, Michael Butler)*

Tap WF5 8JS [The Green]: Retro refurbishment by Ossett, their ales and guest beers, friendly service and locals, several wines by the glass, flagstones and open fire; open all day Thurs-Sun *(the Didler)*

OVERTON [SE2516]

Black Swan WF4 4RF [off A642 Wakefield—Huddersfield; Green Lane]: Traditional local, two cosy knocked-together low-beamed rooms full of brasses and bric-a-brac, well kept John Smiths, popular Thurs quiz night *(Michael Butler)*

OXENHOPE [SE0434]

☆ *Dog & Gun* BD22 9SN [off B6141 towards Denholme]: Beautifully placed roomy 17th-c moorland pub, smartly extended and comfortable, with good varied generous food from sandwiches to lots of fish and Sun roasts (worth booking then), thriving atmosphere, cheerful landlord and attentive staff, full Timothy Taylors range kept well, beamery, copper, brasses, plates and jugs, big log fire each end, padded settles and stools, wonderful views; five bedrooms in adjoining hotel *(Gordon and Margaret Ormondroyd, John and Eleanor Holdsworth, Pat and Tony Martin, Andy and Jill Kassube)*

POOL [SE2445]

White Hart LS21 1LH [just off A658 S of Harrogate, A659 E of Otley]: Well maintained M&B dining pub, enjoyable food all day inc cheaper fixed-price menu, efficient service, good choice of wines by the glass, Greene King and Timothy Taylors, stylishly simple bistro eating areas, armchairs and sofas on bar's flagstones and bare boards; tables outside *(Ros Lawler, Gordon and Margaret Ormonroyd, Michael Butler, John and Eleanor Holdsworth, LYM)*

PUDSEY [SE2131]
Bankhouse LS28 8DY [Scholebroke Lane]: Welcoming modernised Tudor-style pub, enjoyable food from shortish menu, Black Sheep and guest beers, several nooks and alcoves, warm lighting and comfortable chairs; dogs welcome, front terrace picnic-sets, lovely valley views, good walking country *(Jeremy Akeroyd, John and Eleanor Holdsworth)*

REDMIRE [SE0491]
Bolton Arms DL8 4EA: Nicely refurbished village inn with convivial landlord, good food cooked by landlady, well kept ales inc Black Sheep, comfortable carpeted bar, attractive dining room, darts, exemplary lavatories; disabled facilities, small garden with quoits, handy for Wensleydale Railway and Bolton Castle, good walks, three courtyard bedrooms *(Michael Tack)*

REETH [SE0399]
Kings Arms DL11 6SY [Market Pl (B6270)]: Friendly beamed village pub with dining area facing green, good reasonably priced food, Black Sheep, Theakstons and a guest beer, good wines and coffee, pine pews around walls, log fire in 18th-c stone inglenook, quieter room behind; children welcome, tables outside, bedrooms *(Bruce and Sharon Eden)*

RIBBLEHEAD [SD7678]
Station Inn LA6 3AS [B6255 Ingleton—Hawes]: Great spot up on the moors by Ribblehead Viaduct (Settle—Carlisle trains), friendly licensees doing varied food from good ciabattas up, log fire, real ales, low-priced wine and coffee, simple public bar with darts and pool, dining room with viaduct mural (the bar has relevant photographs, some you can buy); piped music, TV; children welcome, picnic-sets outside, five bedrooms (some sharing bath), bunkhouse, open all day *(Ann and Tony Bennett-Hughes, BB)*

RIPON [SE3171]
☆ *One-Eyed Rat* HG4 1LQ [Allhallowgate]: Friendly little bare-boards pub with numerous real ales inc Black Sheep and Everards, farm cider, lots of bottled beers and country wines, long narrow bar with fire, fresh flowers, cigarette cards, framed beer mats, bank notes and old pictures, no food but may be free black pudding, pool; pleasant outside area, open all day Sat, cl wkdy lunchtimes *(Alan Thwaite)*

Unicorn HG4 1BP [Market Pl E]: Hotel's traditional bar (Crudd's Bar), popular and cheerful with good mix of customers, well kept Black Sheep ales, enjoyable bar meals, friendly service, also lounge bar and restaurant; 30 bedrooms *(Janet and Peter Race, Chris Flynn, Wendy Jones)*

Water Rat HG4 1QW [Bondgate Green, off B6265]: Prettily set by footbridge over River Skell, charming view of cathedral, ducks and

weir from riverside terrace, friendly service, good choice of well kept ales, reliable straightforward food *(Janet and Peter Race)*

RISHWORTH [SE0318]
Malthouse HX6 4QB [Oldham Rd (A672 S of Ripponden)]: Smart modern dining pub with good affordably priced food, well kept Timothy Taylors Landlord, good helpful service, log fires; disabled access, five bedrooms, open all day *(Gordon and Margaret Ormondroyd, John and Eleanor Holdsworth)*

☆ *Old Bore* HX6 4QU [Oldham Rd (A672)]: Comfortable and quirkily stylish country dining pub, good interesting seasonal food, all home-made inc breads and ice-cream, not cheap but some deals, good choice of wines by the glass, Timothy Taylors and guests, friendly helpful staff, beams and standing timbers, plenty of bric-a-brac and old prints, mixed furnishings, woodburners; busy at wknds so best to book then; outside picnic-sets, cl 8pm Sun evening *(Andy and Jill Kassube, Pat and Tony Martin, Gordon and Margaret Ormondroyd)*

ROBIN HOOD'S BAY [NZ9504]
Bay Hotel YO22 4SJ [The Dock, Bay Town]: Friendly old village inn at end of the 191-mile coast-to-coast walk, fine sea views from cosy picture-window upstairs bar (Wainwright bar downstairs open too if busy), three real ales, log fires, good value home-made food in bar and separate dining area; tables outside, cosy bedrooms, open all day *(Mrs Romey Heaton, the Didler, David and Sue Smith)*

SALTAIRE [SE1437]
Fannys BD18 3JN: Cosy and friendly bare-boards alehouse on two floors, gas lighting, log fire, brewery memorabilia, half a dozen well kept ales, bottled beers and farm ciders; can be crowded wknd evenings; open all day, cl Mon lunchtime *(David Bishop, Neil Whitehead, Victoria Anderson)*

SAWDON [TA9484]
☆ *Anvil* YO13 9DY [Main St]: Pretty high-raftered former smithy with friendly staff, enjoyable good value food (not Sun evening) from chef/landlord, well kept Black Sheep and guest ales, good range of wines, immaculate housekeeping, feature smith's hearth and woodburner, lower-ceilinged second bar leading through to small neat dining room, turkey carpet throughout; comfortable warm bedrooms, cl Mon *(Keith and Margaret Kettell, BB)*

SCARBOROUGH [TA0388]
Lord Rosebery YO11 1JW [Westborough]: Lived-in Wetherspoons in former local Liberal HQ (and Co-op), galleried upper bar, good beer range, enjoyable quickly served food inc Sun roast, good staff, local prints; busy and lively evenings; disabled facilities, open all day *(Pete Coxon, David Carr)*

Valley YO11 2LX [Valley Rd]: L-shaped bar with banquettes, great choice of well kept changing ales and farm ciders, bottled belgians, friendly licensees, may be food, beer festivals; open all day (Bruce Bird, Dave and Shirley Shaw)

SCAWTON [SE5483]

☆ **Hare** YO7 2HG [off A170 Thirsk—Helmsley]: Attractive popular dining pub in quiet spot, good carefully cooked well presented food inc plenty of fish and a good vegetarian choice, enthusiastic hospitable landlord and friendly staff, good wines by the glass, three well kept ales inc Black Sheep and Timothy Taylors, stripped pine tables, heavy beams and some flagstones, old-fashioned range and woodburner, William Morris wallpaper, appealing prints and old books; children welcome, wrought-iron garden furniture, open all day in summer, cl Mon (LYM, Brian and Pat Wardrobe)

SETTLE [SD8163]

☆ **Golden Lion** BD24 9DU [B6480 (main rd through town), off A65 bypass]: Warm friendly old-fashioned atmosphere in market-town inn with grand staircase sweeping down into baronial-style high-beamed hall bar, lovely log fire, comfortably worn settles, plush seats, brass, prints and plates on dark panelling; enjoyable good value food (all day wknds) inc interesting specials, well kept Thwaites, decent wines by the glass, splendid dining room; public bar with darts, pool, games machines and TV; children in eating area, 12 good-sized comfortable bedrooms, hearty breakfast, open all day (Martin Smith, Neil and Anita Christopher, LYM)

SHEFFIELD [SK3487]

Bath S3 7QL [Victoria St, off Glossop Rd]: Two small colourfully restored bare-boards rooms with friendly staff, well kept Abbeydale, Acorn, Tetleys and guests from central servery, lunchtime bar food (not Sat), nice woodwork, tiles and glass; open all day, cl Sun lunchtime (the Didler)

Corner Pin S4 7QN [Carlisle St East]: Restored 19th-c pub with good range of ales (many local), bar food changing daily, basic locals' bar, quiet lounge; open all day (the Didler)

Gardeners Rest S3 8AT [Neepsend Lane]: Finally open again after 2007 floods, welcoming beer-enthusiast landlord serving his own good Sheffield ales from new light wood counter, also several changing guests tapped from the cask, farm cider and continental beers, no food, old brewery memorabilia, changing local artwork, daily papers, games inc bar billiards, live music; children welcome (till 9pm) and well behaved dogs, disabled facilities, back conservatory and tables out overlooking River Don, open all day Fri-Sun, from 3pm other days (David Carr, the Didler, Simon Wigglesworth-Baker)

Harlequin S3 8GG [Nursery St]: Comfortable and welcoming open-plan corner pub, own Sheffield ales (brewed nearby) and eight regularly changing guests, also imports and farm cider, decent pub food inc Sun roasts, live music Sat night, beer festivals; dogs

welcome, children till 7pm, outside seating, open all day (the Didler)

☆ **Hillsborough** S6 2UB [Langsett Rd/Wood St; by Primrose View tram stop]: Chatty and friendly pub-in-hotel, eight beers inc own microbrews and quickly changing guests, good wine and soft drinks choice, generous good value food inc Sun roasts, daily papers, open fire, bare-boards bar, lounge, views to ski slope from attractive back conservatory and terrace tables; silent TV; children and dogs welcome, six good value bedrooms, covered parking, open all day (the Didler, JJW, CMW, David Carr)

Ranmoor S10 3GD [Fulwood Rd]: Comfortable open-plan Victorian local with good value home cooking (not Sun, Mon), well kept Abbeydale and guest ales, piano (often played); pleasant garden, open all day (the Didler)

Rawson Spring S6 2LN [Langsett Rd]: Popular airy Wetherspoons in former swimming baths, their usual value, well kept changing ales, impressive décor with unusual skylights (the Didler, JJW, CMW)

Rising Sun S10 3QA [Fulwood Rd]: Friendly drinkers' pub with up to 14 ales inc full Abbeydale range (many more during summer beer festival), bottled beers, decent food, large lounge with games and reference books; dogs welcome, nice back garden, open all day (the Didler, Mr and Mrs Alesbrook, James A Waller)

Rutland Arms S1 2BS [Brown St/Arundel Lane]: Comfortable one-room corner pub with handsome façade, seven changing ales, real cider, food all day (not Sun); tables in compact garden, handy for the Crucible and station, bedrooms (the Didler)

Sheffield Tap S1 2BP [Platform 1B]: Newly opened station bar in restored Victorian refreshment room, already popular for its huge choice of world beers on tap and in bottles (even a mongolian lager), also Thornbridge ales with guests such as BrewDog and Marble, helpful staff may offer tasters, panini; open all day (Ian and Helen Stafford, the Didler)

Stag S11 8YL [Psalter Lane]: Relaxed pub with friendly helpful staff, four real ales inc Greene King Old Speckled Hen, good soft drinks choice, enjoyable home-made food (all day wknds) from sandwiches up, two dining areas and conservatory; children welcome, garden picnic-sets, play area, open all day (JJW, CMW, Giles and Annie Francis)

Three Merry Lads S10 4LJ [W on Redmires Rd]: Enjoyable good value food inc children's meals and popular all-day Sun carvery, also some unusual things, four ales inc Kelham Island, good wine and soft drinks choice, good service, chatty bar and dining extension with uninterrupted views, open fire; piped music (live Thurs), TV, games machine, darts; garden with terrace picnic-sets and play area, open all day wknds (JJW, CMW)

Union S11 9EF [Union Rd, Netheredge]: Well run and spotless with enjoyable good value home-made lunchtime food, well kept ales, lots of bric-a-brac *(Peter F Marshall)*

University Arms S3 7HG [Brook Hill]: Former university staff club, well kept Thornbridge and great range of changing guests, decent food, back conservatory and small garden, some live music; open all day, cl Sun *(the Didler)*

Walkley Cottage S6 5DD [Bole Hill Rd]: Friendly busy 1930s pub with seven ales, farm cider, good coffee and other drinks choice, decent home-made food (not Sun evening) inc bargain OAP lunch and Sun roasts, daily papers; no credit cards, piped music, TV, pool; children and dogs welcome, disabled access, views from picnic-sets in small back garden, play area, lovely hanging baskets, open all day *(JJW, CMW)*

☆ *Wellington* S3 7EQ [Henry St; Shalesmoor tram stop right outside]: Unpretentious relaxed pub with up to ten changing beers inc own bargain Little Ale Cart brews, bottled imports, real cider, coal fire in lounge, photographs of old Sheffield, daily papers, pub games, friendly staff; tables out behind, open all day but afternoon break on Sun *(the Didler, Martin Grosberg, David Carr)*

SHEPLEY [SE1809]

☆ *Farmers Boy* HD8 8AP [links A629 and A635, from village centre by Black Bull]: Good if pricey food in comfortably modern barn restaurant at back, friendly efficient service, welcoming cottage-conversion beamed bar, well kept Black Sheep and Tetleys; terrace *(David and Cathrine Whiting, Stu Mac, Michael Butler)*

SHIPLEY [SE1437]

Fannys Ale & Cider House BD18 3JN [Saltaire Rd]: Interesting gaslit roadside local, well kept Saltaire and many changing guests, foreign beers and farm cider, open fires, upstairs room; open all day Fri and Sat, cl Mon lunchtime *(the Didler, James Stretton)*

SKIPTON [SD9851]

Woolly Sheep BD23 1HY [Sheep St]: Big bustling pub with full Timothy Taylors range, prompt friendly enthusiastic service, two beamed bars off flagstoned passage, exposed brickwork, stone fireplace, lots of sheep prints and bric-a-brac, daily papers, attractive and comfortable raised lunchtime dining area, good value food (plenty for children); unobtrusive piped music; spacious pretty garden, six good value bedrooms, good breakfast *(Stuart Paulley, Mrs Hazel Rainer)*

SLAITHWAITE [SE0513]

Rose & Crown HD7 5XA [Cop Hill, up Nabbs Lane then Holme Lane]: Good value popular home-made food in cosy isolated pub with great Colne Valley and Pennine views, beers such as Black Sheep, Daleside, Goose Eye and Timothy Taylors, three rooms inc restaurant, log fire, chatty cheery staff, upstairs function room; good walks, open all day *(Gordon and Margaret Ormondroyd, Andy and Jill Kassube)*

SNAITH [SE6422]

Brewers Arms DN14 9JS [Pontefract Rd]: Converted mill brewing its own good range of distinctive beers, generous home-made food, open-plan bar and conservatory-style dining area, old well, open fireplace; children welcome in eating areas *(Ross Gibbins, LYM)*

STAINFORTH [SD8267]

Craven Heifer BD24 9PB [B6479 Settle—Horton-in-Ribblesdale]: Friendly Dales village local, small, cosy and clean, with well kept Thwaites, reasonably priced food, roaring log fire; good walks *(Neil and Anita Christopher)*

STILLINGTON [SE5867]

White Bear YO61 1JU [Main St]: Cosy olde-worlde village pub, warm and friendly, with enjoyable fairly priced pubby food (not Sun evening), good choice of beers, reasonably priced wines by the glass; children welcome, cl Mon *(Mr and Mrs D J Nash, Edward Pearce, Giles and Annie Francis)*

STOKESLEY [NZ5208]

☆ *White Swan* TS9 5BL [West End]: Good Captain Cook ales brewed in attractive flower-clad pub, three relaxing seating areas in L-shaped bar, log fire, lots of brass on elegant dark panelling, lovely bar counter carving, assorted memorabilia and unusual clock, no food, live music, beer festivals; open all day *(the Didler, Blaise Vyner)*

SUTTON-ON-THE-FOREST [SE5864]

☆ *Blackwell Ox* YO61 1DT [just off B1363, 5.7 miles N of York ring road; Huby Road]: Neatly kept, extended roadside inn, L-shaped bar with beam-and-plank ceiling, dark shiny tables on polished boards, long table and settle against one wall, horse pictures and photographs, winter fire, Black Sheep, Copper Dragon, John Smiths and Timothy Taylors Landlord, well described wines by the glass, two-room front dining area with sofas on pale floorboards, food (not Sun evening) can be good and interesting; piped music, small TV; children welcome, circular picnic-sets on terrace, bedrooms, open all day *(Pete Coxon, LYM)*

TERRINGTON [SE6770]

☆ *Bay Horse* YO60 6PP [W of Malton]: Friendly newish landlord at 17th-c pub with cosy log-fire lounge bar, own Storyteller ales and guest like Wylam, several wines by the glass, over 30 whiskies, enjoyable home-made seasonal food inc good set Sun lunch (best to book), refurbished dining area, conservatory with old farm tools, traditional games in public bar; children and dogs welcome, garden tables, unspoilt village, may be cl lunchtimes Mon-Weds winter, open all day Thurs-Sun *(Pat and Tony Martin, Alex and Claire Pearse, Christopher Turner, LYM)*

THORALBY [SE9986]

George DL8 3SU: Welcoming prettily set Dales village pub, two spotless cosy linked areas with enjoyable sensibly priced bar food from sandwiches to steaks, four well kept ales inc Black Sheep, interesting bric-a-brac, coal fire and woodburner, some banquettes, darts and dominoes; walkers welcome, dogs on leads, terrace tables, two bedrooms, cl Mon lunchtime *(Ewan and Moira McCall, Lynda and Trevor Smith)*

THORNTON [SE0933]

☆ *Ring o' Bells* BD13 3QL [Hill Top Rd, off B6145 W of Bradford]: 19th-c moortop dining pub very popular for reliably good home-made food inc bargain early-bird deals, separate sittings Sat night and Sun lunch (best to book), three Black Sheep ales and Courage Directors, large spotless bar, elegant restaurant with linen tablecloths, pleasant conservatory lounge; wide views towards Shipley and Bingley *(Margaret White, Steve Narey, Stanley and Annie Matthews, John and Eleanor Holdsworth)*

White Horse BD13 3SJ [Well Heads]: Refurbished pub popular for its wide choice of good value generous food and five well kept Timothy Taylors ales *(John and Eleanor Holdsworth, Andrew Bosi)*

THORNTON IN LONSDALE [SD6873]

Marton Arms LA6 3PB [off A65 just NW of Ingleton]: Good choice of beers such as Black Sheep, Coniston Bluebird and Sharps Doom Bar, 280 whiskies, generous wholesome food, friendly hard-working staff, beamed bar with stripped pine tables and chairs, pews and built-in seats in airy main part, flagstoned public bar with darts and piped music, log fires; picnic-sets on front terrace and at back, great walking country, 13th-c church opp, comfortable bedrooms *(LYM, Jo Lilley, Simon Calvert, Ian Herdman, Mike and Shelley Woodroffe)*

THORNTON-LE-CLAY [SE6865]

☆ *White Swan* YO60 7TG [off A64 York— Malton; Low St]: Comfortable welcoming early 19th-c family-run dining pub, good generous food such as local sausages with different types of mash, Sun roasts, John Smiths and a guest, decent wines, reasonable prices, beams and brasses, board games and toys; children welcome, disabled access, neat grounds with terrace tables, duck pond, herb and vegetable gardens, orchard, two summerhouses, donkey paddock, attractive countryside nr Castle Howard, cl all day Mon *(Michael Page, Kate Dobson, Paul Tutill, Rev Giles Galley, Ian Maclaren)*

THRESHFIELD [SD9863]

Old Hall Inn BD23 5HB [B6160/B6265 just outside Grassington]: Popular place with three old-world linked rooms inc smart candlelit dining room, well kept John Smiths, Timothy Taylors and Theakstons, helpful friendly staff, enjoyable food, nice coffee, log fires, high beam-and-plank ceiling, cushioned wall pews, tall well blacked kitchen range; children in eating area, neat garden *(John and Eleanor Holdsworth, Bruce and Sharon Eden, Greta and Christopher Wells, Gordon and Margaret Ormondroyd, LYM)*

THUNDER BRIDGE [SE1811]

Woodman HD8 0PX [off A629 Huddersfield— Sheffield]: Two roomy spotless bars, low

beams and heavy wooden tables, fresh décor, welcoming service, enjoyable good value food, well kept Timothy Taylors and Tetleys, upstairs restaurant; tables outside, 12 good bedrooms in adjoining cottages *(Gordon and Margaret Ormondroyd, John and Eleanor Holdsworth)*

TOCKWITH [SE4652]

Spotted Ox YO26 7PY [Westfield Rd, off B1224]: Welcoming traditional beamed village local, three areas off central bar, well kept ales inc Tetleys carefully served the old-fashioned way, good choice of enjoyable sensibly priced home-made food, attentive staff, relaxed atmosphere, interesting local history; open all day Fri-Sun *(Les and Sandra Brown)*

TOPCLIFFE [SE4076]

Angel YO7 3RW [off A1, take A168 to Thirsk, after 3 miles follow signs for Topcliffe; Long St]: Big bustling place with well kept Camerons ales, enjoyable pubby food, separately themed areas inc softly lit stripped-stone faux-irish bar, also billiards room and two dining rooms; piped music, no credit cards; tables outside, bedrooms *(William and Ann Reid, Gerry and Rosemary Dobson)*

WAKEFIELD [SE3320]

Fernandes Brewery Tap WF1 1UA [Avison Yard, Kirkgate]: Owned by Ossett but still brewing Fernandes ales in cellar, interesting guest beers, bottled imports, farm ciders, new ground-floor bar with flagstones, bare brick and panelling, original raftered top-floor bar with unusual breweriana; cl Mon-Thurs lunchtime, open all day Fri-Sun with some lunchtime food *(the Didler)*

Harrys Bar WF1 1EL [Westgate]: Cheery well run one-room local, Bobs, Ossett, Timothy Taylors and guests, free buffet early Fri evening, stripped brick walls, open fire; small back garden, open all day Sun, cl lunchtime other days *(the Didler)*

Henry Boons WF2 9SR [Westgate]: Two-room bare-boards tap for Clarks Brewery, also several guests beers and bottled imports, friendly staff, barrel tables and breweriana, side pool area; gets busy late on with young people, juke box, machines, live bands; open all day *(the Didler)*

O'Donoghues WF1 1DL [George St]: Warm welcome, comfy sofas and chatty locals, well kept East Coast and guests such as Bobs, Leeds and Roosters (regular beer festivals), basic décor, open fires, live music Fri and Sat *(the Didler)*

WALTON [SE4447]

Fox & Hounds LS23 7DQ [Hall Park Rd, off back rd Wetherby—Tadcaster]: Popular dining pub with enjoyable food from good sandwiches up (best to book Sun lunch), well kept John Smiths and guest such as Black Sheep or Caledonian Deuchars IPA, good service, thriving atmosphere *(Robert Wivell, Greta and Christopher Wells, Pat and Graham Williamson, Ian and Jane Haslock)*

WEAVERTHORPE [SE9670]

☆ **Blue Bell** YO17 8EX: Upscale country dining pub with really good beautifully presented food, fine choice of wines, well kept Black Sheep and Timothy Taylors Landlord, pre-meal home-made crisps and dips, cosy cheerful bar with unusual collection of bottles and packaging, open fire, intimate back restaurant, charming efficient waitresses; 12 bedrooms, good breakfast, interesting village (Marlene and Jim Godfrey, Pat and Graham Williamson)

WELBURN [SE7168]

Crown & Cushion YO60 7DZ [off A64]: Welcoming 18th-c beamed village pub with two cosy rooms separated by central bar, log fires, well kept Tetleys and two guests, good value enjoyable home-made food (not Sun and Mon evenings) from sandwiches to local game and Sun roasts, more extensive evening choice; piped music; children welcome, picnic-sets out at front and in attractive small back garden with terrace, handy for Castle Howard, open all day wknds (Robert Wivell, Dr and Mrs Jackson, LYM, Michael Butler, Andy and Jill Kassube)

WENSLEY [SE0989]

Three Horseshoes DL8 4HJ: Three smartly simple flagstoned rooms, friendly helpful staff, warm fire, four well kept Wensleydale ales, straightforward food (not Sun evening); spotless outside lavatories; tables outside, open all day (Mr and Mrs Maurice Thompson)

WEST HADDLESEY [SE5626]

George & Dragon YO8 8OA [Main St]: Lively little country pub with three well kept ales inc local Brown Cow White Dragon, decent generous pubby food (not Mon) inc nice home-made pies; occasional beer festivals; closed wkdy lunchtimes, open all day wknds, late closing Fri and Sat (Barbarrick)

WEST TANFIELD [SE2678]

Bruce Arms HG4 5JJ [Main St (A6108 N of Ripon)]: Comfortable welcoming pub under new licensees, good affordable food, well kept Black Sheep and Copper Dragon, flagstones and log fires; two bedrooms, cl Sun evening and Mon (Andy and Jill Kassube, LYM)

Bull HG4 5JQ [Church St (A6108 N of Ripon)]: Open-plan but with the feel of two smallish rooms, snug and cosy, with warm Victorian décor and comfortable pub furniture; popular food all day inc good baguettes and some enterprising hot dishes, well kept Black Sheep ales, decent wines, quick pleasant service, small restaurant; children allowed away from bar, tables on terraces in attractive garden behind sloping steeply to River Ure and its old bridge (Earl and Chris Pick, BB)

WEST WITTON [SE0588]

☆ **Wensleydale Heifer** DL8 4LS [A684 W of Leyburn]: Stylish restaurant-with-rooms rather than pub, good fresh fish/seafood and some local meat, good wines, cosy informal upmarket food bar and extensive main formal restaurant, friendly helpful service; nice

bedrooms (back ones are quietest), good big breakfast (Edward Mirzoeff, BB, David and Cathrine Whiting)

WESTOW [SE7565]

Blacksmiths Inn YO60 7NE [off A64 York—Malton; Main St]: 18th-c inn reopened under good new landlord, attractive beamed bar, woodburner in big inglenook, good choice of beers and above average pub food, darts and dominoes, restaurant; picnic-sets on side terrace, separate bedroom block (LYM, Christopher Turner)

WETHERBY [SE4048]

Muse Café LS22 6NQ [Bank St]: Very popular bistro-bar with good brasserie food inc early-bird deals, good range of well kept ales, continental lagers, decent wine list, nice coffee, young friendly helpful staff, simple smart décor; seats outside, open all day (WW, Danny Savage, Stuart Paulley, Michael Butler)

WHITBY [NZ9011]

Black Horse YO22 4BH [Church St]: Small two-room pub tastefully refurbished to reflect its age (gas lamps, stained glass), well kept changing ales such as Adnams, Black Dog Rhatas, Timothy Taylors Landlord and Tetleys Imperial, enterprising (using yorkshire produce) tapas, friendly staff, seafaring memorabilia (Eric Ruff, the Didler, Stephen Corfield)

WHIXLEY [SE4457]

Anchor YO26 8AG [New Rd, E of village (1st left turn heading N from Green Hamerton on B6265)]: Family-friendly pub with traditional generous food inc bargain lunchtime carvery particularly popular with OAPs, friendly young staff, John Smiths and Tetleys, straightforward main eating extension, original core with some character and coal fire in small lounge (Mrs Joy Griffiths)

WIGGLESWORTH [SD8056]

Plough BD23 4RJ [B6478, off A65 S of Settle]: Reopened after major refurbishment, light airy and comfortable, with good home-made food and friendly efficient service, local ales, good wines by the glass, panoramic Dales views; bedrooms (Mike and Shelley Woodroffe, John and Sylvia Harrop)

YORK [SE5951]

☆ **Ackhorne** YO1 6LN [St Martins Lane, Micklegate]: Proper unspoilt relaxed pub with six good changing mainly Yorkshire ales, up to four farm ciders, perry, country wines, foreign bottled beers, bargain basic food (not Sun) from good choice of sandwiches up, friendly helpful family service, beams, bare boards, panelling, stained glass, leather wall seats, old range and open fire, Civil War prints, bottles and jugs, carpeted snug, daily papers, traditional games; silenced games machine; suntrap back terrace, smokers' shelter, open all day (Mrs Hazel Rainer, Michael Butler, the Didler, Pete Coxon, Bruce Bird, Dennis Jones, Eric Larkham, John Ainscough, WW)

Bay Horse YO30 7BH [Marygate]: Large open-plan mock-Tudor pub comfortably refurbished by the Little Tap chain, six well kept changing ales (beer festivals), tea/coffee, fresh food from sandwiches up; piped music, TV; seats out in front, three bedrooms *(the Didler)*

☆ *Black Swan* YO1 7PR [Peaseholme Green (inner ring road)]: Striking timbered and jettied Tudor building, compact panelled front bar, crooked-floored central hall with fine period staircase, black-beamed back bar with vast inglenook, good choice of real ales, basic low-priced food, decent wines, jazz and folk nights; piped music; useful car park, open all day *(the Didler, Pete Coxon, WW, Marlene and Jim Godfrey, LYM)*

☆ *Blue Bell* YO1 9TF [Fossgate]: Delightfully old-fashioned Edwardian pub, very friendly and chatty, with well kept ales such as Adnams Bitter, Black Sheep, Caledonian Deuchars IPA and Timothy Taylors Landlord, good value sandwiches till 5pm (not Sun), daily papers, tiny tiled-floor front bar with roaring fire, panelled ceiling, stained glass, bar pots and decanters, corridor to small back room, hatch service, lamps and candles, pub games; may be piped music and may not welcome children; open all day *(Mark Walker, WW, the Didler, Pete Coxon, Eric Ruff, Eric Larkham, Greta and Christopher Wells)*

☆ *Brigantes* YO1 6JX [Micklegate]: Comfortably traditional Market Town Taverns bar/bistro, eight well kept mainly yorkshire ales, good range of bottled beers, good wines and coffee, enjoyable unpretentious brasserie food all day inc snacks and sandwiches, friendly helpful staff, simple pleasant décor, upstairs dining room; open all day *(WW, Pat and Tony Martin, the Didler, Pete Coxon, Bruce Bird, Brian and Janet Ainscough, Eric Larkham)*

Dormouse YO30 5PA [Shipton Rd, Clifton Park]: Purpose-built Vintage Inn set down leafy driveway, spacious and comfortable, with friendly efficient staff, Thwaites and guest ales, wide choice of good value wines, competetively priced pubby food and specials; good disabled access *(Peter and Anne Hollindale)*

Golden Lion YO1 8BG [Church St]: Big, comfortable and popular open-plan pub done up in bare-boards Edwardian style (in fact first licensed 1771), beams, plenty of lamps, old photographs and brewery signs, eight ales inc Wentworth and York, good range of wines by the glass, sensible food all day from good sandwiches up, pleasant young staff; piped music, can be lively wknds; children welcome, open all day *(Mark Walker, David Carr, Dr Kevan Tucker, WW)*

Golden Slipper YO1 7LG [Goodramgate]: Dating from 15th c, unpretentious bar and three comfortably old-fashioned small rooms, one lined with books, cheerful efficient staff, good cheap plain lunchtime food from sandwiches up inc an OAP special, John Smiths and up to three other beers; TV;

tables in back courtyard *(David Carr, Jeremy King, Pete Coxon, Mark Walker)*

Guy Fawkes YO1 7HP [High Petergate]: Friendly pub in splendid spot next to Minster, dark panelled interior with small bar to the left and two sizeable rooms to right, good real ale choice, decent food inc bargain Sun lunch; bedrooms *(Dr Kevan Tucker)*

Kings Arms YO1 9SN [King's Staithe, by Clifford St]: Fine riverside position (prone to flooding – past water levels shown), bowed black beams, flagstones, lunchtime food from sandwiches up, Sam Smiths; picnic-sets out on cobbled waterside terrace, open all day *(Jeremy King, LYM)*

Lamb & Lion YO1 7EH [High Petergate]: Sparse furnishings and low lighting inc candles giving a spartan Georgian feel, friendly helpful service, up to four well kept changing regional ales, enjoyable simple food (not Fri-Sun evenings, all day summer Mon-Thurs), pews and long tables in bar, compact rooms off dark corridors; steep steps up to small attractive garden below city wall and looking up to Minster (barbecues), 12 bedrooms *(David Carr, Eric Larkham, Alan Thwaite, WW)*

☆ *Last Drop* YO1 8BN [Colliergate]: Basic traditional York Brewery pub, their own beers and one or two well kept guests, samples offered by friendly knowledgeable young staff, decent wines and country wines, nice fresh good value food (12-4) inc sandwiches and shared platters, big windows, bare boards, barrel tables and comfortable seats (some up a few steps); no children, can get very busy lunchtime, they may ask to keep a credit card while you eat, attic lavatories; tables out behind, open all day *(Ian and Jane Haslock, Phil and Jane Hodson, WW, the Didler, Dennis Jones, Rob and Catherine Dunster, Eric Larkham)*

Lendal Cellars YO1 8AA [Lendal]: Split-level ale house in broad-vaulted 17th-c cellars, stripped brickwork, stone floor, linked rooms and alcoves, good choice of changing ales and wines by the glass, foreign bottled beers, farm cider, decent coffee, enjoyable generous pub food all day, friendly helpful staff; piped music; no dogs; children allowed if eating, open all day *(the Didler, Edward Pearce, Jeremy King, LYM)*

Minster Inn YO30 7BH [Marygate]: Multi-roomed Edwardian local, bric-a-brac and dark old settles, fires and woodburners, corridor to distinctive back room, friendly staff, well kept changing Marstons-related ales, sandwiches, table games; children welcome, tables out behind *(the Didler, Dr Kevan Tucker)*

Old White Swan YO1 7LF [Goodramgate]: Bustling spacious pub with Victorian, Georgian and Tudor themed bars, popular lunchtime food inc nine types of sausage, Black Sheep and several other well kept ales, good whisky choice, pleasant young staff, central glass-covered courtyard good for families; piped and frequent live music, big-screen sports TV, games machines, Mon quiz; open all day (WW, Lawrence Miller, Jeremy King, Mark Walker)

Phoenix YO1 9PT [George St]: Unpretentious and friendly with proper front public bar and comfortable back horseshoe-shaped lounge, wide choice of well kept ales, live jazz Sun evening; beer garden, handy for Barbican (Rick Howell)

Pivo Café YO1 8BB: Old black and white pub close to the Shambles, extensive range of foreign beers on tap or bottled, also Thornbridge ales and guests, friendly knowledgeable staff, small narrow bar, more seats upstairs (anon)

Punch Bowl YO1 8AN [Stonegate]: Bustling old black and white fronted pub, friendly helpful service, wide range of generous bargain food all day, small panelled rooms off corridor, TV in beamed one on left of food servery, well kept ales such as Black Sheep Leeds, John Smiths and Thornbridge, good wine choice; piped music, games machines, regular quiz nights; open all day (Jeremy King, Edna Jones, David Carr, Phil and Jane Hodson)

Rook & Gaskill YO10 3WP [Lawrence St]: Traditional Castle Rock pub with up to a dozen ales inc guests like York, enjoyable food (not Sun), dark wood tables, banquettes, chairs and high stools, conservatory; open all day (David Carr, WW, the Didler, Pete Coxon, Eric Larkham)

Swan YO23 1JH [Bishopgate St, Clementhorpe]: Unspoilt 1930s pub (recently Grade II listed), friendly and chatty, hatch service to two small rooms off main bar, great staff, several changing ales and ciders; busy with young people wknds; small pleasant walled garden, nr city walls, cl wkdy lunchtime, open all day wknds (the Didler, David Carr)

☆ **Tap & Spile** YO31 7PB [Monkgate]: Friendly open-plan late Victorian pub with Roosters and other mainly northern ales, farm cider and country wines, decent wines by the glass, bookshelves, games in raised back area, cheap straightforward lunchtime bar

food (not Mon); children in eating area, garden and heated terrace, open all day (LYM, David Carr, the Didler, Pete Coxon, WW)

☆ **Three Legged Mare** YO1 7EN [High Petergate]: Bustling light and airy modern café-bar with York Brewery's full range kept well, plenty of belgian beers, quick friendly young staff, interesting sandwiches and some basic lunchtime hot food, low prices, back conservatory; no children; disabled facilities (other lavatories down spiral stairs), back garden with replica gallows after which pub is named, open all day (WW, Eric Larkham, Phil and Jane Hodson, Donna and Roger, David Carr)

Three Tuns YO1 9NR [Coppergate]: Sizeable lively open-plan pub, four well kept ales such as Wychwood and Jennings, decent generous food from sandwiches up, efficient staff; no credit cards; hanging baskets outside, open all day, handy for Jorvik Centre (Dennis Jones, Rob and Catherine Dunster)

☆ **York Brewery Tap** YO1 6JT [Toft Green, Micklegate]: Members only for York Brewery's upstairs lounge (annual fee £3 unless you live in Yorkshire or go on brewery tour), their own full cask range in top condition, also bottled beers, nice clubby atmosphere with friendly staff happy to talk about the beers, lots of breweriana and view of brewing plant, comfortable settees and armchairs, magazines and daily papers, brewery shop; no food; children allowed, open all day except Sun evening (the Didler, Pete Coxon, Ian and Nita Cooper)

Yorkshire Terrier YO1 8AS [Stonegate]: Behind York Brewery shop front, smallish well worn-in bar with their full beer range and guests, tasting trays of four one-third pints, interesting bottled beers, winter mulled wine, dining room upstairs (where the lavatories are – there's a stair lift) allowing children, limited range of food inc bargain curry and pint Weds evening, small conservatory; handy for Minster, open all day (Derek and Sylvia Stephenson, David Carr, Pete Coxon, Eric Larkham, Andy Lickfold, the Didler, Pat and Tony Martin)

London

Particularly with regard to Central London, it's worth noting that to enjoy pubs here at their best you ought to avoid mid-lunchtime or early evening sessions when they tend to be absolutely packed. And while service is almost unfailingly efficient, you can't fully appreciate the charms or often extraordinary décor then. There are some real architectural gems that will amaze first-time visitors and pubs of real age and character with long historical backgrounds: the Black Friar, Cittie of Yorke, Dog & Duck, Guinea, Jerusalem Tavern, the Lamb, Old Bank of England, Olde Cheshire Cheese, Princess Louise and the Salisbury (all Central London), the Dove, the Warrington and Windsor Castle (in West London), Grapes (in East London) and the Cutty Sark and George (South London). With so very many customers and pubs that are often run by managers who change frequently, it is unusual to find long-serving, hands-on landlords or landladies who offer a genuinely warm and caring welcome. But there are exceptions – head for the Olde Mitre and the Seven Stars (Central London), the Anglesea Arms, the Churchill Arms and the Colton Arms (West London). For real ale fans, many pubs in the city stock a fine range of changing, well kept beers (at a price), but those Main Entries with a larger choice than normal include the Grapes, the Harp, the Jerusalem Tavern, the Lamb, Lamb & Flag, Lord Moon of the Mall, Olde Mitre and the Salisbury (in Central London), the Angelsea Arms, the White Horse and the Windsor Castle (in West London), Spaniards Inn (North London), Market Porter, Royal Oak and Telegraph (South London). Pub bar food in Central London is often surprisingly good value but perhaps not a gastronomic experience, though it's certainly worth visiting the Eagle and the Seven Stars (in Central London) and you can be sure of imaginative meals at the Atlas, the Duke of Sussex, the Princess Victoria and the White Horse (all in West London) and the Bull & Last, Chapel and organic Duke of Cambridge (North London). Standing out from the rest, the Havelock Tavern (West London) is our London Dining Pub of the Year 2011.

CENTRAL LONDON

MAP 13

Argyll Arms   🍺   £

Argyll Street; ⊖ *Oxford Circus, opposite tube side exit; W1F 7TP*

Unexpectedly individual pub with interesting little front rooms, appealing range of beers and good value food all day

Run with a lot of energy by the new landlady, this busy pub is handy for Oxford Circus. There's a surprising amount of genuine character in the three atmospheric and secluded little front cubicle rooms – essentially unchanged since they were built in the 1860s. All oddly angular, they're made by wooden partitions with impressive frosted and engraved glass. A long mirrored corridor leads to the spacious back room; newspapers to read, fruit machines and piped music. Fullers London Pride, Greene King IPA, Timothy Taylors Landlord and up to four guests on handpump and quite a few malt whiskies. The quieter upstairs bar, with theatrical photographs, overlooks the pedestrianised street – and the Palladium theatre, if you can see through the impressive foliage outside the window.

🍴 **Well liked bar food includes sandwiches, ploughman's, breakfast (until noon), various platters, a sausage menu with choices like cumberland, wild boar and so forth, aberdeen angus burger with toppings, a vegetarian dish, gammon and free-range eggs, steak in ale pie, and puddings such as banoffi pie.** *Starters/Snacks: £2.95 to £3.50. Main Courses: £5.95 to £9.95. Puddings: £3.50*

Mitchells & Butlers ~ Manager Christine Bateman ~ Real ale ~ Bar food (10am-10pm) ~ Restaurant ~ (020) 7734 6117 ~ Children in upstairs bar ~ Open 10am-11.30pm(midnight Fri and Sat)

Recommended by Derek Thomas, Michael Dandy, Ros Lawler, Mrs Hazel Rainer, Joe Green, Andrea Rampley, the Didler, Mike and Sue Loseby, Peter Dandy, Ian Phillips, Tracey and Stephen Groves, Dr and Mrs M E Wilson, Tim Maddison

Bishops Finger ♀

West Smithfield – opposite Bart's Hospital; ⊖ ⇌ Farringdon; EC1A 9JR

Nicely civilised little pub with a particularly welcoming atmosphere and good beers

Efficiently run and neatly kept, this is a smartly civilised little pub close to Smithfield Market. The well laid-out bar room has cream walls, big windows, fresh flowers on elegant tables, polished bare floorboards, a few pillars and cushioned chairs under one wall lined with framed prints of the market. It does get busy at lunchtime and after work but can be rather relaxed and peaceful at other times; the atmosphere is friendly and welcoming. Shepherd Neame Bitter and Spitfire and two seasonal brews on handpump, six wines by the glass, half a dozen malt whiskies, and several ports and champagnes; prompt, efficient service. There are a few tables outside.

🍴 **Most people go for one of the ten or so varieties of sausage, all served with mash, but they also do sandwiches, home-made burgers, fresh beer-battered haddock, a steak of the day and specials; in the upstairs dining room there's a two- and three-course set menu.** *Starters/Snacks: £4.50 to £4.95. Main Courses: £5.95 to £12.95. Puddings: £4.95*

Shepherd Neame ~ Manager Paul Potts ~ Real ale ~ Bar food (12-3, 6-9 (not Fri evening or weekends)) ~ (020) 7248 2341 ~ Children welcome ~ Open 11-11; closed weekends and bank hols

Recommended by Donna and Roger, Mayur Shah, Ian Phillips, Peter Dandy, Michael Dandy

Black Friar

Queen Victoria Street; ⊖ Mansion House, St Paul's, Temple (not Sundays) ⇌ Blackfriars; EC4V 4EG

Remarkable art nouveau décor, a good choice of beers, friendly atmosphere and popular food all day

Built on the site of a 13th-c Dominican Priory this well run pub is an architectural gem that includes some of the best Edwardian bronze and marble art nouveau work to be found anywhere. The inner back room (known as the Grotto) has big bas-relief friezes of jolly monks set into richly coloured florentine marble walls, an opulent marble-pillared inglenook fireplace, a low vaulted mosaic ceiling, gleaming mirrors, seats built into rich golden marble recesses and tongue-in-cheek verbal embellishments such as Silence is Golden and Finery is Foolish. See if you can spot the opium-smoking hints modelled into the fireplace of the front room. The other large room has a fireplace and plenty of seats and tables. Fullers London Pride, Sharps Doom Bar and Timothy Taylors Landlord on handpump, over a dozen wines by the glass and several malt whiskies; piped music. Despite the crowds (both tourists and business people), service is friendly and extremely efficient. In the evenings, lots of people spill out on to the wide forecourt, near the approach to Blackfriars Bridge; there's some smart furniture out here. Please note that Blackfriars tube station is closed until late 2011, so we've suggested alternatives.

🍴 They specialise in pies such as roasted butternut squash, steak in ale, ham hock and pea and chicken, bacon and cheese; other traditional bar food, served all day, includes sandwiches, ploughman's, sharing platters, a meaty or vegetarian breakfast, chicken caesar salad, fish and chips, lincolnshire sausage whirl and steaks; Sunday roasts. *Starters/Snacks: £3.95 to £5.95. Main Courses: £5.95 to £10.95. Puddings: £4.00*

Mitchells & Butlers ~ Manager Cecilia Soderholm ~ Real ale ~ Bar food (10-10; 12-9 Sun) ~ (020) 7236 5474 ~ Children welcome if quiet ~ Open 10am-11pm; 12-10 Sun

Recommended by Dr and Mrs A K Clarke, N R White, John Saville, Russell and Alison Hunt, John Wooll, the Didler, Dave Braisted, Barry Collett, Tom McLean, Mrs Hazel Rainer, Ian Phillips

Cittie of Yorke 🍺

High Holborn – find it by looking out for its big black and gold clock; ⊖ *Chancery Lane (not Sundays), Holborn; WC1V 6BN*

Bustling old pub where the splendid back bar with its old-fashioned cubicles rarely fails to impress – and the beer is refreshingly low priced

A pub has stood on this site since 1430, though the current building owes more to the 1695 coffee house erected here behind a garden; it was reconstructed in Victorian times, using 17th-c materials and parts. The impressive back bar is the place to head for as it's rather like a baronial hall, with an extraordinarily extended bar counter stretching off into the distance. There are thousand-gallon wine vats resting above the gantry, big, bulbous lights hanging from the soaring high-raftered roof and a nice glow from the fire. It can get busy in the evenings with a fine mix of customers from students to lawyers and City types, but there's plenty of space to absorb the crowds – and indeed it's at the busiest times that the pub is at its most magnificent (it never feels quite right when it's quiet). Most people tend to congregate in the middle, so you should still be able to bag one of the intimate, old-fashioned and ornately carved booths that run along both sides. Cheap Sam Smiths OB on handpump. The triangular Waterloo fireplace, with grates on all three sides and a figure of Peace among laurels, used to stand in the Hall of Gray's Inn Common Room until less obtrusive heating was introduced. A smaller, comfortable panelled room has lots of little prints of York and attractive brass lights, while the ceiling of the entrance hall has medieval-style painted panels and plaster York roses. Fruit machine.

🍴 Under the new licensee, bar food includes soup, chicken caesar salad, bangers and mash, steak in ale pie, a good chilli, and puddings such as jam sponge and sticky toffee pudding. *Starters/Snacks: £2.50 to £4.50. Main Courses: £5.50 to £7.95. Puddings: £2.50*

Sam Smiths ~ Manager Adele Merjanic ~ Real ale ~ Bar food (12-3, 6-9.30; not Sun) ~ (020) 7242 7670 ~ Children welcome ~ Open 11.30(12 Sat)-11; closed Sun

Recommended by Jeremy King, Neil Whitehead, Victoria Anderson, Chris Sale, Di and Mike Gillam, the Didler, Ian Phillips, N R White, Barry Collett, Michael Dandy, Anthony Longden, Pete Coxon

Coopers Arms

Flood Street; ⊖ *Sloane Square, but quite a walk; SW3 5TB*

Well positioned pub with real ales and decent food, and a useful bolthole for Kings Road shoppers

As we went to press, this spacious and pubby place was closed for a couple of months for refurbishment. The open-plan bar has had interesting furnishings such as kitchen chairs and other seats on the floorboards, a mix of nice old good-sized tables and a pre-war sideboard and dresser; also, LNER posters and maps of Chelsea and the Thames on the walls, an enormous railway clock and a fireplace – all watched over by the heads of a moose and a tusky boar. Wells & Youngs Bitter and Special and three guests on handpump, and quite a few wines by the glass. There are seats in the courtyard garden.

🍴 Bar food includes sandwiches, soup, haddock and salmon fishcakes, beer-battered fish and chips, speciality sausages, a risotto of the day, burger with bacon and cheese, various sharing boards, steak and kidney pie, and puddings such as fruit crumble and sticky toffee pudding; Sunday roasts. *Starters/Snacks: £4.15 to £7.50. Main Courses: £9.50 to £14.60. Puddings: £4.65 to £5.20*

Youngs ~ Manager Sarah Pledger ~ Real ale ~ Bar food (all day) ~ (020) 7376 3120 ~
Well behaved children allowed until 7pm ~ Dogs allowed in bar ~ Open 11-11(10.30 Sun)

Recommended by Tracey and Stephen Groves, Peter

Cross Keys
Lawrence Street; ⊖ *Sloane Square, but some distance away; SW3 5NB*

Bustling Chelsea landmark with a friendly bar, airy back restaurant, attentive staff, real ales and modern bar food

With good modern food and several real ales, this bustling 18th-c pub is especially busy in the evenings and at weekends. It's a civilised and friendly place with a roomy, high-ceilinged bar, sofas around low tables, settles and dining chairs on the flagstones, two open fires and a good mix of customers. The light and airy conservatory-style back restaurant has a fully retractable roof. Courage Directors, Sharps Doom Bar and a changing guest beer on handpump, and a quite a choice of wines by the glass from an extensive list; attentive young staff; piped music. More reports please.

🍴 **Interesting bar food might include dressed cornish crab on bruschetta with saffron aioli, asparagus with hollandaise, their much-enjoyed japanese-style wagyu burger with truffle fries, grilled wild bass, rib-eye steak, and puddings like valrhona chocolate fondant with vanilla ice-cream.** *Starters/Snacks: £6.00 to £8.50. Main Courses: £11.50 to £21.00. Puddings: £6.00 to £7.50*

Free house ~ Licensee John Bond ~ Bar food (12-3, 6-10.30(9 Sun)) ~ Restaurant ~ (020) 7349 9111 ~ Children welcome ~ Dogs allowed in bar ~ Open 12-midnight; closed bank hols

Recommended by Peter, BOB

Dog & Duck 🍺 £
Bateman Street, on corner with Frith Street; ⊖ *Tottenham Court Road, Leicester Square; W1D 3AJ*

Tiny Soho pub squeezing in bags of character, with unusual old tiles and mosaics, good beers and a warmly welcoming atmosphere

'The best pub in Soho' and 'Never fails to please' are just two comments from readers about this unchanging little pub. Afternoons are probably the best time to fully appreciate the décor, which has some interesting detail and individual touches; it does get very busy indeed in the evenings. On the floor near the door is an engaging mosaic showing a dog with its tongue out in hot pursuit of a duck; the same theme is embossed on some of the shiny tiles that frame the heavy old advertising mirrors. There are some high stools by the ledge along the back wall, further seats in a slightly roomier area at one end, and a fire in winter; the piped music is usually drowned out by the good-natured chatter. There's also a rather cosy upstairs bar where there's often some free space. Fullers London Pride, Greene King IPA and a couple of guest beers from breweries such as Hook Norton and Sharps on handpump from the unusual little bar counter, maybe Addlestone's cider, and quite a few wines by the glass. In good weather, most people tend to spill on to the bustling street.

🍴 **They specialise in sausages, served all day here, from a choice of a dozen including cumberland, bloody mary, wild mushrooms and black pepper and wild boar, pork and apple; also, sandwiches, beer-battered fish, a meaty or vegetarian breakfast, gammon and free-range eggs, steaks, and puddings.** *Starters/Snacks: £3.95 to £4.75. Main Courses: £5.95 to £9.95. Puddings: £3.75*

Mitchells & Butlers ~ Manager Natalie Hubbard ~ Real ale ~ Bar food (all day) ~ (020) 7494 0697 ~ Children allowed in dining room ~ Dogs allowed in bar ~ Open 10am-11pm(11.30 Sat; 10.30 Sun)

Recommended by Mike Gorton, the Didler, Richard Endacott, Jeremy King, LM, Lawrence R Cotter, Simon Collett-Jones

---

Prices of main dishes sometimes now don't include vegetables – if in doubt, ask.

Eagle 🍽 ⚲

Farringdon Road; opposite Bowling Green Lane car park; ⊖ ⇄ Farringdon, Old Street; EC1R 3AL

Busy, noisy gastropub with gutsy mediterranean cooking, a couple of real ales and quite a few wines by the glass

It's hard to believe that it's 20 years since London's first gastropub opened its doors – but the place is as popular as ever. To be sure of a table you must arrive before serving time starts and on weekday lunchtimes, especially, dishes from the blackboard menu can run out or change fairly quickly. The open-plan room is dominated by a giant open range and it's all pretty busy, noisy and slightly scruffy for some tastes. Furnishings are basic and well worn – school chairs, a random assortment of tables, a couple of sofas on bare boards and modern paintings on the walls (there's an art gallery upstairs, with direct access from the bar). Wells & Youngs Eagle and Bombardier on handpump, good wines including around 16 by the glass and decent coffee; piped music (sometimes loud). Not the ideal choice for a quiet dinner or a smart night out – but great fun; it's generally quieter at weekends. More reports please.

🍽 **Quickly changing dishes from a short choice of gutsy, mediterranean-style food might include hearty soups, a popular steak sandwich, tapas, risottos, pasta with chicken livers and sage, mutton and aubergine tagine, gilthead bream with spinach and romesco sauce, pork and cockles alentejo-style, and puddings such as lemon and almond cake with mascarpone and berries.** *Starters/Snacks: £6.00 to £9.50. Main Courses: £8.50 to £15.00. Puddings: £4.00*

Free house ~ Licensee Michael Belben ~ Real ale ~ Bar food (12.30-3(3.30 weekends), 6.30-10.30; not Sun evening) ~ (020) 7837 1353 ~ Children welcome ~ Dogs welcome ~ Open 12-11(5 Sun); closed Sun evening, bank hols, one week Christmas

Recommended by Dr and Mrs A K Clarke

Grapes 🍺 £

Shepherd Market; ⊖ Green Park, Hyde Park Corner; W1J 7QQ

Genuinely old-fashioned and individual, and always packed in the evenings for the six real ales and thai food

There's a lot of character in this pleasingly old-fashioned pub with its Victorian décor and artefacts, and the six real ales and popular thai food certainly draw in the crowds. It's especially busy in the evenings (though this somehow adds to the allure) and generally quieter at lunchtime. The dimly lit bar has plenty of well worn plush red furnishings, stuffed birds and fish in glass display cases, wooden floors and panelling, a welcoming coal fire and a snug little alcove at the back; readers like the seats on the raised platform by the window. Fullers London Pride, Sharps Doom Bar and guests like Adnams Best, Cottage Champflower Ale, Sambrooks Wandle Ale and Shepherd Neame Spitfire on handpump, several wines by the glass and several malt whiskies. You'll generally see smart-suited drinkers spilling on to the square outside.

🍽 **There's a huge choice of thai dishes cooked by a thai chef and set meals for two or more people, as well as some traditional english dishes like sausage and mash, a pie, and battered cod and chips.** *Starters/Snacks: £2.95 to £3.95. Main Courses: £5.95 to £7.95. Puddings: £2.95 to £3.95*

Free house ~ Licensees John Shannon, Chavdar Anin ~ Real ale ~ Bar food (12-3.30, 5-9.30; 12-6 Sun) ~ Restaurant ~ (020) 7493 4216 ~ Children allowed in bar until 6pm weekdays; any time at weekends ~ Open 11.30-11; 12-10.30 Sun

Recommended by N R White, Darren Le Poidevin, the Didler, Tracey and Stephen Groves, Ian Phillips, Lawrence R Cotter, Peter Dandy, Michael Dandy

---

A few pubs try to make you leave a credit card at the bar, as a sort of deposit if you order food. This is a bad practice, and the banks and credit card firms warn you not to let your card go like this.

Guinea

Bruton Place; ⊖ Bond Street, Green Park, Piccadilly Circus, Oxford Circus; W1J 6NL

Prize-winning steak and kidney pie, and four real ales in a tiny old-fashioned pub with friendly staff and a bustling atmosphere

The hanging baskets outside this 17th-c pub are lovely and it's in this little mews that most customers – suited workers, tourists and diners for the upmarket restaurant – tend to gather at peak times, as it's almost standing room only inside. The look of the place is appealingly simple: bare boards, yellow walls, old-fashioned prints and a red-planked ceiling with raj fans. Three cushioned wooden seats and tables are tucked to the left of the entrance to the bar, with a couple more in a snug area at the back, underneath a big old clock; most people tend to prop themselves against a little shelf running along the side of the small room. Friendly, cheery staff serve Wells & Youngs Bitter, Special and seasonal brews from the striking bar counter, which has some nice wrought-iron work above it. Take care to pick the right entrance – it's all too easy to walk into the upscale Guinea Grill which takes up much of the same building; uniformed doormen will politely redirect you if you've picked the door to that by mistake. No children.

🍴 **The only bar food is the famous lunchtime steak and kidney pie and some sandwiches; the adjacent restaurant serves the famous pie too, as well as a full – if not cheap – à la carte menu.** *Main Courses: £3.50 to £8.50*

Youngs ~ Manager Carl Smith ~ Real ale ~ Bar food (12.30-9; not weekends) ~ Restaurant ~ (020) 7409 1728 ~ Children in restaurant if over 10 ~ Open 11.30-11; 6-11 Sat; closed Sat lunchtime, all day Sun and bank hols

Recommended by N R White, Michael Dandy, Peter Dandy, the Didler, Michael and Alison Sandy, Mike Gorton

Harp £

47 Chandos Place; ⊖ ⇌ Charing Cross, Leicester Square; WC2N 4HS

Quietly civilised little pub with eight real ales, friendly service, a cheerful atmosphere, and nice sausages

The long-serving landlady and her staff in this busy little pub (now a free house) are unfailingly cheerful and welcoming, and the eight real ales on handpump are particularly well kept and quickly changing. There's usually three from Dark Star, one from Harveys, two from Sambrooks and one or two from Twickenham; farm cider and perry, and quite a few malt whiskies. The atmosphere in the long narrow bar is chatty and informal, there are lots of high bar stools along the wall counter and around elbow tables, big mirrors on the red walls, some lovely front stained glass and lots of interesting, if not always well executed, star portraits. If it's not too busy, you may be able to get one of the prized seats looking out through the front windows. Upstairs, a little room has comfortable furniture and a window looking over the road below; if the bar gets too crowded, customers spill out into the back alley.

🍴 **Bar food consists of good changing sausages such as boar and apple, pork, port and stilton, venison and redcurrant, lamb and mint and so forth, served in baps with lots of fried onions.** *Starters/Snacks: £2.50 to £3.50*

Free house ~ Licensee Bridget Walsh ~ Real ale ~ Bar food (12-4; not Sun) ~ (020) 7836 0291 ~ Open 10.30am-11pm; 12-10.30 Sun

Recommended by Matt and Vicky Wharton, Tim Maddison, Joe Green, Mike Gorton, Donna and Roger, Barbarrick, Michael and Alison Sandy

Jerusalem Tavern ★

Britton Street; ⊖ ⇌ Farringdon; EC1M 5UQ

A London favourite, delightfully atmospheric, even at its busiest, with the full range of splendid St Peters beers, good lunchtime food and helpful staff

A real favourite with many of our readers, this is a very well run and genuinely interesting pub – and always packed with customers. It's the only place to stock the whole range of brews from the Suffolk-based St Peters other than the brewery itself, with half a dozen tapped from casks behind the little bar counter, and the rest available in their elegant, distinctively shaped bottles. Depending on the season you'll find St Peters Best, Golden Ale, Grapefruit, Organic Best, and two other changing guests from their range, and you can buy them to take away too. Particularly inviting on a cold winter's evening when there are coal fires and candlelight, the pub is a vivid re-creation of a dark 18th-c tavern, seeming so genuinely old that you'd hardly guess the work was done only a few years ago. The current building was developed around 1720, originally as a merchant's house, then becoming a clock and watchmaker's. It still has the shopfront added in 1810, immediately behind which is a light little room with a couple of wooden tables and benches, and some remarkable old tiles on the walls at either side. This leads to the tiny dimly lit bar, which has a couple of unpretentious tables on the bare boards, and another up some stairs on a discreetly precarious-feeling, though perfectly secure, balcony – a prized vantage point. A plainer back room has a few more tables, a fireplace and a stuffed fox in a case. Staff are always friendly and attentive, even at peak times when it can get horribly crowded. There are some wooden benches outside on the pavement. The brewery's headquarters in South Elmham is a Main Entry in our Suffolk chapter. No children.

🍴 Blackboards list the well liked weekly-changing lunchtime bar food: ploughman's, wild mushrooms on sour dough toast, full english breakfast, very good home-made minted lamb burger with chilli aioli, roast pork and apple sandwiches with crackling, gammon and organic eggs, steak in ale stew with dumplings, and rib-eye steak. *Starters/Snacks: £5.00 to £7.00. Main Courses: £6.80 to £12.00.*

St Peters ~ Manager David Hart ~ Real ale ~ Bar food (12-3; not evenings) ~ (020) 7490 4281 ~ Dogs welcome ~ Open 11-11; closed weekends, bank hols, 24 Dec-2 Jan

Recommended by the Didler, Mike Gorton, Dominic McGonigal, Mayur Shah, Peter Dandy, Anthony Longden, Giles and Annie Francis, Tom McLean, Donna and Roger

Lamb ★ 🍺

Lamb's Conduit Street; ✚ Holborn, Russell Square; WC1N 3LZ

Famously unspoilt Victorian pub, full of character, with unique fittings and atmosphere

Thankfully nothing changes here and it's still a splendid place to unwind in the afternoon (it does get very busy in the evening). There's a great deal of character and plenty to look at, especially the unique Victorian fittings – the highlight being the bank of cut-glass swivelling snob-screens all the way round the U-shaped bar counter. Sepia photographs of 1890s actresses on the ochre-panelled walls and traditional cast-iron-framed tables with neat brass rails around the rim add to the overall effect. Up to seven real ales on handpump like Wells & Youngs Bitter, Bombardier, Special and Waggle Dance, plus three guests and a good choice of malt whiskies. No machines or music. There's a snug little room at the back, slatted wooden seats out in front and more in a little courtyard beyond. Like the street, the pub is named for the kentish clothmaker William Lamb who brought fresh water to Holborn in 1577. No children. The Foundling Museum is nearby.

🍴 Bar food includes sandwiches and wraps, platters, salads like niçoise or chicken and bacon, bangers and mash with red onion gravy, sweet potato curry, all-day breakfast, steak in ale or fish pie, gammon and free-range eggs, and puddings such as coffee crème brûlée and apple pie. *Starters/Snacks: £3.40 to £7.05. Main Courses: £7.95 to £12.95. Puddings: £4.70*

Youngs ~ Manager Mr L Tuohy ~ Real ale ~ Bar food (12-9) ~ (020) 7405 0713 ~ Children allowed until 5pm and only in dining area ~ Open 12-11 Mon-Weds; 12-midnight Thurs-Sat; 12-11.30 Sun

Recommended by Derek and Sylvia Stephenson, James A Waller, John and Gloria Isaacs, Ros Lawler, Roy Hoing, the Didler, Dr and Mrs A K Clarke, Eddie Edwards

---

Places with gardens or terraces usually let children sit there – we note in the text the very few exceptions that don't.

Lamb & Flag 🍺 £

Rose Street, off Garrick Street; ✦ *Leicester Square, Covent Garden; WC2E 9EB*

Historic yet unpretentious, full of character and atmosphere and with six real ales; especially busy in the evening

Even though this tucked-away old pub is always packed with customers, service from the friendly staff remains efficient and friendly. It's an unspoilt and, in places, rather basic old tavern, and the more spartan front room leads into a snugly atmospheric low-ceilinged back bar with high-backed black settles and an open fire. In Regency times this was known as the Bucket of Blood, thanks to the bare-knuckle prize-fights held here. Half a dozen well kept real ales typically include Courage Directors, Greene King Abbot and Old Speckled Hen, Harveys Best and Wells & Youngs Bitter and Special on handpump, and there are a good few malt whiskies. The upstairs Dryden Room is often less crowded and has more seats (though fewer beers). The pub has a lively and well documented history: Dryden was nearly beaten to death by hired thugs outside, and Dickens made fun of the Middle Temple lawyers who frequented it when he was working in nearby Catherine Street.

🍴 **A short choice of simple food is served upstairs, lunchtimes only: soup, baked potatoes, and a few daily changing specials like cottage pie, cauliflower cheese and fish and chips.** *Starters/Snacks: £4.00 to £5.75. Main Courses: £6.50 to £8.50. Puddings: £2.40 to £3.50*

Free house ~ Licensees Terry Archer and Adrian and Sandra Zimmerman ~ Real ale ~ Bar food (12-3(4.30 weekends) ~ (020) 7497 9504 ~ Children in upstairs dining room lunchtime only ~ Live jazz Sun evening ~ Open 11-11; 11-11.40 Fri and Sat; 12-10.30 Sun; closed 25-26 Dec, 1 Jan

Recommended by N R White, the Didler, Mike and Sue Loseby, Donna and Roger, Anthony Longden, Bruce Bird, Barry and Anne, Ian Phillips, John and Sharon Hancock

Lord Moon of the Mall 🍺 £

Whitehall; ✦ ⇌ *Charing Cross; SW1A 2DY*

Superior Wetherspoons pub with excellent value food and drink in a perfect location close to all the sights

This nicely converted former bank offers incredible value food and drink considering this is Central London. Up to nine real ales are kept on handpump which might include Greene King Abbot and Ruddles Best, Highgate Black Pig, Hook Norton Old Hooky, Marstons Pedigree, Mauldons Silver Adder, Roosters Patriot, Thwaites Highwayman and York Centurions Ghost Ale. The impressive main room has a splendid high ceiling and quite an elegant feel, with old prints, big arched windows looking out over Whitehall and a huge painting that seems to show a well-to-do 18th-c gentleman; in fact it's Tim Martin, founder of the Wetherspoons chain. Once through an arch, the style is more recognisably Wetherspoons, with a couple of neatly tiled areas and bookshelves opposite the long bar; silenced fruit machines, trivia and a cash machine. The back doors (now only an emergency exit) were apparently built as a secret entrance for the bank's account holders living in Buckingham Palace (Edward VII had an account here from the age of three). As you come out, Nelson's Column is immediately to the left, and Big Ben a walk of ten minutes or so to the right.

🍴 **Good value bar food from the standard Wetherspoons menu includes sandwiches, filled baked potatoes, ploughman's, soup, ham and free-range eggs, moroccan meatballs with couscous, various burgers, sweet chilli noodles, chicken, chorizo and spinach pasta, mixed grill, and puddings like profiteroles and vanilla cheesecake.** *Starters/Snacks: £2.79 to £6.49. Main Courses: £3.99 to £8.09. Puddings: £1.99 to £3.99*

Wetherspoons ~ Manager Mark Pringle ~ Real ale ~ Bar food (9am-11pm) ~ (020) 7839 7701 ~ Children allowed if eating ~ Dogs welcome ~ Open 9am-11.30pm(midnight Fri and Sat; 11pm Sun)

Recommended by Dave Irving, Jenny Huggins, Dr and Mrs A K Clarke, Ian Phillips, Katrin Schmidt, Jeremy King, Andy Lickfold, Michael Dandy, Dr and Mrs M E Wilson

Old Bank of England ♀

Fleet Street; ⊖ Chancery Lane (not Sundays), Temple (not Sundays) ⇌ Blackfriars; EC4A 2LT

Dramatically converted former bank building, with gleaming chandeliers in impressive, soaring bar, well kept Fullers beers, and good pies

It's best to visit this former subsidiary branch of the Bank of England during the day when things are quieter – it rarely fails to impress visitors. It's a rather austere italianate building with a soaring, spacious bar which has three gleaming chandeliers hanging from the exquisitely plastered ceiling, high above an unusually tall island bar counter, crowned with a clock. The end wall has big paintings and murals that look like 18th-c depictions of Justice, but in fact feature members of the Fuller, Smith and Turner families, who run the brewery the pub belongs to. There are well polished dark wooden furnishings, plenty of framed prints, and, despite the grandeur, some surprisingly cosy corners, with screens between some of the tables creating an unexpectedly intimate feel which readers really enjoy. Tables in a quieter galleried section upstairs offer a bird's-eye view of the action, and some smaller rooms (used mainly for functions) open off. Fullers Chiswick, Discovery, ESB, London Pride and seasonal brews on handpump, a good choice of malt whiskies and a dozen wines by the glass. At lunchtimes the piped music is generally classical or easy listening; it's louder and livelier in the evenings. There's also a garden with seats (one of the few pubs in the area to have one). Pies have a long if rather dubious pedigree in this area; it was in the vaults and tunnels below the Old Bank and the surrounding buildings that Sweeney Todd butchered the clients destined to provide the fillings in his mistress Mrs Lovett's nearby pie shop.

🍴 Available all day, the good bar food has an emphasis on well liked home-made pies such as sweet potato and goats cheese, chicken and asparagus, lamb, shallot and mint and steak in ale, but also includes sandwiches, ploughman's, soup, sausages and mash, proper burgers, fish and chips, puddings like cherry bakewell pudding, and popular afternoon teas. *Starters/Snacks: £4.25 to £6.25. Main Courses: £8.50 to £9.75. Puddings: £4.55 to £4.75*

Fullers ~ Manager Jo Farquhar ~ Real ale ~ Bar food (12-9) ~ (020) 7430 2255 ~ Children welcome ~ Dogs allowed in bar ~ Live jazz last Weds of the month ~ Open 11-11; closed weekends, bank hols

Recommended by Neil Whitehead, Victoria Anderson, Dr and Mrs A K Clarke, Peter, the Didler, Michael Dandy, Peter Dandy, Barry Collett, Michael and Alison Sandy, Donna and Roger

Olde Cheshire Cheese

Wine Office Court, off 145 Fleet Street; ⊖ Chancery Lane (not Sundays), Temple (not Sundays) ⇌ Blackfriars; EC4A 2BU

Much bigger than it looks and soaked in history, with lots of warmly old-fashioned rooms, cheap Sam Smiths beer and a convivial atmosphere

It might be best to avoid early evening visits to this 17th-c former chop house as the place is packed out then with office workers and legal types, and service can struggle to cope. At less busy times, it's fun to wander through the warren of dark, historic and unpretentious rooms with bare wooden benches built into the walls, bare boards and, on the ground floor, high beams, crackly old black varnish, Victorian paintings on dark brown walls and big open winter fires. A particularly snug room is the tiny one on the right as you enter, but the most rewarding bit is the Cellar Bar, down steep narrow stone steps that look as if they're only going to lead to the loo, but in fact take you to an unexpected series of cosy areas with stone walls and ceilings, and some secluded alcoves. The back bar is noisy and usually crowded and a bit like a drinking barn. Sam Smiths OB on handpump, as usual for this brewery, extraordinarily well priced. In the early 20th c, the pub was well known for its famous parrot that for over 40 years entertained princes, ambassadors and other distinguished guests; she's still around today, stuffed and silent, in the restaurant on the ground floor.

🍴 Bar food includes smoked salmon and dill terrine, fish and chips, roast beef, steak and kidney pudding, lamb shank, and puddings such as chocolate fudge cake and bread and butter pudding; the cellar serves a lunchtime pie and mash buffet. *Starters/Snacks: £4.25 to £6.50. Main Courses: £7.50 to £13.00. Puddings: £4.25*

Sam Smiths ~ Manager Gordon Garrity ~ Real ale ~ Bar food (12-10; not Sun evening) ~
Restaurant ~ (020) 7353 6170 ~ Children allowed in eating area lunchtime only ~
Open 11.30(12 Sat)-11; 12-4 Sun; closed Sun evening

Recommended by Tracey and Stephen Groves, Neil Whitehead, Victoria Anderson, N R White, the Didler,
John Wooll, Jeremy King, Peter Dandy, Lawrence R Cotter, LM

Olde Mitre 🍺 £

Ely Place; the easiest way to find it is from the narrow passageway beside 8 Hatton Garden;
⊖ *Chancery Lane (not Sundays); EC1N 6SJ*

**Hard to find but well worth it – an unspoilt old pub with a lovely atmosphere, unusual
guest beers and bargain toasted sandwiches**

It's all too rare in London to find proper hands-on licensees who genuinely care for their
pub and their customers – but Mr and Mrs Scott do just that and our readers love it. It's
an unspoilt and tucked-away little place and a real refuge from the modern city nearby.
The cosy small rooms have lots of dark panelling as well as antique settles and –
particularly in the popular back room, where there are more seats – old local pictures and
so forth. It gets good-naturedly packed between 12.30 and 2.15, filling up again in the
early evening, but in the early afternoons and by around 9pm becomes a good deal more
tranquil. An upstairs room, mainly used for functions, may double as an overflow at peak
periods. Adnams Broadside, Caledonian Deuchars IPA, Fullers London Pride and Gales
Seafarer and guests like Dark Star Hophead and Kelham Island Pale Rider on handpump;
they hold three beer festivals a year (phone for details). No music, TV or machines – the
only games here are cribbage and dominoes. There's some space for outside drinking by
the pot plants and jasmine in the narrow yard between the pub and St Ethelreda's church
(which is worth a look). Note the pub doesn't open weekends. The iron gates that guard
one entrance to Ely Place are a reminder of the days when the law in this district was
administered by the Bishops of Ely. The best approach is from Hatton Garden, walking up
the right-hand side away from Chancery Lane; an easily missed sign on a lamp post
points the way down a narrow alley. No children.

🍴 **Served all day, bar snacks are limited to scotch eggs, pork pies and sausage rolls, and
really good value toasted sandwiches with cheese, ham, pickle or tomato.** *Starters/Snacks:*
£0.75 to £1.85

Fullers ~ Managers Eamon and Kathy Scott ~ Real ale ~ Bar food (11.30-9.30) ~ (020) 7405 4751
~ Open 11-11; closed weekends and bank hols

Recommended by the Didler, Mike Gorton, Jim Frame, Richard Endacott, Tracey and Stephen Groves, Ross Balaam,
John and Gloria Isaacs, Ian Phillips, N R White, Lawrence R Cotter, Anthony Longden, Barbarrick, Tom McLean,
K Almond, Darren Le Poidevin, Donna and Roger, Michael Dandy

Princess Louise

High Holborn; ⊖ *Holborn, Chancery Lane (not Sundays); WC1V 7EP*

Beautifully refurbished Victorian gin-palace with fabulously extravagant décor

The gloriously opulent main bar in this splendid Victorian gin-palace is worth visiting for its
amazing décor – and its well kept and very cheap Sam Smiths OB on handpump. There are
wood and glass partitions in lots of different areas, splendid etched and gilt mirrors, brightly
coloured and fruity-shaped tiles, and slender portland stone columns soaring towards the
lofty and deeply moulded plaster ceiling. Even the gents' has its own preservation order.
There's also a welcoming winter fire. It's generally quite crowded on early weekday evenings
(for some, adding to the appeal), but is usually quieter later on. No children.

🍴 **Bar food includes pies, fish and chips, sausage and mash, gammon and egg, steaks, and
puddings like jam roly-poly.** *Starters/Snacks: £2.75 to £3.00. Main Courses: £4.75 to £6.25.*
Puddings: £2.75

Sam Smiths ~ Manager Campbell Mackay ~ Real ale ~ Bar food (12-2.30, 6-8.30; not Fri and not
weekends) ~ (020) 7405 8816 ~ Open 11.30-11; 12-11(10.30 Sun) Sat

Recommended by Roger Shipperley, David M Smith, Tracey and Stephen Groves, Joe Green, the Didler,
Tim Maddison, Mayur Shah, Ian Phillips, Barry Collett, Eleanor Dandy, Anthony Longden, Barbarrick, Pete Coxon

Red Lion 🍺

Duke of York Street; ⊖ Piccadilly Circus; SW1Y 6JP

Remarkably preserved Victorian pub, all gleaming mirrors and polished mahogany, though right in the heart of town, so does get busy

You can best appreciate the charms of this smart and pretty little pub during the afternoon, as it fills up quickly in the early evening with after-work drinkers, shoppers and tourists. But when it does get very crowded, the many customers are happy to spill out on to the pavement by the mass of foliage and flowers cascading down the wall. When it was built, its profusion of mirrors was said to enable the landlord to keep a watchful eye on local prostitutes, but the gleaming glasswork isn't the only feature of note: the series of small rooms also has a good deal of polished mahogany, as well as cut and etched windows, and a striking ornamental plaster ceiling. Fullers Chiswick, ESB, Discovery and London Pride and Gales HSB and Seafarers on handpump. Diners have priority on a few of the front tables. No children.

🍴 **Simple bar food includes sandwiches, filled baked potatoes, salads, bangers and mash, pies like steak in ale and popular fish and chips.** *Starters/Snacks: £4.95 to £6.00. Main Courses: £7.95 to £12.00*

Fullers ~ Manager Sara Bird ~ Real ale ~ Bar food (all day weekdays (snacks in evening); 12-6 Sat) ~ (020) 7321 0782 ~ Dogs allowed in bar ~ Open 11.30-11; closed Sun, bank hols

Recommended by Ian Phillips, Dr and Mrs A K Clarke, the Didler, N R White, Val and Alan Green, Michael Dandy, Andrea Rampley, Barry and Anne

Salisbury 🍷 🍺

St Martins Lane; ⊖ ≷ Leicester Square, Charing Cross; WC2N 4AP

Gleaming Victorian pub surviving unchanged in the heart of the West End, good atmosphere, wide choice of drinks and tasty bar food

What really strikes our readers about this bustling pub is the genuinely warm and friendly welcome they all get from the enthusiastic landlord and his young staff – and the pubby food is good and well priced, too. There's a wealth of cut glass and mahogany and the busily pubby main bar is perhaps best enjoyed mid-afternoon on a weekday – it can be rather packed in the early evening. A curved upholstered wall seat creates the impression of several distinct areas, framed by wonderfully ornate bronze light fittings shaped like ethereal nymphs each holding stems of flowers; there are only four of these, but mirrors all around make it seem as though there are more, and that the room extends much further than it does. A back room, popular for eating, has plenty more glasswork, and there's a separate little side room with its own entrance. On the walls are old photographs and prints, and, tucked behind the main door, a well known picture of Marianne Faithfull taken here in 1966; Richard Burton and Liz Taylor had their wedding drinks in the main bar and there's a picture in the back room of Dylan Thomas enjoying a drink here in 1941. Every inch of the walls and ceiling around the stairs down to the lavatories is coated with theatre posters (the pub is right in the heart of theatreland). Purity Mad Goose, St Austell Tribute, Timothy Taylors Landlord, Wadworths 6X and Wells & Youngs Bombardier and London Gold on handpump, as well as a dozen wines by the glass, coffees, winter hot toddies and summer Pimms. There are fine details on the exterior of the building too, and tables in a pedestrianised side alley.

🍴 **Good bar food includes sandwiches, filled baked potatoes, soup, various sharing plates, speciality pies and sausages, fish and chips and plenty of pasta dishes and salads.** *Starters/Snacks: £2.25 to £4.50. Main Courses: £7.25 to £10.20. Puddings: £2.95 to £5.25*

Punch ~ Manager Jas Teensa ~ Real ale ~ Bar food (12-9.30(9 Sun)) ~ (020) 7836 5863 ~ Children allowed until 5pm ~ Open 11-11(11.30 Thurs, midnight Fri and Sat); 12-10.30 Sun

Recommended by Tracey and Stephen Groves, Anthony and Marie Lewis, Mike Gorton, Joe Green, the Didler, David and Sue Smith, Donna and Roger

---

We list pubs that serve food all day on at least some days at the end of the book.

Seven Stars ◖

Carey Street; ⊖ Holborn (just as handy from Temple or Chancery Lane (both stations closed Sundays), but the walk through Lincoln's Inn Fields can be rather pleasant); WC2A 2JB

Quirky pub with cheerful staff, an interesting mix of customers, and good choice of drinks and food

This is an interesting and characterful little pub with cheerful staff and a fine choice of food and drink. There's always a good mix of customers – though as it faces the back of the Law Courts, it's a favourite with lawyers and reporters covering notable trials; there are plenty of caricatures of barristers and judges on the red-painted walls of the two main rooms. There are also posters of legal-themed british films, big ceiling fans and a relaxed, intimate atmosphere; checked tablecloths add a quirky, almost continental touch. A third area is in what was formerly a legal wig shop next door – it still retains the original frontage, with a neat display of wigs in the window. Despite the extra space, the pub can fill up very quickly, with lots of the tables snapped up by people here for the often individual food. Adnams Best and Broadside, Dark Star Hophead and Wells & Youngs Bitter on handpump, and a particularly good dry Martini. On busy evenings there's an overflow of customers on to the quiet road in front; things generally quieten down after 8pm and there can be a nice, sleepy atmosphere some afternoons. The Elizabethan stairs up to the lavatories are rather steep, but there's a good strong handrail. Tom Paine, the large and somewhat po-faced pub cat, still remains very much a centre of attention. The licensees have a second pub, the Bountiful Cow, on Eagle Street, near Holborn tube station, which specialises in beef. No children.

🍴 **Good, interesting food chosen and cooked according to the landlady's whim and fancy might include bruschetta with different toppings, a swedish dish of potato, anchovy, cream and dill, napoli sausage with mash, three-meat meatloaf, vegetarian chinese stir fry, home-made meat pies, a large hamburger with trimmings, roast guinea fowl in lemony jus, chargrilled fish of the day, and posh ice-cream.** *Main Courses: £8.50 to £15.00. Puddings: £6.00*

Enterprise ~ Lease Roxy Beaujolais ~ Real ale ~ Bar food (all day) ~ (020) 7242 8521 ~ Open 11-11; 12-11(10.30 Sun) Sat; closed some bank hols (usually including Christmas)

Recommended by LM, Edward Mirzoeff, N R White, Dr and Mrs A K Clarke, Donna and Roger, Joe Green, the Didler, Tim Maddison, Eddie Edwards, Ian Martin, Tracey and Stephen Groves

Star ◖

Belgrave Mews West, behind the German Embassy, off Belgrave Square; ⊖ Knightsbridge, Hyde Park Corner; SW1X 8HT

Bustling local with restful bar, upstairs dining room, Fullers ales, well liked bar food and colourful hanging baskets

Although there are many loyal regulars in this classy, friendly pub, visitors are made just as welcome. The small bar is a pleasant place with sash windows, stools by the counter on the wooden floor, a restful feel outside peak times and Fullers Chiswick, Discovery, ESB and London Pride, with a changing guest beer on handpump and quite a choice of whiskies. An arch leads to the main seating area with well polished tables and chairs, and good lighting; there's also an upstairs dining room. The astonishing array of hanging baskets and flowering tubs are a lovely sight in summer. It's said that this is the pub where the Great Train Robbery was planned.

🍴 **Well liked bar food includes sandwiches, ploughman's, soup, potted pork with toast and pickles, mussels steamed in white wine with chilli and ginger, hand-made burger with bacon, cheese and gherkins, goats cheese and braised shallot tart, beer-battered cod and chips with mushy peas, smoked chicken, leek and mushroom pie, pork belly with creamed savoy cabbage, and puddings like steamed chocolate pudding with berry compote and crêpes suzette.** *Starters/Snacks: £4.00 to £6.00. Main Courses: £8.00 to £12.30. Puddings: £4.00 to £5.50*

Fullers ~ Managers Jason and Karen Tinklin ~ Real ale ~ Bar food (12-4, 5-9; 12-5 Sun; no food Sat) ~ Restaurant ~ (020) 7235 3019 ~ Children welcome ~ Dogs welcome ~ Open 11(12 Sat)-11; 12-10.30 Sun

Recommended by Tracey and Stephen Groves, the Didler, Mike Tucker, N R White, Lawrence R Cotter

EAST LONDON

MAP 12

Crown ♀

Grove Road/Old Ford Road; ⊖ *Mile End; E3 5SN*

Civilised bar in dining pub with interesting food and a choice of moods in the upstairs dining rooms

With the feel of a comfy modern house, this relaxed dining pub has an informal bar with fashionable furnishings, Adnams Broadside, Redemption Pale Ale and Sharps Doom Bar on handpump, and a good choice of wines by the glass. There are high bar stools covered with faux animal hides by the simple bar counter, two-person stools in the same material around chunky pine tables on the polished boards, candles in coloured glass holders, a big bay window with a comfortable built-in seated area with cushions in browns, pinks and greens, a brown leather sofa beside a couple of cream easy chairs, and a scattering of books and objects on open shelves; piped music. Upstairs, the three individually decorated dining areas – again, with simple, contemporary but stylish furniture on carpeted or wooden floors – overlook Victoria Park. More reports please.

🍴 As well as lunchtime sandwiches served with chips, bar food might include chicken liver salad with pancetta and raspberry vinegar, baby spinach salad with marinated artichokes and feta, cheese and bacon burger, roast pork fillet with smoked black pudding and horseradish mash, bass with risotto cake, baby pak choi and sweet chilli sauce, braised ox cheek with swede and cider jus, and sirloin steak with green peppercorn sauce. *Starters/Snacks: £5.95 to £6.95. Main Courses: £8.95 to £14.95. Puddings: £5.00*

Geronimo Inns ~ Lease Finlay MacLeod ~ Real ale ~ Bar food (12-3(4 Sat), 7-10; 12-8 Sun) ~ Restaurant ~ (020) 8880 7261 ~ Children welcome ~ Dogs welcome ~ Open 12-11(10.30 Sun)

Recommended by Simon Rodway, BOB

Grapes

Narrow Street; ⊖ ⇌ *Limehouse (or Westferry on the Docklands Light Railway); the Limehouse link has made it hard to find by car – turn off Commercial Road at signs for Rotherhithe Tunnel, then from the Tunnel Approach slip road, fork left leading into Branch Road, turn left and then left again into Narrow Street; E14 8BP*

Relaxed waterside pub with timeless London feel, particularly appealing cosy back room, helpful friendly staff, well liked Sunday roasts, and good upstairs fish restaurant

Though much brushed up, this 16th-c riverside pub remains almost exactly as Charles Dickens knew it – all the more remarkable considering the ultra-modern buildings that now surround it. It has bags of atmosphere, a good mix of customers and friendly service. The chatty, partly panelled bar has lots of prints, mainly of actors, and old local maps, as well as some elaborately etched windows, plates along a shelf, and newspapers to read; the cosy back part has a winter open fire. Adnams Best, Marstons Pedigree, Timothy Taylors Landlord, and a guest such as Wells & Youngs Kew Gold on handpump and Addlestone's cider; board games. The upstairs fish restaurant, with fine views of the river, is highly thought-of. The pub was a favourite with Rex Whistler, who used it as the viewpoint for his rather special river paintings. In summer, the small balcony at the back is a fine spot for a sheltered waterside drink. Steps lead down to the foreshore where you can catch the Canary Wharf ferry. No children, but they do have a bowl of water for dogs.

🍴 Generous helpings of bar food includes sandwiches, soup, a tankard of whitebait, sausage and mash with onion gravy, very good fish and chips, home-made fishcake with caper sauce, and puddings like apple crumble and bread and butter pudding; Sunday roast is highly regarded (no other meals then). The fish restaurant is pricier. *Starters/Snacks: £4.00 to £6.00. Main Courses: £7.95 to £8.25. Puddings: £4.00*

Free house ~ Licensee Barbara Haigh ~ Real ale ~ Bar food (12-2.30, 6.30-9.30; 12-3.30 Sun; not Sun evening) ~ Restaurant ~ (020) 7987 4396 ~ Dogs allowed in bar ~ Open 12-3.30, 5.30-11; 12-11 Sat; 12-10.30 Sun

Recommended by Michael and Deborah Ethier, Peter, Donna and Roger, Mike Gorton, N R White, Barry and Anne, John Saville, Clare Graham, John and Gloria Isaacs

Gun 🍴 🍷

27 Coldharbour; ◆ Blackwall on the DLR is probably closest, although the slightly longer walk from Canary Wharf has splendid Dockland views; E14 9NS

Top-notch gastropub, pricey but worth it, great views from the riverside terrace, plenty of character and history, well chosen wines

The terrace at this busy riverside pub is a delight: long and narrow, with plenty of smart wooden tables and uninterrupted views of the Dome (O2) across a broad sweep of the Thames. Heaters and huge umbrellas make it welcoming whatever the weather. The building was lovingly restored by its owners after a fire destroyed much of the building that Nelson and Lady Hamilton knew (they often had their assignations upstairs). Unusually, the dining room takes up most of the characterful front bar, with smart white tablecloths and napkins on all but a handful of the tables; there's a relaxed chatty feel nonetheless. There are a couple of big framed naval prints on the white walls, piles of logs in two arched alcoves, candles, a smart oak bar counter, and perhaps an elaborate flower display on the window sill. Towards the terrace is a busy flagstoned bar for drinkers, with antique guns on the wall, and no tables except for a large barrel in the centre of the room. It shares a fireplace with a warm inviting room next door, which has a couple of leather sofas and armchairs, a stuffed boar's head, some modern prints and well stocked bookshelves, and views onto the terrace. Friendly aproned staff serve three real ales such as Adnams, Fullers London Pride and Greene King Abbot, and a good choice of wines. In summer, when it's not raining, they open up another terrace as a portuguese barbecue. They may occasionally close the pub on Saturdays for weddings, and will keep your credit card if you want to run a tab.

🍴 The bar menu includes oysters, fish finger sandwich, macaroni cheese, shepherd's pie, beef shin burger, and puddings such as lemon parfait and dark and white chocolate terrine with cherry compote. The food on the pricier more elaborate restaurant menu is very good. *Starters/Snacks: £3.95 to £8.00. Main Courses: £12.50 to £14.50. Puddings: £5.50*

Free house ~ Licensees Ed and Tom Martin ~ Real ale ~ Bar food (12-3(4 Sat), 6-10.30;11-4, 6.30-9.30 Sun) ~ Restaurant ~ (020) 7515 5222 ~ Children in bar till 8pm ~ Dogs welcome ~ Open 11am-midnight(11pm Sun)

Recommended by Jamie May, N R White, LM

Narrow 🍴 🍷

Narrow Street; ◆ ⇌ Limehouse; E14 8DJ

Stylish and popular, good food and wines by the glass, seats outside on waterside terrace

The simple but smart bar area here retains a pubby feel with white walls and ceilings, dark blue doors and woodwork, two mosaic-tiled fireplaces, each with a mirror above, a couple of hat stands, bar stools at the counter, and some colourfully striped armchairs; piped music. Adnams Bitter, Greene King St Edmunds and a guests on handpump, a good range of bottled beers, a fine wine list, and quite a choice of spirits and cocktails. The dining room is white too, with a glass skylight and big window, the floors are polished wood, and the furnishings simple, matching and dark; on the walls are maps and prints of the area, a boat and a couple of oars. This room opens on to the sizeable terrace where there are plenty of riverside tables with views around a breezy bend of the Thames.

🍴 A handful of bar snacks include soft herring roe on toast, salt beef sandwich, fish and chips with mushy peas, sausage and mash, beetroot and goats cheese curd salad and ham, egg and chips. The pricier restaurant menu has a few more dishes. *Starters/Snacks: £4.00 to £13.00*

Free house ~ Licensee Simon Brencher ~ Real ale ~ Bar food (12-3(4 Sat, Sun), 6(5.30 Sat, Sun)-11(10.30 Sun)) ~ Restaurant ~ (020) 7592 7950 ~ Children welcome ~ Open 12-11(10.30 Sun)

Recommended by John Saville, Mike Gorton

There are report forms at the back of the book.

Prospect of Whitby

Wapping Wall; ⊖ Wapping; E1W 3SH

Waterside pub with colourful history and good river views – welcoming to visitors and families

This ancient place (it claims to be the oldest pub on the Thames, dating back to 1520) is upbeat and friendly and is quite a hit with the tourists. For a while it was better known as the Devil's Tavern, thanks to its popularity with smugglers and other ne'er-do-wells. Pepys and Dickens both regularly popped in, Turner came for weeks at a time to study the scene, and in the 17th c the notorious 'Hanging' Judge Jeffreys was able to combine two of his pastimes by enjoying a drink at the back while looking down over the grisly goings-on in Execution Dock. There are plenty of beams, bare boards, panelling and flagstones in the L-shaped bar (where the long pewter counter is over 400 years old), and from tables in the waterfront courtyard, you get an unbeatable river view towards Docklands. Half a dozen real ales include Fullers London Pride, Greene King IPA and Sharps Doom Bar with guests such as Adnams Explorer, Butcombe Gold and Greene King Suffolk Swift on handpump; lots of wines by the glass, very helpful, efficient staff; piped music and games machine.

🍴 Bar food includes sandwiches, sharing plates, pies like chicken and leek or steak and ale, fish and chips, a good range of burgers, caesar salad, and puddings such as chocolate fudge cake and treacle sponge pudding. *Starters/Snacks: £1.75 to £4.95. Main Courses: £6.75 to £10.45. Puddings: £2.95 to £3.95*

Punch ~ Manager John Towler ~ Real ale ~ Bar food (12-10(9 Sun)) ~ (020) 7481 1095 ~ Children must be dining after 5.30pm ~ Open 12(11 Sat)-11(10.30 Sun)

Recommended by Ross Balaam, Donna and Roger, the Didler, Bill Adie, Barry and Anne

NORTH LONDON

MAP 12

Bull & Last

Highgate Road; ⊖ Kentish Town – then a 20-minute walk; NW5 1QS

Really distinctive food in this bustling Highgate local; good range of drinks and friendly, chatty atmosphere

Traditional with a stylish twist, this nicely refurbished cornerhouse is charmingly animated with a real mix of customers and age groups. Its single room has big windows that overlook the street, and at the far end a wooden wall has a brick fireplace, a faded map of London and a collection of tankards; the wooden planked ceiling has colonial-style fans. Above the bar are three stuffed bulls' heads, as well as a blackboard listing their suppliers; there are a couple of stuffed pheasants beside the open kitchen. Friendly staff serve Black Sheep, Purity Mad Goose, Sharps Doom Bar, Timothy Taylors Landlord, home-made sloe gin and mulled wine in winter, and the good wine list includes several carefully selected ports and dessert wines by the glass. There are some rather nice plants by the door, and hanging baskets above picnic-sets on the street.

🍴 Food here is well sourced and prepared. The menus, though a little pricey, are full of imaginative and unusual touches: bar snacks, for example, include pigs ears for dogs. They do takeaway tubs of their home-made ice-cream, and can prepare picnic hampers to take to Hampstead Heath; you can get various coffees to take away too. Dishes might include garlic snails with bacon salad, pigeon and pistachio terrine, veal ragoût with pappardelle and taleggio, smoked eel, horseradish, egg and beetroot salad, charcuterie board, fish stew, gnocchi with mushrooms, curd cheese, roast ceps purée and parmesan, cod and chips with pea purée, rump of lamb with potato and bacon confit, celeriac and wild garlic, and puddings such as rhubarb clafoutis with stem ginger ice-cream, baked chocolate mousse with cinnamon crisps and prune and armagnac ice-cream. *Starters/Snacks: £4.00 to £10.00. Main Courses: £12.00 to £22.50. Puddings: £5.00 to £8.00*

Free house ~ Licensees Ollie Pudney and Freddie Fleming ~ Real ale ~ Bar food (12-3(4 Sat, Sun), 6.30-10; 7-9.30 Sun) ~ Restaurant ~ (020) 7267 8955 ~ Accompanied children welcome away from bar ~ Dogs welcome ~ Quiz Sun evening ~ Open 12-11(midnight Sat, 10.30 Sun)

Recommended by Richard Greaves

Chapel 🍽 🍷

Chapel Street; ⊖ Edgware Road; NW1 5DP

Very good food in a lively modern gastropub; it does get busy and sometimes noisy – all part of the atmosphere

A long-standing favourite with local office workers, you will normally find this bustling gastropub astir with a vibrant cosmopolitan hum. It's perhaps more relaxed and civilised at lunchtime and is altogether busier and louder in the evenings when there is a more even split between diners and drinkers, and the music is more noticeable, especially at weekends. You may have to wait for a table during busier periods. Rejuvenated some 15 years by its current licensees, the cream-painted rooms are light and spacious and dominated by the open kitchen, and the furnishings are smart but simple, with plenty of plain wooden tables around the bar, a couple of comfortable sofas at the lounge end and a big fireplace. Adnams Best and Greene King IPA are on handpump, and there is a jolly good choice of wines by the glass, cappuccino and espresso, fresh orange juice, and a choice of tisanes. A real bonus is the sizeable back garden with picnic-sets and other seats on wooden decking under large heated umbrellas. More reports please.

🍴 As well as lunchtime open sandwiches, the interesting food includes an extensive choice of antipasti and canapés and changing dishes such as tomato, tarragon and chorizo soup, spanish dried beef with fois gras and truffle oil, linguini with chilli, parsley, broccoli and parmesan, home-made burger, grilled chicken breast with parsnip mash and honey-glazed vegetables and thyme jus, poached bass, spaghetti bolognese, springbok wellington with truffle mash, rib-eye steak, and puddings such as apple crumble and custard, banoffi pie and warm chocolate and almond tart. *Starters/Snacks: £4.00 to £7.50. Main Courses: £19.00. Puddings: £4.00 to £5.50*

Free house ~ Licensee Lakis Hondrogiannis ~ Real ale ~ Bar food (12-2.30(3 Sun), 7-10) ~ (020) 7402 9220 ~ Children welcome ~ Dogs welcome ~ Open 12-11(10.30 Sun)

Recommended by Phil and Jane Hodson, Kevin Thomas, Nina Randall, Bruce and Sharon Eden

Drapers Arms 🍽 🍷

Far west end of Barnsbury Street; ⊖ ⇌ Highbury & Islington; N1 1ER

Streamlined place with good mix of drinkers and diners, thoughtful choice of beers, wines and imaginative modern food, and seats in the attractive back garden

This simply refurbished but stylish Georgian townhouse is run by enthusiastic young owners who are keen that it remains a proper pub where customers can pop in for a drink and a chat with friends and family, have an easy meal or enjoy a celebration in the chic upstairs dining room. The spreading bar has a mix of elegant dark wooden tables and dining chairs on bare boards, an arresting bright green-painted counter contrasting with soft duck-egg walls, gilt mirrors over smart fireplaces, a sofa and some comfortable chairs. Harveys Best and a couple of guests such as Brakspears and Sambrooks Wandle on handpump, and carefully chosen wines by the glass (about 20), carafe or bottle. Upstairs, the dining room has similar tables and chairs on a striking chequerboard-painted wood floor; piped music and board games. The back terrace is most attractive with white or green benches and chairs around zinc-topped tables (each set with a church candle), flagstones and large parasols; more reports please.

🍴 Good modern cooking might include sandwiches, ploughman's, smoked haddock and bacon chowder, grilled razor clams with red onions, garlic and thyme, pork, pigeon and foie gras terrine, braised lamb with chickpeas, tomato and watercress, rabbit and mushroom pie (for two or three), and puddings such as blood orange posset, chocolate pot and chocolate chip cookie. *Starters/Snacks: £3.50 to £7.00. Main Courses: £8.50 to £14.00. Puddings: £5.00 to £6.50*

Free house ~ Licensees Ben Maschler and Nick Gibson ~ Real ale ~ Bar food (12-3(4 Sun), 6-10.30(9.30 Sun)) ~ Restaurant ~ (020) 7619 0348 ~ Children welcome, but after 6pm must be seated and eating ~ Dogs allowed in bar ~ Open 11-11

Recommended by BOB

Duke of Cambridge 🍴 🍷 ☕

St Peters Street; ⊖ Angel, though 15 minutes' walk away; N1 8JT

Trail-blazing organic pub with carefully sourced, imaginative food, excellent range of drinks, and a nice, chatty atmosphere with the feel of a comfortably upmarket local

The licensee at this, London's first organic pub is passionate about the environment. She holds various advisory roles and the pub has been certified by the Soil Association. They try to reuse and recycle as much as possible and even the real ales (Pitfield East Kent Goldings, Eco and St Peters Best) are organic. They also have organic draught lagers and cider, organic spirits, a wide range of organic wines (many of which are available by the glass), quite a few teas and coffees, and a spicy ginger ale. The atmosphere is warmly inviting, and it's the kind of place that somehow encourages conversation, with a steady stream of civilised chat from the varied customers. The big, busy main room is simply decorated and furnished with lots of chunky wooden tables, pews and benches on bare boards, a couple of big metal vases with colourful flowers, and daily papers. A corridor leads off past a few tables and an open kitchen to a couple of smaller candlelit rooms, more formally set for eating, and a conservatory. It's worth arriving early to eat, as they can get very busy.

🍽 Using top-quality seasonal food from small producers, the good, interesting bar food might include gazpacho with mint salsa, pork rillettes on toast with pickled cucumber, fried cuttlefish with gremolata, main courses such as sardines with lentils and braised radicchio with mint and anchovy salsa, chicken and mushroom pie, potato, aubergine, red pepper and feta gratin with watercress pea sprout salad, and puddings such as apricot cheesecake and lavender crème brûlée. *Starters/Snacks: £5.75 to £12.50. Main Courses: £11.75 to £22.00. Puddings: £6.00*

Free house ~ Licensee Geetie Singh ~ Real ale ~ Bar food (12.30-3(3.30 weekends), 6.30-10.30(10 Sun)) ~ Restaurant ~ (020) 7359 3066 ~ Children welcome ~ Dogs welcome ~ Open 12-11(10.30 Sun)

Recommended by John M Murphy, Tracey and Stephen Groves, Dr and Mrs M E Wilson

Flask 🍷

Flask Walk; ⊖ Hampstead; NW3 1HE

Good local feel, real ales, a fine choice of wines by the glass and traditional food

The name of this place is a reminder of the days when it distributed mineral water from Hampstead's springs. Recently smartened up a little, the unassuming bar here still has the feel of a peaceful old local (a popular haunt of Hampstead artists, actors and local characters) and is properly old-fashioned with a nice old wooden counter and pubby tables and chairs. A unique Victorian screen divides this from the smart but cosy lounge at the front, with red plush banquettes curving around the panelled walls and an attractive fireplace. There are more old wooden tables and dining chairs on rugs or on the dark floorboards, lots of little prints on the walls, and quite a few wine and champagne bottles dotted about. Wells & Youngs Bitter, Special and Bombardier on handpump, around 30 wines by the glass and quite a few malt whiskies; piped music and TV. Outside in the alley, there are several seats and tables.

🍽 Good wholesome food includes sandwiches, various sharing boards, summer salads, steak in ale pie, fish pie, ham and free-range eggs, a pie of the day, lamb shoulder cooked in mint sauce, good chicken breast with lemon and thyme with sweet potato wedges, roasted vegetables and goats cheese with basil and pine nut dressing, beer-battered haddock, and puddings such as sticky toffee pudding. *Starters/Snacks: £4.15 to £7.95. Main Courses: £10.20 to £13.95. Puddings: £4.65 to £5.20*

Youngs ~ Manager Claudia McCarthy-Malcher ~ Real ale ~ Bar food (12-3, 6-10; 12-10 Fri, Sat; 12-9 Sun) ~ (020) 7435 4580 ~ Children welcome till 8pm ~ Dogs welcome ~ Open 11-11 (midnight Fri and Sat); 12-10.30 Sun

Recommended by N R White, Donna and Roger, the Didler, Tracey and Stephen Groves, John and Gloria Isaacs

Holly Bush ♀ ◧

Holly Mount; ⊖ Hampstead; NW3 6SG

Unique village local, with good food and drinks, and a lovely unspoilt feel

Now owned by Fullers, this timeless old favourite was originally a stable block and is tucked away among some of Hampstead's most villagey streets. The proudly old-fashioned front bar has a dark sagging ceiling, brown and cream panelled walls (decorated with old advertisements and a few hanging plates), open fires, bare boards, and secretive bays formed by partly glazed partitions. Slightly more intimate, the back room, named after the painter George Romney, has an embossed red ceiling, panelled and etched-glass alcoves, and ochre-painted brick walls covered with small prints; lots of board and card games. Butcombe, Fullers London Pride, Discovery and Seafarers and Harveys are on handpump; plenty of whiskies and a good wine list. The upstairs dining room has table service at the weekend, as does the rest of the pub on a Sunday. There are benches on the pavement outside.

🍴 Conveniently served all day at weekends, bar food includes imaginative dishes such as rabbit terrine, quail pie with beetroot and feta salad, tea-smoked salmon, beef and ale pie, bass and crushed new potatoes, steak with rosemary chips and béarnaise sauce, and puddings such as crackling chocolate mousse and summer fruit jelly with clotted cream. *Starters/Snacks: £4.00 to £8.00. Main Courses: £8.00 to £18.00. Puddings: £4.00 to £5.00*

Fullers ~ Manager Nicolai Outzen ~ Real ale ~ Bar food (12-4, 6-10; all day weekends) ~ Restaurant ~ (020) 7435 2892 ~ Children welcome till 7pm ~ Dogs welcome ~ Open 12-11(10.30 Sun)

Recommended by N R White, Tim Maddison, the Didler, John Wooll, Barry Collett

Marquess Tavern ♀

Canonbury Street/Marquess Road; ⊖ ⇌ Highbury & Islington; N1 2TB

Popular gastropub, imaginative cooking, good range of drinks, and the feel of a proper local in the front bar

This imposing Victorian building stands square and alone in a nice villagey corner of Islington. Inside, the bar is reassuringly traditional and fairly plain, with bare boards and a mix of candlelit wooden tables arranged around a big, horseshoe servery; there's a fireplace either side, one topped by a very tall mirror, as well as an old leather sofa and faded old pictures. You can eat either in the bar or in the slightly more formal back dining room, feeling much brighter with its white paint and skylight; it has an impressive brass chandelier. Wells & Youngs Bitter, Special and London Gold are on handpump alongside quite a few bottled beers and around 50 malt whiskies; piped music. Picnic-sets behind railings by the road in front. Note: they don't open weekday lunchtimes.

🍴 Carefully sourced produce goes into the modern cooking: starters such as chilled pea and mint soup with cream, white cromer crab and brown meat mousse with fennel and orange salad, samphire omelette, venison and mushroom pie, rainbow trout with soused vegetables, clams and sorrel, well hung rib-eye steak, and puddings such as black forest trifle. *Starters/Snacks: £4.50 to £6.50. Main Courses: £9.50 to £17.00. Puddings: £4.50 to £6.00*

Youngs ~ Tenant Damien Geninazza ~ Real ale ~ Bar food (6-10(8.30 Sun)) ~ Restaurant ~ (020) 7354 2975 ~ Children welcome ~ Dogs welcome ~ Open 5-11; 12-12 Sat; 12-10.30 Sun; closed weekday lunchtimes

Recommended by Steve Kirby

Please tell us if the décor, atmosphere, food or drink at a pub is different from our description. We rely on readers' reports to keep us up to date: feedback@goodguides.com, or (no stamp needed) The Good Pub Guide, FREEPOST TN1569, Wadhurst, E Sussex TN5 7BR.

Spaniards Inn ◧

Spaniards Lane; ⊖ *Hampstead (but some distance away) or from Golders Green tube station take 220 bus; NW3 7JJ*

Busy old pub with lots of character and history, delightful garden, and a wide range of drinks and good food

Situated right next to Hampstead Heath, with a big rather charming garden, this historic former toll house really does feel like a country pub. The garden is nicely arranged in a series of areas separated by careful planting of shrubs, and there's a crazy-paved terrace with slatted wooden tables and chairs, and a flagstoned walk around a small raised area with roses; a side arbour has wisteria, clematis and hops. As it's popular with families and those with dogs (they even have a dog wash) you may need to move fast to bag a table. There's an outside bar, regular summer barbecues and an area for smokers. Dating back to 1585, the pub is well known for its tales of hauntings and highwaymen (some of which are best taken with a very large pinch of salt), and the low-ceilinged oak-panelled rooms are attractive and full of character, with open fires, genuinely antique winged settles, candle-shaped lamps in shades and snug little alcoves. There's an impressive range of drinks with half a dozen ales including Adnams Best, Fullers London Pride, Timothy Taylors Landlord and three guests such as Bass, Greene King Old Speckled Hen and Sharps Doom Bar on handpump, a couple of ciders, quite a few continental draught lagers and wines by the glass. The car park fills up fast and other parking nearby is difficult.

⏛ **Served all day, enjoyable unfussy bar food includes lunchtime sandwiches and ploughman's, salt and pepper squid, caesar salad, sausage and mash, pasta of the day, tasty fish and chips, rib-eye steak, and puddings like chocolate sponge and apple crumble.** *Starters/Snacks: £4.20 to £6.50. Main Courses: £7.00 to £11.00. Puddings: £3.50 to £6.00*

Mitchells & Butlers ~ Manager Olivier Jolly ~ Real ale ~ Bar food (12-10) ~ (020) 8731 8406 ~ Children welcome ~ Dogs welcome ~ Open 12-11

Recommended by N R White, John Wooll, Karen Eliot, David Jackson, Jo Lilley, Simon Calvert

SOUTH LONDON   TQ4963   MAP 12

Bo-Peep

Chelsfield; 1.7 miles from M25 junction 4; Hewitts Road, which is the last road off exit roundabout; BR6 7QL

Useful M25, country-feeling meal-stop

Very low old beams and an enormous inglenook dominate the carpeted bar at this 16th-c suburban dining pub. Prettily candlelit at night, two cosy little rooms for dining open off, one with smart cushions and a wooden floor. There's also an airy side room with new dark wood round tables and chairs looking over the country lane. Do look out for Milo, the licensees' miniature english bull terrier, who must love living round here. Adnams, Courage Best and Harveys Sussex are on handpump, and service is cheerfully efficient; piped easy listening. A big brick terrace behind has lots of picnic-sets; more reports please.

⏛ **As well as ploughman's and sandwiches, other reliable home-made dishes might include dolcelatte, pear and walnut salad, fried whitebait, pâté, chicken caesar salad, scampi, fillets of bass on fennel and pea velouté, fish and chips, rib-eye steak, and puddings such as spotted dick and custard, profiteroles and pear and strawberry crumble.** *Starters/Snacks: £5.95 to £9.00. Main Courses: £8.00 to £16.00. Puddings: £1.95 to £4.50*

Enterprise ~ Tenants Kate Mansfield, Graham Buckley ~ Real ale ~ Bar food (12-2, 6-9; 12-5 Sun, not Sun evening) ~ Restaurant ~ (01959) 534457 ~ Children welcome ~ Dogs allowed in bar ~ Open 11-11(10.30 Sun)

Recommended by BOB, Guy Vowles, N R White, Tony Brace

Crown & Greyhound ♀

Dulwich Village; ⇌ North Dulwich; SE21 7BJ

Comfortable Victorian pub with a big back garden, good beers and a popular Sunday carvery

Known locally as the Dog, this lively pub was built at the turn of the last century to replace two inns that had stood here previously, hence the unusual name. It's big and busy (especially in the evenings) but if you want a peaceful pint you can still tuck yourself into a quiet corner. With a Victorian elegance and plenty to look at throughout its period interior, its spacious rooms have some quite ornate plasterwork and lamps over on the right, and a variety of nicely distinct seating areas, some with traditional upholstered and panelled settles, others with stripped kitchen tables on stripped boards. There's a coal-effect gas fire and some old prints; piped music and board games. Real ales include Fullers London Pride, Harveys and a couple of guests such as Sambrooks Wandle on handpump, alongside a good range of draught lagers and ciders, and just under two dozen wines by the glass. They hold an Easter beer festival and a summer cider festival. It's handy for walks through the park and Dulwich Picture Gallery, and boasts a very pleasant back garden, with tables shaded by a chestnut tree, and a fence with murals painted by local schoolchildren; barbecues on summer weekends. A big back dining room and conservatory open onto here, leading from the pleasantly furnished roomy main bar at the front.

🍴 Bar food includes sandwiches, ploughman's, burgers, calamari, nachos, sausage and sage mash, fish and chips, steak, mushroom and ale pie, stuffed red pepper, and puddings such as lemon tart and eton mess. It's best to arrive early for the popular Sunday carvery as they don't take bookings. *Starters/Snacks: £3.25 to £5.25. Main Courses: £6.50 to £10.95. Puddings: £3.50 to £3.75*

Mitchells & Butlers ~ Manager Anthony Worms ~ Real ale ~ Bar food (12-10(11 Fri, Sat, 9.30 Sun)) ~ (020) 8299 4976 ~ Children welcome ~ Dogs welcome ~ Open 11-11(12 Thurs-Sat, 10.30 Sun)

Recommended by Giles and Annie Francis, Bill Adie, Tracey and Stephen Groves, John Saville, Jim and Frances Gowers

Cutty Sark

Ballast Quay, off Lassell Street; ⇌ Maze Hill, from London Bridge; or from the river front, walk past the Yacht in Crane Street and Trinity Hospital; SE10 9PD

Interesting old tavern with genuinely unspoilt bar, great Thames views, organic wines, and a wide range of fairly straightforward but popular food

Readers love this enjoyable white-painted Thames-side pub with its great river views, pubby atmosphere and tasty traditional food. Reached by a winding central staircase, the upstairs room feels just like a ship's deck. The prize seat, in a big bow window that juts out over the pavement, has splendid views of the river and O2 Arena. Alive with young people on Friday and Saturday evenings and at the weekends, but surprisingly quiet some weekday lunchtimes, the dark flagstoned bar has a genuinely old-fashioned feel, with rough brick walls, wooden settles, barrel tables, open fires, low lighting and narrow openings to tiny side snugs. Five real ales are likely to include Fullers London Pride and Seafarers alongside three guests, with a good choice of malt whiskies and a range of organic wines; piped music. There's a busy riverside terrace across the narrow cobbled lane; morris dancers occasionally drop by. Parking is limited nearby – though, unusually for London, if you can bag a space it's free.

🍴 Bar food includes sandwiches, prawn cocktail, whitebait, ploughman's, chicken caesar salad, sausage and mash, steak and ale pie, battered haddock and chips, vegetable wellington, scampi, knickerbocker glory and chocolate fudge cake. *Starters/Snacks: £4.50 to £6.95. Main Courses: £8.95 to £12.95. Puddings: £4.95*

Free house ~ Licensee Stewart Turdy ~ Real ale ~ Bar food (12-9(10 Sat)) ~ (020) 8858 3146 ~ Children welcome ~ Dogs welcome ~ Open 11-11; 12-10.30 Sun

Recommended by Ross Balaam, Robert Gomme, the Didler, John Saville, Susan and John Douglas, Nick Patton

Fire Station ♀
Waterloo Road; ⊖ *Waterloo, Southwark* ⇌ *Waterloo East; SE1 8SB*

Unusual conversion of former fire station, with lively after-work atmosphere (it does get crowded then), and good food all day

The energetic atmosphere and loud acoustics at this conversion of the former LCC central fire station give it quite a young appeal. The bar is two huge knocked-through tiled rooms (a little like an old-fashioned public bath), with lots of wooden tables and a mix of chairs, a couple of pews and worn leather armchairs, some sizeable plants, and distinctive box-shaped floral lampshades hanging from the high ceilings; the back wall has three back-lit mirrored panels, and, as a token to its former life, some red fire buckets on a shelf. The back dining room has smarter chairs and tables. Fullers London Pride, Marstons Pedigree and a guest such as Brakspear are on handpump, they've an excellent choice of wines, and a good range of spirits and cocktails. There are tables in front and picnic-sets in a scruffy side alley; handy for the Old Vic.

🍴 **They serve breakfast from 9am, then have a pubby all-day menu with charcuterie, half a pint of prawns, red thai mussel curry, beef carpaccio, battered haddock with mushy peas, fish of the day, aubergine, spinach and mozzarella lasagne, roast chicken breast with roast hazelnuts and mustard sauce, home-made burger, and puddings such as raspberry cheesecake with hazelnut praline and white chocolate and vanilla bean panna cotta with Pimms-infused blueberries.** *Starters/Snacks: £4.50 to £7.95. Main Courses: £11.95 to £19.50. Puddings: £4.50 to £5.50*

Marstons ~ Manager Jess Manterfield ~ Real ale ~ Bar food (9-10.30) ~ Restaurant ~ (020) 7620 2226 ~ Children welcome ~ Open 9-midnight
Recommended by Michael and Alison Sandy, Ian Phillips, Eleanor Dandy, Dr Ron Cox

Founders Arms ♀
Hopton Street (Bankside); ⊖ *St Paul's (and cross the Millennium Bridge), Southwark* ⇌ *Blackfriars, and cross Blackfriars Bridge; SE1 9JH*

Superb location, with outstanding terrace views along the Thames, and handy for south bank attractions; decent efficiently served food

'Possibly the ugliest pub in the *Guide* but great view' are the words of one reader about this modern building which sits on the Thames' south side of the embankment. Taking in St Paul's, the Millennium Bridge, and even the Tower of London way off in the distance, it's probably the best view you'll find at any pub along the river. Seemingly always busy, it's popular with city types, tourists, theatre and gallery goers, who in summer spill onto the nearby pavement and walls. Charles Wells Bombardier, Wells & Youngs Bitter and Special and a guest are served from the modern bar counter which angles along one side of the glass-walled interior, and you can have most of the wines on their list by the glass. Efficient, cheerful service; piped music.

🍴 **Available all day (with breakfast at 9am at the weekend), and served without too much waiting around, the very useful menu might include sandwiches, ciabattas, moules frites, charcuterie, fish and cheeseboards to share, warm goats cheese salad, beer-battered fish, slow-roasted pork belly, beef, mushroom and ale pie and baked sweet potato topped with vegetable and bean chilli.** *Starters/Snacks: £4.95 to £8.95. Main Courses: £8.45 to £14.95. Puddings: £3.95*

Youngs ~ Manager Paul Raynor ~ Real ale ~ Bar food (12-10) ~ (020) 7928 1899 ~ Children welcome away from bar ~ Open 10(9 Sat, Sun)-11(midnight Fri, Sat)
Recommended by Val and Alan Green, N R White, Dr and Mrs A K Clarke, Howard and Margaret Buchanan, Tracey and Stephen Groves, John Saville, the Didier, Mike and Sue Losey, John Wooll, Kevin Thomas, Nina Randall, Ian Phillips, Michael Doswell, Chris and Angela Buckell

---

The letters and figures after the name of each town are its Ordnance Survey map reference. 'Using the *Guide*' at the beginning of the book explains how it helps you find a pub, in road atlases or on large-scale maps as well as on our own maps.

Fox & Hounds 🍴 ☿

Latchmere Road; ⇌ Clapham Junction; SW11 2JU

Victorian local standing out for its excellent mediterranean cooking

The spacious, straightforward bar at this big Victorian local has bare boards, mismatched tables and chairs, two narrow pillars supporting the dark red ceiling, photographs on the walls and big windows overlooking the street (the view partially obscured by colourful window boxes). There are fresh flowers and daily papers on the bar, and a view of the kitchen behind. Two rooms lead off, one more cosy with its red leatherette sofas. The varied piped music fits in rather well. It can fill quickly with customers in for the good mediterranean food, though it's still very much the kind of place where locals happily come to drink. Fullers London Pride, Harveys and a guest such as Caledonian Deuchars IPA are on handpump, and the carefully chosen wine list (which includes over a dozen by the glass) is written out on a blackboard; TV. The garden has big parasols and heaters for winter; more reports please.

🍽 Changing every day, a typical menu might include **puy lentil soup with cumin and sour cream, bruschetta, butternut squash and feta salad with garlic, mint, chilli and paprika, penne with italian sausage ragoût, salmon and dill fishcakes with wilted spinach and hollandaise, roast veal chop with artichokes, peas, broad beans and sage butter, roast duck breast with roasted red pepper jus, rib-eye steak with salsa verde, and puddings such as apple and date crumble with butterscotch ice-cream.** *Starters/Snacks: £5.00 to £8.00. Main Courses: £7.50 to £15.50. Puddings: £4.50*

Free house ~ Licensees Richard and George Manners ~ Real ale ~ Bar food (12.30-3(4 Sat) Fri; 6.30(6 Sat)-10; 12.30-10 Sun; not Mon-Thurs lunchtimes) ~ (020) 7924 5483 ~ Children welcome till 7pm ~ Dogs welcome ~ Open 12-3, 5-11; 12-11 Fri, Sat; 12-10.30 Sun; closed Mon lunchtime

Recommended by BOB

George ★

Off 77 Borough High Street; ⊖ ⇌ Borough, London Bridge; SE1 1NH

Beautifully preserved 16th-c coaching inn, with lots of tables in bustling courtyard to take in the galleried exterior

This splendidly preserved building is well known (and can attract lots of tourists) for its stunning tiers of exterior open galleries, and is perhaps the country's best example of an historic coaching inn. Tables in the cobbled courtyard (with a summer bar) give you plenty of time to take it all in. Mentioned in *Little Dorrit* and owned by the National Trust, the building dates from the 16th c, but was rebuilt to the original plan after the great Southwark fire of 1676. What survives today is only a third of the original building; it was 'mercilessly reduced', as E V Lucas put it, during the period when it was owned by the Great Northern Railway Company. Unless you know where you're going you may well miss it, as apart from the great gates and sign there's little to indicate that such a gem still exists tucked away behind the less auspicious-looking buildings on the busy high street. The row of no-frills ground-floor rooms and bars all have square-latticed windows, black beams, bare floorboards, some panelling, plain oak or elm tables and old-fashioned built-in settles, along with a 1797 'Act of Parliament' clock, dimpled glass lantern-lamps, and so forth. The best seats indoors are in a snug room nearest the street, where there's an ancient beer engine that looks like a cash register. An impressive central staircase goes up to a series of dining-rooms and to a balcony. Drinks include Fullers London Pride and a couple of guests such as Gales Seafarer and St Austell Tribute, mulled wine in winter, and tea and coffee; darts, trivia games machine.

🍽 Good value bar food includes **sandwiches, ham, egg and chips, sausage and mash, fish and chips, lasagne, lamb shank with minted gravy, beef and ale pie, salads, roast mediterranean vegetable risotto, and puddings like spotted dick and chocolate brownie.** *Starters/Snacks: £2.95 to £5.95. Main Courses: £7.95 to £9.45. Puddings: £4.50 to £4.95*

Greene King ~ Manager Scott Masterson ~ Real ale ~ Bar food (12-9(5 Sun); not Sun evening) ~ Restaurant (5-10 (not Sun)) ~ (020) 7407 2056 ~ Children welcome away from bar ~ Open 11-11.30; 12-10.30 Sun

Recommended by Dr and Mrs A K Clarke, Darren Le Poidevin, N R White, the Didler, Mike and Sue Loseby, Mayur Shah, Rob and Catherine Dunster, Howard and Margaret Buchanan

Greenwich Union ◀
Royal Hill; ⊖ ⇄ Greenwich; SE10 8RT

Enterprising pub with distinctive beers from small local Meantime Brewery, plus other unusual drinks, and good, popular food

As one of just two taps for the small Meantime Brewery in nearby Charlton, this nicely renovated friendly pub stocks all their distinctive unpasteurised beers. The range includes a traditional pale ale (served cool, under pressure), a mix of proper pilsners, lagers and wheat beers, one a deliciously refreshing raspberry flavour, and a stout. The friendly, knowledgeable staff will generally offer small tasters to help you choose. They also have Harveys Best and Dark Star Hophead on handpump, and a draught cider, as well as a helpfully annotated list of unusual bottled beers. The rest of the drinks may be unfamiliar too, as they try to avoid the more common brands. Perhaps feeling a little more like a bar than a pub, the long, narrow stone-flagged room has several different parts: a simple area at the front with a few wooden chairs and tables, a stove and newspapers, then, past the counter with its headings recalling the branding of the brewery's first beers, several brown leather cushioned pews and armchairs under framed editions of *Picture Post* on the yellow walls; piped music, TV. Beyond here, a much lighter, more modern-feeling conservatory has comfortable brown leather wall benches, a few original pictures and paintings, and white fairy lights under the glass roof; it leads out to an appealing terrace with green picnic-sets and a couple of old-fashioned lamp posts. The fence at the end is painted to resemble a poppy field, and the one at the side a wheat field. Though there are plenty of tables out here, it can get busy in summer (as can the whole pub on weekday evenings). In front are a couple of tables overlooking the street. The pub is slightly removed from Greenwich's many attractions and there's a particularly good traditional cheese shop as you walk towards the pub.

🍴 **Good popular food from a seasonally changing menu that might include lunchtime sandwiches, watermelon and feta salad, smoked haddock parcel, pork and apple burger with apple sauce, aubergine and courgette lasagne, butternut squash and leek dumplings with stilton sauce, well hung steaks, and puddings such as vanilla panna cotta with strawberry compote and chocolate ice-cream and rhubarb and amaretto tiramisu.** *Starters/Snacks: £2.50 to £5.00. Main Courses: £6.50 to £15.95. Puddings: £3.95 to £5.95*

Free house ~ Licensee Andrew Ward ~ Real ale ~ Bar food (12-4, 5.30-10; 12-10 Sat, Sun) ~ (020) 8692 6258 ~ Children welcome ~ Dogs welcome ~ Open 12-11; 11-11 Sat; 12-10.30 Sun
Recommended by Nick Patton, Michael and Deborah Ethier, the Didler, N R White

Market Porter ◀
Stoney Street; ⊖ ⇄ Borough, London Bridge; SE1 9AA

Up to ten unusual real ales in a very popular, properly pubby place opening at 6am for workers at the neighbouring market

They can serve up to 60 different guest beers a week through the 11 handpumps at this no-frills down-to-earth pub. Very well kept alongside Harveys, they are sourced from all sorts of often far-flung brewers – to name but a few: Beowulf, Cotleigh, Elland, Hop Back, Oakham and RCH. During the week, workers and porters from Borough Market come here for a very early drink, it then tends to be quieter in the afternoons, getting crowded and noisy with good-natured chatter at the end of the working day. Service is particularly helpful and friendly at all times. Unpretentious and fun, the main part of the bar is pretty manly and straightforward with bare boards, rough wooden ceiling beams with beer barrels balanced on them, a heavy wooden counter with a beamed gantry, cushioned bar stools, an open fire, and 1920s-style wall lamps – it gets more old-fashioned the further you venture in; piped music. In warmer weather, drinkers spill out on to the street.

🍴 **Just a handful of good value pubby dishes include sandwiches, panini, cod and chips, sausage and mash, steak, ale and mushroom pie, scampi, spinach and ricotta tortellini and chilli.** *Starters/Snacks: £3.25 to £5.95. Main Courses: £6.75 to £8.95*

Free house ~ Licensee Sarah Nixon ~ Real ale ~ Bar food (12-3; not Sat) ~ Restaurant ~
(020) 7407 2495 ~ Children welcome Sat, Sun till 7pm ~ Dogs welcome ~ Open 6-9am weekdays,
then 11-11; 12-11 Sat; 12-10.30 Sun

*Recommended by Ian Phillips, N R White, Joe Green, the Didler, Mike and Sue Loseby, Mayur Shah, Peter Dandy,
Mike Gorton, E McCall, T McLean, D Irving*

Old Jail

*Jail Lane, Biggin Hill (first turn E off A233 S of airport and industrial estate, towards
Berry's Hill and Cudham); no station near; TN16 3AX*

**Popular country pub close to the city, with big family garden and RAF memorabilia in its
traditional bars**

The lovely big garden with well spaced picnic-sets on the grass, several substantial trees
and a nicely maintained play area, mean this good all-rounder is popular with families,
especially at weekends, when it can get very busy. At these times they might limit food
to the snack menu if you haven't booked. Inside, several traditional beamed and low-
ceilinged rooms ramble around a central servery, the nicest parts being the two cosy little
areas to the right of the front entrance; divided by dark timbers, one has a very big
inglenook fireplace with lots of logs and brasses, and the other has a cabinet of Battle of
Britain plates – a reference perhaps to the pub's popularity with RAF pilots based at
nearby Biggin Hill. Other parts have wartime prints and plates too, especially around the
edge of the dining room, up a step beyond a second, smaller fireplace. There's also a
plainer, flagstoned room. Fullers London Pride, Harveys and Shepherd Neame Spitfire are
on handpump; discreet piped music, board games. With nice hanging baskets in front,
the attractive building wasn't itself part of any jail, but was a beef shop until becoming a
pub in 1869. More reports please.

🍴 The standard menu has good value sandwiches, baked potatoes and ploughman's, and
there's a wide choice of good, blackboard specials which might include local sausages
with mash and red onion gravy, chicken tarragon with bacon and onion potato cake, slow-
cooked beef with new potatoes and swede mash, pork belly with black pudding and red
wine jus, rib-eye steak, and puddings such as white chocolate raspberry cheesecake and
Baileys crème brûlée; they do a choice of roasts on Sunday. *Starters/Snacks: £4.25 to £5.25.
Main Courses: £7.95 to £16.95. Puddings: £3.95 to £4.25*

Punch ~ Lease Richard Hards ~ Real ale ~ Bar food (12-2.30(3 Sat, Sun), 7-9.30; not Sun evening) ~
(01959) 572979 ~ Children welcome ~ Dogs welcome ~ Open 11.30-3, 6-11; 12-11 Sat; 12-10.30 Sun

Recommended by Chris Pluthero, B and M Kendall, LM

Royal Oak 🍺

Tabard Street/Nebraska Street; ⊖ ⇄ Borough, London Bridge; SE1 4JU

**Old-fashioned Harveys corner house with all their beers excellently kept; good, honest
food too**

'Quite quirky and unexpected and one of London's best kept secrets' is just one of the
cheery reports we've had from the many readers who love this very enjoyable old-
fashioned corner house. Slightly off the beaten track, in rather unprepossessing
surroundings, this is the only London pub belonging to Sussex brewer Harveys – needless
to say, they stock the full range. The brewery transformed the pub when they took over,
and painstakingly re-created the look and feel of a traditional London alehouse – you'd
never imagine it wasn't like this all along. Filled with the sounds of happy chat, two busy
little L-shaped rooms meander around the central wooden servery, which has a fine old
clock in the middle. They're done out in a cosy, traditional style with patterned rugs on
the wooden floors, plates running along a delft shelf, black and white scenes or period
sheet music on the red-painted walls, and an assortment of wooden tables and chairs;
disabled ramp available on the Nebraska Street entrance.

🍴 Honest, good value, pubby bar food includes impressive doorstep sandwiches, and
generously served daily specials such as cod and chips, or pies such as vegetable and
stilton, lamb and apricot, or steak and ale pie; Sunday roasts. *Starters/Snacks: £4.00 to
£5.95. Main Courses: £7.45 to £11.95. Puddings: £4.50*

Harveys ~ Managers John Porteous, Frank Taylor ~ Real ale ~ Bar food (12-2.30, 5-9.30; 12-4.30 Sun) ~ (020) 7357 7173 ~ Children welcome ~ Dogs welcome ~ Open 11(12 Sat)-11; 12-6 Sun; closed Sun evening and bank hols

Recommended by Brian and Rosalie Laverick, Simon and Mandy King, the Didler, Mike and Sue Loseby, Mayur Shah, Andy Lickfold, Susan and John Douglas, John Saville, N R White

Telegraph 🍺

Telegraph Road; ⇌ Putney ⊖ East Putney, Southfields but quite a walk; SW15 3TU

A good summer pub, with plenty of outdoor seats and a rural feel; nicely reworked inside too, with excellent choice of beers, reliable food, and good live blues on Fridays

This attractively located pub is named after the Admiralty telegraph station that used to stand nearby, one of a chain of ten between Chelsea and Portsmouth (on a clear day, a message could be sent between the two in 15 minutes). They like to call it 'a country pub in London', and walking past the cricket played on the heath nearby, or sitting at one of the many tables on the grass in front, it seems no idle boast. It's the outdoor space that for most visitors is the main draw, and on fine weekends it can get very busy indeed out here, with families and dogs a big part of the mix. Some tables are nicely sheltered under big trees (the pergola is slightly less effective), and there are a couple of quirky cow-print sofas under a little verandah by the entrance. The two modernised rooms inside have plenty of comfortable leather armchairs and sofas, and lots of framed period prints and advertisements. The long main bar on the left also has quite a variety of wooden furnishings, including some unusually high tables and stools, and a rather grand dining table at one end; there's a TV for sport, rugs on the polished wooden floor, and an appealing little alcove rather like a private lounge, with a fireplace and a table of newspapers; piped music, TV and board games. As well as Weltons Semaphore and St Austell Tribute, four regularly changing real ales might be from brewers such as Downton, Tintagel and Twickenham. There's a good wine list too. On Friday nights they run a blues bar of some renown, featuring international artists specialising in vintage acoustic blues. One reader tells us it can attract groups of quite lively families in the evening.

🍴 **Bar food includes sharing platters, starters such as thai spiced fishcakes, cajun spiced calamari, goats cheese, beetroot and oregano risotto, burgers, spit roast chicken, roast suckling pig, fish and chips, sausages of the day and well hung steaks.** *Starters/Snacks: £4.25 to £7.00. Main Courses: £9.00 to £18.75. Puddings: £5.50 to £6.95*

Free house ~ Licensee Nick Stafford ~ Real ale ~ Bar food (12-9) ~ (020) 8788 2011 ~ Children welcome ~ Dogs welcome ~ Blues Fri evening ~ Open 12(11 Sat)-12(10.30 Sun)

Recommended by LM, Michael Dandy, John Styles, Shanonne Parsons, Harry Hersom, Colin McKerrow, Peter Dandy, George Wallace

White Cross 🍷

Water Lane; ⊖ ⇌ Richmond; TW9 1TH

Thames-side pub with paved waterside area and cosy bar

Given the terrific river views from the very pleasant garden in front of this superbly positioned place it's not surprising that it gets quite busy here in summer, when it can even feel like a cosmopolitan seaside resort. There's an outside bar and they may use plastic glasses for outside drinking. Boats leave from immediately outside for Kingston and Hampton Court, and it's not unknown for the water to reach right up the steps into the bar and cut off the towpath at the front – if you're leaving your car by the river, check tide times so as not to return to find it marooned in a rapidly swelling pool of water. But this place is equally special in winter, with its two chatty main rooms having something of the air of the hotel this once was, with local prints and photographs, an old-fashioned wooden island servery, and a good mix of variously aged customers. Two of the three cosy log fires have mirrors above them – unusually, the third is below a window. Wells & Youngs Bitter, Special and Bombardier, a seasonal Youngs beer and a couple of guests such as Hook Norton Old Hooky are on handpump, with a dozen or so carefully chosen wines by the glass. A bright and airy upstairs room has lots more tables, and a pretty cast-iron balcony opening off, with a splendid view down to the water; piped music in some areas, TV.

🍴 Served all day from a food counter (thus eliminating a wait even when it's busy) bar food includes sandwiches, wraps and baked potatoes, salads, sharing plates, sausage and mash, pie of the day, rump steak, and (in summer) scones and clotted cream. *Starters/Snacks: £4.30 to £6.95. Main Courses: £7.95 to £10.95. Puddings: £4.50 to £4.85*

Youngs ~ Manager Alex Gibson ~ Real ale ~ Bar food (12-10(9 Sun)) ~ (020) 8940 6844 ~ Children welcome in upstairs room till 6pm ~ Dogs welcome ~ Open 11-11; 12-10.30 Sun

Recommended by N R White, the Didler, Thurstan Johnston, Ian Phillips, Michael Butler

WEST LONDON   MAP 13

Anglesea Arms 🍷 🍴
Selwood Terrace; ⊖ South Kensington; SW7 3QG

Busy Victorian pub with good range of beers, enjoyably chatty atmosphere in the evenings (when it can get packed)

This is an enjoyable pub, very well run by a friendly licensee and her helpful staff. At peak times you'll need to move fast to grab a seat, but most people seem happy leaning on the central elbow tables. When it's not so busy, the characterful bar has an air of faded late-Victorian grandeur with its heavy portraits, large brass chandeliers, panelling, dark painted ceilings and big windows with swagged curtains. It has a mix of cast-iron tables on the bare wood-strip floor and at one end several booths with partly glazed screens have worn leather pews and spindleback chairs; TV. A good choice of half a dozen real ales on handpump takes in Adnams Bitter and Broadside, Fullers London Pride, Sambrooks Wandle and a couple of guests such as Sharps Doom Bar and Timothy Taylors Landlord; also, around 20 malt whiskies, and a varied wine list of about 30 wines by the glass. Down some steps, there's a newly refurbished dining room. In summer, the place to be is on the leafy and heated front terrace.

🍴 Interesting bar food includes soup, pigeon, guinea fowl and duck terrine with pear and date chutney, crispy fried baby squid with risotto nero, a charcuterie plate, home-made burger with smoked cheddar, spinach, sun-dried tomato and goats cheese lasagne, toulouse sausages with shallot gravy, steak in Guinness pie, grilled lemon sole in caper and chervil butter, and puddings such as panna cotta with rhubarb and double chocolate brownie. *Starters/Snacks: £4.45 to £6.95. Main Courses: £10.95 to £16.95. Puddings: £3.50 to £5.00*

Free house ~ Licensee Emma Whittingham ~ Real ale ~ Bar food (12-3, 6-10) ~ Restaurant ~ (020) 7373 7960 ~ Children welcome ~ Dogs allowed in bar ~ Open 11-11; 12-10.30 Sun

Recommended by the Didler, N R White, Barry and Anne, John and Jill Perkins, Tracey and Stephen Groves

Atlas 🍴 🍷
Seagrave Road; ⊖ West Brompton; SW6 1RX

Popular modern cooking and a fine choice of drinks in a busy pub; handy for Earls Court

With good food and a fine choice of drinks, this tucked-away pub is always busy. The long, simple, knocked-together bar has plenty of panelling and dark wooden wall benches, a couple of brick fireplaces, a mix of school chairs and well spaced tables. Fullers London Pride, St Austell Tribute, Sharps Doom Bar and a guest beer on handpump, a carefully chosen wine list with plenty by the glass and big mugs of coffee; friendly service. The piped music covers a real cross section – on various visits we've come across everything from salsa and jazz to vintage TV themes; board games. Outside is an attractively planted narrow and heated side terrace with an overhead awning. They will ask to keep your credit card if you run a tab.

🍴 Enjoyable modern bar food includes sandwiches, soup, warm pork rillettes with beetroot and apple rémoulade and sherry syrup, caesar salad with parmesan croûtons and chicken, an antipasti plate to share, baked polenta gnocchi with butternut squash, mint, chilli and feta, italian sausages with red onion marmalade, rare-grilled tuna with peperonata, pine nuts, balsamic and sorrel, lamb chump with pancetta and sage and sun-dried tomato jus, and puddings such as profiteroles with chocolate sauce and crème brûlée. *Starters/Snacks: £5.00 to £8.00. Main Courses: £11.50 to £15.50. Puddings: £4.50*

Enterprise ~ Lease Craig Fleeton, Richard and George Manners ~ Real ale ~ Bar food (12-2.30, 6-10; 12-10 Sun) ~ (020) 7385 9129 ~ Children welcome till 7pm ~ Dogs welcome ~ Open 12-11 (10.30 Sun)
Recommended by Evelyn and Derek Walter, Nigel and Sue Foster, Robert Lester

Bulls Head ◀
Strand-on-the-Green; ⊖ Gunnersbury, Chiswick Park ⇌ Kew Bridge; W4 3PQ

Cosy old Thames-side pub with tables by the river, with atmospheric little rooms, half a dozen real ales and pubby all-day food

In warm weather you can sit at the tables in front of this riverside pub or on the towpath and enjoy the Thames views. You have the same view from inside too – if you are lucky enough to bag one of the highly prized tables by the little windows. A series of beamed rooms rambles up and down steps, with plenty of polished dark wood and old-fashioned benches built into the simple panelling. The black-panelled alcoves make snug cubby-holes, and there are lots of empty wine bottles dotted around. The building itself is actually very old – it served as Cromwell's HQ several times during the Civil War. Adnams Best, Courage Directors, Greene King Old Speckled Hen and a seasonal beer from Batemans on handpump, up to 20 wines by the glass and maybe summer Pimms; friendly service and newspapers to read. The hanging baskets are most attractive.

🍴 Served all day, the pubby bar food includes ploughman's, platters like farmhouse or mezze, fresh mussels, steak in ale pie, beer-battered fish and chips, specials like lemon, courgette and monkfish skewers, and puddings such as chocolate fudge cake with black cherry compote; popular Sunday roasts. *Starters/Snacks: £2.99 to £4.99. Main Courses: £6.99 to £12.39. Puddings: £2.99 to £4.90*

Punch ~ Manager Julie Whittingham ~ Real ale ~ Bar food (12-10(9.30 Sun)) ~ (020) 8994 1204 ~ Children welcome ~ Open 12-11(10.30 Sun)
Recommended by N R White

Churchill Arms ♀ ◀ £
Kensington Church Street; ⊖ Notting Hill Gate, Kensington High Street; W8 7LN

Cheery irish landlord at bustling and friendly local with very well kept beers and excellent thai food; even at its most crowded, it stays relaxed and welcoming

The façade of this friendly old local has almost disappeared behind the glorious display of 85 window boxes and 42 hanging baskets; it really is quite a sight. The pub has been run for 26 years now by a buoyantly enthusiastic and amiable irish landlord who is always very much in evidence, mixing with customers and making everyone feel at home. Another of Mr O'Brien's hobbies (apart from the amazing floral display) is collecting butterflies – you'll see a variety of prints and books on the subject dotted around the bar. He doesn't stop there though – the pub is also filled with countless lamps, miners' lights, horse tack, bedpans and brasses hanging from the ceiling, a couple of interesting carved figures and statuettes behind the central bar counter, prints of american presidents, and lots of Churchill memorabilia. Well kept Fullers Chiswick, ESB, London Pride and Fullers seasonal beers on handpump and two dozen wines by the glass. The spacious and rather smart plant-filled dining conservatory may be used for hatching butterflies, but is better known for its big choice of excellent thai food. Look out for special events and decorations around Christmas, Hallowe'en, St Patrick's Day, St George's Day, and Churchill's birthday (30 November) – along with more people than you'd ever imagine could feasibly fit inside this place; they have their own cricket and football teams. There can be quite an overspill onto the street, where there are some chrome tables and chairs.

🍴 Good quality and splendid value, the conservatory has authentic thai food with everything from a proper thai curry to various rice, noodle and stir-fried dishes. At lunchtimes they usually also have a very few traditional dishes such as fish and chips or sausage and chips, and they do a good value Sunday roast. *Starters/Snacks: £2.50 to £4.50. Main Courses: £6.50. Puddings: £2.50*

Fullers ~ Manager Gerry O'Brien ~ Real ale ~ Bar food (12-10(9.30 Sun)) ~ Restaurant ~ (020) 7727 4242 ~ Children welcome ~ Dogs welcome ~ Open 11-11(midnight Thurs-Sat); 12-10.30 Sun

Recommended by LM, Peter, the Didler, Tracey and Stephen Groves

Colton Arms

Greyhound Road; ⊖ Barons Court, West Kensington; W14 9SD

Unspoilt little pub kept unchanged thanks to its dedicated landlord; it's peaceful and genuinely old-fashioned with well kept beer

The long-serving landlord has been running this unchanging and unspoilt little gem since 1963, though he is now helped by his son. It's like an old-fashioned country pub and the main U-shaped front bar has a log fire blazing in winter, highly polished brasses, a fox's mask, hunting crops and plates decorated with hunting scenes on the walls, and a remarkable collection of handsomely carved antique oak furniture. That room is small enough, but the two back rooms, each with their own little serving counter with a bell to ring for service, are tiny. Fullers London Pride, Sharps Doom Bar and a guest such as Hogs Back TEA on handpump. When you pay, note the old-fashioned brass-bound till. Pull the curtain aside for the door out to a charming back terrace with a neat rose arbour. The pub is next to the Queens Club tennis courts and gardens.

🍴 **Just sandwiches, weekday lunchtimes only.** *Starters/Snacks: £3.50*

Enterprise ~ Lease N J and J A Nunn ~ Real ale ~ Bar food (weekday lunchtimes only) ~ No credit cards ~ (020) 7385 6956 ~ Children welcome till 7pm ~ Dogs allowed in bar ~ Open 12-3(4 Sat), 6(7 Sat)-11.30; 12-4, 7-11 Sun

Recommended by Susan and John Douglas, Giles and Annie Francis, Barbarrick

Dove

Upper Mall; ⊖ Ravenscourt Park, Stamford Brook, Hammersmith; W6 9TA

One of London's best-known pubs with a lovely riverside terrace, cosily traditional front bar and an interesting history

This 17th-c riverside pub is in the *Guinness World Records* book for having the smallest bar room – the front snug is a mere 4'2" by 7'10". This little room is cosy and traditional with black panelling and red leatherette cushioned built-in wall settles and stools around dimpled copper tables; it leads to a bigger, similarly furnished room with old framed advertisements and photographs of the pub. That opens onto the terrace, where the main flagstoned area, down some steps, has a verandah and some highly prized tables looking over the low river wall to the Thames reach just above Hammersmith Bridge. There's a tiny exclusive area up a spiral staircase, a prime spot for watching the rowing crews out on the water. Fullers Chiswick, Discovery, ESB and London Pride on handpump and over 20 wines by the glass (including champagne and fizz). The pub has played host to many writers, actors and artists over the years and there's a rather fascinating framed list of them all on a wall. It's said to be where *Rule Britannia* was composed and it was a favourite with Turner, who painted the view of the Thames from the delightful back terrace, and with Graham Greene. The street itself is associated with the foundation of the Arts and Crafts movement – William Morris's old residence (open certain afternoons) is nearby.

🍴 **Under the new licensee, bar food now includes lunchtime sandwiches, box-baked camembert with red onion and cider chutney, chicken and ham hock terrine with pear and mint ice-cream, various sharing boards, chicken caesar salad, chargrilled burger with cheese and bacon, sausages with onion gravy, goats cheese, onion, spinach and walnut tart, beer-battered cod and chips, pork fillet stuffed with black pudding and apple purée with madeira jus, and puddings such as raspberry pavlova and sticky toffee pudding.** *Starters/Snacks: £6.00 to £9.00. Main Courses: £7.50 to £16.50. Puddings: £6.00*

Fullers ~ Manager Garry Wood ~ Real ale ~ Bar food (12-3, 6-9; 12-9(7 Sun) Sat) ~ Restaurant ~
(020) 8748 9474 ~ Dogs welcome ~ Live band once a month ~ Open 11-11;
12-10.30 Sun
Recommended by N R White, Peter Dandy, Dominic McGonigal, the Didler

Duke of Sussex 🍽 🍷 🍺

South Parade; ⊖ Chiswick Park ⇌ South Acton,; W4 5LF

**Attractively restored Victorian local with interesting bar food, a good choice of drinks and
a lovely big garden**

A huge bonus for this carefully restored Victorian pub is the most unexpected big back
garden. With plenty of tables, nicely laid out plants and carefully positioned lighting, it's
a real oasis – though it can get packed on sunny days. Inside, the smartly refurbished bar
is simple and classy with huge windows, some original etched glass and a big horseshoe-
shaped counter where a large vase of flowers adds a splash of vibrancy to the otherwise
dark colours. The lighting is mostly modern but there are a few standard lamps and table
lamps which, at night, create a warm yellow glow that from the street makes the place
look warmly inviting. Leading off is a carefully restored room used mainly for eating,
again with plenty of simple wooden furnishings, but also a few little booths, chandeliers
and a splendid skylight framed by colourfully painted cherubs. There are a couple of big
mirrors, one above a small tiled fireplace and lots of black and white local photos. Fullers
Chiswick and a couple of guests such as Hop Back Thaiphoon and Robinsons Dragon Fire
on handpump, quite a choice of wines including half-bottle carafes, draught lagers,
bottled trappist beers and Aspall's cider. More reports please.

🍴 **Enjoyable bar food with some spanish influences includes soup, razor clams in
chilli and garlic, devilled duck livers on toast, ham hash cake with a poached egg,
vegetable paella, chicken or steak pie, braised cuttlefish with chickpeas, braised rabbit
with pancetta, fish and chips with pea purée, old spot pork belly with escalivada and
salsa picante, and puddings like chocolate and caramel tart and crema catalana.**
Starters/Snacks: £3.75 to £6.50. Main Courses: £9.50 to £15.00. Puddings: £5.00

Free house ~ Licensees Mike Buurman and Chris Payne ~ Real ale ~ Bar food (12-10.30;
not Mon lunchtime) ~ Restaurant ~ (020) 8742 8801 ~ Children welcome if well behaved ~
Dogs welcome ~ Open 12-11.30(midnight Sat, 11 Sun)
Recommended by Simon Rodway

Havelock Tavern 🍽 🍷

Masbro Road; ⊖ ⇌ Kensington (Olympia); W14 0LS
LONDON DINING PUB OF THE YEAR

**Popular gastropub with a friendly, often vibrant, atmosphere, very good food and well
chosen wines**

There's always a nice mix of customers at this informal and chatty dining pub –
especially on weekend lunchtimes. The light and airy L-shaped bar is plain and unfussy
with bare boards and long wooden tables that you may end up sharing at busy times.
Until 1932 this blue-tiled building was two separate shops and it still has huge shop-
front windows. A second little room with pews leads to a small paved terrace with
benches, a tree and wall climbers. Friendly staff serve Sharps Doom Bar and a couple of
guests beers like Purity Pure Ubu and Sambrooks Wandle Ale on handpump at the elegant
modern bar counter, as well as a good range of well chosen wines with around a dozen by
the glass; mulled wine in winter and maybe home-made elderflower soda in summer;
backgammon, chess, Scrabble and other board games. More reports please.

🍴 **Interesting modern food might include soup, duck liver and foie gras parfait with gherkins
and chutney, deep-fried monkfish cheeks and tiger prawns with sweet chilli dipping sauce,
lamb, fig and mint tagine with couscous, yoghurt and coriander, aubergine, sweet potato and
spinach lasagne with parmesan and mozzarella, pork tenderloin with puy lentils, bacon, leeks
and spinach, gilt-head bream with wild mushrooms, salsify, jerusalem artichoke and braised
cherry tomatoes, and puddings like sauternes and caramel custard and mixed fruit crumble.**
Starters/Snacks: £4.50 to £8.00. Main Courses: £8.50 to £13.50. Puddings: £4.00 to £4.50

Free house ~ Licensees Helen Watson and Andrew Cooper ~ Real ale ~ Bar food (12.30-2.30(3 Sun), 7-10(9.30 Sun)) ~ (020) 7603 5374 ~ Children welcome ~ Dogs welcome ~ Open 11-11; 12-10.30 Sun
Recommended by Derek Thomas, Martin and Karen Wake

Portobello Gold ♀

Middle of Portobello Road; ⊖ Notting Hill Gate, Ladbroke Grove; W11 2QB

Engaging combination of pub, hotel, restaurant with a relaxed atmosphere, a wide choice of enjoyable food (especially in the attractive dining conservatory) and an excellent range of drinks; bedrooms

Usefully opening early for morning coffee, pastry and the papers, this is an enterprising and almost bohemian place with a monthly art and photographic exhibition and regular live music. Our favourite part is the exotic-seeming dining room with its big tropical plants, an impressive wall-to-wall mirror, comfortable chairs, stained wooden tables and a cage of vocal canaries adding to the outdoor effect – in summer, they open up the sliding roof. The smaller front bar has a nice old fireplace, cushioned banquettes and, more unusually, several Internet terminals (which disappear in the evening). It's all very relaxed, cheerful and informal, though can get a bit rushed when they're busy in the evening. Fullers London Pride and Harveys Best on handpump, several draught belgian beers, Thatcher's farm cider, a good selection of bottled beers from around the world, a wide range of interesting tequilas and other well sourced spirits, and a particularly good wine list (with just under two dozen by the glass) which can be attributed to the landlady who has written books on matching wine with food. They also have a cigar menu; piped music, TV, chess, backgammon. The back garden has seats and tables for dining and there are one or two tables and chairs on the pretty street outside. Some of the bedrooms are small (you might get the best price by booking online) and there's a spacious apartment with a rooftop terrace and putting green. Parking nearby is restricted but you can usually find a space (not so easily on Saturdays during the day).

⑪ **Interesting bar food includes dips and nibbles, toasties, fajitas and nachos, soup, oysters with a choice of dressings, salads with toppings such as jalapenos, sour cream, avocado and so forth, wild boar and apple sausages with parsley mash and gravy, beefburger with home-made chips, pasta with puttanesca sauce, warm seafood salad, beef, Guinness and oyster pie, fish and chips in tempura beer batter, aberdeen angus rib-eye steak, and puddings such as apple crumble and banoffi pie. They have a two- and three-course set menu; also cream teas and Sunday roasts.** *Starters/Snacks: £5.00 to £11.50. Main Courses: £9.00 to £16.00. Puddings: £4.50 to £5.00.*

Enterprise ~ Lease Michael Bell and Linda Johnson-Bell ~ Real ale ~ Bar food (11.30am-11.15pm) ~ Restaurant ~ (020) 7460 4910 ~ Children welcome ~ Dogs allowed in bedrooms ~ Live music Sun evening ~ Open 10am-11.30; 9am-12.30am Sat; 10am-10.30pm Sun ~ Bedrooms: /£75S(£160B)
Recommended by Darren Le Poidevin, Dave Braisted

Princess Victoria ♀

217 Uxbridge Road; ⊖ Shepherd's Bush; W12 9DH

Exceptional food and drink in carefully restored Victorian gin-palace; plenty of space and a pretty courtyard garden

This imposing Victorian gin-palace is a terrific place for a drink or a meal and our readers love it. There's a carefully restored and rather grand bar with oil paintings on the slate-coloured walls, comfortable leather wall seating in the same colour on the parquet flooring, fresh flowers, a couple of stuffed animal heads, a small fireplace with a gilt-edged mirror above it and a handsome horseshoe-shaped marble-topped bar counter where they serve Fullers London Pride, Harvest Best and Timothy Taylors Landlord on handpump; there's a fantastic, carefully chosen wine list with 36 wines by the glass, 28 malt whiskies and lots of gins, armagnacs and cognacs. They have a wine and cigar shop, too. The large dining room has plenty of original features including two ornate stucco roof lights, an interesting collection of old wooden chairs and tables (one table seats 14) and more oil paintings, mirrors and candlelight. The pretty little back terrace has nice white wrought-iron tables and chairs. The Saturday artisan market held in front of the building is exceedingly popular.

🍴 **Produce is carefully sourced for the excellent food which ranges from bar snacks to imaginative full meals: deep-fried pigs cheek with gribiche sauce, home-made scotch egg, soup, potted dorset crab with green bean and endive salad, rock oysters with shallot vinegar, butternut squash, spinach and ricotta gnocchi with pickled wild mushrooms, wild garlic and parmesan oil, braised rabbit and smoked ham hock pasta with chanterelles, broad beans and salsa verde, sea trout with steamed mussels, macaroni and smoked ham and vegetable chowder, and puddings such as chocolate and caramelised peanut tart with peanut butter ice-cream and rhubarb crème brulée; they also offer a two-and three-course set lunch.** *Starters/Snacks: £3.50 to £8.50. Main Courses: £12.50 to £17.50. Puddings: £5.00*

Enterprise ~ Lease James McLean ~ Real ale ~ Bar food (12-3(4.30 Sun), 6.30-10.30(9 Sun)) ~ (020) 8749 5886 ~ Children allowed if dining ~ Dogs allowed in bar ~ Open 11.30am-midnight (11pm Sun)

Recommended by Sophie Harrowes

Warrington ♀
Warrington Crescent; ⊖ Maida Vale; W9 1EH

Beautifully refurbished Victorian gin-palace with extraordinary décor and a short but good menu

The good modern food in this opulent art nouveau building – owned by Gordon Ramsay – continues to draw in customers – but the pub itself is well worth a look, too. A splendid marble and mahogany bar counter is topped by an extraordinary structure that's rather like a cross between a carousel and a ship's hull, with cherubs thrown in for good measure. Throughout are elaborately patterned tiles, ceilings and stained glass, and a remarkable number of big lamps and original light fittings; there's a small coal fire and two exquisitely tiled pillars. The drawings of nubile young women here and above a row of mirrors on the opposite wall are later additions, very much in keeping with the overall style and hinting at the days when the building's trade was rather less respectable than today. Adnams Best, Fullers London Pride, Greene King IPA and a guest beer on handpump. Several unusual bottled beers and a dozen or so wines by the glass from a fine list. More reports please.

🍴 **A short choice of interesting bar food includes devilled whitebait, chips with curry sauce, braised ox cheek, ploughman's, grilled mushrooms on toast with a poached egg, watercress and garlic butter, a burger, pea, broad bean, marjoram and parmesan risotto, sea trout with spiced lentils and gremolata, lamb rump with creamed onions and garlic mash, rib of beef with chips and home-made tomato sauce, and puddings such as eton mess and steamed chocolate and banana pudding with coconut ice-cream; they also offer a two- and three-course set menu.** *Starters/Snacks: £3.50 to £11.00. Main Courses: £8.95 to £22.00. Puddings: £6.00*

Free house ~ Licensee David Martin ~ Real ale ~ Bar food (12.30-2, 6-10(10.30 Fri and Sat); 12-2.30, 6-9 Sun; not Mon-Weds lunch) ~ Restaurant (6-10.30) ~ (020) 7592 7960 ~ Children welcome till 7pm ~ Open 12-11(midnight Fri and Sat, 10.30 Sun)

Recommended by Peter Dandy

White Horse ♀
Parsons Green; ⊖ Parsons Green; SW6 4UL

Cheerfully relaxed local with a big terrace, an excellent range of carefully sourced drinks and very good food

This easy-going pub remains as enjoyable as ever, with friendly, efficient staff and a pleasantly upmarket and chatty atmosphere. The stylishly modernised U-shaped bar has plenty of sofas and wooden tables, huge windows with slatted wooden blinds and winter coal and log fires – one in an elegant marble fireplace. The pub is usually busy (and can feel crowded at times) but you'll rarely have to wait too long to be served. An impressive range of drinks takes in Harveys and half a dozen or so nicely varied guests on handpump from brewers such as Breconshire, Crouch Vale, Oakham, Sarah Hughes and Westerham, two dozen well chosen draught beers from overseas (usually belgian and german but occasionally from further afield), 15 trappist beers, around 120 other foreign bottled beers, a perry on handpump, ten or so malt whiskies, and a constantly expanding range of about 70 good, interesting and reasonably priced wines. They have quarterly beer festivals, often spotlighting regional breweries. The pub overlooks the green and has plenty of seats on the front terrace, with something of a continental feel on summer evenings and at weekends; they have barbecues out here most sunny evenings.

🍴 **Good, interesting bar food includes sandwiches, deep-fried lambs tongue with gribiche sauce, treacle-cured salmon with pickled cucumber, mussels and cockles with pancetta, cider and cream, cumberland sausage with creamy leeks and beer gravy, butternut squash and pea parcels with a pear and feta salad, baked cod with crispy squid, chorizo and smoked paprika mayonnaise, warm salad of rabbit, bacon, artichokes and a truffled egg, grilled bass with tagliatelle, crab and pepper sauce and pea shoots, and puddings like gooseberry cheesecake and blueberry and almond tart.** *Starters/Snacks: £4.50 to £6.75. Main Courses: £10.50 to £14.75. Puddings: £4.95*

Mitchells & Butlers ~ Manager Dan Fox ~ Real ale ~ Bar food (9.30am-10.30pm) ~ Restaurant ~ (020) 7736 2115 ~ Children welcome ~ Dogs welcome ~ Open 9.30am-11.30pm(midnight Thurs-Sat)

Recommended by the Didler, Tracey and Stephen Groves, N R White

Windsor Castle

Campden Hill Road; ⊖ *Holland Park, Notting Hill Gate; W8 7AR*

Genuinely unspoilt, with lots of atmosphere in the tiny, dark rooms and a bustling summer garden; good beers and reliable food

The back garden here is easily one of the city's best pub gardens. It's always busy out here when the sun's shining, but there's quite a secluded feel thanks to the high ivy-covered sheltering walls. They have a summer bar as well as heaters for cooler days and lots of tables and chairs on the flagstones. Inside, there's a lot of character and genuine old-fashioned charm, with a wealth of dark oak furnishings, high-backed sturdy built-in elm benches, time-smoked ceilings, soft lighting and a coal-effect fire. Three of the tiny unspoilt rooms have their own entrance from the street, but it's much more fun trying to navigate through the minuscule doors between them inside (one leads to a cosy pre-war-style dining room). Usually fairly quiet at lunchtime, it tends to be packed most evenings. Fullers London Pride and Timothy Taylors Landlord are well kept alongside guests such as Greene King Abbot, Harveys Best and Hop Back Summer Lightning on handpump, draught ciders, decent house wines, various malt whiskies, jugs of Pimms in summer and perhaps mulled wine in winter.

🍴 **Good quality, reasonably priced bar food includes sandwiches, soup, baked camembert with rosemary and garlic, beer-battered fish and chips, grilled goats cheese salad with beetroot, parsnip crisps and toasted pine nuts, a wide choice of sausages with red onion gravy, honey-roast pork belly with sweet roast gravy and colcannon, lamb chops with redcurrant gravy, and puddings such as chocolate pudding and apple and blackberry crumble.** *Starters/Snacks: £3.25 to £4.50. Main Courses: £6.50 to £11.25. Puddings: £3.80*

Mitchells & Butlers ~ Manager James Platford ~ Real ale ~ Bar food (12-3, 5-10, 12-10(9 Sun) Fri, Sat) ~ (020) 7243 8797 ~ Children welcome till 7pm ~ Dogs welcome ~ Open 12-11(10.30 Sun)

Recommended by the Didler, N R White, LM, Darren Le Poidevin

If a pub tries to make you leave a credit card behind the bar, be on your guard. The credit card firms and banks which issue them condemn this practice. After all, the publican who asks you to do this is in effect saying: 'I don't trust you'. Have you any more reason to trust his staff? If your card is used fraudulently while you have let it be kept out of your sight, the card company could say you've been negligent yourself – and refuse to make good your losses. So say that they can 'swipe' your card instead, but must hand it back to you. Please let us know if a pub does try to keep your card.

LUCKY DIP

Besides the fully inspected pubs, you might like to try these Lucky Dips recommended to us and described by readers (if you do, please send us reports: feedback@goodguides.com).

CENTRAL LONDON

E2

Sun E2 0AN [Bethnal Green Rd]: Welcoming and much improved, good choice of drinks inc real ales such as Wychwood Hobgoblin, cosy relaxed atmosphere, candles on tables, newspapers; open all day, till late Fri, Sat (BOB)

EC1

Butchers Hook & Cleaver EC1A 9DY [West Smithfield]: Fullers bank conversion with their full range kept well, all-day pubby food inc good choice of pies, breakfast from 7.30am, friendly staff, daily papers; relaxed atmosphere, nice mix of chairs inc some button-back leather armchairs, wrought-iron spiral stairs to pleasant mezzanine with waitress service; piped music, big-screen sports TV; open all day, cl wknds (DC, Peter Dandy, Michael Dandy, BB)

Coach & Horses EC1R 3DJ [Ray St]: Enterprising food inc good Sun lunch, well kept ales, good wines by the glass, quick friendly service; gets busy with office workers; courtyard tables (Keith and Inga Davis-Rutter, Gordon Tong)

Fox & Anchor EC1M 6AA [Charterhouse St]: Long, slender all-wood bar with narrow tables, small back snugs, interesting paintings, period prints and Edwardian photographs, mainstream ales in metal tankards (Chris Sale, Peter Dandy)

Gunmakers EC1R 5ET [Eyre St Hill]: Two-room Victorian pub, four well kept changing ales, friendly knowledgeable staff, traditional food with a few twists; dogs welcome, open all day wkdys, cl wknds (Barbarrick)

☆ *Hand & Shears* EC1A 7JA [Middle St]: Traditional panelled Smithfield pub dating from the 16th c, three basic bright rooms and small snug off central servery, bustling at lunchtime, quiet evenings; Adnams and Courage Directors, quick friendly service, interesting bric-a-brac and old photographs, short choice of low-priced pub food; open all day, cl wknds (Peter Dandy, LYM)

Melton Mowbray EC1N 2LE [Marlborough Court, Holborn]: Large busy pastiche of Edwardian pub with Fullers ales, good food service (Melton Mowbray pies among other dishes); lots of woodwork, etched glass, mix of furniture inc front button-back banquettes, bare booths below small mezzanine gallery; opens out in summer to pavement café tables (Michael Dandy, Peter Dandy)

Sekforde Arms EC1R 0HA [Sekforde St]: Small unspoilt and comfortably simple corner local with friendly landlord, Wells & Youngs ales and a guest, simple good value standard food, nice pictures inc Spy caricatures, upstairs restaurant (not always open); darts, cards and board games; pavement tables (the Didler, Tim Maddison)

Three Kings EC1R 0DY [Clerkenwell Close]: Cosy old no-frills pub with plenty of atmosphere, especially when candlelit in winter, ales such as Wells & Youngs Bombardier, some interesting food, well run and efficient even when busy; rhino head above open fire, two more small rooms upstairs (Tim Maddison, Ian Martin)

Water Poet EC1 6BX [Folgate St]: Big rambling pub with bohemian feel, enjoyable food in bar and dining room, Fullers ESB and London Pride, good wines, welcoming hard-working attentive staff, good mix of customers; some comfortable sofas on wood floor, basement bar/function room, pool room, comedy club; sports TV; enclosed garden with covered area, barbecue, open all day (Chris Gant, Neil Hardwick)

EC2

Railway Tavern EC2M 7NX [Liverpool St]: Light and airy, with high ceilings and vast front windows, Greene King ales and several wines by the glass from long bar, pubby food from sandwiches inc sharing platters, second room upstairs; TVs and machines; pavement tables (Michael Dandy, Jeremy King)

EC3

☆ *Counting House* EC3V 3PD [Cornhill]: Spacious bank conversion retaining original Victorian character, impressive glass dome and grand ceiling, chandeliers, rich polished mahogany, mosaics, island bar topped with four-sided clock, gallery seating; Fullers ale range kept well, food inc pies, efficient service; open all day, cl wknds (Peter Dandy, N R White, Barbarrick)

Elephant EC3M 5BA [Fenchurch St]: Small ground-floor bar, larger basement lounge, well kept Wells & Youngs ales, good sandwiches and other mainly snacky food, friendly helpful staff; piped music; cl wknds (Tony and Wendy Hobden, Ian Phillips)

Jamaica Wine House EC3V 9DS [St Michael's Alley, Cornhill]: 19th-c pub on the site of London's first coffee house, in a warren of small alleys; traditional Victorian décor with ornate ceilings, oak-panelled bar, booths and bare boards, Shepherd Neame ales and wide choice of wines, food in downstairs lunchtime dining area, friendly helpful service, bustling atmosphere (quietens after 8pm); cl wknds (N R White)

☆ *Lamb* EC3V 1LR [Leadenhall Market]: Well run stand-up bar, staff always polite and efficient even when very busy with sharp City lads, Wells & Youngs ales, good choice of wines by the glass; bare boards, engraved glass, plenty of ledges and shelves, spiral stairs up to tables and seating in small light and airy carpeted gallery overlooking market's central crossing, corner servery doing good lunchtime carvery, baguettes, sharing platters, brunches from 10am; separate stairs to nice bright dining room (not cheap), also basement bar with shiny wall tiling and own entrance; discreet TV, silenced games machine; lots of tables outside after 4pm when stalls pack up – crowds here in warmer months; open all day, cl wknds *(Derek Thomas, Ian Phillips, BB, N R White)*

Ship EC3V 0BP [Talbot Court, off Eastcheap]: Interesting bare-boards pub, quieter upstairs with old prints and dark décor, friendly staff, several well kept ales, simple low-priced lunchtime food; alley overflow, open all day, cl wknds *(Richard Endacott)*

Simpsons Tavern EC3V 9DR [just off Cornhill]: Pleasingly old-fashioned place founded in 1757, rather clubby small panelled bar serving Bass and a guest such as Harveys, stairs down to another bar with snacks, traditional chophouse with upright stall seating (expect to share a table) and similar upstairs restaurant, good value traditional dishes such as braised oxtail stew, steak and kidney pie and Lancashire hot pot; open wkdy lunchtimes and from 8am Tues-Fri for breakfast *(Peter Dandy, Barbarrick)*

Swan EC3V 1LY [Ship Tavern Passage, off Gracechurch St]: Bustling narrow flagstoned bar, particularly well kept Fullers ales, proper hands-on landlord and friendly chatty service, generous lunchtime sandwiches and snacks; neatly kept Victorian panelled décor, low lighting, larger carpeted upstairs bar; silent corner TV; covered alley used by smokers, usually cl 9pm, cl wknds *(N R White)*

EC4

☆ *Banker* EC4R 3TE [Cousin Lane, by Cannon St Station]: Attractive multi-level pub just below Cannon St railway bridge, stripped brick, mirrors and big chandelier in high-ceilinged bar, steps up to two small rooms (one very cosy, with leather sofas – you can hear the trains rumbling overhead), linking to long narrow glass-fronted room with thrilling Thames view shared by small outdoor deck; good range of Fullers ales and of wines by the glass, enjoyable food inc sharing plates (some nice cheeses), may be spit roasts, smart attentive staff, relaxed chatty atmosphere, framed banknotes and railway posters; open all day *(Dr and Mrs A K Clarke, BB)*

Old Bell EC4Y 1DH [Fleet St, nr Ludgate Circus]: 17th-c tavern backing on to St Bride's, heavy black beams, flagstones, brass-topped tables, dim lighting, stained-glass bow window; good changing choice of ales from island servery (can try before you buy), friendly efficient young foreign staff, usual food, coal fire, cheerful atmosphere; piped music; covered heated

outside area *(BB, N R White, the Didler)*

Paternoster EC4M 7DZ [Queens Head Passage]: In modern development in sight of St Paul's, Wells & Youngs ales, good choice of food and of wines by the glass, good coffee, some sofas; TV, games *(Michael Dandy, Peter Dandy)*

Witness Box EC4Y 0BH [Tudor St]: Open-plan with dark timber and mixed wooden furnishings, welcoming efficient service, generous food inc early breakfast, well kept ales such as Harviestoun Bitter & Twisted and Shepherd Neame Spitfire; bigger basement bar with some easy chairs; popular with legal fraternity *(LM)*

SE1

Rake SE1 9AG [Winchester Walk]: Tiny, discreetly modern bar with amazing bottled beer range in wall-wide cooler, as well as half a dozen continental lagers on tap and perhaps a couple of rare real ales, good friendly service; fair-sized terrace with decking and heated marquee *(Tracey and Stephen Groves, Mike and Sue Loseby)*

SW1

Adam & Eve SW1H 9EX [Petty France]: Spotless Victorian pub with brown anaglypta ceiling, big light windows, etched-glass screens and dark furniture; Adnams and Wells & Youngs, well priced pubby food from sandwiches up, friendly service; piped music, TV and games machine *(Ian Phillips, Michael Dandy)*

☆ *Albert* SW1H 0NP [Victoria St]: Handsome contrast to the cliffs of dark glass around it; busy open-plan airy bar with cut and etched windows, gleaming mahogany, ornate ceiling, solid comfortable furnishings, enjoyable pubby food all day from sandwiches up, well kept Fullers London Pride, Wells & Youngs Bombardier and guests, 24 wines by the glass, efficient cheerful service; handsome staircase lined with portraits of prime ministers up to carvery/dining room; piped music, games machine, lavatories down steep stairs; children welcome if eating, open all day from 8am (breakfast till noon) *(Michael Dandy, LYM, BB, Mike and Sue Loseby, Phil Bryant, Ian Phillips, Mike Tucker, John and Gloria Isaacs, Terry and Nickie Williams)*

☆ *Buckingham Arms* SW1H 9EU [Petty France]: Welcoming bow-windowed 18th-c local, good value pubby food from back open kitchen, Wells & Youngs ales and guests from a long bar, good wines by the glass; elegant mirrors and woodwork, unusual side corridor fitted out with elbow ledge for drinkers; TVs; dogs welcome, handy for Buckingham Palace, Westminster Abbey and St James's Park, open all day *(LYM, Dr and Mrs M E Wilson, Michael Dandy, Dr and Mrs A K Clarke, the Didler)*

Cask SW1V 2EE [Charlwood St/Tachbrook St]: Modern, bright and spacious with simple comfortable furnishings, Dark Star and changing small brewery guests, continental beers, enjoyable food, friendly helpful service *(N R White)*

Cask & Glass SW1E 5HN [Palace St]: Snug one-room traditional pub with good range of Shepherd Neame ales, friendly staff and atmosphere, good value lunchtime sandwiches, old prints and shiny black panelling; quiet corner TV; hanging baskets and a few tables outside, handy for Queen's Gallery *(N R White, Richard Tilbrook)*

Clarence SW1A 2HP [Whitehall]: Civilised olde-worlde beamed pub with well spaced tables, varied seating inc tub chairs and banquettes, ales such as Adnams, Sambrooks and Sharps, decent wines by the glass; friendly chatty landlord, popular reasonably priced food all day from snacks up, upstairs dining area; pavement tables *(Dr and Mrs M E Wilson, Ian Phillips)*

Feathers SW1H 0BH [Broadway]: Large comfortable pub, a Scotland Yard local, with atrium and upstairs dining area, good choice of low-priced pubby food from sandwiches up, six well kept ales inc Fullers London Pride, Sharps Doom Bar and Timothy Taylors Landlord, several wines by the glass; piped music; open all day (from 8am for breakfast) *(BB, Michael Dandy, Dr and Mrs M E Wilson)*

☆ **Fox & Hounds** SW1W 8HR [Passmore St/ Graham Terrace]: Small convivial local, Wells & Youngs ales, warm red décor with big hunting prints, old sepia photographs and toby jugs, wall benches and sofas, book-lined back room, hanging plants under attractive skylight, old-effect gas fire, some low-priced pubby food, friendly staff; can get crowded with after-work drinkers *(Jeremy King, the Didler, N R White)*

Golden Lion SW1Y 6QY [King St]: Busy bow-fronted Victorian pub opp Christie's auction rooms, well kept Fullers, Greene King and Wells & Youngs from decorative servery, decent wines by the glass, good value food, friendly service; ornate 1900s Jacobean décor and dark panelling, upstairs bar; piped music *(Dr and Mrs A K Clarke)*

☆ **Grenadier** SW1X 7NR [Wilton Row; the turning off Wilton Crescent looks prohibitive, but the barrier and watchman are there to keep out cars]: Cosy old mews pub with lots of character and military history, but not much space (avoid 5-7pm); simple unfussy bar, stools and wooden benches, four ales such as Batemans, Fullers, Hop Back and Wells & Youngs from rare pewter-topped counter, famous bloody marys, may be bar food, intimate back restaurant (best to book); no mobiles or photography; children (over 8) and dogs allowed, sentry box and single table outside, open all day *(LM, LYM, Lawrence R Cotter, Mike and Sue Loseby, N R White)*

Grosvenor SW1V 3LA [Grosvenor Rd]: Chatty traditional local across from river (no views); friendly staff and helpful landlord, hearty good value pub food, fire; pool and summer

table tennis; some tables out by road, secluded beer garden *(Ros Lawler, Louise McKee, Jake Lingwood, KJ)*

Jugged Hare SW1V 1DX [Vauxhall Bridge Rd/Rochester Row]: Popular Fullers Ale & Pie pub in former colonnaded bank with balustraded balcony, chandelier, dark wood, old London photographs and busts, back room; good service, reasonably priced food from sandwiches up inc a pie range; piped music, silent fruit machine; open all day *(Jeremy King, N R White, the Didler, BB)*

☆ **Morpeth Arms** SW1P 4RW [Millbank]: Sparkling clean Victorian pub facing Thames, roomy and comfortable, some etched and cut glass, old books and prints, photographs, earthenware jars and bottles; well kept Wells & Youngs and a guest, decent choice of wines and of good value food all day, good welcoming service even at busy lunchtimes, upstairs dining room; games machine, may be unobtrusive sports TV, young evening crowd; seats outside (a lot of traffic), handy for Tate Britain *(BB, Dr and Mrs A K Clarke, the Didler, Ros Lawler, N R White)*

☆ **Nags Head** SW1X 8ED [Kinnerton St; Knightsbridge]: Unspoilt little mews pub, low-ceilinged panelled front room with unusual sunken counter, log-effect gas fire in old range, narrow passage down to even smaller bar, Adnams from 19th-c handpumps, all-day pubby food; theatrical mementoes, old what-the-butler-saw machine and one-armed bandit, no mobiles; individual piped music; well behaved children and dogs allowed, a few seats outside, open all day *(LYM, Tich Critchlow, N R White, the Didler)*

Orange SW1W 8NE [Pimlico Rd]: Refurbished gastropub with good choice of enjoyable food inc wood-fired pizzas, friendly attentive staff, real ales, linked light and airy rooms with rustic furniture and relaxed weathered feel; children welcome, four bedrooms, open all day from 8am *(Miss Jennifer Harvey, Mr Stuart Brown, LYM)*

Red Lion SW1A 2NH [Parliament St]: Congenial pub by Houses of Parliament, used by Foreign Office staff and MPs, soft lighting, parliamentary cartoons and prints; Fullers/Gales beers and decent wines from long bar, good range of food, efficient staff, also cellar bar and small narrow upstairs dining room, outside seating *(N R White, Dr and Mrs A K Clarke, BB, Michael Dandy)*

Sanctuary House SW1H 9LA [Tothill St]: Pub/hotel's roomy high-ceilinged bar with Fullers ales, pubby food from sandwiches to speciality pies and good fish and chips, cheerful helpful staff; plenty of tables, nice stools and armchairs, raised and balustraded back area with monkish mural, ornate outside scrollwork; piped music; children welcome, 30 or more bedrooms, open all day *(Dr and Mrs A K Clarke, Michael Dandy)*

Speaker SW1P 2HA [Great Peter St]: Pleasant chatty atmosphere in unpretentious smallish corner pub, well kept Shepherd Neame Spitfire, Wells & Youngs and quickly changing guests, lots of whiskies, limited popular food inc good sandwiches, friendly helpful staff, panelling, political cartoons and prints; open all day, cl Sat, Sun evening (N R White)

Thomas Cubitt SW1W 9PA [Elizabeth St]: Popular tastefully refurbished dining pub with floor-to-ceiling french doors opening to street, oak floors, panelling and open fires; food in bar or upstairs dining room, good mix of customers (Derek Thomas)

Westminster Arms SW1P 3AT [Storey's Gate]: Busy pub nr Westminster Abbey and Houses of Parliament, six well kept Shepherd Neame ales, several malt whiskies, straightforward all-day food (not wknd evenings), rather sparse bar with old-fashioned furnishings, panelling, wine bar downstairs (may close early if quiet); piped music; children welcome lunchtime in upstairs eating area, tables outside, open all day, cl Sun evening (Michael Dandy, Dr and Mrs A K Clarke, Rob and Catherine Dunster, Edward Mirzoeff, LYM, N R White)

SW3

Hour Glass SW3 2DY [Brompton Rd]: Small welcoming pub handy for the V&A and other nearby museums, well kept Adnams and Fullers London Pride, good value pubby food (not Sun); sports TV; pavement picnic-sets (LM)

W1

Clachan W1B 5QH [Kingly St]: Ornate plaster ceiling supported by two large fluted and decorated pillars (used to be owned by Liberty), comfortable screened leather banquettes, smaller drinking alcove up three or four steps; well kept changing ales such as Caledonian Deuchars IPA, Fullers and Sharps Doom Bar from handsome counter, reasonably priced food from sandwiches up; can get busy, but very relaxed in afternoons (DM, Michael Dandy, BB)

Cock W1W 8QE [Great Portland St]: Big corner local with enormous lamps over picnic-sets outside, florid Victorian/Edwardian décor with gleaming mahogany and plasterwork, some cut and etched glass, high tiled ceiling and mosaic floor, velvet curtains, coal-effect gas fires, upstairs lounge; cheap Sam Smiths OB from all four handpumps, friendly efficient service, reasonably priced food (not Fri-Sun evenings); open all day (the Didler, Tracey and Stephen Groves, BB, John and Gloria Isaacs)

De Hems W1D 5BW [Macclesfield St]: Typical London pub recycled as pastiche of a dutch bar (but roomier and less intimate), old dutch engravings, panelled walls, mixed tables on bare boards, big continental founts and good range of interesting bottled beers, dutch-influenced food, friendly service; can get very busy (DM, Jeremy King, N R White)

French House W1D 5BG [Dean St]: Character pub with impressive range of wines and bottled beers, other unusual drinks, some draught beers (no pint glasses), lively chatty atmosphere – mainly standing room; windows keeping good eye on passers-by, theatre memorabilia, efficient friendly staff, good food in upstairs restaurant, no mobile phones; can get very busy evenings; open all day (Ros Lawler, Jeremy King, Terry and Nickie Williams, DM, Tim Maddison, John and Gloria Isaacs)

George W1W 7LQ [Great Portland St]: Solid old-fashioned pub with lots of mahogany, chandeliers and engraved mirrors, narrow with limited seating, Greene King and guest ales, standard pubby food from sandwiches up, bustling chatty atmosphere (Tracey and Stephen Groves)

Jack Horner W1T 7QN [Tottenham Court Rd]: Fullers bank conversion with full range of their ales from island counter, pie-based food, friendly helpful service, tables in quiet areas, lots of woodwork, photographs of old London; piped music (Jeremy King, Dr and Mrs M E Wilson, Fergus McDonald, Simon Collett-Jones)

Red Lion W1B 5PR [Kingly St]: Dark panelling, narrow front bar with deep leather banquettes, back bar with darts; basic bargain food in comfortable upstairs lounge, cheap Sam Smiths keg beers (Michael Dandy, DC, Jeremy King, BB)

Shakespeares Head W1F 7HZ [Great Marlborough St]: Panelled pub dating from the early 18th c, soft lighting, dark beams, deep red and green décor, Fullers London Pride, Shepherd Neame Spitfire and Wells & Youngs Bitter, standard pubby food from sandwiches up, good friendly staff, upstairs dining room; popular with young people (Michael Dandy, Stephen Moss, Terry and Nickie Williams)

Yorkshire Grey W1W 7AX [Langham St]: Small bare-boards corner pub with nice period feel, well kept cheap Sam Smiths OBB, lots of wood, BBC radio memorabilia, comfortable seating inc snug little parlour, friendly staff, attractively priced bar lunches, upstairs room; open all day (Tracey and Stephen Groves, Jake Lingwood, John and Gloria Isaacs)

W2

Mad Bishop & Bear W2 1HB [Paddington Station]: Up escalators from concourse, full Fullers range and a guest beer, good wine choice, good value standard food quickly served inc breakfast (7.30am on); ornate plasterwork, etched mirrors and fancy lamps, parquet, tiles and carpet, booths with leather banquettes, lots of wood and prints, train departures' screen; sports TV, piped music, games machine; open all day, tables out overlooking concourse (Dr and Mrs A K Clarke, Donna and Roger, Joe Green, Jeremy King, Michael Dandy, Dave Irving, Jenny Huggins, BB, Tracey and Stephen Groves)

☆ **Victoria** W2 2NH [Strathearn Pl]: Well run pub with lots of Victorian pictures and memorabilia, cast-iron fireplaces, gilded mirrors and mahogany panelling, brass mock-gas lamps above attractive horseshoe bar, bare boards and banquettes; relaxed chatty atmosphere, good service, full Fullers ale range kept well, good choice of wines by the glass, well priced food counter; upstairs has leather club chairs in small library/snug (and, mostly used for private functions now, replica of Gaiety Theatre bar, all gilt and red plush); quiet piped music, TV (off unless people ask); pavement picnic-sets, open all day *(LYM, N R White, Ian Herdman)*

WC1

Calthorpe Arms WC1X 8JR [Grays Inn Rd]: Plush wall seats, well kept Wells & Youngs ales, popular generous food upstairs lunchtime and evening, good staff; pavement tables, open all day *(the Didler)*
Dolphin WC1R 4PF [Red Lion St]: Small one-bar corner pub with high stools and wide shelves around the walls, old photographs, horsebrasses, hanging copper pots and pans and so forth, simple wkdy lunchtime food, well kept Adnams and Greene King; open all day wkdys and most Sat lunchtimes *(the Didler, Tracey and Stephen Groves)*
Museum Tavern WC1B 3BA [Museum St/Great Russell St]: Traditional high-ceilinged ornate Victorian pub facing British Museum, busy lunchtime and early evening, but can be quite peaceful other times, good choice of well kept beers inc some unusual ones, several wines by the glass, good hot drinks, straightforward food from end servery; one or two tables out under gas lamps, open all day *(LYM, Michael Butler, Pete Coxon, Tracey and Stephen Groves, Dr and Mrs M E Wilson)*
Rugby WC1N 3ES [Great James St]: Sizeable pub with Shepherd Neame ales from central servery, decent usual food, good service, darts, appropriate photographs; pleasant terrace *(the Didler, Ian Martin)*

WC2

Bear & Staff WC2H 7AX [Bear St]: Traditional Nicholsons corner pub with six well kept changing ales, standard pubby food from sandwiches and sharing platters up, upstairs dining room named after Charlie Chaplin who used the pub *(Terry and Nickie Williams, Michael Dandy)*
☆ *Chandos* WC2N 4ER [St Martins Lane]: Busy bare-boards bar with snug cubicles, lots of theatre memorabilia on stairs up to smarter more comfortable lounge, with opera photographs, low wooden tables, panelling, leather sofas, coloured windows; cheap Sam Smiths OBB, prompt cheerful service, bargain food, air conditioning, darts; can get packed early evening; piped music and games machines; note the automaton on the roof (working 10-2 and 4-9); children upstairs till 6pm, open all day from 9am (for breakfast) *(Ian Phillips, Mrs Hazel Rainer, Bruce Bird, Michael Dandy, LYM, Michael and Alison Sandy)*

Coal Hole WC2R 0DW [Strand]: Chatty and comfortable front bar, softly lit relaxed downstairs dining bar with wall reliefs, mock-baronial high ceiling and raised back gallery, basement snug; Fullers London Pride, Greene King IPA and Timothy Taylors Landlord, decent wines by the glass, bargain pubby food *(BB, Michael Dandy, Dr and Mrs A K Clarke, Bernard Stradling)*
Edgar Wallace WC2R 3JE [Essex St]: Simple spacious open-plan pub dating from the 18th c, up to eight well kept ales inc Adnams, a beer brewed for them by Nethergate and several unusual guests, friendly efficient service, good value all-day food inc doorstep sandwiches, half-panelled walls and red ceilings; interesting old London and Edgar Wallace memorabilia (pub renamed in 1975 to mark his centenary), friendly chatty atmosphere; open all day, cl wknds *(LM, N R White, Michael and Alison Sandy)*
George WC2R 1AP [Strand]: Timbered pub nr law courts, long narrow bare-boards bar, Fullers London Pride, Sharps Doom Bar and Wells & Youngs Bitter, good choice of wines by the glass, sandwiches and limited basic hot food, upstairs bar with carvery *(Pete Coxon, Michael Dandy)*
Lyceum WC2R 0HS [Strand]: Panelling and pleasantly simple furnishings downstairs, several small discreet booths, steps up to a bigger alcove with darts, food in much bigger upstairs panelled lounge with deep button-back leather settees and armchairs, low-priced Sam Smiths beer, civilised atmosphere *(Chris Sale, Mike and Eleanor Anderson)*
Marquess of Anglesey WC2E 7AU [Bow St/Russell St]: Light and airy, with Wells & Youngs and a guest beer, decent food inc interesting specials, friendly staff, a couple of big sofas, more room upstairs *(Michael Dandy)*
Nags Head WC2E 8BT [James St/Neal St]: Etched brewery mirrors, red ceiling, mahogany furniture, some partitioned booths, lots of old local prints, reasonably priced bar lunches from separate side counter, friendly staff, three McMullens ales; open all day *(Michael Dandy, Meg and Colin Hamilton)*
☆ *Porterhouse* WC2E 7NA [Maiden Lane]: Good daytime pub (can be packed evenings), London outpost of Dublin's Porterhouse microbrewery, their interesting if pricey draught beers inc Porter and two Stouts (comprehensive tasting tray), also their TSB real ale and a guest, lots of bottled imports, good choice of wines by the glass, reasonably priced food from soup and open sandwiches up with some emphasis on rock oysters; shiny three-level labyrinth of stairs (lifts for disabled), galleries and copper ducting and piping, some nice design touches, sonorous openwork clock, neatly cased bottled beer displays; piped music, irish live music, big-screen sports TV

(repeated in gents'); tables on front terrace, open all day (Michael and Alison Sandy, Jeremy King, BB)

☆ **Sherlock Holmes** WC2N 5DB [Northumberland St; aka Northumberland Arms]: Fine collection of Holmes' memorabilia, also silent videos of black and white Holmes' films; well kept Greene King ales, usual furnishings, quick service at good value lunchtime food counter, friendly young staff; much quieter upstairs restaurant by replica of Holmes's study; tables out in front (Phil and Jane Hodson, BB)

☆ **Ship & Shovell** WC2N 5PH [Craven Passage, off Craven St]: Well kept Badger ales and a guest, good friendly staff, decent reasonably priced food inc wide range of baguettes etc; brightly lit with dark wood, etched mirrors and interesting mainly naval pictures, plenty of tables, open fire, compact back section, separate partitioned bar across *Underneath the Arches* alley; TV; open all day, cl Sun (Ian Phillips, Michael and Alison Sandy, N R White, the Didler, Andrea Rampley, Joe Green, Tim Maddison)

Wellington WC2R 0HS [Strand/Wellington St]: Long narrow corner pub with room upstairs, Black Sheep, Fullers London Pride and Timothy Taylors Landlord, several wines by the glass, wide choice of low-priced standard food till 5, friendly staff; tables outside (Michael Dandy)

White Lion WC2E 8NS [James St]: Panelling, bare boards, Fullers London Pride, Timothy Taylors Landlord and guest ales, low-priced standard pubby food from sandwiches up, dining room upstairs (Michael Dandy)

EAST LONDON

E1

Captain Kidd E1W 2NE [Wapping High St]: Great Thames views from large open-plan nautical-theme pub's jutting bay windows' in a renovated Docklands warehouse stripped back to beams and basics; good choice of inexpensive bar food all day, pricier restaurant upstairs, cheap Sam Smiths keg beers, nice wines, obliging bow-tied staff, lively bustle; sports TV; dogs welcome, chunky tables on roomy back waterside terrace (John Wooll)

☆ **Dickens Inn** E1W 1UH [Marble Quay, St Katharines Way]: Outstanding position looking over smart docklands marina to Tower Bridge; bare boards, baulks and timbers, wide choice of enjoyable food inc good Sun roasts (pizza/pasta upstairs, smarter restaurant above that), friendly helpful staff, real ales such as Adnams, Greene King and Wells & Youngs, decent wines by the glass; piped music, machines; tables outside (N R White, John Saville, the Didler, LYM)

E11

Birkbeck Tavern E11 4HL [Langthorne Rd]: Interesting high-ceilinged two-room local,

good value snacks and well kept ales; children allowed in nice garden with plenty of tables (Jeremy King)

E14

Bootys E14 8BP [Narrow St]: 19th-c bar with reasonably priced home-made food all day, Brakspears ales, good choice of wines by the glass, friendly staff, spectacular Thames (and London Marathon) view, live jazz Sat night (Martin Davies)

NORTH LONDON

N1

Alwyne Castle N1 2LY [St Pauls Rd; opp Highbury Grove]: Laid-back friendly atmosphere, tasty good value food all day from snacks to burgers and sharing plates, Sun roasts, conservatory; Tues quiz night, Fri DJ; dogs welcome, children after 7pm; disabled facilities, big garden with summer barbecues, open all day (Ros Lawler)

Angelic N1 0RJ [Liverpool Rd]: Large nicely updated pub popular for its food (should book wknds) inc shortish tapas menu and unusual things like quail raised pie and pigs trotters stuffed with black pudding, vegetarian options too; good choice of drinks inc plenty of wines by the glass, juice bar, good friendly service; thoughtful piped music (Ros Lawler)

Charles Lamb N1 8DE [Elia St]: Small friendly backstreet pub with well kept Fullers Chiswick, Timothy Taylors Landlord and a guest, some interesting imports on tap or bottled, good choice of wines by the glass, good blackboard food; big windows, polished boards and simple traditional furniture; piped jazz; tables outside (John M Murphy, Kevin Booker)

Compass N1 9PZ [Penton St]: Redone corner pub/restaurant, mix of old tables and chairs in big bare-boards bar, reasonably priced home-made food (all day Sat) such as wood pigeon with broad beans and hearty fish stew from an open kitchen, three regularly changing ales, scrumpy, some unusual bottled beers; pavement tables, open all day (Michael and Maggie Betton)

Compton Arms N1 2XD [Compton Avenue, off Canonbury Rd]: Tiny villagey local under new licensee, simply furnished unpretentious low-ceilinged rooms, Greene King and guests; sports TV, can be busy Arsenal match days; dogs welcome, tables under big sycamore tree and glass-covered area, open all day (LYM)

Duke of Wellington N1 4BL [Balls Pond Rd]: Welcoming pub with Sambrooks Wandle and three changing guests (beer festivals), enjoyable food Sat brunch and Sun roasts, warm winter fires; regular live music, comedy nights and film screenings; cl till 3pm, open all day wknds (Andrew Boss)

Fellow N1 9AA : Contemporary pub/restaurant, popular and relaxed, with enjoyable unusual food (not cheap and they add a service charge), real ales and good choice of wines, friendly staff coping at busy times, upstairs cocktail bar (DJ nights Thurs, Fri); piped music; roof terrace *(Adam Madai)*

☆ *Island Queen* N1 8HD [Noel Rd]: Fine high-ceilinged Victorian pub handy for Camden Passage antiques area, Fullers London Pride, a guest ale, lots of imported beers and good value wines from island bar, sensibly short choice of fresh often unusual food, pleasant staff and laid-back atmosphere; dark wood and big decorative mirrors, intimate back area, upstairs room; popular wknd evenings with young crowd; children welcome *(Tracey and Stephen Groves, Christopher Armitage, LYM)*

Lord Clyde N1 3PB [Essex Rd]: Civilised dining pub with mix of furnishings inc some comfortable sofas, Harveys and a guest ale, reasonable prices *(Andrew Bosi)*

Old Queens Head N1 8LN [Essex Rd]: Bustling old Islington pub fashionably redone and attracting a trendy crowd, lots going on inc live music, DJs and comedy nights; food (all day wknds) from snacks up, good choice of wines by the glass inc champagne, cocktails; under-18s till 7pm, pavement picnic-sets, small courtyard behind, open all day till late (2am wknds) *(Ros Lawler)*

Wenlock Arms N1 7TA [Wenlock Rd]: Lived-in local in a bleak bit of London, friendly service, half a dozen or more well kept changing ales from central servery (always a Mild), farm cider and perry, foreign bottled beers, doorstep sandwiches (good salt beef), alcove seating, coal fires; darts, back pool table, Fri, Sat jazz nights, piano Sun afternoon; piped music; open all day *(Joe Green, the Didler, Bruce Bird, Roger Shipperley)*

N7

Duchess of Kent N7 8PR [Liverpool Rd]: Relaxed and comfortably refurbished Geronimo Inn, good food and service, well kept beers, nice wines *(Steve and Hilary Nelson)*

N14

Cherry Tree N14 6EN [The Green]: Roomy beamed Vintage Inn with wide choice of wines by the glass and reasonably priced ales, good value food all day from breakfast on, good service, mix of big tables, some leather chesterfields; children welcome, tables out behind, bedrooms in adjacent Innkeepers Lodge, open all day *(Colin Moore)*

N19

St Johns N19 5QU [Junction Rd]: Well run dining pub, enjoyable generous blackboard food, well kept ales and reasonably priced wines, good service even when busy *(Howard and Lorna Lambert)*

NW1

Betjeman Arms NW1 2QL [St Pancras Station]: Good all-rounder with outside seating area facing Eurostar trains *(Derek Thomas)*

Bree Louise NW1 2HH [Cobourg St/Euston St]: Partly divided open-plan bar with half a dozen or more interesting real ales, food emphasising pies (Mon-Thurs bargains), basic décor with prints, UK flags, mixed used furnishings; can get very busy early evening; open all day *(Martin Grosberg, Lynda Payton, Sam Samuells, Joe Green, Bruce Bird)*

☆ *Doric Arch* NW1 2DN [Eversholt St]: Virtually part of Euston Station, up stairs from bus terminus with raised back part overlooking it; well kept Fullers and guests such as Kelham Island, Weston's farm cider, friendly helpful staff, enjoyable well priced pubby food lunchtime and from 4pm wkdys (12-5pm wknds), pleasantly nostalgic atmosphere and some quiet corners; intriguing train and other transport memorabilia inc big clock at entrance, downstairs restaurant; discreet sports TV, machines; lavatories on combination lock; open all day *(BB, Dr and Mrs A K Clarke, Tracey and Stephen Groves, Joe Green, the Didler, Ian Phillips, Ian and Helen Stafford, Jeremy King)*

Edinboro Castle NW1 7RU [Mornington Terrace/Delancy St]: Open-plan bare-boards pub with reasonably priced pubby food (all day, mainly roasts Sun) from open kitchen, lots of wines by the glass, ales such as Fullers London Pride and Sharps; relaxed young atmosphere, unusual décor with long patterned curtains and beaded lampshades, nicely worn-in furniture, raised skylit back area with small fireplace; piped music can be loud; children welcome, big suntrap garden with bar, regular summer barbecues, open all day *(Jeremy King)*

☆ *Engineer* NW1 8JH [Gloucester Avenue]: Mix of foodies and drinkers in big informal L-shaped bar, lively and popular, with good interesting food (not cheap), St Peters Organic and Wells & Youngs Bombardier, enterprising wine list, good range of spirits; handsome original woodwork and rather unusual décor, individual more ornate candlelit rooms upstairs (may need to book); piped and live music; children welcome, attractive garden, handy for Primrose Hill, open all day from 9am *(Jeremy King, BB)*

Euston Flyer NW1 2RA [Euston Rd, opp British Library]: Big welcoming open-plan pub, Fullers/Gales beers, good choice of standard food all day, relaxed lunchtime atmosphere; plenty of light wood, carpet or boarded floors, mirrors, photographs of old London, smaller raised areas, big doors open to street in warm weather; piped music, Sky TV, silent games machine; can get packed evenings; open all day, cl 8.30pm Sun *(Michael and Alison Sandy, the Didler, Stephen and Jean Curtis, Jeremy King)*

Pembroke Castle NW1 8JA : Popular split-level bare-boards pub, Greene King IPA and Bombardier, decent quickly served food inc Sun roasts, short wine list (but most by the glass), newspapers; upstairs dining/function room; piped music, TV, Mon quiz ; spacious beer garden *(Jeremy King)*

Somerstown Coffee House NW1 1HS [Chalton St]: French-run dining pub with good affordable brasserie food, well kept Wells & Youngs ales, pubby atmosphere with mixed furniture inc old chapel chairs on bare boards, black and white pictures on dark panelling; tables out at front and back, open all day *(Vanessa Le Tort)*

NW3

Washington NW3 4UE [Englands Lane]: Ornate Victorian pub with burgundy and gilt ceiling, etched glass and mirrors, stools around central dark wood servery, mixed furniture inc sofas at back; well kept Timothy Taylors Landlord and guests, good choice of wines by the glass, food inc bargain wkdy deals, relaxed atmosphere; soft piped music, Tues quiz night; comedy nights (1st Sun of month) in cellar bar; well behaved dogs allowed, some street tables *(Jeremy King)*

SOUTH LONDON

SE1

Anchor SE1 9EF [Bankside]: In great spot nr Thames with river views from upper floors and roof terrace, extensively refurbished with beams, stripped brickwork and old-world corners, well kept Fullers London Pride and Greene King IPA, good choice of wines by the glass, popular fish and chip bar inc takeaways, other good value all-day food inc breakfast and tearoom; piped music; provision for children, disabled access, bedrooms in friendly quiet Premier Travel Inn behind, open all day *(Michael Doswell, Mike and Sue Loseby, N R White, Phil and Jane Hodson, Paul Humphreys, Ian Phillips, LYM)*

Anchor & Hope SE1 8LP [The Cut]: Busy informal bare-boards gastropub, contrasting reports on food from excellent to rough and ready, prices can be high and service erratic; well kept Wells & Youngs and guests, wine by tumbler or carafe, plain bar with big windows and mix of furniture inc elbow tables, curtained-off dining part with tight-packed scrubbed tables, small open kitchen area and contemporary art on purple walls; children and dogs welcome, cl Sun evening and Mon lunchtime, otherwise open all day *(Ian Phillips, LYM, Mike and Sue Loseby, Jeremy King, Eleanor Dandy, Susan and John Douglas, Edward Mirzoeff)*

Boot & Flogger SE1 1TA [Redcross Way]: Wine bar rather than pub with old-fashioned gentleman's club feel, low lighting, dark panelling, leather armchairs, enjoyable pubby food, no beer; shuts at 8pm *(Christopher Turner)*

Bridge House SE1 2UP [Tower Bridge Rd]: Modern upmarket Adnams bar with young chatty atmosphere, their full range and good wine choice, good value generous food, friendly service, downstairs dining area *(N R White)*

Doggetts Coat & Badge SE1 9UD [by Blackfriars Bridge]: Well run modern pub on four floors with good Thames views, well kept interesting beers, pleasant service, usual food inc range of pies; nice outside drinking area, *(Ian Phillips, BB)*

Garrison SE1 3XB [Bermondsey St]: Interesting pub with scrubbed tables upstairs, cinema downstairs, good reasonably priced food, more emphasis on wine than beer, buzzy atmosphere *(Mrs Jane Kingsbury, Mike and Sue Loseby)*

Goldsmith SE1 0EF [Southwark Bridge Rd]: Recently reopened as pub/dining room, well kept Adnams Best, Wadworths 6X and a guest, imaginative wine list with many by the glass, enjoyable sensibly priced food *(Mike and Sue Loseby)*

Hide Bar SE1 3XF [Bermondsey St]: Cocktail bar with vast collection of spirits and fine range of wines inc champagnes by the glass, local Meantime ales, food from sandwiches up with things to share *(BOB)*

☆ **Kings Arms** SE1 8TB [Roupell St]: Proper corner local, bustling and friendly, curved servery dividing traditional bar and lounge, Fullers London Pride, Greene King IPA, Sharps Doom Bar and Wells & Youngs Bombardier, good wine and malt whisky choice, good friendly service, flame-effect fires, food from thai dishes to good Sun roast; big back extension with conservatory/courtyard dining area, long central table and high side tables, attractive local prints and eccentric bric-a-brac; piped music; open all day *(N R White, Colin and Louise English)*

☆ **Lord Clyde** SE1 1ER [Clennam St]: Neat panelled L-shaped local in same friendly efficient family for over 50 years, well kept Adnams Best, Fullers London Pride, Greene King IPA, Shepherd Neame Spitfire and Wells & Youngs, simple food from good salt beef sandwiches up (wkdy lunchtimes, early evenings); darts in small hatch-service back public bar; outside seating, striking tiled façade, open all day, till 6pm Sun *(Mike and Sue Loseby, N R White)*

Mad Hatter SE1 9NY [Stamford St, Blackfriars Rd end]: Smartly Edwardianised, with stained glass, coaching prints, books and interesting hats, good range of food, Fullers ales, fine choice of wines by the glass, helpful staff *(Tracey and Stephen Groves, N R White)*

SE5

Hoopers Bar SE5 8DH [Ivanhoe Rd]: Traditional Victorian corner pub with good range of changing ales from smaller brewers (beer festivals), over 50 bottled beers, accommodating landlord, quiet side snug, live jazz/blues (Fri, Sat); sports TV *(H D Thompson)*

SE10

Trafalgar SE10 9NW [Park Row]: Substantial 18th-c building with splendid river views from big windows directly above water in four still quite elegant if worn rooms inc end dining room, all with oak panelling and good maritime and local prints; three well kept ales, popular food all day from standard menu (more interesting in dining room), good house wines, brisk friendly service, good atmosphere, though spacious bars can get packed Fri and Sat evenings; piped music; children welcome, tables out by Nelson statue, handy for Maritime Museum *(Mike Gorton, BB)*

Yacht SE10 9NP [Crane St]: Neatly modernised with great river views from spacious room a few steps up from bar, good choice of reasonably priced food, four well kept ales, cosy banquettes, light wood panelling, portholes, yacht pictures; cheerful hanging baskets out at front *(John Saville)*

SE11

Prince of Wales SE11 4EA [Cleaver Sq]: Comfortably traditional little Edwardian pub in smart quiet Georgian square, well kept Shepherd Neame ales, bar food from good sandwiches up, friendly landlord and staff, arch to small saloon; pavement seats, boules available to play in the square *(Tim Maddison, BB)*

SE16

☆ *Mayflower* SE16 4NF [Rotherhithe St]: Unchanging cosy old riverside pub in unusual street with lovely early 18th-c church; wide choice of enjoyable generous food all day, black beams, panelling, nautical bric-a-brac, high-backed settles and coal fires, good Thames views from upstairs restaurant (cl Sat lunchtime); Greene King ales, good coffee and good value wines, friendly service; piped music; children welcome, nice jetty/terrace over water, open all day *(LYM, N R White, the Didler)*

SE18

Bull SE18 3HP [Shooters Hill]: Neat and friendly two-bar local, plusher at back, well kept changing ales such as Courage Best, Fullers ESB, Harveys Best, St Austell Tribute, Sharps Doom Bar and Wells & Youngs Best; no piped music; dogs welcome, by entry to ancient Oxleas Woods *(Michael and Deborah Ethier)*

SE22

Bishop SE22 8EW [Lordship Lane]: Lively contemporary dining pub with good food and friendly staff, several real ales; piped music; children and dogs welcome, small outside area at back *(Jake Lingwood, Jamie Ross)*

SE24

Commercial SE24 0JT [Railton Rd (opp Herne Hill Station)]: Popular pub with Marstons, Wells & Youngs Bombardier and two changing guests, roomy and comfortable with sofas and easy chairs, daily papers, buzzy young atmosphere; Sky TV *(Giles and Annie Francis)*

Prince Regent SE24 0NJ [Dulwich Rd]: Good range of changing ales, belgian beers, friendly staff; books on window sills, good if not cheap changing menu, dining area downstairs, lively atmosphere *(Bill Adie, Tansy Spinks, Nick Rampley)*

SE26

☆ *Dulwich Wood House* SE26 6RS [Sydenham Hill]: Extended, well refurbished Youngs pub in Victorian lodge gatehouse complete with turret, nice local atmosphere, friendly service, decent food cooked to order; steps up to entrance (and stiff walk up from station); big pleasant back garden with old-fashioned street lamps and barbecues, handy for Dulwich Wood *(Ian and Nita Cooper, B J Harding)*

SW8

Priory Arms SW8 2PB [Lansdowne Way]: Friendly little local with wide range of well kept changing ales, continental beers too on tap and in bottle, enjoyable reasonably priced pubby food inc good Sun roasts; packed old corner bookshelf, lots of games *(Gillian Rodgers, Susan and John Douglas)*

SW11

Falcon SW11 1RU [St Johns Hill]: Edwardian pub with several beers inc well kept Fullers London Pride from remarkably long light oak bar, bargain pub food such as pie and mash, friendly service, lively front bar, period partitions, cut glass and mirrors, quieter back dining area, daily papers; big-screen TV *(N R White, Tim Loryman, Vickie Metcalfe)*

SW13

Red Lion SW13 9RU [Castelnau]: Spaciously refurbished Fullers pub with impressive Victorian woodwork, decent food inc sandwiches, children's helpings and popular Sun lunch, friendly staff, good choice of reasonably priced wines by the glass; three separate areas, comfortable fireside sofas, relaxed atmosphere; big garden with good play area and barbecue *(Richard Tilbrook, BB)*

SW14

Victoria SW14 7RT [West Temple Sheen]: Contemporary styling with emphasis on conservatory restaurant, Fullers London Pride and Timothy Taylors Landlord in small wood-floored bar with leather sofas and wood-burning stoves, not cheap food inc breakfast Sat and all day Sun; piped music; dogs welcome, children's play area in nice garden, comfortable bedrooms, open all day *(BB, Noel Ferrin, LYM)*

SW15

☆ *Bricklayers Arms* SW15 1DD [down cul-de-sac off Lower Richmond Rd, nr Putney Bridge]: Small welcoming traditional local with well kept Timothy Taylors range and guest ales such as Sambrooks, real cider and perry, efficient friendly young staff, no food; painted tables on bare boards, woodburner, dim lighting, old local photographs; piped music, sports TV; side terrace, open all day (*N R White, Peter Dandy, Susan and John Douglas, LM, Sue Demont, Tim Barrow, P Dawn, Gavin Robinson*)

Dukes Head SW15 1JN [Lower Richmond Rd, nr Putney Bridge]: Smartly modernised and expanded Victorian pub, comfortable furnishings in knocked-together front bars and trendy downstairs cocktail bar in long-disused skittle alley (very popular wknds); good range of well presented pubby food all day inc sharing platters and snacks, Wells & Youngs ales, lots of wines by glass, light and airy back dining room with great river views, friendly service; plastic glasses for outside terrace or riverside pavement across the road; children welcome (highchairs and smaller helpings), open all day (*Peter Dandy, N R White, BB*)

Green Man SW15 3NG [Wildcroft Rd, Putney Heath]: Small friendly old local by Putney Heath, nicely redecorated rooms and alcoves, good choice of enjoyable food, well kept Wells & Youngs ales with a guest such as St Austell; TV; attractive back garden with decking, also some seats out front near the road, open all day (*Peter Dandy, LYM, Michael Dandy*)

Half Moon SW15 1EU [Lower Richmond Rd]: Good long-standing music venue (saved recently from gastropub conversion), well kept Wells & Youngs ales from elegant curved counter in nicely decorated bar, simple food inc Sun roasts with free live jazz, friendly atmosphere, back music room; wheelchair access, terrace tables, heated smokers' shelter (*Tracey and Stephen Groves, Michael Dandy*)

SW16

Earl Ferrers SW16 6JF [Ellora Rd]: Opened-up Streatham corner local, Sambrooks and several other well kept ales like Ascot, Pilgrim and Twickenham (tasters offered), some interesting food as well as pub favourites and Sun roasts; good informal service, mixed tables and chairs, sofas, old photographs; piped music – live every other Sun, quiz night Weds, pool and darts; children welcome, some tables outside with tractor seat stools, open all day excluding Mon, Tues lunchtimes (*Richard Warrick, LM, Tim Fairhurst*)

SW18

☆ *Cats Back* SW18 1NN [Point Pleasant]: Distinctive backstreet haven with well kept ales such as Sambrooks Wandle, real ciders, good choice of wines by the glass,

reasonably priced food (till 10.30pm) from good sandwiches up in bar and popular upstairs restaurant with art gallery, friendly efficient service; motley furnishings from pews and scrubbed pine tables to pensioned-off chairs and sofas, loads of bric-a-brac, dimmed chandeliers and lit candelabra, customers in keeping with the eccentric décor, blazing fire in small fireplace; interesting piped music such as East European folk – live music too; pavement tables and diverse chairs, open all day (*BB, LM, Peter Dandy*)

SW19

Alexandra SW19 7NE [Wimbledon Hill Rd]: Large busy Youngs pub with reasonably priced beer inc guests and a good wine choice from the central bar, enjoyable food from sandwiches to good Sun roasts, friendly alert service; comfortably up-to-date décor in linked rooms inc bare-boards dining areas; sports TVs; attractive roof terrace, tables also out in mews (*B J Harding, Tracey and Stephen Groves, Michael Dandy, Peter Dandy*)

Crooked Billet SW19 4RQ [Wimbledon Common]: 18th-c pub popular for its position by the common, lovely spot in summer; Wells & Youngs ales, good choice of wines, decent food in bar or dining room, friendly helpful staff, nice furnishings inc high-backed settles on broad polished oak boards, interesting old prints, daily papers; plastic glasses for outdoor drinking; children welcome, open all day (*N R White*)

☆ *Rose & Crown* SW19 5BA [Wimbledon High St]: Comfortably refurbished 17th-c Youngs pub, alcove seating in roomy bar, old prints inc interesting religious texts and drawings, friendly attentive staff, pubby food inc enjoyable Sun lunch, back dining conservatory; partly covered former coachyard, bedrooms (*LYM, Colin McKerrow, Conor McGaughey, Michael Dandy, Peter Dandy*)

Sultan SW19 1BN [Norman Rd]: Proper drinking pub hidden in a tangle of suburban roads, good real ales, friendly locals, big scrubbed tables, darts in public bar; nice beer garden (*BOB*)

WEST LONDON

SW6

Harwood Arms SW6 1QP [Walham Grove]: Interesting bare-boards gastropub, good bar snacks as well as enterprising pricey full meals, friendly helpful staff; separate eating area, real ales such as Fullers London Pride in proper bar area with leather sofas, young lively atmosphere; cl Mon lunchtime (*Antony O'Brien, Katharine Cowherd*)

Wheatsheaf SW6 5NT [Fulham Rd, opp Fire Station and Parsons Green Lane]: Big open-plan pub with some leather settees, high tables/stools and more orthodox tables and chairs, tall wine racks at back, mainly pale boards; Greene King ales, decent quite adventurous pub food inc deals, friendly service (can be slow); enclosed back garden with sports TVs in covered area (LM)

SW7
Queens Arms SW7 5QL [Queens Gate Mews]: Victorian corner pub with open-plan bare-boards bar, good value home-made pubby food, good wines by the glass, ales inc Adnams IPA and Fullers London Pride; disabled facilities, handy for the Albert Hall, open all day (LM, N R White)

W3
Rocket W3 6BD [Churchfield Rd]: Large pub doing enjoyable well priced food inc generous Sun lunch, good smiling service, Timothy Taylors Landlord, resplendent bar with chandeliers, interesting array of tables and chairs, dining room; more tables out on verandah (David and Sue Smith)

W4
☆ **Bell & Crown** W4 3PF [Strand on the Green]: Well run Fullers local, good friendly staff, enjoyable sensibly priced food, panelling and log fire, great Thames views from back bar and conservatory, lots of atmosphere; dogs welcome, terrace and towpath area, good walks, open all day (N R White, Bob and Angela Brooks)
Swan W4 5HH [Evershed Walk, Acton Lane]: Enjoyable food inc some interesting dishes, informal style, friendly staff, good range of wines by the glass, three real ales; they may try to keep your credit card while you eat; dogs very welcome, children till 7.30pm, good spacious garden (Catherine Woodman, Antony O'Brien, Simon Rodway)

W6
Andover Arms W6 0DL [Cardross St/Aldensley Rd]: Small sympathetically refurbished backstreet Hammersmith pub, pleasantly busy, with well kept Fullers ales inc seasonal ones; good wines, above-average pubby food, live jazz (Antony O'Brien)
☆ **Anglesea Arms** W6 0UR [Wingate Rd; Ravenscourt Park]: Good interesting food inc wkdy set lunches in homely bustling pub, welcoming staff, good choice of wines by the glass and of real ales; close-set tables in dining room facing kitchen, roaring fire in simply decorated panelled bar; children welcome, tables out by quiet street, open all day (Nigel and Sue Foster, the Didler, David Gunn, LYM)

W7
Fox W7 2PJ [Green Lane]: Friendly open-plan 19th-c local in quiet cul-de-sac nr Grand Union Canal; Black Sheep, Fullers London Pride, Timothy Taylors Landlord and Twickenham ales, decent wines, well priced food inc popular Sun lunch and good vegetarian options; panelling and stained glass one end, wildlife pictures and big fish tank, farm tools hung from ceiling; darts

end; dogs welcome, small side garden, towpath walks (Catherine Woodman)

W8
☆ **Scarsdale** W8 6HE [Edwardes Sq]: Busy Georgian pub in lovely leafy square, stripped-wood floors, fireplaces with good coal-effect gas fires, various knick-knacks; well kept Fullers/Gales ales from ornate bar counter, enjoyable good value pubby food, friendly helpful service; nice tree-shaded front courtyard, open all day (LYM, Barbarrick, Jill Bickerton)
☆ **Uxbridge Arms** W8 7TQ [Uxbridge St]: Friendly and cottagey backstreet local with three brightly furnished linked areas, well kept Fullers and a guest, good choice of bottled beers, china, prints and photographs; sports TV; open all day (the Didler)

W14
Cumberland Arms W14 8SZ [North End Rd]: Spacious pub with nice range of good reasonably priced food, efficient friendly service, well kept Fullers London Pride, Harveys Best and a guest beer, good wine choice; piped music (Nigel and Sue Foster)

OUTER LONDON

BECKENHAM [TQ3769]
Jolly Woodman BR3 6NR [Chancery Lane]: Small friendly old-fashioned local in conservation area, five or so good changing real ales, welcoming friendly service, good value lunchtime sandwiches or hot home-made specials; flower-filled back yard and pavement tables, open all day, cl Mon lunchtime (N R White, B J Harding)
BRENTFORD [TQ1878]
Express TW8 0EW [Kew Bridge Rd]: Well kept pub close to the station, gently traditional, with Bass and Wells & Youngs Bitter, peaceful relaxed atmosphere; nice garden (Barbarrick)
CROYDON [TQ3466]
Claret CR0 7AA [5 Bingham Corner, Lower Addiscombe Rd]: One-room pub with half a dozen good changing ales, wknd snacks; sports TV; dogs welcome, garden overlooking Tramlink station, open all day (Tim Mountain)
Glamorgan CR0 6BE [Cherry Orchard Rd]: Smart bright refurbishment, ales inc Harveys, popular food served by friendly staff, back dining area; can get busy with office workers; terrace behind, open all day wkdys, from 4pm wknds (N R White)
Sandrock CR0 5HA [Upper Shirley Rd]: Geared for dining but still popular with drinkers, good value enterprising food in back dining room, upmarket atmosphere with good friendly service, real ales such as Adnams and Harveys in more traditional front bar, good choice of wines by the glass, open all day (Alan Gull, N R White)

ENFIELD [TQ3599]

Pied Bull EN2 9HE [Bulls Cross, Bullsmoor Lane, W of A10; handy for M25 junction 25]: Welcoming red-tiled 17th-c pub spruced up by new management, low beam-and-plank ceilings, lots of comfortable little rooms and extensions, well kept ales such as Fullers London Pride and Greene King IPA, enjoyable home-made food inc lunchtime deals; conservatory, pleasant terrace, open all day (David Jackson)

HAMPTON COURT [TQ1668]

☆ *Kings Arms* KT8 9DD [Hampton Court Rd, by Lion Gate]: Civilised well run pub by Hampton Court itself (so popular with tourists), comfortable furnishings inc sofas in back area, attractive Farrow & Ball colours, good open fires, lots of oak panelling, beams and some stained glass; well kept Badger beers, good choice of wines by the glass, friendly service, sensibly priced pubby food from sandwiches up, restaurant too; piped music; children and dogs welcome, picnic-sets on roadside front terrace, limited parking, charming new bedrooms, open all day (Susan and John Douglas, LYM, David and Ruth Shillitoe)

HAREFIELD [TQ0590]

Coy Carp UB9 6HZ [Copperhill Lane]: Well refurbished Vintage Inn, recycled beams, alcoves, log fire, their usual wide choice of well cooked all-day food at reasonable prices, good range of wines, well kept ales such as Adnams Explorer, efficient friendly staff; garden tables, lovely spot by Grand Union Canal lock (Ross Balaam)

HARLINGTON [TQ0877]

Pheasant UB3 5LX [West End Lane]: Busy friendly pub with good varied choice of generous food at fair prices, three real ales, sizeable restaurant; they may try to keep your credit card while you eat; terrace picnic-sets (Barrie and Mary Crees, Daniel Canwell, Andy and Jill Kassube)

ILFORD [TQ4188]

Red House IG4 5BG [Redbridge Lane E; just off A12, handy for M11 via A406]: Popular multi-level Beefeater with friendly service, good value food, spacious bar area (for drinkers only); disabled facilities, bedrooms in adjoining Premier Inn (Robert Lester)

KINGSTON [TQ1869]

Albert KT2 7PX [Kingston Hill]: Recently refurbished sizeable Youngs pub close to Richmond Park, their ales and guests kept well, good choice of wines by the glass, food from sandwiches and light meals up; garden bar and heated courtyard (Fergus McDonald, Michael Dandy)

Boaters KT2 5AU [Canbury Gardens (park in Lower Ham Rd if you can)]: Family-friendly pub by the Thames, half a dozen real ales, variety of good value food inc vegetarian, efficient staff, comfortable banquettes in quiet charming bar, newspapers, Sun Jazz; smart riverside terrace, in small park, ideal for children in summer (Ian Phillips)

Gazebo KT1 1QN [Riverside Walk/Kings Passage; alley off Thames St by toy shop, or from Kingston Bridge]: Sam Smiths pub with terrific river views upstairs, lots of tables out on balcony and terrace, usual good value beer and food (Fergus McDonald)

LONGFORD [TQ0576]

White Horse UB7 0EE [Bath Rd, off A3044 (and A4)]: Brasses on low 17th-c black beams, fireplace between the two spotless areas, comfortable seats, cosy and friendly with pot plants in windows and rustic decorations such as antique rifles and equestrian bronzes; popular food from hearty traditional things to curries and thai dishes (booking advised), good service, three well kept ales such as Fullers, Ringwood and Wells & Youngs; piped music, games machine; flower tubs and picnic-sets outside, one in a little barn, surprisingly villagey surroundings despite the parking meters, open all day (Andy and Jill Kassube)

NORWOOD GREEN [TQ1378]

Plough UB2 4LG [Tentelow Lane (A4127)]: Attractive old-fashioned low-beamed décor, cheerful villagey feel in cosy main bar and two rooms off, well kept Fullers ales, welcoming efficient service, enjoyable food (not Sun evening, Mon); children welcome, disabled facilities, nice garden with bowling green dating from the 14th c, quite handy for Osterley Park, open all day (Ruth Green)

PETERSHAM [TQ1873]

Dysart Arms TW10 7AA [Petersham Rd]: Stylish and airy Arts & Crafts dining pub, bleached refectory tables on huge pale flagstones, grand wrought-iron chandeliers, leaded windows, log fire in chunky stone fireplace; good creative modern cooking inc wkdy set menu and some lighter dishes, ales such as Adnams and Harveys from oak bar, good choice of wines, cocktails; live jazz and classical music (Bechstein grand); well behaved children welcome away from bar (no under-12s after 7.30pm), tables in newly landscaped garden, opp gate to Richmond Park (Simon and Mandy King, Susan and John Douglas, LM)

PINNER [TQ1289]

Queens Head HA5 5PJ [High St]: Traditional panelled local dating from the 16th c, welcoming bustle, interesting décor, well kept Adnams, Greene King, Wells & Youngs Bombardier and two guests, simple good value bar food; useful car park (Brian Glozier)

RICHMOND [TQ1774]

Princes Head TW9 1LX [The Green]: Large unspoilt open-plan pub overlooking cricket green nr theatre, clean and well run, with low-ceilinged panelled areas off big island bar, full Fullers range in top condition, popular imaginative food; friendly young staff and chatty locals, coal-effect fire; over-21s only, seats outside – fine spot (Ian Phillips, Richard and Sissel Harris, N R White)

Rose & Crown TW9 3AH [Kew Green]: Popular part 17th-c Chef & Brewer handy for Kew Gardens, dark interior with panelling and old prints in small linked rooms, lit candles and log fires; their usual food, Fullers London Pride and guests, friendly service; raised front terrace overlooking cricket green, tree-shaded back terrace, open all day *(Susan and John Douglas)*

White Swan TW9 1PG [Old Palace Lane]: Small cottagey pub, civilised and relaxed, with rustic dark-beamed open-plan bar, good friendly service, well kept ales such as Fullers London Pride, St Austell Tribute and Timothy Taylors Landlord, fresh wholesome bar lunches, coal-effect fires, popular upstairs restaurant; piped music; children allowed in back conservatory, some seats on narrow paved area at front, more in pretty walled back terrace below railway *(Meg and Colin Hamilton, N R White, LM, LYM)*

Dukes Head TW10 6AZ [The Vineyard]: Warm homely pub with well kept Fullers ales and guests such as Twickenham, enjoyable home-made food inc good value specials, cheerful public bar and quieter lounge; nice bedrooms *(Fergus McDonald, Simon Le Fort)*

SURBITON [TQ1868]

Wagon & Horses KT6 4TW [Surbiton Hill Rd]: Roomy traditional local refurbished and opened out into four areas, Wells & Youngs ales and guests, decent wine by the glass, generous food, friendly service; no piped music, sports TV; back terrace *(Tom and Ruth Rees)*

TEDDINGTON [TQ1671]

Anglers TW11 9NR [Broom Rd]: Large refurbished Fullers pub in good spot on Thames at Teddington Lock; lots of different seating areas, upstairs restaurant, decent food, attentive pleasant service; big garden popular summer evenings and wknds, well placed for footpath walk from Hampton Court *(Mayur Shah)*

Tide End Cottage TW11 9NN [Broom Rd/ Ferry Rd, nr bridge at Teddington Lock]: Low-ceilinged pub (newish management) in Victorian cottage terrace next to Teddington Studios; two rooms united by big log-effect gas fire, well kept Greene King ales and a guest, decent low-priced bar food to numbered tables from sandwiches up; lots of river, fishing and rowing memorabilia and photographs, interesting Dunkirk evacuation link, back dining extension; piped music, TV, minimal parking; children (till 7.30pm) and dogs welcome, small terraces front and back, open all day *(Ian Phillips, Clare Carter, Chris Evans)*

TWICKENHAM [TQ1673]

White Swan TW1 3DN [Riverside]: Refurbished 17th-c Thames-side pub up steep anti-flood steps, enjoyable food and friendly helpful staff; waterside terrace across quiet lane *(Mrs Barbara Dale, LYM)*

WOODFORD GREEN [TQ3991]

Cricketers IG8 9HQ [High Rd]: Two-bar pub with Winston Churchill memorabilia, enjoyable reasonably priced food (get there early to be sure of the specials), good friendly management; Sun quiz night (no food then); dogs welcome *(Robert Lester)*

Three Jolly Wheelers IG8 8AS [Chigwell Rd (A113)]: Sizeable 19th-c Vintage Inn, carpet, bare boards and flagstones, painted panelling, comfortable seats by open fires, ales such as Caledonian Deuchars IPA and Greene King, good value all-day food from sandwiches up in bar and restaurant; piped music, children welcome, front terrace, bedrooms, open all day *(Robert Lester)*

Please tell us if any Lucky Dips deserve to be upgraded to a Main Entry – and why: feedback@goodguides.com, or (no stamp needed) The Good Pub Guide, FREEPOST TN1569, Wadhurst, E Sussex TN5 7BR.

Scotland

Scotland's two main cities have a notable clutch of exceptionally fine drinking haunts, many with terrific choices of beer, malt whiskies or both, and some with very well preserved interiors: notable ones this year are the Abbotsford, the Bow Bar, the Café Royal and Kays Bar in Edinburgh, and the Bon Accord in Glasgow, where the Babbity Bowster is also enjoyed for its reasonably priced continental-scottish food. Generally we don't receive as many reports for Scotland as we do for many other parts of the country, but pubs we know are doing well at the moment are the Applecross Inn at the extraordinarily remote coastal village of Applecross, the nicely unchanged Fishermans Tavern at Broughty Ferry, the bustling George at Inveraray, the homely Cross Keys at Kippen, the harbourside Selkirk Arms at Kirkcudbright (with beers brewed for the pub and well-liked food), the comfortable Burts Hotel in Melrose (where the food is particularly enjoyable), the memorably located Plockton Hotel at Plockton – which is our Scotland Dining Pub 2011 – and the remote but ever-popular Stein Inn at Stein on the Isle of Skye.

ABOYNE

Boat 🛏️
Charlestown Road (B968, just off A93); AB34 5EL

Friendly riverside pub, open all day, and with bedrooms

Enjoyed by readers for food, drink and accommodation, this welcoming place has fine views across the River Dee. Inside, you are now greeted by the presence of a model train chugging its way around at just below ceiling height. The partly carpeted bar – with a counter running along through the narrower linking section – also has scottish pictures and brasses, a woodburning stove in a stone fireplace, and games in the public-bar end; piped music and games machine. Spiral stairs take you up to a roomy additional dining area. They have three guests such as Belhaven St Andrews, Deeside Lulach and Inveralmond Ossian's Ale on handpump, as well as some 30 malt whiskies. There are six comfortable and well equipped bedrooms.

🍽 Tasty bar food includes a lunchtime menu with soup, sandwiches, ploughman's and dishes like thai chicken skewers, battered haddock, steak pie as well as several vegetarian dishes; the more elaborate seasonal evening menu includes items such as seared king prawns, poached pear with blue cheese and walnuts, main courses like grilled fillet of salmon, and puddings like chocolate cheesecake and banana bavarois; children's menu. *Starters/Snacks: £2.95 to £4.95. Main Courses: £6.25 to £14.95. Puddings: £3.25 to £5.95*

Free house ~ Licensees Wilson and Jacqui Clark ~ Real ale ~ Bar food (12-2(2.30 Sat), 5.30-9(9.30 Sat)) ~ Restaurant ~ (01339) 886137 ~ Children welcome ~ Dogs allowed in bar ~ Open 11-11(12 Fri, Sat) ~ Bedrooms: /£59.95B
Recommended by Christine and Neil Townend, Graham Keithley, J F M and M West

APPLECROSS

NG7144   MAP 11

Applecross Inn ★ ⇌

Off A896 S of Shieldaig; IV54 8LR

Wonderfully remote pub on famously scenic route on west coast; particularly friendly welcome, and good seafood

The reward for one of Britain's most adventurous and often hair-raising drives – across wild, remote country and the spectacular Pass of the Cattle (Beallach na Ba) – is this marvellously situated and warmly welcoming pub. Tables in the nice shoreside garden enjoy magnificent views across to the Cuillin Hills on Skye. With a friendly mix of locals and visitors, the no-nonsense but welcoming bar has a woodburning stove, exposed stone walls and upholstered pine furnishings on the stone floor; Isle of Skye Hebridean Gold and Red Cuillin, and over 50 malt whiskies. There's pool (winter only), TV, board games and juke box (musicians may take over instead); some disabled facilities. The alternative route here, along the single-track lane winding round the coast from just south of Shieldaig, has equally glorious sea loch and then sea views nearly all the way.

🍴 **Particularly liked by readers is the fresh locally caught seafood, which usually includes lobster cocktail, prawns in hot lemon and garlic butter, scallops with crispy bacon and garlic butter, battered haddock, dressed crab and oysters. As well as good sandwiches and ploughman's, other dishes might be warm goats cheese salad, sirloin steak, chicken breast with garlic, green thai curry, gammon and egg, and puddings such as hot chocolate fudge cake.** *Starters/Snacks: £3.50 to £8.95. Main Courses: £8.95 to £16.95. Puddings: £4.25 to £6.50*

Free house ~ Licensee Judith Fish ~ Real ale ~ Bar food (12-9) ~ (01520) 744262 ~ Children welcome until 9pm ~ Dogs welcome ~ Occasional live traditional music ~ Open 11-11.30; 11am-midnight Sat; 12.30-11 Sun ~ Bedrooms: £70B/£100B

Recommended by Martin Stafford, Brian Abbott, Sylvia and Tony Birbeck, Michael and Maggie Betton, Barry Collett, Dave and Shirley Shaw, Mr and Mrs M Stratton, the Dutchman

BADACHRO

NG7873   MAP 11

Badachro Inn 🍽

2.5 miles S of Gairloch village turn off A832 on to B8056, then after another 3.25 miles turn right in Badachro to the quay and inn; IV21 2AA

Convivial waterside pub with chatty local atmosphere, great views and excellent fresh seafood

The bayside position here is really striking with views of Loch Gairloch, and you might spot seals or even otters in the water. It's in a tiny village on a quiet road that comes to a dead end a few miles further on at the lovely Redpoint beach. They have three pub moorings (free for visitors) and showers are available at a small charge. Sailing visitors and chatty locals mix happily in the welcoming bar which can get quite busy in summer (some interesting photographs and collages on the walls, and Sunday newspapers). Friendly staff serve beers from An Teallach, Caledonian and Crofters, and they've over 50 malt whiskies and a good changing wine list, with several by the glass; piped music and darts. The quieter dining area on the left has big tables by a huge log fire and there's a dining conservatory overlooking the bay. Look out for the sociable pub spaniel Kenzie. Nautically styled decking, with even sails and rigging, runs right down to the water's edge, making the most of the outlook.

🍴 **Featuring locally caught seafood and smoked produce, with the good fresh fish earning the place its Food Award, enjoyable dishes might include snacks such as sandwiches, hot panini with interesting fillings, baked potatoes, baguettes, specials like soup, smoked salmon, roast leg of lamb, baked halibut, local prawns or scallops, sausages and mash, and puddings such as chocolate fondant or butterscotch and almond pudding.** *Starters/Snacks: £3.25 to £6.95. Main Courses: £9.95 to £14.95. Puddings: £5.25 to £5.95*

You can send reports directly to us at feedback@goodguides.com

Free house ~ Licensee Martyn Pearson ~ Real ale ~ Bar food (12(12.30 Sun)-3, 6-9) ~ (01445) 741255 ~ Children welcome ~ Dogs welcome ~ Open 12-12; 12.30-11 Sun ~ Bedrooms: /£70B

Recommended by Sylvia and Tony Birbeck, Pat and Stewart Gordon

BROUGHTY FERRY

NO4630   MAP 11

Fishermans Tavern ♀ ◼ £

Fort Street; turning off shore road; DD5 2AD

Friendly, unchanged pub with good choice of beers and bargain food

This welcoming and unpretentious place is within steps of the beach and began life as a row of fishermen's cottages. On the right, a secluded lounge area with an open coal fire runs into a little carpeted snug with nautical tables, light pink soft fabric seating, basket-weave wall panels and beige lamps. The carpeted back bar (popular with diners) has a Victorian fireplace, dominoes, TV, fruit machine and a coal fire. The good range of drinks includes six guest ales such as Caledonian Deuchars IPA, Greene King IPA and Speckled Hen, Timothy Taylors Landlord and Harviestoun Bitter & Twisted on handpump, ten wines by the glass and a good range of malt whiskies, and they have about 40 beers at their May festival. On summer evenings there are tables on the front pavement or you can sit out in the secluded walled garden. They have disabled lavatories and baby changing facilities.

🍴 **Very reasonably priced pubby bar food includes baguettes, steak pie, fish pie, burgers, macaroni cheese, scampi, sausage and mash, chocolate fudge cake and sticky toffee pudding.** *Starters/Snacks: £2.99 to £3.69. Main Courses: £5.25 to £6.99. Puddings: £3.29*

Belhaven (Greene King) ~ Manager Tracey Cooper ~ Real ale ~ Bar food (12-8) ~ (01382) 775941 ~ Children welcome if eating ~ Dogs allowed in bar ~ Scots fiddle music Thurs night from 10pm, Mon quiz ~ Open 11-midnight Mon-Weds; 11-1am Thurs-Sat; 11am-midnight Sun ~ Bedrooms: £39B/£64B

Recommended by Alistair and Kay Butler, Joe Green

EDINBURGH

NT2574   MAP 11

Abbotsford

Rose Street; E end, beside South St David Street; EH2 2PR

Bustling, friendly city pub with period features, changing beers and good value food

Very little has changed in over a century at this handsome Edwardian city pub. It has a green and gold plaster-moulded high ceiling and, perched at its centre on a sea of red flooring, a hefty highly polished island bar ornately carved from dark spanish mahogany. Stools around the bar, and long wooden tables and leatherette benches running the lengths of the dark wooden high-panelled walls, keep it feeling pubby. Up to five changing real ales, usually scottish and served from a set of air pressure tall founts might be from Atlas, Hadrian & Border, Strathaven and Stewart along with around 50 malt whiskies. The smarter upstairs restaurant, with its white tablecloths, black walls and high ornate white ceilings, looks impressive.

🍴 **Bar food includes soup, game terrine, smoked salmon platter, haggis, neeps and tatties, battered haddock, steak pie, goats cheese and vine tomato quiche, rump steak, and good home-made puddings like apple and rhubarb crumble and crème brûlée.** *Starters/Snacks: £3.50 to £5.25. Main Courses: £7.95 to £13.95. Puddings: £3.95 to £6.50*

Stewart ~ Licensee Daniel Jackson ~ Real ale ~ Bar food (12(12.30 Sun)-10) ~ Restaurant (12-2.15, 5.30-9.30) ~ (0131) 225 5276 ~ Children over 5 allowed in restaurant ~ Open 11(12.30 Sun)-11 (midnight Fri, Sat)

Recommended by Michael Dandy, Andy and Claire Barker, Joe Green, the Didler, Simon Daws, Donna and Roger, Comus and Sarah Elliott, Mark Walker, Jeremy King

Bow Bar ★ ◀

West Bow; EH1 2HH

Eight splendidly kept beers – and lots of malts – in well run and friendly alehouse of considerable character

One reader was particularly pleased to find that this bastion of simple stand-up drinking continues unchanged as a prime example of an Edinburgh drinking room. The neatly kept rectangular bar stars an impressive carved mahogany gantry, and from the tall 1920s founts on the bar counter knowledgeable staff dispense eight superbly kept beers with Caledonian Deuchars IPA, Stewarts 80/-, Timothy Taylors Landlord alongside various changing guests such as Fyne Avalanche, Highland Dark Munro, Stewarts Edinburgh Gold and York Guzzler. Also on offer are some 200 malts, including five 'malts of the moment' and a good choice of rums, some 25 international bottled beers and gins. A fine collection of enamel advertising signs and handsome antique brewery mirrors festoons the walls, with sturdy leatherette wall seats and heavy narrow tables on its wooden floor, and café-style bar seats; free wi-fi access.

🍴 **Lunchtime snacks are limited to tasty pies.** *Starters/Snacks: £2.00*

Free house ~ Licensee Helen McLoughlin ~ Real ale ~ Bar food (12-2; not Sun) ~ (0131) 226 7667 ~ Dogs welcome ~ Open 12-11.30; 12.30-11 Sun
Recommended by Joe Green, the Didler, Simon Daws, Donna and Roger, Barbarrick, Andy and Jill Kassube, Mark Walker, Andy and Claire Barker

Café Royal

West Register Street; EH2 2AA

Stunning listed interior, bustling atmosphere and rewarding food

Often very busy, particularly at lunchtimes (when the acoustics lend themselves to a lively lunch rather than intimate chat), the dazzlingly opulent Victorian interior here dates from 1863. It was built with no expense spared – with state-of-the art plumbing and gas fittings that were probably the pride and joy of its owner, Robert Hume, who was a local plumber. Its floors and stairway are laid with marble, chandeliers hang from the magnificent plasterwork ceilings, and the substantial island bar is graced by a carefully re-created gantry. The high-ceilinged vienna café-style rooms have a particularly impressive series of highly detailed Doulton tilework portraits of historical innovators Watt, Faraday, Stephenson, Caxton, Benjamin Franklin and Robert Peel (forget police – his importance here is as the introducer of calico printing), and the stained-glass well in the restaurant is worth a look. Alongside a decent choice of wines, with several by the glass, they've 20 malt whiskies and Caledonian Deuchars IPA and three guests from breweries such as Harviestoun, Kelburn and Stewarts on handpump; piped music and TV when there's rugby on.

🍴 **Bar food includes some seafood: mussels (half a kilo, or a kilo – that's a lot of mussels), fine oysters with lovely bread, cullen skink and fish pie, as well as sandwiches, smoked beetroot and goats cheese salad, haggis with whisky cream pie, beef and ale pie, and steak, with puddings such as raspberry cranachan with heather honey and oats, chocolate marquise with caramelised bananas, and a local cheese plate.** *Starters/Snacks: £4.65 to £5.40. Main Courses: £7.65 to £11.80. Puddings: £4.50 to £6.50*

Punch ~ Manager Valerie Graham ~ Real ale ~ Bar food (11-10) ~ Restaurant ~ (0131) 556 1884 ~ Children welcome in restaurant ~ Open 11(12.30 Sun)-11(1am Sat)
Recommended by Eithne Dandy, Andy and Claire Barker, Mark Walker, Michael Dandy, Christine and Neil Townend, Joe Green, the Didler, Simon Daws, Peter Dandy, Donna and Roger, Michael Butler, Barry Collett, Dr Kevan Tucker, E McCall, T McLean, D Irving, Jeremy King, Janet and Peter Race, Michael and Alison Sandy, Pat and Stewart Gordon, David M Smith

---

Cribbage is a card game using a block of wood with holes for matchsticks or special pins to score with; regulars in cribbage pubs are usually happy to teach strangers how to play.

Guildford Arms 🍺

West Register Street; EH2 2AA

Busy and friendly, with spectacular Victorian décor and an extraordinary range of real ales

It's worth keeping an eye out for the regular beer festivals here at this marvellously preserved Victorian pub, where they hold two 11-day festivals featuring over 50 brews, and monthly mini beer festivals with four beers from one brewery – £2.25 a pint as we go to press. This bustling, sumptuously fitted bar is a memorable place for a drink. Even in between those dates, the regular range of ten beers served by hard-working, knowledgeable staff is extremely impressive – typically Caledonian Deuchars IPA, Fyne Avalanche, Harviestoun Bitter & Twisted and Orkney Dark Island, with quickly changing guests from brewers such as Green Jack, Inveralmond, RCH, Traquair and Stewart; the helpful, friendly staff may offer a taste before you buy. Beyond its elaborate façade, the interior is opulently excessive with ornate painted plasterwork, dark mahogany fittings, heavy swagged velvet curtains at the huge arched windows and a busy patterned carpet. The snug little upstairs gallery restaurant, with strongly contrasting modern décor, gives a fine dress-circle view of the main bar (notice the lovely old mirror decorated with two tigers on the way up). Also, they do a good range of wines by the glass and two dozen or so malt whiskies; board games, TV, fruit machine, piped music.

🍴 Straightforward bar food includes sandwiches, soup, steak and ale pie, breaded haddock, rump steak, vegetable curry, specials such as fillet of organic salmon with mushroom cream sauce, and puddings like french apple tart; in the evenings, food from the same menu is served only in the gallery restaurant. *Starters/Snacks: £4.00 to £7.00. Main Courses: £8.00 to £17.00. Puddings: £4.50*

Stewart ~ Lease Steve Jackson ~ Real ale ~ Bar food (12-2.30, 5.30-9.30; 12-3, 5.30-10 Fri, Sat; 12.30-3, 5.30-9.30 Sun) ~ Restaurant (12(12.30 Sun)-2.30, 6-9.30(10 Fri, Sat)) ~ (0131) 556 4312 ~ Children over 5 allowed only in restaurant ~ Live music during Festival ~ Open 11-11(12 Fri, Sat); 12.30-11 Sun

Recommended by Mark Walker, Janet and Peter Race, Jeremy King, Joe Green, the Didler, Simon Daws, Donna and Roger, Dr Kevan Tucker, Barbarrick, E McCall, T McLean, D Irving, Michael Dandy, Andy and Claire Barker

Kays Bar 🍺 £

Jamaica Street W; off India Street; EH3 6HF

Cosy, enjoyably chatty back-street pub with excellent choice of well kept beers

'No music, no fruit machines, just heaven' commented one reader – this traditional, warmly welcoming and admirably gimmick-free local has a fine range of drinks. They stock a great range of beers and whiskies, including more than 70 malts between eight and 50 years old and ten blended whiskies, and superbly well kept on handpump Caledonian Deuchars IPA and Theakstons Best alongside five or six guests from brewers such as Belhaven, Fyne and Timothy Taylor. The interior is decked out with various casks and vats, old wine and spirits merchant notices, gas-type lamps, well worn red plush wall banquettes and stools around cast-iron tables, and red pillars supporting a red ceiling. A quiet panelled back room (a bit like a library) leads off, with a narrow plank-panelled pitched ceiling and a collection of books ranging from dictionaries to ancient steam-train books for boys; lovely warming coal fire in winter. In days past, the pub was owned by John Kay, a whisky and wine merchant; wine barrels were hoisted up to the first floor and dispensed through pipes attached to nipples which can still be seen around the light rose. Service is friendly, obliging and occasionally idiosyncratic; TV (which one reader found rather obtrusive), dominoes and cribbage, Scrabble and backgammon. On rugby club nights, it can be very busy here.

🍴 Straightforward but good value lunchtime bar food includes soup, sandwiches, haggis and neeps, mince and tatties, steak pie, beefburger and chips, and chicken balti. *Starters/Snacks: £2.50. Main Courses: £3.00 to £6.00. Puddings: £3.00*

Free house ~ Licensee David Mackenzie ~ Real ale ~ Bar food (12(12.30 Sun)-3) ~ (0131) 225 1858 ~ Dogs allowed in bar ~ Open 11am-midnight(1am Fri, Sat); 12.30-11 Sun

Recommended by Peter F Marshall, the Didler, Donna and Roger, David and Sue Atkinson, Barbarrick

Starbank 🍺 £

Laverockbank Road, off Starbank Road, just off A901 Granton—Leith; EH5 3BZ

Eight real ales, good value food and great views at cheery pub

Nicely relaxed, this is a fine spot to enjoy a drink while taking in the terrific views over the Firth of Forth. The long light and airy bare-boarded bar is uncluttered, comfortably elegant and friendly, with Belhaven 80/, Greene King Abot and IPA, Timothy Taylors Landlord, a changing beer from Belhaven or Greene King and three guests on handpump, several wines by the glass and a good selection of malt whiskies. You can eat in the conservatory restaurant, and there's a sheltered back terrace; TV and piped music. Dogs must be on a lead. Parking is on the adjacent hilly street. More reports please.

🍽 **Good-value bar food includes lunchtime sandwiches, soup, cullen skink, king prawn and crayfish cocktail, haggis, neaps and tatties, steak and ale pie and fish and chips; at weekends they open at 10am to serve breakfast.** *Starters/Snacks: £2.99 to £4.99. Main Courses: £5.99 to £12.99. Puddings: £2.99 to £3.99*

Belhaven (Greene King) ~ Manager Adam Tod ~ Real ale ~ Bar food (12-2.30, 5-8; 12-9 Fri; 10-9 Sat, 10-8 Sun) ~ (0131) 552 4141 ~ Children welcome till 9pm if dining ~ Open 11-11 (12 Fri, Sat); 12.30-midnight Sun

Recommended by Jeremy King, Ken Richards

ELIE   NO4999   MAP 11

Ship 🛏

The Toft, off A917 (High Street) towards harbour; KY9 1DT

Friendly seaside inn with views over bay, unspoilt bar and warming fires

This is well positioned for enjoying a drink overlooking the sandy bay, towards the stone pier and old granary. The unspoilt, villagey beamed bar has a buoyantly nautical feel, with friendly locals, warming winter coal fires, partly panelled walls studded with old prints and maps, Caledonian Deuchars IPA, several wines by the glass, and half a dozen malt whiskies. There's also a simple carpeted back room; cards, dominoes and shut the box. The pub is very much a cheery part of the local community; the pub's own cricket team often play on the beach. They've recently bought the Golf Tavern at Earlsferry, at the other end of the village. The comfortable bedrooms are in a guesthouse next door. More reports please.

🍽 **Bar food can be tasty and includes lunchtime open sandwiches, soup, steak and Guinness pie, fish and chips, and specials; children's menu.** *Starters/Snacks: £3.00 to £6.50. Main Courses: £9.50 to £18.50. Puddings: £4.50*

Free house ~ Licensees Richard and Jill Philip ~ Real ale ~ Bar food ~ Restaurant ~ (01333) 330246 ~ Children welcome but not in bar ~ Dogs allowed in bar ~ Open 11am-midnight (1am Fri, Sat); 12.30-midnight Sun ~ Bedrooms: £55B/£80B

Recommended by Ken Richards, Dave Braisted

FORTROSE   NH7256   MAP 11

Anderson 🍺

Union Street, off A832; IV10 8TD

Friendly American licensees in seaside hotel with fine range of drinks and good, interesting bar food; bedrooms

The fine range of drinks and particularly good food are making quite a name for this former coaching inn in a quiet seaside village. It's run by a friendly, approachable american couple who have tremendous enthusiasm for what they do. Mr Anderson loves beer and has one of the largest collection of belgian beers in the UK – as well as keeping Abbeydale Deception, Broughton Old Jock and a changing guest on handpump. Also,

200 malt whiskies and quite a choice of wines (much loved by Peanut their tortoiseshell cat). There's a homely bar and a light and airy dining room with an open fire, lots of puzzle-type games, piped music, games machine, darts and a juke box. The pub rescue dog is called Betty and they keep hens in the garden.

🍴 Using the best local produce and cooked by Mrs Anderson, the good bar food might include soup, diver-caught scallops with fresh crab and prawns in mornay sauce, ham hock terrine with piccalilli sauce, savoury doughballs, a changing tapas plate, beef, chicken or veggie burgers with toppings, steak and mushroom in ale pudding, nut wellington, barbecue free-range corn-fed chicken, flame-grilled lamb rump steak with wild garlic sauce, chocolate and chilli venison and monkfish wrapped in pancetta with a tomato and fennel sauce. *Starters/Snacks: £4.00 to £7.50. Main Courses: £6.50 to £22.00. Puddings: £4.50*

Free House ~ Licensee Jim Anderson ~ Real ale ~ Bar food (6-9; 1-9 Sun; not Mon-Sat lunchtimes) ~ Restaurant ~ (01381) 620236 ~ Children welcome ~ Dogs allowed in bar and bedrooms ~ Open 4-11.30; 12.30-11.30 Sun; closed lunchtimes except Sun ~ Bedrooms: £49B/£80B

Recommended by Iain and Nancy Taylor

GAIRLOCH   NG8075   MAP 11

Old Inn ♀ 🍺
Just off A832/B8021; IV21 2BD

Quietly positioned old inn with local fish and seafood; good beers

This year they've installed a brewhouse here at this country inn and now have their own Erradale in addition to An Teallach Crofters, Black Sheep and Isle of Skye Blind Piper (a blend of Isle of Skye ales made for the pub and named after a famed 17th-c local piper); one of these may be replaced by their new Flowerdale summer ale or a winter warmer called Slattadale; quite a few fairly priced wines by the glass, around 20 malt whiskies and speciality coffees. The relaxed public bar is popular with chatty locals and is quite traditional, with paintings and murals on exposed stone walls and stools lined up along the counter; board games, TV, fruit machine and juke box. There are picnic-sets prettily placed by the trees that line the stream flowing past under an old stone bridge. Credit (but not debit) cards incur a surcharge of £1.75. More reports please.

🍴 They have their own smokery and bake their own bread; as well as fresh local fish such as sole, scallops or lobster, the menu usually includes dishes such as soup, cullen skink, fish and chips, wild mushroom or lamb burger, steak and ale pie, and puddings. *Starters/Snacks: £4.95 to £5.95. Main Courses: £8.75 to £16.95. Puddings: £4.50 to £5.95*

Free house ~ Licensees Alastair and Ute Pearson ~ Real ale ~ Bar food (12-9; not 2.30-5 in winter) ~ Restaurant ~ (01445) 712006 ~ Children welcome ~ Dogs allowed in bar and bedrooms ~ Live music Fri evening ~ Open 11am-11.45pm; 12-11.15 Sun ~ Bedrooms: £57B/£99B

Recommended by Sylvia and Tony Birbeck, Martin Stafford, J K Parry

GATEHOUSE OF FLEET   NX6056   MAP 9

Masonic Arms 🍽 ♀
Ann Street, off B727; DG7 2HU

Flower-bedecked pub with good, very popular food, relaxed traditional bar and stylish dining area

There's a good choice of places to sit and enjoy a drink or a meal at this spacious dining pub. The comfortable two-room bar still feels quite pubby, with well kept Caledonian Deuchars IPA and a beer brewed for them by Sulwath on handpump, a good choice of whiskies, wines by the glass, traditional seating, pictures on its lightly timbered walls and blue and white plates on a delft shelf; piped music, games machine and pool. It opens into an airily attractive conservatory, with comfortable cane bucket chairs around good tables on terracotta tiles, pot plants and colourful pictures on one wall, which in turn opens through into a contemporary restaurant, with high-backed dark leather chairs around modern tables on bare boards. There are picnic-sets under cocktail parasols out in the neatly kept sheltered garden and seats out in front. This is an appealing small town, between the Solway Firth and the Galloway Forest Park.

🍴 **The ambitious food is quite a draw here, so it's worth booking. As well as lunchtime baguettes, there might be haggis and tattie scone tower with Drambuie sauce, wild mushroom and ricotta tart, fish and chips, daube of galloway beef, thai-style chicken or vegetable stir fry, roast duck breast, seared fillet of bass, steaks, and puddings such as white chocolate and apricot crème brûlée and stem ginger, lime and honey cheesecake.** Starters/Snacks: £3.95 to £8.50. Main Courses: £9.95 to £18.95. Puddings: £4.00 to £6.00

Challenger Inns ~ Lease Daniel Cipa ~ Real ale ~ Bar food (12-2, 6-9) ~ Restaurant ~ (01557) 814335 ~ Children not allowed in bar after 9pm ~ Dogs allowed in bar ~ Folk music Thurs night ~ Open 11.30-2, 5.30-11; 11.30-11 Sat, Sun; closed middle two weeks of Nov

Recommended by GSB, Richard J Holloway, Joe Green

GLASGOW
NS5965 MAP 11

Babbity Bowster 🍴 ♀
Blackfriars Street; G1 1PE

A Glasgow institution: friendly, comfortable and sometimes lively mix of traditional and modern, with almost a continental feel; good food

There's a distinctive blend of traditional scottish and modern french in this comfortably informal open-plan bar in the Merchant City. A big ceramic of a kilted dancer and piper in the bar illustrates the mildly cheeky 18th-c lowland wedding pipe tune (Bab at the Bowster) from which the pub takes its name – the friendly landlord or his staff will be happy to explain further. The simply decorated light interior has fine tall windows, well lit photographs and big pen-and-wash drawings of the city, its people and musicians, dark grey stools and wall seats around dark grey tables on the stripped wooden boards, and a peat fire. The bar opens on to a pleasant terrace with tables under cocktail parasols, trellised vines and shrubs; they may have barbecues out here in summer. You'll find Caledonian Deuchars IPA, Kelburn Misty Law and a guest from a brewer such as Red Squirrel on air pressure tall fount, and a remarkably sound collection of wines and malt whiskies; good tea and coffee, too. On Saturday evenings, they have live traditional scottish music, while at other times you may find games of boules in progress outside. Note the bedroom price is for the room only.

🍴 **A short but interesting and reasonably priced bar menu includes scottish and french items such as hearty home-made soup, cullen skink, potted rabbit, croques monsieur, haggis, neeps and tatties (they also do a vegetarian version), stovies, mussels, a pie of the day, platter of scottish smoked salmon, and a daily special such as fried french black pudding with mash, onion and white wine gravy. The airy upstairs restaurant has more elaborate meals.** Starters/Snacks: £4.50 to £7.95. Main Courses: £5.50 to £11.95. Puddings: £3.95 to £4.25

Free house ~ Licensee Fraser Laurie ~ Real ale ~ Bar food (12-10; 10-10 Sun) ~ Restaurant ~ (0141) 552 5055 ~ Children welcome ~ Live traditional music on Sat ~ Open 11am(10 Sun)-midnight ~ Bedrooms: £45S/£60S

Recommended by Dr and Mrs A K Clarke, Andy and Jill Kassube, Barry Collett

Bon Accord 🍺 £
North Street; G3 7DA

Fabulous choice of drinks, with an impressive choice of whiskies, ten real ales, a good welcome and bargain food

Several hundred real ales sourced from breweries around Britain feature each year here on handpump, with Caledonian Deuchars IPA and Marstons Pedigree as house beers alongside daily changing guest beers from breweries such as Dark Star, Fyne, Kelburn, Theakstons and Timothy Taylor; 11 wines by the glass and continental bottled beers. They also have a staggering number of malts, with 240 currently available, as well as lots of gins, vodkas and rums. With a good mix of customers, the interior is neatly kept; partly polished bare-boards and partly carpeted, with a mix of tables and chairs, terracotta walls and pot plants throughout; TV, fruit machine, board games and piped music.

🍴 **Very reasonably priced bar food includes baguettes, baked potatoes, lasagne, steaks, burgers, scampi and steak pie; they do a bargain two-course lunch.** *Starters/Snacks: £1.90 to £3.30. Main Courses: £4.50 to £7.95. Puddings: £1.50 to £1.95*

Scottish Courage ~ Licensee Paul McDonagh ~ Real ale ~ Bar food (12(12.30 Sun)-8) ~ (0141) 248 4427 ~ Children welcome until 8pm ~ Quiz Weds, live band Sat ~ Open 11am-midnight; 12.30-11 Sun

Recommended by Barry Collett

Counting House 🍺 £
St Vincent Place/George Square; G1 2DH

Impressive Wetherspoons conversion of former bank with impressive range of beers and good value food all day

The very reasonable prices surely contribute to drawing the crowd into this impressively converted bank, but even when really busy the atmosphere remains civilised – no music but just the relaxed hubbub of conversation; staff are friendly and efficient. The imposing interior rises into a lofty, richly decorated coffered ceiling which culminates in a great central dome, with well lit nubile caryatids doing a fine supporting job in the corners. You'll also find the sort of decorative glasswork that nowadays seems more appropriate to a landmark pub than to a bank, as well as wall safes, plenty of prints and local history, and big windows overlooking George Square. Away from the bar, several areas have solidly comfortable seating, while a series of smaller rooms – once the managers' offices – lead around the perimeter of the building. Some of these are surprisingly cosy, one is like a well stocked library, and a few are themed with pictures and prints of historical characters such as Walter Scott or Mary, Queen of Scots. The central island servery has a fine choice of real ales on handpump with Greene King Abbot and IPA (the latter at the bargain price of £1.59 a pint as we go to press), alongside half a dozen guests from all sorts of far-flung little brewers such as Arundel, Brains, Harviestoun, Holdens and Oakleaf. They also do a good choice of bottled beers, 35 malt whiskies and seven wines by the glass. More reports please.

🍴 **Served all day, the usual wide choice of straightforward bargain Wetherspoons food includes baguettes and wraps, nachos, beef in ale pie, haggis, neeps and tatties, chilli con carne, breaded scampi, steaks, pasta, sausages and mash, Sunday roasts, and children's meals. Steak night is Tuesday, with curry club on Thursday.** *Starters/Snacks: £2.79 to £8.99. Main Courses: £2.99 to £8.99. Puddings: £1.99 to £3.99*

Wetherspoons ~ Manager Rhoda Thompson ~ Real ale ~ Bar food (9am-10pm) ~ (0141) 225 0160 ~ Children welcome if eating ~ Open 9am-midnight

Recommended by Dr and Mrs A K Clarke

GLENCOE   NN1058   MAP 11
Clachaig
Old Glencoe Road, behind NTS Visitor Centre; PH49 4HX

Climbers' and walkers' haunt with fine selection of scottish beers and malts

Placed right in the middle of the scenic grandeur of Glencoe, this isolated pub is a welcoming place to come into if you've been out touring the area or tackling one of the challenging mountain walks nearby. You'll often encounter hikers, mountain bikers and climbers swapping the day's experiences over a pint by the log fire in the Boots Bar, which hosts live bands on Saturday nights. There's also a pine-panelled, slate-floored snug and a lounge with a mix of dining chairs and leather sofas, and with walls hung with photos signed by famous climbers. Half a dozen changing scottish ales on handpump include brews like Bridge of Allan Lomond Gold and Sporran Warmer, and

Williams Birds and Bees, Ceilidh and Midnight Sun, alongside 180 malts and several wines by the glass. Piped music, TV, games machine, pool, juke box and board games. We imagine this would be a useful base and would welcome reports from readers who stay here; the pub also runs self-catering properties in the area.

🍴 **Tasty bar food includes smoked shetland salmon, nachos, steak in ale pie, meat or vegetarian haggis, neeps and tatties, venison casserole, sirloin steak, cajun salmon, fish and chips, various burgers, and puddings like clootie dumpling or apple crumble; children's menu.** *Starters/Snacks: £2.25 to £5.65. Main Courses: £6.95 to £16.45. Puddings: £3.95 to £4.75*

Free house ~ Licensees Guy and Edward Daynes ~ Real ale ~ Bar food (12-9) ~ (01855) 811252 ~ Children allowed in lounge ~ Dogs welcome ~ Live music Sat night ~ Open 11(12.30 Sun)-11(11.30 Sat); closed 24-27 Dec ~ Bedrooms: £44S/£88S(£92B)

Recommended by D and K, Gwyn and Anne Wake

HOUSTON   NS4066   MAP 11

Fox & Hounds ♀ 🍺

South Street at junction with Main Street (B789, off B790 at Langbank signpost E of Bridge of Weir); PA6 7EN

Village pub with award-winning beers from their own brewery as well as interesting food

The same family has run this welcoming village pub for many years. It is home to the Houston Brewery, and the five constantly changing own-brew beers might feature Blonde Bombshell, Jock Frost, Killellan, Peters Well, Texas or Warlock Stout – you can look through a window in the bar to the little brewery where they are produced; also 12 wines by the glass and more than 100 malt whiskies. The clean plush hunting-theme lounge has comfortable seats by a fire and polished brass and copper; piped music. Popular with a younger crowd, the lively downstairs bar has a large-screen TV, pool, juke box and fruit machines. At the back is a covered and heated area with decking.

🍴 **Served upstairs (downstairs they only do substantial sandwiches), a good choice of enjoyable bar food might include soup, barbecued pork chops marinated in sweet mustard and herbs, mussels, aubergine pie, sausage and mash, haddock and chips, scampi tails dipped in Houston ale batter, steak in ale pie, steaks, and puddings such as apple crumble or warm chocolate fudge cake.** *Starters/Snacks: £3.00 to £10.00. Main Courses: £7.00 to £18.00. Puddings: £3.00 to £4.50*

Own brew ~ Licensee Jonathan Wengel ~ Real ale ~ Bar food (12-10(9 Sun)) ~ Restaurant ~ (01505) 612448 ~ Children in lounge till 8pm and restaurant till 10pm ~ Dogs allowed in bar ~ Open 12(12.30 Sat, Sun)-10(9 Sun)

Recommended by Richard J Holloway, Dr and Mrs A K Clarke, Andy and Jill Kassube, David Hoult, Ken Richards, Ailsa Russell

INNERLEITHEN   NT3336   MAP 9

Traquair Arms 🛏

B709, just off A72 Peebles—Galashiels; follow signs for Traquair House; EH44 6PD

Attractively modernised inn, popular with families, with friendly welcome and nice food

This comfortably refurbished village inn in the Borders is a convivial all-rounder. It is one of only three places where you can taste draught Traquair ale, which is produced using original oak vessels in the 18th-c brewhouse at nearby Traquair House. They also stock Caledonian Deuchars IPA, Timothy Taylors Landlord and several malt whiskies; piped music, TV. There's a relaxed light and airy bistro-style restaurant with high chairs, and a warming log fire. The garden at the back has picnic-sets and a big tree on a neatly kept lawn. Bedrooms are comfortable, clean and fresh.

Tipping is not normal for bar meals, and not usually expected.

🍴 Tasty bar food might include sandwiches, ciabattas, cullen skink, chicken and haggis with whisky sauce, steak and ale pie, beefburger topped with bacon and cheese, grilled pork chops with black pudding and apple mash, and traditional puddings like chocolate and hazelnut brownie. *Starters/Snacks: £3.95 to £4.25. Main Courses: £8.25 to £14.25. Puddings: £4.25*

Free house ~ Licensee Dave Rogers ~ Real ale ~ Bar food (12-2, 5-9; 12-9 Sat, Sun) ~ Restaurant ~ (01896) 830229 ~ Children welcome ~ Dogs allowed in bar and bedrooms ~ Open 11(12 Sun)-midnight ~ Bedrooms: £50S/£80B

Recommended by Joe Green, the Didler

INVERARAY
NN0908   MAP 11

George £ 🛏

Main Street E; PA32 8TT

Well placed and attractive, with atmospheric old bar, enjoyable food and pleasant garden; comfortable bedrooms

Extremely popular at holiday times, this Georgian hotel is at the hub of this appealing little town by Loch Fyne. Oozing a sense of the past, the dark bustling pubby bar has bare stone walls and shows plenty of age in its exposed joists, old tiles and big flagstones. It has antique settles, cushioned stone slabs along the walls, carved wooden benches, nicely grained wooden-topped cast-iron tables and four cosy log fires. The bar carries over 100 malt whiskies and a beer from Fyne Ales with a guest from a brewery such as Houston on handpump; darts. A smarter flagstoned restaurant has french windows that open to tables tucked into nice private corners on a series of well laid-out terraces. The bedrooms are comfortable, individually decorated, have jacuzzis or four-poster beds and are reached by a grand wooden staircase. The hotel is ideally placed for Inveraray Castle and for a range of good local walks.

🍴 Served all day, enjoyable bar food (you order at the table) typically includes soup, starters like oat-crumbed brie fritters with gooseberry jelly or smoked scottish salmon with dill crème fraîche, main courses like battered haddock, mussels with chips, haggis, neeps and tatties, roast free-range chicken breast and sage and onion stuffed leg, or grilled goats cheese with red onion marmalade, with home-made puddings. *Starters/Snacks: £3.95 to £5.95. Main Courses: £6.50 to £14.95. Puddings: £3.95 to £4.75*

Free house ~ Licensee Donald Clark ~ Real ale ~ Bar food (12-9) ~ (01499) 302111 ~ No children in cocktail bar after 10pm ~ Dogs welcome ~ Live entertainment Fri, Sat ~ Open 11am-1am ~ Bedrooms: £35B/£70B

Recommended by Brian Abbott, Alistair and Kay Butler, Mr and Mrs Richard Osborne, Andy and Jill Kassube, Cedric Robertshaw

ISLE OF WHITHORN
NX4736   MAP 9

Steam Packet ♀ 🛏

Harbour Row; DG8 8LL

Unfussy inn with splendid views of working harbour from bar; bedrooms and good food

This welcoming, family-run inn has a tranquil harbourside position. The comfortable low-ceilinged bar is split into two: on the right, plush button-back banquettes and boat pictures, and on the left, green leatherette stools around cast-iron-framed tables on big stone tiles, and a woodburning stove in the bare stone wall. Bar food can be served in the lower-beamed dining room, which has excellent colour wildlife photographs, rugs on its wooden floor, and a solid fuel stove, and there's also a small eating area off the lounge bar, as well as a conservatory. Four guests from brewers such as Arran, Atlas, Kelburn and Northumberland are kept alongside the Timothy Taylors Landlord on handpump, and they've quite a few malt whiskies and a good wine list; board games and pool table. There are white tables and chairs in the garden. This is an enchanting spot near the end of the Machars peninsula at the most southerly point of Scotland and you can walk from here up to the remains of St Ninian's Kirk, on a headland behind the village. More reports please.

🍴 **Bar food includes lunchtime baguettes, sandwiches and baked potatoes, starters like soup, thai beef salad, haggis-stuffed mushroom deep fried in yeast batter or mussels in cream and white wine sauce, main courses like fish and chips, steak pie and braised lamb shank; Sunday lunch features a three-course buffet for £10.** *Starters/Snacks: £3.95 to £5.95. Main Courses: £6.50 to £18.95. Puddings: £2.75 to £3.95*

Free house ~ Licensee Alastair Scoular ~ Real ale ~ Bar food (12-2, 6.30-9) ~ Restaurant ~ (01988) 500334 ~ Children welcome but not in bar ~ Dogs allowed in bar and bedrooms ~ Open 11(12 Sun)-11; closed 2.30-6 Tues-Thurs in winter ~ Bedrooms: £30B/£60B

Recommended by Christine and Neil Townend, the Didler

KILMAHOG   NN6008   MAP 11

Lade ♀ 🍺

A84 just NW of Callander, by A821 junction; FK17 8HD

Lively and pubby, with own-brew beers and shop specialising in scottish brews; lovely garden, and good home-made food

There's a strong scottish theme here, both in the traditional scottish music at weekends and in the scottish real ale shop with over 130 bottled brews from microbreweries around Scotland. In the bar they always have their own WayLade, LadeBack and LadeOut on handpump, along with nine wines by the glass and about 40 malts; beer festival in late August to early September. There's plenty of character in the several small beamed areas – cosy with red walls, panelling, stripped stone and decorated with highland prints and works by local artists; piped music, cards and board games. A big windowed restaurant (with a more ambitious menu) opens on to a terrace and a pleasant garden with three fish ponds and a bird-feeding station.

🍴 **Using local ingredients, food includes soup, sandwiches, battered haggis balls, fresh battered haddock, steak and ale pie, thai spiced vegetable curry, roasted salmon with tomato polenta and red pepper coulis, and puddings like sticky toffee pudding and chocolate fudge cake. They do smaller portions of many dishes for children and pensioners.** *Starters/Snacks: £3.00 to £7.00. Main Courses: £7.00 to £18.00. Puddings: £1.50 to £6.00*

Own brew ~ Licensees Frank and Rita Park ~ Real ale ~ Bar food (12-3, 5-9; 12-9 Sat, 12.30-9 Sun) ~ Restaurant ~ (01877) 330152 ~ Children welcome ~ Dogs allowed in bar ~ Live music Fri and Sat evenings ~ Open 12-11(1am Fri, Sat); 12-10.30 Sun

Recommended by Simon Rodway, Michael Butler

KIPPEN   NS6594   MAP 11

Cross Keys 🛏

Main Street; village signposted off A811 W of Stirling; FK8 3DN

Cosy 18th-c inn, popular with locals and visitors; enjoyable food

A welcoming place to eat, drink or stay the night, this homely inn has a timelessly stylish bar with attractive dark panelling and subdued lighting. A straightforward lounge has a good log fire, and there's a coal fire in the attractive family dining room. Harviestoun Bitter & Twisted and a guest such as Caledonian Deuchars IPA are on handpump, several malts and wines by the glass; board games and piped music. Tables in the garden have good views towards the Trossachs.

🍴 **Well liked bar food might include lunchtime sandwiches, soup, smoked mackerel pâté with beetroot chutney, fried salmon fillet, guinea fowl breast with israeli couscous, fish and chips, sausages and mash, and puddings like lemon and lime crème brûlée and rhubarb and almond crumble tart.** *Starters/Snacks: £4.00 to £6.00. Main Courses: £8.00 to £18.00. Puddings: £5.00 to £7.00*

Free house ~ Licensees Debby McGregor and Brian Horsburgh ~ Real ale ~ Bar food (12-2.30,
5-9; 12-9 Sat; 12-8 Sun) ~ (01786) 870293 ~ Children welcome till 9pm ~ Dogs welcome ~
Open 12-3, 5-11; 12-1am Sat; 12-11 Sun; closed Mon ~ Bedrooms: £50S/£80S

*Recommended by Michael Butler, Neil and Anita Christopher, Dr and Mrs A K Clarke, Lucien Perring, Justin and
Emma King, Simon Rodway*

KIRK YETHOLM
NT8328   MAP 10

Border 🛏

Village signposted off B6352/B6401 crossroads, SE of Kelso; The Green; TD5 8PQ

Welcoming hotel with good inventive food and a renowned objective for walkers

You may well meet weary walkers at this friendly village inn – they'll have completed the
Pennine Way National Trail, which runs 256 miles from Derbyshire to end here. The author
of the classic guide to the Pennine Way, Alfred Wainwright, was keen to reward anyone
who walked the entire length of the trail with a free drink. He left some money here to
cover the bill, but it has long since run out, and the pub now generously foots the bill.
They have a couple of beers on handpump – usually from Broughton brewery plus another
scottish beer such as Cairngorm Trade Winds, decent wines by the glass and a good range
of malt whiskies and bottled beers. The cheerfully unpretentious bar has beams and
flagstones, a log fire, a signed photograph of Wainwright and other souvenirs of the
Pennine Way, and appropriate borders scenery etchings and murals; snug side rooms lead
off. There's a roomy dining room, a comfortable lounge with a second log fire, and a neat
conservatory; piped music, TV, darts, board games, children's games and books, and
there's a water bowl for dogs. A sheltered back terrace has picnic-sets and a play area,
and the colourful window boxes and floral tubs make a very attractive display outside.
The bedrooms are comfortable.

🍴 **Using carefully sourced ingredients (including local fish, game, organic pork and
organic free-range eggs), food from the seasonal menu is inventive without being at all
pretentious and might feature lunchtime sandwiches and baguettes, soup, smoked
salmon, cullen skink, goats cheese and red onion tart, mussels, marinated border lamb,
pheasant breasts, wild boar and apple sausages and mash, steaks and roasted pork fillet.**
Starters/Snacks: £3.25 to £5.95. Main Courses: £8.95 to £14.95. Puddings: £3.25 to £4.55

Free house ~ Licensees Philip and Margaret Blackburn ~ Real ale ~ Bar food (12-2, 6-9(8.30 winter))
~ Restaurant ~ (01573) 420237 ~ Children welcome away from public bar ~ Open 11-11(midnight
Sat); may close earlier in winter ~ Bedrooms: £45B/£90B

Recommended by Dave Braisted, Comus and Sarah Elliott, C A Hall, the Didler

KIRKCUDBRIGHT
NX6850   MAP 9

Selkirk Arms

High Street; DG6 4JG

Well run hotel with good service, enjoyable imaginative food and local sports bar

This comfortable hotel has two beers brewed for it: Geltsdale Galloway Stargazer (so
named because of the Galloway Forest Park's status as one of the world's best places for
star-gazing – it's the country's first designated Dark Sky Park); and The Grace, brewed by
Sulwath and so named because of a strong tradition that Burns, a regular visitor,
composed the Selkirk Grace here (though a rival school of thought is that he did so while
staying at St Mary's Isle with Lord Daer, Selkirk's son). The bars range from the very
simple locals' front bar which has its own street entrance to a welcoming partitioned
high-ceilinged lounge bar at the heart of the hotel, with comfortable upholstered
armchairs and wall banquettes and original paintings which are for sale; piped music and
TV. There's also a bistro and restaurant. Service is thoughtful and efficient and there's a
nice friendly atmosphere. A neatly set-out garden has smart wooden furniture with
contrasting blue umbrellas and a 15th-c font. This is a pleasant spot, right by the mouth
of the Dee, within sight of fishing boats and the quay.

🍴 Food in the locals bar is limited to items like sandwiches, burgers and fish and chips, but the enjoyable food served in the bistro might include starters like baked crottin of goats cheese, rillette of duck confit, filo parcel of haggis on clapshot with whisky jus, king scallops and belly pork roast fillet of salmon on crab risotto, steaks, and puddings like rhubarb crème brûlée or lemon tart with blackcurrant sorbet. *Starters/Snacks: £3.95 to £6.95. Main Courses: £10.95 to £16.95. Puddings: £4.95 to £5.95*

Free house ~ Licensees Douglas McDavid and Chris Walker ~ Real ale ~ Bar food ~ Restaurant ~ (01557) 330402 ~ Children welcome but not in sports bar ~ Dogs welcome ~ Open 11-11(midnight Sat) ~ Bedrooms: £75B/£102B

Recommended by Sheila Topham, Chris Clark, the Didler, Janet and Peter Race, Malcolm M Stewart

LINLITHGOW   NS0077   MAP 11

Four Marys 🍺 £

High Street; 2 miles from M9 junction 3 (and little further from junction 4) – town signposted; EH49 7ED

Well cared-for old pub with Mary, Queen of Scots memorabilia, excellent range of beers, and good food and service

Full of historic character inside and out, this highly evocative 16th-c place has a compelling sense of the past. It takes its name from the four ladies-in-waiting of Mary, Queen of Scots, born at nearby Linlithgow Palace in 1542. Accordingly, the pub is stashed with mementoes of the ill-fated queen, such as pictures and written records, a piece of bed curtain said to be hers, part of a 16th-c cloth and swansdown vest of the type she's likely to have worn and a facsimile of her death-mask. Spotlessly kept, the L-shaped bar has mahogany dining chairs around stripped period and antique tables, a couple of attractive antique corner cupboards, and an elaborate Victorian dresser serving as a bar gantry. The walls are mainly stripped stone, including some remarkable masonry in the inner area; piped music. Up to eight real ales are kept on handpump, with Belhaven Four Marys, 80/- and St Andrews, Caledonian Deuchars IPA, Greene King IPA and three guests; they also have a good range of malt whiskies (including a bargain malt of the month) and several wines by the glass. During their May and October beer festivals, they have 20 real ale pumps and live entertainment. There's an outdoor smoking area with heaters, tables and chairs. Parking can be difficult, but the pub is handy for the station.

🍴 Generously served good value bar food (with around half a dozen dishes qualifying for our Bargain Award) typically includes sandwiches, baked potatoes, grilled goats cheese, nachos, haddock and chips, steak pie, cajun chicken penne, macaroni cheese, haggis, neeps and tatties, sirloin steak, burgers, and puddings such as strawberry brownie cheesecake or bread and butter pudding. *Starters/Snacks: £3.95 to £4.95. Main Courses: £5.95 to £13.99. Puddings: £3.95 to £4.95*

Belhaven (Greene King) ~ Managers Eve and Ian Forrest ~ Real ale ~ Bar food (12(12.30 Sun)-9) ~ Restaurant ~ (01506) 842171 ~ Children in dining area until 9.30pm ~ Open 11(12.30 Sun)-midnight(1am Fri, Sat)

Recommended by Richard J Holloway, Peter F Marshall

MEIKLEOUR   NO1539   MAP 11

Meikleour Hotel 🛏

A984 W of Coupar Angus; PH2 6EB

Friendly and well run, with good bar food and real ales, comfortable bedrooms

Run by obliging staff, this is a pleasant base for rural Perthshire. You can look out to distant hills by sitting outside this creeper-covered early 19th-c inn on Victorian-style seats out in a small colonnaded verandah, or at tables and picnic-sets under tall conifers on the gently sloping lawn of a garden sheltered by clipped box. The main lounge bar is basically two rooms, both with oil-burning fires. One is carpeted and decorated in gentle toning colours, with comfortable seating and an elegant white-painted fireplace, the other is broadly similar, again with well padded seats, but with a stone floor. There is a modicum of fishing equipment (the River Tay is nearby) and pictures of fishing and shooting scenes. They have two beers from Inveralmond and other breweries, one of which, Lure of Meikleour, is brewed especially for them. The elegant fully panelled restaurant specialises in local game and fish; piped music. If you stay, the breakfast is good. Don't miss the spectacular nearby beech hedge, planted over 250 years ago and said to be the grandest in the world. More reports please.

🍴 Local suppliers are listed on the menus, which feature fish from Aberdeen quayside, soft fruit berries from Blairgowrie in summer and game from local shoots. Lighter lunchtime bar options include sandwiches, baked potatoes and a children's menu; the main menu might offer soup, prawn and crayfish cocktail, chicken liver pâté, fried haddock, steaks, and specials like roast shoulder of lamb; puddings like chocolate and pecan pie or eve's pudding. *Starters/Snacks: £3.75 to £5.95. Main Courses: £8.95 to £14.95. Puddings: £4.75 to £4.95*

Free house ~ Licensee Kia Mathieson ~ Real ale ~ Bar food (12.15-2.30, 6.30-9) ~ Restaurant ~ (01250) 883206 ~ Children welcome ~ Dogs allowed in bedrooms ~ Open 11-3, 6-10; 11-10.45 Sat; 12-11.45 Sun; closed 25-30 Dec ~ Bedrooms: £80B/£130B

Recommended by Christine and Neil Townend

MELROSE   NT5433   MAP 9

Burts Hotel 🍴 🛏

B6374, Market Square; TD6 9PL

Comfortably civilised town-centre hotel with tasty food and lots of malt whiskies

'Just as a hotel should be run' remarked one reader of this rather sophisticated place in the middle of this handsome town in the Borders. It's very well run with comfortable rooms and emphasis on fairly unpubby food that is served by polite smartly uniformed staff. Pleasantly informal and inviting, the lounge bar has lots of cushioned wall seats and windsor armchairs, and scottish prints on the walls; piped music. There are 80 malt whiskies to choose from, Caledonian Deuchars IPA, 80/-, Timothy Taylors Landlord and a guest on handpump, several wines by the glass from a good wine list and a farm cider. In summer you can sit out in the well tended garden and the abbey ruins are within strolling distance.

🍴 Enjoyable (but not cheap) bar food might include lunchtime sandwiches, soup, caramelised onion and goats cheese tart, thai prawn cakes, battered haddock, lamb shank, eyemouth scampi tails, honey and mustard-glazed pork fillet, beefburger, vegetable pie with chive mash, and puddings such as dark chocolate tart or sticky toffee pudding. *Starters/Snacks: £3.50 to £8.25. Main Courses: £10.50 to £9.95. Puddings: £5.75 to £6.75*

Free house ~ Licensees Graham and Nick Henderson ~ Real ale ~ Bar food (12-2, 6-9.30(10 Fri, Sat)) ~ Restaurant ~ (01896) 822285 ~ Children welcome but must be over 12 in restaurant ~ Dogs allowed in bar and bedrooms ~ Open 11-2.30, 5-11; 12-2.30, 6-11 Sun; closed 26 Dec, 3-8 Jan ~ Bedrooms: £70B/£130B

Recommended by J K Parry, Comus and Sarah Elliott, Mike and Lynn Robinson, Di and Mike Gillam, Tom and Rosemary Hall, Pat and Stewart Gordon, John and Sylvia Harrop, Malcolm Wood, Ken Richards

PITLOCHRY   NN9459   MAP 11

Moulin 🍺

Kirkmichael Road, Moulin; A924 NE of Pitlochry centre; PH16 5EH

Attractive 17th-c inn with own-brewed beers and nicely pubby bar; comfortable bedrooms

The four own-brew ales here are very well kept in this hotel in the village square: Ale of Atholl, Braveheart, Light and the stronger Old Remedial served here on handpump are brewed in the little stables across the street; they also have around 40 malt whiskies and a good choice of wines by the glass and carafe. Although much extended over the years, the lively bar, in the oldest part of the building, still seems an entity in itself, nicely pubby, with plenty of character. Above the fireplace in the smaller room is an interesting painting of the village before the road was built (Moulin used to be a bustling market town, far busier than upstart Pitlochry), while the bigger carpeted area has a good few tables and cushioned banquettes in little booths divided by stained-glass country scenes, another big fireplace, some exposed stonework, fresh flowers, antique golf clubs and local and sporting prints around the walls; bar billiards and board games; there's also a restaurant. On a gravelled area and surrounded by tubs of flowers, picnic-sets outside look across to the village kirk and there are excellent walks nearby.

⊺⊺ **The extensive bar menu features fish caught in the River Tay and highland game, with baked potatoes and sandwiches served right through the afternoon, and dishes such as such as cullen skink, rabbit casserole, haggis, neeps and tatties, steak and ale pie, a platter of local smoked meats with oatcakes and rowan sauce, fish and chips, grilled salmon steak with lemon and herb butter sauce, stuffed peppers, game casserole, fried strips of venison with mushrooms and their own beer, and puddings like bread and butter pudding or raspberry crumble; more expensive fare is served in the restaurant.** *Starters/Snacks: £3.50 to £7.95. Main Courses: £6.95 to £15.00. Puddings: £3.00 to £4.50*

Own brew ~ Licensee Heather Reeves ~ Real ale ~ Bar food (12-9.30) ~ Restaurant ~ (01796) 472196 ~ Children welcome ~ Open 11-11(11.45 Fri, Sat) ~ Bedrooms: £55B/£70B

Recommended by S G N Bennett, Pat and Stewart Gordon, the Dutchman, Glenn and Evette Booth, Mrs Hazel Rainer, J K Parry

PLOCKTON   NG8033   MAP 11

Plockton Hotel ★ ⑪ 🛏

Village signposted from A87 near Kyle of Lochalsh; IV52 8TN
SCOTLAND DINING PUB OF THE YEAR

Welcoming loch-side hotel with wonderful views, excellent food and particularly friendly staff – a real favourite with many readers

This much-liked hotel occupies a row of waterfront houses in a National Trust for Scotland conservation village on a sheltered bay on Loch Carron. With a buoyant, bustling atmosphere, the comfortably furnished lounge bar has window seats looking out to the boats on the water, as well as antiqued dark red leather seating around neat Regency-style tables on a tartan carpet, three model ships set into the woodwork, and partly panelled stone walls. The separate public bar has darts, pool, board games, TV and piped music. Drinks include local Plockton Bay and a guest such as Hebridean Clansman on handpump, 30 malt whiskies and a short wine list. Most of the comfortable bedrooms (it's worth booking well ahead) are in the adjacent building – one has a balcony and woodburning stove and half of them have extraordinary views over the loch, and you can expect good breakfasts. Tables in the front garden look out past the village's trademark palm trees and colourfully flowering shrub-lined shore, across the sheltered anchorage to the rugged mountainous surrounds of Loch Carron; a stream runs down the hill into a pond in the attractive back garden. A hotel nearby changed its name a few years ago to the Plockton Inn, so don't get the two confused.

⊺⊺ **Especially strong on fresh local seafood, enjoyable bar food includes lunchtime panini and baps, cream of smoked fish soup, langoustines, goats cheese salad, seafood bake, venison casserole, a vegetarian dish of the day, dressed crab, mussels, scallops and lamb chops; children's menu.** *Starters/Snacks: £3.50 to £9.95. Main Courses: £7.95 to £22.95. Puddings: £3.00 to £4.95*

Free house ~ Licensee Alan Pearson ~ Real ale ~ Bar food (12(12.30 Sun)-2.15, 6-10) ~ Restaurant ~ (01599) 544274 ~ Children welcome, but not in bar after 10pm ~ Live entertainment Weds evenings in summer ~ Open 11-midnight; 12.30-11 Sun ~ Bedrooms: £55B/£120B

Recommended by Joan and Tony Walker, Martin Stafford, Cedric Robertshaw, Mr R Croker, Ms C Crew

---

If we know a pub has an outdoor play area for children, we mention it.

PORT CHARLOTTE NR2558 MAP 11

Port Charlotte Hotel 🛏️

Main Street, Isle of Islay; PA48 7TU

Exceptional collection of local malts, cheery bar, lots of seafood, lovely views and comfortable bedrooms

The position here on Islay is very special, with sweeping views over Loch Indaal and across to the peaks of Jura and a sandy beach within strolling distance. Port Charlotte, the most beautiful of Islay's carefully planned Georgian villages, was built originally as a distillery village (its own Lochindaal distillery closed in 1929, though the island still has another eight), and pride of place in the rounded central bar at this friendly hotel goes to an exceptional collection of about 140 Islay and rare Islay malts. The friendly staff will give you a menu to help you choose a malt; also Black Sheep and local Islay Angus Og and Saligo, and good wines by the glass. Light and airy with big windows, the bar is fairly pubby, with a good log and peat fire, well padded wall seats, the usual chairs on bare boards and modern art. The comfortable and relaxed back lounge has a case of books about the area, and there is a good restaurant. The roomy conservatory, with well upholstered seats around its tables, opens on to a garden with more seats. More reports please.

🍴 The island has good local lamb and beef, so even the straightforward dishes are full of flavour. There is often local seafood, too – maybe scallops, oysters, langoustines and a seafood stew. Other dishes might include chicken curry, vegetable stir fry, saddle of venison, and puddings such as apple and plum crumble. *Starters/Snacks: £4.25 to £9.75. Main Courses: £8.95 to £18.95. Puddings: £4.95 to £5.50*

Free house ~ Licensee Graham Allison ~ Real ale ~ Bar food (12-2, 5.30-8.30) ~ Restaurant ~ (01496) 850360 ~ Children welcome, but not in bar after 10pm ~ Dogs allowed in bedrooms ~ Traditional live music weekly ~ Open 12-1am ~ Bedrooms: £95B/£160B

Recommended by Chris Evans, Alistair and Kay Butler, Richard J Holloway

SHIELDAIG NG8153 MAP 11

Tigh an Eilean Hotel 🛏️

Village signposted just off A896 Lochcarron—Gairloch; IV54 8XN

Exceptional views, open all day, good beers and well liked food, especially seafood

In quintessential highland scenery, this comfortable hotel and bar look out on to Loch Shieldaig (which merges into Loch Torridon), with its spectacular backdrop of mountain peaks. On two storeys and separate from the hotel, the recently built bar has an open staircase, dining on the first floor and a decked balcony with a magnificent loch and village view. It's gently contemporary and nicely relaxed with timbered floors, timber boarded walls, shiny bolts through exposed timber roof beams and an open kitchen. Isle of Skye Black Cuillin and Blaven are on handpump, alongside up to ten wines by the glass; board games, pool, newspapers, TV, darts, wi-fi and piped music. Tables outside in a sheltered little courtyard are well placed to enjoy the gorgeous position. Next door, the bedrooms are comfortable and peaceful. More reports please.

🍴 Featuring seafood straight off the fishing boat, food might include sandwiches, crab cakes, garlic and chilli seared scallops, local mussels, fish and chips, seafood stew, fisherman's pie, bream with lemon and garlic butter, rib-eye steak, burgers, pizzas from a pizza oven, and puddings such as apricot tart and cloutie dumpling with whisky custard. *Starters/Snacks: £4.00 to £8.25. Main Courses: £6.50 to £15.00. Puddings: £4.00 to £5.00*

Free house ~ Licensee Cathryn Field ~ Real ale ~ Bar food (12-9 (winter 12-3, 6-9)) ~ Restaurant ~ (01520) 755251 ~ Children welcome but not in bar after 9pm ~ Dogs welcome ~ Traditional live folk music some weekends and holidays ~ Open 11-11 ~ Bedrooms: £75B/£160B

Recommended by Martin Stafford, Will Stevens, Mr and Mrs M Stratton

SLIGACHAN

NG4930   MAP 11

Sligachan Hotel 🛏

A87 Broadford—Portree, junction with A863; IV47 8SW

Summer-opening mountain hotel in the Cuillins with walkers' bar and plusher side; food all day, impressive range of whiskies and useful children's play area

Its position right in the heart of the Cuillins is good reason to seek out this climbers' haunt – it has some of the most testing walks in Britain on its doorstep. The huge modern pine-clad main bar, falling somewhere between an original basic climbers' bar and the plusher more sedate hotel side, is spaciously open to its ceiling rafters and has geometrically laid out dark tables and chairs on neat carpets; pool. The splendid range of 300 malt whiskies makes a most impressive display behind the bar counter at one end, where they also serve their own Cuillin Black Face, Eagle, Glamaig, Pinnacle, Skye and scottish guest beers such as Caledonian Deuchars IPA. It can get quite lively in here some nights, but there is a more sedate lounge bar with leather bucket armchairs on plush carpets and a coal fire; piped highland and islands music. A feature here is the little museum charting the history of the island, and children should be delighted with the big play area which can be watched from the bar. There are tables out in a garden, and as well as self-catering accommodation they've a campsite with caravan hook-ups across the road.

🍴 **Just the sort of pubby food you might want after a good walk, the short bar menu includes sandwiches (during the day only), fish and chips, venison burger, lamb and ale pie, penne with tomato sauce, a couple of daily specials, and home-made cakes with tea or coffee; more elaborate meals in hotel restaurant.** *Starters/Snacks: £3.90 to £6.50. Main Courses: £8.00 to £9.90. Puddings: £3.00 to £4.50*

Own brew ~ Licensee Sandy Coghill ~ Real ale ~ Bar food (8am-late) ~ Restaurant ~ (01478) 650204 ~ Children welcome ~ Dogs allowed in bar ~ Live music some nights ~ Open 8am-midnight; 11-11 Sun; closed Nov-Mar ~ Bedrooms: £49B/£98B

Recommended by Dave Braisted, Tracey and Stephen Groves

STEIN

NG2656   MAP 11

Stein Inn 🛏

End of B886 N of Dunvegan in Waternish, off A850 Dunvegan—Portree; OS Sheet 23 map reference 263564; IV55 8GA

Lovely setting on northern corner of Skye, welcoming 18th-c inn with good, simple food and lots of whiskies; rewarding place to stay

Rather surprisingly considering its remote location in northern Skye, quite a few people – locals as well as visitors – often beat a path to this friendly inn, in an untouched hamlet by a water inlet. The unpretentious original public bar has great character, with its sturdy country furnishings, flagstone floor, beam and plank ceiling, partly panelled stripped-stone walls and coal fire in a grate between the two rooms. There's a games area with pool table, darts, board games, dominoes and cribbage, and maybe piped music. Caledonian Deuchars IPA and a couple of local guests from brewers such as Black Isle and Isle of Skye are kept on handpump, 125 malts and, in summer, they have several wines by the glass. Good service from smartly uniformed staff. There's a lively children's inside play area and showers for yachtsmen. All the bedrooms have sea views and breakfasts are good – it's well worth pre-ordering the tasty smoked kippers if you stay.

🍴 **Using local fish and highland meat, the short choice of good, simple and very sensibly priced food includes items like sandwiches including haggis and beer toastie, mussels, scallops, fish of the day, pork chop, breast of duck with garlic cider cream sauce, steak in ale pie, venison pie, battered haddock, stuffed aubergine, langoustines, steak, and puddings such as seasonal fruit crumble and sticky toffee pudding.** *Starters/Snacks: £3.95 to £9.50. Main Courses: £5.95 to £15.75. Puddings: £3.50 to £6.25*

It's very helpful if you let us know up-to-date food prices when you report on pubs.

Free house ~ Licensees Angus and Teresa Mcghie ~ Real ale ~ Bar food (12(12.30 Sun)-4, 6-9.30(9 Sun)) ~ Restaurant ~ (01470) 592362 ~ Children welcome until 10pm ~ Dogs welcome ~ Open 11-midnight; 12.30-11 Sun; 12-11 Mon-Sat and 1.30-10 Sun in winter ~ Bedrooms: £38.50S/£68S(£100B)

Recommended by Sylvia and Tony Birbeck, Ian and Barbara Rankin, Joan and Tony Walker, Dave Braisted

SWINTON

NT8347 MAP 10

Wheatsheaf ⑪ ♓ ⌫

A6112 N of Coldstream; TD11 3JJ

Upmarket restaurant with imaginative, elaborate food – not cheap; good range of drinks, well chosen wines and comfortable bedrooms

They have now added a lounge for informal drinking, with darts and TV, at this civilised dining pub so it's perfectly feasible just to pop in at any time for a drink even though the accent here is firmly on the very good food. Caledonian Deuchars IPA is on handpump alongside 40 malt whiskies and a choice of 50 wines (with a dozen by the glass). The carefully thought-out main lounge area has an attractive long oak settle and comfortable armchairs, with sporting prints and plates on the bottle-green wall covering; a small lower-ceilinged part by the counter has pubbier furnishings and small agricultural prints on the walls, especially sheep. A further lounge area has a fishing-theme décor (with a detailed fishing map of the River Tweed). The front conservatory has a vaulted pine ceiling and walls of local stone; piped music. Breakfasts are good, with freshly squeezed orange juice. The building is nicely set in a pretty village surrounded by rolling countryside, just a few miles from the River Tweed.

⑪ Skilfully prepared with fresh local ingredients, and available in the bar or in the dining areas, food might include starters such as soup, chicken liver pâté, grilled goats cheese with marinated sweet peppers, smoked duck, main courses such as steak and ale pie, corn-fed chicken breast stuffed with mozzarella and sun-dried tomato wrapped in prosciutto, grilled fillet of bream, loin of roe deer venison, haddock and chips, and puddings such as vanilla crème brûlée with rhubarb in rosewater and hot sticky ginger and pear pudding with warm fudge sauce. *Starters/Snacks: £3.95 to £7.95. Main Courses: £8.95 to £18.95. Puddings: £4.95 to £6.95*

Free house ~ Licensees Chris and Jan Winson ~ Real ale ~ Bar food (12-2, 6-9(8.30 Sun)) ~ Restaurant ~ (01890) 860257 ~ No children under 6 after 7pm ~ Open 11(12 Sun)-11 ~ Bedrooms: £75B/£112B

Recommended by Dr Peter D Smart, James A Waller, Christine and Malcolm Ingram

THORNHILL

NS6699 MAP 11

Lion & Unicorn

A873; FK8 3PJ

Busy, interesting pub with emphasis on its good home-made food, well liked locally

As we went to press, this friendly family-owned inn was up for sale, so we're keeping our fingers crossed that if it changes hands it will continue as it has been for many years. The bar at the back is nicely pubby with some exposed stone walls, wood floor and stools lined along the counter. It opens to a games room with a pool table, juke box, fruit machine, darts, TV and board games. The more restauranty feeling carpeted front room has pub furniture, usually set for dining, a beamed ceiling and – as evidence of the building's 17th-c origins – an original massive fireplace with a log fire in a high brazier, almost big enough to drive a car into. One or two real ales such as Caledonian Deuchars IPA and Harviestoun Bitter & Twisted are on handpump (it's cheaper in the public bar than it is in the lounge), and they've a good choice of malt whiskies; play area in the garden and piped music. More reports please.

⑪ Served all day, enjoyable bar food has included baked potatoes, starters like soup, haggis won tons, tempura-battered prawns, main courses such as steak pie, meat or vegetable lasagne, battered haddock, lamb shank, beef stroganoff, roast pork belly with cider and apple sauce, smoked fishcakes, steaks, vegetable stir fry, and puddings like apple and toffee brioche or rhubarb crumble. *Starters/Snacks: £3.25 to £4.95. Main Courses: £7.50 to £24.95. Puddings: £3.25 to £4.25*

Free house ~ Licensees Fiona and Bobby Stevenson ~ Real ale ~ Bar food (12(12.30 Sun)-9) ~ Restaurant ~ (01786) 850204 ~ Children welcome until 9pm ~ Open 11am(12.30 Sun)-midnight (1 Sat) ~ Bedrooms: £55B/£75B

Recommended by the Dutchman, Dr and Mrs A K Clarke

WEEM   NN8449   MAP 11

Ailean Chraggan 🍽 ⚲
B846; PH15 2LD

Changing range of well sourced creative food in homely family-run hotel

As well as a very good wine list and a selection of some 100 malt whiskies, they have a couple of beers from the local Inveralmond Brewery on handpump in this friendly hotel. Chatty locals gather in the simple bar and there's a neatly laid old-fashioned dining room; winter darts and board games; good breakfasts; one reader found service was a little slow. There are lovely views from its two flower-filled terraces to the mountains beyond the Tay, and up to Ben Lawers – the highest peak in this part of Scotland and the owners can arrange fishing nearby.

🍽 As well as sandwiches, the changing menu, served in either the comfortably carpeted modern lounge or the dining room, might include starters such as cullen skink, moules marinière, gravadlax, main courses like roast fillet of pork, sirloin steak with hand-cut chips, potato gnocchi with wild mushroom and spinach sauce, breast of chicken stuffed with haggis, and puddings like lavender crème brûlée and raspberry cranachan. *Starters/Snacks: £3.25 to £6.95. Main Courses: £7.95 to £17.95. Puddings: £3.95 to £4.95*

Free house ~ Licensee Alastair Gillespie ~ Real ale ~ Bar food ~ Restaurant ~ (01887) 820346 ~ Children welcome ~ Dogs allowed in bar and bedrooms ~ Open 11-11 ~ Bedrooms: £57.50B/£105B

Recommended by Mrs Hazel Rainer, Peter Martin, Brian Abbott, Sylvia and Tony Birbeck, Kevin and Rose Lemin, Andy and Claire Barker, J R and P D Holt

LUCKY DIP

Besides the fully inspected pubs, you might like to try these Lucky Dips recommended to us and described by readers (if you do, please send us reports: feedback@goodguides.com).

ABERDEENSHIRE

ABERDEEN [NJ9305]
Grill AB11 6BA [Union St]: Old-fashioned traditional local with enormous range of whiskies, well kept Caledonian 80/- and guest beers, polished dark panelling, basic snacks; open all day *(Joe Green, the Didler, Dr and Mrs A K Clarke)*
Old Blackfriars AB11 5BB [Castle St]: Welcoming and cosy ancient building on two levels, several well kept mainly scottish beers, interesting food, good service, plenty of character *(Mike and Lynn Robinson)*
☆ *Prince of Wales* AB10 1HF [St Nicholas Lane]: Eight changing ales from individual and convivial old tavern's very long bar counter, bargain hearty food, flagstones, pews and screened booths, smarter lounge; children welcome lunchtime in eating area, open all day from 10am *(LYM, Dr and Mrs A K Clarke, the Didler, Joe Green)*

GLENKINDIE [NJ4413]
Glenkindie Arms AB33 8SX [A97]: Small 17th-c pub with chef/landlord doing good imaginative locally sourced food, two local beers and often an own-brewed ale, 40 whiskies, reasonably priced wines, open fire, restaurant; no dogs; children welcome, side terrace, three bedrooms, open all day *(David and Betty Gittins)*
MILLTOWN OF ROTHIEMAY [NJ5448]
Forbes Arms AB54 7LT: Two neatly renovated bars in popular riverside hotel, two well kept ales, honest pub food (not Mon or Tues lunchtimes), cheerful owners, restaurant; children welcome, garden picnic-sets, six bedrooms *(Anthony Sharp)*
OLDMELDRUM [NJ8127]
☆ *Redgarth* AB51 0DJ [Kirk Brae]: Good-sized comfortable lounge, traditional décor and subdued lighting, three real ales, good range

of malt whiskies, enjoyable good value food, cheerful attentive service, restaurant; gorgeous views to Bennachie, immaculate bedrooms (which get booked quickly) (David and Betty Gittins)

ARGYLL

BRIDGE OF ORCHY [NN2939]
☆ *Bridge of Orchy Hotel* PA36 4AB [A82 Tyndrum—Glencoe]: Spectacular spot on West Highland Way, comfortable and lively with good choice of well kept ales, house wines and malt whiskies, friendly young staff, fairly priced food in bar and restaurant, interesting mountain photographs; lovely bedrooms, good value bunkhouse (Michael and Maggie Betton)
COLINTRAIVE [NS0473]
Colintraive Hotel PA22 3AS [opp the Maids of Bute]: Small friendly hotel (former 18th-c hunting lodge) in lovely remote spot by ferry to Rhubodach on Bute, good food (not cheap) inc local seafood in small log-fire bar or more formal restaurant, well kept Fyne ales; children and dogs welcome, four bedrooms, wonderful views across the Kyles, moorings (the Dutchman, V and E A Bolton)
CONNEL [NM9034]
Oyster PA37 1PJ: 18th-c pub opp former ferry slipway, lovely view across the water (especially at sunset), decent-sized bar with friendly highland atmosphere, log fire in stone fireplace, good standard food, keg beers but good range of wines and malts; sports TV, pool and darts; modern hotel part next door with separate restaurant (J K Parry, D and K)
CRINAN [NR7894]
Crinan Hotel PA31 8SR [B841, off A816]: Elegant hotel by Crinan Canal's entrance basin, picture-window views of fishing boats and yachts wandering out towards the Hebrides, smart nautical cocktail bar, simple snug public bar opening on to side terrace, coffee shop with sandwiches etc, good if pricey restaurant, good wines, whiskies and soft drinks (keg beer), efficient helpful staff; children and dogs welcome, 20 comfortable bedrooms, good breakfast, open all day (Dr D J and Mrs S C Walker, Dave Braisted, LYM)
LOCHGOILHEAD [NN1901]
Shorehouse PA24 8AA: Picturesque inn (former 19th-c manse) at head of Loch Goil, well kept local Fyne ales, good selection of food (not Mon-Thurs lunchtimes) inc local fish and wood-fired lunchtime pizzas, wonderful views from newly built timber restaurant and terrace, compact windowless bar with woodburner, traditional music nights; four bedrooms, cl Mon and Tues (Andy and Jill Kassube)
OBAN [NM8530]
Cuan Mor PA34 5SD [George St]: Contemporary quayside bar/restaurant with good choice of fairly priced food all day, real

ales inc own brews, friendly service; children welcoming, some seats outside (Derek and Sylvia Stephenson)
OTTER FERRY [NR9384]
Oystercatcher PA21 2DH [B8000]: Friendly family-run pub/restaurant in old building in outstanding spot overlooking Loch Fyne, good locally sourced food, well kept ales from pine-clad bar inc nearby Fyne, decent wine list; lots of tables out on spit, free moorings (Patrick and Lynn Billyeald)
PORT APPIN [NM9045]
Pier House PA38 4DE: Beautiful location, small bar with attractive terrace, very good picture-window seafood restaurant looking across to Lismore and beyond, helpful friendly staff; bedrooms, good breakfast (Gordon Nicholson)

AYRSHIRE

AYR [NS3321]
West Kirk KA7 1BX [Sandgate]: Outstanding Wetherspoons conversion of a former church, keeping its original stained glass, pulpit, balconies, doors and so forth; good value interesting real ales and their usual food (Dr and Mrs A K Clarke)
SYMINGTON [NS3831]
Wheatsheaf KA1 5QB [just off A77 Ayr—Kilmarnock; Main St]: Rambling 17th-c pub in quiet pretty village, charming and cosy, two dining rooms with wide blackboard choice of consistently good original food served all day especially fish (must book wknds), quick friendly service, racehorse décor; keg beers; attractively set tables outside, open all day (Christine and Malcolm Ingram)

BANFFSHIRE

PORTSOY [NJ5866]
Shore AB45 2QR [Church St]: Small 17th-c harbourside pub, low-ceilinged bare-boards L-shaped bar with dark bentwood seats, masses of nautical and other bric-a-brac, prints and pictures, good value straightforward food cooked with flair, well kept ales such as Caledonian Deuchars IPA, friendly staff and chatty regulars, darts; subdued piped music, small TV (Mike and Lynn Robinson, Jules Akel)

DUMFRIESSHIRE

DUMFRIES [NX9776]
☆ *Cavens Arms* DG1 2AH [Buccleuch St]: Good home-made food all day (not Mon) from pubby standards to imaginative dishes using prime ingredients, up to eight well kept interesting ales, Aspall's and Stowford Press cider, fine choice of malts, friendly landlord and good helpful staff, civilised front part with lots of wood, drinkers' area at back with bar stools, banquettes and traditional cast-iron tables; can get very busy (efficient

table-queuing system – they were also expanding into next-door property as we went to press); discreet TV, no under-14s or dogs; disabled access, open all day *(Joe Green, Deirdre Holding, the Didler)*

Coach & Horses DG1 2RS [Whitesands]: Popular flagstoned bar with simple furnishings, open fire, well kept Bass, good value inventive food from upstairs dining room, more elaborate evening menu, good friendly service; sports TVs; open all day *(the Didler)*

Globe DG1 2JA [High St]: Proper town pub with strong Burns connections, especially in old-fashioned dark-panelled 17th-c snug and little museum of a room beyond; main part more modern in feel, good value bar and restaurant food, good choice of local ales and whiskies, friendly service, juke box; children in eating areas, side terrace seating, open all day *(M J Winterton, the Didler, LYM)*

Ship DG1 2PY: Small traditional pub with interesting interior, well kept Caledonian Deuchars IPA, Greene King Abbot, Theakstons XB and Wells & Youngs Bombardier; open all day *(the Didler)*

GLENCAPLE [NX9968]

Nith DG1 4RE: Hotel with basic public bar (hatch service to sunny corner room), more comfortable lounge, picture-window dining room looking over river towards Criffel's hoary top, enjoyable quickly served food, keg beer; spacious bedrooms, good breakfast *(Bren and Val Speed)*

MOFFAT [NT0805]

Buccleuch Arms DG10 9ET [High St]: Friendly rather old-fashioned Georgian coaching inn with roomy carpeted bar and lounge areas, open fire, good food using local produce (suppliers listed), informal upstairs restaurant, interesting wines by the glass, good choice of malts and bottled beers, cocktails; keg beer, soft piped music, Sky TV; dogs welcome, garden, 16 bedrooms, open all day *(Joe Green)*

MONIAIVE [NX7790]

Craigdarroch Arms DG3 4HN [High St]: Log fire public bar, lounge bar and minimalist restaurant with dark leather chairs, enjoyable good value food (Thurs evening to Sun), Belhaven and John Smiths beers; children and dogs welcome, disabled access, ten bedrooms *(M J Winterton)*

DUNBARTONSHIRE

ARROCHAR [NN2903]

Village Inn G83 7AX [A814, just off A83 W of Loch Lomond]: Friendly, cosy and interesting with well kept local Fyne and changing guests, enjoyable home-made hearty food in simple all-day dining area with heavy beams, bare boards, some panelling and big open fire, steps down to unpretentious bar, several dozen malts, good coffee, fine sea and hill views; piped music, juke box, can be loud on busy summer Sats;

children welcome in eating areas till 8pm, tables out on deck and lawn, comfortable bedrooms inc spacious ones in former back barn, good breakfast, open all day *(Tracey and Stephen Groves, LYM, Andy and Jill Kassube)*

BALLOCH [NS3982]

Balloch Hotel G83 8LQ [just N of A811]: Vintage Inn superbly placed by River Leven's exit from Loch Lomond, early 18th-c with traditional décor and furnishings in interlinking rooms, beams and open fire, helpful young staff, good range of wines by the glass, well kept Caledonian Deuchars IPA, Fullers London Pride and Marstons Pedigree, good choice of decent reasonably priced food all day; children welcome, 14 bedrooms, open all day *(Phil Bryant)*

LUSS [NS3498]

Inverbeg Inn G83 8PD [A82 about 3 miles N]: Fully refurbished inn across road from Loch Lomond with tables overlooking it, decent choice of enjoyable food all day inc local fish in lounge and restaurant, well kept real ales, good range of whiskies, friendly attentive staff; children welcome, private jetty with boat trips, bedrooms inc eight in water's-edge lodge – great views *(LYM, Andy and Jill Kassube)*

EAST LOTHIAN

GIFFORD [NT5367]

Tweeddale Arms EH41 4QU [S of Haddington; High St (B6355)]: Old refurbished coaching inn peacefully set overlooking attractive village green, enjoyable home-made food using local produce, comfortable lounge bar with open fire, real ales such as Broughton Clipper, good choice of malts, restaurant, public bar (no children); dogs welcome, picnic-sets in small garden behind, 13 bedrooms, open all day *(LYM, Russel and Liz Stewart)*

GULLANE [NT4882]

☆ *Old Clubhouse* EH31 2AF [East Links Rd]: Two spotless bars with Victorian pictures and cartoons, stuffed birds, pre-war sheet music and other memorabilia, open fires, good choice of enjoyable well priced food, four ales inc Caledonian Deuchars IPA and 80/-, nice house wines, fast friendly service, views over golf links to Lammermuirs; children welcome, open all day *(Comus and Sarah Elliott, Ken Richards)*

FIFE

CERES [NO3911]

Meldrums KY15 5NA [Main St]: 19th-c coaching inn popular for good choice of enjoyable reasonably priced bar lunches in roomy clean and attractive beamed dining lounge, well kept Caledonian Deuchars IPA, good friendly service even when busy (best to book Sun lunch), cottagey parlour bar; seven well appointed bedrooms, charming village nr Wemyss Pottery *(Lucien Perring)*

INVERNESS-SHIRE

AVIEMORE [NH8612]
Cairngorm PH22 1PE [Grampian Rd (A9)]: Large flagstoned bar in traditional hotel, lively and friendly, with prompt helpful service, good value bar food using local produce, Cairngorm Gold and Stag, good choice of other drinks, informal dining lounge/conservatory; sports TV; children welcome, comfortable bedrooms *(George Atkinson, Joe Green)*

FORT WILLIAM [NN1274]
Ben Nevis Inn PH33 6TE [N off A82: Achintee]: Roomy well converted raftered stone barn in stunning spot by path up to Ben Nevis, good mainly straightforward food (lots of walkers so best to book), an ale such as Isle of Skye, prompt cheery service, bare-boards dining area with steps up to bar, live music; seats out at front and back, bunkhouse below, open all day Apr-Oct, otherwise cl Mon-Weds *(Mike Proctor, Phil Bryant, Michael and Maggie Betton, John Fiander)*

GLEN SHIEL [NH0711]
☆ *Cluanie Inn* IV63 7YW [A87 Invergarry—Kyle of Lochalsh, on Loch Cluanie]: Welcoming inn in lovely isolated setting by Loch Cluanie, stunning views, friendly table service for drinks inc well kept Isle of Skye, fine malt range, big helpings of enjoyable food inc good local venison in three knocked-together rooms with dining chairs around polished tables, overspill into restaurant, warm log fire, chatty parrots in lobby (mind your fingers); children and dogs welcome, big comfortable pine-furnished modern bedrooms, bunkhouse, great breakfasts inc for non-residents *(Brian Abbott, Sylvia and Tony Birbeck, Michael and Maggie Betton)*

GLENFINNAN [NM9080]
Glenfinnan House PH37 4LT: Beautifully placed 18th-c hotel by Loch Shiel, traditional bar with well kept Glenfinnan Standard and enjoyable food, restaurant, some live folk music; lawns down to the water, bedrooms, may be closed during winter *(anon)*

INVERIE [NG7500]
☆ *Old Forge* PH41 4PL: Utterly remote waterside stone pub with fabulous views, comfortable mix of old furnishings, lots of charts and sailing prints, open fire, buoyant atmosphere, good reasonably priced bar food inc fresh seafood and unusual dishes like haggis lasagne, two well kept changing ales in season, lots of whiskies, good wine choice, restaurant extension, occasional live music and ceilidhs (instruments provided); the snag's getting there – boat (jetty moorings and new pier), Mallaig foot ferry three days a week, or 15-mile walk through Knoydart from nearest road; open all day, late wknds *(Peter Meister)*

INVERNESS [NH6644]
Castle Tavern IV2 4SA [1-2 View Pl, top of Castle St]: Welcoming bare-boards bar with good range of mainly scottish ales inc one brewed for them by Isle of Skye, fine whisky choice, knowledgeable friendly staff, good fairly priced pubby food from local produce, informal upstairs restaurant; terrace, river and castle views *(Mike Proctor, Joe Green, Derek and Sylvia Stephenson, John Fiander, E Michael Holdsworth)*

Clachnaharry Inn IV3 8RB [High St, Clachnaharry (A862 NW of city)]: Under new management; beamed bar with five real ales, friendly atmosphere, good well presented affordable food, log fire, bottom lounge with woodburner and picture windows looking over Beauly Firth; terrace overlooking railway, lovely walks by big flight of Caledonian Canal locks *(John Fiander)*

Snow Goose IV2 7PA [Stoneyfield, about 0.25 miles E of A9/A96 roundabout]: Useful Vintage Inn dining pub, the most northerly of this chain, extended and well laid out with country-feel room areas, beams, flagstones and log fires, soft lighting, interesting décor, their standard all-day food (inc huge sandwiches till 5pm), decent wines by the glass, Caledonian and Timothy Taylors; lots of tables in nice garden, comfortable bedrooms in adjacent Travelodge *(Jules Akel, J F M and M West)*

LAGGAN [NN2996]
Eagle on the Water PH34 4EA [Laggan Locks, NW of Loch Lochy]: Converted dutch barge on Caledonian Canal, small, cosy and friendly, with ales such as Orkney, evening meals must be booked by 4pm; no credit cards or landline *(Dave Braisted)*

NEWTONMORE [NN7198]
Glen PH20 1DD [Main St]: Straightforward village bar with golfing memorabilia, old plates and pictures, three well kept ales inc Cairngorm Trade Winds, Weston's cider, good choice of bar food, friendly staff, pool in separate room, hotel-style dining room *(Neil and Anita Christopher)*

KINCARDINESHIRE

CATTERLINE [NO8678]
☆ *Creel* AB39 2UL: Good generous imaginative food (all day Sun) especially soups and local fish/seafood in big plain but comfortable lounge with woodburner, plenty of tables, several real ales and many unusual bottled beers, good wine choice, friendly welcoming service, small second bar, compact sea-view restaurant (same menu, booking advised); bedrooms, nice clifftop position in old fishing village, open all day Sun *(Allison Kerr, Mike and Lynn Robinson)*

KIRKCUDBRIGHTSHIRE

CASTLE DOUGLAS [NX7662]
Sulwath Brewery DG7 1DT [King St]: Bar attached to this small brewery, four Sulwath ales in top condition and their bottled

beers, baguettes, stools and barrel tables, off-sales and souvenirs, brewery tours at 1pm wkdys; cl evenings and Sun *(the Didler)*

HAUGH OF URR [NX8066]

☆ *Laurie Arms* DG7 3YA [B794 N of Dalbeattie; Main St]: Neatly kept and attractively decorated 19th-c pub, a few tables in log-fire bar with steps up to similar area, decent food from bar snacks to steaks, good changing real ales, decent wines by the glass, welcoming attentive service, restaurant, games room with darts, pool and juke box, splendid Bamforth comic postcards in the gents'; tables out at front and on sheltered terrace behind, open all day wknds *(Joe Green, LYM)*

KIPPFORD [NX8355]

☆ *Anchor* DG5 4LN [off A710 S of Dalbeattie]: New management for popular waterfront inn overlooking yachting estuary and peaceful hills, nautical theme décor with panelling and slight 1960s feel, good fire in small traditional back bar with old local photographs (dogs welcome here), more tables in area off, simple bright roomy dining room, enjoyable pubby food inc signature seafood chowder, quick cheerful service, two or three ales inc Sulwath, lots of malts, lounge bar (closed out of season); piped music, TV; children and dogs welcome, front terrace tables, good walks and bird-watching, on Seven Stanes cycle route, open all day in summer *(LYM, Chris Clark, Margaret and Peter Staples)*

LANARKSHIRE

BEARSDEN [NS5573]

Burnbrae G61 3DQ [Milngavie Rd; A81]: Well run Chef & Brewer with enjoyable food and good attentive service, well kept ales, good choice of wines by the glass; children welcome, disabled facilities, heated terrace, Premier Inn bedrooms, open all day *(Peter Reynolds)*

GLASGOW [NS5964]

☆ *Horseshoe* G2 5AE [Drury St, nr Central Station]: Classic high-ceilinged standing-room pub with enormous island bar, gleaming mahogany and mirrors, snob screens, other high Victorian features and interesting music-hall era memorabilia and musical instruments; friendly staff and atmosphere, well priced ales inc Caledonian Deuchars IPA and 80/-, lots of malt whiskies, bargain simple food served speedily in plainer upstairs bar and restaurant (children allowed here), inc long-served McGhees hot pies; sports TVs, silent fruit machine, piped music; open all day (breakfast from 9pm) *(Jeremy King, Joe Green, LYM)*

Ingram G1 3BX [Queen St]: Civilised and well run Greene King (Belhaven) pub with perhaps two guest beers, several dozen malt whiskies ranked along island bar, good lunchtime ciabattas and bargain generous home-made hot dishes, dark panelling and

some unusual wall covering using old filing cabinet fronts, interesting *Daily Herald* papers from 1953 (pub's opening) lining narrow stairs down to lavatories; TVs and games machines *(Joe Green, Dr and Mrs A K Clarke, Andy and Jill Kassube)*

Pot Still G2 2TH [Hope St]: Comfortable and welcoming traditional pub with hundreds of malt whiskies, bare boards and dark panelling, raised back seating area, changing real ales such as Houston and Kelburn, interesting bottled beers, decent wines, knowledgeable friendly staff; open all day *(Andy and Jill Kassube, BB)*

Sloans G2 8BG [Argyle Arcade]: Restored Grade A listed building over three floors, many original features inc fine mahogany staircase, etched glass, ornate woodwork and moulded ceilings, good choice of food from sandwiches up in ground floor bar/bistro and upstairs restaurant, events in impressive barrel-vaulted parquet-floored ballroom; children welcome, courtyard tables *(Andy and Jill Kassube)*

MIDLOTHIAN

BALERNO [NT1566]

Johnsburn House EH14 7BB [Johnsburn Rd]: Handsome old-fashioned beamed bar in former 18th-c mansion with masterpiece 1911 ceiling by Robert Lorimer; Caledonian Deuchars IPA and interesting changing ales, coal fire, panelled dining lounge with good food inc shellfish and game, more formal evening dining rooms; children and dogs welcome, open all day *(the Didler)*

DALKEITH [NT3367]

Blacksmiths Forge EH22 1DU [Newmills Rd]: Newish Wetherspoons with usual good value food and well kept ales, friendly welcoming staff, some quiet areas (perhaps not wknds), subdued lighting; silent TVs, no dogs; children welcome, terrace seating *(Andy and Jill Kassube)*

Sun EH22 4TR [(A7 S)]: Recently refurbished dining pub/boutique hotel, enjoyable food inc some unusual choices and nice puddings, early-bird deals Mon-Thurs, changing ales such as Caledonian, Innis & Gunn and Timothy Taylors; courtyard garden, five individually styled bedrooms, good generous breakfast *(Andy and Jill Kassube)*

EDINBURGH [NT2473]

Barony EH1 3RJ [Broughton St]: L-shaped Victorian pub with ornate tiles, mahogany, mirrors and brass, coal fire, well kept ales, good value food from sandwiches to haggis; live music Sat; open all day *(Andy and Jill Kassube)*

☆ *Bennets* EH3 9LG [Leven St]: Ornate Victorian bar with original glass, mirrors, arcades, fine panelling and tiles, friendly service, real ales inc Caledonian Deuchars IPA from tall founts, masses of malt whiskies, bar snacks and bargain homely lunchtime dishes (not Sun), second bar with counter salvaged from old ship; children allowed in eating area, open all day, cl Sun (*LYM, the Didler*)

Berts Bar EH3 7NG [William St]: Modern pub done in traditional style, up to ten well kept ales such as Arran, Broughton and Harviestoun, reasonably priced food inc popular pie menu, long narrow bar, room off with nice tiled fireplace (*Andy and Jill Kassube*)

☆ **Canny Man's** EH10 4QU [Morningside Rd; aka Volunteer Arms]: Utterly individual and distinctive, saloon, lounge and snug with fascinating bric-a-brac, ceiling papered with sheet music, huge range of appetising smorgasbord, very efficient friendly service, lots of whiskies, good wines, well kept ales such as Caledonian Deuchars IPA, cheap children's drinks, no credit cards, mobile phones or backpackers; courtyard tables (*Mr and Mrs Richard Osborne, Dr and Mrs R G J Telfer*)

Cask & Barrel EH1 3RZ [Broughton St]: Bareboards traditional Victorian drinkers' pub with some fine features, up to eight mainly scottish ales inc Caledonian 80/- from U-shaped bar, helpful service, good value bar food especially stovies Mon-Fri; sports TVs (*Andy and Jill Kassube, BB*)

Cloisters EH3 9JH [Brougham St]: Friendly and interesting ex-parsonage alehouse with great range of changing beers, dozens of malts, several wines by the glass, decent food till 4pm (6pm Tues-Thurs) from toasties to Sun roasts, pews and bar gantry recycled from redundant church, bare boards and lots of brewery mirrors; lavatories down spiral stairs, folk music Fri and Sat; dogs welcome, open all day (*the Didler, Darren Le Poidevin*)

☆ **Ensign Ewart** EH1 2PE [Lawnmarket, Royal Mile; last pub on right before Castle]: Charming dimly lit old-world pub handy for Castle (so gets busy), beams peppered with brasses, huge painting of Ewart at Waterloo capturing french banner, assorted furniture inc elbow tables, friendly efficient staff, well kept Caledonian, plenty of whiskies, simple enjoyable food; piped music – traditional most nights, games machine, keypad entry to lavatories; open all day (*Christine and Neil Townend, Peter F Marshall, Jeremy King*)

☆ **Halfway House** EH1 1BX [Fleshmarket Close (steps between Cockburn St and Market St, opp Waverley Station)]: Tiny one-room pub off steep steps, a few round tables, railway memorabilia, four ales, good range of malt whiskies, good value all-day food; 60s/70s juke box, small TV; dogs and children welcome (*Joe Green, Jeremy King*)

Jolly Judge EH1 2PB [James Court, by 495 Lawnmarket]: Small comfortable basement of 16th-c tenement with traditional fruit-and-flower-painted wooden ceiling, welcoming relaxed atmosphere, Belhaven and McEwans ales, good range of malts, lunchtime bar meals (children allowed then) and afternoon snacks, nice log fire;

open all day, cl Sun lunchtime (*Peter and Giff Bennett, LYM*)

Oxford EH2 4JB [Young St]: Friendly no-frills pub with two well kept wall settles and friendly locals in tiny bustling bar, steps up to quieter back room with dominoes, lino floor, well kept Caledonian Deuchars IPA and Belhaven 80/-, good whisky range, cheap filled cobs; links with scottish writers and artists (*Peter F Marshall, LYM*)

Royal McGregor EH1 1QS [High St]: Family-run long modern traditional-style bar with raised back area, enjoyable food all day (10-10) from massive breakfasts to good value set meals, well kept scottish ales such as Inveralmond, good coffee, friendly staff, Georgian Edinburgh prints; unobtrusive piped music, TV; pavement tables, open all day (*Michael and Alison Sandy, Peter F Marshall, Derek and Sylvia Stephenson*)

Standing Order EH2 2JP [George St]: Grand Wetherspoons bank conversion in three elegant Georgian houses, imposing columns, enormous main room with elaborate colourful ceiling, lots of tables, smaller side booths, other rooms inc two with floor-to-ceiling bookshelves, comfortable clubby seats, Adam fireplace and portraits; real ales inc some interesting ones from long counter; sports TV, wknd live music, gets very busy particularly Sat night; disabled facilities, open all day till 1am (*Donna and Roger, Michael and Alison Sandy, BB*)

Whiski EH1 1SG [High St]: Bar with over 250 whiskies, Belhaven and Caledonian 80/-, fresh food all day inc lunchtime specials and children's meals, live traditional music Tues and Sat evenings; open all day, till late Fri and Sat (*anon*)

MUSSELBURGH [NT3372]

Volunteer Arms EH21 6JE [North High St; aka Staggs]: In same family since 1858, unspoilt busy bar, dark panelling, old brewery mirrors, great gantry with ancient casks, Caledonian Deuchars IPA and a guest beer, overflow lounge wknds; dogs welcome, open all day (*Joe Green, the Didler*)

PERTHSHIRE

BLAIR ATHOLL [NN8765]

☆ **Atholl Arms** PH18 5SG: Sizeable hotel's cosy stable-theme bar in lovely setting nr castle, four local Moulin ales, good well priced food all day from sandwiches to interesting dishes, local meat and wild salmon, helpful friendly staff, open fire; 31 good value bedrooms, open all day (*Joe Green, Jules Akel*)

BRIG O' TURK [NN5306]

☆ **Byre** FK17 8HT [A821 Callander—Trossachs, just outside village]: Beautifully placed byre conversion with new owners, enjoyable food inc good local trout and some imaginative dishes, friendly staff, flagstoned log-fire bar, roomier high-raftered restaurant area; tables out on extensive decking, good walks, open all day (*LYM, Mr and Mrs P Morris*)

DUNKELD [NO0242]
Taybank PH8 0AQ [Tay Terrace]: Traditional
pub with view over Tay and Georgian bridge,
good value home-made food inc stovies, well
kept Atlas and Timothy Taylors, regular
scottish music open sessions and
workshops (instruments provided)
(Jules Akel)

DUNNING [NO0114]
Kirkstyle PH2 0RR [B9141, off A9 S of Perth;
Kirkstyle Sq]: Unpretentious olde-worlde
streamside pub with chatty landlady and
regulars, log fire in snug bar, good real ale
and whisky choice, enjoyable generous
home-made food inc interesting dishes (book
in season), good service, charming
flagstoned and stripped-stone back
restaurant *(Jules Akel, Andy and
Jill Kassube)*

KILLIN [NN5732]
Falls of Dochart FK21 8SL [Gray St]:
Popular former coaching inn overlooking the
falls, welcoming landlord, big log fire in
attractive flagstoned bar, well kept ales,
good imaginative home-made food all day,
piped traditional music; dogs welcome,
bedrooms *(Peter Martin, Kevin and
Rose Lemin)*

KIRKTON OF GLENISLA [NO2160]
☆ *Glenisla Hotel* PH11 8PH [B951 N of
Kirriemuir and Alyth]: Lively local
atmosphere and good log fire in hotel's
beamed bar, real ales such as Houston and
Inveralmond (beer festivals), enjoyable
hearty food using local produce, good
friendly service, comfortable sunny lounge,
attractive high-ceilinged dining room,
functions in converted stable block; piped
and some live traditional music; children and
dogs welcome, decent clean bedrooms, good
walks, open all day in season
(Mrs Diana Robertson, LYM)

LOGIERAIT [NN9751]
Logierait Inn PH9 0LJ [Off A9 towards
Aberfeldy]: Well refurbished pub dating from
early 18th c, warm welcome, open fire, good
choice of enjoyable food, Inveralmond ales,
no piped music *(Jules Akel)*

PITLOCHRY [NN9163]
☆ *Killiecrankie Hotel* PH16 5LG [Killiecrankie,
off A9 N]: Comfortable and splendidly placed
country hotel smartened up under current
owner, attractive panelled bar, airy and
relaxed conservatory, good nicely varied and
reasonably priced food here and in
restaurant, smiling efficient service, well
kept ales, good choice of wines; children in
eating areas, extensive peaceful grounds and
dramatic views, bedrooms *(LYM, Joan and
Tony Walker)*

RENFREWSHIRE

GOUROCK [NS2477]
Spinnaker PA19 1BU: Small Victorian terrace
hotel with spectacular Firth of Clyde views,
well kept Belhaven, home-made standard
food inc children's menu, friendly chatty

staff; eight bedrooms *(E McCall, T McLean,
D Irving)*

ROSS-SHIRE

ACHILTIBUIE [NC0208]
Summer Isles IV26 2YQ: Locally popular
small bar attached to hotel, good fresh food
all day from sandwiches up inc notable
seafood, real ales, lovely views of the
Summer Isles from small terrace; hotel side
with its separate restaurant closes during
winter *(J F M and M West)*

ALTANDHU [NB9812]
Fuaran IV26 2YR [15 miles off A835 N of
Ullapool]: Splendidly remote, in gorgeous
coastal scenery, enjoyable food inc good
local fish/seafood, takeaways too, McEwans
beer, good whiskies and wine by the glass,
open fire, old local photographs, farm tools,
antlers and bagpipes; beautiful Summer Isles
views from decking *(J F M and M West)*

ANNAT [NG8854]
Torridon Inn IV22 2EY [off A896]: Converted
outbuildings of imposing lochside hotel set
in 58-acre grounds, friendly and comfortable
with leather sofas and open fires, nice
straightforward food, up to four well kept
beers, conservatory; children welcome,
spectacular scenery, 12 bedrooms, may be
closed winter at least Mon-Weds (main hotel
has 19 more expensive bedrooms, an
upmarket restaurant and a very well stocked
whisky bar) *(Michael and Maggie Betton)*

AULTGUISH INN [NH3570]
Aultguish Hotel IV23 2PQ [A835]: Isolated
highland inn nr Loch Glascarnoch,
chef/landlord doing good imaginative food
(scottish and italian), a beer from An
Teallach, plenty of wines with emphasis on
italian, reasonable prices, friendly service,
open fire burning most of the year; children
and dogs welcome, bedrooms and bunkhouse
(David and Carole Sayliss, David Taylor, LYM)

GLENELG [NG8119]
☆ *Glenelg Inn* IV40 8JR [unmarked rd from
Shiel Bridge (A87) towards Skye]:
Unpretentious mountain cabin-like bar in
smart hotel reached by dramatic drive with
spectacular views of Loch Duich to Skye, big
fireplace, black and white photographs, just
a few tables, may have two real ales, fresh
local food inc venison and seafood, dining
room, pool; may be piped music (usually
scottish); children and dogs welcome, lovely
garden, views from some bedrooms, summer
ferry to Skye, open all day *(LYM, Ian and
Deborah Carrington)*

PLOCKTON [NG8033]
☆ *Plockton Inn* IV52 8TW [Innes St;
unconnected to Plockton Hotel]: Situated nr
the harbour in this lovely village, congenial
bustling atmosphere even in winter, good
well priced food with emphasis on local
fish/seafood (some from back smokery),
friendly efficient service, well kept changing
beers, good range of malts, lively public bar
with regular traditional music; seats out on

decking, 14 bedrooms (some in annexe over road) *(Ian and Deborah Carrington, Dave Braisted)*

POOLEWE [NB8580]

Poolewe IV22 2JX: Former 16th-c coaching inn with Loch Ewe views, enjoyable food in bar/bistro from baguettes to specials inc local fish, friendly service, An Teallach and Orkney ales, over 60 malt whiskies, log fires, interesting juke box (may be live folk music), restaurant; children very welcome, handy for Inverewe Garden (NT for Scotand), bedrooms, open all day *(BB, Sylvia and Tony Birbeck)*

ROXBURGHSHIRE

ANCRUM [NT6224]

Cross Keys TD8 6XH [off A68 Jedburgh—Edinburgh]: Pleasant village green setting, friendly landlord, well kept Broughton and guests, small panelled locals' bar with sewing-machine tables and open fire, linked lounge/dining areas (one with original overhead tracks for carrying beer to the cellar), enjoyable home-made food; garden, open all day wknds *(the Didler)*

MELROSE [NT5434]

George & Abbotsford TD6 9PD [High St]: Civilised bar and lounge areas in comfortable hotel, friendly staff, enjoyable freshly made all-day food, good choice of beers such as Cairngorm and Traquair plus some english ones (summer beer festival), decent wines, quite a few malt whiskies, restaurant; no dogs; 30 bedrooms, small shop selling wide range of bottled beers, open all day *(the Didler)*

TOWN YETHOLM [NT8128]

Plough TD5 8RF [High St]: Welcoming unpretentious pub facing green, good honest food inc nice steaks, well kept ales *(C A Hall)*

STIRLINGSHIRE

DRYMEN [NS4788]

Winnock G63 0BL [just off A811; The Square]: Well kept Caledonian 80/- in big Best Western's modern split-level stripped-stone and beamed lounge bar, blazing log fires, leather sofas and easy chairs, neat helpful young staff, good choice of malt whiskies, steps down to popular restaurant area; piped music; big garden, 48 bedrooms *(Dr and Mrs A K Clarke)*

STIRLING [NS7993]

☆ *Portcullis* FK8 1EG [Castle Wynd]: Attractive former 18th-c school below castle, overlooking town and surroundings, entry through high-walled courtyard, spacious and elegant high-ceilinged stripped-stone bar with central pillar, inglenooks and brocades, friendly helpful staff, nice choice of sandwiches and good generous pubby hot dishes (not Mon evening, best to book other evenings), Isle of Skye Red Cuillin and

Orkney Dark Island from handsome counter, good choice of whiskies; lush sheltered terrace garden, good bedrooms and breakfast *(Pete Coxon, Jim Sargent)*

SUTHERLAND

LAIRG [NC5224]

☆ *Crask Inn* IV27 4AB [A836 13 miles N towards Altnaharra]: Remote homely inn on single-track road through peaceful moorland, good simple food cooked by landlady inc their own lamb (the friendly hard-working licensees keep sheep on this working croft), comfortably basic bar with large peat stove to dry the sheepdogs, Black Isle organic bottled beers, interesting books, piano, pleasant separate dining room, no piped music; dogs welcome, three or four bedrooms (lights out when generator goes off), simple nearby bunkhouse *(Jules Akel)*

LOCHINVER [NC0922]

Caberfeidh IV27 4JY: Cosy bar, pleasant dining room, shortish menu with emphasis on local seafood, up to five well kept beers inc McEwans, charming landlord and staff; harbourside garden *(Stephen McNees)*

WIGTOWNSHIRE

BLADNOCH [NX4254]

Bladnoch Inn DG8 9AB: Cheerful bar, neat and bright, with eating area, enjoyable well prepared pubby food from sandwiches up, friendly obliging service, restaurant; keg beer, piped radio; children and dogs welcome, picturesque riverside setting across from Bladnoch distillery (tours), good value bedrooms *(Richard J Holloway, Mr and Mrs P G Mitchell)*

CREEBRIDGE [NX4165]

Creebridge House Hotel DG8 6NP [Minnigaff, just E of Newton Stewart]: Sizeable welcoming country house hotel, good food from shortish menu in brasserie and more formal restaurant, popular carpeted bar, well kept ales; piped music; children in eating areas, tables on front terrace by croquet lawn, bedrooms *(Leslie and Barbara Owen, LYM)*

PORT LOGAN [NX0940]

☆ *Port Logan Inn* DG9 9NG [Laigh St]: Lovely sea-view spot in pretty fishing harbour, family-run and welcoming, well kept ales such as Caledonian Deuchars IPA or Sulwath Criffel, lots of malt whiskies, enjoyable food inc local fish and game, log fire, old local photographs and electronic equipment; handy for Logan Botanic Garden, bedrooms *(Alistair and Kay Butler, Mark O'Sullivan, Derek Roughton)*

STRANRAER [NX0660]

Grapes DG9 7HY [Bridge St]: Busy old local, traditional and basic, with welcoming landlord, a well kept real ale and great range of malts; mini beer festival May; open all day *(the Didler)*

SCOTTISH ISLANDS

ARRAN

BRODICK [NS0136]
Brodick Bar KA28 8BU [Alma Rd]: Simple modern bar tucked away off seafront, relaxed atmosphere, wide choice of food sensibly priced food in restaurant, efficient friendly service, Caledonian ales, several malt whiskies *(Ken Richards, Will Stevens, R L Borthwick)*

KILMORY [NR9521]
Lagg KA27 8PQ: Relaxing old-fashioned streamside inn, interesting food in lively bar and dining room, friendly service; attractive garden with peacocks, delightful view, bedrooms, good breakfast *(MJVK, John Coatsworth)*

COLONSAY

SCALASAIG [NR3893]
☆ *Colonsay* PA61 7YP: Haven for ramblers and birders, cool and trendy décor with log fires, interesting old islander pictures, pastel walls and polished painted boards, bar with sofas, board games, enjoyable food from soup and toasties to fresh seafood, game and venison, good local Colonsay ale, lots of malt whiskies, informal restaurant; children and dogs welcome, pleasant views from gardens, comfortable bedrooms *(David Hoult)*

ISLAY

BOWMORE [NR3159]
Lochside Hotel PA43 7LB [Shore St]: Neatly modernised family-run hotel (for sale as we went to press), well kept Islay beers and great collection of Islay malts, enjoyable straightforward food inc local fish and lamb, good friendly service, two bars, bright conservatory-style back restaurant with lovely Loch Indaal views, traditional music Sat night; ten bedrooms *(David Hoult, Richard J Holloway)*

PORTNAHAVEN [NN1652]
An Tighe Seinnse PA47 7SJ [Queen St]: Friendly end-of-terrace harbourside pub tucked away in remote attractive fishing village, cosy bar with room off, open fire, good food inc local seafood, good choice of malts, bottled local Islay ales *(David Hoult, T A R Curran)*

MULL

DERVAIG [NM4251]
☆ *Bellachroy* PA75 6QW: Island's oldest inn recently refurbished by friendly licensees, good pub and restaurant food inc local seafood and plenty of other fresh produce, reasonable prices and generous helpings, good choice of beers, whiskies and wine, traditional bar, informal dining area and lounge used more by residents, nice spot in sleepy village; children and dogs welcome, six comfortable bedrooms, open all year *(Mr and Mrs Richard Osborne, Barry Collett, Mr and Mrs M Stratton)*

ORKNEY

DOUNBY [HY3001]
Merkister KW17 2LF [S by Harray Loch]: Fishing hotel in great location on the loch shores, bar dominated by prize catches, good food here and in pricey restaurant inc hand-dived scallops and local aberdeen angus steaks, Belhaven and McEwans ales; 16 bedrooms *(Dave Braisted)*

KETTLETOFT [HY6503]
Kettleloft KW17 2BJ [Sanday]: Great views over seal colony from bar windows, friendly landlord, enjoyable pubby food, Highland Scapa ale; bedrooms *(Dave Braisted)*

KIRKWALL [HY4411]
Kirkwall Hotel KW15 1LE [Harbour St]: Large Victorian building overlooking harbour, good food inc local specialities in bar and restaurant, dozens of malt whiskies, friendly well organised staff; 37 bedrooms *(Roger Amey)*

PAPA WESTRAY [HY4905]
Beltane House KW17 2BU: Also houses this little island's store and self catering/hostel accommodation, Highland and Orkney ales, bar food; only open Sat evening *(Dave Braisted)*

SKYE

PORTREE [NG4843]
Bosville IV51 9DG [Bosville Terrace]: Well looked-after hotel not far from main square and overlooking harbour, decent inexpensive food, Isle of Skye beers, good friendly service *(Derek and Sylvia Stephenson)*

Please keep sending us reports. We rely on readers for news of new discoveries, and particularly for news of changes – however slight – at the fully described pubs: feedback@goodguides.com, or (no stamp needed) The Good Pub Guide, FREEPOST TN1569, Wadhurst, E Sussex TN5 7BR.

Wales

Four new entries in Wales this year are the well run Crown at Pantygelli, the smart contemporary Daffodil in Penrhiwllan, the relaxed and pubby Black Lion at Pontrhydfendigaid and the beachside Ship at Tresaith. There's plenty of interesting places to stay here, nearly all of them in terrific surroundings. Most notably, the stylish Harbourmaster at Aberaeron and the personable Penhelig Arms at Aberdovey are in locations by the sea, the remote Hand in Llanarmon Dyffryn Ceiriog is sublimely peaceful and for something completely different, the much loved Pen-y-Gwryd at Llanberis is a famously eccentric climbing hotel, and with just the right attitude coming from the landlord, the enjoyable Stackpole Inn at Stackpole gets a new Stay Award this year. Of the four contenders for Dining Pub of the Year, the beautifully kept Pant-yr-Ochain at Gresford, the charmingly located Corn Mill at Llangollen and the Cross Foxes at Overton Bridge (stunning views) are all Brunning & Price pubs – a tremendous accolade to the success of this small chain. However, after much deliberation, the brilliantly run Griffin at Felinfach, with produce from its own organic garden, is our Wales Dining Pub for 2011. Other places that we'd like to pick out as special are the Bear at Crickhowell, a good all-rounder with a particularly nice bar if you are staying, the lovely old unspoilt Cresselly Arms at Cresswell Quay and the Star at Talybont-on-Usk, with its seemingly permanent beer festival.

ABERAERON   SN4562   MAP 6

Harbourmaster ⓘⓟ ♀ 🛏

Harbour Lane; SA46 0BA

Stylish, thriving waterside dining pub/hotel, interesting food (at a price), up-to-date bedrooms

Most evenings, the freshly turned out bar at this painted waterside hotel hums with lively conversation. It's cleanly decorated, with blue walls, a zinc-clad counter, an assortment of leather sofas, a stuffed albatross reputed to have collided with a ship belonging to the owner's great-grandfather, and has french windows. A large minimalist dining area has modern light wood furniture on light wood floors against aqua-blue walls, while there's also a four-seater cwtch, or snug, within the former porch; piped music and TV. Purple Moose Glaslyn and a beer brewed by them for the pub are on handpump, and they've a good wine list, with a dozen sold by the glass. The owners are chatty and welcoming, and if you stay, the breakfasts are good; disabled access. The hotel (which was extended into a former grain warehouse) is one of an array of colourwashed buildings overlooking an attractive yacht-filled harbour and you can sit outside on a bench near the road.

🍴 The usually enjoyable bar food, featuring welsh recipes, seasonal and often local ingredients, includes oysters, potted crab with sourdough, duck liver parfait with toasted brioche and red onion and apricot compote, chicken breast with tarragon jus and creamed leeks, brill fillet with sweet potato rösti, spinach and chorizo, caramelised red pepper, cheese and onion tartlet, fish of the day, steaks, and puddings such as chocolate brownie sundae and crème brûlée. *Starters/Snacks: £4.50 to £12.00. Main Courses: £9.00 to £17.50. Puddings: £5.50*

Free house ~ Licensees Glyn and Menna Heulyn ~ Real ale ~ Bar food (12-2.30, 6-9) ~ Restaurant ~ (01545) 570755 ~ Children over 5 if staying ~ Open 8am-11pm ~ Bedrooms: £60S/£130B

Recommended by Martin Cawley, Mr and Mrs P R Thomas, Di and Mike Gillam, Mike and Mary Carter, the Didler, Blaise Vyner

ABERDOVEY
SN6196   MAP 6

Penhelig Arms

Opposite Penhelig railway station; LL35 0LT

Fine harbourside location, enjoyable food and a nice place to stay

We like the way the fisherman's bar at this personable waterside hotel has been brought up to date – there's been no sweeping through with a completely modern interior, just a gentle take on the traditional with particularly bright red built-in banquettes and stools, a warm fire in the remaining stud of stone wall, some panelling and a new counter and back display. Efficient and genuinely friendly bar staff serve Brains Bitter, Rev James and a guest from a brewery such as Greene King Abbot, two dozen malt whiskies and a good wine selection with 18 by the glass. The bedrooms are comfortable (some have balconies overlooking the estuary) but the ones nearest the road can be noisy.

🍴 Readers have praised the food here, which, in addition to lunchtime sandwiches, might include starters such as grilled sardines, antipasti, smoked mackerel pâté and cod and chorizo fishcake, main courses such as cajun spiced swordfish with lemon mayonnaise, pork tenderloin in brandy and mushroom sauce, home-made burger, fried chicken fillet with mushroom and pea risotto and pesto, cod and king prawn stew with tomatoes, peppers and chorizo, rib-eye steak, and puddings such as warm chocolate and cherry fondant, banoffi pie and caramelised lemon tart. *Starters/Snacks: £2.00 to £10.95. Main Courses: £8.95 to £17.95. Puddings: £4.95 to £6.00*

Brains ~ Manager Carl Rowlands ~ Real ale ~ Bar food (12-2, 6-9) ~ Restaurant ~ (01654) 767215 ~ Children welcome ~ Dogs welcome ~ Open 11-11(10.30 in winter; midnight Sat); 12-10.30 Sun ~ Bedrooms: £60S(£60B)/£100S(£100B)

Recommended by B and M Kendall, Mike and Mary Carter, David Glynne-Jones, Dr Kevan Tucker, S J and C C Davidson, John Burgess, Steve Whalley, Neil Kellett

ABERGAVENNY
SO3111   MAP 6

Hardwick 🍴 🍷

Hardwick; B4598 SE, off A40 at A465/A4042 exit – coming from E on A40, go right round the exit system, as B4598 is final road out; NP7 9AA

Noteworthy food in smartly simple dining pub, good beers and wines too

Emphasis at this well run dining pub is almost exclusively on the jolly good (though not cheap) imaginative menu. You will need to book. The bar, with a small functional corner server (Rhymney Bevans and a guest such as Breconshire Pale Ale, local bottled ciders and an ample selection of good interesting wines by the glass, in a choice of glass sizes), is a simple room with spindleback chairs around pub tables, and some stripped brickwork around a disused fireplace. The better of the two dining rooms feels more pubby, given its dark beams, a winged high-backed settle by the end serving counter, and another facing a small pew across one table tucked in by a huge fireplace, and a nice mix of other tables and chairs on bare boards with a big rug (the lack of soft furnishings here can make the acoustics rather lively). The second dining room, in a carpeted extension, is lighter and simpler, more modern in style, with big windows; there is some interesting artwork. Service is welcoming and helpful; there may be piped music. They have teak tables and chairs out under umbrellas by the car park, and the garden is neatly kept.

They are in the process of extending the bar and creating bedrooms, which should be open by the time this edition is published.

🍴 Owner-chef Stephen Terry uses carefully selected, largely local ingredients to create supercharged variations on familiar dishes and more original recipes. The extensive lunch and dinner menus might include provençale-style fish soup, starters like confit duck hash with fried local duck egg, salad of buffalo mozzarella with polenta croûtons, anchovies and sun-dried tomato, or mussels on bruschetta, and main courses such as fried sea trout with roasted beetroot, sauté new potatoes, smoked bacon, rocket and horseradish, home-made local gloucester old spot pork meatballs in tomato sauce with penne pasta, and roast boneless wing of skate with wild garlic mash, carrots and braised fennel; puddings like sticky toffee and medjool date loaf with toffee sauce, or vanilla panna cotta with rhubarb jelly and stem ginger shortbread. Children's menu, fixed-price two- and three-course lunches; Sunday roasts. *Starters/Snacks: £6.00 to £11.00. Main Courses: £13.00 to £21.00. Puddings: £6.00 to £7.00*

Free house ~ Licensees Stephen and Joanna Terry ~ Real ale ~ Bar food (12-5, 6.30-9.45; not Sun evening) ~ Restaurant ~ (01873) 854220 ~ Children welcome ~ Open 12-3, 6.30-11.30; 12-3 Sun; closed Mon (except bank hols)
Recommended by Dr Kevan Tucker, Joyce and Maurice Cottrell, Maurice and Gill McMahon, Duncan Cloud, Ian Herdman

BEAUMARIS   SH6076   MAP 6

Olde Bulls Head ♀ 🛏

Castle Street; LL58 8AP

Interesting historic pub with brasserie food, accommodation and wines

This cosy inn near the castle has a simple bar, a relaxed brasserie and a smart upstairs restaurant. Since it was built in 1472, it's been used by a great range of people, including Samuel Johnson and Charles Dickens, both of whom would find much of it familiar today. The low-beamed bar is a nicely rambling place, with plenty of interesting reminders of the town's past: a rare 17th-c brass water clock, a bloodthirsty crew of cutlasses and even an oak ducking stool tucked among the snug alcoves. There are also lots of copper and china jugs, comfortable low-seated settles, leather-cushioned window seats, a good log fire, and Bass, Hancocks and a guest such as Conwy Rampart on handpump. Quite a contrast, the busy brasserie behind is lively and stylishly modern, with a wine list including around 20 available by the glass; the exceptionally good restaurant list runs to 120 bottles. The entrance to the pretty courtyard is closed by what has been listed in the *Guinness World Records* book as the biggest simple-hinged door in Britain (11 feet wide and 13 feet high). Named after characters in Dickens's novels, the bedrooms are very well equipped; some are traditional, and others more up to date, and there are also bedrooms in the Townhouse, an adjacent property with disabled access. More reports on the food please.

🍴 Soup and sandwiches are served in the bar. The brasserie menu includes terrine of chicken, bacon and tarragon with tomato chutney, spinach and cumin falafels with tzatziki, smoked pork loin with roast hazelnut salad and apple and sultana compote, venison, mushroom and root vegetable casserole, pork and leek sausages with grain mustard and leek mash, macaroni cheese, mushroom risotto, fish and chips and rib-eye steak. *Starters/Snacks: £2.95 to £6.40. Main Courses: £7.95 to £16.50. Puddings: £4.75 to £5.95*

Free house ~ Licensee David Robertson ~ Real ale ~ Bar food (12-2(3 Sun), 6-9) ~ Restaurant ~ (01248) 810329 ~ Children welcome ~ Open 11-11; 12-10.30 Sun ~ Bedrooms: £80B/£110B
Recommended by Mrs Angela Graham, Brian and Anna Marsden, Lucie Merrick, Peter and Josie Fawcett, Neil Whitehead, Victoria Anderson

---

Post Office address codings confusingly give the impression that some pubs are in Gwent or Powys, Wales, when they're really in Gloucestershire or Shropshire (which is where we list them).

CAPEL CURIG

SH7257 MAP 6

Bryn Tyrch 🛏️

A5 E; LL24 0EL

Perfectly placed for the mountains of Snowdonia, welcoming licensees, pleasant bedrooms and interesting food

The relaxed bar at this well placed inn has big menu blackboards, leather sofas round low tables, an eclectic mix of pine tables, some rescued from a local church on its bare boards, and a coal fire. The plainer hikers' bar has large, communal tables and natural stone walls. Great Orme Cambria and Orme are on handpump and they've quite a few malt whiskies, including some local ones; board games. You can take in the terrific views from the large picture windows that run the length of one wall – looking across the road to picnic-sets on a floodlit patch of grass by a stream running down to a couple of lakes, and the peaks of the Carneddau, Tryfan and Glyders in close range. There are also tables on a steep little garden at the side and on a terrace off the breakfast room. Some of the country-style bedrooms have views.

🍽️ Bar food includes lunchtime fried pigeon breast, beetroot and pancetta tart, scallop, shitake mushroom and duck confit ravioli with sweet corn purée, smoked chicken and crayfish cocktail with roast red pepper mayonnaise, fish pie, spinach and feta parcel with tzatziki, mushroom and butternut squash, fish and chips, steak and ale pie, lamb burger. Starters/Snacks: £5.50 to £9.50. Main Courses: £9.95 to £19.50. Puddings: £3.95 to £5.00

Free house ~ Licensees Rachel and Neil Roberts ~ Real ale ~ Bar food (12-3(during summer holidays); 6-9) ~ (01690) 720223 ~ Children welcome ~ Open 4.30-11pm(opens midday during summer holidays); 12-11 Sat, Sun; closed first three weeks of Jan ~ Bedrooms: £49.50B/£79.50B

Recommended by Mrs J Skinner, Mike and Eleanor Anderson, John and Bryony Coles, Trudie Hudson

CAREW

SN0403 MAP 6

Carew Inn

A4075, just off A477; SA70 8SL

Appealing cottagey atmosphere, pleasant gardens, good pubby food

Both gardens at this stone-built pub have terrific views. From the front, you can see down to the river, where a tidal watermill is open for afternoon summer visits, and from the back, across to the imposing ruins of Carew Castle and a remarkable 9th-c Celtic cross. It's been run by the same owner-managers for over 19 years. It has open fires in winter, and the landlady is chatty and attentive. The little panelled public bar is unpretentious but welcoming, with nice old bentwood stools at the curved counter, mixed tables and chairs on bare boards, and there's a neat area for dining. The upstairs dining rooms have been freshly decorated with colour photographs of local scenes on cream walls, sky-blue tongue-and-groove wood partitions and black leather chairs at black tables. The homely upstairs dining room has more black leather chairs at new dark wood tables (with little vases of flowers) on bare boards. Beers include Brains Rev James and Worthington, and perhaps a guest beer from a brewer such as Evan Evans on handpump; piped music, darts and outdoor pool table. The back garden has outdoor heating in summer, and it's safely enclosed for small children to play, with a colourful plastic wendy house, climbing frame, slide and other toys.

'Children welcome' means the pub says it lets children inside without any special restriction. If it allows them in, but to restricted areas such as an eating area or family room, we specify this. Places with separate restaurants often let children use them, hotels usually let them into public areas such as lounges. Some pubs impose an evening time limit – let us know if you find one earlier than 9pm.

ⓘ Served by friendly staff, the well liked bar food includes lunchtime ploughman's, sandwiches and baguettes, mussels, starters such as nachos, garlic mushrooms or smoked mackerel pâté, main courses such as steak and ale pie or curry of the day, ostrich strips fried with mushrooms, cream and madeira sauce, stuffed chicken breast wrapped in puff pastry, rib-eye steak and salmon fillet with sun-dried tomato and prawn sauce, and puddings such as syrup sponge and raspberry fool; Sunday roasts; *Starters/Snacks: £3.50 to £5.95. Main Courses: £7.95 to £18.95. Puddings: £1.95 to £4.95*

Free house ~ Licensee Mandy Scourfield ~ Real ale ~ Bar food (12-2(2.30 summer, Easter and Christmas), 6-9) ~ Restaurant ~ (01646) 651267 ~ Children welcome away from public bar ~ Dogs allowed in bar ~ Live music and BBQ Thurs and Sun during summer holidays ~ Open 10.30(11 Sun)-11(11.30 Sat)

Recommended by Colin Moore, Di and Mike Gillam, the Didler, Norma and David Hardy

COLWYN BAY   SH8478   MAP 6

Pen-y-Bryn ⓘ 🍷 🍺

B5113 Llanwrst Road, on southern outskirts; when you see the pub, turn off into Wentworth Avenue for its car park; LL29 6DD

Modern pub in great position overlooking the bay, reliable food all day, good range of drinks, obliging staff

The light and airy open-plan interior at this single-storey pub has big windows looking far across the bay and to the Great Orme. Extending around the three long sides of the bar counter, the mix of seating and well spaced tables, oriental rugs on pale stripped boards, shelves of books, welcoming coal fires, a profusion of pictures, big pot plants, careful lighting and dark green school radiators, are all typical of the pubs in this small, well received chain. Friendly interested young staff serve Flowers Original, Phoenix Brunning & Price and Thwaites Original, three or four changing guests such as Great Orme Best, Greene King Old Speckled Hen, Hook Norton Old Hooky and Weetwood Cheshire Cat on handpump, well chosen good value wines including 20 by the glass, and more than 60 malts; board games and piped music. Outside there are sturdy tables and chairs on a side terrace and a lower one by a lawn with picnic-sets.

ⓘ Served all day, the reliable and much-liked food from their changing menu could typically include substantial sandwiches, ploughman's with welsh cheeses, starters and light dishes such as charcuterie for two, wild mushroom gnocchi with sage butter and parmesan, potted rabbit and pork belly with pumpkin and ginger pickle, venison and game pie with cranberries, main courses such as butternut squash and goats cheese cannelloni, sausage and mash, twice roasted chinese pork with stir-fried vegetables and noodles, chilli beef pie, braised shoulder of lamb with mint gravy, and puddings such as apple pie and custard, vanilla panna cotta with rhubarb compote and dark chocolate brownie with chocolate sauce. *Starters/Snacks: £4.50 to £9.95. Main Courses: £8.95 to £15.95. Puddings: £4.25 to £5.25*

Brunning & Price ~ Licensees Graham Arathoon and Graham Price ~ Real ale ~ Bar food (12-9.30(9 Sun)) ~ (01492) 533360 ~ Children welcome till 7.30pm ~ Open 12-11(10.30 Sun)

Recommended by Mike and Mary Carter, Mr and Mrs Ian King, Frank Blanchard

CRESSWELL QUAY   SN0506   MAP 6

Cresselly Arms

Village signposted from A4075; SA68 0TE

Marvellously simple alehouse, with benches outside overlooking a tidal creek

This wonderfully shambolic old tavern (in the words of one reader) is beautifully positioned by the water and within the Pembrokeshire National Park. Lovers of unchanged, down-to-earth rustic pubs should surely beat a path to its door. Often full of locals (the licensees are a pillar to the local community), the two simple and comfortably old-fashioned communicating rooms have a relaxed and jaunty air, as well as red and black floor tiles, built-in wall benches, kitchen chairs and plain tables, an open fire in one room, a working Aga in the other, and a high beam-and-plank ceiling hung with lots of pictorial china. A third red-carpeted room is more conventionally furnished, with red-cushioned mate's chairs around neat tables. Worthington BB and a winter guest beer are tapped straight from the cask into glass jugs by the landlord, whose presence is a key ingredient of the atmosphere. If you time the tides right, you can arrive by boat; seats outside make the most of the view. No children.

🍴 **No food, except filled rolls on Saturday mornings.**

Free house ~ Licensees Maurice and Janet Cole ~ Real ale ~ No credit cards ~ (01646) 651210 ~ Open 12-3, 5-11; 11-11 Sat; 12-10.30 Sun

Recommended by Mark Farrington, Mrs P Bishop, the Didler, Giles and Annie Francis, Julian Distin, Blaise Vyner

CRICKHOWELL   SO2118   MAP 6

Bear ★ ♀ 🛏

Brecon Road; A40; NP8 1BW

Civilised and interesting inn with splendid, old-fashioned bar area warmed by a log fire, good and sensibly priced food, comfortable bedrooms

Readers continue to enjoy this fine old inn which is consistently praised for its thoroughly convivial atmosphere and efficient staff. Its comfortably furnished, heavily beamed lounge has fresh flowers on tables, lots of little plush-seated bentwood armchairs and handsome cushioned antique settles, and a window seat looking down on the market square. Up by the great roaring log fire, a big sofa and leather easy chairs are spread among rugs on the oak parquet floor. Other good antiques include a fine oak dresser filled with pewter mugs and brassware, a longcase clock and interesting prints. Bass, Brains Rev James, Rhymney Bitter and a guest such as Carlsberg Ansells on handpump, as well as 40 malt whiskies, vintage and late-bottled ports, unusual wines (with several by the glass) and liqueurs; disabled lavatories. It is a welcoming place to stay – some refurbished bedrooms are in a country style, though the older rooms have antiques, and breakfast is excellent; more expensive rooms have jacuzzis and four-poster beds. Readers tell us the staff are especially welcoming to dogs.

🍴 **Enjoyable bar food from a changing menu (with sandwiches and baguettes) might include starters and light meals such as chicken liver parfait, duck breast salad, chicken and leek pie, salmon fishcakes, fish pie, faggots in onion gravy, asparagus, mushroom and apricot risotto, scampi, baked cod fillet on spinach topped with tomatoes and basil, sirloin steak, and puddings like strawberry pavlova.** *Starters/Snacks: £4.50 to £8.50. Main Courses: £8.25 to £17.50. Puddings: £4.50 to £6.50*

Free house ~ Licensee Judy Hindmarsh ~ Real ale ~ Bar food (12-2.15, 6(7 Sun)-9.30) ~ Restaurant ~ (01873) 810408 ~ Children welcome (over 7 in restaurant) ~ Dogs allowed in bar and bedrooms ~ Open 11-3, 6-11; 12-3, 7-10.30 Sun ~ Bedrooms: £73S(£94B)/£90S(£99B)

Recommended by Mr and Mrs P J Fisk, Joyce and Maurice Cottrell, Roy Charlton, David Jackman, Guy Vowles, Gareth Lewis, Reg Fowle, Helen Rickwood, Sue Cane, Colin Moore, Roy Hoing, Mike and Mary Carter, Mr and Mrs C Gothard, Tom and Ruth Rees, B and M Kendall, Bob and Angela Brooks, Maurice and Gill McMahon, Simon and Mandy King, Barry and Anne, Ken and Barbara Turner, Michael Mellers, David and Lin Short

Nantyffin Cider Mill 🍴 ♀

A40/A479 NW; NP8 1LP

Foody and discerning; former drovers' inn with imaginative brasserie food and interesting drinks

You can see the old cider press that gives this pink-painted 16th-c drovers' inn its name in the high-raftered stone barn that is now a striking restaurant. There is quite some emphasis on the food, which does attract customers from quite a radius, so you will need to book. With warm grey stonework, the bar has good solid comfortable wooden tables and chairs and a woodburner in a fine broad fireplace. The counter at one end of the main open-plan area serves welsh beers such as Felinfoel Double Dragon and Rhymney

Hobby Horse on handpump, and appropriately, farm cider, as well as thoughtfully chosen new world wines (a few by the glass or half-bottle), Pimms and home-made elderflower and lemonade in summer, organic farmhouse apple juice, and hot punch and mulled wine in winter. A ramp makes disabled access easy. Tables on the lawn make the most of the rural River Usk views; they may ask to retain your credit card if you run a tab.

🍴 **Largely featuring meat and poultry, as well as lunchtime sandwiches, the seasonally changing menus of carefully presented food might include summer greens risotto, a smoked fish platter, salads, steak, ale and mushroom cobbler, provençale fish casserole, baked hake, leek and caerphilly thermidor, home-made burger in olive focaccia, liver and bacon, leek and welsh cheese tart, pork and leek sausages, rib-eye steak, and puddings such as crème brûlée and sticky toffee pudding.** *Starters/Snacks: £4.75 to £7.95. Main Courses: £9.50 to £18.95. Puddings: £5.25 to £5.50*

Free house ~ Licensees Vic and Ann Williams ~ Real ale ~ Bar food (12-3, 6(7 Sun)-9) ~ Restaurant ~ (01873) 810775 ~ Children welcome ~ Dogs allowed in bar ~ Open 12-3, 6-11(7-10.30 Sun); closed Mon (except bank hols), and Sun evening Oct-Mar

Recommended by Simon Daws, Rodney and Norma Stubington, Gareth Lewis, Mike and Mary Carter, Guy Vowles, Michael Mellers, Steve and Liz Tilley

EAST ABERTHAW   ST0366   MAP 6

Blue Anchor 🍺

B4265; CF62 3DD

Ancient thatched pub with five real ales

It's the appealing warren of little rooms and cosy corners in this character-laden, 600-year-old tavern that provide its appeal. The building has massive walls, low-beamed rooms and tiny doorways, with open fires everywhere, including one in an inglenook with antique oak seats built into its stripped stonework. Other seats and tables are worked into a series of chatty little alcoves, and the more open front bar still has an ancient lime-ash floor. Brains Bitter, Theakstons Old Peculier, Wadworths 6X and Wye Valley Hereford Pale Ale on handpump, alongside a changing guest, perhaps from Cottage; games machine. Rustic seats shelter peacefully among tubs and troughs of flowers outside, with more stone tables on a newer terrace. The pub can get very full in the evenings and on summer weekends, and it's used as a base by a couple of local motorbike clubs. From here a path leads to the shingly flats of the estuary.

🍴 **Bar food includes baguettes, soup of the day, gammon, egg and pineapple, scampi, beef stew, red onion and goats cheese tart, daily specials, and puddings such as baked vanilla cheesecake with rum bananas and chocolate brownie.** *Starters/Snacks: £3.75 to £5.50. Main Courses: £7.95 to £10.95. Puddings: £3.95*

Free house ~ Licensee Jeremy Coleman ~ Real ale ~ Bar food (12.30-2.30, 6-9; not Sun evening) ~ Restaurant ~ (01446) 750329 ~ Children welcome ~ Dogs allowed in bar ~ Open 11-11; 12-10.30 Sun

Recommended by H L Dennis, Prof Kenneth Surin, R T and J C Moggridge

FELINFACH   SO0933   MAP 6

Griffin 🍽 🍷 🍺 🛏

A470 NE of Brecon; LD3 0UB

WALES DINING PUB OF THE YEAR

A classy dining pub for enjoying good, unpretentious cooking featuring lots of home-grown vegetables; upbeat rustic décor, nice bedrooms

A tremendously good all-rounder, this friendly, accomplished dining pub pays close attention to getting every aspect of its business just right, and looks after its guests extremely well. They stock a terrific range of drinks, serve great, carefully sourced food, care about the children and dogs that visit them and set a relaxed atmosphere; this is a lovely place to stay – nothing is missed. The back bar is quite pubby in an up-to-date way: three leather sofas sit around a low table on pitted quarry tiles, by a high slate hearth with a log fire, and behind them mixed stripped seats around scrubbed kitchen tables on bare boards, and a bright blue-and-ochre colour scheme, with some modern prints. The acoustics are pretty lively, due to so much bare flooring and uncurtained windows; maybe piped radio. The two smallish front dining rooms that link through to the back bar are attractive: on the left, mixed dining chairs around mainly stripped tables on flagstones, and white-painted rough stone walls, with a cream-coloured Aga in a big stripped-stone embrasure; on the right, similar furniture on bare boards, big modern prints on terracotta walls and smart dark curtains. Efficient staff serve a fine array of drinks, including a thoughtful choice of wines (with 20 by the glass and carafe), welsh spirits, cocktails, an award-winning local bottled cider, locally sourced apple juice, unusual continental and local bottled beers, sherries and Breconshire Bishop Gower's Well, Otley O1, Tomos Watkins Cwrw Braf, Wye Valley Bitter, with a guest such as Tomos Watkins OSB, on handpump. Good wheelchair access and outside tables. Bedrooms are comfortable and tastefully decorated, and the hearty breakfasts nicely informal: you make your own toast on the Aga and help yourself to home-made marmalade and jam. They are particularly welcoming to visiting dogs (giving them biscuits and bowls of water).

📕 Using organic produce from the pub's own kitchen garden (from which the surplus is often for sale) and eggs from their own hens, not cheap but consistently good food from the lunch and evening menus might include ploughman's, warm foie gras with figs, red wine caramel and toasted onion brioche, soused herring with potato and beetroot salad, smoked haddock, sweetcorn and pancetta chowder, bass with potato and garlic purée, oxtail and mushrooms, grey mullet with borlotti bean casserole, rib-eye beef with onion confit and purée, duck breast with peppercorn sauce, puddings such as spiced prune parkin and toasted almond cream and vanilla crème brûlée with shortbread and mulled wine, and a british cheeseboard. *Starters/Snacks: £5.00 to £8.00. Main Courses: £9.00 to £15.00. Puddings: £6.00*

Free house ~ Licensees Charles and Edmund Inkin and Julie Bell ~ Real ale ~ Bar food (12-2.30, 6-9) ~ Restaurant ~ (01874) 620111 ~ Children welcome ~ Dogs welcome ~ Live music alternate Sun lunchtimes ~ Open 11.30-11pm; closed one week in Jan ~ Bedrooms: £85B/£115B

Recommended by James Paterson, Rodney and Norma Stubington, Simon Daws, MLR, K Hunt, M Smith, Mike and Mary Carter, David and Cathrine Whiting, G M Benson, Dr Kevan Tucker, R T and J C Moggridge

GRESFORD
SJ3453   MAP 6

Pant-yr-Ochain 🍽 🍷 🍺

Off A483 on N edge of Wrexham: at roundabout take A5156 (A534) towards Nantwich, then first left towards the Flash; LL12 8TY

Thoughtfully run, gently refined dining pub with rooms, good food all day, very wide range of drinks, pretty lakeside garden

For several readers this 16th-c former country house is their favourite pub, with one telling us they feel it's the best in the Brunning & Price chain in Wales, and another that it's the best Brunning & Price in the UK. As well as thoughtfully prepared food, they have a terrific range of drinks that includes Flowers Original, Timothy Taylors Landlord and Phoenix Brunning & Price Original and a couple of guests from brewers such as Derby and Three Tuns, a good range of decent wines (strong on upfront new world ones), with 27 by the glass, and around 100 malt whiskies. It has been nicely refurbished inside: the light and airy rooms are stylishly decorated, with a wide range of interesting prints and bric-a-brac on walls and on shelves, and a good mix of individually chosen country furnishings, including comfortable seats for relaxing as well as more upright ones for eating, and there's a recently rebuilt conservatory as well as a good open fire; one area is set out as a library, with floor-to-ceiling bookshelves. Disabled access is good. The particularly charming garden has solid wooden furniture overlooking a pretty lake frequented by waterfowl, mature trees and shrubs, lovely herbaceous borders and thriving box-edged herb beds.

📕 Good food from a well balanced daily changing menu, and using free-range eggs and chicken, includes sandwiches, ploughman's, starters and lighter choices such as mushroom and tarragon soup, seared scallops with carrot cumin purée, smoked haddock and spinach risotto with poached egg, main courses such as aubergine, squash and almond tagine with apricot couscous and fried okra, steak, ale and mushroom pie, pork and leek sausages, home-made burger, honey and sesame chicken breast with mushroom and ginger noodle broth and coriander dumplings, fish and chips, and puddings such as berry panna cotta with berry compote and bread and butter pudding. *Starters/Snacks: £4.50 to £7.75. Main Courses: £8.75 to £16.95. Puddings: £4.85 to £5.50*

Brunning & Price ~ Licensee James Meakin ~ Real ale ~ Bar food (12-9.30(9 Sun)) ~ (01978) 853525 ~ Children welcome ~ Dogs allowed in bar ~ Open 12-11(10.30 Sun)

Recommended by Peter and Josie Fawcett, Adair Cameron, Bruce and Sharon Eden, Roger and Anne Newbury, Clive Watkin, David Hunt, Mr and Mrs D Hammond, Mike Horgan, Maurice and Gill McMahon

HAY-ON-WYE   SO2242   MAP 6

Blue Boar

Castle Street/Oxford Road; HR3 5DF

Generous home cooking in dual-personality pub – low-lit medieval bar, light and airy modern dining area

The particularly friendly new licensees and the irregular shape of the bar with its cosy corners, its candlelight or shaded table lamps, squared dark ply panelling and good winter fire in the handsome Edwardian fireplace, make for a relaxed atmosphere at this genuinely characterful pub. There are pews, country chairs and stools at the counter, which has Bass, Blue Boar (which is Hydes IPA, named for the pub), Flowers Original, Timothy Taylors Landlord, a good choice of wines by the glass and whiskies, and bottled Dunkerton's organic cider and perry; good service. Quite different in colour and mood, the long open café dining room is flooded with light from big sash windows, fresh cheery décor and bright tablecloths. There's a fire here too, and local artwork for sale; good coffees and teas; interesting piped music or Radio Four. The secluded, tree-shaded garden has tables for diners.

🍴 Enjoyable bar food typically includes sandwiches, soup of the day, moules marinière, baked camembert with gherkins and spicy sausage, chicken and leek pie, toulouse sausages on tomato, caper and red onion salad with crusty bread, summer pudding, apple pie and a cheeseboard. They also do breakfasts first thing. *Starters/Snacks: £3.95 to £9.95. Main Courses: £8.95 to £14.95. Puddings: £4.50*

Free house ~ Licensees John, Lucy and Alex Golsworthy ~ Real ale ~ Bar food (9-9(9.30 weekends)) ~ (01497) 820884 ~ Children welcome ~ Dogs welcome ~ Open 9-11

Recommended by Reg Fowle, Helen Rickwood, Michael Butler, Mike and Eleanor Anderson, Andy Lickfold, Sue Demont, Tim Barrow, David Howe, Brian and Jacky Wilson

LITTLE HAVEN   SM8512   MAP 6

St Brides Inn

St Brides Road – in village itself, not St Brides hamlet further W; SA62 3UN

Cheerful seaside inn, tasty food and a log fire

Well positioned, just 20 metres from the Pembrokeshire Coast Path, this quiet little place has a sheltered, suntrap, terraced garden across the road with troughs of colourful plants. There's a neat stripped-stone bar and linking carpeted dining area, and a good log fire. Banks's and Marstons Pedigree are kept on handpump, and several malt whiskies are available. A curious well in a back corner grotto is thought to be partly Roman; piped music and TV. The two bright bedrooms (in a separate building) have pine furniture; we would welcome reports from readers who stay here.

🍴 As well as sandwiches and ploughman's, reasonably priced bar food might include spiced salmon and prawn fishcakes with sweet chilli dip, chicken liver pâté, filo parcels stuffed with spinach, mushrooms and pine nuts with red pepper sauce, rib-eye steak, and local seafood such as dressed crab, crab thermidor, mackerel, pollack and battered cod, with puddings such as Baileys cheesecake and limoncello tartufo. They may barbecue outside on nice days. *Starters/Snacks: £4.10 to £5.95. Main Courses: £8.25 to £15.25. Puddings: £4.25 to £4.50*

Marstons ~ Lease Keith Gardham ~ Real ale ~ Bar food (12-2, 6-9) ~ Restaurant ~ No credit cards ~ (01437) 781266 ~ Children welcome ~ Dogs allowed in bar ~ Open 9am-midnight in summer; 11.30-3, 6-11 in winter; closed Mon lunchtime and Sun evening in winter ~ Bedrooms: £50S/£70S
Recommended by Pat Crabb

LLANARMON DYFFRYN CEIRIOG   SJ1532   MAP 6

Hand 🛏

On B4500 from Chirk; LL20 7LD

Comfortable rural hotel in a remote valley; cosy low-beamed bar area, good bedrooms

At the heart of the upper Ceiriog Valley and set against the backdrop of the Berwyn Mountains, this peaceful inn and former farmhouse is a delightful place to stay: 'The only thing I could hear from my bed was an owl' commented one reader. Happy and welcoming staff help towards the warm atmosphere. The black-beamed, carpeted bar on the left of the broad-flagstoned entrance hall has a hearty log fire in its inglenook fireplace, a mixture of chairs and settles, and old prints on its cream walls, with bar stools along the modern bar counter, which has Weetwood Cheshire Cat and a guest such as Stonehouse Station Bitter on handpump, several malt whiskies and reasonably priced wines by the glass. Round the corner is the largely stripped-stone dining room, with a woodburning stove and carpeted floor; TV, darts and pool in games room. Bedrooms are attractive and spacious, and breakfasts are very satisfying; the residents' lounge on the right is comfortable and attractive. There are tables out on a crazy-paved front terrace, with more in the garden, which has flower beds around another sheltered terrace.

🍴 Besides lunchtime sandwiches and ploughman's, dishes on a seasonally changing menu using named local suppliers might include tomato and chilli risotto, welsh cakes with welsh rarebit and home-made piccalilli, lasagne, steak baguette, sausage and mash, gammon pie, seared duck breast on confit duck risotto with pink peppercorn sauce, braised lamb with black pudding, wild mushrooms and pancetta, salmon fillet with sautéed leeks and caper berries, and puddings such as chocolate crème brûlée with wild berry compote and baked vanilla cheesecake with mango coulis and honeycomb ice-cream. *Starters/Snacks: £4.50 to £7.00. Main Courses: £13.00 to £19.00. Puddings: £3.50 to £5.50*

Free house ~ Licensees Gaynor and Martin de Luchi ~ Bar food (12-2.20(12.30-2.45 Sun), 6.30—8.45) ~ Restaurant ~ (01691) 600666 ~ Children welcome ~ Dogs welcome ~ Open 11(12 Sun)-11(12.30 Sat) ~ Bedrooms: £65B/£110B
Recommended by K and J Whitehead, James Barnes, Mike and Mary Carter, John and Joan Nash, Lois Dyer, Clive Watkin, BOB, Stuart Pugh, Simon Daws

LLANBERIS   SH6655   MAP 6

Pen-y-Gwryd 🛏

Nant Gwynant; at junction of A498 and A4086, ie across mountains from Llanberis – OS Sheet 115 map reference 660558; LL55 4NT

In the hands of the same family since 1947, an illustrious favourite with the mountain fraternity, with a slightly eccentric but cheerily simple atmosphere

Mentioned in the Everest Museum in Darjeeling, this long-established climbers' haunt, isolated among the high mountains of Snowdonia, was used as a training base for the 1953 Everest team. Their fading signatures can still be made out, scrawled on the ceiling, and among the memorabilia is the rope that connected Hilary and Tenzing on top of the mountain. One snug little room in the homely slate-floored log cabin bar has built-in wall benches and sturdy country chairs. From here you can look out on the surrounding mountain landscape, including to precipitous Moel Siabod beyond the lake opposite. A smaller room has a worthy collection of illustrious boots from famous climbs, and a cosy panelled smoke room has more fascinating climbing mementoes and equipment; darts, pool, board games and table tennis. Purple Moose Cwrw Glaslyn and Cwrw Madogs are on handpump and they've several malts. Staying here in the comfortable but basic bedrooms can be quite an experience, and the excellent, traditional breakfast is served at 8.30am (they may serve earlier but certainly not after the breakfast gong); dogs £2 a night. The inn has its own chapel (built for the millennium and dedicated by the Archbishop of Wales), sauna and outdoor natural pool, and the garden overlooks a lake. More reports please.

⊞ The short choice of simple, good-value home-made lunchtime bar food (you order it through a hatch) might include sandwiches, soup, chicken liver pâté, a platter of cold meats, roast lamb or welsh black beef, slow-braised pork, salmon steak or cheese and onion tart; puddings such as chocolate pudding or apple and blackberry pie. The five-course fixed-price meal in the evening restaurant, presenting a similarly hearty range of fare, is signalled by a gong at 7.30pm – if you're late, you'll miss it, and there's no evening bar food. *Starters/Snacks: £4.00 to £7.00. Main Courses: £6.00 to £9.00. Puddings: £2.00 to £4.00*

Free house ~ Licensee Jane Pullee ~ Real ale ~ Bar food (lunchtimes only) ~ (01286) 870211 ~ Children welcome but not in private bar after dinner ~ Dogs allowed in bar and bedrooms ~ Open 11-11; closed all Nov-Dec, and mid-week Jan-Feb ~ Bedrooms: £40/£80(£96B)

Recommended by John and Enid Morris, Neil and Brenda Skidmore, W N F Boughey, Tim Maddison, John and Joan Nash, Dr J Barrie Jones, Giles Smith, Sandra Kiely

LLANDUDNO JUNCTION   SH8180   MAP 6

Queens Head ⊕ ♀

Glanwydden; heading towards Llandudno on B5115 from Colwyn Bay, turn left into Llanrhos Road at roundabout as you enter the Penrhyn Bay speed limit; Glanwydden is signposted as the first left turn off this; LL31 9JP

Food all day at weekends at this comfortably modern dining pub

Despite the emphasis on dining at this big friendly place, you are equally welcome if you're just popping in for a drink, and you'll find Adnams and a guest or two such as Great Orme·Best on handpump, as well as decent wines (including some unusual ones and 11 by the glass), several malt whiskies and good coffee. The spacious modern lounge bar – partly divided by a white wall of broad arches – has brown plush wall banquettes and windsor chairs around neat black tables, and there's a little public bar; unobtrusive piped music. There's an outdoor seating area, available for smokers. Northern Snowdonia is in easy reach, and you can rent the pretty stone cottage (which sleeps two) across the road.

⊞ Dishes from the well presented and efficiently served menu include sandwiches, fish soup, smoked duck breast with apple chutney, fried brie with cranberry and orange chutney, parma ham and melon with pickled pineapple jam, jamaican chicken curry, liver and bacon, home-made burger, steak on ciabatta, butternut squash risotto, fish and chips, baked cod topped with welsh rarebit with creamy leeks, seafood vol-au-vent, game pie and local pheasant with cranberry and port wine jus and bread sauce; good Sunday roast. *Starters/Snacks: £4.35 to £7.50. Main Courses: £9.95 to £21.95. Puddings: £4.75*

Free house ~ Licensees Robert and Sally Cureton ~ Real ale ~ Bar food (12-2, 6-9; 12-9 Sat, Sun) ~ Restaurant ~ (01492) 546570 ~ Children welcome ~ Open 11-3, 6-11; 11.30-11 Sat; 11.30-10.30 Sun

Recommended by Roger Noyes, Mike Proctor, Owen Davies, Dave Johnson, Heather McQuillan, M J Winterton, Joan E Hilditch

---

Bedroom prices normally include full english breakfast, VAT and any inclusive service charge that we know of. Prices before the '/' are for single rooms, after for two people in double or twin (B includes a private bath, S a private shower). If there is no '/', the prices are only for twin or double rooms (as far as we know there are no singles).

LLANELIAN-YN-RHOS
SH8676 MAP 6

White Lion
Signed off A5830 (shown as B5383 on some maps) and B5381, S of Colwyn Bay; LL29 8YA

Pretty pub with friendly staff, pleasantly traditional bar and roomy dining area

This cheery village inn comprises two distinct parts, each with its own personality, linked by a broad flight of steps. Up at the top is a neat and very spacious dining area, while down at the other end is a traditional old bar, with antique high-backed settles angling snugly around a big fireplace, and flagstones by the counter where they serve Marstons Burton and Pedigree and a guest from a brewer such as Purple Moose; on the left, another dining area has jugs hanging from the beams and teapots above the window. Prompt service, good wine list with several by the glass, and malt whiskies; piped music. There are tables in an attractive courtyard (also used for parking) next to the church. More up-to-date reports please, especially on the food.

🍴 **Food includes sandwiches, baguettes and ciabattas, pâté, garlic mushrooms, black pudding and smoked bacon salad, steak and kidney pie, daily roast, home-made cheeseburger, chicken curry, chicken breast topped with smoked bacon, cheese and mushrooms in cider, rosemary and sage sauce, scampi, fish stew, battered hake and chips, macaroni cheese and steaks.** *Starters/Snacks: £4.50 to £6.25. Main Courses: £7.50 to £15.99. Puddings: £2.95 to £5.25*

Free house ~ Licensee Simon Cole ~ Real ale ~ Bar food (12-2, 6-9; 12-2.30, 6-10.30 Sun) ~ Restaurant ~ (01492) 515807 ~ Live jazz every Tues evening, bluegrass Weds ~ Open 12-3, 6-11(midnight Sat); 12-4, 6-10.30 Sun; closed Mon except bank hols
Recommended by Michael and Jenny Back, Noel Grundy, Mr and Mrs B Hobden

LLANFERRES
SJ1860 MAP 6

Druid
A494 Mold—Ruthin; CH7 5SN

Warmly welcoming 17th-c inn with beams, antique settles and a log fire in the bar; well liked food and wonderful views

There are superb hill walks around here, along the Offa's Dyke Path and up to the summit of Moel Famau. From tables outside at the front and from the broad bay window in the civilised, smallish plush lounge, you get choice views of the Alyn Valley and the Clwydian Hills. The hills are also in sight from the bigger beamed back bar, with its two handsome antique oak settles and pleasant mix of more modern furnishings. There's a quarry-tiled area by the log fire, and a three-legged cat, Chu. Marstons Burton and a couple of guests from breweries such as Jennings and Ringwood are on handpump alongside an extensive array of malt whiskies. A games room has darts and pool, along with board games; piped music, TV.

🍴 **Readers have commented on the wide choice of food (which you can eat in the bar or restaurant), which might feature several soups, filled baps, steak and ale pie, poached cod loin with parmesan crust, leek and mushroom pie, grilled leg of welsh lamb, sirloin steak with wild mushroom sauce, or mushrooms stuffed with stilton; daily specials; children's menu.** *Starters/Snacks: £3.95 to £5.95. Main Courses: £9.95 to £19.95. Puddings: £4.25*

Union Pub Company ~ Lease James Dolan ~ Real ale ~ Bar food (12-3, 6-9; 12-9 Thurs-Sun and bank hols) ~ Restaurant ~ (01352) 810225 ~ Children welcome ~ Dogs allowed in bar and bedrooms ~ Open 12-3, 5.30-11; 12-11 Thurs-Sat and bank hols; 12-10.30 Sun ~ Bedrooms: £48S/£70S
Recommended by Jacqui Atlas, KC, Anne Morgan, Maurice and Gill McMahon

---

If you have to cancel a reservation for a bedroom or restaurant, please telephone or write to warn them. You may lose your deposit if you've paid one.

LLANFRYNACH   SO0725   MAP 6

White Swan ♀

Village signposted from B4558, off A40 E of Brecon – take second turn to village, which is also signed to pub; LD3 7BZ

Comfortably upmarket country dining pub with a pretty terrace

The original part of the beamed bar at this cosy place has stripped stone and flagstones, with sturdy oak tables and nice carver chairs in a polished country-kitchen style, a woodburning stove, and leather sofas and armchairs in groups around low tables. On handpump are Brains Bitter, Breconshire Brecon County and Rhymney Bitter; good wines and coffees; piped music. The greater part of the building, however, consists of the apricot-walled high-ceilinged extension which is light and airy, with bare boards and different sets of chairs around each table. The charming secluded back terrace has stone and wood tables with the choice of sun or shade, and is attractively divided into sections by low plantings and climbing shrubs. From here, there are plenty of undemanding saunters along the towpath of the Monmouthshire and Brecon Canal or more energetic hikes up the main Brecon Beacons summits.

⊞ The good food is very much the centre of attention, with changing lunch menus and à la carte evening fare. As well as ploughman's, soup and baguette and salads, dishes might include pigeon breast wrapped in creamed leeks and parma ham in puff pastry with red wine and chilli dressing, purple sprouting, spinach and cheese tart, mushrooms stuffed with mediterranean vegetables with welsh rarebit, duck breast on sauté sugar snaps, spring onion and asparagus, beef and venison pie with rosemary roasted potato, sauté calves liver and bacon, cajun spiced chicken breast with roast pepper risotto and spicy tomato juice, and puddings such as strawberry and rhubarb crumble with strawberry and vanilla panna cotta and strawberry yoghurt ice-cream and chilled lemon tart with lime mousse and lemon curd ice-cream with meringue nest. *Starters/Snacks: £4.95 to £6.95. Main Courses: £10.25 to £15.95. Puddings: £5.00 to £5.65*

Free house ~ Licensee Richard Griffiths ~ Real ale ~ Bar food (12-2(2.30 Sun), 7-9(8.30 Sun)) ~ Restaurant ~ (01874) 665276 ~ Children welcome (not Sat evening in restaurant) ~ Open 11.30-3, 6.30-11.30(10.30 Sun); closed Mon, Tues and first two weeks in Jan

Recommended by the Brewers, David and Cathrine Whiting, Julia and Richard Tredgett, John and Joan Nash, Dr Kevan Tucker, G M Benson

LLANGOLLEN   SJ2142   MAP 6

Corn Mill ⊞ ♀ ◀

Dee Lane, very narrow lane off Castle Street (A539) just S of bridge; nearby parking can be tricky, may be best to use public park on Parade Street/East Street and walk; LL20 8PN

Excellent on all counts, with personable young staff, super food all day, good beers, and a fascinating riverside building

Jutting over the River Dee, which rushes over its rocky bed, this admirable all-rounder is housed in a restored mill. An area with decking and teak tables and chairs looks across the river to the steam trains puffing away at the nearby station and maybe a horse-drawn barge on the Llangollen Canal. Quite a bit of the mill machinery remains – most obviously the great waterwheel, still turning – but the place has been interestingly refitted with pale pine flooring on stout beams, a striking open stairway with gleaming timber and tensioned steel rails, and mainly stripped-stone walls. A bustling chatty atmosphere greets you, with quick service from plenty of pleasant young staff, good-sized dining tables, big rugs, thoughtfully chosen pictures (many to do with water) and lots of pot plants. One of the two serving bars, away from the water, has a much more local feel, with pews on dark slate flagstones, daily papers, and regulars on the bar stools. As well as Phoenix Brunning & Price, they have a great range of drinks, with four guest ales from brewers such as Brimstage, Conway, Derby and Facers, around 50 sensibly priced malt whiskies and a decent wine choice. The pub can get busy, so it might be worth booking if you're planning to eat.

🏠 Good food – served all day – from a daily changing menu includes sandwiches, ploughman's, soup, lighter dishes like wild mushrooms on toast or smoked haddock chowder, and main courses such as braised shoulder of lamb, good fishcakes, local trout with braised fennel, or butternut squash risotto; puddings like mango and coconut cheesecake or bara brith bread and butter pudding; welsh and english cheeseboard. *Starters/Snacks: £4.50 to £9.25. Main Courses: £8.75 to £16.50. Puddings: £4.95 to £5.25*

Brunning & Price ~ Licensee Andrew Barker ~ Real ale ~ Bar food (12-9.30(9 Sun)) ~ (01978) 869555 ~ Children welcome ~ Open 12-11(10.30 Sun)

Recommended by Bruce and Sharon Eden, Earl and Chris Pick, Bob and Laura Brock, Neil Whitehead, Victoria Anderson, Michael Butler, Brian Brooks, Tony and Wendy Hobden, Clive Watkin, John and Verna Aspinall, Phil and Jane Hodson, Peter and Josie Fawcett

MAENTWROG
SH6640   MAP 6

Grapes
A496; village signed from A470; LL41 4HN

Lively inn with good mix of customers, pleasant garden views; accommodation

The cheery new landlord at this rambling old inn is looking forward to introducing an open mike night on Friday as a showcase for the area's local musicians. It's already a lively place, with the pubic bar often frequented by welsh-speaking locals – you may even be addressed in welsh when they greet you. Four beers on handpump are all from Evan Evans – Best, Cwrw, Warrior and a changing monthly ale. All three bars are partly filled with stripped pitch-pine pews, settles, pillars and carvings, mostly salvaged from chapels; elsewhere are soft furnishings. Two woodburning stoves are on the go in winter – there's one in the great hearth of the restaurant; piped music, darts; disabled lavatories. From the good-sized conservatory you can see trains on the Ffestiniog Railway puffing through the wood, beyond the pleasant back terrace and walled garden. More reports please – we've had none on the bedrooms since recent refurbishment.

🍴 The seasonal menu includes smoked mackerel with gooseberry purée, spicy barbecue ribs, pheasant and walnut salad, chicken kiev with blue cheese sauce, lamb shank with rosemary, local catch of the day, chickpea and aubergine curry with chilli cornbread, grilled halloumi salad, and puddings such as raspberry cheesecake and apple and gooseberry bread and butter pudding. *Starters/Snacks: £4.50 to £6.50. Main Courses: £8.95 to £15.95. Puddings: £4.50 to £4.75*

Evan Evans ~ Manager Steven Davies ~ Real ale ~ Bar food (12-2.30, 6-9) ~ Restaurant ~ (01766) 590208 ~ Children welcome ~ Dogs welcome ~ Live music alternate Sat, open mike Fri ~ Open 11-midnight ~ Bedrooms: £60B/£98B

Recommended by Martin Owen, Michelle Jones

MOLD
SJ2465   MAP 6

Glasfryn 🍴 �ू 🍺
N of the centre on Raikes Lane (parallel to the A5119), just past the well signposted Theatr Clwyd; CH7 6LR

Open-plan bistro-style pub with inventive, upmarket food available all day, nice décor, wide drinks' choice

In winter, the roaring fire between two main high-ceilinged rooms at this excellent Brunning & Price is a welcome sight. This is a lively place run with considerable verve by enthusiastic and friendly staff. Its open-plan interior feels spacious but there are plenty of nice quiet corners. Decorated in this fine chain's successful style, it has a mix of informal, attractive, country furnishings on warm-toned rugs on bare boards, and plenty of closely hung pictures. Besides 25 wines by the glass, local apple juice, farm cider and around 100 whiskies, they've 11 beers on handpump, with Facers Flintshire, Flowers Original, Greene King IPA and Purple Moose Snowdonia, alongside swiftly changing guests such as Greene King Abbot, Ruddles County and Titanic Lifeboat. On warm days, the large terrace in front of the pub makes an idyllic place to sit out by the wooden tables – you get sweeping views of the Clwydian Hills. Theatr Clwyd is just across the road.

🍴 From a daily changing menu, the full choice of good, well prepared food is available all day and includes sandwiches, ploughman's, soup, starters and lighter dishes like sticky pork ribs or smoked salmon and avocado salad, and main courses such as beer-battered haddock, braised shoulder of lamb, or smoked haddock and salmon fishcakes; puddings such as lemon posset or dark chocolate tart. *Starters/Snacks: £4.95 to £8.25. Main Courses: £9.25 to £15.95. Puddings: £4.85 to £5.25*

Brunning & Price ~ Licensee James Meakin ~ Real ale ~ Bar food (12-9.30(9 Sun)) ~ (01352) 750500 ~ Children welcome away from bar ~ Dogs allowed in bar ~ Open 11.30-11; 12-10.30 Sun

Recommended by Bruce and Sharon Eden, Brian Brooks, Clive Watkin, Steve Whalley, Chris Flynn, Wendy Jones, Dave Braisted, Peter and Josie Fawcett

MONKNASH   SS9170   MAP 6

Plough & Harrow 🍺

Signposted Marcross, Broughton off B4265 St Brides Major—Llantwit Major – turn left at end of Water Street; OS Sheet 170 map reference 920706; CF71 7QQ

Old building full of history and character, with a good choice of real ales

Enchantingly ancient-feeling and part of a former monastic grange – the walls and dovecote of which are still in evidence – this makes the ideal stopping point if you're visiting the spectacular stretch of coastal cliffs nearby, and you can walk from here to the lighthouse at Nash Point. Built with massively thick stone walls, the dimly lit unspoilt main bar used to be the scriptures room and mortuary. The heavily black-beamed ceiling has ancient ham hooks, an intriguing arched doorway to the back, and a comfortably informal mix of furnishings that includes three fine stripped pine settles on the broad flagstones. There's a log fire in a huge fireplace with a side bread oven large enough to feed a village. The room on the left has lots of Wick Rugby Club memorabilia (it's their club room); daily papers, piped music and darts. It can get crowded at weekends, when it's popular with families (they do children's helpings). Up to five real ales on handpump or tapped from the cask include Bass and Wye Valley HPA alongside two or three changing guests. They also have a good range of local farm cider and welsh and malt whiskies; helpful service from knowledgeable staff. There are picnic-sets in the front garden (with a covered area available to smokers), which has a boules pitch, and they hold barbecues out here in summer. Dogs are welcome in the bar – but not while food is being served.

🍴 Bar food includes sandwiches and dishes such as faggots and mushy peas, ham, egg and chips, butternut squash casserole, salmon and coriander fishcakes, and puddings such as lemon cheesecake and chocolate truffle torte. *Starters/Snacks: £3.00 to £5.95. Main Courses: £6.95 to £14.95. Puddings: £3.95*

Free house ~ Licensee Gareth Davies ~ Real ale ~ Bar food (12-2.30(5 Sat), 6-9; not Sun evening) ~ Restaurant ~ (01656) 890209 ~ Children welcome until 9pm (must be accompanied in bar) ~ Live music Sat evening ~ Open 12-11

Recommended by the Brewers, Prof Kenneth Surin

NEWPORT   SN0539   MAP 6

Golden Lion 🛏

East Street (A487); SA42 0SY

Nicely redone, friendly local, with tasty food and pleasant staff

Some imaginative refurbishments at this pleasant country hotel have cleverly kept a traditional pubby bar alongside the stylish dining room, and it's now a much nicer place to stay. The bar has a welcoming local atmosphere in its cosy series of beamed rooms, some with distinctive old settles, and locally brewed Gwaun Valley Light Ale and a couple of guests such as Black Sheep Golden Sheep and Houston Blonde Bombshell on handpump; pool, darts, juke box, TV and games machine. The revamped dining room has elegant blond wood oak furniture, whitewashed walls and potted plants. There are tables outside at the front and in a side garden; good disabled access and facilities.

🍴 **Enjoyable, carefully presented food includes lunchtime sandwiches, ploughman's and pizzas, as well as starters such as smoked mackerel with citrus mayonnaise, spring rolls with sweet chilli dip, antipasti, main courses such as haddock in coriander batter, pork tenderloin with wholegrain mustard and chorizo sauce, thai chicken, steak and ale pie, roasted mediterranean vegetables with wild rice, home-made burgers, steaks, and puddings such as eton mess, chocolate truffle and apple and mixed berry crumble with almond and coconut topping.** *Starters/Snacks: £4.25 to £7.95. Main Courses: £7.95 to £21.95. Puddings: £4.50 to £7.95*

Free house ~ Licensee Daron Paish ~ Real ale ~ Bar food (12-2.30(2 winter), 6-9) ~ Restaurant ~ (01239) 820321 ~ Children welcome ~ Dogs allowed in bar ~ Open midday-2am ~ Bedrooms: £60B/£85B

Recommended by Ellie O'Mahoney, Brian and Jacky Wilson, R T and J C Moggridge, M E and F J Thomasson

OLD RADNOR   SO2459   MAP 6

Harp 🍴 🛏

Village signposted off A44 Kington—New Radnor in Walton; LD8 2RH

Delightfully placed inn with cottagey bar and comfortable bedrooms; tasty food

One couple visiting this lovely old inn found the public bar full of happy farmers who'd just finished their yearly lambing. Loved equally by locals and tourists, it has high-backed settles, an antique reader's chair and other elderly chairs around a log fire; board games, cribbage. The snug slate-floored lounge has a handsome curved antique settle, a log fire in a fine inglenook, and lots of local books and guides for residents; a dining area is off to the right. They have two changing real ales from brewers such as Hobsons and Wye Valley, five farm ciders and perries, local apple juice and several malt whiskies, and hold a beer and cider festival in June; friendly, helpful service. The pub is in a glorious hilltop position at the end of a lane in a tiny village, and tables on the grassy area beneath a sycamore tree look across to the high massif of Radnor Forest. The impressive village church is worth a look for its interesting early organ case (Britain's oldest), fine rood screen and ancient font. New licensees were taking over just as we went to press, so do please let us know what you think of the new regime.

🍴 **Featuring produce from the publicans' own garden and other carefully sourced ingredients, including lamb from the local butcher's own flock, the well liked food typically includes Saturday lunchtime baguettes, soups, starters like venison and juniper berry terrine or parma ham with rocket and mango, and main courses such as welsh black rump steak, fried haddock with puy lentils, cassoulet, duck breast, and spinach and ricotta cannelloni; puddings such as chocolate brownie or apple and pear crumble.** *Starters/Snacks: £4.25 to £6.50. Main Courses: £8.95 to £15.95. Puddings: £4.95 to £5.95*

Free house ~ Licensees Chris Ireland and Angela Lyne ~ Real ale ~ Bar food (12-2 Sat, Sun; 6-9) ~ Restaurant ~ (01544) 350655 ~ Children welcome ~ Dogs allowed in bar ~ Open 6-11; 12-3, 6-11 Sat, Sun; closed weekday lunchtimes, all day Mon (except bank hols) ~ Bedrooms: £45B/£75B

Recommended by Chris Wall

Several well known guide books make establishments pay for entry, either directly or as a fee for inspection. These fees can run to many hundreds of pounds. We do not. Unlike other guides, we never take payment for entries. We never accept a free meal, free drink, or any other freebie from a pub. We do not accept any sponsorship – let alone from commercial schemes linked to the pub trade. All our entries depend solely on merit.

OVERTON BRIDGE   SJ3542 MAP 6

Cross Foxes 🍴 ☂

A539 W of Overton, near Erbistock; LL13 0DR

Terrific river views from well run 18th-c coaching inn with good food and extensive drinks' range

The River Dee sweeps past below this well placed Brunning & Price pub. One light and airy dining room has a curved wall of great big sash windows with really lovely views over the water, as do good oak chairs and tables on a raised terrace; picnic-sets down on a lawn are even closer to the water. The ancient low-beamed bar, with its red tiled floor, dark timbers, a warm fire in the big inglenook and built-in old pews, is more traditional than you'd usually expect from this small chain, though the characteristic turkey rugs and frame-to-frame pictures are present, as they are in the dining areas. Friendly competent staff serve Brakspear, Jennings Cumberland and a couple of guests such as Ringwood Fortyniner and Wychwood Hobgoblin from handpumps, 51 malts, an excellent range of armagnacs and a changing choice of around 27 wines by the glass.

🍴 As well as sandwiches, carefully prepared bar food from a tempting menu might include ploughman's, gravadlax with celeriac and caper coleslaw, potted duck and rabbit with pear chutney, smoked chicken salad with chicory, orange and caramelised chestnuts, blue cheese rarebit on walnut toast, minted pea, broad bean and feta puffpastry tart with olive salad, charcuterie board, moroccan lamb shank with apricot couscous, spiced chickpea cakes with butternut squash sauce and stir-fried vegetables, battered haddock, pasta with pork meatballs and tomato and chorizo sauce, coq au vin with tarragon mash, rump steak, and puddings such as ginger cheesecake with poached rhubarb, earl grey panna cotta with lemon and honey coulis and shortbread and chocolate brownie with coconut ice-cream. *Starters/Snacks: £4.50 to £9.25. Main Courses: £8.50 to £16.95. Puddings: £4.50 to £5.25*

Brunning & Price ~ Manager Ian Pritchard-Jones ~ Real ale ~ Bar food (12-9.30(9 Sun)) ~ (01978) 780380 ~ Children welcome ~ Dogs allowed in bar ~ Open 12-11(10.30 Sun)
Recommended by Jenny Williams, S P Watkin, P A Taylor, T M Griffiths, Brian and Anna Marsden

PANTYGELLI   SO3017 MAP 6

Crown ☂ 🍺

Old Hereford Road N of Abergavenny; off A40 by war memorial via Penypound, passing leisure centre; Pantygelli also signposted from A465; NP7 7HR

Prettily placed country pub, attractive inside and out, with good food and drinks

A good many devotees regularly make their way to this deeply tucked-away pub, both in the evening and at lunchtime – a sure sign of quality. Comfortable wrought-iron and wicker chairs on the flower-filled front terrace look up from this lush valley to the lower slopes of the Black Mountains; a smaller back terrace is surrounded by lavender. Inside, the neat and efficient staff take their cue from the friendly hands-on family owners, giving a warmly welcoming atmosphere. The dark flagstoned bar, with sturdy timber props and beams, has a piano at the back, darts opposite, a log fire in the stone fireplace, and – from its slate-roofed counter – well kept Bass, Rhymney Best, Tomos Watkins OSB and Wye Valley HPA on handpump, Stowford Press farm cider, good wines by the glass and decent coffees. On the left are four smallish, linked, carpeted dining rooms, the front pair separated by a massive stone chimneybreast; thoughtfully chosen individual furnishings and lots of attractive prints by local artists make it all thoroughly civilised; piped music.

🍴 Bar food includes baguettes and ciabattas, prawn cocktail, chicken caesar salad, country terrine, garlic mushrooms, goats cheese risotto, steak and ale pie, scampi, rib-eye steak, and puddings such as rhubarb brûlée with shortbread, panettone bread and butter pudding and chocolate orange pot with tuile biscuit. *Starters/Snacks: £4.50 to £13.50. Main Courses: £9.50 to £18.00. Puddings: £5.25*

Free house ~ Licensees Steve, Cherrie and Carys Chadwick ~ Real ale ~ Bar food ~
(01873) 853314 ~ Children welcome ~ Dogs welcome ~ Open 12-2.30(3 weekends), 6-11(10.30
Sun); closed Mon lunchtime
Recommended by Reg Fowle, Helen Rickwood, Trevor Swindells, David Whiter

PENRHIWLLAN   SN3641   MAP 6

Daffodil ♀
A475 Newcastle Emlyn—Lampeter; SA44 5NG

**Smart contemporary open-plan dining pub with comfortable welcoming bar, peaceful views
from back decking**

Friendly helpful staff are quick to make newcomers feel at home here – aided by the
comfort of the scatter-cushioned sofas and leather tub chairs on the bar's pale limestone
floor; the dozy pub labrador likes the one nearest the woodburning stove. The striking
granite-panelled counter, with a row of bar chairs, serves a good choice of wines by the
glass as well as Evan Evans BB and Cwrw and Greene King Abbot on handpump, and one
of two lower-ceilinged end rooms, each with a big oriental rug, has darts. Bare stone or
pastel-painted walls have just a few decorations, mainly larger-than-life plaster face
masks. Down a couple of steps are two light, airy and comfortable dining rooms; the one
with picture windows looking past the nicely furnished back decking to the peaceful
valley view is right by the open kitchen, which can seem a bit noisy on quiet days. There
is perky but unobtrusive piped music; lighting throughout is good, with excellent use of
daytime natural light.

🍴 **The specials' board tends to be strong on fish, perhaps sewin fishcakes, john dory,
plaice, ling and stir-fried squid, and the regular menu might have sharing platters,
barbecue pork spare ribs, chicken, pork and pistachio terrine, home-made burger, linguine
with mushroom and smoked bacon ragoût, braised lamb shank with moroccan spices,
curried nut terrine with tomato salsa, and puddings such as crumbles, cheesecakes and
pavlovas.** *Starters/Snacks: £4.25 to £5.50. Main Courses: £7.25 to £12.75. Puddings: £4.25 to
£4.75*

Free house ~ Licensee David Brookes ~ Real ale ~ Bar food (12-2, 6-9) ~ Restaurant ~
(01559) 370343 ~ Children welcome ~ Open 11.30-3, 5.30-11
Recommended by Paul Wright, Peter Hobson, Ruth Green

PONTRHYDFENDIGAID   SN7366   MAP 6

Black Lion 🛏
Just off B4343 Tregaron—Devil's Bridge; SY25 6BE

**Relaxed and chatty country inn with enjoyable sensibly priced food and good value
bedrooms; open evenings only**

In good walking country, this is just a few fields away from the abbey ruins of Strata
Florida. In the evenings all the tables in the smallish main bar are set for the popular
food, but even then you can expect to see locals on the bar stools, enjoying the Felinfoel
Double Dragon on handpump, and the happy informal atmosphere is very much that of a
good pub rather than just some eating place. There are dark beams and floorboards, a lot
of stripped stone, a pleasing variety of different seats, and a woodburning stove in a vast
fireplace with big swinging pot-irons as well as the copper, brass and other metal
ornaments on its double white mantelpiece. They have decent wines by the glass, service
is good, and piped music very unobtrusive; a tiled back room has pool. There are picnic-
sets out in front by the quiet lane, with another in the back courtyard, and more in an
informal tree-shaded garden. If you stay (the rooms are in a separate back block), the
friendly landlord cooks a good breakfast.

🍴 **A sensibly modest, changing choice of freshly made food includes a good homely soup
such as leek and potato, welsh cheese and onion tart, spicy meatballs in tomato sauce
baked with mozzarella, king prawns in filo pastry with sweet chilli dip, sausage and mash,**

vegetable lasagne, steak and ale pie, roast duck breast with port and redcurrant sauce, sirloin steak, and puddings such as apple and blackberry crumble and raspberry and white chocolate tart, and a welsh cheese platter. *Starters/Snacks: £3.50 to £4.55. Main Courses: £10.95 to £12.95. Puddings: £3.50 to £4.50*

Free house ~ Licensees Dominic and Claire Ward ~ Real ale ~ (01974) 831624 ~ Children welcome ~ Dogs welcome ~ Open 5pm-midnight ~ Bedrooms: £75B/£35B

Recommended by Mrs J Main, Ralph Wilmot

PORTH DINLLAEN   SH2741   MAP 6

Ty Coch

Beach car park signposted from Morfa Nefyn, then a 15-minute walk; LL53 6DB

Idyllic location right on the beach, far from the roads; simple fresh lunches

At low tide you can walk along a beach backed by low grassy hills and sand cliffs to get to this beautifully placed pub (otherwise you can walk across via the golf course). Said to have been used by 17th-c smugglers and pirates, with an open coal fire burning at one end of the bar, its interior is crammed with a wonderful miscellany of nautical paraphernalia. Every inch of the walls and beams are hung with pewter, riding lights, navigation lamps, lanterns, small fishing nets, old miners' and railway lamps, copper utensils, an ale-yard, and lots of RNLI photographs and memorabilia; there are ships in bottles, a working barometer, a Caernarfon grandfather clock, and simple furnishings. They are now serving real ales. As we went to press they were from Jennings and Purple Moose, and they also keep a range of bottled beers. Drinks are served in plastic as they are concerned about glass on the beach. More reports please, and do note the very limited winter opening times.

🍴 From a short menu, simple lunchtime bar food includes sandwiches, soup, baked potatoes, mussels in garlic butter, pies, warm melted brie with chutney topping, ham or beef salad and local mussels. *Starters/Snacks: £4.50 to £9.50. Main Courses: £9.50 to £11.95*

Free house ~ Licensee Mrs Brione Webley ~ Real ale ~ Bar food (12-2.30) ~ (01758) 720498 ~ Children welcome ~ Dogs welcome ~ Open 11-11(4 Sun); only open 12-4 Oct-Easter

Recommended by Rodney and Norma Stubington, Mike and Eleanor Anderson, Tim Maddison

PORTHGAIN   SM8132   MAP 6

Sloop

Off A487 St David's—Fishguard; SA62 5BN

Thoroughly nautical pub in wonderful coastal setting, fresh fish in season, efficient service even at busy times

This friendly tavern, snuggled down in a cove wedged tightly between headlands on a dramatic section of the Pembrokeshire Coast Path, has outstanding cliff walks in either direction – eastwards towards Trevine or southwestwards to Abereiddy. Inside, it retains some local atmosphere with all its seafaring memorabilia. The walls of the plank-ceilinged bar hang with lobster pots and fishing nets, ships' clocks and lanterns, and even relics from wrecks along this stretch of the shoreline. Down a step, another room leads round to a decent-sized eating area, with simple wooden chairs and tables, cushioned wall seats, and a freezer with ice-creams for children. On handpump are Brains Rev James, Felinfoel Double Dragon and Greene King IPA, and wine by the glass in three different sized glasses.There's a well segregated games room (used mainly by children) which has a juke box, pool and darts. At the height of summer (when it can draw the crowds) they may extend food serving times. Tables on the terrace overlook the harbour, with outdoor heaters for cooler weather. They don't have bedrooms but let a cottage in the village.

🍴 Rather than having a number for food service, many of the tables are named after a wrecked ship. Well prepared bar food includes fresh fish (caught by their own fishing business) such as crab, lobster, scallops and mackerel, according to season. The menu might also feature lunchtime sandwiches, soup, welsh black rib-eye steak or sirloin steak, burgers, and specials such as fried chicken breast topped with creamed leeks, mushroom, tomato, spring onion and herb risotto, fried bream with mediterranean vegetables and horseradish cream sauce and roast rump of lamb, and puddings such as vanilla and milk chocolate panna cotta with malted biscuits and meringue nest with chantilly cream and summer fruit coulis. *Starters/Snacks: £3.90 to £6.15. Main Courses: £5.35 to £18.20. Puddings: £3.90 to £4.50*

Free house ~ Licensee Matthew Blakiston ~ Real ale ~ Bar food (9.30-11(breakfast), 12-2.30, 6-9.30) ~ Restaurant ~ (01348) 831449 ~ Children under 16 must be accompanied ~ Open 9.30am-midnight(1am Fri, Sat)

Recommended by Theo, Anne and Jane Gaskin, Di and Mike Gillam, Ann and Tony Bennett-Hughes, Simon Watkins, R T and J C Moggridge, David Hoult

RED WHARF BAY
SH5281 MAP 6

Ship ♀ ◀

Village signposted off B5025 N of Pentraeth; LL75 8RJ

Nicely old-fashioned inside, with good drinks; sweeping coastal views from benches outside

This long, whitewashed, 16th-c house stands right on Anglesey's north coast, and on fine days there are plenty of takers for tables outside that get terrific views of miles of tidal sands, fringed by dunes and headlands, and a bay often dotted with yachts. It's cosily old-fashioned inside, with lots of nautical bric-a-brac in big rooms on each side of the busy stone-built bar counter, both with long cushioned varnished pews built around the walls, glossily varnished cast-iron-framed tables and roaring fires; piped Classic FM (in lounge only). Adnams, Tetleys and a guest such as Timothy Taylors on handpump, over 50 malt whiskies, and a wider choice of wines than is usual for the area (with about ten by the glass). If you want to run a tab, they'll ask to keep your credit card behind the bar in a locked numbered box (to which you are given the key).

Using food sourced in Anglesey wherever possible, the changing bar menu includes soup, lunchtime sandwiches, starters like smoked haddock rarebit or goats cheese and field mushroom crostini, and main courses such as baked half-shoulder of welsh lamb, fish of the day and smoked trout and poached salmon salad; puddings like chocolate orange panna cotta and sticky toffee pudding; children's menu. *Starters/Snacks: £4.95 to £7.95. Main Courses: £9.95 to £14.95. Puddings: £4.50 to £5.95*

Free house ~ Licensee Neil Kenneally ~ Real ale ~ Bar food (12-2.30, 6-9(5.30-9.30 Sat); 12-9 Sun) ~ Restaurant ~ (01248) 852568 ~ Children welcome ~ Open 11-11(11.30 Sat)

Recommended by Jill and Julian Tasker, John and Enid Morris, Mike Proctor, Gordon and Margaret Ormondroyd, Neil Whitehead, Victoria Anderson

RHYD-Y-MEIRCH
S02907 MAP 6

Goose & Cuckoo ◀

Upper Llanover signposted up narrow track off A4042 S of Abergavenny; after 0.5 miles take first left, then keep on up (watch for handwritten Goose signs at the forks); NP7 9ER

Remote single-room pub looking over a picturesque valley just inside the Brecon Beacons National Park; good drinks' range

Near the end of a tiny lane, this simple place above the Usk Valley is well positioned for walks along the nearby Monmouthshire and Brecon Canal towpath or over the hilltops towards Blorenge and Blaenavon. It is essentially one small rustically furnished room with a woodburner in an arched stone fireplace. A small picture-window extension makes the most of the view down the valley. They have Newmans Red Stag, Rhymney Bitter and a couple of guests such as Bullmastiff Jack the Lad and Otley Boss on handpump, as well as more than 80 whiskies; daily papers, cribbage, darts and board games. Some rather ad hoc picnic-sets are set out on the gravel below. The licensees keep sheep, geese and chickens, and may have honey for sale.

🍽 The choice of simple food, cooked in an Aga, includes filled home-made rolls, soups, pies such as chicken and ham or steak and kidney, and hot dishes like cajun chicken and liver and bacon casserole; puddings and home-made ice-cream; Sunday roast (bookings only). *Starters/Snacks: £2.50 to £3.50. Main Courses: £7.00 to £8.50. Puddings: £3.00*

Free house ~ Licensees Michael and Carol Langley ~ Real ale ~ Bar food ~ No credit cards ~ (01873) 880277 ~ Children welcome ~ Dogs welcome ~ Open 11-3, 7-11; 11-11 Sat; 12-10.30 Sun; closed Mon except bank hols ~ Bedrooms: £30S/£60S

Recommended by Reg Fowle, Helen Rickwood, Howard Deacon, Guy Vowles

ROSEBUSH   SN0729   MAP 6

Tafarn Sinc

B4329 Haverfordwest—Cardigan; SA66 7QU

Unique 19th-c curio, a slice of social and industrial history

Run in quite a firmly idiosyncratic way and laden with strong character, this is one of the most eccentric pub buildings in all of Wales. A maroon-painted corrugated iron shed, it was built in 1876 as a very basic hotel for a halt for a long-defunct railway serving quarries beneath the Preseli Hills. The halt itself has been more or less re-created, even down to life-size dummy passengers waiting out on the platform; the sizeable garden is periodically enlivened by the sounds of steam trains chuffing through – actually broadcast from a replica signal box. Inside is really interesting, almost a museum of local history, with sawdust on the floor, hams and goodness-knows-what-else hung from the ceiling, and an appealingly buoyant atmosphere, and you will hear Welsh spoken here. The bar has plank panelling, an informal mix of old chairs and pews, a woodburner, and Cwrw Tafarn Sinc (brewed specially for the pub), Brains Rev James and a guest on handpump; piped music, darts, games machine, board games and TV.

🍽 Basic food includes home-made faggots with mushy peas, gammon steak with pineapple, vegetable lasagne, lamb burgers, steaks, and puddings. *Main Courses: £9.80 to £16.50. Puddings: £2.90 to £4.50*

Free house ~ Licensee Hafwen Davies ~ Real ale ~ Bar food (12-2, 6-9) ~ Restaurant ~ (01437) 532214 ~ Children welcome ~ Open 12-11 (midnight Sat); closed Mon

Recommended by the Didler, Ann and Tony Bennett-Hughes, John Hancock, John and Enid Morris, R T and J C Moggridge

SKENFRITH   SO4520   MAP 6

Bell 🍴 ♇ 🛏

Just off B4521, NE of Abergavenny and N of Monmouth; NP7 8UH

Elegant but relaxed, generally much praised for classy though pricey food and excellent accommodation

For a special occasion, head for the big bare-boards dining area at the back of this smart country inn. It's neat, light and airy, with dark country-kitchen chairs and rush-seat dining chairs, church candles and flowers on the dark tables, canary walls and a cream ceiling, and brocaded curtains on sturdy big-ring rails. The flagstoned bar on the left has a rather similar décor, with old local and school photographs, a couple of pews plus tables and café chairs. From an attractive bleached oak bar counter, Kingstone Gold, Wye Valley Bitter and a guest like Timothy Taylors Landlord are on handpump, plus bottled local cider. They have good wines by the glass and half-bottle, and a decent range of brandies. The lounge bar on the right, opening into the dining area, has a nice jacobean-style carved settle and a housekeeper's chair by a log fire in the big fireplace. There are good solid round picnic-sets as well as the usual rectangular ones out on the terrace, with steps up to a sloping lawn; it's a quiet spot. The bedrooms are comfortable, with thoughtful touches. Disabled access is good. The pub is handy for the Three Castles area of the Marches and is within sight of the massive ruins of Skenfrith Castle.

🍴 **Food here is prepared using named local suppliers of carefully chosen fresh ingredients and own-grown vegetables, soft fruit and herbs from their kitchen garden, which is officially classed as organic, and which guests are welcome to look around.** As well as lunchtime sandwiches, the changing menus (not cheap) might include scallops with fennel purée, garden shoots and candied orange, potted pork with piccalilli and apple and thyme purée, charcuterie, pea and baby broad bean risotto, rib-eye steak with béarnaise sauce, confit duck leg with braised pak choi and soy and orange sauce, tomato panna cotta with courgettes, roast tomato and basil tagliatelle, and puddings such as white chocolate and raspberry mousse and beetroot parfait with beetroot crisps, candied orange and beetroot and blackcurrant sorbet. *Starters/Snacks: £6.00 to £11.00. Main Courses: £12.00 to £18.00. Puddings: £6.00*

Free house ~ Licensees William and Janet Hutchings ~ Real ale ~ Bar food (12-2.30, 7-9.30(9 Sun)) ~ (01600) 750235 ~ Children welcome ~ Dogs allowed in bar and bedrooms ~ Open 11-11; 12-10 Sun; closed Tues Nov-Easter, and last week Jan and first week Feb ~ Bedrooms: £75B/£110B

Recommended by Michael and Jenny Back, Dr and Mrs Michael Smith, Maurice and Gill McMahon, John Wooll, Pauline Jones, LM

STACKPOLE
SR9896   MAP 6

Stackpole Inn 🛏

Village signposted off B4319 S of Pembroke; SA71 5DF

Enjoyable food, friendly service and usefully placed for exploring the Stackpole Estate

On jolly good form at the moment, this cottagey inn gains a Stay Award this year for its airy seaside-themed bedrooms, and is just a hair's breadth off a Food Award. Perhaps next year, with enough feedback from readers... One spacious area has pine tables, chairs and a pool table, but the major part of the pub, L-shaped on four different levels, is given over to diners, with neat light oak furnishings, and ash beams and low ceilings to match; piped music. Brains Rev James and a guest from a brewer such as Red Fox are on handpump, with 14 wines by the glass and several malt whiskies. There are tables out in the attractive gardens, with colourful flower beds and mature trees around the car park. From here you can walk across sandy beaches, through the woodland, around the lily ponds or along the craggy cliffs of the Stackpole Estate.

🍴 **With fresh fish delivered daily from Milford Haven, the impressive food might include** filled couronnes, smoked salmon on potato blini, chicken liver parfait with pear chutney, fishcakes with lemon butter sauce, scampi, tuna niçoise, local dressed crab, roast chicken breast with butternut, garlic and herb purée, seared welsh lamb with moroccan couscous and tomato jus, sea bass fillet with fennel and saffron risotto, spinach, roast garlic and stilton crêpes, and puddings such as mixed berry fruit pudding with mascarpone chantilly cream, raspberry crème brûlée with raspberry sorbet and tiramisu with Amaretto cream; **Sunday roasts.** *Starters/Snacks: £4.95 to £7.95. Main Courses: £11.90 to £19.90. Puddings: £4.50 to £6.50*

Free house ~ Licensees Gary and Becky Evans ~ Real ale ~ Bar food (12-2(2.30 Sun), 6.30-9) ~ Restaurant ~ (01646) 672324 ~ Children welcome ~ Dogs allowed in bar ~ Open 12-3, 6-11; 12-11 Sat; 12-3, 6-11 Sun; closed Sun evening Oct-Mar ~ Bedrooms: £55S/£80S

Recommended by Alan Skingsley, Brian and Jacky Wilson, Pat Crabb, Simon Daws, Richard Cole, Julia Morris, Fergus Dowding, Geoff and Linda Payne, John and Enid Morris, Ken and Barbara Turner, Mrs P Bishop, Mark Farrington

---

Stars after the name of a pub show exceptional quality. One star means most people (after reading the report to see just why the star has been won) would think a special trip worth while. Two stars mean that the pub is really outstanding – for its particular qualities it could hardly be bettered.

TALYBONT-ON-USK

Star 🍺

B4558; LD3 7YX

500 real ales a year at this traditional canalside local with walkers' appeal

The energetic landlord at this old-fashioned canalside inn tells us it's a constant beer festival at his place, and especially at weekends. Sourced from brewers just down the road and as far flung as Scotland, London and the west country, half a dozen constantly changing beers might just be from Fullers, Otley, Wye Valley and Marble or Slaters – just might be, that is. Also a farm cider on handpump. Unashamedly stronger on character than on creature comforts, there's always an interesting mix of customers including walkers and locals with their dogs in the several plainly furnished pubby rooms which radiate from the central servery, including a brightly lit games area with pool, fruit machine, TV and juke box; cheering winter fires, one in a splendid stone fireplace. There are picnic-sets in the sizeable tree-ringed garden from which a path leads down to the river. This simple but beautifully set village, with the Monmouthshire and Brecon Canal running through (you can walk along the tow path), is surrounded by the Brecon Beacons National Park. If you want to stay here at the weekend, it must be for two nights.

🍴 **Reasonably priced, straightforward changing bar food includes sandwiches, steak and ale pie, home-made burger, vegetable lasagne, cod and chips, sea trout, curries, venison faggots, and puddings such as sticky toffee pudding and crumbles.** *Starters/Snacks: £3.95 to £6.50. Main Courses: £6.50 to £13.95. Puddings: £3.95 to £4.50*

Punch ~ Lease Ian and Anna Bell ~ Real ale ~ Bar food (12-2(2.30 Sat, Sun), 6(6.30 Sun)-9) ~ (01874) 676635 ~ Children welcome ~ Dogs allowed in bar ~ Live music last Fri of the month, quiz Tues in winter ~ Open 11-11(12 Sat, Sun); 11-3, 5-11(midnight Sun) in winter ~ Bedrooms: /£55S

Recommended by D Crook

TRESAITH

Ship ★

Off A487 E of Cardigan; bear right in village and keep on down – pub's car park fills up quickly; SA43 2JL

Charming pub in splendid setting overlooking broad sandy surfing beach, enjoyable food, nice terrace; seaview bedrooms

We have not yet heard from anyone using the bedrooms, but would expect this to be a nice place to stay: the views are great, not just the beach but the cliffs on either side, one with a high waterfall – we saw a peregrine falcon swoop past, and some say they've spotted dolphins and seals. Teak tables and chairs under a glass canopy on heated front decking, and unusual picnic-sets on a two-level terrace, make the most of this, and picture windows open the views to the front dining area, too. Behind here is a winter log fire, with some chunky pine tables, tub armchairs and sofas in the carpeted part on the right, and large attractive local photographs. They have Brains Rev James and a guest such as Buckleys Best on handpump, and a good choice of wines by the glass and other drinks; the young staff are friendly, cheerful and efficient. Two back rooms, possibly a quieter escape in summer, are appealing, especially the one on the right with its striking blue and red décor, bright flooring tiles, old-fashioned range stove, and snug alcove with a shelf of board games. There are good coast walks from this steep little village.

🍴 **Popular for its fresh fish and hot seafood platter, the menu here might include whitebait, sardines grilled with garlic and tomato, garlic mushrooms, calamari, antipasti, honey glazed king prawns, bream roasted with chilli and lime, battered haddock, plaice in breadcrumbs and parsley, baked chicken and goats cheese with a white sauce, mushroom and stilton bake, vegan salad, rib-eye steak, and puddings such as jam roly-poly and profiteroles.** *Starters/Snacks: £5.00 to £7.00. Main Courses: £7.00 to £17.00. Puddings: £5.00*

Brains ~ Manager Carl O'Shaughnessy ~ Real ale ~ Bar food (8am-11am, midday-3pm, 5pm-9pm; 12-9 in summer) ~ (01239) 811816 ~ Children welcome ~ Open 8am-11pm ~ Bedrooms: /£59.95B

Recommended by Gareth Lewis, Julia Morris

TY'N-Y-GROES
SH7773 MAP 6

Groes
B5106 N of village; LL32 8TN

Lots of antiques in beamed northern Snowdonia hotel

This gracious old hotel has an idyllic back garden with flower-filled hayracks; there are more seats on the flower-decked roadside. Past the hot stove in the entrance area, the rambling, low-beamed and thick-walled rooms are nicely decorated with antique settles and an old sofa, old clocks, portraits, hats and tins hanging from the walls, and fresh flowers. A fine antique fireback is built into one wall, perhaps originally from the formidable fireplace in the back bar, which houses a collection of stone cats as well as cheerful winter log fires. You might find a harpist playing here on certain days. There is also an airy and verdant conservatory. From the family's own Great Orme brewery, a couple of miles away, are Great Orme and Groes Ale (brewed for the pub), and several bottled Great Orme beers too; piped music. The spotless, well equipped bedroom suites (some have terraces or balconies) have gorgeous views. They also rent out a well appointed wooden cabin, and a cottage in the historic centre of Conwy. Dogs are allowed in some bedrooms and in certain areas of the bar. More up-to-date reports please.

🍴 Using local lamb, salmon and game, and herbs from the hotel garden, bar food includes sandwiches, goats cheese and beetroot salad, garlic king prawns, baked mushroom with garlic, stilton and home-made bread, seafood pie, chicken curry, sausage and mash, beefburger, mixed vegetable risotto cakes with tomato and basil sauce, shepherd's pie, rib-eye steak, and puddings such as apple and cinnamon crumble, orange cheesecake and treacle tart. *Starters/Snacks: £5.00 to £18.00. Main Courses: £8.00 to £24.00. Puddings: £5.00 to £7.00*

Free house ~ Licensee Dawn Humphreys ~ Real ale ~ Bar food ~ Restaurant ~ (01492) 650545 ~ Children welcome if eating until 7.30pm ~ Dogs allowed in bar and bedrooms ~ Open 12-3, 6.30-11 ~ Bedrooms: £85B/£105B

Recommended by Susan and Nigel Brookes, Mike Horgan, Margaret and Jeff Graham, Mike and Mary Carter, Tony and Shirley Albert, Noel Grundy, W N F Boughey, Peter Holmes, Maurice and Gill McMahon, Phil and Jane Hodson, Joan E Hilditch, Simon Daws

USK
SO3700 MAP 6

Nags Head ♀
The Square; NP15 1BH

Spotlessly kept by the same family for 43 years, traditional in style and hearty welcome, with good food and drinks

With as warm a reception as could be hoped for, the beautifully kept traditional main bar is cheerily chatty, with lots of well polished tables and chairs packed under its beams (some with farming tools), lanterns or horsebrasses and harness attached, as well as leatherette wall benches, and various sets of sporting prints and local pictures – look out for the original deeds to the pub. Tucked away at the front is an intimate little corner with some african masks, while on the other side of the room a passageway leads to a new dining area converted from the old coffee bar; piped music. There may be prints for sale, and perhaps a knot of sociable locals. They do ten wines by the glass, along with Brains Bitter, Bread of Heaven, Rev James and SA on handpump. The centre of Usk is full of pretty hanging baskets and flowers in summer, and the church is well worth a look.

🍴 Huge helpings of reasonably priced popular food includes soup, grilled sardines, frogs' legs in hot provençale sauce, rabbit pie, steak pie, chicken in red wine, faggots, and vegetable pancake, with specials such as brace of boned quail with stuffing and sauce or poached salmon. You can book tables, some of which may be candlelit at night; nice, proper linen napkins. *Starters/Snacks: £4.50 to £6.50. Main Courses: £7.75 to £16.50. Puddings: £4.00 to £4.75.*

Free house ~ Licensee the Key family ~ Real ale ~ Bar food (11.30-2, 5.30-9) ~ Restaurant ~ (01291) 672820 ~ Children welcome ~ Dogs welcome ~ Open 10.30-2.30, 5.30(5 Sat)-11; 10.30-3, 5.30-10 Sun

Recommended by Eryl and Keith Dykes, Gareth Lewis, M G Hart, Reg Fowle, Helen Rickwood, Mr and Mrs C Gothard, Meg and Colin Hamilton, John and Joan Nash, Sue and Ken Le Prevost

LUCKY DIP

Besides the fully inspected pubs, you might like to try these Lucky Dips recommended to us and described by readers (if you do, please send us reports: feedback@goodguides.com).

ANGLESEY

RHOSCOLYN [SH2675]
White Eagle LL65 2NJ [off B4545 S of Holyhead]: Splendid remote setting with panoramic views towards Snowdonia from dining area, modern redevelopment with relaxed upmarket feel, good imaginative varied food (all day in summer) using local ingredients, well kept ales such as Conwyn, Marstons and Weetwood, friendly helpful staff; children welcome, good large garden, lane down to beach, open all day in summer *(Margaret and Trefor Howorth, Emily Carr, J D C Smellie)*

CLWYD

CARROG [SJ1143]
Grouse LL21 9AT [B5436, signed off A5 Llangollen—Corwen]: Small unpretentious pub with superb views over River Dee and beyond from bay window and balcony, Lees ales, enjoyable food all day from sandwiches up, reasonable prices, friendly helpful staff, local pictures; pool in games room, piped music; narrow turn into car park; children welcome, wheelchair access (side door a bit narrow), tables in pretty walled garden (covered terrace for smokers), handy for Llangollen steam railway, bedrooms *(John Francis, Mr and Mrs M Stratton)*
CHIRK [SJ2937]
Hand LL14 5EY [Church St]: Refurbished 17th-c coaching inn under new local ownership, three comfortable open-plan rooms rambling around servery, wide choice of food from sandwiches and pub staples up, children's dishes, good attentive service; Stonehouse Station and two guest ales, tea lounge and dining room as well as more formal restaurant; games area in public bar; dogs welcome, garden picnic-sets, 15 bedrooms, open all day *(LYM, Roger M Hancock)*
CILCAIN [SJ1765]
☆ *White Horse* CH7 5NN [signed from A494 W of Mold; The Square]: Homely country

local well looked after by friendly long-serving landlord, several unspoilt rooms, low joists, mahogany and oak settles, two blazing fires, old photographs, interesting changing ales, good choice of enjoyable home-made food inc vegetarian; quarry-tiled back bar allowing dogs and muddy boots, pub games, cat; no children inside; picnic-sets outside, delightful village *(Rosemary Kirkus, LYM, Maurice and Gill McMahon)*
COEDWAY [SJ3414]
Old Hand & Diamond SY5 9AR [B4393 W of Shrewsbury]: Beams, panelling, stripped stone and inglenook log fire in carpeted bar, friendly licensees and staff, enjoyable well priced food from familiar favourites to interesting specials, three real ales, nice wine, light and airy restaurant with local pictures; children welcome, tables under cocktail parasols on side terrace, lots of climbing roses and hanging baskets, play area, seven comfortable beamed bedrooms *(Jennifer Banks)*
LLANNEFYDD [SH9870]
☆ *Hawk & Buckle* LL16 5ED [NW of Henllan]: Welcoming village inn, high up with a sweeping panorama over Irish Sea to Blackpool Tower; long knocked-through black-beamed lounge bar with comfortable settles and log fire, a changing real ale, enjoyable food, restaurant; children welcome away from bar, good bedrooms, open all day wknds, cl Mon-Weds lunchtimes *(LYM, John and Eileen Mennear)*
MOLD [SJ1962]
We Three Loggerheads CH7 5LH [Ruthin Rd (A494, 3 miles towards Ruthin)]: Comfortable and friendly 17th-c coaching inn opp entrance to Loggerheads Country Park; two-level bar, good choice of enjoyable fairly priced food all day, well kept real ales, spacious raftered back restaurant; piped music; side terrace overlooking little River Alyn *(LYM)*
RUABON [SJ3043]
Bridge End LL14 6DA [Bridge St]: Proper old-fashioned pub now owned by McGivern, their ales and guests, decent wines,

enthusiastic staff, basic home-made food, open fires; folk music Weds evening, Thurs quiz; open all day wknds and from 5pm wkdys *(Mrs Ginny Weston)*

SANDYCROFT [SJ3366]

Bridge CH5 2QN [Chester Rd (B5129)]: Open-plan pub with Black Sheep and Cumberland ales (sample glasses provided), good choice of enjoyable food inc unusual things like soup served in a hollowed cottage loaf, friendly helpful staff; conservatory-style dining extension with iron pillars, pool room; sports TVs; children welcome, terrace with cane furniture, more tables and play area on lawn, open all day, till late Fri, Sat *(Neil and Anita Christopher)*

ST GEORGE [SH9775]

☆ *Kinmel Arms* LL22 9BP [off A547 or B5381 SE of Abergele]: Dining pub tucked away in attractive village, several neat and tidy refurbished rooms, nice mix of tables and chairs, rugs on stripped wood, wide range of good affordable modern food from lunchtime baguettes and dutch-style open sandwiches up, friendly prompt service; changing well kept ales such as Cains and Facers, good choice of wines by the glass, conservatory; four good bedrooms, cl Sun, Mon *(Nick Sanders, Tony and Shirley Albert)*

TAL-Y-CAFN [SH7871]

☆ *Tal-y-Cafn Hotel* LL28 5RR [A470 Conway—Llanwrst]: Useful hotel for northern Snowdonia, with enormous inglenook in traditional turkey carpeted bar with fireplace, straightforward bar food, Boddingtons, Black Sheep and Tetleys; piped music, TV, rustic tables and large play area in spacious hedged garden, bedrooms *(Susan and Nigel Brookes, LYM, W N F Boughey)*

DYFED

ABERAERON [SN4462]

Cadwgan Arms SA46 0AU [Market St]: Small late 18th-c pub opp harbour, basic with friendly regulars, well kept Brains and changing microbrews, interesting old photographs, open fire; nice outside drinking area, open all day except Mon lunchtime *(the Didler)*

ABERCYCH [SN2539]

☆ *Nags Head* SA37 0HJ [off B4332 Cenarth—Boncath]: Tucked-away riverside pub with dimly lit beamed and flagstoned bar, big fireplace, stripped wood tables, clocks showing time around the world, piano, hundreds of beer bottles, photographs of locals and a coracle on brick and stone walls, even a large stuffed rat, may have own-brew beer with guests like Brains and Shepherd Neame, two sizeable dining areas; piped music, TV; children and dogs welcome, benches in garden overlooking river, play area, open all day Sun, cl Mon *(John and Enid Morris, Brian Brooks, BB, Gareth Lewis, Colin Moore, John and Fiona McIlwain, LYM)*

ABERGORLECH [SN5833]

☆ *Black Lion* SA32 7SN [B4310]: Friendly old coaching inn in fine rural position, traditionally furnished, stripped-stone bar with flagstones, coal stove, oak furniture and high-backed black settles, copper pans on beams, old jugs on shelves, fresh flowers, local paintings; dining extension with french windows opening on to enclosed garden, one Rhymney ale and a guest, good varied choice of inexpensive food; piped music; children and dogs welcome, lovely views of Cothi Valley from sloping garden, open all day wknds *(LYM, Mike and Eleanor Anderson, Peter and Carol Heaton)*

ABERYSTWYTH [SN6777]

Yr Hen Orsaf SY23 1LN [Alexandra Rd]: High-ceilinged air-conditioned Wetherspoons in concourse of Cambrian Railways station, cheap food and beer, efficient friendly service even at busy times, several different areas, platform view; TVs; terrace tables by the buffer stops, open all day from breakfast *(Dennis Jones, B and M Kendall)*

ANGLE [SM8703]

☆ *Old Point House* SA71 5AS [signed off B4320 in village, along long rough waterside track]: Idyllic spot overlooking sheltered anchorage (getting there inc a long waterside drive is part of the pleasure); friendly down-to-earth atmosphere, good simple food (almost all fresh local fish), Felinfoel Double Dragon, cheap soft drinks, flagstoned bar with open fire, small lounge bar, lots of charm and character, run by local lifeboat coxswain – many photographs and charts; home-made chutneys and sauces for charity, resident labradors; plenty of picnic-sets outside *(Julian Distin, BB)*

BROAD HAVEN [SM8614]

☆ *Druidstone Hotel* SA62 3NE [N of village on coast rd, bear left for about 1.5 miles then follow sign left to Druidston Haven – inn a sharp left turn after another 0.5 miles; OS Sheet 157 map ref 862168, marked as Druidston Villa]: Cheerfully informal, the family's former country house in a grand spot above the sea, individualistic and relaxed, terrific views, inventive cooking with fresh often organic ingredients (should book), helpful efficient service, folksy cellar bar with local ale tapped from the cask, country wines and other drinks; ceilidhs and folk events, friendly pub dogs (others welcome), all sorts of sporting activities from boules to sand-yachting; attractive high-walled garden, spacious homely bedrooms, even an eco-friendly chalet, cl Nov and Jan, restaurant cl Sun evening *(Pauline and Derek Hodgkiss, Colin Moore, Geoff and Linda Payne, John and Enid Morris, Blaise Vyner, LYM)*

CAIO [SN6739]

Brunant Arms SA19 8RD [off A482 Llanwrda—Lampeter]: Unpretentious and interestingly furnished village pub, comfortable and friendly, with nice log fire, good choice of local ales, enjoyable regularly changing home-made food from baguettes up, stripped-stone public bar with games inc pool; juke box, TV; children and dogs welcome, small Perspex-roofed verandah and lower terrace, has been open all day wknds *(LYM, David and Lin Short, the Didler)*

CWM GWAUN [SN0333]

☆ *Dyffryn Arms* SA65 9SE [Cwm Gwaun and Pontfaen signed off B4313 E of Fishguard]: Classic rural time warp, virtually the social centre for this lush green valley, very relaxed, basic and idiosyncratic, with much-loved veteran landlady (her farming family have run it since 1840, and she's been in charge for well over one-third of that time); 1920s front parlour with plain deal furniture and draughts boards inlaid into tables, coal fire, well kept Bass served by jug through sliding hatch, low prices, World War I prints and posters, darts, duck eggs for sale; lovely outside view, open more or less all day (may close if no customers) *(MLR, Colin Moore, the Didler, Ann and Tony Bennett-Hughes, Giles and Annie Francis, LYM)*

FELINDRE FARCHOG [SN0939]

☆ *Olde Salutation* SA41 3UY [A487 Newport—Cardigan]: Attractive roadside pub, comfortable and neatly kept traditional lounge bar, popular food inc local beef, Brains Rev James, Felinfoel Double Dragon and a guest, good wines by the glass, friendly landlord, conservatory restaurant; disabled facilities, picnic-sets outside, comfortable bedrooms, fishing and good walks by nearby River Nevern, cl Tues, open all day wknds *(Colin Moore, BB)*

FISHGUARD [SM9537]

☆ *Fishguard Arms* SA65 9HJ [Main St (A487)]: Tiny unspoilt pub; front bar with changing jug-served ales from unusually high counter, chatty landlord and friendly staff, open fire, rugby photographs, woodburner and traditional games in back room, no food; open all day, cl Weds evening *(Giles and Annie Francis, LYM, the Didler)*

Royal Oak SA65 9HA [Market Sq, Upper Town]: Dark beams, stripped stone and panelling, big picture-window dining extension, pictures and tapestry commemorating defeat here of bizarre french raid in 1797, Brains and changing guest beers from bar counter carved with a welsh dragon; generous good value fresh food, woodburner, bar billiards; games machine; pleasant terrace, open all day *(MLR, the Didler, Ann and Tony Bennett-Hughes, BB)*

Ship SA65 9ND [Newport Rd, Lower Town]: Cheerful atmosphere and seafaring locals in ancient dimly lit red-painted pub nr old harbour; friendly staff, well kept ales such as Bass and Theakstons tapped from the cask, homely food from sandwiches and cawl up, coal fire, lots of boat pictures, model ships, photos of Richard Burton, piano; children welcome, toys provided *(LYM, Giles and Annie Francis)*

FRESHWATER EAST [SS0298]

Freshwater Inn SA71 5LE [Jason Rd]: Built in 1912 as a country club, lovely coastal views, friendly staff, reasonably priced home-made food, Felinfoel and guest ales, lounge, dining room and public bar; children and dogs welcome, tables in nice garden, open all day summer *(Louise Harris)*

HAVERFORDWEST [SM9515]

☆ *Georges* SA61 1NH [Market St]: Unique in its mix of good value café and wines by the glass, Brains Rev James and Greene King Old Speckled Hen, enterprising soft drinks, and attractive post-hippy things for sale (glass mobiles, crystals, carvings, buddha figurines etc); quick cheerful service even when busy, interesting home-made food, two floors of booth seating, well reproduced piped music; no dogs; lovely walled garden, open 10.30-5.30pm, all day Sat, cl Sun *(BB)*

LITTLE HAVEN [SM8512]

☆ *Castle Inn* SA62 3UF: Welcoming pub well placed by the green looking over sandy bay (lovely sunsets); enjoyable food inc pizzas and good local fish, Marstons ales, good choice of wines by the glass, tea and cafetière coffee, bare-boards bar and carpeted dining area with big oak tables, beams, some stripped stone, castle prints; pool in back area; children welcome, front picnic-sets, open all day *(John Hancock, John and Fiona McIlwain, Mrs Barbara Barret, Pat Crabb)*

☆ *Swan* SA62 3UL [Point Rd]: Attractively refurbished seaside pub overlooking sandy bay, emphasis on enjoyable if not cheap upscale food, up-to-date bar with leather sofas and comfortable alcove seating on wood-laminate floor, nice views from window tables, fires each end; Brains and guest ales, good but expensive wines, young staff, upstairs dining room *(LYM, Mrs Barbara Barret, Geoff and Linda Payne, John and Enid Morris, Ann and Tony Bennett-Hughes)*

LLANDDAROG [SN5016]

☆ *Butchers Arms* SA32 8NS: Ancient heavily black-beamed local with three intimate eating areas off small central bar, welcoming with charming service, enjoyable generous food at reasonable prices, Felinfoel ales tapped from the cask, good wines by the glass; conventional pub furniture, gleaming brass, candles in bottles, open woodburner in biggish fireplace; piped music; children welcome, tables outside, nice window boxes, cl Mon *(BB, Dr and Mrs A K Clarke, Tom Evans, Michael and Alison Sandy)*

☆ *White Hart* SA32 8NT [off A48 E of Carmarthen, via B4310; aka Yr Hydd Gwyn]: Ancient thatched pub with own-brew beers using water from 300-ft borehole, lots of engaging bric-a-brac and antiques inc suit of armour, 17th-c carved settles by huge log fire, interestingly furnished high-raftered dining room, generous bar food, Zac the macaw and Bendy the galah; piped music, no dogs inside; children welcome, disabled access (ramps provided), picnic-sets on front terrace and in back garden, play area, small farmyard, cl Weds (Robert Turnham, Michael and Alison Sandy, Dr and Mrs A K Clarke, Di and Mike Gillam, Mr and Mrs P R Thomas, Glenys and John Roberts, LYM)

LLANDEILO [SN6222]

White Horse SA19 6EN [Rhosmaen St]: Friendly well run 16th-c local, several linked bare-boards rooms, fine range of Evan Evans ales, nice mix of customers, woodburner in stone fireplace; piped music and occasionally live, games machine, TV; tables outside front and back, open all day (the Didler)

LLANDOVERY [SN7634]

Red Lion SA20 0AA [Market Sq]: One basic welcoming room with no bar, changing ales tapped from cask, jovial characterful landlord; restricted opening – may be just Sat, and Fri evening (BB, the Didler)

MATHRY [SM8831]

Farmers Arms SA62 5HB [Brynamlwg, off A487 Fishguard—St David's]: Creeper-covered pub with beams, flagstones and dark woodwork in basic homely bar, friendly staff and locals, log fires, good value pubby food from sandwiches and baked potatoes up, Brains Rev James, Felinfoel Double Dragon and a guest, fair range of reasonably priced wines; children welcome in large vine-covered dining conservatory (simple rather than smart); piped music; tables in small walled garden, nearby campsite, open all day, has been cl till 4pm Mon-Weds in winter (Ann and Tony Bennett-Hughes)

NEWCASTLE EMLYN [SN3041]

Red Cow SA38 9EH: Traditional stone pub close to the bridge, sympathetically reworked as stylish simply furnished dining pub, good french/welsh cooking from short menu, bar with small seating area; cl Mon, Tues (Chris Wall)

PONTRHYDFENDIGAID [SN7366]

Red Lion SY25 6BH [Bridge St (B4343 Tregaron—Devil's Bridge)]: Friendly new local licensees and appealing simple refurbishment, stripped kitchen tables in comfortable inglenook bar, pubby food, well kept Felinfoel Double Dragon; games bar with pool, darts, juke box and big-screen TV; informal streamside garden, good value bedrooms (BB)

PORTHGAIN [SM8132]

Shed SA62 5BN: In what looks to be a seaside former boat shed, not a pub but does sell beer and is well worth knowing for good seafood in upstairs evening bistro (not winter Sun-Weds), daytime tearoom (Simon Watkins, Blaise Vyner)

RHANDIRMWYN [SN7843]

Royal Oak SA20 0NY: Newish owners for this friendly 17th-c stone-built inn in remote and peaceful walking country, comfortable traditional bar with log fire, four well kept changing ales, may be a perry, reasonably priced straightforward food (welsh black beef recommended), big dining area, pool room; dogs and children welcome, hill views from

garden and bedrooms, handy for Brecon Beacons (Mike and Eleanor Anderson, BB)

ST DAVID'S [SM7525]

☆ *Farmers Arms* SA62 6RF [Goat St]: Bustling old-fashioned low-ceilinged pub by cathedral gate, cheerful and unpretentiously pubby, mainly drinking on the left and eating on the right, central servery with well kept Brains Rev James, generous tasty good value food from baguettes and ploughman's with local cheeses to steaks and Sun lunch; lively friendly young staff, chatty landlord and locals, pool room; they may try to keep your credit card while you eat; TV for rugby; cathedral view from large tables on big back suntrap terrace, open all day (John and Fiona McIlwain, John Hancock, Geoff and Linda Payne, Simon Watkins)

TREGARON [SN6859]

Talbot SY25 6JL [The Square]: Character beamed bar with cosy rooms off, good value food, friendly service, well kept ales; pleasant garden, interesting town, bedrooms, open all day in summer (Mr E Fullilove)

GLAMORGAN

BLACK PILL [SS6190]

Woodman SA3 5AS [Mumbles Rd (A4067 Swansea—Mumbles)]: Attractive relaxed old seafront dining pub, well divided inside, with good value food all day from good sandwiches and baguettes to fresh local fish, Courage Directors and guests such as Adnams and Greene King, nice choice of wines by the glass, good service; hundreds of wine bottles above panelled dado, airy restaurant and conservatory; car park across busy road; children welcome in some areas, next to beautiful Clyne Gardens (great rhododendrons in May) (Richard Hodges)

CAERPHILLY [ST1484]

☆ *Black Cock* CF83 1NF [Watford; Tongwynlais exit from M4 junction 32, then right just after church]: Welcoming, well run, beamed country pub with series of interconnecting rooms, large back dining extension, good choice of enjoyable pub food all day (not Sun evening) inc children's and OAP menus; well kept ales such as Hancocks HB, Theakstons Old Peculier and Wickwar BOB, cheerful staff, woodburners, newspapers; piped music and some live; dogs welcome in bar, disabled access, sizeable terraced garden among trees with barbecue and good play area; up in the hills just below Caerphilly Common, popular with walkers and riders (there's a hitching rail), bedrooms, campsite, open all day (BB, Chris and Angela Buckell, Dr A J and Mrs Tompsett)

CARDIFF [ST1776]

Black Pig CF11 9HW [Sophia Close; aka Y Mochyn Du]: Enjoyable home-made food, well kept Brains and Vale of Glamorgan, good welcoming atmosphere, interesting décor; terrace tables, open all day (Dr and Mrs A K Clarke, the Didler, Andy and Jill Kassube)

☆ *Cayo Arms* CF11 9LL [Cathedral Rd]: Helpful young staff, well kept Marstons and Tomos Watkins, enjoyable good value standard food all day from ciabattas up inc Sun lunch, daily papers, pubby front bar with comfortable side area in Edwardian style, more modern back dining area; piped music, big-screen TV in one part, very busy wknds; tables out in front, more in yard behind (with parking), good value bedrooms, open all day *(Dr and Mrs A K Clarke, the Didler, Andy and Jill Kassube)*

Cottage CF10 1AA [St Mary St, nr Howells]: Proper down-to-earth pub with good value generous home-made food inc bargain all-day breakfast, good cheerful service, full Brains range kept well, decent choice of wines; long bar with narrow frontage and back eating area, lots of polished wood, glass and mirrors, old photographs, relaxed friendly atmosphere even on Fri and Sat when crowded (gets packed on rugby international days); open all day *(Alan and Eve Harding, Joan and Michel Hooper-Immins)*

Goat Major CF10 1PU [High St, opp castle]: Smartly refurbished and named for Royal Welsh Regiment mascot (plenty of pictures), Victorian-style décor, Brains full range kept well, knowledgeable landlord may offer tasters, pleasant helpful young staff, bargain pubby food all day inc good pies; panelling and some armchairs; open all day *(Tony and Wendy Hobden, Bruce Bird, Phil and Sally Gorton)*

Vulcan CF24 2FH [Adam St]: Largely untouched Victorian local surrounded by redevelopment, jovial landlord, well kept Brains, good value lunches (not Sun) in sedate lounge with some original features inc an ornate fireplace; maritime pictures in lively public bar with traditional games and juke box; open all day, cl Sun evening *(Dr and Mrs A K Clarke, the Didler)*

Yard CF10 1AD [St Mary St]: Unusual conversion of the loading bay of Brains' original brewery (the well kept ales now come from the nearby former Hancocks' brewery), good reasonably priced food especially chargrills cooked in front of you, good service; functional décor using some original girders etc, upper gallery with Brains' family portraits in comfortable 'board room'; piped music may be loud, lighting dim; courtyard tables, open all day till late *(Prof Kenneth Surin, Andy and Jill Kassube)*

KENFIG [SS8081]

☆ *Prince of Wales* CF33 4PR [2.2 miles from M4 junction 37; A4229 towards Porthcawl, then right when dual carriageway narrows on bend, signed Maudlam and Kenfig]: Ancient local with plenty of individuality by historic sand dunes; cheerful welcoming landlord, well kept Bass and Worthington tapped from cask and usually two guests, good choice of malts, decent wines, enjoyable generous straightforward food at low prices; chatty panelled room off main bar, log fires, stripped stone, lots of wreck pictures,

traditional games, small upstairs dining room for summer and busy wknds (should book); big-screen TV for special sports events; children and (in non-carpet areas) dogs welcome, handy for nature reserve (orchids Jun) *(Phil and Sally Gorton, the Didler, John and Joan Nash, LYM)*

LLANCARFAN [ST0570]

Fox & Hounds CF62 3AD [signed off A4226; can also be reached from Bonvilston or B4265 via Llancadle]: Good carefully cooked food using local ingredients inc fresh fish, welsh black beef and farmhouse cheeses, in neat comfortably modernised village pub; friendly open-plan bar rambling through arches, coal fire, Brains Bitter and Rev James kept well, good wine choice, traditional settles and plush banquettes, candlelit bistro with woodburners, simple end family room; children welcome, unobtrusive piped music; tables out behind, pretty streamside setting by interesting church, eight comfortable bedrooms, good breakfast, open all day wknds *(Rainer Gliss, Tony and Gill Powell, Fergus Dowding, Bill and Jackie Parfitt, BB)*

LLANDAFF [ST1577]

Butchers Arms CF5 2DZ [High St]: Popular and welcoming three-room pub, two or more well kept ales, enjoyable lunchtime food; can get packed on rugby match days; walled beer garden, open all day *(James Morris)*

LLANGYNWYD [SS8588]

Old House CF34 9SB [off A4063 S of Maesteg; pub behind church, nearly a mile W of modern village]: Pretty thatched and beamed dining pub, enjoyable generous food especially fish, cheerful prompt staff, well kept Flowers, decent wines by the glass, good choice of malt whiskies; huge fireplace, attractive conservatory extension; children welcome, garden tables, nearby large churchyard and valley views worth a look *(John and Joan Nash, LYM)*

LLANMADOC [SS4493]

Britannia SA3 1DB [the Gower, nr Whiteford Burrows – NT]: Busy summer pub right out on the peninsula, locally sourced food, well kept beers, nice coffee, gleaming copper stove in beamed and tiled bar, steps up to stripped-stone dining area; children welcome, tables out in front and in big garden behind, great estuary views, lovely walks *(BB, E McCall, T McLean, D Irving)*

LLWYDCOED [SN9905]

Red Cow CF44 0YE [Merthyr Rd (B4276 N of Aberdare)]: Traditional local doing well under newish people, well kept ales such as Adnams Broadside, Brains SA and Greene King Old Speckled Hen, decent wine choice, enjoyable good value straightforward food; lively quiz night Mon; big back garden *(John and Joan Nash)*

OGMORE [SS8876]

☆ *Pelican* CF32 0QP: Nice spot above ruined castle, attractive rambling revamp with plenty of beamery and bare boards, enjoyable well presented food, good real ale choice, cheerful service, welcoming open fire; they may try to keep your credit card while you eat; rather grand smokers' hut; tables on side terrace, lovely views, quite handy for the beaches, open all day *(K Almond, Glenys and John Roberts, R C Vincent, LYM)*

OLDWALLS [SS4891]

Greyhound SA3 1HA: Good value generous food with two-for-one wkdy bargains and good Sun roasts, busy but spacious beamed and dark-panelled 1970s-style plush lounge bar and restaurant, four well kept ales, good coffee inc decaf, decent wine; hot coal fires, friendly staff, back bar with display cases; big tree-shaded garden with terrace picnic-sets, play area and good views *(Richard Hodges)*

REYNOLDSTON [SS4889]

King Arthur SA3 1AD [Higher Green, off A4118]: Cheerful pub/hotel with timbered main bar and hall, back family summer dining area (games room with pool in winter), popular good value food from lunchtime baguettes to Sun roasts, friendly helpful staff coping well when busy, Breconshire, Felinfoel and Tomos Watkins, country-house bric-a-brac, log fire; lively local atmosphere in evenings, piped music; tables out on green, play area, open all day, bedrooms *(Dr and Mrs A K Clarke, Ian Scott-Thompson, Steff Rees, LYM)*

RHOSSILI [SS4188]

Worms Head Hotel SA3 1PP: Large throughput of summer customers inc walkers for separate unpretentious two-bar pub part of 17-bedroom hotel, relatively modern with stunning views over bay and three-mile sweep of beach from eating area and picnic-sets on clifftop terrace; varied menu, friendly staff, two Tomos Watkin ales *(B and F A Hannam)*

ST HILARY [ST0173]

☆ *Bush* CF71 7DP [off A48 E of Cowbridge]: This cosy 17th-c thatched pub, a favourite of *The Good Pub Guide* and its readers for many years, was gutted by fire in September 2009; the owners have vowed to rebuild it, but it seems unlikely that the pub could reopen before 2011 *(LYM)*

GWENT

ABERGAVENNY [SO2914]

Hen & Chickens NP7 5EG [Flannel St]: Popular traditional local with wholesome cheap lunchtime food (not Sun), friendly efficient staff, well kept Brains and a guest from the bar unusually set against street windows, mugs of tea and coffee, interesting side areas with some nice stripped masonry, pews and wonky tables on wood or tiled floors; darts, cards and dominoes, Sun jazz; TV; very busy on market day, they ask to keep a credit card if running a tab; summer pavement tables *(Reg Fowle, Helen Rickwood, the Didler, Chris Flynn, Wendy Jones, John Wooll)*

BETTWS NEWYDD [SO3606]

Black Bear NP15 1JN [off B4598 N of Usk]: Welcoming cottage-style pub in tranquil village, nice local atmosphere, well kept ales, food inc excellent ploughman's, comfortable bar with mixed furniture, fresh flowers and lots of brasses; picnic-sets in sloping side garden, lovely church, cl Sun evening, Mon and Tues *(R T and J C Moggridge, BB)*

CAERLEON [ST3490]

☆ *Bell* NP18 1QQ [off M4 junction 24 via B4237 and B4236; Bulmore Rd]: Nicely furnished linked beamed areas, good food inc some interesting welsh dishes, well kept ales such as Bath and Vale of Glamorgan, farm cider, daily papers, big open fireplace; good Weds folk night, jazz Sun afternoon; unobtrusive piped music; children welcome, pretty back terrace with koi tank, open all day *(Andy and Jill Kassube, BB, Roger Jones)*

Wheatsheaf NP18 1LT [Llanhennock, N]: Unspoilt ancient-seeming pub with lovely Usk Valley views, cosy friendly bar and snug, old local photographs, good collection of small plates and mugs, popular bargain home-made lunches Mon-Sat, changing well kept ales such as Cwmbran and Otley, log fire; children welcome, garden tables, boules *(Andy and Jill Kassube, Ian Barker)*

CHEPSTOW [ST5394]

Boat NP16 5HH [The Back]: Interesting building at castle end of town, bar with a couple of chesterfields, upstairs room with panoramic views across the Wye, separate dining room, four real ales inc Bass and Brains, good range of enjoyable pub food from ciabattas up, boating/marine memorabilia, spotlessly clean; tables out by river, open all day *(Ewan and Moira McCall, John Wooll)*

Coach & Horses NP16 5LN [Welsh St, just outside Town Arch]: Family-run coaching inn with busy local atmosphere, well kept Brains and guests (beer/cider festival start of July), straightforward good value food from shortish menu, friendly young staff; split-level rooms, beams, two log-effect gas fires, Donald McGill postcards in lavatories, friendly ghost called Sarah; children welcome, dogs, too, outside of food hours, walled garden behind with huge umbrella and heated smokers' shelter, six bedrooms, open all day *(John Wooll)*

GROSMONT [SO4024]

Angel NP7 8EP: Friendly 17th-c local owned by village co-operative, rustic interior with simple wooden furniture, Fullers, Tomos Watkins and Wye Valley ales, farm ciders, decent good value straightforward bar food (not Sun, Mon); pool room with darts, live music (instruments provided); no lavatories – public ones close by; a couple of garden tables and boules behind, seats out by ancient market cross on attractive steep single street in sight of castle, open all day Sat, cl Mon lunchtime *(BB, MLR, Reg Fowle, Helen Rickwood, GSB, R T and J C Moggridge)*

LLANDENNY [SO4103]

☆ *Raglan Arms* NP15 1DL: Well run dining pub with good interesting fresh food, home-baked bread, nice wines, Wye Valley Butty Bach, good friendly staff; big pine tables and a couple of leather sofas in linked dining rooms leading through to conservatory, log fire in flagstoned bar's handsome stone fireplace, pastel paintwork giving slight scandinavian feel, relaxed informal atmosphere; garden tables, cl Mon (*James Paterson, BB, Reg Fowle, Helen Rickwood*)

LLANDEWI SKIRRID [SO3421]

☆ *Walnut Tree* NP7 8AW [B4521]: Appealing dining place with veteran chef producing some very good if not cheap food, good wines, pleasantly relaxed and individual service, fireside seats and small tables in little flagstoned bar, airy informal main dining room; children welcome, cl Sun and Mon (*J E Shackleton, LYM*)

LLANTHONY [SO2827]

☆ *Priory Hotel* NP7 7NN [aka Abbey Hotel, Llanthony Priory; off A465, back road Llanvihangel Crucorney—Hay]: Magical setting for plain bar in dimly lit vaulted, flagstoned crypt of graceful ruined Norman abbey, lovely in summer, with lawns around and the peaceful border hills beyond; well kept real ales such as Felinfoel and Newmans, summer farm cider, good coffee, simple lunchtime bar food (can be a long queue on fine summer days, but number system then works well), evening restaurant; occasional live music; no dogs or children; four bedrooms in restored parts of abbey walls, open all day Sat and summer Sun, cl Mon-Thurs, Fri lunchtime and Sun evening, great walks (*MLR, LYM, Reg Fowle, Helen Rickwood, the Didler*)

LLANTRISANT FAWR [ST3997]

☆ *Greyhound* NP15 1LE [off A449 nr Usk]: Prettily set 17th-c country inn with relaxed homely feel in three linked beamed rooms (steps between two), nice mix of furnishings and rustic decorations, consistently good home cooking at sensible prices, good sandwiches, efficient service, two or more well kept ales, decent wines by the glass; log fires, colourful prints in pleasant grey-panelled dining room; attractive garden with big fountain, hill views, adjoining pine shop, good bedrooms in small attached motel (*BB, Colin Moore, Colin McKerrow, Tony and Gill Powell*)

LLANVIHANGEL GOBION [SO3409]

Charthouse NP7 9AY [A40/B4598, E of Abergavenny]: Civilised and welcoming, with good sensibly priced food inc welsh black beef, attentive service, real ales, nautical memorabilia; outside seats, distant hill views (*Eryl and Keith Dykes, BB*)

MONMOUTH [SO5012]

Robin Hood NP25 3EQ [Monnow St]: Ancient pub with low-beamed panelled bar, popular home-made food from sandwiches up, well kept ales inc Bass and Greene King, friendly service, restaurant; tables outside, play area (*Dave Braisted, George Atkinson*)

NEWPORT [ST3188]

Olde Murenger House NP20 1GA [High St]: Fine 16th-c building with ancient dark woodwork, bargain Sam Smiths; open all day (*the Didler*)

PANDY [SO3322]

Park Hotel NP7 8DS: Georgian hotel rather than pub, but worth knowing for its enjoyable food inc authentic austrian and german dishes in new bistro-style restaurant, vegetarian and children's choices too, decent wine, well kept Wye Valley Butty Bach in airy bar (dogs allowed here), friendly helpful service; garden with Black Mountains' view, eight bedrooms (*Dennis Jenkin*)

PONTYPOOL [ST3398]

Carpenters Arms NP4 0TH [Coed-y-Paen, just SE of Llandegfedd Reservoir]: Pretty country pub recently extended, enjoyable imaginative food, good choice of well kept ales and wine; children welcome, pleasant seating outside, good walking/cycling country (*Julia and Richard Tredgett*)

RAGLAN [SO4107]

Beaufort Arms NP15 2DY [High St]: Old-fashioned pub/hotel (former 16th-c coaching inn), attentive friendly staff, comfortable and roomy characterful beamed bars, well kept Brains and other regional ales, good range of locally sourced food reasonably priced bar snacks, set-price Sun lunch in brasserie, log fire; piped music; children welcome, 15 bedrooms (*Andy and Jill Kassube, Reg Fowle, Helen Rickwood, Eryl and Keith Dykes*)

☆ *Clytha Arms* NP7 9BW [Clytha, off Abergavenny road — former A40, now declassified]: Upmarket place on edge of Clytha Park, light and airy with good mix of old country furniture on scrubbed wood floors, window seats and warming fires, bar food (not Sun evening, Mon lunchtime) inc tapas, pricier more elaborate menu in contemporary restaurant, well kept Evan Evans, Felinfoel, Rhymney and three quickly changing guests, farm ciders and perhaps own perry (occasional beer/cider festivals), also good choice of wines and malts; darts, shove-ha'penny and bar billiards, unusual murals in lavatories; large-screen TV for rugby; children and dogs welcome, long heated verandahs, bedrooms, good welsh breakfast, cl Mon lunchtime (*Anne Helne, J K Parry, Dr Kevan Tucker, the Didler, Dr A Y Drummond, Richard Cole, Peter Dearing, LYM, G M Benson*)

SHIRENEWTON [ST4793]

Tredegar Arms NP16 6RQ [signed off B4235 just W of Chepstow]: Popular pub with welcoming landlady and cheery staff, bright and clean, with good choice of well cooked/presented food, real ales in good condition; sheltered courtyard, bedrooms (*Mrs Lynda Bryan-Brown, LYM*)

ST ARVANS [ST5196]

Piercefield NP16 6EJ: Modern décor and setting in roomy comfortable country-style dining pub, enjoyable generous food at sensible prices inc good cheese selection, Brains ales, friendly efficient staff; handy for walkers and Chepstow races *(Mike and Mary Carter, Reg Fowle, Helen Rickwood)*

TINTERN [SO5300]

Abbey NP6 6SF [Monmouth Rd]: Early 19th-c hotel opp the abbey, spacious bar with tables set for dining but welcoming drinkers, short choice of interesting home-made seasonal food inc hefty sandwiches, friendly helpful staff, well kept Wye Valley Butty Bach and a summer guest, restaurant; children welcome, dogs in bar, disabled access, picnic-sets on front lawn, 23 bedrooms *(Dennis Jenkin)*

☆ *Anchor* NP16 6TE: Prime spot by the abbey, friendly new owners and good speedy service, good value food, well kept Wye Valley and a guest ale, Weston's Old Rosie cider; great medieval stone mill in heavy-beamed main bar, flagstones and stripped stone, separate café and restaurant; children and dogs welcome, extensive lawn with sturdy play area and further grounds, River Wye just behind, open all day *(Mr and Mrs D J Nash, Dave Irving, Jenny Huggins, Geoff Dawe, BB)*

Wye Valley Hotel NP16 6SQ [A466 at Catbrook junction]: Pubby bar doing decent food from sandwiches up, well kept Wye Valley ales, good service, delft shelves with beer bottles, adjacent restaurant; bedrooms *(D Crook)*

TRELLECK [SO5005]

Lion NP25 4PA [B4293 6 miles S of Monmouth]: Open-plan bar with one or two low black beams, comfortably worn-in mix of furnishings, two log fires, several changing real ales such as Potbelly and Wye Valley, wide range of good inexpensive food inc hungarian and thai specialities, Fri evening fish and chips, even basket meals; cribbage, dominoes, shove-ha'penny and table skittles; piped music, TV; children and dogs welcome, picnic-sets and aviary out on grass, side courtyard overlooking church, bedrooms in separate cottage, cl Sun evening, open all day summer Sats *(LM, LYM, R T and J C Moggridge)*

USK [SO3700]

Cross Keys NP15 1BG [Bridge St]: Small friendly two-bar stone pub dating from the 14th c, wide choice of popular good value food from baguettes and baked potatoes to restaurant dishes, two well kept ales, oak beams; interesting *Last Supper* tapestry, nice log fire in handsome fireplace, lots of brass, copper and old photographs, wall plaques marking past flood levels; sports TV; back terrace, disabled access, comfortable bedrooms, good breakfast, open all day *(Phil and Jane Hodson)*

☆ *Royal Hotel* NP15 1AT [New Market St]: Comfortable and genuinely traditional with old pictures and old-fashioned fireplaces, generous home-made food (not Sun night, should book evenings) inc good steaks and

fresh fish, reasonable prices, at least three mainly local ales kept well in deep cellar, friendly service, good buzzy local atmosphere; may be piped music, outside gents', upstairs ladies'; well behaved children welcome, handy for Rural Life Museum, cl Mon inc bank hols *(Chris Flynn, Wendy Jones, LYM, Ian Barker)*

GWYNEDD

CAPEL CURIG [SH7357]

Tyn y Coed LL24 0EE: Friendly pub across road from River Llugwy, enjoyable, straightforward, good value food inc sandwiches, Flowers IPA and Shepherd Neame Spitfire kept well, pool room; pleasant terrace, bedrooms *(Rita and Keith Pollard)*

CONWY [SH7878]

Bridge Hotel LL32 8LD [Rose Hill St]: Neat corner pub with Marstons-related ales and a guest, food from sandwiches up (no evening meals,) bar and dining area separated by big two-sided fireplace; bedrooms, open all day *(Tony and Wendy Hobden)*

LLANDUDNO [SH7882]

Albert LL30 2TW [Madoc St]: Friendly, roomy pub comfortably furnished, good staff, fairly priced standard food from sandwiches up, four well kept ales; children and dogs welcome, covered area for smokers, open all day *(Dennis Jones, Sally Matson, Tony and Wendy Hobden)*

Palladium LL30 2DD [Gloddaeth St]: Spacious Wetherspoons in beautifully restored former theatre, boxes and seats intact, spectacular ceilings, quick friendly helpful service, good value food and drinks inc good choice of real ales, plenty of seating *(John Dwane, John Fiander, Tony and Wendy Hobden)*

LLANENGAN [SH2826]

Sun LL53 7LG: Friendly and cosy Robinsons pub in small village nr spectacular sandy Hell's Mouth beach; three real ales, enjoyable family food, reasonable prices, lifeboatman landlord; large partly covered terrace and garden (very popular with children) with outdoor summer bar and pool table, bedrooms *(anon)*

LLANUWCHLLYN [SH8730]

Eagles LL23 7UB [aka Eryrod; A494/B4403]: Family-run and welcoming with good reasonably priced food from sandwiches up (bilingual menu), small front bar and plush back lounge, neat décor with beams, some stripped stone and open fire, back picture-window view of mountains with Lake Bala in distance; Theakstons Best, limited wine choice in small bottles; picnic-sets under parasols on flower-filled back terrace, cl lunchtime Mon-Weds *(Mike and Mary Carter)*

PENMAENPOOL [SH6918]

George III LL40 1YD [just off A493, nr Dolgellau]: Attractive inn worth knowing for lovely views over Mawddach estuary from the civilised partly panelled upstairs bar opening into cosy inglenook lounge; beamed and flagstoned downstairs bar for peak times, usual bar food, a real ale such as Black Sheep, restaurant, dogs and children welcome, sheltered terrace, good bedrooms inc some in a converted station (line now a walkway), open all day *(Tony and Jill Radnor, Mr and Mrs M Stratton, LYM)*

PORTHMADOG [SH5639]

Royal Sportsman LL49 9HB [High St]: Extensively refurbished early Victorian hotel with enjoyable food from interesting snacks up, popular bar and comfortable lounge with leather armchairs and sofas, restaurant, good friendly staff, well kept changing ales inc local Purple Moose, ten wines by the glass, cocktails, log fire; dogs very welcome (the house sheepdog is Gelert), pretty terrace, 28 updated bedrooms *(Mr and Mrs M Stratton)*

Spooners LL49 9NF [Harbour Station]: Platform café/bar at steam line terminus; lots of railway memorabilia inc a former working engine (*Princess*) in one corner, six changing ales (usually local Purple Moose), good value pub food inc popular Sun lunch, evening meals Thurs-Sat (other days too in high season); overflow into station buffet; children welcome, platform tables, open all day *(Tony and Wendy Hobden)*

TREFRIW [SH7863]

Old Ship LL27 0JH: Particularly well kept Marstons-related beers and local guests such as Conwy, good choice of wines, friendly staff, enjoyable generous fresh pubby food from baguettes up inc good fish and chips, log fire, cheerful local atmosphere, restaurant with inglenook; children welcome *(Martin Cawley, Jan Bertenshaw)*

POWYS

ABEREDW [SO0847]

Seven Stars LD2 3UW [just off B4567 SE of Builth Wells]: Cosy attractive local, good generous honest food from sandwiches up with wider evening choice, two well kept changing ales such as Felinfoel Double Dragon and Wadworths 6X, friendly service; low beams and stripped stone, log fire, local pictures and antiques, small games room with darts and pool, restaurant; children and dogs welcome, disabled facilities, three bedrooms *(anon)*

BERRIEW [SJ1800]

Lion SY21 8PQ [B4390; village signed off A483 Welshpool—Newtown]: Black and white beamed 17th-c coaching inn in attractive riverside village (with lively sculpture gallery), friendly welcome from mother and daughter team; old-fashioned inglenook public bar and partly stripped-stone lounge, enjoyable home-made food here or in restaurant from sandwiches to good fresh fish, helpful cheerful service, well kept Banks's and Jennings, decent house wines, dominoes; quiet piped music; children welcome, dogs in bar, seven bedrooms, open all day Fri, Sat *(LYM, David Glynne-Jones,*

Patrick and Daphne Darley, B and M Kendall)

BRECON [SO0428]

Clarence LD3 7ED [Watton]: Modernised pub with friendly licensees, three well kept ales inc Wye Valley Butty Bach, decent good value pubby food, used as a venue during Brecon Jazz Festival; good beer garden *(Tim Williams)*

George LD3 7LD [George St]: Comfortable old coaching inn, four well kept Evan Evans ales, decent reasonably priced food all day inc breakfast, cheerful efficient service, log-effect gas fires in long bar, dining conservatory; tables in flower-filled back courtyard *(Brian Brooks, David Heath, Howard Deacon)*

Tipple 'n' Tiffin LD3 7EW [Theatr Brycheiniog]: Café-style theatre bar in a great position overlooking canal basin, tapas and sharing plates *(Meg and Colin Hamilton)*

CARNO [SN9696]

Aleppo Merchant SY17 5LL [A470 Newtown—Machynlleth]: Good value pub food from sandwiches up (open for breakfast too), helpful friendly staff, Boddingtons and Tetleys; plushly modernised stripped-stone bar, peaceful lounge on right with open fire, restaurant (well behaved children allowed here), back extension with big-screen TV in games room; piped music; disabled access, steps up to tables in attractively enlarged garden, bedrooms, nice countryside, open all day *(LYM, Michael and Jenny Back)*

CRICKHOWELL [SO2118]

Bridge End NP8 1AR [Bridge St]: Friendly 16th-c coaching inn by many-arched bridge over the Usk, popular with locals; Brains and other ales, enjoyable food from good value lunchtime baguettes up, good service, restaurant; small beer garden across road overlooking river, three bedrooms *(Barry and Anne)*

Dragon NP8 1BE [High St]: Refurbished old inn (more hotel/restaurant than pub but with small bar), good choice of enjoyable well presented food from reasonably priced bar meals up, prompt friendly service, Brains Rev James, log fire; 15 comfortable bedrooms *(Eryl and Keith Dykes, Guy Vowles)*

☆ *White Hart* NP8 1DL [Brecon Rd (A40 W)]: Stripped stone, beams and flagstones, good value food from lunchtime sandwiches up inc several welsh specialities, Brains ales and a guest, friendly staff, bar with end eating area, sizeable restaurant; pub games; may be piped music; children in eating areas, some tables outside, open all day Sat *(LYM, Bob and Angela Brooks)*

DERWENLAS [SN7299]

☆ *Black Lion* SY20 8TN [A487 just S of Machynlleth]: Cosy 16th-c country pub, good range of enjoyable well priced food inc nice children's menu, friendly staff coping well at busy times, Wye Valley Butty Bach and a guest, decent wines; heavy black beams, thick walls and black timbering, attractive pictures and lion models, tartan carpet over big slate flagstones, good log fire; piped music; garden behind with play area and steps up into woods, limited parking, bedrooms *(Dr Kevan Tucker, B and M Kendall, BB)*

DINAS MAWDDWY [SH8514]

Red Lion SY20 9JA [off A470 (N of A458 junction)]: Two small traditional front bars and more modern back extension, changing ales inc some from small local brewers, good generous home-made food, reasonable prices; pub name in welsh (Llew Coch) *(Gwyn and Anne Wake, Keith and Ann Arnold)*

GLADESTRY [SO2355]

Royal Oak HR5 3NR [B4594]: Village pub on Offa's Dyke Path with friendly licensees, simple stripped-stone slate-floor walkers' bar, beams hung with tankards and lanterns, piano, darts, turkey-carpeted lounge, open fires, two Golden Valley ales, basic bar food; no credit cards; children welcome, dogs in bar (and in bedrooms by arrangement), sheltered back garden, camping, open all day (may close if quiet but will reopen if you ring the bell) *(Mrs P Sumner, LYM, Dr Kevan Tucker)*

GLASBURY [SO1839]

Harp HR3 5NR [B4350 towards Hay, just N of A438]: Welcoming, relaxed and homely with good value pubby food cooked by landlady inc proper pies, log-fire lounge with eating areas, airy bar, real ales; picture windows over wooded garden sloping to River Wye; terrace tables, campsite and canoeing, river-view bedrooms *(MLR, LYM)*

GUILSFIELD [SJ2111]

Oak SY21 9NH: Friendly chatty village local, well kept beer, generous home-made food, separate dining room *(Pete Yearsley)*

HAY-ON-WYE [SO2342]

☆ *Kilverts* HR3 5AG [Bell Bank/Bear St]: High-beamed bar in friendly hotel (some recent refurbishment), five well kept ales such as Breconshire, Hobsons and Wye Valley, several wines by the glass, good food inc nice steak and kidney pudding; children welcome, front flagstoned courtyard, pretty terraced back garden (no dogs allowed) with fountain, comfortable bedrooms, good breakfast, open all day *(Barry and Anne, Steve and Liz Tilley, John and Bryony Coles, David Jackman, LYM, Bob and Angela Brooks, Dr Kevan Tucker, Andy Lickfold)*

☆ *Old Black Lion* HR3 5AD [Lion St]: Comfortable low-beamed bar with old pine tables and an original fireplace, mostly laid out for dining, bar and restaurant food available throughout; Wye Valley (labelled as Old Black Lion) and a guest such as Brains Rev James, efficient service; no dogs; children over 5 allowed if eating, sheltered back terrace, bedrooms (some above bar), open all day *(Reg Fowle, Helen Rickwood, LYM, Guy Vowles, Dr Kevan Tucker, Mike and Eleanor Anderson, Sue Demont, Tim Barrow, Pete Coxon)*

☆ *Three Tuns* HR3 5DB [Broad St]: Good affordable food (not Sun evening) inc lovely home-baked bread in big pub with low black beams, inglenook woodburners, lighter sofa

area, ancient stairs to raftered restaurant, well kept ales inc Three Tuns and Wye Valley, good wine choice, friendly efficient service; no dogs; children welcome, disabled facilities, sheltered courtyard, open all day wknds, cl Mon, Tues *(Brian and Jacky Wilson, Guy Vowles, Howard Deacon, BB)*

Wheatsheaf HR3 5AA [Lion St]: Beamed pub with bric-a-brac in nooks and crannies, two well kept Golden Valley ales, enjoyable attractively priced home-made food, cheerful staff, settee and end woodburner, pink-walled dining area with light wood furniture and some stripped masonry; pool room; very lively wknds *(Dr Kevan Tucker)*

HUNDRED HOUSE [SO1154]

Hundred House Inn LD1 5RY [A481 NE Builth Wells]: Two-room roadside country pub, welcoming landlord, two well kept changing ales, low-priced food inc lunchtime specials; garden picnic-sets *(MLR)*

LLANGYNIDR [SO1519]

Red Lion NP8 1NT [off B4558; Duffryn Rd]: Creeper-covered family-run 16th-c inn, attractively furnished bow-windowed bar with good log fire, chatty locals, well kept Breconshire ales and a guest, decent local food from lunchtime rolls up; games room; dogs welcome, sheltered pretty garden, bedrooms *(Steve and Liz Tilley, Paul J Robinshaw)*

MACHYNLLETH [SH7400]

Skinners Arms SY20 8AJ [Penrallt St]: Two comfortable bar areas, efficient young staff, friendly locals, good choice of well kept ales, generous good value home-made food inc sandwiches, welcoming log fire; open all day *(Anne Morris)*

☆ *Wynnstay Arms* SY20 8AE [Maengwyn St]: Civilised market-town hotel, softly lit and welcoming, with good choice of enjoyable food and well kept ales in busy little bare-boards annexe bar, stone fireplace with big copper kettle, comfortable hotel lounge, restaurant; courtyard tables, bedrooms *(B and M Kendall)*

MIDDLETOWN [SJ3012]

Breidden SY21 8EL [A458 Welshpool—Shrewsbury]: Well kept ales such as Adnams, Bass and Shepherd Neame, varied choice of food from well prepared pubby things to chinese, japanese and thai dishes; also takeaway service; decent-sized garden with play area *(Keith and Ann Arnold)*

PAINSCASTLE [SO1646]

☆ *Roast Ox* LD2 3JL [off A470 Brecon—Builth Wells, or from A438 at Clyro]: Well restored pub with beams, flagstones, stripped stone, appropriate simple furnishings and some rustic bric-a-brac, well kept ales such as Black Country and Hook Norton Old Hooky tapped from the cask, extensive range of ciders, decent roasts as well as other enjoyable hearty food inc good lunchtime baps, friendly prompt service; dogs welcome, picnic-sets outside, attractive hill country, ten simple, comfortable bedrooms *(Guy Vowles, Reg Fowle, Helen Rickwood, Geoffrey Hughes, LYM)*

PEN-Y-CAE [SN8313]
Ancient Briton SA9 1YY [Brecon Rd]:
Friendly opened-up roadside pub with
reasonably priced food, well kept ales inc
Wye Valley and often interesting guests,
good service; outside seats and play area,
camping, handy for Dan-yr-Ogof caves and
Carig-y-Nos country park, open all day *(MLR)*

TALGARTH [SO1729]
Castle Inn LD3 0EP [Pengenffordd, A479 3
miles S]: Beautifully located roadside inn at
head of Rhiangoll Valley, handy for Black
Mountains walks inc nearby Castell Dinas and
Waun Fach; small friendly bar with well kept
Rhymney, Wye Valley and a guest, larger
dining room, good choice of enjoyable well
priced local food inc steaks on hot rocks, big
log fire, suit of armour; children welcome,
picnic-sets in sheltered garden, four
comfortable bedrooms, neat bunkhouses,
camping, cl Mon, Tues and wkdy lunchtimes,
open all day wknds *(Howard Beamish,
Nick and Sandra Blaney, Matthew Shackle,
Dallas Berry, Howard Deacon, MLR)*

TALYBONT-ON-USK [SO1122]
White Hart LD3 7JD: Comfortable stone-
built coaching inn with big relaxed bar
divided by working fireplace from beamed
dining area, good home-made food inc all-
day Sun roast, half a dozen well kept
changing ales, Thatcher's farm cider,
welcoming knowledgeable landlord; on Taff
Trail, some tables out by Monmouthshire and
Brecon Canal *(the Didler)*

Please tell us if the décor, atmosphere, food or drink at a pub is different from
our description. We rely on readers' reports to keep us up to date:
feedback@goodguides.com, or (no stamp needed)
The Good Pub Guide, FREEPOST TN1569, Wadhurst, E Sussex TN5 7BR.

A Little Further Afield

The stars beside the pubs recommended below signify those which we and readers judge to be of full Main Entry quality. This year we are not printing Lucky Dip pubs for other overseas countries, but hope eventually to add a greatly expanded Overseas section to our website. So please keep the Overseas recommendations coming!

CHANNEL ISLANDS

GUERNSEY

FOREST
Deerhound GY8 0AN [Le Bourg]: Spacious dining pub with refurbished modern interior, good choice of popular food inc daily specials, beers such as Jersey Liberation, good-sized bar area, friendly helpful service; terrace tables, handy for airport (N R White)

KING'S MILLS
☆ *Fleur du Jardin* GY5 7JT [King's Mills Road]: Lovely country hotel in attractive walled garden, relaxing low-beamed flagstoned bar with good log fire, old prints and subdued lighting, unusually good food strong on local produce and seafood, friendly helpful service, several real ales such as Adnams Broadside and Jersey Liberation, good choice of wines by the glass, local cider, restaurant; piped music; children and dogs welcome, plenty of tables on back terrace, clean comfortable bedrooms, open all day (Steve Kirby, Simon Taylor, LYM, N R White)

ST PETER PORT
La Piette GY1 2BQ [St Georges Esplanade]: Seafront hotel's comfortable chatty lounge bar, food from snacks and pizzas up, bistro; no real ale; view across road to neighbouring islands, bedrooms, open all day (N R White)
Swan GY1 1WA [St Julians Ave]: Well run traditional town pub with two bars, one more for eating, good food using local meat and fish, Randall's Patois ale, Victorian-style wallpaper and furnishings, panelling, soft lighting, upstairs restaurant (N R White)

TORTEVAL
Imperial GY8 0PS [Pleinmont (coast rd, nr Pleinmont Point)]: Good choice of enjoyable food from sandwiches to good seafood and traditional Guernsey bean jar (popular local dish) in dining room which, like the neat and tidy lounge bar, has a great sea view over Rocquaine Bay, locals bar; suntrap garden, bedrooms in separate hotel part, handy for good beach (Roger and Anne Newbury, Gordon Neighbour)

JERSEY

GOREY
Moorings JE3 6EW [Gorey Pier]: Hotel's small front bar leading to bistro-style eating area, Jersey Special and Theakstons, good seafood choice, separate restaurant; harbour-view tables outside, 15 bedrooms, many with sea view, good breakfast (Michael Dandy, Col and Mrs Patrick Kaye)

ST AUBIN
Boat House JE3 8BS [North Quay]: Modern steel and timber clad harbourside building, light and airy with spacious bar and upstairs brasserie, Marstons-related ales, great views; balcony, seats outside (Michael Dandy)
☆ *Old Court House Inn* JE3 8AB [Harbour Blvd]: Pubby low-beamed downstairs bar with open fire, other rambling areas inc smarter bar partly built from schooner's gig, food from pubby snacks to lots of good fresh fish, well kept Jersey Special, nice wines by the glass, handsome upstairs restaurant, glorious views across harbour to St Helier, board games; piped music, TV; children welcome, comfortable bedrooms, open all day (Lynda Payton, Sam Samuells, LYM, Michael Dandy, Col and Mrs Patrick Kaye, David Hoult)

ST BRELADE
☆ *Old Portelet Inn* JE3 8AJ [Rte de Noirmont, Portelet Bay]: Family-friendly place with generous pubby food (something virtually all day) quickly served by neat staff, good choice of wines by the glass, beers under light pressure, huge log fire in olde-worlde low-beamed bar, supervised indoor play area, another outside, board games in loft bar, big

barn restaurant; games machine, pool, piped music, can get very busy; children and dogs welcome, disabled facilities, attractive terrace and sizeable landscaped garden, long steps down to beach, open all day *(LYM, D Goodger)*

ST HELIER

☆ *Lamplighter* JE2 3NJ [Mulcaster St]: Small pub with half a dozen well kept ales inc local Liberation, local cider, over 40 malt whiskies, bargain simple food such as crab sandwiches, heavy timbers, rough panelling and scrubbed pine tables; sports TV, can get very busy early evening; interesting façade (with only Union Flag visible during Nazi occupation), open all day *(Lynda Payton, Sam Samuells, David Hoult, Joan and Michel Hooper-Immins, LYM)*

ST MARY

St Marys JE3 3DF [La rue des Buttes]: Locally popular for good food, with good choice of beers inc Jersey Liberation, reasonably priced wines, great log fire, pool and TV in public bar; children welcome in restaurant, dogs in bars, seats in front garden and back courtyard, opp attractive church, open all day
(Michael Dandy, Jenny and Brian Seller)

ST OUENS BAY

☆ *La Pulente* JE3 8HG [start of Five Mile Rd; OS map reference 562488]: Comfortable lounge and conservatory overlooking Jersey's longest beach (stunning sunsets), enjoyable food (not Sun evening in winter), friendly atmosphere and staff, well kept Bass, restaurant; piped music; children welcome, terrace tables, open all day *(LYM, Michael Dandy, Jo Lilley, Simon Calvert, BB)*

ST BRELADE

Lighthouse JE3 8HN: Sizeable place refurbished in contemporary style, lunchtime sandwiches, baguettes and light meals, more evening choice, friendly helpful staff, restaurant with large sliding windows and views of Corbiere Lighthouse; TV; seats outside, serviced apartments
(Michael Dandy)

IRELAND (NORTHERN)

BALLYMENA

Grouse [Ballymoney St]: Centrally placed bar/restaurant with good choice of enjoyable well priced food from snacks up, friendly service, evening entertainment
(Clare McIlraith)

BALLYNURE

Ballad [Main St]: Old community-spirited village pub saved from redevelopment, clean and caringly run by welcoming landlady, good beer and wine, nice log fire, friendly staff *(Paul McTrustry)*

BELFAST

Botanic [Malone Rd]: Cavernous pub with

ales such as Hilden and Whitewater from main room's curving counter, low-priced food, coal fire in cosy front bar with panelled ceiling and nicely carved bar; live music, popular with students *(Andy and Jill Kassube)*

☆ *Crown* [Great Victoria St, opp Europa Hotel]: Restored ornate 19th-c National Trust gin palace well worth sampling, lively and bustling, with pillared entrance, opulent tiles outside and in, elaborately coloured windows, dark brown curlicued ceiling, handsome mirrors, gleaming intricately carved woodwork, ten snug booths with little doors and bells for waiter service, gas lighting, mosaic tiled floor, three well kept ales inc Whitewater from imposing granite-top counter with colourful tiled facing, food upstairs from good Irish stew to local oysters; can be incredibly noisy, very wide range of customers; open all day *(Andy and Jill Kassube, Jeremy King, Paul Humphreys, BB)*

John Hewitt [Donegall St]: In cathedral quarter, traditional high-ceilinged interior, good food, Hilden, Whitewater and guest ales, open fires, live music *(Andy and Jill Kassube)*

McHughs [Queens Sq]: Extensively restored and extended (dates from 1711), with eclectic design in several linked rooms, comfortable leather chairs and settles around marble-top tables, enjoyable food inc steaks cooked on hot rocks, Whitewater ales, good choice of wines *(Andy and Jill Kassube)*

Morning Star [Pottingers Entry (between Ann St and High St)]: Former coaching inn with large island bar, settles, mahogany stools at high tables, terrazzo floor, snug and side rooms, enjoyable food from home-made sausages to fresh fish and speciality steaks (inc crocodile and kangaroo), buffet lunch (Mon-Sat), cosy upstairs restaurant; some pavement seats *(Andy and Jill Kassube)*

IRELAND (REPUBLIC)

BRAY

Porterhouse [Strand Rd]: Large dimly lit rather rambling seafront pub with various areas (some raised) off large central bar, own-brewed beers inc three stouts, foreign bottled beers, enjoyable food all day; 16 bedrooms *(Jeremy King)*

DUBLIN

Temple Bar [Temple Bar]: Rambling multi-levelled, many-roomed tourist pub on cobbled street corner, fast friendly service even on lively wknd nights, spirits bottles packed to the ceiling, lots of old Guinness advertisements, good live music from 4pm; tables in big yard *(Jeremy King)*

You can send reports directly to us at feedback@goodguides.com

Pubs Serving Food All Day

We list here all the pubs that have told us they plan to serve food all day, even if it's only one day of the week. The individual entries for the pubs themselves show the actual details.

BEDFORDSHIRE
Bletsoe, Falcon
Ireland, Black Horse
Northill, Crown
Woburn, Birch

BERKSHIRE
Cookham Dean, Chequers
Hurley, Olde Bell
Sonning, Bull
White Waltham, Beehive

BUCKINGHAMSHIRE
Coleshill, Harte & Magpies
Dorney, Pineapple
Forty Green, Royal Standard of England
Grove, Grove Lock
Lacey Green, Pink & Lily
Penn Street, Hit or Miss
Wooburn Common, Chequers

CAMBRIDGESHIRE
Cambridge, Cambridge Blue, Eagle
Elton, Black Horse
Pampisford, Chequers
Peterborough, Brewery Tap
Stilton, Bell

CHESHIRE
Aldford, Grosvenor Arms
Astbury, Egerton Arms
Aston, Bhurtpore
Bickley Moss, Cholmondeley Arms
Bunbury, Dysart Arms
Burleydam, Combermere Arms
Burwardsley, Pheasant
Chester, Mill, Old Harkers Arms
Eaton, Plough
Lach Dennis, Duke of Portland
Macclesfield, Sutton Hall
Mobberley, Roebuck
Peover Heath, Dog
Plumley, Smoker
Prestbury, Legh Arms
Tarporley, Rising Sun
Willington, Boot

CORNWALL
Crafthole, Finnygook

Lanlivery, Crown
Mitchell, Plume of Feathers
Morwenstow, Bush
Mylor Bridge, Pandora
Porthtowan, Blue
Watergate Bay, Beach Hut

CUMBRIA
Beetham, Wheatsheaf
Bouth, White Hart
Cartmel Fell, Masons Arms
Coniston, Black Bull
Crosthwaite, Punch Bowl
Elterwater, Britannia
Ings, Watermill
Keswick, Dog & Levens, Strickland Arms
Ravenstonedale, Black Swan
Seathwaite, Newfield Inn
Threlkeld, Horse & Farrier

DERBYSHIRE
Alderwasley, Bear
Beeley, Devonshire Arms
Chelmorton, Church Inn
Denby, Bulls Head
Derby, Brunswick
Fenny Bentley, Coach & Horses
Hathersage, Plough, Scotsmans Pack
Hayfield, Lantern Pike, Royal
Hope, Cheshire Cheese
Ladybower Reservoir, Ladybower Inn, Yorkshire Bridge
Litton, Red Lion

DEVON
Avonwick, Turtley Corn Mill
Cockwood, Anchor
Drewsteignton, Drewe Arms
Exeter, Imperial
Noss Mayo, Ship
Postbridge, Warren House
Rockbeare, Jack in the Green
Sidbury, Hare & Hounds
Sidford, Blue Ball

DORSET
Tarrant Monkton, Langton Arms
Worth Matravers, Square & Compass

ESSEX
Aythorpe Roding, Axe & Compasses
Peldon, Rose
Stow Maries, Prince of Wales

GLOUCESTERSHIRE
Almondsbury, Bowl
Brimpsfield, Golden Heart
Broad Campden, Bakers Arms
Coates, Tunnel House
Didmarton, Kings Arms
Ford, Plough
Guiting Power, Hollow Bottom
Nailsworth, Egypt Mill, Weighbridge
Sheepscombe, Butchers Arms

HAMPSHIRE
Bransgore, Three Tuns
Bucklers Hard, Master Builders House
Colden Common, Fishers Pond
Dunbridge, Mill Arms
Ellisfield, Fox
Hamble, Bugle
Littleton, Running Horse
Lymington, Ship
Portsmouth, Old Customs House
Southsea, Wine Vaults
Wherwell, Mayfly

HERTFORDSHIRE
Aldbury, Greyhound, Valiant Trooper
Ashwell, Three Tuns
Harpenden, White Horse

ISLE OF WIGHT
Arreton, White Lion
Cowes, Folly
Hulverstone, Sun
Ningwood, Horse & Groom
Shorwell, Crown
Ventnor, Spyglass

KENT
Brookland, Woolpack
Hawkhurst, Great House
Hodsoll Street, Green Man
Hollingbourne, Windmill
Langton Green, Hare
Penshurst, Bottle House
Shipbourne, Chaser
Stowting, Tiger

LANCASHIRE
Barrow, Eagle
Bashall Eaves, Red Pump
Bispham Green, Eagle & Child
Broughton, Plough at Eaves
Chipping, Dog & Partridge
Denshaw, Rams Head
Great Mitton, Three Fishes
Lancaster, Borough
Liverpool, Philharmonic Dining Rooms
Longridge, Derby Arms
Lydgate, White Hart
Manchester, Dukes 92, Marble Arch
Nether Burrow, Highwayman
Pleasington, Clog & Billycock
Ramsbottom, Fishermans Retreat

Stalybridge, Station Buffet
Uppermill, Church Inn
Waddington, Lower Buck
Wheatley Lane, Old Sparrow Hawk
Wheelton, Dressers Arms
Yealand Conyers, New Inn

LEICESTERSHIRE AND RUTLAND
Coleorton, George
Lyddington, Marquess of Exeter
Swithland, Griffin
Upper Hambleton, Finchs Arms
Woodhouse Eaves, Wheatsheaf

LINCOLNSHIRE
Allington, Welby Arms
Billingborough, Fortescue Arms
Kirkby la Thorpe, Queens Head
Lincoln, Wig & Mitre
Stamford, George of Stamford

NORFOLK
Aylsham, Black Boys
Brancaster Staithe, Jolly Sailors, White Horse
Edgefield, Pigs
Larling, Angel
Morston, Anchor
Stiffkey, Red Lion
Stow Bardolph, Hare Arms
Swanton Morley, Darbys
Woodbastwick, Fur & Feather

NORTHAMPTONSHIRE
Ashby St Ledgers, Olde Coach House
Aynho, Great Western Arms
East Haddon, Red Lion
Oundle, Ship

NORTHUMBRIA
Blanchland, Lord Crewe Arms
Carterway Heads, Manor House Inn
Corbridge, Angel
Great Whittington, Queens Head
Greta Bridge, Morritt Arms
Lesbury, Coach
New York, Shiremoor Farm
Newburn, Keelman
Stannington, Ridley Arms
Weldon Bridge, Anglers Arms

NOTTINGHAMSHIRE
Beeston, Victoria
Caunton, Caunton Beck
Harby, Bottle & Glass
Nottingham, Bell, Lincolnshire Poacher,
    Olde Trip to Jerusalem

OXFORDSHIRE
Bloxham, Joiners Arms
Kingham, Plough
Oxford, Bear, Turf Tavern
Satwell, Lamb
Stanton St John, Talk House

SHROPSHIRE
Bromfield, Clive
Chetwynd Aston, Fox
Leebotwood, Pound

Shrewsbury, Armoury
Stiperstones, Stiperstones Inn

SOMERSET
Hinton St George, Lord Poulett Arms
Keynsham, Lock-Keeper
Stanton Wick, Carpenters Arms
Wells, City Arms

STAFFORDSHIRE
Lichfield, Boat, Queens Head
Salt, Holly Bush
Wrinehill, Hand & Trumpet

SUFFOLK
Chelmondiston, Butt & Oyster
Snape, Plough & Sail
Stoke-by-Nayland, Crown
Waldringfield, Maybush

SURREY
Blindley Heath, Red Barn
Buckland, Jolly Farmers
Cobham, Cricketers
Elstead, Mill at Elstead
Outwood, Bell

SUSSEX
Alfriston, George
Arlington, Old Oak
Berwick, Cricketers Arms
Blackboys, Blackboys Inn
Charlton, Fox Goes Free
Chiddingly, Six Bells
East Chiltington, Jolly Sportsman
East Dean, Star & Garter
Horsham, Black Jug
Icklesham, Queens Head
Mayfield, Rose & Crown
Ringmer, Cock
Rye, Ypres Castle
Sidlesham, Crab & Lobster
Wilmington, Giants Rest

WARWICKSHIRE
Barford, Granville
Birmingham, Old Joint Stock
Henley-in-Arden, Blue Bell
Hunningham, Red Lion
Long Compton, Red Lion
Welford-on-Avon, Bell

WILTSHIRE
Bradford-on-Avon, Castle
Brinkworth, Three Crowns
Seend, Barge

YORKSHIRE
Appleton-le-Moors, Moors
Beck Hole, Birch Hall
Blakey Ridge, Lion
Bradfield, Strines Inn

Broughton, Bull
Byland Abbey, Abbey Inn
Elslack, Tempest Arms
Grinton, Bridge Inn
Halifax, Shibden Mill
Hartshead, Gray Ox
Hetton, Angel
Kettlesing, Queens Head
Ledsham, Chequers
Linton in Craven, Fountaine
Long Preston, Maypole
Whitby, Duke of York
Widdop, Pack Horse

LONDON
Central London, Argyll Arms, Black Friar, Coopers Arms, Dog & Duck, Guinea, Lamb, Lord Moon of the Mall, Old Bank of England, Olde Cheshire Cheese, Olde Mitre, Red Lion, Salisbury, Seven Stars
East London, Crown, Prospect of Whitby
North London, Flask, Holly Bush, Spaniards Inn
South London, Bo-Peep, Crown & Greyhound, Cutty Sark, Fire Station, Founders Arms, Fox & Hounds, George, Greenwich Union, Telegraph, White Cross
West London, Atlas, Bulls Head, Churchill Arms, Dove, Duke of Sussex, Portobello Gold, Warrington, White Horse, Windsor Castle

SCOTLAND
Applecross, Applecross Inn
Broughty Ferry, Fishermans Tavern
Edinburgh, Abbotsford, Café Royal, Starbank
Gairloch, Old Inn
Glasgow, Babbity Bowster, Bon Accord, Counting House
Glencoe, Clachaig
Houston, Fox & Hounds
Innerleithen, Traquair Arms
Inveraray, George
Kilmahog, Lade
Kippen, Cross Keys
Linlithgow, Four Marys
Pitlochry, Moulin
Shieldaig, Tigh an Eilean Hotel
Sligachan, Sligachan Hotel
Thornhill, Lion & Unicorn

WALES
Colwyn Bay, Pen-y-Bryn
Gresford, Pant-yr-Ochain
Hay-on-Wye, Blue Boar
Llandudno Junction, Queens Head
Llanferres, Druid
Llangollen, Corn Mill
Red Wharf Bay, Ship
Tresaith, Ship

Pubs Near Motorway Junctions

The number at the start of each line is the number of the junction. Detailed directions are given in the Main Entry for each pub. In this section, to help you find the pubs quickly before you're past the junction, we give the name of the chapter where you'll find the text.

M1
9: Redbourn, Cricketers (Herts) 3.2 miles
13: Woburn, Birch (Beds) 3.5 miles
16: Nether Heyford, Olde Sun (Northants) 1.8 miles
18: Crick, Red Lion (Northants) 1 mile; Kilsby, George (Northants) 2.6 miles; Ashby St Ledgers, Olde Coach House (Northants) 4 miles

M3
3: West End, Inn at West End (Surrey) 2.4 miles
9: Winchester, Willow Tree (Hants) 1 mile; Easton, Chestnut Horse (Hants) 3.6 miles
10: Winchester, Black Boy (Hants) 1 mile

M4
7: Dorney, Pineapple (Bucks) 2.4 miles
9: Bray, Crown (Berks) 1.75 miles; Bray, Hinds Head (Berks) 1.75 miles
11: Shinfield, Magpie & Parrot (Berks) 2.6 miles
13: Winterbourne, Winterbourne Arms (Berks) 3.7 miles
17: Norton, Vine Tree (Wilts) 4 miles

M5
4: Holy Cross, Bell & Cross (Worcs) 4 miles
16: Almondsbury, Bowl (Gloucs) 1.25 miles
19: Portishead, Windmill (Somerset) 3.7 miles; Clapton-in-Gordano, Black Horse (Somerset) 4 miles
25: Wrantage, Canal Inn (Somerset) 4 miles
26: Clayhidon, Merry Harriers (Devon) 3.1 miles

28: Broadhembury, Drewe Arms (Devon) 5 miles
30: Topsham, Bridge Inn (Devon) 2.25 miles; Woodbury Salterton, Diggers Rest (Devon) 3.5 miles

M6
T6: Lichfield, Boat (Staffs) 3.8 miles
4: Shustoke, Griffin (Warks) 5 miles
16: Barthomley, White Lion (Cheshire) 1 mile
19: Plumley, Smoker (Cheshire) 2.5 miles
33: Bay Horse, Bay Horse (Lancs) 1.2 miles
35: Yealand Conyers, New Inn (Lancs) 3 miles
36: Levens, Strickland Arms (Cumbria) 4 miles
40: Yanwath, Gate Inn (Cumbria) 2.25 miles

M9
3: Linlithgow, Four Marys (Scotland) 2 miles

M11
1: Histon, Red Lion (Cambs) 3.7 miles
7: Hastingwood, Rainbow & Dove (Essex) 0.25 miles
8: Birchanger, Three Willows (Essex) 0.8 miles
9: Hinxton, Red Lion (Cambs) 2 miles; Great Chesterford, Crown & Thistle (Essex) 1.5 miles
10: Duxford, John Barleycorn (Cambs) 1.8 miles; Pampisford, Chequers (Cambs) 2.6 miles; Thriplow, Green Man (Cambs) 3 miles

M20
8: Hollingbourne, Windmill (Kent) 1 mile
11: Stowting, Tiger (Kent) 3.7 miles

M25

4: South London, Bo-Peep (London) 1.7 miles
10: Cobham, Cricketers (Surrey) 3.75 miles
18: Chenies, Red Lion (Bucks) 2 miles; Flaunden, Bricklayers Arms (Herts) 4 miles
20: Chandlers Cross, Clarendon (Herts) 3 miles
21A: Potters Crouch, Holly Bush (Herts) 2.3 miles

M27

1: Fritham, Royal Oak (Hants) 4 miles
8: Hamble, Bugle (Hants) 3 miles

M40

2: Hedgerley, White Horse (Bucks) 2.4 miles; Forty Green, Royal Standard of England (Bucks) 3.5 miles
6: Lewknor, Olde Leathern Bottel (Oxfordshire) 0.5 miles; Cuxham, Half Moon (Oxfordshire) 4 miles
12: Gaydon, Malt Shovel (Warks) 0.9 miles

15: Barford, Granville (Warks) 1.7 miles
16: Henley-in-Arden, Blue Bell (Warks) 3.3 miles

M42

6: Hampton in Arden, White Lion (Warks) 1.25 miles

M50

1: Baughton, Jockey (Worcs) 4 miles

M53

3: Barnston, Fox & Hounds (Lancs) 3 miles

M55

1: Broughton, Plough at Eaves (Lancs) 3.25 miles

M61

8: Wheelton, Dressers Arms (Lancs) 2.1 miles

M62

22: Denshaw, Rams Head (Lancs) 2 miles
25: Hartshead, Gray Ox (Yorkshire) 3.5 miles

Please keep sending us reports. We rely on readers for news of new discoveries, and particularly for news of changes – however slight – at the fully described pubs: feedback@goodguides.com, or (no stamp needed) The Good Pub Guide, FREEPOST TN1569, Wadhurst, E Sussex TN5 7BR.

Report Forms

We need to know about pubs in this edition, pubs worthy of inclusion and ones that should not be included. Sometimes pubs are dropped simply because very few readers have written to us about them. You can use the cut-out forms on the following pages, the card in the middle of the book, email us at **feedback@goodguides.com** or write to us and we'll gladly send you more forms:

The Good Pub Guide
FREEPOST TN1569
WADHURST
East Sussex TN5 7BR

Though we try to answer all letters, please understand if there's a delay (particularly in summer, our busiest period). We'll assume we can print your name or initials as a recommender unless you tell us otherwise.

MAIN ENTRY OR LUCKY DIP?

Please try to gauge whether a pub should be a Main Entry or Lucky Dip (and tick the relevant box). Main entries need qualities that would make it worth other readers' while to travel some distance to them. If a pub is an entirely new recommendation, the Lucky Dip may be the best place for it to start its career in the *Guide* – to encourage other readers to report on it.

The more detail you can put into your description of a pub, the better. Any information on how good the landlord or landlady is, what it looks like inside, what you like about the atmosphere and character, the quality and type of food, whether the real ale is well kept and which real ales are available, whether bedrooms are available, and how big/attractive the garden is. Other things that help (if possible) include prices for food and bedrooms, food service and opening hours, and if children or dogs are welcome.

If the food or accommodation are outstanding, tick the **FOOD AWARD** or the **STAY AWARD** box.

If you're in a position to gauge a pub's suitability or otherwise for **disabled people**, do please tell us about that.

If you can, give the full address or directions for any pub not yet in the *Guide* – best of all please give us its postcode. If we can't find a pub's postcode, we don't include it in the *Guide*.

I have been to the following pubs in *The Good Pub Guide 2011* in the last few months, found them as described, and confirm that they deserve continued inclusion:

Continued overleaf
PLEASE GIVE YOUR NAME AND ADDRESS ON THE BACK OF THIS FORM

Pubs visited continued...

Your own name and address *(block capitals please)*

....

....

....

....

Postcode

In returning this form I confirm my agreement that the information I provide may be used by The Random House Group Ltd, its assignees and/or licensees in any media or medium whatsoever.

Please return to
The Good Pub Guide,
FREEPOST TN1569,
WADHURST,
East Sussex
TN5 7BR

IF YOU PREFER, YOU CAN SEND US REPORTS
BY EMAIL:
feedback@goodguides.com

I have been to the following pubs in *The Good Pub Guide 2011* in the last few months, found them as described, and confirm that they deserve continued inclusion:

Continued overleaf

PLEASE GIVE YOUR NAME AND ADDRESS ON THE BACK OF THIS FORM

Pubs visited continued...

Your own name and address *(block capitals please)*

Postcode

In returning this form I confirm my agreement that the information I provide may be used by The Random House Group Ltd, its assignees and/or licensees in any media or medium whatsoever.

Please return to
The Good Pub Guide,
FREEPOST TN1569,
WADHURST,
East Sussex
TN5 7BR

IF YOU PREFER, YOU CAN SEND US REPORTS
BY EMAIL:
feedback@goodguides.com

REPORT ON (PUB'S NAME)

Pub's address

☐ **YES** MAIN ENTRY ☐ **YES** LUCKY DIP ☐ **NO** DON'T INCLUDE
Please tick one of these boxes to show your verdict, and give reasons and descriptive
comments, prices etc

☐ DESERVES **FOOD** award ☐ DESERVES **PLACE-TO-STAY** award 2011:1

PLEASE GIVE YOUR NAME AND ADDRESS ON THE BACK OF THIS FORM

✂️ -

REPORT ON (PUB'S NAME)

Pub's address

☐ **YES** MAIN ENTRY ☐ **YES** LUCKY DIP ☐ **NO** DON'T INCLUDE
Please tick one of these boxes to show your verdict, and give reasons and descriptive
comments, prices etc

☐ DESERVES **FOOD** award ☐ DESERVES **PLACE-TO-STAY** award 2011:2

PLEASE GIVE YOUR NAME AND ADDRESS ON THE BACK OF THIS FORM

IF YOU PREFER, YOU CAN SEND US REPORTS BY EMAIL:
feedback@goodguides.com

REPORT ON _____ (PUB'S NAME)

Pub's address _____

☐ **YES** MAIN ENTRY   ☐ **YES** LUCKY DIP   ☐ **NO** DON'T INCLUDE
Please tick one of these boxes to show your verdict, and give reasons and descriptive
comments, prices etc

☐ DESERVES **FOOD** award   ☐ DESERVES **PLACE-TO-STAY** award   2011:3
PLEASE GIVE YOUR NAME AND ADDRESS ON THE BACK OF THIS FORM

✂ -

REPORT ON _____ (PUB'S NAME)

Pub's address _____

☐ **YES** MAIN ENTRY   ☐ **YES** LUCKY DIP   ☐ **NO** DON'T INCLUDE
Please tick one of these boxes to show your verdict, and give reasons and descriptive
comments, prices etc

☐ DESERVES **FOOD** award   ☐ DESERVES **PLACE-TO-STAY** award   2011:4
PLEASE GIVE YOUR NAME AND ADDRESS ON THE BACK OF THIS FORM

Your own name and address *(block capitals please)*
In returning this form I confirm my agreement that the information I provide may be used by
The Random House Group Ltd, its assignees and/or licensees in any media or medium whatsoever.

DO NOT USE THIS SIDE OF THE PAGE FOR WRITING ABOUT PUBS

By returning this form, you consent to the collection, recording and use of the information you submit, by The Random House Group
Ltd. Any personal details which you provide from which we can identify you are held and processed in accordance with the
Data Protection Act 1998 and will not be passed on to any third parties. The Random House Group Ltd may wish to send
you further information on their associated products. Please tick box if you do not wish to receive any such information.

Your own name and address *(block capitals please)*
In returning this form I confirm my agreement that the information I provide may be used by
The Random House Group Ltd, its assignees and/or licensees in any media or medium whatsoever.

DO NOT USE THIS SIDE OF THE PAGE FOR WRITING ABOUT PUBS

By returning this form, you consent to the collection, recording and use of the information you submit, by The Random House Group
Ltd. Any personal details which you provide from which we can identify you are held and processed in accordance with the
Data Protection Act 1998 and will not be passed on to any third parties. The Random House Group Ltd may wish to send
you further information on their associated products. Please tick box if you do not wish to receive any such information.

IF YOU PREFER, YOU CAN SEND US REPORTS BY EMAIL:
feedback@goodguides.com

REPORT ON _____ (PUB'S NAME)

....

Pub's address

....

☐ **YES** MAIN ENTRY   ☐ **YES** LUCKY DIP   ☐ **NO** DON'T INCLUDE
Please tick one of these boxes to show your verdict, and give reasons and descriptive
comments, prices etc

☐ DESERVES **FOOD** award   ☐ DESERVES **PLACE-TO-STAY** award   2011:5

PLEASE GIVE YOUR NAME AND ADDRESS ON THE BACK OF THIS FORM

....✂

REPORT ON _____ (PUB'S NAME)

....

Pub's address

....

☐ **YES** MAIN ENTRY   ☐ **YES** LUCKY DIP   ☐ **NO** DON'T INCLUDE
Please tick one of these boxes to show your verdict, and give reasons and descriptive
comments, prices etc

☐ DESERVES **FOOD** award   ☐ DESERVES **PLACE-TO-STAY** award   2011:6

PLEASE GIVE YOUR NAME AND ADDRESS ON THE BACK OF THIS FORM

Your own name and address *(block capitals please)*

In returning this form I confirm my agreement that the information I provide may be used by
The Random House Group Ltd, its assignees and/or licensees in any media or medium whatsoever.

DO NOT USE THIS SIDE OF THE PAGE FOR WRITING ABOUT PUBS

Your own name and address *(block capitals please)*

In returning this form I confirm my agreement that the information I provide may be used by
The Random House Group Ltd, its assignees and/or licensees in any media or medium whatsoever.

DO NOT USE THIS SIDE OF THE PAGE FOR WRITING ABOUT PUBS

IF YOU PREFER, YOU CAN SEND US REPORTS BY EMAIL:
feedback@goodguides.com

REPORT ON   (PUB'S NAME)

Pub's address

☐ **YES** MAIN ENTRY   ☐ **YES** LUCKY DIP   ☐ **NO** DON'T INCLUDE
Please tick one of these boxes to show your verdict, and give reasons and descriptive comments, prices etc

☐ DESERVES **FOOD** award   ☐ DESERVES **PLACE-TO-STAY** award   2011:7

PLEASE GIVE YOUR NAME AND ADDRESS ON THE BACK OF THIS FORM

✂ -

REPORT ON   (PUB'S NAME)

Pub's address

☐ **YES** MAIN ENTRY   ☐ **YES** LUCKY DIP   ☐ **NO** DON'T INCLUDE
Please tick one of these boxes to show your verdict, and give reasons and descriptive comments, prices etc

☐ DESERVES **FOOD** award   ☐ DESERVES **PLACE-TO-STAY** award   2011:8

PLEASE GIVE YOUR NAME AND ADDRESS ON THE BACK OF THIS FORM

Your own name and address *(block capitals please)*

In returning this form I confirm my agreement that the information I provide may be used by
The Random House Group Ltd, its assignees and/or licensees in any media or medium whatsoever.

DO NOT USE THIS SIDE OF THE PAGE FOR WRITING ABOUT PUBS

By returning this form, you consent to the collection, recording and use of the information you submit, by The Random House Group Ltd. Any personal details which you provide from which we can identify you are held and processed in accordance with the Data Protection Act 1998 and will not be passed on to any third parties. The Random House Group Ltd may wish to send you further information on their associated products. Please tick box if you do not wish to receive any such information.

IF YOU PREFER, YOU CAN SEND US REPORTS BY EMAIL:
feedback@goodguides.com

REPORT ON (PUB'S NAME)

Pub's address

☐ **YES** MAIN ENTRY   ☐ **YES** LUCKY DIP   ☐ **NO** DON'T INCLUDE
Please tick one of these boxes to show your verdict, and give reasons and descriptive comments, prices etc

☐ DESERVES **FOOD** award   ☐ DESERVES **PLACE-TO-STAY** award   2011:9

PLEASE GIVE YOUR NAME AND ADDRESS ON THE BACK OF THIS FORM

✂- -

REPORT ON (PUB'S NAME)

Pub's address

☐ **YES** MAIN ENTRY   ☐ **YES** LUCKY DIP   ☐ **NO** DON'T INCLUDE
Please tick one of these boxes to show your verdict, and give reasons and descriptive comments, prices etc

☐ DESERVES **FOOD** award   ☐ DESERVES **PLACE-TO-STAY** award   2011:10

PLEASE GIVE YOUR NAME AND ADDRESS ON THE BACK OF THIS FORM

Your own name and address *(block capitals please)*

In returning this form I confirm my agreement that the information I provide may be used by
The Random House Group Ltd, its assignees and/or licensees in any media or medium whatsoever.

DO NOT USE THIS SIDE OF THE PAGE FOR WRITING ABOUT PUBS

✂ ....

Your own name and address *(block capitals please)*

In returning this form I confirm my agreement that the information I provide may be used by
The Random House Group Ltd, its assignees and/or licensees in any media or medium whatsoever.

DO NOT USE THIS SIDE OF THE PAGE FOR WRITING ABOUT PUBS

By returning this form, you consent to the collection, recording and use of the information you submit, by The Random House Group Ltd. Any personal details which you provide from which we can identify you are held and processed in accordance with the Data Protection Act 1998 and will not be passed on to any third parties. The Random House Group Ltd may wish to send you further information on their associated products. Please tick box if you do not wish to receive any such information.

IF YOU PREFER, YOU CAN SEND US REPORTS BY EMAIL:
feedback@goodguides.com

REPORT ON (PUB'S NAME)

Pub's address

☐ **YES** MAIN ENTRY ☐ **YES** LUCKY DIP ☐ **NO** DON'T INCLUDE
Please tick one of these boxes to show your verdict, and give reasons and descriptive comments, prices etc

☐ DESERVES **FOOD** award ☐ DESERVES **PLACE-TO-STAY** award 2011:11

PLEASE GIVE YOUR NAME AND ADDRESS ON THE BACK OF THIS FORM

✂ -

REPORT ON (PUB'S NAME)

Pub's address

☐ **YES** MAIN ENTRY ☐ **YES** LUCKY DIP ☐ **NO** DON'T INCLUDE
Please tick one of these boxes to show your verdict, and give reasons and descriptive comments, prices etc

☐ DESERVES **FOOD** award ☐ DESERVES **PLACE-TO-STAY** award 2011:12

PLEASE GIVE YOUR NAME AND ADDRESS ON THE BACK OF THIS FORM

Your own name and address *(block capitals please)*

In returning this form I confirm my agreement that the information I provide may be used by
The Random House Group Ltd, its assignees and/or licensees in any media or medium whatsoever.

DO NOT USE THIS SIDE OF THE PAGE FOR WRITING ABOUT PUBS

Your own name and address *(block capitals please)*

In returning this form I confirm my agreement that the information I provide may be used by
The Random House Group Ltd, its assignees and/or licensees in any media or medium whatsoever.

DO NOT USE THIS SIDE OF THE PAGE FOR WRITING ABOUT PUBS

IF YOU PREFER, YOU CAN SEND US REPORTS BY EMAIL:
feedback@goodguides.com

REPORT ON (PUB'S NAME)

Pub's address

☐ **YES** MAIN ENTRY ☐ **YES** LUCKY DIP ☐ **NO** DON'T INCLUDE
Please tick one of these boxes to show your verdict, and give reasons and descriptive comments, prices etc

☐ DESERVES **FOOD award** ☐ DESERVES **PLACE-TO-STAY award** 2011:13

PLEASE GIVE YOUR NAME AND ADDRESS ON THE BACK OF THIS FORM

--✂

REPORT ON (PUB'S NAME)

Pub's address

☐ **YES** MAIN ENTRY ☐ **YES** LUCKY DIP ☐ **NO** DON'T INCLUDE
Please tick one of these boxes to show your verdict, and give reasons and descriptive comments, prices etc

☐ DESERVES **FOOD award** ☐ DESERVES **PLACE-TO-STAY award** 2011:14

PLEASE GIVE YOUR NAME AND ADDRESS ON THE BACK OF THIS FORM

Your own name and address *(block capitals please)*
In returning this form I confirm my agreement that the information I provide may be used by
The Random House Group Ltd, its assignees and/or licensees in any media or medium whatsoever.

DO NOT USE THIS SIDE OF THE PAGE FOR WRITING ABOUT PUBS

✂ ....

Your own name and address *(block capitals please)*
In returning this form I confirm my agreement that the information I provide may be used by
The Random House Group Ltd, its assignees and/or licensees in any media or medium whatsoever.

DO NOT USE THIS SIDE OF THE PAGE FOR WRITING ABOUT PUBS

IF YOU PREFER, YOU CAN SEND US REPORTS BY EMAIL:
feedback@goodguides.com

REPORT ON (PUB'S NAME)

Pub's address

☐ **YES** MAIN ENTRY ☐ **YES** LUCKY DIP ☐ **NO** DON'T INCLUDE
Please tick one of these boxes to show your verdict, and give reasons and descriptive
comments, prices etc

☐ DESERVES **FOOD award** ☐ DESERVES **PLACE-TO-STAY award** 2011:15
PLEASE GIVE YOUR NAME AND ADDRESS ON THE BACK OF THIS FORM

✂ ---

REPORT ON (PUB'S NAME)

Pub's address

☐ **YES** MAIN ENTRY ☐ **YES** LUCKY DIP ☐ **NO** DON'T INCLUDE
Please tick one of these boxes to show your verdict, and give reasons and descriptive
comments, prices etc

☐ DESERVES **FOOD award** ☐ DESERVES **PLACE-TO-STAY award** 2011:16
PLEASE GIVE YOUR NAME AND ADDRESS ON THE BACK OF THIS FORM

Your own name and address *(block capitals please)*

In returning this form I confirm my agreement that the information I provide may be used by
The Random House Group Ltd, its assignees and/or licensees in any media or medium whatsoever.

DO NOT USE THIS SIDE OF THE PAGE FOR WRITING ABOUT PUBS

✂ ....

Your own name and address *(block capitals please)*

In returning this form I confirm my agreement that the information I provide may be used by
The Random House Group Ltd, its assignees and/or licensees in any media or medium whatsoever.

DO NOT USE THIS SIDE OF THE PAGE FOR WRITING ABOUT PUBS

IF YOU PREFER, YOU CAN SEND US REPORTS BY EMAIL:
feedback@goodguides.com

REPORT ON   (PUB'S NAME)

Pub's address

☐ **YES** MAIN ENTRY   ☐ **YES** LUCKY DIP   ☐ **NO** DON'T INCLUDE
Please tick one of these boxes to show your verdict, and give reasons and descriptive
comments, prices etc

☐ DESERVES **FOOD** award   ☐ DESERVES **PLACE-TO-STAY** award   2011:17

PLEASE GIVE YOUR NAME AND ADDRESS ON THE BACK OF THIS FORM

--------------------------------✂

REPORT ON   (PUB'S NAME)

Pub's address

☐ **YES** MAIN ENTRY   ☐ **YES** LUCKY DIP   ☐ **NO** DON'T INCLUDE
Please tick one of these boxes to show your verdict, and give reasons and descriptive
comments, prices etc

☐ DESERVES **FOOD** award   ☐ DESERVES **PLACE-TO-STAY** award   2011:18

PLEASE GIVE YOUR NAME AND ADDRESS ON THE BACK OF THIS FORM

Your own name and address *(block capitals please)*

In returning this form I confirm my agreement that the information I provide may be used by
The Random House Group Ltd, its assignees and/or licensees in any media or medium whatsoever.

DO NOT USE THIS SIDE OF THE PAGE FOR WRITING ABOUT PUBS

✂ ....

Your own name and address *(block capitals please)*

In returning this form I confirm my agreement that the information I provide may be used by
The Random House Group Ltd, its assignees and/or licensees in any media or medium whatsoever.

DO NOT USE THIS SIDE OF THE PAGE FOR WRITING ABOUT PUBS

IF YOU PREFER, YOU CAN SEND US REPORTS BY EMAIL:
feedback@goodguides.com

REPORT ON   (PUB'S NAME)

Pub's address

☐ **YES** MAIN ENTRY   ☐ **YES** LUCKY DIP   ☐ **NO** DON'T INCLUDE
Please tick one of these boxes to show your verdict, and give reasons and descriptive comments, prices etc

☐ DESERVES **FOOD** award   ☐ DESERVES **PLACE-TO-STAY** award   2011:19

PLEASE GIVE YOUR NAME AND ADDRESS ON THE BACK OF THIS FORM

✂

REPORT ON   (PUB'S NAME)

Pub's address

☐ **YES** MAIN ENTRY   ☐ **YES** LUCKY DIP   ☐ **NO** DON'T INCLUDE
Please tick one of these boxes to show your verdict, and give reasons and descriptive comments, prices etc

☐ DESERVES **FOOD** award   ☐ DESERVES **PLACE-TO-STAY** award   2011:20

PLEASE GIVE YOUR NAME AND ADDRESS ON THE BACK OF THIS FORM

✂ ···

IF YOU PREFER, YOU CAN SEND US REPORTS BY EMAIL:
feedback@goodguides.com

REPORT ON (PUB'S NAME)

Pub's address

☐ **YES** MAIN ENTRY   ☐ **YES** LUCKY DIP   ☐ **NO** DON'T INCLUDE

Please tick one of these boxes to show your verdict, and give reasons and descriptive comments, prices etc

☐ DESERVES **FOOD award**   ☐ DESERVES **PLACE-TO-STAY award**   2011:21

PLEASE GIVE YOUR NAME AND ADDRESS ON THE BACK OF THIS FORM

✂ -

REPORT ON (PUB'S NAME)

Pub's address

☐ **YES** MAIN ENTRY   ☐ **YES** LUCKY DIP   ☐ **NO** DON'T INCLUDE

Please tick one of these boxes to show your verdict, and give reasons and descriptive comments, prices etc

☐ DESERVES **FOOD award**   ☐ DESERVES **PLACE-TO-STAY award**   2011:22

PLEASE GIVE YOUR NAME AND ADDRESS ON THE BACK OF THIS FORM

REPORT ON (PUB'S NAME)

Pub's address

☐ **YES** MAIN ENTRY ☐ **YES** LUCKY DIP ☐ **NO** DON'T INCLUDE
Please tick one of these boxes to show your verdict, and give reasons and descriptive comments, prices etc

☐ DESERVES **FOOD** award ☐ DESERVES **PLACE-TO-STAY** award 2011:23

PLEASE GIVE YOUR NAME AND ADDRESS ON THE BACK OF THIS FORM

✂ ....

REPORT ON (PUB'S NAME)

Pub's address

☐ **YES** MAIN ENTRY ☐ **YES** LUCKY DIP ☐ **NO** DON'T INCLUDE
Please tick one of these boxes to show your verdict, and give reasons and descriptive comments, prices etc

☐ DESERVES **FOOD** award ☐ DESERVES **PLACE-TO-STAY** award 2011:24

PLEASE GIVE YOUR NAME AND ADDRESS ON THE BACK OF THIS FORM

Your own name and address *(block capitals please)*
In returning this form I confirm my agreement that the information I provide may be used by
The Random House Group Ltd, its assignees and/or licensees in any media or medium whatsoever.

DO NOT USE THIS SIDE OF THE PAGE FOR WRITING ABOUT PUBS

✂ ....

Your own name and address *(block capitals please)*
In returning this form I confirm my agreement that the information I provide may be used by
The Random House Group Ltd, its assignees and/or licensees in any media or medium whatsoever.

DO NOT USE THIS SIDE OF THE PAGE FOR WRITING ABOUT PUBS

IF YOU PREFER, YOU CAN SEND US REPORTS BY EMAIL:
feedback@goodguides.com